THE NEW AMERICAN EPHEMERIS

2020-2030

Longitude, Declination, Latitude and Daily Aspectarian

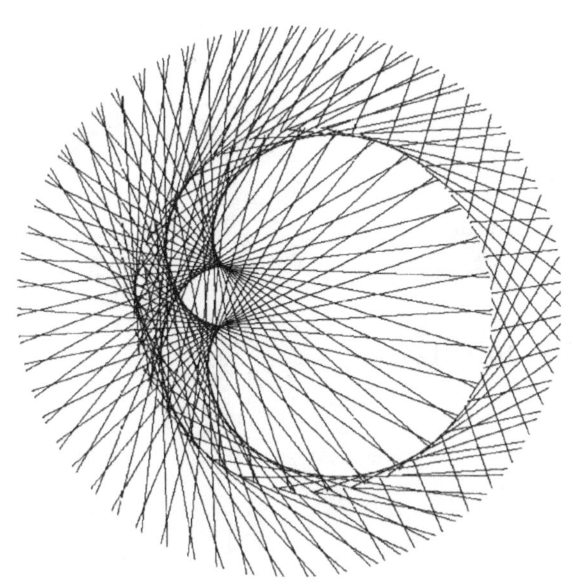

RIQUE POTTENGER
based on the earlier work of
Neil F. Michelsen

The New American Ephemeris 2020-2030
Longitude, Declination & Latitude

Published by ACS Publications, Starcrafts LLC
68 A Fogg Rd., Epping, NH 03042

First Printing 2019

Compiled and Programmed by Rique Pottenger
Based on the earlier work of Neil F. Michelsen

Cover and layout design by Molly Sullivan

The mandala shown on the cover and title page is from Neil F. Michelsen's Table of Planetary Phenomena. It shows the heliocentric orbital pattern made by Venus and Earth

Library of Congress Control Number: 2019912514

ISBN: 978-1934-976-68-5

Printed in the United States of America

Introducing The New American Ephemeris 2020-2030

This book is an updated version of the series of decade ephemerides, beginning with The American Ephemeris 1931-1940, compiled and programmed by Neil F. Michelsen and published by his company, ACS Publications. Earlier, in 1976, Neil had published the first fully computer-generated ephemeris, The American Ephemeris 1931 to 1980 & Book of Tables. More versions followed over the years until Michelsen's death in 1990. Since then, Rique Pottenger has revised and updated all of the Michelsen references as needed. He first extended Michelsen's last version for 1981-1990 by programming and compiling The American Ephemeris 1991-2000 for ACS. With this publication, Rique has included features that he'd added to Starcrafts Publishing's 2006 release, The New American Ephemeris 2007-2020.

Books from the "decade ephemeris" series, as we who were then at ACS always referred to the 10 year publications, have always been particular favorites of mine. Even though I've always had the full century books in multiples at both home and office, I've found the current decade book to be the easiest to have close at hand during a consultation, or to take along on a trip, for quick reference to transits. This thinner, lightweight book is easy to slip into my briefcase. Most valuable for all, though, to a great many astrologers, is that these books include not only the daily longitude tables found in all ephemerides in the series, but they also have declination and latitude tables, and a daily aspectarian.

The New American Ephemeris Features

Because of interest in the features included in our prior full 21st century "New American" we have decided to make this volume "a decade plus." The previous ephemeris gave 14 years of listings from 2007 to 2020. This new ephemeris has 11 years of transits from 2020-2030. Apart from the symmetry of beginning and ending each decade with a zero, we are starting in 2020 instead of 2021 for those persons who may not have bought the previous ephemeris which will be running out in 2020.

Ceres and Chiron are still in the daily longitude positions, and the position of Eris is shown once per month. Pallas, Juno, and Vesta are shown at five day intervals. In the Declination and Latitude tables, Uranus, Neptune, and Pluto were formerly shown at five day intervals. Now you'll also find Chiron, the three asteroids, and Eris there. The Daily Aspectarian includes Ceres and Chiron. Other features include the improved calculation formula for the Galactic Center. The table on the right is provided for those who wish to use it to convert from UT to ET. We have omitted other tables included in the back of former versions as unnecessary today for most users. We hope you will find this book to be a valuable addition to your reference library.

The Kuiper Belt planets, Haumea and Makemake, have been known to mankind for more than a decade. Rique Pottenger has calculated the longitudes and declinations of these dwarf planets, and we have included his work in this new section. Astrologers are still the discussing the meanings of these planets. Haumea is named after a Hawaiian fertility goddess. Makemake is named after the Easter Island god of ecology. To help you understand their roles in your chart and the charts of others, we present these positions so that you can determine the aspects and see what periods of your life were touched by the transits of these two bodies

—Maria Kay Simms

Universal to Ephemeris Time Correction (ΔT)

Add to Universal Time Entries for January 1st

YEAR	SECONDS	YEAR	SECONDS	YEAR	SECONDS	YEAR	SECONDS
1860	8	1910	10	1960	33	2010	66
1861	8	1911	12	1961	34	2011	66
1862	8	1912	13	1962	34	2012	67
1863	7	1913	15	1963	34	2013	67
1864	6	1914	16	1964	35	2014	67
1865	6	1915	17	1965	36	2015	68
1866	5	1916	18	1966	37	2016	68
1867	4	1917	19	1967	37	2017	69
1868	3	1918	20	1968	38	2018	69
1869	2	1919	21	1969	39	2019	69
1870	2	1920	21	1970	40		
1871	0	1921	22	1971	41		
1872	-1	1922	22	1972	42		
1873	-1	1923	23	1973	43		
1874	-3	1924	23	1974	44		
1875	-3	1925	24	1975	45		
1876	-4	1926	24	1976	46		
1877	-5	1927	24	1977	48		
1878	-5	1928	24	1978	49		
1879	-5	1929	24	1979	50		
1880	-5	1930	24	1980	51		
1881	-5	1931	24	1981	51		
1882	-5	1932	24	1982	52		
1883	-5	1933	24	1983	53		
1884	-5	1934	24	1984	54		
1885	-6	1935	24	1985	54		
1886	-6	1936	24	1986	55		
1887	-6	1937	24	1987	55		
1888	-6	1938	24	1988	56		
1889	-6	1939	24	1989	56		
1890	-6	1940	24	1990	57		
1891	-6	1941	25	1991	58		
1892	-6	1942	25	1992	58		
1893	-7	1943	26	1993	59		
1894	-6	1944	26	1994	60		
1895	-6	1945	27	1995	61		
1896	-6	1946	27	1996	62		
1897	-6	1947	28	1997	62		
1898	-5	1948	28	1998	63		
1899	-4	1949	29	1999	63		
1900	-3	1950	29	2000	64		
1901	-2	1951	30	2001	64		
1902	0	1952	30	2002	64		
1903	1	1953	30	2003	64		
1904	3	1954	31	2004	65		
1905	4	1955	31	2005	65		
1906	5	1956	31	2006	65		
1907	6	1957	32	2007	65		
1908	8	1958	32	2008	65		
1909	9	1959	33	2009	66		

About Rique Pottenger

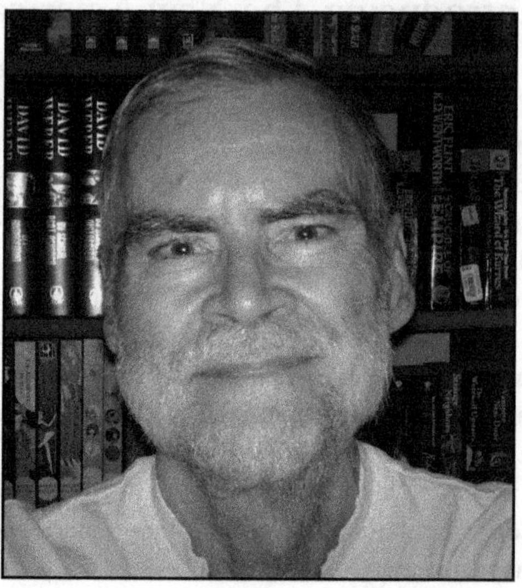

Rique Pottenger was born on September 16, 1949 in Tucson, Arizona at 6:18 am. He has a B.Sc. in Math and Astronomy from the University of Arizona and an M.S. in Computer Science from UCLA. Though never formally trained in astrology, he has absorbed quite a bit of it over the years, as he is the eldest son of Zipporah Dobyns. Maritha Pottenger is his sister. Rique had intended to become a mathematician until he discovered computer programming, and he has now been a programmer for more than 40 years. He has written programs for machines from 8 to 32 bits, running under many different operating systems.

From 1984 to 2004, Rique was employed at Astro Computing Services and ACS Publications where he programmed some of the company's most popular interpreted reports. After the death of founder Neil F. Michelsen in 1990, Rique became responsible for maintaining and improving Astro's production programs. This included his taking the major role in implementing Michelsen's wishes to switch from main frame computers to a modern and faster Windows based PC network. After designing and programming the new system, and recommending new equipment, Rique then trained the staff in how to use the new system. Later, Rique programmed the company's Electronic Astrologer software series. He also assumed responsibility for maintaining and improving the ACS Atlas database. Rique is now retired and lives with his cats in Opelika, Alabama.

Other Titles by Rique Pottenger

The Asteroid Ephemeris 1900-2050 with Chiron and the Black Moon
The American Ephemeris 2001-2010
The New American Ephemeris 2007-2020
The New American Ephemeris for the 21st Century 2000-2100 at Midnight
The New American Ephemeris Trans-Century Edition 1950-2050, Midnight and Noon

And Revisions to:

The American Ephemeris for the 20th Century 1900-2000, Midnight and Noon
The American Ephemeris for the 21st Century 2000-2050, Midnight and Noon
Tables of Planetary Phenomena

KEY TO THE EPHEMERIS
EPHEMERIDENSCHLÜSSEL
COMMENT COMPRENDRE LES EPHEMERIDES
CLAVE PARA LAS EFEMERIDES

Planets	Planeten	Planètes	Los Planetas
☉ Sun	☉ Sonne	☉ Soleil	☉ El Sol
☽ Moon	☽ Mond	☽ Lune	☽ La luna
☊ Moon's node	☊ Knotenpunkt des Mondes	☊ Le noeud lunaire	☊ El nodo lunar
☿ Mercury	☿ Merkur	☿ Mercure	☿ Mercurio
♀ Venus	♀ Venus	♀ Vénus	♀ Venus
♂ Mars	♂ Mars	♂ Mars	♂ Marte
♃ Jupiter	♃ Jupiter	♃ Jupiter	♃ Júpiter
♄ Saturn	♄ Saturn	♄ Saturne	♄ Saturno
♅ Uranus	♅ Uranus	♅ Uranus	♅ Urano
♆ Neptune	♆ Neptun	♆ Neptune	♆ Neptuno
♇ Pluto	♇ Pluto	♇ Pluton	♇ Plutón
⚳ Ceres	⚳ Ceres	⚳ Ceres	⚳ Ceres
⚴ Pallas	⚴ Pallas	⚴ Pallas	⚴ Pallas
⚵ Juno	⚵ Juno	⚵ Juno	⚵ Juno
⚶ Vesta	⚶ Vesta	⚶ Vesta	⚶ Vesta
⯰ Eris	⯰ Eris	⯰ Eris	⯰ Eris
🝻 Haumea	🝻 Haumea	🝻 Haumea	🝻 Haumea
🝼 Makemake	🝼 Makemake	🝼 Makemake	🝼 Makemake

Signs	Tierkreiszeichen	Signes	Los Signos
♈ Aries	♈ Widder	♈ Bélier	♈ Aries
♉ Taurus	♉ Stier	♉ Taureau	♉ Tauro
♊ Gemini	♊ Zwillinge	♊ Gémeaux	♊ Géminis
♋ Cancer	♋ Krebs	♋ Cancer	♋ Cáncer
♌ Leo	♌ Löwe	♌ Lion	♌ Leo
♍ Virgo	♍ Jungfrau	♍ Vierge	♍ Virgo
♎ Libra	♎ Waage	♎ Balance	♎ Libra
♏ Scorpio	♏ Skorpion	♏ Scorpion	♏ Escorpion
♐ Sagittarius	♐ Schütze	♐ Sagittaire	♐ Sagitario
♑ Capricorn	♑ Steinbock	♑ Capricorne	♑ Capricornio
♒ Aquarius	♒ Wassermann	♒ Verseau	♒ Acuario
♓ Pisces	♓ Fische	♓ Poissons	♓ Piscis

Major Aspects	Wichtige Aspekte	Aspects Majeurs	Los aspectos mayores
☌ conjunction	☌ Konjunktion	☌ conjonction	☌ la conjunción
⚹ sextile	⚹ Sextaler	⚹ sextil	⚹ el sextil
□ square	□ Quadratisch	□ carré	□ la cuadratura
△ trine	△ Trigon	△ trigon	△ el trígono
☍ opposition	☍ Opposition	☍ opposition	☍ la oposición

Minor Aspects	Unwichtige Aspekte	Aspects Mineurs	Los aspectos menores
⚼ sesquisquare	⚼ Anderthalbquadratisch	⚼ sesquicarré	⚼ la sesquicuadratura
⚻ quincunx	⚻ Quincunx	⚻ quinconce	⚻ el quinconce
⚺ semisextile	⚺ Halbsextal	⚺ semisextil	⚺ el semisextil
∠ semisquare	∠ Halbquadratisch	∠ semicarré	∠ el semicuadratura

Aspects in Declination	Aspekte in Deklination	Aspects en declination	Los aspectos en declinación
∥ parallel	∥ Parallel	∥ paralléle	∥ paralelo
⋕ contraparallel	⋕ Gegenparallel	⋕ contreparalléle	⋕ contraparalelo

In the Longitude box, shaded positions are retrograde, and unshaded positions are direct. D indicates stationary going direct. R indicates stationary going retrograde, except on the second day of the month, where it merely indicates retrograde, unless the first day of the month is not shaded, in which case the R indicates stationary going retrograde after all.

Im Länge Kasten, Positionen mit die Schattierung rückläufig sind, und Positionen ohne Schattierung direkt sind. D zeigt feststehend geht direkt an. R zeigt feststehend geht rückläufig an, außer auf dem zweiten Tag des Monats, wo es nur rückläufig anzeigt, es sei denn der erste Tag vom Monat keine Schattierung hat, in dem der R doch feststehend geht rückläufig anzeigt.

Dans la boîte de Longitude, les positions avec ombragers sont rétrogrades, et les positions sans ombragers pas sont directes. D indique tourner à l'arrêt direct. R indique tourner à l'arrêt rétrograde, sauf sur le deuxième jour du mois, où il indique simplement rétrograde, à moins que le premier jour du mois n'est pas ombragé, dans lequel reconnaît le R indique tourner à l'arrêt rétrograde après tout.

En la caja de la Longitud, las posiciones dadas sombra son las posiciones retrógradas y sin sombrear son directas. D indica la curva inmóvil dirige. R indica la curva inmóvil retrógrado, menos en el segundo día del mes, donde solamente indica retrógrado, a menos que el primer día del mes no sea dado sombra, en que embala la R indica la curva inmóvil retrógrado.

Moon Phenomena
● new Moon
☽ first quarter
O full
☾ third quarter
● Solar eclipse
T = Total
P = Partial
A = Annular
● Lunar eclipse
T = Total
P = Partial
A = Appulse

Mondersheinungen
Neumond
erstes Viertel
Vollmond
letztes Viertel
Sonnenfinsternis
T = totale
P = partielle
A = ringförmig
Mondfinsternis
T = totale
P = partielle
A = appulse

Phénomènes Lunaires
nouvelle Lune
premier quartier
pleine Lune
dernier quartier
éclipse du Soleil
T = totale
P = partielle
A = annulaire
éclipse de la Lune
T = totale
P = partielle
A = appulse

Fenómenos Lunares
la luna nueva
la creciente
la luna llena
la luna menguante
el eclipse solar
T = total
P = parcial
A = annular
el eclipse lunar
T = total
P = parcial
A = acercamiento

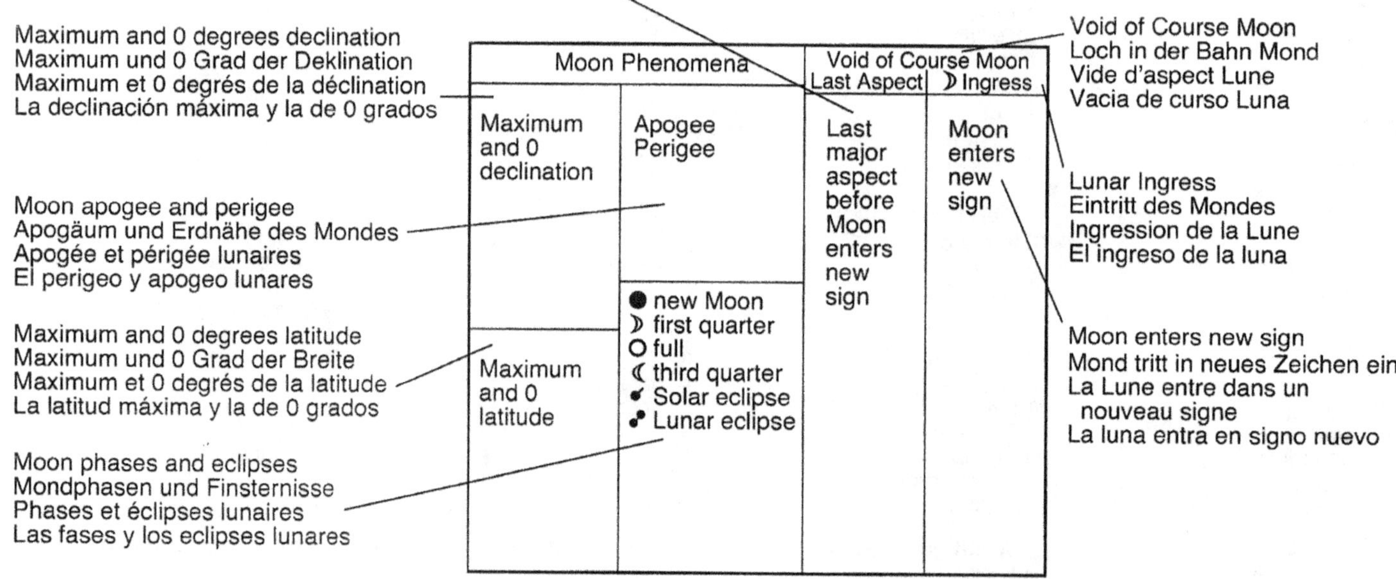

Sidereal Times are given for midnight (0h) Ephemeris Time at 0° longitude (Greenwich).
All planetary positions are given for midnight (0h) Ephemeris Time except Moon 12 hour positions which are given for noon Ephemeris Time.
Aspect and Moon phenomena times are given in Ephemeris Time.

Sternzeiten sind für Null Uhr Mitternacht (0h) Ephemeriden–Zeit bei 0° geographische Länge (Greenwich) angegeben.
Alle Stellungen der Gestirne für 0 Uhr Mitternacht Ephemeriden–Zeit mit Ausnahme der Mond 12–Stunden Positionen, die für 12 Uhr mittags Ephemeriden–Zeit angegeben sind.
Aspekt– und Monderscheinungszeiten sind in Ephemeriden–Zeit angegeben.

Temps Sidéraux donnés pour minuit (0h) Temps Ephéméride a 0° de longitude (Greenwich).
Toutes les positions planétaires sont données pour minuit (0h) Temps Ephéméride, sauf pour les positions lunaires de 12 Heures indiquées pour midi, Temps Ephéméride.
Les heures des aspects et des phénomènes lunaires sont données en Temps Ephéméride.

El Tiempo sidereal dado es el de medianoche (0h) Tiempo de Efemérides a 0° longitud (en Greenwich).
Todas las posiciones planetarias son calculadas a la medianoche (0h) Tiempo de Efemérides, con la excepción de las posiciones de la luna de 12 horas calculadas al mediodía Tiempo de Efemérides.
La hora de los fenómenos de la luna y de los aspectos es dada en Tiempo de Efemérides.

January 2020

LONGITUDE

Day	Sid.Time	☉	☽	☽ 12 hour	Mean ☊	True ☊	☿	♀	♂	⚳	♃	♄	⚷	♅	♆	♇
	h m s	° ' "	° ' "	° ' "	° '	° '	° '	° '	° '	° '	° '	° '	° '	° '	° '	° '
1 W	6 40 28	10♑00 31	16♓07 44	22♓04 31	8♋14.3	8♋23.0	4♑22.9	14♒24.5	28♏23.0	17♑54.3	6♑40.2	21♑23.7	1♈35.8	2♉41.6	16♓15.9	22♑23.1
2 Th	6 44 25	11 01 41	28 00 35	3♈56 32	8 11.1	8R 22.8	5 57.6	15 38.0	29 03.4	18 18.3	6 54.0	21 30.7	1 36.8	2R 41.1	16 17.0	22 25.1
3 F	6 48 21	12 02 51	9♈52 55	15 50 21	8 07.9	8D 22.7	7 32.5	16 51.5	29 43.8	18 42.3	7 07.9	21 37.8	1 37.9	2 40.7	16 18.2	22 27.1
4 Sa	6 52 18	13 04 01	21 49 26	27 50 45	8 04.7	8 22.8	9 07.8	18 04.9	0♐24.2	19 06.2	7 21.7	21 44.8	1 39.1	2 40.3	16 19.5	22 29.1
5 Su	6 56 14	14 05 10	3♉54 51	10♉02 19	8 01.6	8 23.1	10 43.5	19 18.3	1 04.6	19 30.2	7 35.5	21 51.9	1 40.3	2 40.0	16 20.7	22 31.1
6 M	7 00 11	15 06 19	16 13 39	22 29 18	7 58.4	8 23.7	12 19.4	20 31.6	1 45.0	19 54.2	7 49.3	21 58.9	1 41.6	2 39.7	16 22.0	22 33.1
7 Tu	7 04 07	16 07 28	28 49 41	5♊15 08	7 55.2	8 24.5	13 55.8	21 44.9	2 25.5	20 18.2	8 03.0	22 06.0	1 42.9	2 39.4	16 23.3	22 35.1
8 W	7 08 04	17 08 36	11♊45 54	18 22 09	7 52.0	8 25.3	15 32.6	22 58.1	3 05.9	20 42.2	8 16.8	22 13.1	1 44.3	2 39.2	16 24.7	22 37.1
9 Th	7 12 01	18 09 45	25 03 56	1♋51 11	7 48.8	8R 26.0	17 09.8	24 11.3	3 46.4	21 06.1	8 30.6	22 20.2	1 45.7	2 39.1	16 26.1	22 39.1
10 F	7 15 57	19 10 53	8♋43 44	15 41 18	7 45.7	8 26.2	18 47.3	25 24.4	4 26.9	21 30.1	8 44.3	22 27.3	1 47.2	2 39.0	16 27.5	22 41.1
11 Sa	7 19 54	20 12 00	22 43 29	29 49 45	7 42.5	8 25.9	20 25.4	26 37.4	5 07.5	21 54.1	8 58.0	22 34.4	1 48.7	2D 39.0	16 28.9	22 43.1
12 Su	7 23 50	21 13 08	6♌59 30	14♌12 04	7 39.3	8 24.9	22 03.8	27 50.4	5 48.0	22 18.1	9 11.7	22 41.5	1 50.3	2 39.0	16 30.4	22 45.1
13 M	7 27 47	22 14 15	21 26 44	28 42 42	7 36.1	8 23.4	23 42.7	29 03.3	6 28.6	22 42.1	9 25.4	22 48.6	1 51.9	2 39.1	16 31.9	22 47.2
14 Tu	7 31 43	23 15 22	5♍59 14	13♍15 36	7 33.0	8 21.4	25 22.1	0♓16.2	7 09.2	23 06.0	9 39.1	22 55.7	1 53.6	2 39.2	16 33.4	22 49.2
15 W	7 35 40	24 16 28	20 31 06	27 45 07	7 29.8	8 19.5	27 01.9	1 29.0	7 49.9	23 30.0	9 52.7	23 02.8	1 55.3	2 39.4	16 34.9	22 51.2
16 Th	7 39 36	25 17 35	4♎57 06	12♎06 37	7 26.6	8 17.9	28 42.2	2 41.7	8 30.5	23 53.9	10 06.4	23 10.0	1 57.0	2 39.6	16 36.5	22 53.2
17 F	7 43 33	26 18 41	19 13 18	26 16 52	7 23.4	8D 17.0	0♒23.0	3 54.3	9 11.2	24 17.9	10 20.0	23 17.1	1 58.8	2 39.9	16 38.1	22 55.2
18 Sa	7 47 30	27 19 48	3♏17 09	10♏14 01	7 20.3	8 16.9	2 04.2	5 06.9	9 51.9	24 41.8	10 33.5	23 24.2	2 00.7	2 40.2	16 39.7	22 57.2
19 Su	7 51 26	28 20 54	17 07 25	23 57 20	7 17.1	8 17.7	3 45.8	6 19.5	10 32.6	25 05.8	10 47.1	23 31.3	2 02.6	2 40.6	16 41.3	22 59.2
20 M	7 55 23	29 22 00	0♐43 49	7♐26 54	7 13.9	8 19.1	5 27.9	7 31.9	11 13.3	25 29.7	11 00.6	23 38.4	2 04.5	2 41.1	16 43.0	23 01.2
21 Tu	7 59 19	0♒23 05	14 06 39	20 43 09	7 10.7	8 20.7	7 10.3	8 44.3	11 54.1	25 53.6	11 14.1	23 45.5	2 06.5	2 41.5	16 44.7	23 03.2
22 W	8 03 16	1 24 10	27 16 28	3♑46 39	7 07.6	8R 21.9	8 53.1	9 56.6	12 34.9	26 17.6	11 27.6	23 52.5	2 08.6	2 42.1	16 46.4	23 05.2
23 Th	8 07 12	2 25 15	10♑13 46	16 37 53	7 04.4	8 22.3	10 36.2	11 08.8	13 15.7	26 41.5	11 41.0	23 59.6	2 10.7	2 42.7	16 48.1	23 07.2
24 F	8 11 09	3 26 19	22 59 03	29 17 18	7 01.2	8 21.5	12 19.5	12 21.0	13 56.5	27 05.3	11 54.4	24 06.7	2 12.8	2 43.3	16 49.9	23 09.2
25 Sa	8 15 06	4 27 23	5♒32 43	11♒45 21	6 58.0	8 19.2	14 02.9	13 33.0	14 37.3	27 29.2	12 07.8	24 13.7	2 15.0	2 44.0	16 51.7	23 11.2
26 Su	8 19 02	5 28 25	17 55 19	24 02 42	6 54.9	8 15.6	15 46.4	14 45.0	15 18.2	27 53.1	12 21.1	24 20.8	2 17.2	2 44.8	16 53.5	23 13.2
27 M	8 22 59	6 29 27	0♓07 41	6♓10 25	6 51.7	8 10.8	17 29.8	15 56.9	15 59.0	28 16.9	12 34.4	24 27.8	2 19.5	2 45.6	16 55.3	23 15.2
28 Tu	8 26 55	7 30 27	12 11 08	18 10 07	6 48.5	8 05.4	19 12.9	17 08.7	16 39.9	28 40.7	12 47.6	24 34.8	2 21.7	2 46.5	16 57.1	23 17.1
29 W	8 30 52	8 31 27	24 07 39	0♈04 06	6 45.3	7 59.9	20 55.6	18 20.4	17 20.8	29 04.5	13 00.8	24 41.8	2 24.1	2 47.4	16 59.0	23 19.1
30 Th	8 34 48	9 32 25	5♈59 52	11 55 24	6 42.1	7 54.9	22 37.7	19 32.0	18 01.7	29 28.3	13 14.0	24 48.7	2 26.5	2 48.3	17 00.9	23 21.0
31 F	8 38 45	10♒33 23	17 51 10	23 47 42	6♋39.0	7♋51.1	24♒18.9	20♓43.5	18♐42.7	29♑52.1	13♑27.1	24♑55.7	2♈28.9	2♉49.3	17♓02.8	23♑23.0

1st of Month

Julian Day # 2458849.5
Obliquity 23°26'10"
SVP 4♓59'06"
GC 27♐07.1
Eris 23♈13.9R

Day	⚴	Day	⚵	Day	⚶
1	22♐51.6	1	17♒21.8	1	12♉06.4
6	24 56.0	6	18 20.7	6	12 16.3
11	26 59.2	11	19 12.9	11	12 36.5
16	29 01.0	16	19 57.9	16	13 06.4
21	1♑01.5	21	20 35.3	21	13 45.5
26	3 00.2	26	21 04.5	26	14 33.1
31	4 57.1	31	21 25.1	31	15 28.6

DECLINATION and LATITUDE

Day	☉ Decl	☽ Decl	☽ Lat	☽ 12h Decl	☿ Decl	☿ Lat	♀ Decl	♀ Lat	♂ Decl	♂ Lat	⚳ Decl	⚳ Lat	♃ Decl	♃ Lat	♄ Decl	♄ Lat
1 W	23S04	9S59	4S54	7S48	24S38	1S16	18S16	1S50	19S27	0N22	26S13	4S01	23S11	0N05	21S41	0N03
2 Th	22 59	5 34	5 12	3 16	24 40	1 21	17 54	1 50	19 36	0 21	26 11	4 02	23 10	0 05	21 40	0 03
3 F	22 53	0 57	5 17	1N24	24 40	1 26	17 31	1 49	19 45	0 20	26 09	4 03	23 10	0 05	21 39	0 03
4 Sa	22 48	3N44	5 08	6 03	24 38	1 31	17 08	1 48	19 55	0 20	26 06	4 04	23 09	0 05	21 38	0 03
5 Su	22 41	8 20	4 46	10 33	24 35	1 36	16 44	1 48	20 03	0 19	26 04	4 06	23 08	0 05	21 37	0 03
6 M	22 35	12 41	4 11	14 43	24 31	1 40	16 20	1 47	20 12	0 19	26 02	4 07	23 07	0 05	21 36	0 03
7 Tu	22 28	16 36	3 22	18 19	24 26	1 44	15 55	1 46	20 21	0 18	25 60	4 08	23 07	0 05	21 35	0 03
8 W	22 20	19 50	2 23	21 07	24 18	1 47	15 30	1 45	20 29	0 17	25 57	4 10	23 06	0 05	21 34	0 03
9 Th	22 12	22 07	1 13	22 49	24 10	1 51	15 05	1 44	20 38	0 17	25 55	4 11	23 05	0 05	21 33	0 03
10 F	22 04	23 11	0N02	23 11	23 60	1 54	14 39	1 42	20 46	0 16	25 52	4 12	23 04	0 04	21 32	0 02
11 Sa	21 55	22 48	1 18	22 04	23 48	1 57	14 13	1 41	20 54	0 15	25 50	4 14	23 04	0 04	21 30	0 02
12 Su	21 46	20 58	2 31	19 31	23 35	1 59	13 47	1 40	21 02	0 15	25 47	4 15	23 03	0 04	21 29	0 02
13 M	21 36	17 45	3 36	15 43	23 21	2 01	13 20	1 38	21 09	0 14	25 44	4 16	23 02	0 04	21 28	0 02
14 Tu	21 26	13 27	4 27	10 59	23 04	2 03	12 53	1 36	21 17	0 14	25 41	4 18	23 01	0 04	21 27	0 02
15 W	21 15	8 22	5 01	5 38	22 47	2 04	12 25	1 35	21 24	0 13	25 38	4 19	23 00	0 04	21 26	0 02
16 Th	21 05	2 51	5 15	0 03	22 28	2 05	11 57	1 33	21 31	0 12	25 36	4 20	22 59	0 04	21 25	0 02
17 F	20 53	2S44	5 10	5S28	22 07	2 06	11 29	1 31	21 38	0 12	25 33	4 22	22 58	0 04	21 24	0 02
18 Sa	20 41	8 07	4 46	10 38	21 45	2 06	11 01	1 29	21 45	0 11	25 30	4 23	22 57	0 04	21 23	0 02
19 Su	20 29	13 00	4 06	15 11	21 21	2 06	10 32	1 27	21 51	0 10	25 27	4 24	22 56	0 04	21 21	0 02
20 M	20 17	17 09	3 13	18 53	20 55	2 05	10 03	1 25	21 58	0 09	25 23	4 26	22 55	0 04	21 20	0 02
21 Tu	20 04	20 21	2 10	21 31	20 28	2 04	9 34	1 23	22 04	0 09	25 20	4 27	22 54	0 03	21 19	0 02
22 W	19 51	22 24	1 01	22 58	19 60	2 02	9 05	1 20	22 10	0 08	25 17	4 29	22 53	0 03	21 18	0 02
23 Th	19 37	23 13	0S10	23 09	19 30	1 60	8 35	1 18	22 16	0 07	25 14	4 30	22 52	0 03	21 17	0 02
24 F	19 23	22 47	1 19	22 08	18 59	1 57	8 05	1 15	22 22	0 07	25 10	4 31	22 51	0 03	21 16	0 01
25 Sa	19 09	21 12	2 24	20 02	18 26	1 54	7 35	1 13	22 27	0 06	25 07	4 33	22 50	0 03	21 15	0 01
26 Su	18 54	18 38	3 20	17 02	17 51	1 50	7 05	1 10	22 32	0 05	25 03	4 34	22 49	0 03	21 13	0 01
27 M	18 39	15 16	4 06	13 21	17 16	1 45	6 35	1 08	22 38	0 04	24 60	4 36	22 48	0 03	21 12	0 01
28 Tu	18 23	11 19	4 41	9 11	16 39	1 40	6 04	1 05	22 42	0 04	24 56	4 37	22 46	0 03	21 11	0 01
29 W	18 08	6 58	5 03	4 42	16 00	1 34	5 33	1 02	22 47	0 03	24 53	4 39	22 45	0 03	21 10	0 01
30 Th	17 52	2 23	5 12	0 04	15 21	1 28	5 03	0 59	22 52	0 02	24 49	4 40	22 44	0 03	21 09	0 01
31 F	17S35	2N16	5S07	4N35	14S41	1S20	4S32	0S56	22S56	0N01	24S45	4S41	22S43	0N03	21S08	0N01

Day	⚷ Decl	⚷ Lat	♅ Decl	♅ Lat	♆ Decl	♆ Lat	♇ Decl	♇ Lat
1	3N19	2N55	11N57	0S30	6S22	1S02	22S13	0S39
6	3 20	2 54	11 56	0 29	6 19	1 01	22 12	0 40
11	3 22	2 53	11 56	0 29	6 17	1 01	22 11	0 40
16	3 24	2 52	11 56	0 29	6 14	1 01	22 10	0 40
21	3 27	2 51	11 57	0 29	6 10	1 01	22 08	0 41
26	3 31	2 50	11 58	0 29	6 07	1 01	22 07	0 41
31	3N34	2N49	12N00	0S29	6S03	1S01	22S06	0S42

Day	⚴ Decl	⚴ Lat	⚵ Decl	⚵ Lat	⚶ Decl	⚶ Lat	Eris Decl	Eris Lat
1	3N40	26N57	5S15	1N41	9N12	6S34	1S55	11S46
6	3 48	27 09	5 23	1 57	9 34	6 14	1 55	11 45
11	3 58	27 23	5 27	2 14	9 59	5 55	1 54	11 45
16	4 11	27 37	5 28	2 31	10 26	5 36	1 53	11 44
21	4 27	27 53	5 25	2 49	10 54	5 18	1 53	11 43
26	4 46	28 10	5 19	3 08	11 25	5 01	1 52	11 42
31	5N07	28N28	5S08	3N28	11N56	4S44	1S51	11S42

Moon Phenomena

Max/0 Decl (dy hr mn)
3 4:52 0 N
10 6:04 23N13
16 12:13 0 S
23 3:36 23S13
30 12:19 0 N

Max/0 Lat (dy hr mn)
2 20:58 5S17
9 23:30 0 N
16 5:36 5N16
22 20:33 0 S
30 3:52 5S12

Perigee/Apogee (dy hr m kilometers)
2 1:31 a 404580
13 20:22 p 365960
29 21:28 a 405392

PH (dy hr mn)
☽ 3 4:47 12♈15
○ 10 19:22 20♋00
☊ 10 19:11 A 0.895
☾ 17 13:00 26♎52
● 24 21:43 4♒22

Void of Course Moon

Last Aspect			☽ Ingress
2 2:15	♂ △	♈	2 4:02
4 1:19	♇ □	♉	4 16:16
6 12:09	♇ △	♊	7 2:12
8 22:17	♀ △	♋	9 8:44
10 23:59	♇ ☍	♌	11 12:17
13 13:43	♀ ☍	♍	13 14:08
15 12:13	☿ △	♎	15 15:44
17 13:00	☉ □	♏	17 18:22
19 21:23	☉ ⚹	♐	19 22:42
21 4:47	♆ □	♑	22 5:01
24 2:10	♄ ☌	♒	24 13:22
25 19:08	☿ ☌	♓	26 23:45
29 1:10	♄ ⚹	♈	29 11:52

DAILY ASPECTARIAN

1 W ☽☌♆ 0:16 · ☽∠♅ 3:09 · ☽⚹⚳ 3:42 · ☽⚹♄ 10:44 · ☽⚹♇ 12:40 · ☽∥♆ 19:46

2 Th ☽△♂ 2:15 · ☽∠♀ 5:55 · ☽☌⚷ 7:18 · ☽⊻♅ 9:27 · ☽#⚷ 11:44 · ♀⊻♆ 12:57 · ☿☌♃ 16:43 · ☽□♃ 18:20 · ☽□☿ 18:33 · ♀∠⚷ 19:30

3 F ☊ D 4:28 · ☉□☽ 4:47 · ♂ ♐ 9:39 · ☽⚼♂ 10:21 · ☽⊻♆ 12:57 · ☽⚹♀ 15:39 · ☽□⚳ 18:22 · ☽∥⚷ 21:56 · ☽□♄ 23:51

4 Sa ☽□♇ 1:19 · ☽#♆ 13:30 · ☽⚻♂ 18:04 · ☽∠♆ 18:55 · ☽⊻⚷ 19:34 · ☽☌♅ 21:32

5 Su ♀⊻⚳ 5:47 · ☽△♃ 7:21 · ☽△☿ 15:19 · ☽∥♅ 19:43 · ☉△☽ 21:38 · ♂△⚷ 21:54

6 M ☽⚹♆ 0:16 · ☽∠⚷ 0:54 · ☽△⚳ 7:18 · ☽□♀ 9:09 · ☽△♄ 11:08 · ☽△♇ 12:09 · ☽⚼♃ 12:52 · ☽#♀ 20:00

7 Tu ☽⚼☿ 0:13 · ☉⚼☽ 4:41 · ☽⚹⚷ 5:25 · ☉⚹♆ 6:22 · ☽☍♂ 7:07 · ☽⊻♅ 7:10 · ♀⊻♄ 7:40 · ♂⚻♅ 8:15 · ☽⚼⚳ 12:29 · ☽⚼♄ 15:34 · ☽⚼♇ 16:21 · ♀⊻♇ 16:55 · ☽⚻♃ 17:29

8 W ☽#♂ 6:08 · ♀∠♃ 7:33 · ☽⚻☿ 7:51 · ☽□♆ 8:28 · ☉⚻☽ 10:36 · ☽∠♅ 10:42 · ☿⚹♆ 13:04 · ☽⚻⚳ 16:42 · ☽#♄ 16:45 · ☽⚻♄ 19:05 · ☽⚻♇ 19:41 · ☽△♀ 22:17

9 Th ☽#♇ 0:58 · ☉#☽ 1:06 · ☉∥♇ 2:47 · ☽□⚷ 11:52 · ☽⚹♅ 13:24 · ☽⚻♂ 16:10 · ☽#♃ 19:22 · ☊ R 23:37

10 F ☽☍♃ 0:01 · ☽⚼♀ 3:11 · ☽△♆ 13:20 · ☉☌☿ 15:21 · ☿∠♂ 16:33 · ☽#♃ 17:03 · ☉∠♂ 18:44 · ☽⚼♂ 19:21 · ☉☍☽ 19:22 · ☽☍☿ 19:34 · ☽☍⚳ 22:34 · ☽☍♄ 23:44 · ☽☍♇ 23:59

11 Sa ♅ D 1:50 · ☽⚻♀ 7:13 · ☽#♇ 10:28 · ☽⚼♆ 14:48 · ☉#☽ 15:00 · ☽△⚷ 15:21 · ☽□♅ 16:44 · ☽#♄ 18:42 · ☽△♂ 21:55 · ☽#♂ 23:26

12 Su ☽⚻♃ 3:44 · ☿☌⚳ 4:35 · ☿☌♄ 9:52 · ☿☌♇ 10:15 · ☽⚻♆ 15:51 · ☽⚼⚷ 16:24 · ♄☌♇ 17:00

13 M ☉⚻☽ 1:24 · ☽⚻⚳ 2:08 · ☽⚻♇ 2:13 · ☽⚻♄ 2:17 · ☽⚻☿ 4:14 · ☽⚼♃ 5:00 · ⚳☌♇ 5:34 · ⚳☌♄ 9:22 · ☉☌♇ 13:22 · ☽☍♀ 13:43 · ☉☌♄ 15:17 · ☽⚻⚷ 17:14 · ☉☌⚳ 17:58 · ☽△♅ 18:30 · ♀ ♓ 18:40 · ☉∥♄ 20:58

14 Tu ☽□♂ 2:01 · ☽⚼♇ 3:02 · ☽#♀ 3:08 · ☽⚼♄ 3:14 · ☽⚼⚳ 3:35 · ☉⚼☽ 4:01 · ☿∥♃ 5:09 · ☽△♃ 6:08 · ☽∥♅ 7:26 · ☽⚼☿ 8:10 · ☉∥♂ 12:27 · ☽☍♆ 17:29 · ☽⚼♅ 19:16

15 W ♂∠♇ 0:49 · ☽△♇ 3:53 · ☽△♄ 4:14 · ☽△⚳ 5:05 · ♂∥♄ 5:39 · ☉△☽ 6:42 · ♀⊻⚷ 8:53 · ♂∠♄ 9:18 · ☽#♆ 9:25 · ☽△☿ 12:13 · ☽☍⚷ 18:59 · ☽⚻♀ 19:53 · ☽⚻♅ 20:10 · ☽∥⚷ 21:38 · ♀⚹♅ 23:19

16 Th ♀#♅ 0:58 · ☽⚹♂ 6:15 · ☽□♃ 8:46 · ☿ ♒ 18:32 · ☽⚻♆ 19:37 · ☿∥♇ 21:11 · ☽⚼♀ 23:25

17 F ☽#⚷ 2:57 · ☽□♇ 6:17 · ☽□♄ 6:57 · ☽∠♂ 8:51 · ☽□⚳ 8:52 · ♂∠⚳ 9:39 · ☉□☽ 13:00 · ☊ D 13:03 · ☽∥♆ 15:17 · ☿∠♆ 18:06 · ☽⚼♆ 21:12 · ☽□☿ 21:37 · ☽⚻⚷ 21:48 · ☽☍♅ 22:56 · ☿⚹⚷ 23:09 · ☿∥♂ 23:45

18 Sa ☽△♀ 3:27 · ☿□♅ 8:33 · ⚴ ♑ 10:34 · ☽⊻♂ 11:57 · ☽∥♀ 12:37 · ☽⚹♃ 12:46 · ☽#♅ 18:30 · ☿∥♄ 23:13 · ☽△♆ 23:14 · ☽⚼⚷ 23:52

19 Su ☽⚹♇ 10:19 · ☽⚹♄ 11:20 · ♂⊻♃ 12:47 · ☽⚹⚳ 14:26 · ☽∠♃ 15:29 · ☉⚹☽ 21:23

20 M ☽△⚷ 2:24 · ☽⚻♅ 3:29 · ☽⚹☿ 9:41 · ♀∠♇ 10:00 · ☽∠♇ 13:04 · ☽□♀ 13:21 · ☽∠♄ 14:16 · ☉ ♒ 14:56 · ☽∠⚳ 18:01 · ☽⊻♃ 18:43 · ☽☌♂ 19:48 · ☉∥☽ 21:43

21 Tu ♀∠♄ 0:26 · ☽∥☿ 1:01 · ☉∠☽ 2:30 · ☽□♆ 4:47 · ☽⚼♅ 6:30 · ☽∥♄ 9:40 · ♂∥♇ 16:09 · ☽⊻♇ 16:18 · ☽∠☿ 16:51 · ☽⊻♄ 17:43 · ☽∥♇ 19:59 · ☽∥♂ 20:15 · ☽⊻⚳ 22:08

22 W ☉⊻☽ 8:15 · ☉∠♆ 8:59 · ☽□⚷ 9:00 · ☽∥♃ 9:48 · ☽△♅ 10:01 · ☉∥☿ 13:51 · ☉⚹⚷ 18:04 · ☊ R 20:35

23 Th ☽⊻☿ 0:48 · ☽⚹♀ 1:53 · ☽☌♃ 2:46 · ☽⊻♂ 5:59 · ☉□♅ 6:56 · ☽⚹♆ 12:21 · ♀⚹♃ 13:08 · ♀∠⚳ 16:13 · ☿⊻♃ 17:18 · ☽∥♃ 22:21

24 F ☽☌♇ 0:19 · ☿⊻♀ 1:08 · ☽☌♄ 2:10 · ☽∥♂ 7:45 · ☽☌⚳ 8:03 · ☽∠♀ 9:11 · ☽∠♂ 11:59 · ☽∥♇ 12:02 · ☽∠♆ 16:54 · ☽⚹⚷ 17:39 · ☽□♅ 18:36 · ☉☌☽ 21:43 · ☽∥♄ 23:31

25 Sa ☽⊻♃ 12:57 · ☿⚹♂ 13:11 · ☽⊻♀ 17:09 · ☽⚹♂ 18:36 · ☽☌☿ 19:08 · ☉∥☽ 21:36 · ☽⊻♆ 21:59 · ☽∠⚷ 22:45

26 Su ☽∥☿ 7:19 · ☽⊻♇ 10:24 · ☽⊻♄ 12:43 · ☿⊻♆ 15:51 · ☽∠♃ 18:51 · ☽⊻⚳ 20:14 · ☿∠⚷ 21:33

27 M ♀□♂ 1:38 · ☽⊻⚷ 4:22 · ☽⚹♅ 5:13 · ☉⊻☽ 13:48 · ☽∠♇ 16:11 · ☽∠♄ 18:44 · ♀☌♆ 20:01 · ☽#♅ 20:07 · ♀∥♆ 23:02

28 Tu ☽⚹♃ 1:14 · ☽∠⚳ 3:06 · ☽□♂ 9:31 · ☽☌♆ 9:35 · ♂□♆ 10:35 · ☽☌♀ 11:03 · ☽∠♅ 11:13 · ♀∠♅ 12:47 · ♂∥♃ 16:10 · ☽⊻☿ 16:28 · ☽⚹♇ 22:22 · ☉∠☽ 22:40

29 W ☽⚹♄ 1:10 · ☽∥♆ 4:44 · ☽∥♀ 8:25 · ☽⚹⚳ 10:20 · ♂⚼♅ 15:56 · ☽☌⚷ 16:47 · ☽⊻♅ 17:32 · ☽#⚷ 17:56

30 Th ☽∠☿ 3:51 · ☉⚹☽ 7:51 · ☿⊻♇ 10:27 · ☽□♃ 14:56 · ☽⊻♆ 22:22

31 F ☽△♂ 1:50 · ☽⊻♀ 6:27 · ☽∥⚷ 6:47 · ⚳ ♒ 8:02 · ☿⊻♄ 9:27 · ☽#♀ 10:32 · ☽□♇ 11:12 · ☽□♄ 14:25 · ☽⚹☿ 15:11 · ☽#♆ 19:38

February 2020

LONGITUDE

Day	Sid.Time	☉	☽	☽ 12 hour	Mean ☊	True ☊	☿	♀	♂	⚳	♃	♄	⚷	♅	♆	♇
	h m s	° ' "	° ' "	° ' "	° '	° '	° '	° '	° '	° '	° '	° '	° '	° '	° '	° '
1 Sa	8 42 41	11♒34 19	29♈45 34	5♉45 20	6♋35.8	7♋48.7	25♒58.9	21♓54.9	19♐23.6	0♒15.8	13♑40.1	25♑02.6	2♈31.3	2♉50.4	17♓04.7	23♑24.9
2 Su	8 46 38	12 35 14	11♉47 36	17 52 59	6 32.6	7D 47.8	27 37.4	23 06.2	20 04.6	0 39.5	13 53.2	25 09.5	2 33.8	2 51.5	17 06.7	23 26.9
3 M	8 50 34	13 36 07	24 02 07	0♊15 34	6 29.4	7 48.4	29 14.0	24 17.4	20 45.6	1 03.2	14 06.1	25 16.4	2 36.4	2 52.6	17 08.6	23 28.8
4 Tu	8 54 31	14 36 59	6♊33 57	12 57 46	6 26.2	7 49.8	0♓48.2	25 28.5	21 26.6	1 26.8	14 19.0	25 23.3	2 39.0	2 53.9	17 10.6	23 30.7
5 W	8 58 28	15 37 50	19 27 31	26 03 36	6 23.1	7 51.5	2 19.5	26 39.5	22 07.6	1 50.5	14 31.9	25 30.1	2 41.6	2 55.1	17 12.6	23 32.6
6 Th	9 02 24	16 38 40	2♋46 19	9♋35 48	6 19.9	7R 52.6	3 47.4	27 50.3	22 48.6	2 14.1	14 44.7	25 36.9	2 44.2	2 56.4	17 14.6	23 34.5
7 F	9 06 21	17 39 28	16 32 07	23 35 07	6 16.7	7 52.3	5 11.3	29 01.0	23 29.7	2 37.7	14 57.5	25 43.7	2 46.9	2 57.8	17 16.6	23 36.3
8 Sa	9 10 17	18 40 15	0♌44 27	7♌59 39	6 13.5	7 50.3	6 30.5	0♈11.6	24 10.8	3 01.2	15 10.2	25 50.5	2 49.6	2 59.2	17 18.7	23 38.2
9 Su	9 14 14	19 41 00	15 19 59	22 44 36	6 10.4	7 46.3	7 44.2	1 22.0	24 51.9	3 24.7	15 22.9	25 57.2	2 52.4	3 00.6	17 20.7	23 40.1
10 M	9 18 10	20 41 44	0♍12 29	7♍42 30	6 07.2	7 40.5	8 51.8	2 32.3	25 33.0	3 48.2	15 35.4	26 03.9	2 55.1	3 02.1	17 22.8	23 41.9
11 Tu	9 22 07	21 42 27	15 13 28	22 44 11	6 04.0	7 33.6	9 52.5	3 42.5	26 14.1	4 11.7	15 48.0	26 10.6	2 57.9	3 03.7	17 24.9	23 43.7
12 W	9 26 04	22 43 09	0♎13 28	7♎40 14	6 00.8	7 26.6	10 45.5	4 52.6	26 55.3	4 35.1	16 00.4	26 17.2	3 00.8	3 05.3	17 27.0	23 45.6
13 Th	9 30 00	23 43 49	15 03 34	22 22 40	5 57.7	7 20.3	11 30.2	6 02.5	27 36.5	4 58.5	16 12.8	26 23.8	3 03.7	3 06.9	17 29.1	23 47.4
14 F	9 33 57	24 44 28	29 36 55	6♏45 53	5 54.5	7 15.7	12 05.8	7 12.2	28 17.7	5 21.9	16 25.2	26 30.4	3 06.6	3 08.6	17 31.2	23 49.1
15 Sa	9 37 53	25 45 06	13♏49 19	20 47 07	5 51.3	7D 13.1	12 31.8	8 21.8	28 58.9	5 45.2	16 37.5	26 36.9	3 09.5	3 10.3	17 33.4	23 50.9
16 Su	9 41 50	26 45 43	27 39 18	4♐26 02	5 48.1	7 12.4	12 47.8	9 31.2	29 40.1	6 08.5	16 49.7	26 43.4	3 12.5	3 12.1	17 35.5	23 52.7
17 M	9 45 46	27 46 19	11♐07 34	17 44 11	5 44.9	7 13.0	12R 53.4	10 40.6	0♑21.4	6 31.7	17 01.8	26 49.9	3 15.5	3 13.9	17 37.7	23 54.4
18 Tu	9 49 43	28 46 54	24 16 14	0♑44 05	5 41.8	7 14.2	12 48.6	11 49.8	1 02.6	6 55.0	17 13.9	26 56.3	3 18.5	3 15.8	17 39.9	23 56.1
19 W	9 53 39	29 47 28	7♑08 05	13 28 37	5 38.6	7R 14.8	12 33.4	12 58.8	1 43.9	7 18.1	17 25.9	27 02.7	3 21.5	3 17.7	17 42.1	23 57.9
20 Th	9 57 36	0♓48 00	19 46 00	26 00 32	5 35.4	7 13.9	12 08.3	14 07.6	2 25.2	7 41.3	17 37.8	27 09.0	3 24.6	3 19.6	17 44.3	23 59.6
21 F	10 01 33	1 48 31	2♒12 31	8♒22 12	5 32.2	7 10.8	11 33.8	15 16.3	3 06.6	8 04.4	17 49.7	27 15.3	3 27.7	3 21.6	17 46.5	24 01.2
22 Sa	10 05 29	2 49 00	14 29 46	20 35 26	5 29.1	7 05.1	10 50.9	16 24.8	3 47.9	8 27.4	18 01.5	27 21.6	3 30.8	3 23.6	17 48.7	24 02.9
23 Su	10 09 26	3 49 28	26 39 21	2♓41 39	5 25.9	6 56.7	10 00.6	17 33.1	4 29.3	8 50.5	18 13.2	27 27.8	3 34.0	3 25.7	17 50.9	24 04.5
24 M	10 13 22	4 49 54	8♓42 30	14 42 02	5 22.7	6 46.2	9 04.3	18 41.2	5 10.6	9 13.4	18 24.8	27 33.9	3 37.2	3 27.8	17 53.1	24 06.2
25 Tu	10 17 19	5 50 19	20 40 23	26 37 43	5 19.5	6 34.4	8 03.6	19 49.2	5 52.0	9 36.3	18 36.3	27 40.0	3 40.4	3 30.0	17 55.4	24 07.8
26 W	10 21 15	6 50 42	2♈34 14	8♈30 08	5 16.3	6 22.3	6 59.9	20 57.0	6 33.4	9 59.2	18 47.8	27 46.1	3 43.6	3 32.2	17 57.6	24 09.4
27 Th	10 25 12	7 51 02	14 25 41	20 21 10	5 13.2	6 10.9	5 54.9	22 04.5	7 14.8	10 22.0	18 59.1	27 52.1	3 46.8	3 34.4	17 59.8	24 10.9
28 F	10 29 08	8 51 21	26 16 56	2♉13 21	5 10.0	6 01.2	4 50.3	23 11.9	7 56.2	10 44.8	19 10.4	27 58.1	3 50.1	3 36.7	18 02.1	24 12.5
29 Sa	10 33 05	9♓51 39	8♉10 53	14 10 00	5♋06.8	5♋53.9	3♓47.6	24♈19.0	8♑37.6	11♒07.5	19♑21.6	28♑04.0	3♈53.4	3♉39.0	18♓04.3	24♑14.0

1st of Month

Julian Day # 2458880.5
Obliquity 23°26[illegible]1"
SVP 4♓59[illegible]1"
GC 27♐07.2
Eris 23♈15.7

Day	⚴	⚵	⚶
1	5♑20.2	21♎28.1	15♉40.6
6	7 14.6	21 37.9	16 44.8
11	9 06.6	21 38.3R	17 55.5
16	10 56.3	21 29.3R	19 12.1
21	12 43.3	21 10.6R	20 34.2
26	14 27.3	20 42.3R	22 01.3

DECLINATION and LATITUDE

Day	☉ Decl	☽ Decl	☽ Lat	☽ 12h Decl	☿ Decl	☿ Lat	♀ Decl	♀ Lat	♂ Decl	♂ Lat	⚳ Decl	⚳ Lat	♃ Decl	♃ Lat	♄ Decl	♄ Lat
1 Sa	17S19	6N52	4S49	9N06	13S59	1S12	4S01	0S53	23S00	0N01	24S42	4S43	22S42	0N02	21S06	0N01
2 Su	17 02	11 16	4 19	13 20	13 17	1 03	3 30	0 49	23 04	0S00	24 38	4 44	22 40	0 02	21 05	0 01
3 M	16 44	15 17	3 36	17 06	12 35	0 54	2 58	0 46	23 08	0 01	24 34	4 46	22 39	0 02	21 04	0 01
4 Tu	16 27	18 44	2 42	20 11	11 52	0 43	2 27	0 43	23 11	0 02	24 30	4 47	22 38	0 02	21 03	0 01
5 W	16 09	21 23	1 39	22 19	11 09	0 32	1 56	0 39	23 15	0 03	24 26	4 49	22 37	0 02	21 02	0 01
6 Th	15 51	22 57	0 28	23 15	10 26	0 20	1 24	0 36	23 18	0 03	24 22	4 50	22 35	0 02	21 00	0 01
7 F	15 32	23 11	0N47	22 46	9 43	0 07	0 53	0 32	23 21	0 04	24 18	4 52	22 34	0 02	20 59	0 00
8 Sa	15 14	21 57	2 01	20 47	9 02	0N06	0 22	0 28	23 23	0 05	24 14	4 54	22 33	0 02	20 58	0 00
9 Su	14 55	19 14	3 09	17 23	8 21	0 20	0N10	0 25	23 26	0 06	24 10	4 55	22 31	0 02	20 57	0 00
10 M	14 36	15 13	4 05	12 49	7 42	0 35	0 41	0 21	23 28	0 07	24 06	4 57	22 30	0 02	20 56	0 00
11 Tu	14 16	10 12	4 45	7 27	7 05	0 50	1 13	0 17	23 30	0 07	24 02	4 58	22 29	0 01	20 55	0 00
12 W	13 56	4 35	5 06	1 40	6 31	1 06	1 44	0 13	23 32	0 08	23 58	4 60	22 27	0 01	20 53	0 00
13 Th	13 37	1S14	5 05	4S06	5 59	1 22	2 16	0 09	23 34	0 09	23 53	5 01	22 26	0 01	20 52	0 00
14 F	13 16	6 53	4 45	9 33	5 30	1 38	2 47	0 05	23 36	0 10	23 49	5 03	22 24	0 01	20 51	0S00
15 Sa	12 56	12 02	4 08	14 21	5 06	1 54	3 18	0 01	23 37	0 11	23 45	5 05	22 23	0 01	20 50	0 00
16 Su	12 35	16 26	3 17	18 17	4 45	2 10	3 49	0N03	23 38	0 12	23 41	5 06	22 22	0 01	20 49	0 00
17 M	12 15	19 52	2 16	21 10	4 29	2 26	4 20	0 07	23 39	0 13	23 36	5 08	22 20	0 01	20 48	0 00
18 Tu	11 54	22 10	1 09	22 51	4 17	2 40	4 51	0 12	23 39	0 13	23 32	5 10	22 19	0 01	20 46	0 00
19 W	11 33	23 14	0 01	23 18	4 10	2 54	5 22	0 16	23 40	0 14	23 27	5 11	22 17	0 01	20 45	0 00
20 Th	11 11	23 05	1S07	22 34	4 08	3 07	5 53	0 20	23 40	0 15	23 23	5 13	22 16	0 01	20 44	0 00
21 F	10 50	21 46	2 10	20 43	4 11	3 18	6 24	0 25	23 40	0 16	23 18	5 15	22 14	0 01	20 43	0 01
22 Sa	10 28	19 26	3 06	17 57	4 18	3 27	6 54	0 29	23 40	0 17	23 14	5 16	22 13	0 00	20 42	0 01
23 Su	10 06	16 16	3 52	14 25	4 30	3 34	7 25	0 34	23 40	0 18	23 09	5 18	22 12	0 00	20 41	0 01
24 M	9 44	12 27	4 28	10 21	4 47	3 39	7 55	0 38	23 39	0 19	23 05	5 20	22 10	0 00	20 40	0 01
25 Tu	9 22	8 10	4 52	5 54	5 06	3 42	8 25	0 43	23 38	0 20	23 00	5 22	22 09	0 00	20 38	0 01
26 W	8 60	3 36	5 02	1 16	5 29	3 43	8 55	0 48	23 37	0 21	22 56	5 23	22 07	0 00	20 37	0 01
27 Th	8 37	1N04	5 00	3N25	5 54	3 42	9 24	0 52	23 36	0 22	22 51	5 25	22 06	0S00	20 36	0 01
28 F	8 15	5 43	4 45	7 59	6 21	3 38	9 54	0 57	23 35	0 23	22 46	5 27	22 04	0 00	20 35	0 01
29 Sa	7S52	10N11	4S17	12N17	6S49	3N33	10N23	1N02	23S33	0S24	22S42	5S29	22S03	0S00	20S34	0S01

Day	⚷ Decl	⚷ Lat	♅ Decl	♅ Lat	♆ Decl	♆ Lat	♇ Decl	♇ Lat
1	3N35	2N49	12N00	0S29	6S02	1S01	22S06	0S42
6	3 40	2 48	12 03	0 28	5 58	1 01	22 05	0 42
11	3 44	2 47	12 05	0 28	5 54	1 01	22 03	0 43
16	3 49	2 47	12 08	0 28	5 50	1 01	22 02	0 43
21	3 55	2 46	12 12	0 28	5 46	1 01	22 01	0 44
26	4N00	2N45	12N15	0S28	5S42	1S01	22S01	0S44

Day	⚴ Decl	⚴ Lat	⚵ Decl	⚵ Lat	⚶ Decl	⚶ Lat	Eris Decl	Eris Lat
1	5N11	28N32	5S06	3N32	12N03	4S41	1S50	11S41
6	5 35	28 52	4 50	3 52	12 36	4 25	1 49	11 41
11	6 02	29 13	4 31	4 14	13 09	4 11	1 48	11 40
16	6 31	29 35	4 07	4 35	13 44	3 56	1 47	11 39
21	7 02	29 59	3 40	4 57	14 18	3 43	1 45	11 38
26	7N35	30N23	3S09	5N20	14N53	3S30	1S44	11S38

Moon Phenomena

Max/0 Decl
dy hr mn
6 16:10 23N16
12 18:54 0 S
19 8:55 23S19
26 18:30 0 N

Perigee/Apogee
dy hr m kilometers
10 20:29 p 360463
26 11:35 a 406278

Max/0 Lat
dy hr mn
6 9:00 0 N
12 11:33 5N08
19 0:13 0 S
26 7:34 5S03

PH dy hr mn
☽ 2 1:43 12♉40
○ 9 7:34 20♌00
☾ 15 22:18 26♏41
● 23 15:33 4♓29

Void of Course Moon

Last Aspect	☽ Ingress
31 15:11 ☿ ⚹	♉ 1 0:29
3 11:29 ☿ □	♊ 3 11:30
5 14:21 ♀ □	♋ 5 19:04
7 15:44 ♄ ☍	♌ 7 22:46
9 16:10 ♂ △	♍ 9 23:40
11 18:27 ♂ □	♎ 11 23:38
13 21:41 ♂ ⚹	♏ 14 0:39
15 22:21 ♄ ⚹	♐ 16 4:08
18 9:04 ☉ ⚹	♑ 18 10:38
20 14:19 ♄ ☌	♒ 20 19:43
22 4:09 ♀ ⚹	♓ 23 6:38
25 14:13 ♄ ⚹	♈ 25 18:48
28 3:26 ♄ □	♉ 28 7:31

DAILY ASPECTARIAN

1 Sa ☽□⚳ 1:03; ☽∠♆ 4:40; ☽⊻⚷ 5:33; ☽☌♅ 6:11; ☽⚼♂ 9:50; ☽∠♀ 15:53; ♀#⚷ 19:06

2 Su ☊ D 1:29; ☉□☽ 1:43; ☽△♃ 4:13; ☽∥♅ 4:18; ♀⚹♇ 7:08; ☽#☿ 10:00; ☽⚹♆ 10:31; ☽∠⚷ 11:25; ☽⊼♂ 17:15; ☿∠♃ 21:43; ☽△♇ 22:55

3 M ☽⚹♀ 0:33; ☽△♄ 2:25; ☉#☽ 8:48; ☽⚼♃ 9:57; ☽□☿ 11:29; ☿ ♓ 11:39; ☽△⚳ 13:57; ☉⊻♃ 15:01; ☽⚹⚷ 16:32; ☽⊻♅ 17:02; ☿#♅ 18:29; ♀⚹♄ 22:03

4 Tu ☽⚼♇ 3:41; ☽⚼♄ 7:15; ☿⊻⚳ 13:34; ☽⊼♃ 14:46; ☉△☽ 16:21; ☽⚼⚳ 19:02; ☽□♆ 19:51; ☽#♄ 20:14; ☽∠♅ 21:10

5 W ☽☍♂ 5:08; ☿⊻⚷ 6:06; ☽⊼♇ 7:28; ☽#♇ 8:37; ☿⚹♅ 9:44; ☽⊼♄ 11:05; ☽□♀ 14:21; ☽#♃ 16:39; ☉⚼☽ 21:50; ☽⊼⚳ 23:01; ☽□⚷ 23:56

6 Th ☽⚹♅ 0:18; ⚳∠♆ 0:36; ☽△☿ 2:01; ☊ R 9:02; ☉⊻♆ 14:41; ☽☍♃ 21:15

7 F ☽△♆ 1:16; ☉⊼☽ 2:04; ☉∠⚷ 3:04; ♂⊻♇ 4:04; ☽⚼☿ 6:54; ⚳⚹⚷ 10:37; ☽☍♇ 12:04; ☽⊼♂ 12:27; ☽#♃ 15:38; ☽☍♄ 15:44; ♀ ♈ 20:04; ⚳□♅ 21:48; ☽#♇ 22:34; ☽△♀ 23:00

8 Sa ☽⚼♆ 2:37; ☽△⚷ 3:29; ☽□♅ 3:44; ☽☍⚳ 3:54; ☽#♄ 10:18; ☽⊼☿ 10:27; ☽⚼♂ 14:38; ⚵ R 18:00

9 Su ☽⊼♃ 0:05; ☽⚼♀ 1:50; ☽⊼♆ 3:17; ☽⚼⚷ 4:08; ☉☍☽ 7:34; ☽⊼♇ 13:31; ☽△♂ 16:10; ☽⊼♄ 17:18; ☿∠♇ 20:13

10 M ☽⚼♃ 0:37; ☉#☽ 3:28; ☽⊼♀ 4:03; ☽⊼⚷ 4:21; ☽△♅ 4:32; ☽⊼⚳ 5:55; ♀☌⚷ 8:07; ♀⊻♅ 10:25; ☽⚼♇ 13:37; ☽☍☿ 14:52; ☽∥♅ 15:25; ☽⚼♄ 17:29; ♂⊻♄ 21:31

11 Tu ☽△♃ 0:56; ☽☍♆ 3:30; ☽⚼♅ 4:32; ☽⚼⚳ 6:31; ☉⊼☽ 11:06; ☽△♇ 13:37; ♀⚹⚳ 15:00; ☽#☿ 15:04; ☽△♄ 17:38; ☽□♂ 18:27; ☽#♆ 18:32

12 W ☽∥⚷ 3:25; ☽☍⚷ 4:30; ☽⊼♅ 4:37; ☽△⚳ 7:12; ☽☍♀ 8:07; ☽∥♀ 10:47; ☉⚼☽ 12:58; ☽⊼☿ 17:56; ☿∠♄ 19:34

13 Th ☉⊻♇ 1:27; ☽□♃ 1:55; ☽⊼♆ 3:58; ☽#♀ 4:41; ☿∥♆ 5:06; ☽#⚷ 10:38; ☽□♇ 14:22; ☉△☽ 15:18; ☽∥☿ 18:27; ☽□♄ 18:47; ☽∥♆ 19:34; ☽⚼☿ 19:39; ☽⚹♂ 21:41

14 F ☽⚼♆ 4:52; ☽⊼⚷ 5:52; ☽☍♅ 5:55; ☽□⚳ 9:55; ☽⊼♀ 13:53; ☽△☿ 21:44

15 Sa ☽∠♂ 0:17; ☽#♅ 0:26; ☉∥☽ 4:13; ☽⚹♃ 4:53; ☽△♆ 6:26; ☽⚼⚷ 7:29; ♅⊻⚷ 16:11; ☽⚹♇ 17:22; ☽⚼♀ 18:00; ☉□☽ 22:18; ☽⚹♄ 22:21; ☊ D 22:22; ☉⊻♄ 22:58

16 Su ♀∥⚷ 0:05; ☽⊻♂ 3:44; ☽∠♃ 7:29; ☽⊼♅ 9:50; ☽△⚷ 9:51; ♂ ♑ 11:34; ♂∥⚳ 12:13; ☽⚹⚳ 15:30; ☽∠♇ 20:00; ☽△♀ 23:07

17 M ☿ R 0:55; ☽∠♄ 1:17; ☽□☿ 3:11; ☿#♀ 4:22; ☉#♅ 6:29; ☽∥♄ 8:16; ☽⊻♃ 10:53; ☽□♆ 11:50; ☽⚼♅ 12:56; ☽∠⚳ 19:32; ☽∥♇ 22:17; ☽⊻♇ 23:23

18 Tu ☽∥♃ 2:14; ☽⊻♄ 4:59; ☉⚹☽ 9:04; ☽☌♂ 13:17; ☽△♅ 16:46; ☽□⚷ 16:53; ☿⊻♀ 17:04

19 W ☊ R 0:14; ☽⊻⚳ 0:20; ☉ ♓ 4:58; ☽⚹☿ 9:58; ☽□♀ 12:10; ☉∠☽ 15:46; ♀#♆ 19:15; ☽☌♃ 19:51; ☽⚹♆ 20:06; ☿∠♄ 23:32

20 Th ☽☌♇ 8:08; ☽∠☿ 13:35; ☽☌♄ 14:19; ♃⚹♆ 15:57; ☽∥♃ 17:16; ☽∥♇ 20:34; ☉⊻☽ 23:09

21 F ☽∠♆ 1:06; ☽⊻♂ 1:51; ☽□♅ 2:15; ☽⚹⚷ 2:27; ♂△♅ 9:11; ☽☌⚳ 11:47; ☽∥♄ 12:10; ♂□⚷ 13:17; ☽⊻☿ 17:16

22 Sa ☽⚹♀ 4:09; ☉∠♃ 6:08; ☽⊻♆ 6:32; ☽⊻♃ 7:03; ☽∠⚷ 7:56; ☽∠♂ 8:58; ☉⚹♅ 14:14; ☉⊻⚷ 17:31; ☽⊻♇ 18:53

23 Su ☽⊻♄ 1:37; ♀⊻♆ 6:28; ☽∠♀ 12:56; ☽∠♃ 13:16; ☽⚹♅ 13:30; ☽⊻⚷ 13:48; ☉☌☽ 15:33; ☽⚹♂ 16:31; ♀□♃ 17:00; ☿⊻⚳ 21:20; ☿∠♇ 23:17

24 M ☽☌☿ 0:40; ☽∠♇ 0:47; ☽⊻⚳ 1:04; ☽#♅ 1:15; ☽∠♄ 7:47; ☉∥☽ 16:50; ☽☌♆ 18:27; ☽∠♅ 19:37; ☽⚹♃ 19:46; ☽⊻♀ 22:06; ☽#♀ 22:47

25 Tu ☉⚹♂ 2:07; ☽⚹♇ 6:59; ☽∠⚳ 8:11; ☽∥♆ 13:06; ☽⚹♄ 14:13; ☽∥☿ 15:00; ☽#⚷ 21:55

26 W ☉☌☿ 1:46; ☽⊻♅ 1:58; ☽☌⚷ 2:21; ☉#♀ 2:21; ☿⚹♂ 6:00; ☽⊻☿ 8:13; ☽□♂ 8:34; ☉⊻☽ 9:27; ☿∠♀ 11:24; ☿∥♆ 11:54; ☽⚹⚳ 15:30

27 Th ☽⊻♆ 7:15; ☽□♃ 9:23; ☽∠☿ 12:03; ☽∥⚷ 15:16; ☽☌♀ 17:07; ☉∠☽ 18:38; ☽□♇ 19:48; ☽#♆ 23:43

28 F ☽□♄ 3:26; ☽#☿ 3:42; ☉∠♇ 8:37; ☉#☽ 12:24; ☿∠♃ 12:51; ☽∠♆ 13:41; ☽☌♅ 14:51; ☽⊻⚷ 15:19; ☽⚹☿ 15:52; ☿⊻⚷ 21:51; ♀□♇ 22:09

29 Sa ☽△♂ 0:57; ☽∥♀ 1:19; ☿⚹♅ 3:14; ☉⚹☽ 3:41; ☽□⚳ 6:06; ☽∥♅ 12:05; ☽⚹♆ 19:51; ☽∠⚷ 21:31; ☽△♃ 22:42

LONGITUDE

Day	Sid.Time	☉	☽	☽ 12 hour	Mean☊	True☊	☿	♀	♂	⚳	♃	♄	⚷	♅	♆	♇
	h m s	° ' "	° ' "	° ' "	° '	° '	° '	° '	° '	° '	° '	° '	° '	° '	° '	° '
1 Su	10 37 01	10♓51 54	20♉11 12	26♉15 05	5♋03.6	5♋49.2	2♓48.0	25♈26.0	9♑19.0	11♒30.2	19♑32.7	28♑09.9	3♈56.7	3♉41.4	18♓06.6	24♑15.5
2 M	10 40 58	11 52 07	2♊22 12	8♊33 12	5 00.5	5D 47.0	1R 52.7	26 32.7	10 00.5	11 52.8	19 43.7	28 15.7	4 00.0	3 43.8	18 08.9	24 17.0
3 Tu	10 44 55	12 52 18	14 48 40	21 09 16	4 57.3	5 46.5	1 02.6	27 39.1	10 42.0	12 15.4	19 54.6	28 21.4	4 03.3	3 46.2	18 11.1	24 18.5
4 W	10 48 51	13 52 27	27 35 34	4♋08 07	4 54.1	5R 46.9	0 18.4	28 45.4	11 23.4	12 37.9	20 05.4	28 27.1	4 06.7	3 48.7	18 13.4	24 19.9
5 Th	10 52 48	14 52 34	10♋47 26	17 33 53	4 50.9	5 47.0	29♒40.6	29 51.4	12 04.9	13 00.3	20 16.2	28 32.8	4 10.0	3 51.2	18 15.7	24 21.3
6 F	10 56 44	15 52 39	24 27 45	1♌29 08	4 47.7	5 45.6	29 09.5	0♉57.1	12 46.4	13 22.7	20 26.8	28 38.4	4 13.4	3 53.7	18 18.0	24 22.7
7 Sa	11 00 41	16 52 42	8♌37 56	15 53 52	4 44.6	5 42.0	28 45.2	2 02.6	13 27.9	13 45.1	20 37.3	28 43.9	4 16.8	3 56.3	18 20.3	24 24.1
8 Su	11 04 37	17 52 42	23 16 25	0♍44 48	4 41.4	5 35.6	28 27.7	3 07.8	14 09.4	14 07.3	20 47.8	28 49.4	4 20.2	3 58.9	18 22.5	24 25.5
9 M	11 08 34	18 52 41	8♍18 01	15 54 53	4 38.2	5 26.8	28 17.0	4 12.8	14 51.0	14 29.6	20 58.1	28 54.8	4 23.7	4 01.5	18 24.8	24 26.8
10 Tu	11 12 30	19 52 38	23 34 02	1♎14 00	4 35.0	5 16.3	28D 12.8	5 17.4	15 32.5	14 51.7	21 08.3	29 00.1	4 27.1	4 04.2	18 27.1	24 28.1
11 W	11 16 27	20 52 32	8♎53 19	16 30 33	4 31.9	5 05.4	28 14.9	6 21.8	16 14.1	15 13.8	21 18.4	29 05.4	4 30.5	4 06.9	18 29.4	24 29.4
12 Th	11 20 24	21 52 25	24 04 21	1♏33 33	4 28.7	4 55.4	28 23.0	7 25.9	16 55.7	15 35.8	21 28.4	29 10.7	4 34.0	4 09.6	18 31.6	24 30.7
13 F	11 24 20	22 52 16	8♏57 14	16 14 38	4 25.5	4 47.3	28 36.9	8 29.6	17 37.3	15 57.8	21 38.4	29 15.8	4 37.5	4 12.4	18 33.9	24 31.9
14 Sa	11 28 17	23 52 05	23 25 18	0♐28 57	4 22.3	4 41.9	28 56.1	9 33.1	18 18.9	16 19.7	21 48.2	29 20.9	4 40.9	4 15.1	18 36.2	24 33.1
15 Su	11 32 13	24 51 53	7♐25 32	14 15 09	4 19.1	4 39.0	29 20.5	10 36.2	19 00.5	16 41.5	21 57.8	29 25.9	4 44.4	4 18.0	18 38.4	24 34.3
16 M	11 36 10	25 51 39	20 58 06	27 34 44	4 16.0	4D 38.1	29 49.6	11 39.1	19 42.1	17 03.3	22 07.4	29 30.9	4 47.9	4 20.8	18 40.7	24 35.5
17 Tu	11 40 06	26 51 24	4♑05 29	10♑30 53	4 12.8	4R 38.1	0♓23.3	12 41.5	20 23.8	17 25.0	22 16.9	29 35.8	4 51.4	4 23.7	18 43.0	24 36.6
18 W	11 44 03	27 51 06	16 51 28	23 07 44	4 09.6	4 37.7	1 01.2	13 43.7	21 05.4	17 46.6	22 26.2	29 40.6	4 54.9	4 26.6	18 45.2	24 37.7
19 Th	11 47 59	28 50 47	29 20 15	5♒29 30	4 06.4	4 35.8	1 43.0	14 45.5	21 47.1	18 08.2	22 35.5	29 45.4	4 58.5	4 29.5	18 47.5	24 38.8
20 F	11 51 56	29 50 27	11♒35 58	17 40 05	4 03.3	4 31.4	2 28.5	15 46.9	22 28.8	18 29.6	22 44.6	29 50.1	5 02.0	4 32.5	18 49.7	24 39.9
21 Sa	11 55 53	0♈50 04	23 42 14	29 42 47	4 00.1	4 24.0	3 17.5	16 47.9	23 10.5	18 51.0	22 53.5	29 54.7	5 05.5	4 35.5	18 52.0	24 40.9
22 Su	11 59 49	1 49 39	5♓42 01	11♓40 12	3 56.9	4 13.7	4 09.8	17 48.6	23 52.1	19 12.4	23 02.4	29 59.3	5 09.0	4 38.5	18 54.2	24 41.9
23 M	12 03 46	2 49 13	17 37 35	23 34 21	3 53.7	4 00.9	5 05.1	18 48.9	24 33.8	19 33.6	23 11.1	0♒03.7	5 12.6	4 41.5	18 56.5	24 42.9
24 Tu	12 07 42	3 48 44	29 30 41	5♈26 45	3 50.5	3 46.4	6 03.4	19 48.7	25 15.5	19 54.8	23 19.7	0 08.1	5 16.1	4 44.6	18 58.7	24 43.9
25 W	12 11 39	4 48 14	11♈22 41	17 18 41	3 47.4	3 31.5	7 04.3	20 48.1	25 57.2	20 15.8	23 28.2	0 12.4	5 19.6	4 47.7	19 00.9	24 44.8
26 Th	12 15 35	5 47 41	23 14 54	29 11 31	3 44.2	3 17.4	8 07.9	21 47.1	26 38.9	20 36.8	23 36.6	0 16.7	5 23.2	4 50.8	19 03.1	24 45.7
27 F	12 19 32	6 47 07	5♉08 46	11♉06 55	3 41.0	3 05.2	9 13.9	22 45.6	27 20.6	20 57.8	23 44.8	0 20.8	5 26.7	4 53.9	19 05.3	24 46.6
28 Sa	12 23 28	7 46 30	17 06 14	23 07 05	3 37.8	2 55.6	10 22.2	23 43.7	28 02.3	21 18.6	23 52.9	0 24.9	5 30.2	4 57.0	19 07.5	24 47.4
29 Su	12 27 25	8 45 51	29 09 49	5♊14 53	3 34.6	2 49.0	11 32.8	24 41.2	28 44.0	21 39.3	24 00.8	0 28.9	5 33.7	5 00.2	19 09.7	24 48.2
30 M	12 31 21	9 45 10	11♊22 44	17 33 54	3 31.5	2 45.2	12 45.5	25 38.3	29 25.7	22 00.0	24 08.6	0 32.9	5 37.3	5 03.4	19 11.8	24 49.0
31 Tu	12 35 18	10♈44 26	23 48 53	0♋08 16	3♋28.3	2♋43.8	14♓00.3	26♉34.8	0♒07.4	22♒20.5	24♑16.3	0♒36.7	5♈40.8	5♉06.6	19♓14.0	24♑49.8

1st of Month

Julian Day # 2458909.5
Obliquity 23°26'12"
SVP 4♓58'58"
GC 27♐07.3
Eris 23♈26.3

Day	⚴
1	15♑48.1
6	17 26.1
11	19 00.4
16	20 30.8
21	21 56.8
26	23 18.1
31	24 34.2

Day	⚵
1	20♎13.0R
6	19 28.7R
11	18 36.4R
16	17 37.3R
21	16 32.7R
26	15 23.9R
31	14 12.8R

Day	⚶
1	23♉14.2
6	24 49.2
11	26 27.9
16	28 10.1
21	29 55.4
26	1♊43.6
31	3 34.4

DECLINATION and LATITUDE

Day	☉ Decl	☽ Decl	☽ Lat	☽ 12h Decl	☿ Decl	☿ Lat	♀ Decl	♀ Lat	♂ Decl	♂ Lat	⚳ Decl	⚳ Lat	♃ Decl	♃ Lat	♄ Decl	♄ Lat
1 Su	7S29	14N18	3S38	16N10	7S17	3N25	10N52	1N07	23S31	0S25	22S37	5S31	22S01	0S00	20S33	0S01
2 M	7 07	17 53	2 48	19 26	7 45	3 16	11 21	1 12	23 29	0 26	22 32	5 32	21 60	0 00	20 32	0 01
3 Tu	6 44	20 46	1 49	21 52	8 13	3 05	11 50	1 16	23 27	0 27	22 28	5 34	21 58	0 01	20 31	0 01
4 W	6 21	22 41	0 43	23 18	8 39	2 54	12 18	1 21	23 24	0 28	22 23	5 36	21 57	0 01	20 30	0 01
5 Th	5 57	23 26	0N27	23 19	9 04	2 41	12 46	1 26	23 22	0 29	22 18	5 38	21 55	0 01	20 28	0 02
6 F	5 34	22 49	1 37	21 58	9 27	2 28	13 14	1 31	23 19	0 30	22 13	5 40	21 54	0 01	20 27	0 02
7 Sa	5 11	20 45	2 45	19 11	9 49	2 14	13 41	1 36	23 16	0 31	22 09	5 42	21 52	0 01	20 26	0 02
8 Su	4 47	17 16	3 43	15 04	10 08	2 00	14 08	1 41	23 12	0 32	22 04	5 44	21 51	0 01	20 25	0 02
9 M	4 24	12 36	4 28	9 55	10 25	1 46	14 35	1 46	23 09	0 33	21 59	5 46	21 49	0 01	20 24	0 02
10 Tu	4 01	7 04	4 55	4 06	10 40	1 32	15 01	1 51	23 05	0 34	21 54	5 47	21 48	0 01	20 23	0 02
11 W	3 37	1 05	5 00	1S57	10 52	1 17	15 28	1 56	23 01	0 35	21 49	5 49	21 46	0 01	20 22	0 02
12 Th	3 13	4S55	4 45	7 48	11 03	1 03	15 53	2 01	22 57	0 36	21 45	5 51	21 45	0 02	20 21	0 02
13 F	2 50	10 32	4 10	13 05	11 11	0 50	16 19	2 06	22 53	0 37	21 40	5 53	21 43	0 02	20 20	0 02
14 Sa	2 26	15 24	3 19	17 29	11 17	0 36	16 44	2 11	22 49	0 38	21 35	5 55	21 42	0 02	20 19	0 02
15 Su	2 02	19 16	2 19	20 46	11 21	0 23	17 09	2 16	22 44	0 39	21 30	5 57	21 41	0 02	20 18	0 02
16 M	1 39	21 56	1 12	22 48	11 22	0 10	17 33	2 20	22 39	0 40	21 25	5 59	21 39	0 02	20 17	0 02
17 Tu	1 15	23 20	0 03	23 32	11 22	0S02	17 57	2 25	22 34	0 41	21 21	6 02	21 38	0 02	20 16	0 02
18 W	0 51	23 26	1S04	23 02	11 20	0 14	18 21	2 30	22 29	0 42	21 16	6 04	21 36	0 02	20 15	0 03
19 Th	0 28	22 21	2 07	21 24	11 15	0 25	18 44	2 35	22 23	0 43	21 11	6 06	21 35	0 02	20 15	0 03
20 F	0 04	20 13	3 02	18 48	11 09	0 36	19 07	2 40	22 18	0 44	21 06	6 08	21 34	0 02	20 14	0 03
21 Sa	0N20	17 12	3 48	15 26	11 01	0 47	19 29	2 45	22 12	0 46	21 01	6 10	21 32	0 03	20 13	0 03
22 Su	0 44	13 30	4 24	11 27	10 52	0 57	19 51	2 50	22 06	0 47	20 57	6 12	21 31	0 03	20 12	0 03
23 M	1 07	9 18	4 47	7 03	10 40	1 06	20 13	2 54	21 59	0 48	20 52	6 14	21 29	0 03	20 11	0 03
24 Tu	1 31	4 45	4 58	2 25	10 27	1 15	20 34	2 59	21 53	0 49	20 47	6 16	21 28	0 03	20 10	0 03
25 W	1 55	0 03	4 56	2N19	10 12	1 23	20 54	3 04	21 46	0 50	20 42	6 19	21 27	0 03	20 09	0 03
26 Th	2 18	4N40	4 42	6 59	9 56	1 31	21 15	3 09	21 40	0 51	20 38	6 21	21 25	0 03	20 08	0 03
27 F	2 42	9 14	4 14	11 25	9 38	1 39	21 34	3 13	21 33	0 52	20 33	6 23	21 24	0 03	20 08	0 03
28 Sa	3 05	13 29	3 36	15 26	9 19	1 46	21 54	3 18	21 26	0 54	20 28	6 25	21 23	0 03	20 07	0 03
29 Su	3 28	17 15	2 47	18 53	8 58	1 52	22 12	3 22	21 18	0 55	20 23	6 28	21 22	0 03	20 06	0 03
30 M	3 52	20 19	1 50	21 32	8 36	1 58	22 31	3 27	21 11	0 56	20 19	6 30	21 20	0 04	20 05	0 04
31 Tu	4N15	22N31	0S47	23N12	8S12	2S04	22N48	3N31	21S03	0S57	20S14	6S32	21S19	0S04	20S05	0S04

Day	⚷ Decl	⚷ Lat	♅ Decl	♅ Lat	♆ Decl	♆ Lat	♇ Decl	♇ Lat
1	4N05	2N45	12N19	0S28	5S38	1S01	21S60	0S45
6	4 11	2 44	12 23	0 28	5 34	1 01	21 59	0 45
11	4 18	2 44	12 27	0 28	5 29	1 01	21 58	0 46
16	4 24	2 43	12 32	0 27	5 25	1 01	21 58	0 47
21	4 31	2 43	12 37	0 27	5 21	1 01	21 57	0 47
26	4 38	2 42	12 42	0 27	5 16	1 01	21 57	0 48
31	4N44	2N42	12N48	0S27	5S12	1S01	21S57	0S48

Day	⚴ Decl	⚴ Lat	⚵ Decl	⚵ Lat	⚶ Decl	⚶ Lat	Eris Decl	Eris Lat
1	8N03	30N44	2S41	5N38	15N20	3S21	1S43	11S37
6	8 40	31 12	2 04	5 60	15 55	3 09	1 41	11 37
11	9 19	31 41	1 21	6 21	16 28	2 58	1 40	11 36
16	9 59	32 11	0 43	6 42	17 02	2 48	1 38	11 36
21	10 41	32 43	0 00	7 02	17 34	2 37	1 37	11 35
26	11 24	33 16	0N43	7 21	18 06	2 28	1 35	11 35
31	12N09	33N50	1N26	7N38	18N36	2S18	1S34	11S35

Moon Phenomena

Max/0 Decl

dy	hr mn	
5	1:35	23N27
11	4:16	0 S
17	14:02	23S32
25	0:14	0 N

Max/0 Lat

dy	hr mn	
4	15:00	0 N
10	18:07	5N01
17	1:01	0 S
24	8:27	4S59
31	16:52	0 N

Perigee/Apogee

dy	hr m		kilometers
10	6:31	p	357126
24	15:24	a	406692

PH	dy	hr mn	
☽	2	19:59	12♊42
○	9	17:49	19♍37
☾	16	9:35	26♐16
●	24	9:29	4♈12

Void of Course Moon

Last Aspect				☽ Ingress		
1	15:53	♄	△	♊	1	19:22
4	2:21	♀	⚹	♋	4	4:26
6	7:13	♄	☍	♌	6	9:29
8	8:14	☿	☍	♍	8	10:48
10	8:33	♄	△	♎	10	10:04
12	8:13	♄	□	♏	12	9:29
14	10:07	♄	⚹	♐	14	11:10
16	9:35	☉	□	♑	16	16:26
19	0:49	♄	☌	♒	19	1:17
20	9:01	♀	□	♓	21	12:34
23	14:52	♂	⚹	♈	24	0:59
26	7:18	♂	□	♉	26	13:38
28	23:06	♂	△	♊	29	1:39
30	15:11	♆	□	♋	31	11:44

DAILY ASPECTARIAN

1 Su ☉∥☿ 5:49; ☽△♇ 8:05; ☽⚼♂ 8:41; ☽⚺♀ 11:26; ☽△♄ 15:53; ☽□☿ 23:06; ♃∥♇ 23:45

2 M ☉⚺⚳ 0:27; ☽⚺♅ 2:40; ☽⚹⚷ 3:11; ☽⚼♃ 4:40; ☽⚼♇ 13:26; ☽⚻♂ 15:40; ☽△⚳ 18:58; ☽∠♀ 19:29; ☊ D 19:46; ☉□☽ 19:59; ☽⚼♄ 21:12; ☽⋕♄ 21:34

3 Tu ☽□♆ 6:25; ☽∠♅ 7:32; ☽⚻♃ 9:48; ☉∠♄ 12:51; ☽⋕♃ 13:13; ☽⋕♇ 13:39; ♀□♄ 16:46; ☽⚻♇ 17:56; ☽⋕⚳ 19:16

4 W ☽⚼⚳ 0:04; ☽⚻♄ 1:36; ☽⚹♀ 2:21; ♀∥♅ 2:56; ☽△☿ 4:45; ☿ R ♒ 11:09; ☽⚹♅ 11:27; ☽□⚷ 12:00; ☊ R 15:02; ☽⋕♂ 18:02; ☿⚹♀ 21:25

5 Th ☽☍♂ 2:26; ♀ ♉ 3:08; ☽⚻⚳ 4:04; ☉∠♀ 4:56; ☽⚼☿ 6:38; ☉△☽ 7:50; ☽⋕♂ 10:34; ☽△♆ 13:15; ☽☍♃ 16:57; ☽☍♇ 23:51

6 F ☉∥♆ 0:30; ☽☍♄ 7:13; ☽⚻☿ 7:48; ☽⋕⚳ 9:16; ☽⋕♇ 11:47; ☉⚼☽ 11:48; ☽□♀ 12:01; ☽⋕♃ 12:57; ☽⚼♆ 15:06; ☽□♅ 16:07; ☽△⚷ 16:41

7 Sa ☿⚺♄ 1:09; ☽⋕♄ 2:36; ☿∠♂ 6:44; ☽⚻♂ 8:24; ☽☍⚳ 8:42; ☉⚻☽ 14:36; ☽⚻♆ 16:02; ☽⚼⚷ 17:35; ☽⚻♃ 19:56; ♂⚺⚳ 21:23

8 Su ☽⚻♇ 1:52; ♀∠♆ 5:37; ☽☍☿ 8:14; ☽⚻♄ 8:59; ☽⚼♂ 9:55; ☉☌♆ 12:24; ☽∥♀ 15:16; ☽△♀ 17:01; ☽△♅ 17:12; ☽⚻⚷ 17:47; ♀☌♅ 19:39; ☽⚼♃ 20:16

9 M ☽∥♅ 0:48; ⚳∥♇ 1:46; ☽⚼♇ 1:49; ☉∠♅ 3:42; ♀⚺⚷ 4:16; ☉⋕⚷ 8:34; ☽⚼♄ 8:54; ☽⋕☿ 9:23; ☽⚻⚳ 10:00; ☽△♂ 10:49; ☽☍♆ 15:58; ☽⚼♅ 16:56; ☉☍☽ 17:49; ☽⚼♀ 18:29; ☽△♃ 20:09

10 Tu ☽△♇ 1:25; ☿ D 3:50; ☽⋕♆ 6:23; ☽⚻☿ 7:16; ☽△♄ 8:33; ☽⚼⚳ 10:06; ☽∥⚷ 11:16; ☉⋕☽ 13:14; ☽⚻♅ 16:29; ☽☍⚷ 17:06; ☽⚻♀ 19:44

11 W ☽⚼☿ 6:54; ☽△⚳ 10:14; ☽□♂ 12:07; ☉⚹♃ 12:28; ☽⚻♆ 15:10; ☉∥☽ 17:32; ☽□♃ 19:49; ☉⚻☽ 20:15; ☽⋕⚷ 21:31; ⚳∥♃ 22:00

12 Th ☽□♇ 0:42; ☽∥♆ 2:15; ☽△☿ 6:59; ☽□♄ 8:13; ☽⚼♆ 15:13; ☽☍♅ 16:15; ☽⚻⚷ 16:56; ☉⚼☽ 22:06; ☽☍♀ 23:11

13 F ☽∥☿ 3:01; ☽⋕♅ 9:09; ☽□⚳ 11:50; ☽⚹♂ 15:01; ☽△♆ 15:54; ☽⚼⚷ 17:42; ☽⚹♃ 21:15

14 Sa ☉△☽ 0:49; ☽⚹♇ 1:55; ☽⋕♀ 8:23; ☽□☿ 9:37; ☽⚹♄ 10:07; ♂⚹♆ 10:33; ☉⚹♇ 16:48; ☽∠♂ 17:46; ☽⚻♅ 18:33; ☽△⚷ 19:19; ☽∠♃ 23:11

15 Su ☽∠♇ 3:45; ☿⚺♄ 5:51; ☽⚻♀ 6:02; ☽∥♄ 8:02; ☽∠♄ 12:24; ☽⚹⚳ 16:47; ☽∥⚳ 18:34; ☽□♆ 19:53; ☽∥♃ 20:50; ☽⚼♅ 21:05; ☽⚺♂ 21:36

16 M ☽∥♇ 0:20; ☽⚺♃ 2:07; ☽⚺♇ 6:34; ☿ ♓ 7:44; ☽∥♂ 9:10; ☉□☽ 9:35; ☊ D 9:39; ☽⚼♀ 11:12; ☽⚺♄ 15:39; ☽⚹☿ 16:50; ☽∠⚳ 20:49

17 Tu ☽△♅ 0:34; ☊ R 1:04; ☽□⚷ 1:26; ☽△♀ 17:32; ☽∠☿ 22:19

18 W ☽⚺⚳ 1:48; ☽⚹♆ 3:38; ☽☌♂ 8:34; ☽☌♃ 10:48; ☽☌♇ 14:55; ☉⚹☽ 22:58; ☽∥♂ 23:24

19 Th ☽☌♄ 0:49; ☽⚺☿ 4:55; ☽∥♇ 5:19; ☽∠♆ 8:42; ☽∥♃ 10:03; ☽□♅ 10:05; ☽⚹⚷ 11:02; ☽∥⚳ 14:55; ☉⚹♄ 23:51; ☽∥♄ 23:52

20 F ☉ ♈ 3:51; ☉∠☽ 6:58; ☽⋕♀ 8:26; ☽□♀ 9:01; ♂☌♃ 11:36; ☽☌⚳ 14:03; ☽⚺♆ 14:21; ☽∠⚷ 16:47; ☽⚺♃ 22:22; ☽⚺♂ 22:53

21 Sa ⚳⚺♆ 1:12; ☽⚺♇ 1:57; ⚶ ♊ 5:11; ☽⚺♄ 12:29; ☉⚺☽ 15:32; ☽☌☿ 20:40; ☽⚹♅ 21:52; ☽⚺⚷ 22:53

22 Su ♄ ♒ 3:59; ☽∠♃ 4:45; ☽⋕♅ 5:06; ☽∠♂ 6:46; ☽∠♇ 8:03; ☿⚹♅ 13:20; ☽∥☿ 16:02; ☽∠♄ 18:48; ♀⋕♄ 22:11

23 M ☽⚹♀ 2:37; ☽☌♆ 2:40; ♀⚹♆ 3:09; ☿⚺⚷ 3:20; ☽⚺⚳ 4:01; ☽∠♅ 4:11; ♂☌♇ 5:22; ♂∥♇ 7:59; ☽⚹♃ 11:21; ☽⚹♇ 14:20; ☽⚹♂ 14:52; ☽∥♆ 21:10

24 Tu ☽⋕⚷ 0:53; ☽⚹♄ 1:16; ♀□⚳ 3:47; ☉☌☽ 9:29; ☽⚺♅ 10:37; ☽∠⚳ 11:15; ☽∠♀ 11:42; ☽☌⚷ 11:42; ♀∠⚷ 11:44; ♀⋕⚳ 12:33; ☽⚺☿ 14:28; ☉⋕☽ 15:17; ☉⚺♅ 23:45

25 W ⚳∠⚷ 5:11; ☉∥☽ 10:48; ☉☌⚷ 13:28; ☽⚺♆ 15:30; ☉∠⚳ 17:14; ☽⚹⚳ 18:31; ☽⚺♀ 20:47; ☽∠☿ 23:44; ☽∥⚷ 23:46

26 Th ☽□♃ 0:44; ☽□♇ 3:04; ☽⋕♆ 3:05; ☽□♂ 7:18; ☿∠♃ 12:02; ♀⋕♃ 12:24; ☽□♄ 14:16; ☽∠♆ 21:52; ♀⋕♂ 22:34; ☽☌♅ 23:30

27 F ☽⚺⚷ 0:36; ☽⋕☿ 2:01; ☉⚺☽ 3:36; ☽⚹☿ 9:04; ☿∠♇ 11:43; ☽∥♅ 19:36

28 Sa ☽⚹♆ 4:03; ♀△♃ 4:25; ♀⋕♇ 4:28; ☽∠⚷ 6:49; ☽□⚳ 8:39; ♂∥♃ 10:33; ☉∠☽ 12:20; ☽△♃ 13:40; ☽☌♀ 14:21; ☽△♇ 15:21; ☽△♂ 23:06

29 Su ☽△♄ 2:37; ♀△♇ 2:58; ☽⚺♅ 11:34; ☽⚹⚷ 12:41; ☽⚼♃ 19:35; ☉⚹☽ 20:33; ☽⚼♇ 20:57; ☽⋕♄ 21:56; ☽⋕⚳ 23:55

30 M ☽□☿ 2:59; ☽⚼♂ 6:17; ☽⋕♂ 7:47; ☽⚼♄ 8:09; ☽⋕♃ 9:47; ☽□♆ 15:11; ☽⋕♇ 16:42; ☽∠♅ 16:52; ♂ ♒ 19:44; ☽△⚳ 21:06

31 Tu ☽⚻♃ 0:53; ☽⚻♇ 1:56; ☽⚺♀ 5:41; ☽∥♀ 5:44; ☽⚻♂ 12:40; ☽⚻♄ 12:57; ☊ D 16:50; ♂☌♄ 18:32; ☽⚹♅ 21:25; ☽□⚷ 22:30

April 2020 LONGITUDE

Day	Sid.Time	☉	☽	☽ 12 hour	Mean☊	True☊	☿	♀	♂	⚳	♃	♄	⚷	♅	♆	♇
	h m s	° ' "	° ' "	° ' "	° '	° '	° '	° '	° '	° '	° '	° '	° '	° '	° '	° '
1 W	12 39 15	11♈43 40	6♋32 36	13♋02 27	3♋25.1	2♋43.6	15♓17.0	27♉30.8	0♒49.1	22♒41.0	24♑23.8	0♒40.5	5♈44.3	5♉09.8	19♓16.1	24♑50.5
2 Th	12 43 11	12 42 52	19 38 19	26 20 40	3 21.9	2R 43.5	16 35.6	28 26.2	1 30.8	23 01.4	24 31.2	0 44.2	5 47.8	5 13.1	19 18.3	24 51.2
3 F	12 47 08	13 42 02	3♌09 53	10♌06 13	3 18.8	2 42.3	17 56.0	29 21.1	2 12.5	23 21.6	24 38.4	0 47.8	5 51.3	5 16.3	19 20.4	24 51.9
4 Sa	12 51 04	14 41 09	17 09 47	24 20 31	3 15.6	2 39.1	19 18.2	0♊15.3	2 54.2	23 41.8	24 45.5	0 51.3	5 54.8	5 19.6	19 22.5	24 52.6
5 Su	12 55 01	15 40 14	1♍38 07	9♍02 05	3 12.4	2 33.2	20 42.2	1 08.9	3 35.9	24 01.9	24 52.5	0 54.7	5 58.3	5 22.9	19 24.6	24 53.2
6 M	12 58 57	16 39 16	16 31 40	24 05 54	3 09.2	2 25.0	22 07.9	2 01.9	4 17.6	24 21.9	24 59.3	0 58.1	6 01.8	5 26.2	19 26.7	24 53.8
7 Tu	13 02 54	17 38 17	1♎43 35	9♎23 21	3 06.1	2 14.9	23 35.3	2 54.1	4 59.3	24 41.8	25 05.9	1 01.3	6 05.3	5 29.5	19 28.8	24 54.4
8 W	13 06 50	18 37 15	17 03 47	24 43 23	3 02.9	2 04.3	25 04.3	3 45.7	5 41.0	25 01.5	25 12.4	1 04.5	6 08.8	5 32.8	19 30.8	24 54.9
9 Th	13 10 47	19 36 11	2♏20 41	9♏54 21	2 59.7	1 54.4	26 34.9	4 36.5	6 22.7	25 21.2	25 18.8	1 07.6	6 12.2	5 36.1	19 32.8	24 55.4
10 F	13 14 44	20 35 05	17 23 12	24 46 15	2 56.5	1 46.4	28 07.1	5 26.6	7 04.4	25 40.8	25 25.0	1 10.6	6 15.7	5 39.5	19 34.9	24 55.9
11 Sa	13 18 40	21 33 58	2♐02 46	9♐12 12	2 53.3	1 40.8	29 41.0	6 15.9	7 46.1	26 00.3	25 31.0	1 13.5	6 19.1	5 42.9	19 36.9	24 56.3
12 Su	13 22 37	22 32 48	16 14 18	23 08 59	2 50.2	1 37.8	1♈16.4	7 04.5	8 27.8	26 19.6	25 36.9	1 16.3	6 22.5	5 46.2	19 38.9	24 56.7
13 M	13 26 33	23 31 37	29 56 22	6♑36 41	2 47.0	1D 36.9	2 53.4	7 52.2	9 09.6	26 38.9	25 42.7	1 19.1	6 26.0	5 49.6	19 40.8	24 57.1
14 Tu	13 30 30	24 30 24	13♑10 21	19 37 50	2 43.8	1R 37.2	4 32.0	8 39.0	9 51.2	26 58.0	25 48.2	1 21.7	6 29.4	5 53.0	19 42.8	24 57.5
15 W	13 34 26	25 29 10	25 59 39	2♒16 24	2 40.6	1 37.5	6 12.2	9 24.9	10 32.9	27 17.0	25 53.7	1 24.3	6 32.8	5 56.4	19 44.8	24 57.8
16 Th	13 38 23	26 27 54	8♒28 39	14 37 01	2 37.5	1 36.8	7 53.9	10 10.0	11 14.6	27 35.9	25 58.9	1 26.7	6 36.1	5 59.8	19 46.7	24 58.1
17 F	13 42 19	27 26 36	20 42 05	26 44 24	2 34.3	1 34.1	9 37.3	10 54.0	11 56.3	27 54.7	26 04.0	1 29.1	6 39.5	6 03.3	19 48.6	24 58.4
18 Sa	13 46 16	28 25 16	2♓44 30	8♓42 52	2 31.1	1 29.0	11 22.2	11 37.1	12 38.0	28 13.4	26 08.9	1 31.4	6 42.8	6 06.7	19 50.5	24 58.7
19 Su	13 50 13	29 23 55	14 39 58	20 36 11	2 27.9	1 21.4	13 08.8	12 19.2	13 19.6	28 31.9	26 13.6	1 33.6	6 46.1	6 10.1	19 52.3	24 58.9
20 M	13 54 09	0♉22 31	26 31 53	2♈27 24	2 24.7	1 11.7	14 57.0	13 00.1	14 01.3	28 50.3	26 18.2	1 35.7	6 49.5	6 13.6	19 54.2	24 59.1
21 Tu	13 58 06	1 21 06	8♈23 00	14 18 57	2 21.6	1 00.6	16 46.8	13 40.0	14 42.9	29 08.6	26 22.6	1 37.7	6 52.7	6 17.0	19 56.0	24 59.2
22 W	14 02 02	2 19 39	20 15 27	26 12 42	2 18.4	0 49.1	18 38.2	14 18.7	15 24.5	29 26.8	26 26.9	1 39.6	6 56.0	6 20.4	19 57.8	24 59.3
23 Th	14 05 59	3 18 11	2♉10 53	8♉10 10	2 15.2	0 38.1	20 31.3	14 56.2	16 06.1	29 44.8	26 30.9	1 41.4	6 59.3	6 23.9	19 59.6	24 59.4
24 F	14 09 55	4 16 40	14 10 43	20 12 42	2 12.0	0 28.6	22 26.0	15 32.5	16 47.6	0♓02.7	26 34.8	1 43.1	7 02.5	6 27.3	20 01.4	24 59.5
25 Sa	14 13 52	5 15 08	26 16 20	2♊21 48	2 08.8	0 21.3	24 22.3	16 07.5	17 29.2	0 20.5	26 38.5	1 44.7	7 05.7	6 30.8	20 03.1	24R 59.5
26 Su	14 17 48	6 13 33	8♊29 21	14 39 15	2 05.7	0 16.5	26 20.2	16 41.1	18 10.7	0 38.1	26 42.0	1 46.2	7 08.9	6 34.3	20 04.8	24 59.5
27 M	14 21 45	7 11 57	20 51 48	27 07 20	2 02.5	0D 14.1	28 19.7	17 13.3	18 52.2	0 55.6	26 45.4	1 47.7	7 12.1	6 37.7	20 06.5	24 59.5
28 Tu	14 25 42	8 10 19	3♋26 11	9♋48 45	1 59.3	0 13.6	0♉20.8	17 44.1	19 33.7	1 12.9	26 48.6	1 49.0	7 15.2	6 41.2	20 08.2	24 59.5
29 W	14 29 38	9 08 39	16 15 26	22 46 37	1 56.1	0 14.4	2 23.3	18 13.4	20 15.1	1 30.1	26 51.6	1 50.2	7 18.3	6 44.6	20 09.9	24 59.4
30 Th	14 33 35	10♉06 56	29 22 43	6♌04 03	1♋53.0	0♋15.5	4♉27.3	18♊41.1	20♒56.6	1♓47.2	26♑54.4	1♒51.4	7♈21.4	6♉48.1	20♓11.5	24♑59.3

1st of Month

Julian Day # 2458940.5
Obliquity 23°26'12"
SVP 4♓58'55"
GC 27♐07.3
Eris 23♈44.3

Day	⚴	⚵	⚶
1	24♑48.8	13♎58.5R	3♊56.9
6	25 58.3	12 47.2R	5 50.5
11	27 01.8	11 37.5R	7 46.1
16	27 58.9	10 31.0R	9 43.7
21	28 49.0	9 29.4R	11 42.9
26	29 31.6	8 33.8R	13 43.8

DECLINATION and LATITUDE

Day	☉ Decl	☽ Decl	☽ Lat	☽ 12h Decl	☿ Decl	☿ Lat	♀ Decl	♀ Lat	♂ Decl	♂ Lat	⚳ Decl	⚳ Lat	♃ Decl	♃ Lat	♄ Decl	♄ Lat
1 W	4N38	23N37	0N20	23N42	7S47	2S09	23N06	3N35	20S55	0S58	20S09	6S35	21S18	0S04	20S04	0S04
2 Th	5 01	23 27	1 28	22 52	7 20	2 13	23 23	3 40	20 47	0 59	20 05	6 37	21 17	0 04	20 03	0 04
3 F	5 24	21 56	2 34	20 40	6 52	2 17	23 39	3 44	20 39	1 01	20 00	6 39	21 16	0 04	20 02	0 04
4 Sa	5 47	19 03	3 32	17 08	6 23	2 21	23 55	3 48	20 31	1 02	19 56	6 42	21 14	0 04	20 02	0 04
5 Su	6 10	14 55	4 19	12 27	5 53	2 24	24 10	3 52	20 22	1 03	19 51	6 44	21 13	0 04	20 01	0 04
6 M	6 33	9 46	4 50	6 54	5 22	2 26	24 25	3 56	20 13	1 04	19 47	6 47	21 12	0 04	20 00	0 04
7 Tu	6 55	3 55	5 01	0 52	4 49	2 28	24 39	3 60	20 05	1 06	19 42	6 49	21 11	0 05	19 60	0 04
8 W	7 18	2S13	4 51	5S16	4 15	2 30	24 53	4 04	19 56	1 07	19 38	6 52	21 10	0 05	19 59	0 04
9 Th	7 40	8 13	4 20	11 01	3 40	2 31	25 06	4 07	19 46	1 08	19 33	6 54	21 09	0 05	19 59	0 04
10 F	8 02	13 38	3 32	16 01	3 04	2 31	25 19	4 11	19 37	1 09	19 29	6 57	21 08	0 05	19 58	0 04
11 Sa	8 24	18 07	2 30	19 55	2 26	2 31	25 31	4 14	19 28	1 11	19 25	6 59	21 07	0 05	19 57	0 05
12 Su	8 46	21 23	1 21	22 31	1 48	2 31	25 43	4 17	19 18	1 12	19 20	7 02	21 06	0 05	19 57	0 05
13 M	9 08	23 17	0 09	23 43	1 08	2 30	25 54	4 21	19 08	1 13	19 16	7 04	21 05	0 05	19 56	0 05
14 Tu	9 30	23 48	1S01	23 33	0 28	2 28	26 05	4 24	18 58	1 14	19 12	7 07	21 04	0 06	19 56	0 05
15 W	9 51	23 00	2 06	22 10	0N14	2 26	26 15	4 27	18 48	1 16	19 08	7 10	21 03	0 06	19 55	0 05
16 Th	10 13	21 05	3 03	19 45	0 56	2 23	26 25	4 29	18 38	1 17	19 03	7 12	21 03	0 06	19 55	0 05
17 F	10 34	18 07	3 50	16 30	1 40	2 20	26 34	4 32	18 28	1 18	18 59	7 15	21 02	0 06	19 55	0 05
18 Sa	10 55	14 38	4 26	12 38	2 24	2 17	26 42	4 34	18 17	1 20	18 55	7 18	21 01	0 06	19 54	0 05
19 Su	11 16	10 30	4 51	8 17	3 09	2 13	26 50	4 37	18 07	1 21	18 51	7 20	21 00	0 06	19 54	0 05
20 M	11 36	6 00	5 02	3 40	3 55	2 08	26 58	4 39	17 56	1 22	18 47	7 23	20 60	0 06	19 53	0 05
21 Tu	11 57	1 17	5 01	1N06	4 42	2 03	27 05	4 41	17 45	1 24	18 43	7 26	20 59	0 06	19 53	0 05
22 W	12 17	3N30	4 46	5 51	5 30	1 57	27 11	4 43	17 34	1 25	18 39	7 29	20 58	0 07	19 53	0 05
23 Th	12 37	8 10	4 19	10 25	6 18	1 51	27 17	4 44	17 23	1 26	18 36	7 32	20 58	0 07	19 52	0 06
24 F	12 57	12 35	3 41	14 38	7 07	1 45	27 23	4 45	17 12	1 28	18 32	7 35	20 57	0 07	19 52	0 06
25 Sa	13 16	16 32	2 51	18 17	7 56	1 38	27 28	4 47	17 00	1 29	18 28	7 37	20 56	0 07	19 52	0 06
26 Su	13 36	19 51	1 54	21 11	8 46	1 30	27 32	4 47	16 49	1 30	18 24	7 40	20 56	0 07	19 51	0 06
27 M	13 55	22 17	0 50	23 08	9 36	1 22	27 36	4 48	16 37	1 32	18 21	7 43	20 55	0 07	19 51	0 06
28 Tu	14 14	23 41	0N17	23 56	10 26	1 14	27 40	4 49	16 25	1 33	18 17	7 46	20 55	0 07	19 51	0 06
29 W	14 32	23 51	1 25	23 27	11 17	1 05	27 42	4 49	16 14	1 34	18 14	7 49	20 54	0 08	19 51	0 06
30 Th	14N51	22N44	2N30	21N40	12N08	0S56	27N45	4N49	16S02	1S36	18S10	7S52	20S54	0S08	19S51	0S06

Day	⚷ Decl	⚷ Lat	♅ Decl	♅ Lat	♆ Decl	♆ Lat	♇ Decl	♇ Lat
1	4N46	2N42	12N49	0S27	5S11	1S01	21S57	0S48
6	4 52	2 42	12 54	0 27	5 07	1 01	21 57	0 49
11	4 59	2 42	13 00	0 27	5 03	1 02	21 57	0 49
16	5 06	2 42	13 06	0 27	4 60	1 02	21 57	0 50
21	5 12	2 42	13 11	0 27	4 56	1 02	21 58	0 51
26	5 19	2 42	13 17	0 27	4 53	1 02	21 58	0 51

Day	⚴ Decl	⚴ Lat	⚵ Decl	⚵ Lat	⚶ Decl	⚶ Lat	Eris Decl	Eris Lat
1	12N18	33N57	1N34	7N41	18N42	2S17	1S34	11S35
6	13 03	34 33	2 15	7 55	19 11	2 08	1 32	11 34
11	13 50	35 15	2 53	8 08	19 38	1 59	1 31	11 34
16	14 36	35 49	3 29	8 18	20 05	1 51	1 30	11 34
21	15 23	36 29	4 01	8 27	20 29	1 43	1 28	11 34
26	16 09	37 09	4 28	8 34	20 52	1 35	1 27	11 34

Moon Phenomena

Max/0 Decl
dy hr mn
1 9:14 23N42
7 15:21 0 S
13 21:01 23S48
21 6:27 0 N
28 15:23 23N56

Max/0 Lat
dy hr mn
7 0:49 5N01
13 3:00 0 S
20 9:19 5S03
27 17:55 0 N

Perigee/Apogee
dy hr m kilometers
7 18:10 p 356910
20 19:01 a 406462

PH dy hr mn
☽ 1 10:22 12♋09
○ 8 2:36 18♎44
☾ 14 22:57 25♑27
● 23 2:27 3♉24
☽ 30 20:39 10♌57

Void of Course Moon

Last Aspect	☽ Ingress
2 16:50 ♀ ⚹	♌ 2 18:27
3 19:30 ☉ △	♍ 4 21:20
6 13:30 ♃ △	♎ 6 21:17
8 12:51 ♃ □	♏ 8 20:18
10 19:36 ☿ △	♐ 10 20:36
12 11:47 ☉ △	♑ 13 0:06
14 23:49 ♃ ☌	♒ 15 7:38
17 14:35 ☉ ⚹	♓ 17 18:31
19 23:32 ♃ ⚹	♈ 20 7:01
22 12:33 ♃ □	♉ 22 19:37
25 0:44 ♃ △	♊ 25 7:21
27 17:01 ☿ ⚹	♋ 27 17:29
29 19:31 ♃ ☍	♌ 30 1:07

DAILY ASPECTARIAN

1 W
☽⚼⚳ 2:11
☿∠♄ 7:36
☉∥⚷ 8:09
☊R 10:17
☉□☽ 10:22
☽∠♀ 11:52
☽△☿ 17:52
☿∠♂ 20:58
☽△♆ 23:24

2 Th
☽∥♀ 1:34
☽⊼⚳ 6:14
☽☍♃ 8:50
☉#♆ 9:08
☽☍♇ 9:21
⚳∥♄ 10:54
☽⚹♀ 16:50
☽☍♄ 19:50
☽☍♂ 22:14
☽⚼☿ 23:33
☽#♇ 23:51

3 F
☽⚼♆ 2:03
☽□♅ 3:41
☽△⚷ 4:42
☽#♃ 6:47
☽#♂ 12:40
☽#♄ 16:58
♀ ♊ 17:12
☽#⚳ 17:36
☉△☽ 19:30

4 Sa
☿☌♆ 1:16
☽⊼♆ 3:44
☽⊼☿ 3:59
☽⚼⚷ 6:19
☽☍⚳ 11:11
☽⊼♃ 12:47
☽⊼♇ 12:54
☉#☿ 16:24
♀△♄ 17:11
☿∠♅ 18:17
☉⚼☽ 22:19
☽⊼♄ 22:49
☽□♀ 23:09

5 Su
♃☌♇ 2:46
☽⊼♂ 3:21
☽△♅ 6:07
☽⊼⚷ 7:05
☽∥♅ 9:54
☽⚼♇ 13:23
☽⚼♃ 13:27
☽⚼♄ 23:06

6 M
☉⊼☽ 0:13
☽⚼♂ 4:36
☽☍♆ 4:39
♂∠♆ 5:29
☽⚼♅ 6:14
☽☍☿ 9:50
☿∥♆ 10:55
☉∥☽ 12:39
☽⊼⚳ 12:42
☽△♇ 13:16
☽△♃ 13:30
☽#♆ 19:15
☽#☿ 20:05
☽∥⚷ 20:08
☿#⚷ 20:36
☽△♄ 22:53

7 Tu
☽△♀ 1:57
☽△♂ 5:21
☽⊼♅ 5:55
☽☍⚷ 6:52
☽⚼⚳ 12:45
♂∥♄ 14:02
⚳⊻♇ 15:42
♂□♅ 18:52
☿⚹♇ 21:29
☿⊻⚳ 23:04

8 W
☿⚹♃ 2:21
☉☍☽ 2:36
☽⚼♀ 2:49
☽⊼♆ 3:51
☽∥☿ 7:17
☽#⚷ 10:41
☽∥♆ 11:19
☽□♇ 12:19
☽△⚳ 12:45
☽□♃ 12:51
☽⊼☿ 13:55
♂⚹⚷ 17:25
⚳⊻♃ 19:38
☉#☽ 21:37
☽□♄ 22:04
☉⊻♆ 22:35

9 Th
☉∠♀ 0:59
☽⚼♆ 3:30
☽⊼♀ 3:48
☽☍♅ 5:11
☽⊼⚷ 6:08
☽□♂ 6:42
☽⚼☿ 16:21
☽#♅ 20:55

10 F
☽△♆ 3:33
☉⊼☽ 5:33
☽⚼⚷ 6:18
♀⊻♅ 6:41
☽⚹♇ 12:16
☽⚹♃ 13:09
☽□⚳ 13:48
☽△☿ 19:36
☽⚹♄ 22:38

11 Sa
♀⚹⚷ 1:40
☿ ♈ 4:49
☽⊼♅ 6:09
☽△⚷ 7:10
☽☍♀ 7:29
☉⚼☽ 8:07
☽∥⚳ 8:15
☽∥♂ 8:23
☽⚹♂ 10:04
☽∥♄ 12:17
☽∠♇ 13:15
♂∥⚳ 14:14
☽∠♃ 14:20
☽∥♃ 21:29
☿⚹♄ 23:59

12 Su
☽∠♄ 0:03
☽∥♇ 5:35
☽□♆ 5:54
☽⚼♅ 7:53
☉△☽ 11:47
☽∠♂ 13:13
☽⊻♇ 15:10
☽⊻♃ 16:27
☽⚹⚳ 18:01

13 M
♆#⚷ 0:25
☽⊻♄ 2:28
☊D 2:58
☽□☿ 6:01
☽△♅ 10:38
☽□⚷ 11:44
☽⊼♀ 15:11
☽⊻♂ 17:34
☽∠⚳ 21:43

14 Tu
☉□♇ 11:08
☽⚹♆ 12:11
☿⊻♅ 20:07
☽⚼♀ 20:49
☽☌♇ 22:03
☉□☽ 22:57
☊R 23:09
☽☌♃ 23:49

15 W
☽⊻⚳ 2:31
☿☌⚷ 5:03
☽☌♄ 10:22
☉□♃ 11:00
☽∥♇ 14:38
☽∠♆ 16:49
♀⚼♇ 17:36
☽□♅ 19:10
☽⚹⚷ 20:21
☽⚹☿ 22:42

16 Th
☽∥♃ 0:23
☽△♀ 3:30
☽☌♂ 5:43
☽∥♄ 10:41
☽∥⚳ 18:04
☽∥♂ 22:07
☽⊻♆ 22:14

17 F
☽∠⚷ 1:54
♀⚼♃ 6:12
☽⊻♇ 8:29
☽∠☿ 9:06
☽⊻♃ 10:44
☉⚹☽ 14:35
☽☌⚳ 14:43
☉⚹⚳ 16:52
☽⊻♄ 21:33

18 Sa
☿⚹♀ 5:37
☽⚹♅ 6:48
☽⊻⚷ 8:01
☽#♅ 9:00
☽∠♇ 14:33
☽∠♃ 17:01
☽□♀ 18:58
☉#☽ 20:07
☽⊻☿ 20:23
☽⊻♂ 21:08
☉∠☽ 23:25

19 Su
☽∠♄ 3:50
☿⚹♂ 3:56
☿∠⚳ 6:14
☽☌♆ 10:33
☽∠♅ 13:12
☉ ♉ 14:47
☽⚹♇ 20:52
☽⚹♃ 23:32

20 M
☽#⚷ 4:12
☽⊻⚳ 4:48
☽∠♂ 5:21
☽∥♆ 5:27
☉⊻☽ 8:29
☽#☿ 9:10
☽⚹♄ 10:17
☽⊻♅ 19:44
☽☌⚷ 20:56

21 Tu
☉□♄ 7:01
☿#♆ 7:02
☽⚹♀ 11:18
☽∠⚳ 11:57
☽⚹♂ 13:36
☿∥⚷ 15:45
☽☌☿ 20:07
☽⊻♆ 23:24

22 W
☽#♆ 7:14
☽∥⚷ 8:50
☽□♇ 9:32
☽∥☿ 12:14
☽□♃ 12:33
☿⊻♆ 17:12
☽⚹⚳ 18:59
☽∠♀ 19:15
☽□♄ 23:01

23 Th
☉☌☽ 2:27
☽∠♆ 5:39
☽☌♅ 8:30
☽⊻⚷ 9:41
⚳ ♓ 20:21

24 F
☉∥☽ 2:16
☽⊻♀ 2:51
☽∥♅ 3:51
☽□♂ 5:32
☽⚹♆ 11:39
☽∠⚷ 15:42
☉∠♆ 18:55
☽⊻☿ 19:31
☽△♇ 21:28
☉∥♅ 23:37

25 Sa
☽△♃ 0:44
☽#♂ 2:56
☿□♇ 7:37
☽□⚳ 8:13
☽△♄ 10:48
☽#⚳ 13:06
♇R 18:55
☉⊻☽ 19:12
☽⊻♅ 20:14
☽⚹⚷ 21:22

26 Su
☽#♄ 0:08
☽⚼♇ 2:56
♀⚼♄ 3:55
☿□♃ 4:32
☽⚼♃ 6:17
☽∠☿ 6:37
☉☌♅ 9:02
☽#♃ 9:32
☽⚼♄ 16:08
☽☌♀ 16:40
☽△♂ 19:56
☽#♇ 20:16
☽□♆ 22:33

27 M
☉⊻⚷ 0:03
☽∠♅ 1:29
☉∠☽ 2:47
☽⊼♇ 7:56
☽⊼♃ 11:21
☽⚹☿ 17:01
☊D 17:54
☽△⚳ 19:42
☿ ♉ 19:54
☽⊼♄ 20:56

28 Tu
☽⚼♂ 2:15
☽⚹♅ 6:10
☽□⚷ 7:14
☉⚹☽ 9:40
☿⚹⚳ 11:55
☿□♄ 17:29
♂⊻♆ 20:49

29 W
☽⚼⚳ 0:28
☽⊻♀ 3:46
☽△♆ 7:13
☽⊼♂ 7:47
☿∠♀ 12:34
☽☍♇ 16:02
☽☍♃ 19:31

30 Th
♀ ♒ 0:31
☽⊼⚳ 4:26
☽☍♄ 4:28
⚳⊻♄ 6:21
☽∠♀ 8:00
☿∠♆ 8:36
☽#♇ 8:49
☽⚼♆ 10:28
☽□☿ 10:48
☽□♅ 13:22
☽△⚷ 14:21
☽#♃ 19:03
☊R 20:35
☉□☽ 20:39

May 2020

LONGITUDE

Day	Sid.Time	☉	☽	☽ 12 hour	Mean ☊	True ☊	☿	♀	♂	⚳	♃	♄	⚷	♅	♆	♇
	h m s	° ' "	° ' "	° ' "	° '	° '	° '	° '	° '	° '	° '	° '	° '	° '	° '	° '
1 F	14 37 31	11♉05 12	12♌50 58	19♌43 41	1♋49.8	0♋15.9	6♉32.6	19♊07.1	21♒38.0	2♓04.1	26♑57.0	1♒52.4	7♈24.5	6♉51.5	20♓13.1	24♑59.1
2 Sa	14 41 28	12 03 25	26 42 20	3♍46 56	1 46.6	0R 14.9	8 39.2	19 31.5	22 19.4	2 20.8	26 59.5	1 53.3	7 27.5	6 55.0	20 14.7	24R 59.0
3 Su	14 45 24	13 01 36	10♍57 21	18 13 16	1 43.4	0 12.0	10 46.8	19 54.1	23 00.7	2 37.4	27 01.7	1 54.2	7 30.5	6 58.4	20 16.3	24 58.8
4 M	14 49 21	13 59 46	25 34 12	2♎59 29	1 40.3	0 07.3	12 55.4	20 14.8	23 42.0	2 53.8	27 03.8	1 54.9	7 33.5	7 01.8	20 17.8	24 58.6
5 Tu	14 53 17	14 57 53	10♎28 15	17 59 31	1 37.1	0 01.3	15 04.7	20 33.7	24 23.3	3 10.1	27 05.7	1 55.6	7 36.5	7 05.3	20 19.3	24 58.3
6 W	14 57 14	15 55 58	25 32 07	3♏04 52	1 33.9	29♊54.7	17 14.6	20 50.7	25 04.6	3 26.2	27 07.4	1 56.1	7 39.4	7 08.7	20 20.8	24 58.0
7 Th	15 01 11	16 54 02	10♏36 32	18 05 54	1 30.7	29 48.4	19 24.7	21 05.7	25 45.8	3 42.2	27 08.9	1 56.6	7 42.3	7 12.1	20 22.2	24 57.7
8 F	15 05 07	17 52 04	25 31 50	2♐53 20	1 27.5	29 43.3	21 34.9	21 18.6	26 27.1	3 58.0	27 10.3	1 56.9	7 45.2	7 15.5	20 23.7	24 57.4
9 Sa	15 09 04	18 50 04	10♐09 33	17 19 49	1 24.4	29 40.0	23 44.9	21 29.3	27 08.2	4 13.6	27 11.4	1 57.2	7 48.1	7 18.9	20 25.1	24 57.0
10 Su	15 13 00	19 48 03	24 23 39	1♑20 45	1 21.2	29D 38.6	25 54.4	21 38.0	27 49.4	4 29.1	27 12.4	1 57.3	7 50.9	7 22.3	20 26.5	24 56.6
11 M	15 16 57	20 46 01	8♑11 02	14 54 31	1 18.0	29 38.7	28 03.1	21 44.4	28 30.5	4 44.4	27 13.2	1R 57.4	7 53.7	7 25.7	20 27.8	24 56.2
12 Tu	15 20 53	21 43 57	21 31 24	28 02 00	1 14.8	29 39.9	0♊10.7	21 48.5	29 11.6	4 59.5	27 13.8	1 57.4	7 56.4	7 29.1	20 29.2	24 55.8
13 W	15 24 50	22 41 52	4♒26 42	10♒45 59	1 11.7	29 41.4	2 16.9	21R 50.3	29 52.6	5 14.4	27 14.2	1 57.3	7 59.2	7 32.4	20 30.5	24 55.3
14 Th	15 28 46	23 39 46	17 00 22	23 10 25	1 08.5	29R 42.6	4 21.5	21 49.8	0♓33.6	5 29.2	27R 14.4	1 57.0	8 01.8	7 35.8	20 31.7	24 54.8
15 F	15 32 43	24 37 38	29 16 43	5♓19 51	1 05.3	29 42.7	6 24.2	21 46.9	1 14.6	5 43.8	27 14.4	1 56.7	8 04.5	7 39.1	20 33.0	24 54.3
16 Sa	15 36 40	25 35 29	11♓20 25	17 18 57	1 02.1	29 41.4	8 24.7	21 41.6	1 55.5	5 58.1	27 14.2	1 56.3	8 07.1	7 42.5	20 34.2	24 53.7
17 Su	15 40 36	26 33 19	23 16 02	29 12 10	0 59.0	29 38.6	10 23.0	21 33.9	2 36.4	6 12.3	27 13.9	1 55.8	8 09.7	7 45.8	20 35.4	24 53.2
18 M	15 44 33	27 31 08	5♈07 50	11♈03 30	0 55.8	29 34.5	12 18.8	21 23.8	3 17.2	6 26.3	27 13.3	1 55.1	8 12.3	7 49.1	20 36.5	24 52.6
19 Tu	15 48 29	28 28 55	16 59 35	22 56 26	0 52.6	29 29.6	14 12.0	21 11.3	3 57.9	6 40.2	27 12.6	1 54.4	8 14.8	7 52.4	20 37.7	24 51.9
20 W	15 52 26	29 26 42	28 54 25	4♉53 48	0 49.4	29 24.3	16 02.4	20 56.4	4 38.7	6 53.8	27 11.6	1 53.6	8 17.3	7 55.7	20 38.8	24 51.3
21 Th	15 56 22	0♊24 27	10♉54 53	16 57 52	0 46.2	29 19.2	17 50.0	20 39.1	5 19.3	7 07.2	27 10.5	1 52.7	8 19.7	7 58.9	20 39.8	24 50.6
22 F	16 00 19	1 22 11	23 02 57	29 10 20	0 43.1	29 14.8	19 34.6	20 19.5	5 59.9	7 20.4	27 09.2	1 51.7	8 22.1	8 02.2	20 40.9	24 49.9
23 Sa	16 04 15	2 19 53	5♊20 09	11♊32 33	0 39.9	29 11.7	21 16.2	19 57.6	6 40.4	7 33.4	27 07.7	1 50.6	8 24.5	8 05.4	20 41.9	24 49.2
24 Su	16 08 12	3 17 34	17 47 40	24 05 37	0 36.7	29D 09.9	22 54.7	19 33.6	7 20.9	7 46.2	27 06.0	1 49.4	8 26.9	8 08.6	20 42.9	24 48.4
25 M	16 12 09	4 15 15	0♋26 32	6♋50 34	0 33.5	29 09.4	24 30.1	19 07.5	8 01.2	7 58.7	27 04.2	1 48.1	8 29.2	8 11.8	20 43.8	24 47.6
26 Tu	16 16 05	5 12 53	13 17 50	19 48 28	0 30.4	29 10.0	26 02.4	18 39.4	8 41.6	8 11.1	27 02.1	1 46.8	8 31.4	8 15.0	20 44.7	24 46.8
27 W	16 20 02	6 10 31	26 22 38	3♌00 27	0 27.2	29 11.3	27 31.4	18 09.5	9 21.8	8 23.2	26 59.8	1 45.3	8 33.6	8 18.1	20 45.6	24 46.0
28 Th	16 23 58	7 08 06	9♌42 04	16 27 37	0 24.0	29 12.8	28 57.2	17 37.9	10 02.0	8 35.1	26 57.4	1 43.7	8 35.8	8 21.3	20 46.5	24 45.2
29 F	16 27 55	8 05 41	23 17 10	0♍10 47	0 20.8	29 13.9	0♋19.7	17 04.8	10 42.1	8 46.8	26 54.8	1 42.1	8 38.0	8 24.4	20 47.3	24 44.3
30 Sa	16 31 51	9 03 14	7♍08 28	14 10 08	0 17.7	29R 14.5	1 38.9	16 30.3	11 22.1	8 58.2	26 52.0	1 40.3	8 40.0	8 27.5	20 48.1	24 43.4
31 Su	16 35 48	10♊00 45	21 15 40	28 24 49	0♋14.5	29♊14.2	2♋54.7	15♊54.8	12♓02.0	9♓09.4	26♑49.0	1♒38.5	8♈42.1	8♉30.5	20♓48.9	24♑42.5

1st of Month

Julian Day #
2458970.5
Obliquity
23°26'12"
SVP 4♓58'51"
GC 27♐07.4
Eris 24♈03.8

Day	⚴	⚵	⚶
1	0♒06.1	7♎45.5R	15♊46.1
6	0 32.1	7 05.1R	17 49.6
11	0 49.2	6 33.0R	19 54.3
16	0 56.8	6 09.5R	22 00.0
21	0 54.5R	5 54.7R	24 06.6
26	0 41.9R	5 48.6R	26 14.2
31	0 19.0R	5 50.9	28 22.4

DECLINATION and LATITUDE

Day	☉ Decl	☽ Decl	☽ Lat	☽ 12h Decl	☿ Decl	☿ Lat	♀ Decl	♀ Lat	♂ Decl	♂ Lat	⚳ Decl	⚳ Lat	♃ Decl	♃ Lat	♄ Decl	♄ Lat
1 F	15N09	20N17	3N29	18N36	12N58	0S46	27N47	4N48	15S50	1S37	18S07	7S55	20S54	0S08	19S51	0S06
2 Sa	15 27	16 38	4 17	14 24	13 49	0 36	27 48	4 47	15 37	1 39	18 04	7 58	20 53	0 08	19 50	0 06
3 Su	15 45	11 56	4 51	9 17	14 38	0 26	27 49	4 46	15 25	1 40	18 01	8 02	20 53	0 08	19 50	0 06
4 M	16 02	6 27	5 07	3 31	15 28	0 16	27 49	4 45	15 13	1 41	17 58	8 05	20 53	0 08	19 50	0 07
5 Tu	16 19	0 30	5 03	2S32	16 16	0 05	27 49	4 43	15 00	1 43	17 54	8 08	20 53	0 08	19 50	0 07
6 W	16 36	5S33	4 38	8 29	17 04	0N05	27 48	4 41	14 48	1 44	17 51	8 11	20 52	0 09	19 50	0 07
7 Th	16 53	11 18	3 54	13 55	17 50	0 16	27 47	4 39	14 35	1 46	17 49	8 14	20 52	0 09	19 50	0 07
8 F	17 09	16 19	2 54	18 27	18 35	0 26	27 45	4 36	14 23	1 47	17 46	8 18	20 52	0 09	19 50	0 07
9 Sa	17 25	20 16	1 44	21 44	19 18	0 37	27 42	4 33	14 10	1 49	17 43	8 21	20 52	0 09	19 50	0 07
10 Su	17 41	22 51	0 28	23 35	19 59	0 47	27 39	4 29	13 57	1 50	17 40	8 24	20 52	0 09	19 50	0 07
11 M	17 57	23 57	0S46	23 58	20 39	0 57	27 36	4 25	13 44	1 51	17 38	8 27	20 52	0 09	19 50	0 07
12 Tu	18 12	23 38	1 56	22 58	21 16	1 06	27 31	4 21	13 31	1 53	17 35	8 31	20 52	0 10	19 50	0 07
13 W	18 27	22 01	2 58	20 49	21 51	1 16	27 26	4 16	13 18	1 54	17 33	8 34	20 52	0 10	19 51	0 07
14 Th	18 41	19 23	3 49	17 44	22 24	1 24	27 21	4 10	13 05	1 56	17 30	8 38	20 52	0 10	19 51	0 07
15 F	18 55	15 55	4 29	13 57	22 54	1 33	27 15	4 04	12 51	1 57	17 28	8 41	20 52	0 10	19 51	0 08
16 Sa	19 09	11 52	4 56	9 41	23 21	1 40	27 08	3 58	12 38	1 59	17 26	8 45	20 53	0 10	19 51	0 08
17 Su	19 23	7 25	5 10	5 05	23 46	1 47	27 01	3 51	12 25	2 00	17 24	8 48	20 53	0 10	19 51	0 08
18 M	19 36	2 42	5 10	0 19	24 08	1 53	26 53	3 44	12 11	2 02	17 22	8 52	20 53	0 10	19 51	0 08
19 Tu	19 49	2N06	4 57	4N29	24 28	1 59	26 44	3 36	11 58	2 03	17 20	8 55	20 53	0 11	19 52	0 08
20 W	20 02	6 51	4 32	9 09	24 45	2 04	26 34	3 27	11 44	2 05	17 18	8 59	20 54	0 11	19 52	0 08
21 Th	20 14	11 24	3 54	13 32	24 60	2 08	26 24	3 18	11 31	2 06	17 16	9 03	20 54	0 11	19 52	0 08
22 F	20 26	15 33	3 05	17 25	25 12	2 11	26 13	3 09	11 17	2 08	17 15	9 06	20 54	0 11	19 53	0 08
23 Sa	20 38	19 06	2 07	20 36	25 22	2 13	26 01	2 59	11 04	2 09	17 13	9 10	20 55	0 11	19 53	0 08
24 Su	20 49	21 51	1 02	22 51	25 30	2 15	25 49	2 48	10 50	2 11	17 12	9 14	20 55	0 11	19 53	0 08
25 M	20 60	23 33	0N07	23 58	25 35	2 16	25 36	2 37	10 36	2 12	17 11	9 18	20 56	0 12	19 54	0 09
26 Tu	21 10	24 03	1 17	23 48	25 38	2 16	25 22	2 25	10 22	2 14	17 09	9 21	20 56	0 12	19 54	0 09
27 W	21 20	23 14	2 24	22 20	25 40	2 15	25 07	2 13	10 09	2 15	17 08	9 25	20 57	0 12	19 55	0 09
28 Th	21 30	21 06	3 25	19 35	25 39	2 13	24 52	2 01	9 55	2 17	17 07	9 29	20 58	0 12	19 55	0 09
29 F	21 39	17 46	4 15	15 42	25 37	2 11	24 36	1 48	9 41	2 18	17 07	9 33	20 58	0 12	19 55	0 09
30 Sa	21 48	13 24	4 52	10 54	25 33	2 07	24 20	1 35	9 27	2 20	17 06	9 37	20 59	0 12	19 56	0 09
31 Su	21N57	8N15	5N12	5N27	25N27	2N03	24N02	1N21	9S13	2S21	17S05	9S41	20S60	0S13	19S56	0S09

Day	⚷ Decl	⚷ Lat	♅ Decl	♅ Lat	♆ Decl	♆ Lat	♇ Decl	♇ Lat
1	5N25	2N42	13N23	0S27	4S50	1S02	21S59	0S52
6	5 31	2 42	13 28	0 27	4 47	1 02	21 60	0 52
11	5 37	2 42	13 34	0 27	4 44	1 03	22 01	0 53
16	5 42	2 42	13 39	0 27	4 42	1 03	22 02	0 54
21	5 47	2 42	13 45	0 27	4 40	1 03	22 03	0 54
26	5 52	2 43	13 50	0 27	4 38	1 03	22 04	0 55
31	5N57	2N43	13N55	0S27	4S37	1S03	22S05	0S55

Day	⚴ Decl	⚴ Lat	⚵ Decl	⚵ Lat	⚶ Decl	⚶ Lat	Eris Decl	Eris Lat
1	16N55	37N50	4N52	8N38	21N13	1S28	1S26	11S34
6	17 39	38 31	5 10	8 42	21 32	1 21	1 25	11 34
11	18 22	39 12	5 25	8 43	21 50	1 14	1 24	11 34
16	19 03	39 52	5 34	8 44	22 05	1 07	1 23	11 34
21	19 41	40 32	5 40	8 43	22 19	0 60	1 22	11 34
26	20 16	41 10	5 41	8 42	22 30	0 53	1 21	11 34
31	20N47	41N46	5N38	8N40	22N39	0S47	1S21	11S34

Moon Phenomena

Max/0 Decl

dy	hr mn	
5	1:59	0 S
11	6:16	24S00
18	13:32	0 N
25	21:14	24N03

Perigee/Apogee

dy	hr m		kilometers
6	3:04	p	359656
18	7:46	a	405582

Max/0 Lat

dy	hr mn	
4	7:20	5N08
10	9:03	0 S
17	12:50	5S11
24	21:35	0 N
31	13:22	5N15

PH

PH	dy	hr mn	
○	7	10:46	17♏20
☾	14	14:04	24♒14
●	22	17:40	2♊05
☽	30	3:31	9♍12

Void of Course Moon

Last Aspect				☽ Ingress		
1	16:05	♂	☍	♍	2	5:36
4	2:26	♃	△	♎	4	7:11
6	2:32	♃	□	♏	6	7:06
8	2:40	♃	⚹	♐	8	7:16
10	6:12	♂	⚹	♑	10	9:40
12	10:31	♃	☌	♒	12	15:40
14	14:04	☉	□	♓	15	1:26
17	8:00	♃	⚹	♈	17	13:37
19	20:34	♃	□	♉	20	2:12
22	8:02	♃	△	♊	22	13:37
24	11:11	☿	☌	♋	24	23:10
27	1:07	♃	☍	♌	27	6:34
28	13:31	♀	⚹	♍	29	11:41
31	9:18	♃	△	♎	31	14:39

DAILY ASPECTARIAN

1 F	☽ # ♄	3:24
	☿ ☌ ♅	3:42
	☿ ⚺ ⚷	10:06
	☽ ⚹ ♀	11:17
	☿ ∥ ♅	11:56
	☽ ⚻ ♆	12:52
	☽ # ⚳	15:20
	☽ ☍ ♂	16:05
	☽ ⚼ ⚷	16:41
	☽ ⚻ ♇	21:03
2 Sa	☽ ⚻ ♃	0:29
	♂ ∠ ⚷	5:07
	☽ # ♂	5:52
	☉ ∥ ☽	6:07
	☉ # ♂	8:15
	☽ ⚻ ♄	8:49
	☽ ☍ ⚳	9:46
	☽ ∥ ☿	12:45
	☽ ∥ ♅	16:57
	☽ △ ♅	17:20
	☽ ⚻ ⚷	18:14
	☽ ⚼ ♇	22:23
	☽ △ ☿	23:39
3 Su	☽ ⚼ ♃	1:47
	☉ △ ☽	3:41
	☽ ⚼ ♄	9:50
	☽ □ ♀	15:07
	☽ ☍ ♆	15:23
	☿ # ♂	18:11
	☽ ⚼ ♅	18:13
	☽ ⚻ ♂	20:49
	☽ △ ♇	23:02
4 M	☽ △ ♃	2:26
	♀ □ ♆	3:54
	☽ ∥ ⚷	4:02
	☽ ⚼ ☿	4:28
	☉ ⚼ ☽	5:56
	☽ # ♆	6:49
	☽ △ ♄	10:16
	☽ ⚻ ⚳	12:04
	☽ ⚻ ♅	18:34
	☽ ☍ ⚷	19:24
	☉ ☌ ☿	21:42
	☽ ⚼ ♂	22:11
5 Tu	☉ ∥ ☿	2:32
	☊ R ♊	4:41
	☉ ⚻ ☽	7:40
	☽ ⚻ ☿	8:35
	☽ ⚼ ⚳	12:30
	☽ ⚻ ♆	15:44
	☽ △ ♀	16:24
	♂ ⚺ ♇	20:12
	☽ ∥ ♆	20:54
	☽ □ ♇	23:06
	☽ △ ♂	23:14
	☽ # ⚷	23:51
6 W	☽ □ ♃	2:32
	☽ □ ♄	10:11
	☽ △ ⚳	12:48
	☽ ⚼ ♆	15:38
	☽ ⚼ ♀	16:41
	☽ ☍ ♅	18:33
	☽ ⚻ ⚷	19:21
	☿ # ⚳	23:21
7 Th	☽ # ♅	10:00
	☿ ⚹ ♆	10:43
	☉ ☍ ☽	10:46
	☽ ∥ ♂	14:35
	☽ △ ♆	15:41
	☽ ☍ ☿	16:31
	☽ ⚻ ♀	17:05
	☽ ⚼ ⚷	19:29
	☿ ⚺ ♀	20:40
	☽ ⚹ ♇	23:04
8 F	☽ □ ♂	1:34
	☽ ⚹ ♃	2:40
	☉ # ☽	4:49
	☽ ∥ ⚳	7:52
	☽ ⚹ ♄	10:28
	☿ ∠ ⚷	13:15
	☽ □ ⚳	14:01
	☽ # ☿	15:49
	☽ ⚻ ♅	19:16
	☽ △ ⚷	20:05
	☽ ∥ ♄	21:00
	☽ ∠ ♇	23:39
9 Sa	♂ ⚺ ♃	1:55
	☽ ∠ ♃	3:23
	☽ ∥ ♃	4:37
	☽ ∠ ♄	11:22
	☿ △ ♇	13:18
	☽ ∥ ♇	14:39
	☉ ⚻ ☽	15:36
	☽ □ ♆	17:15
	☿ # ♄	18:36
	☽ ☍ ♀	19:15
	☽ ⚼ ♅	20:32
	☉ # ⚳	22:53
10 Su	☽ ⚺ ♇	0:57
	☽ ⚻ ☿	3:04
	☽ ⚺ ♃	4:50
	☽ ⚹ ♂	6:12
	☊ D	9:01
	☽ ⚺ ♄	13:04
	☿ △ ♃	14:37
	☉ ⚹ ♆	16:17
	☽ ⚹ ⚳	17:49
	☉ ⚼ ☽	19:25
	☽ △ ♅	22:40
	☽ □ ⚷	23:29
11 M	♄ R	4:10
	☿ □ ♂	7:34
	☿ # ♃	8:20
	☽ ∠ ♂	10:00
	☽ ⚼ ☿	10:19
	♂ # ♅	16:57
	☽ ∠ ⚳	21:09
	☿ ♊	21:59
	☽ ⚹ ♆	22:06
12 Tu	☉ △ ☽	0:25
	☽ ⚻ ♀	0:31
	☉ ⚺ ♀	1:59
	☽ ☌ ♇	6:15
	☽ ☌ ♃	10:31
	☽ ⚺ ♂	14:57
	☽ △ ☿	19:08
	☽ ☌ ♄	19:19
	☿ △ ♄	20:15
13 W	☽ ∥ ♇	0:06
	☽ # ☿	1:31
	☽ ⚺ ⚳	1:32
	☽ ∠ ♆	2:01
	♂ ♓	4:18
	☽ ⚼ ♀	4:32
	☽ □ ♅	5:53
	☽ ⚹ ⚷	6:44
	♀ R	6:46
	☿ # ♇	7:09
	☉ ∠ ⚷	7:31
	☽ ∥ ♃	11:31
	☽ ∥ ♄	20:17
14 Th	☉ # ☽	4:51
	☽ ⚺ ♆	6:51
	☽ △ ♀	9:21
	☽ ∠ ⚷	11:46
	☽ ∥ ⚳	13:43
	☉ □ ☽	14:04
	☊ R	14:17
	♃ R	14:33
	☿ □ ⚳	14:59
	☽ ⚺ ♇	15:24
	☽ ⚺ ♃	19:59
15 F	☽ ☌ ♂	4:07
	☽ ⚺ ♄	5:16
	☉ △ ♇	6:51
	☽ ☌ ⚳	13:03
	☽ # ♅	13:48
	☿ ⚺ ♅	15:18
	☽ ⚹ ♅	16:42
	☽ □ ☿	16:59
	☽ ⚺ ⚷	17:32
	☽ ∥ ♂	19:25
	☿ ⚹ ⚷	20:23
	☽ ∠ ♇	21:07
16 Sa	♂ ⚺ ♄	0:26
	☽ ∠ ♃	1:48
	☽ ∠ ♄	11:14
	☿ ⚼ ♇	17:55
	☽ ☌ ♆	18:35
	☽ □ ♀	20:36
	☽ ∠ ♅	22:59
17 Su	☽ ⚹ ♇	3:16
	☉ ⚹ ☽	7:14
	☽ ⚹ ♃	8:00
	⚴ R	8:30
	☽ # ⚷	8:42
	☽ ∥ ♆	14:00
	☉ △ ♃	16:41
	☽ ⚹ ♄	17:30
	☽ ⚺ ♂	20:02
	☿ ⚼ ♃	22:51
18 M	☽ ⚺ ⚳	2:42
	☽ ⚺ ♅	5:28
	☽ ☌ ⚷	6:15
	☉ ∠ ☽	16:17
	☽ ⚹ ☿	17:18
19 Tu	☽ ∠ ♂	4:13
	☉ # ♄	4:56
	☽ ⚺ ♆	7:21
	☽ ⚹ ♀	8:18
	☽ ∠ ⚳	9:37
	☽ # ♆	12:56
	☽ □ ♇	15:52
	☽ ∥ ⚷	18:29
	☽ □ ♃	20:34
20 W	☉ ⚺ ☽	1:10
	☽ ∠ ☿	5:03
	☽ □ ♄	5:59
	☿ ⚼ ♄	11:15
	☽ ⚹ ♂	12:11
	☽ ∠ ♆	13:31
	☽ ∠ ♀	13:46
	☉ ♊	13:50
	☽ ⚹ ⚳	16:18
	☽ ☌ ♅	18:08
	☽ ⚺ ⚷	18:50
	♀ □ ♆	23:04
21 Th	☽ # ♂	0:37
	☽ ∥ ♅	13:17
	☽ ⚺ ☿	16:02
	☽ ⚺ ♀	18:47
	☽ ⚹ ♆	19:20
22 F	☽ ∠ ⚷	0:38
	☽ △ ♇	3:30
	☽ △ ♃	8:02
	☿ ☌ ♀	8:42
	☽ # ⚳	10:48
	☉ △ ♄	12:03
	☿ □ ♆	15:44
	☽ △ ♄	17:13
	☉ ☌ ☽	17:40
23 Sa	☽ □ ♂	2:45
	☽ □ ⚳	4:23
	☽ ⚺ ♅	5:22
	☽ ⚹ ⚷	5:58
	☽ # ♄	6:03
	☽ ⚼ ♇	8:40
	☽ ⚼ ♃	13:06
	☉ ∥ ☽	13:12
	☽ # ♃	14:55
	☽ ⚼ ♄	22:09
24 Su	☽ # ♇	2:18
	☽ ☌ ♀	3:16
	☿ ∠ ♅	3:34
	☽ □ ♆	5:35
	☽ ∠ ♅	10:14
	☽ ☌ ☿	11:11
	☽ ⚻ ♇	13:20
	☉ # ♃	15:24
	☽ ⚻ ♃	17:39
	☊ D	21:33
	♂ ☌ ⚳	21:50
25 M	☿ ∥ ♀	1:07
	☽ ⚻ ♄	2:33
	☿ ⚻ ♇	4:27
	♂ ⚹ ♅	6:49
	☉ ⚺ ☽	7:44
	☽ △ ⚳	14:21
	☽ ⚹ ♅	14:35
	☽ △ ♂	14:59
	☽ □ ⚷	15:07
	♂ ⚺ ⚷	17:36
26 Tu	☽ ⚺ ♀	9:32
	⚳ ⚹ ♅	10:23
	☽ △ ♆	13:44
	☉ ∠ ☽	13:45
	☿ ⚻ ♃	15:36
	☽ ⚼ ⚳	18:28
	☽ ⚼ ♂	20:08
	☽ ☍ ♇	21:04
27 W	☽ ☍ ♃	1:07
	☽ ⚺ ☿	2:20
	⚵ D	2:52
	☽ ☍ ♄	9:43
	☽ ∠ ♀	11:49
	♂ ∠ ♇	14:10
	☽ # ♇	14:46
	☽ ⚼ ♆	16:58
	☉ ⚹ ☽	19:04
	☉ ∥ ☽	20:40
	☽ □ ♅	21:35
	☽ ⚻ ⚳	21:59
	☽ △ ⚷	22:01
28 Th	☽ ⚻ ♂	0:37
	☽ # ♃	1:14
	⚳ ⚺ ⚷	1:47
	☽ ∠ ☿	8:26
	☽ # ♄	9:31
	☽ ⚹ ♀	13:31
	☿ ♋	18:10
	☽ ⚻ ♆	19:37
29 F	☽ ⚼ ⚷	0:36
	☽ ⚻ ♇	2:32
	☽ # ⚳	4:00
	☽ ⚻ ♃	6:18
	☉ ⚺ ♅	8:14
	☽ ⚹ ☿	13:34
	☉ ⚹ ⚷	13:58
	☽ ⚻ ♄	14:36
	♀ ⚼ ♄	16:44
	☉ □ ⚳	21:24
	☽ ∥ ♅	21:31
30 Sa	☿ ⚻ ♄	0:26
	☽ △ ♅	2:16
	☽ ⚻ ⚷	2:37
	☽ ☍ ⚳	3:11
	☊ R	3:26
	☉ □ ☽	3:31
	☽ ⚼ ♇	4:25
	☽ ☍ ♂	7:35
	☽ ⚼ ♃	8:03
	☽ □ ♀	15:20
	☽ ⚼ ♄	16:13
	☉ ⚼ ♇	16:30
	♂ ∠ ♃	16:45
	☽ # ♂	19:29
	☽ ☍ ♆	23:15
31 Su	☽ ⚼ ♅	3:48
	☽ △ ♇	5:47
	☽ △ ♃	9:18
	☽ ∥ ⚷	9:52
	☽ # ♆	15:31
	☽ △ ♄	17:21
	☽ □ ☿	21:17

June 2020

LONGITUDE

Day	Sid.Time	☉	☽	☽ 12 hour	Mean☊	True☊	☿	♀	♂	⚳	♃	♄	⚷	♅	♆	♇
	h m s	° ′ ″	° ′ ″	° ′ ″	° ′	° ′	° ′	° ′	° ′	° ′	° ′	° ′	° ′	° ′	° ′	° ′
1 M	16 39 44	10♊58 15	5♎37 14	12♎52 30	0♋11.3	29♊13.0	4♋07.1	15♊18.3	12♓41.9	9♓20.4	26♑45.9	1♒36.6	8♈44.1	8♉33.6	20♓49.6	24♑41.6
2 Tu	16 43 41	11 55 44	20 10 03	27 29 14	0 08.1	29R 11.3	5 16.0	14R 41.2	13 21.6	9 31.1	26R 42.6	1R 34.6	8 46.1	8 36.6	20 50.3	24R 40.6
3 W	16 47 38	12 53 12	4♏49 22	12♏09 37	0 04.9	29 09.2	6 21.4	14 03.6	14 01.3	9 41.6	26 39.1	1 32.5	8 48.0	8 39.6	20 51.0	24 39.6
4 Th	16 51 34	13 50 38	19 29 10	26 47 12	0 01.8	29 07.3	7 23.2	13 25.8	14 40.9	9 51.9	26 35.4	1 30.3	8 49.9	8 42.6	20 51.6	24 38.6
5 F	16 55 31	14 48 03	4♐02 52	11♐15 24	29♊58.6	29 05.8	8 21.3	12 48.1	15 20.5	10 01.9	26 31.6	1 28.1	8 51.7	8 45.5	20 52.2	24 37.6
6 Sa	16 59 27	15 45 28	18 24 06	25 28 22	29 55.4	29D 05.0	9 15.7	12 10.7	15 59.9	10 11.6	26 27.6	1 25.7	8 53.5	8 48.5	20 52.8	24 36.6
7 Su	17 03 24	16 42 51	2♑27 41	9♑21 41	29 52.2	29 04.8	10 06.2	11 33.9	16 39.2	10 21.1	26 23.4	1 23.3	8 55.3	8 51.4	20 53.3	24 35.5
8 M	17 07 20	17 40 14	16 10 06	22 52 48	29 49.1	29 05.2	10 52.8	10 57.9	17 18.5	10 30.4	26 19.1	1 20.8	8 57.0	8 54.2	20 53.8	24 34.5
9 Tu	17 11 17	18 37 36	29 29 47	6♒01 10	29 45.9	29 06.0	11 35.5	10 22.8	17 57.6	10 39.3	26 14.6	1 18.2	8 58.7	8 57.1	20 54.3	24 33.4
10 W	17 15 13	19 34 58	12♒27 07	18 47 56	29 42.7	29 06.9	12 14.0	9 49.0	18 36.7	10 48.0	26 09.9	1 15.6	9 00.3	8 59.9	20 54.8	24 32.3
11 Th	17 19 10	20 32 18	25 04 00	1♓15 44	29 39.5	29 07.8	12 48.4	9 16.7	19 15.6	10 56.5	26 05.1	1 12.8	9 01.9	9 02.7	20 55.2	24 31.1
12 F	17 23 07	21 29 39	7♓23 36	13 28 08	29 36.4	29 08.3	13 18.5	8 45.9	19 54.5	11 04.6	26 00.1	1 10.0	9 03.4	9 05.5	20 55.6	24 30.0
13 Sa	17 27 03	22 26 58	19 29 53	25 29 25	29 33.2	29R 08.6	13 44.2	8 16.9	20 33.2	11 12.5	25 55.0	1 07.1	9 04.9	9 08.2	20 55.9	24 28.8
14 Su	17 31 00	23 24 18	1♈27 16	7♈24 03	29 30.0	29 08.5	14 05.6	7 49.8	21 11.8	11 20.1	25 49.7	1 04.2	9 06.3	9 10.9	20 56.2	24 27.6
15 M	17 34 56	24 21 37	13 20 19	19 16 36	29 26.8	29 08.2	14 22.4	7 24.8	21 50.3	11 27.4	25 44.3	1 01.1	9 07.7	9 13.6	20 56.5	24 26.4
16 Tu	17 38 53	25 18 55	25 13 27	1♉11 21	29 23.7	29 07.8	14 34.8	7 01.9	22 28.6	11 34.5	25 38.8	0 58.0	9 09.0	9 16.2	20 56.8	24 25.2
17 W	17 42 49	26 16 13	7♉10 48	13 12 14	29 20.5	29 07.4	14 42.5	6 41.2	23 06.8	11 41.2	25 33.1	0 54.8	9 10.3	9 18.8	20 57.0	24 24.0
18 Th	17 46 46	27 13 31	19 16 02	25 22 34	29 17.3	29 07.1	14R 45.7	6 22.8	23 44.9	11 47.6	25 27.3	0 51.6	9 11.5	9 21.4	20 57.2	24 22.8
19 F	17 50 42	28 10 49	1♊32 07	7♊44 59	29 14.1	29D 07.0	14 44.4	6 06.7	24 22.9	11 53.8	25 21.3	0 48.3	9 12.7	9 24.0	20 57.3	24 21.5
20 Sa	17 54 39	29 08 06	14 01 20	20 21 21	29 10.9	29 07.0	14 38.7	5 53.0	25 00.7	11 59.6	25 15.2	0 44.9	9 13.9	9 26.5	20 57.4	24 20.2
21 Su	17 58 36	0♋05 23	26 45 08	3♋12 43	29 07.8	29R 07.0	14 28.5	5 41.7	25 38.3	12 05.1	25 09.0	0 41.5	9 15.0	9 29.0	20 57.5	24 18.9
22 M	18 02 32	1 02 39	9♋44 07	16 19 19	29 04.6	29 06.9	14 14.2	5 32.8	26 15.8	12 10.4	25 02.7	0 38.0	9 16.0	9 31.4	20 57.6	24 17.7
23 Tu	18 06 29	1 59 55	22 58 11	29 40 39	29 01.4	29 06.8	13 55.9	5 26.3	26 53.2	12 15.3	24 56.2	0 34.4	9 17.0	9 33.8	20R 57.6	24 16.3
24 W	18 10 25	2 57 10	6♌26 32	13♌15 39	28 58.2	29 06.5	13 33.9	5 22.1	27 30.3	12 19.8	24 49.7	0 30.8	9 18.0	9 36.2	20 57.6	24 15.0
25 Th	18 14 22	3 54 25	20 07 50	27 02 49	28 55.1	29 06.0	13 08.4	5D 20.3	28 07.3	12 24.1	24 43.0	0 27.1	9 18.9	9 38.5	20 57.6	24 13.7
26 F	18 18 18	4 51 40	4♍00 25	11♍00 21	28 51.9	29 05.4	12 39.9	5 20.8	28 44.2	12 28.0	24 36.3	0 23.4	9 19.7	9 40.8	20 57.5	24 12.4
27 Sa	18 22 15	5 48 53	18 02 22	25 06 12	28 48.7	29 04.9	12 08.8	5 23.6	29 20.8	12 31.6	24 29.4	0 19.6	9 20.5	9 43.1	20 57.4	24 11.0
28 Su	18 26 12	6 46 07	2♎11 34	9♎18 12	28 45.5	29D 04.6	11 35.7	5 28.6	29 57.3	12 34.9	24 22.4	0 15.7	9 21.2	9 45.3	20 57.2	24 09.6
29 M	18 30 08	7 43 19	16 25 45	23 33 56	28 42.4	29 04.7	11 00.9	5 35.7	0♈33.6	12 37.9	24 15.4	0 11.9	9 21.9	9 47.5	20 57.0	24 08.3
30 Tu	18 34 05	8♋40 31	0♏42 24	7♏50 46	28♊39.2	29♊05.2	10♋25.1	5♊45.1	1♈09.7	12♓40.5	24♑08.3	0♒07.9	9♈22.6	9♉49.7	20♓56.8	24♑06.9

1st of Month

Julian Day # 2459001.5
Obliquity 23°26'12"
SVP 4♓58'57"
GC 27♐07.5
Eris 24♈21.2

Day	⚴
1	0♒13.2R
6	29♑37.9R
11	28 52.7R
16	27 58.0R
21	26 54.6R
26	25 43.9R

Day	⚵
1	5♎52.3
6	6 04.2
11	6 23.7
16	6 50.3
21	7 23.7
26	8 03.4

Day	⚶
1	28♊48.1
6	0♋57.1
11	3 06.7
16	5 16.7
21	7 27.2
26	9 38.1

DECLINATION and LATITUDE

Day	☉ Decl	☽ Decl	☽ Lat	☽ 12h Decl	☿ Decl	☿ Lat	♀ Decl	♀ Lat	♂ Decl	♂ Lat	⚳ Decl	⚳ Lat	♃ Decl	♃ Lat	♄ Decl	♄ Lat
1 M	22N05	2N34	5N13	0S23	25N20	1N58	23N45	1N08	8S59	2S23	17S05	9S45	21S01	0S13	19S57	0S09
2 Tu	22 13	3S20	4 54	6 15	25 12	1 52	23 27	0 54	8 45	2 24	17 04	9 49	21 01	0 13	19 57	0 09
3 W	22 20	9 06	4 16	11 49	25 02	1 46	23 08	0 40	8 31	2 26	17 04	9 53	21 02	0 13	19 58	0 09
4 Th	22 28	14 23	3 22	16 42	24 52	1 38	22 50	0 25	8 18	2 27	17 04	9 57	21 03	0 13	19 59	0 09
5 F	22 34	18 46	2 14	20 31	24 40	1 30	22 31	0 11	8 04	2 29	17 04	10 01	21 04	0 13	19 59	0 10
6 Sa	22 41	21 57	0 59	23 02	24 27	1 21	22 12	0S03	7 50	2 30	17 04	10 05	21 05	0 14	19 60	0 10
7 Su	22 46	23 43	0S19	24 03	24 14	1 11	21 53	0 17	7 36	2 32	17 04	10 09	21 06	0 14	20 00	0 10
8 M	22 52	23 60	1 33	23 36	23 60	1 00	21 34	0 31	7 22	2 33	17 04	10 14	21 07	0 14	20 01	0 10
9 Tu	22 57	22 52	2 40	21 50	23 45	0 49	21 16	0 45	7 08	2 35	17 05	10 18	21 08	0 14	20 02	0 10
10 W	23 02	20 33	3 38	19 01	23 29	0 37	20 57	0 58	6 54	2 36	17 05	10 22	21 09	0 14	20 02	0 10
11 Th	23 06	17 17	4 23	15 23	23 14	0 24	20 39	1 12	6 40	2 38	17 06	10 27	21 10	0 14	20 03	0 10
12 F	23 10	13 21	4 54	11 11	22 57	0 11	20 22	1 25	6 26	2 39	17 07	10 31	21 11	0 15	20 04	0 10
13 Sa	23 13	8 56	5 12	6 38	22 41	0S03	20 05	1 37	6 12	2 41	17 08	10 35	21 12	0 15	20 05	0 10
14 Su	23 16	4 16	5 16	1 52	22 24	0 17	19 49	1 50	5 59	2 42	17 09	10 40	21 13	0 15	20 05	0 10
15 M	23 19	0N33	5 07	2N57	22 07	0 32	19 33	2 01	5 45	2 44	17 10	10 44	21 14	0 15	20 06	0 11
16 Tu	23 21	5 20	4 45	7 41	21 51	0 48	19 18	2 13	5 31	2 45	17 11	10 48	21 16	0 15	20 07	0 11
17 W	23 23	9 58	4 10	12 11	21 34	1 04	19 04	2 24	5 17	2 47	17 13	10 53	21 17	0 15	20 08	0 11
18 Th	23 24	14 17	3 23	16 15	21 17	1 20	18 50	2 34	5 04	2 48	17 14	10 57	21 18	0 16	20 08	0 11
19 F	23 25	18 04	2 27	19 42	21 01	1 37	18 38	2 44	4 50	2 50	17 16	11 02	21 19	0 16	20 09	0 11
20 Sa	23 26	21 07	1 23	22 17	20 45	1 53	18 26	2 53	4 36	2 51	17 18	11 06	21 21	0 16	20 10	0 11
21 Su	23 26	23 11	0 13	23 47	20 30	2 10	18 16	3 02	4 23	2 53	17 20	11 11	21 22	0 16	20 11	0 11
22 M	23 26	24 03	0N59	23 60	20 15	2 26	18 06	3 11	4 09	2 54	17 22	11 16	21 23	0 16	20 12	0 11
23 Tu	23 25	23 35	2 08	22 51	20 01	2 42	17 57	3 19	3 56	2 56	17 25	11 20	21 25	0 16	20 13	0 11
24 W	23 24	21 46	3 12	20 22	19 47	2 58	17 49	3 26	3 42	2 57	17 27	11 25	21 26	0 16	20 13	0 11
25 Th	23 23	18 40	4 06	16 42	19 35	3 14	17 41	3 33	3 29	2 59	17 30	11 29	21 27	0 17	20 14	0 12
26 F	23 21	14 29	4 47	12 04	19 23	3 28	17 35	3 40	3 16	3 00	17 32	11 34	21 29	0 17	20 15	0 12
27 Sa	23 19	9 30	5 11	6 47	19 12	3 42	17 30	3 46	3 03	3 02	17 35	11 39	21 30	0 17	20 16	0 12
28 Su	23 16	3 58	5 16	1 05	19 02	3 55	17 25	3 52	2 49	3 03	17 38	11 43	21 31	0 17	20 17	0 12
29 M	23 13	1S48	5 02	4S41	18 53	4 06	17 21	3 57	2 36	3 05	17 41	11 48	21 33	0 17	20 18	0 12
30 Tu	23N09	7S30	4N30	10S13	18N46	4S17	17N18	4S02	2S23	3S06	17S45	11S53	21S34	0S18	20S19	0S12

Day	⚷ Decl	⚷ Lat	♅ Decl	♅ Lat	♆ Decl	♆ Lat	♇ Decl	♇ Lat
1	5N58	2N43	13N56	0S27	4S36	1S03	22S06	0S55
6	6 02	2 43	14 01	0 27	4 35	1 04	22 07	0 56
11	6 05	2 44	14 05	0 27	4 35	1 04	22 09	0 57
16	6 08	2 44	14 09	0 27	4 34	1 04	22 10	0 57
21	6 11	2 44	14 13	0 27	4 34	1 04	22 12	0 58
26	6 13	2 45	14 17	0 27	4 34	1 05	22 13	0 58

Day	⚴ Decl	⚴ Lat	⚵ Decl	⚵ Lat	⚶ Decl	⚶ Lat	Eris Decl	Eris Lat
1	20N53	41N52	5N37	8N40	22N41	0S45	1S21	11S35
6	21 19	42 25	5 30	8 37	22 47	0 39	1 20	11 35
11	21 40	42 53	5 20	8 35	22 52	0 32	1 20	11 35
16	21 55	43 17	5 07	8 31	22 54	0 26	1 19	11 36
21	22 04	43 35	4 51	8 28	22 54	0 20	1 19	11 36
26	22 06	43 47	4 33	8 25	22 52	0 14	1 19	11 36

Moon Phenomena

Max/0 Decl
dy hr mn
1 10:27 0 S
7 16:24 24S04
14 21:17 0 N
22 3:56 24N04
28 16:31 0 S

Max/0 Lat
dy hr mn
6 18:11 0 S
13 19:21 5S17
21 4:25 0 N
27 18:44 5N17

Perigee/Apogee
dy hr m kilometers
3 3:40 p 364367
15 0:58 a 404595
30 2:14 p 368958

PH dy hr mn
○ 5 19:14 15♐34
• 5 19:26 A 0.568
☾ 13 6:25 22♓42
● 21 6:43 0♋21
• 21 401:15A 00'38"
☽ 28 8:17 7♎06

Void of Course Moon

Last Aspect	☽ Ingress
2 10:41 ♃ □	♏ 2 16:07
4 11:38 ♃ ⚹	♐ 4 17:18
6 4:12 ♆ □	♑ 6 19:45
8 18:07 ♃ ☌	♒ 9 0:55
10 14:36 ☉ △	♓ 11 9:33
13 12:46 ♃ ⚹	♈ 13 21:04
16 0:51 ♃ □	♉ 16 9:37
18 12:03 ♃ △	♊ 18 21:01
20 21:49 ♂ □	♋ 21 6:03
23 7:21 ♂ △	♌ 23 12:34
24 5:35 ♅ □	♍ 25 17:06
27 20:03 ♂ ☍	♎ 27 20:18
29 13:03 ♃ □	♏ 29 22:49

DAILY ASPECTARIAN

1 M
☉⋕♇ 1:16
☽⚻♅ 4:53
☽☍⚷ 5:10
☽⚻⚳ 6:14
☉△☽ 9:29
☽⚻♂ 12:16
☽△♀ 15:21
☉⚼♃ 18:48

2 Tu
☽⚻♆ 1:06
☽∥♆ 5:11
☽⚼⚳ 7:13
☽□♇ 7:23
☽□♃ 10:41
☽⋕⚷ 10:51
☉⚼☽ 11:52
☽⚼♂ 14:04
☽⚼♀ 14:58
☽□♄ 18:39
⚳∠♇ 19:47
☽∥♂ 21:38

3 W
♀□♂ 0:42
⚴R♑ 0:56
☽⚼♆ 1:41
☽△☿ 2:42
☽☍♅ 6:18
☽⚻⚷ 6:31
☽△⚳ 8:04
☉⚻☽ 14:07
☽⚻♀ 14:29
☽△♂ 15:45
☉☌♀ 17:45
⚶ ♋ 18:56
☽⋕♅ 22:07

4 Th
☽△♆ 2:15
☽⚼☿ 5:06
☽⚼⚷ 7:09
☽⚹♇ 8:28
☽⚹♃ 11:38
☽∥⚳ 14:02
☽⚹♄ 19:44
☉∥♀ 20:57

5 F
☽⚻☿ 7:39
☽⚻♅ 7:52
☽△⚷ 8:01
☽∥♄ 8:09
☽∠♇ 9:16
☽□⚳ 10:04
☿⚹♅ 11:06
☽∠♃ 12:24
☿□⚷ 13:42
☽☍♀ 13:59
☽∥♃ 16:19
☉☍☽ 19:14
☽□♂ 19:45
☽∠♄ 20:41

6 Sa
☽∥♇ 1:36
☽⋕♀ 2:09
☽□♆ 4:12
♀⋕♇ 6:20
☉⋕☽ 8:01
☽⚼♅ 9:12
☽⚺♇ 10:31
☽⚺♃ 13:37
♂∠♄ 14:51
☉⚼♄ 16:10
☊D 18:05
☉□♂ 19:12
☽⚺♄ 22:09

7 Su
♀⚼♃ 7:52
☿△⚳ 9:18
☽△♅ 11:09
☽□⚷ 11:15
☽⚹⚳ 13:54
☽☍☿ 14:07
☽⚻♀ 15:12

8 M
☽⋕☿ 0:22
☽⋕☿ 0:24
☿⚺♀ 1:30
☽⚹♂ 2:08
☉⚻☽ 2:53
☽⚹♆ 8:27
♀□⚳ 14:54
☽☌♇ 15:02
☽⚼♀ 16:50
☽∠⚳ 16:56
☽☌♃ 18:07
☉⋕☽ 22:55

9 Tu
☽☌♄ 3:18
☽∠♂ 6:41
☉⚼☽ 8:11
☽∥♇ 8:52
♀⋕♃ 9:45
☽∠♆ 11:48
☽□♅ 17:31
☽⚹⚷ 17:32
☽∥♃ 18:43
☽△♀ 19:16
☽⋕♀ 19:57
☽⚺⚳ 20:52
☽⚻☿ 23:34

10 W
☽∥♄ 4:07
♅⚺⚷ 7:22
☽⚺♂ 12:17
♀⚼♇ 12:45
☉△☽ 14:36
☽⚺♆ 16:02
☽∠⚷ 22:00
☽⚺♇ 22:57

11 Th
☽∥⚳ 1:13
☽⚺♃ 1:57
☽⚼☿ 5:32
☉∥☿ 9:05
☉□♆ 9:39
♀⚺♅ 9:51
♀⚹⚷ 10:51
☽⚺♄ 11:52
⚳∠♃ 15:44
☽⋕♅ 19:39

12 F
☽□♀ 2:36
☽⚺⚷ 3:17
☽⚹♅ 3:21
☽∠♇ 4:09
☽∠♃ 7:04
☽☌⚳ 7:21
☽△☿ 12:08
☽∠♄ 17:17

13 Sa
♀⋕♄ 0:35
☽☌♂ 2:14
☽☌♆ 2:52
☉□☽ 6:25
☊R 6:37
☽∠♅ 9:19
♂⋕⚷ 9:48
☽⚹♇ 9:57
☽⚹♃ 12:46
♂☌♆ 14:14
☽⋕⚷ 14:37
☽∥♂ 14:52
☽∥♆ 22:26
☽⚹♄ 23:14

14 Su
☽⚹♀ 12:25
☽☌⚷ 15:28
☽⚺♅ 15:39
☽⚺⚳ 20:10
☉∠♅ 20:28
☿⋕♇ 20:36

15 M
☉⚻♇ 1:59
☽□☿ 2:08
☽⚺♆ 15:22
☽∠♀ 17:45
☽⚺♂ 18:09
☽⋕♆ 20:07
☽□♇ 22:23

16 Tu
☉⚹☽ 0:12
☽□♃ 0:51
☽⋕♂ 0:51
☽∠⚳ 2:45
☽∥⚷ 4:04
☉⚻♃ 7:34
☽□♄ 11:30
☽∠♆ 21:32
☽⚺♀ 23:02

17 W
☽∠♂ 1:58
☽⚺⚷ 3:59
☽☌♅ 4:16
☉∠☽ 8:51
☽⚹⚳ 9:04
☽⚹☿ 15:04
☿⋕♃ 23:09
☽∥♅ 23:27

18 Th
☽⚹♆ 3:19
☿R 5:00
☽⚹♂ 9:18
☽∠⚷ 9:42
☽△♇ 10:02
☽△♃ 12:03
☉⚺☽ 16:56
☽⋕⚳ 18:33
☽∠☿ 20:32
☽△♄ 22:35
♂⚹♇ 23:10

19 F
♂∠♅ 0:44
☽∥♀ 3:47
☽☌♀ 8:41
☽⚹⚷ 14:50
☽⚼♇ 15:04
☽⚺♅ 15:13
☽⋕♄ 15:45
☽⚼♃ 16:52
☽□⚳ 20:06
☽∥☿ 21:05
☊D 21:59

20 Sa
☽⚺☿ 1:10
☽⋕♃ 2:13
☽⚼♄ 3:16
♂∥♆ 3:50
♂⚹♃ 7:57
☽⋕♇ 11:00
☽□♆ 13:08
☽⚻♇ 19:27
☽∠♅ 19:45
☽⚻♃ 21:02
☉ ♋ 21:45
☽□♂ 21:49

21 Su
☉∥☽ 4:29
☊R 5:20
☉☌☽ 6:43
☽⚻♄ 7:18
☉⚻♄ 14:15
☽⚺♀ 16:23
☽□⚷ 23:08
☽⚹♅ 23:37

22 M
☽△⚳ 4:29
☿⋕♄ 5:18
☽☌☿ 8:02
☽∠♀ 19:28
☽△♆ 20:23

23 Tu
☽☍♇ 2:20
☉∥☽ 3:16
☽☍♃ 3:30
♆R 4:33
☽△♂ 7:21
☽⚼⚳ 7:43
☽☍♄ 13:32
☉⚺☽ 17:21
☽⋕♇ 19:26
☽⚹♀ 22:07
☽⚼♆ 23:09

24 W
☽⋕♃ 3:04
☽△⚷ 5:03
☽□♅ 5:35
☽⚻⚳ 10:25
☽⚼♂ 11:11
☽⚺☿ 12:10
☽⋕♄ 12:59
☽∥☿ 17:23
☉∠☽ 21:43

25 Th
☽⚻♆ 1:27
☽∥♀ 6:18
♀D 6:49
☽⚻♇ 7:06
☽⋕⚳ 7:14
☽⚼⚷ 7:17
☽⚻♃ 7:54
☽∠☿ 13:26
☽⚻♂ 14:30
☽⚻♄ 17:48

26 F
☽∥♅ 1:03
☉⚹☽ 1:35
☽□♀ 2:18
♀⋕⚳ 7:27
☿△⚳ 8:23
☽⚼♇ 8:54
☽⚻⚷ 9:08
☽⚼♃ 9:31
☽△♅ 9:46
☉⚺♀ 12:43
☽⚹☿ 14:19
☽☍⚳ 14:34
☽⚼♄ 19:24

27 Sa
☽☍♆ 4:58
☽△♇ 10:25
☽△♃ 10:52
☽⚼♅ 11:23
☽∥⚷ 14:21
☽☍♂ 20:03
☽△♄ 20:45
☽⋕♆ 21:25

28 Su
♂ ♈ 1:46
☽⋕♂ 4:58
☽△♀ 5:35
☊D 8:08
☉□☽ 8:17
♂⚹♄ 11:00
☽☍⚷ 12:06
☽⚻♅ 12:48
☽□☿ 15:15
☽⚻⚳ 17:35

29 M
☽∥♂ 3:12
☽⚼♀ 7:05
☽⚻♆ 7:36
☽∥♆ 11:34
☽□♇ 12:56
☽□♃ 13:03
☽⋕⚷ 18:36
☽⚼⚳ 18:53
☽□♄ 23:02

30 Tu
☽⚻♂ 0:48
♃☌♇ 5:48
☽⚻♀ 8:35
☽⚼♆ 8:48
☉△☽ 14:21
☽⚻⚷ 14:35
☽☍♅ 15:22
☽△☿ 15:40
☉□⚷ 17:50
☽△⚳ 20:11
☿⚹♅ 22:14

LONGITUDE

Day	Sid.Time	☉	☽	☽ 12 hour	Mean ☊	True ☊	☿	♀	♂
	h m s	° ' "	° ' "	° ' "	° '	° '	° '	° '	° '
1 W	18 38 01	9♋37 43	14♏58 41	22♏05 45	28♊36.0	29♊05.9	9♋49.0	5♊56.5	1♈45.7
2 Th	18 41 58	10 34 55	29 11 32	6♐15 38	28 32.8	29 06.8	9R 13.0	6 09.9	2 21.4
3 F	18 45 54	11 32 06	13♐17 38	20 17 05	28 29.7	29 07.6	8 38.0	6 25.3	2 57.0
4 Sa	18 49 51	12 29 17	27 13 37	4♑06 51	28 26.5	29R 08.0	8 04.3	6 42.7	3 32.3
5 Su	18 53 47	13 26 28	10♑56 26	17 42 04	28 23.3	29 07.7	7 32.7	7 01.9	4 07.5
6 M	18 57 44	14 23 39	24 23 33	1♒00 40	28 20.1	29 06.7	7 03.8	7 22.9	4 42.4
7 Tu	19 01 41	15 20 49	7♒33 21	14 01 32	28 17.0	29 05.0	6 37.9	7 45.6	5 17.1
8 W	19 05 37	16 18 01	20 25 18	26 44 44	28 13.8	29 02.7	6 15.6	8 10.0	5 51.6
9 Th	19 09 34	17 15 12	3♓00 03	9♓11 31	28 10.6	29 00.1	5 57.4	8 36.1	6 25.9
10 F	19 13 30	18 12 23	15 19 26	21 24 13	28 07.4	28 57.6	5 43.5	9 03.7	7 00.0
11 Sa	19 17 27	19 09 35	27 26 17	3♈26 07	28 04.2	28 55.5	5 34.2	9 32.9	7 33.7
12 Su	19 21 23	20 06 48	9♈24 15	15 21 13	28 01.1	28D 54.1	5D 29.9	10 03.5	8 07.3
13 M	19 25 20	21 04 01	21 17 36	27 13 59	27 57.9	28 53.6	5 30.7	10 35.4	8 40.6
14 Tu	19 29 16	22 01 14	3♉10 57	9♉09 07	27 54.7	28 54.1	5 36.7	11 08.8	9 13.6
15 W	19 33 13	22 58 28	15 09 03	21 11 20	27 51.5	28 55.3	5 48.1	11 43.4	9 46.3
16 Th	19 37 10	23 55 43	27 16 30	3♊25 03	27 48.4	28 56.9	6 04.9	12 19.3	10 18.8
17 F	19 41 06	24 52 58	9♊37 28	15 54 07	27 45.2	28 58.5	6 27.3	12 56.4	10 50.9
18 Sa	19 45 03	25 50 14	22 15 23	28 41 29	27 42.0	28R 59.5	6 55.1	13 34.7	11 22.8
19 Su	19 48 59	26 47 30	5♋12 38	11♋48 53	27 38.8	28 59.5	7 28.5	14 14.0	11 54.4
20 M	19 52 56	27 44 48	18 30 14	25 16 33	27 35.6	28 58.2	8 07.3	14 54.4	12 25.6
21 Tu	19 56 52	28 42 05	2♌07 37	9♌03 04	27 32.5	28 55.6	8 51.5	15 35.9	12 56.5
22 W	20 00 49	29 39 23	16 02 31	23 05 26	27 29.3	28 51.8	9 41.2	16 18.3	13 27.1
23 Th	20 04 45	0♌36 42	0♍11 15	7♍19 23	27 26.1	28 47.2	10 36.2	17 01.6	13 57.3
24 F	20 08 42	1 34 00	14 29 10	21 40 00	27 22.9	28 42.5	11 36.4	17 45.9	14 27.2
25 Sa	20 12 39	2 31 20	28 51 15	6♎02 21	27 19.8	28 38.4	12 41.8	18 31.1	14 56.7
26 Su	20 16 35	3 28 39	13♎12 48	20 22 09	27 16.6	28 35.5	13 52.3	19 17.0	15 25.9
27 M	20 20 32	4 25 59	27 30 01	4♏36 06	27 13.4	28D 34.0	15 07.8	20 03.8	15 54.7
28 Tu	20 24 28	5 23 20	11♏40 08	18 41 58	27 10.2	28 34.0	16 28.1	20 51.4	16 23.1
29 W	20 28 25	6 20 40	25 41 26	2♐38 26	27 07.1	28 35.0	17 53.2	21 39.7	16 51.2
30 Th	20 32 21	7 18 02	9♐32 53	16 24 45	27 03.9	28 36.4	19 22.8	22 28.8	17 18.8
31 F	20 36 18	8♌15 24	23 13 55	0♑00 22	27♊00.7	28♊37.4	20♋56.7	23♊18.6	17♈46.1

Day	⚳	♃	♄	⚷	♅	♆	♇
	° '	° '	° '	° '	° '	° '	° '
1 W	12♓42.8	24♑01.1	0♒04.0	9♈23.2	9♉51.8	20♓56.6	24♑05.5
2 Th	12 44.7	23R 53.8	29♑59.9	9 23.7	9 53.9	20R 56.3	24R 04.1
3 F	12 46.4	23 46.5	29R 55.9	9 24.2	9 55.9	20 56.0	24 02.7
4 Sa	12 47.6	23 39.1	29 51.8	9 24.6	9 57.9	20 55.7	24 01.3
5 Su	12 48.6	23 31.7	29 47.7	9 25.0	9 59.9	20 55.3	23 59.9
6 M	12 49.1	23 24.2	29 43.5	9 25.3	10 01.8	20 54.9	23 58.5
7 Tu	12R 49.4	23 16.6	29 39.3	9 25.6	10 03.7	20 54.5	23 57.0
8 W	12 49.3	23 09.0	29 35.1	9 25.8	10 05.5	20 54.1	23 55.6
9 Th	12 48.8	23 01.4	29 30.8	9 26.0	10 07.3	20 53.6	23 54.2
10 F	12 48.0	22 53.7	29 26.5	9 26.1	10 09.1	20 53.1	23 52.7
11 Sa	12 46.8	22 46.0	29 22.2	9R 26.2	10 10.8	20 52.5	23 51.3
12 Su	12 45.2	22 38.3	29 17.9	9 26.2	10 12.4	20 51.9	23 49.8
13 M	12 43.3	22 30.6	29 13.5	9 26.2	10 14.1	20 51.3	23 48.4
14 Tu	12 41.1	22 22.9	29 09.1	9 26.1	10 15.6	20 50.7	23 46.9
15 W	12 38.5	22 15.1	29 04.7	9 26.0	10 17.2	20 50.0	23 45.5
16 Th	12 35.5	22 07.4	29 00.3	9 25.8	10 18.7	20 49.3	23 44.0
17 F	12 32.2	21 59.7	28 55.9	9 25.6	10 20.1	20 48.6	23 42.6
18 Sa	12 28.5	21 52.0	28 51.5	9 25.3	10 21.5	20 47.8	23 41.1
19 Su	12 24.4	21 44.3	28 47.1	9 24.9	10 22.9	20 47.1	23 39.7
20 M	12 20.0	21 36.6	28 42.6	9 24.5	10 24.2	20 46.3	23 38.2
21 Tu	12 15.3	21 29.0	28 38.2	9 24.1	10 25.5	20 45.4	23 36.8
22 W	12 10.1	21 21.3	28 33.7	9 23.6	10 26.7	20 44.6	23 35.4
23 Th	12 04.7	21 13.8	28 29.3	9 23.1	10 27.9	20 43.7	23 33.9
24 F	11 58.8	21 06.3	28 24.9	9 22.5	10 29.0	20 42.7	23 32.5
25 Sa	11 52.7	20 58.8	28 20.4	9 21.8	10 30.1	20 41.8	23 31.1
26 Su	11 46.2	20 51.4	28 16.0	9 21.1	10 31.1	20 40.8	23 29.6
27 M	11 39.3	20 44.0	28 11.6	9 20.3	10 32.1	20 39.8	23 28.2
28 Tu	11 32.2	20 36.8	28 07.2	9 19.5	10 33.0	20 38.8	23 26.8
29 W	11 24.7	20 29.6	28 02.8	9 18.7	10 33.9	20 37.8	23 25.4
30 Th	11 16.8	20 22.4	27 58.5	9 17.8	10 34.7	20 36.7	23 24.0
31 F	11♓08.7	20♑15.4	27♑54.2	9♈16.8	10♉35.5	20♓35.6	23♑22.6

1st of Month

Julian Day # 2459031.5
Obliquity 23°26'[illegible]2"
SVP 4♓58'[illegible]1"
GC 27♐07.5
Eris 24♈31.5

Day	⚴	Day	⚵	Day	⚶
1	24♑27.3R	1	8♎48.9	1	11♋49.3
6	23 06.8R	6	9 39.9	6	14 00.6
11	21 44.1R	11	10 35.9	11	16 12.1
16	20 21.3R	16	11 36.4	16	18 23.8
21	19 00.4R	21	12 41.3	21	20 35.5
26	17 43.5R	26	13 50.2	26	22 47.2
31	16 32.2R	31	15 02.7	31	24 58.8

DECLINATION and LATITUDE

Day	☉ Decl	☽ Decl	☽ Lat	☽ 12h Decl	☿ Decl	☿ Lat	♀ Decl	♀ Lat	♂ Decl	♂ Lat	⚳ Decl	⚳ Lat	♃ Decl	♃ Lat	♄ Decl	♄ Lat
1 W	23N05	12S49	3N41	15S13	18N39	4S26	17N15	4S06	2S10	3S08	17S48	11S57	21S36	0S18	20S20	0S12
2 Th	23 01	17 24	2 38	19 20	18 34	4 34	17 14	4 10	1 58	3 09	17 52	12 02	21 37	0 18	20 21	0 12
3 F	22 56	20 58	1 27	22 16	18 30	4 40	17 13	4 13	1 45	3 11	17 55	12 07	21 38	0 18	20 22	0 12
4 Sa	22 51	23 14	0 11	23 50	18 28	4 44	17 13	4 17	1 32	3 12	17 59	12 12	21 40	0 18	20 23	0 12
5 Su	22 45	24 04	1S05	23 56	18 26	4 47	17 13	4 20	1 20	3 14	18 03	12 16	21 41	0 18	20 24	0 12
6 M	22 40	23 27	2 15	22 39	18 27	4 49	17 14	4 22	1 07	3 15	18 07	12 21	21 43	0 18	20 25	0 13
7 Tu	22 33	21 33	3 16	20 10	18 28	4 49	17 15	4 24	0 55	3 17	18 12	12 26	21 44	0 19	20 26	0 13
8 W	22 27	18 34	4 06	16 46	18 31	4 47	17 17	4 26	0 42	3 18	18 16	12 31	21 46	0 19	20 27	0 13
9 Th	22 19	14 48	4 43	12 42	18 35	4 44	17 20	4 28	0 30	3 20	18 21	12 35	21 47	0 19	20 28	0 13
10 F	22 12	10 29	5 06	8 11	18 40	4 39	17 23	4 29	0 18	3 21	18 25	12 40	21 48	0 19	20 29	0 13
11 Sa	22 04	5 50	5 15	3 26	18 46	4 33	17 26	4 30	0 06	3 23	18 30	12 45	21 50	0 19	20 30	0 13
12 Su	21 56	1 01	5 09	1N24	18 53	4 26	17 30	4 31	0N06	3 24	18 35	12 50	21 51	0 19	20 31	0 13
13 M	21 47	3N48	4 51	6 10	19 01	4 18	17 34	4 31	0 18	3 25	18 40	12 54	21 53	0 19	20 32	0 13
14 Tu	21 38	8 29	4 20	10 44	19 11	4 09	17 38	4 31	0 29	3 27	18 45	12 59	21 54	0 20	20 33	0 13
15 W	21 29	12 54	3 38	14 57	19 20	3 59	17 43	4 31	0 41	3 28	18 50	13 04	21 55	0 20	20 34	0 13
16 Th	21 19	16 52	2 45	18 37	19 31	3 47	17 48	4 31	0 52	3 30	18 56	13 08	21 57	0 20	20 35	0 13
17 F	21 09	20 10	1 44	21 31	19 41	3 36	17 53	4 30	1 03	3 31	19 01	13 13	21 58	0 20	20 36	0 14
18 Sa	20 59	22 36	0 37	23 24	19 52	3 23	17 58	4 30	1 15	3 32	19 07	13 17	21 60	0 20	20 37	0 14
19 Su	20 48	23 54	0N34	24 04	20 04	3 10	18 03	4 29	1 26	3 34	19 13	13 22	22 01	0 20	20 38	0 14
20 M	20 37	23 53	1 45	23 21	20 15	2 57	18 09	4 28	1 36	3 35	19 19	13 27	22 02	0 20	20 39	0 14
21 Tu	20 25	22 28	2 51	21 14	20 26	2 43	18 15	4 26	1 47	3 36	19 25	13 31	22 04	0 21	20 40	0 14
22 W	20 13	19 40	3 49	17 48	20 37	2 28	18 20	4 25	1 58	3 38	19 31	13 36	22 05	0 21	20 41	0 14
23 Th	20 01	15 40	4 34	13 18	20 47	2 14	18 26	4 23	2 08	3 39	19 37	13 40	22 06	0 21	20 41	0 14
24 F	19 49	10 45	5 02	8 02	20 57	1 59	18 32	4 21	2 18	3 40	19 43	13 44	22 08	0 21	20 42	0 14
25 Sa	19 36	5 13	5 11	2 20	21 06	1 45	18 38	4 19	2 29	3 42	19 50	13 49	22 09	0 21	20 43	0 14
26 Su	19 23	0S35	5 01	3S29	21 13	1 30	18 44	4 17	2 39	3 43	19 56	13 53	22 10	0 21	20 44	0 14
27 M	19 09	6 20	4 33	9 06	21 20	1 15	18 50	4 15	2 48	3 44	20 03	13 57	22 11	0 21	20 45	0 14
28 Tu	18 55	11 43	3 48	14 11	21 25	1 01	18 55	4 13	2 58	3 46	20 09	14 01	22 13	0 21	20 46	0 15
29 W	18 41	16 26	2 49	18 27	21 28	0 47	19 01	4 10	3 08	3 47	20 16	14 05	22 14	0 22	20 47	0 15
30 Th	18 27	20 12	1 42	21 39	21 30	0 33	19 06	4 07	3 17	3 48	20 23	14 09	22 15	0 22	20 48	0 15
31 F	18N12	22S47	0N29	23S34	21N29	0S19	19N12	4S05	3N26	3S49	20S29	14S13	22S16	0S22	20S49	0S15

Day	⚷ Decl	⚷ Lat	♅ Decl	♅ Lat	♆ Decl	♆ Lat	♇ Decl	♇ Lat
1	6N15	2N45	14N20	0S27	4S35	1S05	22S15	0S59
6	6 16	2 46	14 24	0 27	4 36	1 05	22 17	0 59
11	6 17	2 46	14 26	0 27	4 37	1 05	22 19	0 60
16	6 17	2 46	14 29	0 27	4 38	1 05	22 20	1 00
21	6 17	2 47	14 31	0 27	4 40	1 06	22 22	1 01
26	6 16	2 47	14 32	0 27	4 42	1 06	22 24	1 01
31	6N15	2N48	14N34	0S28	4S44	1S06	22S25	1S01

Day	⚴ Decl	⚴ Lat	⚵ Decl	⚵ Lat	⚶ Decl	⚶ Lat	Eris Decl	Eris Lat
1	22N02	43N53	4N12	8N22	22N47	0S07	1S19	11S37
6	21 50	43 52	3 49	8 19	22 41	0 01	1 19	11 37
11	21 32	43 43	3 25	8 16	22 32	0N05	1 19	11 38
16	21 07	43 27	2 59	8 13	22 22	0 11	1 19	11 38
21	20 35	43 03	2 31	8 10	22 09	0 18	1 20	11 38
26	19 57	42 32	2 02	8 08	21 54	0 24	1 20	11 39
31	19N14	41N55	1N33	8N06	21N38	0N30	1S21	11S39

Moon Phenomena

Max/0 Decl

dy	hr mn	
5	1:36	24S04
12	5:03	0 N
19	11:53	24N04
25	21:35	0 S

Max/0 Lat

dy	hr mn	
4	3:19	0 S
11	2:58	5S15
18	12:34	0 N
24	23:39	5N11
31	9:33	0 S

Perigee/Apogee

dy	hr m		kilometers
12	19:28	a	404198
25	5:03	p	368361

PH	dy	hr mn	
○	5	4:46	13♑38
(eclipse)	5	4:31	A 0.354
☾	12	23:30	21♈03
●	20	17:34	28♋27
☽	27	12:34	4♏56

Void of Course Moon

Last Aspect				☽ Ingress		
2	1:22	♄	⚹	♐	2	1:22
3	13:07	♆	□	♑	4	4:49
6	9:36	♄	☌	♒	6	10:09
7	4:39	♅	□	♓	8	18:14
11	3:50	♄	⚹	♈	11	5:07
13	15:55	♄	□	♉	13	17:35
16	3:22	♄	△	♊	16	5:20
17	21:16	♆	□	♋	18	14:25
20	17:56	♄	☍	♌	20	20:17
22	0:28	♀	⚹	♍	22	23:41
24	23:09	♄	△	♎	25	1:55
27	1:10	♄	□	♏	27	4:13
29	4:02	♄	⚹	♐	29	7:26
31	0:09	♀	☍	♑	31	11:59

DAILY ASPECTARIAN

1 W ☉☌☿ 2:54; ☽⚼♂ 3:08; ☉⚹♅ 6:08; ☽⋕♅ 7:33; ☽△♆ 10:03; ☽⚹♃ 15:07; ☽⚹♇ 15:21; ☽⚼⚷ 15:53; ☽⚼☿ 15:55; ☿□⚷ 16:57; ☉⚼☽ 17:27; ☽⋕♀ 23:01; ♄R♑ 23:39

2 Th ☽⚹♄ 1:22; ☽∥⚳ 2:46; ☽△♂ 5:36; ☽⋕☿ 6:56; ☽☍♀ 12:03; ☽∠♃ 16:21; ☽⚻☿ 16:21; ☽∠♇ 16:45; ☽△⚷ 17:21; ☽⚻♅ 18:15; ☽∥♄ 19:19; ☉⚻☽ 20:46; ☽□⚳ 23:06

3 F ☽∠♄ 2:47; ☽∥♃ 5:55; ☽∥♇ 12:00; ☽□♆ 13:07; ☽⚺♃ 17:52; ☽⚺♇ 18:27; ☉⋕☽ 18:57; ☽⚼♅ 20:04

4 Sa ☊R 3:25; ☽⚺♄ 4:34; ☉△⚳ 7:51; ☽□♂ 11:29; ☽⚻♀ 16:57; ☽☍☿ 18:14; ☽□⚷ 21:19; ☽△♅ 22:20

5 Su ☽⚹⚳ 3:18; ☉☍☽ 4:46; ☿⚺♀ 14:46; ☽⚹♆ 17:45; ☽⚼♀ 20:17; ☽☌♃ 22:14; ☽☌♇ 23:15

6 M ☽∠⚳ 6:12; ☽☌♄ 9:36; ☉⋕☽ 12:29; ☽∥♇ 16:16; ☽⚹♂ 19:38; ☽∠♆ 20:58; ☽∥♃ 22:07; ☽⚻☿ 22:21

7 Tu ☽△♀ 0:23; ☽⚹⚷ 3:27; ⚳R 4:02; ☽□♅ 4:39; ☽⚺⚳ 9:46; ☽∥♄ 9:52; ☉⚻☽ 15:38; ♀⚼♃ 23:15

8 W ☽⋕☿ 0:24; ☽∠♂ 0:52; ☽⚺♆ 0:54; ☽⚼☿ 1:33; ☽∥⚳ 2:04; ☽⚺♃ 5:07; ☽⚺♇ 6:37; ☽∠⚷ 7:36; ☽⋕♀ 8:35; ☿□♂ 10:43; ☽⚺♄ 17:20; ☉⚼☽ 22:26

9 Th ☽⋕♅ 2:12; ☉⋕♇ 4:37; ☽△☿ 5:36; ☽⚺♂ 6:57; ☽∠♃ 9:38; ☽□♀ 11:16; ☽∠♇ 11:25; ☽⚺⚷ 12:28; ☽⚹♅ 13:51; ♀⚼♇ 15:05; ☽☌⚳ 19:03; ☽∠♄ 22:17

10 F ☉△☽ 6:10; ☽☌♆ 10:58; ☽⚹♃ 14:48; ☽⚹♇ 16:53; ♀⚹⚷ 18:38; ☽∠♅ 19:29; ☽⋕⚷ 21:42

11 Sa ☽⚹♄ 3:50; ☽∥♆ 6:06; ☽□☿ 16:10; ⚷R 21:10; ☽☌♂ 21:17

12 Su ☽☌⚷ 0:04; ☽⚹♀ 1:23; ☽⚺♅ 1:37; ☽⋕♂ 4:24; ☽∥♂ 5:46; ☽⚺⚳ 6:44; ♀⚺♅ 7:13; ☿D 8:28; ☉⋕♃ 11:02; ☉△♆ 18:44; ☽⚺♆ 23:07; ☉□☽ 23:30; ☊D 23:38

13 M ☽□♃ 2:26; ☽⋕♆ 4:08; ☽□♇ 5:04; ☽∠♀ 9:06; ☽∥⚷ 12:35; ☽∠⚳ 12:57; ☽□♄ 15:55

14 Tu ☽⚹☿ 4:57; ☽∠♆ 5:21; ☉☍♃ 8:00; ♂☌⚷ 9:09; ☽⚺⚷ 12:34; ☽⚺♂ 12:44; ☽☌♅ 14:15; ☽⚺♀ 16:48; ☽⚹⚳ 19:00

15 W ☽∥♅ 9:09; ☽⚹♆ 11:17; ☽∠☿ 11:29; ☽△♃ 13:57; ☉⚹☽ 16:51; ☽△♇ 17:03; ☽∠⚷ 18:24; ☉☍♇ 19:14; ☽∠♂ 19:58; ♂⚺♅ 23:56

16 Th ☽△♄ 3:22; ☽∥♀ 6:22; ♀□⚳ 9:43; ☽⋕⚳ 14:45; ☽⚺☿ 17:41; ☽⚼♃ 18:59; ☽∥☿ 19:52; ☽⚼♇ 22:15; ☽⚹⚷ 23:37

17 F ☉∠☽ 0:32; ☽⚺♅ 1:22; ☽⚹♂ 2:27; ☽⋕♄ 3:35; ☽□⚳ 5:33; ☽☌♀ 6:41; ☉∥☽ 8:02; ☽⚼♄ 8:12; ☽⋕♃ 16:55; ☽⋕♇ 21:00; ☽□♆ 21:16; ☽⚻♃ 23:16

18 Sa ☽⚻♇ 2:40; ☽∠♅ 5:49; ☉⚺☽ 7:14; ♀⚼♄ 9:17; ☽⚻♄ 12:14; ☊R 12:37

19 Su ☽☌☿ 4:20; ☽□⚷ 7:39; ☽⚹♅ 9:25; ☽□♂ 12:40; ☽△⚳ 13:00; ☉⚼⚳ 14:23; ☽⚺♀ 17:13; ☉⋕♄ 20:13; ♂⚺⚳ 20:15

20 M ☽△♆ 4:02; ☽☍♃ 5:28; ☽☍♇ 9:06; ☽⚼⚳ 15:32; ☉☌☽ 17:34; ☽☍♄ 17:56; ☽∠♀ 21:11; ☉☍♄ 22:29; ☉∥☿ 22:54

21 Tu ☽⋕♇ 1:04; ☽⋕♃ 4:15; ☽⚼♆ 6:18; ☽⚺☿ 12:23; ☽△⚷ 12:36; ☽□♅ 14:23; ☿□⚷ 15:52; ☽⋕♄ 16:34; ☽∥☿ 17:22; ☽⚻⚳ 17:24; ☽△♂ 19:24; ☉∥☽ 19:44

22 W ☽⚹♀ 0:28; ☽⋕⚳ 1:02; ☽⚻♆ 8:00; ☽∥♀ 8:30; ☉ ♌ 8:38; ☽⚻♃ 8:58; ☿⋕♄ 9:04; ☽⚻♇ 12:49; ☽⚼⚷ 14:12; ☽∠☿ 15:42; ☿⚹♅ 20:26; ☽⚻♄ 21:09; ☽⚼♂ 21:51

23 Th ☉⚺☽ 0:46; ☽∥♅ 5:56; ☽⚼♃ 10:05; ☽⚼♇ 14:04; ☽⚻⚷ 15:27; ☽△♅ 17:17; ☽⚹☿ 18:48; ☽☍⚳ 19:50; ☽⚼♄ 22:13; ☽⚻♂ 23:57

24 F ☉∠☽ 3:44; ☽□♀ 5:47; ☉⋕⚳ 6:44; ☿△⚳ 7:43; ☽☍♆ 10:24; ☽△♃ 10:58; ☽△♇ 15:06; ☽⚼♅ 18:24; ☽∥⚷ 19:33; ☽△♄ 23:09

25 Sa ☽⋕♆ 2:11; ☉⚹☽ 6:34; ☽∥♂ 11:04; ☽☍⚷ 17:33; ☽⚻♅ 19:29; ☽⚻⚳ 21:36

26 Su ☽□☿ 1:12; ☽☍♂ 3:51; ☽⋕♂ 8:44; ☽△♀ 10:46; ☽⚻♆ 12:31; ☽□♃ 12:43; ☽∥♆ 17:06; ☽□♇ 17:13; ☽⚼⚳ 22:35; ☽⋕⚷ 23:42

27 M ☽□♄ 1:10; ☊D 12:22; ☉□☽ 12:34; ☽⚼♀ 13:32; ☽⚼♆ 13:47; ♃⚹♆ 16:08; ♀⚻♃ 17:37; ♀□♆ 17:49; ☽⚻⚷ 20:01; ☿□♂ 21:47; ☽☍♅ 22:06; ☽△⚳ 23:47; ☉∥♀ 23:52

28 Tu ☉⚼♆ 6:22; ☽⚻♂ 8:19; ☽△☿ 9:05; ☽⋕♅ 13:55; ☽⚹♃ 15:09; ☽△♆ 15:19; ☽⚻♀ 16:39; ☽⚹♇ 20:06; ☽⚼⚷ 21:38

29 W ☽⚹♄ 4:02; ☽⚼♂ 11:00; ☉⋕☽ 12:41; ☽⚼☿ 13:55; ☽⋕♀ 16:04; ☽∠♃ 16:48; ☉△☽ 19:48; ☽∠♇ 22:00; ☽△⚷ 23:34

30 Th ☽∥⚳ 1:22; ☽⚻♅ 1:48; ☽□⚳ 3:00; ☽∥♄ 4:43; ☽∠♄ 5:57; ☽⋕☿ 10:36; ☽△♂ 14:03; ☿☍♃ 14:18; ☽∥♃ 18:07; ☿△♆ 18:46; ☽⚺♃ 18:48; ☽□♆ 19:21; ☽⚻☿ 19:26; ☽∥♇ 19:50

31 F ☉⚼☽ 0:03; ☽☍♀ 0:09; ☽⚺♇ 0:15; ♀⚻♇ 1:52; ☽⚼♅ 4:11; ☽⚺♄ 8:13; ☊R 9:35; ☉∠♀ 10:49

August 2020

LONGITUDE

Day	Sid.Time	☉	☽	☽ 12 hour	Mean☊	True☊	☿	♀	♂	⚳	♃	♄	⚷	♅	♆	♇
	h m s	° ' "	° ' "	° ' "	° '	° '	° '	° '	° '	° '	° '	° '	° '	° '	° '	° '
1 Sa	20 40 14	9♌12 46	6♑44 01	13♑24 46	26♊57.5	28♊37.2	22♋34.8	24♊09.1	18♈12.9	11♓00.3	20♑08.5	27♑49.8	9♈15.9	10♉36.3	20♓34.5	23♑21.2
2 Su	20 44 11	10 10 10	20 02 33	26 37 16	26 54.4	28R 35.3	24 16.8	25 00.2	18 39.3	10R 51.5	20R 01.6	27R 45.6	9R 14.8	10 37.0	20R 33.3	23R 19.8
3 M	20 48 08	11 07 34	3♒08 50	9♒37 10	26 51.2	28 31.4	26 02.4	25 52.0	19 05.3	10 42.5	19 54.9	27 41.3	9 13.7	10 37.6	20 32.2	23 18.5
4 Tu	20 52 04	12 04 58	16 02 12	22 23 54	26 48.0	28 25.6	27 51.3	26 44.3	19 30.8	10 33.1	19 48.2	27 37.1	9 12.6	10 38.2	20 31.0	23 17.1
5 W	20 56 01	13 02 24	28 42 15	4♓57 18	26 44.8	28 18.4	29 43.2	27 37.3	19 55.9	10 23.5	19 41.6	27 32.9	9 11.4	10 38.7	20 29.8	23 15.8
6 Th	20 59 57	13 59 51	11♓09 09	17 17 53	26 41.6	28 10.2	1♌37.8	28 30.9	20 20.5	10 13.6	19 35.2	27 28.7	9 10.2	10 39.2	20 28.5	23 14.4
7 F	21 03 54	14 57 19	23 23 45	29 26 58	26 38.5	28 02.1	3 34.6	29 25.0	20 44.7	10 03.4	19 28.9	27 24.6	9 08.9	10 39.7	20 27.3	23 13.1
8 Sa	21 07 50	15 54 48	5♈27 50	11♈26 44	26 35.3	27 54.8	5 33.4	0♋19.7	21 08.3	9 53.0	19 22.7	27 20.5	9 07.5	10 40.1	20 26.0	23 11.8
9 Su	21 11 47	16 52 18	17 24 04	23 20 19	26 32.1	27 49.0	7 33.8	1 14.9	21 31.5	9 42.3	19 16.6	27 16.4	9 06.2	10 40.4	20 24.7	23 10.5
10 M	21 15 43	17 49 50	29 15 59	5♉11 38	26 28.9	27 45.0	9 35.3	2 10.6	21 54.1	9 31.3	19 10.6	27 12.4	9 04.8	10 40.7	20 23.4	23 09.2
11 Tu	21 19 40	18 47 23	11♉07 50	17 05 12	26 25.7	27D 43.0	11 37.7	3 06.9	22 16.2	9 20.2	19 04.8	27 08.4	9 03.3	10 41.0	20 22.1	23 07.9
12 W	21 23 37	19 44 57	23 04 23	29 06 00	26 22.6	27 42.7	13 40.6	4 03.5	22 37.8	9 08.8	18 59.1	27 04.5	9 01.8	10 41.2	20 20.7	23 06.6
13 Th	21 27 33	20 42 33	5♊10 43	11♊19 09	26 19.4	27 43.5	15 43.7	5 00.7	22 58.8	8 57.1	18 53.5	27 00.6	9 00.2	10 41.3	20 19.4	23 05.4
14 F	21 31 30	21 40 10	17 31 54	23 49 31	26 16.2	27R 44.5	17 46.7	5 58.3	23 19.2	8 45.3	18 48.1	26 56.8	8 58.7	10 41.5	20 18.0	23 04.1
15 Sa	21 35 26	22 37 49	0♋12 33	6♋41 23	26 13.0	27 44.9	19 49.5	6 56.3	23 39.0	8 33.3	18 42.8	26 53.0	8 57.0	10R 41.5	20 16.6	23 02.9
16 Su	21 39 23	23 35 30	13 16 21	19 57 42	26 09.9	27 43.7	21 51.8	7 54.8	23 58.3	8 21.1	18 37.7	26 49.3	8 55.3	10 41.5	20 15.1	23 01.7
17 M	21 43 19	24 33 11	26 45 29	3♌39 37	26 06.7	27 40.4	23 53.3	8 53.6	24 16.9	8 08.7	18 32.7	26 45.6	8 53.6	10 41.5	20 13.7	23 00.5
18 Tu	21 47 16	25 30 55	10♌39 54	17 45 54	26 03.5	27 34.8	25 54.1	9 52.9	24 34.9	7 56.2	18 27.9	26 42.0	8 51.9	10 41.4	20 12.3	22 59.4
19 W	21 51 12	26 28 39	24 57 03	2♍12 37	26 00.3	27 27.2	27 53.8	10 52.5	24 52.3	7 43.5	18 23.3	26 38.4	8 50.1	10 41.2	20 10.8	22 58.2
20 Th	21 55 09	27 26 25	9♍31 44	16 53 27	25 57.2	27 18.2	29 52.5	11 52.5	25 09.0	7 30.7	18 18.8	26 34.9	8 48.2	10 41.0	20 09.3	22 57.1
21 F	21 59 06	28 24 12	24 16 44	1♎40 33	25 54.0	27 08.9	1♍50.1	12 52.8	25 25.0	7 17.8	18 14.4	26 31.5	8 46.3	10 40.8	20 07.8	22 55.9
22 Sa	22 03 02	29 22 01	9♎03 53	16 25 49	25 50.8	27 00.5	3 46.5	13 53.5	25 40.3	7 04.8	18 10.3	26 28.1	8 44.4	10 40.5	20 06.3	22 54.8
23 Su	22 06 59	0♍19 50	23 45 31	1♏02 16	25 47.6	26 53.9	5 41.6	14 54.5	25 55.0	6 51.7	18 06.3	26 24.8	8 42.5	10 40.1	20 04.8	22 53.7
24 M	22 10 55	1 17 41	8♏15 31	15 24 51	25 44.4	26 49.6	7 35.4	15 55.9	26 09.0	6 38.5	18 02.4	26 21.6	8 40.5	10 39.7	20 03.2	22 52.7
25 Tu	22 14 52	2 15 33	22 30 00	29 30 50	25 41.3	26D 47.5	9 27.9	16 57.6	26 22.2	6 25.2	17 58.8	26 18.4	8 38.5	10 39.3	20 01.7	22 51.6
26 W	22 18 48	3 13 26	6♐27 19	13♐19 32	25 38.1	26 47.2	11 19.1	17 59.5	26 34.7	6 11.9	17 55.3	26 15.3	8 36.4	10 38.8	20 00.1	22 50.6
27 Th	22 22 45	4 11 21	20 07 35	26 51 40	25 34.9	26R 47.6	13 08.9	19 01.8	26 46.5	5 58.6	17 52.0	26 12.3	8 34.3	10 38.3	19 58.6	22 49.6
28 F	22 26 41	5 09 17	3♑31 58	10♑08 42	25 31.7	26 47.6	14 57.5	20 04.4	26 57.6	5 45.3	17 48.9	26 09.3	8 32.2	10 37.7	19 57.0	22 48.6
29 Sa	22 30 38	6 07 14	16 42 05	23 12 19	25 28.6	26 46.0	16 44.7	21 07.3	27 07.9	5 31.9	17 46.0	26 06.5	8 30.0	10 37.1	19 55.4	22 47.6
30 Su	22 34 35	7 05 12	29 39 32	6♒03 55	25 25.4	26 42.0	18 30.7	22 10.4	27 17.4	5 18.6	17 43.2	26 03.7	8 27.8	10 36.4	19 53.8	22 46.7
31 M	22 38 31	8♍03 12	12♒25 33	18 44 33	25♊22.2	26♊35.2	20♍15.3	23♋13.9	27♈26.2	5♓05.3	17♑40.7	26♑00.9	8♈25.6	10♉35.7	19♓52.2	22♑45.8

1st of Month

Julian Day #
2459062.5
Obliquity
23°26'12"
SVP 4♓58'56"
GC 27♐07.6
Eris 24♈32.9R

Day	⚴
1	16♑ 18.8R
6	15 16.2R
11	14 21.9R
16	13 36.7R
21	13 01.0R
26	12 35.2R
31	12 19.2R
	⚵
1	15♎ 17.6
6	16 34.0
11	17 53.4
16	19 15.6
21	20 40.4
26	22 07.5
31	23 36.6
	⚶
1	25♋ 25.1
6	27 36.5
11	29 47.7
16	1♌ 58.6
21	4 09.1
26	6 19.1
31	8 28.6

DECLINATION and LATITUDE

Day	☉ Decl	☽ Decl	☽ Lat	☽12h Decl	☿ Decl	☿ Lat	♀ Decl	♀ Lat	♂ Decl	♂ Lat	⚳ Decl	⚳ Lat	♃ Decl	♃ Lat	♄ Decl	♄ Lat
1 Sa	17N57	23S60	0S44	24S05	21N27	0S06	19N17	4S02	3N35	3S51	20S36	14S17	22S17	0S22	20S50	0S15
2 Su	17 42	23 49	1 53	23 13	21 22	0N06	19 22	3 59	3 44	3 52	20 43	14 21	22 18	0 22	20 51	0 15
3 M	17 26	22 18	2 56	21 06	21 14	0 18	19 27	3 55	3 53	3 53	20 50	14 25	22 19	0 22	20 52	0 15
4 Tu	17 10	19 39	3 48	17 58	21 04	0 30	19 32	3 52	4 01	3 54	20 57	14 29	22 21	0 22	20 53	0 15
5 W	16 54	16 06	4 28	14 04	20 52	0 40	19 36	3 49	4 10	3 55	21 04	14 32	22 22	0 22	20 54	0 15
6 Th	16 38	11 55	4 54	9 39	20 37	0 50	19 40	3 45	4 18	3 56	21 11	14 36	22 23	0 22	20 55	0 15
7 F	16 21	7 18	5 06	4 55	20 19	0 60	19 44	3 42	4 26	3 58	21 18	14 39	22 24	0 23	20 56	0 15
8 Sa	16 04	2 30	5 05	0 03	19 59	1 08	19 48	3 38	4 33	3 59	21 25	14 42	22 25	0 23	20 57	0 15
9 Su	15 47	2N22	4 50	4N46	19 36	1 15	19 51	3 34	4 41	3 60	21 32	14 45	22 26	0 23	20 57	0 16
10 M	15 29	7 07	4 22	9 24	19 10	1 22	19 54	3 31	4 48	4 01	21 39	14 49	22 27	0 23	20 58	0 16
11 Tu	15 11	11 37	3 44	13 44	18 42	1 28	19 57	3 27	4 56	4 02	21 46	14 52	22 27	0 23	20 59	0 16
12 W	14 53	15 43	2 55	17 33	18 12	1 33	19 60	3 23	5 03	4 03	21 54	14 54	22 28	0 23	20 60	0 16
13 Th	14 35	19 13	1 58	20 42	17 40	1 37	20 02	3 19	5 10	4 04	22 01	14 57	22 29	0 23	21 01	0 16
14 F	14 17	21 57	0 55	22 57	17 06	1 40	20 04	3 15	5 16	4 05	22 08	14 60	22 30	0 23	21 02	0 16
15 Sa	13 58	23 39	0N13	24 04	16 30	1 43	20 05	3 11	5 23	4 05	22 15	15 02	22 31	0 23	21 02	0 16
16 Su	13 39	24 08	1 22	23 52	15 52	1 44	20 06	3 06	5 29	4 06	22 21	15 05	22 32	0 23	21 03	0 16
17 M	13 20	23 14	2 29	22 15	15 13	1 45	20 06	3 02	5 35	4 07	22 28	15 07	22 32	0 23	21 04	0 16
18 Tu	13 01	20 54	3 28	19 13	14 33	1 46	20 07	2 58	5 40	4 08	22 35	15 09	22 33	0 24	21 05	0 16
19 W	12 41	17 14	4 17	14 58	13 51	1 45	20 06	2 54	5 46	4 09	22 42	15 11	22 34	0 24	21 05	0 16
20 Th	12 22	12 28	4 49	9 46	13 08	1 44	20 06	2 49	5 51	4 10	22 49	15 13	22 35	0 24	21 06	0 16
21 F	12 02	6 55	5 03	3 58	12 25	1 43	20 05	2 45	5 56	4 10	22 55	15 15	22 35	0 24	21 07	0 16
22 Sa	11 42	0 58	4 57	2S03	11 41	1 40	20 03	2 40	6 01	4 11	23 02	15 17	22 36	0 24	21 08	0 16
23 Su	11 21	5S01	4 31	7 54	10 56	1 38	20 01	2 36	6 06	4 12	23 08	15 18	22 37	0 24	21 08	0 17
24 M	11 01	10 39	3 48	13 14	10 11	1 34	19 59	2 31	6 10	4 12	23 14	15 20	22 37	0 24	21 09	0 17
25 Tu	10 40	15 37	2 52	17 46	9 25	1 31	19 56	2 27	6 15	4 13	23 21	15 21	22 38	0 24	21 10	0 17
26 W	10 19	19 39	1 46	21 13	8 39	1 27	19 52	2 22	6 19	4 13	23 27	15 22	22 38	0 24	21 10	0 17
27 Th	9 58	22 29	0 35	23 24	7 53	1 22	19 49	2 18	6 22	4 14	23 33	15 23	22 39	0 24	21 11	0 17
28 F	9 37	23 59	0S36	24 13	7 07	1 17	19 44	2 13	6 26	4 14	23 39	15 24	22 39	0 24	21 12	0 17
29 Sa	9 16	24 06	1 44	23 40	6 20	1 12	19 40	2 09	6 29	4 15	23 44	15 24	22 40	0 24	21 12	0 17
30 Su	8 54	22 54	2 45	21 51	5 34	1 06	19 34	2 04	6 32	4 15	23 50	15 25	22 40	0 24	21 13	0 17
31 M	8N33	20S32	3S37	18S59	4N47	1N01	19N29	1S59	6N35	4S15	23S55	15S25	22S40	0S25	21S13	0S17

Day	⚷ Decl	⚷ Lat	♅ Decl	♅ Lat	♆ Decl	♆ Lat	♇ Decl	♇ Lat
1	6N14	2N48	14N34	0S28	4S45	1S06	22S26	1S02
6	6 12	2 48	14 35	0 28	4 47	1 06	22 27	1 02
11	6 10	2 48	14 35	0 28	4 50	1 06	22 29	1 02
16	6 07	2 49	14 35	0 28	4 53	1 06	22 30	1 03
21	6 04	2 49	14 35	0 28	4 56	1 07	22 32	1 03
26	5 60	2 49	14 34	0 28	4 59	1 07	22 33	1 04
31	5N56	2N49	14N33	0S28	5S02	1S07	22S34	1S04

Day	⚴ Decl	⚴ Lat	⚵ Decl	⚵ Lat	⚶ Decl	⚶ Lat	Eris Decl	Eris Lat
1	19N04	41N47	1N27	8N05	21N34	0N32	1S21	11S39
6	18 15	41 03	0 56	8 03	21 16	0 38	1 22	11 40
11	17 23	40 15	0 25	8 02	20 55	0 45	1 22	11 40
16	16 27	39 22	0S07	8 00	20 33	0 52	1 23	11 41
21	15 29	38 26	0 40	7 59	20 10	0 58	1 24	11 41
26	14 29	37 28	1 13	7 58	19 45	1 05	1 25	11 41
31	13N29	36N29	1S45	7N58	19N19	1N13	1S26	11S42

Moon Phenomena

Max/0 Decl

dy	hr mn	
1	8:45	24S05
8	12:17	0 N
15	20:40	24N09
22	3:50	0 S
28	14:05	24S13

Max/0 Lat

dy	hr mn	
7	9:06	5S07
14	19:24	0 N
21	4:37	5N04
27	11:54	0 S

Perigee/Apogee

dy	hr m		kilometers
9	13:51	a	404657
21	10:58	p	363516

PH	dy	hr mn	
○	3	16:00	11♒46
☾	11	16:46	19♉28
●	19	2:43	26♌35
☽	25	17:59	2♐59

Void of Course Moon

Last Aspect				☽ Ingress		
2	14:01	♄	☌	♒	2	18:12
4	21:47	♀	△	♓	5	2:29
7	12:55	♀	□	♈	7	13:06
9	19:51	♄	□	♉	10	1:29
12	7:56	♄	△	♊	12	13:47
14	11:20	♂	⚹	♋	14	23:37
17	0:00	♄	☍	♌	17	5:40
19	5:39	☿	☌	♍	19	8:21
21	3:38	♄	△	♎	21	9:17
23	4:21	♄	□	♏	23	10:17
25	6:28	♄	⚹	♐	25	12:50
27	12:01	♂	△	♑	27	17:38
29	19:32	♂	□	♒	30	0:38

DAILY ASPECTARIAN

1 Sa: ☉△⚷ 1:16; ☽□⚷ 4:32; ☉⚻☽ 4:47; ☽△♅ 6:57; ☽⚹⚳ 7:35; ☿☍♇ 10:53; ☽□♂ 21:24; ☽☌♃ 23:58

2 Su: ☽⚹♆ 0:56; ☽☌♇ 5:59; ☽☍☿ 8:54; ☽⚻♀ 9:40; ☽∠⚳ 10:29; ☉□♅ 11:20; ☽☌♄ 14:01; ☉⚻⚳ 14:57; ♀∠♅ 17:18; ☿⚺♀ 19:28; ☿⚼⚳ 19:54; ☽∥♇ 22:24; ☽∥♃ 23:44

3 M: ☽∠♆ 4:25; ⚳∥♄ 7:47; ☽⚹⚷ 11:15; ☽#☿ 11:25; ⚳⚹♅ 11:50; ☽∥⚳ 13:48; ☽⚺⚳ 13:52; ☽□♅ 13:53; ☽∥♄ 14:01; ☽⚼♀ 15:22; ☉☍☽ 16:00; ☿☍♄ 21:01

4 Tu: ☽#♀ 0:54; ☽⚹♂ 6:46; ☽⚺♃ 7:02; ☽⚺♆ 8:26; ☿#⚳ 9:34; ♂□♃ 13:08; ☽⚺♇ 13:39; ☽∠⚷ 15:25; ☉#☽ 18:38; ☿#♄ 20:58; ☽△♀ 21:47; ☽⚺♄ 21:48; ♀⚻♄ 22:08

5 W: ☽⚻☿ 2:17; ☿ ♌ 3:33; ☽#♅ 9:05; ☽∠♃ 11:24; ☽∠♂ 12:22; ☽∠♇ 18:22; ☽⚺⚷ 20:09; ☽☌⚳ 22:14; ☽⚹♅ 23:02

6 Th: ☽∠♄ 2:34; ☉⚻☽ 6:01; ♂⚺♆ 7:32; ☽⚼☿ 12:42; ☽⚹♃ 16:21; ☽☌♆ 18:13; ☽⚺♂ 18:36; ☽⚹♇ 23:39

7 F: ☽∠♅ 4:29; ☽#⚷ 5:36; ☽⚹♄ 7:54; ☽∥♆ 12:34; ☽□♀ 12:55; ☽#♂ 14:03; ☉⚼☽ 14:08; ♀ ♋ 15:22; ☿⚼♆ 22:32

8 Sa: ☽△☿ 0:13; ☽☌⚷ 7:20; ☽⚺⚳ 8:44; ☿∥♀ 9:54; ☽⚺♅ 10:27; ☉△☽ 22:50

9 Su: ☽□♃ 3:45; ☽⚺♆ 6:04; ☽☌♂ 8:36; ☽□♇ 11:39; ☽∥♂ 11:54; ☽#♆ 12:16; ☽∠⚳ 14:33; ☿△⚷ 18:04; ☽∥⚷ 19:10; ☽□♄ 19:51; ☿⚻⚳ 23:17

10 M: ♂#♆ 3:07; ☽⚹♀ 6:24; ☽∠♆ 12:22; ☿□♅ 12:53; ☽⚺⚷ 19:49; ☽⚹⚳ 20:26; ☽☌♅ 23:06

11 Tu: ☽□☿ 1:13; ☉⚻♃ 6:36; ⚶ ♌ 11:18; ☽∠♀ 15:16; ☽△♃ 15:53; ☉□☽ 16:46; ☊ D 16:53; ☽∥♅ 17:07; ☽⚹♆ 18:33; ☉∥☽ 19:18; ☽⚺♂ 23:05

12 W: ☽△♇ 0:04; ☽∠⚷ 1:54; ☽△♄ 7:56; ☽∥☿ 14:17; ☉⚻♆ 14:34; ⚳⚺⚷ 16:39; ☽⚼♃ 21:29; ☽⚺♀ 23:39; ☉∥♅ 23:51

13 Th: ♃∥♇ 5:22; ☽∠♂ 5:39; ☽⚼♇ 5:42; ☽∥♀ 6:26; ♂□♇ 7:15; ☽□⚳ 7:16; ☽⚹⚷ 7:28; ☽⚺♅ 10:47; ☽⚼♄ 13:16; ☽#♄ 14:55

14 F: ☽⚹☿ 0:34; ☽#⚳ 2:04; ☽⚻♃ 2:25; ☽□♆ 5:17; ☽#♇ 6:13; ☽#♃ 6:20; ☉⚹☽ 8:34; ☽⚻♇ 10:33; ☽⚹♂ 11:20; ☿⚻♃ 11:30; ☽∠♅ 15:32; ☽⚻♄ 17:48; ☊ R 19:26; ♂∠⚳ 19:39

15 Sa: ☿⚻♆ 5:15; ☽∠☿ 10:09; ☉⚻♇ 10:14; ☽☌♀ 13:27; ♅ R 14:28; ☉∠☽ 14:49; ☽△⚳ 15:11; ☽□⚷ 16:06; ☽⚹♅ 19:19

16 Su: ☉⚼⚷ 8:01; ♀△⚳ 8:53; ☽☍♃ 9:34; ☽△♆ 12:30; ☿⚻♇ 13:40; ☉△♂ 14:03; ☽☍♇ 17:25; ☽⚼⚳ 17:44; ☽⚺☿ 18:05; ☽□♂ 19:33; ☉⚺☽ 19:50; ♀□⚷ 24:00

17 M: ☽☍♄ 0:00; ☿⚼⚷ 0:04; ☿∠♀ 0:07; ☿△♂ 5:30; ⚳∥♇ 7:56; ☽#♃ 8:44; ☽#⚳ 9:05; ☽#♇ 9:08; ☽⚼♆ 14:40; ☉☌☿ 15:08; ⚳∥♃ 16:19; ⚳∠♇ 17:22; ☽⚻⚳ 19:25; ☽△⚷ 20:56; ☿∥♅ 22:20; ☽⚺♀ 22:34; ☽#♄ 22:34

18 Tu: ☽□♅ 0:03; ☽∥♀ 5:55; ☿⚻♄ 9:18; ☽⚻♃ 13:06; ☽⚻♆ 16:04; ♀⚹♅ 19:29; ☽⚻♇ 20:43; ☽⚼⚷ 22:09; ☽△♂ 23:52

19 W: ☽∠♀ 1:39; ☉☌☽ 2:43; ☽⚻♄ 2:47; ☉⚻♄ 3:50; ☽☌☿ 5:39; ☽⚼♃ 13:52; ☽∥♅ 13:52; ☽∥☿ 20:19; ☽☍⚳ 20:45; ☽⚼♇ 21:25; ☽⚻⚷ 22:49

20 Th: ☉∥☽ 0:29; ☽⚼♂ 1:02; ☿ ♍ 1:31; ☽△♅ 1:53; ☽⚼♄ 3:20; ☽⚹♀ 4:07; ☽△♃ 14:15; ☽☍♆ 17:17; ☽△♇ 21:49

21 F: ☽⚻♂ 1:53; ☽⚼♅ 2:16; ☽∥⚷ 3:30; ☽△♄ 3:38; ☽∥♂ 3:56; ☉⚺☽ 7:09; ☽#♆ 8:05; ☽⚺☿ 14:07; ☿⚼♃ 16:46; ☽⚻⚳ 20:49; ☉∥☿ 23:22; ☽☍⚷ 23:28

22 Sa: ☽⚻♅ 2:37; ♂∥⚷ 7:02; ☽□♀ 8:27; ☉∠☽ 9:14; ☽□♃ 14:47; ☉ ♍ 15:46; ☽⚻♆ 17:59; ☽∠☿ 18:13; ☽⚼⚳ 20:56; ☽□♇ 22:35; ☽∥♆ 23:44

23 Su: ☽☍♂ 3:36; ☽#⚷ 4:12; ☽□♄ 4:21; ☽#♂ 4:32; ☉⚹☽ 11:36; ☿☍⚳ 13:13; ☽⚼♆ 18:40; ☽△⚳ 21:21; ☽#☿ 22:10; ☽⚹☿ 22:43

24 M: ☽⚻⚷ 0:42; ☉#☽ 1:32; ☿⚼♇ 3:38; ☽☍♅ 4:01; ☿⚻⚷ 13:37; ☽△♀ 13:53; ☽⚹♃ 16:22; ♂□♄ 18:21; ☽#♅ 18:36; ☽△♆ 19:49

25 Tu: ☽⚹♇ 0:37; ☽⚼⚷ 1:56; ☽⚹♄ 6:28; ☽⚻♂ 6:43; ☿△♅ 15:19; ☉⚼♃ 16:54; ☽⚼♀ 17:31; ☊ D 17:46; ☽∠♃ 17:54; ☉□☽ 17:59; ♀☍♃ 22:27; ☿⚼♄ 23:12; ☽□⚳ 23:34

26 W: ☽#♀ 1:36; ☽∠♇ 2:25; ☽△⚷ 3:44; ☿⚼♂ 3:49; ☽⚻♅ 7:18; ☽∠♄ 8:20; ☽⚼♂ 9:04; ☽□☿ 9:48; ☽∥♄ 11:39; ☽⚺♃ 20:01; ☽⚻♀ 21:54; ☽□♆ 23:44

27 Th: ☽∥♇ 0:47; ☽∥♃ 1:52; ☽⚺♇ 4:47; ☽⚼♅ 9:48; ☽⚺♄ 10:47; ☊ R 11:55; ☽△♂ 12:01; ☽∥⚳ 15:30; ♀△♆ 21:14

28 F: ☉△☽ 3:10; ☽⚹⚳ 3:57; ☽□⚷ 9:03; ☉☍⚳ 12:07; ☽△♅ 12:52; ♀⚼⚳ 12:53; ☿∥♂ 19:35; ☉∠♀ 23:47

29 Sa: ☽△☿ 0:06; ☽☌♃ 1:57; ☽⚹♆ 5:55; ☽∠⚳ 6:56; ☉⚼☽ 8:48; ☽☍♀ 8:52; ☽∥⚳ 9:39; ☽☌♇ 11:13; ☿∥⚷ 11:58; ☿△♃ 13:29; ☽☌♄ 17:19; ☽□♂ 19:32

30 Su: ☽∥♃ 3:01; ☽∥♇ 4:17; ☽⚼☿ 8:21; ☽∠♆ 9:47; ☽⚺⚳ 10:24; ♀☍♇ 13:32; ☉⚻☽ 15:04; ☿#♆ 16:27; ☽⚹⚷ 16:28; ☉⚼♇ 16:54; ☽∥♄ 18:04; ☿☍♆ 18:45; ☽□♅ 20:32

31 M: ☽#♀ 8:39; ☉⚻⚷ 8:56; ☽⚺♃ 9:56; ☽⚺♆ 14:07; ☽⚻☿ 17:15; ☽⚺♇ 19:39; ☽∠⚷ 20:53; ☽⚻♀ 22:29

LONGITUDE

Day	Sid.Time	☉	☽	☽ 12 hour	Mean☊	True☊	☿	♀	♂	⚳	♃	♄	⚷	♅	♆	♇
	h m s	° ' "	° ' "	° ' "	° '	° '	° '	° '	° '	° '	° '	° '	° '	° '	° '	° '
1 Tu	22 42 28	9♍01 13	25♒00 58	1♓14 52	25♊19.0	26♊25.7	21♍58.7	24♋17.6	27♈34.1	4♓52.0	17♑38.3	25♑58.3	8♈23.4	10♉34.9	19♓50.6	22♑44.9
2 W	22 46 24	9 59 16	7♓26 20	13 35 23	25 15.8	26R 14.1	23 40.8	25 21.5	27 41.3	4R 38.8	17R 36.1	25R 55.7	8R 21.1	10R 34.1	19R 49.0	22R 44.0
3 Th	22 50 21	10 57 20	19 42 06	25 46 35	25 12.7	26 01.1	25 21.7	26 25.8	27 47.7	4 25.7	17 34.1	25 53.3	8 18.8	10 33.2	19 47.3	22 43.1
4 F	22 54 17	11 55 26	1♈48 58	7♈49 23	25 09.5	25 48.0	27 01.3	27 30.3	27 53.2	4 12.6	17 32.2	25 50.9	8 16.4	10 32.3	19 45.7	22 42.3
5 Sa	22 58 14	12 53 34	13 48 03	19 45 13	25 06.3	25 35.9	28 39.7	28 35.0	27 57.9	3 59.6	17 30.6	25 48.5	8 14.1	10 31.3	19 44.1	22 41.5
6 Su	23 02 10	13 51 44	25 41 12	1♉36 19	25 03.1	25 25.7	0♎17.0	29 40.0	28 01.7	3 46.8	17 29.2	25 46.3	8 11.7	10 30.3	19 42.4	22 40.7
7 M	23 06 07	14 49 56	7♉31 01	13 25 45	25 00.0	25 17.9	1 53.0	0♌45.2	28 04.7	3 34.0	17 27.9	25 44.1	8 09.2	10 29.3	19 40.8	22 39.9
8 Tu	23 10 04	15 48 09	19 21 01	25 17 22	24 56.8	25 12.9	3 27.9	1 50.7	28 06.9	3 21.4	17 26.8	25 42.1	8 06.8	10 28.2	19 39.1	22 39.2
9 W	23 14 00	16 46 25	1♊15 25	7♊15 46	24 53.6	25 10.3	5 01.6	2 56.3	28R 08.1	3 08.9	17 26.0	25 40.1	8 04.3	10 27.0	19 37.5	22 38.4
10 Th	23 17 57	17 44 43	13 19 05	19 26 03	24 50.4	25 09.5	6 34.1	4 02.3	28 08.5	2 56.6	17 25.3	25 38.2	8 01.9	10 25.8	19 35.8	22 37.8
11 F	23 21 53	18 43 03	25 37 18	1♋53 31	24 47.2	25 09.5	8 05.5	5 08.4	28 08.0	2 44.4	17 24.8	25 36.4	7 59.4	10 24.6	19 34.2	22 37.1
12 Sa	23 25 50	19 41 25	8♋15 19	14 43 17	24 44.1	25 09.1	9 35.8	6 14.7	28 06.6	2 32.5	17 24.5	25 34.7	7 56.8	10 23.3	19 32.5	22 36.4
13 Su	23 29 46	20 39 49	21 17 52	27 59 30	24 40.9	25 07.3	11 04.8	7 21.3	28 04.3	2 20.7	17D 24.4	25 33.1	7 54.3	10 22.0	19 30.9	22 35.8
14 M	23 33 43	21 38 15	4♌48 25	11♌44 43	24 37.7	25 03.1	12 32.8	8 28.0	28 01.2	2 09.1	17 24.5	25 31.6	7 51.7	10 20.7	19 29.2	22 35.2
15 Tu	23 37 39	22 36 43	18 48 19	25 58 53	24 34.5	24 56.3	13 59.5	9 35.0	27 57.1	1 57.8	17 24.8	25 30.1	7 49.1	10 19.3	19 27.6	22 34.7
16 W	23 41 36	23 35 13	3♍15 56	10♍38 43	24 31.4	24 47.0	15 25.1	10 42.1	27 52.2	1 46.6	17 25.2	25 28.8	7 46.5	10 17.8	19 25.9	22 34.1
17 Th	23 45 33	24 33 45	18 06 17	25 37 30	24 28.2	24 36.1	16 49.4	11 49.5	27 46.3	1 35.8	17 25.9	25 27.6	7 43.9	10 16.4	19 24.3	22 33.6
18 F	23 49 29	25 32 20	3♎11 08	10♎45 51	24 25.0	24 24.7	18 12.6	12 57.0	27 39.7	1 25.1	17 26.8	25 26.4	7 41.3	10 14.8	19 22.6	22 33.1
19 Sa	23 53 26	26 30 55	18 20 19	25 53 14	24 21.8	24 14.1	19 34.4	14 04.7	27 32.1	1 14.8	17 27.8	25 25.4	7 38.7	10 13.3	19 21.0	22 32.7
20 Su	23 57 22	27 29 33	3♏23 25	10♏49 51	24 18.6	24 05.6	20 55.0	15 12.5	27 23.7	1 04.7	17 29.1	25 24.4	7 36.0	10 11.7	19 19.3	22 32.3
21 M	0 01 19	28 28 13	18 11 42	25 28 19	24 15.5	23 59.8	22 14.2	16 20.6	27 14.5	0 54.8	17 30.5	25 23.5	7 33.3	10 10.1	19 17.7	22 31.9
22 Tu	0 05 15	29 26 54	2♐39 17	9♐44 19	24 12.3	23 56.6	23 32.1	17 28.8	27 04.6	0 45.3	17 32.2	25 22.8	7 30.7	10 08.4	19 16.1	22 31.5
23 W	0 09 12	0♎25 37	16 43 23	23 36 32	24 09.1	23D 55.5	24 48.4	18 37.1	26 53.8	0 36.1	17 34.0	25 22.1	7 28.0	10 06.7	19 14.5	22 31.1
24 Th	0 13 08	1 24 22	0♑23 58	7♑05 57	24 05.9	23R 55.5	26 03.3	19 45.7	26 42.3	0 27.2	17 36.0	25 21.6	7 25.3	10 04.9	19 12.9	22 30.8
25 F	0 17 05	2 23 08	13 42 49	20 14 57	24 02.8	23 55.1	27 16.6	20 54.4	26 30.0	0 18.6	17 38.2	25 21.1	7 22.6	10 03.2	19 11.2	22 30.5
26 Sa	0 21 01	3 21 56	26 42 45	3♒06 35	23 59.6	23 53.4	28 28.2	22 03.2	26 17.1	0 10.3	17 40.6	25 20.7	7 19.9	10 01.3	19 09.7	22 30.3
27 Su	0 24 58	4 20 46	9♒26 51	15 43 54	23 56.4	23 49.2	29 38.0	23 12.2	26 03.4	0 02.3	17 43.2	25 20.5	7 17.2	9 59.5	19 08.1	22 30.0
28 M	0 28 55	5 19 38	21 58 02	28 09 33	23 53.2	23 42.2	0♏45.9	24 21.3	25 49.2	29♒54.7	17 46.0	25 20.3	7 14.5	9 57.6	19 06.5	22 29.8
29 Tu	0 32 51	6 18 31	4♓18 43	10♓25 44	23 50.0	23 32.4	1 51.8	25 30.6	25 34.3	29 47.4	17 49.0	25D 20.2	7 11.8	9 55.7	19 04.9	22 29.7
30 W	0 36 48	7♎17 26	16 30 47	22 34 04	23♊46.9	23♊20.4	2♏55.5	26♌40.1	25♈18.8	29♒40.4	17♑52.1	25♑20.3	7♈09.1	9♉53.8	19♓03.4	22♑29.5

1st of Month

Julian Day #
2459093.5
Obliquity
23°26'13"
SVP 4♓58'52"
GC 27♐07.7
Eris 24♈24.5R

Day	⚴
1	12♑17.1R
6	12 12.4R
11	12 16.8
16	12 29.9
21	12 51.2
26	13 20.3

Day	⚵
1	23♎54.7
6	25 26.1
11	26 59.3
16	28 34.1
21	0♏10.2
26	1 47.6

Day	⚶
1	8♌54.4
6	11 03.0
11	13 10.9
16	15 17.9
21	17 23.9
26	19 28.7

DECLINATION and LATITUDE

Day	☉ Decl	☽ Decl	☽ Lat	☽12h Decl	☿ Decl	☿ Lat	♀ Decl	♀ Lat	♂ Decl	♂ Lat	⚳ Decl	⚳ Lat	♃ Decl	♃ Lat	♄ Decl	♄ Lat
1 Tu	8N11	17S13	4S17	15S16	4N01	0N54	19N22	1S55	6N38	4S15	24S00	15S25	22S41	0S25	21S14	0S17
2 W	7 49	13 11	4 45	10 58	3 15	0 48	19 16	1 50	6 40	4 15	24 06	15 26	22 41	0 25	21 14	0 17
3 Th	7 27	8 39	4 59	6 16	2 29	0 41	19 08	1 45	6 43	4 16	24 11	15 26	22 41	0 25	21 15	0 17
4 F	7 05	3 51	4 59	1 24	1 43	0 35	19 01	1 41	6 44	4 16	24 15	15 25	22 42	0 25	21 15	0 17
5 Sa	6 43	1N03	4 46	3N29	0 57	0 28	18 52	1 36	6 46	4 15	24 20	15 25	22 42	0 25	21 16	0 17
6 Su	6 21	5 53	4 20	8 13	0 12	0 21	18 44	1 32	6 48	4 15	24 24	15 25	22 42	0 25	21 16	0 17
7 M	5 58	10 29	3 44	12 40	0S33	0 13	18 34	1 27	6 49	4 15	24 29	15 24	22 43	0 25	21 17	0 18
8 Tu	5 36	14 43	2 57	16 38	1 17	0 06	18 25	1 22	6 50	4 15	24 33	15 23	22 43	0 25	21 17	0 18
9 W	5 13	18 24	2 03	19 59	2 01	0S02	18 14	1 18	6 51	4 15	24 37	15 22	22 43	0 25	21 18	0 18
10 Th	4 51	21 22	1 02	22 31	2 45	0 09	18 04	1 13	6 51	4 14	24 41	15 22	22 43	0 25	21 18	0 18
11 F	4 28	23 24	0N02	24 01	3 28	0 17	17 52	1 09	6 51	4 14	24 44	15 20	22 43	0 25	21 19	0 18
12 Sa	4 05	24 19	1 09	24 18	4 11	0 25	17 41	1 04	6 52	4 13	24 47	15 19	22 43	0 25	21 19	0 18
13 Su	3 42	23 57	2 13	23 14	4 53	0 33	17 28	0 59	6 51	4 12	24 51	15 18	22 43	0 25	21 19	0 18
14 M	3 19	22 11	3 13	20 47	5 35	0 41	17 16	0 55	6 51	4 12	24 54	15 16	22 43	0 25	21 20	0 18
15 Tu	2 56	19 02	4 03	16 59	6 16	0 49	17 02	0 51	6 50	4 11	24 56	15 15	22 43	0 25	21 20	0 18
16 W	2 33	14 39	4 40	12 04	6 56	0 57	16 49	0 46	6 49	4 10	24 59	15 13	22 43	0 25	21 20	0 18
17 Th	2 10	9 17	4 58	6 20	7 36	1 04	16 34	0 42	6 48	4 09	25 01	15 11	22 43	0 25	21 21	0 18
18 F	1 46	3 16	4 57	0 10	8 15	1 12	16 20	0 37	6 47	4 08	25 03	15 09	22 43	0 25	21 21	0 18
19 Sa	1 23	2S57	4 34	6S01	8 54	1 20	16 05	0 33	6 46	4 06	25 05	15 07	22 43	0 25	21 21	0 18
20 Su	0 60	8 59	3 53	11 48	9 32	1 28	15 49	0 29	6 44	4 05	25 07	15 05	22 43	0 26	21 21	0 18
21 M	0 37	14 25	2 57	16 48	10 08	1 36	15 33	0 24	6 42	4 03	25 09	15 03	22 43	0 26	21 21	0 18
22 Tu	0 13	18 54	1 50	20 41	10 45	1 44	15 16	0 20	6 40	4 02	25 10	15 00	22 43	0 26	21 22	0 18
23 W	0S10	22 09	0 38	23 15	11 20	1 51	14 59	0 16	6 38	4 00	25 11	14 58	22 42	0 26	21 22	0 18
24 Th	0 34	24 00	0S34	24 24	11 54	1 59	14 42	0 12	6 35	3 58	25 12	14 55	22 42	0 26	21 22	0 18
25 F	0 57	24 26	1 43	24 07	12 28	2 06	14 24	0 08	6 33	3 57	25 13	14 53	22 42	0 26	21 22	0 19
26 Sa	1 20	23 30	2 44	22 34	13 00	2 13	14 06	0 04	6 30	3 54	25 13	14 50	22 42	0 26	21 22	0 19
27 Su	1 44	21 21	3 36	19 54	13 32	2 21	13 47	0N00	6 27	3 52	25 14	14 47	22 41	0 26	21 22	0 19
28 M	2 07	18 13	4 16	16 21	14 02	2 27	13 28	0 04	6 24	3 50	25 14	14 44	22 41	0 26	21 22	0 19
29 Tu	2 30	14 20	4 44	12 10	14 32	2 34	13 09	0 08	6 21	3 48	25 14	14 41	22 41	0 26	21 23	0 19
30 W	2S54	9S54	4S58	7S33	14S60	2S41	12N49	0N12	6N18	3S45	25S13	14S38	22S40	0S26	21S23	0S19

Day	⚷ Decl	⚷ Lat	♅ Decl	♅ Lat	♆ Decl	♆ Lat	♇ Decl	♇ Lat
1	5N55	2N49	14N33	0S28	5S03	1S07	22S34	1S04
6	5 50	2 49	14 32	0 28	5 06	1 07	22 35	1 04
11	5 45	2 49	14 30	0 28	5 09	1 07	22 36	1 05
16	5 40	2 49	14 28	0 28	5 13	1 07	22 37	1 05
21	5 35	2 49	14 25	0 28	5 16	1 07	22 38	1 05
26	5 29	2 48	14 22	0 28	5 19	1 07	22 38	1 06

Day	⚴ Decl	⚴ Lat	⚵ Decl	⚵ Lat	⚶ Decl	⚶ Lat	Eris Decl	Eris Lat
1	13N16	36N17	1S52	7N58	19N13	1N14	1S26	11S42
6	12 16	35 16	2 25	7 57	18 45	1 21	1 27	11 42
11	11 16	34 16	2 58	7 58	18 17	1 29	1 28	11 42
16	10 17	33 15	3 31	7 58	17 47	1 37	1 29	11 42
21	9 19	32 16	4 03	7 59	17 17	1 45	1 30	11 43
26	8 23	31 18	4 35	7 60	16 46	1 53	1 31	11 43

Moon Phenomena

Max/0 Decl
dy hr mn
4 18:51 0 N
12 5:24 24N21
18 12:37 0 S
24 19:12 24S27

Perigee/Apogee
dy hr m kilometers
6 6:30 a 405606
18 13:49 p 359087

PH dy hr mn
○ 2 5:23 10♓12
☾ 10 9:27 18♊08
● 17 11:01 25♍01
☽ 24 1:56 1♑29

Max/0 Lat
dy hr mn
3 12:16 5S00
10 23:07 0 N
17 10:15 5N00
23 12:34 0 S
30 13:18 5S00

Void of Course Moon

Last Aspect	☽ Ingress
1 4:57 ♂ ✱	♓ 1 9:35
3 14:35 ♀ △	♈ 3 20:23
6 4:46 ♂ ☌	♉ 6 8:45
8 12:48 ♄ △	♊ 8 21:29
11 4:49 ♂ ✱	♋ 11 8:24
13 12:06 ♂ □	♌ 13 15:34
15 15:11 ♂ △	♍ 15 18:38
17 11:43 ♄ △	♎ 17 18:57
19 14:30 ♂ ☍	♏ 19 18:34
21 18:14 ☉ ✱	♐ 21 19:33
23 17:33 ♂ △	♑ 23 23:17
26 3:37 ☿ □	♒ 26 6:09
28 7:19 ♂ ✱	♓ 28 15:35

DAILY ASPECTARIAN

1 Tu
☽⊻♄ 1:50
☽✱♂ 4:57
☿△♇ 10:43
☽∠♃ 14:39
☽#♅ 16:15
☽☌⚳ 18:40

2 W
☽∠♇ 0:34
☽⊻⚷ 1:46
☉☍☽ 5:23
☽✱♅ 6:05
☽⚼♀ 6:14
☽∠♄ 6:47
☽∠♂ 10:20
♀☍♄ 12:19
☉△♅ 14:10
☽✱♃ 19:49
☉⚼♄ 22:23

3 Th
☽☌♆ 0:10
☿⚼♅ 2:44
☽✱♇ 5:57
☉#☽ 6:35
☿△♄ 7:24
☽#♂ 9:46
☽∠♅ 11:33
☽✱♄ 12:11
☽☍☿ 12:58
☽#⚷ 13:59
☽△♀ 14:35
☽⊻♂ 16:08
☽∥♆ 17:57

4 F
☽⊻⚳ 4:41
♀□♂ 9:13
☽#☿ 12:23
☽☌⚷ 12:52
☿⚻♂ 13:16
☽⊻♅ 17:25
☿✱♀ 20:33
☉∥♂ 20:57
☉⚻☽ 22:01
☽∥☿ 23:35

5 Sa
☉⚼♂ 1:55
☽□♃ 7:27
☽∠⚳ 10:17
☽⊻♆ 11:56
☽□♇ 17:55
☿ ♎ 19:47
☽#♆ 20:03
☽∥⚷ 23:46

6 Su
☽□♄ 0:10
⚴ D 1:07
☉∥☽ 2:11
☽∥♂ 4:39
☽☌♂ 4:46
☉⚼☽ 7:01
♀ ♌ 7:23
☽□♀ 8:53
☽⚻☿ 10:47
☽✱⚳ 16:07
☽∠♆ 18:15

7 M
☽⊻⚷ 1:17
☽☌♅ 6:01
☉∥⚷ 10:10
☉△☽ 16:10
☽△♃ 20:09
☽⚼☿ 21:56
☿⚻⚳ 22:32
☽∥♅ 22:47

8 Tu
☽✱♆ 0:37
☽△♇ 6:40
☽∠⚷ 7:35
☽△♄ 12:48
☽⊻♂ 17:43
☽∥♀ 22:53

9 W
☽⚼♃ 2:21
☽✱♀ 3:43
☽□⚳ 3:43
♀⚻⚳ 3:51
☉#♆ 5:27
☽△☿ 8:39
☽⚼♇ 12:44
☽✱⚷ 13:34
☉△♃ 16:05
☽⊻♅ 18:18
☽⚼♄ 18:43
♂ R 22:24
☽#♄ 23:25
☽∠♂ 23:39

10 Th
☽⚻♃ 8:04
☉□☽ 9:27
♀⚼♆ 11:54
☽□♆ 12:17
☽∠♀ 12:20
☽#♇ 13:03
☽#♃ 14:28
☽⚻♇ 18:12
☿☍⚷ 22:25
☽∠♅ 23:36
☽⚻♄ 23:58

11 F
☽✱♂ 4:49
☽△⚳ 13:24
☽⊻♀ 19:52
☉☍♆ 20:27
☉#☿ 21:46
☽□⚷ 23:25

12 Sa
☽□☿ 2:50
☽✱♅ 3:58
☿⚻♅ 12:36
⚳∠♃ 16:23
☽⚼⚳ 16:55
☽☍♃ 16:55
☽△♆ 20:46
☉✱☽ 22:46

13 Su
♃ D 0:42
☽☍♇ 2:21
☽☍♄ 7:38
☿∥♆ 10:09
♀△⚷ 11:26
☽□♂ 12:06
☽#♃ 18:22
☽⚻⚳ 19:25
☽#♇ 19:36
☽⚼♆ 23:27

14 M
☉∠☽ 3:26
☿#⚷ 4:12
☽△⚷ 5:18
☽☌♀ 6:55
☽#♄ 7:36
☽□♅ 9:35
☽✱☿ 14:55
☽⚻♃ 21:39
☉△♇ 23:10

15 Tu
☽⚻♆ 1:06
☽⚻♇ 6:20
☽⚼⚷ 6:43
☉⊻☽ 6:51
☽⚻♄ 11:11
☽∥♀ 12:19
☽△♂ 15:11
♀□♅ 15:31
☽∠☿ 18:49
☿#♂ 20:00
☽☍⚳ 21:35
☽⚼♃ 22:37

16 W
☽∥♅ 0:54
☽⚼♇ 7:01
☽⚻⚷ 7:20
☽△♅ 11:25
☽⚼♄ 11:43
☽⊻♀ 13:05
☽⚼♂ 15:29
☿⚼⚳ 20:32
☽⊻☿ 21:44
☽△♃ 22:55

17 Th
☽☍♆ 2:05
☽#☿ 6:11
☽△♇ 7:07
☽∥♂ 10:07
☿□♃ 10:36
☉☌☽ 11:01
☽⚼♅ 11:25
☽△♄ 11:43
☽∥⚷ 14:44
☽∠♀ 15:02
☽⚻♂ 15:18
☽#♆ 16:21
☉⚼♅ 17:01
☽⚻⚳ 21:14
☉△♄ 21:37

18 F
☉∥☽ 6:11
☽☍⚷ 7:07
☽⚻♅ 11:10
☽✱♀ 16:42
☉#☽ 18:18
☿⚻♆ 20:07
☽⚼⚳ 20:43
☽□♃ 22:37

19 Sa
☽⚻♆ 1:36
☽☌☿ 2:09
☽□♇ 6:41
☽∥♆ 8:56
☽#⚷ 10:22
☽□♄ 11:15
☉⊻☽ 13:54
☽☍♂ 14:30
☽#♂ 14:53
☽△⚳ 20:20
☉⚻♂ 21:56

20 Su
☽⚼♆ 1:30
☽∥☿ 2:31
☽⚻⚷ 6:45
☽☍♅ 10:57
⚵ ♏ 11:20
☉∠☽ 15:44
☽□♀ 20:43
☽✱♃ 22:52

21 M
☽#♅ 0:01
☽△♆ 1:48
☽#♀ 5:16
☿□♇ 5:22
☽✱♇ 7:08
☽⚼⚷ 7:09
☽⊻☿ 7:18
☽✱♄ 11:52
☽⚻♂ 14:47
☉✱☽ 18:14
☽□⚳ 20:51
☽∠♃ 23:48

22 Tu
♀⚻♃ 1:14
☽△⚷ 8:11
☽∠♇ 8:14
☽∠☿ 10:57
☽⚻♅ 12:40
☽∠♄ 13:05
☉ ♎ 13:32
☽⚼♂ 15:48
☽∥♄ 17:15

23 W
☽⊻♃ 1:28
☽△♀ 3:35
☉⚻⚳ 3:43
☽□♆ 4:22
☽∥♇ 4:50
☽∥♃ 5:37
☽⊻♇ 10:05
☿□♄ 10:39
☊ D 12:29
♀⚻♆ 12:47
☽⚼♅ 14:37
☽⊻♄ 15:05
☽✱☿ 15:32
☽△♂ 17:33

24 Th
☽✱⚳ 0:06
☊ R 1:52
☉□☽ 1:56
☽⚼♀ 8:31
☿☍♂ 10:54
☽□⚷ 12:32
☽△♅ 17:21

25 F
♀∥♅ 1:41
☽∠⚳ 2:53
☽☌♃ 7:13
☽✱♆ 10:01
☽⚻♀ 14:30
☽☌♇ 16:11
☽☌♄ 21:27
☽□♂ 23:13

26 Sa
☽□☿ 3:37
♀⚼⚷ 5:36
☽⊻⚳ 6:24
♀⚻♇ 9:23
☽∥♃ 10:30
☽∥♇ 11:08
☉△☽ 13:31
☽∠♆ 13:57
☽✱⚷ 19:55
☽∥♄ 23:49

27 Su
☽□♅ 1:02
⚳ R♒ 7:09
☿#♀ 7:19
☿△⚳ 7:38
☿ ♏ 7:42
☽⊻♃ 15:53
☽⊻♆ 18:30
☉⚼☽ 20:34

28 M
☽∠⚷ 0:32
☽⊻♇ 1:01
☽☍♀ 5:06
☽⊻♄ 6:31
☽✱♂ 7:19
☿#♅ 14:55
☽☌⚳ 15:15
☽△☿ 18:45
♀⚻♄ 20:24
☽∠♃ 21:04
☽∥☿ 22:59
☽#♅ 23:56

29 Tu
♀△♂ 1:02
☉⚻☽ 4:15
♄ D 5:13
☽⊻⚷ 5:38
☽∠♇ 6:14
☽#♀ 7:15
☽✱♅ 10:59
☽∠♄ 11:49
☽∠♂ 12:02
☉☍⚷ 20:45
♂□♄ 21:51

30 W
☽✱♃ 2:42
☽⚼☿ 3:03
☽☌♆ 5:01
☽✱♇ 11:51
☽∠♅ 16:35
☽⊻♂ 17:05
☽✱♄ 17:31
☽#♂ 18:28
☽⚻♀ 22:18
☽#⚷ 22:43
☽∥♆ 22:51

October 2020

LONGITUDE

Day	Sid.Time	☉	☽	☽ 12 hour	Mean☊	True☊	☿	♀	♂	⚳	♃	♄	⚷	♅	♆	♇
	h m s	° ' "	° ' "	° ' "	° '	° '	° '	° '	° '	° '	° '	° '	° '	° '	° '	° '
1 Th	0 40 44	8♎16 23	28♓35 42	4♈35 51	23♊43.7	23♊07.0	3♏56.9	27♌49.7	25♈02.8	29♒33.8	17♑55.4	25♑20.4	7♈06.4	9♉51.8	19♓01.8	22♑29.4
2 F	0 44 41	9 15 22	10♈34 38	16 32 14	23 40.5	22R 53.5	4 55.7	28 59.4	24R 46.3	29R 27.5	17 58.9	25 20.6	7R 03.7	9R 49.8	19R 00.3	22R 29.3
3 Sa	0 48 37	10 14 23	22 28 47	28 24 29	23 37.3	22 40.8	5 51.8	0♍09.3	24 29.4	29 21.6	18 02.6	25 20.9	7 01.0	9 47.8	18 58.8	22 29.2
4 Su	0 52 34	11 13 26	4♉19 34	10♉14 16	23 34.1	22 30.1	6 44.9	1 19.3	24 11.9	29 16.0	18 06.5	25 21.4	6 58.3	9 45.7	18 57.3	22D 29.2
5 M	0 56 30	12 12 32	16 08 54	22 03 49	23 31.0	22 21.9	7 34.8	2 29.4	23 54.2	29 10.8	18 10.5	25 21.9	6 55.6	9 43.6	18 55.8	22 29.2
6 Tu	1 00 27	13 11 39	27 59 23	3♊56 03	23 27.8	22 16.5	8 21.2	3 39.7	23 36.0	29 05.9	18 14.8	25 22.5	6 52.9	9 41.5	18 54.3	22 29.2
7 W	1 04 24	14 10 49	9♊54 17	15 54 38	23 24.6	22 13.7	9 03.8	4 50.2	23 17.6	29 01.4	18 19.2	25 23.2	6 50.2	9 39.3	18 52.8	22 29.3
8 Th	1 08 20	15 10 01	21 57 39	28 03 56	23 21.4	22D 13.0	9 42.1	6 00.7	22 58.9	28 57.3	18 23.7	25 24.1	6 47.5	9 37.2	18 51.4	22 29.4
9 F	1 12 17	16 09 16	4♋14 06	10♋28 47	23 18.3	22 13.4	10 15.9	7 11.2	22 40.0	28 53.5	18 28.5	25 25.0	6 44.8	9 35.0	18 50.0	22 29.5
10 Sa	1 16 13	17 08 32	16 48 35	23 14 08	23 15.1	22R 13.7	10 44.6	8 22.2	22 21.0	28 50.1	18 33.4	25 26.0	6 42.2	9 32.8	18 48.5	22 29.6
11 Su	1 20 10	18 07 51	29 45 58	6♌24 35	23 11.9	22 13.1	11 07.9	9 33.1	22 01.8	28 47.1	18 38.5	25 27.1	6 39.5	9 30.5	18 47.1	22 29.8
12 M	1 24 06	19 07 13	13♌10 22	20 03 34	23 08.7	22 10.6	11 25.3	10 44.2	21 42.6	28 44.4	18 43.8	25 28.4	6 36.9	9 28.3	18 45.8	22 30.0
13 Tu	1 28 03	20 06 36	27 04 19	4♍12 29	23 05.6	22 05.8	11 36.2	11 55.3	21 23.4	28 42.1	18 49.2	25 29.7	6 34.3	9 26.0	18 44.4	22 30.3
14 W	1 31 59	21 06 02	11♍27 47	18 49 42	23 02.4	21 58.7	11R 40.2	13 06.6	21 04.2	28 40.2	18 54.8	25 31.1	6 31.7	9 23.7	18 43.1	22 30.5
15 Th	1 35 56	22 05 30	26 17 26	3♎50 02	22 59.2	21 50.1	11 36.7	14 18.0	20 45.2	28 38.6	19 00.6	25 32.6	6 29.1	9 21.4	18 41.7	22 30.8
16 F	1 39 53	23 05 01	11♎26 17	19 04 53	22 56.0	21 40.8	11 25.4	15 29.5	20 26.3	28 37.4	19 06.5	25 34.2	6 26.5	9 19.1	18 40.4	22 31.1
17 Sa	1 43 49	24 04 33	26 44 24	4♏23 25	22 52.8	21 32.2	11 05.7	16 41.0	20 07.6	28 36.6	19 12.6	25 35.9	6 24.0	9 16.7	18 39.2	22 31.5
18 Su	1 47 46	25 04 07	12♏00 32	19 34 28	22 49.7	21 25.2	10 37.6	17 52.8	19 49.1	28D 36.1	19 18.9	25 37.7	6 21.4	9 14.3	18 37.9	22 31.9
19 M	1 51 42	26 03 44	27 04 05	4♐28 27	22 46.5	21 20.5	10 00.7	19 04.6	19 31.0	28 36.1	19 25.3	25 39.6	6 18.9	9 12.0	18 36.7	22 32.3
20 Tu	1 55 39	27 03 22	11♐46 51	18 58 48	22 43.3	21D 18.2	9 15.4	20 16.5	19 13.3	28 36.4	19 31.9	25 41.7	6 16.4	9 09.6	18 35.4	22 32.7
21 W	1 59 35	28 03 02	26 03 59	3♑02 20	22 40.1	21 17.9	8 21.8	21 28.4	18 55.9	28 37.0	19 38.6	25 43.8	6 13.9	9 07.2	18 34.3	22 33.2
22 Th	2 03 32	29 02 44	9♑53 53	16 38 50	22 37.0	21 18.8	7 20.9	22 40.5	18 39.0	28 38.0	19 45.5	25 46.0	6 11.5	9 04.8	18 33.1	22 33.7
23 F	2 07 28	0♏02 28	23 17 31	29 50 19	22 33.8	21R 19.7	6 13.6	23 52.7	18 22.6	28 39.4	19 52.5	25 48.3	6 09.1	9 02.3	18 31.9	22 34.3
24 Sa	2 11 25	1 02 13	6♒17 40	12♒40 03	22 30.6	21 19.8	5 01.4	25 05.0	18 06.7	28 41.2	19 59.7	25 50.6	6 06.7	8 59.9	18 30.8	22 34.8
25 Su	2 15 22	2 02 00	18 57 57	25 11 53	22 27.4	21 18.1	3 46.2	26 17.3	17 51.3	28 43.3	20 07.1	25 53.1	6 04.3	8 57.4	18 29.7	22 35.4
26 M	2 19 18	3 01 48	1♓22 18	7♓29 40	22 24.2	21 14.4	2 30.2	27 29.7	17 36.6	28 45.7	20 14.6	25 55.7	6 01.9	8 55.0	18 28.7	22 36.0
27 Tu	2 23 15	4 01 38	13 34 25	19 36 56	22 21.1	21 08.6	1 15.5	28 42.2	17 22.5	28 48.5	20 22.2	25 58.4	5 59.6	8 52.5	18 27.6	22 36.7
28 W	2 27 11	5 01 30	25 37 36	1♈36 44	22 17.9	21 01.0	0 04.5	29 54.8	17 09.0	28 51.7	20 30.0	26 01.1	5 57.3	8 50.1	18 26.6	22 37.3
29 Th	2 31 08	6 01 24	7♈34 38	13 31 34	22 14.7	20 52.4	28♎59.4	1♎07.5	16 56.2	28 55.2	20 37.9	26 04.0	5 55.1	8 47.6	18 25.6	22 38.1
30 F	2 35 04	7 01 19	19 27 47	25 23 30	22 11.5	20 43.6	28 02.2	2 20.3	16 44.1	28 59.0	20 46.0	26 06.9	5 52.8	8 45.1	18 24.6	22 38.8
31 Sa	2 39 01	8♏01 17	1♉18 56	7♉14 18	22♊08.4	20♊35.4	27♎14.4	3♎33.1	16♈32.6	29♒03.2	20♑54.2	26♑09.9	5♈50.6	8♉42.7	18♓23.7	22♑39.5

1st of Month

Julian Day # 2459123.5
Obliquity 23°26'13"
SVP 4♓58'29"
GC 27♐07.7
Eris 24♈09.5R

Day	⚴	⚵	⚶
1	13♑56.5	3♏26.1	21♌32.2
6	14 39.3	5 05.5	23 34.2
11	15 28.3	6 45.8	25 34.6
16	16 23.0	8 26.8	27 33.2
21	17 22.9	10 08.4	29 29.7
26	18 27.6	11 50.5	1♍23.8
31	19 36.6	13 32.8	3 15.3

DECLINATION and LATITUDE

Day	☉ Decl	☽ Decl	☽ Lat	☽ 12h Decl	☿ Decl	☿ Lat	♀ Decl	♀ Lat	♂ Decl	♂ Lat	⚳ Decl	⚳ Lat	♃ Decl	♃ Lat	♄ Decl	♄ Lat
1 Th	3S17	5S08	4S59	2S41	15S27	2S47	12N28	0N16	6N14	3S43	25S13	14S35	22S40	0S26	21S23	0S19
2 F	3 40	0 13	4 47	2N15	15 52	2 53	12 08	0 19	6 11	3 40	25 12	14 32	22 39	0 26	21 23	0 19
3 Sa	4 03	4N42	4 22	7 06	16 16	2 58	11 46	0 23	6 07	3 37	25 11	14 29	22 39	0 26	21 23	0 19
4 Su	4 26	9 25	3 45	11 40	16 39	3 03	11 25	0 26	6 04	3 34	25 10	14 25	22 39	0 26	21 23	0 19
5 M	4 50	13 48	2 59	15 49	16 60	3 08	11 03	0 30	5 60	3 31	25 09	14 22	22 38	0 26	21 23	0 19
6 Tu	5 13	17 41	2 05	19 22	17 19	3 12	10 41	0 33	5 56	3 28	25 08	14 18	22 37	0 26	21 22	0 19
7 W	5 35	20 52	1 05	22 08	17 36	3 16	10 18	0 37	5 53	3 25	25 06	14 15	22 37	0 26	21 22	0 19
8 Th	5 58	23 10	0 01	23 56	17 51	3 19	9 56	0 40	5 49	3 21	25 04	14 11	22 36	0 26	21 22	0 19
9 F	6 21	24 26	1N04	24 37	18 04	3 21	9 32	0 43	5 45	3 18	25 03	14 08	22 36	0 26	21 22	0 19
10 Sa	6 44	24 29	2 07	24 01	18 15	3 23	9 09	0 47	5 41	3 15	25 00	14 04	22 35	0 26	21 22	0 19
11 Su	7 07	23 14	3 06	22 06	18 23	3 23	8 45	0 50	5 38	3 11	24 58	14 01	22 34	0 26	21 22	0 19
12 M	7 29	20 39	3 57	18 53	18 28	3 23	8 21	0 53	5 34	3 07	24 56	13 57	22 34	0 26	21 22	0 19
13 Tu	7 52	16 48	4 36	14 28	18 31	3 22	7 57	0 56	5 30	3 03	24 53	13 53	22 33	0 26	21 21	0 19
14 W	8 14	11 52	4 59	9 05	18 30	3 20	7 32	0 58	5 27	2 60	24 50	13 50	22 32	0 26	21 21	0 19
15 Th	8 36	6 07	5 04	3 02	18 25	3 16	7 07	1 01	5 23	2 56	24 47	13 46	22 31	0 26	21 21	0 20
16 F	8 58	0S07	4 47	3S18	18 17	3 11	6 42	1 04	5 20	2 52	24 44	13 42	22 31	0 26	21 21	0 20
17 Sa	9 20	6 26	4 09	9 28	18 04	3 04	6 17	1 07	5 16	2 48	24 41	13 38	22 30	0 26	21 20	0 20
18 Su	9 42	12 21	3 14	15 02	17 48	2 56	5 51	1 09	5 13	2 44	24 38	13 34	22 29	0 26	21 20	0 20
19 M	10 04	17 27	2 06	19 34	17 27	2 46	5 25	1 12	5 10	2 40	24 34	13 30	22 28	0 26	21 20	0 20
20 Tu	10 25	21 21	0 51	22 46	17 01	2 34	4 59	1 14	5 07	2 35	24 30	13 27	22 27	0 27	21 20	0 20
21 W	10 47	23 48	0S26	24 27	16 31	2 21	4 33	1 16	5 05	2 31	24 27	13 23	22 26	0 27	21 19	0 20
22 Th	11 08	24 42	1 38	24 35	15 56	2 06	4 07	1 19	5 02	2 27	24 23	13 19	22 25	0 27	21 19	0 20
23 F	11 29	24 07	2 43	23 19	15 18	1 49	3 40	1 21	5 00	2 23	24 18	13 15	22 24	0 27	21 18	0 20
24 Sa	11 50	22 13	3 38	20 51	14 37	1 30	3 13	1 23	4 58	2 19	24 14	13 11	22 23	0 27	21 18	0 20
25 Su	12 11	19 15	4 20	17 28	13 53	1 11	2 46	1 25	4 56	2 14	24 10	13 07	22 22	0 27	21 18	0 20
26 M	12 31	15 29	4 50	13 23	13 08	0 51	2 19	1 27	4 54	2 10	24 05	13 03	22 21	0 27	21 17	0 20
27 Tu	12 52	11 09	5 05	8 49	12 23	0 30	1 52	1 29	4 53	2 06	24 01	12 59	22 20	0 27	21 17	0 20
28 W	13 12	6 26	5 07	3 59	11 39	0 09	1 25	1 30	4 52	2 02	23 56	12 55	22 19	0 27	21 16	0 20
29 Th	13 32	1 31	4 55	0N58	10 57	0N11	0 57	1 32	4 51	1 57	23 51	12 51	22 18	0 27	21 16	0 20
30 F	13 51	3N27	4 30	5 53	10 18	0 30	0 30	1 33	4 50	1 53	23 46	12 47	22 16	0 27	21 15	0 20
31 Sa	14S11	8N16	3S54	10N35	9S44	0N48	0N02	1N35	4N50	1S49	23S41	12S43	22S15	0S27	21S15	0S20

Day	⚷ Decl	⚷ Lat	♅ Decl	♅ Lat	♆ Decl	♆ Lat	♇ Decl	♇ Lat
1	5N24	2N48	14N19	0S28	5S22	1S07	22S39	1S06
6	5 18	2 48	14 16	0 28	5 25	1 07	22 39	1 06
11	5 12	2 47	14 13	0 28	5 28	1 07	22 39	1 06
16	5 06	2 47	14 09	0 28	5 30	1 07	22 39	1 07
21	5 01	2 46	14 05	0 28	5 33	1 07	22 39	1 07
26	4 56	2 45	14 01	0 28	5 35	1 07	22 39	1 07
31	4N50	2N45	13N57	0S28	5S37	1S07	22S39	1S08

Day	⚴ Decl	⚴ Lat	⚵ Decl	⚵ Lat	⚶ Decl	⚶ Lat	Eris Decl	Eris Lat
1	7N30	30N21	5S07	8N01	16N15	2N02	1S32	11S43
6	6 38	29 26	5 38	8 03	15 43	2 11	1 33	11 43
11	5 50	28 33	6 08	8 05	15 11	2 20	1 34	11 43
16	5 04	27 41	6 37	8 07	14 40	2 30	1 35	11 42
21	4 21	26 51	7 06	8 10	14 09	2 40	1 36	11 42
26	3 41	26 04	7 34	8 13	13 38	2 51	1 37	11 42
31	3N04	25N18	8S00	8N16	13N08	3N02	1S38	11S42

Moon Phenomena

Max/0 Decl

dy	hr mn	
2	1:01	0 N
9	13:06	24N37
15	23:32	0 S
22	2:06	24S42
29	7:18	0 N

Max/0 Lat

dy	hr mn	
8	0:31	0 N
14	16:56	5N04
20	15:55	0 S
27	14:54	5S08

Perigee/Apogee

dy	hr m		kilometers
3	17:24	a	406322
16	23:47	p	356912
30	18:47	a	406395

PH	dy	hr mn	
○	1	21:06	9♈08
☾	10	0:41	17♋10
●	16	19:32	23♎53
☽	23	13:24	0♒36
○	31	14:50	8♉38

Void of Course Moon

Last Aspect		☽ Ingress	
30 17:31	♄ ⚹	♈	1 2:48
3 5:48	♄ □	♉	3 15:14
5 18:42	♄ △	♊	6 4:04
8 1:58	♂ ⚹	♋	8 15:47
10 16:05	♄ ☍	♌	11 0:26
12 14:31	♂ △	♍	13 4:57
14 22:48	♄ △	♎	15 5:55
16 22:13	♄ □	♏	17 5:07
18 21:44	♄ ⚹	♐	19 4:44
21 3:39	☉ ⚹	♑	21 6:45
23 4:36	♄ ☌	♒	23 12:18
24 21:55	♂ ⚹	♓	25 21:19
28 0:47	♄ ⚹	♈	28 8:46
30 16:14	☿ ☍	♉	30 21:20

DAILY ASPECTARIAN

1 Th	☽ ⚺ ⚳	1:55
	☿ ⚼ ♆	1:56
	☉ ∥ ☽	8:24
	☽ ⚻ ☿	11:40
	☽ ☌ ⚷	16:58
	♆ ⋕ ⚷	21:04
	☉ ☍ ☽	21:06
	☽ ⚺ ♅	22:30
2 F	☽ ⚼ ♀	7:37
	☽ ∠ ⚳	7:45
	♀ ☍ ⚳	8:53
	☉ ⚻ ♅	13:32
	☽ □ ♃	15:00
	☽ ⚺ ♆	16:57
	☉ ⋕ ☽	20:33
	♀ ♍	20:49
3 Sa	☽ □ ♇	0:01
	☽ ∥ ⚷	3:15
	☽ ⋕ ♆	3:26
	☽ ☌ ♂	3:58
	☽ □ ♄	5:48
	☽ ∥ ♂	7:00
	♃ ∥ ♇	11:04
	☽ ⚹ ⚳	13:49
	☽ △ ♀	17:14
	☽ ∠ ♆	23:15
4 Su	☽ ☍ ☿	5:18
	☽ ⚺ ⚷	5:21
	☿ ⚻ ⚷	5:56
	☽ ∥ ♀	9:49
	☽ ☌ ♅	11:00
	♇ D	13:34
	☉ ⚻ ☽	15:17
5 M	☽ ∥ ♅	2:44
	☽ △ ♃	4:08
	☽ ⚹ ♆	5:38
	☽ ∠ ⚷	11:41
	☽ △ ♇	12:52
	♀ ⚼ ♃	14:56
	☽ ⚺ ♂	15:20
	☽ △ ♄	18:42
	☽ ⋕ ☿	21:21
6 Tu	☉ ⚼ ☽	0:27
	☽ □ ⚳	2:14
	☉ ⋕ ⚷	5:16
	☽ ⚼ ♃	10:41
	☽ □ ♀	12:42
	☉ ∥ ♆	13:18
	☽ ⚹ ⚷	17:52
	☽ ⚼ ♇	19:09
	☉ ⚼ ⚳	20:27
	☽ ∠ ♂	20:51
	☽ ⚻ ☿	22:13
	☽ ⚺ ♅	23:30
7 W	☽ ⚼ ♄	0:58
	☽ ⋕ ♄	4:34
	☉ △ ☽	9:19
	☉ ⋕ ♂	15:20
	☽ ⚻ ♃	16:54
	☽ ⋕ ♃	17:08
	☽ ⋕ ♇	17:37
	☽ □ ♆	17:52
	☿ ☍ ♅	20:57
8 Th	☊ D	0:30
	☽ ⚻ ♇	1:03
	☽ ⚹ ♂	1:58
	☽ ∠ ♅	5:14
	☽ ⚼ ☿	5:41
	☽ ⚻ ♄	6:47
	☽ △ ⚳	13:40
	♀ ⚻ ⚷	15:19
9 F	☽ □ ⚷	4:50
	♀ ⚼ ♇	6:09
	☽ ⚹ ♀	6:17
	♀ ⚼ ♂	7:39
	☽ ⚹ ♅	10:15
	☽ △ ☿	12:04
	♂ □ ♇	13:10
	☽ ⚼ ⚳	18:24
10 Sa	☉ □ ☽	0:41
	☊ R	0:52
	☽ ☍ ♃	3:18
	☽ △ ♆	3:45
	☽ □ ♂	10:06
	☽ ☍ ♇	10:38
	☽ ∠ ♀	13:29
	☽ ☍ ♄	16:05
	☽ ⚻ ⚳	22:13
	♀ △ ♅	23:10
11 Su	☽ ⋕ ♇	6:35
	☽ ⚼ ♆	7:16
	☽ ⋕ ♃	7:26
	☽ △ ⚷	12:24
	☉ □ ♃	13:36
	☉ ⚻ ♆	15:32
	☽ □ ♅	17:29
	☽ ⋕ ♄	18:26
	♀ ⚼ ♄	18:34
	☽ ⚺ ♀	19:17
	☽ □ ☿	20:51
12 M	♃ ⚹ ♆	7:07
	☽ ⚻ ♆	9:44
	☽ ⚻ ♃	9:46
	☉ ⚹ ☽	11:10
	☽ ⋕ ☿	14:17
	☽ △ ♂	14:31
	☽ ⚼ ⚷	14:38
	☽ ⚻ ♇	16:12
	☿ ⚹ ♀	16:40
	☽ ⚻ ♄	21:19
13 Tu	☉ ⋕ ♀	2:39
	☽ ☍ ⚳	2:45
	♂ ⋕ ♆	8:26
	☽ ⚼ ♃	11:25
	☽ ∥ ♅	13:22
	☉ ∠ ☽	14:30
	☽ ⚼ ♂	15:17
	☽ ⚻ ⚷	15:53
	☽ ⚼ ♇	17:29
	☽ △ ♅	20:36
	☽ ⚼ ♄	22:27
	☉ ☍ ♂	23:27
14 W	☽ ⚹ ☿	0:20
	☿ R	1:06
	☽ ☌ ♀	2:56
	☽ ☍ ♆	11:48
	☽ △ ♃	12:13
	☉ ⋕ ☽	14:34
	☽ ⚻ ♂	15:18
	☉ ⚺ ☽	16:47
	☽ △ ♇	17:56
	☽ ∥ ♀	19:41
	☽ ⚼ ♅	20:55
	☽ △ ♄	22:48
15 Th	☽ ∠ ☿	0:31
	☽ ⋕ ♆	2:26
	☽ ∥ ♂	2:54
	☽ ⚻ ⚳	3:45
	☽ ∥ ⚷	3:54
	☉ □ ♇	10:16
	☽ ☍ ⚷	16:09
	☽ ⚻ ♅	20:40
	☽ ⚺ ☿	23:59
16 F	☽ ⚼ ⚳	3:26
	☽ ⚺ ♀	6:54
	☽ ⚻ ♆	11:21
	☽ □ ♃	12:07
	☽ ☍ ♂	13:51
	☽ □ ♇	17:24
	☽ ⋕ ⚷	18:51
	☉ ☌ ☽	19:32
	☽ ⋕ ♂	19:35
	☽ ∥ ♆	20:27
	☽ □ ♄	22:13
	☽ ⋕ ♀	23:27
17 Sa	☽ △ ⚳	2:56
	☽ ∠ ♀	8:25
	☽ ⚼ ♆	10:50
	☉ ∥ ☽	12:14
	☽ ⚻ ⚷	15:07
	☽ ☍ ♅	19:38
	☽ ☌ ☿	21:53
18 Su	☽ ⋕ ♅	7:48
	☽ ⚹ ♀	10:06
	☽ △ ♆	10:29
	☽ ⚹ ♃	11:40
	☽ ⚻ ♂	12:09
	☉ □ ♄	13:59
	☽ ⚼ ⚷	14:48
	♀ ☍ ♆	14:50
	☽ ⚹ ♇	16:44
	⚳ D	17:01
	♀ ⋕ ♆	18:09
	☽ ⚹ ♄	21:44
	☉ ⚺ ☽	22:16
	☽ ∥ ☿	23:57
19 M	☽ □ ⚳	2:28
	♂ □ ♃	5:39
	♀ ⚻ ♂	7:04
	♀ △ ♃	7:36
	☽ ⚼ ♂	11:50
	☽ ∠ ♃	12:00
	☽ △ ⚷	14:58
	♀ ∥ ♂	15:32
	☽ ∠ ♇	17:01
	☽ ⚻ ♅	19:41
	☽ ⚺ ☿	20:03
	♀ ∥ ⚷	21:21
	☽ ∠ ♄	22:12
	☽ ∥ ♄	23:47
20 Tu	☉ ∠ ☽	0:29
	☿ ☍ ♅	2:55
	☽ ∥ ♃	8:58
	☽ ∥ ♇	10:53
	☽ □ ♆	11:20
	☽ △ ♂	12:10
	☽ ⚺ ♃	13:02
	☽ □ ♀	15:29
	☊ D	15:53
	☽ ⚺ ♇	18:02
	☽ ∠ ☿	19:41
	☽ ⚼ ♅	20:42
	☽ ⚺ ♄	23:25
21 W	☉ ⚹ ☽	3:39
	☽ ⚹ ⚳	4:22
	☽ ∥ ⚳	11:11
	☉ △ ⚳	13:53
	☽ □ ⚷	17:31
	☽ ⚹ ☿	19:50
	☿ ∠ ♀	20:32
	♀ △ ♇	21:43
	☽ △ ♅	22:34
22 Th	☽ ∠ ⚳	6:38
	⚶ ♍	7:39
	♂ ⚺ ♆	9:11
	☽ □ ♂	15:17
	☽ ⚹ ♆	15:24
	☽ ☌ ♃	17:45
	☽ ∥ ⚳	19:39
	☽ ☌ ♇	22:41
	☉ ♏	23:01
23 F	☽ △ ♀	1:11
	☿ ⚻ ⚷	1:36
	♀ ⚼ ♅	3:06
	☽ ☌ ♄	4:36
	☽ ⚺ ⚳	9:51
	☊ R	13:19
	☉ □ ☽	13:24
	☽ ∠ ♆	18:49
	☽ ∥ ♇	19:34
	☽ □ ☿	21:50
	☽ ∥ ♃	22:16
	☽ ⚹ ⚷	23:39
24 Sa	☽ □ ♅	5:03
	♂ ∥ ⚷	6:20
	☽ ⚼ ♀	7:52
	☽ ∥ ♄	8:17
	♀ △ ♄	15:42
	☿ ⋕ ♅	19:04
	☽ ⚹ ♂	21:55
	☽ ⚺ ♆	23:06
25 Su	☽ ⚺ ♃	2:14
	☽ ∠ ⚷	4:02
	☿ ⚼ ♆	5:17
	☽ ⚺ ♇	6:58
	☽ ⚺ ♄	13:23
	☽ ⚻ ♀	15:38
	☉ ☌ ☿	18:24
	☽ ☌ ⚳	18:54
26 M	☽ △ ☿	2:00
	☽ ∠ ♂	2:22
	☉ △ ☽	3:32
	☽ ∠ ♃	7:39
	☽ ⋕ ♅	8:27
	☽ ⚺ ⚷	9:06
	☉ ⚼ ♆	10:35
	☽ ∠ ♇	12:13
	☉ ∥ ☿	13:23
	☽ ⚹ ♅	14:45
	☉ ∥ ☽	15:29
	☽ ∥ ☿	16:07
	☽ ∠ ♄	18:50
27 Tu	♀ ⚻ ⚳	2:10
	☽ ⚼ ☿	4:50
	☽ ⚺ ♂	7:24
	☽ ☌ ♆	9:41
	☉ ⚼ ☽	11:48
	☽ ⚹ ♃	13:39
	☽ ⚹ ♇	17:59
	☽ ∠ ♅	20:26
28 W	☽ ⚹ ♄	0:47
	☿ R ♎	1:35
	☿ ⚺ ♀	1:39
	♀ ♎	1:42
	☽ ∥ ♆	4:07
	☽ ⚺ ⚳	6:31
	☽ ⋕ ⚷	7:35
	☽ ⋕ ♂	7:44
	☽ ⚻ ☿	8:09
	☽ ☍ ♀	9:33
	☉ ⚻ ☽	20:35
	☽ ☌ ⚷	20:40
	☉ ⚻ ⚷	21:33
29 Th	☿ △ ⚳	1:34
	☽ ⚺ ♅	2:27
	☽ ⋕ ♀	2:56
	☽ ∥ ♀	10:55
	☽ ∠ ⚳	12:52
	☽ ☌ ♂	18:34
	☽ ⚺ ♆	21:52
30 F	☽ □ ♃	2:40
	☽ □ ♇	6:27
	☽ ∥ ♂	6:48
	☽ ∥ ⚷	6:55
	☉ ⋕ ♅	8:00
	☽ ⋕ ♆	10:38
	☽ □ ♄	13:31
	☽ ☍ ☿	16:14
	☽ ⚹ ⚳	19:23
31 Sa	☽ ∠ ♆	4:12
	☽ ⚻ ♀	5:03
	☽ ⋕ ☿	6:49
	☽ ⚺ ⚷	9:09
	☉ ☍ ☽	14:50
	☽ ☌ ♅	14:56
	☉ ☍ ♅	15:54

LONGITUDE

November 2020

Day	Sid.Time	☉	☽	☽ 12 hour	Mean☊	True☊	☿	♀	♂	⚳	♃	♄	⚷	♅	♆	♇
	h m s	° ' "	° ' "	° ' "	° '	° '	° '	° '	° '	° '	° '	° '	° '	° '	° '	° '
1 Su	2 42 57	9♏01 16	13♉09 47	19♉05 37	22♊05.2	20♊28.5	26♎37.2	4♎46.0	16♈22.0	29♒07.7	21♑02.5	26♑13.1	5♈48.5	8♉40.2	18♓22.8	22♑40.3
2 M	2 46 54	10 01 17	25 02 00	0♊59 13	22 02.0	20R 23.5	26R 11.3	5 59.1	16R 12.0	29 12.6	21 11.0	26 16.3	5R 46.3	8R 37.7	18R 21.9	22 41.2
3 Tu	2 50 50	11 01 20	6♊57 31	12 57 12	21 58.8	20 20.5	25D 57.0	7 12.1	16 02.9	29 17.7	21 19.6	26 19.6	5 44.2	8 35.3	18 21.0	22 42.0
4 W	2 54 47	12 01 25	18 58 36	25 02 05	21 55.6	20D 19.5	25 54.2	8 25.3	15 54.4	29 23.2	21 28.4	26 22.9	5 42.2	8 32.8	18 20.2	22 42.9
5 Th	2 58 44	13 01 32	1♋08 02	7♋16 54	21 52.5	20 20.0	26 02.6	9 38.5	15 46.8	29 29.0	21 37.2	26 26.4	5 40.2	8 30.3	18 19.4	22 43.8
6 F	3 02 40	14 01 42	13 29 07	19 45 10	21 49.3	20 21.5	26 21.5	10 51.8	15 40.0	29 35.2	21 46.3	26 30.0	5 38.2	8 27.9	18 18.6	22 44.7
7 Sa	3 06 37	15 01 53	26 05 31	2♌30 40	21 46.1	20 23.1	26 50.1	12 05.2	15 33.9	29 41.6	21 55.4	26 33.6	5 36.2	8 25.4	18 17.9	22 45.7
8 Su	3 10 33	16 02 06	9♌01 05	15 37 12	21 42.9	20R 24.3	27 27.7	13 18.6	15 28.7	29 48.4	22 04.7	26 37.3	5 34.3	8 23.0	18 17.2	22 46.6
9 M	3 14 30	17 02 21	22 19 22	29 07 54	21 39.8	20 24.4	28 13.4	14 32.1	15 24.2	29 55.5	22 14.0	26 41.1	5 32.4	8 20.5	18 16.5	22 47.7
10 Tu	3 18 26	18 02 38	6♍03 00	13♍04 42	21 36.6	20 23.1	29 06.2	15 45.7	15 20.5	0♓02.9	22 23.6	26 45.0	5 30.6	8 18.1	18 15.9	22 48.7
11 W	3 22 23	19 02 58	20 12 56	27 27 26	21 33.4	20 20.4	0♏05.3	16 59.3	15 17.7	0 10.5	22 33.2	26 49.0	5 28.8	8 15.7	18 15.3	22 49.7
12 Th	3 26 20	20 03 19	4♎47 43	12♎13 08	21 30.2	20 16.5	1 09.9	18 13.0	15 15.7	0 18.5	22 42.9	26 53.1	5 27.0	8 13.3	18 14.7	22 50.8
13 F	3 30 16	21 03 42	19 42 52	27 15 53	21 27.1	20 12.2	2 19.3	19 26.8	15 14.4	0 26.8	22 52.8	26 57.2	5 25.3	8 10.9	18 14.1	22 51.9
14 Sa	3 34 13	22 04 07	4♏51 22	12♏27 06	21 23.9	20 08.1	3 32.8	20 40.6	15D 14.0	0 35.4	23 02.8	27 01.4	5 23.7	8 08.5	18 13.6	22 53.1
15 Su	3 38 09	23 04 34	20 02 48	27 36 50	21 20.7	20 04.8	4 49.7	21 54.4	15 14.4	0 44.2	23 12.9	27 05.7	5 22.1	8 06.1	18 13.1	22 54.3
16 M	3 42 06	24 05 02	5♐08 02	12♐35 17	21 17.5	20 02.7	6 09.7	23 08.4	15 15.6	0 53.4	23 23.1	27 10.1	5 20.5	8 03.8	18 12.6	22 55.4
17 Tu	3 46 02	25 05 32	19 57 39	27 14 21	21 14.3	20D 02.1	7 32.2	24 22.3	15 17.6	1 02.8	23 33.4	27 14.5	5 18.9	8 01.4	18 12.2	22 56.7
18 W	3 49 59	26 06 04	4♑24 50	11♑28 41	21 11.2	20 02.6	8 56.7	25 36.3	15 20.3	1 12.5	23 43.9	27 19.0	5 17.5	7 59.1	18 11.8	22 57.9
19 Th	3 53 55	27 06 37	18 25 42	25 15 50	21 08.0	20 03.9	10 23.1	26 50.4	15 23.9	1 22.5	23 54.4	27 23.7	5 16.0	7 56.8	18 11.5	22 59.2
20 F	3 57 52	28 07 11	1♒59 12	8♒36 01	21 04.8	20 05.5	11 50.9	28 04.5	15 28.2	1 32.7	24 05.1	27 28.3	5 14.6	7 54.5	18 11.2	23 00.5
21 Sa	4 01 49	29 07 46	15 06 38	21 31 27	21 01.6	20 06.8	13 19.9	29 18.6	15 33.3	1 43.3	24 15.9	27 33.1	5 13.3	7 52.3	18 10.9	23 01.8
22 Su	4 05 45	0♐08 23	27 50 57	4♓05 39	20 58.5	20R 07.4	14 49.9	0♏32.8	15 39.1	1 54.0	24 26.7	27 37.9	5 12.0	7 50.0	18 10.6	23 03.1
23 M	4 09 42	1 09 00	10♓16 05	16 22 47	20 55.3	20 07.1	16 20.8	1 47.1	15 45.7	2 05.1	24 37.7	27 42.8	5 10.8	7 47.8	18 10.4	23 04.5
24 Tu	4 13 38	2 09 39	22 26 19	28 27 13	20 52.1	20 05.9	17 52.3	3 01.3	15 53.0	2 16.4	24 48.7	27 47.7	5 09.6	7 45.6	18 10.2	23 05.8
25 W	4 17 35	3 10 19	4♈26 00	10♈23 09	20 48.9	20 03.9	19 24.3	4 15.6	16 01.0	2 27.9	24 59.9	27 52.8	5 08.4	7 43.4	18 10.0	23 07.2
26 Th	4 21 31	4 11 00	16 19 10	22 14 27	20 45.8	20 01.6	20 56.7	5 30.0	16 09.7	2 39.7	25 11.2	27 57.9	5 07.3	7 41.3	18 09.9	23 08.7
27 F	4 25 28	5 11 42	28 09 26	4♉04 29	20 42.6	19 59.0	22 29.5	6 44.3	16 19.1	2 51.7	25 22.5	28 03.0	5 06.3	7 39.2	18 09.8	23 10.1
28 Sa	4 29 24	6 12 26	9♉59 55	15 56 04	20 39.4	19 56.7	24 02.5	7 58.8	16 29.2	3 04.0	25 33.9	28 08.2	5 05.3	7 37.1	18 09.8	23 11.6
29 Su	4 33 21	7 13 10	21 53 13	27 51 37	20 36.2	19 54.9	25 35.7	9 13.2	16 39.9	3 16.5	25 45.5	28 13.5	5 04.3	7 35.0	18D 09.8	23 13.0
30 M	4 37 18	8♐13 56	3♊51 30	9♊53 05	20♊33.0	19♊53.8	27♏09.1	10♏27.7	16♈51.2	3♓29.2	25♑57.1	28♑18.9	5♈03.4	7♉33.0	18♓09.8	23♑14.6

1st of Month

Julian Day # 2459154.5
Obliquity 23°26'13"
SVP 4♓58'26"
GC 27♐07.8
Eris 23♈51.2R

Day	⚴	Day	⚵	Day	⚶
1	19♑50.9	1	13♏53.3	1	3♍37.3
6	21 04.7	6	15 35.8	6	5 25.3
11	22 22.1	11	17 18.4	11	7 10.2
16	23 42.7	16	19 01.0	16	8 51.4
21	25 06.4	21	20 43.3	21	10 28.6
26	26 32.7	26	22 25.2	26	12 01.3

DECLINATION and LATITUDE

Day	☉ Decl	☽ Decl	☽ Lat	☽ 12h Decl	☿ Decl	☿ Lat	♀ Decl	♀ Lat	♂ Decl	♂ Lat	⚳ Decl	⚳ Lat	♃ Decl	♃ Lat	♄ Decl	♄ Lat
1 Su	14S30	12N48	3S08	14N54	9S15	1N05	0S25	1N36	4N49	1S45	23S35	12S40	22S14	0S27	21S14	0S20
2 M	14 49	16 52	2 13	18 40	8 52	1 20	0 53	1 38	4 49	1 41	23 28	12 36	22 13	0 27	21 14	0 20
3 Tu	15 08	20 17	1 12	21 41	8 35	1 33	1 21	1 39	4 50	1 37	23 25	12 32	22 11	0 27	21 13	0 20
4 W	15 27	22 51	0 07	23 46	8 23	1 44	1 49	1 40	4 50	1 32	23 19	12 28	22 10	0 27	21 12	0 20
5 Th	15 45	24 25	0N59	24 45	8 17	1 54	2 16	1 41	4 51	1 28	23 13	12 24	22 09	0 27	21 12	0 20
6 F	16 03	24 48	2 03	24 31	8 17	2 01	2 44	1 42	4 52	1 24	23 08	12 20	22 07	0 27	21 11	0 21
7 Sa	16 21	23 55	3 03	23 00	8 22	2 07	3 12	1 43	4 53	1 20	23 02	12 16	22 06	0 27	21 11	0 21
8 Su	16 38	21 47	3 55	20 15	8 31	2 12	3 40	1 44	4 55	1 17	22 56	12 13	22 04	0 27	21 10	0 21
9 M	16 55	18 25	4 36	16 19	8 44	2 15	4 08	1 44	4 57	1 13	22 49	12 09	22 03	0 27	21 09	0 21
10 Tu	17 12	13 59	5 03	11 25	9 01	2 17	4 35	1 45	4 59	1 09	22 43	12 05	22 01	0 27	21 09	0 21
11 W	17 29	8 40	5 13	5 45	9 21	2 17	5 03	1 45	5 01	1 05	22 37	12 01	21 60	0 27	21 08	0 21
12 Th	17 45	2 44	5 03	0S22	9 44	2 17	5 31	1 46	5 04	1 02	22 31	11 58	21 58	0 27	21 07	0 21
13 F	18 01	3S30	4 33	6 36	10 09	2 15	5 58	1 46	5 07	0 58	22 24	11 54	21 57	0 27	21 06	0 21
14 Sa	18 17	9 38	3 43	12 31	10 37	2 13	6 26	1 46	5 10	0 54	22 18	11 50	21 55	0 27	21 06	0 21
15 Su	18 32	15 13	2 37	17 40	11 05	2 10	6 53	1 47	5 13	0 51	22 11	11 46	21 53	0 27	21 05	0 21
16 M	18 47	19 49	1 21	21 38	11 35	2 06	7 20	1 47	5 17	0 47	22 04	11 43	21 52	0 27	21 04	0 21
17 Tu	19 02	23 03	0 00	24 04	12 06	2 02	7 47	1 47	5 21	0 44	21 57	11 39	21 50	0 27	21 03	0 21
18 W	19 17	24 40	1S18	24 51	12 37	1 58	8 14	1 47	5 25	0 41	21 50	11 36	21 48	0 27	21 02	0 21
19 Th	19 31	24 39	2 30	24 04	13 09	1 52	8 41	1 47	5 29	0 37	21 43	11 32	21 46	0 27	21 01	0 21
20 F	19 44	23 08	3 31	21 55	13 42	1 47	9 08	1 46	5 34	0 34	21 36	11 28	21 45	0 27	21 01	0 21
21 Sa	19 58	20 25	4 19	18 42	14 14	1 41	9 34	1 46	5 39	0 31	21 29	11 25	21 43	0 27	20 60	0 21
22 Su	20 11	16 47	4 52	14 43	14 46	1 35	10 01	1 46	5 44	0 28	21 22	11 21	21 41	0 28	20 59	0 21
23 M	20 23	12 31	5 11	10 12	15 19	1 28	10 27	1 45	5 49	0 25	21 15	11 18	21 39	0 28	20 58	0 21
24 Tu	20 36	7 50	5 15	5 23	15 51	1 22	10 53	1 45	5 55	0 22	21 07	11 14	21 37	0 28	20 57	0 21
25 W	20 47	2 55	5 06	0 26	16 22	1 15	11 18	1 44	6 00	0 19	20 60	11 11	21 35	0 28	20 56	0 21
26 Th	20 59	2N03	4 43	4N31	16 53	1 08	11 44	1 43	6 06	0 16	20 52	11 08	21 33	0 28	20 55	0 21
27 F	21 10	6 57	4 09	9 19	17 24	1 02	12 09	1 43	6 13	0 13	20 45	11 04	21 31	0 28	20 54	0 21
28 Sa	21 21	11 36	3 23	13 47	17 54	0 55	12 34	1 42	6 19	0 11	20 37	11 01	21 29	0 28	20 53	0 22
29 Su	21 31	15 50	2 29	17 45	18 23	0 47	12 58	1 41	6 26	0 08	20 29	10 57	21 27	0 28	20 52	0 22
30 M	21S41	19N29	1S28	21N01	18S52	0N40	13S23	1N40	6N32	0S05	20S21	10S54	21S25	0S28	20S51	0S22

Day	⚷ Decl	⚷ Lat	♅ Decl	♅ Lat	♆ Decl	♆ Lat	♇ Decl	♇ Lat
1	4N49	2N44	13N57	0S28	5S37	1S07	22S39	1S08
6	4 45	2 44	13 53	0 28	5 38	1 06	22 38	1 08
11	4 40	2 43	13 49	0 28	5 40	1 06	22 38	1 08
16	4 36	2 42	13 45	0 28	5 41	1 06	22 37	1 09
21	4 32	2 41	13 41	0 28	5 41	1 06	22 36	1 09
26	4 29	2 40	13 38	0 28	5 41	1 06	22 35	1 09

Day	⚴ Decl	⚴ Lat	⚵ Decl	⚵ Lat	⚶ Decl	⚶ Lat	Eris Decl	Eris Lat
1	2N56	25N09	8S05	8N17	13N02	3N04	1S38	11S42
6	2 23	24 26	8 31	8 21	12 33	3 16	1 39	11 41
11	1 53	23 45	8 55	8 25	12 06	3 28	1 39	11 41
16	1 25	23 05	9 17	8 30	11 40	3 41	1 40	11 40
21	1 01	22 28	9 39	8 35	11 15	3 55	1 40	11 40
26	0 40	21 52	9 59	8 40	10 53	4 09	1 40	11 39

Moon Phenomena

Max/0 Decl (dy hr mn)	Perigee/Apogee (dy hr m kilometers)
5 19:31 24N49	14 11:44 p 357842
12 10:34 0 S	27 0:30 a 405894
18 11:35 24S51	
25 14:04 0 N	

Max/0 Lat (dy hr mn)	PH dy hr mn
4 2:41 0 N	☾ 8 13:47 16♌37
11 0:13 5N13	● 15 5:08 23♏18
17 0:08 0 S	☽ 22 4:46 0♓20
23 19:22 5S16	○ 30 9:31 8♊38
	☍ 30 9:44 A 0.828

Void of Course Moon

Last Aspect	☽ Ingress
2 2:31 ♄ △	♊ 2 10:01
4 13:50 ☿ △	♋ 4 21:47
7 1:28 ☿ □	♌ 7 7:19
9 11:06 ☿ ⚹	♍ 9 13:31
11 11:00 ♄ △	♎ 11 16:11
13 11:34 ♄ □	♏ 13 16:20
15 11:14 ♄ ⚹	♐ 15 15:48
17 7:56 ♀ ⚹	♑ 17 16:36
19 16:31 ☉ ⚹	♒ 19 20:26
21 0:50 ♂ ⚹	♓ 22 4:07
24 10:46 ♄ ⚹	♈ 24 15:06
26 23:47 ♄ □	♉ 27 3:44
29 12:50 ♄ △	♊ 29 16:17

DAILY ASPECTARIAN

1 Su
♂ ∥ ⚷ 2:38
☽ ⚺ ♂ 6:24
☽ ∥ ♅ 6:24
☉ ⋕ ☽ 10:27
☽ ⚹ ♆ 10:33
☽ ⚼ ♀ 14:53
☽ ∠ ⚷ 15:25
☽ △ ♃ 16:08
☿ □ ♄ 19:07
☽ △ ♇ 19:15
♀ ☍ ⚷ 19:56

2 M
☽ ⚻ ☿ 2:16
☽ △ ♄ 2:31
☽ □ ⚳ 8:29
☽ ∠ ♂ 12:16
☽ ⚹ ⚷ 21:33
☽ ⚼ ♃ 22:43

3 Tu
☽ △ ♀ 0:33
☽ ⚼ ♇ 1:29
☽ ⚺ ♅ 3:15
☽ ⋕ ♄ 7:45
☽ ⚼ ☿ 7:55
☽ ⚼ ♄ 8:47
☉ ⚻ ☽ 8:53
☽ ⋕ ♃ 16:42
☿ D 17:51
☽ ⚹ ♂ 17:58
☽ ⋕ ♇ 21:34
☽ □ ♆ 22:44

4 W
♀ ⚻ ♅ 2:23
☊ D 2:40
☽ ⚻ ♃ 5:01
☽ ⋕ ⚳ 5:21
☽ ⚻ ♇ 7:25
☽ ∠ ♅ 9:02
☽ △ ☿ 13:50
☽ ⚻ ♄ 14:44
☉ ⚼ ☽ 17:21
☽ △ ⚳ 20:44

5 Th
☽ □ ⚷ 8:50
☽ ⚹ ♅ 14:20
☽ □ ♀ 18:23

6 F
☉ △ ☽ 1:08
☽ ⚼ ⚳ 2:08
☽ □ ♂ 4:09
☿ □ ♄ 9:13
☽ △ ♆ 9:14
☽ ☍ ♃ 16:02
☽ ☍ ♇ 17:42

7 Sa
☽ ☍ ♄ 0:53
☽ □ ☿ 1:28
☽ ⚻ ⚳ 6:49
☉ ⚻ ♂ 11:42
☽ ⋕ ⚳ 12:19
☽ ⚼ ♆ 13:27
☽ ⋕ ♇ 15:57
☽ △ ⚷ 17:41
☽ ⋕ ♃ 21:20
☽ □ ♅ 22:50

8 Su
☽ ⋕ ♄ 5:04
☽ ⚹ ♀ 8:37
☽ △ ♂ 11:40
☉ □ ☽ 13:47
☊ R 14:00
☽ ⚻ ♆ 16:47
☽ ⚼ ⚷ 20:50
☽ ⚻ ♃ 23:50

9 M
☽ ⚻ ♇ 0:50
☽ ⚻ ♄ 7:45
☉ ⋕ ☽ 8:11
♀ ⚼ ⚳ 8:28
☽ ⚹ ☿ 11:06
☽ ☍ ⚳ 13:30
☽ ∠ ♀ 13:57
☽ ⚼ ♂ 14:09
⚳ ♓ 14:49
♀ ☍ ♂ 16:10
☽ ⚻ ⚷ 23:04

10 Tu
☽ ∥ ♅ 0:46
☽ ⚼ ♃ 2:20
☽ ⚼ ♇ 3:02
☽ △ ♅ 3:51
♀ ⋕ ⚷ 4:43
☉ △ ♆ 5:13
☽ ⚼ ♄ 9:47
☽ ∠ ☿ 14:44
☽ ⚻ ♂ 15:46
☽ ⚺ ♀ 18:05
☽ ☍ ♆ 20:43
☽ ⋕ ☿ 21:14
⚳ ∥ ♇ 21:42
☉ ⚹ ☽ 21:54
☿ ♏ 21:57
♀ ⋕ ♂ 22:15

11 W
☿ △ ⚳ 2:19
☽ △ ♃ 3:56
☽ △ ♇ 4:21
☽ ⚼ ♅ 5:03
☽ △ ♄ 11:00
☽ ⋕ ♆ 12:22
☽ ⋕ ♀ 13:46
☽ ∥ ♂ 14:51
☽ ∥ ⚷ 16:24
☽ ⚻ ⚳ 16:37
♂ ∠ ⚳ 17:02
☽ ⚺ ☿ 17:36

12 Th
☉ ∠ ☽ 0:27
♀ ⚻ ♆ 0:32
☽ ☍ ⚷ 1:04
☽ ⚻ ♅ 5:32
♀ ∥ ♆ 8:03
☉ ⚼ ⚷ 9:10
☽ ☍ ♂ 16:51
☽ ⚼ ⚳ 17:07
☽ ⚻ ♆ 21:38
♃ ☌ ♇ 21:40
☽ ☌ ♀ 23:32

13 F
☉ ⚺ ☽ 2:18
☽ ⋕ ⚷ 4:22
☽ □ ♇ 5:01
☽ □ ♃ 5:06
☽ ⋕ ♂ 6:15
☽ ∥ ♆ 8:21
☽ ∥ ♀ 10:17
☽ □ ♄ 11:34
☽ △ ⚳ 17:12
☿ ⚼ ♆ 17:54
☽ ⚼ ♆ 21:26
☽ ☌ ☿ 21:45

14 Sa
♂ D 0:37
☽ ⚻ ⚷ 0:51
☽ ∥ ☿ 4:19
☽ ☍ ♅ 5:11
☽ ⚻ ♂ 16:24
☽ ⋕ ♅ 17:24
☉ ⚹ ♇ 19:49
☽ △ ♆ 21:07

15 Su
☽ ⚼ ⚷ 0:30
☽ ⚺ ♀ 3:12
☉ ⚹ ♃ 3:59
☽ ⚹ ♇ 4:32
☽ ⚹ ♃ 5:04
☉ ☌ ☽ 5:08
☿ ⚻ ⚷ 9:37
☽ ⚹ ♄ 11:14
☽ ⚼ ♂ 16:12
☽ □ ⚳ 17:09
☉ ∥ ☽ 17:39
♀ □ ♇ 19:44

16 M
☽ △ ⚷ 0:20
☽ ⚺ ☿ 1:49
☽ ∠ ♇ 4:29
☽ ⚻ ♅ 4:41
☽ ∠ ♀ 5:16
☽ ∠ ♃ 5:17
♀ □ ♃ 5:34
☽ ∥ ♄ 7:59
☽ ∠ ♄ 11:23
☽ ∥ ♃ 13:40
☽ ∥ ⚳ 14:52
☽ △ ♂ 16:22
☽ ∥ ♇ 19:58
☽ □ ♆ 21:08

17 Tu
☊ D 0:05
☽ ∠ ☿ 4:41
☽ ⚺ ♇ 4:54
☽ ⚼ ♅ 5:01
☽ ⚺ ♃ 5:59
☽ ⚹ ♀ 7:56
☿ ☍ ♅ 8:09
☉ ⚺ ☽ 9:05
☽ ⚺ ♄ 12:04
☽ ⚹ ⚳ 18:33

18 W
☽ □ ⚷ 1:29
☽ △ ♅ 6:02
☽ ⚹ ☿ 8:33
⚳ ∥ ♃ 10:24
☉ ∠ ☽ 12:14
☽ □ ♂ 18:43
☽ ∠ ⚳ 20:23
☽ ⚹ ♆ 23:35

19 Th
☉ ⚹ ♄ 7:19
☽ ☌ ♇ 8:00
☽ ☌ ♃ 9:44
♀ □ ♄ 11:30
☽ ☌ ♄ 15:52
☽ □ ♀ 16:17
☉ ⚹ ☽ 16:31
☽ ⚺ ⚳ 23:12

20 F
☿ ⋕ ♅ 0:24
☽ ∠ ♆ 2:10
☉ ⚺ ♀ 4:46
☽ ∥ ♇ 5:35
☽ ⚹ ⚷ 5:53
☽ □ ♅ 10:42
☽ ∥ ♃ 13:38
☽ ∥ ⚳ 15:17
☽ ∥ ♄ 19:35
☽ □ ☿ 20:17

21 Sa
☽ ⚹ ♂ 0:50
☉ ∥ ☽ 3:08
☽ ⚺ ♆ 5:43
☽ ∠ ⚷ 9:32
♂ ⋕ ♆ 11:33
♀ ♏ 13:23
☽ ⚺ ♇ 14:52
☽ ⚺ ♃ 17:26
☉ ♐ 20:41
☽ ⚺ ♄ 23:35

22 Su
☊ R 4:40
☉ □ ☽ 4:46
☽ ∠ ♂ 5:25
☽ △ ♀ 5:44
☽ ☌ ⚳ 7:53
☽ ∥ ☿ 10:21
☉ ⚼ ♂ 13:37
☿ ⚻ ♂ 14:01
☽ ⚺ ⚷ 14:07
☽ ⋕ ♅ 17:46
☽ ⚹ ♅ 19:12
☽ ∠ ♇ 19:43
☽ ∠ ♃ 22:44

23 M
☽ ∠ ♄ 4:49
♀ △ ⚳ 6:52
☽ ∥ ♀ 9:52
☽ ⚺ ♂ 10:53
☽ △ ☿ 13:39
☽ ⚼ ♀ 14:15
☽ ☌ ♆ 15:32

24 Tu
☽ ∠ ♅ 0:38
☽ ⚹ ♇ 1:19
♀ ⚼ ♆ 2:52
☉ □ ⚳ 3:16
☿ △ ♆ 4:41
☽ ⚹ ♃ 4:48
☽ ⋕ ♂ 9:16
☽ ∥ ♆ 10:32
☽ ⚹ ♄ 10:46
☽ ⋕ ⚷ 16:21
☽ ⚺ ⚳ 19:59
☉ △ ☽ 21:14
☽ ⚻ ♀ 23:37
☽ ⚼ ☿ 23:56

25 W
☽ ☌ ⚷ 1:25
☽ ⚺ ♅ 6:36
☿ ⚼ ⚷ 11:20
⚳ ∥ ♄ 13:58
☉ ∥ ⚳ 15:39
☉ ∥ ♄ 16:33
♀ ⚻ ⚷ 16:48
☽ ☌ ♂ 23:41

26 Th
☽ ∠ ⚳ 2:46
☽ ⚺ ♆ 3:44
☉ ⚼ ☽ 6:21
☽ ⚻ ☿ 10:47
☽ ∥ ⚷ 11:48
☽ □ ♇ 13:52
☽ ⋕ ♆ 17:46
☽ □ ♃ 18:16
☽ ∥ ♂ 20:16
☉ △ ⚷ 21:53
☽ □ ♄ 23:47

27 F
☽ ⚹ ⚳ 9:42
☽ ∠ ♆ 10:09
☿ ⚹ ♇ 10:40
☽ ⚺ ⚷ 14:04
☉ ⚻ ☽ 15:36
♀ ☍ ♅ 17:12
☽ ☌ ♅ 19:12
☽ ☍ ♀ 19:26

28 Sa
☽ ⋕ ♀ 5:48
☽ ∥ ♅ 11:02
☽ ⚺ ♂ 13:19
☉ ∥ ♃ 16:05
☽ ⚹ ♆ 16:30
☽ ∠ ⚷ 20:21

29 Su
♆ D 0:37
☽ △ ♇ 2:41
☿ ⚹ ♃ 2:52
☽ △ ♃ 7:55
☉ ⚻ ♅ 8:21
☽ ☍ ☿ 8:34
☽ △ ♄ 12:50
☽ ⋕ ☿ 18:52
☽ ∠ ♂ 19:56
☽ □ ⚳ 23:15

30 M
☉ ∠ ♇ 0:15
☽ ⚹ ⚷ 2:23
☽ ⋕ ⚳ 6:21
☽ ⚺ ♅ 7:20
☽ ⚼ ♇ 8:45
☉ ☍ ☽ 9:31
☽ ⋕ ♄ 10:31
♀ ⋕ ♅ 12:21
☽ ⚼ ♃ 14:21
☽ ⚻ ♀ 14:39
☽ ⋕ ♃ 15:09
☉ ⋕ ☽ 18:53
☽ ⚼ ♄ 18:57
☿ ⚹ ♄ 19:02

December 2020

LONGITUDE

Day	Sid.Time	☉	☽	☽ 12 hour	Mean☊	True☊	☿	♀	♂	⚳	♃	♄	⚷	♅	♆	♇
	h m s	° ' "	° ' "	° ' "	° '	° '	° '	° '	° '	° '	° '	° '	° '	° '	° '	° '
1 Tu	4 41 14	9♐14 43	15♊56 35	22♊02 11	20♊29.9	19♊53.3	28♏42.5	11♏42.2	17♈03.2	3♓42.2	26♑08.8	28♑24.3	5♈02.6	7♉31.0	18♓09.8	23♑16.1
2 W	4 45 11	10 15 31	28 10 06	4♋20 30	20 26.7	19D 53.3	0♐16.1	12 56.8	17 15.8	3 55.3	26 20.6	28 29.8	5R 01.8	7R 29.0	18 09.9	23 17.6
3 Th	4 49 07	11 16 21	10♋33 37	16 49 38	20 23.5	19 53.9	1 49.7	14 11.4	17 29.0	4 08.7	26 32.5	28 35.3	5 01.1	7 27.1	18 10.0	23 19.2
4 F	4 53 04	12 17 11	23 08 47	29 31 16	20 20.3	19 54.6	3 23.4	15 26.0	17 42.7	4 22.4	26 44.4	28 40.9	5 00.4	7 25.2	18 10.2	23 20.8
5 Sa	4 57 00	13 18 03	5♌57 19	12♌27 10	20 17.2	19 55.4	4 57.1	16 40.7	17 57.1	4 36.2	26 56.5	28 46.6	4 59.8	7 23.3	18 10.4	23 22.4
6 Su	5 00 57	14 18 57	19 01 02	25 39 09	20 14.0	19 56.0	6 30.8	17 55.4	18 12.0	4 50.2	27 08.6	28 52.3	4 59.2	7 21.5	18 10.6	23 24.0
7 M	5 04 53	15 19 51	2♍21 41	9♍08 49	20 10.8	19 56.4	8 04.5	19 10.1	18 27.5	5 04.5	27 20.8	28 58.1	4 58.7	7 19.7	18 10.9	23 25.7
8 Tu	5 08 50	16 20 47	16 00 39	22 57 14	20 07.6	19R 56.5	9 38.3	20 24.9	18 43.4	5 18.9	27 33.1	29 03.9	4 58.2	7 17.9	18 11.2	23 27.3
9 W	5 12 47	17 21 44	29 58 32	7♎04 26	20 04.5	19 56.4	11 12.1	21 39.7	19 00.0	5 33.6	27 45.4	29 09.8	4 57.8	7 16.1	18 11.5	23 29.0
10 Th	5 16 43	18 22 42	14♎14 43	21 29 01	20 01.3	19 56.3	12 45.9	22 54.5	19 17.0	5 48.4	27 57.9	29 15.7	4 57.4	7 14.4	18 11.8	23 30.7
11 F	5 20 40	19 23 42	28 46 54	6♏07 46	19 58.1	19D 56.2	14 19.8	24 09.3	19 34.5	6 03.5	28 10.4	29 21.7	4 57.1	7 12.8	18 12.2	23 32.4
12 Sa	5 24 36	20 24 43	13♏30 55	20 55 34	19 54.9	19 56.2	15 53.7	25 24.2	19 52.6	6 18.7	28 22.9	29 27.7	4 56.9	7 11.2	18 12.7	23 34.1
13 Su	5 28 33	21 25 44	28 20 50	5♐45 47	19 51.8	19 56.3	17 27.7	26 39.0	20 11.1	6 34.2	28 35.6	29 33.8	4 56.7	7 09.6	18 13.1	23 35.8
14 M	5 32 29	22 26 47	13♐09 28	20 30 56	19 48.6	19R 56.4	19 01.7	27 53.9	20 30.1	6 49.8	28 48.3	29 40.0	4 56.6	7 08.1	18 13.6	23 37.6
15 Tu	5 36 26	23 27 51	27 49 17	5♑03 42	19 45.4	19 56.4	20 35.9	29 08.9	20 49.6	7 05.6	29 01.1	29 46.1	4D 56.5	7 06.6	18 14.2	23 39.4
16 W	5 40 22	24 28 55	12♑13 27	19 17 58	19 42.2	19 56.1	22 10.1	0♐23.8	21 09.5	7 21.6	29 13.9	29 52.4	4 56.5	7 05.1	18 14.7	23 41.2
17 Th	5 44 19	25 30 00	26 16 45	3♒09 30	19 39.1	19 55.6	23 44.5	1 38.8	21 29.9	7 37.8	29 26.8	29 58.7	4 56.5	7 03.7	18 15.4	23 43.0
18 F	5 48 16	26 31 06	9♒56 01	16 36 18	19 35.9	19 54.9	25 19.0	2 53.7	21 50.7	7 54.1	29 39.8	0♒05.0	4 56.6	7 02.3	18 16.0	23 44.8
19 Sa	5 52 12	27 32 11	23 10 26	29 38 36	19 32.7	19 53.9	26 53.6	4 08.7	22 11.9	8 10.6	29 52.8	0 11.4	4 56.7	7 01.0	18 16.7	23 46.6
20 Su	5 56 09	28 33 17	6♓01 07	12♓18 24	19 29.5	19 53.0	28 28.4	5 23.7	22 33.6	8 27.3	0♒05.9	0 17.8	4 56.9	6 59.7	18 17.4	23 48.4
21 M	6 00 05	29 34 23	18 30 54	24 39 07	19 26.3	19D 52.4	0♑03.4	6 38.7	22 55.6	8 44.2	0 19.1	0 24.2	4 57.2	6 58.5	18 18.1	23 50.3
22 Tu	6 04 02	0♑35 30	0♈43 38	6♈45 01	19 23.2	19 52.1	1 38.6	7 53.8	23 18.0	9 01.2	0 32.3	0 30.7	4 57.5	6 57.3	18 18.9	23 52.1
23 W	6 07 58	1 36 37	12 43 52	18 40 48	19 20.0	19 52.4	3 13.9	9 08.8	23 40.8	9 18.3	0 45.5	0 37.2	4 57.8	6 56.1	18 19.7	23 54.0
24 Th	6 11 55	2 37 43	24 36 23	0♉31 14	19 16.8	19 53.2	4 49.5	10 23.8	24 04.0	9 35.7	0 58.8	0 43.8	4 58.2	6 55.0	18 20.5	23 55.9
25 F	6 15 51	3 38 50	6♉25 54	12 20 56	19 13.6	19 54.5	6 25.3	11 38.9	24 27.5	9 53.1	1 12.2	0 50.4	4 58.7	6 54.0	18 21.4	23 57.8
26 Sa	6 19 48	4 39 58	18 16 50	24 14 05	19 10.5	19 55.9	8 01.3	12 54.0	24 51.4	10 10.8	1 25.6	0 57.0	4 59.2	6 53.0	18 22.3	23 59.7
27 Su	6 23 45	5 41 05	0♊13 07	6♊14 20	19 07.3	19 57.2	9 37.6	14 09.1	25 15.6	10 28.5	1 39.0	1 03.7	4 59.8	6 52.0	18 23.2	24 01.6
28 M	6 27 41	6 42 13	12 18 04	18 24 36	19 04.1	19R 58.1	11 14.1	15 24.1	25 40.2	10 46.5	1 52.5	1 10.4	5 00.5	6 51.1	18 24.2	24 03.5
29 Tu	6 31 38	7 43 20	24 34 12	0♋47 03	19 00.9	19 58.2	12 50.9	16 39.2	26 05.0	11 04.5	2 06.1	1 17.1	5 01.2	6 50.2	18 25.2	24 05.5
30 W	6 35 34	8 44 28	7♋03 18	13 23 02	18 57.8	19 57.3	14 28.0	17 54.4	26 30.2	11 22.7	2 19.7	1 23.9	5 01.9	6 49.4	18 26.2	24 07.4
31 Th	6 39 31	9♑45 36	19 46 19	26 13 08	18♊54.6	19♊55.5	16♑05.3	19♐09.5	26♈55.7	11♓41.1	2♒33.3	1♒30.7	5♈02.7	6♉48.7	18♓27.3	24♑09.3

1st of Month

Julian Day #
2459184.5
Obliquity
23°26'13"
SVP 4♓58'21"
GC 27♐07.9
Eris 23♈35.9R

Day	⚴
1	28♑01.3
6	29 32.2
11	1♒04.9
16	2 39.5
21	4 15.5
26	5 52.9
31	7 31.3

Day	⚵
1	24♏06.6
6	25 47.4
11	27 27.4
16	29 06.4
21	0♐44.4
26	2 21.0
31	3 56.1

Day	⚶
1	13♍29.1
6	14 51.4
11	16 07.8
16	17 17.6
21	18 20.0
26	19 14.5
31	20 00.4

DECLINATION and LATITUDE

Day	☉ Decl	☽ Decl	☽ Lat	☽12h Decl	☿ Decl	☿ Lat	♀ Decl	♀ Lat	♂ Decl	♂ Lat	⚳ Decl	⚳ Lat	♃ Decl	♃ Lat	♄ Decl	♄ Lat
1 Tu	21S50	22N20	0S22	23N24	19S20	0N33	13S47	1N39	6N39	0S03	20S14	10S51	21S22	0S28	20S50	0S22
2 W	21 59	24 11	0N46	24 41	19 47	0 26	14 10	1 38	6 46	0 00	20 06	10 48	21 20	0 28	20 49	0 22
3 Th	22 08	24 53	1 52	24 46	20 13	0 19	14 34	1 36	6 54	0N02	19 58	10 44	21 18	0 28	20 48	0 22
4 F	22 16	24 19	2 54	23 33	20 38	0 12	14 57	1 35	7 01	0 04	19 50	10 41	21 16	0 28	20 47	0 22
5 Sa	22 24	22 28	3 49	21 06	21 02	0 05	15 19	1 34	7 09	0 07	19 42	10 38	21 14	0 28	20 46	0 22
6 Su	22 31	19 26	4 33	17 30	21 25	0S02	15 41	1 33	7 17	0 09	19 33	10 35	21 11	0 28	20 44	0 22
7 M	22 38	15 20	5 03	12 57	21 48	0 09	16 03	1 31	7 24	0 11	19 25	10 32	21 09	0 28	20 43	0 22
8 Tu	22 44	10 23	5 17	7 39	22 09	0 15	16 25	1 30	7 33	0 13	19 17	10 29	21 07	0 28	20 42	0 22
9 W	22 50	4 47	5 13	1 50	22 29	0 22	16 46	1 28	7 41	0 16	19 09	10 26	21 04	0 28	20 41	0 22
10 Th	22 56	1S10	4 50	4S11	22 48	0 29	17 06	1 26	7 49	0 18	19 00	10 23	21 02	0 28	20 40	0 22
11 F	23 01	7 11	4 08	10 06	23 06	0 35	17 26	1 25	7 58	0 20	18 52	10 20	20 59	0 28	20 39	0 22
12 Sa	23 05	12 53	3 09	15 30	23 23	0 41	17 46	1 23	8 06	0 22	18 43	10 17	20 57	0 28	20 37	0 22
13 Su	23 10	17 53	1 57	19 59	23 38	0 48	18 05	1 21	8 15	0 24	18 35	10 14	20 54	0 28	20 36	0 22
14 M	23 13	21 45	0 38	23 09	23 53	0 54	18 24	1 19	8 24	0 25	18 26	10 11	20 52	0 28	20 35	0 22
15 Tu	23 17	24 09	0S44	24 43	24 06	0 60	18 42	1 17	8 33	0 27	18 17	10 08	20 49	0 28	20 34	0 22
16 W	23 19	24 53	2 01	24 37	24 18	1 05	19 00	1 16	8 42	0 29	18 09	10 05	20 46	0 29	20 32	0 22
17 Th	23 22	23 59	3 08	22 59	24 28	1 11	19 17	1 14	8 51	0 31	17 60	10 02	20 44	0 29	20 31	0 22
18 F	23 23	21 40	4 03	20 04	24 37	1 16	19 34	1 12	9 01	0 32	17 51	9 60	20 41	0 29	20 30	0 23
19 Sa	23 25	18 15	4 43	16 14	24 45	1 21	19 50	1 09	9 10	0 34	17 42	9 57	20 38	0 29	20 29	0 23
20 Su	23 26	14 04	5 08	11 47	24 52	1 26	20 06	1 07	9 20	0 36	17 33	9 54	20 36	0 29	20 27	0 23
21 M	23 26	9 24	5 17	6 57	24 57	1 31	20 21	1 05	9 29	0 37	17 24	9 51	20 33	0 29	20 26	0 23
22 Tu	23 26	4 28	5 11	1 58	25 01	1 36	20 35	1 03	9 39	0 39	17 15	9 49	20 30	0 29	20 25	0 23
23 W	23 26	0N32	4 52	3N02	25 04	1 40	20 49	1 01	9 49	0 40	17 06	9 46	20 27	0 29	20 23	0 23
24 Th	23 25	5 29	4 21	7 53	25 05	1 44	21 02	0 59	9 59	0 42	16 57	9 43	20 25	0 29	20 22	0 23
25 F	23 23	10 13	3 38	12 28	25 05	1 48	21 15	0 56	10 09	0 43	16 48	9 41	20 22	0 29	20 20	0 23
26 Sa	23 21	14 36	2 47	16 36	25 03	1 51	21 27	0 54	10 19	0 45	16 39	9 38	20 19	0 29	20 19	0 23
27 Su	23 19	18 27	1 47	20 07	24 60	1 55	21 38	0 52	10 29	0 46	16 30	9 36	20 16	0 29	20 18	0 23
28 M	23 16	21 34	0 42	22 47	24 55	1 58	21 49	0 49	10 39	0 47	16 21	9 33	20 13	0 29	20 16	0 23
29 Tu	23 13	23 45	0N25	24 25	24 49	2 00	21 59	0 47	10 50	0 49	16 11	9 31	20 10	0 29	20 15	0 23
30 W	23 09	24 48	1 33	24 51	24 41	2 03	22 09	0 44	10 60	0 50	16 02	9 28	20 07	0 29	20 13	0 23
31 Th	23S05	24N34	2N37	23N58	24S32	2S05	22S18	0N42	11N10	0N51	15S53	9S26	20S04	0S29	20S12	0S23

Day	⚷ Decl	⚷ Lat	♅ Decl	♅ Lat	♆ Decl	♆ Lat	♇ Decl	♇ Lat
1	4N26	2N39	13N35	0S28	5S41	1S06	22S34	1S09
6	4 24	2 38	13 32	0 28	5 41	1 06	22 33	1 10
11	4 22	2 37	13 29	0 28	5 40	1 05	22 32	1 10
16	4 21	2 36	13 27	0 27	5 39	1 05	22 31	1 11
21	4 20	2 35	13 25	0 27	5 38	1 05	22 30	1 11
26	4 20	2 34	13 23	0 27	5 36	1 05	22 29	1 11
31	4N21	2N33	13N22	0S27	5S34	1S05	22S27	1S12

Day	⚴ Decl	⚴ Lat	⚵ Decl	⚵ Lat	⚶ Decl	⚶ Lat	Eris Decl	Eris Lat
1	0N21	21N18	10S17	8N46	10N34	4N24	1S41	11S39
6	0 06	20 46	10 34	8 53	10 16	4 41	1 41	11 38
11	0S07	20 15	10 49	9 00	10 02	4 57	1 41	11 37
16	0 17	19 46	11 02	9 08	9 51	5 15	1 41	11 37
21	0 24	19 18	11 14	9 16	9 44	5 34	1 40	11 36
26	0 29	18 51	11 24	9 24	9 41	5 54	1 40	11 35
31	0S31	18N26	11S32	9N34	9N42	6N15	1S40	11S34

Moon Phenomena

Max/0 Decl
dy hr mn
3 1:24 24N53
9 19:22 0 S
15 22:26 24S53
22 21:25 0 N
30 7:55 24N52

Max/0 Lat
dy hr mn
1 7:47 0 N
8 6:49 5N18
14 11:04 0 S
21 2:39 5S17
28 15:03 0 N

Perigee/Apogee
dy hr m kilometers
12 20:43 p 361774
24 16:33 a 405010

PH dy hr mn
☾ 8 0:38 16♍22
● 14 16:18 23♐08
● 14 974:39T 02'10"
☽ 21 23:42 0♈35
○ 30 3:29 8♋53

Void of Course Moon

Last Aspect	☽ Ingress
1 4:23 ♆ □	♋ 2 3:34
4 10:30 ♄ ☍	♌ 4 12:54
5 22:29 ♂ △	♍ 6 19:47
8 22:36 ♄ △	♎ 9 0:02
11 0:57 ♄ □	♏ 11 2:00
13 1:59 ♄ ✶	♐ 13 2:40
14 16:18 ☉ ☌	♑ 15 3:36
17 5:36 ♃ ☌	♒ 17 6:28
19 8:46 ☉ ✶	♓ 19 12:40
21 10:26 ♇ ✶	♈ 21 22:33
23 22:52 ♂ ☌	♉ 24 10:57
26 11:33 ♇ △	♊ 26 23:34
29 3:02 ♂ ✶	♋ 29 10:29
31 13:46 ♂ □	♌ 31 18:59

DAILY ASPECTARIAN

1 Tu
☽✶♂ 2:14
☽⫲♇ 2:29
☽□♆ 4:23
☊ D 7:42
☽∠♅ 12:54
☽⚻♇ 14:27
☿ ♐ 19:52
☽⚻♃ 20:23
☽⚼♀ 23:31

2 W
☽⚻♄ 0:39
☽⚻☿ 4:41
☽△⚳ 11:24
☽□⚷ 13:19
☿∥⚳ 13:20
☽✶♅ 18:02

3 Th
☉⚻☽ 1:29
☽△♀ 7:44
☉∠♃ 7:55
☿⚼♂ 11:46
☽□♂ 13:30
☽⚼☿ 13:42
☽△♆ 14:33
☽⚼⚳ 16:43

4 F
☽☍♇ 0:23
☽☍♃ 6:53
☿∥♄ 8:10
☉⚼☽ 8:29
☽☍♄ 10:30
☿□⚳ 17:43
☽⚼♆ 18:49
☽⚻⚳ 21:27
☽△☿ 21:53
☽△⚷ 22:13
☽⫲♇ 23:10

5 Sa
☿△⚷ 0:41
☉⫲☽ 0:45
☽□♅ 2:39
☿∥♃ 10:34
☽⫲☿ 11:02
☽⫲♃ 11:06
☉∠♄ 12:24
☽⫲♄ 14:41
☉△☽ 14:42
♂⚺♆ 21:45
☽□♀ 21:48
☽⚻♆ 22:28
☽△♂ 22:29
☽⫲⚳ 23:09

6 Su
☽⚼⚷ 1:46
♀△♆ 4:54
♀⚻♂ 6:42
☽⚻♇ 7:57
☉∥♇ 8:05
☿⚻♅ 12:44
⚳⚺⚷ 14:37
☽⚻♃ 14:54
☽⚻♄ 17:54
☽⫲♀ 20:28

7 M
☽⚼♂ 1:59
☽⚻⚷ 4:38
☽☍⚳ 4:54
☿∠♇ 5:30
☽△♅ 8:47
☽∥♅ 9:15
☽⚼♇ 10:45
☽□☿ 11:25
♀ ♒ 12:15
♀⚼⚷ 15:30
☽⚼♃ 17:53
☽⚼♄ 20:35

8 Tu
☉□☽ 0:38
☊ R 0:53
☽☍♆ 3:46
☽⚻♂ 4:48
☽✶♀ 8:23
☽⚼♅ 10:51
☽∥♂ 12:09
☽△♇ 12:53
☽△♃ 20:10
☽⫲♆ 20:20
☽△♄ 22:36

9 W
☽∥⚷ 1:41
☿∥♇ 4:33
☽☍⚷ 8:26
☽⚻⚳ 9:37
☽⚻♅ 12:18
☽∠♀ 12:23
☉□♆ 19:42
☽✶☿ 21:14

10 Th
☿∠♃ 3:32
☽⚻♆ 6:34
☉✶☽ 7:23
☽☍♂ 8:32
☽⚼⚳ 11:04
♀✶♇ 11:53
☽⫲⚷ 12:44
☉∥☿ 14:20
☽□♇ 15:22
☽⚺♀ 15:41
☽∥♆ 17:55
☽□♃ 22:59

11 F
☿∠♄ 0:31
☽□♄ 0:57
☽∠☿ 1:00
☽⫲♂ 3:15
☉△♂ 6:02
☽⚼♆ 7:14
☉∠☽ 9:51
☽⚻⚷ 10:05
☊ D 11:37
☽△⚳ 12:05
☽☍♅ 13:44

12 Sa
☽⫲♅ 2:37
☽⚺☿ 4:19
☽△♆ 7:37
☽⚼⚷ 10:25
☽⚻♂ 10:31
☉⚺☽ 11:59
☽✶♇ 16:18
☽☌♀ 21:00

13 Su
☽✶♃ 0:24
☽∥♀ 1:11
☽✶♄ 1:59
☽∥⚳ 3:39
☽△⚷ 10:40
☽⚼♂ 11:18
☿□♆ 11:40
☽□⚳ 13:33
☽⚻♅ 14:14
☽∥♄ 15:51
☽∠♇ 16:38
☉⚼♅ 16:49
☽∥♃ 17:44

14 M
☽∠♃ 1:04
♀∥⚳ 1:47
☽∠♄ 2:28
☽∥♇ 6:14
☽□♆ 8:16
☽☌☿ 10:43
☊ R 11:30
☽△♂ 12:15
☉∥☽ 13:05
☽⚼♅ 14:38
☉☌☽ 16:18
☽⚺♇ 17:08
♀✶♃ 20:59
☽∥☿ 23:07

15 Tu
⚳✶♅ 1:19
☽⚺♃ 2:00
☽⚺♀ 2:24
☽⚺♄ 3:14
☿△♂ 4:25
☉⚺♇ 4:40
☽□⚷ 11:48
♀✶♄ 13:01
☽△♅ 15:23
☽✶⚳ 15:41
♀ ♐ 16:22
⚷ D 22:18
☿⚼♅ 22:44

16 W
☽∠♀ 5:53
☽✶♆ 10:13
☽□♂ 15:33
☽∥☿ 16:34
☽∠⚳ 17:35
☽⚺☿ 19:04
☽☌♇ 19:34
☉⚺☽ 22:33
☿⚺♇ 23:36

17 Th
♄ ♒ 5:05
☽☌♃ 5:36
☽☌♄ 6:29
☉∥☽ 7:43
☽✶♀ 10:17
☽∠♆ 12:11
☽✶⚷ 15:09
☽∥♇ 16:33
☽□♅ 18:52
☽⚺⚳ 20:18

18 F
☽∠☿ 0:46
☉∠☽ 3:04
☽∥♃ 7:41
☽∥♄ 9:01
☽∥♀ 14:23
☽⚺♆ 15:02
⚵ ♐ 17:26
☽∠⚷ 18:05
☽✶♂ 22:09

19 Sa
☽⚺♇ 1:07
☽∥⚳ 3:29
☽✶☿ 7:50
☉✶☽ 8:46
☽⚺♃ 12:40
☽⚺♄ 13:08
♃ ♒ 13:08
♀△⚷ 15:24
☽⚺⚷ 21:58
☽□♀ 22:41

20 Su
☽✶♅ 1:51
☽∠♂ 3:01
☉☌☿ 3:27
☽⫲♅ 3:29
☽☌⚳ 4:44
☽∠♇ 5:19
☽∠♃ 17:41
☽∠♄ 17:55
☿ ♑ 23:08
☽⫲♂ 23:34
☽☌♆ 23:35

21 M
☿⚺♃ 4:36
☿⚺♄ 5:38
♀⚻♅ 6:13
☽∠♅ 6:44
♀∥♄ 7:45
☽⚺♂ 8:53
⚳∠♇ 9:45
☉ ♑ 10:03
☽✶♇ 10:26
♀∥♃ 16:56
♃☌♄ 18:22
☽∥♆ 18:29
☉⚺♄ 21:53
☉⚺♃ 22:23
☊ D 23:31
☽✶♄ 23:34
☽✶♃ 23:37
☉□☽ 23:42

22 Tu
☽⫲⚷ 0:39
☽□☿ 2:06
☽☌⚷ 8:25
♀⚼♂ 11:08
☽⚺♅ 12:23
☽△♀ 15:58
☽⚺⚳ 16:57
♀∠♇ 19:09

23 W
♀□⚳ 3:57
☽⚺♆ 11:18
♂□♇ 14:54
☽∥⚷ 18:22
☽□♇ 22:38
☽☌♂ 22:52
☽∠⚳ 23:58

24 Th
☽⫲♆ 0:37
☽⚼♀ 1:48
☿□⚷ 2:12
☽□♄ 12:32
☽□♃ 13:11
☽∠♆ 17:45
☉△☽ 17:49
☽⚺⚷ 21:03
☽∥♂ 23:36
☽△☿ 23:59

25 F
☽☌♅ 0:57
☿△♅ 7:06
☽✶⚳ 7:11
☽⚻♀ 11:50
☽∥♅ 17:04
♃∥♄ 18:52

26 Sa
☽✶♆ 0:11
☉⚼☽ 3:04
☽∠⚷ 3:27
☉□⚷ 7:38
☽⚼☿ 11:03
☽△♇ 11:33
☽⫲⚳ 11:50
☽⚺♂ 13:43

27 Su
☽△♄ 1:42
☽△♃ 2:55
☽✶⚷ 9:32
☉⚻☽ 11:54
☽⫲♃ 12:58
☽⚺♅ 13:14
☽⫲♄ 13:19
☿✶⚳ 15:33
☽⚼♇ 17:35
☽∠♂ 20:40
☽□⚳ 20:55
☽⚻☿ 21:35

28 M
☽⫲♀ 2:29
☉△♅ 3:27
☽☍♀ 6:48
☽⚼♄ 7:41
☽⫲♇ 8:36
☽⚼♃ 9:10
☽□♆ 12:00
☊ R 15:07
♀∠♄ 16:14
☉⫲☽ 17:06
☽∠♅ 18:42
♂∠⚳ 22:13
☽⚻♇ 23:04

29 Tu
☽✶♂ 3:02
♀∠♃ 10:28
☽⚻♄ 13:05
☽⚻♃ 14:48
☽⫲☿ 20:01
☽□⚷ 20:08
☽✶♅ 23:34

30 W
☉☍☽ 3:29
☽△⚳ 8:25
♀□♆ 10:20
☽☍☿ 16:05
☽△♆ 21:32
☽⚻♀ 22:44

31 Th
☽⫲☿ 1:18
☽☍♇ 8:11
☽⚼⚳ 13:10
☽□♂ 13:46
☽☍♄ 21:58

January 2021

LONGITUDE

Day	Sid.Time	☉	☽	☽ 12 hour	Mean☊	True☊	☿	♀	♂	⚳	♃	♄	⚷	♅	♆	♇
	h m s	° ' "	° ' "	° ' "	° '	° '	° '	° '	° '	° '	° '	° '	° '	° '	° '	° '
1 F	6 43 27	10♑46 44	2♌43 29	9♌17 16	18♊51.4	19♊52.7	17♑42.8	20♐24.6	27♈21.4	11♓59.6	2♒47.0	1♒37.5	5♈03.6	6♉48.0	18♓28.4	24♑11.3
2 Sa	6 47 24	11 47 53	15 54 26	22 34 51	18 48.2	19R 49.3	19 20.6	21 39.8	27 47.5	12 18.2	3 00.7	1 44.3	5 04.5	6R 47.3	18 29.5	24 13.2
3 Su	6 51 21	12 49 01	29 18 24	6♍04 58	18 45.1	19 45.8	20 58.6	22 54.9	28 13.8	12 36.9	3 14.4	1 51.2	5 05.4	6 46.7	18 30.7	24 15.2
4 M	6 55 17	13 50 10	12♍54 25	19 46 36	18 41.9	19 42.6	22 36.8	24 10.1	28 40.4	12 55.8	3 28.2	1 58.1	5 06.4	6 46.1	18 31.9	24 17.2
5 Tu	6 59 14	14 51 19	26 41 25	3♎38 42	18 38.7	19 40.3	24 15.2	25 25.2	29 07.3	13 14.8	3 42.0	2 05.0	5 07.5	6 45.6	18 33.1	24 19.1
6 W	7 03 10	15 52 28	10♎38 20	17 40 10	18 35.5	19D 39.2	25 53.7	26 40.4	29 34.4	13 33.9	3 55.9	2 11.9	5 08.6	6 45.1	18 34.3	24 21.1
7 Th	7 07 07	16 53 37	24 44 03	1♏49 46	18 32.3	19 39.3	27 32.2	27 55.6	0♉01.8	13 53.1	4 09.8	2 18.9	5 09.8	6 44.7	18 35.6	24 23.1
8 F	7 11 03	17 54 47	8♏57 08	16 05 52	18 29.2	19 40.4	29 10.7	29 10.8	0 29.4	14 12.5	4 23.7	2 25.9	5 11.0	6 44.4	18 36.9	24 25.1
9 Sa	7 15 00	18 55 57	23 15 39	0♐26 09	18 26.0	19 41.9	0♒49.1	0♑26.0	0 57.2	14 32.0	4 37.6	2 32.9	5 12.3	6 44.1	18 38.3	24 27.1
10 Su	7 18 56	19 57 07	7♐36 55	14 47 30	18 22.8	19R 43.3	2 27.4	1 41.2	1 25.3	14 51.6	4 51.6	2 39.9	5 13.6	6 43.8	18 39.6	24 29.1
11 M	7 22 53	20 58 16	21 57 22	29 05 57	18 19.6	19 43.7	4 05.3	2 56.4	1 53.7	15 11.3	5 05.6	2 47.0	5 15.0	6 43.6	18 41.0	24 31.1
12 Tu	7 26 50	21 59 26	6♑12 41	13♑16 56	18 16.5	19 42.7	5 42.7	4 11.6	2 22.2	15 31.1	5 19.7	2 54.0	5 16.4	6 43.5	18 42.4	24 33.1
13 W	7 30 46	23 00 36	20 18 09	27 15 46	18 13.3	19 39.9	7 19.5	5 26.9	2 51.0	15 51.1	5 33.7	3 01.1	5 17.9	6 43.4	18 43.9	24 35.1
14 Th	7 34 43	24 01 45	4♒09 17	10♒58 18	18 10.1	19 35.4	8 55.4	6 42.1	3 20.0	16 11.1	5 47.8	3 08.2	5 19.4	6D 43.3	18 45.4	24 37.1
15 F	7 38 39	25 02 54	17 42 27	24 21 30	18 06.9	19 29.5	10 30.2	7 57.3	3 49.2	16 31.3	6 01.9	3 15.3	5 21.0	6 43.3	18 46.9	24 39.1
16 Sa	7 42 36	26 04 02	0♓55 21	7♓23 57	18 03.8	19 23.1	12 03.6	9 12.5	4 18.7	16 51.5	6 16.0	3 22.4	5 22.6	6 43.4	18 48.4	24 41.1
17 Su	7 46 32	27 05 09	13 47 23	20 05 52	18 00.6	19 16.7	13 35.2	10 27.8	4 48.3	17 11.9	6 30.2	3 29.5	5 24.3	6 43.5	18 49.9	24 43.1
18 M	7 50 29	28 06 16	26 19 39	2♈29 08	17 57.4	19 11.2	15 04.7	11 43.0	5 18.1	17 32.4	6 44.3	3 36.6	5 26.0	6 43.7	18 51.5	24 45.1
19 Tu	7 54 25	29 07 21	8♈34 45	14 37 01	17 54.2	19 07.1	16 31.6	12 58.2	5 48.1	17 52.9	6 58.5	3 43.7	5 27.8	6 43.9	18 53.1	24 47.1
20 W	7 58 22	0♒08 26	20 36 29	26 33 45	17 51.0	19D 04.8	17 55.3	14 13.4	6 18.3	18 13.6	7 12.7	3 50.9	5 29.6	6 44.1	18 54.8	24 49.1
21 Th	8 02 19	1 09 31	2♉29 26	8♉24 13	17 47.9	19 04.2	19 15.3	15 28.6	6 48.7	18 34.3	7 26.9	3 58.0	5 31.5	6 44.5	18 56.4	24 51.0
22 F	8 06 15	2 10 34	14 18 44	20 13 40	17 44.7	19 05.0	20 31.0	16 43.8	7 19.2	18 55.2	7 41.1	4 05.2	5 33.4	6 44.8	18 58.1	24 53.0
23 Sa	8 10 12	3 11 36	26 09 37	2♊07 16	17 41.5	19 06.5	21 41.7	17 59.0	7 49.9	19 16.1	7 55.3	4 12.3	5 35.4	6 45.3	18 59.8	24 55.0
24 Su	8 14 08	4 12 37	8♊07 12	14 09 57	17 38.3	19R 08.0	22 46.5	19 14.3	8 20.8	19 37.1	8 09.5	4 19.5	5 37.4	6 45.7	19 01.5	24 57.0
25 M	8 18 05	5 13 38	20 16 05	26 26 01	17 35.2	19 08.5	23 44.6	20 29.5	8 51.8	19 58.2	8 23.8	4 26.6	5 39.4	6 46.3	19 03.3	24 59.0
26 Tu	8 22 01	6 14 37	2♋40 10	8♋58 49	17 32.0	19 07.5	24 35.3	21 44.7	9 22.9	20 19.4	8 38.0	4 33.7	5 41.5	6 46.9	19 05.0	25 00.9
27 W	8 25 58	7 15 36	15 22 12	21 50 27	17 28.8	19 04.3	25 17.7	22 59.9	9 54.3	20 40.7	8 52.3	4 40.9	5 43.6	6 47.5	19 06.8	25 02.9
28 Th	8 29 54	8 16 33	28 23 34	5♌01 31	17 25.6	18 58.8	25 50.9	24 15.1	10 25.7	21 02.0	9 06.5	4 48.0	5 45.8	6 48.2	19 08.7	25 04.9
29 F	8 33 51	9 17 30	11♌44 05	18 31 01	17 22.5	18 51.3	26 14.2	25 30.2	10 57.3	21 23.4	9 20.8	4 55.2	5 48.0	6 48.9	19 10.5	25 06.8
30 Sa	8 37 48	10 18 25	25 21 56	2♍16 25	17 19.3	18 42.5	26R 27.0	26 45.4	11 29.1	21 44.9	9 35.0	5 02.3	5 50.3	6 49.7	19 12.3	25 08.8
31 Su	8 41 44	11♒19 20	9♍13 58	16 14 04	17♊16.1	18♊33.3	26♒28.8	28♑00.6	12♉00.9	22♓06.5	9♒49.3	5♒09.4	5♈52.6	6♉50.6	19♓14.2	25♑10.7

1st of Month

Julian Day # 2459215.5
Obliquity 23°26'13"
SVP 4♓58'15"
GC 27♐08.0
Eris 23♈27.7R

Day	⚴
1	7♒51.1
6	9 30.7
11	11 11.1
16	12 52.1
21	14 33.5
26	16 15.2
31	17 57.0

Day	⚵
1	4♐15.0
6	5 48.1
11	7 19.4
16	8 48.5
21	10 15.3
26	11 39.5
31	13 00.8

Day	⚶
1	20♍08.5
6	20 43.1
11	21 07.5
16	21 21.0
21	21 23.0R
26	21 13.3R
31	20 51.7R

DECLINATION and LATITUDE

Day	☉ Decl	☽ Decl	☽ Lat	☽ 12h Decl	☿ Decl	☿ Lat	♀ Decl	♀ Lat	♂ Decl	♂ Lat	⚳ Decl	⚳ Lat	♃ Decl	♃ Lat	♄ Decl	♄ Lat
1 F	22S60	23N01	3N34	21N46	24S21	2S06	22S26	0N39	11N21	0N52	15S43	9S23	20S01	0S29	20S10	0S23
2 Sa	22 55	20 13	4 21	18 23	24 09	2 07	22 34	0 37	11 31	0 53	15 34	9 21	19 58	0 29	20 09	0 23
3 Su	22 49	16 18	4 55	14 00	23 55	2 08	22 40	0 35	11 42	0 55	15 24	9 18	19 55	0 30	20 08	0 23
4 M	22 43	11 31	5 12	8 52	23 39	2 09	22 47	0 32	11 52	0 56	15 15	9 16	19 51	0 30	20 06	0 23
5 Tu	22 37	6 05	5 12	3 13	23 22	2 09	22 52	0 29	12 03	0 57	15 05	9 14	19 48	0 30	20 05	0 24
6 W	22 30	0 17	4 53	2S39	23 04	2 08	22 57	0 27	12 13	0 58	14 56	9 12	19 45	0 30	20 03	0 24
7 Th	22 22	5S35	4 17	8 28	22 44	2 07	23 01	0 24	12 24	0 59	14 46	9 09	19 42	0 30	20 02	0 24
8 F	22 14	11 14	3 25	13 52	22 22	2 06	23 04	0 22	12 35	0 60	14 37	9 07	19 39	0 30	20 00	0 24
9 Sa	22 06	16 20	2 20	18 33	21 59	2 04	23 07	0 19	12 45	1 01	14 27	9 05	19 35	0 30	19 58	0 24
10 Su	21 57	20 30	1 06	22 07	21 34	2 01	23 09	0 17	12 56	1 02	14 17	9 03	19 32	0 30	19 57	0 24
11 M	21 48	23 24	0S12	24 17	21 08	1 58	23 10	0 14	13 07	1 03	14 08	9 00	19 29	0 30	19 55	0 24
12 Tu	21 39	24 46	1 29	24 51	20 41	1 54	23 11	0 12	13 17	1 04	13 58	8 58	19 25	0 30	19 54	0 24
13 W	21 29	24 32	2 39	23 49	20 12	1 49	23 11	0 09	13 28	1 04	13 48	8 56	19 22	0 30	19 52	0 24
14 Th	21 18	22 45	3 39	21 23	19 42	1 44	23 10	0 06	13 39	1 05	13 38	8 54	19 19	0 30	19 51	0 24
15 F	21 07	19 43	4 25	17 49	19 11	1 38	23 08	0 04	13 50	1 06	13 28	8 52	19 15	0 30	19 49	0 24
16 Sa	20 56	15 44	4 55	13 29	18 38	1 31	23 06	0 01	14 00	1 07	13 19	8 50	19 12	0 30	19 48	0 24
17 Su	20 44	11 08	5 09	8 41	18 05	1 24	23 03	0S01	14 11	1 08	13 09	8 48	19 08	0 30	19 46	0 24
18 M	20 32	6 10	5 08	3 38	17 31	1 15	22 59	0 04	14 22	1 08	12 59	8 46	19 05	0 31	19 44	0 24
19 Tu	20 20	1 05	4 53	1N27	16 56	1 06	22 55	0 06	14 33	1 09	12 49	8 44	19 01	0 31	19 43	0 24
20 W	20 07	3N57	4 25	6 24	16 21	0 56	22 49	0 09	14 43	1 10	12 39	8 42	18 58	0 31	19 41	0 24
21 Th	19 54	8 48	3 46	11 06	15 45	0 45	22 44	0 11	14 54	1 11	12 29	8 40	18 54	0 31	19 40	0 25
22 F	19 40	13 18	2 58	15 23	15 10	0 33	22 37	0 14	15 05	1 11	12 19	8 38	18 51	0 31	19 38	0 25
23 Sa	19 26	17 19	2 01	19 06	14 35	0 20	22 30	0 16	15 15	1 12	12 09	8 36	18 47	0 31	19 36	0 25
24 Su	19 12	20 41	0 59	22 03	14 01	0 06	22 22	0 19	15 26	1 13	11 59	8 34	18 43	0 31	19 35	0 25
25 M	18 58	23 11	0N06	24 03	13 28	0N09	22 13	0 21	15 36	1 13	11 49	8 32	18 40	0 31	19 33	0 25
26 Tu	18 43	24 37	1 12	24 53	12 57	0 24	22 04	0 24	15 47	1 14	11 39	8 31	18 36	0 31	19 31	0 25
27 W	18 27	24 49	2 17	24 25	12 28	0 40	21 54	0 26	15 58	1 14	11 29	8 29	18 33	0 31	19 30	0 25
28 Th	18 12	23 40	3 15	22 35	12 01	0 57	21 44	0 28	16 08	1 15	11 19	8 27	18 29	0 31	19 28	0 25
29 F	17 56	21 11	4 05	19 28	11 37	1 14	21 32	0 31	16 19	1 16	11 08	8 25	18 25	0 31	19 26	0 25
30 Sa	17 39	17 28	4 41	15 14	11 16	1 32	21 20	0 33	16 29	1 16	10 58	8 23	18 21	0 31	19 25	0 25
31 Su	17S23	12N46	5N02	10N07	10S59	1N49	21S08	0S35	16N39	1N17	10S48	8S22	18S18	0S32	19S23	0S25

Day	⚷ Decl	⚷ Lat	♅ Decl	♅ Lat	♆ Decl	♆ Lat	♇ Decl	♇ Lat
1	4N21	2N33	13N21	0S27	5S33	1S05	22S27	1S12
6	4 22	2 32	13 21	0 27	5 31	1 05	22 26	1 12
11	4 23	2 31	13 20	0 27	5 28	1 05	22 24	1 13
16	4 26	2 30	13 20	0 27	5 25	1 05	22 23	1 13
21	4 28	2 29	13 21	0 26	5 22	1 04	22 22	1 13
26	4 31	2 28	13 22	0 26	5 18	1 04	22 20	1 14
31	4N35	2N27	13N23	0S26	5S15	1S04	22S19	1S14

Day	⚴ Decl	⚴ Lat	⚵ Decl	⚵ Lat	⚶ Decl	⚶ Lat	Eris Decl	Eris Lat
1	0S31	18N21	11S33	9N36	9N43	6N19	1S39	11S34
6	0 31	17 58	11 39	9 46	9 49	6 41	1 39	11 34
11	0 28	17 35	11 43	9 56	10 00	7 04	1 38	11 33
16	0 23	17 14	11 45	10 08	10 16	7 27	1 37	11 32
21	0 16	16 54	11 45	10 20	10 37	7 51	1 36	11 31
26	0 06	16 34	11 44	10 33	11 03	8 15	1 35	11 30
31	0N04	16N16	11S40	10N46	11N34	8N39	1S34	11S30

Moon Phenomena

Max/0 Decl
dy hr mn
6 1:11 0 S
12 8:18 24S52
19 5:08 0 N
26 15:40 24N54

Perigee/Apogee
dy hr m kilometers
9 15:38 p 367389
21 13:12 a 404357

PH dy hr mn
☾ 6 9:38 16♎17
● 13 5:01 23♑13
☽ 20 21:03 1♉02
○ 28 19:17 9♌06

Max/0 Lat
dy hr mn
4 11:51 5N14
10 20:16 0 S
17 10:22 5S11
24 21:48 0 N
31 15:48 5N06

Void of Course Moon

Last Aspect	☽ Ingress
2 22:01 ♂ △	♍ 3 1:14
4 21:35 ♀ □	♎ 5 5:43
7 5:56 ♀ ⚹	♏ 7 8:55
9 2:00 ♇ ⚹	♐ 9 11:16
10 18:30 ♅ ☍	♑ 11 13:31
13 7:23 ♇ ☌	♒ 13 16:45
14 9:29 ☿ ☌	♓ 15 22:18
18 3:46 ☉ ⚹	♈ 18 7:08
20 8:30 ♇ □	♉ 20 18:57
22 21:29 ♇ △	♊ 23 7:44
25 7:18 ☿ △	♋ 25 18:53
27 17:56 ♇ ☍	♌ 28 2:55
30 1:54 ☿ ☍	♍ 30 8:04

DAILY ASPECTARIAN

1 F	☽☍♃	0:07
	☉#☽	0:17
	☽⚼♆	1:23
	♀∥♇	2:56
	☽△⚷	4:17
	☽⚼♀	5:27
	☽#♀	5:43
	☽#♇	5:52
	☽□♅	7:27
	☿⚹♆	11:19
	☉⚻☽	15:56
	☽⚻⚳	17:19
2 Sa	☽#♄	0:29
	☽#♃	1:49
	♀⚼♅	2:23
	☽⚻♆	4:40
	☽⚻☿	7:03
	☽⚼⚷	7:31
	☽△♀	11:25
	☽⚻♇	14:58
	☉⚹⚳	17:08
	☉⚼☽	21:08
	☽△♂	22:01
3 Su	☽⚻♄	4:34
	☽#⚳	5:00
	☽⚻♃	7:06
	☽⚻⚷	10:16
	☽△♅	13:13
	☽⚼☿	13:26
	☽∥♅	15:14
	☉∥♀	17:10
	☽⚼♇	17:38
	☽∥♂	22:23
4 M	☽☍⚳	0:02
	☽⚼♂	1:23
	☉△☽	1:46
	♀⚺♇	2:20
	♃∠♆	6:59
	☽⚼♄	7:10
	☽☍♆	9:51
	☽⚼♃	9:53
	☽⚼♅	15:27
	☽△☿	19:13
	☽△♇	19:53
	☽□♀	21:35
5 Tu	☿☌♇	0:59
	☽#♆	2:23
	☽⚻♂	4:21
	☽∥⚷	7:15
	☽△♄	9:23
	☽△♃	12:18
	☽☍⚷	14:34
	☽⚻♅	17:21
6 W	☽⚻⚳	5:07
	☿∥♀	7:01
	☉□☽	9:38
	☊ D	9:45
	☉∥♇	13:17
	☽⚻♆	13:33
	☽#⚷	19:00
	♂ ♉	22:28
	☽□♇	23:24
	☽∥♆	23:40
7 Th	☽□☿	5:22
	☽⚹♀	5:56
	☽⚼⚳	7:11
	☽☍♂	9:16
	☽□♄	12:55
	☽⚼♆	15:00
	☽□♃	16:12
	☽⚻⚷	17:39
	☽☍♅	20:17
	☿∥♇	20:40
8 F	☿⚺♀	0:05
	☿∠⚳	0:32
	☽#♂	6:13
	☽△⚳	9:02
	☽#♅	9:31
	☽∠♀	9:38
	☿ ♒	12:01
	☉∥☿	12:48
	☽∥⚳	15:01
	♀ ♑	15:42
	☉⚹☽	16:12
	☽△♆	16:15
	☉⚹♆	16:54
	☽⚼⚷	18:53
9 Sa	☽⚹♇	2:00
	☿□♂	2:46
	☽⚺♀	13:09
	☽⚻♂	13:18
	☽⚹☿	14:16
	☽⚹♄	15:39
	♀△♂	15:54
	☽∥♃	17:56
	☉∠☽	19:12
	☽⚹♃	19:19
	☽△⚷	20:00
	☽∥♄	20:29
	☽⚻♅	22:31
10 Su	☽∠♇	3:08
	☿☌♄	3:18
	☽∥☿	6:46
	☉∥☽	10:09
	☽□⚳	12:24
	☽∥♇	14:26
	☽⚼♂	15:14
	☽∠♄	16:57
	☿∠♆	17:57
	☽□♆	18:30
	☽∠☿	18:35
	☊ R	20:19
	♀⚺♄	20:40
	☽∠♃	20:50
	☽∥♀	21:35
	☉⚺☽	22:13
	☽⚼♅	23:37
11 M	☽⚺♇	4:19
	☽△♂	17:17
	☿☌♃	17:21
	☿⚹⚷	17:24
	♃⚹⚷	17:49
	☽⚺♄	18:22
	☽☌♀	20:16
	☽□⚷	22:25
	☽⚺♃	22:29
	☽⚺☿	23:03
12 Tu	☽△♅	0:52
	♂∥♅	6:32
	☿□♅	15:01
	☽⚹⚳	16:12
	♀□⚷	21:05
	☽⚹♆	21:18
13 W	♀⚺♃	2:41
	☉☌☽	5:01
	☽☌♇	7:23
	♂□♄	11:03
	☿∥♄	16:37
	☽∠⚳	18:41
	☽∥♀	19:49
	☽☌♄	22:12
	☽□♂	22:31
	☽∠♆	23:18
	♂#⚳	23:19
14 Th	♀△♅	0:23
	☽⚹⚷	2:03
	☽☌♃	2:56
	☽∥♇	3:27
	☽□♅	4:30
	☽⚺♀	4:55
	♅ D	8:37
	☽☌☿	9:29
	☉∥☽	13:21
	☉☌♇	14:20
	☿∥♃	20:04
	☽⚺⚳	21:49
	♂∠♆	21:56
	☽∥♄	23:19
15 F	☽⚺♆	1:56
	☽∥♃	3:08
	☽∥☿	4:11
	☽∠⚷	4:46
	☽∠♀	10:27
	☽⚺♇	12:34
	☉⚺☽	14:22
	⚳#♅	19:36
16 Sa	☽⚺♄	4:34
	☽⚹♂	6:30
	☽⚺⚷	8:15
	☽#♂	8:58
	☽⚺♃	10:05
	☽⚹♅	10:45
	☽#♅	12:47
	☽∥⚳	13:25
	☽∠♇	16:19
	☽⚹♀	17:03
	☉∠☽	20:30
	☽⚺☿	23:34
17 Su	☽☌⚳	6:39
	☽∠♄	9:01
	☽☌♆	9:36
	☽∠♂	11:55
	☽∠♃	14:59
	☽∠♅	15:07
	☽⚹♇	20:57
	♃□♅	22:51
18 M	☽∥♆	3:41
	☉⚹☽	3:46
	♂⚺⚷	6:45
	☽#⚷	8:10
	☽∠☿	8:17
	☽⚹♄	14:21
	☽☌⚷	17:50
	☽⚺♂	18:17
	☽⚺♅	20:21
	☽⚹♃	20:46
19 Tu	⚶ R	8:55
	☽□♀	9:44
	☽⚹☿	17:55
	☽⚺⚳	19:05
	☽⚺♆	20:35
	☉ ♒	20:41
20 W	☽∥⚷	2:29
	☽#♆	6:55
	☿⚺⚳	7:13
	☽□♇	8:30
	♄∠♆	16:59
	☿⚺♆	18:05
	♂☌♅	20:39
	☊ D	20:50
	☉□☽	21:03
21 Th	☽∠⚳	2:16
	☽∠♆	2:57
	☽□♄	3:01
	☽⚺⚷	6:10
	☽☌♅	8:38
	☽☌♂	9:10
	☽□♃	10:16
	☽#⚳	18:44
22 F	☽∥♅	0:16
	☿∠⚷	0:48
	☿#♂	2:52
	⚳☌♆	3:39
	☉∥♄	4:55
	☽△♀	5:29
	☽#☿	9:22
	☽⚹♆	9:28
	☽⚹⚳	9:38
	☽∥♂	10:38
	☽∠⚷	12:42
	☽□☿	14:00
	⚳∠♄	17:25
	☽△♇	21:29
23 Sa	♂□♃	7:50
	☽#♃	9:37
	☉#☽	13:30
	☽⚼♀	15:20
	☉△☽	15:28
	☽#♄	15:33
	☽△♄	16:20
	☽⚹⚷	19:00
	☉∠♆	19:30
	♀⚹♆	19:50
	☽⚺♅	21:17
24 Su	☽△♃	0:05
	☽⚺♂	0:28
	☉☌♄	3:03
	♀∥♇	3:29
	☽⚼♇	3:39
	♀⚹⚳	10:08
	☽#♀	14:15
	☉∠⚳	14:43
	☽#♇	14:52
	☽□♆	21:37
	☊ R	21:50
	☽⚼♄	22:22
	☽□⚳	23:24
	☉⚼☽	23:55
25 M	☽⚻♀	0:29
	☽∠♅	2:56
	☿#♅	4:57
	☽⚼♃	6:13
	☽△☿	7:18
	☽∠♂	7:19
	☽⚻♇	9:13
	☉⚹⚷	10:30
26 Tu	☽⚻♄	3:39
	☽□⚷	5:47
	☉⚻☽	7:25
	☽⚹♅	7:50
	☽⚻♃	11:34
	☉□♅	12:49
	☽⚹♂	13:18
	☉∥♃	13:22
	☽⚼☿	13:57
	☿⚺♇	14:36
27 W	☽△♆	6:59
	☽△⚳	10:08
	☽☍♀	15:38
	☽☍♇	17:56
	☽⚻☿	19:11
28 Th	☽⚼♆	10:26
	☽☍♄	11:42
	☽△⚷	13:22
	☽⚼⚳	14:11
	☽#♇	14:25
	☽□♅	15:12
	♀☌♇	16:19
	☉☍☽	19:17
	☽☍♃	19:40
	☽#♀	20:59
	☽□♂	22:33
29 F	☉☌♃	1:41
	☽#♄	12:15
	☽⚻♆	13:11
	☽⚼⚷	16:03
	☿⚺♀	17:20
	☽⚻⚳	17:30
	☽#♃	18:47
	☉#☽	22:53
	☽⚻♇	23:37
30 Sa	☽☍☿	1:54
	☽⚻♀	2:40
	☽∥♂	5:14
	⚳∠♅	5:32
	☿ R	15:53
	☽⚻♄	16:55
	☽⚻⚷	18:12
	☽△♅	19:53
	☽∥♅	21:03
31 Su	☽⚻♃	1:02
	☽⚼♇	1:38
	☉⚻☽	3:52
	☽△♂	4:58
	☽⚼♀	7:07
	☽#☿	8:34
	☽#⚳	9:16
	☽☍♆	17:10
	☽⚼♄	18:51
	☽⚼♅	21:36
	☽☍⚳	22:36

February 2021

LONGITUDE

Day	Sid.Time	☉	☽	☽ 12 hour	Mean ☊	True ☊	☿	♀	♂	⚳	♃	♄	⚷	♅	♆	♇	1st of Month
	h m s	° ' "	° ' "	° ' "	° '	° '	° '	° '	° '	° '	° '	° '	° '	° '	° '	° '	
1 M	8 45 41	12♒20 13	23♍16 11	0♎19 47	17♊12.9	18♊24.7	26♒19.4	29♑15.8	12♉32.9	22♓28.2	10♒03.5	5♒16.5	5♈54.9	6♉51.5	19♓16.1	25♑12.6	Julian Day #
2 Tu	8 49 37	13 21 06	7♎24 23	14 29 32	17 09.7	18R 17.8	25R 58.7	0♒31.0	13 05.0	22 49.9	10 17.8	5 23.6	5 57.3	6 52.4	19 18.0	25 14.5	2459246.5
3 W	8 53 34	14 21 58	21 34 50	28 39 57	17 06.6	18 13.2	25 27.1	1 46.2	13 37.3	23 11.7	10 32.0	5 30.7	5 59.7	6 53.4	19 20.0	25 16.5	Obliquity
4 Th	8 57 30	15 22 49	5♏44 36	12♏48 37	17 03.4	18D 10.8	24 45.4	3 01.3	14 09.6	23 33.6	10 46.2	5 37.8	6 02.2	6 54.4	19 21.9	25 18.4	23°26'14"
5 F	9 01 27	16 23 40	19 51 48	26 54 03	17 00.2	18 10.5	23 54.5	4 16.5	14 42.1	23 55.5	11 00.5	5 44.9	6 04.7	6 55.5	19 23.9	25 20.3	SVP 4♓58'50"
6 Sa	9 05 23	17 24 29	3♐55 16	10♐55 22	16 57.0	18 11.1	22 55.8	5 31.7	15 14.7	24 17.5	11 14.7	5 52.0	6 07.2	6 56.7	19 25.9	25 22.1	GC 27♐08.0 Eris 23♈29.7
7 Su	9 09 20	18 25 18	17 54 16	24 51 50	16 53.9	18R 11.6	21 51.0	6 46.9	15 47.4	24 39.6	11 28.9	5 59.0	6 09.8	6 57.9	19 27.9	25 24.0	Day ⚴
8 M	9 13 17	19 26 06	1♑47 58	8♑42 27	16 50.7	18 10.8	20 42.0	8 02.1	16 20.2	25 01.7	11 43.1	6 06.0	6 12.4	6 59.1	19 29.9	25 25.9	1 18♒17.4
9 Tu	9 17 13	20 26 53	15 35 08	22 25 43	16 47.5	18 07.7	19 30.7	9 17.2	16 53.2	25 23.9	11 57.3	6 13.1	6 15.0	7 00.4	19 31.9	25 27.7	6 19 59.2
10 W	9 21 10	21 27 39	29 13 58	5♒59 33	16 44.3	18 01.8	18 19.2	10 32.4	17 26.2	25 46.2	12 11.5	6 20.1	6 17.7	7 01.8	19 34.0	25 29.6	11 21 41.0
11 Th	9 25 06	22 28 23	12♒42 12	19 21 37	16 41.2	17 53.1	17 09.4	11 47.5	17 59.4	26 08.5	12 25.7	6 27.0	6 20.4	7 03.2	19 36.1	25 31.4	16 23 22.4
12 F	9 29 03	23 29 06	25 57 30	2♓29 39	16 38.0	17 42.2	16 02.9	13 02.7	18 32.6	26 30.9	12 39.8	6 34.0	6 23.2	7 04.6	19 38.1	25 33.2	21 25 03.4
13 Sa	9 32 59	24 29 48	8♓57 51	15 22 00	16 34.8	17 29.9	15 01.2	14 17.8	19 06.0	26 53.4	12 54.0	6 40.9	6 26.0	7 06.1	19 40.2	25 35.0	26 26 43.8
14 Su	9 36 56	25 30 28	21 42 03	27 58 02	16 31.6	17 17.6	14 05.4	15 33.0	19 39.4	27 15.9	13 08.1	6 47.8	6 28.8	7 07.6	19 42.3	25 36.8	
15 M	9 40 52	26 31 07	4♈10 06	10♈18 25	16 28.4	17 06.2	13 16.4	16 48.1	20 13.0	27 38.4	13 22.2	6 54.7	6 31.6	7 09.2	19 44.5	25 38.6	⚵
16 Tu	9 44 49	27 31 44	16 23 17	22 25 05	16 25.3	16 56.9	12 34.8	18 03.2	20 46.6	28 01.0	13 36.3	7 01.6	6 34.5	7 10.8	19 46.6	25 40.4	1 13♐16.8
17 W	9 48 46	28 32 19	28 24 13	4♉21 12	16 22.1	16 50.1	12 00.8	19 18.3	21 20.3	28 23.7	13 50.3	7 08.4	6 37.4	7 12.5	19 48.7	25 42.1	6 14 34.4
18 Th	9 52 42	29 32 53	10♉16 35	16 10 59	16 18.9	16 46.0	11 34.6	20 33.4	21 54.1	28 46.4	14 04.3	7 15.2	6 40.3	7 14.2	19 50.9	25 43.8	11 15 48.6
19 F	9 56 39	0♓33 25	22 05 02	27 59 23	16 15.7	16D 44.2	11 16.1	21 48.5	22 28.0	29 09.2	14 18.3	7 22.0	6 43.3	7 16.0	19 53.1	25 45.5	16 16 59.0
20 Sa	10 00 35	1 33 55	3♊54 45	9♊51 48	16 12.6	16 43.9	11 05.1	23 03.5	23 02.0	29 32.0	14 32.3	7 28.8	6 46.3	7 17.8	19 55.2	25 47.2	21 18 05.3
21 Su	10 04 32	2 34 23	15 51 16	21 53 49	16 09.4	16R 44.1	11D 01.4	24 18.6	23 36.0	29 54.8	14 46.3	7 35.5	6 49.3	7 19.7	19 57.4	25 48.9	26 19 07.2
22 M	10 08 28	3 34 49	28 00 06	4♋10 45	16 06.2	16 43.6	11 04.5	25 33.6	24 10.1	0♈17.7	15 00.2	7 42.2	6 52.4	7 21.6	19 59.6	25 50.6	
23 Tu	10 12 25	4 35 14	10♋26 18	16 47 16	16 03.0	16 41.5	11 14.1	26 48.7	24 44.3	0 40.7	15 14.1	7 48.8	6 55.5	7 23.5	20 01.8	25 52.2	⚶
24 W	10 16 21	5 35 37	23 14 01	29 46 51	15 59.8	16 36.9	11 29.8	28 03.7	25 18.6	1 03.7	15 27.9	7 55.5	6 58.6	7 25.5	20 04.1	25 53.9	1 20♍45.9R
25 Th	10 20 18	6 35 58	6♌25 54	13♌11 11	15 56.7	16 29.5	11 51.2	29 18.7	25 52.9	1 26.7	15 41.7	8 02.1	7 01.7	7 27.5	20 06.3	25 55.5	6 20 10.1R
26 F	10 24 15	7 36 16	20 02 33	26 59 41	15 53.5	16 19.6	12 17.9	0♓33.7	26 27.3	1 49.8	15 55.5	8 08.6	7 04.8	7 29.6	20 08.5	25 57.1	11 19 23.1R
27 Sa	10 28 11	8 36 34	4♍02 08	11♍09 18	15 50.3	16 07.9	12 49.6	1 48.7	27 01.8	2 12.9	16 09.2	8 15.1	7 08.0	7 31.7	20 10.8	25 58.6	16 18 25.8R
28 Su	10 32 08	9♓36 49	18 20 25	25 34 39	15♊47.1	15♊55.6	13♒25.8	3♓03.7	27♉36.3	2♈36.0	16♒23.0	8♒21.6	7♈11.2	7♉33.8	20♓13.0	26♑00.2	21 17 19.9R 26 16 07.3R

DECLINATION and LATITUDE

Day	☉ Decl	☽ Decl	☽ Lat	☽ 12h Decl	☿ Decl	☿ Lat	♀ Decl	♀ Lat	♂ Decl	♂ Lat	⚳ Decl	⚳ Lat	♃ Decl	♃ Lat	♄ Decl	♄ Lat
1 M	17S06	7N20	5N05	4N27	10S46	2N06	20S55	0S37	16N50	1N17	10S38	8S20	18S14	0S32	19S21	0S25
2 Tu	16 49	1 29	4 49	1S29	10 37	2 23	20 41	0 39	16 60	1 18	10 28	8 18	18 10	0 32	19 20	0 25
3 W	16 31	4S27	4 16	7 22	10 32	2 39	20 26	0 42	17 10	1 18	10 18	8 17	18 06	0 32	19 18	0 26
4 Th	16 13	10 11	3 27	12 52	10 32	2 54	20 11	0 44	17 20	1 19	10 07	8 15	18 03	0 32	19 17	0 26
5 F	15 55	15 22	2 26	17 39	10 37	3 07	19 56	0 46	17 30	1 19	9 57	8 13	17 59	0 32	19 15	0 26
6 Sa	15 37	19 42	1 16	21 26	10 45	3 18	19 40	0 48	17 40	1 20	9 47	8 12	17 55	0 32	19 13	0 26
7 Su	15 18	22 52	0 02	23 56	10 57	3 28	19 23	0 50	17 50	1 20	9 37	8 10	17 51	0 32	19 12	0 26
8 M	14 59	24 38	1S12	24 56	11 12	3 35	19 05	0 52	18 00	1 20	9 26	8 08	17 47	0 32	19 10	0 26
9 Tu	14 40	24 51	2 21	24 24	11 30	3 39	18 48	0 54	18 10	1 21	9 16	8 07	17 43	0 32	19 08	0 26
10 W	14 21	23 34	3 20	22 25	11 49	3 41	18 29	0 56	18 20	1 21	9 06	8 05	17 40	0 33	19 07	0 26
11 Th	14 01	20 57	4 08	19 14	12 10	3 41	18 10	0 57	18 30	1 21	8 56	8 04	17 36	0 33	19 05	0 26
12 F	13 41	17 16	4 41	15 07	12 32	3 39	17 51	0 59	18 39	1 22	8 45	8 02	17 32	0 33	19 03	0 26
13 Sa	13 21	12 49	4 59	10 24	12 55	3 34	17 31	1 01	18 49	1 22	8 35	8 01	17 28	0 33	19 02	0 26
14 Su	13 01	7 54	5 01	5 21	13 17	3 28	17 10	1 03	18 58	1 23	8 25	7 59	17 24	0 33	18 60	0 26
15 M	12 41	2 46	4 49	0 11	13 38	3 20	16 49	1 04	19 08	1 23	8 14	7 58	17 20	0 33	18 58	0 26
16 Tu	12 20	2N23	4 24	4N54	13 59	3 11	16 28	1 06	19 17	1 23	8 04	7 56	17 16	0 33	18 57	0 27
17 W	11 59	7 22	3 47	9 45	14 18	3 00	16 06	1 07	19 26	1 24	7 54	7 55	17 12	0 33	18 55	0 27
18 Th	11 38	12 02	3 01	14 12	14 36	2 49	15 43	1 09	19 35	1 24	7 43	7 53	17 08	0 33	18 53	0 27
19 F	11 16	16 14	2 07	18 07	14 53	2 37	15 21	1 10	19 44	1 24	7 33	7 52	17 04	0 33	18 52	0 27
20 Sa	10 55	19 49	1 08	21 08	15 08	2 24	14 57	1 12	19 53	1 24	7 23	7 51	17 00	0 34	18 50	0 27
21 Su	10 33	22 36	0 05	23 39	15 21	2 12	14 34	1 13	20 02	1 25	7 12	7 49	16 56	0 34	18 48	0 27
22 M	10 12	24 25	0N59	24 53	15 33	1 59	14 10	1 14	20 11	1 25	7 02	7 48	16 52	0 34	18 47	0 27
23 Tu	9 50	25 03	2 02	24 54	15 43	1 46	13 45	1 15	20 20	1 25	6 52	7 47	16 48	0 34	18 45	0 27
24 W	9 28	24 24	3 00	23 34	15 51	1 33	13 20	1 16	20 28	1 25	6 41	7 45	16 44	0 34	18 43	0 27
25 Th	9 05	22 23	3 51	20 53	15 57	1 20	12 55	1 17	20 37	1 25	6 31	7 44	16 40	0 34	18 42	0 27
26 F	8 43	19 04	4 30	16 57	16 02	1 07	12 30	1 18	20 45	1 26	6 21	7 43	16 36	0 34	18 40	0 27
27 Sa	8 20	14 35	4 54	11 59	16 05	0 55	12 04	1 19	20 53	1 26	6 10	7 41	16 32	0 34	18 39	0 28
28 Su	7S58	9N13	5N00	6N17	16S07	0N42	11S38	1S20	21N01	1N26	6S00	7S40	16S28	0S35	18S37	0S28

Day	⚷ Decl	⚷ Lat	♅ Decl	♅ Lat	♆ Decl	♆ Lat	♇ Decl	♇ Lat
1	4N36	2N27	13N23	0S26	5S14	1S04	22S19	1S14
6	4 40	2 26	13 25	0 26	5 10	1 04	22 17	1 15
11	4 44	2 25	13 28	0 26	5 06	1 04	22 16	1 15
16	4 49	2 25	13 30	0 26	5 02	1 04	22 15	1 16
21	4 55	2 24	13 33	0 26	4 58	1 04	22 14	1 17
26	5N00	2N23	13N37	0S25	4S53	1S04	22S13	1S17

Day	⚴ Decl	⚴ Lat	⚵ Decl	⚵ Lat	⚶ Decl	⚶ Lat	Eris Decl	Eris Lat
1	0N07	16N13	11S39	10N49	11N41	8N44	1S34	11S29
6	0 20	15 55	11 33	11 04	12 17	9 08	1 33	11 29
11	0 34	15 39	11 25	11 19	12 56	9 30	1 32	11 28
16	0 51	15 23	11 16	11 35	13 38	9 51	1 31	11 27
21	1 08	15 09	11 05	11 52	14 21	10 10	1 29	11 27
26	1N27	14N54	10S51	12N10	15N05	10N26	1S28	11S26

Moon Phenomena

Max/0 Decl

dy	hr mn	
2	6:00	0 S
8	15:32	24S57
15	12:51	0 N
23	0:13	25N03

Max/0 Lat

dy	hr mn	
7	0:30	0 S
13	15:46	5S02
21	1:46	0 N
27	20:03	5N00

Perigee/Apogee

dy	hr m		kilometers
3	19:04	p	370116
18	10:23	a	404465

PH	dy	hr mn	
☾	4	17:38	16♏08
●	11	19:07	23♒17
☽	19	18:48	1♊21
○	27	8:18	8♍57

Void of Course Moon

Last Aspect			☽ Ingress		
1	11:11	♀ △	♎	1	11:26
3	6:16	☿ △	♏	3	14:16
5	9:21	♇ ✶	♐	5	17:18
7	6:17	☿ ✶	♑	7	20:53
9	17:23	♇ ☌	♒	10	1:21
11	19:07	☉ ☌	♓	12	7:24
14	7:30	♇ ✶	♈	14	15:55
17	0:18	☉ ✶	♉	17	3:13
19	7:29	♇ △	♊	19	16:05
21	18:40	♀ △	♋	22	3:54
24	4:55	♇ ☍	♌	24	12:24
26	11:33	♂ □	♍	26	17:08
28	15:59	♂ △	♎	28	19:18

DAILY ASPECTARIAN

1 M
☽⚼♃ 3:06
☽△♇ 3:19
☽⚻☿ 5:06
☉⚼☽ 7:27
☽⚼♂ 7:34
☽⋕♆ 8:47
☉□♂ 10:35
☽△♀ 11:11
☽∥⚷ 11:21
♀ ♒ 14:07
☉⋕♂ 14:13
☽△♄ 20:34
☽☍⚷ 21:32
☽⚻♅ 23:06

2 Tu
☽△♃ 4:59
☽⚼☿ 5:52
☽⚻♂ 10:00
☉△☽ 10:51
☽⚻♆ 20:11

3 W
☽⋕⚷ 0:42
☽⚻⚳ 2:48
☽∥♆ 3:04
☽□♇ 6:16
☽△☿ 6:16
☿⚺♇ 6:23
☽□♀ 18:56
☽⚼♆ 21:39
☽∥⚳ 23:46
☽□♄ 23:48

4 Th
☽⚻⚷ 0:30
☽∥☿ 1:35
☽☍♅ 1:59
☽⚼⚳ 4:54
☽□♃ 8:41
☽⋕♅ 14:35
☽☍♂ 14:52
☉□☽ 17:38
☊ D 17:42
☽△♆ 23:12
☿⚺⚳ 23:40

5 F
☽⚼⚷ 2:05
♀∠♆ 2:25
☉∥☽ 2:38
☽□☿ 6:28
☽△⚳ 7:06
☽✶♇ 9:21
☽⋕♂ 11:38
☽∥♃ 13:37
☽∥♄ 21:05
☽∥♀ 23:48

6 Sa
☽✶♀ 3:01
☽✶♄ 3:21
☽△⚷ 3:47
☽⚻♅ 5:11
♀☌♄ 7:08
☽∠♇ 11:04
♀✶⚷ 11:44
☽✶♃ 12:46
☽∥♇ 18:49
☽⚻♂ 20:13

7 Su
☊ R 0:32
☉✶☽ 0:58
♂⋕♃ 1:20
☽□♆ 2:42
♀□♅ 3:34
☽∠♄ 5:21
☽✶☿ 6:17
☽⚼♅ 7:00
☽∠♀ 7:20
☽□⚳ 11:58
☽⚺♇ 12:57
☿∠⚷ 13:56
☽∠♃ 15:03
♀∥♄ 17:23
☽⚼♂ 23:10

8 M
☉⚺♆ 1:33
☉∠☽ 4:56
☽∠☿ 6:14
☽⚺♄ 7:32
☽□⚷ 7:40
☽△♅ 9:01
☽⚺♀ 11:55
☉☌☿ 13:49
☽⚺♃ 17:33
☿⚺♆ 23:36

9 Tu
☽△♂ 2:22
⚳✶♇ 4:28
☽⚺☿ 6:20
☽✶♆ 6:56
☉⚺☽ 9:12
♄✶⚷ 11:00
☽☌♇ 17:23
☽✶⚳ 17:43
☉∠⚷ 19:54

10 W
♀∠⚳ 6:17
♀⋕♂ 7:45
☽∠♆ 9:29
☿□♂ 12:17
☽✶⚷ 12:35
☽☌♄ 12:43
☽∥♇ 13:17
☽□♅ 13:52
☽∠⚳ 21:07
☽☌♀ 22:12
☽☌♃ 23:30

11 Th
☽☌☿ 7:23
☽□♂ 9:56
☽⚺♆ 12:28
☽∥♄ 13:02
♀☌♃ 15:01
☽∠⚷ 15:39
☽⋕♂ 15:58
☉☌☽ 19:07
☽∥♀ 20:18
☽∥♃ 22:26
☽⚺♇ 23:16

12 F
☽⚺⚳ 1:03
☉⋕♅ 15:33
☽⚺⚷ 19:16
☽⚺♄ 19:43
☽✶♅ 20:32
☽⋕♅ 20:39
☉∥☽ 21:04
☽∥☿ 23:34

13 Sa
☽∠♇ 3:02
♀∥♃ 4:03
☽⚺♃ 7:30
☿☌♀ 7:49
☽⚺☿ 10:33
☽⚺♀ 11:05
☉∥☿ 15:03
☽✶♂ 19:56
☽☌♆ 20:12
☽∥⚳ 21:30

14 Su
☽∠♄ 0:11
☽∠♅ 0:49
♂✶♆ 2:14
☉⚺♇ 2:35
♂⋕♄ 3:26
☽✶♇ 7:30
☉⚺☽ 7:55
☽☌⚳ 10:59
☽∠♃ 12:34
☽∠☿ 13:16
☽∥♆ 13:23
☿⋕♅ 14:02
☽⋕⚷ 14:34
☽∠♀ 18:53
☿☌♃ 21:41

15 M
☽∠♂ 2:08
☽☌⚷ 4:37
☽✶♄ 5:24
☽⚺♅ 5:50
☿∠⚳ 13:51
☉∠☽ 15:41
☽✶☿ 16:51
☽✶♃ 18:23

16 Tu
☽✶♀ 3:41
☽⚺♆ 6:45
☽⚺♂ 9:09
☽∥⚷ 11:39
☽⋕♆ 12:34
☉⚺⚳ 18:33
☽□♇ 18:34
☽⚺⚳ 23:59

17 W
☉✶☽ 0:18
☽⋕⚳ 2:32
♀⚺♆ 10:01
☽∠♆ 12:58
♂∠⚷ 13:18
☽⚺⚷ 16:40
☽□♄ 17:49
☽☌♅ 17:49
♄□♅ 19:10
☉⋕☽ 21:59

18 Th
☽□☿ 2:34
☽∠⚳ 7:20
☽□♃ 7:52
☽∥♅ 8:10
☉ ♓ 10:45
☽⋕☿ 15:19
☽⋕♀ 19:04
☽✶♆ 19:31
♀∠⚷ 22:17
☽∠⚷ 23:16
☽□♀ 23:22

19 F
☽☌♂ 0:49
☽⋕♃ 5:05
☽△♇ 7:29
☽✶⚳ 14:50
☽⋕♄ 16:55
☿∥♀ 17:19
☊ D 18:36
☉□☽ 18:48
♀□♂ 23:05

20 Sa
☽∥♂ 0:31
⚳∠♃ 0:52
☽✶⚷ 5:48
☽⚺♅ 6:51
☽△♄ 7:16
☽⚼♇ 13:53
☽△☿ 14:21
☽⋕♇ 20:16
☽△♃ 21:48

21 Su
☿ D 0:53
☊ R 1:47
⚳ ♈ 5:24
☽□♆ 8:11
☽∠♅ 12:53
☽⚼♄ 13:30
☽⚺♂ 16:07
☽△♀ 18:40
☽⚻♇ 19:46
☽⚼☿ 20:12

22 M
☽⚼♃ 3:59
☽□⚳ 4:37
♀⚺♇ 5:32
☉△☽ 11:48
♆⋕⚷ 12:24
☽□⚷ 17:15
☽✶♅ 18:10
☽⚻♄ 18:57
☽∠♂ 22:36

23 Tu
☽⚻☿ 1:33
☽⚼♀ 2:54
☽⚻♃ 9:15
♀⋕♅ 10:07
☽△♆ 18:07
☉⚼☽ 18:42

24 W
☽✶♂ 4:00
☽☍♇ 4:55
☽⚻♀ 9:48
☽△⚳ 14:45
☽⚼♆ 21:37

25 Th
☉⚻☽ 0:19
☽△⚷ 1:04
☽⋕♇ 1:27
☽□♅ 1:50
♂△♇ 1:53
☽☍♄ 2:53
☽☍☿ 9:57
☉⚺⚷ 10:48
♀ ♓ 13:13
☽∥♂ 13:21
☽☍♃ 16:41
☽⚼⚳ 18:14
☉✶♅ 21:14

26 F
☽⚻♆ 0:10
☽⋕♄ 2:22
☽⚼⚷ 3:33
☽⚻♇ 10:14
☽□♂ 11:33
☽⋕♃ 14:02
☉⚺♄ 14:26
☽⋕☿ 16:35
☽☍♀ 19:51
☽⚻⚳ 20:49

27 Sa
☽∥♅ 4:33
☽⚻⚷ 5:15
☽△♅ 5:55
☽⚻♄ 7:11
☉☍☽ 8:18
♀⚺⚳ 11:11
☽⚼♇ 11:43
☽⋕♀ 12:41
☽⚻☿ 15:26
☽⚻♃ 20:41

28 Su
☽☍♆ 3:08
☉⋕☽ 5:32
☽⚼♅ 7:02
☽⚼♄ 8:24
☽△♇ 12:44
☽⋕⚳ 13:31
☽△♂ 15:59
☽∥⚷ 16:55
☽⚼☿ 17:31
☽⋕♆ 17:44
☽⚼♃ 21:55

LONGITUDE

Day	Sid.Time	☉	☽	☽ 12 hour	Mean☊	True☊	☿	♀	♂	⚳	♃	♄	⚷	♅	♆	♇
	h m s	° ' "	° ' "	° ' "	° '	° '	° '	° '	° '	° '	° '	° '	° '	° '	° '	° '
1 M	10 36 04	10♓37 02	2♎51 08	10♎08 55	15♊44.0	15♊43.9	14♒06.2	4♓18.6	28♉10.8	2♈59.2	16♒36.6	8♒28.0	7♈14.4	7♉36.0	20♓15.2	26♑01.7
2 Tu	10 40 01	11 37 14	17 27 07	24 44 54	15 40.8	15R 34.3	14 50.6	5 33.6	28 45.5	3 22.4	16 50.2	8 34.4	7 17.6	7 38.2	20 17.5	26 03.3
3 W	10 43 57	12 37 24	2♏01 29	9♏16 15	15 37.6	15 27.3	15 38.7	6 48.5	29 20.2	3 45.7	17 03.8	8 40.8	7 20.9	7 40.5	20 19.8	26 04.7
4 Th	10 47 54	13 37 33	16 28 39	23 38 18	15 34.4	15 23.2	16 30.1	8 03.5	29 54.9	4 08.9	17 17.4	8 47.1	7 24.2	7 42.8	20 22.0	26 06.2
5 F	10 51 50	14 37 41	0♐44 55	7♐48 21	15 31.2	15 21.5	17 24.7	9 18.4	0♊29.7	4 32.3	17 30.9	8 53.4	7 27.4	7 45.2	20 24.3	26 07.7
6 Sa	10 55 47	15 37 46	14 48 30	21 45 24	15 28.1	15 21.2	18 22.2	10 33.3	1 04.6	4 55.6	17 44.3	8 59.6	7 30.8	7 47.5	20 26.6	26 09.1
7 Su	10 59 44	16 37 51	28 39 04	5♑29 38	15 24.9	15 21.0	19 22.5	11 48.2	1 39.5	5 19.0	17 57.8	9 05.8	7 34.1	7 50.0	20 28.8	26 10.5
8 M	11 03 40	17 37 54	12♑17 11	19 01 48	15 21.7	15 19.6	20 25.4	13 03.1	2 14.5	5 42.4	18 11.1	9 11.9	7 37.4	7 52.4	20 31.1	26 11.9
9 Tu	11 07 37	18 37 55	25 43 36	2♒22 38	15 18.5	15 15.8	21 30.7	14 18.0	2 49.5	6 05.9	18 24.4	9 18.0	7 40.8	7 54.9	20 33.4	26 13.3
10 W	11 11 33	19 37 54	8♒58 57	15 32 31	15 15.4	15 09.0	22 38.2	15 32.9	3 24.6	6 29.3	18 37.7	9 24.0	7 44.2	7 57.4	20 35.7	26 14.6
11 Th	11 15 30	20 37 52	22 03 22	28 31 24	15 12.2	14 59.2	23 47.9	16 47.7	3 59.7	6 52.9	18 50.9	9 30.0	7 47.6	8 00.0	20 37.9	26 16.0
12 F	11 19 26	21 37 48	4♓56 36	11♓18 52	15 09.0	14 47.1	24 59.7	18 02.6	4 34.8	7 16.4	19 04.1	9 36.0	7 51.0	8 02.6	20 40.2	26 17.3
13 Sa	11 23 23	22 37 42	17 38 10	23 54 27	15 05.8	14 33.4	26 13.3	19 17.4	5 10.1	7 39.9	19 17.2	9 41.9	7 54.4	8 05.2	20 42.5	26 18.6
14 Su	11 27 19	23 37 34	0♈07 42	6♈17 57	15 02.6	14 19.5	27 28.9	20 32.2	5 45.3	8 03.5	19 30.2	9 47.7	7 57.8	8 07.9	20 44.8	26 19.8
15 M	11 31 16	24 37 24	12 25 15	18 29 46	14 59.5	14 06.5	28 46.1	21 47.1	6 20.7	8 27.1	19 43.2	9 53.5	8 01.3	8 10.6	20 47.1	26 21.0
16 Tu	11 35 13	25 37 12	24 31 38	0♉31 08	14 56.3	13 55.6	0♓05.1	23 01.8	6 56.0	8 50.7	19 56.2	9 59.2	8 04.7	8 13.3	20 49.3	26 22.2
17 W	11 39 09	26 36 58	6♉28 34	12 24 17	14 53.1	13 47.3	1 25.7	24 16.6	7 31.4	9 14.4	20 09.0	10 04.8	8 08.2	8 16.1	20 51.6	26 23.4
18 Th	11 43 06	27 36 41	18 18 44	24 12 23	14 49.9	13 42.0	2 47.9	25 31.4	8 06.9	9 38.1	20 21.8	10 10.5	8 11.7	8 18.9	20 53.9	26 24.6
19 F	11 47 02	28 36 23	0♊05 46	5♊59 30	14 46.8	13 39.2	4 11.7	26 46.1	8 42.3	10 01.7	20 34.6	10 16.0	8 15.1	8 21.7	20 56.1	26 25.7
20 Sa	11 50 59	29 36 02	11 54 10	17 50 27	14 43.6	13D 38.4	5 36.9	28 00.8	9 17.9	10 25.5	20 47.2	10 21.5	8 18.6	8 24.5	20 58.4	26 26.8
21 Su	11 54 55	0♈35 40	23 49 00	29 50 32	14 40.4	13R 38.6	7 03.6	29 15.5	9 53.4	10 49.2	20 59.8	10 26.9	8 22.1	8 27.4	21 00.6	26 27.9
22 M	11 58 52	1 35 14	5♋55 44	12♋05 17	14 37.2	13 38.7	8 31.7	0♈30.2	10 29.0	11 12.9	21 12.4	10 32.3	8 25.6	8 30.3	21 02.9	26 29.0
23 Tu	12 02 48	2 34 47	18 19 49	24 39 58	14 34.0	13 37.5	10 01.3	1 44.9	11 04.6	11 36.7	21 24.9	10 37.6	8 29.1	8 33.2	21 05.1	26 30.0
24 W	12 06 45	3 34 17	1♌06 16	7♌39 09	14 30.9	13 34.3	11 32.2	2 59.5	11 40.3	12 00.4	21 37.3	10 42.8	8 32.6	8 36.2	21 07.4	26 31.0
25 Th	12 10 42	4 33 45	14 18 57	21 05 51	14 27.7	13 28.7	13 04.6	4 14.2	12 16.0	12 24.2	21 49.6	10 48.0	8 36.2	8 39.2	21 09.6	26 32.0
26 F	12 14 38	5 33 11	27 59 53	5♍00 53	14 24.5	13 20.8	14 38.3	5 28.8	12 51.7	12 48.0	22 01.8	10 53.1	8 39.7	8 42.2	21 11.8	26 32.9
27 Sa	12 18 35	6 32 34	12♍08 32	19 22 14	14 21.3	13 11.2	16 13.3	6 43.4	13 27.5	13 11.8	22 14.0	10 58.2	8 43.2	8 45.2	21 14.1	26 33.8
28 Su	12 22 31	7 31 56	26 41 17	4♎04 45	14 18.2	13 00.8	17 49.8	7 57.9	14 03.2	13 35.6	22 26.1	11 03.2	8 46.7	8 48.3	21 16.3	26 34.7
29 M	12 26 28	8 31 15	11♎31 36	19 00 41	14 15.0	12 50.9	19 27.6	9 12.5	14 39.0	13 59.4	22 38.1	11 08.1	8 50.2	8 51.3	21 18.5	26 35.6
30 Tu	12 30 24	9 30 32	26 30 51	4♏00 53	14 11.8	12 42.6	21 06.8	10 27.0	15 14.9	14 23.2	22 50.1	11 12.9	8 53.7	8 54.4	21 20.7	26 36.4
31 W	12 34 21	10♈29 47	11♏29 42	18 56 17	14♊08.6	12♊36.7	22♓47.3	11♈41.5	15♊50.7	14♈47.0	23♒01.9	11♒17.7	8♈57.3	8♉57.6	21♓22.8	26♑37.3

1st of Month

Julian Day # 2459274.5
Obliquity 23°26'14"
SVP 4♓58'07"
GC 27♐08.1
Eris 23♈40.0

Day	⚴	Day	⚵	Day	⚶
1	27♒43.7	1	19♐42.1	1	15♍21.6R
6	29 22.9	6	20 36.2	6	14 03.3R
11	1♓01.3	11	21 24.9	11	12 44.8R
16	2 38.5	16	22 07.7	16	11 29.0R
21	4 14.6	21	22 44.4	21	10 18.5R
26	5 49.3	26	23 14.4	26	9 15.5R
31	7 22.5	31	23 37.5	31	8 21.9R

DECLINATION and LATITUDE

Day	☉ Decl	☽ Decl	☽ Lat	☽ 12h Decl	☿ Decl	☿ Lat	♀ Decl	♀ Lat	♂ Decl	♂ Lat	⚳ Decl	⚳ Lat	♃ Decl	♃ Lat	♄ Decl	♄ Lat
1 M	7S35	3N16	4N47	0N11	16S06	0N31	11S11	1S21	21N09	1N26	5S50	7S39	16S24	0S35	18S35	0S28
2 Tu	7 12	2S55	4 16	5S58	16 05	0 19	10 44	1 22	21 17	1 27	5 40	7 38	16 20	0 35	18 34	0 28
3 W	6 49	8 56	3 27	11 46	16 01	0 08	10 17	1 23	21 25	1 27	5 29	7 37	16 16	0 35	18 32	0 28
4 Th	6 26	14 26	2 26	16 52	15 56	0S03	9 50	1 23	21 33	1 27	5 19	7 35	16 12	0 35	18 31	0 28
5 F	6 03	19 04	1 16	20 57	15 50	0 14	9 22	1 24	21 40	1 27	5 09	7 34	16 08	0 35	18 29	0 28
6 Sa	5 40	22 31	0 03	23 45	15 42	0 24	8 55	1 24	21 48	1 27	4 58	7 33	16 04	0 35	18 28	0 28
7 Su	5 17	24 35	1S10	25 04	15 32	0 33	8 27	1 25	21 55	1 27	4 48	7 32	16 00	0 35	18 26	0 28
8 M	4 53	25 09	2 17	24 51	15 21	0 43	7 58	1 25	22 02	1 28	4 38	7 31	15 56	0 36	18 25	0 28
9 Tu	4 30	24 12	3 16	23 13	15 09	0 52	7 30	1 26	22 09	1 28	4 28	7 30	15 52	0 36	18 23	0 29
10 W	4 06	21 55	4 03	20 20	14 55	1 00	7 01	1 26	22 16	1 28	4 17	7 28	15 49	0 36	18 22	0 29
11 Th	3 43	18 31	4 37	16 29	14 40	1 08	6 32	1 26	22 23	1 28	4 07	7 27	15 45	0 36	18 20	0 29
12 F	3 19	14 17	4 56	11 56	14 23	1 16	6 03	1 26	22 30	1 28	3 57	7 26	15 41	0 36	18 19	0 29
13 Sa	2 56	9 29	4 60	6 57	14 05	1 23	5 34	1 26	22 36	1 28	3 47	7 25	15 37	0 36	18 17	0 29
14 Su	2 32	4 22	4 49	1 46	13 45	1 30	5 04	1 26	22 43	1 28	3 36	7 24	15 33	0 36	18 16	0 29
15 M	2 08	0N50	4 25	3N25	13 25	1 37	4 35	1 26	22 49	1 28	3 26	7 23	15 29	0 36	18 14	0 29
16 Tu	1 44	5 57	3 49	8 25	13 03	1 43	4 05	1 26	22 55	1 28	3 16	7 22	15 25	0 37	18 13	0 29
17 W	1 21	10 47	3 03	13 03	12 39	1 48	3 35	1 26	23 01	1 28	3 06	7 21	15 21	0 37	18 11	0 29
18 Th	0 57	15 12	2 10	17 11	12 14	1 53	3 05	1 26	23 07	1 29	2 56	7 20	15 17	0 37	18 10	0 29
19 F	0 33	19 00	1 11	20 38	11 48	1 58	2 35	1 25	23 13	1 29	2 46	7 19	15 13	0 37	18 09	0 30
20 Sa	0 10	22 04	0 09	23 15	11 21	2 03	2 05	1 25	23 18	1 29	2 35	7 18	15 09	0 37	18 07	0 30
21 Su	0N14	24 11	0N54	24 51	10 53	2 06	1 35	1 24	23 24	1 29	2 25	7 17	15 05	0 37	18 06	0 30
22 M	0 38	25 14	1 56	25 18	10 23	2 10	1 05	1 24	23 29	1 29	2 15	7 16	15 01	0 37	18 04	0 30
23 Tu	1 02	25 03	2 53	24 28	9 52	2 13	0 35	1 23	23 34	1 29	2 05	7 15	14 57	0 38	18 03	0 30
24 W	1 25	23 33	3 44	22 19	9 20	2 16	0 05	1 23	23 39	1 29	1 55	7 14	14 54	0 38	18 02	0 30
25 Th	1 49	20 45	4 25	18 53	8 46	2 18	0N26	1 22	23 44	1 29	1 45	7 13	14 50	0 38	18 00	0 30
26 F	2 12	16 44	4 52	14 19	8 11	2 19	0 56	1 21	23 48	1 29	1 35	7 12	14 46	0 38	17 59	0 30
27 Sa	2 36	11 40	5 03	8 49	7 36	2 21	1 26	1 21	23 53	1 29	1 25	7 11	14 42	0 38	17 58	0 30
28 Su	2 59	5 49	4 55	2 42	6 59	2 21	1 56	1 20	23 57	1 29	1 15	7 11	14 38	0 38	17 57	0 31
29 M	3 23	0S28	4 26	3S40	6 21	2 22	2 27	1 19	24 02	1 29	1 05	7 10	14 35	0 39	17 55	0 31
30 Tu	3 46	6 49	3 40	9 52	5 41	2 21	2 57	1 18	24 06	1 29	0 55	7 09	14 31	0 39	17 54	0 31
31 W	4N09	12S47	2N38	15S29	5S01	2S21	3N27	1S17	24N10	1N29	0S45	7S08	14S27	0S39	17S53	0S31

Day	⚷ Decl	⚷ Lat	♅ Decl	♅ Lat	♆ Decl	♆ Lat	♇ Decl	♇ Lat
1	5N04	2N23	13N39	0S25	4S51	1S04	22S13	1S17
6	5 10	2 22	13 43	0 25	4 46	1 04	22 12	1 18
11	5 16	2 22	13 47	0 25	4 42	1 04	22 11	1 19
16	5 22	2 21	13 51	0 25	4 37	1 04	22 10	1 19
21	5 29	2 21	13 56	0 25	4 33	1 04	22 10	1 20
26	5 35	2 20	14 01	0 25	4 28	1 04	22 10	1 20
31	5N42	2N20	14N06	0S25	4S24	1S04	22S09	1S21

Day	⚴ Decl	⚴ Lat	⚵ Decl	⚵ Lat	⚶ Decl	⚶ Lat	Eris Decl	Eris Lat
1	1N38	14N46	10S43	12N22	15N30	10N35	1S27	11S26
6	1 59	14 33	10 27	12 41	16 11	10 46	1 26	11 25
11	2 20	14 21	10 13	13 01	16 49	10 53	1 24	11 25
16	2 42	14 09	9 51	13 22	17 22	10 57	1 23	11 24
21	3 04	13 57	9 31	13 44	17 49	10 58	1 21	11 24
26	3 27	13 47	9 10	14 07	18 11	10 55	1 20	11 23
31	3N51	13N36	8S48	14N30	18N26	10N49	1S18	11S23

Moon Phenomena

Max/0 Decl (dy hr mn)
1 12:41 0 S
7 20:41 25S09
14 20:07 0 N
22 8:36 25N19
28 22:14 0 S

Max/0 Lat (dy hr mn)
6 0:57 0 S
12 18:15 5S00
20 3:32 0 N
27 1:44 5N03

Perigee/Apogee (dy hr m kilometers)
2 5:19 p 365425
18 5:04 a 405252
30 6:17 p 360312

PH (dy hr mn)
☾ 6 1:31 15♐42
● 13 10:22 23♓04
☽ 21 14:42 1♋12
○ 28 18:49 8♎18

Void of Course Moon

Last Aspect	☽ Ingress
2 14:11 ♇ □	♏ 2 20:39
4 16:11 ♇ ✱	♐ 4 22:44
6 9:45 ♆ □	♑ 7 2:21
9 0:54 ♇ ☌	♒ 9 7:42
11 3:33 ♆ ☌	♓ 11 14:45
13 16:39 ♇ ✱	♈ 13 23:45
16 3:41 ♇ □	♉ 16 10:57
18 20:41 ☉ ✱	♊ 18 23:48
21 12:05 ♀ □	♋ 21 12:19
23 15:27 ♇ ☍	♌ 23 21:57
25 13:29 ♃ ☍	♍ 26 3:27
27 23:49 ♇ △	♎ 28 5:23
30 0:09 ♇ □	♏ 30 5:34

DAILY ASPECTARIAN

1 M ☽☍⚳ 0:14, ☽⚻♀ 2:38, ☽☍⚷ 7:15, ☽⚻♅ 7:50, ☽△♄ 9:18, ☉∠♇ 10:06, ☉⚻☽ 13:43, ☽⚼♂ 17:41, ☽△☿ 19:29, ☽△♃ 22:58

2 Tu ☽⚻♆ 4:41, ☽⚼♀ 5:35, ☽∥♆ 7:30, ☽⋕⚷ 8:32, ☽∥⚳ 10:30, ☽□♇ 14:11, ☉∥☽ 15:57, ☉⚼☽ 16:12, ☽⚻♂ 19:23

3 W ☽⚻⚳ 2:57, ☽∥♀ 5:16, ☽⚼♆ 5:29, ☽△♀ 8:40, ☽⚻⚷ 8:51, ☽☍♅ 9:23, ♀⊻⚷ 10:50, ☽□♄ 11:06, ♀✱♅ 17:10, ☉△☽ 18:53, ☽⋕♅ 20:33

4 Th ☽□☿ 0:03, ☽□♃ 1:23, ♂ ♊ 3:31, ☽⚼⚳ 4:36, ☽△♆ 6:32, ☽∥☿ 7:09, ☽∥♃ 8:31, ☽⚼⚷ 9:58, ♀⊻♄ 15:15, ☽✱♇ 16:11, ☽∥♄ 20:44, ☽☍♂ 23:33

5 F ⚳⋕⚷ 0:42, ☿☌♃ 3:28, ☽△⚳ 6:37, ☽△⚷ 11:27, ☽⚻♅ 11:57, ☽✱♄ 13:57, ☽□♀ 15:59, ☽∠♇ 17:43, ☽⋕♂ 17:53, ☽∥♇ 21:16

6 Sa ☉□☽ 1:31, ☽✱♃ 5:08, ☽✱☿ 6:37, ☽□♆ 9:45, ♀∠♇ 11:42, ☽⚼♅ 13:50, ☽∠♄ 16:00, ☽⊻♇ 19:40

7 Su ☽⚻♂ 5:30, ☉⋕⚷ 5:43, ⚳∥♆ 7:21, ☽∠♃ 7:41, ☽∠☿ 10:51, ☽□⚳ 12:02, ☽□⚷ 15:43, ☽△♅ 16:10, ☽⊻♄ 18:30, ♀ ♓ 21:07

8 M ☽✱♀ 1:30, ☿⊻♆ 2:13, ☽⚼♂ 9:12, ☉∥♆ 9:29, ☿∠⚳ 9:56, ☉✱☽ 10:16, ☽⊻♃ 10:40, ☽✱♆ 14:42, ☽⊻☿ 15:46, ☉⊻♃ 17:05

9 Tu ☽☌♇ 0:54, ☉∥⚳ 4:04, ♂⋕♇ 6:35, ☽∠♀ 7:06, ☽△♂ 13:24, ☉∠☽ 15:26, ☽∠♆ 17:49, ☽✱⚳ 19:19, ☽⋕♂ 21:05, ☽∥♇ 21:42, ☽✱⚷ 21:43, ☽□♅ 22:08

10 W ☽☌♄ 0:46, ☿∠⚷ 2:11, ☽⊻♀ 13:17, ☽☌♃ 17:59, ☉⊻☽ 21:09, ☽⊻♆ 21:22, ☽∠⚳ 23:40

11 Th ☉☌♆ 0:02, ☽∥♄ 1:07, ☽∠⚷ 1:22, ☽☌☿ 3:33, ☽⊻♇ 7:49, ☽∥♃ 16:23, ☽□♂ 23:17, ☽∥☿ 23:25

12 F ☽⋕♅ 2:32, ☽⊻⚳ 4:31, ☽⊻⚷ 5:29, ☽✱♅ 5:51, ☽⊻♄ 8:50, ☽∠♇ 11:58, ♀⊻♃ 23:54

13 Sa ☿⊻♇ 1:42, ☽⊻♃ 3:12, ☽☌♀ 3:30, ☽☌♆ 5:53, ☉☌☽ 10:22, ☽∠♅ 10:28, ☉∠♅ 11:33, ♀⋕⚷ 12:04, ☽∠♄ 13:38, ☽✱♇ 16:39, ⚳☌⚷ 17:13, ☽⊻☿ 18:18, ☿⋕♅ 19:32, ☽⋕⚷ 19:35, ☽∥♀ 20:24, ☽∥♆ 22:41

14 Su ☽∥⚳ 3:37, ♀☌♆ 4:09, ⚳⊻♅ 5:01, ☽∠♃ 8:39, ☉∥☽ 9:09, ☽✱♂ 11:29, ☽☌⚷ 15:20, ☽⊻♅ 15:38, ☽☌⚳ 15:57, ☽✱♄ 18:59, ♀∥♆ 21:08

15 M ☽∠☿ 2:58, ☉⋕☽ 5:35, ☉∠♄ 7:08, ☽⋕⚳ 11:42, ☽✱♃ 14:42, ☽⋕♀ 15:55, ☽⊻♆ 16:36, ☽⋕♆ 17:41, ☽∠♂ 18:34, ☽⊻♀ 20:40, ☽∥⚷ 21:12, ☿ ♓ 22:28

16 Tu ☉⊻☽ 2:23, ☽□♇ 3:41, ♀∠♅ 3:49, ☽✱☿ 12:32, ☉✱♇ 18:27, ☽∠♆ 22:45

17 W ☽⊻♂ 2:14, ☽⊻⚷ 3:22, ☽☌♅ 3:38, ☽⊻⚳ 5:47, ☽∠♀ 6:20, ☽□♄ 7:21, ☽⋕☿ 9:00, ☉∠☽ 11:21, ☽∥♅ 16:31, ♀∠♄ 16:45

18 Th ☽⋕♃ 0:30, ♂✱⚷ 3:36, ☽□♃ 4:15, ☽✱♆ 5:17, ♂⊻♅ 8:49, ☽∠⚷ 9:59, ♀∥⚳ 11:39, ☽∠⚳ 13:19, ☽✱♀ 16:25, ☽△♇ 16:31, ♀✱♇ 17:21, ☽⋕♄ 18:12, ☉✱☽ 20:41

19 F ☽□☿ 9:29, ☽✱⚷ 16:41, ☽⊻♅ 16:53, ☽☌♂ 18:26, ⚳✱♄ 18:48, ☽△♄ 20:51, ☽✱⚳ 20:54, ☽⚼♇ 23:04

20 Sa ☽⋕♇ 0:59, ☊ D 3:31, ☉ ♈ 9:39, ☽∥♂ 13:10, ☽△♃ 18:15, ☽□♆ 18:22, ☽∠♅ 23:17

21 Su ♃⊻♆ 1:52, ☽⚼♄ 3:17, ☽⚻♇ 5:18, ☽□♀ 12:05, ♀ ♈ 14:17, ☊ R 14:33, ☉□☽ 14:42, ☿⊻⚷ 22:17, ☿✱♅ 23:36

22 M ☽⚼♃ 0:33, ♂△♄ 2:36, ☽□⚷ 4:55, ☽✱♅ 5:03, ☽△☿ 5:47, ☽⚻♄ 9:04, ☽⊻♂ 9:20, ☽□⚳ 10:39, ☉⋕♀ 12:06

23 Tu ☽△♆ 5:15, ☽⚻♃ 5:58, ☿⊻♄ 10:13, ☽⚼☿ 14:22, ☽∠♂ 15:21, ☽☍♇ 15:27, ♂⚼♇ 17:33, ☽∥♂ 22:59, ☿∠♇ 23:40

24 W ☿□♂ 3:27, ☽△♀ 3:51, ☉△☽ 4:55, ☽⚼♆ 9:14, ☿⊻⚳ 9:56, ☽⋕♇ 13:19, ☽△⚷ 13:41, ☽□♅ 13:47, ☽☍♄ 17:39, ☽✱♂ 20:10, ☽△⚳ 20:28, ☉⋕⚳ 21:24, ☽⚻☿ 21:30

25 Th ☽⚼♀ 9:36, ☉⚼☽ 10:02, ☽⚻♆ 12:08, ☽☍♃ 13:29, ☽⚼⚷ 16:27, ♂✱⚳ 16:29, ☽⋕♄ 17:11, ☽⚻♇ 21:30, ☽⚼⚳ 23:39

26 F ☉☌♀ 6:59, ☽⋕♃ 9:59, ☽∥♅ 13:24, ☉⚻☽ 13:53, ☽⚻♀ 14:01, ☽⚻⚷ 18:14, ☽△♅ 18:18, ☽⚻♄ 22:02, ☽⚼♇ 23:02, ♀⋕⚳ 23:26

27 Sa ☽⚻⚳ 1:49, ☽□♂ 2:17, ☽☍☿ 7:38, ♀∠♃ 11:47, ☽☍♆ 15:06, ☽⚻♃ 16:57, ☽⋕☿ 18:54, ☽⚼♅ 19:16, ☉∠♃ 21:03, ☽⚼♄ 22:57, ☽△♇ 23:49

28 Su ☽∥⚷ 0:45, ☽⋕♆ 5:21, ☉∥☽ 10:17, ☽∥♀ 13:49, ♀☌⚷ 16:29, ♀⊻♅ 16:54, ☽⚼♃ 17:39, ☽⋕⚳ 17:58, ☉☍☽ 18:49, ☽☍⚷ 19:39, ☽⚻♅ 19:41, ☽☍♀ 19:56, ☽△♄ 23:22

29 M ☽∥⚳ 2:16, ☽☍⚳ 4:04, ☽△♂ 5:13, ☽⋕♀ 8:02, ☉☌⚷ 8:10, ☉⊻♅ 8:35, ☉⋕☽ 11:39, ☽⚻☿ 14:17, ☽∥♆ 14:53, ☽⚻♆ 15:43, ☽△♃ 18:02, ☽⋕⚷ 19:37, ☽∥☿ 20:06

30 Tu ☽□♇ 0:09, ☿⋕⚷ 0:33, ☿☌♆ 3:25, ☽⚼♂ 6:13, ☽⚼♆ 15:46, ♀✱♄ 15:48, ☽⚼☿ 17:18, ☽⚻⚷ 19:54, ☽☍♅ 19:55, ☉⚻☽ 22:17, ☽□♄ 23:41

31 W ☽⚻♀ 0:21, ☿⊻♃ 3:55, ☽⚻⚳ 5:26, ☽⋕♅ 5:44, ☽∥♃ 7:13, ☽⚻♂ 7:18, ☉⋕♆ 14:52, ☽△♆ 16:00, ☿∠♅ 17:06, ♅⊻⚷ 18:12, ☽□♃ 18:53, ☉⋕☿ 19:14, ☽⚼⚷ 20:13, ☽△☿ 20:37, ☉✱♄ 21:06, ☿∥♆ 21:48, ☽∥♄ 23:35

April 2021

LONGITUDE

Day	Sid.Time	☉	☽	☽ 12 hour	Mean☊	True ☊	☿	♀	♂	⚳	♃	♄	⚷	♅	♆	♇
	h m s	° ' "	° ' "	° ' "	° '	° '	° '	° '	° '	° '	° '	° '	° '	° '	° '	° '
1 Th	12 38 17	11♈29 00	26♏19 46	3♐39 26	14♊05.4	12♊33.4	24♓29.2	12♈56.0	16♊26.6	15♈10.9	23♒13.7	11♒22.4	9♈00.8	9♉00.7	21♓25.0	26♑38.0
2 F	12 42 14	12 28 12	10♐54 44	18 05 18	14 02.3	12D 32.4	26 12.6	14 10.5	17 02.5	15 34.7	23 25.4	11 27.0	9 04.3	9 03.9	21 27.2	26 38.8
3 Sa	12 46 10	13 27 21	25 10 52	2♑11 22	13 59.1	12 32.8	27 57.3	15 25.0	17 38.4	15 58.6	23 37.0	11 31.6	9 07.8	9 07.0	21 29.3	26 39.5
4 Su	12 50 07	14 26 30	9♑06 49	15 57 18	13 55.9	12R 33.5	29 43.5	16 39.4	18 14.4	16 22.5	23 48.6	11 36.1	9 11.3	9 10.2	21 31.5	26 40.2
5 M	12 54 04	15 25 36	22 43 01	29 24 10	13 52.7	12 33.3	1♈31.1	17 53.9	18 50.4	16 46.3	24 00.0	11 40.5	9 14.8	9 13.5	21 33.6	26 40.9
6 Tu	12 58 00	16 24 41	6♒01 00	12♒33 47	13 49.6	12 31.5	3 20.1	19 08.3	19 26.4	17 10.2	24 11.4	11 44.8	9 18.4	9 16.7	21 35.7	26 41.6
7 W	13 01 57	17 23 43	19 02 46	25 28 12	13 46.4	12 27.3	5 10.5	20 22.7	20 02.4	17 34.1	24 22.6	11 49.1	9 21.9	9 20.0	21 37.8	26 42.2
8 Th	13 05 53	18 22 44	1♓50 18	8♓09 18	13 43.2	12 20.8	7 02.5	21 37.1	20 38.5	17 58.0	24 33.8	11 53.3	9 25.3	9 23.2	21 39.9	26 42.8
9 F	13 09 50	19 21 43	14 25 21	20 38 39	13 40.0	12 12.4	8 55.8	22 51.5	21 14.6	18 21.9	24 44.9	11 57.4	9 28.8	9 26.5	21 42.0	26 43.3
10 Sa	13 13 46	20 20 41	26 49 19	2♈57 31	13 36.8	12 02.9	10 50.6	24 05.9	21 50.7	18 45.7	24 55.8	12 01.4	9 32.3	9 29.8	21 44.1	26 43.9
11 Su	13 17 43	21 19 36	9♈03 23	15 07 02	13 33.7	11 53.0	12 46.9	25 20.2	22 26.8	19 09.6	25 06.7	12 05.4	9 35.8	9 33.1	21 46.1	26 44.4
12 M	13 21 39	22 18 29	21 08 37	27 08 18	13 30.5	11 43.9	14 44.6	26 34.5	23 03.0	19 33.5	25 17.5	12 09.3	9 39.2	9 36.5	21 48.1	26 44.9
13 Tu	13 25 36	23 17 20	3♉06 15	9♉02 43	13 27.3	11 36.2	16 43.7	27 48.8	23 39.2	19 57.4	25 28.2	12 13.0	9 42.7	9 39.8	21 50.2	26 45.3
14 W	13 29 33	24 16 10	14 57 54	20 52 06	13 24.1	11 30.6	18 44.2	29 03.1	24 15.4	20 21.3	25 38.7	12 16.8	9 46.1	9 43.2	21 52.2	26 45.7
15 Th	13 33 29	25 14 57	26 45 39	2♊38 54	13 21.0	11 27.2	20 45.9	0♉17.4	24 51.6	20 45.1	25 49.2	12 20.4	9 49.5	9 46.5	21 54.1	26 46.1
16 F	13 37 26	26 13 42	8♊32 17	14 26 13	13 17.8	11D 25.9	22 49.0	1 31.6	25 27.9	21 09.0	25 59.6	12 23.9	9 53.0	9 49.9	21 56.1	26 46.5
17 Sa	13 41 22	27 12 25	20 21 13	26 17 49	13 14.6	11 26.2	24 53.1	2 45.8	26 04.1	21 32.9	26 09.8	12 27.4	9 56.4	9 53.3	21 58.1	26 46.8
18 Su	13 45 19	28 11 06	2♋16 34	8♋18 04	13 11.4	11 27.5	26 58.4	4 00.1	26 40.4	21 56.7	26 20.0	12 30.7	9 59.8	9 56.7	22 00.0	26 47.1
19 M	13 49 15	29 09 45	14 22 56	20 31 46	13 08.2	11 29.0	29 04.5	5 14.2	27 16.7	22 20.6	26 30.0	12 34.0	10 03.1	10 00.1	22 01.9	26 47.4
20 Tu	13 53 12	0♉08 22	26 45 12	3♌03 50	13 05.1	11R 29.9	1♉11.4	6 28.4	27 53.0	22 44.4	26 39.9	12 37.2	10 06.5	10 03.5	22 03.8	26 47.6
21 W	13 57 08	1 06 56	9♌28 14	15 58 54	13 01.9	11 29.6	3 18.9	7 42.5	28 29.4	23 08.2	26 49.7	12 40.3	10 09.8	10 07.0	22 05.7	26 47.8
22 Th	14 01 05	2 05 28	22 36 15	29 20 39	12 58.7	11 27.7	5 26.8	8 56.7	29 05.7	23 32.1	26 59.4	12 43.4	10 13.2	10 10.4	22 07.5	26 48.0
23 F	14 05 02	3 03 58	6♍12 16	13♍11 10	12 55.5	11 24.2	7 34.7	10 10.8	29 42.1	23 55.9	27 09.0	12 46.3	10 16.5	10 13.8	22 09.4	26 48.2
24 Sa	14 08 58	4 02 26	20 17 11	27 30 02	12 52.4	11 19.5	9 42.5	11 24.8	0♋18.4	24 19.7	27 18.5	12 49.2	10 19.8	10 17.3	22 11.2	26 48.3
25 Su	14 12 55	5 00 51	4♎49 09	12♎13 51	12 49.2	11 14.1	11 49.9	12 38.9	0 54.8	24 43.4	27 27.8	12 51.9	10 23.1	10 20.7	22 13.0	26 48.4
26 M	14 16 51	5 59 15	19 43 11	27 16 07	12 46.0	11 08.9	13 56.5	13 52.9	1 31.2	25 07.2	27 37.0	12 54.6	10 26.3	10 24.2	22 14.8	26 48.4
27 Tu	14 20 48	6 57 36	4♏51 26	12♏27 54	12 42.8	11 04.5	16 02.1	15 06.9	2 07.6	25 31.0	27 46.1	12 57.2	10 29.5	10 27.6	22 16.5	26R 48.5
28 W	14 24 44	7 55 56	20 04 15	27 39 13	12 39.6	11 01.6	18 06.4	16 20.9	2 44.1	25 54.7	27 55.1	12 59.6	10 32.8	10 31.1	22 18.3	26 48.5
29 Th	14 28 41	8 54 14	5♐11 40	12♐40 33	12 36.5	11D 00.2	20 09.0	17 34.9	3 20.5	26 18.4	28 03.9	13 02.0	10 36.0	10 34.5	22 20.0	26 48.5
30 F	14 32 37	9♉52 31	20 05 02	27 24 22	12♊33.3	11♊00.4	22♉09.6	18♉48.9	3♋57.0	26♈42.1	28♒12.7	13♒04.4	10♈39.1	10♉38.0	22♓21.7	26♑48.4

1st of Month

Julian Day # 2459305.5
Obliquity 23°26'15"
SVP 4♓58'04"
GC 27♐08.2
Eris 23♈57.9

Day	⚴	⚵	⚶
1	7♓41.0	23♒41.2	8♍12.5R
6	9 12.2	23 55.4	7 31.8R
11	10 41.6	24 01.8	7 02.8R
16	12 09.0	24 00.0R	6 46.1R
21	13 34.1	23 49.9R	6 41.7
26	14 56.7	23 31.6R	6 49.3

DECLINATION and LATITUDE

Day	☉ Decl	☽ Decl	☽ Lat	☽12h Decl	☿ Decl	☿ Lat	♀ Decl	♀ Lat	♂ Decl	♂ Lat	⚳ Decl	⚳ Lat	♃ Decl	♃ Lat	♄ Decl	♄ Lat
1 Th	4N33	17S57	1N26	20S06	4S20	2S20	3N57	1S16	24N13	1N29	0S36	7S07	14S23	0S39	17S52	0S31
2 F	4 56	21 56	0 09	23 24	3 37	2 18	4 27	1 14	24 17	1 29	0 26	7 06	14 20	0 39	17 51	0 31
3 Sa	5 19	24 28	1S07	25 08	2 54	2 16	4 57	1 13	24 20	1 29	0 16	7 05	14 16	0 39	17 49	0 31
4 Su	5 42	25 24	2 17	25 17	2 09	2 13	5 26	1 12	24 24	1 29	0 06	7 05	14 12	0 40	17 48	0 31
5 M	6 04	24 47	3 18	23 55	1 23	2 10	5 56	1 11	24 27	1 29	0N04	7 04	14 09	0 40	17 47	0 31
6 Tu	6 27	22 45	4 06	21 17	0 37	2 07	6 25	1 09	24 30	1 29	0 13	7 03	14 05	0 40	17 46	0 32
7 W	6 50	19 33	4 41	17 37	0N11	2 02	6 55	1 08	24 32	1 29	0 23	7 02	14 02	0 40	17 45	0 32
8 Th	7 12	15 30	5 01	13 13	0 59	1 58	7 24	1 06	24 35	1 29	0 33	7 02	13 58	0 40	17 44	0 32
9 F	7 35	10 50	5 06	8 20	1 49	1 53	7 53	1 05	24 37	1 29	0 42	7 01	13 54	0 40	17 43	0 32
10 Sa	7 57	5 47	4 56	3 12	2 39	1 47	8 22	1 03	24 40	1 29	0 52	7 00	13 51	0 41	17 42	0 32
11 Su	8 19	0 35	4 33	2N01	3 30	1 41	8 51	1 02	24 42	1 29	1 02	6 59	13 47	0 41	17 41	0 32
12 M	8 41	4N35	3 57	7 06	4 22	1 34	9 19	1 00	24 44	1 29	1 11	6 59	13 44	0 41	17 40	0 32
13 Tu	9 03	9 32	3 12	11 53	5 14	1 27	9 47	0 58	24 45	1 28	1 21	6 58	13 41	0 41	17 39	0 32
14 W	9 25	14 07	2 18	16 13	6 07	1 20	10 15	0 57	24 47	1 28	1 30	6 57	13 37	0 41	17 38	0 33
15 Th	9 46	18 09	1 19	19 55	7 00	1 12	10 43	0 55	24 49	1 28	1 40	6 56	13 34	0 42	17 37	0 33
16 F	10 07	21 28	0 16	22 48	7 54	1 03	11 11	0 53	24 50	1 28	1 49	6 56	13 31	0 42	17 36	0 33
17 Sa	10 29	23 53	0N48	24 43	8 48	0 54	11 38	0 51	24 51	1 28	1 59	6 55	13 27	0 42	17 36	0 33
18 Su	10 50	25 16	1 51	25 31	9 42	0 45	12 05	0 49	24 52	1 28	2 08	6 54	13 24	0 42	17 35	0 33
19 M	11 11	25 28	2 49	25 06	10 36	0 35	12 32	0 47	24 53	1 28	2 17	6 54	13 21	0 42	17 34	0 33
20 Tu	11 31	24 25	3 41	23 26	11 30	0 25	12 58	0 45	24 53	1 28	2 27	6 53	13 18	0 43	17 33	0 33
21 W	11 52	22 07	4 24	20 31	12 23	0 15	13 24	0 43	24 54	1 28	2 36	6 52	13 14	0 43	17 32	0 33
22 Th	12 12	18 37	4 55	16 27	13 16	0 04	13 50	0 41	24 54	1 28	2 45	6 52	13 11	0 43	17 32	0 34
23 F	12 32	14 02	5 10	11 23	14 08	0N06	14 15	0 39	24 54	1 28	2 54	6 51	13 08	0 43	17 31	0 34
24 Sa	12 52	8 33	5 07	5 34	14 60	0 17	14 40	0 37	24 54	1 28	3 04	6 51	13 05	0 43	17 30	0 34
25 Su	13 12	2 27	4 45	0S44	15 50	0 28	15 05	0 34	24 54	1 27	3 13	6 50	13 02	0 44	17 30	0 34
26 M	13 31	3S57	4 04	7 08	16 38	0 39	15 29	0 32	24 53	1 27	3 22	6 49	12 59	0 44	17 29	0 34
27 Tu	13 50	10 14	3 05	13 12	17 25	0 49	15 53	0 30	24 53	1 27	3 31	6 49	12 56	0 44	17 28	0 34
28 W	14 09	15 58	1 52	18 27	18 11	0 60	16 17	0 28	24 52	1 27	3 40	6 48	12 53	0 44	17 28	0 34
29 Th	14 28	20 39	0 32	22 28	18 54	1 10	16 40	0 25	24 51	1 27	3 49	6 48	12 50	0 44	17 27	0 35
30 F	14N46	23S53	0S50	24S53	19N35	1N20	17N03	0S23	24N50	1N27	3N58	6S47	12S48	0S45	17S27	0S35

Day	⚷ Decl	⚷ Lat	♅ Decl	♅ Lat	♆ Decl	♆ Lat	♇ Decl	♇ Lat
1	5N43	2N20	14N07	0S25	4S23	1S04	22S09	1S21
6	5 50	2 20	14 12	0 25	4 19	1 05	22 09	1 22
11	5 56	2 20	14 17	0 24	4 15	1 05	22 09	1 23
16	6 03	2 19	14 22	0 24	4 11	1 05	22 10	1 23
21	6 10	2 19	14 28	0 24	4 08	1 05	22 10	1 24
26	6 16	2 19	14 33	0 24	4 04	1 05	22 11	1 25

Day	⚴ Decl	⚴ Lat	⚵ Decl	⚵ Lat	⚶ Decl	⚶ Lat	Eris Decl	Eris Lat
1	3N55	13N34	8S44	14N35	18N29	10N48	1S18	11S23
6	4 19	13 24	8 20	14 58	18 36	10 39	1 17	11 23
11	4 43	13 15	7 57	15 22	18 38	10 29	1 15	11 22
16	5 06	13 05	7 32	15 47	18 33	10 17	1 14	11 22
21	5 30	12 56	7 08	16 10	18 22	10 04	1 13	11 22
26	5 53	12 48	6 44	16 34	18 07	9 50	1 11	11 22

Moon Phenomena

Max/0 Decl (dy hr mn)
4 2:05 25S25
11 2:43 0 N
18 16:03 25N32
25 9:15 0 S

Perigee/Apogee (dy hr m kilometers)
14 17:47 a 406119
27 15:24 p 357383

PH (dy hr mn)
☾ 4 10:04 14♑51
● 12 2:32 22♈25
☽ 20 7:00 0♌25
○ 27 3:33 7♏06

Max/0 Lat (dy hr mn)
2 2:43 0 S
8 19:48 5S06
16 5:54 0 N
23 8:55 5N11
29 9:19 0 S

Void of Course Moon

Last Aspect	☽ Ingress
1 0:30 ♇ ⚹	♐ 1 6:00
3 5:25 ☿ □	♑ 3 8:14
5 7:06 ♇ ☌	♒ 5 13:05
7 10:06 ♃ ☌	♓ 7 20:32
9 23:49 ♇ ⚹	♈ 10 6:12
12 12:08 ☿ ☌	♉ 12 17:45
15 0:01 ♇ △	♊ 15 6:36
17 15:04 ☉ ⚹	♋ 17 19:26
20 0:05 ♇ ☍	♌ 20 6:12
22 12:06 ♂ ⚹	♍ 22 13:09
24 10:51 ♇ △	♎ 24 16:07
26 12:41 ♃ △	♏ 26 16:19
28 12:33 ♃ □	♐ 28 15:44
30 13:28 ♃ ⚹	♑ 30 16:17

DAILY ASPECTARIAN

1 Th ☉⚼☽ 0:16; ☽⚹♇ 0:30; ☽⚼♀ 2:52; ☽⚼⚳ 6:28; ☿#♀ 7:36; ♀#♆ 20:46; ☽⚻♅ 20:55; ☽△⚷ 20:56

2 F ☽⚹♄ 0:54; ☽∠♇ 1:13; ☽ǁ♇ 1:38; ☊D 2:42; ☉△☽ 2:47; ☿∠♄ 3:29; ☽△♀ 5:57; ☿⚹♇ 6:05; ☽△⚳ 8:01; ☽☍♂ 10:41; ☽□♆ 17:43; ☽⚹♃ 21:18; ☽⚼♅ 22:11; ☽#♂ 22:14

3 Sa ☽∠♄ 2:18; ☽⊻♇ 2:31; ☽□☿ 5:25; ♀☌⚳ 15:57; ☽∠♃ 23:28

4 Su ☽△♅ 0:06; ☽□⚷ 0:08; ☿ ♈ 3:42; ☽⊻♄ 4:22; ☉ǁ⚷ 6:11; ☉□☽ 10:04; ☊R 10:15; ☽□⚳ 13:08; ♃#♅ 13:45; ☽□♀ 14:34; ☽⚻♂ 16:47; ♀ǁ⚷ 17:40; ☽⚹♆ 21:56

5 M ☽⊻♃ 2:20; ☽#♂ 5:05; ☽☌♇ 7:06; ☽⚹☿ 18:20; ☽⚼♂ 20:59

6 Tu ☽∠♆ 1:04; ☽ǁ♇ 5:05; ☽□♅ 5:59; ☽⚹⚷ 6:02; ☉ǁ♀ 6:08; ☿#⚳ 9:47; ☽☌♄ 10:33; ♀⚹♂ 11:19; ☉⚹☽ 20:41; ☽⚹⚳ 21:10; ♃∠⚷ 21:36

7 W ☽△♂ 1:56; ☽∠☿ 2:27; ☽⚹♀ 2:45; ☽⊻♆ 4:50; ☉☌⚳ 7:05; ☿ǁ⚳ 7:37; ☽∠⚷ 9:58; ☽☌♃ 10:06; ☽ǁ♄ 11:16; ☽⊻♇ 14:20

8 Th ♀⊻♆ 0:56; ☽∠⚳ 2:12; ☉∠☽ 3:10; ☽#♅ 6:44; ☽ǁ♃ 8:15; ☽∠♀ 10:04; ☽⊻☿ 11:37; ☽⚹♅ 14:25; ☽⊻⚷ 14:29; ☽∠♇ 18:49; ☽⊻♄ 19:15

9 F ☿⊻♅ 6:38; ☿☌⚷ 7:09; ☽⊻⚳ 7:51; ☉⊻☽ 10:20; ☿∠♃ 11:23; ☽#♀ 12:56; ☽□♂ 13:50; ☽☌♆ 14:05; ☉#☽ 14:33; ☽⊻♀ 18:06; ♂□♆ 19:19; ☽∠♅ 19:27; ☽⊻♃ 20:16; ☽#⚷ 23:24; ☽⚹♇ 23:49

10 Sa ☽∠♄ 0:24; ☽ǁ♆ 7:04; ☽#☿ 12:30; ☿⚹♄ 15:10; ♀⚹♃ 18:54; ☽#⚳ 22:02

11 Su ☽⊻♅ 0:59; ☽☌⚷ 1:04; ☽∠♃ 2:07; ☽⚹♄ 6:02; ☽ǁ⚳ 7:42; ☽☌☿ 8:47; ☉⊻♆ 11:11; ☽☌⚳ 20:44; ☿#♆ 20:47; ☽#♆ 22:25; ☽ǁ☿ 22:45

12 M ☽⊻♆ 1:19; ☉☌☽ 2:32; ♀□♇ 3:22; ☽⚹♂ 4:01; ☽ǁ⚷ 6:35; ☽⚹♃ 8:25; ⚵ R 10:14; ☽□♇ 11:13; ☽☌♀ 12:08; ☉ǁ☽ 21:21

13 Tu ☽ǁ♀ 1:23; ☽∠♆ 7:33; ☽∠♂ 11:48; ☽☌♅ 13:19; ☽⊻⚷ 13:25; ☽□♄ 18:31; ☿ǁ⚷ 21:04; ☽#♃ 21:16; ☉⚹♂ 23:10

14 W ☽ǁ♅ 1:12; ☽⊻☿ 9:15; ☽⊻⚳ 11:20; ☽⚹♆ 14:05; ♀ ♉ 18:23; ☽⊻♂ 19:55; ☽∠⚷ 20:02; ♂∠♅ 20:18; ☽#♄ 20:35; ☉⊻☽ 20:38; ☽□♃ 22:03; ☿☌⚳ 23:48

15 Th ☽△♇ 0:01; ☽⊻♀ 8:02; ☿⊻♆ 13:33; ☉⚹♃ 17:00; ☽∠⚳ 18:58; ☽∠☿ 22:13

16 F ☽⊻♅ 2:39; ☽⚹⚷ 2:45; ☊D 5:53; ☉∠☽ 5:58; ☽#♇ 5:59; ☽⚼♇ 6:35; ☽△♄ 7:54; ☉□♇ 13:28; ☽∠♀ 18:08

17 Sa ☽⚹⚳ 2:30; ☽□♆ 3:16; ♂△♃ 5:15; ☽∠♅ 9:12; ☽⚹☿ 11:06; ☽△♃ 11:54; ☽☌♂ 12:09; ☽⚻♇ 12:59; ☽⚼♄ 14:24; ☽ǁ♂ 14:37; ☉⚹☽ 15:04; ☿⚹♃ 16:01; ☿⚹♂ 19:10; ☿□♇ 21:50

18 Su ⚳⊻♆ 3:35; ☽⚹♀ 3:50; ♂⚻♇ 4:27; ☽⚹♅ 15:20; ☽□⚷ 15:26; ☽⚼♃ 18:15; ☽⚻♄ 20:25

19 M ☉☌☿ 1:51; ☿ ♉ 10:30; ♂⚼♄ 12:34; ☽△♆ 14:57; ☽□⚳ 16:02; ☽ǁ♂ 16:31; ☉ ♉ 20:35; ☽⚻♃ 23:50

20 Tu ☽☍♇ 0:05; ☉ǁ☿ 1:02; ☽⊻♂ 2:16; ☊R 6:55; ☉□☽ 7:00; ⚶D 7:07; ☽□☿ 10:09; ♀∠♆ 11:45; ♀#♃ 15:56; ♃⊻♇ 19:10; ☽⚼♆ 19:34; ☽□♀ 20:22; ☽#♇ 23:37

21 W ☽□♅ 1:12; ☽△⚷ 1:18; ☽☍♄ 5:57; ☽∠♂ 7:47; ☿#♃ 21:51; ☽⚻♆ 23:08

22 Th ☽△⚳ 1:43; ☽⚼⚷ 4:42; ☽#♄ 6:12; ☽⚻♇ 7:30; ☽☍♃ 7:56; ☽⚹♂ 12:06; ☉△☽ 18:07; ☿∠♆ 19:11; ☽ǁ♅ 21:45; ☽ǁ♀ 23:00; ☽ǁ☿ 23:33

23 F ♀☌♅ 1:02; ♀⊻⚷ 1:56; ☽△☿ 2:48; ☽#♃ 4:12; ☽⚼⚳ 4:51; ☿ǁ♀ 6:19; ☉ǁ☽ 6:30; ☽△♅ 6:58; ☽⚻⚷ 7:03; ☽△♀ 7:31; ☽⚼♇ 9:38; ☿ǁ♅ 10:17; ☽⚻♄ 11:20; ♂ ♋ 11:50; ♀ǁ♅ 14:38; ☉⚼☽ 21:45

24 Sa ☽☍♆ 3:11; ☿☌♅ 6:43; ☽⚻⚳ 6:56; ☿⊻⚷ 7:12; ☽⚼♅ 8:22; ☽⚼☿ 8:39; ☽ǁ⚷ 9:21; ☽△♇ 10:51; ☽⚼♀ 11:09; ☽⚻♃ 11:48; ☽⚼♄ 12:34; ☉#♃ 13:56; ☽□♂ 17:20; ☽#♆ 17:44; ☽ǁ⚳ 21:10

25 Su ☉⚻☽ 0:20; ♀□♄ 4:23; ☽⚻♅ 9:00; ☽☍⚷ 9:03; ☿□♄ 11:59; ☽⚼♃ 12:30; ☽△♄ 13:04; ☽⚻☿ 13:14; ☽⚻♀ 13:49; ☽#⚳ 21:46; ☿☌♀ 22:20

26 M ☽ǁ♆ 0:28; ☽⚻♆ 4:02; ☽#⚷ 8:44; ☽☍⚳ 8:49; ☽□♇ 11:16; ☽△♃ 12:41; ☽△♂ 19:31

27 Tu ☿#♄ 1:29; ☉☍☽ 3:33; ☽⚼♆ 3:49; ☉∠♆ 8:01; ☽☍♅ 8:52; ☽⚻⚷ 8:55; ☽ǁ♃ 10:49; ☽□♄ 12:48; ☉#☽ 15:34; ☽☍♀ 17:36; ☿∠♂ 17:52; ☽#♅ 17:54; ♇R 20:04; ☽⚼♂ 20:09; ☽☍☿ 20:25

28 W ☽#♀ 1:36; ☽△♆ 3:32; ☽ǁ♄ 7:03; ☽⚼⚷ 8:41; ☽⚻⚳ 9:29; ☽⚹♇ 10:40; ☽□♃ 12:33; ☽#☿ 12:33; ☽⚻♂ 20:55

29 Th ☉⚻☽ 6:21; ☽⚻♅ 8:39; ☽△⚷ 8:41; ☊D 9:17; ☽ǁ♇ 9:59; ☽⚼⚳ 10:04; ☽∠♇ 10:36; ☉ǁ♅ 11:50; ☽⚹♄ 12:37; ☽⚻♀ 21:45

30 F ☿⚹♆ 2:28; ☽□♆ 3:43; ☽⚻☿ 3:55; ♀∠♂ 5:11; ⚳□♇ 6:20; ☉⚼☽ 8:24; ☽⚼♅ 9:07; ⚳#♆ 10:05; ☽#♂ 10:59; ☽⊻♇ 11:01; ☽△⚳ 11:09; ☽∠♄ 13:08; ☽⚹♃ 13:28; ☉☌♅ 19:55; ☉⊻⚷ 20:18; ☽☍♂ 23:52

LONGITUDE

Day	Sid.Time	☉	☽	☽ 12 hour	Mean☊	True☊	☿	♀	♂	⚳	♃	♄	⚷	♅	♆	♇
	h m s	° ' "	° ' "	° ' "	° '	° '	° '	° '	° '	° '	° '	° '	° '	° '	° '	° '
1 Sa	14 36 34	10♉50 46	4♑38 03	11♑45 44	12♊30.1	11♊01.5	24♉08.0	20♉02.8	4♋33.4	27♈05.8	28♒21.2	13♒06.6	10♈42.3	10♉41.4	22♓23.3	26♑48.3
2 Su	14 40 31	11 48 59	18 47 13	25 42 27	12 26.9	11 03.0	26 03.9	21 16.7	5 09.9	27 29.5	28 29.7	13 08.7	10 45.4	10 44.9	22 25.0	26R 48.2
3 M	14 44 27	12 47 11	2♒31 31	9♒14 37	12 23.8	11R 04.1	27 57.0	22 30.6	5 46.4	27 53.2	28 38.0	13 10.7	10 48.5	10 48.4	22 26.6	26 48.1
4 Tu	14 48 24	13 45 22	15 51 58	22 23 55	12 20.6	11 04.5	29 47.2	23 44.5	6 22.9	28 16.8	28 46.2	13 12.7	10 51.6	10 51.8	22 28.2	26 48.0
5 W	14 52 20	14 43 31	28 50 49	5♓13 04	12 17.4	11 03.7	1♊34.2	24 58.4	6 59.4	28 40.5	28 54.3	13 14.5	10 54.7	10 55.3	22 29.8	26 47.8
6 Th	14 56 17	15 41 39	11♓31 02	17 45 08	12 14.2	11 01.7	3 18.0	26 12.3	7 36.0	29 04.1	29 02.2	13 16.2	10 57.7	10 58.7	22 31.3	26 47.5
7 F	15 00 13	16 39 45	23 55 45	0♈03 15	12 11.1	10 58.7	4 58.3	27 26.1	8 12.5	29 27.7	29 10.0	13 17.9	11 00.7	11 02.2	22 32.9	26 47.3
8 Sa	15 04 10	17 37 49	6♈08 01	12 10 23	12 07.9	10 55.1	6 35.1	28 39.9	8 49.1	29 51.3	29 17.6	13 19.4	11 03.7	11 05.6	22 34.3	26 47.0
9 Su	15 08 06	18 35 52	18 10 39	24 09 09	12 04.7	10 51.4	8 08.2	29 53.7	9 25.6	0♉14.8	29 25.1	13 20.9	11 06.6	11 09.1	22 35.8	26 46.7
10 M	15 12 03	19 33 54	0♉06 10	6♉01 58	12 01.5	10 47.9	9 37.6	1♊07.5	10 02.2	0 38.3	29 32.5	13 22.2	11 09.6	11 12.5	22 37.3	26 46.4
11 Tu	15 16 00	20 31 54	11 56 49	17 50 59	11 58.3	10 45.1	11 03.2	2 21.3	10 38.8	1 01.8	29 39.7	13 23.5	11 12.5	11 15.9	22 38.7	26 46.0
12 W	15 19 56	21 29 53	23 44 45	29 38 21	11 55.2	10 43.2	12 25.0	3 35.0	11 15.5	1 25.3	29 46.7	13 24.7	11 15.3	11 19.4	22 40.1	26 45.6
13 Th	15 23 53	22 27 50	5♊32 05	11♊26 14	11 52.0	10D 42.3	13 42.7	4 48.8	11 52.1	1 48.8	29 53.6	13 25.7	11 18.2	11 22.8	22 41.5	26 45.2
14 F	15 27 49	23 25 46	17 21 07	23 17 04	11 48.8	10 42.3	14 56.5	6 02.5	12 28.7	2 12.2	0♓00.4	13 26.7	11 21.0	11 26.2	22 42.8	26 44.8
15 Sa	15 31 46	24 23 40	29 14 27	5♋13 37	11 45.6	10 43.1	16 06.2	7 16.2	13 05.4	2 35.6	0 07.0	13 27.6	11 23.8	11 29.6	22 44.1	26 44.3
16 Su	15 35 42	25 21 33	11♋14 59	17 18 59	11 42.5	10 44.3	17 11.8	8 29.9	13 42.1	2 58.9	0 13.4	13 28.4	11 26.5	11 33.0	22 45.4	26 43.8
17 M	15 39 39	26 19 23	23 26 04	29 36 40	11 39.3	10 45.6	18 13.2	9 43.5	14 18.8	3 22.3	0 19.7	13 29.0	11 29.2	11 36.4	22 46.7	26 43.3
18 Tu	15 43 35	27 17 13	5♌51 18	12♌10 24	11 36.1	10 46.8	19 10.4	10 57.2	14 55.5	3 45.6	0 25.9	13 29.6	11 31.9	11 39.7	22 47.9	26 42.8
19 W	15 47 32	28 15 00	18 34 28	25 03 51	11 32.9	10R 47.5	20 03.2	12 10.8	15 32.2	4 08.9	0 31.8	13 30.1	11 34.6	11 43.1	22 49.1	26 42.2
20 Th	15 51 29	29 12 46	1♍39 06	8♍20 25	11 29.8	10 47.6	20 51.6	13 24.4	16 08.9	4 32.1	0 37.6	13 30.5	11 37.2	11 46.4	22 50.3	26 41.6
21 F	15 55 25	0♊10 30	15 08 06	22 02 19	11 26.6	10 47.3	21 35.6	14 38.0	16 45.6	4 55.3	0 43.3	13 30.8	11 39.8	11 49.8	22 51.4	26 41.0
22 Sa	15 59 22	1 08 12	29 03 05	6♎10 19	11 23.4	10 46.5	22 15.1	15 51.5	17 22.3	5 18.5	0 48.8	13 30.9	11 42.3	11 53.1	22 52.5	26 40.3
23 Su	16 03 18	2 05 53	13♎23 43	20 42 53	11 20.2	10 45.6	22 50.0	17 05.0	17 59.1	5 41.6	0 54.1	13R 31.0	11 44.8	11 56.4	22 53.6	26 39.6
24 M	16 07 15	3 03 32	28 07 12	5♏35 54	11 17.0	10 44.7	23 20.3	18 18.6	18 35.8	6 04.7	0 59.2	13 31.0	11 47.3	11 59.7	22 54.7	26 38.9
25 Tu	16 11 11	4 01 10	13♏08 02	20 42 34	11 13.9	10 44.0	23 45.9	19 32.0	19 12.6	6 27.8	1 04.2	13 30.9	11 49.7	12 02.9	22 55.7	26 38.2
26 W	16 15 08	4 58 46	28 18 22	5♐54 13	11 10.7	10D 43.6	24 06.8	20 45.5	19 49.3	6 50.8	1 09.0	13 30.7	11 52.1	12 06.2	22 56.7	26 37.5
27 Th	16 19 04	5 56 21	13♐28 55	21 01 19	11 07.5	10 43.5	24 22.9	21 59.0	20 26.1	7 13.8	1 13.7	13 30.4	11 54.5	12 09.4	22 57.7	26 36.7
28 F	16 23 01	6 53 56	28 30 21	5♑55 02	11 04.3	10 43.6	24 34.3	23 12.4	21 02.9	7 36.7	1 18.2	13 30.0	11 56.8	12 12.7	22 58.6	26 35.9
29 Sa	16 26 58	7 51 29	13♑14 34	20 28 18	11 01.2	10 43.9	24R 41.0	24 25.8	21 39.7	7 59.7	1 22.5	13 29.5	11 59.1	12 15.9	22 59.5	26 35.1
30 Su	16 30 54	8 49 01	27 35 45	4♒36 37	10 58.0	10 44.1	24 43.0	25 39.2	22 16.5	8 22.5	1 26.6	13 28.9	12 01.3	12 19.1	23 00.4	26 34.3
31 M	16 34 51	9♊46 32	11♒30 45	18 18 09	10♊54.8	10♊44.2	24♊40.5	26♊52.6	22♋53.3	8♉45.4	1♓30.6	13♒28.3	12♈03.6	12♉22.2	23♓01.2	26♑33.4

1st of Month

Julian Day #
2459335.5
Obliquity
23°26'04"
SVP 4♓58'00"
GC 27♐08.2
Eris 24♈17.4

Day	⚴	Day	⚵	Day	⚶
1	16♓16.8	1	23♐04.9R	1	7♍08.5
6	17 34.0	6	22 30.2R	6	7 38.8
11	18 48.2	11	21 47.8R	11	8 19.4
16	19 58.9	16	20 58.2R	16	9 09.8
21	21 06.0	21	20 02.5R	21	10 09.3
26	22 09.1	26	19 01.7R	26	11 17.2
31	23 08.1	31	17 57.0R	31	12 32.8

DECLINATION and LATITUDE

Day	☉ Decl	☽ Decl	☽ Lat	☽12h Decl	☿ Decl	☿ Lat	♀ Decl	♀ Lat	♂ Decl	♂ Lat	⚳ Decl	⚳ Lat	♃ Decl	♃ Lat	♄ Decl	♄ Lat
1 Sa	15N05	25S27	2S06	25S35	20N15	1N29	17N25	0S21	24N48	1N27	4N07	6S46	12S45	0S45	17S26	0S35
2 Su	15 23	25 18	3 13	24 37	20 51	1 38	17 47	0 18	24 47	1 27	4 15	6 46	12 42	0 45	17 26	0 35
3 M	15 40	23 35	4 06	22 14	21 26	1 46	18 08	0 16	24 45	1 27	4 24	6 45	12 39	0 45	17 25	0 35
4 Tu	15 58	20 36	4 44	18 44	21 57	1 54	18 29	0 14	24 43	1 26	4 33	6 45	12 37	0 46	17 25	0 35
5 W	16 15	16 40	5 07	14 26	22 27	2 01	18 50	0 11	24 41	1 26	4 42	6 44	12 34	0 46	17 24	0 35
6 Th	16 32	12 05	5 14	9 37	22 54	2 07	19 09	0 09	24 39	1 26	4 50	6 44	12 32	0 46	17 24	0 35
7 F	16 49	7 06	5 06	4 31	23 18	2 13	19 29	0 06	24 37	1 26	4 59	6 43	12 29	0 46	17 24	0 36
8 Sa	17 05	1 55	4 44	0N41	23 40	2 17	19 48	0 04	24 34	1 26	5 08	6 43	12 27	0 46	17 23	0 36
9 Su	17 21	3N16	4 10	5 49	23 59	2 21	20 06	0 02	24 32	1 26	5 16	6 42	12 24	0 47	17 23	0 36
10 M	17 37	8 18	3 26	10 42	24 16	2 24	20 24	0N01	24 29	1 26	5 25	6 42	12 22	0 47	17 23	0 36
11 Tu	17 53	13 00	2 32	15 11	24 31	2 26	20 41	0 03	24 26	1 25	5 33	6 41	12 20	0 47	17 23	0 36
12 W	18 08	17 13	1 32	19 05	24 43	2 28	20 58	0 06	24 23	1 25	5 42	6 41	12 17	0 47	17 22	0 36
13 Th	18 23	20 45	0 29	22 13	24 54	2 28	21 14	0 08	24 19	1 25	5 50	6 40	12 15	0 48	17 22	0 36
14 F	18 38	23 27	0N37	24 25	25 02	2 27	21 29	0 11	24 16	1 25	5 58	6 40	12 13	0 48	17 22	0 37
15 Sa	18 52	25 07	1 41	25 32	25 08	2 26	21 44	0 13	24 12	1 25	6 07	6 39	12 11	0 48	17 22	0 37
16 Su	19 06	25 38	2 41	25 27	25 12	2 24	21 59	0 16	24 08	1 25	6 15	6 39	12 09	0 48	17 22	0 37
17 M	19 20	24 56	3 35	24 07	25 15	2 20	22 12	0 18	24 04	1 24	6 23	6 39	12 07	0 49	17 22	0 37
18 Tu	19 33	23 00	4 20	21 36	25 15	2 16	22 25	0 21	23 60	1 24	6 31	6 38	12 05	0 49	17 22	0 37
19 W	19 46	19 54	4 54	17 57	25 14	2 10	22 38	0 23	23 56	1 24	6 39	6 38	12 03	0 49	17 22	0 37
20 Th	19 59	15 45	5 13	13 20	25 11	2 04	22 50	0 25	23 51	1 24	6 47	6 37	12 01	0 49	17 22	0 37
21 F	20 11	10 43	5 16	7 55	25 07	1 57	23 01	0 28	23 46	1 24	6 55	6 37	11 59	0 50	17 22	0 38
22 Sa	20 23	4 59	5 01	1 56	25 01	1 49	23 11	0 30	23 41	1 24	7 03	6 37	11 58	0 50	17 22	0 38
23 Su	20 35	1S11	4 27	4S19	24 54	1 40	23 21	0 33	23 36	1 23	7 11	6 36	11 56	0 50	17 22	0 38
24 M	20 46	7 27	3 35	10 30	24 46	1 29	23 30	0 35	23 31	1 23	7 19	6 36	11 54	0 50	17 22	0 38
25 Tu	20 57	13 26	2 27	16 11	24 36	1 18	23 39	0 37	23 26	1 23	7 26	6 35	11 53	0 51	17 22	0 38
26 W	21 08	18 40	1 09	20 51	24 25	1 07	23 47	0 40	23 20	1 23	7 34	6 35	11 51	0 51	17 23	0 38
27 Th	21 18	22 40	0S15	24 05	24 13	0 54	23 54	0 42	23 15	1 23	7 42	6 35	11 50	0 51	17 23	0 38
28 F	21 28	25 03	1 37	25 34	23 60	0 40	24 00	0 44	23 09	1 22	7 49	6 34	11 49	0 51	17 23	0 39
29 Sa	21 37	25 37	2 51	25 14	23 45	0 26	24 06	0 47	23 03	1 22	7 57	6 34	11 47	0 52	17 23	0 39
30 Su	21 46	24 26	3 52	23 16	23 30	0 11	24 11	0 49	22 57	1 22	8 05	6 34	11 46	0 52	17 24	0 39
31 M	21N55	21S46	4S37	19S60	23N15	0S05	24N15	0N51	22N50	1N22	8N12	6S33	11S45	0S52	17S24	0S39

Day	⚷ Decl	⚷ Lat	♅ Decl	♅ Lat	♆ Decl	♆ Lat	♇ Decl	♇ Lat
1	6N22	2N19	14N39	0S24	4S01	1S05	22S11	1S25
6	6 28	2 19	14 44	0 24	3 58	1 05	22 12	1 26
11	6 34	2 19	14 49	0 24	3 55	1 06	22 13	1 27
16	6 40	2 19	14 55	0 24	3 53	1 06	22 14	1 27
21	6 45	2 19	14 60	0 24	3 51	1 06	22 15	1 28
26	6 50	2 20	15 05	0 24	3 49	1 06	22 17	1 28
31	6N55	2N20	15N10	0S24	3S47	1S06	22S18	1S29

Day	⚴ Decl	⚴ Lat	⚵ Decl	⚵ Lat	⚶ Decl	⚶ Lat	Eris Decl	Eris Lat
1	6N15	12N39	6S20	16N56	17N46	9N35	1S10	11S22
6	6 37	12 31	5 57	17 18	17 21	9 21	1 09	11 22
11	6 58	12 22	5 36	17 37	16 52	9 06	1 08	11 22
16	7 17	12 14	5 16	17 54	16 20	8 52	1 07	11 22
21	7 36	12 06	4 57	18 09	15 44	8 37	1 06	11 22
26	7 52	11 58	4 41	18 21	15 05	8 23	1 05	11 22
31	8N08	11N49	4S28	18N30	14N23	8N10	1S05	11S23

Moon Phenomena

Max/0 Decl
dy hr mn
1 9:40 25S35
8 8:51 0 N
15 22:24 25N38
22 19:29 0 S
28 19:26 25S39

Perigee/Apogee
dy hr m kilometers
11 21:54 a 406512
26 1:51 p 357312

PH dy hr mn
☾ 3 19:51 13♒35
● 11 19:01 21♉18
☽ 19 19:14 29♌01
○ 26 11:15 5♐26
● 26 11:20 T 1.009

Max/0 Lat
dy hr mn
5 23:05 5S14
13 10:31 0 N
20 16:21 5N17
26 19:38 0 S

Void of Course Moon

Last Aspect	☽ Ingress
2 14:39 ☿ △	♒ 2 19:32
5 0:07 ♃ ☌	♓ 5 2:10
7 7:37 ♀ ⚹	♈ 7 11:54
9 22:51 ♃ ⚹	♉ 9 23:48
12 12:24 ♃ □	♊ 12 12:44
14 10:52 ♆ □	♋ 15 1:32
17 6:24 ♇ ☍	♌ 17 12:45
19 19:14 ☉ □	♍ 19 21:00
21 19:57 ♇ △	♎ 22 1:37
23 21:38 ♇ □	♏ 24 3:02
25 21:21 ♇ ⚹	♐ 26 2:40
27 17:37 ☿ ☍	♑ 28 2:25
29 22:16 ♇ ☌	♒ 30 4:05

DAILY ASPECTARIAN

1 Sa
☽⚼♀ 0:45
♀#♄ 1:13
☽⚼☿ 8:45
☽△♅ 10:14
☽□⚷ 10:15
☉△☽ 11:13
☽⚺♄ 14:20
☽∠♃ 14:51
☿∠⚷ 20:02

2 Su
☽△♀ 4:43
☽⚹♆ 6:17
☿△♇ 9:20
☽#♂ 9:48
☽☌♇ 13:55
☽△☿ 14:39
☽□⚳ 15:34
☽⚺♃ 17:04
♀⚹♆ 22:40
☿⚺⚳ 22:58

3 M
☽⚻♂ 6:03
☽∠♆ 8:47
☿□♃ 9:35
☉□♄ 10:03
♅⚺⚷ 10:47
☽∥♇ 12:17
☽⚹⚷ 14:53
☽□♅ 14:53
☽#☿ 15:33
☽☌♄ 19:09
☉□☽ 19:51
☊ R 20:05

4 Tu
☿ ♊ 2:50
☽⚼♂ 10:37
☿#♇ 11:30
☽⚺♆ 12:09
☽#♀ 12:25
☽□♀ 16:01
☽∠⚷ 18:30
☽∥♄ 19:48
☽⚺♇ 20:10
☽⚹⚳ 23:40

5 W
☽☌♃ 0:07
☉#☽ 2:08
☽□☿ 5:56
☽#♅ 10:30
☽△♂ 16:09
♀∠⚷ 19:04
⚳⚹♃ 21:08
☽∥♃ 21:45
☽⚺⚷ 22:56
☽⚹♅ 22:58

6 Th
☽∠♇ 0:32
☽⚺♄ 3:22
☽∠⚳ 5:03
☉⚹☽ 8:42
♀△♇ 11:26
☽☌♆ 21:18

7 F
☽#⚷ 2:49
☽∠♅ 4:08
☽⚹♇ 5:35
☽⚹♀ 7:37
☽∠♄ 8:34
☽#⚳ 9:35
☽⚺♃ 10:22
☽⚺⚳ 11:12
☽∥♆ 14:37
☉∠☽ 16:29

8 Sa
☽⚹☿ 1:02
☽□♂ 5:36
⚳ ♉ 8:55
☽☌⚷ 9:50
☽⚺♅ 9:54
♀□♃ 13:39
☽⚹♄ 14:19
☽∠♃ 16:24
☽∠♀ 16:41

9 Su
☉⚺☽ 0:55
♀ ♊ 2:02
☉#♄ 2:28
☽#♆ 3:09
☽⚺♆ 8:53
☽∥⚳ 9:42
♀⚺⚳ 10:04
☽∠☿ 11:24
☽∥⚷ 15:30
☽□♇ 17:17
☽⚹♃ 22:51

10 M
☽☌⚳ 1:07
☽⚺♀ 2:18
☿⚺♂ 11:49
☽∠♆ 15:15
☿∥♂ 16:49
☽#♃ 20:26
☽⚹♂ 21:13
☽⚺☿ 21:57
☽⚺⚷ 22:30
☽☌♅ 22:37

11 Tu
☿⚹⚷ 2:45
☽□♄ 2:56
☿⚺♅ 3:49
☽∥♅ 10:01
☿⚼♇ 12:22
☉☌☽ 19:01
☽⚹♆ 21:48
♂□⚷ 23:55

12 W
☽#♄ 0:59
♂⚹♅ 2:49
☽∠⚷ 5:08
☽∠♂ 5:24
☽△♇ 6:08
☉∥☽ 6:11
☽□♃ 12:24
☽⚺⚳ 16:10
☿△♄ 18:35
☽☌♀ 22:22

13 Th
☽∥♀ 4:04
☉⚹♆ 5:46
☊ D 10:29
☽⚹⚷ 11:46
☽⚺♅ 11:56
☽#♇ 12:04
☽⚼♇ 12:38
☽⚺♂ 13:35
☽△♄ 16:04
☽☌☿ 18:34
♃ ♓ 22:37
☽∠⚳ 23:41

14 F
☽∥♂ 9:32
☽□♆ 10:52
☉⚺☽ 13:23
☽∠♅ 18:27
☽⚻♇ 18:58
☽⚼♄ 22:26

15 Sa
☽∥☿ 0:23
☽△♃ 1:47
☽⚹⚳ 6:57
♂⚻♄ 14:50
☽⚺♀ 17:54
☉∠☽ 22:05

16 Su
☽□⚷ 0:23
☽⚹♅ 0:36
☽⚻♄ 4:25
☽☌♂ 5:07
☽⚼♃ 7:56
☽⚺☿ 12:52
☽∥☿ 17:50
☽△♆ 22:43

17 M
☽∠♀ 2:48
♀#♇ 3:27
☉∠⚷ 4:17
☉⚹☽ 6:06
☿∠⚳ 6:09
☽☍♇ 6:24
☉△♇ 9:50
☽∥♂ 13:08
☽⚻♃ 13:30
☽□⚳ 19:52
☽∠☿ 20:31

18 Tu
☽⚼♆ 3:43
☽∥♀ 4:53
☽#♇ 6:48
☽⚹♀ 10:44
☽△⚷ 10:50
☽□♅ 11:05
♀⚹⚷ 11:45
☽☍♄ 14:30
♀⚺♅ 14:32
♀⚼♇ 14:45
☽⚺♂ 18:02
♂⚼♃ 23:44

19 W
☉∥☽ 0:52
☽⚹☿ 2:56
☽⚻♆ 7:53
⚳∥⚷ 13:03
☽⚼⚷ 14:49
☽⚻♇ 14:59
☽#♄ 15:21
☊ R 19:11
☉□☽ 19:14
☽☍♃ 22:08
☽∠♂ 23:03

20 Th
♀△♄ 2:00
☽∥♅ 3:56
☽△⚳ 5:21
☽⚻⚷ 17:52
☽⚼♇ 17:56
☽△♅ 18:10
☽#♃ 18:14
☉ ♊ 19:38
☽⚻♄ 21:09
☽□♀ 23:02

21 F
☽⚹♂ 2:58
☽⚼⚳ 8:35
☽□☿ 11:48
☽☍♆ 13:26
☉□♃ 15:05
☽∥⚳ 15:47
☽∥⚷ 16:47
☽△♇ 19:57
☽⚼♅ 20:18
☽⚼♄ 23:05

22 Sa
☽⚻♃ 3:00
☉△☽ 3:47
☽#♆ 4:33
☽⚻⚳ 10:51
☽☍⚷ 21:16
☽⚻♅ 21:35

23 Su
☽△♄ 0:12
☿□♆ 2:44
☽⚼♃ 4:09
☉⚼☽ 6:31
☽△♀ 6:37
☽□♂ 7:52
♄ R 9:20
☽∥♆ 10:06
☽⚻♆ 15:34
☽△☿ 16:00
☽#⚷ 21:29
☽□♇ 21:38
☽#⚳ 23:27

24 M
♀∥♂ 1:28
☽△♃ 4:38
☉⚻☽ 8:29
☽⚼♀ 9:05
♀⚺♂ 11:17
☽☍⚳ 13:06
☽⚼♆ 15:42
☽⚼☿ 16:52
☽∥♃ 17:34
☽⚻⚷ 21:55
☽☍♅ 22:16

25 Tu
☽□♄ 0:36
☽#♅ 7:03
☽△♂ 10:02
☽⚻♀ 11:02
☉∠♂ 13:08
☽△♆ 15:31
☽⚻☿ 17:14
☽∥♄ 17:37
☽⚹♇ 21:21
☽⚼⚷ 21:43

26 W
☽□♃ 4:31
☽⚼♂ 10:43
☉☍☽ 11:15
☽⚻⚳ 13:50
☉#☽ 14:19
☊ D 19:23
☽∠♇ 21:02
☽∥♇ 21:12
☽△⚷ 21:30
☽⚻♅ 21:53

27 Th
☽⚹♄ 0:02
☽#♂ 4:21
♀∠⚳ 7:03
☽#♀ 10:44
☽⚻♂ 11:32
☽#☿ 12:17
☽⚼⚳ 14:18
☽☍♀ 14:44
☽□♆ 15:07
☽☍☿ 17:37
♀□♆ 19:26
☽⚺♇ 20:56
☽⚼♅ 21:55
☿∥♀ 23:19
☽∠♄ 23:59

28 F
☽⚹♃ 4:32
☉⚻☽ 14:33
☽△⚳ 15:10
☽□⚷ 21:55
☽△♅ 22:23
⚳∠♆ 23:49

29 Sa
☽⚺♄ 0:25
☽∠♃ 5:12
☿☌♀ 5:14
☉⚺⚳ 5:40
☽☍♂ 14:37
☽⚹♆ 16:15
☉⚼☽ 17:09
☽⚻☿ 19:08
☽⚻♀ 20:24
☽☌♇ 22:16
☿ R 22:35

30 Su
☽#♀ 2:48
☽⚺♃ 6:36
☽#☿ 10:50
☽#♂ 15:19
♀⚻♇ 17:48
☽∠♆ 17:54
☽□⚳ 19:03
☽∥♇ 20:01
☉△☽ 20:44
☽⚼☿ 20:48
☉#☽ 22:58

31 M
☽⚼♀ 0:42
☽⚹⚷ 0:58
☽□♅ 1:31
☽☌♄ 3:26
♂△♆ 5:17
♀∠♅ 10:08
☽⚺♆ 20:29
☽⚻♂ 21:12
☽△☿ 23:15

June 2021

LONGITUDE

Day	Sid.Time	☉	☽	☽ 12 hour	Mean☊	True☊	☿	♀	♂	⚳	♃	♄	⚷	♅	♆	♇
	h m s	° ' "	° ' "	° ' "	° '	° '	° '	° '	° '	° '	° '	° '	° '	° '	° '	° '
1 Tu	16 38 47	10♊44 03	24♒58 56	1♓33 23	10♊51.6	10♊44.3	24♊33.5	28♊05.9	23♋30.1	9♉08.2	1♓34.4	13♒27.5	12♈05.7	12♉25.4	23♓02.0	26♑32.5
2 W	16 42 44	11 41 32	8♓01 48	14 24 36	10 48.5	10D 44.3	24R 22.3	29 19.3	24 07.0	9 30.9	1 38.0	13R 26.6	12 07.9	12 28.5	23 02.8	26R 31.6
3 Th	16 46 40	12 39 01	20 42 15	26 55 13	10 45.3	10 44.3	24 07.0	0♋32.6	24 43.8	9 53.6	1 41.4	13 25.6	12 09.9	12 31.6	23 03.6	26 30.7
4 F	16 50 37	13 36 29	3♈04 02	9♈09 13	10 42.1	10 44.4	23 48.0	1 45.9	25 20.7	10 16.3	1 44.6	13 24.6	12 12.0	12 34.7	23 04.3	26 29.7
5 Sa	16 54 33	14 33 56	15 11 18	21 10 47	10 38.9	10 44.7	23 25.6	2 59.2	25 57.6	10 38.9	1 47.7	13 23.4	12 14.0	12 37.8	23 05.0	26 28.8
6 Su	16 58 30	15 31 23	27 08 09	3♉03 54	10 35.7	10 45.2	23 00.1	4 12.5	26 34.4	11 01.5	1 50.6	13 22.1	12 16.0	12 40.8	23 05.6	26 27.8
7 M	17 02 27	16 28 49	8♉58 28	14 52 17	10 32.6	10 45.8	22 31.9	5 25.7	27 11.3	11 24.0	1 53.3	13 20.8	12 17.9	12 43.8	23 06.3	26 26.8
8 Tu	17 06 23	17 26 14	20 45 45	26 39 14	10 29.4	10 46.3	22 01.7	6 39.0	27 48.3	11 46.5	1 55.8	13 19.3	12 19.8	12 46.8	23 06.9	26 25.7
9 W	17 10 20	18 23 39	2♊33 06	8♊27 38	10 26.2	10R 46.7	21 29.7	7 52.2	28 25.2	12 08.9	1 58.1	13 17.8	12 21.6	12 49.8	23 07.4	26 24.7
10 Th	17 14 16	19 21 03	14 23 10	20 19 58	10 23.0	10 46.8	20 56.7	9 05.4	29 02.1	12 31.3	2 00.2	13 16.2	12 23.4	12 52.8	23 08.0	26 23.6
11 F	17 18 13	20 18 26	26 18 19	2♋18 27	10 19.9	10 46.4	20 23.1	10 18.6	29 39.1	12 53.6	2 02.2	13 14.5	12 25.1	12 55.7	23 08.4	26 22.5
12 Sa	17 22 09	21 15 48	8♋20 37	14 25 04	10 16.7	10 45.6	19 49.6	11 31.7	0♌16.0	13 15.9	2 03.9	13 12.7	12 26.8	12 58.6	23 08.9	26 21.4
13 Su	17 26 06	22 13 10	20 32 03	26 41 48	10 13.5	10 44.2	19 16.7	12 44.9	0 53.0	13 38.1	2 05.5	13 10.8	12 28.5	13 01.5	23 09.3	26 20.3
14 M	17 30 02	23 10 31	2♌54 34	9♌10 35	10 10.3	10 42.6	18 44.9	13 58.0	1 30.0	14 00.3	2 06.8	13 08.8	12 30.1	13 04.3	23 09.7	26 19.2
15 Tu	17 33 59	24 07 51	15 30 07	21 53 27	10 07.2	10 40.8	18 14.9	15 11.1	2 07.0	14 22.4	2 08.0	13 06.7	12 31.7	13 07.1	23 10.1	26 18.0
16 W	17 37 56	25 05 09	28 20 48	4♍52 26	10 04.0	10 39.2	17 47.0	16 24.2	2 44.0	14 44.4	2 09.0	13 04.5	12 33.2	13 09.9	23 10.4	26 16.9
17 Th	17 41 52	26 02 28	11♍28 35	18 09 29	10 00.8	10 38.1	17 21.9	17 37.3	3 21.0	15 06.4	2 09.8	13 02.3	12 34.6	13 12.6	23 10.7	26 15.7
18 F	17 45 49	26 59 45	24 55 19	1♎46 12	9 57.6	10D 37.6	16 59.9	18 50.3	3 58.1	15 28.3	2 10.4	13 00.0	12 36.1	13 15.4	23 11.0	26 14.5
19 Sa	17 49 45	27 57 01	8♎42 13	15 43 21	9 54.5	10 37.8	16 41.3	20 03.3	4 35.1	15 50.1	2 10.8	12 57.6	12 37.4	13 18.1	23 11.2	26 13.2
20 Su	17 53 42	28 54 17	22 49 33	0♏00 34	9 51.3	10 38.7	16 26.6	21 16.3	5 12.2	16 11.9	2R 11.0	12 55.1	12 38.8	13 20.7	23 11.4	26 12.0
21 M	17 57 38	29 51 31	7♏16 07	14 35 45	9 48.1	10 39.9	16 15.9	22 29.2	5 49.2	16 33.6	2 11.1	12 52.5	12 40.0	13 23.4	23 11.6	26 10.8
22 Tu	18 01 35	0♋48 45	21 58 53	29 24 50	9 44.9	10 41.1	16D 09.5	23 42.2	6 26.3	16 55.3	2 10.9	12 49.9	12 41.3	13 26.0	23 11.8	26 09.5
23 W	18 05 32	1 45 59	6♐52 46	14♐21 46	9 41.7	10R 41.7	16 07.6	24 55.1	7 03.4	17 16.9	2 10.5	12 47.1	12 42.4	13 28.5	23 11.9	26 08.2
24 Th	18 09 28	2 43 12	21 50 52	29 19 01	9 38.6	10 41.5	16 10.3	26 08.0	7 40.5	17 38.4	2 10.0	12 44.3	12 43.6	13 31.1	23 11.9	26 06.9
25 F	18 13 25	3 40 25	6♑45 12	14♑08 25	9 35.4	10 40.1	16 17.7	27 20.8	8 17.6	17 59.9	2 09.2	12 41.5	12 44.7	13 33.6	23R 12.0	26 05.7
26 Sa	18 17 21	4 37 37	21 27 44	28 42 20	9 32.2	10 37.7	16 29.9	28 33.6	8 54.7	18 21.3	2 08.3	12 38.5	12 45.7	13 36.0	23 12.0	26 04.3
27 Su	18 21 18	5 34 49	5♒51 31	12♒54 44	9 29.0	10 34.5	16 46.8	29 46.5	9 31.8	18 42.6	2 07.2	12 35.5	12 46.7	13 38.5	23 12.0	26 03.0
28 M	18 25 14	6 32 01	19 51 36	26 41 54	9 25.9	10 30.9	17 08.5	0♌59.2	10 09.0	19 03.9	2 05.9	12 32.4	12 47.6	13 40.9	23 11.9	26 01.7
29 Tu	18 29 11	7 29 13	3♓25 34	10♓02 38	9 22.7	10 27.5	17 35.0	2 12.0	10 46.1	19 25.0	2 04.4	12 29.2	12 48.5	13 43.3	23 11.8	26 00.4
30 W	18 33 07	8♋26 25	16 33 21	22 58 00	9♊19.5	10♊24.7	18♊06.2	3♌24.7	11♌23.3	19♉46.1	2♓02.7	12♒26.0	12♈49.4	13♉45.6	23♓11.7	25♑59.0

1st of Month

Julian Day #
2459366.5
Obliquity
23°26'14"
SVP 4♓57'55"
GC 27♐08.3
Eris 24♈34.9

Day	⚴
1	23♓19.3
6	24 12.7
11	25 01.0
16	25 43.8
21	26 20.8
26	26 51.6

Day	⚵
1	17♐43.7R
6	16 36.2R
11	15 28.1R
16	14 21.0R
21	13 16.4R
26	12 15.8R

Day	⚶
1	12♍48.8
6	14 12.7
11	15 43.2
16	17 19.6
21	19 01.4
26	20 48.2

DECLINATION and LATITUDE

Day	☉ Decl	☽ Decl	☽ Lat	☽ 12h Decl	☿ Decl	☿ Lat	♀ Decl	♀ Lat	♂ Decl	♂ Lat	⚳ Decl	⚳ Lat	♃ Decl	♃ Lat	♄ Decl	♄ Lat
1 Tu	22N03	17S59	5S06	15S48	22N58	0S21	24N19	0N53	22N44	1N22	8N19	6S33	11S44	0S52	17S24	0S39
2 W	22 11	13 28	5 17	11 01	22 41	0 38	24 22	0 56	22 37	1 21	8 27	6 33	11 43	0 53	17 25	0 39
3 Th	22 19	8 29	5 13	5 53	22 23	0 55	24 24	0 58	22 31	1 21	8 34	6 32	11 42	0 53	17 25	0 39
4 F	22 26	3 17	4 54	0 40	22 05	1 13	24 25	0 60	22 24	1 21	8 41	6 32	11 41	0 53	17 26	0 40
5 Sa	22 33	1N57	4 22	4N31	21 47	1 30	24 26	1 02	22 17	1 21	8 48	6 32	11 40	0 53	17 26	0 40
6 Su	22 39	7 02	3 40	9 29	21 28	1 47	24 26	1 04	22 09	1 21	8 55	6 31	11 39	0 54	17 27	0 40
7 M	22 45	11 50	2 48	14 05	21 09	2 04	24 25	1 06	22 02	1 20	9 03	6 31	11 39	0 54	17 27	0 40
8 Tu	22 51	16 11	1 49	18 09	20 51	2 21	24 24	1 08	21 54	1 20	9 10	6 31	11 38	0 54	17 28	0 40
9 W	22 56	19 55	0 46	21 30	20 33	2 37	24 22	1 10	21 47	1 20	9 16	6 31	11 37	0 55	17 28	0 40
10 Th	23 01	22 51	0N20	23 58	20 15	2 53	24 19	1 11	21 39	1 20	9 23	6 30	11 37	0 55	17 29	0 40
11 F	23 05	24 48	1 25	25 22	19 58	3 07	24 15	1 13	21 31	1 19	9 30	6 30	11 36	0 55	17 29	0 41
12 Sa	23 09	25 37	2 27	25 34	19 42	3 21	24 11	1 15	21 23	1 19	9 37	6 30	11 36	0 55	17 30	0 41
13 Su	23 13	25 13	3 23	24 32	19 27	3 34	24 06	1 17	21 15	1 19	9 44	6 30	11 36	0 56	17 31	0 41
14 M	23 16	23 34	4 10	22 18	19 13	3 45	24 00	1 18	21 06	1 19	9 50	6 29	11 35	0 56	17 31	0 41
15 Tu	23 18	20 45	4 46	18 56	19 00	3 56	23 54	1 20	20 58	1 19	9 57	6 29	11 35	0 56	17 32	0 41
16 W	23 21	16 52	5 09	14 36	18 49	4 04	23 47	1 22	20 49	1 18	10 03	6 29	11 35	0 56	17 33	0 41
17 Th	23 23	12 08	5 16	9 29	18 39	4 12	23 39	1 23	20 40	1 18	10 10	6 29	11 35	0 57	17 34	0 41
18 F	23 24	6 42	5 07	3 49	18 31	4 18	23 30	1 25	20 31	1 18	10 16	6 28	11 35	0 57	17 35	0 42
19 Sa	23 25	0 50	4 39	2S12	18 25	4 23	23 21	1 26	20 22	1 18	10 23	6 28	11 35	0 57	17 35	0 42
20 Su	23 26	5S14	3 55	8 15	18 20	4 26	23 11	1 27	20 13	1 17	10 29	6 28	11 36	0 58	17 36	0 42
21 M	23 26	11 11	2 54	13 60	18 17	4 28	23 01	1 29	20 04	1 17	10 35	6 28	11 36	0 58	17 37	0 42
22 Tu	23 26	16 37	1 42	19 01	18 16	4 29	22 50	1 30	19 54	1 17	10 41	6 28	11 36	0 58	17 38	0 42
23 W	23 26	21 07	0 21	22 51	18 16	4 28	22 38	1 31	19 45	1 17	10 47	6 27	11 36	0 58	17 39	0 42
24 Th	23 25	24 12	1S01	25 07	18 18	4 26	22 26	1 32	19 35	1 16	10 53	6 27	11 37	0 59	17 40	0 42
25 F	23 23	25 34	2 19	25 34	18 22	4 23	22 12	1 33	19 25	1 16	10 59	6 27	11 37	0 59	17 41	0 42
26 Sa	23 21	25 07	3 26	24 14	18 27	4 19	21 59	1 34	19 15	1 16	11 05	6 27	11 38	0 59	17 42	0 43
27 Su	23 19	22 59	4 19	21 23	18 34	4 14	21 44	1 35	19 05	1 16	11 11	6 27	11 39	0 60	17 43	0 43
28 M	23 17	19 30	4 54	17 23	18 42	4 08	21 30	1 36	18 55	1 15	11 17	6 26	11 39	0 60	17 44	0 43
29 Tu	23 14	15 05	5 12	12 39	18 52	4 01	21 14	1 36	18 44	1 15	11 23	6 26	11 40	1 00	17 45	0 43
30 W	23N10	10S06	5S12	7S29	19N03	3S53	20N58	1N37	18N34	1N15	11N28	6S26	11S41	1S00	17S46	0S43

Day	⚷ Decl	⚷ Lat	♅ Decl	♅ Lat	♆ Decl	♆ Lat	♇ Decl	♇ Lat
1	6N56	2N20	15N11	0S24	3S47	1S07	22S18	1S29
6	6 60	2 20	15 15	0 24	3 46	1 07	22 20	1 30
11	7 04	2 20	15 20	0 24	3 45	1 07	22 21	1 30
16	7 07	2 21	15 24	0 24	3 44	1 07	22 23	1 31
21	7 10	2 21	15 28	0 24	3 44	1 07	22 25	1 32
26	7 12	2 21	15 32	0 24	3 44	1 08	22 26	1 32

Day	⚴ Decl	⚴ Lat	⚵ Decl	⚵ Lat	⚶ Decl	⚶ Lat	Eris Decl	Eris Lat
1	8N10	11N47	4S25	18N31	14N14	8N07	1S05	11S23
6	8 23	11 39	4 15	18 35	13 29	7 54	1 04	11 23
11	8 34	11 29	4 09	18 36	12 42	7 41	1 04	11 23
16	8 42	11 20	4 05	18 33	11 53	7 29	1 03	11 24
21	8 47	11 10	4 05	18 27	11 02	7 17	1 03	11 24
26	8 49	10 59	4 08	18 17	10 10	7 06	1 03	11 24

Moon Phenomena

Max/0 Decl
dy hr mn
4 15:02 0 N
12 4:09 25N38
19 3:18 0 S
25 5:52 25S38

Max/0 Lat
dy hr mn
2 5:05 5S18
9 16:43 0 N
16 22:29 5N16
23 6:08 0 S
29 12:43 5S14

Perigee/Apogee
dy hr m kilometers
8 2:28 a 406228
23 9:56 p 359960

PH dy hr mn
☾ 2 7:26 11♓59
● 10 10:54 19♊47
● 10 643:05A 03'51"
☽ 18 3:55 27♍09
○ 24 18:41 3♑28

Void of Course Moon

Last Aspect			☽ Ingress	
1 6:15	♀	△	♓	1 9:09
3 11:12	♇	⚹	♈	3 18:00
5 22:48	♂	□	♉	6 5:47
8 15:08	♂	⚹	♊	8 18:49
10 17:39	♆	□	♋	11 7:24
13 11:17	♇	☍	♌	13 18:24
15 17:28	☉	⚹	♍	16 3:03
18 3:55	☉	□	♎	18 8:55
20 10:53	☉	△	♏	20 11:59
22 6:44	♇	⚹	♐	22 12:57
24 2:10	♆	□	♑	24 13:06
26 12:51	♀	☍	♒	26 14:10
27 19:09	☿	△	♓	28 17:52

DAILY ASPECTARIAN

1 Tu	☊R	1:29
	☽⚺♇	2:50
	☽∥♄	3:17
	☽∠⚷	3:51
	☽△♀	6:15
	♀⚼♄	6:58
	☽☌♃	12:05
	☽#♅	15:12
	☿∠⚳	18:10
	☉⚼♇	19:55
2 W	☽⚼♂	2:08
	☽⚹⚳	2:52
	☽∠♇	6:33
	☿⚺♂	7:15
	☉□☽	7:26
	☊D	7:26
	☽⚺⚷	7:43
	☿∥♂	7:45
	☽⚹♅	8:23
	☽∥♃	8:38
	☽⚺♄	10:10
	☉⚹⚷	11:24
	♀ ♋	13:20
	☉⚺♅	20:44
	☽#⚳	23:35
3 Th	☉#♇	0:19
	☉∥☿	4:12
	☽☌♆	4:32
	☿#♇	5:41
	☽□☿	6:25
	☽#⚷	7:04
	☽△♂	8:10
	☽∠⚳	8:20
	☽⚹♇	11:12
	☽∠♅	13:14
	☽∠♄	14:55
	☉△♄	19:07
	☉∥♂	20:12
	☽□♀	21:10
	☽⚺♃	21:24
	☽∥♆	21:45
	♀△♃	23:34
4 F	☽⚺⚳	14:40
	♂#♇	14:55
	☽☌⚷	18:06
	☽⚺♅	18:53
	☽⚹♄	20:25
	☉⚹☽	22:39
5 Sa	☽∠♃	3:13
	☽#♆	8:28
	☽⚺♆	15:51
	☽⚹☿	15:58
	☿□♆	19:06
	♂☍♇	19:46
	☽□♇	22:39
	☽□♂	22:48
	☽∥⚷	23:48
6 Su	☉∠☽	7:27
	☽∥⚳	9:27
	☽⚹♃	9:34
	☽⚹♀	15:58
	☽∠☿	21:11
	☽∠♆	22:14
	☽#♃	22:59
7 M	☽☌⚳	5:06
	☽⚺⚷	6:47
	☽☌♅	7:40
	☽□♄	8:53
	☉⚺☽	16:38
	☽∥♅	18:45
8 Tu	☽∠♀	2:01
	☽⚺☿	2:28
	☽⚹♆	4:48
	☽#♄	7:42
	☽△♇	11:31
	☽∠⚷	13:25
	☽⚹♂	15:08
	☽□♃	22:49
9 W	☽∥☿	4:10
	☽⚺♀	12:03
	☽∥♂	13:42
	⚳⚺⚷	14:46
	☊R	16:48
	☽⚼♇	17:57
	☽#♇	19:16
	☽⚹⚷	19:57
	☽⚺⚳	20:06
	☽⚺♅	20:56
	☽△♄	21:45
	☽∠♂	23:15
10 Th	☉∥☽	1:35
	☉☌☽	10:54
	☽☌☿	12:38
	☽∥♀	16:03
	☽□♆	17:39
11 F	☽⚻♇	0:08
	☉☌☿	1:14
	⚳☌♅	2:33
	☽∠♅	3:16
	☽∠⚳	3:17
	☽⚼♄	3:52
	☽⚺♂	7:04
	☽△♃	11:29
	♂ ♌	13:35
	⚳□♄	20:47
12 Sa	☽☌♀	7:00
	☽□⚷	8:08
	☽⚹♅	9:12
	☽⚻♄	9:36
	☽⚹⚳	10:02
	☽⚼♃	17:15
	♀□⚷	18:29
	☽⚺☿	21:39
13 Su	☉⚺☽	3:34
	☽△♆	5:07
	♀⚹♅	5:39
	♀⚻♄	8:16
	☽☍♇	11:17
	☽∥♀	18:46
	☽☌♂	21:09
	☽⚻♃	22:28
	☉□♆	23:41
14 M	♀⚹⚳	1:03
	☽∠☿	1:33
	☉∥☽	3:03
	☽⚼♆	10:04
	☉∠☽	10:55
	☽#♇	11:18
	☽△⚷	18:22
	☽□♅	19:29
	☽☍♄	19:29
	☽□⚳	21:48
	♄□♅	22:02
	☽∥♂	22:21
	☽⚺♀	23:20
15 Tu	♂⚻♃	0:40
	☽⚹☿	4:59
	☽∥☿	12:07
	☽⚻♆	14:24
	☉⚹☽	17:28
	☽⚻♇	20:11
	☽#♄	20:13
	☽⚼⚷	22:32
16 W	☿∠♂	1:08
	☽∠♀	6:13
	☽☍♃	7:01
	☽∥♅	7:51
	☽⚺♂	8:29
	♀⚼♃	14:53
	☿⚺♀	20:12
	☽⚼♇	23:37
17 Th	☽⚻⚷	1:59
	☽#♃	2:32
	☽⚻♄	2:49
	☽△♅	3:08
	☉⚻♇	5:25
	☽△⚳	6:43
	☽∥⚳	8:49
	☽□☿	10:17
	☽⚹♀	12:08
	☽∠♂	12:56
	☽☍♆	20:56
	☽∥⚷	22:11
18 F	☽△♇	2:19
	☊D	3:49
	☉□☽	3:55
	☽⚼♄	5:24
	☽⚼♅	5:53
	☽⚼⚳	10:00
	☽#♆	12:18
	☽⚻♃	12:43
	☉∥♀	14:47
	☽⚹♂	16:33
19 Sa	☉⚼♄	0:13
	☽☍⚷	6:44
	☽△♄	7:16
	☽⚻♅	7:54
	☉∠♅	9:15
	☽⚻⚳	12:31
	☽△☿	13:24
	☽⚼♃	14:29
	☽∥♆	18:03
	☽□♀	21:08
20 Su	☽⚻♆	0:37
	☽□♇	5:39
	☽#⚷	7:36
	☿⚺⚳	10:28
	☉△☽	10:53
	☽⚼☿	14:11
	♃R	15:06
	☽△♃	15:36
	☽#⚳	21:27
	☽□♂	21:31
21 M	☽⚼♆	1:31
	☽∥♃	1:42
	☉ ♋	3:33
	☽⚻⚷	8:52
	☽□♄	9:10
	☽☍♅	10:04
	☉⚼☽	13:17
	♀△♆	13:58
	☽⚻☿	14:36
	☽☍⚳	15:35
	☽#♅	18:39
22 Tu	☽△♆	1:58
	☽△♀	3:02
	☽∥♄	4:55
	☽⚹♇	6:44
	☽#☿	8:05
	☽⚼⚷	9:14
	☉⚻☽	15:13
	☽#♂	16:15
	☽□♃	16:27
	☿D	22:01
23 W	☽△♂	0:18
	☽⚼♀	5:18
	☊R	6:12
	☽∠♇	6:49
	☽∥♇	8:49
	☽△⚷	9:21
	☽⚹♄	9:27
	☽#♀	9:44
	☉△♃	10:12
	☽⚻♅	10:36
	☽☍☿	14:51
	☉#☽	16:34
	☽⚻⚳	17:05
	☉∠⚳	20:48
	♀☍♇	23:40
	♀#♇	23:41
24 Th	☽⚼♂	1:23
	☽□♆	2:10
	♄⚹⚷	4:31
	☽⚺♇	6:51
	☽⚻♀	7:29
	☽∠♄	9:26
	☽⚼♅	10:45
	☽⚹♃	16:35
	☽⚼⚳	17:47
	☉☍☽	18:41
	♂⚼♆	20:23
25 F	☽⚻♂	2:36
	☽⚺♄	9:36
	☽□⚷	9:44
	☽△♅	11:05
	☽⚻☿	15:43
	☽∠♃	16:55
	☽△⚳	18:46
	♆R	19:22
26 Sa	☽⚹♆	2:52
	☽☌♇	7:37
	☽☍♀	12:51
	☽⚼☿	16:59
	☽⚺♃	17:43
	☉#☽	21:01
	☉⚻☽	23:30
27 Su	☽∠♆	3:58
	☽∥♇	4:16
	♀ ♌	4:28
	☽☍♂	6:31
	☽#♀	10:14
	☽☌♄	11:25
	☽⚹⚷	11:47
	☽□♅	13:17
	☽△☿	19:09
	☽□⚳	22:35
28 M	☉⚼☽	3:08
	☽#♂	3:39
	☽#☿	4:30
	☽⚺♆	5:50
	☽∥♄	10:07
	☽⚺♇	10:48
	☽∠⚷	13:57
	☿∥♂	14:45
	♀⚻♃	21:32
	☽#♅	21:34
	☽☌♃	21:35
	☽⚻♀	21:35
29 Tu	☉△☽	7:55
	☿∠♀	12:57
	☽∠♇	13:44
	☽⚻♂	13:59
	☽⚺♄	16:25
	☽∥♃	16:36
	☽⚺⚷	17:05
	☽#⚳	17:41
	☽⚹♅	18:49
30 W	☽□☿	3:01
	☽⚼♀	3:49
	☽⚹⚳	6:10
	☽☌♆	12:26
	☽#⚷	13:07
	☽⚹♇	17:41
	☽⚼♂	19:26
	☽∠♄	20:23
	☽∠♅	23:04

LONGITUDE

Day	Sid.Time	☉	☽	☽ 12 hour	Mean☊	True☊	☿	♀	♂	⚳	♃	♄	⚷	♅	♆	♇
	h m s	° ' "	° ' "	° ' "	° '	° '	° '	° '	° '	° '	° '	° '	° '	° '	° '	° '
1 Th	18 37 04	9♋23 37	29♓16 59	5♈30 49	9♊16.3	10♊23.1	18♊42.1	4♌37.4	12♌00.4	20♉07.2	2♓00.8	12♒22.7	12♈50.1	13♉47.9	23♓11.5	25♑57.6
2 F	18 41 01	10 20 49	11♈40 00	17 45 08	9 13.2	10D 22.6	19 22.7	5 50.1	12 37.6	20 28.1	1R 58.7	12R 19.3	12 50.9	13 50.1	23R 11.4	25R 56.3
3 Sa	18 44 57	11 18 02	23 46 49	29 45 39	9 10.0	10 23.2	20 07.9	7 02.8	13 14.8	20 49.0	1 56.4	12 15.9	12 51.6	13 52.3	23 11.1	25 54.9
4 Su	18 48 54	12 15 14	5♉42 16	11♉37 16	9 06.8	10 24.7	20 57.6	8 15.4	13 52.1	21 09.8	1 54.0	12 12.4	12 52.2	13 54.5	23 10.9	25 53.5
5 M	18 52 50	13 12 27	17 31 13	23 24 44	9 03.6	10 26.4	21 51.8	9 28.0	14 29.3	21 30.5	1 51.3	12 08.8	12 52.8	13 56.7	23 10.6	25 52.1
6 Tu	18 56 47	14 09 40	29 18 19	5♊12 29	9 00.5	10R 27.8	22 50.5	10 40.6	15 06.6	21 51.1	1 48.5	12 05.2	12 53.3	13 58.8	23 10.3	25 50.7
7 W	19 00 43	15 06 53	11♊07 42	17 04 24	8 57.3	10 28.4	23 53.5	11 53.2	15 43.8	22 11.6	1 45.5	12 01.5	12 53.8	14 00.8	23 09.9	25 49.3
8 Th	19 04 40	16 04 07	23 02 56	29 03 40	8 54.1	10 27.6	25 00.8	13 05.7	16 21.1	22 32.1	1 42.3	11 57.8	12 54.2	14 02.9	23 09.6	25 47.9
9 F	19 08 36	17 01 21	5♋06 53	11♋12 48	8 50.9	10 25.1	26 12.4	14 18.3	16 58.4	22 52.4	1 38.9	11 54.0	12 54.6	14 04.9	23 09.2	25 46.5
10 Sa	19 12 33	17 58 35	17 21 39	23 33 33	8 47.8	10 20.9	27 28.2	15 30.8	17 35.8	23 12.7	1 35.3	11 50.2	12 54.9	14 06.8	23 08.7	25 45.0
11 Su	19 16 30	18 55 49	29 48 39	6♌07 00	8 44.6	10 15.2	28 48.1	16 43.2	18 13.1	23 32.9	1 31.6	11 46.3	12 55.2	14 08.7	23 08.3	25 43.6
12 M	19 20 26	19 53 03	12♌28 39	18 53 39	8 41.4	10 08.7	0♋12.1	17 55.6	18 50.5	23 52.9	1 27.7	11 42.3	12 55.4	14 10.6	23 07.7	25 42.2
13 Tu	19 24 23	20 50 17	25 22 00	1♍53 41	8 38.2	10 01.8	1 40.1	19 08.0	19 27.8	24 12.9	1 23.6	11 38.4	12 55.6	14 12.4	23 07.2	25 40.7
14 W	19 28 19	21 47 32	8♍28 42	15 07 03	8 35.0	9 55.5	3 12.0	20 20.4	20 05.2	24 32.8	1 19.3	11 34.3	12 55.7	14 14.2	23 06.7	25 39.3
15 Th	19 32 16	22 44 46	21 48 43	28 33 41	8 31.9	9 50.5	4 47.7	21 32.7	20 42.6	24 52.6	1 14.9	11 30.3	12R 55.8	14 15.9	23 06.1	25 37.9
16 F	19 36 12	23 42 00	5♎21 58	12♎13 33	8 28.7	9 47.2	6 27.1	22 45.1	21 20.0	25 12.3	1 10.3	11 26.1	12 55.8	14 17.6	23 05.4	25 36.4
17 Sa	19 40 09	24 39 15	19 08 27	26 06 36	8 25.5	9D 45.7	8 10.0	23 57.3	21 57.4	25 31.8	1 05.5	11 22.0	12 55.7	14 19.2	23 04.8	25 35.0
18 Su	19 44 05	25 36 29	3♏07 59	10♏12 30	8 22.3	9 45.8	9 56.4	25 09.5	22 34.9	25 51.3	1 00.6	11 17.8	12 55.7	14 20.9	23 04.1	25 33.5
19 M	19 48 02	26 33 44	17 20 00	24 30 17	8 19.2	9 46.7	11 45.9	26 21.7	23 12.3	26 10.6	0 55.5	11 13.6	12 55.5	14 22.4	23 03.4	25 32.1
20 Tu	19 51 59	27 30 59	1♐43 03	8♐57 57	8 16.0	9R 47.7	13 38.5	27 33.9	23 49.8	26 29.9	0 50.3	11 09.3	12 55.3	14 23.9	23 02.7	25 30.7
21 W	19 55 55	28 28 14	16 14 30	23 32 08	8 12.8	9 47.8	15 33.8	28 46.0	24 27.3	26 49.0	0 45.0	11 05.1	12 55.1	14 25.4	23 01.9	25 29.2
22 Th	19 59 52	29 25 30	0♑50 13	8♑08 01	8 09.6	9 46.1	17 31.6	29 58.1	25 04.8	27 08.0	0 39.4	11 00.8	12 54.8	14 26.8	23 01.1	25 27.8
23 F	20 03 48	0♌22 46	15 24 46	22 39 39	8 06.5	9 42.3	19 31.6	1♍10.1	25 42.3	27 27.0	0 33.8	10 56.4	12 54.4	14 28.2	23 00.3	25 26.3
24 Sa	20 07 45	1 20 02	29 51 53	7♒00 39	8 03.3	9 36.2	21 33.6	2 22.2	26 19.8	27 45.8	0 28.0	10 52.1	12 54.0	14 29.6	22 59.4	25 24.9
25 Su	20 11 41	2 17 19	14♒05 16	21 05 06	8 00.1	9 28.5	23 37.0	3 34.1	26 57.4	28 04.4	0 22.0	10 47.7	12 53.6	14 30.9	22 58.6	25 23.5
26 M	20 15 38	3 14 37	27 59 38	4♓48 30	7 56.9	9 19.9	25 41.8	4 46.0	27 35.0	28 23.0	0 15.9	10 43.3	12 53.1	14 32.1	22 57.7	25 22.1
27 Tu	20 19 34	4 11 55	11♓31 27	18 08 23	7 53.7	9 11.4	27 47.4	5 57.9	28 12.5	28 41.4	0 09.7	10 38.9	12 52.5	14 33.3	22 56.7	25 20.6
28 W	20 23 31	5 09 14	24 39 20	1♈04 27	7 50.6	9 04.0	29 53.6	7 09.8	28 50.1	28 59.7	0 03.4	10 34.5	12 51.9	14 34.5	22 55.8	25 19.2
29 Th	20 27 28	6 06 35	7♈24 02	13 38 27	7 47.4	8 58.2	2♌00.1	8 21.6	29 27.8	29 17.9	29♒57.0	10 30.1	12 51.3	14 35.6	22 54.8	25 17.8
30 F	20 31 24	7 03 56	19 48 10	25 53 43	7 44.2	8 54.6	4 06.7	9 33.3	0♍05.4	29 36.0	29 50.4	10 25.6	12 50.6	14 36.6	22 53.8	25 16.4
31 Sa	20 35 21	8♌01 18	1♉55 42	7♉54 44	7♊41.0	8♊52.9	6♌12.9	10♍45.1	0♍43.1	29♉53.9	29♒43.7	10♒21.2	12♈49.8	14♉37.6	22♓52.7	25♑15.0

1st of Month
Julian Day # 2459396.5
Obliquity 23°26'4"
SVP 4♓57'50"
GC 27♐08.4
Eris 24♈45.3

Day	⚴
1	27♓15.7
6	27 32.6
11	27 41.9
16	27 43.3R
21	27 36.3R
26	27 20.8R
31	26 56.6R

Day	⚵
1	11♐20.3R
6	10 31.1R
11	9 49.1R
16	9 14.8R
21	8 48.7R
26	8 31.1R
31	8 21.9R

Day	⚶
1	22♍39.5
6	24 35.0
11	26 34.5
16	28 37.6
21	0♎44.0
26	2 53.5
31	5 05.8

DECLINATION and LATITUDE

Day	☉ Decl	☽ Decl	☽ Lat	☽ 12h Decl	☿ Decl	☿ Lat	♀ Decl	♀ Lat	♂ Decl	♂ Lat	⚳ Decl	⚳ Lat	♃ Decl	♃ Lat	♄ Decl	♄ Lat
1 Th	23N06	4S50	4S57	2S10	19N14	3S44	20N41	1N38	18N23	1N15	11N34	6S26	11S42	1S01	17S47	0S43
2 F	23 02	0N29	4 29	3N07	19 27	3 35	20 24	1 38	18 12	1 14	11 40	6 26	11 43	1 01	17 48	0 43
3 Sa	22 57	5 41	3 49	8 11	19 40	3 25	20 06	1 39	18 01	1 14	11 45	6 26	11 44	1 01	17 49	0 44
4 Su	22 52	10 36	2 59	12 55	19 54	3 14	19 48	1 39	17 50	1 14	11 50	6 26	11 45	1 01	17 50	0 44
5 M	22 47	15 06	2 02	17 08	20 09	3 03	19 29	1 39	17 39	1 13	11 56	6 25	11 46	1 02	17 51	0 44
6 Tu	22 41	19 01	1 01	20 42	20 24	2 51	19 09	1 40	17 28	1 13	12 01	6 25	11 48	1 02	17 52	0 44
7 W	22 35	22 10	0N04	23 24	20 39	2 39	18 49	1 40	17 17	1 13	12 06	6 25	11 49	1 02	17 53	0 44
8 Th	22 28	24 20	1 08	25 06	20 54	2 27	18 29	1 40	17 05	1 13	12 11	6 25	11 50	1 02	17 55	0 44
9 F	22 21	25 31	2 10	25 37	21 09	2 14	18 08	1 40	16 54	1 12	12 17	6 25	11 52	1 03	17 56	0 44
10 Sa	22 14	25 24	3 07	24 53	21 24	2 01	17 47	1 40	16 42	1 12	12 22	6 25	11 53	1 03	17 57	0 44
11 Su	22 06	24 02	3 56	22 53	21 38	1 48	17 25	1 40	16 30	1 12	12 27	6 25	11 55	1 03	17 58	0 44
12 M	21 58	21 27	4 34	19 44	21 51	1 35	17 02	1 40	16 19	1 12	12 31	6 25	11 57	1 04	17 59	0 45
13 Tu	21 49	17 46	4 59	15 34	22 04	1 22	16 39	1 39	16 07	1 11	12 36	6 25	11 58	1 04	18 01	0 45
14 W	21 40	13 10	5 09	10 36	22 16	1 08	16 16	1 39	15 54	1 11	12 41	6 24	12 00	1 04	18 02	0 45
15 Th	21 31	7 53	5 03	5 03	22 26	0 55	15 53	1 39	15 42	1 11	12 46	6 24	12 02	1 04	18 03	0 45
16 F	21 22	2 09	4 39	0S49	22 35	0 42	15 29	1 38	15 30	1 10	12 50	6 24	12 04	1 05	18 04	0 45
17 Sa	21 12	3S48	3 60	6 45	22 42	0 29	15 04	1 38	15 18	1 10	12 55	6 24	12 06	1 05	18 05	0 45
18 Su	21 01	9 39	3 05	12 27	22 47	0 17	14 39	1 37	15 05	1 10	12 60	6 24	12 08	1 05	18 07	0 45
19 M	20 50	15 07	1 58	17 34	22 51	0 04	14 14	1 36	14 53	1 09	13 04	6 24	12 10	1 05	18 08	0 45
20 Tu	20 39	19 48	0 44	21 43	22 52	0N08	13 48	1 35	14 40	1 09	13 08	6 24	12 12	1 06	18 09	0 45
21 W	20 28	23 18	0S35	24 30	22 51	0 19	13 23	1 34	14 27	1 09	13 13	6 24	12 14	1 06	18 11	0 46
22 Th	20 16	25 17	1 51	25 38	22 47	0 30	12 56	1 33	14 14	1 09	13 17	6 24	12 16	1 06	18 12	0 46
23 F	20 04	25 31	2 60	24 59	22 41	0 40	12 30	1 32	14 01	1 08	13 21	6 24	12 18	1 06	18 13	0 46
24 Sa	19 52	24 01	3 56	22 41	22 32	0 50	12 03	1 31	13 48	1 08	13 25	6 24	12 21	1 06	18 14	0 46
25 Su	19 39	21 01	4 37	19 03	22 20	0 59	11 36	1 30	13 35	1 08	13 30	6 24	12 23	1 07	18 16	0 46
26 M	19 26	16 52	5 00	14 29	22 06	1 07	11 08	1 29	13 22	1 07	13 34	6 24	12 25	1 07	18 17	0 46
27 Tu	19 12	11 57	5 06	9 19	21 49	1 14	10 40	1 27	13 09	1 07	13 38	6 24	12 28	1 07	18 18	0 46
28 W	18 59	6 38	4 55	3 55	21 30	1 21	10 12	1 26	12 55	1 07	13 41	6 23	12 30	1 07	18 20	0 46
29 Th	18 45	1 12	4 30	1N30	21 08	1 27	9 44	1 24	12 42	1 06	13 45	6 23	12 33	1 08	18 21	0 46
30 F	18 30	4N10	3 52	6 45	20 43	1 32	9 16	1 23	12 28	1 06	13 49	6 23	12 35	1 08	18 22	0 46
31 Sa	18N16	9N15	3S05	11N39	20N16	1N36	8N47	1N21	12N15	1N06	13N53	6S23	12S38	1S08	18S23	0S47

Day	⚷ Decl	⚷ Lat	♅ Decl	♅ Lat	♆ Decl	♆ Lat	♇ Decl	♇ Lat
1	7N14	2N21	15N35	0S24	3S44	1S08	22S28	1S33
6	7 16	2 22	15 39	0 24	3 45	1 08	22 30	1 33
11	7 17	2 22	15 42	0 24	3 46	1 08	22 32	1 34
16	7 17	2 22	15 44	0 25	3 48	1 09	22 34	1 34
21	7 17	2 23	15 46	0 25	3 49	1 09	22 35	1 35
26	7 17	2 23	15 48	0 25	3 51	1 09	22 37	1 35
31	7N16	2N23	15N50	0S25	3S53	1S09	22S39	1S36

Day	⚴ Decl	⚴ Lat	⚵ Decl	⚵ Lat	⚶ Decl	⚶ Lat	Eris Decl	Eris Lat
1	8N48	10N47	4S14	18N04	9N15	6N55	1S03	11S25
6	8 43	10 35	4 23	17 48	8 20	6 44	1 03	11 25
11	8 34	10 21	4 36	17 30	7 23	6 34	1 03	11 26
16	8 21	10 06	4 51	17 10	6 24	6 23	1 03	11 26
21	8 03	9 49	5 08	16 49	5 25	6 14	1 04	11 27
26	7 40	9 30	5 27	16 27	4 25	6 04	1 04	11 27
31	7N11	9N10	5S49	16N04	3N25	5N55	1S05	11S27

Moon Phenomena

Max/0 Decl
dy hr mn
1 21:46 0 N
9 10:05 25N37
16 8:42 0 S
22 15:11 25S38
29 5:17 0 N

Perigee/Apogee
dy hr m kilometers
5 14:48 a 405340
21 10:26 p 364523

Max/0 Lat
dy hr mn
6 22:41 0 N
14 2:37 5N09
20 13:23 0 S
26 19:52 5S06

PH dy hr mn
☾ 1 21:12 10♈14
● 10 1:18 18♋02
☽ 17 10:12 25♎04
○ 24 2:38 1♒26
☾ 31 13:17 8♉33

Void of Course Moon

Last Aspect	☽ Ingress
30 17:41 ♇ ✶	♈ 1 1:22
3 4:16 ♇ □	♉ 3 12:29
5 16:58 ♇ △	♊ 6 1:25
8 4:21 ♅ ✶	♋ 8 13:52
10 16:11 ♇ ☍	♌ 11 0:22
12 12:30 ♂ ☌	♍ 13 8:32
15 6:47 ♇ △	♎ 15 14:33
17 11:05 ♇ □	♏ 17 18:39
19 16:31 ☉ △	♐ 19 21:09
21 22:27 ♀ △	♑ 21 22:37
23 16:35 ♇ ☌	♒ 24 0:14
25 23:15 ♂ ☍	♓ 26 3:31
28 1:14 ♇ ✶	♈ 28 9:59
30 19:39 ♃ ✶	♉ 30 20:09

DAILY ASPECTARIAN

1 Th ☽∥♆ 4:54 · ☽⊻♃ 5:13 · ☽△♀ 11:23 · ☽∠⚳ 11:34 · ♂☍♄ 13:09 · ☉□☽ 21:12 · ☊D 21:21

2 F ☽✶♄ 1:17 · ☽△♂ 1:59 · ☽☌⚷ 2:19 · ☽⊻♅ 4:17 · ♂△⚷ 8:43 · ☽∠♃ 10:26 · ☽#♆ 14:55 · ☽✶☿ 16:13 · ☽⊻⚳ 17:55 · ⚳#♃ 19:08 · ☽⊻♆ 22:49

3 Sa ☽□♇ 4:16 · ☽∥⚷ 7:28 · ☽✶♃ 16:20 · ☿∥♀ 19:10 · ♀⚼♆ 22:30 · ☉⚻♄ 22:52

4 Su ☽∠☿ 0:34 · ♂#♄ 0:51 · ♂□♅ 1:41 · ☽∠♆ 5:01 · ☽□♀ 5:46 · ☽#♃ 5:55 · ☽∥⚳ 6:28 · ☿⊻⚳ 9:04 · ☽□♄ 13:07 · ☉✶☽ 14:27 · ☽⊻⚷ 14:33 · ☉□⚷ 15:40 · ☽☌♅ 16:42 · ☽□♂ 17:29

5 M ☽∥♅ 3:04 · ☽☌⚳ 8:22 · ☽⊻☿ 9:38 · ☽✶♆ 11:31 · ☽∥♂ 14:30 · ☽#♄ 16:31 · ☽△♇ 16:58 · ☉✶♅ 19:15 · ☽∠⚷ 21:07 · ☉∠☽ 23:41

6 Tu ☽∥♀ 0:54 · ☽□♃ 5:04 · ☿□♆ 7:41 · ☽∥☿ 10:35 · ☊R 22:43 · ☽⚼♇ 23:23

7 W ☽✶♀ 1:42 · ☽△♄ 1:48 · ♀☍♄ 2:37 · ☽#♇ 3:05 · ☽✶⚷ 3:35 · ☉∥☽ 3:36 · ☽⊻♅ 5:51 · ☉⊻☽ 8:45 · ☽✶♂ 9:48 · ☉#♇ 15:19 · ♀△⚷ 20:10 · ☽⊻⚳ 22:56

8 Th ☽□♆ 0:13 · ☽☌☿ 4:21 · ☽⚻♇ 5:29 · ☽⚼♄ 7:47 · ☽∠♀ 11:12 · ☽∠♅ 12:00 · ☉⚼♃ 15:07 · ☿⚻♇ 15:37 · ☽△♃ 17:10 · ☽∠♂ 17:27 · ♀□♅ 19:26 · ☉⊻♂ 20:30

9 F ☽∠⚳ 5:36 · ☿⚼♄ 12:41 · ♀#♄ 13:03 · ☽⚻♄ 13:17 · ☽□⚷ 15:20 · ☽✶♅ 17:39 · ⚳✶♆ 19:23 · ☽⊻♀ 20:01 · ☽⚼♃ 22:30

10 Sa ☽⊻♂ 0:29 · ☉☌☽ 1:18 · ☽△♆ 11:12 · ☽✶⚳ 11:39 · ☽☍♇ 16:11 · ☽⊻☿ 21:50

11 Su ☽⚻♃ 3:16 · ☿∠♅ 6:08 · ☽#♇ 15:08 · ☽⚼♆ 15:49 · ☉∥☽ 19:44 · ☿ ♋ 20:36 · ☽∥☿ 21:02 · ☽☍♄ 22:33

12 M ☽△⚷ 0:50 · ☽□♅ 3:12 · ☽∠☿ 5:45 · ☉∥☿ 7:25 · ☽☌♀ 11:15 · ☽☌♂ 12:30 · ☉⊻☽ 14:57 · ☿△♃ 19:46 · ☽⚻♆ 19:51 · ☽□⚳ 21:49 · ☽#♄ 22:34

13 Tu ☽⚻♇ 0:35 · ☽⚼⚷ 4:43 · ☽∥♀ 6:45 · ☽∥♂ 9:33 · ☽☍♃ 11:01 · ☽∥♅ 11:12 · ☽✶☿ 13:06 · ♀☌♂ 13:34 · ☉∠☽ 20:42

14 W ☽∥⚳ 2:16 · ☽⚼♇ 3:56 · ☽#♃ 5:30 · ☽⚻♄ 5:35 · ⚴R 7:41 · ☽⚻⚷ 8:03 · ☽△♅ 10:26 · ♂∥♅ 21:21 · ☽⊻♂ 21:56 · ☽⊻♀ 23:29

15 Th ☉✶☽ 1:48 · ☽☍♆ 2:18 · ☽∥⚷ 2:33 · ☽△⚳ 5:36 · ☽△♇ 6:47 · ☽⚼♄ 8:19 · ♀∥♅ 8:47 · ☉△♆ 8:50 · ☽⚼♅ 13:16 · ☽⚻♃ 16:39 · ⚷R 16:42 · ☽#♆ 17:15 · ☿#♇ 20:56 · ♀∥♂ 21:06 · ☿∠♂ 21:20

16 F ☽∠♂ 1:47 · ☽□☿ 2:10 · ☽∠♀ 4:35 · ♀⚻♆ 6:43 · ☽⚼⚳ 8:41 · ☽△♄ 10:34 · ☽☍⚷ 13:14 · ☽⚻♅ 15:38 · ☽⚼♃ 18:45

17 Sa ☽∥♆ 0:00 · ⚳△♇ 3:37 · ☽✶♂ 5:05 · ☽⚻♆ 6:47 · ☽✶♀ 9:05 · ☊D 10:02 · ☉□☽ 10:12 · ☽□♇ 11:05 · ☽⚻⚳ 11:16 · ☽#⚷ 14:11 · ☽△♃ 20:24 · ☉☍♇ 22:48

18 Su ♀⚻♇ 7:49 · ☽⚼♆ 8:22 · ☿∠♀ 8:42 · ☉✶⚳ 9:23 · ☽∥♃ 10:38 · ☽△☿ 13:14 · ☽□♄ 13:46 · ☽#⚳ 14:34 · ☿∠⚳ 14:43 · ☽⚻⚷ 16:35 · ☿⚻♄ 17:15 · ♂⚻♆ 18:23 · ♀□⚳ 18:57 · ☽☍♅ 19:01 · ☽#♀ 20:15 · ☽#♂ 22:57

19 M ☽#♅ 3:04 · ⚶ ♎ 6:32 · ☽△♆ 9:34 · ☽□♂ 10:17 · ☽✶♇ 13:42 · ☿□⚷ 14:53 · ☽∥♄ 14:58 · ☽☍⚳ 15:07 · ☽□♀ 16:28 · ☉△☽ 16:31 · ☽⚼⚷ 17:42 · ☽⚼☿ 18:07 · ☉⊻♀ 19:18 · ☽□♃ 22:33

20 Tu ☉#☽ 4:55 · ♀⚼⚷ 7:06 · ☿✶♅ 9:39 · ☊R 13:25 · ☽∠♇ 14:32 · ☽✶♄ 15:32 · ☽∥♇ 18:17 · ☽△⚷ 18:31 · ☉⚼☽ 19:07 · ☽#☿ 20:17 · ☽⚻♅ 21:00 · ☽⚻☿ 22:43

21 W ☿⚼♃ 2:11 · ♀∥⚳ 7:41 · ☽□♆ 11:10 · ☽△♂ 14:07 · ☽⊻♇ 15:11 · ☽∠♄ 16:07 · ☽⚻⚳ 17:47 · ☉⚻☽ 21:31 · ☽⚼♅ 21:43 · ☽△♀ 22:27 · ☽✶♃ 23:42

22 Th ♀ ♍ 0:38 · ♀☍♃ 12:46 · ♂⚻♇ 14:10 · ☉ ♌ 14:28 · ☽⚼♂ 15:53 · ☽⊻♄ 16:40 · ☽⚼⚳ 19:00 · ☽□⚷ 19:52 · ☽△♅ 22:26

23 F ☽∠♃ 0:15 · ☽⚼♀ 1:22 · ☉⚻♃ 4:11 · ☽☍☿ 7:55 · ♀#♃ 9:24 · ☿#♇ 12:27 · ☽✶♆ 12:34 · ☽☌♇ 16:35 · ☽⚻♂ 17:50 · ☽△⚳ 20:25

24 Sa ☽⊻♃ 1:00 · ☉☍☽ 2:38 · ☽⚻♀ 4:35 · ⚳∠⚷ 10:22 · ☽∥♇ 12:34 · ☽∠♆ 13:38 · ☽#☿ 14:02 · ☿△♆ 16:36 · ☽☌♄ 18:26 · ☽✶⚷ 21:58

25 Su ☽□♅ 0:44 · ♂∥⚳ 7:47 · ☉#☽ 9:01 · ☽⊻♆ 15:15 · ☽∥♄ 16:23 · ☽⚻☿ 19:17 · ☽⊻♇ 19:26 · ☿☍♇ 20:16 · ☽☍♂ 23:15 · ☽∠⚷ 23:49

26 M ☽□⚳ 0:42 · ☽☌♃ 3:57 · ☽#♅ 5:24 · ☉⚻☽ 9:56 · ♂⚼⚷ 11:24 · ☽☍♀ 13:05 · ☽#⚳ 16:13 · ☽#♂ 18:09 · ☽∥♃ 21:38 · ☽∠♇ 21:53 · ☽⊻♄ 22:26

27 Tu ☽⊻⚷ 2:26 · ☽⚼☿ 2:43 · ☽✶♅ 5:29 · ☽#♀ 6:27 · ☿⊻♂ 6:49 · ☿✶⚳ 12:02 · ☉⚼☽ 15:02 · ☽☌♆ 20:48 · ☽#⚷ 21:10

28 W ☿ ♌ 1:13 · ☽✶♇ 1:14 · ☽∠♄ 1:42 · ☿⚻♃ 1:46 · ☽⚻♂ 8:12 · ☽✶⚳ 8:18 · ☽∠♅ 9:12 · ☽⊻♃ 10:00 · ☽△☿ 11:43 · ♂□⚳ 11:52 · ☽∥♆ 12:13 · ♃R♒ 12:44 · ☉△☽ 21:20

29 Th ☽⚻♀ 2:02 · ☽✶♄ 5:54 · ☽☌⚷ 10:28 · ☽∠⚳ 13:36 · ♂#♃ 13:44 · ☽⊻♅ 13:52 · ☽⚼♂ 14:19 · ☽∠♃ 14:25 · ♂☍♃ 15:51 · ♂ ♍ 20:34 · ☽#♆ 22:42

30 F ☽⊻♆ 6:04 · ☽⚼♀ 10:22 · ☽□♇ 10:45 · ☉#♄ 12:13 · ⚳□♃ 14:04 · ♀⚼♇ 14:08 · ☽∥⚷ 14:27 · ♀⚻♄ 16:28 · ☽✶♃ 19:39 · ☽⊻⚳ 19:51 · ☉⚼♆ 20:29 · ☽△♂ 21:27 · ☽∥♀ 21:55

31 Sa ⚳ ♊ 8:14 · ☽□☿ 10:25 · ☽∠♆ 11:55 · ☉□☽ 13:17 · ☊D 13:25 · ☽∥♂ 14:21 · ☽□♄ 16:49 · ☽#♃ 17:13 · ☿⚼♆ 18:53 · ☽△♀ 19:42 · ☽⊻⚷ 21:54

August 2021

LONGITUDE

Day	Sid.Time	☉	☽	☽ 12 hour	Mean☊	True☊	☿	♀	♂	⚳	♃	♄	⚷	♅	♆	♇
	h m s	° ' "	° ' "	° ' "	° '	° '	° '	° '	° '	° '	° '	° '	° '	° '	° '	° '
1 Su	20 39 17	8♌58 41	13♉51 29	19♉46 36	7♊37.9	8♊52.8	8♌18.7	11♍56.7	1♍20.7	0♊11.7	29♒36.9	10♒16.7	12♈49.0	14♉38.6	22♓51.7	25♑13.6
2 M	20 43 14	9 56 06	25 40 47	1♊34 40	7 34.7	8 53.5	10 23.8	13 08.4	1 58.4	0 29.3	29R 30.0	10R 12.2	12R 48.1	14 39.5	22R 50.6	25R 12.2
3 Tu	20 47 10	10 53 31	7♊28 55	13 24 10	7 31.5	8R 54.0	12 28.0	14 20.0	2 36.2	0 46.8	29 23.0	10 07.8	12 47.2	14 40.4	22 49.5	25 10.8
4 W	20 51 07	11 50 58	19 20 59	25 19 56	7 28.3	8 53.5	14 31.2	15 31.6	3 13.9	1 04.2	29 15.9	10 03.3	12 46.3	14 41.2	22 48.4	25 09.4
5 Th	20 55 03	12 48 26	1♋21 30	7♋26 07	7 25.2	8 51.1	16 33.2	16 43.1	3 51.7	1 21.4	29 08.7	9 58.8	12 45.3	14 42.0	22 47.2	25 08.1
6 F	20 59 00	13 45 55	13 34 11	19 45 59	7 22.0	8 46.2	18 34.1	17 54.6	4 29.5	1 38.5	29 01.4	9 54.4	12 44.2	14 42.7	22 46.0	25 06.7
7 Sa	21 02 57	14 43 25	26 01 44	2♌21 35	7 18.8	8 38.9	20 33.5	19 06.0	5 07.3	1 55.4	28 54.1	9 49.9	12 43.1	14 43.4	22 44.8	25 05.4
8 Su	21 06 53	15 40 57	8♌45 37	15 13 47	7 15.6	8 29.4	22 31.6	20 17.4	5 45.1	2 12.2	28 46.7	9 45.5	12 42.0	14 44.0	22 43.6	25 04.1
9 M	21 10 50	16 38 29	21 46 02	28 22 10	7 12.4	8 18.4	24 28.3	21 28.8	6 22.9	2 28.8	28 39.2	9 41.1	12 40.8	14 44.6	22 42.4	25 02.7
10 Tu	21 14 46	17 36 02	5♍01 59	11♍45 13	7 09.3	8 07.0	26 23.5	22 40.1	7 00.8	2 45.2	28 31.6	9 36.7	12 39.5	14 45.1	22 41.1	25 01.4
11 W	21 18 43	18 33 37	18 31 34	25 20 44	7 06.1	7 56.3	28 17.2	23 51.3	7 38.7	3 01.5	28 24.0	9 32.3	12 38.3	14 45.6	22 39.8	25 00.1
12 Th	21 22 39	19 31 12	2♎12 24	9♎06 16	7 02.9	7 47.4	0♍09.5	25 02.5	8 16.6	3 17.6	28 16.3	9 27.9	12 36.9	14 46.0	22 38.5	24 58.8
13 F	21 26 36	20 28 48	16 02 05	22 59 35	6 59.7	7 40.9	2 00.2	26 13.7	8 54.6	3 33.6	28 08.6	9 23.6	12 35.5	14 46.3	22 37.2	24 57.6
14 Sa	21 30 32	21 26 25	29 58 34	6♏58 53	6 56.6	7 37.1	3 49.4	27 24.8	9 32.5	3 49.4	28 00.9	9 19.2	12 34.1	14 46.7	22 35.9	24 56.3
15 Su	21 34 29	22 24 03	14♏00 22	21 02 55	6 53.4	7D 35.5	5 37.2	28 35.8	10 10.5	4 05.0	27 53.1	9 14.9	12 32.6	14 46.9	22 34.5	24 55.1
16 M	21 38 26	23 21 42	28 06 26	5♐10 48	6 50.2	7R 35.4	7 23.4	29 46.8	10 48.5	4 20.4	27 45.3	9 10.7	12 31.1	14 47.2	22 33.1	24 53.8
17 Tu	21 42 22	24 19 23	12♐15 53	19 21 31	6 47.0	7 35.4	9 08.2	0♎57.7	11 26.5	4 35.6	27 37.4	9 06.4	12 29.6	14 47.4	22 31.7	24 52.6
18 W	21 46 19	25 17 04	26 27 31	3♑33 36	6 43.8	7 34.4	10 51.6	2 08.6	12 04.5	4 50.7	27 29.6	9 02.2	12 28.0	14 47.5	22 30.3	24 51.4
19 Th	21 50 15	26 14 46	10♑39 26	17 44 39	6 40.7	7 31.2	12 33.5	3 19.4	12 42.6	5 05.6	27 21.7	8 58.1	12 26.3	14 47.6	22 28.9	24 50.2
20 F	21 54 12	27 12 29	24 48 48	1♒51 22	6 37.5	7 25.4	14 13.9	4 30.2	13 20.7	5 20.3	27 13.8	8 54.0	12 24.7	14R 47.6	22 27.4	24 49.1
21 Sa	21 58 08	28 10 14	8♒51 50	15 49 39	6 34.3	7 16.8	15 53.0	5 40.9	13 58.8	5 34.7	27 06.0	8 49.9	12 22.9	14 47.6	22 26.0	24 47.9
22 Su	22 02 05	29 07 59	22 44 17	29 35 14	6 31.1	7 05.9	17 30.6	6 51.5	14 36.9	5 49.0	26 58.1	8 45.8	12 21.2	14 47.5	22 24.5	24 46.8
23 M	22 06 01	0♍05 47	6♓22 03	13♓04 21	6 28.0	6 53.8	19 06.8	8 02.0	15 15.0	6 03.1	26 50.3	8 41.8	12 19.4	14 47.4	22 23.0	24 45.6
24 Tu	22 09 58	1 03 35	19 41 52	26 14 25	6 24.8	6 41.7	20 41.6	9 12.5	15 53.2	6 17.0	26 42.4	8 37.9	12 17.5	14 47.2	22 21.5	24 44.5
25 W	22 13 55	2 01 25	2♈41 55	9♈04 25	6 21.6	6 30.7	22 15.1	10 22.9	16 31.4	6 30.7	26 34.6	8 33.9	12 15.6	14 47.0	22 20.0	24 43.5
26 Th	22 17 51	2 59 17	15 22 03	21 35 05	6 18.4	6 21.7	23 47.2	11 33.3	17 09.6	6 44.2	26 26.8	8 30.1	12 13.7	14 46.7	22 18.5	24 42.4
27 F	22 21 48	3 57 10	27 43 51	3♉48 46	6 15.2	6 15.3	25 17.8	12 43.6	17 47.9	6 57.5	26 19.1	8 26.3	12 11.8	14 46.4	22 16.9	24 41.3
28 Sa	22 25 44	4 55 05	9♉50 20	15 49 07	6 12.1	6 11.5	26 47.1	13 53.8	18 26.1	7 10.6	26 11.3	8 22.5	12 09.8	14 46.0	22 15.4	24 40.3
29 Su	22 29 41	5 53 02	21 45 42	27 40 46	6 08.9	6 09.8	28 15.0	15 04.0	19 04.4	7 23.4	26 03.7	8 18.8	12 07.7	14 45.6	22 13.8	24 39.3
30 M	22 33 37	6 51 01	3♊34 57	9♊28 58	6 05.7	6 09.4	29 41.5	16 14.1	19 42.7	7 36.0	25 56.1	8 15.2	12 05.7	14 45.1	22 12.2	24 38.3
31 Tu	22 37 34	7♍49 01	15 23 29	21 19 12	6♊02.5	6♊09.3	1♎06.6	17♎24.1	20♍21.1	7♊48.4	25♒48.5	8♒11.6	12♈03.6	14♉44.6	22♓10.6	24♑37.4

1st of Month

Julian Day # 2459427.5
Obliquity 23°26'05"
SVP 4♓57'05"
GC 27♐08.4
Eris 24♈46.8R

Day	⚴
1	26♓50.7R
6	26 15.9R
11	25 32.4R
16	24 40.7R
21	23 41.5R
26	22 35.6R
31	21 24.2R

Day	⚵
1	8♐21.1R
6	8 21.9
11	8 31.0
16	8 48.0
21	9 12.5
26	9 44.3
31	10 22.8

Day	⚶
1	5♎32.5
6	7 48.0
11	10 05.9
16	12 26.1
21	14 48.3
26	17 12.5
31	19 38.5

DECLINATION and LATITUDE

Day	☉ Decl	☽ Decl	☽ Lat	☽12h Decl	☿ Decl	☿ Lat	♀ Decl	♀ Lat	♂ Decl	♂ Lat	⚳ Decl	⚳ Lat	♃ Decl	♃ Lat	♄ Decl	♄ Lat
1 Su	18N01	13N56	2S10	16N04	19N48	1N40	8N18	1N19	12N01	1N05	13N56	6S23	12S40	1S08	18S25	0S47
2 M	17 45	18 02	1 10	19 50	19 17	1 43	7 49	1 17	11 47	1 05	13 60	6 23	12 43	1 08	18 26	0 47
3 Tu	17 30	21 26	0 08	22 48	18 44	1 44	7 19	1 15	11 33	1 05	14 04	6 23	12 45	1 09	18 27	0 47
4 W	17 14	23 56	0N56	24 48	18 10	1 46	6 50	1 13	11 19	1 04	14 07	6 23	12 48	1 09	18 29	0 47
5 Th	16 58	25 23	1 57	25 40	17 34	1 46	6 20	1 11	11 05	1 04	14 10	6 23	12 51	1 09	18 30	0 47
6 F	16 42	25 38	2 54	25 16	16 56	1 46	5 50	1 09	10 51	1 04	14 14	6 23	12 53	1 09	18 31	0 47
7 Sa	16 25	24 36	3 43	23 36	16 18	1 45	5 20	1 07	10 37	1 03	14 17	6 23	12 56	1 09	18 32	0 47
8 Su	16 08	22 18	4 23	20 42	15 38	1 44	4 50	1 04	10 23	1 03	14 20	6 23	12 59	1 09	18 34	0 47
9 M	15 51	18 49	4 50	16 41	14 58	1 42	4 20	1 02	10 08	1 03	14 23	6 23	13 02	1 10	18 35	0 47
10 Tu	15 33	14 20	5 02	11 48	14 16	1 39	3 49	0 60	9 54	1 02	14 27	6 23	13 05	1 10	18 36	0 47
11 W	15 16	9 06	4 57	6 16	13 34	1 36	3 19	0 57	9 40	1 02	14 30	6 23	13 07	1 10	18 38	0 47
12 Th	14 58	3 20	4 36	0 21	12 51	1 32	2 48	0 54	9 25	1 02	14 33	6 23	13 10	1 10	18 39	0 48
13 F	14 40	2S39	3 58	5S38	12 08	1 28	2 18	0 52	9 11	1 01	14 36	6 23	13 13	1 10	18 40	0 48
14 Sa	14 21	8 34	3 05	11 24	11 25	1 24	1 47	0 49	8 56	1 01	14 38	6 23	13 16	1 10	18 41	0 48
15 Su	14 03	14 06	2 02	16 38	10 41	1 19	1 16	0 46	8 41	1 01	14 41	6 23	13 19	1 10	18 42	0 48
16 M	13 44	18 55	0 50	20 57	9 56	1 14	0 45	0 43	8 27	1 00	14 44	6 23	13 21	1 11	18 44	0 48
17 Tu	13 25	22 40	0S25	24 02	9 12	1 08	0 14	0 40	8 12	1 00	14 47	6 23	13 24	1 11	18 45	0 48
18 W	13 06	25 02	1 38	25 36	8 27	1 02	0S17	0 37	7 57	0 60	14 49	6 23	13 27	1 11	18 46	0 48
19 Th	12 46	25 46	2 45	25 29	7 43	0 56	0 48	0 34	7 42	0 59	14 52	6 23	13 30	1 11	18 47	0 48
20 F	12 26	24 48	3 42	23 44	6 58	0 49	1 19	0 31	7 27	0 59	14 55	6 23	13 33	1 11	18 48	0 48
21 Sa	12 07	22 18	4 25	20 33	6 13	0 43	1 50	0 28	7 12	0 59	14 57	6 23	13 35	1 11	18 49	0 48
22 Su	11 46	18 31	4 51	16 16	5 29	0 36	2 20	0 25	6 57	0 58	14 59	6 23	13 38	1 11	18 50	0 48
23 M	11 26	13 49	5 01	11 15	4 44	0 28	2 51	0 22	6 42	0 58	15 02	6 23	13 41	1 11	18 52	0 48
24 Tu	11 06	8 34	4 53	5 50	4 00	0 21	3 22	0 18	6 27	0 58	15 04	6 23	13 44	1 11	18 53	0 48
25 W	10 45	3 04	4 30	0 18	3 16	0 13	3 53	0 15	6 12	0 57	15 06	6 23	13 47	1 11	18 54	0 48
26 Th	10 24	2N27	3 55	5N07	2 33	0 05	4 24	0 11	5 57	0 57	15 09	6 23	13 49	1 12	18 55	0 48
27 F	10 04	7 44	3 08	10 14	1 50	0S03	4 54	0 08	5 41	0 56	15 11	6 23	13 52	1 12	18 56	0 48
28 Sa	9 42	12 38	2 15	14 53	1 07	0 11	5 25	0 04	5 26	0 56	15 13	6 22	13 55	1 12	18 57	0 48
29 Su	9 21	16 59	1 16	18 55	0 24	0 19	5 55	0 01	5 11	0 56	15 15	6 22	13 57	1 12	18 58	0 48
30 M	8 60	20 39	0 14	22 10	0S18	0 28	6 26	0S03	4 55	0 55	15 17	6 22	13 60	1 12	18 59	0 48
31 Tu	8N38	23N27	0N49	24N29	0S60	0S36	6S56	0S07	4N40	0N55	15N19	6S22	14S03	1S12	18S60	0S49

Day	⚷ Decl	⚷ Lat	♅ Decl	♅ Lat	♆ Decl	♆ Lat	♇ Decl	♇ Lat
1	7N16	2N23	15N50	0S25	3S54	1S09	22S39	1S36
6	7 14	2 23	15 51	0 25	3 56	1 09	22 41	1 36
11	7 12	2 24	15 52	0 25	3 59	1 10	22 43	1 36
16	7 09	2 24	15 52	0 25	4 01	1 10	22 44	1 37
21	7 06	2 24	15 53	0 25	4 04	1 10	22 45	1 37
26	7 03	2 24	15 52	0 25	4 07	1 10	22 47	1 37
31	6N59	2N24	15N52	0S25	4S11	1S10	22S48	1S38

Day	⚴ Decl	⚴ Lat	⚵ Decl	⚵ Lat	⚶ Decl	⚶ Lat	Eris Decl	Eris Lat
1	7N05	9N05	5S53	15N60	3N12	5N53	1S05	11S28
6	6 30	8 42	6 16	15 37	2 11	5 45	1 06	11 28
11	5 50	8 17	6 40	15 14	1 09	5 36	1 06	11 28
16	5 04	7 49	7 05	14 51	0 07	5 28	1 07	11 29
21	4 13	7 19	7 31	14 28	0S55	5 19	1 08	11 29
26	3 17	6 46	7 58	14 06	1 58	5 11	1 09	11 29
31	2N17	6N11	8S24	13N44	2S60	5N04	1S10	11S30

Moon Phenomena

Max/0 Decl

dy hr mn	
5 16:48	25N41
12 13:25	0 S
18 22:22	25S46
25 13:17	0 N

Max/0 Lat

dy hr mn	
3 2:53	0 N
10 5:27	5N02
16 16:05	0 S
23 0:56	5S01
30 5:15	0 N

Perigee/Apogee

dy hr m		kilometers
2 7:36	a	404408
17 9:17	p	369124
30 2:23	a	404099

PH	dy hr mn	
●	8 13:51	16♌14
☽	15 15:21	23♏01
○	22 12:03	29♒37
☾	30 7:14	7♊09

Void of Course Moon

Last Aspect			☽ Ingress
2 7:42	♃ □	♊	2 8:47
4 19:39	♃ △	♋	4 21:18
6 22:13	♇ ☍	♌	7 7:33
9 12:24	♃ ☍	♍	9 14:57
11 11:23	♇ △	♎	11 20:09
13 20:40	♃ △	♏	14 0:02
16 3:06	♀ ✶	♐	16 3:13
18 1:44	♃ ✶	♑	18 5:59
20 0:00	♇ ☌	♒	20 8:50
22 12:03	☉ ☍	♓	22 12:44
24 9:14	♇ ✶	♈	24 18:58
26 21:16	♃ ✶	♉	27 4:28
29 15:00	☿ △	♊	29 16:43

DAILY ASPECTARIAN

1 Su ☽∥⚳ 0:04 · ☽☌♅ 1:35 · ☽∥♅ 10:41 · ☉☌☿ 14:09 · ♀⚻⚷ 17:18 · ☽✶♆ 18:14 · ☿☍♄ 21:51 · ☉∥☽ 22:20 · ☽△♇ 23:02

2 M ☽#♄ 2:33 · ☽∠⚷ 4:19 · ☉☍♄ 6:16 · ☽∥☿ 7:04 · ☽□♃ 7:42 · ☽☌⚳ 10:02 · ☽□♂ 13:32 · ⚵ D 23:44

3 Tu ☊ R 2:54 · ♀∥⚷ 3:39 · ☿△⚷ 3:42 · ☽△♄ 5:20 · ☽⚼♇ 5:28 · ♀△♅ 6:55 · ☉✶☽ 7:31 · ☽#♇ 10:43 · ☽✶⚷ 10:44 · ☿#♄ 11:18 · ☽✶☿ 12:14 · ☽⚺♅ 14:35 · ☽□♀ 15:26

4 W ☿□♅ 1:58 · ☽□♆ 6:56 · ☽⚼♄ 11:22 · ☽⚻♇ 11:38 · ☉∠☽ 16:20 · ☽△♃ 19:39 · ☽∠♅ 20:42 · ☉△⚷ 22:42 · ☽⚺⚳ 24:00

5 Th ☽∠☿ 0:28 · ☿⚺♀ 4:45 · ☽✶♂ 5:14 · ☽⚻♄ 16:53 · ☽□⚷ 22:23

6 F ☉⚺☽ 0:25 · ☽⚼♃ 0:53 · ☽✶♅ 2:13 · ☽∠⚳ 6:06 · ☽✶♀ 9:19 · ☽⚺☿ 11:32 · ☽∠♂ 12:05 · ☉∥☿ 16:21 · ☽△♆ 17:44 · ☽☍♇ 22:13 · ☉□♅ 23:58

7 Sa ☽⚻♃ 5:24 · ☽✶⚳ 11:26 · ☿∥♅ 16:00 · ☽∠♀ 16:51 · ☽⚺♂ 18:05 · ☽#♇ 20:38 · ☽⚼♆ 22:04

8 Su ☽☍♄ 1:51 · ☿⚻♆ 2:26 · ☽△⚷ 7:19 · ☽□♅ 11:05 · ☉☌☽ 13:51 · ☉∥♅ 22:42 · ☽⚺♀ 23:25

9 M ☽#♄ 1:23 · ☽⚻♆ 1:43 · ☽☌☿ 5:46 · ☽⚻♇ 5:58 · ☿⚻♇ 7:04 · ☽⚼⚷ 10:44 · ☽☍♃ 12:24 · ☽∥♅ 16:20 · ♀#♆ 17:17 · ☉∥☽ 17:30 · ☿∥⚳ 18:31 · ☽□⚳ 19:49 · ☽∥⚳ 23:30

10 Tu ♀☍♆ 0:21 · ☽∥☿ 0:23 · ☽☌♂ 3:43 · ☽#♃ 6:01 · ☽⚻♄ 8:08 · ☽⚼♇ 8:54 · ☽⚻⚷ 13:35 · ☿⚼⚷ 15:50 · ☽△♅ 17:20 · ☽∥♂ 21:25

11 W ☉⚺☽ 0:04 · ☿☍♃ 1:21 · ☽☍♆ 7:17 · ☽∥⚷ 8:06 · ☽☌♀ 10:17 · ☽⚼♄ 10:32 · ☽△♇ 11:23 · ♀⚼♄ 13:00 · ☿#♃ 14:12 · ☽⚻♃ 17:11 · ☽⚼♅ 19:44 · ☽⚺☿ 19:52 · ☽#♆ 21:22 · ☿ ♍ 21:58 · ♀△♇ 22:47

12 Th ☽△⚳ 1:56 · ☽∥♀ 2:22 · ☉∠☽ 4:20 · ☽⚺♂ 11:04 · ☽△♄ 12:34 · ☽☍⚷ 18:03 · ☽⚼♃ 19:03 · ☽⚻♅ 21:49 · ☽#♀ 22:41

13 F ☽∠☿ 1:56 · ☽⚼⚳ 4:27 · ☉∥⚳ 4:42 · ☽∥♆ 5:24 · ☉✶☽ 8:14 · ☽⚻♆ 11:20 · ☽∠♂ 14:13 · ☽□♇ 15:22 · ♂⚻♄ 16:28 · ☽#⚷ 18:15 · ☽⚺♀ 19:12 · ☽△♃ 20:40 · ☿□⚳ 23:59

14 Sa ☽#♂ 1:28 · ☽⚻⚳ 6:43 · ☽✶☿ 7:34 · ☽#☿ 10:37 · ♀⚻♃ 10:59 · ☽⚼♆ 13:02 · ♂⚼♇ 14:33 · ☽□♄ 15:55 · ☽✶♂ 17:09 · ☽∥♃ 20:22 · ☽⚻⚷ 21:31 · ☽∠♀ 23:14 · ☉#☽ 23:44

15 Su ☽☍♅ 1:19 · ☽#⚳ 2:43 · ☉⚻♆ 4:15 · ☽#♅ 8:19 · ☽△♆ 14:34 · ☊ D 15:09 · ☉□☽ 15:21 · ☽✶♇ 18:33 · ☽∥♄ 22:55 · ☽⚼⚷ 23:00 · ☽□♃ 23:24

16 M ♀⚼♅ 0:07 · ☽✶♀ 3:06 · ♀ ♎ 4:28 · ☽☍⚳ 10:46 · ☊ R 16:08 · ☽□☿ 17:58 · ☽✶♄ 18:41 · ☽∠♇ 19:58 · ☽□♂ 22:33 · ☿⚻♄ 23:36

17 Tu ☽△⚷ 0:23 · ☽∥♇ 0:32 · ☉#♃ 0:38 · ☽⚻♅ 4:16 · ☿⚼♇ 10:09 · ☉⚻♇ 13:33 · ☽□♆ 17:20 · ☽∠♄ 19:56 · ☽⚺♇ 21:18 · ☉△☽ 21:52

18 W ☽✶♃ 1:44 · ☽⚼♅ 5:38 · ♃∠⚷ 6:08 · ☽□♀ 10:29 · ♂⚻⚷ 14:10 · ☽⚻⚳ 14:25 · ☽⚺♄ 21:09 · ☿⚻⚷ 22:20

19 Th ☿∥♂ 0:18 · ☉⚼☽ 1:04 · ☽∠♃ 2:51 · ☽□⚷ 3:01 · ☿☌♂ 3:29 · ☽△♂ 3:38 · ☽△☿ 3:39 · ☽△♅ 7:00 · ☽⚼⚳ 16:16 · ☿∥⚷ 19:10 · ☽✶♆ 20:00

20 F ☽☌♇ 0:00 · ☉☍♃ 0:30 · ♅ R 1:41 · ☽⚺♃ 4:05 · ☉⚻☽ 4:22 · ☉⚼⚷ 4:55 · ☽⚼♂ 6:18 · ☿△♅ 8:07 · ☽⚼☿ 8:32 · ☽△♀ 18:02 · ☽△⚳ 18:16 · ☽∥♇ 20:27 · ♀△⚳ 21:24 · ☽∠♆ 21:33 · ☽☌♄ 23:57

21 Sa ☽✶⚷ 6:02 · ☽⚻♂ 9:14 · ☽□♅ 10:13 · ♂∥⚷ 10:14 · ☽⚻☿ 13:43 · ☽∥♄ 22:12 · ☽⚼♀ 22:19 · ☽⚺♆ 23:26

22 Su ☽⚺♇ 3:34 · ♂△♅ 6:39 · ☽☌♃ 7:20 · ☽∠⚷ 8:03 · ☉☍☽ 12:03 · ☽#♅ 13:58 · ☽#⚳ 18:13 · ☉ ♍ 21:36 · ☽□⚳ 23:26

23 M ☽∥♃ 0:40 · ☽⚻♀ 3:15 · ☽⚺♄ 4:08 · ☽∠♇ 6:03 · ☽⚺⚷ 10:38 · ☉#☽ 11:54 · ♀△♄ 12:49 · ☽✶♅ 15:06 · ☽☍♂ 16:44 · ☿#♆ 20:53

24 Tu ☽☍☿ 2:04 · ☽☌♆ 4:51 · ☽#⚷ 6:37 · ☽∠♄ 7:10 · ☽✶♇ 9:14 · ☽#♂ 9:45 · ☿#♀ 12:14 · ☽⚺♃ 12:44 · ☽∠♅ 18:34 · ☽∥♆ 19:27 · ☽∥♀ 20:44 · ☉⚻☽ 22:38 · ☽#☿ 22:56

25 W ☿☍♆ 1:15 · ☽✶⚳ 7:17 · ♀∥♆ 10:57 · ☽✶♄ 10:59 · ☽☍♀ 15:58 · ☽∠♃ 16:35 · ☽☌⚷ 18:01 · ☿⚼♄ 19:42 · ♀⚼♃ 22:00 · ☽⚺♅ 22:52

26 Th ☽∥☿ 0:25 · ☽⚻♂ 3:38 · ☉⚼☽ 5:28 · ☽#♆ 7:30 · ☽#♀ 9:38 · ☽∠⚳ 12:31 · ☽⚺♆ 13:23 · ♀☍⚷ 13:25 · ☿△♇ 14:24 · ☽∥♂ 15:00 · ☽□♇ 18:03 · ☽⚻☿ 18:34 · ☽∥⚷ 20:45 · ☽✶♃ 21:16

27 F ☉∥☽ 10:23 · ☽⚼♂ 10:33 · ☉△☽ 13:21 · ☿⚻♃ 15:06 · ☽⚺⚳ 18:35 · ☽∠♆ 18:51 · ☽□♄ 21:05

28 Sa ♀#♂ 0:33 · ☽⚼☿ 4:27 · ☽⚺⚷ 4:38 · ☽#♃ 6:46 · ☽⚻♀ 9:01 · ☽☌♅ 9:53 · ☽∥⚳ 13:56 · ☽∥♅ 17:28 · ♀⚻♅ 17:45 · ☽△♂ 18:15

29 Su ☽✶♆ 0:57 · ☽△♇ 5:51 · ☽□♃ 8:37 · ☽∠⚷ 10:51 · ☽#♄ 12:24 · ☽△☿ 15:00 · ☽⚼♀ 18:42

30 M ☿⚼♅ 1:01 · ☿ ♎ 5:11 · ☉□☽ 7:14 · ☽☌⚳ 8:19 · ☽△♄ 9:27 · ☽⚼♇ 12:18 · ☽✶⚷ 17:15 · ☽#♇ 17:40 · ☽⚺♅ 22:41 · ☉□⚳ 23:40

31 Tu ♀#⚷ 2:01 · ☽△♀ 4:31 · ☉⚻♄ 8:47 · ☽□♂ 10:37 · ☽□♆ 13:42 · ☽⚼♄ 15:42 · ☽⚻♇ 18:38 · ☽△♃ 20:50

September 2021

LONGITUDE

Day	Sid.Time	☉	☽	☽ 12 hour	Mean☊	True☊	☿	♀	♂	⚳	♃	♄	⚷	♅	♆	♇
	h m s	° ' "	° ' "	° ' "	° '	° '	° '	° '	° '	° '	° '	° '	° '	° '	° '	° '
1 W	22 41 30	8♍47 04	27♊16 48	3♋16 55	5♊59.4	6♊08.4	2♎30.2	18♎34.1	20♍59.5	8♊00.5	25♒41.0	8♒08.0	12♈01.4	14♉44.1	22♓09.1	24♑36.4
2 Th	22 45 27	9 45 08	9♋20 11	15 27 07	5 56.2	6R 05.8	3 52.3	19 44.0	21 37.9	8 12.4	25R 33.6	8R 04.6	11R 59.3	14R 43.4	22R 07.5	24R 35.5
3 F	22 49 24	10 43 15	21 38 16	27 54 01	5 53.0	6 00.7	5 12.9	20 53.8	22 16.3	8 24.1	25 26.2	8 01.2	11 57.1	14 42.8	22 05.8	24 34.6
4 Sa	22 53 20	11 41 23	4♌14 43	10♌40 35	5 49.8	5 53.0	6 32.0	22 03.5	22 54.8	8 35.5	25 18.9	7 57.8	11 54.9	14 42.1	22 04.2	24 33.7
5 Su	22 57 17	12 39 33	17 11 45	23 48 13	5 46.7	5 42.9	7 49.5	23 13.2	23 33.2	8 46.7	25 11.7	7 54.6	11 52.6	14 41.3	22 02.6	24 32.8
6 M	23 01 13	13 37 45	0♍29 53	7♍16 30	5 43.5	5 31.2	9 05.3	24 22.8	24 11.8	8 57.6	25 04.6	7 51.4	11 50.3	14 40.5	22 01.0	24 32.0
7 Tu	23 05 10	14 35 58	14 07 43	21 03 05	5 40.3	5 18.9	10 19.4	25 32.3	24 50.3	9 08.3	24 57.6	7 48.2	11 48.0	14 39.7	21 59.3	24 31.2
8 W	23 09 06	15 34 14	28 02 06	5♎04 10	5 37.1	5 07.3	11 31.8	26 41.8	25 28.9	9 18.7	24 50.7	7 45.2	11 45.6	14 38.8	21 57.7	24 30.4
9 Th	23 13 03	16 32 30	12♎08 39	19 14 58	5 33.9	4 57.5	12 42.2	27 51.1	26 07.5	9 28.8	24 43.9	7 42.2	11 43.3	14 37.8	21 56.0	24 29.6
10 F	23 16 59	17 30 49	26 22 29	3♏30 39	5 30.8	4 50.4	13 50.8	29 00.4	26 46.1	9 38.7	24 37.2	7 39.3	11 40.9	14 36.8	21 54.4	24 28.9
11 Sa	23 20 56	18 29 09	10♏38 59	17 47 02	5 27.6	4 46.1	14 57.2	0♏09.6	27 24.7	9 48.2	24 30.6	7 36.5	11 38.4	14 35.8	21 52.7	24 28.2
12 Su	23 24 53	19 27 31	24 54 28	2♐00 59	5 24.4	4D 44.3	16 01.5	1 18.7	28 03.4	9 57.5	24 24.2	7 33.7	11 36.0	14 34.7	21 51.1	24 27.5
13 M	23 28 49	20 25 55	9♐06 23	16 10 29	5 21.2	4R 44.1	17 03.4	2 27.7	28 42.1	10 06.6	24 17.8	7 31.0	11 33.5	14 33.6	21 49.4	24 26.8
14 Tu	23 32 46	21 24 20	23 13 13	0♑14 26	5 18.0	4 44.2	18 02.9	3 36.6	29 20.8	10 15.3	24 11.6	7 28.5	11 31.0	14 32.4	21 47.8	24 26.2
15 W	23 36 42	22 22 46	7♑14 06	14 12 08	5 14.9	4 43.5	18 59.8	4 45.4	29 59.6	10 23.7	24 05.6	7 26.0	11 28.5	14 31.2	21 46.1	24 25.6
16 Th	23 40 39	23 21 15	21 08 25	28 02 49	5 11.7	4 40.7	19 53.8	5 54.1	0♎38.4	10 31.9	23 59.6	7 23.5	11 26.0	14 30.0	21 44.5	24 25.0
17 F	23 44 35	24 19 44	4♒55 13	11♒45 25	5 08.5	4 35.4	20 44.9	7 02.7	1 17.2	10 39.7	23 53.8	7 21.2	11 23.5	14 28.7	21 42.8	24 24.4
18 Sa	23 48 32	25 18 16	18 33 13	25 18 22	5 05.3	4 27.5	21 32.6	8 11.2	1 56.0	10 47.3	23 48.2	7 18.9	11 20.9	14 27.3	21 41.2	24 23.9
19 Su	23 52 28	26 16 49	2♓00 37	8♓39 44	5 02.2	4 17.4	22 16.9	9 19.6	2 34.9	10 54.5	23 42.7	7 16.8	11 18.3	14 25.9	21 39.5	24 23.4
20 M	23 56 25	27 15 24	15 15 29	21 47 39	4 59.0	4 06.1	22 57.5	10 27.9	3 13.8	11 01.4	23 37.3	7 14.7	11 15.7	14 24.5	21 37.9	24 22.9
21 Tu	0 00 22	28 14 00	28 17 12	4♈40 36	4 55.8	3 54.7	23 34.0	11 36.0	3 52.7	11 08.0	23 32.1	7 12.7	11 13.1	14 23.1	21 36.2	24 22.4
22 W	0 04 18	29 12 39	11♈01 13	17 17 56	4 52.6	3 44.3	24 06.1	12 44.0	4 31.6	11 14.3	23 27.1	7 10.8	11 10.5	14 21.6	21 34.6	24 22.0
23 Th	0 08 15	0♎11 19	23 30 48	29 40 01	4 49.4	3 35.8	24 33.5	13 52.0	5 10.6	11 20.3	23 22.2	7 09.0	11 07.8	14 20.0	21 33.0	24 21.6
24 F	0 12 11	1 10 02	5♉45 46	11♉48 24	4 46.3	3 29.7	24 55.8	14 59.7	5 49.6	11 25.9	23 17.5	7 07.3	11 05.2	14 18.4	21 31.3	24 21.2
25 Sa	0 16 08	2 08 47	17 48 15	23 45 47	4 43.1	3 26.1	25 12.6	16 07.4	6 28.7	11 31.3	23 13.0	7 05.6	11 02.5	14 16.8	21 29.7	24 20.8
26 Su	0 20 04	3 07 34	29 41 29	5♊35 53	4 39.9	3D 24.7	25 23.6	17 15.0	7 07.7	11 36.2	23 08.6	7 04.1	10 59.8	14 15.2	21 28.1	24 20.5
27 M	0 24 01	4 06 23	11♊29 34	17 23 11	4 36.7	3 24.9	25R 28.3	18 22.4	7 46.9	11 40.9	23 04.4	7 02.7	10 57.2	14 13.5	21 26.5	24 20.2
28 Tu	0 27 57	5 05 15	23 17 21	29 12 44	4 33.6	3 25.8	25 26.3	19 29.7	8 26.0	11 45.1	23 00.4	7 01.3	10 54.5	14 11.7	21 24.9	24 20.0
29 W	0 31 54	6 04 09	5♋10 03	11♋09 56	4 30.4	3R 26.3	25 17.4	20 36.8	9 05.2	11 49.1	22 56.5	7 00.1	10 51.8	14 10.0	21 23.3	24 19.7
30 Th	0 35 51	7♎03 05	17 13 04	23 20 05	4♊27.2	3♊25.7	25♎01.1	21♏43.8	9♎44.4	11♊52.7	22♒52.9	6♒58.9	10♈49.1	14♉08.2	21♓21.7	24♑19.5

1st of Month

Julian Day # 2459458.5
Obliquity 23°26'15"
SVP 4♓57'31"
GC 27♐08.5
Eris 24♈38.7R

Day	⚴
1	21♓09.4R
6	19 53.2R
11	18 34.8R
16	17 15.9R
21	15 58.5R
26	14 44.1R

Day	⚵
1	10♐31.3
6	11 17.5
11	12 09.7
16	13 07.6
21	14 10.6
26	15 18.5

Day	⚶
1	20♎07.9
6	22 35.9
11	25 05.5
16	27 36.6
21	0♏09.0
26	2 42.5

DECLINATION and LATITUDE

Day	☉ Decl	☽ Decl	☽ Lat	☽12h Decl	☿ Decl	☿ Lat	♀ Decl	♀ Lat	♂ Decl	♂ Lat	⚳ Decl	⚳ Lat	♃ Decl	♃ Lat	♄ Decl	♄ Lat
1 W	8N17	25N14	1N49	25N42	1S41	0S45	7S26	0S10	4N24	0N55	15N21	6S22	14S05	1S12	19S01	0S49
2 Th	7 55	25 52	2 46	25 43	2 21	0 53	7 56	0 14	4 09	0 54	15 23	6 22	14 08	1 12	19 02	0 49
3 F	7 33	25 15	3 36	24 28	3 01	1 02	8 26	0 18	3 53	0 54	15 25	6 22	14 10	1 12	19 03	0 49
4 Sa	7 11	23 21	4 17	21 56	3 41	1 11	8 56	0 22	3 38	0 53	15 27	6 22	14 13	1 12	19 04	0 49
5 Su	6 49	20 13	4 45	18 13	4 19	1 19	9 25	0 26	3 22	0 53	15 28	6 22	14 15	1 12	19 04	0 49
6 M	6 26	15 58	4 60	13 29	4 57	1 28	9 55	0 30	3 07	0 53	15 30	6 22	14 18	1 12	19 05	0 49
7 Tu	6 04	10 49	4 57	7 59	5 34	1 37	10 24	0 34	2 51	0 52	15 32	6 22	14 20	1 12	19 06	0 49
8 W	5 41	5 01	4 37	1 59	6 11	1 46	10 53	0 38	2 35	0 52	15 33	6 22	14 22	1 12	19 07	0 49
9 Th	5 19	1S06	4 00	4S12	6 46	1 54	11 21	0 42	2 20	0 51	15 35	6 21	14 24	1 12	19 08	0 49
10 F	4 56	7 15	3 08	10 13	7 21	2 03	11 50	0 46	2 04	0 51	15 37	6 21	14 27	1 12	19 09	0 49
11 Sa	4 33	13 03	2 04	15 43	7 54	2 11	12 18	0 50	1 48	0 51	15 38	6 21	14 29	1 12	19 09	0 49
12 Su	4 10	18 09	0 52	20 20	8 27	2 19	12 46	0 54	1 32	0 50	15 40	6 21	14 31	1 12	19 10	0 49
13 M	3 47	22 12	0S23	23 43	8 58	2 28	13 14	0 58	1 17	0 50	15 41	6 21	14 33	1 12	19 11	0 49
14 Tu	3 24	24 52	1 36	25 37	9 29	2 36	13 41	1 02	1 01	0 49	15 42	6 21	14 35	1 12	19 11	0 49
15 W	3 01	25 58	2 43	25 53	9 58	2 44	14 09	1 06	0 45	0 49	15 44	6 20	14 37	1 12	19 12	0 49
16 Th	2 38	25 24	3 40	24 32	10 25	2 51	14 35	1 10	0 29	0 49	15 45	6 20	14 39	1 12	19 13	0 49
17 F	2 15	23 17	4 23	21 44	10 51	2 58	15 02	1 14	0 14	0 48	15 46	6 20	14 41	1 12	19 13	0 49
18 Sa	1 52	19 52	4 51	17 46	11 16	3 05	15 28	1 18	0S02	0 48	15 48	6 20	14 43	1 12	19 14	0 49
19 Su	1 29	15 27	5 02	12 59	11 39	3 12	15 54	1 23	0 18	0 47	15 49	6 19	14 45	1 12	19 14	0 49
20 M	1 05	10 22	4 57	7 40	11 60	3 18	16 20	1 27	0 34	0 47	15 50	6 19	14 46	1 12	19 15	0 49
21 Tu	0 42	4 55	4 36	2 08	12 19	3 24	16 45	1 31	0 50	0 47	15 51	6 19	14 48	1 12	19 16	0 49
22 W	0 19	0N39	4 02	3N24	12 36	3 30	17 10	1 35	1 06	0 46	15 52	6 19	14 50	1 12	19 16	0 49
23 Th	0S05	6 05	3 16	8 42	12 50	3 34	17 35	1 39	1 21	0 46	15 54	6 18	14 51	1 11	19 16	0 49
24 F	0 28	11 12	2 22	13 35	13 02	3 38	17 59	1 43	1 37	0 45	15 55	6 18	14 53	1 11	19 17	0 49
25 Sa	0 51	15 49	1 23	17 53	13 11	3 42	18 22	1 47	1 53	0 45	15 56	6 17	14 54	1 11	19 17	0 49
26 Su	1 15	19 46	0 20	21 26	13 18	3 44	18 46	1 51	2 09	0 44	15 57	6 17	14 55	1 11	19 18	0 49
27 M	1 38	22 52	0N43	24 04	13 21	3 45	19 09	1 56	2 25	0 44	15 58	6 17	14 57	1 11	19 18	0 49
28 Tu	2 01	25 01	1 45	25 40	13 20	3 46	19 31	1 60	2 41	0 44	15 59	6 16	14 58	1 11	19 18	0 49
29 W	2 25	26 02	2 42	26 06	13 16	3 45	19 53	2 04	2 56	0 43	15 60	6 16	14 59	1 11	19 19	0 49
30 Th	2S48	25N51	3N33	25N17	13S08	3S43	20S15	2S08	3S12	0N43	16N01	6S15	15S00	1S11	19S19	0S49

Day	⚷ Decl	⚷ Lat	♅ Decl	♅ Lat	♆ Decl	♆ Lat	♇ Decl	♇ Lat
1	6N58	2N24	15N51	0S25	4S11	1S10	22S48	1S38
6	6 53	2 24	15 50	0 25	4 14	1 10	22 49	1 38
11	6 49	2 24	15 49	0 25	4 18	1 10	22 50	1 38
16	6 44	2 24	15 47	0 25	4 21	1 10	22 51	1 38
21	6 39	2 24	15 45	0 25	4 24	1 10	22 52	1 39
26	6 33	2 24	15 43	0 25	4 28	1 10	22 52	1 39

Day	⚴ Decl	⚴ Lat	⚵ Decl	⚵ Lat	⚶ Decl	⚶ Lat	Eris Decl	Eris Lat
1	2N04	6N04	8S29	13N40	3S12	5N02	1S10	11S30
6	0 60	5 26	8 56	13 19	4 14	4 54	1 11	11 30
11	0S07	4 46	9 22	12 59	5 15	4 47	1 12	11 30
16	1 16	4 06	9 48	12 40	6 16	4 40	1 13	11 30
21	2 24	3 24	10 13	12 22	7 16	4 32	1 14	11 31
26	3 32	2 42	10 38	12 04	8 15	4 25	1 15	11 31

Moon Phenomena

Max/0 Decl

dy	hr mn	
2	0:25	25N52
8	19:42	0 S
15	3:46	25S59
21	21:10	0 N
29	8:28	26N07

Max/0 Lat

dy	hr mn	
6	8:47	5N01
12	16:36	0 S
19	4:03	5S02
26	7:34	0 N

Perigee/Apogee

dy	hr m		kilometers
11	10:05	p	368462
26	21:45	a	404640

PH	dy	hr mn	
●	7	0:53	14♍38
☽	13	20:41	21♐16
○	20	23:56	28♓14
☾	29	1:58	6♋09

Void of Course Moon

Last Aspect	☽ Ingress
31 20:50 ♃ △	♋ 1 5:27
3 5:39 ♇ ☍	♌ 3 15:59
5 14:23 ♃ ☍	♍ 5 23:07
7 19:25 ♂ ☌	♎ 8 3:22
10 4:49 ♀ ☌	♏ 10 6:06
12 5:34 ♂ ✶	♐ 12 8:36
14 10:59 ☉ □	♑ 14 11:35
16 5:41 ♇ ☌	♒ 16 15:24
18 9:16 ♃ ☌	♓ 18 20:24
20 23:56 ☉ ☍	♈ 21 3:14
23 2:06 ☿ ☍	♉ 23 12:39
25 13:10 ♇ △	♊ 26 0:38
28 4:19 ☿ △	♋ 28 13:35

DAILY ASPECTARIAN

1 W: ☽∠♅ 4:55; ⚳△♄ 11:40; ☽□☿ 11:48; ♂#♆ 19:38; ☉⚼♇ 20:04; ☽⚻♄ 21:31; ☽⚺⚳ 21:44; ☉#♀ 23:20

2 Th: ☉✶☽ 0:53; ☽⚼♃ 2:23; ☽□⚷ 5:12; ☽✶♅ 10:34; ♂☍♆ 17:44; ☽□♀ 22:25

3 F: ☽△♆ 0:53; ☽✶♂ 1:17; ☽∠⚳ 3:27; ☽☍♇ 5:39; ☽⚻♃ 7:14; ☉∠☽ 8:30; ☿#♂ 22:48

4 Sa: ♀⚻♆ 0:14; ♂⚼♄ 1:46; ☽✶☿ 4:46; ☽#♇ 4:49; ☽⚼♆ 5:17; ☉⚻⚷ 5:21; ☽☍♄ 6:56; ☽∠♂ 7:13; ☽✶⚳ 8:15; ☽△⚷ 14:15; ☉⚺☽ 15:00; ☉∥⚷ 17:25; ☽□♅ 19:25; ☿∥♆ 20:33

5 Su: ☿△♄ 1:32; ☽#♄ 6:59; ☽⚻♆ 8:48; ☽∠☿ 11:19; ☽✶♀ 12:00; ☽⚺♂ 12:08; ☽⚻♇ 13:20; ♀⚼⚳ 13:43; ☽☍♃ 14:23; ♀⚺♂ 15:27; ☽⚼⚷ 17:29; ☿△⚳ 21:08

6 M: ☽∥♅ 0:37; ☽∥⚳ 2:17; ♀□♇ 3:08; ☽#♃ 8:08; ♂△♇ 12:21; ☽⚻♄ 12:58; ♀△♃ 13:06; ☽□⚳ 15:10; ☽⚼♇ 15:57; ☽⚺☿ 16:42; ☽∠♀ 17:09; ☿⚼♃ 17:29; ☽⚻⚷ 19:57

7 Tu: ☉☌☽ 0:53; ☽△♅ 0:56; ☉△♅ 1:30; ☽#♀ 1:40; ♂⚻♃ 3:51; ☉#☿ 11:59; ☽☍♆ 13:35; ☽⚼♄ 14:58; ☽∥⚷ 16:34; ☽△♇ 17:57; ☽⚻♃ 18:34; ☽☌♂ 19:25; ☽#☿ 19:47; ☉∥☽ 21:09; ☽⚺♀ 21:30

8 W: ☽⚼♅ 2:45; ☽#♆ 3:01; ☿☍⚷ 4:31; ☽∥♂ 10:03; ☽△♄ 16:30; ☽△⚳ 19:26; ☽⚼♃ 19:57; ☽☍⚷ 23:17

9 Th: ☽☌☿ 1:02; ⚳⚼♇ 1:50; ☿#⚷ 3:01; ☽⚻♅ 4:12; ☽#♂ 4:32; ☉⚺☽ 7:59; ☽∥♆ 12:19; ☉#☽ 15:24; ☽⚻♆ 16:30; ☽□♇ 20:49; ☽⚼⚳ 21:03; ☽△♃ 21:04; ☽#⚷ 22:20

10 F: ☽∥☿ 0:25; ☽⚺♂ 0:42; ☽☌♀ 4:49; ☉∠☽ 11:05; ☿⚻♅ 16:18; ☽⚼♆ 17:40; ☽□♄ 18:54; ☽∥♀ 20:28; ♀ ♏ 20:40; ☽⚻⚳ 22:34

11 Sa: ☽⚻⚷ 1:40; ☽∠♂ 3:06; ☽∥♃ 6:23; ☽☍♅ 6:38; ☽⚺☿ 7:50; ♃⚺♇ 10:07; ☽#⚳ 11:41; ☽#♅ 12:28; ☉✶☽ 14:09; ☉#♆ 15:47; ☽△♆ 18:52; ☽□♃ 23:09; ☽✶♇ 23:15

12 Su: ☽⚼⚷ 2:51; ☽∥♄ 5:25; ☽✶♂ 5:34; ☽∠☿ 11:09; ☽⚺♀ 11:46; ☊ D 16:35; ☽✶♄ 21:19

13 M: ☽∠♇ 0:35; ☽☍⚳ 1:43; ☽△⚷ 4:09; ☽∥♇ 4:46; ☽⚻♅ 9:15; ☽✶☿ 14:32; ☽∠♀ 15:27; ☊ R 20:35; ☉□☽ 20:41; ☽□♆ 21:35; ☽∠♄ 22:44

14 Tu: ☽✶♃ 1:39; ☽⚺♇ 2:04; ♂⚼♅ 6:58; ☉☍♆ 9:22; ☽⚼♅ 10:47; ☽□♂ 10:59; ☽✶♀ 19:22

15 W: ♂ ♎ 0:15; ☽⚺♄ 0:20; ☉⚼♄ 1:15; ☽∠♃ 3:10; ☽⚻⚳ 5:29; ☽□⚷ 7:17; ☽△♅ 12:32; ☽□☿ 21:42

16 Th: ☽✶♆ 1:02; ♀∥♃ 3:33; ☉△☽ 4:08; ☽⚺♃ 4:55; ☽☌♇ 5:41; ☽⚼⚳ 7:42; ☉⚻♃ 14:19; ♀⚼♆ 17:12; ☽△♂ 17:20

17 F: ☉△♇ 1:54; ☽∠♆ 3:08; ☽∥♇ 3:37; ⚳∥♅ 4:01; ☽□♀ 4:04; ☽☌♄ 4:15; ♀□♄ 6:16; ☉⚼☽ 8:19; ☽△⚳ 10:10; ☽✶⚷ 11:19; ☽□♅ 16:46; ☽⚼♂ 20:59

18 Sa: ☽∥♄ 3:48; ☿⚻♆ 4:19; ☽⚺♆ 5:33; ☽△☿ 5:37; ☽☌♃ 9:16; ☽⚺♇ 10:22; ☉⚻☽ 12:56; ☽∠⚷ 13:49; ♀#♅ 16:19; ♀#⚳ 18:46; ☽∥♀ 21:56; ☽#⚳ 22:13; ☽#♅ 22:27

19 Su: ☽⚻♂ 1:05; ☽∥♃ 3:30; ☽⚺♄ 9:28; ☽⚼☿ 10:02; ☽∠♇ 13:19; ☽△♀ 14:27; ☽□⚳ 16:13; ☽⚺⚷ 16:44; ☽∥☿ 17:02; ☽✶♅ 22:27

20 M: ☽☌♆ 11:41; ☽∠♄ 12:48; ♀⚻⚳ 13:06; ☽⚻☿ 14:52; ☽⚺♃ 15:17; ♀⚻⚷ 16:14; ☽#⚷ 16:28; ☽✶♇ 16:46; ⚶ ♏ 16:58; ☉#♂ 19:20; ☽⚼♀ 20:36; ☿△♃ 22:54; ☉☍☽ 23:56

21 Tu: ☽∠♅ 2:05; ☽∥♆ 2:10; ☽☍♂ 11:04; ⚳✶⚷ 13:29; ☽✶♄ 16:44; ☽∥♂ 16:48; ☽∠♃ 19:09; ☉#☽ 19:30; ☉∥☽ 22:38

22 W: ☽☌⚷ 0:18; ☽✶⚳ 0:25; ☽#♂ 2:00; ☉⚼♅ 3:33; ☽⚻♀ 3:35; ☽⚺♅ 6:21; ☿□♇ 13:13; ☽#♆ 16:32; ☉ ♎ 19:22; ☽⚺♆ 20:12; ☽✶♃ 23:43

23 Th: ☽□♇ 1:39; ☽☍☿ 2:06; ☽∥⚷ 2:20; ☽∠⚳ 5:32; ♀☍♅ 9:42; ☉⚻☽ 14:09

24 F: ☽⚻♂ 0:08; ☽∠♆ 1:30; ☽□♄ 2:41; ☽#☿ 9:31; ☽⚺⚷ 10:32; ☽⚺⚳ 11:20; ☽☌♅ 16:57; ☽#♃ 18:57; ☽☍♀ 20:17; ☉⚼☽ 22:34; ☽∥♅ 23:28

25 Sa: ☽∥⚳ 0:38; ☽✶♆ 7:24; ☽⚼♂ 7:49; ☽□♃ 10:50; ☽△♇ 13:10; ☽⚻☿ 15:11; ☽∠⚷ 16:33; ☽#♀ 16:45; ☽#♄ 20:55; ♂△♄ 21:51

26 Su: ☊ D 7:34; ☉△☽ 7:36; ☽△♄ 14:58; ☽△♂ 16:00; ☽⚼♇ 19:37; ☽⚼☿ 21:55; ☽✶⚷ 22:54; ☽#♇ 24:00

27 M: ☽☌⚳ 0:23; ☿ R 5:11; ☽⚺♅ 5:33; ♂⚼♃ 9:45; ♀∥♄ 10:07; ☽⚻♀ 15:29; ☽□♆ 20:12; ☽⚼♄ 21:26; ☽△♃ 23:26

28 Tu: ☽⚻♇ 2:07; ☽△☿ 4:19; ☽∠♅ 11:56

29 W: ☽⚼♀ 0:59; ☉□☽ 1:58; ☊ R 2:10; ☽⚻♄ 3:40; ☽⚼♃ 5:32; ☽□♂ 8:18; ☽□⚷ 11:21; ☽⚺⚳ 13:22; ♀△♆ 16:15; ☽✶♅ 17:55; ☉△♄ 22:21

30 Th: ☽△♆ 8:08; ☽△♀ 9:45; ☽⚻♃ 11:04; ☽☍♇ 13:56; ☽□☿ 14:50; ☽∠⚳ 18:58; ☉⚼♃ 19:08; ♀□♃ 23:32

October 2021

LONGITUDE

Day	Sid.Time	☉	☽	☽ 12 hour	Mean ☊	True ☊	☿	♀	♂	⚳	♃	♄	⚷	♅	♆	♇
	h m s	° ' "	° ' "	° ' "	° '	° '	° '	° '	° '	° '	° '	° '	° '	° '	° '	° '
1 F	0 39 47	8♎02 03	29♋31 36	5♌48 08	4♊24.0	3♊23.3	24♎37.3	22♏50.7	10♎23.6	11♊55.9	22♒49.4	6♒57.9	10♈46.4	14♉06.3	21♓20.1	24♑19.3
2 Sa	0 43 44	9 01 04	12♌10 10	18 38 05	4 20.9	3R 18.7	24R 05.8	23 57.5	11 02.9	11 58.7	22R 46.1	6R 56.9	10R 43.7	14R 04.5	21R 18.6	24R 19.2
3 Su	0 47 40	10 00 06	25 12 10	1♍52 32	4 17.7	3 12.1	23 26.7	25 04.0	11 42.2	12 01.2	22 43.0	6 56.0	10 40.9	14 02.5	21 17.0	24 19.1
4 M	0 51 37	10 59 11	8♍39 13	15 32 05	4 14.5	3 04.1	22 40.2	26 10.5	12 21.5	12 03.3	22 40.0	6 55.3	10 38.2	14 00.6	21 15.5	24 19.0
5 Tu	0 55 33	11 58 19	22 30 49	29 34 59	4 11.3	2 55.4	21 46.9	27 16.8	13 00.9	12 05.1	22 37.3	6 54.6	10 35.5	13 58.6	21 13.9	24 18.9
6 W	0 59 30	12 57 28	6♎44 00	13♎57 08	4 08.1	2 47.2	20 47.3	28 22.9	13 40.3	12 06.4	22 34.8	6 54.0	10 32.8	13 56.6	21 12.4	24D 18.9
7 Th	1 03 26	13 56 39	21 13 36	28 32 30	4 05.0	2 40.3	19 42.7	29 28.8	14 19.7	12 07.4	22 32.4	6 53.6	10 30.1	13 54.6	21 10.9	24 18.9
8 F	1 07 23	14 55 53	5♏52 57	13♏14 03	4 01.8	2 35.4	18 34.3	0♐34.6	14 59.2	12 08.0	22 30.3	6 53.2	10 27.4	13 52.6	21 09.4	24 18.9
9 Sa	1 11 19	15 55 08	20 34 57	27 54 51	3 58.6	2D 32.9	17 23.8	1 40.2	15 38.7	12R 08.2	22 28.3	6 52.9	10 24.7	13 50.5	21 08.0	24 18.9
10 Su	1 15 16	16 54 25	5♐13 04	12♐29 00	3 55.4	2 32.3	16 12.9	2 45.6	16 18.2	12 08.1	22 26.6	6 52.8	10 22.0	13 48.4	21 06.5	24 19.0
11 M	1 19 13	17 53 45	19 42 12	26 52 16	3 52.2	2 33.1	15 03.6	3 50.8	16 57.8	12 07.5	22 25.0	6D 52.7	10 19.3	13 46.2	21 05.1	24 19.1
12 Tu	1 23 09	18 53 06	3♑58 56	11♑02 02	3 49.1	2 34.4	13 57.9	4 55.9	17 37.4	12 06.6	22 23.7	6 52.8	10 16.6	13 44.1	21 03.6	24 19.3
13 W	1 27 06	19 52 28	18 01 29	24 57 13	3 45.9	2R 35.1	12 57.8	6 00.7	18 17.0	12 05.2	22 22.5	6 52.9	10 14.0	13 41.9	21 02.2	24 19.4
14 Th	1 31 02	20 51 53	1♒49 16	8♒37 39	3 42.7	2 34.5	12 04.9	7 05.3	18 56.7	12 03.5	22 21.6	6 53.1	10 11.3	13 39.7	21 00.9	24 19.6
15 F	1 34 59	21 51 19	15 22 26	22 03 41	3 39.5	2 32.2	11 20.6	8 09.7	19 36.4	12 01.4	22 20.8	6 53.5	10 08.7	13 37.4	20 59.5	24 19.9
16 Sa	1 38 55	22 50 46	28 41 29	5♓15 53	3 36.4	2 28.1	10 46.3	9 13.8	20 16.1	11 58.9	22 20.3	6 53.9	10 06.1	13 35.2	20 58.1	24 20.1
17 Su	1 42 52	23 50 16	11♓46 57	18 14 43	3 33.2	2 22.4	10 22.5	10 17.7	20 55.9	11 56.0	22 19.9	6 54.5	10 03.4	13 32.9	20 56.8	24 20.4
18 M	1 46 48	24 49 47	24 39 16	1♈00 37	3 30.0	2 15.9	10D 09.8	11 21.4	21 35.7	11 52.7	22D 19.8	6 55.1	10 00.8	13 30.6	20 55.5	24 20.7
19 Tu	1 50 45	25 49 20	7♈18 49	13 33 57	3 26.8	2 09.3	10 08.3	12 24.8	22 15.5	11 49.0	22 19.8	6 55.9	9 58.2	13 28.3	20 54.2	24 21.1
20 W	1 54 42	26 48 55	19 46 05	25 55 19	3 23.6	2 03.3	10 17.7	13 27.9	22 55.3	11 44.9	22 20.1	6 56.7	9 55.7	13 25.9	20 52.9	24 21.5
21 Th	1 58 38	27 48 32	2♉01 47	8♉05 37	3 20.5	1 58.5	10 37.7	14 30.8	23 35.2	11 40.4	22 20.5	6 57.7	9 53.1	13 23.6	20 51.7	24 21.9
22 F	2 02 35	28 48 12	14 07 01	20 06 14	3 17.3	1 55.2	11 07.7	15 33.4	24 15.2	11 35.6	22 21.2	6 58.7	9 50.6	13 21.2	20 50.4	24 22.3
23 Sa	2 06 31	29 47 53	26 03 32	1♊59 14	3 14.1	1D 53.7	11 46.9	16 35.7	24 55.1	11 30.3	22 22.1	6 59.8	9 48.1	13 18.9	20 49.2	24 22.8
24 Su	2 10 28	0♏47 36	7♊53 42	13 47 21	3 10.9	1 53.7	12 34.5	17 37.7	25 35.1	11 24.7	22 23.1	7 01.1	9 45.6	13 16.5	20 48.1	24 23.3
25 M	2 14 24	1 47 22	19 40 36	25 33 58	3 07.8	1 54.9	13 29.7	18 39.4	26 15.2	11 18.6	22 24.4	7 02.4	9 43.1	13 14.1	20 46.9	24 23.8
26 Tu	2 18 21	2 47 09	1♋27 57	7♋23 07	3 04.6	1 56.6	14 31.7	19 40.7	26 55.2	11 12.2	22 25.8	7 03.9	9 40.7	13 11.6	20 45.8	24 24.3
27 W	2 22 17	3 46 59	13 20 04	19 19 22	3 01.4	1 58.4	15 39.6	20 41.8	27 35.3	11 05.4	22 27.5	7 05.4	9 38.2	13 09.2	20 44.7	24 24.9
28 Th	2 26 14	4 46 51	25 21 40	1♌27 33	2 58.2	1R 59.7	16 52.7	21 42.5	28 15.5	10 58.3	22 29.3	7 07.1	9 35.8	13 06.8	20 43.6	24 25.5
29 F	2 30 11	5 46 46	7♌37 39	13 52 32	2 55.1	2 00.1	18 10.2	22 42.8	28 55.7	10 50.7	22 31.4	7 08.8	9 33.5	13 04.3	20 42.5	24 26.2
30 Sa	2 34 07	6 46 42	20 12 47	26 38 52	2 51.9	1 59.3	19 31.5	23 42.8	29 35.9	10 42.8	22 33.7	7 10.7	9 31.1	13 01.9	20 41.5	24 26.8
31 Su	2 38 04	7♏46 40	3♍11 13	9♍50 10	2♊48.7	1♊57.4	20♎56.1	24♐42.4	0♏16.2	10♊34.5	22♒36.1	7♒12.6	9♈28.8	12♉59.4	20♓40.5	24♑27.5

1st of Month

Julian Day #
2459488.5
Obliquity
23°26'6"
SVP 4♓57'7"
GC 27♐08.6
Eris 24♈23.7R

Day	⚴
1	13♓34.4R
6	12 30.7R
11	11 34.3R
16	10 46.3R
21	10 07.1R
26	9 37.1R
31	9 16.6R

Day	⚵
1	16♐31.0
6	17 47.7
11	19 08.4
16	20 32.9
21	22 00.6
26	23 31.6
31	25 05.5

Day	⚶
1	5♏17.3
6	7 53.2
11	10 30.1
16	13 07.8
21	15 46.4
26	18 25.6
31	21 05.6

DECLINATION and LATITUDE

Day	☉ Decl	☽ Decl	☽ Lat	☽ 12h Decl	☿ Decl	☿ Lat	♀ Decl	♀ Lat	♂ Decl	♂ Lat	⚳ Decl	⚳ Lat	♃ Decl	♃ Lat	♄ Decl	♄ Lat
1 F	3S11	24N24	4N15	23N13	12S56	3S39	20S36	2S12	3S28	0N42	16N02	6S15	15S01	1S11	19S19	0S49
2 Sa	3 34	21 43	4 46	19 56	12 39	3 34	20 57	2 16	3 44	0 42	16 02	6 14	15 02	1 11	19 20	0 49
3 Su	3 58	17 53	5 04	15 34	12 18	3 27	21 17	2 19	3 60	0 41	16 03	6 14	15 03	1 11	19 20	0 49
4 M	4 21	13 02	5 05	10 18	11 53	3 18	21 37	2 23	4 15	0 41	16 04	6 13	15 04	1 11	19 20	0 49
5 Tu	4 44	7 24	4 49	4 22	11 23	3 07	21 56	2 27	4 31	0 41	16 05	6 12	15 05	1 10	19 20	0 49
6 W	5 07	1 14	4 15	1S57	10 49	2 55	22 15	2 31	4 47	0 40	16 06	6 12	15 06	1 10	19 20	0 49
7 Th	5 30	5S07	3 24	8 16	10 11	2 40	22 33	2 35	5 02	0 40	16 07	6 11	15 06	1 10	19 20	0 49
8 F	5 53	11 18	2 19	14 11	9 30	2 24	22 51	2 38	5 18	0 39	16 08	6 10	15 07	1 10	19 21	0 49
9 Sa	6 16	16 52	1 04	19 17	8 47	2 07	23 08	2 42	5 34	0 39	16 08	6 10	15 07	1 10	19 21	0 49
10 Su	6 39	21 24	0S14	23 11	8 02	1 48	23 25	2 46	5 49	0 38	16 09	6 09	15 08	1 10	19 21	0 49
11 M	7 01	24 34	1 32	25 32	7 17	1 28	23 41	2 49	6 05	0 38	16 10	6 08	15 08	1 10	19 21	0 49
12 Tu	7 24	26 05	2 42	26 11	6 33	1 07	23 57	2 53	6 20	0 37	16 11	6 07	15 09	1 10	19 21	0 49
13 W	7 46	25 53	3 42	25 10	5 50	0 47	24 12	2 56	6 36	0 37	16 11	6 06	15 09	1 09	19 21	0 49
14 Th	8 09	24 05	4 27	22 40	5 11	0 26	24 26	2 59	6 51	0 36	16 12	6 05	15 09	1 09	19 21	0 49
15 F	8 31	20 57	4 57	18 58	4 35	0 06	24 40	3 03	7 07	0 36	16 13	6 04	15 09	1 09	19 20	0 49
16 Sa	8 53	16 46	5 10	14 23	4 04	0N13	24 53	3 06	7 22	0 35	16 13	6 03	15 09	1 09	19 20	0 49
17 Su	9 15	11 51	5 06	9 13	3 39	0 30	25 06	3 09	7 38	0 35	16 14	6 02	15 09	1 09	19 20	0 49
18 M	9 37	6 31	4 47	3 46	3 18	0 47	25 18	3 12	7 53	0 35	16 15	6 01	15 09	1 09	19 20	0 49
19 Tu	9 59	0 60	4 14	1N46	3 04	1 02	25 30	3 15	8 08	0 34	16 16	5 60	15 09	1 09	19 20	0 49
20 W	10 20	4N30	3 30	7 09	2 55	1 15	25 41	3 18	8 24	0 34	16 16	5 58	15 09	1 09	19 20	0 49
21 Th	10 42	9 44	2 36	12 12	2 52	1 27	25 51	3 20	8 39	0 33	16 17	5 57	15 09	1 08	19 19	0 49
22 F	11 03	14 33	1 36	16 44	2 55	1 37	26 01	3 23	8 54	0 33	16 18	5 56	15 08	1 08	19 19	0 49
23 Sa	11 24	18 45	0 32	20 34	3 02	1 46	26 10	3 26	9 09	0 32	16 18	5 54	15 08	1 08	19 19	0 49
24 Su	11 45	22 10	0N33	23 32	3 14	1 53	26 19	3 28	9 24	0 32	16 19	5 53	15 07	1 08	19 18	0 49
25 M	12 06	24 38	1 36	25 28	3 31	1 58	26 27	3 30	9 39	0 31	16 20	5 52	15 07	1 08	19 18	0 49
26 Tu	12 26	26 01	2 35	26 16	3 51	2 02	26 34	3 32	9 54	0 31	16 20	5 50	15 06	1 08	19 18	0 49
27 W	12 47	26 14	3 28	25 52	4 14	2 05	26 41	3 35	10 09	0 30	16 21	5 48	15 05	1 08	19 17	0 49
28 Th	13 07	25 13	4 13	24 15	4 41	2 07	26 47	3 37	10 24	0 30	16 22	5 47	15 05	1 07	19 17	0 49
29 F	13 27	22 59	4 47	21 26	5 09	2 08	26 52	3 38	10 38	0 29	16 23	5 45	15 04	1 07	19 16	0 49
30 Sa	13 47	19 37	5 08	17 32	5 40	2 07	26 57	3 40	10 53	0 29	16 23	5 43	15 03	1 07	19 16	0 49
31 Su	14S06	15N13	5N15	12N42	6S13	2N06	27S01	3S42	11S08	0N28	16N24	5S41	15S02	1S07	19S16	0S49

Day	⚷ Decl	⚷ Lat	♅ Decl	♅ Lat	♆ Decl	♆ Lat	♇ Decl	♇ Lat
1	6N28	2N23	15N40	0S25	4S31	1S10	22S53	1S39
6	6 22	2 23	15 37	0 25	4 34	1 10	22 53	1 39
11	6 16	2 23	15 34	0 25	4 37	1 10	22 53	1 40
16	6 11	2 22	15 31	0 25	4 39	1 10	22 53	1 40
21	6 05	2 22	15 27	0 25	4 42	1 10	22 53	1 40
26	5 60	2 21	15 24	0 25	4 44	1 10	22 53	1 40
31	5N54	2N20	15N20	0S25	4S46	1S10	22S52	1S40

Day	⚴ Decl	⚴ Lat	⚵ Decl	⚵ Lat	⚶ Decl	⚶ Lat	Eris Decl	Eris Lat
1	4S37	1N59	11S01	11N47	9S13	4N18	1S16	11S31
6	5 40	1 18	11 24	11 31	10 10	4 11	1 17	11 31
11	6 39	0 37	11 46	11 16	11 06	4 04	1 18	11 31
16	7 34	0S03	12 06	11 01	12 00	3 58	1 19	11 30
21	8 25	0 41	12 25	10 48	12 52	3 51	1 20	11 30
26	9 10	1 18	12 43	10 34	13 43	3 44	1 21	11 30
31	9S50	1S53	12S59	10N22	14S32	3N38	1S21	11S30

Moon Phenomena

Max/0 Decl
dy hr mn
6 4:40 0 S
12 9:10 26S12
19 4:18 0 N
26 16:07 26N17

Max/0 Lat
dy hr mn
3 14:14 5N07
9 19:36 0 S
16 6:51 5S10
23 11:49 0 N
30 21:46 5N15

Perigee/Apogee
dy hr m kilometers
8 17:29 p 363388
24 15:29 a 405614

PH dy hr mn
● 6 11:07 13♎25
☽ 13 3:26 20♑01
○ 20 14:58 27♈26
☾ 28 20:06 5♌37

Void of Course Moon

Last Aspect			☽ Ingress		
30 14:50	☿	□	♌	1	0:55
2 23:44	♀	□	♍	3	8:39
5 8:47	♀	⚹	♎	5	12:42
7 5:04	♇	□	♏	7	14:23
9 6:06	♇	⚹	♐	9	15:25
11 4:32	♃	⚹	♑	11	17:16
13 10:54	♇	☌	♒	13	20:48
15 12:34	☉	△	♓	16	2:23
17 23:25	♇	⚹	♈	18	10:05
20 14:58	☉	☍	♉	20	20:00
22 20:36	♇	△	♊	23	7:58
25 14:12	♂	△	♋	25	21:01
28 6:03	♂	□	♌	28	9:08
30 7:06	♀	△	♍	30	18:11

DAILY ASPECTARIAN

1 F
☽⚼♆ 12:59
♂☍⚷ 13:01
☽☍♄ 14:11
☿□♇ 14:27
☽#♇ 14:55
☉⚹☽ 17:35
☽△⚷ 21:18
☽⚹♂ 21:47
☽⚹⚳ 23:39

2 Sa
☿⚺♀ 1:58
☽□♅ 3:33
☽#♀ 4:58
♀⚹♇ 7:49
☉∠♀ 11:24
☽#♄ 15:43
☽⚻♆ 16:53
☽☍♃ 19:30
☽⚹☿ 20:58
☽⚻♇ 22:24
☉∠☽ 23:36
☽□♀ 23:44

3 Su
☽⚼⚷ 0:52
☽∠♂ 2:51
☉‖♂ 6:04
☽‖⚳ 9:34
☽‖♅ 11:39
♂△⚳ 12:18
♀⚼⚷ 12:48
☽#♃ 14:30
☉☍⚷ 15:52
☽⚻♄ 20:57
☽∠☿ 22:22

4 M
☿△♃ 0:06
☽⚼♇ 1:10
☽⚻⚷ 3:28
☉⚺☽ 4:24
☽#☿ 5:40
☽□⚳ 5:58
☽⚺♂ 6:48
☽△♅ 9:20
☉‖♆ 12:27
☽☍♆ 21:49
☽⚺☿ 22:50
☽⚼♄ 22:58

5 Tu
☽⚻♃ 0:11
☉△⚳ 2:49
☽△♇ 3:04
♂‖♆ 3:19
☽‖⚷ 4:04
☽⚹♀ 8:47
☉#☽ 9:56
☽#♂ 10:56
☽⚼♅ 10:57
☽#♆ 11:14
☿⚻♆ 13:54

6 W
☽△♄ 0:17
☽⚼♃ 1:24
☽☍⚷ 6:20
☽△⚳ 8:57
♂⚻♅ 9:28
☉☌☽ 11:07
☽⚻♅ 11:57
☽∠♀ 11:58
☽☌♂ 12:05
♀∠♂ 15:45
♇ D 18:30
☽☌☿ 21:41
☽‖♆ 21:54
☉⚻♅ 23:12
☽‖♂ 23:40
☽⚻♆ 23:56

7 Th
☉‖☽ 1:31
☽△♃ 2:09
☽#⚷ 4:38
☽□♇ 5:04
☽⚼⚳ 9:41
♀ ♐ 11:22
☽⚺♀ 14:38
☽‖☿ 17:35

8 F
☽⚼♆ 0:27
☽□♄ 1:38
♀‖♇ 2:43
☉☌♂ 4:02
☽⚻⚷ 7:27
☽⚻⚳ 10:13
☽☍♅ 13:01
☽⚺♂ 15:33
☉⚺☽ 15:50
☽‖♃ 16:06
☽#♅ 18:11
☽⚺☿ 19:11
☽#⚳ 20:39

9 Sa
☽△♆ 0:54
⚳ R 1:32
☉#⚷ 2:45
☽□♃ 3:05
☽⚹♇ 6:06
☿∠♀ 7:39
☽⚼⚷ 7:53
☽‖♄ 12:19
☉☌☿ 16:19
☽∠♂ 17:16
☽∠☿ 17:54
☉∠☽ 18:10
☊ D 19:35
☽☌♀ 19:38
☿☌♂ 22:50

10 Su
☽⚹♄ 2:44
☽∠♇ 6:46
☽△⚷ 8:28
☽‖♇ 9:51
☽☍⚳ 11:25
☽⚻♅ 14:10
☽‖♀ 15:15
☽⚹☿ 16:50
☽⚹♂ 19:13
☉⚹☽ 20:46

11 M
☽□♆ 2:18
♄ D 2:18
☽∠♄ 3:38
☽⚹♃ 4:32
☉‖☿ 5:34
☽⚺♇ 7:43
☽⚼♅ 15:09
♂#⚷ 16:17

12 Tu
☽⚺♀ 1:45
☽⚺♄ 4:55
☿‖♂ 4:56
☿⚻♅ 5:31
☽∠♃ 5:47
☿#⚷ 9:58
☽□⚷ 10:40
☽⚻⚳ 13:49
☽□☿ 15:52
☽△♅ 16:35

13 W
☽□♂ 0:28
☊ R 3:23
☉□☽ 3:26
☽⚹♆ 5:12
☽∠♀ 5:36
☽⚺♃ 7:31
☽☌♇ 10:54
☽⚼⚳ 15:41
♀⚹♄ 19:28
☽‖♀ 20:50

14 Th
☿△⚳ 0:41
☉⚻♆ 3:33
☽∠♆ 7:22
☽☌♄ 8:55
☽⚹♀ 10:04
☽‖♇ 10:18
☽⚹⚷ 14:43
☽△☿ 17:10
☽△⚳ 18:03
☽□♅ 20:53
☿‖♆ 21:29

15 F
☽△♂ 7:59
☽‖♄ 9:49
☽⚺♆ 10:03
☉△♃ 11:47
☽☌♃ 12:30
☉△☽ 12:34
☽⚺♇ 16:06
☽∠⚷ 17:31
☽⚼☿ 18:54

16 Sa
♀∠♇ 2:23
☽#⚳ 2:46
☽#♅ 6:25
☽‖♃ 8:11
☽⚼♂ 12:39
☽⚺♄ 15:01
☉⚼☽ 18:07
♀△⚷ 18:50
☽∠♇ 19:29
☽⚺⚷ 20:49
☽□♀ 21:01
☽⚻☿ 21:28

17 Su
☽□⚳ 0:17
♂⚻♆ 0:33
☿⚹♀ 1:25
☽⚹♅ 3:16
☉‖☽ 11:08
☉□♇ 12:14
☽☌♆ 17:01
☽⚻♂ 17:57
☽‖♂ 18:15
☽∠♄ 18:52
☽⚺♃ 19:38
☽⚹♇ 23:25

18 M
☉⚻☽ 0:21
☽#⚷ 1:40
♃ D 5:31
☽∠♅ 7:15
☽‖♆ 8:03
♀☍⚳ 11:12
☽‖☿ 14:40
☿ D 15:18
☽⚹♄ 23:16

19 Tu
☽∠♃ 0:02
♂△♃ 2:38
☽☌⚷ 5:04
☽☍☿ 5:27
☽⚹⚳ 8:35
☽△♀ 10:41
☽⚺♅ 11:47
☽#☿ 17:12
☉⚼⚳ 22:29
♀⚻♅ 23:17

20 W
☽#♆ 0:52
☽⚺♆ 2:10
☽⚹♃ 5:00
☽☍♂ 6:29
☽‖⚷ 7:11
☽□♇ 8:57
☽∠⚳ 13:32
☉☍☽ 14:58
☽⚼♀ 18:35
☽#♂ 18:37

21 Th
☉#☽ 4:56
☽∠♆ 7:34
☽□♄ 9:46
☽⚺⚷ 15:30
☽⚻☿ 17:45
☽⚺⚳ 19:00
☽☌♅ 22:29

22 F
☽#♃ 3:08
☽⚻♀ 3:09
♂□♇ 4:21
☽‖♅ 4:47
☽‖⚳ 9:32
☽⚹♆ 13:28
☿△⚳ 15:37
☽□♃ 16:33
☽△♇ 20:36
☽∠⚷ 21:28
☽⚻♂ 21:34

23 Sa
☽⚼☿ 1:33
☽#♄ 3:35
☉ ♏ 4:52
☉⚻☽ 8:15
☊ D 11:49
☽△♄ 22:13

24 Su
☽⚼♇ 3:02
☽⚹⚷ 3:47
☽⚼♂ 5:48
☽#♇ 6:03
☽☌⚳ 7:06
☽△☿ 10:18
☽⚺♅ 10:55
☉⚼☽ 17:34
☿⚻♅ 17:46
☽☍♀ 21:43

25 M
♂⚼⚳ 1:48
☽□♆ 2:15
☽⚼♄ 4:50
☽△♃ 5:34
☽⚻♇ 9:38
☽△♂ 14:12
☽∠♅ 17:22

26 Tu
☉△☽ 2:56
☽⚻♄ 11:23
☽⚼♃ 12:07
☽□⚷ 16:35
☽⚺⚳ 19:32
☽⚹♅ 23:38

27 W
♀□♆ 1:07
☽□☿ 5:11
☽△♆ 14:49
☽⚻♀ 16:05
☽⚻♃ 18:17
☽☍♇ 22:09

28 Th
☽∠⚳ 1:12
☿‖♆ 3:40
☽□♂ 6:03
♀∠♄ 10:03
♀⚹♃ 19:17
☉□☽ 20:06
☽⚼♆ 20:17
☊ R 20:21
☉⚼♆ 22:20
☽☍♄ 23:04

29 F
☽⚼♀ 0:11
☽#♇ 0:54
☽△⚷ 3:43
☽⚹⚳ 6:08
☽□♅ 10:26
☽⚹☿ 22:33

30 Sa
☽⚻♆ 0:54
☽#♄ 2:08
☽☍♃ 4:25
☽△♀ 7:06
☽⚻♇ 7:55
☽⚼⚷ 8:02
☉□♄ 9:55
☿#⚷ 10:47
♂ ♏ 14:22
♀⚺♇ 17:55
☽‖⚳ 18:05
☽⚹♂ 18:23
☿⚻♆ 19:41
☽‖♅ 23:28

31 Su
☽#♃ 0:56
☉#☽ 5:06
☽⚺☿ 5:35
☽⚻♄ 7:18
☉⚹☽ 8:59
☽⚻⚷ 11:20
☽⚼♇ 11:20
☽□⚳ 13:11
☽△♅ 17:34
☽#♂ 18:11
☽∠♂ 22:47

LONGITUDE

Day	Sid.Time	☉	☽	☽ 12 hour	Mean☊	True☊	☿	♀	♂	⚳	♃	♄	⚷	♅	♆	♇
	h m s	° ' "	° ' "	° ' "	° '	° '	° '	° '	° '	° '	° '	° '	° '	° '	° '	° '
1 M	2 42 00	8♏46 41	16♍35 56	23♍28 36	2♊45.5	1♊54.7	22♎23.3	25♐41.7	0♏56.5	10♊25.9	22♒38.7	7♒14.6	9♈26.5	12♉56.9	20♓39.5	24♑28.3
2 Tu	2 45 57	9 46 44	0♎28 05	7♎34 09	2 42.3	1R 51.5	23 52.7	26 40.5	1 36.8	10R 16.9	22 41.6	7 16.8	9R 24.3	12R 54.5	20R 38.5	24 29.0
3 W	2 49 53	10 46 49	14 46 23	22 04 12	2 39.2	1 48.4	25 24.0	27 38.9	2 17.2	10 07.6	22 44.6	7 19.0	9 22.0	12 52.0	20 37.6	24 29.8
4 Th	2 53 50	11 46 56	29 26 51	6♏53 26	2 36.0	1 45.8	26 56.8	28 36.9	2 57.6	9 57.9	22 47.8	7 21.3	9 19.8	12 49.5	20 36.7	24 30.6
5 F	2 57 46	12 47 04	14♏22 57	21 54 18	2 32.8	1 44.1	28 30.7	29 34.3	3 38.0	9 47.9	22 51.3	7 23.8	9 17.7	12 47.0	20 35.8	24 31.4
6 Sa	3 01 43	13 47 15	29 26 23	6♐58 03	2 29.6	1D 43.5	0♏05.6	0♑31.4	4 18.5	9 37.6	22 54.9	7 26.3	9 15.6	12 44.5	20 35.0	24 32.3
7 Su	3 05 40	14 47 27	14♐28 14	21 55 58	2 26.5	1 43.8	1 41.1	1 28.0	4 59.0	9 27.0	22 58.7	7 28.9	9 13.5	12 42.1	20 34.2	24 33.2
8 M	3 09 36	15 47 42	29 20 22	6♑40 42	2 23.3	1 44.7	3 17.2	2 24.1	5 39.6	9 16.0	23 02.7	7 31.6	9 11.4	12 39.6	20 33.4	24 34.1
9 Tu	3 13 33	16 47 57	13♑56 22	21 06 56	2 20.1	1 45.9	4 53.7	3 19.6	6 20.2	9 04.8	23 06.9	7 34.4	9 09.4	12 37.1	20 32.7	24 35.1
10 W	3 17 29	17 48 14	28 12 05	5♒11 41	2 16.9	1 46.9	6 30.5	4 14.5	7 00.8	8 53.3	23 11.2	7 37.3	9 07.4	12 34.7	20 31.9	24 36.0
11 Th	3 21 26	18 48 33	12♒05 40	18 54 06	2 13.8	1R 47.5	8 07.3	5 08.9	7 41.5	8 41.6	23 15.8	7 40.3	9 05.5	12 32.2	20 31.2	24 37.0
12 F	3 25 22	19 48 53	25 37 08	2♓14 57	2 10.6	1 47.6	9 44.3	6 02.7	8 22.2	8 29.6	23 20.5	7 43.4	9 03.6	12 29.7	20 30.6	24 38.1
13 Sa	3 29 19	20 49 14	8♓47 50	15 16 04	2 07.4	1 47.0	11 21.2	6 55.8	9 02.9	8 17.3	23 25.4	7 46.5	9 01.7	12 27.3	20 29.9	24 39.1
14 Su	3 33 15	21 49 36	21 39 58	27 59 50	2 04.2	1 46.0	12 58.1	7 48.3	9 43.7	8 04.9	23 30.5	7 49.8	8 59.9	12 24.8	20 29.3	24 40.2
15 M	3 37 12	22 50 00	4♈16 00	10♈28 48	2 01.0	1 44.8	14 34.9	8 40.1	10 24.5	7 52.2	23 35.8	7 53.1	8 58.1	12 22.4	20 28.8	24 41.3
16 Tu	3 41 09	23 50 26	16 38 31	22 45 28	1 57.9	1 43.6	16 11.5	9 31.2	11 05.3	7 39.3	23 41.3	7 56.6	8 56.4	12 20.0	20 28.2	24 42.4
17 W	3 45 05	24 50 52	28 49 56	4♉52 10	1 54.7	1 42.6	17 48.0	10 21.5	11 46.2	7 26.2	23 46.9	8 00.1	8 54.7	12 17.6	20 27.7	24 43.6
18 Th	3 49 02	25 51 21	10♉52 26	16 51 01	1 51.5	1 41.9	19 24.3	11 11.1	12 27.1	7 13.0	23 52.7	8 03.7	8 53.0	12 15.2	20 27.3	24 44.7
19 F	3 52 58	26 51 50	22 48 08	28 44 02	1 48.3	1D 41.5	21 00.4	11 59.8	13 08.1	6 59.6	23 58.6	8 07.4	8 51.4	12 12.8	20 26.8	24 45.9
20 Sa	3 56 55	27 52 22	4♊38 59	10♊33 15	1 45.2	1 41.5	22 36.3	12 47.8	13 49.0	6 46.1	24 04.8	8 11.2	8 49.8	12 10.5	20 26.4	24 47.2
21 Su	4 00 51	28 52 55	16 27 05	22 20 48	1 42.0	1 41.6	24 12.1	13 34.8	14 30.1	6 32.4	24 11.1	8 15.0	8 48.3	12 08.1	20 26.0	24 48.4
22 M	4 04 48	29 53 29	28 14 42	4♋09 07	1 38.8	1 41.8	25 47.6	14 21.0	15 11.1	6 18.6	24 17.6	8 19.0	8 46.9	12 05.8	20 25.7	24 49.7
23 Tu	4 08 44	0♐54 05	10♋04 24	16 00 57	1 35.6	1R 41.9	27 23.0	15 06.2	15 52.3	6 04.8	24 24.2	8 23.0	8 45.4	12 03.5	20 25.4	24 51.0
24 W	4 12 41	1 54 43	21 59 11	27 59 31	1 32.5	1 42.0	28 58.1	15 50.4	16 33.4	5 50.8	24 31.0	8 27.1	8 44.0	12 01.2	20 25.1	24 52.3
25 Th	4 16 38	2 55 22	4♌02 26	10♌08 24	1 29.3	1 41.9	0♐33.1	16 33.6	17 14.6	5 36.8	24 37.9	8 31.3	8 42.7	11 58.9	20 24.9	24 53.7
26 F	4 20 34	3 56 03	16 17 55	22 31 31	1 26.1	1 41.7	2 08.0	17 15.7	17 55.8	5 22.7	24 45.1	8 35.6	8 41.4	11 56.6	20 24.7	24 55.0
27 Sa	4 24 31	4 56 45	28 49 40	5♍12 53	1 22.9	1D 41.6	3 42.7	17 56.7	18 37.1	5 08.6	24 52.3	8 39.9	8 40.2	11 54.4	20 24.5	24 56.4
28 Su	4 28 27	5 57 29	11♍41 36	18 16 17	1 19.7	1 41.6	5 17.2	18 36.6	19 18.4	4 54.5	24 59.8	8 44.4	8 39.0	11 52.2	20 24.4	24 57.8
29 M	4 32 24	6 58 15	24 57 15	1♎44 48	1 16.6	1 41.8	6 51.7	19 15.3	19 59.7	4 40.4	25 07.4	8 48.9	8 37.9	11 50.0	20 24.3	24 59.3
30 Tu	4 36 20	7♐59 02	8♎39 05	15 40 09	1♊13.4	1♊42.3	8♐26.0	19♑52.8	20♏41.1	4♊26.3	25♒15.1	8♒53.5	8♈36.8	11♉47.9	20♓24.2	25♑00.7

1st of Month

Julian Day #
2459519.5
Obliquity
23°26'16"
SVP 4♓57'54"
GC 27♐08.7
Eris 24♈05.4R

Day	⚴
1	9♓13.6R
6	9 04.4R
11	9 04.6
16	9 13.8
21	9 31.6
26	9 57.6

Day	⚵
1	25♐24.6
6	27 01.9
11	28 41.6
16	0♑23.7
21	2 07.8
26	3 53.9

Day	⚶
1	21♏37.6
6	24 18.3
11	26 59.5
16	29 41.0
21	2♐22.8
26	5 04.8

DECLINATION and LATITUDE

Day	☉ Decl	☽ Decl	☽ Lat	☽ 12h Decl	☿ Decl	☿ Lat	♀ Decl	♀ Lat	♂ Decl	♂ Lat	⚳ Decl	⚳ Lat	♃ Decl	♃ Lat	♄ Decl	♄ Lat
1 M	14S26	9N58	5N05	7N04	6S47	2N04	27S05	3S43	11S22	0N28	16N25	5S39	15S01	1S07	19S15	0S49
2 Tu	14 45	4 03	4 37	0 55	7 23	2 02	27 08	3 44	11 37	0 27	16 25	5 37	15 00	1 07	19 14	0 49
3 W	15 03	2S16	3 51	5S28	7 59	1 59	27 11	3 46	11 51	0 27	16 26	5 35	14 59	1 07	19 14	0 49
4 Th	15 22	8 38	2 49	11 43	8 36	1 55	27 12	3 47	12 05	0 26	16 27	5 33	14 58	1 06	19 13	0 49
5 F	15 40	14 39	1 35	17 22	9 13	1 51	27 14	3 47	12 20	0 26	16 27	5 31	14 57	1 06	19 13	0 49
6 Sa	15 59	19 49	0 13	21 57	9 51	1 46	27 14	3 48	12 34	0 25	16 28	5 29	14 55	1 06	19 12	0 49
7 Su	16 16	23 42	1S10	25 01	10 29	1 41	27 14	3 49	12 48	0 25	16 29	5 27	14 54	1 06	19 11	0 49
8 M	16 34	25 53	2 27	26 18	11 07	1 36	27 14	3 49	13 02	0 24	16 30	5 24	14 52	1 06	19 11	0 49
9 Tu	16 51	26 14	3 33	25 45	11 44	1 30	27 13	3 49	13 16	0 23	16 30	5 22	14 51	1 06	19 10	0 49
10 W	17 08	24 50	4 24	23 33	12 22	1 24	27 11	3 49	13 30	0 23	16 31	5 19	14 49	1 06	19 09	0 49
11 Th	17 25	21 56	4 59	20 03	12 59	1 18	27 09	3 49	13 43	0 22	16 32	5 17	14 48	1 06	19 08	0 49
12 F	17 41	17 55	5 15	15 36	13 36	1 12	27 06	3 49	13 57	0 22	16 33	5 14	14 46	1 05	19 08	0 49
13 Sa	17 58	13 08	5 15	10 33	14 12	1 05	27 03	3 48	14 10	0 21	16 33	5 12	14 44	1 05	19 07	0 49
14 Su	18 13	7 52	4 58	5 09	14 48	0 59	26 59	3 47	14 24	0 21	16 34	5 09	14 42	1 05	19 06	0 49
15 M	18 29	2 24	4 28	0N21	15 23	0 52	26 55	3 46	14 37	0 20	16 35	5 06	14 41	1 05	19 05	0 49
16 Tu	18 44	3N05	3 45	5 45	15 58	0 45	26 50	3 45	14 50	0 20	16 36	5 03	14 39	1 05	19 04	0 49
17 W	18 59	8 22	2 53	10 53	16 31	0 38	26 45	3 44	15 04	0 19	16 37	5 00	14 37	1 05	19 03	0 49
18 Th	19 13	13 18	1 53	15 34	17 04	0 32	26 39	3 42	15 17	0 19	16 38	4 57	14 35	1 05	19 02	0 49
19 F	19 27	17 41	0 49	19 36	17 37	0 25	26 33	3 40	15 30	0 18	16 38	4 54	14 32	1 04	19 01	0 49
20 Sa	19 41	21 20	0N16	22 50	18 08	0 18	26 26	3 38	15 42	0 18	16 39	4 51	14 30	1 04	19 00	0 49
21 Su	19 54	24 06	1 21	25 05	18 39	0 11	26 19	3 36	15 55	0 17	16 40	4 48	14 28	1 04	18 59	0 49
22 M	20 08	25 48	2 22	26 13	19 08	0 04	26 12	3 33	16 08	0 16	16 41	4 45	14 26	1 04	18 58	0 49
23 Tu	20 20	26 20	3 18	26 09	19 37	0S03	26 04	3 30	16 20	0 16	16 42	4 41	14 23	1 04	18 57	0 49
24 W	20 33	25 40	4 05	24 53	20 05	0 09	25 56	3 27	16 32	0 15	16 43	4 38	14 21	1 04	18 56	0 49
25 Th	20 44	23 48	4 42	22 27	20 32	0 16	25 47	3 24	16 45	0 14	16 44	4 34	14 19	1 04	18 55	0 49
26 F	20 56	20 49	5 07	18 57	20 57	0 23	25 38	3 20	16 57	0 14	16 45	4 31	14 16	1 03	18 54	0 49
27 Sa	21 07	16 50	5 18	14 31	21 22	0 29	25 28	3 16	17 09	0 13	16 46	4 27	14 14	1 03	18 53	0 49
28 Su	21 18	11 60	5 13	9 19	21 46	0 36	25 19	3 12	17 21	0 13	16 47	4 24	14 11	1 03	18 52	0 49
29 M	21 28	6 28	4 52	3 31	22 09	0 42	25 08	3 07	17 32	0 12	16 48	4 20	14 08	1 03	18 50	0 49
30 Tu	21S38	0N28	4N14	2S38	22S30	0S48	24S58	3S02	17S44	0N12	16N49	4S16	14S06	1S03	18S49	0S49

Day	⚷ Decl	⚷ Lat	♅ Decl	♅ Lat	♆ Decl	♆ Lat	♇ Decl	♇ Lat
1	5N53	2N20	15N19	0S25	4S46	1S10	22S52	1S40
6	5 48	2 19	15 16	0 25	4 48	1 10	22 52	1 41
11	5 44	2 19	15 12	0 25	4 49	1 10	22 51	1 41
16	5 39	2 18	15 08	0 25	4 50	1 09	22 50	1 41
21	5 35	2 17	15 05	0 25	4 51	1 09	22 49	1 41
26	5 32	2 16	15 01	0 25	4 52	1 09	22 49	1 42

Day	⚴ Decl	⚴ Lat	⚵ Decl	⚵ Lat	⚶ Decl	⚶ Lat	Eris Decl	Eris Lat
1	9S57	1S60	13S02	10N20	14S41	3N36	1S22	11S30
6	10 31	2 33	13 16	10 08	15 27	3 30	1 22	11 29
11	11 00	3 04	13 29	9 57	16 11	3 23	1 23	11 29
16	11 24	3 33	13 40	9 46	16 53	3 17	1 23	11 28
21	11 43	4 01	13 49	9 36	17 32	3 10	1 24	11 28
26	11 58	4 28	13 56	9 27	18 08	3 03	1 24	11 27

Moon Phenomena

Max/0 Decl
dy hr mn
2 15:28 0 S
8 16:34 26S19
15 10:28 0 N
22 22:46 26N21
30 1:49 0 S

Perigee/Apogee
dy hr m kilometers
5 22:19 p 358845
21 2:14 a 406279

PH dy hr mn
● 4 21:16 12♏40
☽ 11 12:47 19♒21
○ 19 8:59 27♉14
◐ 19 9:04 P 0.974
☾ 27 12:29 5♍28

Max/0 Lat
dy hr mn
6 3:39 0 S
12 11:10 5S17
19 18:00 0 N
27 5:25 5N18

Void of Course Moon

Last Aspect	☽ Ingress
1 17:01 ♀ □	♎ 1 23:12
3 22:33 ♀ ✱	♏ 4 0:54
5 16:11 ♇ ✱	♐ 6 0:54
7 13:45 ♃ ✱	♑ 8 1:05
9 17:53 ♇ ☌	♒ 10 3:04
11 19:53 ♃ ☌	♓ 12 7:55
14 5:41 ♇ ✱	♈ 14 15:49
16 15:52 ♇ □	♉ 17 2:19
19 8:59 ☉ ☍	♊ 19 14:34
21 15:53 ♃ △	♋ 22 3:34
24 5:47 ♇ ☍	♌ 24 16:00
26 16:25 ♃ ☍	♍ 27 2:13
29 0:04 ♇ △	♎ 29 8:56

DAILY ASPECTARIAN

1 M: ☿△♃ 4:19; ☽☍♆ 7:06; ☽⚼♄ 9:53; ☽⚻♃ 10:36; ☽⚺☿ 11:19; ☽#☿ 11:58; ☉∠☽ 13:29; ☽△♇ 13:44; ☉⚻⚷ 15:21; ☽∥⚷ 16:48; ☽□♀ 17:01; ☽⚼♅ 19:38; ☽#♆ 21:09

2 Tu: ☽⚺♂ 2:03; ☿□♇ 9:40; ☉⚻⚳ 10:27; ☽△♄ 11:33; ☽⚼♃ 12:15; ☽☍⚷ 15:02; ☽△⚳ 16:22; ☉⚺☽ 16:52; ☉∥♃ 18:34; ☿⚼⚳ 20:07; ☽⚻♅ 20:51

3 W: ♀⚼♅ 5:11; ☽∥♆ 9:26; ☽⚻♆ 9:38; ☽△♃ 13:09; ☽#⚷ 13:24; ☽□♇ 15:58; ☽⚼⚳ 16:48; ☉#♅ 17:40; ☽☌☿ 19:28; ☽✱♀ 22:33; ☽∥☿ 23:50

4 Th: ☽☌♂ 5:57; ☽⚼♆ 9:56; ☽□♄ 12:47; ☽∥♂ 14:02; ☽⚻⚷ 15:53; ☽⚻⚳ 16:45; ☉☌☽ 21:16; ☽☍♅ 21:27; ☉☍♅ 23:59

5 F: ☽∠♀ 0:20; ☽∥♃ 1:15; ☽#♅ 2:39; ☉∥☽ 4:40; ☽#⚳ 7:52; ☽△♆ 9:54; ♀ ♑ 10:45; ☽□♃ 13:34; ☽⚼⚷ 15:46; ☽✱♇ 16:11; ☽∥♄ 20:49; ☿ ♏ 22:36

6 Sa: ☽⚺☿ 1:10; ☽⚺♀ 1:51; ☊ D 3:36; ☽⚺♂ 8:07; ⚳⚼♇ 11:06; ☽✱♄ 12:47; ☽△⚷ 15:37; ☿✱♀ 16:00; ☽☍⚳ 16:04; ☽∠♇ 16:07; ☽∥♇ 17:57; ☽⚻♅ 21:10

7 Su: ☉⚺☽ 0:33; ☽∠☿ 3:59; ☽∠♂ 9:17; ☽□♆ 9:48; ☽∠♄ 12:56; ☽✱♃ 13:45; ☽⚺♇ 16:15; ☉#⚳ 17:41; ♂⚼♆ 20:25; ☽⚼♅ 21:17

8 M: ☉∠☽ 2:33; ☽☌♀ 5:20; ☽✱☿ 7:14; ♀ D 9:24; ☽✱♂ 10:50; ⚳✱⚷ 12:10; ☽⚺♄ 13:26; ☽∠♃ 14:19; ☽⚻⚳ 16:04; ☽□⚷ 16:06; ☽△♅ 21:49

9 Tu: ☉✱☽ 5:07; ☿⚼♆ 9:36; ☽✱♆ 11:02; ☽⚺♃ 15:27; ☽⚼⚳ 16:47; ☽☌♇ 17:53

10 W: ☽⚺♀ 11:05; ☽∠♆ 12:34; ☿☌♂ 12:58; ☽□♂ 15:56; ☽□☿ 16:09; ☽☌♄ 16:16; ☿□♄ 17:05; ☽∥♇ 17:29; ☽△⚳ 18:09; ☽✱⚷ 18:46; ♂□♄ 23:15

11 Th: ☽□♅ 0:46; ☿⚻⚳ 7:33; ☊ R 12:47; ☉□☽ 12:47; ☿⚻⚷ 14:07; ☽⚺♆ 14:52; ☽∠♀ 15:14; ☽∥♄ 17:20; ☽☌♃ 19:53; ☽∠⚷ 21:12; ☽⚺♇ 22:14

12 F: ☉∥☽ 1:10; ♂⚻⚳ 3:22; ☽#⚳ 7:13; ☽#♅ 14:07; ☽∥♃ 16:14; ☉△♆ 16:25; ☽∥♂ 19:14; ☽∥☿ 19:25; ☽✱♀ 20:19; ☽⚺♄ 22:07; ☿∥♂ 22:09; ☽□⚳ 23:05; ♂⚻⚷ 23:20

13 Sa: ☽⚺⚷ 0:26; ☽△♂ 0:29; ☽∠♇ 1:35; ☽△☿ 5:24; ☽✱♅ 6:45; ☿☍♅ 15:58; ☿∥♃ 20:27; ☽☌♆ 21:47

14 Su: ☉△☽ 0:20; ♀⚺♄ 0:44; ☽∠♄ 2:12; ☽⚺♃ 3:30; ☽✱♇ 5:41; ☽⚼♂ 6:07; ♀⚻⚳ 6:09; ☽#⚷ 9:41; ☽∠♅ 10:51; ☽∥♆ 13:22; ☽⚼☿ 13:42; ☿#♅ 14:28; ⚵ ♑ 20:24; ♀∠♃ 21:46; ⚳△♄ 22:35

15 M: ♂∥♃ 5:13; ☽✱⚳ 6:50; ☽✱♄ 7:01; ☉⚼☽ 7:29; ♀□⚷ 8:08; ☽∠♃ 8:25; ☽☌⚷ 9:03; ☽□♀ 9:07; ☽⚻♂ 12:33; ☽⚺♅ 15:38; ☉□♃ 19:59; ☽⚻☿ 22:59

16 Tu: ☉⚼⚷ 2:18; ☽⚺♆ 7:30; ☽#♆ 7:53; ☽∥⚷ 11:31; ☽∠⚳ 11:35; ☽✱♃ 13:56; ⚶ ♐ 14:08; ☉⚻☽ 15:24; ☽□♇ 15:52; ☉✱♇ 21:03

17 W: ☿#⚳ 4:00; ♂#♅ 6:43; ☉∥♄ 6:58; ☽∠♆ 13:10; ☽⚺⚳ 16:49; ♂☍♅ 17:24; ☽□♄ 18:21; ☽⚺⚷ 20:01

18 Th: ☽△♀ 0:40; ♃∠⚷ 1:06; ☽☌♅ 2:45; ☽☍♂ 3:21; ☽#♃ 6:38; ☽∥♅ 9:31; ☽#♂ 10:58; ☿△♆ 15:39; ☽∥⚳ 17:58; ☽✱♆ 19:15; ☽☍☿ 19:49; ☽#☿ 23:32

19 F: ☽∠⚷ 2:08; ☽□♃ 2:24; ☽△♇ 3:59; ♀△♅ 6:09; ☽#♄ 8:12; ☉☍☽ 8:59; ☽⚼♀ 9:06; ☉#☽ 11:44; ☉∠♀ 15:27; ☊ D 17:54

20 Sa: ☽☌⚳ 4:13; ☽△♄ 7:13; ☽✱⚷ 8:29; ☽⚼♇ 10:27; ☽#♇ 11:55; ☽⚺♅ 15:15; ☽⚻♀ 17:45; ☿⚼⚷ 18:08; ☽⚻♂ 19:47; ☿□♃ 23:44

21 Su: ☽□♆ 8:06; ☿✱♇ 9:15; ☽⚼♄ 13:55; ☽△♃ 15:53; ☿∥♄ 16:11; ☽⚻♇ 17:02; ☽⚻☿ 18:14; ☽∠♅ 21:40

22 M: ☉ ♐ 2:35; ☉⚻☽ 3:40; ☽⚼♂ 4:11; ☽#♀ 9:12; ☽⚺⚳ 16:04; ☽⚻♄ 20:34; ☽□⚷ 21:20; ☽⚼♃ 22:38

23 Tu: ☽✱♅ 4:00; ☽⚼☿ 5:23; ☽☍♀ 10:50; ☽△♂ 12:25; ☉⚼☽ 12:52; ☽#♀ 17:41; ☊ R 19:49; ☽△♆ 20:51; ☽∠⚳ 21:46

24 W: ☽⚻♃ 5:07; ☽☍♇ 5:47; ☿ ♐ 15:38; ☽△☿ 16:03; ☉△☽ 21:35; ♂#⚳ 22:49

25 Th: ☽⚼♆ 2:43; ☽✱⚳ 3:03; ☽☍♄ 8:53; ☽#♇ 8:59; ☽△⚷ 9:11; ☽□♅ 15:33; ☉∥☿ 21:45; ☽#☿ 23:10; ☉#☽ 23:15

26 F: ☽⚻♀ 1:59; ☽□♂ 3:21; ☿∠♀ 3:29; ☽⚻♆ 7:56; ☽#♄ 12:19; ☽⚼⚷ 14:12; ☽☍♃ 16:25; ☽⚻♇ 16:36; ☽#♂ 22:23

27 Sa: ☽∥⚳ 0:21; ♄✱⚷ 1:05; ☉☍⚳ 3:49; ☽⚼♀ 8:11; ☽∥♅ 9:33; ☽□☿ 10:29; ☽□⚳ 11:39; ☉□☽ 12:29; ☊ D 12:32; ☽#♃ 13:32; ♃⚺♇ 16:17; ☽⚻⚷ 18:24; ☽⚻♄ 18:31; ☿☍⚳ 18:59; ☽⚼♇ 20:48

28 Su: ☽△♅ 0:19; ☽△♀ 13:16; ☽✱♂ 14:38; ☽☍♆ 15:51; ☽⚼♄ 21:57

29 M: ☽△♇ 0:04; ☽⚻♃ 0:18; ☽⚼♅ 3:20; ☽∥⚷ 4:00; ☉☌☿ 4:41; ☽#♆ 6:36; ♀⚼⚳ 11:37; ♂△♆ 14:11; ☽△⚳ 16:49; ☽∠♂ 18:36; ☉✱☽ 22:45; ☽✱☿ 23:35; ☽☍⚷ 23:56

30 Tu: ☽△♄ 0:25; ☿△⚷ 2:42; ☽⚼♃ 2:47; ☽⚻♅ 5:23; ☿✱♄ 7:20; ☉△⚷ 14:39; ☽⚼⚳ 18:04; ☽□♀ 19:57; ☽⚻♆ 19:59; ☿∥♇ 20:25; ☽∥♆ 20:31; ♀✱♆ 20:47; ☽⚺♂ 21:30; ☽#⚷ 22:54; ☉✱♄ 23:16

December 2021

LONGITUDE

Day	Sid.Time	☉	☽	☽ 12 hour	Mean☊	True☊	☿	♀	♂	⚳	♃	♄	⚷	♅	♆	♇
	h m s	° ' "	° ' "	° ' "	° '	° '	° '	° '	° '	° '	° '	° '	° '	° '	° '	° '
1 W	4 40 17	8♐59 50	22♎47 55	0♏02 05	1♊10.2	1♊43.0	10♐00.3	20♑28.9	21♏22.6	4♊12.3	25♒23.0	8♒58.1	8♈35.7	11♉45.7	20♓24.2	25♑02.2
2 Th	4 44 13	10 00 40	7♏22 13	14 47 42	1 07.0	1 43.6	11 34.5	21 03.7	22 04.0	3R 58.3	25 31.0	9 02.8	8R 34.8	11R 43.6	20D 24.1	25 03.7
3 F	4 48 10	11 01 32	22 17 42	29 51 16	1 03.9	1R 44.1	13 08.6	21 37.1	22 45.5	3 44.3	25 39.2	9 07.6	8 33.8	11 41.5	20 24.2	25 05.2
4 Sa	4 52 07	12 02 24	7♐27 18	15♐04 34	1 00.7	1 44.2	14 42.7	22 09.1	23 27.1	3 30.5	25 47.6	9 12.5	8 32.9	11 39.5	20 24.3	25 06.7
5 Su	4 56 03	13 03 18	22 41 50	0♑17 50	0 57.5	1 43.7	16 16.8	22 39.5	24 08.7	3 16.8	25 56.1	9 17.5	8 32.1	11 37.5	20 24.4	25 08.3
6 M	5 00 00	14 04 13	7♑51 20	15 21 13	0 54.3	1 42.5	17 50.8	23 08.4	24 50.3	3 03.2	26 04.7	9 22.5	8 31.3	11 35.5	20 24.5	25 09.9
7 Tu	5 03 56	15 05 09	22 46 29	0♒06 18	0 51.2	1 40.9	19 24.9	23 35.6	25 32.0	2 49.7	26 13.5	9 27.6	8 30.6	11 33.5	20 24.7	25 11.4
8 W	5 07 53	16 06 06	7♒20 01	14 27 10	0 48.0	1 39.1	20 59.0	24 01.1	26 13.7	2 36.4	26 22.4	9 32.8	8 30.0	11 31.6	20 24.9	25 13.1
9 Th	5 11 49	17 07 03	21 27 30	28 20 54	0 44.8	1 37.4	22 33.0	24 24.8	26 55.4	2 23.3	26 31.4	9 38.0	8 29.4	11 29.7	20 25.1	25 14.7
10 F	5 15 46	18 08 01	5♓07 25	11♓47 15	0 41.6	1 36.2	24 07.2	24 46.6	27 37.2	2 10.4	26 40.6	9 43.3	8 28.8	11 27.9	20 25.4	25 16.3
11 Sa	5 19 43	19 09 00	18 20 42	24 48 09	0 38.5	1D 35.8	25 41.3	25 06.6	28 19.0	1 57.6	26 49.9	9 48.6	8 28.3	11 26.0	20 25.7	25 18.0
12 Su	5 23 39	20 09 59	1♈10 04	7♈26 55	0 35.3	1 36.1	27 15.5	25 24.5	29 00.8	1 45.1	26 59.3	9 54.0	8 27.8	11 24.3	20 26.1	25 19.7
13 M	5 27 36	21 10 58	13 39 15	19 47 35	0 32.1	1 37.2	28 49.7	25 40.4	29 42.7	1 32.8	27 08.9	9 59.5	8 27.4	11 22.5	20 26.4	25 21.4
14 Tu	5 31 32	22 11 58	25 52 27	1♉54 23	0 28.9	1 38.8	0♑24.0	25 54.2	0♐24.6	1 20.8	27 18.6	10 05.1	8 27.1	11 20.8	20 26.9	25 23.1
15 W	5 35 29	23 12 59	7♉53 52	13 51 24	0 25.7	1 40.5	1 58.4	26 05.8	1 06.6	1 09.0	27 28.4	10 10.7	8 26.8	11 19.1	20 27.3	25 24.8
16 Th	5 39 25	24 14 00	19 47 24	25 42 17	0 22.6	1 41.9	3 32.7	26 15.1	1 48.6	0 57.5	27 38.4	10 16.3	8 26.6	11 17.5	20 27.8	25 26.5
17 F	5 43 22	25 15 02	1♊36 27	7♊30 15	0 19.4	1R 42.4	5 07.1	26 22.2	2 30.6	0 46.2	27 48.4	10 22.1	8 26.4	11 15.9	20 28.3	25 28.3
18 Sa	5 47 18	26 16 05	13 23 59	19 17 58	0 16.2	1 41.8	6 41.5	26 26.9	3 12.7	0 35.3	27 58.6	10 27.8	8 26.3	11 14.3	20 28.9	25 30.1
19 Su	5 51 15	27 17 08	25 12 27	1♋07 42	0 13.0	1 39.8	8 15.9	26R 29.2	3 54.8	0 24.7	28 08.9	10 33.7	8D 26.2	11 12.8	20 29.5	25 31.8
20 M	5 55 12	28 18 11	7♋03 56	13 01 22	0 09.9	1 36.5	9 50.3	26 29.0	4 37.0	0 14.3	28 19.3	10 39.6	8 26.2	11 11.4	20 30.1	25 33.6
21 Tu	5 59 08	29 19 16	19 00 15	25 00 46	0 06.7	1 32.0	11 24.6	26 26.4	5 19.1	0 04.3	28 29.9	10 45.5	8 26.2	11 09.9	20 30.7	25 35.5
22 W	6 03 05	0♑20 21	1♌03 11	7♌07 42	0 03.5	1 26.8	12 58.7	26 21.3	6 01.4	29♉54.7	28 40.5	10 51.5	8 26.3	11 08.6	20 31.4	25 37.3
23 Th	6 07 01	1 21 26	13 14 35	19 24 07	0 00.3	1 21.4	14 32.7	26 13.7	6 43.7	29 45.3	28 51.3	10 57.6	8 26.5	11 07.2	20 32.2	25 39.1
24 F	6 10 58	2 22 32	25 36 35	1♍52 17	29♉57.2	1 16.5	16 06.4	26 03.6	7 26.0	29 36.4	29 02.1	11 03.7	8 26.7	11 05.9	20 32.9	25 41.0
25 Sa	6 14 54	3 23 39	8♍11 35	14 34 47	29 54.0	1 12.6	17 39.7	25 51.0	8 08.3	29 27.7	29 13.1	11 09.8	8 27.0	11 04.7	20 33.7	25 42.8
26 Su	6 18 51	4 24 46	21 02 17	27 34 24	29 50.8	1 10.1	19 12.6	25 35.9	8 50.7	29 19.5	29 24.2	11 16.0	8 27.3	11 03.4	20 34.5	25 44.7
27 M	6 22 47	5 25 54	4♎11 30	10♎53 53	29 47.6	1D 09.2	20 44.9	25 18.5	9 33.1	29 11.6	29 35.3	11 22.3	8 27.7	11 02.3	20 35.4	25 46.6
28 Tu	6 26 44	6 27 02	17 41 51	24 35 36	29 44.5	1 09.6	22 16.4	24 58.6	10 15.6	29 04.0	29 46.6	11 28.5	8 28.1	11 01.2	20 36.3	25 48.4
29 W	6 30 41	7 28 11	1♏35 15	8♏40 50	29 41.3	1 11.0	23 47.0	24 36.6	10 58.1	28 56.9	29 58.0	11 34.9	8 28.6	11 00.1	20 37.2	25 50.3
30 Th	6 34 37	8 29 21	15 52 13	23 09 10	29 38.1	1 12.5	25 16.5	24 12.3	11 40.7	28 50.2	0♓09.5	11 41.3	8 29.1	10 59.1	20 38.1	25 52.2
31 F	6 38 34	9♑30 31	0♐31 13	7♐57 47	29♉34.9	1♊13.2	26♑44.5	23♑46.0	12♐23.3	28♉43.8	0♓21.1	11♒47.7	8♈29.7	10♉58.1	20♓39.1	25♑54.2

1st of Month

Julian Day # 2459549.5
Obliquity 23°26'35"
SVP 4♓57'29"
GC 27♐08.7
Eris 23♈50.1R

Day	⚴	Day	⚵	Day	⚶
1	10♓31.4	1	5♑41.9	1	7♐47.1
6	11 12.5	6	7 31.5	6	10 29.5
11	12 00.6	11	9 22.7	11	13 11.8
16	12 55.1	16	11 15.2	16	15 54.0
21	13 55.5	21	13 09.0	21	18 36.0
26	15 01.5	26	15 03.8	26	21 17.8
31	16 12.7	31	16 59.7	31	23 59.3

DECLINATION and LATITUDE

Day	☉ Decl	☽ Decl	☽ Lat	☽12h Decl	☿ Decl	☿ Lat	♀ Decl	♀ Lat	♂ Decl	♂ Lat	⚳ Decl	⚳ Lat	♃ Decl	♃ Lat	♄ Decl	♄ Lat
1 W	21S48	5S46	3N20	8S52	22S50	0S54	24S47	2S57	17S55	0N11	16N51	4S13	14S03	1S03	18S48	0S49
2 Th	21 57	11 54	2 11	14 48	23 10	1 00	24 36	2 51	18 07	0 11	16 52	4 09	13 60	1 03	18 47	0 49
3 F	22 06	17 30	0 52	19 57	23 28	1 06	24 25	2 45	18 18	0 10	16 53	4 05	13 57	1 03	18 46	0 49
4 Sa	22 14	22 04	0S32	23 49	23 45	1 12	24 14	2 39	18 29	0 10	16 54	4 01	13 54	1 03	18 44	0 49
5 Su	22 22	25 08	1 54	25 58	24 00	1 17	24 02	2 32	18 40	0 09	16 55	3 57	13 51	1 02	18 43	0 49
6 M	22 29	26 19	3 07	26 11	24 15	1 22	23 50	2 25	18 50	0 08	16 57	3 54	13 48	1 02	18 42	0 49
7 Tu	22 36	25 34	4 07	24 31	24 28	1 27	23 38	2 18	19 01	0 08	16 58	3 50	13 45	1 02	18 40	0 49
8 W	22 43	23 05	4 49	21 19	24 40	1 32	23 26	2 10	19 11	0 07	16 60	3 46	13 42	1 02	18 39	0 49
9 Th	22 49	19 16	5 12	16 59	24 51	1 37	23 14	2 02	19 22	0 07	17 01	3 42	13 39	1 02	18 37	0 49
10 F	22 54	14 32	5 16	11 56	24 60	1 42	23 02	1 53	19 32	0 06	17 02	3 37	13 35	1 02	18 36	0 49
11 Sa	22 60	9 16	5 03	6 31	25 08	1 46	22 49	1 44	19 42	0 05	17 04	3 33	13 32	1 02	18 35	0 49
12 Su	23 04	3 45	4 36	0 59	25 14	1 50	22 37	1 35	19 52	0 05	17 05	3 29	13 29	1 02	18 33	0 49
13 M	23 09	1N46	3 55	4N28	25 20	1 54	22 24	1 25	20 01	0 04	17 07	3 25	13 25	1 02	18 32	0 49
14 Tu	23 12	7 07	3 05	9 40	25 23	1 57	22 11	1 15	20 11	0 04	17 09	3 21	13 22	1 01	18 30	0 49
15 W	23 16	12 08	2 08	14 27	25 26	2 00	21 59	1 04	20 20	0 03	17 10	3 17	13 18	1 01	18 29	0 49
16 Th	23 19	16 38	1 05	18 39	25 26	2 03	21 46	0 53	20 29	0 02	17 12	3 13	13 15	1 01	18 27	0 49
17 F	23 21	20 28	0 01	22 05	25 26	2 06	21 33	0 42	20 38	0 02	17 14	3 09	13 11	1 01	18 26	0 49
18 Sa	23 23	23 28	1N04	24 35	25 24	2 08	21 21	0 30	20 47	0 01	17 16	3 04	13 08	1 01	18 24	0 49
19 Su	23 25	25 27	2 06	26 01	25 20	2 10	21 08	0 17	20 55	0 00	17 18	3 00	13 04	1 01	18 23	0 49
20 M	23 26	26 17	3 02	26 15	25 15	2 11	20 56	0 04	21 04	0S00	17 20	2 56	13 00	1 01	18 21	0 49
21 Tu	23 26	25 54	3 51	25 15	25 09	2 12	20 43	0N09	21 12	0 01	17 22	2 52	12 57	1 01	18 19	0 49
22 W	23 26	24 19	4 30	23 05	25 01	2 13	20 31	0 22	21 20	0 01	17 24	2 48	12 53	1 01	18 18	0 49
23 Th	23 26	21 35	4 57	19 50	24 51	2 13	20 18	0 36	21 28	0 02	17 26	2 44	12 49	1 01	18 16	0 49
24 F	23 25	17 51	5 11	15 40	24 40	2 13	20 06	0 51	21 36	0 03	17 28	2 39	12 45	1 00	18 14	0 49
25 Sa	23 24	13 17	5 10	10 45	24 27	2 12	19 54	1 05	21 43	0 03	17 30	2 35	12 41	1 00	18 13	0 49
26 Su	23 22	8 03	4 54	5 15	24 13	2 11	19 42	1 20	21 50	0 04	17 33	2 31	12 37	1 00	18 11	0 49
27 M	23 20	2 21	4 22	0S37	23 57	2 09	19 31	1 35	21 57	0 05	17 35	2 27	12 33	1 00	18 09	0 49
28 Tu	23 17	3S38	3 35	6 38	23 40	2 06	19 19	1 51	22 04	0 05	17 37	2 23	12 29	1 00	18 08	0 49
29 W	23 14	9 36	2 35	12 30	23 22	2 03	19 08	2 06	22 11	0 06	17 40	2 19	12 25	1 00	18 06	0 49
30 Th	23 10	15 16	1 23	17 51	23 02	1 59	18 57	2 22	22 18	0 07	17 42	2 15	12 21	0 60	18 04	0 49
31 F	23S06	20S12	0N04	22S14	22S41	1S55	18S46	2N37	22S24	0S07	17N45	2S11	12S17	0S60	18S02	0S49

Day	⚷ Decl	⚷ Lat	♅ Decl	♅ Lat	♆ Decl	♆ Lat	♇ Decl	♇ Lat
1	5N29	2N15	14N58	0S25	4S52	1S09	22S47	1S42
6	5 26	2 14	14 55	0 25	4 51	1 09	22 46	1 42
11	5 24	2 14	14 52	0 25	4 51	1 09	22 45	1 42
16	5 23	2 13	14 50	0 25	4 50	1 09	22 44	1 43
21	5 22	2 12	14 47	0 25	4 48	1 08	22 42	1 43
26	5 21	2 11	14 45	0 24	4 47	1 08	22 41	1 43
31	5N21	2N10	14N44	0S24	4S45	1S08	22S40	1S44

Day	⚴ Decl	⚴ Lat	⚵ Decl	⚵ Lat	⚶ Decl	⚶ Lat	Eris Decl	Eris Lat
1	12S08	4S53	14S01	9N18	18S42	2N57	1S24	11S27
6	12 15	5 17	14 04	9 10	19 13	2 50	1 25	11 26
11	12 17	5 40	14 06	9 02	19 40	2 44	1 25	11 26
16	12 17	6 02	14 05	8 54	20 05	2 37	1 24	11 25
21	12 13	6 23	14 02	8 47	20 27	2 30	1 24	11 24
26	12 06	6 44	13 58	8 41	20 46	2 24	1 24	11 23
31	11S56	7S04	13S51	8N34	21S01	2N17	1S24	11S23

Moon Phenomena

Max/0 Decl
dy hr mn
6 2:32 26S20
12 16:16 0 N
20 4:36 26N18
27 9:30 0 S

Perigee/Apogee
dy hr m kilometers
4 10:05 p 356800
18 2:16 a 406320

Max/0 Lat
dy hr mn
3 14:59 0 S
9 17:45 5S17
17 0:13 0 N
24 10:48 5N13
31 1:08 0 S

PH dy hr mn
● 4 7:44 12♐22
● 4 454:36T 01'55"
☽ 11 1:37 19♓13
○ 19 4:37 27♊29
☾ 27 2:25 5♎32

Void of Course Moon

Last Aspect				☽ Ingress		
1	4:21	♃ △		♏	1	11:57
3	5:23	♃ □		♐	3	12:14
5	5:09	♃ ✱		♑	5	11:32
7	4:43	♂ ✱		♒	7	11:50
9	10:01	♂ □		♓	9	14:54
11	19:41	♂ △		♈	11	21:47
14	2:53	♃ ✱		♉	14	8:12
16	16:10	♃ □		♊	16	20:44
19	6:03	♃ △		♋	19	9:43
21	14:45	♀ ☍		♌	21	21:55
24	6:41	♃ ☍		♍	24	8:25
26	8:41	♇ △		♎	26	16:25
28	21:12	♃ △		♏	28	21:17
30	17:11	☿ ✱		♐	30	23:09

DAILY ASPECTARIAN

1 W: ☿∠♇ 0:29; ☉∠☽ 2:09; ☽□♇ 3:44; ☽∠☿ 4:08; ☽△♃ 4:21; ♆ D 13:23; ☽⚻⚳ 18:33; ☽⚼♆ 20:48
2 Th: ☉∠♇ 1:13; ☽⚻⚷ 1:58; ☿⚻♅ 2:16; ☽□♄ 2:44; ☉⚺☽ 4:36; ☽☍♅ 7:02; ☽⚺☿ 7:37; ☽∥♃ 8:33; ☽#♅ 12:39; ☽△♆ 20:59; ☽#⚳ 21:09; ☽✱♀ 22:53
3 F: ☽☌♂ 0:46; ☽⚼⚷ 2:01; ☽∥♂ 3:54; ☽✱♇ 4:27; ☽□♃ 5:23; ☽∥♄ 5:58; ☊ R 15:05; ☉⚻♅ 15:15; ☽☍⚳ 17:52; ☽∠♀ 23:30
4 Sa: ☉∥☽ 1:02; ☽△⚷ 1:43; ☽✱♄ 2:47; ♂⚼⚷ 3:19; ☽∠♇ 4:12; ☽∥♇ 4:33; ☽⚻♅ 6:36; ☉☌☽ 7:44; ☽∥☿ 12:35; ☽☌☿ 12:44; ☽∥♀ 14:26; ☽□♆ 20:23; ☽⚺♀ 23:56
5 Su: ☿∥♀ 1:36; ☽⚺♂ 2:23; ☽∠♄ 2:32; ☽⚺♇ 3:51; ☽✱♃ 5:09; ☽⚼♅ 6:11; ♂∥♄ 6:23; ☽⚻⚳ 16:29
6 M: ☽□⚷ 1:04; ☽⚺♄ 2:26; ☽∠♂ 3:19; ☽∠♃ 5:12; ☽△♅ 5:57; ☉⚺☽ 10:40; ♂✱♇ 11:42; ☽⚼⚳ 16:06; ☽⚺☿ 17:54; ☽✱♆ 20:10
7 Tu: ☽☌♀ 1:22; ☽☌♇ 3:57; ☽✱♂ 4:43; ☽⚺♃ 5:41; ☽∥☿ 11:33; ☉∠☽ 12:52; ☿□♆ 15:17; ☽△⚳ 16:15; ☽∠♆ 20:48; ☽∥♀ 21:07; ☽∠☿ 21:28
8 W: ☽✱⚷ 1:57; ☽∥♇ 2:21; ☉∥☽ 2:38; ☽☌♄ 3:44; ♂□♃ 6:23; ☽□♅ 7:02; ☉∥♇ 11:31; ☉✱☽ 15:58; ☽⚺♆ 22:12; ☽∥♂ 23:28
9 Th: ☽✱☿ 2:08; ☽∥♄ 3:30; ☽∠⚷ 3:31; ☽⚺♀ 5:16; ☽⚺♇ 6:35; ☽☌♃ 8:54; ☽□♂ 10:01; ☽#⚳ 11:47; ☽□⚳ 18:50; ☽#♅ 22:20
10 F: ☽∥♃ 4:28; ☽⚺⚷ 6:01; ☽⚺♄ 8:19; ☽∠♀ 8:35; ☽∠♇ 9:16; ☿∠♄ 9:46; ☉∥♀ 9:46; ☽✱♅ 11:23; ☿⚺♀ 12:51; ☿⚺♇ 17:57
11 Sa: ☊ D 1:29; ☉□☽ 1:37; ☽☌♆ 3:51; ♀∥♇ 8:04; ☿⚼♅ 11:11; ☽∠♄ 12:06; ☽✱♀ 12:53; ☽✱♇ 12:58; ☽∠♅ 15:02; ☽□☿ 15:34; ☽⚺♃ 16:00; ♀☌♇ 16:30; ☽#⚷ 16:52; ☽∥♆ 19:16; ☿✱♃ 19:25; ☽△♂ 19:41
12 Su: ☽✱⚳ 1:05; ☉□♆ 6:22; ☽☌⚷ 13:57; ☽✱♄ 16:51; ☽⚺♅ 19:35; ☽∠♃ 21:02
13 M: ☽⚼♂ 2:11; ☽∠⚳ 5:33; ♂ ♐ 9:54; ☽⚺♆ 13:17; ☽#♆ 13:38; ☉△☽ 16:04; ☽∥⚷ 16:07; ☿ ♑ 17:53; ☽□♇ 23:02
14 Tu: ☽□♀ 0:04; ☿⚺♂ 0:17; ☽✱♃ 2:53; ☽⚻♂ 9:34; ☽△☿ 10:21; ☽⚺⚳ 10:42; ☿⚻⚳ 12:50; ☽∠♆ 19:06
15 W: ☉⚼☽ 0:42; ♂☍⚳ 1:04; ☽⚺⚷ 1:06; ☽□♄ 4:37; ☽#♃ 5:56; ☽☌♅ 6:52; ☽∥♅ 14:00; ☽⚼☿ 21:06
16 Th: ☽✱♆ 1:22; ☽∥⚳ 3:19; ☽∠⚷ 7:24; ☉⚻☽ 9:52; ☽#♄ 10:43; ☽△♇ 11:30; ☽△♀ 13:15; ☽□♃ 16:10; ☽☌⚳ 22:19
17 F: ☊ R 0:14; ☽#♂ 1:11; ☽☍♂ 1:57; ☉∠♄ 3:03; ☉⚺♇ 5:22; ☽#♀ 7:23; ☽⚻☿ 8:15; ☽✱⚷ 13:54; ☽#♇ 17:17; ☽△♄ 17:59; ☽⚼♇ 18:05; ☽⚺♅ 19:37; ☽⚼♀ 20:00; ☉#☽ 23:14; ☉⚼♅ 23:20
18 Sa: ☉⚺♀ 4:29; ☽□♆ 14:25; ☽#☿ 22:20
19 Su: ☽⚻♇ 0:39; ☽⚼♄ 0:43; ☽∠♅ 2:02; ☽⚻♀ 2:36; ☿□⚷ 2:36; ☉☍☽ 4:37; ☽△♃ 6:03; ☽⚺⚳ 10:24; ♀ R 10:37; ♀∥♂ 14:35; ⚷ D 16:34; ☽⚻♂ 18:45
20 M: ☉✱♃ 0:33; ☽□⚷ 2:46; ☽☍☿ 6:26; ☽⚻♄ 7:18; ☽✱♅ 8:18; ☽⚼♃ 12:47; ☿⚺♄ 13:23; ☽∠⚳ 16:13; ☿△♅ 20:19
21 Tu: ☽⚼♂ 2:48; ☽△♆ 3:01; ⚳ R♉ 10:40; ☽☍♇ 13:11; ☽#☿ 14:44; ☽☍♀ 14:45; ☉⚻⚳ 15:17; ☉ ♑ 16:00; ☽⚻♃ 19:13; ☽✱⚳ 21:46; ☉⚻☽ 22:27
22 W: ☉#☽ 8:48; ☽⚼♆ 8:51; ☽△♂ 10:26; ☿∠♃ 12:02; ☽△⚷ 14:35; ☽#♇ 15:16; ☽☍♄ 19:29; ☽□♅ 19:51
23 Th: ☽#♂ 0:51; ☽⚻☿ 2:55; ☿⚼⚳ 2:57; ☉⚼☽ 6:38; ☽#♀ 9:27; ☽⚻♆ 14:13; ☽⚼⚷ 19:50; ☽#♄ 21:45
24 F: ☽⚻♇ 0:08; ☽⚻♀ 0:51; ☽∥⚳ 2:12; ☽☍♃ 6:41; ♄□♅ 7:18; ☽□⚳ 7:35; ☽⚼☿ 12:02; ☉△☽ 14:06; ☽∥♅ 16:39; ☽□♂ 23:53
25 Sa: ☽⚻⚷ 0:29; ☽#♃ 2:56; ☽⚼♇ 4:46; ☽⚼♀ 4:55; ☽△♅ 5:26; ☽⚻♄ 5:39; ♂△⚷ 10:38; ♀☌♇ 12:03; ⚳□♃ 18:07; ☽△☿ 20:10; ☽☍♆ 23:09
26 Su: ☽△♀ 8:13; ☽△♇ 8:41; ☽⚼♅ 9:13; ☽⚼♄ 9:41; ☽∥⚷ 11:33; ☽#♆ 13:58; ☽△⚳ 15:02; ☽⚻♃ 15:33; ☿✱♆ 21:30
27 M: ☉□☽ 2:25; ☊ D 2:35; ☽☍⚷ 7:40; ☽✱♂ 10:08; ☽⚻♅ 12:14; ☽△♄ 12:56; ♀∠♂ 17:33; ☽⚼⚳ 17:40; ☽⚼♃ 18:48
28 Tu: ☽∥♆ 4:32; ☽⚻♆ 5:05; ☽#⚷ 6:53; ☽□☿ 8:58; ☽□♀ 12:21; ☽∠♂ 13:51; ☽□♇ 14:08; ♂∠♇ 19:24; ☽⚻⚳ 19:32; ☽△♃ 21:12
29 W: ♂⚻♅ 1:05; ♃ ♓ 4:11; ☽⚼♆ 6:51; ☿☌♀ 10:29; ☉✱☽ 10:44; ☽∥♃ 11:31; ☽⚻⚷ 11:40; ☉∥☿ 12:21; ☽☍♅ 15:52; ☽⚺♂ 16:40; ☽□♄ 16:59; ☽#♅ 21:38; ☉□⚷ 23:54
30 Th: ♂✱♄ 0:23; ☽△♆ 7:53; ☿☌♇ 9:55; ☽#⚳ 11:23; ☽⚼⚷ 12:33; ☽∥♄ 12:59; ☽✱♀ 13:20; ☉∠☽ 13:29; ☽✱♇ 16:29; ☽∥♀ 16:46; ☽✱☿ 17:11; ☽☍⚳ 21:07; ☽□♃ 23:43
31 F: ☊ R 1:10; ☿∥♇ 1:19; ☽△⚷ 12:52; ☽∠♀ 12:53; ☽∥♂ 13:26; ☽∥☿ 13:32; ☿∥♂ 14:22; ☽∥♇ 14:46; ☉⚺☽ 15:32; ☽∠♇ 16:45; ☽⚻♅ 16:48; ☉∥☽ 17:25; ☽✱♄ 18:16; ☽∠☿ 19:58; ☽☌♂ 20:02; ☿∠♂ 21:13

LONGITUDE — January 2022

Day	Sid.Time	☉	☽	☽ 12 hour	Mean ☊	True ☊	☿	♀	♂	⚳	♃	♄	⚷	♅	♆	♇
	h m s	° ' "	° ' "	° ' "	° '	° '	° '	° '	° '	° '	° '	° '	° '	° '	° '	° '
1 Sa	6 42 30	10♑31 41	15♐28 04	23♐01 07	29♉31.7	1♊12.4	28♑10.9	23♑17.7	13♐05.9	28♉37.9	0♓32.7	11♒54.2	8♈30.4	10♉57.2	20♓40.1	25♑56.1
2 Su	6 46 27	11 32 52	0♑35 49	8♑11 00	29 28.6	1R 09.7	29 35.2	22R 47.7	13 48.6	28R 32.3	0 44.5	12 00.7	8 31.1	10R 56.3	20 41.2	25 58.0
3 M	6 50 23	12 34 03	15 45 21	23 17 39	29 25.4	1 04.9	0♒57.1	22 16.1	14 31.3	28 27.2	0 56.4	12 07.2	8 31.8	10 55.5	20 42.3	25 59.9
4 Tu	6 54 20	13 35 14	0♒46 38	8♒11 13	29 22.2	0 58.5	2 16.1	21 43.1	15 14.1	28 22.4	1 08.3	12 13.8	8 32.6	10 54.7	20 43.4	26 01.9
5 W	6 58 17	14 36 25	15 30 24	22 43 24	29 19.1	0 51.3	3 31.7	21 08.8	15 56.8	28 18.1	1 20.4	12 20.4	8 33.5	10 54.0	20 44.5	26 03.8
6 Th	7 02 13	15 37 35	29 49 37	6♓48 40	29 15.9	0 44.3	4 43.2	20 33.6	16 39.7	28 14.2	1 32.5	12 27.1	8 34.4	10 53.3	20 45.7	26 05.8
7 F	7 06 10	16 38 45	13♓40 22	20 24 43	29 12.7	0 38.4	5 50.1	19 57.6	17 22.5	28 10.7	1 44.7	12 33.8	8 35.4	10 52.6	20 46.9	26 07.8
8 Sa	7 10 06	17 39 55	27 01 54	3♈32 13	29 09.5	0 34.1	6 51.5	19 21.1	18 05.4	28 07.7	1 57.0	12 40.5	8 36.4	10 52.1	20 48.2	26 09.7
9 Su	7 14 03	18 41 04	9♈56 06	16 14 04	29 06.3	0D 31.9	7 46.7	18 44.4	18 48.3	28 05.0	2 09.4	12 47.3	8 37.5	10 51.5	20 49.4	26 11.7
10 M	7 17 59	19 42 13	22 26 44	28 34 41	29 03.2	0 31.5	8 34.8	18 07.6	19 31.3	28 02.8	2 21.8	12 54.1	8 38.6	10 51.1	20 50.7	26 13.7
11 Tu	7 21 56	20 43 21	4♉38 36	10♉39 09	29 00.0	0 32.4	9 15.0	17 31.2	20 14.3	28 01.0	2 34.4	13 00.9	8 39.8	10 50.6	20 52.0	26 15.6
12 W	7 25 52	21 44 29	16 36 59	22 32 44	28 56.8	0 33.7	9 46.3	16 55.2	20 57.3	27 59.6	2 47.0	13 07.8	8 41.1	10 50.3	20 53.4	26 17.6
13 Th	7 29 49	22 45 37	28 27 02	4♊20 27	28 53.6	0R 34.5	10 07.9	16 20.0	21 40.4	27 58.6	2 59.7	13 14.6	8 42.4	10 49.9	20 54.8	26 19.6
14 F	7 33 45	23 46 43	10♊13 33	16 06 48	28 50.5	0 33.9	10R 18.9	15 45.8	22 23.5	27D 58.0	3 12.4	13 21.5	8 43.7	10 49.7	20 56.2	26 21.6
15 Sa	7 37 42	24 47 50	22 00 41	27 55 34	28 47.3	0 31.3	10 18.7	15 12.8	23 06.6	27 57.8	3 25.3	13 28.5	8 45.1	10 49.5	20 57.6	26 23.5
16 Su	7 41 39	25 48 55	3♋51 50	9♋49 47	28 44.1	0 26.1	10 07.0	14 41.3	23 49.8	27 58.1	3 38.1	13 35.4	8 46.5	10 49.3	20 59.1	26 25.5
17 M	7 45 35	26 50 00	15 49 39	21 51 38	28 40.9	0 18.4	9 43.4	14 11.4	24 33.0	27 58.7	3 51.1	13 42.4	8 48.0	10 49.2	21 00.6	26 27.5
18 Tu	7 49 32	27 51 05	27 55 55	4♌02 37	28 37.8	0 08.6	9 08.3	13 43.3	25 16.3	27 59.8	4 04.1	13 49.4	8 49.6	10D 49.1	21 02.1	26 29.5
19 W	7 53 28	28 52 09	10♌11 50	16 23 37	28 34.6	29♉57.3	8 22.3	13 17.2	25 59.6	28 01.3	4 17.2	13 56.4	8 51.2	10 49.1	21 03.6	26 31.5
20 Th	7 57 25	29 53 12	22 38 02	28 55 09	28 31.4	29 45.5	7 26.4	12 53.2	26 42.9	28 03.1	4 30.4	14 03.5	8 52.8	10 49.2	21 05.2	26 33.5
21 F	8 01 21	0♒54 15	5♍15 00	11♍37 40	28 28.2	29 34.5	6 22.1	12 31.5	27 26.3	28 05.4	4 43.6	14 10.5	8 54.5	10 49.3	21 06.8	26 35.4
22 Sa	8 05 18	1 55 18	18 03 14	24 31 47	28 25.0	29 25.1	5 11.4	12 12.0	28 09.7	28 08.0	4 56.9	14 17.6	8 56.2	10 49.4	21 08.4	26 37.4
23 Su	8 09 15	2 56 20	1♎03 28	7♎38 25	28 21.9	29 18.1	3 56.5	11 55.0	28 53.1	28 11.1	5 10.2	14 24.7	8 58.0	10 49.6	21 10.0	26 39.4
24 M	8 13 11	3 57 21	14 16 50	20 58 54	28 18.7	29 13.9	2 39.6	11 40.4	29 36.6	28 14.5	5 23.6	14 31.8	8 59.8	10 49.9	21 11.7	26 41.4
25 Tu	8 17 08	4 58 22	27 44 48	4♏34 44	28 15.5	29D 12.0	1 23.1	11 28.2	0♑20.1	28 18.3	5 37.1	14 38.9	9 01.7	10 50.2	21 13.4	26 43.3
26 W	8 21 04	5 59 22	11♏28 53	18 27 20	28 12.3	29 11.9	0 09.2	11 18.6	1 03.7	28 22.5	5 50.6	14 46.0	9 03.6	10 50.5	21 15.1	26 45.3
27 Th	8 25 01	7 00 23	25 30 10	2♐37 20	28 09.2	29R 12.3	28♑59.9	11 11.5	1 47.3	28 27.1	6 04.1	14 53.2	9 05.6	10 50.9	21 16.8	26 47.2
28 F	8 28 57	8 01 22	9♐48 41	17 03 58	28 06.0	29 12.0	27 56.6	11 06.9	2 30.9	28 32.0	6 17.7	15 00.3	9 07.6	10 51.4	21 18.6	26 49.2
29 Sa	8 32 54	9 02 21	24 22 45	1♑44 27	28 02.8	29 09.7	27 00.7	11D 04.8	3 14.6	28 37.3	6 31.4	15 07.5	9 09.6	10 51.9	21 20.4	26 51.2
30 Su	8 36 50	10 03 20	9♑08 22	16 33 36	27 59.6	29 04.7	26 12.8	11 05.1	3 58.3	28 43.0	6 45.1	15 14.7	9 11.7	10 52.5	21 22.2	26 53.1
31 M	8 40 47	11♒04 17	23 59 12	1♒24 06	27♉56.5	28♉56.8	25♑33.6	11♑07.8	4♑42.1	28♉49.0	6♓58.9	15♒21.9	9♈13.9	10♉53.1	21♓24.0	26♑55.0

1st of Month

Julian Day #
2459580.5
Obliquity
23°26'[illegible]5"
SVP 4♓57'23"
GC 27♐08.8
Eris 23♈41.7R

Day	⚴
1	16♓27.5
6	17 44.6
11	19 06.0
16	20 31.5
21	22 00.8
26	23 33.6
31	25 09.8

Day	⚵
1	17♑23.0
6	19 19.9
11	21 17.6
16	23 15.8
21	25 14.5
26	27 13.6
31	29 13.1

Day	⚶
1	24♐31.6
6	27 12.5
11	29 52.9
16	2♑32.6
21	5 11.5
26	7 49.6
31	10 26.8

DECLINATION and LATITUDE

Day	☉ Decl	☽ Decl	☽ Lat	☽ 12h Decl	☿ Decl	☿ Lat	♀ Decl	♀ Lat	♂ Decl	♂ Lat	⚳ Decl	⚳ Lat	♃ Decl	♃ Lat	♄ Decl	♄ Lat
1 Sa	23S01	23S55	1S17	25S11	22S18	1S49	18S35	2N53	22S30	0S08	17N48	2S07	12S13	0S60	18S01	0S49
2 Su	22 56	25 59	2 33	26 18	21 55	1 43	18 25	3 09	22 36	0 09	17 50	2 03	12 08	0 60	17 59	0 49
3 M	22 51	26 07	3 38	25 27	21 30	1 36	18 14	3 24	22 42	0 09	17 53	1 59	12 04	0 60	17 57	0 49
4 Tu	22 45	24 20	4 28	22 48	21 05	1 28	18 04	3 39	22 47	0 10	17 56	1 55	11 60	0 60	17 55	0 50
5 W	22 38	20 56	4 58	18 45	20 39	1 19	17 55	3 54	22 52	0 11	17 59	1 51	11 55	0 60	17 53	0 50
6 Th	22 31	16 21	5 09	13 46	20 12	1 09	17 45	4 09	22 57	0 11	18 02	1 47	11 51	0 59	17 52	0 50
7 F	22 24	11 03	5 01	8 15	19 46	0 59	17 37	4 23	23 02	0 12	18 05	1 43	11 47	0 59	17 50	0 50
8 Sa	22 16	5 25	4 37	2 34	19 19	0 47	17 28	4 37	23 07	0 13	18 08	1 39	11 42	0 59	17 48	0 50
9 Su	22 08	0N16	3 59	3N03	18 52	0 34	17 20	4 51	23 11	0 13	18 11	1 35	11 38	0 59	17 46	0 50
10 M	21 59	5 47	3 11	8 25	18 26	0 20	17 12	5 03	23 15	0 14	18 14	1 31	11 33	0 59	17 44	0 50
11 Tu	21 50	10 57	2 15	13 21	18 01	0 05	17 04	5 16	23 19	0 15	18 18	1 27	11 29	0 59	17 42	0 50
12 W	21 41	15 37	1 15	17 43	17 37	0N11	16 57	5 27	23 23	0 15	18 21	1 24	11 24	0 59	17 40	0 50
13 Th	21 31	19 38	0 11	21 21	17 15	0 28	16 51	5 38	23 27	0 16	18 25	1 20	11 19	0 59	17 38	0 50
14 F	21 21	22 50	0N52	24 05	16 55	0 46	16 45	5 48	23 30	0 17	18 28	1 16	11 15	0 59	17 36	0 50
15 Sa	21 10	25 04	1 53	25 47	16 38	1 04	16 39	5 57	23 33	0 17	18 32	1 13	11 10	0 59	17 34	0 50
16 Su	20 59	26 12	2 49	26 18	16 23	1 23	16 34	6 06	23 36	0 18	18 35	1 09	11 05	0 59	17 32	0 50
17 M	20 47	26 06	3 38	25 36	16 11	1 41	16 29	6 13	23 38	0 19	18 39	1 05	11 01	0 59	17 30	0 50
18 Tu	20 35	24 47	4 18	23 40	16 03	1 60	16 25	6 20	23 41	0 19	18 43	1 02	10 56	0 59	17 29	0 50
19 W	20 23	22 16	4 46	20 37	15 58	2 17	16 22	6 27	23 43	0 20	18 46	0 58	10 51	0 59	17 27	0 50
20 Th	20 10	18 43	5 01	16 35	15 56	2 34	16 19	6 32	23 45	0 21	18 50	0 55	10 46	0 59	17 25	0 50
21 F	19 57	14 16	5 02	11 46	15 57	2 49	16 16	6 36	23 46	0 22	18 54	0 51	10 41	0 59	17 23	0 50
22 Sa	19 44	9 08	4 48	6 23	16 01	3 03	16 14	6 40	23 48	0 22	18 58	0 48	10 36	0 59	17 21	0 50
23 Su	19 30	3 32	4 19	0 38	16 08	3 14	16 12	6 44	23 49	0 23	19 02	0 44	10 31	0 59	17 19	0 50
24 M	19 16	2S19	3 35	5S16	16 16	3 23	16 11	6 46	23 50	0 24	19 06	0 41	10 26	0 59	17 16	0 50
25 Tu	19 01	8 12	2 39	11 03	16 27	3 29	16 10	6 48	23 51	0 24	19 10	0 38	10 21	0 59	17 14	0 50
26 W	18 46	13 48	1 33	16 24	16 39	3 33	16 10	6 49	23 51	0 25	19 14	0 34	10 16	0 59	17 12	0 50
27 Th	18 31	18 49	0 20	20 59	16 52	3 34	16 10	6 49	23 51	0 26	19 18	0 31	10 11	0 58	17 10	0 51
28 F	18 16	22 51	0S56	24 22	17 05	3 33	16 10	6 49	23 51	0 27	19 23	0 28	10 06	0 58	17 08	0 51
29 Sa	17 60	25 28	2 10	26 09	17 19	3 30	16 11	6 49	23 51	0 27	19 27	0 25	10 01	0 58	17 06	0 51
30 Su	17 44	26 22	3 15	26 06	17 33	3 25	16 12	6 48	23 51	0 28	19 31	0 22	9 56	0 58	17 04	0 51
31 M	17S27	25S22	4S08	24S12	17S46	3N19	16S13	6N46	23S50	0S29	19N36	0S18	9S51	0S58	17S02	0S51

Day	⚷ Decl	⚷ Lat	♅ Decl	♅ Lat	♆ Decl	♆ Lat	♇ Decl	♇ Lat
1	5N21	2N10	14N44	0S24	4S44	1S08	22S39	1S44
6	5 22	2 09	14 43	0 24	4 42	1 08	22 38	1 44
11	5 24	2 08	14 42	0 24	4 40	1 08	22 36	1 44
16	5 25	2 07	14 42	0 24	4 37	1 08	22 35	1 45
21	5 28	2 06	14 42	0 24	4 33	1 08	22 33	1 45
26	5 31	2 05	14 42	0 24	4 30	1 07	22 32	1 46
31	5N34	2N04	14N43	0S23	4S27	1S07	22S31	1S46

Day	⚴ Decl	⚴ Lat	⚵ Decl	⚵ Lat	⚶ Decl	⚶ Lat	Eris Decl	Eris Lat
1	11S54	7S08	13S49	8N33	21S04	2N16	1S23	11S23
6	11 42	7 27	13 40	8 27	21 16	2 09	1 23	11 22
11	11 27	7 46	13 29	8 22	21 25	2 02	1 22	11 21
16	11 10	8 04	13 16	8 17	21 30	1 55	1 21	11 20
21	10 51	8 23	13 01	8 12	21 33	1 47	1 21	11 19
26	10 31	8 41	12 44	8 07	21 32	1 40	1 20	11 19
31	10S10	8S59	12S26	8N03	21S29	1N33	1S19	11S18

Moon Phenomena

Max/0 Decl

dy hr mn	
2 13:36	26S18
8 22:52	0 N
16 10:19	26N18
23 14:33	0 S
29 23:24	26S22

Max/0 Lat

dy hr mn	
6 1:33	5S09
13 4:20	0 N
20 13:24	5N04
27 6:16	0 S

Perigee/Apogee

dy hr m		kilometers
1 22:57	p	358033
14 9:27	a	405804
30 7:12	p	362255

PH	dy hr mn	
●	2 18:35	12♑20
☽	9 18:12	19♈27
○	17 23:50	27♋51
☾	25 13:42	5♏33

Void of Course Moon

Last Aspect			☽ Ingress	
1 8:17	♆	□	♑	1 23:03
3 16:22	♇	☌	♒	3 22:45
5 0:46	♂	⚹	♓	6 0:18
7 22:24	♇	⚹	♈	8 5:27
10 7:24	♇	□	♉	10 14:48
12 19:40	♇	△	♊	13 3:09
15 2:23	♂	☍	♋	15 16:12
17 23:50	☉	☍	♌	18 4:04
20 8:17	♂	△	♍	20 14:03
22 19:47	♂	□	♎	22 22:04
24 22:11	♇	□	♏	25 3:58
27 5:29	☿	⚹	♐	27 7:36
28 19:01	♆	□	♑	29 9:10
31 4:45	♇	☌	♒	31 9:44

DAILY ASPECTARIAN

1 Sa
☿△⚳ 7:08
☽□♆ 8:17
☉△♅ 9:51
☽⚺♀ 12:03
☽⚼♅ 16:38
☽⚺♇ 16:39
☽∠♄ 18:17
☽⚻⚳ 20:46
☽⚺☿ 22:14

2 Su
☽⚹♃ 0:14
☿ ♒ 7:11
☉⚺♄ 12:13
☽□⚷ 12:32
♂∥♇ 12:41
☽△♅ 16:21
☽⚺♄ 18:12
☉☌☽ 18:35
☽⚼⚳ 20:22
☽⚺♂ 21:57
☿⚺♃ 23:45

3 M
☽∠♃ 0:18
☽⚹♆ 7:53
☽☌♀ 10:00
☽☌♇ 16:22
☉∥♂ 19:04
☉⚼⚳ 19:20
⚳⋕♄ 20:00
☽△⚳ 20:09
☽∠♂ 23:05

4 Tu
☽⚺♃ 0:35
☽☌☿ 2:38
☽∠♆ 8:00
☽∥♂ 11:50
☽⚹⚷ 12:36
☉∥☽ 12:49
☽∥♇ 13:09
♀⋕⚳ 16:04
☽□♅ 16:26
☽☌♄ 18:45
☉⚺☽ 22:24

5 W
☉∥♇ 0:13
☽⚹♂ 0:46
☽∥☿ 1:49
♀∥♄ 4:28
☽⚺♆ 8:42
☽⚺♀ 9:00
☽∠⚷ 13:25
☽⋕⚳ 15:48
♀⚹♆ 16:04
☽∥♄ 16:33
☽∥♀ 16:52
☽⚺♇ 17:40
☽□⚳ 21:19

6 Th
☉∠☽ 1:28
☽☌♃ 2:58
☽⋕♅ 7:42
☽⚺☿ 9:08
☽∠♀ 9:26
☽⚺⚷ 15:05
☽⚹♅ 19:05
☽∠♇ 19:31
☽∥♃ 20:47
☽⚺♄ 22:02
☿∠♆ 22:49

7 F
☉∠♃ 2:56
☉⚹☽ 5:42
☽□♂ 6:56
☽⚹♀ 10:42
☽☌♆ 12:41
☽∠☿ 13:51
☽∠♅ 21:53
☽⚹♇ 22:24

8 Sa
☽⋕⚷ 0:09
☽∠♄ 1:11
☽⚹⚳ 2:00
☽∥♆ 3:05
☽⚺♃ 9:12
☽⚹☿ 19:38
☽☌⚷ 21:31
♀⚺♂ 22:49

9 Su
☉☌♀ 0:49
☽⚺♅ 1:45
☽⚹♄ 5:28
☽∠⚳ 5:57
☉⚺♂ 9:33
☽∠♃ 14:00
☽□♀ 16:02
☽△♂ 17:59
☊ D 18:02
☉□☽ 18:12
☽⋕♆ 19:05
☽⚺♆ 20:53
☽∥⚷ 22:16

10 M
☿⚹⚷ 2:08
☽□♇ 7:24
☿⋕⚳ 9:41
☽⚺⚳ 10:56
☽⚹♃ 19:49
♀∠♃ 22:25

11 Tu
☽⚼♂ 1:15
☽∠♆ 2:26
☽⋕♃ 2:34
☉⚹♆ 3:29
⚶ ♑ 5:20
☽⚺⚷ 8:02
☽□☿ 9:39
☽☌♅ 12:23
☽□♄ 16:54
☽∥♅ 19:03
☿∥♄ 20:34
♂□♆ 21:44

12 W
☽△♀ 0:35
☽⋕♀ 7:23
☽⚹♆ 8:40
☽⚻♂ 9:20
☽⋕☿ 10:30
☉△☽ 11:21
☽⋕♄ 11:40
☽∠⚷ 14:20
☽∥⚳ 16:07
☽△♇ 19:40
☽☌⚳ 23:02

13 Th
☊ R 4:21
☽⚼♀ 5:36
☽□♃ 9:25
☉⋕☽ 12:39
☉⚼☽ 20:46
☽⚹⚷ 20:56
☽⋕♇ 21:55

14 F
☽△☿ 0:11
☽⚺♅ 1:14
☽⚼♇ 2:19
☽⋕♂ 6:12
☽△♄ 6:27
☽⚻♀ 10:47
☿ R 11:43
☿∥♀ 20:41
⚳ D 21:21
☽□♆ 21:52

15 Sa
☽☍♂ 2:23
☉⚻☽ 6:11
☽⚼☿ 6:38
☽∠♅ 7:44
☽⚻♇ 8:55
☽⚺⚳ 12:05
☽⚼♄ 13:14
☽△♃ 23:32

16 Su
☽□⚷ 9:54
☽⚻☿ 12:13
☽⚹♅ 13:59
☉☌♇ 14:52
☽∠⚳ 18:18
☽⚻♄ 19:43
☽☍♀ 20:51

17 M
☿∠♂ 3:23
☽⚼♃ 6:08
☽△♆ 10:20
☽⚻♂ 18:25
♀⚺♄ 19:45
☽☍♇ 21:09
☉☍☽ 23:50

18 Tu
☽⚹⚳ 0:08
☉△⚳ 3:30
☿⚹⚷ 10:05
☽⋕♂ 11:44
☽⚻♃ 12:16
♅ D 15:28
☽⚼♆ 15:55
♂⚼♅ 18:12
☊R♉ 18:22
☽☍☿ 20:40
☽△⚷ 21:23
☽⋕♇ 21:39

19 W
☽□♅ 1:12
☽⚼♂ 1:39
☽⚻♀ 5:48
☽☍♄ 7:20
☉⋕☽ 14:21
♀⚼⚳ 14:38
♂⚺♇ 18:31
☽⚻♆ 21:02
☽∥⚳ 23:16

20 Th
☽⚼⚷ 2:23
☉ ♒ 2:40
☽⚻♇ 7:31
☽⋕♄ 7:33
☽△♂ 8:17
☽⚼♀ 9:45
☽□⚳ 10:23
☽⋕♀ 13:37
☉⚻☽ 15:03
☽⋕☿ 15:28
☽∥♅ 21:51
☽☍♃ 23:00

21 F
☽⚻☿ 1:56
☿∠♆ 5:15
☽⚻⚷ 6:55
☽△♅ 10:29
☽⚼♇ 11:58
☽△♀ 13:20
☽⚻♄ 16:55
☽⋕♃ 17:17
☉⚼☽ 21:43
♂⚻⚳ 23:01

22 Sa
☽⚼☿ 3:38
☿⚺♃ 4:01
☽☍♆ 5:45
☽⚼♅ 14:23
☽∥⚷ 15:51
☽△♇ 15:54
☽△⚳ 18:43
☽□♂ 19:47
☽⋕♆ 19:49
☽⚼♄ 20:57

23 Su
☉△☽ 3:44
☽△☿ 4:48
☽⚻♃ 7:38
☉☌☿ 10:29
☿∥♀ 11:27
☽☍⚷ 14:26
☽⚻♅ 17:47
☽□♀ 19:23
♂∠♄ 20:49
☽⚼⚳ 22:07

24 M
☽△♄ 0:27
☽∥♆ 8:56
☽⚼♃ 11:08
☽⚻♆ 12:24
☉⋕⚳ 12:48
♂ ♑ 12:54
☽⋕⚷ 12:55
☽□♇ 22:11

25 Tu
☽⚻⚳ 0:59
☽⚹♂ 4:49
☽□☿ 5:52
☽∥♃ 8:56
☿⚺♂ 12:47
☉□☽ 13:42
☊ D 13:48
☽△♃ 14:03
☽⚼♆ 14:54
☉⚺♃ 19:33
☽⚻⚷ 19:48
☽☍♅ 22:54
☽⚹♀ 23:42

26 W
☿R♑ 3:06
☽⋕♅ 4:04
☽□♄ 5:43
☉∠♆ 6:22
☽∠♂ 8:20
☽∥♀ 10:50
☽∥☿ 13:45
☽∥♄ 15:45
☽△♆ 16:49
☽⚼⚷ 21:36
☉∥☽ 22:32

27 Th
☽∠♀ 1:10
☽⚹♇ 2:11
☽⋕⚳ 2:38
☽☍⚳ 5:01
☽⚹☿ 5:29
☊ R 6:18
☽⚺♂ 11:10
☿△⚳ 11:17
☽□♃ 18:03
☉⚹☽ 20:48
☽∥♇ 21:47
☽△⚷ 22:52

28 F
☽⚻♅ 1:44
☽⚺♀ 2:09
☽∠♇ 3:20
☿∥♄ 4:31
☽∠☿ 4:52
☽∥♂ 7:41
☽⚹♄ 8:40
☽□♆ 19:01
☉∠☽ 23:24

29 Sa
☽⚼♅ 2:26
☉⚹⚷ 2:58
☽⚺♇ 4:03
☽⚺☿ 4:04
☿☌♇ 4:17
☽⚻⚳ 6:58
♀ D 8:47
☽∠♄ 9:27
☽☌♂ 15:11
☽⚹♃ 20:04

30 Su
☽□⚷ 0:05
☉⚺☽ 1:36
☽△♅ 2:49
☽☌♀ 3:09
☽⚼⚳ 7:27
☉∥☿ 8:28
☽⚺♄ 9:57
☉□♅ 19:33
☽⚹♆ 19:49
☽∠♃ 20:42

31 M
☉⚺♀ 1:30
☽☌☿ 2:27
☽☌♇ 4:45
☽△⚳ 7:52
☽∥♂ 15:06
☽⚺♂ 18:15
☽∠♆ 20:09
☽⚺♃ 21:24

February 2022

LONGITUDE

Day	Sid.Time	☉	☽	☽ 12 hour	Mean ☊	True ☊	☿	♀	♂	⚳	♃	♄	⚷	♅	♆	♇
	h m s	° E "	° E "	° E "	° E	° E	° E	° E	° E	° E	° E	° E	° E	° E	° E	° E
1 Tu	8 44 44	12♒05 14	8♒47 13	16♒07 28	27♉53.3	28♉46.5	25♑03.1	11♑12.9	5♑25.8	28♉55.5	7♓12.7	15♒29.1	9♈16.1	10♉53.8	21♓25.9	26♑57.0
2 W	8 48 40	13 06 09	23 23 49	0♓35 22	27 50.1	28R 34.8	24R 41.3	11 20.3	6 09.6	29 02.2	7 26.5	15 36.3	9 18.3	10 54.5	21 27.7	26 58.9
3 Th	8 52 37	14 07 04	7♓41 21	14 41 10	27 46.9	28 23.0	24 27.9	11 30.0	6 53.5	29 09.3	7 40.4	15 43.5	9 20.6	10 55.3	21 29.6	27 00.8
4 F	8 56 33	15 07 57	21 34 24	28 20 49	27 43.7	28 12.4	24D 22.7	11 41.8	7 37.4	29 16.8	7 54.4	15 50.7	9 22.9	10 56.1	21 31.5	27 02.7
5 Sa	9 00 30	16 08 49	5♈00 22	11♈33 10	27 40.6	28 04.0	24 25.1	11 55.8	8 21.3	29 24.6	8 08.3	15 57.9	9 25.2	10 57.0	21 33.5	27 04.6
6 Su	9 04 26	17 09 39	17 59 30	24 19 44	27 37.4	27 58.2	24 34.7	12 11.8	9 05.2	29 32.7	8 22.4	16 05.0	9 27.6	10 57.9	21 35.4	27 06.5
7 M	9 08 23	18 10 28	0♉34 23	6♉44 00	27 34.2	27 55.1	24 50.9	12 29.9	9 49.2	29 41.2	8 36.4	16 12.2	9 30.1	10 58.9	21 37.4	27 08.4
8 Tu	9 12 19	19 11 16	12 49 14	18 50 46	27 31.0	27D 53.9	25 13.2	12 49.8	10 33.2	29 50.0	8 50.5	16 19.4	9 32.5	11 00.0	21 39.3	27 10.3
9 W	9 16 16	20 12 02	24 49 17	0♊45 29	27 27.9	27R 53.8	25 41.3	13 11.7	11 17.2	29 59.1	9 04.6	16 26.6	9 35.0	11 01.0	21 41.3	27 12.1
10 Th	9 20 13	21 12 47	6♊40 06	12 33 48	27 24.7	27 53.7	26 14.5	13 35.4	12 01.2	0♊08.6	9 18.7	16 33.8	9 37.6	11 02.2	21 43.4	27 14.0
11 F	9 24 09	22 13 30	18 27 15	24 21 05	27 21.5	27 52.2	26 52.5	14 00.8	12 45.3	0 18.3	9 32.9	16 41.0	9 40.2	11 03.4	21 45.4	27 15.8
12 Sa	9 28 06	23 14 11	0♋15 53	6♋12 12	27 18.3	27 48.6	27 34.9	14 28.0	13 29.5	0 28.4	9 47.1	16 48.2	9 42.8	11 04.6	21 47.4	27 17.6
13 Su	9 32 02	24 14 51	12 10 31	18 11 15	27 15.2	27 42.2	28 21.3	14 56.7	14 13.6	0 38.8	10 01.4	16 55.3	9 45.5	11 05.9	21 49.5	27 19.4
14 M	9 35 59	25 15 30	24 14 44	0♌21 17	27 12.0	27 33.0	29 11.3	15 27.1	14 57.8	0 49.5	10 15.6	17 02.5	9 48.1	11 07.2	21 51.6	27 21.2
15 Tu	9 39 55	26 16 07	6♌31 07	12 44 21	27 08.8	27 21.2	0♒04.8	15 58.9	15 42.0	1 00.4	10 29.9	17 09.6	9 50.9	11 08.6	21 53.7	27 23.0
16 W	9 43 52	27 16 42	19 01 04	25 21 18	27 05.6	27 07.7	1 01.3	16 32.2	16 26.3	1 11.7	10 44.2	17 16.8	9 53.6	11 10.0	21 55.8	27 24.8
17 Th	9 47 48	28 17 16	1♍44 58	8♍11 59	27 02.4	26 53.6	2 00.7	17 06.9	17 10.6	1 23.2	10 58.5	17 23.9	9 56.4	11 11.5	21 57.9	27 26.6
18 F	9 51 45	29 17 48	14 42 13	21 15 31	26 59.3	26 40.2	3 02.8	17 43.0	17 54.9	1 35.0	11 12.9	17 31.0	9 59.2	11 13.0	22 00.0	27 28.3
19 Sa	9 55 42	0♓18 19	27 51 42	4♎30 36	26 56.1	26 28.6	4 07.3	18 20.4	18 39.2	1 47.1	11 27.3	17 38.1	10 02.1	11 14.6	22 02.1	27 30.0
20 Su	9 59 38	1 18 48	11♎12 05	17 56 00	26 52.9	26 19.8	5 14.1	18 59.0	19 23.6	1 59.5	11 41.7	17 45.1	10 05.0	11 16.2	22 04.3	27 31.8
21 M	10 03 35	2 19 16	24 42 16	1♏30 49	26 49.7	26 14.1	6 23.0	19 38.8	20 08.0	2 12.1	11 56.1	17 52.2	10 07.9	11 17.9	22 06.5	27 33.5
22 Tu	10 07 31	3 19 43	8♏21 37	15 14 39	26 46.5	26 11.2	7 33.9	20 19.8	20 52.5	2 25.0	12 10.5	17 59.2	10 10.8	11 19.6	22 08.6	27 35.1
23 W	10 11 28	4 20 08	22 09 58	29 07 33	26 43.4	26 10.4	8 46.7	21 01.9	21 36.9	2 38.2	12 24.9	18 06.3	10 13.8	11 21.3	22 10.8	27 36.8
24 Th	10 15 24	5 20 32	6♐07 25	13♐09 35	26 40.2	26 10.4	10 01.3	21 45.0	22 21.4	2 51.6	12 39.4	18 13.3	10 16.8	11 23.1	22 13.0	27 38.5
25 F	10 19 21	6 20 55	20 13 58	27 20 27	26 37.0	26 09.8	11 17.5	22 29.2	23 06.0	3 05.3	12 53.8	18 20.2	10 19.8	11 25.0	22 15.2	27 40.1
26 Sa	10 23 17	7 21 17	4♑28 49	11♑38 48	26 33.8	26 07.6	12 35.3	23 14.3	23 50.6	3 19.2	13 08.3	18 27.2	10 22.9	11 26.9	22 17.4	27 41.7
27 Su	10 27 14	8 21 37	18 50 00	26 01 54	26 30.7	26 02.7	13 54.6	24 00.4	24 35.2	3 33.4	13 22.8	18 34.1	10 25.9	11 28.8	22 19.6	27 43.3
28 M	10 31 11	9♓21 55	3♒13 56	10♒25 26	26♉27.5	25♉54.9	15♒15.4	24♑47.3	25♑19.8	3♊47.8	13♓37.3	18♒41.0	10♈29.0	11♉30.8	22♓21.9	27♑44.9

1st of Month

Julian Day #
2459611.5
Obliquity
23°26'6"
SVP 4♓57'7"
GC 27♐08.9
Eris 23♈43.5

Day	⚴
1	25♓29.4
6	27 09.3
11	28 51.9
16	0♈37.2
21	2 24.9
26	4 14.9

Day	⚵
1	29♑37.0
6	1♒36.6
11	3 36.2
16	5 35.8
21	7 35.1
26	9 34.2

Day	⚶
1	10♑58.2
6	13 34.0
11	16 08.7
16	18 42.0
21	21 13.9
26	23 44.3

DECLINATION and LATITUDE

Day	☉ Decl	☽ Decl	☽ Lat	☽ 12h Decl	☿ Decl	☿ Lat	♀ Decl	♀ Lat	♂ Decl	♂ Lat	⚳ Decl	⚳ Lat	♃ Decl	♃ Lat	♄ Decl	♄ Lat
1 Tu	17S10	22S37	4S43	20S41	17S60	3N11	16S15	6N44	23S49	0S29	19N40	0S15	9S46	0S58	17S00	0S51
2 W	16 53	18 26	5 00	15 57	18 12	3 02	16 17	6 42	23 48	0 30	19 44	0 12	9 41	0 58	16 58	0 51
3 Th	16 36	13 17	4 57	10 28	18 24	2 52	16 19	6 39	23 46	0 31	19 49	0 09	9 36	0 58	16 56	0 51
4 F	16 18	7 35	4 37	4 39	18 35	2 41	16 21	6 36	23 45	0 32	19 54	0 06	9 30	0 58	16 54	0 51
5 Sa	15 60	1 43	4 02	1N12	18 46	2 31	16 23	6 32	23 43	0 32	19 58	0 03	9 25	0 58	16 52	0 51
6 Su	15 41	4N03	3 15	6 50	18 55	2 19	16 26	6 29	23 41	0 33	20 03	0 00	9 20	0 58	16 50	0 51
7 M	15 23	9 30	2 19	12 02	19 04	2 08	16 28	6 24	23 38	0 34	20 07	0N02	9 15	0 58	16 48	0 51
8 Tu	15 04	14 26	1 19	16 40	19 11	1 56	16 31	6 20	23 36	0 35	20 12	0 05	9 09	0 58	16 45	0 51
9 W	14 45	18 42	0 16	20 33	19 18	1 44	16 33	6 15	23 33	0 35	20 17	0 08	9 04	0 58	16 43	0 51
10 Th	14 26	22 11	0N46	23 34	19 23	1 33	16 36	6 11	23 29	0 36	20 22	0 11	8 59	0 58	16 41	0 51
11 F	14 06	24 42	1 47	25 34	19 27	1 21	16 38	6 06	23 26	0 37	20 26	0 14	8 53	0 58	16 39	0 51
12 Sa	13 46	26 09	2 42	26 25	19 30	1 10	16 41	6 00	23 23	0 37	20 31	0 17	8 48	0 58	16 37	0 52
13 Su	13 26	26 23	3 31	26 03	19 32	0 58	16 43	5 55	23 19	0 38	20 36	0 19	8 43	0 58	16 35	0 52
14 M	13 06	25 23	4 11	24 25	19 33	0 47	16 46	5 49	23 15	0 39	20 41	0 22	8 37	0 58	16 33	0 52
15 Tu	12 46	23 10	4 40	21 37	19 32	0 37	16 48	5 43	23 10	0 40	20 46	0 25	8 32	0 58	16 31	0 52
16 W	12 25	19 49	4 57	17 46	19 30	0 26	16 50	5 37	23 06	0 40	20 50	0 27	8 26	0 58	16 29	0 52
17 Th	12 04	15 30	4 59	13 02	19 27	0 16	16 52	5 31	23 01	0 41	20 55	0 30	8 21	0 58	16 27	0 52
18 F	11 43	10 24	4 45	7 39	19 23	0 06	16 53	5 25	22 56	0 42	21 00	0 32	8 15	0 58	16 25	0 52
19 Sa	11 22	4 46	4 17	1 50	19 17	0S04	16 55	5 19	22 51	0 43	21 05	0 35	8 10	0 58	16 22	0 52
20 Su	11 00	1S09	3 34	4S09	19 11	0 13	16 56	5 13	22 45	0 43	21 10	0 37	8 05	0 58	16 20	0 52
21 M	10 39	7 07	2 38	10 01	19 02	0 23	16 57	5 06	22 39	0 44	21 15	0 40	7 59	0 58	16 18	0 52
22 Tu	10 17	12 50	1 33	15 29	18 53	0 31	16 57	4 60	22 33	0 45	21 20	0 42	7 54	0 58	16 16	0 52
23 W	9 55	17 58	0 21	20 13	18 42	0 40	16 58	4 53	22 27	0 46	21 25	0 45	7 48	0 58	16 14	0 52
24 Th	9 33	22 11	0S52	23 51	18 30	0 48	16 58	4 47	22 21	0 46	21 30	0 47	7 43	0 58	16 12	0 53
25 F	9 11	25 08	2 04	26 01	18 17	0 56	16 58	4 40	22 14	0 47	21 35	0 50	7 37	0 58	16 10	0 53
26 Sa	8 49	26 29	3 08	26 31	18 02	1 03	16 57	4 33	22 07	0 48	21 40	0 52	7 31	0 58	16 08	0 53
27 Su	8 26	26 05	4 01	25 13	17 46	1 10	16 56	4 26	22 00	0 49	21 45	0 54	7 26	0 58	16 06	0 53
28 M	8S03	23S56	4S38	22S17	17S29	1S17	16S55	4N20	21S53	0S49	21N50	0N57	7S20	0S59	16S04	0S53

Day	⚷ Decl	⚷ Lat	♅ Decl	♅ Lat	♆ Decl	♆ Lat	♇ Decl	♇ Lat
1	5N35	2N04	14N43	0S23	4S26	1S07	22S30	1S46
6	5 38	2 04	14 45	0 23	4 22	1 07	22 29	1 47
11	5 43	2 03	14 47	0 23	4 18	1 07	22 28	1 47
16	5 47	2 02	14 49	0 23	4 14	1 07	22 26	1 48
21	5 52	2 01	14 51	0 23	4 10	1 07	22 25	1 49
26	5N58	2N01	14N54	0S23	4S05	1S07	22S24	1S49

Day	⚴ Decl	⚴ Lat	⚵ Decl	⚵ Lat	⚶ Decl	⚶ Lat	Eris Decl	Eris Lat
1	10S05	9S03	12S22	8N02	21S28	1N31	1S18	11S18
6	9 42	9 21	12 01	7 59	21 22	1 24	1 17	11 17
11	9 18	9 39	11 39	7 55	21 12	1 16	1 16	11 16
16	8 53	9 57	11 15	7 51	21 01	1 08	1 15	11 16
21	8 27	10 15	10 49	7 48	20 47	0 60	1 13	11 15
26	8S00	10S34	10S22	7N45	20S31	0N51	1S12	11S14

Moon Phenomena

Max/0 Decl

dy	hr mn	
5	7:02	0 N
12	16:47	26N26
19	19:22	0 S
26	6:34	26S33

Max/0 Lat

dy	hr mn	
2	8:31	5S01
9	6:13	0 N
16	15:04	5N00
23	6:55	0 S

Perigee/Apogee

dy	hr m		kilometers
11	2:38	a	404896
26	22:26	p	367789

PH	dy	hr mn	
●	1	5:47	12♒20
☽	8	13:51	19♉46
○	16	16:58	28♌00
☾	23	22:34	5♐17

Void of Course Moon

Last Aspect				☽ Ingress		
1	11:02	♄	☌	♓	2	11:01
4	9:42	♇	⚹	♈	4	14:58
6	17:22	♇	□	♉	6	22:54
9	4:49	♇	△	♊	9	10:28
11	8:24	☉	△	♋	11	23:28
14	10:28	☿	☍	♌	14	11:18
16	16:58	☉	☍	♍	16	20:44
18	23:21	♇	△	♎	19	3:52
21	5:03	♇	□	♏	21	9:20
23	9:25	♇	⚹	♐	23	13:30
25	3:26	♆	□	♑	25	16:29
27	14:51	♇	☌	♒	27	18:37

DAILY ASPECTARIAN

1 Tu	☽∥♇	0:45
	☽⚹⚷	0:47
	☽□♅	3:27
	☽⚺♀	3:59
	☉☌☽	5:47
	☽☌♄	11:02
	☉∥♄	16:02
	☽#⚳	17:18
	☽∠♂	20:06
	☽⚺♆	20:47
	⚵ ♒	23:06
2 W	☽∥☿	1:08
	☽∠⚷	1:31
	☽⚺☿	2:06
	☽∠♀	4:57
	☽⚺♇	5:59
	☽∥♄	7:17
	☉∥☽	8:06
	☽□⚳	9:29
	☽∥♀	10:25
	☽#♅	17:35
	☽⚹♂	22:34
	☽☌♃	23:58
3 Th	☽⚺⚷	2:50
	☽∠☿	3:00
	☽⚹♅	5:32
	☽⚹♀	6:36
	☽∠♇	7:25
	☉⚺☽	11:53
	☽⚺♄	13:55
	☽∥♃	15:56
	☉∥♀	20:13
	☽☌♆	23:55
4 F	☿ D	4:14
	☽⚹☿	4:57
	☽∠♅	7:43
	☽#⚷	8:03
	☽⚹♇	9:42
	☽∥♆	13:05
	♂⚹♃	13:39
	☽⚹⚳	13:48
	☉∠☽	16:27
	☽∠♄	16:38
	☉☌♄	19:06
5 Sa	☽⚺♃	5:49
	☽□♂	6:28
	☽☌⚷	8:06
	☽⚺♅	10:54
	☽□♀	12:57
	☽∠⚳	17:29
	☽⚹♄	20:23
	☉⚹☽	22:18
6 Su	☽#♆	1:19
	☽⚺♆	6:49
	☽∥⚷	6:50
	☽∠♃	10:22
	☽□☿	12:43
	♂□⚷	12:58
	☽□♇	17:22
	☽⚺⚳	22:16
	☽#♃	22:52
7 M	☽∠♆	11:49
	☽⚹♃	15:59
	☽⚺⚷	17:30
	☽△♂	19:14
	☽☌♅	20:23
8 Tu	☽△♀	0:01
	☽∥♅	1:43
	☉#☽	3:08
	☽□♄	7:02
	☽#♀	11:17
	☽#♄	12:27
	☊ D	13:39
	☉□☽	13:51
	♂△♅	14:58
	☽⚹♆	17:41
	☉#♅	22:58
	☽∠⚷	23:31
9 W	☽△☿	1:50
	⚳ ♊	2:14
	☽⚼♂	3:09
	☽#☿	3:46
	☽△♇	4:49
	☊ R	6:14
	☽⚼♀	7:02
	☽∥⚳	10:21
	☽☌⚳	10:34
10 Th	☽#♇	2:17
	☽□♃	5:29
	☽⚹⚷	6:02
	☽⚺♅	8:54
	☽⚼☿	9:49
	☽#♂	11:01
	☽⚼♇	11:21
	☽⚻♂	11:37
	☉⚺♆	12:30
	☽⚻♀	14:37
	☽△♄	20:21
11 F	♀∥♄	4:00
	☽□♆	6:44
	☉△☽	8:24
	☿☌♇	14:05
	♃⚺⚷	15:02
	☽∠♅	15:29
	☽⚻♇	17:58
	☽⚻☿	18:12
12 Sa	☽⚺⚳	0:26
	☽⚼♄	3:09
	☉⚼☽	17:35
	☽□⚷	19:08
	☽△♃	19:36
	☽⚹♅	21:50
13 Su	☽☍♂	4:22
	☽☍♀	5:47
	☽∠⚳	7:02
	☽⚻♄	9:35
	☉∠⚷	12:40
	☽△♆	19:16
14 M	☽⚼♃	2:02
	☉⚻☽	2:11
	⚴ ♈	5:54
	☽☍♇	6:08
	☽☍☿	10:28
	☽⚹⚳	13:07
	☿ ♒	21:55
	☽#♂	23:57
15 Tu	☽⚼♆	0:44
	♀⚼⚳	1:42
	☽#♇	5:52
	☽△⚷	6:28
	☽⚻♃	7:50
	☽□♅	8:57
	♂⚼⚳	13:21
	☽∥⚳	17:32
	☽⚻♂	18:47
	☽⚻♀	19:03
	☽☍♄	20:39
16 W	☽#☿	1:55
	☉⚺♇	3:19
	☿△⚳	5:18
	☽⚻♆	5:33
	☽⚼⚷	11:10
	♀☌♂	14:30
	☽⚻♇	15:55
	☽#♀	16:57
	☉☍☽	16:58
	☽#♄	19:04
	☽□⚳	23:19
17 Th	☽⚻☿	0:32
	☽⚼♀	0:43
	☽⚼♂	0:51
	☽∥♅	3:22
	♂⚺♄	8:36
	♀⚺♄	14:10
	☽⚻⚷	15:17
	☽☍♃	17:27
	☽△♅	17:34
	☉#☽	17:40
	☽⚼♇	19:53
18 F	♃⚹♅	0:14
	☽⚻♄	5:12
	☽△♀	5:48
	☽△♂	6:14
	☽⚼☿	6:40
	☽#♃	9:32
	☽☍♆	13:23
	☉ ♓	16:44
	☽∥⚷	19:36
	☽⚼♅	21:04
	☽△♇	23:21
19 Sa	☽#♆	2:25
	☉⚻☽	4:47
	☽△⚳	7:12
	☽⚼♄	8:42
	☽△☿	12:19
	☽☍⚷	21:59
20 Su	☽⚻♅	0:07
	☽⚻♃	0:54
	☉⚼☽	9:51
	☽⚼⚳	10:29
	☽△♄	11:47
	☽∥♆	12:04
	☽□♀	14:35
	☽□♂	15:26
	☽#⚷	18:56
	☽⚻♆	19:24
	☉□⚳	20:25
21 M	☽∥♃	3:29
	☽⚼♃	4:00
	☽□♇	5:03
	☽⚻⚳	13:25
	☉∥☽	13:45
	☉△☽	14:29
	☿∠♆	15:14
	☽⚼♆	21:52
	☽□☿	22:29
22 Tu	☽⚻⚷	3:11
	☽☍♅	5:11
	☽△♃	6:47
	☽#♅	9:08
	☽∥♄	15:34
	☽□♄	16:54
	☽∥♀	19:01
	☽⚹♀	21:56
	☽⚹♂	23:00
23 W	☽△♆	0:01
	☽∥☿	3:38
	☽⚼⚷	5:19
	♂∥♇	9:16
	☽⚹♇	9:25
	☽☍⚳	18:19
	♂⚹♆	19:13
	☽#⚳	19:31
	♃∠♇	22:18
	☉□☽	22:34
24 Th	☽∥♂	1:01
	☽∠♀	1:08
	☽∥♇	1:29
	☽∠♂	2:14
	☿⚹⚷	5:07
	☽△⚷	7:07
	☽⚹☿	7:19
	☽⚻♅	9:00
	☽∠♇	11:08
	☽□♃	11:20
	♀⚹♆	16:05
	☽⚹♄	20:46
25 F	☿□♅	2:23
	☽□♆	3:26
	☽⚺♀	4:01
	☽⚺♂	5:07
	☽⚼♅	10:28
	☽∠☿	11:15
	☽⚺♇	12:34
	☽⚻⚳	22:01
	☽∠♄	22:16
26 Sa	☉⚹☽	5:11
	☽□⚷	9:55
	☽△♅	11:42
	☿⚺♃	12:17
	☽⚹♃	14:44
	☽⚺☿	14:57
	☽⚼⚳	23:32
	☽⚺♄	23:33
27 Su	☽⚹♆	5:50
	☉∠☽	8:07
	☽☌♀	9:07
	☽☌♂	10:07
	☽☌♇	14:51
	☽∠♃	16:11
28 M	☽△⚳	0:57
	♂#⚳	4:59
	☽∠♆	6:55
	☉⚺☽	11:00
	☽∥♇	11:14
	☽⚹⚷	12:09
	☽□♅	13:51
	☽#⚳	14:31
	☽∥♂	15:03
	☽⚺♃	17:39
	☽☌☿	22:12

LONGITUDE

Day	Sid.Time	☉	☽	☽ 12 hour	Mean☊	True☊	☿	♀	♂	⚳	♃	♄	⚷	♅	♆	♇
	h m s	° E "	° E "	° E "	° E	° E	° E	° E	° E	° E	° E	° E	° E	° E	° E	° E
1 Tu	10 35 07	10♓22 12	17♒35 39	24♒43 50	26♉24.3	25♉44.7	16♒37.6	25♑35.1	26♑04.4	4♊02.4	13♓51.8	18♒47.9	10♈32.2	11♉32.8	22♓24.1	27♑46.5
2 W	10 39 04	11 22 28	1♓49 15	8♓51 09	26 21.1	25R 33.0	18 01.1	26 23.8	26 49.1	4 17.3	14 06.3	18 54.8	10 35.3	11 34.8	22 26.3	27 48.0
3 Th	10 43 00	12 22 41	15 48 55	22 41 57	26 18.0	25 21.1	19 25.9	27 13.2	27 33.8	4 32.4	14 20.9	19 01.6	10 38.5	11 36.9	22 28.6	27 49.5
4 F	10 46 57	13 22 53	29 29 50	6♈12 15	26 14.8	25 10.1	20 52.0	28 03.4	28 18.5	4 47.8	14 35.4	19 08.4	10 41.7	11 39.1	22 30.8	27 51.1
5 Sa	10 50 53	14 23 03	12♈49 00	19 20 04	26 11.6	25 01.2	22 19.3	28 54.3	29 03.3	5 03.3	14 49.9	19 15.2	10 44.9	11 41.3	22 33.1	27 52.5
6 Su	10 54 50	15 23 11	25 45 31	2♉05 34	26 08.4	24 54.9	23 47.9	29 45.9	29 48.1	5 19.1	15 04.4	19 21.9	10 48.1	11 43.5	22 35.4	27 54.0
7 M	10 58 46	16 23 16	8♉20 33	14 30 51	26 05.2	24 51.3	25 17.6	0♒38.1	0♒32.9	5 35.1	15 18.9	19 28.6	10 51.4	11 45.7	22 37.6	27 55.4
8 Tu	11 02 43	17 23 20	20 37 01	26 39 33	26 02.1	24D 50.0	26 48.5	1 31.0	1 17.7	5 51.3	15 33.5	19 35.3	10 54.7	11 48.0	22 39.9	27 56.9
9 W	11 06 39	18 23 22	2♊39 07	8♊36 20	25 58.9	24 50.1	28 20.6	2 24.6	2 02.5	6 07.7	15 48.0	19 41.9	10 58.0	11 50.4	22 42.2	27 58.3
10 Th	11 10 36	19 23 21	14 31 52	20 26 25	25 55.7	24R 50.7	29 53.9	3 18.7	2 47.4	6 24.3	16 02.5	19 48.5	11 01.3	11 52.8	22 44.4	27 59.7
11 F	11 14 33	20 23 19	26 20 41	2♋15 19	25 52.5	24 50.6	1♓28.3	4 13.4	3 32.3	6 41.2	16 17.0	19 55.1	11 04.6	11 55.2	22 46.7	28 01.0
12 Sa	11 18 29	21 23 14	8♋11 00	14 08 22	25 49.4	24 48.9	3 03.9	5 08.6	4 17.2	6 58.2	16 31.5	20 01.6	11 08.0	11 57.6	22 49.0	28 02.3
13 Su	11 22 26	22 23 07	20 07 59	26 10 25	25 46.2	24 45.1	4 40.7	6 04.4	5 02.1	7 15.4	16 46.0	20 08.1	11 11.4	12 00.1	22 51.3	28 03.7
14 M	11 26 22	23 22 58	2♌16 10	8♌25 37	25 43.0	24 38.9	6 18.6	7 00.7	5 47.0	7 32.8	17 00.4	20 14.5	11 14.7	12 02.6	22 53.6	28 05.0
15 Tu	11 30 19	24 22 47	14 39 10	20 57 02	25 39.8	24 30.5	7 57.7	7 57.5	6 32.0	7 50.3	17 14.9	20 20.9	11 18.1	12 05.2	22 55.8	28 06.2
16 W	11 34 15	25 22 33	27 19 25	3♍46 23	25 36.6	24 20.5	9 38.0	8 54.8	7 17.0	8 08.1	17 29.3	20 27.2	11 21.5	12 07.8	22 58.1	28 07.5
17 Th	11 38 12	26 22 18	10♍17 56	16 53 58	25 33.5	24 10.0	11 19.5	9 52.5	8 02.0	8 26.0	17 43.8	20 33.6	11 25.0	12 10.4	23 00.4	28 08.7
18 F	11 42 08	27 22 00	23 34 16	0♎18 35	25 30.3	23 59.8	13 02.2	10 50.7	8 47.0	8 44.1	17 58.2	20 39.8	11 28.4	12 13.1	23 02.7	28 09.9
19 Sa	11 46 05	28 21 40	7♎06 36	13 57 56	25 27.1	23 51.2	14 46.1	11 49.3	9 32.1	9 02.4	18 12.6	20 46.0	11 31.8	12 15.7	23 04.9	28 11.0
20 Su	11 50 02	29 21 19	20 52 11	27 48 55	25 23.9	23 44.7	16 31.3	12 48.3	10 17.2	9 20.9	18 27.0	20 52.2	11 35.3	12 18.5	23 07.2	28 12.2
21 M	11 53 58	0♈20 55	4♏47 44	11♏48 15	25 20.8	23 40.7	18 17.7	13 47.8	11 02.3	9 39.5	18 41.4	20 58.3	11 38.7	12 21.2	23 09.5	28 13.3
22 Tu	11 57 55	1 20 30	18 50 05	25 52 56	25 17.6	23D 39.2	20 05.3	14 47.6	11 47.4	9 58.3	18 55.7	21 04.4	11 42.2	12 24.0	23 11.7	28 14.4
23 W	12 01 51	2 20 03	2♐56 30	10♐00 33	25 14.4	23 39.4	21 54.3	15 47.8	12 32.5	10 17.2	19 10.0	21 10.4	11 45.7	12 26.8	23 14.0	28 15.5
24 Th	12 05 48	3 19 34	17 04 53	24 09 18	25 11.2	23 40.4	23 44.5	16 48.4	13 17.7	10 36.3	19 24.4	21 16.4	11 49.2	12 29.6	23 16.2	28 16.5
25 F	12 09 44	4 19 04	1♑13 39	8♑17 46	25 08.0	23R 41.1	25 36.0	17 49.3	14 02.9	10 55.6	19 38.6	21 22.4	11 52.7	12 32.5	23 18.5	28 17.6
26 Sa	12 13 41	5 18 32	15 21 29	22 24 36	25 04.9	23 40.7	27 28.8	18 50.5	14 48.1	11 15.0	19 52.9	21 28.2	11 56.2	12 35.4	23 20.7	28 18.6
27 Su	12 17 37	6 17 58	29 26 56	6♒28 13	25 01.7	23 38.5	29 22.8	19 52.1	15 33.3	11 34.5	20 07.1	21 34.1	11 59.7	12 38.3	23 23.0	28 19.5
28 M	12 21 34	7 17 22	13♒28 11	20 26 31	24 58.5	23 34.1	1♈18.2	20 54.0	16 18.5	11 54.2	20 21.4	21 39.8	12 03.2	12 41.3	23 25.2	28 20.5
29 Tu	12 25 31	8 16 45	27 22 52	4♓16 53	24 55.3	23 28.0	3 14.8	21 56.2	17 03.7	12 14.1	20 35.5	21 45.5	12 06.7	12 44.3	23 27.4	28 21.4
30 W	12 29 27	9 16 05	11♓08 12	17 56 26	24 52.2	23 20.8	5 12.6	22 58.7	17 49.0	12 34.1	20 49.7	21 51.2	12 10.2	12 47.3	23 29.6	28 22.3
31 Th	12 33 24	10♈15 24	24 41 16	1♈22 24	24♉49.0	23♉13.3	7♈11.7	24♒01.5	18♒34.3	12♊54.2	21♓03.8	21♒56.8	12♈13.7	12♉50.3	23♓31.8	28♑23.1

1st of Month

Julian Day #
2459639.5
Obliquity
23°26'07"
SVP 4♓57'04"
GC 27♐08.9
Eris 23♈53.7

Day	⚴	⚵	⚶
1	5♈22.0	10♒45.5	25♑13.7
6	7 15.4	12 43.9	27 41.2
11	9 10.8	14 41.6	0♒06.8
16	11 08.0	16 38.6	2 30.2
21	13 06.8	18 34.8	4 51.3
26	15 07.3	20 30.0	7 10.1
31	17 09.4	22 24.1	9 26.2

DECLINATION and LATITUDE

Day	☉ Decl	☽ Decl	☽ Lat	☽ 12h Decl	☿ Decl	☿ Lat	♀ Decl	♀ Lat	♂ Decl	♂ Lat	⚳ Decl	⚳ Lat	♃ Decl	♃ Lat	♄ Decl	♄ Lat
1 Tu	7S41	20S17	4S58	18S00	17S11	1S24	16S53	4N13	21S45	0S50	21N55	0N59	7S15	0S59	16S02	0S53
2 W	7 18	15 29	4 59	12 46	16 51	1 30	16 51	4 06	21 37	0 51	22 00	1 01	7 09	0 59	15 60	0 53
3 Th	6 55	9 56	4 42	6 60	16 30	1 35	16 48	3 59	21 29	0 52	22 05	1 03	7 04	0 59	15 58	0 53
4 F	6 32	4 01	4 09	1 02	16 08	1 41	16 45	3 52	21 21	0 52	22 10	1 06	6 58	0 59	15 56	0 53
5 Sa	6 09	1N56	3 24	4N50	15 44	1 46	16 42	3 45	21 13	0 53	22 15	1 08	6 53	0 59	15 54	0 53
6 Su	5 46	7 39	2 28	10 21	15 19	1 50	16 38	3 39	21 04	0 54	22 20	1 10	6 47	0 59	15 52	0 54
7 M	5 22	12 55	1 27	15 19	14 53	1 54	16 34	3 32	20 55	0 55	22 25	1 12	6 41	0 59	15 50	0 54
8 Tu	4 59	17 33	0 22	19 34	14 26	1 58	16 29	3 25	20 46	0 55	22 30	1 14	6 36	0 59	15 48	0 54
9 W	4 35	21 22	0N42	22 56	13 57	2 02	16 24	3 18	20 37	0 56	22 35	1 17	6 30	0 59	15 46	0 54
10 Th	4 12	24 15	1 43	25 17	13 27	2 05	16 19	3 11	20 27	0 57	22 40	1 19	6 25	0 59	15 44	0 54
11 F	3 48	26 03	2 40	26 31	12 56	2 07	16 13	3 05	20 18	0 58	22 45	1 21	6 19	0 59	15 42	0 54
12 Sa	3 25	26 40	3 30	26 32	12 24	2 10	16 06	2 58	20 08	0 58	22 50	1 23	6 13	0 59	15 40	0 54
13 Su	3 01	26 04	4 11	25 18	11 50	2 12	15 59	2 51	19 58	0 59	22 55	1 25	6 08	0 59	15 38	0 54
14 M	2 38	24 13	4 42	22 51	11 15	2 13	15 52	2 44	19 47	0 60	22 60	1 27	6 02	0 59	15 36	0 54
15 Tu	2 14	21 13	4 60	19 18	10 39	2 14	15 44	2 38	19 37	1 01	23 05	1 29	5 57	0 59	15 34	0 55
16 W	1 50	17 09	5 04	14 47	10 02	2 15	15 36	2 31	19 26	1 01	23 09	1 31	5 51	0 59	15 32	0 55
17 Th	1 27	12 13	4 52	9 29	9 23	2 15	15 27	2 24	19 15	1 02	23 14	1 33	5 46	0 59	15 30	0 55
18 F	1 03	6 37	4 25	3 38	8 44	2 14	15 18	2 18	19 04	1 03	23 19	1 35	5 40	0 59	15 28	0 55
19 Sa	0 39	0 35	3 43	2S30	8 03	2 13	15 08	2 11	18 53	1 03	23 24	1 37	5 34	0 59	15 26	0 55
20 Su	0 15	5S34	2 46	8 37	7 21	2 12	14 58	2 05	18 42	1 04	23 29	1 39	5 29	0 60	15 24	0 55
21 M	0N08	11 33	1 40	14 22	6 38	2 10	14 47	1 59	18 30	1 05	23 33	1 41	5 23	0 60	15 23	0 55
22 Tu	0 32	17 01	0 26	19 25	5 53	2 08	14 36	1 52	18 18	1 06	23 38	1 43	5 18	0 60	15 21	0 55
23 W	0 56	21 34	0S50	23 23	5 08	2 05	14 25	1 46	18 06	1 06	23 43	1 44	5 12	0 60	15 19	0 55
24 Th	1 19	24 51	2 03	25 55	4 21	2 02	14 13	1 40	17 54	1 07	23 47	1 46	5 07	0 60	15 17	0 56
25 F	1 43	26 34	3 08	26 47	3 34	1 59	14 00	1 34	17 42	1 08	23 52	1 48	5 01	0 60	15 15	0 56
26 Sa	2 07	26 34	4 02	25 55	2 45	1 54	13 47	1 27	17 29	1 09	23 56	1 50	4 56	0 60	15 14	0 56
27 Su	2 30	24 51	4 41	23 24	1 55	1 50	13 34	1 21	17 16	1 09	24 01	1 52	4 50	1 00	15 12	0 56
28 M	2 54	21 37	5 03	19 32	1 05	1 44	13 20	1 15	17 04	1 10	24 05	1 54	4 45	1 00	15 10	0 56
29 Tu	3 17	17 11	5 07	14 38	0 13	1 38	13 06	1 09	16 51	1 11	24 10	1 55	4 39	1 00	15 08	0 56
30 W	3 40	11 55	4 54	9 04	0N40	1 32	12 51	1 04	16 37	1 11	24 14	1 57	4 34	1 00	15 07	0 56
31 Th	4N04	6S08	4S23	3S10	1N33	1S25	12S36	0N58	16S24	1S12	24N19	1N59	4S28	1S00	15S05	0S57

Day	⚷ Decl	⚷ Lat	♅ Decl	♅ Lat	♆ Decl	♆ Lat	♇ Decl	♇ Lat
1	6N01	2N00	14N56	0S23	4S03	1S07	22S24	1S49
6	6 07	1 60	14 60	0 23	3 58	1 07	22 23	1 50
11	6 13	1 59	15 03	0 22	3 54	1 07	22 22	1 51
16	6 19	1 59	15 07	0 22	3 49	1 07	22 21	1 51
21	6 25	1 58	15 11	0 22	3 45	1 07	22 21	1 52
26	6 32	1 58	15 16	0 22	3 40	1 07	22 20	1 53
31	6N38	1N58	15N20	0S22	3S36	1S07	22S20	1S53

Day	⚴ Decl	⚴ Lat	⚵ Decl	⚵ Lat	⚶ Decl	⚶ Lat	Eris Decl	Eris Lat
1	7S44	10S45	10S06	7N43	20S20	0N46	1S11	11S14
6	7 17	11 04	9 37	7 41	20 01	0 37	1 10	11 13
11	6 50	11 24	9 07	7 38	19 40	0 28	1 08	11 13
16	6 23	11 43	8 36	7 36	19 18	0 19	1 07	11 12
21	5 56	12 04	8 04	7 33	18 54	0 09	1 05	11 12
26	5 30	12 24	7 31	7 31	18 30	0S01	1 04	11 12
31	5S03	12S45	6S57	7N29	18S05	0S11	1S02	11S11

Moon Phenomena

Max/0 Decl

dy hr mn	
4 16:08	0 N
12 0:15	26N40
19 2:18	0 S
25 11:54	26S47

Perigee/Apogee

dy hr m	kilometers
10 23:05	a 404268
23 23:39	p 369760

Max/0 Lat

dy hr mn	
1 13:32	5S01
8 8:22	0 N
15 18:29	5N04
22 8:13	0 S
28 17:17	5S08

PH	dy hr mn	
●	2 17:36	12♓07
☽	10 10:47	19♊50
○	18 7:19	27♍40
☾	25 5:38	4♑33

Void of Course Moon

Last Aspect			☽ Ingress	
1 2:02	♄	☌	♓	1 20:55
3 21:46	♂	✶	♈	4 0:54
6 4:03	♇	□	♉	6 8:01
8 14:36	♇	△	♊	8 18:41
10 16:44	♆	□	♋	11 7:25
13 15:45	♇	☍	♌	13 19:33
15 10:57	♄	☍	♍	16 5:00
18 8:12	♇	△	♎	18 11:27
20 12:41	♇	□	♏	20 15:46
22 16:02	♇	✶	♐	22 19:00
24 13:00	☿	□	♑	24 21:55
26 23:52	☿	✶	♒	27 0:56
28 14:12	♄	☌	♓	29 4:33
31 6:38	♇	✶	♈	31 9:32

DAILY ASPECTARIAN

1 Tu
☽☌♄ 2:02
☉⚺⚷ 4:11
☽⚺♆ 8:06
☽∠⚷ 13:25
☽⚺♀ 14:15
☽⚺♂ 15:03
☽∥☿ 17:09
☽⚺♇ 17:10
☽∥♀ 17:35
☽∥♄ 21:37

2 W
☿∥♀ 0:26
☽#♅ 2:25
☉∠♀ 2:50
☽□⚳ 4:17
☉✶♅ 5:06
☉∥♃ 11:55
☽⚺⚷ 15:02
☿☌♄ 16:34
☽✶♅ 16:44
☽∠♀ 17:24
☉☌☽ 17:36
☽∠♂ 18:04
☽∠♇ 18:49
☽☌♃ 21:25

3 Th
☽⚺♄ 5:38
☽⚺☿ 7:01
♂☌♇ 8:44
☉∠♇ 10:59
☽☌♆ 11:39
☽∥♃ 11:55
☉∥☽ 13:11
☽#⚷ 15:45
☉∠♂ 17:15
♀☌♇ 17:57
☽∠♅ 18:57
☽✶♇ 21:04
☽✶♀ 21:16
☽✶♂ 21:46

4 F
☽∥♆ 0:04
☽∠♄ 8:22
☽✶⚳ 9:39
☽∠☿ 12:47
☿∥♄ 13:34
☽☌⚷ 20:13
☽⚺♅ 21:56

5 Sa
☉⚺☽ 3:07
☉#⚷ 3:10
☽⚺♃ 3:46
☿⚺♆ 3:51
☽#♆ 8:25
☽✶♄ 11:57
☽∠⚳ 13:37
☉☌♃ 14:08
☉#☽ 16:24
☽∥⚷ 17:21
☽⚺♆ 18:03
☽✶☿ 19:50
☽#♃ 20:18

6 Su
☽□♇ 4:03
♂ ♒ 6:24
♀ ♒ 6:31
♀☌♂ 7:14
☽□♂ 8:07
☽□♀ 8:08
☽∠♃ 8:19
☉∠☽ 9:30
⚳#♇ 11:34
♀∠♃ 11:50
♂∠♃ 12:58
☿#♅ 17:42
☽⚺⚳ 18:34
☽∠♆ 22:37

7 M
☽⚺⚷ 4:54
☽☌♅ 6:39
☽#☿ 8:55
☿∠⚷ 9:17
☽∥♅ 10:24
☽✶♃ 13:51
☽#♄ 14:32
☉✶☽ 17:04
☽#♀ 18:17
☽□♄ 21:57

8 Tu
☽✶♆ 4:04
☊ D 8:23
☽∠⚷ 10:33
☽□☿ 14:06
☽△♇ 14:36
☿⚺♇ 18:07
☽#♂ 19:01
☽△♂ 22:42
☽△♀ 23:28

9 W
☽☌⚳ 7:10
☽#♇ 7:27
☽∥⚳ 9:25
☽✶⚷ 16:51
☽⚺♅ 18:36
☽⚼♇ 20:53

10 Th
☿ ♓ 1:33
☽□♃ 3:08
☽⚼♂ 7:04
☽⚼♀ 8:19
☊ R 10:37
☉□☽ 10:47
☽△♄ 10:49
☉⚺♄ 11:18
☽□♆ 16:44
⚶ ♒ 18:23
☉∥♆ 18:31

11 F
☽∠♅ 1:10
☽⚻♇ 3:24
☽△☿ 12:02
☽⚻♂ 15:35
☽⚻♀ 17:20
☽⚼♄ 17:33
☽⚺⚳ 21:29
♃#⚷ 22:19

12 Sa
☽□⚷ 5:59
☽✶♅ 7:39
☽△♃ 17:08
☽⚼☿ 22:57

13 Su
☽⚻♄ 0:00
☽∠⚳ 4:20
☉△☽ 4:53
☽△♆ 5:26
☿⚺♂ 9:45
☉☌♆ 11:44
☽☍♇ 15:45
☽⚼♃ 23:29

14 M
☽☍♂ 7:19
☽⚻☿ 9:06
☽☍♀ 10:01
☽✶⚳ 10:32
☽∥⚳ 10:35
☽⚼♆ 11:00
☉⚼☽ 12:57
☽#♇ 15:51
☽△⚷ 17:32
☽□♅ 19:03
♀△⚳ 19:38
☿□⚳ 21:50
♀∠♆ 23:16
☿⚺♀ 23:52

15 Tu
☽⚻♃ 5:04
☽#♂ 10:36
☽☍♄ 10:57
☽⚻♆ 15:47
☉⚻☽ 20:02
☽⚼⚷ 22:11

16 W
☽⚻♇ 1:30
☽#♀ 8:13
☽#♄ 8:21
☽∥♅ 10:18
♀∥♄ 13:47
☽⚻♂ 19:36
☽□⚳ 20:30
♂∠♆ 23:05
☽⚻♀ 23:10

17 Th
☿⚺⚷ 1:19
☽⚻⚷ 2:03
☽☍☿ 2:09
☽△♅ 3:26
☽⚼♇ 5:12
☿✶♅ 12:15
☽☍♃ 13:45
☽#☿ 14:01
☽⚻♄ 18:45
☉∠♅ 20:14
♂△⚳ 21:24
☽☍♆ 23:03

18 F
☽⚼♂ 0:24
☽∥⚷ 1:02
☿∠♇ 1:48
☽#♃ 3:54
☽⚼♀ 4:23
☽⚼♅ 6:32
☉☍☽ 7:19
☽△♇ 8:12
☽#♆ 11:25
♀✶⚷ 16:25
☉✶♇ 19:38
♀#♅ 20:38
☽⚼♄ 21:37
☉#☽ 23:44

19 Sa
☽△⚳ 3:28
☽△♂ 4:30
☉∥☽ 4:32
☽☍⚷ 7:47
☽△♀ 8:54
☽⚻♅ 9:03
♀□♅ 11:18
☽⚻☿ 15:21
☽∥♆ 16:56
☽⚻♃ 19:44
☽∥♃ 23:39

20 Su
☽△♄ 0:00
☽#⚷ 3:15
☽⚻♆ 3:54
☽⚼⚳ 6:09
☽∥☿ 6:15
☽□♇ 12:41
☉ ♈ 15:35
☉⚻☽ 15:47
☽⚼☿ 21:03
☽⚼♃ 22:04

21 M
☽⚼♆ 5:47
☿☌♃ 6:07
☿#⚷ 6:37
☽⚻⚳ 8:31
☽□♂ 11:18
☽⚻⚷ 11:47
☽☍♅ 12:59
☽∥♀ 13:24
☽#♅ 15:40
☽∥♄ 16:23
☽□♀ 16:35
☉⚼☽ 19:26
♂✶⚷ 21:01

22 Tu
☽△♃ 0:10
☽△☿ 2:27
☽□♄ 3:51
☽∥♂ 6:02
☽△♆ 7:27
☊ D 8:13
☽⚼⚷ 13:27
☿⚺♄ 13:49
☽✶♇ 16:02
♂□♅ 20:45
☿∥♃ 21:28
☉△☽ 22:53

23 W
☽∥♇ 4:54
☽☍⚳ 12:45
☽#⚳ 14:50
☽△⚷ 15:02
☽⚻♅ 16:11
☽✶♂ 17:13
☽∠♇ 17:32
☿☌♆ 17:45
☽✶♀ 23:30

24 Th
☽□♃ 4:01
☽✶♄ 7:10
☽□♆ 10:32
☽□☿ 13:00
☽⚼♅ 17:43
☽⚺♇ 19:01
☽∠♂ 20:06
☿∥♆ 20:11

25 F
☽∠♀ 2:55
♄#♅ 4:04
☉□☽ 5:38
☊ R 5:50
☽∠♄ 8:48
☽⚻⚳ 16:51
☽□⚷ 18:10
☽△♅ 19:17
☽⚺♂ 23:00

26 Sa
☿∠♅ 1:27
☽⚺♀ 6:23
☽✶♃ 7:50
☽⚺♄ 10:28
☿✶♇ 10:36
☉#☿ 12:38
☽✶♆ 13:38
☽⚼⚳ 18:59
☽☌♇ 22:05
☽✶☿ 23:52

27 Su
☽#⚳ 7:04
☉∠♄ 7:12
♀⚺♃ 7:35
☿ ♈ 7:46
☽∠♃ 9:51
☉✶☽ 12:36
☽∠♆ 15:19
☽∥♇ 19:25
☽△⚳ 21:15
☽✶⚷ 21:33
☽□♅ 22:39

28 M
☿∠♂ 0:06
☽☌♂ 5:09
☽∠☿ 5:39
☽⚺♃ 12:03
⚳✶⚷ 13:10
☽☌♀ 13:49
☽☌♄ 14:12
☉∠☽ 16:21
☽⚺♆ 17:11
♀☌♄ 19:28
☽∠⚷ 23:32

29 Tu
☽⚺♇ 1:42
☽∥♂ 1:45
☽#♅ 8:52
☽∥♄ 9:44
☽⚺☿ 11:53
☽∥♀ 19:43
☉⚺☽ 20:28
☉#♆ 20:32

30 W
☽⚺⚷ 1:50
☽□⚳ 2:35
☽✶♅ 2:55
☽∠♇ 3:56
♀⚺♆ 12:17
☽⚺♂ 12:29
☽☌♃ 17:26
⚳⚺♅ 18:29
☽⚺♄ 19:05
☿∠♄ 20:52
☽☌♆ 21:56
☽#⚷ 21:59
☽⚺♀ 22:43

31 Th
☽∠♅ 5:40
☽✶♇ 6:38
☽∥♃ 6:52
☉#☽ 7:53
☽∥♆ 10:17
☽#☿ 16:05
☽∠♂ 16:56
☉#♃ 20:24
☽∠♄ 22:15

April 2022

LONGITUDE

Day	Sid.Time	☉	☽	☽ 12 hour	Mean ☊	True ☊	☿	♀	♂	⚳	♃	♄	⚷	♅	♆	♇
	h m s	° ' "	° ' "	° ' "	° '	° '	° '	° '	° '	° '	° '	° '	° '	° '	° '	° '
1 F	12 37 20	11♈14 40	7♈59 33	14♈32 33	24♉45.8	23♉06.4	9♈11.8	25♒04.5	19♒19.5	13♊14.5	21♓17.9	22♒02.3	12♈17.3	12♉53.3	23♓34.0	28♑24.0
2 Sa	12 41 17	12 13 55	21 01 16	27 25 40	24 42.6	23R 00.8	11 13.0	26 07.8	20 04.8	13 34.9	21 32.0	22 07.8	12 20.8	12 56.4	23 36.2	28 24.8
3 Su	12 45 13	13 13 08	3♉45 45	10♉01 40	24 39.4	22 57.1	13 15.2	27 11.3	20 50.1	13 55.5	21 46.0	22 13.2	12 24.3	12 59.5	23 38.4	28 25.6
4 M	12 49 10	14 12 18	16 13 36	22 21 48	24 36.3	22D 55.3	15 18.3	28 15.0	21 35.4	14 16.2	22 00.0	22 18.6	12 27.8	13 02.6	23 40.6	28 26.3
5 Tu	12 53 06	15 11 26	28 26 37	4♊28 28	24 33.1	22 55.2	17 22.1	29 19.0	22 20.7	14 37.0	22 13.9	22 23.9	12 31.3	13 05.8	23 42.7	28 27.1
6 W	12 57 03	16 10 33	10♊27 47	16 25 05	24 29.9	22 56.4	19 26.4	0♓23.3	23 06.0	14 58.0	22 27.8	22 29.1	12 34.9	13 09.0	23 44.9	28 27.8
7 Th	13 01 00	17 09 36	22 20 55	28 15 52	24 26.7	22 58.1	21 31.2	1 27.7	23 51.4	15 19.0	22 41.7	22 34.2	12 38.4	13 12.1	23 47.0	28 28.4
8 F	13 04 56	18 08 38	4♋10 33	10♋05 34	24 23.6	22 59.7	23 36.0	2 32.4	24 36.7	15 40.2	22 55.5	22 39.3	12 41.9	13 15.3	23 49.1	28 29.1
9 Sa	13 08 53	19 07 38	16 01 34	21 59 11	24 20.4	23R 00.6	25 40.8	3 37.2	25 22.0	16 01.5	23 09.3	22 44.4	12 45.4	13 18.6	23 51.2	28 29.7
10 Su	13 12 49	20 06 35	27 59 02	4♌01 43	24 17.2	23 00.3	27 45.1	4 42.3	26 07.4	16 22.9	23 23.1	22 49.3	12 48.9	13 21.8	23 53.3	28 30.3
11 M	13 16 46	21 05 29	10♌07 50	16 17 53	24 14.0	22 58.6	29 48.8	5 47.5	26 52.7	16 44.5	23 36.8	22 54.2	12 52.4	13 25.1	23 55.4	28 30.8
12 Tu	13 20 42	22 04 22	22 32 23	28 51 44	24 10.8	22 55.6	1♉51.5	6 52.9	27 38.1	17 06.1	23 50.4	22 59.0	12 55.9	13 28.3	23 57.5	28 31.4
13 W	13 24 39	23 03 12	5♍16 15	11♍46 12	24 07.7	22 51.5	3 52.8	7 58.5	28 23.4	17 27.9	24 04.0	23 03.8	12 59.4	13 31.6	23 59.6	28 31.9
14 Th	13 28 35	24 02 00	18 21 44	25 02 53	24 04.5	22 47.0	5 52.4	9 04.3	29 08.8	17 49.8	24 17.6	23 08.5	13 02.9	13 34.9	24 01.6	28 32.3
15 F	13 32 32	25 00 46	1♎49 33	8♎41 33	24 01.3	22 42.6	7 50.0	10 10.3	29 54.1	18 11.7	24 31.1	23 13.1	13 06.3	13 38.2	24 03.6	28 32.8
16 Sa	13 36 29	25 59 29	15 38 35	22 40 11	23 58.1	22 38.8	9 45.2	11 16.4	0♓39.5	18 33.8	24 44.5	23 17.6	13 09.8	13 41.6	24 05.6	28 33.2
17 Su	13 40 25	26 58 11	29 45 53	6♏55 02	23 55.0	22 36.1	11 37.7	12 22.7	1 24.8	18 56.0	24 57.9	23 22.1	13 13.2	13 44.9	24 07.6	28 33.6
18 M	13 44 22	27 56 51	14♏07 01	21 21 08	23 51.8	22D 34.8	13 27.1	13 29.1	2 10.2	19 18.3	25 11.2	23 26.4	13 16.7	13 48.3	24 09.6	28 33.9
19 Tu	13 48 18	28 55 29	28 36 40	5♐52 55	23 48.6	22 34.6	15 13.2	14 35.7	2 55.6	19 40.6	25 24.5	23 30.8	13 20.1	13 51.6	24 11.5	28 34.2
20 W	13 52 15	29 54 05	13♐09 13	20 24 56	23 45.4	22 35.5	16 55.8	15 42.5	3 40.9	20 03.1	25 37.8	23 35.0	13 23.5	13 55.0	24 13.5	28 34.5
21 Th	13 56 11	0♉52 40	27 39 31	4♑52 28	23 42.2	22 36.8	18 34.5	16 49.4	4 26.3	20 25.7	25 51.0	23 39.2	13 26.9	13 58.4	24 15.4	28 34.8
22 F	14 00 08	1 51 13	12♑03 21	19 11 48	23 39.1	22 38.1	20 09.2	17 56.5	5 11.0	20 48.4	26 04.1	23 43.2	13 30.3	14 01.8	24 17.3	28 35.1
23 Sa	14 04 04	2 49 44	26 17 33	3♒20 20	23 35.9	22R 38.9	21 39.7	19 03.7	5 57.1	21 11.1	26 17.1	23 47.2	13 33.7	14 05.2	24 19.2	28 35.3
24 Su	14 08 01	3 48 14	10♒20 00	17 16 25	23 32.7	22 38.9	23 05.8	20 11.0	6 42.4	21 34.0	26 30.1	23 51.2	13 37.0	14 08.7	24 21.1	28 35.5
25 M	14 11 58	4 46 42	24 09 28	0♓59 07	23 29.5	22 38.0	24 27.3	21 18.5	7 27.8	21 56.9	26 43.1	23 55.0	13 40.4	14 12.1	24 22.9	28 35.6
26 Tu	14 15 54	5 45 08	7♓45 18	14 27 59	23 26.4	22 36.4	25 44.3	22 26.0	8 13.2	22 20.0	26 55.9	23 58.8	13 43.7	14 15.5	24 24.8	28 35.7
27 W	14 19 51	6 43 33	21 07 11	27 42 52	23 23.2	22 34.4	26 56.5	23 33.7	8 58.5	22 43.1	27 08.7	24 02.4	13 47.0	14 19.0	24 26.6	28 35.8
28 Th	14 23 47	7 41 56	4♈15 04	10♈43 47	23 20.0	22 32.2	28 03.8	24 41.6	9 43.9	23 06.3	27 21.5	24 06.0	13 50.3	14 22.4	24 28.4	28 35.9
29 F	14 27 44	8 40 17	17 09 04	23 30 57	23 16.8	22 30.2	29 06.3	25 49.5	10 29.2	23 29.6	27 34.2	24 09.5	13 53.6	14 25.9	24 30.1	28R 35.9
30 Sa	14 31 40	9♉38 37	29 49 31	6♉04 50	23♉13.6	22♉28.8	0♊03.7	26♓57.5	11♓14.5	23♊53.0	27♓46.8	24♒13.0	13♈56.8	14♉29.3	24♓31.9	28♑35.9

1st of Month

Julian Day # 2459670.5
Obliquity 23°26[illegible]7"
SVP 4♓57[illegible]1"
GC 27♐09.0
Eris 24♈11.5

Day	⚴	Day	⚵	Day	⚶
1	17♈34.0	1	22♒46.8	1	9♒53.0
6	19 37.9	6	24 39.3	6	12 05.6
11	21 43.1	11	26 30.3	11	14 15.0
16	23 49.6	16	28 19.7	16	16 20.9
21	25 57.3	21	0♓07.2	21	18 23.2
26	28 06.3	26	1 52.8	26	20 21.6

DECLINATION and LATITUDE

Day	☉ Decl	☽ Decl	☽ Lat	☽ 12h Decl	☿ Decl	☿ Lat	♀ Decl	♀ Lat	♂ Decl	♂ Lat	⚳ Decl	⚳ Lat	♃ Decl	♃ Lat	♄ Decl	♄ Lat
1 F	4N27	0S11	3S39	2N46	2N27	1S18	12S21	0N52	16S11	1S13	24N23	2N01	4S23	1S01	15S03	0S57
2 Sa	4 50	5N40	2 44	8 28	3 22	1 10	12 05	0 46	15 57	1 13	24 27	2 02	4 17	1 01	15 02	0 57
3 Su	5 13	11 10	1 42	13 43	4 17	1 02	11 48	0 41	15 43	1 14	24 32	2 04	4 12	1 01	15 00	0 57
4 M	5 36	16 07	0 36	18 19	5 13	0 53	11 32	0 35	15 29	1 15	24 36	2 06	4 06	1 01	14 58	0 57
5 Tu	5 59	20 18	0N30	22 04	6 09	0 44	11 14	0 30	15 15	1 16	24 40	2 08	4 01	1 01	14 57	0 57
6 W	6 22	23 34	1 34	24 49	7 05	0 34	10 57	0 25	15 01	1 16	24 44	2 09	3 55	1 01	14 55	0 57
7 Th	6 44	25 46	2 34	26 26	8 01	0 24	10 39	0 20	14 47	1 17	24 48	2 11	3 50	1 01	14 54	0 58
8 F	7 07	26 48	3 26	26 52	8 57	0 14	10 21	0 14	14 32	1 18	24 52	2 13	3 45	1 01	14 52	0 58
9 Sa	7 29	26 37	4 10	26 03	9 53	0 03	10 02	0 09	14 18	1 18	24 56	2 14	3 39	1 01	14 51	0 58
10 Su	7 52	25 12	4 44	24 02	10 48	0N08	9 43	0 04	14 03	1 19	24 60	2 16	3 34	1 01	14 49	0 58
11 M	8 14	22 36	5 05	20 53	11 42	0 19	9 24	0S01	13 48	1 20	25 04	2 18	3 29	1 02	14 48	0 58
12 Tu	8 36	18 55	5 13	16 43	12 36	0 30	9 04	0 05	13 33	1 20	25 07	2 19	3 23	1 02	14 46	0 58
13 W	8 58	14 19	5 05	11 42	13 28	0 41	8 44	0 10	13 18	1 21	25 11	2 21	3 18	1 02	14 45	0 58
14 Th	9 19	8 56	4 42	6 01	14 18	0 53	8 24	0 15	13 03	1 22	25 15	2 23	3 13	1 02	14 44	0 59
15 F	9 41	2 60	4 03	0S06	15 07	1 04	8 03	0 19	12 47	1 22	25 18	2 24	3 08	1 02	14 42	0 59
16 Sa	10 02	3S15	3 09	6 23	15 55	1 14	7 42	0 24	12 32	1 23	25 22	2 26	3 02	1 02	14 41	0 59
17 Su	10 24	9 29	2 02	12 29	16 40	1 25	7 21	0 28	12 16	1 23	25 26	2 27	2 57	1 02	14 39	0 59
18 M	10 45	15 20	0 46	17 59	17 23	1 35	6 59	0 32	12 01	1 24	25 29	2 29	2 52	1 02	14 38	0 59
19 Tu	11 05	20 23	0S33	22 29	18 04	1 45	6 37	0 36	11 45	1 25	25 32	2 31	2 47	1 02	14 37	0 59
20 W	11 26	24 13	1 51	25 32	18 43	1 54	6 15	0 40	11 29	1 25	25 36	2 32	2 42	1 03	14 36	0 59
21 Th	11 47	26 26	3 01	26 53	19 19	2 02	5 53	0 44	11 13	1 26	25 39	2 34	2 37	1 03	14 34	0 60
22 F	12 07	26 52	3 60	26 25	19 52	2 10	5 30	0 48	10 57	1 27	25 42	2 35	2 32	1 03	14 33	0 60
23 Sa	12 27	25 31	4 43	24 14	20 23	2 17	5 07	0 52	10 41	1 27	25 45	2 37	2 26	1 03	14 32	0 60
24 Su	12 47	22 35	5 08	20 38	20 52	2 24	4 44	0 56	10 25	1 28	25 48	2 38	2 21	1 03	14 31	1 00
25 M	13 07	18 25	5 15	15 59	21 18	2 29	4 21	0 59	10 08	1 28	25 51	2 40	2 16	1 03	14 30	1 00
26 Tu	13 26	13 22	5 05	10 37	21 41	2 34	3 58	1 03	9 52	1 29	25 54	2 41	2 11	1 03	14 29	1 00
27 W	13 46	7 46	4 37	4 52	22 02	2 38	3 34	1 06	9 35	1 30	25 57	2 43	2 06	1 04	14 28	1 01
28 Th	14 05	1 55	3 56	1N01	22 20	2 40	3 10	1 09	9 19	1 30	25 60	2 45	2 02	1 04	14 27	1 01
29 F	14 23	3N55	3 03	6 45	22 36	2 42	2 46	1 12	9 02	1 31	26 03	2 46	1 57	1 04	14 26	1 01
30 Sa	14N42	9N30	2S02	12N08	22N49	2N43	2S22	1S15	8S45	1S31	26N05	2N48	1S52	1S04	14S25	1S01

Day	⚷ Decl	⚷ Lat	♅ Decl	♅ Lat	♆ Decl	♆ Lat	♇ Decl	♇ Lat
1	6N40	1N58	15N21	0S22	3S35	1S07	22S20	1S54
6	6 46	1 57	15 26	0 22	3 31	1 08	22 20	1 54
11	6 53	1 57	15 31	0 22	3 27	1 08	22 20	1 55
16	6 59	1 57	15 36	0 22	3 23	1 08	22 20	1 56
21	7 06	1 57	15 41	0 22	3 19	1 08	22 21	1 56
26	7 12	1 56	15 46	0 22	3 16	1 08	22 21	1 57

Day	⚴ Decl	⚴ Lat	⚵ Decl	⚵ Lat	⚶ Decl	⚶ Lat	Eris Decl	Eris Lat
1	4S58	12S50	6S50	7N29	17S59	0S14	1S02	11S11
6	4 33	13 12	6 16	7 27	17 38	0 25	1 01	11 11
11	4 08	13 34	5 42	7 25	17 08	0 36	0 59	11 11
16	3 45	13 57	5 07	7 23	16 42	0 48	0 58	11 10
21	3 22	14 21	4 32	7 21	16 16	1 00	0 57	11 10
26	3 00	14 45	3 57	7 19	15 51	1 13	0 55	11 10

Moon Phenomena

Max/0 Decl
dy hr mn
1 0:46 0 N
8 8:16 26N53
15 11:35 0 S
21 17:39 26S56
28 7:51 0 N

Perigee/Apogee
dy hr m kilometers
7 19:12 a 404437
19 15:15 p 365146

Max/0 Lat
dy hr mn
4 13:06 0 N
12 0:45 5N13
18 14:02 0 S
24 21:21 5S15

PH dy hr mn
● 1 6:26 11♈31
☽ 9 6:49 19♋24
○ 16 18:56 26♎46
☾ 23 11:58 3♒19
● 30 20:29 10♉28
• 30 1242:3P 0.640

Void of Course Moon

Last Aspect	☽ Ingress
2 13:52 ♇ □	♉ 2 16:51
5 1:54 ♀ □	♊ 5 3:05
7 3:16 ♂ △	♋ 7 15:31
10 1:02 ♇ ☍	♌ 10 4:01
12 10:18 ♂ ☍	♍ 12 14:09
14 18:13 ♇ △	♎ 14 20:47
16 21:58 ♇ □	♏ 17 0:24
18 23:56 ♇ ✶	♐ 19 2:18
20 20:57 ♃ □	♑ 21 3:53
23 3:54 ♇ ☌	♒ 23 6:18
25 0:35 ☿ □	♓ 25 10:16
27 13:37 ♇ ✶	♈ 27 16:11
29 21:40 ♇ □	♉ 30 0:20

DAILY ASPECTARIAN

1 F: ☽☌☿ 2:36; ☽∠♀ 4:08; ☉☌☽ 6:26; ☽☌⚷ 7:53; ☽⚺♅ 9:00; ☽✶⚳ 9:52; ⚳⚼♇ 11:36; ☽∥☿ 12:41; ☽#♆ 15:20; ☽#♃ 18:21; ☉∥☽ 20:17; ☿∠♀ 21:49; ☽✶♂ 22:08

2 Sa: ☽⚺♃ 0:58; ☽✶♄ 2:05; ☉☌⚷ 2:58; ☽∥⚷ 4:19; ☽⚺♆ 4:50; ☿#♆ 5:25; ☽✶♀ 10:25; ☿☌⚷ 13:43; ☽□♇ 13:52; ☽∠⚳ 14:34; ☉⚺♅ 18:11; ☿⚺♅ 20:51; ☿#♃ 21:55; ☉☌☿ 23:12

3 Su: ☽#♀ 2:47; ♀∠⚷ 5:12; ☽∠♃ 5:51; ☽∠♆ 9:22; ☿✶⚳ 9:27; ☽⚺⚷ 16:40; ☽☌♅ 17:48; ☽#♄ 18:13; ☉⚺☽ 19:44; ☽⚺⚳ 20:05; ☽∥♅ 20:21; ☽#♂ 20:56; ☽⚺☿ 21:51

4 M: ☉✶⚳ 2:26; ♀⚺♇ 4:17; ♂#♅ 8:04; ☽□♂ 11:10; ☽✶♃ 11:30; ☽□♄ 11:59; ☊ D 13:06; ☽✶♆ 14:38; ☉∥☿ 16:58; ♂⚺♃ 18:48; ☽∠⚷ 22:10

5 Tu: ☽△♇ 0:01; ♂☌♄ 1:52; ☽□♀ 1:54; ☉∠☽ 3:46; ☽∠☿ 9:25; ☽#♇ 14:02; ♀ ♓ 15:19; ☿∥⚷ 15:49

6 W: ♃⚺♄ 3:25; ☽✶⚷ 4:17; ☽⚺♅ 5:26; ☽⚼♇ 6:03; ☽☌⚳ 9:21; ♂∥♄ 10:44; ☽∥⚳ 11:30; ☉✶☽ 12:33; ♂⚺♆ 21:35; ☽✶☿ 21:58

7 Th: ☽△♄ 0:27; ☽□♃ 0:43; ☽□♆ 2:55; ☽△♂ 3:16; ☉∥⚷ 3:32; ☽∠♅ 11:56; ☽⚻♇ 12:26; ☿✶♄ 12:39; ☿⚺♃ 15:15; ☽△♀ 20:21

8 F: ☿⚺♆ 2:34; ☽⚼♄ 7:07; ☽⚼♂ 11:47; ☽□⚷ 17:22; ☿✶♂ 18:20; ☽✶♅ 18:29; ☽⚺⚳ 24:00

9 Sa: ☿#♀ 3:00; ☽⚼♀ 5:45; ☊ R 6:43; ☉□☽ 6:49; ☽⚻♄ 13:36; ☽△♃ 14:38; ☽△♆ 15:48; ☽⚻♂ 20:02; ☽□☿ 23:27

10 Su: ☽☍♇ 1:02; ☽∥⚳ 2:11; ☽∠⚳ 6:58; ☿□♇ 8:47; ☽⚻♀ 14:39; ☽⚼♃ 20:58; ☽⚼♆ 21:38

11 M: ☽#♇ 1:57; ☿ ♉ 2:11; ☽△⚷ 5:23; ☽□♅ 6:26; ♃∥♆ 9:29; ☽✶⚳ 13:14; ☉△☽ 23:02

12 Tu: ☽☍♄ 0:51; ☽⚻♃ 2:32; ☽⚻♆ 2:43; ☿∠⚳ 3:30; ♂∠⚷ 10:14; ☽⚼⚷ 10:17; ☽☍♂ 10:18; ☽⚻♇ 11:22; ♃☌♆ 14:44; ☉#♀ 16:11; ☽∥♅ 17:58; ☿#♂ 20:29; ☽△☿ 20:56; ☽#♄ 21:53

13 W: ☉✶♄ 0:15; ☽∥☿ 3:26; ♂⚺♇ 4:31; ☽#♂ 5:00; ☽☍♀ 5:29; ☉⚼☽ 5:35; ☽⚻⚷ 14:18; ☽⚼♇ 15:14; ☽△♅ 15:17; ☉∠♀ 16:08; ☉∥☽ 22:27; ☽□⚳ 23:01; ☉⚺♆ 23:50

14 Th: ☽#♀ 2:24; ☽⚼☿ 5:19; ☽∥⚷ 8:12; ☉⚺♃ 8:15; ☽⚻♄ 8:39; ☽☍♆ 10:12; ☽☍♃ 10:50; ☉⚻☽ 10:59; ☿#♄ 11:51; ☽△♇ 18:13; ☽⚼♅ 18:21; ☽⚻♂ 20:25; ☽#♆ 22:25; ☽#♃ 23:28

15 F: ♂ ♓ 3:07; ☽⚼♄ 11:14; ☽⚻☿ 12:13; ☿∥♅ 14:12; ☿∠♆ 15:33; ☽⚻♀ 15:49; ☽☍⚷ 19:43; ☽⚻♅ 20:38; ☽∥♃ 23:13; ☿∠♃ 23:50

16 Sa: ☽⚼♂ 0:02; ☽∥♆ 0:31; ☽△⚳ 5:08; ☽△♄ 13:08; ☽#⚷ 14:21; ☽⚻♆ 14:27; ☽⚻♃ 15:46; ☽∥♀ 16:08; ☉☍☽ 18:56; ☽⚼♀ 19:38; ☽□♇ 21:58

17 Su: ☽△♂ 2:56; ☉#☽ 3:49; ☽⚼⚳ 7:11; ☽∥♂ 10:40; ☽⚼♆ 15:44; ☽⚼♃ 17:21; ♀⚺⚷ 19:15; ☽∥♄ 21:00; ♀#⚷ 21:08; ☿⚺⚷ 21:36; ☽⚻⚷ 22:36; ☽☍☿ 22:44; ☽△♀ 22:52; ☽☍♅ 23:29

18 M: ☿✶♀ 1:10; ☽#♅ 1:19; ♀∠♇ 1:44; ☿☌♅ 4:53; ♀✶♅ 7:16; ☽⚻⚳ 8:50; ☽#☿ 10:36; ☊ D 14:01; ☉□♇ 15:15; ☽□♄ 15:32; ☽△♆ 16:41; ☽△♃ 18:38; ☽⚼⚷ 23:33; ☽✶♇ 23:56

19 Tu: ☉⚻☽ 0:33; ☽□♂ 7:31; ☽∥♇ 11:10

20 W: ☽△⚷ 0:24; ☽∠♇ 0:42; ☽⚻♅ 1:16; ☉#♂ 1:49; ☉ ♉ 2:25; ☉⚼☽ 3:06; ☽□♀ 4:34; ☽⚻☿ 7:03; ☽☍⚳ 11:42; ☽#⚳ 12:57; ⚵ ♓ 15:52; ☽✶♄ 17:20; ☽□♆ 18:21; ☽□♃ 20:57

21 Th: ☽⚺♇ 1:32; ☽⚼♅ 2:12; ☉△☽ 5:44; ☽⚼☿ 11:04; ☽✶♂ 11:54; ☽∠♄ 18:24

22 F: ☽□⚷ 2:26; ☽△♅ 3:19; ☽✶♀ 10:44; ☿⚺⚳ 13:42; ☽∠♂ 14:27; ☽⚻⚳ 15:07; ☽△☿ 15:15; ☽⚺♄ 19:44; ☽✶♆ 20:39; ☽#⚳ 21:22; ☽✶♃ 23:59

23 Sa: ☽☌♇ 3:54; ☉□☽ 11:58; ☊ R 12:14; ☽∠♀ 14:23; ☽⚼⚳ 17:21; ☽⚺♂ 17:25; ☽∠♆ 22:18

24 Su: ☽∥♇ 1:35; ☽∠♃ 2:03; ☽✶⚷ 5:41; ☽□♅ 6:36; ☽#☿ 9:40; ☿□♄ 13:51; ☽⚺♀ 18:35; ☽△⚳ 20:02; ☿✶♆ 22:38; ☽☌♄ 23:35

25 M: ☽⚺♆ 0:24; ☽□☿ 0:35; ☽⚺♃ 4:34; ☽⚺♇ 7:47; ☽∠⚷ 7:57; ☽#♅ 13:02; ☽∥♄ 18:58; ☉✶☽ 20:10; ♀□⚳ 20:44; ☉#☽ 23:42

26 Tu: ☽☌♂ 0:53; ☽∠♇ 10:26; ☽⚺⚷ 10:43; ☽✶♅ 11:41; ☽∥♂ 15:59

27 W: ☉∠☽ 1:11; ☽#⚷ 2:15; ☽□⚳ 2:59; ☽☌♀ 4:51; ☿✶♃ 5:13; ☽⚺♄ 5:20; ☽☌♆ 6:03; ♀⚺♄ 10:44; ☽☌♃ 11:08; ☽✶☿ 11:36; ☽✶♇ 13:37; ☽∠♅ 15:00; ☽∥♀ 18:33; ☽∥♆ 18:37; ♀☌♆ 19:13; ♀∥♆ 19:36; ☽∥♃ 23:34

28 Th: ☿#♇ 2:09; ☉⚺☽ 6:53; ☽∠♄ 9:01; ☽⚺♂ 10:46; ☿△♇ 12:06; ☽#♃ 15:57; ☉∠⚳ 16:41; ☽∠☿ 17:48; ☽☌⚷ 17:52; ☿∠⚷ 18:41; ☽⚺♅ 18:53; ☽#♀ 19:32; ☽#♆ 21:09

29 F: ☉#♄ 2:33; ☽✶⚳ 12:20; ☽✶♄ 13:17; ☽⚺♆ 13:54; ☽∥⚷ 14:16; ☽∠♂ 16:44; ☽⚺♀ 18:00; ♇ R 18:38; ☽⚺♃ 20:02; ☽#♂ 20:51; ☉∠♆ 21:08; ☽□♇ 21:40; ☿ ♊ 22:24

30 Sa: ☽⚺☿ 0:29; ⚴ ♉ 8:51; ☽∠⚳ 17:59; ☽∠♆ 18:42; ☉☌☽ 20:29; ♀☌♃ 21:15; ☽#♄ 22:50; ☽✶♂ 23:24; ⚳△♄ 23:50

LONGITUDE

May 2022

Day	Sid.Time	☉	☽	☽ 12 hour	Mean☊	True☊	☿	♀	♂	⚳	♃	♄	⚷	♅	♆	♇
	h m s	° ' "	° ' "	° ' "	° '	° '	° '	° '	° '	° '	° '	° '	° '	° '	° '	° '
1 Su	14 35 37	10♉36 55	12♉17 01	18♉26 13	23♉10.5	22♉28.0	0♊56.0	28♓05.7	11♓59.8	24♊16.4	27♓59.3	24♒16.3	14♈00.1	14♉32.8	24♓33.6	28♑35.9
2 M	14 39 33	11 35 12	24 32 38	0♊36 26	23 07.3	22D 27.8	1 43.2	29 13.9	12 45.1	24 40.0	28 11.7	24 19.6	14 03.3	14 36.2	24 35.3	28R 35.9
3 Tu	14 43 30	12 33 26	6♊37 54	12 37 17	23 04.1	22 28.1	2 25.1	0♈22.2	13 30.4	25 03.6	28 24.1	24 22.7	14 06.5	14 39.7	24 37.0	28 35.8
4 W	14 47 27	13 31 39	18 34 56	24 31 13	23 00.9	22 28.8	3 01.8	1 30.7	14 15.7	25 27.3	28 36.4	24 25.8	14 09.6	14 43.2	24 38.6	28 35.7
5 Th	14 51 23	14 29 50	0♋26 30	6♋21 15	22 57.8	22 29.6	3 33.3	2 39.2	15 00.9	25 51.1	28 48.7	24 28.8	14 12.8	14 46.6	24 40.3	28 35.6
6 F	14 55 20	15 27 59	12 15 55	18 11 00	22 54.6	22 30.5	3 59.4	3 47.8	15 46.2	26 14.9	29 00.8	24 31.7	14 15.9	14 50.1	24 41.9	28 35.4
7 Sa	14 59 16	16 26 06	24 07 02	0♌04 32	22 51.4	22 31.1	4 20.2	4 56.5	16 31.4	26 38.9	29 12.9	24 34.5	14 19.0	14 53.6	24 43.5	28 35.2
8 Su	15 03 13	17 24 11	6♌04 06	12 06 16	22 48.2	22 31.5	4 35.6	6 05.3	17 16.6	27 02.9	29 24.9	24 37.2	14 22.1	14 57.0	24 45.0	28 35.0
9 M	15 07 09	18 22 14	18 11 38	24 20 45	22 45.1	22R 31.6	4 45.9	7 14.2	18 01.7	27 26.9	29 36.8	24 39.9	14 25.2	15 00.5	24 46.6	28 34.7
10 Tu	15 11 06	19 20 15	0♍34 10	6♍52 23	22 41.9	22 31.5	4R 50.9	8 23.1	18 46.9	27 51.0	29 48.6	24 42.4	14 28.2	15 04.0	24 48.1	28 34.5
11 W	15 15 02	20 18 15	13 15 53	19 45 04	22 38.7	22 31.3	4 50.9	9 32.2	19 32.0	28 15.2	0♈00.3	24 44.9	14 31.2	15 07.4	24 49.6	28 34.2
12 Th	15 18 59	21 16 12	26 20 16	3♎01 43	22 35.5	22 31.2	4 45.9	10 41.3	20 17.1	28 39.5	0 11.9	24 47.2	14 34.2	15 10.9	24 51.0	28 33.8
13 F	15 22 56	22 14 08	9♎49 32	16 43 45	22 32.3	22D 31.1	4 36.3	11 50.5	21 02.2	29 03.8	0 23.5	24 49.5	14 37.1	15 14.3	24 52.5	28 33.5
14 Sa	15 26 52	23 12 02	23 44 13	0♏50 39	22 29.2	22 31.1	4 22.1	12 59.7	21 47.3	29 28.2	0 35.0	24 51.6	14 40.0	15 17.8	24 53.9	28 33.1
15 Su	15 30 49	24 09 54	8♏02 37	15 19 32	22 26.0	22R 31.2	4 03.9	14 09.0	22 32.3	29 52.7	0 46.3	24 53.7	14 42.9	15 21.2	24 55.3	28 32.7
16 M	15 34 45	25 07 45	22 40 42	0♐05 16	22 22.8	22 31.2	3 41.8	15 18.5	23 17.3	0♋17.2	0 57.6	24 55.7	14 45.8	15 24.6	24 56.6	28 32.2
17 Tu	15 38 42	26 05 34	7♐32 18	15 00 48	22 19.6	22 31.1	3 16.3	16 27.9	24 02.3	0 41.7	1 08.8	24 57.6	14 48.6	15 28.1	24 57.9	28 31.8
18 W	15 42 38	27 03 22	22 29 44	29 58 06	22 16.5	22 30.9	2 48.0	17 37.5	24 47.3	1 06.4	1 19.9	24 59.4	14 51.4	15 31.5	24 59.2	28 31.3
19 Th	15 46 35	28 01 09	7♑24 53	14♑49 13	22 13.3	22 30.4	2 17.3	18 47.1	25 32.2	1 31.0	1 30.9	25 01.1	14 54.2	15 34.9	25 00.5	28 30.8
20 F	15 50 31	28 58 54	22 10 17	29 27 24	22 10.1	22 29.7	1 44.7	19 56.8	26 17.2	1 55.8	1 41.8	25 02.7	14 57.0	15 38.3	25 01.8	28 30.2
21 Sa	15 54 28	29 56 39	6♒40 01	13♒47 44	22 06.9	22 29.1	1 10.8	21 06.6	27 02.0	2 20.6	1 52.6	25 04.2	14 59.7	15 41.7	25 03.0	28 29.7
22 Su	15 58 25	0♊54 22	20 50 17	27 47 31	22 03.8	22D 28.6	0 36.4	22 16.4	27 46.9	2 45.4	2 03.3	25 05.7	15 02.4	15 45.1	25 04.2	28 29.1
23 M	16 02 21	1 52 04	4♓39 22	11♓25 56	22 00.6	22 28.5	0 01.8	23 26.3	28 31.7	3 10.4	2 13.9	25 07.0	15 05.0	15 48.5	25 05.3	28 28.5
24 Tu	16 06 18	2 49 45	18 07 20	24 43 46	21 57.4	22 28.8	29♉27.8	24 36.3	29 16.5	3 35.3	2 24.4	25 08.2	15 07.6	15 51.8	25 06.5	28 27.8
25 W	16 10 14	3 47 25	1♈15 30	7♈42 48	21 54.2	22 29.6	28 55.0	25 46.3	0♈01.3	4 00.3	2 34.8	25 09.3	15 10.2	15 55.2	25 07.6	28 27.2
26 Th	16 14 11	4 45 04	14 05 58	20 25 18	21 51.1	22 30.6	28 23.8	26 56.4	0 46.0	4 25.4	2 45.0	25 10.3	15 12.7	15 58.5	25 08.6	28 26.5
27 F	16 18 07	5 42 42	26 41 07	2♉53 43	21 47.9	22 31.7	27 54.8	28 06.5	1 30.7	4 50.5	2 55.2	25 11.3	15 15.2	16 01.8	25 09.7	28 25.7
28 Sa	16 22 04	6 40 19	9♉03 23	15 10 25	21 44.7	22 32.6	27 28.5	29 16.7	2 15.3	5 15.7	3 05.2	25 12.1	15 17.7	16 05.1	25 10.7	28 25.0
29 Su	16 26 00	7 37 56	21 15 05	27 17 38	21 41.5	22R 33.0	27 05.2	0♉27.0	2 59.9	5 40.9	3 15.2	25 12.8	15 20.1	16 08.4	25 11.7	28 24.2
30 M	16 29 57	8 35 31	3♊18 18	9♊17 22	21 38.3	22 32.7	26 45.4	1 37.3	3 44.5	6 06.2	3 25.0	25 13.5	15 22.5	16 11.7	25 12.6	28 23.4
31 Tu	16 33 54	9♊33 05	15 15 03	21 11 36	21♉35.2	22♉31.5	26♉29.3	2♉47.6	4♈29.0	6♋31.5	3♈34.7	25♒14.0	15♈24.9	16♉14.9	25♓13.6	28♑22.6

1st of Month

Julian Day # 2459700.5
Obliquity 23°26'07"
SVP 4♓57'07"
GC 27♐09.1
Eris 24♈31.1

Day	⚴	Day	⚵	Day	⚶
1	0♉16.5	1	3♓36.1	1	22♒15.6
6	2 27.8	6	5 16.9	6	24 04.9
11	4 40.1	11	6 55.0	11	25 49.0
16	6 53.5	16	8 30.0	16	27 27.7
21	9 07.8	21	10 01.7	21	29 00.4
26	11 23.2	26	11 29.8	26	0♓26.7
31	13 39.4	31	12 53.8	31	1 46.0

DECLINATION and LATITUDE

Day	☉ Decl	☽ Decl	☽ Lat	☽12h Decl	☿ Decl	☿ Lat	♀ Decl	♀ Lat	♂ Decl	♂ Lat	⚳ Decl	⚳ Lat	♃ Decl	♃ Lat	♄ Decl	♄ Lat
1 Su	15N00	14N38	0S56	16N57	22N60	2N43	1S57	1S18	8S29	1S32	26N08	2N49	1S47	1S04	14S24	1S01
2 M	15 18	19 05	0N12	21 01	23 08	2 41	1 33	1 21	8 12	1 32	26 10	2 51	1 42	1 04	14 23	1 01
3 Tu	15 36	22 42	1 18	24 07	23 14	2 39	1 08	1 24	7 55	1 33	26 13	2 52	1 37	1 05	14 22	1 02
4 W	15 54	25 16	2 20	26 08	23 18	2 35	0 43	1 27	7 38	1 33	26 15	2 54	1 33	1 05	14 21	1 02
5 Th	16 11	26 42	3 15	26 57	23 20	2 31	0 18	1 29	7 21	1 34	26 17	2 55	1 28	1 05	14 20	1 02
6 F	16 28	26 54	4 02	26 32	23 19	2 25	0N07	1 32	7 04	1 35	26 20	2 57	1 23	1 05	14 19	1 02
7 Sa	16 45	25 52	4 39	24 54	23 16	2 18	0 32	1 34	6 47	1 35	26 22	2 58	1 19	1 05	14 19	1 02
8 Su	17 02	23 40	5 04	22 09	23 11	2 09	0 57	1 36	6 30	1 36	26 24	2 59	1 14	1 05	14 18	1 02
9 M	17 18	20 23	5 16	18 23	23 03	2 00	1 22	1 38	6 12	1 36	26 26	3 01	1 09	1 06	14 17	1 03
10 Tu	17 34	16 10	5 14	13 45	22 54	1 50	1 47	1 40	5 55	1 37	26 28	3 02	1 05	1 06	14 16	1 03
11 W	17 49	11 09	4 57	8 23	22 43	1 38	2 13	1 42	5 38	1 37	26 29	3 04	1 00	1 06	14 16	1 03
12 Th	18 05	5 29	4 24	2 29	22 29	1 25	2 38	1 44	5 21	1 37	26 31	3 05	0 56	1 06	14 15	1 03
13 F	18 20	0S35	3 36	3S43	22 14	1 12	3 04	1 46	5 03	1 38	26 33	3 07	0 51	1 06	14 14	1 03
14 Sa	18 34	6 50	2 33	9 56	21 57	0 57	3 29	1 47	4 46	1 38	26 34	3 08	0 47	1 06	14 14	1 04
15 Su	18 49	12 56	1 20	15 48	21 39	0 42	3 54	1 49	4 28	1 39	26 36	3 10	0 43	1 07	14 13	1 04
16 M	19 03	18 27	0S01	20 51	21 19	0 26	4 20	1 50	4 11	1 39	26 37	3 11	0 38	1 07	14 13	1 04
17 Tu	19 17	22 55	1 22	24 37	20 58	0 09	4 45	1 52	3 54	1 40	26 39	3 13	0 34	1 07	14 12	1 04
18 W	19 30	25 52	2 39	26 39	20 35	0S08	5 11	1 53	3 36	1 40	26 40	3 14	0 30	1 07	14 12	1 04
19 Th	19 43	26 58	3 44	26 46	20 12	0 25	5 36	1 54	3 19	1 41	26 41	3 15	0 26	1 07	14 12	1 04
20 F	19 56	26 07	4 34	25 01	19 49	0 43	6 01	1 55	3 01	1 41	26 42	3 17	0 21	1 08	14 11	1 05
21 Sa	20 08	23 31	5 05	21 41	19 25	1 00	6 27	1 56	2 44	1 41	26 43	3 18	0 17	1 08	14 11	1 05
22 Su	20 20	19 33	5 17	17 10	19 01	1 18	6 52	1 57	2 26	1 42	26 44	3 20	0 13	1 08	14 11	1 05
23 M	20 32	14 36	5 10	11 54	18 37	1 35	7 17	1 58	2 09	1 42	26 45	3 21	0 09	1 08	14 10	1 05
24 Tu	20 43	9 05	4 46	6 12	18 13	1 51	7 42	1 58	1 51	1 43	26 46	3 23	0 05	1 08	14 10	1 05
25 W	20 54	3 17	4 07	0 22	17 51	2 07	8 07	1 59	1 34	1 43	26 46	3 24	0 01	1 09	14 10	1 06
26 Th	21 05	2N32	3 17	5N22	17 29	2 23	8 32	1 59	1 16	1 43	26 47	3 25	0N03	1 09	14 10	1 06
27 F	21 15	8 08	2 18	10 48	17 09	2 37	8 56	1 60	0 59	1 44	26 48	3 27	0 06	1 09	14 10	1 06
28 Sa	21 25	13 21	1 14	15 44	16 50	2 50	9 21	1 60	0 42	1 44	26 48	3 28	0 10	1 09	14 09	1 06
29 Su	21 35	17 57	0 07	19 59	16 32	3 03	9 45	1 60	0 24	1 44	26 48	3 30	0 14	1 09	14 09	1 06
30 M	21 44	21 47	0N59	23 21	16 17	3 14	10 10	2 00	0 07	1 45	26 49	3 31	0 18	1 10	14 09	1 06
31 Tu	21N53	24N39	2N02	25N40	16N04	3S24	10N34	2S00	0N11	1S45	26N49	3N32	0N21	1S10	14S09	1S07

Day	⚷ Decl	⚷ Lat	♅ Decl	♅ Lat	♆ Decl	♆ Lat	♇ Decl	♇ Lat
1	7N19	1N56	15N51	0S22	3S12	1S08	22S22	1S58
6	7 25	1 56	15 57	0 22	3 09	1 08	22 23	1 59
11	7 30	1 56	16 02	0 22	3 06	1 09	22 24	1 59
16	7 36	1 56	16 07	0 22	3 04	1 09	22 25	2 00
21	7 42	1 56	16 12	0 22	3 01	1 09	22 26	2 01
26	7 47	1 56	16 17	0 21	2 59	1 09	22 27	2 02
31	7N51	1N56	16N21	0S21	2S58	1S09	22S29	2S02

Day	⚴ Decl	⚴ Lat	⚵ Decl	⚵ Lat	⚶ Decl	⚶ Lat	Eris Decl	Eris Lat
1	2S40	15S11	3S23	7N17	15S27	1S27	0S54	11S10
6	2 22	15 37	2 49	7 15	15 05	1 41	0 53	11 10
11	2 05	16 03	2 15	7 13	14 44	1 56	0 52	11 10
16	1 50	16 31	1 43	7 11	14 25	2 12	0 51	11 10
21	1 37	16 60	1 11	7 09	14 08	2 28	0 50	11 11
26	1 26	17 30	0 41	7 06	13 53	2 45	0 50	11 11
31	1S17	18S00	0S12	7N03	13S42	3S03	0S49	11S11

Moon Phenomena

Max/0 Decl
dy hr mn
5 15:55 26N58
12 21:43 0 S
19 1:24 26S58
25 13:30 0 N

Max/0 Lat
dy hr mn
1 19:55 0 N
9 8:28 5N17
15 23:45 0 S
22 2:49 5S17
29 2:35 0 N

Perigee/Apogee
dy hr m kilometers
5 12:47 a 405284
17 15:28 p 360302

PH dy hr mn
☽ 9 0:23 18♌23
○ 16 4:15 25♏18
☍ 16 4:13 T 1.413
☾ 22 18:44 1♓39
● 30 11:31 9♊03

Void of Course Moon

Last Aspect	☽ Ingress
2 10:14 ♀ ✶	♊ 2 10:48
4 20:38 ♃ □	♋ 4 23:06
7 10:27 ♃ △	♌ 7 11:51
9 12:40 ♄ ☍	♍ 9 22:54
12 4:01 ♇ △	♎ 12 6:36
14 8:08 ♇ □	♏ 14 10:35
16 9:29 ♇ ✶	♐ 16 11:52
18 4:01 ♄ ✶	♑ 18 12:03
20 12:01 ☉ △	♒ 20 12:54
22 7:20 ♄ ☌	♓ 22 15:51
24 21:35 ♂ ☌	♈ 24 21:41
27 3:21 ♇ □	♉ 27 6:24
29 14:12 ♇ △	♊ 29 17:24

DAILY ASPECTARIAN

1 Su: ☽∠♃ 1:24; ☽∠♀ 1:44; ☉∥☽ 2:00; ☽⚺⚷ 3:21; ☽☌♅ 4:25; ☽∥♅ 6:14; ♀✶♇ 10:38; ♀∥♃ 12:44; ⚳□♆ 18:51; ☊D 19:54; ☽□♄ 23:34

2 M: ☽✶♆ 0:05; ☽⚺⚳ 0:15; ☽✶♃ 7:21; ☽△♇ 8:01; ♀∠♅ 8:16; ☽∠⚷ 8:58; ☽✶♀ 10:14; ☽☌☿ 15:06; ♀ ♈ 16:12; ☽#♇ 21:33

3 Tu: ♂∠♇ 2:51; ☽∥☿ 4:28; ☉⚺☽ 12:55; ☽⚼♇ 13:57; ☽□♂ 14:43; ☽✶⚷ 15:03; ☽⚺♅ 16:11; ♂⚺⚷ 20:34; ♃✶♇ 22:35

4 W: ☉∥♅ 0:53; ☉∠♃ 2:30; ☽△♄ 11:52; ☽□♆ 12:17; ☽☌⚳ 14:22; ☽∥⚳ 14:32; ♂✶♅ 15:48; ☉⚺⚷ 16:34; ☽⚻♇ 20:15; ☽□♃ 20:38; ♂#⚷ 20:39; ☉∠☽ 21:55; ☽∠♅ 22:39

5 Th: ☽□♀ 4:58; ☽⚺☿ 6:35; ☉☌♅ 7:23; ☽⚼♄ 18:25

6 F: ☽□⚷ 4:05; ☽✶♅ 5:14; ☿✶♀ 6:02; ☉✶☽ 7:04; ☽△♂ 7:35; ☽∠☿ 14:04; ☽∥⚳ 15:53

7 Sa: ☽⚻♄ 0:56; ☽△♆ 1:14; ☽⚺⚳ 5:17; ☽☍♇ 9:00; ☉✶♂ 9:49; ☽△♃ 10:27; ☽⚼♂ 15:54; ☽✶☿ 21:00

8 Su: ☽△♀ 0:03; ☽∥☿ 4:16; ☽⚼♆ 7:21; ☽#♇ 10:17; ☽∠⚳ 12:18; ♀#♃ 13:47; ☽△⚷ 16:33; ☽⚼♃ 16:50; ☽□♅ 17:42; ☽⚻♂ 23:39

9 M: ☉□☽ 0:23; ☊R 0:30; ☽⚼♀ 8:43; ☽☍♄ 12:40; ☽⚻♆ 12:52; ☉∥☽ 17:00; ☽✶⚳ 18:36; ☽⚻♇ 20:10; ☽⚼⚷ 21:53; ☽⚻♃ 22:31

10 Tu: ☽∥♅ 0:47; ☽□☿ 8:11; ☽#♄ 9:28; ☿R 11:49; ☽⚻♀ 16:20; ♃ ♈ 23:23

11 W: ☽⚼♇ 0:34; ☽⚻⚷ 2:21; ☽△♅ 3:28; ♀∠♄ 4:34; ☽☍♂ 12:18; ☉△☽ 14:03; ☽∥⚷ 15:38; ⚳⚻♇ 18:29; ♃∠♅ 20:53; ☽⚻♄ 21:11; ☽☍♆ 21:18

12 Th: ☽#♂ 0:38; ☽△♇ 4:01; ☽□⚳ 4:19; ☽⚼♅ 6:57; ☽☍♃ 7:03; ☿#♇ 8:52; ☽#♆ 9:37; ☽∥♀ 10:41; ☽△☿ 14:55; ☽#♃ 18:20; ☉⚼☽ 19:06; ☽⚼♄ 24:00

13 F: ☽∥♃ 1:02; ♀#♆ 1:37; ☽☍♀ 3:51; ☊D 7:05; ☽☍⚷ 8:23; ☽⚻♅ 9:28; ☽∥♆ 9:35; ☽#♀ 10:11; ☽∥♂ 16:23; ☽⚼☿ 16:41; ☽⚻♂ 20:29; ☉⚻☽ 23:01

14 Sa: ☽△♄ 1:55; ☽⚻♆ 1:58; ☽#⚷ 2:48; ☽□♇ 8:08; ☽△⚳ 9:59; ☽⚻♃ 11:43; ☽⚻☿ 17:32; ☽⚼♂ 23:07

15 Su: ☽⚼♆ 3:07; ☽∥♄ 5:19; ⚳ ♋ 7:12; ☽⚻♀ 10:56; ☽⚻⚷ 11:02; ☽⚼⚳ 11:35; ☽☍♅ 12:06; ♀☌⚷ 12:14; ☽⚼♃ 12:54; ☽#♅ 13:21; ☉□♄ 18:50; ♀#♂ 19:06; ☉✶♆ 19:16; ☊R 23:57

16 M: ☽△♂ 1:03; ♀⚺♅ 2:15; ☉#☽ 2:59; ☽□♄ 3:40; ☽△♆ 3:41; ☉☍☽ 4:15; ⚳∠♅ 8:31; ☽✶♇ 9:29; ☽⚼⚷ 11:31; ☽⚻⚳ 12:40; ☽⚼♀ 13:24; ☽#☿ 13:28; ☽△♃ 13:35; ☽☍☿ 17:20; ☽∥♇ 20:53

17 Tu: ☽∠♇ 9:37; ☽△⚷ 11:43; ☽⚻♅ 12:47; ☽△♀ 15:32; ♄⚺♆ 15:40

18 W: ☿∠♀ 2:32; ☽□♂ 3:52; ☽□♆ 4:00; ☽✶♄ 4:01; ♂☌♆ 6:34; ♂⚺♄ 6:44; ☉⚻☽ 7:50; ☽⚺♇ 9:40; ☽#⚳ 12:34; ☽⚼♅ 12:57; ☽☍⚳ 14:13; ☽□♃ 14:22; ☽⚻☿ 16:01; ⚳□♃ 23:44

19 Th: ☽∠♄ 4:13; ☉⚼☽ 9:42; ☽□⚷ 12:10; ☉△♇ 12:12; ☽△♅ 13:17; ☽#⚳ 13:53; ☽⚼☿ 15:27; ☉∥☿ 19:19; ☿⚺⚳ 19:24; ☽□♀ 20:03; ♂∥♆ 23:15

20 F: ☿✶♃ 1:34; ☽✶♆ 4:42; ☽⚺♄ 4:44; ☽✶♂ 7:08; ☽☌♇ 10:25; ☉△☽ 12:01; ☽△☿ 15:12; ☽✶♃ 15:55; ☽⚻⚳ 16:35

21 Sa: ☉∠⚷ 1:19; ☉ ♊ 1:24; ☽∠♆ 5:41; ☽∥♇ 7:20; ☽∠♂ 9:31; ☽✶⚷ 14:05; ☽□♅ 15:17; ☽∠♃ 17:27; ☽⚼⚳ 18:34; ☉☌☿ 19:19; ☉#☽ 19:54

22 Su: ☽✶♀ 2:41; ☽#☿ 3:05; ☽⚺♆ 7:18; ☽☌♄ 7:20; ☽⚺♂ 12:40; ☽⚺♇ 13:12; ☽∠⚷ 15:58; ☽□☿ 16:13; ☽#♅ 16:32; ☉□☽ 18:44; ☊D 18:51; ☽⚺♃ 19:41; ☽△⚳ 21:19; ☿∠⚷ 21:56; ♂✶♇ 22:17

23 M: ☿R♉ 1:16; ☽∥♄ 1:58; ☽∠♀ 7:19; ☉✶♃ 11:06; ☽∠♇ 15:38; ☽⚺⚷ 18:35; ☽✶♅ 19:55

24 Tu: ♀∥⚷ 2:41; ☿✶♂ 3:28; ☽#♀ 5:23; ☽#⚷ 5:35; ⚶ ♓ 9:47; ♀⚺♆ 10:31; ♀✶♄ 11:07; ☽☌♆ 12:43; ☽⚺♄ 12:46; ☽⚺♀ 12:55; ☽✶♇ 18:50; ☽✶☿ 19:51; ☽☌♂ 21:35; ♂ ♈ 23:19; ☽∠♅ 23:22

25 W: ☽∥♆ 1:11; ☽☌♃ 2:29; ☉✶☽ 5:04; ☽□⚳ 5:16; ☽∥♂ 7:26; ☉⚺⚳ 9:31; ☽#♃ 13:27; ☽∥♃ 13:34; ☽∠♄ 16:36; ☽#♂ 19:02; ☿△♇ 21:50; ☽∠☿ 22:43

26 Th: ☽#♆ 1:55; ☽☌⚷ 2:07; ☽⚺♅ 3:34; ♂∠♅ 7:14; ☉∠☽ 11:36; ☽⚺♆ 21:04; ☽✶♄ 21:07; ☿⚺♀ 21:08; ☽∥⚷ 22:29

27 F: ☽⚺☿ 2:17; ☽☌♀ 3:02; ☽□♇ 3:21; ☽∥♀ 3:51; ♀□♇ 6:30; ☽⚺♂ 9:55; ☽⚺♃ 12:13; ☽✶⚳ 16:20; ☉⚺☽ 18:57

28 Sa: ☽∠♆ 2:12; ☽#♄ 3:59; ☽⚺⚷ 12:17; ☽☌♅ 13:51; ♀ ♉ 14:47; ☽∥♅ 15:03; ☽∥☿ 16:41; ☽∠♂ 17:09; ☽∠♃ 17:59; ☽∠⚳ 22:50

29 Su: ☊R 2:36; ☽✶♆ 7:50; ☽□♄ 7:52; ♂☌♃ 10:32; ☽☌☿ 11:16; ♂#♃ 11:38; ☽△♇ 14:12; ☽∠⚷ 18:08; ☿∥♅ 18:52; ☽⚺♀ 20:16; ☉∥☽ 23:39

30 M: ☽✶♃ 0:14; ☽✶♂ 0:56; ☽#♇ 5:06; ☽⚺⚳ 5:49; ☉☌☽ 11:31; ☽⚼♇ 20:14

31 Tu: ☽✶⚷ 0:20; ☽⚺♅ 2:01; ☽∠♀ 5:42; ♀⚺♃ 18:35; ♂∥♃ 18:38; ☽□♆ 20:11; ☽△♄ 20:11; ♄⚺♆ 22:04; ☽⚺☿ 22:20

LONGITUDE

Day	Sid.Time	☉	☽	☽ 12 hour	Mean☊	True☊	☿	♀	♂	⚳	♃	♄	⚷	♅	♆	♇
	h m s	° ' "	° ' "	° ' "	° '	° '	° '	° '	° '	° '	° '	° '	° '	° '	° '	° '
1 W	16 37 50	10♊30 37	27♉07 17	3♋02 21	21♉32.0	22♉29.5	26♉17.1	3♉58.0	5♈13.5	6♋56.9	3♈44.3	25♒14.4	15♈27.2	16♉18.2	25♓14.5	28♑21.8
2 Th	16 41 47	11 28 09	8♋57 05	14 51 48	21 28.8	22R 26.8	26R 09.2	5 08.5	5 57.9	7 22.3	3 53.8	25 14.8	15 29.5	16 21.4	25 15.3	28R 21.0
3 F	16 45 43	12 25 40	20 46 48	26 42 27	21 25.6	22 23.7	26D 05.5	6 19.0	6 42.3	7 47.8	4 03.1	25 15.0	15 31.8	16 24.6	25 16.2	28 20.1
4 Sa	16 49 40	13 23 09	2♌39 07	8♌37 13	21 22.5	22 20.5	26 06.2	7 29.5	7 26.6	8 13.3	4 12.3	25R 15.1	15 34.0	16 27.8	25 17.0	28 19.2
5 Su	16 53 36	14 20 37	14 37 10	20 39 27	21 19.3	22 17.6	26 11.4	8 40.1	8 10.9	8 38.8	4 21.4	25 15.2	15 36.1	16 31.0	25 17.7	28 18.3
6 M	16 57 33	15 18 04	26 44 31	2♍52 53	21 16.1	22 15.4	26 21.1	9 50.8	8 55.1	9 04.4	4 30.4	25 15.1	15 38.3	16 34.1	25 18.5	28 17.3
7 Tu	17 01 29	16 15 30	9♍05 04	15 21 34	21 12.9	22D 14.3	26 35.3	11 01.4	9 39.2	9 30.0	4 39.2	25 15.0	15 40.3	16 37.3	25 19.2	28 16.4
8 W	17 05 26	17 12 55	21 42 54	28 09 32	21 09.8	22 14.1	26 53.9	12 12.1	10 23.3	9 55.7	4 47.9	25 14.7	15 42.4	16 40.4	25 19.8	28 15.4
9 Th	17 09 23	18 10 18	4♎41 55	11♎20 28	21 06.6	22 14.9	27 17.0	13 22.9	11 07.4	10 21.4	4 56.5	25 14.4	15 44.4	16 43.5	25 20.5	28 14.4
10 F	17 13 19	19 07 40	18 05 28	24 57 10	21 03.4	22 16.3	27 44.4	14 33.7	11 51.4	10 47.1	5 05.0	25 13.9	15 46.3	16 46.5	25 21.1	28 13.3
11 Sa	17 17 16	20 05 02	1♏55 39	9♏00 53	21 00.2	22 17.8	28 16.1	15 44.6	12 35.3	11 12.9	5 13.3	25 13.4	15 48.3	16 49.6	25 21.7	28 12.3
12 Su	17 21 12	21 02 22	16 12 40	23 30 36	20 57.0	22R 18.7	28 52.0	16 55.5	13 19.2	11 38.7	5 21.5	25 12.7	15 50.1	16 52.6	25 22.2	28 11.2
13 M	17 25 09	21 59 41	0♐54 08	8♐22 30	20 53.9	22 18.6	29 32.0	18 06.4	14 03.0	12 04.6	5 29.5	25 12.0	15 52.0	16 55.6	25 22.7	28 10.2
14 Tu	17 29 05	22 57 00	15 54 46	23 29 51	20 50.7	22 17.1	0♊16.1	19 17.4	14 46.8	12 30.4	5 37.4	25 11.1	15 53.7	16 58.5	25 23.2	28 09.1
15 W	17 33 02	23 54 18	1♑06 33	8♑43 36	20 47.5	22 14.2	1 04.2	20 28.4	15 30.5	12 56.4	5 45.2	25 10.2	15 55.5	17 01.5	25 23.7	28 08.0
16 Th	17 36 59	24 51 36	16 19 41	23 53 33	20 44.3	22 10.1	1 56.2	21 39.5	16 14.1	13 22.3	5 52.8	25 09.2	15 57.2	17 04.4	25 24.1	28 06.8
17 F	17 40 55	25 48 52	1♒24 02	8♒50 06	20 41.2	22 05.5	2 52.0	22 50.6	16 57.7	13 48.3	6 00.3	25 08.1	15 58.8	17 07.3	25 24.5	28 05.7
18 Sa	17 44 52	26 46 09	16 10 52	23 25 39	20 38.0	22 01.0	3 51.6	24 01.8	17 41.2	14 14.3	6 07.6	25 06.9	16 00.4	17 10.1	25 24.8	28 04.5
19 Su	17 48 48	27 43 25	0♓34 00	7♓35 35	20 34.8	21 57.3	4 54.8	25 13.0	18 24.7	14 40.4	6 14.8	25 05.6	16 02.0	17 13.0	25 25.1	28 03.3
20 M	17 52 45	28 40 41	14 30 20	21 18 17	20 31.6	21 54.9	6 01.7	26 24.2	19 08.1	15 06.4	6 21.8	25 04.2	16 03.5	17 15.8	25 25.4	28 02.2
21 Tu	17 56 41	29 37 56	27 59 38	4♈34 41	20 28.5	21D 54.0	7 12.1	27 35.5	19 51.4	15 32.5	6 28.7	25 02.7	16 05.0	17 18.6	25 25.7	28 00.9
22 W	18 00 38	0♋35 11	11♈03 49	17 27 31	20 25.3	21 54.4	8 26.1	28 46.9	20 34.6	15 58.7	6 35.4	25 01.1	16 06.4	17 21.3	25 25.9	27 59.7
23 Th	18 04 34	1 32 26	23 46 14	0♉00 31	20 22.1	21 55.7	9 43.5	29 58.2	21 17.8	16 24.9	6 42.0	24 59.4	16 07.8	17 24.0	25 26.1	27 58.5
24 F	18 08 31	2 29 42	6♉10 51	12 17 46	20 18.9	21 57.2	11 04.4	1♊09.7	22 00.9	16 51.1	6 48.4	24 57.6	16 09.1	17 26.7	25 26.3	27 57.2
25 Sa	18 12 28	3 26 56	18 21 45	24 23 15	20 15.8	21R 58.1	12 28.7	2 21.1	22 43.9	17 17.3	6 54.7	24 55.8	16 10.4	17 29.4	25 26.4	27 56.0
26 Su	18 16 24	4 24 11	0♊22 44	6♊20 36	20 12.6	21 57.8	13 56.4	3 32.6	23 26.9	17 43.5	7 00.8	24 53.8	16 11.6	17 32.0	25 26.5	27 54.7
27 M	18 20 21	5 21 26	12 17 12	18 12 53	20 09.4	21 55.7	15 27.4	4 44.2	24 09.7	18 09.8	7 06.7	24 51.8	16 12.8	17 34.6	25 26.5	27 53.4
28 Tu	18 24 17	6 18 41	24 07 57	0♋02 42	20 06.2	21 51.6	17 01.7	5 55.8	24 52.5	18 36.2	7 12.5	24 49.7	16 13.9	17 37.2	25R 26.6	27 52.1
29 W	18 28 14	7 15 55	5♋57 22	11 52 11	20 03.1	21 45.4	18 39.3	7 07.4	25 35.2	19 02.5	7 18.1	24 47.5	16 15.0	17 39.7	25 26.6	27 50.8
30 Th	18 32 10	8♋13 09	17 47 23	23 43 11	19♉59.9	21♉37.7	20♊20.0	8♊19.1	26♈17.8	19♋28.9	7♈23.5	24♒45.2	16♈16.0	17♉42.2	25♓26.5	27♑49.4

1st of Month

Julian Day # 2459731.5
Obliquity 23°26'16"
SVP 4♓57'02"
GC 27♐09.1
Eris 24♈48.7

Day	⚴	Day	⚵	Day	⚶
1	14♉06.8	1	13♓10.1	1	2♓00.9
6	16 24.2	6	14 28.7	6	3 10.9
11	18 42.3	11	15 42.3	11	4 12.4
16	21 01.3	16	16 50.6	16	5 05.1
21	23 21.0	21	17 52.8	21	5 48.1
26	25 41.5	26	18 48.6	26	6 20.9

DECLINATION and LATITUDE

Day	☉ Decl	☽ Decl	☽ Lat	☽ 12h Decl	☿ Decl	☿ Lat	♀ Decl	♀ Lat	♂ Decl	♂ Lat	⚳ Decl	⚳ Lat	♃ Decl	♃ Lat	♄ Decl	♄ Lat
1 W	22N01	26N24	2N59	26N49	15N52	3S33	10N57	1S60	0N28	1S45	26N49	3N34	0N25	1S10	14S09	1S07
2 Th	22 09	26 56	3 49	26 45	15 43	3 41	11 21	1 60	0 45	1 45	26 49	3 35	0 28	1 10	14 09	1 07
3 F	22 17	26 15	4 28	25 27	15 36	3 47	11 45	1 60	1 03	1 46	26 49	3 37	0 32	1 10	14 10	1 07
4 Sa	22 24	24 22	4 56	23 01	15 31	3 52	12 08	1 59	1 20	1 46	26 49	3 38	0 35	1 11	14 10	1 07
5 Su	22 31	21 25	5 12	19 34	15 28	3 57	12 31	1 59	1 37	1 46	26 48	3 39	0 39	1 11	14 10	1 08
6 M	22 38	17 30	5 13	15 15	15 27	3 60	12 54	1 58	1 54	1 47	26 48	3 41	0 42	1 11	14 10	1 08
7 Tu	22 44	12 49	5 01	10 13	15 29	4 01	13 16	1 58	2 11	1 47	26 48	3 42	0 45	1 11	14 10	1 08
8 W	22 49	7 29	4 34	4 38	15 32	4 02	13 38	1 57	2 28	1 47	26 47	3 44	0 49	1 12	14 11	1 08
9 Th	22 55	1 41	3 52	1S19	15 37	4 02	14 00	1 56	2 45	1 47	26 46	3 45	0 52	1 12	14 11	1 08
10 F	22 60	4S22	2 57	7 25	15 45	4 01	14 22	1 55	3 02	1 47	26 46	3 46	0 55	1 12	14 11	1 09
11 Sa	23 04	10 26	1 50	13 21	15 54	3 59	14 44	1 54	3 19	1 48	26 45	3 48	0 58	1 12	14 12	1 09
12 Su	23 08	16 09	0 33	18 45	16 04	3 56	15 05	1 53	3 36	1 48	26 44	3 49	1 01	1 13	14 12	1 09
13 M	23 12	21 06	0S47	23 08	16 17	3 52	15 25	1 52	3 53	1 48	26 43	3 51	1 04	1 13	14 12	1 09
14 Tu	23 15	24 46	2 06	25 59	16 30	3 47	15 46	1 51	4 10	1 48	26 42	3 52	1 07	1 13	14 13	1 09
15 W	23 18	26 42	3 16	26 55	16 45	3 41	16 06	1 50	4 26	1 48	26 41	3 54	1 10	1 13	14 13	1 09
16 Th	23 20	26 38	4 13	25 50	17 02	3 35	16 26	1 49	4 43	1 48	26 40	3 55	1 13	1 14	14 14	1 10
17 F	23 22	24 35	4 52	22 55	17 19	3 28	16 45	1 47	4 60	1 49	26 38	3 56	1 15	1 14	14 14	1 10
18 Sa	23 24	20 55	5 10	18 36	17 38	3 21	17 04	1 46	5 16	1 49	26 37	3 58	1 18	1 14	14 15	1 10
19 Su	23 25	16 04	5 08	13 22	17 57	3 13	17 23	1 44	5 32	1 49	26 36	3 59	1 21	1 14	14 16	1 10
20 M	23 26	10 31	4 48	7 37	18 17	3 04	17 41	1 43	5 49	1 49	26 34	4 01	1 23	1 15	14 16	1 10
21 Tu	23 26	4 39	4 12	1 42	18 38	2 55	17 59	1 41	6 05	1 49	26 32	4 02	1 26	1 15	14 17	1 11
22 W	23 26	1N15	3 24	4N08	18 60	2 45	18 16	1 40	6 21	1 49	26 31	4 03	1 28	1 15	14 18	1 11
23 Th	23 26	6 57	2 27	9 39	19 21	2 35	18 33	1 38	6 37	1 49	26 29	4 05	1 30	1 15	14 18	1 11
24 F	23 25	12 15	1 25	14 42	19 43	2 24	18 49	1 36	6 53	1 49	26 27	4 06	1 33	1 16	14 19	1 11
25 Sa	23 24	16 59	0 20	19 05	20 05	2 13	19 05	1 34	7 09	1 49	26 25	4 08	1 35	1 16	14 20	1 11
26 Su	23 22	20 58	0N45	22 38	20 27	2 02	19 21	1 32	7 25	1 49	26 23	4 09	1 37	1 16	14 21	1 11
27 M	23 20	24 03	1 48	25 12	20 49	1 51	19 36	1 30	7 41	1 49	26 21	4 10	1 39	1 16	14 21	1 12
28 Tu	23 17	26 03	2 45	26 37	21 10	1 39	19 51	1 28	7 56	1 49	26 18	4 12	1 41	1 17	14 22	1 12
29 W	23 14	26 53	3 35	26 50	21 31	1 27	20 05	1 26	8 12	1 49	26 16	4 13	1 43	1 17	14 23	1 12
30 Th	23N11	26N28	4N15	25N49	21N51	1S15	20N18	1S24	8N27	1S49	26N13	4N15	1N45	1S17	14S24	1S12

Day	⚷ Decl	⚷ Lat	♅ Decl	♅ Lat	♆ Decl	♆ Lat	♇ Decl	♇ Lat
1	7N52	1N56	16N22	0S21	2S57	1S10	22S29	2S02
6	7 57	1 56	16 27	0 21	2 56	1 10	22 31	2 03
11	8 01	1 57	16 31	0 21	2 55	1 10	22 32	2 04
16	8 04	1 57	16 35	0 22	2 54	1 10	22 34	2 04
21	8 07	1 57	16 39	0 22	2 54	1 10	22 36	2 05
26	8 10	1 57	16 43	0 22	2 54	1 11	22 38	2 06

Day	⚴ Decl	⚴ Lat	⚵ Decl	⚵ Lat	⚶ Decl	⚶ Lat	Eris Decl	Eris Lat
1	1S16	18S06	0S06	7N02	13S40	3S07	0S49	11S11
6	1 10	18 38	0N20	6 59	13 33	3 26	0 48	11 11
11	1 06	19 11	0 45	6 55	13 29	3 47	0 48	11 12
16	1 06	19 45	1 07	6 51	13 29	4 08	0 47	11 12
21	1 08	20 21	1 26	6 45	13 34	4 30	0 47	11 12
26	1 13	20 57	1 42	6 40	13 43	4 53	0 47	11 13

Moon Phenomena

Max/0 Decl
dy hr mn
1 22:31 26N56
9 6:45 0 S
15 11:03 26S55
21 18:54 0 N
29 4:05 26N54

Max/0 Lat
dy hr mn
5 15:12 5N14
12 10:03 0 S
18 9:37 5S12
25 7:11 0 N

Perigee/Apogee
dy hr m kilometers
2 1:14 a 406192
14 23:25 p 357433
29 6:09 a 406581

PH dy hr mn
☽ 7 14:50 16♍51
○ 14 11:53 23♐25
☾ 21 3:12 29♓46
● 29 2:53 7♋23

Void of Course Moon

Last Aspect	☽ Ingress
31 20:11 ♆ □	♋ 1 5:50
3 15:16 ♇ ☍	♌ 3 18:39
5 23:13 ☿ □	♍ 6 6:23
8 12:10 ♇ △	♎ 8 15:24
10 17:38 ♇ □	♏ 10 20:42
12 21:41 ♆ △	♐ 12 22:33
14 14:59 ♆ □	♑ 14 22:15
16 18:43 ♇ ☌	♒ 16 21:45
18 18:51 ☉ △	♓ 18 23:02
21 3:12 ☉ □	♈ 21 3:38
23 8:04 ♇ □	♉ 23 11:59
25 19:04 ♇ △	♊ 25 23:14
28 2:39 ♆ □	♋ 28 11:55

DAILY ASPECTARIAN

1 W
☽⚻♇ 2:31
☽∠♅ 8:31
☽∥⚳ 11:46
☽□♃ 13:36
☽✶♀ 15:25
☽□♂ 17:32
☽☌⚳ 20:40

2 Th
☽⚼♄ 2:38
☽∠☿ 4:26
☉⚺☽ 5:34
☽∥⚳ 9:19
☽□⚷ 13:19
☽✶♅ 15:06

3 F
☿ D 8:01
☽⚻♄ 9:03
☽△♆ 9:06
☽✶☿ 10:45
☉∠☽ 14:38
☽☍♇ 15:16
♀⚺♂ 21:19
☉⚼♇ 22:22

4 Sa
☽△♃ 3:10
☽△♂ 10:16
☽□♀ 10:48
☽⚺⚳ 11:37
☽⚼♆ 15:21
☽#♇ 16:02
☉∥☽ 16:11
☉#♇ 20:48
♄ R 21:48
♀✶⚳ 23:19
☉✶☽ 23:24

5 Su
☽△⚷ 1:58
☽□♅ 3:48
☽⚼♃ 9:33
☽⚼♂ 18:05
☽∠⚳ 18:34
☽☍♄ 21:04
☽⚻♆ 21:11
☽□☿ 23:13

6 M
☽⚻♇ 3:02
☽∥♅ 5:44
☽⚼⚷ 7:39
☉✶⚷ 8:45
♀∠♆ 9:31
☽∥☿ 10:54
♂□⚳ 12:04
☽⚻♃ 15:20
☽#♄ 17:24
☽∥♀ 21:57

7 Tu
☽✶⚳ 0:50
☽⚻♂ 1:10
☽△♀ 4:07
☽⚼♇ 8:01
☉⚺♅ 9:37
☽⚻⚷ 12:38
☽△♅ 14:27
☊ D 14:42
☉□☽ 14:50
♂∠♄ 19:20
☽∥⚷ 21:53

8 W
☽⚻♄ 6:36
☽☍♆ 6:46
☽△☿ 9:57
☽⚼♀ 11:15
☽△♇ 12:10
⚳⚼♄ 17:32
☽⚼♅ 18:33
☽#♆ 19:00
☽∥♂ 19:52

9 Th
☽☍♃ 0:27
☽∥♃ 3:16
☽⚼♄ 10:01
☽#♃ 10:16
☽□⚳ 10:34
♀#♄ 11:36
☽☍♂ 12:17
♂#♆ 13:44
☽⚼☿ 14:09
☽⚻♀ 17:09
☽∥♆ 18:18
☽#♂ 18:31
☽☍⚷ 19:53
☽⚻♅ 21:40

10 F
☉△☽ 1:58
☽△♄ 12:28
☽⚻♆ 12:42
☽#⚷ 14:19
☽⚻☿ 17:28
☽□♇ 17:38
☿△♇ 21:22

11 Sa
♀⚺⚷ 1:17
☽⚻♃ 5:39
☉⚼☽ 5:45
☽⚼♆ 14:16
☽∥♄ 15:31
☽△⚳ 16:10
☽⚻♂ 18:57
☽#♀ 18:59
♀☌♅ 22:59
☽⚻⚷ 23:23
☽#☿ 23:38

12 Su
☽☍♅ 1:06
☽☍♀ 1:17
☽#♅ 1:42
☽⚼♃ 6:54
☉⚻☽ 8:31
☊ R 10:05
☽□♄ 14:46
☽△♆ 15:02
☽⚼⚳ 17:37
☽✶♇ 19:35
☽⚼♂ 20:51
☽☍☿ 21:41
☽⚼⚷ 23:56

13 M
☽△♃ 7:27
☽∥♇ 8:22
☉#☽ 12:38
☿ ♊ 15:28
☽⚻⚳ 18:26
☽∠♇ 19:37
☽△♂ 22:07
☽△⚷ 23:58

14 Tu
☽⚻♅ 1:41
☿∥♅ 5:47
☽⚻♀ 5:48
☉☍☽ 11:53
☽✶♄ 14:39
☽□♆ 14:59
☽⚺♇ 19:19
☿∠⚷ 19:38
☽#⚳ 23:26
☽#⚳ 23:27
☽⚻☿ 23:56

15 W
☽⚼♅ 1:27
♀∠♃ 6:21
☽□♃ 7:23
☽⚼♀ 7:27
☽∠♄ 14:16
♂☌⚷ 14:18
☽☍⚳ 19:11
☽□⚷ 23:24
☽□♂ 23:51

16 Th
☽⚼☿ 1:01
☽△♅ 1:11
☉△♄ 7:14
☽△♀ 9:10
♀∥♅ 12:28
☉□♆ 13:43
☽⚺♄ 14:00
☽✶♆ 14:25
☉⚻☽ 14:27
☽☌♇ 18:43

17 F
☽△☿ 2:31
♂⚺♅ 5:39
☽✶♃ 7:29
☉#☽ 8:56
☽∥♇ 14:13
☽∠♆ 14:34
☉⚼☽ 16:17
☽⚻⚳ 20:43
☽✶⚷ 23:43

18 Sa
☽□♅ 1:38
☽✶♂ 2:37
☽∠♃ 8:14
☽□♀ 14:11
☽☌♄ 14:48
☽⚺♆ 15:20
☽#☿ 15:44
☽#♀ 18:17
☉△☽ 18:51
☽⚺♇ 19:46
☽#♅ 21:26
♀□♄ 21:33
☽⚼⚳ 22:26

19 Su
☽∠⚷ 0:48
♀✶♆ 4:07
☽∠♂ 5:06
☽□☿ 8:02
☽∥♄ 8:05
☉⚻♇ 8:11
☽⚺♃ 9:46
☽∠♇ 21:26

20 M
☽△⚳ 1:05
☽⚺⚷ 2:44
☽✶♅ 4:52
☿✶♃ 7:45
☽⚺♂ 8:37
☽#⚷ 9:56
☽#♂ 18:28
☽⚺♄ 18:42
☽☌♆ 19:22
☽✶♀ 23:12

21 Tu
☽✶♇ 0:02
☉□☽ 3:12
☊ D 3:22
☽∥♆ 7:08
☽∠♅ 7:52
♀△♇ 8:25
☉ ♋ 9:15
☽#♃ 13:00
☽☌♃ 15:38
☽✶☿ 18:35
☽∠♄ 22:03

22 W
☽∥♃ 0:55
☽∠♀ 5:36
☽#♆ 6:49
⚳□⚷ 7:29
☽☌⚷ 9:28
☽□⚳ 9:32
☽⚺♅ 11:51
☽☌♂ 19:00
☽∥♂ 22:32

23 Th
♀ ♊ 0:36
☽∠☿ 2:03
☽✶♄ 2:20
☽⚺♆ 3:11
☽∥⚷ 5:16
☽□♇ 8:04
☽⚺♀ 13:12
☉✶☽ 16:13
☉∠♅ 22:42
♀∠⚷ 23:48

24 F
☽⚺♃ 1:14
☽∠♆ 8:21
☽#♄ 10:08
☽⚺☿ 10:50
☽⚺⚷ 19:39
☽✶⚳ 21:47
♀∠⚳ 21:58
☽☌♅ 22:16
☽∥♅ 22:30

25 Sa
☉∠☽ 0:11
☽∠♃ 7:07
☊ R 7:12
☿⚼♇ 7:26
☽⚺♂ 9:15
⚳✶♅ 12:17
☽∥♀ 12:55
☽□♄ 13:03
☽✶♆ 14:06
☽△♇ 19:04
☽∥☿ 20:11

26 Su
☽∠⚷ 1:38
☽∠⚳ 4:54
☽☌♀ 7:04
☉⚺☽ 8:48
☽#♇ 11:59
☽✶♃ 13:28
☽∠♂ 17:17
☉∥☽ 17:43

27 M
☽⚼♇ 1:13
☽☌☿ 7:23
☽✶⚷ 7:57
☽⚺♅ 10:45
☿✶⚷ 11:48
☽⚺⚳ 12:21
♂✶♄ 22:30

28 Tu
☽△♄ 1:24
☽✶♂ 1:36
☽□♆ 2:39
☽∥⚳ 4:23
☽⚻♇ 7:34
♆ R 7:56
☿⚺♅ 9:03
☽∠♅ 17:17
♂⚺♆ 19:09
♂∥⚷ 23:24

29 W
☉□♃ 1:01
☽⚺♀ 2:38
☽□♃ 2:45
☉☌☽ 2:53
♀✶♃ 3:53
☿⚺⚳ 7:37
☽⚼♄ 7:45
☉⚺♀ 14:10
☽□⚷ 20:55
☽✶♅ 23:49

30 Th
☽☌⚳ 3:33
☽∥⚳ 5:22
☽⚺☿ 6:01
☽∠♀ 12:26
☽⚻♄ 14:02
☽△♆ 15:29
☽□♂ 18:18
☽☍♇ 20:15

LONGITUDE — July 2022

Day	Sid.Time	☉	☽	☽ 12 hour	Mean ☊	True ☊	☿	♀	♂	⚳	♃	♄	⚷	♅	♆	♇
	h m s	° ' "	° ' "	° ' "	° '	° '	° '	° '	° '	° '	° '	° '	° '	° '	° '	° '
1 F	18 36 07	9♋10 23	29♋39 48	5♌37 27	19♉56.7	21♉28.9	22♊03.8	9♊30.8	27♈00.3	19♋55.2	7♈28.8	24♒42.8	16♈17.0	17♉44.7	25♓26.4	27♑48.1
2 Sa	18 40 03	10 07 37	11♌36 23	17 36 51	19 53.5	21R 19.9	23 50.7	10 42.5	27 42.7	20 21.7	7 33.9	24R 40.3	16 18.0	17 47.1	25R 26.3	27R 46.8
3 Su	18 44 00	11 04 50	23 39 08	29 43 31	19 50.4	21 11.6	25 40.6	11 54.3	28 25.0	20 48.1	7 38.8	24 37.8	16 18.8	17 49.5	25 26.2	27 45.4
4 M	18 47 57	12 02 03	5♍50 22	12♍00 02	19 47.2	21 04.6	27 33.3	13 06.1	29 07.2	21 14.6	7 43.6	24 35.1	16 19.7	17 51.8	25 26.0	27 44.1
5 Tu	18 51 53	12 59 16	18 12 54	24 29 25	19 44.0	20 59.6	29 28.6	14 17.9	29 49.3	21 41.0	7 48.2	24 32.4	16 20.4	17 54.1	25 25.8	27 42.7
6 W	18 55 50	13 56 28	0♎50 00	7♎15 06	19 40.8	20 56.8	1♋26.5	15 29.8	0♉31.4	22 07.5	7 52.6	24 29.7	16 21.2	17 56.4	25 25.6	27 41.3
7 Th	18 59 46	14 53 41	13 45 09	20 20 37	19 37.6	20D 55.9	3 26.7	16 41.7	1 13.3	22 34.0	7 56.8	24 26.8	16 21.9	17 58.7	25 25.3	27 39.9
8 F	19 03 43	15 50 53	27 01 53	3♏49 17	19 34.5	20 56.3	5 29.0	17 53.7	1 55.1	23 00.6	8 00.9	24 23.8	16 22.5	18 00.9	25 25.0	27 38.5
9 Sa	19 07 39	16 48 05	10♏43 05	17 43 27	19 31.3	20R 57.2	7 33.1	19 05.7	2 36.8	23 27.1	8 04.8	24 20.8	16 23.1	18 03.0	25 24.7	27 37.1
10 Su	19 11 36	17 45 16	24 50 24	2♐03 48	19 28.1	20 57.4	9 38.9	20 17.7	3 18.4	23 53.7	8 08.5	24 17.8	16 23.6	18 05.2	25 24.3	27 35.7
11 M	19 15 32	18 42 28	9♐23 19	16 48 26	19 24.9	20 56.1	11 45.9	21 29.8	3 59.9	24 20.3	8 12.0	24 14.6	16 24.1	18 07.3	25 23.9	27 34.3
12 Tu	19 19 29	19 39 40	24 18 25	1♑52 19	19 21.8	20 52.6	13 53.9	22 41.9	4 41.4	24 46.9	8 15.3	24 11.4	16 24.5	18 09.3	25 23.5	27 32.9
13 W	19 23 26	20 36 52	9♑29 02	17 07 18	19 18.6	20 46.8	16 02.6	23 54.0	5 22.7	25 13.5	8 18.5	24 08.1	16 24.9	18 11.3	25 23.1	27 31.5
14 Th	19 27 22	21 34 04	24 45 46	2♒23 00	19 15.4	20 39.0	18 11.7	25 06.2	6 03.9	25 40.1	8 21.4	24 04.7	16 25.2	18 13.3	25 22.6	27 30.1
15 F	19 31 19	22 31 16	9♒57 40	17 28 29	19 12.2	20 30.1	20 20.9	26 18.4	6 44.9	26 06.8	8 24.2	24 01.3	16 25.4	18 15.2	25 22.1	27 28.6
16 Sa	19 35 15	23 28 28	24 54 19	2♓14 14	19 09.1	20 21.2	22 30.0	27 30.7	7 25.9	26 33.4	8 26.8	23 57.8	16 25.7	18 17.1	25 21.5	27 27.2
17 Su	19 39 12	24 25 41	9♓27 29	16 33 36	19 05.9	20 13.4	24 38.6	28 43.0	8 06.8	27 00.1	8 29.2	23 54.3	16 25.8	18 19.0	25 21.0	27 25.8
18 M	19 43 08	25 22 55	23 32 17	0♈23 28	19 02.7	20 07.5	26 46.6	29 55.3	8 47.5	27 26.8	8 31.5	23 50.7	16 25.9	18 20.8	25 20.4	27 24.3
19 Tu	19 47 05	26 20 09	7♈07 17	13 43 59	18 59.5	20 03.8	28 53.7	1♋07.7	9 28.2	27 53.5	8 33.5	23 47.0	16R 26.0	18 22.6	25 19.7	27 22.9
20 W	19 51 01	27 17 24	20 13 59	26 37 45	18 56.3	20D 02.2	0♌59.7	2 20.1	10 08.7	28 20.2	8 35.3	23 43.2	16 26.0	18 24.3	25 19.1	27 21.5
21 Th	19 54 58	28 14 40	2♉55 52	9♉08 56	18 53.2	20 02.0	3 04.6	3 32.6	10 49.0	28 47.0	8 37.0	23 39.5	16 26.0	18 26.0	25 18.4	27 20.0
22 F	19 58 55	29 11 56	15 17 35	21 22 27	18 50.0	20R 02.4	5 08.2	4 45.1	11 29.3	29 13.7	8 38.4	23 35.6	16 25.9	18 27.6	25 17.6	27 18.6
23 Sa	20 02 51	0♌09 14	27 24 09	3♊23 19	18 46.8	20 02.3	7 10.4	5 57.7	12 09.4	29 40.5	8 39.7	23 31.7	16 25.7	18 29.2	25 16.9	27 17.2
24 Su	20 06 48	1 06 32	9♊20 30	15 16 15	18 43.6	20 00.6	9 11.0	7 10.3	12 49.4	0♌07.2	8 40.7	23 27.8	16 25.5	18 30.7	25 16.1	27 15.7
25 M	20 10 44	2 03 51	21 11 04	27 05 24	18 40.5	19 56.6	11 10.2	8 22.9	13 29.2	0 34.0	8 41.6	23 23.8	16 25.3	18 32.2	25 15.3	27 14.3
26 Tu	20 14 41	3 01 11	2♋59 40	8♋54 13	18 37.3	19 50.0	13 07.7	9 35.6	14 09.0	1 00.8	8 42.2	23 19.8	16 25.0	18 33.7	25 14.5	27 12.9
27 W	20 18 37	3 58 31	14 49 21	20 45 22	18 34.1	19 40.6	15 03.6	10 48.3	14 48.5	1 27.6	8 42.7	23 15.7	16 24.6	18 35.1	25 13.6	27 11.4
28 Th	20 22 34	4 55 52	26 42 29	2♌40 54	18 30.9	19 29.1	16 57.8	12 01.0	15 27.9	1 54.4	8R 43.0	23 11.6	16 24.2	18 36.5	25 12.7	27 10.0
29 F	20 26 30	5 53 14	8♌40 47	14 42 17	18 27.8	19 16.1	18 50.3	13 13.8	16 07.2	2 21.3	8 43.1	23 07.4	16 23.7	18 37.8	25 11.8	27 08.6
30 Sa	20 30 27	6 50 37	20 45 33	26 50 41	18 24.6	19 02.8	20 41.2	14 26.7	16 46.3	2 48.1	8 42.9	23 03.2	16 23.2	18 39.1	25 10.9	27 07.2
31 Su	20 34 24	7♌48 01	2♍57 52	9♍07 13	18♉21.4	18♉50.2	22♌30.4	15♋39.5	17♉25.3	3♌14.9	8♈42.6	22♒59.0	16♈22.7	18♉40.3	25♓09.9	27♑05.8

1st of Month

Julian Day # 2459761.5
Obliquity 23°26'6"
SVP 4♓56'56"
GC 27♐09.2
Eris 24♈59.3

Day	⚴	⚵	⚶
1	28♉02.7	19♓37.1	6♓42.7
6	0♊24.5	20 17.9	6 53.0
11	2 46.8	20 50.3	6 51.6R
16	5 09.6	21 13.7	6 38.2R
21	7 32.8	21 27.6	6 13.0R
26	9 56.4	21 31.4R	5 36.2R
31	12 20.1	21 24.5R	4 48.6R

DECLINATION and LATITUDE

Day	☉ Decl	☽ Decl	☽ Lat	☽ 12h Decl	☿ Decl	☿ Lat	♀ Decl	♀ Lat	♂ Decl	♂ Lat	⚳ Decl	⚳ Lat	♃ Decl	♃ Lat	♄ Decl	♄ Lat
1 F	23N07	24N52	4N45	23N38	22N09	1S03	20N31	1S22	8N43	1S49	26N11	4N16	1N47	1S18	14S25	1S12
2 Sa	23 03	22 08	5 02	20 24	22 27	0 50	20 44	1 20	8 58	1 49	26 08	4 18	1 49	1 18	14 26	1 12
3 Su	22 59	18 27	5 06	16 18	22 44	0 38	20 56	1 18	9 13	1 49	26 06	4 19	1 50	1 18	14 27	1 13
4 M	22 54	13 58	4 57	11 28	22 59	0 26	21 07	1 15	9 28	1 49	26 03	4 21	1 52	1 18	14 28	1 13
5 Tu	22 48	8 51	4 33	6 06	23 12	0 14	21 18	1 13	9 43	1 49	26 00	4 22	1 53	1 19	14 29	1 13
6 W	22 43	3 16	3 56	0 22	23 23	0 03	21 29	1 11	9 58	1 49	25 57	4 23	1 55	1 19	14 30	1 13
7 Th	22 36	2S34	3 06	5S32	23 32	0N09	21 38	1 08	10 12	1 48	25 54	4 25	1 56	1 19	14 31	1 13
8 F	22 30	8 28	2 05	11 22	23 39	0 20	21 47	1 06	10 27	1 48	25 51	4 26	1 58	1 20	14 33	1 13
9 Sa	22 23	14 10	0 55	16 50	23 43	0 30	21 56	1 04	10 41	1 48	25 48	4 28	1 59	1 20	14 34	1 14
10 Su	22 16	19 19	0S21	21 32	23 45	0 40	22 04	1 01	10 55	1 48	25 45	4 29	2 00	1 20	14 35	1 14
11 M	22 08	23 27	1 37	25 00	23 44	0 50	22 11	0 59	11 10	1 48	25 41	4 31	2 01	1 20	14 36	1 14
12 Tu	21 60	26 07	2 48	26 46	23 41	0 58	22 18	0 56	11 24	1 48	25 38	4 32	2 02	1 21	14 37	1 14
13 W	21 51	26 54	3 49	26 32	23 35	1 07	22 24	0 53	11 38	1 47	25 34	4 34	2 03	1 21	14 39	1 14
14 Th	21 43	25 40	4 34	24 19	23 26	1 14	22 30	0 51	11 51	1 47	25 31	4 35	2 04	1 21	14 40	1 14
15 F	21 33	22 32	4 59	20 24	23 14	1 21	22 35	0 48	12 05	1 47	25 27	4 37	2 05	1 22	14 41	1 15
16 Sa	21 24	17 58	5 03	15 18	22 59	1 27	22 39	0 46	12 18	1 47	25 23	4 38	2 06	1 22	14 42	1 15
17 Su	21 14	12 27	4 47	9 29	22 42	1 32	22 43	0 43	12 32	1 46	25 19	4 39	2 06	1 22	14 44	1 15
18 M	21 04	6 27	4 14	3 24	22 23	1 37	22 46	0 40	12 45	1 46	25 16	4 41	2 07	1 23	14 45	1 15
19 Tu	20 53	0 21	3 28	2N39	22 01	1 40	22 48	0 38	12 58	1 46	25 12	4 42	2 07	1 23	14 46	1 15
20 W	20 42	5N34	2 32	8 23	21 37	1 43	22 50	0 35	13 11	1 46	25 08	4 44	2 08	1 23	14 48	1 15
21 Th	20 31	11 05	1 30	13 38	21 11	1 46	22 51	0 32	13 24	1 45	25 03	4 45	2 08	1 23	14 49	1 15
22 F	20 19	16 01	0 25	18 13	20 43	1 47	22 51	0 30	13 37	1 45	24 59	4 47	2 09	1 24	14 51	1 16
23 Sa	20 07	20 13	0N39	21 59	20 13	1 48	22 51	0 27	13 49	1 45	24 55	4 48	2 09	1 24	14 52	1 16
24 Su	19 55	23 31	1 41	24 46	19 41	1 48	22 50	0 24	14 02	1 44	24 51	4 50	2 09	1 24	14 53	1 16
25 M	19 42	25 46	2 37	26 27	19 08	1 47	22 49	0 22	14 14	1 44	24 46	4 52	2 09	1 25	14 55	1 16
26 Tu	19 29	26 51	3 27	26 56	18 34	1 46	22 47	0 19	14 26	1 44	24 42	4 53	2 09	1 25	14 56	1 16
27 W	19 16	26 43	4 07	26 11	17 59	1 44	22 44	0 16	14 38	1 43	24 37	4 55	2 09	1 25	14 58	1 16
28 Th	19 02	25 21	4 37	24 14	17 22	1 42	22 40	0 13	14 50	1 43	24 32	4 56	2 09	1 25	14 59	1 16
29 F	18 48	22 50	4 55	21 11	16 45	1 39	22 36	0 11	15 02	1 42	24 28	4 58	2 09	1 26	15 01	1 16
30 Sa	18 34	19 19	5 00	17 13	16 06	1 35	22 31	0 08	15 13	1 42	24 23	4 59	2 08	1 26	15 02	1 17
31 Su	18N19	14N56	4N51	12N30	15N27	1N31	22N26	0S05	15N25	1S41	24N18	5N01	2N08	1S26	15S04	1S17

Day	⚷ Decl	⚷ Lat	♅ Decl	♅ Lat	♆ Decl	♆ Lat	♇ Decl	♇ Lat
1	8N12	1N57	16N47	0S22	2S54	1S11	22S40	2S06
6	8 14	1 57	16 50	0 22	2 54	1 11	22 41	2 07
11	8 15	1 58	16 53	0 22	2 55	1 11	22 43	2 07
16	8 16	1 58	16 55	0 22	2 56	1 12	22 45	2 08
21	8 17	1 58	16 58	0 22	2 58	1 12	22 47	2 08
26	8 16	1 58	16 60	0 22	2 60	1 12	22 49	2 09
31	8N16	1N58	17N02	0S22	3S02	1S12	22S51	2S09

Day	⚴ Decl	⚴ Lat	⚵ Decl	⚵ Lat	⚶ Decl	⚶ Lat	Eris Decl	Eris Lat
1	1S22	21S35	1N55	6N33	13S57	5S17	0S47	11S13
6	1 33	22 14	2 04	6 25	14 15	5 41	0 47	11 13
11	1 48	22 55	2 08	6 16	14 39	6 06	0 47	11 14
16	2 06	23 36	2 08	6 06	15 07	6 31	0 47	11 14
21	2 28	24 20	2 02	5 54	15 40	6 56	0 48	11 15
26	2 53	25 04	1 51	5 40	16 17	7 21	0 48	11 15
31	3S22	25S51	1N34	5N24	16S57	7S45	0S49	11S16

Moon Phenomena

Max/0 Decl

dy	hr mn	
6	13:32	0 S
12	21:19	26S55
19	1:24	0 N
26	9:19	26N57

Perigee/Apogee

dy	hr m		kilometers
13	9:07	p	357269
26	10:23	a	406275

Max/0 Lat

dy	hr mn	
2	19:11	5N07
9	17:28	0 S
15	16:42	5S04
22	9:22	0 N
29	20:41	5N00

PH	dy	hr mn	
☽	7	2:15	14♎59
○	13	18:39	21♑21
☾	20	14:20	27♈52
●	28	17:56	5♌39

Void of Course Moon

Last Aspect			☽ Ingress		
30 20:15	♇	☍	♌	1	0:41
3 10:00	♂	△	♍	3	12:32
5 18:05	♇	△	♎	5	22:26
8 1:05	♇	□	♏	8	5:16
10 4:35	♇	⚹	♐	10	8:35
12 1:44	♆	□	♑	12	9:02
14 4:18	♇	☌	♒	14	8:14
16 4:38	♀	△	♓	16	8:19
18 6:44	♇	⚹	♈	18	11:19
20 14:20	☉	□	♉	20	18:24
22 23:46	♇	△	♊	23	5:12
25 8:16	♆	□	♋	25	17:55
28 0:55	♇	☍	♌	28	6:37
30 4:30	♄	☍	♍	30	18:12

DAILY ASPECTARIAN

1 F
☉⚼♄ 13:02
☽△♃ 15:50
☉∥☽ 16:43
☽∠☿ 17:29
☽#♇ 19:59
☉⚺☽ 20:47
☽⚼♆ 21:40
☽∥☿ 21:49
☽⚹♀ 22:00

2 Sa
♂□♇ 2:15
☽∥♀ 9:19
☽△⚷ 9:23
☿△♄ 10:40
☽□♅ 12:23
☽⚺⚳ 18:08
☿#♇ 18:44
☿□♆ 20:54
☽⚼♃ 22:00

3 Su
☽☍♄ 1:56
☽⚻♆ 3:32
☽⚹☿ 4:44
☉∠☽ 5:13
☽⚻♇ 8:06
☽∥♅ 9:16
☽△♂ 10:00
☽⚼⚷ 15:09
♀⚼♇ 16:46
☉∥☿ 17:46
☽#♄ 21:28

4 M
☽∠⚳ 0:49
☿⚻♇ 2:14
☽⚻♃ 3:43
☉⚹☽ 13:04
☽⚼♇ 13:24
☽□♀ 15:39
☽⚼♂ 17:04
☽∥♂ 20:16
☽⚻⚷ 20:23
☽△♅ 23:24

5 Tu
☽∥⚷ 2:44
♀ ♊ 3:17
♂ ♉ 6:05
☿ ♋ 6:26
☿⚹♂ 6:38
☽⚹⚳ 6:53
☽⚻♄ 12:03
☽☍♆ 13:47
☽△♇ 18:05
☽⚻♂ 23:23

6 W
♀∠♂ 1:15
☽□☿ 1:21
☽#♆ 1:32
☉#♇ 3:56
☽⚼♅ 3:58
☽∥♃ 5:38
☽☍♃ 13:14
☽⚼♄ 16:06
♀⚹⚷ 17:18
☿∠♅ 18:20
☽#♃ 21:26

7 Th
☽∥♆ 1:23
☊ D 2:07
☉□☽ 2:15
☽☍⚷ 4:47
☽△♀ 5:55
☽⚻♅ 7:44
☽□⚳ 16:33
☽△♄ 19:19
☽⚻♆ 21:07
⚶ R 21:31
☽#⚷ 23:03

8 F
☽□♇ 1:05
♀⚺♅ 2:29
☽#♂ 8:29
☽☍♂ 9:07
☽⚼♀ 11:22
☉□⚷ 13:24
☽△☿ 17:32
☽⚻♃ 19:25
☽⚼♆ 23:28

9 Sa
☽∥♄ 1:43
☿□♃ 6:15
☽⚻⚷ 9:43
☉△☽ 11:11
☽#♅ 12:07
☽☍♅ 12:35
☽⚻♀ 15:39
☊ R 17:30
☿⚼♄ 20:05
☽⚼♃ 21:08
☽△⚳ 22:22
☽□♄ 23:06
☽⚼☿ 23:37

10 Su
☽△♆ 0:57
☽⚹♇ 4:35
☉⚹♅ 8:40
☽⚼⚷ 10:54
☉⚼☽ 14:03
☽⚻♂ 14:45
☽#♀ 15:36
☉#☽ 15:46
☉∥♀ 18:21
☽∥♇ 19:09
⚳⚻♄ 19:26
☽△♃ 22:03
☽⚼⚳ 23:55

11 M
☽#☿ 1:59
☽⚻☿ 4:30
☽∠♇ 5:09
☽△⚷ 11:21
☽⚻♅ 14:09
☉⚻☽ 16:04
☽⚼♂ 16:16
☽#⚳ 18:19
☽☍♀ 21:13
☽⚹♄ 23:49

12 Tu
☽⚻⚳ 0:47
☽□♆ 1:44
☽⚺♇ 5:09
☽⚼♅ 14:03
☽△♂ 17:14
☽□♃ 22:09
☽∠♄ 23:27

13 W
☿□⚷ 4:09
♀△♄ 4:29
⚳△♆ 8:29
☽□⚷ 10:54
☽☍☿ 12:00
☽△♅ 13:42
☉☍☽ 18:39
☽⚺♄ 22:56

14 Th
☿⚹♅ 0:18
☽⚻♀ 0:35
☽⚹♆ 0:58
☽☍⚳ 1:28
☽#⚳ 1:34
☽☌♇ 4:18
♀□♆ 5:25
♀⚺⚳ 17:53
☽□♂ 18:40
☽#☿ 19:21
☽⚹♃ 21:31
☽∥♇ 22:43
☽#♀ 23:46

15 F
☽∠♆ 0:39
☽⚼♀ 2:20
☉#☽ 5:59
☽⚹⚷ 10:19
☽□♅ 13:17
☽⚻☿ 19:26
☉⚻☽ 21:31
☽∠♃ 21:38
☽☌♄ 22:29
♀⚻♇ 22:52

16 Sa
☽⚺♆ 0:44
☽⚻⚳ 2:46
☽⚺♇ 4:09
☽△♀ 4:38
☽#♅ 4:48
☽∠⚷ 10:40
☉⚻♄ 11:36
☽∥♄ 14:30
☿⚻♄ 15:56
☉☌☿ 19:39
☿#♇ 19:44
☽⚹♂ 21:38
☽⚺♃ 22:22
☿∥♀ 23:29
☽#♂ 23:41
☉⚼☽ 23:57

17 Su
☽⚼☿ 0:22
☽⚼⚳ 4:25
☽∠♇ 4:59
☿△♆ 7:54
☽⚺⚷ 11:47
♂⚺♃ 14:00
☽⚹♅ 15:02
☽#⚷ 16:50
⚳☍♇ 21:53
☉△♆ 22:56

18 M
☽∠♂ 0:28
☽⚺♄ 0:32
♀ ♋ 1:33
♀#♇ 1:39
☽☌♆ 3:08
☉△☽ 3:27
☽△☿ 6:41
☽⚹♇ 6:44
☿☍♇ 7:02
☽△⚳ 7:03
☿☌⚳ 9:36
☽□♀ 12:16
☽∥♆ 13:45
☽#♃ 17:01
☽∠♅ 17:17

19 Tu
☽☌♃ 2:36
☽∠♄ 2:59
☽⚺♂ 4:28
☽∥♃ 9:56
☿ ♌ 12:36
☽#♆ 13:17
⚷ R 15:23
☽☌⚷ 16:58
☽⚺♅ 20:36

20 W
☉☍♇ 1:40
♂∠♆ 6:04
☽⚹♄ 6:29
☽⚺♆ 9:31
☽∥⚷ 11:32
☽□♇ 13:21
☉□☽ 14:20
☊ D 14:28
☽□⚳ 15:48
♀∠♅ 21:45

21 Th
☽□☿ 0:20
☽⚹♀ 1:18
☽⚺♃ 10:59
♃∠♄ 11:18
☽∥♂ 11:22
☿⚺♀ 13:04
☽∠♆ 14:14
☽☌♂ 16:07
☽#♄ 17:57

22 F
☉☌⚳ 1:24
☽⚺⚷ 2:14
☽∥♅ 5:05
☽☌♅ 6:15
☊ R 9:23
☽∠♀ 9:46
☽□♄ 16:19
☽∠♃ 16:32
☽⚹♆ 19:46
☉ ♌ 20:08
☉∥☽ 23:25
☽△♇ 23:46

23 Sa
☽∥☿ 0:01
☽⚹⚳ 4:43
☉⚹☽ 5:59
☉∥☿ 7:36
☽∠⚷ 8:04
⚳ ♌ 17:30
☿△♃ 17:53
☽#♇ 18:12
☽∥♀ 18:32
☽⚺♀ 19:07
☽⚹♃ 22:40
☽⚹☿ 23:37

24 Su
☽⚼♇ 5:54
☽⚺♂ 7:28
☽∠⚳ 12:09
☽∥⚳ 12:21
☿⚼♆ 12:59
☽⚹⚷ 14:20
☉∠☽ 14:54
☽⚺♅ 18:37

25 M
♀⚼♄ 0:17
♀#♇ 2:14
☽△♄ 4:28
♀□♃ 6:14
⚵ R 6:50
☽□♆ 8:16
☽∠☿ 12:09
☽⚻♇ 12:17
☽∠♂ 15:43
☽⚺⚳ 19:49

26 Tu
☉⚺☽ 0:03
☽∠♅ 1:09
☽⚼♄ 10:46
☽□♃ 11:36
☽☌♀ 14:56
☿□♂ 19:14
☽⚹♂ 23:58

27 W
☽⚺☿ 0:34
☽□⚷ 3:13
☽⚹♅ 7:38
☿△⚷ 16:56
☽⚻♄ 16:57
☽△♆ 20:59

28 Th
☽☍♇ 0:55
☽∥⚳ 9:13
☽☌⚳ 10:51
☿∥♅ 13:35
☉☌☽ 17:56
♃ R 20:39
☿□♅ 21:17
♂#♄ 22:00

29 F
☽#♇ 0:00
☽△♃ 0:05
☽∥♀ 1:51
☽⚼♆ 3:01
♂⚺⚷ 10:00
☽⚺♀ 10:05
☽△⚷ 15:21
☽□♂ 15:39
☽□♅ 19:49
☽☌☿ 23:50

30 Sa
☽☍♄ 4:30
☉∥☽ 4:42
☽⚼♃ 5:50
☽⚻♆ 8:43
☽⚻♇ 12:31
☽∥♅ 13:03
☽∠♀ 18:59
☽⚼⚷ 20:54
☽∥☿ 20:58
☽∥♂ 21:42
☽#♄ 23:23

31 Su
☽⚺⚳ 0:35
☿∥♂ 1:10
☿☍♄ 6:06
☉⚺☽ 10:14
☽⚻♃ 11:12
☿#♄ 13:31
♀□⚷ 14:06
☿⚼♃ 16:01
☽⚼♇ 17:45
☉△♃ 22:37

August 2022

LONGITUDE

Day	Sid.Time h m s	☉ ° ' "	☽ ° ' "	☽ 12 hour ° ' "	Mean☊ ° '	True☊ ° '	☿ ° '	♀ ° '	♂ ° '	⚳ ° '	♃ ° '	♄ ° '	⚷ ° '	♅ ° '	♆ ° '	♇ ° '
1 M	20 38 20	8♌45 25	15♍18 55	21♍33 09	18♉18.2	18♉39.5	24♌17.9	16♋52.4	18♉04.1	3♌41.7	8♈42.1	22♒54.7	16♈22.1	18♉41.5	25♓08.9	27♑04.4
2 Tu	20 42 17	9 42 49	27 50 10	4♎10 11	18 15.0	18R 31.3	26 03.7	18 05.4	18 42.8	4 08.6	8R 41.4	22R 50.4	16R 21.4	18 42.6	25R 07.9	27R 03.0
3 W	20 46 13	10 40 15	10♎33 32	17 00 29	18 11.9	18 26.0	27 47.9	19 18.3	19 21.2	4 35.4	8 40.4	22 46.1	16 20.7	18 43.7	25 06.8	27 01.6
4 Th	20 50 10	11 37 41	23 31 24	0♏06 38	18 08.7	18 23.2	29 30.5	20 31.3	19 59.6	5 02.3	8 39.3	22 41.7	16 19.9	18 44.7	25 05.8	27 00.2
5 F	20 54 06	12 35 08	6♏46 30	13 31 20	18 05.5	18 22.3	1♍11.4	21 44.4	20 37.7	5 29.1	8 38.0	22 37.3	16 19.1	18 45.7	25 04.7	26 58.8
6 Sa	20 58 03	13 32 35	20 21 26	27 17 01	18 02.3	18 22.3	2 50.6	22 57.5	21 15.7	5 55.9	8 36.5	22 32.9	16 18.2	18 46.7	25 03.5	26 57.5
7 Su	21 01 59	14 30 03	4♐18 13	11♐25 02	17 59.2	18 21.8	4 28.3	24 10.6	21 53.5	6 22.8	8 34.8	22 28.5	16 17.3	18 47.6	25 02.4	26 56.1
8 M	21 05 56	15 27 32	18 37 22	25 54 53	17 56.0	18 19.7	6 04.3	25 23.7	22 31.1	6 49.6	8 32.9	22 24.1	16 16.4	18 48.4	25 01.2	26 54.8
9 Tu	21 09 53	16 25 02	3♑17 08	10♑43 27	17 52.8	18 15.3	7 38.7	26 36.9	23 08.6	7 16.5	8 30.8	22 19.6	16 15.4	18 49.2	25 00.1	26 53.4
10 W	21 13 49	17 22 32	18 12 59	25 44 41	17 49.6	18 08.1	9 11.4	27 50.2	23 45.9	7 43.3	8 28.5	22 15.2	16 14.3	18 50.0	24 58.9	26 52.1
11 Th	21 17 46	18 20 04	3♒17 25	10♒49 56	17 46.5	17 58.7	10 42.6	29 03.4	24 23.0	8 10.2	8 26.0	22 10.7	16 13.2	18 50.7	24 57.6	26 50.8
12 F	21 21 42	19 17 36	18 20 58	25 49 14	17 43.3	17 47.8	12 12.1	0♌16.7	24 59.9	8 37.0	8 23.4	22 06.2	16 12.0	18 51.3	24 56.4	26 49.5
13 Sa	21 25 39	20 15 10	3♓13 34	10♓32 57	17 40.1	17 36.8	13 39.9	1 30.1	25 36.7	9 03.9	8 20.5	22 01.7	16 10.8	18 51.9	24 55.1	26 48.2
14 Su	21 29 35	21 12 45	17 46 31	24 53 35	17 36.9	17 26.9	15 06.1	2 43.5	26 13.2	9 30.7	8 17.5	21 57.2	16 09.6	18 52.5	24 53.8	26 46.9
15 M	21 33 32	22 10 21	1♈53 43	8♈46 40	17 33.7	17 19.1	16 30.6	3 56.9	26 49.6	9 57.5	8 14.2	21 52.7	16 08.3	18 53.0	24 52.5	26 45.7
16 Tu	21 37 28	23 07 58	15 32 23	22 10 59	17 30.6	17 13.8	17 53.5	5 10.3	27 25.7	10 24.4	8 10.8	21 48.2	16 07.0	18 53.4	24 51.2	26 44.4
17 W	21 41 25	24 05 37	28 42 45	5♉08 06	17 27.4	17 10.9	19 14.5	6 23.8	28 01.7	10 51.2	8 07.2	21 43.7	16 05.6	18 53.8	24 49.8	26 43.2
18 Th	21 45 22	25 03 17	11♉27 32	17 41 37	17 24.2	17D 10.0	20 33.8	7 37.4	28 37.5	11 18.0	8 03.4	21 39.2	16 04.1	18 54.2	24 48.4	26 41.9
19 F	21 49 18	26 01 00	23 50 59	29 56 18	17 21.0	17R 10.0	21 51.3	8 51.0	29 13.0	11 44.8	7 59.5	21 34.8	16 02.7	18 54.5	24 47.1	26 40.7
20 Sa	21 53 15	26 58 43	5♊58 13	11♊57 25	17 17.9	17 09.7	23 06.9	10 04.6	29 48.3	12 11.7	7 55.3	21 30.3	16 01.1	18 54.7	24 45.6	26 39.5
21 Su	21 57 11	27 56 29	17 54 33	23 50 15	17 14.7	17 08.2	24 20.6	11 18.2	0♊23.4	12 38.5	7 51.0	21 25.8	15 59.6	18 54.9	24 44.2	26 38.3
22 M	22 01 08	28 54 16	29 45 07	5♋39 43	17 11.5	17 04.6	25 32.2	12 31.9	0 58.3	13 05.3	7 46.5	21 21.4	15 58.0	18 55.1	24 42.8	26 37.2
23 Tu	22 05 04	29 52 05	11♋34 33	17 30 06	17 08.3	16 58.4	26 41.8	13 45.7	1 33.0	13 32.1	7 41.8	21 16.9	15 56.3	18 55.2	24 41.3	26 36.0
24 W	22 09 01	0♍49 55	23 26 46	29 24 55	17 05.2	16 49.6	27 49.3	14 59.4	2 07.4	13 58.9	7 37.0	21 12.5	15 54.6	18R 55.2	24 39.9	26 34.9
25 Th	22 12 57	1 47 47	5♌24 52	11♌26 50	17 02.0	16 38.5	28 54.6	16 13.3	2 41.6	14 25.6	7 32.0	21 08.1	15 52.9	18 55.2	24 38.4	26 33.8
26 F	22 16 54	2 45 40	17 31 02	23 37 38	16 58.8	16 25.9	29 57.3	17 27.1	3 15.5	14 52.4	7 26.8	21 03.8	15 51.1	18 55.2	24 36.9	26 32.7
27 Sa	22 20 51	3 43 35	29 46 42	5♍58 21	16 55.6	16 13.0	0♎57.6	18 41.0	3 49.2	15 19.2	7 21.5	20 59.4	15 49.3	18 55.1	24 35.4	26 31.6
28 Su	22 24 47	4 41 32	12♍12 37	18 29 32	16 52.4	16 00.8	1 55.3	19 54.9	4 22.6	15 45.9	7 16.0	20 55.1	15 47.5	18 55.0	24 33.9	26 30.5
29 M	22 28 44	5 39 30	24 49 06	1♎11 22	16 49.3	15 50.3	2 50.2	21 08.8	4 55.7	16 12.6	7 10.3	20 50.8	15 45.6	18 54.8	24 32.3	26 29.5
30 Tu	22 32 40	6 37 29	7♎36 22	14 04 08	16 46.1	15 42.4	3 42.2	22 22.8	5 28.6	16 39.4	7 04.6	20 46.6	15 43.6	18 54.5	24 30.8	26 28.4
31 W	22 36 37	7♍35 30	20 34 45	27 08 20	16♉42.9	15♉37.3	4♎31.0	23♌36.8	6♊01.2	17♌06.1	6♈58.6	20♒42.4	15♈41.7	18♉54.2	24♓29.2	26♑27.4

1st of Month

Julian Day #
2459792.5
Obliquity
23°26'[illegible]7"
SVP 4♓56'51"
GC 27♐09.3
Eris 25♈00.9R

Day	⚴	⚵	⚶
1	12♊48.9	21♓21.8R	4♓37.9R
6	15 12.6	21 01.9R	3 39.0R
11	17 36.3	20 31.4R	2 32.8R
16	19 59.6	19 50.4R	1 21.2R
21	22 22.6	18 59.8R	0 06.6R
26	24 44.9	18 00.5R	28♒51.7R
31	27 06.2	16 54.1R	27 39.0R

DECLINATION and LATITUDE

Day	☉ Decl	☽ Decl	☽ Lat	☽12h Decl	☿ Decl	☿ Lat	♀ Decl	♀ Lat	♂ Decl	♂ Lat	⚳ Decl	⚳ Lat	♃ Decl	♃ Lat	♄ Decl	♄ Lat
1 M	18N04	9N55	4N29	7N13	14N47	1N27	22N20	0S03	15N36	1S41	24N13	5N02	2N07	1S27	15S05	1S17
2 Tu	17 49	4 26	3 53	1 34	14 07	1 22	22 13	0 00	15 47	1 40	24 08	5 04	2 07	1 27	15 07	1 17
3 W	17 34	1S20	3 06	4S15	13 26	1 17	22 05	0N03	15 58	1 40	24 03	5 05	2 06	1 27	15 08	1 17
4 Th	17 18	7 10	2 07	10 02	12 45	1 11	21 57	0 05	16 08	1 39	23 58	5 07	2 05	1 28	15 10	1 17
5 F	17 02	12 49	1 01	15 29	12 04	1 05	21 49	0 08	16 19	1 39	23 53	5 09	2 05	1 28	15 11	1 17
6 Sa	16 45	18 00	0S10	20 19	11 22	0 58	21 39	0 10	16 30	1 38	23 48	5 10	2 04	1 28	15 13	1 17
7 Su	16 29	22 22	1 23	24 06	10 40	0 51	21 29	0 13	16 40	1 38	23 42	5 12	2 03	1 28	15 14	1 17
8 M	16 12	25 29	2 32	26 27	9 58	0 44	21 19	0 15	16 50	1 37	23 37	5 13	2 02	1 29	15 16	1 18
9 Tu	15 55	26 57	3 33	26 58	9 16	0 37	21 08	0 18	16 60	1 37	23 31	5 15	2 01	1 29	15 18	1 18
10 W	15 38	26 30	4 21	25 33	8 34	0 29	20 56	0 21	17 10	1 36	23 26	5 17	1 60	1 29	15 19	1 18
11 Th	15 20	24 08	4 51	22 17	7 53	0 21	20 43	0 23	17 19	1 35	23 20	5 18	1 58	1 29	15 21	1 18
12 F	15 02	20 05	5 00	17 34	7 11	0 13	20 30	0 25	17 29	1 35	23 15	5 20	1 57	1 30	15 22	1 18
13 Sa	14 44	14 49	4 49	11 53	6 30	0 04	20 17	0 28	17 38	1 34	23 09	5 21	1 56	1 30	15 24	1 18
14 Su	14 26	8 49	4 20	5 41	5 48	0S04	20 02	0 30	17 47	1 33	23 03	5 23	1 54	1 30	15 25	1 18
15 M	14 07	2 32	3 35	0N36	5 07	0 13	19 48	0 33	17 57	1 33	22 58	5 25	1 53	1 31	15 27	1 18
16 Tu	13 48	3N40	2 39	6 39	4 27	0 22	19 32	0 35	18 05	1 32	22 52	5 26	1 51	1 31	15 28	1 18
17 W	13 29	9 31	1 36	12 14	3 47	0 31	19 16	0 37	18 14	1 31	22 46	5 28	1 50	1 31	15 30	1 18
18 Th	13 10	14 47	0 30	17 09	3 07	0 40	18 60	0 39	18 23	1 31	22 40	5 30	1 48	1 31	15 31	1 18
19 F	12 51	19 18	0N35	21 14	2 28	0 50	18 43	0 42	18 31	1 30	22 34	5 31	1 46	1 32	15 33	1 18
20 Sa	12 31	22 54	1 38	24 19	1 49	0 59	18 25	0 44	18 39	1 29	22 28	5 33	1 44	1 32	15 34	1 19
21 Su	12 11	25 28	2 35	26 19	1 12	1 09	18 07	0 46	18 48	1 28	22 22	5 35	1 42	1 32	15 36	1 19
22 M	11 51	26 51	3 25	27 06	0 34	1 19	17 49	0 48	18 56	1 27	22 15	5 36	1 40	1 32	15 37	1 19
23 Tu	11 31	27 01	4 06	26 38	0S02	1 28	17 30	0 50	19 03	1 27	22 09	5 38	1 38	1 33	15 39	1 19
24 W	11 11	25 57	4 37	24 57	0 38	1 38	17 10	0 52	19 11	1 26	22 03	5 40	1 36	1 33	15 40	1 19
25 Th	10 50	23 41	4 55	22 08	1 13	1 48	16 50	0 54	19 18	1 25	21 57	5 42	1 34	1 33	15 42	1 19
26 F	10 29	20 21	5 01	18 20	1 47	1 58	16 29	0 56	19 26	1 24	21 50	5 43	1 32	1 33	15 43	1 19
27 Sa	10 08	16 07	4 53	13 42	2 20	2 07	16 08	0 58	19 33	1 23	21 44	5 45	1 29	1 33	15 45	1 19
28 Su	9 47	11 09	4 31	8 27	2 52	2 17	15 47	0 59	19 40	1 22	21 37	5 47	1 27	1 34	15 46	1 19
29 M	9 26	5 39	3 55	2 47	3 22	2 27	15 25	1 01	19 47	1 21	21 31	5 49	1 25	1 34	15 48	1 19
30 Tu	9 05	0S09	3 07	3S06	3 52	2 36	15 03	1 03	19 54	1 20	21 24	5 50	1 22	1 34	15 49	1 19
31 W	8N43	6S03	2N09	8S57	4S20	2S46	14N40	1N05	20N00	1S19	21N18	5N52	1N20	1S34	15S50	1S19

Day	⚷ Decl	⚷ Lat	♅ Decl	♅ Lat	♆ Decl	♆ Lat	♇ Decl	♇ Lat
1	8N15	1N58	17N02	0S22	3S02	1S12	22S51	2S09
6	8 14	1 58	17 03	0 22	3 04	1 12	22 53	2 09
11	8 12	1 59	17 04	0 22	3 07	1 13	22 54	2 10
16	8 10	1 59	17 05	0 22	3 10	1 13	22 56	2 10
21	8 07	1 59	17 06	0 22	3 12	1 13	22 58	2 10
26	8 04	1 59	17 06	0 22	3 15	1 13	22 59	2 11
31	8N00	1N59	17N05	0S22	3S19	1S13	23S00	2S11

Day	⚴ Decl	⚴ Lat	⚵ Decl	⚵ Lat	⚶ Decl	⚶ Lat	Eris Decl	Eris Lat
1	3S29	26S00	1N30	5N21	17S05	7S49	0S49	11S16
6	4 02	26 48	1 05	5 03	17 47	8 11	0 49	11 16
11	4 40	27 38	0 34	4 42	18 30	8 31	0 50	11 16
16	5 21	28 29	0S03	4 19	19 12	8 49	0 51	11 17
21	6 06	29 22	0 46	3 53	19 53	9 03	0 52	11 17
26	6 55	30 16	1 35	3 25	20 31	9 15	0 52	11 17
31	7S47	31S12	2S29	2N55	21S05	9S23	0S53	11S18

Moon Phenomena

Max/0 Decl (dy hr mn)
2 18:30 0 S
9 6:35 27S01
15 9:42 0 N
22 15:09 27N06
29 23:22 0 S

Max/0 Lat (dy hr mn)
5 20:32 0 S
11 23:08 5S00
18 10:59 0 N
25 21:54 5N01

Perigee/Apogee (dy hr m kilometers)
10 17:10 p 359831
22 21:54 a 405417

PH (dy hr mn)
☽ 5 11:08 13♏02
○ 12 1:37 19♒21
☾ 19 4:37 26♉12
● 27 8:18 4♍04

Void of Course Moon

Last Aspect	☽ Ingress
1 22:30 ♇ △	♎ 2 4:07
4 6:21 ♇ □	♏ 4 11:48
6 11:25 ♇ ✶	♐ 6 16:40
8 10:31 ♆ □	♑ 8 18:40
10 16:41 ♀ ☍	♒ 10 18:46
12 11:08 ♂ □	♓ 12 18:45
14 15:12 ♇ ✶	♈ 14 20:44
16 20:19 ♇ □	♉ 17 2:23
19 11:07 ♂ ☌	♊ 19 12:07
21 22:08 ☉ ✶	♋ 22 0:30
24 9:41 ☿ ✶	♌ 24 13:10
26 6:56 ♄ ☍	♍ 27 0:26
29 3:09 ♇ △	♎ 29 9:46
31 10:45 ♇ □	♏ 31 17:12

DAILY ASPECTARIAN

1 M: ☽⚻⚷ 2:02; ☽✶♀ 3:20; ☽△♂ 5:36; ☽△♅ 6:31; ☽∠⚳ 6:45; ☽∥⚷ 7:27; ☿⚻♆ 11:25; ☽⚻♄ 14:31; ☉∠☽ 17:34; ☽☍♆ 18:51; ☽⊻☿ 20:05; ☽△♇ 22:30; ♂☌♅ 23:54

2 Tu: ☽#♆ 5:50; ☽∥♃ 9:45; ☉⚼♆ 10:17; ☽⚼♅ 11:09; ☽⚼♂ 11:44; ☽✶⚳ 12:23; ♀✶♅ 12:26; ☿⚻♇ 13:25; ☽⚼♄ 18:48; ☽☍♃ 20:29

3 W: ☉✶☽ 0:14; ♀✶♂ 2:01; ☽#♃ 3:09; ☽∠☿ 4:50; ☽∥♆ 7:03; ☽☍⚷ 10:46; ☽⚻♅ 15:12; ☽⚻♂ 17:11; ☽□♀ 17:55; ☽△♄ 22:29

4 Th: ☽⚻♆ 2:52; ☽#⚷ 4:30; ☽□♇ 6:21; ☿ ♍ 6:59; ☽✶☿ 12:30; ☽#☿ 21:04; ☽□⚳ 21:37; ☉∥♅ 21:54

5 F: ☿⚼⚷ 1:50; ☽⚻♃ 3:19; ☽⚼♆ 5:53; ☽∥♄ 10:40; ☉□☽ 11:08; ♀⚻♄ 16:24; ☽#♂ 16:25; ☽⚻⚷ 16:55; ☉#☽ 18:15; ☽#♅ 19:22; ☽☍♅ 21:14

6 Sa: ☽☍♂ 1:39; ☽□♄ 3:48; ☽△♀ 4:58; ☽⚼♃ 5:38; ☽△♆ 8:09; ☽✶♇ 11:25; ☉∥♂ 14:15; ☽⚼⚷ 18:52; ☽#♀ 18:53

7 Su: ☽□☿ 0:19; ☽∥♇ 3:22; ☽△⚳ 3:38; ☽△♃ 7:13; ☽#⚳ 8:47; ☽⚼♀ 9:00; ☽∠♇ 12:51; ♀△♆ 16:44; ☉△☽ 18:22; ♂□♄ 19:58; ☽△⚷ 20:06

8 M: ☽⚻♅ 0:18; ☽⚼⚳ 5:27; ☽✶♄ 6:12; ☽⚻♂ 6:43; ☽□♆ 10:31; ☽⚻♀ 12:10; ☽⊻♇ 13:37; ☿⊻⚳ 16:03; ☉△⚷ 20:02; ☉⚼☽ 20:45

9 Tu: ☽⚼♅ 0:52; ♀☍♇ 5:19; ☽∠♄ 6:30; ☽⚻⚳ 6:39; ☽△☿ 7:52; ☽⚼♂ 8:11; ☽□♃ 8:25; ♂∥♅ 10:27; ☿⚻♃ 13:07; ♂∠♃ 13:27; ☽□⚷ 20:51; ☉⚻☽ 22:34

10 W: ☽△♅ 0:59; ☽⊻♄ 6:24; ☽△♂ 9:14; ☽⚼☿ 10:36; ☽✶♆ 10:46; ☿∥⚷ 12:37; ☽☌♇ 13:46; ☽☍♀ 16:41; ☉#♄ 23:07

11 Th: ☽#⚳ 5:35; ☽☍⚳ 8:00; ☽✶♃ 8:09; ☽∥♇ 8:12; ☽∠♆ 10:36; ☉□♅ 12:55; ⚳△♃ 12:55; ☽⚻☿ 13:07; ☿⚼♇ 17:59; ♀ ♌ 18:31; ☽✶⚷ 20:34; ☽#♀ 21:43; ♂✶♆ 21:45

12 F: ☽□♅ 0:49; ☉☍☽ 1:37; ☽☌♄ 5:59; ☽∠♃ 8:04; ☽⊻♆ 10:34; ☽□♂ 11:08; ☽#♂ 12:02; ☽⊻♇ 13:36; ☽#♅ 14:12; ☽∠⚷ 20:41; ☽⚻♀ 20:56; ☽∥♄ 21:33

13 Sa: ☉#☽ 0:21; ☽⊻♃ 8:20; ☽⚻⚳ 9:52; ☽∠♇ 14:03; ☽☍☿ 19:03; ☽⊻⚷ 21:18; ☽⚼♀ 23:54

14 Su: ☽✶♅ 1:51; ☽#⚷ 2:27; ☉⚻☽ 6:11; ☽⊻♄ 6:59; ☽⚼⚳ 11:44; ☽☌♆ 11:59; ☽#☿ 12:57; ☽✶♂ 14:54; ☽✶♇ 15:12; ☉☍♄ 17:12; ☿⚻⚷ 17:42; ⚳⚼♆ 19:42; ♂△♇ 21:29; ☽∥♆ 21:39

15 M: ☽#♃ 2:30; ☽∠♅ 3:27; ☽△♀ 3:54; ⚳#♇ 6:52; ☽∠♄ 8:37; ☉⚼☽ 9:53; ☽☌♃ 11:00; ☽△⚳ 14:34; ☽∥♃ 16:54; ☽∠♂ 18:12; ☽#♆ 21:58

16 Tu: ☽☌⚷ 1:02; ☉⚼♃ 1:07; ☽∥☿ 2:46; ☽⚻☿ 4:42; ☽⊻♅ 6:02; ☽✶♄ 11:15; ☉△☽ 14:49; ☽⊻♆ 16:51; ☿△♅ 17:47; ☽∥⚷ 18:14; ☽□♇ 20:19; ☽⊻♂ 22:40

17 W: ☽⚼☿ 11:31; ☽□♀ 15:55; ☉∥☽ 16:44; ☽⊻♃ 17:33; ☉⚻♆ 17:58; ☽∠♆ 20:51; ☿#♆ 21:54; ☽□⚳ 23:41

18 Th: ☽#♄ 3:38; ♀△♃ 8:04; ☽⊻⚷ 8:50; ☊ D 11:00; ☽∥♅ 11:40; ☽☌♅ 14:21; ☿⚻♄ 19:07; ☽∥♂ 19:20; ☽□♄ 19:35; ☽△☿ 19:39; ☽∥♀ 20:48; ☽∠♃ 22:20

19 F: ☽✶♆ 1:50; ☉□☽ 4:37; ☊ R 4:46; ☽△♇ 5:33; ♀∥♂ 10:58; ☽☌♂ 11:07; ☽∠⚷ 14:10; ☉⚻♇ 16:11; ♀⚼♆ 17:57; ☽∥⚳ 20:44

20 Sa: ☽#♇ 0:22; ☿∥♃ 3:31; ☽✶♃ 3:53; ♂ ♊ 7:57; ☽✶♀ 9:10; ☽⚼♇ 11:23; ☽✶⚳ 12:58; ☽✶⚷ 20:08

21 Su: ☽⊻♅ 2:02; ☽△♄ 7:05; ☿☍♆ 7:42; ⚶ R♒ 10:34; ☽□♆ 13:48; ☽□☿ 14:30; ☽⚻♇ 17:39; ☽∠♀ 18:58; ☽∠⚳ 20:29; ☉✶☽ 22:08; ♂∠⚷ 23:46

22 M: ☽⊻♂ 2:36; ☽∠♅ 8:28; ☽⚼♄ 13:20; ☽□♃ 16:11; ♀☌⚳ 17:03; ☿△♇ 22:00

23 Tu: ☉ ♍ 3:17; ☽⊻⚳ 4:08; ☽⊻♀ 4:56; ☉∠☽ 7:16; ☽□⚷ 8:49; ☽∠♂ 10:35; ☽✶♅ 14:52; ☽⚻♄ 19:31

24 W: ☉⚼⚷ 1:54; ☽△♆ 2:27; ♀∥♅ 5:18; ☽☍♇ 6:18; ☽✶☿ 9:41; ♅ R 13:55; ☉⊻☽ 16:08; ♀△⚷ 17:32; ☽✶♂ 18:18

25 Th: ☽△♃ 4:12; ☽#♇ 5:44; ☽⚼♆ 8:24; ☿#♃ 13:48; ☽∥⚳ 13:50; ☽∠☿ 18:28; ☽☌⚳ 18:35; ☿∠⚳ 20:40; ☽△⚷ 20:43; ☽☌♀ 23:51

26 F: ☿ ♎ 1:04; ☽□♅ 2:46; ☽∥♂ 5:28; ☽☍♄ 6:56; ☽⚼♃ 9:37; ☽⚻♆ 13:54; ☽⚻♇ 17:41; ☽∥♅ 18:49; ☽∥♀ 23:50

27 Sa: ☽#♄ 1:52; ☽⚼⚷ 2:01; ☽⊻☿ 2:30; ♀□♅ 4:35; ☉□♂ 5:29; ☽□♂ 8:12; ☉☌☽ 8:18; ☽⚻♃ 14:34; ☽⚼♇ 22:39

28 Su: ♀#♄ 0:45; ⚳△⚷ 1:17; ☉∥☽ 6:31; ☽⚻⚷ 6:50; ☽⊻⚳ 7:03; ☽△♅ 12:48; ☽∥⚷ 13:49; ☽⊻♀ 16:18; ☽⚻♄ 16:31; ♀☍♄ 18:29; ☿∥♆ 19:57; ☽☍♆ 23:28

29 M: ☽△♇ 3:09; ☽#☿ 8:47; ☽#♆ 9:51; ☽∠⚳ 12:28; ☽☌☿ 16:12; ☽⚼♅ 17:06; ☽∥♃ 17:44; ♀⚼♃ 18:31; ☽△♂ 19:51; ☽⚼♄ 20:36; ☉⊻☽ 22:01; ☽☍♃ 23:01; ☽∠♀ 23:32

30 Tu: ☽#♃ 4:54; ☿⚼♅ 5:54; ☉⚻♃ 10:10; ☽∥♆ 12:49; ☽☍⚷ 15:02; ☽∥☿ 16:23; ☽✶⚳ 17:22; ☽⚻♅ 20:55

31 W: ☽△♄ 0:14; ☽⚼♂ 0:51; ☉∠☽ 3:59; ☽✶♀ 6:08; ☽⚻♆ 7:09; ☽#⚷ 8:02; ☉#☽ 10:23; ☽□♇ 10:45; ♀⚻♆ 16:38

LONGITUDE — September 2022

Day	Sid.Time	☉	☽	☽ 12 hour	Mean☊	True☊	☿	♀	♂	⚳	♃	♄	⚷	♅	♆	♇
	h m s	° ' "	° ' "	° ' "	° '	° '	° '	° '	° '	° '	° '	° '	° '	° '	° '	° '
1 Th	22 40 33	8♍33 32	3♏44 59	10♏24 52	16♉39.7	15♉34.8	5♎16.5	24♌50.9	6♊33.6	17♌32.7	6♈52.5	20♒38.2	15♈39.6	18♉53.9	24♓27.6	26♑26.5
2 F	22 44 30	9 31 36	17 08 08	23 54 56	16 36.5	15D34.2	5 58.5	26 04.9	7 05.6	17 59.4	6R46.3	20R34.0	15R37.6	18R53.5	24R26.0	26R25.5
3 Sa	22 48 26	10 29 41	0♐45 28	7♐39 49	16 33.4	15R34.6	6 36.7	27 19.0	7 37.4	18 26.1	6 40.0	20 29.9	15 35.5	18 53.0	24 24.5	26 24.5
4 Su	22 52 23	11 27 48	14 38 06	21 40 19	16 30.2	15 34.8	7 10.9	28 33.2	8 08.9	18 52.7	6 33.5	20 25.9	15 33.4	18 52.5	24 22.9	26 23.6
5 M	22 56 20	12 25 56	28 46 24	5♑56 12	16 27.0	15 33.7	7 40.8	29 47.3	8 40.1	19 19.3	6 26.9	20 21.9	15 31.3	18 52.0	24 21.3	26 22.7
6 Tu	23 00 16	13 24 06	13♑09 24	20 25 34	16 23.8	15 30.5	8 06.1	1♍01.5	9 10.9	19 45.9	6 20.2	20 17.9	15 29.1	18 51.4	24 19.6	26 21.9
7 W	23 04 13	14 22 16	27 44 09	5♒04 27	16 20.7	15 25.0	8 26.5	2 15.7	9 41.5	20 12.5	6 13.3	20 14.0	15 26.9	18 50.8	24 18.0	26 21.0
8 Th	23 08 09	15 20 29	12♒25 40	19 46 53	16 17.5	15 17.4	8 41.7	3 30.0	10 11.8	20 39.0	6 06.4	20 10.2	15 24.7	18 50.1	24 16.4	26 20.2
9 F	23 12 06	16 18 43	27 07 10	4♓25 32	16 14.3	15 08.5	8 51.5	4 44.2	10 41.8	21 05.5	5 59.3	20 06.4	15 22.4	18 49.3	24 14.8	26 19.4
10 Sa	23 16 02	17 16 58	11♓41 02	18 52 48	16 11.1	14 59.4	8R55.4	5 58.5	11 11.4	21 32.0	5 52.2	20 02.6	15 20.1	18 48.6	24 13.1	26 18.6
11 Su	23 19 59	18 15 15	26 00 02	3♈02 05	16 08.0	14 51.1	8 53.2	7 12.9	11 40.7	21 58.5	5 44.9	19 58.9	15 17.8	18 47.7	24 11.5	26 17.8
12 M	23 23 55	19 13 34	9♈58 27	16 48 47	16 04.8	14 44.6	8 44.7	8 27.2	12 09.7	22 25.0	5 37.6	19 55.3	15 15.4	18 46.9	24 09.8	26 17.1
13 Tu	23 27 52	20 11 55	23 32 54	0♉10 46	16 01.6	14 40.3	8 29.6	9 41.6	12 38.3	22 51.4	5 30.2	19 51.7	15 13.0	18 45.9	24 08.2	26 16.3
14 W	23 31 49	21 10 18	6♉42 29	13 08 17	15 58.4	14D38.3	8 07.8	10 56.0	13 06.6	23 17.8	5 22.6	19 48.2	15 10.6	18 45.0	24 06.5	26 15.6
15 Th	23 35 45	22 08 43	19 28 32	25 43 40	15 55.2	14 38.1	7 39.3	12 10.5	13 34.5	23 44.2	5 15.1	19 44.8	15 08.2	18 43.9	24 04.9	26 15.0
16 F	23 39 42	23 07 10	1♊54 11	8♊00 39	15 52.1	14 39.0	7 04.1	13 25.0	14 02.1	24 10.6	5 07.4	19 41.4	15 05.8	18 42.9	24 03.2	26 14.3
17 Sa	23 43 38	24 05 40	14 03 41	20 03 55	15 48.9	14R40.1	6 22.3	14 39.5	14 29.2	24 36.9	4 59.7	19 38.1	15 03.3	18 41.8	24 01.6	26 13.7
18 Su	23 47 35	25 04 11	26 01 59	1♋58 33	15 45.7	14 40.6	5 34.5	15 54.0	14 56.0	25 03.2	4 51.9	19 34.8	15 00.8	18 40.6	23 59.9	26 13.1
19 M	23 51 31	26 02 45	7♋54 14	13 49 40	15 42.5	14 39.7	4 41.2	17 08.6	15 22.4	25 29.5	4 44.1	19 31.7	14 58.3	18 39.4	23 58.3	26 12.6
20 Tu	23 55 28	27 01 21	19 45 27	25 42 08	15 39.4	14 36.9	3 43.3	18 23.2	15 48.4	25 55.7	4 36.2	19 28.6	14 55.7	18 38.2	23 56.6	26 12.0
21 W	23 59 24	27 59 59	1♌40 15	7♌40 16	15 36.2	14 32.2	2 41.7	19 37.8	16 14.0	26 21.9	4 28.3	19 25.5	14 53.2	18 36.9	23 54.9	26 11.5
22 Th	0 03 21	28 58 39	13 42 36	19 47 39	15 33.0	14 25.8	1 37.6	20 52.4	16 39.2	26 48.1	4 20.3	19 22.6	14 50.6	18 35.6	23 53.3	26 11.0
23 F	0 07 18	29 57 21	25 55 41	2♍06 57	15 29.8	14 18.1	0 32.6	22 07.1	17 03.9	27 14.2	4 12.3	19 19.7	14 48.0	18 34.2	23 51.7	26 10.6
24 Sa	0 11 14	0♎56 06	8♍21 38	14 39 51	15 26.6	14 10.0	29♍28.2	23 21.8	17 28.2	27 40.4	4 04.3	19 16.9	14 45.4	18 32.8	23 50.0	26 10.1
25 Su	0 15 11	1 54 52	21 01 40	27 27 03	15 23.5	14 02.4	28 26.0	24 36.5	17 52.0	28 06.4	3 56.3	19 14.2	14 42.8	18 31.4	23 48.4	26 09.7
26 M	0 19 07	2 53 41	3♎55 59	10♎28 21	15 20.3	13 55.9	27 27.6	25 51.2	18 15.3	28 32.5	3 48.2	19 11.6	14 40.1	18 29.9	23 46.7	26 09.3
27 Tu	0 23 04	3 52 31	17 04 02	23 42 54	15 17.1	13 51.2	26 34.6	27 06.0	18 38.2	28 58.4	3 40.2	19 09.0	14 37.5	18 28.3	23 45.1	26 09.0
28 W	0 27 00	4 51 23	0♏24 48	7♏09 32	15 13.9	13D48.5	25 48.5	28 20.8	19 00.6	29 24.4	3 32.1	19 06.6	14 34.8	18 26.8	23 43.5	26 08.7
29 Th	0 30 57	5 50 18	13 56 59	20 46 59	15 10.7	13 47.7	25 10.4	29 35.6	19 22.5	29 50.3	3 24.1	19 04.2	14 32.1	18 25.2	23 41.9	26 08.4
30 F	0 34 53	6♎49 14	27 39 25	4♐34 07	15♉07.6	13♉48.4	24♍41.2	0♎50.4	19♊43.9	0♍16.2	3♈16.1	19♒01.9	14♈29.4	18♉23.5	23♓40.3	26♑08.1

1st of Month
Julian Day # 2459823.5
Obliquity 23°26'[illegible]8"
SVP 4♓56'[illegible]7"
GC 27♐09.4
Eris 24♈52.9R

Day	⚴
1	27♊34.4
6	29 54.1
11	2♋12.2
16	4 28.4
21	6 42.2
26	8 53.0

Day	⚵
1	16♓40.2R
6	15 28.2R
11	14 14.1R
16	13 00.4R
21	11 49.6R
26	10 44.2R

Day	⚶
1	27♒25.0R
6	26 18.4R
11	25 19.3R
16	24 29.2R
21	23 49.3R
26	23 20.6R

DECLINATION and LATITUDE

Day	☉ Decl	☽ Decl	☽ Lat	☽ 12h Decl	☿ Decl	☿ Lat	♀ Decl	♀ Lat	♂ Decl	♂ Lat	⚳ Decl	⚳ Lat	♃ Decl	♃ Lat	♄ Decl	♄ Lat
1 Th	8N22	11S47	1N02	14S31	4S46	2S55	14N17	1N06	20N07	1S18	21N11	5N54	1N17	1S34	15S52	1S19
2 F	7 60	17 05	0S08	19 28	5 11	3 04	13 53	1 08	20 13	1 17	21 04	5 56	1 14	1 35	15 53	1 19
3 Sa	7 38	21 37	1 20	23 29	5 34	3 12	13 29	1 09	20 19	1 16	20 58	5 58	1 12	1 35	15 54	1 19
4 Su	7 16	25 01	2 28	26 10	5 55	3 21	13 05	1 11	20 25	1 15	20 51	5 59	1 09	1 35	15 56	1 19
5 M	6 54	26 55	3 29	27 13	6 14	3 29	12 40	1 12	20 31	1 14	20 44	6 01	1 06	1 35	15 57	1 19
6 Tu	6 31	27 03	4 17	26 26	6 31	3 36	12 15	1 13	20 37	1 13	20 37	6 03	1 03	1 35	15 58	1 19
7 W	6 09	25 21	4 50	23 50	6 46	3 43	11 50	1 14	20 43	1 12	20 31	6 05	1 00	1 36	15 60	1 19
8 Th	5 47	21 56	5 04	19 40	6 58	3 50	11 24	1 16	20 48	1 11	20 24	6 07	0 58	1 36	16 01	1 19
9 F	5 24	17 07	4 58	14 20	7 07	3 55	10 58	1 17	20 54	1 10	20 17	6 09	0 55	1 36	16 02	1 19
10 Sa	5 01	11 22	4 32	8 17	7 13	4 00	10 31	1 18	20 59	1 09	20 10	6 11	0 52	1 36	16 03	1 19
11 Su	4 39	5 06	3 50	1 54	7 16	4 04	10 05	1 19	21 04	1 08	20 03	6 13	0 49	1 36	16 04	1 19
12 M	4 16	1N16	2 55	4N24	7 15	4 07	9 38	1 20	21 09	1 06	19 56	6 14	0 46	1 36	16 06	1 19
13 Tu	3 53	7 26	1 51	10 20	7 11	4 09	9 11	1 21	21 14	1 05	19 49	6 16	0 43	1 36	16 07	1 19
14 W	3 30	13 05	0 42	15 39	7 02	4 09	8 43	1 21	21 19	1 04	19 42	6 18	0 40	1 36	16 08	1 19
15 Th	3 07	18 01	0N26	20 09	6 50	4 08	8 16	1 22	21 24	1 03	19 35	6 20	0 36	1 37	16 09	1 19
16 F	2 44	22 02	1 32	23 39	6 34	4 06	7 48	1 23	21 28	1 01	19 28	6 22	0 33	1 37	16 10	1 19
17 Sa	2 21	24 60	2 32	26 02	6 13	4 01	7 19	1 23	21 33	0 60	19 21	6 24	0 30	1 37	16 11	1 19
18 Su	1 58	26 47	3 24	27 12	5 49	3 55	6 51	1 24	21 37	0 59	19 13	6 26	0 27	1 37	16 12	1 19
19 M	1 34	27 19	4 07	27 07	5 20	3 47	6 22	1 24	21 41	0 57	19 06	6 28	0 24	1 37	16 13	1 19
20 Tu	1 11	26 36	4 40	25 46	4 48	3 37	5 54	1 25	21 45	0 56	18 59	6 30	0 21	1 37	16 14	1 19
21 W	0 48	24 40	5 00	23 16	4 13	3 26	5 25	1 25	21 50	0 54	18 52	6 32	0 18	1 37	16 15	1 19
22 Th	0 24	21 37	5 08	19 43	3 35	3 12	4 56	1 25	21 54	0 53	18 45	6 34	0 14	1 37	16 16	1 19
23 F	0 01	17 36	5 02	15 17	2 55	2 56	4 26	1 26	21 57	0 51	18 38	6 36	0 11	1 37	16 17	1 19
24 Sa	0S22	12 47	4 41	10 07	2 14	2 39	3 57	1 26	22 01	0 50	18 30	6 38	0 08	1 37	16 18	1 19
25 Su	0 46	7 20	4 07	4 27	1 32	2 21	3 27	1 26	22 05	0 48	18 23	6 41	0 05	1 37	16 18	1 19
26 M	1 09	1 29	3 19	1S32	0 51	2 02	2 58	1 26	22 09	0 47	18 16	6 43	0 01	1 37	16 19	1 19
27 Tu	1 32	4S33	2 20	7 33	0 12	1 42	2 28	1 26	22 12	0 45	18 08	6 45	0S02	1 37	16 20	1 19
28 W	1 56	10 29	1 12	13 20	0N25	1 22	1 58	1 26	22 16	0 44	18 01	6 47	0 05	1 37	16 21	1 19
29 Th	2 19	16 02	0S01	18 34	0 59	1 02	1 28	1 26	22 19	0 42	17 54	6 49	0 08	1 37	16 21	1 19
30 F	2S42	20S51	1S15	22S52	1N28	0S42	0N58	1N25	22N22	0S40	17N47	6N51	0S11	1S37	16S22	1S19

Day	⚷ Decl	⚷ Lat	♅ Decl	♅ Lat	♆ Decl	♆ Lat	♇ Decl	♇ Lat
1	7N59	1N59	17N05	0S22	3S19	1S13	23S00	2S11
6	7 55	1 59	17 04	0 22	3 23	1 13	23 01	2 11
11	7 51	1 59	17 03	0 22	3 26	1 13	23 02	2 11
16	7 46	1 59	17 02	0 22	3 29	1 13	23 03	2 12
21	7 41	1 58	17 00	0 22	3 32	1 13	23 04	2 12
26	7 36	1 58	16 58	0 22	3 36	1 13	23 05	2 12

Day	⚴ Decl	⚴ Lat	⚵ Decl	⚵ Lat	⚶ Decl	⚶ Lat	Eris Decl	Eris Lat
1	7S58	31S24	2S40	2N49	21S11	9S25	0S54	11S18
6	8 55	32 22	3 38	2 16	21 39	9 29	0 55	11 18
11	9 56	33 21	4 38	1 42	22 01	9 31	0 56	11 18
16	10 60	34 22	5 39	1 07	22 17	9 29	0 57	11 18
21	12 07	35 25	6 38	0 32	22 27	9 26	0 58	11 19
26	13 17	36 30	7 36	0S04	22 32	9 20	0 59	11 19

Moon Phenomena

Max/0 Decl
dy hr mn
5 13:53 27S13
11 19:11 0 N
18 22:12 27N19
26 5:55 0 S

Max/0 Lat
dy hr mn
1 21:13 0 S
8 4:38 5S04
14 14:50 0 N
22 1:25 5N08
28 23:44 0 S

Perigee/Apogee
dy hr m kilometers
7 18:20 p 364494
19 14:45 a 404554

PH dy hr mn
☽ 3 18:09 11♐14
○ 10 10:00 17♓41
☾ 17 21:53 24♊59
● 25 21:56 2♎49

Void of Course Moon

Last Aspect			☽ Ingress	
2 17:23	♀	□	♐	2 22:41
5 1:52	♀	△	♑	5 2:04
6 21:44	♇	☌	♒	7 3:42
8 12:35	♄	☌	♓	9 4:43
11 0:30	♇	⚹	♈	11 6:48
13 4:54	♇	□	♉	13 11:40
15 13:00	♇	△	♊	15 20:17
17 21:53	☉	□	♋	18 8:00
20 15:58	☉	⚹	♌	20 20:39
22 11:08	♄	☍	♍	23 7:55
25 12:50	☿	☌	♎	25 16:44
27 16:22	♇	□	♏	27 23:16
29 21:21	♇	⚹	♐	30 4:05

DAILY ASPECTARIAN

1 Th
☽ ⚺ ☿ 2:55
☽ ⚻ ♂ 5:17
☽ ⚻ ♃ 5:36
☉ ⚹ ☽ 9:21
☽ ⋕ ♀ 10:12
☽ ⚼ ♆ 10:16
☿ ⚼ ♄ 11:02
♂ ⚹ ♃ 11:53
☽ ∥ ♄ 18:17
☊ D 21:14
☽ ⚻ ⚷ 21:19

2 F
☽ ⋕ ♅ 0:00
☉ ∥ ⚷ 1:20
☽ □ ⚳ 1:34
☽ ☍ ♅ 3:07
☽ □ ♄ 6:03
♀ ⚻ ♇ 6:35
☽ ∠ ☿ 7:09
☽ ⚼ ♃ 8:09
☽ △ ♆ 12:53
☽ ⚹ ♇ 16:24
☽ ⋕ ♂ 16:27
☽ □ ♀ 17:23
☽ ⋕ ⚳ 20:18
☽ ⚼ ⚷ 23:43

3 Sa
☿ ☍ ♃ 1:50
☽ ∥ ♇ 8:51
☽ △ ♃ 10:12
☽ ⚹ ☿ 10:38
☽ ☍ ♂ 12:24
☊ R 18:02
☉ □ ☽ 18:09
☽ ∠ ♇ 18:26
☉ ⚼ ♇ 22:18
⚳ □ ♅ 23:51

4 Su
☽ △ ⚷ 1:34
☽ ⚻ ♅ 7:14
☽ △ ⚳ 7:29
☽ ⚹ ♄ 9:51
☽ □ ♆ 16:33
☽ ⚺ ♇ 19:58

5 M
☽ △ ♀ 1:52
♀ ♍ 4:06
☽ ⚼ ♅ 8:32
☽ ⚼ ⚳ 9:36
☽ ∠ ♄ 11:00
☽ □ ♃ 12:45
♀ ⚼ ⚷ 13:49
☽ □ ☿ 15:22
☽ ⚻ ♂ 17:10

6 Tu
☉ ⋕ ☿ 0:02
☉ △ ☽ 0:26
♂ ∥ ⚳ 0:33
☽ □ ⚷ 3:51
⚴ ♋ 5:05
☽ ⚼ ♀ 5:11
☽ △ ♅ 9:24
☽ ⚻ ⚳ 11:15
☽ ⚺ ♄ 11:44
☽ ⚹ ♆ 18:23
☽ ⚼ ♂ 18:50
☽ ☌ ♇ 21:44

7 W
⚳ ☍ ♄ 1:13
☉ ⚼ ☽ 2:52
☽ ⚻ ♀ 8:05
☽ ⚹ ♃ 13:46
☽ ∥ ♇ 17:19
☽ △ ☿ 17:49
☽ ∠ ♆ 18:52
☽ △ ♂ 20:14

8 Th
☉ ⚻ ⚷ 1:40
☽ ⚹ ⚷ 4:51
☉ ⚻ ☽ 5:05
☽ ⋕ ♂ 6:03
☽ ⋕ ⚳ 8:32
☽ □ ♅ 10:27
☽ ☌ ♄ 12:35
☽ ☍ ⚳ 13:50
☽ ∠ ♃ 14:03
☽ ⚼ ☿ 18:37
☽ ⚺ ♆ 19:18
⚳ ⚼ ♃ 19:34
☽ ⚺ ♇ 22:42

9 F
☽ ⋕ ♅ 0:16
☽ ∥ ♄ 4:48
☽ ∠ ⚷ 5:19
☽ ☍ ♀ 13:41
☽ ⚺ ♃ 14:28
☽ ⚻ ☿ 19:25
♀ ⚻ ♃ 22:08
☽ □ ♂ 23:09
☽ ∠ ♇ 23:23

10 Sa
☽ ⋕ ♀ 3:35
☿ R 3:39
♂ ⚼ ♇ 5:42
☽ ⚺ ⚷ 6:04
☉ ☍ ☽ 10:00
☽ ⚹ ♅ 11:52
☽ ⋕ ⚷ 13:37
☽ ⚺ ♄ 13:54
☽ ∥ ☿ 15:54
☽ ⚻ ⚳ 16:59
☽ ☌ ♆ 20:57

11 Su
☽ ⚹ ♇ 0:30
☉ ⋕ ☽ 1:51
☽ ∥ ♆ 6:17
☉ △ ♅ 13:10
☽ ∠ ♅ 13:18
☽ ∠ ♄ 15:17
☽ ⋕ ♃ 16:15
☽ ☌ ♃ 16:32
☽ ⚼ ⚳ 19:25
☽ ⚻ ♀ 21:06
☽ ☍ ☿ 21:54
☽ ∥ ♃ 22:05

12 M
☽ ⚹ ♂ 3:57
☿ ⚺ ♀ 4:50
☽ ⋕ ♆ 8:19
☽ ☌ ⚷ 9:14
☉ ∥ ☽ 10:49
☽ ⚺ ♅ 15:28
☉ ⚻ ♄ 16:10
☽ ⚹ ♄ 17:26
☉ ⚻ ☽ 17:33
☽ △ ⚳ 22:43
☽ ⋕ ☿ 23:00

13 Tu
☽ ⚺ ♆ 1:03
☽ ∥ ⚷ 1:34
☽ ⚼ ♀ 2:16
☽ □ ♇ 4:54
☽ ∥ ♀ 6:38
☽ ∠ ♂ 7:39
☿ ∠ ⚳ 19:18
☽ ⚺ ♃ 21:34
☉ ⚼ ☽ 22:56

14 W
☉ ⋕ ♆ 2:13
☽ ⚻ ☿ 2:33
☽ ∠ ♆ 4:27
♀ ⚼ ♇ 6:16
☽ △ ♀ 8:43
☽ ⚺ ♂ 12:24
☽ ⋕ ♄ 14:24
☊ D 14:50
☽ ⚺ ⚷ 15:48
☽ ∥ ♅ 18:54
☽ ☌ ♅ 22:35

15 Th
☽ □ ♄ 0:31
☽ ∠ ♃ 1:28
☉ △ ☽ 5:32
☽ ⚼ ☿ 5:50
☽ ∥ ⚳ 8:25
☽ □ ⚳ 8:28
☽ ⚹ ♆ 8:48
☽ △ ♇ 13:00
⚳ ⚻ ♆ 17:42
☽ ∥ ♂ 20:09
☽ ∠ ⚷ 20:29

16 F
♀ ∥ ⚷ 1:17
☽ ⚹ ♃ 6:15
☽ ⋕ ♇ 7:19
☽ △ ☿ 9:37
☽ ⚼ ♇ 18:22
♀ □ ♂ 18:50
☉ ☍ ♆ 22:22

17 Sa
☽ ☌ ♂ 0:53
☽ □ ♀ 1:19
☽ ⚹ ⚷ 1:58
♀ ⚻ ⚷ 7:25
☽ ⚺ ♅ 9:15
☽ △ ♄ 11:05
☽ □ ♆ 19:55
☉ □ ☽ 21:53
☽ ⚹ ⚳ 21:57
☊ R 22:05
☉ ⚺ ⚳ 23:16

18 Su
☽ ⚻ ♇ 0:22
♂ ⚹ ⚷ 3:56
☽ ∠ ♅ 15:25
☽ ⚼ ♄ 17:12
☽ □ ♃ 17:39
☽ □ ☿ 17:57
☿ ☍ ♃ 22:35

19 M
☉ △ ♇ 3:59
☿ ⚼ ♄ 4:20
☽ ∠ ⚳ 5:27
☽ □ ⚷ 14:16
☽ ⚺ ♂ 15:42
☽ ⚹ ♀ 20:54
☽ ⚹ ♅ 21:44
☽ ⚻ ♄ 23:26

20 Tu
☿ ⚼ ♅ 2:04
♀ △ ♅ 4:46
☽ △ ♆ 8:26
☽ ⚺ ⚳ 12:56
☽ ☍ ♇ 13:00
⚳ ⚻ ♇ 14:38
☉ ⚹ ☽ 15:58
♀ ⚻ ♄ 20:13
☽ ∠ ♂ 23:05

21 W
☽ ⚹ ☿ 1:53
☽ △ ♃ 5:33
☽ ∠ ♀ 6:37
♃ ∠ ♄ 13:09
☽ ⋕ ♇ 13:35
☽ ⚼ ♆ 14:27
☽ ∥ ♂ 22:10

22 Th
☉ ∠ ☽ 0:35
☿ ∥ ♆ 1:02
☽ △ ⚷ 2:14
☽ ∠ ☿ 5:18
☽ ⚹ ♂ 6:01
☽ □ ♅ 9:37
☽ ⚼ ♃ 10:59
☽ ☍ ♄ 11:08
☉ ∥ ♃ 12:02
☽ ⚺ ♀ 15:43
☽ ∥ ⚳ 18:11
☽ ⚻ ♆ 19:59

23 F
☽ ⚻ ♇ 0:29
☉ ♎ 1:05
☽ ☌ ⚳ 2:38
☽ ∥ ♅ 3:15
☉ ☌ ☿ 6:51
☽ ⋕ ♄ 6:56
☽ ⚼ ⚷ 7:30
☽ ⚺ ☿ 8:15
☉ ⚺ ☽ 8:30
☉ ⋕ ♃ 10:59
☿ R♍ 12:06
☽ ⚻ ♃ 15:51

24 Sa
☽ ⚼ ♇ 5:21
♀ ☍ ♆ 8:52
☽ ⚻ ⚷ 12:08
☽ □ ♂ 17:52
♀ ⋕ ♆ 17:56
☽ △ ♅ 19:18
☽ ⚻ ♄ 20:39
☽ ∥ ⚷ 22:49

25 Su
☽ ☍ ♆ 5:12
☿ ⚺ ⚳ 5:27
☽ ☌ ♀ 7:25
☽ △ ♇ 9:36
☽ ☌ ☿ 12:50
☽ ⚺ ⚳ 13:41
☽ ⋕ ♆ 15:29
☉ ∥ ☿ 17:20
☽ ∥ ♀ 17:29
☉ ☌ ☽ 21:56
☽ ⚼ ♅ 23:12
☽ ☍ ♃ 23:46

26 M
☽ ⚼ ♄ 0:29
☉ ⋕ ☽ 1:15
☽ ⋕ ☿ 2:49
♀ △ ♇ 5:47
☽ ∥ ♃ 5:53
☽ ⋕ ♃ 5:58
☽ ∥ ☿ 8:24
☉ ∥ ☽ 11:13
♂ ⚺ ♅ 14:15
☉ ⚼ ♅ 14:24
☽ ⋕ ♀ 16:21
☿ ☌ ♀ 18:00
☽ ∠ ⚳ 18:12
☉ ☍ ♃ 19:34
☽ ☍ ⚷ 19:35
☽ ∥ ♆ 20:15

27 Tu
☽ ⚻ ♅ 2:32
☽ △ ♂ 2:55
☽ △ ♄ 3:46
☿ ∥ ♃ 6:00
☉ ⚼ ♄ 6:27
☿ ⋕ ♃ 9:34
☽ ⚻ ♆ 12:02
☽ ⋕ ⚷ 12:05
☿ △ ♇ 12:57
☽ ⚺ ☿ 16:11
☽ □ ♇ 16:22
☽ ⚺ ♀ 19:56
☽ ⚹ ⚳ 22:09

28 W
☉ ⋕ ♀ 1:05
☽ ⚻ ♃ 5:31
♂ △ ♄ 5:50
☽ ⚼ ♂ 6:35
☉ ⚺ ☽ 8:32
⚳ ⚼ ⚷ 8:45
☽ ⚼ ♆ 14:45
☽ ∠ ☿ 17:37
♃ ∠ ♅ 19:59
☊ D 23:45

29 Th
☽ ⚻ ⚷ 1:02
☽ ∠ ♀ 1:15
☽ ∥ ♄ 1:28
☽ ⋕ ♅ 4:14
♀ ⚺ ⚳ 7:14
☽ ⚼ ♃ 7:45
♀ ♎ 7:50
☽ ☍ ♅ 7:50
☽ ⋕ ⚳ 8:33
☽ □ ♄ 8:58
⚳ ♍ 9:00
☽ ⚻ ♂ 9:47
☿ ∥ ♀ 11:42
☉ ∠ ☽ 13:02
☽ △ ♆ 17:04
☽ ⚹ ☿ 18:59
☽ ⚹ ♇ 21:21

30 F
☽ ⚼ ⚷ 3:11
☽ □ ⚳ 4:41
☽ ⚹ ♀ 6:05
☽ ⋕ ♂ 9:01
☽ △ ♃ 9:39
☽ ∥ ♇ 13:25
☉ ⚹ ☽ 17:06
☽ ∠ ♇ 23:20

October 2022

LONGITUDE

Day	Sid.Time	☉	☽	☽ 12 hour	Mean ☊	True ☊	☿	♀	♂	⚳	♃	♄	⚷	♅	♆	♇
	h m s	° ' "	° ' "	° ' "	° '	° '	° '	° '	° '	° '	° '	° '	° '	° '	° '	° '
1 Sa	0 38 50	7♎48 12	11♐31 00	18♐29 57	15♉04.4	13♉49.8	24♍21.9	2♎05.2	20♊04.8	0♍42.0	3♈08.1	18♒59.7	14♈26.8	18♉21.8	23♓38.7	26♑07.9
2 Su	0 42 47	8 47 11	25 30 50	2♑33 32	15 01.2	13 51.1	24D 12.7	3 20.1	20 25.2	1 07.8	3R 00.1	18R 57.6	14R 24.1	18R 20.1	23R 37.1	26R 07.6
3 M	0 46 43	9 46 13	9♑37 52	16 43 39	14 58.0	13R 51.7	24 14.0	4 34.9	20 45.0	1 33.5	2 52.2	18 55.6	14 21.4	18 18.4	23 35.5	26 07.5
4 Tu	0 50 40	10 45 16	23 50 38	0♒58 32	14 54.9	13 51.0	24 25.6	5 49.8	21 04.3	1 59.2	2 44.3	18 53.7	14 18.7	18 16.6	23 33.9	26 07.3
5 W	0 54 36	11 44 21	8♒07 01	15 15 38	14 51.7	13 48.9	24 47.3	7 04.7	21 23.1	2 24.8	2 36.4	18 51.8	14 15.9	18 14.7	23 32.4	26 07.2
6 Th	0 58 33	12 43 28	22 23 57	29 31 28	14 48.5	13 45.4	25 18.8	8 19.6	21 41.3	2 50.4	2 28.6	18 50.1	14 13.2	18 12.9	23 30.8	26 07.1
7 F	1 02 29	13 42 36	6♓37 37	13♓41 52	14 45.3	13 41.1	25 59.5	9 34.5	21 58.9	3 15.9	2 20.9	18 48.4	14 10.5	18 11.0	23 29.3	26 07.0
8 Sa	1 06 26	14 41 46	20 43 39	27 42 26	14 42.2	13 36.6	26 48.7	10 49.5	22 15.9	3 41.4	2 13.2	18 46.9	14 07.8	18 09.0	23 27.8	26D 07.0
9 Su	1 10 22	15 40 58	4♈37 44	11♈29 06	14 39.0	13 32.5	27 45.8	12 04.4	22 32.4	4 06.8	2 05.6	18 45.4	14 05.1	18 07.1	23 26.2	26 07.0
10 M	1 14 19	16 40 12	18 16 10	24 58 38	14 35.8	13 29.4	28 49.9	13 19.4	22 48.2	4 32.2	1 58.1	18 44.0	14 02.4	18 05.1	23 24.8	26 07.0
11 Tu	1 18 15	17 39 28	1♉36 20	8♉09 10	14 32.6	13D 27.6	0♎00.4	14 34.4	23 03.4	4 57.5	1 50.6	18 42.8	13 59.7	18 03.1	23 23.3	26 07.0
12 W	1 22 12	18 38 46	14 37 08	21 00 18	14 29.4	13 27.1	1 16.5	15 49.4	23 18.0	5 22.7	1 43.3	18 41.6	13 56.9	18 01.0	23 21.8	26 07.1
13 Th	1 26 09	19 38 07	27 18 52	3♊33 06	14 26.3	13 27.7	2 37.4	17 04.4	23 32.0	5 47.9	1 36.0	18 40.5	13 54.2	17 58.9	23 20.4	26 07.2
14 F	1 30 05	20 37 29	9♊43 20	15 49 57	14 23.1	13 29.1	4 02.5	18 19.4	23 45.3	6 13.1	1 28.8	18 39.6	13 51.5	17 56.8	23 18.9	26 07.4
15 Sa	1 34 02	21 36 54	21 53 26	27 54 15	14 19.9	13 30.8	5 31.2	19 34.5	23 57.9	6 38.1	1 21.7	18 38.7	13 48.9	17 54.7	23 17.5	26 07.5
16 Su	1 37 58	22 36 21	3♋52 59	9♋50 10	14 16.7	13 32.3	7 02.8	20 49.5	24 09.8	7 03.2	1 14.8	18 37.9	13 46.2	17 52.6	23 16.1	26 07.7
17 M	1 41 55	23 35 51	15 46 25	21 42 18	14 13.6	13R 33.3	8 36.9	22 04.6	24 21.0	7 28.1	1 07.9	18 37.2	13 43.5	17 50.4	23 14.7	26 07.9
18 Tu	1 45 51	24 35 23	27 38 28	3♌35 29	14 10.4	13 33.5	10 12.9	23 19.7	24 31.5	7 53.0	1 01.1	18 36.7	13 40.9	17 48.2	23 13.4	26 08.2
19 W	1 49 48	25 34 57	9♌33 57	15 34 26	14 07.2	13 32.8	11 50.6	24 34.8	24 41.3	8 17.8	0 54.5	18 36.2	13 38.2	17 45.9	23 12.0	26 08.5
20 Th	1 53 45	26 34 33	21 37 28	27 43 35	14 04.0	13 31.4	13 29.5	25 49.9	24 50.3	8 42.6	0 48.0	18 35.8	13 35.6	17 43.7	23 10.7	26 08.8
21 F	1 57 41	27 34 11	3♍53 12	10♍06 45	14 00.8	13 29.3	15 09.4	27 05.0	24 58.5	9 07.3	0 41.7	18 35.5	13 32.9	17 41.4	23 09.4	26 09.1
22 Sa	2 01 38	28 33 52	16 24 33	22 46 52	13 57.7	13 27.1	16 50.0	28 20.2	25 06.0	9 31.9	0 35.4	18 35.4	13 30.3	17 39.1	23 08.1	26 09.5
23 Su	2 05 34	29 33 35	29 13 54	5♎45 45	13 54.5	13 25.0	18 31.0	29 35.3	25 12.7	9 56.4	0 29.3	18D 35.3	13 27.7	17 36.8	23 06.8	26 09.9
24 M	2 09 31	0♏33 20	12♎22 25	19 03 51	13 51.3	13 23.2	20 12.3	0♏50.5	25 18.6	10 20.8	0 23.4	18 35.3	13 25.2	17 34.5	23 05.6	26 10.3
25 Tu	2 13 27	1 33 07	25 49 53	2♏40 16	13 48.1	13 22.1	21 53.8	2 05.6	25 23.7	10 45.2	0 17.6	18 35.5	13 22.6	17 32.1	23 04.4	26 10.8
26 W	2 17 24	2 32 56	9♏34 40	16 32 44	13 45.0	13D 21.6	23 35.2	3 20.8	25 28.0	11 09.5	0 11.9	18 35.7	13 20.1	17 29.7	23 03.2	26 11.3
27 Th	2 21 20	3 32 47	23 33 59	0♐37 57	13 41.8	13 21.7	25 16.6	4 36.0	25 31.4	11 33.7	0 06.5	18 36.1	13 17.5	17 27.4	23 02.0	26 11.8
28 F	2 25 17	4 32 40	7♐44 07	14 51 59	13 38.6	13 22.3	26 57.7	5 51.2	25 34.0	11 57.9	0 01.1	18 36.5	13 15.1	17 25.0	23 00.9	26 12.3
29 Sa	2 29 13	5 32 35	22 01 01	29 10 44	13 35.4	13 23.0	28 38.7	7 06.4	25 35.8	12 21.9	29♓56.0	18 37.1	13 12.6	17 22.5	22 59.7	26 12.9
30 Su	2 33 10	6 32 31	6♑20 37	13♑30 16	13 32.2	13 23.7	0♏19.3	8 21.6	25R 36.7	12 45.9	29 51.0	18 37.7	13 10.1	17 20.1	22 58.7	26 13.5
31 M	2 37 07	7♏32 29	20 39 14	27 47 12	13♉29.1	13♉24.1	1♏59.6	9♏36.8	25♊36.8	13♍09.7	29♓46.2	18♒38.5	13♈07.7	17♉17.7	22♓57.6	26♑14.1

1st of Month

Julian Day #
2459853.5
Obliquity
23°26[illegible]8"
SVP 4♓56[illegible]4"
GC 27♐09.4
Eris 24♈38.0R

Day	⚴
1	11♋00.3
6	13 03.4
11	15 01.7
16	16 54.4
21	18 40.5
26	20 19.1
31	21 48.9

Day	⚵
1	9♓46.4R
6	8 58.4R
11	8 21.2R
16	7 55.9R
21	7 43.1R
26	7 43.0
31	7 55.6

Day	⚶
1	23♒03.5R
6	22 58.2
11	23 04.5
16	23 21.8
21	23 49.8
26	24 27.7
31	25 15.2

DECLINATION and LATITUDE

Day	☉ Decl	☽ Decl	☽ Lat	☽ 12h Decl	☿ Decl	☿ Lat	♀ Decl	♀ Lat	♂ Decl	♂ Lat	⚳ Decl	⚳ Lat	♃ Decl	♃ Lat	♄ Decl	♄ Lat
1 Sa	3S06	24S34	2S25	25S53	1N54	0S22	0N28	1N25	22N26	0S39	17N39	6N53	0S14	1S37	16S23	1S19
2 Su	3 29	26 49	3 28	27 19	2 15	0 04	0S02	1 25	22 29	0 37	17 32	6 56	0 18	1 37	16 23	1 19
3 M	3 52	27 23	4 18	26 59	2 30	0N14	0 32	1 24	22 32	0 35	17 25	6 58	0 21	1 37	16 24	1 19
4 Tu	4 15	26 09	4 53	24 53	2 40	0 30	1 02	1 24	22 35	0 33	17 17	6 60	0 24	1 37	16 25	1 19
5 W	4 39	23 14	5 11	21 13	2 45	0 45	1 32	1 23	22 38	0 32	17 10	7 02	0 27	1 37	16 25	1 19
6 Th	5 02	18 54	5 09	16 19	2 45	0 59	2 02	1 23	22 41	0 30	17 03	7 04	0 30	1 37	16 26	1 19
7 F	5 25	13 32	4 48	10 34	2 40	1 11	2 32	1 22	22 44	0 28	16 56	7 07	0 33	1 37	16 26	1 19
8 Sa	5 47	7 30	4 09	4 21	2 31	1 21	3 02	1 21	22 47	0 26	16 48	7 09	0 36	1 37	16 27	1 19
9 Su	6 10	1 10	3 17	1N59	2 16	1 31	3 32	1 20	22 50	0 24	16 41	7 11	0 39	1 37	16 27	1 19
10 M	6 33	5N06	2 14	8 07	1 58	1 38	4 02	1 19	22 53	0 22	16 34	7 14	0 42	1 37	16 27	1 19
11 Tu	6 56	11 01	1 05	13 46	1 36	1 45	4 32	1 19	22 55	0 20	16 27	7 16	0 45	1 37	16 28	1 19
12 W	7 18	16 20	0N06	18 40	1 11	1 50	5 02	1 18	22 58	0 18	16 19	7 18	0 48	1 37	16 28	1 19
13 Th	7 41	20 47	1 16	22 38	0 42	1 54	5 32	1 16	23 01	0 16	16 12	7 21	0 50	1 36	16 28	1 19
14 F	8 03	24 12	2 20	25 29	0 11	1 57	6 01	1 15	23 04	0 14	16 05	7 23	0 53	1 36	16 29	1 18
15 Sa	8 26	26 27	3 16	27 06	0S22	1 59	6 31	1 14	23 07	0 12	15 58	7 26	0 56	1 36	16 29	1 18
16 Su	8 48	27 26	4 03	27 26	0 58	1 60	7 00	1 13	23 09	0 09	15 51	7 28	0 58	1 36	16 29	1 18
17 M	9 10	27 08	4 39	26 30	1 35	1 60	7 29	1 12	23 12	0 07	15 43	7 30	1 01	1 36	16 29	1 18
18 Tu	9 32	25 35	5 03	24 23	2 13	1 59	7 58	1 10	23 15	0 05	15 36	7 33	1 04	1 36	16 29	1 18
19 W	9 53	22 54	5 15	21 11	2 53	1 58	8 27	1 09	23 17	0 03	15 29	7 35	1 06	1 36	16 29	1 18
20 Th	10 15	19 13	5 12	17 02	3 33	1 55	8 56	1 08	23 20	0 00	15 22	7 38	1 09	1 36	16 29	1 18
21 F	10 36	14 40	4 56	12 08	4 14	1 53	9 24	1 06	23 23	0N02	15 15	7 40	1 11	1 35	16 29	1 18
22 Sa	10 58	9 26	4 25	6 36	4 56	1 49	9 53	1 05	23 25	0 05	15 08	7 43	1 13	1 35	16 29	1 18
23 Su	11 19	3 41	3 40	0 40	5 38	1 45	10 21	1 03	23 28	0 07	15 01	7 46	1 16	1 35	16 29	1 18
24 M	11 40	2S23	2 43	5S27	6 20	1 41	10 48	1 01	23 31	0 09	14 54	7 48	1 18	1 35	16 29	1 18
25 Tu	12 01	8 30	1 36	11 29	7 02	1 37	11 16	0 60	23 33	0 12	14 47	7 51	1 20	1 35	16 29	1 18
26 W	12 21	14 21	0 21	17 04	7 44	1 32	11 43	0 58	23 36	0 15	14 40	7 53	1 22	1 35	16 29	1 18
27 Th	12 42	19 34	0S56	21 49	8 26	1 26	12 10	0 56	23 39	0 17	14 33	7 56	1 24	1 34	16 29	1 18
28 F	13 02	23 45	2 11	25 20	9 08	1 21	12 37	0 54	23 42	0 20	14 26	7 59	1 26	1 34	16 29	1 18
29 Sa	13 22	26 30	3 18	27 14	9 49	1 15	13 04	0 52	23 44	0 22	14 19	8 01	1 28	1 34	16 29	1 18
30 Su	13 42	27 30	4 13	27 19	10 30	1 09	13 30	0 51	23 47	0 25	14 13	8 04	1 30	1 34	16 28	1 18
31 M	14S02	26S40	4S52	25S35	11S11	1N03	13S55	0N49	23N50	0N28	14N06	8N07	1S31	1S34	16S28	1S18

Day	⚷ Decl	⚷ Lat	♅ Decl	♅ Lat	♆ Decl	♆ Lat	♇ Decl	♇ Lat
1	7N30	1N58	16N56	0S22	3S39	1S13	23S05	2S12
6	7 25	1 58	16 54	0 22	3 42	1 13	23 05	2 12
11	7 19	1 57	16 51	0 22	3 45	1 13	23 05	2 12
16	7 14	1 57	16 48	0 22	3 48	1 13	23 05	2 12
21	7 08	1 56	16 45	0 22	3 50	1 13	23 05	2 12
26	7 03	1 56	16 42	0 22	3 53	1 13	23 05	2 13
31	6N57	1N55	16N38	0S22	3S55	1S13	23S04	2S13

Day	⚴ Decl	⚴ Lat	⚵ Decl	⚵ Lat	⚶ Decl	⚶ Lat	Eris Decl	Eris Lat
1	14S30	37S35	8S30	0S39	22S31	9S13	0S60	11S19
6	15 45	38 43	9 19	1 12	22 25	9 04	1 01	11 19
11	17 02	39 51	10 03	1 45	22 14	8 55	1 02	11 19
16	18 21	41 00	10 41	2 15	21 58	8 45	1 03	11 18
21	19 41	42 10	11 13	2 44	21 39	8 34	1 04	11 18
26	21 01	43 21	11 38	3 11	21 16	8 24	1 04	11 18
31	22S21	44S33	11S56	3S36	20S50	8S13	1S05	11S18

Moon Phenomena

Max/0 Decl

dy	hr mn	
2	19:30	27S25
9	4:26	0 N
16	6:16	27N28
23	14:38	0 S
30	1:06	27S30

Max/0 Lat

dy	hr mn	
5	9:32	5S12
11	21:50	0 N
19	7:57	5N15
26	6:32	0 S

Perigee/Apogee

dy	hr m		kilometers
4	16:35	p	369325
17	10:21	a	404325
29	14:37	p	368291

PH	dy	hr mn	
☽	3	0:15	9♑47
○	9	20:56	16♈33
☾	17	17:16	24♋19
●	25	10:50	2♏00
•	25	661:21P	0.862

Void of Course Moon

Last Aspect				☽ Ingress		
1	21:47	☿	□	♑	2	7:39
4	3:50	♇	☌	♒	4	10:22
5	22:47	♂	△	♓	6	12:48
8	11:12	☿	☍	♈	8	15:58
10	14:03	♇	□	♉	10	21:05
12	21:43	♇	△	♊	13	5:09
15	4:12	♂	☌	♋	15	16:12
17	20:58	♇	☍	♌	18	4:46
20	10:36	☉	✶	♍	20	16:27
22	18:19	♇	△	♎	23	1:25
25	0:37	♇	□	♏	25	7:20
27	4:29	♇	✶	♐	27	10:56
29	13:11	♃	□	♑	29	13:23
31	15:16	♃	✶	♒	31	15:44

DAILY ASPECTARIAN

1 Sa
☽△⚷ 5:01
♀⋕♃ 9:59
☽⚻♅ 11:45
☽✶♄ 12:49
☽☍♂ 15:05
♀☍♃ 18:13
☽□♆ 20:46
☽□☿ 21:47

2 Su
♀⚼♅ 0:01
☽⚺♇ 1:03
☿ D 9:09
☽△⚳ 9:52
☉∥♆ 11:11
♀⚼♄ 11:43
☽□♃ 12:38
☽⚼♅ 13:18
♀∥♃ 14:04
☽∠♄ 14:21
☽□♀ 14:36

3 M
☊ R 0:13
☉□☽ 0:15
☽□⚷ 7:58
☽⚼⚳ 12:05
☽△♅ 14:38
☽⚺♄ 15:40
☽⚻♂ 19:13
☽✶♆ 23:32

4 Tu
☽△☿ 1:00
☽☌♇ 3:50
☽⚻⚳ 14:07
☽✶♃ 14:50
☽⚼♂ 21:02
☽△♀ 22:05

5 W
☽∠♆ 0:43
☽∥♇ 0:56
☽⚼☿ 2:54
☽⋕♂ 3:43
☉△☽ 6:32
⚳⚻♃ 8:22
☽✶⚷ 10:18
☽∠♃ 15:48
☽□♅ 16:59
☽☌♄ 18:01
⚶ D 18:11
☽△♂ 22:47

6 Th
☽⚼♀ 1:43
☽⚺♆ 1:52
☽⚻☿ 5:08
☽⚺♇ 6:16
☽⋕⚳ 8:56
☽⋕♅ 9:27
☉⚼☽ 9:38
☽∠⚷ 11:27
☽∥♄ 11:31
☽⚺♃ 16:50
☽☍⚳ 18:08

7 F
☿△♇ 3:57
☿⋕♀ 5:07
☽⚻♀ 5:29
☽∠♇ 7:37
⚳∥♅ 8:59
☉☍⚷ 10:50
☽⚺⚷ 12:46
☉⚻☽ 12:55
☽✶♅ 19:36
☽⚺♄ 20:41

8 Sa
☽⋕⚷ 0:27
☽□♂ 2:41
☽☌♆ 4:41
☉∥☽ 6:09
☽✶♇ 9:15
☽☍☿ 11:12
☽∥♆ 14:21
☽∥♀ 15:43
☽☌♃ 19:38
☽⋕☿ 19:39
☽∠♅ 21:23
♇ D 21:58
☽∠♄ 22:29
☽⚻⚳ 23:04

9 Su
☽∥♃ 1:58
☽⋕♃ 6:57
♀∥♆ 9:19
☽∥☿ 12:31
☽☍♀ 14:21
☽☌⚷ 16:32
☽⋕♆ 18:43
☽⋕♀ 19:31
☉☍☽ 20:56
☽⚺♅ 23:40

10 M
☽✶♄ 0:50
☽⚼⚳ 2:20
☉⋕☽ 6:06
☽✶♂ 8:15
☽∥⚷ 8:50
☽⚺♆ 9:10
♀☍⚷ 13:16
☽□♇ 14:03
⚳⋕♄ 20:28
☽⚻☿ 20:48
☿ ♎ 23:52

11 Tu
☽⚺♃ 0:26
☽△⚳ 6:20
☉⚻♅ 9:14
☽∠♂ 12:03
☽∠♆ 12:25
☊ D 21:51
☽⚺⚷ 22:45
☉⋕⚷ 23:44
☽∥⚳ 23:59

12 W
☽⋕♄ 0:42
☉△♄ 1:08
☽⚻♀ 2:30
☽∥♅ 2:32
☽⚼☿ 3:27
☽∠♃ 3:54
♂□♆ 5:48
☽☌♅ 6:21
☿☍♃ 7:25
☽□♄ 7:38
☉⚻☽ 8:11
☽✶♆ 16:26
☽⚺♂ 16:40
☿⋕♃ 18:00
☽△♇ 21:43

13 Th
☽∠⚷ 3:02
☿⚼♅ 6:02
☽✶♃ 8:09
☽⚼♀ 10:10
☽△☿ 11:30
☽∥♂ 14:57
☽⋕♇ 15:16
☉⚼☽ 15:19
☽□⚳ 16:56
♀⚻♅ 16:59
☿⚼♄ 17:42

14 F
☽⚼♇ 2:44
♀△♄ 6:22
☽✶⚷ 8:05
♂⋕♇ 13:32
☽⚺♅ 16:08
☽△♄ 17:34
☽△♀ 18:52
☉△☽ 23:24

15 Sa
☉∠⚳ 0:51
☽□♆ 2:47
☽☌♂ 4:12
☽⚻♇ 8:27
☽□♃ 18:45
☽∠♅ 21:59
☽⚼♄ 23:30

16 Su
☿⚺⚳ 0:08
☿∥♃ 0:37
☽✶⚳ 6:37
☽□☿ 7:20
♀⋕⚷ 10:40
☉⚻♆ 15:40
☽□⚷ 19:52

17 M
☽✶♅ 4:10
☽⚻♄ 5:45
♀∠⚳ 11:15
☽∠⚳ 14:02
☽□♀ 14:15
☽△♆ 15:05
☉□☽ 17:16
☊ R 17:34
☽⚺♂ 17:37
☽☍♇ 20:58
♀⚻♆ 22:01
☉△♂ 22:07

18 Tu
☽△♃ 6:45
☽∥♂ 21:07
☽⚼♆ 21:16
☽⚺⚳ 21:22
☽⋕♇ 22:37

19 W
☽∠♂ 0:15
♀△♂ 2:22
☽✶☿ 5:17
☽△⚷ 8:07
☽⚼♃ 12:33
☉□♇ 13:34
☽□♅ 16:18
☽☍♄ 18:01

20 Th
☿☍⚷ 1:25
☽⚻♆ 3:04
♀□♇ 6:04
☽✶♂ 6:24
☽⚻♇ 8:54
☽✶♀ 9:14
☿∥♆ 9:56
☉✶☽ 10:36
☽∥♅ 13:31
☽⚼⚷ 13:39
☽⋕♄ 14:52
☽∠☿ 15:37
☽⚻♃ 17:51
☽∥⚳ 21:05

21 F
☽☌⚳ 10:26
☽⚼♇ 14:00
☽∠♀ 17:31
☉⋕☽ 17:40
☉∠☽ 18:08
☽⚻⚷ 18:30
☽⋕♀ 22:12

22 Sa
☽⚺☿ 0:55
☽△♅ 2:21
☽⚻♄ 4:07
☽∥⚷ 9:54
☿⚻♅ 11:25
☽☍♆ 12:38
☽□♂ 16:29
☽⋕☿ 16:53
☽△♇ 18:19
☉☌♀ 21:19
☽⋕♆ 23:16

23 Su
☉⚺☽ 0:39
☽⚺♀ 0:44
☿△♄ 1:01
☽☍♃ 2:18
♄ D 4:09
☽⚼♅ 6:13
♀ ♏ 7:53
☽⚼♄ 8:01
☽⋕♃ 9:36
☉ ♏ 10:37
⚵ D 13:06
♀⚻♃ 15:59
☽∥♃ 19:42
☽⚺⚳ 20:13
☉⚻♃ 20:22

24 M
☽☍⚷ 1:53
☽∥♆ 5:47
☽⚻♅ 9:19
☽△♄ 11:09
☽☌☿ 16:02
☽∥☿ 17:28
☽⋕⚷ 18:20
☽⚻♆ 19:08
☽△♂ 23:14
☽∠⚳ 23:52

25 Tu
☽□♇ 0:37
☿⋕⚷ 0:48
☽⚻♃ 7:47
☉☌☽ 10:50
☽∥♀ 12:05
☽☌♀ 12:06
☉∥☽ 15:05
☿⚻♆ 16:31
☽⚼♆ 21:22

26 W
☽⋕⚳ 1:20
☽⚼♂ 1:33
⚳⚼♇ 1:45
☽✶⚳ 2:49
☽⚻⚷ 6:28
☊ D 6:33
☽∥♄ 9:22
☽⚼♃ 9:37
☽⋕♅ 10:17
☽☍♅ 13:35
☽□♄ 15:31
☽△♆ 23:06

27 Th
☽⚺☿ 3:18
☽⚻♂ 3:21
☿△♂ 3:38
☽✶♇ 4:29
☽⚼⚷ 8:01
☽△♃ 11:02
☿□♇ 13:10
☉⚺☽ 18:13
☽∥♇ 19:35
☽⚺♀ 20:31
☽⋕♂ 23:35

28 F
☿∠⚳ 0:02
♃R♓ 5:11
☽∠♇ 5:51
☽□⚳ 7:20
☽∠☿ 8:04
☽△⚷ 9:15
☽⚻♅ 16:14
☽✶♄ 18:18
☉∠☽ 21:21

29 Sa
☽∠♀ 0:10
☽□♆ 1:38
☽☍♂ 6:00
☽⚺♇ 7:02
☽✶☿ 12:35
☽□♃ 13:11
♀⚼♆ 16:47
☽⚼♅ 17:18
☿⚻♃ 17:33
☿ ♏ 19:23
☽∠♄ 19:27

30 Su
☉✶☽ 0:21
☽✶♀ 3:42
☽△⚳ 11:04
☽□⚷ 11:24
♂ R 13:27
☽△♅ 18:23
☽⚺♄ 20:37
⚳⚻⚷ 22:09

31 M
☽✶♆ 3:52
☉⋕⚳ 3:54
♀⋕⚳ 7:47
☽⚻♂ 8:20
☽☌♇ 9:24
☉⚼♆ 9:52
☽⚼⚳ 13:00
☽✶♃ 15:16
♀⚼♂ 18:57
☽□☿ 21:38

LONGITUDE — November 2022

Day	Sid.Time	☉	☽	☽ 12 hour	Mean ☊	True ☊	☿	♀	♂	⚳	♃	♄	⚷	♅	♆	♇
	h m s	° ' "	° ' "	° ' "	° '	° '	° '	° '	° '	° '	° '	° '	° '	° '	° '	° '
1 Tu	2 41 03	8♏32 29	4♒53 48	11♒58 45	13♉25.9	13♉24.4	3♏39.5	10♏52.0	25♊35.9	13♍33.5	29♓41.5	18♒39.4	13♈05.3	17♉15.3	22♓56.5	26♑14.8
2 W	2 45 00	9 32 30	19 01 49	26 02 46	13 22.7	13R 24.3	5 19.1	12 07.3	25R 34.3	13 57.2	29R 37.1	18 40.3	13R 03.0	17R 12.8	22R 55.5	26 15.5
3 Th	2 48 56	10 32 33	3♓01 23	9♓57 30	13 19.5	13 24.1	6 58.2	13 22.5	25 31.7	14 20.8	29 32.8	18 41.4	13 00.6	17 10.3	22 54.5	26 16.2
4 F	2 52 53	11 32 37	16 50 57	23 41 35	13 16.4	13 23.9	8 36.9	14 37.7	25 28.3	14 44.3	29 28.7	18 42.5	12 58.3	17 07.9	22 53.6	26 17.0
5 Sa	2 56 49	12 32 42	0♈29 16	7♈13 51	13 13.2	13D 23.7	10 15.2	15 52.9	25 24.0	15 07.6	29 24.8	18 43.8	12 56.0	17 05.4	22 52.6	26 17.7
6 Su	3 00 46	13 32 50	13 55 14	20 33 18	13 10.0	13 23.7	11 53.1	17 08.1	25 18.8	15 30.9	29 21.1	18 45.2	12 53.8	17 02.9	22 51.7	26 18.5
7 M	3 04 42	14 32 59	27 07 58	3♉39 10	13 06.8	13 23.7	13 30.6	18 23.4	25 12.7	15 54.1	29 17.5	18 46.7	12 51.5	17 00.4	22 50.8	26 19.3
8 Tu	3 08 39	15 33 10	10♉06 51	16 31 01	13 03.7	13R 23.8	15 07.7	19 38.6	25 05.8	16 17.2	29 14.2	18 48.2	12 49.3	16 58.0	22 50.0	26 20.2
9 W	3 12 36	16 33 22	22 51 40	29 08 52	13 00.5	13 23.8	16 44.4	20 53.9	24 58.0	16 40.2	29 11.0	18 49.9	12 47.2	16 55.5	22 49.1	26 21.1
10 Th	3 16 32	17 33 37	5♊22 44	11♊33 23	12 57.3	13 23.5	18 20.7	22 09.1	24 49.3	17 03.0	29 08.1	18 51.7	12 45.1	16 53.0	22 48.3	26 22.0
11 F	3 20 29	18 33 53	17 41 02	23 45 54	12 54.1	13 23.0	19 56.7	23 24.3	24 39.7	17 25.8	29 05.3	18 53.5	12 43.0	16 50.5	22 47.6	26 22.9
12 Sa	3 24 25	19 34 11	29 48 16	5♋48 29	12 50.9	13 22.2	21 32.3	24 39.6	24 29.3	17 48.4	29 02.8	18 55.5	12 40.9	16 48.0	22 46.8	26 23.9
13 Su	3 28 22	20 34 31	11♋46 55	17 43 58	12 47.8	13 21.3	23 07.6	25 54.9	24 18.1	18 11.0	29 00.4	18 57.6	12 38.9	16 45.5	22 46.1	26 24.9
14 M	3 32 18	21 34 53	23 40 07	29 35 51	12 44.6	13 20.3	24 42.6	27 10.1	24 05.9	18 33.4	28 58.2	18 59.7	12 36.9	16 43.1	22 45.4	26 25.9
15 Tu	3 36 15	22 35 16	5♌31 42	11♌28 11	12 41.4	13 19.4	26 17.3	28 25.4	23 53.0	18 55.7	28 56.3	19 02.0	12 35.0	16 40.6	22 44.8	26 26.9
16 W	3 40 12	23 35 42	17 25 54	23 25 25	12 38.2	13D 18.9	27 51.7	29 40.7	23 39.2	19 17.8	28 54.5	19 04.4	12 33.1	16 38.1	22 44.2	26 28.0
17 Th	3 44 08	24 36 09	29 27 21	5♍32 15	12 35.1	13 18.9	29 25.9	0♐56.0	23 24.6	19 39.9	28 53.0	19 06.8	12 31.2	16 35.7	22 43.6	26 29.1
18 F	3 48 05	25 36 38	11♍40 42	17 53 16	12 31.9	13 19.4	0♐59.8	2 11.2	23 09.3	20 01.8	28 51.6	19 09.4	12 29.4	16 33.2	22 43.0	26 30.2
19 Sa	3 52 01	26 37 09	24 10 27	0♎32 44	12 28.7	13 20.3	2 33.4	3 26.5	22 53.2	20 23.6	28 50.5	19 12.0	12 27.6	16 30.8	22 42.5	26 31.4
20 Su	3 55 58	27 37 42	7♎00 30	13 34 04	12 25.5	13 21.6	4 06.9	4 41.8	22 36.3	20 45.2	28 49.6	19 14.8	12 25.9	16 28.3	22 42.0	26 32.5
21 M	3 59 54	28 38 17	20 13 40	26 59 25	12 22.4	13 22.8	5 40.1	5 57.1	22 18.8	21 06.7	28 48.8	19 17.6	12 24.2	16 25.9	22 41.6	26 33.7
22 Tu	4 03 51	29 38 53	3♏51 17	10♏49 08	12 19.2	13R 23.7	7 13.2	7 12.4	22 00.5	21 28.1	28 48.3	19 20.5	12 22.6	16 23.5	22 41.1	26 34.9
23 W	4 07 47	0♐39 31	17 52 40	25 01 25	12 16.0	13 23.8	8 46.1	8 27.7	21 41.7	21 49.3	28D 48.0	19 23.6	12 21.0	16 21.1	22 40.8	26 36.2
24 Th	4 11 44	1 40 10	2♐14 50	9♐32 10	12 12.8	13 23.0	10 18.8	9 43.0	21 22.2	22 10.4	28 47.9	19 26.7	12 19.4	16 18.7	22 40.4	26 37.4
25 F	4 15 40	2 40 51	16 52 36	24 15 15	12 09.6	13 21.3	11 51.3	10 58.3	21 02.1	22 31.3	28 48.0	19 29.9	12 17.9	16 16.4	22 40.1	26 38.7
26 Sa	4 19 37	3 41 33	1♑39 07	9♑03 15	12 06.5	13 18.7	13 23.7	12 13.6	20 41.6	22 52.1	28 48.3	19 33.2	12 16.4	16 14.0	22 39.8	26 40.0
27 Su	4 23 34	4 42 17	16 26 42	23 48 35	12 03.3	13 15.8	14 55.9	13 28.9	20 20.5	23 12.7	28 48.9	19 36.6	12 15.0	16 11.7	22 39.5	26 41.4
28 M	4 27 30	5 43 01	1♒08 06	8♒24 32	12 00.1	13 12.9	16 27.9	14 44.3	19 59.1	23 33.1	28 49.6	19 40.1	12 13.6	16 09.4	22 39.3	26 42.7
29 Tu	4 31 27	6 43 47	15 37 21	22 46 05	11 56.9	13 10.7	17 59.8	15 59.6	19 37.2	23 53.4	28 50.6	19 43.7	12 12.3	16 07.1	22 39.1	26 44.1
30 W	4 35 23	7♐44 33	29 50 27	6♓50 16	11♉53.8	13♉09.4	19♐31.5	17♐14.9	19♊15.0	24♍13.6	28♓51.7	19♒47.3	12♈11.0	16♉04.9	22♓39.0	26♑45.5

1st of Month

Julian Day # 2459884.5
Obliquity 23°26'07"
SVP 4♓56'30"
GC 27♐09.5
Eris 24♈19.7R

Day	⚴
1	22♋05.7
6	23 23.5
11	24 29.9
16	25 23.5
21	26 02.8
26	26 26.3

Day	⚵
1	7♓59.7
6	8 27.2
11	9 06.4
16	9 56.7
21	10 57.6
26	12 08.5

Day	⚶
1	25♒25.7
6	26 23.6
11	27 29.3
16	28 42.2
21	0♓01.8
26	1 27.5

DECLINATION and LATITUDE

Day	☉ Decl	☽ Decl	☽ Lat	☽ 12h Decl	☿ Decl	☿ Lat	♀ Decl	♀ Lat	♂ Decl	♂ Lat	⚳ Decl	⚳ Lat	♃ Decl	♃ Lat	♄ Decl	♄ Lat
1 Tu	14S21	24S06	5S13	22S16	11S51	0N57	14S21	0N47	23N52	0N31	13N59	8N10	1S33	1S33	16S28	1S17
2 W	14 40	20 06	5 15	17 41	12 30	0 50	14 46	0 45	23 55	0 33	13 53	8 12	1 35	1 33	16 27	1 17
3 Th	14 59	15 02	4 59	12 13	13 09	0 44	15 11	0 43	23 58	0 36	13 46	8 15	1 36	1 33	16 27	1 17
4 F	15 18	9 15	4 25	6 12	13 47	0 37	15 35	0 40	24 01	0 39	13 39	8 18	1 37	1 33	16 26	1 17
5 Sa	15 36	3 07	3 36	0 00	14 25	0 30	15 59	0 38	24 03	0 42	13 33	8 21	1 39	1 32	16 26	1 17
6 Su	15 54	3N05	2 36	6N07	15 02	0 24	16 22	0 36	24 06	0 45	13 26	8 24	1 40	1 32	16 26	1 17
7 M	16 12	9 04	1 29	11 53	15 38	0 17	16 45	0 34	24 09	0 48	13 20	8 27	1 41	1 32	16 25	1 17
8 Tu	16 30	14 34	0 18	17 03	16 13	0 10	17 08	0 32	24 12	0 51	13 14	8 30	1 42	1 32	16 24	1 17
9 W	16 47	19 20	0N52	21 22	16 47	0 03	17 30	0 30	24 14	0 54	13 07	8 33	1 43	1 31	16 24	1 17
10 Th	17 04	23 09	1 59	24 39	17 21	0S03	17 52	0 27	24 17	0 57	13 01	8 36	1 44	1 31	16 23	1 17
11 F	17 21	25 50	2 59	26 43	17 53	0 10	18 13	0 25	24 20	0 60	12 55	8 39	1 45	1 31	16 23	1 17
12 Sa	17 37	27 16	3 50	27 30	18 25	0 17	18 34	0 23	24 22	1 03	12 49	8 42	1 46	1 31	16 22	1 17
13 Su	17 54	27 24	4 30	26 59	18 56	0 23	18 54	0 20	24 25	1 06	12 43	8 45	1 47	1 30	16 21	1 17
14 M	18 09	26 15	4 58	25 15	19 26	0 30	19 14	0 18	24 27	1 09	12 37	8 48	1 47	1 30	16 21	1 17
15 Tu	18 25	23 57	5 14	22 24	19 55	0 36	19 33	0 16	24 30	1 12	12 31	8 51	1 48	1 30	16 20	1 17
16 W	18 40	20 37	5 16	18 37	20 23	0 43	19 52	0 13	24 32	1 15	12 25	8 54	1 48	1 30	16 19	1 17
17 Th	18 55	16 24	5 04	14 01	20 50	0 49	20 10	0 11	24 35	1 18	12 19	8 57	1 49	1 29	16 18	1 16
18 F	19 10	11 28	4 39	8 47	21 16	0 55	20 27	0 09	24 37	1 21	12 13	9 01	1 49	1 29	16 17	1 16
19 Sa	19 24	5 59	3 60	3 05	21 40	1 01	20 44	0 06	24 39	1 24	12 08	9 04	1 49	1 29	16 16	1 16
20 Su	19 38	0 06	3 08	2S56	22 04	1 07	21 01	0 04	24 41	1 27	12 02	9 07	1 49	1 29	16 15	1 16
21 M	19 51	5S59	2 05	9 01	22 27	1 13	21 17	0 01	24 43	1 30	11 57	9 10	1 49	1 28	16 15	1 16
22 Tu	20 04	11 59	0 53	14 51	22 49	1 19	21 32	0S01	24 45	1 33	11 51	9 14	1 49	1 28	16 14	1 16
23 W	20 17	17 33	0S25	20 03	23 09	1 24	21 46	0 03	24 47	1 37	11 46	9 17	1 49	1 28	16 13	1 16
24 Th	20 30	22 17	1 42	24 10	23 28	1 30	22 00	0 06	24 49	1 40	11 41	9 21	1 49	1 27	16 12	1 16
25 F	20 42	25 41	2 54	26 45	23 46	1 35	22 13	0 08	24 50	1 42	11 35	9 24	1 49	1 27	16 10	1 16
26 Sa	20 53	27 21	3 55	27 27	24 03	1 40	22 26	0 11	24 52	1 45	11 30	9 27	1 48	1 27	16 09	1 16
27 Su	21 05	27 04	4 41	26 12	24 19	1 44	22 38	0 13	24 53	1 48	11 25	9 31	1 48	1 27	16 08	1 16
28 M	21 15	24 54	5 07	23 12	24 33	1 49	22 49	0 16	24 55	1 51	11 20	9 34	1 47	1 26	16 07	1 16
29 Tu	21 26	21 09	5 14	18 48	24 46	1 53	22 60	0 18	24 56	1 54	11 16	9 38	1 47	1 26	16 06	1 16
30 W	21S36	16S13	5S01	13S27	24S58	1S57	23S10	0S20	24N57	1N57	11N11	9N42	1S46	1S26	16S05	1S16

Day	⚷ Decl	⚷ Lat	♅ Decl	♅ Lat	♆ Decl	♆ Lat	♇ Decl	♇ Lat
1	6N56	1N55	16N38	0S22	3S55	1S13	23S04	2S13
6	6 51	1 55	16 34	0 22	3 57	1 13	23 04	2 13
11	6 46	1 54	16 31	0 22	3 59	1 13	23 03	2 13
16	6 42	1 53	16 27	0 22	3 60	1 13	23 02	2 13
21	6 38	1 52	16 24	0 22	4 01	1 13	23 01	2 13
26	6 34	1 52	16 20	0 22	4 01	1 12	23 00	2 13

Day	⚴ Decl	⚴ Lat	⚵ Decl	⚵ Lat	⚶ Decl	⚶ Lat	Eris Decl	Eris Lat
1	22S37	44S47	11S59	3S41	20S44	8S11	1S05	11S18
6	23 56	45 58	12 10	4 04	20 14	8 00	1 06	11 17
11	25 13	47 08	12 15	4 25	19 41	7 50	1 07	11 17
16	26 28	48 16	12 14	4 45	19 06	7 40	1 07	11 17
21	27 38	49 23	12 08	5 03	18 28	7 30	1 08	11 16
26	28 43	50 26	11 56	5 20	17 48	7 20	1 08	11 16

Moon Phenomena

Max/0 Decl — dy hr mn
- 5 12:00 0 N
- 12 14:22 27N30
- 20 0:23 0 S
- 26 8:34 27S28

Max/0 Lat — dy hr mn
- 1 14:26 5S17
- 8 6:09 0 N
- 15 15:44 5N16
- 22 16:24 0 S
- 28 19:56 5S14

Perigee/Apogee — dy hr m kilometers
- 14 6:41 a 404920
- 26 1:32 p 362827

PH dy hr mn
- ☽ 1 6:38 8♒49
- ○ 8 11:03 16♉01
- • 8 11:00 T 1.359
- ☾ 16 13:28 24♌10
- ● 23 22:58 1♐38
- ☽ 30 14:38 8♓22

Void of Course Moon

Last Aspect	☽ Ingress
2 11:09 ♂ △	♓ 2 18:48
4 22:06 ♃ ☌	♈ 4 23:08
6 22:31 ♇ □	♉ 7 5:16
9 12:01 ♃ ⚹	♊ 9 13:38
11 22:30 ♃ □	♋ 12 0:23
14 10:42 ♃ △	♌ 14 12:49
16 23:57 ☿ □	♍ 17 1:05
19 8:48 ♃ ☍	♎ 19 10:59
21 11:16 ♇ □	♏ 21 17:17
23 18:17 ♃ △	♐ 23 20:17
25 19:23 ♃ □	♑ 25 21:19
27 20:12 ♃ ⚹	♒ 27 22:08
29 6:55 ♄ ☌	♓ 30 0:16

DAILY ASPECTARIAN

1 Tu: ☉∥♀ 0:40; ☽⋕♂ 1:37; ☽∠♆ 5:09; ☉□☽ 6:38; ☊ R 6:57; ☽∥♇ 7:00; ☽⚼♂ 9:39; ☽□♀ 11:06; ☽⚹⚷ 13:51; ☽⚻⚳ 15:06; ☽∠♃ 16:31; ☽□♅ 20:55; ☽☌♄ 23:23

2 W: ☽⚺♆ 6:39; ☽△♂ 11:09; ☽⚺♇ 12:22; ☽∠⚷ 15:24; ☽⋕♅ 16:59; ♀⚻⚷ 17:14; ☽∥♄ 17:41; ☽⚺♃ 18:03; ☽∥♀ 23:25; ☉⚼♂ 23:41

3 Th: ☉∥☽ 0:12; ☽⋕⚳ 5:35; ☽∥☿ 7:15; ☽△☿ 7:44; ☿⚼♆ 13:33; ☉△☽ 14:02; ☽∠♇ 14:17; ☽⚺⚷ 17:15; ☿⋕⚳ 19:40; ☽△♀ 19:44; ☽☍⚳ 20:12; ♀⚼♃ 21:16

4 F: ☽⚹♅ 0:29; ♀⚹⚳ 3:03; ☽⚺♄ 3:15; ☽⋕⚷ 9:23; ☽☌♆ 10:35; ☽⚼☿ 13:29; ☽□♂ 15:03; ☽⚹♇ 16:35; ☉⚼☽ 18:23; ☽∥♆ 20:47; ☽☌♃ 22:06

5 Sa: ☽⚼♀ 0:46; ☿⚼♂ 2:03; ☽∠♅ 2:50; ☽∥♃ 5:38; ☽∠♄ 5:46; ☉⚻⚷ 8:58; ☽⋕♃ 18:26; ☽⚻☿ 19:50; ☊ D 20:32; ☽☌⚷ 22:10; ♀☍♅ 22:23; ☉⚻☽ 23:16

6 Su: ☽⚻⚳ 2:58; ♀∥♄ 3:18; ☽⋕♆ 3:23; ☽⚺♅ 5:38; ☽⚻♀ 6:25; ☽⚹♄ 8:45; ♀⋕♅ 11:54; ☿⚻⚷ 14:35; ☽∥⚷ 14:54; ☽⚺♆ 16:11; ☉⚼♃ 18:10; ☽⚹♂ 20:31; ☽□♇ 22:31

7 M: ☽⚺♃ 3:57; ☽⚼⚳ 7:08; ♀□♄ 7:35; ☿⚼♃ 11:12; ☉∥♄ 16:56; ☽∥⚳ 18:02; ☽∠♆ 19:45; ☽∠♂ 23:58

8 Tu: ☉⋕♅ 3:52; ☽⚺⚷ 5:03; ☊ R 6:07; ☽∠♃ 7:41; ☿∥♄ 8:01; ☽⋕♄ 8:48; ☽⋕☿ 8:54; ☽∥♅ 9:28; ☉⋕☽ 9:50; ☽☍☿ 10:45; ☉☍☽ 11:03; ☽△⚳ 11:56; ☽☌♅ 12:48; ☽⋕♀ 13:28; ☿⋕♅ 13:37; ☽□♄ 16:21; ☉☌☿ 16:44; ☽☍♀ 19:52; ☿⚹⚳ 22:37; ☽⚹♆ 23:55

9 W: ☉∥☿ 0:05; ☿☍♅ 2:41; ☽⚺♂ 3:58; ☉⚹⚳ 4:22; ☽△♇ 6:39; ☉☍♅ 8:27; ☽∠⚷ 9:22; ☽⚹♃ 12:01; ⚳△♅ 14:28; ☽⋕♇ 23:19

10 Th: ☿□♄ 7:53; ☽∥♂ 9:02; ☽⚼♇ 11:39; ♀△♆ 12:23; ☽⚹⚷ 14:18; ☽⚺♅ 22:21; ☽□⚳ 23:29

11 F: ☉⚻☽ 1:53; ☽△♄ 2:23; ☽⚻☿ 5:07; ☉□♄ 8:05; ☽□♆ 10:04; ☽⚻♀ 12:36; ☽☌♂ 13:35; ☽⚻♇ 17:13; ♀⚻♂ 21:08; ☽□♃ 22:30

12 Sa: ☽∠♅ 3:58; ☽⚼♄ 8:15; ☉⚼☽ 10:24; ☽⚼☿ 15:32; ☿△♆ 18:37; ☿∥♀ 19:58; ☽⚼♀ 22:03

13 Su: ☽□⚷ 1:44; ♀⚹♇ 9:42; ☽⚹♅ 10:00; ☽⚹⚳ 13:20; ☽⚻♄ 14:31; ☿⚻♂ 15:48; ☉△☽ 19:23; ☽△♆ 22:09

14 M: ☽⚺♂ 0:51; ☽△☿ 2:26; ☽☍♇ 5:36; ☽△♀ 7:55; ♀⚼⚷ 8:20; ☽△♃ 10:42; ☽∥♂ 19:18; ☽∠⚳ 20:40

15 Tu: ☿⚹♇ 2:28; ☉△♆ 3:45; ☽⚼♆ 4:29; ☽∠♂ 6:39; ☽⋕♇ 7:18; ⚳⚻♄ 7:39; ♀△♃ 9:37; ☽△⚷ 14:12; ☽⚼♃ 16:56; ☿⚼⚷ 19:21; ☽□♅ 22:24

16 W: ☉⚻♂ 1:08; ☽⋕☿ 1:19; ☽☍♄ 3:18; ☽⚺⚳ 3:52; ☽⋕♀ 4:19; ♀ ♐ 6:10; ☽⚻♆ 10:37; ☉⋕☽ 10:59; ☽⚹♂ 12:13; ☉□☽ 13:28; ☊ D 13:36; ☿△♃ 15:44; ☽⚻♇ 18:06; ☽⚼⚷ 20:10; ☽⚻♃ 22:52; ☽∥♅ 23:48; ☽□☿ 23:57

17 Th: ☽⋕♄ 0:32; ☽□♀ 3:16; ☿ ♐ 8:43; ☽∥⚳ 20:29; ☽⚼♇ 23:40

18 F: ☽⚻⚷ 1:34; ☽△♅ 9:24; ☽⚻♄ 14:29; ☽☌⚳ 16:35; ☽∥⚷ 21:09; ☽☍♆ 21:13; ☽□♂ 21:36; ☉⚹♇ 21:39

19 Sa: ☽△♇ 4:27; ☉⚹☽ 5:01; ☽⋕♆ 8:11; ☽☍♃ 8:48; ☽⚼♅ 13:46; ♂□♆ 15:45; ☽⋕♃ 17:05; ☽⚹☿ 17:55; ☽⚼♄ 18:52; ☽⚹♀ 19:16; ☉⚼⚷ 19:27

20 Su: ☽∥♃ 7:36; ☽☍⚷ 9:55; ☉∠☽ 11:09; ☽∥♆ 16:14; ☽⚻♅ 17:12; ⚶ ♓ 21:27; ☽△♄ 22:19

21 M: ☽∠☿ 0:53; ☽∠♀ 1:26; ☽⚺⚳ 1:37; ☽⋕⚷ 2:33; ☽△♂ 3:38; ☉△♃ 4:08; ☽⚻♆ 4:24; ☽□♇ 11:16; ☽⚻♃ 15:12; ☉⚺☽ 16:05; ☿☌♀ 22:56; ☽⋕⚳ 23:30

22 Tu: ☽∠⚳ 4:38; ☽⚼♂ 5:20; ☽⚺♀ 6:22; ☽⚺☿ 6:33; ☽⚼♆ 6:37; ☉ ♐ 8:22; ☿∥♇ 14:19; ☽⚻⚷ 14:38; ☊ R 16:25; ☽⚼♃ 17:05; ☽∥♄ 17:57; ☽⋕♅ 18:41; ♂□⚳ 19:27; ☽☍♅ 21:26

23 W: ☽□♄ 2:34; ☽⚻♂ 6:17; ☽⚹⚳ 6:48; ☽△♆ 8:04; ☉∥☽ 13:49; ☽⚹♇ 14:39; ☽⚼⚷ 15:51; ☽△♃ 18:17; ☽∥♀ 22:20; ☉☌☽ 22:58; ♃ D 23:03

24 Th: ☽∥♇ 4:23; ☽∥☿ 7:58; ☽☌♀ 13:27; ☽☌☿ 14:50; ☽∠♇ 15:27; ☽△⚷ 16:32; ☽⋕♂ 16:52; ☿∠♇ 20:41; ☽⚻♅ 23:01

25 F: ☽⚹♄ 4:17; ☽☍♂ 6:37; ☿△⚷ 6:48; ☽□⚳ 9:24; ☽□♆ 9:25; ⚳☍♆ 9:59; ♀∠♇ 13:06; ☽⚺♇ 15:54; ☽□♃ 19:23; ☽⚼♅ 23:19

26 Sa: ♀△⚷ 0:52; ☉⚺☽ 3:33; ☽∠♄ 4:43; ☽□⚷ 17:12; ☽⚺♀ 18:44; ☽⚺☿ 21:15; ☽△♅ 23:36

27 Su: ☽⚺♄ 5:10; ☉∠☽ 5:42; ☽⚻♂ 6:12; ☽⚹♆ 10:07; ☽△⚳ 11:17; ☽☌♇ 16:44; ☿⚻♅ 19:17; ☽⚹♃ 20:12; ☽∠♀ 21:29; ☽⋕♂ 23:55

28 M: ☽∠☿ 0:36; ☽∥☿ 2:28; ☽⚼♂ 6:11; ☉⚹☽ 8:07; ☽∠♆ 10:45; ☽⚼⚳ 12:32; ☽∥♇ 13:16; ☽∥♀ 13:42; ♂△♄ 17:57; ☽⚹⚷ 18:19; ☽∠♃ 21:02; ☉∥☽ 22:28; ♀∥♇ 22:57

29 Tu: ☽⚹♀ 0:41; ☽□♅ 0:50; ♀⚻♅ 2:20; ☽⚹☿ 4:27; ☽△♂ 6:32; ☽☌♄ 6:55; ☽⚺♆ 11:48; ☽⚻⚳ 14:14; ☽⚺♇ 18:45; ☽∠⚷ 19:29; ☿⋕♂ 20:08; ☿☍♂ 20:31; ☽⚺♃ 22:20; ☽⋕♅ 23:39

30 W: ☽∥♄ 0:38; ☿⚹♄ 4:19; ⚴ R 8:34; ☊ D 14:31; ☉□☽ 14:38; ☽∠♇ 20:33; ☽⚺⚷ 21:14; ☽⋕⚳ 21:43

December 2022

LONGITUDE

Day	Sid.Time	☉	☽	☽ 12 hour	Mean ☊	True ☊	☿	♀	♂	⚳	♃	♄	⚷	♅	♆	♇
	h m s	° ' "	° ' "	° ' "	° '	° '	° '	° '	° '	° '	° '	° '	° '	° '	° '	° '
1 Th	4 39 20	8♐45 21	13♓45 27	20♓36 02	11♉50.6	13♉09.3	21♐03.1	18♐30.2	18♊52.5	24♍33.5	28♓53.1	19♒51.1	12♈09.8	16♉02.6	22♓38.9	26♑46.9
2 F	4 43 16	9 46 09	27 22 06	4♈03 48	11 47.4	13 10.2	22 34.4	19 45.5	18R 29.8	24 53.3	28 54.7	19 54.9	12R 08.6	16R 00.4	22R 38.8	26 48.4
3 Sa	4 47 13	10 46 58	10♈41 21	17 14 56	11 44.2	13 11.7	24 05.5	21 00.7	18 06.9	25 12.9	28 56.4	19 58.8	12 07.5	15 58.2	22 38.7	26 49.8
4 Su	4 51 10	11 47 48	23 44 48	0♉11 11	11 41.1	13 13.4	25 36.3	22 16.0	17 43.9	25 32.3	28 58.4	20 02.8	12 06.4	15 56.0	22D 38.7	26 51.3
5 M	4 55 06	12 48 39	6♉34 18	12 54 21	11 37.9	13R 14.5	27 06.9	23 31.3	17 20.7	25 51.6	29 00.6	20 06.9	12 05.4	15 53.9	22 38.7	26 52.8
6 Tu	4 59 03	13 49 30	19 11 33	25 26 04	11 34.7	13 14.5	28 37.1	24 46.6	16 57.5	26 10.7	29 03.0	20 11.1	12 04.5	15 51.7	22 38.8	26 54.3
7 W	5 02 59	14 50 23	1♊38 04	7♊47 41	11 31.5	13 13.0	0♑06.9	26 01.9	16 34.4	26 29.5	29 05.5	20 15.3	12 03.5	15 49.7	22 38.9	26 55.9
8 Th	5 06 56	15 51 17	13 55 05	20 00 25	11 28.4	13 09.8	1 36.3	27 17.2	16 11.3	26 48.2	29 08.3	20 19.7	12 02.7	15 47.6	22 39.0	26 57.4
9 F	5 10 52	16 52 12	26 03 48	2♋05 24	11 25.2	13 04.9	3 05.1	28 32.4	15 48.3	27 06.7	29 11.3	20 24.1	12 01.9	15 45.6	22 39.1	26 59.0
10 Sa	5 14 49	17 53 07	8♋05 24	14 03 59	11 22.0	12 58.7	4 33.3	29 47.7	15 25.4	27 25.1	29 14.5	20 28.5	12 01.1	15 43.6	22 39.3	27 00.6
11 Su	5 18 45	18 54 04	20 01 23	25 57 51	11 18.8	12 51.7	6 00.7	1♑03.0	15 02.8	27 43.2	29 17.9	20 33.1	12 00.4	15 41.6	22 39.6	27 02.2
12 M	5 22 42	19 55 02	1♌53 42	7♌49 14	11 15.7	12 44.7	7 27.2	2 18.2	14 40.4	28 01.1	29 21.4	20 37.8	11 59.7	15 39.7	22 39.8	27 03.8
13 Tu	5 26 39	20 56 01	13 44 51	19 40 57	11 12.5	12 38.4	8 52.7	3 33.5	14 18.3	28 18.8	29 25.2	20 42.5	11 59.1	15 37.8	22 40.1	27 05.5
14 W	5 30 35	21 57 00	25 38 00	1♍36 31	11 09.3	12 33.3	10 16.9	4 48.8	13 56.5	28 36.2	29 29.2	20 47.3	11 58.6	15 35.9	22 40.4	27 07.2
15 Th	5 34 32	22 58 01	7♍37 00	13 40 02	11 06.1	12 30.0	11 39.7	6 04.0	13 35.1	28 53.5	29 33.3	20 52.1	11 58.1	15 34.0	22 40.8	27 08.8
16 F	5 38 28	23 59 03	19 46 12	25 56 06	11 02.9	12D 28.6	13 00.7	7 19.3	13 14.2	29 10.5	29 37.6	20 57.1	11 57.6	15 32.2	22 41.2	27 10.5
17 Sa	5 42 25	25 00 06	2♎10 19	8♎29 28	10 59.8	12 28.7	14 19.7	8 34.5	12 53.7	29 27.4	29 42.1	21 02.1	11 57.3	15 30.5	22 41.6	27 12.2
18 Su	5 46 21	26 01 09	14 54 07	21 24 47	10 56.6	12 29.9	15 36.4	9 49.8	12 33.7	29 43.9	29 46.9	21 07.1	11 56.9	15 28.7	22 42.1	27 14.0
19 M	5 50 18	27 02 14	28 01 54	4♏45 52	10 53.4	12 31.3	16 50.2	11 05.1	12 14.3	0♎00.3	29 51.8	21 12.3	11 56.6	15 27.0	22 42.6	27 15.7
20 Tu	5 54 14	28 03 19	11♏36 55	18 35 08	10 50.2	12R 32.1	18 00.8	12 20.3	11 55.4	0 16.4	29 56.8	21 17.5	11 56.4	15 25.4	22 43.1	27 17.5
21 W	5 58 11	29 04 26	25 40 27	2♐52 38	10 47.1	12 31.3	19 07.6	13 35.6	11 37.1	0 32.3	0♈02.1	21 22.8	11 56.3	15 23.8	22 43.7	27 19.2
22 Th	6 02 08	0♑05 33	10♐11 11	17 35 25	10 43.9	12 28.4	20 10.1	14 50.8	11 19.5	0 47.9	0 07.5	21 28.2	11 56.2	15 22.2	22 44.3	27 21.0
23 F	6 06 04	1 06 41	25 04 27	2♑37 13	10 40.7	12 23.3	21 07.5	16 06.1	11 02.6	1 03.2	0 13.2	21 33.6	11D 56.1	15 20.7	22 45.0	27 22.8
24 Sa	6 10 01	2 07 49	10♑12 28	17 48 54	10 37.5	12 16.2	21 59.1	17 21.3	10 46.3	1 18.3	0 19.0	21 39.1	11 56.1	15 19.2	22 45.6	27 24.6
25 Su	6 13 57	3 08 58	25 25 08	2♒59 49	10 34.4	12 08.0	22 44.1	18 36.5	10 30.8	1 33.2	0 25.0	21 44.6	11 56.2	15 17.8	22 46.3	27 26.4
26 M	6 17 54	4 10 06	10♒31 44	17 59 43	10 31.2	11 59.8	23 21.7	19 51.8	10 16.1	1 47.8	0 31.1	21 50.2	11 56.3	15 16.4	22 47.1	27 28.3
27 Tu	6 21 50	5 11 15	25 22 51	2♓40 23	10 28.0	11 52.7	23 50.9	21 07.0	10 02.0	2 02.1	0 37.4	21 55.9	11 56.5	15 15.0	22 47.9	27 30.1
28 W	6 25 47	6 12 24	9♓51 47	16 56 45	10 24.8	11 47.5	24 10.8	22 22.2	9 48.8	2 16.1	0 43.9	22 01.6	11 56.7	15 13.7	22 48.7	27 32.0
29 Th	6 29 44	7 13 33	23 55 09	0♈47 01	10 21.7	11 44.6	24R 20.5	23 37.4	9 36.4	2 29.8	0 50.6	22 07.4	11 57.0	15 12.4	22 49.5	27 33.8
30 F	6 33 40	8 14 42	7♈32 32	14 12 01	10 18.5	11D 43.7	24 19.3	24 52.6	9 24.8	2 43.3	0 57.4	22 13.3	11 57.3	15 11.2	22 50.4	27 35.7
31 Sa	6 37 37	9♑15 51	20 45 50	27 14 26	10♉15.3	11♉44.1	24♑06.7	26♑07.7	9♊13.9	2♎56.4	1♈04.4	22♒19.2	11♈57.7	15♉10.0	22♓51.3	27♑37.6

1st of Month

Julian Day # 2459914.5
Obliquity 23°26'37"
SVP 4♓56'35"
GC 27♐09.6
Eris 24♈04.3R

Day	⚴	Day	⚵	Day	⚶
1	26♋32.8R	1	13♓28.7	1	2♓58.8
6	26 21.5R	6	14 57.4	6	4 35.2
11	25 52.1R	11	16 34.1	11	6 16.1
16	25 04.5R	16	18 18.0	16	8 01.1
21	23 59.8R	21	20 08.8	21	9 50.0
26	22 40.1R	26	22 05.9	26	11 42.3
31	21 08.7R	31	24 08.9	31	13 37.8

DECLINATION and LATITUDE

Day	☉ Decl	☽ Decl	☽ Lat	☽ 12h Decl	☿ Decl	☿ Lat	♀ Decl	♀ Lat	♂ Decl	♂ Lat	⚳ Decl	⚳ Lat	♃ Decl	♃ Lat	♄ Decl	♄ Lat
1 Th	21S46	10S33	4S31	7S33	25S09	2S01	23S19	0S23	24N58	1N60	11N06	9N45	1S45	1S26	16S03	1S16
2 F	21 55	4 30	3 46	1 25	25 18	2 04	23 28	0 25	24 58	2 02	11 02	9 49	1 44	1 25	16 02	1 16
3 Sa	22 04	1N38	2 49	4N39	25 26	2 08	23 35	0 27	24 59	2 05	10 57	9 53	1 43	1 25	16 01	1 16
4 Su	22 12	7 36	1 45	10 26	25 32	2 10	23 42	0 30	24 59	2 08	10 53	9 56	1 42	1 25	15 60	1 16
5 M	22 20	13 08	0 37	15 41	25 37	2 13	23 49	0 32	24 60	2 10	10 49	9 60	1 41	1 24	15 58	1 15
6 Tu	22 28	18 03	0N32	20 11	25 41	2 15	23 55	0 34	24 60	2 12	10 45	10 04	1 40	1 24	15 57	1 15
7 W	22 35	22 06	1 39	23 45	25 43	2 17	23 59	0 37	24 60	2 15	10 41	10 08	1 39	1 24	15 55	1 15
8 Th	22 41	25 07	2 40	26 10	25 44	2 18	24 04	0 39	24 60	2 17	10 37	10 11	1 37	1 24	15 54	1 15
9 F	22 47	26 55	3 32	27 20	25 43	2 19	24 07	0 41	24 59	2 19	10 33	10 15	1 36	1 23	15 53	1 15
10 Sa	22 53	27 26	4 15	27 12	25 41	2 19	24 10	0 43	24 59	2 22	10 29	10 19	1 34	1 23	15 51	1 15
11 Su	22 58	26 39	4 46	25 49	25 37	2 19	24 12	0 46	24 59	2 24	10 26	10 23	1 33	1 23	15 50	1 15
12 M	23 03	24 41	5 04	23 17	25 32	2 19	24 13	0 48	24 58	2 26	10 22	10 27	1 31	1 22	15 48	1 15
13 Tu	23 08	21 38	5 10	19 46	25 26	2 18	24 13	0 50	24 57	2 28	10 19	10 31	1 29	1 22	15 47	1 15
14 W	23 12	17 42	5 02	15 27	25 18	2 16	24 13	0 52	24 57	2 29	10 15	10 35	1 27	1 22	15 45	1 15
15 Th	23 15	13 03	4 41	10 30	25 08	2 13	24 12	0 54	24 56	2 31	10 12	10 39	1 26	1 22	15 43	1 15
16 F	23 18	7 50	4 07	5 04	24 58	2 10	24 10	0 56	24 55	2 33	10 09	10 43	1 24	1 21	15 42	1 15
17 Sa	23 21	2 12	3 21	0S42	24 46	2 06	24 08	0 58	24 54	2 34	10 06	10 48	1 22	1 21	15 40	1 15
18 Su	23 23	3S40	2 24	6 37	24 32	2 02	24 04	1 00	24 53	2 36	10 04	10 52	1 19	1 21	15 38	1 15
19 M	23 24	9 34	1 18	12 27	24 18	1 56	24 00	1 02	24 52	2 37	10 01	10 56	1 17	1 21	15 37	1 15
20 Tu	23 25	15 14	0 05	17 53	24 02	1 50	23 56	1 04	24 50	2 39	9 59	11 00	1 15	1 20	15 35	1 15
21 W	23 26	20 19	1S10	22 29	23 46	1 42	23 50	1 06	24 49	2 40	9 56	11 04	1 13	1 20	15 33	1 15
22 Th	23 26	24 20	2 23	25 48	23 28	1 34	23 44	1 08	24 48	2 41	9 54	11 09	1 10	1 20	15 32	1 15
23 F	23 26	26 49	3 28	27 21	23 10	1 24	23 37	1 09	24 46	2 42	9 52	11 13	1 08	1 20	15 30	1 15
24 Sa	23 25	27 22	4 20	26 52	22 52	1 14	23 29	1 11	24 45	2 43	9 50	11 18	1 05	1 19	15 28	1 15
25 Su	23 24	25 51	4 53	24 23	22 33	1 02	23 21	1 13	24 44	2 44	9 48	11 22	1 03	1 19	15 26	1 15
26 M	23 22	22 30	5 06	20 15	22 13	0 49	23 12	1 14	24 43	2 45	9 46	11 26	0 60	1 19	15 24	1 15
27 Tu	23 20	17 24	4 58	14 58	21 54	0 35	23 02	1 16	24 41	2 46	9 45	11 31	0 57	1 18	15 23	1 15
28 W	23 18	12 02	4 30	8 60	21 36	0 20	22 51	1 17	24 40	2 47	9 44	11 36	0 54	1 18	15 21	1 15
29 Th	23 14	5 54	3 47	2 46	21 18	0 03	22 40	1 19	24 39	2 47	9 42	11 40	0 51	1 18	15 19	1 15
30 F	23 11	0N21	2 53	3N25	21 01	0N14	22 28	1 20	24 38	2 48	9 41	11 45	0 48	1 18	15 17	1 15
31 Sa	23S07	6N24	1S50	9N18	20S45	0N33	22S15	1S22	24N36	2N48	9N40	11N49	0S45	1S17	15S15	1S15

Day	⚷ Decl	⚷ Lat	♅ Decl	♅ Lat	♆ Decl	♆ Lat	♇ Decl	♇ Lat
1	6N31	1N51	16N17	0S22	4S01	1S12	22S59	2S14
6	6 28	1 50	16 14	0 22	4 01	1 12	22 58	2 14
11	6 25	1 49	16 11	0 22	4 01	1 12	22 56	2 14
16	6 24	1 49	16 09	0 22	4 00	1 12	22 55	2 14
21	6 22	1 48	16 06	0 22	3 59	1 12	22 54	2 14
26	6 22	1 47	16 04	0 22	3 57	1 11	22 52	2 15
31	6N21	1N46	16N03	0S21	3S56	1S11	22S50	2S15

Day	⚴ Decl	⚴ Lat	⚵ Decl	⚵ Lat	⚶ Decl	⚶ Lat	Eris Decl	Eris Lat
1	29S42	51S26	11S39	5S36	17S06	7S11	1S08	11S15
6	30 33	52 19	11 18	5 50	16 22	7 02	1 08	11 14
11	31 15	53 05	10 53	6 04	15 36	6 54	1 08	11 14
16	31 46	53 43	10 23	6 16	14 49	6 45	1 08	11 13
21	32 06	54 11	9 50	6 28	14 01	6 38	1 08	11 12
26	32 13	54 27	9 14	6 39	13 11	6 30	1 08	11 12
31	32S06	54S29	8S35	6S49	12S19	6S23	1S07	11S11

Moon Phenomena

Max/0 Decl (dy hr mn)
2 17:34 0 N
9 21:27 27N26
17 9:06 0 S
23 18:23 27S25
29 22:39 0 N

Max/0 Lat (dy hr mn)
5 12:39 0 N
12 21:47 5N10
20 1:36 0 S
26 2:20 5S06

Perigee/Apogee (dy hr m kilometers)
12 0:30 a 405868
24 8:28 p 358275

PH (dy hr mn)
○ 8 4:09 16♊02
☾ 16 8:57 24♍22
● 23 10:18 1♑33
☽ 30 1:22 8♈18

Void of Course Moon

Last Aspect	☽ Ingress
2 2:46 ♃ ☌	♈ 2 4:42
4 5:47 ♇ □	♉ 4 11:39
6 19:03 ♃ ⚹	♊ 6 20:50
9 6:15 ♃ □	♋ 9 7:50
11 18:50 ♃ △	♌ 11 20:10
13 15:53 ☉ △	♍ 14 8:47
16 19:14 ♃ ☍	♎ 16 19:50
18 22:37 ♇ □	♏ 19 3:32
21 2:46 ♇ ⚹	♐ 21 7:14
22 20:17 ♆ □	♑ 23 7:51
25 3:12 ♇ ☌	♒ 25 7:15
26 18:21 ♄ ☌	♓ 27 7:35
29 6:22 ♇ ⚹	♈ 29 10:37
31 12:45 ♇ □	♉ 31 17:10

DAILY ASPECTARIAN

1 Th ☽⚹♅ 3:59 · ♀☍♂ 5:29 · ☽□♂ 8:43 · ☽□♀ 9:09 · ☽⚺♄ 10:44 · ☽□☿ 14:25 · ☽☌♆ 15:37 · ☽#⚷ 16:08 · ☽☍⚳ 19:29 · ☽⚹♇ 23:00

2 F ☿□♆ 1:09 · ☽∥♆ 1:51 · ☽☌♃ 2:46 · ♀⚹♄ 3:11 · ☽∠♅ 6:29 · ☽∥♃ 10:48 · ☽∠♄ 13:36

3 Sa ☉△☽ 0:11 · ☽#♃ 0:20 · ☽☌⚷ 2:37 · ☽#♆ 9:29 · ☽⚺♅ 9:37 · ☽⚹♂ 13:12 · ☽⚹♄ 17:07 · ☽∥⚷ 19:26 · ☽△♀ 20:58 · ☽⚺♆ 21:57 · ☿□⚳ 22:40

4 Su ♆D 0:16 · ☉∠♇ 1:25 · ☽⚻⚳ 3:25 · ☽△☿ 3:55 · ☽□♇ 5:47 · ☉⚼☽ 6:09 · ♀□♆ 7:13 · ☉△⚷ 7:14 · ☽⚺♃ 9:45 · ☽∥⚳ 13:48 · ☽∠♂ 16:17 · ☿⚺♇ 20:12

5 M ☽∠♆ 2:02 · ☽⚼♀ 4:05 · ☽⚼⚳ 8:19 · ☽⚺⚷ 10:26 · ☽⚼☿ 11:55 · ☊R 12:40 · ☉⚻☽ 12:51 · ☽#♄ 13:21 · ☽∠♃ 14:09 · ☽∥♅ 14:45 · ☽☌♅ 17:39 · ☽⚺♂ 19:51

6 Tu ☽□♄ 1:55 · ☽⚹♆ 6:38 · ☿□♃ 7:06 · ☽⚻♀ 11:56 · ☽△⚳ 13:47 · ☽△♇ 14:52 · ☽∠⚷ 15:09 · ☽⚹♃ 19:03 · ☽⚻☿ 20:39 · ☿ ♑ 22:09

7 W ☉#☽ 3:23 · ☽#♇ 6:00 · ☿⚼♅ 11:13 · ♀□⚳ 11:45 · ☽#♀ 14:20 · ♀⚺♇ 17:35 · ☽⚼♇ 20:08 · ☽⚹⚷ 20:19 · ☉⚻♅ 22:36 · ☽∥♂ 22:53

8 Th ☽⚺♅ 3:41 · ☉☍☽ 4:09 · ☽☌♂ 4:20 · ☉☍♂ 5:43 · ☽#☿ 6:36 · ☽△♄ 12:43 · ⚳△♇ 12:59 · ☽□♆ 17:14

9 F ☽⚻♇ 1:50 · ☽□⚳ 2:08 · ♂⚺♅ 3:06 · ☽☍♀ 5:30 · ☽□♃ 6:15 · ☽∠♅ 9:19 · ♀□♃ 12:56 · ☽☍☿ 15:56 · ☽⚼♄ 18:44

10 Sa ♀ ♑ 3:55 · ☽□⚷ 7:52 · ☽⚺♂ 14:17 · ☉∥♇ 14:54 · ☽⚹♅ 15:18 · ☿∠♄ 15:59 · ♀⚼♅ 17:21 · ☉⚻☽ 21:32

11 Su ☽⚻♄ 1:04 · ☽△♆ 5:19 · ☽☍♇ 14:12 · ☽#☿ 14:45 · ☽⚹⚳ 15:57 · ☽△♃ 18:50 · ☽∠♂ 19:38 · ☽∥♂ 21:09

12 M ☽⚻♀ 0:56 · ☽#♀ 4:12 · ☉⚼☽ 6:42 · ☽⚼♆ 11:41 · ☽⚻☿ 12:48 · ☉#☽ 13:25 · ☽#♇ 14:41 · ☉⚹♄ 18:13 · ☽△⚷ 20:26 · ☽∠⚳ 23:06

13 Tu ☽⚹♂ 1:06 · ☽⚼♃ 1:22 · ☽□♅ 3:48 · ☽⚼♀ 10:53 · ☽☍♄ 14:10 · ☉△☽ 15:53 · ☽⚻♆ 18:02 · ☽⚼☿ 23:12

14 W ☽⚼⚷ 2:42 · ☽⚻♇ 3:00 · ☽⚺⚳ 6:07 · ☽⚻♃ 7:47 · ☽∥♅ 8:21 · ☽#♄ 10:33 · ☉□♆ 17:11 · ♀∠♄ 19:56 · ☽△♀ 20:33

15 Th ☿□⚷ 5:22 · ☽⚻⚷ 8:38 · ☽⚼♇ 9:01 · ☽△☿ 9:03 · ☽□♂ 11:30 · ☽∥⚳ 13:29 · ☽△♅ 15:43

16 F ☽⚻♄ 2:19 · ☿⚻♂ 3:13 · ☽☍♆ 5:42 · ☽∥⚷ 6:17 · ☿#♂ 6:38 · ☉□☽ 8:57 · ☊D 9:09 · ☽△♇ 14:26 · ☽#♆ 16:30 · ☽☌⚳ 18:40 · ☽☍♃ 19:14 · ☽⚼♅ 20:49

17 Sa ☽#♃ 3:32 · ☽⚼♄ 7:24 · ☽□♀ 13:29 · ☽∥♃ 14:34 · ☽☍⚷ 18:30 · ☽△♂ 19:45 · ☿△♅ 21:38

18 Su ☽⚻♅ 1:04 · ☽∥♆ 1:21 · ☽□☿ 1:27 · ⚳☍♃ 6:02 · ☽#⚷ 11:01 · ☽△♄ 11:32 · ☽⚻♆ 14:22 · ☉⚹☽ 22:04 · ♂⚼♇ 22:21 · ☽⚼♂ 22:36 · ☽□♇ 22:37 · ⚳ ♎ 23:35

19 M ☽#⚳ 1:51 · ☽⚻♃ 3:18 · ☽⚺⚳ 3:37 · ☉⚺♇ 5:27 · ♀□⚷ 16:24 · ☽⚼♆ 17:12 · ♀⚻♂ 17:38 · ♂⚹⚷ 22:40

20 Tu ☽⚻♂ 0:31 · ☽⚻⚷ 0:34 · ☽⚹♀ 1:23 · ☽∥♄ 1:32 · ☊R 1:37 · ☉∠☽ 2:42 · ☽#♅ 3:53 · ☽⚼♃ 5:48 · ☽∠⚳ 6:27 · ☽☍♅ 6:34 · ☽⚹☿ 11:59 · ⚳⚼♅ 12:19 · ♃ ♈ 14:33 · ☿∥♀ 14:39 · ☽□♄ 16:42 · ☽△♆ 19:02

21 W ☽⚼⚷ 2:07 · ☽⚹♇ 2:46 · ☽∠♀ 5:21 · ☉⚺☽ 6:07 · ☽△♃ 7:20 · ☽⚹⚳ 8:16 · ☽∥♇ 14:25 · ☽∠☿ 15:10 · ☉∥☽ 17:52 · ☽∥☿ 18:32 · ☽∥♀ 19:55 · ☉ ♑ 21:49

22 Th ☉□♃ 0:52 · ☽☍♂ 1:49 · ☉∥☿ 2:44 · ☽△⚷ 2:51 · ☽#♂ 3:24 · ☽∠♇ 3:32 · ☉⚼♅ 6:23 · ☽⚺♀ 8:16 · ☽⚻♅ 8:24 · ♀△♅ 9:49 · ☽⚺☿ 17:16 · ☽⚹♄ 18:21 · ☽□♆ 20:17 · ☉□⚳ 22:12

23 F ☽⚺♇ 3:41 · ☽□♃ 8:15 · ☽⚼♅ 8:23 · ⚷D 9:32 · ☽□⚳ 9:41 · ☉☌☽ 10:18 · ☿⚺♄ 13:10 · ☽∠♄ 18:21 · ☿∥♇ 22:34

24 Sa ♃∠♅ 0:44 · ☽⚻♂ 0:53 · ☽□⚷ 2:44 · ☽△♅ 8:03 · ☽☌♀ 12:17 · ☉∥♀ 13:06 · ☽⚺♄ 18:10 · ☽☌☿ 19:33 · ☽⚹♆ 19:49

25 Su ☽⚼♂ 0:09 · ☿⚹♆ 1:18 · ☽☌♇ 3:12 · ☽⚹♃ 7:58 · ☽#♂ 9:31 · ☽△⚳ 9:52 · ☉⚺☽ 13:08 · ☉∥☽ 18:41 · ☽∠♆ 19:37 · ☽∥♀ 19:40 · ☽∥♇ 21:50 · ☽△♂ 23:35

26 M ☽∥☿ 1:42 · ☽⚹⚷ 2:15 · ☽□♅ 7:36 · ☽∠♃ 8:04 · ☽⚼⚳ 10:14 · ☉∠☽ 14:55 · ☽⚺♀ 16:25 · ☽☌♄ 18:21 · ☽⚺♆ 19:47 · ☽⚺☿ 21:25

27 Tu ☽∠⚷ 2:33 · ☽⚺♇ 3:29 · ☽#♅ 7:21 · ☽⚺♃ 8:41 · ☽∥♄ 10:21 · ☽⚻⚳ 11:07 · ♀⚺♄ 16:54 · ☉⚹☽ 17:25 · ☽∠♀ 19:25 · ☽∠☿ 22:50 · ♀∥♇ 23:37 · ☽□♂ 23:55

28 W ☽⚺⚷ 3:31 · ☽∠♇ 4:31 · ♀⚹♆ 8:33 · ☽⚹♅ 9:04 · ☽#⚳ 9:12 · ☽⚺♄ 20:52 · ☉∠♄ 21:20 · ☽☌♆ 22:06 · ☽#⚷ 22:13 · ☽⚹♀ 23:26

29 Th ☽⚹☿ 0:44 · ☽⚹♇ 6:22 · ☽∥♆ 7:31 · ☿R 9:33 · ☽∠♅ 10:58 · ☽☌♃ 12:12 · ☿☌♀ 13:59 · ☽☍⚳ 15:17 · ♀⚼♂ 16:17 · ☽∥♃ 19:30 · ☽∠♄ 23:25

30 F ☊D 1:14 · ☉□☽ 1:22 · ☽#♃ 1:46 · ☽⚹♂ 3:18 · ☽☌⚷ 7:56 · ☽⚺♅ 13:46 · ☽#♆ 14:02 · ☉⚻♂ 23:22 · ☽∥⚷ 23:47

31 Sa ☽⚹♄ 2:53 · ☽⚺♆ 3:52 · ☽□☿ 6:02 · ☽∠♂ 6:19 · ☽□♀ 11:00 · ☽□♇ 12:45 · ☽∥⚳ 13:35 · ☽⚺♃ 19:21 · ☽⚻⚳ 23:04

LONGITUDE

January 2023

Day	Sid.Time	☉	☽	☽ 12 hour	Mean☊	True☊	☿	♀	♂	⚳	♃	♄	⚷	♅	♆	♇
	h m s	° ' "	° ' "	° ' "	° '	° '	° '	° '	° '	° '	° '	° '	° '	° '	° '	° '
1 Su	6 41 33	10♑16 59	3♉38 16	9♉57 50	10♉12.1	11♉45.0	23♑42.1	27♑22.9	9♊04.0	3♎09.3	1♈11.6	22♒25.1	11♈58.1	15♉08.9	22♓52.2	27♑39.5
2 M	6 45 30	11 18 08	16 13 36	22 26 01	10 08.9	11R 45.1	23R 05.8	28 38.0	8R 54.8	3 21.9	1 18.9	22 31.1	11 58.6	15R 07.8	22 53.2	27 41.4
3 Tu	6 49 26	12 19 16	28 35 33	4♊42 33	10 05.8	11 43.6	22 18.1	29 53.2	8 46.4	3 34.2	1 26.4	22 37.2	11 59.2	15 06.7	22 54.2	27 43.3
4 W	6 53 23	13 20 24	10♊47 26	16 50 28	10 02.6	11 39.5	21 20.0	1♒08.3	8 38.9	3 46.1	1 34.0	22 43.3	11 59.8	15 05.7	22 55.2	27 45.2
5 Th	6 57 19	14 21 32	22 51 58	28 52 09	9 59.4	11 32.6	20 13.0	2 23.4	8 32.2	3 57.8	1 41.8	22 49.5	12 00.5	15 04.8	22 56.3	27 47.1
6 F	7 01 16	15 22 40	4♋51 15	10♋49 27	9 56.2	11 23.0	18 59.0	3 38.5	8 26.3	4 09.1	1 49.7	22 55.7	12 01.2	15 03.9	22 57.4	27 49.0
7 Sa	7 05 13	16 23 48	16 46 55	22 43 47	9 53.1	11 11.1	17 40.3	4 53.6	8 21.3	4 20.2	1 57.8	23 02.0	12 02.0	15 03.1	22 58.5	27 51.0
8 Su	7 09 09	17 24 56	28 40 15	4♌36 26	9 49.9	10 57.9	16 19.7	6 08.7	8 17.0	4 30.9	2 06.0	23 08.3	12 02.8	15 02.3	22 59.7	27 52.9
9 M	7 13 06	18 26 04	10♌32 33	16 28 45	9 46.7	10 44.5	14 59.6	7 23.7	8 13.6	4 41.2	2 14.4	23 14.7	12 03.7	15 01.5	23 00.9	27 54.9
10 Tu	7 17 02	19 27 11	22 25 18	28 22 27	9 43.5	10 31.9	13 42.5	8 38.8	8 11.0	4 51.3	2 22.9	23 21.1	12 04.6	15 00.8	23 02.1	27 56.8
11 W	7 20 59	20 28 18	4♍20 30	10♍19 48	9 40.4	10 21.2	12 30.7	9 53.8	8 09.1	5 00.9	2 31.6	23 27.5	12 05.6	15 00.2	23 03.4	27 58.8
12 Th	7 24 55	21 29 26	16 20 44	22 23 46	9 37.2	10 13.1	11 26.0	11 08.8	8D 08.0	5 10.3	2 40.4	23 34.0	12 06.7	14 59.6	23 04.6	28 00.7
13 F	7 28 52	22 30 33	28 29 21	4♎38 01	9 34.0	10 07.8	10 29.5	12 23.8	8 07.8	5 19.3	2 49.4	23 40.5	12 07.8	14 59.0	23 05.9	28 02.7
14 Sa	7 32 48	23 31 40	10♎50 19	17 06 51	9 30.8	10 05.1	9 42.3	13 38.8	8 08.2	5 27.9	2 58.4	23 47.1	12 08.9	14 58.5	23 07.3	28 04.6
15 Su	7 36 45	24 32 47	23 28 10	29 54 52	9 27.7	10D 04.4	9 04.7	14 53.7	8 09.5	5 36.2	3 07.7	23 53.7	12 10.1	14 58.1	23 08.6	28 06.6
16 M	7 40 42	25 33 54	6♏27 31	13♏06 37	9 24.5	10R 04.6	8 36.9	16 08.7	8 11.5	5 44.1	3 17.0	24 00.4	12 11.4	14 57.7	23 10.0	28 08.6
17 Tu	7 44 38	26 35 01	19 52 35	26 45 46	9 21.3	10 04.3	8 18.6	17 23.6	8 14.2	5 51.6	3 26.5	24 07.1	12 12.7	14 57.4	23 11.5	28 10.5
18 W	7 48 35	27 36 07	3♐46 20	10♐54 18	9 18.1	10 02.4	8D 09.4	18 38.6	8 17.7	5 58.7	3 36.1	24 13.8	12 14.0	14 57.1	23 12.9	28 12.5
19 Th	7 52 31	28 37 14	18 09 29	25 31 27	9 14.9	9 58.1	8 09.0	19 53.5	8 21.8	6 05.5	3 45.8	24 20.5	12 15.4	14 56.8	23 14.4	28 14.5
20 F	7 56 28	29 38 20	2♑59 32	10♑32 49	9 11.8	9 50.8	8 16.6	21 08.4	8 26.7	6 11.9	3 55.7	24 27.3	12 16.9	14 56.7	23 15.9	28 16.4
21 Sa	8 00 24	0♒39 26	18 10 10	25 50 15	9 08.6	9 41.0	8 31.7	22 23.2	8 32.3	6 17.9	4 05.7	24 34.2	12 18.4	14 56.5	23 17.4	28 18.4
22 Su	8 04 21	1 40 31	3♒31 36	11♒12 42	9 05.4	9 29.6	8 53.7	23 38.1	8 38.6	6 23.5	4 15.8	24 41.0	12 20.0	14D 56.5	23 19.0	28 20.4
23 M	8 08 17	2 41 35	18 52 00	26 28 05	9 02.2	9 17.9	9 21.9	24 52.9	8 45.6	6 28.6	4 26.1	24 47.9	12 21.6	14 56.4	23 20.6	28 22.3
24 Tu	8 12 14	3 42 39	3♓59 39	11♓25 37	8 59.1	9 07.4	9 55.9	26 07.7	8 53.2	6 33.4	4 36.4	24 54.8	12 23.2	14 56.5	23 22.2	28 24.3
25 W	8 16 11	4 43 41	18 45 09	25 57 36	8 55.9	9 00.0	10 34.9	27 22.5	9 01.5	6 37.8	4 46.9	25 01.8	12 24.9	14 56.5	23 23.8	28 26.3
26 Th	8 20 07	5 44 43	3♈02 39	10♈00 10	8 52.7	8 53.5	11 18.7	28 37.3	9 10.4	6 41.7	4 57.5	25 08.8	12 26.7	14 56.7	23 25.5	28 28.2
27 F	8 24 04	6 45 43	16 50 12	23 33 01	8 49.5	8 50.6	12 06.6	29 52.0	9 20.0	6 45.3	5 08.2	25 15.8	12 28.5	14 56.9	23 27.1	28 30.2
28 Sa	8 28 00	7 46 43	0♉08 58	6♉38 33	8 46.4	8 49.7	12 58.4	1♓06.7	9 30.2	6 48.4	5 19.0	25 22.8	12 30.3	14 57.1	23 28.8	28 32.1
29 Su	8 31 57	8 47 41	13 02 17	19 20 47	8 43.2	8 49.7	13 53.6	2 21.4	9 40.9	6 51.1	5 29.9	25 29.8	12 32.2	14 57.4	23 30.6	28 34.1
30 M	8 35 53	9 48 38	25 34 38	1♊44 28	8 40.0	8 49.1	14 52.0	3 36.0	9 52.3	6 53.4	5 40.9	25 36.9	12 34.2	14 57.7	23 32.3	28 36.0
31 Tu	8 39 50	10♒49 34	7♊50 53	13 54 25	8♉36.8	8♉47.0	15♑53.3	4♓50.7	10♊04.2	6♎55.2	5♈52.0	25♒44.0	12♈36.1	14♉58.1	23♓34.1	28♑37.9

1st of Month

Julian Day # 2459945.5
Obliquity 23°26'[illegible]7"
SVP 4♓56'29"
GC 27♐09.6
Eris 23♈55.8R

Day	⚴	⚵	⚶
1	20♋49.4R	24♓34.1	14♓01.2
6	19 09.8R	26 43.5	15 59.9
11	17 28.6R	28 57.6	18 01.1
16	15 50.6R	1♈16.1	20 04.5
21	14 20.3R	3 38.9	22 09.9
26	13 01.8R	6 05.5	24 17.1
31	11 58.0R	8 35.5	26 25.9

DECLINATION and LATITUDE

Day	☉ Decl	☽ Decl	☽ Lat	☽ 12h Decl	☿ Decl	☿ Lat	♀ Decl	♀ Lat	♂ Decl	♂ Lat	⚳ Decl	⚳ Lat	♃ Decl	♃ Lat	♄ Decl	♄ Lat
1 Su	23S02	12N03	0S43	14N39	20S30	0N52	22S02	1S23	24N35	2N49	9N39	11N54	0S42	1S17	15S13	1S15
2 M	22 57	17 04	0N24	19 18	20 17	1 11	21 48	1 24	24 34	2 49	9 39	11 59	0 39	1 17	15 11	1 15
3 Tu	22 52	21 17	1 29	23 03	20 06	1 31	21 34	1 25	24 33	2 50	9 38	12 03	0 36	1 17	15 09	1 15
4 W	22 46	24 31	2 28	25 42	19 56	1 50	21 19	1 26	24 32	2 50	9 38	12 08	0 33	1 16	15 07	1 15
5 Th	22 40	26 35	3 20	27 09	19 48	2 08	21 03	1 27	24 32	2 50	9 38	12 13	0 29	1 16	15 05	1 15
6 F	22 33	27 24	4 03	27 19	19 42	2 25	20 46	1 28	24 31	2 50	9 38	12 18	0 26	1 16	15 03	1 15
7 Sa	22 26	26 56	4 35	26 14	19 37	2 40	20 29	1 29	24 30	2 50	9 38	12 23	0 23	1 16	15 01	1 15
8 Su	22 18	25 14	4 55	23 57	19 34	2 53	20 12	1 30	24 29	2 50	9 38	12 28	0 19	1 16	14 59	1 15
9 M	22 10	22 25	5 01	20 39	19 33	3 04	19 53	1 31	24 29	2 51	9 38	12 32	0 16	1 15	14 57	1 15
10 Tu	22 02	18 41	4 55	16 31	19 33	3 12	19 35	1 32	24 29	2 51	9 39	12 37	0 12	1 15	14 54	1 15
11 W	21 53	14 12	4 36	11 44	19 34	3 18	19 15	1 32	24 28	2 50	9 40	12 42	0 08	1 15	14 52	1 15
12 Th	21 43	9 08	4 04	6 27	19 36	3 21	18 55	1 33	24 28	2 50	9 41	12 47	0 05	1 15	14 50	1 15
13 F	21 34	3 41	3 21	0 51	19 40	3 22	18 35	1 34	24 28	2 50	9 42	12 52	0 01	1 14	14 48	1 15
14 Sa	21 23	2S01	2 28	4S54	19 45	3 21	18 14	1 34	24 28	2 50	9 43	12 57	0N03	1 14	14 46	1 15
15 Su	21 13	7 46	1 27	10 36	19 50	3 18	17 52	1 35	24 28	2 50	9 44	13 02	0 07	1 14	14 44	1 15
16 M	21 02	13 22	0 19	16 02	19 57	3 13	17 30	1 35	24 28	2 50	9 46	13 07	0 11	1 14	14 41	1 15
17 Tu	20 50	18 32	0S52	20 51	20 04	3 07	17 08	1 35	24 28	2 49	9 48	13 13	0 15	1 14	14 39	1 15
18 W	20 38	22 54	2 02	24 38	20 12	2 60	16 45	1 35	24 28	2 49	9 50	13 18	0 19	1 13	14 37	1 15
19 Th	20 26	26 00	3 07	26 57	20 20	2 52	16 21	1 35	24 29	2 49	9 52	13 23	0 23	1 13	14 35	1 15
20 F	20 14	27 25	4 01	27 23	20 28	2 43	15 58	1 36	24 29	2 48	9 54	13 28	0 27	1 13	14 32	1 15
21 Sa	20 01	26 49	4 39	25 45	20 36	2 34	15 33	1 36	24 30	2 48	9 56	13 33	0 31	1 13	14 30	1 15
22 Su	19 47	24 12	4 58	22 13	20 45	2 24	15 09	1 35	24 30	2 48	9 59	13 38	0 35	1 13	14 28	1 15
23 M	19 33	19 51	4 56	17 11	20 53	2 14	14 43	1 35	24 31	2 47	10 01	13 43	0 39	1 12	14 26	1 15
24 Tu	19 19	14 16	4 33	11 11	21 01	2 04	14 18	1 35	24 32	2 47	10 04	13 48	0 44	1 12	14 23	1 15
25 W	19 05	7 60	3 51	4 45	21 08	1 53	13 52	1 35	24 32	2 46	10 07	13 54	0 48	1 12	14 21	1 15
26 Th	18 50	1 30	2 57	1N44	21 15	1 43	13 26	1 34	24 33	2 46	10 10	13 59	0 52	1 12	14 19	1 15
27 F	18 35	4N52	1 53	7 55	21 21	1 32	12 59	1 34	24 34	2 45	10 14	14 04	0 57	1 12	14 16	1 15
28 Sa	18 19	10 49	0 46	13 33	21 27	1 22	12 32	1 33	24 35	2 45	10 17	14 09	1 01	1 11	14 14	1 15
29 Su	18 04	16 06	0N22	18 27	21 31	1 12	12 05	1 33	24 37	2 44	10 21	14 14	1 06	1 11	14 12	1 15
30 M	17 47	20 34	1 27	22 26	21 35	1 02	11 37	1 32	24 38	2 44	10 25	14 19	1 10	1 11	14 09	1 15
31 Tu	17S31	24N02	2N27	25N21	21S38	0N52	11S09	1S31	24N39	2N43	10N29	14N25	1N15	1S11	14S07	1S15

Day	⚷ Decl	⚷ Lat	♅ Decl	♅ Lat	♆ Decl	♆ Lat	♇ Decl	♇ Lat
1	6N21	1N46	16N02	0S21	3S55	1S11	22S50	2S15
6	6 22	1 45	16 01	0 21	3 53	1 11	22 49	2 15
11	6 23	1 44	15 60	0 21	3 51	1 11	22 47	2 16
16	6 24	1 43	15 59	0 21	3 48	1 11	22 45	2 16
21	6 26	1 43	15 59	0 21	3 45	1 11	22 44	2 17
26	6 29	1 42	15 59	0 21	3 41	1 11	22 42	2 17
31	6N32	1N41	15N60	0S21	3S38	1S10	22S41	2S18

Day	⚴ Decl	⚴ Lat	⚵ Decl	⚵ Lat	⚶ Decl	⚶ Lat	Eris Decl	Eris Lat
1	32S03	54S28	8S26	6S51	12S09	6S22	1S07	11S11
6	31 39	54 13	7 44	7 00	11 16	6 15	1 07	11 10
11	30 60	53 43	6 58	7 09	10 23	6 08	1 06	11 09
16	30 07	52 58	6 11	7 17	9 29	6 02	1 05	11 08
21	29 01	51 57	5 22	7 25	8 34	5 57	1 05	11 08
26	27 42	50 43	4 31	7 33	7 38	5 51	1 04	11 07
31	26S12	49S17	3S38	7S40	6S42	5S46	1S03	11S06

Moon Phenomena

Max/0 Decl (dy hr mn)
6 3:11 27N25
13 15:34 0 S
20 5:06 27S28
26 5:33 0 N

Max/0 Lat (dy hr mn)
1 15:26 0 N
9 0:24 5N01
16 6:33 0 S
22 9:12 5S00
28 16:05 0 N

Perigee/Apogee (dy hr m kilometers)
8 9:20 a 406459
21 20:58 p 356571

PH (dy hr mn)
○ 6 23:09 16♋22
☾ 15 2:11 24♎38
● 21 20:54 1♒33
☽ 28 15:20 8♉26

Void of Course Moon

Last Aspect			☽ Ingress
2 22:18	♇	△	♊ 3 2:45
5 0:09	♆	□	♋ 5 14:16
7 22:24	♇	☍	♌ 8 2:41
10 1:54	♄	☍	♍ 10 15:16
12 23:08	♇	△	♎ 13 2:58
15 8:41	♇	□	♏ 15 12:09
17 14:28	♇	⚹	♐ 17 17:34
19 10:10	♄	⚹	♑ 19 19:13
21 15:53	♇	☌	♒ 21 18:30
23 10:20	♀	☌	♓ 23 17:37
25 16:13	♇	⚹	♈ 25 18:49
27 21:02	♇	□	♉ 27 23:44
30 5:53	♇	△	♊ 30 8:36

DAILY ASPECTARIAN

1 Su ♀☌♇ 5:26; ☽∠♆ 8:02; ☽⊻♂ 10:10; ☉△☽ 13:43; ☽#♄ 14:37; ☊ R 15:26; ☽⊻⚷ 15:50; ☽‖♅ 18:44; ☽☌♅ 21:54

2 M ☽∠♃ 0:10; ☽⚼⚳ 4:12; ☿⚹♆ 6:45; ☽□♄ 12:16; ☽△☿ 12:32; ☽⚹♆ 12:54; ☿⊻♄ 16:00; ☉□⚷ 16:03; ☽#☿ 17:00; ☽∠⚷ 20:52; ☉⚼☽ 21:17; ☽△♇ 22:18

3 Tu ☽#♀ 1:41; ♀ ♒ 2:11; ☽△♀ 2:49; ☽⚹♃ 5:38; ☽△⚳ 9:55; ☽#♇ 10:28; ☉#☽ 10:29; ☉‖♇ 11:09; ☽⚼☿ 15:53; ☽☌♂ 19:48

4 W ☽‖♂ 0:17; ☽⚹⚷ 2:23; ☽⚼♇ 3:54; ☉⊼☽ 5:31; ☽⊻♅ 8:31; ♀⚹♃ 9:09; ☽⚼♀ 11:50; ☽⊼☿ 19:11; ☽△♄ 23:55

5 Th ☽□♆ 0:09; ☽⊼♇ 9:51; ☽∠♅ 14:24; ☉△♅ 16:44; ☽□♃ 17:52; ☽⊼♀ 21:17; ☽□⚳ 22:34

6 F ☽⚼♄ 6:14; ☽⊻♂ 7:09; ♄⊻♆ 7:57; ♀△⚳ 11:29; ☽□⚷ 14:25; ☽⚹♅ 20:31; ☉☍☽ 23:09

7 Sa ☽☍☿ 1:37; ☽△♆ 12:31; ☽⊼♄ 12:43; ☉☌☿ 12:58; ☽∠♂ 13:11; ☽☍♇ 22:24

8 Su ☽△♃ 7:01; ☽‖♂ 7:15; ☽⚹⚳ 11:59; ☽☍♀ 16:53; ☽⚼♆ 18:53; ☽⚹♂ 19:20; ☽#♇ 21:15; ☿△♅ 23:24

9 M ☉#☽ 1:53; ☽△⚷ 3:05; ☽⊼☿ 8:06; ☽□♅ 9:03; ♀∠♆ 12:05; ☽⚼♃ 13:42; ♀△♂ 15:23; ☉⊼☽ 17:27; ☽#♀ 18:15; ☽∠⚳ 18:45; ☽#☿ 18:54

10 Tu ☽⊼♆ 1:14; ☽☍♄ 1:54; ☿‖♀ 2:12; ☽⚼⚷ 9:24; ☽⊼♇ 11:10; ☽⚼☿ 11:30; ☽‖♅ 14:45; ☽⊼♃ 20:19; ☽#♄ 20:33

11 W ☽⊻⚳ 1:22; ☉⚼☽ 2:29; ☽□♂ 7:38; ☿□⚷ 8:50; ☽⊼♀ 12:26; ☽△☿ 14:59; ☽⊼⚷ 15:33; ☽⚼♇ 17:20; ☽△♅ 21:19; ☽‖⚳ 21:32

12 Th ☿⊻♀ 3:03; ☉△☽ 11:09; ☽‖⚷ 12:16; ☽☍♆ 13:22; ☽⊼♄ 14:27; ♀⚹⚷ 18:47; ♂ D 20:58; ☽⚼♀ 21:37; ☽△♇ 23:08; ☽#♆ 23:23

13 F ☽⚼♅ 2:56; ⚵ ♈ 6:32; ☽☍♃ 8:35; ☽☌⚳ 13:30; ☉⚹♆ 14:13; ☉⚼♂ 14:41; ☽‖♃ 15:28; ☽#♃ 15:41; ☽△♂ 18:47; ☽⚼♄ 20:00; ☽□☿ 21:56

14 Sa ☽☍⚷ 2:31; ☽△♀ 5:59; ☉⊻♄ 6:48; ☽‖♆ 7:29; ☽⊼♅ 7:55; ☽#⚷ 18:15; ☽⊼♆ 23:23; ☽⚼♂ 23:25

15 Su ☽△♄ 0:48; ♀□♅ 1:23; ☉□☽ 2:11; ☊ D 2:21; ☿∠♄ 6:58; ☽#⚳ 8:21; ☽□♇ 8:41; ☽⊼♃ 18:08; ☽⊻⚳ 22:40

16 M ☽⚼♆ 3:06; ☽⊼♂ 3:09; ☽⚹☿ 3:48; ☽‖♄ 5:50; ☊ R 6:34; ☽⊼⚷ 10:22; ☽#♅ 11:48; ☽☍♅ 15:18; ☽‖♀ 17:39; ☽□♀ 19:11; ☽⚼♃ 21:27

17 Tu ☽∠⚳ 1:45; ☽△♆ 5:49; ☽∠☿ 5:55; ☿⊼♂ 6:43; ☽□♄ 7:28; ☽‖☿ 8:03; ☉‖☽ 11:27; ☉⚹☽ 12:37; ☽⚼⚷ 12:48; ☽⚹♇ 14:28; ☽‖♇ 23:03; ♀∠♃ 23:06; ☽△♃ 23:42

18 W ☽⚹⚳ 3:46; ☽⊻☿ 7:22; ☽☍♂ 7:40; ☽#♂ 10:45; ☿ D 13:13; ☽△⚷ 14:14; ☉☌♇ 14:46; ☽∠♇ 15:52; ☉∠☽ 15:57; ☽⊼♅ 18:43

19 Th ☽⚹♀ 3:06; ☉‖☿ 7:23; ☽□♆ 8:19; ☽⚹♄ 10:10; ☽⊻♇ 16:25; ☉⊻☽ 18:14; ☽⚼♅ 19:07; ♀#♅ 22:27

20 F ♀⚼⚳ 1:14; ☽□♃ 1:31; ☽□⚳ 5:08; ☽∠♀ 5:28; ☉ ♒ 8:31; ☽☌☿ 8:32; ☽⊼♂ 8:43; ☽∠♄ 10:21; ☽□⚷ 14:46; ☽△♅ 18:56

21 Sa ☿⊼♂ 1:07; ☽⊻♀ 7:11; ☽⚹♆ 8:02; ☽⚼♂ 8:28; ☽⊻♄ 10:06; ☽☌♇ 15:53; ♀⊻♆ 17:44; ☉☌☽ 20:54; ☽#♂ 21:53

22 Su ☽⚹♃ 1:10; ☽△⚳ 4:30; ☽∠♆ 7:29; ☿∠♀ 7:42; ☽△♂ 8:03; ☽⊻☿ 8:38; ☽‖♇ 9:07; ☽⚹⚷ 13:47; ☽□♅ 17:50; ☽‖☿ 19:06; ♀☌♄ 22:14; ♅ D 23:00

23 M ☽∠♃ 0:54; ☉‖☽ 1:27; ☽⚼⚳ 4:08; ☽⊻♆ 7:04; ☽∠☿ 8:59; ☽☌♄ 9:26; ☽☌♀ 10:20; ☽∠⚷ 13:26; ☽⊻♇ 15:03; ☽#♅ 17:02; ♀‖♄ 18:24; ☿∠♄ 23:10; ☉⊻☽ 23:31; ☽‖♄ 23:32; ☽‖♀ 23:54

24 Tu ☽⊻♃ 1:00; ☽⊼⚳ 4:08; ☽□♂ 7:57; ☽⚹☿ 10:00; ☽⊻⚷ 13:35; ☽∠♇ 15:15; ☽#⚳ 16:08; ☽⚹♅ 17:44

25 W ♀∠⚷ 0:47; ☉⚹♃ 1:31; ☉∠☽ 1:44; ☽#⚷ 5:39; ☽☌♆ 7:44; ☽⊻♄ 10:32; ☽⊻♀ 15:46; ☽‖♆ 15:53; ☽⚹♇ 16:13; ☽∠♅ 18:43; ♀⊻♇ 21:01

26 Th ☽#♃ 2:17; ☽☌♃ 3:19; ☉⚹☽ 5:00; ☽☍⚳ 6:18; ☽‖♃ 8:54; ☽⚹♂ 10:41; ☽∠♄ 12:21; ☽□☿ 15:09; ☽☌⚷ 16:18; ☽#♆ 19:25; ☽∠♀ 20:10; ☽⊻♅ 20:40; ☉△⚳ 23:49

27 F ♀ ♓ 2:34; ☽‖⚷ 6:21; ☿□⚷ 10:43; ☽⊻♆ 11:51; ☽∠♂ 13:35; ☽⚹♄ 15:14; ☽□♇ 21:02; ☽‖⚳ 21:46

28 Sa ☽⚹♀ 1:57; ☽#♀ 6:53; ☽⊻♃ 9:40; ☽⊼⚳ 12:21; ☽#♄ 15:01; ☉□☽ 15:20; ☽∠♆ 15:28; ☉∠♆ 17:04; ☽⊻♂ 17:35; ☽⊻⚷ 23:03; ☽‖♅ 23:27

29 Su ☽△☿ 1:45; ☽☌♅ 3:38; ☉#☽ 9:23; ☽∠♃ 14:25; ☽⚼⚳ 16:52; ☽⚹♆ 20:03

30 M ☽□♄ 0:04; ☉△♂ 1:47; ☿△♅ 2:18; ☽∠⚷ 3:52; ☽△♇ 5:53; ☽#☿ 6:29; ☽⚼☿ 9:05; ☽#♇ 13:45; ☽□♀ 17:25; ☽⚹♃ 20:02; ☽△⚳ 22:10

31 Tu ☽☌♂ 4:28; ☽‖♂ 5:24; ☉△☽ 6:26; ☽⚹⚷ 9:26; ☽⚼♇ 11:29; ☽⊻♅ 14:07; ☽⊼☿ 17:29; ♀⊻♃ 23:15

February 2023

LONGITUDE

Day	Sid.Time	☉	☽	☽ 12 hour	Mean☊	True☊	☿	♀	♂	⚳	♃	♄	⚷	♅	♆	♇
	h m s	° E "	° E "	° E "	° E	° E	° E	° E	° E	° E	° E	° E	° E	° E	° E	° E
1 W	8 43 46	11♒50 28	19♊55 38	25♊55 00	8♉33.7	8♉42.3	16♑57.2	6♓05.2	10♊16.7	6♎56.6	6♈03.3	25♒51.1	12♈38.2	14♉58.6	23♓35.9	28♑39.9
2 Th	8 47 43	12 51 22	1♋52 59	7♋49 58	8 30.5	8R 34.6	18 03.4	7 19.8	10 29.7	6 57.6	6 14.6	25 58.2	12 40.2	14 59.1	23 37.7	28 41.8
3 F	8 51 40	13 52 14	13 46 17	19 42 16	8 27.3	8 23.9	19 11.8	8 34.3	10 43.3	6R 58.2	6 26.0	26 05.3	12 42.4	14 59.6	23 39.5	28 43.7
4 Sa	8 55 36	14 53 05	25 38 10	1♌34 12	8 24.1	8 10.9	20 22.3	9 48.8	10 57.3	6 58.3	6 37.5	26 12.5	12 44.5	15 00.3	23 41.4	28 45.6
5 Su	8 59 33	15 53 55	7♌30 33	13 27 23	8 20.9	7 56.3	21 34.6	11 03.2	11 11.9	6 58.0	6 49.2	26 19.7	12 46.7	15 00.9	23 43.3	28 47.5
6 M	9 03 29	16 54 43	19 24 51	25 23 06	8 17.8	7 41.3	22 48.6	12 17.6	11 27.0	6 57.3	7 00.9	26 26.9	12 49.0	15 01.6	23 45.2	28 49.4
7 Tu	9 07 26	17 55 31	1♍22 15	7♍22 30	8 14.6	7 27.3	24 04.3	13 32.0	11 42.5	6 56.1	7 12.7	26 34.1	12 51.3	15 02.4	23 47.1	28 51.3
8 W	9 11 22	18 56 17	13 23 59	19 26 55	8 11.4	7 15.2	25 21.4	14 46.4	11 58.6	6 54.5	7 24.6	26 41.3	12 53.6	15 03.2	23 49.0	28 53.2
9 Th	9 15 19	19 57 02	25 31 32	1♎38 06	8 08.2	7 05.8	26 40.0	16 00.7	12 15.0	6 52.4	7 36.5	26 48.5	12 55.9	15 04.1	23 51.0	28 55.0
10 F	9 19 15	20 57 46	7♎46 56	13 58 23	8 05.1	6 59.6	27 59.9	17 14.9	12 32.0	6 49.9	7 48.6	26 55.7	12 58.4	15 05.0	23 52.9	28 56.9
11 Sa	9 23 12	21 58 29	20 12 50	26 30 43	8 01.9	6 56.2	29 21.0	18 29.2	12 49.3	6 47.0	8 00.7	27 02.9	13 00.8	15 06.0	23 54.9	28 58.7
12 Su	9 27 09	22 59 11	2♏52 30	9♏18 40	7 58.7	6D 55.0	0♒43.4	19 43.4	13 07.1	6 43.6	8 13.0	27 10.2	13 03.3	15 07.0	23 56.9	29 00.6
13 M	9 31 05	23 59 52	15 49 40	22 25 58	7 55.5	6R 55.1	2 07.0	20 57.5	13 25.3	6 39.8	8 25.3	27 17.4	13 05.8	15 08.0	23 59.0	29 02.4
14 Tu	9 35 02	25 00 31	29 08 01	5♐56 11	7 52.3	6 55.2	3 31.6	22 11.6	13 43.9	6 35.6	8 37.7	27 24.7	13 08.4	15 09.2	24 01.0	29 04.2
15 W	9 38 58	26 01 10	12♐50 43	19 51 48	7 49.2	6 54.0	4 57.4	23 25.7	14 02.9	6 30.9	8 50.2	27 31.9	13 11.0	15 10.3	24 03.0	29 06.0
16 Th	9 42 55	27 01 48	26 59 26	4♑13 27	7 46.0	6 50.8	6 24.2	24 39.8	14 22.3	6 25.8	9 02.7	27 39.2	13 13.6	15 11.6	24 05.1	29 07.8
17 F	9 46 51	28 02 24	11♑33 27	18 58 51	7 42.8	6 44.9	7 52.0	25 53.8	14 42.1	6 20.2	9 15.3	27 46.5	13 16.3	15 12.8	24 07.2	29 09.6
18 Sa	9 50 48	29 02 59	26 28 50	4♒02 24	7 39.6	6 36.7	9 20.9	27 07.7	15 02.3	6 14.3	9 28.0	27 53.7	13 19.0	15 14.1	24 09.3	29 11.3
19 Su	9 54 45	0♓03 33	11♒38 20	19 15 19	7 36.5	6 26.8	10 50.7	28 21.7	15 22.8	6 07.9	9 40.8	28 01.0	13 21.7	15 15.5	24 11.4	29 13.1
20 M	9 58 41	1 04 06	26 51 58	4♓26 52	7 33.3	6 16.4	12 21.5	29 35.6	15 43.7	6 01.1	9 53.7	28 08.2	13 24.5	15 16.9	24 13.5	29 14.8
21 Tu	10 02 38	2 04 37	11♓58 42	19 26 14	7 30.1	6 06.9	13 53.3	0♈49.4	16 05.0	5 53.8	10 06.6	28 15.5	13 27.3	15 18.4	24 15.7	29 16.5
22 W	10 06 34	3 05 06	26 48 26	4♈04 29	7 26.9	5 59.3	15 26.0	2 03.2	16 26.6	5 46.2	10 19.6	28 22.7	13 30.1	15 19.9	24 17.8	29 18.2
23 Th	10 10 31	4 05 33	11♈13 44	18 15 49	7 23.8	5 54.2	16 59.8	3 16.9	16 48.5	5 38.2	10 32.6	28 30.0	13 33.0	15 21.5	24 20.0	29 19.9
24 F	10 14 27	5 05 58	25 10 33	1♉57 58	7 20.6	5D 51.7	18 34.4	4 30.6	17 10.7	5 29.8	10 45.7	28 37.2	13 35.9	15 23.1	24 22.1	29 21.6
25 Sa	10 18 24	6 06 22	8♉38 14	15 11 42	7 17.4	5 51.2	20 10.1	5 44.2	17 33.3	5 21.1	10 58.9	28 44.4	13 38.8	15 24.7	24 24.3	29 23.2
26 Su	10 22 20	7 06 44	21 38 47	28 00 00	7 14.2	5 51.9	21 46.7	6 57.8	17 56.2	5 11.9	11 12.1	28 51.7	13 41.8	15 26.4	24 26.5	29 24.9
27 M	10 26 17	8 07 04	4♊15 57	10♊27 15	7 11.0	5R 52.6	23 24.3	8 11.3	18 19.3	5 02.5	11 25.4	28 58.9	13 44.7	15 28.2	24 28.7	29 26.5
28 Tu	10 30 13	9♓07 22	16 34 30	22 38 21	7♉07.9	5♉52.3	25♒02.9	9♈24.8	18♊42.8	4♎52.6	11♈38.7	29♒06.1	13♈47.8	15♉29.9	24♓30.9	29♑28.1

1st of Month

Julian Day #
2459976.5
Obliquity
23°26'38"
SVP 4♓56'23"
GC 27♐09.7
Eris 23♈57.5

Day	⚴
1	11♋47.2R
6	11 03.1R
11	10 36.1R
16	10 25.9R
21	10 31.9
26	10 53.2

Day	⚵
1	9♈05.9
6	11 39.8
11	14 16.5
16	16 55.9
21	19 37.7
26	22 21.7

Day	⚶
1	26♓51.8
6	29 02.2
11	1♈13.8
16	3 26.4
21	5 40.0
26	7 54.3

DECLINATION and LATITUDE

Day	☉	☽		☽ 12h	☿		♀		♂		⚳		♃		♄	
	Decl	Decl	Lat	Decl	Decl	Lat	Decl	Lat	Decl	Lat	Decl	Lat	Decl	Lat	Decl	Lat
1 W	17S14	26N21	3N19	27N03	21S40	0N42	10S41	1S31	24N40	2N43	10N33	14N30	1N19	1S11	14S05	1S15
2 Th	16 57	27 26	4 01	27 30	21 42	0 32	10 12	1 30	24 42	2 42	10 37	14 35	1 24	1 10	14 02	1 15
3 F	16 40	27 15	4 33	26 40	21 42	0 22	9 44	1 29	24 43	2 42	10 42	14 40	1 29	1 10	13 60	1 15
4 Sa	16 22	25 48	4 52	24 38	21 41	0 13	9 15	1 28	24 44	2 41	10 46	14 45	1 33	1 10	13 57	1 15
5 Su	16 04	23 12	4 59	21 32	21 38	0 04	8 45	1 27	24 46	2 40	10 51	14 50	1 38	1 10	13 55	1 15
6 M	15 46	19 38	4 53	17 32	21 35	0S05	8 16	1 25	24 47	2 40	10 56	14 55	1 43	1 10	13 53	1 15
7 Tu	15 28	15 15	4 34	12 49	21 31	0 13	7 46	1 24	24 49	2 39	11 01	14 60	1 48	1 10	13 50	1 15
8 W	15 09	10 15	4 03	7 35	21 25	0 22	7 16	1 23	24 51	2 39	11 06	15 05	1 53	1 09	13 48	1 15
9 Th	14 50	4 50	3 20	2 01	21 18	0 30	6 46	1 22	24 52	2 38	11 11	15 09	1 57	1 09	13 45	1 15
10 F	14 30	0S50	2 28	3S42	21 10	0 38	6 16	1 20	24 54	2 37	11 16	15 14	2 02	1 09	13 43	1 15
11 Sa	14 11	6 33	1 27	9 22	21 01	0 45	5 46	1 19	24 55	2 37	11 22	15 19	2 07	1 09	13 40	1 15
12 Su	13 51	12 08	0 21	14 48	20 51	0 52	5 15	1 17	24 57	2 36	11 27	15 24	2 12	1 09	13 38	1 15
13 M	13 31	17 20	0S47	19 41	20 39	0 59	4 44	1 15	24 59	2 35	11 33	15 28	2 17	1 09	13 36	1 15
14 Tu	13 11	21 50	1 55	23 43	20 26	1 06	4 13	1 14	25 00	2 35	11 39	15 33	2 22	1 09	13 33	1 15
15 W	12 51	25 17	2 58	26 29	20 12	1 12	3 43	1 12	25 02	2 34	11 45	15 37	2 27	1 08	13 31	1 15
16 Th	12 30	27 17	3 53	27 37	19 56	1 18	3 11	1 10	25 04	2 33	11 51	15 42	2 32	1 08	13 28	1 16
17 F	12 09	27 29	4 34	26 51	19 39	1 24	2 40	1 08	25 05	2 33	11 57	15 46	2 37	1 08	13 26	1 16
18 Sa	11 48	25 43	4 58	24 08	19 21	1 30	2 09	1 06	25 07	2 32	12 03	15 50	2 43	1 08	13 23	1 16
19 Su	11 27	22 07	5 01	19 42	19 02	1 35	1 38	1 04	25 09	2 31	12 10	15 55	2 48	1 08	13 21	1 16
20 M	11 06	16 59	4 43	14 01	18 41	1 40	1 07	1 02	25 10	2 31	12 16	15 59	2 53	1 08	13 18	1 16
21 Tu	10 44	10 51	4 06	7 34	18 19	1 44	0 35	0 60	25 12	2 30	12 22	16 03	2 58	1 08	13 16	1 16
22 W	10 22	4 12	3 12	0 50	17 56	1 48	0 04	0 58	25 13	2 29	12 29	16 06	3 03	1 07	13 13	1 16
23 Th	10 01	2N29	2 07	5N44	17 31	1 52	0N28	0 55	25 15	2 29	12 35	16 10	3 09	1 07	13 11	1 16
24 F	9 38	8 52	0 57	11 50	17 05	1 56	0 59	0 53	25 16	2 28	12 42	16 14	3 14	1 07	13 09	1 16
25 Sa	9 16	14 37	0N15	17 11	16 38	1 59	1 30	0 51	25 18	2 27	12 49	16 17	3 19	1 07	13 06	1 16
26 Su	8 54	19 31	1 23	21 35	16 10	2 01	2 02	0 48	25 19	2 27	12 55	16 21	3 24	1 07	13 04	1 16
27 M	8 32	23 23	2 26	24 53	15 40	2 04	2 33	0 46	25 21	2 26	13 02	16 24	3 30	1 07	13 01	1 16
28 Tu	8S09	26N05	3N20	26N57	15S09	2S06	3N04	0S43	25N22	2N25	13N09	16N27	3N35	1S07	12S59	1S16

Day	⚷		♅		♆		♇	
	Decl	Lat	Decl	Lat	Decl	Lat	Decl	Lat
1	6N33	1N41	15N60	0S21	3S37	1S10	22S40	2S18
6	6 36	1 40	16 01	0 20	3 33	1 10	22 39	2 18
11	6 40	1 40	16 02	0 20	3 29	1 10	22 37	2 19
16	6 44	1 39	16 04	0 20	3 25	1 10	22 36	2 19
21	6 49	1 38	16 06	0 20	3 21	1 10	22 35	2 20
26	6N54	1N38	16N09	0S20	3S17	1S10	22S34	2S21

Day	⚴		⚵		⚶		Eris	
	Decl	Lat	Decl	Lat	Decl	Lat	Decl	Lat
1	25S53	48S59	3S27	7S41	6S31	5S45	1S02	11S06
6	24 13	47 20	2 34	7 47	5 35	5 40	1 01	11 05
11	22 25	45 33	1 39	7 53	4 38	5 35	1 00	11 05
16	20 31	43 40	0 44	7 59	3 41	5 31	0 59	11 04
21	18 34	41 43	0N12	8 04	2 45	5 26	0 57	11 03
26	16S36	39S42	1N08	8S09	1S48	5S22	0S56	11S03

Moon Phenomena

Max/0 Decl
dy hr mn
2 8:18 27N31
9 20:32 0 S
16 14:35 27S38
22 15:01 0 N

Max/0 Lat
dy hr mn
5 0:51 4N59
12 7:33 0 S
18 15:54 5S02
24 18:59 0 N

Perigee/Apogee
dy hr m kilometers
4 8:56 a 406477
19 9:07 p 358272

PH dy hr mn
○ 5 18:30 16♌41
☾ 13 16:02 24♏40
● 20 7:07 1♓22
☽ 27 8:07 8♊27

Void of Course Moon

Last Aspect	☽ Ingress
1 11:59 ♄ △	♋ 1 20:13
4 6:20 ♇ ☍	♌ 4 8:50
6 14:17 ♄ ☍	♍ 6 21:15
9 6:41 ♇ △	♎ 9 8:48
11 16:42 ♇ □	♏ 11 18:36
13 23:53 ♇ ⚹	♐ 14 1:32
16 1:07 ♄ ⚹	♑ 16 5:01
18 4:19 ♇ ☌	♒ 18 5:36
20 2:01 ♄ ☌	♓ 20 4:57
22 4:07 ♇ ⚹	♈ 22 5:15
24 7:23 ♇ □	♉ 24 8:30
26 14:44 ♇ △	♊ 26 15:49

DAILY ASPECTARIAN

1 W
♀#⚳ 5:53
☽□♆ 7:22
☽△♄ 11:59
☉⚼☽ 15:09
♀⚻⚳ 16:47
☽⚻♇ 17:34
☉⚹⚷ 19:28
☽∠♅ 20:10

2 Th
☽□♃ 8:56
☽□⚳ 10:15
☽△♀ 12:16
☽⚺♂ 17:43
☽⚼♄ 18:31
☽□⚷ 21:50

3 F
☉⚻☽ 0:13
☽⚹♅ 2:28
☽☍☿ 12:10
⚳ R 19:14
☽△♆ 20:03
☽⚼♀ 22:08

4 Sa
☽∠♂ 0:40
☽⚻♄ 1:10
☉□♅ 2:52
☽☍♇ 6:20
☽∥♂ 10:55
☽△♃ 22:35
☽⚹⚳ 22:54

5 Su
☽⚼♆ 2:27
♀□♂ 3:30
☽#♇ 4:10
☉#♅ 4:29
☽⚹♂ 7:36
☽⚻♀ 7:59
☽△⚷ 10:40
☽#☿ 11:25
☽□♅ 15:09
⚳☍♃ 17:12
☉☍☽ 18:30

6 M
☽∠⚳ 5:06
☽⚼♃ 5:19
☽⚻☿ 7:38
☽⚻♆ 8:45
♀⚺⚷ 10:26
☽☍♄ 14:17
☽⚼⚷ 16:56
☿⚹♆ 18:27
☽⚻♇ 18:57
☽∥♅ 20:03
☉#☽ 22:52

7 Tu
♀∠♇ 6:23
☽#♄ 7:08
☽⚺⚳ 11:06
☽⚻♃ 11:52
☽⚼☿ 17:13
☽∥⚳ 20:12
☽□♂ 21:06
☽⚻⚷ 22:59

8 W
☽⚼♇ 0:58
☽☍♀ 3:02
☽△♅ 3:17
⚶ ♈ 4:48
♀⚹♅ 5:30
☉⚻☽ 11:59
☽#♀ 14:45
☽∥⚷ 16:12
☽☍♆ 20:41

9 Th
☽△☿ 2:31
☽⚻♄ 2:33
☿⚺♄ 2:50
☽#♆ 5:40
♀#⚷ 6:01
☽△♇ 6:41
☽⚼♅ 8:56
☽∥♃ 12:06
☿⚼♂ 13:24
☉⚼☽ 20:08
☽☌⚳ 22:09

10 F
☽☍♃ 0:03
☽#♃ 5:09
☽⚼♄ 8:08
☽△♂ 9:26
☽☍⚷ 10:06
☽∥♆ 11:11
☽⚻♅ 14:10
☿☌♇ 17:17
☉⚼⚳ 19:41
☽⚻♀ 20:19
☽∥♀ 20:56

11 Sa
☽#⚷ 0:29
☉△☽ 3:40
☽⚻♆ 7:05
☿ ♒ 11:23
☽△♄ 13:09
☽⚼♂ 14:50
☽□♇ 16:42
♂⚹⚷ 18:04
☽□☿ 19:28
☽#⚳ 20:58

12 Su
☽⚼♀ 3:50
☽∥♄ 6:38
☉∠♃ 6:50
☽⚺⚳ 7:10
☉∥☽ 7:14
☊ D 7:35
☽⚻♃ 10:08
☽⚼♆ 11:21
☽#♅ 17:51
☉∥♄ 18:16
☽⚻⚷ 18:58
☽⚻♂ 19:29
☽☍♅ 22:44
☉⚺♆ 23:38

13 M
☽△♀ 10:18
☽∠⚳ 10:33
☽⚼♃ 14:00
☽△♆ 14:50
☉□☽ 16:02
☊ R 16:10
☽∥☿ 16:25
☽□♄ 20:54
☽⚼⚷ 22:13
☽⚹♇ 23:53

14 Tu
☽∥♇ 4:44
☽⚹☿ 8:41
☽⚹⚳ 13:04
☽△♃ 16:57
☽#♂ 21:52

15 W
☽△⚷ 0:35
☽☍♂ 2:07
☽∠♇ 2:10
☽⚻♅ 4:00
♂⚼♇ 4:11
♀☌♆ 12:26
♀∥♆ 12:58
☽∠☿ 13:32
☽□♆ 19:07
☽□♀ 19:44

16 Th
☉⚹☽ 0:04
☿△⚳ 0:24
☽⚹♄ 1:07
☽⚺♇ 3:34
☽⚼♅ 5:20
⚴ D 14:27
☽□⚳ 15:32
☉☌♄ 16:50
☽⚺☿ 17:19
☽□♃ 20:12

17 F
♀#♃ 1:55
☽∠♄ 2:00
☉∠☽ 2:35
☽□⚷ 2:47
☽⚻♂ 5:13
☉∠⚷ 5:45
☽△♅ 5:56
☉#⚳ 10:47
☽⚹♆ 20:17
☿∠♆ 20:49

18 Sa
☽⚹♀ 1:07
☿⚹♃ 2:15
☽⚺♄ 2:16
☉⚺♇ 3:24
☽☌♇ 4:19
☉⚺☽ 4:23
☽#♂ 4:56
☽⚼♂ 5:47
♂⚺♅ 14:52
☽△⚳ 15:22
♀⚺♄ 16:33
☽∠♆ 20:08
☽⚹♃ 20:52
☽∥♇ 21:20
☉ ♓ 22:35
☽☌☿ 22:37

19 Su
☽⚹⚷ 2:43
☽∠♀ 2:57
☽□♅ 5:43
☽△♂ 6:02
☽⚼⚳ 14:51
☽∥☿ 16:08
♀⚹♇ 17:06
☽⚺♆ 19:49
☽∠♃ 20:51

20 M
☽☌♄ 2:01
☽∠⚷ 2:27
☽#♅ 3:42
☽⚺♇ 3:46
☽⚺♀ 4:41
☉☌☽ 7:07
♀ ♈ 7:57
♀∠♅ 13:43
☽⚻⚳ 14:23
☽∥♄ 14:51
☿⚹⚷ 17:00
☽#⚳ 18:24
☽⚺♃ 20:58

21 Tu
☉∥☽ 0:27
☽⚺⚷ 2:22
☽⚺☿ 3:25
☽∠♇ 3:41
☽⚹♅ 5:21
☽□♂ 6:45
☽#⚷ 14:38
☽☌♆ 19:53
☿□♅ 22:23

22 W
☽⚺♄ 2:36
☽∥♆ 3:06
☽#♃ 4:03
☽⚹♇ 4:07
☽∠♅ 5:49
☽∠☿ 6:41
☽☌♀ 9:27
☉⚺☽ 11:08
☽#♀ 14:08
☽☍⚳ 14:42
☽∥♀ 16:02
☿△♂ 20:15
☽☌♃ 22:49

23 Th
☽∥♃ 2:25
☽#♆ 3:03
☽∠♄ 3:53
☽☌⚷ 3:57
☽⚺♅ 7:02
☽⚹♂ 9:46
☽⚹☿ 11:04
☉∠☽ 14:29
☽∥⚷ 16:17
♄∠⚷ 16:31
☽⚺♆ 22:35

24 F
☉#☽ 2:54
☽⚹♄ 6:07
☽□♇ 7:23
☉⚻⚳ 8:18
☽∠♂ 12:44
☽∥⚳ 15:58
♀☍⚳ 17:16
☽#♄ 17:25
☽⚻⚳ 18:08
☽⚺♀ 18:14
♃#♆ 18:57
☊ D 18:59
☉⚹☽ 19:03

25 Sa
☽∠♆ 1:24
☿⚼⚳ 2:31
☽⚺♃ 4:20
☽∥♅ 7:00
☽#☿ 8:34
☽⚺⚷ 9:11
☽☌♅ 12:26
☽⚺♂ 16:52
☽⚼⚳ 21:19

26 Su
☽□☿ 0:17
☽∠♀ 0:39
☿#♅ 0:49
☽⚹♆ 5:16
☽∠♃ 8:44
☿∠♀ 11:13
☽∠⚷ 13:23
☽□♄ 13:46
☽△♇ 14:44
☉⚺♀ 16:13
☽#♇ 18:15
⚳#♄ 22:01

27 M
☽△⚳ 1:29
☊ R 7:58
☉□☽ 8:07
☽⚹♀ 8:26
☽⚹♃ 14:09
☿⚺♆ 16:04
☽∥♂ 16:28
☽⚹⚷ 18:31
☽⚼♇ 19:51
☽⚺♅ 21:53

28 Tu
☽☌♂ 4:22
♀#♆ 8:05
☽□♆ 15:47
☽△☿ 19:29

LONGITUDE

March 2023

Day	Sid.Time	☉	☽	☽ 12 hour	Mean☊	True☊	☿	♀	♂	⚳	♃	♄	⚷	♅	♆	♇
	h m s	° ' "	° ' "	° ' "	° '	° '	° '	° '	° '	° '	° '	° '	° '	° '	° '	° '
1 W	10 34 10	10♓07 38	28♊39 25	4♋38 19	7♉04.7	5♉50.3	26♒42.5	10♈38.2	19♊06.6	4♎42.5	11♈52.1	29♒13.2	13♈50.8	15♉31.8	24♓33.1	29♑29.7
2 Th	10 38 07	11 07 52	10♋35 35	16 31 46	7 01.5	5R46.0	28 23.1	11 51.6	19 30.6	4R32.0	12 05.6	29 20.4	13 53.9	15 33.7	24 35.4	29 31.3
3 F	10 42 03	12 08 04	22 27 21	28 22 47	6 58.3	5 39.4	0♓04.7	13 04.9	19 54.9	4 21.2	12 19.1	29 27.6	13 57.0	15 35.6	24 37.6	29 32.8
4 Sa	10 46 00	13 08 13	4♌18 27	10♌14 44	6 55.2	5 30.8	1 47.4	14 18.1	20 19.4	4 10.1	12 32.7	29 34.7	14 00.1	15 37.5	24 39.8	29 34.3
5 Su	10 49 56	14 08 21	16 11 54	22 10 14	6 52.0	5 21.1	3 31.2	15 31.3	20 44.3	3 58.7	12 46.3	29 41.8	14 03.2	15 39.6	24 42.1	29 35.9
6 M	10 53 53	15 08 27	28 09 57	4♍11 15	6 48.8	5 10.9	5 16.0	16 44.4	21 09.3	3 47.1	12 59.9	29 48.9	14 06.4	15 41.6	24 44.3	29 37.3
7 Tu	10 57 49	16 08 31	10♍14 16	16 19 10	6 45.6	5 01.3	7 01.9	17 57.4	21 34.6	3 35.1	13 13.6	29 56.0	14 09.6	15 43.7	24 46.6	29 38.8
8 W	11 01 46	17 08 33	22 26 04	28 35 05	6 42.4	4 53.2	8 48.9	19 10.4	22 00.2	3 23.0	13 27.4	0♓03.1	14 12.8	15 45.8	24 48.8	29 40.3
9 Th	11 05 42	18 08 34	4♎46 19	10♎59 55	6 39.3	4 47.0	10 37.0	20 23.3	22 25.9	3 10.6	13 41.1	0 10.1	14 16.0	15 48.0	24 51.1	29 41.7
10 F	11 09 39	19 08 32	17 16 01	23 34 46	6 36.1	4 43.2	12 26.2	21 36.2	22 51.9	2 58.0	13 55.0	0 17.1	14 19.2	15 50.2	24 53.3	29 43.1
11 Sa	11 13 36	20 08 29	29 56 21	6♏20 59	6 32.9	4D41.6	14 16.6	22 49.0	23 18.1	2 45.2	14 08.8	0 24.1	14 22.5	15 52.4	24 55.6	29 44.5
12 Su	11 17 32	21 08 24	12♏48 53	19 20 18	6 29.7	4 41.8	16 08.0	24 01.7	23 44.5	2 32.2	14 22.7	0 31.1	14 25.8	15 54.7	24 57.9	29 45.9
13 M	11 21 29	22 08 17	25 55 29	2♐34 41	6 26.6	4 43.0	18 00.6	25 14.3	24 11.2	2 19.1	14 36.7	0 38.0	14 29.1	15 57.1	25 00.2	29 47.2
14 Tu	11 25 25	23 08 09	9♐18 09	16 06 06	6 23.4	4 44.4	19 54.3	26 26.9	24 38.0	2 05.7	14 50.7	0 44.9	14 32.4	15 59.4	25 02.4	29 48.5
15 W	11 29 22	24 07 59	22 58 41	29 56 01	6 20.2	4R45.1	21 49.0	27 39.4	25 05.1	1 52.3	15 04.7	0 51.8	14 35.8	16 01.8	25 04.7	29 49.9
16 Th	11 33 18	25 07 47	6♑58 06	14♑04 50	6 17.0	4 44.5	23 44.9	28 51.9	25 32.3	1 38.8	15 18.8	0 58.7	14 39.1	16 04.3	25 07.0	29 51.1
17 F	11 37 15	26 07 34	21 15 59	28 31 13	6 13.8	4 42.2	25 41.7	0♉04.3	25 59.7	1 25.1	15 32.8	1 05.5	14 42.5	16 06.8	25 09.3	29 52.4
18 Sa	11 41 11	27 07 19	5♒50 01	13♒11 42	6 10.7	4 38.2	27 39.4	1 16.6	26 27.4	1 11.4	15 47.0	1 12.3	14 45.9	16 09.3	25 11.6	29 53.6
19 Su	11 45 08	28 07 03	20 35 31	28 00 33	6 07.5	4 33.2	29 38.1	2 28.8	26 55.2	0 57.6	16 01.1	1 19.1	14 49.3	16 11.8	25 13.8	29 54.8
20 M	11 49 05	29 06 44	5♓25 48	12♓50 16	6 04.3	4 27.6	1♈37.5	3 41.0	27 23.2	0 43.7	16 15.3	1 25.8	14 52.7	16 14.4	25 16.1	29 56.0
21 Tu	11 53 01	0♈06 24	20 12 54	27 32 43	6 01.1	4 22.5	3 37.5	4 53.0	27 51.4	0 29.8	16 29.5	1 32.5	14 56.2	16 17.0	25 18.4	29 57.2
22 W	11 56 58	1 06 01	4♈48 47	12♈00 19	5 58.0	4 18.5	5 38.1	6 05.0	28 19.7	0 16.0	16 43.8	1 39.2	14 59.6	16 19.7	25 20.6	29 58.3
23 Th	12 00 54	2 05 37	19 06 37	26 07 12	5 54.8	4 16.0	7 38.9	7 17.0	28 48.2	0 02.1	16 58.0	1 45.8	15 03.1	16 22.3	25 22.9	29 59.4
24 F	12 04 51	3 05 10	3♉01 41	9♉49 54	5 51.6	4D15.1	9 39.9	8 28.8	29 16.9	29♍48.3	17 12.3	1 52.4	15 06.5	16 25.1	25 25.2	0♒00.5
25 Sa	12 08 47	4 04 42	16 31 47	23 07 26	5 48.4	4 15.6	11 40.8	9 40.6	29 45.8	29 34.5	17 26.6	1 58.9	15 10.0	16 27.8	25 27.4	0 01.6
26 Su	12 12 44	5 04 11	29 37 05	6♊01 02	5 45.2	4 17.0	13 41.4	10 52.3	0♋14.8	29 20.8	17 40.9	2 05.4	15 13.5	16 30.6	25 29.7	0 02.6
27 M	12 16 40	6 03 38	12♊19 42	18 33 34	5 42.1	4 18.7	15 41.2	12 03.9	0 44.0	29 07.2	17 55.3	2 11.9	15 17.0	16 33.4	25 31.9	0 03.6
28 Tu	12 20 37	7 03 03	24 43 09	0♋49 01	5 38.9	4 20.1	17 40.0	13 15.4	1 13.3	28 53.7	18 09.6	2 18.3	15 20.5	16 36.2	25 34.2	0 04.6
29 W	12 24 34	8 02 25	6♋51 45	12 51 57	5 35.7	4R20.7	19 37.5	14 26.8	1 42.8	28 40.3	18 24.0	2 24.7	15 24.0	16 39.1	25 36.4	0 05.6
30 Th	12 28 30	9 01 45	18 50 14	24 47 10	5 32.5	4 20.3	21 33.2	15 38.1	2 12.4	28 27.1	18 38.4	2 31.0	15 27.5	16 42.0	25 38.7	0 06.5
31 F	12 32 27	10♈01 03	0♌43 20	6♌39 17	5♉29.4	4♉18.7	23♈26.8	16♉49.3	2♋42.1	28♍14.1	18♈52.8	2♓37.3	15♈31.0	16♉44.9	25♓40.9	0♒07.4

1st of Month

Julian Day # 2460004.5
Obliquity 23°26'18"
SVP 4♓56'20"
GC 27♐09.8
Eris 24♈07.5

Day	⚴
1	11♋12.9
6	11 56.0
11	12 50.9
16	13 56.2
21	15 11.0
26	16 34.0
31	18 04.4

Day	⚵
1	24♈01.1
6	26 48.2
11	29 37.0
16	2♉27.3
21	5 18.9
26	8 11.8
31	11 05.6

Day	⚶
1	9♈15.2
6	11 30.5
11	13 46.1
16	16 02.2
21	18 18.5
26	20 35.0
31	22 51.6

DECLINATION and LATITUDE

Day	☉ Decl	☽ Decl	☽ Lat	☽ 12h Decl	☿ Decl	☿ Lat	♀ Decl	♀ Lat	♂ Decl	♂ Lat	⚳ Decl	⚳ Lat	♃ Decl	♃ Lat	♄ Decl	♄ Lat
1 W	7S46	27N30	4N04	27N43	14S36	2S07	3N35	0S40	25N24	2N25	13N15	16N30	3N40	1S07	12S56	1S16
2 Th	7 23	27 37	4 37	27 11	14 03	2 09	4 07	0 38	25 25	2 24	13 22	16 33	3 46	1 06	12 54	1 17
3 F	7 01	26 27	4 57	25 26	13 28	2 09	4 38	0 35	25 26	2 23	13 29	16 36	3 51	1 06	12 51	1 17
4 Sa	6 38	24 07	5 05	22 33	12 51	2 10	5 09	0 32	25 27	2 23	13 35	16 38	3 56	1 06	12 49	1 17
5 Su	6 14	20 45	4 60	18 43	12 14	2 10	5 39	0 29	25 28	2 22	13 42	16 40	4 02	1 06	12 47	1 17
6 M	5 51	16 31	4 42	14 07	11 35	2 09	6 10	0 27	25 29	2 21	13 49	16 43	4 07	1 06	12 44	1 17
7 Tu	5 28	11 35	4 10	8 56	10 55	2 08	6 41	0 24	25 30	2 20	13 55	16 45	4 13	1 06	12 42	1 17
8 W	5 05	6 11	3 27	3 21	10 13	2 07	7 11	0 21	25 31	2 20	14 02	16 47	4 18	1 06	12 39	1 17
9 Th	4 41	0 28	2 34	2S27	9 31	2 05	7 41	0 18	25 32	2 19	14 08	16 48	4 23	1 06	12 37	1 17
10 F	4 18	5S21	1 33	8 14	8 47	2 02	8 12	0 15	25 33	2 18	14 14	16 50	4 29	1 06	12 35	1 17
11 Sa	3 54	11 03	0 26	13 47	8 01	1 59	8 42	0 12	25 34	2 18	14 21	16 51	4 34	1 06	12 32	1 17
12 Su	3 31	16 23	0S44	18 49	7 15	1 56	9 11	0 09	25 34	2 17	14 27	16 52	4 40	1 05	12 30	1 17
13 M	3 07	21 03	1 52	23 03	6 28	1 52	9 41	0 05	25 35	2 16	14 33	16 53	4 45	1 05	12 27	1 18
14 Tu	2 43	24 45	2 56	26 07	5 39	1 48	10 10	0 02	25 35	2 16	14 39	16 54	4 51	1 05	12 25	1 18
15 W	2 20	27 07	3 52	27 41	4 49	1 43	10 39	0N01	25 36	2 15	14 45	16 55	4 56	1 05	12 23	1 18
16 Th	1 56	27 50	4 35	27 30	3 58	1 37	11 08	0 04	25 36	2 14	14 50	16 55	5 02	1 05	12 20	1 18
17 F	1 32	26 43	5 02	25 29	3 06	1 31	11 37	0 07	25 36	2 14	14 56	16 56	5 07	1 05	12 18	1 18
18 Sa	1 09	23 49	5 10	21 45	2 13	1 24	12 05	0 11	25 37	2 13	15 02	16 56	5 13	1 05	12 16	1 18
19 Su	0 45	19 20	4 58	16 37	1 20	1 17	12 33	0 14	25 37	2 12	15 07	16 56	5 18	1 05	12 13	1 18
20 M	0 21	13 39	4 26	10 29	0 25	1 10	13 01	0 17	25 37	2 12	15 12	16 55	5 24	1 05	12 11	1 18
21 Tu	0N03	7 12	3 37	3 50	0N30	1 01	13 28	0 20	25 36	2 11	15 17	16 55	5 29	1 05	12 09	1 18
22 W	0 26	0 26	2 34	2N56	1 26	0 53	13 55	0 24	25 36	2 11	15 22	16 54	5 35	1 05	12 07	1 19
23 Th	0 50	6N13	1 22	9 24	2 22	0 43	14 22	0 27	25 36	2 10	15 27	16 53	5 40	1 05	12 04	1 19
24 F	1 14	12 25	0 07	15 15	3 19	0 33	14 49	0 30	25 35	2 09	15 31	16 52	5 46	1 05	12 02	1 19
25 Sa	1 37	17 51	1N07	20 11	4 16	0 23	15 15	0 34	25 35	2 09	15 35	16 51	5 51	1 05	11 60	1 19
26 Su	2 01	22 15	2 14	24 01	5 12	0 13	15 41	0 37	25 34	2 08	15 39	16 49	5 57	1 04	11 58	1 19
27 M	2 24	25 28	3 13	26 35	6 09	0 02	16 06	0 41	25 33	2 07	15 43	16 48	6 02	1 04	11 55	1 19
28 Tu	2 48	27 22	4 02	27 48	7 05	0N10	16 31	0 44	25 33	2 07	15 47	16 46	6 08	1 04	11 53	1 19
29 W	3 11	27 54	4 39	27 40	8 00	0 21	16 56	0 47	25 32	2 06	15 51	16 44	6 13	1 04	11 51	1 19
30 Th	3 35	27 06	5 02	26 14	8 55	0 33	17 20	0 51	25 31	2 05	15 54	16 42	6 19	1 04	11 49	1 20
31 F	3N58	25N05	5N13	23N40	9N48	0N45	17N44	0N54	25N29	2N05	15N57	16N39	6N24	1S04	11S47	1S20

Day	⚷ Decl	⚷ Lat	♅ Decl	♅ Lat	♆ Decl	♆ Lat	♇ Decl	♇ Lat
1	6N58	1N37	16N10	0S20	3S14	1S10	22S33	2S21
6	7 03	1 37	16 13	0 20	3 10	1 10	22 32	2 22
11	7 09	1 36	16 17	0 20	3 05	1 10	22 31	2 22
16	7 15	1 36	16 20	0 20	3 01	1 10	22 31	2 23
21	7 21	1 35	16 24	0 19	2 56	1 10	22 30	2 24
26	7 27	1 35	16 28	0 19	2 52	1 10	22 30	2 24
31	7N34	1N35	16N32	0S19	2S48	1S10	22S29	2S25

Day	⚴ Decl	⚴ Lat	⚵ Decl	⚵ Lat	⚶ Decl	⚶ Lat	Eris Decl	Eris Lat
1	15S24	38S29	1N41	8S12	1S14	5S20	0S55	11S02
6	13 26	36 28	2 36	8 16	0 18	5 16	0 54	11 02
11	11 30	34 28	3 31	8 20	0N38	5 13	0 52	11 01
16	9 37	32 29	4 25	8 24	1 33	5 09	0 51	11 01
21	7 48	30 33	5 18	8 27	2 28	5 06	0 50	11 00
26	6 04	28 40	6 10	8 30	3 21	5 03	0 48	10 60
31	4S25	26S51	7N01	8S33	4N15	4S60	0S47	10S59

Moon Phenomena

Max/0 Decl (dy hr mn)
1 14:07 27N43
9 1:55 0 S
15 21:41 27S50
22 1:33 0 N
28 21:28 27N54

Max/0 Lat (dy hr mn)
4 2:25 5N05
11 8:54 0 S
17 22:04 5S10
24 2:09 0 N
31 7:15 5N14

Perigee/Apogee (dy hr m kilometers)
3 18:01 a 405888
19 15:14 p 362700
31 11:18 a 404917

PH (dy hr mn)
○ 7 12:42 16♍40
☾ 15 2:09 24♐13
● 21 17:24 0♈50
☽ 29 2:34 8♋09

Void of Course Moon

Last Aspect	☽ Ingress
1 1:08 ♄ △	♋ 1 2:41
3 14:24 ♇ ☍	♌ 3 15:17
6 3:20 ♄ ☍	♍ 6 3:40
8 14:08 ♇ △	♎ 8 14:45
10 23:38 ♇ □	♏ 11 0:07
13 7:00 ♇ ⚹	♐ 13 7:22
15 8:51 ☉ □	♑ 15 12:07
17 14:15 ♇ ☌	♒ 17 14:26
19 10:34 ♂ △	♓ 19 15:13
21 15:59 ♇ ⚹	♈ 21 16:02
23 17:14 ♂ ⚹	♉ 23 18:43
25 16:20 ♆ ⚹	♊ 26 0:43
28 1:40 ♆ □	♋ 28 10:23
30 13:47 ♆ △	♌ 30 22:32

DAILY ASPECTARIAN

1 W: ☽△♄ 1:08; ☽⚻♇ 1:41; ☿∠♃ 2:40; ☽∠♅ 3:46; ♀∥♃ 4:25; ☽□⚳ 11:58

2 Th: ☉△☽ 1:11; ☽□♀ 2:51; ☽□♃ 3:05; ♀☌♃ 5:37; ☽Q☿ 6:34; ☽□⚷ 6:42; ☿∠⚷ 7:31; ☽Q♄ 7:39; ☽⚹♅ 10:04; ☿☌♄ 14:35; ☿⚺♇ 16:22; ☽⚺♂ 18:40; ☿ ♓ 22:53; ☿#⚳ 23:25

3 F: ☉#⚷ 0:50; ☽△♆ 4:25; ☉⚺♃ 5:41; ☉Q☽ 10:21; ☽∥♂ 11:48; ☽⚻♄ 14:20; ☽☍♇ 14:24; ♀☌⚷ 17:49; ☽⚻☿ 18:03; ♄⚺♇ 22:27; ☽⚹⚳ 23:43

4 Sa: ☿∥♄ 1:37; ☽∠♂ 2:08; ♀∠♄ 6:01; ☽Q♆ 10:52; ☽#♇ 12:05; ☽△♃ 16:58; ☉⚻☽ 19:28; ☽△⚷ 19:40; ☉⚺⚷ 21:50; ☽△♀ 22:29; ☽□♅ 22:55

5 Su: ♀⚺♅ 2:47; ☽∠⚳ 5:30; ☿⚻⚳ 5:42; ☽⚹♂ 9:27; ☉∠♇ 11:16; ☉#♀ 15:35; ☽⚻♆ 17:07; ☽Q♃ 23:40

6 M: ☽∥♅ 1:29; ☽Q⚷ 1:53; ☽⚻♇ 2:55; ☽☍♄ 3:20; ☽Q♀ 7:56; ☽⚺⚳ 11:01; ☽∥⚳ 13:14; ☉⚹♅ 13:43; ☽☍☿ 16:33; ☽#♄ 18:48

7 Tu: ☽#☿ 3:34; ☽⚻♃ 6:01; ☽⚻⚷ 7:47; ☽Q♇ 8:43; ☽△♅ 10:52; ☉☍☽ 12:42; ♄ ♓ 13:36; ☽⚻♀ 16:54; ♀∥⚷ 19:12; ☽∥♀ 20:01; ☽∥⚷ 20:05; ☽□♂ 23:07

8 W: ☽☍♆ 4:40; ☉#☽ 5:02; ☽∥♃ 7:52; ☽#♆ 12:55; ☽△♇ 14:08; ☽⚻♄ 15:00; ☽Q♅ 16:17; ☽☌⚳ 20:58

9 Th: ☽⚻☿ 13:11; ☽∥♆ 14:44; ☉#♃ 14:52; ☽☍♃ 17:29; ☽☍⚷ 18:21; ☉∥☽ 19:55; ☽Q♄ 20:11; ☽#♃ 20:20; ☽⚻♅ 21:16

10 F: ☉⚻☽ 3:53; ☽#⚷ 7:24; ☽☍♀ 9:08; ☽△♂ 11:02; ☿#♀ 11:14; ☽∥☿ 12:38; ☽#♀ 12:59; ☽⚻♆ 14:31; ☿⚺♃ 22:05; ☽Q☿ 22:32; ☽□♇ 23:38

11 Sa: ☽△♄ 0:53; ☿⚺⚷ 1:20; ☽⚺⚳ 5:12; ☿∠♇ 6:07; ☽∥♄ 6:26; ☊ D 8:56; ☉Q☽ 10:34; ☽#⚳ 14:51; ♀⚹♂ 15:06; ☽Q♂ 16:11; ⚵ ♉ 16:16; ☽Q♆ 18:42; ☿⚹♅ 21:06; ☽#♅ 23:34

12 Su: ☿#⚷ 2:30; ☽⚻♃ 2:56; ☽⚻⚷ 3:00; ☽☍♅ 5:44; ♃☌⚷ 6:54; ☽△☿ 7:09; ☽∠⚳ 8:33; ☉△☽ 16:33; ♀⚺♆ 19:10; ☽⚻♂ 20:44; ☽△♆ 22:19; ☽⚻♀ 22:38

13 M: ☉∥♆ 3:50; ☽Q⚷ 6:28; ☽Q♃ 6:47; ☽⚹♇ 7:00; ☽□♄ 8:35; ☽∥♇ 8:37; ☽⚹⚳ 11:21

14 Tu: ☽Q♀ 4:10; ☽#♂ 7:02; ☽△⚷ 9:18; ☽∠♇ 9:45; ☽△♃ 9:58; ☽⚻♅ 11:50; ☿#♃ 20:55; ☽□☿ 21:39; ♂□♆ 23:40

15 W: ☉□☽ 2:09; ☊ R 2:21; ☽□♆ 3:39; ☽☍♂ 3:46; ☽△♀ 8:51; ☽⚺♇ 11:50; ☽⚹♄ 13:42; ☽Q♅ 13:55; ☽□⚳ 15:05; ☉☌♆ 23:40

16 Th: ☽□⚷ 13:01; ☽□♃ 14:18; ☽∠♄ 15:18; ☽△♅ 15:23; ☿☌♆ 17:14; ☉□♂ 18:11; ♀□♇ 20:00; ♀ ♉ 22:35

17 F: ☿∥♆ 2:56; ☿□♂ 4:50; ☽⚹♆ 6:28; ☽⚻♂ 8:05; ☽⚹☿ 8:29; ☉⚹☽ 8:39; ☉☌☿ 10:46; ☽#♂ 10:57; ☽☌♇ 14:15; ☽□♀ 15:52; ☽⚺♄ 16:21; ☽△⚳ 16:30; ♀⚹♄ 22:26; ♀⚻⚳ 22:33; ⚳⚻♄ 22:54

18 Sa: ⚳Q♅ 3:04; ☽∠♆ 7:08; ☽∥♇ 7:52; ♀#♄ 8:31; ☽Q♂ 9:28; ☉∠☽ 11:00; ☽∠☿ 12:50; ☽⚹⚷ 14:36; ☽⚹♃ 16:28; ☽Q⚳ 16:36; ☽□♅ 16:51

19 Su: ☿⚹♇ 3:25; ☿ ♈ 4:25; ☽⚺♆ 7:32; ☽△♂ 10:34; ☽#♅ 12:59; ☉⚺☽ 13:03; ☿☍⚳ 14:20; ☽∠⚷ 14:59; ☽⚺♇ 15:06; ☽⚻⚳ 16:31; ☽⚺☿ 16:53; ☽∠♃ 17:08; ☽☌♄ 17:29; ☽#⚳ 17:54; ☿∠♅ 19:16; ☽⚹♀ 20:55; ☿⚺♄ 21:31; ♃⚺♅ 22:07

20 M: ☽#♀ 2:18; ☉∥☿ 2:57; ☽∥♄ 5:40; ☉#☿ 14:04; ☽⚺⚷ 15:22; ☽∠♇ 15:25; ☽⚹♅ 17:35; ☽⚺♃ 17:50; ☉⚹♇ 20:13; ☉ ♈ 21:26; ☽∠♀ 23:25; ☽#⚷ 23:27

21 Tu: ☽#♃ 6:03; ☉☍⚳ 7:39; ☽☌♆ 8:21; ♃∠♄ 9:27; ☽□♂ 12:56; ☽∥♆ 15:12; ☽⚹♇ 15:59; ☽☍⚳ 16:36; ☉☌☽ 17:24; ☽∠♅ 18:13; ☽⚺♄ 18:44; ☽#☿ 20:54

22 W: ☉#☽ 0:00; ☽☌☿ 1:35; ☽⚺♀ 2:18; ☉∥☽ 3:18; ☉∠♅ 5:45; ☽∥☿ 7:44; ☽#♆ 11:58; ☿⚺♀ 13:15; ☉⚺♄ 15:01; ☽☌⚷ 17:06; ☽⚺♅ 19:21; ☽∠♄ 19:59; ☽☌♃ 20:18; ☽∥♃ 21:56

23 Th: ⚳ R♍ 3:39; ⚳△♇ 4:16; ☽∥⚷ 4:23; ☽⚺♆ 10:46; ♇ ♒ 12:14; ☿#♆ 13:27; ☽⚹♂ 17:14; ☽⚻⚳ 18:28; ☽□♇ 18:44; ☽⚹♄ 21:58; ☽#♄ 22:27

24 F: ☉⚺☽ 0:07; ☊ D 2:10; ☽☌♀ 10:32; ☽∥♀ 10:59; ☽∠♆ 13:05; ☽∥⚳ 13:25; ☽⚺☿ 13:46; ☽∥♅ 17:25; ♂□⚳ 17:39; ☽Q⚳ 20:32; ☽∠♂ 20:42; ☽⚺⚷ 21:32; ☽☌♅ 23:53

25 Sa: ☽⚺♃ 1:41; ☉∠☽ 4:59; ♂ ♋ 11:46; ♂⚻♇ 13:35; ♀∠♆ 16:11; ☽⚹♆ 16:20; ☽∠☿ 21:57; ♀∥⚳ 22:46; ☽△⚳ 23:30

26 Su: ☽△♇ 0:48; ☽∠⚷ 1:08; ☽⚺♂ 1:13; ☽#♇ 1:30; ☽□♄ 4:39; ☽∠♃ 5:50; ☉⚹☽ 11:05; ☿☌⚷ 18:59; ☿∥♃ 20:52; ☽⚺♀ 23:27

27 M: ☽∥♂ 0:51; ☽Q♇ 5:15; ☽⚹⚷ 5:42; ☽⚹☿ 7:40; ☽⚺♅ 8:10; ☿⚺♅ 10:46; ☽⚹♃ 10:59; ☿∠♄ 19:21; ♀∥♅ 22:26

28 Tu: ☽□♆ 1:40; ☉#♆ 2:11; ☿☌♃ 6:52; ☽∠♀ 7:42; ☽□⚳ 8:04; ☽⚻♇ 10:33; ♀Q⚳ 10:51; ☿∥⚷ 11:04; ☽☌♂ 13:20; ☽∠♅ 13:37; ☽△♄ 15:05; ♂∠♅ 20:42

29 W: ☊ R 2:29; ☉□☽ 2:34; ☽⚹♀ 16:51; ☽□⚷ 17:10; ☽⚹♅ 19:41; ♀⚺⚷ 20:14; ☽Q♄ 21:19; ☽□♃ 23:36

30 Th: ☽□☿ 6:31; ☽△♆ 13:47; ☽⚹⚳ 19:04; ♂△♄ 19:05; ☽∥♂ 20:05; ♀☌♅ 22:27; ☽☍♇ 22:47

31 F: ☽⚻♄ 3:53; ☽⚺♂ 4:11; ☽Q♆ 20:12; ☉△☽ 20:30; ☽#♇ 20:35

April 2023

LONGITUDE

Day	Sid.Time	☉	☽	☽ 12 hour	Mean☊	True☊	☿	♀	♂	⚳	♃	♄	⚷	♅	♆	♇
	h m s	° ' "	° ' "	° ' "	° '	° '	° '	° '	° '	° '	° '	° '	° '	° '	° '	° '
1 Sa	12 36 23	11♈00 18	12♌35 33	18♌32 36	5♉26.2	4♉16.1	25♈17.8	18♉00.5	3♋12.0	28♍01.2	19♈07.3	2♓43.5	15♈34.5	16♉47.9	25♓43.1	0♒08.3
2 Su	12 40 20	11 59 31	24 30 53	0♍30 49	5 23.0	4R 12.8	27 05.9	19 11.5	3 42.0	27R 48.5	19 21.7	2 49.7	15 38.0	16 50.8	25 45.3	0 09.2
3 M	12 44 16	12 58 42	6♍32 47	12 37 04	5 19.8	4 09.2	28 50.6	20 22.4	4 12.2	27 36.0	19 36.1	2 55.9	15 41.6	16 53.8	25 47.5	0 10.0
4 Tu	12 48 13	13 57 51	18 43 57	24 53 39	5 16.6	4 05.8	0♉31.6	21 33.2	4 42.5	27 23.7	19 50.6	3 02.0	15 45.1	16 56.9	25 49.7	0 10.8
5 W	12 52 09	14 56 57	1♎06 22	7♎22 13	5 13.5	4 03.0	2 08.5	22 44.0	5 12.9	27 11.7	20 05.0	3 08.0	15 48.6	16 59.9	25 51.9	0 11.6
6 Th	12 56 06	15 56 02	13 41 19	20 03 42	5 10.3	4 01.1	3 41.0	23 54.6	5 43.4	26 59.9	20 19.5	3 14.0	15 52.1	17 03.0	25 54.1	0 12.3
7 F	13 00 02	16 55 04	26 29 26	2♏58 30	5 07.1	4D 00.1	5 08.8	25 05.1	6 14.0	26 48.4	20 34.0	3 20.0	15 55.7	17 06.1	25 56.2	0 13.0
8 Sa	13 03 59	17 54 04	9♏30 53	16 06 34	5 03.9	4 00.0	6 31.6	26 15.5	6 44.7	26 37.2	20 48.4	3 25.8	15 59.2	17 09.2	25 58.4	0 13.7
9 Su	13 07 56	18 53 03	22 45 30	29 27 37	5 00.8	4 00.7	7 49.1	27 25.7	7 15.6	26 26.2	21 02.9	3 31.7	16 02.7	17 12.3	26 00.5	0 14.4
10 M	13 11 52	19 52 00	6♐12 52	13♐01 12	4 57.6	4 01.7	9 01.1	28 35.9	7 46.6	26 15.6	21 17.4	3 37.5	16 06.3	17 15.5	26 02.6	0 15.0
11 Tu	13 15 49	20 50 55	19 52 31	26 46 44	4 54.4	4 02.9	10 07.5	29 46.0	8 17.7	26 05.2	21 31.9	3 43.2	16 09.8	17 18.7	26 04.8	0 15.7
12 W	13 19 45	21 49 48	3♑43 45	10♑43 27	4 51.2	4 03.8	11 08.1	0♊55.9	8 48.9	25 55.2	21 46.4	3 48.8	16 13.3	17 21.9	26 06.9	0 16.2
13 Th	13 23 42	22 48 39	17 45 39	24 50 09	4 48.1	4R 04.2	12 02.7	2 05.8	9 20.2	25 45.5	22 00.8	3 54.5	16 16.8	17 25.1	26 09.0	0 16.8
14 F	13 27 38	23 47 29	1♒56 44	9♒05 07	4 44.9	4 04.2	12 51.3	3 15.5	9 51.6	25 36.1	22 15.3	4 00.0	16 20.3	17 28.3	26 11.0	0 17.3
15 Sa	13 31 35	24 46 17	16 14 55	23 25 46	4 41.7	4 03.7	13 33.6	4 25.1	10 23.1	25 27.1	22 29.8	4 05.5	16 23.8	17 31.6	26 13.1	0 17.8
16 Su	13 35 32	25 45 04	0♓37 12	7♓48 43	4 38.5	4 02.9	14 09.8	5 34.6	10 54.7	25 18.5	22 44.3	4 10.9	16 27.3	17 34.9	26 15.1	0 18.3
17 M	13 39 28	26 43 48	14 59 47	22 09 48	4 35.3	4 02.0	14 39.7	6 43.9	11 26.4	25 10.2	22 58.7	4 16.3	16 30.8	17 38.2	26 17.2	0 18.7
18 Tu	13 43 25	27 42 31	29 18 13	6♈24 26	4 32.2	4 01.2	15 03.3	7 53.2	11 58.2	25 02.2	23 13.2	4 21.6	16 34.3	17 41.5	26 19.2	0 19.1
19 W	13 47 21	28 41 12	13♈27 53	20 28 03	4 29.0	4 00.6	15 20.6	9 02.3	12 30.1	24 54.7	23 27.6	4 26.8	16 37.8	17 44.8	26 21.2	0 19.5
20 Th	13 51 18	29 39 51	27 24 27	4♉16 40	4 25.8	4D 00.4	15 31.8	10 11.3	13 02.1	24 47.6	23 42.1	4 32.0	16 41.2	17 48.1	26 23.2	0 19.9
21 F	13 55 14	0♉38 29	11♉04 24	17 47 23	4 22.6	4 00.4	15R 36.9	11 20.1	13 34.2	24 40.8	23 56.5	4 37.1	16 44.7	17 51.5	26 25.2	0 20.2
22 Sa	13 59 11	1 37 04	24 25 28	0♊58 36	4 19.4	4 00.5	15 36.1	12 28.8	14 06.4	24 34.5	24 10.9	4 42.1	16 48.1	17 54.8	26 27.1	0 20.5
23 Su	14 03 07	2 35 37	7♊26 49	13 50 15	4 16.3	4 00.7	15 29.6	13 37.4	14 38.6	24 28.5	24 25.3	4 47.1	16 51.6	17 58.2	26 29.0	0 20.7
24 M	14 07 04	3 34 09	20 09 04	26 23 35	4 13.1	4R 00.8	15 17.6	14 45.8	15 11.0	24 23.0	24 39.7	4 52.0	16 55.0	18 01.6	26 31.0	0 21.0
25 Tu	14 11 00	4 32 38	2♋34 09	8♋41 09	4 09.9	4 00.8	15 00.5	15 54.1	15 43.4	24 17.9	24 54.1	4 56.8	16 58.4	18 05.0	26 32.9	0 21.2
26 W	14 14 57	5 31 05	14 45 03	20 46 22	4 06.7	4 00.7	14 38.7	17 02.2	16 16.0	24 13.2	25 08.4	5 01.6	17 01.8	18 08.4	26 34.7	0 21.4
27 Th	14 18 54	6 29 30	26 45 37	2♌43 21	4 03.6	4D 00.6	14 12.7	18 10.2	16 48.6	24 08.9	25 22.8	5 06.3	17 05.2	18 11.8	26 36.6	0 21.5
28 F	14 22 50	7 27 53	8♌40 09	14 36 35	4 00.4	4 00.6	13 42.9	19 18.0	17 21.3	24 05.0	25 37.1	5 10.9	17 08.6	18 15.2	26 38.4	0 21.7
29 Sa	14 26 47	8 26 14	20 33 15	26 30 43	3 57.2	4 00.7	13 10.0	20 25.6	17 54.1	24 01.5	25 51.4	5 15.4	17 11.9	18 18.7	26 40.3	0 21.7
30 Su	14 30 43	9♉24 33	2♍29 33	8♍30 16	3♉54.0	4♉01.0	12♉34.6	21♊33.1	18♋26.9	23♍58.5	26♈05.7	5♓19.9	17♈15.2	18♉22.1	26♓42.1	0♒21.8

1st of Month

Julian Day # 2460035.5
Obliquity 23°26'09"
SVP 4♓56'06"
GC 27♐09.8
Eris 24♈25.3

Day	⚴
1	18♋23.3
6	20 01.1
11	21 44.3
16	23 32.2
21	25 24.2
26	27 19.9

Day	⚵
1	11♉40.5
6	14 35.3
11	17 30.8
16	20 26.9
21	23 23.5
26	26 20.4

Day	⚶
1	23♈18.9
6	25 35.3
11	27 51.7
16	0♉07.9
21	2 23.9
26	4 39.5

DECLINATION and LATITUDE

Day	☉ Decl	☽ Decl	☽ Lat	☽12h Decl	☿ Decl	☿ Lat	♀ Decl	♀ Lat	♂ Decl	♂ Lat	⚳ Decl	⚳ Lat	♃ Decl	♃ Lat	♄ Decl	♄ Lat
1 Sa	4N21	21N59	5N10	20N05	10N40	0N57	18N07	0N58	25N28	2N04	15N60	16N37	6N30	1S04	11S45	1S20
2 Su	4 44	17 58	4 54	15 40	11 30	1 08	18 30	1 01	25 27	2 03	16 02	16 34	6 35	1 04	11 43	1 20
3 M	5 08	13 13	4 25	10 37	12 19	1 20	18 52	1 04	25 25	2 03	16 05	16 31	6 41	1 04	11 40	1 20
4 Tu	5 30	7 53	3 44	5 04	13 05	1 31	19 14	1 08	25 23	2 02	16 07	16 28	6 46	1 04	11 38	1 20
5 W	5 53	2 11	2 51	0S45	13 49	1 43	19 36	1 11	25 22	2 02	16 08	16 25	6 52	1 04	11 36	1 20
6 Th	6 16	3S43	1 50	6 40	14 31	1 53	19 57	1 14	25 20	2 01	16 10	16 22	6 57	1 04	11 34	1 21
7 F	6 39	9 35	0 41	12 25	15 10	2 03	20 17	1 18	25 18	2 00	16 12	16 18	7 03	1 04	11 32	1 21
8 Sa	7 01	15 08	0S30	17 43	15 47	2 13	20 38	1 21	25 16	1 60	16 13	16 15	7 08	1 04	11 30	1 21
9 Su	7 24	20 06	1 42	22 15	16 21	2 22	20 57	1 24	25 13	1 59	16 14	16 11	7 14	1 04	11 28	1 21
10 M	7 46	24 07	2 49	25 39	16 52	2 30	21 16	1 27	25 11	1 58	16 14	16 07	7 19	1 04	11 26	1 21
11 Tu	8 08	26 50	3 47	27 36	17 20	2 37	21 34	1 31	25 08	1 58	16 15	16 03	7 24	1 04	11 24	1 21
12 W	8 30	27 56	4 33	27 50	17 46	2 44	21 52	1 34	25 06	1 57	16 15	15 59	7 30	1 04	11 22	1 22
13 Th	8 52	27 16	5 04	26 17	18 08	2 49	22 10	1 37	25 03	1 57	16 15	15 55	7 35	1 04	11 21	1 22
14 F	9 14	24 51	5 16	23 03	18 27	2 54	22 27	1 40	24 60	1 56	16 15	15 50	7 41	1 04	11 19	1 22
15 Sa	9 36	20 53	5 09	18 24	18 43	2 57	22 43	1 43	24 57	1 55	16 14	15 46	7 46	1 04	11 17	1 22
16 Su	9 57	15 40	4 43	12 42	18 56	2 59	22 58	1 46	24 54	1 55	16 13	15 41	7 51	1 04	11 15	1 22
17 M	10 18	9 35	3 59	6 21	19 06	3 00	23 13	1 49	24 51	1 54	16 12	15 36	7 57	1 04	11 13	1 22
18 Tu	10 39	3 02	3 01	0N18	19 13	2 60	23 28	1 52	24 47	1 54	16 11	15 31	8 02	1 04	11 11	1 22
19 W	11 00	3N36	1 51	6 51	19 16	2 58	23 42	1 55	24 44	1 53	16 10	15 27	8 07	1 04	11 10	1 23
20 Th	11 21	9 59	0 37	12 58	19 17	2 55	23 55	1 58	24 40	1 52	16 08	15 22	8 13	1 04	11 08	1 23
21 F	11 42	15 46	0N39	18 21	19 14	2 51	24 08	2 01	24 36	1 52	16 06	15 16	8 18	1 04	11 06	1 23
22 Sa	12 02	20 40	1 51	22 42	19 09	2 45	24 20	2 03	24 32	1 51	16 04	15 11	8 23	1 04	11 05	1 23
23 Su	12 22	24 26	2 55	25 49	19 00	2 38	24 31	2 06	24 28	1 51	16 01	15 06	8 29	1 04	11 03	1 23
24 M	12 42	26 52	3 49	27 34	18 49	2 30	24 42	2 09	24 24	1 50	15 59	15 01	8 34	1 04	11 02	1 23
25 Tu	13 02	27 55	4 30	27 55	18 34	2 20	24 52	2 11	24 19	1 49	15 56	14 55	8 39	1 04	10 60	1 24
26 W	13 22	27 35	4 59	26 55	18 18	2 09	25 01	2 14	24 15	1 49	15 53	14 50	8 44	1 04	10 58	1 24
27 Th	13 41	25 56	5 14	24 41	17 58	1 57	25 10	2 16	24 10	1 48	15 49	14 44	8 50	1 04	10 57	1 24
28 F	14 00	23 10	5 16	21 24	17 36	1 44	25 18	2 18	24 05	1 48	15 46	14 39	8 55	1 04	10 55	1 24
29 Sa	14 19	19 26	5 04	17 16	17 13	1 30	25 26	2 21	24 01	1 47	15 42	14 33	9 00	1 04	10 54	1 24
30 Su	14N38	14N55	4N39	12N25	16N48	1N14	25N33	2N23	23N56	1N46	15N38	14N28	9N05	1S04	10S52	1S25

Day	⚷ Decl	⚷ Lat	♅ Decl	♅ Lat	♆ Decl	♆ Lat	♇ Decl	♇ Lat
1	7N35	1N35	16N33	0S19	2S47	1S10	22S29	2S25
6	7 42	1 34	16 37	0 19	2 42	1 10	22 29	2 26
11	7 48	1 34	16 42	0 19	2 38	1 11	22 29	2 27
16	7 55	1 34	16 46	0 19	2 34	1 11	22 29	2 28
21	8 01	1 33	16 51	0 19	2 30	1 11	22 30	2 28
26	8 07	1 33	16 56	0 19	2 27	1 11	22 30	2 29

Day	⚴ Decl	⚴ Lat	⚵ Decl	⚵ Lat	⚶ Decl	⚶ Lat	Eris Decl	Eris Lat
1	4S06	26S29	7N11	8S34	4N25	4S59	0S46	10S59
6	2 34	24 45	7 59	8 36	5 17	4 57	0 45	10 59
11	1 08	23 05	8 46	8 38	6 08	4 54	0 44	10 59
16	0N12	21 29	9 30	8 40	6 58	4 52	0 42	10 59
21	1 25	19 57	10 12	8 41	7 46	4 49	0 41	10 59
26	2 32	18 29	10 52	8 42	8 34	4 47	0 40	10 58

Moon Phenomena

Max/0 Decl
dy hr mn
5 8:55 0 S
12 3:11 27S57
18 10:57 0 N
25 5:54 27N58

Max/0 Lat
dy hr mn
7 13:53 0 S
14 3:35 5S16
20 11:32 0 N
27 14:36 5N17

Perigee/Apogee
dy hr m kilometers
16 2:25 p 367969
28 6:44 a 404297

PH dy hr mn
○ 6 4:36 16♎07
☾ 13 9:13 23♑11
● 20 4:14 29♈50
● 20 257:56AT01'16"
☽ 27 21:21 7♌21

Void of Course Moon

Last Aspect	☽ Ingress
2 6:04 ☿ △	♍ 2 10:58
4 13:51 ♆ ☍	♎ 4 21:52
6 12:44 ♃ ☍	♏ 7 6:30
9 9:10 ♀ ☍	♐ 9 12:58
11 10:49 ♆ □	♑ 11 17:34
13 14:15 ♆ ✶	♒ 13 20:43
15 15:17 ☉ ✶	♓ 15 22:58
17 18:58 ♆ ☌	♈ 18 1:10
20 4:14 ☉ ☌	♉ 20 4:31
22 3:42 ♀ ✶	♊ 22 10:12
24 12:16 ♆ □	♋ 24 19:00
26 23:42 ♆ △	♌ 27 6:31
29 10:54 ♃ △	♍ 29 19:00

DAILY ASPECTARIAN

1 Sa ☽∠⚳ 0:51; ☿⚺♆ 5:41; ☽△⚷ 6:03; ♀∠♂ 6:45; ☽□♅ 8:31; ☽∠♂ 11:48; ☽□♀ 12:08; ☽△♃ 13:26; ☽∥♀ 21:20

2 Su ☽⚻♆ 2:30; ♀⚺♃ 4:20; ☉⚼☽ 5:24; ☿⋕♄ 5:48; ☽△☿ 6:04; ☽⚺⚳ 6:29; ☽∥♅ 7:27; ☿⚻⚳ 8:38; ☽∥⚳ 10:05; ☽⚻♇ 11:18; ☽⚼⚷ 12:18; ☽☍♄ 16:45; ☽✶♂ 19:09; ☽⚼♃ 20:04

3 M ☽∥☿ 3:40; ☽⋕♄ 7:13; ☉⚻☽ 13:50; ☿ ♉ 16:23; ☽⚼☿ 16:44; ☽⚼♇ 17:02; ☽⚻⚷ 18:08; ☿□♇ 18:56; ☽△♅ 20:30

4 Tu ☽∥⚷ 1:02; ☽⚻♃ 2:13; ☽∥♃ 4:44; ☽△♀ 6:05; ☉∥☽ 9:31; ☽☍♆ 13:51; ☽☌⚳ 16:35; ☽⋕♆ 21:46; ☽△♇ 22:14

5 W ☽⚼♅ 1:43; ☽⚻☿ 2:17; ☽⚻♄ 3:56; ☽□♂ 8:13; ☽⚼♀ 14:00; ☿✶♄ 16:22; ☽∥♆ 19:55; ☉☌⚷ 22:19

6 Th ☽☍⚷ 4:08; ☉☍☽ 4:36; ☽⚻♅ 6:22; ☽⚼♄ 8:38; ☉⋕☽ 11:05; ☽☍♃ 12:44; ☽⋕♃ 13:23; ☽⋕⚷ 16:16; ☽⚻♀ 21:07; ☽⚻♆ 22:58

7 F ☽⚺⚳ 0:35; ☉⚺♅ 4:44; ☽□♇ 6:55; ☽∥♄ 8:12; ☽△♄ 12:45; ☊ D 13:56; ☽☍☿ 17:54; ♀✶♆ 17:59; ☽△♂ 18:43

8 Sa ☽⚼♆ 2:40; ☽⋕☿ 3:18; ☽∠⚳ 3:47; ☽⋕⚳ 4:54; ♀△⚳ 6:24; ☿✶♂ 6:30; ☽⋕♅ 6:57; ☉∥♃ 9:32; ☽⚻⚷ 11:50; ☽☍♅ 13:57; ☉∠♄ 14:21; ☉⚻☽ 16:28; ☿∥⚳ 18:24; ☽⚻♃ 20:52; ☽⚼♂ 23:04

9 Su ☽⋕♀ 4:57; ☽△♆ 5:51; ☽✶⚳ 6:31; ☽☍♀ 9:10; ☽✶♇ 13:24; ☽∥♇ 13:25; ☿∥♅ 14:40; ☽⚼⚷ 14:53; ☽□♄ 19:23; ☉⚼☽ 21:26

10 M ☽⚼♃ 0:08; ☉∥⚷ 0:47; ☽⚻♂ 2:52; ☽⚻☿ 5:25; ☽⋕♂ 7:55; ☽∠♇ 15:56; ☽△⚷ 17:29; ☽⚻♅ 19:30

11 Tu ⚳☍♆ 0:52; ☉△☽ 1:50; ☽△♃ 2:56; ♀ ♊ 4:48; ☽⚼☿ 9:52; ♀△♇ 10:16; ☽□⚳ 10:40; ☽□♆ 10:49; ☽⚺♇ 18:02; ☽⚻♀ 18:44; ☿⚼⚳ 19:27; ☽⚼♅ 21:38; ☉☌♃ 22:08; ☿∠♆ 23:28

12 W ☽✶♄ 0:09; ♀∠⚷ 6:17; ☽☍♂ 9:04; ☽△☿ 13:36; ☽□⚷ 21:28; ☽⚼♀ 22:46; ☽△♅ 23:25

13 Th ☽∠♄ 1:58; ☽□♃ 7:21; ☉□☽ 9:13; ☊ R 9:37; ☽△⚳ 13:25; ☽✶♆ 14:15; ☽☌♇ 21:12; ☽⋕♂ 22:54

14 F ☽△♀ 2:24; ☽⚺♄ 3:29; ♀⋕♇ 3:50; ☽⚻♂ 13:48; ☽⚼⚳ 14:23; ☽⋕♀ 14:33; ☽∥♇ 15:15; ☽∠♆ 15:33; ♀□♄ 16:40; ☽□☿ 19:17

15 Sa ☽✶⚷ 0:15; ☽□♅ 2:09; ☽⋕☿ 10:04; ☽✶♃ 10:37; ☉⚻⚳ 14:31; ☽⚻⚳ 15:13; ☉✶☽ 15:17; ☽⚼♂ 15:51; ☽⚺♆ 16:42; ⚶ ♉ 17:02; ☽⋕♅ 19:16; ☽⋕⚳ 21:37; ☽⚺♇ 23:28

16 Su ☽∠⚷ 1:24; ☽☌♄ 5:59; ☽□♀ 9:00; ☽∠♃ 12:05; ☉⚺♆ 12:44; ☽∥♄ 17:45; ☽△♂ 17:50; ☉∠☽ 18:09; ♃∥⚷ 18:40; ☉⋕☽ 21:25; ☽✶☿ 23:25

17 M ☽∠♇ 0:32; ☽⚺⚷ 2:33; ☽✶♅ 4:26; ☽⋕♃ 6:02; ☽⋕⚷ 6:09; ☽⚺♃ 13:36; ☽☍⚳ 16:53; ☽☌♆ 18:58; ☉⚺☽ 21:07

18 Tu ☽∠☿ 1:18; ☽✶♇ 1:43; ☽∥♆ 1:47; ☽∠♅ 5:44; ☽⚺♄ 8:35; ♀∠♃ 8:47; ☽✶♀ 15:48; ☽⋕♆ 20:06; ☽□♂ 22:18

19 W ☽⚺☿ 3:16; ☽☌⚷ 5:26; ☽⚺♅ 7:21; ☉⋕♄ 9:51; ☽∠♄ 10:19; ☽∥⚷ 16:19; ☽∥♃ 17:05; ☽☌♃ 17:28; ☽⚻⚳ 19:30; ☽∠♀ 19:48; ☽⚺♆ 22:13

20 Th ☉☌☽ 4:14; ☽⋕♄ 4:31; ☽□♇ 5:06; ☉∥☽ 5:46; ☉ ♉ 8:15; ☊ D 11:39; ☽✶♄ 12:32; ☉□♇ 16:28; ☽⚼⚳ 21:33

21 F ☽⚺♀ 0:30; ☽∠♆ 0:37; ☽∥⚳ 1:28; ☽✶♂ 4:38; ☽∥♅ 4:55; ☽☌☿ 8:07; ☿ R 8:36; ☽⚺⚷ 10:10; ☽☌♅ 12:10; ☽∥☿ 16:11; ☽⚺♃ 23:33

22 Sa ☽△⚳ 0:16; ☽✶♆ 3:42; ☽∠♂ 8:56; ☽⋕♇ 10:43; ☽△♇ 10:50; ☽∠⚷ 13:35; ☉⚺☽ 14:15; ☽□♄ 19:01; ♀∥♂ 19:02

23 Su ☽∥♂ 0:18; ☽∥♀ 0:46; ☽∠♃ 3:46; ⚳⚻♃ 3:49; ☽☌♀ 12:44; ☽⚺♂ 14:08; ☽⚼♇ 14:52; ☽⚺☿ 14:55; ☽✶⚷ 17:48; ☽⚺♅ 19:56; ☉∠☽ 20:44

24 M ☿✶♂ 3:20; ☽□⚳ 8:04; ☽✶♃ 8:50; ☿⚺♀ 9:06; ☊ R 11:43; ☽□♆ 12:16; ♀⚼♇ 12:24; ♀⚺♂ 16:51; ☽∠☿ 19:08; ☽⚻♇ 19:41

25 Tu ☽∠♅ 1:01; ☉✶☽ 4:12; ☽△♄ 4:41; ☉✶♄ 10:49; ☽✶☿ 23:48; ♀✶⚷ 23:51

26 W ☽☌♂ 3:09; ☽□⚷ 4:33; ☽⚺♀ 5:01; ☽✶♅ 6:47; ☽⚼♄ 10:35; ☽✶⚳ 18:47; ☽□♃ 21:10; ☽△♆ 23:42

27 Th ♀⚺♅ 0:37; ☽☍♇ 7:14; ☽∥♀ 7:15; ♂□⚷ 13:36; ☽∠♀ 14:15; ☽∥♂ 16:44; ☽⚻♄ 16:55; ☊ D 20:47; ☉□☽ 21:21

28 F ☽∠⚳ 0:50; ☽⋕♇ 4:41; ☽⚼♆ 6:01; ☽□☿ 9:45; ☽△⚷ 17:12; ☽⚺♂ 18:23; ☽□♅ 19:27; ☽✶♀ 23:43

29 Sa ☽⚺⚳ 6:58; ☽△♃ 10:54; ☽⚻♆ 12:21; ☿∥♅ 13:08; ☽∥♅ 13:27; ☽∥☿ 13:29; ☉⚼⚳ 13:47; ☽⚻♇ 19:44; ♂✶♅ 20:06; ☽∥⚳ 20:20; ☽⚼⚷ 23:31

30 Su ☉∥☽ 1:20; ☽∠♂ 2:00; ☽☍♄ 5:43; ☉△☽ 15:00; ☽⚼♃ 17:29; ☽△♆ 19:07; ☽⋕♄ 19:13

LONGITUDE

Day	Sid.Time	☉	☽	☽ 12 hour	Mean☊	True☊	☿	♀	♂	⚳	♃	♄	⚷	♅	♆	♇
	h m s	° ' "	° ' "	° ' "	° '	° '	° '	° '	° '	° '	° '	° '	° '	° '	° '	° '
1 M	14 34 40	10♉22 49	14♍33 23	20♍39 24	3♉50.9	4♉01.6	11♉57.3	22♊40.4	18♋59.8	23♍55.9	26♈19.9	5♓24.3	17♈18.6	18♉25.6	26♓43.8	0♒21.8
2 Tu	14 38 36	11 21 04	26 48 44	3♎01 45	3 47.7	4 02.3	11R 19.0	23 47.5	19 32.8	23R 53.7	26 34.1	5 28.6	17 21.8	18 29.0	26 45.6	0R 21.9
3 W	14 42 33	12 19 17	9♎18 47	15 40 05	3 44.5	4 03.0	10 40.1	24 54.5	20 05.9	23 51.9	26 48.3	5 32.8	17 25.1	18 32.5	26 47.3	0 21.8
4 Th	14 46 29	13 17 27	22 05 52	28 36 12	3 41.3	4R 03.6	10 01.6	26 01.2	20 39.0	23 50.5	27 02.5	5 37.0	17 28.4	18 35.9	26 49.0	0 21.8
5 F	14 50 26	14 15 36	5♏11 10	11♏50 40	3 38.1	4 03.8	9 23.9	27 07.8	21 12.2	23 49.6	27 16.6	5 41.1	17 31.6	18 39.4	26 50.7	0 21.7
6 Sa	14 54 23	15 13 44	18 34 37	25 22 48	3 35.0	4 03.5	8 47.9	28 14.1	21 45.4	23D 49.0	27 30.7	5 45.1	17 34.8	18 42.9	26 52.4	0 21.6
7 Su	14 58 19	16 11 49	2♐14 55	9♐10 39	3 31.8	4 02.6	8 14.0	29 20.3	22 18.8	23 48.9	27 44.8	5 49.0	17 38.0	18 46.3	26 54.0	0 21.5
8 M	15 02 16	17 09 53	16 09 35	23 11 18	3 28.6	4 01.2	7 42.8	0♋26.3	22 52.2	23 49.2	27 58.9	5 52.8	17 41.2	18 49.8	26 55.7	0 21.3
9 Tu	15 06 12	18 07 56	0♑15 18	7♑21 08	3 25.4	3 59.4	7 14.8	1 32.0	23 25.6	23 49.9	28 12.9	5 56.6	17 44.4	18 53.3	26 57.3	0 21.1
10 W	15 10 09	19 05 57	14 28 17	21 36 18	3 22.3	3 57.7	6 50.4	2 37.6	23 59.2	23 51.0	28 26.9	6 00.3	17 47.5	18 56.7	26 58.8	0 20.9
11 Th	15 14 05	20 03 57	28 44 48	5♒53 07	3 19.1	3 56.2	6 29.9	3 42.9	24 32.8	23 52.5	28 40.9	6 03.9	17 50.6	19 00.2	27 00.4	0 20.7
12 F	15 18 02	21 01 55	13♒01 07	20 08 22	3 15.9	3D 55.4	6 13.5	4 48.1	25 06.4	23 54.3	28 54.8	6 07.4	17 53.7	19 03.7	27 01.9	0 20.4
13 Sa	15 21 59	21 59 53	27 14 32	4♓19 22	3 12.7	3 55.3	6 01.5	5 53.0	25 40.1	23 56.6	29 08.7	6 10.8	17 56.8	19 07.2	27 03.4	0 20.1
14 Su	15 25 55	22 57 49	11♓22 36	18 24 02	3 09.6	3 56.0	5 54.0	6 57.6	26 13.9	23 59.3	29 22.5	6 14.1	17 59.8	19 10.7	27 04.9	0 19.8
15 M	15 29 52	23 55 43	25 23 27	2♈20 39	3 06.4	3 57.1	5D 51.0	8 02.1	26 47.7	24 02.4	29 36.3	6 17.4	18 02.8	19 14.1	27 06.3	0 19.4
16 Tu	15 33 48	24 53 37	9♈15 28	16 07 43	3 03.2	3 58.5	5 52.7	9 06.3	27 21.6	24 05.8	29 50.1	6 20.6	18 05.8	19 17.6	27 07.8	0 19.0
17 W	15 37 45	25 51 29	22 57 14	29 43 51	3 00.0	3R 59.6	5 59.0	10 10.2	27 55.6	24 09.7	0♉03.8	6 23.6	18 08.8	19 21.0	27 09.2	0 18.6
18 Th	15 41 41	26 49 20	6♉27 23	13♉07 42	2 56.8	3 59.9	6 09.9	11 13.9	28 29.6	24 13.9	0 17.5	6 26.6	18 11.7	19 24.5	27 10.5	0 18.2
19 F	15 45 38	27 47 09	19 44 39	26 18 07	2 53.7	3 59.1	6 25.2	12 17.4	29 03.7	24 18.5	0 31.1	6 29.5	18 14.6	19 28.0	27 11.9	0 17.7
20 Sa	15 49 34	28 44 57	2♊48 01	9♊14 17	2 50.5	3 57.0	6 45.1	13 20.6	29 37.9	24 23.5	0 44.7	6 32.3	18 17.5	19 31.4	27 13.2	0 17.2
21 Su	15 53 31	29 42 44	15 36 53	21 55 53	2 47.3	3 53.8	7 09.2	14 23.5	0♌12.1	24 28.9	0 58.3	6 35.1	18 20.3	19 34.9	27 14.5	0 16.7
22 M	15 57 28	0♊40 30	28 11 20	4♋23 22	2 44.1	3 49.7	7 37.6	15 26.1	0 46.3	24 34.6	1 11.8	6 37.7	18 23.1	19 38.3	27 15.8	0 16.2
23 Tu	16 01 24	1 38 14	10♋32 12	16 38 03	2 41.0	3 45.2	8 10.1	16 28.4	1 20.6	24 40.7	1 25.2	6 40.2	18 25.9	19 41.7	27 17.0	0 15.6
24 W	16 05 21	2 35 56	22 41 15	28 42 09	2 37.8	3 40.7	8 46.6	17 30.5	1 55.0	24 47.1	1 38.6	6 42.7	18 28.7	19 45.1	27 18.2	0 15.0
25 Th	16 09 17	3 33 37	4♌41 08	10♌38 40	2 34.6	3 36.8	9 27.0	18 32.2	2 29.4	24 53.9	1 51.9	6 45.0	18 31.4	19 48.5	27 19.4	0 14.4
26 F	16 13 14	4 31 17	16 35 16	22 31 26	2 31.4	3 34.0	10 11.1	19 33.6	3 03.9	25 01.0	2 05.2	6 47.3	18 34.1	19 51.9	27 20.5	0 13.8
27 Sa	16 17 10	5 28 55	28 27 44	4♍24 46	2 28.3	3D 32.5	10 58.9	20 34.6	3 38.4	25 08.5	2 18.5	6 49.4	18 36.7	19 55.3	27 21.6	0 13.1
28 Su	16 21 07	6 26 31	10♍23 07	16 23 23	2 25.1	3 32.3	11 50.2	21 35.3	4 13.0	25 16.3	2 31.6	6 51.5	18 39.3	19 58.7	27 22.7	0 12.4
29 M	16 25 03	7 24 06	22 26 12	28 32 09	2 21.9	3 33.2	12 45.0	22 35.7	4 47.6	25 24.5	2 44.8	6 53.5	18 41.9	20 02.0	27 23.8	0 11.7
30 Tu	16 29 00	8 21 40	4♎41 48	10♎55 42	2 18.7	3 34.8	13 43.2	23 35.7	5 22.3	25 33.0	2 57.8	6 55.4	18 44.4	20 05.4	27 24.8	0 11.0
31 W	16 32 57	9♊19 12	17 14 21	23 38 10	2♉15.5	3♉36.3	14♉44.6	24♋35.3	5♌57.0	25♍41.8	3♉10.8	6♓57.1	18♈47.0	20♉08.7	27♓25.8	0♒10.2

1st of Month
Julian Day #
2460065.5
Obliquity
23°26'[illegible]8"
SVP 4♓56'[illegible]3"
GC 27♐09.9
Eris 24♈44.9

Day	⚴
1	29♋18.7
6	1♌20.2
11	3 24.0
16	5 29.8
21	7 37.4
26	9 46.6
31	11 57.2

Day	⚵
1	29♉17.4
6	2♊14.5
11	5 11.5
16	8 08.4
21	11 05.1
26	14 01.4
31	16 57.2

Day	⚶
1	6♉54.7
6	9 09.4
11	11 23.6
16	13 37.1
21	15 50.1
26	18 02.3
31	20 13.6

DECLINATION and LATITUDE

Day	☉ Decl	☽ Decl	☽ Lat	☽ 12h Decl	☿ Decl	☿ Lat	♀ Decl	♀ Lat	♂ Decl	♂ Lat	⚳ Decl	⚳ Lat	♃ Decl	♃ Lat	♄ Decl	♄ Lat
1 M	14N56	9N47	4N01	7N02	16N21	0N58	25N39	2N25	23N50	1N46	15N34	14N22	9N10	1S04	10S51	1S25
2 Tu	15 14	4 12	3 12	1 18	15 53	0 42	25 45	2 27	23 45	1 45	15 30	14 16	9 15	1 04	10 49	1 25
3 W	15 32	1S39	2 13	4S38	15 25	0 25	25 49	2 29	23 40	1 45	15 25	14 11	9 21	1 04	10 48	1 25
4 Th	15 50	7 35	1 06	10 30	14 56	0 07	25 54	2 31	23 34	1 44	15 21	14 05	9 26	1 04	10 46	1 25
5 F	16 07	13 21	0S06	16 04	14 28	0S10	25 57	2 33	23 28	1 44	15 16	13 59	9 31	1 04	10 45	1 26
6 Sa	16 24	18 38	1 19	20 58	14 00	0 27	26 00	2 35	23 22	1 43	15 11	13 54	9 36	1 04	10 44	1 26
7 Su	16 41	23 03	2 30	24 49	13 33	0 44	26 02	2 36	23 16	1 42	15 06	13 48	9 41	1 04	10 43	1 26
8 M	16 58	26 14	3 32	27 15	13 07	1 01	26 04	2 38	23 10	1 42	15 00	13 42	9 46	1 04	10 41	1 26
9 Tu	17 14	27 49	4 23	27 56	12 43	1 17	26 05	2 39	23 04	1 41	14 55	13 36	9 51	1 04	10 40	1 26
10 W	17 30	27 35	4 57	26 46	12 20	1 33	26 05	2 40	22 58	1 41	14 49	13 30	9 56	1 04	10 39	1 27
11 Th	17 45	25 32	5 14	23 53	11 60	1 47	26 05	2 42	22 51	1 40	14 43	13 25	10 01	1 04	10 38	1 27
12 F	18 01	21 53	5 11	19 33	11 41	2 01	26 04	2 43	22 45	1 40	14 37	13 19	10 05	1 04	10 37	1 27
13 Sa	18 16	16 58	4 50	14 09	11 25	2 14	26 02	2 44	22 38	1 39	14 31	13 13	10 10	1 04	10 36	1 27
14 Su	18 31	11 09	4 11	8 03	11 11	2 26	25 60	2 45	22 31	1 38	14 24	13 07	10 15	1 04	10 35	1 27
15 M	18 45	4 51	3 17	1 36	10 60	2 37	25 57	2 46	22 24	1 38	14 18	13 01	10 20	1 04	10 34	1 28
16 Tu	18 59	1N39	2 12	4N51	10 51	2 48	25 53	2 46	22 17	1 37	14 11	12 56	10 25	1 04	10 33	1 28
17 W	19 13	7 59	1 00	11 01	10 44	2 57	25 49	2 47	22 09	1 37	14 04	12 50	10 29	1 04	10 32	1 28
18 Th	19 27	13 53	0N14	16 34	10 40	3 05	25 44	2 47	22 02	1 36	13 58	12 44	10 34	1 04	10 31	1 28
19 F	19 40	19 03	1 25	21 16	10 38	3 12	25 39	2 48	21 54	1 36	13 50	12 38	10 39	1 04	10 30	1 28
20 Sa	19 53	23 03	2 32	24 49	10 39	3 18	25 33	2 48	21 46	1 35	13 43	12 33	10 44	1 04	10 29	1 29
21 Su	20 05	26 07	3 29	27 04	10 42	3 23	25 27	2 48	21 39	1 34	13 36	12 27	10 48	1 04	10 28	1 29
22 M	20 17	27 40	4 14	27 54	10 47	3 27	25 19	2 48	21 31	1 34	13 28	12 21	10 53	1 04	10 27	1 29
23 Tu	20 29	27 44	4 47	27 20	10 54	3 31	25 12	2 48	21 23	1 33	13 21	12 16	10 58	1 05	10 27	1 29
24 W	20 41	26 34	5 07	25 30	11 03	3 33	25 03	2 47	21 14	1 33	13 13	12 10	11 02	1 05	10 26	1 29
25 Th	20 52	24 08	5 12	22 32	11 15	3 35	24 55	2 47	21 06	1 32	13 05	12 04	11 07	1 05	10 25	1 30
26 F	21 03	20 42	5 04	18 39	11 28	3 35	24 45	2 46	20 57	1 32	12 57	11 59	11 11	1 05	10 25	1 30
27 Sa	21 13	16 26	4 43	14 03	11 43	3 35	24 35	2 46	20 49	1 31	12 49	11 53	11 16	1 05	10 24	1 30
28 Su	21 23	11 32	4 10	8 53	11 59	3 34	24 25	2 45	20 40	1 31	12 41	11 48	11 20	1 05	10 23	1 30
29 M	21 33	6 09	3 26	3 20	12 17	3 32	24 14	2 44	20 31	1 30	12 33	11 42	11 24	1 05	10 23	1 31
30 Tu	21 42	0 27	2 31	2S29	12 37	3 30	24 03	2 42	20 22	1 29	12 25	11 37	11 29	1 05	10 22	1 31
31 W	21N51	5S25	1N28	8S20	12N58	3S27	23N51	2N41	20N13	1N29	12N16	11N31	11N33	1S05	10S22	1S31

Day	⚷ Decl	⚷ Lat	♅ Decl	♅ Lat	♆ Decl	♆ Lat	♇ Decl	♇ Lat
1	8N14	1N33	17N01	0S19	2S23	1S11	22S31	2S30
6	8 20	1 33	17 05	0 19	2 20	1 11	22 32	2 31
11	8 26	1 33	17 10	0 19	2 17	1 11	22 33	2 32
16	8 31	1 33	17 15	0 19	2 14	1 12	22 34	2 32
21	8 37	1 33	17 20	0 19	2 12	1 12	22 35	2 33
26	8 42	1 32	17 24	0 19	2 10	1 12	22 36	2 34
31	8N47	1N32	17N29	0S19	2S08	1S12	22S38	2S35

Day	⚴ Decl	⚴ Lat	⚵ Decl	⚵ Lat	⚶ Decl	⚶ Lat	Eris Decl	Eris Lat
1	3N33	17S05	11N29	8S43	9N20	4S45	0S38	10S58
6	4 28	15 45	12 03	8 43	10 04	4 43	0 37	10 58
11	5 17	14 29	12 34	8 44	10 47	4 41	0 36	10 58
16	5 60	13 17	13 03	8 43	11 29	4 40	0 35	10 59
21	6 37	12 07	13 28	8 43	12 08	4 38	0 34	10 59
26	7 10	11 01	13 50	8 42	12 47	4 36	0 34	10 59
31	7N37	9S58	14N09	8S41	13N23	4S35	0S33	10S59

Moon Phenomena

Max/0 Decl (dy hr mn)
2 17:17 0 S
9 8:58 27S56
15 17:55 0 N
22 14:08 27N54
30 1:50 0 S

Perigee/Apogee (dy hr m kilometers)
11 5:06 p 369343
26 1:40 a 404508

PH (dy hr mn)
○ 5 17:35 14♏58
◐ 5 17:24 A 0.963
☾ 12 14:29 21♒37
● 19 15:54 28♉25
☽ 27 15:23 6♍06

Max/0 Lat (dy hr mn)
4 21:58 0 S
11 8:43 5S15
17 19:37 0 N
24 21:52 5N12

Void of Course Moon

Last Aspect	☽ Ingress
1 23:54 ♆ ☍	♎ 2 6:10
4 9:18 ♃ ☍	♏ 4 14:33
6 14:39 ♅ △	♐ 6 20:05
8 20:29 ♃ △	♑ 8 23:34
10 23:53 ♃ □	♒ 11 2:07
13 3:16 ♃ ✶	♓ 13 4:40
15 2:58 ♆ ☌	♈ 15 7:57
17 5:12 ♂ △	♉ 17 12:29
19 17:52 ♂ ✶	♊ 19 18:49
21 22:13 ♆ □	♋ 22 3:30
24 9:13 ♆ △	♌ 24 14:36
26 6:39 ♅ □	♍ 27 3:06
29 9:47 ♆ ☍	♎ 29 14:52
31 14:55 ♀ □	♏ 31 23:46

DAILY ASPECTARIAN

1 M
☽⚼♇ 1:36
☽∥♃ 2:40
☽⚻⚷ 5:27
☽∥⚷ 6:50
☽△♅ 7:40
☿∠♆ 8:08
☽✶♂ 9:09
♇ R 17:10
☽□♀ 17:32
☽☌⚳ 18:20
☉⚼☽ 23:02
☽⚼☿ 23:05
☉☌☿ 23:29
☽⚻♃ 23:31
☽☍♆ 23:54

2 Tu
♀□⚳ 2:08
⚵ ♊ 4:51
☽△♇ 6:52
☽⫲♆ 7:35
☉∠♆ 10:25
☽⚼♅ 12:56
☽⚻♄ 16:47
☉∥⚳ 16:55
⚴ ♌ 17:04
☉∥☿ 20:18
♃⚺♆ 22:05
☿∥⚳ 23:27

3 W
☽⚻☿ 2:27
☽∥♆ 2:52
☉⚻☽ 6:10
☿∠♀ 10:23
☽☍⚷ 15:21
☽⚻♅ 17:27
☽□♂ 21:11
☽⚼♄ 21:14
♂⚼♄ 22:20

4 Th
☽⫲⚷ 2:52
☽⚺⚳ 3:14
☽⫲♃ 7:38
☽△♀ 7:56
☽⚻♆ 8:44
☽☍♃ 9:18
☽∥♄ 13:03
☽□♇ 15:13
♀□♆ 17:41
☊ R 21:56

5 F
☽△♄ 0:54
♀✶♃ 4:04
☽⫲☿ 4:28
☽∠⚳ 6:34
☽☍☿ 7:16
☽⫲⚳ 8:15
☽⚼♆ 12:02
☉⫲☽ 12:55
☽⚼♀ 13:38
☽⫲♅ 16:40
☉☍☽ 17:35
☽⚻⚷ 22:14
☿⚼⚳ 23:13

6 Sa
☽☍♅ 0:15
☽△♂ 5:52
☽✶⚳ 9:15
☽△♆ 14:39
☽⚻♃ 16:01
☽⚻♀ 18:29
⚳ D 19:25
☽✶♇ 20:42
☽∥♇ 20:50

7 Su
☽⚼⚷ 0:40
☽⫲♂ 1:21
☽□♄ 6:13
☽⚼♂ 9:09
☽⚻☿ 9:59
♀ ♋ 14:26
☽⚼♃ 18:27
♀⚻♇ 22:11
☽⫲♀ 22:22
☽∠♇ 22:37

8 M
☉⚻☽ 1:51
☽△⚷ 2:37
☽⚻♅ 4:35
☽⚼☿ 10:49
☽⚻♂ 11:56
☽□⚳ 13:05
☉⚺⚷ 13:42
☉∥♅ 15:17
☽□♆ 18:24
☽△♃ 20:29

9 Tu
☽⚺♇ 0:10
☽☍♀ 2:21
☉⚼☽ 5:14
☽⚼♅ 6:10
☽✶♄ 9:40
☽△☿ 11:29
♂✶⚳ 17:54
☉☌♅ 19:57

10 W
☽□⚷ 5:37
☽△♅ 7:34
☉△☽ 8:21
☽∠♄ 11:02
☽△⚳ 15:48
☽☍♂ 16:39
☽⫲♀ 19:08
☽✶♆ 21:04
☽□♃ 23:53

11 Th
☽☌♇ 2:41
♀∠♅ 6:43
☽⚻♀ 9:02
☽⚺♄ 12:21
☽□☿ 12:46
☽⚼⚳ 17:04
☽⫲♂ 18:56
☽∥♇ 20:13
☽∠♆ 22:20

12 F
☽✶⚷ 8:15
☿✶♄ 8:43
☽□♅ 10:13
☽⚼♀ 12:22
☉□☽ 14:29
☊ D 14:36
☉⫲☽ 18:22
☽⚻⚳ 18:24
☽⚻♂ 21:14
☽⫲♅ 22:56
☽⚺♆ 23:41

13 Sa
☿✶♀ 2:45
☽✶♃ 3:16
☽⚺♇ 5:14
♀△♄ 6:58
☽∠⚷ 9:42
☽⫲⚳ 10:40
☽✶☿ 14:45
☽☌♄ 15:13
♂⫲♇ 15:41
☽△♀ 15:52
☽⚼♂ 23:45
☽⫲☿ 23:53

14 Su
☽∥♄ 2:17
☽⫲♃ 3:29
☽∠♃ 5:12
☽∠♇ 6:45
☽⫲⚷ 10:17
☽⚺⚷ 11:21
☽✶♅ 13:23
☽∠☿ 16:13
☉✶☽ 21:18
☽☍⚳ 21:40

15 M
☽△♂ 2:31
☉△⚳ 2:56
☽☌♆ 2:58
☿ D 3:18
☽⚺♃ 7:23
☽✶♇ 8:30
☽∥♆ 9:38
♂△♆ 13:46
☽∠♅ 15:20
☽⚺☿ 18:06
☽⚺♄ 18:55
☽□♀ 23:43

16 Tu
☉∠☽ 1:11
☽⫲♆ 2:12
☽☌⚷ 15:30
♃ ♉ 17:21
☽⚺♅ 17:38
☽∠♄ 21:14

17 W
☽⚻⚳ 2:09
☽∥⚷ 2:10
☉⚺☽ 5:31
☽⚺♆ 7:26
♃⫲♄ 9:03
☽□♂ 9:11
☽⫲♄ 10:01
☽∥♃ 10:02
☽∥☿ 10:44
☽☌♃ 12:48
☽□♇ 13:01
☊ R 19:36
☽☌☿ 23:28
☽✶♄ 23:59

18 Th
☽∥⚳ 0:19
♃□♇ 1:12
☽⚼⚳ 5:00
☉✶♆ 9:01
☽✶♀ 9:19
☽∠♆ 10:18
☽∥♅ 15:23
☿∥♃ 20:47
☽⚺⚷ 21:16
☽☌♅ 23:29

19 F
☉∥☽ 3:24
☿✶♄ 6:41
☽△⚳ 8:24
☽✶♆ 13:40
☽∠♀ 15:02
☽∥♂ 15:19
☉☌☽ 15:54
☽✶♂ 17:52
☽△♇ 19:21
☽⫲♇ 19:59
☽⚺♃ 20:08

20 Sa
☽∠⚷ 0:55
☽□♄ 6:59
☽⚺☿ 7:34
♂ ♌ 15:33
☽∥♀ 17:39
☽⚺♀ 21:29
☽∠♂ 23:11
☽⚼♇ 23:22

21 Su
☽∠♃ 0:41
♂☍♇ 3:13
☽✶⚷ 5:11
☉ ♊ 7:10
☽⚺♅ 7:33
☽∠☿ 12:54
☉△♇ 14:00
☽□⚳ 17:00
☽□♆ 22:13

22 M
☽⚻♇ 4:01
☉⚺☽ 5:12
☽⚺♂ 5:14
☽✶♃ 5:55
☉✶♂ 5:58
☽∠♅ 12:33
☽△♄ 16:25
☉⚺♃ 16:57
☽✶☿ 19:08

23 Tu
♂□♃ 5:14
☽☌♀ 12:46
☉∠☽ 13:02
☽□⚷ 15:37
☿∥♃ 18:05
☽✶♅ 18:09
☽⚼♄ 22:03

24 W
☽✶⚳ 4:13
☽△♆ 9:13
☽☍♇ 15:05
☽∥♀ 17:03
☽□♃ 18:14
☽☌♂ 19:22
☉✶☽ 21:32
☉∠⚷ 23:01
♀□⚷ 23:40

25 Th
☽⚻♄ 4:10
☉∠♀ 9:07
☽□☿ 10:12
☽∠⚳ 10:36
☽⫲♇ 11:29
☽⚼♆ 15:25
☉∥♂ 17:33
☿⚼⚳ 17:41
☉∥☽ 21:56
☽∥♂ 22:18

26 F
☽△⚷ 4:01
☽⚺♀ 6:34
☽□♅ 6:39
♀✶♅ 7:38
☽⚺⚳ 17:13
☽∥♅ 18:48
☽⚻♆ 21:46

27 Sa
☽⚻♇ 3:33
☽△♃ 7:54
☽⚼⚷ 10:26
☽⚺♂ 10:59
☊ D 15:15
☉□☽ 15:23
☽∠♀ 15:40
☽☍♄ 16:54
☽∥⚳ 18:25
☽∥☿ 21:59

28 Su
☽∥♃ 0:54
☽△☿ 3:08
☽⫲♄ 5:15
♀⚼♄ 6:39
☽⚼♇ 9:38
☉□♄ 10:47
☽∥⚷ 12:39
☽⚼♃ 14:32
☿∠♆ 14:41
☽⚻⚷ 16:34
☽∠♂ 18:30
☽△♅ 19:13

29 M
☽✶♀ 0:20
☽☌⚳ 5:56
☽☍♆ 9:47
☽⚼☿ 11:21
☿∥⚳ 13:40
☽△♇ 15:14
☽⫲♆ 16:59
☽⚻♃ 20:35

30 Tu
☽⚼♅ 0:46
☽✶♂ 1:22
☽⚻♄ 4:19
☉△☽ 7:40
☽∥♆ 10:35
☽⚻☿ 18:51

31 W
☽☍⚷ 2:55
☽⚻♅ 5:30
☽⚼♄ 8:53
☽⫲⚷ 13:52
☉⚼☽ 14:20
☽□♀ 14:55
☽⚺⚳ 16:01
☽⚻♆ 19:04
☽∥♄ 20:24

June 2023

LONGITUDE

Day	Sid.Time	☉	☽	☽ 12 hour	Mean☊	True☊	☿	♀	♂	⚳	♃	♄	⚷	♅	♆	♇
	h m s	° ' "	° ' "	° ' "	° '	° '	° '	° '	° '	° '	° '	° '	° '	° '	° '	° '
1 Th	16 36 53	10♊16 43	0♏07 30	6♏42 38	2♉12.4	3♉37.2	15♉49.2	25♋34.5	6♌31.8	25♍50.9	3♉23.7	6♓58.8	18♈49.4	20♉12.0	27♓26.8	0♒09.4
2 F	16 40 50	11 14 12	13 23 42	20 10 44	2 09.2	3R 36.9	16 56.9	26 33.3	7 06.6	26 00.3	3 36.6	7 00.4	18 51.9	20 15.4	27 27.6	0R 08.6
3 Sa	16 44 46	12 11 41	27 03 38	4♐02 09	2 06.0	3 34.9	18 07.7	27 31.7	7 41.5	26 10.1	3 49.4	7 01.9	18 54.3	20 18.6	27 28.6	0 07.8
4 Su	16 48 43	13 09 08	11♐05 53	18 14 18	2 02.8	3 31.1	19 21.4	28 29.6	8 16.4	26 20.1	4 02.2	7 03.3	18 56.6	20 21.9	27 29.5	0 06.9
5 M	16 52 39	14 06 35	25 26 45	2♑42 28	1 59.7	3 25.9	20 38.1	29 27.1	8 51.3	26 30.5	4 14.9	7 04.6	18 59.0	20 25.2	27 30.4	0 06.1
6 Tu	16 56 36	15 04 00	10♑00 35	17 20 14	1 56.5	3 19.8	21 57.7	0♌24.2	9 26.3	26 41.1	4 27.5	7 05.8	19 01.2	20 28.4	27 31.2	0 05.2
7 W	17 00 32	16 01 25	24 40 30	2♒00 29	1 53.3	3 13.6	23 20.2	1 20.8	10 01.4	26 52.0	4 40.0	7 06.9	19 03.5	20 31.7	27 32.0	0 04.3
8 Th	17 04 29	16 58 49	9♒19 22	16 36 26	1 50.1	3 08.1	24 45.5	2 16.9	10 36.5	27 03.2	4 52.5	7 08.0	19 05.7	20 34.9	27 32.7	0 03.3
9 F	17 08 26	17 56 13	23 51 01	1♓02 37	1 47.0	3 04.1	26 13.7	3 12.5	11 11.6	27 14.7	5 04.9	7 08.9	19 07.9	20 38.1	27 33.5	0 02.4
10 Sa	17 12 22	18 53 36	8♓10 50	15 15 24	1 43.8	3D 01.9	27 44.6	4 07.6	11 46.8	27 26.5	5 17.3	7 09.7	19 10.0	20 41.2	27 34.1	0 01.4
11 Su	17 16 19	19 50 58	22 16 09	29 13 01	1 40.6	3 01.5	29 18.3	5 02.2	12 22.0	27 38.5	5 29.5	7 10.4	19 12.1	20 44.4	27 34.8	0 00.4
12 M	17 20 15	20 48 20	6♈05 59	12♈55 09	1 37.4	3 02.2	0♊54.7	5 56.2	12 57.3	27 50.8	5 41.7	7 11.0	19 14.1	20 47.5	27 35.4	29♑59.4
13 Tu	17 24 12	21 45 41	19 40 35	26 22 28	1 34.3	3 03.3	2 33.9	6 49.6	13 32.6	28 03.4	5 53.8	7 11.5	19 16.2	20 50.6	27 36.0	29 58.4
14 W	17 28 08	22 43 02	3♉00 54	9♉36 03	1 31.1	3R 03.9	4 15.8	7 42.5	14 07.9	28 16.2	6 05.9	7 12.0	19 18.1	20 53.7	27 36.6	29 57.3
15 Th	17 32 05	23 40 22	16 08 02	22 37 00	1 27.9	3 03.0	6 00.4	8 34.7	14 43.4	28 29.3	6 17.8	7 12.3	19 20.0	20 56.7	27 37.1	29 56.2
16 F	17 36 01	24 37 42	29 03 01	5♊26 11	1 24.7	3 00.2	7 47.7	9 26.4	15 18.8	28 42.6	6 29.7	7 12.5	19 21.9	20 59.8	27 37.6	29 55.1
17 Sa	17 39 58	25 35 02	11♊46 34	18 04 13	1 21.6	2 54.9	9 37.6	10 17.3	15 54.3	28 56.2	6 41.5	7R 12.6	19 23.7	21 02.8	27 38.1	29 54.0
18 Su	17 43 55	26 32 21	24 19 11	0♋31 33	1 18.4	2 47.4	11 30.0	11 07.6	16 29.9	29 10.0	6 53.2	7 12.6	19 25.5	21 05.8	27 38.5	29 52.9
19 M	17 47 51	27 29 39	6♋41 21	12 48 43	1 15.2	2 38.2	13 24.9	11 57.2	17 05.5	29 24.1	7 04.8	7 12.6	19 27.3	21 08.8	27 38.9	29 51.8
20 Tu	17 51 48	28 26 57	18 53 43	24 56 32	1 12.0	2 27.9	15 22.2	12 46.1	17 41.1	29 38.4	7 16.3	7 12.4	19 29.0	21 11.7	27 39.3	29 50.6
21 W	17 55 44	29 24 15	0♌57 21	6♌56 24	1 08.9	2 17.6	17 21.8	13 34.2	18 16.8	29 52.9	7 27.8	7 12.1	19 30.6	21 14.6	27 39.7	29 49.4
22 Th	17 59 41	0♋21 31	12 53 58	18 50 23	1 05.7	2 08.3	19 23.5	14 21.6	18 52.5	0♎07.7	7 39.1	7 11.7	19 32.2	21 17.5	27 40.0	29 48.3
23 F	18 03 37	1 18 47	24 46 02	0♍41 21	1 02.5	2 00.6	21 27.3	15 08.1	19 28.3	0 22.7	7 50.4	7 11.3	19 33.8	21 20.4	27 40.2	29 47.1
24 Sa	18 07 34	2 16 02	6♍36 48	12 32 56	0 59.3	1 55.1	23 32.8	15 53.7	20 04.1	0 37.9	8 01.6	7 10.7	19 35.3	21 23.2	27 40.5	29 45.8
25 Su	18 11 30	3 13 17	18 30 17	24 29 28	0 56.1	1 51.9	25 39.9	16 38.5	20 39.9	0 53.3	8 12.6	7 10.0	19 36.8	21 26.0	27 40.7	29 44.6
26 M	18 15 27	4 10 31	0♎31 06	6♎35 49	0 53.0	1D 50.7	27 48.3	17 22.4	21 15.8	1 09.0	8 23.6	7 09.2	19 38.2	21 28.8	27 40.8	29 43.4
27 Tu	18 19 24	5 07 45	12 44 15	18 57 03	0 49.8	1 50.8	29 57.8	18 05.3	21 51.7	1 24.8	8 34.5	7 08.4	19 39.6	21 31.5	27 41.0	29 42.1
28 W	18 23 20	6 04 57	25 14 50	1♏38 11	0 46.6	1R 51.4	2♋08.0	18 47.2	22 27.7	1 40.9	8 45.2	7 07.4	19 40.9	21 34.2	27 41.1	29 40.8
29 Th	18 27 17	7 02 10	8♏07 36	14 43 32	0 43.4	1 51.4	4 18.8	19 28.1	23 03.7	1 57.1	8 55.9	7 06.4	19 42.2	21 36.9	27 41.2	29 39.5
30 F	18 31 13	7♋59 22	21 26 18	28 16 05	0♉40.3	1♉49.8	6♋29.9	20♌07.9	23♌39.7	2♎13.6	9♉06.5	7♓05.2	19♈43.4	21♉39.6	27♓41.2	29♑38.2

1st of Month

Julian Day #
2460096.5
Obliquity
23°26'08"
SVP 4♓56'08"
GC 27♐10.0
Eris 25♈02.5

Day	⚴	Day	⚵	Day	⚶
1	12♌23.4	1	17♊32.3	1	20♉39.7
6	14 35.3	6	20 27.5	6	22 49.9
11	16 48.1	11	23 22.0	11	24 59.2
16	19 01.8	16	26 15.7	16	27 07.4
21	21 16.3	21	29 08.7	21	29 14.5
26	23 31.4	26	2♋00.8	26	1♊20.2

DECLINATION and LATITUDE

Day	☉ Decl	☽ Decl	☽ Lat	☽12h Decl	☿ Decl	☿ Lat	♀ Decl	♀ Lat	♂ Decl	♂ Lat	⚳ Decl	⚳ Lat	♃ Decl	♃ Lat	♄ Decl	♄ Lat
1 Th	21N59	11S13	0N19	14S01	13N20	3S23	23N38	2N40	20N04	1N28	12N08	11N26	11N38	1S05	10S22	1S31
2 F	22 07	16 42	0S53	19 13	13 43	3 18	23 26	2 38	19 55	1 28	11 59	11 21	11 42	1 05	10 21	1 31
3 Sa	22 15	21 31	2 04	23 32	14 08	3 13	23 12	2 36	19 45	1 27	11 50	11 15	11 46	1 05	10 21	1 32
4 Su	22 23	25 14	3 09	26 32	14 33	3 08	22 59	2 34	19 35	1 27	11 41	11 10	11 50	1 05	10 21	1 32
5 M	22 30	27 25	4 04	27 50	14 60	3 01	22 45	2 32	19 26	1 26	11 33	11 05	11 55	1 05	10 20	1 32
6 Tu	22 36	27 46	4 44	27 13	15 27	2 54	22 30	2 30	19 16	1 26	11 24	10 60	11 59	1 06	10 20	1 32
7 W	22 42	26 11	5 05	24 43	15 55	2 47	22 15	2 27	19 06	1 25	11 14	10 54	12 03	1 06	10 20	1 33
8 Th	22 48	22 51	5 07	20 37	16 23	2 39	21 60	2 25	18 56	1 24	11 05	10 49	12 07	1 06	10 20	1 33
9 F	22 53	18 06	4 49	15 21	16 52	2 30	21 44	2 22	18 46	1 24	10 56	10 44	12 11	1 06	10 19	1 33
10 Sa	22 58	12 24	4 13	9 20	17 21	2 21	21 28	2 19	18 35	1 23	10 47	10 39	12 15	1 06	10 19	1 33
11 Su	23 03	6 09	3 22	2 57	17 51	2 12	21 12	2 16	18 25	1 22	10 37	10 34	12 19	1 06	10 19	1 33
12 M	23 07	0N17	2 20	3N28	18 21	2 02	20 55	2 12	18 14	1 22	10 28	10 29	12 23	1 06	10 19	1 34
13 Tu	23 11	6 36	1 12	9 37	18 50	1 52	20 38	2 09	18 04	1 21	10 18	10 24	12 27	1 06	10 19	1 34
14 W	23 14	12 31	0 00	15 15	19 20	1 42	20 21	2 05	17 53	1 21	10 09	10 19	12 31	1 06	10 19	1 34
15 Th	23 17	17 47	1N10	20 05	19 49	1 31	20 04	2 01	17 42	1 21	9 59	10 14	12 34	1 06	10 19	1 34
16 F	23 20	22 08	2 15	23 55	20 17	1 20	19 46	1 57	17 31	1 20	9 49	10 10	12 38	1 06	10 20	1 35
17 Sa	23 22	25 22	3 12	26 30	20 45	1 09	19 28	1 52	17 20	1 20	9 40	10 05	12 42	1 07	10 20	1 35
18 Su	23 24	27 18	3 59	27 44	21 12	0 58	19 09	1 48	17 09	1 19	9 30	9 60	12 46	1 07	10 20	1 35
19 M	23 25	27 50	4 34	27 35	21 38	0 47	18 51	1 43	16 58	1 18	9 20	9 55	12 49	1 07	10 20	1 35
20 Tu	23 26	26 59	4 56	26 05	22 03	0 35	18 32	1 38	16 46	1 18	9 10	9 51	12 53	1 07	10 20	1 35
21 W	23 26	24 53	5 04	23 25	22 27	0 24	18 14	1 32	16 35	1 17	8 60	9 46	12 57	1 07	10 21	1 36
22 Th	23 26	21 43	4 59	19 47	22 48	0 12	17 55	1 27	16 23	1 17	8 50	9 41	13 00	1 07	10 21	1 36
23 F	23 26	17 40	4 41	15 23	23 08	0 01	17 35	1 21	16 11	1 16	8 40	9 37	13 04	1 07	10 21	1 36
24 Sa	23 25	12 58	4 11	10 25	23 26	0N10	17 16	1 15	15 59	1 16	8 30	9 32	13 07	1 07	10 22	1 36
25 Su	23 24	7 46	3 30	5 02	23 42	0 20	16 57	1 09	15 48	1 15	8 19	9 28	13 11	1 07	10 22	1 37
26 M	23 22	2 13	2 39	0S37	23 56	0 31	16 37	1 03	15 35	1 15	8 09	9 23	13 14	1 08	10 23	1 37
27 Tu	23 20	3S30	1 40	6 22	24 07	0 40	16 18	0 56	15 23	1 14	7 59	9 19	13 17	1 08	10 23	1 37
28 W	23 18	9 13	0 35	12 01	24 15	0 50	15 58	0 49	15 11	1 14	7 48	9 15	13 21	1 08	10 24	1 37
29 Th	23 15	14 45	0S33	17 20	24 21	0 59	15 39	0 42	14 59	1 13	7 38	9 10	13 24	1 08	10 25	1 37
30 F	23N12	19S46	1S42	21S59	24N24	1N07	15N19	0N35	14N46	1N13	7N28	9N06	13N27	1S08	10S25	1S38

Day	⚷ Decl	⚷ Lat	♅ Decl	♅ Lat	♆ Decl	♆ Lat	♇ Decl	♇ Lat
1	8N48	1N32	17N30	0S19	2S07	1S12	22S38	2S35
6	8 52	1 32	17 34	0 19	2 06	1 13	22 40	2 36
11	8 57	1 32	17 38	0 19	2 05	1 13	22 42	2 36
16	9 00	1 32	17 42	0 19	2 04	1 13	22 43	2 37
21	9 04	1 33	17 46	0 19	2 03	1 13	22 45	2 38
26	9 07	1 33	17 50	0 19	2 03	1 14	22 47	2 38

Day	⚴ Decl	⚴ Lat	⚵ Decl	⚵ Lat	⚶ Decl	⚶ Lat	Eris Decl	Eris Lat
1	7N42	9S46	14N12	8S41	13N30	4S35	0S33	10S59
6	8 03	8 46	14 27	8 40	14 04	4 33	0 32	10 59
11	8 20	7 49	14 38	8 39	14 37	4 32	0 32	10 60
16	8 33	6 54	14 46	8 37	15 07	4 31	0 31	11 00
21	8 41	6 02	14 51	8 35	15 36	4 30	0 31	11 00
26	8 46	5 11	14 53	8 33	16 02	4 29	0 31	11 01

Moon Phenomena

Max/0 Decl
dy hr mn
5 16:23 27S52
11 22:58 0 N
18 21:06 27N50
26 9:23 0 S

Perigee/Apogee
dy hr m kilometers
6 23:07 p 364862
22 18:32 a 405384

Max/0 Lat
dy hr mn
1 6:24 0 S
7 13:55 5S09
14 0:06 0 N
21 2:39 5N04
28 12:25 0 S

PH dy hr mn
○ 4 3:43 13♐18
☾ 10 19:33 19♓40
● 18 4:38 26♊43
☽ 26 7:51 4♎29

Void of Course Moon

Last Aspect			☽ Ingress		
3	0:52	♀ △	♐	3	5:05
5	3:25	♆ □	♑	5	7:32
7	4:41	♅ ⚹	♒	7	8:43
9	4:25	♀ □	♓	9	10:15
11	13:21	♇ ⚹	♈	11	13:22
13	18:28	♇ □	♉	13	18:32
16	1:38	♇ △	♊	16	1:47
18	6:25	♆ □	♋	18	10:59
20	21:44	♇ ☍	♌	20	22:05
22	17:02	♅ □	♍	23	10:36
25	22:25	♇ △	♎	25	22:58
28	8:20	♇ □	♏	28	8:57
30	14:21	♇ ⚹	♐	30	15:01

DAILY ASPECTARIAN

1 Th
☽□♇ 0:04
☽#♃ 1:44
☽#⚳ 3:45
☽☍♃ 6:05
☊ R 6:24
♀⚹⚳ 7:57
☽#☿ 9:41
☽□♂ 12:12
☽△♄ 12:31
♂⚻♄ 19:32
☽∠⚳ 19:41
☉⚻☽ 19:51
☽⚼♆ 22:20

2 F
☽#♅ 3:47
☽☍☿ 6:54
☽⚻⚷ 9:43
☽☍♅ 12:11
☽#♂ 15:00
☽⚹⚳ 22:26
♀△♆ 22:44

3 Sa
☽△♆ 0:43
☽△♀ 0:52
☉#☽ 4:21
☽⚹♇ 5:18
☽∥♇ 6:33
⚳∥♃ 7:39
☽#♀ 9:24
☽⚼⚷ 11:48
☽⚻♃ 11:49
☿⚺⚷ 15:47
☽□♄ 17:08
☽△♂ 19:01

4 Su
☉☍☽ 3:43
☽⚼♀ 4:20
☽∠♇ 6:46
☽△⚷ 13:13
☽⚼♃ 13:32
☽⚻☿ 15:13
☽⚻♅ 15:37
☿☌♅ 19:50
☽⚼♂ 21:15

5 M
☽□⚳ 1:47
☽□♆ 3:25
☽⚻♀ 7:06
☽⚺♇ 7:42
♀#♇ 8:10
♀ ♌ 13:48
☽△♃ 14:45
♀☍♇ 16:06
☽⚼♅ 16:31
☉∥♀ 17:04
☽⚼☿ 18:29
☽⚹♄ 19:13
☽⚻♂ 23:01

6 Tu
☉⚼♇ 0:29
☉⚻☽ 8:52
☽□⚷ 14:48
☉#♇ 15:15
☽△♅ 17:12
☽∠♄ 19:49
☽△☿ 21:35

7 W
☽△⚳ 3:38
☽⚹♆ 4:41
☽☌♇ 8:49
☉⚼☽ 11:07
☽☍♀ 11:40
☽□♃ 16:36
☽⚺♄ 20:24

8 Th
☉#☽ 0:15
☽∥♇ 0:59
☽☍♂ 2:12
☽⚼⚳ 4:33
☽#♀ 5:05
☽∠♆ 5:18
☉△☽ 13:30
☽⚹⚷ 16:09
☽□♅ 18:39
☽#♂ 20:53

9 F
☽#♅ 2:13
☽□☿ 4:25
☽#☿ 5:03
☽⚻⚳ 5:44
☽⚺♆ 6:11
☽⚺♇ 10:19
☽⚻♀ 16:42
☽∠⚷ 17:13
☿△⚳ 18:34
☽⚹♃ 19:03
☿⚹♆ 21:16
☽☌♄ 22:17

10 Sa
☽#♃ 0:37
☽⚻♂ 6:21
☽#⚳ 6:34
☉⚹⚷ 7:08
☽∥♄ 8:10
☽∠♇ 11:35
☿∥♅ 13:24
☽#⚷ 13:30
⚳☍♆ 16:16
☽⚺⚷ 18:43
☉□☽ 19:33
☊ D 19:43
☽⚼♀ 19:54
☽∠♃ 20:54
☽⚹♅ 21:22

11 Su
♂⚼♆ 8:53
☽☌♆ 9:10
☽⚼♂ 9:11
☽☍⚳ 9:25
♇R♑ 9:48
☿△♇ 10:27
☿ ♊ 10:28
☽⚹♇ 13:21
☽⚹☿ 13:45
☽∥♆ 15:14
♀□♃ 15:41
♂∠⚳ 17:14
☿∥♂ 20:19
☉∠♃ 20:29
☽⚺♃ 23:17
☽∠♅ 23:27
☉⚺♅ 23:38
☽△♀ 23:42

12 M
☽⚺♄ 1:54
☽#♆ 6:44
☽△♂ 12:37
☽∠☿ 19:42
⚳#♄ 21:47
☽☌⚷ 23:16

13 Tu
☽⚺♅ 2:05
☉⚹☽ 4:01
☽∠♄ 4:30
☽∥⚷ 9:24
♀⚻♄ 10:00
☽⚺♆ 14:13
☽∥⚳ 14:25
☽#♄ 14:52
☽⚻⚳ 15:16
☽□♇ 18:28
☉∠♀ 21:10
☽∥♃ 24:00

14 W
☊ R 0:06
☿∠⚷ 0:32
☽⚺☿ 2:37
☽☌♃ 5:41
☽⚹♄ 7:37
☽□♀ 9:09
☉∠☽ 9:14
☽∠♆ 17:32
☽⚼⚳ 19:03
☽□♂ 21:17
☽∥♅ 23:35
☽∥♂ 23:38

15 Th
♂∥♅ 1:11
☿⚺♃ 4:26
☽⚺⚷ 5:56
☿∥♀ 7:43
☽☌♅ 8:56
☽∥♀ 11:06
☽∥☿ 11:47
☉⚺☽ 15:05
☿□♄ 16:11
☽⚹♆ 21:20
☽△⚳ 23:21

16 F
☽△♇ 1:38
☽#♇ 3:45
☉∥☽ 7:56
☽∠⚷ 10:00
☽⚺♃ 14:13
☽□♄ 15:21
☽☌☿ 19:13
☽⚹♀ 20:59

17 Sa
☽⚼♇ 5:56
☽⚹♂ 8:15
☽⚹⚷ 14:34
☿⚹♀ 15:30
♄ R 17:29
☽⚺♅ 17:47
☽∠♃ 19:15

18 Su
☽∠♀ 3:44
☉☌☽ 4:38
☽□♆ 6:25
☽□⚳ 9:33
☽⚻♇ 10:44
☽∠♂ 14:35
☽∠♅ 22:56

19 M
☽⚹♃ 0:47
☽△♄ 1:01
☉□♆ 3:55
☽⚺♀ 11:03
☽⚺☿ 15:42
♃⚹♄ 15:54
☿⚼♇ 17:39
♀⚼♆ 20:37
☽⚺♂ 21:29

20 Tu
☽□⚷ 1:10
☽⚹♅ 4:34
☽⚼♄ 6:34
⚳∥⚷ 15:45
☽△♆ 17:25
⚳△♇ 18:42
☉⚺☽ 20:38
☽☍♇ 21:44
☽⚹⚳ 21:49

21 W
☽∠☿ 3:23
☉⚻♇ 10:21
⚳ ♎ 11:31
☉∥☽ 11:53
☽⚻♄ 12:31
☽□♃ 13:16
☉ ♋ 14:59
☿⚹♂ 15:24
☉□⚳ 16:11
☽#♇ 16:51
☽∥☿ 17:13
☿#♇ 20:46
☽⚼♆ 23:32

22 Th
☿⚹⚷ 1:43
☽☌♀ 3:09
☽∠⚳ 4:36
☉∠☽ 5:24
♀∥♅ 9:10
⚵ ♋ 11:41
☽☌♂ 12:43
☽△⚷ 13:27
☽⚹☿ 15:52
☽□♅ 17:02
⚶ ♊ 19:18
☿⚺♅ 22:38
☽∥♅ 23:20

23 F
☽∥♀ 0:29
♂△⚷ 3:54
☽⚻♆ 5:53
☽∥♂ 8:15
☽⚻♇ 10:09
♀∠⚳ 11:25
☽⚺⚳ 11:37
☉⚹☽ 14:26
☿∠♃ 17:29
☽⚼⚷ 19:54
☉∥☿ 22:13
☽∥♃ 23:15

24 Sa
☽☍♄ 1:09
☽△♃ 2:54
☽#♄ 12:13
☽⚼♇ 16:26
☽∥⚷ 18:01
☽⚺♀ 20:00
☽∥⚳ 21:25

25 Su
☽⚻⚷ 2:14
☽⚺♂ 4:34
☽△♅ 5:54
☽⚼♃ 9:35
☽□☿ 17:26
☽☍♆ 18:22
☽△♇ 22:25
☿□♆ 22:37

26 M
☽#♆ 0:45
☽☌⚳ 1:17
☽∠♀ 3:54
☊ D 7:43
☉□☽ 7:51
♂□♅ 9:24
☽⚼♅ 11:49
☽∠♂ 11:56
☽⚻♄ 13:05
☽⚻♃ 15:45
☽∥♆ 17:58
☿⚻♇ 21:08

27 Tu
☿ ♋ 0:25
☽⚹♀ 10:58
☽☍⚷ 13:23
☽⚻♅ 16:59
☽⚼♄ 18:05
☽#⚳ 18:12
☿□⚳ 18:18
☽⚹♂ 18:27
☽#⚷ 23:36

28 W
☽⚻♆ 4:36
☽∥♄ 5:01
☽□♇ 8:20
☽⚺⚳ 12:20
☊ R 12:25
☉∠♅ 12:53
☽△☿ 15:33
☽#♃ 17:58
☉△☽ 21:50
☽△♄ 22:08

29 Th
☽#♂ 1:02
☽☍♃ 1:30
☉△♄ 1:44
☿∠♀ 2:27
☽#♀ 3:52
☽⚼♆ 8:19
♀△⚷ 8:42
☽#♅ 14:34
☽∠⚳ 16:20
☽⚻⚷ 20:57
☽□♀ 21:34

30 F
☽⚼☿ 0:08
☽☍♅ 0:24
☿∠♅ 1:48
☉⚼☽ 2:57
☽□♂ 4:07
☿△♄ 6:25
☽△♆ 10:59
☽⚹♇ 14:21
☽∥♇ 16:59
☉#☽ 19:03
☽⚹⚳ 19:15
♆ R 21:08
☽⚼⚷ 23:11

LONGITUDE

Day	Sid.Time	☉	☽	☽ 12 hour	Mean ☊	True ☊	☿	♀	♂	⚳	♃	♄	⚷	♅	♆	♇
	h m s	° E "	° E "	° E "	° E	° E	° E	° E	° E	° E	° E	° E	° E	° E	° E	° E
1 Sa	18 35 10	8♋56 34	5♐12 57	12♐16 44	0♉37.1	1♉46.0	8♋40.9	20♌46.6	24♌15.8	2♎30.2	9♉16.9	7♓04.0	19♈44.6	21♉42.2	27♓41.2	29♑36.9
2 Su	18 39 06	9 53 45	19 27 06	26 43 30	0 33.9	1R 39.8	10 51.5	21 24.1	24 51.9	2 47.0	9 27.3	7R 02.6	19 45.7	21 44.8	27R 41.2	29R 35.6
3 M	18 43 03	10 50 56	4♑05 12	11♑31 16	0 30.7	1 31.4	13 01.6	22 00.4	25 28.1	3 04.0	9 37.6	7 01.2	19 46.8	21 47.3	27 41.1	29 34.3
4 Tu	18 47 00	11 48 07	19 00 36	26 32 02	0 27.6	1 21.7	15 10.9	22 35.5	26 04.3	3 21.2	9 47.7	6 59.7	19 47.8	21 49.8	27 41.1	29 33.0
5 W	18 50 56	12 45 18	4♒04 18	11♒36 08	0 24.4	1 11.7	17 19.2	23 09.3	26 40.5	3 38.6	9 57.8	6 58.1	19 48.8	21 52.3	27 40.9	29 31.6
6 Th	18 54 53	13 42 29	19 06 20	26 33 50	0 21.2	1 02.7	19 26.3	23 41.7	27 16.8	3 56.1	10 07.7	6 56.3	19 49.8	21 54.8	27 40.8	29 30.3
7 F	18 58 49	14 39 40	3♓57 41	11♓17 05	0 18.0	0 55.6	21 32.1	24 12.8	27 53.1	4 13.9	10 17.5	6 54.5	19 50.6	21 57.2	27 40.6	29 28.9
8 Sa	19 02 46	15 36 52	18 31 29	25 40 29	0 14.9	0 50.9	23 36.3	24 42.4	28 29.4	4 31.7	10 27.2	6 52.7	19 51.5	21 59.6	27 40.4	29 27.5
9 Su	19 06 42	16 34 03	2♈43 51	9♈41 33	0 11.7	0 48.6	25 39.0	25 10.5	29 05.8	4 49.8	10 36.8	6 50.7	19 52.3	22 01.9	27 40.2	29 26.2
10 M	19 10 39	17 31 16	16 33 39	23 20 20	0 08.5	0D 48.0	27 40.0	25 37.1	29 42.2	5 08.0	10 46.2	6 48.6	19 53.0	22 04.2	27 39.9	29 24.8
11 Tu	19 14 35	18 28 28	0♉01 52	6♉38 33	0 05.3	0R 48.1	29 39.3	26 02.1	0♍18.7	5 26.4	10 55.6	6 46.4	19 53.7	22 06.5	27 39.6	29 23.4
12 W	19 18 32	19 25 41	13 10 45	19 38 49	0 02.1	0 47.7	1♌36.8	26 25.4	0 55.2	5 44.9	11 04.8	6 44.2	19 54.3	22 08.7	27 39.2	29 22.0
13 Th	19 22 29	20 22 55	26 03 07	2♊23 59	29♈59.0	0 45.6	3 32.4	26 47.0	1 31.8	6 03.6	11 13.9	6 41.9	19 54.9	22 10.9	27 38.8	29 20.6
14 F	19 26 25	21 20 09	8♊41 44	14 56 40	29 55.8	0 41.1	5 26.3	27 06.9	2 08.4	6 22.5	11 22.9	6 39.4	19 55.4	22 13.1	27 38.4	29 19.2
15 Sa	19 30 22	22 17 24	21 09 02	27 19 03	29 52.6	0 33.7	7 18.2	27 24.9	2 45.0	6 41.5	11 31.7	6 36.9	19 55.9	22 15.2	27 38.0	29 17.8
16 Su	19 34 18	23 14 39	3♋26 54	9♋32 46	29 49.4	0 23.5	9 08.3	27 41.0	3 21.7	7 00.6	11 40.5	6 34.3	19 56.3	22 17.3	27 37.5	29 16.3
17 M	19 38 15	24 11 54	15 36 46	21 39 05	29 46.3	0 11.2	10 56.5	27 55.2	3 58.4	7 19.9	11 49.0	6 31.7	19 56.7	22 19.4	27 37.0	29 14.9
18 Tu	19 42 11	25 09 10	27 39 48	3♌40 26	29 43.1	29♈57.6	12 42.8	28 07.4	4 35.2	7 39.4	11 57.5	6 28.9	19 57.0	22 21.4	27 36.5	29 13.5
19 W	19 46 08	26 06 26	9♌37 06	15 33 59	29 39.9	29 43.8	14 27.3	28 17.5	5 12.0	7 59.0	12 05.8	6 26.1	19 57.3	22 23.3	27 36.0	29 12.1
20 Th	19 50 04	27 03 42	21 29 58	27 25 17	29 36.7	29 31.1	16 09.8	28 25.5	5 48.9	8 18.7	12 14.0	6 23.2	19 57.5	22 25.2	27 35.4	29 10.7
21 F	19 54 01	28 00 59	3♍20 12	9♍15 03	29 33.6	29 20.3	17 50.6	28 31.3	6 25.7	8 38.6	12 22.0	6 20.2	19 57.6	22 27.1	27 34.8	29 09.2
22 Sa	19 57 58	28 58 16	15 10 13	21 06 06	29 30.4	29 12.1	19 29.4	28 34.9	7 02.7	8 58.6	12 29.9	6 17.2	19 57.7	22 29.0	27 34.1	29 07.8
23 Su	20 01 54	29 55 34	27 03 10	3♎01 57	29 27.2	29 06.7	21 06.4	28R 36.2	7 39.6	9 18.7	12 37.7	6 14.0	19R 57.8	22 30.8	27 33.4	29 06.4
24 M	20 05 51	0♌52 51	9♎03 00	15 06 53	29 24.0	29 03.9	22 41.5	28 35.2	8 16.6	9 38.9	12 45.3	6 10.8	19 57.8	22 32.5	27 32.7	29 04.9
25 Tu	20 09 47	1 50 09	21 14 15	27 25 42	29 20.8	29 02.9	24 14.7	28 31.8	8 53.7	9 59.3	12 52.8	6 07.5	19 57.7	22 34.2	27 32.0	29 03.5
26 W	20 13 44	2 47 28	3♏41 53	10♏03 26	29 17.7	29 02.8	25 46.1	28 26.1	9 30.8	10 19.8	13 00.1	6 04.2	19 57.6	22 35.9	27 31.2	29 02.1
27 Th	20 17 40	3 44 47	16 30 56	23 04 56	29 14.5	29 02.5	27 15.5	28 17.9	10 07.9	10 40.5	13 07.3	6 00.8	19 57.5	22 37.5	27 30.4	29 00.7
28 F	20 21 37	4 42 06	29 45 53	6♐34 07	29 11.3	29 00.8	28 43.1	28 07.4	10 45.0	11 01.2	13 14.3	5 57.3	19 57.3	22 39.1	27 29.6	28 59.2
29 Sa	20 25 33	5 39 26	13♐29 52	20 33 08	29 08.1	28 56.9	0♍08.7	27 54.4	11 22.2	11 22.1	13 21.2	5 53.8	19 57.0	22 40.6	27 28.8	28 57.8
30 Su	20 29 30	6 36 46	27 43 46	5♑01 23	29 05.0	28 50.6	1 32.4	27 39.1	11 59.5	11 43.0	13 27.9	5 50.2	19 56.7	22 42.1	27 27.9	28 56.4
31 M	20 33 27	7♌34 07	12♑25 20	19 54 46	29♈01.8	28♈41.9	2♍54.0	27♌21.4	12♍36.7	12♎04.1	13♉34.5	5♓46.5	19♈56.4	22♉43.5	27♓27.0	28♑55.0

1st of Month

Julian Day # 2460126.5
Obliquity 23°26'18"
SVP 4♓56'02"
GC 27♐10.0
Eris 25♈13.2

Day	⚴	⚵	⚶
1	25♌47.0	4♋51.8	3♊24.6
6	28 03.0	7 41.8	5 27.5
11	0♍19.4	10 30.6	7 28.8
16	2 36.2	13 18.3	9 28.5
21	4 53.3	16 04.7	11 26.2
26	7 10.7	18 49.7	13 22.0
31	9 28.2	21 33.2	15 15.5

DECLINATION and LATITUDE

Day	☉ Decl	☽ Decl	☽ Lat	☽ 12h Decl	☿ Decl	☿ Lat	♀ Decl	♀ Lat	♂ Decl	♂ Lat	⚳ Decl	⚳ Lat	♃ Decl	♃ Lat	♄ Decl	♄ Lat
1 Sa	23N08	23S55	2S47	25S31	24N24	1N15	14N60	0N27	14N34	1N12	7N17	9N02	13N31	1S08	10S26	1S38
2 Su	23 04	26 45	3 44	27 32	24 21	1 22	14 40	0 19	14 21	1 11	7 07	8 58	13 34	1 08	10 27	1 38
3 M	22 60	27 51	4 28	27 39	24 15	1 28	14 30	0 11	14 09	1 11	6 56	8 53	13 37	1 08	10 27	1 38
4 Tu	22 55	26 57	4 55	25 46	24 07	1 33	14 01	0 02	13 56	1 10	6 46	8 49	13 40	1 09	10 28	1 39
5 W	22 50	24 07	5 01	22 03	23 56	1 38	13 42	0S06	13 43	1 10	6 35	8 45	13 43	1 09	10 29	1 39
6 Th	22 44	19 38	4 47	16 56	23 43	1 42	13 23	0 15	13 30	1 09	6 24	8 41	13 46	1 09	10 30	1 39
7 F	22 38	13 59	4 13	10 53	23 27	1 45	13 04	0 24	13 17	1 09	6 14	8 37	13 49	1 09	10 31	1 39
8 Sa	22 31	7 40	3 24	4 23	23 09	1 48	12 45	0 34	13 04	1 08	6 03	8 33	13 52	1 09	10 31	1 39
9 Su	22 25	1 06	2 23	2N10	22 48	1 50	12 27	0 44	12 51	1 08	5 52	8 29	13 55	1 09	10 32	1 40
10 M	22 17	5N22	1 15	8 27	22 26	1 51	12 08	0 54	12 37	1 07	5 41	8 25	13 57	1 09	10 33	1 40
11 Tu	22 10	11 25	0 04	14 13	22 02	1 51	11 50	1 04	12 24	1 07	5 31	8 21	14 00	1 10	10 34	1 40
12 W	22 02	16 50	1N05	19 13	21 36	1 51	11 32	1 15	12 11	1 06	5 20	8 17	14 03	1 10	10 35	1 40
13 Th	21 54	21 22	2 09	23 14	21 08	1 50	11 15	1 26	11 57	1 06	5 09	8 14	14 05	1 10	10 36	1 40
14 F	21 45	24 49	3 06	26 04	20 39	1 48	10 57	1 37	11 43	1 05	4 58	8 10	14 08	1 10	10 37	1 41
15 Sa	21 36	27 01	3 52	27 36	20 09	1 46	10 40	1 48	11 30	1 04	4 47	8 06	14 11	1 10	10 39	1 41
16 Su	21 26	27 51	4 28	27 45	19 37	1 43	10 24	1 60	11 16	1 04	4 36	8 02	14 13	1 10	10 40	1 41
17 M	21 16	27 20	4 50	26 34	19 05	1 39	10 08	2 12	11 02	1 03	4 25	7 59	14 16	1 11	10 41	1 41
18 Tu	21 06	25 31	4 59	24 10	18 31	1 35	9 52	2 24	10 48	1 03	4 14	7 55	14 18	1 11	10 42	1 41
19 W	20 56	22 35	4 55	20 45	17 57	1 31	9 37	2 37	10 34	1 02	4 03	7 51	14 20	1 11	10 43	1 42
20 Th	20 45	18 43	4 38	16 31	17 21	1 26	9 22	2 49	10 20	1 02	3 52	7 48	14 23	1 11	10 45	1 42
21 F	20 33	14 09	4 09	11 38	16 46	1 20	9 08	3 02	10 06	1 01	3 41	7 44	14 25	1 11	10 46	1 42
22 Sa	20 22	9 04	3 29	6 23	16 09	1 15	8 55	3 15	9 52	1 01	3 30	7 41	14 27	1 11	10 47	1 42
23 Su	20 10	3 37	2 40	0 50	15 32	1 08	8 42	3 28	9 38	1 00	3 19	7 37	14 30	1 11	10 49	1 42
24 M	19 58	1S60	1 44	4S50	14 55	1 01	8 30	3 42	9 23	0 60	3 08	7 34	14 32	1 12	10 50	1 42
25 Tu	19 45	7 39	0 41	10 25	14 17	0 54	8 18	3 55	9 09	0 59	2 57	7 30	14 34	1 12	10 51	1 43
26 W	19 32	13 08	0S25	15 45	13 40	0 47	8 07	4 09	8 54	0 59	2 46	7 27	14 36	1 12	10 53	1 43
27 Th	19 19	18 14	1 31	20 32	13 02	0 39	7 57	4 23	8 40	0 58	2 35	7 23	14 38	1 12	10 54	1 43
28 F	19 05	22 37	2 35	24 26	12 24	0 30	7 48	4 36	8 25	0 57	2 24	7 20	14 40	1 12	10 56	1 43
29 Sa	18 51	25 55	3 32	27 02	11 46	0 22	7 40	4 50	8 11	0 57	2 12	7 17	14 42	1 13	10 57	1 43
30 Su	18 37	27 43	4 18	27 56	11 08	0 13	7 32	5 03	7 56	0 56	2 01	7 14	14 43	1 13	10 58	1 44
31 M	18N23	27S39	4S49	26S52	10N30	0N04	7N25	5S17	7N41	0N56	1N50	7N10	14N45	1S13	10S60	1S44

Day	⚷ Decl	⚷ Lat	♅ Decl	♅ Lat	♆ Decl	♆ Lat	♇ Decl	♇ Lat
1	9N09	1N33	17N53	0S19	2S03	1S14	22S49	2S39
6	9 11	1 33	17 57	0 19	2 03	1 14	22 51	2 39
11	9 13	1 33	17 60	0 19	2 04	1 14	22 53	2 40
16	9 14	1 33	18 02	0 19	2 05	1 15	22 55	2 41
21	9 14	1 33	18 05	0 19	2 06	1 15	22 57	2 41
26	9 14	1 33	18 07	0 19	2 08	1 15	22 59	2 41
31	9N14	1N33	18N09	0S19	2S10	1S15	23S01	2S42

Day	⚴ Decl	⚴ Lat	⚵ Decl	⚵ Lat	⚶ Decl	⚶ Lat	Eris Decl	Eris Lat
1	8N48	4S23	14N51	8S31	16N27	4S28	0S31	11S01
6	8 46	3 36	14 46	8 28	16 50	4 27	0 31	11 02
11	8 41	2 51	14 37	8 25	17 11	4 26	0 31	11 02
16	8 34	2 08	14 26	8 23	17 29	4 26	0 31	11 02
21	8 24	1 25	14 12	8 20	17 46	4 25	0 32	11 03
26	8 11	0 45	13 55	8 17	18 02	4 25	0 32	11 03
31	7N57	0S05	13N35	8S13	18N15	4S24	0S33	11S04

Moon Phenomena

Max/0 Decl (dy hr mn)
3 1:28 27S51
9 4:01 0 N
16 2:39 27N52
23 15:31 0 S
30 11:15 27S56

Max/0 Lat (dy hr mn)
4 19:28 5S02
11 1:24 0 N
18 4:31 4N59
25 15:07 0 S

Perigee/Apogee (dy hr m kilometers)
4 22:26 p 360150
20 6:58 a 406289

PH dy hr mn
○ 3 11:40 11♑19
☾ 10 1:49 17♈36
● 17 18:33 24♋56
☽ 25 22:08 2♏43

Void of Course Moon

Last Aspect	☽ Ingress
2 13:34 ♆ □	♑ 2 17:21
4 16:47 ♇ ☌	♒ 4 17:31
6 13:43 ♂ ☍	♓ 6 17:34
8 18:23 ♇ ⚹	♈ 8 19:20
10 23:12 ♀ □	♉ 10 23:57
13 6:12 ♇ △	♊ 13 7:27
15 12:37 ♀ ⚹	♋ 15 17:15
18 3:07 ♇ ☍	♌ 18 4:41
20 14:10 ♀ ☌	♍ 20 17:14
23 4:07 ♇ △	♎ 23 5:55
25 15:06 ♇ □	♏ 25 16:56
27 22:37 ♇ ⚹	♐ 28 0:25
29 23:52 ♀ △	♑ 30 3:45

DAILY ASPECTARIAN

1 Sa: ☽□♄ 3:09; ☽⋕☿ 3:18; ☉☌☿ 5:07; ☉⚻☽ 6:49; ☽⚻☿ 6:59; ☽⚻♃ 7:01; ☿⚹♃ 7:11; ☿∠♂ 8:51; ☉⚹♃ 10:27; ☽∠♇ 15:54; ☉∠♂ 21:54

2 Su: ☽△⚷ 0:31; ☽△♀ 3:23; ☽⚻♅ 3:49; ☽⚼♃ 8:22; ☽△♂ 9:20; ☽□♆ 13:34; ♀□♅ 14:35; ☽⚺♇ 16:40; ☽□⚳ 22:19

3 M: ☽⚼♅ 4:23; ☽⚹♄ 4:44; ☽⚼♀ 4:55; ☽△♃ 9:03; ☽⚼♂ 10:44; ☉☍☽ 11:40; ☽☍☿ 16:51

4 Tu: ☽□⚷ 1:16; ☽△♅ 4:31; ☽∠♄ 4:45; ☽⚻♀ 5:57; ☽⚻♂ 11:44; ☽⚹♆ 13:50; ☽☌♇ 16:47; ☉⋕♇ 19:23; ♀∥♂ 20:27; ♀∥♃ 23:07; ☽△⚳ 23:18

5 W: ♂∥♃ 0:11; ☽⋕☿ 1:10; ☽⚺♄ 4:36; ☽∥♇ 7:36; ☉⋕☽ 7:54; ☽□♃ 9:29; ☽∠♆ 13:43; ☉⚻☽ 14:47; ☽⚼⚳ 23:43

6 Th: ☽⚻☿ 0:37; ☽⚹⚷ 1:10; ☿□⚷ 4:29; ☽□♅ 4:31; ☽⋕♅ 7:37; ☽☍♀ 7:39; ☽☍♂ 13:43; ☽⚺♆ 13:48; ♂⚻♆ 15:49; ☉⚼☽ 16:32; ☽⚺♇ 16:44

7 F: ☽⚻⚳ 0:27; ☽⋕♃ 0:41; ☽∠⚷ 1:26; ☽⋕♂ 2:53; ☽⋕♀ 3:49; ☿⚼♄ 4:16; ☽☌♄ 4:48; ☽⚼☿ 4:54; ☿⚹♅ 4:56; ☽⚹♃ 10:29; ☽∥♄ 13:23; ☽∠♇ 17:15; ☽⋕⚷ 18:20; ☉△☽ 18:49

8 Sa: ☽⚺⚷ 2:14; ☽⚹♅ 5:49; ☽⋕⚳ 6:07; ☽△☿ 9:57; ☽⚻♀ 10:44; ☽∠♃ 11:46; ☽☌♆ 15:23; ☿⚺♀ 16:46; ☽⚻♂ 17:31; ☽⚹♇ 18:23; ☿⋕♇ 19:39; ☽∥♆ 20:29

9 Su: ☽☍⚳ 3:41; ☽⚺♄ 7:03; ☽∠♅ 7:25; ☽⋕♆ 11:38; ♂⚻♇ 12:55; ☽⚼♀ 13:16; ☽⚺♃ 13:45; ☽⚼♂ 20:35; ☿△♆ 23:58

10 M: ☽∥⚳ 1:13; ☉□☽ 1:49; ☊ D 1:58; ☽☌⚷ 5:52; ⚴ ♍ 6:57; ☽∠♄ 9:15; ☽⚺♅ 9:46; ♂ ♍ 11:41; ☉∥☿ 12:39; ☽∥⚷ 15:00; ☽△♀ 16:35; ☽⚺♆ 19:44; ☽⋕♄ 20:30; ☿☍♇ 20:49; ☽□♇ 22:51; ☽□☿ 23:12

11 Tu: ☽△♂ 0:32; ☊ R 1:23; ☽∥♀ 1:39; ☽∥♂ 3:58; ☿ ♌ 4:12; ☽⚻⚳ 10:02; ☽∥♃ 11:08; ☿⚺♂ 11:37; ☽⚹♄ 12:12; ☽☌♃ 20:05; ☽∠♆ 23:02

12 W: ☽∥♅ 5:46; ☉□⚷ 12:07; ☽⚺⚷ 12:29; ☉⚹☽ 12:31; ☽⚼⚳ 14:24; ☽☌♅ 16:43; ☽∥☿ 22:50

13 Th: ☽□♀ 1:25; ☽⚹♆ 3:00; ☉∥☽ 3:08; ☽△♇ 6:12; ☽⋕♇ 9:45; ☽□♂ 10:52; ☽⚹☿ 16:41; ☽∠⚷ 16:48; ☉∠☽ 19:07; ☽△⚳ 19:27; ☽□♄ 20:07

14 F: ☽⚺♃ 5:13; ☉⚼♄ 7:45; ☽⚼♇ 10:47; ☿⚹⚳ 14:27; ☿⚻♄ 15:18; ⚳⚻♄ 18:57; ☽⚹⚷ 21:38; ☉⚹♅ 23:04

15 Sa: ☽⚺♅ 2:09; ☉⚺☽ 2:24; ♀⋕♄ 2:25; ☽∠☿ 2:38; ☽∠♃ 10:35; ☽⚹♀ 12:28; ☽□♆ 12:37; ☽⚻♇ 15:50; ♀⚻♆ 18:43; ☽⚹♂ 23:49

16 Su: ☽△♄ 6:07; ☽□⚳ 7:12; ☽∠♅ 7:34; ☽⚺☿ 13:09; ☽⚹♃ 16:24; ☽∠♀ 18:34; ⚳⚼♅ 23:12

17 M: ☽∠♂ 7:02; ☽□⚷ 8:36; ☽⚼♄ 11:43; ☿□♃ 12:50; ☽⚹♅ 13:22; ☉☌☽ 18:33; ☊R♈ 19:47; ☿⚼♆ 22:34; ☽△♆ 23:53

18 Tu: ☽⚺♀ 0:56; ☽☍♇ 3:07; ♂⋕♄ 9:38; ♂⚼⚷ 14:19; ☽⚺♂ 14:38; ☽⚻♄ 17:37; ☿∥♅ 19:06; ☽⚹⚳ 20:37; ☽⋕♇ 21:27

19 W: ☽□♃ 5:03; ☽⚼♆ 6:00; ☽☌☿ 11:24; ☉∥☽ 11:26; ☽△⚷ 20:53

20 Th: ☽□♅ 1:52; ☽∥♅ 3:37; ☽∠⚳ 3:47; ☽∥☿ 8:40; ☉⚺☽ 12:16; ☽⚻♆ 12:20; ☉△♆ 13:08; ♀∥⚷ 13:52; ☽☌♀ 14:10; ☽⚻♇ 15:32; ♂☍♄ 20:40; ☽∥♃ 22:41

21 F: ☽⚼⚷ 3:18; ☽☍♄ 6:04; ☽☌♂ 6:37; ☽⚺⚳ 11:05; ☉⚺♀ 13:40; ☽⋕♄ 16:07; ☽△♃ 18:32; ☽∥♂ 20:10; ☉∠☽ 21:21; ☽⚼♇ 21:54; ☽∥⚷ 23:12

22 Sa: ☽∥♀ 0:42; ☉☍♇ 3:54; ☿△⚷ 6:58; ☽⚻⚷ 9:42; ☽⚺☿ 10:08; ♃∠♆ 11:48; ☽△♅ 14:50

23 Su: ☽☍♆ 1:01; ☽⚼♃ 1:10; ☽∥⚳ 1:22; ♀ R 1:34; ☉ ♌ 1:52; ☽⚺♀ 3:07; ☽△♇ 4:07; ☉⚹☽ 6:17; ☽⋕♆ 6:29; ⚷ R 12:43; ☽⚻♄ 18:19; ☽∠☿ 20:54; ☽⚼♅ 21:00; ☿□♅ 21:40; ☽⚺♂ 22:23

24 M: ☽∥♆ 0:31; ☽☌⚳ 1:13; ☽⋕⚳ 4:39; ☽⚻♃ 7:25; ☽∠♀ 8:57; ☿∥♃ 14:09; ♂∥⚷ 14:48; ☽☍⚷ 21:31; ☽⚼♄ 23:47

25 Tu: ☽⚻♅ 2:36; ☽⋕♀ 2:44; ☽∠♂ 5:26; ☽⋕♂ 6:11; ☽⚹☿ 6:40; ☽⋕⚷ 6:51; ☽⚻♆ 12:11; ☽∥♄ 13:56; ☽⚹♀ 14:01; ☿∠⚳ 15:02; ☽□♇ 15:06; ☉□☽ 22:08

26 W: ☽⋕☿ 2:07; ☽△♄ 4:29; ☽⋕♃ 6:41; ☽⚹♂ 11:32; ☽⚺⚳ 12:51; ☽⚼♆ 16:35; ☽☍♃ 17:40; ☽⋕♅ 23:29

27 Th: ☿⚻♆ 4:01; ☉⋕☽ 5:16; ☽⚻⚷ 6:19; ☽☍♅ 11:12; ☿☌♀ 15:17; ☽∠⚳ 17:07; ☽△♆ 19:57; ☽□♀ 21:07; ☽□☿ 21:55; ☽⚹♇ 22:37

28 F: ☽∥♇ 2:21; ☿⚻♇ 4:25; ☽⚼⚷ 9:10; ☉△☽ 9:23; ☽□♄ 10:53; ☽□♂ 20:10; ☽⚹⚳ 20:14; ☿ ♍ 21:32; ♂⚺⚳ 23:45; ☽⚻♃ 23:45

29 Sa: ☽∠♇ 0:48; ☉⚻♄ 5:39; ⚳⋕♆ 6:49; ☽△⚷ 10:59; ☉⚼☽ 13:03; ☽⚻♅ 15:36; ☽□♆ 23:34; ☽△♀ 23:52

30 Su: ☽⚼♃ 1:14; ☽⚺♇ 2:00; ☿⋕♄ 5:37; ☽△☿ 6:57; ☽⚹♄ 13:16; ☉⚻☽ 15:36; ☽⚼♅ 16:23; ♀⚻♆ 16:26; ☽□⚳ 23:25; ☽⚼♀ 23:54

31 M: ☽△♂ 0:19; ☽△♃ 1:52; ☽⚼☿ 9:39; ♀∠⚳ 10:16; ☽□⚷ 12:02; ☽∠♄ 13:19; ☽△♅ 16:30; ☉∥♅ 21:44; ☽⚻♀ 23:18; ☽⚹♆ 23:56

August 2023

LONGITUDE

Day	Sid.Time	☉	☽	☽ 12 hour	Mean☊	True☊	☿	♀	♂	⚳	♃	♄	⚷	♅	♆	♇
	h m s	° ' "	° ' "	° ' "	° '	° '	° '	° '	° '	° '	° '	° '	° '	° '	° '	° '
1 Tu	20 37 23	8♌31 28	27♑28 37	5♒05 37	28♈58.6	28♈31.7	4♍13.7	27♌01.5	13♍14.1	12♎25.3	13♉40.9	5♓42.8	19♈56.0	22♉44.9	27♓26.1	28♑53.6
2 W	20 41 20	9 28 51	12♒44 25	20 23 34	28 55.4	28R 21.2	5 31.3	26R 39.3	13 51.4	12 46.6	13 47.2	5R 39.0	19R 55.5	22 46.3	27R 25.1	28R 52.2
3 Th	20 45 16	10 26 14	28 01 38	5♓37 15	28 52.3	28 11.5	6 46.7	26 15.0	14 28.8	13 08.0	13 53.3	5 35.2	19 55.0	22 47.6	27 24.1	28 50.8
4 F	20 49 13	11 23 38	13♓09 11	20 36 25	28 49.1	28 03.8	8 00.0	25 48.6	15 06.2	13 29.5	13 59.2	5 31.3	19 54.4	22 48.8	27 23.1	28 49.4
5 Sa	20 53 09	12 21 03	27 58 06	5♈13 37	28 45.9	27 58.6	9 11.0	25 20.3	15 43.7	13 51.2	14 05.0	5 27.3	19 53.8	22 50.1	27 22.1	28 48.0
6 Su	20 57 06	13 18 29	12♈22 34	19 24 47	28 42.7	27 55.9	10 19.8	24 50.3	16 21.2	14 12.9	14 10.6	5 23.3	19 53.1	22 51.2	27 21.0	28 46.7
7 M	21 01 02	14 15 56	26 20 13	3♉09 03	28 39.5	27D 55.2	11 26.1	24 18.6	16 58.7	14 34.7	14 16.1	5 19.3	19 52.4	22 52.3	27 19.9	28 45.3
8 Tu	21 04 59	15 13 25	9♉51 32	16 28 01	28 36.4	27R 55.3	12 29.9	23 45.5	17 36.3	14 56.6	14 21.4	5 15.2	19 51.6	22 53.4	27 18.8	28 43.9
9 W	21 08 56	16 10 55	22 58 57	29 24 46	28 33.2	27 55.2	13 31.1	23 11.2	18 14.0	15 18.6	14 26.5	5 11.1	19 50.8	22 54.4	27 17.7	28 42.6
10 Th	21 12 52	17 08 26	5♊45 58	12♊03 02	28 30.0	27 53.8	14 29.7	22 35.9	18 51.6	15 40.7	14 31.4	5 06.9	19 50.0	22 55.4	27 16.6	28 41.2
11 F	21 16 49	18 05 59	18 16 25	24 26 36	28 26.8	27 50.1	15 25.3	21 59.7	19 29.4	16 02.9	14 36.2	5 02.7	19 49.0	22 56.3	27 15.4	28 39.9
12 Sa	21 20 45	19 03 34	0♋33 58	6♋38 56	28 23.7	27 43.9	16 18.0	21 22.9	20 07.1	16 25.2	14 40.8	4 58.5	19 48.1	22 57.2	27 14.2	28 38.6
13 Su	21 24 42	20 01 09	12 41 50	18 42 59	28 20.5	27 35.1	17 07.6	20 45.7	20 44.9	16 47.6	14 45.2	4 54.2	19 47.1	22 58.0	27 13.0	28 37.3
14 M	21 28 38	20 58 46	24 42 39	0♌41 05	28 17.3	27 24.3	17 53.9	20 08.5	21 22.8	17 10.0	14 49.4	4 49.9	19 46.0	22 58.8	27 11.7	28 36.0
15 Tu	21 32 35	21 56 24	6♌38 31	12 35 08	28 14.1	27 12.2	18 36.7	19 31.3	22 00.7	17 32.6	14 53.5	4 45.5	19 44.9	22 59.5	27 10.5	28 34.7
16 W	21 36 31	22 54 04	18 31 08	24 26 42	28 11.0	27 00.1	19 15.9	18 54.5	22 38.6	17 55.2	14 57.4	4 41.1	19 43.7	23 00.2	27 09.2	28 33.4
17 Th	21 40 28	23 51 44	0♍22 02	6♍17 19	28 07.8	26 48.8	19 51.2	18 18.2	23 16.6	18 18.0	15 01.0	4 36.7	19 42.5	23 00.9	27 07.9	28 32.2
18 F	21 44 25	24 49 26	12 12 46	18 08 38	28 04.6	26 39.2	20 22.4	17 42.7	23 54.6	18 40.8	15 04.5	4 32.3	19 41.2	23 01.4	27 06.6	28 30.9
19 Sa	21 48 21	25 47 09	24 05 11	0♎02 44	28 01.4	26 32.1	20 49.3	17 08.2	24 32.6	19 03.7	15 07.9	4 27.8	19 39.9	23 02.0	27 05.2	28 29.7
20 Su	21 52 18	26 44 53	6♎01 37	12 02 13	27 58.2	26 27.5	21 11.7	16 35.0	25 10.7	19 26.6	15 11.0	4 23.3	19 38.6	23 02.4	27 03.8	28 28.4
21 M	21 56 14	27 42 39	18 04 59	24 10 21	27 55.1	26D 25.3	21 29.3	16 03.1	25 48.9	19 49.7	15 13.9	4 18.9	19 37.2	23 02.9	27 02.5	28 27.2
22 Tu	22 00 11	28 40 26	0♏18 50	6♏30 58	27 51.9	26 25.0	21 41.9	15 32.9	26 27.1	20 12.8	15 16.7	4 14.4	19 35.7	23 03.3	27 01.1	28 26.0
23 W	22 04 07	29 38 13	12 47 16	19 08 18	27 48.7	26 25.8	21R 49.2	15 04.3	27 05.3	20 36.0	15 19.3	4 09.8	19 34.2	23 03.6	26 59.7	28 24.9
24 Th	22 08 04	0♍36 02	25 34 37	2♐06 43	27 45.5	26R 26.5	21 51.0	14 37.7	27 43.6	20 59.3	15 21.6	4 05.3	19 32.7	23 03.9	26 58.2	28 23.7
25 F	22 12 00	1 33 53	8♐45 04	15 30 04	27 42.4	26 26.4	21 47.2	14 13.0	28 21.9	21 22.6	15 23.8	4 00.8	19 31.1	23 04.1	26 56.8	28 22.5
26 Sa	22 15 57	2 31 44	22 21 59	29 21 00	27 39.2	26 24.6	21 37.6	13 50.5	29 00.2	21 46.0	15 25.8	3 56.2	19 29.5	23 04.3	26 55.3	28 21.4
27 Su	22 19 54	3 29 37	6♑27 05	13♑40 03	27 36.0	26 20.8	21 22.0	13 30.1	29 38.6	22 09.5	15 27.6	3 51.7	19 27.9	23 04.4	26 53.8	28 20.3
28 M	22 23 50	4 27 31	20 59 30	28 24 48	27 32.8	26 15.1	21 00.5	13 12.0	0♎17.1	22 33.0	15 29.2	3 47.2	19 26.2	23 04.5	26 52.4	28 19.2
29 Tu	22 27 47	5 25 26	5♒55 08	13♒29 26	27 29.7	26 08.0	20 33.0	12 56.3	0 55.5	22 56.6	15 30.6	3 42.6	19 24.4	23R 04.5	26 50.8	28 18.1
30 W	22 31 43	6 23 23	21 06 31	28 45 03	27 26.5	26 00.5	19 59.6	12 42.9	1 34.0	23 20.3	15 31.8	3 38.1	19 22.6	23 04.5	26 49.3	28 17.1
31 Th	22 35 40	7♍21 21	6♓23 40	14♓00 58	27♈23.3	25♈53.6	19♍20.7	12♌31.9	2♎12.6	23♎44.0	15♉32.8	3♓33.5	19♈20.8	23♉04.4	26♓47.8	28♑16.0

1st of Month

Julian Day # 2460157.5
Obliquity 23°26'18"
SVP 4♓55'56"
GC 27♐10.1
Eris 25♈15.1R

Day	⚴	⚵	⚶
1	9♍55.7	22♋05.7	15♊37.9
6	12 13.3	24 47.4	17 28.5
11	14 31.1	27 27.5	19 16.6
16	16 49.0	0♌05.9	21 01.8
21	19 06.9	2 42.5	22 43.8
26	21 24.9	5 17.2	24 22.4
31	23 42.8	7 49.9	25 57.3

DECLINATION and LATITUDE

Day	☉ Decl	☽ Decl	☽ Lat	☽12h Decl	☿ Decl	☿ Lat	♀ Decl	♀ Lat	♂ Decl	♂ Lat	⚳ Decl	⚳ Lat	♃ Decl	♃ Lat	♄ Decl	♄ Lat
1 Tu	18N08	25S34	5S01	23S49	9N52	0S06	7N19	5S30	7N26	0N55	1N39	7N07	14N47	1S13	11S01	1S44
2 W	17 53	21 38	4 51	19 06	9 15	0 15	7 14	5 43	7 12	0 55	1 28	7 04	14 49	1 13	11 03	1 44
3 Th	17 37	16 15	4 21	13 09	8 38	0 25	7 10	5 56	6 57	0 54	1 17	7 01	14 50	1 13	11 05	1 44
4 F	17 22	9 54	3 33	6 32	8 01	0 35	7 07	6 09	6 42	0 54	1 05	6 58	14 52	1 14	11 06	1 44
5 Sa	17 06	3 07	2 31	0N17	7 25	0 46	7 05	6 21	6 27	0 53	0 54	6 54	14 53	1 14	11 08	1 44
6 Su	16 49	3N38	1 21	6 54	6 50	0 56	7 04	6 33	6 12	0 53	0 43	6 51	14 55	1 14	11 09	1 45
7 M	16 33	10 02	0 08	12 60	6 15	1 07	7 03	6 44	5 56	0 52	0 32	6 48	14 56	1 14	11 11	1 45
8 Tu	16 16	15 46	1N03	18 18	5 40	1 18	7 04	6 55	5 41	0 51	0 21	6 45	14 58	1 14	11 13	1 45
9 W	15 59	20 36	2 09	22 36	5 07	1 29	7 05	7 05	5 26	0 51	0 10	6 42	14 59	1 15	11 14	1 45
10 Th	15 42	24 19	3 06	25 44	4 34	1 40	7 08	7 14	5 11	0 50	0S02	6 39	15 00	1 15	11 16	1 45
11 F	15 24	26 48	3 54	27 32	4 02	1 51	7 11	7 23	4 56	0 50	0 13	6 36	15 02	1 15	11 18	1 45
12 Sa	15 07	27 56	4 29	27 58	3 32	2 02	7 15	7 31	4 40	0 49	0 24	6 33	15 03	1 15	11 19	1 45
13 Su	14 48	27 41	4 52	27 04	3 02	2 13	7 19	7 38	4 25	0 49	0 35	6 30	15 04	1 15	11 21	1 45
14 M	14 30	26 08	5 02	24 54	2 34	2 24	7 25	7 45	4 09	0 48	0 46	6 27	15 05	1 15	11 23	1 46
15 Tu	14 12	23 25	4 58	21 41	2 07	2 35	7 31	7 50	3 54	0 48	0 58	6 25	15 06	1 16	11 24	1 46
16 W	13 53	19 44	4 41	17 35	1 42	2 46	7 37	7 55	3 38	0 47	1 09	6 22	15 07	1 16	11 26	1 46
17 Th	13 34	15 17	4 13	12 50	1 18	2 57	7 44	7 59	3 23	0 47	1 20	6 19	15 08	1 16	11 28	1 46
18 F	13 15	10 15	3 33	7 35	0 56	3 08	7 52	8 02	3 07	0 46	1 31	6 16	15 09	1 16	11 29	1 46
19 Sa	12 55	4 51	2 44	2 04	0 36	3 18	8 00	8 04	2 52	0 45	1 42	6 13	15 09	1 16	11 31	1 46
20 Su	12 36	0S46	1 47	3S35	0 18	3 28	8 09	8 05	2 36	0 45	1 53	6 11	15 10	1 17	11 33	1 46
21 M	12 16	6 24	0 44	9 11	0 02	3 38	8 17	8 05	2 21	0 44	2 04	6 08	15 11	1 17	11 35	1 46
22 Tu	11 56	11 54	0S21	14 32	0S11	3 47	8 26	8 05	2 05	0 44	2 16	6 05	15 11	1 17	11 36	1 46
23 W	11 36	17 03	1 27	19 25	0 22	3 56	8 36	8 04	1 49	0 43	2 27	6 02	15 12	1 17	11 38	1 47
24 Th	11 16	21 35	2 30	23 31	0 30	4 04	8 45	8 02	1 33	0 43	2 38	5 60	15 12	1 17	11 40	1 47
25 F	10 55	25 10	3 27	26 30	0 35	4 11	8 54	7 59	1 18	0 42	2 49	5 57	15 13	1 18	11 42	1 47
26 Sa	10 34	27 27	4 15	27 60	0 37	4 18	9 04	7 56	1 02	0 42	2 60	5 54	15 13	1 18	11 43	1 47
27 Su	10 14	28 05	4 49	27 42	0 36	4 23	9 13	7 52	0 46	0 41	3 11	5 52	15 14	1 18	11 45	1 47
28 M	9 53	26 50	5 05	25 29	0 32	4 27	9 23	7 47	0 30	0 41	3 22	5 49	15 14	1 18	11 47	1 47
29 Tu	9 31	23 40	5 02	21 27	0 23	4 30	9 32	7 42	0 15	0 40	3 33	5 47	15 14	1 18	11 48	1 47
30 W	9 10	18 51	4 38	15 56	0 12	4 31	9 41	7 36	0S01	0 39	3 44	5 44	15 14	1 19	11 50	1 47
31 Th	8N49	12S47	3S54	9S27	0N04	4S31	9N50	7S30	0S17	0N39	3S55	5N42	15N14	1S19	11S52	1S47

Day	⚷ Decl	⚷ Lat	♅ Decl	♅ Lat	♆ Decl	♆ Lat	♇ Decl	♇ Lat
1	9N14	1N33	18N09	0S19	2S10	1S15	23S01	2S42
6	9 13	1 33	18 11	0 19	2 12	1 15	23 03	2 42
11	9 11	1 33	18 12	0 19	2 15	1 16	23 05	2 43
16	9 09	1 33	18 13	0 19	2 18	1 16	23 06	2 43
21	9 07	1 33	18 14	0 19	2 20	1 16	23 08	2 43
26	9 04	1 33	18 14	0 19	2 23	1 16	23 09	2 43
31	9N00	1N33	18N14	0S19	2S26	1S16	23S11	2S44

Day	⚴ Decl	⚴ Lat	⚵ Decl	⚵ Lat	⚶ Decl	⚶ Lat	Eris Decl	Eris Lat
1	7N54	0N03	13N31	8S13	18N17	4S24	0S33	11S04
6	7 37	0 41	13 08	8 09	18 28	4 24	0 33	11 04
11	7 19	1 19	12 43	8 06	18 38	4 23	0 34	11 04
16	6 59	1 56	12 16	8 02	18 46	4 23	0 35	11 05
21	6 38	2 32	11 47	7 59	18 52	4 23	0 35	11 05
26	6 16	3 07	11 16	7 55	18 57	4 23	0 36	11 05
31	5N53	3N42	10N43	7S51	19N00	4S22	0S37	11S06

Moon Phenomena

Max/0 Decl

dy	hr mn	
5	11:00	0 N
12	7:36	28N00
19	20:47	0 S
26	20:19	28S06

Perigee/Apogee

dy	hr m		kilometers
2	5:53	p	357314
16	11:55	a	406635
30	15:55	p	357185

PH	dy	hr mn	
○	1	18:33	9♒16
☾	8	10:30	15♉39
●	16	9:39	23♌17
☽	24	9:58	1♐00
○	31	1:37	7♓25

Max/0 Lat

dy	hr mn	
1	1:39	5S01
7	2:47	0 N
14	5:19	5N02
21	16:24	0 S
28	8:27	5S07

Void of Course Moon

Last Aspect			☽ Ingress		
1	2:14	♇ ☌	♒	1	3:59
2	21:17	♀ ☍	♓	3	3:07
5	1:22	♇ ✱	♈	5	3:20
7	4:14	♇ □	♉	7	6:26
9	10:40	♇ △	♊	9	13:06
11	17:28	♆ □	♋	11	22:53
14	7:48	♇ ☍	♌	14	10:37
16	9:39	☉ ☌	♍	16	23:15
19	8:52	♇ △	♎	19	11:55
21	20:32	☉ ✱	♏	21	23:23
24	5:11	♇ ✱	♐	24	8:09
26	11:57	♂ □	♑	26	13:06
28	11:50	♇ ☌	♒	28	14:33
30	3:05	♅ □	♓	30	13:58

DAILY ASPECTARIAN

1 Tu	☽⚼♂ 1:15; ☽☌♇ 2:14; ☽⚻☿ 11:38; ☽⚺♄ 12:55; ☿⚼⚷ 12:55; ☽∥♇ 16:37; ♀∥♂ 17:10; ☉☍☽ 18:33; ♂△♃ 20:46; ☽∠♆ 23:30
2 W	☽△⚳ 0:04; ♂⚼♇ 0:30; ☿∥⚷ 0:50; ☽□♃ 1:39; ☽⚻♂ 1:49; ☿☍♄ 2:19; ☽✱⚷ 11:16; ☽□♅ 15:45; ☽#♅ 16:02; ☉#☽ 18:04; ☽☍♀ 21:17; ☽⚺♆ 23:01
3 Th	☽⚼⚳ 0:10; ☽⚺♇ 1:17; ☽#♃ 5:32; ☽∠⚷ 10:53; ☽☌♄ 11:54; ☽☍☿ 15:04; ☽∥♄ 19:39; ☉⚻☽ 21:00
4 F	☽⚻⚳ 0:33; ☽∠♇ 1:04; ☽✱♃ 1:21; ☽#⚷ 2:27; ☽☍♂ 3:16; ☽#☿ 7:25; ☽#♀ 10:00; ☽⚺⚷ 10:52; ☽#♂ 11:53; ☽✱♅ 15:36; ☽⚻♀ 19:50; ☉⚼☽ 22:55; ☽☌♆ 23:01
5 Sa	☉⚼♆ 0:26; ☽✱♇ 1:22; ☽∠♃ 1:51; ☽∥♆ 3:14; ☽#⚳ 8:02; ☽⚺♄ 12:20; ☽∥⚳ 13:49; ☿∥♀ 14:03; ☽∠♅ 16:23; ☽#♆ 18:51; ☽⚼♀ 19:52; ☽⚻☿ 20:15; ⚳⚻♃ 20:42
6 Su	☉△☽ 1:42; ☽⚺♃ 3:04; ☽☍⚳ 3:12; ☽⚻♂ 7:04; ☽∥♂ 9:00; ☽∥☿ 10:44; ☽∥♀ 12:35; ☽☌⚷ 12:48; ☽∠♄ 13:37; ☽⚺♅ 17:58; ☽△♀ 20:36; ☽∥⚷ 20:47
7 M	☉□♃ 0:04; ☽⚼☿ 0:11; ☽⚺♆ 1:44; ☊ D 2:48; ☽□♇ 4:14; ☽#♄ 4:35; ☽⚼♂ 10:24; ☉✱⚳ 12:38; ☽✱♄ 15:47; ☽∥♃ 20:25; ☿∥♂ 22:43
8 Tu	☉∥☽ 2:11; ☽∠♆ 4:26; ☽△☿ 5:11; ☽☌♃ 8:12; ☽⚻⚳ 9:29; ☉□☽ 10:30; ☊ R 10:37; ☽∥♅ 11:27; ☽△♂ 14:48; ☽⚺⚷ 18:13; ☽☌♅ 23:52
9 W	☽□♀ 0:22; ☿⚼♇ 4:31; ☽✱♆ 8:01; ☽△♇ 10:40; ♀□♅ 11:10; ☽⚼⚳ 14:06; ☽#♇ 15:03; ☽∠⚷ 22:14; ☽□♄ 22:46
10 Th	☿△♃ 0:49; ☽⚼♇ 15:07; ☽⚺♃ 16:52; ☽□☿ 18:03; ☽△⚳ 19:34; ☉✱☽ 23:38
11 F	☽□♂ 2:29; ☽✱⚷ 2:59; ☽✱♀ 6:53; ☽⚺♅ 9:05; ♂⚻⚷ 12:12; ☽□♆ 17:28; ☽⚻♇ 20:14; ☽∠♃ 22:15
12 Sa	☉∥♃ 4:49; ☿⚺⚳ 6:02; ☉∠☽ 7:28; ☽△♄ 8:38; ☽∠♀ 10:55; ☽∠♅ 14:36; ☉△⚷ 18:14
13 Su	♀⚺♂ 0:16; ☽✱♃ 4:07; ☽□⚳ 8:25; ☽✱☿ 9:27; ☉☌♀ 11:17; ☽□⚷ 14:07; ☽⚼♄ 14:17; ☽⚺♀ 15:18; ☉⚺☽ 15:52; ☽✱♂ 16:57; ☽✱♅ 20:32
14 M	☽△♆ 4:59; ☽☍♇ 7:48; ♀△⚷ 14:56; ☿#♆ 15:19; ☽∠☿ 17:31; ☽⚻♄ 20:14
15 Tu	☽∠♂ 0:47; ☽#♇ 2:18; ♄∠⚷ 4:41; ☉⚺♂ 5:11; ☽⚼♆ 11:09; ☽□♃ 16:45; ☿⚺♀ 17:06; ⚵ ♌ 19:30; ☽✱⚳ 22:45
16 W	☽☌♀ 0:45; ☽⚺☿ 1:36; ☽△⚷ 2:27; ☉□♅ 2:36; ☽∥♅ 8:35; ☽⚺♂ 8:49; ☽□♅ 9:05; ☉☌☽ 9:39; ♂△♅ 13:55; ☽⚻♆ 17:27; ☿⚻⚷ 18:03; ☽⚻♇ 20:18; ☿#⚳ 22:46
17 Th	♀✱⚳ 0:05; ☽∥♃ 0:45; ☽∠⚳ 6:08; ☽☍♄ 8:33; ☽⚼⚷ 8:47; ☉∥☽ 9:01; ☽#♄ 18:20
18 F	☽⚼♇ 2:38; ☽∥⚷ 5:05; ☽△♃ 5:49; ☽∥♀ 10:31; ☽⚺♀ 10:37; ☽⚺⚳ 13:31; ☽⚻⚷ 15:06; ☽☌☿ 17:10; ☽△♅ 21:52
19 Sa	☽☌♂ 0:59; ☉⚺☽ 3:44; ☽☍♆ 6:02; ☽△♇ 8:52; ☽∥♂ 8:59; ☽#♆ 10:53; ☽⚼♃ 12:14; ☽#⚳ 13:06; ☽∠♀ 15:29; ☽∥☿ 19:16; ☽⚻♄ 20:44; ⚳⚼♄ 21:08; ☽#☿ 22:08
20 Su	☽⚼♅ 4:02; ☽∥⚳ 4:57; ☽∥♆ 6:40; ☽#♂ 7:28; ☉⚻♆ 7:42; ⚳☍⚷ 11:45; ☉∠☽ 12:25; ☽⚻♃ 18:20; ☽✱♀ 20:09
21 M	♂#♆ 0:20; ☽⚼♄ 2:25; ☽☍⚷ 3:02; ☽☌⚳ 3:34; ☽⚺☿ 6:51; ☽#♀ 8:20; ☽⚻♅ 9:48; ☽#⚷ 11:39; ♂#⚳ 14:30; ☽⚺♂ 16:03; ☊ D 16:26; ☽⚻♆ 17:35; ☉⚻♇ 18:09; ☽□♇ 20:21; ☉✱☽ 20:32; ☽∥♄ 22:39
22 Tu	☉#☽ 0:07; ☽△♄ 7:34; ♀□♃ 12:18; ⚳∥♆ 12:21; ☽∠☿ 12:30; ☽#♃ 15:04; ♂☍♆ 20:35; ☉#♄ 21:36; ☽⚼♆ 22:30; ☽∠♂ 22:36
23 W	☽□♀ 4:11; ☽☍♃ 4:49; ☽#♅ 5:53; ☉ ♍ 9:02; ☽⚻⚷ 12:47; ☽⚺⚳ 15:12; ☽✱☿ 17:05; ☽☍♅ 19:20; ☿ R 20:01
24 Th	☽△♆ 2:34; ☽✱♂ 4:10; ☽✱♇ 5:11; ☽∥♇ 9:36; ☊ R 9:49; ☉□☽ 9:58; ☽□♄ 15:30; ☽⚼⚷ 16:23; ☽∠⚳ 19:36
25 F	♂△♇ 0:24; ☽∠♇ 8:14; ☽△♀ 9:28; ☽⚻♃ 11:51; ☿⚺⚳ 18:18; ☽△⚷ 19:01; ♀∠♂ 20:06; ☽□☿ 22:44; ☽✱⚳ 22:56; ♀∥⚷ 23:37
26 Sa	☽⚻♅ 1:13; ☽□♆ 7:50; ☽⚺♇ 10:17; ☽⚼♀ 10:52; ☽□♂ 11:57; ☽⚼♃ 13:52; ☉△☽ 18:40; ☽✱♄ 19:40
27 Su	☽⚼♅ 2:43; ☉☍♄ 8:29; ☽⚻♀ 11:29; ♂ ♎ 13:21; ☽△♃ 14:59; ☽∠♄ 20:25; ☿#♂ 21:01; ☉⚼☽ 21:20; ☽□⚷ 21:28; ☉⚼⚷ 23:27
28 M	☽△☿ 0:02; ☽□⚳ 2:36; ☽△♅ 3:23; ♂⚼♃ 7:52; ☽✱♆ 9:30; ☽☌♇ 11:50; ☽△♂ 15:40; ☽⚺♄ 20:30; ☉⚻☽ 23:09; ☉∥♀ 23:24; ☽⚼☿ 23:26
29 Tu	♅ R 2:40; ☽∥♇ 2:53; ⚳⚻♅ 8:01; ☽∠♆ 9:23; ☽☍♀ 10:57; ☽□♃ 15:12; ☽⚼♂ 16:32; ☽✱⚷ 21:17; ☽⚻☿ 22:19
30 W	☽#♅ 2:38; ☽□♅ 3:05; ☽△⚳ 3:36; ☿∥♂ 8:25; ☽⚺♆ 8:57; ☉∥⚷ 10:15; ☽⚺♇ 11:15; ☽#♃ 14:45; ☽⚻♂ 17:08; ☽☌♄ 19:34; ☽∠⚷ 20:47; ☿⚻⚷ 23:57
31 Th	☉☍☽ 1:37; ☽∥♄ 3:21; ☽⚼⚳ 3:47; ☽⚻♀ 9:34; ☽#♀ 10:24; ☽∠♇ 10:48; ☽#⚷ 13:34; ☽✱♃ 14:26; ☉#☽ 15:02; ☽☍☿ 19:30; ☽⚺⚷ 20:23

LONGITUDE — September 2023

Day	Sid.Time	☉	☽	☽ 12 hour	Mean ☊	True ☊	☿	♀	♂	⚳	♃	♄	⚷	♅	♆	♇
	h m s	° ' "	° ' "	° ' "	° '	° '	° '	° '	° '	° '	° '	° '	° '	° '	° '	° '
1 F	22 39 36	8♍19 20	21♓35 37	29♓06 27	27♈20.1	25♈48.2	18♍36.7	12♌23.4	2♎51.2	24♎07.8	15♉33.6	3♓29.0	19♈18.9	23♉04.3	26♓46.3	28♑15.0
2 Sa	22 43 33	9 17 21	6♈32 25	13♈52 41	27 16.9	25R 44.7	17R 48.0	12R 17.3	3 29.8	24 31.7	15 34.2	3R 24.5	19R 17.0	23R 04.1	26R 44.7	28R 14.0
3 Su	22 47 29	10 15 24	21 06 36	28 13 46	27 13.8	25D 43.2	16 55.5	12 13.6	4 08.5	24 55.6	15 34.7	3 20.0	19 15.1	23 03.9	26 43.1	28 13.0
4 M	22 51 26	11 13 29	5♉13 57	12♉07 06	27 10.6	25 43.4	15 59.9	12D 12.2	4 47.2	25 19.5	15R 34.9	3 15.5	19 13.1	23 03.6	26 41.6	28 12.1
5 Tu	22 55 23	12 11 36	18 53 20	25 32 55	27 07.4	25 44.6	15 02.4	12 13.3	5 26.0	25 43.6	15 34.9	3 11.1	19 11.1	23 03.3	26 40.0	28 11.1
6 W	22 59 19	13 09 45	2♊06 11	8♊33 34	27 04.2	25R 45.9	14 04.0	12 16.6	6 04.8	26 07.6	15 34.7	3 06.6	19 09.1	23 03.0	26 38.4	28 10.2
7 Th	23 03 16	14 07 56	14 55 33	21 12 39	27 01.1	25 46.4	13 06.0	12 22.3	6 43.7	26 31.8	15 34.3	3 02.2	19 07.0	23 02.5	26 36.8	28 09.3
8 F	23 07 12	15 06 09	27 25 23	3♋34 19	26 57.9	25 45.5	12 09.6	12 30.2	7 22.6	26 56.0	15 33.8	2 57.8	19 04.8	23 02.1	26 35.2	28 08.4
9 Sa	23 11 09	16 04 24	9♋39 59	15 42 52	26 54.7	25 43.0	11 16.3	12 40.2	8 01.6	27 20.2	15 33.0	2 53.4	19 02.7	23 01.6	26 33.5	28 07.6
10 Su	23 15 05	17 02 41	21 43 28	27 42 14	26 51.5	25 38.7	10 27.3	12 52.4	8 40.6	27 44.5	15 32.0	2 49.1	19 00.5	23 01.0	26 31.9	28 06.7
11 M	23 19 02	18 01 00	3♌39 37	9♌35 58	26 48.3	25 33.0	9 43.8	13 06.7	9 19.6	28 08.9	15 30.8	2 44.8	18 58.3	23 00.4	26 30.3	28 05.9
12 Tu	23 22 58	18 59 21	15 31 41	21 27 04	26 45.2	25 26.5	9 06.8	13 22.9	9 58.7	28 33.3	15 29.4	2 40.5	18 56.0	22 59.7	26 28.7	28 05.2
13 W	23 26 55	19 57 44	27 22 24	3♍17 58	26 42.0	25 19.7	8 37.3	13 41.1	10 37.9	28 57.8	15 27.8	2 36.2	18 53.8	22 59.0	26 27.0	28 04.4
14 Th	23 30 52	20 56 09	9♍14 01	15 10 46	26 38.8	25 13.5	8 16.0	14 01.1	11 17.1	29 22.3	15 26.0	2 32.0	18 51.4	22 58.2	26 25.4	28 03.6
15 F	23 34 48	21 54 36	21 08 27	27 07 16	26 35.6	25 08.4	8D 03.6	14 23.0	11 56.3	29 46.8	15 24.0	2 27.9	18 49.1	22 57.4	26 23.7	28 02.9
16 Sa	23 38 45	22 53 04	3♎07 26	9♎09 11	26 32.5	25 04.7	8 00.3	14 46.7	12 35.6	0♏11.4	15 21.8	2 23.7	18 46.7	22 56.6	26 22.1	28 02.2
17 Su	23 42 41	23 51 35	15 12 44	21 18 20	26 29.3	25D 02.7	8 06.4	15 12.0	13 14.9	0 36.1	15 19.4	2 19.7	18 44.3	22 55.7	26 20.4	28 01.6
18 M	23 46 38	24 50 07	27 26 16	3♏36 49	26 26.1	25 02.3	8 22.0	15 38.9	13 54.3	1 00.8	15 16.8	2 15.6	18 41.9	22 54.7	26 18.7	28 00.9
19 Tu	23 50 34	25 48 41	9♏50 18	16 07 02	26 22.9	25 03.1	8 47.0	16 07.5	14 33.7	1 25.5	15 14.0	2 11.7	18 39.5	22 53.7	26 17.1	28 00.3
20 W	23 54 31	26 47 17	22 27 23	28 51 42	26 19.7	25 04.6	9 21.0	16 37.6	15 13.2	1 50.3	15 11.1	2 07.7	18 37.0	22 52.7	26 15.4	27 59.7
21 Th	23 58 27	27 45 54	5♐20 21	11♐53 40	26 16.6	25 06.2	10 03.8	17 09.1	15 52.7	2 15.1	15 07.9	2 03.9	18 34.5	22 51.6	26 13.8	27 59.1
22 F	0 02 24	28 44 34	18 32 00	25 15 37	26 13.4	25R 07.4	10 54.9	17 42.1	16 32.2	2 40.0	15 04.5	2 00.1	18 32.0	22 50.5	26 12.1	27 58.6
23 Sa	0 06 21	29 43 14	2♑04 46	8♑59 33	26 10.2	25 07.7	11 53.7	18 16.4	17 11.8	3 04.8	15 01.0	1 56.3	18 29.5	22 49.3	26 10.4	27 58.1
24 Su	0 10 17	0♎41 57	16 00 03	23 06 11	26 07.0	25 07.0	12 59.7	18 52.0	17 51.5	3 29.8	14 57.3	1 52.6	18 26.9	22 48.1	26 08.8	27 57.6
25 M	0 14 14	1 40 41	0♒17 42	7♒34 15	26 03.9	25 05.1	14 12.2	19 28.9	18 31.2	3 54.7	14 53.3	1 49.0	18 24.3	22 46.8	26 07.1	27 57.1
26 Tu	0 18 10	2 39 27	14 55 18	22 20 09	26 00.7	25 02.6	15 30.5	20 07.1	19 10.9	4 19.8	14 49.2	1 45.4	18 21.7	22 45.5	26 05.5	27 56.7
27 W	0 22 07	3 38 15	29 47 59	7♓17 48	25 57.5	24 59.7	16 54.1	20 46.4	19 50.7	4 44.8	14 44.9	1 41.9	18 19.1	22 44.1	26 03.9	27 56.3
28 Th	0 26 03	4 37 04	14♓48 35	22 19 12	25 54.3	24 57.0	18 22.1	21 26.9	20 30.5	5 09.9	14 40.5	1 38.5	18 16.5	22 42.7	26 02.2	27 55.9
29 F	0 30 00	5 35 55	29 48 32	7♈15 30	25 51.1	24 54.9	19 54.3	22 08.5	21 10.4	5 34.9	14 35.8	1 35.1	18 13.9	22 41.3	26 00.6	27 55.6
30 Sa	0 33 56	6♎34 49	14♈39 04	21 58 21	25♈48.0	24♈53.8	21♍29.7	22♌51.2	21♎50.3	6♏00.1	14♉31.0	1♓31.8	18♈11.2	22♉39.8	25♓59.0	27♑55.2

1st of Month

Julian Day # 2460188.5
Obliquity 23°26'19"
SVP 4♓55'52"
GC 27♐10.2
Eris 25♈07.2R

Day	⚴	⚵	⚶
1	24♍10.3	8♌20.2	26♊15.8
6	26 28.1	10 50.4	27 45.8
11	28 45.8	13 18.4	29 11.4
16	1♎03.4	15 44.1	0♋31.9
21	3 20.9	18 07.3	1 47.1
26	5 38.1	20 27.9	2 56.3

DECLINATION and LATITUDE

Day	☉ Decl	☽ Decl	☽ Lat	☽ 12h Decl	☿ Decl	☿ Lat	♀ Decl	♀ Lat	♂ Decl	♂ Lat	⚳ Decl	⚳ Lat	♃ Decl	♃ Lat	♄ Decl	♄ Lat
1 F	8N27	5S59	2S53	2S28	0N22	4S29	9N59	7S23	0S33	0N38	4S06	5N39	15N14	1S19	11S54	1S47
2 Sa	8 05	1N02	1 42	4N30	0 45	4 26	10 07	7 16	0 49	0 38	4 17	5 37	15 14	1 19	11 55	1 47
3 Su	7 43	7 51	0 25	11 03	1 10	4 20	10 15	7 09	1 05	0 37	4 28	5 34	15 14	1 19	11 57	1 47
4 M	7 21	14 04	0N51	16 52	1 39	4 12	10 23	7 01	1 20	0 37	4 39	5 32	15 14	1 20	11 59	1 47
5 Tu	6 59	19 24	2 02	21 39	2 09	4 03	10 30	6 53	1 36	0 36	4 50	5 29	15 14	1 20	12 00	1 47
6 W	6 37	23 35	3 04	25 12	2 42	3 52	10 37	6 45	1 52	0 36	5 00	5 27	15 14	1 20	12 02	1 47
7 Th	6 15	26 29	3 55	27 24	3 16	3 39	10 44	6 37	2 08	0 35	5 11	5 24	15 13	1 20	12 04	1 47
8 F	5 52	27 58	4 33	28 11	3 52	3 24	10 50	6 28	2 24	0 34	5 22	5 22	15 13	1 20	12 05	1 47
9 Sa	5 30	28 02	4 58	27 34	4 27	3 08	10 56	6 19	2 40	0 34	5 33	5 20	15 13	1 21	12 07	1 47
10 Su	5 07	26 46	5 09	25 41	5 01	2 50	11 01	6 10	2 56	0 33	5 44	5 17	15 12	1 21	12 08	1 47
11 M	4 44	24 18	5 07	22 40	5 35	2 32	11 06	6 01	3 12	0 33	5 54	5 15	15 12	1 21	12 10	1 47
12 Tu	4 21	20 49	4 51	18 45	6 06	2 13	11 10	5 52	3 28	0 32	6 05	5 13	15 11	1 21	12 11	1 47
13 W	3 59	16 30	4 23	14 06	6 35	1 53	11 14	5 43	3 43	0 32	6 16	5 10	15 11	1 21	12 13	1 47
14 Th	3 36	11 34	3 44	8 55	7 01	1 34	11 17	5 34	3 59	0 31	6 27	5 08	15 10	1 21	12 15	1 47
15 F	3 13	6 11	2 54	3 23	7 24	1 14	11 20	5 24	4 15	0 31	6 37	5 06	15 09	1 22	12 16	1 47
16 Sa	2 49	0 33	1 57	2S19	7 43	0 55	11 22	5 15	4 31	0 30	6 48	5 03	15 08	1 22	12 18	1 47
17 Su	2 26	5S10	0 54	7 60	7 58	0 36	11 24	5 06	4 47	0 29	6 58	5 01	15 07	1 22	12 19	1 47
18 M	2 03	10 46	0S13	13 27	8 09	0 18	11 25	4 56	5 03	0 29	7 09	4 59	15 07	1 22	12 20	1 47
19 Tu	1 40	16 02	1 20	18 28	8 15	0 01	11 26	4 47	5 18	0 28	7 20	4 57	15 06	1 22	12 22	1 47
20 W	1 17	20 43	2 25	22 45	8 17	0N15	11 26	4 38	5 34	0 28	7 30	4 55	15 05	1 22	12 23	1 47
21 Th	0 53	24 32	3 23	26 00	8 15	0 29	11 26	4 28	5 50	0 27	7 40	4 52	15 03	1 23	12 25	1 47
22 F	0 30	27 08	4 13	27 54	8 08	0 43	11 25	4 19	6 06	0 27	7 51	4 50	15 02	1 23	12 26	1 47
23 Sa	0 07	28 15	4 49	28 09	7 57	0 55	11 23	4 10	6 21	0 26	8 01	4 48	15 01	1 23	12 27	1 47
24 Su	0S17	27 37	5 10	26 37	7 42	1 07	11 21	4 01	6 37	0 25	8 12	4 46	14 60	1 23	12 29	1 47
25 M	0 40	25 11	5 13	23 19	7 24	1 17	11 18	3 52	6 53	0 25	8 22	4 44	14 59	1 23	12 30	1 47
26 Tu	1 03	21 04	4 56	18 28	7 01	1 25	11 15	3 43	7 08	0 24	8 32	4 42	14 57	1 23	12 31	1 47
27 W	1 27	15 34	4 19	12 26	6 36	1 33	11 11	3 34	7 24	0 24	8 43	4 40	14 56	1 23	12 32	1 47
28 Th	1 50	9 06	3 23	5 39	6 07	1 39	11 07	3 25	7 39	0 23	8 53	4 38	14 55	1 24	12 34	1 47
29 F	2 13	2 08	2 14	1N25	5 35	1 44	11 02	3 16	7 55	0 23	9 03	4 35	14 53	1 24	12 35	1 47
30 Sa	2S37	4N55	0S56	8N19	5N02	1N48	10N57	3S07	8S10	0N22	9S13	4N33	14N52	1S24	12S36	1S47

Day	⚷ Decl	⚷ Lat	♅ Decl	♅ Lat	♆ Decl	♆ Lat	♇ Decl	♇ Lat
1	8N60	1N33	18N14	0S19	2S27	1S16	23S11	2S44
6	8 56	1 33	18 14	0 19	2 30	1 16	23 12	2 44
11	8 52	1 33	18 13	0 19	2 34	1 16	23 13	2 44
16	8 47	1 33	18 13	0 19	2 37	1 17	23 14	2 44
21	8 42	1 33	18 11	0 19	2 40	1 17	23 15	2 44
26	8 37	1 32	18 09	0 19	2 44	1 17	23 15	2 44

Day	⚴ Decl	⚴ Lat	⚵ Decl	⚵ Lat	⚶ Decl	⚶ Lat	Eris Decl	Eris Lat
1	5N49	3N48	10N36	7S50	19N01	4S22	0S37	11S06
6	5 25	4 23	10 01	7 46	19 03	4 22	0 38	11 06
11	5 01	4 56	9 26	7 42	19 04	4 22	0 39	11 06
16	4 37	5 30	8 49	7 39	19 04	4 22	0 40	11 06
21	4 13	6 03	8 11	7 35	19 04	4 22	0 41	11 07
26	3 50	6 36	7 32	7 31	19 03	4 21	0 42	11 07

Moon Phenomena

Max/0 Decl
dy hr mn
1 20:26 0 N
8 13:14 28N11
16 2:18 0 S
23 3:37 28S16
29 7:12 0 N

Max/0 Lat
dy hr mn
3 7:45 0 N
10 7:49 5N10
17 19:19 0 S
24 15:21 5S14
30 16:50 0 N

Perigee/Apogee
dy hr m kilometers
12 15:44 a 406291
28 1:00 p 359912

PH dy hr mn
☾ 6 22:22 14♊04
● 15 1:41 21♍59
☽ 22 19:33 29♐32
○ 29 9:59 6♈00

Void of Course Moon

Last Aspect	☽ Ingress
1 10:37 ♇ ⚹	♈ 1 13:26
3 11:58 ♇ □	♉ 3 15:01
5 16:47 ♇ △	♊ 5 20:08
7 22:23 ♆ □	♋ 8 5:01
10 12:48 ♇ ☍	♌ 10 16:37
12 15:07 ♅ □	♍ 13 5:19
15 13:51 ♇ △	♎ 15 17:46
18 1:10 ♇ □	♏ 18 4:59
20 10:23 ♇ ⚹	♐ 20 14:07
22 19:33 ☉ □	♑ 22 20:21
24 20:07 ♇ ☌	♒ 24 23:31
26 12:40 ♅ □	♓ 27 0:19
28 20:59 ♇ ⚹	♈ 29 0:18

DAILY ASPECTARIAN

1 F
☽⚹♅ 2:21
☽⚻⚳ 4:09
☽∥⚳ 6:18
☽☌♆ 8:15
☽Q♀ 9:11
☽⚹♇ 10:37
☽∥♆ 12:04
☽∠♃ 14:21
☽∥♂ 17:54
☽#☿ 18:13
☽☍♂ 18:51
☽⚺♄ 18:57
♂⚻♄ 21:02
☽∥☿ 22:56
☽#♂ 23:11

2 Sa
☽∠♅ 2:29
☉⚻☽ 4:48
☽#♆ 4:55
☽△♀ 9:20
☉∠⚳ 10:03
☿#♂ 10:56
☽#⚳ 11:33
☽⚺♃ 14:48
☽⚻☿ 17:26
☽∠♄ 19:24
☽☌⚷ 20:54
☉∥☽ 23:33

3 Su
☽⚺♅ 3:17
☽∥⚷ 4:07
☽☍⚳ 6:36
☉Q☽ 7:29
☊ D 7:47
☽∥♀ 9:08
☽⚺♆ 9:25
☽□♇ 11:58
☽#♄ 15:33
☽Q☿ 17:11
☽⚹♄ 20:37
☽⚻♂ 23:12

4 M
♀ D 1:21
☽∥♃ 4:53
☿△♃ 10:30
☉△☽ 11:14
☽∠♆ 11:14
☽□♀ 12:10
♃ R 14:12
☽△☿ 17:37
☽☌♃ 18:07
☽∥♅ 18:19

5 Tu
☽⚺⚷ 0:32
☉⚺♀ 0:43
☽Q♂ 2:54
☽☌♅ 7:29
☽⚻⚳ 12:43
☽⚹♆ 14:00
☿#♆ 15:13
☽△♇ 16:47
☽#♇ 21:27

6 W
☉Q♇ 0:11
☽□♄ 1:51
☽∠⚷ 3:47
☽△♂ 7:46
☉☌☿ 11:10
☽Q⚳ 17:22
☽⚹♀ 19:07
☽Q♇ 20:39
☽□☿ 20:47
☉□☽ 22:22
☊ R 22:33
☿Q♇ 22:34

7 Th
☽⚺♃ 1:14
⚳⚻♆ 4:38
☽⚹⚷ 7:58
☽⚺♅ 15:31
☿⚺♀ 16:19
☽□♆ 22:23
☽△⚳ 23:01

8 F
☽∠♀ 0:09
☽⚻♇ 1:24
☿∠⚳ 4:09
☽∠♃ 6:06
☽△♄ 10:45
☉△♃ 11:14
♂∥♆ 11:56
☽□♂ 20:35
☽∠♅ 20:46
☉#⚳ 21:37
♂Q♅ 23:59

9 Sa
☽⚹☿ 2:58
☽⚺♀ 6:03
☽⚹♃ 11:39
☉⚹☽ 13:50
☽Q♄ 16:14
☽□⚷ 18:35

10 Su
☉∥☿ 2:25
☽⚹♅ 2:35
☽∠☿ 7:02
☽△♆ 9:37
☽□⚳ 12:30
☽☍♇ 12:48
⚳□♇ 21:10
☽⚻♄ 22:10
☉∠☽ 22:35

11 M
☿⚺♂ 7:23
☽#♇ 8:11
☽⚺☿ 11:38
☽⚹♂ 12:07
☽Q♆ 15:49
☽☌♀ 19:33
☉⚻⚷ 22:41
☿#⚳ 22:51
☽□♃ 23:55

12 Tu
☽△⚷ 6:53
☉⚺☽ 7:38
☽∥♅ 14:58
☽□♅ 15:07
☽∠♂ 20:16
☽⚻♆ 22:08

13 W
☽⚻♇ 1:25
☽⚹⚳ 3:20
☽∥♃ 6:44
☉#♂ 9:23
☽☍♄ 10:32
☽Q⚷ 13:10
♀ ♎ 16:39
☽#♄ 20:51
☽☌☿ 22:06
⚶ ♋ 23:30

14 Th
☽∥♀ 1:15
☽⚺♂ 4:23
☽Q♇ 7:43
☽⚺♀ 9:57
☽∠⚳ 10:44
☽△♃ 12:29
☽∥⚷ 12:29
☽∥☿ 19:01
☽⚻⚷ 19:21
☽#⚳ 22:10

15 F
☉☌☽ 1:41
☽△♅ 3:39
☽#♂ 7:56
☽☍♆ 10:31
⚳ ♏ 12:51
☉∥☽ 13:41
☽△♇ 13:51
☽#♆ 15:18
☽∠♀ 17:05
☽⚺⚳ 17:56
☽Q♃ 18:30
☿ D 20:22
☽⚻♄ 22:33

16 Sa
☉△♅ 1:25
☽Q♅ 9:35
☽⚺☿ 9:46
☉#♆ 12:41
☉#☽ 13:15
☽∥♆ 13:18
☽☌♂ 19:54
☽∥♂ 22:17
☽⚹♀ 23:58

17 Su
☽⚻♃ 0:13
☽Q♄ 4:09
♀□♃ 6:11
☽☍⚷ 6:56
☽∥⚳ 7:54
☽#☿ 12:19
☽⚻♅ 15:10
☽#⚷ 15:17
☽∠☿ 15:50
☉⚺☽ 18:29
☊ D 19:21
☽⚻♆ 21:49

18 M
☽□♇ 1:07
☽#♀ 2:54
☽∥♄ 7:00
☽☌⚳ 7:12
☽△♄ 9:20
☽#♃ 19:34
☽⚹☿ 21:53

19 Tu
☉∠☽ 2:01
☽Q♆ 2:46
☽⚺♂ 9:32
☽☍♃ 10:17
☽#♅ 10:34
☉☍♆ 11:19
☽□♀ 12:30
☽⚻⚷ 16:46
♂⚻♃ 22:49

20 W
☽☍♅ 0:48
☽△♆ 7:07
☉⚹☽ 8:48
☽⚹♇ 10:23
⚳△♄ 14:36
☽∥♇ 15:09
☽∠♂ 15:18
☽□♄ 17:59
☽⚺⚳ 18:07
☽Q⚷ 20:45

21 Th
☉△♇ 5:22
☽□☿ 9:14
☽∠♇ 13:58
☽⚻♃ 17:48
☽⚹♂ 20:13
☽∠⚳ 22:23
☽△♀ 22:26
☽△⚷ 24:00

22 F
☽⚻♅ 7:41
☽□♆ 13:38
♂Q♄ 15:24
☽⚺♇ 16:47
☊ R 19:31
☉□☽ 19:33
☿#⚳ 19:50
☽Q♃ 20:24
☽⚹♄ 23:45

23 Sa
☽⚹⚳ 1:48
☽Q♀ 2:11
☉Q♃ 6:50
☉ ♎ 6:51
♀△⚷ 8:18
☽Q♅ 9:58
☽△☿ 18:25
☽△♃ 22:14
☿Q♇ 23:17

24 Su
☽∠♄ 1:29
☽□♂ 3:18
☽□⚷ 4:08
☽⚻♀ 5:05
☽△♅ 11:28
☽⚹♆ 17:04
☽☌♇ 20:07
♂☍⚷ 20:07
☽Q☿ 22:01

25 M
☉△☽ 2:27
☽⚺♄ 2:31
☉⚻♄ 3:11
☽□⚳ 6:09
☿△♃ 12:11
☽∥♇ 12:22
☽∠♆ 17:46
☿#♂ 19:50
☽□♃ 23:50

26 Tu
☽⚻☿ 1:03
☉Q☽ 4:45
☽⚹⚷ 5:34
☽△♂ 7:14
☽☍♀ 8:48
⚳#⚷ 10:35
☽□♅ 12:40
☽#♅ 13:23
☽⚺♆ 18:01
☽⚺♇ 21:01

27 W
☽#♃ 2:32
☽☌♄ 3:02
☽∠⚷ 5:37
☉⚻☽ 6:35
☽△⚳ 8:09
☽Q♂ 8:27
☽∥♄ 11:34
☽#♀ 16:43
☽∠♇ 21:00
☿⚻⚷ 22:31
☽⚹♃ 23:47

28 Th
☽∥⚳ 0:47
☽#⚷ 1:50
☽∥♂ 4:54
☽⚺⚷ 5:31
☽☍☿ 6:19
☽Q⚳ 8:48
☽⚻♂ 9:32
☽⚻♀ 11:07
☽#☿ 11:14
☽⚹♅ 12:36
☽☌♆ 17:55
☽⚹♇ 20:59
☽∥♆ 21:52
☉⚺⚳ 23:18
☽∠♃ 23:40
☉∥☽ 23:41

29 F
☽⚺♄ 2:51
☽⚻⚳ 9:34
☉☍☽ 9:59
☽Q♀ 12:24
☽∠♅ 12:41
☿∠⚳ 14:00
☉#☽ 15:38
☽#♆ 16:37
♀□♅ 17:54
☽⚺♃ 23:47

30 Sa
☽∥☿ 0:22
☽∠♄ 3:03
☽☌⚷ 5:46
☿⚺♂ 8:36
☉∥♆ 9:56
☽#♂ 11:58
☽☍♂ 12:21
☽⚻☿ 12:38
☽∥⚷ 12:50
☽⚺♅ 13:07
☽△♀ 14:10
☽#⚳ 15:41
☊ D 16:53
☿△♅ 16:57
☽⚺♆ 18:36
☽∥♀ 21:21
☽□♇ 21:51

October 2023

LONGITUDE

Day	Sid.Time	⊙	☽	☽ 12 hour	Mean ☊	True ☊	☿	♀	♂	⚳	♃	♄	⚷	♅	♆	♇
	h m s	° E "	° E "	° E "	° E	° E	° E	° E	° E	° E	° E	° E	° E	° E	° E	° E
1 Su	0 37 53	7♎33 44	29♈12 33	6♉21 05	25♈44.8	24♈53.6	23♍07.9	23♌34.9	22♎30.3	6♏25.2	14♉26.1	1♓28.5	18♈08.6	22♉38.3	25♓57.3	27♑54.9
2 M	0 41 50	8 32 41	13♉23 30	20 19 29	25 41.6	24 54.2	24 48.4	24 19.5	23 10.3	6 50.4	14R 20.9	1R 25.4	18R 05.9	22R 36.8	25R 55.7	27R 54.7
3 Tu	0 45 46	9 31 41	27 08 56	3♊51 51	25 38.4	24 55.3	26 30.7	25 05.2	23 50.3	7 15.7	14 15.6	1 22.3	18 03.2	22 35.2	25 54.1	27 54.4
4 W	0 49 43	10 30 43	10♊28 23	16 58 48	25 35.3	24 56.5	28 14.5	25 51.8	24 30.4	7 40.9	14 10.1	1 19.3	18 00.5	22 33.5	25 52.5	27 54.2
5 Th	0 53 39	11 29 47	23 23 27	29 42 46	25 32.1	24 57.6	29 59.3	26 39.3	25 10.6	8 06.2	14 04.5	1 16.4	17 57.8	22 31.9	25 50.9	27 54.0
6 F	0 57 36	12 28 54	5♋57 13	12♋07 19	25 28.9	24R 58.2	1♎44.9	27 27.6	25 50.8	8 31.5	13 58.7	1 13.5	17 55.1	22 30.2	25 49.4	27 53.9
7 Sa	1 01 32	13 28 03	18 13 38	24 16 44	25 25.7	24 58.2	3 31.0	28 16.8	26 31.1	8 56.8	13 52.8	1 10.8	17 52.4	22 28.4	25 47.8	27 53.8
8 Su	1 05 29	14 27 14	0♌17 10	6♌15 31	25 22.5	24 57.7	5 17.3	29 06.7	27 11.4	9 22.2	13 46.7	1 08.1	17 49.7	22 26.6	25 46.2	27 53.7
9 M	1 09 25	15 26 28	12 12 19	18 08 05	25 19.4	24 56.8	7 03.8	29 57.4	27 51.7	9 47.6	13 40.4	1 05.5	17 46.9	22 24.8	25 44.7	27 53.6
10 Tu	1 13 22	16 25 43	24 03 21	29 58 34	25 16.2	24 55.7	8 50.2	0♍48.9	28 32.1	10 13.0	13 34.1	1 03.0	17 44.2	22 23.0	25 43.2	27 53.5
11 W	1 17 19	17 25 01	5♍54 11	11♍50 37	25 13.0	24 54.6	10 36.3	1 41.1	29 12.6	10 38.5	13 27.5	1 00.5	17 41.5	22 21.1	25 41.7	27D 53.5
12 Th	1 21 15	18 24 22	17 48 13	23 47 21	25 09.8	24 53.6	12 22.2	2 34.0	29 53.1	11 03.9	13 20.9	0 58.2	17 38.7	22 19.2	25 40.1	27 53.5
13 F	1 25 12	19 23 44	29 48 18	5♎51 19	25 06.7	24 52.9	14 07.6	3 27.5	0♏33.7	11 29.4	13 14.1	0 55.9	17 36.0	22 17.2	25 38.7	27 53.6
14 Sa	1 29 08	20 23 08	11♎56 40	18 04 32	25 03.5	24 52.5	15 52.6	4 21.7	1 14.3	11 54.9	13 07.2	0 53.8	17 33.3	22 15.2	25 37.2	27 53.6
15 Su	1 33 05	21 22 35	24 15 06	0♏28 30	25 00.3	24D 52.3	17 37.1	5 16.5	1 54.9	12 20.5	13 00.2	0 51.7	17 30.6	22 13.2	25 35.7	27 53.7
16 M	1 37 01	22 22 03	6♏44 53	13 04 22	24 57.1	24 52.4	19 21.0	6 11.9	2 35.6	12 46.0	12 53.1	0 49.7	17 27.8	22 11.1	25 34.3	27 53.9
17 Tu	1 40 58	23 21 34	19 27 02	25 52 59	24 53.9	24 52.5	21 04.3	7 07.8	3 16.4	13 11.6	12 45.9	0 47.8	17 25.1	22 09.1	25 32.8	27 54.0
18 W	1 44 54	24 21 07	2♐22 18	8♐55 05	24 50.8	24R 52.6	22 47.0	8 04.4	3 57.2	13 37.2	12 38.5	0 46.1	17 22.4	22 07.0	25 31.4	27 54.2
19 Th	1 48 51	25 20 41	15 31 22	22 11 14	24 47.6	24 52.6	24 29.1	9 01.4	4 38.0	14 02.8	12 31.1	0 44.4	17 19.7	22 04.8	25 30.0	27 54.4
20 F	1 52 47	26 20 17	28 54 43	5♑41 53	24 44.4	24 52.5	26 10.5	9 59.0	5 18.9	14 28.4	12 23.6	0 42.8	17 17.0	22 02.7	25 28.7	27 54.7
21 Sa	1 56 44	27 19 56	12♑32 44	19 27 14	24 41.2	24 52.4	27 51.4	10 57.1	5 59.9	14 54.0	12 16.0	0 41.3	17 14.3	22 00.5	25 27.3	27 55.0
22 Su	2 00 41	28 19 35	26 25 21	3♒26 58	24 38.1	24D 52.3	29 31.6	11 55.7	6 40.9	15 19.7	12 08.3	0 39.9	17 11.7	21 58.3	25 26.0	27 55.3
23 M	2 04 37	29 19 17	10♒31 55	17 40 00	24 34.9	24 52.4	1♏11.2	12 54.7	7 21.9	15 45.3	12 00.6	0 38.6	17 09.0	21 56.1	25 24.7	27 55.6
24 Tu	2 08 34	0♏19 00	24 50 52	2♓04 10	24 31.7	24 52.7	2 50.2	13 54.2	8 03.0	16 11.0	11 52.7	0 37.4	17 06.4	21 53.8	25 23.4	27 56.0
25 W	2 12 30	1 18 44	9♓19 26	16 36 08	24 28.5	24 53.2	4 28.6	14 54.2	8 44.2	16 36.7	11 44.9	0 36.3	17 03.7	21 51.6	25 22.1	27 56.4
26 Th	2 16 27	2 18 31	23 53 38	1♈11 16	24 25.3	24 53.8	6 06.4	15 54.5	9 25.3	17 02.4	11 36.9	0 35.3	17 01.1	21 49.3	25 20.8	27 56.8
27 F	2 20 23	3 18 19	8♈28 20	15 44 06	24 22.2	24 54.4	7 43.7	16 55.4	10 06.6	17 28.1	11 29.0	0 34.4	16 58.5	21 46.9	25 19.6	27 57.3
28 Sa	2 24 20	4 18 09	22 57 48	0♉08 44	24 19.0	24R 54.7	9 20.4	17 56.6	10 47.9	17 53.8	11 20.9	0 33.6	16 55.9	21 44.6	25 18.4	27 57.7
29 Su	2 28 16	5 18 01	7♉16 13	14 19 38	24 15.8	24 54.5	10 56.6	18 58.2	11 29.2	18 19.5	11 12.9	0 32.9	16 53.4	21 42.3	25 17.2	27 58.2
30 M	2 32 13	6 17 54	21 18 29	28 12 19	24 12.6	24 53.7	12 32.3	20 00.2	12 10.6	18 45.2	11 04.8	0 32.3	16 50.8	21 39.9	25 16.1	27 58.8
31 Tu	2 36 10	7♏17 50	5♊00 49	11♊43 47	24♈09.5	24♈52.3	14♏07.5	21♍02.6	12♏52.0	19♏10.9	10♉56.7	0♓31.8	16♈48.3	21♉37.5	25♓14.9	27♑59.3

1st of Month

Julian Day #
2460218.5
Obliquity
23°26[illegible]9"
SVP 4♓55[illegible]9"
GC 27♐10.3
Eris 24♈52.4R

Day	⚴
1	7♎55.0
6	10 11.6
11	12 27.8
16	14 43.7
21	16 59.0
26	19 13.7
31	21 27.8

Day	⚵
1	22♌45.6
6	25 00.5
11	27 12.2
16	29 20.6
21	1♍25.4
26	3 26.4
31	5 23.3

Day	⚶
1	3♋59.2
6	4 55.1
11	5 43.4
16	6 23.5
21	6 54.7
26	7 16.4
31	7 28.1

DECLINATION and LATITUDE

Day	⊙ Decl	☽ Decl	☽ Lat	☽ 12h Decl	☿ Decl	☿ Lat	♀ Decl	♀ Lat	♂ Decl	♂ Lat	⚳ Decl	⚳ Lat	♃ Decl	♃ Lat	♄ Decl	♄ Lat
1 Su	3S00	11N34	0N24	14N38	4N25	1N51	10N51	2S58	8S26	0N21	9S23	4N31	14N50	1S24	12S37	1S47
2 M	3 23	17 27	1 40	20 01	3 47	1 53	10 44	2 50	8 41	0 21	9 33	4 29	14 48	1 24	12 38	1 47
3 Tu	3 47	22 16	2 49	24 11	3 08	1 54	10 37	2 41	8 56	0 20	9 43	4 27	14 47	1 24	12 39	1 47
4 W	4 10	25 45	3 46	26 57	2 27	1 54	10 30	2 33	9 11	0 20	9 53	4 25	14 45	1 24	12 40	1 47
5 Th	4 33	27 46	4 30	28 13	1 45	1 54	10 22	2 25	9 27	0 19	10 03	4 23	14 43	1 24	12 41	1 47
6 F	4 56	28 17	4 59	28 00	1 02	1 53	10 13	2 17	9 42	0 19	10 13	4 21	14 41	1 24	12 42	1 47
7 Sa	5 19	27 23	5 14	26 27	0 18	1 51	10 04	2 08	9 57	0 18	10 23	4 19	14 40	1 25	12 43	1 47
8 Su	5 42	25 13	5 15	23 43	0S27	1 48	9 54	2 01	10 12	0 17	10 33	4 17	14 38	1 25	12 44	1 47
9 M	6 05	21 58	5 02	20 00	1 12	1 45	9 44	1 53	10 27	0 17	10 42	4 15	14 36	1 25	12 45	1 47
10 Tu	6 28	17 51	4 37	15 31	1 57	1 42	9 33	1 45	10 42	0 16	10 52	4 13	14 34	1 25	12 46	1 47
11 W	6 50	13 03	3 59	10 27	2 42	1 38	9 22	1 37	10 57	0 16	11 02	4 12	14 32	1 25	12 46	1 46
12 Th	7 13	7 45	3 11	4 59	3 27	1 34	9 10	1 30	11 12	0 15	11 11	4 10	14 30	1 25	12 47	1 46
13 F	7 35	2 08	2 15	0S44	4 12	1 29	8 58	1 22	11 27	0 15	11 21	4 08	14 28	1 25	12 48	1 46
14 Sa	7 58	3S38	1 11	6 31	4 57	1 24	8 45	1 15	11 41	0 14	11 30	4 06	14 25	1 25	12 49	1 46
15 Su	8 20	9 21	0 03	12 07	5 42	1 19	8 32	1 08	11 56	0 13	11 40	4 04	14 23	1 25	12 49	1 46
16 M	8 42	14 48	1S05	17 20	6 27	1 13	8 18	1 01	12 10	0 13	11 49	4 02	14 21	1 25	12 50	1 46
17 Tu	9 04	19 43	2 12	21 53	7 11	1 07	8 04	0 54	12 25	0 12	11 59	4 00	14 19	1 25	12 50	1 46
18 W	9 26	23 48	3 13	25 25	7 55	1 01	7 49	0 47	12 39	0 12	12 08	3 58	14 17	1 25	12 51	1 46
19 Th	9 48	26 43	4 06	27 39	8 38	0 55	7 34	0 40	12 54	0 11	12 17	3 56	14 14	1 25	12 52	1 46
20 F	10 10	28 11	4 45	28 18	9 21	0 49	7 18	0 34	13 08	0 10	12 26	3 55	14 12	1 25	12 52	1 46
21 Sa	10 31	27 59	5 10	27 14	10 03	0 42	7 02	0 27	13 22	0 10	12 36	3 53	14 10	1 25	12 52	1 46
22 Su	10 53	26 03	5 17	24 28	10 45	0 36	6 46	0 21	13 36	0 09	12 45	3 51	14 08	1 25	12 53	1 45
23 M	11 14	22 29	5 05	20 10	11 26	0 29	6 29	0 15	13 50	0 09	12 54	3 49	14 05	1 25	12 53	1 45
24 Tu	11 35	17 33	4 35	14 40	12 06	0 23	6 12	0 09	14 04	0 08	13 03	3 47	14 03	1 25	12 54	1 45
25 W	11 56	11 34	3 47	8 19	12 46	0 16	5 54	0 03	14 18	0 07	13 12	3 46	14 00	1 25	12 54	1 45
26 Th	12 16	4 56	2 44	1 29	13 25	0 09	5 36	0N03	14 31	0 07	13 21	3 44	13 58	1 25	12 54	1 45
27 F	12 37	1N59	1 30	5N25	14 03	0 03	5 18	0 09	14 45	0 06	13 29	3 42	13 56	1 25	12 54	1 45
28 Sa	12 57	8 46	0 11	11 58	14 40	0S04	4 59	0 15	14 58	0 06	13 38	3 40	13 53	1 25	12 55	1 45
29 Su	13 17	15 01	1N08	17 49	15 17	0 11	4 40	0 20	15 12	0 05	13 47	3 38	13 51	1 25	12 55	1 45
30 M	13 37	20 21	2 21	22 35	15 53	0 18	4 21	0 25	15 25	0 05	13 56	3 37	13 48	1 25	12 55	1 45
31 Tu	13S57	24N29	3N24	26N00	16S28	0S24	4N01	0N31	15S38	0N04	14S04	3N35	13N46	1S25	12S55	1S45

Day	⚷ Decl	⚷ Lat	♅ Decl	♅ Lat	♆ Decl	♆ Lat	♇ Decl	♇ Lat
1	8N32	1N32	18N07	0S19	2S47	1S17	23S16	2S44
6	8 27	1 32	18 05	0 19	2 50	1 17	23 16	2 44
11	8 21	1 31	18 03	0 19	2 53	1 17	23 16	2 44
16	8 15	1 31	18 00	0 19	2 56	1 16	23 16	2 44
21	8 10	1 31	17 58	0 19	2 59	1 16	23 16	2 44
26	8 04	1 30	17 55	0 19	3 01	1 16	23 15	2 44
31	7N59	1N30	17N52	0S19	3S03	1S16	23S15	2S44

Day	⚴ Decl	⚴ Lat	⚵ Decl	⚵ Lat	⚶ Decl	⚶ Lat	Eris Decl	Eris Lat
1	3N26	7N09	6N53	7S27	19N02	4S21	0S43	11S07
6	3 03	7 43	6 14	7 22	19 01	4 20	0 44	11 07
11	2 41	8 16	5 34	7 18	18 60	4 19	0 45	11 07
16	2 20	8 49	4 55	7 14	18 59	4 18	0 46	11 07
21	1 60	9 23	4 16	7 10	18 59	4 17	0 47	11 06
26	1 41	9 57	3 37	7 06	18 60	4 15	0 48	11 06
31	1N24	10N31	2N60	7S01	19N01	4S13	0S49	11S06

Moon Phenomena

Max/0 Decl
dy hr mn
5 20:31 28N18
13 8:55 0 S
20 9:15 28S19
26 17:08 0 N

Perigee/Apogee
dy hr m kilometers
10 3:43 a 405425
26 3:03 p 364873

PH dy hr mn
☾ 6 13:49 13♋03
● 14 17:56 21♎08
● 14 1080:4A 05[illegible]7"
☽ 22 3:31 28♑28
○ 28 20:25 5♉09
● 28 20:15 P 0.122

Max/0 Lat
dy hr mn
7 13:22 5N17
15 1:12 0 S
21 21:21 5S17
28 3:15 0 N

Void of Course Moon

Last Aspect			☽ Ingress	
30 21:51	♇	□	♉ 1	1:19
3 1:21	♇	△	♊ 3	5:04
5 6:36	♀	⚹	♋ 5	12:33
7 19:13	♇	☍	♌ 7	23:26
10 9:38	♂	⚹	♍ 10	12:03
12 20:12	♇	△	♎ 13	0:23
15 7:02	♇	□	♏ 15	11:05
17 15:45	♇	⚹	♐ 17	19:38
19 19:03	⊙	⚹	♑ 20	1:56
22 6:02	☿	□	♒ 22	6:07
23 19:05	♅	□	♓ 24	8:34
26 6:40	♇	⚹	♈ 26	10:03
28 8:21	♇	□	♉ 28	11:45
30 11:37	♇	△	♊ 30	15:09

DAILY ASPECTARIAN

1 Su	⊙⚼♅	1:49
	☽⚹♄	3:47
	☽#♄	4:03
	♂⚻♅	4:40
	♂#⚷	9:24
	☿⚺♀	11:39
	☽☍⚳	12:29
	☽∥♃	12:47
	⊙⚻☽	15:06
	☽⚼☿	17:02
	☽∠♆	19:47
2 M	☽☌♃	1:38
	☽∥♅	2:58
	☽⚺⚷	8:06
	⊙#☿	9:19
	☿☍♆	15:36
	☽☌♅	15:58
	☽⚻♂	17:51
	⊙⚼☽	19:01
	☽□♀	20:08
	☽⚹♆	21:48
	☽△☿	22:43
3 Tu	☽△♇	1:21
	☽#♇	6:00
	☽□♄	7:30
	☽∠⚷	10:30
	☿#♆	11:31
	☽⚻⚳	18:45
	☿△♇	19:21
	☽⚼♂	22:08
4 W	⊙△☽	0:05
	♀⚻♆	0:22
	☽⚼♇	4:28
	☽⚺♃	6:45
	☿⚼♃	12:07
	☽⚹⚷	13:52
	☽⚺♅	22:23
	☽⚼⚳	23:26
5 Th	☿ ♎	0:10
	☽△♂	3:34
	☽□♆	4:38
	☽⚹♀	6:36
	☽⚻♇	8:33
	☽∠♃	10:42
	☽□☿	14:34
	☽△♄	14:56
	☿⚻♄	17:04
	⊙∠♀	20:59
	♂⚻♆	23:11
	♀#⚳	23:58
6 F	☽∠♅	3:00
	☽△⚳	5:10
	♀⚻♇	12:51
	☽∠♀	13:34
	⊙□☽	13:49
	☊ R	14:11
	☽⚹♃	15:31
	☽⚼♄	19:59
	☽□⚷	23:18
7 Sa	♀#♂	6:32
	☽⚹♅	8:23
	⊙⚻♃	9:05
	☽△♆	15:00
	☽□♂	17:26
	☽☍♇	19:13
	☽⚺♀	21:28
8 Su	☽⚻♄	1:42
	☽⚹☿	11:48
	☽#♇	15:15
	☽□⚳	18:57
	☽⚼♆	21:03
9 M	♂□♇	1:06
	♀ ♍	1:12
	☽□♃	2:57
	☿⚼♅	4:40
	⊙⚹☽	7:08
	☽△⚷	11:15
	⊙⚼♄	15:09
	☽□♅	20:37
	☽∥♅	22:54
	☽∠☿	23:29
10 Tu	☽⚻♆	3:22
	♀☍♄	6:12
	☽⚻♇	7:47
	☽⚹♂	9:38
	☽☍♄	14:08
	☽☌♀	14:47
	⊙∠☽	16:18
	☽∥♃	16:52
	☽⚼⚷	17:31
11 W	☿⚺⚳	0:38
	♇ D	1:12
	☽#♄	1:18
	⚳⚼♆	2:50
	☿∥♆	5:57
	⊙☍⚷	6:22
	☽#⚳	9:07
	☽#♂	9:19
	☽⚹⚳	9:56
	☽⚺☿	11:09
	☽⚼♇	14:07
	☽△♃	15:07
	☽∥♀	17:33
	☽∠♂	17:47
	☽∥⚷	21:28
	♂∥⚳	22:10
	☽⚻⚷	23:41
12 Th	⊙⚺☽	1:19
	♀⚼⚷	2:03
	⊙#☽	2:13
	♂ ♏	4:05
	☽△♅	9:02
	☿⚻♃	12:33
	☽☍♆	15:43
	☽#☿	16:18
	☽∠⚳	17:09
	☽△♇	20:12
	☽#♆	20:47
	☽⚼♃	20:54
13 F	☽⚺♂	1:36
	☽⚻♄	2:14
	☽⚺♀	7:50
	♂△♄	12:30
	☽⚼♅	14:47
	☽∥♆	21:00
	☽⚺⚳	23:56
14 Sa	☿⚼♄	0:16
	☽⚻♃	2:17
	☽∥☿	6:20
	☽⚼♄	7:43
	☽☌☿	8:59
	☽☍⚷	10:57
	☽∠♀	15:40
	⊙☌☽	17:56
	⊙∥☽	19:23
	☽#⚷	19:27
	☽⚻♅	20:04
	⊙#⚷	20:17
	☽#♀	20:38
	☿☍⚷	22:32
15 Su	☊ D	1:26
	☽⚻♆	2:36
	☽□♇	7:02
	⊙#♀	7:36
	☽∥⚳	10:17
	☽∥♂	11:40
	☽△♄	12:43
	☽∥♄	15:07
	☽☌♂	15:37
	⊙⚻♅	19:45
	☽#♃	21:59
	☽⚹♀	22:52
16 M	♀∥⚷	4:22
	⚳☍♃	5:11
	☽⚼♆	7:15
	☽☍♃	11:32
	☽☌⚳	11:49
	☽#♅	15:14
	☽⚻⚷	20:12
17 Tu	☽⚺☿	3:30
	☽☍♅	5:02
	⊙⚺☽	7:55
	☽△♆	11:21
	⚵ ♍	13:28
	☿⚻♅	14:49
	☽⚹♇	15:45
	☽∥♇	20:31
	☽□♄	21:03
	☿#♀	21:38
18 W	☽⚼⚷	0:00
	☽⚺♂	3:04
	☿∠♀	9:12
	☿#⚷	9:57
	☽□♀	11:16
	☽∠☿	11:24
	☊ R	12:50
	⊙∠☽	13:50
	☽⚻♃	18:36
	☽∠♇	19:16
	♂∥♄	20:28
	☽⚺⚳	21:14
19 Th	☽△⚷	3:15
	⊙⚻♆	3:41
	☽∠♂	7:49
	☽⚻♅	11:47
	☿⚻♆	14:13
	☽□♆	17:54
	☽⚹☿	18:26
	⊙⚹☽	19:03
	☽⚼♃	21:19
	☽⚺♇	22:13
20 F	☽∠⚳	1:02
	☽⚹♄	3:11
	⊙☌☿	5:39
	☽⚹♂	11:55
	☽⚼♅	14:20
	☽△♀	21:00
	☽△♃	23:31
21 Sa	☿□♇	0:52
	☽⚹⚳	4:14
	☽∠♄	5:28
	☽□⚷	8:08
	⊙□♇	14:10
	☽△♅	16:22
	☽⚹♆	22:18
22 Su	☽⚼♀	0:56
	☽☌♇	2:34
	☊ D	2:44
	⊙□☽	3:31
	♀△♃	4:34
	☽□☿	6:02
	☿ ♏	6:50
	☽⚺♄	7:15
	⊙∥☿	9:47
	☿△♄	16:14
	☽□♂	18:22
	☽∥♇	19:34
	⚳∥♄	22:22
	☽∠♆	23:48
23 M	♀⚼♇	0:22
	☽□♃	2:28
	☽⚻♀	4:19
	☽□⚳	9:04
	☽⚹⚷	11:06
	⊙ ♏	16:22
	☽□♅	19:05
	☽#♅	22:21
	♂#♃	22:25
24 Tu	☽⚺♆	0:54
	☽⚺♇	5:08
	⊙△♄	7:15
	☽☌♄	9:35
	⊙△☽	9:46
	☽∠⚷	12:01
	☽∥♂	13:53
	☽#♃	14:34
	☽△☿	14:58
	☽∥⚳	17:57
	☽∥♄	18:58
	☽∥☿	19:55
	⊙∥☽	22:43
	☽△♂	22:59
25 W	☽⚹♃	3:58
	☿∥♄	5:03
	☽∠♇	5:58
	☽☍♀	9:53
	⊙⚼☽	12:22
	☽△⚳	12:23
	☽⚺⚷	12:43
	☽#⚷	12:49
	☽⚼☿	18:50
	☽⚹♅	20:36
	☿∥⚳	20:47
	☽#♀	21:30
	⚳⚻⚷	22:57
26 Th	☽⚼♂	0:55
	☽☌♆	2:23
	☽∠♃	4:26
	☽∥♆	6:40
	☽⚹♇	6:40
	☽⚺♄	11:00
	☽⚼⚳	13:48
	⊙⚻☽	14:52
	☿#♃	19:40
	☽∠♅	21:13
	☽⚻☿	22:37
27 F	♀⚻⚷	1:11
	☽⚻♂	2:50
	☽#♆	3:38
	☽⚺♃	4:55
	♂⚼♆	7:22
	☽∥♀	11:06
	☽∠♄	11:43
	☽☌⚷	14:01
	☽⚻♀	15:01
	☽⚻⚳	15:19
	⊙∥♄	20:46
	☽∥⚷	21:23
	☽⚺♅	21:59
	♀⚹⚳	22:06
28 Sa	☊ R	3:11
	☽⚺♆	3:54
	☽□♇	8:21
	☽⚹♄	12:41
	☿⚼♆	14:17
	☽#♄	15:37
	♂☍♃	16:04
	⊙#☽	16:42
	☽⚼♀	18:00
	☿∥♂	18:33
	☽#⚳	18:56
	☽∥♃	19:20
	⊙☍☽	20:25
29 Su	☽#♂	0:48
	☽#☿	1:16
	☿☍♃	3:46
	☽∠♆	5:07
	☽☌♃	6:38
	☽☍☿	7:02
	☽☍♂	7:31
	⚳#♃	8:08
	☽∥♅	12:16
	☿☌♂	14:23
	☽⚺⚷	16:20
	☽☍⚳	19:27
	☽△♀	21:34
30 M	☽☌♅	0:37
	☽⚹♆	6:52
	☽△♇	11:37
	⊙#♃	12:01
	☽#♇	15:58
	☽□♄	16:05
	☽∠⚷	18:21
31 Tu	⊙⚻☽	4:23
	☽⚺♃	10:29
	♀△♅	12:52
	☽⚼♇	14:17
	☽⚻♂	14:49
	⊙∥⚳	16:11
	☽⚻☿	18:32
	☽⚹⚷	21:07

LONGITUDE

Day	Sid.Time	☉	☽	☽ 12 hour	Mean☊	True☊	☿	♀	♂	⚳	♃	♄	⚷	♅	♆	♇
	h m s	° ' "	° ' "	° ' "	° '	° '	° '	° '	° '	° '	° '	° '	° '	° '	° '	° '
1 W	2 40 06	8♏17 48	18♊21 09	24♊52 56	24♈06.3	24♈50.5	15♏42.2	22♍05.4	13♏33.5	19♏36.7	10♉48.5	0♓31.4	16♈45.8	21♉35.1	25♓13.8	27♑59.9
2 Th	2 44 03	9 17 48	1♋19 16	7♋40 23	24 03.1	24R 48.6	17 16.4	23 08.5	14 15.0	20 02.4	10R 40.4	0R 31.1	16R 43.3	21R 32.7	25R 12.7	28 00.6
3 F	2 47 59	10 17 50	13 56 36	20 08 19	23 59.9	24 46.7	18 50.3	24 11.9	14 56.6	20 28.2	10 32.2	0 30.9	16 40.9	21 30.3	25 11.7	28 01.2
4 Sa	2 51 56	11 17 55	26 16 00	2♌20 09	23 56.8	24 45.3	20 23.6	25 15.7	15 38.3	20 53.9	10 24.1	0D 30.8	16 38.4	21 27.8	25 10.6	28 01.9
5 Su	2 55 52	12 18 01	8♌21 20	14 20 07	23 53.6	24D 44.6	21 56.6	26 19.9	16 20.0	21 19.7	10 15.9	0 30.8	16 36.0	21 25.4	25 09.6	28 02.6
6 M	2 59 49	13 18 09	20 17 06	26 12 55	23 50.4	24 44.7	23 29.2	27 24.3	17 01.7	21 45.4	10 07.8	0 31.0	16 33.7	21 22.9	25 08.6	28 03.4
7 Tu	3 03 45	14 18 20	2♍08 08	8♍03 24	23 47.2	24 45.6	25 01.4	28 29.1	17 43.5	22 11.2	9 59.7	0 31.2	16 31.3	21 20.5	25 07.7	28 04.1
8 W	3 07 42	15 18 32	13 59 16	19 56 19	23 44.0	24 47.1	26 33.2	29 34.1	18 25.3	22 37.0	9 51.6	0 31.5	16 29.0	21 18.0	25 06.8	28 04.9
9 Th	3 11 39	16 18 47	25 55 05	1♎56 04	23 40.9	24 48.8	28 04.6	0♎39.4	19 07.2	23 02.7	9 43.5	0 32.0	16 26.7	21 15.5	25 05.9	28 05.7
10 F	3 15 35	17 19 03	7♎59 43	14 06 26	23 37.7	24 50.3	29 35.6	1 45.0	19 49.2	23 28.5	9 35.5	0 32.5	16 24.4	21 13.0	25 05.0	28 06.6
11 Sa	3 19 32	18 19 21	20 16 35	26 30 26	23 34.5	24R 51.2	1♐06.3	2 50.9	20 31.2	23 54.3	9 27.5	0 33.2	16 22.2	21 10.5	25 04.1	28 07.4
12 Su	3 23 28	19 19 41	2♏48 13	9♏10 05	23 31.3	24 51.0	2 36.6	3 57.0	21 13.2	24 20.0	9 19.5	0 33.9	16 20.0	21 08.1	25 03.3	28 08.3
13 M	3 27 25	20 20 03	15 36 07	22 06 19	23 28.2	24 49.6	4 06.6	5 03.4	21 55.3	24 45.8	9 11.7	0 34.8	16 17.9	21 05.6	25 02.5	28 09.3
14 Tu	3 31 21	21 20 27	28 40 38	5♐18 56	23 25.0	24 46.8	5 36.1	6 10.1	22 37.5	25 11.6	9 03.8	0 35.7	16 15.7	21 03.1	25 01.8	28 10.2
15 W	3 35 18	22 20 53	12♐01 02	18 46 42	23 21.8	24 42.9	7 05.3	7 16.9	23 19.7	25 37.3	8 56.1	0 36.8	16 13.6	21 00.6	25 01.1	28 11.2
16 Th	3 39 14	23 21 20	25 35 39	2♑27 33	23 18.6	24 38.3	8 34.0	8 24.0	24 02.0	26 03.1	8 48.4	0 38.0	16 11.6	20 58.1	25 00.4	28 12.2
17 F	3 43 11	24 21 48	9♑22 07	16 18 59	23 15.5	24 33.7	10 02.3	9 31.3	24 44.3	26 28.8	8 40.8	0 39.2	16 09.6	20 55.6	24 59.7	28 13.2
18 Sa	3 47 08	25 22 18	23 17 49	0♒18 20	23 12.3	24 29.7	11 30.1	10 38.9	25 26.6	26 54.6	8 33.3	0 40.6	16 07.6	20 53.1	24 59.1	28 14.3
19 Su	3 51 04	26 22 49	7♒20 12	14 23 11	23 09.1	24 26.8	12 57.5	11 46.6	26 09.0	27 20.3	8 25.9	0 42.1	16 05.7	20 50.6	24 58.5	28 15.4
20 M	3 55 01	27 23 22	21 26 59	28 31 24	23 05.9	24D 25.4	14 24.2	12 54.5	26 51.5	27 46.0	8 18.6	0 43.7	16 03.8	20 48.1	24 57.9	28 16.5
21 Tu	3 58 57	28 23 55	5♓36 13	12♓41 13	23 02.8	24 25.5	15 50.4	14 02.7	27 34.0	28 11.7	8 11.4	0 45.4	16 01.9	20 45.7	24 57.4	28 17.6
22 W	4 02 54	29 24 30	19 46 13	26 50 58	22 59.6	24 26.6	17 15.9	15 11.0	28 16.5	28 37.4	8 04.4	0 47.2	16 00.1	20 43.2	24 56.9	28 18.8
23 Th	4 06 50	0♐25 05	3♈55 16	10♈58 52	22 56.4	24 28.1	18 40.6	16 19.5	28 59.1	29 03.1	7 57.4	0 49.0	15 58.3	20 40.8	24 56.4	28 20.0
24 F	4 10 47	1 25 42	18 01 27	25 02 43	22 53.2	24R 29.2	20 04.5	17 28.2	29 41.7	29 28.7	7 50.5	0 51.0	15 56.6	20 38.3	24 56.0	28 21.2
25 Sa	4 14 44	2 26 20	2♉02 21	8♉59 56	22 50.0	24 29.1	21 27.4	18 37.1	0♐24.4	29 54.4	7 43.8	0 53.1	15 54.9	20 35.9	24 55.5	28 22.4
26 Su	4 18 40	3 27 00	15 55 08	22 47 31	22 46.9	24 27.3	22 49.3	19 46.2	1 07.2	0♐20.0	7 37.2	0 55.3	15 53.3	20 33.5	24 55.2	28 23.7
27 M	4 22 37	4 27 41	29 36 45	6♊22 26	22 43.7	24 23.4	24 10.0	20 55.4	1 50.0	0 45.7	7 30.7	0 57.6	15 51.7	20 31.1	24 54.8	28 24.9
28 Tu	4 26 33	5 28 23	13♊04 16	19 41 59	22 40.5	24 17.5	25 29.2	22 04.8	2 32.8	1 11.3	7 24.4	1 00.0	15 50.1	20 28.7	24 54.5	28 26.2
29 W	4 30 30	6 29 06	26 15 23	2♋44 20	22 37.3	24 10.2	26 46.9	23 14.4	3 15.7	1 36.9	7 18.2	1 02.5	15 48.6	20 26.3	24 54.3	28 27.5
30 Th	4 34 26	7♐29 51	9♋08 49	15 28 50	22♈34.2	24♈02.2	28♐02.7	24♎24.2	3♐58.6	2♐02.4	7♉12.2	1♓05.0	15♈47.1	20♉23.9	24♓54.0	28♑28.9

1st of Month

Julian Day #
2460249.5
Obliquity
23°26'[illegible]9"
SVP 4♓55'[illegible]5"
GC 27♐10.3
Eris 24♈34.1R

Day	⚴
1	21♎54.6
6	24 07.8
11	26 20.2
16	28 31.7
21	0♏42.2
26	2 51.4

Day	⚵
1	5♍46.1
6	7 37.7
11	9 24.6
16	11 06.3
21	12 42.4
26	14 12.4

Day	⚶
1	7♋29.2
6	7 28.3R
11	7 16.3R
16	6 53.1R
21	6 18.8R
26	5 34.0R

DECLINATION and LATITUDE

Day	☉ Decl	☽ Decl	☽ Lat	☽ 12h Decl	☿ Decl	☿ Lat	♀ Decl	♀ Lat	♂ Decl	♂ Lat	⚳ Decl	⚳ Lat	♃ Decl	♃ Lat	♄ Decl	♄ Lat
1 W	14S16	27N09	4N14	27N54	17S02	0S31	3N41	0N36	15S51	0N03	14S13	3N33	13N43	1S25	12S55	1S44
2 Th	14 35	28 16	4 50	28 14	17 36	0 38	3 21	0 41	16 04	0 03	14 21	3 31	13 41	1 25	12 55	1 44
3 F	14 54	27 51	5 10	27 07	18 08	0 44	3 00	0 46	16 17	0 02	14 30	3 30	13 38	1 25	12 55	1 44
4 Sa	15 13	26 04	5 16	24 43	18 40	0 51	2 39	0 50	16 30	0 02	14 38	3 28	13 36	1 25	12 55	1 44
5 Su	15 32	23 07	5 07	21 16	19 10	0 57	2 18	0 55	16 42	0 01	14 46	3 26	13 34	1 25	12 55	1 44
6 M	15 50	19 14	4 45	17 00	19 40	1 03	1 56	0 59	16 55	0 00	14 54	3 25	13 31	1 24	12 55	1 44
7 Tu	16 08	14 37	4 11	12 06	20 09	1 10	1 35	1 04	17 07	0S00	15 03	3 23	13 29	1 24	12 54	1 44
8 W	16 26	9 29	3 27	6 45	20 37	1 16	1 13	1 08	17 19	0 01	15 11	3 21	13 26	1 24	12 54	1 44
9 Th	16 43	3 58	2 33	1 07	21 03	1 22	0 50	1 12	17 31	0 01	15 19	3 20	13 24	1 24	12 54	1 44
10 F	17 00	1S46	1 32	4S40	21 29	1 27	0 28	1 16	17 43	0 02	15 27	3 18	13 21	1 24	12 54	1 43
11 Sa	17 17	7 32	0 25	10 22	21 54	1 33	0 05	1 20	17 55	0 03	15 35	3 16	13 19	1 24	12 53	1 43
12 Su	17 34	13 08	0S44	15 47	22 17	1 38	0S18	1 23	18 07	0 03	15 43	3 15	13 17	1 24	12 53	1 43
13 M	17 50	18 17	1 52	20 37	22 40	1 44	0 41	1 27	18 18	0 04	15 50	3 13	13 14	1 24	12 52	1 43
14 Tu	18 06	22 42	2 55	24 32	23 01	1 49	1 04	1 30	18 30	0 04	15 58	3 11	13 12	1 23	12 52	1 43
15 W	18 21	26 02	3 50	27 10	23 21	1 53	1 27	1 34	18 41	0 05	16 06	3 10	13 10	1 23	12 51	1 43
16 Th	18 37	27 55	4 33	28 14	23 40	1 58	1 51	1 37	18 52	0 06	16 13	3 08	13 07	1 23	12 51	1 43
17 F	18 52	28 07	5 01	27 33	23 58	2 02	2 15	1 40	19 03	0 06	16 21	3 06	13 05	1 23	12 50	1 43
18 Sa	19 06	26 33	5 12	25 08	24 15	2 07	2 38	1 43	19 14	0 07	16 28	3 05	13 03	1 23	12 50	1 42
19 Su	19 21	23 20	5 04	21 12	24 30	2 10	3 02	1 45	19 25	0 07	16 36	3 03	13 01	1 23	12 49	1 42
20 M	19 35	18 44	4 38	16 02	24 45	2 14	3 26	1 48	19 35	0 08	16 43	3 01	12 58	1 22	12 48	1 42
21 Tu	19 48	13 06	3 55	10 00	24 57	2 17	3 50	1 51	19 45	0 09	16 50	2 60	12 56	1 22	12 48	1 42
22 W	20 01	6 47	2 58	3 28	25 09	2 20	4 15	1 53	19 55	0 09	16 57	2 58	12 54	1 22	12 47	1 42
23 Th	20 14	0 07	1 50	3N14	25 19	2 22	4 39	1 55	20 05	0 10	17 04	2 57	12 52	1 22	12 46	1 42
24 F	20 27	6N32	0 35	9 44	25 28	2 24	5 03	1 57	20 15	0 10	17 11	2 55	12 50	1 22	12 45	1 42
25 Sa	20 39	12 49	0N41	15 44	25 36	2 26	5 27	1 59	20 25	0 11	17 18	2 53	12 48	1 21	12 45	1 42
26 Su	20 51	18 25	1 54	20 51	25 42	2 27	5 52	2 01	20 34	0 12	17 25	2 52	12 46	1 21	12 44	1 42
27 M	21 02	22 59	2 59	24 47	25 46	2 28	6 16	2 03	20 44	0 12	17 32	2 50	12 44	1 21	12 43	1 41
28 Tu	21 13	26 13	3 53	27 16	25 50	2 28	6 40	2 05	20 53	0 13	17 39	2 49	12 43	1 21	12 42	1 41
29 W	21 23	27 56	4 33	28 12	25 52	2 28	7 04	2 06	21 02	0 13	17 45	2 47	12 41	1 20	12 41	1 41
30 Th	21S34	28N05	4N58	27N35	25S52	2S27	7S29	2N08	21S10	0S14	17S52	2N45	12N39	1S20	12S40	1S41

Day	⚷ Decl	⚷ Lat	♅ Decl	♅ Lat	♆ Decl	♆ Lat	♇ Decl	♇ Lat
1	7N58	1N30	17N51	0S19	3S04	1S16	23S15	2S44
6	7 53	1 29	17 48	0 19	3 06	1 16	23 14	2 44
11	7 48	1 28	17 45	0 19	3 07	1 16	23 13	2 45
16	7 43	1 28	17 41	0 19	3 09	1 16	23 12	2 45
21	7 39	1 27	17 38	0 19	3 10	1 16	23 11	2 45
26	7 35	1 27	17 35	0 19	3 10	1 15	23 10	2 45

Day	⚴ Decl	⚴ Lat	⚵ Decl	⚵ Lat	⚶ Decl	⚶ Lat	Eris Decl	Eris Lat
1	1N21	10N38	2N52	7S01	19N02	4S12	0S49	11S06
6	1 05	11 13	2 16	6 56	19 05	4 09	0 50	11 05
11	0 52	11 49	1 41	6 52	19 10	4 05	0 50	11 05
16	0 41	12 25	1 07	6 47	19 16	4 00	0 51	11 05
21	0 31	13 02	0 36	6 42	19 23	3 55	0 51	11 04
26	0 25	13 40	0 06	6 37	19 32	3 48	0 52	11 04

Moon Phenomena

Max/0 Decl
dy hr mn
2 5:16 28N18
9 16:38 0 S
16 14:46 28S15
23 0:26 0 N
29 14:13 28N12

Max/0 Lat
dy hr mn
3 21:02 5N16
11 8:50 0 S
18 2:03 5S12
24 11:03 0 N

Perigee/Apogee
dy hr m kilometers
6 21:50 a 404568
21 21:03 p 369818

PH dy hr mn
☾ 5 8:38 12♌40
● 13 9:29 20♏44
☽ 20 10:51 27♒51
○ 27 9:17 4♊51

Void of Course Moon

Last Aspect	☽ Ingress
1 12:38 ♆ □	♋ 1 21:31
4 3:29 ♇ ☍	♌ 4 7:22
6 7:26 ☿ □	♍ 6 19:40
9 4:56 ☿ ⚹	♎ 9 8:09
11 15:07 ♇ □	♏ 11 18:40
13 23:05 ♇ ⚹	♐ 14 2:24
15 22:58 ♆ □	♑ 16 7:43
18 8:29 ♇ ☌	♒ 18 11:29
20 10:51 ☉ □	♓ 20 14:30
22 15:11 ♂ △	♈ 22 17:21
24 17:42 ♇ □	♉ 24 20:30
26 21:53 ♇ △	♊ 27 0:41
29 1:04 ☿ ☍	♋ 29 6:55

DAILY ASPECTARIAN

1 W
☽⊼⚳ 2:23
☽⚺♅ 5:54
☽□♀ 7:27
☉⚼☽ 9:50
☽□♆ 12:38
☽∠♃ 13:35
☿⊼⚷ 15:46
☽⊼♇ 17:48
☽⚼♂ 19:54
☽△♄ 22:30

2 Th
☽⚼☿ 2:02
☽⚼⚳ 7:15
☽∠♅ 9:50
☿#♅ 10:38
☉△☽ 16:24
☽⚹♃ 17:32
♀#♆ 19:02
☉⚼♆ 21:35

3 F
⚶ R 1:51
☽△♂ 2:03
☽⚼♄ 3:02
☉☍♃ 5:04
☽□⚷ 5:16
☽△☿ 10:50
☽△⚳ 13:06
☽⚹♅ 14:37
☽⚹♀ 21:50
☽△♆ 21:52
♀☍♆ 22:07

4 Sa
♀⚼♃ 2:46
☽☍♇ 3:29
♄ D 7:04
☽⊼♄ 8:23
☿☌⚳ 10:47
☿☍♅ 16:08
☽#♇ 23:07

5 Su
☽⚼♆ 3:37
☽□♃ 3:47
⚳☍♅ 4:52
☽∠♀ 6:33
☉□☽ 8:38
♂⊼⚷ 8:45
☊ D 8:47
☽△⚷ 16:30
☽□♂ 17:01
♃∠♆ 21:05
☽#☿ 21:46

6 M
☽□♅ 2:13
☽□⚳ 3:05
☽□☿ 7:26
☽‖♅ 7:50
☽⊼♆ 9:49
☽#♂ 11:55
♀△♇ 14:39
☽⊼♇ 15:45
☽⚺♀ 15:51
☉#☽ 16:55
☽☍♄ 20:43
☽#⚳ 21:58
☽⚼⚷ 22:46

7 Tu
☿△♆ 1:38
☽‖♃ 5:34
☽#♄ 8:15
☽△♃ 15:45
☽⚼♇ 22:10

8 W
☉⚹☽ 2:55
☽⊼⚷ 5:01
☽‖⚷ 7:15
☽⚹♂ 9:30
♀ ♎ 9:32
☽△♅ 14:41
☽⚹⚳ 18:02
♀⊼♄ 21:15
☽⚼♃ 21:38
☽☍♆ 22:22

9 Th
☿⚹♇ 0:18
☉⊼⚷ 3:03
☽#♆ 3:35
☽△♇ 4:21
☽⚹☿ 4:56
☽⊼♄ 9:13
☽☌♀ 10:24
☉∠☽ 11:44
☽‖♀ 14:03
☽∠♂ 17:20
☽#♀ 18:54
☽⚼♅ 20:30

10 F
☽∠⚳ 0:59
☽⊼♃ 3:07
♂#♅ 3:35
☽‖♆ 5:36
☿ ♐ 6:26
☽∠☿ 14:46
☽⚼♄ 14:49
☿□♄ 15:08
☽☍⚷ 16:26
☉⚺☽ 19:53

11 Sa
☽⚺♂ 0:30
☽#⚷ 1:06
☽⊼♅ 1:44
☿⚼⚷ 4:07
☽⚺⚳ 7:15
☊ R 8:49
☽⊼♆ 9:14
☽□♇ 15:07
☽△♄ 19:45
♂☍♅ 21:13
☽‖♄ 22:55
☽⚺☿ 23:35

12 Su
☽#♃ 0:39
☽⚺♀ 2:23
☽‖⚳ 11:58
☽☍♃ 12:10
☽⚼♆ 13:39
☉#♅ 14:49
☽#♅ 21:13
☉‖☽ 21:37

13 M
☽‖♂ 0:06
☽⊼⚷ 1:17
☽∠♀ 9:00
☉☌☽ 9:29
☽☍♅ 10:06
☽☌♂ 12:20
⚳△♆ 15:09
☽△♆ 17:22
☉☍♅ 17:22
☽☌⚳ 17:26
♀⚼♅ 21:35
☽⚹♇ 23:05

14 Tu
☽‖☿ 2:07
☽‖♇ 3:08
☽□♄ 3:29
☽⚼⚷ 4:40
☿‖♇ 13:26
☽☌☿ 14:05
☽⚹♀ 14:46
☽⊼♃ 18:33

15 W
☽∠♇ 2:05
☽△⚷ 7:28
☿⚹♀ 12:50
☉∠♀ 14:23
☽⊼♅ 15:53
☉⚺☽ 19:45
☽⚼♃ 20:53
☽⚺♂ 21:07
☽□♆ 22:58

16 Th
☽⚺⚳ 0:50
☿⊼♃ 3:36
☽⚺♇ 4:35
♀⊼♃ 7:50
☽⚹♄ 8:50
☽⚼♅ 18:03
☽△♃ 22:49
☉∠☽ 23:59

17 F
☽□♀ 0:17
☽∠♂ 0:40
☽⚺☿ 1:18
☽∠⚳ 3:46
♂△♆ 8:37
☽∠♄ 10:53
☽□⚷ 11:42
♀∠♂ 12:22
☉△♆ 14:53
☽△♅ 19:52

18 Sa
☽⚹♆ 2:53
☉⚹☽ 3:50
☽⚹♂ 3:53
☉☌♂ 5:44
☽∠☿ 6:08
☽⚹⚳ 6:23
☽☌♇ 8:29
☽⚺♄ 12:39
☽‖☿ 16:59

19 Su
☽‖♇ 0:51
☽□♃ 1:51
☽∠♆ 4:29
☿∠♇ 5:01
♀‖♆ 7:02
☽△♀ 8:13
♀ ♏ 9:04
☽⚹☿ 10:40
☽⚹⚷ 14:52
♀∠⚳ 19:09
☽‖♂ 20:09
☉‖☽ 20:14
☽□♅ 22:54

20 M
☉‖♂ 3:12
☽#♅ 4:59
☽⚺♆ 5:58
☽‖⚳ 8:52
☽□♂ 9:40
☊ D 10:45
☉□☽ 10:51
☽□⚳ 11:03
☽⚺♇ 11:36
☽⚼♀ 11:55
☉☌⚳ 15:36
☽☌♄ 15:46
☽∠⚷ 16:16
☉⚹♇ 21:28

21 Tu
☽#♃ 0:39
☽‖♄ 1:13
☿△⚷ 3:10
☽⚹♃ 4:21
⚳⚹♇ 5:48
☽∠♇ 13:03
☽⊼♀ 15:33
☽⚺⚷ 17:38
☽□☿ 19:17
☽#⚷ 20:51

22 W
♂⚹♇ 1:19
☽⚹♅ 1:36
☽∠♃ 5:33
☽‖♀ 8:41
☽☌♆ 8:46
♀⚼♄ 13:01
☽‖♆ 13:05
☉ ♐ 14:04
☽⚹♇ 14:30
☽△♂ 15:11
☽△⚳ 15:29
♀☍⚷ 16:46
☉△☽ 17:36
☽⚺♄ 18:43

23 Th
☽∠♅ 2:59
♂☌⚳ 5:38
☽⚺♃ 6:48
☉□♄ 9:48
☽#♆ 11:47
☉⚼⚷ 12:47
☽⚼⚳ 17:46
☽⚼♂ 18:01
☽#♀ 18:15
☽∠♄ 20:17
☽☌⚷ 20:27
☉⚼☽ 21:04
☽☍♀ 22:58

24 F
☽△☿ 3:53
☽‖⚷ 3:59
☽⚺♅ 4:27
☿⊼♅ 9:28
♂ ♐ 10:16
☊ R 11:03
☽⚺♆ 11:48
☽□♇ 17:42
☽⊼⚳ 20:13
☽⊼♂ 21:03
☽⚹♄ 22:01
☽#♄ 23:41
☽‖♃ 23:56

25 Sa
☉⊼☽ 0:44
⚳ ♐ 5:15
☽⚼☿ 8:27
☽☌♃ 9:44
♄∠⚷ 11:13
☽∠♆ 13:36
♂⚼⚷ 16:29
♂□♄ 16:58
☽#⚳ 19:19
☽‖♅ 20:10
☿⚼♃ 20:41
☽⚺⚷ 23:57

26 Su
☽⊼♀ 7:20
☽☌♅ 8:04
☽#♂ 10:56
☉#☽ 12:31
☽⊼☿ 13:22
☽⚹♆ 15:44
♀⊼♅ 15:51
☽△♇ 21:53

27 M
☽#♇ 1:09
☽☍⚳ 2:06
☽∠⚷ 2:12
☽□♄ 2:23
☽☍♂ 4:09
⚳⚼⚷ 5:18
⚳#♅ 7:44
☉☍☽ 9:17
☽⚼♀ 12:15
⚳□♄ 12:19
☿□♆ 13:29
☽⚺♃ 13:55
☽#☿ 20:25

28 Tu
☽⚼♇ 0:40
☽⚹⚷ 4:59
☽⚺♅ 13:23
☽∠♃ 16:48
☽△♀ 17:56
☽□♆ 21:31

29 W
♃#♄ 0:05
☽☍☿ 1:04
☽⊼♇ 4:04
☽△♄ 8:52
☽⊼⚳ 10:15
☽⊼♂ 13:44
☽∠♅ 16:59
☉⊼♃ 17:39
☽⚹♃ 20:22
☉⊼☽ 20:38

30 Th
♀#⚷ 3:20
☿⚺♇ 8:36
♀⊼♆ 10:14
☽□⚷ 12:34
☽⚼♄ 13:12
☽⚼⚳ 15:30
☽⚼♂ 19:49
☽⚹♅ 21:21

December 2023

LONGITUDE

Day	Sid.Time	☉	☽	☽ 12 hour	Mean☊	True☊	☿	♀	♂	⚳	♃	♄	⚷	♅	♆	♇
	h m s	° ′ ″	° ′ ″	° ′ ″	° ′	° ′	° ′	° ′	° ′	° ′	° ′	° ′	° ′	° ′	° ′	° ′
1 F	4 38 23	8♐30 37	21♋44 33	27♋56 10	22♈31.0	23♈54.4	29♐16.5	25♎34.0	4♐41.6	2♐28.0	7♉06.3	1♓07.7	15♈45.7	20♉21.6	24♓53.8	28♑30.3
2 Sa	4 42 19	9 31 25	4♌03 59	10♌08 22	22 27.8	23R 47.6	0♑27.8	26 44.1	5 24.7	2 53.5	7R 00.6	1 10.5	15R 44.4	20R 19.3	24R 53.6	28 31.6
3 Su	4 46 16	10 32 14	16 09 45	22 08 39	22 24.6	23 42.4	1 36.4	27 54.3	6 07.8	3 19.1	6 55.0	1 13.4	15 43.0	20 17.0	24 53.5	28 33.1
4 M	4 50 13	11 33 04	28 05 36	4♍01 13	22 21.5	23 39.2	2 41.7	29 04.6	6 50.9	3 44.6	6 49.6	1 16.3	15 41.8	20 14.7	24 53.4	28 34.5
5 Tu	4 54 09	12 33 56	9♍56 05	15 50 54	22 18.3	23D 37.9	3 43.5	0♏15.1	7 34.1	4 10.0	6 44.3	1 19.4	15 40.6	20 12.4	24 53.3	28 35.9
6 W	4 58 06	13 34 49	21 46 17	27 42 56	22 15.1	23 38.2	4 41.1	1 25.7	8 17.3	4 35.5	6 39.3	1 22.5	15 39.4	20 10.2	24D 53.3	28 37.4
7 Th	5 02 02	14 35 43	3♎41 30	9♎42 37	22 11.9	23 39.4	5 33.9	2 36.4	9 00.6	5 00.9	6 34.4	1 25.8	15 38.3	20 08.0	24 53.3	28 38.9
8 F	5 05 59	15 36 38	15 46 56	21 55 01	22 08.7	23R 40.6	6 21.2	3 47.3	9 44.0	5 26.4	6 29.6	1 29.1	15 37.2	20 05.8	24 53.3	28 40.4
9 Sa	5 09 55	16 37 35	28 07 24	4♏24 32	22 05.6	23 40.7	7 02.4	4 58.3	10 27.4	5 51.7	6 25.1	1 32.5	15 36.2	20 03.6	24 53.4	28 41.9
10 Su	5 13 52	17 38 33	10♏46 49	17 14 30	22 02.4	23 39.1	7 36.6	6 09.4	11 10.8	6 17.1	6 20.7	1 36.1	15 35.2	20 01.5	24 53.5	28 43.5
11 M	5 17 48	18 39 32	23 47 47	0♐26 43	21 59.2	23 35.2	8 03.0	7 20.6	11 54.3	6 42.4	6 16.5	1 39.7	15 34.3	19 59.4	24 53.6	28 45.0
12 Tu	5 21 45	19 40 33	7♐11 13	14 01 05	21 56.0	23 28.7	8 20.7	8 31.9	12 37.9	7 07.8	6 12.5	1 43.4	15 33.4	19 57.3	24 53.8	28 46.6
13 W	5 25 42	20 41 34	20 55 58	27 55 23	21 52.9	23 20.2	8R 28.9	9 43.4	13 21.5	7 33.0	6 08.7	1 47.2	15 32.6	19 55.3	24 54.0	28 48.2
14 Th	5 29 38	21 42 36	4♑58 46	12♑05 27	21 49.7	23 10.2	8 26.7	10 54.9	14 05.1	7 58.3	6 05.1	1 51.0	15 31.9	19 53.2	24 54.3	28 49.8
15 F	5 33 35	22 43 39	19 14 43	26 25 47	21 46.5	23 00.1	8 13.5	12 06.5	14 48.8	8 23.5	6 01.7	1 55.0	15 31.2	19 51.2	24 54.6	28 51.5
16 Sa	5 37 31	23 44 42	3♒37 54	10♒50 20	21 43.3	22 50.8	7 48.9	13 18.3	15 32.5	8 48.7	5 58.5	1 59.1	15 30.6	19 49.3	24 54.9	28 53.1
17 Su	5 41 28	24 45 46	18 02 27	25 13 38	21 40.2	22 43.5	7 12.6	14 30.1	16 16.3	9 13.9	5 55.5	2 03.2	15 30.0	19 47.4	24 55.2	28 54.8
18 M	5 45 24	25 46 50	2♓23 25	9♓31 24	21 37.0	22 38.8	6 25.0	15 42.0	17 00.1	9 39.0	5 52.7	2 07.4	15 29.4	19 45.5	24 55.6	28 56.5
19 Tu	5 49 21	26 47 54	16 37 17	23 40 54	21 33.8	22D 36.5	5 26.8	16 54.0	17 44.0	10 04.1	5 50.1	2 11.7	15 29.0	19 43.6	24 56.0	28 58.2
20 W	5 53 17	27 48 59	0♈42 06	7♈40 52	21 30.6	22 36.1	4 19.3	18 06.0	18 27.9	10 29.1	5 47.7	2 16.1	15 28.5	19 41.8	24 56.5	28 59.9
21 Th	5 57 14	28 50 04	14 37 10	21 31 01	21 27.5	22R 36.5	3 04.4	19 18.2	19 11.9	10 54.1	5 45.5	2 20.5	15 28.2	19 40.0	24 57.0	29 01.6
22 F	6 01 11	29 51 09	28 22 29	5♉11 35	21 24.3	22 36.5	1 44.3	20 30.4	19 55.9	11 19.1	5 43.5	2 25.1	15 27.8	19 38.3	24 57.5	29 03.4
23 Sa	6 05 07	0♑52 15	11♉58 19	18 42 40	21 21.1	22 34.9	0 21.8	21 42.7	20 39.9	11 44.0	5 41.7	2 29.7	15 27.6	19 36.6	24 58.0	29 05.1
24 Su	6 09 04	1 53 21	25 24 37	2♊04 04	21 17.9	22 30.8	28♐59.5	22 55.1	21 24.0	12 08.9	5 40.1	2 34.4	15 27.4	19 34.9	24 58.6	29 06.9
25 M	6 13 00	2 54 27	8♊40 56	15 15 05	21 14.8	22 23.7	27 40.3	24 07.5	22 08.2	12 33.8	5 38.7	2 39.2	15 27.2	19 33.3	24 59.3	29 08.7
26 Tu	6 16 57	3 55 33	21 46 22	28 14 39	21 11.6	22 13.7	26 26.6	25 20.1	22 52.4	12 58.6	5 37.6	2 44.0	15 27.1	19 31.7	24 59.9	29 10.5
27 W	6 20 53	4 56 40	4♋39 49	11♋01 44	21 08.4	22 01.5	25 20.3	26 32.7	23 36.6	13 23.3	5 36.6	2 48.9	15D 27.1	19 30.1	25 00.6	29 12.3
28 Th	6 24 50	5 57 47	17 20 20	23 35 36	21 05.2	21 48.0	24 23.1	27 45.3	24 20.9	13 48.1	5 35.9	2 53.9	15 27.1	19 28.6	25 01.3	29 14.1
29 F	6 28 47	6 58 54	29 47 32	5♌56 14	21 02.1	21 34.5	23 35.8	28 58.1	25 05.2	14 12.7	5 35.3	2 59.0	15 27.2	19 27.2	25 02.1	29 15.9
30 Sa	6 32 43	8 00 01	12♌01 51	18 04 36	20 58.9	21 22.2	22 59.0	0♐10.9	25 49.6	14 37.4	5 35.0	3 04.1	15 27.3	19 25.8	25 02.9	29 17.8
31 Su	6 36 40	9♑01 09	24 04 48	0♍02 46	20♈55.7	21♈12.0	22♐32.8	1♐23.8	26♐34.0	15♐02.0	5♉34.9	3♓09.3	15♈27.5	19♉24.4	25♓03.7	29♑19.6

1st of Month

Julian Day #
2460279.5
Obliquity
23°26′[illegible]8″
SVP 4♓55′[illegible]0″
GC 27♐10.4
Eris 24♈18.6R

Day	⚴
1	4♏59.4
6	7 05.9
11	9 10.9
16	11 14.1
21	13 15.3
26	15 14.3
31	17 11.0

Day	⚵
1	15♍36.2
6	16 53.0
11	18 02.3
16	19 03.6
21	19 56.2
26	20 39.7
31	21 13.5

Day	⚶
1	4♋39.3R
6	3 35.8R
11	2 25.2R
16	1 09.4R
21	29♊50.7R
26	28 31.7R
31	27 14.6R

DECLINATION and LATITUDE

Day	☉ Decl	☽ Decl	☽ Lat	☽ 12h Decl	☿ Decl	☿ Lat	♀ Decl	♀ Lat	♂ Decl	♂ Lat	⚳ Decl	⚳ Lat	♃ Decl	♃ Lat	♄ Decl	♄ Lat
1 F	21S43	26N45	5N08	25N35	25S51	2S25	7S53	2N09	21S19	0S15	17S59	2N44	12N37	1S20	12S39	1S41
2 Sa	21 53	24 09	5 03	22 27	25 49	2 23	8 17	2 10	21 27	0 15	18 05	2 42	12 36	1 20	12 38	1 41
3 Su	22 02	20 31	4 45	18 24	25 45	2 20	8 41	2 11	21 35	0 16	18 11	2 41	12 34	1 20	12 37	1 41
4 M	22 10	16 07	4 15	13 41	25 40	2 16	9 05	2 12	21 43	0 16	18 18	2 39	12 33	1 19	12 35	1 41
5 Tu	22 18	11 08	3 34	8 29	25 34	2 11	9 29	2 13	21 51	0 17	18 24	2 37	12 31	1 19	12 34	1 41
6 W	22 26	5 46	2 43	2 59	25 26	2 05	9 53	2 14	21 59	0 18	18 30	2 36	12 30	1 19	12 33	1 40
7 Th	22 33	0 09	1 46	2S42	25 17	1 58	10 16	2 14	22 06	0 18	18 36	2 34	12 28	1 18	12 32	1 40
8 F	22 40	5S33	0 42	8 23	25 07	1 50	10 40	2 15	22 13	0 19	18 42	2 33	12 27	1 18	12 30	1 40
9 Sa	22 46	11 11	0S24	13 53	24 56	1 41	11 03	2 15	22 20	0 19	18 48	2 31	12 26	1 18	12 29	1 40
10 Su	22 52	16 29	1 31	18 57	24 44	1 31	11 26	2 16	22 27	0 20	18 54	2 30	12 25	1 18	12 28	1 40
11 M	22 57	21 13	2 34	23 14	24 30	1 19	11 49	2 16	22 33	0 21	18 60	2 28	12 24	1 17	12 26	1 40
12 Tu	23 02	24 59	3 31	26 23	24 16	1 06	12 12	2 16	22 40	0 21	19 05	2 27	12 23	1 17	12 25	1 40
13 W	23 07	27 24	4 17	28 00	24 02	0 52	12 35	2 16	22 46	0 22	19 11	2 25	12 22	1 17	12 23	1 40
14 Th	23 11	28 09	4 49	27 50	23 46	0 36	12 57	2 16	22 52	0 22	19 17	2 23	12 21	1 17	12 22	1 40
15 F	23 14	27 03	5 03	25 50	23 30	0 19	13 19	2 15	22 57	0 23	19 22	2 22	12 20	1 16	12 20	1 40
16 Sa	23 17	24 10	4 59	22 09	23 14	0 01	13 41	2 15	23 03	0 24	19 28	2 20	12 19	1 16	12 19	1 39
17 Su	23 20	19 47	4 35	17 08	22 57	0N18	14 03	2 15	23 08	0 24	19 33	2 19	12 18	1 16	12 17	1 39
18 M	23 22	14 16	3 54	11 13	22 39	0 38	14 24	2 14	23 13	0 25	19 38	2 17	12 18	1 15	12 16	1 39
19 Tu	23 24	8 02	2 59	4 46	22 22	0 58	14 45	2 13	23 18	0 25	19 43	2 16	12 17	1 15	12 14	1 39
20 W	23 25	1 28	1 54	1N51	22 04	1 18	15 06	2 13	23 22	0 26	19 48	2 14	12 17	1 15	12 12	1 39
21 Th	23 26	5N07	0 42	8 18	21 47	1 37	15 26	2 12	23 26	0 27	19 53	2 13	12 16	1 14	12 11	1 39
22 F	23 26	11 22	0N31	14 18	21 30	1 55	15 46	2 11	23 30	0 27	19 58	2 11	12 16	1 14	12 09	1 39
23 Sa	23 26	17 02	1 41	19 32	21 14	2 12	16 06	2 10	23 34	0 28	20 03	2 09	12 15	1 14	12 07	1 39
24 Su	23 25	21 47	2 45	23 44	20 59	2 27	16 25	2 09	23 38	0 28	20 08	2 08	12 15	1 14	12 05	1 39
25 M	23 24	25 21	3 39	26 37	20 45	2 40	16 44	2 08	23 41	0 29	20 13	2 06	12 15	1 13	12 04	1 39
26 Tu	23 23	27 30	4 20	28 01	20 33	2 50	17 03	2 06	23 44	0 30	20 17	2 05	12 15	1 13	12 02	1 39
27 W	23 21	28 08	4 47	27 53	20 24	2 58	17 21	2 05	23 47	0 30	20 22	2 03	12 15	1 13	12 00	1 38
28 Th	23 18	27 16	4 60	26 18	20 16	3 03	17 39	2 03	23 50	0 31	20 26	2 02	12 15	1 12	11 58	1 38
29 F	23 15	25 02	4 58	23 29	20 11	3 06	17 57	2 02	23 52	0 31	20 31	2 00	12 15	1 12	11 56	1 38
30 Sa	23 12	21 41	4 42	19 40	20 08	3 07	18 14	2 00	23 54	0 32	20 35	1 59	12 15	1 12	11 54	1 38
31 Su	23S08	17N28	4N13	15N07	20S08	3N06	18S30	1N59	23S56	0S32	20S40	1N57	12N16	1S11	11S52	1S38

Day	⚷ Decl	⚷ Lat	♅ Decl	♅ Lat	♆ Decl	♆ Lat	♇ Decl	♇ Lat
1	7N31	1N26	17N32	0S19	3S11	1S15	23S09	2S45
6	7 28	1 25	17 29	0 19	3 11	1 15	23 08	2 45
11	7 26	1 24	17 26	0 19	3 11	1 15	23 06	2 45
16	7 24	1 24	17 24	0 19	3 10	1 15	23 05	2 45
21	7 22	1 23	17 21	0 19	3 09	1 15	23 03	2 45
26	7 21	1 22	17 19	0 18	3 08	1 14	23 01	2 46
31	7N20	1N22	17N17	0S18	3S06	1S14	22S60	2S46

Day	⚴ Decl	⚴ Lat	⚵ Decl	⚵ Lat	⚶ Decl	⚶ Lat	Eris Decl	Eris Lat
1	0N21	14N19	0S21	6S32	19N42	3S40	0S52	11S03
6	0 19	14 59	0 45	6 26	19 53	3 30	0 52	11 02
11	0 21	15 41	1 06	6 20	20 05	3 20	0 52	11 02
16	0 25	16 23	1 24	6 14	20 18	3 08	0 52	11 01
21	0 33	17 07	1 38	6 07	20 31	2 56	0 52	11 00
26	0 44	17 52	1 48	5 59	20 44	2 42	0 52	10 60
31	0N59	18N39	1S54	5S51	20N57	2S27	0S51	10S59

Moon Phenomena

Max/0 Decl
dy hr mn
7 0:37 0 S
13 21:54 28S10
20 5:18 0 N
26 21:52 28N09

Max/0 Lat
dy hr mn
1 4:08 5N08
8 15:25 0 S
15 6:13 5S04
21 13:55 0 N
28 8:24 5N01

Perigee/Apogee
dy hr m kilometers
4 18:43 a 404345
16 18:54 p 367902

PH dy hr mn
☾ 5 5:50 12♍49
● 12 23:33 20♐40
☽ 19 18:40 27♓35
○ 27 0:34 4♋58

Void of Course Moon

Last Aspect	☽ Ingress
1 13:08 ♇ ☍	♌ 1 16:02
4 2:12 ♀ ⚹	♍ 4 3:51
6 13:51 ♇ △	♎ 6 16:36
9 1:06 ♇ □	♏ 9 3:36
11 8:58 ♇ ⚹	♐ 11 11:12
13 6:50 ♆ □	♑ 13 15:33
15 16:05 ♇ ☌	♒ 15 17:57
17 12:05 ☉ ⚹	♓ 17 19:59
19 21:05 ♇ ⚹	♈ 19 22:48
22 2:48 ☉ △	♉ 22 2:51
24 6:41 ♇ △	♊ 24 8:16
26 7:57 ☿ ☍	♋ 26 15:16
28 22:58 ♇ ☍	♌ 29 0:24
31 5:19 ♂ △	♍ 31 11:54

DAILY ASPECTARIAN

1 F
☉⚼☽ 3:43
☽△♆ 6:06
☽□♀ 8:10
☽⋕☿ 9:39
☽☍♇ 13:08
☿ ♑ 14:33
☽⚻☿ 16:11
☽⚻♄ 18:18
☽△⚳ 21:37

2 Sa
☽△♂ 2:49
☽□♃ 5:46
☽⋕♇ 7:17
☽⚼♆ 11:31
☉△☽ 11:46
☉⋕☽ 15:05
☿⚹♄ 15:28
☽⋕♂ 17:44
☽△⚷ 23:07

3 Su
☽⚼☿ 0:59
☽□♅ 8:14
☽⋕⚳ 12:51
♀□♇ 13:31
☽∥♅ 16:48
☽⚻♆ 17:32
♂⚻♃ 23:21

4 M
☽⚻♇ 0:59
☽⚹♀ 2:12
☽⚼⚷ 5:15
☽☍♄ 6:28
☽△☿ 10:13
☽□⚳ 11:52
☽⋕♄ 17:18
☽∥♃ 17:31
☽△♃ 17:34
♀ ♏ 18:52
☽□♂ 18:53

5 Tu
☉□☽ 5:50
☊ D 6:03
☽⋕♀ 7:02
☽⚼♇ 7:27
☽⚻⚷ 11:38
☽∠♀ 11:59
☽∥⚷ 16:30
☿⚺⚳ 19:35
☽△♅ 20:46
♀△♄ 22:53
☽⚼♃ 23:46

6 W
☉∠♇ 1:03
☽☍♆ 6:18
☽⋕♆ 11:08
☿⚼♅ 12:26
♆ D 13:23
☽△♇ 13:51
☽⚻♄ 19:27
☽⚺♀ 21:35

7 Th
☽⚹⚳ 2:45
☽⚼♅ 2:52
☽□☿ 4:01
☽⚻♃ 5:43
☽⚹♂ 11:17
☽∥♆ 14:00
☉⚹☽ 23:38
☽☍⚷ 23:41

8 F
☉△⚷ 0:13
☽⚼♄ 1:23
☿△♃ 4:10
☽⋕⚷ 8:00
☽⚻♅ 8:26
☽∠⚳ 9:27
☊ R 15:25
☽⚻♆ 17:46
☽∠♂ 18:33
☽∥♀ 23:25

9 Sa
☽□♇ 1:06
☽⋕♃ 5:28
☽∥♄ 5:42
☽△♄ 6:35
☉∠☽ 7:18
☽☌♀ 14:25
☽⚺⚳ 15:16
☽☍♃ 15:43
☽⚹☿ 17:48
☽⚼♆ 22:20

10 Su
☽⚺♂ 0:48
⚳⚻♃ 2:55
♀☍♃ 3:36
♀⚺⚳ 4:02
☽⋕♅ 4:33
☽⚻⚷ 8:56
☽∥⚳ 12:00
☉⚺☽ 13:49
☽☍♅ 17:04
☽∠☿ 22:36

11 M
☽△♆ 2:00
☽∥♂ 8:00
☽⚹♇ 8:58
☉∥☽ 10:28
☽∥♇ 11:08
☽⚼⚷ 12:13
☽□♄ 14:14
☽∥☿ 19:13
☿⚹♀ 19:18
☽⚻♃ 22:17
☽☌⚳ 23:54

12 Tu
☽⚺☿ 2:05
☽⚺♀ 2:36
☉⚻♅ 6:23
☽☌♂ 10:07
♀⋕♃ 10:35
☽∠♇ 11:36
♀∥♄ 12:41
☽△⚷ 14:40
☉∥♇ 17:56
☽⚻♅ 22:15
☉☌☽ 23:33

13 W
☽⚼♃ 0:22
♀⚼♆ 3:35
☽□♆ 6:50
☽∠♀ 7:08
☿ R 7:10
☉⚼♃ 10:05
☽⚺♇ 13:32
♂∠♇ 15:17
☽⚹♄ 18:40
☽⚼♅ 23:51

14 Th
☽△♃ 1:52
☽⚺⚳ 5:13
☽☌☿ 5:48
☽⚹♀ 10:56
☽⚺♂ 16:10
☽□⚷ 17:46
☿⚺⚳ 18:23
☽∠♄ 20:05

15 F
☽△♅ 1:01
☉⚺☽ 6:16
☽∠⚳ 7:08
☽⚹♆ 9:28
☽☌♇ 16:05
☽∠♂ 18:35
♃⋕♄ 18:58
☉∥☿ 19:12
☽⚺♄ 21:15
♂△⚷ 22:56

16 Sa
☽□♃ 3:53
☉∥☽ 5:25
☽∥☿ 6:18
☽⚺☿ 6:43
☽∥♇ 6:45
☽∥♂ 6:47
♂∥♇ 8:21
☽⚹⚳ 8:53
☉∠☽ 9:10
☽∠♆ 10:28
☿∥♂ 11:45
☿∥♇ 12:53
☽□♀ 17:34
☽⚹⚷ 19:46
☽⚹♂ 20:54

17 Su
☽∥⚳ 1:05
☽□♅ 2:55
☉□♆ 3:44
☽∠☿ 6:37
☽⋕♅ 10:56
☽⚺♆ 11:30
☉⚹☽ 12:05
☽⚺♇ 18:12
♀⚻⚷ 19:51
☽∠⚷ 20:49
☽∥♀ 23:29
☽☌♄ 23:33

18 M
☽⚹♃ 5:51
☽⚹☿ 6:22
☽⋕♃ 7:50
☽∥♄ 7:59
☽□⚳ 12:35
☿△♃ 14:29
☽∠♇ 19:30
☽⚺⚷ 22:04

19 Tu
☽△♀ 0:31
☽□♂ 1:59
☽⋕⚷ 2:26
☽⚹♅ 5:16
☽∠♃ 7:08
☽☌♆ 14:09
☿⚼♅ 16:07
☽∥♆ 17:52
☊ D 18:34
☉□☽ 18:40
☽⚹♇ 21:05

20 W
☽⚺♄ 2:42
☽⚼♀ 4:30
☽□☿ 5:43
☽∠♅ 6:51
☽⚺♃ 8:44
⚶ R♊ 9:57
☿∠♀ 12:05
☽⋕♆ 16:46
☽△⚳ 17:22
♀⚺♂ 18:39
☉∥♂ 21:17

21 Th
☽☌⚷ 1:28
☉⚺♇ 4:40
☽∠♄ 4:45
♀☍♅ 7:05
☽△♂ 8:24
☽∥⚷ 8:27
☽⚺♅ 8:45
☽⚻♀ 8:55
☿⚹♄ 12:34
☊ R 13:54
♂⚻♅ 14:45
☽⚺♆ 18:01
☽⚼⚳ 20:17

22 F
☽□♇ 1:12
☉△☽ 2:48
☽⋕♄ 3:07
☉ ♑ 3:28
☽∥♃ 3:35
☽△☿ 5:22
☽⚹♄ 7:09
☽⚼♂ 12:12
☽☌♃ 12:55
☉☌☿ 18:55
☽⋕♀ 19:34
☽∠♆ 20:26
☽⚻⚳ 23:34

23 Sa
♂⚼♃ 0:55
☽∥♅ 1:25
☽⚼☿ 5:28
☽⚺⚷ 6:12
☿R♐ 6:19
☉⚼☽ 7:30
☽☌♅ 13:35
☽⋕⚳ 14:55
☽⚻♂ 16:23
☽☍♀ 19:05
☽⋕☿ 19:48
☿⚺♇ 21:52
☽⚹♆ 23:13

24 Su
☽⚻☿ 5:51
☽△♇ 6:41
☽⋕♇ 7:31
☽∠⚷ 9:05
☉⋕☽ 9:59
☽⋕♂ 11:33
☉⚻☽ 12:39
☽□♄ 12:59
☉⚹♄ 17:29
☽⚺♃ 18:29

25 M
☽☍⚳ 7:19
☽⚼♇ 10:00
☽⚹⚷ 12:22
♀△♆ 17:16
☽⚺♅ 19:52
☽∠♃ 21:53

26 Tu
☽☍♂ 2:09
☽□♆ 5:59
☽⚻♀ 7:16
☽☍☿ 7:57
☿⚺♀ 11:19
☽⚻♇ 13:46
☉⚼♅ 13:50
♀⋕♅ 20:24
☽△♄ 20:31
☽∠♅ 23:42

27 W
☉☍☽ 0:34
☽⚹♃ 1:47
☿∥⚳ 3:02
⚷ D 3:11
☿□♆ 7:44
☽⚼♀ 14:21
☉△♃ 15:29
☽⚻⚳ 17:02
☽□⚷ 20:24

28 Th
☿☌♂ 0:32
☽⚼♄ 1:05
☽⚹♅ 4:05
☽⚻☿ 12:41
☽⚻♂ 14:18
☽△♆ 14:46
☽△♀ 22:13
♂□♆ 22:17
☽⚼⚳ 22:50
☽☍♇ 22:58

29 F
⚳∠♇ 3:21
♀⚹♇ 6:02
☽⚻♄ 6:16
☽⋕♂ 9:08
☽□♃ 11:19
☉⋕☽ 13:52
☉⚻☽ 15:20
☽⋕♇ 15:23
☽⚼☿ 16:22
☽⚼♆ 20:05
♀ ♐ 20:25
☽⚼♂ 21:28

30 Sa
☽△⚳ 5:19
♀⚼⚷ 5:26
☽⋕⚳ 6:35
☽△⚷ 6:47
☽⋕☿ 9:24
☽□♅ 14:40
☽⋕♀ 18:50
☽△☿ 21:01
☉⚼☽ 23:52

31 Su
☽∥♅ 0:59
☽⚻♆ 1:58
♃ D 2:42
☽△♂ 5:19
☽⚻♇ 10:35
☽⚼⚷ 12:50
☽□♀ 16:24
☽☍♄ 18:25
☽△♃ 23:11

January 2024

LONGITUDE

Day	Sid.Time	☉	☽	☽ 12 hour	Mean ☊	True ☊	☿	♀	♂	⚳	♃	♄	⚷	♅	♆	♇
	h m s	° ′ ″	° ′ ″	° ′ ″	° ′	° ′	° ′	° ′	° ′	° ′	° ′	° ′	° ′	° ′	° ′	° ′
1 M	6 40 36	10♑02 18	5♍58 58	11♍53 51	20♈52.5	21♈04.6	22♐16.9	2♐36.7	27♐18.5	15♐26.5	5♉34.9	3♓14.6	15♈27.8	19♉23.0	25♓04.6	29♑21.5
2 Tu	6 44 33	11 03 26	17 47 59	23 41 57	20 49.3	20R 59.9	22D 10.9	3 49.7	28 03.0	15 51.0	5 35.2	3 20.0	15 28.0	19R 21.7	25 05.5	29 23.3
3 W	6 48 29	12 04 35	29 36 22	5♎31 54	20 46.2	20 57.7	22 14.3	5 02.7	28 47.5	16 15.4	5 35.7	3 25.4	15 28.4	19 20.5	25 06.4	29 25.2
4 Th	6 52 26	13 05 44	11♎29 15	17 29 06	20 43.0	20 57.1	22 26.2	6 15.8	29 32.1	16 39.8	5 36.4	3 30.8	15 28.8	19 19.3	25 07.3	29 27.1
5 F	6 56 22	14 06 53	23 32 11	29 39 10	20 39.8	20 57.2	22 46.0	7 29.0	0♑16.8	17 04.2	5 37.3	3 36.4	15 29.3	19 18.1	25 08.3	29 29.0
6 Sa	7 00 19	15 08 03	5♏50 44	12♏07 30	20 36.6	20 56.5	23 12.9	8 42.2	1 01.5	17 28.5	5 38.5	3 42.0	15 29.8	19 17.0	25 09.3	29 30.9
7 Su	7 04 16	16 09 13	18 30 02	24 58 48	20 33.5	20 54.2	23 46.3	9 55.5	1 46.2	17 52.7	5 39.8	3 47.6	15 30.4	19 16.0	25 10.4	29 32.8
8 M	7 08 12	17 10 23	1♐34 11	8♐16 25	20 30.3	20 49.3	24 25.5	11 08.8	2 31.0	18 16.9	5 41.3	3 53.4	15 31.0	19 15.0	25 11.5	29 34.7
9 Tu	7 12 09	18 11 33	15 05 34	22 01 33	20 27.1	20 41.5	25 09.9	12 22.1	3 15.8	18 41.0	5 43.1	3 59.2	15 31.7	19 14.0	25 12.6	29 36.6
10 W	7 16 05	19 12 43	29 04 05	6♑12 41	20 23.9	20 31.2	25 58.9	13 35.5	4 00.7	19 05.1	5 45.0	4 05.0	15 32.4	19 13.1	25 13.7	29 38.5
11 Th	7 20 02	20 13 54	13♑26 42	20 45 18	20 20.8	20 19.2	26 52.1	14 49.0	4 45.6	19 29.1	5 47.1	4 10.9	15 33.2	19 12.2	25 14.9	29 40.5
12 F	7 23 58	21 15 04	28 07 29	5♒32 12	20 17.6	20 06.7	27 49.0	16 02.4	5 30.5	19 53.0	5 49.5	4 16.9	15 34.1	19 11.4	25 16.1	29 42.4
13 Sa	7 27 55	22 16 13	12♒58 19	20 24 41	20 14.4	19 55.1	28 49.2	17 16.0	6 15.5	20 16.9	5 52.1	4 22.9	15 35.0	19 10.6	25 17.4	29 44.3
14 Su	7 31 51	23 17 22	27 50 14	5♓13 59	20 11.2	19 45.7	29 52.3	18 29.5	7 00.6	20 40.7	5 54.8	4 29.0	15 35.9	19 09.9	25 18.6	29 46.3
15 M	7 35 48	24 18 30	12♓35 04	19 52 48	20 08.1	19 39.1	0♑58.2	19 43.1	7 45.6	21 04.5	5 57.8	4 35.1	15 36.9	19 09.3	25 19.9	29 48.2
16 Tu	7 39 45	25 19 38	27 06 38	4♈16 11	20 04.9	19 35.5	2 06.4	20 56.7	8 30.7	21 28.2	6 00.9	4 41.3	15 38.0	19 08.6	25 21.2	29 50.2
17 W	7 43 41	26 20 45	11♈21 16	18 21 45	20 01.7	19D 34.2	3 16.8	22 10.3	9 15.9	21 51.8	6 04.2	4 47.6	15 39.1	19 08.1	25 22.6	29 52.1
18 Th	7 47 38	27 21 51	25 17 41	2♉09 12	19 58.5	19R 34.1	4 29.1	23 24.0	10 01.0	22 15.3	6 07.8	4 53.8	15 40.3	19 07.6	25 24.0	29 54.1
19 F	7 51 34	28 22 57	8♉56 26	15 39 38	19 55.3	19 33.8	5 43.2	24 37.7	10 46.3	22 38.8	6 11.5	5 00.2	15 41.5	19 07.1	25 25.4	29 56.0
20 Sa	7 55 31	29 24 01	22 19 02	28 54 51	19 52.2	19 32.1	6 58.9	25 51.4	11 31.5	23 02.2	6 15.5	5 06.6	15 42.8	19 06.7	25 26.8	29 58.0
21 Su	7 59 27	0♒25 05	5♊27 20	11♊56 41	19 49.0	19 27.8	8 16.1	27 05.2	12 16.8	23 25.5	6 19.6	5 13.0	15 44.1	19 06.3	25 28.3	29 59.9
22 M	8 03 24	1 26 08	18 23 04	24 46 39	19 45.8	19 20.6	9 34.6	28 19.0	13 02.1	23 48.8	6 23.9	5 19.5	15 45.5	19 06.0	25 29.8	0♒01.9
23 Tu	8 07 20	2 27 10	1♋07 32	7♋25 48	19 42.6	19 10.5	10 54.5	29 32.8	13 47.5	24 12.0	6 28.4	5 26.0	15 46.9	19 05.8	25 31.3	0 03.8
24 W	8 11 17	3 28 11	13 41 31	19 54 45	19 39.5	18 58.1	12 15.4	0♑46.6	14 32.9	24 35.1	6 33.0	5 32.5	15 48.4	19 05.6	25 32.8	0 05.8
25 Th	8 15 14	4 29 11	26 05 31	2♌13 54	19 36.3	18 44.4	13 37.5	2 00.4	15 18.3	24 58.1	6 37.9	5 39.1	15 49.9	19 05.5	25 34.4	0 07.7
26 F	8 19 10	5 30 11	8♌19 55	14 23 41	19 33.1	18 30.5	15 00.6	3 14.3	16 03.8	25 21.0	6 42.9	5 45.8	15 51.5	19 05.4	25 36.0	0 09.7
27 Sa	8 23 07	6 31 10	20 25 17	26 24 54	19 29.9	18 17.8	16 24.7	4 28.2	16 49.3	25 43.9	6 48.1	5 52.5	15 53.1	19D 05.3	25 37.6	0 11.6
28 Su	8 27 03	7 32 07	2♍22 43	8♍18 59	19 26.8	18 07.1	17 49.8	5 42.2	17 34.9	26 06.7	6 53.5	5 59.2	15 54.8	19 05.3	25 39.3	0 13.6
29 M	8 31 00	8 33 05	14 13 59	20 08 05	19 23.6	17 59.2	19 15.7	6 56.1	18 20.4	26 29.4	6 59.1	6 05.9	15 56.5	19 05.4	25 40.9	0 15.5
30 Tu	8 34 56	9 34 01	26 01 41	1♎55 15	19 20.4	17 54.1	20 42.5	8 10.1	19 06.1	26 52.0	7 04.8	6 12.7	15 58.3	19 05.5	25 42.6	0 17.4
31 W	8 38 53	10♒34 56	7♎49 17	13 44 21	19♈17.2	17♈51.6	22♑10.1	9♑24.1	19♑51.7	27♐14.6	7♉10.8	6♓19.5	16♈00.1	19♉05.7	25♓44.3	0♒19.4

1st of Month

Julian Day # 2460310.5
Obliquity 23°26[illegible]8"
SVP 4♓55[illegible]4"
GC 27♐10.5
Eris 24♈09.9R

Day	⚴	⚵	⚶
1	17♏34.1	21♍19.1	26♊59.7R
6	19 27.6	21 40.5	25 48.1R
11	21 18.3	21 51.1	24 43.3R
16	23 05.7	21 50.4R	23 47.0R
21	24 49.6	21 38.4R	23 00.7R
26	26 29.6	21 15.1R	22 25.1R
31	28 05.3	20 40.8R	22 00.6R

DECLINATION and LATITUDE

Day	☉ Decl	☽ Decl	☽ Lat	☽ 12h Decl	☿ Decl	☿ Lat	♀ Decl	♀ Lat	♂ Decl	♂ Lat	⚳ Decl	⚳ Lat	♃ Decl	♃ Lat	♄ Decl	♄ Lat
1 M	23S04	12N38	3N34	10N02	20S09	3N04	18S46	1N57	23S58	0S33	20S44	1N56	12N16	1S11	11S50	1S38
2 Tu	22 59	7 22	2 46	4 38	20 13	2 60	19 02	1 55	23 59	0 34	20 48	1 54	12 16	1 11	11 48	1 38
3 W	22 53	1 51	1 50	0S58	20 18	2 55	19 17	1 53	24 00	0 34	20 52	1 52	12 17	1 11	11 46	1 38
4 Th	22 48	3S47	0 50	6 35	20 25	2 49	19 31	1 51	24 01	0 35	20 56	1 51	12 17	1 10	11 44	1 38
5 F	22 41	9 21	0S14	12 04	20 33	2 42	19 46	1 49	24 02	0 35	20 60	1 49	12 18	1 10	11 42	1 38
6 Sa	22 35	14 42	1 18	17 13	20 42	2 34	19 59	1 47	24 02	0 36	21 04	1 48	12 18	1 10	11 40	1 38
7 Su	22 28	19 35	2 20	21 45	20 51	2 26	20 12	1 45	24 02	0 37	21 07	1 46	12 19	1 09	11 38	1 38
8 M	22 20	23 41	3 17	25 20	21 02	2 18	20 25	1 43	24 02	0 37	21 11	1 45	12 20	1 09	11 36	1 38
9 Tu	22 12	26 39	4 05	27 35	21 12	2 09	20 37	1 41	24 02	0 38	21 15	1 43	12 21	1 09	11 34	1 38
10 W	22 04	28 06	4 40	28 08	21 23	1 60	20 48	1 38	24 01	0 38	21 18	1 41	12 22	1 08	11 31	1 37
11 Th	21 55	27 42	4 58	26 46	21 33	1 51	20 59	1 36	23 60	0 39	21 22	1 40	12 23	1 08	11 29	1 37
12 F	21 46	25 23	4 57	23 33	21 44	1 41	21 09	1 34	23 59	0 39	21 25	1 38	12 24	1 08	11 27	1 37
13 Sa	21 36	21 20	4 36	18 46	21 54	1 32	21 19	1 31	23 57	0 40	21 29	1 37	12 25	1 07	11 25	1 37
14 Su	21 26	15 56	3 57	12 52	22 03	1 23	21 28	1 29	23 56	0 41	21 32	1 35	12 26	1 07	11 22	1 37
15 M	21 15	9 38	3 02	6 18	22 13	1 14	21 37	1 26	23 54	0 41	21 35	1 33	12 27	1 07	11 20	1 37
16 Tu	21 04	2 55	1 56	0N28	22 21	1 04	21 44	1 24	23 51	0 42	21 38	1 32	12 29	1 07	11 18	1 37
17 W	20 53	3N50	0 43	7 06	22 29	0 55	21 52	1 21	23 49	0 42	21 41	1 30	12 30	1 06	11 16	1 37
18 Th	20 41	10 15	0N30	13 15	22 36	0 46	21 58	1 18	23 46	0 43	21 44	1 29	12 32	1 06	11 13	1 37
19 F	20 29	16 04	1 41	18 39	22 42	0 37	22 04	1 16	23 43	0 43	21 47	1 27	12 33	1 06	11 11	1 37
20 Sa	20 17	20 59	2 44	23 02	22 47	0 28	22 10	1 13	23 40	0 44	21 50	1 25	12 35	1 05	11 08	1 37
21 Su	20 04	24 46	3 37	26 10	22 51	0 20	22 14	1 10	23 36	0 44	21 53	1 24	12 36	1 05	11 06	1 37
22 M	19 50	27 13	4 18	27 54	22 54	0 11	22 18	1 07	23 33	0 45	21 56	1 22	12 38	1 05	11 04	1 37
23 Tu	19 37	28 12	4 46	28 08	22 57	0 03	22 22	1 04	23 29	0 45	21 58	1 21	12 40	1 04	11 01	1 37
24 W	19 23	27 42	4 59	26 55	22 58	0S05	22 25	1 02	23 24	0 46	22 01	1 19	12 41	1 04	10 59	1 37
25 Th	19 08	25 48	4 58	24 24	22 58	0 13	22 27	0 59	23 20	0 47	22 03	1 17	12 43	1 04	10 56	1 37
26 F	18 54	22 44	4 43	20 49	22 57	0 21	22 28	0 56	23 15	0 47	22 06	1 16	12 45	1 04	10 54	1 37
27 Sa	18 39	18 43	4 15	16 26	22 54	0 29	22 29	0 53	23 10	0 48	22 08	1 14	12 47	1 03	10 51	1 37
28 Su	18 23	13 60	3 37	11 27	22 51	0 36	22 29	0 50	23 05	0 48	22 11	1 12	12 49	1 03	10 49	1 37
29 M	18 07	8 48	2 49	6 05	22 46	0 43	22 28	0 47	22 59	0 49	22 13	1 11	12 51	1 03	10 46	1 37
30 Tu	17 51	3 19	1 53	0 31	22 40	0 50	22 27	0 44	22 53	0 49	22 15	1 09	12 53	1 03	10 44	1 37
31 W	17S35	2S17	0N53	5S05	22S33	0S56	22S25	0N41	22S47	0S50	22S17	1N07	12N56	1S02	10S41	1S37

Day	⚷ Decl	⚷ Lat	♅ Decl	♅ Lat	♆ Decl	♆ Lat	♇ Decl	♇ Lat
1	7N20	1N21	17N17	0S18	3S06	1S14	22S59	2S46
6	7 21	1 21	17 15	0 18	3 03	1 14	22 58	2 46
11	7 21	1 20	17 14	0 18	3 01	1 14	22 56	2 47
16	7 22	1 19	17 13	0 18	2 58	1 14	22 54	2 47
21	7 24	1 19	17 13	0 18	2 56	1 14	22 53	2 47
26	7 26	1 18	17 13	0 18	2 52	1 13	22 51	2 48
31	7N29	1N17	17N13	0S18	2S49	1S13	22S49	2S48

Day	⚴ Decl	⚴ Lat	⚵ Decl	⚵ Lat	⚶ Decl	⚶ Lat	Eris Decl	Eris Lat
1	1N02	18N49	1S55	5S49	20N60	2S24	0S51	10S59
6	1 21	19 38	1 54	5 40	21 13	2 09	0 51	10 58
11	1 44	20 29	1 49	5 30	21 26	1 54	0 50	10 57
16	2 10	21 21	1 38	5 18	21 39	1 39	0 49	10 57
21	2 41	22 16	1 22	5 06	21 51	1 24	0 49	10 56
26	3 15	23 13	1 00	4 52	22 04	1 10	0 48	10 55
31	3N54	24N11	0S33	4S37	22N16	0S56	0S47	10S54

Moon Phenomena

Max/0 Decl

dy	hr mn	
3	7:54	0 S
10	7:05	28S10
16	10:19	0 N
23	3:42	28N13
30	14:13	0 S

Max/0 Lat

dy	hr mn	
4	18:54	0 S
11	11:08	5S00
17	14:05	0 N
24	10:00	5N00
31	20:19	0 S

Perigee/Apogee

dy	hr m		kilometers
1	15:29	a	404908
13	10:37	p	362270
29	8:15	a	405777

PH	dy	hr mn	
☾	4	3:32	13♎15
●	11	11:58	20♑44
☽	18	3:54	27♈32
○	25	17:55	5♌15

Void of Course Moon

Last Aspect				☽ Ingress		
2	23:37	♇	△	♎	3	0:48
5	11:42	♇	□	♏	5	12:41
7	20:23	♇	⚹	♐	7	21:10
9	18:26	☿	☌	♑	10	1:34
12	2:34	♇	☌	♒	12	3:02
13	10:00	♅	□	♓	14	3:30
16	4:34	♇	⚹	♈	16	4:50
18	8:04	♇	□	♉	18	8:13
20	13:58	☉	△	♊	20	13:59
22	20:41	♀	☍	♋	22	21:52
24	22:59	♆	△	♌	25	7:38
26	21:20	♅	□	♍	27	19:12
29	23:21	♆	☍	♎	30	8:05

DAILY ASPECTARIAN

1 M: ⚳△⚷ 1:14; ☽∥♃ 1:44; ☽#♄ 3:45; ☉△☽ 9:00; ♀□♄ 13:27; ☽⚼♇ 17:03; ☽⚻⚷ 19:15; ☽□⚳ 19:54; ☉∥♇ 21:59

2 Tu: ☽∥⚷ 0:07; ☿ D 3:09; ☽△♅ 3:10; ☽⚼♃ 5:40; ☽□☿ 8:55; ☽☍♆ 14:51; ☽#♆ 18:42; ☽□♂ 22:14; ☽△♇ 23:37

3 W: ☽⚻♄ 7:48; ☽⚼♅ 9:35; ♀⚻♃ 10:56; ☽⚻♃ 12:08; ☽⚹♀ 12:17; ☽∥♆ 21:00; ♂⚺♇ 21:10

4 Th: ☉□☽ 3:32; ☽☍⚷ 8:00; ☽⚹⚳ 10:43; ☽⚼♄ 14:09; ♂ ♑ 14:59; ☽#⚷ 15:16; ☽⚻♅ 15:38; ☽∠♀ 21:41; ☽⚹☿ 22:26

5 F: ☽⚻♆ 3:10; ☽∥♄ 10:18; ☽□♇ 11:42; ☽#♃ 13:03; ☽⚹♂ 14:04; ☽∠⚳ 17:16; ☽△♄ 19:50; ☽☍♃ 23:36

6 Sa: ☽∠☿ 4:45; ☽⚺♀ 6:04; ☽⚼♆ 8:16; ☉□⚷ 8:36; ☽#♅ 12:11; ☽⚻⚷ 18:23; ☉⚹☽ 19:13; ☽∠♂ 20:34; ☽⚺⚳ 22:48

7 Su: ☽☍♅ 1:26; ☽∥♀ 3:31; ☽∥☿ 7:12; ☽∥⚳ 8:32; ☽⚺☿ 10:16; ☽△♆ 12:22; ☉∥☽ 15:43; ☽∥♇ 19:14; ☽⚹♇ 20:23; ☽⚼⚷ 22:06

8 M: ☉∠☽ 1:11; ☽⚺♂ 1:48; ☽∥♂ 2:19; ☽□♄ 4:12; ☽⚻♃ 7:25; ☽☌♀ 18:46; ☽∠♇ 23:09

9 Tu: ☽△⚷ 0:46; ☿□♆ 1:25; ☉⚺☽ 5:49; ☽☌⚳ 6:25; ☽⚻♅ 7:11; ☿∥⚳ 8:59; ☽⚼♃ 9:46; ☽□♆ 17:28; ☽☌☿ 18:26; ☉⚺⚳ 19:03; ☉∠♄ 20:40

10 W: ☉△♅ 0:08; ☽⚺♇ 0:58; ♂⚹♄ 2:41; ♂⚼♅ 6:31; ⚳⚻♅ 7:44; ☽⚹♄ 8:30; ☽⚼♅ 8:39; ☽☌♂ 8:47; ☽△♃ 11:15; ♀∠♇ 21:09

11 Th: ☽⚺♀ 2:28; ☽□⚷ 3:29; ☽△♅ 9:27; ☽∠♄ 9:29; ☽⚺⚳ 10:12; ☉☌☽ 11:58; ♀△⚷ 14:37; ☽⚹♆ 19:21; ☽⚺☿ 23:28

12 F: ☉∥☿ 2:15; ☽☌♇ 2:34; ☽∠♀ 5:09; ☽∥♂ 9:28; ☽⚺♄ 10:02; ♂△♃ 10:43; ☽∠⚳ 11:15; ☽□♃ 12:30; ☽⚺♂ 12:35; ☽∥♇ 15:36; ☽∠♆ 19:40; ☽∥☿ 21:13; ☉∥☽ 22:37; ☽∥⚳ 23:17

13 Sa: ☽∥♀ 0:05; ☽∠☿ 1:28; ☽⚹⚷ 4:13; ⚵ R 4:56; ☽⚹♀ 7:33; ☽□♅ 10:00; ☽⚹⚳ 12:07; ☉∥⚳ 13:13; ☽∠♂ 14:05; ☉⚺☽ 16:06; ☽#♅ 18:39; ☽⚺♆ 19:54; ☉∥♀ 21:09; ☿⚺♇ 21:41

14 Su: ☿ ♑ 2:51; ☽⚺♇ 3:08; ☽⚹☿ 3:33; ☽∠⚷ 4:29; ☽☌♄ 10:51; ♀⚻♅ 13:04; ☽⚹♃ 13:09; ☽#♃ 13:35; ☽⚹♂ 15:42; ⚳⚼♃ 16:13; ♀∥⚳ 16:58; ☽∥♄ 17:42; ☉∠☽ 18:15

15 M: ☽∠♇ 3:39; ☽⚺⚷ 4:59; ☽#⚷ 8:12; ☽⚹♅ 10:48; ☽□♀ 12:49; ☽∠♃ 13:50; ☽□⚳ 14:22; ☉⚹☽ 20:48; ☽☌♆ 21:04; ☽∥♆ 23:48

16 Tu: ☉⚹♆ 0:39; ♀⚼♃ 1:26; ☽⚹♇ 4:34; ☽□☿ 9:06; ☽∠♅ 11:47; ☽⚺♄ 12:48; ☽⚺♃ 15:00; ♀☌⚳ 15:06; ☽□♂ 20:15; ☽#♆ 20:54

17 W: ☽☌⚷ 7:21; ☽∥⚷ 13:03; ☽⚺♅ 13:19; ☊ D 14:08; ☽∠♄ 14:35; ☿⚼♅ 16:59; ☽△⚳ 18:34; ☽△♀ 20:23

18 Th: ☽⚺♆ 0:11; ☊ R 3:43; ☽#♄ 3:46; ☉□☽ 3:54; ☽□♇ 8:04; ☿⚹♄ 8:50; ☽∥♃ 9:04; ☽⚹♄ 16:58; ☽△☿ 17:43; ☽☌♃ 19:06; ☽⚼⚳ 21:38

19 F: ☽⚼♀ 1:21; ☽∠♆ 2:39; ☽△♂ 3:27; ☽∥♅ 5:12; ☿△♃ 9:32; ☽⚺⚷ 12:05; ♀□♆ 15:50; ☽☌♅ 18:13; ☉#☽ 20:22; ☽⚼☿ 23:20

20 Sa: ☽⚻⚳ 1:21; ☽#⚳ 4:49; ☽⚹♆ 5:41; ☽#♀ 6:48; ☽⚻♀ 7:05; ☽⚼♂ 8:06; ☽#☿ 10:38; ☽#♇ 11:02; ☉☌♇ 13:47; ☽△♇ 13:57; ☉△☽ 13:58; ☉ ♒ 14:08; ☽∠⚷ 15:19; ☽#♂ 15:52; ☽□♄ 23:33

21 Su: ♇ ♒ 0:51; ☽⚺♃ 1:37; ☽⚻☿ 5:46; ☿∥♇ 8:05; ☽⚻♂ 13:24; ☽⚼♇ 17:43; ☽⚹⚷ 19:05; ☉⚼☽ 20:03

22 M: ☽⚺♅ 1:20; ☽∠♃ 5:41; ☽☍⚳ 10:30; ☽□♆ 13:23; ☽☍♀ 20:41; ☽⚻♇ 21:59

23 Tu: ☉⚻☽ 2:44; ☽∠♅ 5:39; ☽△♄ 8:16; ♀ ♑ 8:51; ☽⚹♃ 10:14; ♀⚺♇ 10:23; ☽☍☿ 20:54

24 W: ☽☍♂ 1:45; ☽□⚷ 4:05; ☽⚹♅ 10:25; ☽⚼♄ 13:20; ☽⚻⚳ 21:44; ☽△♆ 22:59

25 Th: ☽☍♇ 7:54; ☽⚻♀ 12:51; ♂□⚷ 17:16; ☉☍☽ 17:55; ☽⚻♄ 18:53; ☽#♂ 20:22; ☽□♃ 20:47; ☽#☿ 22:34; ☽#♇ 23:13

26 F: ☽#♀ 1:45; ☽#⚳ 4:06; ☽⚼⚳ 4:07; ☽⚼♆ 4:29; ☉⚺♄ 6:54; ☿□⚷ 14:50; ☽△⚷ 14:57; ☽⚻☿ 14:57; ☽⚻♂ 16:21; ♀⚼♅ 16:34; ⚳□♆ 16:54; ☽□♅ 21:20; ☽⚼♀ 21:53

27 Sa: ☉#☽ 0:24; ☉□♃ 7:20; ♅ D 7:37; ☽∥♅ 7:59; ☽⚻♆ 10:27; ☽△⚳ 10:59; ☿☌♂ 15:00; ☽⚻♇ 19:39; ☽⚼⚷ 21:02

28 Su: ☽⚼♂ 0:26; ☽⚼☿ 1:02; ☿∥♇ 2:22; ☽∥♃ 5:33; ♀⚹♄ 6:05; ☽☍♄ 7:21; ☽△♀ 7:29; ☽△♃ 9:11; ☉⚻☽ 11:24; ☽#♄ 15:00; ☿△♅ 21:08

29 M: ♀△♃ 1:03; ☽⚼♇ 2:05; ☽⚻⚷ 3:29; ☽∥⚷ 5:54; ☽△♂ 8:56; ☽△♅ 9:53; ☽△☿ 11:39; ☽⚼♃ 15:54; ☉⚼☽ 20:45; ☽☍♆ 23:21; ♂△♅ 23:42

30 Tu: ☽□⚳ 1:46; ☽#♆ 2:06; ☽△♇ 8:42; ☿∠♄ 9:01; ♂∥♇ 16:15; ☽⚼♅ 16:25; ☽⚻♄ 20:56; ☽⚻♃ 22:41

31 W: ☽∥♆ 2:15; ☽□♀ 3:35; ☉∠♆ 3:49; ☉△☽ 6:08; ☽☍⚷ 16:37; ☊ D 20:20; ☽#⚷ 22:26; ☽⚻♅ 22:49

February 2024

LONGITUDE

Day	Sid.Time	☉	☽	☽ 12 hour	Mean ☊	True ☊	☿	♀	♂	⚳	♃	♄	⚷	♅	♆	♇
	h m s	° ' "	° ' "	° ' "	° '	° '	° '	° '	° '	° '	° '	° '	° '	° '	° '	° '
1 Th	8 42 49	11♒35 51	19♎41 02	25♎39 59	19♈14.0	17♈51.1	23♑38.5	10♑38.1	20♑37.4	27♐37.0	7♉16.8	6♓26.4	16♈02.0	19♉05.9	25♓46.1	0♒21.3
2 F	8 46 46	12 36 45	1♏41 51	7♏47 18	19 10.9	17R 51.6	25 07.8	11 52.1	21 23.1	27 59.4	7 23.1	6 33.3	16 03.9	19 06.2	25 47.8	0 23.2
3 Sa	8 50 43	13 37 38	13 57 01	20 11 42	19 07.7	17 52.0	26 37.8	13 06.2	22 08.9	28 21.6	7 29.5	6 40.2	16 05.9	19 06.5	25 49.6	0 25.1
4 Su	8 54 39	14 38 31	26 31 57	2♐58 22	19 04.5	17 51.2	28 08.6	14 20.3	22 54.7	28 43.8	7 36.1	6 47.2	16 07.9	19 06.9	25 51.4	0 27.0
5 M	8 58 36	15 39 23	9♐31 28	16 11 40	19 01.3	17 48.5	29 40.1	15 34.4	23 40.5	29 05.9	7 42.8	6 54.2	16 09.9	19 07.3	25 53.3	0 28.9
6 Tu	9 02 32	16 40 14	22 59 14	29 54 19	18 58.2	17 43.4	1♒12.4	16 48.5	24 26.4	29 27.9	7 49.7	7 01.2	16 12.0	19 07.8	25 55.1	0 30.8
7 W	9 06 29	17 41 04	6♑56 51	14♑06 34	18 55.0	17 36.1	2 45.5	18 02.6	25 12.3	29 49.8	7 56.8	7 08.2	16 14.1	19 08.3	25 57.0	0 32.7
8 Th	9 10 25	18 41 53	21 22 59	28 45 24	18 51.8	17 27.1	4 19.4	19 16.8	25 58.2	0♑11.6	8 04.1	7 15.3	16 16.3	19 08.9	25 58.9	0 34.6
9 F	9 14 22	19 42 41	6♒12 54	13♒44 24	18 48.6	17 17.6	5 54.1	20 30.9	26 44.2	0 33.3	8 11.4	7 22.4	16 18.6	19 09.6	26 00.8	0 36.5
10 Sa	9 18 19	20 43 28	21 18 40	28 54 23	18 45.5	17 08.6	7 29.5	21 45.1	27 30.2	0 54.9	8 19.0	7 29.5	16 20.8	19 10.3	26 02.7	0 38.3
11 Su	9 22 15	21 44 13	6♓30 15	14♓04 55	18 42.3	17 01.3	9 05.7	22 59.2	28 16.2	1 16.4	8 26.7	7 36.6	16 23.1	19 11.0	26 04.6	0 40.2
12 M	9 26 12	22 44 57	21 37 13	29 06 04	18 39.1	16 56.3	10 42.7	24 13.4	29 02.2	1 37.8	8 34.5	7 43.8	16 25.5	19 11.8	26 06.6	0 42.0
13 Tu	9 30 08	23 45 39	6♈30 34	13♈50 01	18 35.9	16D 53.8	12 20.5	25 27.6	29 48.3	1 59.0	8 42.5	7 51.0	16 27.9	19 12.7	26 08.6	0 43.8
14 W	9 34 05	24 46 20	21 03 55	28 11 56	18 32.7	16 53.4	13 59.2	26 41.8	0♒34.4	2 20.2	8 50.6	7 58.2	16 30.3	19 13.6	26 10.6	0 45.7
15 Th	9 38 01	25 46 59	5♉13 54	12♉09 51	18 29.6	16 54.3	15 38.7	27 56.0	1 20.5	2 41.2	8 58.9	8 05.4	16 32.8	19 14.5	26 12.6	0 47.5
16 F	9 41 58	26 47 37	18 59 52	25 44 11	18 26.4	16R 55.3	17 19.0	29 10.2	2 06.6	3 02.2	9 07.3	8 12.6	16 35.3	19 15.5	26 14.6	0 49.3
17 Sa	9 45 54	27 48 12	2♊23 06	8♊56 56	18 23.2	16 55.4	19 00.2	0♒24.4	2 52.8	3 23.0	9 15.9	8 19.8	16 37.8	19 16.6	26 16.7	0 51.1
18 Su	9 49 51	28 48 46	15 26 04	21 50 52	18 20.0	16 53.9	20 42.3	1 38.6	3 39.0	3 43.7	9 24.6	8 27.1	16 40.4	19 17.7	26 18.7	0 52.8
19 M	9 53 48	29 49 19	28 11 43	4♋28 58	18 16.9	16 50.3	22 25.3	2 52.8	4 25.2	4 04.3	9 33.4	8 34.4	16 43.0	19 18.8	26 20.8	0 54.6
20 Tu	9 57 44	0♓49 49	10♋42 58	16 54 02	18 13.7	16 44.5	24 09.2	4 07.1	5 11.4	4 24.7	9 42.4	8 41.6	16 45.7	19 20.0	26 22.9	0 56.3
21 W	10 01 41	1 50 18	23 02 28	29 08 32	18 10.5	16 37.1	25 54.0	5 21.3	5 57.7	4 45.1	9 51.5	8 48.9	16 48.4	19 21.3	26 25.0	0 58.1
22 Th	10 05 37	2 50 45	5♌12 27	11♌14 29	18 07.3	16 28.7	27 39.8	6 35.5	6 44.0	5 05.3	10 00.7	8 56.2	16 51.1	19 22.6	26 27.1	0 59.8
23 F	10 09 34	3 51 10	17 14 48	23 13 36	18 04.2	16 20.2	29 26.5	7 49.8	7 30.3	5 25.4	10 10.0	9 03.5	16 53.8	19 24.0	26 29.2	1 01.5
24 Sa	10 13 30	4 51 33	29 11 05	5♍07 27	18 01.0	16 12.4	1♓14.1	9 04.0	8 16.6	5 45.3	10 19.5	9 10.8	16 56.6	19 25.4	26 31.4	1 03.2
25 Su	10 17 27	5 51 55	11♍02 54	16 57 38	17 57.8	16 05.9	3 02.7	10 18.2	9 02.9	6 05.2	10 29.1	9 18.2	16 59.5	19 26.8	26 33.5	1 04.9
26 M	10 21 23	6 52 15	22 51 54	28 45 59	17 54.6	16 01.2	4 52.2	11 32.5	9 49.3	6 24.9	10 38.8	9 25.5	17 02.3	19 28.3	26 35.7	1 06.5
27 Tu	10 25 20	7 52 34	4♎40 09	10♎34 45	17 51.4	15D 58.6	6 42.7	12 46.7	10 35.7	6 44.4	10 48.6	9 32.8	17 05.2	19 29.8	26 37.9	1 08.1
28 W	10 29 16	8 52 50	16 30 09	22 26 45	17 48.3	15 57.9	8 34.0	14 01.0	11 22.1	7 03.9	10 58.6	9 40.1	17 08.1	19 31.4	26 40.0	1 09.8
29 Th	10 33 13	9♓53 06	28 24 59	4♏25 21	17♈45.1	15♈58.6	10♓26.3	15♒15.3	12♒08.5	7♑23.1	11♉08.7	9♓47.5	17♈11.0	19♉33.1	26♓42.2	1♒11.4

1st of Month

Julian Day #
2460341.5
Obliquity
23°26'[illegible]9"
SVP 4♓55'[illegible]8"
GC 27♐10.5
Eris 24♈11.4

Day	⚴
1	28♏23.9
6	29 54.0
11	1♐19.0
16	2 38.1
21	3 51.0
26	4 57.1

Day	⚵
1	20♍32.6R
6	19 45.9R
11	18 49.8R
16	17 45.8R
21	16 35.8R
26	15 21.7R

Day	⚶
1	21♊57.0R
6	21 46.0R
11	21 46.2
16	21 57.3
21	22 18.7
26	22 49.9

DECLINATION and LATITUDE

Day	☉ Decl	☽ Decl	☽ Lat	☽ 12h Decl	☿ Decl	☿ Lat	♀ Decl	♀ Lat	♂ Decl	♂ Lat	⚳ Decl	⚳ Lat	♃ Decl	♃ Lat	♄ Decl	♄ Lat
1 Th	17S18	7S51	0S10	10S34	22S24	1S03	22S23	0N38	22S41	0S50	22S19	1N06	12N58	1S02	10S39	1S37
2 F	17 01	13 12	1 13	15 45	22 14	1 09	22 19	0 35	22 35	0 51	22 22	1 04	13 00	1 02	10 36	1 37
3 Sa	16 44	18 10	2 15	20 25	22 03	1 15	22 15	0 32	22 28	0 51	22 24	1 02	13 03	1 01	10 34	1 37
4 Su	16 26	22 29	3 11	24 18	21 51	1 20	22 11	0 29	22 21	0 52	22 26	1 00	13 05	1 01	10 31	1 37
5 M	16 09	25 50	3 60	27 02	21 37	1 26	22 06	0 26	22 13	0 52	22 27	0 59	13 07	1 01	10 28	1 37
6 Tu	15 50	27 52	4 37	28 17	21 22	1 31	21 60	0 23	22 06	0 53	22 29	0 57	13 10	1 01	10 26	1 37
7 W	15 32	28 14	4 59	27 44	21 05	1 35	21 53	0 20	21 58	0 53	22 31	0 55	13 12	1 00	10 23	1 37
8 Th	15 13	26 44	5 04	25 17	20 48	1 40	21 46	0 17	21 50	0 54	22 33	0 53	13 15	1 00	10 21	1 37
9 F	14 54	23 22	4 48	21 03	20 29	1 44	21 38	0 15	21 42	0 54	22 35	0 52	13 18	0 60	10 18	1 37
10 Sa	14 35	18 23	4 13	15 25	20 08	1 48	21 29	0 12	21 33	0 55	22 36	0 50	13 20	0 60	10 15	1 37
11 Su	14 16	12 12	3 19	8 49	19 46	1 51	21 20	0 09	21 25	0 55	22 38	0 48	13 23	0 59	10 13	1 37
12 M	13 56	5 20	2 11	1 48	19 23	1 54	21 10	0 06	21 16	0 56	22 39	0 46	13 26	0 59	10 10	1 37
13 Tu	13 36	1N44	0 56	5N12	18 58	1 57	21 00	0 03	21 06	0 56	22 41	0 45	13 28	0 59	10 07	1 37
14 W	13 16	8 34	0N22	11 47	18 32	1 60	20 49	0S00	20 57	0 57	22 42	0 43	13 31	0 59	10 05	1 37
15 Th	12 55	14 47	1 37	17 35	18 05	2 02	20 37	0 03	20 47	0 57	22 44	0 41	13 34	0 58	10 02	1 37
16 F	12 35	20 06	2 44	22 19	17 36	2 04	20 25	0 06	20 38	0 58	22 45	0 39	13 37	0 58	9 59	1 37
17 Sa	12 14	24 14	3 40	25 48	17 06	2 05	20 12	0 09	20 27	0 58	22 46	0 37	13 40	0 58	9 57	1 37
18 Su	11 53	27 00	4 23	27 50	16 35	2 06	19 59	0 11	20 17	0 59	22 48	0 35	13 43	0 58	9 54	1 37
19 M	11 32	28 18	4 52	28 23	16 02	2 06	19 45	0 14	20 07	0 59	22 49	0 34	13 46	0 57	9 51	1 37
20 Tu	11 11	28 06	5 06	27 28	15 28	2 07	19 30	0 17	19 56	0 60	22 50	0 32	13 49	0 57	9 48	1 37
21 W	10 49	26 30	5 06	25 14	14 52	2 06	19 15	0 20	19 45	0 60	22 51	0 30	13 52	0 57	9 46	1 37
22 Th	10 28	23 41	4 52	21 53	14 15	2 06	18 59	0 22	19 34	1 00	22 53	0 28	13 55	0 57	9 43	1 37
23 F	10 06	19 52	4 25	17 40	13 37	2 04	18 43	0 25	19 22	1 01	22 54	0 26	13 58	0 56	9 40	1 37
24 Sa	9 44	15 17	3 46	12 47	12 57	2 03	18 26	0 27	19 11	1 01	22 55	0 24	14 02	0 56	9 38	1 37
25 Su	9 22	10 10	2 58	7 28	12 16	2 01	18 08	0 30	18 59	1 02	22 56	0 22	14 05	0 56	9 35	1 37
26 M	8 59	4 42	2 02	1 54	11 33	1 58	17 51	0 33	18 47	1 02	22 57	0 20	14 08	0 56	9 32	1 37
27 Tu	8 37	0S55	1 01	3S44	10 49	1 55	17 32	0 35	18 35	1 03	22 58	0 18	14 11	0 56	9 29	1 37
28 W	8 14	6 32	0S03	9 17	10 04	1 51	17 13	0 37	18 23	1 03	22 59	0 16	14 15	0 55	9 27	1 37
29 Th	7S52	11S58	1S07	14S33	9S18	1S47	16S54	0S40	18S10	1S03	22S60	0N14	14N18	0S55	9S24	1S37

Day	⚷ Decl	⚷ Lat	♅ Decl	♅ Lat	♆ Decl	♆ Lat	♇ Decl	♇ Lat
1	7N30	1N17	17N13	0S18	2S48	1S13	22S49	2S48
6	7 33	1 17	17 13	0 18	2 45	1 13	22 47	2 49
11	7 37	1 16	17 14	0 17	2 41	1 13	22 46	2 49
16	7 41	1 15	17 16	0 17	2 37	1 13	22 44	2 50
21	7 45	1 15	17 17	0 17	2 33	1 13	22 43	2 51
26	7N50	1N14	17N19	0S17	2S28	1S13	22S42	2S51

Day	⚴ Decl	⚴ Lat	⚵ Decl	⚵ Lat	⚶ Decl	⚶ Lat	Eris Decl	Eris Lat
1	4N02	24N24	0S27	4S33	22N19	0S53	0S46	10S54
6	4 46	25 25	0N08	4 16	22 32	0 39	0 45	10 53
11	5 33	26 29	0 46	3 58	22 44	0 27	0 44	10 53
16	6 25	27 35	1 30	3 38	22 57	0 15	0 43	10 52
21	7 20	28 43	2 16	3 16	23 10	0 03	0 42	10 51
26	8N19	29N53	3N05	2S54	23N22	0N07	0S40	10S51

Moon Phenomena

Max/0 Decl

dy	hr mn	
6	17:04	28S19
12	18:06	0 N
19	8:42	28N23
26	20:06	0 S

Max/0 Lat

dy	hr mn	
7	17:36	5S05
13	17:04	0 N
20	11:35	5N08
27	22:55	0 S

Perigee/Apogee

dy	hr m		kilometers
10	18:54	p	358092
25	15:00	a	406312

PH	dy	hr mn	
☾	2	23:19	13♏36
●	9	23:00	20♒41
☽	16	15:02	27♉26
○	24	12:32	5♍23

Void of Course Moon

Last Aspect				☽ Ingress		
1	9:04	☿	□	♏	1	20:38
4	3:25	☿	⚹	♐	4	6:29
6	5:07	♆	□	♑	6	12:10
8	7:53	♂	☌	♒	8	14:01
9	23:00	☉	☌	♓	10	13:44
12	12:33	♂	⚹	♈	12	13:27
14	10:22	♀	□	♉	14	15:03
16	15:02	☉	□	♊	16	19:41
19	3:22	☉	△	♋	19	3:26
21	6:39	♆	△	♌	21	13:42
23	4:19	♅	□	♍	24	1:39
26	7:36	♆	☍	♎	26	14:31
27	18:23	♀	△	♏	29	3:10

DAILY ASPECTARIAN

- **1 Th**: ☽□♂ 2:01; ☽⚼♄ 3:34; ☿∥♀ 5:22; ☉#♅ 7:47; ☽□☿ 9:04; ☿∥⚳ 9:28; ☽⚻♆ 12:14; ☽∥♄ 12:15; ♀∥⚳ 14:26; ☽⚹⚳ 16:24; ☽□♇ 21:24; ☽#♃ 23:03
- **2 F**: ♂∠♄ 6:17; ☽△♄ 9:40; ☿⚹♆ 10:56; ☽☍♃ 11:18; ☉∠⚳ 14:04; ☉∥☽ 17:12; ☽⚼♆ 17:55; ☽#♅ 19:11; ☽⚹♀ 22:11; ☽∠⚳ 22:49; ☉□☽ 23:19; ☊ R 23:28
- **3 Sa**: ☽⚻⚷ 4:09; ☽☍♅ 9:56; ♂∥⚳ 11:09; ☽⚹♂ 16:44; ☽∥☿ 20:22; ☽∥♀ 22:14; ☽△♆ 22:44; ☽∥♂ 23:13; ☽∥⚳ 23:41
- **4 Su**: ☽∥♇ 2:01; ☽⚹☿ 3:25; ☽⚺⚳ 4:14; ☽∠♀ 5:49; ☽⚹♇ 7:20; ☽⚼⚷ 8:37; ☿⚺⚳ 12:13; ☽□♄ 19:11; ☽⚻♃ 20:41; ☽∠♂ 22:22
- **5 M**: ☿ ♒ 5:11; ☉⚺♀ 9:04; ☽∠☿ 10:28; ☽∠♇ 10:45; ♀□⚷ 11:51; ☉⚹☽ 11:56; ☽△⚷ 11:59; ☽⚺♀ 11:59; ☉⚹⚷ 12:28; ☿☌♇ 12:59; ☽⚻♅ 17:12; ☽⚼♃ 23:43
- **6 Tu**: ☽⚺♂ 2:41; ☽□♆ 5:07; ⚴ ♐ 8:10; ☽☌⚳ 11:33; ☽⚺♇ 13:04; ☽⚺☿ 16:00; ☉∠☽ 16:12; ☽⚼♅ 19:14
- **7 W**: ☽⚹♄ 0:19; ☽△♃ 1:42; ⚳ ♑ 11:13; ☽□⚷ 15:34; ☉⚺☽ 19:16; ☽☌♀ 20:14; ☽△♅ 20:20; ♀△♅ 21:27
- **8 Th**: ♂⚹♆ 0:21; ☽∠♄ 1:26; ☽⚹♆ 7:31; ☽☌♂ 7:53; ⚶ D 9:42; ☉□♅ 10:47; ☽⚺⚳ 14:41; ☽☌♇ 14:58; ☽☌☿ 23:26
- **9 F**: ☽⚺♄ 1:52; ☽□♃ 3:11; ☽∥♇ 3:17; ⚳⚺♇ 3:50; ☽∥⚳ 4:19; ☽∠♆ 7:41; ☽∥♂ 9:07; ☽∥♀ 9:26; ☽∠⚳ 15:15; ☽∥☿ 15:45; ☽⚹⚷ 16:07; ☽□♅ 20:37; ☉☌☽ 23:00
- **10 Sa**: ☿⚺♄ 0:00; ☽⚺♀ 0:45; ☽#♅ 4:45; ☽⚺♆ 7:30; ☽⚺♂ 10:18; ☿□♃ 13:26; ☽⚺♇ 14:46; ☽⚹⚳ 15:32; ☽∠⚷ 15:54; ♀∠♄ 15:54; ☉∥☽ 15:59; ☽#♃ 19:43
- **11 Su**: ☽☌♄ 1:46; ☽∠♀ 2:33; ☽⚹♃ 3:06; ☽⚺☿ 4:35; ☽∥♄ 7:11; ☽∠♂ 11:17; ☽∠♇ 14:33; ☽⚺⚷ 15:42; ☽#⚷ 16:11; ☽⚹♅ 20:08
- **12 M**: ☉⚺☽ 1:56; ☽∠♃ 3:09; ☽⚹♀ 4:32; ☿∠♆ 6:00; ☽☌♆ 7:12; ☽∠☿ 7:21; ☽∥♆ 9:05; ☽⚹♂ 12:33; ☽⚹♇ 14:37; ☽□⚳ 16:29; ☽∠♅ 20:16
- **13 Tu**: ☽⚺♄ 2:12; ☽#♆ 3:08; ☽⚺♃ 3:37; ☉∠☽ 3:57; ♂ ♒ 6:06; ☉#♃ 7:54; ☽⚹☿ 10:45; ♀⚹♆ 13:37; ☽☌⚷ 16:24; ☊ D 17:05; ☽∥⚷ 20:41; ☽⚺♅ 20:56
- **14 W**: ☽∠♄ 3:13; ☽#♄ 5:32; ♂☌♇ 6:07; ☉⚹☽ 6:41; ☽⚺♆ 8:36; ☽□♀ 10:22; ☽□♇ 16:23; ☉#☽ 16:53; ☽□♂ 16:57; ☽∥♃ 19:00; ☽△⚳ 19:32
- **15 Th**: ☽⚹♄ 4:58; ☽☌♃ 6:32; ☽∠♆ 10:22; ☉⚺♆ 10:29; ☽∥♅ 10:35; ☽#☿ 13:08; ☿⚹⚷ 13:17; ⚳∥♇ 13:53; ☽⚺⚷ 19:44; ☽□☿ 20:37; ☽⚼⚳ 22:15
- **16 F**: ☽☌♅ 0:28; ☽#♀ 1:34; ☽#♂ 2:37; ☿∠⚳ 12:55; ☽⚹♆ 12:57; ☽#♇ 14:26; ☽#⚳ 14:36; ☊ R 14:54; ☉□☽ 15:02; ♀ ♒ 16:06; ☿#♅ 16:21; ☽△♀ 20:03; ☽△♇ 21:13; ☽∠⚷ 22:38
- **17 Sa**: ☽△♂ 0:57; ☽⚻⚳ 1:52; ☿□♅ 3:54; ♀☌♇ 8:50; ☽□♄ 10:58; ☽⚺♃ 12:43
- **18 Su**: ☽⚼♇ 0:50; ☽⚹⚷ 2:19; ☽⚼♀ 2:30; ♂⚺⚳ 4:25; ☽⚼♂ 6:23; ☽⚺♅ 7:13; ☽△☿ 11:23; ☽∠♃ 17:02; ☽□♆ 20:29
- **19 M**: ☉△☽ 3:22; ☉ ♓ 4:14; ☽⚻♇ 5:11; ☽⚻♀ 9:55; ☽☍⚳ 11:32; ☽∠♅ 11:42; ☽⚻♂ 12:40; ⚳⚼♅ 18:09; ☽△♄ 20:03; ☽⚼☿ 20:30; ☽⚹♃ 22:02
- **20 Tu**: ☉⚺♇ 2:40; ♀⚺⚳ 7:52; ☉⚼☽ 10:48; ☽□⚷ 11:46; ☽⚹♅ 16:46; ☉∠⚷ 23:12
- **21 W**: ☽⚼♄ 1:32; ☽⚻☿ 6:34; ☽△♆ 6:39; ☿⚺♆ 7:12; ☽☍♇ 15:39; ☉⚻☽ 18:54; ☽⚻⚳ 23:45
- **22 Th**: ☽☍♀ 3:04; ☽☍♂ 3:14; ☽#⚳ 5:33; ☽#♇ 6:40; ♀☌♂ 7:16; ☽⚻♄ 7:29; ☽□♃ 9:40; ☿#♃ 11:27; ☽⚼♆ 12:27; ☽△⚷ 23:18
- **23 F**: ☽#♂ 2:54; ☽□♅ 4:19; ☽⚼⚳ 6:33; ☽#♀ 6:50; ☿ ♓ 7:30; ☽∥♅ 13:50; ☽⚻♆ 18:37; ☿⚺♇ 21:32
- **24 Sa**: ♀⚺♄ 2:27; ☽⚻♇ 3:47; ☽☍☿ 4:53; ☽⚼⚷ 5:36; ☽∥♃ 6:04; ☉∥♄ 7:42; ☿∠⚷ 9:41; ☉☍☽ 12:32; ☽#☿ 12:58; ☽△⚳ 13:40; ☽⚻♂ 19:40; ☽☍♄ 20:25; ☽⚻♀ 22:19; ☽△♃ 22:51
- **25 Su**: ☽#♄ 2:40; ☉#☽ 3:54; ♀□♃ 4:02; ☉⚹⚳ 7:50; ♂⚺♄ 9:21; ☽⚼♇ 10:14; ☽∥⚷ 10:26; ☽⚻⚷ 12:07; ☽△♅ 17:05
- **26 M**: ♀∠♆ 1:04; ☽⚼♂ 4:15; ☽⚼♃ 5:44; ☽☍♆ 7:36; ☽⚼♀ 8:21; ☽#♆ 9:36; ☽△♇ 16:48; ☽⚼♅ 23:39
- **27 Tu**: ☿⚹⚳ 0:28; ☽□⚳ 4:20; ☽⚻☿ 4:55; ☽∥♆ 6:31; ☉⚻☽ 7:07; ♂□♃ 8:31; ☽⚻♄ 10:01; ☽⚻♃ 12:39; ☽△♂ 12:52; ♀#♅ 15:11; ☽△♀ 18:23; ☊ D 22:57
- **28 W**: ☽☍⚷ 1:17; ☽#⚷ 5:49; ☽⚻♅ 6:07; ☉∥☽ 6:57; ☉☌☿ 8:44; ♂∠♆ 9:44; ☽∥♄ 12:37; ☽∥☿ 13:35; ☿☌♄ 15:09; ☉⚼☽ 16:16; ☽⚼♄ 16:39; ☽⚼☿ 16:54; ☽⚻♆ 20:33; ☿∥♄ 20:51; ☉☌♄ 21:27; ☉#⚷ 22:36
- **29 Th**: ☽□♇ 5:34; ☿⚹♃ 9:54; ☽#♃ 10:56; ☽⚹⚳ 18:22; ☽∥♀ 21:54; ☽△♄ 22:53

LONGITUDE

Day	Sid.Time	☉	☽	☽ 12 hour	Mean ☊	True ☊	☿	♀	♂	⚳	♃	♄	⚷	♅	♆	♇
	h m s	° ' "	° ' "	° ' "	° '	° '	° '	° '	° '	° '	° '	° '	° '	° '	° '	° '
1 F	10 37 10	10♓53 19	10♏28 21	16♏34 31	17♈41.9	16♈00.2	12♓19.4	16♒29.5	12♒55.0	7♑42.3	11♉18.8	9♓54.8	17♈14.0	19♉34.8	26♓44.4	1♒13.0
2 Sa	10 41 06	11 53 32	22 44 24	28 58 35	17 38.7	16 01.9	14 13.3	17 43.8	13 41.5	8 01.3	11 29.1	10 02.1	17 17.0	19 36.5	26 46.6	1 14.5
3 Su	10 45 03	12 53 42	5♐17 36	11♐42 01	17 35.5	16R 03.1	16 07.9	18 58.1	14 28.0	8 20.2	11 39.5	10 09.4	17 20.1	19 38.3	26 48.9	1 16.1
4 M	10 48 59	13 53 52	18 12 20	24 49 00	17 32.4	16 03.3	18 03.2	20 12.4	15 14.5	8 38.9	11 50.1	10 16.8	17 23.1	19 40.1	26 51.1	1 17.6
5 Tu	10 52 56	14 54 00	1♑32 23	8♑22 44	17 29.2	16 02.1	19 59.0	21 26.6	16 01.0	8 57.5	12 00.7	10 24.1	17 26.2	19 41.9	26 53.3	1 19.2
6 W	10 56 52	15 54 06	15 20 11	22 24 43	17 26.0	15 59.6	21 55.2	22 40.9	16 47.5	9 15.9	12 11.4	10 31.4	17 29.3	19 43.9	26 55.6	1 20.7
7 Th	11 00 49	16 54 11	29 36 07	6♒53 59	17 22.8	15 56.0	23 51.7	23 55.2	17 34.1	9 34.2	12 22.2	10 38.7	17 32.5	19 45.8	26 57.8	1 22.1
8 F	11 04 45	17 54 14	14♒17 41	21 46 26	17 19.7	15 51.9	25 48.2	25 09.5	18 20.7	9 52.3	12 33.2	10 46.0	17 35.6	19 47.8	27 00.1	1 23.6
9 Sa	11 08 42	18 54 15	29 19 15	6♓54 59	17 16.5	15 48.0	27 44.5	26 23.8	19 07.3	10 10.2	12 44.2	10 53.3	17 38.8	19 49.8	27 02.3	1 25.1
10 Su	11 12 39	19 54 14	14♓32 24	22 10 12	17 13.3	15 44.8	29 40.4	27 38.1	19 53.9	10 28.0	12 55.3	11 00.6	17 42.0	19 51.9	27 04.6	1 26.5
11 M	11 16 35	20 54 12	29 47 04	7♈21 46	17 10.1	15 42.8	1♈35.6	28 52.3	20 40.5	10 45.6	13 06.5	11 07.9	17 45.2	19 54.0	27 06.8	1 27.9
12 Tu	11 20 32	21 54 07	14♈53 09	22 20 12	17 07.0	15D 42.1	3 29.8	0♓06.6	21 27.1	11 03.1	13 17.9	11 15.1	17 48.5	19 56.2	27 09.1	1 29.3
13 W	11 24 28	22 54 01	29 42 04	6♉58 06	17 03.8	15 42.5	5 22.5	1 20.9	22 13.7	11 20.3	13 29.3	11 22.4	17 51.8	19 58.4	27 11.4	1 30.6
14 Th	11 28 25	23 53 52	14♉07 49	21 10 57	17 00.6	15 43.7	7 13.4	2 35.2	23 00.4	11 37.4	13 40.8	11 29.6	17 55.0	20 00.6	27 13.7	1 31.9
15 F	11 32 21	24 53 41	28 07 22	4♊57 05	16 57.4	15 45.2	9 02.0	3 49.4	23 47.0	11 54.4	13 52.4	11 36.8	17 58.4	20 02.9	27 15.9	1 33.3
16 Sa	11 36 18	25 53 29	11♊40 17	18 17 13	16 54.2	15 46.4	10 48.0	5 03.7	24 33.7	12 11.1	14 04.0	11 44.0	18 01.7	20 05.2	27 18.2	1 34.6
17 Su	11 40 14	26 53 13	24 48 13	1♋13 42	16 51.1	15R 46.9	12 30.7	6 17.9	25 20.3	12 27.7	14 15.8	11 51.2	18 05.0	20 07.6	27 20.5	1 35.8
18 M	11 44 11	27 52 56	7♋34 06	13 49 54	16 47.9	15 46.6	14 09.8	7 32.2	26 07.0	12 44.0	14 27.6	11 58.3	18 08.4	20 10.0	27 22.8	1 37.1
19 Tu	11 48 08	28 52 36	20 01 35	26 09 38	16 44.7	15 45.5	15 44.7	8 46.4	26 53.7	13 00.2	14 39.6	12 05.5	18 11.8	20 12.4	27 25.0	1 38.3
20 W	11 52 04	29 52 14	2♌14 32	8♌16 43	16 41.5	15 43.7	17 15.1	10 00.6	27 40.3	13 16.2	14 51.6	12 12.6	18 15.2	20 14.9	27 27.3	1 39.5
21 Th	11 56 01	0♈51 50	14 16 38	20 14 43	16 38.4	15 41.5	18 40.3	11 14.9	28 27.0	13 32.1	15 03.7	12 19.7	18 18.6	20 17.4	27 29.6	1 40.7
22 F	11 59 57	1 51 23	26 11 20	2♍06 51	16 35.2	15 39.3	20 00.1	12 29.1	29 13.7	13 47.7	15 15.8	12 26.8	18 22.0	20 20.0	27 31.9	1 41.8
23 Sa	12 03 54	2 50 55	8♍01 38	13 55 58	16 32.0	15 37.3	21 14.0	13 43.3	0♓00.4	14 03.1	15 28.0	12 33.8	18 25.4	20 22.5	27 34.1	1 42.9
24 Su	12 07 50	3 50 24	19 50 10	25 44 31	16 28.8	15 35.7	22 21.7	14 57.5	0 47.1	14 18.3	15 40.3	12 40.8	18 28.9	20 25.1	27 36.4	1 44.1
25 M	12 11 47	4 49 51	1♎39 16	7♎34 42	16 25.6	15 34.7	23 22.8	16 11.7	1 33.7	14 33.3	15 52.7	12 47.8	18 32.3	20 27.8	27 38.7	1 45.1
26 Tu	12 15 43	5 49 16	13 31 05	19 28 39	16 22.5	15D 34.3	24 17.0	17 25.9	2 20.4	14 48.2	16 05.2	12 54.8	18 35.8	20 30.4	27 40.9	1 46.2
27 W	12 19 40	6 48 39	25 27 40	1♏28 26	16 19.3	15 34.5	25 04.2	18 40.1	3 07.1	15 02.8	16 17.7	13 01.7	18 39.3	20 33.1	27 43.2	1 47.2
28 Th	12 23 37	7 48 00	7♏31 13	13 36 19	16 16.1	15 35.0	25 44.2	19 54.2	3 53.8	15 17.2	16 30.2	13 08.6	18 42.8	20 35.9	27 45.4	1 48.2
29 F	12 27 33	8 47 19	19 44 03	25 54 45	16 12.9	15 35.7	26 16.8	21 08.4	4 40.5	15 31.3	16 42.9	13 15.5	18 46.3	20 38.7	27 47.7	1 49.2
30 Sa	12 31 30	9 46 36	2♐08 46	8♐26 27	16 09.8	15 36.4	26 42.0	22 22.6	5 27.2	15 45.3	16 55.6	13 22.3	18 49.8	20 41.5	27 49.9	1 50.1
31 Su	12 35 26	10♈45 52	14 48 10	21 14 16	16♈06.6	15♈36.9	26♈59.7	23♓36.8	6♓13.9	15♑59.1	17♉08.4	13♓29.2	18♈53.3	20♉44.3	27♓52.2	1♒51.1

1st of Month

Julian Day # 2460370.5
Obliquity 23°26'19"
SVP 4♓55'25"
GC 27♐10.6
Eris 24♈21.9

Day	⚴	⚵	⚶
1	5♐44.7	14♍20.9R	23♊21.4
6	6 37.0	13 04.9R	24 08.5
11	7 20.6	11 50.9R	25 03.7
16	7 54.9	10 41.1R	26 06.2
21	8 19.2	9 37.4R	27 15.5
26	8 32.8	8 41.2R	28 31.1
31	8 35.2R	7 53.5R	29 52.3

DECLINATION and LATITUDE

Day	☉ Decl	☽ Decl	☽ Lat	☽ 12h Decl	☿ Decl	☿ Lat	♀ Decl	♀ Lat	♂ Decl	♂ Lat	⚳ Decl	⚳ Lat	♃ Decl	♃ Lat	♄ Decl	♄ Lat
1 F	7S29	17S01	2S10	19S20	8S31	1S42	16S34	0S42	17S57	1S04	23S01	0N12	14N21	0S55	9S21	1S37
2 Sa	7 06	21 29	3 08	23 24	7 42	1 37	16 14	0 45	17 44	1 04	23 01	0 10	14 25	0 55	9 18	1 37
3 Su	6 43	25 05	3 58	26 28	6 52	1 31	15 53	0 47	17 31	1 05	23 02	0 08	14 28	0 54	9 16	1 37
4 M	6 20	27 31	4 37	28 12	6 01	1 24	15 31	0 49	17 18	1 05	23 03	0 06	14 31	0 54	9 13	1 37
5 Tu	5 57	28 29	5 03	28 20	5 09	1 17	15 10	0 51	17 04	1 05	23 04	0 04	14 35	0 54	9 10	1 38
6 W	5 34	27 45	5 13	26 41	4 16	1 10	14 48	0 53	16 51	1 06	23 05	0 02	14 38	0 54	9 08	1 38
7 Th	5 10	25 12	5 04	23 16	3 23	1 01	14 25	0 55	16 37	1 06	23 06	0S00	14 42	0 54	9 05	1 38
8 F	4 47	20 56	4 36	18 15	2 28	0 53	14 02	0 57	16 23	1 06	23 06	0 02	14 45	0 53	9 02	1 38
9 Sa	4 23	15 16	3 48	12 01	1 33	0 43	13 39	0 59	16 09	1 07	23 07	0 04	14 49	0 53	8 59	1 38
10 Su	3 60	8 36	2 43	5 02	0 38	0 33	13 15	1 01	15 55	1 07	23 08	0 06	14 52	0 53	8 57	1 38
11 M	3 36	1 25	1 27	2N13	0N17	0 23	12 51	1 03	15 40	1 08	23 09	0 09	14 56	0 53	8 54	1 38
12 Tu	3 13	5N48	0 05	9 16	1 13	0 12	12 27	1 05	15 25	1 08	23 09	0 11	14 60	0 53	8 51	1 38
13 W	2 49	12 33	1N16	15 39	2 08	0 00	12 02	1 07	15 11	1 08	23 10	0 13	15 03	0 52	8 49	1 38
14 Th	2 25	18 28	2 30	21 00	3 03	0N12	11 37	1 08	14 56	1 09	23 11	0 15	15 07	0 52	8 46	1 38
15 F	2 02	23 12	3 33	25 03	3 57	0 24	11 12	1 10	14 41	1 09	23 12	0 17	15 10	0 52	8 43	1 38
16 Sa	1 38	26 30	4 22	27 35	4 50	0 36	10 46	1 12	14 25	1 09	23 12	0 20	15 14	0 52	8 41	1 38
17 Su	1 14	28 15	4 55	28 32	5 42	0 49	10 20	1 13	14 10	1 09	23 13	0 22	15 18	0 52	8 38	1 38
18 M	0 51	28 25	5 13	27 57	6 32	1 02	9 54	1 15	13 54	1 10	23 14	0 24	15 21	0 52	8 35	1 39
19 Tu	0 27	27 08	5 15	26 00	7 20	1 14	9 27	1 16	13 39	1 10	23 15	0 27	15 25	0 51	8 33	1 39
20 W	0 03	24 34	5 03	22 53	8 07	1 27	9 00	1 17	13 23	1 10	23 15	0 29	15 29	0 51	8 30	1 39
21 Th	0N21	20 58	4 38	18 51	8 51	1 40	8 33	1 18	13 07	1 11	23 16	0 31	15 32	0 51	8 27	1 39
22 F	0 44	16 33	4 01	14 07	9 33	1 52	8 06	1 20	12 51	1 11	23 17	0 34	15 36	0 51	8 25	1 39
23 Sa	1 08	11 33	3 13	8 53	10 12	2 04	7 39	1 21	12 35	1 11	23 18	0 36	15 40	0 51	8 22	1 39
24 Su	1 32	6 08	2 18	3 20	10 47	2 15	7 11	1 22	12 19	1 11	23 18	0 38	15 44	0 50	8 20	1 39
25 M	1 55	0 31	1 16	2S20	11 20	2 26	6 43	1 23	12 02	1 12	23 19	0 41	15 47	0 50	8 17	1 39
26 Tu	2 19	5S10	0 11	7 57	11 50	2 36	6 15	1 24	11 46	1 12	23 20	0 43	15 51	0 50	8 14	1 39
27 W	2 42	10 42	0S55	13 21	12 16	2 45	5 47	1 25	11 29	1 12	23 21	0 46	15 55	0 50	8 12	1 39
28 Th	3 06	15 54	1 59	18 18	12 38	2 53	5 18	1 25	11 12	1 12	23 22	0 48	15 58	0 50	8 09	1 40
29 F	3 29	20 32	2 59	22 34	12 57	3 00	4 50	1 26	10 55	1 13	23 23	0 51	16 02	0 50	8 07	1 40
30 Sa	3 52	24 22	3 51	25 53	13 11	3 06	4 21	1 27	10 38	1 13	23 24	0 53	16 06	0 50	8 04	1 40
31 Su	4N16	27S06	4S33	27S58	13N22	3N11	3S52	1S27	10S21	1S13	23S25	0S56	16N10	0S49	8S02	1S40

Day	⚷ Decl	⚷ Lat	♅ Decl	♅ Lat	♆ Decl	♆ Lat	♇ Decl	♇ Lat
1	7N54	1N14	17N21	0S17	2S25	1S13	22S41	2S52
6	7 60	1 13	17 24	0 17	2 20	1 13	22 40	2 53
11	8 05	1 13	17 27	0 17	2 16	1 13	22 39	2 53
16	8 11	1 12	17 30	0 17	2 11	1 13	22 38	2 54
21	8 17	1 12	17 33	0 17	2 07	1 13	22 37	2 55
26	8 23	1 11	17 37	0 16	2 02	1 13	22 37	2 56
31	8N30	1N11	17N40	0S16	1S58	1S13	22S37	2S56

Day	⚴ Decl	⚴ Lat	⚵ Decl	⚵ Lat	⚶ Decl	⚶ Lat	Eris Decl	Eris Lat
1	9N09	30N51	3N46	2S36	23N32	0N15	0S39	10S50
6	10 14	32 04	4 36	2 13	23 44	0 25	0 38	10 50
11	11 22	33 19	5 26	1 49	23 55	0 34	0 36	10 49
16	12 33	34 35	6 14	1 26	24 06	0 43	0 35	10 49
21	13 46	35 52	6 60	1 03	24 15	0 51	0 33	10 48
26	15 00	37 09	7 41	0 40	24 24	0 58	0 32	10 48
31	16N15	38N25	8N19	0S19	24N32	1N06	0S30	10S48

Moon Phenomena

Max/0 Decl

dy	hr mn	
5	1:59	28S29
11	4:39	0 N
17	14:40	28N32
25	2:10	0 S

Max/0 Lat

dy	hr mn	
6	1:07	5S13
12	1:19	0 N
18	15:44	5N16
26	4:09	0 S

Perigee/Apogee

dy	hr m		kilometers
10	7:05	p	356900
23	15:46	a	406295

PH	dy	hr mn	
☾	3	15:25	13♐32
●	10	9:02	20♓17
☽	17	4:12	27♊04
○	25	7:01	5♎07
☍ (eclipse)	25	7:14	A 0.956

Void of Course Moon

Last Aspect			☽ Ingress	
2 7:49	♆	△	♐	2 13:57
4 15:42	♆	□	♑	4 21:16
6 19:36	♆	✶	♒	7 0:40
8 18:57	♀	☌	♓	9 1:05
10 19:47	♆	☌	♈	11 0:20
12 11:09	♂	✶	♉	13 0:29
14 22:30	♆	✶	♊	15 3:17
17 4:44	♆	□	♋	17 9:42
19 18:53	☉	△	♌	19 19:34
22 6:35	♂	☍	♍	22 7:43
24 15:50	♆	☍	♎	24 20:39
26 23:10	☿	☍	♏	27 9:04
29 15:41	♆	△	♐	29 19:53

DAILY ASPECTARIAN

1 F: ☉△☽ 0:54; ☽☍♃ 1:41; ☽⋕♅ 1:42; ☽⚼♆ 2:31; ☽△☿ 4:19; ☽∥♂ 4:32; ☽□♂ 5:09; ☉✶♃ 12:16; ☿⚺♂ 12:43; ☽□♀ 13:10; ☽⚻⚷ 13:21; ♀✶⚷ 14:59; ☿⋕⚷ 17:36; ☽☍♅ 17:54

2 Sa: ☽∠⚳ 0:34; ☽∥♇ 7:17; ☽△♆ 7:49; ☽∥⚳ 9:33; ☽✶♇ 16:21; ☽⚼⚷ 18:23; ☽△⚷ 22:29; ☽□☿ 23:40

3 Su: ☿∠♇ 1:44; ☽⚺⚳ 5:52; ☉∥☿ 7:43; ☽□♄ 9:13; ☽⚻♃ 12:05; ♀□♅ 13:19; ☉□☽ 15:25; ☿⚺⚷ 15:27; ☊ R 15:37; ♂⋕♅ 15:40; ☽✶♂ 18:13; ☽∠♇ 20:29

4 M: ☽⚻♅ 2:41; ♃∠♆ 2:58; ☽✶♀ 4:02; ☽□♆ 15:42; ☽⚼♃ 15:50; ☿✶♅ 20:25; ☽∠♂ 23:01; ☽⚺♇ 23:37

5 Tu: ☽⚼♅ 5:35; ☽∠♀ 9:29; ☽☌⚳ 13:18; ☽✶♄ 15:39; ☽△♃ 18:32

6 W: ☉✶☽ 1:02; ☽⚺♂ 2:38; ☽□⚷ 3:41; ☽△♅ 7:29; ♀⋕♃ 8:37; ☉∠♇ 10:53; ☽✶☿ 12:56; ☽⚺♀ 13:38; ☽∠♄ 17:22; ☽✶♆ 19:36; ♂✶⚷ 23:05

7 Th: ☿⚺♀ 2:01; ☽☌♇ 2:56; ☉∠☽ 4:05; ☽∥⚳ 12:53; ☽∥♇ 15:18; ☉⚺⚷ 16:09; ♀∠⚳ 16:39; ☽⚺⚳ 16:41; ☽∠☿ 17:30; ☽⚺♄ 18:15; ☽∠♆ 20:17; ☽□♃ 21:09

8 F: ☿∥♆ 4:24; ☽✶⚷ 5:20; ☉⚺☽ 6:13; ☽☌♂ 6:52; ☽□♅ 8:51; ☿☌♆ 15:07; ☽⋕♅ 15:27; ☽∠⚳ 17:17; ☽☌♀ 18:57; ☽⚺♆ 20:22; ☽∥♂ 20:25; ☽⚺☿ 21:08; ☿∠♃ 23:56

9 Sa: ☽⋕♃ 1:42; ☽⚺♇ 3:19; ☽∠⚷ 5:17; ☽∥♀ 6:28; ♀⚺♆ 12:51; ☽✶⚳ 17:28; ☽☌♄ 18:24; ☽✶♃ 21:25; ☽∥♄ 22:47; ♂□♅ 22:57; ☉✶♅ 23:02; ☉⚺♂ 23:21

10 Su: ☽⋕⚷ 1:47; ☽∠♇ 3:00; ☿ ♈ 4:04; ☽⚺⚷ 4:59; ☽✶♅ 8:24; ☽⚺♂ 8:53; ☉☌☽ 9:02; ☉∥☽ 16:20; ☽☌♆ 19:47; ☽∥♆ 21:11; ☽∠♃ 21:19; ☿✶♇ 22:22; ☽⚺♀ 22:26

11 M: ☽✶♇ 2:40; ☽☌☿ 3:16; ☽⋕☿ 3:17; ☽∥☿ 6:25; ☽∠♅ 8:07; ☽∠♂ 9:50; ☽⋕♆ 12:07; ☉⋕☽ 15:45; ☽□⚳ 17:45; ☽⚺♄ 18:09; ☽⚺♃ 21:26; ♀ ♓ 21:52

12 Tu: ☽∠♀ 0:24; ☊ D 1:21; ☽☌⚷ 4:43; ☽∥⚷ 7:59; ☽⚺♅ 8:09; ☽⋕♄ 10:31; ☽✶♂ 11:09; ☉⚺☽ 12:07; ☽∠♄ 18:31; ☿∠♅ 18:44; ☽⚺♆ 19:53; ☽⋕♀ 22:10

13 W: ☿⋕♆ 2:40; ☽✶♀ 2:57; ☽□♇ 2:59; ♀⚺♇ 3:12; ⚳✶♄ 4:55; ♂⋕♃ 9:35; ☽⋕♂ 9:44; ☽∥♃ 9:44; ☽⚺☿ 10:44; ☉⋕☿ 12:36; ☉∠☽ 14:34; ☽✶♄ 19:31; ☽∥♅ 19:38; ☽△⚳ 19:42; ☽∠♆ 20:47; ☽☌♃ 23:14

14 Th: ☽⚺⚷ 6:27; ♀∠⚷ 6:44; ☽☌♅ 10:01; ☉∥♆ 12:57; ☽∠☿ 15:51; ☽□♂ 16:02; ☉✶☽ 17:58; ☿∠♂ 18:06; ☽⋕♇ 20:45; ☽⚼⚳ 21:50; ☽✶♆ 22:30; ☽⋕⚳ 23:57

15 F: ☽△♇ 6:01; ☽∠⚷ 8:32; ☽□♀ 11:01; ☽✶☿ 22:12

16 Sa: ☽□♄ 0:07; ☽⚻⚳ 0:57; ☽⚺♃ 4:23; ☽⚼♇ 8:54; ☽✶⚷ 11:35; ☿⚺♄ 13:58; ☽⚺♅ 15:21; ☿□⚳ 23:08

17 Su: ☽△♂ 1:03; ☊ R 4:12; ☉□☽ 4:12; ☽□♆ 4:44; ☽∠♃ 8:27; ☉☌♆ 11:24; ☽⚻♇ 12:43; ☽∠♅ 19:25; ☽△♀ 23:56

18 M: ☿⚺♃ 5:03; ☽⚼♂ 7:14; ☽△♄ 8:30; ☽☍⚳ 10:06; ☽✶♃ 13:26; ☽□☿ 14:30; ☽□⚷ 20:26

19 Tu: ☽✶♅ 0:21; ☽⚼♀ 8:08; ☽⚼♄ 13:58; ☽⚻♂ 14:22; ☽△♆ 14:31; ♂⚺♆ 16:58; ☉△☽ 18:53; ☽☍♇ 22:51; ☉∠♃ 23:40

20 W: ☉ ♈ 3:08; ☿∥⚷ 4:57; ☽⋕⚳ 9:29; ☿⋕♄ 11:44; ☽⋕♇ 13:44; ☽⚻♀ 17:14; ☿☌⚷ 17:28; ☿⋕♀ 17:59; ☽⚻♄ 20:03; ☽⚼♆ 20:25; ☽⚻⚳ 22:29

21 Th: ☽□♃ 1:36; ☉⚼☽ 3:28; ♂∠⚳ 3:55; ♀∥♄ 5:51; ☽△⚷ 8:08; ☽△☿ 9:58; ☽□♅ 12:08; ♀⋕⚷ 13:45; ☽∥♅ 18:51; ☉✶♇ 20:04; ♀☌♄ 23:11

22 F: ☽⚻♆ 2:43; ☽∥♃ 4:42; ☽⚼⚳ 5:23; ☿⚺♅ 6:28; ☽☍♂ 6:35; ☽⚻♇ 11:10; ☉⚻☽ 12:32; ☽⚼⚷ 14:37; ☽⋕♂ 18:58; ☽⚼☿ 19:57; ♂ ♓ 23:48

23 Sa: ☽∥☿ 5:31; ♀✶⚳ 8:05; ☽☍♄ 9:19; ☽△⚳ 12:31; ☽☍♀ 12:55; ☽⋕♄ 14:22; ☽∥⚷ 14:24; ☽△♃ 15:23; ♄⋕⚷ 16:24; ☽⚼♇ 17:41; ☽⋕♀ 19:03; ☽⚻⚷ 21:14

24 Su: ☽△♅ 1:11; ☽⚻☿ 5:38; ☽☍♆ 15:50; ♀✶♃ 16:38; ☽⋕♆ 17:27; ☉∥☽ 18:26; ☽⚼♃ 22:24; ☽⚻♂ 23:48

25 M: ☽△♇ 0:12; ♂⚺♇ 5:59; ☉☍☽ 7:01; ☽⚼♅ 7:45; ☉⋕♆ 7:55; ☽∥♆ 10:48; ♀∠♇ 10:59; ☉⋕☽ 11:02; ☉∠♅ 16:02; ☿⋕♂ 21:52; ☽⚻♄ 22:46

26 Tu: ☽□⚳ 2:39; ☊ D 4:15; ☽∥♀ 4:18; ☽⚻♃ 5:16; ☽⚼♂ 8:14; ☽⚻♀ 8:48; ☽☍⚷ 10:17; ☽∥♄ 13:08; ☽⋕⚷ 13:56; ☽⚻♅ 14:07; ☽☍☿ 23:10; ♀⚺⚷ 23:44

27 W: ☽∥♂ 3:21; ☽⚻♆ 4:32; ☽⚼♄ 5:11; ☽⋕☿ 7:35; ☽□♇ 12:38; ☽△♂ 16:19; ♂∠⚷ 17:52; ☽⚼♀ 18:14

28 Th: ☽⋕♃ 0:24; ☉⚻☽ 0:36; ☽⋕♅ 8:38; ☽⚼♆ 10:22; ☽△♄ 11:12; ♀✶♅ 14:00; ☽✶⚳ 15:36; ☽☍♃ 18:00; ☽⚻⚷ 22:07

29 F: ☽☍♅ 1:47; ☽△♀ 3:03; ☉⚼☽ 8:34; ☽∥♇ 12:18; ☽⚻☿ 13:11; ⚴ R 13:18; ☽△♆ 15:41; ☽∥⚳ 17:18; ☽∠⚳ 21:17; ☽✶♇ 23:24

30 Sa: ☽⚼⚷ 3:14; ☽□♂ 6:44; ☉⋕♀ 13:20; ☉△☽ 15:45; ☽⚼☿ 18:37; ☽□♄ 21:30

31 Su: ☽⚺⚳ 2:15; ☽∠♇ 3:50; ☽⚻♃ 4:27; ☽△⚷ 7:40; ⚶ ♋ 11:03; ☽⚻♅ 11:07; ☽□♀ 18:07; ☽△☿ 22:55

April 2024

LONGITUDE

Day	Sid.Time	☉	☽	☽ 12 hour	Mean☊	True ☊	☿	♀	♂	⚳	♃	♄	⚷	♅	♆	♇
	h m s	° ' "	° ' "	° ' "	° '	° '	° '	° '	° '	° '	° '	° '	° '	° '	° '	° '
1 M	12 39 23	11♈45 06	27♐45 06	4♑21 00	16♈03.4	15♈37.2	27♈10.0	24♓50.9	7♓00.6	16♑12.6	17♉21.2	13♓35.9	18♈56.8	20♉47.1	27♓54.4	1♒52.0
2 Tu	12 43 19	12 44 18	11♑02 14	17 49 02	16 00.2	15R 37.4	27R 13.1	26 05.1	7 47.3	16 25.9	17 34.1	13 42.7	19 00.4	20 50.0	27 56.6	1 52.9
3 W	12 47 16	13 43 28	24 41 34	1♒39 54	15 57.0	15 37.3	27 09.1	27 19.3	8 34.0	16 39.0	17 47.0	13 49.4	19 03.9	20 53.0	27 58.8	1 53.7
4 Th	12 51 12	14 42 37	8♒43 59	15 53 39	15 53.9	15D 37.2	26 58.3	28 33.4	9 20.7	16 51.8	18 00.0	13 56.1	19 07.4	20 55.9	28 01.0	1 54.5
5 F	12 55 09	15 41 44	23 08 35	0♓28 21	15 50.7	15 37.2	26 41.1	29 47.6	10 07.4	17 04.4	18 13.1	14 02.7	19 11.0	20 58.9	28 03.2	1 55.3
6 Sa	12 59 06	16 40 49	7♓52 20	15 19 46	15 47.5	15 37.3	26 18.0	1♈01.7	10 54.1	17 16.7	18 26.2	14 09.3	19 14.5	21 01.9	28 05.4	1 56.1
7 Su	13 03 02	17 39 52	22 49 47	0♈21 24	15 44.3	15 37.4	25 49.4	2 15.9	11 40.7	17 28.8	18 39.4	14 15.9	19 18.1	21 04.9	28 07.6	1 56.8
8 M	13 06 59	18 38 53	7♈53 32	15 25 04	15 41.2	15R 37.5	25 16.1	3 30.0	12 27.4	17 40.7	18 52.6	14 22.4	19 21.6	21 07.9	28 09.8	1 57.5
9 Tu	13 10 55	19 37 52	22 54 55	0♉22 00	15 38.0	15 37.5	24 38.8	4 44.1	13 14.0	17 52.2	19 05.9	14 28.8	19 25.2	21 11.0	28 11.9	1 58.2
10 W	13 14 52	20 36 49	7♉45 21	15 04 05	15 34.8	15 37.3	23 58.2	5 58.2	14 00.7	18 03.6	19 19.2	14 35.3	19 28.7	21 14.1	28 14.1	1 58.9
11 Th	13 18 48	21 35 45	22 17 27	29 24 54	15 31.6	15 36.7	23 15.2	7 12.3	14 47.3	18 14.7	19 32.5	14 41.6	19 32.2	21 17.2	28 16.2	1 59.5
12 F	13 22 45	22 34 38	6♊26 00	13♊20 31	15 28.4	15 36.0	22 30.6	8 26.4	15 33.9	18 25.5	19 46.0	14 48.0	19 35.8	21 20.3	28 18.3	2 00.1
13 Sa	13 26 41	23 33 29	20 08 20	26 49 30	15 25.3	15 35.1	21 45.3	9 40.5	16 20.5	18 36.0	19 59.4	14 54.3	19 39.3	21 23.5	28 20.4	2 00.7
14 Su	13 30 38	24 32 17	3♋24 13	9♋52 46	15 22.1	15 34.3	21 00.2	10 54.6	17 07.1	18 46.3	20 12.9	15 00.5	19 42.9	21 26.7	28 22.5	2 01.2
15 M	13 34 35	25 31 04	16 15 30	22 32 54	15 18.9	15D 33.7	20 16.1	12 08.6	17 53.7	18 56.3	20 26.4	15 06.7	19 46.4	21 29.9	28 24.6	2 01.8
16 Tu	13 38 31	26 29 48	28 45 27	4♌53 42	15 15.7	15 33.6	19 33.8	13 22.7	18 40.2	19 06.0	20 40.0	15 12.8	19 50.0	21 33.1	28 26.7	2 02.3
17 W	13 42 28	27 28 30	10♌58 12	16 59 32	15 12.6	15 34.0	18 53.9	14 36.7	19 26.8	19 15.5	20 53.6	15 18.9	19 53.5	21 36.4	28 28.7	2 02.7
18 Th	13 46 24	28 27 10	22 58 16	28 55 00	15 09.4	15 34.8	18 17.1	15 50.7	20 13.3	19 24.6	21 07.3	15 25.0	19 57.0	21 39.6	28 30.8	2 03.1
19 F	13 50 21	29 25 47	4♍50 14	10♍44 32	15 06.2	15 36.0	17 44.0	17 04.8	20 59.8	19 33.5	21 20.9	15 30.9	20 00.5	21 42.9	28 32.8	2 03.6
20 Sa	13 54 17	0♉24 22	16 38 24	22 32 17	15 03.0	15 37.3	17 14.9	18 18.8	21 46.3	19 42.1	21 34.7	15 36.9	20 04.0	21 46.2	28 34.8	2 03.9
21 Su	13 58 14	1 22 55	28 26 38	4♎21 53	14 59.9	15 38.5	16 50.2	19 32.8	22 32.7	19 50.4	21 48.4	15 42.7	20 07.5	21 49.5	28 36.8	2 04.3
22 M	14 02 10	2 21 26	10♎18 22	16 16 26	14 56.7	15R 39.2	16 30.2	20 46.8	23 19.2	19 58.3	22 02.2	15 48.6	20 11.0	21 52.8	28 38.8	2 04.6
23 Tu	14 06 07	3 19 56	22 16 24	28 18 30	14 53.5	15 39.1	16 15.0	22 00.7	24 05.6	20 06.0	22 16.0	15 54.3	20 14.5	21 56.1	28 40.7	2 04.9
24 W	14 10 03	4 18 23	4♏22 59	10♏30 04	14 50.3	15 38.2	16 04.8	23 14.7	24 52.0	20 13.4	22 29.8	16 00.0	20 18.0	21 59.5	28 42.7	2 05.1
25 Th	14 14 00	5 16 48	16 39 55	22 52 41	14 47.1	15 36.3	15D 59.6	24 28.7	25 38.4	20 20.5	22 43.7	16 05.7	20 21.4	22 02.8	28 44.6	2 05.4
26 F	14 17 57	6 15 12	29 08 31	5♐27 32	14 44.0	15 33.5	15 59.4	25 42.6	26 24.7	20 27.3	22 57.5	16 11.2	20 24.9	22 06.2	28 46.5	2 05.6
27 Sa	14 21 53	7 13 34	11♐49 49	18 15 30	14 40.8	15 30.3	16 04.2	26 56.6	27 11.1	20 33.8	23 11.5	16 16.8	20 28.3	22 09.6	28 48.4	2 05.8
28 Su	14 25 50	8 11 54	24 44 40	1♑17 24	14 37.6	15 26.9	16 13.8	28 10.5	27 57.4	20 39.9	23 25.4	16 22.2	20 31.7	22 13.0	28 50.3	2 05.9
29 M	14 29 46	9 10 13	7♑53 47	14 33 54	14 34.4	15 23.9	16 28.2	29 24.4	28 43.7	20 45.7	23 39.4	16 27.6	20 35.1	22 16.4	28 52.1	2 06.0
30 Tu	14 33 43	10♉08 30	21 17 50	28 05 37	14♈31.3	15♈21.7	16♈47.2	0♉38.4	29♓30.0	20♑51.2	23♉53.3	16♓33.0	20♈38.5	22♉19.8	28♓53.9	2♒06.1

1st of Month

Julian Day # 2460401.5
Obliquity 23°26'19"
SVP 4♓55'21"
GC 27♐10.7
Eris 24♈39.7

Day	⚴
1	8♐34.3R
6	8 22.5R
11	7 58.5R
16	7 22.3R
21	6 34.2R
26	5 34.9R

Day	⚵
1	7♍45.0R
6	7 08.5R
11	6 41.8R
16	6 25.1R
21	6 18.1R
26	6 20.7

Day	⚶
1	0♋09.1
6	1 36.5
11	3 08.7
16	4 45.1
21	6 25.5
26	8 09.4

DECLINATION and LATITUDE

Day	☉ Decl	☽ Decl	☽ Lat	☽ 12h Decl	☿ Decl	☿ Lat	♀ Decl	♀ Lat	♂ Decl	♂ Lat	⚳ Decl	⚳ Lat	♃ Decl	♃ Lat	♄ Decl	♄ Lat
1 M	4N39	28S28	5S02	28S33	13N29	3N15	3S24	1S28	10S04	1S13	23S25	0S59	16N13	0S49	7S59	1S40
2 Tu	5 02	28 14	5 17	27 30	13 32	3 17	2 55	1 28	9 47	1 14	23 26	1 01	16 17	0 49	7 57	1 40
3 W	5 25	26 20	5 14	24 45	13 32	3 17	2 25	1 29	9 30	1 14	23 27	1 04	16 21	0 49	7 54	1 40
4 Th	5 48	22 46	4 52	20 26	13 27	3 16	1 56	1 29	9 12	1 14	23 29	1 07	16 25	0 49	7 52	1 40
5 F	6 11	17 46	4 12	14 49	13 18	3 14	1 27	1 29	8 55	1 14	23 30	1 09	16 29	0 49	7 49	1 41
6 Sa	6 33	11 38	3 15	8 15	13 06	3 10	0 58	1 30	8 37	1 14	23 31	1 12	16 32	0 48	7 47	1 41
7 Su	6 56	4 44	2 03	1 08	12 50	3 04	0 28	1 30	8 20	1 14	23 32	1 15	16 36	0 48	7 45	1 41
8 M	7 18	2N28	0 43	6N03	12 31	2 57	0N01	1 30	8 02	1 15	23 33	1 18	16 40	0 48	7 42	1 41
9 Tu	7 41	9 32	0N40	12 52	12 09	2 48	0 30	1 30	7 44	1 15	23 34	1 20	16 44	0 48	7 40	1 41
10 W	8 03	15 59	1 60	18 51	11 44	2 37	0 60	1 30	7 26	1 15	23 36	1 23	16 47	0 48	7 37	1 41
11 Th	8 25	21 24	3 10	23 36	11 17	2 26	1 29	1 30	7 09	1 15	23 37	1 26	16 51	0 48	7 35	1 41
12 F	8 47	25 26	4 06	26 50	10 49	2 13	1 59	1 29	6 51	1 15	23 38	1 29	16 55	0 48	7 33	1 42
13 Sa	9 09	27 50	4 47	28 24	10 19	1 59	2 28	1 29	6 33	1 15	23 40	1 32	16 58	0 48	7 31	1 42
14 Su	9 31	28 34	5 10	28 19	9 48	1 44	2 57	1 29	6 15	1 15	23 41	1 35	17 02	0 47	7 28	1 42
15 M	9 52	27 42	5 17	26 44	9 17	1 28	3 27	1 28	5 57	1 15	23 43	1 38	17 06	0 47	7 26	1 42
16 Tu	10 13	25 27	5 09	23 53	8 46	1 12	3 56	1 28	5 38	1 16	23 44	1 41	17 10	0 47	7 24	1 42
17 W	10 34	22 04	4 47	20 02	8 15	0 55	4 25	1 27	5 20	1 16	23 46	1 44	17 13	0 47	7 22	1 42
18 Th	10 55	17 50	4 12	15 27	7 46	0 38	4 54	1 27	5 02	1 16	23 48	1 47	17 17	0 47	7 19	1 42
19 F	11 16	12 57	3 27	10 20	7 18	0 22	5 23	1 26	4 44	1 16	23 50	1 50	17 21	0 47	7 17	1 43
20 Sa	11 37	7 38	2 34	4 52	6 51	0 05	5 52	1 25	4 25	1 16	23 51	1 53	17 24	0 47	7 15	1 43
21 Su	11 57	2 03	1 34	0S47	6 26	0S11	6 21	1 25	4 07	1 16	23 53	1 56	17 28	0 47	7 13	1 43
22 M	12 17	3S38	0 30	6 27	6 04	0 27	6 49	1 24	3 49	1 16	23 55	1 59	17 32	0 46	7 11	1 43
23 Tu	12 37	9 14	0S37	11 57	5 44	0 43	7 18	1 23	3 30	1 16	23 57	2 03	17 35	0 46	7 09	1 43
24 W	12 57	14 35	1 42	17 04	5 26	0 58	7 46	1 22	3 12	1 16	23 59	2 06	17 39	0 46	7 07	1 43
25 Th	13 17	19 25	2 43	21 34	5 11	1 12	8 14	1 21	2 54	1 16	24 01	2 09	17 43	0 46	7 05	1 44
26 F	13 36	23 30	3 37	25 10	4 59	1 25	8 42	1 20	2 35	1 16	24 04	2 12	17 46	0 46	7 03	1 44
27 Sa	13 55	26 32	4 22	27 34	4 49	1 38	9 10	1 19	2 17	1 16	24 06	2 16	17 50	0 46	7 01	1 44
28 Su	14 14	28 14	4 54	28 31	4 42	1 50	9 37	1 17	1 58	1 16	24 08	2 19	17 53	0 46	6 59	1 44
29 M	14 33	28 23	5 12	27 51	4 37	2 01	10 04	1 16	1 40	1 16	24 11	2 22	17 57	0 46	6 57	1 44
30 Tu	14N51	26S54	5S13	25S33	4N35	2S11	10N32	1S15	1S22	1S16	24S13	2S26	18N01	0S46	6S55	1S45

Day	⚷ Decl	⚷ Lat	♅ Decl	♅ Lat	♆ Decl	♆ Lat	♇ Decl	♇ Lat
1	8N31	1N11	17N41	0S16	1S57	1S13	22S37	2S57
6	8 37	1 11	17 45	0 16	1 53	1 13	22 37	2 57
11	8 44	1 10	17 49	0 16	1 49	1 13	22 37	2 58
16	8 50	1 10	17 53	0 16	1 45	1 13	22 37	2 59
21	8 56	1 10	17 58	0 16	1 41	1 14	22 37	2 60
26	9 03	1 09	18 02	0 16	1 37	1 14	22 38	3 01

Day	⚴ Decl	⚴ Lat	⚵ Decl	⚵ Lat	⚶ Decl	⚶ Lat	Eris Decl	Eris Lat
1	16N30	38N40	8N26	0S15	24N33	1N07	0S30	10S48
6	17 45	39 54	8 58	0N06	24 40	1 14	0 29	10 47
11	18 59	41 06	9 26	0 25	24 45	1 20	0 27	10 47
16	20 10	42 14	9 49	0 43	24 48	1 27	0 26	10 47
21	21 19	43 17	10 07	0 59	24 50	1 33	0 25	10 47
26	22 23	44 15	10 20	1 15	24 50	1 38	0 24	10 47

Moon Phenomena

Max/0 Decl
dy hr mn
1 8:53 28S34
7 15:47 0 N
13 22:33 28N34
21 8:41 0 S
28 14:20 28S31

Max/0 Lat
dy hr mn
2 8:08 5S18
8 12:20 0 N
14 22:41 5N17
22 10:46 0 S
29 13:27 5S14

Perigee/Apogee
dy hr m kilometers
7 17:52 p 358853
20 2:12 a 405623

PH dy hr mn
☾ 2 3:16 12♑52
● 8 18:22 19♈24
● 8 1098:29 T 04'28"
☽ 15 19:14 26♋18
○ 23 23:50 4♏18

Void of Course Moon

Last Aspect			☽ Ingress		
1	0:17	♆ □	♑	1	4:06
3	5:42	♆ ⚹	♒	3	9:09
5	5:41	☿ ⚹	♓	5	11:14
7	8:28	♆ ☌	♈	7	11:26
9	2:40	☿ ☌	♉	9	11:24
11	10:05	♆ ⚹	♊	11	13:00
13	14:47	♆ □	♋	13	17:46
15	23:23	♆ △	♌	16	2:25
18	12:03	☉ △	♍	18	14:12
21	0:21	♆ ☍	♎	21	3:09
22	23:25	♀ ☍	♏	23	15:21
25	23:18	♆ △	♐	26	1:38
28	7:32	♆ □	♑	28	9:39
30	15:20	♂ ⚹	♒	30	15:21

DAILY ASPECTARIAN

1 M ☽□♆ 0:17 · ☽⚺♇ 7:31 · ☽⚼♃ 8:31 · ☽⚼♅ 14:39 · ☽⚹♂ 17:50 · ☿R 22:16

2 Tu ☉□☽ 3:16 · ☊R 4:28 · ☽⚹♄ 4:48 · ☽☌⚳ 9:43 · ☽△♃ 11:45 · ☽□⚷ 14:09 · ☽△♅ 17:21 · ☿⚺♀ 21:00 · ☽∠♂ 21:56

3 W ☉⚺♄ 2:43 · ☽□☿ 4:13 · ☽⚹♀ 4:59 · ☽⚹♆ 5:42 · ☽∠♄ 7:11 · ☽☌♇ 12:24 · ♀☌♆ 13:12 · ☽∥⚳ 20:00

4 Th ☽∥♇ 0:54 · ☽⚺♂ 1:05 · ♀∥♆ 1:28 · ☽∠♆ 7:13 · ☽⚺♄ 8:48 · ☽∠♀ 8:52 · ☉⚹☽ 10:46 · ☽⚺⚳ 13:49 · ☽□♃ 15:44 · ☽⚹⚷ 17:26 · ☽□♅ 20:25 · ☊D 22:42

5 F ☽⋕♅ 0:08 · ♀ ♈ 4:01 · ☽⋕♃ 5:20 · ☽⚹☿ 5:41 · ☽⚺♆ 8:04 · ☽⚺♀ 11:53 · ☉∠☽ 13:15 · ☽⚺♇ 14:22 · ☽∠⚳ 14:49 · ☽∠⚷ 18:06 · ☽⋕☿ 18:22

6 Sa ♂⋕⚷ 0:11 · ☽☌♂ 5:09 · ☽∠☿ 5:22 · ☿∠♂ 7:48 · ☽☌♄ 10:11 · ☽⋕⚷ 10:40 · ☽∥♂ 11:10 · ☽∥♄ 13:41 · ☽∠♇ 14:35 · ☉⚺☽ 15:10 · ☽⚹⚳ 15:20 · ☉⋕☽ 16:55 · ☽⚹♃ 17:14 · ♀⚹♇ 17:47 · ☽⚺⚷ 18:20 · ☉□⚳ 18:22 · ☽⚹♅ 21:12

7 Su ☽⚺☿ 4:37 · ☽☌♆ 8:28 · ☽∥♆ 9:37 · ☽⚹♇ 14:33 · ☽∥♀ 15:15 · ☽⋕♀ 16:15 · ☽☌♀ 16:23 · ☽∠♃ 17:31 · ☽∠♅ 21:11 · ☽⋕♆ 21:56

8 M ☉⚺♃ 7:12 · ☽⚺♂ 7:40 · ♀∠♃ 8:55 · ☽⚺♄ 10:24 · ☊R 12:04 · ☽□⚳ 15:49 · ☉∥☽ 17:12 · ☽⋕♄ 17:32 · ☽⚺♃ 17:47 · ☽⋕♂ 18:01 · ☉☌☽ 18:22 · ☽☌⚷ 18:22 · ☉☌⚷ 18:30 · ☽∥⚷ 21:01 · ☽⚺♅ 21:13 · ☉⋕♄ 23:05

9 Tu ☉⋕♂ 2:07 · ☽☌☿ 2:40 · ♂∥♄ 6:58 · ☽⚺♆ 8:31 · ☽∥☿ 8:50 · ☽∠♂ 9:02 · ☽∠♄ 10:39 · ☽□♇ 14:36 · ☽⚺♀ 20:49

10 W ☽∥♃ 3:17 · ♀∠♅ 5:22 · ☽∥♅ 7:32 · ☽∠♆ 9:00 · ☽⚹♂ 10:50 · ☽⚹♄ 11:17 · ☉⚺♅ 16:01 · ☽△⚳ 17:10 · ☽☌♃ 19:21 · ☽⚺⚷ 19:23 · ♂☌♄ 20:37 · ☽☌♅ 22:19 · ☉⚺☽ 22:45 · ♃⚺⚷ 23:16 · ☽∠♀ 23:51

11 Th ☽⚺☿ 1:32 · ☽⋕♇ 6:21 · ☽⚹♆ 10:05 · ☽⋕⚳ 12:10 · ♀⋕♆ 15:20 · ☽△♇ 16:24 · ☽⚼⚳ 18:46 · ☽∠⚷ 20:50 · ☉∥⚷ 21:34 · ☉☌☿ 23:04

12 F ☽∠☿ 1:46 · ☉∠☽ 2:07 · ☽⚹♀ 3:48 · ☽□♄ 14:40 · ☽□♂ 16:52 · ☽⚼♇ 18:27 · ☽⚻⚳ 21:14 · ☽⚹⚷ 23:08 · ☽⚺♃ 23:44

13 Sa ☽⚺♅ 2:15 · ☽⚹☿ 2:44 · ☉⚹☽ 6:36 · ☿⚺♅ 10:49 · ☽□♆ 14:47 · ♂∠♇ 20:57 · ☽⚻♇ 21:28

14 Su ☽∠♃ 3:24 · ☽∠♅ 5:38 · ☉∥☿ 7:57 · ☽□♀ 15:25 · ☿⚺♃ 19:39 · ☽△♄ 21:49

15 M ☽△♂ 3:19 · ☽☍⚳ 5:10 · ☽□⚷ 6:43 · ☽□☿ 7:13 · ☽⚹♃ 8:06 · ☽⚹♅ 10:02 · ☿☌⚷ 15:24 · ☊D 18:56 · ☉□☽ 19:14 · ☿∥⚷ 20:45 · ☽△♆ 23:23

16 Tu ☽⚼♄ 2:52 · ☽☍♇ 6:24 · ☽⚼♂ 10:15 · ☽⋕⚳ 12:53 · ☿□⚳ 13:20 · ☿⚺♂ 14:47 · ♂⚹⚳ 16:42 · ☽⋕♇ 20:33

17 W ☽⚼♆ 5:00 · ☽△♀ 8:04 · ☽⚻♄ 8:43 · ♀⚺♄ 14:54 · ♂⚺⚷ 14:55 · ☽△☿ 15:02 · ☽⚻⚳ 16:45 · ☽△⚷ 17:54 · ☽⚻♂ 18:05 · ☽□♃ 20:12 · ☽□♅ 21:21 · ☽∥♅ 23:31

18 Th ☉⚺♆ 1:32 · ☽∥♃ 2:47 · ♀⋕♂ 4:03 · ☽⚻♆ 11:13 · ☉△☽ 12:03 · ☽⚼♀ 17:45 · ☽⚻♇ 18:22 · ☽⚼☿ 19:55 · ☽⚼⚳ 23:26

19 F ☿⋕♄ 0:21 · ☽⚼⚷ 0:21 · ☉∥☽ 7:17 · ☿☌♀ 9:01 · ☉ ♉ 14:01 · ♂⚹♃ 15:30 · ☽∥⚷ 18:22 · ☉⚼☽ 21:16 · ☽☍♄ 21:54 · ♂⚹♅ 23:57

20 Sa ☽⚼♇ 0:52 · ☽⚻☿ 1:12 · ☽⋕♄ 1:42 · ☽∥☿ 3:43 · ☽⚻♀ 3:48 · ☉∠♄ 5:42 · ☽△⚳ 6:18 · ☽⚻⚷ 7:00 · ☽∥♀ 7:06 · ☽△♃ 10:15 · ☽△♅ 10:29 · ☽☍♂ 11:10 · ☽⋕♂ 14:42

21 Su ☽☍♆ 0:21 · ☽⋕♆ 1:36 · ♃☌♅ 2:28 · ☿∥♀ 2:45 · ♀□⚳ 6:24 · ☉⚻☽ 6:30 · ☽△♇ 7:22 · ♀☌⚷ 11:50 · ☽∥♆ 15:44 · ☉□♇ 17:03 · ☽⚼♅ 17:03 · ☽⚼♃ 17:16

22 M ☽∥♂ 0:45 · ⚵D 3:00 · ☽⋕☿ 9:45 · ☊R 10:42 · ☽⚻♄ 11:09 · ☽☍☿ 12:11 · ☽⋕♀ 14:49 · ☽∥♄ 15:01 · ♀⋕♄ 17:04 · ☽□⚳ 19:37 · ☽☍⚷ 19:55 · ♀⚺♅ 22:26 · ☽⋕⚷ 22:54 · ☽⚻♅ 23:19 · ☽☍♀ 23:25 · ☽⚻♃ 23:59

23 Tu ☽⚻♂ 3:53 · ♀⚺♃ 6:05 · ☽⚻♆ 12:46 · ☉⋕☽ 16:02 · ☽⚼♄ 17:16 · ☽□♇ 19:28 · ☉☍☽ 23:50

24 W ☿⚺♄ 9:15 · ☽⚼♂ 11:29 · ☽⋕♃ 15:03 · ☽⋕♅ 16:43 · ☽⚼♆ 18:18 · ☽⚻☿ 22:42 · ☽△♄ 22:53

25 Th ⚳□⚷ 6:16 · ☽⚻⚷ 7:10 · ☽⚹⚳ 7:11 · ☽☍♅ 10:27 · ☽☍♃ 11:56 · ☿D 12:55 · ☽⚻♀ 16:43 · ☽∥♇ 18:23 · ☽△♂ 18:26 · ☽△♆ 23:18

26 F ☽⚼☿ 3:32 · ☽∥⚳ 3:52 · ☽⚹♇ 5:37 · ☽⚼⚷ 11:58 · ☽∠⚳ 12:06 · ☉⚻☽ 14:37 · ♀∥⚷ 18:58

27 Sa ☽⚼♀ 0:14 · ☽△☿ 8:01 · ☽□♄ 8:23 · ☽∠♇ 9:50 · ♀⚺♂ 12:37 · ☽△⚷ 16:11 · ☽⚺⚳ 16:24 · ☽⚻♅ 19:19 · ☉⚼☽ 20:55 · ☽⚻♃ 21:31

28 Su ☽□♂ 6:16 · ☽△♀ 6:57 · ☽□♆ 7:32 · ♀⚺♆ 13:14 · ☽⚺♇ 13:29 · ☿⚺♄ 22:50 · ☽⚼♅ 22:52

29 M ☽⚼♃ 1:24 · ☉△☽ 2:29 · ♂☌♆ 4:32 · ♂∥♆ 7:05 · ♀ ♉ 11:32 · ☽⚹♄ 15:30 · ☽□☿ 15:46 · ☽□⚷ 22:50 · ☽☌⚳ 23:12

30 Tu ☽△♅ 1:50 · ☽△♃ 4:40 · ☽⚹♆ 13:27 · ☽⚹♂ 15:20 · ♂ ♈ 15:34 · ☽□♀ 18:05 · ☽∠♄ 18:10 · ☽☌♇ 19:02 · ♀∠♄ 19:05 · ☽∥⚳ 21:08

LONGITUDE

Day	Sid.Time	☉	☽	☽ 12 hour	Mean☊	True☊	☿	♀	♂	⚳	♃	♄	⚷	♅	♆	♇
	h m s	° ' "	° ' "	° ' "	° '	° '	° '	° '	° '	° '	° '	° '	° '	° '	° '	° '
1 W	14 37 39	11♉06 45	4♒57 19	11♒52 54	14♈28.1	15♈20.6	17♈10.7	1♉52.3	0♈16.3	20♑56.4	24♉07.3	16♓38.3	20♈41.9	22♉23.3	28♓55.8	2♒06.2
2 Th	14 41 36	12 04 59	18 55 22	25 55 38	14 24.9	15D 20.6	17 38.5	3 06.2	1 02.5	21 01.3	24 21.4	16 43.5	20 45.3	22 26.7	28 57.5	2R 06.2
3 F	14 45 33	13 03 12	3♓02 32	10♓12 51	14 21.7	15 21.5	18 10.5	4 20.1	1 48.7	21 05.8	24 35.4	16 48.6	20 48.6	22 30.1	28 59.3	2 06.2
4 Sa	14 49 29	14 01 23	17 26 18	24 42 27	14 18.5	15 23.0	18 46.6	5 34.0	2 34.9	21 09.9	24 49.5	16 53.7	20 52.0	22 33.6	29 01.1	2 06.2
5 Su	14 53 26	14 59 33	2♈00 50	9♈20 51	14 15.4	15R 24.2	19 26.4	6 48.0	3 21.0	21 13.7	25 03.5	16 58.7	20 55.3	22 37.0	29 02.8	2 06.2
6 M	14 57 22	15 57 41	16 41 49	24 02 59	14 12.2	15 24.7	20 10.0	8 01.8	4 07.1	21 17.2	25 17.6	17 03.6	20 58.6	22 40.5	29 04.5	2 06.1
7 Tu	15 01 19	16 55 48	1♉23 32	8♉42 37	14 09.0	15 23.9	20 57.2	9 15.7	4 53.2	21 20.3	25 31.7	17 08.5	21 01.9	22 44.0	29 06.2	2 06.0
8 W	15 05 15	17 53 53	15 59 24	23 13 03	14 05.8	15 21.4	21 47.7	10 29.6	5 39.3	21 23.1	25 45.8	17 13.3	21 05.1	22 47.5	29 07.8	2 05.9
9 Th	15 09 12	18 51 57	0♊22 48	7♊27 58	14 02.7	15 17.5	22 41.6	11 43.5	6 25.3	21 25.5	25 59.9	17 18.0	21 08.4	22 50.9	29 09.5	2 05.7
10 F	15 13 08	19 49 59	14 27 58	21 22 23	13 59.5	15 12.4	23 38.6	12 57.4	7 11.3	21 27.6	26 14.1	17 22.7	21 11.6	22 54.4	29 11.1	2 05.5
11 Sa	15 17 05	20 47 59	28 10 52	4♋53 17	13 56.3	15 06.8	24 38.7	14 11.2	7 57.2	21 29.3	26 28.2	17 27.2	21 14.8	22 57.9	29 12.7	2 05.3
12 Su	15 21 02	21 45 58	11♋29 34	17 59 50	13 53.1	15 01.5	25 41.7	15 25.1	8 43.1	21 30.7	26 42.4	17 31.8	21 17.9	23 01.4	29 14.2	2 05.0
13 M	15 24 58	22 43 54	24 24 18	0♌43 17	13 50.0	14 57.0	26 47.6	16 38.9	9 29.0	21 31.7	26 56.5	17 36.2	21 21.1	23 04.9	29 15.8	2 04.8
14 Tu	15 28 55	23 41 49	6♌57 11	13 06 31	13 46.8	14 54.0	27 56.2	17 52.8	10 14.8	21 32.3	27 10.7	17 40.5	21 24.2	23 08.4	29 17.3	2 04.5
15 W	15 32 51	24 39 43	19 11 48	25 13 38	13 43.6	14D 52.5	29 07.6	19 06.6	11 00.6	21R 32.6	27 24.8	17 44.8	21 27.3	23 11.8	29 18.8	2 04.1
16 Th	15 36 48	25 37 34	1♍12 38	7♍09 26	13 40.4	14 52.5	0♉21.5	20 20.4	11 46.4	21 32.5	27 39.0	17 49.0	21 30.4	23 15.3	29 20.2	2 03.8
17 F	15 40 44	26 35 24	13 04 41	18 59 01	13 37.3	14 53.6	1 38.0	21 34.2	12 32.1	21 32.0	27 53.2	17 53.1	21 33.4	23 18.8	29 21.7	2 03.4
18 Sa	15 44 41	27 33 12	24 53 03	0♎47 25	13 34.1	14 55.1	2 57.1	22 48.0	13 17.8	21 31.2	28 07.3	17 57.1	21 36.5	23 22.3	29 23.1	2 03.0
19 Su	15 48 37	28 30 58	6♎42 41	12 39 23	13 30.9	14R 56.4	4 18.6	24 01.8	14 03.4	21 30.0	28 21.5	18 01.1	21 39.5	23 25.8	29 24.5	2 02.6
20 M	15 52 34	29 28 42	18 38 02	24 39 06	13 27.7	14 56.6	5 42.5	25 15.6	14 49.0	21 28.4	28 35.6	18 05.0	21 42.4	23 29.2	29 25.8	2 02.1
21 Tu	15 56 31	0♊26 26	0♏42 58	6♏49 59	13 24.5	14 55.2	7 08.8	26 29.4	15 34.6	21 26.5	28 49.8	18 08.7	21 45.4	23 32.7	29 27.2	2 01.6
22 W	16 00 27	1 24 07	13 00 26	19 14 32	13 21.4	14 51.9	8 37.5	27 43.2	16 20.1	21 24.2	29 03.9	18 12.4	21 48.3	23 36.2	29 28.5	2 01.1
23 Th	16 04 24	2 21 48	25 32 26	1♐54 14	13 18.2	14 46.5	10 08.5	28 56.9	17 05.5	21 21.6	29 18.1	18 16.1	21 51.2	23 39.6	29 29.7	2 00.6
24 F	16 08 20	3 19 27	8♐19 56	14 49 29	13 15.0	14 39.4	11 41.9	0♊10.7	17 51.0	21 18.5	29 32.2	18 19.6	21 54.0	23 43.1	29 31.0	2 00.0
25 Sa	16 12 17	4 17 05	21 22 47	27 59 42	13 11.8	14 31.1	13 17.6	1 24.4	18 36.4	21 15.2	29 46.3	18 23.1	21 56.8	23 46.5	29 32.2	1 59.4
26 Su	16 16 13	5 14 41	4♑40 03	11♑23 37	13 08.7	14 22.6	14 55.7	2 38.2	19 21.7	21 11.4	0♊00.4	18 26.4	21 59.6	23 50.0	29 33.4	1 58.8
27 M	16 20 10	6 12 17	18 10 10	24 59 29	13 05.5	14 14.8	16 36.0	3 52.0	20 07.0	21 07.3	0 14.5	18 29.7	22 02.4	23 53.4	29 34.6	1 58.2
28 Tu	16 24 06	7 09 52	1♒51 20	8♒45 31	13 02.3	14 08.5	18 18.7	5 05.7	20 52.2	21 02.8	0 28.6	18 32.9	22 05.1	23 56.8	29 35.7	1 57.5
29 W	16 28 03	8 07 26	15 41 50	22 40 07	12 59.1	14 04.2	20 03.7	6 19.5	21 37.5	20 58.0	0 42.7	18 36.0	22 07.8	24 00.2	29 36.8	1 56.8
30 Th	16 32 00	9 04 58	29 40 12	6♓41 58	12 56.0	14D 02.1	21 50.9	7 33.2	22 22.6	20 52.8	0 56.8	18 39.1	22 10.5	24 03.6	29 37.9	1 56.1
31 F	16 35 56	10♊02 30	13♓45 15	20 49 57	12♈52.8	14♈01.7	23♉40.5	8♊47.0	23♈07.7	20♑47.2	1♊10.8	18♓42.0	22♈13.1	24♉07.0	29♓38.9	1♒55.4

1st of Month

Julian Day # 2460431.5
Obliquity 23°26'19"
SVP 4♓55'17"
GC 27♐10.7
Eris 24♈59.3

Day	⚴	✱	⚶
1	4♐25.4R	6♍32.3	9♋56.7
6	3 07.2R	6 52.4	11 46.9
11	1 42.3R	7 20.6	13 40.0
16	0 13.1R	7 56.3	15 35.7
21	28♏42.3R	8 39.0	17 33.7
26	27 12.6R	9 28.0	19 33.8
31	25 46.3R	10 22.8	21 36.0

DECLINATION and LATITUDE

Day	☉ Decl	☽ Decl	☽ Lat	☽ 12h Decl	☿ Decl	☿ Lat	♀ Decl	♀ Lat	♂ Decl	♂ Lat	⚳ Decl	⚳ Lat	♃ Decl	♃ Lat	♄ Decl	♄ Lat
1 W	15N10	23S49	4S56	21S44	4N35	2S21	10N58	1S14	1S03	1S16	24S16	2S29	18N04	0S45	6S53	1S45
2 Th	15 28	19 19	4 22	16 37	4 38	2 29	11 25	1 12	0 45	1 16	24 19	2 33	18 08	0 45	6 51	1 45
3 F	15 45	13 41	3 32	10 32	4 42	2 37	11 51	1 11	0 26	1 16	24 21	2 36	18 11	0 45	6 49	1 45
4 Sa	16 03	7 14	2 28	3 48	4 50	2 44	12 17	1 09	0 08	1 16	24 24	2 40	18 15	0 45	6 47	1 45
5 Su	16 20	0 19	1 13	3N12	4 59	2 50	12 43	1 08	0N10	1 16	24 27	2 43	18 18	0 45	6 46	1 46
6 M	16 37	6N40	0N07	10 04	5 10	2 55	13 09	1 06	0 29	1 16	24 30	2 47	18 22	0 45	6 44	1 46
7 Tu	16 54	13 19	1 26	16 22	5 24	2 60	13 34	1 04	0 47	1 15	24 33	2 50	18 25	0 45	6 42	1 46
8 W	17 10	19 10	2 39	21 40	5 39	3 04	13 59	1 03	1 06	1 15	24 36	2 54	18 28	0 45	6 41	1 46
9 Th	17 26	23 50	3 41	25 36	5 56	3 07	14 23	1 01	1 24	1 15	24 39	2 58	18 32	0 45	6 39	1 46
10 F	17 42	26 58	4 28	27 54	6 15	3 09	14 47	0 59	1 42	1 15	24 43	3 01	18 35	0 45	6 37	1 47
11 Sa	17 57	28 23	4 58	28 27	6 35	3 11	15 11	0 57	2 00	1 15	24 46	3 05	18 39	0 45	6 36	1 47
12 Su	18 12	28 06	5 11	27 22	6 57	3 12	15 34	0 56	2 19	1 15	24 50	3 09	18 42	0 44	6 34	1 47
13 M	18 27	26 16	5 07	24 52	7 21	3 12	15 57	0 54	2 37	1 15	24 53	3 13	18 45	0 44	6 33	1 47
14 Tu	18 42	23 11	4 49	21 16	7 46	3 11	16 20	0 52	2 55	1 15	24 57	3 16	18 49	0 44	6 31	1 47
15 W	18 56	19 08	4 17	16 50	8 13	3 10	16 42	0 50	3 13	1 14	25 01	3 20	18 52	0 44	6 30	1 48
16 Th	19 10	14 24	3 35	11 50	8 39	3 08	17 04	0 48	3 31	1 14	25 04	3 24	18 55	0 44	6 28	1 48
17 F	19 24	9 17	2 44	6 27	9 08	3 06	17 25	0 46	3 49	1 14	25 08	3 28	18 58	0 44	6 27	1 48
18 Sa	19 37	3 40	1 47	0 51	9 38	3 03	17 46	0 44	4 07	1 14	25 12	3 32	19 02	0 44	6 25	1 48
19 Su	19 50	1S59	0 45	4S49	10 08	2 59	18 06	0 42	4 25	1 14	25 16	3 36	19 05	0 44	6 24	1 48
20 M	20 02	7 37	0S20	10 22	10 40	2 55	18 26	0 39	4 42	1 14	25 20	3 40	19 08	0 44	6 23	1 49
21 Tu	20 15	13 02	1 24	15 37	11 13	2 50	18 46	0 37	5 00	1 13	25 25	3 44	19 11	0 44	6 21	1 49
22 W	20 26	18 03	2 26	20 20	11 46	2 45	19 05	0 35	5 18	1 13	25 29	3 48	19 14	0 44	6 20	1 49
23 Th	20 38	22 24	3 21	24 14	12 20	2 39	19 23	0 33	5 35	1 13	25 33	3 52	19 17	0 44	6 19	1 49
24 F	20 49	25 46	4 08	26 59	12 55	2 33	19 41	0 31	5 53	1 13	25 38	3 56	19 21	0 43	6 18	1 50
25 Sa	20 60	27 51	4 42	28 19	13 30	2 26	19 59	0 28	6 11	1 12	25 42	3 60	19 24	0 43	6 17	1 50
26 Su	21 10	28 23	5 02	28 02	14 06	2 19	20 16	0 26	6 28	1 12	25 47	4 04	19 27	0 43	6 16	1 50
27 M	21 21	27 15	5 06	26 04	14 43	2 11	20 32	0 24	6 45	1 12	25 51	4 08	19 30	0 43	6 14	1 50
28 Tu	21 30	24 29	4 52	22 33	15 19	2 02	20 48	0 22	7 02	1 12	25 56	4 12	19 33	0 43	6 13	1 51
29 W	21 40	20 17	4 21	17 44	15 56	1 54	21 03	0 19	7 20	1 11	26 01	4 16	19 36	0 43	6 12	1 51
30 Th	21 49	14 56	3 35	11 56	16 33	1 45	21 17	0 17	7 37	1 11	26 06	4 20	19 39	0 43	6 11	1 51
31 F	21N57	8S46	2S35	5S29	17N09	1S35	21N32	0S15	7N54	1S11	26S11	4S24	19N42	0S43	6S11	1S51

Day	⚷ Decl	⚷ Lat	♅ Decl	♅ Lat	♆ Decl	♆ Lat	♇ Decl	♇ Lat
1	9N09	1N09	18N07	0S16	1S33	1S14	22S38	3S02
6	9 15	1 09	18 11	0 16	1 30	1 14	22 39	3 03
11	9 21	1 09	18 15	0 16	1 27	1 14	22 40	3 03
16	9 27	1 09	18 20	0 16	1 24	1 15	22 41	3 04
21	9 32	1 08	18 24	0 16	1 22	1 15	22 43	3 05
26	9 37	1 08	18 29	0 16	1 19	1 15	22 44	3 06
31	9N42	1N08	18N33	0S16	1S17	1S15	22S46	3S07

Day	⚴ Decl	⚴ Lat	✱ Decl	✱ Lat	⚶ Decl	⚶ Lat	Eris Decl	Eris Lat
1	23N22	45N06	10N30	1N29	24N48	1N44	0S22	10S47
6	24 15	45 49	10 35	1 43	24 44	1 49	0 21	10 47
11	25 00	46 23	10 36	1 55	24 38	1 55	0 20	10 47
16	25 38	46 49	10 33	2 07	24 31	1 60	0 19	10 47
21	26 08	47 05	10 27	2 18	24 21	2 05	0 18	10 47
26	26 29	47 11	10 18	2 28	24 09	2 10	0 18	10 47
31	26N41	47N09	10N06	2N37	23N55	2N14	0S17	10S47

Moon Phenomena

Max/0 Decl (dy hr mn)
5 1:04 0 N
11 7:42 28N29
18 15:36 0 S
25 19:51 28S25

Perigee/Apogee (dy hr m kilometers)
5 22:05 p 363164
17 19:00 a 404639

Max/0 Lat (dy hr mn)
5 21:54 0 N
12 6:27 5N11
19 16:36 0 S
26 17:08 5S06

PH (dy hr mn)
☾ 1 11:28 11♒35
● 8 3:23 18♉02
☽ 15 11:49 25♌08
○ 23 13:54 2♐55
☾ 30 17:14 9♓46

Void of Course Moon

Last Aspect	☽ Ingress
2 9:30 ♃ □	♓ 2 18:53
4 19:07 ♆ ☌	♈ 4 20:42
6 5:58 ♆ ☌	♉ 6 21:43
8 21:56 ♆ ⚹	♊ 8 23:22
11 1:50 ♆ □	♋ 11 3:14
13 9:14 ♆ △	♌ 13 10:37
15 16:42 ♃ □	♍ 15 21:34
18 3:23 ☉ △	♎ 18 10:24
19 15:49 ♂ ☍	♏ 20 22:35
23 7:29 ♆ △	♐ 23 8:25
25 14:48 ♆ □	♑ 25 15:37
27 20:03 ♆ ⚹	♒ 27 20:46
29 14:21 ♅ □	♓ 30 0:34

DAILY ASPECTARIAN

1 W: ♀□♇ 4:31; ☽∥♇ 6:58; ☉□☽ 11:28; ☊ D 11:36; ☽∠♆ 15:34; ☽∠♂ 18:52; ☽⊻♄ 20:18; ☽⚹☿ 21:49; ♃∥♅ 22:51

2 Th: ☽⚹⚷ 3:13; ☽⊻⚳ 3:41; ☽⋕♃ 5:23; ☽⋕♅ 5:26; ☽□♅ 6:07; ☽□♃ 9:30; ☉⋕☽ 16:02; ☽⊻♆ 17:10; ♇ R 17:47; ☽⊻♂ 21:49; ☽⊻♇ 22:25

3 F: ☽∠☿ 0:14; ☽⚹♀ 2:23; ☽∠⚷ 4:40; ☽∠⚳ 5:09; ☽⋕♀ 6:35; ♂⚹♇ 9:07; ☽⋕⚷ 16:53; ☉⚹☽ 17:56; ☽☌♄ 23:06; ☽∠♇ 23:27; ☉∠♆ 23:52

4 Sa: ☽∥♄ 1:33; ☽⊻☿ 2:19; ☽∠♀ 5:39; ☽⊻⚷ 5:41; ☽⚹⚳ 6:11; ☽⋕☿ 8:16; ☽⚹♅ 8:30; ☽⚹♃ 12:23; ☽☌♆ 19:07; ☽∥♆ 19:53; ☉∠☽ 20:27

5 Su: ☽⚹♇ 0:09; ☽⋕♂ 0:27; ☽∥♂ 1:45; ☽☌♂ 2:19; ☽⋕♆ 6:14; ☽⊻♀ 8:33; ☽∠♅ 9:12; ☽∠♃ 13:23; ☽∥☿ 18:39; ☊ R 21:53; ☉⊻☽ 22:43

6 M: ☽⋕♄ 0:13; ☽⊻♄ 0:36; ☽☌☿ 5:58; ☽☌⚷ 7:01; ☽□⚳ 7:31; ☽∥⚷ 9:08; ☽⊻♅ 9:48; ♄∠♇ 11:51; ☽⊻♃ 14:16; ☽⊻♆ 20:15

7 Tu: ☽∥♀ 1:02; ☽□♇ 1:09; ☽∠♄ 1:14; ☿☌⚷ 2:28; ☉⚹♄ 5:43; ☽⊻♂ 6:02; ☿□⚳ 11:53; ☽☌♀ 14:06; ☉∥☽ 14:54; ☽∥♅ 19:47; ☽∥♃ 20:53; ☽∠♆ 20:55

8 W: ☽⚹♄ 2:03; ☉☌☽ 3:23; ☽∠♂ 8:10; ☽⊻⚷ 8:29; ☽△⚳ 8:59; ☽⊻☿ 10:16; ☽☌♅ 11:20; ☽☌♃ 16:31; ☽⋕♇ 17:16; ☽⚹♆ 21:56

9 Th: ☽△♇ 2:53; ☿⊻♅ 4:18; ☽⋕⚳ 5:21; ♂⋕♆ 5:32; ☽∠⚷ 9:47; ☽⚼⚳ 10:15; ☽⚹♂ 10:49; ☽∠☿ 13:16; ☽⊻♀ 21:09

10 F: ☽⚼♇ 4:33; ☽□♄ 5:04; ☉⊻☽ 10:01; ☽⚹⚷ 11:44; ☽⚻⚳ 12:11; ☽⊻♅ 14:45; ☽⚹☿ 17:14; ☽⊻♃ 20:55

11 Sa: ☿⋕♄ 0:22; ♂∠♅ 0:23; ♀∠♆ 0:29; ☽□♆ 1:50; ☽∠♀ 1:58; ☽⚻♇ 6:58; ☉⊻⚷ 11:44; ☉∠☽ 14:43; ☉△⚳ 17:32; ☽∠♅ 17:39; ☽□♂ 18:38

12 Su: ☽∠♃ 0:24; ☉∥♅ 6:45; ☽⚹♀ 7:59; ☽△♄ 11:12; ☽□⚷ 18:14; ☽☍⚳ 18:35; ☉⚹☽ 20:36; ☽⚹♅ 21:30

13 M: ☿⊻♃ 4:02; ☽⚹♃ 4:54; ☽□☿ 4:58; ☽△♆ 9:14; ☉☌♅ 9:15; ☽⋕⚳ 11:37; ☽☍♇ 14:36; ☽⚼♄ 15:42; ♀⚹♄ 19:46

14 Tu: ☽⋕♇ 3:16; ☽△♂ 6:50; ☽⚼♆ 14:21; ☉∥♃ 14:48; ☽⚻♄ 21:07; ☽□♀ 23:49

15 W: ☉∥☽ 1:03; ☽∥♃ 1:27; ☿⊻♆ 3:46; ☽∥♅ 4:22; ☽△⚷ 4:30; ☽⚻⚳ 4:39; ⚳ R 5:35; ☽□♅ 7:59; ☊ D 11:41; ☽∥♀ 11:48; ☉□☽ 11:49; ☽⚼♂ 14:29; ☽□♃ 16:42; ☿ ♉ 17:06; ☽⚻♆ 20:14; ☽△☿ 22:05

16 Th: ☽⚻♇ 1:43; ☽⚼⚷ 10:44; ☽⚼⚳ 10:45; ⚳□⚷ 14:27; ⚴ R♏ 17:24; ☽∥⚷ 22:44; ☽⚻♂ 22:49; ♀△⚳ 23:17; ♀⊻⚷ 23:44

17 F: ☽∥☿ 0:12; ☿□♇ 7:45; ☽⚼♇ 8:05; ☽⚼☿ 8:07; ☽☍♄ 9:49; ☽⋕♄ 12:04; ♂∠♃ 16:02; ☿∥⚷ 16:46; ☽△⚳ 17:10; ☽⚻⚷ 17:18; ☽△♀ 19:16; ☽△♅ 20:55; ☽∥♂ 22:11

18 Sa: ☿∠♄ 0:01; ☉△☽ 5:54; ☽△♃ 6:43; ☽☍♆ 9:10; ☽⋕♆ 9:44; ♀☌♅ 11:42; ☽△♇ 14:33; ☽⚻☿ 18:30; ☉☌♃ 18:47; ☽∥♆ 21:26

19 Su: ☽⚼♅ 3:29; ☽⚼♀ 5:14; ☽⋕♂ 10:53; ☽⚼♃ 13:41; ☉⚼☽ 14:56; ☽☍♂ 15:49; ☊ R 16:35; ☽∥♄ 18:43; ♀∥♅ 20:09; ☉⚹♆ 22:46; ☽⚻♄ 22:53

20 M: ☽□⚳ 5:40; ☽☍⚷ 6:10; ☽⋕⚷ 8:19; ☽⚻♅ 9:44; ☉ ♊ 13:01; ☽⚻♀ 14:42; ☽⋕☿ 14:50; ☽⚻♃ 20:12; ☽⚻♆ 21:30; ☉⚻☽ 23:25

21 Tu: ☽□♇ 2:35; ☽⚼♄ 4:48; ☽☍☿ 14:19; ☉∠♂ 16:02

22 W: ☽⋕♅ 1:51; ☽⚼♆ 2:50; ☽⋕♀ 5:40; ☽⋕♃ 6:11; ☽⚻♂ 6:50; ☽△♄ 10:04; ☉⋕☽ 13:11; ♀∥♃ 14:46; ☉△♇ 15:15; ☽⚹⚳ 16:05; ☽⚻⚷ 16:58; ☽☍♅ 20:25

23 Th: ☽∥♇ 2:00; ☽☍♀ 7:08; ☽☍♃ 7:14; ☽△♆ 7:29; ♀☌♃ 8:30; ♀⚹♆ 10:52; ☽⚹♇ 12:11; ☽⚼♂ 13:08; ☉☍☽ 13:54; ☽∠⚳ 20:15; ♀ ♊ 20:31; ☽⚼⚷ 21:20; ♃⚹♆ 21:45; ☽∥⚳ 22:46

24 F: ☽⚻☿ 7:06; ☽∠♇ 15:59; ♂⊻♄ 16:24; ☽□♄ 18:30; ☽△♂ 18:38; ☽⊻⚳ 23:46

25 Sa: ☽△⚷ 1:02; ☽⚻♅ 4:23; ♂⋕♄ 7:58; ♀△♇ 11:17; ☽⚼☿ 14:17; ☽□♆ 14:48; ☽⚻♃ 15:29; ☿∠♆ 18:32; ☽⊻♇ 19:11; ☽⚻♀ 19:59; ♃ ♊ 23:16

26 Su: ☉⚻☽ 1:07; ☽⚼♅ 7:28; ☽⚼♃ 18:44; ☽△☿ 20:50; ☉⚼⚳ 22:04

27 M: ☽⚹♄ 0:35; ☽⚼♀ 1:21; ☽□♂ 3:38; ☽☌⚳ 5:11; ☉⚼☽ 5:45; ☽□⚷ 6:50; ☽△♅ 10:07; ☽∥⚳ 13:23; ☽⚹♆ 20:03; ☽△♃ 21:33; ☉∠⚷ 21:56

28 Tu: ☽☌♇ 0:11; ☽∠♄ 2:58; ☿⚹♄ 3:23; ♂□⚳ 5:05; ☽△♀ 6:11; ☉△☽ 9:55; ☽∥♇ 10:51; ☉⋕☽ 17:08; ♀⚼⚳ 17:27; ☽⋕♀ 20:20; ☽∠♆ 22:08

29 W: ☽⋕♃ 3:21; ☽⊻♄ 5:01; ☽⋕♅ 8:25; ☽□☿ 8:37; ☽⊻⚳ 9:01; ☽⚹♂ 10:47; ☽⚹⚷ 11:07; ☿△⚳ 11:40; ☽□♅ 14:21; ♀∠♂ 15:07; ♀∠⚷ 16:20; ♂☌⚷ 17:09; ☽⋕☿ 17:54; ☽⊻♆ 23:56

30 Th: ☽□♃ 2:13; ☽⊻♇ 3:52; ☿⊻⚷ 4:26; ☽∠⚳ 10:32; ☿⊻♂ 11:55; ☽∠⚷ 12:51; ☽∠♂ 13:54; ☽□♀ 14:44; ☉□☽ 17:14; ☊ D 17:25; ☽⋕⚷ 20:32

31 F: ☽⋕♂ 3:07; ☽∠♇ 5:22; ☿☌♅ 5:55; ☽☌♄ 8:25; ☽∥♄ 9:33; ☽⚹⚳ 11:51; ☽⊻⚷ 14:23; ☽⊻♂ 16:46; ☽⚹♅ 17:38; ☽⚹☿ 19:21

June 2024

LONGITUDE

Day	Sid.Time	☉	☽	☽ 12 hour	Mean ☊	True ☊	☿	♀	♂	⚳	♃	♄	⚷	♅	♆	♇
	h m s	° E "	° E "	° E "	° E	° E	° E	° E	° E	° E	° E	° E	° E	° E	° E	° E
1 Sa	16 39 53	11♊00 02	27♓55 53	5♈02 54	12♈49.6	14♈02.4	25♉32.3	10♊00.7	23♈52.8	20♑41.3	1♊24.9	18♓44.8	22♈15.7	24♉10.4	29♓40.0	1♒54.6
2 Su	16 43 49	11 57 32	12♈10 45	19 19 10	12 46.4	14R 03.0	27 26.3	11 14.5	24 37.8	20R 35.1	1 38.9	18 47.6	22 18.3	24 13.8	29 40.9	1R 53.9
3 M	16 47 46	12 55 02	26 27 49	3♉36 18	12 43.2	14 02.4	29 22.6	12 28.2	25 22.8	20 28.5	1 52.9	18 50.2	22 20.8	24 17.1	29 41.9	1 53.1
4 Tu	16 51 42	13 52 31	10♉44 10	17 50 55	12 40.1	13 59.7	1♊21.0	13 41.9	26 07.7	20 21.5	2 06.9	18 52.8	22 23.3	24 20.4	29 42.8	1 52.2
5 W	16 55 39	14 49 59	24 55 58	1♊58 47	12 36.9	13 54.6	3 21.4	14 55.7	26 52.6	20 14.2	2 20.9	18 55.3	22 25.8	24 23.8	29 43.7	1 51.4
6 Th	16 59 35	15 47 26	8♊58 45	15 55 19	12 33.7	13 47.0	5 23.9	16 09.5	27 37.4	20 06.6	2 34.8	18 57.6	22 28.2	24 27.1	29 44.6	1 50.5
7 F	17 03 32	16 44 53	22 47 59	29 36 17	12 30.5	13 37.5	7 28.2	17 23.2	28 22.1	19 58.7	2 48.8	18 59.9	22 30.5	24 30.4	29 45.4	1 49.6
8 Sa	17 07 29	17 42 19	6♋19 51	12♋58 25	12 27.4	13 27.0	9 34.2	18 36.9	29 06.8	19 50.4	3 02.7	19 02.1	22 32.9	24 33.7	29 46.2	1 48.7
9 Su	17 11 25	18 39 44	19 31 49	26 00 01	12 24.2	13 16.6	11 41.7	19 50.7	29 51.5	19 41.8	3 16.5	19 04.2	22 35.2	24 36.9	29 47.0	1 47.8
10 M	17 15 22	19 37 08	2♌23 05	8♌41 10	12 21.0	13 07.4	13 50.6	21 04.4	0♉36.0	19 32.9	3 30.4	19 06.2	22 37.5	24 40.2	29 47.7	1 46.9
11 Tu	17 19 18	20 34 30	14 54 34	21 03 39	12 17.8	13 00.0	16 00.6	22 18.2	1 20.5	19 23.7	3 44.2	19 08.1	22 39.7	24 43.4	29 48.5	1 45.9
12 W	17 23 15	21 31 52	27 08 50	3♍10 40	12 14.7	12 55.0	18 11.5	23 31.9	2 05.0	19 14.3	3 58.0	19 09.9	22 41.9	24 46.6	29 49.1	1 44.9
13 Th	17 27 11	22 29 13	9♍09 42	15 06 33	12 11.5	12 52.3	20 23.1	24 45.6	2 49.4	19 04.5	4 11.8	19 11.6	22 44.0	24 49.8	29 49.8	1 43.9
14 F	17 31 08	23 26 33	21 01 52	26 56 19	12 08.3	12D 51.5	22 35.0	25 59.3	3 33.7	18 54.5	4 25.5	19 13.3	22 46.1	24 53.0	29 50.4	1 42.8
15 Sa	17 35 04	24 23 52	2♎50 34	8♎45 19	12 05.1	12R 51.6	24 47.0	27 13.0	4 18.0	18 44.2	4 39.2	19 14.8	22 48.2	24 56.1	29 51.0	1 41.8
16 Su	17 39 01	25 21 09	14 41 14	20 38 58	12 02.0	12 51.8	26 58.8	28 26.8	5 02.2	18 33.6	4 52.8	19 16.2	22 50.2	24 59.2	29 51.5	1 40.7
17 M	17 42 58	26 18 27	26 39 08	2♏42 19	11 58.8	12 51.0	29 10.2	29 40.5	5 46.4	18 22.8	5 06.5	19 17.5	22 52.1	25 02.3	29 52.0	1 39.6
18 Tu	17 46 54	27 15 43	8♏49 03	14 59 47	11 55.6	12 48.4	1♋20.8	0♋54.2	6 30.4	18 11.8	5 20.1	19 18.7	22 54.1	25 05.4	29 52.5	1 38.5
19 W	17 50 51	28 12 59	21 14 56	27 34 47	11 52.4	12 43.3	3 30.5	2 07.9	7 14.5	18 00.5	5 33.6	19 19.9	22 55.9	25 08.5	29 53.0	1 37.4
20 Th	17 54 47	29 10 14	3♐59 34	10♐29 22	11 49.2	12 35.7	5 39.1	3 21.6	7 58.4	17 49.0	5 47.1	19 20.9	22 57.8	25 11.5	29 53.4	1 36.3
21 F	17 58 44	0♋07 28	17 04 13	23 43 58	11 46.1	12 25.8	7 46.2	4 35.3	8 42.3	17 37.4	6 00.6	19 21.8	22 59.6	25 14.5	29 53.8	1 35.1
22 Sa	18 02 40	1 04 42	0♑28 26	7♑17 16	11 42.9	12 14.5	9 51.9	5 49.0	9 26.1	17 25.5	6 14.0	19 22.6	23 01.3	25 17.5	29 54.1	1 34.0
23 Su	18 06 37	2 01 56	14 10 05	21 06 25	11 39.7	12 02.7	11 55.9	7 02.7	10 09.9	17 13.4	6 27.4	19 23.4	23 03.1	25 20.5	29 54.5	1 32.8
24 M	18 10 34	2 59 09	28 05 43	5♒07 27	11 36.5	11 51.8	13 58.1	8 16.4	10 53.6	17 01.2	6 40.8	19 24.0	23 04.7	25 23.4	29 54.8	1 31.6
25 Tu	18 14 30	3 56 22	12♒11 03	19 15 59	11 33.4	11 42.7	15 58.5	9 30.2	11 37.3	16 48.9	6 54.1	19 24.5	23 06.3	25 26.3	29 55.0	1 30.4
26 W	18 18 27	4 53 35	26 21 46	3♓27 58	11 30.2	11 36.2	17 56.9	10 43.9	12 20.8	16 36.3	7 07.4	19 25.0	23 07.9	25 29.2	29 55.2	1 29.2
27 Th	18 22 23	5 50 47	10♓34 11	17 40 07	11 27.0	11 32.4	19 53.3	11 57.6	13 04.3	16 23.7	7 20.6	19 25.3	23 09.4	25 32.1	29 55.4	1 27.9
28 F	18 26 20	6 48 00	24 45 31	1♈50 11	11 23.8	11D 30.8	21 47.6	13 11.3	13 47.8	16 10.9	7 33.8	19 25.5	23 10.9	25 34.9	29 55.6	1 26.7
29 Sa	18 30 16	7 45 13	8♈54 00	15 56 49	11 20.7	11R 30.6	23 39.9	14 25.0	14 31.1	15 58.0	7 46.9	19R 25.7	23 12.3	25 37.7	29 55.7	1 25.4
30 Su	18 34 13	8♋42 26	22 58 35	29 59 10	11♈17.5	11♈30.4	25♋30.1	15♋38.7	15♉14.4	15♑45.0	8♊00.0	19♓25.7	23♈13.7	25♉40.5	29♓55.8	1♒24.1

1st of Month

Julian Day # 2460462.5
Obliquity 23°26'9"
SVP 4♓55'2"
GC 27♐10.8
Eris 25♈16.9

Day	⚴		Day	⚵		Day	⚶
1	25♏29.7R		1	10♍34.4		1	22♋00.6
6	24 10.8R		6	11 35.7		6	24 05.0
11	23 00.3R		11	12 41.8		11	26 11.1
16	21 59.7R		16	13 52.3		16	28 18.8
21	21 10.0R		21	15 06.8		21	0♌27.9
26	20 31.8R		26	16 24.9		26	2 38.3

DECLINATION and LATITUDE

Day	☉ Decl	☽ Decl	☽ Lat	☽ 12h Decl	☿ Decl	☿ Lat	♀ Decl	♀ Lat	♂ Decl	♂ Lat	⚳ Decl	⚳ Lat	♃ Decl	♃ Lat	♄ Decl	♄ Lat
1 Sa	22N06	2S08	1S25	1N16	17N46	1S25	21N45	0S12	8N11	1S10	26S16	4S28	19N45	0S43	6S10	1S51
2 Su	22 13	4N40	0 10	7 60	18 22	1 15	21 58	0 10	8 27	1 10	26 21	4 32	19 47	0 43	6 09	1 52
3 M	22 21	11 14	1N06	14 20	18 58	1 05	22 10	0 07	8 44	1 10	26 26	4 36	19 50	0 43	6 08	1 52
4 Tu	22 28	17 13	2 18	19 53	19 33	0 54	22 22	0 05	9 01	1 09	26 31	4 40	19 53	0 43	6 07	1 52
5 W	22 35	22 14	3 20	24 16	20 07	0 43	22 33	0 03	9 17	1 09	26 36	4 44	19 56	0 43	6 06	1 52
6 Th	22 41	25 55	4 10	27 09	20 40	0 33	22 43	0 00	9 34	1 09	26 41	4 49	19 59	0 43	6 06	1 53
7 F	22 47	27 58	4 44	28 21	21 12	0 22	22 52	0N02	9 50	1 08	26 46	4 53	20 01	0 43	6 05	1 53
8 Sa	22 52	28 18	5 01	27 50	21 42	0 11	23 01	0 04	10 06	1 08	26 52	4 57	20 04	0 43	6 04	1 53
9 Su	22 57	26 59	5 02	25 47	22 11	0N00	23 10	0 07	10 22	1 08	26 57	5 01	20 07	0 43	6 04	1 53
10 M	23 02	24 17	4 47	22 29	22 38	0 11	23 17	0 09	10 38	1 07	27 02	5 05	20 10	0 43	6 03	1 54
11 Tu	23 06	20 28	4 18	18 15	23 03	0 21	23 24	0 12	10 54	1 07	27 08	5 09	20 12	0 42	6 03	1 54
12 W	23 10	15 53	3 38	13 22	23 26	0 31	23 31	0 14	11 10	1 06	27 13	5 13	20 15	0 42	6 02	1 54
13 Th	23 14	10 45	2 49	8 03	23 47	0 41	23 36	0 16	11 25	1 06	27 19	5 17	20 17	0 42	6 02	1 54
14 F	23 17	5 18	1 54	2 30	24 04	0 51	23 41	0 19	11 41	1 06	27 24	5 21	20 20	0 42	6 01	1 55
15 Sa	23 19	0S19	0 53	3S08	24 20	0 60	23 45	0 21	11 56	1 05	27 29	5 25	20 22	0 42	6 01	1 55
16 Su	23 21	5 56	0S10	8 42	24 32	1 08	23 49	0 23	12 11	1 05	27 35	5 29	20 25	0 42	6 01	1 55
17 M	23 23	11 24	1 13	14 02	24 42	1 16	23 52	0 26	12 26	1 04	27 40	5 33	20 27	0 42	6 00	1 55
18 Tu	23 25	16 32	2 13	18 55	24 49	1 23	23 54	0 28	12 41	1 04	27 46	5 37	20 30	0 42	6 00	1 56
19 W	23 26	21 06	3 09	23 05	24 53	1 30	23 55	0 30	12 56	1 03	27 51	5 40	20 32	0 42	6 00	1 56
20 Th	23 26	24 49	3 56	26 14	24 54	1 35	23 56	0 32	13 11	1 03	27 56	5 44	20 35	0 42	5 60	1 56
21 F	23 26	27 20	4 32	28 02	24 53	1 40	23 56	0 35	13 25	1 02	28 02	5 48	20 37	0 42	5 60	1 56
22 Sa	23 26	28 21	4 55	28 14	24 49	1 45	23 55	0 37	13 39	1 02	28 07	5 52	20 39	0 42	5 60	1 57
23 Su	23 25	27 40	5 01	26 40	24 42	1 48	23 54	0 39	13 54	1 01	28 12	5 55	20 42	0 42	5 60	1 57
24 M	23 24	25 16	4 49	23 27	24 33	1 51	23 52	0 41	14 08	1 01	28 17	5 59	20 44	0 42	5 60	1 57
25 Tu	23 23	21 18	4 20	18 50	24 22	1 53	23 49	0 43	14 22	1 00	28 23	6 03	20 46	0 42	5 60	1 57
26 W	23 21	16 05	3 35	13 08	24 08	1 55	23 45	0 45	14 36	0 60	28 28	6 06	20 49	0 42	5 60	1 58
27 Th	23 19	10 00	2 36	6 45	23 52	1 55	23 41	0 47	14 49	0 59	28 33	6 10	20 51	0 42	5 60	1 58
28 F	23 16	3 25	1 27	0 03	23 34	1 55	23 36	0 49	15 03	0 59	28 38	6 13	20 53	0 42	5 60	1 58
29 Sa	23 13	3N19	0 14	6N38	23 15	1 55	23 30	0 51	15 16	0 58	28 43	6 17	20 55	0 42	6 00	1 58
30 Su	23N09	9N52	1N00	12N58	22N54	1N53	23N24	0N53	15N29	0S58	28S48	6S20	20N57	0S42	6S00	1S59

Day	⚷ Decl	⚷ Lat	♅ Decl	♅ Lat	♆ Decl	♆ Lat	♇ Decl	♇ Lat
1	9N43	1N08	18N34	0S16	1S17	1S15	22S46	3S07
6	9 48	1 08	18 38	0 16	1 15	1 15	22 48	3 08
11	9 52	1 08	18 42	0 16	1 14	1 16	22 50	3 08
16	9 56	1 08	18 46	0 16	1 13	1 16	22 51	3 09
21	9 59	1 08	18 49	0 16	1 12	1 16	22 53	3 10
26	10 02	1 08	18 53	0 16	1 12	1 16	22 55	3 11

Day	⚴ Decl	⚴ Lat	⚵ Decl	⚵ Lat	⚶ Decl	⚶ Lat	Eris Decl	Eris Lat
1	26N42	47N07	10N03	2N39	23N52	2N15	0S17	10S47
6	26 44	46 55	9 48	2 48	23 36	2 20	0 16	10 48
11	26 37	46 35	9 30	2 56	23 17	2 25	0 16	10 48
16	26 23	46 08	9 10	3 04	22 56	2 29	0 15	10 48
21	26 01	45 36	8 48	3 11	22 33	2 34	0 15	10 49
26	25 33	44 58	8 24	3 18	22 08	2 38	0 15	10 49

Moon Phenomena

Max/0 Decl

dy	hr mn	
1	7:31	0 N
7	16:36	28N22
14	22:39	0 S
22	2:39	28S21
28	12:11	0 N

Max/0 Lat

dy	hr mn	
2	3:09	0 N
8	12:42	5N03
15	20:19	0 S
22	20:22	5S01
29	4:27	0 N

Perigee/Apogee

dy	hr m		kilometers
2	7:17	p	368103
14	13:36	a	404074
27	11:31	p	369286

PH	dy	hr mn	
●	6	12:39	16♊18
☽	14	5:20	23♍39
○	22	1:09	1♑07
☾	28	21:55	7♈40

Void of Course Moon

Last Aspect				☽ Ingress		
1	2:56	♆	☌	♈	1	3:29
2	22:05	♂	☌	♉	3	5:56
5	8:10	♆	⚹	♊	5	8:37
7	12:17	♆	□	♋	7	12:42
9	19:07	♆	△	♌	9	19:30
11	19:18	♅	□	♍	12	5:40
14	17:55	♆	☍	♎	14	18:13
17	6:06	☿	△	♏	17	6:39
19	16:20	♆	△	♐	19	16:33
21	22:59	♆	□	♑	21	23:10
24	3:07	♆	⚹	♒	24	3:15
25	22:31	♅	□	♓	26	6:09
28	8:46	♆	☌	♈	28	8:53
30	4:58	☿	□	♉	30	12:01

DAILY ASPECTARIAN

1 Sa: ☽☌♆ 2:56; ☽∥♆ 2:59; ☽⚹♃ 5:58; ☽⚹♇ 6:42; ♂⚺♅ 10:08; ☽#♆ 12:02; ☽∠♅ 19:01; ☽⚹♀ 22:16; ☉⚹☽ 23:36

2 Su: ☽∠☿ 0:30; ☊ R 3:08; ☽#♄ 5:18; ☽∠♃ 7:38; ☿∥♅ 8:31; ☽⚺♄ 11:09; ☽□⚳ 14:01; ☽∥♂ 14:17; ☽☌⚷ 17:04; ☽∥⚷ 18:26; ☽⚺♅ 20:20; ☽☌♂ 22:05

3 M: ♃△♇ 0:14; ☽∠♀ 1:51; ☉∠☽ 2:37; ☿⚹♆ 3:58; ☽⚺♆ 5:26; ☽⚺☿ 5:40; ☿ ♊ 7:38; ☽□♇ 9:06; ☽⚺♃ 9:15; ☽∠♄ 12:26

4 Tu: ☽⚺♀ 5:28; ☉⚺☽ 5:40; ☽∥♅ 6:06; ☿△♇ 6:13; ☽∠♆ 6:43; ☿☌♃ 10:24; ☽∥☿ 11:46; ☽∥♃ 12:10; ☽⚹♄ 13:47; ☿∥♃ 15:30; ☉☌♀ 15:33; ☽△⚳ 16:07; ☽⚺⚷ 19:44; ☽☌♅ 23:05

5 W: ☽∥♀ 1:46; ☉∥☽ 1:56; ☽#♇ 3:06; ☽⚺♂ 3:29; ☽⚹♆ 8:10; ☽△♇ 11:47; ☉∥♀ 12:03; ☽☌♃ 12:51; ☽☌☿ 16:48; ☽⚼⚳ 17:25; ☿⚼⚳ 20:50; ☽∠⚷ 21:24

6 Th: ☽∠♂ 6:39; ☽#⚳ 7:20; ☉☌☽ 12:39; ♀#♇ 12:39; ♀⚼♇ 13:13; ☽⚼♇ 13:35; ☽☌♀ 13:37; ☽□♄ 17:20; ☽⚻⚳ 19:07; ♂∥⚷ 22:11; ☽⚹⚷ 23:29

7 F: ☿∠⚷ 0:28; ☉⚼♇ 1:57; ☽⚺♅ 3:01; ☉#♇ 6:31; ☽⚹♂ 10:23; ☽□♆ 12:17; ☽⚻♇ 15:56; ☽⚺♃ 18:01

8 Sa: ☽∠♅ 5:50; ☽⚺☿ 6:56; ♀□♄ 8:27; ♀⚻⚳ 21:25; ♂⚺♆ 21:34; ☽∠♃ 21:39; ☉⚺☽ 22:17; ☽△♄ 23:09

9 Su: ☽☍⚳ 0:18; ☽#⚳ 0:25; ☽⚺♀ 0:38; ♂ ♉ 4:36; ☽□⚷ 5:40; ☽⚹♅ 9:28; ☉□♄ 10:37; ☽∠☿ 15:58; ☽△♆ 19:07; ☽□♂ 20:25; ☉⚻⚳ 22:29; ☽☍♇ 22:52

10 M: ☽⚹♃ 2:10; ☽⚼♄ 3:16; ☉∠☽ 4:35; ☽∥♀ 6:37; ☽∠♀ 7:46; ☉∥☽ 8:22; ☽#♇ 9:54; ☽∥☿ 9:57; ☿#♇ 10:23; ☽⚼♆ 23:48

11 Tu: ☽∥♃ 1:30; ☽⚹☿ 2:36; ☉∥☿ 3:32; ☿∠♂ 5:33; ♀⚹⚷ 7:13; ☽⚻♄ 8:15; ☿⚼♇ 8:15; ☽⚻⚳ 8:38; ☽∥♅ 9:40; ☉⚹☽ 11:59; ♂□♇ 13:23; ☽△⚷ 15:11; ☽⚹♀ 16:03; ☽□♅ 19:18

12 W: ☽⚻♆ 5:19; ☿∥♀ 7:10; ⚳⚹♄ 9:05; ☽⚻♇ 9:08; ☽△♂ 10:28; ☿⚻⚳ 10:40; ☿□♄ 10:49; ☽□♃ 13:51; ☽⚼⚳ 13:56; ⚳⚼♃ 16:37; ☽∥♂ 21:07; ☽⚼⚷ 21:07

13 Th: ♀⚺♅ 1:26; ☽∥⚷ 3:50; ☉⚹⚷ 6:25; ☽⚼♇ 15:16; ☽⚼♂ 18:40; ☽△⚳ 19:45; ☽☍♄ 20:19; ☽#♄ 20:50

14 F: ☿⚹⚷ 2:03; ☽⚻⚷ 3:32; ☽□☿ 3:52; ☊ D 5:12; ☉□☽ 5:20; ☽△♅ 7:51; ☽□♀ 11:14; ☉☌☿ 16:34; ☽#♆ 17:27; ☽☍♆ 17:55; ☽△♇ 21:40; ♂∠♄ 22:11

15 Sa: ☿⚺♅ 1:42; ☽⚻♂ 3:09; ☽△♃ 3:45; ☽∥♆ 3:50; ☉⚺♅ 14:17; ☽⚼♅ 14:27; ♂⚺♃ 16:38; ☊ R 20:18

16 Su: ☽∥♄ 0:19; ☽□⚳ 7:41; ☽⚻♄ 9:15; ☽⚼♃ 10:40; ☽☍⚷ 16:26; ☽#⚷ 17:27; ☽⚻♅ 20:46; ☉△☽ 23:15

17 M: ♀□♆ 3:47; ☽#♂ 4:53; ☽△☿ 6:06; ♀ ♋ 6:21; ☽⚻♆ 6:23; ☽△♀ 6:41; ☿□♆ 7:42; ☿ ♋ 9:08; ☽□♇ 9:55; ☿☌♀ 12:44; ☽⚼♄ 15:09; ☽⚻♃ 17:03; ☽☍♂ 19:11

18 Tu: ☿⚻♇ 3:14; ☉⚼☽ 7:16; ☽#♅ 11:22; ☽⚼♆ 11:46; ♀⚻♇ 14:14; ☽⚼♀ 15:15; ☽⚼☿ 17:40; ☽⚹⚳ 17:53; ☽△♄ 20:20; ☽#♃ 20:46

19 W: ☽⚻⚷ 3:13; ☽☍♅ 7:26; ☽∥♇ 10:41; ☉⚻☽ 14:16; ☉#☽ 14:17; ☽△♆ 16:20; ☽#♀ 17:39; ☽⚹♇ 19:33; ☽∠⚳ 21:51; ⚶ ♌ 22:12; ☽⚻♀ 22:42

20 Th: ☽#☿ 0:44; ☿⚺♃ 1:42; ☽☍♃ 3:23; ☽⚻☿ 3:41; ☽⚼⚷ 7:22; ☽⚻♂ 7:49; ☉□♆ 18:13; ☉ ♋ 20:52; ☽∠♇ 23:07

21 F: ☽⚺⚳ 0:59; ☽□♄ 4:09; ☽△⚷ 10:42; ☽⚼♂ 12:38; ☽∥⚳ 12:53; ☽⚻♅ 14:45; ☿⚹♂ 16:24; ☽□♆ 22:59

22 Sa: ☉☍☽ 1:09; ☽⚺♇ 1:56; ☿∠♅ 5:03; ♀⚺♃ 9:57; ☽⚻♃ 10:19; ☽☍♀ 10:21; ☉⚻♇ 12:02; ☽∥⚳ 13:47; ☽△♂ 16:38; ☽⚼♅ 17:19; ☽☍☿ 19:26

23 Su: ☽☌⚳ 5:13; ☽⚹♄ 9:03; ☽⚼♃ 12:48; ☽□⚷ 15:23; ☽△♅ 19:21

24 M: ☽⚹♆ 3:07; ☽#☿ 5:16; ☽☌♇ 5:51; ☉⚻☽ 8:58; ☽#♀ 9:35; ☽∠♄ 10:46; ☉#☽ 12:22; ☽△♃ 14:53; ☽∥♇ 15:10; ☽⚻♀ 19:01; ☽□♂ 23:00

25 Tu: ☽#♃ 2:39; ☽∠♆ 4:38; ☽⚻☿ 7:28; ☽⚺⚳ 7:44; ☿☍⚳ 9:12; ☽#♅ 11:47; ☽⚺♄ 12:15; ☉⚼☽ 12:16; ☽⚹⚷ 18:32; ♀∠♅ 19:02; ☽□♅ 22:31; ☽⚼♀ 22:50

26 W: ☽#♂ 5:57; ☽⚺♆ 6:01; ☽⚺♇ 8:39; ☽∠⚳ 8:44; ☽⚼☿ 12:54; ☉△☽ 15:27; ☿△♄ 18:11; ☽□♃ 18:28; ☽∠⚷ 19:55; ☽#⚷ 23:51

27 Th: ☽△♀ 2:34; ☽⚹♂ 4:27; ☽⚹⚳ 9:42; ☽∠♇ 9:57; ☽∥♄ 14:45; ☽☌♄ 14:58; ☽△☿ 18:12; ☿∥♀ 20:46; ☽⚺⚷ 21:20

28 F: ☽⚹♅ 1:24; ☽∠♂ 7:13; ☽∥♆ 7:55; ☽☌♆ 8:46; ☿∠♃ 11:07; ☽⚹♇ 11:19; ☽#♆ 16:27; ☿□⚷ 18:00; ☉□☽ 21:55; ☽⚹♃ 22:04; ☊ D 22:11

29 Sa: ☉⚺♃ 0:55; ☽∠♅ 2:57; ☉∥☿ 2:58; ☊ R 4:18; ♀⚹♂ 4:51; ☽#♄ 9:42; ☽⚺♂ 10:05; ☽□♀ 10:17; ☽□⚳ 11:51; ♂∠♆ 13:39; ☽⚺♄ 17:56; ♄ R 19:08; ☿#♇ 20:17

30 Su: ☽∠♃ 0:02; ☽☌⚷ 0:26; ☽∥⚷ 0:47; ♀☍⚳ 1:44; ☿⚹♅ 2:21; ☽⚺♅ 4:38; ☽□☿ 4:58; ☽⚺♆ 11:54; ♂△⚳ 13:02; ☽□♇ 14:24; ☽∠♄ 19:37; ☽∥♂ 23:11

LONGITUDE

July 2024

Day	Sid.Time	☉	☽	☽ 12 hour	Mean ☊	True ☊	☿	♀	♂	⚳	♃	♄	⚷	♅	♆	♇
	h m s	° ' "	° ' "	° ' "	° '	° '	° '	° '	° '	° '	° '	° '	° '	° '	° '	° '
1 M	18 38 09	9♋39 39	6♉58 28	13♉56 23	11♈14.3	11♈29.0	27♋18.2	16♋52.5	15♉57.7	15♑32.0	8♊13.0	19♓25.6	23♈15.1	25♉43.2	29♓55.9	1♒22.9
2 Tu	18 42 06	10 36 52	20 52 43	27 47 17	11 11.1	11R 25.4	29 04.1	18 06.2	16 40.8	15R 18.8	8 26.0	19R 25.4	23 16.3	25 45.9	29R 55.9	1R 21.6
3 W	18 46 03	11 34 05	4♊39 50	11♊30 06	11 08.0	11 19.1	0♌48.0	19 19.9	17 23.9	15 05.6	8 38.9	19 25.2	23 17.6	25 48.6	29 55.9	1 20.3
4 Th	18 49 59	12 31 19	18 17 48	25 02 37	11 04.8	11 09.9	2 29.7	20 33.7	18 06.9	14 52.4	8 51.8	19 24.8	23 18.8	25 51.3	29 55.9	1 18.9
5 F	18 53 56	13 28 33	1♋44 15	8♋22 25	11 01.6	10 58.6	4 09.3	21 47.4	18 49.9	14 39.2	9 04.6	19 24.3	23 19.9	25 53.9	29 55.8	1 17.6
6 Sa	18 57 52	14 25 46	14 56 50	21 27 20	10 58.4	10 46.1	5 46.7	23 01.1	19 32.7	14 25.9	9 17.3	19 23.8	23 21.0	25 56.5	29 55.7	1 16.3
7 Su	19 01 49	15 23 00	27 53 46	4♌16 02	10 55.3	10 33.6	7 22.0	24 14.9	20 15.5	14 12.7	9 30.0	19 23.1	23 22.1	25 59.0	29 55.6	1 14.9
8 M	19 05 45	16 20 14	10♌34 10	16 48 14	10 52.1	10 22.3	8 55.2	25 28.6	20 58.2	13 59.5	9 42.7	19 22.3	23 23.0	26 01.5	29 55.4	1 13.6
9 Tu	19 09 42	17 17 28	22 58 25	29 04 59	10 48.9	10 13.0	10 26.2	26 42.3	21 40.8	13 46.3	9 55.2	19 21.5	23 24.0	26 04.0	29 55.2	1 12.2
10 W	19 13 38	18 14 41	5♍08 15	11♍08 36	10 45.7	10 06.3	11 55.0	27 56.1	22 23.3	13 33.1	10 07.7	19 20.5	23 24.9	26 06.5	29 55.0	1 10.8
11 Th	19 17 35	19 11 55	17 06 32	23 02 34	10 42.5	10 02.2	13 21.6	29 09.8	23 05.8	13 20.1	10 20.2	19 19.4	23 25.7	26 08.9	29 54.7	1 09.4
12 F	19 21 32	20 09 08	28 57 16	4♎51 15	10 39.4	10D 00.3	14 45.9	0♌23.6	23 48.2	13 07.1	10 32.5	19 18.3	23 26.5	26 11.2	29 54.4	1 08.1
13 Sa	19 25 28	21 06 22	10♎45 10	16 39 41	10 36.2	9R 59.9	16 08.1	1 37.3	24 30.4	12 54.2	10 44.8	19 17.0	23 27.2	26 13.6	29 54.1	1 06.7
14 Su	19 29 25	22 03 35	22 35 29	28 33 16	10 33.0	10 00.0	17 27.9	2 51.0	25 12.6	12 41.4	10 57.1	19 15.7	23 27.9	26 15.9	29 53.7	1 05.3
15 M	19 33 21	23 00 49	4♏33 42	10♏37 28	10 29.8	9 59.5	18 45.3	4 04.7	25 54.7	12 28.7	11 09.2	19 14.2	23 28.5	26 18.1	29 53.3	1 03.9
16 Tu	19 37 18	23 58 02	16 45 09	22 57 22	10 26.7	9 57.5	20 00.4	5 18.5	26 36.8	12 16.2	11 21.3	19 12.7	23 29.1	26 20.4	29 52.9	1 02.5
17 W	19 41 14	24 55 16	29 14 37	5♐37 20	10 23.5	9 53.3	21 13.0	6 32.2	27 18.7	12 03.8	11 33.4	19 11.0	23 29.6	26 22.6	29 52.5	1 01.1
18 Th	19 45 11	25 52 30	12♐05 52	18 40 25	10 20.3	9 46.7	22 23.1	7 45.9	28 00.6	11 51.6	11 45.3	19 09.3	23 30.1	26 24.7	29 52.0	0 59.6
19 F	19 49 07	26 49 44	25 21 05	2♑07 50	10 17.1	9 37.8	23 30.6	8 59.6	28 42.4	11 39.5	11 57.2	19 07.5	23 30.5	26 26.8	29 51.5	0 58.2
20 Sa	19 53 04	27 46 59	9♑00 28	15 58 37	10 14.0	9 27.5	24 35.5	10 13.3	29 24.0	11 27.7	12 09.0	19 05.6	23 30.9	26 28.9	29 50.9	0 56.8
21 Su	19 57 01	28 44 14	23 01 50	0♒09 27	10 10.8	9 16.7	25 37.5	11 27.1	0♊05.7	11 16.0	12 20.7	19 03.6	23 31.2	26 30.9	29 50.4	0 55.4
22 M	20 00 57	29 41 29	7♒20 47	14 35 02	10 07.6	9 06.6	26 36.7	12 40.8	0 47.2	11 04.5	12 32.3	19 01.5	23 31.5	26 32.9	29 49.8	0 54.0
23 Tu	20 04 54	0♌38 45	21 51 20	29 08 51	10 04.4	8 58.2	27 32.9	13 54.5	1 28.6	10 53.2	12 43.9	18 59.3	23 31.7	26 34.9	29 49.1	0 52.6
24 W	20 08 50	1 36 02	6♓26 45	13♓44 17	10 01.3	8 52.3	28 26.0	15 08.2	2 09.9	10 42.2	12 55.4	18 57.1	23 31.9	26 36.8	29 48.5	0 51.1
25 Th	20 12 47	2 33 19	21 00 45	28 15 33	9 58.1	8 48.9	29 15.9	16 21.9	2 51.2	10 31.4	13 06.8	18 54.7	23 32.0	26 38.6	29 47.8	0 49.7
26 F	20 16 43	3 30 37	5♈28 14	12♈38 24	9 54.9	8D 47.8	0♍02.4	17 35.6	3 32.3	10 20.8	13 18.1	18 52.3	23R 32.1	26 40.5	29 47.1	0 48.3
27 Sa	20 20 40	4 27 56	19 45 47	26 50 12	9 51.7	8 48.0	0 45.4	18 49.3	4 13.4	10 10.5	13 29.3	18 49.7	23 32.1	26 42.3	29 46.3	0 46.9
28 Su	20 24 36	5 25 16	3♉51 32	10♉49 45	9 48.5	8R 48.4	1 24.7	20 03.0	4 54.4	10 00.4	13 40.4	18 47.1	23 32.0	26 44.0	29 45.5	0 45.5
29 M	20 28 33	6 22 37	17 44 49	24 36 45	9 45.4	8 47.9	2 00.2	21 16.7	5 35.3	9 50.6	13 51.5	18 44.4	23 31.9	26 45.7	29 44.7	0 44.1
30 Tu	20 32 30	7 20 00	1♊25 35	8♊11 20	9 42.2	8 45.5	2 31.7	22 30.4	6 16.1	9 41.1	14 02.4	18 41.7	23 31.8	26 47.3	29 43.9	0 42.6
31 W	20 36 26	8♌17 23	14 54 02	21 33 41	9♈39.0	8♈40.8	2♍58.9	23♌44.1	6♊56.8	9♑31.9	14♊13.3	18♓38.8	23♈31.6	26♉49.0	29♓43.0	0♒41.2

1st of Month

Julian Day #
2460492.5
Obliquity
23°26[illegible]8"
SVP 4♓55[illegible]6"
GC 27♐10.9
Eris 25♈27.4

Day	⚴
1	20♏05.2R
6	19 50.2R
11	19 46.6
16	19 53.9
21	20 11.4
26	20 38.6
31	21 14.6

Day	⚵
1	17♍46.3
6	19 10.8
11	20 38.0
16	22 07.7
21	23 39.7
26	25 13.7
31	26 49.5

Day	⚶
1	4♌50.0
6	7 02.9
11	9 16.9
16	11 31.9
21	13 47.8
26	16 04.6
31	18 22.2

DECLINATION and LATITUDE

Day	☉ Decl	☽ Decl	☽ Lat	☽ 12h Decl	☿ Decl	☿ Lat	♀ Decl	♀ Lat	♂ Decl	♂ Lat	⚳ Decl	⚳ Lat	♃ Decl	♃ Lat	♄ Decl	♄ Lat
1 M	23N05	15N54	2N10	18N36	22N31	1N51	23N17	0N55	15N42	0S57	28S53	6S23	20N59	0S42	6S01	1S59
2 Tu	23 01	21 03	3 12	23 13	22 07	1 48	23 09	0 57	15 55	0 56	28 58	6 27	21 01	0 42	6 01	1 59
3 W	22 56	25 02	4 02	26 28	21 41	1 45	23 01	0 59	16 08	0 56	29 02	6 30	21 03	0 42	6 01	1 59
4 Th	22 51	27 31	4 37	28 09	21 14	1 41	22 52	1 01	16 20	0 55	29 07	6 33	21 05	0 42	6 02	1 60
5 F	22 45	28 22	4 56	28 10	20 47	1 36	22 42	1 02	16 33	0 55	29 11	6 36	21 07	0 42	6 02	1 60
6 Sa	22 39	27 34	4 59	26 35	20 18	1 31	22 32	1 04	16 45	0 54	29 16	6 39	21 09	0 42	6 02	2 00
7 Su	22 33	25 16	4 47	23 39	19 49	1 26	22 21	1 06	16 57	0 53	29 20	6 42	21 11	0 42	6 03	2 00
8 M	22 26	21 45	4 20	19 39	19 18	1 19	22 09	1 07	17 09	0 53	29 25	6 45	21 13	0 42	6 03	2 01
9 Tu	22 19	17 21	3 42	14 54	18 47	1 13	21 56	1 09	17 21	0 52	29 29	6 48	21 15	0 42	6 04	2 01
10 W	22 12	12 19	2 53	9 39	18 16	1 06	21 43	1 10	17 32	0 51	29 33	6 50	21 17	0 42	6 05	2 01
11 Th	22 04	6 54	1 58	4 07	17 44	0 58	21 30	1 12	17 44	0 51	29 37	6 53	21 19	0 42	6 05	2 01
12 F	21 56	1 18	0 58	1S31	17 12	0 50	21 16	1 13	17 55	0 50	29 41	6 56	21 21	0 42	6 06	2 02
13 Sa	21 47	4S19	0S04	7 06	16 39	0 41	21 01	1 15	18 06	0 50	29 45	6 58	21 22	0 42	6 07	2 02
14 Su	21 38	9 49	1 06	12 28	16 07	0 32	20 45	1 16	18 17	0 49	29 48	7 00	21 24	0 42	6 07	2 02
15 M	21 29	15 02	2 07	17 28	15 34	0 23	20 29	1 17	18 27	0 48	29 52	7 03	21 26	0 42	6 08	2 02
16 Tu	21 19	19 45	3 02	21 51	15 01	0 13	20 12	1 18	18 38	0 47	29 56	7 05	21 27	0 41	6 09	2 03
17 W	21 09	23 44	3 50	25 21	14 28	0 03	19 55	1 20	18 48	0 47	29 59	7 07	21 29	0 41	6 10	2 03
18 Th	20 58	26 40	4 28	27 39	13 56	0S08	19 38	1 21	18 58	0 46	30 02	7 09	21 31	0 41	6 11	2 03
19 F	20 47	28 14	4 53	28 25	13 24	0 18	19 19	1 22	19 08	0 45	30 05	7 12	21 32	0 41	6 12	2 03
20 Sa	20 36	28 09	5 02	27 27	12 52	0 30	19 00	1 23	19 18	0 45	30 09	7 14	21 34	0 41	6 13	2 04
21 Su	20 25	26 18	4 54	24 43	12 20	0 41	18 41	1 23	19 27	0 44	30 11	7 15	21 35	0 41	6 14	2 04
22 M	20 13	22 44	4 27	20 23	11 49	0 53	18 21	1 24	19 37	0 43	30 14	7 17	21 37	0 41	6 15	2 04
23 Tu	20 01	17 44	3 42	14 48	11 19	1 05	18 01	1 25	19 46	0 42	30 17	7 19	21 38	0 41	6 16	2 04
24 W	19 48	11 40	2 43	8 23	10 49	1 17	17 40	1 25	19 55	0 42	30 20	7 21	21 40	0 41	6 17	2 05
25 Th	19 35	4 59	1 33	1 33	10 20	1 29	17 18	1 26	20 04	0 41	30 22	7 22	21 41	0 41	6 18	2 05
26 F	19 22	1N54	0 18	5N18	9 52	1 42	16 57	1 27	20 12	0 40	30 25	7 24	21 43	0 41	6 19	2 05
27 Sa	19 09	8 38	0N58	11 49	9 25	1 54	16 34	1 28	20 21	0 39	30 27	7 26	21 44	0 41	6 20	2 05
28 Su	18 55	14 50	2 10	17 38	8 60	2 07	16 11	1 28	20 29	0 38	30 29	7 27	21 45	0 41	6 22	2 05
29 M	18 41	20 12	3 12	22 28	8 35	2 20	15 48	1 28	20 37	0 38	30 31	7 28	21 47	0 41	6 23	2 06
30 Tu	18 26	24 24	4 03	26 12	8 12	2 32	15 25	1 29	20 45	0 37	30 33	7 30	21 48	0 41	6 24	2 06
31 W	18N12	27N12	4N39	28N01	7N51	2S45	15N01	1N29	20N53	0S36	30S35	7S31	21N49	0S41	6S25	2S06

Day	⚷ Decl	⚷ Lat	♅ Decl	♅ Lat	♆ Decl	♆ Lat	♇ Decl	♇ Lat
1	10N05	1N08	18N56	0S16	1S12	1S17	22S57	3S11
6	10 07	1 08	18 59	0 16	1 12	1 17	22 60	3 12
11	10 09	1 08	19 02	0 16	1 13	1 17	23 02	3 12
16	10 10	1 08	19 05	0 16	1 14	1 17	23 04	3 13
21	10 11	1 07	19 07	0 16	1 15	1 18	23 06	3 13
26	10 11	1 07	19 09	0 16	1 17	1 18	23 08	3 14
31	10N11	1N07	19N11	0S16	1S18	1S18	23S10	3S14

Day	⚴ Decl	⚴ Lat	⚵ Decl	⚵ Lat	⚶ Decl	⚶ Lat	Eris Decl	Eris Lat
1	24N59	44N18	7N58	3N25	21N41	2N43	0S15	10S49
6	24 20	43 34	7 31	3 31	21 13	2 47	0 15	10 50
11	23 37	42 48	7 02	3 37	20 42	2 52	0 15	10 50
16	22 50	42 01	6 33	3 43	20 09	2 57	0 15	10 50
21	22 00	41 13	6 02	3 49	19 34	3 01	0 16	10 51
26	21 09	40 25	5 29	3 55	18 58	3 06	0 16	10 51
31	20N15	39N37	4N57	4N01	18N20	3N10	0S16	10S52

Moon Phenomena

Max/0 Decl
dy hr mn
5 0:03 28N22
12 5:34 0 S
19 10:59 28S25
25 17:23 0 N

Max/0 Lat
dy hr mn
5 16:29 5N00
12 22:28 0 S
20 0:46 5S02
26 5:34 0 N

Perigee/Apogee
dy hr m kilometers
12 8:12 a 404360
24 5:42 p 364919

PH dy hr mn
● 5 22:59 14♋23
☽ 13 22:50 22♎01
○ 21 10:18 29♑09
☾ 28 2:53 5♉32

Void of Course Moon

Last Aspect	☽ Ingress
2 15:44 ♆ ✶	♊ 2 15:51
4 20:45 ♆ □	♋ 4 20:53
7 3:49 ♆ △	♌ 7 3:57
9 6:05 ♅ □	♍ 9 13:49
12 1:56 ♆ ☍	♎ 12 2:08
13 22:50 ☉ □	♏ 14 14:54
17 1:12 ♆ △	♐ 17 1:26
19 7:59 ♆ □	♑ 19 8:15
21 11:27 ♆ ✶	♒ 21 11:44
23 9:59 ☿ ☍	♓ 23 13:24
25 14:33 ♆ ☌	♈ 25 14:53
26 22:16 ♀ △	♉ 27 17:24
29 21:01 ♆ ✶	♊ 29 21:29

DAILY ASPECTARIAN

1 M ☽⚺♃ 2:10 · ♃∠⚷ 4:14 · ☉✶☽ 4:58 · ☽∥♅ 13:34 · ☽∠♆ 13:43 · ☽△⚳ 14:31 · ☽☌♂ 16:20 · ☽✶♀ 18:44 · ☽✶♄ 21:29 · ☽∥♃ 23:49

2 Tu ☉∠♅ 3:59 · ☽⚺⚷ 4:09 · ☽∥☿ 5:09 · ☽☌♅ 8:31 · ☉∠☽ 8:50 · ☽#♇ 10:33 · ☉∥☽ 10:37 · ♆ R 10:43 · ☽∥♀ 11:17 · ☿△♆ 11:54 · ☿ ♌ 12:51 · ☉#♇ 14:07 · ☽✶♆ 15:44 · ☽⚼⚳ 16:09 · ☽✶☿ 16:17 · ☽△♇ 18:12 · ☽∠♀ 23:22

3 W ♀△♄ 1:42 · ☽∠⚷ 6:22 · ♀#♇ 6:54 · ☽☌♃ 7:06 · ☿☍♇ 7:28 · ☉⚺☽ 13:02 · ☽⚻⚳ 18:02 · ☽⚼♇ 20:30 · ☽∠☿ 22:23 · ☽⚺♂ 23:40

4 Th ☽□♄ 1:59 · ☽⚺♀ 4:25 · ☉∥♀ 5:16 · ☿∥♃ 7:21 · ☽✶⚷ 8:56 · ☽⚺♅ 13:30 · ☽□♆ 20:45 · ☽⚻♇ 23:12

5 F ☿⚼♄ 3:40 · ☽∠♂ 3:59 · ☽⚺☿ 4:58 · ☽⚺♃ 13:30 · ☽∠♅ 16:39 · ♂✶♄ 19:03 · ☉☌☽ 22:59 · ☽☍⚳ 23:04

6 Sa ☉☍⚳ 0:03 · ♀□⚷ 6:34 · ☽△♄ 8:11 · ☽✶♂ 8:57 · ☽□⚷ 15:32 · ☽☌♀ 16:28 · ☽∠♃ 17:33 · ☽✶♅ 20:25

7 Su ☽△♆ 3:49 · ♀∠♃ 5:57 · ☽☍♇ 6:17 · ☽⚼♄ 12:13 · ☽#♇ 16:15 · ☉∥☽ 19:42 · ☽☌☿ 20:24 · ☽∥♀ 21:31 · ☽✶♃ 22:20

8 M ☽∥♃ 3:09 · ☽⚻⚳ 6:27 · ☽⚼♆ 8:22 · ♀✶♅ 11:05 · ☉⚺☽ 12:01 · ☿∥♅ 13:40 · ☿✶♃ 14:27 · ☽∥♅ 15:24 · ☽∥☿ 15:38 · ☽⚻♄ 16:58 · ☽□♂ 21:19

9 Tu ☽∥♂ 0:00 · ☽△⚷ 0:50 · ☽□♅ 6:05 · ☽⚺♀ 8:08 · ☽⚼⚳ 11:11 · ☽⚻♆ 13:39 · ☽⚻♇ 16:10 · ☉∠☽ 19:55

10 W ⚴ D 2:47 · ☽⚼⚷ 6:33 · ☽∥⚷ 9:48 · ☽□♃ 10:09 · ☽⚺☿ 15:25 · ☽△⚳ 16:32 · ☽∠♀ 17:23 · ☽⚼♇ 22:05 · ☿⚻⚳ 23:38

11 Th ☿∥♂ 0:15 · ☉△♄ 3:06 · ☽#♄ 3:32 · ☽☍♄ 4:28 · ☉✶☽ 4:35 · ♂⚺⚷ 11:30 · ☽⚻⚷ 12:48 · ☽△♂ 12:53 · ♀△♆ 14:33 · ♀ ♌ 16:20 · ♀∥♃ 16:39 · ☽△♅ 18:22

12 F ☽#♆ 0:23 · ☽∠☿ 1:52 · ☽☍♆ 1:56 · ☿⚼♆ 2:26 · ☽✶♀ 3:16 · ☽△♇ 4:25 · ☽∥♆ 10:46 · ♀☍♇ 14:13 · ☽⚼♂ 21:18 · ☊ D 22:31 · ☽△♃ 23:59

13 Sa ☽⚼♅ 0:58 · ☽□⚳ 4:18 · ☽∥♄ 7:45 · ☽✶☿ 12:20 · ☽⚻♄ 17:17 · ☊ R 22:37 · ☉□☽ 22:50

14 Su ☽#⚷ 1:32 · ☽☍⚷ 1:46 · ☽⚻♂ 5:37 · ☽⚼♃ 6:53 · ☽⚻♅ 7:25 · ☽⚻♆ 14:41 · ☽□♇ 17:02 · ☽□♀ 22:56 · ☽⚼♄ 23:21

15 M ☽#☿ 2:20 · ♀⚼♄ 3:01 · ☉∥♃ 6:04 · ☿⚻♄ 8:58 · ☉□⚷ 11:45 · ☽⚻♃ 13:16 · ♂☌♅ 14:06 · ☽✶⚳ 15:23 · ☽#♂ 17:46 · ☽⚼♆ 20:21 · ☽#♅ 20:23

16 Tu ☽#♀ 2:23 · ☽△♄ 4:46 · ☽□☿ 7:00 · ☉#☽ 8:29 · ☽#♃ 9:43 · ☽⚻⚷ 13:01 · ☉△☽ 15:05 · ♂⚼⚳ 17:24 · ☽☍♅ 18:32 · ☽∥♇ 19:35 · ☽∠⚳ 19:55 · ☽☍♂ 20:07

17 W ☽△♆ 1:12 · ☽✶♇ 3:21 · ☽△♀ 15:09 · ☽⚼⚷ 17:21 · ☉⚼☽ 21:34 · ☽☍♃ 23:22 · ☽⚺⚳ 23:34

18 Th ⚳⚻♃ 6:16 · ☽∠♇ 7:07 · ☽□♄ 12:50 · ☉✶♅ 14:01 · ♂∥♅ 19:37 · ☽△☿ 20:25 · ☽△⚷ 20:42 · ☽⚼♀ 21:20 · ☿△⚷ 23:58

19 F ☽⚻♅ 1:57 · ☉⚻☽ 2:50 · ☉∠♃ 3:56 · ☽⚻♂ 6:17 · ☽□♆ 7:59 · ♀∥♂ 9:26 · ☽⚺♇ 9:56 · ♀∥♅ 16:06 · ⚳⚼♅ 21:51

20 Sa ☽⚼☿ 1:06 · ☽⚻♀ 2:18 · ☽☌⚳ 4:11 · ☽⚼♅ 4:17 · ☽⚻♃ 5:30 · ☽⚼♂ 9:47 · ♂✶♆ 15:18 · ☽✶♄ 17:17 · ♂ ♊ 20:44 · ♀⚻⚳ 20:53

21 Su ☽□⚷ 0:50 · ☽⚻☿ 4:43 · ☽△♅ 5:54 · ☽⚼♃ 7:23 · ☉☍☽ 10:18 · ☽✶♆ 11:27 · ☽△♂ 12:30 · ☿⚼⚳ 12:55 · ☽☌♇ 13:16 · ☽∠♄ 18:29 · ♀✶♃ 20:44 · ☽∥♇ 21:55 · ☿□♅ 22:22

22 M ☉△♆ 3:26 · ♂△♇ 3:49 · ☽#♃ 5:54 · ☽⚺⚳ 6:07 · ☉ ♌ 7:46 · ☽△♃ 8:44 · ☽☍♀ 9:40 · ☽∠♆ 12:24 · ☉#☽ 13:20 · ☽#♂ 15:11 · ☽#♅ 17:48 · ☽⚺♄ 19:17 · ☽#♀ 22:42

23 Tu ☽✶⚷ 2:45 · ☉☍♇ 5:39 · ☽∠⚳ 6:33 · ☽□♅ 7:48 · ☽☍☿ 9:59 · ☽⚺♆ 13:06 · ☽⚺♇ 14:49 · ☉⚻☽ 15:29 · ☉∥♂ 16:34 · ☽□♂ 16:37 · ♀⚼♆ 17:39

24 W ☽#☿ 3:25 · ☽∠⚷ 3:26 · ☽#⚷ 5:30 · ☽✶⚳ 6:55 · ☽□♃ 10:48 · ☽∠♇ 15:28 · ☽⚻♀ 15:37 · ☉⚼☽ 17:54 · ☽∥♄ 19:25 · ☽☌♄ 20:32

25 Th ☽⚺⚷ 4:10 · ☿∥⚷ 7:54 · ☽✶♅ 9:20 · ☽∥♆ 12:57 · ☽⚻☿ 14:27 · ☽☌♆ 14:33 · ☿⚻♆ 16:01 · ☽✶♇ 16:15 · ☽⚼♀ 18:45 · ☉△☽ 20:30 · ☽✶♂ 20:37 · ☽#♆ 21:49 · ☿ ♍ 22:43

26 F ☉✶♂ 2:34 · ☊ D 5:35 · ☽□⚳ 8:03 · ☉⚼♄ 8:41 · ☽∠♅ 10:24 · ☽✶♃ 13:17 · ⚷ R 14:00 · ☽#♄ 15:40 · ☽⚼☿ 16:54 · ☉∥♅ 21:57 · ☽△♀ 22:16 · ☽⚺♄ 22:26 · ☽∠♂ 23:03

27 Sa ♀⚻♄ 0:08 · ☿⚻♇ 0:51 · ☽∥☿ 2:46 · ☽∥⚷ 5:47 · ☽☌⚷ 6:23 · ☽⚺♅ 11:48 · ☽∠♃ 15:01 · ☽⚺♆ 16:59 · ☽□♇ 18:42 · ☽△☿ 19:37 · ☽∠♄ 23:52

28 Su ☽⚺♂ 1:53 · ☉□☽ 2:53 · ☊ R 2:59 · ☽∥♀ 5:19 · ☽△⚳ 10:27 · ☉∥☽ 17:03 · ☽⚺♃ 17:09 · ☽∠♆ 18:47 · ☽∥♅ 19:03

29 M ☽✶♄ 1:44 · ☽∥♂ 2:11 · ☽□♀ 6:46 · ☽∥♃ 8:14 · ☽⚺⚷ 10:06 · ☽⚼⚳ 12:16 · ☽☌♅ 15:48 · ☽#♇ 16:02 · ☽✶♆ 21:01 · ☽△♇ 22:44

30 Tu ☽□☿ 2:01 · ☽☌♂ 9:02 · ☉✶☽ 11:17 · ☽∠⚷ 12:36 · ☽⚻⚳ 14:30 · ♀△⚷ 19:55 · ☽☌♃ 22:46

31 W ☽⚼♇ 1:25 · ☽□♄ 6:43 · ♀⚼⚳ 13:52 · ☽✶⚷ 15:33 · ☉∠☽ 16:18 · ☽✶♀ 17:34 · ☽⚺♅ 21:34

August 2024

LONGITUDE

Day	Sid.Time	☉	☽	☽ 12 hour	Mean☊	True☊	☿	♀	♂	⚳	♃	♄	⚷	♅	♆	♇
	h m s	° ' "	° ' "	° ' "	° '	° '	° '	° '	° '	° '	° '	° '	° '	° '	° '	° '
1 Th	20 40 23	9♌14 48	28♊10 15	4♋43 44	9♈35.8	8♈33.7	3♍21.8	24♌57.8	7♊37.4	9♑22.9	14♊24.0	18♓35.9	23♈31.3	26♉50.5	29♓42.2	0♒39.8
2 F	20 44 19	10 12 13	11♋14 06	17 41 16	9 32.7	8R 24.8	3 40.2	26 11.5	8 17.9	9R 14.3	14 34.7	18R 32.9	23R 31.0	26 52.0	29R 41.3	0R 38.4
3 Sa	20 48 16	11 09 40	24 05 15	0♌25 59	9 29.5	8 14.8	3 53.8	27 25.2	8 58.3	9 06.0	14 45.3	18 29.8	23 30.6	26 53.5	29 40.3	0 37.0
4 Su	20 52 12	12 07 07	6♌43 28	12 57 44	9 26.3	8 04.8	4 02.5	28 38.9	9 38.5	8 58.0	14 55.7	18 26.6	23 30.2	26 55.0	29 39.3	0 35.7
5 M	20 56 09	13 04 36	19 08 50	25 16 52	9 23.1	7 55.7	4R 06.2	29 52.6	10 18.7	8 50.3	15 06.1	18 23.4	23 29.8	26 56.3	29 38.3	0 34.3
6 Tu	21 00 06	14 02 05	1♍21 58	7♍24 21	9 20.0	7 48.3	4 04.6	1♍06.3	10 58.8	8 43.0	15 16.4	18 20.0	23 29.2	26 57.7	29 37.3	0 32.9
7 W	21 04 02	14 59 35	13 24 16	19 22 01	9 16.8	7 43.1	3 57.8	2 20.0	11 38.8	8 35.9	15 26.5	18 16.7	23 28.7	26 59.0	29 36.3	0 31.5
8 Th	21 07 59	15 57 06	25 17 58	1♎12 31	9 13.6	7 40.1	3 45.6	3 33.7	12 18.6	8 29.2	15 36.6	18 13.2	23 28.0	27 00.2	29 35.2	0 30.2
9 F	21 11 55	16 54 38	7♎06 09	12 59 21	9 10.4	7D 39.2	3 28.1	4 47.4	12 58.4	8 22.9	15 46.5	18 09.7	23 27.4	27 01.4	29 34.1	0 28.8
10 Sa	21 15 52	17 52 11	18 52 41	24 46 43	9 07.2	7 39.7	3 05.3	6 01.0	13 38.0	8 16.9	15 56.3	18 06.1	23 26.6	27 02.5	29 33.0	0 27.5
11 Su	21 19 48	18 49 45	0♏42 05	6♏39 25	9 04.1	7 41.0	2 37.4	7 14.7	14 17.5	8 11.2	16 06.1	18 02.4	23 25.9	27 03.6	29 31.9	0 26.1
12 M	21 23 45	19 47 19	12 39 22	18 42 35	9 00.9	7R 42.1	2 04.5	8 28.3	14 56.9	8 06.0	16 15.7	17 58.7	23 25.0	27 04.7	29 30.7	0 24.8
13 Tu	21 27 41	20 44 55	24 49 42	1♐01 22	8 57.7	7 42.2	1 27.1	9 42.0	15 36.2	8 01.0	16 25.2	17 55.0	23 24.1	27 05.7	29 29.5	0 23.5
14 W	21 31 38	21 42 31	7♐18 10	13 40 37	8 54.5	7 40.8	0 45.6	10 55.6	16 15.4	7 56.4	16 34.5	17 51.1	23 23.2	27 06.6	29 28.3	0 22.2
15 Th	21 35 35	22 40 09	20 09 11	26 44 14	8 51.4	7 37.7	0 00.5	12 09.2	16 54.5	7 52.2	16 43.8	17 47.3	23 22.2	27 07.6	29 27.1	0 20.9
16 F	21 39 31	23 37 47	3♑26 01	10♑14 38	8 48.2	7 32.9	29♌12.6	13 22.9	17 33.5	7 48.3	16 52.9	17 43.3	23 21.2	27 08.4	29 25.8	0 19.6
17 Sa	21 43 28	24 35 27	17 10 04	24 12 04	8 45.0	7 26.9	28 22.6	14 36.5	18 12.3	7 44.8	17 01.9	17 39.3	23 20.2	27 09.2	29 24.5	0 18.3
18 Su	21 47 24	25 33 07	1♒20 17	8♒34 09	8 41.8	7 20.4	27 31.3	15 50.1	18 51.0	7 41.7	17 10.8	17 35.3	23 19.0	27 10.0	29 23.2	0 17.1
19 M	21 51 21	26 30 49	15 52 57	23 15 49	8 38.7	7 14.2	26 39.8	17 03.6	19 29.6	7 38.9	17 19.6	17 31.2	23 17.9	27 10.7	29 21.9	0 15.8
20 Tu	21 55 17	27 28 32	0♓41 47	8♓09 48	8 35.5	7 09.2	25 49.1	18 17.2	20 08.1	7 36.4	17 28.2	17 27.1	23 16.6	27 11.4	29 20.6	0 14.6
21 W	21 59 14	28 26 17	15 38 48	23 07 43	8 32.3	7 05.8	25 00.2	19 30.8	20 46.5	7 34.4	17 36.8	17 22.9	23 15.4	27 12.0	29 19.3	0 13.4
22 Th	22 03 10	29 24 02	0♈35 32	8♈01 20	8 29.1	7D 04.3	24 14.2	20 44.3	21 24.7	7 32.6	17 45.1	17 18.7	23 14.1	27 12.5	29 17.9	0 12.2
23 F	22 07 07	0♍21 50	15 24 18	22 43 44	8 25.9	7 04.3	23 31.9	21 57.9	22 02.8	7 31.3	17 53.4	17 14.4	23 12.7	27 13.0	29 16.5	0 11.0
24 Sa	22 11 03	1 19 39	29 59 07	7♉10 02	8 22.8	7 05.5	22 54.5	23 11.4	22 40.8	7 30.3	18 01.5	17 10.1	23 11.3	27 13.5	29 15.1	0 09.8
25 Su	22 15 00	2 17 30	14♉16 12	21 17 29	8 19.6	7 06.8	22 22.6	24 24.9	23 18.7	7 29.6	18 09.5	17 05.8	23 09.8	27 13.9	29 13.7	0 08.7
26 M	22 18 57	3 15 22	28 13 47	5♊05 10	8 16.4	7R 07.8	21 57.2	25 38.5	23 56.5	7D 29.3	18 17.3	17 01.4	23 08.3	27 14.3	29 12.2	0 07.5
27 Tu	22 22 53	4 13 17	11♊51 44	18 33 37	8 13.2	7 07.6	21 38.7	26 52.0	24 34.1	7 29.4	18 25.1	16 57.0	23 06.8	27 14.6	29 10.8	0 06.4
28 W	22 26 50	5 11 13	25 10 59	1♋44 05	8 10.1	7 06.1	21D 27.7	28 05.5	25 11.6	7 29.8	18 32.6	16 52.6	23 05.2	27 14.9	29 09.3	0 05.3
29 Th	22 30 46	6 09 12	8♋13 06	14 38 16	8 06.9	7 03.2	21 24.6	29 19.0	25 48.9	7 30.6	18 40.1	16 48.1	23 03.6	27 15.1	29 07.8	0 04.2
30 F	22 34 43	7 07 12	20 59 49	27 17 57	8 03.7	6 59.1	21 29.6	0♎32.5	26 26.1	7 31.7	18 47.3	16 43.6	23 01.9	27 15.2	29 06.3	0 03.1
31 Sa	22 38 39	8♍05 13	3♌32 52	9♌44 47	8♈00.5	6♈54.3	21♌43.0	1♎45.9	27♊03.2	7♑33.2	18♊54.5	16♓39.1	23♈00.2	27♉15.3	29♓04.8	0♒02.1

1st of Month

Julian Day #
2460523.5
Obliquity
23°26'[illegible]9"
SVP 4♓55'[illegible]1"
GC 27♐11.0
Eris 25♈29.1R

Day	⚴	⚵	⚶
1	21♏22.8	27♍08.9	18♌49.8
6	22 08.7	28 46.8	21 08.4
11	23 02.2	0♎26.1	23 27.6
16	24 02.5	2 06.8	25 47.4
21	25 09.1	3 48.6	28 07.8
26	26 21.3	5 31.4	0♍28.6
31	27 38.7	7 15.1	2 50.0

DECLINATION and LATITUDE

Day	☉ Decl	☽ Decl	☽ Lat	☽ 12h Decl	☿ Decl	☿ Lat	♀ Decl	♀ Lat	♂ Decl	♂ Lat	⚳ Decl	⚳ Lat	♃ Decl	♃ Lat	♄ Decl	♄ Lat
1 Th	17N56	28N25	4N60	28N25	7N31	2S58	14N36	1N29	21N00	0S35	30S37	7S32	21N50	0S41	6S27	2S06
2 F	17 41	28 01	5 04	27 14	7 12	3 10	14 11	1 29	21 07	0 34	30 39	7 33	21 52	0 41	6 28	2 06
3 Sa	17 26	26 06	4 53	24 39	6 56	3 22	13 46	1 29	21 14	0 34	30 41	7 34	21 53	0 41	6 30	2 07
4 Su	17 10	22 55	4 28	20 55	6 42	3 34	13 20	1 29	21 21	0 33	30 42	7 35	21 54	0 42	6 31	2 07
5 M	16 53	18 43	3 50	16 21	6 30	3 45	12 55	1 29	21 28	0 32	30 44	7 36	21 55	0 42	6 32	2 07
6 Tu	16 37	13 50	3 02	11 12	6 21	3 56	12 28	1 29	21 35	0 31	30 45	7 37	21 56	0 42	6 34	2 07
7 W	16 20	8 28	2 07	5 42	6 14	4 06	12 02	1 29	21 41	0 30	30 46	7 38	21 57	0 42	6 35	2 07
8 Th	16 03	2 53	1 06	0 03	6 09	4 16	11 35	1 29	21 47	0 29	30 47	7 38	21 58	0 42	6 37	2 08
9 F	15 46	2S46	0 03	5S34	6 07	4 24	11 07	1 28	21 53	0 28	30 48	7 39	21 59	0 42	6 38	2 08
10 Sa	15 29	8 19	1S00	11 01	6 09	4 32	10 40	1 28	21 59	0 28	30 49	7 40	22 00	0 42	6 40	2 08
11 Su	15 11	13 37	2 01	16 06	6 13	4 38	10 12	1 27	22 04	0 27	30 50	7 40	22 01	0 42	6 42	2 08
12 M	14 53	18 27	2 58	20 39	6 20	4 43	9 44	1 27	22 10	0 26	30 51	7 41	22 02	0 42	6 43	2 08
13 Tu	14 35	22 39	3 47	24 25	6 29	4 47	9 16	1 26	22 15	0 25	30 52	7 41	22 03	0 42	6 45	2 09
14 W	14 16	25 55	4 27	27 07	6 42	4 48	8 47	1 26	22 20	0 24	30 53	7 41	22 04	0 42	6 47	2 09
15 Th	13 57	27 59	4 55	28 28	6 58	4 49	8 18	1 25	22 25	0 23	30 53	7 42	22 05	0 42	6 48	2 09
16 F	13 39	28 32	5 09	28 11	7 16	4 47	7 49	1 24	22 30	0 22	30 54	7 42	22 06	0 42	6 50	2 09
17 Sa	13 19	27 23	5 05	26 08	7 36	4 44	7 20	1 23	22 34	0 21	30 54	7 42	22 07	0 42	6 52	2 09
18 Su	13 00	24 28	4 43	22 23	7 58	4 38	6 51	1 22	22 38	0 20	30 55	7 43	22 08	0 42	6 53	2 09
19 M	12 41	19 56	4 02	17 09	8 23	4 31	6 21	1 21	22 42	0 19	30 55	7 43	22 09	0 42	6 55	2 09
20 Tu	12 21	14 06	3 05	10 50	8 48	4 22	5 51	1 20	22 46	0 18	30 55	7 43	22 09	0 42	6 57	2 10
21 W	12 01	7 25	1 54	3 53	9 14	4 11	5 22	1 19	22 50	0 17	30 56	7 43	22 10	0 42	6 59	2 10
22 Th	11 41	0 18	0 35	3N16	9 41	3 59	4 51	1 18	22 54	0 16	30 56	7 43	22 11	0 42	7 00	2 10
23 F	11 21	6N46	0N45	10 09	10 08	3 45	4 21	1 16	22 57	0 15	30 56	7 43	22 12	0 42	7 02	2 10
24 Sa	11 00	13 22	2 02	16 23	10 35	3 29	3 51	1 15	23 00	0 14	30 56	7 43	22 12	0 42	7 04	2 10
25 Su	10 40	19 08	3 09	21 35	11 00	3 13	3 20	1 13	23 03	0 13	30 56	7 43	22 13	0 42	7 06	2 10
26 M	10 19	23 43	4 04	25 30	11 25	2 56	2 50	1 12	23 06	0 12	30 56	7 43	22 14	0 42	7 08	2 10
27 Tu	9 58	26 53	4 43	27 52	11 48	2 38	2 19	1 10	23 09	0 11	30 56	7 43	22 14	0 42	7 09	2 10
28 W	9 37	28 27	5 06	28 37	12 09	2 20	1 49	1 09	23 11	0 10	30 56	7 43	22 15	0 42	7 11	2 11
29 Th	9 15	28 23	5 13	27 46	12 27	2 01	1 18	1 07	23 13	0 09	30 55	7 43	22 16	0 42	7 13	2 11
30 F	8 54	26 48	5 03	25 30	12 43	1 43	0 47	1 05	23 16	0 08	30 55	7 42	22 16	0 42	7 15	2 11
31 Sa	8N32	23N54	4N40	22N02	12N56	1S24	0N16	1N03	23N18	0S07	30S55	7S42	22N17	0S42	7S17	2S11

Day	⚷ Decl	⚷ Lat	♅ Decl	♅ Lat	♆ Decl	♆ Lat	♇ Decl	♇ Lat
1	10N11	1N07	19N12	0S16	1S19	1S18	23S10	3S14
6	10 10	1 07	19 13	0 16	1 21	1 18	23 12	3 15
11	10 08	1 07	19 15	0 16	1 23	1 19	23 14	3 15
16	10 07	1 07	19 16	0 16	1 26	1 19	23 15	3 15
21	10 04	1 07	19 17	0 16	1 29	1 19	23 17	3 15
26	10 02	1 07	19 17	0 16	1 32	1 19	23 18	3 16
31	9N59	1N07	19N17	0S16	1S35	1S19	23S20	3S16

Day	⚴ Decl	⚴ Lat	⚵ Decl	⚵ Lat	⚶ Decl	⚶ Lat	Eris Decl	Eris Lat
1	20N04	39N28	4N50	4N02	18N12	3N11	0S17	10S52
6	19 10	38 41	4 16	4 07	17 32	3 16	0 17	10 52
11	18 14	37 55	3 42	4 13	16 51	3 21	0 18	10 53
16	17 19	37 10	3 07	4 18	16 08	3 25	0 19	10 53
21	16 24	36 26	2 31	4 24	15 24	3 30	0 19	10 53
26	15 29	35 44	1 56	4 29	14 39	3 35	0 20	10 54
31	14N35	35N03	1N20	4N35	13N53	3N40	0S21	10S54

Moon Phenomena

Max/0 Decl

dy	hr mn	
1	5:53	28N28
8	12:13	0 S
15	20:07	28S33
22	1:01	0 N
28	10:59	28N37

Max/0 Lat

dy	hr mn	
1	18:51	5N05
9	1:07	0 S
16	7:14	5S09
22	10:28	0 N
28	21:51	5N13

Perigee/Apogee

dy	hr m		kilometers
9	1:33	a	405297
21	5:03	p	360198

PH	dy	hr mn	
●	4	11:14	12♌34
☽	12	15:20	20♏24
○	19	18:27	27♒15
☾	26	9:27	3♊38

Void of Course Moon

Last Aspect			☽ Ingress		
1 2:47	♆	□	♋	1	3:20
3 10:33	♆	△	♌	3	11:11
5 15:17	♅	□	♍	5	21:18
8 8:41	♆	☍	♎	8	9:33
9 21:46	☉	⚹	♏	10	22:35
13 9:02	♆	△	♐	13	10:02
15 16:53	☿	△	♑	15	17:52
17 20:44	♆	⚹	♒	17	21:46
19 18:27	☉	☍	♓	19	22:53
21 21:55	♆	☌	♈	21	23:03
23 12:46	☿	△	♉	24	0:01
26 1:42	♆	⚹	♊	26	3:05
28 7:15	♆	□	♋	28	8:49
30 15:26	♆	△	♌	30	17:10

DAILY ASPECTARIAN

1 Th
☽□♆ 2:47
☉⚻⚳ 2:57
☽⚻♇ 4:33
☽⚹☿ 9:44
☽⚺♂ 18:16
☽☍⚳ 20:21
☉⚺☽ 21:56
☽∠♀ 23:55

2 F
☽∠♅ 1:10
☽⚺♃ 6:17
♂∠⚷ 7:44
♀□♅ 13:28
☽△♄ 13:33
☽∠☿ 14:06
☽□⚷ 22:55
☽∠♂ 23:46

3 Sa
♂⚻⚳ 3:50
☽⚹♅ 5:18
☽⚺♀ 6:58
☽△♆ 10:33
☽∠♃ 10:52
☽☍♇ 12:20
☽⚼♄ 17:45
☽⚺☿ 18:49
☽⋕♇ 22:13

4 Su
☽⚻⚳ 4:15
☽⚹♂ 5:55
☽∥♃ 6:15
☽∥♂ 9:15
☉☌☽ 11:14
☽⚼♆ 15:15
☽⚹♃ 16:02
♀⚻♆ 19:25
☿⋕♄ 19:41
☽∥♅ 21:24
☽⚻♄ 22:32

5 M
♀ ♍ 2:24
☿ R 4:57
☽△⚷ 8:30
☽⚼⚳ 9:05
☉∥☽ 9:53
♀⚻♇ 13:19
☽□♅ 15:17
☽⚻♆ 20:33
☽⚻♇ 22:23
☽☌♀ 23:26

6 Tu
☽☌☿ 5:20
☽∥♀ 6:48
☽⚼⚷ 14:09
☉⚼♆ 14:27
☽△⚳ 14:28
☽∥⚷ 16:36
☽□♂ 20:16

7 W
☉⚺☽ 3:28
☽□♃ 4:09
☽⚼♇ 4:15
☽⋕♄ 8:07
☽☍♄ 9:45
☽∥☿ 9:53
♃⚼♇ 10:29
☉⚹♃ 13:38
☽⚻⚷ 20:18

8 Th
☿☌♀ 3:13
☽△♅ 3:28
☽⋕♆ 6:25
☽☍♆ 8:41
☽△♇ 10:33
☉∠☽ 12:30
☽⚺☿ 16:48
☽∥♆ 18:02
☽⚺♀ 18:44

9 F
☊ D 1:09
☽□⚳ 2:35
☽⚼♅ 10:03
☽△♂ 12:41
☽⋕☿ 14:25
⚵ ♎ 16:37
☽∥♄ 16:43
☽△♃ 17:56
☉⚹☽ 21:46
☽⚻♄ 22:26
☽∠☿ 22:27

10 Sa
☽∠♀ 4:52
☉⚻♄ 5:27
☽⋕⚷ 8:06
♂∥♃ 8:14
☽☍⚷ 9:17
☽⋕♀ 9:36
☽⚻♅ 16:37
☽⚼♂ 20:59
☽⚻♆ 21:38
☽□♇ 23:28

11 Su
☽⚼♃ 0:49
♀∥⚷ 3:12
☽⚹☿ 3:43
☽⚼♄ 4:42
☉⋕☽ 7:04
☽⚹♀ 14:41
☽⚹⚳ 14:58
♀△⚳ 17:11
♀⚼⚷ 22:56

12 M
☽⚼♆ 3:41
☽⋕♅ 4:14
☽⚻♂ 4:49
☽⚻♃ 7:15
☽△♄ 10:30
☊ R 15:10
☉□☽ 15:20
♂⚼♇ 16:27
☽⋕♃ 20:18
☽∠⚳ 20:29
☽⚻⚷ 21:13
☽⋕♂ 21:27

13 Tu
☽∥♇ 3:50
☽☍♅ 4:25
☽△♆ 9:02
☽⚹♇ 10:46
☽□☿ 12:10

14 W
☽⚺⚳ 1:12
☽⚼⚷ 2:03
☽□♀ 7:34
☿⋕♄ 8:06
☿⚻♇ 13:04
☽∠♇ 15:08
♂☌♃ 15:23
☽☍♃ 17:36
☽☍♂ 17:42
☽□♄ 19:40

15 Th
☿R♌ 0:17
☉⚼⚳ 4:42
☉△☽ 4:58
☽△⚷ 5:53
☽⚻♅ 12:43
☽□♆ 16:52
☽△☿ 16:53
☉△⚷ 17:14
☿⚻♆ 17:20
☽⚺♇ 18:28

16 F
♂□♄ 5:31
☽☌⚳ 7:41
☉⚼☽ 9:52
☽⚼♅ 15:19
☿∥♀ 16:29
☽⚼☿ 17:50
☽△♀ 19:09
☽⚻♃ 23:46

17 Sa
☽⚹♄ 0:50
☽⚻♂ 1:52
☽□⚷ 10:31
♀⚼♇ 13:26
☉⚻☽ 13:35
☽△♅ 17:00
☽⚻☿ 17:58
☽⚹♆ 20:44
♀⋕♄ 22:05
☽☌♇ 22:14
☽⚼♀ 23:05

18 Su
☽⚼♃ 1:25
☽∠♄ 2:05
☽⚼♂ 4:23
☽∥♇ 7:08
☿□♅ 9:48
☽⋕♂ 10:26
☽⚺⚳ 10:31
☽⋕♃ 13:15
☽∠♆ 21:31

19 M
☉☌☿ 1:59
☽⚻♀ 2:06
☽△♃ 2:23
☽⚺♄ 2:39
☽⋕♅ 2:58
♀□♃ 5:54
☽△♂ 6:09
♀☍♄ 8:31
☽∠⚳ 10:58
☽⚹⚷ 12:02
☽☍☿ 16:33
☉□♅ 16:47
☽□♅ 18:21
☉☍☽ 18:27
♃□♄ 21:47
☽⚺♆ 21:49
☽⚺♇ 23:16

20 Tu
☉⋕☽ 6:53
☽⚹⚳ 11:05
☽∠⚷ 12:10
☽⋕⚷ 14:42
☽⋕☿ 18:02
☽∠♇ 23:19

21 W
☽∥♄ 1:29
☽☌♄ 2:46
☽□♃ 3:11
☽☍♀ 6:45
☽⋕♀ 7:32
☽□♂ 8:35
☽⚺⚷ 12:11
☽⚻☿ 14:16
☽⚹♅ 18:33
☽∥♆ 20:02
☉⚻♆ 21:30
☽☌♆ 21:55
☉⚻☽ 21:57
☽⚹♇ 23:22

22 Th
☽⋕♆ 6:01
☊ D 10:30
☽□⚳ 11:13
☽⚼☿ 13:19
☉ ♍ 14:56
☽∥♀ 16:16
☽∠♅ 18:48
☉⚻♇ 19:35
☿∥⚷ 19:46
☉⚼☽ 23:56

23 F
☽⋕♄ 0:57
☽⚺♄ 2:59
♀□♂ 3:22
☽⚹♃ 4:06
☽⚹♂ 11:22
☽∥⚷ 11:40
☽⚻♀ 11:44
☿△⚷ 12:22
☽△☿ 12:46
☽☌⚷ 12:47
☽∥☿ 12:50
☉∥☽ 15:34
☽⚺♅ 19:25
☿⚺♀ 20:16
☽⚺♆ 22:47
♀⚻⚷ 23:58

24 Sa
☽□♇ 0:18
☉△☽ 2:24
☽∠♄ 3:37
☿⚹♂ 4:32
☽∠♃ 5:07
☽△⚳ 12:33
☉∥☿ 13:06
☽∠♂ 13:28
☽⚼♀ 15:01
☿⚼⚳ 18:13
♂⚹⚷ 18:35
⚶ ♍ 23:39
☽∠♆ 23:56

25 Su
☽∥♅ 0:43
☽⚹♄ 4:47
☽⚺♃ 6:41
☽□☿ 13:26
☽⚼⚳ 14:04
☽⚺⚷ 15:12
☽∥♃ 15:23
☽⚺♂ 16:13
☽△♀ 19:04
☽∥♂ 20:15
☽⋕♇ 21:30
☽☌♅ 22:17

26 M
☽⚹♆ 1:42
☽△♇ 3:18
⚳ D 7:38
☉□☽ 9:27
☊ R 9:38
☽⚻⚳ 16:14
☽∠⚷ 17:21
☉∥⚷ 19:58

27 Tu
☽⚼♇ 5:47
♀△♅ 7:25
☽□♄ 9:03
☽☌♃ 11:51
☽⚹☿ 17:19
☽⚹⚷ 20:12

28 W
☽☌♂ 0:01
☽⚺♅ 3:46
☽□♀ 5:52
☽□♆ 7:15
☽⚻♇ 8:58
♀⋕♆ 12:05
☉⚹☽ 19:51
♀☍♆ 20:26
☽∠☿ 20:38
☿ D 21:15
☽☍⚳ 22:41

29 Th
☽∠♅ 7:32
♀ ♎ 13:24
♀△♇ 14:33
☽△♄ 15:59
☽⚺♃ 19:47

30 F
☽⚺☿ 0:57
☉∠☽ 2:18
☽□⚷ 3:51
☉△⚳ 10:24
☽⚺♂ 10:53
☽⚹♅ 11:55
☽△♆ 15:26
☽☍♇ 17:15
☽⚹♀ 20:12
☽⚼♄ 20:22
☉⚼⚷ 21:59

31 Sa
☽∠♃ 0:42
☽⋕♇ 3:48
☽∥♂ 4:00
☽⚻⚳ 7:46
♂⚺♅ 7:54
☉⚺☽ 9:31
☽∥♃ 10:28
☽∠♂ 17:21
☽⚼♆ 20:24

September 2024

LONGITUDE

Day	Sid.Time	☉	☽	☽ 12 hour	Mean☊	True☊	☿	♀	♂	⚳	♃	♄	⚷	♅	♆	♇
	h m s	° ' "	° ' "	° ' "	° '	° '	° '	° '	° '	° '	° '	° '	° '	° '	° '	° '
1 Su	22 42 36	9♍03 17	15♌53 53	22♌00 22	7♈57.3	6♈49.5	22♌04.7	2♎59.4	27♊40.1	7♑35.0	19♊01.5	16♓34.6	22♈58.4	27♉15.4	29♓03.3	0♒01.0
2 M	22 46 33	10 01 22	28 04 25	4♍06 14	7 54.2	6R 45.2	22 34.6	4 12.9	28 16.9	7 37.2	19 08.3	16R 30.0	22R 56.6	27R 15.4	29R 01.7	0R 00.0
3 Tu	22 50 29	10 59 29	10♍06 02	16 04 01	7 51.0	6 41.9	23 12.8	5 26.3	28 53.5	7 39.7	19 15.0	16 25.5	22 54.8	27 15.4	29 00.2	29♑59.0
4 W	22 54 26	11 57 38	22 00 27	27 55 34	7 47.8	6 39.7	23 58.9	6 39.8	29 30.0	7 42.5	19 21.5	16 20.9	22 52.9	27 15.3	28 58.6	29 58.0
5 Th	22 58 22	12 55 48	3♎49 40	9♎43 05	7 44.6	6D 38.8	24 52.6	7 53.2	0♋06.4	7 45.7	19 27.9	16 16.3	22 51.0	27 15.1	28 57.0	29 57.1
6 F	23 02 19	13 54 00	15 36 08	21 29 14	7 41.5	6 39.1	25 53.7	9 06.6	0 42.5	7 49.3	19 34.1	16 11.7	22 49.0	27 14.9	28 55.5	29 56.1
7 Sa	23 06 15	14 52 13	27 22 47	3♏17 14	7 38.3	6 40.2	27 01.6	10 20.0	1 18.6	7 53.1	19 40.1	16 07.1	22 47.0	27 14.7	28 53.9	29 55.2
8 Su	23 10 12	15 50 28	9♏13 05	15 10 48	7 35.1	6 41.8	28 15.9	11 33.4	1 54.4	7 57.3	19 46.0	16 02.5	22 45.0	27 14.4	28 52.3	29 54.3
9 M	23 14 08	16 48 45	21 10 57	27 14 05	7 31.9	6 43.4	29 36.1	12 46.7	2 30.1	8 01.8	19 51.7	15 57.9	22 42.9	27 14.0	28 50.7	29 53.4
10 Tu	23 18 05	17 47 03	3♐20 45	9♐31 32	7 28.7	6 44.6	1♍01.7	14 00.1	3 05.7	8 06.7	19 57.3	15 53.3	22 40.8	27 13.6	28 49.0	29 52.6
11 W	23 22 01	18 45 23	15 46 59	22 07 39	7 25.6	6R 45.2	2 32.1	15 13.4	3 41.1	8 11.8	20 02.7	15 48.7	22 38.7	27 13.2	28 47.4	29 51.8
12 Th	23 25 58	19 43 44	28 34 01	5♑06 32	7 22.4	6 45.0	4 06.7	16 26.7	4 16.3	8 17.3	20 07.9	15 44.2	22 36.5	27 12.7	28 45.8	29 50.9
13 F	23 29 55	20 42 07	11♑45 34	18 31 24	7 19.2	6 44.0	5 45.1	17 40.0	4 51.3	8 23.1	20 13.0	15 39.6	22 34.3	27 12.2	28 44.2	29 50.2
14 Sa	23 33 51	21 40 31	25 24 10	2♒23 53	7 16.0	6 42.5	7 26.6	18 53.3	5 26.2	8 29.2	20 17.9	15 35.0	22 32.1	27 11.6	28 42.5	29 49.4
15 Su	23 37 48	22 38 58	9♒30 24	16 43 25	7 12.9	6 40.8	9 10.8	20 06.6	6 00.9	8 35.6	20 22.6	15 30.5	22 29.8	27 10.9	28 40.9	29 48.7
16 M	23 41 44	23 37 25	24 02 24	1♓26 42	7 09.7	6 39.1	10 57.2	21 19.8	6 35.5	8 42.3	20 27.1	15 25.9	22 27.5	27 10.2	28 39.2	29 48.0
17 Tu	23 45 41	24 35 54	8♓55 28	16 27 42	7 06.5	6 37.8	12 45.2	22 33.1	7 09.8	8 49.3	20 31.5	15 21.4	22 25.2	27 09.5	28 37.6	29 47.3
18 W	23 49 37	25 34 26	24 02 18	1♈38 05	7 03.3	6D 37.0	14 34.6	23 46.3	7 44.0	8 56.6	20 35.7	15 16.9	22 22.8	27 08.7	28 35.9	29 46.6
19 Th	23 53 34	26 32 58	9♈13 52	16 48 26	7 00.1	6 36.8	16 25.0	24 59.4	8 18.0	9 04.2	20 39.7	15 12.5	22 20.5	27 07.9	28 34.2	29 46.0
20 F	23 57 30	27 31 33	24 20 41	1♉49 33	6 57.0	6 37.1	18 16.0	26 12.6	8 51.9	9 12.1	20 43.5	15 08.0	22 18.0	27 07.0	28 32.6	29 45.3
21 Sa	0 01 27	28 30 11	9♉14 10	16 33 47	6 53.8	6 37.7	20 07.4	27 25.8	9 25.5	9 20.2	20 47.2	15 03.6	22 15.6	27 06.1	28 30.9	29 44.7
22 Su	0 05 24	29 28 50	23 47 49	0♊55 51	6 50.6	6 38.4	21 58.9	28 38.9	9 59.0	9 28.7	20 50.7	14 59.2	22 13.1	27 05.1	28 29.3	29 44.2
23 M	0 09 20	0♎27 32	7♊57 38	14 53 04	6 47.4	6 38.9	23 50.3	29 52.0	10 32.2	9 37.4	20 53.9	14 54.9	22 10.7	27 04.1	28 27.6	29 43.6
24 Tu	0 13 17	1 26 16	21 42 10	28 25 05	6 44.3	6R 39.3	25 41.5	1♏05.1	11 05.3	9 46.4	20 57.0	14 50.6	22 08.2	27 03.0	28 25.9	29 43.1
25 W	0 17 13	2 25 02	5♋02 03	11♋33 23	6 41.1	6 39.3	27 32.3	2 18.2	11 38.2	9 55.6	21 00.0	14 46.3	22 05.6	27 01.9	28 24.3	29 42.6
26 Th	0 21 10	3 23 50	17 59 25	24 20 34	6 37.9	6 39.2	29 22.6	3 31.3	12 10.8	10 05.1	21 02.7	14 42.0	22 03.1	27 00.8	28 22.6	29 42.2
27 F	0 25 06	4 22 41	0♌37 15	6♌49 54	6 34.7	6 39.0	1♎12.3	4 44.3	12 43.3	10 14.9	21 05.2	14 37.8	22 00.5	26 59.5	28 21.0	29 41.7
28 Sa	0 29 03	5 21 34	12 58 57	19 04 49	6 31.6	6 38.8	3 01.4	5 57.4	13 15.6	10 25.0	21 07.5	14 33.7	21 57.9	26 58.3	28 19.3	29 41.3
29 Su	0 32 59	6 20 29	25 07 54	1♍08 36	6 28.4	6D 38.7	4 49.7	7 10.4	13 47.6	10 35.3	21 09.7	14 29.6	21 55.3	26 57.0	28 17.7	29 40.9
30 M	0 36 56	7♎19 26	7♍07 18	13 04 20	6♈25.2	6♈38.7	6♎37.2	8♏23.4	14♋19.4	10♑45.8	21♊11.6	14♓25.5	21♈52.7	26♉55.7	28♓16.1	29♑40.6

1st of Month

Julian Day #
2460554.5
Obliquity
23°26'[illegible]9"
SVP 4♓54'56"
GC 27♐11.0
Eris 25♈21.1R

Day	⚴
1	27♏54.8
6	29 17.9
11	0♐45.3
16	2 16.5
21	3 51.2
26	5 29.0

Day	⚵
1	7♎35.9
6	9 20.6
11	11 05.9
16	12 51.8
21	14 38.0
26	16 24.5

Day	⚶
1	3♏18.3
6	5 40.1
11	8 02.2
16	10 24.6
21	12 47.1
26	15 09.8

DECLINATION and LATITUDE

Day	☉ Decl	☽ Decl	☽ Lat	☽ 12h Decl	☿ Decl	☿ Lat	♀ Decl	♀ Lat	♂ Decl	♂ Lat	⚳ Decl	⚳ Lat	♃ Decl	♃ Lat	♄ Decl	♄ Lat
1 Su	8N10	19N56	4N03	17N39	13N07	1S06	0S15	1N02	23N19	0S06	30S54	7S42	22N17	0S42	7S19	2S11
2 M	7 49	15 13	3 16	12 38	13 14	0 48	0 46	0 60	23 21	0 05	30 54	7 42	22 18	0 42	7 20	2 11
3 Tu	7 27	9 57	2 21	7 12	13 17	0 31	1 17	0 58	23 23	0 03	30 54	7 41	22 18	0 42	7 22	2 11
4 W	7 05	4 24	1 20	1 33	13 18	0 15	1 48	0 56	23 24	0 02	30 53	7 41	22 19	0 42	7 24	2 11
5 Th	6 42	1S17	0 16	4S07	13 13	0N01	2 19	0 54	23 25	0 01	30 53	7 41	22 19	0 42	7 26	2 11
6 F	6 20	6 54	0S49	9 38	13 08	0 15	2 49	0 51	23 26	0 00	30 52	7 40	22 20	0 42	7 28	2 11
7 Sa	5 58	12 17	1 52	14 50	12 57	0 29	3 20	0 49	23 27	0N01	30 51	7 40	22 20	0 42	7 30	2 11
8 Su	5 35	17 15	2 50	19 32	12 43	0 41	3 51	0 47	23 28	0 02	30 51	7 40	22 21	0 42	7 31	2 11
9 M	5 12	21 37	3 42	23 30	12 26	0 53	4 22	0 45	23 28	0 03	30 50	7 39	22 21	0 42	7 33	2 12
10 Tu	4 50	25 09	4 24	26 31	12 06	1 03	4 52	0 42	23 29	0 05	30 49	7 39	22 21	0 42	7 35	2 12
11 W	4 27	27 35	4 56	28 18	11 42	1 13	5 23	0 40	23 29	0 06	30 49	7 38	22 22	0 42	7 37	2 12
12 Th	4 04	28 39	5 13	28 37	11 15	1 21	5 53	0 37	23 29	0 07	30 48	7 38	22 22	0 42	7 39	2 12
13 F	3 41	28 09	5 15	27 16	10 46	1 28	6 24	0 35	23 29	0 08	30 47	7 37	22 22	0 42	7 41	2 12
14 Sa	3 18	25 58	4 60	24 15	10 14	1 34	6 54	0 32	23 29	0 09	30 46	7 37	22 23	0 42	7 42	2 12
15 Su	2 55	22 09	4 26	19 41	9 39	1 39	7 24	0 30	23 29	0 11	30 45	7 37	22 23	0 42	7 44	2 12
16 M	2 32	16 53	3 35	13 49	9 03	1 43	7 54	0 27	23 28	0 12	30 44	7 36	22 23	0 42	7 46	2 12
17 Tu	2 09	10 30	2 28	7 01	8 24	1 46	8 24	0 25	23 28	0 13	30 43	7 36	22 24	0 42	7 48	2 12
18 W	1 46	3 26	1 09	0N14	7 44	1 48	8 53	0 22	23 27	0 14	30 42	7 35	22 24	0 42	7 49	2 12
19 Th	1 22	3N53	0N15	7 28	7 03	1 50	9 23	0 19	23 26	0 16	30 41	7 35	22 24	0 43	7 51	2 12
20 F	0 59	10 56	1 37	14 14	6 20	1 50	9 52	0 16	23 25	0 17	30 40	7 34	22 24	0 43	7 53	2 12
21 Sa	0 36	17 17	2 52	20 03	5 36	1 50	10 21	0 14	23 24	0 18	30 39	7 33	22 25	0 43	7 55	2 12
22 Su	0 12	22 29	3 53	24 33	4 51	1 49	10 50	0 11	23 23	0 19	30 38	7 33	22 25	0 43	7 56	2 12
23 M	0S11	26 13	4 39	27 28	4 05	1 47	11 18	0 08	23 22	0 21	30 36	7 32	22 25	0 43	7 58	2 12
24 Tu	0 34	28 17	5 07	28 40	3 19	1 45	11 46	0 05	23 21	0 22	30 35	7 32	22 25	0 43	7 60	2 12
25 W	0 58	28 38	5 18	28 12	2 33	1 43	12 14	0 02	23 19	0 23	30 34	7 31	22 25	0 43	8 01	2 12
26 Th	1 21	27 22	5 12	26 13	1 46	1 39	12 42	0S01	23 18	0 25	30 33	7 31	22 26	0 43	8 03	2 12
27 F	1 44	24 44	4 50	22 60	0 59	1 36	13 10	0 04	23 16	0 26	30 31	7 30	22 26	0 43	8 05	2 12
28 Sa	2 08	21 01	4 16	18 49	0 12	1 32	13 37	0 07	23 14	0 28	30 30	7 30	22 26	0 43	8 06	2 12
29 Su	2 31	16 27	3 31	13 57	0S35	1 27	14 04	0 10	23 12	0 29	30 28	7 29	22 26	0 43	8 08	2 12
30 M	2S54	11N19	2N37	8N37	1S22	1N22	14S30	0S13	23N10	0N30	30S27	7S28	22N26	0S43	8S09	2S12

Day	⚷ Decl	⚷ Lat	♅ Decl	♅ Lat	♆ Decl	♆ Lat	♇ Decl	♇ Lat
1	9N58	1N07	19N17	0S16	1S35	1S19	23S20	3S16
6	9 54	1 07	19 17	0 16	1 38	1 19	23 21	3 16
11	9 50	1 06	19 17	0 16	1 42	1 19	23 22	3 16
16	9 46	1 06	19 16	0 16	1 45	1 20	23 23	3 16
21	9 41	1 06	19 15	0 16	1 48	1 20	23 24	3 16
26	9 36	1 06	19 14	0 16	1 52	1 20	23 24	3 16

Day	⚴ Decl	⚴ Lat	⚵ Decl	⚵ Lat	⚶ Decl	⚶ Lat	Eris Decl	Eris Lat
1	14N24	34N55	1N13	4N36	13N44	3N41	0S21	10S54
6	13 31	34 15	0 37	4 42	12 56	3 46	0 22	10 54
11	12 40	33 38	0 01	4 47	12 08	3 51	0 23	10 54
16	11 50	33 02	0S35	4 53	11 19	3 57	0 24	10 54
21	11 01	32 28	1 10	4 59	10 29	4 02	0 25	10 55
26	10 15	31 55	1 45	5 05	9 39	4 08	0 26	10 55

Moon Phenomena

Max/0 Decl
dy hr mn
4 18:35 0 S
12 4:44 28S41
18 11:15 0 N
24 16:53 28N42

Max/0 Lat
dy hr mn
5 5:45 0 S
12 14:58 5S17
18 19:52 0 N
25 2:58 5N18

Perigee/Apogee
dy hr m kilometers
5 14:55 a 406211
18 13:24 p 357291

PH dy hr mn
● 3 1:57 11♍04
☽ 11 6:07 19♐00
○ 18 2:36 25♓41
• 18 2:45 P 0.085
☾ 24 18:51 2♋12

Void of Course Moon

Last Aspect	☽ Ingress
2 0:26 ♂ ⚹	♍ 2 3:50
4 16:08 ♇ △	♎ 4 16:13
7 5:10 ♇ □	♏ 7 5:20
9 17:13 ♇ ⚹	♐ 9 17:27
12 0:22 ♆ □	♑ 12 2:39
14 7:36 ♇ ☌	♒ 14 7:55
16 5:05 ♅ □	♓ 16 9:40
18 9:04 ♇ ⚹	♈ 18 9:25
20 8:40 ♇ □	♉ 20 9:04
22 10:15 ☉ △	♊ 22 10:25
24 12:00 ♆ □	♋ 24 14:51
26 22:13 ♇ ☍	♌ 26 22:48
29 3:37 ♅ □	♍ 29 9:43

DAILY ASPECTARIAN

1 Su: ☽⚻♄ 1:19; ☽∥♅ 3:31; ☽∠♀ 4:33; ☽⚹♃ 6:11; ♂#♇ 8:02; ☽☌☿ 12:38; ☽⚼⚳ 13:11; ☽△⚷ 13:53; ♅ R 15:19; ☽□♅ 22:23

2 M: ♇R♑ 0:11; ☽⚹♂ 0:26; ☽⚻♆ 1:54; ☿⚼⚳ 1:54; ☽⚻♇ 3:49; ☽∥☿ 9:09; ☽⚺♀ 13:36; ☿△⚷ 13:48; ☽△⚳ 19:06; ☽⚼⚷ 19:38

3 Tu: ☽∥⚷ 0:04; ☉☌☽ 1:57; ♂□♆ 4:11; ☉#♄ 4:26; ☽⚼♇ 9:48; ☽#♄ 11:12; ☉∥☽ 11:43; ☽☍♄ 12:38; ♀∥♆ 15:44; ☽□♃ 18:36

4 W: ☽⚻⚷ 1:46; ☽⚺☿ 4:18; ☽#♀ 10:05; ☽△♅ 10:38; ☽#♆ 11:43; ☽☍♆ 14:06; ☽□♂ 16:01; ☽△♇ 16:08; ♂⚻♇ 18:00; ♂ ♋ 19:47; ♀□⚳ 21:27

5 Th: ☽∥♆ 1:28; ☽∥♀ 4:46; ☊ D 5:48; ☽□⚳ 8:03; ☽☌♀ 9:14; ☽∠☿ 13:28; ☽⚼♅ 17:10; ☉⚺☽ 20:13; ☉#☽ 21:42

6 F: ☽⚻♄ 1:12; ☽∥♄ 2:28; ☽△♃ 8:09; ☽#⚷ 13:11; ☽☍⚷ 14:40; ☽⚹☿ 23:12; ☽⚻♅ 23:43

7 Sa: ☉⚼♇ 1:13; ☽#☿ 3:00; ☽⚻♆ 3:05; ☿□♅ 4:22; ☽□♇ 5:10; ☉∠☽ 5:31; ☽⚼♄ 7:33; ☽△♂ 8:25; ☽⚼♃ 14:55; ☽⚹⚳ 21:26

8 Su: ☉☍♄ 4:36; ☽⚺♀ 5:15; ☽⚼♆ 9:21; ♀ ♐ 10:31; ☽#♅ 10:40; ☿⚻♆ 10:53; ♀⚼♅ 13:21; ☽△♄ 13:39; ☉⚹☽ 14:30; ☽⚼♂ 16:16; ☽⚻♃ 21:21

9 M: ☽⚻⚷ 3:02; ☽∠⚳ 3:42; ☽#♃ 4:29; ☿⚻♇ 4:56; ☿ ♍ 6:51; ☽∥♇ 11:02; ☽#♂ 11:47; ☽☍♅ 12:00; ☽∠♀ 14:32; ☽△♆ 15:08; ☽⚹♇ 17:13; ☽□☿ 18:51; ☉#♀ 22:47; ☽⚻♂ 23:29

10 Tu: ☽⚼⚷ 8:24; ☽⚺⚳ 9:20; ☽∠♇ 22:15; ☽⚹♀ 22:49

11 W: ☽□♄ 0:03; ☊ R 6:06; ☉□☽ 6:07; ☽☍♃ 8:08; ♀⚻♄ 10:53; ☽△⚷ 12:56; ☽⚻♅ 21:29

12 Th: ☽□♆ 0:22; ☽⚺♇ 2:22; ☿⚹♂ 3:43; ☉□♃ 10:54; ☽☍♂ 10:58; ☽△☿ 11:37; ☽☌⚳ 17:53

13 F: ☽⚼♅ 0:48; ☽⚹♄ 6:54; ☽□♀ 11:31; ☽⚻♃ 15:04; ☉△☽ 17:02; ☽⚼☿ 18:08; ☽□⚷ 19:02

14 Sa: ☿⚼⚷ 1:15; ☽△♅ 3:05; ☽⚹♆ 5:41; ☽☌♇ 7:36; ☽∠♄ 8:51; ☿△⚳ 15:25; ☽#♂ 16:39; ☽⚼♃ 17:01; ☽∥♇ 17:14; ☽⚻♂ 17:53; ☿∥⚷ 18:55; ☉⚻⚷ 20:23; ☉⚼☽ 20:39; ☽⚺⚳ 22:27; ☽#♃ 22:45; ☽⚻☿ 23:23

15 Su: ♀△♃ 5:36; ☽∠♆ 6:57; ☽⚺♄ 9:56; ☽#♅ 13:50; ♀∥♄ 17:11; ☽△♃ 18:06; ☽△♀ 19:10; ☽⚼♂ 19:50; ☽⚹⚷ 21:26; ☉⚻☽ 23:16; ☽∠⚳ 23:27

16 M: ☽□♅ 5:05; ☽⚺♆ 7:29; ☽⚺♇ 9:20; ☽△♂ 21:04; ♀☍⚷ 21:30; ☽∠⚷ 21:36; ☽⚼♀ 21:37; ☽⚹⚳ 23:50

17 Tu: ☿#♀ 0:16; ☽#⚷ 2:39; ☽∥♀ 6:51; ☽☍☿ 6:57; ☽#☿ 8:03; ☽∠♇ 9:20; ☽∥♄ 9:21; ☽☌♄ 10:12; ☽□♃ 18:32; ☿#♄ 21:04; ☽⚺⚷ 21:23; ☉#♆ 23:08; ☽⚻♀ 23:32

18 W: ☉☍☽ 2:36; ☿⚼♇ 2:36; ☽⚹♅ 4:54; ☽∥♆ 5:26; ☉#☽ 5:48; ☽☌♆ 7:12; ☿☍♄ 8:52; ☽⚹♇ 9:04; ☉∥☽ 16:10; ☽#♆ 17:05; ☊ D 19:59; ☽□♂ 22:28; ☽□⚳ 23:45

19 Th: ☽∠♅ 4:35; ☽⚺♄ 9:25; ☽∥☿ 9:36; ☽⚻☿ 12:58; ☽#♄ 13:21; ☉△♅ 14:05; ♀#⚷ 16:16; ☽⚹♃ 18:12; ☽∥⚷ 19:40; ☽#♀ 19:56; ☽☌⚷ 20:45

20 F: ☽☍♀ 3:15; ☽⚺♅ 4:26; ☉⚻☽ 5:27; ☽⚺♆ 6:43; ☽□♇ 8:40; ☽∠♄ 9:14; ☽⚼☿ 16:22; ♀⚻♅ 17:37; ☽∠♃ 18:23; ♂☍⚳ 19:00

21 Sa: ☽△⚳ 0:10; ☉☍♆ 0:18; ☽⚹♂ 0:19; ☽∠♆ 6:59; ☉⚼☽ 7:28; ☽∥♅ 8:25; ☿□♃ 8:51; ☽⚹♄ 9:29; ♂#♇ 12:20; ☽⚺♃ 19:04; ☽△☿ 20:32; ♀⚻♆ 20:55; ☽⚺⚷ 21:23; ☽∥♃ 23:38

22 Su: ☽⚼⚳ 1:09; ☽∠♂ 2:04; ☿⚻⚷ 3:00; ☽∥♂ 4:57; ☽#♇ 5:02; ☽☌♅ 5:30; ☉△♇ 6:13; ☽⚹♆ 7:51; ☽⚻♀ 8:54; ☽△♇ 9:58; ☉△☽ 10:15; ☉ ♎ 12:45; ♀□♇ 21:16; ☽∠⚷ 22:40

23 M: ♀⚼♄ 0:53; ♀ ♏ 2:37; ☽⚻⚳ 2:54; ☽⚺♂ 4:38; ☽⚼♇ 11:43; ☽□♄ 11:59; ☽⚼♀ 13:08; ☽☌♃ 22:40

24 Tu: ☽⚹⚷ 0:46; ☽□☿ 8:15; ☽⚺♅ 9:32; ☽□♆ 12:00; ☽⚻♇ 14:20; ☿△♅ 17:28; ☽△♀ 18:31; ☉□☽ 18:51; ☊ R 19:40

25 W: ☽☍⚳ 9:06; ☿☍♆ 11:08; ☉⚺♀ 11:28; ☽☌♂ 12:41; ☽∠♅ 12:52; ♂∠♅ 16:50; ☽△♄ 17:53; ☿#♆ 21:06; ♄∠♇ 23:10

26 Th: ☿△♇ 4:15; ☽⚺♃ 5:46; ☽□⚷ 7:38; ☿ ♎ 8:10; ☉#☿ 8:31; ☽⚹♅ 17:04; ☽△♆ 19:39; ☽⚼♄ 22:07; ☽☍♇ 22:13

27 F: ☽⚹☿ 1:19; ☉⚹☽ 7:52; ☉∥♆ 8:28; ☽□♀ 8:48; ☽#♇ 9:19; ☽∥♂ 10:20; ☽∠♃ 10:35; ☽∥♃ 15:33; ☽⚻⚳ 18:55

28 Sa: ☽⚺♂ 0:34; ☽⚼♆ 0:40; ☽⚻♄ 3:05; ♀⚼♃ 3:27; ☽∥♅ 9:53; ☽∠☿ 11:39; ☉∠☽ 15:49; ☽⚹♃ 16:06; ☽△⚷ 17:39

29 Su: ☽⚼⚳ 0:55; ☽□♅ 3:37; ☽⚻♆ 6:17; ☽∠♂ 7:38; ☊ D 8:00; ☽⚻♇ 9:04; ☽#♀ 10:33; ☽⚺☿ 22:49; ☽⚼⚷ 23:31

30 M: ☉⚺☽ 0:27; ☽⚹♀ 2:51; ♂△♄ 4:07; ☽△⚳ 7:27; ☽∥⚷ 7:58; ☽#♄ 13:56; ☽☍♄ 14:39; ☽⚹♂ 15:12; ☽⚼♇ 15:14; ☿∥♆ 16:47; ☉☌☿ 21:11

October 2024

LONGITUDE

Day	Sid.Time	☉	☽	☽ 12 hour	Mean☊	True☊	☿	♀	♂	⚳	♃	♄	⚷	♅	♆	♇
	h m s	° ' "	° ' "	° ' "	° '	° '	° '	° '	° '	° '	° '	° '	° '	° '	° '	° '
1 Tu	0 40 53	8♎18 25	19♍00 03	24♍54 45	6♈22.0	6♈38.8	8♎24.0	9♏36.4	14♋51.0	10♑56.6	21♊13.4	14♓21.5	21♈50.0	26♉54.3	28♓14.4	29♑40.3
2 W	0 44 49	9 17 27	0♎48 45	6♎42 20	6 18.8	6R 38.9	10 10.0	10 49.3	15 22.3	11 07.7	21 14.9	14R 17.6	21R 47.4	26R 52.9	28R 12.8	29R 40.0
3 Th	0 48 46	10 16 30	12 35 46	18 29 20	6 15.7	6 38.9	11 55.1	12 02.3	15 53.4	11 19.0	21 16.3	14 13.7	21 44.7	26 51.4	28 11.2	29 39.7
4 F	0 52 42	11 15 36	24 23 20	0♏18 00	6 12.5	6 38.7	13 39.4	13 15.2	16 24.3	11 30.5	21 17.5	14 09.8	21 42.0	26 49.9	28 09.6	29 39.4
5 Sa	0 56 39	12 14 43	6♏13 40	12 10 37	6 09.3	6 38.2	15 22.8	14 28.1	16 55.0	11 42.3	21 18.4	14 06.0	21 39.3	26 48.4	28 08.0	29 39.2
6 Su	1 00 35	13 13 53	18 09 10	24 09 40	6 06.1	6 37.4	17 05.5	15 41.0	17 25.3	11 54.3	21 19.2	14 02.3	21 36.6	26 46.8	28 06.4	29 39.0
7 M	1 04 32	14 13 04	0♐12 28	6♐17 56	6 02.9	6 36.4	18 47.3	16 53.9	17 55.5	12 06.6	21 19.7	13 58.7	21 33.9	26 45.2	28 04.8	29 38.9
8 Tu	1 08 28	15 12 18	12 26 28	18 38 28	5 59.8	6 35.3	20 28.3	18 06.7	18 25.4	12 19.0	21 20.1	13 55.1	21 31.2	26 43.5	28 03.2	29 38.8
9 W	1 12 25	16 11 33	24 54 22	1♑14 35	5 56.6	6 34.4	22 08.6	19 19.5	18 55.0	12 31.7	21R 20.3	13 51.5	21 28.4	26 41.8	28 01.6	29 38.6
10 Th	1 16 22	17 10 50	7♑39 31	14 09 36	5 53.4	6D 33.7	23 48.0	20 32.3	19 24.4	12 44.6	21 20.2	13 48.1	21 25.7	26 40.1	28 00.1	29 38.6
11 F	1 20 18	18 10 09	20 45 11	27 26 37	5 50.2	6 33.6	25 26.7	21 45.1	19 53.4	12 57.8	21 20.0	13 44.7	21 23.0	26 38.3	27 58.6	29 38.5
12 Sa	1 24 15	19 09 29	4♒14 08	11♒07 56	5 47.1	6 34.0	27 04.7	22 57.8	20 22.3	13 11.1	21 19.5	13 41.4	21 20.2	26 36.5	27 57.0	29D 38.5
13 Su	1 28 11	20 08 51	18 08 04	25 14 31	5 43.9	6 34.8	28 41.9	24 10.5	20 50.8	13 24.6	21 18.9	13 38.2	21 17.5	26 34.6	27 55.5	29 38.5
14 M	1 32 08	21 08 15	2♓27 04	9♓45 22	5 40.7	6 35.9	0♏18.4	25 23.2	21 19.1	13 38.4	21 18.0	13 35.0	21 14.7	26 32.8	27 54.0	29 38.6
15 Tu	1 36 04	22 07 41	17 08 54	24 36 59	5 37.5	6 37.0	1 54.2	26 35.9	21 47.0	13 52.3	21 17.0	13 31.9	21 12.0	26 30.9	27 52.5	29 38.6
16 W	1 40 01	23 07 08	2♈08 45	9♈43 12	5 34.3	6R 37.5	3 29.4	27 48.5	22 14.7	14 06.5	21 15.7	13 28.9	21 09.2	26 28.9	27 51.1	29 38.7
17 Th	1 43 57	24 06 38	17 19 13	24 55 36	5 31.2	6 37.3	5 03.9	29 01.1	22 42.1	14 20.8	21 14.3	13 26.0	21 06.5	26 26.9	27 49.6	29 38.9
18 F	1 47 54	25 06 09	2♉31 07	10♉04 32	5 28.0	6 36.2	6 37.7	0♐13.6	23 09.2	14 35.4	21 12.6	13 23.2	21 03.7	26 24.9	27 48.2	29 39.0
19 Sa	1 51 51	26 05 43	17 34 43	25 00 34	5 24.8	6 34.2	8 10.9	1 26.2	23 36.0	14 50.1	21 10.8	13 20.4	21 01.0	26 22.9	27 46.8	29 39.2
20 Su	1 55 47	27 05 18	2♊21 13	9♊35 54	5 21.6	6 31.5	9 43.5	2 38.7	24 02.4	15 05.0	21 08.8	13 17.7	20 58.3	26 20.8	27 45.4	29 39.4
21 M	1 59 44	28 04 56	16 44 03	23 45 18	5 18.5	6 28.6	11 15.5	3 51.1	24 28.6	15 20.1	21 06.5	13 15.1	20 55.5	26 18.7	27 44.0	29 39.7
22 Tu	2 03 40	29 04 37	0♋39 28	7♋26 33	5 15.3	6 26.0	12 46.9	5 03.6	24 54.4	15 35.4	21 04.1	13 12.6	20 52.8	26 16.6	27 42.6	29 39.9
23 W	2 07 37	0♏04 19	14 06 39	20 40 04	5 12.1	6 24.0	14 17.7	6 16.0	25 19.9	15 50.8	21 01.4	13 10.2	20 50.1	26 14.5	27 41.3	29 40.2
24 Th	2 11 33	1 04 04	27 07 09	3♌28 22	5 08.9	6D 23.1	15 48.0	7 28.3	25 45.0	16 06.5	20 58.6	13 07.9	20 47.4	26 12.3	27 39.9	29 40.6
25 F	2 15 30	2 03 51	9♌44 14	15 55 18	5 05.8	6 23.3	17 17.6	8 40.7	26 09.8	16 22.3	20 55.6	13 05.7	20 44.7	26 10.1	27 38.6	29 40.9
26 Sa	2 19 26	3 03 40	22 02 09	28 05 23	5 02.6	6 24.4	18 46.7	9 53.0	26 34.2	16 38.2	20 52.3	13 03.5	20 42.1	26 07.9	27 37.3	29 41.3
27 Su	2 23 23	4 03 31	4♍05 34	10♍03 18	4 59.4	6 26.1	20 15.1	11 05.3	26 58.3	16 54.4	20 48.9	13 01.5	20 39.4	26 05.6	27 36.1	29 41.7
28 M	2 27 20	5 03 25	15 59 08	21 53 35	4 56.2	6 27.9	21 43.0	12 17.5	27 22.0	17 10.7	20 45.3	12 59.5	20 36.7	26 03.3	27 34.8	29 42.2
29 Tu	2 31 16	6 03 20	27 47 09	3♎40 17	4 53.0	6R 29.2	23 10.2	13 29.8	27 45.3	17 27.2	20 41.5	12 57.7	20 34.1	26 01.0	27 33.6	29 42.7
30 W	2 35 13	7 03 18	9♎33 26	15 26 57	4 49.9	6 29.5	24 36.8	14 41.9	28 08.2	17 43.8	20 37.5	12 55.9	20 31.5	25 58.7	27 32.4	29 43.2
31 Th	2 39 09	8♏03 18	21 21 13	27 16 30	4♈46.7	6♈28.4	26♏02.8	15♐54.1	28♋30.7	18♑00.6	20♊33.4	12♓54.3	20♈28.9	25♉56.4	27♓31.2	29♑43.7

1st of Month

Julian Day # 2460584.5
Obliquity 23°26'20"
SVP 4♓54'53"
GC 27♐11.1
Eris 25♈06.2R

Day	⚴	Day	⚵	Day	⚶
1	7♐09.7	1	18♎11.2	1	17♍32.5
6	8 53.0	6	19 58.1	6	19 55.3
11	10 38.6	11	21 44.9	11	22 17.8
16	12 26.4	16	23 31.5	16	24 40.2
21	14 15.9	21	25 17.9	21	27 02.2
26	16 07.2	26	27 03.9	26	29 23.9
31	17 59.9	31	28 49.4	31	1♎45.1

DECLINATION and LATITUDE

Day	☉ Decl	☽ Decl	☽ Lat	☽ 12h Decl	☿ Decl	☿ Lat	♀ Decl	♀ Lat	♂ Decl	♂ Lat	⚳ Decl	⚳ Lat	♃ Decl	♃ Lat	♄ Decl	♄ Lat
1 Tu	3S18	5N50	1N37	3N01	2S09	1N17	14S56	0S16	23N08	0N32	30S26	7S28	22N26	0S43	8S11	2S12
2 W	3 41	0 10	0 32	2S40	2 55	1 12	15 22	0 19	23 06	0 33	30 24	7 27	22 26	0 43	8 12	2 11
3 Th	4 04	5S29	0S33	8 15	3 42	1 06	15 48	0 22	23 04	0 35	30 22	7 27	22 26	0 43	8 14	2 11
4 F	4 27	10 57	1 37	13 34	4 28	1 00	16 13	0 25	23 02	0 36	30 21	7 26	22 26	0 43	8 15	2 11
5 Sa	4 50	16 04	2 37	18 25	5 13	0 54	16 38	0 28	22 59	0 38	30 19	7 26	22 26	0 43	8 16	2 11
6 Su	5 13	20 36	3 31	22 36	5 58	0 48	17 02	0 31	22 57	0 39	30 17	7 25	22 26	0 43	8 18	2 11
7 M	5 36	24 21	4 16	25 51	6 43	0 42	17 26	0 34	22 54	0 41	30 16	7 24	22 26	0 43	8 19	2 11
8 Tu	5 59	27 04	4 50	27 58	7 27	0 35	17 49	0 37	22 52	0 42	30 14	7 24	22 26	0 43	8 21	2 11
9 W	6 22	28 31	5 11	28 42	8 11	0 29	18 12	0 41	22 49	0 44	30 12	7 23	22 26	0 43	8 22	2 11
10 Th	6 45	28 30	5 17	27 54	8 54	0 22	18 35	0 44	22 47	0 45	30 10	7 23	22 26	0 43	8 23	2 11
11 F	7 08	26 54	5 08	25 31	9 36	0 15	18 57	0 47	22 44	0 47	30 08	7 22	22 26	0 43	8 24	2 11
12 Sa	7 30	23 45	4 41	21 37	10 18	0 09	19 19	0 50	22 41	0 48	30 06	7 22	22 26	0 43	8 25	2 11
13 Su	7 52	19 10	3 58	16 24	10 59	0 02	19 40	0 53	22 39	0 50	30 05	7 21	22 26	0 43	8 27	2 11
14 M	8 15	13 22	2 58	10 07	11 40	0S05	20 01	0 56	22 36	0 51	30 03	7 21	22 26	0 43	8 28	2 11
15 Tu	8 37	6 42	1 46	3 09	12 19	0 12	20 21	0 59	22 33	0 53	30 00	7 20	22 26	0 43	8 29	2 10
16 W	8 59	0N28	0 25	4N07	12 59	0 19	20 41	1 02	22 30	0 55	29 58	7 19	22 26	0 43	8 30	2 10
17 Th	9 21	7 42	0N59	11 12	13 37	0 26	20 60	1 05	22 27	0 56	29 56	7 19	22 26	0 43	8 31	2 10
18 F	9 43	14 31	2 18	17 36	14 15	0 33	21 18	1 08	22 24	0 58	29 54	7 18	22 26	0 43	8 32	2 10
19 Sa	10 05	20 23	3 27	22 50	14 52	0 40	21 36	1 11	22 22	0 60	29 52	7 18	22 26	0 43	8 33	2 10
20 Su	10 26	24 54	4 21	26 31	15 28	0 46	21 54	1 14	22 19	1 02	29 50	7 17	22 26	0 43	8 34	2 10
21 M	10 48	27 42	4 57	28 25	16 03	0 53	22 11	1 17	22 16	1 03	29 47	7 17	22 25	0 43	8 35	2 10
22 Tu	11 09	28 40	5 14	28 28	16 37	0 60	22 27	1 20	22 13	1 05	29 45	7 16	22 25	0 43	8 36	2 10
23 W	11 30	27 52	5 12	26 53	17 11	1 06	22 42	1 22	22 10	1 07	29 42	7 16	22 25	0 43	8 36	2 10
24 Th	11 51	25 33	4 55	23 56	17 44	1 13	22 57	1 25	22 07	1 09	29 40	7 15	22 25	0 43	8 37	2 09
25 F	12 11	22 02	4 24	19 56	18 16	1 19	23 12	1 28	22 04	1 10	29 38	7 15	22 25	0 43	8 38	2 09
26 Sa	12 32	17 38	3 41	15 12	18 47	1 25	23 26	1 31	22 01	1 12	29 35	7 14	22 24	0 43	8 39	2 09
27 Su	12 52	12 38	2 49	9 58	19 17	1 32	23 39	1 34	21 58	1 14	29 32	7 14	22 24	0 43	8 39	2 09
28 M	13 12	7 13	1 50	4 26	19 46	1 38	23 51	1 36	21 56	1 16	29 30	7 13	22 24	0 43	8 40	2 09
29 Tu	13 32	1 37	0 48	1S13	20 14	1 43	24 03	1 39	21 53	1 18	29 27	7 13	22 24	0 43	8 40	2 09
30 W	13 52	4S03	0S17	6 50	20 41	1 49	24 14	1 41	21 50	1 20	29 24	7 12	22 23	0 43	8 41	2 09
31 Th	14S12	9S34	1S21	12S14	21S07	1S54	24S25	1S44	21N47	1N22	29S22	7S12	22N23	0S43	8S42	2S08

Day	⚷ Decl	⚷ Lat	♅ Decl	♅ Lat	♆ Decl	♆ Lat	♇ Decl	♇ Lat
1	9N31	1N05	19N12	0S16	1S55	1S20	23S25	3S16
6	9 26	1 05	19 11	0 16	1 58	1 20	23 25	3 16
11	9 20	1 05	19 09	0 16	2 01	1 20	23 25	3 16
16	9 15	1 04	19 06	0 16	2 04	1 19	23 25	3 16
21	9 09	1 04	19 04	0 16	2 07	1 19	23 25	3 16
26	9 04	1 04	19 02	0 16	2 10	1 19	23 24	3 16
31	8N59	1N03	18N59	0S16	2S12	1S19	23S24	3S16

Day	⚴ Decl	⚴ Lat	⚵ Decl	⚵ Lat	⚶ Decl	⚶ Lat	Eris Decl	Eris Lat
1	9N30	31N24	2S20	5N11	8N49	4N14	0S27	10S55
6	8 47	30 54	2 54	5 18	7 58	4 20	0 28	10 55
11	8 07	30 26	3 27	5 24	7 07	4 26	0 29	10 55
16	7 28	29 59	4 00	5 31	6 17	4 32	0 30	10 54
21	6 52	29 34	4 32	5 38	5 26	4 38	0 31	10 54
26	6 19	29 10	5 03	5 45	4 36	4 45	0 32	10 54
31	5N47	28N47	5S33	5N53	3N46	4N52	0S33	10S54

Moon Phenomena

Max/0 Decl
dy hr mn
2 0:44 0 S
9 11:45 28S42
15 22:26 0 N
22 0:44 28N40
29 6:49 0 S

Max/0 Lat
dy hr mn
2 11:53 0 S
9 21:58 5S17
16 7:06 0 N
22 10:11 5N15
29 17:45 0 S

Perigee/Apogee
dy hr m kilometers
2 19:40 a 406516
17 0:52 p 357175
29 22:51 a 406161

PH dy hr mn
● 2 18:50 10♎04
● 2 11 26:1A 07'25"
☽ 10 18:56 17♑58
○ 17 11:28 24♈35
☾ 24 8:04 1♌24

Void of Course Moon

Last Aspect			☽ Ingress
1 21:40	♇	△	♎ 1 22:21
4 10:42	♇	□	♏ 4 11:23
6 22:54	♇	⚹	♐ 6 23:35
9 5:55	♆	□	♑ 9 9:39
11 15:54	♇	☌	♒ 11 16:32
13 14:12	♅	□	♓ 13 19:56
15 20:01	♇	⚹	♈ 15 20:35
17 19:28	♇	□	♉ 17 20:01
19 19:35	♇	△	♊ 19 20:08
21 21:01	☉	△	♋ 21 22:51
24 4:49	♇	☍	♌ 24 5:25
26 8:05	♅	□	♍ 26 15:49
29 3:56	♇	△	♎ 29 4:31
31 16:58	♇	□	♏ 31 17:30

DAILY ASPECTARIAN

1 Tu ☽□♃ 4:31 · ☽⚻⚷ 5:44 · ☉#☽ 10:07 · ☽∠♀ 12:41 · ☽#☿ 13:46 · ☽△♅ 16:01 · ☽#♆ 16:36 · ☽☍♆ 18:43 · ☽△♇ 21:40

2 W ♀⚹⚳ 7:08 · ☽∥♆ 8:53 · ☊R 11:32 · ☿□⚳ 14:44 · ☽∥☿ 15:10 · ☉∥☽ 17:31 · ☉☌☽ 18:50 · ☽□⚳ 21:21 · ☽☌☿ 22:23 · ☽⚼♅ 22:30 · ☽⊻♀ 22:44 · ☿⚼♅ 23:10

3 Th ☽⚻♄ 3:18 · ☿⊻♀ 5:28 · ☽□♂ 7:01 · ☽∥♄ 11:56 · ☽#⚷ 17:22 · ☽△♃ 17:42 · ☽☍⚷ 18:33 · ♀⚼♆ 22:11 · ☉∥☿ 23:39

4 F ☽⚻♅ 4:57 · ☿⚻♄ 6:47 · ☉□⚳ 7:33 · ☽⚻♆ 7:38 · ☽⚼♄ 9:39 · ☽□♇ 10:42 · ☉⚼♅ 13:35 · ♀△♄ 17:05

5 Sa ☽⚼♃ 0:10 · ☽∥♀ 3:03 · ⚳⚼♅ 10:45 · ☽⚹⚳ 11:14 · ☉⊻☽ 13:14 · ☽⚼♆ 13:54 · ☽△♄ 15:47 · ☽#♅ 16:03 · ☽☌♀ 18:29 · ☽⊻☿ 21:31 · ☽△♂ 22:28

6 Su ☽⚻♃ 6:20 · ☿□♂ 6:38 · ☽⚻⚷ 6:53 · ☽#♃ 11:01 · ☽#♂ 14:08 · ☽☍♅ 17:10 · ☽∥♇ 17:23 · ☽∠⚳ 17:45 · ☉⚻♄ 18:29 · ☽△♆ 19:48 · ☉∠☽ 21:52 · ☽⚹♇ 22:54

7 M ☽⚼♂ 5:36 · ☽∠☿ 8:12 · ☽⚼⚷ 12:29 · ☽⊻⚳ 23:45

8 Tu ☽□♄ 2:51 · ☽∠♇ 4:17 · ☉⚹☽ 5:50 · ♀△♂ 10:23 · ☽⚻♂ 12:04 · ☽⊻♀ 12:10 · ☿△♃ 12:24 · ☿☍⚷ 14:37 · ☽☍♃ 17:11 · ☽△⚷ 17:28 · ☽⚹☿ 17:55

9 W ☽⚻♅ 3:24 · ☽□♆ 5:55 · ☿∥♄ 6:24 · ♃R 7:06 · ☽⊻♇ 8:59 · ☽∠♀ 19:38

10 Th ☽⚼♅ 7:24 · ☽☌⚳ 9:34 · ☽⚹♄ 11:18 · ☿#⚷ 15:19 · ♀⚻♃ 15:45 · ♀⚻⚷ 16:58 · ☊D 18:36 · ☉□☽ 18:56 · ☽☍♂ 22:23

11 F ☽⚻♃ 1:03 · ☽□⚷ 1:08 · ☽⚹♀ 1:59 · ☽□☿ 9:36 · ☽△♅ 10:32 · ♀#♅ 12:20 · ☽⚹♆ 12:55 · ☽∠♄ 14:15 · ☽☌♇ 15:54 · ☿⚻♅ 17:12

12 Sa ♇D 0:35 · ☽∥♇ 2:00 · ☽⚼♃ 3:39 · ☽#♂ 6:16 · ♃⚹⚷ 7:33 · ☽#♃ 7:35 · ☿⚻♆ 12:42 · ☽∠♆ 15:06 · ☽⊻⚳ 15:47 · ☽⊻♄ 16:20 · ☽∥♀ 21:47 · ☿⚼♄ 23:06

13 Su ☽#♅ 0:08 · ☉△☽ 3:40 · ☽⚻♂ 4:45 · ☽⚹⚷ 5:20 · ☽△♃ 5:23 · ☽□♀ 11:09 · ☿□♇ 14:04 · ☽□♅ 14:12 · ☽⊻♆ 16:27 · ☽∠⚳ 17:34 · ⚳⚹♄ 19:12 · ☽⊻♇ 19:21 · ☿ ♏ 19:25 · ☽△☿ 20:00 · ♂□⚷ 20:37 · ♂⊻♃ 23:09

14 M ☉☍⚷ 2:30 · ☉△♃ 3:53 · ☽∥☿ 5:49 · ☽∠⚷ 6:14 · ☉⚼☽ 6:31 · ☽⚼♂ 6:35 · ☉□♂ 8:17 · ☉∥♄ 14:44 · ☽#⚷ 15:02 · ☉∥☽ 17:41 · ☽∥♄ 17:50 · ☽☌♄ 18:10 · ☽⚹⚳ 18:37 · ☽∠♇ 19:57 · ♀☍♅ 22:23 · ☽⚼☿ 23:33

15 Tu ☽⊻⚷ 6:30 · ☽□♃ 6:39 · ☽△♂ 7:42 · ☉⚻☽ 8:35 · ☽⚹♅ 15:00 · ☽∥♆ 15:36 · ☽△♀ 16:30 · ☽☌♆ 17:11 · ☽⚹♇ 20:01

16 W ♀△♆ 0:50 · ☽⚻☿ 2:23 · ☽#♆ 5:16 · ☊R 7:03 · ☽∠♅ 14:45 · ☉#⚷ 16:26 · ☽⊻♄ 17:53 · ☽⚼♀ 18:20 · ☽□⚳ 19:14

17 Th ☽#♄ 2:45 · ☽∥⚷ 5:10 · ☉#☽ 5:54 · ☽☌⚷ 5:57 · ☽⚹♃ 6:10 · ♀∠⚳ 8:10 · ☽□♂ 8:45 · ☉☍☽ 11:28 · ♂∥♃ 12:03 · ♀⚹♇ 12:32 · ☽⊻♅ 14:22 · ☽⊻♆ 16:33 · ☽∠♄ 17:29 · ☿⚼♃ 17:41 · ☽□♇ 19:28 · ♀ ♐ 19:29 · ☽⚻♀ 20:04 · ☽#☿ 22:54

18 F ☽∠♃ 5:51 · ☽☍☿ 7:16 · ☽∠♆ 16:20 · ☽⚹♄ 17:14 · ☽∥♅ 18:14 · ☽△⚳ 19:32

19 Sa ☽⊻⚷ 5:31 · ☽⊻♃ 5:47 · ☽#♀ 6:06 · ☉⚻♅ 6:41 · ☽∥♂ 9:25 · ☽∥♃ 9:52 · ☽⚹♂ 10:01 · ☽☌♅ 14:12 · ☉⚻☽ 14:46 · ☽#♇ 15:08 · ☽⚹♆ 16:29 · ☽△♇ 19:35 · ☽⚼⚳ 20:13

20 Su ☽☍♀ 0:31 · ☽∠⚷ 5:57 · ☽∠♂ 11:25 · ☽⚻☿ 13:41 · ☉⚻♆ 15:45 · ☉⚼☽ 17:23 · ☽□♄ 18:08 · ☽⚼♇ 20:30 · ☽⚻⚳ 21:35

21 M ☉⚼♄ 3:56 · ♀#♂ 6:25 · ☽⚹⚷ 7:07 · ☽☌♃ 7:26 · ☽⊻♂ 13:40 · ☽⊻♅ 16:23 · ☽⚼☿ 18:21 · ☽□♆ 18:52 · ☉△☽ 21:01 · ♀#♃ 21:41 · ☽⚻♇ 22:16 · ☿⚼♆ 22:53

22 Tu ☿△♄ 6:36 · ☽⚻♀ 8:31 · ☉□♇ 14:17 · ♀⚼⚷ 15:44 · ☽∠♅ 18:50 · ☉ ♏ 22:16 · ☽△♄ 22:18

23 W ☽△☿ 0:23 · ☽☍⚳ 3:13 · ☽□⚷ 12:16 · ☽⊻♃ 12:37 · ☽⚼♀ 14:27 · ☽☌♂ 21:21 · ☽⚹♅ 22:18

24 Th ☽△♆ 1:01 · ☽⚼♄ 1:54 · ☽☍♇ 4:49 · ☿⚹⚳ 5:59 · ☉□☽ 8:04 · ☊D 8:12 · ☽#♇ 15:29 · ☽∠♃ 16:43 · ☽#♀ 17:15 · ☽△♀ 21:45 · ☽∥♃ 21:45 · ☽∥♂ 23:49

25 F ♂⚹♅ 0:14 · ☽⚼♆ 5:37 · ☽⚻♄ 6:29 · ☽⚻⚳ 13:10 · ☽□☿ 16:42 · ☽∥♅ 16:51 · ☽#☿ 18:45 · ♀∥♇ 21:18 · ☽△⚷ 21:23 · ☽⚹♃ 21:43

26 Sa ☽□♅ 8:05 · ☽⊻♂ 9:17 · ☽⚻♆ 11:03 · ☿#♅ 11:37 · ☽⚻♇ 15:12 · ☽⚼⚳ 19:31 · ☉#☽ 22:57 · ☉⚹☽ 23:56

27 Su ☽⚼⚷ 3:08 · ☿⚻⚷ 6:25 · ⚶ ♎ 6:36 · ☿⚻♃ 8:51 · ☽□♀ 15:41 · ☽∥⚷ 16:06 · ☽∠♂ 16:25 · ☽#♄ 17:44 · ☽☍♄ 17:57 · ☽⚼♇ 21:24

28 M ♀⚼♂ 2:11 · ☽△⚳ 2:29 · ☉∠☽ 9:02 · ☽⚻⚷ 9:22 · ☽□♃ 9:38 · ♂△♆ 12:32 · ☽⚹☿ 13:17 · ♀□♄ 13:36 · ☉⚼♃ 15:48 · ☽△♅ 20:24 · ☽#♆ 21:34 · ☽☍♆ 23:32 · ☽⚹♂ 23:56

29 Tu ☽△♇ 3:56 · ♂⚼♄ 12:01 · ☽∥♆ 16:06 · ☊R 17:43 · ☉⊻☽ 18:26

30 W ☽∠☿ 0:08 · ♀∠♇ 0:24 · ☽⚼♅ 2:53 · ☽⚻♄ 6:52 · ☽⚹♀ 11:40 · ☽□⚳ 17:03 · ☽∥♄ 20:06 · ☽#⚷ 21:22 · ☽☍⚷ 22:14 · ☿☍♅ 22:16 · ☽△♃ 22:23

31 Th ☽⚻♅ 9:16 · ☽⊻☿ 10:49 · ☽⚻♆ 12:29 · ☽⚼♄ 13:15 · ☽□♂ 14:58 · ☽□♇ 16:58 · ☽∠♀ 21:30 · ☉∥☽ 22:34

LONGITUDE

Day	Sid.Time	☉	☽	☽ 12 hour	Mean ☊	True ☊	☿	♀	♂	⚳	♃	♄	⚷	♅	♆	♇
	h m s	° ' "	° ' "	° ' "	° '	° '	° '	° '	° '	° '	° '	° '	° '	° '	° '	° '
1 F	2 43 06	9♏03 19	3♏13 07	9♏11 16	4♈43.5	6♈25.6	27♏28.0	17♐06.2	28♋52.7	18♑17.5	20♊29.0	12♓52.7	20♈26.3	25♉54.0	27♓30.1	29♑44.3
2 Sa	2 47 02	10 03 23	15 11 13	21 13 07	4 40.3	6R 21.1	28 52.5	18 18.3	29 14.4	18 34.7	20R 24.5	12R 51.2	20R 23.8	25R 51.7	27R 28.9	29 44.8
3 Su	2 50 59	11 03 28	27 17 11	3♐23 33	4 37.2	6 15.3	0♐16.3	19 30.3	29 35.6	18 51.9	20 19.8	12 49.9	20 21.2	25 49.3	27 27.8	29 45.5
4 M	2 54 55	12 03 36	9♐32 24	15 43 53	4 34.0	6 08.7	1 39.2	20 42.3	29 56.4	19 09.3	20 14.9	12 48.6	20 18.7	25 46.9	27 26.8	29 46.1
5 Tu	2 58 52	13 03 45	21 58 11	28 15 28	4 30.8	6 02.0	3 01.3	21 54.3	0♌16.8	19 26.9	20 09.8	12 47.5	20 16.2	25 44.5	27 25.7	29 46.8
6 W	3 02 49	14 03 56	4♑35 55	10♑59 45	4 27.6	5 55.9	4 22.3	23 06.2	0 36.7	19 44.6	20 04.6	12 46.4	20 13.7	25 42.0	27 24.7	29 47.5
7 Th	3 06 45	15 04 08	17 27 11	23 58 27	4 24.4	5 51.1	5 42.3	24 18.0	0 56.1	20 02.4	19 59.2	12 45.5	20 11.3	25 39.6	27 23.7	29 48.2
8 F	3 10 42	16 04 22	0♒33 47	7♒13 26	4 21.3	5 48.1	7 01.2	25 29.9	1 15.0	20 20.4	19 53.7	12 44.6	20 08.9	25 37.2	27 22.7	29 49.0
9 Sa	3 14 38	17 04 37	13 57 36	20 46 31	4 18.1	5D 46.8	8 18.8	26 41.6	1 33.5	20 38.5	19 48.0	12 43.9	20 06.5	25 34.7	27 21.8	29 49.8
10 Su	3 18 35	18 04 54	27 40 20	4♓39 09	4 14.9	5 47.2	9 34.9	27 53.3	1 51.5	20 56.7	19 42.1	12 43.2	20 04.1	25 32.2	27 20.9	29 50.6
11 M	3 22 31	19 05 12	11♓42 58	18 51 45	4 11.7	5 48.4	10 49.5	29 05.0	2 09.0	21 15.1	19 36.1	12 42.7	20 01.8	25 29.7	27 20.0	29 51.4
12 Tu	3 26 28	20 05 31	26 05 16	3♈23 13	4 08.6	5R 49.6	12 02.3	0♑16.6	2 25.9	21 33.6	19 29.9	12 42.2	19 59.5	25 27.3	27 19.1	29 52.3
13 W	3 30 24	21 05 52	10♈45 05	18 10 16	4 05.4	5 49.8	13 13.1	1 28.1	2 42.4	21 52.2	19 23.6	12 41.9	19 57.2	25 24.8	27 18.3	29 53.2
14 Th	3 34 21	22 06 14	25 37 57	3♉07 14	4 02.2	5 48.2	14 21.7	2 39.5	2 58.3	22 10.9	19 17.2	12 41.6	19 55.0	25 22.3	27 17.5	29 54.1
15 F	3 38 18	23 06 38	10♉37 05	18 06 23	3 59.0	5 44.4	15 27.8	3 50.9	3 13.7	22 29.8	19 10.6	12D 41.6	19 52.8	25 19.8	27 16.7	29 55.0
16 Sa	3 42 14	24 07 04	25 34 01	2♊58 50	3 55.9	5 38.5	16 31.1	5 02.3	3 28.5	22 48.8	19 03.9	12 41.6	19 50.6	25 17.3	27 16.0	29 56.0
17 Su	3 46 11	25 07 31	10♊19 48	17 35 57	3 52.7	5 30.8	17 31.1	6 13.5	3 42.8	23 07.9	18 57.1	12 41.7	19 48.5	25 14.8	27 15.3	29 57.0
18 M	3 50 07	26 08 00	24 46 28	1♋50 44	3 49.5	5 22.4	18 27.6	7 24.7	3 56.4	23 27.1	18 50.2	12 41.9	19 46.4	25 12.3	27 14.6	29 58.0
19 Tu	3 54 04	27 08 30	8♋48 17	15 38 51	3 46.3	5 14.3	19 19.9	8 35.9	4 09.5	23 46.4	18 43.1	12 42.2	19 44.4	25 09.8	27 14.0	29 59.1
20 W	3 58 00	28 09 02	22 22 22	28 58 54	3 43.2	5 07.4	20 07.6	9 46.9	4 22.1	24 05.9	18 36.0	12 42.6	19 42.4	25 07.3	27 13.4	0♒00.2
21 Th	4 01 57	29 09 36	5♌28 43	11♌52 10	3 40.0	5 02.3	20 50.2	10 57.9	4 33.9	24 25.4	18 28.7	12 43.1	19 40.4	25 04.8	27 12.8	0 01.3
22 F	4 05 53	0♐10 12	18 09 43	24 21 56	3 36.8	4 59.5	21 26.9	12 08.8	4 45.2	24 45.1	18 21.3	12 43.7	19 38.4	25 02.3	27 12.2	0 02.4
23 Sa	4 09 50	1 10 49	0♍29 24	6♍32 48	3 33.6	4D 58.6	21 57.0	13 19.7	4 55.8	25 04.9	18 13.8	12 44.5	19 36.5	24 59.8	27 11.7	0 03.5
24 Su	4 13 47	2 11 28	12 32 48	18 30 05	3 30.4	4 59.0	22 19.8	14 30.4	5 05.8	25 24.7	18 06.3	12 45.3	19 34.7	24 57.3	27 11.2	0 04.7
25 M	4 17 43	3 12 09	24 25 19	0♎19 12	3 27.3	5R 00.0	22 34.4	15 41.1	5 15.1	25 44.7	17 58.6	12 46.2	19 32.8	24 54.8	27 10.7	0 05.9
26 Tu	4 21 40	4 12 51	6♎12 21	12 05 22	3 24.1	5 00.4	22R 40.2	16 51.7	5 23.7	26 04.8	17 50.9	12 47.3	19 31.1	24 52.4	27 10.3	0 07.1
27 W	4 25 36	5 13 35	17 58 51	23 53 19	3 20.9	4 59.4	22 36.4	18 02.2	5 31.6	26 24.9	17 43.1	12 48.4	19 29.3	24 49.9	27 09.9	0 08.4
28 Th	4 29 33	6 14 20	29 49 14	5♏47 00	3 17.7	4 56.1	22 22.3	19 12.6	5 38.8	26 45.2	17 35.3	12 49.7	19 27.6	24 47.5	27 09.6	0 09.6
29 F	4 33 29	7 15 07	11♏47 00	17 49 32	3 14.6	4 50.2	21 57.4	20 23.0	5 45.3	27 05.6	17 27.3	12 51.0	19 26.0	24 45.0	27 09.2	0 10.9
30 Sa	4 37 26	8♐15 55	23 54 50	0♐03 04	3♈11.4	4♈41.6	21♐21.5	21♑33.2	5♌51.1	27♑26.1	17♊19.3	12♓52.5	19♈24.4	24♉42.6	27♓08.9	0♒12.2

1st of Month

Julian Day #
2460615.5
Obliquity
23°26[illegible]9"
SVP 4♓54[illegible]9"
GC 27♐11.2
Eris 24♈47.8R

Day	⚴
1	18♐22.6
6	20 16.9
11	22 12.3
16	24 08.5
21	26 05.5
26	28 03.2

Day	⚵
1	29♎10.5
6	0♏55.3
11	2 39.3
16	4 22.4
21	6 04.4
26	7 45.2

Day	⚶
1	2♎13.3
6	4 33.8
11	6 53.4
16	9 12.0
21	11 29.7
26	13 46.1

DECLINATION and LATITUDE

Day	☉ Decl	☽ Decl	☽ Lat	☽ 12h Decl	☿ Decl	☿ Lat	♀ Decl	♀ Lat	♂ Decl	♂ Lat	⚳ Decl	⚳ Lat	♃ Decl	♃ Lat	♄ Decl	♄ Lat
1 F	14S31	14S48	2S21	17S14	21S32	1S60	24S35	1S46	21N45	1N24	29S19	7S12	22N23	0S43	8S42	2S08
2 Sa	14 50	19 30	3 16	21 36	21 56	2 05	24 44	1 49	21 42	1 26	29 16	7 11	22 23	0 43	8 42	2 08
3 Su	15 09	23 29	4 02	25 07	22 19	2 10	24 52	1 51	21 40	1 28	29 13	7 11	22 22	0 43	8 43	2 08
4 M	15 27	26 28	4 38	27 30	22 41	2 14	24 60	1 53	21 37	1 30	29 10	7 10	22 22	0 43	8 43	2 08
5 Tu	15 46	28 12	5 01	28 33	23 01	2 18	25 07	1 56	21 35	1 32	29 07	7 10	22 22	0 43	8 43	2 08
6 W	16 04	28 32	5 10	28 07	23 21	2 22	25 13	1 58	21 33	1 34	29 04	7 09	22 21	0 43	8 44	2 08
7 Th	16 21	27 19	5 04	26 09	23 39	2 26	25 19	2 00	21 30	1 36	29 01	7 09	22 21	0 43	8 44	2 07
8 F	16 39	24 37	4 42	22 44	23 56	2 29	25 24	2 02	21 28	1 38	28 57	7 09	22 21	0 43	8 44	2 07
9 Sa	16 56	20 32	4 04	18 02	24 12	2 32	25 28	2 04	21 26	1 40	28 54	7 08	22 20	0 43	8 44	2 07
10 Su	17 13	15 17	3 12	12 18	24 26	2 34	25 31	2 06	21 24	1 42	28 51	7 08	22 20	0 43	8 44	2 07
11 M	17 30	9 07	2 07	5 48	24 39	2 37	25 34	2 08	21 23	1 44	28 48	7 07	22 19	0 43	8 44	2 07
12 Tu	17 46	2 22	0 53	1N09	24 51	2 38	25 36	2 10	21 21	1 47	28 44	7 07	22 19	0 43	8 44	2 07
13 W	18 02	4N40	0N27	8 09	25 01	2 39	25 37	2 11	21 19	1 49	28 41	7 07	22 18	0 43	8 44	2 06
14 Th	18 18	11 32	1 45	14 47	25 10	2 39	25 38	2 13	21 18	1 51	28 37	7 06	22 18	0 43	8 44	2 06
15 F	18 33	17 48	2 57	20 33	25 17	2 39	25 37	2 15	21 16	1 53	28 34	7 06	22 18	0 42	8 44	2 06
16 Sa	18 48	22 58	3 56	24 59	25 23	2 38	25 36	2 16	21 15	1 56	28 30	7 06	22 17	0 42	8 44	2 06
17 Su	19 03	26 35	4 38	27 43	25 27	2 37	25 35	2 17	21 14	1 58	28 26	7 05	22 17	0 42	8 44	2 06
18 M	19 17	28 22	5 02	28 32	25 30	2 35	25 32	2 19	21 13	2 00	28 23	7 05	22 16	0 42	8 44	2 06
19 Tu	19 31	28 14	5 06	27 31	25 31	2 31	25 29	2 20	21 12	2 03	28 19	7 05	22 16	0 42	8 43	2 05
20 W	19 45	26 24	4 53	24 56	25 31	2 27	25 25	2 21	21 12	2 05	28 15	7 05	22 15	0 42	8 43	2 05
21 Th	19 58	23 11	4 25	21 10	25 29	2 22	25 21	2 22	21 11	2 08	28 11	7 04	22 14	0 42	8 43	2 05
22 F	20 11	18 57	3 44	16 33	25 25	2 16	25 15	2 23	21 11	2 10	28 07	7 04	22 14	0 42	8 42	2 05
23 Sa	20 24	14 01	2 54	11 23	25 19	2 08	25 09	2 24	21 11	2 13	28 03	7 04	22 13	0 42	8 42	2 05
24 Su	20 36	8 40	1 58	5 53	25 12	1 59	25 03	2 24	21 11	2 15	27 59	7 03	22 13	0 42	8 41	2 05
25 M	20 48	3 05	0 57	0 15	25 03	1 49	24 55	2 25	21 11	2 18	27 55	7 03	22 12	0 42	8 41	2 04
26 Tu	20 59	2S34	0S06	5S22	24 52	1 38	24 47	2 26	21 11	2 20	27 51	7 03	22 12	0 42	8 40	2 04
27 W	21 10	8 07	1 09	10 48	24 38	1 25	24 38	2 26	21 12	2 23	27 47	7 03	22 11	0 41	8 40	2 04
28 Th	21 21	13 25	2 09	15 55	24 23	1 10	24 29	2 26	21 12	2 25	27 43	7 03	22 10	0 41	8 39	2 04
29 F	21 31	18 16	3 03	20 28	24 06	0 54	24 18	2 27	21 13	2 28	27 38	7 02	22 10	0 41	8 38	2 04
30 Sa	21S41	22S28	3S50	24S14	23S46	0S37	24S08	2S27	21N14	2N30	27S34	7S02	22N09	0S41	8S38	2S04

Day	⚷ Decl	⚷ Lat	♅ Decl	♅ Lat	♆ Decl	♆ Lat	♇ Decl	♇ Lat
1	8N57	1N03	18N58	0S16	2S12	1S19	23S23	3S16
6	8 52	1 03	18 56	0 16	2 14	1 19	23 23	3 16
11	8 47	1 02	18 53	0 16	2 16	1 19	23 22	3 16
16	8 43	1 02	18 50	0 16	2 18	1 19	23 21	3 16
21	8 38	1 01	18 47	0 16	2 19	1 19	23 20	3 16
26	8 34	1 00	18 44	0 16	2 19	1 18	23 18	3 16

Day	⚴ Decl	⚴ Lat	⚵ Decl	⚵ Lat	⚶ Decl	⚶ Lat	Eris Decl	Eris Lat
1	5N42	28N43	5S39	5N54	3N36	4N53	0S33	10S54
6	5 13	28 22	6 08	6 02	2 47	5 01	0 34	10 53
11	4 48	28 03	6 35	6 11	1 59	5 08	0 34	10 53
16	4 25	27 45	7 01	6 19	1 12	5 16	0 35	10 53
21	4 04	27 28	7 26	6 28	0 25	5 24	0 35	10 52
26	3 46	27 12	7 49	6 38	0S20	5 32	0 36	10 52

Moon Phenomena

Max/0 Decl

dy	hr mn	
5	17:11	28S35
12	8:06	0 N
18	10:20	28N32
25	13:06	0 S

Max/0 Lat

dy	hr mn	
6	2:30	5S10
12	15:59	0 N
18	17:53	5N07
25	21:33	0 S

Perigee/Apogee

dy	hr m		kilometers
14	11:17	p	360114
26	11:57	a	405313

PH	dy	hr mn	
●	1	12:48	9♏35
☽	9	5:57	17♒20
○	15	21:30	24♉01
☾	23	1:29	1♍15

Void of Course Moon

Last Aspect				☽ Ingress		
3	4:52	♇	✱	♐	3	5:21
5	10:25	♆	□	♑	5	15:18
7	22:39	♇	☌	♒	7	22:59
10	0:25	♀	✱	♓	10	4:01
12	6:14	♇	✱	♈	12	6:27
14	6:51	♇	□	♉	14	7:00
16	7:04	♇	△	♊	16	7:10
18	4:10	♆	□	♋	18	8:51
20	11:21	☉	△	♌	20	13:52
22	13:16	♅	□	♍	22	23:02
25	5:36	♆	☍	♎	25	11:21
27	9:15	☿	✱	♏	28	0:22
30	6:20	♆	△	♐	30	11:54

DAILY ASPECTARIAN

1 F
☿ △ ♆ 0:35
☽ ⚼ ♃ 4:32
☿ ⋕ ♂ 11:19
☉ ☌ ☽ 12:48
☽ ⚼ ♆ 18:36
☽ △ ♄ 19:21
☽ ⋕ ♅ 21:03

2 Sa
☽ ⚺ ♀ 6:54
☽ ✱ ⚳ 6:55
♀ ⚺ ⚳ 7:10
♃ ✱ ⚷ 8:13
☿ △ ♂ 8:23
☽ ⚻ ♃ 10:19
☽ ⚻ ⚷ 10:20
☽ ⋕ ♂ 12:29
☿ ✱ ♇ 15:04
☽ ∥ ☿ 15:35
☽ ⋕ ♃ 16:45
☿ ♐ 19:19
☽ ☍ ♅ 21:07
☽ ∥ ♇ 23:22

3 Su
☽ △ ♆ 0:21
☿ ⋕ ♃ 3:29
☽ △ ♂ 4:41
☽ ✱ ♇ 4:52
☽ ☌ ☿ 6:38
⚵ ♏ 8:36
☽ ∥ ♀ 10:35
♂ ☍ ♇ 11:38
☽ ∠ ⚳ 13:14
♀ ☍ ♃ 15:26
☽ ⚼ ⚷ 15:47
♀ △ ⚷ 16:23

4 M
♂ ♌ 4:11
☉ ⚺ ☽ 5:20
☽ □ ♄ 6:20
☉ ⚼ ♆ 9:05
☽ ∠ ♇ 10:09
☽ ⚼ ♂ 10:46
☉ △ ♄ 17:37
☽ ⚺ ⚳ 19:03
☽ ☍ ♃ 20:34
☽ △ ⚷ 20:45
☽ ☌ ♀ 23:52

5 Tu
☽ ⚻ ♅ 7:11
☽ □ ♆ 10:25
☉ ∠ ☽ 12:38
☽ ⚺ ♇ 14:54
☽ ⚻ ♂ 16:16
☽ ⚺ ☿ 23:31

6 W
☿ ∥ ♇ 2:31
☿ ∠ ⚳ 8:31
☽ ⚼ ♅ 11:25
☿ ⚼ ⚷ 14:56
☽ ✱ ♄ 15:18
☉ ✱ ☽ 19:13
⚳ ⚻ ♃ 20:44

7 Th
☽ ⚻ ♃ 4:39
☽ ☌ ⚳ 4:53
☽ □ ⚷ 5:02
☽ ∠ ☿ 6:41
⚳ □ ⚷ 10:30
☽ ⚺ ♀ 13:52
☽ △ ♅ 15:02
☽ ✱ ♆ 18:13
☽ ∥ ♀ 18:24
☽ ∠ ♄ 18:53
☽ ☌ ♇ 22:39

8 F
☽ ☍ ♂ 1:16
♀ ⚻ ♅ 2:21
☽ ∥ ☿ 4:19
☽ ⚼ ♃ 7:46
☽ ∥ ♇ 8:10
☽ ✱ ☿ 12:53
☽ ⋕ ♃ 14:18
☽ ⋕ ♂ 19:14
☽ ∠ ♀ 19:35
☽ ∠ ♆ 21:10
☽ ⚺ ♄ 21:49

9 Sa
☊ D 5:50
☉ □ ☽ 5:57
☽ ⋕ ♅ 8:02
☽ △ ♃ 10:13
☽ ✱ ⚷ 10:48
☽ ⚺ ⚳ 12:02
♀ □ ♆ 13:17
☉ ∥ ☽ 16:06
☽ □ ♅ 20:19
☽ ⚺ ♆ 23:26

10 Su
☽ ✱ ♀ 0:25
☽ ⚺ ♇ 3:45
☽ ⚻ ♂ 7:22
☽ ∠ ⚷ 12:41
☽ ∠ ⚳ 14:31
☽ □ ☿ 22:21

11 M
☽ ⋕ ⚷ 1:14
☽ ∥ ♄ 1:25
☽ ☌ ♄ 1:41
☽ ∠ ♇ 5:18
☽ ⚼ ♂ 9:19
☉ ⚻ ♃ 11:10
☽ □ ♃ 13:08
☉ △ ☽ 13:18
☽ ⚺ ⚷ 13:55
♀ ⚺ ♇ 15:46
☽ ✱ ⚳ 16:20
♀ ♑ 18:27
☉ ⚻ ⚷ 21:42
☽ ✱ ♅ 22:57

12 Tu
☽ ∥ ♆ 0:18
☽ ☌ ♆ 2:02
☽ ✱ ♇ 6:14
☽ □ ♀ 7:31
☽ △ ♂ 10:38
☿ □ ♄ 13:23
☽ ⋕ ♆ 15:51
☉ ⚼ ☽ 15:52
☊ R 15:58
☽ ∠ ♅ 23:27

13 W
☽ ⚺ ♄ 3:09
☽ △ ☿ 4:20
☽ ✱ ♃ 13:52
☽ ⋕ ♄ 14:04
☽ ∥ ⚷ 14:06
☽ ☌ ⚷ 14:50
☉ ⚻ ☽ 17:55
☽ □ ⚳ 18:20
☽ ⚺ ♅ 23:35

14 Th
♄ ⋕ ⚷ 2:33
☽ ⚺ ♆ 2:40
☉ ✱ ⚳ 2:43
☽ ∠ ♄ 3:18
☽ ⚼ ☿ 6:28
☽ □ ♇ 6:51
♀ ⚻ ♂ 8:03
☿ ∠ ♇ 11:48
☽ □ ♂ 11:58
☽ △ ♀ 12:14
☽ ∠ ♃ 13:46

15 F
☽ ∠ ♆ 2:39
☉ ⋕ ☽ 3:18
☽ ✱ ♄ 3:19
☽ ∥ ♅ 4:22
☽ ⚻ ☿ 8:22
☽ ⚺ ♃ 13:37
☽ ⚼ ♀ 14:20
♄ D 14:21
☽ ⚺ ⚷ 14:49
☽ ∥ ♂ 15:22
☽ △ ⚳ 19:28
☽ ∥ ♃ 20:27
☉ ☍ ☽ 21:30
☽ ☌ ♅ 23:33

16 Sa
☽ ⋕ ♇ 2:06
☉ ⋕ ♅ 2:38
☽ ✱ ♆ 2:44
☽ △ ♇ 7:04
☽ ✱ ♂ 13:01
☽ ∠ ⚷ 15:00
☽ ⋕ ☿ 15:03
☽ ⋕ ♀ 16:10
☽ ⚻ ♀ 16:42
☽ ⚼ ⚳ 20:19

17 Su
☉ ☍ ♅ 2:46
☽ □ ♄ 3:53
☽ ⚼ ♇ 7:37
☽ ☍ ☿ 12:43
☽ ∠ ♂ 14:05
☽ ☌ ♃ 14:08
☽ ✱ ⚷ 15:38
♂ ∠ ♃ 16:39
☽ ⚻ ⚳ 21:43

18 M
☽ ⋕ ⚳ 0:31
☽ ⋕ ⚳ 0:31
☽ ⚺ ♅ 0:43
☉ ⚻ ☽ 2:28
☽ □ ♆ 4:10
☽ ⚻ ♇ 8:48
☿ ☍ ♃ 8:56
☿ ∥ ♀ 11:02
☽ ⚺ ♂ 15:51
☿ ⚼ ♂ 17:26
☽ ☍ ♀ 23:36

19 Tu
☉ △ ♆ 2:09
☽ ∠ ♅ 2:22
☉ ⚼ ☽ 6:17
☽ △ ♄ 6:49
☿ △ ⚷ 11:30
☽ ⚺ ♃ 17:18
☽ □ ⚷ 19:14
☽ ⚻ ☿ 19:44
♇ ♒ 20:30

20 W
☽ ☍ ⚳ 3:11
☽ ✱ ♅ 4:57
♀ ⚼ ♅ 6:39
☽ ⋕ ☿ 7:39
☽ ⋕ ♀ 8:33
☽ △ ♆ 8:47
☽ ⚼ ♄ 9:41
☉ △ ☽ 11:21
☽ ☍ ♇ 13:54
☽ ∠ ♃ 20:19
☽ ☌ ♂ 22:17
☽ ⋕ ♇ 23:03

21 Th
☽ ⚼ ☿ 0:42
☽ ∥ ♃ 5:47
☽ ⚻ ♀ 11:21
☽ ∥ ♂ 11:55
☽ ⚼ ♆ 12:39
☽ ⚻ ♄ 13:37
☉ ⋕ ☽ 17:44
☉ ♐ 19:58
☉ ✱ ♇ 20:51

22 F
☽ ✱ ♃ 0:22
☽ ∥ ♅ 0:54
☽ △ ⚷ 2:50
☽ △ ☿ 6:38
♀ ✱ ♄ 11:56
☽ ⚻ ⚳ 13:06
☽ □ ♅ 13:16
☽ ⚻ ♆ 17:32
⚳ △ ♅ 18:34
☽ ⚼ ♀ 19:18
☽ ⚻ ♇ 23:09

23 Sa
☉ □ ☽ 1:29
☊ D 1:42
☽ ⚼ ⚷ 8:08
☽ ⚺ ♂ 8:55
☽ ⚼ ⚳ 19:36
☽ ⋕ ♄ 23:53

24 Su
☽ ∥ ⚷ 0:17
☽ ☍ ♄ 0:25
☽ △ ♀ 4:22
☽ ⚼ ♇ 5:06
☽ □ ♃ 11:05
☽ ⚻ ⚷ 14:08
☽ ∠ ♂ 15:26
☽ □ ☿ 20:11

25 M
☽ △ ♅ 1:00
☽ △ ⚳ 2:46
☽ ⋕ ♆ 3:14
☽ ☍ ♆ 5:36
☽ △ ♇ 11:34
☉ ✱ ☽ 19:33
☊ R 21:32
☽ ✱ ♂ 22:20
☽ ∥ ♆ 22:59

26 Tu
☿ R 2:43
☉ ⚼ ⚷ 7:00
☽ ⚼ ♅ 7:27
☽ ⚻ ♄ 13:27
♀ ⚻ ♃ 18:09
☽ △ ♃ 23:28

27 W
☽ □ ♀ 0:08
☿ ∥ ♀ 1:10
☽ ⋕ ⚷ 1:57
☽ ∥ ♄ 2:25
☉ ⋕ ♂ 2:57
☽ ☍ ⚷ 3:04
☉ ∠ ☽ 5:00
☉ △ ♂ 8:08
☽ ✱ ☿ 9:15
☽ ⚻ ♅ 13:52
☽ □ ⚳ 17:37
☽ ⚻ ♆ 18:38
☽ ⚼ ♄ 19:58

28 Th
☽ □ ♇ 0:41
♀ □ ⚷ 5:00
☽ ⚼ ♃ 5:31
☽ □ ♂ 11:50
☉ ⚺ ☽ 14:06
☽ ∠ ☿ 14:43

29 F
☽ ⚼ ♆ 0:44
☽ △ ♄ 2:08
☽ ⋕ ♅ 2:16
⚳ ✱ ♆ 4:13
☽ ⚻ ♃ 11:09
☽ ⚻ ⚷ 15:09
☽ ⋕ ♂ 16:27
☽ ✱ ♀ 18:52
☉ ∥ ☽ 18:58
☽ ⚺ ☿ 19:14
☿ ⚺ ♀ 21:27
☽ ⋕ ♃ 22:03

30 Sa
☽ ☍ ♅ 1:33
☽ ∥ ♇ 5:25
☽ △ ♆ 6:20
☽ ✱ ⚳ 7:06
☽ ∥ ☿ 7:55
☽ ∥ ♀ 10:40
☽ ✱ ♇ 12:19
☿ ⚼ ♂ 14:35
☽ ⚼ ⚷ 20:25
⚴ ♑ 22:39
☽ △ ♂ 23:25

December 2024

LONGITUDE

Day	Sid.Time	☉	☽	☽ 12 hour	Mean☊	True☊	☿	♀	♂	⚳	♃	♄	⚷	♅	♆	♇
	h m s	° ′ "	° ′ "	° ′ "	° ′	° ′	° ′	° ′	° ′	° ′	° ′	° ′	° ′	° ′	° ′	° ′
1 Su	4 41 22	9♐16 45	6♐14 21	12♐28 46	3♈08.2	4♈30.7	20♐34.6	22♑43.4	5♌56.2	27♑46.6	17♊11.3	12♓54.1	19♈22.8	24♉40.2	27♓08.7	0♒13.5
2 M	4 45 19	10 17 36	18 46 20	25 07 02	3 05.0	4R 18.4	19R 37.5	23 53.4	6 00.4	28 07.3	17R 03.3	12 55.8	19R 21.3	24R 37.8	27R 08.5	0 14.9
3 Tu	4 49 16	11 18 28	1♑30 48	7♑57 35	3 01.9	4 05.9	18 31.1	25 03.3	6 04.0	28 28.0	16 55.2	12 57.5	19 19.9	24 35.5	27 08.3	0 16.3
4 W	4 53 12	12 19 21	14 27 19	20 59 54	2 58.7	3 54.2	17 17.1	26 13.2	6 06.7	28 48.8	16 47.0	12 59.4	19 18.4	24 33.1	27 08.1	0 17.7
5 Th	4 57 09	13 20 15	27 35 19	4♒13 29	2 55.5	3 44.4	15 57.5	27 22.9	6 08.7	29 09.7	16 38.9	13 01.4	19 17.1	24 30.8	27 08.0	0 19.1
6 F	5 01 05	14 21 09	10♒54 26	17 38 09	2 52.3	3 37.3	14 35.0	28 32.5	6R 09.9	29 30.7	16 30.7	13 03.5	19 15.8	24 28.4	27 07.9	0 20.5
7 Sa	5 05 02	15 22 05	24 24 41	1♓14 05	2 49.2	3 33.1	13 12.4	29 42.0	6 10.3	29 51.8	16 22.5	13 05.7	19 14.5	24 26.1	27D 07.9	0 22.0
8 Su	5 08 58	16 23 01	8♓06 27	15 01 50	2 46.0	3D 31.3	11 52.3	0♒51.3	6 09.8	0♒13.0	16 14.3	13 08.0	19 13.3	24 23.9	27 07.9	0 23.5
9 M	5 12 55	17 23 58	22 00 19	29 01 53	2 42.8	3R 31.2	10 37.5	2 00.5	6 08.6	0 34.2	16 06.2	13 10.4	19 12.1	24 21.6	27 07.9	0 25.0
10 Tu	5 16 51	18 24 55	6♈06 33	13♈14 12	2 39.6	3 31.3	9 30.1	3 09.6	6 06.6	0 55.5	15 58.0	13 12.9	19 11.0	24 19.4	27 07.9	0 26.5
11 W	5 20 48	19 25 53	20 24 37	27 37 32	2 36.4	3 30.4	8 32.0	4 18.5	6 03.7	1 16.9	15 49.8	13 15.5	19 10.0	24 17.2	27 08.0	0 28.0
12 Th	5 24 45	20 26 51	4♉52 31	12♉09 02	2 33.3	3 27.3	7 44.2	5 27.3	6 00.0	1 38.4	15 41.7	13 18.2	19 08.9	24 15.0	27 08.1	0 29.6
13 F	5 28 41	21 27 51	19 26 26	26 43 58	2 30.1	3 21.3	7 07.5	6 35.9	5 55.5	1 59.9	15 33.6	13 20.9	19 08.0	24 12.8	27 08.3	0 31.2
14 Sa	5 32 38	22 28 51	4♊00 47	11♊16 01	2 26.9	3 12.4	6 42.1	7 44.3	5 50.2	2 21.5	15 25.5	13 23.8	19 07.1	24 10.7	27 08.5	0 32.7
15 Su	5 36 34	23 29 51	18 28 45	25 38 09	2 23.7	3 01.2	6D 27.7	8 52.6	5 44.0	2 43.1	15 17.5	13 26.8	19 06.2	24 08.6	27 08.7	0 34.4
16 M	5 40 31	24 30 53	2♋43 25	9♋43 49	2 20.6	2 48.7	6 23.8	10 00.7	5 37.0	3 04.9	15 09.5	13 29.9	19 05.4	24 06.6	27 09.0	0 36.0
17 Tu	5 44 27	25 31 55	16 38 48	23 27 56	2 17.4	2 36.3	6 30.0	11 08.7	5 29.2	3 26.7	15 01.6	13 33.1	19 04.7	24 04.5	27 09.3	0 37.6
18 W	5 48 24	26 32 57	0♌10 57	6♌47 44	2 14.2	2 25.2	6 45.2	12 16.4	5 20.5	3 48.5	14 53.8	13 36.3	19 04.0	24 02.5	27 09.6	0 39.3
19 Th	5 52 21	27 34 01	13 18 19	19 42 53	2 11.0	2 16.4	7 08.9	13 24.0	5 10.9	4 10.5	14 46.0	13 39.7	19 03.4	24 00.5	27 10.0	0 40.9
20 F	5 56 17	28 35 05	26 01 45	2♍15 20	2 07.9	2 10.4	7 40.0	14 31.4	5 00.6	4 32.4	14 38.2	13 43.1	19 02.8	23 58.6	27 10.4	0 42.6
21 Sa	6 00 14	29 36 10	8♍24 08	14 28 43	2 04.7	2 07.0	8 17.9	15 38.5	4 49.4	4 54.5	14 30.6	13 46.7	19 02.3	23 56.7	27 10.8	0 44.3
22 Su	6 04 10	0♑37 16	20 29 43	26 27 50	2 01.5	2 05.8	9 01.9	16 45.5	4 37.4	5 16.6	14 23.0	13 50.3	19 01.8	23 54.8	27 11.3	0 46.0
23 M	6 08 07	1 38 22	2♎23 45	8♎18 11	1 58.3	2 05.6	9 51.1	17 52.3	4 24.6	5 38.8	14 15.5	13 54.0	19 01.4	23 53.0	27 11.8	0 47.8
24 Tu	6 12 03	2 39 30	14 11 49	20 05 23	1 55.2	2 05.3	10 45.1	18 58.8	4 10.9	6 01.0	14 08.1	13 57.8	19 01.0	23 51.2	27 12.3	0 49.5
25 W	6 16 00	3 40 37	25 59 33	1♏54 58	1 52.0	2 03.9	11 43.3	20 05.2	3 56.5	6 23.3	14 00.8	14 01.7	19 00.7	23 49.4	27 12.9	0 51.3
26 Th	6 19 56	4 41 46	7♏52 14	13 51 54	1 48.8	2 00.3	12 45.1	21 11.3	3 41.3	6 45.6	13 53.6	14 05.7	19 00.5	23 47.7	27 13.5	0 53.0
27 F	6 23 53	5 42 55	19 54 29	26 00 25	1 45.6	1 53.9	13 50.2	22 17.2	3 25.4	7 08.0	13 46.5	14 09.8	19 00.3	23 46.0	27 14.1	0 54.8
28 Sa	6 27 50	6 44 04	2♐10 01	8♐23 36	1 42.4	1 44.6	14 58.1	23 22.8	3 08.7	7 30.5	13 39.6	14 14.0	19 00.1	23 44.3	27 14.8	0 56.6
29 Su	6 31 46	7 45 14	14 41 20	21 03 18	1 39.3	1 32.9	16 08.5	24 28.2	2 51.3	7 52.9	13 32.7	14 18.2	19D 00.1	23 42.7	27 15.5	0 58.4
30 M	6 35 43	8 46 25	27 29 32	3♑59 55	1 36.1	1 19.5	17 21.1	25 33.3	2 33.2	8 15.5	13 26.0	14 22.5	19 00.0	23 41.2	27 16.3	1 00.2
31 Tu	6 39 39	9♑47 35	10♑34 19	17 12 30	1♈32.9	1♈05.6	18♐35.8	26♒38.1	2♌14.5	8♒38.1	13♊19.4	14♓26.9	19♈00.1	23♉39.6	27♓17.1	1♒02.1

1st of Month

Julian Day #
2460645.5
Obliquity
23°26[illegible]8"
SVP 4♓54[illegible]4"
GC 27♐11.2
Eris 24♈32.5R

Day	⚴	⚵	⚶
1	0♑01.3	9♏24.7	16♎01.1
6	1 59.9	11 02.7	18 14.5
11	3 58.5	12 38.8	20 26.1
16	5 57.3	14 13.1	22 35.5
21	7 55.9	15 45.2	24 42.8
26	9 54.4	17 15.1	26 47.4
31	11 52.6	18 42.3	28 49.2

DECLINATION and LATITUDE

Day	☉ Decl	☽ Decl	☽ Lat	☽ 12h Decl	☿ Decl	☿ Lat	♀ Decl	♀ Lat	♂ Decl	♂ Lat	⚳ Decl	⚳ Lat	♃ Decl	♃ Lat	♄ Decl	♄ Lat
1 Su	21S50	25S44	4S27	26S56	23S24	0S18	23S56	2S27	21N16	2N33	27S29	7S02	22N08	0S41	8S37	2S03
2 M	21 59	27 48	4 51	28 19	23 01	0N01	23 44	2 27	21 17	2 36	27 25	7 02	22 08	0 41	8 36	2 03
3 Tu	22 08	28 28	5 02	28 13	22 35	0 22	23 31	2 26	21 19	2 38	27 20	7 02	22 07	0 41	8 35	2 03
4 W	22 16	27 35	4 57	26 33	22 08	0 42	23 18	2 26	21 21	2 41	27 16	7 01	22 06	0 41	8 34	2 03
5 Th	22 24	25 10	4 37	23 25	21 40	1 02	23 04	2 26	21 23	2 44	27 11	7 01	22 06	0 41	8 34	2 03
6 F	22 31	21 21	4 01	19 00	21 12	1 22	22 49	2 25	21 25	2 47	27 06	7 01	22 05	0 40	8 33	2 03
7 Sa	22 38	16 24	3 12	13 34	20 44	1 40	22 34	2 24	21 28	2 49	27 02	7 01	22 04	0 40	8 32	2 02
8 Su	22 45	10 33	2 10	7 23	20 17	1 56	22 18	2 23	21 31	2 52	26 57	7 01	22 04	0 40	8 31	2 02
9 M	22 50	4 06	1 01	0 45	19 53	2 11	22 02	2 22	21 34	2 55	26 52	7 01	22 03	0 40	8 29	2 02
10 Tu	22 56	2N38	0N14	6N01	19 31	2 23	21 45	2 21	21 37	2 58	26 47	7 01	22 02	0 40	8 28	2 02
11 W	23 01	9 20	1 28	12 33	19 12	2 33	21 27	2 20	21 40	3 00	26 42	7 01	22 02	0 40	8 27	2 02
12 Th	23 06	15 37	2 38	18 29	18 57	2 41	21 09	2 19	21 44	3 03	26 37	7 00	22 01	0 40	8 26	2 02
13 F	23 10	21 05	3 37	23 21	18 46	2 47	20 50	2 17	21 48	3 06	26 32	7 00	22 00	0 39	8 25	2 01
14 Sa	23 13	25 15	4 23	26 44	18 38	2 50	20 31	2 16	21 52	3 09	26 27	7 00	21 59	0 39	8 24	2 01
15 Su	23 17	27 46	4 51	28 20	18 34	2 52	20 12	2 14	21 56	3 12	26 22	7 00	21 59	0 39	8 22	2 01
16 M	23 19	28 25	5 00	28 02	18 34	2 52	19 52	2 12	22 00	3 14	26 16	7 00	21 58	0 39	8 21	2 01
17 Tu	23 22	27 13	4 52	26 01	18 36	2 50	19 31	2 10	22 05	3 17	26 11	7 00	21 57	0 39	8 20	2 01
18 W	23 24	24 27	4 26	22 35	18 41	2 47	19 10	2 08	22 10	3 20	26 06	7 00	21 57	0 39	8 18	2 01
19 Th	23 25	20 28	3 48	18 08	18 49	2 43	18 49	2 06	22 15	3 23	26 00	7 00	21 56	0 38	8 17	2 01
20 F	23 26	15 38	2 58	13 01	18 59	2 38	18 27	2 04	22 20	3 25	25 55	7 00	21 55	0 38	8 15	2 00
21 Sa	23 26	10 18	2 02	7 31	19 11	2 33	18 04	2 01	22 25	3 28	25 49	7 00	21 54	0 38	8 14	2 00
22 Su	23 26	4 42	1 01	1 52	19 24	2 26	17 42	1 59	22 31	3 31	25 44	7 00	21 54	0 38	8 12	2 00
23 M	23 26	0S59	0S02	3S48	19 38	2 19	17 19	1 56	22 36	3 33	25 38	7 00	21 53	0 38	8 11	1 60
24 Tu	23 25	6 35	1 04	9 18	19 53	2 12	16 55	1 53	22 42	3 36	25 33	7 00	21 52	0 38	8 09	1 60
25 W	23 23	11 57	2 03	14 30	20 08	2 05	16 31	1 50	22 48	3 38	25 27	7 00	21 52	0 37	8 07	1 60
26 Th	23 21	16 56	2 57	19 12	20 24	1 57	16 07	1 47	22 54	3 41	25 21	7 00	21 51	0 37	8 06	1 59
27 F	23 19	21 19	3 44	23 13	20 40	1 49	15 43	1 43	23 00	3 43	25 15	7 00	21 50	0 37	8 04	1 59
28 Sa	23 16	24 52	4 22	26 15	20 56	1 40	15 18	1 40	23 07	3 46	25 09	7 00	21 50	0 37	8 02	1 59
29 Su	23 13	27 19	4 47	28 03	21 11	1 32	14 52	1 36	23 13	3 48	25 03	7 00	21 49	0 37	8 01	1 59
30 M	23 09	28 24	4 59	28 22	21 27	1 24	14 27	1 32	23 20	3 50	24 57	7 01	21 48	0 36	7 59	1 59
31 Tu	23S05	27S56	4S56	27S06	21S42	1N15	14S01	1S28	23N26	3N53	24S51	7S01	21N48	0S36	7S57	1S59

Day	⚷ Decl	⚷ Lat	♅ Decl	♅ Lat	♆ Decl	♆ Lat	♇ Decl	♇ Lat
1	8N31	0N60	18N41	0S16	2S20	1S18	23S17	3S16
6	8 27	0 59	18 38	0 16	2 20	1 18	23 16	3 16
11	8 25	0 59	18 35	0 16	2 20	1 18	23 14	3 16
16	8 22	0 58	18 33	0 15	2 19	1 18	23 12	3 16
21	8 20	0 57	18 31	0 15	2 18	1 18	23 11	3 16
26	8 19	0 57	18 28	0 15	2 17	1 17	23 09	3 16
31	8N19	0N56	18N27	0S15	2S16	1S17	23S07	3S16

Day	⚴ Decl	⚴ Lat	⚵ Decl	⚵ Lat	⚶ Decl	⚶ Lat	Eris Decl	Eris Lat
1	3N31	26N58	8S11	6N47	1S03	5N41	0S36	10S51
6	3 19	26 44	8 31	6 58	1 45	5 50	0 36	10 50
11	3 09	26 32	8 49	7 08	2 26	5 59	0 36	10 50
16	3 02	26 21	9 06	7 20	3 04	6 09	0 36	10 49
21	2 57	26 12	9 20	7 32	3 41	6 20	0 36	10 48
26	2 55	26 03	9 33	7 44	4 15	6 30	0 36	10 48
31	2N56	25N56	9S44	7N57	4S47	6N42	0S35	10S47

Moon Phenomena

Max/0 Decl
dy hr mn
2 22:25 28S28
9 14:39 0 N
15 20:09 28N26
22 19:52 0 S
30 5:01 28S26

Max/0 Lat
dy hr mn
3 4:45 5S02
9 19:37 0 N
16 0:09 5N00
22 23:23 0 S
30 6:58 5S00

Perigee/Apogee
dy hr m kilometers
12 13:21 p 365363
24 7:26 a 404483

PH dy hr mn
● 1 6:23 9♐33
☽ 8 15:28 17♓02
○ 15 9:03 23♊53
☾ 22 22:19 1♎34
● 30 22:28 9♑44

Void of Course Moon

Last Aspect	☽ Ingress
2 15:48 ♆ □	♑ 2 21:10
4 23:35 ♀ ☌	♒ 5 4:22
7 0:03 ♅ □	♓ 7 9:50
9 8:46 ♆ ☌	♈ 9 13:39
10 22:15 ☉ △	♉ 11 15:56
13 12:40 ♆ ⚹	♊ 13 17:23
15 14:33 ♆ □	♋ 15 19:22
17 18:35 ♆ △	♌ 17 23:40
20 5:21 ☉ △	♍ 20 7:38
22 13:28 ♆ ☍	♎ 22 19:09
24 10:45 ♀ △	♏ 25 8:07
27 14:25 ♆ △	♐ 27 19:48
29 23:35 ♆ □	♑ 30 4:38

DAILY ASPECTARIAN

1 Su ☽∠♀ 3:09; ☉☌☽ 6:23; ☿∥♇ 7:40; ⚳∠♄ 9:26; ☽□♄ 12:50; ☽∠⚳ 12:55; ☽∠♇ 17:17; ☽∥⚳ 18:23; ☽☍♃ 20:46

2 M ☽△⚷ 1:06; ☽☌☿ 1:30; ☽⚼♂ 4:16; ☿△⚷ 6:17; ☽⚺♀ 10:40; ☽⚻♅ 11:03; ♀△♅ 14:44; ☽□♆ 15:48; ☽⚺⚳ 18:08; ☉⋕♃ 21:25; ☽⚺♇ 21:40

3 Tu ☽⚻♂ 8:31; ☽⚼♅ 14:59; ☉∥☿ 18:30; ☉⚺☽ 19:44; ☽⚹♄ 21:18

4 W ☿⋕♃ 1:30; ♀∥♇ 2:39; ☽⚻♃ 4:14; ☽∥⚳ 4:20; ☽⚺☿ 4:44; ☽□⚷ 8:54; ☿☍♃ 10:17; ☉□♄ 16:19; ☽△♅ 18:26; ♀⚹♆ 18:53; ☽⚹♆ 23:10; ☽☌♀ 23:35

5 Th ☽∠♄ 0:47; ☉∠☽ 1:28; ☽☌⚳ 2:56; ☽☌♇ 4:57; ☽∠☿ 5:32; ☽⚼♃ 7:17; ☿∠♇ 11:03; ☽∥♇ 12:58; ☿⋕♂ 13:35; ♀∠♄ 13:41; ☽∥♀ 15:09; ☽☍♂ 15:29; ☉∥☽ 17:38; ☽⋕♃ 19:57; ☽⋕♂ 23:40

6 F ☽∥☿ 0:58; ☿∠⚳ 1:00; ☽∠♆ 2:11; ☉☌☿ 2:19; ☽⚺♄ 3:51; ☉∠⚳ 5:46; ☽⚹☿ 5:57; ☉⚹☽ 6:39; ☿∠♀ 9:51; ☽△♃ 9:54; ☽⋕♅ 13:47; ☽⚹⚷ 14:52; ☉∥♀ 19:17; ♂ R 23:34; ☉∠♇ 23:58

7 Sa ☽□♅ 0:03; ☿□♄ 1:55; ☽⚺♆ 4:48; ♀☌⚳ 4:54; ♀ ♒ 6:14; ⚳ ♒ 9:17; ☽⚺⚳ 9:51; ☽⚺♀ 10:10; ☽⚺♇ 10:30; ♀☌♇ 14:09; ☽∠⚷ 17:14; ☽⚻♂ 20:37; ☉☍♃ 20:59; ♆ D 23:45

8 Su ☽□☿ 5:59; ♀⚼♃ 7:08; ☽∥♄ 7:48; ☽⋕⚷ 8:04; ☽☌♄ 8:45; ☽∠⚳ 12:39; ☽∠♇ 12:39; ⚳☌♇ 12:47; ☽□♃ 13:57; ☽∠♀ 14:38; ☊ D 15:23; ☉□☽ 15:28; ☽⚺⚷ 19:12; ♀⋕♃ 21:50; ☽⚼♂ 22:32

9 M ☽⚹♅ 4:01; ☽∥♆ 6:21; ☽☌♆ 8:46; ☽⚹♇ 14:23; ☽⚹⚳ 15:00; ☽⚹♀ 18:34; ☊ R 19:36; ☽⋕♆ 22:55

10 Tu ☽△♂ 0:00; ⚳⚼♃ 2:00; ☽△☿ 5:20; ☽∠♅ 5:24; ♀⋕♂ 9:08; ☽⚺♄ 12:00; ☽⚹♃ 16:25; ☉△⚷ 17:50; ☽∥⚷ 20:38; ☽⋕♄ 20:48; ☽☌⚷ 21:56; ☉△☽ 22:15

11 W ☽⚼☿ 4:54; ☽⚺♅ 6:26; ☽⚺♆ 11:11; ☽∠♄ 13:05; ☽□♇ 16:44; ☽∠♃ 17:09; ☽□⚳ 18:31; ☉∠♀ 22:46

12 Th ☉⚼☽ 1:01; ☽□♀ 1:02; ☽□♂ 1:51; ☽⚻☿ 4:31; ♀☍♂ 10:47; ☽∠♆ 11:59; ☉⚼♂ 12:12; ☽∥♅ 12:26; ☽⋕☿ 13:34; ☽⚹♄ 13:56; ☽⚺♃ 17:40; ☽⋕♀ 22:55; ☽⚺⚷ 23:30

13 F ☉⚻☽ 3:35; ☽∥♂ 3:39; ☽∥♃ 4:40; ♃⚼♇ 6:05; ☿⚹♀ 7:46; ☽☌♅ 7:50; ☉⋕☽ 11:08; ☽⋕♇ 11:17; ☽⚹♆ 12:40; ☽△♇ 18:16; ☽△⚳ 21:12; ☉∥♇ 21:32

14 Sa ☽∠⚷ 0:10; ☽⚹♂ 2:59; ☽☍☿ 4:21; ☽△♀ 6:41; ☽⋕⚳ 9:07; ♄⋕⚷ 12:47; ☽□♄ 15:35; ☽☌♃ 18:44; ☽⚼♇ 19:09; ☽⚼⚳ 22:42

15 Su ☽⚹⚷ 1:03; ☽∠♂ 3:44; ☉☍☽ 9:03; ☽⚺♅ 9:28; ☽⚼♀ 9:49; ♂∥♃ 13:44; ☽□♆ 14:33; ☉⚻♅ 14:45; ☽⚻♇ 20:23; ☿ D 20:57

16 M ☽⚻⚳ 0:38; ☽⚺♂ 4:54; ☽⚻☿ 6:18; ☽∠♅ 10:54; ☽⚻♀ 13:36; ☽△♄ 18:35; ☽⚺♃ 21:12

17 Tu ☽□⚷ 4:15; ☽⚼☿ 8:39; ☽⋕⚳ 10:49; ☽⚹♅ 13:03; ☉⚻☽ 16:57; ☽△♆ 18:35; ☽⚼♄ 21:09; ♀∠♆ 21:35; ☽∠♃ 23:29

18 W ☽☍♇ 0:51; ☽☍⚳ 6:45; ☉⋕☽ 6:57; ☽⋕♇ 8:15; ☽☌♂ 9:14; ☽△☿ 12:16; ☽∥♂ 14:12; ☉□♆ 14:30; ☽∥♃ 15:48; ☽⚼♆ 21:53; ☉⚼☽ 22:31; ☿∥♀ 23:31

19 Th ☽☍♀ 0:12; ☽⚻♄ 0:40; ☽⚹♃ 2:42; ♀⚺♄ 5:53; ☽⋕☿ 8:17; ☽⋕♀ 9:18; ☽∥♅ 10:03; ☽△⚷ 10:45; ♀⋕♅ 19:15; ☽□♅ 20:05

20 F ☽⚻♆ 2:12; ♀△♃ 2:12; ☉△☽ 5:21; ☽⚻♇ 9:02; ☽⚼⚷ 15:28; ☽⚻⚳ 16:57; ☽⚺♂ 17:06; ♂☍⚳ 20:22; ☽□☿ 23:47

21 Sa ☽∥⚷ 8:30; ☽⋕♄ 9:01; ☉ ♑ 9:22; ☽☍♄ 10:40; ☽□♃ 11:56; ☽⚼♇ 14:32; ☽⚻♀ 15:46; ☽⚻⚷ 21:04; ☽∠♂ 22:17; ☽⚼⚳ 23:33

22 Su ☉⚺♇ 3:33; ☽△♅ 6:51; ☽⋕♆ 10:09; ☽☍♆ 13:28; ☽△♇ 20:45; ☉□☽ 22:19

23 M ☽⚼♀ 1:04; ☽⚹♂ 4:01; ☽∥♆ 5:37; ☽△⚳ 6:49; ☽⚼♅ 13:09; ☽⚹☿ 16:23; ☽⚻♄ 23:31; ☽△♃ 23:52

24 Tu ♀⚹⚷ 0:47; ☽∥♄ 6:52; ☽⋕⚷ 7:40; ☽☍⚷ 9:49; ☽△♀ 10:45; ☽⚻♅ 19:36; ♃□♄ 22:01

25 W ☽∠☿ 1:37; ☽⚻♆ 2:29; ☉⚻♂ 5:01; ☽⚼♃ 6:04; ☽⚼♄ 6:11; ☽□♇ 9:53; ☽□♂ 15:45; ☉⚹☽ 17:01; ☽∥♀ 20:15; ☽□⚳ 21:42

26 Th ☽⋕♅ 8:02; ☽⚼♆ 8:44; ☽⚺☿ 10:44; ☽⚻♃ 11:56; ☽△♄ 12:32; ☽∥☿ 19:55; ☽⚻⚷ 22:13; ☿☍♃ 22:49

27 F ☉∠☽ 1:44; ☽⋕♃ 3:12; ☽□♀ 5:09; ☿□♄ 7:30; ☽☍♅ 7:35; ☽⋕♂ 10:58; ☽∥♇ 11:32; ☉∥☽ 12:33; ☽△♆ 14:25; ☽⚹♇ 21:37

28 Sa ☽△♂ 1:51; ☽∥⚳ 2:15; ☽⚼⚷ 3:33; ♂⋕♇ 5:31; ♀□♅ 7:43; ☉⚺☽ 9:36; ☽⚹⚳ 10:37; ☿∠♇ 20:32; ☽☍♃ 21:51; ☉⋕♂ 22:57; ☽□♄ 23:16

29 Su ☽∠♇ 2:26; ☽☌☿ 3:02; ☉⚺⚳ 4:47; ☽⚼♂ 5:51; ☽△⚷ 8:08; ☽∠⚳ 15:53; ☽⚻♅ 16:56; ☽⚹♀ 20:04; ⚷ D 21:14; ☉⚼♅ 22:00; ☽□♆ 23:35

30 M ☿⚼♂ 3:08; ☽⚺♇ 6:30; ☉∥♇ 8:27; ☽⚻♂ 9:08; ☽⚺⚳ 20:22; ☽⚼♅ 20:32; ☉☌☽ 22:28

31 Tu ☽∠♀ 2:06; ☽⚻♃ 4:57; ☽⚹♄ 7:04; ☿△⚷ 7:42; ☿⋕♃ 9:15; ♀⚺♆ 14:39; ☽□⚷ 15:13; ☽⚺☿ 16:01; ☽△♅ 23:31

LONGITUDE

January 2025

Day	Sid.Time	☉	☽	☽ 12 hour	Mean ☊	True ☊	☿	♀	♂	⚳	♃	♄	⚷	♅	♆	♇
	h m s	° ' "	° ' "	° ' "	° '	° '	° '	° '	° '	° '	° '	° '	° '	° '	° '	° '
1 W	6 43 36	10♑48 46	23♑54 10	0♒39 01	1♈29.7	0♈52.7	19♐52.1	27♒42.7	1♌55.1	9♒00.7	13♊12.9	14♓31.4	19♈00.2	23♉38.2	27♓17.9	1♒03.9
2 Th	6 47 32	11 49 57	7♒26 42	14 16 51	1 26.6	0R 41.7	21 10.1	28 46.9	1R 35.1	9 23.4	13R 06.6	14 36.0	19 00.3	23R 36.7	27 18.7	1 05.7
3 F	6 51 29	12 51 07	21 09 10	28 03 19	1 23.4	0 33.6	22 29.4	29 50.9	1 14.6	9 46.2	13 00.4	14 40.7	19 00.5	23 35.3	27 19.6	1 07.6
4 Sa	6 55 25	13 52 18	4♓59 03	11♓56 09	1 20.2	0 28.7	23 50.0	0♓54.6	0 53.5	10 08.9	12 54.4	14 45.4	19 00.8	23 34.0	27 20.5	1 09.5
5 Su	6 59 22	14 53 28	18 54 25	25 53 44	1 17.0	0D 26.4	25 11.7	1 57.9	0 32.0	10 31.7	12 48.5	14 50.2	19 01.1	23 32.6	27 21.4	1 11.3
6 M	7 03 19	15 54 37	2♈54 01	9♈55 11	1 13.9	0R 26.0	26 34.5	3 00.9	0 10.0	10 54.6	12 42.8	14 55.1	19 01.5	23 31.4	27 22.4	1 13.2
7 Tu	7 07 15	16 55 47	16 57 10	23 59 54	1 10.7	0 26.2	27 58.1	4 03.5	29♋47.6	11 17.5	12 37.3	15 00.1	19 01.9	23 30.2	27 23.4	1 15.1
8 W	7 11 12	17 56 56	1♉03 18	8♉07 14	1 07.5	0 25.6	29 22.7	5 05.7	29 24.8	11 40.4	12 31.9	15 05.1	19 02.4	23 29.0	27 24.4	1 17.0
9 Th	7 15 08	18 58 04	15 11 31	22 15 54	1 04.3	0 23.0	0♑48.0	6 07.6	29 01.8	12 03.4	12 26.7	15 10.2	19 02.9	23 27.9	27 25.5	1 18.9
10 F	7 19 05	19 59 12	29 20 05	6♊23 41	1 01.2	0 17.8	2 14.1	7 09.1	28 38.4	12 26.4	12 21.6	15 15.4	19 03.5	23 26.8	27 26.6	1 20.8
11 Sa	7 23 01	21 00 19	13♊26 15	20 27 18	0 58.0	0 09.8	3 41.0	8 10.1	28 14.9	12 49.4	12 16.7	15 20.7	19 04.2	23 25.8	27 27.8	1 22.7
12 Su	7 26 58	22 01 26	27 26 17	4♋22 42	0 54.8	29♓59.6	5 08.4	9 10.8	27 51.1	13 12.5	12 12.0	15 26.0	19 04.9	23 24.8	27 28.9	1 24.6
13 M	7 30 55	23 02 33	11♋16 00	18 05 41	0 51.6	29 48.1	6 36.5	10 11.0	27 27.3	13 35.6	12 07.5	15 31.4	19 05.6	23 23.8	27 30.1	1 26.5
14 Tu	7 34 51	24 03 39	24 51 19	1♌32 31	0 48.5	29 36.5	8 05.3	11 10.7	27 03.3	13 58.7	12 03.1	15 36.8	19 06.4	23 23.0	27 31.3	1 28.5
15 W	7 38 48	25 04 45	8♌09 02	14 40 40	0 45.3	29 26.1	9 34.6	12 10.0	26 39.3	14 21.9	11 59.0	15 42.4	19 07.3	23 22.1	27 32.6	1 30.4
16 Th	7 42 44	26 05 50	21 07 23	27 29 11	0 42.1	29 17.7	11 04.5	13 08.8	26 15.3	14 45.1	11 55.0	15 48.0	19 08.2	23 21.3	27 33.9	1 32.3
17 F	7 46 41	27 06 55	3♍46 14	9♍58 47	0 38.9	29 11.9	12 35.0	14 07.0	25 51.3	15 08.3	11 51.2	15 53.6	19 09.2	23 20.6	27 35.2	1 34.2
18 Sa	7 50 37	28 08 00	16 07 09	22 11 45	0 35.8	29 08.7	14 06.0	15 04.8	25 27.4	15 31.5	11 47.6	15 59.3	19 10.2	23 19.9	27 36.5	1 36.2
19 Su	7 54 34	29 09 04	28 13 06	4♎11 43	0 32.6	29D 07.7	15 37.6	16 02.0	25 03.7	15 54.8	11 44.2	16 05.1	19 11.3	23 19.3	27 37.9	1 38.1
20 M	7 58 30	0♒10 07	10♎08 13	16 03 13	0 29.4	29 08.2	17 09.8	16 58.6	24 40.2	16 18.1	11 41.0	16 10.9	19 12.5	23 18.7	27 39.3	1 40.0
21 Tu	8 02 27	1 11 11	21 57 24	27 51 25	0 26.2	29R 09.1	18 42.5	17 54.7	24 16.9	16 41.4	11 37.9	16 16.8	19 13.6	23 18.2	27 40.7	1 42.0
22 W	8 06 24	2 12 14	3♏45 57	9♏41 43	0 23.0	29 09.5	20 15.9	18 50.2	23 53.8	17 04.7	11 35.1	16 22.8	19 14.9	23 17.7	27 42.1	1 43.9
23 Th	8 10 20	3 13 16	15 39 22	21 39 33	0 19.9	29 08.5	21 49.7	19 45.0	23 31.1	17 28.1	11 32.5	16 28.8	19 16.2	23 17.2	27 43.6	1 45.8
24 F	8 14 17	4 14 19	27 42 52	3♐49 54	0 16.7	29 05.4	23 24.2	20 39.2	23 08.8	17 51.5	11 30.1	16 34.9	19 17.5	23 16.9	27 45.1	1 47.8
25 Sa	8 18 13	5 15 20	10♐01 07	16 16 59	0 13.5	29 00.1	24 59.3	21 32.8	22 46.9	18 14.9	11 27.8	16 41.0	19 18.9	23 16.5	27 46.7	1 49.7
26 Su	8 22 10	6 16 22	22 37 50	29 03 55	0 10.3	28 52.7	26 35.0	22 25.6	22 25.4	18 38.3	11 25.8	16 47.2	19 20.4	23 16.3	27 48.2	1 51.7
27 M	8 26 06	7 17 22	5♑35 21	12♑12 11	0 07.2	28 43.9	28 11.3	23 17.8	22 04.4	19 01.7	11 24.0	16 53.4	19 21.9	23 16.0	27 49.8	1 53.6
28 Tu	8 30 03	8 18 22	18 54 19	25 41 32	0 04.0	28 34.6	29 48.3	24 09.1	21 43.9	19 25.2	11 22.3	16 59.7	19 23.4	23 15.9	27 51.4	1 55.5
29 W	8 33 59	9 19 21	2♒33 31	9♒29 50	0 00.8	28 25.8	1♒25.8	24 59.8	21 23.9	19 48.7	11 20.9	17 06.1	19 25.0	23 15.8	27 53.0	1 57.4
30 Th	8 37 56	10 20 19	16 29 58	23 33 22	29♓57.6	28 18.4	3 04.1	25 49.6	21 04.6	20 12.2	11 19.7	17 12.5	19 26.7	23D 15.7	27 54.7	1 59.4
31 F	8 41 53	11♒21 16	0♓39 24	7♓47 26	29♓54.5	28♓13.1	4♒43.0	26♓38.5	20♋45.9	20♒35.7	11♊18.7	17♓18.9	19♈28.4	23♉15.7	27♓56.4	2♒01.3

1st of Month

Julian Day #
2460676.5
Obliquity
23°26'38"
SVP 4♓54'38"
GC 27♐11.3
Eris 24♈23.9R

Day	⚴	⚵	⚶
1	12♑16.2	18♏59.5	29♎13.2
6	14 13.8	20 23.3	1♏11.0
11	16 10.8	21 44.0	3 05.1
16	18 07.0	23 01.2	4 55.3
21	20 02.3	24 14.8	6 41.0
26	21 56.7	25 24.3	8 21.8
31	23 49.9	26 29.5	9 57.1

DECLINATION and LATITUDE

Day	☉ Decl	☽ Decl	☽ Lat	☽ 12h Decl	☿ Decl	☿ Lat	♀ Decl	♀ Lat	♂ Decl	♂ Lat	⚳ Decl	⚳ Lat	♃ Decl	♃ Lat	♄ Decl	♄ Lat
1 W	22S60	25S52	4S37	24S15	21S56	1N07	13S35	1S24	23N33	3N55	24S45	7S01	21N47	0S36	7S55	1S59
2 Th	22 55	22 18	4 01	20 01	22 10	0 58	13 09	1 20	23 39	3 57	24 39	7 01	21 47	0 36	7 53	1 59
3 F	22 49	17 28	3 12	14 41	22 24	0 50	12 42	1 16	23 46	3 59	24 33	7 01	21 46	0 36	7 51	1 58
4 Sa	22 43	11 42	2 10	8 34	22 36	0 42	12 16	1 11	23 53	4 01	24 27	7 01	21 46	0 35	7 49	1 58
5 Su	22 36	5 19	1 01	1 60	22 48	0 33	11 49	1 07	23 59	4 03	24 21	7 01	21 45	0 35	7 47	1 58
6 M	22 29	1N21	0N13	4N42	22 58	0 25	11 21	1 02	24 06	4 05	24 14	7 01	21 44	0 35	7 45	1 58
7 Tu	22 22	7 59	1 26	11 12	23 08	0 17	10 54	0 57	24 12	4 06	24 08	7 02	21 44	0 35	7 43	1 58
8 W	22 14	14 15	2 35	17 08	23 17	0 09	10 27	0 52	24 19	4 08	24 02	7 02	21 43	0 35	7 41	1 58
9 Th	22 06	19 48	3 34	22 11	23 25	0 02	9 59	0 46	24 25	4 09	23 55	7 02	21 43	0 34	7 39	1 58
10 F	21 57	24 14	4 20	25 55	23 31	0S06	9 31	0 41	24 31	4 11	23 49	7 02	21 43	0 34	7 37	1 58
11 Sa	21 48	27 12	4 50	28 03	23 37	0 13	9 03	0 35	24 38	4 12	23 42	7 02	21 42	0 34	7 35	1 57
12 Su	21 38	28 27	5 02	28 23	23 41	0 21	8 35	0 30	24 44	4 13	23 36	7 03	21 42	0 34	7 33	1 57
13 M	21 28	27 53	4 56	26 57	23 44	0 28	8 07	0 24	24 50	4 15	23 29	7 03	21 41	0 34	7 30	1 57
14 Tu	21 18	25 39	4 34	23 59	23 46	0 35	7 39	0 18	24 55	4 16	23 22	7 03	21 41	0 33	7 28	1 57
15 W	21 07	22 02	3 57	19 50	23 47	0 42	7 11	0 12	25 01	4 16	23 16	7 03	21 41	0 33	7 26	1 57
16 Th	20 56	17 26	3 08	14 51	23 47	0 48	6 42	0 05	25 06	4 17	23 09	7 04	21 40	0 33	7 24	1 57
17 F	20 44	12 10	2 11	9 23	23 45	0 54	6 14	0N01	25 12	4 18	23 02	7 04	21 40	0 33	7 21	1 57
18 Sa	20 32	6 32	1 09	3 40	23 42	1 01	5 46	0 08	25 17	4 18	22 55	7 04	21 40	0 33	7 19	1 57
19 Su	20 20	0 47	0 05	2S05	23 37	1 07	5 17	0 15	25 22	4 19	22 48	7 04	21 40	0 32	7 17	1 57
20 M	20 07	4S55	0S59	7 41	23 32	1 12	4 49	0 21	25 26	4 19	22 42	7 05	21 39	0 32	7 14	1 56
21 Tu	19 54	10 24	1 59	13 01	23 25	1 18	4 20	0 29	25 31	4 19	22 35	7 05	21 39	0 32	7 12	1 56
22 W	19 40	15 31	2 55	17 53	23 17	1 23	3 52	0 36	25 35	4 20	22 28	7 05	21 39	0 32	7 10	1 56
23 Th	19 26	20 05	3 43	22 06	23 07	1 28	3 24	0 43	25 39	4 20	22 21	7 06	21 39	0 31	7 07	1 56
24 F	19 12	23 54	4 22	25 27	22 56	1 33	2 56	0 51	25 43	4 20	22 14	7 06	21 39	0 31	7 05	1 56
25 Sa	18 57	26 44	4 50	27 41	22 43	1 37	2 27	0 58	25 47	4 19	22 07	7 07	21 39	0 31	7 02	1 56
26 Su	18 42	28 18	5 05	28 32	22 29	1 41	1 59	1 06	25 50	4 19	21 59	7 07	21 39	0 31	6 60	1 56
27 M	18 27	28 23	5 04	27 49	22 14	1 45	1 32	1 14	25 53	4 19	21 52	7 07	21 39	0 31	6 57	1 56
28 Tu	18 11	26 51	4 48	25 28	21 57	1 48	1 04	1 22	25 56	4 18	21 45	7 08	21 39	0 30	6 55	1 56
29 W	17 55	23 43	4 14	21 36	21 39	1 52	0 36	1 31	25 59	4 18	21 38	7 08	21 39	0 30	6 52	1 56
30 Th	17 39	19 09	3 25	16 26	21 20	1 55	0 09	1 39	26 01	4 17	21 31	7 08	21 39	0 30	6 50	1 56
31 F	17S22	13S28	2S23	10S19	20S59	1S57	0N19	1N48	26N03	4N16	21S23	7S09	21N39	0S30	6S47	1S56

Day	⚷ Decl	⚷ Lat	♅ Decl	♅ Lat	♆ Decl	♆ Lat	♇ Decl	♇ Lat
1	8N18	0N56	18N26	0S15	2S15	1S17	23S07	3S16
6	8 18	0 56	18 25	0 15	2 13	1 17	23 05	3 17
11	8 19	0 55	18 23	0 15	2 11	1 17	23 03	3 17
16	8 20	0 54	18 22	0 15	2 08	1 17	23 01	3 17
21	8 21	0 54	18 22	0 15	2 06	1 16	22 60	3 18
26	8 23	0 53	18 21	0 15	2 02	1 16	22 58	3 18
31	8N26	0N53	18N21	0S15	1S59	1S16	22S56	3S19

Day	⚴ Decl	⚴ Lat	⚵ Decl	⚵ Lat	⚶ Decl	⚶ Lat	Eris Decl	Eris Lat
1	2N56	25N54	9S46	7N60	4S54	6N44	0S35	10S47
6	2 60	25 48	9 54	8 14	5 23	6 56	0 35	10 46
11	3 06	25 43	9 60	8 29	5 50	7 08	0 34	10 45
16	3 14	25 39	10 04	8 44	6 14	7 21	0 33	10 45
21	3 25	25 36	10 06	9 00	6 35	7 34	0 32	10 44
26	3 38	25 35	10 05	9 17	6 54	7 48	0 31	10 43
31	3N53	25N34	10S02	9N35	7S09	8N03	0S30	10S42

Moon Phenomena

Max/0 Decl
dy hr mn
5 19:10 0 N
12 4:25 28N28
19 3:16 0 S
26 13:22 28S32

Max/0 Lat
dy hr mn
5 19:47 0 N
12 4:21 5N02
19 1:49 0 S
26 11:32 5S06

Perigee/Apogee
dy hr m kilometers
8 0:02 p 370171
8 0:02 p 370171
21 4:55 a 404297

PH dy hr mn
☽ 6 23:57 16♈56
○ 13 22:28 24♋00
☾ 21 20:32 2♏03
● 29 12:37 9♒51

Void of Course Moon

Last Aspect			☽ Ingress	
1 6:03	♆	⚹	♒	1 10:51
3 4:14	♅	□	♓	3 15:22
5 14:31	♆	☌	♈	5 19:02
7 21:17	♂	□	♉	7 22:12
9 22:51	♂	⚹	♊	10 1:08
12 0:05	♆	□	♋	12 4:25
14 4:47	♆	△	♌	14 9:13
16 4:11	♅	□	♍	16 16:47
19 2:02	☉	△	♎	19 3:34
21 4:35	♂	□	♏	21 16:21
24 0:04	♆	△	♐	24 4:30
26 9:41	♆	□	♑	26 13:44
28 15:50	♆	⚹	♒	28 19:33
30 11:30	♅	□	♓	30 22:54

DAILY ASPECTARIAN

1 W ☽⚹♆ 6:03; ☽⚺♀ 7:22; ☽⚼♃ 7:37; ☽∥⚳ 8:47; ☽∠♄ 10:04; ☽☌♇ 12:46; ☽☍♂ 13:54; ☽⋕♂ 16:07; ☽∥♇ 19:15; ☉∥☽ 20:21; ☽∠☿ 21:31

2 Th ☽∥☿ 0:39; ☽⋕♃ 2:53; ☽☌⚳ 3:31; ☉⚺☽ 8:20; ☽∠♆ 8:34; ☽△♃ 9:53; ☽⚺♄ 12:38; ☽⋕♅ 19:39; ☽⚹⚷ 20:16; ⚶ ♏ 23:16

3 F ☽⚹☿ 2:35; ☉⚻♃ 3:20; ♀ ♓ 3:25; ☽□♅ 4:14; ♂☍♇ 7:23; ☽⚺♆ 10:45; ☉∠☽ 12:34; ☽☌♀ 16:22; ☽⚻♂ 17:06; ☽⚺♇ 17:22; ☿⚻♅ 19:20; ☽∥♀ 21:39; ☽∠⚷ 22:19; ♀⚻♂ 23:42

4 Sa ♀⚺♇ 5:48; ☉∥☿ 9:07; ☽⚺⚳ 9:10; ☽⋕⚷ 12:59; ☽□♃ 13:35; ☽∥♄ 14:52; ☉⚹☽ 16:33; ☽☌♄ 16:57; ☽⚼♂ 18:21; ☽∠♇ 19:19; ☉⚹♄ 22:37

5 Su ☽⚺⚷ 0:11; ☽⚹♅ 7:57; ☿∠⚳ 8:04; ☽∥♆ 11:11; ☽∠⚳ 11:41; ☽□☿ 11:59; ☽☌♆ 14:31; ☽△♂ 19:26; ☊D 19:49; ☽⚹♇ 21:07

6 M ☽⚺♀ 0:13; ☽⋕♆ 3:06; ☽∠♅ 9:36; ♂R♋ 10:45; ♂⚼♄ 13:06; ☿□♆ 13:57; ☽⚹⚳ 14:04; ☿∥♇ 15:42; ♂⋕⚳ 16:01; ☽⚹♃ 16:40; ☽⚺♄ 20:39; ☽⋕♄ 23:00; ♀∠⚷ 23:23; ☊R 23:48; ☉□☽ 23:57

7 Tu ☽∥⚷ 1:10; ☽☌⚷ 3:33; ☽∠♀ 3:52; ☽⋕♀ 10:09; ☽⚺♅ 11:08; ☽⚺♆ 17:47; ☽∠♃ 18:03; ☽△☿ 20:50; ☽□♂ 21:17; ☽∠♄ 22:20

8 W ☽□♇ 0:23; ☿⚻♂ 0:29; ☽⚹♀ 7:24; ☿ ♑ 10:31; ☽∥♅ 17:32; ☽□⚳ 18:32; ☽∠♆ 19:18; ☽⚺♃ 19:22; ☽⚹♄ 23:58

9 Th ☽⚼☿ 1:09; ☉□⚷ 1:55; ☽⚺⚷ 6:33; ☉△☽ 6:54; ☿⚺♇ 8:49; ☽∥♃ 9:33; ☉⋕☽ 11:13; ☽☌♅ 14:01; ☽⋕♇ 16:56; ☽⋕☿ 19:30; ⚳△♃ 19:54; ☽⚹♆ 20:47; ☽⋕⚳ 21:27; ☽⚹♂ 22:51

10 F ⚳∠♆ 0:15; ☽∥♂ 1:58; ☽△♇ 3:25; ☽⚻☿ 5:29; ☽∠⚷ 8:02; ☉⚼☽ 10:21; ☽□♀ 14:19; ☽☌♃ 22:02; ☽△⚳ 22:55; ☽∠♂ 23:41

11 Sa ☽□♄ 3:17; ☽⚼♇ 5:02; ☽⚹⚷ 9:38; ☿∥⚳ 11:46; ☉⚻☽ 13:58; ☉⋕♃ 15:03; ☽⚺♅ 17:05; ☊R♓ 23:04

12 Su ☽□♆ 0:05; ☽⚺♂ 0:42; ☽⚼⚳ 1:22; ☽⚻♇ 6:52; ♀⋕⚷ 13:46; ☽☍☿ 14:54; ☽∠♅ 19:00; ♂△♆ 21:17; ☽△♀ 21:57

13 M ☽⚺♃ 1:30; ☽⚻⚳ 4:12; ☽△♄ 7:31; ☉△♅ 8:15; ☽□⚷ 13:47; ☽⚹♅ 21:23; ☉☍☽ 22:28

14 Tu ♂∠♃ 0:11; ☽⚼♀ 2:33; ☽☌♂ 3:49; ☽∠♃ 3:54; ☿⚼♅ 4:43; ☽△♆ 4:47; ☽∥♂ 5:22; ♀∥♄ 9:50; ☽⚼♄ 10:24; ☽☍♇ 11:54; ☽⋕☿ 13:22; ♀⚼♂ 15:08; ☽⋕⚳ 16:28; ☽⋕♇ 18:06; ♀□♃ 19:49

15 W ☽∥♃ 2:03; ☽⚻☿ 2:57; ☉⋕☽ 5:24; ☽⚹♃ 7:00; ☽⚻♀ 7:58; ☽⚼♆ 8:04; ☽☍⚳ 11:46; ☽⚻♄ 14:00; ☽∥♅ 19:24; ☽△⚷ 20:17

16 Th ☉☍♂ 2:40; ☽□♅ 4:11; ☽⚺♂ 9:22; ☉⚻☽ 10:11; ☽⚼☿ 10:35; ☽⚻♆ 12:10; ☿⚻♃ 12:52; ☉⚼♃ 18:11; ☽⚻♇ 19:46

17 F ☽⚼⚷ 0:44; ⚳∥♇ 4:14; ☉⚹♆ 11:21; ☽∠♂ 13:17; ☽□♃ 15:34; ☽∥⚷ 16:25; ☉⚼☽ 17:37; ☽△☿ 19:29; ☽⋕♄ 20:42; ☽☍♀ 21:47; ☽⚻⚳ 22:48; ☽☍♄ 23:45

18 Sa ☽⚼♇ 0:57; ☽⋕♀ 3:33; ☽⚻⚷ 6:01; ☽△♅ 14:15; ☽⚹♂ 17:54; ☽⋕♆ 18:27; ♀⚺⚳ 18:51; ☽☍♆ 22:49

19 Su ♀☌♄ 1:27; ☊D 1:51; ☉△☽ 2:02; ☽⚼⚳ 5:35; ☿⚺⚳ 5:59; ☽△♇ 6:52; ☿⚹♄ 7:39; ☽∥♆ 12:06; ⚳⚺♄ 14:12; ♀∠♇ 15:49; ☿⚹♀ 16:33; ☉ ♒ 20:01; ☽⚼♅ 20:19; ☽∥♀ 23:36

20 M ☽△♃ 3:07; ☽∥♄ 9:57; ☽⚻♄ 12:22; ☽△⚳ 12:56; ☽⋕⚷ 14:54; ☽⚻♀ 15:04; ☽□☿ 16:24; ☽☍⚷ 18:26

21 Tu ☉∠♄ 2:28; ☽⚻♅ 2:44; ☽□♂ 4:35; ☿□⚷ 8:07; ☽⚼♃ 9:28; ☽⚻♆ 11:40; ☉☌♇ 12:30; ☽⚼♄ 19:07; ☽□♇ 19:52; ☉□☽ 20:32; ☊R 20:42

22 W ☽⚼♀ 0:09; ♀⚺⚷ 11:02; ☽⋕♅ 14:33; ☽⚻♃ 15:45; ☽⚼♆ 18:06; ☉∥☽ 20:35

23 Th ☽△♄ 1:40; ☽□⚳ 3:45; ☽⚻⚷ 7:15; ☽△♀ 8:52; ☽⋕♃ 9:11; ☽∥⚳ 13:08; ☽⚹☿ 14:11; ♂⚹♅ 15:09; ☽△♂ 15:14; ☽☍♅ 15:14; ☽∥♇ 17:38; ☽∥☿ 17:40; ☿∥♇ 18:11; ☿☍♂ 20:50; ☿△♅ 22:09

24 F ☽△♆ 0:04; ☽⚹♇ 8:03; ☽⚼⚷ 12:55; ☉⚹☽ 13:57; ☽⋕♂ 14:33; ☽⚼♂ 19:48; ☽∠☿ 23:56

25 Sa ☽☍♃ 2:46; ☽□♄ 12:52; ☽∠♇ 13:04; ☽⚹⚳ 16:14; ☽△⚷ 17:47; ☉∠☽ 21:13; ♀∥♆ 21:22; ☿⚼♃ 21:45; ☽□♀ 23:35; ☽⚻♂ 23:37; ♀△♂ 23:55

26 Su ☽⚻♅ 1:12; ☽⚺☿ 8:26; ☽□♆ 9:41; ☽⚺♇ 17:12; ☿⚹♆ 18:34; ☽∠⚳ 21:03; ♀⚹♅ 23:12

27 M ♄∠♇ 0:47; ☉⚺☽ 3:22; ☽⚼♅ 4:53; ☉⋕♅ 8:51; ☽⚻♃ 10:32; ☽⚹♄ 20:34; ⚳⚹⚷ 22:04

28 Tu ☽□⚷ 0:52; ☽⚺⚳ 0:57; ☿ ♒ 2:54; ☽☍♂ 4:54; ☽△♅ 7:43; ☽⋕♂ 8:13; ☽⚹♀ 9:54; ☽⚼♃ 13:10; ☽⚹♆ 15:50; ☽☌☿ 21:46; ⚳⋕♃ 22:00; ☽☌♇ 22:57; ☽∠♄ 23:12

29 W ☿⋕♃ 1:02; ☿∥⚳ 2:55; ☽∥♇ 4:35; ☿☌♇ 7:54; ☿∠♄ 10:32; ☽⋕♃ 11:44; ☽∥⚳ 12:07; ☽∥☿ 12:33; ☉☌☽ 12:37; ☽∠♀ 13:40; ☽△♃ 15:10; ☽∠♆ 17:51

30 Th ☽⚺♄ 1:13; ☽⋕♅ 3:39; ☽⚹⚷ 5:02; ☽☌⚳ 6:29; ☉∥☽ 7:07; ☽⚻♂ 7:37; ☽□♅ 11:30; ♅D 16:24; ☽⚺♀ 16:49; ☽⚺♆ 19:24; ☉△♃ 23:00

31 F ☽⚺♇ 2:18; ♂⚻⚳ 5:51; ☽∠⚷ 6:26; ☽⚺☿ 7:44; ☽⚼♂ 8:25; ☽□♃ 17:53; ☽⋕⚷ 18:53; ☉⚺☽ 19:21

February 2025

LONGITUDE

Day	Sid.Time	☉	☽	☽ 12 hour	Mean☊	True☊	☿	♀	♂	⚳	♃	♄	⚷	♅	♆	♇
	h m s	° ' "	° ' "	° ' "	° '	° '	° '	° '	° '	° '	° '	° '	° '	° '	° '	° '
1 Sa	8 45 49	12♒22 12	14♓56 51	22♓07 04	29♓51.3	28♓10.1	6♒22.6	27♓26.6	20♋27.8	20♒59.2	11♊17.9	17♓25.4	19♈30.1	23♉15.7	27♓58.1	2♒03.2
2 Su	8 49 46	13 23 07	29 17 31	6♈27 44	29 48.1	28D 09.4	8 03.0	28 13.8	20R 10.4	21 22.7	11R 17.3	17 31.9	19 31.9	23 15.8	27 59.8	2 05.1
3 M	8 53 42	14 24 00	13♈37 16	20 45 47	29 44.9	28 10.1	9 44.0	29 00.0	19 53.7	21 46.2	11 16.9	17 38.5	19 33.8	23 16.0	28 01.6	2 07.0
4 Tu	8 57 39	15 24 52	27 53 00	4♉58 40	29 41.7	28 11.4	11 25.8	29 45.2	19 37.7	22 09.8	11D 16.7	17 45.1	19 35.7	23 16.2	28 03.3	2 08.9
5 W	9 01 35	16 25 43	12♉02 36	19 04 39	29 38.6	28R 12.4	13 08.3	0♈29.4	19 22.4	22 33.3	11 16.7	17 51.8	19 37.6	23 16.4	28 05.1	2 10.8
6 Th	9 05 32	17 26 32	26 04 43	3♊02 39	29 35.4	28 12.1	14 51.5	1 12.5	19 07.9	22 56.9	11 17.0	17 58.5	19 39.6	23 16.8	28 06.9	2 12.7
7 F	9 09 28	18 27 19	9♊58 21	16 51 42	29 32.2	28 10.1	16 35.5	1 54.5	18 54.2	23 20.5	11 17.4	18 05.2	19 41.6	23 17.1	28 08.8	2 14.6
8 Sa	9 13 25	19 28 06	23 42 36	0♋30 53	29 29.0	28 06.3	18 20.3	2 35.4	18 41.2	23 44.0	11 18.0	18 12.0	19 43.7	23 17.5	28 10.6	2 16.4
9 Su	9 17 22	20 28 50	7♋16 25	13 59 02	29 25.9	28 00.9	20 05.9	3 15.0	18 29.0	24 07.6	11 18.9	18 18.8	19 45.8	23 18.0	28 12.5	2 18.3
10 M	9 21 18	21 29 34	20 38 35	27 14 55	29 22.7	27 54.7	21 52.2	3 53.3	18 17.6	24 31.2	11 19.9	18 25.7	19 48.0	23 18.5	28 14.4	2 20.2
11 Tu	9 25 15	22 30 15	3♌47 53	10♌17 22	29 19.5	27 48.4	23 39.2	4 30.4	18 07.0	24 54.7	11 21.1	18 32.6	19 50.2	23 19.1	28 16.3	2 22.0
12 W	9 29 11	23 30 56	16 43 17	23 05 35	29 16.3	27 42.7	25 27.0	5 06.0	17 57.2	25 18.3	11 22.6	18 39.5	19 52.5	23 19.7	28 18.3	2 23.8
13 Th	9 33 08	24 31 34	29 24 16	5♍39 22	29 13.2	27 38.2	27 15.5	5 40.3	17 48.2	25 41.9	11 24.2	18 46.5	19 54.7	23 20.4	28 20.2	2 25.7
14 F	9 37 04	25 32 12	11♍51 00	17 59 19	29 10.0	27 35.3	29 04.6	6 13.1	17 40.0	26 05.5	11 26.0	18 53.5	19 57.1	23 21.1	28 22.2	2 27.5
15 Sa	9 41 01	26 32 48	24 04 33	0♎06 58	29 06.8	27D 34.1	0♓54.4	6 44.3	17 32.5	26 29.0	11 28.1	19 00.5	19 59.5	23 21.9	28 24.2	2 29.3
16 Su	9 44 57	27 33 22	6♎06 54	12 04 44	29 03.6	27 34.4	2 44.7	7 14.0	17 25.9	26 52.6	11 30.3	19 07.5	20 01.9	23 22.7	28 26.2	2 31.1
17 M	9 48 54	28 33 56	18 00 53	23 55 52	29 00.4	27 35.7	4 35.5	7 42.1	17 20.0	27 16.2	11 32.7	19 14.6	20 04.3	23 23.6	28 28.2	2 32.9
18 Tu	9 52 51	29 34 28	29 50 11	5♏44 23	28 57.3	27 37.5	6 26.7	8 08.4	17 15.0	27 39.7	11 35.3	19 21.7	20 06.8	23 24.6	28 30.2	2 34.6
19 W	9 56 47	0♓34 58	11♏39 03	17 34 48	28 54.1	27 39.3	8 18.2	8 33.0	17 10.7	28 03.3	11 38.1	19 28.8	20 09.3	23 25.5	28 32.3	2 36.4
20 Th	10 00 44	1 35 28	23 32 15	29 32 01	28 50.9	27R 40.5	10 09.7	8 55.8	17 07.2	28 26.9	11 41.1	19 36.0	20 11.9	23 26.6	28 34.3	2 38.1
21 F	10 04 40	2 35 56	5♐34 44	11♐40 59	28 47.7	27 40.8	12 01.2	9 16.7	17 04.5	28 50.4	11 44.3	19 43.2	20 14.5	23 27.7	28 36.4	2 39.9
22 Sa	10 08 37	3 36 23	17 51 23	24 06 28	28 44.6	27 39.9	13 52.4	9 35.6	17 02.5	29 14.0	11 47.7	19 50.4	20 17.2	23 28.8	28 38.5	2 41.6
23 Su	10 12 33	4 36 49	0♑26 43	6♑52 33	28 41.4	27 38.0	15 43.1	9 52.6	17 01.4	29 37.5	11 51.2	19 57.6	20 19.8	23 30.0	28 40.6	2 43.3
24 M	10 16 30	5 37 13	13 24 19	20 02 14	28 38.2	27 35.2	17 33.0	10 07.5	17D 00.9	0♓01.0	11 55.0	20 04.8	20 22.6	23 31.2	28 42.8	2 45.0
25 Tu	10 20 26	6 37 36	26 46 25	3♒36 52	28 35.0	27 32.1	19 21.7	10 20.2	17 01.2	0 24.6	11 58.9	20 12.1	20 25.3	23 32.5	28 44.9	2 46.7
26 W	10 24 23	7 37 57	10♒33 25	17 35 45	28 31.9	27 29.0	21 08.9	10 30.8	17 02.3	0 48.1	12 03.0	20 19.4	20 28.1	23 33.9	28 47.0	2 48.3
27 Th	10 28 20	8 38 17	24 43 28	1♓55 57	28 28.7	27 26.5	22 54.2	10 39.2	17 04.0	1 11.6	12 07.3	20 26.7	20 30.9	23 35.3	28 49.2	2 50.0
28 F	10 32 16	9♓38 35	9♓12 30	16 32 21	28♓25.5	27♓24.9	24♓37.0	10♈45.2	17♋06.5	1♓35.1	12♊11.8	20♓34.0	20♈33.8	23♉36.7	28♓51.4	2♒51.6

1st of Month

Julian Day # 2460707.5
Obliquity 23°26'39"
SVP 4♓54'32"
GC 27♐11.4
Eris 24♈25.6

Day	⚴		⚵		⚶
1	24♑12.4		26♏42.0		10♏15.4
6	26 04.0		27 41.3		11 43.3
11	27 54.1		28 35.5		13 04.4
16	29 42.6		29 24.2		14 18.2
21	1♒29.3		0♐06.8		15 23.9
26	3 14.1		0 43.2		16 20.7

DECLINATION and LATITUDE

Day	☉ Decl	☽ Decl	☽ Lat	☽ 12h Decl	☿ Decl	☿ Lat	♀ Decl	♀ Lat	♂ Decl	♂ Lat	⚳ Decl	⚳ Lat	♃ Decl	♃ Lat	♄ Decl	♄ Lat
1 Sa	17S05	7S01	1S11	3S38	20S36	1S59	0N46	1N56	26N05	4N15	21S16	7S09	21N39	0S30	6S44	1S56
2 Su	16 48	0 11	0N06	3N15	20 12	2 01	1 13	2 05	26 07	4 15	21 09	7 10	21 39	0 29	6 42	1 55
3 M	16 31	6N39	1 23	9 57	19 47	2 03	1 39	2 14	26 09	4 14	21 01	7 10	21 39	0 29	6 39	1 55
4 Tu	16 13	13 07	2 34	16 06	19 20	2 04	2 06	2 23	26 10	4 12	20 54	7 11	21 39	0 29	6 37	1 55
5 W	15 55	18 52	3 35	21 21	18 52	2 05	2 32	2 33	26 11	4 11	20 47	7 11	21 39	0 29	6 34	1 55
6 Th	15 36	23 32	4 23	25 22	18 22	2 05	2 58	2 42	26 12	4 10	20 39	7 12	21 40	0 28	6 31	1 55
7 F	15 18	26 48	4 55	27 50	17 51	2 05	3 23	2 52	26 13	4 09	20 32	7 12	21 40	0 28	6 29	1 55
8 Sa	14 59	28 26	5 09	28 36	17 18	2 05	3 48	3 02	26 13	4 08	20 24	7 13	21 40	0 28	6 26	1 55
9 Su	14 40	28 20	5 06	27 39	16 44	2 04	4 13	3 11	26 14	4 06	20 17	7 13	21 41	0 28	6 23	1 55
10 M	14 20	26 34	4 47	25 08	16 09	2 02	4 37	3 21	26 14	4 05	20 09	7 14	21 41	0 28	6 20	1 55
11 Tu	14 01	23 23	4 12	21 21	15 32	2 00	5 01	3 31	26 14	4 03	20 02	7 14	21 41	0 27	6 18	1 55
12 W	13 41	19 04	3 25	16 36	14 53	1 58	5 25	3 42	26 14	4 02	19 54	7 15	21 42	0 27	6 15	1 55
13 Th	13 21	13 59	2 28	11 15	14 13	1 55	5 48	3 52	26 14	4 00	19 46	7 16	21 42	0 27	6 12	1 55
14 F	13 00	8 26	1 25	5 33	13 32	1 51	6 11	4 02	26 13	3 59	19 39	7 16	21 43	0 27	6 09	1 55
15 Sa	12 40	2 39	0 19	0S16	12 49	1 47	6 33	4 13	26 12	3 57	19 31	7 17	21 43	0 27	6 07	1 55
16 Su	12 19	3S09	0S47	5 59	12 06	1 43	6 54	4 23	26 12	3 56	19 23	7 17	21 44	0 26	6 04	1 55
17 M	11 58	8 46	1 50	11 27	11 20	1 38	7 15	4 34	26 11	3 54	19 16	7 18	21 44	0 26	6 01	1 55
18 Tu	11 37	14 02	2 48	16 29	10 34	1 32	7 35	4 45	26 10	3 52	19 08	7 19	21 45	0 26	5 58	1 55
19 W	11 16	18 48	3 39	20 56	9 46	1 25	7 55	4 55	26 09	3 51	19 00	7 19	21 45	0 26	5 55	1 55
20 Th	10 55	22 52	4 21	24 34	8 58	1 18	8 14	5 06	26 07	3 49	18 53	7 20	21 46	0 26	5 53	1 55
21 F	10 33	26 01	4 52	27 11	8 08	1 11	8 32	5 17	26 06	3 47	18 45	7 21	21 46	0 25	5 50	1 55
22 Sa	10 11	28 02	5 10	28 32	7 18	1 02	8 49	5 28	26 05	3 45	18 37	7 21	21 47	0 25	5 47	1 55
23 Su	9 49	28 41	5 14	28 26	6 27	0 53	9 06	5 39	26 03	3 44	18 29	7 22	21 48	0 25	5 44	1 55
24 M	9 27	27 47	5 03	26 44	5 35	0 44	9 22	5 50	26 01	3 42	18 21	7 23	21 48	0 25	5 41	1 55
25 Tu	9 05	25 18	4 35	23 28	4 43	0 33	9 37	6 00	25 59	3 40	18 14	7 23	21 49	0 25	5 38	1 55
26 W	8 42	21 17	3 51	18 46	3 51	0 22	9 51	6 11	25 57	3 38	18 06	7 24	21 50	0 24	5 35	1 55
27 Th	8 20	15 58	2 51	12 54	2 59	0 11	10 04	6 22	25 55	3 36	17 58	7 25	21 51	0 24	5 33	1 55
28 F	7S57	9S39	1S39	6S14	2S07	0N01	10N16	6N32	25N53	3N34	17S50	7S26	21N51	0S24	5S30	1S55

Day	⚷ Decl	⚷ Lat	♅ Decl	♅ Lat	♆ Decl	♆ Lat	♇ Decl	♇ Lat
1	8N26	0N52	18N21	0S15	1S58	1S16	22S56	3S19
6	8 29	0 52	18 22	0 14	1 55	1 16	22 54	3 19
11	8 33	0 51	18 22	0 14	1 51	1 16	22 52	3 20
16	8 37	0 51	18 23	0 14	1 47	1 16	22 51	3 20
21	8 41	0 50	18 25	0 14	1 43	1 16	22 49	3 21
26	8N46	0N50	18N26	0S14	1S39	1S16	22S48	3S22

Day	⚴ Decl	⚴ Lat	⚵ Decl	⚵ Lat	⚶ Decl	⚶ Lat	Eris Decl	Eris Lat
1	3N56	25N34	10S01	9N39	7S12	8N06	0S30	10S42
6	4 14	25 35	9 56	9 57	7 23	8 21	0 29	10 42
11	4 34	25 37	9 48	10 17	7 32	8 37	0 28	10 41
16	4 56	25 40	9 38	10 38	7 38	8 53	0 27	10 40
21	5 19	25 44	9 25	10 59	7 40	9 10	0 25	10 40
26	5N44	25N49	9S11	11N21	7S39	9N27	0S24	10S39

Moon Phenomena

Max/0 Decl

dy	hr mn	
2	0:39	0 N
8	10:31	28N36
15	10:56	0 S
22	22:25	28S41

Max/0 Lat

dy	hr mn	
1	22:06	0 N
8	7:42	5N10
15	6:56	0 S
22	18:43	5S15

Perigee/Apogee

dy	hr m		kilometers
2	2:48	p	367457
18	1:11	a	404882

PH	dy	hr mn	
☽	5	8:03	16♉46
○	12	13:55	24♌06
☾	20	17:34	2♐20
●	28	0:46	9♓41

Void of Course Moon

Last Aspect			☽ Ingress		
1 22:07	♀	☌	♈	2	1:11
3 10:21	♂	□	♉	4	3:35
6 3:31	♆	⚹	♊	6	6:45
8 7:53	♆	□	♋	8	11:05
10 13:51	♆	△	♌	10	17:02
12 19:13	☿	☍	♍	13	1:08
15 8:37	♆	☍	♎	15	11:46
17 23:25	☉	△	♏	18	0:20
20 10:07	♆	△	♐	20	12:56
22 20:40	♆	□	♑	22	23:10
25 3:29	♆	⚹	♒	25	5:41
26 22:06	♅	□	♓	27	8:48

DAILY ASPECTARIAN

1 Sa
☽∥♄ 1:00
☽∠♇ 3:32
☽☌♄ 4:11
☽⚺⚷ 7:38
☉∠♀ 7:51
☽△♂ 9:03
☽⚺⚳ 10:24
☽∠☿ 12:11
☽⚹♅ 13:55
☉∠♆ 14:33
♀☌♆ 16:34
☽∥♆ 17:49
☽⋕♀ 20:39
☽☌♆ 21:50
☽☌♀ 22:07
☊ D 22:07
☉∠☽ 22:22

2 Su
☽⚹♇ 4:41
☽∥♀ 5:13
☽⋕♆ 7:28
☽∠⚳ 12:12
☽∠♅ 15:01
☽⚹☿ 16:37
☽⚹♃ 20:05

3 M
☽⋕♄ 0:01
☉⚹☽ 1:24
☽∥⚷ 6:33
☽⚺♄ 6:48
☽☌⚷ 10:00
☽□♂ 10:21
☽⚹⚳ 14:05
♀⋕♆ 15:33
☽⚺♅ 16:13
☽∠♃ 21:18
☿△♃ 21:53

4 Tu
☽⚺♆ 0:17
♂□⚷ 2:46
☽⚺♀ 3:20
☽□♇ 7:14
♀ ♈ 7:58
☽∠♄ 8:18
♃ D 9:41
☉⋕☽ 11:51
☽∥♅ 21:43
☽⚺♃ 22:42
☿∠♆ 23:15

5 W
☽⋕☿ 0:01
☽∠♆ 1:47
☽□☿ 2:07
☽∠♀ 6:12
☊ R 7:56
☉□☽ 8:03
☽⋕⚳ 8:52
☽⚹♄ 10:00
☽⚹♂ 12:18
☽⚺⚷ 12:58
☽∥♃ 13:36
☽□⚳ 18:28
☽☌♅ 19:12
☽⋕♇ 20:20

6 Th
☿⋕♅ 0:30
☽⚹♆ 3:31
☽⚹♀ 9:18
☽△♇ 10:35
☽∠♂ 13:39
☉⚺♄ 14:11
☽∠⚷ 14:50
☽∥♂ 18:40
⚳□♅ 20:33

7 F
☽☌♃ 2:17
☿∠♀ 7:12
☉⚻♂ 8:43
♀⚹♇ 12:16
☽⚼♇ 12:42
☽△☿ 13:12
☽□♄ 14:16
☽⚺♂ 15:20
☉△☽ 15:58
☽⚹⚷ 17:00
☿⚺♄ 21:59
☽⚺♅ 23:16

8 Sa
☽△⚳ 0:03
☿⚻♂ 4:16
☉⚹⚷ 6:23
☽□♆ 7:53
☽⚻♇ 15:09
☽□♀ 16:29
☿⚹⚷ 19:22
☽⚼☿ 19:33
☉⚼☽ 20:33

9 Su
☽∠♅ 1:50
☽⚼⚳ 3:24
☽⚺♃ 7:13
☉☌☿ 12:09
♂△♄ 13:16
☽☌♂ 19:49
☽△♄ 19:58
☽□⚷ 22:28

10 M
☉⚻☽ 1:40
☽⚻☿ 2:34
☽∥♂ 3:06
☽⚹♅ 4:50
☽⚻⚳ 7:15
☽∠♃ 10:21
☽△♆ 13:51
☿□♅ 19:29
☽☍♇ 21:22
☽⚼♄ 23:32

11 Tu
☽△♀ 1:22
☽⋕♇ 3:08
☽∥♃ 10:03
☽⚹♃ 14:00
☽⚼♆ 17:36
☉□♅ 19:31
☽⋕⚳ 19:38
☿☌⚳ 21:32

12 W
☽⚺♂ 2:17
☽∥♅ 3:29
☽⚻♄ 3:40
☽△⚷ 5:57
☽⚼♀ 6:39
☽□♅ 12:27
☉☍☽ 13:55
☽☍⚳ 16:43
☽☍☿ 19:13
☽⚻♆ 21:57
☽⋕☿ 22:48

13 Th
☉⋕☽ 3:03
☽⚻♇ 5:48
☽∠♂ 6:26
☽⚼⚷ 10:36
☽⚻♀ 12:35
☿⚺♆ 14:31
♀⋕♄ 22:55
☽□♃ 23:11
☽∥⚷ 23:20

14 F
☽∥♀ 8:50
☽⋕♄ 9:34
☽⚼♇ 10:59
☽⚹♂ 11:15
☿ ♓ 12:08
☽☍♄ 13:54
☽⚻⚷ 15:55
☉☌⚳ 21:34
☽△♅ 22:36

15 Sa
☽⋕♆ 3:31
☽⚻⚳ 4:56
☉⚻☽ 5:21
☊ D 6:58
☽☍♆ 8:37
☉∥☿ 9:55
☽⚻☿ 16:02
☽△♇ 16:47
☽∥♆ 18:20
☿⚼♂ 20:08
☿⚺♇ 20:59

16 Su
☽☍♀ 2:20
☽⚼♅ 4:33
☽△♃ 10:53
☽⚼⚳ 11:59
☽∥♄ 12:14
☉⚼☽ 14:10
☽⋕♀ 17:00
⚴ ♒ 19:28
☉⚺♆ 21:39
☽□♂ 22:38
☽⋕⚷ 23:26

17 M
☽⚻♄ 2:31
☽⚼☿ 3:47
☽☍⚷ 4:11
☿∠⚷ 6:22
☽∥☿ 10:03
☽⚻♅ 10:55
☉∥☽ 13:29
☽⚼♃ 17:22
☽△⚳ 19:26
☽⚻♆ 21:17
☉△☽ 23:25

18 Tu
☽□♇ 5:35
☽⚼♄ 9:18
☉ ♓ 10:08
☽△☿ 15:56
♀∠♅ 16:12
☽⚻♀ 17:29
☽⋕♅ 21:53
☽⚻♃ 23:58

19 W
☽∥⚳ 1:06
☽⚼♆ 3:50
☿⚺♀ 4:03
☽△♂ 11:08
☽△♄ 16:00
☽⋕♃ 17:00
☽⚻⚷ 17:15
☽∥♇ 23:46
☽☍♅ 23:49

20 Th
☽⚼♀ 0:49
⚵ ♐ 3:32
⚳⚺♆ 8:21
☿⋕⚷ 8:25
☽△♆ 10:07
☽□⚳ 10:10
☉⚼♂ 12:01
☿⋕♀ 15:39
☽⚼♂ 17:05
☉□☽ 17:34
☊ R 17:47
☽⚹♇ 18:13
☿□♃ 20:15
☽⚼⚷ 23:20

21 F
☽⋕♂ 0:45
☉⚺♇ 1:36
☽△♀ 7:29
☽☍♃ 12:10
♀∥⚷ 13:18
☽□☿ 14:54
☽⚻♂ 22:26
☽∠♇ 23:41

22 Sa
☽□♄ 3:52
☽△⚷ 4:42
☽⚻♅ 10:49
☽□♆ 20:40
☽⚹⚳ 22:24

23 Su
☽⚺♇ 4:17
☉⚹☽ 8:28
⚳⋕♅ 11:47
☽⚼♅ 15:02
☿△♂ 16:59
☽□♀ 17:53
☉∠⚷ 17:54
☿∥♄ 21:06
☽⚻♃ 21:16
⚳ ♓ 22:56

24 M
♂ D 2:01
☿∠♇ 2:41
☽∠⚳ 3:01
☉⋕♀ 3:20
☽☍♂ 6:33
☽⚹☿ 8:43
☽⚹♄ 12:11
☽□⚷ 12:39
☉∠☽ 14:06
☽△♅ 18:15
☽⋕♂ 18:34

25 Tu
☽⚼♃ 0:22
☽⚹♆ 3:29
☽⚺⚳ 6:35
☽☌♇ 10:34
☿☌♄ 12:03
☿⚺⚷ 14:34
☽∠♄ 14:53
☽∠☿ 15:17
☽∥♇ 15:52
☉⚺☽ 18:34
☉⋕⚷ 20:27
☽⋕♃ 21:10
☽⚹♀ 23:56

26 W
☽△♃ 2:34
☽∠♆ 5:32
☽⚻♂ 11:04
☽⋕♅ 13:28
☽∥⚳ 15:21
☽⚺♄ 16:45
☽⚹⚷ 16:54
☽⚺☿ 20:31
☽□♅ 22:06

27 Th
☽∠♀ 1:34
☽⚺♆ 6:51
☿⚹♅ 9:39
☽☌⚳ 11:04
☽⚼♂ 12:15
☽⚺♇ 13:31
☽∠⚷ 17:59
☽⋕♀ 21:50
♄⚺⚷ 22:42

28 F
☉☌☽ 0:46
☽⚺♀ 2:33
☽⋕⚷ 3:01
☽□♃ 4:56
☉∥☽ 6:21
☽△♂ 12:58
☽∠♇ 14:11
☿∥♆ 14:29
☽∥♄ 14:38
☽⚺⚷ 18:37
☽☌♄ 18:43
☽⚹♅ 23:33

LONGITUDE

March 2025

Day	Sid.Time	☉	☽	☽ 12 hour	Mean☊	True☊	☿	♀	♂	⚳	♃	♄	⚷	♅	♆	♇
	h m s	° E "	° E "	° E "	° E	° E	° E	° E	° E	° E	° E	° E	° E	° E	° E	° E
1 Sa	10 36 13	10♓38 51	23♓54 35	1♈18 19	28♓22.3	27♓24.2	26♓17.0	10♈48.9	17♋09.7	1♓58.5	12♊16.4	20♓41.3	20♈36.6	23♉38.2	28♓53.5	2♒53.2
2 Su	10 40 09	11 39 05	8♈42 36	16 06 34	28 19.1	27D 24.4	27 53.6	10R 50.1	17 13.6	2 22.0	12 21.3	20 48.7	20 39.6	23 39.7	28 55.7	2 54.8
3 M	10 44 06	12 39 18	23 29 21	0♉50 11	28 16.0	27 25.2	29 26.1	10 49.0	17 18.2	2 45.4	12 26.3	20 56.0	20 42.5	23 41.3	28 57.9	2 56.4
4 Tu	10 48 02	13 39 28	8♉08 23	15 23 22	28 12.8	27 26.3	0♈54.1	10 45.3	17 23.5	3 08.8	12 31.5	21 03.4	20 45.5	23 42.9	29 00.1	2 57.9
5 W	10 51 59	14 39 37	22 34 42	29 42 01	28 09.6	27 27.3	2 17.0	10 39.2	17 29.4	3 32.2	12 36.8	21 10.8	20 48.5	23 44.6	29 02.3	2 59.5
6 Th	10 55 55	15 39 43	6♊45 04	13♊43 42	28 06.4	27R 27.9	3 34.2	10 30.5	17 36.0	3 55.6	12 42.3	21 18.1	20 51.5	23 46.3	29 04.6	3 01.0
7 F	10 59 52	16 39 47	20 37 51	27 27 32	28 03.2	27 28.0	4 45.1	10 19.3	17 43.3	4 19.0	12 48.0	21 25.5	20 54.6	23 48.1	29 06.8	3 02.5
8 Sa	11 03 49	17 39 49	4♋12 48	10♋53 45	28 00.1	27 27.6	5 49.2	10 05.6	17 51.1	4 42.3	12 53.9	21 32.9	20 57.7	23 49.9	29 09.0	3 04.0
9 Su	11 07 45	18 39 49	17 30 32	24 03 17	27 56.9	27 26.8	6 46.0	9 49.4	17 59.6	5 05.6	12 59.9	21 40.3	21 00.8	23 51.7	29 11.3	3 05.5
10 M	11 11 42	19 39 47	0♌32 12	6♌57 27	27 53.7	27 25.8	7 35.1	9 30.8	18 08.6	5 28.9	13 06.1	21 47.7	21 03.9	23 53.6	29 13.5	3 06.9
11 Tu	11 15 38	20 39 42	13 19 14	19 37 42	27 50.5	27 24.9	8 16.1	9 09.8	18 18.3	5 52.2	13 12.4	21 55.1	21 07.1	23 55.5	29 15.8	3 08.4
12 W	11 19 35	21 39 36	25 53 03	2♍05 28	27 47.4	27 24.1	8 48.8	8 46.4	18 28.5	6 15.4	13 18.9	22 02.6	21 10.3	23 57.5	29 18.0	3 09.8
13 Th	11 23 31	22 39 27	8♍15 08	14 22 13	27 44.2	27 23.5	9 12.9	8 20.9	18 39.3	6 38.6	13 25.5	22 10.0	21 13.5	23 59.6	29 20.3	3 11.1
14 F	11 27 28	23 39 16	20 26 55	26 29 27	27 41.0	27D 23.3	9 28.3	7 53.3	18 50.6	7 01.8	13 32.3	22 17.4	21 16.7	24 01.6	29 22.6	3 12.5
15 Sa	11 31 24	24 39 04	2♎30 01	8♎28 50	27 37.8	27 23.3	9R 35.0	7 23.8	19 02.5	7 25.0	13 39.3	22 24.8	21 20.0	24 03.7	29 24.8	3 13.9
16 Su	11 35 21	25 38 49	14 26 10	20 22 18	27 34.6	27 23.4	9 33.2	6 52.4	19 14.9	7 48.1	13 46.3	22 32.2	21 23.2	24 05.9	29 27.1	3 15.2
17 M	11 39 18	26 38 32	26 17 31	2♏12 10	27 31.5	27R 23.5	9 23.0	6 19.5	19 27.8	8 11.2	13 53.6	22 39.6	21 26.5	24 08.1	29 29.4	3 16.5
18 Tu	11 43 14	27 38 14	8♏06 35	14 01 12	27 28.3	27 23.5	9 04.9	5 45.3	19 41.2	8 34.3	14 01.0	22 47.0	21 29.8	24 10.3	29 31.6	3 17.8
19 W	11 47 11	28 37 54	19 56 24	25 52 39	27 25.1	27 23.4	8 39.4	5 09.8	19 55.1	8 57.4	14 08.5	22 54.3	21 33.2	24 12.6	29 33.9	3 19.0
20 Th	11 51 07	29 37 32	1♐50 27	7♐50 16	27 21.9	27 23.2	8 07.2	4 33.4	20 09.4	9 20.4	14 16.2	23 01.7	21 36.5	24 14.9	29 36.2	3 20.3
21 F	11 55 04	0♈37 09	13 52 40	19 58 09	27 18.8	27 22.9	7 29.0	3 56.3	20 24.3	9 43.4	14 24.0	23 09.1	21 39.9	24 17.2	29 38.5	3 21.5
22 Sa	11 59 00	1 36 43	26 07 17	2♑20 37	27 15.6	27D 22.8	6 45.7	3 18.7	20 39.6	10 06.3	14 31.9	23 16.5	21 43.3	24 19.6	29 40.7	3 22.7
23 Su	12 02 57	2 36 16	8♑38 40	15 01 56	27 12.4	27 22.8	5 58.3	2 40.9	20 55.3	10 29.2	14 40.0	23 23.8	21 46.7	24 22.0	29 43.0	3 23.8
24 M	12 06 53	3 35 47	21 30 53	28 05 55	27 09.2	27 23.1	5 08.0	2 03.2	21 11.5	10 52.1	14 48.3	23 31.2	21 50.1	24 24.5	29 45.3	3 25.0
25 Tu	12 10 50	4 35 17	4♒47 21	11♒35 24	27 06.1	27 23.6	4 15.8	1 25.8	21 28.2	11 15.0	14 56.6	23 38.5	21 53.6	24 27.0	29 47.6	3 26.1
26 W	12 14 47	5 34 45	18 30 11	25 31 39	27 02.9	27 24.3	3 22.8	0 48.9	21 45.2	11 37.8	15 05.1	23 45.8	21 57.0	24 29.5	29 49.8	3 27.2
27 Th	12 18 43	6 34 10	2♓39 37	9♓53 43	26 59.7	27 25.1	2 30.2	0 12.8	22 02.7	12 00.6	15 13.7	23 53.1	22 00.5	24 32.1	29 52.1	3 28.3
28 F	12 22 40	7 33 34	17 13 26	24 38 04	26 56.5	27R 25.6	1 39.0	29♓37.8	22 20.6	12 23.3	15 22.5	24 00.4	22 04.0	24 34.7	29 54.4	3 29.3
29 Sa	12 26 36	8 32 56	2♈06 45	9♈38 28	26 53.3	27 25.7	0 50.0	29 04.0	22 38.9	12 46.0	15 31.3	24 07.7	22 07.4	24 37.3	29 56.6	3 30.3
30 Su	12 30 33	9 32 16	17 12 08	24 46 34	26 50.2	27 25.2	0 04.2	28 31.6	22 57.5	13 08.6	15 40.3	24 14.9	22 10.9	24 40.0	29 58.9	3 31.3
31 M	12 34 29	10♈31 34	2♉20 34	9♉52 59	26♓47.0	27♓24.1	29♓22.3	28♓00.8	23♋16.6	13♓31.2	15♊49.4	24♓22.2	22♈14.5	24♉42.7	0♈01.1	3♒32.3

1st of Month

Julian Day # 2460735.5
Obliquity 23°26'09"
SVP 4♓54'28"
GC 27♐11.4
Eris 24♈35.7

Day	⚴
1	4♒16.0
6	5 57.2
11	7 36.0
16	9 12.2
21	10 45.6
26	12 15.9
31	13 43.0

Day	⚵
1	1♐01.7
6	1 26.9
11	1 44.6
16	1 54.7
21	1 56.7R
26	1 50.5R
31	1 35.8R

Day	⚶
1	16♏50.2
6	17 31.3
11	18 01.6
16	18 20.6
21	18 27.8
26	18 22.6R
31	18 04.9R

DECLINATION and LATITUDE

Day	☉ Decl	☽ Decl	☽ Lat	☽ 12h Decl	☿ Decl	☿ Lat	♀ Decl	♀ Lat	♂ Decl	♂ Lat	⚳ Decl	⚳ Lat	♃ Decl	♃ Lat	♄ Decl	♄ Lat
1 Sa	7S34	2S43	0S19	0N51	1S16	0N14	10N27	6N42	25N51	3N33	17S42	7S26	21N52	0S24	5S27	1S55
2 Su	7 12	4N24	1N02	7 54	0 26	0 27	10 36	6 53	25 49	3 31	17 34	7 27	21 53	0 24	5 24	1 55
3 M	6 49	11 17	2 19	14 30	0N23	0 40	10 45	7 02	25 46	3 29	17 27	7 28	21 54	0 23	5 21	1 55
4 Tu	6 26	17 29	3 27	20 12	1 11	0 54	10 53	7 12	25 44	3 27	17 19	7 29	21 55	0 23	5 18	1 55
5 W	6 02	22 36	4 20	24 39	1 57	1 08	10 59	7 21	25 41	3 25	17 11	7 30	21 56	0 23	5 15	1 55
6 Th	5 39	26 18	4 57	27 32	2 40	1 22	11 04	7 30	25 39	3 24	17 03	7 30	21 57	0 23	5 12	1 55
7 F	5 16	28 20	5 15	28 42	3 21	1 35	11 07	7 39	25 36	3 22	16 55	7 31	21 57	0 23	5 09	1 55
8 Sa	4 52	28 37	5 15	28 07	3 59	1 49	11 09	7 47	25 33	3 20	16 47	7 32	21 58	0 22	5 07	1 55
9 Su	4 29	27 13	4 58	25 57	4 34	2 03	11 10	7 55	25 30	3 18	16 39	7 33	21 59	0 22	5 04	1 55
10 M	4 06	24 21	4 26	22 29	5 05	2 16	11 09	8 02	25 27	3 16	16 31	7 34	22 00	0 22	5 01	1 55
11 Tu	3 42	20 21	3 41	18 00	5 33	2 29	11 06	8 09	25 24	3 15	16 24	7 35	22 01	0 22	4 58	1 55
12 W	3 18	15 30	2 46	12 51	5 57	2 40	11 03	8 14	25 21	3 13	16 16	7 36	22 02	0 22	4 55	1 55
13 Th	2 55	10 05	1 44	7 15	6 17	2 51	10 57	8 20	25 18	3 11	16 08	7 37	22 03	0 22	4 52	1 55
14 F	2 31	4 22	0 38	1 28	6 32	3 01	10 50	8 24	25 14	3 09	15 60	7 38	22 04	0 21	4 49	1 55
15 Sa	2 08	1S26	0S28	4S18	6 43	3 10	10 42	8 28	25 11	3 08	15 52	7 38	22 05	0 21	4 46	1 55
16 Su	1 44	7 07	1 33	9 53	6 49	3 18	10 32	8 31	25 07	3 06	15 44	7 39	22 06	0 21	4 43	1 55
17 M	1 20	12 32	2 34	15 05	6 50	3 24	10 21	8 33	25 04	3 04	15 36	7 40	22 07	0 21	4 41	1 55
18 Tu	0 56	17 29	3 27	19 43	6 47	3 28	10 08	8 34	25 00	3 02	15 28	7 41	22 08	0 21	4 38	1 55
19 W	0 33	21 46	4 12	23 37	6 40	3 31	9 54	8 34	24 56	3 01	15 21	7 42	22 09	0 21	4 35	1 55
20 Th	0 09	25 12	4 47	26 32	6 28	3 32	9 39	8 33	24 53	2 59	15 13	7 43	22 10	0 20	4 32	1 55
21 F	0N15	27 34	5 09	28 17	6 12	3 31	9 23	8 31	24 49	2 57	15 05	7 44	22 12	0 20	4 29	1 55
22 Sa	0 38	28 40	5 17	28 41	5 52	3 28	9 05	8 29	24 45	2 56	14 57	7 46	22 13	0 20	4 26	1 55
23 Su	1 02	28 20	5 11	27 36	5 29	3 24	8 47	8 25	24 41	2 54	14 49	7 47	22 14	0 20	4 23	1 55
24 M	1 26	26 29	4 50	24 60	5 03	3 17	8 28	8 20	24 36	2 52	14 41	7 48	22 15	0 20	4 20	1 56
25 Tu	1 49	23 09	4 12	20 57	4 35	3 09	8 08	8 15	24 32	2 51	14 34	7 49	22 16	0 20	4 18	1 56
26 W	2 13	18 27	3 20	15 39	4 05	2 59	7 47	8 08	24 28	2 49	14 26	7 50	22 17	0 19	4 15	1 56
27 Th	2 36	12 36	2 13	9 20	3 34	2 48	7 26	8 01	24 23	2 48	14 18	7 51	22 18	0 19	4 12	1 56
28 F	2 60	5 55	0 56	2 22	3 02	2 36	7 05	7 53	24 19	2 46	14 10	7 52	22 19	0 19	4 09	1 56
29 Sa	3 23	1N14	0N26	4N51	2 30	2 22	6 44	7 44	24 14	2 44	14 03	7 53	22 20	0 19	4 06	1 56
30 Su	3 47	8 25	1 47	11 51	1 59	2 08	6 22	7 35	24 10	2 43	13 55	7 54	22 21	0 19	4 04	1 56
31 M	4N10	15N08	3N02	18N10	1N28	1N52	6N00	7N25	24N05	2N41	13S47	7S56	22N23	0S19	4S01	1S56

Day	⚷ Decl	⚷ Lat	♅ Decl	♅ Lat	♆ Decl	♆ Lat	♇ Decl	♇ Lat
1	8N49	0N49	18N27	0S14	1S36	1S16	22S47	3S22
6	8 54	0 49	18 30	0 14	1 32	1 16	22 46	3 23
11	8 59	0 49	18 32	0 14	1 27	1 16	22 45	3 24
16	9 05	0 48	18 35	0 14	1 23	1 16	22 44	3 24
21	9 11	0 48	18 37	0 14	1 18	1 16	22 44	3 25
26	9 17	0 47	18 41	0 13	1 14	1 16	22 43	3 26
31	9N23	0N47	18N44	0S13	1S09	1S16	22S43	3S27

Day	⚴ Decl	⚴ Lat	⚵ Decl	⚵ Lat	⚶ Decl	⚶ Lat	Eris Decl	Eris Lat
1	6N00	25N52	9S01	11N35	7S37	9N38	0S23	10S39
6	6 28	25 59	8 43	11 58	7 31	9 56	0 22	10 38
11	6 57	26 07	8 22	12 22	7 22	10 13	0 20	10 38
16	7 27	26 16	8 00	12 47	7 11	10 30	0 19	10 37
21	7 59	26 27	7 36	13 12	6 56	10 47	0 17	10 37
26	8 31	26 38	7 10	13 37	6 40	11 03	0 16	10 36
31	9N05	26N51	6S43	14N02	6S21	11N17	0S15	10S36

Moon Phenomena

Max/0 Decl

dy hr mn	
1 9:09	0 N
7 15:44	28N43
14 18:05	0 S
22 6:39	28S43
28 19:54	0 N

Max/0 Lat

dy hr mn	
1 5:40	0 N
7 12:01	5N17
14 13:47	0 S
22 2:26	5S17
28 16:29	0 N

Perigee/Apogee

dy hr m		kilometers
1 21:23	p	361965
17 16:38	a	405753
30 5:26	p	358131

PH	dy hr mn	
☽	6 16:33	16♊21
○	14 6:56	23♍57
●	14 7:00	T 1.179
☾	22 11:31	2♑05
●	29 10:59	9♈00
●	29 10:48:35	P 0.938

Void of Course Moon

Last Aspect			☽ Ingress		
1 8:06	♆	☌	♈	1	9:53
2 13:53	♂	□	♉	3	10:38
5 10:55	♆	⚹	♊	5	12:30
7 14:58	♆	□	♋	7	16:30
9 21:33	♆	△	♌	9	23:00
11 20:17	♅	□	♍	12	7:57
14 17:49	♆	☍	♎	14	19:00
16 9:54	♂	□	♏	17	7:32
19 19:29	♆	△	♐	19	20:18
22 6:54	♆	□	♑	22	7:30
24 15:02	♆	⚹	♒	24	15:26
26 10:16	♅	□	♓	26	19:33
28 20:31	♆	☌	♈	28	20:37
30 9:19	♂	□	♉	30	20:17

DAILY ASPECTARIAN

1 Sa
☽ ∥ ♆ 3:46
☉ ⚺ ♀ 4:09
☽ ☌ ☿ 4:20
☽ ∥ ☿ 5:32
☊ D 5:44
☽ ☌ ♆ 8:06
☽ ⋕ ☿ 11:59
☽ ⚺ ⚳ 13:26
♂ ⚼ ⚳ 13:40
☽ ⋕ ♆ 14:29
☽ ⚹ ♇ 14:35
☽ ∠ ♅ 23:55

2 Su
♀ R 0:37
☽ ⋕ ♄ 3:21
☽ ☌ ♀ 3:27
☉ ⚺ ☽ 5:07
☽ ⚹ ♃ 5:56
☉ ⋕ ☽ 9:03
☽ □ ♂ 13:53
☽ ∠ ⚳ 14:25
☽ ∥ ⚷ 15:17
☿ ☌ ♆ 16:23
☉ □ ♃ 18:20
☽ ☌ ⚷ 19:27
☽ ⚺ ♄ 19:48
☽ ∥ ♀ 22:03

3 M
☽ ⚺ ♅ 0:19
☽ ∠ ♃ 6:29
☉ ∠ ☽ 7:18
☽ ⚺ ♆ 8:58
☿ ♈ 9:05
☽ ⚺ ☿ 10:48
⚳ ⚺ ♇ 12:02
☽ □ ♇ 15:29
☽ ⚹ ⚳ 15:34
☽ ∠ ♄ 20:32
☽ ⋕ ⚳ 23:18

4 Tu
☽ ∥ ♅ 4:15
☽ ⚺ ♀ 4:18
☽ ⚺ ♃ 7:17
☽ ∠ ♆ 9:43
☉ ⚹ ☽ 9:48
☿ ⋕ ♆ 11:27
☽ ∠ ☿ 14:14
☽ ⚹ ♂ 15:26
☽ ∥ ♃ 20:26
☽ ⚺ ⚷ 21:01
☽ ⚹ ♄ 21:38

5 W
☽ ⋕ ♇ 0:55
☽ ☌ ♅ 1:58
☽ ∠ ♀ 5:07
☽ ⚹ ♆ 10:55
☿ ⚹ ♇ 13:14
☽ ∠ ♂ 16:52
☽ △ ♇ 17:37
☽ ⚹ ☿ 18:03
☽ ∥ ♂ 18:56
☽ □ ⚳ 19:03
☽ ∠ ⚷ 22:28

6 Th
☽ ⚹ ♀ 6:22
☽ ☌ ♃ 10:18
☿ ⚺ ⚳ 10:25
☉ □ ☽ 16:33
☊ R 16:42
☽ ⚺ ♂ 18:53
☽ ⚼ ♇ 19:29

7 F
☽ ⚹ ⚷ 0:29
☽ □ ♄ 1:24
☽ ⚺ ♅ 5:34
☉ ∥ ♄ 7:33
☽ □ ♆ 14:58
☽ ⚻ ♇ 21:57

8 Sa
☽ △ ⚳ 0:54
☽ □ ☿ 3:06
☉ △ ♂ 5:14
☽ ∠ ♅ 8:18
☉ ∠ ♇ 9:55
☽ □ ♀ 10:21
☽ ⚺ ♃ 15:44
☉ ⋕ ☿ 21:56

9 Su
☽ ☌ ♂ 0:54
☉ △ ☽ 2:17
☽ ⚼ ⚳ 4:52
☽ □ ⚷ 6:26
☽ △ ♄ 7:41
☽ ⚹ ♅ 11:40
☽ ∥ ♂ 15:52
☽ ∠ ♃ 19:26
☿ ⋕ ♄ 20:34
☽ △ ♆ 21:33

10 M
☽ ☍ ♇ 4:49
☉ ⚼ ☽ 8:21
☽ ⚻ ⚳ 9:31
☽ ⋕ ♇ 10:20
☽ ⚼ ♄ 11:49
☽ △ ☿ 13:57
☽ ∥ ♃ 14:44
☽ △ ♀ 16:22
☽ ⚹ ♃ 23:47

11 Tu
☽ ⚼ ♆ 1:48
☽ ∥ ♅ 9:23
☽ ⚺ ♂ 9:36
☉ ⚺ ⚷ 11:35
♀ ∠ ♅ 13:44
☽ △ ⚷ 14:55
☉ ⚻ ☽ 15:11
☽ ⚻ ♄ 16:33
⚳ ∠ ⚷ 17:49
☽ ⚼ ☿ 19:51
☽ ⚼ ♀ 20:04
☽ □ ♅ 20:17
☽ ⋕ ⚳ 20:20
☿ ☌ ♀ 22:56

12 W
☽ ⚻ ♆ 6:37
☿ ∠ ♅ 8:27
☉ ☌ ♄ 10:30
☽ ⚻ ♇ 14:06
☽ ∠ ♂ 14:54
☽ ⚼ ⚷ 20:01
☽ ∥ ♀ 20:12
☽ ☍ ⚳ 20:45

13 Th
☽ ⚻ ♀ 0:11
☽ ⚻ ☿ 1:56
☽ ∥ ⚷ 4:30
☽ □ ♃ 10:14
☽ ∥ ☿ 15:22
☽ ⚼ ♇ 19:34
☽ ⚹ ♂ 20:46
☽ ⋕ ♄ 22:08

14 F
☽ ⚻ ⚷ 1:39
☽ ☍ ♄ 3:41
☉ ☍ ☽ 6:56
☽ △ ♅ 7:07
☉ ⋕ ☽ 8:14
☉ ⚹ ♅ 9:18
☽ ⋕ ♆ 12:18
☊ D 14:08
☽ ☍ ♆ 17:49
♀ ⚺ ⚳ 23:27
☽ ∥ ♆ 23:51

15 Sa
☽ △ ♇ 1:28
☉ ∥ ☽ 2:43
☿ R 6:47
☽ ☍ ♀ 9:25
☽ ⚻ ⚳ 10:11
☽ ⚼ ♅ 13:13
☽ ∥ ♄ 13:52
☽ ☍ ☿ 14:13
☽ △ ♃ 22:39
☽ ⋕ ☿ 22:39

16 Su
☽ ⋕ ⚷ 8:32
☽ □ ♂ 9:54
☽ ☍ ⚷ 14:07
☽ ⋕ ♀ 14:26
☽ ⚻ ♄ 16:33
☽ ⚼ ⚳ 17:30
☽ ⚻ ♅ 19:37
☉ ∥ ♆ 22:22

17 M
☉ ⚻ ☽ 0:47
☽ ⚼ ♃ 5:20
☽ ⚻ ♆ 6:31
☽ ∥ ⚳ 14:11
☽ □ ♇ 14:12
☊ R 17:33
☿ ∠ ♅ 18:29
☽ ⚻ ♀ 19:26
☽ ⚼ ♄ 23:20

18 Tu
☽ △ ⚳ 0:58
☽ ⚻ ☿ 1:55
☽ ⋕ ♅ 5:52
☉ ⚼ ☽ 10:02
☽ ⚻ ♃ 12:07
☽ ⚼ ♆ 13:04
☿ ⚺ ⚳ 15:32
☽ △ ♂ 23:57

19 W
☽ ⚼ ♀ 0:26
☽ ⋕ ♃ 2:25
☽ ⚻ ⚷ 3:17
☽ △ ♄ 6:04
☽ ∥ ♇ 6:05
☽ ⚼ ☿ 7:13
☽ ☍ ♅ 8:40
⚵ R 18:01
☉ △ ☽ 19:09
☽ △ ♆ 19:29
☽ ⋕ ♂ 21:25
☉ ☌ ♆ 23:26

20 Th
☽ ⚹ ♇ 3:00
☽ △ ♀ 5:11
☽ ⚼ ♂ 6:47
☉ ♈ 9:03
☽ ⚼ ⚷ 9:36
☽ △ ☿ 11:57
☽ □ ⚳ 15:29

21 F
☽ ☍ ♃ 1:03
☽ ∠ ♇ 8:51
⚶ R 10:12
☽ ⚻ ♂ 13:08
♀ ∥ ⚷ 15:22
☽ △ ⚷ 15:23
☽ □ ♄ 18:24
☽ ⚻ ♅ 20:30
♀ ⚹ ♇ 21:33

22 Sa
☽ □ ♆ 6:54
☊ D 11:09
☉ □ ☽ 11:31
☽ □ ♀ 13:11
☽ ⚺ ♇ 14:00
☽ □ ☿ 19:14

23 Su
☉ ☌ ♀ 1:09
☽ ⚼ ♅ 1:22
☽ ⚹ ⚳ 3:35
☽ ⚻ ♃ 11:26
☉ ⋕ ♆ 13:49
☉ ⚹ ♇ 19:33
☽ ☍ ♂ 23:24

24 M
☽ □ ⚷ 0:35
☽ ⚹ ♄ 3:42
☽ △ ♅ 5:19
☽ ∠ ⚳ 8:12
☽ ⋕ ♂ 15:01
☽ ⚹ ♆ 15:02
☽ ⚼ ♃ 15:14
☽ ⚹ ♀ 18:16
☉ ☌ ☿ 19:49
☽ ☌ ♇ 21:35
☽ ⚹ ☿ 23:07
☉ ⚹ ☽ 23:37

25 Tu
☽ ∥ ♇ 2:29
☽ ⋕ ♃ 5:01
☽ ∠ ♄ 6:53
☽ ⚺ ⚳ 11:44
☿ ⋕ ♄ 15:40
☽ ∠ ♆ 17:38
☽ △ ♃ 18:02
☽ ∠ ♀ 19:33
☿ ⚹ ♇ 22:03
☽ ⋕ ♅ 22:57
☽ ∠ ☿ 23:48

26 W
☉ ∠ ☽ 3:50
☽ ⚻ ♂ 5:42
☽ ⚹ ⚷ 5:56
☽ ⚺ ♄ 9:05
☽ □ ♅ 10:16
☽ ∥ ⚳ 17:15
☽ ⚺ ♆ 19:19
☽ ⚺ ♀ 20:04
♂ □ ⚷ 20:14
☽ ⚺ ☿ 23:45

27 Th
☽ ⚺ ♇ 1:21
☉ ⚺ ☽ 6:59
☽ ∠ ⚷ 7:15
☽ ⚼ ♂ 7:27
♀ R ♓ 8:42
☽ ⋕ ⚷ 12:05
♀ ☌ ♆ 13:15
☽ ☌ ⚳ 15:53
☽ ⋕ ♀ 19:43
☽ □ ♃ 20:57

28 F
☉ ∥ ☿ 0:56
☽ ∠ ♇ 2:03
☽ ∥ ♄ 6:02
☽ ⚺ ⚷ 7:53
☽ △ ♂ 8:28
☉ ⋕ ☽ 9:22
☽ ⋕ ☿ 10:33
☽ ☌ ♄ 11:05
☽ ⚹ ♅ 11:57
☽ ∥ ♆ 15:57
☊ R 16:23
☽ ☌ ♀ 19:18
☽ ☌ ♆ 20:31
☽ ☌ ☿ 22:03
☽ ⋕ ♆ 23:49

29 Sa
☽ ⚹ ♇ 2:14
☽ ∥ ☿ 3:55
☉ ∥ ☽ 7:33
☽ ⋕ ♄ 9:27
☉ ☌ ☽ 10:59
☽ ∠ ♅ 12:00
☽ ⚺ ⚳ 17:24
☽ ∥ ♀ 17:25
☽ ⚹ ♃ 21:33

30 Su
☿ R ♓ 2:19
☿ ☌ ♆ 2:48
☉ ∠ ♅ 3:16
☽ ∥ ⚷ 3:17
☽ ☌ ⚷ 7:55
☽ □ ♂ 9:19
☽ ⚺ ♄ 11:15
☽ ⚺ ♅ 11:52
♆ ♈ 12:01
☉ ⋕ ♄ 15:28
☽ ⚺ ♀ 17:21
☽ ∠ ⚳ 17:47
☽ ⋕ ⚳ 19:05
☽ ⚺ ☿ 19:29
☽ ⚺ ♆ 20:18
☽ ∠ ♃ 21:34

31 M
☽ □ ♇ 1:54
☽ ∠ ♄ 11:16
☉ ⚺ ☽ 13:57
☽ ∥ ♅ 14:26
☿ ⋕ ♆ 15:59
☽ ∠ ♀ 16:28
☽ ⚹ ⚳ 18:16
☽ ∠ ☿ 18:24
☽ ∠ ♆ 20:16
☽ ⚺ ♃ 21:44

April 2025

LONGITUDE

Day	Sid.Time	☉	☽	☽ 12 hour	Mean☊	True☊	☿	♀	♂	⚳	♃	♄	⚷	♅	♆	♇
	h m s	° E "	° E "	° E "	° E	° E	° E	° E	° E	° E	° E	° E	° E	° E	° E	° E
1 Tu	12 38 26	11 ♈ 30 50	17 ♉ 22 43	24 ♉ 48 45	26 ♓ 43.8	27 ♓ 22.4	28 ♓ 44.8	27 ♓ 31.8	23 ♋ 36.0	13 ♓ 53.8	15 ♊ 58.7	24 ♓ 29.4	22 ♈ 18.0	24 ♉ 45.4	0 ♈ 03.4	3 ♒ 33.2
2 W	12 42 22	12 30 03	2 ♊ 10 15	9 ♊ 26 32	26 40.6	27R 20.6	28R 12.2	27R 04.7	23 55.8	14 16.3	16 08.0	24 36.6	22 21.5	24 48.2	0 05.6	3 34.1
3 Th	12 46 19	13 29 15	16 37 05	23 41 32	26 37.5	27 18.9	27 44.7	26 39.7	24 16.0	14 38.8	16 17.5	24 43.7	22 25.0	24 51.0	0 07.8	3 35.0
4 F	12 50 15	14 28 24	0 ♋ 39 42	7 ♋ 31 35	26 34.3	27 17.7	27 22.7	26 16.8	24 36.5	15 01.2	16 27.1	24 50.9	22 28.6	24 53.8	0 10.1	3 35.9
5 Sa	12 54 12	15 27 31	14 17 14	20 56 53	26 31.1	27D 17.2	27 06.3	25 56.2	24 57.3	15 23.6	16 36.8	24 58.0	22 32.1	24 56.6	0 12.3	3 36.7
6 Su	12 58 09	16 26 35	27 30 48	3 ♌ 59 22	26 27.9	27 17.5	26 55.5	25 37.8	25 18.5	15 45.9	16 46.6	25 05.1	22 35.7	24 59.5	0 14.5	3 37.6
7 M	13 02 05	17 25 37	10 ♌ 22 57	16 41 58	26 24.7	27 18.6	26D 50.2	25 21.9	25 40.0	16 08.2	16 56.5	25 12.1	22 39.3	25 02.4	0 16.7	3 38.3
8 Tu	13 06 02	18 24 37	22 56 54	29 08 09	26 21.6	27 20.1	26 50.4	25 08.4	26 01.8	16 30.4	17 06.5	25 19.2	22 42.8	25 05.4	0 18.9	3 39.1
9 W	13 09 58	19 23 34	5 ♍ 16 09	11 ♍ 21 19	26 18.4	27 21.7	26 55.9	24 57.3	26 23.9	16 52.6	17 16.6	25 26.2	22 46.4	25 08.3	0 21.1	3 39.8
10 Th	13 13 55	20 22 29	17 24 04	23 24 44	26 15.2	27R 22.8	27 06.6	24 48.7	26 46.3	17 14.7	17 26.8	25 33.2	22 50.0	25 11.3	0 23.2	3 40.5
11 F	13 17 51	21 21 22	29 23 42	5 ♎ 21 15	26 12.0	27 23.2	27 22.4	24 42.5	27 09.0	17 36.7	17 37.2	25 40.1	22 53.5	25 14.3	0 25.4	3 41.2
12 Sa	13 21 48	22 20 13	11 ♎ 17 43	17 13 22	26 08.9	27 22.3	27 42.9	24 38.8	27 32.0	17 58.7	17 47.6	25 47.0	22 57.1	25 17.4	0 27.5	3 41.9
13 Su	13 25 44	23 19 02	23 08 27	29 03 14	26 05.7	27 20.2	28 08.1	24D 37.5	27 55.2	18 20.7	17 58.1	25 53.9	23 00.7	25 20.4	0 29.7	3 42.5
14 M	13 29 41	24 17 49	4 ♏ 57 58	10 ♏ 52 53	26 02.5	27 16.8	28 37.6	24 38.6	28 18.8	18 42.6	18 08.7	26 00.7	23 04.2	25 23.5	0 31.8	3 43.1
15 Tu	13 33 38	25 16 34	16 48 14	22 44 17	25 59.3	27 12.4	29 11.4	24 42.0	28 42.6	19 04.4	18 19.4	26 07.5	23 07.8	25 26.6	0 33.9	3 43.7
16 W	13 37 34	26 15 17	28 41 18	4 ♐ 39 34	25 56.1	27 07.3	29 49.2	24 47.7	29 06.6	19 26.2	18 30.2	26 14.3	23 11.4	25 29.8	0 36.0	3 44.2
17 Th	13 41 31	27 13 59	10 ♐ 39 24	16 41 09	25 53.0	27 02.1	0 ♈ 30.8	24 55.7	29 30.9	19 47.9	18 41.1	26 21.1	23 15.0	25 32.9	0 38.1	3 44.7
18 F	13 45 27	28 12 39	22 45 10	28 51 50	25 49.8	26 57.4	1 16.1	25 05.9	29 55.5	20 09.5	18 52.1	26 27.8	23 18.5	25 36.1	0 40.2	3 45.2
19 Sa	13 49 24	29 11 17	5 ♑ 01 34	11 ♑ 14 49	25 46.6	26 53.8	2 04.8	25 18.2	0 ♌ 20.3	20 31.1	19 03.1	26 34.4	23 22.1	25 39.3	0 42.3	3 45.7
20 Su	13 53 20	0 ♉ 09 53	17 32 00	23 53 37	25 43.4	26 51.5	2 56.8	25 32.6	0 45.4	20 52.6	19 14.3	26 41.0	23 25.6	25 42.5	0 44.3	3 46.1
21 M	13 57 17	1 08 28	0 ♒ 20 05	6 ♒ 51 51	25 40.3	26D 50.7	3 51.9	25 49.0	1 10.6	21 14.1	19 25.5	26 47.6	23 29.2	25 45.8	0 46.3	3 46.5
22 Tu	14 01 13	2 07 01	13 29 20	20 12 52	25 37.1	26 51.2	4 50.1	26 07.4	1 36.2	21 35.5	19 36.8	26 54.2	23 32.8	25 49.0	0 48.4	3 46.9
23 W	14 05 10	3 05 32	27 02 46	3 ♓ 59 11	25 33.9	26 52.5	5 51.1	26 27.6	2 01.9	21 56.8	19 48.2	27 00.7	23 36.3	25 52.3	0 50.4	3 47.2
24 Th	14 09 07	4 04 02	11 ♓ 02 13	18 11 46	25 30.7	26 53.9	6 54.9	26 49.7	2 27.9	22 18.1	19 59.7	27 07.1	23 39.8	25 55.6	0 52.3	3 47.5
25 F	14 13 03	5 02 30	25 27 36	2 ♈ 49 17	25 27.5	26R 54.6	8 01.3	27 13.5	2 54.1	22 39.3	20 11.3	27 13.5	23 43.4	25 58.9	0 54.3	3 47.8
26 Sa	14 17 00	6 00 56	10 ♈ 16 11	17 47 31	25 24.4	26 54.0	9 10.3	27 38.9	3 20.5	23 00.4	20 22.9	27 19.9	23 46.9	26 02.2	0 56.3	3 48.1
27 Su	14 20 56	6 59 21	25 22 14	2 ♉ 59 13	25 21.2	26 51.5	10 21.8	28 06.0	3 47.1	23 21.4	20 34.6	27 26.2	23 50.4	26 05.6	0 58.2	3 48.3
28 M	14 24 53	7 57 44	10 ♉ 37 11	18 14 47	25 18.0	26 47.2	11 35.6	28 34.7	4 13.9	23 42.4	20 46.4	27 32.4	23 53.9	26 08.9	1 00.1	3 48.5
29 Tu	14 28 49	8 56 05	25 50 42	3 ♊ 23 39	25 14.8	26 41.4	12 51.8	29 04.8	4 40.9	24 03.3	20 58.3	27 38.6	23 57.4	26 12.3	1 02.0	3 48.7
30 W	14 32 46	9 ♉ 54 25	10 ♊ 52 25	18 16 01	25 ♓ 11.7	26 ♓ 35.0	14 ♈ 10.2	29 ♓ 36.4	5 ♌ 08.1	24 ♓ 24.1	21 ♊ 10.2	27 ♓ 44.8	24 ♈ 00.8	26 ♉ 15.7	1 ♈ 03.9	3 ♒ 48.8

1st of Month

Julian Day #
2460766.5
Obliquity
23°26E9"
SVP 4♓54E25"
GC 27♐11.5
Eris 24♈53.5

Day	⚴
1	13♒59.9
6	15 22.6
11	16 41.4
16	17 55.9
21	19 06.0
26	20 11.2

Day	⚵
1	1♐31.9R
6	1 07.1R
11	0 34.2R
16	29♏53.6R
21	29 05.9R
26	28 11.7R

Day	⚶
1	17♏59.9R
6	17 27.6R
11	16 43.9R
16	15 50.0R
21	14 47.5R
26	13 38.4R

DECLINATION and LATITUDE

Day	☉ Decl	☽ Decl	☽ Lat	☽12h Decl	☿ Decl	☿ Lat	♀ Decl	♀ Lat	♂ Decl	♂ Lat	⚳ Decl	⚳ Lat	♃ Decl	♃ Lat	♄ Decl	♄ Lat
1 Tu	4N33	20N54	4N03	23N17	0N59	1N37	5N39	7N14	24N00	2N40	13S39	7S57	22N24	0S18	3S58	1S56
2 W	4 56	25 16	4 46	26 49	0 31	1 21	5 18	7 03	23 55	2 38	13 32	7 58	22 25	0 18	3 55	1 56
3 Th	5 19	27 55	5 11	28 32	0 06	1 05	4 57	6 51	23 50	2 37	13 24	7 59	22 26	0 18	3 52	1 56
4 F	5 42	28 42	5 16	28 24	0S18	0 49	4 37	6 39	23 45	2 35	13 16	8 00	22 27	0 18	3 50	1 56
5 Sa	6 05	27 41	5 02	26 35	0 39	0 33	4 18	6 26	23 40	2 34	13 09	8 02	22 28	0 18	3 47	1 57
6 Su	6 28	25 07	4 33	23 22	0 57	0 18	3 59	6 13	23 34	2 32	13 01	8 03	22 29	0 18	3 44	1 57
7 M	6 51	21 21	3 51	19 06	1 13	0 03	3 40	6 00	23 29	2 31	12 54	8 04	22 30	0 18	3 42	1 57
8 Tu	7 13	16 41	2 59	14 07	1 26	0S12	3 23	5 47	23 23	2 30	12 46	8 06	22 32	0 17	3 39	1 57
9 W	7 35	11 25	1 59	8 39	1 37	0 26	3 06	5 34	23 18	2 28	12 39	8 07	22 33	0 17	3 36	1 57
10 Th	7 58	5 49	0 55	2 57	1 45	0 40	2 50	5 20	23 12	2 27	12 31	8 08	22 34	0 17	3 34	1 57
11 F	8 20	0 04	0S11	2S48	1 51	0 53	2 36	5 07	23 06	2 25	12 24	8 10	22 35	0 17	3 31	1 57
12 Sa	8 42	5S38	1 16	8 25	1 54	1 05	2 22	4 53	23 00	2 24	12 16	8 11	22 36	0 17	3 28	1 57
13 Su	9 04	11 07	2 17	13 43	1 55	1 17	2 09	4 40	22 54	2 23	12 09	8 12	22 37	0 17	3 26	1 57
14 M	9 25	16 11	3 12	18 31	1 53	1 28	1 57	4 26	22 48	2 21	12 02	8 14	22 38	0 17	3 23	1 58
15 Tu	9 47	20 40	3 59	22 37	1 49	1 38	1 46	4 13	22 42	2 20	11 54	8 15	22 39	0 16	3 20	1 58
16 W	10 08	24 20	4 35	25 48	1 43	1 47	1 36	3 60	22 36	2 18	11 47	8 17	22 40	0 16	3 18	1 58
17 Th	10 29	26 59	4 60	27 52	1 35	1 56	1 27	3 47	22 29	2 17	11 40	8 18	22 41	0 16	3 15	1 58
18 F	10 50	28 25	5 11	28 38	1 24	2 05	1 19	3 34	22 23	2 16	11 33	8 19	22 42	0 16	3 13	1 58
19 Sa	11 11	28 30	5 09	27 59	1 12	2 12	1 13	3 21	22 16	2 15	11 25	8 21	22 43	0 16	3 10	1 58
20 Su	11 32	27 07	4 52	25 54	0 57	2 19	1 07	3 09	22 09	2 13	11 18	8 22	22 44	0 16	3 08	1 58
21 M	11 52	24 19	4 21	22 25	0 41	2 25	1 02	2 56	22 02	2 12	11 11	8 24	22 46	0 16	3 05	1 59
22 Tu	12 13	20 12	3 35	17 42	0 23	2 31	0 58	2 44	21 56	2 11	11 04	8 25	22 47	0 15	3 03	1 59
23 W	12 33	14 56	2 36	11 56	0 04	2 36	0 55	2 32	21 49	2 09	10 57	8 27	22 48	0 15	3 00	1 59
24 Th	12 52	8 45	1 25	5 24	0N18	2 40	0 53	2 21	21 41	2 08	10 50	8 29	22 49	0 15	2 58	1 59
25 F	13 12	1 56	0 08	1N37	0 40	2 44	0 52	2 09	21 34	2 07	10 43	8 30	22 50	0 15	2 55	1 59
26 Sa	13 32	5N10	1N12	8 42	1 05	2 47	0 52	1 58	21 27	2 06	10 36	8 32	22 51	0 15	2 53	1 59
27 Su	13 51	12 07	2 28	15 23	1 31	2 49	0 53	1 47	21 19	2 05	10 29	8 33	22 51	0 15	2 51	1 59
28 M	14 10	18 24	3 35	21 08	1 58	2 51	0 54	1 36	21 12	2 03	10 22	8 35	22 52	0 15	2 48	1 60
29 Tu	14 29	23 31	4 26	25 29	2 26	2 52	0 57	1 26	21 04	2 02	10 16	8 37	22 53	0 15	2 46	1 60
30 W	14N47	26N59	4N58	27N60	2N56	2S53	1N00	1N16	20N56	2N01	10S09	8S38	22N54	0S14	2S44	1S60

Day	⚷ Decl	⚷ Lat	♅ Decl	♅ Lat	♆ Decl	♆ Lat	♇ Decl	♇ Lat
1	9N24	0N47	18N44	0S13	1S08	1S16	22S43	3S27
6	9 31	0 46	18 48	0 13	1 04	1 16	22 43	3 28
11	9 37	0 46	18 52	0 13	0 60	1 16	22 43	3 29
16	9 43	0 46	18 55	0 13	0 56	1 16	22 43	3 30
21	9 50	0 45	18 59	0 13	0 52	1 16	22 43	3 31
26	9 56	0 45	19 03	0 13	0 48	1 16	22 44	3 32

Day	⚴ Decl	⚴ Lat	⚵ Decl	⚵ Lat	⚶ Decl	⚶ Lat	Eris Decl	Eris Lat
1	9N11	26N53	6S38	14N07	6S18	11N20	0S14	10S36
6	9 46	27 07	6 09	14 31	5 57	11 32	0 13	10 36
11	10 20	27 22	5 40	14 54	5 37	11 41	0 12	10 35
16	10 55	27 38	5 11	15 16	5 16	11 47	0 10	10 35
21	11 31	27 55	4 41	15 37	4 57	11 50	0 09	10 35
26	12 06	28 14	4 13	15 55	4 38	11 49	0 08	10 35

Moon Phenomena

Max/0 Decl
dy hr mn
3 22:04 28N42
11 0:18 0 S
18 13:13 28S38
25 6:33 0 N

Max/0 Lat
dy hr mn
3 18:11 5N16
10 19:58 0 S
18 8:13 5S12
25 2:22 0 N

Perigee/Apogee
dy hr m kilometers
13 22:49 a 406295
27 16:19 p 357123

PH dy hr mn
☽ 5 2:16 15♋33
○ 13 0:23 23♎20
☾ 21 1:37 1♒12
● 27 19:32 7♉47

Void of Course Moon

Last Aspect	☽ Ingress
1 17:44 ☿ ⚹	♊ 1 20:27
3 18:28 ☿ □	♋ 3 22:51
5 22:56 ☿ △	♌ 6 4:35
8 4:09 ♅ □	♍ 8 13:41
10 19:50 ☿ ☍	♎ 11 1:13
13 10:02 ♂ □	♏ 13 13:55
16 2:25 ☿ △	♐ 16 2:38
18 11:39 ☉ △	♑ 18 14:13
20 17:22 ♄ ⚹	♒ 20 23:23
22 21:57 ♅ □	♓ 23 5:08
25 2:58 ♀ ☌	♈ 25 7:25
26 16:19 ♃ ⚹	♉ 27 7:18
29 5:19 ♀ ⚹	♊ 29 6:36

DAILY ASPECTARIAN

1 Tu ☽∥♃ 7:22 · ☽⚺⚷ 7:58 · ☽#♇ 8:58 · ☽⚹♂ 10:16 · ☽⚹♄ 11:34 · ☽☌♅ 11:57 · ☽∥♂ 15:46 · ☉∠☽ 15:49 · ☽⚹♀ 15:55 · ☽⚹☿ 17:44 · ☽⚹♆ 20:35

2 W ☽△♇ 2:18 · ☽∠⚷ 8:35 · ☽∠♂ 11:25 · ☉∥♀ 11:53 · ☉⚹☽ 18:21 · ☽□⚳ 20:36 · ☽☌♃ 23:27

3 Th ☽⚼♇ 3:19 · ☽⚹⚷ 9:52 · ☽⚺♂ 13:18 · ☽□♄ 13:54 · ☽⚺♅ 14:02 · ☽□♀ 16:38 · ☽□☿ 18:28 · ☽□♆ 23:08

4 F ☽⚻♇ 5:07 · ☽∠♅ 16:15 · ♄⚹♅ 16:22 · ☉⚺⚳ 21:26 · ♂⚹♅ 23:06

5 Sa ♂△♄ 1:09 · ☊D 2:01 · ☽△⚳ 2:02 · ☉□☽ 2:16 · ☽⚺♃ 4:13 · ☽□⚷ 14:57 · ☽⚹♅ 19:21 · ☽△♄ 19:30 · ☽☌♂ 19:50 · ☽△♀ 20:37 · ☽△☿ 22:56

6 Su ☽△♆ 5:03 · ☽⚼⚳ 6:11 · ☽∠♃ 7:59 · ☿∥♆ 9:23 · ☉⚹♃ 9:46 · ☽∥♂ 10:56 · ☽☍♇ 11:20 · ♀△♂ 12:15 · ☽#♇ 16:03 · ☽∥♃ 17:18 · ♀#♄ 22:02 · ☽⚼♄ 23:39 · ☽⚼♀ 23:58

7 M ☽⚼☿ 2:44 · ☽⚼♆ 9:19 · ♀☌♄ 11:02 · ☿D 11:09 · ☽⚻⚳ 11:15 · ☽⚹♃ 12:38 · ☽∥♅ 13:28 · ☉△☽ 14:32 · ☽△⚷ 23:33

8 Tu ☽□♅ 4:09 · ☽⚻♀ 4:10 · ☽⚻♄ 4:38 · ♀⚹♅ 4:49 · ☽⚺♂ 6:09 · ☽⚻☿ 7:34 · ☽⚻♆ 14:20 · ☽#⚳ 18:28 · ☽⚻♇ 20:51 · ☉⚼☽ 22:08

9 W ☽⚼⚷ 4:57 · ☽∥⚷ 8:01 · ☽∠♂ 12:28 · ☉∥☽ 15:30 · ☽☍⚳ 23:41

10 Th ☽□♃ 0:06 · ☽⚼♇ 2:32 · ☉⚻☽ 6:27 · ☽#♄ 9:32 · ☽⚻⚷ 10:54 · ☽∥♀ 13:02 · ☽☍♀ 14:40 · ☽△♅ 15:37 · ☽☍♄ 16:27 · ☽#☿ 16:42 · ☽⚹♂ 19:21 · ☽☍☿ 19:50 · ☊R 19:55 · ☽#♆ 20:09

11 F ⚳□♃ 0:55 · ☽☍♆ 2:04 · ☽∥♆ 4:26 · ☽∥☿ 8:07 · ☽△♇ 8:39 · ☽#♀ 10:42 · ☽∥♄ 14:54 · ☽⚼♅ 21:57

12 Sa ☽△♃ 13:21 · ☽⚻⚳ 13:58 · ☉#☽ 14:11 · ☉☌⚷ 16:01 · ☽#⚷ 17:28 · ☽☍⚷ 23:44

13 Su ☉☍☽ 0:23 · ♀D 1:04 · ☽⚻♀ 3:01 · ☽⚻♅ 4:29 · ☽∥⚳ 4:37 · ☽⚻♄ 5:39 · ☽□♂ 10:02 · ☽⚻☿ 10:33 · ☽⚻♆ 14:58 · ☽⚼♃ 20:15 · ☽⚼⚳ 21:22 · ☽□♇ 21:28

14 M ⚳∠♇ 0:36 · ☉⚺♀ 8:53 · ☽⚼♀ 9:32 · ☿#♀ 11:59 · ☽⚼♄ 12:23 · ☽#♅ 14:06 · ☉∥⚷ 18:21 · ☽⚼☿ 18:26 · ♂#♇ 21:12 · ☽⚼♆ 21:29

15 Tu ☽⚻♃ 3:07 · ☉⚺♅ 4:21 · ☽△⚳ 4:44 · ⚵R♏ 6:32 · ♂∥♃ 8:53 · ☽#♂ 12:13 · ☽#♃ 12:19 · ☽∥♇ 12:39 · ☽⚻⚷ 12:51 · ☽△♀ 16:05 · ☽☍♅ 17:32 · ☉⚻☽ 18:39 · ☽△♄ 19:01 · ☉⚺♄ 23:33

16 W ☽△♂ 0:53 · ☽△☿ 2:25 · ☽△♆ 3:52 · ☿ ♈ 6:26 · ☽⚹♇ 10:09 · ☽⚼⚷ 19:10

17 Th ☉⚼☽ 3:25 · ☿☌♆ 4:12 · ☽⚼♂ 7:57 · ♃⚼♇ 8:17 · ☽∠♇ 16:06 · ☽☍♃ 16:12 · ☽□⚳ 18:43

18 F ☽△⚷ 1:06 · ♂ ♌ 4:22 · ☽□♀ 4:41 · ☽⚻♅ 5:38 · ☽□♄ 7:22 · ♃#♇ 10:24 · ☉△☽ 11:39 · ☽⚻♂ 14:34 · ☽□♆ 15:34 · ☽□☿ 17:52 · ☿#♀ 20:31 · ☽⚺♇ 21:33

19 Sa ☽⚼♅ 10:55 · ☉#⚳ 12:18 · ☉ ♉ 19:57 · ♂△♆ 22:54

20 Su ☽⚻♃ 3:17 · ☽⚹⚳ 6:31 · ☿∥♆ 8:08 · ☽□⚷ 11:11 · ☉⚺♆ 14:37 · ☽⚹♀ 15:25 · ☽△♅ 15:28 · ☽⚹♄ 17:22 · ♀⚹♅ 18:22 · ☿⚹♇ 21:41

21 M ☽⚹♆ 0:49 · ☉□♂ 1:35 · ☽☍♂ 1:37 · ☉□☽ 1:37 · ☊D 1:45 · ☽☌♇ 6:21 · ☽⚹☿ 7:01 · ☽⚼♃ 7:39 · ☽#♃ 9:56 · ☽∥♇ 10:13 · ☽∠⚳ 11:09 · ☽#♂ 14:32 · ☽∠♀ 19:38 · ☽∠♄ 21:07

22 Tu ☽∠♆ 4:10 · ☽#♅ 5:54 · ☽△♃ 11:05 · ☽∠☿ 12:14 · ☽⚺⚳ 14:49 · ☽⚹⚷ 17:57 · ☽□♅ 21:57 · ☽⚺♀ 22:57 · ☽⚺♄ 23:56

23 W ☽⚺♆ 6:36 · ☽⚻♂ 8:55 · ☉#☽ 9:08 · ☉⚹☽ 11:15 · ☽⚺♇ 11:40 · ☽∥⚳ 16:04 · ☽⚺☿ 16:26 · ☉□♇ 17:11 · ☽#⚷ 19:47 · ☽∠⚷ 19:58

24 Th ☽⚼♂ 11:07 · ☽∠♇ 13:00 · ☉∠☽ 14:25 · ☽□♃ 15:11 · ☽☌⚳ 19:16 · ☽∥♄ 20:33 · ☽⚺⚷ 21:08

25 F ♀☌♄ 0:03 · ☽⚹♅ 0:52 · ☊R 2:21 · ☽☌♄ 2:55 · ☽☌♀ 2:58 · ☽#♀ 3:35 · ☽∥♆ 3:49 · ☽#☿ 4:02 · ☉∠♃ 4:30 · ☿#♆ 7:54 · ☽☌♆ 8:55 · ☽#♆ 9:16 · ☽∥☿ 9:21 · ☽∥♀ 9:29 · ☿∥♀ 11:43 · ☽△♂ 12:30 · ☽⚹♇ 13:35 · ☽#♄ 16:19 · ☉⚺☽ 16:41 · ☽☌☿ 22:05

26 Sa ☽∠♅ 1:14 · ☽⚹♃ 16:19 · ☽∥⚷ 16:20 · ☽#⚳ 18:20 · ☽⚺⚳ 20:45 · ☽☌⚷ 21:34

27 Su ♂☍♇ 1:07 · ☽⚺♅ 1:09 · ☽⚺♄ 3:17 · ☽⚺♀ 4:27 · ☉∥☽ 6:36 · ☽⚺♆ 8:51 · ☽□♇ 13:17 · ☽□♂ 13:39 · ☿∠♅ 15:00 · ☽∠♃ 16:17 · ☉☌☽ 19:32 · ☽∠⚳ 20:55

28 M ☽⚺☿ 1:40 · ☽∥♅ 2:50 · ☽∠♄ 3:02 · ☽∠♀ 4:48 · ☽∠♆ 8:29 · ☽∥♂ 11:58 · ⚳⚺⚷ 15:50 · ☽⚺♃ 16:12 · ☽#♇ 19:49 · ☽∥♃ 20:37 · ☽⚺⚷ 21:00 · ☽⚹⚳ 21:06

29 Tu ☽☌♅ 0:34 · ☽⚹♄ 2:52 · ☽∠☿ 3:30 · ☉∠⚳ 4:36 · ☽⚹♀ 5:19 · ☽⚹♆ 8:15 · ☽△♇ 12:40 · ☽⚹♂ 14:30 · ☿#♄ 14:59 · ☽∠⚷ 21:00 · ☉⚺☽ 22:20

30 W ☽⚹☿ 5:51 · ☽⚼♇ 12:54 · ☽∠♂ 15:33 · ☽☌♃ 16:59 · ♀ ♈ 17:17 · ☽⚹⚷ 21:32 · ☽□⚳ 22:37

LONGITUDE

May 2025

Day	Sid.Time	☉	☽	☽ 12 hour	Mean ☊	True ☊	☿	♀	♂	⚳	♃	♄	⚷	♅	♆	♇
	h m s	° ' "	° ' "	° ' "	° '	° '	° '	° '	° '	° '	° '	° '	° '	° '	° '	° '
1 Th	14 36 42	10♉52 42	25♊33 35	2♋44 30	25♓08.5	26♓28.7	15♈30.7	0♈09.4	5♌35.6	24♓44.8	21♊22.2	27♓50.9	24♈04.3	26♉19.0	1♈05.8	3♒48.9
2 F	14 40 39	11 50 58	9♋48 22	16 44 57	25 05.3	26R 23.4	16 53.5	0 43.6	6 03.2	25 05.5	21 34.2	27 57.0	24 07.8	26 22.5	1 07.6	3 49.0
3 Sa	14 44 36	12 49 11	23 34 15	0♌16 25	25 02.1	26 19.8	18 18.3	1 19.2	6 31.0	25 26.0	21 46.4	28 03.0	24 11.2	26 25.9	1 09.4	3 49.1
4 Su	14 48 32	13 47 23	6♌51 44	13 20 35	24 59.0	26D 18.1	19 45.1	1 56.0	6 59.0	25 46.5	21 58.6	28 08.9	24 14.6	26 29.3	1 11.2	3R 49.1
5 M	14 52 29	14 45 32	19 43 29	26 00 58	24 55.8	26 18.0	21 14.1	2 33.9	7 27.1	26 06.9	22 10.8	28 14.8	24 18.0	26 32.7	1 13.0	3 49.1
6 Tu	14 56 25	15 43 39	2♍13 37	8♍22 00	24 52.6	26 18.9	22 45.0	3 13.0	7 55.5	26 27.2	22 23.1	28 20.6	24 21.4	26 36.2	1 14.8	3 49.1
7 W	15 00 22	16 41 45	14 26 46	20 28 28	24 49.4	26R 20.1	24 17.9	3 53.2	8 24.0	26 47.4	22 35.5	28 26.4	24 24.8	26 39.6	1 16.5	3 49.1
8 Th	15 04 18	17 39 48	26 27 41	2♎24 58	24 46.2	26 20.7	25 52.9	4 34.5	8 52.6	27 07.6	22 47.9	28 32.1	24 28.1	26 43.1	1 18.2	3 49.0
9 F	15 08 15	18 37 50	8♎20 48	14 15 39	24 43.1	26 19.8	27 29.8	5 16.7	9 21.4	27 27.6	23 00.4	28 37.7	24 31.5	26 46.5	1 19.9	3 48.9
10 Sa	15 12 11	19 35 50	20 09 58	26 04 06	24 39.9	26 16.9	29 08.7	5 59.9	9 50.4	27 47.5	23 12.9	28 43.3	24 34.8	26 50.0	1 21.6	3 48.7
11 Su	15 16 08	20 33 48	1♏58 25	7♏53 12	24 36.7	26 11.7	0♉49.5	6 44.1	10 19.6	28 07.4	23 25.5	28 48.9	24 38.1	26 53.5	1 23.2	3 48.6
12 M	15 20 05	21 31 45	13 48 43	19 45 13	24 33.5	26 04.1	2 32.4	7 29.1	10 48.9	28 27.2	23 38.1	28 54.3	24 41.4	26 57.0	1 24.8	3 48.4
13 Tu	15 24 01	22 29 40	25 42 54	1♐41 57	24 30.4	25 54.7	4 17.2	8 15.1	11 18.3	28 46.8	23 50.8	28 59.7	24 44.6	27 00.4	1 26.4	3 48.2
14 W	15 27 58	23 27 33	7♐42 32	13 44 50	24 27.2	25 44.1	6 04.1	9 01.9	11 47.9	29 06.4	24 03.6	29 05.1	24 47.9	27 03.9	1 28.0	3 47.9
15 Th	15 31 54	24 25 26	19 49 00	25 55 14	24 24.0	25 33.2	7 52.9	9 49.4	12 17.6	29 25.8	24 16.4	29 10.4	24 51.1	27 07.4	1 29.6	3 47.6
16 F	15 35 51	25 23 16	2♑03 41	8♑14 36	24 20.8	25 23.1	9 43.7	10 37.8	12 47.5	29 45.2	24 29.2	29 15.6	24 54.3	27 10.9	1 31.1	3 47.3
17 Sa	15 39 47	26 21 06	14 28 12	20 44 44	24 17.7	25 14.6	11 36.5	11 26.9	13 17.5	0♈04.5	24 42.1	29 20.7	24 57.5	27 14.4	1 32.6	3 47.0
18 Su	15 43 44	27 18 54	27 04 30	3♒27 49	24 14.5	25 08.3	13 31.2	12 16.7	13 47.7	0 23.6	24 55.0	29 25.8	25 00.6	27 17.9	1 34.1	3 46.7
19 M	15 47 40	28 16 41	9♒55 01	16 26 26	24 11.3	25 04.5	15 27.9	13 07.2	14 18.0	0 42.7	25 08.0	29 30.8	25 03.8	27 21.4	1 35.5	3 46.3
20 Tu	15 51 37	29 14 27	23 02 26	29 43 22	24 08.1	25D 03.0	17 26.5	13 58.3	14 48.4	1 01.6	25 21.0	29 35.7	25 06.9	27 24.9	1 36.9	3 45.9
21 W	15 55 34	0♊12 12	6♓29 32	13♓21 12	24 04.9	25 02.9	19 27.0	14 50.1	15 19.0	1 20.5	25 34.0	29 40.6	25 09.9	27 28.4	1 38.3	3 45.5
22 Th	15 59 30	1 09 56	20 18 34	27 21 43	24 01.8	25R 03.4	21 29.3	15 42.6	15 49.6	1 39.2	25 47.1	29 45.4	25 13.0	27 31.9	1 39.7	3 45.0
23 F	16 03 27	2 07 38	4♈30 37	11♈45 06	23 58.6	25 03.1	23 33.3	16 35.6	16 20.5	1 57.8	26 00.3	29 50.1	25 16.0	27 35.4	1 41.1	3 44.5
24 Sa	16 07 23	3 05 20	19 04 49	26 29 13	23 55.4	25 01.2	25 39.0	17 29.1	16 51.4	2 16.3	26 13.4	29 54.7	25 19.0	27 38.8	1 42.4	3 44.0
25 Su	16 11 20	4 03 01	3♉57 36	11♉29 01	23 52.2	24 56.7	27 46.1	18 23.3	17 22.5	2 34.7	26 26.6	29 59.3	25 22.0	27 42.3	1 43.7	3 43.5
26 M	16 15 16	5 00 40	19 02 25	26 36 35	23 49.1	24 49.7	29 54.6	19 17.9	17 53.7	2 52.9	26 39.9	0♈03.8	25 24.9	27 45.8	1 44.9	3 42.9
27 Tu	16 19 13	5 58 19	4♊10 16	11♊42 09	23 45.9	24 40.6	2♊04.2	20 13.0	18 25.0	3 11.1	26 53.1	0 08.2	25 27.8	27 49.3	1 46.2	3 42.3
28 W	16 23 09	6 55 57	19 10 59	26 35 35	23 42.7	24 30.3	4 14.8	21 08.6	18 56.5	3 29.1	27 06.4	0 12.6	25 30.7	27 52.8	1 47.4	3 41.7
29 Th	16 27 06	7 53 33	3♋54 57	11♋08 14	23 39.5	24 20.0	6 26.2	22 04.7	19 28.1	3 47.0	27 19.8	0 16.8	25 33.6	27 56.2	1 48.6	3 41.1
30 F	16 31 03	8 51 08	18 14 50	25 14 18	23 36.4	24 11.0	8 38.0	23 01.3	19 59.7	4 04.7	27 33.1	0 21.0	25 36.4	27 59.7	1 49.7	3 40.4
31 Sa	16 34 59	9♊48 42	2♌06 28	8♌51 17	23♓33.2	24♓04.0	10♊50.1	23♈58.2	20♌31.6	4♈22.3	27♊46.5	0♈25.1	25♈39.2	28♉03.1	1♈50.8	3♒39.7

1st of Month

Julian Day # 2460796.5
Obliquity 23°26'19"
SVP 4♓54'21"
GC 27♐11.6
Eris 25♈13.0

Day	⚴	⚵	⚶
1	21♒11.2	27♏12.1R	12♏25.3R
6	22 05.6	26 08.5R	11 11.1R
11	22 53.9	25 02.1R	9 58.7R
16	23 35.8	23 54.6R	8 50.6R
21	24 10.9	22 47.4R	7 49.4R
26	24 38.7	21 41.9R	6 56.9R
31	24 58.7	20 39.7R	6 15.0R

DECLINATION and LATITUDE

Day	☉ Decl	☽ Decl	☽ Lat	☽ 12h Decl	☿ Decl	☿ Lat	♀ Decl	♀ Lat	♂ Decl	♂ Lat	⚳ Decl	⚳ Lat	♃ Decl	♃ Lat	♄ Decl	♄ Lat
1 Th	15N05	28N31	5N09	28N32	3N27	2S53	1N04	1N06	20N48	1N60	10S02	8S40	22N55	0S14	2S42	2S00
2 F	15 23	28 04	5 01	27 11	3 59	2 52	1 09	0 56	20 40	1 59	9 56	8 42	22 56	0 14	2 39	2 00
3 Sa	15 41	25 54	4 35	24 16	4 32	2 51	1 14	0 47	20 32	1 57	9 49	8 44	22 57	0 14	2 37	2 00
4 Su	15 59	22 21	3 55	20 11	5 07	2 49	1 20	0 37	20 24	1 56	9 42	8 45	22 58	0 14	2 35	2 01
5 M	16 16	17 49	3 05	15 18	5 42	2 47	1 27	0 28	20 16	1 55	9 36	8 47	22 59	0 14	2 33	2 01
6 Tu	16 33	12 39	2 06	9 54	6 18	2 44	1 35	0 20	20 07	1 54	9 30	8 49	22 60	0 14	2 30	2 01
7 W	16 50	7 06	1 04	4 16	6 56	2 41	1 43	0 11	19 59	1 53	9 23	8 51	23 00	0 14	2 28	2 01
8 Th	17 06	1 24	0S01	1S28	7 34	2 37	1 52	0 03	19 50	1 52	9 17	8 53	23 01	0 13	2 26	2 01
9 F	17 22	4S18	1 04	7 05	8 13	2 32	2 01	0S05	19 41	1 51	9 11	8 54	23 02	0 13	2 24	2 01
10 Sa	17 38	9 48	2 04	12 26	8 52	2 27	2 11	0 13	19 32	1 50	9 04	8 56	23 03	0 13	2 22	2 02
11 Su	17 53	14 58	2 59	17 21	9 33	2 22	2 22	0 20	19 24	1 48	8 58	8 58	23 03	0 13	2 20	2 02
12 M	18 09	19 35	3 46	21 37	10 14	2 16	2 33	0 27	19 14	1 47	8 52	9 00	23 04	0 13	2 18	2 02
13 Tu	18 24	23 27	4 23	25 02	10 55	2 09	2 45	0 34	19 05	1 46	8 46	9 02	23 05	0 13	2 16	2 02
14 W	18 38	26 21	4 49	27 22	11 37	2 02	2 57	0 41	18 56	1 45	8 40	9 04	23 06	0 13	2 14	2 02
15 Th	18 53	28 04	5 02	28 26	12 20	1 55	3 09	0 48	18 47	1 44	8 34	9 06	23 06	0 13	2 12	2 03
16 F	19 07	28 27	5 02	28 07	13 02	1 47	3 22	0 54	18 37	1 43	8 28	9 08	23 07	0 12	2 10	2 03
17 Sa	19 20	27 25	4 47	26 22	13 45	1 38	3 36	1 00	18 28	1 42	8 22	9 10	23 08	0 12	2 09	2 03
18 Su	19 34	24 58	4 19	23 15	14 28	1 30	3 50	1 06	18 18	1 41	8 17	9 12	23 08	0 12	2 07	2 03
19 M	19 47	21 14	3 36	18 56	15 11	1 20	4 04	1 12	18 08	1 40	8 11	9 14	23 09	0 12	2 05	2 03
20 Tu	19 59	16 23	2 42	13 36	15 54	1 11	4 19	1 18	17 58	1 39	8 05	9 16	23 09	0 12	2 03	2 04
21 W	20 12	10 38	1 37	7 30	16 37	1 01	4 34	1 23	17 48	1 38	7 60	9 18	23 10	0 12	2 01	2 04
22 Th	20 24	4 14	0 25	0 52	17 19	0 51	4 50	1 28	17 38	1 37	7 54	9 20	23 10	0 12	1 60	2 04
23 F	20 35	2N34	0N50	5N59	18 00	0 41	5 05	1 33	17 28	1 36	7 49	9 22	23 11	0 12	1 58	2 04
24 Sa	20 46	9 23	2 04	12 41	18 41	0 30	5 21	1 38	17 17	1 35	7 44	9 25	23 11	0 12	1 56	2 05
25 Su	20 57	15 50	3 11	18 46	19 20	0 20	5 38	1 42	17 07	1 34	7 38	9 27	23 12	0 11	1 55	2 05
26 M	21 08	21 25	4 06	23 43	19 59	0 09	5 54	1 47	16 57	1 33	7 33	9 29	23 12	0 11	1 53	2 05
27 Tu	21 18	25 37	4 43	27 03	20 36	0N01	6 11	1 51	16 46	1 32	7 28	9 31	23 12	0 11	1 52	2 05
28 W	21 28	27 59	5 01	28 25	21 11	0 12	6 28	1 55	16 35	1 31	7 23	9 34	23 13	0 11	1 50	2 05
29 Th	21 37	28 20	4 58	27 46	21 45	0 22	6 46	1 59	16 24	1 30	7 18	9 36	23 13	0 11	1 49	2 06
30 F	21 47	26 45	4 36	25 20	22 17	0 33	7 03	2 02	16 13	1 29	7 13	9 38	23 14	0 11	1 47	2 06
31 Sa	21N55	23N34	3N58	21N30	22N46	0N42	7N21	2S06	16N02	1N28	7S08	9S40	23N14	0S11	1S46	2S06

Day	⚷ Decl	⚷ Lat	♅ Decl	♅ Lat	♆ Decl	♆ Lat	♇ Decl	♇ Lat
1	10N02	0N45	19N07	0S13	0S44	1S17	22S44	3S32
6	10 08	0 45	19 11	0 13	0 41	1 17	22 45	3 33
11	10 14	0 44	19 15	0 13	0 38	1 17	22 46	3 34
16	10 20	0 44	19 19	0 13	0 35	1 17	22 47	3 35
21	10 25	0 44	19 23	0 13	0 32	1 17	22 49	3 36
26	10 30	0 44	19 27	0 13	0 29	1 18	22 50	3 37
31	10N35	0N43	19N31	0S13	0S27	1S18	22S52	3S38

Day	⚴ Decl	⚴ Lat	⚵ Decl	⚵ Lat	⚶ Decl	⚶ Lat	Eris Decl	Eris Lat
1	12N41	28N33	3S45	16N11	4S23	11N43	0S06	10S35
6	13 15	28 53	3 18	16 24	4 11	11 33	0 05	10 35
11	13 49	29 14	2 54	16 35	4 02	11 19	0 04	10 35
16	14 21	29 36	2 33	16 42	3 58	11 02	0 03	10 35
21	14 52	29 58	2 14	16 45	3 59	10 41	0 02	10 35
26	15 22	30 21	1 58	16 46	4 05	10 17	0 02	10 35
31	15N49	30N44	1S46	16N43	4S17	9N52	0S01	10S35

Moon Phenomena

Max/0 Decl
dy hr mn
1 6:25 28N35
8 5:52 0 S
15 18:31 28S29
22 15:02 0 N
28 16:04 28N27

Perigee/Apogee
dy hr m kilometers
11 0:48 a 406244
26 1:35 p 359023

PH dy hr mn
☽ 4 13:53 14♌21
○ 12 16:57 22♏13
☾ 20 12:00 29♒43
● 27 3:04 6♊06

Max/0 Lat
dy hr mn
1 1:31 5N09
7 23:46 0 S
15 11:07 5S04
22 8:05 0 N
28 8:30 5N02

Void of Course Moon

Last Aspect	☽ Ingress
1 3:50 ♄ □	♋ 1 7:24
3 8:03 ♄ △	♌ 3 11:30
5 13:05 ♅ □	♍ 5 19:41
8 4:12 ♄ ☍	♎ 8 7:07
10 6:19 ♃ △	♏ 10 19:59
13 6:38 ♄ △	♐ 13 8:36
15 18:30 ♄ □	♑ 15 19:59
18 4:28 ♄ ⚹	♒ 18 5:31
20 12:00 ☉ □	♓ 20 12:30
22 16:08 ♄ ☌	♈ 22 16:27
24 11:45 ♃ ⚹	♉ 24 17:39
26 13:53 ♅ ☌	♊ 26 17:23
28 13:02 ♃ ☌	♋ 28 17:34
30 16:52 ♅ ⚹	♌ 30 20:18

DAILY ASPECTARIAN

1 Th ☉∠☽ 0:34; ⚳⋕⚷ 0:49; ☽⚺♅ 1:16; ☽□♄ 3:50; ☽□♀ 7:58; ☽□♆ 9:15; ☽⚻♇ 13:49; ☽⚺♂ 17:23

2 F ☽∠♅ 2:42; ☉⚹☽ 3:46; ☽□☿ 13:39; ♀☌♆ 17:08; ☽⚺♃ 20:46

3 Sa ☽□⚷ 1:06; ☽△⚳ 3:24; ☽⚹♅ 5:07; ☉∠♄ 6:20; ☽△♄ 8:03; ☽△♆ 13:38; ☽△♀ 14:34; ☽☍♇ 18:26; ☽∥♃ 20:20; ☽⋕♇ 21:39; ♂∠♃ 23:22

4 Su ☽∠♃ 0:13; ☽☌♂ 0:14; ☽⚼⚳ 7:25; ☽∥♂ 11:12; ☽⚼♄ 11:44; ☊ D 13:46; ☉□☽ 13:53; ♇ R 15:28; ☽∥♅ 17:16; ☽⚼♆ 17:22; ☽⚼♀ 19:42

5 M ☽△☿ 3:15; ☽⚹♃ 4:44; ☉∥☽ 7:05; ☽△⚷ 8:45; ☽⚻⚳ 12:32; ☽□♅ 13:05; ☽⚻♄ 16:25; ☿⚹♃ 17:23; ☽⚻♆ 22:05

6 Tu ☽⚻♀ 2:02; ☽⚻♇ 3:06; ☽∥⚷ 11:00; ☽⚺♂ 11:35; ☽⚼☿ 12:21; ⚳⚹♅ 12:47; ☉∠♆ 13:14; ☽⚼⚷ 14:01; ☽⋕⚳ 14:04; ♀⚹♇ 21:33

7 W ☽∥☿ 0:40; ☿☌⚷ 1:49; ☉△☽ 4:51; ☽⚼♇ 8:41; ☽□♃ 16:31; ☽∠♂ 18:36; ☽⋕♄ 19:37; ☽⚻⚷ 19:59; ☽∥♀ 22:05; ☽⚻☿ 22:39; ☊ R 23:44

8 Th ☽△♅ 0:31; ☽☍⚳ 1:22; ☽⋕♆ 3:07; ☽☍♄ 4:12; ☽∥♆ 8:36; ☽☍♆ 9:47; ☿⚺♅ 12:57; ☉⚼☽ 13:36; ☽⋕♀ 14:05; ☽△♇ 14:50; ☽∥♄ 16:02; ☽☍♀ 17:23; ☿⚺⚳ 23:20

9 F ☽⚹♂ 2:08; ☽⚼♅ 6:59; ☿⚺♄ 17:32; ☽⋕☿ 19:17; ☽∥⚳ 20:48; ☉⚻☽ 22:44

10 Sa ☽⋕⚷ 1:50; ☿⋕⚳ 6:09; ☽△♃ 6:19; ☽☍⚷ 9:01; ☿ ♉ 12:16; ☽⚻♅ 13:37; ☽⚻⚳ 15:57; ☽⚻♄ 17:32; ♀⋕♄ 20:39; ☽☍☿ 21:17; ☽⚻♆ 22:48

11 Su ☽□♇ 3:44; ☿⚺♆ 8:02; ☽⚻♀ 10:19; ☽⚼♃ 13:20; ☉⋕☽ 15:43; ☽□♂ 17:40; ♂∥♅ 20:08; ☽⋕♂ 22:11; ☽⋕♅ 22:16; ☽⚼⚳ 23:15

12 M ☽⚼♄ 0:11; ☿∥⚷ 0:44; ☽⚼♆ 5:16; ☉☍☽ 16:57; ☿□♇ 17:24; ☽⚼♀ 18:42; ☽∥♇ 19:24; ☽⚻♃ 20:11; ☽⋕♃ 21:27; ☽⚻⚷ 22:02

13 Tu ☽☍♅ 2:36; ☽△⚳ 6:20; ☽△♄ 6:38; ☽△♆ 11:30; ☽⚹♇ 16:12; ☽⚻☿ 20:09; ⚳☌♄ 21:48

14 W ☽△♀ 2:49; ☽⚼⚷ 4:11; ☽△♂ 8:29; ☉∥♂ 17:58; ☉⚺♃ 19:10; ☽∠♇ 21:59

15 Th ☽⚼☿ 7:06; ☽☍♃ 8:55; ☉⚻☽ 9:50; ☽△⚷ 9:57; ☉⚺⚷ 11:17; ☽⚻♅ 14:26; ☽⚼♂ 15:19; ☽□♄ 18:30; ☽□⚳ 19:23; ☿∠♃ 20:29; ☽□♆ 22:56

16 F ☽⚺♇ 3:22; ☉⚼☽ 17:30; ☽△☿ 17:31; ☽□♀ 17:47; ⚳ ♈ 18:24; ☽⚼♅ 19:42; ☿⚺♀ 20:25; ☽⚻♂ 21:39; ☉∥♅ 23:47

17 Sa ☉∠♀ 17:06; ☽⚻♃ 19:51; ☽□⚷ 20:05; ☉☌♅ 23:33

18 Su ☽△♅ 0:25; ☉△☽ 0:29; ♀∠♅ 0:38; ☽⚹♄ 4:28; ☿□♂ 4:37; ☽⚹⚳ 6:25; ☽⚹♆ 8:28; ☿∠♄ 11:47; ☽☌♇ 12:35; ☽⋕♃ 12:42; ♃⚹⚷ 13:45; ☽∥♇ 14:50

19 M ☽⚼♃ 0:24; ☿∠⚳ 3:36; ☽⚹♀ 6:19; ☉⋕☽ 7:26; ☽☍♂ 8:24; ☽∠♄ 8:31; ☽⋕♅ 9:51; ☽∠⚳ 10:56; ☽□☿ 12:01; ♂⚼♄ 12:06; ☽∠♆ 12:18; ☿∠♆ 13:54; ☽⋕♂ 16:26

20 Tu ☽⋕☿ 1:54; ☽⚹⚷ 3:45; ☽△♃ 4:14; ☽□♅ 7:54; ☉⚹♄ 9:40; ☽∠♀ 11:23; ☽⚺♄ 11:51; ☉□☽ 12:00; ☊ D 12:12; ☽⚺⚳ 14:40; ☽⚺♆ 15:24; ☉ ♊ 18:56; ☽⚺♇ 19:10

21 W ☽⋕⚷ 0:51; ☽∠⚷ 6:28; ☽∥⚳ 10:16; ☽⚺♀ 15:33; ☽⚻♂ 15:59; ☽∠♇ 21:20; ☽⋕♀ 21:55

22 Th ⚳☌♆ 0:42; ☽⚹☿ 2:22; ♀△♂ 7:43; ☽∥♄ 8:01; ☊ R 8:04; ☽⚺⚷ 8:24; ☿∥♂ 8:59; ☽□♃ 9:29; ☽⚹♅ 12:20; ☉⚹♆ 12:41; ☽∥♆ 13:12; ☽☌♄ 16:08; ☽⋕♆ 16:51; ☉⚹⚳ 17:59; ☽⚼♂ 18:30; ☽☌♆ 19:16; ☽☌⚳ 19:39; ☉⚹☽ 19:44; ☽⋕♄ 21:56; ☽⚹♇ 22:43

23 F ☽∠☿ 7:51; ☽∥♀ 9:12; ☽∠♅ 13:26; ♂⚼♆ 16:42; ☽⋕⚳ 18:11; ☿⚺⚷ 20:07; ☽△♂ 20:14; ☽☌♀ 21:14; ☉∠☽ 22:16

24 Sa ☽∥⚷ 3:55; ☿⚺♃ 7:17; ☽☌⚷ 10:09; ☽⚹♃ 11:45; ☽⚺☿ 12:25; ☽⚺♅ 13:55; ☉△♇ 15:56; ☽⚺♄ 17:36; ☽⚺♆ 20:25; ☽⚺⚳ 21:44; ☿☌♅ 23:16; ☽□♇ 23:37

25 Su ☉⚺☽ 0:09; ♄ ♈ 3:37; ☿∥♅ 3:53; ☽∥♂ 4:59; ☽∠♃ 12:07; ☽∥♅ 14:59; ☽∥☿ 16:26; ☽∠♄ 17:39; ☽∠♆ 20:22; ☽□♂ 22:07; ☽∠⚳ 22:08; ♂⚼⚳ 22:36; ☉∥☽ 22:36

26 M ☽⚺♀ 0:26; ☿ ♊ 1:00; ☿⚹♄ 1:47; ☽⋕♇ 7:12; ☽∥♃ 9:12; ☽⚺⚷ 10:08; ☽⚺♃ 12:16; ☽☌♅ 13:53; ☽⚹♄ 17:34; ☽☌☿ 20:06; ☽⚹♆ 20:11; ☿⚹♆ 20:38; ☽⚹⚳ 22:24; ☽△♇ 23:16

27 Tu ☽∠♀ 1:46; ☉☌☽ 3:04; ☽∠⚷ 10:03; ☿⚹⚳ 14:16; ☿△♇ 17:57; ☽⚼♇ 23:13; ☽⚹♂ 23:36

28 W ☽⚹♀ 3:23; ☽⚹⚷ 10:17; ☽☌♃ 13:02; ☽⚺♅ 14:09; ⚳⚹♇ 16:22; ☉∥☿ 16:25; ☽□♄ 18:00; ☽□♆ 20:32; ☽⚻♇ 23:37; ☽□⚳ 23:47

29 Th ☽∠♂ 0:57; ☽⚺☿ 4:55; ☉⚺☽ 7:03; ☿∠♀ 12:17; ☽∠♅ 15:05

30 F ☽⚺♂ 3:06; ☉☌☿ 4:14; ☽□♀ 8:46; ☉∠☽ 10:19; ♀⋕⚳ 10:29; ☽∠☿ 10:58; ☽□⚷ 12:41; ☽⚺♃ 16:17; ☽⚹♅ 16:52; ☽△♄ 21:01; ☿∠⚷ 21:59; ☽△♆ 23:32

31 Sa ☽∥♃ 1:58; ☽☍♇ 2:45; ☽△⚳ 4:06; ☽⋕♇ 4:14; ☽∥☿ 4:18; ☿⋕♇ 4:51; ☉∥☽ 9:21; ☉⚹☽ 14:47; ☽⚹☿ 18:39; ☽∠♃ 19:24; ☉∠⚷ 22:07; ☽∥♅ 22:20

June 2025

LONGITUDE

Day	Sid.Time	☉	☽	☽ 12 hour	Mean☊	True☊	☿	♀	♂	⚳	♃	♄	⚷	♅	♆	♇
	h m s	° ' "	° ' "	° ' "	° '	° '	° '	° '	° '	° '	° '	° '	° '	° '	° '	° '
1 Su	16 38 56	10♊46 14	15♌28 57	21♌59 47	23♓30.0	23♓59.5	13♊02.1	24♈55.6	21♌03.5	4♈39.8	28♊00.0	0♈29.2	25♈41.9	28♉06.6	1♈51.9	3♒39.0
2 M	16 42 52	11 43 45	28 24 11	4♍42 42	23 26.8	23R 57.2	15 13.7	25 53.4	21 35.5	4 57.2	28 13.4	0 33.1	25 44.6	28 10.0	1 53.0	3R 38.3
3 Tu	16 46 49	12 41 14	10♍55 56	17 04 30	23 23.7	23D 56.6	17 24.8	26 51.6	22 07.6	5 14.4	28 26.9	0 36.9	25 47.3	28 13.4	1 54.0	3 37.6
4 W	16 50 45	13 38 43	23 09 05	29 10 20	23 20.5	23R 56.7	19 35.0	27 50.1	22 39.9	5 31.4	28 40.3	0 40.7	25 50.0	28 16.8	1 55.0	3 36.8
5 Th	16 54 42	14 36 10	5♎08 56	11♎05 31	23 17.3	23 56.3	21 44.1	28 49.0	23 12.2	5 48.3	28 53.9	0 44.4	25 52.6	28 20.2	1 56.0	3 36.0
6 F	16 58 39	15 33 36	17 00 43	22 55 07	23 14.1	23 54.5	23 51.8	29 48.3	23 44.7	6 05.1	29 07.4	0 48.0	25 55.2	28 23.6	1 56.9	3 35.2
7 Sa	17 02 35	16 31 00	28 49 14	4♏43 36	23 10.9	23 50.4	25 58.0	0♉47.9	24 17.2	6 21.8	29 20.9	0 51.5	25 57.7	28 26.9	1 57.9	3 34.3
8 Su	17 06 32	17 28 24	10♏38 38	16 34 46	23 07.8	23 43.6	28 02.5	1 47.8	24 49.9	6 38.2	29 34.5	0 55.0	26 00.2	28 30.3	1 58.7	3 33.4
9 M	17 10 28	18 25 47	22 32 18	28 31 32	23 04.6	23 34.1	0♋05.1	2 48.1	25 22.6	6 54.6	29 48.1	0 58.3	26 02.7	28 33.6	1 59.6	3 32.6
10 Tu	17 14 25	19 23 09	4♐32 43	10♐36 02	23 01.4	23 22.4	2 05.7	3 48.7	25 55.4	7 10.8	0♋01.7	1 01.6	26 05.1	28 37.0	2 00.4	3 31.7
11 W	17 18 21	20 20 30	16 41 38	22 49 38	22 58.2	23 09.3	4 04.2	4 49.6	26 28.4	7 26.8	0 15.3	1 04.7	26 07.5	28 40.3	2 01.2	3 30.7
12 Th	17 22 18	21 17 50	29 00 05	5♑13 05	22 55.1	22 55.9	6 00.5	5 50.8	27 01.4	7 42.7	0 28.9	1 07.8	26 09.9	28 43.6	2 02.0	3 29.8
13 F	17 26 14	22 15 10	11♑28 24	17 46 52	22 51.9	22 43.3	7 54.5	6 52.3	27 34.5	7 58.4	0 42.5	1 10.8	26 12.2	28 46.9	2 02.7	3 28.8
14 Sa	17 30 11	23 12 29	24 07 45	0♒30 22	22 48.7	22 32.5	9 46.2	7 54.1	28 07.8	8 13.9	0 56.2	1 13.7	26 14.5	28 50.1	2 03.4	3 27.8
15 Su	17 34 08	24 09 47	6♒57 50	13 27 14	22 45.5	22 24.4	11 35.5	8 56.1	28 41.1	8 29.3	1 09.9	1 16.5	26 16.7	28 53.4	2 04.0	3 26.8
16 M	17 38 04	25 07 05	19 59 43	26 35 27	22 42.4	22 19.1	13 22.4	9 58.4	29 14.5	8 44.5	1 23.5	1 19.2	26 19.0	28 56.6	2 04.7	3 25.8
17 Tu	17 42 01	26 04 23	3♓14 37	9♓57 24	22 39.2	22 16.4	15 06.9	11 01.0	29 48.0	8 59.6	1 37.2	1 21.9	26 21.1	28 59.8	2 05.3	3 24.8
18 W	17 45 57	27 01 40	16 44 02	23 34 40	22 36.0	22 15.6	16 49.0	12 03.8	0♍21.5	9 14.5	1 50.9	1 24.4	26 23.2	29 03.0	2 05.8	3 23.7
19 Th	17 49 54	27 58 57	0♈29 29	7♈28 35	22 32.8	22 15.6	18 28.6	13 06.8	0 55.2	9 29.2	2 04.6	1 26.8	26 25.3	29 06.2	2 06.4	3 22.6
20 F	17 53 50	28 56 14	14 31 59	21 39 38	22 29.7	22 15.1	20 05.8	14 10.1	1 29.0	9 43.7	2 18.3	1 29.2	26 27.3	29 09.3	2 06.9	3 21.5
21 Sa	17 57 47	29 53 30	28 51 20	6♉06 46	22 26.5	22 12.9	21 40.5	15 13.7	2 02.8	9 58.0	2 32.0	1 31.4	26 29.3	29 12.5	2 07.4	3 20.4
22 Su	18 01 43	0♋50 47	13♉25 28	20 46 48	22 23.3	22 08.3	23 12.7	16 17.4	2 36.8	10 12.2	2 45.7	1 33.6	26 31.3	29 15.6	2 07.8	3 19.3
23 M	18 05 40	1 48 03	28 10 01	5♊34 14	22 20.1	22 01.0	24 42.4	17 21.4	3 10.8	10 26.1	2 59.4	1 35.6	26 33.2	29 18.6	2 08.2	3 18.2
24 Tu	18 09 37	2 45 19	12♊58 26	20 21 36	22 16.9	21 51.6	26 09.6	18 25.5	3 44.9	10 39.9	3 13.1	1 37.6	26 35.1	29 21.7	2 08.6	3 17.0
25 W	18 13 33	3 42 35	27 42 40	5♋00 36	22 13.8	21 40.8	27 34.3	19 29.9	4 19.1	10 53.5	3 26.8	1 39.5	26 36.9	29 24.8	2 08.9	3 15.8
26 Th	18 17 30	4 39 51	12♋14 28	19 23 26	22 10.6	21 29.9	28 56.3	20 34.5	4 53.4	11 06.8	3 40.5	1 41.3	26 38.7	29 27.8	2 09.2	3 14.6
27 F	18 21 26	5 37 06	26 26 49	3♌24 07	22 07.4	21 20.2	0♌15.8	21 39.2	5 27.8	11 20.0	3 54.2	1 42.9	26 40.4	29 30.8	2 09.5	3 13.4
28 Sa	18 25 23	6 34 21	10♌14 59	16 59 16	22 04.2	21 12.5	1 32.5	22 44.1	6 02.2	11 32.9	4 07.9	1 44.5	26 42.1	29 33.7	2 09.8	3 12.2
29 Su	18 29 19	7 31 36	23 36 58	0♍08 16	22 01.1	21 07.3	2 46.6	23 49.2	6 36.8	11 45.7	4 21.6	1 46.0	26 43.7	29 36.7	2 10.0	3 11.0
30 M	18 33 16	8♋28 49	6♍33 26	12 52 53	21♓57.9	21♓04.6	3♌57.8	24♉54.5	7♍11.4	11♈58.2	4♋35.3	1♈47.3	26♈45.3	29♉39.6	2♈10.1	3♒09.7

1st of Month

Julian Day # 2460827.5
Obliquity 23°26'8"
SVP 4♓54'6"
GC 27♐11.7
Eris 25♈30.7

Day	⚴	Day	⚵	Day	⚶
1	25♒01.7	1	20♏27.8R	1	6♏08.0R
6	25 11.8	6	19 31.3R	6	5 40.2R
11	25 13.4R	11	18 40.7R	11	5 24.7R
16	25 06.1R	16	17 56.9R	16	5 21.7
21	24 49.7R	21	17 20.4R	21	5 30.8
26	24 24.0R	26	16 51.7R	26	5 51.8

DECLINATION and LATITUDE

Day	☉ Decl	☽ Decl	☽ Lat	☽ 12h Decl	☿ Decl	☿ Lat	♀ Decl	♀ Lat	♂ Decl	♂ Lat	⚳ Decl	⚳ Lat	♃ Decl	♃ Lat	♄ Decl	♄ Lat
1 Su	22N04	19N12	3N09	16N43	23N13	0N52	7N39	2S09	15N51	1N27	7S04	9S43	23N15	0S11	1S44	2S06
2 M	22 12	14 05	2 11	11 20	23 38	1 01	7 57	2 12	15 40	1 26	6 59	9 45	23 15	0 11	1 43	2 07
3 Tu	22 19	8 31	1 08	5 40	24 00	1 10	8 15	2 15	15 29	1 25	6 54	9 48	23 15	0 11	1 42	2 07
4 W	22 26	2 47	0 04	0S06	24 19	1 18	8 34	2 18	15 17	1 24	6 50	9 50	23 15	0 10	1 40	2 07
5 Th	22 33	2S57	0S59	5 46	24 36	1 25	8 52	2 20	15 06	1 23	6 46	9 52	23 16	0 10	1 39	2 07
6 F	22 39	8 31	1 59	11 11	24 50	1 32	9 10	2 23	14 54	1 22	6 41	9 55	23 16	0 10	1 38	2 08
7 Sa	22 45	13 45	2 53	16 12	25 01	1 39	9 29	2 25	14 42	1 22	6 37	9 57	23 16	0 10	1 37	2 08
8 Su	22 51	18 30	3 40	20 38	25 09	1 44	9 48	2 27	14 31	1 21	6 33	9 60	23 16	0 10	1 36	2 08
9 M	22 56	22 33	4 18	24 15	25 15	1 49	10 06	2 29	14 19	1 20	6 29	10 02	23 16	0 10	1 35	2 08
10 Tu	23 01	25 42	4 44	26 52	25 18	1 53	10 25	2 31	14 07	1 19	6 25	10 05	23 16	0 10	1 34	2 09
11 W	23 05	27 43	4 58	28 14	25 19	1 56	10 44	2 33	13 55	1 18	6 21	10 08	23 17	0 10	1 32	2 09
12 Th	23 09	28 24	4 58	28 13	25 17	1 59	11 03	2 34	13 43	1 17	6 17	10 10	23 17	0 10	1 31	2 09
13 F	23 13	27 40	4 44	26 45	25 12	2 00	11 22	2 35	13 30	1 16	6 13	10 13	23 17	0 10	1 31	2 09
14 Sa	23 16	25 29	4 16	23 54	25 06	2 01	11 40	2 37	13 18	1 15	6 10	10 16	23 17	0 09	1 30	2 10
15 Su	23 19	21 59	3 35	19 48	24 57	2 02	11 59	2 38	13 06	1 14	6 06	10 18	23 17	0 09	1 29	2 10
16 M	23 21	17 22	2 42	14 42	24 47	2 01	12 18	2 39	12 53	1 14	6 03	10 21	23 17	0 09	1 28	2 10
17 Tu	23 23	11 51	1 39	8 50	24 34	2 00	12 36	2 39	12 41	1 13	5 60	10 24	23 17	0 09	1 27	2 10
18 W	23 24	5 41	0 29	2 27	24 20	1 58	12 55	2 40	12 28	1 12	5 56	10 26	23 17	0 09	1 26	2 11
19 Th	23 25	0N52	0N43	4N11	24 04	1 55	13 13	2 41	12 15	1 11	5 53	10 29	23 16	0 09	1 26	2 11
20 F	23 26	7 30	1 55	10 44	23 47	1 52	13 32	2 41	12 02	1 10	5 50	10 32	23 16	0 09	1 25	2 11
21 Sa	23 26	13 53	3 00	16 51	23 28	1 48	13 50	2 41	11 49	1 09	5 47	10 35	23 16	0 09	1 24	2 11
22 Su	23 26	19 36	3 55	22 05	23 09	1 44	14 08	2 41	11 36	1 08	5 44	10 38	23 16	0 09	1 24	2 12
23 M	23 26	24 13	4 36	25 58	22 48	1 38	14 26	2 41	11 23	1 08	5 42	10 41	23 16	0 09	1 23	2 12
24 Tu	23 25	27 16	4 57	28 05	22 26	1 32	14 44	2 41	11 10	1 07	5 39	10 44	23 16	0 08	1 23	2 12
25 W	23 23	28 24	4 59	28 13	22 03	1 26	15 01	2 41	10 57	1 06	5 36	10 47	23 15	0 08	1 22	2 13
26 Th	23 21	27 33	4 42	26 26	21 39	1 19	15 18	2 41	10 44	1 05	5 34	10 50	23 15	0 08	1 22	2 13
27 F	23 19	24 54	4 07	23 01	21 15	1 11	15 36	2 40	10 30	1 04	5 32	10 53	23 15	0 08	1 21	2 13
28 Sa	23 17	20 51	3 18	18 27	20 50	1 03	15 53	2 40	10 17	1 03	5 30	10 56	23 14	0 08	1 21	2 13
29 Su	23 13	15 51	2 20	13 07	20 25	0 54	16 09	2 39	10 03	1 02	5 27	10 59	23 14	0 08	1 20	2 14
30 M	23N10	10N17	1N16	7N23	19N59	0N44	16N26	2S38	9N49	1N02	5S25	11S02	23N14	0S08	1S20	2S14

Day	⚷ Decl	⚷ Lat	♅ Decl	♅ Lat	♆ Decl	♆ Lat	♇ Decl	♇ Lat
1	10N36	0N43	19N32	0S13	0S27	1S18	22S52	3S38
6	10 41	0 43	19 36	0 13	0 25	1 18	22 54	3 39
11	10 45	0 43	19 39	0 13	0 24	1 18	22 56	3 40
16	10 49	0 43	19 43	0 13	0 23	1 19	22 58	3 41
21	10 53	0 43	19 47	0 13	0 22	1 19	22 60	3 41
26	10 56	0 42	19 50	0 13	0 21	1 19	23 02	3 42

Day	⚴ Decl	⚴ Lat	⚵ Decl	⚵ Lat	⚶ Decl	⚶ Lat	Eris Decl	Eris Lat
1	15N54	30N48	1S44	16N42	4S19	9N46	0S01	10S36
6	16 18	31 11	1 36	16 36	4 36	9 19	0 00	10 36
11	16 39	31 32	1 32	16 27	4 58	8 51	0N00	10 36
16	16 57	31 53	1 31	16 16	5 24	8 23	0 01	10 36
21	17 10	32 13	1 34	16 03	5 53	7 55	0 01	10 37
26	17 19	32 30	1 41	15 49	6 26	7 27	0 01	10 37

Moon Phenomena

Max/0 Decl (dy hr mn)
4 11:36 0 S
11 23:44 28S24
18 20:53 0 N
25 1:33 28N24

Perigee/Apogee (dy hr m kilometers)
7 10:45 a 405553
23 4:45 p 363180

Max/0 Lat (dy hr mn)
4 1:35 0 S
11 12:25 5S00
18 9:42 0 N
24 14:16 5N01

PH dy hr mn
☽ 3 3:42 12♍50
○ 11 7:45 20♐39
☾ 18 19:20 27♓48
● 25 10:33 4♋08

Void of Course Moon

Last Aspect	☽ Ingress
1 23:39 ♃ ✶	♍ 2 3:01
4 11:13 ♃ □	♎ 4 13:39
7 1:06 ♃ △	♏ 7 2:24
9 12:08 ♅ ☍	♐ 9 14:57
11 19:59 ♂ △	♑ 12 1:56
14 8:53 ♅ △	♒ 14 11:01
16 17:32 ♂ ☍	♓ 16 18:10
18 21:35 ♅ ✶	♈ 18 23:09
21 1:50 ☉ ✶	♉ 21 1:54
23 1:52 ♅ ☌	♊ 23 2:58
23 8:27 ♂ □	♋ 25 3:45
27 5:17 ♅ ✶	♌ 27 6:06
29 11:04 ♅ □	♍ 29 11:45

DAILY ASPECTARIAN

1 Su	☽⚼♄ 0:00; ☿∥♃ 1:17; ☽⚼♆ 2:32; ☽⚼⚳ 7:51; ☽☌♂ 10:42; ♃⚺♅ 15:49; ☽∥♂ 16:34; ☽△♀ 18:53; ☽△⚷ 18:59; ♀☌⚷ 20:12; ☽□♅ 23:33; ☽✶♃ 23:39
2 M	☽⚻♄ 4:05; ☽⚻♆ 6:36; ☽⚻♇ 9:56; ☽⚻⚳ 12:45; ☽∥⚷ 15:02; ☽⚼⚷ 23:43
3 Tu	☽∥♀ 1:04; ☽⚼♀ 1:57; ☊ D 3:37; ☉□☽ 3:42; ☽⋕⚳ 6:53; ☿⚼♇ 13:19; ☽⚼♇ 15:02; ☽□☿ 15:25; ☽⚺♂ 22:59
4 W	☊ R 1:31; ☽⋕♄ 4:38; ☽⚻⚷ 5:21; ☽⋕♆ 9:49; ☽⚻♀ 10:09; ☽△♅ 10:16; ☽□♃ 11:13; ♀⚺♅ 11:34; ☽∥♆ 13:24; ☽☍♄ 15:06; ☽☍♆ 17:32; ☽∥♄ 18:33; ☽△♇ 20:53
5 Th	☽☍⚳ 1:21; ♀✶♃ 2:33; ☽∠♂ 6:27; ☽∥⚳ 16:06; ☽⚼♅ 16:37; ☉△☽ 20:48; ☿✶♂ 22:11
6 F	☽⋕♀ 3:07; ♀ ♉ 4:44; ☽⋕⚷ 9:44; ☽✶♂ 14:20; ☽△☿ 16:57; ☽☍⚷ 18:10; ☽⚻♅ 23:14; ☿✶⚷ 23:56
7 Sa	☽△♃ 1:06; ♀⚺♄ 1:33; ☽⚻♄ 4:10; ☽☍♀ 4:23; ☽⋕♂ 4:26; ☉⚼☽ 5:58; ☽⚻♆ 6:24; ☽□♇ 9:39; ☽⚻⚳ 15:41
8 Su	♀⚺♆ 4:25; ☿⚺♅ 5:33; ☽⚼☿ 5:52; ☽⋕♅ 6:13; ☽⚼♃ 8:06; ☽⚼♄ 10:43; ☽⚼♆ 12:49; ☉⚻☽ 15:01; ☉⋕♇ 18:05; ☿☌♃ 20:13; ☽⚼⚳ 22:42; ☿ ♋ 22:59
9 M	☽∥♇ 2:25; ☉⋕☽ 2:37; ☉⚼♇ 2:48; ☽⋕♃ 4:53; ☽□♂ 5:58; ☽⚻⚷ 7:04; ⚴ R 9:42; ☿□♄ 10:50; ☽☍♅ 12:08; ☽⚻♃ 14:50; ☽△♄ 16:58; ♀□♇ 17:22; ☽⚻☿ 18:09; ☽△♆ 18:57; ☽⋕☿ 20:26; ♃ ♋ 21:03; ☽✶♇ 21:59; ☽⚻♀ 22:24; ☿□♆ 22:56
10 Tu	☽△⚳ 5:21; ♂△⚷ 7:38; ☽⚼⚷ 13:00; ☿⚻♇ 17:14
11 W	♀∥⚷ 1:41; ☽∠♇ 3:34; ☽⚼♀ 6:42; ☉☍☽ 7:45; ☽△⚷ 18:29; ☿✶♀ 19:42; ☽△♂ 19:59; ☽⚻♅ 23:28
12 Th	☽☍♃ 2:55; ☽□♄ 4:08; ☽□♆ 5:52; ☽⚺♇ 8:40; ☽△♀ 14:23; ☽☍☿ 15:57; ☽□⚳ 17:09
13 F	☿□⚳ 0:58; ☽⚼♂ 2:12; ☽⚼♅ 4:25; ☉⚻☽ 22:07
14 Sa	☽⋕☿ 3:18; ☽□⚷ 3:59; ☉∥♃ 7:11; ☽⚻♂ 7:52; ☽△♅ 8:53; ♀⚺⚳ 10:15; ☽⚻♃ 13:00; ☽✶♄ 13:22; ☽✶♆ 14:53; ☉⋕☽ 15:58; ☽⋕♃ 16:05; ☽☌♇ 17:28; ⚶ D 18:01; ☽∥♇ 18:10
15 Su	☽✶⚳ 2:53; ☽□♀ 3:58; ☉⚼☽ 4:24; ♂□♅ 9:48; ☽⚻☿ 9:56; ☽⋕♅ 12:29; ♃□♄ 14:37; ☽∠♄ 17:15; ☽⚼♃ 17:17; ☽∠♆ 18:39
16 M	☽∠⚳ 6:58; ☿∠♅ 8:03; ☉△☽ 10:03; ☽✶⚷ 11:32; ☽□♅ 16:19; ☿∠♂ 17:31; ☽☍♂ 17:32; ☽⚼☿ 17:32; ☽⋕♂ 20:28; ☽⚺♄ 20:37; ☽△♃ 21:02; ☽⋕♀ 21:03; ☽⚺♆ 21:55
17 Tu	☽⚺♇ 0:18; ♀∥♂ 3:14; ☽⋕⚷ 4:06; ☉✶⚷ 7:17; ♂ ♍ 8:37; ☽⚺⚳ 10:29; ☽∠⚷ 14:31; ☉∠♀ 14:54; ☽✶♀ 15:03; ☽∥⚳ 23:03
18 W	☽△☿ 0:10; ☽∠♇ 2:55; ☽∥♄ 15:42; ☽⚺⚷ 16:56; ☉□☽ 19:20; ☽∠♀ 19:33; ☽∥♆ 19:33; ☽✶♅ 21:35; ☽⋕♆ 22:13
19 Th	☽⚻♂ 0:46; ☽☌♄ 1:39; ☽⋕♄ 2:03; ☽□♃ 2:47; ☽☌♆ 2:47; ♃□♆ 3:17; ☽✶♇ 4:58; ☽☌⚳ 15:42; ☽⋕⚳ 18:01; ☽⚺♀ 23:20; ☽∠♅ 23:21
20 F	♂⚻♄ 0:10; ☽⚼♂ 3:26; ☉⚺♅ 5:48; ☽□☿ 10:33; ☽∥⚷ 12:30; ☽∥♂ 16:20; ☽☌⚷ 20:03; ☽∥♀ 23:48
21 Sa	☽⚺♅ 0:35; ☉✶☽ 1:50; ☉∥☿ 2:38; ☉ ♋ 2:43; ♂⚻♆ 3:15; ☽⚺♄ 4:26; ☽⚺♆ 5:25; ☽△♂ 5:30; ☽✶♃ 6:11; ☽□♇ 7:25; ☿∥♃ 15:10; ☽⚺⚳ 18:38
22 Su	☽∥♅ 0:49; ☉∠☽ 4:14; ☽☌♀ 5:03; ☽∠♄ 5:08; ☽∠♆ 6:03; ♀∠♄ 6:17; ☽∠♃ 7:12; ☿⋕♇ 9:48; ♂✶♃ 10:33; ☽∥☿ 16:23; ☽⋕♇ 16:55; ☽✶☿ 17:46; ☽∥♃ 18:22; ☉□♄ 18:37; ♀∠♆ 19:02; ☉∥☽ 19:18; ☽∠⚳ 19:30; ☽⚺⚷ 21:23
23 M	☽☌♅ 1:52; ♂⚻♇ 5:01; ☽✶♄ 5:34; ☉⚺☽ 6:18; ☽✶♆ 6:26; ☽⚺♃ 7:56; ☽△♇ 8:19; ☽□♂ 8:27; ☉□♆ 8:30; ♀∠♃ 18:06; ☽✶⚳ 20:12; ☽∠☿ 20:45; ☽∠⚷ 21:44
24 Tu	♃⚻♇ 6:17; ☿□⚷ 7:17; ☽⚼♇ 8:37; ☽⚺♀ 9:33; ☉⚻♇ 13:01; ☉☌♃ 15:18; ☽✶⚷ 22:12; ☽⚺☿ 23:45
25 W	♂∥⚷ 2:27; ☽⚺♅ 2:48; ☽□♄ 6:29; ☽□♆ 7:17; ☽⚻♇ 9:07; ☽☌♃ 9:34; ☉☌☽ 10:33; ☽✶♂ 11:18; ☽∠♀ 12:03; ☽□⚳ 22:05
26 Th	☽∠♅ 3:44; ☿✶♅ 9:46; ☽∠♂ 13:23; ☉✶♂ 14:12; ☽✶♀ 15:09; ☿ ♌ 19:10
27 F	☽□⚷ 0:23; ☽✶♅ 5:17; ☽☌☿ 7:14; ☽△♄ 9:06; ☽△♆ 9:51; ☉∥☽ 10:21; ☽∥♃ 10:42; ☽☍♇ 11:41; ☽⋕♇ 11:55; ☽⚺♃ 13:05; ☽⚺♂ 16:16; ☉⚺☽ 17:03
28 Sa	☽∥☿ 0:07; ☽△⚳ 2:20; ☿△♄ 3:54; ☽∥♅ 5:07; ☽⚼♄ 11:35; ☿△♆ 11:59; ☽⚼♆ 12:19; ☽∠♃ 16:08; ☉∥♃ 19:11; ☉∠☽ 21:52; ☽∥♀ 22:42
29 Su	☽□♀ 0:24; ☽△⚷ 5:43; ☽⚼⚳ 5:52; ☿☍♇ 7:58; ☽□♅ 11:04; ☽⚻♄ 15:03; ☽⚻♆ 15:47; ☽⚻♇ 17:39; ☽⚺☿ 18:39; ☽✶♃ 20:14; ☽∥⚷ 21:08
30 M	☽☌♂ 1:15; ☽∥♂ 2:00; ☉✶☽ 3:56; ☿∥♅ 5:52; ☽⚼⚷ 9:52; ☽⚻⚳ 10:26; ☿⚺♃ 16:17; ☽⋕⚳ 20:11; ☽⚼♇ 22:07

LONGITUDE

Day	Sid.Time	☉	☽	☽ 12 hour	Mean ☊	True ☊	☿	♀	♂	⚳	♃	♄	⚷	♅	♆	♇
	h m s	° ' "	° ' "	° ' "	° '	° '	° '	° '	° '	° '	° '	° '	° '	° '	° '	° '
1 Tu	18 37 13	9♋26 03	19♍07 06	25♍16 39	21♓54.7	21♓03.8	5♌06.3	25♉59.9	7♍46.1	12♈10.5	4♋49.0	1♈48.6	26♈46.8	29♉42.5	2♈10.3	3♒08.5
2 W	18 41 09	10 23 16	1♎22 10	7♎24 16	21 51.5	21R 04.0	6 11.8	27 05.6	8 20.9	12 22.6	5 02.6	1 49.8	26 48.3	29 45.3	2 10.4	3R 07.2
3 Th	18 45 06	11 20 29	13 23 37	19 20 55	21 48.4	21 04.1	7 14.2	28 11.3	8 55.7	12 34.5	5 16.3	1 50.9	26 49.8	29 48.1	2 10.5	3 05.9
4 F	18 49 02	12 17 41	25 16 48	1♏11 55	21 45.2	21 03.3	8 13.6	29 17.2	9 30.6	12 46.2	5 29.9	1 51.8	26 51.2	29 50.9	2R 10.5	3 04.6
5 Sa	18 52 59	13 14 54	7♏06 53	13 02 19	21 42.0	21 00.6	9 09.9	0♊23.3	10 05.6	12 57.6	5 43.5	1 52.7	26 52.5	29 53.7	2 10.5	3 03.3
6 Su	18 56 55	14 12 06	18 58 43	24 56 37	21 38.8	20 55.6	10 02.8	1 29.6	10 40.7	13 08.8	5 57.2	1 53.5	26 53.8	29 56.4	2 10.5	3 02.0
7 M	19 00 52	15 09 17	0♐56 27	6♐58 35	21 35.7	20 48.2	10 52.3	2 36.0	11 15.9	13 19.8	6 10.8	1 54.1	26 55.1	29 59.1	2 10.5	3 00.7
8 Tu	19 04 48	16 06 29	13 03 23	19 11 05	21 32.5	20 38.8	11 38.2	3 42.5	11 51.1	13 30.5	6 24.3	1 54.7	26 56.3	0♊01.8	2 10.4	2 59.4
9 W	19 08 45	17 03 41	25 21 54	1♑35 57	21 29.3	20 28.2	12 20.6	4 49.2	12 26.4	13 41.0	6 37.9	1 55.2	26 57.4	0 04.4	2 10.3	2 58.0
10 Th	19 12 42	18 00 53	7♑53 21	14 14 05	21 26.1	20 17.1	12 59.1	5 56.0	13 01.8	13 51.2	6 51.5	1 55.6	26 58.5	0 07.1	2 10.1	2 56.7
11 F	19 16 38	18 58 05	20 38 10	27 05 31	21 23.0	20 06.7	13 33.7	7 03.0	13 37.2	14 01.2	7 05.0	1 55.8	26 59.6	0 09.6	2 09.9	2 55.3
12 Sa	19 20 35	19 55 17	3♒36 03	10♒09 40	21 19.8	19 58.0	14 04.2	8 10.1	14 12.7	14 11.0	7 18.5	1 56.0	27 00.6	0 12.2	2 09.7	2 54.0
13 Su	19 24 31	20 52 29	16 46 15	23 25 40	21 16.6	19 51.5	14 30.5	9 17.3	14 48.3	14 20.5	7 32.0	1R 56.1	27 01.5	0 14.7	2 09.5	2 52.6
14 M	19 28 28	21 49 41	0♓07 51	6♓52 42	21 13.4	19 47.5	14 52.5	10 24.7	15 24.0	14 29.7	7 45.5	1 56.0	27 02.4	0 17.2	2 09.2	2 51.2
15 Tu	19 32 24	22 46 54	13 40 09	20 30 08	21 10.2	19D 45.8	15 10.0	11 32.2	15 59.7	14 38.7	7 58.9	1 55.9	27 03.3	0 19.6	2 08.9	2 49.8
16 W	19 36 21	23 44 08	27 22 39	4♈17 40	21 07.1	19 45.8	15 22.9	12 39.9	16 35.4	14 47.4	8 12.3	1 55.7	27 04.1	0 22.0	2 08.6	2 48.4
17 Th	19 40 17	24 41 22	11♈15 08	18 15 03	21 03.9	19 46.6	15 31.0	13 47.6	17 11.4	14 55.8	8 25.7	1 55.3	27 04.8	0 24.4	2 08.2	2 47.0
18 F	19 44 14	25 38 37	25 17 20	2♉21 52	21 00.7	19R 47.1	15R 34.4	14 55.2	17 47.3	15 04.0	8 39.1	1 54.9	27 05.5	0 26.7	2 07.8	2 45.6
19 Sa	19 48 11	26 35 53	9♉28 30	16 36 59	20 57.5	19 46.4	15 32.9	16 03.6	18 23.3	15 11.8	8 52.4	1 54.3	27 06.2	0 29.0	2 07.4	2 44.2
20 Su	19 52 07	27 33 09	23 47 01	0♊58 12	20 54.4	19 43.8	15 26.6	17 11.7	18 59.4	15 19.4	9 05.7	1 53.7	27 06.7	0 31.3	2 06.9	2 42.8
21 M	19 56 04	28 30 26	8♊10 03	15 22 00	20 51.2	19 39.2	15 15.4	18 20.0	19 35.6	15 26.7	9 19.0	1 53.0	27 07.3	0 33.5	2 06.4	2 41.4
22 Tu	20 00 00	29 27 44	22 33 26	29 43 40	20 48.0	19 32.7	14 59.4	19 28.4	20 11.8	15 33.8	9 32.3	1 52.1	27 07.8	0 35.7	2 05.9	2 40.0
23 W	20 03 57	0♌25 03	6♋52 01	13♋57 46	20 44.8	19 25.2	14 38.7	20 36.9	20 48.1	15 40.5	9 45.5	1 51.2	27 08.2	0 37.8	2 05.3	2 38.6
24 Th	20 07 53	1 22 23	21 00 16	27 58 56	20 41.7	19 17.5	14 13.6	21 45.5	21 24.5	15 46.9	9 58.7	1 50.2	27 08.6	0 39.9	2 04.7	2 37.2
25 F	20 11 50	2 19 43	4♌53 13	11♌42 41	20 38.5	19 10.7	13 44.2	22 54.2	22 01.0	15 53.0	10 11.8	1 49.0	27 08.9	0 42.0	2 04.1	2 35.8
26 Sa	20 15 46	3 17 03	18 27 03	25 06 06	20 35.3	19 05.3	13 10.9	24 03.0	22 37.5	15 58.8	10 24.9	1 47.8	27 09.2	0 44.0	2 03.5	2 34.4
27 Su	20 19 43	4 14 24	1♍39 45	8♍08 04	20 32.1	19 01.9	12 34.3	25 11.9	23 14.1	16 04.3	10 38.0	1 46.5	27 09.4	0 46.0	2 02.8	2 33.0
28 M	20 23 40	5 11 46	14 31 10	20 49 21	20 29.0	19D 00.4	11 54.7	26 20.9	23 50.7	16 09.5	10 51.0	1 45.0	27 09.6	0 48.0	2 02.1	2 31.5
29 Tu	20 27 36	6 09 08	27 02 55	3♎12 18	20 25.8	19 00.6	11 12.8	27 30.0	24 27.4	16 14.4	11 04.0	1 43.5	27 09.7	0 49.9	2 01.4	2 30.1
30 W	20 31 33	7 06 31	9♎17 59	15 20 30	20 22.6	19 01.8	10 29.2	28 39.2	25 04.2	16 19.0	11 17.0	1 41.9	27R 09.8	0 51.7	2 00.6	2 28.7
31 Th	20 35 29	8♌03 54	21 20 25	27 18 21	20♓19.4	19♓03.3	9♌44.7	29♉48.5	25♍41.1	16♈23.2	11♋29.9	1♈40.1	27♈09.8	0♊53.5	1♈59.8	2♒27.3

1st of Month

Julian Day #
2460857.5
Obliquity
23°26'8"
SVP 4♓54'0"
GC 27♐11.7
Eris 25♈41.4

Day	⚴
1	23♒49.1R
6	23 05.4R
11	22 13.4R
16	21 13.7R
21	20 07.4R
26	18 55.6R
31	17 39.9R

Day	⚵
1	16♏31.1R
6	16 18.8R
11	16 14.5R
16	16 18.2
21	16 29.5
26	16 48.2
31	17 13.9

Day	⚶
1	6♏24.2
6	7 07.5
11	8 00.7
16	9 03.1
21	10 14.1
26	11 33.1
31	12 59.3

DECLINATION and LATITUDE

Day	☉ Decl	☽ Decl	☽ Lat	☽ 12h Decl	☿ Decl	☿ Lat	♀ Decl	♀ Lat	♂ Decl	♂ Lat	⚳ Decl	⚳ Lat	♃ Decl	♃ Lat	♄ Decl	♄ Lat
1 Tu	23N06	4N28	0N10	1N32	19N33	0N34	16N42	2S38	9N36	1N01	5S24	11S05	23N13	0S08	1S20	2S14
2 W	23 02	1S23	0S55	4S15	19 07	0 24	16 58	2 37	9 22	1 00	5 22	11 08	23 13	0 08	1 20	2 14
3 Th	22 57	7 04	1 56	9 48	18 40	0 13	17 14	2 36	9 08	0 59	5 20	11 11	23 12	0 08	1 20	2 15
4 F	22 52	12 26	2 51	14 57	18 14	0 02	17 29	2 34	8 54	0 58	5 19	11 14	23 12	0 07	1 19	2 15
5 Sa	22 47	17 20	3 39	19 33	17 48	0S10	17 44	2 33	8 40	0 58	5 17	11 17	23 11	0 07	1 19	2 15
6 Su	22 41	21 35	4 18	23 25	17 22	0 22	17 59	2 32	8 26	0 57	5 16	11 21	23 11	0 07	1 19	2 16
7 M	22 35	24 60	4 45	26 19	16 57	0 35	18 13	2 30	8 12	0 56	5 15	11 24	23 10	0 07	1 19	2 16
8 Tu	22 28	27 20	5 00	28 02	16 32	0 48	18 27	2 29	7 58	0 55	5 14	11 27	23 10	0 07	1 19	2 16
9 W	22 21	28 23	5 02	28 23	16 07	1 01	18 41	2 27	7 44	0 54	5 13	11 30	23 09	0 07	1 19	2 16
10 Th	22 14	28 01	4 49	27 16	15 43	1 15	18 55	2 25	7 30	0 54	5 12	11 34	23 09	0 07	1 19	2 17
11 F	22 06	26 10	4 22	24 42	15 20	1 29	19 08	2 24	7 15	0 53	5 11	11 37	23 08	0 07	1 20	2 17
12 Sa	21 58	22 55	3 40	20 49	14 58	1 43	19 20	2 22	7 01	0 52	5 10	11 40	23 07	0 07	1 20	2 17
13 Su	21 49	18 27	2 47	15 51	14 37	1 57	19 32	2 20	6 46	0 51	5 10	11 44	23 07	0 07	1 20	2 17
14 M	21 40	13 02	1 43	10 03	14 17	2 11	19 44	2 18	6 32	0 51	5 10	11 47	23 06	0 07	1 20	2 18
15 Tu	21 31	6 55	0 33	3 42	13 58	2 26	19 56	2 16	6 17	0 50	5 09	11 51	23 05	0 06	1 21	2 18
16 W	21 21	0 25	0N41	2N53	13 40	2 40	20 06	2 13	6 03	0 49	5 09	11 54	23 05	0 06	1 21	2 18
17 Th	21 11	6N11	1 53	9 25	13 24	2 55	20 17	2 11	5 48	0 48	5 09	11 57	23 04	0 06	1 21	2 19
18 F	21 01	12 33	2 59	15 33	13 10	3 09	20 27	2 09	5 33	0 47	5 09	12 01	23 03	0 06	1 22	2 19
19 Sa	20 50	18 21	3 54	20 54	12 57	3 22	20 37	2 07	5 18	0 47	5 10	12 04	23 02	0 06	1 22	2 19
20 Su	20 39	23 10	4 36	25 05	12 46	3 36	20 46	2 04	5 04	0 46	5 10	12 08	23 02	0 06	1 23	2 19
21 M	20 28	26 37	5 01	27 42	12 37	3 49	20 54	2 02	4 49	0 45	5 10	12 11	23 01	0 06	1 23	2 20
22 Tu	20 16	28 19	5 06	28 28	12 30	4 01	21 03	1 59	4 34	0 44	5 11	12 15	22 60	0 06	1 24	2 20
23 W	20 04	28 08	4 53	27 26	12 25	4 12	21 10	1 56	4 19	0 44	5 12	12 18	22 59	0 06	1 24	2 20
24 Th	19 51	26 06	4 21	24 29	12 22	4 22	21 17	1 54	4 04	0 43	5 13	12 22	22 58	0 06	1 25	2 20
25 F	19 38	22 31	3 35	20 16	12 22	4 32	21 24	1 51	3 49	0 42	5 14	12 26	22 57	0 06	1 26	2 21
26 Sa	19 25	17 47	2 37	15 07	12 23	4 40	21 30	1 48	3 34	0 41	5 15	12 29	22 56	0 05	1 26	2 21
27 Su	19 12	12 19	1 32	9 25	12 27	4 47	21 36	1 46	3 18	0 41	5 16	12 33	22 55	0 05	1 27	2 21
28 M	18 58	6 28	0 24	3 29	12 32	4 52	21 41	1 43	3 03	0 40	5 17	12 36	22 54	0 05	1 28	2 21
29 Tu	18 44	0 31	0S43	2S26	12 40	4 56	21 45	1 40	2 48	0 39	5 19	12 40	22 53	0 05	1 29	2 22
30 W	18 30	5S20	1 48	8 10	12 50	4 58	21 49	1 37	2 33	0 38	5 21	12 44	22 52	0 05	1 30	2 22
31 Th	18N15	10S54	2S46	13S31	13N01	4S58	21N52	1S34	2N17	0N38	5S22	12S47	22N51	0S05	1S31	2S22

Day	⚷ Decl	⚷ Lat	♅ Decl	♅ Lat	♆ Decl	♆ Lat	♇ Decl	♇ Lat
1	10N59	0N42	19N53	0S13	0S21	1S19	23S04	3S43
6	11 01	0 42	19 56	0 13	0 21	1 20	23 06	3 43
11	11 03	0 42	19 59	0 13	0 22	1 20	23 08	3 44
16	11 05	0 42	20 01	0 13	0 22	1 20	23 10	3 44
21	11 06	0 42	20 04	0 13	0 24	1 20	23 12	3 45
26	11 06	0 41	20 06	0 13	0 25	1 21	23 14	3 45
31	11N06	0N41	20N08	0S13	0S27	1S21	23S16	3S46

Day	⚴ Decl	⚴ Lat	⚵ Decl	⚵ Lat	⚶ Decl	⚶ Lat	Eris Decl	Eris Lat
1	17N24	32N45	1S50	15N33	7S02	6N60	0N01	10S37
6	17 22	32 57	2 03	15 17	7 41	6 34	0 01	10 38
11	17 15	33 05	2 18	14 60	8 22	6 08	0 01	10 38
16	17 02	33 08	2 35	14 43	9 04	5 44	0 01	10 39
21	16 43	33 07	2 55	14 26	9 48	5 21	0 01	10 39
26	16 17	32 60	3 16	14 09	10 33	4 59	0 00	10 39
31	15N45	32N47	3S39	13N52	11S19	4N38	0S00	10S40

Moon Phenomena

Max/0 Decl
dy hr mn
1 18:18 0 S
9 5:56 28S26
16 1:31 0 N
22 9:34 28N28
29 2:04 0 S

Max/0 Lat
dy hr mn
1 3:46 0 S
8 14:38 5S03
15 10:42 0 N
21 19:01 5N07
28 8:32 0 S

Perigee/Apogee
dy hr m kilometers
5 2:30 a 404626
20 13:56 p 368042

PH dy hr mn
☽ 2 19:31 11♎10
○ 10 20:38 18♑50
☾ 18 0:39 25♈40
● 24 19:12 2♌08

Void of Course Moon

Last Aspect	☽ Ingress
1 20:48 ♅ △	♎ 1 21:18
2 19:31 ☉ □	♏ 4 9:34
6 22:05 ♅ ☍	♐ 6 22:07
7 21:31 ♂ □	♑ 9 8:56
10 20:38 ☉ ☍	♒ 11 17:22
12 19:46 ♅ □	♓ 13 23:46
15 17:11 ☉ △	♈ 16 4:33
18 0:39 ☉ □	♉ 18 8:00
20 6:45 ☉ ⚹	♊ 20 10:23
21 19:53 ♂ □	♋ 22 12:27
24 0:43 ♂ ⚹	♌ 24 15:30
26 11:03 ♀ ⚹	♍ 26 20:57
29 0:58 ♀ □	♎ 29 5:44
30 4:00 ♃ □	♏ 31 17:26

DAILY ASPECTARIAN

1 Tu	☽∠☿ 2:06; ☊ D 3:48; ☉⋕♇ 12:35; ☽⋕♄ 12:50; ☽△♀ 14:44; ☽⚻⚷ 14:59; ☽⋕♆ 16:52; ♀⚺⚷ 17:33; ☽∥♆ 19:45; ☽△♅ 20:48; ☽∥♄ 23:47
2 W	☽☍♄ 0:55; ☽☍♆ 1:36; ☽△♇ 3:28; ☽□♃ 7:26; ♀∠⚳ 7:38; ☽⚹☿ 10:31; ☽⚺♂ 14:35; ☽∥⚳ 16:38; ☊ R 19:20; ☉□☽ 19:31; ☽☍⚳ 22:20; ☽⚼♀ 23:33
3 Th	☽⚼♅ 2:51; ☽⋕♂ 8:41; ☽⋕⚷ 17:25; ☽∠♂ 22:22
4 F	☽☍⚷ 3:12; ☽⚻♀ 8:57; ☽⚻♅ 9:18; ♀☌♅ 12:46; ☽⚻♄ 13:22; ☽⚻♆ 13:59; ☉□⚳ 14:57; ♀ ♊ 15:32; ☽□♇ 15:47; ☽△♃ 21:08; ♆ R 21:35
5 Sa	☽⋕♀ 2:12; ☽⋕☿ 2:13; ☿∥♀ 2:18; ☽□☿ 4:30; ☽⚹♂ 6:21; ☽⚻⚳ 12:02; ☉△☽ 13:31; ☽⋕♅ 14:06; ☽⚼♄ 19:47; ☽⚼♆ 20:22
6 Su	☽⚼♃ 4:03; ☉⋕☽ 6:49; ♀⚹♄ 8:44; ☽∥♇ 9:50; ☽⋕♃ 10:23; ♀⚹♆ 14:48; ☽⚻⚷ 15:57; ☽⚼⚳ 18:42; ☉∠♅ 19:32; ☽☍♅ 22:05; ☉⚼☽ 22:18
7 M	☽△♄ 1:55; ☽△♆ 2:28; ☽☍♀ 3:38; ☽⚹♇ 4:07; ♅ ♊ 7:46; ♀△♇ 8:45; ☽⚻♃ 10:37; ☽△☿ 21:02; ☽□♂ 21:31; ☽⚼⚷ 21:48
8 Tu	☽△⚳ 0:54; ♂⚼⚷ 3:37; ☉⚻☽ 6:30; ☽∠♇ 9:39
9 W	☽△⚷ 3:05; ☽⚼☿ 4:02; ☽⚻♅ 9:06; ☽□♄ 12:37; ☽□♆ 13:06; ☽⚺♇ 14:36; ☽⚻♀ 19:55; ☽☍♃ 22:00
10 Th	☽⚻☿ 10:07; ☽△♂ 10:12; ☽□⚳ 11:26; ☽⚼♅ 13:42; ☉☍☽ 20:38
11 F	♀⚺♃ 0:54; ♃⋕♇ 1:58; ☽⚼♀ 2:53; ⚵ D 4:03; ☽□⚷ 11:50; ☽⚼♂ 15:32; ☽△♅ 17:44; ☽⚹♄ 20:56; ☽⚹♆ 21:21; ♂⚻⚳ 22:22; ☽∥♇ 22:36; ☽⋕♃ 22:42; ☽☌♇ 22:43
12 Sa	☉⋕☽ 5:53; ☽⚻♃ 6:55; ☿△⚳ 8:59; ☽△♀ 9:09; ☽⋕♅ 16:21; ☽⋕♀ 18:53; ☽⚹⚳ 19:33; ☽☍☿ 19:46; ☽⚻♂ 20:16
13 Su	☽∠♄ 0:18; ☽∠♆ 0:42; ♄ R 4:08; ☉⚻☽ 7:59; ☽⚼♃ 10:34; ☽⚹⚷ 18:28; ☽⋕☿ 18:29; ☽∠⚳ 22:51
14 M	☽□♅ 0:17; ☽⚺♄ 3:13; ☽⚺♆ 3:36; ☽⚺♇ 4:51; ☽⋕⚷ 7:57; ☉⚼☽ 12:49; ☽△♃ 13:47; ☽□♀ 19:54; ☽∠⚷ 21:09
15 Tu	☽⚺⚳ 1:44; ☽⋕♂ 2:29; ☽⚻☿ 2:41; ☽☍♂ 4:17; ☽∥⚳ 6:37; ☽∠♇ 7:18; ☊ D 10:43; ♀∠⚷ 11:09; ♀∥♅ 12:06; ☉△☽ 17:11; ☽∥♄ 20:37; ☽⚺⚷ 23:28
16 W	☽∥♆ 0:10; ☽⋕♆ 2:53; ☽⚹♅ 5:13; ☽⚼☿ 5:17; ☽⋕♄ 6:25; ☽☌♄ 7:54; ☽☌♆ 8:16; ☽⚹♇ 9:25; ☽□♃ 19:04; ☽⋕⚳ 20:15; ☽∥♂ 22:40
17 Th	☽⚹♀ 4:45; ☽☌⚳ 6:23; ☽∠♅ 7:09; ☽△☿ 7:22; ☽⚻♂ 10:38; ☽∥⚷ 18:19; ♂⚼♇ 22:55
18 F	☉□☽ 0:39; ☊ R 0:45; ☽∥☿ 2:18; ☽☌⚷ 3:04; ♀⚹⚳ 3:22; ☿ R 4:46; ☽∠♀ 8:33; ☽⚺♅ 8:46; ☽⚺♄ 11:14; ☽⚺♆ 11:36; ☽□♇ 12:39; ☽⚼♂ 13:17; ☿⚹♀ 13:38; ☽⚹♃ 22:58
19 Sa	☽∥♅ 7:50; ☽⚺⚳ 9:42; ☽□☿ 10:09; ☽∥♀ 10:53; ☉∥☽ 11:13; ☽⚺♀ 12:01; ☽∠♄ 12:29; ☉□⚷ 12:49; ☽∠♆ 12:50; ♂⋕⚳ 14:04; ☽△♂ 15:38; ☉∥♀ 15:56; ☽∥♃ 23:11
20 Su	☽⋕♇ 0:09; ☽∠♃ 0:32; ☽⚺⚷ 5:34; ☉⚹☽ 6:45; ☿△⚳ 10:01; ♀⚼♇ 10:44; ☽∠⚳ 11:01; ☽☌♅ 11:17; ☽⚹♄ 13:32; ☽⚹♆ 13:54; ☽△♇ 14:53
21 M	☽⚺♃ 1:57; ☽∠⚷ 6:36; ☉∠☽ 9:32; ☽⚹☿ 11:37; ☽⚹⚳ 12:14; ☽⚼♇ 15:51; ☽☌♀ 18:24; ☽□♂ 19:53
22 Tu	☽⚹⚷ 7:39; ⚳∠♅ 9:56; ☽∠☿ 12:10; ☉⚺☽ 12:23; ☽⚺♅ 13:29; ☉ ♌ 13:31; ☽□♄ 15:35; ☽□♆ 15:58; ☽⚻♇ 16:54; ☉∥♅ 22:05
23 W	☽☌♃ 4:57; ☉⚹♅ 5:33; ♀□♂ 8:24; ☽⚺☿ 12:48; ☽∠♅ 14:52; ☽□⚳ 15:01
24 Th	☽⚹♂ 0:43; ☽⚺♀ 1:24; ☽□⚷ 10:33; ☉△♄ 11:25; ☽⚹♅ 16:41; ☉△♆ 17:33; ☽△♄ 18:39; ☽△♆ 19:05; ☉☌☽ 19:12; ☽⋕♇ 19:51; ☽☍♇ 20:01; ☽∥♃ 21:29
25 F	☽∠♂ 3:54; ☽∠♀ 5:46; ☽∥♀ 6:01; ☉☍♇ 6:34; ☽⚺♃ 9:29; ☽∥♅ 12:53; ☽☌☿ 14:59; ☉∥☽ 15:52; ☽△⚳ 19:33; ☽⚼♄ 21:03; ☽⚼♆ 21:31
26 Sa	☽⚺♂ 7:52; ☽⚹♀ 11:03; ☽∠♃ 12:47; ☽△⚷ 15:44; ☽□♅ 22:21; ☽⚼⚳ 22:54; ☽∥☿ 23:30
27 Su	☽⚻♄ 0:12; ☽⚻♆ 0:42; ☽⚻♇ 1:38; ☽∥⚷ 5:05; ☉⚺☽ 5:08; ☽⚹♃ 16:58; ☽⚺☿ 19:20; ☽⚼⚷ 19:33
28 M	☽⚻⚳ 3:08; ☽⋕⚳ 4:43; ☽⚼♇ 5:42; ☿∠♀ 7:21; ☊ D 8:33; ☉∠☽ 11:42; ☽∥♂ 14:21; ♀⚹⚷ 16:56; ☽☌♂ 18:44; ☽⋕♄ 20:05; ☽∠☿ 22:28
29 Tu	☽⚻⚷ 0:13; ☽⋕♆ 0:19; ☽□♀ 0:58; ☿⚺♃ 3:45; ☽∥♆ 3:49; ☽△♅ 7:23; ☽∥♄ 8:06; ☽☍♄ 9:05; ☽☍♆ 9:41; ☽△♇ 10:36; ☽⋕♂ 12:55; ☉⚹☽ 19:18
30 W	☽∥⚳ 0:02; ☽⚹☿ 2:13; ☽□♃ 4:00; ☿∠♂ 7:23; ☽⚼♅ 13:04; ☽☍⚳ 14:02; ⚷ R 14:43
31 Th	☽⋕⚷ 0:57; ♀ ♋ 3:58; ☽⚺♂ 9:13; ☽⋕☿ 10:08; ☽☍⚷ 11:43; ☽△♀ 18:53; ☽⚻♅ 19:17; ☽⚻♄ 20:45; ☽⚻♆ 21:27; ☽□♇ 22:21; ♀⚺♅ 23:04; ☉☌☿ 23:42

August 2025

LONGITUDE

Day	Sid.Time	☉	☽	☽ 12 hour	Mean☊	True☊	☿	♀	♂	⚳	♃	♄	⚷	♅	♆	♇
	h m s	° ' "	° ' "	° ' "	° '	° '	° '	° '	° '	° '	° '	° '	° '	° '	° '	° '
1 F	20 39 26	9♌01 18	3♏14 54	9♏10 43	20♓16.2	19♓04.4	9♌00.1	0♋57.9	26♍18.0	16♈27.1	11♋42.8	1♈38.3	27♈09.7	0♊55.3	1♈59.0	2♒25.9
2 Sa	20 43 22	9 58 43	15 06 25	21 02 37	20 13.1	19R 04.4	8R 16.1	2 07.4	26 55.0	16 30.7	11 55.6	1R 36.4	27R 09.6	0 57.0	1R 58.1	2R 24.5
3 Su	20 47 19	10 56 08	26 59 55	2♐58 54	20 09.9	19 03.0	7 33.6	3 17.0	27 32.1	16 33.9	12 08.3	1 34.4	27 09.5	0 58.7	1 57.2	2 23.1
4 M	20 51 15	11 53 33	9♐00 06	15 04 01	20 06.7	19 00.0	6 53.4	4 26.7	28 09.2	16 36.8	12 21.1	1 32.3	27 09.3	1 00.3	1 56.3	2 21.7
5 Tu	20 55 12	12 51 00	21 11 05	27 21 42	20 03.5	18 55.6	6 16.3	5 36.5	28 46.4	16 39.4	12 33.7	1 30.2	27 09.0	1 01.9	1 55.4	2 20.3
6 W	20 59 09	13 48 27	3♑36 11	9♑54 46	20 00.4	18 50.3	5 43.1	6 46.4	29 23.6	16 41.6	12 46.3	1 27.9	27 08.7	1 03.5	1 54.5	2 19.0
7 Th	21 03 05	14 45 55	16 17 40	22 44 57	19 57.2	18 44.6	5 14.3	7 56.3	0♎00.9	16 43.5	12 58.9	1 25.5	27 08.3	1 05.0	1 53.5	2 17.6
8 F	21 07 02	15 43 24	29 16 39	5♒52 41	19 54.0	18 39.2	4 50.7	9 06.4	0 38.3	16 45.1	13 11.4	1 23.1	27 07.9	1 06.5	1 52.5	2 16.2
9 Sa	21 10 58	16 40 54	12♒32 57	19 17 14	19 50.8	18 34.7	4 32.7	10 16.5	1 15.7	16 46.3	13 23.9	1 20.6	27 07.5	1 07.9	1 51.5	2 14.9
10 Su	21 14 55	17 38 25	26 05 17	2♓56 47	19 47.7	18 31.5	4 20.8	11 26.8	1 53.2	16 47.1	13 36.3	1 17.9	27 06.9	1 09.2	1 50.4	2 13.5
11 M	21 18 51	18 35 57	9♓51 25	16 48 49	19 44.5	18D 29.9	4D 15.3	12 37.1	2 30.8	16R 47.6	13 48.6	1 15.2	27 06.4	1 10.6	1 49.3	2 12.2
12 Tu	21 22 48	19 33 30	23 48 36	0♈50 24	19 41.3	18 29.8	4 16.6	13 47.5	3 08.4	16 47.8	14 00.9	1 12.4	27 05.7	1 11.8	1 48.2	2 10.8
13 W	21 26 44	20 31 04	7♈53 52	14 58 38	19 38.1	18 30.7	4 24.8	14 58.0	3 46.1	16 47.6	14 13.2	1 09.6	27 05.1	1 13.1	1 47.1	2 09.5
14 Th	21 30 41	21 28 40	22 04 22	29 10 45	19 34.9	18 32.1	4 40.2	16 08.6	4 23.9	16 47.0	14 25.3	1 06.6	27 04.3	1 14.2	1 45.9	2 08.2
15 F	21 34 38	22 26 18	6♉17 30	13♉24 19	19 31.8	18 33.4	5 02.7	17 19.3	5 01.7	16 46.0	14 37.4	1 03.6	27 03.6	1 15.4	1 44.7	2 06.9
16 Sa	21 38 34	23 23 57	20 30 56	27 37 05	19 28.6	18R 34.1	5 32.4	18 30.1	5 39.6	16 44.7	14 49.5	1 00.5	27 02.7	1 16.5	1 43.6	2 05.6
17 Su	21 42 31	24 21 37	4♊42 28	11♊46 50	19 25.4	18 33.8	6 09.3	19 41.0	6 17.5	16 43.1	15 01.5	0 57.3	27 01.8	1 17.5	1 42.3	2 04.3
18 M	21 46 27	25 19 20	18 49 54	25 51 21	19 22.2	18 32.4	6 53.2	20 51.9	6 55.6	16 41.1	15 13.4	0 54.0	27 00.9	1 18.5	1 41.1	2 03.0
19 Tu	21 50 24	26 17 03	2♋50 54	9♋48 13	19 19.1	18 30.1	7 44.1	22 03.0	7 33.7	16 38.7	15 25.2	0 50.7	26 59.9	1 19.4	1 39.8	2 01.7
20 W	21 54 20	27 14 49	16 43 02	23 35 00	19 15.9	18 27.3	8 41.7	23 14.1	8 11.8	16 35.9	15 37.0	0 47.3	26 58.9	1 20.3	1 38.5	2 00.5
21 Th	21 58 17	28 12 36	0♌23 51	7♌09 20	19 12.7	18 24.3	9 45.9	24 25.3	8 50.0	16 32.8	15 48.7	0 43.8	26 57.8	1 21.2	1 37.2	1 59.2
22 F	22 02 13	29 10 24	13 51 11	20 29 14	19 09.5	18 21.7	10 56.3	25 36.6	9 28.3	16 29.3	16 00.4	0 40.3	26 56.7	1 22.0	1 35.9	1 58.0
23 Sa	22 06 10	0♍08 14	27 03 18	3♍33 20	19 06.4	18 19.8	12 12.7	26 47.9	10 06.7	16 25.4	16 11.9	0 36.7	26 55.5	1 22.7	1 34.6	1 56.8
24 Su	22 10 07	1 06 05	9♍59 17	16 21 10	19 03.2	18D 18.8	13 34.7	27 59.4	10 45.1	16 21.1	16 23.4	0 33.0	26 54.3	1 23.4	1 33.2	1 55.6
25 M	22 14 03	2 03 58	22 39 05	28 53 11	19 00.0	18 18.7	15 01.9	29 10.9	11 23.6	16 16.5	16 34.8	0 29.2	26 53.0	1 24.1	1 31.8	1 54.4
26 Tu	22 18 00	3 01 52	5♎03 41	11♎10 52	18 56.8	18 19.3	16 34.0	0♌22.5	12 02.1	16 11.6	16 46.1	0 25.4	26 51.7	1 24.6	1 30.4	1 53.2
27 W	22 21 56	3 59 47	17 15 03	23 16 37	18 53.6	18 20.4	18 10.5	1 34.1	12 40.7	16 06.2	16 57.4	0 21.6	26 50.3	1 25.2	1 29.0	1 52.1
28 Th	22 25 53	4 57 44	29 16 01	5♏13 41	18 50.5	18 21.6	19 51.0	2 45.8	13 19.4	16 00.6	17 08.5	0 17.6	26 48.9	1 25.7	1 27.6	1 50.9
29 F	22 29 49	5 55 42	11♏10 10	17 05 58	18 47.3	18 22.8	21 34.9	3 57.6	13 58.2	15 54.5	17 19.6	0 13.7	26 47.4	1 26.1	1 26.1	1 49.8
30 Sa	22 33 46	6 53 41	23 01 39	28 57 47	18 44.1	18 23.6	23 21.8	5 09.5	14 37.0	15 48.1	17 30.6	0 09.6	26 45.9	1 26.5	1 24.7	1 48.7
31 Su	22 37 42	7♍51 42	4♐54 58	10♐53 47	18♓40.9	18♓24.0	25♌11.3	6♌21.4	15♎15.8	15♈41.4	17♋41.5	0♈05.5	26♈44.4	1♊26.8	1♈23.2	1♒47.6

1st of Month

Julian Day #
2460888.5
Obliquity
23°26'8"
SVP 4♓54'5"
GC 27♐11.8
Eris 25♈43.2R

Day	⚴
1	17♒24.5R
6	16 06.3R
11	14 48.0R
16	13 31.3R
21	12 17.9R
26	11 09.2R
31	10 06.7R

Day	⚵
1	17♏19.9
6	17 53.7
11	18 33.6
16	19 19.4
21	20 10.6
26	21 06.9
31	22 08.0

Day	⚶
1	13♏17.4
6	14 51.6
11	16 31.8
16	18 17.4
21	20 08.0
26	22 03.2
31	24 02.7

DECLINATION and LATITUDE

Day	☉ Decl	☽ Decl	☽ Lat	☽ 12h Decl	☿ Decl	☿ Lat	♀ Decl	♀ Lat	♂ Decl	♂ Lat	⚳ Decl	⚳ Lat	♃ Decl	♃ Lat	♄ Decl	♄ Lat
1 F	18N00	15S60	3S37	18S19	13N14	4S56	21N55	1S31	2N02	0N37	5S24	12S51	22N50	0S05	1S32	2S22
2 Sa	17 45	20 29	4 18	22 26	13 29	4 53	21 57	1 28	1 47	0 36	5 26	12 55	22 49	0 05	1 33	2 23
3 Su	17 29	24 10	4 48	25 38	13 44	4 48	21 59	1 25	1 31	0 35	5 29	12 58	22 48	0 05	1 34	2 23
4 M	17 13	26 50	5 06	27 44	14 01	4 41	22 00	1 22	1 16	0 35	5 31	13 02	22 47	0 05	1 35	2 23
5 Tu	16 57	28 19	5 11	28 32	14 18	4 32	22 01	1 19	1 00	0 34	5 33	13 05	22 46	0 05	1 36	2 23
6 W	16 41	28 24	5 01	27 53	14 36	4 22	22 00	1 16	0 45	0 33	5 36	13 09	22 45	0 04	1 37	2 24
7 Th	16 24	27 01	4 36	25 46	14 54	4 11	21 60	1 12	0 29	0 33	5 38	13 13	22 44	0 04	1 38	2 24
8 F	16 07	24 09	3 57	22 13	15 12	3 58	21 59	1 09	0 14	0 32	5 41	13 16	22 43	0 04	1 39	2 24
9 Sa	15 50	19 59	3 04	17 27	15 30	3 44	21 57	1 06	0S02	0 31	5 44	13 20	22 42	0 04	1 40	2 24
10 Su	15 33	14 42	1 59	11 44	15 47	3 29	21 54	1 03	0 17	0 30	5 47	13 24	22 41	0 04	1 42	2 25
11 M	15 15	8 36	0 47	5 21	16 04	3 13	21 51	0 60	0 33	0 30	5 50	13 27	22 39	0 04	1 43	2 25
12 Tu	14 57	2 01	0N29	1N22	16 19	2 57	21 47	0 56	0 48	0 29	5 53	13 31	22 38	0 04	1 44	2 25
13 W	14 39	4N44	1 44	8 03	16 33	2 40	21 43	0 53	1 04	0 28	5 57	13 34	22 37	0 04	1 46	2 25
14 Th	14 21	11 17	2 54	14 22	16 46	2 23	21 38	0 50	1 20	0 28	6 00	13 38	22 36	0 04	1 47	2 25
15 F	14 02	17 17	3 53	19 57	16 58	2 06	21 33	0 47	1 35	0 27	6 04	13 41	22 35	0 04	1 48	2 26
16 Sa	13 43	22 20	4 37	24 23	17 07	1 49	21 27	0 43	1 51	0 26	6 08	13 45	22 33	0 03	1 50	2 26
17 Su	13 24	26 04	5 05	27 21	17 15	1 32	21 20	0 40	2 07	0 25	6 11	13 48	22 32	0 03	1 51	2 26
18 M	13 05	28 11	5 14	28 34	17 20	1 15	21 13	0 37	2 22	0 25	6 15	13 52	22 31	0 03	1 53	2 26
19 Tu	12 45	28 29	5 04	27 57	17 23	0 59	21 05	0 34	2 38	0 24	6 19	13 55	22 30	0 03	1 54	2 27
20 W	12 26	26 58	4 37	25 36	17 24	0 43	20 56	0 30	2 54	0 23	6 24	13 59	22 28	0 03	1 56	2 27
21 Th	12 06	23 52	3 54	21 50	17 22	0 27	20 47	0 27	3 09	0 23	6 28	14 02	22 27	0 03	1 57	2 27
22 F	11 46	19 31	2 59	16 59	17 18	0 12	20 38	0 24	3 25	0 22	6 32	14 05	22 26	0 03	1 59	2 27
23 Sa	11 25	14 17	1 55	11 27	17 10	0N02	20 28	0 21	3 41	0 21	6 37	14 09	22 25	0 03	2 01	2 27
24 Su	11 05	8 32	0 46	5 33	16 60	0 16	20 17	0 17	3 56	0 21	6 41	14 12	22 23	0 03	2 02	2 27
25 M	10 44	2 33	0S24	0S27	16 47	0 28	20 05	0 14	4 12	0 20	6 46	14 15	22 22	0 03	2 04	2 28
26 Tu	10 24	3S24	1 31	6 19	16 30	0 40	19 53	0 11	4 28	0 19	6 51	14 18	22 21	0 03	2 05	2 28
27 W	10 03	9 08	2 33	11 51	16 11	0 51	19 41	0 08	4 44	0 18	6 55	14 21	22 19	0 02	2 07	2 28
28 Th	9 41	14 27	3 28	16 54	15 49	1 01	19 28	0 05	4 59	0 18	7 00	14 24	22 18	0 02	2 09	2 28
29 F	9 20	19 10	4 12	21 16	15 25	1 10	19 14	0 02	5 15	0 17	7 05	14 27	22 17	0 02	2 11	2 28
30 Sa	8 59	23 08	4 46	24 47	14 57	1 18	19 00	0N01	5 31	0 16	7 10	14 30	22 15	0 02	2 12	2 28
31 Su	8N37	26S10	5S08	27S15	14N27	1N25	18N45	0N04	5S46	0N16	7S15	14S33	22N14	0S02	2S14	2S29

Day	⚷ Decl	⚷ Lat	♅ Decl	♅ Lat	♆ Decl	♆ Lat	♇ Decl	♇ Lat
1	11N06	0N41	20N08	0S13	0S27	1S21	23S17	3S46
6	11 06	0 41	20 10	0 13	0 29	1 21	23 19	3 46
11	11 05	0 41	20 11	0 13	0 31	1 21	23 21	3 46
16	11 03	0 41	20 13	0 13	0 34	1 22	23 22	3 47
21	11 01	0 40	20 14	0 13	0 36	1 22	23 24	3 47
26	10 59	0 40	20 14	0 13	0 39	1 22	23 25	3 47
31	10N56	0N40	20N15	0S13	0S42	1S22	23S27	3S47

Day	⚴ Decl	⚴ Lat	⚵ Decl	⚵ Lat	⚶ Decl	⚶ Lat	Eris Decl	Eris Lat
1	15N38	32N44	3S44	13N48	11S29	4N34	0S00	10S40
6	14 59	32 23	4 08	13 32	12 15	4 14	0 01	10 40
11	14 15	31 57	4 34	13 16	13 02	3 54	0 02	10 41
16	13 25	31 25	5 00	13 01	13 48	3 36	0 02	10 41
21	12 32	30 48	5 28	12 46	14 35	3 19	0 03	10 41
26	11 35	30 05	5 55	12 32	15 20	3 02	0 04	10 42
31	10N36	29N19	6S23	12N19	16S05	2N47	0S05	10S42

Moon Phenomena

Max/0 Decl
dy hr mn
5 13:32 28S32
12 7:10 0 N
18 15:49 28N35
25 10:13 0 S

Max/0 Lat
dy hr mn
4 19:37 5S11
11 14:53 0 N
17 23:30 5N14
24 15:43 0 S

Perigee/Apogee
dy hr m kilometers
1 20:38 a 404160
14 18:00 p 369288
29 15:35 a 404546

PH dy hr mn
☽ 1 12:42 9♏32
○ 9 7:56 17♒00
☾ 16 5:13 23♉36
● 23 6:08 0♍23
☽ 31 6:26 8♐07

Void of Course Moon

Last Aspect		☽ Ingress	
3 1:08	♂ ⚹	♐ 3	6:02
5 15:30	♂ □	♑ 5	17:05
6 17:41	♃ ☍	♒ 8	1:19
9 7:56	☉ ☍	♓ 10	6:51
11 6:56	♃ △	♈ 12	10:34
13 22:55	☉ △	♉ 14	13:23
16 5:13	☉ □	♊ 16	16:02
18 11:54	☉ ⚹	♋ 18	19:06
20 12:28	♀ ☌	♌ 20	23:18
21 18:15	☿ ☌	♍ 23	5:25
25 13:55	♀ ⚹	♎ 25	14:09
27 2:08	☿ ⚹	♏ 28	1:28
30 0:48	☿ □	♐ 30	14:06

DAILY ASPECTARIAN

1 F
☉#☽ 9:44
☽□☿ 10:58
☊R 12:32
☉□☽ 12:42
♀□♄ 13:35
☽∠♂ 17:11
☽△♃ 17:27
♀□♆ 20:50
☽#♅ 22:04

2 Sa
☽⚻⚳ 2:51
☽⚼♄ 3:02
☽⚼♆ 3:46
☽⚼♀ 4:31
♀⚻♇ 5:47
☽#♀ 9:02
♂⚻⚷ 9:26
☽#♃ 14:31
☽∥♇ 17:46
♂#♄ 20:43

3 Su
☽⚼♃ 0:17
☽⚻⚷ 0:19
☽⚹♂ 1:08
☽☍♅ 8:00
☽△♄ 9:09
☽⚼⚳ 9:12
☽△♆ 9:56
☽⚹♇ 10:47
☽⚻♀ 13:57
☽△☿ 20:01

4 M
☉△☽ 6:13
☽⚼⚷ 6:15
☽⚻♃ 6:45
☉⚺♃ 14:45
☽△⚳ 15:06
☽∠♇ 16:29

5 Tu
☽⚼☿ 0:10
☿⚺♀ 9:10
☽△⚷ 11:35
☉⚼☽ 14:01
☽□♂ 15:30
☽⚻♅ 19:07
☽□♄ 19:55
☽□♆ 20:45
☽⚺♇ 21:32

6 W
☽⚻☿ 3:53
☽☍♀ 6:40
☽☍♃ 17:41
☉⚻☽ 20:54
♂ ♎ 23:24
☽⚼♅ 23:36

7 Th
♂#♆ 0:10
☽□⚳ 0:48
☉∠♂ 17:54
☽□⚷ 20:04

8 F
☽△♂ 2:36
☽△♅ 3:21
☽⚹♄ 3:50
☽⚹♆ 4:44
☽∥♇ 5:23
☽☌♇ 5:27
☽#♃ 9:09
☽☍☿ 9:53
☽#♀ 13:28
☉⚼♄ 15:52
♂△♅ 18:46
☽⚻♀ 19:32
☽#♅ 22:58

9 Sa
☽⚻♃ 1:33
☉△⚳ 2:17
♂☍♄ 2:53
☉⚼♆ 4:20
☽∠♄ 6:45
☽⚼♂ 6:57
☽⚹⚳ 7:32
☽∠♆ 7:41
☉☍☽ 7:56
☉∥☿ 13:58
☽#☿ 19:35
☉#☽ 20:12
♂☍♆ 22:14

10 Su
☽⚼♀ 0:41
☽⚹⚷ 1:48
☽⚼♃ 4:29
☽□♅ 8:53
☽⚺♄ 9:06
☽∠⚳ 9:59
☽⚺♆ 10:03
☽⚻♂ 10:38
☽⚺♇ 10:43
♂△♇ 12:30
☽⚻☿ 14:19
☽#⚷ 14:33
♂∥♆ 21:32

11 M
☽∠⚷ 3:53
☽△♀ 5:13
☽△♃ 6:56
☿D 7:31
☽∥⚳ 10:08
☽⚺⚳ 11:58
☽∠♇ 12:39
☊D 14:55
☉⚻☽ 16:11
☽⚼☿ 16:12
⚳R 21:37

12 Tu
☽∥♄ 0:59
♄⚹♅ 3:33
☽∥♂ 4:08
☽∥♆ 5:17
♀☌♃ 5:31
☽⚺⚷ 5:37
☽#♆ 9:03
☽#♂ 10:26
☽☌♄ 12:35
☽⚹♅ 12:38
☽#♄ 13:23
☽☌♆ 13:37
☽⚹♇ 14:16
☽☍♂ 16:39
☽△☿ 18:00
☉⚼☽ 19:40

13 W
☽#⚳ 4:24
☽□♃ 10:52
☽□♀ 13:04
☽∠♅ 14:07
☽☌⚳ 15:04
☉△☽ 22:55
☽∥⚷ 23:10

14 Th
♀∠♅ 1:56
☽☌⚷ 8:26
☉∥☽ 11:18
♀□⚳ 12:52
☽⚺♄ 15:12
☽⚺♅ 15:30
☽⚺♆ 16:21
☽□♇ 16:58
☽⚻♂ 21:46
☽□☿ 21:50
☽∥☿ 22:37

15 F
☿⚹♂ 2:06
☽∥♅ 13:15
☽⚹♃ 14:15
☽∠♄ 16:25
☽∠♆ 17:37
☽⚺⚳ 17:39
☽∥♀ 19:28
☽⚹♀ 20:18
♂∥♄ 22:09

16 Sa
☽⚼♂ 0:15
☽∥♃ 1:13
☉□☽ 5:13
☊R 5:25
☽#♇ 5:50
☽⚺⚷ 11:01
☽∠♃ 15:57
☽⚹♄ 17:40
☽☌♅ 18:12
☽⚹♆ 18:55
☽∠⚳ 18:57
☽△♇ 19:32
☽∠♀ 23:57

17 Su
☽⚹☿ 2:35
☽△♂ 2:49
☽∠⚷ 12:25
☽⚺♃ 17:46
☽⚹⚳ 20:21
☽⚼♇ 20:58

18 M
☽⚺♀ 3:47
☽∠☿ 5:32
☿⚹♂ 5:34
☉⚹☽ 11:54
☽⚹⚷ 13:58
☽□♄ 20:34
☽⚺♅ 21:23
☽□♆ 21:58
☽⚻♇ 22:36

19 Tu
☽□♂ 8:31
☽⚺☿ 9:01
☉∠☽ 15:39
☉△⚷ 17:31
☽☌♃ 22:03
☽∠♅ 23:20
☽□⚳ 23:48

20 W
☽☌♀ 12:28
☽□⚷ 17:57
☉⚺☽ 19:51

21 Th
☽△♄ 0:35
☽⚹♅ 1:42
☽△♆ 2:10
☽☍♇ 2:49
☽#♇ 2:56
☽∥♃ 8:33
☽⚹♂ 15:45
☽∥♀ 18:11
☽☌☿ 18:15
☽∥♅ 20:27

22 F
☽⚼♄ 3:16
☽⚺♃ 3:56
☽△⚳ 4:44
☽⚼♆ 4:57
☽∥☿ 10:50
☽∠♂ 20:15
☉ ♍ 20:35
☽⚺♀ 23:29
☽△⚷ 23:46

23 Sa
♀□⚷ 2:30
☉☌☽ 6:08
☽⚻♄ 6:31
☽∠♃ 7:45
☽□♅ 7:59
☽⚼⚳ 8:00
☽⚻♆ 8:19
☽⚻♇ 9:00
☉⚻♄ 11:06
☉∥☽ 12:53
⚳∠♅ 13:10
☽∥⚷ 13:53
⚳□♃ 20:36

24 Su
♃∠♅ 0:02
☽⚺♂ 1:31
☽⚼⚷ 3:36
☉⚼⚳ 5:48
♀∥♅ 5:54
☉∥⚷ 6:13
☽∠♀ 6:14
☉□♅ 7:16
☽#⚳ 7:21
☽⚺☿ 7:36
☉∠♃ 8:57
☉⚻♆ 10:59
☽⚻⚳ 11:56
☽⚹♃ 12:15
☽⚼♇ 13:04
☊D 15:47
☽#♂ 17:40
☉⚻♇ 20:07

25 M
☽#♄ 1:56
☿⚼♄ 6:57
☽#♆ 7:37
☽⚻⚷ 8:07
☽∥♆ 12:49
☽⚹♀ 13:55
☽☍♄ 15:01
☽∠☿ 16:13
♀ ♌ 16:28
☽△♅ 16:53
☽☍♆ 17:06
☽△♇ 17:50
☿△⚳ 18:33
☽∥♄ 18:37
☉⚺☽ 19:42
☿⚼♆ 23:06

26 Tu
♀△♄ 0:57
☿⚺♃ 3:29
☽∥♂ 4:32
☽∥⚳ 14:26
☽☌♂ 14:27
♀⚹♅ 20:59
☽☍⚳ 21:45
♀△♆ 22:19
☽⚼♅ 22:21
☽□♃ 23:24

27 W
☽⚹☿ 2:08
☉#☽ 3:43
☉∠☽ 3:46
♀☍♇ 5:55
☽#⚷ 8:02
☽☍⚷ 19:05

28 Th
☽⚻♄ 2:03
☽⚻♅ 4:21
☽⚻♆ 4:24
☽□♇ 5:11
☽#☿ 6:09
☽□♀ 7:49
☉⚹☽ 12:29

29 F
♅⚹♆ 0:10
☽#♀ 0:20
☽#♅ 5:59
☽⚺♂ 5:59
☽⚼♄ 8:10
☽⚻⚳ 9:30
☽⚼♆ 10:38
☽△♃ 12:39
☽#♃ 18:12

30 Sa
☽□☿ 0:48
☽∥♇ 2:06
☽⚻⚷ 7:33
☽∠♂ 14:05
☽△♄ 14:20
☽⚼⚳ 15:34
☽△♆ 16:54
☽☍♅ 17:01
☽⚹♇ 17:43
☽⚼♃ 19:27

31 Su
☽△♀ 3:13
☉□☽ 6:26
☊R 6:28
♂☍⚳ 13:21
☽⚼⚷ 13:39
☿△⚷ 19:45
☽△⚳ 21:21
☽⚹♂ 21:54
☽∠♇ 23:44

LONGITUDE

Day	Sid.Time	☉	☽	☽ 12 hour	Mean☊	True☊	☿	♀	♂	⚳	♃	♄	⚷	♅	♆	♇
	h m s	° ' "	° ' "	° ' "	° '	° '	° '	° '	° '	° '	° '	° '	° '	° '	° '	° '
1 M	22 41 39	8♍49 44	16♐54 49	22♐58 38	18♓37.7	18♓23.9	27♌02.9	7♌33.5	15♎54.8	15♈34.3	17♋52.3	0♈01.4	26♈42.8	1♊27.1	1♈21.7	1♒46.6
2 Tu	22 45 36	9 47 48	29 05 46	5♑16 44	18 34.6	18R 23.4	28 56.2	8 45.5	16 33.8	15R 26.9	18 03.1	29♓57.2	26R 41.1	1 27.4	1R 20.2	1R 45.5
3 W	22 49 32	10 45 53	11♑32 00	17 52 00	18 31.4	18 22.6	0♍50.7	9 57.7	17 12.8	15 19.1	18 13.7	29R 53.0	26 39.4	1 27.6	1 18.7	1 44.5
4 Th	22 53 29	11 43 59	24 17 02	0♒47 24	18 28.2	18 21.8	2 46.1	11 09.9	17 51.9	15 11.0	18 24.2	29 48.7	26 37.7	1 27.7	1 17.1	1 43.5
5 F	22 57 25	12 42 07	7♒23 16	14 04 42	18 25.0	18 21.0	4 42.2	12 22.2	18 31.1	15 02.6	18 34.7	29 44.4	26 35.9	1 27.8	1 15.6	1 42.5
6 Sa	23 01 22	13 40 16	20 51 40	27 44 02	18 21.9	18 20.5	6 38.5	13 34.5	19 10.3	14 53.9	18 45.0	29 40.1	26 34.1	1R 27.8	1 14.0	1 41.5
7 Su	23 05 18	14 38 27	4♓41 32	11♓43 47	18 18.7	18D 20.1	8 34.9	14 47.0	19 49.6	14 44.8	18 55.3	29 35.7	26 32.3	1 27.8	1 12.5	1 40.5
8 M	23 09 15	15 36 40	18 50 20	26 00 36	18 15.5	18 20.1	10 31.0	15 59.5	20 29.0	14 35.5	19 05.5	29 31.3	26 30.4	1 27.7	1 10.9	1 39.6
9 Tu	23 13 11	16 34 54	3♈13 55	10♈29 36	18 12.3	18 20.1	12 26.8	17 12.0	21 08.4	14 25.8	19 15.5	29 26.8	26 28.4	1 27.6	1 09.3	1 38.7
10 W	23 17 08	17 33 10	17 46 54	25 05 03	18 09.1	18R 20.2	14 22.1	18 24.6	21 47.9	14 15.9	19 25.5	29 22.3	26 26.5	1 27.5	1 07.7	1 37.8
11 Th	23 21 05	18 31 28	2♉23 19	9♉40 59	18 06.0	18 20.2	16 16.8	19 37.3	22 27.4	14 05.7	19 35.3	29 17.8	26 24.4	1 27.2	1 06.1	1 36.9
12 F	23 25 01	19 29 48	16 57 23	24 11 57	18 02.8	18 20.1	18 10.6	20 50.1	23 07.0	13 55.2	19 45.1	29 13.3	26 22.4	1 27.0	1 04.5	1 36.1
13 Sa	23 28 58	20 28 11	1♊24 08	8♊33 31	17 59.6	18 20.0	20 03.7	22 02.9	23 46.7	13 44.4	19 54.7	29 08.7	26 20.3	1 26.7	1 02.8	1 35.2
14 Su	23 32 54	21 26 35	15 39 45	22 42 35	17 56.4	18D 19.9	21 55.8	23 15.8	24 26.4	13 33.4	20 04.2	29 04.1	26 18.2	1 26.3	1 01.2	1 34.4
15 M	23 36 51	22 25 02	29 41 48	6♋37 17	17 53.3	18 19.9	23 47.1	24 28.8	25 06.2	13 22.1	20 13.7	28 59.5	26 16.0	1 25.9	0 59.6	1 33.7
16 Tu	23 40 47	23 23 31	13♋28 59	20 16 53	17 50.1	18 20.2	25 37.3	25 41.9	25 46.1	13 10.6	20 23.0	28 54.9	26 13.8	1 25.4	0 57.9	1 32.9
17 W	23 44 44	24 22 02	27 01 00	3♌41 22	17 46.9	18 20.6	27 26.5	26 54.9	26 26.0	12 58.8	20 32.2	28 50.3	26 11.6	1 24.9	0 56.3	1 32.2
18 Th	23 48 40	25 20 35	10♌18 04	16 51 11	17 43.7	18 21.3	29 14.7	28 08.1	27 06.0	12 46.9	20 41.3	28 45.7	26 09.4	1 24.3	0 54.7	1 31.5
19 F	23 52 37	26 19 10	23 20 48	29 47 02	17 40.6	18 22.0	1♎01.9	29 21.3	27 46.1	12 34.7	20 50.2	28 41.0	26 07.1	1 23.7	0 53.0	1 30.8
20 Sa	23 56 34	27 17 47	6♍09 57	12♍29 41	17 37.4	18R 22.5	2 48.0	0♍34.6	28 26.2	12 22.3	20 59.1	28 36.4	26 04.8	1 23.1	0 51.3	1 30.1
21 Su	0 00 30	28 16 27	18 46 20	25 00 02	17 34.2	18 22.7	4 33.1	1 47.9	29 06.4	12 09.8	21 07.8	28 31.7	26 02.4	1 22.3	0 49.7	1 29.5
22 M	0 04 27	29 15 08	1♎10 54	7♎19 06	17 31.0	18 22.4	6 17.3	3 01.3	29 46.7	11 57.0	21 16.4	28 27.0	26 00.0	1 21.6	0 48.0	1 28.8
23 Tu	0 08 23	0♎13 51	13 24 48	19 28 12	17 27.8	18 21.5	8 00.4	4 14.8	0♏27.0	11 44.2	21 24.8	28 22.4	25 57.6	1 20.8	0 46.3	1 28.2
24 W	0 12 20	1 12 36	25 29 30	1♏28 58	17 24.7	18 20.0	9 42.5	5 28.2	1 07.4	11 31.2	21 33.2	28 17.7	25 55.2	1 19.9	0 44.7	1 27.7
25 Th	0 16 16	2 11 23	7♏26 53	13 23 34	17 21.5	18 18.0	11 23.7	6 41.8	1 47.8	11 18.0	21 41.4	28 13.1	25 52.7	1 19.0	0 43.0	1 27.1
26 F	0 20 13	3 10 12	19 19 23	25 14 42	17 18.3	18 15.8	13 03.9	7 55.4	2 28.4	11 04.8	21 49.4	28 08.4	25 50.2	1 18.0	0 41.4	1 26.6
27 Sa	0 24 09	4 09 02	1♐09 58	7♐05 38	17 15.1	18 13.5	14 43.1	9 09.0	3 08.9	10 51.4	21 57.4	28 03.8	25 47.7	1 17.0	0 39.7	1 26.1
28 Su	0 28 06	5 07 55	13 02 12	19 00 11	17 11.9	18 11.7	16 21.5	10 22.7	3 49.6	10 38.0	22 05.2	27 59.2	25 45.2	1 16.0	0 38.0	1 25.7
29 M	0 32 02	6 06 49	25 00 07	1♑02 34	17 08.8	18D 10.4	17 58.9	11 36.5	4 30.3	10 24.5	22 12.9	27 54.6	25 42.6	1 14.9	0 36.4	1 25.3
30 Tu	0 35 59	7♎05 45	7♑08 06	13 17 17	17♓05.6	18♓10.0	19♎35.5	12♍50.3	5♏11.0	10♈11.0	22♋20.4	27♓50.0	25♈40.1	1♊13.8	0♈34.7	1♒24.8

1st of Month

Julian Day # 2460919.5
Obliquity 23°26'09"
SVP 4♓54'01"
GC 27♐11.9
Eris 25♈35.3R

Day	⚴
1	9♒55.0R
6	9 01.3R
11	8 15.7R
16	7 38.8R
21	7 10.7R
26	6 51.6R

Day	⚵
1	22♏20.8
6	23 27.2
11	24 37.6
16	25 51.8
21	27 09.4
26	28 30.4

Day	⚶
1	24♏27.0
6	26 31.1
11	28 38.5
16	0♐49.1
21	3 02.7
26	5 18.9

DECLINATION and LATITUDE

Day	☉ Decl	☽ Decl	☽ Lat	☽ 12h Decl	☿ Decl	☿ Lat	♀ Decl	♀ Lat	♂ Decl	♂ Lat	⚳ Decl	⚳ Lat	♃ Decl	♃ Lat	♄ Decl	♄ Lat
1 M	8N16	28S03	5S17	28S30	13N55	1N31	18N30	0N08	6S02	0N15	7S21	14S35	22N13	0S02	2S16	2S29
2 Tu	7 54	28 37	5 11	28 23	13 20	1 36	18 14	0 10	6 17	0 14	7 26	14 38	22 11	0 02	2 18	2 29
3 W	7 32	27 46	4 51	26 48	12 44	1 40	17 58	0 13	6 33	0 13	7 31	14 41	22 10	0 02	2 19	2 29
4 Th	7 10	25 28	4 17	23 47	12 05	1 43	17 41	0 16	6 49	0 13	7 36	14 43	22 09	0 02	2 21	2 29
5 F	6 48	21 46	3 28	19 27	11 25	1 45	17 24	0 19	7 04	0 12	7 42	14 46	22 07	0 02	2 23	2 29
6 Sa	6 25	16 51	2 27	14 00	10 43	1 47	17 06	0 22	7 20	0 12	7 47	14 48	22 06	0 01	2 25	2 29
7 Su	6 03	10 57	1 15	7 44	10 01	1 47	16 48	0 25	7 35	0 11	7 53	14 50	22 05	0 01	2 27	2 29
8 M	5 40	4 22	0N03	0 56	9 17	1 47	16 29	0 28	7 51	0 10	7 58	14 52	22 04	0 01	2 29	2 30
9 Tu	5 18	2N32	1 22	5N59	8 32	1 47	16 10	0 30	8 06	0 10	8 04	14 54	22 02	0 01	2 31	2 30
10 W	4 55	9 23	2 36	12 39	7 46	1 45	15 50	0 33	8 21	0 09	8 09	14 56	22 01	0 01	2 32	2 30
11 Th	4 32	15 45	3 41	18 38	7 00	1 43	15 30	0 36	8 37	0 08	8 15	14 58	21 60	0 01	2 34	2 30
12 F	4 09	21 13	4 31	23 30	6 13	1 41	15 09	0 38	8 52	0 08	8 20	14 60	21 58	0 01	2 36	2 30
13 Sa	3 47	25 23	5 03	26 52	5 26	1 38	14 48	0 41	9 07	0 07	8 26	15 01	21 57	0 01	2 38	2 30
14 Su	3 24	27 55	5 17	28 30	4 39	1 35	14 27	0 43	9 22	0 06	8 31	15 03	21 56	0 01	2 40	2 30
15 M	3 01	28 37	5 11	28 17	3 51	1 31	14 05	0 46	9 38	0 06	8 37	15 04	21 54	0 01	2 42	2 30
16 Tu	2 37	27 31	4 47	26 21	3 04	1 26	13 43	0 48	9 53	0 05	8 42	15 06	21 53	0 00	2 44	2 30
17 W	2 14	24 48	4 08	22 56	2 16	1 22	13 20	0 51	10 08	0 04	8 48	15 07	21 52	0 00	2 46	2 30
18 Th	1 51	20 48	3 16	18 25	1 29	1 17	12 57	0 53	10 23	0 04	8 53	15 08	21 51	0 00	2 48	2 30
19 F	1 28	15 51	2 14	13 00	0 41	1 12	12 33	0 55	10 38	0 03	8 59	15 09	21 49	0 00	2 49	2 30
20 Sa	1 05	10 17	1 07	7 22	0S06	1 06	12 10	0 57	10 53	0 02	9 04	15 09	21 48	0N00	2 51	2 31
21 Su	0 41	4 25	0S02	1 26	0 53	1 00	11 46	0 59	11 08	0 02	9 09	15 10	21 47	0 00	2 53	2 31
22 M	0 18	1S33	1 10	4S29	1 40	0 54	11 21	1 01	11 23	0 01	9 15	15 10	21 46	0 00	2 55	2 31
23 Tu	0S06	7 21	2 14	10 08	2 26	0 48	10 56	1 03	11 37	0 00	9 20	15 11	21 44	0 00	2 57	2 31
24 W	0 29	12 49	3 11	15 22	3 12	0 42	10 31	1 05	11 52	0S00	9 25	15 11	21 43	0 00	2 59	2 31
25 Th	0 52	17 46	3 59	19 58	3 58	0 35	10 06	1 07	12 07	0 01	9 30	15 11	21 42	0 01	3 01	2 31
26 F	1 16	21 59	4 36	23 46	4 43	0 29	9 40	1 09	12 21	0 02	9 35	15 11	21 41	0 01	3 03	2 31
27 Sa	1 39	25 18	5 02	26 35	5 28	0 22	9 14	1 11	12 36	0 02	9 40	15 11	21 40	0 01	3 04	2 31
28 Su	2 02	27 33	5 14	28 13	6 12	0 15	8 48	1 13	12 50	0 03	9 45	15 11	21 39	0 01	3 06	2 31
29 M	2 26	28 33	5 13	28 33	6 56	0 08	8 21	1 14	13 05	0 03	9 50	15 10	21 37	0 01	3 08	2 31
30 Tu	2S49	28S13	4S58	27S31	7S39	0N01	7N54	1N16	13S19	0S04	9S54	15S09	21N36	0N01	3S10	2S31

Day	⚷ Decl	⚷ Lat	♅ Decl	♅ Lat	♆ Decl	♆ Lat	♇ Decl	♇ Lat
1	10N55	0N40	20N15	0S13	0S43	1S22	23S27	3S47
6	10 52	0 40	20 15	0 13	0 46	1 22	23 28	3 47
11	10 48	0 39	20 15	0 13	0 49	1 22	23 29	3 47
16	10 44	0 39	20 14	0 13	0 53	1 22	23 30	3 47
21	10 40	0 39	20 14	0 13	0 56	1 22	23 31	3 47
26	10 35	0 39	20 13	0 13	0 59	1 22	23 32	3 47

Day	⚴ Decl	⚴ Lat	⚵ Decl	⚵ Lat	⚶ Decl	⚶ Lat	Eris Decl	Eris Lat
1	10N24	29N09	6S29	12N16	16S14	2N44	0S05	10S42
6	9 22	28 18	6 57	12 03	16 58	2 29	0 06	10 42
11	8 20	27 24	7 24	11 51	17 40	2 14	0 07	10 42
16	7 19	26 29	7 52	11 40	18 21	2 01	0 08	10 42
21	6 18	25 32	8 19	11 29	19 00	1 48	0 09	10 43
26	5 18	24 35	8 46	11 19	19 38	1 35	0 10	10 43

Moon Phenomena

Max/0 Decl

dy	hr mn	
1	21:57	28S38
8	15:14	0 N
14	21:08	28N38
21	17:45	0 S
29	6:00	28S36

Max/0 Lat

dy	hr mn	
1	2:57	5S17
7	23:09	0 N
14	4:32	5N17
20	23:15	0 S
28	10:21	5S15

Perigee/Apogee

dy	hr m		kilometers
10	12:11	p	364780
26	9:47	a	405546

PH	dy	hr mn	
○	7	18:10	15♓23
●	7	18:13	T 1.362
☾	14	10:34	21♊52
●	21	19:55	29♍05
●	21	1183:0P	0.855
☽	29	23:55	7♑06

Void of Course Moon

Last Aspect			☽ Ingress	
2 1:40	♄	□	♑	2 1:46
4 10:09	♄	⚹	♒	4 10:33
5 20:53	♂	△	♓	6 15:55
8 17:45	♄	☌	♈	8 18:38
10 6:55	♂	☍	♉	10 20:05
12 20:15	♄	⚹	♊	12 21:39
14 22:48	♄	□	♋	15 0:31
17 3:15	♄	△	♌	17 5:21
19 12:23	♀	☌	♍	19 12:24
21 19:55	☉	☌	♎	21 21:42
23 16:03	♃	□	♏	24 9:01
26 17:45	♄	△	♐	26 21:38
29 5:45	♄	□	♑	29 9:56

DAILY ASPECTARIAN

1 M
☽⚻♃ 1:56
♄R♓ 8:08
☽⚼♀ 12:24
☽△⚷ 19:18
♂⚼♅ 20:03
☽△☿ 23:38

2 Tu
☽□♄ 1:40
☽□♆ 4:21
☽⚻♅ 4:36
☽⚺♇ 5:11
☿⚻♄ 12:22
☿ ♍ 13:24
☿⚼⚳ 17:50
☽⚻♀ 20:41
☉△☽ 22:25

3 W
☉∦⚳ 0:40
☿⚻♆ 5:45
☽□⚳ 7:07
☿□♅ 7:41
☽⚼♅ 9:21
☽⚼☿ 9:39
☿⚻♇ 11:06
☽□♂ 11:21
☽☍♃ 12:51
☉⚼⚷ 21:29

4 Th
☿∠♂ 1:48
☽□⚷ 4:20
☉⚼☽ 4:54
☿∠♃ 8:40
☽⚹♄ 10:09
☽⚹♆ 12:53
☽△♅ 13:14
☉∦♂ 13:29
☽☌♇ 13:41
☽∥♇ 14:01
☽⚻☿ 18:18
☽∦♃ 22:01

5 F
♂□♃ 3:00
☽∦♅ 8:03
☽☍♀ 9:50
☉⚻☽ 10:17
☽∠♄ 13:06
☽⚹⚳ 13:34
☽∠♆ 15:51
☿∥⚷ 19:05
☽⚻♃ 20:14
☽△♂ 20:53
☽∦♀ 22:50

6 Sa
♅R 4:53
☉⚺♀ 9:39
☽⚹⚷ 9:57
☽⚺♄ 15:16
☽∠⚳ 15:35
☽⚺♆ 18:01
☽□♅ 18:27
☽⚺♇ 18:49
♀⚼♄ 20:29
☽⚼♃ 22:40
♀△⚳ 23:22

7 Su
☽⚼♂ 0:15
☽∦⚷ 0:23
☉⚻⚳ 2:16
☽∦☿ 4:01
☽☍☿ 7:42
☽∥⚳ 11:18
☽∠⚷ 11:39
☽∥♂ 12:03
☽⚺⚳ 16:55
☉☍☽ 18:10
☽⚻♀ 18:46
☉∦☽ 19:07
☽∠♇ 20:20
☊D 23:33

8 M
☽△♃ 0:26
☽⚻♂ 2:54
♀⚼♆ 3:42
☽∥♄ 6:37
☿⚼⚷ 12:05
☽∥♆ 12:30
☽⚺⚷ 12:48
☽☌♄ 17:45
☽∦♆ 17:59
♂∥⚳ 18:14
☽☌♆ 20:34
☽⚹♅ 21:04
☽⚹♇ 21:22
☽⚼♀ 22:08
☽∦♄ 23:55

9 Tu
☉⚼♇ 1:32
☉∥☽ 9:05
☿∦♂ 10:16
☿∦⚳ 13:22
☽⚻☿ 17:32
☽☌⚳ 18:17
☽∥☿ 18:51
☽∦⚳ 19:33
☽∦♂ 20:11
☽∠♅ 21:49
☿⚻⚳ 22:48
☉⚻☽ 23:36

10 W
☽△♀ 1:08
☽□♃ 2:44
☽∥⚷ 5:11
☽☍♂ 6:55
☽☌⚷ 14:12
☊R 18:18
☽⚺♄ 18:57
☽⚺♆ 21:53
☽⚼☿ 21:54
☽⚺♅ 22:28
☽□♇ 22:44
☽∥♀ 23:02
♀⚺♃ 23:14

11 Th
☉⚼☽ 2:00
☿⚼♇ 4:12
☽⚺⚳ 19:03
☽∥♅ 19:19
☽∠♄ 19:30
☽∠♆ 22:33

12 F
☽△☿ 2:19
☽∥♃ 3:45
☉△☽ 4:30
☽⚹♃ 4:41
☽□♀ 7:00
☉⚹♃ 7:31
☽⚻♂ 10:42
☽∦♇ 12:02
☽⚺⚷ 15:35
☽∠⚳ 19:37
☽⚹♄ 20:15
☿⚹♃ 21:54
☽⚹♆ 23:25

13 Sa
☽☌♅ 0:04
☽△♇ 0:19
☽∠♃ 5:56
☉☌☿ 10:53
☽⚼♂ 12:58
☽∠⚷ 16:39
☽⚹⚳ 20:29

14 Su
☽⚼♇ 1:33
⚶ ♐ 3:11
☽⚺♃ 7:35
☊D 9:46
☉□☽ 10:34
☽□☿ 12:18
☽⚹♀ 14:11
☽△♂ 15:42
☽⚹⚷ 18:07
☽□♄ 22:48

15 M
☽□♆ 2:14
☽⚺♅ 3:00
☽⚻♇ 3:13
☉∦♄ 17:54
☽∠♀ 18:38
☽□⚳ 23:28

16 Tu
☿⚺♀ 3:00
☿⚺♂ 3:02
♀⚹♂ 3:05
☽∠♅ 5:10
☿⚻⚷ 7:51
☿∦♄ 9:40
♀△⚷ 10:12
☽☌♃ 12:19
♂☍⚷ 15:48
☉⚹☽ 18:54
☽□⚷ 22:32
☽□♂ 22:54
☽⚺♀ 23:48

17 W
☽⚹☿ 0:53
☉∥☿ 1:49
☽△♄ 3:15
☽△♆ 7:01
☽⚹♅ 7:54
☽☍♇ 8:06
☽∦♇ 8:32
☿☍♄ 17:48
♀⚼⚳ 18:01
☽∥♃ 18:18

18 Th
☉∠☽ 0:05
☽∥♅ 2:56
☽△⚳ 4:28
☽⚼♄ 6:17
☽∠☿ 8:21
☿ ♎ 10:07
☽⚼♆ 10:15
♀⚻♄ 11:35
☿∦♆ 17:17
☉⚻⚷ 19:14
☽⚺♃ 19:18
☿☍♆ 22:02

19 F
☿△♅ 4:53
☽△⚷ 5:08
♂∦⚷ 5:18
☉⚺☽ 5:59
☿△♇ 6:28
☽⚼⚳ 7:45
☽⚹♂ 8:41
☽⚻♄ 9:53
☽☌♀ 12:23
♀ ♍ 12:40
☽⚻♆ 14:02
☽□♅ 15:00
☽⚻♇ 15:14
☽∥♀ 15:32
☽⚺☿ 16:39
☽∦♂ 21:38
☽∥⚷ 22:23
☽∠♃ 23:39

20 Sa
☽∦⚳ 4:59
♀⚻♆ 5:22
♂⚻♄ 5:25
☽⚼⚷ 9:17
☉∦♆ 9:19
☽⚻⚳ 11:35
☽∠♂ 14:34
♀□♅ 15:43
♀⚻♇ 18:01
☽⚼♇ 19:38
☉∦☿ 19:54
☊R 23:08

21 Su
☿∥♆ 1:23
☽⚹♃ 4:35
☉☍♄ 5:47
☽∦♄ 6:05
☽∦☿ 12:32
☽⚻⚷ 13:58
☽∦♆ 13:58
☉∥☽ 16:02
☽☍♄ 18:43
☉∦☽ 19:16
☉☌☽ 19:55
☽⚺♂ 21:07
☽∥♆ 21:33
♀∦♂ 23:04
☽☍♆ 23:16

22 M
☽△♅ 0:21
☽∥☿ 0:34
☽△♇ 0:35
☽⚺♀ 3:59
☽∥♄ 5:37
♂ ♏ 7:56
☽☌☿ 11:37
☉ ♎ 18:20
☽☍⚳ 20:45

23 Tu
☽⚼♅ 5:48
☽∥⚳ 8:37
♂⚻♆ 11:02
☽∠♀ 12:52
☉☍♆ 12:55
☽∦⚷ 14:07
☽∦♀ 14:24
☽□♃ 16:03
☿∥♄ 16:39
☉⚺♂ 17:12
♀∥⚷ 18:20
☽∥♂ 19:28

24 W
☽☍⚷ 0:51
☉△♅ 2:56
☽⚻♄ 5:34
☉△♇ 6:06
♂⚻♅ 7:16
☽⚻♆ 10:30
☽⚻♅ 11:41
♂□♇ 11:53
☽□♇ 11:57
☽☌♂ 11:57
☉⚺☽ 12:29
☽⚹♀ 22:19
☿☍⚳ 22:49
♀∠♃ 23:51

25 Th
☉∥♆ 6:38
☽⚻⚳ 7:38
☽⚺☿ 9:16
☽⚼♄ 11:34
☽∦♅ 13:23
☽⚼♆ 16:40
☉∠☽ 21:27
☽∦♃ 22:07

26 F
♀∦⚳ 3:42
☽△♃ 5:07
☽∥♇ 10:17
☽⚻⚷ 13:09
☽⚼⚳ 13:26
☽△♄ 17:45
☽∠☿ 20:36
☽△♆ 22:59

27 Sa
☽☍♅ 0:14
☽⚹♇ 0:33
☽⚺♂ 4:16
☉⚹☽ 6:35
☽⚼♃ 11:51
☽□♀ 18:01
☽△⚳ 19:15
☽⚼⚷ 19:25
☿⚼♅ 22:40

28 Su
♀⚻⚳ 4:12
☽∠♇ 6:49
♀⚼⚷ 7:03
☽⚹☿ 7:45
☽∠♂ 12:21
☽⚻♃ 18:22

29 M
☽△⚷ 1:24
☽□♄ 5:45
☽□♆ 11:07
☽⚻♅ 12:23
☽⚺♇ 12:44
☽⚹♂ 19:57
☊D 23:39
☉□☽ 23:55

30 Tu
☿∦♀ 5:15
☽□⚳ 5:51
☽△♀ 12:21
☽⚼♅ 17:40
☉∥♄ 23:25

October 2025

LONGITUDE

Day	Sid.Time	☉	☽	☽ 12 hour	Mean☊	True☊	☿	♀	♂	⚳	♃	♄	⚷	♅	♆	♇
	h m s	° ' "	° ' "	° ' "	° '	° '	° '	° '	° '	° '	° '	° '	° '	° '	° '	° '
1 W	0 39 56	8♎04 42	19♑30 42	25♑48 52	17♓02.4	18♓10.4	21♎11.1	14♍04.1	5♏51.8	9♈57.4	22♋27.8	27♓45.5	25♈37.5	1♊12.6	0♈33.1	1♒24.5
2 Th	0 43 52	9 03 42	2♒12 18	8♒41 27	16 59.2	18 11.6	22 45.9	15 18.0	6 32.7	9R 43.8	22 35.0	27R 41.0	25R 34.8	1R 11.3	0R 31.4	1R 24.1
3 F	0 47 49	10 02 43	15 16 42	21 58 22	16 56.1	18 13.0	24 19.9	16 32.0	7 13.7	9 30.2	22 42.1	27 36.5	25 32.2	1 10.1	0 29.8	1 23.8
4 Sa	0 51 45	11 01 46	28 46 36	5♓41 29	16 52.9	18 14.5	25 53.0	17 46.0	7 54.7	9 16.6	22 49.1	27 32.0	25 29.6	1 08.8	0 28.2	1 23.5
5 Su	0 55 42	12 00 50	12♓42 56	19 50 42	16 49.7	18R 15.3	27 25.3	19 00.0	8 35.7	9 03.0	22 55.9	27 27.6	25 26.9	1 07.4	0 26.6	1 23.2
6 M	0 59 38	12 59 57	27 04 20	4♈23 17	16 46.5	18 15.2	28 56.8	20 14.1	9 16.9	8 49.5	23 02.6	27 23.2	25 24.2	1 06.0	0 24.9	1 23.0
7 Tu	1 03 35	13 59 05	11♈46 46	19 13 53	16 43.3	18 13.8	0♏27.5	21 28.2	9 58.0	8 36.0	23 09.1	27 18.8	25 21.5	1 04.5	0 23.3	1 22.8
8 W	1 07 31	14 58 16	26 43 35	4♉14 47	16 40.2	18 11.1	1 57.4	22 42.3	10 39.3	8 22.6	23 15.5	27 14.5	25 18.8	1 03.1	0 21.7	1 22.6
9 Th	1 11 28	15 57 28	11♉46 17	19 16 58	16 37.0	18 07.5	3 26.4	23 56.6	11 20.6	8 09.2	23 21.7	27 10.2	25 16.1	1 01.5	0 20.1	1 22.4
10 F	1 15 25	16 56 43	26 45 42	4♊11 30	16 33.8	18 03.5	4 54.7	25 10.8	12 02.0	7 56.0	23 27.7	27 05.9	25 13.4	1 00.0	0 18.6	1 22.3
11 Sa	1 19 21	17 56 00	11♊33 28	18 50 54	16 30.6	17 59.6	6 22.1	26 25.1	12 43.4	7 42.8	23 33.6	27 01.7	25 10.6	0 58.4	0 17.0	1 22.2
12 Su	1 23 18	18 55 20	26 03 13	3♋10 02	16 27.5	17 56.6	7 48.7	27 39.5	13 24.9	7 29.8	23 39.4	26 57.6	25 07.9	0 56.7	0 15.4	1 22.1
13 M	1 27 14	19 54 42	10♋11 09	17 06 27	16 24.3	17D 54.9	9 14.5	28 53.8	14 06.5	7 16.9	23 45.0	26 53.5	25 05.1	0 55.0	0 13.9	1 22.0
14 Tu	1 31 11	20 54 06	23 56 00	0♌39 59	16 21.1	17 54.5	10 39.4	0♎08.3	14 48.1	7 04.2	23 50.4	26 49.4	25 02.4	0 53.3	0 12.3	1D 22.0
15 W	1 35 07	21 53 32	7♌18 36	13 52 11	16 17.9	17 55.3	12 03.4	1 22.7	15 29.8	6 51.6	23 55.6	26 45.4	24 59.6	0 51.6	0 10.8	1 22.0
16 Th	1 39 04	22 53 01	20 21 05	26 45 38	16 14.8	17 56.9	13 26.5	2 37.3	16 11.5	6 39.2	24 00.7	26 41.5	24 56.8	0 49.8	0 09.3	1 22.1
17 F	1 43 00	23 52 32	3♍06 15	9♍23 17	16 11.6	17 58.4	14 48.7	3 51.8	16 53.4	6 27.0	24 05.6	26 37.6	24 54.1	0 47.9	0 07.8	1 22.1
18 Sa	1 46 57	24 52 05	15 37 06	21 48 01	16 08.4	17R 59.3	16 09.8	5 06.4	17 35.2	6 15.0	24 10.4	26 33.8	24 51.3	0 46.1	0 06.3	1 22.2
19 Su	1 50 54	25 51 40	27 56 23	4♎02 27	16 05.2	17 58.8	17 29.9	6 21.0	18 17.2	6 03.2	24 14.9	26 30.0	24 48.5	0 44.2	0 04.9	1 22.4
20 M	1 54 50	26 51 18	10♎06 30	16 08 45	16 02.0	17 56.5	18 48.8	7 35.7	18 59.2	5 51.6	24 19.3	26 26.3	24 45.7	0 42.2	0 03.4	1 22.5
21 Tu	1 58 47	27 50 57	22 09 27	28 08 46	15 58.9	17 52.1	20 06.6	8 50.4	19 41.3	5 40.3	24 23.5	26 22.7	24 43.0	0 40.2	0 02.0	1 22.7
22 W	2 02 43	28 50 39	4♏06 55	10♏04 05	15 55.7	17 45.9	21 23.1	10 05.1	20 23.4	5 29.2	24 27.6	26 19.1	24 40.2	0 38.2	0 00.6	1 22.9
23 Th	2 06 40	29 50 22	16 00 28	21 56 15	15 52.5	17 38.1	22 38.1	11 19.8	21 05.6	5 18.4	24 31.4	26 15.7	24 37.4	0 36.2	29♓59.2	1 23.1
24 F	2 10 36	0♏50 08	27 51 41	3♐47 00	15 49.3	17 29.6	23 51.7	12 34.6	21 47.9	5 07.9	24 35.1	26 12.2	24 34.7	0 34.2	29 57.8	1 23.4
25 Sa	2 14 33	1 49 55	9♐42 29	15 38 26	15 46.2	17 21.1	25 03.7	13 49.4	22 30.2	4 57.6	24 38.6	26 08.9	24 31.9	0 32.1	29 56.4	1 23.7
26 Su	2 18 29	2 49 45	21 35 13	27 33 12	15 43.0	17 13.4	26 13.8	15 04.3	23 12.6	4 47.6	24 41.9	26 05.6	24 29.2	0 29.9	29 55.1	1 24.0
27 M	2 22 26	3 49 36	3♑32 48	9♑34 30	15 39.8	17 07.2	27 22.0	16 19.1	23 55.0	4 38.0	24 45.0	26 02.5	24 26.4	0 27.8	29 53.8	1 24.4
28 Tu	2 26 23	4 49 28	15 38 47	21 46 11	15 36.6	17 03.0	28 28.0	17 34.0	24 37.5	4 28.6	24 48.0	25 59.4	24 23.7	0 25.6	29 52.5	1 24.8
29 W	2 30 19	5 49 23	27 57 14	4♒12 32	15 33.5	17D 00.9	29 31.6	18 48.9	25 20.1	4 19.6	24 50.7	25 56.3	24 21.0	0 23.4	29 51.2	1 25.2
30 Th	2 34 16	6 49 19	10♒32 38	16 58 05	15 30.3	17 00.7	0♐32.5	20 03.9	26 02.7	4 10.9	24 53.3	25 53.4	24 18.3	0 21.2	29 50.0	1 25.7
31 F	2 38 12	7♏49 16	23 29 26	0♓07 08	15♓27.1	17♓01.5	1♐30.5	21♎18.8	26♏45.4	4♈02.5	24♋55.7	25♓50.5	24♈15.6	0♊19.0	29♓48.7	1♒26.1

1st of Month

Julian Day # 2460949.5
Obliquity 23°26'39"
SVP 4♓53'57"
GC 27♐11.9
Eris 25♈20.5R

Day	⚴
1	6♒41.5R
6	6 40.2
11	6 47.1
16	7 02.1
21	7 24.6
26	7 54.3
31	8 30.7

Day	⚵
1	29♏54.3
6	1♐21.0
11	2 50.3
16	4 21.9
21	5 55.7
26	7 31.5
31	9 09.1

Day	⚶
1	7♐37.7
6	9 58.6
11	12 21.5
16	14 46.4
21	17 12.9
26	19 41.1
31	22 10.7

DECLINATION and LATITUDE

Day	☉ Decl	☽ Decl	☽ Lat	☽ 12h Decl	☿ Decl	☿ Lat	♀ Decl	♀ Lat	♂ Decl	♂ Lat	⚳ Decl	⚳ Lat	♃ Decl	♃ Lat	♄ Decl	♄ Lat
1 W	3S12	26S28	4S29	25S04	8S22	0S06	7N27	1N17	13S33	0S05	9S59	15S09	21N35	0N01	3S12	2S31
2 Th	3 36	23 21	3 47	21 19	9 04	0 13	7 00	1 19	13 47	0 05	10 03	15 08	21 34	0 01	3 14	2 31
3 F	3 59	18 59	2 52	16 23	9 45	0 21	6 33	1 20	14 01	0 06	10 07	15 07	21 33	0 01	3 15	2 31
4 Sa	4 22	13 33	1 45	10 29	10 26	0 28	6 05	1 21	14 15	0 07	10 12	15 05	21 32	0 02	3 17	2 31
5 Su	4 45	7 15	0 30	3 53	11 06	0 35	5 37	1 22	14 29	0 07	10 16	15 04	21 31	0 02	3 19	2 31
6 M	5 08	0 26	0N48	3N05	11 45	0 42	5 09	1 24	14 43	0 08	10 19	15 03	21 30	0 02	3 20	2 31
7 Tu	5 31	6N35	2 06	10 01	12 24	0 49	4 41	1 25	14 56	0 08	10 23	15 01	21 29	0 02	3 22	2 30
8 W	5 54	13 20	3 15	16 28	13 02	0 56	4 12	1 26	15 10	0 09	10 27	14 59	21 28	0 02	3 24	2 30
9 Th	6 17	19 22	4 12	21 56	13 39	1 03	3 44	1 27	15 23	0 10	10 30	14 57	21 27	0 02	3 26	2 30
10 F	6 39	24 09	4 51	25 57	14 16	1 10	3 15	1 27	15 37	0 10	10 33	14 55	21 26	0 02	3 27	2 30
11 Sa	7 02	27 18	5 11	28 10	14 51	1 17	2 46	1 28	15 50	0 11	10 36	14 53	21 25	0 02	3 29	2 30
12 Su	7 25	28 32	5 09	28 26	15 26	1 24	2 18	1 29	16 03	0 12	10 39	14 51	21 25	0 03	3 30	2 30
13 M	7 47	27 51	4 49	26 51	16 00	1 31	1 49	1 30	16 16	0 12	10 42	14 48	21 24	0 03	3 32	2 30
14 Tu	8 09	25 28	4 13	23 46	16 34	1 37	1 19	1 30	16 29	0 13	10 45	14 46	21 23	0 03	3 33	2 30
15 W	8 32	21 44	3 24	19 28	17 06	1 44	0 50	1 31	16 42	0 13	10 47	14 43	21 22	0 03	3 35	2 30
16 Th	8 54	16 60	2 25	14 22	17 37	1 50	0 21	1 31	16 54	0 14	10 49	14 40	21 21	0 03	3 36	2 30
17 F	9 16	11 37	1 20	8 46	18 08	1 56	0S08	1 31	17 07	0 15	10 51	14 37	21 21	0 03	3 38	2 30
18 Sa	9 38	5 52	0 13	2 56	18 37	2 02	0 37	1 32	17 19	0 15	10 53	14 34	21 20	0 03	3 39	2 30
19 Su	9 59	0S00	0S54	2S55	19 06	2 08	1 07	1 32	17 32	0 16	10 55	14 31	21 19	0 03	3 41	2 30
20 M	10 21	5 48	1 57	8 37	19 33	2 14	1 36	1 32	17 44	0 16	10 56	14 28	21 19	0 04	3 42	2 29
21 Tu	10 43	11 20	2 55	13 56	19 60	2 19	2 06	1 32	17 56	0 17	10 58	14 24	21 18	0 04	3 43	2 29
22 W	11 04	16 24	3 44	18 42	20 25	2 24	2 35	1 32	18 08	0 18	10 59	14 21	21 17	0 04	3 45	2 29
23 Th	11 25	20 49	4 23	22 43	20 50	2 29	3 04	1 32	18 19	0 18	10 60	14 17	21 17	0 04	3 46	2 29
24 F	11 46	24 23	4 50	25 48	21 13	2 33	3 33	1 32	18 31	0 19	11 01	14 13	21 16	0 04	3 47	2 29
25 Sa	12 07	26 56	5 05	27 45	21 34	2 37	4 03	1 32	18 43	0 19	11 01	14 10	21 16	0 04	3 48	2 29
26 Su	12 27	28 16	5 07	28 28	21 55	2 41	4 32	1 31	18 54	0 20	11 01	14 06	21 15	0 04	3 50	2 29
27 M	12 48	28 19	4 55	27 49	22 14	2 45	5 01	1 31	19 05	0 21	11 02	14 02	21 15	0 04	3 51	2 29
28 Tu	13 08	26 60	4 30	25 51	22 32	2 47	5 30	1 31	19 16	0 21	11 01	13 58	21 15	0 05	3 52	2 28
29 W	13 28	24 22	3 53	22 36	22 49	2 50	5 59	1 30	19 27	0 22	11 01	13 54	21 14	0 05	3 53	2 28
30 Th	13 47	20 32	3 03	18 12	23 04	2 52	6 27	1 30	19 38	0 22	11 01	13 49	21 14	0 05	3 54	2 28
31 F	14S07	15S38	2S03	12S50	23S17	2S53	6S56	1N29	19S48	0S23	11S00	13S45	21N14	0N05	3S55	2S28

Day	⚷ Decl	⚷ Lat	♅ Decl	♅ Lat	♆ Decl	♆ Lat	♇ Decl	♇ Lat
1	10N30	0N38	20N12	0S13	1S02	1S22	23S32	3S47
6	10 25	0 38	20 10	0 13	1 06	1 22	23 32	3 47
11	10 20	0 38	20 09	0 13	1 09	1 22	23 32	3 47
16	10 14	0 37	20 07	0 13	1 12	1 22	23 32	3 47
21	10 09	0 37	20 05	0 13	1 15	1 22	23 32	3 47
26	10 03	0 36	20 03	0 13	1 17	1 22	23 32	3 46
31	9N58	0N36	20N01	0S13	1S20	1S22	23S31	3S46

Day	⚴ Decl	⚴ Lat	⚵ Decl	⚵ Lat	⚶ Decl	⚶ Lat	Eris Decl	Eris Lat
1	4N21	23N39	9S12	11N10	20S13	1N23	0S11	10S43
6	3 26	22 42	9 38	11 01	20 46	1 11	0 12	10 43
11	2 33	21 47	10 02	10 53	21 17	0 60	0 13	10 43
16	1 44	20 53	10 26	10 45	21 45	0 49	0 14	10 42
21	0 58	20 00	10 49	10 38	22 11	0 39	0 15	10 42
26	0 16	19 09	11 10	10 32	22 34	0 28	0 16	10 42
31	0S24	18N20	11S30	10N26	22S54	0N19	0S17	10S42

Moon Phenomena

Max/0 Decl
dy hr mn
6 1:28 0 N
12 3:15 28N33
18 23:59 0 S
26 12:41 28S27

Max/0 Lat
dy hr mn
5 9:20 0 N
11 10:33 5N13
18 4:35 0 S
25 15:17 5S08

Perigee/Apogee
dy hr m kilometers
8 12:40 p 359823
23 23:32 a 406444

PH dy hr mn
○ 7 3:49 14♈08
☾ 13 18:14 20♋40
● 21 12:26 28♎22
☽ 29 16:22 6♒30

Void of Course Moon

Last Aspect	☽ Ingress
1 15:35 ♄ ⚹	♒ 1 19:53
3 18:16 ☿ △	♓ 4 2:08
6 0:31 ♄ ☌	♈ 6 4:49
7 18:25 ♃ □	♉ 8 5:14
10 0:32 ♄ □	♊ 10 5:13
12 2:57 ♀ □	♋ 12 6:38
14 5:06 ♄ △	♌ 14 10:48
16 5:07 ☉ ⚹	♍ 16 18:07
18 21:12 ♄ ☍	♎ 19 4:03
21 12:26 ☉ ☌	♏ 21 15:43
24 4:15 ♆ △	♐ 24 4:20
26 16:43 ♆ □	♑ 26 16:54
29 3:39 ♆ ⚹	♒ 29 3:56
31 6:16 ♂ □	♓ 31 11:47

DAILY ASPECTARIAN

1 W
☽□☿ 3:40
☽☍♃ 5:42
⚵ ♐ 7:56
☽□⚷ 11:36
☽⚹♄ 15:35
☽⚼♀ 20:04
☽⚹♆ 20:52
☿□♃ 21:00
☽△♅ 22:06
☽☌♇ 22:30
☽∥♇ 22:49

2 Th
☽□♂ 8:30
☽#♃ 10:38
☉☍⚳ 13:15
☽⚹⚳ 13:40
☉△☽ 13:43
☽#♅ 17:59
☽∠♄ 19:11
♀⚼♇ 21:21

3 F
☽∠♆ 0:24
☽⚻♀ 2:30
☽⚻♃ 13:25
☿∥⚳ 14:37
☽∠⚳ 16:13
☿☍⚷ 18:06
☽⚹⚷ 18:15
☽△☿ 18:16
☉⚼☽ 18:48
☽∥♂ 21:12
☽⚺♄ 21:50

4 Sa
☿#⚷ 0:40
☽⚺♆ 2:57
☽□♅ 4:08
☽⚺♇ 4:33
⚴ D 7:18
☽∥☿ 11:02
☽#⚷ 12:10
☽∥⚳ 12:59
☽⚼♃ 15:47
☽△♂ 16:37
☽⚺⚳ 17:52
☽∠⚷ 20:09
☉⚻☽ 22:43
☽⚼☿ 23:27

5 Su
☿⚻♄ 0:33
☽∠♇ 6:12
☽#♀ 6:19
☉∥☽ 8:29
☊ R 9:17
☽☍♀ 11:35
♂⚻⚳ 11:59
☽∥♄ 13:57
☽△♃ 17:17
☽⚼♂ 19:09
☽⚺⚷ 21:15
☽∥♆ 21:42

6 M
☉#♀ 0:28
☽☌♄ 0:31
☽⚻☿ 3:27
☽#♆ 5:13
☽☌♆ 5:29
☽⚹♅ 6:37
☽⚹♇ 7:05
☽#♄ 12:56
☿ ♏ 16:42
☽∥♀ 17:52
☽☌⚳ 18:56
☉#☽ 20:07
☽⚻♂ 20:55
☿⚻♆ 22:55

7 Tu
⚳#⚷ 3:42
☉☍☽ 3:49
☽∠♅ 6:55
☿⚻♅ 9:42
☽∥⚷ 13:17
☽#⚳ 13:24
☿□♇ 14:42
☽⚻♀ 16:59
☽□♃ 18:25
☽☌⚷ 21:45
☽#☿ 22:45

8 W
☽⚺♄ 0:49
☽⚺♆ 5:48
☽⚺♅ 6:54
☽#♂ 7:08
☽□♇ 7:25
☽☍☿ 9:16
♀⚹♃ 11:42
☽⚺⚳ 18:19
☽⚼♀ 19:05
☽☍♂ 23:17

9 Th
☽∠♄ 0:38
☉⚼♅ 1:36
☽∥♅ 3:33
☽∠♆ 5:41
☉⚻☽ 7:09
☽∥♃ 9:35
♀#♄ 14:32
☽∠⚳ 17:56
☽⚹♃ 18:40
☽#♇ 20:27
☽△♀ 21:14
☽⚺⚷ 21:32

10 F
☽⚹♄ 0:32
♀⚻⚷ 0:48
♂⚼♄ 2:05
☽⚹♆ 5:43
☽☌♅ 6:49
☽△♇ 7:26
☉⚼☽ 8:58
☽⚻☿ 14:37
☽⚹⚳ 17:49
☽∠♃ 19:04
☽∠⚷ 21:45

11 Sa
☽⚻♂ 2:00
☽⚼♇ 7:54
♀☍♄ 11:12
☉△☽ 11:15
☽⚼☿ 17:59
☿⚻⚳ 19:25
☽⚺♃ 19:58
☽⚹⚷ 22:28

12 Su
☽□♄ 1:31
☽□♀ 2:57
☽⚼♂ 4:10
☽□♆ 7:04
☽⚺♅ 8:13
☽⚻♇ 8:57
☽□⚳ 19:05
☽△☿ 22:12

13 M
☽△♂ 7:08
♀∠♂ 9:14
☽∠♅ 9:54
☉□☽ 18:14
☊ D 18:20
☿∥♂ 18:20
♀ ♎ 21:20
☽☌♃ 23:50

14 Tu
♀☍♆ 1:17
☽□⚷ 1:57
♇ D 2:55
☽△♄ 5:06
♀#♆ 7:04
☽△♆ 11:09
☽⚹♀ 12:11
☽⚹♅ 12:22
☽☍♇ 13:16
☽#♇ 13:19
♂⚼♆ 13:29
♀△♅ 14:11
☿⚼♄ 19:04
☽△⚳ 23:12
♀△♇ 23:46

15 W
☽∥♃ 1:59
☽⚼♄ 8:05
☽∥♅ 8:37
☽□☿ 9:42
☽⚼♆ 14:23
☽□♂ 15:51
☽∠♀ 18:23
☽#☿ 21:18

16 Th
☽#♂ 0:24
☽⚼⚳ 2:23
☉⚹☽ 5:07
☽⚺♃ 6:53
☽△⚷ 8:34
☽⚻♄ 11:49
☽⚻♆ 18:22
☽□♅ 19:38
☽⚻♇ 20:42

17 F
☽⚺♀ 1:36
☽#⚳ 3:13
☿⚼♆ 5:32
☉□♃ 5:44
☽∥⚷ 5:57
☽⚻⚳ 6:16
☉#☽ 9:21
☽∠♃ 11:30
☉∠☽ 11:58
☽⚼⚷ 12:56
☉☍⚷ 23:41

18 Sa
☽⚹☿ 1:11
☽⚼♇ 1:27
☽⚹♂ 4:02
☊ R 4:33
☽#♄ 9:01
☽⚹♃ 16:44
☽⚻⚷ 17:54
☽#♆ 18:59
♀☍⚳ 19:03
☉⚺☽ 19:34
☽#♀ 19:47
☽☍♄ 21:12

19 Su
☽☍♆ 4:12
☽∥♀ 4:57
☽∥♆ 5:01
☽△♅ 5:29
♀∥♆ 5:39
☽△♇ 6:45
☽∠☿ 10:03
☽∠♂ 11:09
☉#⚷ 12:04
☉⚻♄ 14:32
☽∥♄ 15:11
☽☍⚳ 15:43
☽☌♀ 18:27

20 M
☿☌♂ 6:53
☽⚼♅ 11:05
☽#⚷ 18:45
☽⚺♂ 18:45
☽⚺☿ 19:25
☉∥☽ 21:02
☽∥⚳ 22:22

21 Tu
☽□♃ 4:30
☿#♅ 4:42
☽☍⚷ 5:06
☽⚻♄ 8:25
☿⚼⚳ 9:11
☉☌☽ 12:26
☽⚻♆ 15:45
☽⚻♅ 17:01
☉∥⚳ 18:09
☽□♇ 18:30

22 W
♂⚼⚳ 2:38
☽⚻⚳ 2:43
☽∥♂ 9:21
♆R♓ 9:49
☽⚺♀ 13:27
☽⚼♄ 14:27
☽#♅ 19:40
☽⚼♆ 21:56

23 Th
☽∥☿ 0:05
☽#♃ 2:48
☉⚻♆ 3:27
☉ ♏ 3:52
☽⚼⚳ 8:34
☽☌♂ 10:56
☽☌☿ 14:58
☽△♃ 17:20
☽⚻⚷ 17:22
☽∥♇ 17:37
☉⚻♅ 17:48
☽△♄ 20:39
♃□⚷ 22:19
☽∠♀ 23:21

24 F
☿#♃ 3:49
☽△♆ 4:15
☽☍♅ 5:28
☉⚺☽ 6:35
☽⚹♇ 7:09
♀∥♄ 11:53
☉□♇ 13:26
☿⚻⚷ 13:44
☽△⚳ 14:31
☿△♃ 15:09
☽⚼⚷ 23:39
☽⚼♃ 23:52

25 Sa
☽⚹♀ 9:18
☽∠♇ 13:32
☉∠☽ 15:44
☿△♄ 21:18

26 Su
☽⚺♂ 3:28
☽△⚷ 5:49
☽⚻♃ 6:18
♀⚼♅ 8:00
☽□♄ 9:02
☽⚺☿ 10:20
☽□♆ 16:43
☽⚻♅ 17:51
☽⚺♇ 19:43

27 M
☉⚹☽ 0:37
☽□⚳ 2:08
☽∠♂ 11:22
♂⚻⚷ 16:41
☉⚻⚳ 16:46
☽∠☿ 19:17
☽⚼♅ 23:34

28 Tu
☽□♀ 4:12
♂△♃ 6:20
☽□⚷ 17:03
☽☍♃ 17:58
☽⚹♂ 18:37
☽⚹♄ 20:07

29 W
☽⚹☿ 3:18
☽⚹♆ 3:39
☽△♅ 4:41
☽∥♇ 6:00
☽☌♇ 6:40
☿△♆ 7:27
☽∥☿ 9:57
☿ ♐ 11:03
☽⚹⚳ 12:05
☊ D 16:14
☉□☽ 16:22
♂△♄ 19:07
☿☍♅ 19:37
☽#♃ 20:07

30 Th
☽∠♄ 0:39
☽#♅ 2:46
☽∥♂ 4:38
☽∠♆ 8:01
☽∠⚳ 15:55
☽△♀ 19:36
☿⚹♇ 22:07

31 F
☽⚹⚷ 1:24
☽⚻♃ 2:38
☽⚺♄ 4:16
☉∥☽ 6:13
☽□♂ 6:16
☽⚺♆ 11:26
☽□♅ 12:19
☽⚺♇ 14:22
☽□☿ 15:33
☽⚺⚳ 18:49
☽∥⚳ 19:27
☽#⚷ 23:34

LONGITUDE

November 2025

Day	Sid.Time	☉	☽	☽ 12 hour	Mean☊	True☊	☿	♀	♂	⚳	♃	♄	⚷	♅	♆	♇
	h m s	° ' "	° ' "	° ' "	° '	° '	° '	° '	° '	° '	° '	° '	° '	° '	° '	° '
1 Sa	2 42 09	8♏49 15	6♓51 37	13♓43 11	15♓23.9	17♓02.6	2♐25.2	22♎33.8	27♏28.1	3♈54.5	24♋57.9	25♓47.8	24♈13.0	0♊16.7	29♓47.5	1♒26.6
2 Su	2 46 05	9 49 16	20 41 59	27 48 02	15 20.7	17R 02.9	3 16.2	23 48.8	28 10.9	3R 46.8	24 59.9	25R 45.1	24R 10.3	0R 14.4	29R 46.3	1 27.1
3 M	2 50 02	10 49 18	5♈01 10	12♈20 59	15 17.6	17 01.5	4 03.1	25 03.8	28 53.7	3 39.5	25 01.7	25 42.5	24 07.7	0 12.1	29 45.2	1 27.7
4 Tu	2 53 58	11 49 22	19 46 52	27 17 59	15 14.4	16 57.8	4 45.5	26 18.9	29 36.7	3 32.5	25 03.3	25 40.0	24 05.0	0 09.7	29 44.0	1 28.3
5 W	2 57 55	12 49 28	4♉53 18	12♉31 33	15 11.2	16 51.7	5 22.8	27 33.9	0♐19.6	3 25.9	25 04.7	25 37.6	24 02.4	0 07.4	29 42.9	1 28.9
6 Th	3 01 52	13 49 36	20 11 24	27 51 22	15 08.0	16 43.7	5 54.4	28 49.0	1 02.7	3 19.6	25 05.9	25 35.3	23 59.9	0 05.0	29 41.8	1 29.5
7 F	3 05 48	14 49 45	5♊30 01	13♊05 58	15 04.9	16 34.7	6 19.7	0♏04.1	1 45.8	3 13.7	25 07.0	25 33.0	23 57.3	0 02.6	29 40.8	1 30.2
8 Sa	3 09 45	15 49 57	20 37 55	28 04 47	15 01.7	16 25.8	6 38.2	1 19.3	2 28.9	3 08.2	25 07.8	25 30.9	23 54.8	0 00.2	29 39.7	1 30.9
9 Su	3 13 41	16 50 10	5♋25 42	12♋39 59	14 58.5	16 18.2	6R 49.0	2 34.4	3 12.1	3 03.0	25 08.4	25 28.9	23 52.3	29♉57.8	29 38.7	1 31.6
10 M	3 17 38	17 50 26	19 47 13	26 47 13	14 55.3	16 12.6	6 51.5	3 49.6	3 55.4	2 58.2	25 08.9	25 26.9	23 49.8	29 55.4	29 37.7	1 32.4
11 Tu	3 21 34	18 50 43	3♌39 58	10♌25 39	14 52.2	16 09.4	6 45.1	5 04.8	4 38.7	2 53.8	25R 09.1	25 25.1	23 47.3	29 53.0	29 36.8	1 33.2
12 W	3 25 31	19 51 02	17 04 33	23 37 05	14 49.0	16D 08.3	6 29.2	6 20.0	5 22.1	2 49.8	25 09.1	25 23.3	23 44.9	29 50.5	29 35.8	1 34.0
13 Th	3 29 27	20 51 23	0♍03 45	6♍25 05	14 45.8	16 08.5	6 03.3	7 35.3	6 05.6	2 46.1	25 09.0	25 21.7	23 42.5	29 48.0	29 34.9	1 34.8
14 F	3 33 24	21 51 47	12 41 39	18 54 02	14 42.6	16R 09.0	5 27.3	8 50.5	6 49.1	2 42.9	25 08.6	25 20.2	23 40.1	29 45.6	29 34.1	1 35.7
15 Sa	3 37 21	22 52 12	25 02 46	1♎08 25	14 39.4	16 08.7	4 41.1	10 05.8	7 32.7	2 40.0	25 08.1	25 18.7	23 37.8	29 43.1	29 33.2	1 36.5
16 Su	3 41 17	23 52 38	7♎11 29	13 12 26	14 36.3	16 06.5	3 45.3	11 21.1	8 16.3	2 37.5	25 07.3	25 17.4	23 35.5	29 40.6	29 32.4	1 37.5
17 M	3 45 14	24 53 07	19 11 41	25 09 38	14 33.1	16 01.7	2 40.7	12 36.4	9 00.0	2 35.3	25 06.3	25 16.1	23 33.2	29 38.1	29 31.6	1 38.4
18 Tu	3 49 10	25 53 38	1♏06 37	7♏02 55	14 29.9	15 53.9	1 28.7	13 51.7	9 43.7	2 33.6	25 05.2	25 15.0	23 30.9	29 35.6	29 30.9	1 39.4
19 W	3 53 07	26 54 10	12 58 47	18 54 27	14 26.7	15 43.3	0 11.2	15 07.0	10 27.5	2 32.3	25 03.8	25 14.0	23 28.7	29 33.1	29 30.1	1 40.3
20 Th	3 57 03	27 54 44	24 50 06	0♐45 55	14 23.6	15 30.4	28♏50.4	16 22.4	11 11.4	2 31.3	25 02.2	25 13.0	23 26.5	29 30.6	29 29.4	1 41.4
21 F	4 01 00	28 55 19	6♐42 03	12 38 40	14 20.4	15 16.3	27 29.1	17 37.7	11 55.3	2D 30.7	25 00.5	25 12.2	23 24.4	29 28.0	29 28.8	1 42.4
22 Sa	4 04 56	29 55 56	18 35 55	24 33 59	14 17.2	15 02.0	26 09.8	18 53.1	12 39.3	2 30.5	24 58.5	25 11.5	23 22.3	29 25.5	29 28.1	1 43.5
23 Su	4 08 53	0♐56 34	0♑33 04	6♑33 24	14 14.0	14 48.7	24 55.3	20 08.5	13 23.4	2 30.7	24 56.3	25 10.9	23 20.2	29 23.0	29 27.5	1 44.6
24 M	4 12 50	1 57 13	12 35 14	18 38 52	14 10.9	14 37.6	23 47.8	21 23.9	14 07.5	2 31.3	24 54.0	25 10.4	23 18.2	29 20.5	29 27.0	1 45.7
25 Tu	4 16 46	2 57 54	24 44 40	0♒53 00	14 07.7	14 29.2	22 49.3	22 39.3	14 51.6	2 32.2	24 51.4	25 10.0	23 16.2	29 18.0	29 26.4	1 46.8
26 W	4 20 43	3 58 36	7♒04 18	13 19 02	14 04.5	14 23.8	22 01.2	23 54.7	15 35.8	2 33.6	24 48.7	25 09.7	23 14.2	29 15.5	29 25.9	1 48.0
27 Th	4 24 39	4 59 19	19 37 42	26 00 49	14 01.3	14 21.1	21 24.4	25 10.1	16 20.1	2 35.3	24 45.7	25 09.5	23 12.3	29 13.0	29 25.5	1 49.2
28 F	4 28 36	6 00 03	2♓28 54	9♓02 28	13 58.1	14 20.3	20 59.1	26 25.5	17 04.4	2 37.4	24 42.6	25D 09.5	23 10.4	29 10.5	29 25.0	1 50.4
29 Sa	4 32 32	7 00 48	15 42 00	22 27 56	13 55.0	14 20.3	20D 45.4	27 40.9	17 48.8	2 39.8	24 39.3	25 09.5	23 08.6	29 08.0	29 24.6	1 51.6
30 Su	4 36 29	8♐01 33	29 20 35	6♈20 10	13♓51.8	14♓19.8	20♏42.8	28♏56.4	18♐33.2	2♈42.6	24♋35.8	25♓09.6	23♈06.8	29♉05.5	29♓24.2	1♒52.9

1st of Month

Julian Day #
2460980.5
Obliquity
23°26'38"
SVP 4♓53'53"
GC 27♐12.0
Eris 25♈02.2R

Day	⚴
1	8♒38.8
6	9 22.6
11	10 12.1
16	11 06.9
21	12 06.5
26	13 10.7

Day	⚵
1	9♐28.9
6	11 08.4
11	12 49.5
16	14 31.8
21	16 15.4
26	18 00.1

Day	⚶
1	22♐40.8
6	25 11.9
11	27 44.1
16	0♑17.4
21	2 51.6
26	5 26.6

DECLINATION and LATITUDE

Day	☉ Decl	☽ Decl	☽ Lat	☽ 12h Decl	☿ Decl	☿ Lat	♀ Decl	♀ Lat	♂ Decl	♂ Lat	⚳ Decl	⚳ Lat	♃ Decl	♃ Lat	♄ Decl	♄ Lat
1 Sa	14S26	9S50	0S55	6S41	23S29	2S54	7S25	1N28	19S59	0S24	10S59	13S41	21N13	0N05	3S56	2S28
2 Su	14 45	3 23	0N20	0N00	23 39	2 54	7 53	1 28	20 09	0 24	10 58	13 36	21 13	0 05	3 57	2 28
3 M	15 04	3N27	1 35	6 54	23 47	2 53	8 21	1 27	20 19	0 25	10 57	13 32	21 13	0 05	3 58	2 28
4 Tu	15 23	10 18	2 46	13 35	23 54	2 52	8 49	1 26	20 29	0 25	10 56	13 27	21 13	0 06	3 59	2 27
5 W	15 41	16 43	3 47	19 36	23 58	2 49	9 17	1 25	20 38	0 26	10 54	13 23	21 13	0 06	3 59	2 27
6 Th	15 59	22 10	4 33	24 22	24 00	2 45	9 45	1 24	20 48	0 26	10 52	13 18	21 12	0 06	4 00	2 27
7 F	16 17	26 07	4 59	27 23	24 00	2 41	10 12	1 23	20 57	0 27	10 50	13 13	21 12	0 06	4 01	2 27
8 Sa	16 35	28 09	5 03	28 23	23 58	2 35	10 39	1 22	21 06	0 28	10 48	13 08	21 12	0 06	4 02	2 27
9 Su	16 52	28 07	4 48	27 22	23 53	2 28	11 06	1 21	21 15	0 28	10 46	13 04	21 12	0 06	4 02	2 27
10 M	17 09	26 10	4 14	24 35	23 45	2 19	11 33	1 19	21 24	0 29	10 43	12 59	21 13	0 06	4 03	2 26
11 Tu	17 26	22 40	3 26	20 29	23 34	2 09	11 59	1 18	21 33	0 29	10 40	12 54	21 13	0 07	4 03	2 26
12 W	17 42	18 04	2 28	15 29	23 19	1 58	12 25	1 17	21 41	0 30	10 38	12 49	21 13	0 07	4 04	2 26
13 Th	17 58	12 46	1 25	9 57	23 02	1 45	12 51	1 15	21 49	0 30	10 34	12 44	21 13	0 07	4 04	2 26
14 F	18 14	7 05	0 18	4 10	22 41	1 30	13 17	1 14	21 57	0 31	10 31	12 39	21 13	0 07	4 05	2 26
15 Sa	18 29	1 15	0S47	1S40	22 16	1 13	13 42	1 12	22 05	0 31	10 28	12 34	21 13	0 07	4 05	2 25
16 Su	18 44	4S32	1 49	7 20	21 49	0 56	14 07	1 11	22 13	0 32	10 24	12 29	21 14	0 07	4 06	2 25
17 M	18 59	10 04	2 46	12 42	21 17	0 36	14 31	1 09	22 20	0 33	10 21	12 24	21 14	0 07	4 06	2 25
18 Tu	19 14	15 12	3 34	17 34	20 44	0 17	14 55	1 08	22 27	0 33	10 17	12 19	21 14	0 08	4 06	2 25
19 W	19 28	19 45	4 13	21 45	20 07	0N04	15 19	1 06	22 34	0 34	10 13	12 14	21 15	0 08	4 06	2 25
20 Th	19 42	23 31	4 41	25 03	19 30	0 25	15 43	1 04	22 41	0 34	10 08	12 09	21 15	0 08	4 07	2 24
21 F	19 55	26 18	4 57	27 16	18 52	0 45	16 06	1 02	22 47	0 35	10 04	12 04	21 16	0 08	4 07	2 24
22 Sa	20 08	27 55	4 60	28 15	18 15	1 04	16 28	1 01	22 54	0 35	9 59	11 59	21 16	0 08	4 07	2 24
23 Su	20 21	28 15	4 49	27 55	17 40	1 22	16 50	0 59	22 60	0 36	9 55	11 54	21 17	0 08	4 07	2 24
24 M	20 33	27 15	4 26	26 15	17 08	1 38	17 12	0 57	23 06	0 36	9 50	11 49	21 17	0 08	4 07	2 24
25 Tu	20 45	24 57	3 50	23 20	16 39	1 53	17 33	0 55	23 11	0 37	9 45	11 44	21 18	0 09	4 07	2 23
26 W	20 57	21 27	3 03	19 19	16 15	2 05	17 54	0 53	23 17	0 37	9 40	11 39	21 19	0 09	4 07	2 23
27 Th	21 08	16 56	2 07	14 20	15 56	2 15	18 14	0 51	23 22	0 38	9 35	11 34	21 19	0 09	4 07	2 23
28 F	21 18	11 33	1 02	8 37	15 42	2 23	18 34	0 49	23 27	0 38	9 29	11 29	21 20	0 09	4 06	2 23
29 Sa	21 29	5 32	0N07	2 20	15 32	2 29	18 53	0 47	23 31	0 39	9 24	11 24	21 21	0 09	4 06	2 23
30 Su	21S39	0N56	1N18	4N15	15S28	2N34	19S12	0N44	23S36	0S39	9S18	11S19	21N21	0N09	4S06	2S22

Day	⚷ Decl	⚷ Lat	♅ Decl	♅ Lat	♆ Decl	♆ Lat	♇ Decl	♇ Lat
1	9N57	0N36	20N00	0S13	1S20	1S22	23S31	3S46
6	9 52	0 36	19 58	0 13	1 22	1 22	23 30	3 46
11	9 47	0 35	19 55	0 12	1 24	1 22	23 29	3 46
16	9 42	0 35	19 53	0 12	1 26	1 22	23 28	3 46
21	9 37	0 34	19 50	0 12	1 27	1 22	23 27	3 46
26	9 33	0 34	19 47	0 12	1 28	1 21	23 25	3 46

Day	⚴ Decl	⚴ Lat	⚵ Decl	⚵ Lat	⚶ Decl	⚶ Lat	Eris Decl	Eris Lat
1	0S31	18N10	11S34	10N25	22S57	0N17	0S17	10S42
6	1 06	17 24	11 53	10 19	23 14	0 07	0 17	10 41
11	1 37	16 39	12 10	10 15	23 27	0S02	0 18	10 41
16	2 05	15 55	12 26	10 10	23 37	0 11	0 19	10 41
21	2 30	15 14	12 40	10 07	23 44	0 20	0 19	10 40
26	2 51	14 35	12 53	10 03	23 48	0 28	0 19	10 40

Moon Phenomena

Max/0 Decl
dy hr mn
2 11:59 0 N
8 11:31 28N23
15 5:08 0 S
22 18:01 28S18
29 20:35 0 N

Max/0 Lat
dy hr mn
1 17:45 0 N
7 17:21 5N04
14 6:40 0 S
21 16:57 5S00
28 21:33 0 N

Perigee/Apogee
dy hr m kilometers
5 22:28 p 356834
20 2:50 a 406692

PH dy hr mn
○ 5 13:20 13♉23
☾ 12 5:29 20♌05
● 20 6:48 28♏12
☽ 28 7:00 6♓18

Void of Course Moon

Last Aspect	☽ Ingress
2 15:16 ♆ ☌	♈ 2 15:41
4 11:22 ♀ ☍	♉ 4 16:17
6 14:52 ♆ ✶	♊ 6 15:22
8 14:33 ♆ □	♋ 8 15:07
10 17:24 ♅ ✶	♌ 10 17:35
12 23:31 ♅ □	♍ 12 23:53
15 9:10 ♅ △	♎ 15 9:45
17 11:52 ♃ □	♏ 17 21:46
20 9:26 ♅ ☍	♐ 20 10:27
22 21:49 ♆ □	♑ 22 22:54
25 9:11 ♆ ✶	♒ 25 10:17
27 17:54 ♅ □	♓ 27 19:25
30 0:06 ♆ ☌	♈ 30 1:08

DAILY ASPECTARIAN

1 Sa ☽⚼♀ 1:22; ♂#♅ 3:39; ☉△☽ 3:43; ☿∥♇ 3:54; ☽∠⚷ 4:08; ☽⚼♃ 5:28; ☽∥♀ 8:37; ☽∠♇ 16:43; ☊ R 17:43; ☽∥♄ 21:59

2 Su ☽⚻♀ 5:48; ☽⚺⚷ 5:52; ♀☍⚷ 6:39; ☽∥♆ 7:14; ☽△♃ 7:18; ☉⚼☽ 7:31; ☽☌♄ 8:32; ☿△⚳ 13:17; ☽△♂ 13:18; ☽☌♆ 15:16; ☽✶♅ 16:02; ☽#♆ 16:42; ☽✶♇ 18:06; ☉⚼♄ 21:23; ☽☌⚳ 21:46; ☽△☿ 22:19; ♀□♃ 23:18

3 M ☽#♄ 1:48; ☉⚻☽ 10:12; ♀⚻♄ 11:58; ☽⚼♂ 15:15; ☽∠♅ 16:35; ☽#♀ 18:22; ☽∥⚷ 22:34; ☽⚼☿ 23:58

4 Tu ☽#⚳ 2:15; ♂△♆ 4:00; ☽☌⚷ 6:52; ☽□♃ 8:27; ☽⚺♄ 9:23; ☽☍♀ 11:22; ♂ ♐ 13:02; ☽⚺♆ 15:50; ☽⚻♂ 16:26; ☽⚺♅ 16:30; ♂☍♅ 17:31; ☽□♇ 18:37; ☉#☽ 19:45; ☽⚺⚳ 21:43

5 W ☽⚻☿ 0:48; ☽∠♄ 9:00; ☉☍☽ 13:20; ☽∥♅ 13:39; ☽∠♆ 15:25; ☽#♂ 17:13; ☽∥♃ 19:21; ☽∠⚳ 21:06

6 Th ♀#⚷ 5:54; ☽⚺⚷ 5:57; ☽#♇ 7:03; ☽✶♃ 7:41; ☽✶♄ 8:26; ☽#☿ 9:58; ☽⚻♀ 14:43; ☽✶♆ 14:52; ♂✶♇ 15:12; ☽☌♅ 15:27; ♀⚻♆ 16:38; ☽△♇ 17:43; ☽☍♂ 17:50; ☽✶⚳ 20:27; ☉⚼♆ 20:28; ♀ ♏ 22:41; ♀⚻♅ 23:32

7 F ☽☍☿ 1:20; ☽∠⚷ 5:26; ☽∠♃ 7:17; ☉⚻☽ 15:48; ☽⚼♀ 16:30; ☽⚼♇ 17:25

8 Sa ♅R♉ 2:23; ♀□♇ 3:45; ☽✶⚷ 5:15; ♀∥⚳ 7:13; ☽⚺♃ 7:14; ☽□♄ 7:50; ☽□♆ 14:33; ☽⚺♅ 15:05; ♂#♃ 16:08; ☽⚻♇ 17:36; ☉⚼☽ 17:41; ☽△♀ 18:53; ♂△⚳ 19:28; ☽□⚳ 20:07; ☽⚻♂ 20:10

9 Su ☽⚻☿ 2:18; ♀⚻⚳ 8:34; ☽∠♅ 15:48; ☿ R 19:03; ☉△☽ 20:27; ☽⚼♂ 22:27

10 M ☉⚼⚳ 2:53; ☽⚼☿ 3:31; ♀⚺♂ 4:21; ☽□⚷ 6:53; ☽☌♃ 9:11; ☽△♄ 9:40; ☽△♆ 16:55; ☽✶♅ 17:24; ☽#☿ 18:22; ☽#♇ 19:08; ☽☍♇ 20:17; ☽△⚳ 22:39

11 Tu ☽△♂ 1:49; ☽□♀ 2:45; ☽△☿ 5:22; ☽#♂ 6:10; ☽∥♃ 8:10; ☿∥♇ 8:22; ☽⚼♄ 11:58; ☽∥♅ 14:56; ♃ R 16:43; ☽⚼♆ 19:31

12 W ☽⚼⚳ 1:22; ☉#☽ 1:42; ☿⚺♀ 2:17; ☉□☽ 5:29; ☊ D 5:41; ☽△⚷ 12:12; ☽⚺♃ 14:50; ☽⚻♄ 15:15; ☽⚻♆ 23:06; ☿☌♂ 23:17; ☽□♅ 23:31; ☽#♀ 23:40

13 Th ☽⚻♇ 2:51; ☽⚻⚳ 5:04; ☽#⚳ 9:29; ☽□☿ 10:50; ☽□♂ 12:05; ☽∥⚷ 12:56; ☽✶♀ 15:48; ☽⚼⚷ 16:19; ☽∠♃ 19:07

14 F ☊ R 6:38; ☽⚼♇ 7:32; ☽#♄ 12:21; ☉✶☽ 19:21; ☽⚻⚷ 21:14; ☽#♆ 23:16

15 Sa ☽∠♀ 0:07; ☽✶♃ 0:10; ☽☍♄ 0:31; ♀⚼♄ 4:03; ☿∥♂ 7:57; ☽☍♆ 8:51; ☽△♅ 9:10; ⚶ ♑ 10:26; ☽∥♆ 11:03; ☽△♇ 12:57; ☽☍⚳ 14:58; ☉⚻⚷ 17:26; ☽✶☿ 17:41; ☽∥♄ 22:10

16 Su ☽✶♂ 2:17; ☉∠☽ 3:40; ☽⚺♀ 9:15; ♂⚼⚷ 10:01; ☽⚼♅ 14:53; ☽∠☿ 21:13; ☽#⚷ 22:16

17 M ☽∥⚳ 1:12; ☿△⚳ 1:55; ☿#♃ 2:31; ☉△♃ 5:09; ☽☍⚷ 8:44; ☉△♄ 8:57; ☽∠♂ 10:17; ☽□♃ 11:52; ☽⚻♄ 12:12; ☉⚺☽ 12:30; ☿✶♇ 20:37; ☽⚻♆ 20:47; ☽⚻♅ 20:57; ☽∥♀ 22:29

18 Tu ☽⚺☿ 0:40; ☽□♇ 1:06; ☽⚻⚳ 2:55; ♂⚼♃ 11:24; ♀⚼♆ 12:21; ☽⚼♄ 18:27; ☽⚺♂ 18:34; ☉∥☽ 22:15

19 W ☽#♅ 0:33; ☽∥☿ 1:51; ☽⚼♆ 3:05; ☿R♏ 3:21; ☽☌♀ 4:50; ☽#♃ 8:52; ☽⚼⚳ 9:13; ☿#♅ 10:43; ☿☍♅ 11:46; ☿△♆ 12:23; ☽∥♂ 17:57; ☉∥☿ 18:35; ☽⚻⚷ 21:11; ☽∥♇ 23:31

20 Th ☽△♃ 0:24; ☽△♄ 0:46; ☉☌☽ 6:48; ☽☌☿ 7:16; ☉☌☿ 9:24; ☽△♆ 9:25; ☽☍♅ 9:26; ☽✶♇ 13:53; ♅✶♆ 14:40; ☉#♅ 15:17; ☽△⚳ 15:32; ♀⚼⚳ 21:46

21 F ☽⚼⚷ 3:26; ☽⚼♃ 6:40; ☽☌♂ 11:14; ☉☍♅ 12:27; ☉△♆ 13:06; ☽∠♇ 20:13; ⚳ D 23:58

22 Sa ☽⚺♀ 0:39; ☉ ♐ 1:37; ☽△⚷ 9:34; ☽⚻♃ 12:47; ☽□♄ 13:15; ☽⚺☿ 13:45; ☿△♄ 18:47; ☽⚻♅ 21:40; ☽□♆ 21:49; ☿△♃ 23:38

23 Su ☉⚺☽ 0:51; ☽⚺♇ 2:23; ☽□⚳ 3:56; ☽∠♀ 10:15; ☽∠☿ 17:05; ☉✶♇ 19:21; ☿∥♀ 22:11

24 M ☽⚺♂ 3:15; ☽⚼♅ 3:28; ☉∠☽ 9:26; ☿⚻⚷ 12:06; ☉△⚳ 13:40; ☽✶♀ 19:25; ☽✶☿ 20:29; ☽□⚷ 21:07

25 Tu ☽☍♃ 0:13; ☽✶♄ 0:50; ☿☌♀ 1:53; ☽△♅ 8:53; ☽✶♆ 9:11; ☽∠♂ 10:39; ☽∥♇ 11:24; ♀⚻⚷ 11:27; ☽∥♂ 12:43; ☽☌♇ 13:46; ☽✶⚳ 15:15; ☉✶☽ 17:29

26 W ☽#♃ 0:52; ☉∥☽ 2:52; ☽∠♄ 5:57; ☽#♅ 9:28; ☽∠♆ 14:07; ♀△♃ 16:33; ☽✶♂ 17:22; ☽∥♀ 18:00; ☽∠⚳ 20:08; ♀△♄ 23:49

27 Th ☽□☿ 3:14; ☽∥☿ 5:00; ☽✶⚷ 6:43; ☽⚻♃ 9:37; ☽⚺♄ 10:24; ☽□♀ 11:33; ⚳#⚷ 12:06; ♂∥♇ 15:31; ♂∠♇ 16:12; ☽□♅ 17:54; ☽⚺♆ 18:20; ☽⚺♇ 22:49

28 F ☽⚺⚳ 0:16; ☉#♃ 3:32; ♄ D 3:53; ☉□☽ 7:00; ☽#⚷ 8:22; ☽∥⚳ 8:38; ☽∠⚷ 10:24; ☽⚼♃ 13:10

29 Sa ☽∠♇ 2:04; ☽□♂ 3:59; ☽∥♄ 5:24; ☽△☿ 8:55; ☽⚺⚷ 13:10; ☽∥♆ 15:09; ☽△♃ 15:46; ☽☌♄ 16:43; ☿ D 17:40; ☽△♀ 23:14; ☽✶♅ 23:34

30 Su ☽☌♆ 0:06; ☽#♆ 1:58; ☉⚼⚷ 2:01; ♀☍♅ 2:50; ☽✶♇ 4:23; ☽☌⚳ 5:49; ♀△♆ 8:49; ☽⚼☿ 11:00; ☽#♄ 11:26; ☉△☽ 16:01; ♀ ♐ 20:15

December 2025

LONGITUDE

Day	Sid.Time	☉	☽	☽ 12 hour	Mean ☊	True ☊	☿	♀	♂	⚳	♃	♄	⚷	♅	♆	♇
	h m s	° ' "	° ' "	° ' "	° '	° '	° '	° '	° '	° '	° '	° '	° '	° '	° '	° '
1 M	4 40 26	9♐02 20	13♈26 47	20♈40 17	13♓48.6	14♓17.5	20♏50.7	0♐11.8	19♐17.6	2♈45.8	24♋32.1	25♓09.9	23♈05.1	29♉03.1	29♓23.9	1♒54.2
2 Tu	4 44 22	10 03 08	28 00 22	5♉26 29	13 45.4	14R 12.6	21 08.4	1 27.2	20 02.2	2 49.3	24R 28.2	25 10.2	23R 03.4	29R 00.6	29R 23.6	1 55.5
3 W	4 48 19	11 03 57	12♉57 49	20 33 22	13 42.3	14 04.9	21 35.1	2 42.7	20 46.7	2 53.2	24 24.1	25 10.7	23 01.7	28 58.2	29 23.3	1 56.8
4 Th	4 52 15	12 04 46	28 11 55	5♊52 03	13 39.1	13 54.8	22 09.7	3 58.1	21 31.4	2 57.4	24 19.9	25 11.3	23 00.1	28 55.7	29 23.1	1 58.1
5 F	4 56 12	13 05 37	13♊32 19	21 11 13	13 35.9	13 43.2	22 51.5	5 13.6	22 16.0	3 02.0	24 15.5	25 12.0	22 58.6	28 53.3	29 22.9	1 59.5
6 Sa	5 00 08	14 06 29	28 47 16	6♋19 09	13 32.7	13 31.5	23 39.6	6 29.0	23 00.8	3 06.9	24 10.9	25 12.8	22 57.1	28 50.9	29 22.7	2 00.9
7 Su	5 04 05	15 07 22	13♋45 41	21 05 57	13 29.6	13 21.2	24 33.4	7 44.5	23 45.6	3 12.2	24 06.1	25 13.7	22 55.6	28 48.5	29 22.6	2 02.3
8 M	5 08 01	16 08 16	28 19 13	5♌25 01	13 26.4	13 13.2	25 32.0	9 00.0	24 30.4	3 17.8	24 01.2	25 14.7	22 54.2	28 46.2	29 22.5	2 03.7
9 Tu	5 11 58	17 09 12	12♌23 10	19 13 38	13 23.2	13 07.9	26 34.9	10 15.5	25 15.3	3 23.8	23 56.1	25 15.8	22 52.8	28 43.8	29 22.4	2 05.2
10 W	5 15 55	18 10 08	25 56 36	2♍32 24	13 20.0	13 05.3	27 41.5	11 31.0	26 00.2	3 30.0	23 50.8	25 17.0	22 51.5	28 41.5	29D 22.4	2 06.6
11 Th	5 19 51	19 11 06	9♍01 29	15 24 24	13 16.9	13 04.5	28 51.4	12 46.5	26 45.2	3 36.6	23 45.4	25 18.3	22 50.3	28 39.2	29 22.4	2 08.1
12 F	5 23 48	20 12 05	21 41 44	27 54 09	13 13.7	13 04.5	0♐04.1	14 02.0	27 30.3	3 43.5	23 39.8	25 19.8	22 49.0	28 36.9	29 22.4	2 09.6
13 Sa	5 27 44	21 13 04	4♎02 18	10♎06 50	13 10.5	13 04.0	1 19.2	15 17.5	28 15.4	3 50.8	23 34.1	25 21.3	22 47.9	28 34.6	29 22.5	2 11.2
14 Su	5 31 41	22 14 05	16 08 23	22 07 34	13 07.3	13 01.8	2 36.4	16 33.0	29 00.5	3 58.3	23 28.2	25 22.9	22 46.8	28 32.4	29 22.6	2 12.7
15 M	5 35 37	23 15 07	28 04 57	4♏01 04	13 04.1	12 57.1	3 55.4	17 48.5	29 45.7	4 06.2	23 22.2	25 24.7	22 45.7	28 30.1	29 22.7	2 14.3
16 Tu	5 39 34	24 16 10	9♏56 24	15 51 24	13 01.0	12 49.5	5 16.1	19 04.0	0♑31.0	4 14.4	23 16.0	25 26.5	22 44.7	28 27.9	29 22.9	2 15.8
17 W	5 43 30	25 17 14	21 46 25	27 41 47	12 57.8	12 39.0	6 38.1	20 19.5	1 16.3	4 22.9	23 09.7	25 28.5	22 43.7	28 25.8	29 23.1	2 17.4
18 Th	5 47 27	26 18 19	3♐37 49	9♐34 43	12 54.6	12 26.1	8 01.3	21 35.0	2 01.6	4 31.7	23 03.2	25 30.6	22 42.8	28 23.6	29 23.3	2 19.0
19 F	5 51 24	27 19 24	15 32 41	21 31 54	12 51.4	12 11.9	9 25.6	22 50.6	2 47.0	4 40.7	22 56.6	25 32.7	22 42.0	28 21.5	29 23.6	2 20.7
20 Sa	5 55 20	28 20 31	27 32 29	3♑34 34	12 48.3	11 57.4	10 50.9	24 06.1	3 32.5	4 50.1	22 49.9	25 35.0	22 41.2	28 19.4	29 23.9	2 22.3
21 Su	5 59 17	29 21 37	9♑38 15	15 43 38	12 45.1	11 43.9	12 16.9	25 21.6	4 18.0	4 59.8	22 43.1	25 37.4	22 40.5	28 17.4	29 24.3	2 24.0
22 M	6 03 13	0♑22 45	21 50 52	28 00 24	12 41.9	11 32.5	13 43.7	26 37.2	5 03.5	5 09.8	22 36.1	25 39.9	22 39.8	28 15.3	29 24.7	2 25.6
23 Tu	6 07 10	1 23 52	4♒11 25	10♒25 06	12 38.7	11 23.9	15 11.1	27 52.7	5 49.1	5 20.0	22 29.1	25 42.4	22 39.1	28 13.3	29 25.1	2 27.3
24 W	6 11 06	2 25 00	16 41 21	23 00 26	12 35.6	11 18.4	16 39.0	29 08.2	6 34.7	5 30.5	22 21.9	25 45.1	22 38.6	28 11.4	29 25.5	2 29.0
25 Th	6 15 03	3 26 08	29 22 40	5♓48 23	12 32.4	11D 15.6	18 07.6	0♑23.8	7 20.4	5 41.3	22 14.7	25 47.9	22 38.1	28 09.4	29 26.0	2 30.8
26 F	6 18 59	4 27 16	12♓17 56	18 51 43	12 29.2	11 15.0	19 36.5	1 39.3	8 06.1	5 52.4	22 07.3	25 50.8	22 37.6	28 07.6	29 26.6	2 32.5
27 Sa	6 22 56	5 28 24	25 30 04	2♈13 21	12 26.0	11R 15.4	21 06.0	2 54.8	8 51.9	6 03.7	21 59.8	25 53.7	22 37.2	28 05.7	29 27.1	2 34.2
28 Su	6 26 53	6 29 32	9♈01 53	15 55 55	12 22.9	11 15.6	22 35.8	4 10.3	9 37.7	6 15.3	21 52.3	25 56.8	22 36.8	28 03.9	29 27.7	2 36.0
29 M	6 30 49	7 30 40	22 55 35	0♉00 55	12 19.7	11 14.5	24 06.1	5 25.8	10 23.5	6 27.1	21 44.7	26 00.0	22 36.5	28 02.1	29 28.3	2 37.8
30 Tu	6 34 46	8 31 48	7♉11 47	14 27 56	12 16.5	11 11.3	25 36.7	6 41.3	11 09.4	6 39.2	21 37.0	26 03.2	22 36.3	28 00.3	29 29.0	2 39.5
31 W	6 38 42	9♑32 56	21 48 51	29 13 54	12♓13.3	11♓05.5	27♐07.7	7♑56.8	11♑55.3	6♈51.6	21♋29.3	26♓06.6	22♈36.1	27♉58.6	29♓29.7	2♒41.3

1st of Month

Julian Day #
2461010.5
Obliquity
23°26■8"
SVP 4♓53■8"
GC 27♐12.1
Eris 24♈46.7R

Day	⚴
1	14♒19.0
6	15 31.1
11	16 46.6
16	18 05.3
21	19 26.9
26	20 51.1
31	22 17.8

Day	⚵
1	19♐45.6
6	21 31.8
11	23 18.7
16	25 06.1
21	26 53.9
26	28 42.0
31	0♑30.1

Day	⚶
1	8♑02.3
6	10 38.5
11	13 15.3
16	15 52.4
21	18 30.0
26	21 07.7
31	23 45.5

DECLINATION and LATITUDE

Day	☉ Decl	☽ Decl	☽ Lat	☽12h Decl	☿ Decl	☿ Lat	♀ Decl	♀ Lat	♂ Decl	♂ Lat	⚳ Decl	⚳ Lat	♃ Decl	♃ Lat	♄ Decl	♄ Lat
1 M	21S48	7N34	2N27	10N50	15S27	2N36	19S30	0N42	23S40	0S40	9S12	11S14	21N22	0N10	4S06	2S22
2 Tu	21 57	14 00	3 28	17 01	15 31	2 37	19 48	0 40	23 44	0 40	9 06	11 09	21 23	0 10	4 05	2 22
3 W	22 06	19 49	4 17	22 19	15 38	2 36	20 05	0 38	23 48	0 41	9 00	11 04	21 24	0 10	4 05	2 22
4 Th	22 14	24 27	4 49	26 09	15 49	2 35	20 21	0 36	23 51	0 41	8 54	10 59	21 25	0 10	4 05	2 21
5 F	22 22	27 23	4 60	28 05	16 02	2 32	20 37	0 33	23 54	0 42	8 48	10 54	21 26	0 10	4 04	2 21
6 Sa	22 30	28 15	4 49	27 53	16 17	2 28	20 53	0 31	23 57	0 42	8 41	10 49	21 27	0 10	4 04	2 21
7 Su	22 36	27 01	4 19	25 42	16 35	2 24	21 08	0 29	24 00	0 43	8 35	10 45	21 28	0 10	4 03	2 21
8 M	22 43	23 58	3 33	21 54	16 54	2 19	21 22	0 26	24 03	0 43	8 28	10 40	21 29	0 11	4 02	2 21
9 Tu	22 49	19 33	2 34	16 60	17 14	2 13	21 35	0 24	24 05	0 44	8 21	10 35	21 30	0 11	4 02	2 20
10 W	22 55	14 16	1 29	11 26	17 35	2 07	21 48	0 22	24 07	0 44	8 15	10 30	21 31	0 11	4 01	2 20
11 Th	22 60	8 31	0 21	5 34	17 56	2 01	22 00	0 19	24 09	0 45	8 08	10 25	21 32	0 11	4 00	2 20
12 F	23 05	2 36	0S45	0S21	18 18	1 54	22 12	0 17	24 10	0 45	8 01	10 21	21 33	0 11	3 60	2 20
13 Sa	23 09	3S16	1 48	6 07	18 41	1 47	22 23	0 15	24 11	0 46	7 53	10 16	21 34	0 11	3 59	2 19
14 Su	23 13	8 53	2 45	11 34	19 03	1 40	22 33	0 12	24 12	0 46	7 46	10 11	21 35	0 12	3 58	2 19
15 M	23 16	14 07	3 34	16 32	19 25	1 32	22 43	0 10	24 13	0 46	7 39	10 07	21 37	0 12	3 57	2 19
16 Tu	23 19	18 47	4 13	20 52	19 47	1 25	22 52	0 07	24 13	0 47	7 31	10 02	21 38	0 12	3 56	2 19
17 W	23 21	22 43	4 41	24 21	20 09	1 17	23 00	0 05	24 13	0 47	7 24	9 58	21 39	0 12	3 55	2 19
18 Th	23 23	25 44	4 57	26 49	20 30	1 09	23 08	0 03	24 13	0 48	7 16	9 53	21 40	0 12	3 54	2 18
19 F	23 25	27 37	4 59	28 05	20 51	1 02	23 14	0 00	24 13	0 48	7 09	9 49	21 41	0 12	3 53	2 18
20 Sa	23 26	28 14	4 49	28 02	21 11	0 54	23 21	0S02	24 12	0 49	7 01	9 44	21 43	0 13	3 52	2 18
21 Su	23 26	27 30	4 26	26 38	21 30	0 46	23 26	0 05	24 11	0 49	6 53	9 40	21 44	0 13	3 51	2 18
22 M	23 26	25 27	3 50	23 57	21 49	0 38	23 31	0 07	24 10	0 49	6 45	9 35	21 45	0 13	3 50	2 18
23 Tu	23 26	22 10	3 03	20 08	22 06	0 31	23 35	0 09	24 08	0 50	6 37	9 31	21 47	0 13	3 48	2 17
24 W	23 25	17 51	2 06	15 21	22 23	0 23	23 38	0 12	24 07	0 50	6 29	9 27	21 48	0 13	3 47	2 17
25 Th	23 24	12 40	1 03	9 50	22 39	0 15	23 40	0 14	24 05	0 51	6 21	9 22	21 49	0 13	3 46	2 17
26 F	23 22	6 52	0N06	3 47	22 54	0 08	23 42	0 16	24 02	0 51	6 12	9 18	21 51	0 13	3 45	2 17
27 Sa	23 19	0 38	1 15	2N33	23 08	0 01	23 43	0 19	23 60	0 52	6 04	9 14	21 52	0 14	3 43	2 17
28 Su	23 17	5N45	2 22	8 56	23 20	0S07	23 44	0 21	23 57	0 52	5 56	9 10	21 53	0 14	3 42	2 16
29 M	23 14	12 03	3 23	15 03	23 32	0 14	23 43	0 23	23 54	0 52	5 47	9 05	21 55	0 14	3 40	2 16
30 Tu	23 10	17 53	4 12	20 30	23 43	0 21	23 42	0 26	23 51	0 53	5 39	9 01	21 56	0 14	3 39	2 16
31 W	23S06	22N50	4N47	24N49	23S52	0S28	23S40	0S28	23S47	0S53	5S30	8S57	21N57	0N14	3S37	2S16

Day	⚷ Decl	⚷ Lat	♅ Decl	♅ Lat	♆ Decl	♆ Lat	♇ Decl	♇ Lat
1	9N29	0N33	19N45	0S12	1S29	1S21	23S24	3S46
6	9 26	0 33	19 42	0 12	1 29	1 21	23 22	3 46
11	9 23	0 32	19 40	0 12	1 29	1 21	23 21	3 46
16	9 20	0 32	19 37	0 12	1 29	1 21	23 19	3 46
21	9 18	0 31	19 35	0 12	1 28	1 20	23 17	3 46
26	9 17	0 31	19 33	0 12	1 27	1 20	23 15	3 46
31	9N16	0N30	19N31	0S12	1S25	1S20	23S14	3S46

Day	⚴ Decl	⚴ Lat	⚵ Decl	⚵ Lat	⚶ Decl	⚶ Lat	Eris Decl	Eris Lat
1	3S09	13N57	13S04	10N01	23S48	0S36	0S20	10S39
6	3 24	13 21	13 13	9 58	23 45	0 45	0 20	10 38
11	3 36	12 47	13 20	9 57	23 39	0 53	0 20	10 38
16	3 45	12 14	13 26	9 55	23 30	1 00	0 20	10 37
21	3 51	11 42	13 30	9 55	23 18	1 08	0 20	10 36
26	3 55	11 12	13 32	9 54	23 02	1 16	0 19	10 36
31	3S56	10N43	13S32	9N54	22S43	1S23	0S19	10S35

Moon Phenomena

Max/0 Decl
dy hr mn
5 21:44 28N16
12 10:34 0 S
19 23:08 28S14
27 2:25 0 N

Perigee/Apogee
dy hr m kilometers
4 11:09 p 356968
17 6:10 a 406322

Max/0 Lat
dy hr mn
5 0:17 5N00
11 7:36 0 S
18 17:24 5S00
25 22:04 0 N

PH dy hr mn
○ 4 23:15 13♊04
◐ 11 20:53 20♍04
● 20 1:44 28♐25
☽ 27 19:11 6♈17

Void of Course Moon

Last Aspect	☽ Ingress
1 18:16 ♃ □	♉ 2 3:14
4 1:51 ♆ ⚹	♊ 4 2:49
6 0:56 ♆ □	♋ 6 1:55
8 1:46 ♆ △	♌ 8 2:49
10 4:58 ♅ □	♍ 10 7:21
12 14:52 ♆ ☍	♎ 12 16:05
15 3:37 ♂ ⚹	♏ 15 3:52
17 15:25 ♆ △	♐ 17 16:40
20 3:42 ♆ □	♑ 20 4:54
22 14:45 ♆ ⚹	♒ 22 15:53
24 21:43 ♅ □	♓ 25 1:10
27 7:05 ♆ ☌	♈ 27 8:03
29 2:14 ☿ △	♉ 29 11:58
31 12:26 ♆ ⚹	♊ 31 13:14

DAILY ASPECTARIAN

1 M ☽∠♅ 1:01; ☽⚼♀ 3:12; ☽⋕⚳ 5:53; ☽∥⚷ 7:00; ☽△♂ 10:15; ☉⚼♃ 11:03; ☽⚻☿ 12:30; ☽☌⚷ 15:56; ☽□♃ 18:16; ☉⚼☽ 18:50; ♀⋕♅ 19:13; ☽⚺♄ 19:23

2 Tu ☽⚺♅ 1:37; ☽⚺♆ 2:15; ☽⋕☿ 6:01; ☽⚻♀ 6:06; ☽□♇ 6:21; ☽⚺⚳ 7:49; ♀⚹♇ 9:08; ☽⚼♂ 11:56; ☽∠♄ 19:34; ☉⚻☽ 20:46; ☽∥♅ 23:38

3 W ☽⋕♀ 1:18; ☽∠♆ 2:15; ♀△⚳ 3:32; ☽∥♃ 7:28; ☽∠⚳ 7:50; ☉⋕☽ 11:16; ☽⚻♂ 12:59; ☽☍☿ 14:08; ☽⚺⚷ 15:52; ☽⋕♇ 17:47; ☽⚹♃ 17:58; ☽⚹♄ 19:17; ☽⋕♂ 20:24

4 Th ☽☌♅ 1:08; ☽⚹♆ 1:51; ☽△♇ 5:55; ☽⚹⚳ 7:29; ☽☍♀ 9:50; ☽∠⚷ 15:19; ☽∠♃ 17:20; ☉☍☽ 23:15

5 F ☿⚻⚷ 3:37; ☽⚼♇ 5:25; ☽☍♂ 14:24; ☽⚹⚷ 14:48; ☽⚻☿ 15:26; ☽⚺♃ 16:45; ☽□♄ 18:20; ♂△⚷ 22:05

6 Sa ☽⚺♅ 0:06; ☽□♆ 0:56; ☽⚻♇ 5:08; ☽□⚳ 6:55; ☿△♃ 13:06; ☽⚻♀ 13:24; ☽⚼☿ 16:45

7 Su ☽∠♅ 0:05; ☉⚻☽ 2:23; ♀⚼⚷ 3:28; ♂⚻♃ 9:56; ☽□⚷ 15:00; ☽⚼♀ 16:07; ☽☌♃ 16:52; ☿△♄ 16:59; ☽⚻♂ 17:18; ☽△♄ 18:52; ☽△☿ 19:00; ☽⋕♂ 23:31

8 M ♀⚼♃ 0:22; ☽⚹♅ 0:45; ☽△♆ 1:46; ☽⋕♇ 3:41; ☉⚼☽ 5:06; ☽☍♇ 6:19; ☉⋕☽ 7:17; ☽△⚳ 8:27; ♀⋕♃ 13:15; ☽⋕♀ 14:09; ☽∥♃ 14:12; ☽△♀ 19:57; ☽⚼♂ 20:06; ☽⚼♄ 20:19; ☉∠♇ 22:23; ☽∥♅ 23:24

9 Tu ♂□♄ 0:17; ☽⚼♆ 3:28; ☉△☽ 9:01; ☽⋕☿ 10:16; ☽⚼⚳ 10:37; ☽△⚷ 18:28; ☽⚺♃ 20:15; ☽⚻♄ 22:49

10 W ☽△♂ 0:07; ☽□☿ 3:28; ☽□♅ 4:58; ☽⚻♆ 6:13; ☽⚻♇ 11:14; ♆ D 12:25; ☽⚻⚳ 13:53; ☿☍♅ 20:00; ☽∥⚷ 20:28; ☽⚼⚷ 21:48; ☽∠♃ 23:30

11 Th ☽⋕⚳ 1:37; ☽□♀ 7:48; ☿△♆ 10:20; ☽⚼♇ 15:19; ☽⋕♄ 18:21; ☉□☽ 20:53; ☿ ♐ 22:41

12 F ☽⚻⚷ 2:09; ☽⚹♃ 3:46; ☽⋕♆ 4:31; ☽☍♄ 7:01; ☽□♂ 11:57; ☽△♅ 13:21; ☽☍♆ 14:52; ☽∥♆ 16:38; ☽⚹☿ 18:03; ☽△♇ 20:21; ☽☍⚳ 23:37

13 Sa ☽∥♄ 2:59; ♂⚻♅ 9:45; ☿⚹♇ 16:33; ☽⚼♅ 18:50; ☽∥⚳ 19:13

14 Su ☽⚹♀ 0:55; ☽⋕⚷ 2:03; ☽∠☿ 3:17; ♂□♆ 11:45; ☉△⚷ 12:37; ♀∠♇ 12:54; ☽☍⚷ 13:18; ☉⚹☽ 13:21; ☽□♃ 14:35; ☽⚻♄ 18:36

15 M ☽⚻♅ 0:51; ☉⚻♃ 2:31; ☽⚻♆ 2:37; ☿△⚳ 3:35; ☽⚹♂ 3:37; ♂ ♑ 7:35; ☽□♇ 8:25; ☽∠♀ 10:41; ☽⚻⚳ 12:19; ☿⋕♅ 13:11; ☽⚺☿ 13:19; ☉∠☽ 22:31

16 Tu ☽⚼♄ 1:01; ☉∥♇ 2:10; ☽⋕♅ 4:41; ☽∥☿ 6:12; ☽⚼♆ 9:01; ☽∠♂ 12:05; ☽⋕♃ 16:53; ☽⚼⚳ 19:05; ☽⚺♀ 20:43

17 W ☽⚻⚷ 1:56; ☽∥♀ 2:01; ☽△♃ 2:47; ☽∥♇ 4:08; ☉∥☽ 4:30; ☉□♄ 4:35; ☽△♄ 7:31; ☉⚺☽ 7:47; ☽∥♂ 10:58; ☽☍♅ 13:27; ☽△♆ 15:25; ☿⚼⚷ 18:45; ☽⚺♂ 20:32; ☽⚹♇ 21:20

18 Th ☿⚼♃ 0:30; ☽△⚳ 1:50; ☽⚼⚷ 8:14; ☽⚼♃ 8:51; ♂⚺♇ 9:33; ☽☌☿ 10:03; ♀△⚷ 21:18

19 F ♀⚻♃ 1:46; ☽∠♇ 3:37; ♀∥♇ 12:55; ☽△⚷ 14:19; ☽⚻♃ 14:41; ☽☌♀ 16:20; ☽□♄ 20:05; ☉⚻♅ 23:35

20 Sa ☽⚻♅ 1:33; ☉☌☽ 1:44; ☽□♆ 3:42; ☽⚺♇ 9:38; ☽☌♂ 12:44; ☽□⚳ 14:42

21 Su ☉∥♀ 1:01; ☉□♆ 1:03; ♀□♄ 5:10; ☽⚺☿ 5:55; ☽⚼♅ 7:11; ♃□⚷ 10:10; ☉ ♑ 15:04; ☿⋕♃ 19:02

22 M ☽☍♃ 1:28; ☽□⚷ 1:36; ♂□⚳ 4:14; ☽⚹♄ 7:29; ☽⚺♀ 10:22; ☽∥♂ 10:30; ☽△♅ 12:28; ☽⚹♆ 14:45; ☽∥♀ 14:51; ☽∠☿ 15:12; ☉∥☽ 15:41; ☽∥♇ 16:45; ☉⚺☽ 18:07; ☽☌♇ 20:38

23 Tu ☽∥☿ 0:22; ☽⚹⚳ 2:14; ☽⋕♃ 2:25; ☽⚺♂ 3:21; ♀⚻♅ 6:23; ☽∠♄ 12:36; ☽⋕♅ 15:04; ☽∠♀ 18:35; ☽∠♆ 19:41; ☽⚹☿ 23:55

24 W ☉∠☽ 1:31; ☉⚺♇ 1:38; ♀□♆ 5:32; ☽∠⚳ 7:22; ☽∠♂ 9:53; ☽⚻♃ 10:41; ☽⚹⚷ 11:18; ☿∠♇ 13:51; ♀ ♑ 16:27; ☽⚺♄ 17:15; ☽□♅ 21:43

25 Th ☽⚺♆ 0:06; ☽⚹♀ 2:07; ☽⚺♇ 5:53; ☉⚹☽ 8:14; ☽⚺⚳ 11:57; ☽⋕⚷ 14:16; ☽⚼♃ 14:32; ☽∠⚷ 15:23; ☽⚹♂ 15:46; ☊ D 22:05

26 F ☽∥⚳ 2:38; ☽∠♇ 9:37; ☽∥♄ 12:13; ☽□☿ 15:03; ♀⚺♇ 17:19; ☽△♃ 17:45; ☽⚺⚷ 18:49; ☽∥♆ 20:57

27 Sa ☽☌♄ 0:43; ☽⚹♅ 4:38; ☽☌♆ 7:05; ☽⋕♆ 7:50; ☽⚹♇ 12:39; ☿⚻♃ 13:17; ☿∥♇ 13:18; ☽□♀ 14:35; ☽⋕♄ 16:18; ☉□⚳ 17:05; ☉∥☿ 18:10; ☊ R 19:02; ☽☌⚳ 19:03; ☉□☽ 19:11

28 Su ☿△⚷ 0:16; ☽⋕⚳ 0:38; ☽□♂ 1:06; ☽∠♅ 7:01; ☽∥⚷ 13:15; ☉∥♇ 17:19; ☽□♃ 22:00; ☽☌⚷ 23:28

29 M ☽△☿ 2:14; ☽⚺♄ 5:14; ☽⚺♅ 8:39; ☽⚺♆ 11:06; ⚵ ♑ 14:36; ☽□♇ 16:25; ☿∥♀ 22:34; ☽△♀ 23:05; ☽⚺⚳ 23:05; ♀□⚳ 23:12

30 Tu ☉△☽ 2:23; ☽⚼☿ 6:19; ☽∠♄ 6:24; ☽△♂ 6:55; ☿□♄ 7:16; ☽∥♅ 7:22; ☽∠♆ 12:02; ☿∥♂ 14:51; ☽∥♃ 19:16; ☽⚹♃ 23:28

31 W ☽∠⚳ 0:04; ☽⚺⚷ 1:17; ☉⋕☽ 1:26; ☽⚼♀ 2:01; ☽⋕♇ 2:12; ☽⋕♀ 4:43; ☉⚼☽ 4:46; ☽⋕♂ 5:23; ☽⋕☿ 6:11; ☽⚹♄ 6:59; ☽⚼♂ 8:43; ☽⚻☿ 9:35; ☽☌♅ 9:57; ☽⚹♆ 12:26; ☿⚻♅ 13:09; ☽△♇ 17:36; ☽∠♃ 23:27

LONGITUDE

Day	Sid.Time	☉	☽	☽ 12 hour	Mean ☊	True ☊	☿	♀	♂	⚳	♃	♄	⚷	♅	♆	♇
	h m s	° ' "	° ' "	° ' "	° '	° '	° '	° '	° '	° '	° '	° '	° '	° '	° '	° '
1 Th	6 42 39	10♑34 04	6♊42 13	14♊12 48	12♓10.1	10♓57.6	28♐39.0	9♑12.3	12♑41.3	7♈04.2	21♋21.5	26♓10.0	22♈36.0	27♉57.0	29♓30.4	2♒43.1
2 F	6 46 35	11 35 12	21 44 29	29 16 03	12 07.0	10R 48.3	0♑10.7	10 27.8	13 27.3	7 17.0	21R 13.6	26 13.6	22D 35.9	27R 55.3	29 31.2	2 44.9
3 Sa	6 50 32	12 36 20	6♋46 15	14♋13 49	12 03.8	10 38.8	1 42.8	11 43.3	14 13.3	7 30.1	21 05.7	26 17.2	22 35.9	27 53.7	29 32.0	2 46.8
4 Su	6 54 29	13 37 28	21 37 38	28 56 41	12 00.6	10 30.2	3 15.2	12 58.8	14 59.4	7 43.4	20 57.7	26 20.9	22 36.0	27 52.2	29 32.8	2 48.6
5 M	6 58 25	14 38 36	6♌10 05	13♌17 13	11 57.5	10 23.5	4 48.0	14 14.3	15 45.5	7 56.9	20 49.8	26 24.8	22 36.1	27 50.7	29 33.7	2 50.4
6 Tu	7 02 22	15 39 43	20 17 37	27 11 01	11 54.3	10 19.2	6 21.1	15 29.8	16 31.7	8 10.7	20 41.7	26 28.7	22 36.3	27 49.2	29 34.6	2 52.3
7 W	7 06 18	16 40 51	3♍57 22	10♍36 46	11 51.1	10D 17.3	7 54.6	16 45.3	17 17.8	8 24.6	20 33.7	26 32.7	22 36.5	27 47.8	29 35.5	2 54.1
8 Th	7 10 15	17 41 59	17 09 28	23 35 50	11 47.9	10 17.3	9 28.5	18 00.7	18 04.1	8 38.8	20 25.6	26 36.7	22 36.7	27 46.4	29 36.4	2 56.0
9 F	7 14 11	18 43 07	29 56 22	6♎11 35	11 44.7	10 18.4	11 02.8	19 16.2	18 50.4	8 53.2	20 17.5	26 40.9	22 37.1	27 45.1	29 37.4	2 57.9
10 Sa	7 18 08	19 44 15	12♎22 05	18 28 30	11 41.6	10R 19.5	12 37.5	20 31.7	19 36.7	9 07.8	20 09.4	26 45.2	22 37.5	27 43.8	29 38.4	2 59.7
11 Su	7 22 04	20 45 23	24 31 29	0♏31 41	11 38.4	10 19.7	14 12.7	21 47.2	20 23.0	9 22.7	20 01.3	26 49.5	22 37.9	27 42.6	29 39.5	3 01.6
12 M	7 26 01	21 46 31	6♏29 44	12 26 15	11 35.2	10 18.2	15 48.3	23 02.6	21 09.4	9 37.7	19 53.2	26 53.9	22 38.4	27 41.4	29 40.6	3 03.5
13 Tu	7 29 58	22 47 40	18 21 49	24 17 02	11 32.0	10 14.7	17 24.3	24 18.1	21 55.8	9 52.9	19 45.1	26 58.4	22 38.9	27 40.2	29 41.7	3 05.4
14 W	7 33 54	23 48 48	0♐12 22	6♐08 19	11 28.9	10 09.1	19 00.8	25 33.6	22 42.3	10 08.4	19 37.1	27 03.0	22 39.6	27 39.1	29 42.8	3 07.3
15 Th	7 37 51	24 49 56	12 05 18	18 03 41	11 25.7	10 01.8	20 37.8	26 49.0	23 28.8	10 24.0	19 29.0	27 07.7	22 40.2	27 38.1	29 44.0	3 09.2
16 F	7 41 47	25 51 03	24 03 48	0♑05 54	11 22.5	9 53.3	22 15.2	28 04.5	24 15.3	10 39.8	19 21.0	27 12.4	22 41.0	27 37.1	29 45.2	3 11.1
17 Sa	7 45 44	26 52 11	6♑10 14	12 16 58	11 19.3	9 44.5	23 53.2	29 19.9	25 01.9	10 55.9	19 13.0	27 17.3	22 41.7	27 36.1	29 46.5	3 13.0
18 Su	7 49 40	27 53 18	18 26 13	24 38 06	11 16.2	9 36.3	25 31.7	0♒35.4	25 48.5	11 12.1	19 05.1	27 22.2	22 42.6	27 35.2	29 47.7	3 15.0
19 M	7 53 37	28 54 24	0♒52 40	7♒09 58	11 13.0	9 29.5	27 10.8	1 50.8	26 35.1	11 28.5	18 57.2	27 27.2	22 43.5	27 34.3	29 49.0	3 16.9
20 Tu	7 57 33	29 55 30	13 30 03	19 52 56	11 09.8	9 24.5	28 50.4	3 06.3	27 21.8	11 45.0	18 49.4	27 32.2	22 44.4	27 33.5	29 50.4	3 18.8
21 W	8 01 30	0♒56 35	26 18 39	2♓47 13	11 06.6	9 21.7	0♒30.5	4 21.7	28 08.4	12 01.8	18 41.6	27 37.4	22 45.4	27 32.8	29 51.7	3 20.7
22 Th	8 05 27	1 57 39	9♓18 43	15 53 12	11 03.5	9D 20.8	2 11.2	5 37.1	28 55.1	12 18.7	18 33.9	27 42.6	22 46.5	27 32.1	29 53.1	3 22.6
23 F	8 09 23	2 58 43	22 30 45	29 11 27	11 00.3	9 21.5	3 52.5	6 52.5	29 41.9	12 35.8	18 26.2	27 47.8	22 47.6	27 31.4	29 54.5	3 24.6
24 Sa	8 13 20	3 59 45	5♈55 25	12♈42 44	10 57.1	9 23.0	5 34.3	8 07.9	0♒28.7	12 53.1	18 18.7	27 53.2	22 48.7	27 30.8	29 55.9	3 26.5
25 Su	8 17 16	5 00 47	19 33 30	26 27 47	10 53.9	9 24.5	7 16.8	9 23.3	1 15.4	13 10.5	18 11.2	27 58.6	22 49.9	27 30.2	29 57.4	3 28.4
26 M	8 21 13	6 01 47	3♉25 35	10♉26 53	10 50.7	9R 25.3	8 59.8	10 38.6	2 02.3	13 28.1	18 03.8	28 04.1	22 51.2	27 29.7	29 58.9	3 30.3
27 Tu	8 25 09	7 02 46	17 31 35	24 39 28	10 47.6	9 24.9	10 43.3	11 54.0	2 49.1	13 45.8	17 56.5	28 09.7	22 52.5	27 29.3	0♈00.4	3 32.2
28 W	8 29 06	8 03 45	1♊50 15	9♊03 33	10 44.4	9 23.0	12 27.4	13 09.3	3 36.0	14 03.7	17 49.3	28 15.3	22 53.9	27 28.9	0 02.0	3 34.2
29 Th	8 33 02	9 04 42	16 18 52	23 35 34	10 41.2	9 19.7	14 12.0	14 24.7	4 22.8	14 21.8	17 42.2	28 21.0	22 55.3	27 28.6	0 03.5	3 36.1
30 F	8 36 59	10 05 38	0♋52 59	8♋10 21	10 38.0	9 15.6	15 57.0	15 40.0	5 09.8	14 40.0	17 35.3	28 26.7	22 56.8	27 28.3	0 05.1	3 38.0
31 Sa	8 40 56	11♒06 32	15 26 50	22 41 39	10♓34.9	9♓11.2	17♒42.5	16♒55.3	5♒56.7	14♈58.3	17♋28.4	28♓32.6	22♈58.4	27♉28.0	0♈06.7	3♒39.9

1st of Month

Julian Day #
2461041.5
Obliquity
23°26'■7"
SVP 4♓53'■2"
GC 27♐12.1
Eris 24♈38.0R

Day	⚴
1	22♒35.3
6	24 04.5
11	25 35.5
16	27 08.2
21	28 42.4
26	0♓17.9
31	1 54.6
	⚵
1	0♑51.7
6	2 39.8
11	4 27.7
16	6 15.3
21	8 02.5
26	9 49.0
31	11 34.8
	⚶
1	24♑17.1
6	26 55.0
11	29 32.8
16	2♒10.5
21	4 48.0
26	7 25.2
31	10 02.0

DECLINATION and LATITUDE

Day	☉ Decl	☽ Decl	☽ Lat	☽ 12h Decl	☿ Decl	☿ Lat	♀ Decl	♀ Lat	♂ Decl	♂ Lat	⚳ Decl	⚳ Lat	♃ Decl	♃ Lat	♄ Decl	♄ Lat
1 Th	23S01	26N24	5N03	27N31	24S00	0S34	23S37	0S30	23S43	0S53	5S21	8S53	21N59	0N14	3S36	2S16
2 F	22 56	28 09	4 58	28 14	24 07	0 41	23 34	0 33	23 39	0 54	5 13	8 49	22 00	0 14	3 34	2 15
3 Sa	22 50	27 49	4 33	26 53	24 13	0 47	23 30	0 35	23 35	0 54	5 04	8 45	22 01	0 15	3 33	2 15
4 Su	22 44	25 29	3 50	23 40	24 17	0 53	23 25	0 37	23 30	0 55	4 55	8 41	22 03	0 15	3 31	2 15
5 M	22 38	21 30	2 52	19 03	24 20	0 59	23 19	0 39	23 25	0 55	4 46	8 37	22 04	0 15	3 29	2 15
6 Tu	22 31	16 23	1 45	13 32	24 22	1 05	23 13	0 41	23 20	0 55	4 37	8 33	22 06	0 15	3 27	2 15
7 W	22 24	10 35	0 34	7 34	24 23	1 11	23 06	0 43	23 14	0 56	4 28	8 30	22 07	0 15	3 26	2 14
8 Th	22 16	4 30	0S37	1 27	24 22	1 16	22 59	0 45	23 09	0 56	4 19	8 26	22 08	0 15	3 24	2 14
9 F	22 08	1S34	1 44	4S31	24 20	1 21	22 50	0 47	23 03	0 56	4 10	8 22	22 10	0 15	3 22	2 14
10 Sa	21 59	7 24	2 44	10 11	24 16	1 26	22 41	0 49	22 56	0 57	4 01	8 18	22 11	0 16	3 20	2 14
11 Su	21 50	12 50	3 35	15 21	24 11	1 31	22 31	0 51	22 50	0 57	3 52	8 15	22 12	0 16	3 18	2 14
12 M	21 41	17 43	4 16	19 53	24 05	1 35	22 21	0 53	22 43	0 57	3 43	8 11	22 14	0 16	3 16	2 13
13 Tu	21 31	21 52	4 46	23 37	23 57	1 39	22 10	0 55	22 36	0 58	3 33	8 07	22 15	0 16	3 15	2 13
14 W	21 20	25 07	5 03	26 22	23 48	1 43	21 58	0 57	22 29	0 58	3 24	8 04	22 16	0 16	3 13	2 13
15 Th	21 10	27 19	5 07	27 57	23 37	1 47	21 45	0 59	22 21	0 58	3 15	8 00	22 18	0 16	3 11	2 13
16 F	20 58	28 16	4 58	28 15	23 25	1 50	21 32	1 00	22 13	0 59	3 05	7 57	22 19	0 16	3 08	2 13
17 Sa	20 47	27 53	4 36	27 11	23 11	1 53	21 18	1 02	22 05	0 59	2 56	7 53	22 20	0 17	3 06	2 13
18 Su	20 35	26 08	4 00	24 46	22 56	1 56	21 04	1 04	21 57	0 59	2 46	7 50	22 21	0 17	3 04	2 12
19 M	20 23	23 06	3 13	21 09	22 40	1 59	20 49	1 05	21 49	0 59	2 37	7 46	22 23	0 17	3 02	2 12
20 Tu	20 10	18 56	2 16	16 29	22 21	2 01	20 33	1 07	21 40	0 60	2 27	7 43	22 24	0 17	2 60	2 12
21 W	19 57	13 51	1 10	11 02	22 02	2 02	20 17	1 09	21 31	0 60	2 18	7 39	22 25	0 17	2 58	2 12
22 Th	19 43	8 05	0 00	5 01	21 41	2 04	19 60	1 10	21 21	1 00	2 08	7 36	22 26	0 17	2 56	2 12
23 F	19 30	1 53	1N11	1N18	21 18	2 05	19 42	1 11	21 12	1 00	1 58	7 33	22 27	0 17	2 53	2 12
24 Sa	19 15	4N29	2 20	7 39	20 54	2 05	19 24	1 13	21 02	1 01	1 49	7 29	22 28	0 17	2 51	2 12
25 Su	19 01	10 46	3 22	13 46	20 28	2 05	19 06	1 14	20 52	1 01	1 39	7 26	22 30	0 18	2 49	2 11
26 M	18 46	16 37	4 13	19 17	20 01	2 05	18 46	1 15	20 42	1 01	1 29	7 23	22 31	0 18	2 46	2 11
27 Tu	18 31	21 41	4 50	23 49	19 32	2 04	18 27	1 17	20 32	1 01	1 20	7 20	22 32	0 18	2 44	2 11
28 W	18 15	25 35	5 10	26 57	19 02	2 03	18 07	1 18	20 21	1 02	1 10	7 16	22 33	0 18	2 42	2 11
29 Th	17 59	27 52	5 10	28 19	18 30	2 01	17 46	1 19	20 10	1 02	1 00	7 13	22 34	0 18	2 39	2 11
30 F	17 43	28 17	4 50	27 44	17 57	1 59	17 25	1 20	19 59	1 02	0 50	7 10	22 35	0 18	2 37	2 11
31 Sa	17S26	26N43	4N12	25N15	17S22	1S56	17S03	1S21	19S48	1S02	0S40	7S07	22N36	0N18	2S35	2S11

Day	⚷ Decl	⚷ Lat	♅ Decl	♅ Lat	♆ Decl	♆ Lat	♇ Decl	♇ Lat
1	9N16	0N30	19N31	0S12	1S25	1S20	23S13	3S46
6	9 15	0 30	19 29	0 12	1 23	1 20	23 11	3 46
11	9 15	0 29	19 28	0 12	1 21	1 20	23 09	3 47
16	9 16	0 29	19 26	0 12	1 19	1 19	23 07	3 47
21	9 17	0 28	19 25	0 12	1 16	1 19	23 05	3 47
26	9 19	0 28	19 25	0 11	1 13	1 19	23 04	3 48
31	9N21	0N27	19N25	0S11	1S10	1S19	23S02	3S48

Day	⚴ Decl	⚴ Lat	⚵ Decl	⚵ Lat	⚶ Decl	⚶ Lat	Eris Decl	Eris Lat
1	3S56	10N37	13S32	9N54	22S39	1S25	0S19	10S35
6	3 54	10 09	13 30	9 55	22 17	1 32	0 18	10 34
11	3 50	9 43	13 26	9 56	21 52	1 40	0 18	10 33
16	3 44	9 17	13 20	9 58	21 25	1 47	0 17	10 33
21	3 36	8 52	13 13	9 60	20 55	1 54	0 16	10 32
26	3 26	8 28	13 03	10 03	20 22	2 01	0 15	10 31
31	3S14	8N05	12S53	10N06	19S48	2S09	0S14	10S31

Moon Phenomena

Max/0 Decl

dy	hr mn	
2	8:12	28N16
8	17:46	0 S
16	5:16	28S18
23	7:07	0 N
29	16:55	28N21

Max/0 Lat

dy	hr mn	
1	6:44	5N04
7	11:25	0 S
14	19:54	5S07
22	0:04	0 N
28	12:29	5N12

Perigee/Apogee

dy	hr m		kilometers
1	21:46	p	360349
13	20:48	a	405437
29	21:47	p	365871

PH	dy	hr mn	
○	3	10:04	13♋02
☾	10	15:50	20♎25
●	18	19:53	28♑44
☽	26	4:49	6♉14

Void of Course Moon

Last Aspect			☽ Ingress	
2 12:25	♆	□	♋	2 13:10
4 13:01	♆	△	♌	4 13:45
6 13:06	♅	□	♍	6 16:58
8 23:24	♆	☍	♎	9 0:07
10 17:55	♀	□	♏	11 10:56
13 23:00	♆	△	♐	13 23:35
16 11:20	♆	□	♑	16 11:48
18 21:58	♆	⚹	♒	18 22:19
21 2:18	♅	□	♓	21 6:51
23 13:18	♆	☌	♈	23 13:27
24 21:37	♃	□	♉	25 18:06
27 17:59	♄	⚹	♊	27 20:56
29 19:58	♄	□	♋	29 22:33

DAILY ASPECTARIAN

1 Th
☽⚹⚳ 0:36
☽∠⚷ 1:26
☽⚻♀ 4:22
☉⚻☽ 6:38
♂⚼♅ 7:55
☽⚻♂ 10:05
☿□♆ 13:34
☽⚼♇ 17:37
☿ ♑ 21:12
☽⚺♃ 23:11

2 F
☽⚹⚷ 1:22
☽□♄ 7:11
☽⚺♅ 9:50
☽□♆ 12:25
⚷ D 14:39
☽☍☿ 14:59
☽⚻♇ 17:36

3 Sa
☽□⚳ 1:11
☉⚼♅ 6:40
☽☍♀ 8:41
☽∠♅ 9:50
☉☍☽ 10:04
☽☍♂ 12:38
☿⚺♇ 16:58
♀⚼♅ 21:56
☽☌♃ 22:56

4 Su
☽□⚷ 1:35
☽△♄ 7:46
☽⋕☿ 8:03
☽⚹♅ 10:13
☽△♆ 13:01
☽⋕♂ 13:16
☽⋕♀ 13:47
☽⋕♇ 14:46
☉⋕☽ 17:48
☽☍♇ 18:26
☽∥♃ 21:02
☽⚻☿ 21:26

5 M
☽△⚳ 3:02
☽⚼♄ 8:52
☽∥♅ 9:59
☽⚼♆ 14:11
☽⚻♀ 14:57
☉⚻☽ 15:26
☽⚻♂ 17:09

6 Tu
☽⚺♃ 0:41
☽⚼☿ 2:04
☽△⚷ 4:00
☽⚼⚳ 5:05
♀∥♇ 7:20
☽⚻♄ 10:49
☽□♅ 13:06
☽⚻♆ 16:14
☉☌♀ 16:37
☉⚼☽ 19:37
☽⚼♀ 19:40
☽⚼♂ 20:52
☽⚻♇ 22:07

7 W
☽∠♃ 2:51
☽∥⚷ 5:19
☽⚼⚷ 6:34
☽△☿ 8:03
☽⚻⚳ 8:09
☿□⚳ 9:02
☊ D 11:25
♂∥♇ 15:40

8 Th
☽⋕⚳ 0:45
☉△☽ 1:05
☽⚼♇ 1:26
☽△♀ 1:45
☽△♂ 1:48
♀☌♂ 2:44
☽⋕♄ 4:22
☽⚹♃ 6:00
☽⚻⚷ 10:09
☽⋕♆ 12:21
☽☍♄ 17:47
☉⋕♃ 19:35
☽△♅ 19:51
☽∥♆ 23:14
☽☍♆ 23:24

9 F
☽△♇ 5:48
☽∥♄ 7:16
☽∥⚳ 10:18
☉☌♂ 11:42
☽☍⚳ 17:34
♀☍♃ 17:36

10 Sa
☽□☿ 0:35
☽⚼♅ 0:42
☿⚼♅ 1:34
☽⋕⚷ 7:58
☉☍♃ 8:43
♂☍♃ 14:26
☽□♃ 15:09
☽□♂ 15:13
☉□☽ 15:50
☊ R 15:59
☽□♀ 17:55
☽☍⚷ 20:14

11 Su
☽⚻♄ 4:37
☽⚻♅ 6:21
☽⚻♆ 10:16
♀□⚷ 16:14
☽□♇ 17:04
⚶ ♒ 20:41

12 M
☽⚻⚳ 6:28
☽⋕♅ 9:31
☽⚼♄ 10:59
♀⋕♃ 13:45
☽⚼♆ 16:33
☉□⚷ 20:33
☽⚹☿ 21:45
☉∥☽ 21:52

13 Tu
☽∥♀ 1:49
☽⋕♃ 2:31
☽△♃ 2:47
☽∥♂ 4:42
☽⚹♂ 7:44
☽∥♇ 8:34
☽⚻⚷ 8:42
☉⚹☽ 9:50
☽⚹♀ 13:28
☽⚼⚳ 13:30
☽∥☿ 13:50
☽△♄ 17:34
☽☍♅ 18:50
♂□⚷ 22:35
☽△♆ 23:00

14 W
☽⚹♇ 5:55
☿☍♃ 8:18
☽⚼♃ 8:50
☽∠☿ 8:55
☽⚼⚷ 15:05
☽∠♂ 16:13
☉∠☽ 19:02
☽△⚳ 20:31
☽∠♀ 23:23

15 Th
♀⚹♄ 6:20
♂⋕♃ 9:47
☽∠♇ 12:13
⚳∥♄ 13:43
☽⚻♃ 14:41
♀△♅ 15:23
☽⚺☿ 19:49
☽△⚷ 21:15

16 F
☽⚺♂ 0:25
☉⚺☽ 3:53
☽□♄ 6:18
☿□⚷ 6:22
☽⚻♅ 7:04
☽⚺♀ 8:55
☽□♆ 11:20
☽⚺♇ 18:09

17 Sa
☿∥♇ 7:15
♀⚹♆ 8:35
☽□⚳ 9:34
☉⚹♄ 10:43
☽⚼♅ 12:36
♀ ♒ 12:45
☉△♅ 17:00

18 Su
☽☍♃ 1:15
☿☌♂ 7:42
☽□⚷ 8:17
☽☌♂ 15:13
☽☌☿ 15:49
☽⚹♄ 17:23
☽△♅ 17:40
☉☌☽ 19:53
☽⚹♆ 21:58
☽∥♇ 23:59

19 M
☽☌♀ 2:04
☽∥☿ 3:06
☿⚹♄ 4:10
☽☌♇ 4:37
☽⋕♃ 4:38
☿△♅ 5:39
☽∥♂ 8:25
☽∥♀ 14:48
☉∥☽ 17:09
☽⚹⚳ 20:37
☿⋕♃ 21:16
☽⋕♅ 21:26
☉⚹♆ 21:56
☽∠♄ 22:10

20 Tu
☉ ♒ 1:46
☽∠♆ 2:32
♀☌♇ 4:06
♄⚹♅ 5:21
♂△♅ 5:58
♂⚹♄ 6:03
☽⚻♃ 9:55
☿⚹♆ 14:35
☿ ♒ 16:42
☽⚹⚷ 17:22

21 W
☽∠⚳ 1:22
☽□♅ 2:18
☽⚺♄ 2:27
☽⚺♂ 3:37
☽⚺♆ 6:36
☽⚺☿ 8:57
☉⚺☽ 9:19
☽⚺♇ 13:04
☽⚼♃ 13:32
☉☌☿ 15:50
☽⚺♀ 16:30
☽⋕⚷ 19:09
☽∠⚷ 21:11

22 Th
☊ D 0:04
☽⚺⚳ 5:36
☽∠♂ 8:57
☉∠☽ 15:07
☽∠☿ 16:28
☽∠♇ 16:34
☽△♃ 16:42
☿☌♇ 17:16
⚳∠♅ 18:06
☽∥♄ 20:09
☽∠♀ 22:44
☽∥⚳ 23:38

23 F
☽⚺⚷ 0:30
☽∥♆ 2:24
♂⚹♆ 6:41
☉⋕♅ 7:22
☽⚹♅ 9:00
♂ ♒ 9:18
☽☌♄ 9:34
☉☌♇ 10:30
☿∥♂ 10:30
☽⋕♆ 11:47
☽☌♆ 13:18
☽⚹♂ 13:42
☽⋕⚳ 14:11
☽⋕♄ 17:52
☽⚹♇ 19:35
☉⚹☽ 20:18
♀⋕♅ 22:52
☽⚹☿ 23:17

24 Sa
☽⚹♀ 4:19
☽∠♅ 11:38
☽☌⚳ 12:34
☽∥⚷ 18:20
☽□♃ 21:37

25 Su
♀ ♓ 1:34
☽☌⚷ 5:43
☽⚺♅ 13:47
☽⚺♄ 14:43
☽⚺♆ 18:04
☽□♂ 21:28

26 M
☽□♇ 0:08
☉∥♀ 3:23
☊ R 4:41
☉□☽ 4:49
☽⋕♀ 9:05
☉⋕☽ 9:10
☽□☿ 10:51
☽∥♅ 12:39
☽□♀ 13:32
☽⋕☿ 14:11
☽∠♄ 16:34
☽⚺⚳ 17:30
♆ ♈ 17:38
☽⋕♂ 18:15
☽∠♆ 19:44

27 Tu
☽⚹♃ 0:42
☽∥♃ 4:33
☿⋕♅ 5:58
☽⋕♇ 7:29
☽⚺⚷ 9:01
☽☌♅ 16:44
☽⚹♄ 17:59
⚳∥♆ 19:05
☽∠⚳ 19:16
☽⚹♆ 20:59
♂☌♇ 23:03

28 W
☽∠♃ 1:38
♀∠♄ 2:03
☽△♇ 2:53
☽△♂ 3:06
☽∠⚷ 10:05
☉△☽ 11:08
☿∠♄ 11:38
☽△☿ 20:02
☽△♀ 20:34
☽⚹⚳ 20:42
♀⚹⚳ 22:47

29 Th
☽⚺♃ 2:16
☿⚹⚳ 2:43
☽⚼♇ 3:47
☽⚼♂ 5:21
☿☌♀ 10:18
☽⚹⚷ 10:55
☿∠♆ 11:58
♀∠♆ 12:39
☉⚼☽ 13:45
☽⚺♅ 18:23
☽□♄ 19:58
☽□♆ 22:41
☽⚼♀ 23:37

30 F
☽⚼☿ 0:08
☽⚻♇ 4:32
☽⚻♂ 7:27
☉⚻☽ 16:18
☉∥☿ 18:35
☽∠♅ 19:05
☿⚻♃ 20:59
☽□⚳ 23:12

31 Sa
☽⚻♀ 2:40
☽☌♃ 3:19
☽⚻☿ 4:15
♀⚻♃ 9:40
☽□⚷ 12:29
☽⚹♅ 19:56
☽△♄ 21:53

February 2026

LONGITUDE

Day	Sid.Time	☉	☽	☽ 12 hour	Mean ☊	True ☊	☿	♀	♂	⚳	♃	♄	⚷	♅	♆	♇
	h m s	° E "	° E "	° E "	° E	° E	° E	° E	° E	° E	° E	° E	° E	° E	° E	° E
1 Su	8 44 52	12♒07 26	29♋53 58	7♌03 01	10♓31.7	9♓07.2	19♒28.3	18♒10.6	6♒43.6	15♈16.8	17♋21.6	28♓38.4	22♈59.9	27♉27.8	0♈08.4	3♒41.8
2 M	8 48 49	13 08 18	14♌08 06	21 08 39	10 28.5	9R 04.2	21 14.5	19 25.9	7 30.6	15 35.4	17R 15.0	28 44.4	23 01.6	27R 27.7	0 10.1	3 43.7
3 Tu	8 52 45	14 09 10	28 04 10	4♍54 17	10 25.3	9D 02.5	23 00.8	20 41.1	8 17.6	15 54.2	17 08.5	28 50.4	23 03.2	27 27.6	0 11.8	3 45.6
4 W	8 56 42	15 10 00	11♍38 48	18 17 37	10 22.2	9 02.1	24 47.2	21 56.4	9 04.6	16 13.1	17 02.1	28 56.4	23 05.0	27D 27.6	0 13.5	3 47.5
5 Th	9 00 38	16 10 49	24 50 44	1♎18 19	10 19.0	9 02.9	26 33.5	23 11.6	9 51.6	16 32.2	16 55.9	29 02.5	23 06.7	27 27.6	0 15.2	3 49.4
6 F	9 04 35	17 11 38	7♎40 37	13 57 56	10 15.8	9 04.3	28 19.6	24 26.9	10 38.7	16 51.3	16 49.8	29 08.7	23 08.6	27 27.7	0 17.0	3 51.3
7 Sa	9 08 31	18 12 25	20 10 42	26 19 24	10 12.6	9 06.0	0♓05.2	25 42.1	11 25.8	17 10.6	16 43.8	29 14.9	23 10.4	27 27.8	0 18.7	3 53.2
8 Su	9 12 28	19 13 11	2♏24 31	8♏26 38	10 09.4	9 07.4	1 50.1	26 57.3	12 12.8	17 30.1	16 38.0	29 21.2	23 12.4	27 28.0	0 20.5	3 55.0
9 M	9 16 25	20 13 57	14 26 21	20 24 14	10 06.3	9R 08.2	3 34.1	28 12.5	13 00.0	17 49.6	16 32.4	29 27.5	23 14.3	27 28.2	0 22.4	3 56.9
10 Tu	9 20 21	21 14 41	26 20 54	2♐16 57	10 03.1	9 08.3	5 16.8	29 27.6	13 47.1	18 09.3	16 26.9	29 33.9	23 16.3	27 28.5	0 24.2	3 58.8
11 W	9 24 18	22 15 24	8♐12 59	14 09 35	9 59.9	9 07.5	6 57.8	0♓42.8	14 34.2	18 29.1	16 21.5	29 40.3	23 18.4	27 28.9	0 26.1	4 00.6
12 Th	9 28 14	23 16 07	20 07 16	26 06 35	9 56.7	9 05.9	8 36.7	1 58.0	15 21.4	18 49.0	16 16.3	29 46.8	23 20.5	27 29.2	0 28.0	4 02.4
13 F	9 32 11	24 16 48	2♑07 59	8♑11 55	9 53.6	9 03.9	10 13.0	3 13.1	16 08.6	19 09.1	16 11.3	29 53.4	23 22.6	27 29.7	0 29.9	4 04.3
14 Sa	9 36 07	25 17 28	14 18 46	20 28 52	9 50.4	9 01.7	11 46.3	4 28.2	16 55.8	19 29.2	16 06.5	29 59.9	23 24.8	27 30.2	0 31.8	4 06.1
15 Su	9 40 04	26 18 07	26 42 29	2♒59 49	9 47.2	8 59.7	13 15.8	5 43.3	17 43.0	19 49.5	16 01.8	0♈06.6	23 27.1	27 30.8	0 33.8	4 07.9
16 M	9 44 01	27 18 45	9♒21 02	15 46 12	9 44.0	8 58.0	14 41.1	6 58.4	18 30.2	20 09.9	15 57.3	0 13.2	23 29.4	27 31.4	0 35.7	4 09.7
17 Tu	9 47 57	28 19 21	22 15 22	28 48 28	9 40.9	8 57.0	16 01.4	8 13.5	19 17.4	20 30.4	15 52.9	0 20.0	23 31.7	27 32.0	0 37.7	4 11.5
18 W	9 51 54	29 19 55	5♓25 26	12♓06 07	9 37.7	8D 56.5	17 16.0	9 28.6	20 04.6	20 51.0	15 48.8	0 26.7	23 34.0	27 32.7	0 39.7	4 13.3
19 Th	9 55 50	0♓20 28	18 50 20	25 37 53	9 34.5	8 56.7	18 24.3	10 43.6	20 51.9	21 11.7	15 44.8	0 33.5	23 36.5	27 33.5	0 41.7	4 15.1
20 F	9 59 47	1 21 00	2♈28 30	9♈21 55	9 31.3	8 57.1	19 25.6	11 58.6	21 39.1	21 32.5	15 41.0	0 40.3	23 38.9	27 34.3	0 43.7	4 16.8
21 Sa	10 03 43	2 21 29	16 17 54	23 16 07	9 28.1	8 57.8	20 19.2	13 13.6	22 26.4	21 53.4	15 37.4	0 47.2	23 41.4	27 35.2	0 45.8	4 18.6
22 Su	10 07 40	3 21 57	0♉16 19	7♉18 13	9 25.0	8 58.4	21 04.5	14 28.6	23 13.7	22 14.4	15 34.0	0 54.1	23 43.9	27 36.1	0 47.8	4 20.3
23 M	10 11 36	4 22 23	14 21 32	21 25 58	9 21.8	8 58.8	21 41.0	15 43.6	24 00.9	22 35.5	15 30.7	1 01.1	23 46.5	27 37.1	0 49.9	4 22.0
24 Tu	10 15 33	5 22 47	28 31 16	5♊37 10	9 18.6	8R 59.0	22 08.2	16 58.5	24 48.2	22 56.7	15 27.7	1 08.0	23 49.1	27 38.1	0 52.0	4 23.7
25 W	10 19 29	6 23 10	12♊43 21	19 49 33	9 15.4	8 59.0	22 25.8	18 13.4	25 35.5	23 18.0	15 24.8	1 15.1	23 51.7	27 39.1	0 54.1	4 25.4
26 Th	10 23 26	7 23 30	26 55 28	4♋00 46	9 12.3	8 58.9	22R 33.5	19 28.3	26 22.8	23 39.4	15 22.2	1 22.1	23 54.4	27 40.3	0 56.2	4 27.1
27 F	10 27 23	8 23 48	11♋05 08	18 08 14	9 09.1	8D 58.8	22 31.4	20 43.2	27 10.0	24 00.8	15 19.7	1 29.2	23 57.1	27 41.4	0 58.3	4 28.7
28 Sa	10 31 19	9♓24 05	25 09 43	2♌09 12	9♓05.9	8♓58.8	22♓19.6	21♓58.0	27♒57.3	24♈22.4	15♋17.4	1♈36.3	23♈59.9	27♉42.7	1♈00.5	4♒30.4

1st of Month

Julian Day #
2461072.5
Obliquity
23°26B8"
SVP 4♓53B6"
GC 27♐12.2
Eris 24♈39.6

Day	⚴
1	2♓14.1
6	3 51.9
11	5 30.5
16	7 09.7
21	8 49.5
26	10 29.7

Day	⚵
1	11♑55.8
6	13 40.5
11	15 24.1
16	17 06.5
21	18 47.4
26	20 26.8

Day	⚶
1	10♒33.3
6	13 09.6
11	15 45.3
16	18 20.3
21	20 54.7
26	23 28.3

DECLINATION and LATITUDE

Day	☉ Decl	☽ Decl	☽ Lat	☽ 12h Decl	☿ Decl	☿ Lat	♀ Decl	♀ Lat	♂ Decl	♂ Lat	⚳ Decl	⚳ Lat	♃ Decl	♃ Lat	♄ Decl	♄ Lat
1 Su	17S10	23N24	3N18	21N11	16S46	1S53	16S41	1S22	19S36	1S03	0S31	7S04	22N37	0N18	2S32	2S10
2 M	16 52	18 42	2 12	15 59	16 08	1 49	16 18	1 23	19 24	1 03	0 21	7 01	22 38	0 18	2 30	2 10
3 Tu	16 35	13 05	0 60	10 04	15 29	1 45	15 55	1 23	19 12	1 03	0 11	6 58	22 39	0 19	2 27	2 10
4 W	16 17	6 58	0S14	3 51	14 49	1 39	15 31	1 24	19 00	1 03	0 01	6 55	22 40	0 19	2 25	2 10
5 Th	15 59	0 44	1 26	2S21	14 08	1 34	15 07	1 25	18 48	1 03	0N09	6 52	22 41	0 19	2 22	2 10
6 F	15 41	5S22	2 31	8 17	13 25	1 27	14 43	1 25	18 35	1 04	0 19	6 49	22 41	0 19	2 19	2 10
7 Sa	15 22	11 05	3 27	13 45	12 41	1 20	14 18	1 26	18 22	1 04	0 29	6 46	22 42	0 19	2 17	2 10
8 Su	15 04	16 16	4 13	18 36	11 57	1 12	13 53	1 26	18 09	1 04	0 39	6 44	22 43	0 19	2 14	2 10
9 M	14 44	20 44	4 47	22 39	11 11	1 04	13 27	1 27	17 56	1 04	0 49	6 41	22 44	0 19	2 12	2 09
10 Tu	14 25	24 19	5 08	25 44	10 25	0 54	13 01	1 27	17 43	1 04	0 59	6 38	22 45	0 19	2 09	2 09
11 W	14 06	26 52	5 15	27 42	9 38	0 44	12 35	1 27	17 29	1 04	1 09	6 35	22 45	0 19	2 06	2 09
12 Th	13 46	28 13	5 10	28 24	8 52	0 34	12 08	1 28	17 15	1 04	1 19	6 32	22 46	0 19	2 04	2 09
13 F	13 26	28 16	4 50	27 46	8 05	0 22	11 41	1 28	17 01	1 05	1 29	6 30	22 47	0 19	2 01	2 09
14 Sa	13 05	26 56	4 18	25 47	7 18	0 10	11 14	1 28	16 47	1 05	1 39	6 27	22 47	0 20	1 58	2 09
15 Su	12 45	24 18	3 33	22 30	6 32	0N03	10 47	1 28	16 33	1 05	1 49	6 24	22 48	0 20	1 56	2 09
16 M	12 24	20 26	2 36	18 06	5 47	0 16	10 19	1 28	16 19	1 05	1 59	6 22	22 49	0 20	1 53	2 09
17 Tu	12 03	15 32	1 31	12 46	5 03	0 30	9 51	1 28	16 04	1 05	2 09	6 19	22 49	0 20	1 50	2 09
18 W	11 42	9 49	0 19	6 45	4 21	0 45	9 22	1 28	15 49	1 05	2 19	6 16	22 50	0 20	1 47	2 09
19 Th	11 21	3 35	0N55	0 21	3 40	0 60	8 54	1 27	15 34	1 05	2 29	6 14	22 50	0 20	1 45	2 08
20 F	10 60	2N55	2 07	6N10	3 02	1 15	8 25	1 27	15 19	1 05	2 39	6 11	22 51	0 20	1 42	2 08
21 Sa	10 38	9 22	3 12	12 28	2 27	1 30	7 56	1 27	15 04	1 05	2 49	6 09	22 51	0 20	1 39	2 08
22 Su	10 16	15 26	4 08	18 12	1 55	1 46	7 26	1 26	14 48	1 05	2 60	6 06	22 52	0 20	1 36	2 08
23 M	9 54	20 44	4 48	22 59	1 27	2 01	6 57	1 26	14 33	1 05	3 10	6 03	22 52	0 20	1 33	2 08
24 Tu	9 32	24 53	5 12	26 26	1 03	2 16	6 27	1 25	14 17	1 06	3 20	6 01	22 53	0 20	1 31	2 08
25 W	9 10	27 33	5 16	28 13	0 43	2 30	5 57	1 25	14 01	1 06	3 30	5 59	22 53	0 20	1 28	2 08
26 Th	8 48	28 26	5 02	28 10	0 27	2 43	5 27	1 24	13 45	1 06	3 40	5 56	22 54	0 20	1 25	2 08
27 F	8 25	27 26	4 29	26 16	0 16	2 56	4 57	1 23	13 29	1 06	3 50	5 54	22 54	0 21	1 22	2 08
28 Sa	8S03	24N42	3N40	22N46	0S10	3N08	4S27	1S22	13S13	1S06	3N60	5S51	22N54	0N21	1S19	2S08

Day	⚷ Decl	⚷ Lat	♅ Decl	♅ Lat	♆ Decl	♆ Lat	♇ Decl	♇ Lat
1	9N22	0N27	19N25	0S11	1S09	1S19	23S01	3S48
6	9 24	0 27	19 25	0 11	1 06	1 19	22 60	3 49
11	9 28	0 26	19 25	0 11	1 02	1 19	22 58	3 49
16	9 31	0 26	19 26	0 11	0 58	1 19	22 56	3 50
21	9 35	0 25	19 27	0 11	0 54	1 18	22 55	3 51
26	9N40	0N25	19N28	0S11	0S50	1S18	22S53	3S51

Day	⚴ Decl	⚴ Lat	⚵ Decl	⚵ Lat	⚶ Decl	⚶ Lat	Eris Decl	Eris Lat
1	3S11	8N01	12S50	10N06	19S40	2S10	0S14	10S30
6	2 58	7 38	12 37	10 10	19 03	2 17	0 13	10 30
11	2 43	7 16	12 23	10 14	18 25	2 24	0 12	10 29
16	2 27	6 55	12 07	10 19	17 44	2 32	0 11	10 28
21	2 10	6 34	11 49	10 24	17 02	2 39	0 09	10 28
26	1S52	6N14	11S30	10N30	16S19	2S46	0S08	10S27

Moon Phenomena

Max/0 Decl
dy hr mn
5 2:51 0 S
12 12:49 28S24
19 13:15 0 N
25 23:16 28N26

Max/0 Lat
dy hr mn
3 19:20 0 S
11 1:50 5S15
18 6:20 0 N
24 17:41 5N17

Perigee/Apogee
dy hr m kilometers
10 16:53 a 404575
24 23:15 p 370135

PH dy hr mn
○ 1 22:10 13♌04
☾ 9 12:44 20♏46
● 17 12:02 28♒50
◐ 17 733:04A 02B20"
☽ 24 12:29 5♊54

Void of Course Moon

Last Aspect	☽ Ingress
31 21:53 ♄ △	♌ 1 0:10
2 22:56 ♅ □	♍ 3 3:22
5 7:50 ♄ ☍	♎ 5 9:34
7 12:01 ♀ △	♏ 7 19:14
10 7:02 ♀ □	♐ 10 7:23
12 19:30 ♄ □	♑ 12 19:46
15 1:33 ♅ △	♒ 15 6:18
17 12:02 ☉ ☌	♓ 17 14:10
19 15:24 ♅ ⚹	♈ 19 19:40
21 11:13 ♂ ⚹	♉ 21 23:32
23 22:30 ♅ ☌	♊ 24 2:30
25 23:01 ♂ △	♋ 26 5:12
28 4:22 ♅ ⚹	♌ 28 8:18

DAILY ASPECTARIAN

1 Su
☽△♆ 0:24
☽⋕♇ 2:10
☽∥♃ 4:27
☽☍♇ 6:23
☿∥♀ 8:51
☽☍♂ 12:07
☽⋕♂ 20:36
☽∥♅ 20:42
☉☍☽ 22:10
♂⋕♅ 23:18
☽⚼♄ 23:19

2 M
☽⚼♆ 1:46
☽△⚳ 2:32
☽⚺♃ 5:17
☉⋕☽ 8:36
☽☍♀ 9:57
☽⋕♀ 11:24
☽⋕☿ 12:46
☽☍☿ 13:57
☽△⚷ 15:17
☉∠♄ 15:47
☽□♅ 22:56

3 Tu
☿⚹⚷ 0:34
☽⚻♄ 1:21
☽⚻♆ 3:43
☽⚼⚳ 5:04
☽∠♃ 7:05
☽⚻♇ 10:00
☽∥⚷ 14:40
☽⚼⚷ 17:37
☽⚻♂ 19:07
☊ D 19:21

4 W
☉∠♆ 1:24
♅ D 2:34
☉⚻☽ 6:51
☽⚻⚳ 8:26
☽⚹♃ 9:38
☽⚼♇ 12:56
☽⋕♄ 17:40
☽⚻♀ 20:38
☽⚻⚷ 20:48
♀⚹⚷ 22:24
☽⋕♆ 22:34

5 Th
☽⚼♂ 0:02
☽∥⚳ 2:12
☽⋕⚳ 3:32
☽⚻☿ 3:40
☽△♅ 4:50
☽∥♆ 7:08
☽☍♄ 7:50
☽☍♆ 10:03
☽∥♄ 12:00
☿□♅ 12:15
☉⚹⚳ 12:18
☉⚼☽ 12:47
☉⚻♃ 16:10
☽△♇ 16:46
⚳□♃ 22:33

6 F
☽⚼♀ 3:44
☽△♂ 6:01
☽⚼♅ 9:07
☿⚺♄ 11:51
☽⚼☿ 12:32
☽⋕⚷ 16:47
☽□♃ 17:23
☽☍⚳ 18:02
☉△☽ 19:50
☿ ♓ 22:49

7 Sa
☿⚺♆ 3:09
☽☍⚷ 5:51
☽∥☿ 6:16
☽△♀ 12:01
☽∥♀ 13:27
☽⚻♅ 14:15
☽⚻♄ 17:55
☉∥☽ 18:29
☽⚻♆ 19:54
☿⚼♃ 21:22
☽△☿ 22:40

8 Su
☽□♇ 3:00
☽∥♂ 9:12
♀□♅ 9:50
☿∠⚳ 11:19
☽⋕♅ 16:28
☽□♂ 20:55

9 M
☽⚼♄ 0:02
☽⚼♆ 1:53
☽△♃ 4:11
☿⚺♇ 5:24
☽⚻⚳ 7:00
☽⋕♃ 12:38
☉□☽ 12:44
☊ R 12:59
☽∥♇ 14:14
☽⚻⚷ 17:46

10 Tu
♀⚺♄ 2:11
☽☍♅ 2:17
☽△♄ 6:34
☽□♀ 7:02
⚳⋕♆ 7:59
☽△♆ 8:13
☽⚼♃ 10:14
♀ ♓ 10:20
☽⚼⚳ 14:09
☽⚹♇ 15:28
♀⚺♆ 18:31
☽□☿ 21:03

11 W
☽⚼⚷ 0:11
♂∠♄ 3:36
☿⋕⚷ 5:30
♀⚼♃ 11:33
☽⚹♂ 13:44
☽⚻♃ 16:19
☿∠⚷ 19:57
☽△⚳ 21:18
☽∠♇ 21:49

12 Th
☉⚹⚷ 1:48
♂∠♆ 3:29
☽△⚷ 6:29
☉⚹☽ 6:54
☽⚻♅ 14:46
☽□♄ 19:30
☽□♆ 20:44
☽∠♂ 21:54

13 F
♂⚻♃ 1:16
☽⚹♀ 2:24
☽⚺♇ 3:51
☉∠☽ 15:24
♀⚺♇ 16:45
☽⚹☿ 18:19
☽⚼♅ 20:27

14 Sa
♄ ♈ 0:13
♀∠⚳ 0:26
☽☍♃ 3:29
☽⚺♂ 5:27
☽□⚳ 10:21
☽∠♀ 11:10
☽□⚷ 17:43
☉⚺☽ 23:09

15 Su
☽△♅ 1:33
☽∠☿ 3:22
☽⚹♄ 6:34
☽⚹♆ 7:23
☽∥♇ 9:13
☽⋕♃ 10:05
⚳⋕♄ 12:08
☽☌♇ 14:11
☽⚺♀ 19:02

16 M
☉□♅ 5:03
☽⋕♅ 5:17
☽∠♄ 11:04
☽⚺☿ 11:09
☽∠♆ 11:42
☽⚻♃ 12:16
☽☌♂ 18:10
☽⚹⚳ 20:41
☽∥♂ 21:27
☿△♃ 21:32

17 Tu
☽⚹⚷ 2:21
♀∠⚷ 6:00
☽□♅ 9:41
☉☌☽ 12:02
☽⚺♄ 14:54
♀⋕⚷ 15:18
☽⚺♆ 15:21
☽⚼♃ 15:41
☉∥☽ 15:53
☽⚺♇ 21:49

18 W
☽∠⚳ 0:47
☽⋕⚷ 1:06
☽∥♀ 1:58
☽∠⚷ 5:41
☊ D 6:25
☽☌♀ 8:03
☉ ♓ 15:53
☽△♃ 18:32
☽☌☿ 23:10
☽∥☿ 23:37

19 Th
☽∠♇ 0:44
☽⚺♂ 3:49
☽⋕⚳ 3:57
☽⚺⚳ 4:17
☉⚺♄ 5:49
☽∥♄ 6:52
☽⚺⚷ 8:28
☉⚺♆ 8:43
☉⚼♃ 9:04
☽∥♆ 9:52
☽⚹♅ 15:24
☽⋕♆ 16:37
♂⚹⚳ 17:57
☽⋕♄ 19:32
☿∠♇ 20:15
☽☌♄ 20:49
☽☌♆ 20:56
☉⚺☽ 21:53
☽∥⚳ 23:00

20 F
☽⋕☿ 0:23
☽⚹♇ 3:09
☽∠♂ 7:44
☿⋕⚳ 11:56
♄☌♆ 16:54
☽∠♅ 17:35
☽⚺♀ 18:10
☽⋕♀ 18:56
☽□♃ 22:50

21 Sa
☽∥⚷ 0:50
☉∠☽ 1:58
☉⋕☽ 4:34
☽⚺☿ 7:21
☽☌⚳ 9:53
☽⚹♂ 11:13
☽☌⚷ 12:46
☽⚺♅ 19:25
☽⋕♂ 21:32
☽∠♀ 22:30

22 Su
☽⚺♆ 0:54
☽⚺♄ 1:05
☉⚹☽ 5:42
☽□♇ 6:58
☽∠☿ 10:23
♂⚹⚷ 16:14
☿∥♄ 17:38
☽∥♅ 17:47
♀△♃ 20:03
☉⚺♇ 23:50

23 M
☽⚹♃ 1:57
☽∠♆ 2:30
☽⚹♀ 2:33
☽∠♄ 2:50
☽∥♃ 11:26
☽⋕♇ 11:34
☽⚹☿ 12:52
☽⚺⚳ 14:19
☽⚺⚷ 16:01
☽□♂ 17:20
☉⋕⚷ 18:13
☽☌♅ 22:30

24 Tu
☽∠♃ 3:16
☽⚹♆ 3:59
☽⚹♄ 4:27
☽△♇ 9:57
☉□☽ 12:29
☊ R 13:16
☿∥♆ 13:25
☽∠⚳ 16:20
☽∠⚷ 17:27

25 W
☽⚺♃ 4:32
☽□♀ 10:11
☽⚼♇ 11:21
♃⋕♇ 14:45
☽□☿ 16:35
☽⚹⚳ 18:20
☽⚹⚷ 18:53
☽△♂ 23:01
♀∠♇ 23:36

26 Th
☽⚺♅ 1:16
☽□♆ 6:48
☿ R 6:49
☽□♄ 7:35
☽⚻♇ 12:46
☉△☽ 19:05
⚳☌⚷ 19:14

27 F
☽⚼♂ 1:57
☽∠♅ 2:44
☽☌♃ 7:12
☊ D 13:22
☉∠⚷ 13:54
♂□♅ 16:22
☽△♀ 18:00
☽△☿ 19:14
☽□⚷ 22:00
☉⚼☽ 22:36
☽□⚳ 22:37
☉∠⚳ 22:58

28 Sa
☽⚹♅ 4:22
☽⚻♂ 5:04
☿☌♀ 5:36
☽△♆ 10:03
☽△♄ 11:09
☽∥♃ 11:12
☽⋕♇ 11:22
♀⋕⚳ 16:05
☽☍♇ 16:05
☽⚼☿ 20:25
☽⚼♀ 22:18

March 2026

LONGITUDE

Day	Sid.Time	☉	☽	☽ 12 hour	Mean ☊	True ☊	☿	♀	♂	⚳	♃	♄	⚷	♅	♆	♇
	h m s	° ' "	° ' "	° ' "	° '	° '	° '	° '	° '	° '	° '	° '	° '	° '	° '	° '
1 Su	10 35 16	10♓24 19	9♌06 21	16♌00 49	9♓02.7	8♓58.9	21♓58.4	23♓12.8	28♒44.6	24♈44.0	15♋15.3	1♈43.4	24♈02.7	27♉43.9	1♈02.6	4♒32.0
2 M	10 39 12	11 24 31	22 52 15	29 40 21	8 59.5	8 59.1	21R 28.5	24 27.6	29 31.9	25 05.8	15R 13.4	1 50.6	24 05.5	27 45.3	1 04.8	4 33.6
3 Tu	10 43 09	12 24 41	6♍24 50	13♍05 30	8 56.4	8R 59.2	20 50.5	25 42.3	0♓19.1	25 27.6	15 11.8	1 57.8	24 08.3	27 46.6	1 07.0	4 35.2
4 W	10 47 05	13 24 50	19 42 08	26 14 38	8 53.2	8 59.1	20 05.5	26 57.1	1 06.4	25 49.4	15 10.3	2 05.0	24 11.2	27 48.0	1 09.1	4 36.8
5 Th	10 51 02	14 24 57	2♎42 56	9♎07 03	8 50.0	8 58.8	19 14.6	28 11.8	1 53.7	26 11.4	15 08.9	2 12.2	24 14.1	27 49.5	1 11.3	4 38.4
6 F	10 54 58	15 25 02	15 27 03	21 43 05	8 46.8	8 58.1	18 19.1	29 26.5	2 41.0	26 33.4	15 07.8	2 19.5	24 17.1	27 51.0	1 13.5	4 39.9
7 Sa	10 58 55	16 25 05	27 55 22	4♏04 09	8 43.7	8 57.1	17 20.4	0♈41.1	3 28.2	26 55.5	15 06.9	2 26.8	24 20.0	27 52.6	1 15.7	4 41.4
8 Su	11 02 52	17 25 07	10♏09 47	16 12 38	8 40.5	8 56.0	16 20.0	1 55.7	4 15.5	27 17.7	15 06.2	2 34.1	24 23.0	27 54.2	1 18.0	4 43.0
9 M	11 06 48	18 25 07	22 13 10	28 11 51	8 37.3	8 54.9	15 19.2	3 10.4	5 02.8	27 40.0	15 05.7	2 41.4	24 26.1	27 55.8	1 20.2	4 44.4
10 Tu	11 10 45	19 25 05	4♐09 11	10♐05 44	8 34.1	8 54.0	14 19.5	4 24.9	5 50.0	28 02.3	15 05.4	2 48.8	24 29.1	27 57.5	1 22.4	4 45.9
11 W	11 14 41	20 25 02	16 02 03	21 58 44	8 30.9	8D 53.5	13 22.0	5 39.5	6 37.3	28 24.7	15D 05.2	2 56.1	24 32.2	27 59.3	1 24.7	4 47.4
12 Th	11 18 38	21 24 57	27 56 21	3♑55 31	8 27.8	8 53.6	12 27.9	6 54.0	7 24.5	28 47.2	15 05.3	3 03.5	24 35.4	28 01.1	1 26.9	4 48.8
13 F	11 22 34	22 24 51	9♑56 49	16 00 48	8 24.6	8 54.2	11 38.1	8 08.5	8 11.8	29 09.7	15 05.6	3 10.9	24 38.5	28 02.9	1 29.1	4 50.2
14 Sa	11 26 31	23 24 42	22 08 02	28 19 00	8 21.4	8 55.3	10 53.4	9 23.0	8 59.0	29 32.3	15 06.0	3 18.3	24 41.7	28 04.8	1 31.4	4 51.6
15 Su	11 30 27	24 24 33	4♒34 11	10♒53 58	8 18.2	8 56.7	10 14.3	10 37.5	9 46.3	29 55.0	15 06.7	3 25.8	24 44.9	28 06.7	1 33.7	4 53.0
16 M	11 34 24	25 24 21	17 18 41	23 48 36	8 15.1	8 57.9	9 41.1	11 51.9	10 33.5	0♉17.7	15 07.5	3 33.2	24 48.1	28 08.7	1 35.9	4 54.4
17 Tu	11 38 21	26 24 07	0♓23 52	7♓04 32	8 11.9	8R 58.8	9 14.2	13 06.3	11 20.7	0 40.5	15 08.6	3 40.6	24 51.3	28 10.7	1 38.2	4 55.7
18 W	11 42 17	27 23 52	13 50 34	20 41 46	8 08.7	8 58.9	8 53.6	14 20.7	12 07.9	1 03.4	15 09.8	3 48.1	24 54.6	28 12.7	1 40.5	4 57.0
19 Th	11 46 14	28 23 35	27 37 52	4♈38 29	8 05.5	8 58.1	8 39.4	15 35.0	12 55.1	1 26.3	15 11.2	3 55.6	24 57.9	28 14.8	1 42.7	4 58.3
20 F	11 50 10	29 23 15	11♈43 06	18 51 09	8 02.3	8 56.2	8D 31.4	16 49.3	13 42.3	1 49.3	15 12.9	4 03.0	25 01.2	28 17.0	1 45.0	4 59.6
21 Sa	11 54 07	0♈22 54	26 01 58	3♉14 51	7 59.2	8 53.5	8 29.5	18 03.6	14 29.5	2 12.3	15 14.7	4 10.5	25 04.6	28 19.1	1 47.3	5 00.8
22 Su	11 58 03	1 22 30	10♉29 04	17 43 53	7 56.0	8 50.4	8 33.5	19 17.9	15 16.6	2 35.4	15 16.7	4 18.0	25 07.9	28 21.4	1 49.6	5 02.0
23 M	12 02 00	2 22 05	24 58 37	2♊12 36	7 52.8	8 47.3	8 43.2	20 32.1	16 03.7	2 58.6	15 18.9	4 25.5	25 11.3	28 23.6	1 51.8	5 03.2
24 Tu	12 05 56	3 21 37	9♊25 16	16 36 07	7 49.6	8 44.8	8 58.3	21 46.3	16 50.9	3 21.8	15 21.2	4 33.0	25 14.7	28 25.9	1 54.1	5 04.4
25 W	12 09 53	4 21 07	23 44 41	0♋50 41	7 46.5	8D 43.3	9 18.4	23 00.4	17 37.9	3 45.0	15 23.8	4 40.5	25 18.1	28 28.3	1 56.4	5 05.6
26 Th	12 13 50	5 20 34	7♋53 51	14 53 59	7 43.3	8 42.9	9 43.5	24 14.5	18 25.0	4 08.3	15 26.6	4 48.0	25 21.5	28 30.6	1 58.7	5 06.7
27 F	12 17 46	6 20 00	21 51 01	28 44 51	7 40.1	8 43.6	10 13.1	25 28.6	19 12.1	4 31.7	15 29.5	4 55.5	25 25.0	28 33.1	2 00.9	5 07.8
28 Sa	12 21 43	7 19 22	5♌35 29	12♌22 56	7 36.9	8 45.1	10 47.1	26 42.6	19 59.1	4 55.1	15 32.6	5 02.9	25 28.4	28 35.5	2 03.2	5 08.9
29 Su	12 25 39	8 18 43	19 07 13	25 48 22	7 33.7	8 46.6	11 25.2	27 56.6	20 46.1	5 18.5	15 35.9	5 10.4	25 31.9	28 38.0	2 05.5	5 10.0
30 M	12 29 36	9 18 01	2♍26 26	9♍01 26	7 30.6	8R 47.7	12 07.2	29 10.6	21 33.1	5 42.0	15 39.4	5 17.9	25 35.4	28 40.5	2 07.7	5 11.0
31 Tu	12 33 32	10♈17 17	15 33 24	22 02 21	7♓27.4	8♓47.6	12♓52.8	0♉24.5	22♓20.1	6♉05.5	15♋43.0	5♈25.4	25♈38.9	28♉43.1	2♈10.0	5♒12.0

1st of Month

Julian Day # 2461100.5
Obliquity 23°26'18"
SVP 4♓53'52"
GC 27♐12.3
Eris 24♈49.5

Day	⚴		⚵		⚶
1	11♓29.9	1	21♑25.5	1	25♒00.0
6	13 10.3	6	23 01.8	6	27 32.1
11	14 50.9	11	24 36.0	11	0♓03.2
16	16 31.3	16	26 07.9	16	2 33.3
21	18 11.5	21	27 37.2	21	5 02.2
26	19 51.5	26	29 03.6	26	7 29.8
31	21 30.9	31	0♒26.8	31	9 56.0

DECLINATION and LATITUDE

Day	☉ Decl	☽ Decl	☽ Lat	☽ 12h Decl	☿ Decl	☿ Lat	♀ Decl	♀ Lat	♂ Decl	♂ Lat	⚳ Decl	⚳ Lat	♃ Decl	♃ Lat	♄ Decl	♄ Lat
1 Su	7S40	20N31	2N38	18N00	0S09	3N18	3S57	1S22	12S56	1S06	4N10	5S49	22N54	0N21	1S16	2S08
2 M	7 17	15 17	1 28	12 23	0 13	3 26	3 26	1 21	12 40	1 06	4 20	5 47	22 55	0 21	1 13	2 08
3 Tu	6 54	9 23	0 14	6 18	0 22	3 33	2 55	1 20	12 23	1 06	4 30	5 44	22 55	0 21	1 10	2 08
4 W	6 31	3 10	0S59	0 03	0 35	3 38	2 25	1 19	12 06	1 06	4 40	5 42	22 55	0 21	1 07	2 08
5 Th	6 08	3S02	2 08	6S03	0 53	3 40	1 54	1 17	11 49	1 06	4 50	5 40	22 55	0 21	1 05	2 08
6 F	5 45	8 59	3 09	11 47	1 14	3 41	1 23	1 16	11 32	1 06	4 60	5 37	22 56	0 21	1 02	2 08
7 Sa	5 22	14 27	3 59	16 57	1 38	3 40	0 52	1 15	11 15	1 06	5 10	5 35	22 56	0 21	0 59	2 08
8 Su	4 58	19 15	4 37	21 20	2 04	3 36	0 22	1 14	10 58	1 06	5 20	5 33	22 56	0 21	0 56	2 08
9 M	4 35	23 12	5 03	24 48	2 33	3 30	0N09	1 12	10 41	1 06	5 30	5 30	22 56	0 21	0 53	2 08
10 Tu	4 11	26 08	5 15	27 10	3 03	3 23	0 40	1 11	10 23	1 06	5 40	5 28	22 56	0 21	0 50	2 08
11 W	3 48	27 54	5 14	28 19	3 33	3 14	1 11	1 09	10 06	1 05	5 50	5 26	22 56	0 21	0 47	2 07
12 Th	3 24	28 24	4 59	28 09	4 03	3 03	1 42	1 08	9 48	1 05	5 59	5 24	22 56	0 21	0 44	2 07
13 F	3 01	27 34	4 31	26 29	4 33	2 51	2 13	1 06	9 30	1 05	6 09	5 22	22 56	0 21	0 41	2 07
14 Sa	2 37	25 25	3 51	23 52	5 02	2 39	2 44	1 05	9 13	1 05	6 19	5 20	22 56	0 21	0 38	2 07
15 Su	2 13	22 01	2 59	19 53	5 30	2 25	3 15	1 03	8 55	1 05	6 29	5 17	22 56	0 21	0 35	2 07
16 M	1 50	17 30	1 57	14 53	5 55	2 11	3 45	1 01	8 37	1 05	6 39	5 15	22 56	0 22	0 32	2 07
17 Tu	1 26	12 04	0 47	9 05	6 19	1 56	4 16	0 59	8 19	1 05	6 49	5 13	22 56	0 22	0 29	2 07
18 W	1 02	5 57	0N27	2 42	6 40	1 41	4 46	0 57	8 01	1 05	6 59	5 11	22 56	0 22	0 26	2 07
19 Th	0 38	0N36	1 41	3N56	6 60	1 26	5 17	0 55	7 42	1 05	7 08	5 09	22 56	0 22	0 23	2 07
20 F	0 15	7 15	2 51	10 30	7 16	1 11	5 47	0 54	7 24	1 05	7 18	5 07	22 56	0 22	0 20	2 07
21 Sa	0N09	13 38	3 51	16 36	7 31	0 56	6 17	0 51	7 06	1 05	7 28	5 05	22 56	0 22	0 17	2 07
22 Su	0 33	19 20	4 36	21 48	7 43	0 42	6 47	0 49	6 47	1 04	7 37	5 03	22 55	0 22	0 14	2 07
23 M	0 57	23 56	5 05	25 42	7 52	0 28	7 17	0 47	6 29	1 04	7 47	5 01	22 55	0 22	0 11	2 07
24 Tu	1 20	27 02	5 14	27 57	7 59	0 14	7 47	0 45	6 11	1 04	7 57	4 59	22 55	0 22	0 09	2 07
25 W	1 44	28 20	5 03	28 17	8 04	0 01	8 17	0 43	5 52	1 04	8 06	4 57	22 55	0 22	0 06	2 07
26 Th	2 07	27 46	4 34	26 48	8 07	0S12	8 46	0 41	5 34	1 04	8 16	4 55	22 55	0 22	0 03	2 08
27 F	2 31	25 26	3 49	23 42	8 07	0 24	9 15	0 38	5 15	1 04	8 26	4 53	22 54	0 22	0N00	2 08
28 Sa	2 54	21 39	2 52	19 19	8 05	0 36	9 44	0 36	4 56	1 03	8 35	4 51	22 54	0 22	0 03	2 08
29 Su	3 18	16 46	1 46	14 01	8 01	0 48	10 13	0 34	4 38	1 03	8 45	4 49	22 54	0 22	0 06	2 08
30 M	3 41	11 09	0 35	8 10	7 55	0 58	10 41	0 31	4 19	1 03	8 54	4 47	22 53	0 22	0 09	2 08
31 Tu	4N04	5N08	0S37	2N04	7S47	1S09	11N10	0S29	4S00	1S03	9N04	4S45	22N53	0N22	0N12	2S08

Day	⚷ Decl	⚷ Lat	♅ Decl	♅ Lat	♆ Decl	♆ Lat	♇ Decl	♇ Lat
1	9N42	0N25	19N29	0S11	0S47	1S18	22S52	3S52
6	9 47	0 24	19 30	0 11	0 43	1 18	22 51	3 52
11	9 53	0 24	19 32	0 11	0 38	1 18	22 50	3 54
16	9 58	0 23	19 35	0 11	0 34	1 18	22 49	3 54
21	10 04	0 23	19 37	0 10	0 29	1 18	22 48	3 55
26	10 10	0 23	19 40	0 10	0 25	1 18	22 48	3 56
31	10N15	0N22	19N42	0S10	0S20	1S18	22S47	3S57

Day	⚴ Decl	⚴ Lat	⚵ Decl	⚵ Lat	⚶ Decl	⚶ Lat	Eris Decl	Eris Lat
1	1S41	6N01	11S18	10N33	15S52	2S51	0S07	10S27
6	1 21	5 41	10 57	10 40	15 07	2 58	0 06	10 26
11	1 01	5 22	10 35	10 47	14 21	3 06	0 04	10 26
16	0 41	5 02	10 12	10 55	13 34	3 13	0 03	10 25
21	0 20	4 42	9 48	11 03	12 47	3 21	0 02	10 25
26	0N01	4 23	9 23	11 12	11 59	3 29	0 00	10 24
31	0N22	4N04	8S57	11N21	11S11	3S37	0N01	10S24

Moon Phenomena

Max/0 Decl
dy hr mn
4 12:12 0 S
11 21:04 28S25
18 21:49 0 N
25 4:36 28N22
31 20:04 0 S

Max/0 Lat
dy hr mn
3 4:36 0 S
10 9:34 5S16
17 15:23 0 N
23 22:53 5N14
30 11:35 0 S

Perigee/Apogee
dy hr m kilometers
10 13:44 a 404382
22 11:41 p 366859

PH dy hr mn
○ 3 11:39 12♍54
• 3 11:35 T 1.151
☾ 11 9:40 20♐49
● 19 1:25 28♓27
☽ 25 19:19 5♋09

Void of Course Moon

Last Aspect	☽ Ingress
2 12:29 ♂ ☍	♍ 2 12:35
4 14:54 ♅ △	♎ 4 18:57
5 23:23 ♃ □	♏ 7 4:03
9 11:29 ♅ ☍	♐ 9 15:38
11 9:40 ☉ □	♑ 12 4:08
14 11:34 ♅ △	♒ 14 15:15
16 19:58 ♅ □	♓ 16 23:17
19 1:25 ☉ ☌	♈ 19 4:04
20 9:24 ♀ ☌	♉ 21 6:36
23 5:41 ♅ ☌	♊ 23 8:20
24 22:38 ♀ ⚹	♋ 25 10:34
27 11:41 ♅ ⚹	♌ 27 14:11
29 17:29 ♀ △	♍ 29 19:34

DAILY ASPECTARIAN

1 Su
☉⚻☽ 2:26
☽∥♅ 5:07
☽⚺♃ 10:39
☽⚼♆ 12:05
☽⚼♄ 13:21
♀⚺⚷ 16:37
☽⚻☿ 21:39

2 M
☽△⚷ 2:09
☽⚻♀ 3:05
☽△⚳ 4:01
☽□♅ 8:37
☽#♂ 11:26
☽☍♂ 12:29
☽∠♃ 12:57
♂ ♓ 14:17
☽⚻♆ 14:32
☽⚻♄ 16:00
♀⚺⚳ 17:17
♂⚼♃ 20:22
☽⚻♇ 20:44
☽∥⚷ 22:35

3 Tu
☊ R 4:22
☽⚼⚷ 4:54
☽⚼⚳ 7:28
☉#☽ 10:17
☉☍☽ 11:39
☽⚹♃ 15:47
☽∥⚳ 18:25
☽⚼♇ 23:50

4 W
☽☍☿ 0:40
♂⚺♆ 1:27
☽#♀ 3:11
☽#♄ 7:56
☽⚻⚷ 8:15
☽#♆ 9:22
☽#☿ 9:32
☽⚻⚳ 11:33
☿∥♆ 12:42
☿∠♇ 13:25
☽☍♀ 14:43
☽△♅ 14:54
☽∥♆ 15:02
☽∥☿ 15:09
☽∥♄ 16:26
♀⚹♅ 16:42
☽∥♀ 19:55
☽☍♆ 21:09
☽⚻♂ 22:22
☽☍♄ 23:02

5 Th
☽△♇ 3:36
☽#⚳ 7:19
♂⚺♄ 11:08
☉∥☽ 11:35
☿∥♄ 12:24
☉△♃ 17:15
☽⚼♅ 19:03
☽□♃ 23:23
☉⚻☽ 23:56

6 F
☽#⚷ 3:25
☿∥♀ 4:17
☽⚼♂ 4:33
☽⚻☿ 5:05
☽∥♂ 10:23
♀ ♈ 10:47
☽☍⚷ 17:01
♀∥♄ 18:35
☽☍⚳ 22:00
☽⚻♅ 23:55

7 Sa
☽⚻♀ 5:59
☽⚻♆ 6:32
☉⚼☽ 7:25
☽⚼☿ 7:58
☉#⚳ 8:29
♀∥♆ 8:30
☽⚻♄ 8:55
☉☌☿ 11:03
♀☌♆ 11:28
☽△♂ 11:34
☽□♇ 13:15

8 Su
☽#♅ 1:29
☽△♃ 9:47
☽△☿ 11:18
☽⚼♆ 12:13
♀☌♄ 13:41
♂⚺♇ 14:24
☽⚼♄ 14:51
☽⚼♀ 14:59
☉△☽ 15:43
☽∥♇ 21:34
☽#♃ 22:11

9 M
☽⚻⚷ 4:28
☿△♃ 5:25
☽⚻⚳ 11:17
☽☍♅ 11:29
☽⚼♃ 15:49
☽△♆ 18:23
⚳⚺♅ 18:28
☽△♄ 21:16
♀#♆ 23:07

10 Tu
☽△♀ 0:35
☽⚹♇ 1:14
☽□♂ 3:38
♀#♄ 6:49
♀⚹♇ 6:53
☉∠♇ 8:33
☽⚼⚷ 10:49
☽⚼⚳ 18:32
☽□☿ 19:00
⚶ ♓ 21:27
☽⚻♃ 22:05
☿∠⚳ 23:11

11 W
♃ D 3:31
☉∥☿ 6:29
☽∠♇ 7:36
☊ D 9:40
☉□☽ 9:40
♂#⚷ 16:52
☽△⚷ 17:14

12 Th
☽⚻♅ 0:10
☽△⚳ 1:45
☽□♆ 7:04
☽□♄ 10:22
☽⚺♇ 13:48
☽□♀ 20:00
☽⚹♂ 20:17

13 F
♀⚺♂ 2:53
☽⚹☿ 3:09
☽⚼♅ 6:10
☽☍♃ 10:11
☉#♀ 21:00

14 Sa
☉⚹☽ 2:43
☽∠♂ 3:51
☽□⚷ 5:00
☽∠☿ 6:55
☽△♅ 11:34
☽□⚳ 14:48
☽#♃ 18:13
☽⚹♆ 18:14
☽∥♇ 18:57
☿⚺♀ 19:00
☽⚹♄ 21:48
♂∠⚷ 23:14

15 Su
☽☌♇ 0:36
⚳ ♉ 5:17
♄∥♆ 5:59
☿☌♂ 8:09
☉⚺⚷ 8:37
☉∠☽ 9:58
☽⚺☿ 10:17
☽⚺♂ 10:31
☽⚹♀ 12:43
☽#♅ 13:38
☿∠⚷ 19:04
☽⚻♃ 19:55
☽∠♆ 22:40

16 M
☽∠♄ 2:20
☽⚹⚷ 13:52
☉⚺☽ 16:09
☽∠♀ 19:25
☽□♅ 19:58
☽⚼♃ 23:32

17 Tu
☽⚹⚳ 0:31
♀∠♅ 1:27
☽⚺♆ 2:15
☽⚺♄ 5:58
☽⚺♇ 8:10
☽#⚷ 8:23
☊ R 15:20
☽☌☿ 15:26
☽∥♂ 15:44
☽∠⚷ 17:01
☽#⚳ 20:11
☽☌♂ 20:48
☽∥☿ 21:23

18 W
☽⚺♀ 0:58
☽△♃ 2:20
☽∠⚳ 4:00
☽#♀ 4:03
☽∠♇ 10:43
♀□♃ 16:10
☉∥☽ 19:14
☽⚺⚷ 19:23
☽∥♆ 19:57
☉⚹♅ 20:21
☽∥♄ 20:23
☽#♄ 23:14
☽#♆ 23:42

19 Th
☉#☽ 0:07
☽⚹♅ 1:04
☉☌☽ 1:25
☽⚺⚳ 6:43
☽☌♆ 7:01
☉∥♆ 7:41
☽☌♄ 10:53
☽⚹♇ 12:35
☉∥♄ 17:22
☽∥♀ 18:14
☽⚺☿ 18:38
⚳⚺♆ 19:03

20 F
☽#☿ 0:05
☽∥⚳ 0:11
☽#♂ 0:32
☽∠♅ 2:39
☽⚺♂ 3:33
♂#⚳ 5:12
☿∥♂ 5:34
☽□♃ 5:54
☿#⚳ 7:28
☽☌♀ 9:24
☽∥⚷ 10:19
☉ ♈ 14:47
☿ D 19:34
☽∠☿ 19:46
☽☌⚷ 22:24

21 Sa
☽⚺♅ 3:49
☽∠♂ 6:05
☉#♄ 7:27
☉⚺☽ 7:46
☽⚺♆ 9:36
☽☌⚳ 10:33
☽⚺♄ 13:39
☽□♇ 14:57
☉#♆ 19:38
☽⚹☿ 20:47

22 Su
♀#♂ 0:01
♂△♃ 0:02
☽∥♅ 1:20
☽⚹♃ 7:57
☽⚹♂ 8:23
☉∠☽ 10:28
☽∠♆ 10:32
☉☌♆ 11:20
☽∠♄ 14:43
☽⚺♀ 15:57
☽#♇ 17:24
☽∥♃ 18:04

23 M
☽⚺⚷ 0:21
☽☌♅ 5:41
☽∠♃ 8:53
☽⚹♆ 11:27
☉⚹☽ 13:10
☽⚺⚳ 13:38
☽⚹♄ 15:49
☽△♇ 16:45
☽∠♀ 19:10
☽□☿ 23:14

24 Tu
☉⚺⚳ 0:06
☽∠⚷ 1:23
☽⚺♃ 9:56
♀∥⚳ 11:41
☿#♀ 12:04
☽□♂ 13:08
☿#⚳ 13:39
☽∠⚳ 15:22
☽⚼♇ 17:51
☽⚹♀ 22:38

25 W
☽⚹⚷ 2:38
☽⚺♅ 8:00
☉☌♄ 8:56
☽□♆ 13:54
☽⚹⚳ 17:25
☉⚹♇ 18:18
☽□♄ 18:40
☊ D 19:05
☽⚻♇ 19:15
☉□☽ 19:19

26 Th
☽△☿ 3:14
☽∠♅ 9:38
☽☌♃ 12:59
☿∠♀ 15:22
☽△♂ 19:09
♀☌⚷ 22:46

27 F
☽⚼☿ 6:05
☽□⚷ 6:13
☽□♀ 6:55
☿∠⚷ 9:42
☽⚹♅ 11:41
☽∥♃ 16:54
☽#♇ 17:31
☽△♆ 17:46
♂∠⚳ 19:52
☽□⚳ 22:47
☽⚼♂ 22:52
☽△♄ 23:02
☽☍♇ 23:13

28 Sa
☉△☽ 3:17
♂∠♇ 5:07
☽⚻☿ 9:36
☽∥♅ 10:13
⚳⚺♄ 11:53
⚳□♇ 14:51
☽⚺♃ 17:41
☽⚼♆ 20:22
♄⚹♇ 22:14

29 Su
♀∥⚷ 0:07
☽⚼♄ 1:54
☽⚻♂ 3:08
☉⚼☽ 8:07
⚵ ♒ 8:50
☽△⚷ 11:33
♀⚺♅ 13:53
☽□♅ 17:09
☽△♀ 17:29
☽∠♃ 20:45
☽⚻♆ 23:26

30 M
☽∥♀ 1:43
☽∥⚷ 3:41
☽⚻♇ 5:00
☽⚻♄ 5:15
☽△⚳ 6:07
☽∥⚳ 8:50
☊ R 11:33
☽#☿ 13:17
☉⚻☽ 13:31
☽⚼⚷ 14:56
♀ ♉ 16:02
☽☍☿ 18:45
☉#♂ 21:36
☽⚼♀ 23:42

31 Tu
☽⚹♃ 0:18
☉∥☽ 3:53
☽#♂ 4:38
☽⚼♇ 8:36
☽⚼⚳ 10:34
☽☍♂ 13:22
☽#♆ 18:47
☽⚻⚷ 18:48
☽∥♄ 19:07
☽#♄ 21:01
☽∥♆ 21:20

April 2026

LONGITUDE

Day	Sid.Time	☉	☽	☽ 12 hour	Mean ☊	True ☊	☿	♀	♂	⚳	♃	♄	⚷	♅	♆	♇
	h m s	° ′ ″	° ′ ″	° ′ ″	° ′	° ′	° ′	° ′	° ′	° ′	° ′	° ′	° ′	° ′	° ′	° ′
1 W	12 37 29	11♈16 31	28♍28 18	4♎51 15	7♓24.2	8♓46.1	13♓41.8	1♉38.4	23♓07.0	6♉29.1	15♋46.8	5♈32.9	25♈42.4	28♉45.6	2♈12.2	5♒13.0
2 Th	12 41 25	12 15 42	11♎11 14	17 28 18	7 21.0	8R 42.8	14 34.1	2 52.3	23 54.0	6 52.7	15 50.8	5 40.3	25 45.9	28 48.3	2 14.5	5 13.9
3 F	12 45 22	13 14 52	23 42 28	29 53 50	7 17.9	8 37.9	15 29.5	4 06.1	24 40.9	7 16.3	15 55.0	5 47.8	25 49.4	28 50.9	2 16.7	5 14.9
4 Sa	12 49 19	14 13 59	6♏02 29	12♏08 35	7 14.7	8 31.9	16 27.8	5 19.9	25 27.7	7 40.0	15 59.3	5 55.2	25 53.0	28 53.6	2 19.0	5 15.8
5 Su	12 53 15	15 13 05	18 12 19	24 13 54	7 11.5	8 25.2	17 28.9	6 33.6	26 14.6	8 03.7	16 03.8	6 02.6	25 56.5	28 56.3	2 21.2	5 16.7
6 M	12 57 12	16 12 09	0♐13 37	6♐11 48	7 08.3	8 18.5	18 32.6	7 47.3	27 01.4	8 27.5	16 08.5	6 10.1	26 00.1	28 59.1	2 23.4	5 17.5
7 Tu	13 01 08	17 11 11	12 08 48	18 05 05	7 05.1	8 12.7	19 38.8	9 01.0	27 48.2	8 51.3	16 13.4	6 17.5	26 03.7	29 01.9	2 25.7	5 18.4
8 W	13 05 05	18 10 11	24 01 04	29 57 17	7 02.0	8 08.1	20 47.5	10 14.6	28 35.0	9 15.2	16 18.4	6 24.9	26 07.3	29 04.7	2 27.9	5 19.2
9 Th	13 09 01	19 09 10	5♑54 17	11♑52 37	6 58.8	8 05.3	21 58.4	11 28.2	29 21.8	9 39.1	16 23.5	6 32.3	26 10.8	29 07.5	2 30.1	5 19.9
10 F	13 12 58	20 08 07	17 52 53	23 55 43	6 55.6	8D 04.2	23 11.6	12 41.8	0♈08.5	10 03.0	16 28.9	6 39.6	26 14.4	29 10.4	2 32.3	5 20.7
11 Sa	13 16 54	21 07 02	0♒01 43	6♒11 30	6 52.4	8 04.6	24 26.9	13 55.3	0 55.2	10 26.9	16 34.3	6 47.0	26 18.0	29 13.3	2 34.5	5 21.4
12 Su	13 20 51	22 05 55	12 25 42	18 44 50	6 49.3	8 05.8	25 44.3	15 08.8	1 41.9	10 50.9	16 40.0	6 54.3	26 21.6	29 16.3	2 36.6	5 22.1
13 M	13 24 48	23 04 46	25 09 27	1♓40 00	6 46.1	8R 07.2	27 03.6	16 22.2	2 28.6	11 14.9	16 45.8	7 01.6	26 25.2	29 19.2	2 38.8	5 22.8
14 Tu	13 28 44	24 03 36	8♓16 51	15 00 14	6 42.9	8 07.8	28 24.9	17 35.7	3 15.2	11 39.0	16 51.7	7 08.9	26 28.8	29 22.2	2 41.0	5 23.4
15 W	13 32 41	25 02 24	21 50 17	28 46 57	6 39.7	8 06.9	29 48.1	18 49.0	4 01.8	12 03.1	16 57.8	7 16.2	26 32.5	29 25.2	2 43.1	5 24.1
16 Th	13 36 37	26 01 10	5♈50 04	12♈59 14	6 36.5	8 04.0	1♈13.2	20 02.4	4 48.3	12 27.2	17 04.1	7 23.4	26 36.1	29 28.2	2 45.2	5 24.6
17 F	13 40 34	26 59 54	20 13 53	27 33 17	6 33.4	7 59.0	2 40.1	21 15.7	5 34.9	12 51.3	17 10.5	7 30.7	26 39.7	29 31.3	2 47.3	5 25.2
18 Sa	13 44 30	27 58 36	4♉56 33	12♉22 39	6 30.2	7 52.2	4 08.7	22 28.9	6 21.4	13 15.5	17 17.1	7 37.9	26 43.3	29 34.4	2 49.5	5 25.7
19 Su	13 48 27	28 57 17	19 50 29	27 18 54	6 27.0	7 44.3	5 39.1	23 42.1	7 07.8	13 39.7	17 23.8	7 45.1	26 46.9	29 37.5	2 51.6	5 26.2
20 M	13 52 23	29 55 55	4♊46 47	12♊13 01	6 23.8	7 36.4	7 11.3	24 55.3	7 54.2	14 03.9	17 30.6	7 52.2	26 50.5	29 40.6	2 53.6	5 26.7
21 Tu	13 56 20	0♉54 32	19 36 41	26 56 54	6 20.7	7 29.6	8 45.1	26 08.5	8 40.6	14 28.2	17 37.6	7 59.3	26 54.1	29 43.8	2 55.7	5 27.2
22 W	14 00 17	1 53 06	4♋13 01	11♋24 30	6 17.5	7 24.5	10 20.7	27 21.6	9 27.0	14 52.4	17 44.7	8 06.4	26 57.7	29 47.0	2 57.8	5 27.6
23 Th	14 04 13	2 51 38	18 31 02	25 32 26	6 14.3	7 21.6	11 58.0	28 34.6	10 13.3	15 16.7	17 52.0	8 13.5	27 01.3	29 50.2	2 59.8	5 28.0
24 F	14 08 10	3 50 08	2♌28 37	9♌19 41	6 11.1	7D 20.6	13 37.0	29 47.6	10 59.6	15 41.0	17 59.4	8 20.5	27 04.9	29 53.4	3 01.8	5 28.4
25 Sa	14 12 06	4 48 35	16 05 47	22 47 09	6 08.0	7 21.0	15 17.8	1♊00.6	11 45.8	16 05.4	18 06.9	8 27.5	27 08.5	29 56.6	3 03.8	5 28.7
26 Su	14 16 03	5 47 01	29 24 03	5♍56 49	6 04.8	7R 21.8	17 00.2	2 13.5	12 32.0	16 29.7	18 14.6	8 34.5	27 12.1	29 59.9	3 05.8	5 29.0
27 M	14 19 59	6 45 24	12♍25 44	18 51 08	6 01.6	7 21.9	18 44.3	3 26.3	13 18.2	16 54.1	18 22.4	8 41.4	27 15.7	0♊03.2	3 07.8	5 29.3
28 Tu	14 23 56	7 43 45	25 13 18	1♎32 29	5 58.4	7 20.3	20 30.2	4 39.1	14 04.3	17 18.5	18 30.3	8 48.3	27 19.3	0 06.4	3 09.8	5 29.5
29 W	14 27 52	8 42 04	7♎48 56	14 02 53	5 55.2	7 16.4	22 17.8	5 51.9	14 50.3	17 42.9	18 38.4	8 55.2	27 22.8	0 09.7	3 11.7	5 29.8
30 Th	14 31 49	9♉40 21	20 14 29	26 23 55	5♓52.1	7♓09.9	24♈07.2	7♊04.6	15♈36.4	18♉07.3	18♋46.6	9♈02.0	27♈26.4	0♊13.1	3♈13.6	5♒30.0

1st of Month

Julian Day # 2461131.5
Obliquity 23°26′8″
SVP 4♓53′29″
GC 27♐12.4
Eris 25♈07.2

Day	⚴
1	21♓50.7
6	23 29.4
11	25 07.4
16	26 44.6
21	28 20.9
26	29 55.9

Day	⚵
1	0♒43.0
6	2 02.2
11	3 17.5
16	4 28.7
21	5 35.4
26	6 37.1

Day	⚶
1	10♓25.1
6	12 49.6
11	15 12.5
16	17 33.8
21	19 53.3
26	22 10.9

DECLINATION and LATITUDE

Day	☉ Decl	☽ Decl	☽ Lat	☽ 12h Decl	☿ Decl	☿ Lat	♀ Decl	♀ Lat	♂ Decl	♂ Lat	⚳ Decl	⚳ Lat	♃ Decl	♃ Lat	♄ Decl	♄ Lat
1 W	4N28	1S00	1S45	4S02	7S37	1S18	11N38	0S27	3S41	1S03	9N13	4S43	22N52	0N22	0N15	2S08
2 Th	4 51	6 60	2 47	9 52	7 25	1 27	12 05	0 24	3 23	1 02	9 22	4 41	22 52	0 22	0 18	2 08
3 F	5 14	12 37	3 40	15 13	7 12	1 36	12 33	0 22	3 04	1 02	9 32	4 40	22 52	0 22	0 21	2 08
4 Sa	5 37	17 39	4 22	19 53	6 56	1 44	12 60	0 19	2 45	1 02	9 41	4 38	22 51	0 22	0 24	2 08
5 Su	5 60	21 54	4 51	23 41	6 39	1 51	13 27	0 17	2 26	1 02	9 50	4 36	22 51	0 22	0 27	2 08
6 M	6 22	25 11	5 07	26 25	6 21	1 58	13 53	0 14	2 07	1 01	9 60	4 34	22 50	0 22	0 29	2 08
7 Tu	6 45	27 21	5 09	27 58	6 00	2 04	14 19	0 11	1 49	1 01	10 09	4 32	22 50	0 23	0 32	2 08
8 W	7 07	28 16	4 58	28 14	5 39	2 10	14 45	0 09	1 30	1 01	10 18	4 30	22 49	0 23	0 35	2 08
9 Th	7 30	27 52	4 34	27 11	5 15	2 15	15 11	0 06	1 11	1 01	10 27	4 28	22 48	0 23	0 38	2 08
10 F	7 52	26 11	3 58	24 52	4 51	2 20	15 36	0 03	0 52	1 00	10 36	4 27	22 48	0 23	0 41	2 08
11 Sa	8 14	23 16	3 11	21 22	4 25	2 24	16 00	0 01	0 33	1 00	10 45	4 25	22 47	0 23	0 44	2 08
12 Su	8 36	19 13	2 14	16 50	3 57	2 28	16 25	0N02	0 14	0 60	10 55	4 23	22 46	0 23	0 47	2 08
13 M	8 58	14 14	1 10	11 25	3 29	2 31	16 49	0 05	0N04	0 60	11 04	4 21	22 46	0 23	0 49	2 08
14 Tu	9 20	8 27	0N01	5 20	2 58	2 33	17 12	0 08	0 23	0 59	11 13	4 20	22 45	0 23	0 52	2 09
15 W	9 42	2 07	1 13	1N11	2 27	2 35	17 35	0 10	0 42	0 59	11 21	4 18	22 44	0 23	0 55	2 09
16 Th	10 03	4N31	2 24	7 50	1 55	2 37	17 58	0 13	1 01	0 59	11 30	4 16	22 44	0 23	0 58	2 09
17 F	10 24	11 06	3 27	14 14	1 21	2 38	18 20	0 16	1 19	0 58	11 39	4 14	22 43	0 23	1 01	2 09
18 Sa	10 45	17 12	4 17	19 56	0 46	2 38	18 41	0 19	1 38	0 58	11 48	4 13	22 42	0 23	1 03	2 09
19 Su	11 06	22 22	4 51	24 26	0 10	2 38	19 02	0 21	1 57	0 58	11 57	4 11	22 41	0 23	1 06	2 09
20 M	11 27	26 06	5 06	27 18	0N27	2 37	19 23	0 24	2 15	0 57	12 05	4 09	22 40	0 23	1 09	2 09
21 Tu	11 47	28 00	4 59	28 13	1 05	2 36	19 43	0 27	2 34	0 57	12 14	4 07	22 39	0 23	1 11	2 09
22 W	12 08	27 56	4 33	27 10	1 44	2 34	20 03	0 30	2 53	0 57	12 23	4 06	22 39	0 23	1 14	2 09
23 Th	12 28	25 58	3 51	24 23	2 24	2 32	20 22	0 32	3 11	0 56	12 31	4 04	22 38	0 23	1 17	2 09
24 F	12 48	22 27	2 55	20 14	3 05	2 29	20 41	0 35	3 30	0 56	12 40	4 02	22 37	0 23	1 20	2 09
25 Sa	13 07	17 47	1 51	15 08	3 47	2 26	20 59	0 38	3 48	0 56	12 48	4 01	22 36	0 23	1 22	2 10
26 Su	13 27	12 21	0 43	9 27	4 29	2 22	21 16	0 41	4 06	0 55	12 57	3 59	22 35	0 23	1 25	2 10
27 M	13 46	6 29	0S27	3 28	5 13	2 18	21 33	0 43	4 25	0 55	13 05	3 57	22 34	0 23	1 27	2 10
28 Tu	14 05	0 28	1 34	2S32	5 57	2 13	21 49	0 46	4 43	0 54	13 14	3 56	22 33	0 23	1 30	2 10
29 W	14 24	5S28	2 35	8 20	6 42	2 08	22 05	0 49	5 01	0 54	13 22	3 54	22 32	0 23	1 33	2 10
30 Th	14N43	11S07	3S28	13S45	7N28	2S02	22N20	0N51	5N19	0S54	13N30	3S52	22N31	0N23	1N35	2S10

Day	⚷ Decl	⚷ Lat	♅ Decl	♅ Lat	♆ Decl	♆ Lat	♇ Decl	♇ Lat
1	10N17	0N22	19N43	0S10	0S19	1S18	22S47	3S57
6	10 23	0 22	19 46	0 10	0 15	1 19	22 47	3 58
11	10 29	0 21	19 49	0 10	0 11	1 19	22 47	3 59
16	10 35	0 21	19 52	0 10	0 07	1 19	22 47	3 60
21	10 41	0 21	19 56	0 10	0 03	1 19	22 48	4 01
26	10 48	0 20	19 59	0 10	0N01	1 19	22 48	4 02

Day	⚴ Decl	⚴ Lat	⚵ Decl	⚵ Lat	⚶ Decl	⚶ Lat	Eris Decl	Eris Lat
1	0N26	3N60	8S52	11N23	11S02	3S38	0N02	10S24
6	0 47	3 40	8 26	11 33	10 14	3 47	0 03	10 24
11	1 08	3 20	7 60	11 44	9 26	3 55	0 04	10 24
16	1 28	3 00	7 33	11 55	8 39	4 03	0 06	10 23
21	1 47	2 40	7 07	12 07	7 52	4 12	0 07	10 23
26	2 06	2 19	6 40	12 19	7 06	4 21	0 08	10 23

Moon Phenomena

Max/0 Decl

dy	hr mn	
8	4:51	28S17
15	7:43	0 N
21	11:00	28N12
28	1:51	0 S

Max/0 Lat

dy	hr mn	
6	16:07	5S10
13	23:43	0 N
20	4:31	5N06
26	14:37	0 S

Perigee/Apogee

dy	hr m		kilometers
7	8:32	a	404969
19	6:57	p	361633

PH	dy	hr mn	
○	2	2:13	12♎21
☾	10	4:53	20♑20
●	17	11:53	27♈29
☽	24	2:33	3♌56

Void of Course Moon

Last Aspect				☽ Ingress		
1	0:33	♅	△	♎	1	2:52
2	8:56	♃	□	♏	3	12:12
5	21:30	♅	☍	♐	5	23:33
8	9:53	♂	□	♑	8	12:05
10	22:25	♅	△	♒	10	23:57
13	7:43	♅	□	♓	13	8:57
15	13:08	♅	⚹	♈	15	14:05
17	11:53	☉	☌	♉	17	15:59
19	15:46	♅	☌	♊	19	16:19
20	5:19	♂	⚹	♋	21	17:01
23	19:29	♅	⚹	♌	23	19:42
24	22:22	☿	△	♍	26	1:06
27	11:13	♃	⚹	♎	28	9:04
30	8:53	☿	☍	♏	30	19:03

DAILY ASPECTARIAN

1 W ☽△♅ 0:33 · ☽⚻♀ 6:35 · ☽☍♆ 7:02 · ☽∥♂ 10:07 · ♀⚺♆ 11:20 · ☽△♇ 12:42 · ☽☍♄ 13:26 · ☉#☽ 14:40 · ☽⚻⚳ 15:34

2 Th ☽∥☿ 1:41 · ☉☍☽ 2:13 · ♄#♆ 4:10 · ☽⚼♅ 5:00 · ☽⚻☿ 6:57 · ☽□♃ 8:56 · ☽#⚳ 10:13 · ☽#⚷ 13:55 · ☽#♀ 23:41

3 F ☽⚻♂ 2:00 · ☽☍⚷ 4:07 · ☽⚻♅ 10:00 · ☿△♃ 11:30 · ☽⚼☿ 14:16 · ☉∠♅ 15:20 · ☽⚻♆ 16:42 · ☽☍♀ 22:27 · ☽□♇ 22:28 · ♀□♇ 22:39 · ☽⚻♄ 23:46

4 Sa ☽☍⚳ 3:18 · ☽⚼♂ 9:17 · ☽#♅ 11:15 · ♀⚺♄ 12:48 · ♂⚺⚷ 13:59 · ☉⚻☽ 17:33 · ☽△♃ 19:44 · ☽⚼♆ 22:18 · ☽△☿ 22:26

5 Su ☽⚼♄ 5:42 · ☽∥♇ 5:45 · ☽#♃ 6:08 · ☽⚻⚷ 15:30 · ☽△♂ 17:08 · ☽☍♅ 21:30 · ☉□♃ 22:24 · ☉#☿ 23:00

6 M ☽⚼♃ 1:51 · ☉⚼☽ 2:08 · ☽△♆ 4:21 · ☽⚹♇ 10:11 · ☽△♄ 12:04 · ☽⚻♀ 16:57 · ☽⚻⚳ 17:08 · ♀☌⚳ 19:21 · ☽⚼⚷ 21:48

7 Tu ☽⚻♃ 8:18 · ☉△☽ 11:06 · ☿∠♇ 14:05 · ☽∠♇ 16:31 · ☽□☿ 16:46

8 W ☽⚼⚳ 0:30 · ☽⚼♀ 2:46 · ☽△⚷ 4:16 · ☽□♂ 9:53 · ☽⚻♅ 10:16 · ♂⚹♅ 16:13 · ☽□♆ 17:07 · ⚳∥⚷ 21:37 · ☽⚺♇ 22:51

9 Th ☽□♄ 1:17 · ☽△⚳ 7:48 · ☽△♀ 12:28 · ☽⚼♅ 16:34 · ♂ ♈ 19:37 · ☽☍♃ 21:11

10 F ☉□☽ 4:53 · ☊ D 5:03 · ☽⚹☿ 11:45 · ♂#♄ 12:23 · ☽□⚷ 16:39 · ☽△♅ 22:25

11 Sa ☽⚹♂ 1:52 · ♃#♇ 1:54 · ☽∥♇ 3:11 · ☽#♃ 3:11 · ☽⚹♆ 4:59 · ☽☌♇ 10:24 · ☽⚹♄ 13:16 · ☽∠☿ 20:23 · ☽#♅ 20:46 · ☽□⚳ 20:52

12 Su ☿∠⚳ 2:55 · ☽□♀ 5:44 · ♂∥♆ 6:03 · ☽⚻♃ 8:08 · ☽∠♂ 8:39 · ☽∠♆ 9:53 · ☿⚺⚷ 11:55 · ☽#♀ 12:59 · ☽∠♄ 18:06 · ☉⚹☽ 19:49

13 M ☽⚹⚷ 2:21 · ☽⚺☿ 3:56 · ♂☌♆ 5:31 · ♂#♆ 5:41 · ☽□♅ 7:43 · ♀⚹♃ 8:22 · ☽⚼♃ 12:16 · ☽#⚳ 13:10 · ☽⚺♆ 13:50 · ☽⚺♂ 14:19 · ☽#⚷ 15:39 · ☽⚺♇ 18:47 · ☉#☽ 20:42 · ☽⚺♄ 21:56 · ☊ R 23:42

14 Tu ☉∠☽ 1:31 · ♀∠♆ 1:47 · ☽∠⚷ 5:46 · ☽⚹⚳ 6:13 · ☽△♃ 15:24 · ☿⚹♅ 17:11 · ☽⚹♀ 18:12 · ☽∠♇ 21:29 · ☽∥☿ 22:38

15 W ☿ ♈ 3:23 · ☽#♄ 4:21 · ☽#♂ 4:56 · ☉⚺☽ 5:59 · ☽∥♆ 7:17 · ☽#♆ 8:08 · ☽⚺⚷ 8:11 · ☽∠⚳ 9:17 · ☽∥♂ 10:45 · ☽∥♄ 11:06 · ♀∠♂ 11:26 · ☽⚹♅ 13:08 · ☽☌☿ 15:17 · ☽#☿ 15:20 · ☽☌♆ 18:46 · ♂∥♄ 19:33 · ☽☌♂ 22:10 · ☽∠♀ 22:32 · ☽⚹♇ 23:17

16 Th ☽☌♄ 2:39 · ☽⚺⚳ 11:26 · ☽∠♅ 14:31 · ☉☌⚷ 15:12 · ☽□♃ 18:55 · ♂⚹♇ 18:57 · ☉∥☽ 21:16 · ☽∥⚷ 22:11

17 F ☿#♂ 0:43 · ☽⚺♀ 1:51 · ☿☌♆ 2:03 · ☽∥⚳ 2:08 · ☽☌⚷ 10:35 · ☉☌☽ 11:53 · ☿#♄ 13:12 · ☉∥⚷ 14:47 · ☽⚺♅ 15:15 · ☽⚺♆ 20:34 · ☽⚺☿ 22:34

18 Sa ☽□♇ 0:47 · ☽⚺♂ 2:25 · ♀∠♄ 3:15 · ☽⚺♄ 4:23 · ☽∥♀ 6:49 · ☽∥♅ 11:50 · ☽☌⚳ 13:47 · ☽⚹♃ 20:03 · ☿⚹♇ 20:36 · ☽∠♆ 20:49

19 Su ☽∠☿ 1:27 · ☽∥♃ 1:42 · ☽#♇ 2:16 · ☽∠♂ 3:53 · ☿∥♆ 4:09 · ☽∠♄ 4:43 · ☽☌♀ 6:45 · ☿#♆ 9:13 · ☽⚺⚷ 11:11 · ☉⚺☽ 15:40 · ☽☌♅ 15:46 · ☉⚺♅ 17:23 · ☽∠♃ 20:19 · ☽⚹♆ 20:58 · ♂☌♄ 22:45

20 M ☽△♇ 1:04 · ☉ ♉ 1:40 · ☽⚹☿ 4:20 · ☽⚹♄ 5:01 · ☽⚹♂ 5:19 · ☿☌♄ 11:23 · ☽∠⚷ 11:26 · ☽⚺⚳ 15:25 · ☉∠☽ 17:33 · ☽⚺♃ 20:45 · ☿☌♂ 21:46

21 Tu ☽⚼♇ 1:22 · ☿∥♄ 4:27 · ☽⚺♀ 11:39 · ☽⚹⚷ 11:58 · ♀∥♅ 15:44 · ♀⚺⚷ 15:46 · ☽∠⚳ 16:37 · ☽⚺♅ 16:38 · ☉⚹☽ 19:52 · ☽□♆ 21:55

22 W ☽⚻♇ 2:04 · ☽□♄ 6:32 · ☽□♂ 9:13 · ☽□☿ 11:31 · ☽∠♀ 14:52 · ☽∠♅ 17:45 · ☽⚹⚳ 18:21 · ☽☌♃ 22:53

23 Th ☉⚺♆ 3:29 · ☉∥⚳ 7:22 · ☽□⚷ 14:37 · ☽⚹♀ 18:54 · ☽⚹♅ 19:29 · ☽#♇ 22:00 · ☽∥♃ 23:05

24 F ☽△♆ 0:58 · ♀☌♅ 1:59 · ☊ D 2:27 · ☉□☽ 2:33 · ♀ ♊ 4:05 · ☽☍♇ 5:14 · ☽∥♀ 9:08 · ☽△♄ 10:21 · ☽∥♅ 13:21 · ☽△♂ 15:50 · ☿∠♅ 18:50 · ☽△☿ 22:22 · ☽□⚳ 23:59

25 Sa ☿∥♂ 1:13 · ☽⚼♆ 3:31 · ☽⚺♃ 3:39 · ☽⚼♄ 13:20 · ☿⚺⚳ 14:42 · ☉□♇ 16:34 · ☉∥☽ 19:35 · ☽△⚷ 19:59 · ☽⚼♂ 20:23 · ☽∥⚳ 21:31

26 Su ♅ ♊ 0:51 · ☽□♅ 1:06 · ⚴ ♈ 5:10 · ☽⚼☿ 5:29 · ☽□♀ 5:41 · ☽∥⚷ 6:27 · ☽⚻♆ 6:47 · ☽∠♃ 7:06 · ☿∠♀ 10:21 · ☽⚻♇ 11:09 · ☉△☽ 12:39 · ☊ R 14:35 · ☽⚻♄ 17:00 · ♀⚹♆ 17:44 · ☿□♃ 18:34 · ♀∠♃ 22:33 · ☽⚼⚷ 23:41

27 M ☽⚻♂ 1:44 · ☽∥☿ 4:30 · ☽∥♂ 7:53 · ☽△⚳ 8:37 · ☽⚹♃ 11:13 · ☽⚻☿ 13:40 · ☽⚼♇ 15:05 · ☉⚼☽ 18:54 · ☽∥♄ 19:54

28 Tu ☽∥♆ 1:39 · ☽#♆ 2:03 · ☽⚻⚷ 4:00 · ☽#♄ 7:55 · ☽△♅ 9:19 · ☽⚼⚳ 13:55 · ☽☍♆ 15:08 · ♀△♇ 16:41 · ☽△♇ 19:33 · ☽△♀ 19:52 · ☽#♂ 22:02

29 W ☉⚻☽ 1:51 · ☽☍♄ 2:08 · ☽#☿ 5:54 · ☉⚺♄ 6:07 · ♂∠♅ 10:54 · ☽⚼♅ 14:13 · ☽☍♂ 14:25 · ☽⚻⚳ 19:45 · ☽□♃ 21:07 · ☽#⚷ 22:57

30 Th ☽⚼♀ 3:57 · ⚳∠♆ 6:44 · ☽☍☿ 8:53 · ☽#⚳ 11:07 · ☽☍⚷ 14:06 · ♀∥♃ 16:08 · ☉#☽ 17:34 · ☽⚻♅ 19:34

LONGITUDE

Day	Sid.Time	☉	☽	☽ 12 hour	Mean☊	True ☊	☿	♀	♂	⚳	♃	♄	⚷	♅	♆	♇
	h m s	° ' "	° ' "	° ' "	° '	° '	° '	° '	° '	° '	° '	° '	° '	° '	° '	° '
1 F	14 35 45	10♉38 36	2♏31 19	8♏36 48	5♓48.9	7♓00.8	25♈58.3	8♊17.3	16♈22.4	18♉31.8	18♋54.9	9♈08.8	27♈29.9	0♊16.4	3♈15.5	5♒30.1
2 Sa	14 39 42	11 36 50	14 40 29	20 42 31	5 45.7	6R 49.7	27 51.1	9 29.9	17 08.3	18 56.2	19 03.3	9 15.5	27 33.4	0 19.8	3 17.4	5 30.3
3 Su	14 43 39	12 35 02	26 43 01	2♐42 08	5 42.5	6 37.6	29 45.7	10 42.4	17 54.2	19 20.7	19 11.8	9 22.2	27 37.0	0 23.1	3 19.3	5 30.4
4 M	14 47 35	13 33 12	8♐40 03	14 36 59	5 39.4	6 25.4	1♉42.0	11 54.9	18 40.1	19 45.2	19 20.5	9 28.9	27 40.5	0 26.5	3 21.1	5 30.5
5 Tu	14 51 32	14 31 21	20 33 11	26 28 57	5 36.2	6 14.2	3 40.1	13 07.4	19 25.9	20 09.7	19 29.3	9 35.5	27 44.0	0 29.9	3 23.0	5 30.5
6 W	14 55 28	15 29 28	2♑24 37	8♑20 35	5 33.0	6 04.8	5 39.8	14 19.8	20 11.7	20 34.2	19 38.1	9 42.1	27 47.5	0 33.3	3 24.8	5R 30.6
7 Th	14 59 25	16 27 34	14 17 16	20 15 11	5 29.8	5 57.9	7 41.2	15 32.2	20 57.5	20 58.7	19 47.1	9 48.6	27 50.9	0 36.7	3 26.6	5 30.6
8 F	15 03 21	17 25 38	26 14 49	2♒16 45	5 26.7	5 53.5	9 44.2	16 44.5	21 43.2	21 23.2	19 56.3	9 55.1	27 54.4	0 40.1	3 28.3	5 30.6
9 Sa	15 07 18	18 23 41	8♒21 36	14 29 56	5 23.5	5D 51.5	11 48.7	17 56.8	22 28.8	21 47.8	20 05.5	10 01.6	27 57.8	0 43.6	3 30.1	5 30.5
10 Su	15 11 15	19 21 42	20 42 26	26 59 42	5 20.3	5 51.1	13 54.6	19 09.0	23 14.5	22 12.4	20 14.8	10 08.0	28 01.3	0 47.0	3 31.8	5 30.4
11 M	15 15 11	20 19 42	3♓22 21	9♓50 58	5 17.1	5R 51.3	16 01.9	20 21.2	24 00.0	22 36.9	20 24.2	10 14.3	28 04.7	0 50.5	3 33.5	5 30.3
12 Tu	15 19 08	21 17 41	16 26 03	23 08 02	5 13.9	5 50.9	18 10.3	21 33.3	24 45.6	23 01.5	20 33.8	10 20.6	28 08.1	0 53.9	3 35.2	5 30.2
13 W	15 23 04	22 15 38	29 57 14	6♈53 48	5 10.8	5 49.0	20 19.7	22 45.4	25 31.0	23 26.1	20 43.4	10 26.9	28 11.5	0 57.4	3 36.9	5 30.0
14 Th	15 27 01	23 13 34	13♈57 44	21 08 49	5 07.6	5 44.8	22 29.8	23 57.4	26 16.5	23 50.7	20 53.2	10 33.1	28 14.8	1 00.9	3 38.5	5 29.8
15 F	15 30 57	24 11 29	28 26 37	5♉50 28	5 04.4	5 37.9	24 40.6	25 09.3	27 01.9	24 15.3	21 03.0	10 39.2	28 18.1	1 04.4	3 40.1	5 29.6
16 Sa	15 34 54	25 09 23	13♉19 29	20 52 35	5 01.2	5 28.7	26 51.7	26 21.3	27 47.2	24 39.9	21 13.0	10 45.3	28 21.5	1 07.9	3 41.7	5 29.4
17 Su	15 38 50	26 07 15	28 28 30	6♊05 53	4 58.1	5 18.1	29 02.9	27 33.1	28 32.5	25 04.6	21 23.0	10 51.3	28 24.8	1 11.4	3 43.3	5 29.1
18 M	15 42 47	27 05 06	13♊43 18	21 19 22	4 54.9	5 07.3	1♊13.9	28 44.9	29 17.7	25 29.2	21 33.1	10 57.3	28 28.1	1 14.9	3 44.8	5 28.8
19 Tu	15 46 44	28 02 55	28 52 47	6♋22 22	4 51.7	4 57.6	3 24.4	29 56.7	0♉02.9	25 53.8	21 43.4	11 03.3	28 31.3	1 18.4	3 46.3	5 28.5
20 W	15 50 40	29 00 43	13♋47 08	21 06 20	4 48.5	4 50.0	5 34.1	1♋08.4	0 48.1	26 18.5	21 53.7	11 09.1	28 34.5	1 21.9	3 47.8	5 28.1
21 Th	15 54 37	29 58 29	28 19 23	5♌25 59	4 45.4	4 45.1	7 42.8	2 20.0	1 33.2	26 43.1	22 04.1	11 14.9	28 37.8	1 25.4	3 49.3	5 27.7
22 F	15 58 33	0♊56 13	12♌25 58	19 19 23	4 42.2	4 42.6	9 50.1	3 31.6	2 18.2	27 07.7	22 14.6	11 20.7	28 41.0	1 28.9	3 50.7	5 27.3
23 Sa	16 02 30	1 53 56	26 06 25	2♍47 21	4 39.0	4 41.8	11 55.9	4 43.1	3 03.2	27 32.4	22 25.2	11 26.4	28 44.1	1 32.4	3 52.1	5 26.9
24 Su	16 06 26	2 51 37	9♍22 34	15 52 30	4 35.8	4 41.8	14 00.0	5 54.6	3 48.1	27 57.0	22 35.9	11 32.0	28 47.2	1 35.9	3 53.5	5 26.4
25 M	16 10 23	3 49 17	22 17 37	28 38 24	4 32.6	4 41.2	16 02.0	7 05.9	4 33.0	28 21.6	22 46.6	11 37.6	28 50.4	1 39.4	3 54.9	5 26.0
26 Tu	16 14 19	4 46 55	4♎55 18	11♎08 47	4 29.5	4 38.9	18 01.9	8 17.2	5 17.8	28 46.2	22 57.4	11 43.1	28 53.4	1 42.9	3 56.2	5 25.4
27 W	16 18 16	5 44 31	17 19 16	23 27 10	4 26.3	4 34.2	19 59.5	9 28.5	6 02.5	29 10.9	23 08.3	11 48.5	28 56.5	1 46.4	3 57.5	5 24.9
28 Th	16 22 13	6 42 07	29 32 49	5♏36 32	4 23.1	4 26.6	21 54.6	10 39.7	6 47.3	29 35.5	23 19.3	11 53.9	28 59.5	1 49.9	3 58.8	5 24.3
29 F	16 26 09	7 39 40	11♏38 36	17 39 15	4 19.9	4 16.3	23 47.2	11 50.8	7 31.9	0♊00.1	23 30.4	11 59.2	29 02.5	1 53.4	4 00.0	5 23.8
30 Sa	16 30 06	8 37 13	23 38 42	29 37 09	4 16.8	4 03.9	25 37.2	13 01.8	8 16.5	0 24.7	23 41.5	12 04.4	29 05.5	1 56.9	4 01.3	5 23.2
31 Su	16 34 02	9♊34 45	5♐34 46	11♐31 43	4♓13.6	3♓50.2	27♊24.5	14♋12.8	9♉01.1	0♊49.4	23♋52.8	12♈09.6	29♈08.4	2♊00.4	4♈02.5	5♒22.5

1st of Month

Julian Day #
2461161.5
Obliquity
23°26'08"
SVP 4♓53'26"
GC 27♐12.4
Eris 25♈26.8

Day	⚴	⚵	⚶
1	1♈29.7	7♒33.5	24♓26.4
6	3 02.1	8 24.1	26 39.7
11	4 32.9	9 08.5	28 50.8
16	6 02.0	9 46.2	0♈59.4
21	7 29.2	10 16.6	3 05.3
26	8 54.2	10 39.3	5 08.3
31	10 16.8	10 53.9	7 08.2

DECLINATION and LATITUDE

Day	☉ Decl	☽ Decl	☽ Lat	☽12h Decl	☿ Decl	☿ Lat	♀ Decl	♀ Lat	♂ Decl	♂ Lat	⚳ Decl	⚳ Lat	♃ Decl	♃ Lat	♄ Decl	♄ Lat
1 F	15N01	16S15	4S10	18S34	8N14	1S55	22N34	0N54	5N37	0S53	13N38	3S51	22N29	0N23	1N38	2S10
2 Sa	15 19	20 42	4 40	22 35	9 01	1 49	22 48	0 57	5 55	0 53	13 46	3 49	22 28	0 23	1 40	2 10
3 Su	15 37	24 14	4 57	25 37	9 48	1 41	23 02	0 59	6 13	0 52	13 55	3 48	22 27	0 24	1 43	2 11
4 M	15 54	26 43	5 02	27 30	10 36	1 34	23 14	1 02	6 31	0 52	14 03	3 46	22 26	0 24	1 45	2 11
5 Tu	16 12	27 58	4 53	28 07	11 24	1 25	23 26	1 04	6 49	0 51	14 11	3 44	22 25	0 24	1 48	2 11
6 W	16 29	27 56	4 31	27 26	12 12	1 17	23 37	1 07	7 06	0 51	14 19	3 43	22 23	0 24	1 50	2 11
7 Th	16 45	26 37	3 58	25 29	13 00	1 08	23 48	1 09	7 24	0 51	14 26	3 41	22 22	0 24	1 53	2 11
8 F	17 02	24 04	3 14	22 23	13 48	0 58	23 58	1 12	7 41	0 50	14 34	3 40	22 21	0 24	1 55	2 11
9 Sa	17 18	20 26	2 20	18 15	14 36	0 49	24 07	1 14	7 59	0 50	14 42	3 38	22 20	0 24	1 57	2 11
10 Su	17 34	15 51	1 19	13 15	15 24	0 39	24 16	1 16	8 16	0 49	14 50	3 36	22 18	0 24	1 60	2 12
11 M	17 50	10 28	0 13	7 33	16 11	0 29	24 24	1 19	8 33	0 49	14 58	3 35	22 17	0 24	2 02	2 12
12 Tu	18 05	4 30	0N56	1 21	16 57	0 18	24 31	1 21	8 50	0 48	15 05	3 33	22 15	0 24	2 04	2 12
13 W	18 20	1N53	2 04	5N08	17 42	0 08	24 38	1 23	9 07	0 48	15 13	3 32	22 14	0 24	2 07	2 12
14 Th	18 35	8 23	3 07	11 34	18 26	0N03	24 43	1 26	9 24	0 47	15 20	3 30	22 13	0 24	2 09	2 12
15 F	18 49	14 39	4 00	17 34	19 09	0 13	24 49	1 28	9 41	0 47	15 28	3 29	22 11	0 24	2 11	2 12
16 Sa	19 03	20 16	4 39	22 39	19 50	0 24	24 53	1 30	9 58	0 46	15 35	3 27	22 10	0 24	2 13	2 13
17 Su	19 17	24 40	4 58	26 15	20 30	0 34	24 57	1 32	10 15	0 46	15 42	3 26	22 08	0 24	2 16	2 13
18 M	19 30	27 22	4 57	27 57	21 07	0 44	24 60	1 34	10 31	0 45	15 50	3 24	22 07	0 24	2 18	2 13
19 Tu	19 43	28 01	4 35	27 34	21 43	0 54	25 02	1 36	10 47	0 45	15 57	3 22	22 05	0 24	2 20	2 13
20 W	19 56	26 37	3 54	25 13	22 16	1 03	25 04	1 38	11 04	0 44	16 04	3 21	22 03	0 24	2 22	2 13
21 Th	20 09	23 25	2 59	21 18	22 47	1 12	25 05	1 40	11 20	0 44	16 11	3 19	22 02	0 24	2 24	2 13
22 F	20 21	18 54	1 55	16 18	23 15	1 21	25 05	1 41	11 36	0 43	16 18	3 18	22 00	0 24	2 26	2 14
23 Sa	20 32	13 31	0 45	10 38	23 41	1 29	25 04	1 43	11 52	0 42	16 25	3 16	21 58	0 24	2 28	2 14
24 Su	20 44	7 40	0S25	4 40	24 04	1 36	25 03	1 45	12 07	0 42	16 32	3 15	21 57	0 24	2 30	2 14
25 M	20 55	1 39	1 32	1S20	24 25	1 43	25 01	1 46	12 23	0 42	16 39	3 13	21 55	0 24	2 32	2 14
26 Tu	21 05	4S17	2 32	7 10	24 42	1 49	24 58	1 48	12 39	0 41	16 46	3 12	21 53	0 24	2 34	2 14
27 W	21 16	9 57	3 25	12 37	24 58	1 54	24 55	1 49	12 54	0 40	16 53	3 10	21 51	0 24	2 36	2 15
28 Th	21 26	15 09	4 07	17 31	25 10	1 59	24 51	1 51	13 09	0 40	16 59	3 09	21 50	0 25	2 38	2 15
29 F	21 35	19 43	4 37	21 41	25 20	2 03	24 46	1 52	13 24	0 39	17 06	3 07	21 48	0 25	2 40	2 15
30 Sa	21 44	23 26	4 55	24 56	25 27	2 06	24 41	1 53	13 39	0 39	17 13	3 06	21 46	0 25	2 42	2 15
31 Su	21N53	26S08	4S59	27S04	25N33	2N08	24N35	1N54	13N54	0S38	17N19	3S04	21N44	0N25	2N44	2S15

Day	⚷ Decl	⚷ Lat	♅ Decl	♅ Lat	♆ Decl	♆ Lat	♇ Decl	♇ Lat
1	10N54	0N20	20N03	0S10	0N05	1S19	22S49	4S03
6	10 60	0 20	20 06	0 10	0 09	1 19	22 50	4 04
11	11 06	0 19	20 10	0 10	0 12	1 20	22 51	4 05
16	11 11	0 19	20 14	0 10	0 15	1 20	22 52	4 06
21	11 17	0 19	20 17	0 10	0 18	1 20	22 53	4 07
26	11 22	0 18	20 21	0 10	0 20	1 20	22 55	4 07
31	11N27	0N18	20N24	0S10	0N23	1S20	22S56	4S08

Day	⚴ Decl	⚴ Lat	⚵ Decl	⚵ Lat	⚶ Decl	⚶ Lat	Eris Decl	Eris Lat
1	2N24	1N58	6S15	12N32	6S21	4S30	0N09	10S23
6	2 41	1 37	5 50	12 45	5 36	4 40	0 11	10 23
11	2 57	1 14	5 26	12 59	4 53	4 50	0 12	10 23
16	3 11	0 52	5 03	13 13	4 11	4 60	0 13	10 23
21	3 24	0 28	4 41	13 27	3 31	5 10	0 13	10 23
26	3 35	0 03	4 22	13 41	2 52	5 21	0 14	10 23
31	3N44	0S22	4S05	13N55	2S15	5S32	0N15	10S24

Moon Phenomena

Max/0 Decl
dy hr mn
5 11:23 28S07
12 17:02 0 N
18 19:26 28N03
25 6:37 0 S

Max/0 Lat
dy hr mn
3 19:33 5S02
11 4:37 0 N
17 10:37 5N00
23 15:28 0 S
30 20:33 4S59

Perigee/Apogee
dy hr m kilometers
4 22:31 a 405839
17 13:45 p 358080

PH dy hr mn
○ 1 17:24 11♏21
☾ 9 21:12 19♒15
● 16 20:02 25♉58
☽ 23 11:12 2♍21
○ 31 8:46 9♐56

Void of Course Moon

Last Aspect	☽ Ingress
2 8:49 ♃ △	♐ 3 6:35
4 21:35 ♂ △	♑ 5 19:07
7 14:20 ♂ □	♒ 8 7:29
10 5:10 ♂ ✱	♓ 10 17:41
12 10:05 ♀ □	♈ 13 0:05
14 21:34 ♂ ☌	♉ 15 2:32
17 1:03 ☿ ☌	♊ 17 2:24
17 19:37 ♄ ✱	♋ 19 1:47
20 13:28 ♃ ☌	♌ 21 2:49
21 22:07 ♄ △	♍ 23 6:58
25 0:55 ♃ ✱	♎ 25 14:35
27 11:33 ♃ □	♏ 28 0:54
30 0:06 ♃ △	♐ 30 12:46

DAILY ASPECTARIAN

1 F: ☽⚻♆ 1:27; ☽□♇ 5:52; ☽⚻♀ 12:37; ☽⚻♄ 13:11; ☉☍☽ 17:24; ♀✱♄ 18:46; ☿☌⚷ 20:09; ☽⋕♅ 20:16

2 Sa: ♀⋕♇ 0:56; ☽⚻♂ 5:14; ☽⚼♆ 7:12; ☽☍⚳ 8:46; ☽△♃ 8:49; ⚳✱♃ 10:38; ☽⋕♃ 11:09; ☽∥♇ 13:32; ☽⋕♀ 14:24; ☽⚼♄ 19:16

3 Su: ☽⚻⚷ 1:49; ☿ ♉ 2:58; ☽⚻☿ 7:16; ☽☍♅ 7:23; ☿⚺♅ 7:59; ☽⚼♂ 13:15; ☽△♆ 13:17; ☽⚼♃ 15:11; ☽✱♇ 17:38

4 M: ☽△♄ 1:39; ☽☍♀ 7:17; ☽⚼⚷ 8:07; ☉⚻☽ 10:44; ☿∥⚷ 10:53; ♀∠⚷ 15:51; ☽⚼☿ 19:26; ☿⚺♆ 20:29; ☽△♂ 21:35; ☽⚻♃ 21:49; ☽⚻⚳ 23:11; ☽∠♇ 23:55

5 Tu: ♂□♃ 2:09; ☽△⚷ 14:36; ☉⚼☽ 19:46; ☽⚻♅ 20:14; ☿□♇ 22:09

6 W: ☽□♆ 2:02; ☽⚺♇ 6:16; ☽⚼⚳ 6:37; ☽△☿ 7:56; ☽□♄ 14:53; ♇ R 15:36

7 Th: ♂⚺⚳ 1:24; ☽⚼♅ 2:41; ☽⚻♀ 2:48; ☉△☽ 4:46; ☽☍♃ 11:12; ☽△⚳ 13:56; ☽□♂ 14:20

8 F: ☽⋕♀ 0:45; ☿⚺♄ 2:14; ☽□⚷ 3:20; ☽△♅ 8:51; ☽∥♇ 8:56; ☽⚼♀ 12:09; ☽⋕♃ 12:16; ☽✱♆ 14:24; ☽☌♇ 18:23

9 Sa: ☽⋕♅ 1:39; ☉∠♆ 2:44; ☽✱♄ 3:18; ☿∥⚳ 3:34; ☽□☿ 8:09; ☉⋕☽ 15:57; ☽∠♆ 19:48; ☽△♀ 20:41; ☉□☽ 21:12; ☊ D 21:25; ☽⚻♃ 23:06

10 Su: ☽⋕☿ 1:51; ☽□⚳ 2:58; ☽⋕⚳ 4:40; ☽✱♂ 5:10; ☽∠♄ 8:32; ☽✱⚷ 14:00; ☽□♅ 19:14; ☽⋕⚷ 21:23; ☉⚺♀ 21:30

11 M: ☽⚺♆ 0:21; ♀⚺♃ 1:11; ☉✱♃ 2:15; ♀⚼♇ 3:02; ☽⚼♃ 3:50; ☽⚺♇ 3:58; ☊ R 4:35; ☽⋕♂ 7:34; ☽∠♂ 11:05; ☽⚺♄ 12:49; ☽∠⚷ 17:59

12 Tu: ☽✱☿ 3:44; ☿∠♆ 4:42; ☽∠♇ 7:19; ☽△♃ 7:30; ☽⋕♄ 9:12; ☉✱☽ 9:24; ☽□♀ 10:05; ☽✱⚳ 12:10; ☽⚺♂ 15:45; ☽⋕♆ 16:13; ☽∥♆ 17:50; ☽⚺⚷ 20:54

13 W: ☽∥♄ 0:52; ☽✱♅ 1:45; ☿✱♃ 4:45; ☽☌♆ 6:22; ☽✱♇ 9:36; ☽∠☿ 11:01; ☉∠☽ 13:33; ☽∠⚳ 15:04; ⚶ ♈ 16:18; ☽☌♄ 18:11; ♀⚺⚳ 20:37

14 Th: ☽∠♅ 3:28; ☽∥♂ 4:00; ☉∥☿ 7:06; ☽∥⚷ 10:25; ☽□♃ 11:42; ☉☌☿ 14:25; ☉⚺☽ 16:32; ☽⚺☿ 16:44; ☽⚺⚳ 16:56; ☽✱♀ 18:08; ☿☌⚳ 18:17; ☽☌♂ 21:34; ☽☌⚷ 23:46

15 F: ☉☌⚳ 2:46; ☽∥⚳ 3:18; ☽⚺♅ 4:18; ☽⚺♆ 8:30; ☿∠♄ 11:15; ☽□♇ 11:26; ☿⚺♀ 11:40; ☉∥☽ 18:12; ☽⚺♄ 19:52; ☽∠♀ 20:35; ☽∥☿ 21:44; ☽∥♅ 23:51

16 Sa: ☽∠♆ 8:33; ☽∥♃ 9:22; ☽✱♃ 12:41; ☽⋕♇ 13:12; ☿∥♅ 14:16; ☿⚺♂ 15:30; ☉∠♄ 16:38; ☿⚺⚷ 16:51; ☽☌⚳ 18:29; ♂☌⚷ 19:35; ☽∠♄ 19:51; ☉☌☽ 20:02; ☽⚺♀ 22:25; ☽⚺⚷ 23:54

17 Su: ☽⚺♂ 0:07; ☽☌☿ 1:03; ☽∥♀ 1:57; ☽☌♅ 4:18; ☽✱♆ 8:16; ☿ ♊ 10:28; ☽△♇ 11:02; ☽∠♃ 12:35; ♀✱⚷ 18:05; ☽✱♄ 19:37; ☽∠⚷ 23:36

18 M: ☿☌♅ 0:11; ☽∠♂ 0:57; ☽⚼♇ 10:40; ☽⚺♃ 12:30; ☽⚺⚳ 19:07; ♂ ♉ 22:27; ☉⚺☽ 22:35; ☽✱⚷ 23:26

19 Tu: ♀ ♋ 1:06; ☽☌♀ 1:51; ☽✱♂ 1:58; ☽⚺♅ 3:53; ☿✱♆ 4:06; ♀✱♂ 5:38; ☽□♆ 7:50; ☽⚺☿ 8:28; ☽⚻♇ 10:33; ⚳∠♄ 12:05; ☉⚺⚷ 12:29; ☿∥♃ 14:57; ☽□♄ 19:42; ☽∠⚳ 19:52; ☿△♇ 22:54

20 W: ☉∠☽ 0:24; ☽∠♅ 4:14; ♀⚺♅ 4:45; ☽∥♀ 13:02; ☽∠☿ 13:03; ☽☌♃ 13:28; ☿∠♃ 16:08; ♂∥⚷ 19:07; ♂⚺♅ 19:30; ☽✱⚳ 21:14

21 Th: ☽□⚷ 0:31; ☉ ♊ 0:38; ☉✱☽ 2:58; ☽⋕♇ 3:13; ☽∥☿ 3:23; ☿⋕♇ 4:57; ☽✱♅ 5:14; ☽□♂ 5:44; ☽⚺♀ 7:22; ☽∥♃ 8:07; ☽△♆ 9:17; ☽☍♇ 12:03; ☽∥♅ 17:11; ☉∥☽ 17:13; ☉∥♅ 18:05; ☽✱☿ 18:44; ☽△♄ 22:07

22 F: ♀□♆ 6:33; ☽⚼♆ 11:11; ☽∠♀ 11:37; ☽∥⚳ 11:43; ☉☌♅ 14:27; ☽⚺♃ 17:22; ☿✱♄ 18:04

23 Sa: ☽⚼♄ 0:36; ☽□⚳ 2:38; ☽△⚷ 4:43; ☽∥♂ 6:40; ☽∥⚷ 9:12; ☽□♅ 9:47; ☉□☽ 11:12; ☽△♂ 13:14; ☽⚻♆ 13:59; ♀⚻♇ 14:37; ☽⚻♇ 16:49; ☽✱♀ 17:02; ☽∠♃ 20:42; ☿∠⚷ 21:27

24 Su: ♂⚺♆ 3:00; ☽⚻♄ 4:00; ☽⚼⚷ 8:10; ☽□☿ 10:07; ☽⚼♂ 18:32; ☽∥♄ 20:30; ☽⚼♇ 20:30

25 M: ☽✱♃ 0:55; ☉✱♆ 2:23; ☽∥♆ 5:17; ☽⋕♆ 7:58; ☽△⚳ 11:51; ☽⚻⚷ 12:26; ☽⋕♄ 16:57; ☽△♅ 17:50; ☽☍♆ 22:06; ☉△☽ 23:43

26 Tu: ☽⚻♂ 0:46; ☽△♇ 0:58; ♂□♇ 4:03; ☽□♀ 7:10; ⚳⚺⚷ 8:00; ☽☍♄ 13:12; ☉△♇ 15:54; ☽⚼⚳ 17:41; ☿∥♀ 20:31; ☽⚼♅ 22:56

27 W: ☿⚼♇ 5:14; ☽△☿ 6:12; ☽⋕⚷ 6:24; ☉⚼☽ 7:15; ☽□♃ 11:33; ☽⋕♂ 13:58; ☿∠♂ 21:27; ☽☍⚷ 22:54

28 Th: ☽⚻⚳ 0:05; ☽⚻♅ 4:32; ☽⚻♆ 8:47; ☽⋕⚳ 9:27; ☉⚺♂ 9:34; ☽□♇ 11:35; ☽☍♂ 15:17; ☉⚻☽ 15:23; ☽⚼☿ 17:17; ☿⚺♃ 19:59; ⚳ ♊ 23:53

29 F: ☽△♀ 0:27; ☽⚻♄ 0:41; ♀□♄ 3:04; ☽⋕♅ 3:57; ☉⋕☽ 11:50; ☽⋕♃ 12:36; ☽⚼♆ 14:43; ☽∥♇ 20:22

30 Sa: ☽△♃ 0:06; ☉∠♃ 2:14; ☉∥♃ 3:23; ☽⚻☿ 4:40; ☽⚼♄ 6:56; ☽⋕♀ 9:32; ☽⚼♀ 9:46; ☽⚻⚷ 10:59; ☽☍⚳ 14:05; ☽☍♅ 16:46; ☽⋕☿ 17:34; ☽△♆ 20:54; ☽✱♇ 23:35

31 Su: ☽⚼♃ 6:46; ☽⚻♂ 7:24; ☉☍☽ 8:46; ☽△♄ 13:22; ☽⚼⚷ 17:21; ☽⚻♀ 19:21

June 2026

LONGITUDE

Day	Sid.Time	☉	☽	☽ 12 hour	Mean ☊	True ☊	☿	♀	♂	⚳	♃	♄	⚷	♅	♆	♇
	h m s	° ' "	° ' "	° ' "	° '	° '	° '	° '	° '	° '	° '	° '	° '	° '	° '	° '
1 M	16 37 59	10♊32 15	17♐28 09	23♐24 16	4♓10.4	3♓36.4	29♊09.0	15♋23.7	9♉45.6	1♊14.0	24♋04.0	12♈14.7	29♈11.4	2♊03.8	4♈03.6	5♒21.9
2 Tu	16 41 55	11 29 45	29 20 14	5♑16 17	4 07.2	3R 23.7	0♋50.7	16 34.5	10 30.0	1 38.6	24 15.4	12 19.7	29 14.2	2 07.3	4 04.8	5R 21.2
3 W	16 45 52	12 27 13	11♑12 39	17 09 36	4 04.1	3 12.9	2 29.6	17 45.2	11 14.4	2 03.2	24 26.8	12 24.7	29 17.1	2 10.8	4 05.9	5 20.5
4 Th	16 49 48	13 24 41	23 07 28	29 06 37	4 00.9	3 04.7	4 05.7	18 55.9	11 58.7	2 27.8	24 38.3	12 29.6	29 19.9	2 14.2	4 07.0	5 19.8
5 F	16 53 45	14 22 08	5♒07 27	11♒10 25	3 57.7	2 59.3	5 38.9	20 06.5	12 43.0	2 52.4	24 49.9	12 34.4	29 22.7	2 17.7	4 08.0	5 19.0
6 Sa	16 57 42	15 19 34	17 15 59	23 24 43	3 54.5	2 56.5	7 09.1	21 17.0	13 27.2	3 16.9	25 01.5	12 39.1	29 25.5	2 21.1	4 09.0	5 18.2
7 Su	17 01 38	16 16 59	29 37 09	5♓53 51	3 51.4	2D 55.6	8 36.4	22 27.5	14 11.4	3 41.5	25 13.2	12 43.8	29 28.2	2 24.6	4 10.0	5 17.5
8 M	17 05 35	17 14 24	12♓15 24	18 42 22	3 48.2	2R 55.7	10 00.7	23 37.9	14 55.5	4 06.1	25 25.0	12 48.4	29 30.9	2 28.0	4 11.0	5 16.6
9 Tu	17 09 31	18 11 48	25 15 17	1♈54 39	3 45.0	2 55.6	11 22.1	24 48.1	15 39.5	4 30.6	25 36.8	12 52.9	29 33.5	2 31.4	4 11.9	5 15.8
10 W	17 13 28	19 09 11	8♈40 50	15 34 07	3 41.8	2 54.2	12 40.3	25 58.4	16 23.5	4 55.2	25 48.7	12 57.3	29 36.1	2 34.8	4 12.8	5 14.9
11 Th	17 17 24	20 06 34	22 34 40	29 42 27	3 38.6	2 50.8	13 55.5	27 08.5	17 07.5	5 19.7	26 00.6	13 01.7	29 38.7	2 38.2	4 13.7	5 14.1
12 F	17 21 21	21 03 57	6♉57 12	14♉18 29	3 35.5	2 45.0	15 07.6	28 18.6	17 51.4	5 44.2	26 12.6	13 06.0	29 41.3	2 41.6	4 14.5	5 13.2
13 Sa	17 25 17	22 01 19	21 45 35	29 17 36	3 32.3	2 36.9	16 16.5	29 28.5	18 35.2	6 08.7	26 24.6	13 10.2	29 43.8	2 44.9	4 15.3	5 12.2
14 Su	17 29 14	22 58 41	6♊53 25	14♊31 44	3 29.1	2 27.4	17 22.1	0♌38.4	19 19.0	6 33.2	26 36.8	13 14.3	29 46.2	2 48.3	4 16.1	5 11.3
15 M	17 33 11	23 56 02	22 11 09	29 50 13	3 25.9	2 17.6	18 24.4	1 48.3	20 02.7	6 57.7	26 48.9	13 18.3	29 48.7	2 51.6	4 16.8	5 10.3
16 Tu	17 37 07	24 53 23	7♋27 30	15♋01 41	3 22.8	2 08.7	19 23.2	2 58.0	20 46.3	7 22.2	27 01.1	13 22.3	29 51.1	2 54.9	4 17.6	5 09.4
17 W	17 41 04	25 50 42	22 31 34	29 56 10	3 19.6	2 01.7	20 18.6	4 07.6	21 29.9	7 46.7	27 13.4	13 26.2	29 53.4	2 58.2	4 18.2	5 08.4
18 Th	17 45 00	26 48 01	7♌14 40	14♌26 33	3 16.4	1 57.1	21 10.4	5 17.2	22 13.5	8 11.1	27 25.7	13 30.0	29 55.7	3 01.5	4 18.9	5 07.3
19 F	17 48 57	27 45 20	21 31 27	28 29 14	3 13.2	1D 54.9	21 58.5	6 26.6	22 56.9	8 35.5	27 38.1	13 33.7	29 58.0	3 04.8	4 19.5	5 06.3
20 Sa	17 52 53	28 42 37	5♍19 58	12♍03 51	3 10.1	1 54.6	22 42.9	7 36.0	23 40.3	8 59.9	27 50.5	13 37.3	0♉00.2	3 08.1	4 20.1	5 05.2
21 Su	17 56 50	29 39 54	18 41 11	25 12 24	3 06.9	1R 55.1	23 23.3	8 45.2	24 23.6	9 24.3	28 03.0	13 40.8	0 02.4	3 11.3	4 20.6	5 04.2
22 M	18 00 47	0♋37 09	1♎37 58	7♎58 25	3 03.7	1 55.4	23 59.7	9 54.3	25 06.9	9 48.7	28 15.5	13 44.3	0 04.6	3 14.5	4 21.2	5 03.1
23 Tu	18 04 43	1 34 24	14 14 17	20 26 07	3 00.5	1 54.6	24 32.1	11 03.4	25 50.1	10 13.0	28 28.0	13 47.6	0 06.7	3 17.7	4 21.7	5 02.0
24 W	18 08 40	2 31 39	26 34 26	2♏39 47	2 57.3	1 51.8	25 00.2	12 12.3	26 33.3	10 37.3	28 40.6	13 50.9	0 08.7	3 20.9	4 22.1	5 00.8
25 Th	18 12 36	3 28 53	8♏42 38	14 43 26	2 54.2	1 46.7	25 23.9	13 21.1	27 16.3	11 01.6	28 53.2	13 54.1	0 10.8	3 24.0	4 22.5	4 59.7
26 F	18 16 33	4 26 06	20 42 37	26 40 33	2 51.0	1 39.4	25 43.3	14 29.8	27 59.3	11 25.9	29 05.9	13 57.1	0 12.7	3 27.1	4 22.9	4 58.6
27 Sa	18 20 29	5 23 19	2♐37 34	8♐34 00	2 47.8	1 30.4	25 58.2	15 38.4	28 42.3	11 50.1	29 18.5	14 00.1	0 14.7	3 30.3	4 23.3	4 57.4
28 Su	18 24 26	6 20 32	14 30 07	20 26 09	2 44.6	1 20.3	26 08.5	16 46.9	29 25.2	12 14.4	29 31.3	14 03.0	0 16.6	3 33.3	4 23.6	4 56.2
29 M	18 28 22	7 17 44	26 22 19	2♑18 51	2 41.5	1 10.0	26R 14.2	17 55.2	0♊08.0	12 38.6	29 44.1	14 05.9	0 18.4	3 36.4	4 23.9	4 55.0
30 Tu	18 32 19	8♋14 56	8♑15 55	14 13 44	2♓38.3	1♓00.6	26♋15.3	19♌03.4	0♊50.8	13♊02.7	29♋56.9	14♈08.6	0♉20.2	3♊39.4	4♈24.2	4♒53.8

1st of Month

Julian Day # 2461192.5
Obliquity 23°26'37"
SVP 4♓53'20"
GC 27♐12.5
Eris 25♈44.5

Day	⚴	Day	⚵	Day	⚶
1	10♈33.1	1	10♒55.8	1	7♈31.8
6	11 52.7	6	11 00.1R	6	9 27.9
11	13 09.4	11	10 55.4R	11	11 20.3
16	14 22.9	16	10 41.4R	16	13 08.9
21	15 33.0	21	10 18.0R	21	14 53.2
26	16 39.3	26	9 45.4R	26	16 33.0

DECLINATION and LATITUDE

Day	☉ Decl	☽ Decl	☽ Lat	☽ 12h Decl	☿ Decl	☿ Lat	♀ Decl	♀ Lat	♂ Decl	♂ Lat	⚳ Decl	⚳ Lat	♃ Decl	♃ Lat	♄ Decl	♄ Lat
1 M	22N02	27S40	4S51	27S58	25N35	2N09	24N28	1N55	14N09	0S38	17N25	3S03	21N42	0N25	2N45	2S16
2 Tu	22 10	27 56	4 30	27 35	25 36	2 10	24 20	1 57	14 23	0 37	17 32	3 01	21 40	0 25	2 47	2 16
3 W	22 17	26 54	3 57	25 55	25 35	2 10	24 12	1 57	14 37	0 36	17 38	2 60	21 38	0 25	2 49	2 16
4 Th	22 24	24 38	3 14	23 05	25 31	2 09	24 03	1 58	14 52	0 36	17 44	2 58	21 36	0 25	2 51	2 16
5 F	22 31	21 16	2 21	19 13	25 26	2 07	23 54	1 59	15 06	0 35	17 51	2 57	21 34	0 25	2 52	2 17
6 Sa	22 38	16 58	1 22	14 30	25 19	2 05	23 44	1 60	15 20	0 35	17 57	2 55	21 32	0 25	2 54	2 17
7 Su	22 44	11 53	0 18	9 06	25 11	2 01	23 33	2 00	15 33	0 34	18 03	2 54	21 30	0 25	2 56	2 17
8 M	22 50	6 12	0N49	3 12	25 01	1 57	23 21	2 01	15 47	0 33	18 09	2 52	21 28	0 25	2 57	2 17
9 Tu	22 55	0 07	1 55	3N01	24 49	1 53	23 09	2 01	16 00	0 33	18 15	2 51	21 26	0 25	2 59	2 17
10 W	22 60	6N10	2 57	9 17	24 37	1 47	22 57	2 02	16 14	0 32	18 21	2 49	21 24	0 25	3 00	2 18
11 Th	23 04	12 22	3 51	15 19	24 23	1 41	22 43	2 02	16 27	0 31	18 26	2 48	21 21	0 25	3 02	2 18
12 F	23 08	18 07	4 32	20 42	24 08	1 34	22 29	2 02	16 40	0 31	18 32	2 46	21 19	0 25	3 03	2 18
13 Sa	23 12	22 59	4 57	24 54	23 52	1 26	22 15	2 02	16 52	0 30	18 38	2 45	21 17	0 25	3 04	2 18
14 Su	23 15	26 24	5 01	27 26	23 36	1 18	21 60	2 02	17 05	0 30	18 43	2 43	21 15	0 25	3 06	2 19
15 M	23 18	27 56	4 44	27 54	23 18	1 09	21 44	2 02	17 17	0 29	18 49	2 42	21 12	0 25	3 07	2 19
16 Tu	23 20	27 20	4 07	26 16	23 00	0 59	21 28	2 02	17 30	0 28	18 54	2 40	21 10	0 25	3 08	2 19
17 W	23 22	24 44	3 13	22 47	22 42	0 48	21 11	2 02	17 42	0 28	18 60	2 39	21 08	0 26	3 10	2 19
18 Th	23 24	20 31	2 07	17 57	22 23	0 37	20 54	2 01	17 53	0 27	19 05	2 37	21 05	0 26	3 11	2 20
19 F	23 25	15 12	0 55	12 17	22 04	0 26	20 36	2 01	18 05	0 26	19 10	2 36	21 03	0 26	3 12	2 20
20 Sa	23 26	9 16	0S18	6 12	21 45	0 13	20 18	2 00	18 17	0 26	19 16	2 34	21 01	0 26	3 13	2 20
21 Su	23 26	3 07	1 28	0 03	21 25	0 00	19 59	1 59	18 28	0 25	19 21	2 33	20 58	0 26	3 15	2 20
22 M	23 26	2S58	2 32	5S55	21 06	0S13	19 40	1 59	18 39	0 24	19 26	2 31	20 56	0 26	3 16	2 21
23 Tu	23 26	8 46	3 26	11 31	20 46	0 27	19 20	1 58	18 50	0 24	19 31	2 30	20 53	0 26	3 17	2 21
24 W	23 25	14 07	4 09	16 34	20 27	0 41	19 00	1 57	19 01	0 23	19 36	2 28	20 51	0 26	3 18	2 21
25 Th	23 24	18 50	4 40	20 53	20 08	0 56	18 39	1 56	19 11	0 22	19 41	2 27	20 48	0 26	3 19	2 21
26 F	23 22	22 44	4 59	24 20	19 50	1 11	18 18	1 54	19 22	0 22	19 45	2 25	20 46	0 26	3 20	2 22
27 Sa	23 20	25 39	5 04	26 42	19 32	1 27	17 57	1 53	19 32	0 21	19 50	2 24	20 43	0 26	3 21	2 22
28 Su	23 17	27 27	4 57	27 53	19 14	1 43	17 35	1 52	19 42	0 20	19 55	2 22	20 41	0 26	3 21	2 22
29 M	23 14	27 59	4 36	27 46	18 58	1 58	17 12	1 50	19 52	0 19	19 59	2 20	20 38	0 26	3 22	2 22
30 Tu	23N11	27S14	4S03	26S22	18N42	2S14	16N50	1N48	20N01	0S19	20N04	2S19	20N35	0N26	3N23	2S23

Day	⚷ Decl	⚷ Lat	♅ Decl	♅ Lat	♆ Decl	♆ Lat	♇ Decl	♇ Lat
1	11N28	0N18	20N25	0S10	0N23	1S20	22S57	4S09
6	11 33	0 18	20 28	0 10	0 25	1 21	22 58	4 09
11	11 37	0 18	20 32	0 09	0 27	1 21	23 00	4 10
16	11 41	0 17	20 35	0 09	0 28	1 21	23 02	4 11
21	11 45	0 17	20 38	0 09	0 29	1 21	23 04	4 12
26	11 48	0 17	20 41	0 09	0 29	1 22	23 06	4 13

Day	⚴ Decl	⚴ Lat	⚵ Decl	⚵ Lat	⚶ Decl	⚶ Lat	Eris Decl	Eris Lat
1	3N45	0S27	4S01	13N58	2S08	5S34	0N15	10S24
6	3 52	0 54	3 47	14 12	1 33	5 46	0 16	10 24
11	3 56	1 22	3 36	14 25	1 01	5 58	0 16	10 24
16	3 57	1 51	3 28	14 37	0 30	6 11	0 17	10 24
21	3 56	2 22	3 23	14 47	0 02	6 24	0 17	10 25
26	3 51	2 55	3 23	14 56	0N23	6 37	0 17	10 25

Moon Phenomena

Max/0 Decl

dy	hr mn	
1	16:49	27S59
9	0:28	0 N
15	5:19	27N59
21	12:13	0 S
28	21:59	27S59

Max/0 Lat

dy	hr mn	
7	6:20	0 N
13	17:05	5N02
19	17:58	0 S
26	21:46	5S04

Perigee/Apogee

dy	hr m		kilometers
1	4:34	a	406366
14	23:21	p	357197
28	7:12	a	406265

PH	dy	hr mn	
☾	8	10:02	17♓38
●	15	2:55	24♊03
☽	21	21:57	0♎32
○	29	23:58	8♑15

Void of Course Moon

Last Aspect				☽ Ingress		
31	13:22	♄	△	♑	2	1:20
4	3:05	♃	☍	♒	4	13:47
5	19:52	☉	△	♓	7	0:44
9	0:40	♃	△	♈	9	8:35
11	8:23	♀	□	♉	11	12:29
13	7:31	♃	⚹	♊	13	13:07
15	2:55	☉	☌	♋	15	12:15
17	7:42	♃	☌	♌	17	12:06
19	11:32	☉	⚹	♍	19	14:38
21	17:34	♃	⚹	♎	21	20:56
24	4:12	♃	□	♏	24	6:44
26	17:11	♃	△	♐	26	18:42
28	5:06	♀	△	♑	29	7:20

DAILY ASPECTARIAN

1 M
☿⚹⚷ 0:34
☽∠♇ 5:51
☿ ♋ 11:57
☽⚻♃ 13:33
☽⚼♂ 15:43
☽△⚷ 23:48

2 Tu
♀∠⚳ 2:08
☽☍☿ 3:33
☽⚻⚳ 4:50
☽⚻♅ 5:40
☽□♆ 9:36
♀∠♅ 11:43
☽⚺♇ 12:09
☿⚺⚳ 15:21
☿⚺♅ 19:12
☉⚹♄ 22:50

3 W
☽△♂ 0:04
☽□♄ 2:26
☉⚻☽ 2:44
⚳☌♅ 8:38
☽⚼♅ 12:06
☽⚼⚳ 12:12
☽☍♀ 14:39
☽#☿ 15:47

4 Th
☿□♆ 0:19
☽☍♃ 3:05
☽#♀ 5:01
☉⚼☽ 11:31
☽□⚷ 12:30
☽∥♇ 12:51
☉#☽ 16:08
☽△♅ 18:20
♂⚺♄ 18:46
☿⚻♇ 18:52
☽△⚳ 19:21
☽⚹♆ 22:02
☽#♃ 22:07

5 F
☉∠⚷ 0:15
☽☌♇ 0:23
☽⚻☿ 1:12
☽#♅ 4:53
☽⚹♄ 14:52
☽□♂ 16:01
☽#⚳ 19:01
☉△☽ 19:52
⚵ R 21:57

6 Sa
☽∠♆ 3:42
☽#♂ 7:43
☽⚻♀ 8:41
☽⚼☿ 10:50
☽⚻♃ 15:22
☽∠♄ 20:20
☽⚹⚷ 23:43

7 Su
☽#⚷ 1:24
☽□♅ 5:23
☊ D 6:21
☽□⚳ 8:04
☽⚺♆ 8:43
☽⚺♇ 10:50
☽⚼♀ 16:29
☽△☿ 19:16
☽⚼♃ 20:29

8 M
☽⚺♄ 1:02
☽∠⚷ 4:14
⚳⚹♆ 5:00
☽⚹♂ 5:17
☉□☽ 10:02
☊ R 10:11
☽#♄ 12:55
☽∠♇ 14:53
☽#♆ 22:47
☽△♀ 23:06

9 Tu
☽△♃ 0:40
☽∥♆ 2:07
☽⚺⚷ 7:48
☽∠♂ 10:19
☽∥♄ 11:55
☽⚹♅ 13:09
☽☌♆ 16:06
☽⚹⚳ 17:09
☽⚹♇ 17:57
♀#♇ 18:17
☉∥♀ 19:49
♀☌♃ 20:00

10 W
☉#♇ 0:34
☿□♄ 5:40
☽☌♄ 7:31
☽□☿ 7:41
☽⚺♂ 14:10
☽∠♅ 15:32
⚳△♇ 18:40
☉⚹☽ 19:29
☽∠⚳ 20:03
☽∥⚷ 21:04

11 Th
☉⚼♇ 3:05
☽□♃ 5:53
☽□♀ 8:23
☽☌⚷ 11:56
☽⚺♅ 16:56
☽∥♂ 17:23
☽⚺♆ 19:32
☽□♇ 21:09
☽⚺⚳ 21:56
☉∠☽ 22:26

12 F
☽∥⚳ 1:54
☽⚺♄ 10:05
☽∥♅ 11:17
☽⚹☿ 14:27
☽∥♃ 15:01
☽☌♂ 18:39
☽∠♆ 19:59
☽∥♀ 20:12

13 Sa
☽#♇ 0:14
☉⚺☽ 0:27
☉∥☽ 1:18
☽∥☿ 4:57
♀□⚷ 5:25
☽⚹♃ 7:31
☽∠♄ 10:16
♀ ♌ 10:48
☽⚺⚷ 12:43
☽⚹♀ 13:19
☽∠☿ 16:19
☽☌♅ 17:32
☽⚹♆ 19:52
☽△♇ 21:19
♂∠♆ 22:24
☽☌⚳ 23:27

14 Su
☽∠♃ 7:31
☽⚹♄ 10:01
☿∠♅ 10:30
☽∠⚷ 12:25
☽∠♀ 14:52
☽⚺☿ 17:39
☽⚺♂ 20:29
☽⚼♇ 20:51

15 M
☉∥☿ 0:28
☉☌☽ 2:55
☽⚺♃ 7:21
☽⚹⚷ 12:00
☽⚺♀ 16:20
☽⚺♅ 16:49
☽□♆ 19:00
☽⚻♇ 20:22
☽∠♂ 21:12
☿#♇ 21:44
♀⚹♅ 22:54
☽⚺⚳ 23:51

16 Tu
☽□♄ 9:24
☽∠♅ 16:40
☽☌☿ 20:13
☽⚹♂ 22:16

17 W
☽∠⚳ 0:25
♀△♆ 3:42
☉⚺☽ 5:44
♀∥♃ 5:57
☽☌♃ 7:42
☉∥☽ 8:34
☽#♇ 10:32
☽□⚷ 11:58
☽∥☿ 13:30
☽⚹♅ 17:02
☽△♆ 19:10
☽☌♀ 20:29
☽☍♇ 20:30
♀☍♇ 20:39
☽∥♃ 21:04
☽∥♀ 21:54
☽∥♅ 23:31

18 Th
☽⚹⚳ 1:36
☽∥⚳ 6:44
☉∠☽ 8:07
☽△♄ 10:28
☽∥♂ 11:53
☉⚺♃ 20:08
☽⚼♆ 20:15
♀∥♅ 23:13

19 F
☽⚺☿ 0:49
☽□♂ 2:34
☽⚺♃ 10:41
☉⚹☽ 11:32
☽⚼♄ 12:11
☽∥⚷ 14:14
☽△⚷ 14:37
☊ D 17:59
☽□♅ 20:07
⚷ ♉ 21:22
☽⚻♆ 22:14
☽⚻♇ 23:34

20 Sa
☽⚺♀ 4:24
☽∠☿ 4:27
☽□⚳ 6:43
☽∠♃ 13:37
☽⚻♄ 14:52
☽⚼⚷ 17:21
☽∥♄ 23:32

21 Su
☽⚼♇ 2:32
☉ ♋ 8:26
☽⚹☿ 9:04
☉⚹⚷ 9:49
☽∠♀ 10:13
☽∥♆ 10:19
☽△♂ 11:07
☽#♆ 14:07
☽⚹♃ 17:34
♀⚹⚳ 20:57
☽⚻⚷ 21:04
☊ R 21:47
☉□☽ 21:57

22 M
☽#♄ 1:11
☽△♅ 3:03
☽☍♆ 5:08
☽△♇ 6:26
☿∥♃ 13:51
♀∥⚳ 13:54
☽△⚳ 16:01
☽⚼♂ 17:04
☽⚹♀ 17:16
☽☍♄ 23:08

23 Tu
☽⚼♅ 7:53
☿∥♅ 8:01
☽#⚷ 13:11
☽□☿ 20:48
☽⚼⚳ 22:04
♀∥♂ 23:29
☽⚻♂ 23:58

24 W
☽□♃ 4:12
☽☍⚷ 7:03
☉△☽ 12:44
☽⚻♅ 13:25
☽⚻♆ 15:23
☽□♇ 16:38
☉⚺♅ 21:50
☽#♀ 23:08

25 Th
☽#♂ 2:06
☽⚻⚳ 4:47
☽#⚳ 4:53
☽#☿ 6:57
☽□♀ 10:14
☽⚻♄ 10:24
☽#♅ 10:45
☽#♃ 11:22
♀△♄ 12:03
☉⚼☽ 21:13
☽⚼♆ 21:20
☉□♆ 22:39

26 F
☽∥♇ 2:40
☉#☽ 4:30
☿∥⚳ 4:32
☽△☿ 10:19
☉⚻♇ 13:20
☽☍♂ 15:35
☽⚼♄ 16:39
☽△♃ 17:11
☽⚻⚷ 19:11
☿∥♂ 23:54

27 Sa
☽☍♅ 1:47
☽△♆ 3:34
☽⚹♇ 4:42
☉⚻☽ 6:04
♃∥♅ 9:01
♂∠♄ 10:42
☽⚼☿ 17:07
☽☍⚳ 19:16
☽△♄ 23:05

28 Su
☽⚼♃ 0:02
☽⚼⚷ 1:34
♂⚹♃ 4:52
☽△♀ 5:06
☽∠♇ 10:58
♂ ♊ 19:30
☽⚻☿ 23:44

29 M
♂⚺⚷ 6:06
☽⚻♃ 6:55
☽△⚷ 7:58
☽⚻♂ 8:05
☽⚼♀ 14:37
☽⚻♅ 14:40
☽□♆ 16:13
☽⚺♇ 17:13
☿ R 17:37
☉☍☽ 23:58

30 Tu
♃ ♌ 5:53
♀⚼♆ 7:20
☽⚻⚳ 9:57
☽□♄ 11:52
♂∥⚳ 12:42
☽⚼♂ 16:13
☉#♇ 16:18
☽⚼♅ 20:59
☽⚻♀ 23:58

July 2026

LONGITUDE

Day	Sid.Time	☉	☽	☽ 12 hour	Mean☊	True☊	☿	♀	♂	⚳	♃	♄	⚷	♅	♆	♇
	h m s	° ' "	° ' "	° ' "	° '	° '	° '	° '	° '	° '	° '	° '	° '	° '	° '	° '
1 W	18 36 16	9♋12 08	20♑12 29	26♑12 22	2♓35.1	0♓52.7	26♋11.8	20♌11.5	1♊33.5	13♊26.9	0♌09.7	14♈11.2	0♉22.0	3♊42.5	4♈24.4	4♒52.6
2 Th	18 40 12	10 09 19	2♒13 39	8♒16 33	2 31.9	0R46.8	26R03.7	21 19.5	2 16.1	13 51.0	0 22.6	14 13.7	0 23.7	3 45.4	4 24.6	4R51.3
3 F	18 44 09	11 06 31	14 21 21	20 28 22	2 28.8	0 43.3	25 51.1	22 27.3	2 58.7	14 15.1	0 35.5	14 16.2	0 25.3	3 48.4	4 24.8	4 50.1
4 Sa	18 48 05	12 03 43	26 37 56	2♓50 24	2 25.6	0D41.8	25 34.3	23 35.0	3 41.2	14 39.2	0 48.4	14 18.5	0 27.0	3 51.3	4 24.9	4 48.8
5 Su	18 52 02	13 00 54	9♓06 12	15 25 43	2 22.4	0 42.0	25 13.4	24 42.6	4 23.6	15 03.2	1 01.3	14 20.8	0 28.5	3 54.2	4 25.0	4 47.5
6 M	18 55 58	13 58 06	21 49 25	28 17 41	2 19.2	0 43.2	24 48.7	25 50.1	5 06.0	15 27.2	1 14.3	14 22.9	0 30.0	3 57.1	4 25.0	4 46.3
7 Tu	18 59 55	14 55 19	4♈50 58	11♈29 39	2 16.1	0R44.3	24 20.4	26 57.4	5 48.3	15 51.2	1 27.3	14 25.0	0 31.5	4 00.0	4R25.1	4 45.0
8 W	19 03 51	15 52 31	18 14 04	25 04 29	2 12.9	0 44.7	23 49.1	28 04.5	6 30.6	16 15.2	1 40.4	14 26.9	0 32.9	4 02.8	4 25.1	4 43.7
9 Th	19 07 48	16 49 44	2♉01 03	9♉03 50	2 09.7	0 43.6	23 15.2	29 11.5	7 12.8	16 39.1	1 53.4	14 28.8	0 34.3	4 05.6	4 25.0	4 42.3
10 F	19 11 45	17 46 58	16 12 42	23 27 24	2 06.5	0 40.9	22 39.2	0♍18.4	7 54.9	17 03.0	2 06.5	14 30.5	0 35.6	4 08.4	4 25.0	4 41.0
11 Sa	19 15 41	18 44 12	0♊47 26	8♊12 11	2 03.3	0 36.5	22 01.6	1 25.1	8 37.0	17 26.9	2 19.6	14 32.2	0 36.9	4 11.1	4 24.9	4 39.7
12 Su	19 19 38	19 41 26	15 40 49	23 12 19	2 00.2	0 31.0	21 23.2	2 31.7	9 19.0	17 50.7	2 32.7	14 33.8	0 38.1	4 13.8	4 24.8	4 38.3
13 M	19 23 34	20 38 41	0♋45 35	8♋19 24	1 57.0	0 25.2	20 44.5	3 38.1	10 00.9	18 14.5	2 45.9	14 35.2	0 39.3	4 16.5	4 24.6	4 37.0
14 Tu	19 27 31	21 35 56	15 52 32	23 23 44	1 53.8	0 19.8	20 06.2	4 44.4	10 42.8	18 38.2	2 59.0	14 36.6	0 40.4	4 19.1	4 24.4	4 35.6
15 W	19 31 27	22 33 12	0♌51 51	8♌15 52	1 50.7	0 15.7	19 28.9	5 50.5	11 24.6	19 02.0	3 12.2	14 37.9	0 41.5	4 21.7	4 24.2	4 34.3
16 Th	19 35 24	23 30 27	15 34 51	22 48 07	1 47.5	0 13.2	18 53.4	6 56.4	12 06.3	19 25.6	3 25.4	14 39.0	0 42.5	4 24.3	4 23.9	4 32.9
17 F	19 39 20	24 27 43	29 55 08	6♍55 32	1 44.3	0D12.4	18 20.3	8 02.2	12 47.9	19 49.3	3 38.6	14 40.1	0 43.5	4 26.9	4 23.6	4 31.5
18 Sa	19 43 17	25 24 59	13♍49 12	20 36 05	1 41.1	0 13.0	17 50.1	9 07.8	13 29.5	20 12.8	3 51.9	14 41.0	0 44.4	4 29.4	4 23.3	4 30.1
19 Su	19 47 14	26 22 15	27 16 22	3♎50 18	1 37.9	0 14.4	17 23.5	10 13.1	14 11.0	20 36.4	4 05.1	14 41.9	0 45.3	4 31.8	4 22.9	4 28.8
20 M	19 51 10	27 19 32	10♎18 14	16 40 38	1 34.8	0 15.9	17 00.9	11 18.3	14 52.5	20 59.9	4 18.3	14 42.6	0 46.1	4 34.3	4 22.6	4 27.4
21 Tu	19 55 07	28 16 48	22 57 57	29 10 45	1 31.6	0R16.8	16 42.8	12 23.3	15 33.8	21 23.3	4 31.6	14 43.3	0 46.9	4 36.7	4 22.1	4 26.0
22 W	19 59 03	29 14 05	5♏19 34	11♏24 58	1 28.4	0 16.8	16 29.6	13 28.1	16 15.1	21 46.8	4 44.9	14 43.8	0 47.6	4 39.0	4 21.7	4 24.6
23 Th	20 03 00	0♌11 22	17 27 31	23 27 44	1 25.2	0 15.4	16D21.6	14 32.7	16 56.3	22 10.1	4 58.1	14 44.2	0 48.2	4 41.4	4 21.2	4 23.2
24 F	20 06 56	1 08 40	29 26 09	5♐23 17	1 22.1	0 12.8	16 19.0	15 37.1	17 37.5	22 33.4	5 11.4	14 44.6	0 48.9	4 43.7	4 20.7	4 21.8
25 Sa	20 10 53	2 05 57	11♐19 36	17 15 31	1 18.9	0 09.1	16 22.1	16 41.2	18 18.5	22 56.7	5 24.7	14 44.8	0 49.4	4 45.9	4 20.2	4 20.4
26 Su	20 14 49	3 03 16	23 11 27	29 07 46	1 15.7	0 04.8	16 31.1	17 45.1	18 59.5	23 19.9	5 38.0	14R45.0	0 49.9	4 48.1	4 19.6	4 19.0
27 M	20 18 46	4 00 34	5♑04 49	11♑02 53	1 12.5	0 00.3	16 46.0	18 48.8	19 40.5	23 43.1	5 51.3	14 45.0	0 50.4	4 50.3	4 19.0	4 17.6
28 Tu	20 22 43	4 57 54	17 02 14	23 03 08	1 09.4	29♒56.2	17 06.9	19 52.3	20 21.3	24 06.2	6 04.6	14 44.9	0 50.7	4 52.4	4 18.4	4 16.2
29 W	20 26 39	5 55 14	29 05 48	5♒10 25	1 06.2	29 52.9	17 33.9	20 55.5	21 02.1	24 29.3	6 17.8	14 44.8	0 51.1	4 54.5	4 17.7	4 14.7
30 Th	20 30 36	6 52 34	11♒17 12	17 26 17	1 03.0	29 50.6	18 06.9	21 58.4	21 42.9	24 52.3	6 31.1	14 44.5	0 51.4	4 56.6	4 17.0	4 13.3
31 F	20 34 32	7♌49 56	23 37 54	29 52 10	0♓59.8	29♒49.5	18♋46.1	23♍01.1	22♊23.5	25♊15.3	6♌44.4	14♈44.1	0♉51.6	4♊58.6	4♈16.3	4♒11.9

1st of Month

Julian Day #
2461222.5
Obliquity
23°26'▯7"
SVP 4♓53'▯4"
GC 27♐12.6
Eris 25♈55.3

Day	⚴	⚵	⚶
1	17♈41.4	9♒04.0R	18♈07.9
6	18 39.0	8 14.3R	19 37.5
11	19 31.7	7 17.1R	21 01.5
16	20 18.9	6 13.6R	22 19.2
21	21 00.1	5 05.3R	23 30.0
26	21 34.9	3 54.1R	24 33.6
31	22 02.8	2 41.8R	25 29.3

DECLINATION and LATITUDE

Day	☉ Decl	☽ Decl	☽ Lat	☽ 12h Decl	☿ Decl	☿ Lat	♀ Decl	♀ Lat	♂ Decl	♂ Lat	⚳ Decl	⚳ Lat	♃ Decl	♃ Lat	♄ Decl	♄ Lat
1 W	23N07	25S13	3S20	23S46	18N27	2S30	16N26	1N47	20N11	0S18	20N08	2S17	20N33	0N26	3N24	2S23
2 Th	23 03	22 03	2 27	20 05	18 13	2 46	16 03	1 45	20 20	0 17	20 13	2 16	20 30	0 26	3 25	2 23
3 F	22 58	17 54	1 27	15 32	18 00	3 01	15 39	1 43	20 29	0 17	20 17	2 14	20 27	0 26	3 25	2 23
4 Sa	22 53	12 59	0 22	10 17	17 48	3 16	15 15	1 41	20 38	0 16	20 21	2 13	20 24	0 27	3 26	2 24
5 Su	22 48	7 27	0N45	4 32	17 38	3 31	14 50	1 39	20 46	0 15	20 26	2 11	20 22	0 27	3 27	2 24
6 M	22 42	1 32	1 52	1N31	17 29	3 45	14 25	1 36	20 55	0 14	20 30	2 10	20 19	0 27	3 27	2 24
7 Tu	22 36	4N35	2 54	7 39	17 21	3 58	13 60	1 34	21 03	0 14	20 34	2 08	20 16	0 27	3 28	2 25
8 W	22 30	10 40	3 48	13 36	17 14	4 10	13 34	1 32	21 11	0 13	20 38	2 07	20 13	0 27	3 28	2 25
9 Th	22 23	16 25	4 32	19 03	17 09	4 20	13 09	1 29	21 19	0 12	20 42	2 05	20 10	0 27	3 29	2 25
10 F	22 15	21 28	4 60	23 35	17 06	4 30	12 42	1 26	21 26	0 11	20 46	2 04	20 08	0 27	3 29	2 25
11 Sa	22 08	25 21	5 09	26 43	17 04	4 38	12 16	1 23	21 34	0 11	20 49	2 02	20 05	0 27	3 29	2 26
12 Su	21 60	27 37	4 59	28 01	17 03	4 45	11 49	1 20	21 41	0 10	20 53	2 00	20 02	0 27	3 30	2 26
13 M	21 51	27 53	4 27	27 15	17 03	4 50	11 23	1 17	21 48	0 09	20 57	1 59	19 59	0 27	3 30	2 26
14 Tu	21 42	26 05	3 37	24 28	17 06	4 54	10 55	1 14	21 55	0 08	21 00	1 57	19 56	0 27	3 30	2 27
15 W	21 33	22 27	2 33	20 04	17 09	4 55	10 28	1 11	22 01	0 08	21 04	1 56	19 53	0 27	3 31	2 27
16 Th	21 24	17 25	1 19	14 33	17 14	4 56	10 01	1 08	22 08	0 07	21 07	1 54	19 50	0 27	3 31	2 27
17 F	21 14	11 31	0 02	8 24	17 19	4 54	9 33	1 04	22 14	0 06	21 11	1 52	19 47	0 27	3 31	2 27
18 Sa	21 03	5 14	1S14	2 03	17 26	4 51	9 05	1 01	22 20	0 05	21 14	1 51	19 44	0 27	3 31	2 28
19 Su	20 53	1S05	2 22	4S10	17 34	4 46	8 37	0 57	22 25	0 05	21 17	1 49	19 41	0 28	3 31	2 28
20 M	20 42	7 10	3 21	10 02	17 43	4 40	8 08	0 53	22 31	0 04	21 21	1 48	19 38	0 28	3 31	2 28
21 Tu	20 30	12 47	4 09	15 21	17 53	4 33	7 40	0 49	22 36	0 03	21 24	1 46	19 35	0 28	3 31	2 28
22 W	20 19	17 45	4 44	19 56	18 03	4 24	7 11	0 45	22 41	0 02	21 27	1 44	19 32	0 28	3 31	2 29
23 Th	20 07	21 55	5 05	23 38	18 14	4 14	6 43	0 41	22 46	0 02	21 30	1 43	19 28	0 28	3 31	2 29
24 F	19 54	25 07	5 13	26 18	18 26	4 03	6 14	0 37	22 51	0 01	21 33	1 41	19 25	0 28	3 31	2 29
25 Sa	19 41	27 12	5 07	27 47	18 37	3 51	5 45	0 32	22 55	0 00	21 36	1 39	19 22	0 28	3 31	2 30
26 Su	19 28	28 03	4 48	27 60	18 49	3 38	5 16	0 28	22 60	0N01	21 38	1 38	19 19	0 28	3 30	2 30
27 M	19 15	27 37	4 16	26 54	19 01	3 24	4 47	0 23	23 04	0 02	21 41	1 36	19 16	0 28	3 30	2 30
28 Tu	19 01	25 53	3 34	24 34	19 12	3 10	4 18	0 19	23 08	0 02	21 44	1 35	19 13	0 28	3 30	2 30
29 W	18 47	22 58	2 41	21 06	19 23	2 55	3 49	0 14	23 11	0 03	21 47	1 33	19 09	0 28	3 30	2 31
30 Th	18 33	18 60	1 40	16 41	19 34	2 40	3 19	0 09	23 15	0 04	21 49	1 31	19 06	0 28	3 29	2 31
31 F	18N19	14S11	0S34	11S31	19N44	2S25	2N50	0N04	23N18	0N05	21N52	1S29	19N03	0N29	3N29	2S31

Day	⚷ Decl	⚷ Lat	♅ Decl	♅ Lat	♆ Decl	♆ Lat	♇ Decl	♇ Lat
1	11N51	0N16	20N44	0S09	0N30	1S22	23S09	4S13
6	11 54	0 16	20 47	0 09	0 30	1 22	23 11	4 14
11	11 56	0 16	20 50	0 09	0 30	1 23	23 13	4 15
16	11 58	0 15	20 52	0 09	0 29	1 23	23 15	4 15
21	11 59	0 15	20 54	0 09	0 28	1 23	23 17	4 16
26	11 60	0 15	20 57	0 09	0 27	1 23	23 19	4 16
31	12N00	0N15	20N58	0S09	0N25	1S24	23S22	4S17

Day	⚴ Decl	⚴ Lat	⚵ Decl	⚵ Lat	⚶ Decl	⚶ Lat	Eris Decl	Eris Lat
1	3N44	3S29	3S27	15N03	0N46	6S52	0N17	10S25
6	3 32	4 05	3 35	15 07	1 06	7 06	0 17	10 26
11	3 16	4 43	3 47	15 08	1 22	7 22	0 17	10 26
16	2 57	5 23	4 04	15 06	1 36	7 38	0 17	10 27
21	2 33	6 06	4 25	14 60	1 46	7 54	0 17	10 27
26	2 04	6 51	4 50	14 50	1 53	8 11	0 16	10 27
31	1N30	7S38	5S19	14N36	1N57	8S29	0N16	10S28

Moon Phenomena

Max/0 Decl

dy	hr mn	
6	6:03	0 N
12	15:11	28N02
18	19:49	0 S
26	3:52	28S04

Max/0 Lat

dy	hr mn	
4	7:52	0 N
10	23:42	5N09
17	0:29	0 S
24	1:33	5S13
31	11:54	0 N

Perigee/Apogee

dy	hr m		kilometers
13	7:58	p	359116
25	16:47	a	405547

PH	dy	hr mn	
☾	7	19:30	15♈42
●	14	9:45	21♋59
☽	21	11:07	28♎43
○	29	14:37	6♒30

Void of Course Moon

Last Aspect			☽ Ingress		
1 11:52	☿	☍	♒	1	19:34
3 17:29	♀	☍	♓	4	6:31
6 5:22	☿	△	♈	6	15:08
8 18:43	♀	△	♉	8	20:32
10 10:14	☿	⚹	♊	10	22:43
11 22:13	♄	⚹	♋	12	22:48
14 9:45	☉	☌	♌	14	22:36
15 22:28	♄	△	♍	17	0:08
18 22:14	☉	⚹	♎	19	4:58
21 11:07	☉	□	♏	21	13:36
22 21:50	☿	△	♐	24	1:08
25 14:59	♂	☍	♑	26	13:45
28 6:12	♀	△	♒	29	1:47
30 21:28	♂	△	♓	31	12:15

DAILY ASPECTARIAN

1 W
☽☍☿ 11:52
☽∥♇ 16:31
☽⚼⚳ 17:03
☉⋕☽ 17:03
☽☍♃ 20:15
☽□⚷ 20:21

2 Th
☽△♂ 0:05
♃□⚷ 2:25
☽△♅ 3:03
☽⚹♆ 4:20
☽☌♇ 5:13
☽⋕♅ 8:06
☽⋕♃ 9:42
☽⋕♂ 10:12
☽⋕⚳ 11:05
☉⚻☽ 17:03
♂∥♃ 20:34
☽⋕☿ 23:29
☽△⚳ 23:47
☽⚹♄ 23:50

3 F
⚳⚹♄ 1:10
☽∠♆ 9:56
☽⋕♀ 12:26
☽☍♀ 17:29
☽⚻☿ 22:00

4 Sa
☉⚼☽ 0:54
☽⋕⚷ 4:57
☽∠♄ 5:12
♂☌♅ 6:09
☽⚹⚷ 7:24
☊D 7:52
☽⚻♃ 8:13
⚳∥♃ 10:48
☽□♅ 14:00
☽□♂ 14:27
☽⚺♆ 15:02
☽⚺♇ 15:46

5 Su
♂∥♅ 0:39
♂⚹♆ 0:45
☽⚼☿ 2:04
☉△☽ 8:02
☿⚺♀ 8:07
☽⚺♄ 9:59
☽□⚳ 11:40
☽∠⚷ 12:07
♂△♇ 13:08
☽⚼♃ 13:21
☽⋕♄ 16:22
☽∠♇ 20:10

6 M
⚳∠⚷ 2:59
☽⋕♆ 4:06
☽△☿ 5:22
☽∥♆ 8:00
☽⚻♀ 8:10
☉□♄ 10:48
☽⚺⚷ 16:05
☽△♃ 17:42
☽∥♄ 19:36
☽⚹♅ 22:27
☽☌♆ 23:13
☽⚹♇ 23:49

7 Tu
☽⚹♂ 1:50
♆R 10:56
☽⚼♀ 14:00
☽☌♄ 17:16
☉□☽ 19:30
☊R 19:38
☽⚹⚳ 20:23

8 W
☽∠♅ 1:26
☽∥⚷ 5:02
☽∠♂ 6:05
☽□☿ 9:26
☽∥♀ 11:02
☉⚺⚳ 16:21
☽△♀ 18:43
☽☌⚷ 21:31
☽∠⚳ 23:21
☽□♃ 23:47

9 Th
☽∥☿ 3:14
☽⚺♅ 3:34
☽⚺♆ 4:06
☽□♇ 4:35
♀⚼♄ 6:21
☽⚺♂ 9:20
☽∥♃ 17:15
♀ ♍ 17:23
☿∠♂ 19:12
☽∥⚳ 20:18
☽∥♅ 20:39
☽⚺♄ 21:09
☽∥♂ 23:52

10 F
☽⚺⚳ 1:26
☉⚹☽ 2:48
☉∥☽ 4:10
☽∠♆ 5:20
♀△⚷ 6:19
⚳∠♃ 7:47
☽⋕♇ 9:45
☽⚹☿ 10:14
☽∠♄ 21:57
☽⚺⚷ 23:43

11 Sa
☽□♀ 1:06
☽⚹♃ 2:32
⚳∥♅ 2:46
☉∠☽ 5:07
☽☌♅ 5:32
☽⚹♆ 5:53
☽△♇ 6:16
☽∠☿ 9:41
☉∠♅ 11:51
☽☌♂ 13:17
♀∥⚷ 17:51
☽⚹♄ 22:13
☽∠⚷ 23:56

12 Su
♀⚺♃ 0:28
☽∠♃ 3:01
☽☌⚳ 3:33
☽⚼♇ 6:19
☉⚺☽ 6:50
☽⚺☿ 8:44
☽⚹⚷ 23:50

13 M
☉☌☿ 1:27
☽⚺♃ 3:14
☽⚹♀ 4:55
☉∥♂ 5:01
☽⚺♅ 5:36
☽□♆ 5:47
☽⚻♇ 6:07
♀□♅ 14:28
☽⚺♂ 15:24
♀⚻♆ 16:46
♀⚻♇ 20:53
☽□♄ 21:59

14 Tu
☽⚺⚳ 4:31
☿∠♀ 5:01
☽∠♅ 5:30
☽☌☿ 6:28
☽∠♀ 6:39
☉☌☽ 9:45
☽∠♂ 16:29
☽⋕♇ 19:32
☽□⚷ 23:43

15 W
☽∥♂ 2:14
☽☌♃ 3:50
☿∠♅ 4:26
☉∥☽ 4:53
☽∠⚳ 5:16
☽⚹♅ 5:40
☽△♆ 5:43
☽☍♇ 5:59
☽∥⚳ 7:06
☽∥♅ 8:10
☽⚺♀ 8:42
☿⚺⚳ 10:50
☽∥♃ 13:02
☽⚹♂ 18:00
♅⚹♆ 20:33
☽△♄ 22:28

16 Th
☽∥☿ 0:49
☽⚺☿ 5:16
☽⚼♆ 6:19
☽⚹⚳ 6:33
⚳⚼♇ 6:59
☉⚺☽ 14:08
☽∥⚷ 22:17
☽⚼♄ 23:34

17 F
☊D 0:30
☽△⚷ 1:22
☉∥⚳ 5:05
☽∠☿ 5:37
☽⚺♃ 6:28
☽⚻♆ 7:38
☽□♅ 7:46
☽⚻♇ 7:51
☽∥♀ 8:15
☽☌♀ 15:07
☉∠☽ 17:37
☽□♂ 23:24

18 Sa
☽⚻♄ 1:31
☽⚼⚷ 3:23
♅△♇ 4:47
☽∥♄ 6:28
☽⚹☿ 6:51
☽∠♃ 9:03
☽⚼♇ 10:02
☽□⚳ 11:39
☽∥♆ 18:01
☽⋕♆ 21:38
☉∥♅ 22:03
☉⚹☽ 22:14

19 Su
☽⚻⚷ 6:21
☽⋕♄ 9:25
☽⚹♃ 12:40
☽☍♆ 13:00
☽△♇ 13:10
☽△♅ 13:19
♂⚹♄ 18:12

20 M
☽⚺♀ 2:03
☽⋕♀ 3:43
♃△♆ 7:24
☽☍♄ 8:17
☽△♂ 9:05
☽□☿ 12:20
♃☍♇ 14:47
☽⚼♅ 17:34
☽⋕⚷ 20:27
☽△⚳ 20:53

21 Tu
♂∠⚷ 7:43
☽∠♀ 9:21
☊R 10:58
☉□☽ 11:07
♃⚹♅ 11:12
☽☍⚷ 15:08
☽⚼♂ 15:34
☽⚻♆ 22:07
☽□♇ 22:12
☽⚻♅ 22:40
☽□♃ 22:51

22 W
☽⋕☿ 1:41
☽⚼⚳ 2:57
☿⚺♂ 6:48
☽⋕♃ 9:32
☉⋕☽ 13:30
☽⚹♀ 17:38
☽⋕♅ 17:47
☽⚻♄ 18:35
☉ ♌ 19:14
☽⋕⚳ 21:19
☽△☿ 21:50
☽⚻♂ 22:54

23 Th
☽⚼♆ 3:47
♀⚻♄ 4:20
☽⋕♂ 5:53
☽∥♇ 9:32
☽⚻⚳ 9:43
☉□⚷ 15:37
☿D 22:59

24 F
☽⚼♄ 0:37
☽⚻⚷ 2:47
☉△☽ 3:44
☽⚼☿ 3:47
♀⚼⚷ 4:26
☽△♆ 9:53
☽⚹♇ 9:55
☽☍♅ 10:42
☽△♃ 11:49
☿⚹♀ 16:14

25 Sa
♆⚹♇ 5:50
☽△♄ 6:55
☽⚼⚷ 9:06
☽⚻☿ 10:18
☽□♀ 11:55
☉⚼☽ 12:42
☽☍♂ 14:59
☽∠♇ 16:11
☽⚼♃ 18:44

26 Su
☽☍⚳ 0:18
♂⚼♇ 11:00
☽△⚷ 15:27
♄R 19:57
☉⚻☽ 21:39
☽⚺♇ 22:25
☉∥♃ 22:26
☽□♆ 22:28
☽⚻♅ 23:31

27 M
☽⚻♃ 1:35
☊R♒ 1:43
☉☍♇ 6:56
☉△♆ 7:38
♀⚼♇ 10:37
☉∥☿ 13:45
☽□♄ 19:25
☉⚹♅ 21:38

28 Tu
☽☍☿ 0:10
☿∥♃ 0:35
☽⚼♅ 5:41
☽△♀ 6:12
☽⚻♂ 7:01
☽⚻⚳ 14:33
☽∥♇ 21:18
☽⋕♂ 22:26
☉∠♀ 23:01

29 W
☽□⚷ 3:28
♀□♂ 7:11
☽⋕⚳ 7:43
☉∠♂ 9:59
☽☌♇ 10:09
☽⚹♆ 10:16
♀∠♃ 10:48
☽△♅ 11:31
☉☌♃ 12:19
☽⋕♅ 12:48
♂∠♃ 13:44
☽☍♃ 14:28
☽⚼♂ 14:30
☉☍☽ 14:37
☽⚼♀ 14:45
♀∥♄ 15:44
☽⋕☿ 20:59
☽⚼⚳ 21:08
☽⋕♃ 23:25

30 Th
☉⋕☽ 2:31
☽⚹♄ 6:45
☽⚻☿ 14:02
☽∠♆ 15:34
☽△♂ 21:28
☽⚻♀ 22:42

31 F
☽△⚳ 3:14
☽⋕⚷ 9:51
☽∠♄ 11:44
☊D 11:55
☽⚹⚷ 13:54
☽⚺♇ 20:14
☽⚺♆ 20:24
☽⚼☿ 20:41
☽□♅ 21:49

August 2026

LONGITUDE

Day	Sid.Time	☉	☽	☽ 12 hour	Mean ☊	True ☊	☿	♀	♂	⚳	♃	♄	⚷	♅	♆	♇
	h m s	° ' "	° ' "	° ' "	° '	° '	° '	° '	° '	° '	° '	° '	° '	° '	° '	° '
1 Sa	20 38 29	8♌47 18	6♓09 17	12♓29 26	0♓56.6	29♒49.5	19♋31.2	24♍03.5	23♊04.1	25♊38.2	6♌57.7	14♈43.6	0♉51.8	5♊00.6	4♈15.5	4♒10.5
2 Su	20 42 25	9 44 41	18 52 48	25 19 33	0 53.5	29 50.3	20 22.3	25 05.7	23 44.6	26 01.0	7 11.0	14R 43.0	0 51.9	5 02.5	4R 14.8	4R 09.1
3 M	20 46 22	10 42 05	1♈49 55	8♈24 04	0 50.3	29 51.6	21 19.2	26 07.5	24 25.0	26 23.8	7 24.2	14 42.4	0R 52.0	5 04.4	4 14.0	4 07.7
4 Tu	20 50 18	11 39 30	15 02 12	21 44 27	0 47.1	29 53.0	22 21.9	27 09.1	25 05.4	26 46.5	7 37.5	14 41.6	0 52.0	5 06.3	4 13.1	4 06.3
5 W	20 54 15	12 36 57	28 31 00	5♉21 56	0 43.9	29 54.0	23 30.2	28 10.4	25 45.7	27 09.2	7 50.8	14 40.7	0 52.0	5 08.1	4 12.3	4 05.0
6 Th	20 58 12	13 34 24	12♉17 17	19 17 03	0 40.8	29R 54.4	24 44.0	29 11.4	26 25.9	27 31.8	8 04.0	14 39.7	0 51.9	5 09.8	4 11.4	4 03.6
7 F	21 02 08	14 31 54	26 21 07	3♊29 16	0 37.6	29 54.2	26 03.0	0♎12.0	27 06.0	27 54.4	8 17.3	14 38.6	0 51.7	5 11.5	4 10.5	4 02.2
8 Sa	21 06 05	15 29 24	10♊41 13	17 56 32	0 34.4	29 53.2	27 27.2	1 12.4	27 46.1	28 16.9	8 30.5	14 37.4	0 51.5	5 13.2	4 09.5	4 00.8
9 Su	21 10 01	16 26 56	25 14 42	2♋35 03	0 31.2	29 51.8	28 56.2	2 12.4	28 26.1	28 39.3	8 43.8	14 36.2	0 51.3	5 14.9	4 08.6	3 59.4
10 M	21 13 58	17 24 29	9♋56 53	17 19 22	0 28.1	29 50.3	0♌29.8	3 12.1	29 06.0	29 01.7	8 57.0	14 34.8	0 51.0	5 16.4	4 07.6	3 58.1
11 Tu	21 17 54	18 22 04	24 41 38	2♌02 48	0 24.9	29 49.0	2 07.6	4 11.5	29 45.9	29 23.9	9 10.2	14 33.3	0 50.6	5 18.0	4 06.6	3 56.7
12 W	21 21 51	19 19 39	9♌22 00	16 38 23	0 21.7	29 48.0	3 49.5	5 10.4	0♋25.6	29 46.2	9 23.4	14 31.7	0 50.2	5 19.5	4 05.5	3 55.4
13 Th	21 25 48	20 17 16	23 51 09	0♍59 39	0 18.5	29D 47.5	5 34.9	6 09.1	1 05.3	0♋08.3	9 36.5	14 30.0	0 49.8	5 20.9	4 04.4	3 54.0
14 F	21 29 44	21 14 54	8♍03 16	15 01 35	0 15.3	29 47.6	7 23.6	7 07.3	1 44.9	0 30.4	9 49.7	14 28.3	0 49.3	5 22.3	4 03.3	3 52.7
15 Sa	21 33 41	22 12 33	21 54 15	28 41 05	0 12.2	29 48.0	9 15.2	8 05.1	2 24.4	0 52.4	10 02.8	14 26.4	0 48.7	5 23.7	4 02.2	3 51.4
16 Su	21 37 37	23 10 13	5♎22 02	11♎57 08	0 09.0	29 48.6	11 09.2	9 02.5	3 03.9	1 14.3	10 15.9	14 24.4	0 48.1	5 25.0	4 01.1	3 50.1
17 M	21 41 34	24 07 54	18 26 34	24 50 35	0 05.8	29 49.2	13 05.2	9 59.5	3 43.2	1 36.1	10 29.0	14 22.3	0 47.4	5 26.3	3 59.9	3 48.8
18 Tu	21 45 30	25 05 36	1♏09 32	7♏23 50	0 02.6	29 49.7	15 03.0	10 56.0	4 22.5	1 57.8	10 42.1	14 20.2	0 46.7	5 27.5	3 58.7	3 47.5
19 W	21 49 27	26 03 19	13 33 56	19 40 22	29♒59.5	29 50.0	17 02.0	11 52.1	5 01.7	2 19.5	10 55.1	14 17.9	0 45.9	5 28.6	3 57.5	3 46.2
20 Th	21 53 23	27 01 03	25 43 39	1♐44 21	29 56.3	29R 50.1	19 01.9	12 47.7	5 40.8	2 41.1	11 08.2	14 15.6	0 45.0	5 29.8	3 56.3	3 44.9
21 F	21 57 20	27 58 49	7♐43 03	13 40 19	29 53.1	29 50.0	21 02.4	13 42.8	6 19.8	3 02.6	11 21.2	14 13.2	0 44.2	5 30.8	3 55.0	3 43.7
22 Sa	22 01 16	28 56 35	19 36 41	25 32 44	29 49.9	29D 49.9	23 03.2	14 37.4	6 58.8	3 24.0	11 34.1	14 10.6	0 43.2	5 31.9	3 53.8	3 42.4
23 Su	22 05 13	29 54 23	1♑29 00	7♑25 57	29 46.7	29 49.9	25 04.0	15 31.4	7 37.6	3 45.3	11 47.1	14 08.0	0 42.2	5 32.8	3 52.5	3 41.2
24 M	22 09 10	0♍52 12	13 24 06	19 23 52	29 43.6	29 50.0	27 04.6	16 24.9	8 16.4	4 06.6	12 00.0	14 05.3	0 41.2	5 33.8	3 51.1	3 40.0
25 Tu	22 13 06	1 50 02	25 25 40	1♒29 51	29 40.4	29 50.2	29 04.7	17 17.8	8 55.1	4 27.7	12 12.8	14 02.6	0 40.1	5 34.6	3 49.8	3 38.8
26 W	22 17 03	2 47 54	7♒36 45	13 46 38	29 37.2	29 50.4	1♍04.2	18 10.2	9 33.7	4 48.8	12 25.7	13 59.7	0 39.0	5 35.5	3 48.5	3 37.6
27 Th	22 20 59	3 45 46	19 59 43	26 16 11	29 34.0	29R 50.6	3 03.0	19 01.9	10 12.2	5 09.7	12 38.5	13 56.8	0 37.8	5 36.2	3 47.1	3 36.4
28 F	22 24 56	4 43 40	2♓36 11	8♓59 47	29 30.9	29 50.7	5 00.9	19 52.9	10 50.7	5 30.6	12 51.3	13 53.7	0 36.6	5 37.0	3 45.7	3 35.2
29 Sa	22 28 52	5 41 36	15 27 02	21 57 56	29 27.7	29 50.5	6 57.8	20 43.3	11 29.0	5 51.3	13 04.0	13 50.6	0 35.3	5 37.6	3 44.3	3 34.1
30 Su	22 32 49	6 39 33	28 32 27	5♈10 30	29 24.5	29 49.9	8 53.6	21 33.0	12 07.3	6 12.0	13 16.7	13 47.4	0 33.9	5 38.3	3 42.9	3 32.9
31 M	22 36 45	7♍37 32	11♈52 01	18 36 52	29♒21.3	29♒49.1	10♍48.4	22♎22.0	12♋45.5	6♋32.5	13♌29.3	13♈44.2	0♉32.6	5♊38.8	3♈41.4	3♒31.8

1st of Month

Julian Day # 2461253.5

Obliquity 23°26'[illegible]7"

SVP 4♓53'[illegible]9"

GC 27♐12.6

Eris 25♈57.3R

Day	⚴
1	22♈07.5
6	22 26.2
11	22 36.7
16	22 38.4R
21	22 30.7R
26	22 13.3R
31	21 45.9R

Day	⚵
1	2♒27.3R
6	1 16.1R
11	0 08.1R
16	29♑04.9R
21	28 08.5R
26	27 20.0R
31	26 40.4R

Day	⚶
1	25♈39.4
6	26 24.9
11	27 01.2
16	27 27.5
21	27 43.4
26	27 48.4R
31	27 42.1R

DECLINATION and LATITUDE

Day	☉ Decl	☽ Decl	☽ Lat	☽ 12h Decl	☿ Decl	☿ Lat	♀ Decl	♀ Lat	♂ Decl	♂ Lat	⚳ Decl	⚳ Lat	♃ Decl	♃ Lat	♄ Decl	♄ Lat
1 Sa	18N04	8S43	0N35	5S48	19N53	2S09	2N21	0S01	23N21	0N06	21N54	1S28	18N60	0N29	3N28	2S32
2 Su	17 49	2 49	1 43	0N13	20 01	1 54	1 51	0 06	23 24	0 06	21 57	1 26	18 56	0 29	3 28	2 32
3 M	17 33	3N17	2 47	6 21	20 08	1 38	1 22	0 12	23 26	0 07	21 59	1 24	18 53	0 29	3 27	2 32
4 Tu	17 17	9 22	3 44	12 19	20 13	1 23	0 52	0 17	23 29	0 08	22 01	1 23	18 50	0 29	3 27	2 32
5 W	17 01	15 09	4 30	17 49	20 17	1 07	0 23	0 22	23 31	0 09	22 04	1 21	18 46	0 29	3 26	2 33
6 Th	16 45	20 18	5 01	22 31	20 19	0 52	0S06	0 28	23 33	0 10	22 06	1 19	18 43	0 29	3 26	2 33
7 F	16 28	24 26	5 15	26 00	20 19	0 38	0 36	0 34	23 35	0 10	22 08	1 17	18 40	0 29	3 25	2 33
8 Sa	16 11	27 10	5 10	27 53	20 17	0 23	1 05	0 39	23 36	0 11	22 10	1 16	18 36	0 29	3 24	2 33
9 Su	15 54	28 06	4 46	27 51	20 13	0 10	1 34	0 45	23 38	0 12	22 12	1 14	18 33	0 29	3 24	2 34
10 M	15 37	27 05	4 02	25 51	20 06	0N04	2 03	0 51	23 39	0 13	22 14	1 12	18 30	0 29	3 23	2 34
11 Tu	15 19	24 10	3 02	22 06	19 57	0 16	2 33	0 57	23 40	0 14	22 16	1 10	18 26	0 30	3 22	2 34
12 W	15 01	19 41	1 51	16 60	19 45	0 28	3 02	1 04	23 41	0 15	22 18	1 08	18 23	0 30	3 21	2 34
13 Th	14 43	14 05	0 33	11 01	19 30	0 39	3 31	1 10	23 42	0 15	22 20	1 07	18 19	0 30	3 20	2 35
14 F	14 25	7 51	0S46	4 37	19 13	0 50	3 60	1 16	23 42	0 16	22 21	1 05	18 16	0 30	3 19	2 35
15 Sa	14 06	1 23	1 59	1S49	18 53	0 59	4 28	1 23	23 42	0 17	22 23	1 03	18 12	0 30	3 18	2 35
16 Su	13 48	4S57	3 05	7 59	18 31	1 08	4 57	1 29	23 42	0 18	22 25	1 01	18 09	0 30	3 17	2 36
17 M	13 29	10 54	3 58	13 39	18 05	1 15	5 25	1 36	23 42	0 19	22 26	0 59	18 06	0 30	3 16	2 36
18 Tu	13 09	16 13	4 38	18 35	17 38	1 22	5 54	1 42	23 42	0 20	22 28	0 57	18 02	0 30	3 15	2 36
19 W	12 50	20 45	5 04	22 39	17 08	1 28	6 22	1 49	23 41	0 21	22 30	0 55	17 59	0 30	3 14	2 36
20 Th	12 30	24 18	5 16	25 41	16 35	1 33	6 50	1 56	23 40	0 21	22 31	0 54	17 55	0 30	3 13	2 36
21 F	12 10	26 45	5 14	27 32	16 01	1 37	7 18	2 03	23 39	0 22	22 33	0 52	17 52	0 31	3 12	2 37
22 Sa	11 50	27 59	4 58	28 07	15 25	1 41	7 45	2 10	23 38	0 23	22 34	0 50	17 48	0 31	3 11	2 37
23 Su	11 30	27 56	4 30	27 25	14 47	1 43	8 13	2 17	23 37	0 24	22 35	0 48	17 45	0 31	3 09	2 37
24 M	11 10	26 35	3 50	25 26	14 08	1 45	8 40	2 24	23 36	0 25	22 37	0 46	17 41	0 31	3 08	2 37
25 Tu	10 49	23 59	2 59	22 16	13 27	1 46	9 07	2 31	23 34	0 26	22 38	0 44	17 38	0 31	3 07	2 38
26 W	10 29	20 18	2 00	18 06	12 45	1 46	9 34	2 38	23 32	0 27	22 39	0 42	17 34	0 31	3 06	2 38
27 Th	10 08	15 40	0 54	13 04	12 02	1 46	10 00	2 46	23 30	0 28	22 40	0 40	17 31	0 31	3 04	2 38
28 F	9 47	10 18	0N15	7 25	11 18	1 44	10 27	2 53	23 28	0 28	22 42	0 38	17 27	0 31	3 03	2 38
29 Sa	9 25	4 25	1 25	1 21	10 33	1 43	10 53	3 01	23 26	0 29	22 43	0 36	17 24	0 31	3 02	2 38
30 Su	9 04	1N45	2 32	4N52	9 47	1 41	11 18	3 08	23 23	0 30	22 44	0 34	17 20	0 32	3 00	2 39
31 M	8N43	7N57	3N32	10N58	9N01	1N38	11S44	3S16	23N21	0N31	22N45	0S32	17N17	0N32	2N59	2S39

Day	⚷ Decl	⚷ Lat	♅ Decl	♅ Lat	♆ Decl	♆ Lat	♇ Decl	♇ Lat
1	12N00	0N15	20N59	0S09	0N25	1S24	23S22	4S17
6	11 60	0 14	21 00	0 09	0 23	1 24	23 24	4 17
11	11 59	0 14	21 02	0 09	0 21	1 24	23 26	4 17
16	11 58	0 14	21 03	0 09	0 19	1 24	23 28	4 18
21	11 56	0 13	21 04	0 09	0 16	1 24	23 29	4 18
26	11 54	0 13	21 05	0 09	0 13	1 25	23 31	4 18
31	11N52	0N13	21N06	0S09	0N10	1S25	23S33	4S18

Day	⚴ Decl	⚴ Lat	⚵ Decl	⚵ Lat	⚶ Decl	⚶ Lat	Eris Decl	Eris Lat
1	1N22	7S48	5S25	14N33	1N57	8S33	0N16	10S28
6	0 42	8 39	5 57	14 15	1 56	8 51	0 15	10 28
11	0S04	9 32	6 32	13 54	1 51	9 10	0 15	10 29
16	0 55	10 28	7 08	13 29	1 43	9 29	0 14	10 29
21	1 52	11 26	7 45	13 02	1 30	9 48	0 13	10 29
26	2 55	12 27	8 23	12 32	1 14	10 07	0 12	10 29
31	4S03	13S30	9S00	12N01	0N54	10S26	0N11	10S30

Moon Phenomena

Max/0 Decl

dy hr mn
2 11:07 0 N
8 23:39 28N06
15 5:09 0 S
22 10:56 28S07
29 17:15 0 N

Max/0 Lat

dy hr mn
7 5:58 5N16
13 9:58 0 S
20 8:11 5S17
27 18:47 0 N

Perigee/Apogee

dy hr m kilometers
10 11:19 p 363287
22 8:22 a 404640

PH dy hr mn

☾ 6 2:23 13♉40
● 12 17:38 20♌02
● 12 1067:04 02'[illegible]8"
☽ 20 2:47 27♏08
○ 28 4:20 4♓54
● 28 4:14 P 0.930

Void of Course Moon

Last Aspect	☽ Ingress
2 12:34 ♀ ☍	♈ 2 20:38
4 18:53 ♂ ⚹	♉ 5 2:37
6 23:26 ☿ ⚹	♊ 7 6:09
9 5:28 ♂ ☌	♋ 9 7:47
10 7:31 ♄ □	♌ 11 8:39
12 17:38 ☉ ☌	♍ 13 10:19
13 19:25 ♅ □	♎ 15 14:21
17 11:32 ☉ ⚹	♏ 17 21:47
20 2:47 ☉ □	♐ 20 8:31
22 20:32 ☉ △	♑ 22 21:00
24 6:31 ♀ □	♒ 25 9:03
26 22:01 ♀ △	♓ 27 19:05
28 16:15 ♂ △	♈ 30 2:39

DAILY ASPECTARIAN

1 Sa: ☽⚻♃ 1:34; ☉⚻☽ 5:24; ♂#♇ 9:51; ☿∠♅ 14:42; ☽⊻♄ 16:12; ☽∠⚷ 18:21; ☽#♄ 21:25

2 Su: ☽∠♇ 0:30; ☽△☿ 3:00; ☽#♀ 4:09; ☽⚼♃ 6:16; ☽#♆ 9:31; ☽□♂ 9:34; ☉⚼☽ 11:48; ☽☍♀ 12:34; ☽∥♆ 12:43; ☽□⚳ 13:41; ☽∥♀ 17:01; ☽⊻⚷ 22:14

3 M: ☽∥♄ 0:39; ☽⚹♇ 4:12; ☽☌♆ 4:24; ☽⚹♅ 5:57; ♀□⚳ 10:03; ☽△♃ 10:22; ☉△☽ 17:26; ⚷ R 20:11; ☽☌♄ 23:23

4 Tu: ☉∠⚳ 4:52; ☽∠♅ 9:06; ☽∥⚷ 10:42; ☽□☿ 14:18; ☽⚹♂ 18:53; ☽⚹⚳ 21:32; ☽⚻♀ 23:21; ♀∥♆ 23:40

5 W: ☽☌⚷ 4:08; ☉∥☽ 7:55; ☽□♇ 9:45; ☽⊻♆ 9:58; ☽⊻♅ 11:37; ☽∥♃ 16:18; ☽□♃ 16:35; ☽∠♂ 22:27

6 Th: ☽∥☿ 0:08; ☽∠⚳ 0:26; ☉□☽ 2:23; ☊ R 2:35; ☽⚼♀ 3:32; ☽∥♅ 3:41; ☽⊻♄ 4:05; ☽∥⚳ 9:41; ☽∠♆ 11:50; ♀#♆ 13:25; ☽#♇ 17:17; ☽∥♂ 18:20; ♀ ♎ 19:14; ☽⚹☿ 23:26

7 F: ☽⊻♂ 1:20; ☽⊻⚳ 2:42; ☉△♄ 2:45; ☽∠♄ 5:32; ☽△♀ 6:59; ☽⊻⚷ 7:36; ☽△♇ 12:54; ☽⚹♆ 13:08; ☽☌♅ 14:53; ♀⚻⚷ 15:44; ☽⚹♃ 20:19

8 Sa: ☽∠☿ 3:15; ☽⚹♄ 6:31; ☉⚹☽ 8:31; ☽∠⚷ 8:34; ☿⊻♂ 9:33; ☽⚼♇ 13:45; ☿⊻⚳ 18:05; ☽∠♃ 21:29

9 Su: ☽☌♂ 5:28; ☽☌⚳ 5:44; ☽⊻☿ 6:45; ☽⚹⚷ 9:10; ☉∠☽ 10:51; ☽□♀ 12:13; ☽⚻♇ 14:16; ☽□♆ 14:32; ☽⊻♅ 16:22; ☿ ♌ 16:29; ♂☌⚳ 18:02; ☽⊻♃ 22:21

10 M: ☿□⚷ 5:17; ☽□♄ 7:31; ☉⊻☽ 12:59; ☽∠♅ 16:50; ♀△♇ 18:10; ♀☍♆ 22:03

11 Tu: ☽∥♂ 3:06; ☽#♇ 4:31; ☽⊻⚳ 7:52; ♂ ♋ 8:32; ☽⊻♂ 8:40; ☽□⚷ 10:02; ☽∥⚳ 11:01; ☽☌☿ 13:42; ⚵ R♑ 14:46; ☽☍♇ 15:05; ☽△♆ 15:21; ☽⚹♀ 16:38; ☽⚹♅ 17:21; ☽∥♅ 17:29; ☉⚼♆ 18:13; ☽∥☿ 23:41

12 W: ☽☌♃ 0:02; ☿☍♇ 1:21; ☿△♆ 3:40; ♀△♅ 3:47; ☽∥♃ 6:02; ☽△♄ 8:30; ☽∠⚳ 9:08; ☽∠♂ 10:28; ♂⚹⚷ 14:43; ⚳ ♋ 14:59; ♀#♄ 15:36; ☽⚼♆ 16:03; ☉☌☽ 17:38; ☽∠♀ 19:10; ☿⚹♅ 20:49; ☉∥☽ 21:18

13 Th: ☽∥⚷ 8:18; ☽⚼♄ 9:28; ☊ D 10:01; ☽⚹⚳ 10:50; ☽△⚷ 11:43; ☽⚹♂ 12:45; ☿⚹♀ 16:24; ☽⚻♇ 16:54; ☽⚻♆ 17:12; ☽□♅ 19:25; ☽⊻♀ 22:17; ☽⊻☿ 22:42

14 F: ☽⊻♃ 3:05; ⚴ R 9:40; ☽⚻♄ 11:01; ☽#♀ 13:20; ☽⚼⚷ 13:22; ☽∥♄ 16:51; ☽⚼♇ 18:40; ⚳⚹⚷ 20:05

15 Sa: ☉⊻☽ 0:35; ☽∥♆ 3:58; ☽∠☿ 4:48; ☽∠♃ 5:38; ☽#♆ 6:20; ☿☌♃ 11:24; ☽⚻⚷ 15:47; ☽□⚳ 16:21; ☽#♄ 17:36; ☽□♂ 19:38; ☽△♇ 21:14; ☽☍♆ 21:34; ☽∥♀ 23:58

16 Su: ☽△♅ 0:05; ☉∠☽ 5:29; ☽☌♀ 7:12; ☽⚹♃ 9:04; ☽⚹☿ 12:21; ☽☍♄ 16:29; ☿∥♃ 23:51

17 M: ♂⚻♇ 3:16; ☽⚼♅ 3:44; ☽#⚷ 4:33; ♂□♆ 9:54; ☉#☽ 10:36; ☉⚹☽ 11:32; ☿△♄ 15:28; ♀⚹♃ 16:17; ☽☍⚷ 23:16

18 Tu: ☽△⚳ 1:35; ☽□♇ 5:02; ☽⚻♆ 5:24; ☽#☿ 6:21; ☽△♂ 6:31; ☽⚻♅ 8:16; ☽#♃ 8:59; ☽□♃ 18:45; ☽⊻♀ 20:25

19 W: ☽⚻♄ 1:26; ☽#♅ 1:55; ☿∠⚳ 4:18; ☽⚼⚳ 7:36; ☽□☿ 8:08; ☽⚼♆ 10:34; ☽#⚳ 11:01; ☽⚼♂ 13:25; ♂⊻♅ 17:01; ☽∥♇ 17:48; ☽#♂ 19:13; ☿⚼♆ 22:54

20 Th: ☉□☽ 2:47; ☊ R 3:20; ☽∠♀ 4:28; ☽⚼♄ 7:01; ☽⚻⚷ 10:01; ☽⚻⚳ 14:19; ☽⚹♇ 16:00; ☽△♆ 16:23; ☽☍♅ 19:34; ☽⚻♂ 21:03

21 F: ☿∠♂ 5:07; ☽△♃ 7:27; ♀☍♄ 12:44; ☽△♄ 13:04; ☽⚹♀ 13:05; ☽⚼⚷ 16:09; ☉∥⚷ 17:28; ☽∠♇ 22:10

22 Sa: ☉⚼♄ 5:35; ☽△☿ 8:23; ☽⚼♃ 14:20; ⚳⚻♇ 19:34; ☉△☽ 20:32; ☊ D 21:01; ☽△⚷ 22:26

23 Su: ☉ ♍ 2:20; ☽⊻♇ 4:26; ☽☍⚳ 4:44; ☽□♆ 4:49; ⚳□♆ 7:35; ☽⚻♅ 8:13; ☽☍♂ 13:06; ☉△⚷ 19:31; ☽⚼☿ 20:48; ☽⚻♃ 21:08

24 M: ☽□♄ 1:22; ☉⚼☽ 5:23; ☽□♀ 6:31; ☽⚼♅ 14:20; ☿⚼♄ 23:35

25 Tu: ☽#♂ 3:10; ☽∥♇ 3:32; ☽⚻☿ 8:39; ☽#⚳ 9:35; ☽□⚷ 10:21; ☿ ♍ 11:05; ☉⚻☽ 13:45; ☽☌♇ 16:12; ☽⚹♆ 16:33; ⚶ R 18:00; ☽⚻⚳ 18:21; ☿△⚷ 18:58; ☽#♅ 19:25; ☽△♅ 20:02

26 W: ☽⚻♂ 4:01; ☽☍♃ 9:33; ☽⚹♄ 12:22; ♂#♇ 12:30; ☽#♃ 14:52; ☉⚻♇ 20:11; ☽∠♆ 21:41; ☽△♀ 22:01

27 Th: ☽⚼⚳ 0:20; ☉⚻♆ 0:32; ☉#♀ 3:39; ☿∥⚷ 4:24; ☿⚻♇ 6:43; ☿⚻♆ 8:51; ☽⚼♂ 10:30; ☽∠♄ 17:01; ☉☌☿ 17:05; ☽#⚷ 17:13; ☊ R 18:38; ☽#☿ 19:09; ☽⚹⚷ 20:14; ☿∠♀ 21:08; ☽∥♀ 23:28

28 F: ☽⊻♇ 1:51; ☽⊻♆ 2:11; ☉#☽ 2:23; ☉☍☽ 4:20; ☽⚼♀ 4:36; ☽☍☿ 5:22; ☽△⚳ 5:37; ☽□♅ 5:40; ☿⚹⚳ 7:23; ☿□♅ 7:26; ⚳⊻♅ 7:38; ☽△♂ 16:15; ☿#♀ 17:14; ☽⚻♃ 19:30; ☽⊻♄ 21:02; ♀⚼♅ 21:14; ☉□♅ 22:20

29 Sa: ☽∠⚷ 0:15; ☉∠♀ 5:10; ☽#♄ 5:31; ☽∠♇ 5:45; ☉⚹⚳ 6:16; ☽⚻♀ 10:23; ☽#♆ 16:32; ☽∥♆ 17:57; ☽⚼♃ 23:31

30 Su: ☽⊻⚷ 3:40; ☽∥♄ 4:48; ☽⚹♇ 9:03; ☽☌♆ 9:21; ☽⚹♅ 12:51; ☽□⚳ 14:13; ☉⚻☽ 15:49; ☽⚻☿ 21:47

31 M: ☽□♂ 1:40; ☉∥☽ 2:50; ☽△♃ 2:56; ☽☌♄ 3:19; ☽∥☿ 3:45; ♀#⚷ 7:10; ☽∥⚷ 15:36; ☽∠♅ 15:36; ☽#♀ 16:16; ☉∥☿ 18:13; ☽☍♀ 19:48; ☉⚼☽ 20:33; ♃△♄ 22:18

September 2026

LONGITUDE

Day	Sid.Time	☉	☽	☽ 12 hour	Mean ☊	True ☊	☿	♀	♂	⚳	♃	♄	⚷	♅	♆	♇
	h m s	° ' "	° ' "	° ' "	° '	° '	° '	° '	° '	° '	° '	° '	° '	° '	° '	° '
1 Tu	22 40 42	8♍35 33	25♈24 53	2♉15 57	29♒18.1	29♒48.1	12♍42.0	23♎10.3	13♋23.6	6♋53.0	13♌42.0	13♈40.8	0♉31.1	5♊39.4	3♈40.0	3♒30.7
2 W	22 44 39	9 33 36	9♉09 51	16 06 26	29 15.0	29R 47.0	14 34.4	23 57.8	14 01.6	7 13.3	13 54.6	13R 37.4	0R 29.7	5 39.8	3R 38.5	3R 29.6
3 Th	22 48 35	10 31 40	23 05 28	0♊06 47	29 11.8	29 46.2	16 25.6	24 44.5	14 39.5	7 33.6	14 07.1	13 33.9	0 28.1	5 40.3	3 37.0	3 28.6
4 F	22 52 32	11 29 47	7♊10 07	14 15 15	29 08.6	29D 45.7	18 15.7	25 30.3	15 17.4	7 53.7	14 19.6	13 30.4	0 26.6	5 40.6	3 35.5	3 27.5
5 Sa	22 56 28	12 27 55	21 21 54	28 29 47	29 05.4	29 45.8	20 04.5	26 15.4	15 55.1	8 13.7	14 32.1	13 26.8	0 25.0	5 41.0	3 34.0	3 26.5
6 Su	23 00 25	13 26 06	5♋38 35	12♋47 58	29 02.3	29 46.5	21 52.1	26 59.5	16 32.8	8 33.6	14 44.5	13 23.1	0 23.3	5 41.2	3 32.5	3 25.5
7 M	23 04 21	14 24 19	19 57 32	27 06 52	28 59.1	29 47.5	23 38.5	27 42.8	17 10.4	8 53.4	14 56.8	13 19.3	0 21.6	5 41.5	3 30.9	3 24.5
8 Tu	23 08 18	15 22 33	4♌15 32	11♌23 04	28 55.9	29 48.6	25 23.7	28 25.0	17 47.8	9 13.0	15 09.2	13 15.5	0 19.9	5 41.6	3 29.4	3 23.5
9 W	23 12 14	16 20 50	18 28 59	25 32 47	28 52.7	29R 49.5	27 07.7	29 06.3	18 25.2	9 32.6	15 21.4	13 11.6	0 18.1	5 41.7	3 27.8	3 22.6
10 Th	23 16 11	17 19 08	2♍33 59	9♍32 07	28 49.6	29 49.7	28 50.5	29 46.6	19 02.5	9 52.0	15 33.6	13 07.7	0 16.3	5R 41.8	3 26.2	3 21.7
11 F	23 20 08	18 17 28	16 26 45	23 17 29	28 46.4	29 49.1	0♎32.2	0♏25.8	19 39.7	10 11.2	15 45.8	13 03.6	0 14.4	5 41.8	3 24.6	3 20.7
12 Sa	23 24 04	19 15 50	0♎04 01	6♎46 04	28 43.2	29 47.4	2 12.8	1 03.9	20 16.8	10 30.4	15 57.9	12 59.6	0 12.5	5 41.8	3 23.0	3 19.8
13 Su	23 28 01	20 14 14	13 23 26	19 56 04	28 40.0	29 44.9	3 52.3	1 40.8	20 53.7	10 49.4	16 09.9	12 55.5	0 10.5	5 41.7	3 21.4	3 19.0
14 M	23 31 57	21 12 40	26 23 54	2♏47 03	28 36.8	29 41.7	5 30.6	2 16.5	21 30.6	11 08.3	16 21.9	12 51.3	0 08.5	5 41.6	3 19.8	3 18.1
15 Tu	23 35 54	22 11 07	9♏05 40	15 19 59	28 33.7	29 38.3	7 07.9	2 50.9	22 07.4	11 27.0	16 33.8	12 47.1	0 06.5	5 41.4	3 18.2	3 17.3
16 W	23 39 50	23 09 36	21 30 19	27 37 03	28 30.5	29 35.1	8 44.1	3 24.0	22 44.1	11 45.6	16 45.7	12 42.8	0 04.4	5 41.1	3 16.6	3 16.5
17 Th	23 43 47	24 08 06	3♐47 10	9♐41 32	28 27.3	29 32.6	10 19.2	3 55.8	23 20.6	12 04.0	16 57.5	12 38.5	0 02.3	5 40.8	3 14.9	3 15.7
18 F	23 47 43	25 06 38	15 40 18	21 37 30	28 24.1	29D 31.1	11 53.3	4 26.1	23 57.1	12 22.3	17 09.3	12 34.1	0 00.2	5 40.5	3 13.3	3 15.0
19 Sa	23 51 40	26 05 12	27 33 43	3♑29 33	28 21.0	29 30.7	13 26.3	4 54.9	24 33.5	12 40.4	17 20.9	12 29.7	29♈58.0	5 40.1	3 11.6	3 14.2
20 Su	23 55 37	27 03 48	9♑25 37	15 22 32	28 17.8	29 31.3	14 58.3	5 22.2	25 09.7	12 58.4	17 32.6	12 25.3	29 55.8	5 39.7	3 10.0	3 13.5
21 M	23 59 33	28 02 25	21 20 54	27 21 17	28 14.6	29 32.8	16 29.3	5 47.9	25 45.9	13 16.2	17 44.1	12 20.8	29 53.5	5 39.2	3 08.3	3 12.8
22 Tu	0 03 30	29 01 04	3♒24 15	9♒30 20	28 11.4	29 34.5	17 59.3	6 11.9	26 21.9	13 33.9	17 55.6	12 16.3	29 51.3	5 38.6	3 06.7	3 12.2
23 W	0 07 26	29 59 44	15 39 59	21 53 39	28 08.2	29 36.1	19 28.2	6 34.3	26 57.8	13 51.4	18 07.0	12 11.8	29 48.9	5 38.0	3 05.0	3 11.5
24 Th	0 11 23	0♎58 27	28 11 39	4♓34 18	28 05.1	29R 36.8	20 56.0	6 54.8	27 33.7	14 08.7	18 18.3	12 07.3	29 46.6	5 37.4	3 03.4	3 10.9
25 F	0 15 19	1 57 11	11♓01 47	17 34 11	28 01.9	29 36.2	22 22.8	7 13.4	28 09.4	14 25.9	18 29.6	12 02.7	29 44.2	5 36.7	3 01.7	3 10.3
26 Sa	0 19 16	2 55 57	24 11 33	0♈53 45	27 58.7	29 34.1	23 48.6	7 30.2	28 45.0	14 42.9	18 40.7	11 58.0	29 41.8	5 36.0	3 00.0	3 09.8
27 Su	0 23 12	3 54 44	7♈40 37	14 31 50	27 55.5	29 30.4	25 13.3	7 45.0	29 20.5	14 59.7	18 51.8	11 53.4	29 39.4	5 35.2	2 58.4	3 09.2
28 M	0 27 09	4 53 34	21 27 04	28 25 49	27 52.3	29 25.4	26 36.9	7 57.8	29 55.8	15 16.4	19 02.9	11 48.8	29 36.9	5 34.3	2 56.7	3 08.7
29 Tu	0 31 06	5 52 26	5♉27 36	12♉31 51	27 49.2	29 19.7	27 59.3	8 08.5	0♌31.1	15 32.9	19 13.8	11 44.1	29 34.4	5 33.5	2 55.0	3 08.2
30 W	0 35 02	6♎51 20	19 38 00	26 45 28	27♒46.0	29♒14.0	29♎20.6	8♏17.0	1♌06.2	15♋49.1	19♌24.7	11♈39.4	29♈31.9	5♊32.5	2♈53.4	3♒07.8

1st of Month

Julian Day # 2461284.5
Obliquity 23°26'07"
SVP 4♓53'05"
GC 27♐12.7
Eris 25♈49.5R

Day	⚴
1	21♈39.2R
6	20 59.7R
11	20 10.0R
16	19 10.6R
21	18 02.5R
26	16 46.8R

Day	⚵
1	26♑33.6R
6	26 05.6R
11	25 47.8R
16	25 40.4R
21	25 43.4
26	25 56.5

Day	⚶
1	27♈39.5R
6	27 19.5R
11	26 48.1R
16	26 05.7R
21	25 13.1R
26	24 11.6R

DECLINATION and LATITUDE

Day	☉ Decl	☽ Decl	☽ Lat	☽ 12h Decl	☿ Decl	☿ Lat	♀ Decl	♀ Lat	♂ Decl	♂ Lat	⚳ Decl	⚳ Lat	♃ Decl	♃ Lat	♄ Decl	♄ Lat
1 Tu	8N21	13N53	4N21	16N39	8N15	1N35	12S09	3S23	23N18	0N32	22N46	0S30	17N13	0N32	2N57	2S39
2 W	7 59	19 13	4 56	21 33	7 28	1 31	12 34	3 31	23 15	0 33	22 47	0 27	17 10	0 32	2 56	2 39
3 Th	7 37	23 36	5 14	25 19	6 41	1 27	12 58	3 39	23 12	0 34	22 48	0 25	17 06	0 32	2 54	2 39
4 F	7 15	26 39	5 14	27 35	5 54	1 22	13 22	3 46	23 08	0 35	22 49	0 23	17 03	0 32	2 53	2 40
5 Sa	6 53	28 03	4 54	28 03	5 07	1 17	13 46	3 54	23 05	0 36	22 50	0 21	16 59	0 32	2 51	2 40
6 Su	6 31	27 35	4 16	26 40	4 20	1 12	14 10	4 02	23 01	0 37	22 51	0 19	16 56	0 32	2 50	2 40
7 M	6 08	25 18	3 23	23 22	3 33	1 07	14 33	4 10	22 57	0 38	22 52	0 17	16 52	0 32	2 48	2 40
8 Tu	5 46	21 24	2 17	18 58	2 46	1 01	14 55	4 18	22 53	0 38	22 53	0 15	16 49	0 33	2 46	2 40
9 W	5 23	16 16	1 02	13 23	1 59	0 55	15 17	4 25	22 49	0 39	22 53	0 12	16 45	0 33	2 45	2 41
10 Th	5 01	10 19	0S15	7 10	1 12	0 49	15 39	4 33	22 45	0 40	22 54	0 10	16 42	0 33	2 43	2 41
11 F	4 38	3 58	1 30	0 44	0 26	0 42	16 00	4 41	22 41	0 41	22 55	0 08	16 38	0 33	2 41	2 41
12 Sa	4 15	2S27	2 39	5S35	0S20	0 35	16 21	4 49	22 36	0 42	22 56	0 05	16 35	0 33	2 40	2 41
13 Su	3 52	8 37	3 37	11 31	1 06	0 29	16 42	4 57	22 31	0 43	22 57	0 03	16 31	0 33	2 38	2 41
14 M	3 29	14 16	4 23	16 49	1 51	0 22	17 02	5 05	22 27	0 44	22 57	0 01	16 28	0 33	2 36	2 41
15 Tu	3 06	19 10	4 54	21 17	2 36	0 15	17 21	5 13	22 22	0 45	22 58	0N02	16 24	0 34	2 34	2 41
16 W	2 43	23 08	5 11	24 43	3 21	0 07	17 40	5 20	22 17	0 46	22 59	0 04	16 21	0 34	2 33	2 41
17 Th	2 20	26 00	5 13	26 58	4 05	0S00	17 58	5 28	22 11	0 47	22 60	0 06	16 17	0 34	2 31	2 42
18 F	1 57	27 40	5 02	28 01	4 49	0 07	18 16	5 36	22 06	0 48	23 00	0 09	16 14	0 34	2 29	2 42
19 Sa	1 33	28 02	4 37	27 44	5 32	0 15	18 33	5 43	22 01	0 49	23 01	0 11	16 10	0 34	2 27	2 42
20 Su	1 10	27 07	4 01	26 11	6 15	0 22	18 49	5 51	21 55	0 50	23 02	0 14	16 07	0 34	2 25	2 42
21 M	0 47	24 57	3 14	23 26	6 57	0 30	19 05	5 58	21 49	0 51	23 03	0 16	16 04	0 34	2 23	2 42
22 Tu	0 23	21 38	2 19	19 36	7 38	0 38	19 20	6 06	21 44	0 52	23 03	0 19	16 00	0 34	2 22	2 42
23 W	0 00	17 21	1 16	14 52	8 19	0 45	19 34	6 13	21 38	0 53	23 04	0 21	15 57	0 35	2 20	2 42
24 Th	0S23	12 13	0 08	9 25	8 59	0 53	19 48	6 20	21 32	0 54	23 05	0 24	15 54	0 35	2 18	2 42
25 F	0 47	6 28	1N02	3 26	9 39	1 00	20 00	6 27	21 25	0 55	23 06	0 26	15 50	0 35	2 16	2 42
26 Sa	1 10	0 19	2 10	2N50	10 18	1 08	20 12	6 34	21 19	0 56	23 06	0 29	15 47	0 35	2 14	2 42
27 Su	1 33	5N60	3 13	9 07	10 56	1 15	20 23	6 40	21 13	0 57	23 07	0 32	15 44	0 35	2 12	2 43
28 M	1 57	12 09	4 05	15 04	11 33	1 23	20 34	6 46	21 06	0 58	23 08	0 34	15 40	0 35	2 11	2 43
29 Tu	2 20	17 48	4 44	20 18	12 10	1 30	20 43	6 52	20 60	0 59	23 09	0 37	15 37	0 36	2 09	2 43
30 W	2S43	22N32	5N06	24N27	12S46	1S38	20S51	6S58	20N53	0N60	23N09	0N40	15N34	0N36	2N07	2S43

Day	⚷ Decl	⚷ Lat	♅ Decl	♅ Lat	♆ Decl	♆ Lat	♇ Decl	♇ Lat
1	11N51	0N13	21N06	0S09	0N10	1S25	23S33	4S18
6	11 48	0 12	21 06	0 09	0 07	1 25	23 34	4 18
11	11 44	0 12	21 06	0 09	0 03	1 25	23 35	4 18
16	11 41	0 12	21 06	0 09	0 00	1 25	23 36	4 18
21	11 36	0 11	21 06	0 09	0S03	1 25	23 37	4 18
26	11 32	0 11	21 05	0 09	0 07	1 25	23 38	4 18

Day	⚴ Decl	⚴ Lat	⚵ Decl	⚵ Lat	⚶ Decl	⚶ Lat	Eris Decl	Eris Lat
1	4S17	13S42	9S08	11N55	0N50	10S29	0N11	10S30
6	5 31	14 47	9 44	11 23	0 26	10 47	0 10	10 30
11	6 49	15 51	10 19	10 50	0S00	11 04	0 09	10 30
16	8 11	16 56	10 53	10 18	0 29	11 19	0 08	10 30
21	9 34	17 60	11 24	9 45	0 60	11 32	0 07	10 30
26	10 59	19 01	11 53	9 13	1 31	11 42	0 06	10 31

Moon Phenomena

Max/0 Decl
dy hr mn
5 6:09 28N06
11 14:46 0 S
18 18:50 28S04
26 1:12 0 N

Perigee/Apogee
dy hr m kilometers
6 20:44 p 368259
19 3:01 a 404220

PH dy hr mn
☾ 4 7:52 11♊49
● 11 3:28 18♍26
☽ 18 20:45 25♐57
○ 26 16:50 3♈37

Max/0 Lat
dy hr mn
3 11:24 5N16
9 19:18 0 S
16 15:49 5S14
24 2:41 0 N
30 16:04 5N10

Void of Course Moon

Last Aspect	☽ Ingress
31 19:48 ♀ ☍	♉ 1 8:02
2 10:48 ☿ △	♊ 3 11:48
5 8:41 ♀ △	♋ 5 14:32
7 13:41 ♀ □	♌ 7 16:51
9 18:59 ♀ ⚹	♍ 9 19:36
11 5:53 ♂ ⚹	♎ 11 23:53
13 14:28 ♂ □	♏ 14 6:45
16 3:31 ☉ ⚹	♐ 16 16:42
18 20:45 ☉ □	♑ 19 4:56
21 14:33 ☉ △	♒ 21 17:16
23 8:19 ☿ △	♓ 24 3:25
26 8:33 ♂ △	♈ 26 10:24
28 9:52 ☿ ☍	♉ 28 14:41
29 23:37 ♃ □	♊ 30 17:27

DAILY ASPECTARIAN

1 Tu
☽ ⚼ ☿ 4:39
☽ ☌ ⚷ 8:56
♂ □ ♄ 10:00
☿ ⊼ ♄ 12:10
☿ ⚹ ♂ 13:22
☽ □ ♇ 14:09
☿ ⊻ ♃ 14:23
☽ ⊻ ♆ 14:25
☽ ∥ ♃ 14:26
♂ ⊻ ♃ 17:21
☽ ⊻ ♅ 17:55
☽ ⚹ ⚳ 20:33

2 W
☉ △ ☽ 0:44
☽ ⊻ ♄ 7:41
☽ □ ♃ 8:20
☽ ⚹ ♂ 8:49
☽ ∥ ♅ 9:32
☽ △ ☿ 10:48
☿ ⚼ ⚷ 11:44
☽ ∠ ♆ 16:20
☽ ∥ ⚳ 19:03
☽ ∥ ♂ 21:28
☽ ∠ ⚳ 23:04
☽ # ♇ 23:41

3 Th
☽ ⊼ ♀ 2:59
☽ ∠ ♄ 9:19
☽ ∠ ♂ 11:45
☽ ⊻ ⚷ 12:35
☽ △ ♇ 17:42
☽ ⚹ ♆ 17:56
☽ ☌ ♅ 21:28

4 F
☽ ⊻ ⚳ 1:16
☿ ⚼ ♇ 2:35
☽ ⚼ ♀ 5:59
☊ D 7:44
☉ □ ☽ 7:52
☽ ⚹ ♄ 10:41
☽ ⚹ ♃ 12:18
☽ ∠ ⚷ 13:59
☽ ⊻ ♂ 14:23
☽ ⚼ ♇ 19:05
☽ □ ☿ 21:31

5 Sa
☽ △ ♀ 8:41
☽ ∠ ♃ 13:57
☽ ⚹ ⚷ 15:12
☽ ⊼ ♇ 20:17
☽ □ ♆ 20:29
☉ ⊼ ♄ 22:50

6 Su
☽ ⊻ ♅ 0:04
☽ ☌ ⚳ 5:00
☽ □ ♄ 12:55
☉ ⚹ ☽ 14:01
☽ ⊻ ♃ 15:29
☽ ☌ ♂ 19:07

7 M
☽ ∠ ♅ 1:14
☽ ⚹ ☿ 7:02
☽ # ♇ 11:43
☽ □ ♀ 13:41
☽ ∥ ♂ 15:40
☽ ∥ ⚳ 15:55
☉ ⊻ ♃ 17:00
☉ ∠ ☽ 17:00
☽ □ ⚷ 17:25
☽ ☍ ♇ 22:33
☽ △ ♆ 22:43
☉ ⚼ ⚷ 22:56
☿ ∥ ♄ 23:41

8 Tu
☽ ∥ ♅ 1:34
☽ ⚹ ♅ 2:25
♂ ∥ ⚳ 4:00
☽ ⊻ ⚳ 8:33
☽ ∠ ☿ 11:46
☽ △ ♄ 15:06
☽ ☌ ♃ 18:38
☉ ⊻ ☽ 20:07
☽ ∥ ♃ 21:55
☽ ⊻ ♂ 23:53
☽ ⚼ ♆ 23:58

9 W
☽ # ♀ 3:55
☽ ∠ ⚳ 10:32
☽ ⚼ ♄ 16:26
☽ ⊻ ☿ 16:45
☽ ∥ ⚷ 18:26
☽ ⚹ ♀ 18:59
☊ R 19:16
☽ △ ⚷ 20:05

10 Th
☽ ⊼ ♇ 1:22
☽ ⊼ ♆ 1:30
☽ ∠ ♂ 2:39
☽ □ ♅ 5:23
♀ ♏ 8:08
☽ ⚹ ⚳ 12:52
☿ ♎ 16:22
♀ ☍ ⚷ 17:16
☽ ⊼ ♄ 18:08
♅ R 18:28
☿ ⊼ ⚷ 19:51
☉ ∥ ☽ 21:21
☿ ⊻ ♀ 21:31
☽ ⚼ ⚷ 21:54
☽ ∠ ♀ 22:09
☽ ⊻ ♃ 22:48

11 F
☉ ⚼ ♇ 1:19
☽ ⚼ ♇ 3:19
☉ ☌ ☽ 3:28
☿ ∠ ♃ 3:39
☽ ∥ ♄ 4:46
☽ ⚹ ♂ 5:53
☿ ∥ ♆ 11:49
☽ ∥ ♆ 14:34
☽ # ☿ 14:37
☽ ∥ ☿ 14:57
☽ # ♆ 14:57
☿ # ♆ 14:57

12 Sa
☽ ⊼ ⚷ 0:15
☽ # ♄ 0:45
☽ ∠ ♃ 1:37
☽ ⊻ ♀ 1:52
☽ ☌ ☿ 4:22
☽ △ ♇ 5:49
☽ ☍ ♆ 5:55
☉ # ☽ 6:26
☽ △ ♅ 10:04
♀ # ♃ 13:21
☿ △ ♇ 16:00
♂ ∠ ♅ 16:12
☿ ☍ ♆ 16:39
☽ □ ⚳ 19:13
☽ ☍ ♄ 23:09

13 Su
☽ ⚹ ♃ 5:09
☽ # ⚷ 12:48
☽ ⚼ ♅ 13:24
☉ ⊻ ☽ 13:35
☽ □ ♂ 14:28

14 M
☿ △ ♅ 2:41
☽ ☍ ⚷ 7:00
☽ # ♃ 10:08
☽ ☌ ♀ 11:34
☽ □ ♇ 12:58
☽ ⊼ ♆ 13:00
☽ ∥ ♀ 13:56
☽ ⊼ ♅ 17:31
☽ ⊻ ☿ 19:42
☉ ⚹ ♂ 19:54
☉ ∠ ☽ 20:03
☿ # ♄ 22:52

15 Tu
☽ △ ⚳ 4:38
☽ ⊼ ♄ 7:03
☉ # ☿ 10:27
☽ # ♅ 10:57
☽ □ ♃ 14:37
☽ ⚼ ♆ 17:43
☽ # ♂ 18:23
♀ □ ♇ 18:36
♀ ⊼ ♆ 18:47
☽ # ⚳ 22:57

16 W
♆ ⚹ ♇ 1:48
☽ △ ♂ 2:32
☽ ∥ ♇ 3:20
☉ ⚹ ☽ 3:31
☽ ∠ ☿ 5:01
☽ ⚼ ⚳ 10:35
☉ ∥ ♄ 11:40
☽ ⚼ ♄ 12:07
☽ ⊼ ⚷ 16:48
☽ △ ♆ 23:09
☽ ⚹ ♇ 23:11

17 Th
☽ ⊻ ♀ 0:31
⚵ D 1:11
☽ ☍ ♅ 3:59
☽ ⚼ ♂ 9:48
☽ ⚹ ☿ 15:16
☽ ⊼ ⚳ 17:12
☽ △ ♄ 17:48
☽ ⚼ ⚷ 22:40

18 F
⚷ R ♈ 1:52
☽ △ ♃ 3:02
☽ ∠ ♇ 5:11
☽ ∠ ♀ 7:54
☿ □ ⚳ 9:15
☿ ☍ ♄ 10:02
⚳ □ ♄ 12:37
☽ ⊼ ♂ 17:36
☊ D 20:31
☉ □ ☽ 20:45

19 Sa
☽ △ ⚷ 4:51
☽ ⚼ ♃ 9:51
☽ □ ♆ 11:22
☽ ⊻ ♇ 11:28
☽ ⚹ ♀ 15:29
☽ ⊼ ♅ 16:24

20 Su
☽ □ ♄ 6:01
☽ ☍ ⚳ 7:21
☽ □ ☿ 12:49
♀ ⊼ ♅ 15:50
☽ ⊼ ♃ 16:38
☽ ⚼ ♅ 22:36

21 M
☽ ☍ ♂ 9:18
☽ ∥ ♇ 10:36
☉ △ ☽ 14:33
☽ # ⚳ 14:39
☽ □ ⚷ 16:59
☿ ⚹ ♃ 22:52
☽ ⚹ ♆ 23:25
☽ # ♂ 23:26
☽ ☌ ♇ 23:36

22 Tu
☽ # ♅ 3:22
☽ △ ♅ 4:25
☽ □ ♀ 5:41
☽ ∥ ♀ 12:49
☽ ⚹ ♄ 17:18
☉ # ♆ 19:31
☉ ⊼ ⚷ 19:45
☽ ⊼ ⚳ 20:24
♃ ⚼ ♆ 20:25
☉ ⚼ ☽ 22:35

23 W
☉ ♎ 0:06
☽ ∠ ♆ 4:40
☽ ☍ ♃ 4:49
☉ ∥ ♆ 4:58
☽ # ♃ 6:58
☽ △ ☿ 8:19
☿ ⚼ ♅ 18:56
☽ ∠ ♄ 21:59
☽ ⊼ ♂ 22:44

24 Th
☽ ⚼ ⚳ 1:50
☊ R 2:39
☽ # ⚷ 2:52
☽ ⚹ ⚷ 2:59
☉ ⊼ ☽ 5:41
☽ ⊻ ♆ 9:08
☽ ⊻ ♇ 9:23
☽ ∥ ☿ 12:21
☽ □ ♅ 13:57
☽ ⚼ ☿ 16:23
☽ △ ♀ 16:47

25 F
☽ ⊻ ♄ 1:52
☽ ⚼ ♂ 4:06
☽ △ ⚳ 6:24
☽ ∠ ⚷ 6:48
☽ ∠ ♇ 13:05
☽ ⊼ ♃ 13:53
☽ # ♄ 16:35
☽ ⚼ ♀ 20:53
☉ ∥ ☽ 20:56
☽ ⊼ ☿ 23:14

26 Sa
☽ ∥ ♆ 0:47
☉ ☍ ♆ 1:37
☽ # ♆ 1:38
☉ △ ♇ 5:36
☉ # ☽ 6:01
☽ △ ♂ 8:33
☽ ∥ ♄ 9:40
☽ ⊻ ⚷ 9:50
☽ ☌ ♆ 15:42
☽ ⚹ ♇ 16:01
☉ ☍ ☽ 16:50
☽ ⚼ ♃ 17:11
☽ ⚹ ♅ 20:19
☉ ∠ ♃ 22:33

27 Su
☽ ⊼ ♀ 0:08
☽ ☌ ♄ 7:21
♂ □ ⚷ 12:00
☽ □ ⚳ 13:04
☽ △ ♃ 19:47
☽ # ☿ 21:20
☽ ∥ ⚷ 21:25
☿ # ⚷ 22:07
☽ ∠ ♅ 22:29

28 M
♂ ♌ 2:50
♂ ∥ ♅ 5:38
☽ ☍ ☿ 9:52
☉ # ♄ 13:14
☽ ☌ ⚷ 13:59
☽ ∥ ♃ 14:28
☽ □ ♂ 15:12
☉ △ ♅ 16:23
☽ ⊻ ♆ 19:41
☽ □ ♇ 20:03

29 Tu
☽ ⊻ ♅ 0:10
☉ ⊼ ☽ 0:45
☽ ☍ ♀ 4:37
☽ ⊻ ♄ 10:36
☽ # ♀ 14:31
☽ ∥ ♂ 15:11
☽ ∥ ♅ 15:58
☽ ⚹ ⚳ 17:26
☽ ∠ ♆ 21:04
☽ □ ♃ 23:37

30 W
☿ ☍ ⚷ 3:16
♀ # ♂ 3:28
☽ ∥ ⚳ 3:40
☉ ⚼ ☽ 4:01
☽ # ♇ 6:36
☿ ♏ 11:46
☽ ∠ ♄ 11:46
☽ ⊻ ⚷ 16:37
☽ ⊼ ☿ 18:02
☽ ∠ ⚳ 19:11
☽ ⚹ ♂ 20:08
☽ ⚹ ♆ 22:16
☽ △ ♇ 22:42

October 2026

LONGITUDE

Day	Sid.Time	☉	☽	☽ 12 hour	Mean☊	True☊	☿	♀	♂	⚳	♃	♄	⚷	♅	♆	♇
	h m s	° ' "	° ' "	° ' "	° '	° '	° '	° '	° '	° '	° '	° '	° '	° '	° '	° '
1 Th	0 38 59	7♎50 17	3♊53 43	11♊02 13	27♒42.8	29♒09.2	0♏40.7	8♏23.4	1♌41.3	16♋05.2	19♌35.5	11♈34.7	29♈29.4	5♊31.6	2♈51.7	3♒07.4
2 F	0 42 55	8 49 16	18 10 31	25 18 12	27 39.6	29R 05.7	1 59.5	8 27.5	2 16.2	16 21.2	19 46.2	11R 30.0	29R 26.8	5R 30.5	2R 50.1	3R 06.9
3 Sa	0 46 52	9 48 17	2♋24 57	9♋30 29	27 36.5	29D 04.0	3 17.1	8R 29.4	2 51.0	16 36.9	19 56.8	11 25.3	29 24.3	5 29.5	2 48.4	3 06.6
4 Su	0 50 48	10 47 20	16 34 33	23 37 00	27 33.3	29 03.9	4 33.3	8 28.9	3 25.6	16 52.4	20 07.3	11 20.6	29 21.7	5 28.4	2 46.8	3 06.2
5 M	0 54 45	11 46 26	0♌37 42	7♌36 31	27 30.1	29 04.9	5 48.0	8 26.1	4 00.2	17 07.7	20 17.8	11 15.9	29 19.0	5 27.2	2 45.1	3 05.9
6 Tu	0 58 41	12 45 34	14 33 22	21 28 09	27 26.9	29 06.2	7 01.2	8 20.9	4 34.6	17 22.8	20 28.1	11 11.1	29 16.4	5 26.0	2 43.5	3 05.6
7 W	1 02 38	13 44 44	28 20 46	5♍11 04	27 23.8	29R 06.9	8 12.7	8 13.4	5 08.9	17 37.7	20 38.4	11 06.4	29 13.7	5 24.7	2 41.9	3 05.3
8 Th	1 06 35	14 43 56	11♍58 57	18 44 14	27 20.6	29 06.1	9 22.5	8 03.4	5 43.0	17 52.3	20 48.5	11 01.7	29 11.0	5 23.4	2 40.2	3 05.1
9 F	1 10 31	15 43 11	25 26 47	2♎06 23	27 17.4	29 03.3	10 30.5	7 51.1	6 17.1	18 06.8	20 58.6	10 57.0	29 08.3	5 22.1	2 38.6	3 04.9
10 Sa	1 14 28	16 42 28	8♎42 52	15 16 05	27 14.2	28 58.1	11 36.3	7 36.4	6 50.9	18 21.0	21 08.6	10 52.3	29 05.6	5 20.7	2 37.0	3 04.7
11 Su	1 18 24	17 41 47	21 45 51	28 12 05	27 11.0	28 50.8	12 40.0	7 19.4	7 24.7	18 35.0	21 18.4	10 47.6	29 02.9	5 19.3	2 35.4	3 04.5
12 M	1 22 21	18 41 08	4♏34 41	10♏53 37	27 07.9	28 42.0	13 41.3	7 00.0	7 58.3	18 48.8	21 28.2	10 43.0	29 00.2	5 17.8	2 33.8	3 04.4
13 Tu	1 26 17	19 40 30	17 08 56	23 20 44	27 04.7	28 32.4	14 40.0	6 38.5	8 31.7	19 02.3	21 37.9	10 38.3	28 57.4	5 16.3	2 32.2	3 04.3
14 W	1 30 14	20 39 55	29 29 10	5♐34 28	27 01.5	28 23.1	15 35.8	6 14.8	9 05.0	19 15.6	21 47.4	10 33.7	28 54.6	5 14.7	2 30.7	3 04.2
15 Th	1 34 10	21 39 22	11♐36 56	17 36 55	26 58.3	28 14.9	16 28.5	5 49.0	9 38.2	19 28.6	21 56.9	10 29.1	28 51.9	5 13.1	2 29.1	3 04.1
16 F	1 38 07	22 38 51	23 34 52	29 31 15	26 55.2	28 08.5	17 17.7	5 21.4	10 11.2	19 41.4	22 06.2	10 24.6	28 49.1	5 11.5	2 27.6	3D 04.1
17 Sa	1 42 04	23 38 21	5♑26 37	11♑21 31	26 52.0	28 04.4	18 03.2	4 51.9	10 44.1	19 53.9	22 15.4	10 20.0	28 46.3	5 09.8	2 26.0	3 04.1
18 Su	1 46 00	24 37 53	17 16 34	23 12 24	26 48.8	28D 02.4	18 44.4	4 20.8	11 16.8	20 06.2	22 24.5	10 15.5	28 43.5	5 08.1	2 24.5	3 04.2
19 M	1 49 57	25 37 27	29 09 41	5♒09 06	26 45.6	28 02.1	19 21.1	3 48.2	11 49.3	20 18.2	22 33.5	10 11.1	28 40.7	5 06.4	2 23.0	3 04.2
20 Tu	1 53 53	26 37 03	11♒11 18	17 16 56	26 42.4	28 02.8	19 52.8	3 14.4	12 21.7	20 29.9	22 42.4	10 06.6	28 37.9	5 04.6	2 21.5	3 04.3
21 W	1 57 50	27 36 40	23 26 38	29 41 00	26 39.3	28R 03.6	20 18.8	2 39.5	12 53.9	20 41.4	22 51.2	10 02.2	28 35.1	5 02.8	2 20.1	3 04.5
22 Th	2 01 46	28 36 19	6♓00 33	12♓25 45	26 36.1	28 03.4	20 38.9	2 03.8	13 26.0	20 52.6	22 59.8	9 57.9	28 32.3	5 00.9	2 18.6	3 04.6
23 F	2 05 43	29 36 00	18 56 58	25 34 27	26 32.9	28 01.3	20 52.2	1 27.5	13 57.9	21 03.5	23 08.4	9 53.6	28 29.5	4 59.0	2 17.2	3 04.8
24 Sa	2 09 39	0♏35 42	2♈18 18	9♈08 31	26 29.7	27 56.8	20R 58.4	0 50.8	14 29.6	21 14.1	23 16.8	9 49.3	28 26.7	4 57.1	2 15.7	3 05.0
25 Su	2 13 36	1 35 26	16 04 52	23 07 00	26 26.6	27 49.8	20 56.8	0 14.0	15 01.2	21 24.4	23 25.0	9 45.1	28 23.9	4 55.1	2 14.3	3 05.2
26 M	2 17 32	2 35 13	0♉14 25	7♉26 25	26 23.4	27 40.7	20 46.9	29♎37.4	15 32.6	21 34.5	23 33.2	9 40.9	28 21.1	4 53.1	2 12.9	3 05.5
27 Tu	2 21 29	3 35 01	14 42 12	22 00 50	26 20.2	27 30.3	20 28.2	29 01.2	16 03.8	21 44.2	23 41.2	9 36.8	28 18.3	4 51.1	2 11.6	3 05.8
28 W	2 25 26	4 34 51	29 21 22	6♊42 48	26 17.0	27 19.9	20 00.5	28 25.7	16 34.9	21 53.7	23 49.1	9 32.8	28 15.5	4 49.1	2 10.2	3 06.1
29 Th	2 29 22	5 34 44	14♊04 09	21 24 30	26 13.8	27 10.5	19 23.5	27 51.1	17 05.8	22 02.8	23 56.9	9 28.8	28 12.8	4 47.0	2 08.9	3 06.5
30 F	2 33 19	6 34 38	28 43 03	5♋59 07	26 10.7	27 03.3	18 37.4	27 17.6	17 36.5	22 11.6	24 04.5	9 24.9	28 10.0	4 44.9	2 07.6	3 06.9
31 Sa	2 37 15	7♏34 35	13♋12 09	20 21 43	26♒07.5	26♒58.6	17♏42.5	26♎45.5	18♌07.0	22♋20.1	24♌12.0	9♈21.0	28♈07.2	4♊42.7	2♈06.3	3♒07.3

1st of Month

Julian Day # 2461314.5
Obliquity 23°26'07"
SVP 4♓53'02"
GC 27♐12.8
Eris 25♈34.8R

Day	⚴	Day	⚵	Day	⚶
1	15♈25.0R	1	26♑19.3	1	23♈02.9R
6	13 58.9R	6	26 51.6	6	21 48.8R
11	12 30.6R	11	27 32.8	11	20 31.6R
16	11 02.6R	16	28 22.5	16	19 13.8R
21	9 37.3R	21	29 20.3	21	17 58.1R
26	8 16.9R	26	0♒25.5	26	16 46.9R
31	7 03.3R	31	1 37.7	31	15 42.1R

DECLINATION and LATITUDE

Day	☉ Decl	☽ Decl	☽ Lat	☽12h Decl	☿ Decl	☿ Lat	♀ Decl	♀ Lat	♂ Decl	♂ Lat	⚳ Decl	⚳ Lat	♃ Decl	♃ Lat	♄ Decl	♄ Lat
1 Th	3S07	25N59	5N09	27N06	13S21	1S45	20S58	7S04	20N46	1N01	23N10	0N42	15N31	0N36	2N05	2S43
2 F	3 30	27 47	4 53	27 59	13 55	1 52	21 05	7 09	20 40	1 02	23 11	0 45	15 27	0 36	2 03	2 43
3 Sa	3 53	27 44	4 19	27 02	14 28	1 59	21 10	7 14	20 33	1 03	23 12	0 48	15 24	0 36	2 01	2 43
4 Su	4 16	25 53	3 30	24 20	15 01	2 06	21 14	7 18	20 26	1 04	23 13	0 51	15 21	0 36	1 59	2 43
5 M	4 39	22 25	2 28	20 12	15 32	2 12	21 18	7 22	20 18	1 05	23 14	0 54	15 18	0 36	1 57	2 43
6 Tu	5 02	17 42	1 18	14 60	16 02	2 19	21 18	7 25	20 11	1 06	23 15	0 57	15 15	0 37	1 56	2 43
7 W	5 25	12 07	0 04	9 06	16 32	2 25	21 18	7 28	20 04	1 07	23 16	0 60	15 12	0 37	1 54	2 43
8 Th	5 48	6 00	1S09	2 52	17 00	2 31	21 17	7 31	19 57	1 08	23 17	1 03	15 08	0 37	1 52	2 43
9 F	6 11	0S17	2 17	3S25	17 27	2 37	21 15	7 33	19 49	1 09	23 18	1 06	15 05	0 37	1 50	2 43
10 Sa	6 34	6 28	3 17	9 26	17 53	2 42	21 11	7 34	19 42	1 10	23 19	1 09	15 02	0 37	1 48	2 43
11 Su	6 57	12 16	4 05	14 56	18 18	2 47	21 06	7 35	19 34	1 12	23 20	1 12	14 59	0 37	1 46	2 43
12 M	7 19	17 26	4 40	19 42	18 41	2 52	20 60	7 35	19 27	1 13	23 21	1 15	14 56	0 38	1 45	2 43
13 Tu	7 42	21 45	4 60	23 31	19 03	2 56	20 52	7 34	19 19	1 14	23 22	1 18	14 53	0 38	1 43	2 43
14 W	8 04	25 01	5 06	26 12	19 23	3 00	20 42	7 32	19 11	1 15	23 24	1 21	14 51	0 38	1 41	2 43
15 Th	8 26	27 05	4 58	27 39	19 42	3 04	20 31	7 30	19 03	1 16	23 25	1 24	14 48	0 38	1 39	2 43
16 F	8 49	27 53	4 37	27 48	19 59	3 07	20 19	7 27	18 56	1 17	23 26	1 28	14 45	0 38	1 38	2 43
17 Sa	9 11	27 23	4 04	26 40	20 14	3 09	20 05	7 23	18 48	1 18	23 28	1 31	14 42	0 39	1 36	2 43
18 Su	9 33	25 38	3 20	24 19	20 27	3 11	19 50	7 18	18 40	1 19	23 29	1 34	14 39	0 39	1 34	2 43
19 M	9 54	22 45	2 28	20 55	20 38	3 12	19 33	7 13	18 32	1 20	23 31	1 38	14 36	0 39	1 33	2 42
20 Tu	10 16	18 51	1 29	16 34	20 47	3 12	19 16	7 06	18 24	1 22	23 32	1 41	14 34	0 39	1 31	2 42
21 W	10 37	14 06	0 25	11 27	20 53	3 11	18 57	6 59	18 16	1 23	23 34	1 44	14 31	0 39	1 30	2 42
22 Th	10 59	8 39	0N42	5 44	20 57	3 09	18 36	6 51	18 08	1 24	23 36	1 48	14 28	0 39	1 28	2 42
23 F	11 20	2 42	1 49	0N24	20 58	3 06	18 15	6 42	17 60	1 25	23 37	1 51	14 26	0 40	1 26	2 42
24 Sa	11 41	3N33	2 52	6 42	20 55	3 02	17 53	6 32	17 51	1 26	23 39	1 55	14 23	0 40	1 24	2 42
25 Su	12 02	9 48	3 47	12 51	20 50	2 56	17 30	6 22	17 43	1 27	23 41	1 58	14 21	0 40	1 23	2 42
26 M	12 22	15 45	4 29	18 28	20 40	2 49	17 07	6 11	17 35	1 29	23 43	2 02	14 18	0 40	1 21	2 42
27 Tu	12 43	20 56	4 55	23 07	20 27	2 41	16 43	5 59	17 27	1 30	23 45	2 06	14 16	0 40	1 20	2 42
28 W	13 03	24 55	5 02	26 20	20 10	2 31	16 18	5 47	17 19	1 31	23 47	2 09	14 13	0 41	1 18	2 42
29 Th	13 23	27 17	4 49	27 45	19 48	2 19	15 54	5 34	17 11	1 32	23 49	2 13	14 11	0 41	1 17	2 41
30 F	13 43	27 44	4 18	27 14	19 22	2 05	15 29	5 20	17 02	1 34	23 52	2 17	14 08	0 41	1 15	2 41
31 Sa	14S02	26N16	3N30	24N53	18S52	1S50	15S04	5S06	16N54	1N35	23N54	2N21	14N06	0N41	1N14	2S41

Day	⚷ Decl	⚷ Lat	♅ Decl	♅ Lat	♆ Decl	♆ Lat	♇ Decl	♇ Lat
1	11N27	0N10	21N04	0S09	0S10	1S25	23S38	4S18
6	11 22	0 10	21 03	0 09	0 13	1 25	23 38	4 17
11	11 17	0 10	21 02	0 09	0 16	1 25	23 38	4 17
16	11 12	0 09	21 01	0 09	0 19	1 25	23 38	4 17
21	11 07	0 09	20 59	0 09	0 22	1 25	23 38	4 17
26	11 01	0 09	20 58	0 09	0 25	1 25	23 37	4 17
31	10N56	0N08	20N56	0S09	0S28	1S25	23S37	4S16

Day	⚴ Decl	⚴ Lat	⚵ Decl	⚵ Lat	⚶ Decl	⚶ Lat	Eris Decl	Eris Lat
1	12S22	19S59	12S20	8N42	2S02	11S49	0N05	10S31
6	13 44	20 54	12 44	8 12	2 33	11 53	0 04	10 31
11	15 02	21 43	13 06	7 42	3 01	11 54	0 03	10 30
16	16 15	22 27	13 24	7 14	3 27	11 51	0 02	10 30
21	17 22	23 04	13 39	6 46	3 48	11 44	0 01	10 30
26	18 21	23 36	13 52	6 20	4 06	11 38	0 01	10 30
31	19S12	24S02	14S02	5N55	4S18	11S21	0S00	10S30

Moon Phenomena

Max/0 Decl dy hr mn		
2	11:28	27N59
8	22:54	0 S
16	2:39	27S54
23	10:27	0 N
29	17:32	27N48

Max/0 Lat dy hr mn		
7	1:21	0 S
13	21:52	5S06
21	8:53	0 N
27	20:44	5N02

Perigee/Apogee dy hr m		kilometers
1	20:53	p 369334
16	22:57	a 404642
28	18:07	p 364409

PH	dy	hr mn	
☾	3	13:26	10♋21
●	10	15:51	17♎22
☽	18	16:14	25♑18
○	26	4:13	2♉46

Void of Course Moon

Last Aspect			☽ Ingress		
2	2:43	♃ ✶	♋	2	19:55
3	15:10	♄ □	♌	4	22:55
6	10:23	♃ ☌	♍	7	2:54
7	18:58	☿ ✶	♎	9	8:12
10	23:08	♃ ✶	♏	11	15:22
13	8:47	♃ □	♐	14	1:01
15	21:57	☉ ✶	♑	16	12:58
18	16:14	☉ □	♒	19	1:41
21	8:43	☉ △	♓	21	12:36
23	3:32	☿ △	♈	23	19:55
25	23:01	♀ ☍	♉	25	23:36
27	14:52	♃ □	♊	28	1:03
29	21:45	♀ △	♋	30	2:07

DAILY ASPECTARIAN

1 Th	☽☌♅ 2:44; ☉△☽ 7:07; ☽⚻♀ 7:36; ☽✶♄ 12:50; ☉⚺♀ 14:36; ☽∠⚷ 17:45; ☽⚺⚳ 20:53; ☽⚼☿ 21:49; ☽∠♂ 22:25; ♀⋕♅ 22:45; ☽⚼♇ 23:54
2 F	☽✶♃ 2:43; ☽⚼♀ 8:55; ☿□♂ 9:15; ☿⚻♆ 15:16; ☽✶⚷ 18:56; ☿□♇ 20:44; ♂△♆ 22:19
3 Sa	☽□♆ 0:40; ☽⚺♂ 0:46; ☽⚻♇ 1:10; ☽△☿ 1:37; ☽∠♃ 4:20; ☽⚺♅ 5:12; ♀R 7:17; ☽△♀ 10:17; ♂☍♇ 10:40; ☉□☽ 13:26; ☊D 13:32; ☽□♄ 15:10
4 Su	☽☌⚳ 0:31; ☽⚺♃ 6:07; ☽∠♅ 6:38; ☉☍♄ 12:30; ☿⋕♃ 14:00; ☽⋕♇ 16:37; ☿⚻♅ 17:23; ☽∥⚳ 19:12; ☽□⚷ 21:46
5 M	☽△♆ 3:38; ☽☍♇ 4:14; ☽☌♂ 6:03; ☽⋕♀ 6:21; ☽∥♅ 7:32; ☽✶♅ 8:17; ☽□☿ 9:45; ☽∥♂ 11:45; ☽□♀ 13:21; ☽△♄ 18:12; ☉✶☽ 20:39
6 Tu	☽⚺⚳ 4:59; ☽⚼♆ 5:29; ☽⋕☿ 6:52; ☽☌♃ 10:23; ☽∥♃ 11:03; ☽⚼♄ 20:06
7 W	☿☌♀ 0:12; ☉∠☽ 0:45; ☊R 1:19; ☽△⚷ 1:32; ☽∥⚷ 3:04; ☽⚻♆ 7:37; ☽∠⚳ 7:39; ☽⚻♇ 8:19; ♂✶♅ 10:43; ☽□♅ 12:23; ☽⚺♂ 12:27; ☽✶♀ 17:09; ☽✶☿ 18:58; ☽⚻♄ 22:19
8 Th	☉⋕☽ 0:43; ☽⚼⚷ 3:53; ☉⚺☽ 5:16; ☽✶⚳ 10:39; ☽⚼♇ 10:50; ☽∥♄ 15:52; ☽⚺♃ 15:54; ☽∠♂ 16:13; ☽∠♀ 19:25; ☽⋕♆ 21:56; ☽∥♆ 23:51
9 F	☽∠☿ 0:07; ☽⋕♄ 5:54; ☽⚻⚷ 6:37; ☿⚻♄ 8:57; ☽☍♆ 12:57; ☽△♇ 13:46; ☽△♅ 17:53; ☽∠♃ 19:16; ☽✶♂ 20:27; ☽⚺♀ 22:01
10 Sa	☉∥☽ 0:25; ☽☍♄ 3:55; ☽⚺☿ 5:45; ☉☌☽ 15:51; ☽□⚳ 18:00; ☽⋕⚷ 19:49; ☽⚼♅ 21:20; ♀□♂ 21:32; ☽✶♃ 23:08
11 Su	☽⋕♃ 12:07; ☽☍⚷ 13:32; ♀⋕♅ 15:27; ☽⚻♆ 20:12; ☽□♇ 21:09
12 M	☽⚻♅ 1:21; ☉□⚳ 4:00; ☽☌♀ 4:28; ☽□♂ 6:44; ☽∥☿ 7:03; ☽⋕♂ 10:16; ☽⚻♄ 11:35; ☽∥♀ 18:48; ☽☌☿ 18:50; ☽⋕♅ 19:38
13 Tu	☽⚼♆ 0:45; ☽△⚳ 3:43; ☉⚺☽ 5:18; ☽□♃ 8:47; ☽⋕⚳ 11:01; ☽∥♇ 12:54; ☿⋕♂ 13:38; ☉⚼♅ 14:05; ☽⚼♄ 16:22; ☽⚻⚷ 22:53
14 W	☽△♆ 5:56; ☽✶♇ 7:03; ☽⚼⚳ 9:34; ☽☍♅ 11:20; ☽⚺♀ 12:53; ☉∠☽ 13:16; ☽△♂ 19:52; ☽△♄ 21:46
15 Th	☽⚼⚷ 4:28; ☉✶♃ 8:23; ☽⚺☿ 10:27; ☽∠♇ 12:55; ☽⚻⚳ 16:01; ☽∠♀ 17:45; ☽△♃ 20:59; ☉✶☽ 21:57
16 F	♇D 2:42; ☽⚼♂ 3:24; ☿⚼♆ 4:52; ♂△♄ 8:34; ♀⚻♅ 8:40; ☽△⚷ 10:32; ☿∥♀ 16:37; ☽□♆ 17:55; ☽∠☿ 18:50; ☽⚺♇ 19:11; ☽✶♀ 22:52; ☽⚻♅ 23:26
17 Sa	☽⚼♃ 3:44; ☽□♄ 9:52; ☽⚻♂ 11:15
18 Su	☽✶☿ 3:08; ⚳∠♅ 3:23; ☽⚼♅ 5:47; ☽☍⚳ 5:49; ☽⚻♃ 10:31; ☊D 16:05; ☉□☽ 16:14; ☽∥♇ 17:28; ☽⋕⚳ 18:27; ☽□⚷ 23:02
19 M	☽✶♆ 6:27; ☽☌♇ 7:50; ☽□♀ 8:54; ☽⋕♅ 11:28; ☽△♅ 11:53; ☽∥☿ 13:09; ☽∥♀ 21:30; ☽✶♄ 21:53
20 Tu	☽☍♂ 2:26; ☽⋕♂ 2:31; ♀□♇ 6:57; ☽∠♆ 12:08; ☽□☿ 17:43; ☽⚻⚳ 18:34; ☽⋕♃ 21:59; ☽☍♃ 22:51
21 W	☽∠♄ 3:04; ☉△☽ 8:43; ☊R 8:52; ☽✶⚷ 9:52; ☽⋕⚷ 13:31; ♀⚻♆ 13:40; ☉∥☽ 14:39; ☽△♀ 16:52; ☽⚺♆ 17:01; ☽⚺♇ 18:27; ☽□♅ 22:08; ☉☍⚷ 22:28; ☽⚼⚳ 23:45
22 Th	☽⚺♄ 7:22; ☉⋕⚷ 7:25; ☽∠⚷ 14:00; ☽⚻♂ 14:27; ☉⚼☽ 15:21; ☽⚼♀ 19:38; ☽∠♇ 22:25
23 F	☽△☿ 3:32; ☽△⚳ 3:53; ☽⋕♄ 4:57; ⚳⋕♇ 5:36; ☽⚻♃ 7:42; ☽∥♆ 8:56; ☉ ♏ 9:39; ☽⋕♆ 11:58; ☽∥♄ 15:53; ☽⚺⚷ 17:10; ☽⚼♂ 18:48; ☉⚻☽ 20:44; ☽⚻♀ 21:32; ☽☌♆ 23:55
24 Sa	☽✶♇ 1:23; ⚵ ♒ 2:40; ♀⋕♂ 2:46; ☉☌♀ 3:45; ☽✶♅ 4:39; ☽⚼☿ 6:28; ☿R 7:14; ☽⚼♃ 10:36; ☽☌♄ 13:07; ☽△♂ 22:06
25 Su	☽∥⚷ 4:48; ☽∠♅ 6:33; ☽⚻☿ 8:15; ♀R♎ 9:11; ☽□⚳ 9:12; ☉⋕☽ 9:15; ☽△♃ 12:38; ☉⚻♆ 15:16; ☽∥♃ 17:59; ☽☌⚷ 20:50; ☽☍♀ 23:01
26 M	☽⚺♆ 3:18; ☉☍☽ 4:13; ☽□♇ 4:46; ☽⋕♀ 5:31; ☽⚺♅ 7:44; ☽∥♂ 7:49; ☉□♇ 12:13; ☽⚺♄ 15:38; ☽⋕☿ 21:38
27 Tu	☽∥♅ 0:05; ☽□♂ 2:19; ☽∠♆ 4:05; ☽☍☿ 9:13; ☽✶⚳ 11:40; ☽□♃ 14:52; ☽⋕♇ 15:09; ☽∥⚳ 16:07; ☽∠♄ 16:11; ☽⚺⚷ 22:13; ☽⚻♀ 22:33
28 W	☽✶♆ 4:35; ☉⚻♅ 5:30; ☽△♇ 6:07; ♀☍⚷ 7:36; ☽☌♅ 8:53; ☉⚻☽ 9:09; ☽∠⚳ 12:26; ☽✶♄ 16:33; ☽⚼♀ 22:05; ☽∠⚷ 22:36
29 Th	♂⚼♆ 2:21; ☽✶♂ 5:07; ☽⚼♇ 6:36; ☽⚻☿ 8:18; ☉⚼☽ 11:25; ☽⚺⚳ 13:11; ☽✶♃ 16:18; ☽△♀ 21:45; ☽✶⚷ 23:06
30 F	☽□♆ 5:37; ☽∠♂ 6:39; ☽⚻♇ 7:15; ☽⚼☿ 7:38; ☽⚺♅ 9:56; ☉△☽ 13:57; ☽∠♃ 17:17; ☿□♂ 17:21; ☽□♄ 17:37
31 Sa	☉⋕♃ 4:16; ☽△☿ 7:03; ☽⚺♂ 8:32; ☽∠♅ 10:53; ☿⚼♆ 14:28; ☽☌⚳ 15:29; ☽⚺♃ 18:38; ☽∥⚳ 18:42; ♃⚼♄ 19:15; ☽⋕♇ 20:49; ☽□♀ 22:01

LONGITUDE

November 2026

Day	Sid.Time	☉	☽	☽ 12 hour	Mean ☊	True ☊	☿	♀	♂	⚳	♃	♄	⚷	♅	♆	♇
	h m s	° ' "	° ' "	° ' "	° '	° '	° '	° '	° '	° '	° '	° '	° '	° '	° '	° '
1 Su	2 41 12	8♏34 34	27♋27 34	4♌29 31	26♒04.3	26♒56.5	16♏39.7	26♎14.8	18♌37.3	22♋28.3	24♌19.4	9♈17.2	28♈04.5	4♊40.6	2♈05.0	3♒07.7
2 M	2 45 08	9 34 35	11♌27 34	18 21 44	26 01.1	26D 56.0	15R 30.2	25R 46.0	19 07.4	22 36.1	24 26.6	9R 13.4	28R 01.7	4R 38.4	2R 03.8	3 08.2
3 Tu	2 49 05	10 34 38	25 12 08	1♍58 54	25 58.0	26R 56.2	14 15.7	25 18.9	19 37.3	22 43.7	24 33.7	9 09.8	27 59.0	4 36.2	2 02.6	3 08.7
4 W	2 53 02	11 34 44	8♍42 13	15 22 15	25 54.8	26 55.8	12 58.0	24 53.9	20 07.0	22 50.8	24 40.6	9 06.2	27 56.3	4 33.9	2 01.4	3 09.2
5 Th	2 56 58	12 34 51	21 59 11	28 33 09	25 51.6	26 53.5	11 39.7	24 31.1	20 36.6	22 57.7	24 47.4	9 02.6	27 53.6	4 31.6	2 00.2	3 09.8
6 F	3 00 55	13 35 00	5♎04 15	11♎32 36	25 48.4	26 48.5	10 23.0	24 10.4	21 05.9	23 04.1	24 54.1	8 59.2	27 50.9	4 29.3	1 59.0	3 10.3
7 Sa	3 04 51	14 35 12	17 58 15	24 21 14	25 45.3	26 40.4	9 10.5	23 52.1	21 34.9	23 10.2	25 00.6	8 55.8	27 48.2	4 27.0	1 57.9	3 10.9
8 Su	3 08 48	15 35 25	0♏41 33	6♏59 12	25 42.1	26 29.4	8 04.6	23 36.2	22 03.8	23 16.0	25 06.9	8 52.5	27 45.6	4 24.7	1 56.8	3 11.6
9 M	3 12 44	16 35 40	13 14 11	19 26 31	25 38.9	26 16.3	7 07.0	23 22.6	22 32.4	23 21.4	25 13.1	8 49.2	27 43.0	4 22.3	1 55.7	3 12.2
10 Tu	3 16 41	17 35 57	25 36 12	1♐43 17	25 35.7	26 02.0	6 19.4	23 11.6	23 00.8	23 26.4	25 19.1	8 46.1	27 40.4	4 20.0	1 54.7	3 12.9
11 W	3 20 37	18 36 16	7♐47 53	13 50 06	25 32.5	25 47.8	5 42.8	23 02.9	23 29.0	23 31.1	25 25.0	8 43.0	27 37.8	4 17.6	1 53.6	3 13.6
12 Th	3 24 34	19 36 37	19 50 07	25 48 11	25 29.4	25 35.0	5 17.8	22 56.8	23 56.9	23 35.3	25 30.7	8 40.1	27 35.2	4 15.2	1 52.6	3 14.4
13 F	3 28 31	20 36 59	1♑44 36	7♑39 43	25 26.2	25 24.4	5D 04.5	22 53.1	24 24.6	23 39.2	25 36.3	8 37.2	27 32.7	4 12.8	1 51.7	3 15.2
14 Sa	3 32 27	21 37 22	13 33 56	19 27 44	25 23.0	25 16.6	5 02.6	22D 51.8	24 52.1	23 42.7	25 41.7	8 34.4	27 30.2	4 10.3	1 50.7	3 16.0
15 Su	3 36 24	22 37 47	25 21 39	1♒16 14	25 19.8	25 11.8	5 11.7	22 53.0	25 19.3	23 45.9	25 46.9	8 31.6	27 27.7	4 07.9	1 49.8	3 16.8
16 M	3 40 20	23 38 13	7♒12 06	13 09 54	25 16.7	25 09.5	5 31.1	22 56.5	25 46.2	23 48.6	25 52.0	8 29.0	27 25.2	4 05.4	1 48.9	3 17.7
17 Tu	3 44 17	24 38 41	19 10 20	25 14 03	25 13.5	25 08.8	5 59.9	23 02.4	26 12.9	23 50.9	25 56.9	8 26.5	27 22.8	4 02.9	1 48.1	3 18.5
18 W	3 48 13	25 39 10	1♓21 47	7♓34 13	25 10.3	25 08.8	6 37.2	23 10.5	26 39.3	23 52.8	26 01.7	8 24.1	27 20.4	4 00.5	1 47.2	3 19.4
19 Th	3 52 10	26 39 40	13 51 59	20 15 43	25 07.1	25 08.1	7 22.2	23 20.9	27 05.4	23 54.4	26 06.2	8 21.7	27 18.0	3 58.0	1 46.4	3 20.4
20 F	3 56 06	27 40 12	26 45 57	3♈23 07	25 04.0	25 05.7	8 14.0	23 33.5	27 31.3	23 55.5	26 10.6	8 19.5	27 15.7	3 55.5	1 45.7	3 21.3
21 Sa	4 00 03	28 40 44	10♈07 33	16 59 24	25 00.8	25 00.9	9 11.7	23 48.2	27 56.8	23 56.2	26 14.8	8 17.3	27 13.4	3 53.0	1 44.9	3 22.3
22 Su	4 03 59	29 41 18	23 58 39	1♉05 06	24 57.6	24 53.3	10 14.6	24 05.0	28 22.1	23R 56.5	26 18.9	8 15.3	27 11.1	3 50.5	1 44.2	3 23.3
23 M	4 07 56	0♐41 53	8♉18 17	15 37 34	24 54.4	24 43.3	11 22.0	24 23.9	28 47.1	23 56.4	26 22.8	8 13.3	27 08.9	3 47.9	1 43.5	3 24.4
24 Tu	4 11 53	1 42 30	23 02 05	0♊30 47	24 51.2	24 31.7	12 33.3	24 44.6	29 11.8	23 55.9	26 26.5	8 11.4	27 06.7	3 45.4	1 42.9	3 25.4
25 W	4 15 49	2 43 08	8♊02 29	15 35 52	24 48.1	24 19.9	13 47.9	25 07.3	29 36.3	23 55.0	26 30.0	8 09.7	27 04.5	3 42.9	1 42.3	3 26.5
26 Th	4 19 46	3 43 48	23 09 39	0♋42 31	24 44.9	24 09.3	15 05.4	25 31.8	0♍00.4	23 53.6	26 33.3	8 08.0	27 02.4	3 40.4	1 41.7	3 27.6
27 F	4 23 42	4 44 29	8♋13 17	15 40 52	24 41.7	24 00.8	16 25.3	25 58.1	0 24.2	23 51.9	26 36.5	8 06.5	27 00.3	3 37.9	1 41.1	3 28.7
28 Sa	4 27 39	5 45 11	23 04 24	0♌23 10	24 38.5	23 55.1	17 47.3	26 26.2	0 47.6	23 49.7	26 39.5	8 05.0	26 58.3	3 35.4	1 40.6	3 29.9
29 Su	4 31 35	6 45 55	7♌36 39	14 44 34	24 35.4	23 52.3	19 11.0	26 55.8	1 10.8	23 47.1	26 42.3	8 03.7	26 56.2	3 32.8	1 40.1	3 31.1
30 M	4 35 32	7♐46 41	21 46 45	28 43 14	24♒32.2	23♒51.5	20♏36.2	27♎27.1	1♍33.6	23♋44.0	26♌44.9	8♈02.5	26♈54.3	3♊30.3	1♈39.7	3♒32.3

1st of Month

Julian Day #
2461345.5
Obliquity
23°26'7"
SVP 4♓52'58"
GC 27♐12.8
Eris 25♈16.5R

Day	⚴	Day	⚵	Day	⚶
1	6♈49.6R	1	1♒53.0	1	15♈30.0R
6	5 46.5R	6	3 13.0	6	14 35.3R
11	4 53.6R	11	4 39.1	11	13 50.4R
16	4 11.9R	16	6 11.0	16	13 16.3R
21	3 41.9R	21	7 48.1	21	12 53.5R
26	3 23.8R	26	9 30.1	26	12 42.1R

DECLINATION and LATITUDE

Day	☉ Decl	☽ Decl	☽ Lat	☽ 12h Decl	☿ Decl	☿ Lat	♀ Decl	♀ Lat	♂ Decl	♂ Lat	⚳ Decl	⚳ Lat	♃ Decl	♃ Lat	♄ Decl	♄ Lat
1 Su	14S22	23N07	2N30	21N01	18S18	1S33	14S40	4S52	16N46	1N36	23N56	2N25	14N04	0N41	1N13	2S41
2 M	14 41	18 39	1 21	16 03	17 40	1 15	14 16	4 37	16 38	1 37	23 59	2 28	14 02	0 42	1 11	2 41
3 Tu	14 60	13 16	0 09	10 21	16 60	0 55	13 52	4 23	16 29	1 39	24 02	2 32	13 59	0 42	1 10	2 41
4 W	15 18	7 21	1S02	4 17	16 17	0 35	13 29	4 08	16 21	1 40	24 04	2 36	13 57	0 42	1 09	2 41
5 Th	15 37	1 13	2 08	1S51	15 33	0 14	13 06	3 53	16 13	1 41	24 07	2 40	13 55	0 42	1 08	2 41
6 F	15 55	4S53	3 07	7 49	14 50	0N06	12 44	3 37	16 05	1 42	24 10	2 45	13 53	0 42	1 06	2 40
7 Sa	16 13	10 40	3 55	13 23	14 08	0 27	12 24	3 22	15 57	1 44	24 13	2 49	13 51	0 43	1 05	2 40
8 Su	16 30	15 56	4 30	18 18	13 29	0 46	12 04	3 07	15 49	1 45	24 16	2 53	13 49	0 43	1 04	2 40
9 M	16 48	20 27	4 52	22 22	12 53	1 03	11 45	2 52	15 41	1 46	24 19	2 57	13 47	0 43	1 03	2 40
10 Tu	17 05	24 00	4 60	25 22	12 22	1 20	11 27	2 37	15 32	1 48	24 23	3 01	13 46	0 43	1 02	2 40
11 W	17 22	26 26	4 53	27 11	11 57	1 34	11 10	2 23	15 24	1 49	24 26	3 06	13 44	0 44	1 01	2 39
12 Th	17 38	27 36	4 34	27 42	11 37	1 47	10 54	2 08	15 16	1 50	24 30	3 10	13 42	0 44	0 60	2 39
13 F	17 54	27 28	4 02	26 55	11 22	1 57	10 40	1 54	15 08	1 52	24 33	3 14	13 40	0 44	0 59	2 39
14 Sa	18 10	26 04	3 21	24 56	11 14	2 06	10 26	1 40	15 01	1 53	24 37	3 19	13 39	0 44	0 58	2 39
15 Su	18 26	23 32	2 30	21 52	11 10	2 13	10 14	1 26	14 53	1 55	24 41	3 23	13 37	0 44	0 57	2 39
16 M	18 41	19 59	1 33	17 52	11 12	2 18	10 03	1 13	14 45	1 56	24 45	3 28	13 36	0 45	0 56	2 39
17 Tu	18 56	15 34	0 32	13 06	11 18	2 21	9 53	0 60	14 37	1 57	24 49	3 32	13 34	0 45	0 55	2 38
18 W	19 10	10 29	0N33	7 43	11 28	2 23	9 44	0 47	14 29	1 59	24 53	3 37	13 33	0 45	0 55	2 38
19 Th	19 24	4 51	1 37	1 53	11 42	2 24	9 36	0 34	14 22	2 00	24 57	3 41	13 32	0 45	0 54	2 38
20 F	19 38	1N09	2 39	4N13	11 59	2 23	9 29	0 22	14 14	2 02	25 02	3 46	13 30	0 46	0 53	2 38
21 Sa	19 52	7 17	3 34	10 20	12 19	2 22	9 24	0 10	14 07	2 03	25 06	3 51	13 29	0 46	0 52	2 37
22 Su	20 05	13 18	4 18	16 09	12 41	2 20	9 20	0N01	13 59	2 05	25 11	3 55	13 28	0 46	0 52	2 37
23 M	20 18	18 49	4 48	21 15	13 05	2 16	9 16	0 12	13 52	2 06	25 15	4 00	13 27	0 46	0 51	2 37
24 Tu	20 30	23 22	5 00	25 07	13 30	2 13	9 14	0 23	13 45	2 08	25 20	4 05	13 26	0 46	0 51	2 37
25 W	20 42	26 27	4 52	27 18	13 56	2 08	9 13	0 33	13 38	2 09	25 25	4 10	13 25	0 47	0 50	2 37
26 Th	20 54	27 39	4 23	27 28	14 24	2 03	9 12	0 43	13 31	2 11	25 30	4 14	13 24	0 47	0 50	2 36
27 F	21 05	26 47	3 36	25 37	14 52	1 58	9 13	0 52	13 24	2 12	25 35	4 19	13 23	0 47	0 49	2 36
28 Sa	21 16	24 01	2 35	22 02	15 21	1 52	9 15	1 01	13 17	2 14	25 40	4 24	13 22	0 47	0 49	2 36
29 Su	21 26	19 44	1 25	17 11	15 49	1 46	9 17	1 10	13 10	2 16	25 46	4 29	13 22	0 48	0 49	2 36
30 M	21S36	14N25	0N11	11N31	16S18	1N39	9S20	1N19	13N03	2N17	25N51	4N34	13N21	0N48	0N49	2S35

Day	⚷ Decl	⚷ Lat	♅ Decl	♅ Lat	♆ Decl	♆ Lat	♇ Decl	♇ Lat
1	10N55	0N08	20N55	0S09	0S28	1S25	23S37	4S16
6	10 50	0 08	20 53	0 09	0 30	1 25	23 36	4 16
11	10 45	0 07	20 51	0 09	0 32	1 25	23 35	4 16
16	10 40	0 07	20 49	0 09	0 34	1 24	23 34	4 16
21	10 35	0 07	20 47	0 09	0 36	1 24	23 32	4 16
26	10 31	0 06	20 44	0 09	0 37	1 24	23 31	4 15

Day	⚴ Decl	⚴ Lat	⚵ Decl	⚵ Lat	⚶ Decl	⚶ Lat	Eris Decl	Eris Lat
1	19S22	24S06	14S03	5N50	4S20	11S18	0S00	10S30
6	20 03	24 25	14 09	5 26	4 26	11 02	0 01	10 29
11	20 36	24 39	14 12	5 03	4 26	10 44	0 02	10 29
16	21 00	24 48	14 12	4 40	4 21	10 24	0 02	10 29
21	21 17	24 54	14 09	4 19	4 11	10 04	0 03	10 28
26	21 26	24 56	14 03	3 58	3 56	9 43	0 03	10 28

Moon Phenomena

Max/0 Decl

dy	hr mn	
5	4:44	0 S
12	9:33	27S42
19	19:30	0 N
26	1:56	27N39

Perigee/Apogee

dy	hr m		kilometers
13	17:52	a	405618
25	21:02	p	359349

Max/0 Lat

dy	hr mn	
3	3:04	0 S
10	0:49	5S00
17	11:49	0 N
24	2:22	5N00
30	3:34	0 S

PH	dy	hr mn	
☾	1	20:30	9♌26
●	9	7:03	16♏53
☽	17	11:49	25♒08
○	24	14:55	2♊20

Void of Course Moon

Last Aspect				☽ Ingress		
31	22:01	♀	□	♌	1	4:19
3	0:12	♀	⚹	♍	3	8:29
4	6:59	☿	⚹	♎	5	14:39
7	13:21	♃	⚹	♏	7	22:41
9	23:26	♃	□	♐	10	8:37
12	11:30	♃	△	♑	12	20:28
14	18:57	♀	□	♒	15	9:25
17	14:27	♂	☍	♓	17	21:21
20	1:47	☉	△	♈	20	5:53
22	7:40	♂	△	♉	22	10:11
24	10:10	♂	□	♊	24	11:11
26	5:25	♃	⚹	♋	26	10:52
28	5:41	♀	□	♌	28	11:22
30	10:12	♀	⚹	♍	30	14:14

DAILY ASPECTARIAN

1 Su
☽□⚷ 1:03
☽△♆ 7:52
☽☍♇ 9:40
☉∥♀ 9:59
☽⚹♅ 12:17
☽∥♅ 12:31
☉⚻♄ 16:03
☽△♄ 20:09
☉□☽ 20:30
☊ D 20:40

2 M
☽#☿ 5:16
☽□☿ 6:27
☽∥♂ 9:38
☽⚼♆ 9:43
☽☌♂ 13:50
♀#♃ 15:26
☉#☽ 17:00
☽⚺⚳ 19:36
☽∥♃ 20:54
☽#♀ 21:17
☽⚼♄ 22:11
☽☌♃ 22:52

3 Tu
☽⚹♀ 0:12
☊ R 3:02
☽△⚷ 4:54
☽∥⚷ 9:54
☽⚻♆ 12:05
☽⚻♇ 14:05
☽□♅ 16:37
☿#♂ 21:04
☽∠⚳ 22:27

4 W
☽⚻♄ 0:43
☽∠♀ 2:05
☉⚹☽ 5:35
☽⚹☿ 6:59
☽⚼⚷ 7:35
♀⚹♃ 10:32
☉☌☿ 14:25
☽⚼♇ 17:03
☽⚺♂ 21:24
☉∥☿ 22:40

5 Th
☽∥♄ 0:20
☽⚹⚳ 1:47
☽#♆ 2:46
☽⚺♀ 4:30
☽⚺♃ 5:09
☽∥♆ 6:42
☽∠☿ 7:46
☽#♄ 9:06
☽⚻⚷ 10:45
☉∠☽ 11:04
☽☍♆ 18:19
☽△♇ 20:30
☽△♅ 22:56

6 F
☽∠♂ 1:58
☽☍♄ 7:13
☽⚺☿ 8:59
☽∠♃ 9:01
☉#♂ 9:10
☉⚺☽ 17:08

7 Sa
☽#⚷ 0:37
☽⚼♅ 2:46
☿⚻♄ 5:25
☽⚹♂ 7:03
☽∥♀ 7:07
☽□⚳ 9:51
☿#♃ 10:30
☽☌♀ 10:51
☽⚹♃ 13:21
☽∥☿ 13:42
☽#♃ 14:05
☽☍⚷ 18:27
☽#♂ 23:25

8 Su
☽⚻♆ 2:23
☉∥☽ 3:01
☽□♇ 4:46
☽⚻♅ 7:04
☽☌☿ 13:03
☽⚻♄ 15:33

9 M
♀□⚳ 1:43
☽#♅ 2:30
☉☌☽ 7:03
☽⚼♆ 7:07
☉⚼♆ 7:50
☽□♂ 18:45
☽⚺♀ 19:22
☽△⚳ 19:45
☽⚼♄ 20:26
☽∥♇ 20:44
☽□♃ 23:26

10 Tu
☽#⚳ 3:06
☽⚻⚷ 4:02
♀⚹♂ 6:49
☽△♆ 12:21
☽⚹♇ 14:57
☽☍♅ 17:05
☽⚺☿ 20:03

11 W
☽∠♀ 0:30
☽⚼⚳ 1:26
☽△♄ 1:49
♂⚺⚳ 2:06
☽⚼⚷ 9:34
♂⚼♄ 10:51
☽∠♇ 20:48
☉⚺☽ 23:30

12 Th
☽∠☿ 0:54
☽⚹♀ 6:13
☽⚻⚳ 7:35
☽△♂ 8:36
☽△♃ 11:30
☽△⚷ 15:33
♀#⚷ 18:21

13 F
☽□♆ 0:14
☽⚺♇ 3:04
☽⚻♅ 4:59
☽⚹☿ 6:42
☉∠☽ 8:35
☽□♄ 13:53
☿ D 15:55
☽⚼♂ 16:11
☽⚼♃ 18:07

14 Sa
♀ D 0:29
☽⚼♅ 11:22
☽#⚳ 14:36
☉⚹☽ 17:56
☽□♀ 18:57
☽☍⚳ 20:44
☽∥♇ 23:43
☽⚻♂ 23:55

15 Su
☽⚻♃ 0:52
☽□⚷ 4:15
☉⚺♀ 6:19
☽⚹♆ 13:07
☽☌♇ 16:05
☽△♅ 17:44
☽#♅ 18:50
☽□☿ 20:29
☉⚼♄ 20:30

16 M
☽⚹♄ 2:35
☉△⚳ 4:17
♂☌♃ 6:25
☉∥☽ 7:06
☽∠♆ 19:17

17 Tu
☽#♂ 4:51
☽△♀ 7:45
☽∠♄ 8:26
☽⚻⚳ 9:18
☽#♃ 9:49
☉□☽ 11:49
☽☍♃ 13:30
☽☍♂ 14:27
☽⚹⚷ 16:10
☽∥☿ 19:42
☽#⚷ 23:19

18 W
☽⚺♆ 0:49
☽∥♀ 3:24
☽⚺♇ 3:49
☽□♅ 5:07
☉□♃ 9:40
☽△☿ 10:48
☽⚼♀ 13:20
☽⚺♄ 13:33
☽⚼⚳ 14:33
☽∠⚷ 21:02

19 Th
☽∠♇ 8:25
♂△⚷ 10:43
☉⚻⚷ 14:39
☽#♄ 15:58
☽⚼☿ 17:01
☽∥♆ 17:10
☉□♂ 17:50
☽⚻♀ 18:00
☽△⚳ 18:47
☽#♆ 21:49
☽⚻♃ 22:55
☽∥♄ 22:59

20 F
☽⚺⚷ 0:54
☽⚻♂ 1:26
☉△☽ 1:47
☿⚻♄ 2:18
☽☌♆ 9:04
☽⚹♇ 11:58
☽⚹♅ 12:56
☽☌♄ 20:45
☽⚻☿ 22:13

21 Sa
☽⚼♃ 1:59
☽⚼♂ 5:07
☉⚼☽ 6:44
☽#♀ 8:12
♀□⚳ 12:02
☽∥⚷ 12:58
☽∠♅ 15:13
☽#☿ 21:17
☽□⚳ 23:56

22 Su
☽☍♀ 0:11
☽∥♃ 0:41
☽∥♂ 2:47
☽△♃ 3:59
☽☌⚷ 5:25
⚳ R 5:59
☉ ♐ 7:24
☽△♂ 7:40
☉⚻☽ 10:23
☽⚺♆ 13:05
☽□♇ 15:52
☽⚺♅ 16:33
☽⚺♄ 23:52

23 M
☽☍☿ 5:28
☉#☽ 7:29
☽∥♅ 9:30
☽∠♆ 13:47
☿#♃ 20:21

24 Tu
☉△♆ 0:09
☽∠♄ 0:15
☽#♇ 1:00
☽⚹⚳ 1:27
☽⚻♀ 2:49
☽□♃ 5:30
☽⚺⚷ 6:32
☽□♂ 10:10
☿#♂ 10:43
☽⚹♆ 13:55
☽∥⚳ 14:07
☉☍☽ 14:55
☽△♇ 16:40
☽☌♅ 17:08

25 W
☽⚹♄ 0:11
☽∠⚳ 1:23
☽⚼♀ 3:24
☉#♅ 5:22
☽∠⚷ 6:24
☽⚻☿ 9:59
☽⚼♇ 16:32
☉⚹♇ 17:29
☉☍♅ 22:43
♂ ♍ 23:38

26 Th
☽⚺⚳ 1:10
☽△♀ 3:52
☽⚹♃ 5:25
☽⚹⚷ 6:09
☽⚹♂ 11:11
☽⚼☿ 12:05
☽□♆ 13:34
☽⚻♇ 16:25
☽⚺♅ 16:41
☉⚻☽ 18:02
☽□♄ 23:49

27 F
♂∥♃ 2:07
☿⚼♆ 4:39
☽∠♃ 5:27
☽∥⚳ 11:50
☽∠♂ 11:52
☽△☿ 14:32
☽∠♅ 16:44
☉⚼☽ 19:57

28 Sa
☽☌⚳ 1:14
☽#♇ 3:16
☽□♀ 5:41
☽⚺♃ 5:53
☽□⚷ 6:22
♀⚹♃ 12:06
☽⚺♂ 13:01
⚶ D 13:27
☽△♆ 14:08
☉#☽ 15:35
☽☍♇ 17:11
☽⚹♅ 17:15
☽∥♅ 19:03
☉△☽ 22:29

29 Su
♀☍⚷ 0:18
☽△♄ 0:45
♅△♇ 11:22
☽⚼♆ 15:16
☽#☿ 16:33
☽□☿ 21:45

30 M
☽⚼♄ 2:10
☽⚺⚳ 3:21
☊ D 3:34
☽∥♃ 4:30
☽∥♂ 5:49
☉△♄ 6:07
♂⚻♆ 6:21
☽☌♃ 8:36
☽△⚷ 8:50
☽⚹♀ 10:12
☽∥⚷ 16:18
☽⚻♆ 17:07
☽☌♂ 17:26
☽□♅ 20:18
☽⚻♇ 20:27
☽#♀ 20:30
☉⚼⚳ 21:26

December 2026

LONGITUDE

Day	Sid.Time	☉	☽	☽ 12 hour	Mean☊	True☊	☿	♀	♂	⚳	♃	♄	⚷	♅	♆	♇
	h m s	° ' "	° ' "	° ' "	° '	° '	° '	° '	° '	° '	° '	° '	° '	° '	° '	° '
1 Tu	4 39 29	8♐47 27	5♍34 07	12♍19 40	24♒29.0	23♒51.6	22♏02.6	27♎59.9	1♍56.0	23♋40.6	26♌47.3	8♈01.3	26♈52.3	3♊27.8	1♈39.2	3♒33.5
2 W	4 43 25	9 48 16	19 00 08	25 35 53	24 25.8	23R 51.3	23 30.1	28 34.2	2 18.1	23R 36.7	26 49.6	8R 00.3	26R 50.5	3R 25.3	1R 38.8	3 34.8
3 Th	4 47 22	10 49 06	2♎07 16	8♎34 38	24 22.7	23 49.4	24 58.5	29 09.9	2 39.9	23 32.4	26 51.6	7 59.4	26 48.6	3 22.8	1 38.5	3 36.0
4 F	4 51 18	11 49 57	14 58 20	21 18 42	24 19.5	23 45.0	26 27.6	29 47.0	3 01.2	23 27.6	26 53.5	7 58.5	26 46.8	3 20.3	1 38.2	3 37.3
5 Sa	4 55 15	12 50 50	27 36 01	3♏50 33	24 16.3	23 37.8	27 57.4	0♏25.4	3 22.2	23 22.5	26 55.1	7 57.8	26 45.1	3 17.8	1 37.9	3 38.6
6 Su	4 59 11	13 51 44	10♏02 33	16 12 11	24 13.1	23 27.7	29 27.6	1 05.0	3 42.8	23 16.9	26 56.6	7 57.2	26 43.3	3 15.4	1 37.6	3 40.0
7 M	5 03 08	14 52 39	22 19 38	28 25 03	24 10.0	23 15.6	0♐58.3	1 45.8	4 03.0	23 10.9	26 57.9	7 56.7	26 41.7	3 12.9	1 37.4	3 41.3
8 Tu	5 07 04	15 53 36	4♐28 34	10♐30 17	24 06.8	23 02.3	2 29.4	2 27.8	4 22.8	23 04.5	26 59.0	7 56.4	26 40.1	3 10.5	1 37.2	3 42.7
9 W	5 11 01	16 54 33	16 30 21	22 28 53	24 03.6	22 49.0	4 00.8	3 11.0	4 42.2	22 57.7	26 59.9	7 56.1	26 38.5	3 08.0	1 37.0	3 44.1
10 Th	5 14 58	17 55 32	28 26 03	4♑22 01	24 00.4	22 37.0	5 32.5	3 55.1	5 01.2	22 50.5	27 00.6	7D 55.9	26 37.0	3 05.6	1 36.9	3 45.5
11 F	5 18 54	18 56 31	10♑17 00	16 11 14	23 57.3	22 27.0	7 04.3	4 40.4	5 19.7	22 42.9	27 01.1	7 55.9	26 35.5	3 03.2	1 36.8	3 47.0
12 Sa	5 22 51	19 57 31	22 05 02	27 58 44	23 54.1	22 19.7	8 36.4	5 26.5	5 37.8	22 34.9	27 01.4	7 55.9	26 34.1	3 00.8	1D 36.8	3 48.4
13 Su	5 26 47	20 58 32	3♒52 43	9♒47 25	23 50.9	22 15.2	10 08.7	6 13.7	5 55.4	22 26.5	27R 01.5	7 56.1	26 32.7	2 58.4	1 36.8	3 49.9
14 M	5 30 44	21 59 33	15 43 19	21 40 57	23 47.7	22D 13.2	11 41.1	7 01.7	6 12.6	22 17.8	27 01.4	7 56.4	26 31.4	2 56.1	1 36.8	3 51.4
15 Tu	5 34 40	23 00 35	27 40 53	3♓43 44	23 44.5	22 13.1	13 13.7	7 50.7	6 29.3	22 08.7	27 01.1	7 56.7	26 30.1	2 53.8	1 36.8	3 52.9
16 W	5 38 37	24 01 38	9♓50 08	16 00 42	23 41.4	22 13.9	14 46.4	8 40.4	6 45.5	21 59.2	27 00.6	7 57.2	26 28.9	2 51.4	1 36.9	3 54.5
17 Th	5 42 33	25 02 40	22 16 06	28 36 58	23 38.2	22R 14.6	16 19.2	9 31.0	7 01.3	21 49.3	26 59.9	7 57.9	26 27.7	2 49.2	1 37.1	3 56.0
18 F	5 46 30	26 03 44	5♈03 53	11♈37 24	23 35.0	22 14.2	17 52.2	10 22.3	7 16.5	21 39.2	26 59.1	7 58.6	26 26.6	2 46.9	1 37.2	3 57.6
19 Sa	5 50 27	27 04 47	18 17 59	25 05 57	23 31.8	22 11.9	19 25.3	11 14.5	7 31.3	21 28.6	26 58.0	7 59.4	26 25.5	2 44.6	1 37.4	3 59.2
20 Su	5 54 23	28 05 51	2♉01 30	9♉04 40	23 28.7	22 07.5	20 58.6	12 07.3	7 45.5	21 17.8	26 56.7	8 00.3	26 24.5	2 42.4	1 37.6	4 00.8
21 M	5 58 20	29 06 55	16 15 16	23 32 53	23 25.5	22 01.0	22 32.1	13 00.8	7 59.2	21 06.7	26 55.2	8 01.4	26 23.6	2 40.2	1 37.9	4 02.4
22 Tu	6 02 16	0♑08 00	0♊56 54	8♊26 28	23 22.3	21 53.0	24 05.7	13 55.0	8 12.4	20 55.2	26 53.6	8 02.5	26 22.7	2 38.1	1 38.2	4 04.0
23 W	6 06 13	1 09 05	16 00 30	23 37 46	23 19.1	21 44.7	25 39.5	14 49.9	8 25.0	20 43.5	26 51.7	8 03.8	26 21.8	2 35.9	1 38.5	4 05.7
24 Th	6 10 09	2 10 11	1♋16 54	8♋56 31	23 16.0	21 37.1	27 13.5	15 45.4	8 37.1	20 31.5	26 49.7	8 05.2	26 21.1	2 33.8	1 38.9	4 07.3
25 F	6 14 06	3 11 17	16 35 10	24 11 33	23 12.8	21 31.0	28 47.7	16 41.5	8 48.6	20 19.3	26 47.5	8 06.6	26 20.3	2 31.8	1 39.3	4 09.0
26 Sa	6 18 03	4 12 23	1♌44 25	9♌12 44	23 09.6	21 27.2	0♑22.1	17 38.1	8 59.5	20 06.8	26 45.1	8 08.2	26 19.6	2 29.7	1 39.7	4 10.7
27 Su	6 21 59	5 13 30	16 35 39	23 52 32	23 06.4	21D 25.6	1 56.7	18 35.4	9 09.9	19 54.1	26 42.4	8 09.9	26 19.0	2 27.7	1 40.2	4 12.4
28 M	6 25 56	6 14 37	1♍02 57	8♍06 40	23 03.3	21 25.8	3 31.6	19 33.2	9 19.6	19 41.1	26 39.6	8 11.7	26 18.5	2 25.7	1 40.7	4 14.1
29 Tu	6 29 52	7 15 44	15 03 39	21 53 58	23 00.1	21 27.1	5 06.8	20 31.5	9 28.7	19 28.0	26 36.6	8 13.6	26 17.9	2 23.8	1 41.3	4 15.8
30 W	6 33 49	8 16 53	28 37 51	5♎15 36	22 56.9	21R 28.3	6 42.2	21 30.3	9 37.2	19 14.6	26 33.5	8 15.6	26 17.5	2 21.9	1 41.8	4 17.6
31 Th	6 37 45	9♑18 01	11♎47 38	18 14 21	22♒53.7	21♒28.7	8♑18.0	22♏29.6	9♍45.1	19♋01.1	26♌30.1	8♈17.7	26♈17.1	2♊20.0	1♈42.4	4♒19.3

1st of Month	
Julian Day #	2461375.5
Obliquity	23°26'[illegible]6"
SVP	4♓52'53"
GC	27♐12.9
Eris	25♈00.9R

Day	⚴	⚵	⚶
1	3♈17.6R	11♒16.6	12♈42.0
6	3 22.9	13 07.5	12 52.8
11	3 39.5	15 02.5	13 14.0
16	4 07.0	17 01.2	13 45.3
21	4 44.6	19 03.4	14 25.8
26	5 31.9	21 08.9	15 15.0
31	6 28.2	23 17.4	16 12.1

DECLINATION and LATITUDE

Day	☉ Decl	☽ Decl	☽ Lat	☽12h Decl	☿ Decl	☿ Lat	♀ Decl	♀ Lat	♂ Decl	♂ Lat	⚳ Decl	⚳ Lat	♃ Decl	♃ Lat	♄ Decl	♄ Lat
1 Tu	21S46	8N31	1S02	5N27	16S47	1N33	9S24	1N27	12N57	2N19	25N57	4N39	13N20	0N48	0N48	2S35
2 W	21 55	2 22	2 09	0S42	17 16	1 26	9 29	1 35	12 50	2 20	26 02	4 44	13 20	0 48	0 48	2 35
3 Th	22 04	3S43	3 08	6 40	17 44	1 19	9 35	1 42	12 44	2 22	26 08	4 49	13 19	0 49	0 48	2 35
4 F	22 12	9 31	3 56	12 15	18 12	1 12	9 41	1 50	12 38	2 24	26 14	4 54	13 19	0 49	0 48	2 34
5 Sa	22 20	14 50	4 32	17 15	18 39	1 05	9 48	1 56	12 32	2 25	26 20	4 59	13 19	0 49	0 48	2 34
6 Su	22 28	19 28	4 54	21 27	19 06	0 58	9 56	2 03	12 26	2 27	26 26	5 04	13 18	0 49	0 48	2 34
7 M	22 35	23 12	5 02	24 41	19 32	0 50	10 04	2 09	12 20	2 29	26 32	5 09	13 18	0 50	0 48	2 34
8 Tu	22 41	25 53	4 56	26 46	19 57	0 43	10 13	2 15	12 14	2 30	26 38	5 15	13 18	0 50	0 48	2 33
9 W	22 48	27 20	4 37	27 36	20 22	0 36	10 22	2 21	12 09	2 32	26 44	5 20	13 18	0 50	0 48	2 33
10 Th	22 53	27 31	4 06	27 08	20 46	0 28	10 32	2 26	12 03	2 34	26 50	5 25	13 18	0 50	0 48	2 33
11 F	22 59	26 26	3 24	25 26	21 09	0 21	10 42	2 31	11 58	2 36	26 57	5 30	13 18	0 51	0 48	2 33
12 Sa	23 03	24 09	2 34	22 37	21 30	0 14	10 53	2 36	11 53	2 38	27 03	5 35	13 18	0 51	0 49	2 32
13 Su	23 08	20 51	1 36	18 51	21 51	0 07	11 04	2 41	11 48	2 39	27 10	5 40	13 18	0 51	0 49	2 32
14 M	23 12	16 40	0 35	14 19	22 11	0S00	11 16	2 45	11 44	2 41	27 16	5 45	13 18	0 51	0 49	2 32
15 Tu	23 15	11 49	0N29	9 11	22 30	0 07	11 27	2 49	11 39	2 43	27 23	5 50	13 19	0 52	0 50	2 32
16 W	23 18	6 27	1 33	3 37	22 48	0 14	11 40	2 53	11 35	2 45	27 29	5 55	13 19	0 52	0 50	2 31
17 Th	23 21	0 43	2 34	2N14	23 05	0 21	11 52	2 56	11 31	2 47	27 36	6 00	13 20	0 52	0 51	2 31
18 F	23 23	5N13	3 29	8 10	23 20	0 27	12 05	2 60	11 27	2 49	27 42	6 06	13 20	0 52	0 51	2 31
19 Sa	23 24	11 06	4 15	13 57	23 35	0 34	12 18	3 03	11 23	2 50	27 49	6 11	13 21	0 53	0 52	2 31
20 Su	23 25	16 41	4 48	19 14	23 48	0 40	12 32	3 05	11 19	2 52	27 56	6 16	13 21	0 53	0 52	2 30
21 M	23 26	21 34	5 05	23 36	24 00	0 47	12 45	3 08	11 16	2 54	28 03	6 21	13 22	0 53	0 53	2 30
22 Tu	23 26	25 17	5 03	26 33	24 11	0 53	12 59	3 10	11 13	2 56	28 09	6 25	13 23	0 53	0 54	2 30
23 W	23 26	27 20	4 40	27 37	24 21	0 59	13 13	3 12	11 10	2 58	28 16	6 30	13 24	0 54	0 54	2 30
24 Th	23 25	27 23	3 57	26 36	24 29	1 04	13 27	3 14	11 07	3 00	28 23	6 35	13 25	0 54	0 55	2 29
25 F	23 24	25 20	2 57	23 36	24 36	1 10	13 41	3 16	11 05	3 02	28 29	6 40	13 26	0 54	0 56	2 29
26 Sa	23 22	21 28	1 44	19 00	24 42	1 15	13 56	3 18	11 02	3 04	28 36	6 45	13 27	0 54	0 57	2 29
27 Su	23 20	16 17	0 26	13 21	24 46	1 21	14 10	3 19	11 00	3 06	28 43	6 50	13 28	0 55	0 58	2 29
28 M	23 17	10 18	0S52	7 09	24 49	1 26	14 24	3 20	10 59	3 08	28 49	6 54	13 29	0 55	0 59	2 28
29 Tu	23 14	3 58	2 04	0 48	24 51	1 30	14 39	3 21	10 57	3 10	28 56	6 59	13 30	0 55	0 60	2 28
30 W	23 11	2S20	3 08	5S23	24 51	1 35	14 53	3 22	10 56	3 12	29 02	7 03	13 32	0 55	1 01	2 28
31 Th	23S07	8S20	3S59	11S09	24S50	1S39	15S08	3N23	10N55	3N14	29N09	7N08	13N33	0N56	1N02	2S28

Day	⚷ Decl	⚷ Lat	♅ Decl	♅ Lat	♆ Decl	♆ Lat	♇ Decl	♇ Lat
1	10N27	0N06	20N42	0S09	0S38	1S24	23S30	4S15
6	10 23	0 05	20 40	0 09	0 38	1 24	23 28	4 15
11	10 20	0 05	20 37	0 09	0 38	1 24	23 26	4 15
16	10 17	0 04	20 35	0 09	0 38	1 23	23 24	4 15
21	10 15	0 04	20 33	0 09	0 37	1 23	23 22	4 15
26	10 13	0 04	20 31	0 09	0 36	1 23	23 21	4 15
31	10N12	0N03	20N29	0S08	0S35	1S23	23S19	4S15

Day	⚴ Decl	⚴ Lat	⚵ Decl	⚵ Lat	⚶ Decl	⚶ Lat	Eris Decl	Eris Lat
1	21S28	24S56	13S54	3N38	3S37	9S22	0S03	10S27
6	21 25	24 54	13 42	3 19	3 13	9 01	0 04	10 26
11	21 15	24 50	13 27	3 00	2 46	8 40	0 04	10 26
16	21 00	24 46	13 09	2 42	2 16	8 20	0 04	10 25
21	20 41	24 40	12 49	2 25	1 42	8 01	0 04	10 25
26	20 17	24 35	12 26	2 08	1 06	7 42	0 03	10 24
31	19S50	24S29	12S00	1N51	0S28	7S24	0S03	10S23

Moon Phenomena

Max/0 Decl dy hr mn	
2 9:16	0 S
9 15:20	27S36
17 2:54	0 N
23 12:27	27N37
29 15:04	0 S

Max/0 Lat dy hr mn	
7 1:48	5S02
14 13:04	0 N
21 9:25	5N06
27 7:57	0 S

Perigee/Apogee dy hr m	kilometers
11 6:47 a	406419
24 8:33 p	356655

PH	dy hr mn	
☾	1 6:10	9♍03
●	9 0:53	16♐57
☽	17 5:44	25♓17
○	24 1:29	2♋14
☾	30 19:01	9♎05

Void of Course Moon

Last Aspect	☽ Ingress
2 9:12 ☿ ⚹	♎ 2 20:05
4 22:42 ♃ ⚹	♏ 5 4:36
7 9:09 ♃ □	♐ 7 15:08
9 21:07 ♃ △	♑ 10 3:10
10 19:14 ♄ □	♒ 12 16:07
14 22:41 ♃ ☍	♓ 15 4:37
17 5:44 ☉ □	♈ 17 14:36
19 16:41 ☉ △	♉ 19 20:31
21 17:27 ♃ □	♊ 21 22:28
23 17:02 ♃ ⚹	♋ 23 22:00
25 0:11 ♀ △	♌ 25 21:13
27 16:40 ♃ ☌	♍ 27 22:14
29 10:19 ♀ ⚹	♎ 30 2:28

DAILY ASPECTARIAN

1 Tu ☽⚻♄ 4:20; ⚴ D 4:35; ☽∠⚳ 5:28; ☉□☽ 6:10; ☊ R 6:19; ☽⚼⚷ 11:10; ☽∠♀ 13:47; ☿⚼♄ 15:56; ☽⚼♇ 23:14

2 W ☿△⚳ 1:42; ♃△⚷ 5:22; ☽∥♄ 6:08; ☽⋕♆ 6:49; ☽⚹⚳ 8:20; ☽⚹☿ 9:12; ☽∥♆ 11:45; ☽⋕♄ 12:25; ☽⚻⚷ 14:15; ☽⚺♃ 14:17; ☽⚺♀ 18:17; ☽☍♆ 23:07

3 Th ☽⚺♂ 1:02; ☽△♅ 2:19; ☽△♇ 2:45; ☽☍♄ 10:53; ☽∠☿ 16:32; ☉⚹☽ 17:35; ☽∠♃ 18:11; ☉⚼⚷ 22:48

4 F ☽∥♀ 0:43; ☽⋕⚷ 3:49; ☿⚻⚷ 5:03; ☽∠♂ 5:55; ☽⚼♅ 6:20; ☿□♃ 7:04; ♀ ♏ 8:14; ☽⋕♂ 13:26; ☽□⚳ 15:59; ☽⋕♃ 16:49; ♂□♅ 19:30; ☽☍⚷ 22:23; ☽⚹♃ 22:42

5 Sa ☉∠☽ 0:31; ☽⚺☿ 0:46; ☽☌♀ 5:43; ☽⚻♆ 7:44; ☽⚻♅ 10:55; ☽⚹♂ 11:24; ☽□♇ 11:38; ☽⚻♄ 19:57; ♂⚻♇ 20:25; ☽∥☿ 21:42

6 Su ☽⋕♅ 7:02; ☉⚺☽ 8:06; ☿ ♐ 8:34; ☽⚼♆ 12:49; ♀⚻♆ 19:06; ☉∥☽ 19:22

7 M ☽⚼♄ 1:13; ☽△⚳ 1:40; ☽∥♇ 1:56; ☽⚻⚷ 8:35; ☽□♃ 9:09; ☿△♆ 10:17; ☽△♆ 18:20; ☽☌☿ 19:30; ☽⚺♀ 19:46; ☽☍♅ 21:26; ☽⚹♇ 22:29; ☿⚺♀ 23:14; ☽□♂ 23:48

8 Tu ☽△♄ 6:53; ☽⚼⚳ 7:06; ☿☍♅ 10:30; ☽⋕⚳ 10:35; ☽⚼⚷ 14:17; ☿⚹♇ 19:33; ♀⋕⚷ 22:06; ♀⚻♅ 22:28

9 W ☉☌☽ 0:53; ☽∠♀ 3:35; ☽∠♇ 4:29; ☽⚻⚳ 12:50; ☿□♂ 13:42; ☿⋕♅ 16:14; ♀□♇ 18:39; ☽△⚷ 20:20; ☽△♃ 21:07

10 Th ☽□♆ 6:26; ☽⚻♅ 9:23; ☽⚺♇ 10:47; ☽⚹♀ 11:51; ☽△♂ 13:41; ☽⋕⚳ 16:20; ☽⚺☿ 16:31; ☽□♄ 19:14; ☉∠♇ 20:09; ♄ D 23:32

11 F ☽⚼♃ 3:32; ☿⚼⚳ 9:16; ☿△♄ 13:27; ☽⚼♅ 15:45; ☉⚺☽ 19:16; ☽⚼♂ 20:58

12 Sa ☽☍⚳ 1:00; ☽∠☿ 3:34; ☽∥♇ 5:54; ☉∥☽ 8:33; ☽□⚷ 9:07; ♀⚹♂ 9:16; ☽⚻♃ 10:03; ☽∥☿ 17:55; ☽⚹♆ 19:24; ☽△♅ 22:10; ♆ D 22:19; ☽☌♇ 23:54

13 Su ♃ R 0:58; ☽⋕♅ 1:29; ☽⚻♂ 4:16; ☉∠☽ 4:40; ☽□♀ 5:07; ☽⚹♄ 8:14; ☽⚹☿ 14:37; ☿⚼⚷ 21:31

14 M ☽∠♆ 1:48; ☉∠♀ 4:12; ☉⚻⚳ 6:15; ☊ D 13:04; ☽⚻⚳ 13:04; ☉⚹☽ 13:48; ☽∠♄ 14:32; ☽⋕♃ 16:56; ☽⚹⚷ 21:39; ☽☍♃ 22:41

15 Tu ☽⋕♂ 0:47; ☽∥♀ 1:37; ♀⚻♄ 2:59; ☽⋕⚷ 7:02; ☽⚺♆ 7:49; ☽□♅ 10:19; ☽⚺♇ 12:20; ♀⋕♂ 16:57; ☽☍♂ 17:50; ☽⚼⚳ 18:29; ☽⚺♄ 20:19; ☽△♀ 21:34

16 W ☽∠⚷ 3:12; ☽□☿ 10:58; ♂∠⚳ 12:47; ☽∠♇ 17:37; ☽△⚳ 23:10; ☽⋕♄ 23:27

17 Th ☽∥♆ 0:19; ☽⚼♀ 4:35; ☽⋕♆ 5:28; ☊ R 5:35; ☉□☽ 5:44; ☽∥♄ 6:20; ☽⚺⚷ 7:56; ☽⚻♃ 8:57; ☽☌♆ 17:37; ☽⚹♅ 19:47; ☽⚹♇ 21:57

18 F ☽⚻♂ 4:09; ☉∥☿ 4:11; ☿∥♇ 5:02; ☽☌♄ 5:21; ☉△⚷ 8:50; ☽⚻♀ 10:25; ☉∥♇ 10:25; ☽⚼♃ 12:38; ☿∠♇ 17:08; ☽∥⚷ 20:32; ☉△♃ 21:22; ☽∠♅ 23:01

19 Sa ☽∥♂ 1:10; ☽△☿ 2:15; ☽⋕♀ 5:13; ☽□⚳ 5:34; ☽⚼♂ 7:37; ☽∥♃ 9:26; ☽☌⚷ 14:18; ☽△♃ 15:14; ☉△☽ 16:41; ☽⚺♆ 23:19

20 Su ☽⚺♅ 1:10; ☽□♇ 3:25; ☿⚻⚳ 4:25; ☽⚼☿ 7:35; ☽△♂ 9:56; ☽⚺♄ 10:12; ☽☍♀ 18:15; ☽∥♅ 18:38; ☉⚼☽ 20:10

21 M ☽∠♆ 0:38; ♂⚻♄ 4:14; ☽⚹⚳ 7:54; ☽⋕♇ 10:34; ☉⋕☽ 10:58; ☽∠♄ 11:09; ☽⚻☿ 11:34; ☽⋕☿ 15:28; ☽⚺⚷ 16:37; ☽□♃ 17:27; ☉ ♑ 20:51; ☉⚻☽ 22:35

22 Tu ☽⚹♆ 1:06; ☽☌♅ 2:42; ☽△♇ 5:01; ☽∠⚳ 7:53; ☽⚹♄ 11:23; ☽□♂ 11:47; ☽∠⚷ 16:39; ☽⚻♀ 22:01

23 W ☽⚼♇ 4:53; ☽⚺⚳ 7:20; ☿△⚷ 10:44; ☉□♆ 11:38; ☽⚹⚷ 16:17; ☽☍☿ 16:55; ☽⚹♃ 17:02; ☿△♃ 18:04; ♀⋕♃ 19:58; ☽⚼♀ 23:07

24 Th ☽□♆ 0:34; ☉☍☽ 1:29; ☽⚺♅ 2:00; ☽⚻♇ 4:27; ☉⚻♅ 8:59; ☽□♄ 10:41; ☽⚹♂ 11:38; ☽∠♃ 16:29; ♀⚼♆ 23:05

25 F ☽△♀ 0:11; ☽∠♅ 1:29; ☽⋕☿ 5:15; ☽☌⚳ 5:48; ☽∠♂ 11:32; ☉⋕☽ 13:16; ☽⋕♇ 13:31; ☽□⚷ 15:23; ☽⚺♃ 16:05; ☿ ♑ 18:24; ☽⚻☿ 21:33; ☉⚺♇ 23:19; ☽△♆ 23:53

26 Sa ☽⚹♅ 1:12; ☽☍♇ 3:55; ☉⚻☽ 4:14; ☽∥♅ 4:48; ☽△♄ 10:17; ☽⚺♂ 11:47; ☿□♆ 19:48; ☉∥♇ 22:55

27 Su ☽⚼♆ 0:07; ☽⚼☿ 0:39; ☽□♀ 3:30; ☽⚺⚳ 5:21; ☉⚼☽ 6:25; ☿⚻♅ 7:41; ☊ D 7:56; ☽⋕♀ 8:24; ☽⚼♄ 10:51; ☽∥♃ 11:31; ☽△⚷ 16:03; ☽☌♃ 16:40; ☽∥♂ 21:20

28 M ☽∥⚷ 0:19; ☽⚻♆ 1:04; ☽□♅ 2:19; ♀△⚳ 2:41; ☽△☿ 4:43; ☽⚻♇ 5:24; ☽∠⚳ 6:04; ☉△☽ 9:30; ☿⚺♇ 10:55; ☽⚻♄ 12:10; ☽☌♂ 14:15; ☽⚼⚷ 17:29

29 Tu ☽⚼♇ 7:22; ☽⚹⚳ 7:35; ☽⚹♀ 10:19; ☽∥♄ 11:15; ☽⋕♆ 12:48; ☿∠♀ 16:09; ☽∥♆ 17:19; ☽⋕♄ 18:55; ☽⚻⚷ 19:49; ☽⚺♃ 20:18; ☉□♄ 23:29

30 W ☽☍♆ 5:32; ☽△♅ 6:43; ☽△♇ 10:16; ☽∠♀ 15:26; ☽□☿ 16:40; ☽☍♄ 17:32; ☉□☽ 19:01; ☊ R 19:10; ☽⚺♂ 20:12; ☽∠♃ 23:28; ☿□♄ 23:56

31 Th ☽⋕⚷ 7:52; ☽⚼♅ 10:17; ☽⋕♂ 10:56; ☉△♂ 12:04; ☽□⚳ 13:14; ♀⚼♄ 20:04; ☽⚺♀ 21:42; ☽⋕♃ 22:52; ☿△♂ 23:31

LONGITUDE — January 2027

Day	Sid.Time	☉	☽	☽ 12 hour	Mean☊	True☊	☿	♀	♂	⚳	♃	♄	⚷	♅	♆	♇
	h m s	° ' "	° ' "	° ' "	° '	° '	° '	° '	° '	° '	° '	° '	° '	° '	° '	° '
1 F	6 41 42	10♑19 10	24♎36 14	0♏53 44	22♒50.5	21♒27.5	9♑54.0	23♏29.4	9♍52.3	18♋47.4	26♌26.5	8♈19.9	26♈16.7	2♊18.1	1♈43.1	4♒21.1
2 Sa	6 45 38	11 20 20	7♏07 20	13 17 28	22 47.4	21R 24.5	11 30.4	24 29.6	9 58.8	18R 33.6	26R 22.8	8 22.2	26R 16.4	2R 16.3	1 43.8	4 22.9
3 Su	6 49 35	12 21 30	19 24 35	25 29 04	22 44.2	21 19.6	13 07.1	25 30.2	10 04.6	18 19.6	26 18.9	8 24.7	26 16.2	2 14.6	1 44.5	4 24.7
4 M	6 53 32	13 22 40	1♐31 19	7♐31 39	22 41.0	21 13.2	14 44.2	26 31.3	10 09.8	18 05.6	26 14.8	8 27.2	26 16.0	2 12.8	1 45.2	4 26.5
5 Tu	6 57 28	14 23 51	13 30 23	19 27 49	22 37.8	21 06.1	16 21.7	27 32.8	10 14.2	17 51.5	26 10.5	8 29.8	26 15.9	2 11.1	1 46.0	4 28.3
6 W	7 01 25	15 25 01	25 24 12	1♑19 46	22 34.7	20 58.8	17 59.5	28 34.6	10 18.0	17 37.3	26 06.1	8 32.6	26D 15.9	2 09.5	1 46.8	4 30.1
7 Th	7 05 21	16 26 12	7♑14 45	13 09 22	22 31.5	20 52.3	19 37.6	29 36.8	10 21.0	17 23.0	26 01.5	8 35.4	26 15.9	2 07.9	1 47.7	4 31.9
8 F	7 09 18	17 27 22	19 03 50	24 58 23	22 28.3	20 47.0	21 16.2	0♐39.4	10 23.3	17 08.8	25 56.7	8 38.3	26 15.9	2 06.3	1 48.5	4 33.8
9 Sa	7 13 14	18 28 33	0♒53 15	6♒48 39	22 25.1	20 43.3	22 55.1	1 42.3	10 24.8	16 54.5	25 51.8	8 41.3	26 16.1	2 04.8	1 49.4	4 35.6
10 Su	7 17 11	19 29 43	12 44 53	18 42 15	22 22.0	20D 41.4	24 34.4	2 45.5	10R 25.6	16 40.2	25 46.6	8 44.5	26 16.2	2 03.3	1 50.4	4 37.5
11 M	7 21 07	20 30 52	24 41 04	0♓41 42	22 18.8	20 41.2	26 14.1	3 49.1	10 25.7	16 26.0	25 41.4	8 47.7	26 16.5	2 01.8	1 51.4	4 39.3
12 Tu	7 25 04	21 32 02	6♓44 32	12 49 59	22 15.6	20 42.2	27 54.1	4 52.9	10 24.9	16 11.8	25 35.9	8 51.0	26 16.7	2 00.4	1 52.4	4 41.2
13 W	7 29 01	22 33 10	18 58 31	25 10 36	22 12.4	20 43.9	29 34.4	5 57.1	10 23.4	15 57.7	25 30.4	8 54.4	26 17.1	1 59.1	1 53.4	4 43.1
14 Th	7 32 57	23 34 18	1♈26 43	7♈47 22	22 09.3	20 45.7	1♒15.0	7 01.5	10 21.1	15 43.6	25 24.6	8 58.0	26 17.5	1 57.8	1 54.5	4 44.9
15 F	7 36 54	24 35 26	14 13 01	20 44 09	22 06.1	20R 47.0	2 55.9	8 06.2	10 18.1	15 29.7	25 18.8	9 01.6	26 18.0	1 56.5	1 55.6	4 46.8
16 Sa	7 40 50	25 36 33	27 21 10	4♉04 27	22 02.9	20 47.3	4 37.0	9 11.2	10 14.2	15 15.9	25 12.8	9 05.3	26 18.5	1 55.3	1 56.7	4 48.7
17 Su	7 44 47	26 37 39	10♉54 14	17 50 43	21 59.7	20 46.6	6 18.2	10 16.4	10 09.5	15 02.2	25 06.6	9 09.1	26 19.1	1 54.1	1 57.9	4 50.6
18 M	7 48 43	27 38 44	24 45 54	2♊03 38	21 56.5	20 44.8	7 59.5	11 21.9	10 04.1	14 48.7	25 00.4	9 12.9	26 19.7	1 53.0	1 59.1	4 52.5
19 Tu	7 52 40	28 39 49	9♊19 38	16 41 23	21 53.4	20 42.1	9 40.8	12 27.7	9 57.9	14 35.4	24 54.0	9 16.9	26 20.4	1 51.9	2 00.3	4 54.4
20 W	7 56 36	29 40 53	24 08 11	1♋39 09	21 50.2	20 39.1	11 21.9	13 33.6	9 50.8	14 22.3	24 47.4	9 21.0	26 21.1	1 50.9	2 01.5	4 56.3
21 Th	8 00 33	0♒41 56	9♋13 16	16 49 23	21 47.0	20 36.4	13 02.7	14 39.8	9 43.0	14 09.3	24 40.8	9 25.1	26 21.9	1 49.9	2 02.8	4 58.2
22 F	8 04 30	1 42 58	24 26 14	2♌02 32	21 43.8	20 34.2	14 43.1	15 46.2	9 34.4	13 56.6	24 34.0	9 29.4	26 22.8	1 49.0	2 04.1	5 00.1
23 Sa	8 08 26	2 44 00	9♌37 04	17 08 36	21 40.7	20D 33.0	16 22.8	16 52.9	9 25.0	13 44.1	24 27.2	9 33.7	26 23.7	1 48.1	2 05.5	5 02.0
24 Su	8 12 23	3 45 01	24 36 06	1♍58 37	21 37.5	20 32.8	18 01.6	17 59.7	9 14.7	13 31.9	24 20.2	9 38.1	26 24.7	1 47.3	2 06.9	5 03.9
25 M	8 16 19	4 46 01	9♍15 25	16 25 56	21 34.3	20 33.4	19 39.2	19 06.8	9 03.7	13 19.9	24 13.1	9 42.6	26 25.7	1 46.5	2 08.2	5 05.8
26 Tu	8 20 16	5 47 00	23 29 46	0♎26 44	21 31.1	20 34.5	21 15.4	20 14.0	8 51.9	13 08.3	24 06.0	9 47.2	26 26.8	1 45.8	2 09.7	5 07.7
27 W	8 24 12	6 47 59	7♎16 47	14 00 02	21 28.0	20 35.7	22 49.6	21 21.5	8 39.4	12 56.9	23 58.7	9 51.8	26 27.9	1 45.1	2 11.1	5 09.6
28 Th	8 28 09	7 48 57	20 36 42	27 07 07	21 24.8	20 36.7	24 21.5	22 29.1	8 26.0	12 45.8	23 51.4	9 56.6	26 29.1	1 44.5	2 12.6	5 11.5
29 F	8 32 05	8 49 55	3♏31 41	9♏50 53	21 21.6	20R 37.3	25 50.7	23 36.9	8 11.9	12 35.0	23 43.9	10 01.4	26 30.3	1 43.9	2 14.1	5 13.4
30 Sa	8 36 02	9 50 52	16 05 14	22 15 15	21 18.4	20 37.2	27 16.5	24 44.9	7 57.0	12 24.5	23 36.4	10 06.3	26 31.6	1 43.3	2 15.6	5 15.3
31 Su	8 39 59	10♒51 49	28 21 29	4♐24 28	21♒15.3	20♒36.7	28♒38.3	25♐53.0	7♍41.5	12♋14.4	23♌28.9	10♈11.3	26♈33.0	1♊42.9	2♈17.2	5♒17.3

1st of Month

Julian Day #
2461406.5
Obliquity
23°26'6"
SVP 4♓52'7"
GC 27♐13.0
Eris 24♈52.1R

Day	⚴	⚵	⚶
1	6♈40.5	23♒43.5	16♈24.4
6	7 46.9	25 55.5	17 30.2
11	9 01.2	28 10.3	18 42.7
16	10 22.8	0♓27.6	20 01.2
21	11 51.2	2 47.2	21 25.2
26	13 25.9	5 09.1	22 54.2
31	15 06.5	7 33.0	24 27.7

DECLINATION and LATITUDE

Day	☉ Decl	☽ Decl	☽ Lat	☽12h Decl	☿ Decl	☿ Lat	♀ Decl	♀ Lat	♂ Decl	♂ Lat	⚳ Decl	⚳ Lat	♃ Decl	♃ Lat	♄ Decl	♄ Lat
1 F	23S02	13S49	4S37	16S19	24S47	1S43	15S22	3N23	10N54	3N16	29N15	7N12	13N35	0N56	1N03	2S27
2 Sa	22 57	18 37	5 01	20 42	24 43	1 47	15 36	3 23	10 53	3 18	29 21	7 17	13 36	0 56	1 04	2 27
3 Su	22 52	22 33	5 10	24 08	24 37	1 50	15 51	3 23	10 53	3 21	29 28	7 21	13 38	0 56	1 05	2 27
4 M	22 46	25 26	5 05	26 27	24 30	1 54	16 05	3 23	10 53	3 23	29 34	7 25	13 39	0 57	1 06	2 27
5 Tu	22 40	27 10	4 47	27 33	24 22	1 56	16 19	3 23	10 53	3 25	29 40	7 29	13 41	0 57	1 08	2 26
6 W	22 33	27 38	4 16	27 23	24 12	1 59	16 33	3 23	10 54	3 27	29 46	7 33	13 43	0 57	1 09	2 26
7 Th	22 26	26 49	3 35	25 57	24 00	2 01	16 47	3 22	10 55	3 29	29 52	7 37	13 44	0 57	1 10	2 26
8 F	22 18	24 47	2 44	23 22	23 47	2 03	17 00	3 21	10 56	3 31	29 58	7 41	13 46	0 57	1 12	2 26
9 Sa	22 10	21 41	1 46	19 47	23 32	2 05	17 14	3 21	10 57	3 33	30 03	7 45	13 48	0 58	1 13	2 25
10 Su	22 01	17 41	0 43	15 23	23 16	2 06	17 27	3 20	10 59	3 35	30 09	7 49	13 50	0 58	1 14	2 25
11 M	21 52	12 57	0N22	10 22	22 58	2 07	17 40	3 18	11 01	3 37	30 14	7 52	13 52	0 58	1 16	2 25
12 Tu	21 43	7 41	1 27	4 55	22 39	2 07	17 53	3 17	11 03	3 40	30 20	7 56	13 54	0 58	1 17	2 25
13 W	21 33	2 04	2 29	0N49	22 18	2 07	18 05	3 16	11 05	3 42	30 25	7 59	13 56	0 59	1 19	2 24
14 Th	21 23	3N43	3 26	6 37	21 56	2 06	18 17	3 14	11 08	3 44	30 30	8 03	13 58	0 59	1 21	2 24
15 F	21 12	9 30	4 13	12 18	21 32	2 05	18 29	3 13	11 11	3 46	30 35	8 06	14 00	0 59	1 22	2 24
16 Sa	21 01	15 01	4 49	17 36	21 07	2 04	18 41	3 11	11 15	3 48	30 40	8 09	14 03	0 59	1 24	2 24
17 Su	20 50	20 00	5 10	22 11	20 40	2 02	18 52	3 09	11 18	3 50	30 44	8 12	14 05	0 59	1 26	2 24
18 M	20 38	24 04	5 14	25 37	20 11	1 59	19 03	3 07	11 22	3 52	30 49	8 15	14 07	0 60	1 27	2 23
19 Tu	20 26	26 46	4 59	27 28	19 41	1 56	19 14	3 05	11 26	3 54	30 53	8 18	14 10	0 60	1 29	2 23
20 W	20 13	27 41	4 23	27 24	19 10	1 52	19 24	3 03	11 31	3 56	30 57	8 21	14 12	0 60	1 31	2 23
21 Th	19 60	26 35	3 29	25 17	18 37	1 48	19 34	3 01	11 36	3 58	31 01	8 23	14 14	1 00	1 33	2 23
22 F	19 47	23 31	2 19	21 20	18 03	1 42	19 43	2 58	11 41	3 60	31 05	8 26	14 17	1 00	1 35	2 22
23 Sa	19 33	18 48	1 00	15 60	17 28	1 37	19 53	2 56	11 46	4 02	31 09	8 28	14 19	1 01	1 37	2 22
24 Su	19 19	12 58	0S22	9 47	16 51	1 30	20 01	2 53	11 52	4 03	31 13	8 31	14 22	1 01	1 38	2 22
25 M	19 04	6 32	1 42	3 14	16 14	1 23	20 09	2 51	11 57	4 05	31 16	8 33	14 24	1 01	1 40	2 22
26 Tu	18 49	0S04	2 53	3S17	15 36	1 15	20 17	2 48	12 04	4 07	31 20	8 35	14 27	1 01	1 42	2 22
27 W	18 34	6 25	3 51	9 26	14 57	1 06	20 25	2 45	12 10	4 09	31 23	8 37	14 29	1 01	1 44	2 21
28 Th	18 19	12 17	4 35	14 58	14 17	0 56	20 32	2 42	12 17	4 10	31 26	8 39	14 32	1 01	1 46	2 21
29 F	18 03	17 26	5 03	19 41	13 37	0 46	20 38	2 39	12 23	4 12	31 29	8 41	14 35	1 02	1 49	2 21
30 Sa	17 47	21 41	5 16	23 26	12 57	0 34	20 44	2 36	12 30	4 14	31 32	8 42	14 37	1 02	1 51	2 21
31 Su	17S30	24S54	5S14	26S04	12S17	0S22	20S50	2N33	12N38	4N15	31N34	8N44	14N40	1N02	1N53	2S21

Day	⚷ Decl	⚷ Lat	♅ Decl	♅ Lat	♆ Decl	♆ Lat	♇ Decl	♇ Lat
1	10N12	0N03	20N29	0S08	0S35	1S23	23S18	4S15
6	10 11	0 03	20 27	0 08	0 33	1 22	23 16	4 16
11	10 11	0 02	20 26	0 08	0 31	1 22	23 14	4 16
16	10 11	0 02	20 25	0 08	0 29	1 22	23 12	4 16
21	10 12	0 02	20 24	0 08	0 26	1 22	23 10	4 16
26	10 13	0 01	20 23	0 08	0 23	1 22	23 08	4 17
31	10N15	0N01	20N22	0S08	0S20	1S22	23S06	4S17

Day	⚴ Decl	⚴ Lat	⚵ Decl	⚵ Lat	⚶ Decl	⚶ Lat	Eris Decl	Eris Lat
1	19S45	24S28	11S55	1N48	0S20	7S21	0S03	10S23
6	19 14	24 22	11 26	1 32	0N21	7 03	0 02	10 22
11	18 41	24 16	10 55	1 16	1 03	6 47	0 02	10 22
16	18 05	24 11	10 22	1 00	1 47	6 32	0 01	10 21
21	17 28	24 06	9 47	0 45	2 31	6 17	0 00	10 20
26	16 49	24 02	9 09	0 30	3 17	6 03	0N01	10 19
31	16S08	23S58	8S30	0N15	4N03	5S50	0N02	10S19

Moon Phenomena

Max/0 Decl
dy hr mn
5 20:40 27S38
13 8:38 0 N
19 23:11 27N41
25 23:47 0 S

Perigee/Apogee
dy hr m kilometers
7 8:09 a 406608
21 21:49 p 357285

PH dy hr mn
● 7 20:26 17♑18
☽ 15 20:36 25♈28
○ 22 12:19 2♌14
☾ 29 10:57 9♏18

Max/0 Lat
dy hr mn
3 3:44 5S10
10 15:58 0 N
17 16:58 5N15
23 17:28 0 S
30 8:48 5S17

Void of Course Moon

Last Aspect				☽ Ingress		
1	3:29	♃	⚹	♏	1	10:17
3	13:34	♃	□	♐	3	20:58
6	1:24	♃	△	♑	6	9:18
8	5:12	☿	☌	♒	8	22:12
11	2:00	♃	☍	♓	11	10:37
13	7:33	☉	⚹	♈	13	21:15
15	20:36	☉	□	♉	16	4:45
18	4:59	☉	△	♊	18	8:34
20	1:02	♃	⚹	♋	20	9:22
21	0:47	♂	⚹	♌	22	8:46
23	23:35	♃	☌	♍	24	8:46
25	17:57	♀	□	♎	26	11:13
28	7:47	☿	△	♏	28	17:22
31	0:37	☿	□	♐	31	3:15

DAILY ASPECTARIAN

1 F
☽∠♂ 0:31
☽☍⚷ 3:11
☽⚹♃ 3:29
☽∥♀ 7:42
☽⊼♆ 13:35
☽⊼♅ 14:40
☉☌☿ 17:09
☽□♇ 18:41
☿⚼♃ 22:11

2 Sa
☉⚼♃ 0:55
☽⊼♄ 2:26
☽⚹♂ 5:35
☉⚹☽ 8:56
☽⚹☿ 9:48
☽#♅ 10:38
☽⚼♆ 18:45
☽△⚳ 21:55

3 Su
☉∥☽ 2:12
☽∥♇ 5:22
☽⚼♄ 7:55
☽☌♀ 13:08
☽⊼⚷ 13:33
☽□♃ 13:34
☽∥☿ 15:33
♃△⚷ 16:31
☉∠☽ 17:10
♀□♃ 17:57
♀⊼⚷ 18:02
☽∠☿ 19:54

4 M
☽△♆ 0:28
☽☍♅ 1:23
☽⚼⚳ 3:04
☽⚹♇ 5:50
☽△♄ 13:54
☽□♂ 17:24
☽⚼⚷ 19:30

5 Tu
☉⊻☽ 1:58
☽⊻☿ 6:39
☽⊼⚳ 8:35
☿⚼♅ 11:57
☽∠♇ 12:03
☿☍⚳ 19:15

6 W
☽△♃ 1:24
☽△⚷ 1:45
☽⊻♀ 7:02
⚷ D 11:02
☽□♆ 12:56
☽⊼♅ 13:39
☽⊻♇ 18:29

7 Th
☽□♄ 2:44
☽△♂ 6:19
☽⚼♃ 7:37
♀ ♐ 8:55
☉⚼♅ 15:56
☽∠♀ 16:24
☉☍⚳ 18:05
☽⚼♅ 20:02
☽☍⚳ 20:11
☉☌☽ 20:26

8 F
⚳∠♅ 4:39
☽☌☿ 5:12
☽∥☿ 9:26
☽∥♇ 12:51
☽⚼♂ 12:52
☽⊼♃ 13:53
☽□⚷ 14:38
☉∥☽ 20:37

9 Sa
☽⚹♀ 1:49
☽⚹♆ 1:54
☽△♅ 2:25
♀△♆ 2:46
♀⚼⚳ 3:47
☽☌♇ 7:32
☽#♅ 8:01
♀☍♅ 8:21
☽⚹♄ 15:52
☽⊼♂ 19:19

10 Su
☽∥♀ 1:11
☿∥♇ 2:29
☽⊼⚳ 7:45
☽∠♆ 8:16
☿⚼♂ 12:23
♂ R 13:00
☉⊻☽ 14:52
☊ D 15:58
☿⊼♃ 16:32
☽#♃ 19:36
☽∠♄ 22:13

11 M
☿□⚷ 0:35
☽☍♃ 2:00
☽⚹⚷ 3:11
☽⊻☿ 3:36
☽#♂ 9:02
☽#⚷ 12:53
☽⚼⚳ 13:13
☽⊻♆ 14:20
☽□♅ 14:38
♀⚹♇ 19:28
☽⊻♇ 19:55
☽□♀ 19:58
☉∠☽ 23:33

12 Tu
☽⊻♄ 4:11
☽☍♂ 7:14
☽∠⚷ 8:57
☽∠☿ 14:03
☽△⚳ 18:14

13 W
☽∠♇ 1:27
☽#♄ 3:09
☿ ♒ 6:07
☽∥♆ 6:33
☉⚹☽ 7:33
☽#♆ 10:43
☽⊼♃ 12:32
☽⊻⚷ 14:08
☽∥♄ 14:09
☽⚹☿ 23:34

14 Th
☽☌♆ 0:53
☽⚹♅ 0:59
☽⚹♇ 6:17
☿⚹♆ 9:30
☿△♅ 10:03
☽△♀ 11:32
☽☌♄ 14:17
☽⊼♂ 16:44
☽⚼♃ 16:47

15 F
⚵ ♓ 0:04
☽□⚳ 2:19
☽∥⚷ 2:55
☽∠♅ 5:02
☽∥♂ 7:15
♅⚹♆ 9:32
☉⊼♃ 15:30
☉⚼♂ 15:47
☽⚼♀ 17:46
☽∥♃ 19:35
☽△♃ 20:10
☽⚼♂ 20:12
☊ R 20:28
☉□☽ 20:36
♀△♄ 21:41
☽☌⚷ 22:07

16 Sa
☿☌♇ 2:50
☽⊻♅ 8:10
☽⊻♆ 8:14
☉∥☿ 8:35
☽□♇ 13:20
☽□☿ 14:48
☉□⚷ 16:37
☽#♀ 17:57
☽⊻♄ 20:55
♀□♂ 21:39
☽△♂ 22:42
☽⊼♀ 22:48

17 Su
☽∥♅ 2:07
☽#☿ 3:09
☉#☽ 4:12
☽⚹⚳ 7:03
☽∠♆ 10:30
☿#♅ 13:02
☽#♇ 18:10
☽∠♄ 22:50
♀⚼⚷ 23:10

18 M
☽□♃ 0:11
☽⊻⚷ 2:25
☉△☽ 4:59
☽∠⚳ 8:07
☽☌♅ 11:41
☽⚹♆ 11:53
☽△♇ 16:42
☿⚹♄ 18:07
☽⚹♄ 23:56

19 Tu
☽△☿ 0:39
☽□♂ 1:02
☉#♅ 3:06
☽∠⚷ 3:18
☿⊼♂ 3:48
☽☍♀ 5:32
☉⚼☽ 7:37
☽⊻⚳ 8:28
☿∥♀ 15:53
☽⚼♇ 17:14

20 W
☽⚹♃ 1:02
☽⚹⚷ 3:33
☽⚼☿ 4:01
☉ ♒ 7:31
☉⊼☽ 9:30
☽⊻♅ 12:18
☽□♆ 12:37
♀⊼⚳ 14:45
☽⊼♇ 17:15

21 Th
☽□♄ 0:19
☽∠♃ 0:43
☽⚹♂ 0:47
☽⊼☿ 6:47
☽☌⚳ 7:41
☽⊼♀ 9:16
☽∠♅ 12:00
☿⊼⚳ 14:07

22 F
☽⊻♃ 0:12
☽∠♂ 0:13
☽#♇ 2:07
☉△♅ 2:20
☽□⚷ 3:04
☉∥♀ 3:20
☉⚹♆ 8:31
♂⊼♄ 8:54
♃⚼♄ 10:03
☽⚼♀ 10:47
☽⚹♅ 11:38
☽△♆ 12:04
☉☍☽ 12:19
☽∥♅ 16:40
☽☍♇ 16:43
☽#♀ 19:15
☉#☽ 20:29
☽⊻♂ 23:41
☽△♄ 23:55

23 Sa
☽⊻⚳ 6:28
☽#☿ 6:34
☿∠♆ 10:29
☽⚼♆ 11:56
☽☍☿ 12:07
☽△♀ 12:31
☊ D 17:27
☽∥♃ 18:36
☿⚹♀ 22:34
☽☌♃ 23:35

24 Su
☽⚼♄ 0:03
☽△⚷ 2:56
☽∥♂ 4:11
☽∠⚳ 6:18
☽∥⚷ 10:26
☽□♅ 11:41
☽⊼♆ 12:15
☉⊼☽ 16:01
☽⊼♇ 17:07
☽☌♂ 23:41

25 M
☽⊼♄ 0:45
☽⚼⚷ 3:37
☽⚹⚳ 6:42
☉☌♇ 8:03
☽∥♄ 17:34
☽□♀ 17:57
☽⚼♇ 18:15
☉⚼☽ 19:01
☽⊼☿ 19:41
♀∠♇ 21:41
☽#♆ 22:21

26 Tu
☽⊻♃ 1:02
☽∥♆ 1:13
☽⊼⚷ 5:05
☽#♄ 6:07
☽△♅ 14:17
☽☍♆ 15:01
♀#♅ 17:36
☽△♇ 20:15
☉△☽ 23:05

27 W
☽⚼☿ 1:06
☽⊻♂ 2:24
☽∠♃ 2:59
☽☍♄ 4:37
☽□⚳ 9:58
☽#⚷ 15:18
☿#♃ 15:30
☿☍♃ 16:38
☽⚼♅ 16:57
☽#♂ 23:57

28 Th
☽⚹♀ 3:46
☽∠♂ 5:06
☽⚹♃ 5:54
☽△☿ 7:47
☽∥☿ 7:53
☿∠♄ 9:52
☽#♃ 10:06
☽☍⚷ 10:50
☉⊼♂ 11:53
☽⊼♅ 20:37
☽⊼♆ 21:34

29 F
♀△♃ 2:14
☉∥☽ 2:59
☽□♇ 3:13
☽⚹♂ 8:41
☽∠♀ 10:36
☉□☽ 10:57
☿⚹⚷ 11:07
☊ R 11:12
☽⊼♄ 12:25
☽#♅ 15:58
☽△⚳ 17:00
☽∥♀ 17:57

30 Sa
☿⚼⚳ 2:03
☽⚼♆ 2:17
☉⚹♄ 6:37
☽∥♇ 9:36
☿#♂ 13:41
☽□♃ 14:30
☽⚼♄ 17:43
☽⊻♀ 18:37
☉∠♀ 20:00
☽⊼⚷ 20:26
☽⚼⚳ 21:49

31 Su
☽□☿ 0:37
☽☍♅ 6:38
☽△♆ 7:48
☽⚹♇ 13:47
♀△⚷ 14:20
☽□♂ 18:09
☽△♄ 23:43

February 2027

LONGITUDE

Day	Sid.Time	☉	☽	☽ 12 hour	Mean ☊	True ☊	☿	♀	♂	⚳	♃	♄	⚷	♅	♆	♇
	h m s	° ' "	° ' "	° ' "	° '	° '	° '	° '	° '	° '	° '	° '	° '	° '	° '	° '
1 M	8 43 55	11♒52 45	10♐24 46	16♐22 53	21♒12.1	20♒35.8	29♒55.5	27♐01.3	7♍25.2	12♋04.6	23♌21.2	10♈16.3	26♈34.4	1♊42.5	2♈18.8	5♒19.2
2 Tu	8 47 52	12 53 40	22 19 19	28 14 31	21 08.9	20R 34.7	1♓07.4	28 09.8	7R 08.2	11R 55.2	23R 13.5	10 21.5	26 35.8	1R 42.1	2 20.4	5 21.1
3 W	8 51 48	13 54 34	4♑08 58	10♑03 02	21 05.7	20 33.7	2 13.1	29 18.4	6 50.5	11 46.2	23 05.8	10 26.7	26 37.3	1 41.8	2 22.0	5 22.9
4 Th	8 55 45	14 55 27	15 57 08	21 51 35	21 02.5	20 32.8	3 11.9	0♑27.2	6 32.2	11 37.5	22 58.0	10 32.0	26 38.9	1 41.5	2 23.7	5 24.8
5 F	8 59 41	15 56 20	27 46 43	3♒42 49	20 59.4	20 32.2	4 03.0	1 36.0	6 13.2	11 29.2	22 50.1	10 37.3	26 40.5	1 41.3	2 25.4	5 26.7
6 Sa	9 03 38	16 57 11	9♒40 10	15 39 00	20 56.2	20D 31.9	4 45.7	2 45.1	5 53.6	11 21.3	22 42.3	10 42.7	26 42.1	1 41.1	2 27.1	5 28.6
7 Su	9 07 35	17 58 01	21 39 34	27 42 04	20 53.0	20 31.8	5 19.1	3 54.2	5 33.5	11 13.9	22 34.4	10 48.2	26 43.8	1 41.0	2 28.8	5 30.5
8 M	9 11 31	18 58 50	3♓46 43	9♓53 44	20 49.8	20 31.8	5 42.7	5 03.5	5 12.9	11 06.8	22 26.4	10 53.8	26 45.6	1D 41.0	2 30.5	5 32.3
9 Tu	9 15 28	19 59 37	16 03 18	22 15 40	20 46.7	20R 31.9	5R 56.0	6 12.8	4 51.7	11 00.1	22 18.5	10 59.4	26 47.4	1 41.0	2 32.3	5 34.2
10 W	9 19 24	21 00 23	28 31 02	4♈49 37	20 43.5	20 31.9	5 58.5	7 22.3	4 30.1	10 53.9	22 10.5	11 05.1	26 49.3	1 41.0	2 34.1	5 36.1
11 Th	9 23 21	22 01 08	11♈11 40	17 37 24	20 40.3	20 31.8	5 50.2	8 31.9	4 08.1	10 48.0	22 02.6	11 10.9	26 51.2	1 41.1	2 35.9	5 37.9
12 F	9 27 17	23 01 51	24 07 03	0♉40 52	20 37.1	20 31.6	5 31.2	9 41.6	3 45.7	10 42.6	21 54.6	11 16.7	26 53.1	1 41.3	2 37.8	5 39.8
13 Sa	9 31 14	24 02 33	7♉19 03	14 01 48	20 33.9	20 31.3	5 01.8	10 51.5	3 23.0	10 37.7	21 46.6	11 22.6	26 55.1	1 41.5	2 39.6	5 41.6
14 Su	9 35 10	25 03 13	20 49 17	27 41 36	20 30.8	20D 31.1	4 22.8	12 01.4	2 59.9	10 33.1	21 38.7	11 28.6	26 57.2	1 41.8	2 41.5	5 43.4
15 M	9 39 07	26 03 51	4♊38 47	11♊40 50	20 27.6	20 31.2	3 35.2	13 11.4	2 36.7	10 29.0	21 30.8	11 34.6	26 59.3	1 42.1	2 43.4	5 45.2
16 Tu	9 43 03	27 04 27	18 47 36	25 58 51	20 24.4	20 31.5	2 40.2	14 21.5	2 13.2	10 25.4	21 22.9	11 40.7	27 01.4	1 42.5	2 45.3	5 47.0
17 W	9 47 00	28 05 02	3♋14 15	10♋33 19	20 21.2	20 32.1	1 39.3	15 31.7	1 49.5	10 22.1	21 15.0	11 46.8	27 03.6	1 42.9	2 47.2	5 48.8
18 Th	9 50 57	29 05 35	17 55 27	25 19 58	20 18.1	20 32.9	0 34.3	16 42.0	1 25.7	10 19.3	21 07.2	11 53.0	27 05.8	1 43.4	2 49.2	5 50.6
19 F	9 54 53	0♓06 07	2♌46 02	10♌12 44	20 14.9	20 33.5	29♒26.9	17 52.3	1 01.9	10 17.0	20 59.4	11 59.2	27 08.1	1 43.9	2 51.2	5 52.4
20 Sa	9 58 50	1 06 36	17 39 09	25 04 17	20 11.7	20R 33.9	28 18.9	19 02.8	0 38.0	10 15.0	20 51.7	12 05.5	27 10.4	1 44.5	2 53.2	5 54.2
21 Su	10 02 46	2 07 04	2♍27 10	9♍46 53	20 08.5	20 33.7	27 12.0	20 13.4	0 14.1	10 13.5	20 44.0	12 11.9	27 12.8	1 45.1	2 55.2	5 55.9
22 M	10 06 43	3 07 30	17 02 34	24 13 29	20 05.4	20 32.8	26 07.8	21 24.0	29♌50.3	10 12.5	20 36.4	12 18.3	27 15.2	1 45.8	2 57.2	5 57.7
23 Tu	10 10 39	4 07 55	1♎19 00	8♎18 39	20 02.2	20 31.4	25 07.6	22 34.7	29 26.6	10D 11.8	20 28.8	12 24.7	27 17.6	1 46.6	2 59.2	5 59.4
24 W	10 14 36	5 08 18	15 12 07	21 59 11	19 59.0	20 29.4	24 12.6	23 45.5	29 03.0	10 11.6	20 21.3	12 31.2	27 20.1	1 47.4	3 01.3	6 01.1
25 Th	10 18 32	6 08 40	28 39 50	5♏14 10	19 55.8	20 27.3	23 23.6	24 56.3	28 39.7	10 11.9	20 13.9	12 37.8	27 22.6	1 48.2	3 03.3	6 02.8
26 F	10 22 29	7 09 00	11♏42 24	18 04 51	19 52.6	20 25.4	22 41.3	26 07.3	28 16.5	10 12.5	20 06.5	12 44.4	27 25.2	1 49.1	3 05.4	6 04.5
27 Sa	10 26 26	8 09 19	24 21 55	0♐34 05	19 49.5	20 24.0	22 05.9	27 18.3	27 53.6	10 13.6	19 59.2	12 51.1	27 27.8	1 50.0	3 07.5	6 06.2
28 Su	10 30 22	9♓09 36	6♐41 53	12 45 53	19♒46.3	20♒23.3	21♒37.8	28♑29.4	27♌31.0	10♋15.1	19♌52.1	12♈57.8	27♈30.4	1♊51.0	3♈09.6	6♒07.8

1st of Month

Julian Day # 2461437.5
Obliquity 23°26'[illegible]6"
SVP 4♓52'[illegible]1"
GC 27♐13.1
Eris 24♈53.5

Day	⚴	Day	⚵	Day	⚶
1	15♈27.3	1	8♓02.1	1	24♈46.9
6	17 14.5	6	10 28.5	6	26 25.3
11	19 06.9	11	12 56.7	11	28 07.4
16	21 04.1	16	15 26.7	16	29 52.9
21	23 05.8	21	17 58.3	21	1♉41.3
26	25 11.6	26	20 31.4	26	3 32.4

DECLINATION and LATITUDE

Day	☉ Decl	☽ Decl	☽ Lat	☽ 12h Decl	☿ Decl	☿ Lat	♀ Decl	♀ Lat	♂ Decl	♂ Lat	⚳ Decl	⚳ Lat	♃ Decl	♃ Lat	♄ Decl	♄ Lat
1 M	17S14	26S56	4S58	27S29	11S38	0S09	20S54	2N30	12N45	4N17	31N37	8N46	14N43	1N02	1N55	2S20
2 Tu	16 57	27 42	4 30	27 37	10 60	0N05	20 59	2 27	12 53	4 18	31 39	8 47	14 45	1 02	1 57	2 20
3 W	16 39	27 12	3 50	26 29	10 23	0 19	21 03	2 23	13 01	4 19	31 41	8 48	14 48	1 02	1 59	2 20
4 Th	16 21	25 28	3 00	24 10	9 48	0 35	21 06	2 20	13 09	4 21	31 43	8 50	14 51	1 02	2 02	2 20
5 F	16 03	22 37	2 03	20 49	9 14	0 50	21 09	2 17	13 17	4 22	31 45	8 51	14 53	1 03	2 04	2 20
6 Sa	15 45	18 47	0 60	16 34	8 44	1 07	21 12	2 13	13 25	4 23	31 47	8 52	14 56	1 03	2 06	2 19
7 Su	15 27	14 11	0N06	11 39	8 16	1 23	21 13	2 10	13 33	4 24	31 49	8 53	14 59	1 03	2 08	2 19
8 M	15 08	8 59	1 13	6 14	7 52	1 40	21 15	2 06	13 42	4 25	31 50	8 54	15 01	1 03	2 11	2 19
9 Tu	14 49	3 24	2 17	0 30	7 31	1 57	21 15	2 02	13 51	4 25	31 52	8 55	15 04	1 03	2 13	2 19
10 W	14 30	2N24	3 16	5N19	7 15	2 13	21 15	1 59	13 59	4 26	31 53	8 56	15 07	1 03	2 15	2 19
11 Th	14 10	8 12	4 06	11 01	7 04	2 29	21 15	1 55	14 08	4 27	31 54	8 56	15 09	1 03	2 18	2 19
12 F	13 50	13 46	4 45	16 22	6 56	2 44	21 14	1 51	14 17	4 27	31 55	8 57	15 12	1 03	2 20	2 18
13 Sa	13 30	18 49	5 09	21 04	6 54	2 58	21 12	1 48	14 25	4 28	31 56	8 58	15 15	1 03	2 23	2 18
14 Su	13 10	23 03	5 18	24 45	6 57	3 10	21 10	1 44	14 34	4 28	31 57	8 58	15 17	1 04	2 25	2 18
15 M	12 50	26 07	5 08	27 05	7 04	3 21	21 07	1 40	14 43	4 28	31 58	8 59	15 20	1 04	2 28	2 18
16 Tu	12 29	27 37	4 40	27 41	7 15	3 30	21 04	1 36	14 51	4 28	31 59	8 59	15 23	1 04	2 30	2 18
17 W	12 08	27 17	3 54	26 25	7 30	3 37	21 00	1 33	14 60	4 28	31 59	8 59	15 25	1 04	2 33	2 18
18 Th	11 47	25 04	2 51	23 17	7 49	3 41	20 56	1 29	15 08	4 28	31 60	8 59	15 28	1 04	2 35	2 17
19 F	11 26	21 07	1 37	18 36	8 11	3 43	20 51	1 25	15 17	4 28	32 00	8 60	15 30	1 04	2 38	2 17
20 Sa	11 05	15 48	0 16	12 46	8 34	3 43	20 45	1 21	15 25	4 28	32 01	8 60	15 33	1 04	2 40	2 17
21 Su	10 43	9 35	1S06	6 17	8 59	3 40	20 39	1 17	15 33	4 27	32 01	8 60	15 36	1 04	2 43	2 17
22 M	10 21	2 57	2 22	0S24	9 25	3 36	20 32	1 13	15 41	4 27	32 01	8 60	15 38	1 04	2 46	2 17
23 Tu	9 60	3S41	3 27	6 53	9 51	3 29	20 24	1 09	15 49	4 26	32 01	8 60	15 40	1 04	2 48	2 17
24 W	9 38	9 57	4 18	12 52	10 17	3 21	20 16	1 06	15 57	4 25	32 01	8 60	15 43	1 04	2 51	2 17
25 Th	9 15	15 34	4 54	18 03	10 42	3 11	20 08	1 02	16 04	4 24	32 01	8 60	15 45	1 04	2 54	2 17
26 F	8 53	20 18	5 13	22 16	11 06	3 01	19 59	0 58	16 11	4 23	32 01	8 60	15 48	1 04	2 56	2 16
27 Sa	8 31	23 57	5 15	25 20	11 29	2 49	19 49	0 54	16 18	4 22	32 00	8 59	15 50	1 04	2 59	2 16
28 Su	8S08	26S25	5S04	27S10	11S50	2N36	19S39	0N50	16N25	4N21	31N60	8N59	15N52	1N04	3N02	2S16

Day	⚷ Decl	⚷ Lat	♅ Decl	♅ Lat	♆ Decl	♆ Lat	♇ Decl	♇ Lat
1	10N16	0N01	20N22	0S08	0S20	1S22	23S06	4S17
6	10 18	0 01	20 22	0 08	0 16	1 21	23 04	4 18
11	10 21	0 00	20 22	0 08	0 13	1 21	23 02	4 18
16	10 25	0S00	20 23	0 08	0 09	1 21	23 00	4 19
21	10 28	0 01	20 23	0 08	0 05	1 21	22 59	4 20
26	10N32	0S01	20N24	0S08	0S01	1S21	22S57	4S20

Day	⚴ Decl	⚴ Lat	⚵ Decl	⚵ Lat	⚶ Decl	⚶ Lat	Eris Decl	Eris Lat
1	16S00	23S57	8S22	0N12	4N13	5S47	0N02	10S19
6	15 18	23 54	7 41	0S03	4 60	5 34	0 03	10 18
11	14 36	23 52	6 58	0 17	5 47	5 22	0 04	10 17
16	13 53	23 50	6 13	0 32	6 34	5 11	0 05	10 17
21	13 09	23 48	5 28	0 46	7 22	5 00	0 06	10 16
26	12S25	23S47	4S41	1S00	8N09	4S50	0N08	10S15

Moon Phenomena

Max/0 Decl
dy hr mn
2 2:34 27S43
9 14:05 0 N
16 7:59 27N43
22 10:34 0 S

Max/0 Lat
dy hr mn
6 21:44 0 N
13 23:28 5N18
20 4:42 0 S
26 16:25 5S16

Perigee/Apogee
dy hr m kilometers
3 13:32 a 406189
19 7:32 p 361020

PH dy hr mn
● 6 15:57 17♒38
● 6 960:47A 07'[illegible]51"
☽ 14 8:00 25♉23
○ 20 23:25 2♍06
● 20 23:14 A 0.927
☾ 28 5:18 9♐23

Void of Course Moon

Last Aspect			☽ Ingress		
2 13:06	♀	☌	♑	2	15:34
3 12:54	♄	□	♒	5	4:30
7 1:48	♃	☍	♓	7	16:33
8 3:54	☿	☌	♈	10	2:50
11 21:50	☉	⚹	♉	12	10:46
14 8:00	☉	□	♊	14	16:00
16 14:51	☉	△	♋	16	18:40
17 21:50	♀	☍	♌	18	19:32
20 16:03	☿	☍	♍	20	20:00
22 7:55	♀	△	♎	22	21:46
24 24:00	♂	⚹	♏	25	2:25
27 6:36	♂	□	♐	27	10:54

DAILY ASPECTARIAN

1 M
☿ ♓ 1:27
☽ ⚼ ⚷ 2:20
☉ ⚹ ☽ 3:13
☽ ⚻ ⚳ 3:18
☉ ⚻ ⚳ 4:03
☽ ∠ ♇ 20:00

2 Tu
☽ △ ♃ 1:49
☽ △ ⚷ 8:41
☿ □ ♅ 12:19
☉ ∠ ☽ 12:21
☽ ☌ ♀ 13:06
☽ ⚻ ♅ 19:01
☽ ⚹ ☿ 19:41
☽ □ ♆ 20:22

3 W
☽ ⚺ ♇ 2:31
☿ ⚺ ♆ 3:33
☿ ⋕ ⚷ 4:05
☽ △ ♂ 5:20
☽ ⚼ ♃ 7:56
☽ □ ♄ 12:54
♀ ♑ 14:32
☽ ☍ ⚳ 15:18
☉ ⚺ ☽ 21:43

4 Th
☽ ⚼ ♅ 1:30
☽ ∠ ☿ 4:57
☽ ⚼ ♂ 11:03
☽ ⚻ ♃ 14:05
☽ ∥ ♇ 20:41
☽ □ ⚷ 21:46

5 F
♀ ⚻ ♅ 1:49
☽ △ ♅ 7:54
☽ ⚺ ♀ 8:34
☽ ⚹ ♆ 9:25
☽ ∥ ♀ 9:44
☽ ⚺ ☿ 13:31
☽ ⋕ ♅ 14:45
☽ ☌ ♇ 15:32
☽ ⚻ ♂ 16:36
♀ □ ♆ 17:35

6 Sa
☽ ⚹ ♄ 2:07
☽ ⚻ ⚳ 3:21
☉ ∠ ♆ 12:08
☽ ∠ ♆ 15:38
☉ ☌ ☽ 15:57
☉ ∥ ☽ 17:20
☽ ∠ ♀ 17:55
☽ ⋕ ♃ 20:08
☊ D 21:50

7 Su
☽ ☍ ♃ 1:48
☽ ⋕ ♂ 2:57
♂ ⚻ ♇ 3:17
☿ ☍ ♂ 7:16
☽ ∠ ♄ 8:18
☽ ⚼ ⚳ 9:00
☽ ⚹ ⚷ 10:06
☿ ⚺ ♇ 11:09
☽ ⋕ ⚷ 18:03
☽ □ ♅ 19:52
☽ ⚺ ♆ 21:30

8 M
♀ △ ♂ 2:30
☽ ☍ ♂ 2:45
☽ ⚹ ♀ 2:47
☽ ⚺ ♇ 3:28
☽ ☌ ☿ 3:54
☽ ∥ ☿ 5:17
☉ ⋕ ♃ 7:15
♀ ⚺ ♇ 10:16
♅ D 12:31
☽ ⚺ ♄ 14:04
☽ △ ⚳ 14:15
☽ ∠ ⚷ 15:41
☿ ⚹ ♀ 17:15

9 Tu
⚳ □ ♄ 1:22
☽ ⋕ ♄ 4:52
☉ ⚺ ☽ 8:18
☽ ∠ ♇ 8:46
☽ ⚻ ♃ 11:58
☊ R 12:22
☽ ∥ ♆ 13:09
☽ ⋕ ♆ 15:02
☿ R 17:37
♀ ⚼ ♃ 20:21
☽ ⚺ ⚷ 20:45
☽ ∥ ♄ 23:23

10 W
☽ ⚹ ♅ 6:02
☽ ☌ ♆ 7:44
☽ ⚻ ♂ 11:04
☽ ⚹ ♇ 13:30
☽ ⚺ ☿ 14:04
☉ ∠ ☽ 15:28
☽ ⚼ ♃ 16:16
☽ □ ♀ 18:30
☽ ⋕ ☿ 19:22
☽ □ ⚳ 23:16
☽ ☌ ♄ 23:59

11 Th
☉ ☍ ♃ 0:30
☉ ⋕ ♂ 1:56
☽ ∥ ⚷ 9:08
☽ ∠ ♅ 10:16
☽ ⚼ ♂ 14:23
☿ ⚺ ♇ 15:30
☽ ∠ ☿ 17:33
☽ △ ♃ 19:59
☉ ⚹ ☽ 21:50

12 F
☉ ⋕ ☽ 0:20
☽ ∥ ♂ 2:23
☽ ☌ ⚷ 5:05
☽ ∥ ♃ 6:36
☽ ⚺ ♅ 13:50
☽ ⚺ ♆ 15:34
☽ △ ♂ 17:06
♀ ☍ ⚳ 19:34
☽ ⚹ ☿ 20:03
☽ □ ♇ 21:04

13 Sa
☽ ⚹ ⚳ 5:54
☽ △ ♀ 6:57
☽ ⚺ ♄ 7:20
☽ ∥ ♅ 8:10
♀ □ ♄ 11:41
☽ ⋕ ♀ 12:42
☽ ∠ ♆ 18:28
☽ ⋕ ♇ 23:43

14 Su
☽ □ ♃ 1:26
☊ D 7:23
☉ □ ☽ 8:00
☽ ∠ ⚳ 8:14
☽ ∠ ♄ 9:57
☽ ⚺ ⚷ 10:44
☉ ⚼ ⚳ 11:04
☽ ⚼ ♀ 11:50
♂ ⚻ ♆ 17:37
☽ ☌ ♅ 18:56
☽ □ ♂ 20:36
☽ ⚹ ♆ 20:41
☽ □ ☿ 22:17

15 M
☽ △ ♇ 1:54
☽ ⚺ ⚳ 9:55
☽ ⚹ ♄ 11:54
☽ ∠ ⚷ 12:33
☉ ∠ ♄ 13:31
☽ ⚻ ♀ 15:52
☿ ⚺ ♆ 21:57
☉ ⚹ ⚷ 22:45

16 Tu
☽ ⚼ ♇ 3:21
☽ ⚹ ♃ 4:18
⚶ ♉ 7:58
☽ ⚹ ⚷ 13:46
☉ △ ☽ 14:51
☿ ☍ ♂ 17:43
☽ ⚺ ♅ 21:29
☽ △ ☿ 21:34
☽ ⚹ ♂ 21:44
☿ □ ♅ 22:39
☽ □ ♆ 23:15

17 W
☽ ⚻ ♇ 4:15
☽ ∠ ♃ 4:54
♂ □ ♅ 6:34
☽ ☌ ⚳ 11:39
☿ ∠ ♀ 12:04
☽ □ ♄ 14:06
☉ ⚼ ☽ 17:19
♀ ⚼ ♂ 19:52
☽ ⚼ ☿ 20:27
☽ ∠ ♂ 21:38
☽ ☍ ♀ 21:50
☽ ∠ ♅ 22:03

18 Th
♀ ⚼ ♅ 0:29
☽ ⚺ ♃ 5:08
☿ R♒ 12:17
☽ ⋕ ♇ 13:46
☽ □ ⚷ 14:53
☉ ☌ ☿ 16:40
☽ ⚻ ☿ 19:01
☉ ⚻ ☽ 19:23
☽ ⚺ ♂ 21:16
☉ ♓ 21:35
☽ ⚹ ♅ 22:20

19 F
☽ △ ♆ 0:08
☽ ⋕ ♀ 1:25
☽ ∥ ♅ 3:40
☽ ☍ ♇ 5:01
☽ ⚺ ⚳ 12:05
☽ △ ♄ 14:58
☉ ☍ ♂ 15:52

20 Sa
☽ ⚼ ♆ 0:23
☽ ∥ ♃ 1:00
☽ ∥ ♂ 1:31
☽ ⚻ ♀ 2:27
☊ R 4:41
☽ ☌ ♃ 5:08
☽ ∠ ⚳ 12:16
☉ □ ♅ 15:12
☽ ⚼ ♄ 15:23
☽ △ ⚷ 15:27
☽ ☍ ☿ 16:03
☉ ⋕ ☽ 19:31
☽ ☌ ♂ 20:29
☽ ∥ ⚷ 20:42
☽ □ ♅ 22:51
☉ ☍ ☽ 23:25
☿ ⚹ ⚷ 23:44

21 Su
☿ ∠ ♄ 0:02
☽ ⚻ ♆ 0:46
☽ ⋕ ☿ 2:03
☽ ⚼ ♀ 4:55
☽ ⚻ ♇ 5:42
♀ ⚻ ♃ 9:24
♂ ∥ ♃ 10:31
☽ ⚹ ⚳ 12:43
♂ R♌ 14:15
☉ ⋕ ⚷ 15:57
☽ ⚼ ⚷ 16:03
☽ ⚻ ♄ 16:06
☉ ⚺ ♆ 19:45

22 M
☽ ∥ ♄ 0:39
☽ ⚺ ♃ 5:53
☽ ⚼ ♇ 6:33
☽ △ ♀ 7:55
☽ ⋕ ♆ 10:21
☽ ∥ ♆ 10:47
☽ ⚻ ☿ 14:12
☽ ⚻ ⚷ 17:09
☽ ⋕ ♄ 20:43
☽ ⚺ ♂ 20:54
☿ ⚼ ⚳ 22:14

23 Tu
☽ △ ♅ 0:47
♀ ⋕ ♅ 2:44
☽ ☍ ♆ 2:51
☉ ∥ ☿ 4:09
☉ ⚻ ☽ 5:11
☽ ∠ ♃ 7:04
☽ △ ♇ 8:01
☽ ⚼ ☿ 14:11
☽ □ ⚳ 15:16
☽ ☍ ♄ 19:16
☽ ∠ ♂ 22:02
☉ ∥ ☽ 22:45
⚳ D 23:25

24 W
☽ ∥ ☿ 1:25
☽ ⋕ ⚷ 2:14
☽ ⚼ ♅ 2:48
☿ ⚺ ♀ 5:20
☽ ⚹ ♃ 9:01
☉ ⚼ ☽ 9:25
☿ ⋕ ⚷ 13:16
☽ △ ☿ 15:02
☽ □ ♀ 16:38
☉ ⚺ ♇ 21:36
☽ ☍ ⚷ 21:40
☽ ⚹ ♂ 24:00

25 Th
☽ ⋕ ♃ 0:52
☽ ⋕ ♂ 2:23
☽ ⚻ ♅ 5:43
☽ ⚻ ♆ 8:01
☽ □ ♇ 13:31
☉ △ ☽ 14:49
☽ △ ⚳ 21:12
☽ ∥ ♀ 22:17

26 F
☽ ⋕ ♅ 0:36
☽ ⚻ ♄ 1:57
☽ ⚼ ♆ 12:03
☽ □ ♃ 15:42
☽ ∥ ♇ 16:36
☽ □ ☿ 19:50

27 Sa
☽ ⚼ ⚳ 1:40
♂ ⚼ ♄ 2:05
♀ □ ⚷ 3:19
☽ ⚻ ⚷ 6:00
☽ ⚹ ♀ 6:16
☽ □ ♂ 6:36
☽ ⚼ ♄ 6:47
♀ ⚻ ♂ 9:02
☽ ☍ ♅ 14:29
☽ △ ♆ 17:02
☽ ⚹ ♇ 22:53

28 Su
♂ △ ⚷ 0:35
☉ □ ☽ 5:18
☊ D 5:21
☽ ⚻ ⚳ 7:02
☽ ⚼ ⚷ 11:32
☽ △ ♄ 12:31
☽ ∠ ♀ 14:54

LONGITUDE

March 2027

Day	Sid.Time	☉	☽	☽ 12 hour	Mean ☊	True ☊	☿	♀	♂	⚳	♃	♄	⚷	♅	♆	♇
	h m s	° ' "	° ' "	° ' "	° '	° '	° '	° '	° '	° '	° '	° '	° '	° '	° '	° '
1 M	10 34 19	10♓09 53	18♐46 41	24♐44 54	19♒43.1	20♒23.6	21♒16.9	29♑40.5	27♌08.8	10♋17.0	19♌45.0	13♈04.5	27♈33.1	1♊52.1	3♈11.7	6♒09.5
2 Tu	10 38 15	11 10 07	0♑41 09	6♑36 02	19 39.9	20 24.6	21R 03.1	0♒51.8	26R 47.0	10 19.3	19R 38.0	13 11.3	27 35.8	1 53.2	3 13.9	6 11.1
3 W	10 42 12	12 10 20	12 30 08	18 24 03	19 36.8	20 26.2	20D 56.3	2 03.1	26 25.6	10 22.1	19 31.1	13 18.1	27 38.6	1 54.3	3 16.0	6 12.7
4 Th	10 46 08	13 10 32	24 18 18	0♒13 25	19 33.6	20 28.0	20 56.1	3 14.4	26 04.6	10 25.3	19 24.3	13 25.0	27 41.3	1 55.5	3 18.2	6 14.3
5 F	10 50 05	14 10 42	6♒09 52	12 08 06	19 30.4	20 29.5	21 02.3	4 25.8	25 44.2	10 28.8	19 17.7	13 31.9	27 44.2	1 56.8	3 20.3	6 15.9
6 Sa	10 54 01	15 10 50	18 08 29	24 11 22	19 27.2	20R 30.2	21 14.5	5 37.2	25 24.3	10 32.8	19 11.1	13 38.8	27 47.0	1 58.1	3 22.5	6 17.5
7 Su	10 57 58	16 10 56	0♓17 02	6♓25 44	19 24.0	20 29.8	21 32.4	6 48.7	25 05.0	10 37.2	19 04.7	13 45.8	27 49.9	1 59.4	3 24.7	6 19.0
8 M	11 01 55	17 11 01	12 37 40	18 52 57	19 20.9	20 28.1	21 55.6	8 00.3	24 46.2	10 41.9	18 58.4	13 52.8	27 52.8	2 00.8	3 26.9	6 20.6
9 Tu	11 05 51	18 11 03	25 11 41	1♈33 55	19 17.7	20 25.0	22 23.8	9 11.9	24 28.1	10 47.1	18 52.2	13 59.9	27 55.8	2 02.3	3 29.1	6 22.1
10 W	11 09 48	19 11 04	7♈59 41	14 28 55	19 14.5	20 20.7	22 56.6	10 23.5	24 10.6	10 52.7	18 46.2	14 07.0	27 58.8	2 03.8	3 31.3	6 23.6
11 Th	11 13 44	20 11 03	21 01 36	27 37 38	19 11.3	20 15.8	23 33.8	11 35.2	23 53.8	10 58.6	18 40.3	14 14.1	28 01.8	2 05.3	3 33.5	6 25.1
12 F	11 17 41	21 11 00	4♉16 57	10♉59 27	19 08.2	20 10.7	24 15.1	12 47.0	23 37.8	11 04.9	18 34.6	14 21.3	28 04.8	2 06.9	3 35.8	6 26.5
13 Sa	11 21 37	22 10 54	17 45 02	24 33 35	19 05.0	20 06.3	25 00.1	13 58.7	23 22.4	11 11.6	18 29.0	14 28.5	28 07.9	2 08.6	3 38.0	6 28.0
14 Su	11 25 34	23 10 47	1♊25 02	8♊19 17	19 01.8	20 03.0	25 48.6	15 10.5	23 07.7	11 18.7	18 23.5	14 35.7	28 11.0	2 10.2	3 40.2	6 29.4
15 M	11 29 30	24 10 37	15 16 13	22 15 45	18 58.6	20D 01.2	26 40.5	16 22.4	22 53.8	11 26.1	18 18.2	14 42.9	28 14.2	2 12.0	3 42.5	6 30.8
16 Tu	11 33 27	25 10 26	29 17 46	6♋22 06	18 55.4	20 01.0	27 35.4	17 34.3	22 40.7	11 34.0	18 13.1	14 50.2	28 17.3	2 13.8	3 44.7	6 32.2
17 W	11 37 24	26 10 11	13♋28 37	20 37 04	18 52.3	20 01.9	28 33.3	18 46.2	22 28.3	11 42.1	18 08.1	14 57.5	28 20.5	2 15.6	3 47.0	6 33.5
18 Th	11 41 20	27 09 55	27 47 12	4♌58 41	18 49.1	20 03.3	29 33.9	19 58.2	22 16.7	11 50.6	18 03.2	15 04.8	28 23.8	2 17.4	3 49.2	6 34.9
19 F	11 45 17	28 09 36	12♌11 07	19 24 02	18 45.9	20R 04.5	0♓37.0	21 10.2	22 05.8	11 59.5	17 58.6	15 12.2	28 27.0	2 19.4	3 51.5	6 36.2
20 Sa	11 49 13	29 09 15	26 36 55	3♍49 11	18 42.7	20 04.5	1 42.6	22 22.2	21 55.8	12 08.7	17 54.1	15 19.5	28 30.3	2 21.3	3 53.8	6 37.5
21 Su	11 53 10	0♈08 52	11♍00 11	18 09 16	18 39.6	20 02.8	2 50.5	23 34.2	21 46.5	12 18.2	17 49.7	15 26.9	28 33.5	2 23.3	3 56.0	6 38.8
22 M	11 57 06	1 08 26	25 15 46	2♎19 04	18 36.4	19 59.1	4 00.6	24 46.3	21 38.0	12 28.0	17 45.6	15 34.3	28 36.9	2 25.3	3 58.3	6 40.0
23 Tu	12 01 03	2 07 59	9♎18 32	16 13 39	18 33.2	19 53.5	5 12.8	25 58.5	21 30.3	12 38.2	17 41.6	15 41.7	28 40.2	2 27.4	4 00.6	6 41.3
24 W	12 04 59	3 07 29	23 03 58	29 49 08	18 30.0	19 46.5	6 27.0	27 10.6	21 23.4	12 48.7	17 37.8	15 49.2	28 43.5	2 29.5	4 02.9	6 42.5
25 Th	12 08 56	4 06 58	6♏28 56	13♏03 14	18 26.8	19 38.9	7 43.1	28 22.8	21 17.2	12 59.5	17 34.1	15 56.6	28 46.9	2 31.7	4 05.1	6 43.7
26 F	12 12 53	5 06 25	19 32 02	25 55 28	18 23.7	19 31.5	9 01.0	29 35.0	21 11.9	13 10.6	17 30.6	16 04.1	28 50.3	2 33.9	4 07.4	6 44.8
27 Sa	12 16 49	6 05 50	2♐13 46	8♐27 14	18 20.5	19 25.2	10 20.8	0♓47.3	21 07.3	13 22.1	17 27.4	16 11.6	28 53.7	2 36.1	4 09.7	6 46.0
28 Su	12 20 46	7 05 13	14 36 18	20 41 26	18 17.3	19 20.6	11 42.3	1 59.6	21 03.4	13 33.8	17 24.2	16 19.1	28 57.2	2 38.4	4 12.0	6 47.1
29 M	12 24 42	8 04 35	26 43 11	2♑42 09	18 14.1	19 17.9	13 05.4	3 11.9	21 00.4	13 45.8	17 21.3	16 26.6	29 00.6	2 40.8	4 14.2	6 48.2
30 Tu	12 28 39	9 03 54	8♑38 57	14 34 13	18 11.0	19D 17.0	14 30.2	4 24.2	20 58.1	13 58.1	17 18.6	16 34.1	29 04.1	2 43.1	4 16.5	6 49.3
31 W	12 32 35	10♈03 12	20 28 38	26 22 52	18♒07.8	19♒17.5	15♓56.6	5♓36.6	20♌56.5	14♋10.8	17♌16.0	16♈41.7	29♈07.6	2♊45.5	4♈18.8	6♒50.3

1st of Month
Julian Day #
2461465.5
Obliquity
23°26'36"
SVP 4♓52'37"
GC 27♐13.1
Eris 25♈03.3

Day	⚴
1	26♈29.0
6	28 41.2
11	0♉57.0
16	3 16.3
21	5 38.8
26	8 04.3
31	10 32.8

Day	⚵
1	22♓04.0
6	24 39.5
11	27 16.4
16	29 54.5
21	2♈33.8
26	5 14.2
31	7 55.7

Day	⚶
1	4♉40.2
6	6 35.1
11	8 32.1
16	10 30.9
21	12 31.4
26	14 33.3
31	16 36.5

DECLINATION and LATITUDE

Day	☉ Decl	☽ Decl	☽ Lat	☽ 12h Decl	☿ Decl	☿ Lat	♀ Decl	♀ Lat	♂ Decl	♂ Lat	⚳ Decl	⚳ Lat	♃ Decl	♃ Lat	♄ Decl	♄ Lat
1 M	7S45	27S35	4S38	27S41	12S09	2N23	19S28	0N46	16N32	4N20	31N59	8N59	15N55	1N04	3N04	2S16
2 Tu	7 23	27 28	4 01	26 55	12 26	2 10	19 16	0 42	16 38	4 19	31 59	8 58	15 57	1 04	3 07	2 16
3 W	6 60	26 05	3 15	24 57	12 41	1 56	19 05	0 39	16 44	4 17	31 58	8 58	15 59	1 04	3 10	2 16
4 Th	6 37	23 33	2 19	21 53	12 54	1 42	18 52	0 35	16 50	4 16	31 58	8 58	16 01	1 04	3 13	2 16
5 F	6 14	19 60	1 18	17 53	13 05	1 28	18 39	0 31	16 55	4 14	31 57	8 57	16 03	1 04	3 15	2 16
6 Sa	5 50	15 36	0 13	13 08	13 14	1 15	18 25	0 27	17 01	4 13	31 56	8 57	16 05	1 04	3 18	2 16
7 Su	5 27	10 32	0N54	7 49	13 21	1 02	18 11	0 23	17 06	4 11	31 55	8 56	16 07	1 04	3 21	2 15
8 M	5 04	4 60	1 59	2 06	13 26	0 48	17 57	0 20	17 10	4 09	31 54	8 56	16 09	1 04	3 24	2 15
9 Tu	4 40	0N50	2 59	3N47	13 29	0 36	17 42	0 16	17 15	4 07	31 54	8 55	16 11	1 04	3 27	2 15
10 W	4 17	6 43	3 51	9 36	13 30	0 23	17 26	0 12	17 19	4 05	31 52	8 55	16 13	1 04	3 29	2 15
11 Th	3 53	12 25	4 33	15 07	13 30	0 11	17 10	0 09	17 23	4 03	31 51	8 54	16 15	1 04	3 32	2 15
12 F	3 30	17 39	5 00	20 00	13 27	0S01	16 53	0 05	17 26	4 01	31 50	8 54	16 17	1 04	3 35	2 15
13 Sa	3 06	22 07	5 12	23 56	13 23	0 12	16 36	0 02	17 29	3 59	31 49	8 53	16 18	1 04	3 38	2 15
14 Su	2 42	25 26	5 06	26 34	13 17	0 23	16 19	0S02	17 32	3 57	31 48	8 52	16 20	1 04	3 41	2 15
15 M	2 19	27 18	4 43	27 37	13 09	0 33	16 01	0 05	17 35	3 55	31 46	8 52	16 22	1 04	3 44	2 15
16 Tu	1 55	27 28	4 02	26 53	12 59	0 43	15 42	0 09	17 37	3 52	31 45	8 51	16 23	1 04	3 46	2 15
17 W	1 31	25 51	3 06	24 23	12 48	0 53	15 23	0 12	17 39	3 50	31 44	8 50	16 25	1 04	3 49	2 15
18 Th	1 08	22 32	1 58	20 20	12 36	1 02	15 04	0 15	17 40	3 48	31 42	8 50	16 26	1 04	3 52	2 15
19 F	0 44	17 50	0 43	15 04	12 21	1 11	14 44	0 19	17 42	3 46	31 41	8 49	16 27	1 04	3 55	2 15
20 Sa	0 20	12 05	0S36	8 57	12 06	1 19	14 24	0 22	17 43	3 43	31 39	8 48	16 29	1 04	3 58	2 14
21 Su	0N04	5 43	1 51	2 26	11 48	1 27	14 03	0 25	17 44	3 41	31 37	8 48	16 30	1 04	4 01	2 14
22 M	0 27	0S52	2 59	4S07	11 30	1 34	13 42	0 28	17 44	3 38	31 36	8 47	16 31	1 04	4 04	2 14
23 Tu	0 51	7 17	3 55	10 21	11 10	1 41	13 21	0 31	17 44	3 36	31 34	8 46	16 32	1 04	4 07	2 14
24 W	1 15	13 14	4 36	15 56	10 48	1 47	12 59	0 34	17 44	3 34	31 32	8 45	16 34	1 04	4 10	2 14
25 Th	1 38	18 24	5 01	20 37	10 25	1 53	12 37	0 37	17 44	3 31	31 30	8 45	16 35	1 04	4 12	2 14
26 F	2 02	22 34	5 09	24 12	10 01	1 58	12 15	0 40	17 44	3 29	31 28	8 44	16 36	1 04	4 15	2 14
27 Sa	2 25	25 31	5 01	26 31	9 35	2 03	11 52	0 43	17 43	3 26	31 26	8 43	16 36	1 03	4 18	2 14
28 Su	2 49	27 10	4 39	27 30	9 08	2 08	11 29	0 46	17 42	3 24	31 24	8 42	16 37	1 03	4 21	2 14
29 M	3 12	27 29	4 06	27 09	8 40	2 12	11 05	0 49	17 40	3 21	31 22	8 41	16 38	1 03	4 24	2 14
30 Tu	3 36	26 30	3 22	25 34	8 11	2 15	10 41	0 51	17 39	3 19	31 20	8 41	16 39	1 03	4 27	2 14
31 W	3N59	24S20	2S29	22S51	7S40	2S18	10S17	0S54	17N37	3N16	31N18	8N40	16N40	1N03	4N30	2S14

Day	⚷ Decl	⚷ Lat	♅ Decl	♅ Lat	♆ Decl	♆ Lat	♇ Decl	♇ Lat
1	10N35	0S01	20N25	0S08	0N02	1S21	22S56	4S21
6	10 40	0 01	20 26	0 07	0 06	1 21	22 55	4 21
11	10 45	0 02	20 27	0 07	0 11	1 21	22 54	4 22
16	10 50	0 02	20 29	0 07	0 15	1 21	22 53	4 23
21	10 55	0 03	20 31	0 07	0 20	1 21	22 52	4 24
26	11 01	0 03	20 33	0 07	0 24	1 21	22 51	4 25
31	11N07	0S03	20N36	0S07	0N29	1S21	22S51	4S26

Day	⚴ Decl	⚴ Lat	⚵ Decl	⚵ Lat	⚶ Decl	⚶ Lat	Eris Decl	Eris Lat
1	11S59	23S47	4S12	1S09	8N37	4S44	0N09	10S15
6	11 15	23 46	3 24	1 23	9 23	4 34	0 10	10 14
11	10 31	23 46	2 35	1 38	10 09	4 25	0 11	10 14
16	9 48	23 47	1 45	1 52	10 55	4 16	0 13	10 13
21	9 06	23 48	0 55	2 07	11 39	4 08	0 14	10 13
26	8 24	23 49	0 05	2 21	12 23	3 60	0 16	10 13
31	7S43	23S51	0N45	2S36	13N05	3S52	0N17	10S12

Moon Phenomena

Max/0 Decl

dy	hr mn	
1	9:38	27S41
8	20:37	0 N
15	14:16	27N37
21	20:52	0 S
28	17:39	27S32

Max/0 Lat

dy	hr mn	
6	4:41	0 N
13	4:08	5N12
19	13:07	0 S
25	23:59	5S09

Perigee/Apogee

dy	hr m		kilometers
3	5:42	a	405216
19	4:29	p	366437
31	1:34	a	404326

PH	dy	hr mn	
●	8	9:31	17♓35
☽	15	16:26	24♊52
○	22	10:45	1♎35
☾	30	0:55	9♑06

Void of Course Moon

Last Aspect			☽ Ingress	
1 16:20	♂	△	♑	1 22:37
3 1:39	♄	□	♒	4 11:33
6 14:02	♂	☍	♓	6 23:27
8 9:31	☉	☌	♈	9 9:04
11 5:08	☉	✱	♉	11 16:17
13 13:34	♀	□	♊	13 21:32
15 20:53	♀	△	♋	16 1:12
17 22:53	☉	△	♌	18 3:42
19 16:18	♀	☍	♍	20 5:38
20 9:35	♅	□	♎	22 8:03
24 8:00	♀	△	♏	24 12:19
26 3:05	♂	□	♐	26 19:44
28 12:40	♂	△	♑	29 6:34
30 16:14	♄	□	♒	31 19:21

DAILY ASPECTARIAN

1 M ☽△♃ 1:56; ☉△⚳ 2:57; ☽∠♇ 4:47; ☽✱☿ 4:55; ♀ ♒ 6:33; ☽△♂ 16:20; ☽△⚷ 17:44

2 Tu ☽⊻♀ 0:24; ☽⊼♅ 2:26; ☽□♆ 5:10; ☽⚼♃ 7:56; ☽∠☿ 10:45; ☽⊻♇ 11:11; ☽☍⚳ 19:38; ♀△♅ 21:01; ☽⚼♂ 21:52; ☉✱☽ 23:16

3 W ☽□♄ 1:39; ☽⚼♅ 8:58; ☉∠⚷ 11:48; ☿ D 12:33; ☽⊼♃ 14:08; ☽⊻☿ 17:08

4 Th ♀✱♆ 1:18; ☽⊼♂ 3:30; ☽∥♇ 4:42; ☉⊻♄ 6:31; ☽□⚷ 6:54; ☉∠☽ 8:35; ☽△♅ 15:28; ☽✱♆ 18:17; ☽☌♀ 20:07; ☽#♅ 21:22

5 F ☽☌♇ 0:12; ☽∥♀ 8:13; ☽⊼⚳ 8:44; ☽✱♄ 14:56; ♂∠⚳ 15:26; ☽#♂ 16:51; ☉⊻☽ 17:33; ☽#♃ 21:32

6 Sa ☽∠♆ 0:28; ☽☍♃ 2:04; ☊ R 4:40; ☽☌☿ 6:18; ☽∥☿ 11:16; ♀☌♇ 13:49; ☽☍♂ 14:02; ☽⚼⚳ 14:46; ☽✱⚷ 19:10; ☽∠♄ 20:59; ☽#⚷ 23:22

7 Su ☽□♅ 3:21; ☽⊻♆ 6:08; ☽⊻♇ 11:48; ☽⊻♀ 14:06; ☽△⚳ 20:15; ☉∥☽ 23:41

8 M ☽∠⚷ 0:29; ☽⊻♄ 2:26; ☽#♄ 6:36; ☉☌☽ 9:31; ☽⊼♃ 12:04; ☽∠♇ 16:43; ☽⊻☿ 18:29; ☽#♆ 20:01; ☽∥♆ 21:13; ☽∠♀ 21:55; ⚴ ♉ 22:01; ☽⊼♂ 22:39

9 Tu ☽⊻⚷ 5:11; ☽∥♄ 10:43; ☽✱♅ 12:55; ☉#☽ 14:39; ☉⊼♃ 14:58; ☽☌♆ 15:38; ☽⚼♃ 16:11; ☽✱♇ 21:01; ☽∠☿ 23:54

10 W ☽⚼♂ 2:09; ☽✱♀ 4:54; ☽□⚳ 5:23; ♀#♂ 8:49; ♀⊼⚳ 10:37; ☽☌♄ 11:26; ☽∠♅ 16:47; ☽∥⚷ 16:47; ☽△♃ 19:44; ☉⊻☽ 22:20

11 Th ☽#☿ 4:41; ☽✱☿ 4:52; ☽△♂ 5:08; ☿☍♂ 8:32; ☽☌⚷ 12:47; ☽∥♃ 17:21; ☉#♄ 19:08; ☽⊻♅ 20:06; ♃⚼♆ 20:25; ☽#♀ 20:30; ☽⊻♆ 22:46; ☽∥♂ 22:55

12 F ☉∠☽ 3:41; ☽□♇ 3:53; ☉∠♇ 6:23; ☽✱⚳ 12:16; ☽∥♅ 14:32; ☽□♀ 16:40; ☽⊻♄ 18:09

13 Sa ☽□♃ 1:17; ☽∠♆ 1:34; ☽#♇ 4:53; ☉✱☽ 8:26; ☽□♂ 9:44; ♀✱♄ 11:03; ☽□☿ 13:34; ☽∠⚳ 15:00; ☽⊻⚷ 18:20; ☽∠♄ 20:47; ♀#♃ 22:31; ☉⊼♂ 23:01

14 Su ☽☌♅ 1:19; ☽✱♆ 3:56; ☽△♇ 8:50; ☿⚼⚳ 16:26; ☽⊻⚳ 17:20; ☽∠⚷ 20:29; ☽✱♄ 23:02

15 M ☽△♀ 2:05; ☽✱♃ 5:11; ☽⚼♇ 10:44; ☽✱♂ 12:53; ☊ D 16:14; ☉□☽ 16:26; ☽△☿ 20:53; ☽✱⚷ 22:17

16 Tu ⚵ ♈ 4:09; ☽⊻♅ 5:00; ☽⚼♀ 6:05; ☽∠♃ 6:37; ☽□♆ 7:35; ♀☍♃ 12:06; ☽⊼♇ 12:18; ☽∠♂ 14:00; ☿✱⚷ 18:31; ☽☌⚳ 20:59

17 W ☽⚼☿ 0:08; ♀∠♆ 0:16; ☽□♄ 2:31; ☽∠♅ 6:23; ☽⊻♃ 7:47; ☽⊼♀ 9:43; ☽⊻♂ 14:54; ☽#♇ 21:59; ☉△☽ 22:53

18 Th ☽□⚷ 1:01; ☽⊼☿ 3:12; ☽✱♅ 7:32; ☿ ♓ 10:03; ☽△♆ 10:06; ☽∥♅ 11:09; ☿∠♄ 13:26; ☽☍♇ 14:42; ☽⊻⚳ 23:40

19 F ☽∥♂ 0:35; ☉⚼☽ 1:44; ☽△♄ 5:04; ☽∥♃ 6:03; ☉⊻⚷ 7:24; ☽☌♃ 9:35; ☽⚼♆ 11:08; ☊ R 13:06; ☽#♀ 14:09; ♀☍♂ 16:16; ☽☌♂ 16:18; ☽☍♀ 16:18; ☽#☿ 23:58

20 Sa ☽∠⚳ 0:53; ☉#♆ 1:27; ☽△⚷ 3:09; ☉⊼☽ 4:32; ☽∥⚷ 4:35; ☽⚼♄ 6:14; ☽☍☿ 9:12; ☽□♅ 9:35; ☽⊼♆ 12:10; ☿□♅ 14:11; ☽⊼♇ 16:42; ☉ ♈ 20:26

21 Su ☽✱⚳ 2:12; ☽⚼⚷ 4:18; ☽∥♄ 6:12; ☽⊼♄ 7:31; ☽⊻♃ 11:24; ☉∥♆ 16:55; ☽⚼♇ 17:55; ☽⊻♂ 17:55; ☉∥☽ 19:29; ☽∥♆ 19:37; ☽#♆ 22:06; ☉#☽ 22:25; ☽⊼♀ 23:06; ☿⊻♆ 23:12

22 M ☽⊼⚷ 5:43; ☉☍☽ 10:45; ☽#♄ 11:53; ☽△♅ 12:13; ☽∠♃ 12:42; ☽☍♆ 14:52; ☽⊼☿ 16:17; ☽∠♂ 19:13; ☽△♇ 19:29

23 Tu ☽⚼♀ 3:09; ☽□⚳ 5:50; ☉✱♅ 8:07; ☽☍♄ 11:10; ☉⚼♃ 12:43; ☿#⚷ 12:57; ☽⚼♅ 14:11; ☽∥☿ 14:27; ☽✱♃ 14:30; ☽#⚷ 14:33; ☽⚼☿ 20:52; ☽✱♂ 21:04; ☽∥♀ 23:01

24 W ☿⊻♇ 5:01; ☽△♀ 8:00; ☽☍⚷ 10:05; ♀⚼⚳ 14:53; ☽#♃ 15:00; ☽⊼♅ 16:50; ☉⊼☽ 19:23; ☽⊼♆ 19:39; ☽#♂ 20:38; ☉☌♆ 23:14

25 Th ☽□♇ 0:27; ☽△☿ 2:29; ♀✱⚷ 8:25; ☽#♅ 11:37; ☽△⚳ 12:03; ☽⊼♄ 17:30; ☽□♃ 20:15; ☽⚼♆ 23:14

26 F ☉⚼☽ 1:10; ☽∥♇ 2:00; ☽□♂ 3:05; ♀ ♓ 8:18; ☽⚼⚳ 16:31; ☽⊼⚷ 17:36; ☽□♀ 20:57; ☽⚼♄ 22:00

27 Sa ☉⚼♂ 0:33; ☽☍♅ 0:43; ☽△♆ 3:43; ☉△☽ 8:05; ☽✱♇ 8:45; ♀∠♄ 9:00; ☉✱♇ 16:32; ☽□☿ 17:37; ☽⊼⚳ 21:56; ☽⚼⚷ 22:43

28 Su ☽△♄ 3:24; ☽△♃ 5:29; ☽△♂ 12:40; ♀□♅ 13:19; ☽∠♇ 14:12

29 M ♀#⚷ 0:46; ☽△⚷ 4:36; ☽⚼♃ 11:15; ☽⊼♅ 12:00; ☿△⚳ 13:26; ☽✱♀ 14:28; ☽□♆ 15:08; ☿∠⚷ 16:21; ☽⚼♂ 18:36; ☽⊻♇ 20:18; ♀⊻♆ 21:21

30 Tu ☉□☽ 0:55; ☊ D 1:05; ☽☍⚳ 10:58; ☽✱☿ 13:30; ☽□♄ 16:14; ☽⊼♃ 17:30; ☽⚼♅ 18:27

31 W ☽∠♀ 0:18; ☽⊼♂ 0:57; ☽∥♇ 12:01; ☿⊻♄ 13:30; ☽□⚷ 17:40; ☿⊼♃ 21:07

April 2027

LONGITUDE

Day	Sid.Time	☉	☽	☽ 12 hour	Mean ☊	True ☊	☿	♀	♂	⚳	♃	♄	⚷	♅	♆	♇
	h m s	° ' "	° ' "	° ' "	° '	° '	° '	° '	° '	° '	° '	° '	° '	° '	° '	° '
1 Th	12 36 32	11 ♈ 02 28	2 ♒ 17 34	8 ♒ 13 24	18 ♒ 04.6	19 ♒ 18.7	17 ♓ 24.6	6 ♓ 49.0	20 ♌ 55.7	14 ♋ 23.6	17 ♌ 13.6	16 ♈ 49.2	29 ♈ 11.1	2 ♊ 47.9	4 ♈ 21.0	6 ♒ 51.4
2 F	12 40 28	12 01 43	14 10 57	20 10 49	18 01.4	19R 19.7	18 54.1	8 01.8	20D 55.7	14 36.8	17R 11.4	16 56.8	29 14.6	2 50.4	4 23.3	6 52.4
3 Sa	12 44 25	13 00 55	26 13 32	2 ♓ 19 37	17 58.3	19 19.6	20 25.1	9 13.9	20 56.3	14 50.3	17 09.4	17 04.3	29 18.1	2 52.9	4 25.5	6 53.3
4 Su	12 48 22	14 00 06	8 ♓ 29 27	14 43 25	17 55.1	19 17.6	21 57.6	10 26.4	20 57.7	15 04.0	17 07.6	17 11.9	29 21.7	2 55.5	4 27.8	6 54.3
5 M	12 52 18	14 59 14	21 01 46	27 24 42	17 51.9	19 13.3	23 31.7	11 38.9	20 59.8	15 17.9	17 06.0	17 19.4	29 25.2	2 58.1	4 30.0	6 55.2
6 Tu	12 56 15	15 58 21	3 ♈ 52 18	10 ♈ 24 33	17 48.7	19 06.6	25 07.2	12 51.4	21 02.6	15 32.2	17 04.5	17 27.0	29 28.8	3 00.7	4 32.3	6 56.1
7 W	13 00 11	16 57 26	17 01 22	23 42 33	17 45.5	18 57.9	26 44.2	14 03.9	21 06.1	15 46.7	17 03.3	17 34.6	29 32.4	3 03.3	4 34.5	6 57.0
8 Th	13 04 08	17 56 28	0 ♉ 27 49	7 ♉ 16 51	17 42.4	18 47.9	28 22.7	15 16.4	21 10.3	16 01.4	17 02.2	17 42.2	29 36.0	3 06.0	4 36.8	6 57.8
9 F	13 08 04	18 55 29	14 09 12	21 04 29	17 39.2	18 37.7	0 ♈ 02.7	16 29.0	21 15.2	16 16.5	17 01.3	17 49.7	29 39.6	3 08.7	4 39.0	6 58.7
10 Sa	13 12 01	19 54 28	28 02 11	5 ♊ 01 54	17 36.0	18 28.4	1 44.2	17 41.6	21 20.8	16 31.7	17 00.6	17 57.3	29 43.2	3 11.5	4 41.2	6 59.4
11 Su	13 15 57	20 53 24	12 ♊ 03 09	19 05 34	17 32.8	18 21.0	3 27.2	18 54.1	21 27.0	16 47.2	17 00.1	18 04.9	29 46.8	3 14.2	4 43.4	7 00.2
12 M	13 19 54	21 52 18	26 08 46	3 ♋ 12 26	17 29.6	18 15.9	5 11.6	20 06.8	21 33.8	17 02.9	16 59.8	18 12.4	29 50.4	3 17.0	4 45.6	7 01.0
13 Tu	13 23 51	22 51 10	10 ♋ 16 21	17 20 16	17 26.5	18D 13.3	6 57.6	21 19.4	21 41.3	17 18.9	16D 59.7	18 20.0	29 54.1	3 19.9	4 47.8	7 01.7
14 W	13 27 47	23 50 00	24 24 03	1 ♌ 27 33	17 23.3	18 12.7	8 45.2	22 32.0	21 49.4	17 35.1	16 59.8	18 27.6	29 57.7	3 22.8	4 50.0	7 02.4
15 Th	13 31 44	24 48 47	8 ♌ 30 39	15 33 14	17 20.1	18R 13.1	10 34.2	23 44.6	21 58.1	17 51.5	17 00.1	18 35.1	0 ♉ 01.4	3 25.7	4 52.1	7 03.0
16 F	13 35 40	25 47 32	22 35 11	29 36 20	17 16.9	18 13.2	12 24.8	24 57.3	22 07.4	18 08.2	17 00.5	18 42.7	0 05.0	3 28.6	4 54.3	7 03.7
17 Sa	13 39 37	26 46 14	6 ♍ 36 30	13 ♍ 35 28	17 13.8	18 11.9	14 16.9	26 09.2	22 17.3	18 25.0	17 01.2	18 50.2	0 08.7	3 31.5	4 56.5	7 04.3
18 Su	13 43 33	27 44 55	20 32 58	27 28 40	17 10.6	18 08.3	16 10.6	27 22.6	22 27.8	18 42.1	17 02.0	18 57.7	0 12.3	3 34.5	4 58.6	7 04.9
19 M	13 47 30	28 43 33	4 ♎ 22 15	11 ♎ 13 20	17 07.4	18 01.9	18 05.9	28 35.3	22 38.8	18 59.3	17 03.0	19 05.2	0 16.0	3 37.5	5 00.7	7 05.4
20 Tu	13 51 26	29 42 09	18 01 33	24 46 31	17 04.2	17 52.9	20 02.7	29 48.0	22 50.4	19 16.8	17 04.2	19 12.7	0 19.6	3 40.6	5 02.8	7 05.9
21 W	13 55 23	0 ♉ 40 43	1 ♏ 27 54	8 ♏ 05 23	17 01.0	17 41.7	22 01.0	1 ♈ 00.7	23 02.5	19 34.5	17 05.6	19 20.2	0 23.3	3 43.6	5 04.9	7 06.4
22 Th	13 59 19	1 39 16	14 38 44	21 07 47	16 57.9	17 29.6	24 00.8	2 13.4	23 15.1	19 52.3	17 07.1	19 27.7	0 26.9	3 46.7	5 07.0	7 06.9
23 F	14 03 16	2 37 46	27 32 27	3 ♐ 52 42	16 54.7	17 17.5	26 02.0	3 26.1	23 28.2	20 10.4	17 08.9	19 35.1	0 30.6	3 49.8	5 09.1	7 07.4
24 Sa	14 07 13	3 36 15	10 ♐ 08 39	16 20 28	16 51.5	17 06.7	28 04.7	4 38.9	23 41.8	20 28.6	17 10.8	19 42.5	0 34.3	3 52.9	5 11.2	7 07.8
25 Su	14 11 09	4 34 42	22 28 26	28 32 52	16 48.3	16 58.0	0 ♉ 08.7	5 51.7	23 56.0	20 47.1	17 12.9	19 50.0	0 37.9	3 56.1	5 13.2	7 08.2
26 M	14 15 06	5 33 07	4 ♑ 34 13	10 ♑ 32 58	16 45.2	16 51.8	2 14.0	7 04.4	24 10.6	21 05.7	17 15.2	19 57.4	0 41.6	3 59.2	5 15.2	7 08.5
27 Tu	14 19 02	6 31 31	16 29 39	22 24 53	16 42.0	16 48.2	4 20.3	8 17.2	24 25.7	21 24.5	17 17.6	20 04.8	0 45.2	4 02.4	5 17.3	7 08.9
28 W	14 22 59	7 29 53	28 19 16	4 ♒ 13 30	16 38.8	16D 46.7	6 27.7	9 30.0	24 41.2	21 43.5	17 20.2	20 12.1	0 48.9	4 05.7	5 19.3	7 09.2
29 Th	14 26 55	8 28 14	10 ♒ 08 15	16 04 12	16 35.6	16R 46.4	8 35.9	10 42.8	24 57.2	22 02.6	17 23.0	20 19.5	0 52.5	4 08.9	5 21.2	7 09.4
30 F	14 30 52	9 ♉ 26 33	22 02 03	28 02 28	16 ♒ 32.5	16 ♒ 46.4	10 ♉ 44.7	11 ♈ 55.7	25 ♌ 13.7	22 ♋ 21.9	17 ♌ 26.0	20 ♈ 26.8	0 ♉ 56.1	4 ♊ 12.1	5 ♈ 23.2	7 ♒ 09.7

1st of Month

Julian Day # 2461496.5
Obliquity 23°26'36"
SVP 4♓52'34"
GC 27♐13.2
Eris 25♈20.9

Day	⚴	⚵	⚶
1	11 ♉ 02.9	8 ♈ 28.1	17 ♉ 01.3
6	13 34.7	11 10.8	19 05.9
11	16 09.2	13 54.5	21 11.6
16	18 46.1	16 39.0	23 18.1
21	21 25.4	19 24.2	25 25.4
26	24 06.8	22 10.3	27 33.3

DECLINATION and LATITUDE

Day	☉ Decl	☽ Decl	☽ Lat	☽ 12h Decl	☿ Decl	☿ Lat	♀ Decl	♀ Lat	♂ Decl	♂ Lat	⚳ Decl	⚳ Lat	♃ Decl	♃ Lat	♄ Decl	♄ Lat
1 Th	4N22	21S07	1S31	19S10	7S08	2S21	9S53	0S56	17N35	3N14	31N16	8N39	16N40	1N03	4N33	2S14
2 F	4 45	17 01	0 28	14 41	6 35	2 23	9 28	0 59	17 33	3 12	31 13	8 38	16 41	1 03	4 36	2 14
3 Sa	5 08	12 12	0N37	9 34	6 01	2 25	9 03	1 01	17 30	3 09	31 11	8 38	16 41	1 03	4 39	2 14
4 Su	5 31	6 49	1 41	3 59	5 25	2 26	8 38	1 04	17 27	3 07	31 08	8 37	16 42	1 03	4 41	2 14
5 M	5 54	1 05	2 42	1N52	4 49	2 27	8 13	1 06	17 24	3 04	31 06	8 36	16 42	1 03	4 44	2 14
6 Tu	6 17	4N50	3 35	7 47	4 11	2 27	7 47	1 08	17 21	3 02	31 03	8 35	16 43	1 03	4 47	2 14
7 W	6 40	10 40	4 19	13 28	3 32	2 27	7 21	1 10	17 18	2 59	31 01	8 34	16 43	1 03	4 50	2 14
8 Th	7 02	16 08	4 49	18 38	2 52	2 26	6 55	1 12	17 14	2 57	30 58	8 33	16 43	1 02	4 53	2 14
9 F	7 25	20 54	5 03	22 54	2 11	2 24	6 28	1 14	17 10	2 55	30 55	8 33	16 43	1 02	4 56	2 14
10 Sa	7 47	24 35	4 60	25 55	1 29	2 23	6 02	1 16	17 06	2 52	30 53	8 32	16 43	1 02	4 59	2 14
11 Su	8 09	26 50	4 39	27 20	0 46	2 20	5 35	1 18	17 02	2 50	30 50	8 31	16 44	1 02	5 02	2 14
12 M	8 31	27 23	4 01	26 60	0 03	2 18	5 08	1 20	16 58	2 48	30 47	8 30	16 44	1 02	5 04	2 14
13 Tu	8 53	26 10	3 08	24 54	0N42	2 14	4 41	1 21	16 53	2 45	30 44	8 29	16 43	1 02	5 07	2 14
14 W	9 15	23 16	2 03	21 16	1 28	2 11	4 14	1 23	16 48	2 43	30 41	8 29	16 43	1 02	5 10	2 14
15 Th	9 37	18 58	0 51	16 24	2 15	2 06	3 47	1 25	16 43	2 41	30 38	8 28	16 43	1 02	5 13	2 14
16 F	9 58	13 37	0S23	10 40	3 02	2 01	3 19	1 26	16 38	2 39	30 35	8 27	16 43	1 02	5 16	2 14
17 Sa	10 19	7 36	1 36	4 26	3 51	1 56	2 52	1 28	16 33	2 36	30 32	8 26	16 43	1 02	5 19	2 14
18 Su	10 40	1 15	2 43	1S56	4 40	1 50	2 24	1 29	16 27	2 34	30 28	8 26	16 42	1 01	5 21	2 14
19 M	11 01	5S05	3 39	8 09	5 30	1 44	1 56	1 30	16 22	2 32	30 25	8 25	16 42	1 01	5 24	2 14
20 Tu	11 22	11 06	4 22	13 54	6 20	1 37	1 29	1 31	16 16	2 30	30 22	8 24	16 41	1 01	5 27	2 14
21 W	11 43	16 30	4 50	18 53	7 11	1 30	1 01	1 32	16 10	2 28	30 18	8 23	16 41	1 01	5 30	2 14
22 Th	12 03	21 01	5 01	22 52	8 02	1 22	0 33	1 33	16 03	2 26	30 15	8 22	16 40	1 01	5 32	2 14
23 F	12 23	24 25	4 57	25 39	8 54	1 14	0 05	1 34	15 57	2 23	30 11	8 22	16 40	1 01	5 35	2 14
24 Sa	12 43	26 33	4 38	27 06	9 46	1 05	0N23	1 35	15 51	2 21	30 07	8 21	16 39	1 01	5 38	2 14
25 Su	13 03	27 19	4 06	27 12	10 38	0 56	0 52	1 36	15 44	2 19	30 04	8 20	16 38	1 01	5 41	2 15
26 M	13 22	26 45	3 24	25 60	11 31	0 47	1 20	1 37	15 37	2 17	30 00	8 19	16 37	1 01	5 43	2 15
27 Tu	13 42	24 57	2 33	23 38	12 23	0 37	1 48	1 37	15 30	2 15	29 56	8 19	16 37	1 00	5 46	2 15
28 W	14 01	22 04	1 36	20 16	13 15	0 27	2 16	1 38	15 23	2 13	29 52	8 18	16 36	1 00	5 49	2 15
29 Th	14 20	18 16	0 35	16 05	14 06	0 17	2 44	1 38	15 16	2 11	29 48	8 17	16 35	1 00	5 52	2 15
30 F	14N38	13S43	0N28	11S13	14N57	0S07	3N12	1S39	15N08	2N09	29N44	8N16	16N34	1N00	5N54	2S15

Day	⚷ Decl	⚷ Lat	♅ Decl	♅ Lat	♆ Decl	♆ Lat	♇ Decl	♇ Lat
1	11N08	0S03	20N36	0S07	0N29	1S21	22S51	4S26
6	11 14	0 04	20 39	0 07	0 34	1 21	22 50	4 27
11	11 20	0 04	20 41	0 07	0 38	1 21	22 50	4 28
16	11 26	0 04	20 44	0 07	0 42	1 21	22 50	4 29
21	11 32	0 05	20 47	0 07	0 47	1 21	22 51	4 30
26	11 38	0 05	20 50	0 07	0 50	1 21	22 51	4 31

Day	⚴ Decl	⚴ Lat	⚵ Decl	⚵ Lat	⚶ Decl	⚶ Lat	Eris Decl	Eris Lat
1	7S35	23S51	0N56	2S39	13N14	3S51	0N17	10S12
6	6 56	23 53	1 46	2 53	13 55	3 43	0 19	10 12
11	6 18	23 55	2 36	3 08	14 35	3 36	0 20	10 12
16	5 41	23 57	3 25	3 23	15 13	3 29	0 22	10 11
21	5 06	23 59	4 13	3 38	15 50	3 22	0 23	10 11
26	4 32	24 01	5 01	3 54	16 26	3 16	0 24	10 11

Moon Phenomena

Max/0 Decl
dy hr mn
5 4:24 0 N
11 19:27 27N25
18 4:41 0 S
25 1:40 27S19

Max/0 Lat
dy hr mn
2 10:18 0 N
9 7:40 5N04
15 16:33 0 S
22 5:10 5S01
29 13:25 0 N

Perigee/Apogee
dy hr m kilometers
14 0:37 p 370004
27 21:23 a 404168

PH dy hr mn
● 6 23:52 16♈57
☽ 13 22:58 23♋47
○ 20 22:28 0♏37
☾ 28 20:19 8♒19

Void of Course Moon

Last Aspect	☽ Ingress
2 13:30 ♂ ☍	♓ 3 7:26
5 5:23 ☿ ☌	♈ 5 16:50
7 7:22 ♂ △	♉ 7 23:11
9 12:23 ♂ □	♊ 10 3:22
11 16:11 ☉ ⚹	♋ 12 6:33
13 22:58 ☉ □	♌ 14 9:31
16 5:53 ☉ △	♍ 16 12:41
18 12:58 ♀ ☍	♎ 18 16:23
20 8:41 ♂ ⚹	♏ 20 21:22
22 16:14 ♂ □	♐ 23 4:38
25 2:56 ♂ △	♑ 25 14:53
27 7:20 ♄ □	♒ 28 3:25
30 6:33 ♂ ☍	♓ 30 15:53

DAILY ASPECTARIAN

1 Th: ☽∠☿ 0:16; ♀⊻♇ 0:47; ☽△♅ 1:02; ☽⋕♅ 3:17; ☽⚹♆ 4:11; ☽☌♇ 9:15; ☽⊻♀ 10:12; ☉∥♄ 12:32; ♂ D 14:09; ☉⚹☽ 19:17; ☽⋕♂ 21:08

2 F: ☽⊼⚳ 0:53; ☽⋕♃ 1:46; ☽⚹♄ 5:36; ☽☍♃ 6:01; ☊ R 10:17; ☽∠♆ 10:27; ☽⊻☿ 10:48; ☽☍♂ 13:30

3 Sa: ☉∠☽ 3:51; ☽⋕⚷ 4:43; ☽⚹⚷ 6:06; ☽⚼⚳ 7:15; ☿⊼♂ 8:15; ☽∠♄ 11:37; ♃△♄ 13:00; ☽□♅ 13:08; ☽∥♀ 15:28; ☽⊻♆ 16:09; ☽⊻♇ 20:55; ☉⋕☿ 21:35; ☿∠♇ 23:08

4 Su: ☽☌♀ 4:10; ☉⋕☽ 5:11; ☽∥☿ 6:40; ☽⋕♄ 8:58; ☽∠⚷ 11:22; ☉⊻☽ 11:31; ☽△⚳ 12:54; ☽⊼♃ 16:33; ☽⊻♄ 16:54; ☽⊼♂ 23:56

5 M: ☽∠♇ 1:41; ☽⋕♆ 2:10; ☿⋕♄ 2:42; ☽☌☿ 5:23; ☽∥♆ 6:39; ☉□⚳ 9:59; ☽⊻⚷ 15:49; ☽⚼♃ 20:41; ☽⋕☿ 21:38; ☽⚹♅ 22:24; ☽∥♄ 23:49

6 Tu: ☽☌♆ 1:14; ☽⚼♂ 4:01; ☽⚹♇ 5:39; ☉∥☽ 6:18; ☽⋕♀ 11:12; ☽⊻♀ 18:07; ☽□⚳ 21:43; ☉☌☽ 23:52

7 W: ☽△♃ 0:03; ☽☌♄ 1:00; ☽∠♅ 1:52; ☉△♃ 2:20; ☽∥⚷ 2:28; ☽△♂ 7:22; ♀∠⚷ 9:55; ☉☌♄ 17:19; ☽⊻☿ 19:48; ☉⋕♀ 20:20; ☽☌⚷ 22:28; ☽∠♀ 23:38

8 Th: ☽∥♃ 2:43; ☉∠♅ 4:03; ☽⊻♅ 4:40; ☽∥♂ 5:06; ☽⊻♆ 7:20; ☽□♇ 11:27; ☿⊻⚷ 18:17; ♀△⚳ 18:46; ☽∥♅ 22:42; ☿ ♈ 23:21

9 F: ☽∠☿ 1:46; ☽⚹⚳ 3:45; ☽⚹♀ 4:26; ☽□♃ 4:59; ☽⊻♄ 6:26; ☉⊻☽ 8:55; ☽∠♆ 9:34; ♀⊼♃ 10:35; ☽⋕♇ 11:34; ☽□♂ 12:23

10 Sa: ☽⊻⚷ 2:54; ☿⚼♃ 3:50; ♀⊻♄ 5:49; ☽∠⚳ 6:07; ☽⚹☿ 7:14; ☽∠♄ 8:31; ☽☌♅ 8:53; ☽⚹♆ 11:26; ☉∠☽ 12:41; ☽△♇ 15:22; ☿⚹♅ 20:55

11 Su: ☿⋕♆ 4:29; ☽∠⚷ 4:40; ☽⊻⚳ 8:14; ☽⚹♃ 8:26; ☽⚹♄ 10:22; ☽□♀ 12:46; ☉△♂ 15:27; ☽⚹♂ 16:08; ☉⚹☽ 16:11; ☽⚼♇ 16:58; ☿☌♆ 17:55; ⚳⊻♃ 19:22

12 M: ♀⋕♄ 3:11; ☽⚹⚷ 6:18; ☽∠♃ 9:57; ☽⊻♅ 12:10; ☽□♆ 14:41; ☽□☿ 17:34; ☽∠♂ 17:51; ☽⊼♇ 18:29; ☿⚼♂ 20:02; ☿∥♆ 22:39; ♄∠♅ 23:24

13 Tu: ☿⚹♇ 0:55; ♃ D 2:13; ♀⊼♂ 8:08; ☽⊻♃ 11:25; ☽☌⚳ 12:12; ☽∠♅ 13:44; ☽□♄ 13:49; ♀∠♇ 14:07; ☽⊻♂ 19:35; ☽△♀ 20:32; ☊ D 22:51; ☉□☽ 22:58

14 W: ☽⋕♇ 2:43; ☽□⚷ 9:30; ☽∥♅ 14:58; ⚷ ♉ 15:00; ☽⚹♅ 15:19; ☽△♆ 17:47; ☽☍♇ 21:31

15 Th: ♂∥♃ 0:10; ☽⚼♀ 0:26; ☽△☿ 4:02; ☽∥♃ 10:34; ☽∥♂ 10:43; ☽☌♃ 14:28; ☽⊻⚳ 16:15; ☊ R 16:32; ☽△♄ 17:19; ☽⚼♆ 19:25; ☽☌♂ 23:12

16 F: ☽⊼♀ 4:26; ☿⋕♀ 5:22; ☉△☽ 5:53; ☽∥⚷ 8:55; ☽⚼☿ 9:31; ☽△⚷ 12:52; ☉∥☽ 13:58; ☽∠⚳ 18:25; ☽□♅ 18:42; ☽⚼♄ 19:12; ☽⊼♆ 21:08

17 Sa: ☽⊼♇ 0:48; ☽∥♄ 8:40; ☉⚼☽ 9:32; ⚳∠♅ 11:10; ☽∥☿ 12:38; ☽⚼⚷ 14:44; ☽⊼☿ 15:16; ☽⊻♃ 17:55; ☽⋕♀ 19:20; ☽⚹⚳ 20:44; ☽⊼♄ 21:14

18 Su: ☽∥♆ 1:56; ☽⚼♇ 2:39; ☽⊻♂ 3:21; ☽⋕♆ 7:28; ☿△♃ 10:49; ☽∥♀ 12:49; ☽☍♀ 12:58; ☉⊼☽ 13:25; ☽⊼⚷ 16:49; ☽∠♃ 19:57; ☿∥♄ 21:12; ☽△♅ 22:42

19 M: ☽☍♆ 1:07; ☽⋕♄ 1:13; ☽⋕☿ 1:49; ☽△♇ 4:45; ☽∠♂ 5:48; ☿∠♅ 6:43; ☿□⚳ 12:58; ☿☌♄ 13:04; ☉⊻♀ 14:06; ⚳□♄ 14:12; ☽⚹♃ 22:18

20 Tu: ☽⚼♅ 1:09; ☉⋕☽ 1:10; ☽⋕⚷ 1:43; ☽☍♄ 2:07; ☽□⚳ 2:16; ♀ ♈ 3:58; ☽☍☿ 4:11; ☉ ♉ 7:19; ☽⚹♂ 8:41; ☉∥⚷ 10:57; ♀⊻⚷ 11:00; ☉☌⚷ 16:23; ☽☍⚷ 22:03; ☽⋕♂ 22:24; ☉☍☽ 22:28; ☽⊼♀ 23:06

21 W: ☽⋕♃ 0:52; ☽⊼♅ 4:06; ☽⊼♆ 6:33; ☽□♇ 10:13; ♀⋕♆ 11:45; ☿△♂ 13:48; ♀⚼♃ 21:53; ☽⋕♅ 22:40

22 Th: ☽□♃ 4:34; ☽⚼♀ 5:15; ☽⊼♄ 8:59; ☽△⚳ 9:54; ☽⚼♆ 10:09; ☽∥♇ 11:50; ☽□♂ 16:14; ☽⊼☿ 20:38

23 F: ☽⊼⚷ 5:38; ♀⚹♅ 8:09; ☉⊼☽ 10:26; ☽☍♅ 11:57; ☽△♀ 12:21; ☽⚼♄ 13:29; ☽△♆ 14:28; ☽⚼⚳ 14:50; ☽⚹♇ 18:12

24 Sa: ☽⚼☿ 6:48; ☉⊻♅ 7:14; ☽⚼⚷ 10:33; ♀☌♆ 10:57; ☽△♃ 13:40; ☉⚼☽ 17:50; ☽△♄ 18:46; ☽⊼⚳ 20:36; ☿ ♉ 22:19; ♀∥♆ 22:20; ☽∠♇ 23:20

25 Su: ☽△♂ 2:56; ☿☌⚷ 5:47; ☽△⚷ 16:13; ☉⊻♆ 16:23; ☽△☿ 18:21; ☽⚼♃ 19:21; ☽⊼♅ 22:50

26 M: ♀⚹♇ 1:21; ☽□♆ 1:22; ☉△☽ 2:08; ☿∥⚷ 3:29; ☽⊻♇ 5:09; ☽□♀ 5:35; ☽⚼♂ 9:26; ☿⊻♅ 20:32

27 Tu: ☽⊼♃ 1:37; ☽⚼♅ 5:11; ☽□♄ 7:20; ☽☍⚳ 10:14; ☿⊻♆ 10:55; ☉□♇ 15:26; ☽⊼♂ 16:27; ☽∥♇ 18:12

28 W: ♀⚼♂ 4:43; ☽□⚷ 5:06; ☿□♇ 7:48; ☽⋕♅ 8:14; ☽△♅ 11:47; ☽⚹♆ 14:16; ☽☌♇ 17:57; ☽□☿ 20:11; ☉□☽ 20:19; ☊ D 20:33; ☉☌☿ 21:23

29 Th: ☽⚹♀ 1:18; ☽⋕♃ 9:22; ☉∥☿ 10:14; ☊ R 13:23; ☽☍♃ 14:43; ☽⋕♂ 16:41; ☽⋕☿ 18:49; ☉⋕☽ 19:43; ☽∠♆ 20:41; ☽⚹♄ 20:47

30 F: ☽⊼⚳ 0:41; ☿∥♂ 4:58; ☽☍♂ 6:33; ☽⋕⚷ 9:39; ☽∠♀ 10:53; ☽⚹⚷ 17:50

LONGITUDE

May 2027

Day	Sid.Time	☉	☽	☽ 12 hour	Mean☊	True☊	☿	♀	♂	⚳	♃	♄	⚷	♅	♆	♇
	h m s	° ' "	° ' "	° ' "	° '	° '	° '	° '	° '	° '	° '	° '	° '	° '	° '	° '
1 Sa	14 34 49	10♉24 50	4♓06 07	10♓13 37	16♒29.3	16♒45.5	12♉53.9	13♈08.5	25♌30.6	22♋41.4	17♌29.2	20♈34.1	0♉59.8	4♊15.4	5♈25.2	7♒09.9
2 Su	14 38 45	11 23 06	16 25 30	22 42 17	16 26.1	16R 42.8	15 03.3	14 21.3	25 47.9	23 01.1	17 32.5	20 41.3	1 03.4	4 18.7	5 27.1	7 10.1
3 M	14 42 42	12 21 20	29 04 23	5♈32 06	16 22.9	16 37.6	17 12.6	15 34.2	26 05.6	23 20.9	17 36.0	20 48.6	1 07.0	4 22.0	5 29.0	7 10.3
4 Tu	14 46 38	13 19 33	12♈05 37	18 45 02	16 19.7	16 29.7	19 21.5	16 47.1	26 23.8	23 40.9	17 39.7	20 55.8	1 10.6	4 25.3	5 30.9	7 10.4
5 W	14 50 35	14 17 44	25 30 14	2♉21 03	16 16.6	16 19.5	21 29.7	17 59.9	26 42.3	24 01.0	17 43.5	21 03.0	1 14.2	4 28.7	5 32.8	7 10.5
6 Th	14 54 31	15 15 54	9♉17 06	16 17 54	16 13.4	16 07.8	23 37.0	19 12.8	27 01.3	24 21.3	17 47.5	21 10.2	1 17.8	4 32.0	5 34.6	7 10.6
7 F	14 58 28	16 14 02	23 22 50	0♊31 13	16 10.2	15 55.7	25 42.9	20 25.7	27 20.6	24 41.8	17 51.7	21 17.3	1 21.3	4 35.4	5 36.5	7 10.7
8 Sa	15 02 24	17 12 08	7♊42 16	14 55 13	16 07.0	15 44.5	27 47.4	21 38.6	27 40.4	25 02.4	17 56.0	21 24.4	1 24.9	4 38.8	5 38.3	7R 10.7
9 Su	15 06 21	18 10 13	22 09 15	29 23 36	16 03.9	15 35.4	29 50.0	22 51.5	28 00.5	25 23.1	18 00.5	21 31.5	1 28.5	4 42.2	5 40.1	7 10.7
10 M	15 10 18	19 08 16	6♋37 37	13♋50 39	16 00.7	15 29.0	1♊50.5	24 04.4	28 20.9	25 44.0	18 05.2	21 38.5	1 32.0	4 45.6	5 41.9	7 10.7
11 Tu	15 14 14	20 06 17	21 02 13	28 11 54	15 57.5	15 25.4	3 48.6	25 17.3	28 41.8	26 05.0	18 10.0	21 45.5	1 35.5	4 49.0	5 43.7	7 10.6
12 W	15 18 11	21 04 16	5♌19 24	12♌24 31	15 54.3	15D 24.0	5 44.3	26 30.2	29 03.0	26 26.2	18 15.0	21 52.5	1 39.0	4 52.4	5 45.4	7 10.5
13 Th	15 22 07	22 02 13	19 27 06	26 27 06	15 51.2	15R 23.8	7 37.2	27 43.1	29 24.5	26 47.5	18 20.1	21 59.4	1 42.5	4 55.9	5 47.1	7 10.4
14 F	15 26 04	23 00 09	3♍24 29	10♍19 16	15 48.0	15 23.6	9 27.3	28 56.1	29 46.4	27 09.0	18 25.4	22 06.3	1 46.0	4 59.3	5 48.8	7 10.3
15 Sa	15 30 00	23 58 02	17 11 27	24 01 04	15 44.8	15 22.1	11 14.3	0♉09.0	0♍08.5	27 30.5	18 30.8	22 13.1	1 49.5	5 02.8	5 50.5	7 10.1
16 Su	15 33 57	24 55 54	0♎48 07	7♎32 34	15 41.6	15 18.3	12 58.3	1 21.9	0 31.0	27 52.2	18 36.4	22 19.9	1 52.9	5 06.3	5 52.1	7 09.9
17 M	15 37 53	25 53 43	14 14 22	20 53 28	15 38.4	15 11.7	14 39.0	2 34.8	0 53.8	28 14.1	18 42.1	22 26.7	1 56.3	5 09.7	5 53.7	7 09.7
18 Tu	15 41 50	26 51 32	27 29 44	4♏03 05	15 35.3	15 02.5	16 16.5	3 47.8	1 17.0	28 36.0	18 48.0	22 33.4	1 59.7	5 13.2	5 55.3	7 09.4
19 W	15 45 47	27 49 18	10♏33 24	17 00 33	15 32.1	14 51.2	17 50.6	5 00.7	1 40.4	28 58.1	18 54.1	22 40.1	2 03.1	5 16.7	5 56.9	7 09.2
20 Th	15 49 43	28 47 04	23 24 27	29 45 01	15 28.9	14 38.8	19 21.3	6 13.7	2 04.1	29 20.2	19 00.2	22 46.7	2 06.5	5 20.2	5 58.5	7 08.9
21 F	15 53 40	29 44 48	6♐02 14	12♐16 05	15 25.7	14 26.4	20 48.5	7 26.7	2 28.1	29 42.5	19 06.5	22 53.3	2 09.8	5 23.7	6 00.0	7 08.5
22 Sa	15 57 36	0♊42 30	18 26 39	24 34 02	15 22.6	14 15.2	22 12.3	8 39.6	2 52.4	0♌05.0	19 13.0	22 59.9	2 13.2	5 27.2	6 01.5	7 08.2
23 Su	16 01 33	1 40 12	0♑38 26	6♑40 06	15 19.4	14 06.1	23 32.4	9 52.6	3 16.9	0 27.5	19 19.6	23 06.4	2 16.5	5 30.7	6 03.0	7 07.8
24 M	16 05 29	2 37 52	12 39 21	18 36 32	15 16.2	13 59.4	24 49.0	11 05.6	3 41.7	0 50.1	19 26.3	23 12.9	2 19.8	5 34.2	6 04.4	7 07.4
25 Tu	16 09 26	3 35 31	24 32 06	0♒26 32	15 13.0	13 55.4	26 02.0	12 18.6	4 06.8	1 12.9	19 33.2	23 19.3	2 23.0	5 37.7	6 05.9	7 07.0
26 W	16 13 22	4 33 09	6♒20 22	12 14 11	15 09.9	13D 53.7	27 11.2	13 31.6	4 32.1	1 35.7	19 40.2	23 25.6	2 26.2	5 41.3	6 07.3	7 06.5
27 Th	16 17 19	5 30 46	18 08 37	24 04 17	15 06.7	13 53.5	28 16.7	14 44.6	4 57.7	1 58.7	19 47.3	23 31.9	2 29.5	5 44.8	6 08.6	7 06.0
28 F	16 21 16	6 28 22	0♓01 52	6♓02 03	15 03.5	13R 53.9	29 18.4	15 57.7	5 23.6	2 21.8	19 54.6	23 38.2	2 32.6	5 48.3	6 10.0	7 05.5
29 Sa	16 25 12	7 25 57	12 05 30	18 12 52	15 00.3	13 54.0	0♋16.1	17 10.7	5 49.7	2 44.9	20 02.0	23 44.4	2 35.8	5 51.8	6 11.3	7 05.0
30 Su	16 29 09	8 23 31	24 24 49	0♈41 55	14 57.1	13 52.7	1 10.0	18 23.8	6 16.0	3 08.2	20 09.5	23 50.5	2 38.9	5 55.3	6 12.6	7 04.4
31 M	16 33 05	9♊21 04	7♈04 42	13 33 37	14♒54.0	13♒49.4	1♋59.8	19♉36.8	6♍42.6	3♌31.6	20♌17.1	23♈56.6	2♉42.0	5♊58.8	6♈13.9	7♒03.9

1st of Month

Julian Day # 2461526.5
Obliquity 23°26'15"
SVP 4♓52'50"
GC 27♐13.3
Eris 25♈40.5

Day	⚴
1	26♉50.4
6	29 36.0
11	2♊23.5
16	5 12.6
21	8 03.3
26	10 55.5
31	13 49.1

Day	⚵
1	24♈57.0
6	27 44.4
11	0♉32.4
16	3 20.8
21	6 09.6
26	8 58.9
31	11 48.4

Day	⚶
1	29♉41.7
6	1♊50.7
11	4 00.1
16	6 09.7
21	8 19.5
26	10 29.5
31	12 39.6

DECLINATION and LATITUDE

Day	☉ Decl	☽ Decl	☽ Lat	☽12h Decl	☿ Decl	☿ Lat	♀ Decl	♀ Lat	♂ Decl	♂ Lat	⚳ Decl	⚳ Lat	♃ Decl	♃ Lat	♄ Decl	♄ Lat
1 Sa	14N57	8S36	1N31	5S52	15N46	0N04	3N40	1S39	15N01	2N07	29N40	8N16	16N33	1N00	5N57	2S15
2 Su	15 15	3 03	2 30	0 10	16 35	0 15	4 08	1 39	14 53	2 05	29 36	8 15	16 32	0 60	5 60	2 15
3 M	15 33	2N45	3 24	5N41	17 22	0 25	4 36	1 39	14 45	2 04	29 32	8 14	16 30	0 60	6 02	2 15
4 Tu	15 50	8 36	4 09	11 27	18 08	0 36	5 04	1 40	14 37	2 02	29 28	8 14	16 29	0 60	6 05	2 15
5 W	16 08	14 13	4 41	16 51	18 53	0 46	5 32	1 40	14 29	1 60	29 23	8 13	16 28	0 60	6 07	2 15
6 Th	16 25	19 18	4 58	21 30	19 35	0 56	5 59	1 39	14 21	1 58	29 19	8 12	16 27	0 60	6 10	2 15
7 F	16 42	23 25	4 58	24 60	20 16	1 06	6 27	1 39	14 13	1 56	29 14	8 12	16 25	0 59	6 13	2 15
8 Sa	16 58	26 11	4 39	26 56	20 54	1 16	6 54	1 39	14 04	1 54	29 10	8 11	16 24	0 59	6 15	2 16
9 Su	17 14	27 14	4 02	27 04	21 30	1 25	7 21	1 39	13 56	1 53	29 05	8 10	16 22	0 59	6 18	2 16
10 M	17 30	26 26	3 10	25 21	22 03	1 33	7 49	1 39	13 47	1 51	29 00	8 10	16 21	0 59	6 20	2 16
11 Tu	17 46	23 51	2 05	21 59	22 34	1 41	8 16	1 38	13 38	1 49	28 56	8 09	16 19	0 59	6 23	2 16
12 W	18 01	19 48	0 53	17 20	23 03	1 49	8 42	1 38	13 29	1 47	28 51	8 08	16 18	0 59	6 25	2 16
13 Th	18 17	14 39	0S21	11 47	23 29	1 55	9 09	1 37	13 20	1 46	28 46	8 08	16 16	0 59	6 28	2 16
14 F	18 31	8 48	1 34	5 43	23 52	2 01	9 35	1 37	13 10	1 44	28 41	8 07	16 14	0 59	6 30	2 16
15 Sa	18 46	2 36	2 40	0S31	24 13	2 06	10 02	1 36	13 01	1 42	28 36	8 06	16 12	0 59	6 32	2 16
16 Su	18 60	3S37	3 36	6 39	24 31	2 11	10 28	1 35	12 51	1 41	28 31	8 06	16 10	0 58	6 35	2 16
17 M	19 14	9 35	4 19	12 24	24 47	2 14	10 53	1 34	12 42	1 39	28 25	8 05	16 09	0 58	6 37	2 17
18 Tu	19 27	15 03	4 47	17 30	25 00	2 17	11 19	1 33	12 32	1 37	28 20	8 05	16 07	0 58	6 40	2 17
19 W	19 40	19 44	5 00	21 43	25 12	2 19	11 44	1 32	12 22	1 36	28 15	8 04	16 05	0 58	6 42	2 17
20 Th	19 53	23 22	4 57	24 49	25 21	2 20	12 09	1 31	12 12	1 34	28 09	8 03	16 03	0 58	6 44	2 17
21 F	20 06	25 55	4 40	26 40	25 27	2 21	12 34	1 30	12 02	1 33	28 04	8 03	16 01	0 58	6 47	2 17
22 Sa	20 18	27 05	4 10	27 10	25 32	2 20	12 59	1 29	11 52	1 31	27 58	8 02	15 59	0 58	6 49	2 17
23 Su	20 30	26 54	3 28	26 20	25 35	2 19	13 23	1 28	11 41	1 29	27 53	8 02	15 56	0 58	6 51	2 17
24 M	20 41	25 27	2 38	24 18	25 36	2 16	13 47	1 27	11 31	1 28	27 47	8 01	15 54	0 58	6 53	2 18
25 Tu	20 52	22 52	1 41	21 13	25 36	2 13	14 10	1 25	11 21	1 26	27 41	8 00	15 52	0 58	6 56	2 18
26 W	21 03	19 20	0 40	17 16	25 33	2 09	14 34	1 23	11 10	1 25	27 35	7 60	15 50	0 58	6 58	2 18
27 Th	21 13	15 02	0N23	12 39	25 29	2 04	14 57	1 22	10 59	1 23	27 30	7 59	15 47	0 57	6 60	2 18
28 F	21 23	10 08	1 25	7 31	25 24	1 58	15 19	1 21	10 48	1 22	27 24	7 59	15 45	0 57	7 02	2 18
29 Sa	21 33	4 48	2 25	2 01	25 18	1 51	15 41	1 20	10 37	1 21	27 18	7 58	15 43	0 57	7 04	2 18
30 Su	21 42	0N49	3 19	3N41	25 10	1 44	16 03	1 18	10 26	1 19	27 11	7 58	15 40	0 57	7 06	2 18
31 M	21N51	6N33	4N05	9N24	25N01	1N35	16N25	1S16	10N15	1N18	27N05	7N57	15N38	0N57	7N08	2S19

Day	⚷ Decl	⚷ Lat	♅ Decl	♅ Lat	♆ Decl	♆ Lat	♇ Decl	♇ Lat
1	11N44	0S05	20N53	0S07	0N54	1S22	22S52	4S32
6	11 50	0 06	20 56	0 07	0 58	1 22	22 53	4 33
11	11 56	0 06	20 59	0 07	1 01	1 22	22 54	4 34
16	12 02	0 06	21 02	0 07	1 04	1 22	22 55	4 35
21	12 07	0 07	21 06	0 06	1 07	1 22	22 56	4 36
26	12 12	0 07	21 09	0 06	1 10	1 23	22 58	4 37
31	12N17	0S08	21N12	0S06	1N12	1S23	22S59	4S38

Day	⚴ Decl	⚴ Lat	⚵ Decl	⚵ Lat	⚶ Decl	⚶ Lat	Eris Decl	Eris Lat
1	4S00	24S03	5N48	4S09	16N60	3S10	0N25	10S11
6	3 31	24 05	6 33	4 24	17 32	3 04	0 26	10 11
11	3 03	24 07	7 17	4 40	18 02	2 58	0 27	10 11
16	2 37	24 09	7 59	4 56	18 31	2 52	0 28	10 11
21	2 14	24 10	8 40	5 12	18 58	2 46	0 29	10 11
26	1 54	24 11	9 18	5 28	19 22	2 40	0 30	10 11
31	1S35	24S12	9N54	5S45	19N45	2S35	0N31	10S12

Moon Phenomena

Max/0 Decl

dy	hr mn	
2	12:42	0 N
9	1:39	27N14
15	10:00	0 S
22	8:49	27S10
29	20:32	0 N

Max/0 Lat

dy	hr mn	
6	11:33	5N00
12	17:05	0 S
19	7:51	5S01
26	15:21	0 N

Perigee/Apogee

dy	hr m		kilometers
9	20:10	p	366632
25	15:15	a	404799

PH	dy	hr mn	
●	6	11:00	15♉43
☽	13	4:45	22♌14
○	20	11:00	29♏14
☾	28	13:59	7♓02

Void of Course Moon

Last Aspect			☽ Ingress		
1 20:48	☿	⚹	♈	3	1:44
5 2:10	♂	△	♉	5	7:54
7 6:50	♂	□	♊	7	11:08
9 9:56	♂	⚹	♋	9	13:00
11 7:47	♀	□	♌	11	15:02
13 17:33	♂	☌	♍	13	18:07
15 12:49	☉	△	♎	15	22:35
17 14:57	♄	☍	♏	18	4:34
20 11:00	☉	☍	♐	20	12:28
22 9:00	♄	△	♑	22	22:44
24 21:31	♄	□	♒	25	11:06
27 22:25	☿	△	♓	27	23:56
29 11:05	♀	⚹	♈	30	10:40

DAILY ASPECTARIAN

1 Sa ☽□♅ 0:18; ☽⚺♆ 2:36; ☽∠♄ 2:55; ☉∥♂ 3:59; ☽⚺♇ 6:01; ☿⚺♀ 6:12; ☽⚼⚳ 7:14; ☽#♄ 11:33; ☉⚹☽ 13:25; ⚶ ♊ 17:01; ☽⚺♀ 19:35; ☽#♀ 19:46; ☽⚹☿ 20:48; ☿∥♃ 22:19; ☽∠⚷ 23:17

2 Su ☽⚻♃ 2:09; ☽⚺♄ 8:15; ☽#♆ 8:53; ☽∠♇ 10:59; ☽△⚳ 12:56; ☽∥♆ 16:31; ☽⚻♂ 18:16; ☉∠☽ 20:31

3 M ☽⚺⚷ 3:50; ☿□♃ 4:29; ☽⚼♃ 6:36; ☽∠☿ 7:01; ☽∥♀ 8:13; ☽⚹♅ 9:53; ☽☌♆ 11:56; ☽∥♄ 13:33; ☽⚹♇ 15:01; ☽⚼♂ 22:42

4 Tu ☉⚺☽ 2:25; ☽☌♀ 9:19; ☽△♃ 10:06; ☿∠♆ 13:10; ☽∠♅ 13:15; ☽∥⚷ 13:30; ☽⚺☿ 15:34; ☽☌♄ 16:02; ♀△♃ 18:17; ☿⚺♄ 18:41; ☽□⚳ 21:18

5 W ☽∥♂ 1:10; ☽△♂ 2:10; ☉∥☽ 9:08; ☽☌⚷ 10:06; ☽∥♃ 10:09; ☽⚺♅ 15:46; ☽⚺♆ 17:35; ☽□♇ 20:22

6 Th ☽∥☿ 1:47; ☉∥♃ 2:24; ♀∠♅ 6:38; ☽∥♅ 8:49; ☿⚹⚳ 10:03; ♀∥♄ 10:21; ☉☌☽ 11:00; ☽□♃ 14:37; ⚴ ♊ 17:17; ☽⚺♀ 18:33; ☽∠♆ 19:18; ☽#♇ 20:25; ☽⚺♄ 20:26

7 F ☽⚹⚳ 2:16; ☽☌☿ 4:36; ☽□♂ 6:50; ☽⚺⚷ 13:27; ♀☌♄ 18:49; ☽☌♅ 18:53; ☽⚹♆ 20:33; ☽∠♄ 21:49; ☽∠♀ 22:04; ☿□♂ 22:23; ☽△♇ 23:07

8 Sa ☿∥♅ 2:26; ☽∠⚳ 3:59; ♇ R 12:58; ☽∠⚷ 14:33; ☉⚺☽ 16:55; ☽⚹♃ 17:05; ☉□♃ 19:39; ☽⚹♄ 22:57

9 Su ☽⚼♇ 0:02; ☽⚹♀ 1:16; ☿ ♊ 1:59; ☽⚺⚳ 5:29; ☽⚹♂ 9:56; ☽⚺☿ 14:47; ☽⚹⚷ 15:31; ☽∠♃ 18:06; ☉∠☽ 19:34; ☿⚺⚷ 20:11; ☽⚺♅ 20:53; ☽□♆ 22:27

10 M ⚵ ♉ 0:53; ☽⚻♇ 0:55; ☽∠♂ 11:27; ☽⚺♃ 19:11; ☽∠☿ 19:42; ☽∠♅ 21:57; ☉⚹☽ 22:20

11 Tu ☽□♄ 1:13; ☽#♇ 6:26; ☽∥☿ 7:30; ☽□♀ 7:47; ☽☌⚳ 8:40; ☿☌♅ 12:50; ☽⚺♂ 13:10; ☉∠♆ 15:57; ☿#♇ 16:12; ☽∥♅ 17:37; ☽□⚷ 17:47; ♀□⚳ 22:08; ☽⚹♅ 23:14

12 W ☿⚹♆ 0:14; ☽△♆ 0:44; ☽⚹☿ 0:49; ☽☍♇ 3:08; ☉∥☽ 8:19; ☿∠♄ 15:22; ☽∥♃ 16:50; ☊ D 17:03; ☿△♇ 18:15; ☽☌♃ 22:05; ☉⚺♄ 22:40

13 Th ☽⚼♆ 2:17; ☽△♄ 4:23; ☊ R 4:40; ☉□☽ 4:45; ☽∥♂ 5:46; ☽∥⚷ 11:13; ☽⚺⚳ 12:55; ☽△♀ 15:32; ☽☌♂ 17:33; ☽∥♀ 21:04; ☽△⚷ 21:09

14 F ☽□♅ 2:45; ☽⚻♆ 4:11; ☽⚼♄ 6:28; ☽⚻♇ 6:31; ☽∥♄ 8:56; ☽□☿ 12:04; ♂ ♍ 14:48; ☽∠⚳ 15:36; ☽⚼♀ 20:05; ♀ ♉ 21:03; ☽⚼⚷ 23:21; ♀△♂ 23:47

15 Sa ☽⚺♃ 2:20; ☽∥♆ 5:55; ☽⚼♇ 8:44; ☽⚻♄ 8:54; ☉△☽ 12:49; ☽#♆ 14:07; ☽⚹⚳ 18:40; ☿∠⚳ 22:12; ☽⚺♂ 23:29

16 Su ☽⚻♀ 1:06; ☽⚻⚷ 1:56; ☽∠♃ 5:01; ☽△♅ 7:41; ☽☍♆ 9:02; ♀☌⚷ 10:42; ☽△♇ 11:19; ☽#♄ 11:48; ☉⚼☽ 17:32

17 M ☽△☿ 0:51; ☽∠♂ 3:04; ☽#♀ 5:57; ☽⚹♃ 8:06; ☽#⚷ 10:30; ☽⚼♅ 10:44; ☽#♂ 12:56; ☽☍♄ 14:57; ☉⚻☽ 22:45

18 Tu ☽□⚳ 2:04; ☽#♃ 5:04; ☽⚹♂ 7:08; ☽⚼☿ 7:52; ☽☍⚷ 8:16; ☿∠⚷ 11:20; ☽☍♀ 12:43; ☽⚻♅ 14:13; ☽⚻♆ 15:28; ☽□♇ 17:43; ☉#☽ 23:39

19 W ♀⚺♅ 5:31; ☽#♅ 7:58; ☽⚻☿ 15:23; ☽□♃ 15:40; ☿⚹♃ 17:56; ♀⚺♆ 18:53; ☽⚼♆ 19:25; ☽∥♇ 20:20; ♀∥⚷ 20:30; ☽⚻♄ 22:48

20 Th ♀∥♂ 1:52; ♂△⚷ 2:48; ☉☍☽ 11:00; ☽△⚳ 11:33; ♂∥⚷ 13:21; ☽⚻⚷ 16:34; ☽□♂ 16:57; ♀□♇ 18:04; ☽#☿ 18:18; ☉⚹⚳ 22:29; ☽☍♅ 22:46; ☽△♆ 23:56

21 F ☽⚹♇ 2:07; ☽⚻♀ 3:00; ☽⚼♄ 3:35; ☉ ♊ 6:19; ☽⚼⚳ 17:15; ⚳ ♌ 18:42; ☽⚼⚷ 21:36; ☿⚼♇ 22:49

22 Sa ☽△♃ 1:31; ☽∠♇ 7:13; ☽☍☿ 8:17; ☽△♄ 9:00; ☽⚼♀ 11:21; ☿⚹♄ 15:23; ☽⚻⚳ 23:38

23 Su ☉⚻☽ 2:13; ☽△⚷ 3:16; ☽△♂ 5:26; ☽⚼♃ 7:24; ☽⚻♅ 9:44; ☽□♆ 10:47; ☽⚺♇ 12:55; ☉⚺⚷ 16:00; ☽△♀ 20:30; ☽#☿ 22:14

24 M ☉⚼☽ 10:54; ☽⚼♂ 12:37; ☽⚻♃ 13:49; ☽⚼♅ 16:03; ☽□♄ 21:31; ☽∥♇ 23:22

25 Tu ☽⚻☿ 3:23; ☽#♅ 12:28; ☉#☽ 13:36; ☽☍⚳ 14:01; ☽□⚷ 16:01; ☉△☽ 20:02; ☽⚻♂ 20:12; ☽△♅ 22:40; ☉□♂ 23:15; ☽⚹♆ 23:33

26 W ☽☌♇ 1:34; ☽⚼☿ 13:08; ☉∥♅ 14:23; ☊ D 15:21; ☽□♀ 16:18; ☽#♃ 20:00

27 Th ☽#♀ 0:25; ☽☍♃ 3:22; ☽∠♆ 6:06; ☉☌♅ 6:13; ☽⚹♄ 11:00; ☽#⚷ 14:01; ☉⚹♆ 16:09; ☽#♂ 20:44; ☽△☿ 22:25

28 F ☽⚻⚳ 4:50; ☽⚹⚷ 5:03; ☽☍♂ 11:07; ☽□♅ 11:36; ☽⚺♆ 12:17; ⚳□⚷ 13:04; ☉□☽ 13:59; ☽#♄ 14:02; ☽⚺♇ 14:06; ☊ R 14:11; ☉△♇ 15:21; ☿ ♋ 17:08; ☽∠♄ 17:19

29 Sa ♀∥♃ 1:12; ♂□♅ 2:15; ☽∠⚷ 10:50; ☽⚹♀ 11:05; ☽⚼⚳ 11:27; ☽#♆ 15:29; ☽⚻♃ 15:42; ☽∠♇ 19:30; ♂⚻♆ 20:45; ☽⚺♄ 22:54

30 Su ☽∥♆ 1:35; ☉∠♄ 12:37; ☽□☿ 13:48; ☽⚺⚷ 15:45; ☽△⚳ 17:08; ☽∠♀ 18:54; ☽⚼♃ 20:37; ☽⚹♅ 21:56; ☽☌♆ 22:25; ☽⚻♂ 23:17; ☽⚹♇ 23:58

31 M ☽∥♄ 2:29; ☉⚹☽ 4:34; ♀□♃ 14:48; ☽∥♂ 15:08; ♂⚻♇ 18:39; ☿⚹⚷ 23:47

June 2027

LONGITUDE

Day	Sid.Time	☉	☽	☽ 12 hour	Mean☊	True☊	☿	♀	♂	⚳	♃	♄	⚷	♅	♆	♇
	h m s	° ' "	° ' "	° ' "	° '	° '	° '	° '	° '	° '	° '	° '	° '	° '	° '	° '
1 Tu	16 37 02	10♊18 37	20♈09 00	26♈51 04	14♒50.8	13♒43.9	2♋45.5	20♉49.9	7♍09.4	3♌55.0	20♌24.9	24♈02.7	2♉45.1	6♊02.3	6♈15.1	7♒03.3
2 W	16 40 58	11 16 08	3♉39 53	10♉35 22	14 47.6	13R 36.3	3 27.0	22 03.0	7 36.4	4 18.6	20 32.8	24 08.7	2 48.2	6 05.8	6 16.3	7R 02.6
3 Th	16 44 55	12 13 39	17 37 13	24 45 01	14 44.4	13 27.2	4 04.3	23 16.1	8 03.7	4 42.3	20 40.8	24 14.6	2 51.2	6 09.4	6 17.5	7 02.0
4 F	16 48 51	13 11 09	1♊58 08	9♊15 48	14 41.3	13 17.8	4 37.2	24 29.2	8 31.2	5 06.0	20 48.9	24 20.5	2 54.2	6 12.9	6 18.6	7 01.3
5 Sa	16 52 48	14 08 38	16 37 07	24 01 05	14 38.1	13 09.0	5 05.7	25 42.3	8 58.9	5 29.9	20 57.2	24 26.3	2 57.1	6 16.4	6 19.8	7 00.6
6 Su	16 56 45	15 06 07	1♋26 40	8♋52 48	14 34.9	13 01.8	5 29.8	26 55.4	9 26.9	5 53.8	21 05.6	24 32.0	3 00.1	6 19.8	6 20.9	6 59.9
7 M	17 00 41	16 03 34	16 18 29	23 42 47	14 31.7	12 56.9	5 49.3	28 08.6	9 55.0	6 17.8	21 14.0	24 37.7	3 03.0	6 23.3	6 21.9	6 59.1
8 Tu	17 04 38	17 01 00	1♌04 51	8♌24 01	14 28.6	12D 54.4	6 04.3	29 21.7	10 23.4	6 41.9	21 22.6	24 43.3	3 05.8	6 26.8	6 23.0	6 58.4
9 W	17 08 34	17 58 25	15 39 41	22 51 27	14 25.4	12 53.9	6 14.6	0♊34.9	10 52.0	7 06.1	21 31.3	24 48.9	3 08.7	6 30.3	6 24.0	6 57.6
10 Th	17 12 31	18 55 48	29 59 01	7♍02 13	14 22.2	12 54.6	6R 20.4	1 48.0	11 20.7	7 30.4	21 40.2	24 54.4	3 11.5	6 33.7	6 25.0	6 56.8
11 F	17 16 27	19 53 11	14♍00 58	20 55 17	14 19.0	12R 55.4	6 21.5	3 01.2	11 49.7	7 54.8	21 49.1	24 59.8	3 14.2	6 37.2	6 25.9	6 55.9
12 Sa	17 20 24	20 50 33	27 45 15	4♎31 00	14 15.9	12 55.3	6 18.2	4 14.3	12 18.8	8 19.2	21 58.1	25 05.2	3 17.0	6 40.6	6 26.8	6 55.1
13 Su	17 24 20	21 47 53	11♎12 40	17 50 25	14 12.7	12 53.5	6 10.5	5 27.5	12 48.2	8 43.7	22 07.2	25 10.5	3 19.7	6 44.1	6 27.7	6 54.2
14 M	17 28 17	22 45 12	24 24 26	0♏54 53	14 09.5	12 49.7	5 58.6	6 40.7	13 17.7	9 08.3	22 16.5	25 15.7	3 22.3	6 47.5	6 28.5	6 53.3
15 Tu	17 32 14	23 42 31	7♏21 55	13 45 40	14 06.3	12 43.8	5 42.6	7 53.9	13 47.4	9 32.9	22 25.8	25 20.8	3 25.0	6 50.9	6 29.4	6 52.4
16 W	17 36 10	24 39 49	20 06 17	26 23 52	14 03.1	12 36.4	5 22.9	9 07.1	14 17.3	9 57.7	22 35.3	25 25.9	3 27.5	6 54.3	6 30.2	6 51.4
17 Th	17 40 07	25 37 06	2♐38 33	8♐50 27	14 00.0	12 28.2	4 59.6	10 20.3	14 47.4	10 22.5	22 44.8	25 30.9	3 30.1	6 57.7	6 30.9	6 50.5
18 F	17 44 03	26 34 22	14 59 39	21 06 17	13 56.8	12 19.9	4 33.1	11 33.5	15 17.6	10 47.4	22 54.4	25 35.9	3 32.6	7 01.0	6 31.7	6 49.5
19 Sa	17 48 00	27 31 38	27 10 30	3♑12 28	13 53.6	12 12.5	4 04.3	12 46.8	15 48.0	11 12.3	23 04.1	25 40.7	3 35.1	7 04.4	6 32.4	6 48.5
20 Su	17 51 56	28 28 53	9♑12 21	15 10 23	13 50.4	12 06.5	3 33.0	14 00.0	16 18.6	11 37.3	23 14.0	25 45.5	3 37.5	7 07.7	6 33.0	6 47.5
21 M	17 55 53	29 26 08	21 06 50	27 02 00	13 47.3	12 02.3	3 00.1	15 13.3	16 49.3	12 02.4	23 23.9	25 50.2	3 39.9	7 11.0	6 33.7	6 46.5
22 Tu	17 59 50	0♋23 22	2♒56 12	8♒49 49	13 44.1	12D 00.2	2 26.0	16 26.6	17 20.2	12 27.5	23 33.9	25 54.9	3 42.3	7 14.4	6 34.3	6 45.4
23 W	18 03 46	1 20 36	14 43 16	20 37 02	13 40.9	11 59.7	1 51.3	17 39.9	17 51.3	12 52.8	23 44.0	25 59.4	3 44.6	7 17.6	6 34.8	6 44.3
24 Th	18 07 43	2 17 50	26 31 36	2♓27 30	13 37.7	12 00.6	1 16.7	18 53.2	18 22.5	13 18.0	23 54.1	26 03.9	3 46.9	7 20.9	6 35.4	6 43.3
25 F	18 11 39	3 15 04	8♓25 18	14 25 35	13 34.6	12 02.2	0 42.6	20 06.5	18 53.9	13 43.4	24 04.4	26 08.3	3 49.1	7 24.2	6 35.9	6 42.2
26 Sa	18 15 36	4 12 17	20 28 57	26 36 02	13 31.4	12 03.6	0 09.7	21 19.9	19 25.4	14 08.8	24 14.7	26 12.7	3 51.3	7 27.4	6 36.4	6 41.0
27 Su	18 19 32	5 09 31	2♈47 26	9♈03 44	13 28.2	12R 04.4	29♊38.6	22 33.2	19 57.1	14 34.2	24 25.2	26 16.9	3 53.4	7 30.6	6 36.8	6 39.9
28 M	18 23 29	6 06 44	15 25 29	21 53 13	13 25.0	12 04.0	29 09.8	23 46.6	20 28.9	14 59.7	24 35.7	26 21.1	3 55.5	7 33.8	6 37.2	6 38.8
29 Tu	18 27 25	7 03 57	28 27 20	5♉08 11	13 21.9	12 02.2	28 43.8	25 00.0	21 00.9	15 25.3	24 46.3	26 25.2	3 57.6	7 37.0	6 37.6	6 37.6
30 W	18 31 22	8♋01 11	11♉56 00	18 50 50	13♒18.7	11♒59.0	28♊21.1	26♊13.4	21♍33.1	15♌51.0	24♌56.9	26♈29.2	3♉59.6	7♊40.2	6♈37.9	6♒36.4

1st of Month

Julian Day # 2461557.5
Obliquity 23°26'35"
SVP 4♓52'26"
GC 27♐13.3
Eris 25♈58.3

Day	⚴
1	14♊23.9
6	17 19.0
11	20 15.1
16	23 12.1
21	26 09.8
26	29 08.2

Day	⚵
1	12♉22.4
6	15 12.2
11	18 02.1
16	20 52.0
21	23 41.8
26	26 31.5

Day	⚶
1	13♊05.6
6	15 15.7
11	17 25.8
16	19 35.6
21	21 45.3
26	23 54.7

DECLINATION and LATITUDE

Day	☉ Decl	☽ Decl	☽ Lat	☽12h Decl	☿ Decl	☿ Lat	♀ Decl	♀ Lat	♂ Decl	♂ Lat	⚳ Decl	⚳ Lat	♃ Decl	♃ Lat	♄ Decl	♄ Lat
1 Tu	21N60	12N11	4N39	14N53	24N50	1N26	16N46	1S15	10N04	1N16	26N59	7N57	15N35	0N57	7N11	2S19
2 W	22 08	17 26	4 60	19 48	24 39	1 16	17 06	1 13	9 52	1 15	26 53	7 56	15 32	0 57	7 13	2 19
3 Th	22 15	21 56	5 04	23 47	24 27	1 05	17 26	1 11	9 41	1 13	26 46	7 56	15 30	0 57	7 15	2 19
4 F	22 23	25 16	4 49	26 21	24 14	0 53	17 46	1 09	9 29	1 12	26 40	7 55	15 27	0 57	7 17	2 19
5 Sa	22 30	26 59	4 15	27 09	24 01	0 40	18 05	1 08	9 18	1 11	26 33	7 55	15 24	0 57	7 18	2 19
6 Su	22 36	26 49	3 23	25 60	23 47	0 27	18 24	1 06	9 06	1 09	26 27	7 54	15 22	0 57	7 20	2 20
7 M	22 42	24 43	2 18	23 01	23 32	0 13	18 43	1 04	8 54	1 08	26 20	7 54	15 19	0 57	7 22	2 20
8 Tu	22 48	20 56	1 03	18 33	23 16	0S01	19 00	1 02	8 42	1 07	26 13	7 53	15 16	0 56	7 24	2 20
9 W	22 54	15 54	0S15	13 03	23 01	0 17	19 18	0 60	8 30	1 05	26 06	7 53	15 13	0 56	7 26	2 20
10 Th	22 59	10 04	1 31	6 59	22 45	0 32	19 35	0 58	8 18	1 04	25 59	7 52	15 10	0 56	7 28	2 20
11 F	23 03	3 50	2 39	0 41	22 28	0 49	19 51	0 56	8 06	1 03	25 52	7 52	15 07	0 56	7 30	2 21
12 Sa	23 07	2S26	3 37	5S29	22 12	1 05	20 07	0 53	7 53	1 02	25 45	7 51	15 04	0 56	7 31	2 21
13 Su	23 11	8 27	4 22	11 17	21 56	1 22	20 22	0 51	7 41	1 00	25 38	7 51	15 01	0 56	7 33	2 21
14 M	23 14	13 59	4 52	16 29	21 39	1 39	20 37	0 49	7 28	0 59	25 31	7 51	14 58	0 56	7 35	2 21
15 Tu	23 17	18 47	5 06	20 51	21 23	1 56	20 51	0 47	7 16	0 58	25 24	7 50	14 55	0 56	7 37	2 21
16 W	23 20	22 39	5 05	24 11	21 07	2 13	21 05	0 45	7 03	0 57	25 17	7 50	14 52	0 56	7 38	2 22
17 Th	23 22	25 24	4 49	26 19	20 51	2 30	21 18	0 42	6 50	0 55	25 09	7 49	14 49	0 56	7 40	2 22
18 F	23 24	26 53	4 19	27 08	20 36	2 46	21 30	0 40	6 38	0 54	25 02	7 49	14 45	0 56	7 41	2 22
19 Sa	23 25	27 03	3 39	26 38	20 21	3 01	21 42	0 38	6 25	0 53	24 54	7 48	14 42	0 56	7 43	2 22
20 Su	23 26	25 55	2 48	24 54	20 07	3 16	21 54	0 35	6 12	0 52	24 47	7 48	14 39	0 56	7 44	2 22
21 M	23 26	23 36	1 51	22 04	19 54	3 30	22 04	0 33	5 59	0 51	24 39	7 48	14 36	0 56	7 46	2 23
22 Tu	23 26	20 18	0 49	18 20	19 41	3 44	22 14	0 31	5 46	0 49	24 31	7 47	14 32	0 56	7 47	2 23
23 W	23 26	16 11	0N15	13 53	19 30	3 56	22 24	0 28	5 32	0 48	24 24	7 47	14 29	0 55	7 49	2 23
24 Th	23 25	11 27	1 18	8 54	19 20	4 06	22 33	0 26	5 19	0 47	24 16	7 47	14 25	0 55	7 50	2 23
25 F	23 24	6 16	2 19	3 33	19 10	4 16	22 41	0 23	5 06	0 46	24 08	7 46	14 22	0 55	7 52	2 24
26 Sa	23 22	0 47	3 14	2N00	19 02	4 24	22 48	0 21	4 52	0 45	24 00	7 46	14 19	0 55	7 53	2 24
27 Su	23 20	4N49	4 02	7 36	18 56	4 30	22 55	0 19	4 39	0 44	23 52	7 45	14 15	0 55	7 54	2 24
28 M	23 18	10 22	4 39	13 03	18 51	4 35	23 01	0 16	4 25	0 43	23 44	7 45	14 11	0 55	7 56	2 24
29 Tu	23 15	15 39	5 04	18 06	18 47	4 39	23 07	0 14	4 12	0 41	23 36	7 45	14 08	0 55	7 57	2 24
30 W	23N12	20N22	5N12	22N23	18N45	4S41	23N12	0S11	3N58	0N40	23N28	7N44	14N04	0N55	7N58	2S25

Day	⚷ Decl	⚷ Lat	♅ Decl	♅ Lat	♆ Decl	♆ Lat	♇ Decl	♇ Lat
1	12N18	0S08	21N13	0S06	1N13	1S23	22S60	4S38
6	12 23	0 08	21 16	0 06	1 15	1 23	23 01	4 39
11	12 28	0 08	21 19	0 06	1 17	1 23	23 03	4 40
16	12 32	0 09	21 21	0 06	1 18	1 24	23 05	4 41
21	12 36	0 09	21 24	0 06	1 19	1 24	23 07	4 42
26	12 39	0 10	21 27	0 06	1 20	1 24	23 10	4 43

Day	⚴ Decl	⚴ Lat	⚵ Decl	⚵ Lat	⚶ Decl	⚶ Lat	Eris Decl	Eris Lat
1	1S32	24S12	10N01	5S48	19N50	2S34	0N31	10S12
6	1 17	24 13	10 35	6 04	20 10	2 28	0 32	10 12
11	1 04	24 13	11 06	6 21	20 28	2 23	0 32	10 12
16	0 55	24 12	11 34	6 38	20 44	2 18	0 33	10 12
21	0 48	24 11	11 59	6 55	20 59	2 12	0 33	10 13
26	0 44	24 10	12 21	7 13	21 11	2 07	0 33	10 13

Moon Phenomena

Max/0 Decl
dy hr mn
5 9:55 27N09
11 14:39 0 S
18 14:51 27S09
26 3:24 0 N

Perigee/Apogee
dy hr m kilometers
6 14:55 p 361706
22 5:08 a 405698

PH dy hr mn
● 4 19:41 13♊58
☽ 11 10:57 20♍19
○ 19 0:46 27♐33
☾ 27 4:55 5♈21

Max/0 Lat
dy hr mn
2 16:59 5N04
8 19:25 0 S
15 9:58 5S07
22 18:26 0 N
30 0:05 5N12

Void of Course Moon

Last Aspect	☽ Ingress
1 7:03 ♄ ☌	♉ 1 17:34
3 10:24 ♀ ☌	♊ 3 20:44
5 12:46 ♄ ⚹	♋ 5 21:40
7 20:56 ♀ ⚹	♌ 7 22:14
9 15:23 ♄ △	♍ 10 0:02
11 10:57 ☉ □	♎ 12 3:58
14 1:35 ♄ ☍	♏ 14 10:18
16 4:47 ♃ □	♐ 16 18:55
19 0:46 ☉ ☍	♑ 19 5:37
21 9:38 ♄ □	♒ 21 18:02
23 23:04 ♄ ⚹	♓ 24 7:02
26 18:09 ☿ □	♈ 26 18:37
29 0:29 ☿ ⚹	♉ 29 2:48

DAILY ASPECTARIAN

1 Tu
☽△♃ 0:29
☽∥⚷ 0:33
☽⚺♀ 1:21
☽∠♅ 1:37
☽⚼♂ 3:44
☽☌♄ 7:03
♀∠♆ 8:25
☉∠☽ 9:58
☽∥♃ 15:07
☽∥♀ 22:17
☽☌⚷ 22:29
☽⚹☿ 23:36

2 W
☽□⚳ 1:10
☽⚺♅ 4:15
☽⚺♆ 4:33
☽□♇ 5:52
☽△♂ 7:05
☉⚺☽ 14:08
☽∥♅ 19:50

3 Th
☉∥☽ 2:01
☽∠☿ 2:34
☽□♃ 5:13
☽∠♆ 6:12
☽⋕♇ 6:43
☽☌♀ 10:24
☽⚺♄ 11:14
☽∥☿ 16:00
♀⚺♄ 20:53

4 F
☽⚺⚷ 1:33
☽⚺☿ 4:32
☽⚹⚳ 5:19
☽☌♅ 7:01
☽⚹♆ 7:10
☽△♇ 8:19
☽□♂ 11:08
☽∠♄ 12:12
☽∥⚳ 15:43
☉☌☽ 19:41

5 Sa
☽∠⚷ 2:10
☽∠⚳ 6:28
☽⚹♃ 7:06
☽⚼♇ 8:44
☽⚹♄ 12:46
☽⚺♀ 16:03

6 Su
☽⚹⚷ 2:31
♂⚼♄ 5:32
☽∥⚳ 6:42
☽☌☿ 6:42
☽⚺⚳ 7:23
☽∠♃ 7:34
☽⚺♅ 7:55
☽□♆ 7:55
☽⚻♇ 8:57
♅⚹♆ 10:09
☽⚹♂ 13:20
☽∠♀ 18:26
☉⚺☽ 23:34

7 M
⚳△♆ 4:17
⚳⚹♅ 6:25
☽⚺♃ 8:03
☽∠♅ 8:16
☽∥☿ 9:18
☽⋕♇ 11:53
☉∥☽ 13:34
☽□♄ 13:34
☽∠♂ 14:25
☽⚹♀ 20:56
☽∥♅ 22:10

8 Tu
♃⚼♆ 1:03
☉∠☽ 1:38
☽□⚷ 3:19
☽⚺☿ 8:17
☽△♆ 8:42
☽⚹♅ 8:49
☽∥♀ 9:16
☽☌⚳ 9:28
☽☍♇ 9:39
♀ ♊ 12:34
⚳☍♇ 15:48
☽⚺♂ 15:48
☊ D 19:24
☿⋕♇ 21:27

9 W
☽∥♃ 2:59
☉⚹☽ 4:07
☉∠⚷ 4:31
☉∥☿ 8:08
☽∠☿ 9:23
☽⚼♆ 9:34
☽☌♃ 9:52
☽∥⚷ 14:31
☽△♄ 15:23

10 Th
☽□♀ 3:22
☽△⚷ 5:28
☽∥♂ 7:08
☽∥♄ 10:04
☽⚹☿ 10:50
☽⚻♆ 10:57
☽□♅ 11:14
☽⚻♇ 11:50
☽⚺⚳ 13:11
☽⚼♄ 17:02
☿ R 18:16
☽☌♂ 20:05

11 F
☉⋕♇ 0:43
♀⚺⚷ 4:27
☽⚼⚷ 7:21
☽∥♆ 9:45
☊ R 10:50
☉□☽ 10:57
☽⚺♃ 13:43
☽⚼♇ 13:45
☽∠⚳ 15:58
☽⚻♄ 19:16
☽⋕♆ 19:34

12 Sa
☽⚻⚷ 9:50
☽△♀ 12:39
☽□☿ 15:04
☽☍♆ 15:28
☽△♅ 15:56
☽△♇ 16:16
☽∠♃ 16:34
☽⚹⚳ 19:24
☽⋕♄ 20:18
☽⋕♂ 20:57

13 Su
☉⚼♇ 2:36
☽⚺♂ 2:59
☉⚹♃ 9:39
☿⚺♀ 12:16
♂∥♄ 13:07
☽⋕⚷ 17:18
☽⚼♀ 18:29
☽⚼♅ 19:11
♀⚹♆ 19:58
☽⚹♃ 20:03
☉△☽ 20:44

14 M
☽☍♄ 1:35
♀☌♅ 2:20
♀△♇ 4:05
☽⋕♃ 4:35
☽∠♂ 7:26
☽☍⚷ 16:37
☽△☿ 20:59
☽⚻♆ 22:22
☽⚻♅ 23:02
☽□♇ 23:05

15 Tu
☽⚻♀ 1:06
☉⚼☽ 2:43
☿∥♅ 2:53
☽□⚳ 4:13
♅△♇ 8:14
☽⚹♂ 12:33
☽⋕♀ 12:47
☽⋕☿ 14:20
☽⋕♅ 15:11

16 W
☽⚼☿ 0:31
☿∥♀ 1:40
☽⚼♆ 2:40
☽∥♇ 3:11
☽□♃ 4:47
☉⋕☽ 5:06
☉⚻☽ 9:24
☽⚻♄ 10:13
☉∠⚳ 13:12
☉⚹♄ 21:10
☽⋕⚳ 21:25

17 Th
♀⚹⚳ 1:05
☽⚻⚷ 1:40
♀∠♄ 3:44
☽⚻☿ 4:24
☽△♆ 7:30
☽⚹♇ 8:07
♀∥♅ 8:15
☽☍♅ 8:23
☽⚼♄ 15:22
☽△⚳ 15:30
☽☍♀ 16:33

18 F
☽□♂ 0:37
☽⚼⚷ 6:59
☽∠♇ 13:24
☽△♃ 15:46
☽△♄ 21:01
☽⚼⚳ 22:01

19 Sa
☉☍☽ 0:46
☽△⚷ 12:48
☽☍☿ 13:10
☽□♆ 18:40
☽⚺♇ 19:10
☽⚻♅ 19:49
☿⚹⚷ 20:53
☽⚼♃ 22:01

20 Su
☽⚻⚳ 5:02
☽⚻♀ 10:44
☽⋕⚳ 13:57
☽△♂ 14:56

21 M
☉⋕☽ 1:25
☽⚼♅ 2:11
☽∥♇ 3:58
☽⚻♃ 4:42
☽□♄ 9:38
☽⋕♀ 11:22
☉ ♋ 14:12
☽⋕♅ 16:36
☉⚻☽ 18:22
☽⚼♀ 20:37
☽⚼♂ 22:43
☽⚻☿ 23:01

22 Tu
☽□⚷ 1:34
☽⋕☿ 4:02
☽⚹♆ 7:24
☽☌♇ 7:46
☽△♅ 8:48
☊ D 18:26
☽☍⚳ 20:07

23 W
☉⚼☽ 3:36
☽⚼☿ 4:09
♀□♂ 6:30
☽⚻♂ 6:40
☽△♀ 6:41
☉☌☿ 8:01
☽⋕♃ 9:02
☽∠♆ 13:58
☽⋕⚷ 18:15
☽☍♃ 18:36
♀∠⚷ 21:52
☽⚹♄ 23:04

24 Th
☽△☿ 9:10
☉△☽ 12:42
☽⚹⚷ 14:43
☽⋕♄ 16:48
♂⚼⚷ 20:04
☽⚺♆ 20:20
☽⚺♇ 20:33
☽□♅ 21:57

25 F
☽⋕♂ 5:25
☽∠♄ 5:29
☽⚻⚳ 10:59
☉⚹⚷ 14:51
☽∠⚷ 20:47
☽⋕♆ 21:39
☽☍♂ 21:49

26 Sa
☽□♀ 1:51
☽∠♇ 2:22
♀⚼♇ 6:49
☿R♊ 7:20
☽⚻♃ 7:30
☽∥♆ 9:08
☽⚺♄ 11:18
☽⚼⚳ 17:33
☽□☿ 18:09
☽∥♂ 23:20

27 Su
☿∠⚳ 1:54
☽⚺⚷ 2:07
☉□☽ 4:55
☊ R 5:05
☽☌♆ 7:20
☽⚹♇ 7:25
☽⚹♅ 9:05
♀ ♋ 10:48
☽⚼♃ 12:51
☽∥♄ 13:20
☽△⚳ 23:10

28 M
☽⚻♂ 9:49
☽∥⚷ 10:16
☉□♆ 12:52
☉⚻♇ 13:10
☽∠♅ 13:18
☽∥♃ 16:59
☽⚹♀ 17:04
☽△♃ 17:12
♀⚹♃ 18:45
☽☌♄ 20:17

29 Tu
♆⚹♇ 0:10
☽⚹☿ 0:29
☽☌⚷ 9:56
☽⚼♂ 14:07
☽□♇ 14:38
☽⚺♆ 14:39
☉⚺♅ 14:40
☽∥☿ 15:22
☽⚺♅ 16:28
☉⚹☽ 16:36
♀⋕♇ 21:39
☽∠♀ 22:38
☉∥♀ 23:58

30 W
☉⋕♇ 2:24
♂⚼♇ 2:25
☽∠☿ 2:25
♀⚹♄ 5:27
☽∥♅ 6:28
☽□⚳ 7:02
☽∠♆ 16:47
☉∥☽ 16:59
☽⋕♇ 17:16
☽△♂ 17:18
☽∥♀ 17:38
☽∥⚳ 18:23
☉∠☽ 20:32
☽□♃ 22:43

LONGITUDE

Day	Sid.Time	☉	☽	☽ 12 hour	Mean ☊	True ☊	☿	♀	♂	⚳	♃	♄	⚷	♅	♆	♇
	h m s	° ' "	° ' "	° ' "	° '	° '	° '	° '	° '	° '	° '	° '	° '	° '	° '	° '
1 Th	18 35 18	8♋58 25	25♉52 37	3♊01 06	13♒15.5	11♒54.8	28♊02.0	27♊26.8	22♍05.3	16♌16.7	25♌07.7	26♈33.1	4♉01.6	7♊43.3	6♈38.2	6♒35.2
2 F	18 39 15	9 55 39	10♊15 49	17 36 09	13 12.3	11R 50.2	27R 46.9	28 40.3	22 37.8	16 42.4	25 18.5	26 36.9	4 03.5	7 46.4	6 38.5	6R 34.0
3 Sa	18 43 12	10 52 53	25 01 18	2♋30 19	13 09.2	11 45.8	27 36.0	29 53.7	23 10.4	17 08.2	25 29.4	26 40.7	4 05.4	7 49.5	6 38.8	6 32.8
4 Su	18 47 08	11 50 06	10♋02 06	17 35 31	13 06.0	11 42.3	27D 29.8	1♋07.2	23 43.1	17 34.1	25 40.4	26 44.3	4 07.3	7 52.6	6 39.0	6 31.6
5 M	18 51 05	12 47 20	25 09 24	2♌42 33	13 02.8	11 40.1	27 28.2	2 20.7	24 15.9	18 00.0	25 51.4	26 47.9	4 09.1	7 55.6	6 39.2	6 30.3
6 Tu	18 55 01	13 44 34	10♌13 52	17 42 21	12 59.6	11D 39.4	27 31.6	3 34.2	24 48.9	18 26.0	26 02.6	26 51.4	4 10.8	7 58.6	6 39.3	6 29.1
7 W	18 58 58	14 41 48	25 07 06	2♍27 25	12 56.5	11 39.8	27 39.9	4 47.7	25 22.1	18 52.0	26 13.8	26 54.8	4 12.5	8 01.6	6 39.4	6 27.8
8 Th	19 02 54	15 39 01	9♍42 42	16 52 33	12 53.3	11 41.0	27 53.3	6 01.3	25 55.4	19 18.1	26 25.0	26 58.1	4 14.2	8 04.6	6 39.5	6 26.5
9 F	19 06 51	16 36 14	23 56 42	0♎55 01	12 50.1	11 42.4	28 11.8	7 14.8	26 28.8	19 44.2	26 36.3	27 01.3	4 15.8	8 07.5	6R 39.6	6 25.2
10 Sa	19 10 48	17 33 27	7♎47 31	14 34 17	12 46.9	11R 43.4	28 35.5	8 28.4	27 02.3	20 10.4	26 47.7	27 04.4	4 17.3	8 10.4	6 39.6	6 23.9
11 Su	19 14 44	18 30 39	21 15 30	27 51 25	12 43.7	11 43.7	29 04.3	9 42.0	27 36.0	20 36.6	26 59.2	27 07.5	4 18.8	8 13.3	6 39.6	6 22.6
12 M	19 18 41	19 27 52	4♏22 19	10♏48 32	12 40.6	11 42.9	29 38.2	10 55.6	28 09.8	21 02.9	27 10.7	27 10.4	4 20.3	8 16.2	6 39.5	6 21.3
13 Tu	19 22 37	20 25 05	17 10 23	23 28 14	12 37.4	11 41.2	0♋17.2	12 09.2	28 43.7	21 29.2	27 22.2	27 13.3	4 21.7	8 19.0	6 39.4	6 20.0
14 W	19 26 34	21 22 17	29 42 25	5♐53 17	12 34.2	11 38.8	1 01.2	13 22.8	29 17.7	21 55.5	27 33.9	27 16.0	4 23.0	8 21.8	6 39.3	6 18.6
15 Th	19 30 30	22 19 30	12♐01 09	18 06 20	12 31.0	11 35.9	1 50.3	14 36.4	29 51.9	22 21.9	27 45.6	27 18.7	4 24.3	8 24.5	6 39.2	6 17.3
16 F	19 34 27	23 16 43	24 09 09	0♑09 53	12 27.9	11 33.0	2 44.3	15 50.1	0♎26.2	22 48.3	27 57.3	27 21.2	4 25.6	8 27.3	6 39.0	6 15.9
17 Sa	19 38 23	24 13 56	6♑08 48	12 06 12	12 24.7	11 30.5	3 43.3	17 03.7	1 00.6	23 14.8	28 09.1	27 23.7	4 26.8	8 30.0	6 38.8	6 14.6
18 Su	19 42 20	25 11 10	18 02 18	23 57 25	12 21.5	11 28.6	4 47.0	18 17.4	1 35.1	23 41.3	28 20.9	27 26.1	4 28.0	8 32.7	6 38.5	6 13.2
19 M	19 46 17	26 08 23	29 51 48	5♒45 42	12 18.3	11D 27.4	5 55.6	19 31.1	2 09.7	24 07.8	28 32.8	27 28.3	4 29.1	8 35.3	6 38.3	6 11.9
20 Tu	19 50 13	27 05 37	11♒39 27	17 33 20	12 15.2	11 27.1	7 08.8	20 44.9	2 44.5	24 34.4	28 44.8	27 30.5	4 30.1	8 37.9	6 38.0	6 10.5
21 W	19 54 10	28 02 52	23 27 40	29 22 47	12 12.0	11 27.4	8 26.6	21 58.6	3 19.3	25 01.0	28 56.8	27 32.6	4 31.1	8 40.5	6 37.6	6 09.1
22 Th	19 58 06	29 00 07	5♓19 05	11♓16 56	12 08.8	11 28.2	9 49.0	23 12.3	3 54.3	25 27.7	29 08.9	27 34.6	4 32.1	8 43.0	6 37.3	6 07.7
23 F	20 02 03	29 57 23	17 16 45	23 18 58	12 05.6	11 29.3	11 15.7	24 26.1	4 29.4	25 54.4	29 21.0	27 36.4	4 33.0	8 45.5	6 36.9	6 06.3
24 Sa	20 05 59	0♌54 40	29 24 04	5♈32 29	12 02.4	11 30.3	12 46.7	25 39.9	5 04.6	26 21.1	29 33.1	27 38.2	4 33.8	8 48.0	6 36.4	6 04.9
25 Su	20 09 56	1 51 57	11♈44 43	18 01 16	11 59.3	11 31.2	14 21.9	26 53.7	5 39.9	26 47.9	29 45.3	27 39.9	4 34.6	8 50.4	6 36.0	6 03.5
26 M	20 13 52	2 49 15	24 22 35	0♉49 08	11 56.1	11R 31.6	16 00.9	28 07.6	6 15.3	27 14.7	29 57.5	27 41.5	4 35.4	8 52.8	6 35.5	6 02.2
27 Tu	20 17 49	3 46 34	7♉21 19	13 59 32	11 52.9	11 31.7	17 43.8	29 21.4	6 50.8	27 41.5	0♍09.8	27 43.0	4 36.0	8 55.2	6 34.9	6 00.8
28 W	20 21 46	4 43 55	20 44 03	27 35 03	11 49.7	11 31.5	19 30.1	0♌35.3	7 26.5	28 08.4	0 22.1	27 44.3	4 36.7	8 57.5	6 34.4	5 59.4
29 Th	20 25 42	5 41 16	4♊32 39	11♊36 48	11 46.6	11 31.0	21 19.8	1 49.2	8 02.2	28 35.3	0 34.5	27 45.6	4 37.3	8 59.8	6 33.8	5 58.0
30 F	20 29 39	6 38 38	18 47 16	26 03 43	11 43.4	11 30.5	23 12.4	3 03.1	8 38.1	29 02.2	0 46.9	27 46.8	4 37.8	9 02.0	6 33.2	5 56.6
31 Sa	20 33 35	7♌36 02	3♋25 36	10♋52 13	11♒40.2	11♒30.0	25♋07.7	4♌17.0	9♎14.1	29♌29.2	0♍59.4	27♈47.9	4♉38.3	9♊04.3	6♈32.5	5♒55.2

1st of Month

Julian Day #
2461587.5
Obliquity
23°26'34"
SVP 4♓52'20"
GC 27♐13.4
Eris 26♈09.2

Day	⚴
1	2♋07.1
6	5 06.3
11	8 05.7
16	11 05.1
21	14 04.4
26	17 03.4
31	20 01.9

Day	⚵
1	29♉20.9
6	2♊10.0
11	4 58.5
16	7 46.4
21	10 33.4
26	13 19.6
31	16 04.7

Day	⚶
1	26♊03.8
6	28 12.5
11	0♋20.7
16	2 28.4
21	4 35.4
26	6 41.7
31	8 47.3

DECLINATION and LATITUDE

Day	☉ Decl	☽ Decl	☽ Lat	☽ 12h Decl	☿ Decl	☿ Lat	♀ Decl	♀ Lat	♂ Decl	♂ Lat	⚳ Decl	⚳ Lat	♃ Decl	♃ Lat	♄ Decl	♄ Lat
1 Th	23N08	24N08	5N03	25N31	18N44	4S41	23N16	0S09	3N44	0N39	23N19	7N44	14N01	0N55	7N59	2S25
2 F	23 04	26 31	4 35	27 04	18 45	4 41	23 19	0 06	3 31	0 38	23 11	7 44	13 57	0 55	8 00	2 25
3 Sa	22 59	27 09	3 48	26 43	18 47	4 38	23 22	0 04	3 17	0 37	23 03	7 43	13 53	0 55	8 02	2 25
4 Su	22 55	25 48	2 45	24 24	18 50	4 35	23 24	0 02	3 03	0 36	22 54	7 43	13 49	0 55	8 03	2 26
5 M	22 49	22 34	1 29	20 21	18 55	4 30	23 26	0N01	2 49	0 35	22 46	7 43	13 46	0 55	8 04	2 26
6 Tu	22 44	17 48	0 08	14 60	19 01	4 24	23 27	0 03	2 35	0 34	22 37	7 43	13 42	0 55	8 05	2 26
7 W	22 38	11 60	1S13	8 51	19 08	4 17	23 27	0 06	2 21	0 33	22 29	7 42	13 38	0 55	8 06	2 26
8 Th	22 31	5 38	2 28	2 23	19 16	4 09	23 26	0 08	2 06	0 32	22 20	7 42	13 34	0 55	8 07	2 27
9 F	22 24	0S50	3 32	4S01	19 26	3 60	23 25	0 11	1 52	0 31	22 11	7 42	13 30	0 55	8 08	2 27
10 Sa	22 17	7 06	4 22	10 03	19 36	3 50	23 23	0 13	1 38	0 30	22 02	7 41	13 26	0 55	8 08	2 27
11 Su	22 09	12 51	4 55	15 28	19 47	3 39	23 20	0 15	1 24	0 29	21 54	7 41	13 22	0 55	8 09	2 27
12 M	22 01	17 52	5 12	20 03	19 58	3 28	23 17	0 18	1 09	0 28	21 45	7 41	13 18	0 55	8 10	2 28
13 Tu	21 53	21 58	5 14	23 37	20 10	3 16	23 13	0 20	0 55	0 27	21 36	7 41	13 14	0 55	8 11	2 28
14 W	21 44	24 58	4 60	26 00	20 22	3 04	23 08	0 22	0 40	0 26	21 27	7 40	13 10	0 55	8 12	2 28
15 Th	21 35	26 43	4 32	27 07	20 34	2 51	23 03	0 25	0 26	0 25	21 18	7 40	13 06	0 55	8 12	2 28
16 F	21 26	27 11	3 52	26 55	20 47	2 38	22 57	0 27	0 11	0 24	21 09	7 40	13 02	0 55	8 13	2 29
17 Sa	21 16	26 20	3 03	25 28	20 59	2 24	22 50	0 29	0S03	0 23	20 59	7 40	12 58	0 55	8 14	2 29
18 Su	21 06	24 18	2 06	22 53	21 11	2 11	22 42	0 31	0 18	0 22	20 50	7 39	12 54	0 55	8 14	2 29
19 M	20 55	21 13	1 04	19 20	21 22	1 57	22 34	0 34	0 32	0 21	20 41	7 39	12 50	0 55	8 15	2 29
20 Tu	20 44	17 16	0N01	15 02	21 32	1 43	22 26	0 36	0 47	0 20	20 32	7 39	12 46	0 54	8 15	2 30
21 W	20 33	12 39	1 06	10 10	21 42	1 29	22 16	0 38	1 02	0 19	20 22	7 39	12 41	0 54	8 16	2 30
22 Th	20 21	7 34	2 09	4 54	21 50	1 15	22 06	0 40	1 17	0 18	20 13	7 39	12 37	0 54	8 16	2 30
23 F	20 09	2 10	3 06	0N36	21 57	1 01	21 55	0 42	1 31	0 17	20 03	7 38	12 33	0 54	8 17	2 31
24 Sa	19 57	3N22	3 56	6 08	22 03	0 47	21 44	0 44	1 46	0 16	19 54	7 38	12 29	0 54	8 17	2 31
25 Su	19 45	8 52	4 36	11 33	22 07	0 33	21 32	0 46	2 01	0 15	19 44	7 38	12 24	0 54	8 17	2 31
26 M	19 32	14 09	5 03	16 37	22 09	0 20	21 19	0 48	2 16	0 14	19 35	7 38	12 20	0 54	8 18	2 31
27 Tu	19 18	18 57	5 17	21 05	22 08	0 07	21 06	0 50	2 31	0 13	19 25	7 38	12 16	0 54	8 18	2 32
28 W	19 05	22 58	5 13	24 34	22 06	0N05	20 52	0 52	2 46	0 13	19 16	7 37	12 11	0 54	8 18	2 32
29 Th	18 51	25 50	4 52	26 43	22 01	0 17	20 38	0 54	3 01	0 12	19 06	7 37	12 07	0 54	8 18	2 32
30 F	18 37	27 10	4 13	27 09	21 54	0 28	20 23	0 56	3 16	0 11	18 56	7 37	12 03	0 54	8 19	2 32
31 Sa	18N22	26N40	3N16	25N41	21N44	0N39	20N07	0N57	3S31	0N10	18N46	7N37	11N58	0N54	8N19	2S33

Day	⚷ Decl	⚷ Lat	♅ Decl	♅ Lat	♆ Decl	♆ Lat	♇ Decl	♇ Lat
1	12N42	0S10	21N30	0S06	1N21	1S24	23S12	4S44
6	12 45	0 10	21 32	0 06	1 21	1 25	23 14	4 44
11	12 47	0 11	21 35	0 06	1 21	1 25	23 16	4 45
16	12 49	0 11	21 37	0 06	1 20	1 25	23 19	4 45
21	12 51	0 12	21 39	0 06	1 19	1 25	23 21	4 46
26	12 52	0 12	21 41	0 06	1 18	1 26	23 23	4 46
31	12N52	0S13	21N43	0S06	1N17	1S26	23S25	4S47

Day	⚴ Decl	⚴ Lat	⚵ Decl	⚵ Lat	⚶ Decl	⚶ Lat	Eris Decl	Eris Lat
1	0S42	24S08	12N41	7S30	21N21	2S02	0N33	10S13
6	0 44	24 05	12 57	7 48	21 29	1 57	0 33	10 14
11	0 48	24 02	13 09	8 06	21 34	1 52	0 33	10 14
16	0 55	23 58	13 18	8 24	21 38	1 47	0 33	10 15
21	1 05	23 53	13 24	8 42	21 40	1 41	0 33	10 15
26	1 17	23 48	13 27	9 01	21 40	1 36	0 32	10 15
31	1S32	23S43	13N26	9S20	21N38	1S31	0N32	10S16

Moon Phenomena

Max/0 Decl
dy hr mn
2 19:46 27N10
8 20:52 0 S
15 20:20 27S12
23 9:26 0 N
30 5:45 27N13

Max/0 Lat
dy hr mn
6 2:17 0 S
12 13:40 5S15
19 23:34 0 N
27 7:34 5N18

Perigee/Apogee
dy hr m kilometers
4 20:57 p 358285
19 11:54 a 406216

PH dy hr mn
● 4 3:03 11♋57
☽ 10 18:40 18♎18
○ 18 15:46 25♑49
☊ 18 16:04 A 0.001
☾ 26 16:56 3♉30

Void of Course Moon

Last Aspect			☽ Ingress		
30 22:43	♃	□	♊	1	6:57
3 4:06	☿	☌	♋	3	8:00
5 2:37	♄	□	♌	5	7:41
7 4:12	☿	✶	♍	7	7:58
9 7:30	☿	□	♎	9	10:25
11 14:51	☿	△	♏	11	15:56
13 23:10	♂	✶	♐	14	0:34
16 7:42	♃	△	♑	16	11:40
18 19:07	♄	□	♒	19	0:17
21 11:19	♃	☍	♓	21	13:15
23 15:49	♀	△	♈	24	1:11
26 7:45	♀	□	♉	26	10:29
27 21:29	☿	✶	♊	28	16:11
30 14:50	♄	✶	♋	30	18:26

DAILY ASPECTARIAN

1 Th
☽⚺♄ 1:09
☽⚺♀ 2:54
☽⚺☿ 3:34
♀∥⚳ 6:51
☿☌♀ 9:23
☽⚺⚷ 13:43
☽△♇ 17:54
☽✶♆ 18:01
☽☌♅ 19:53
⚳⫲♇ 20:48
☉⚺☽ 23:24

2 F
☽∠♄ 2:14
⚵ ♊ 3:41
☽✶⚳ 10:52
☉∠♃ 11:51
☽∠⚷ 14:24
☽⚼♇ 18:24
☽□♂ 20:54
☽∥♀ 18:41
☿ D 19:41
☽⫲♇ 19:58
☽∠♅ 20:27
☉∥☽ 22:26
☽✶♂ 22:32
☽∥⚳ 22:47

3 Sa
☽✶♃ 0:46
♀ ♋ 2:03
☽✶♄ 2:40
☽☌☿ 4:06
☽☌♀ 8:31
☽∠⚳ 11:45
☽✶⚷ 14:34
☽⚻♇ 18:25
☽□♆ 18:37
☽⚺♅ 20:33
☉∥⚳ 20:59

4 Su
☽∠♃ 1:02
☉☌☽ 3:03
☽⚺⚳ 12:19

5 M
☽⚺♃ 1:08
☽□♄ 2:37
☽⚺☿ 3:41
☽∥♅ 5:50
☽⚺♀ 12:26
☽□⚷ 14:19
☽☍♇ 18:01
☽△♆ 18:17
☽∥☿ 18:34
♀∠⚳ 19:51
☽✶♅ 20:23
☽∠♂ 23:19

6 Tu
☊ D 2:15
☽∠☿ 3:42
☉⚺☽ 6:01
♀✶⚷ 12:14
☽☌⚳ 13:34
☽∠♀ 14:36
☽∥♃ 17:28
☽⚼♆ 18:23
☽∥⚷ 21:01

7 W
☽⚺♂ 0:25
☽☌♃ 1:50
☽△♄ 2:56
☽✶☿ 4:12
☉∠☽ 8:00
☽∥♄ 14:50
☽△⚷ 14:55
☽✶♀ 17:19
☽⚻♇ 18:35
☽⚻♆ 18:56
☽□♅ 21:16

8 Th
☽⚼♄ 3:47
♀⚻♇ 8:06
☉✶☽ 10:39
♀□♆ 12:29
☽∥♂ 13:33
☽∥♆ 15:52
☽⚼⚷ 16:01
☽⚺⚳ 16:37
☽⚼♇ 19:42

9 F
☽⫲♆ 1:53
☽⫲♂ 3:43
☽☌♂ 4:31
☽⚺♃ 4:37
☽⚻♄ 5:18
☽□☿ 7:30
♂⚺♃ 8:12
☽⚻⚷ 17:51
♀⚺♅ 17:54
☽∠⚳ 19:16
☽△♇ 21:34
☽☍♆ 22:01
♆ R 22:43

10 Sa
☽△♅ 0:40
☽□♀ 1:19
♂⚻♄ 1:41
☽⫲♄ 4:11
⚶ ♋ 4:35
☽∠♃ 7:10
☊ R 18:32
☉□☽ 18:40
☽✶⚳ 22:47
☽⫲⚷ 23:43

11 Su
☽⫲♃ 2:18
☽⚼♅ 3:34
♂∥♆ 5:12
☽✶♃ 10:34
☽☍♄ 10:42
☽⚺♂ 12:03
☽△☿ 14:51
♃△♄ 23:17
☽☍⚷ 23:56

12 M
♀∥♇ 0:58
☽□♇ 3:41
☽⚻♆ 4:15
☽⚻♅ 7:17
☽⫲☿ 12:07
☽△♀ 13:31
☿ ♋ 13:49
☽∠♂ 17:11
☽⚼☿ 20:13
☽⫲♅ 21:30
☽⫲⚳ 21:38
☉⫲☽ 23:28

13 Tu
⚳∥♅ 0:35
♀∠♃ 5:04
☉△☽ 6:40
☽□⚳ 8:30
☽⚼♆ 8:32
☽⫲♀ 8:42
⚳⚼♆ 9:19
☽∥♇ 9:29
☽⚻♄ 19:16
☽□♃ 19:48
☽⚼♀ 21:09
☽✶♂ 23:10

14 W
☽⚻☿ 2:43
☽⚻⚷ 9:05
☽✶♇ 12:48
☽△♆ 13:30
☉⚼☽ 14:02
☽☍♅ 16:54
☉∥♅ 21:24

15 Th
☽⚼♄ 0:35
☉⚺⚳ 1:52
☽⚻♀ 5:40
♂ ♎ 5:42
☽⚼⚷ 14:36
☽∠♇ 18:16
☽△⚳ 21:13
☉⚻☽ 22:07

16 F
☉∠♅ 4:39
☽△♄ 6:24
☽△♃ 7:42
☽□♂ 13:10
☽☍☿ 18:41
☽△⚷ 20:35

17 Sa
☽⚺♇ 0:12
☿∥⚳ 0:35
☽□♆ 1:00
☽⚼⚳ 4:23
☽⚻♅ 4:45
☽⚼♃ 14:21
☿✶⚷ 16:53
☉∥☿ 18:42

18 Su
☽☍♀ 0:34
☽∥♇ 8:26
☽⚼♅ 11:12
☽⚻⚳ 11:54
☽⫲♀ 13:54
☉☍☽ 15:46
☽□♄ 19:07
☽⫲♅ 21:08
☽⚻♃ 21:17
♃∥⚷ 22:57
☽⫲☿ 23:03

19 M
☉⫲☽ 2:05
☽⫲⚳ 3:42
☽△♂ 4:55
☿⚻♇ 5:22
☽□⚷ 9:25
☽☌♇ 12:52
☽⚻☿ 13:44
☽✶♆ 13:47
☿□♆ 14:07
☽△♅ 17:49
☊ D 23:34

20 Tu
☉□♄ 10:50
☽⚼♂ 13:01
☿∥♅ 16:09
☽∠♆ 20:17
☽⚻♀ 20:38
☽⫲⚷ 23:05
☽⫲♃ 23:50
☽⚼☿ 23:58

21 W
☽☍⚳ 3:17
☿⚺♅ 4:16
☽✶♄ 8:18
☉⚻☽ 10:07
☽☍♃ 11:19
☽⫲♄ 20:47
☽⚻♂ 21:00
☽✶⚷ 22:25

22 Th
☽⚺♇ 1:38
☽⚺♆ 2:37
♂⫲♆ 4:10
☉⚺♃ 4:38
☽⚼♀ 6:29
☽□♅ 6:52
☽△☿ 10:17
♀∠♅ 10:20
☽∠♄ 14:38
☿∠⚳ 15:41
☉⚼☽ 18:58
☿∥♀ 21:24

23 F
☉ ♌ 1:06
♂⚻⚷ 2:31
☽∥♂ 2:42
☽⫲♆ 3:43
☽∠⚷ 4:32
☽∠♇ 7:36
☽∥♆ 15:07
☽△♀ 15:49
☽⫲♂ 16:46
☽⚻⚳ 17:46
☽⚺♄ 20:31

24 Sa
☽⚻♃ 0:18
☉△☽ 3:13
♀∥♅ 7:38
☽⚺⚷ 10:06
☽☍♂ 11:39
☽✶♇ 13:02
☽☌♆ 14:04
☽✶♅ 18:23
♀⚺⚳ 21:01
☽∥♄ 21:25

25 Su
☽⚼⚳ 0:06
☉∥⚳ 1:24
☽□☿ 5:46
☽⚼♃ 5:52
☿∠♃ 6:35
♀□♄ 15:21
♂△♇ 15:26
☽∥♃ 15:41
☽∥⚷ 17:59
☽∠♅ 23:04

26 M
♃ ♍ 4:50
☽△⚳ 5:33
☽☌♄ 6:12
☽□♀ 7:45
☽△♃ 10:34
♂☍♆ 13:25
☉□☽ 16:56
☊ R 17:12
☽☌⚷ 18:58
☽□♇ 21:33
☽⚺♆ 22:35
☽⚻♂ 23:02

27 Tu
⚳△♄ 1:21
☉∥☽ 1:50
☽∥⚳ 2:28
☽⚺♅ 2:51
☽∥♀ 11:29
♀ ♌ 12:32
☽∥♅ 15:42
☽∥☿ 18:22
♀⚺♃ 18:52
☉□⚷ 20:56
☽✶☿ 21:29

28 W
☽∠♆ 1:29
☽⫲♇ 3:01
☽⚼♂ 3:09
☽⚺♄ 12:17
☽□⚳ 13:24
☽□♃ 17:05
☽✶♀ 18:52

29 Th
☽⚺⚷ 0:08
☉✶☽ 2:06
☽△♇ 2:25
☽✶♆ 3:27
☽∠☿ 3:31
☽△♂ 6:13
☉☍♇ 6:49
☽☌♅ 7:36
☽∠♄ 13:57
☉△♆ 21:45
☽∠♀ 22:40

30 F
☽∠⚷ 1:24
☽⚼♇ 3:34
☉∠☽ 5:04
☽⚺☿ 8:24
☿∠♅ 10:36
☽✶♄ 14:50
♂△♅ 17:01
☽✶⚳ 17:24
☽✶♃ 19:59

31 Sa
☽⚺♀ 1:31
☽✶⚷ 1:58
☿∥♅ 3:46
☽⚻♇ 4:01
☽□♆ 5:02
♀□⚷ 6:55
☉⚺☽ 7:12
☽⚺♅ 9:08
☽□♂ 9:46
☽∠⚳ 18:20
☽∠♃ 20:28

August 2027

LONGITUDE

Day	Sid.Time	☉	☽	☽ 12 hour	Mean☊	True☊	☿	♀	♂	⚳	♃	♄	⚷	♅	♆	♇
	h m s	° ' "	° ' "	° ' "	° '	° '	° '	° '	° '	° '	° '	° '	° '	° '	° '	° '
1 Su	20 37 32	8♌33 26	18♋22 42	25♋56 04	11♒37.0	11♒29.7	27♋05.4	5♌31.0	9♎50.2	29♌56.2	1♍11.8	27♈48.8	4♉38.7	9♊06.4	6♈31.9	5♒53.8
2 M	20 41 28	9 30 52	3♌31 13	11♌06 57	11 33.9	11D 29.6	29 05.1	6 45.0	10 26.4	0♍23.3	1 24.4	27 49.7	4 39.0	9 08.6	6R 31.2	5R 52.4
3 Tu	20 45 25	10 28 18	18 42 05	26 15 27	11 30.7	11 29.6	1♌06.5	7 59.0	11 02.7	0 50.3	1 36.9	27 50.5	4 39.3	9 10.7	6 30.4	5 51.0
4 W	20 49 21	11 25 45	3♍45 55	11♍12 31	11 27.5	11R 29.6	3 09.1	9 13.0	11 39.1	1 17.4	1 49.5	27 51.1	4 39.6	9 12.7	6 29.7	5 49.6
5 Th	20 53 18	12 23 12	18 34 20	25 50 41	11 24.3	11 29.6	5 12.8	10 27.0	12 15.6	1 44.5	2 02.1	27 51.7	4 39.8	9 14.7	6 28.9	5 48.2
6 F	20 57 15	13 20 41	3♎01 00	10♎04 54	11 21.1	11 29.4	7 17.1	11 41.0	12 52.2	2 11.6	2 14.8	27 52.1	4 39.9	9 16.7	6 28.1	5 46.8
7 Sa	21 01 11	14 18 10	17 02 12	23 52 50	11 18.0	11 29.2	9 21.7	12 55.1	13 28.9	2 38.8	2 27.4	27 52.4	4 40.0	9 18.6	6 27.2	5 45.4
8 Su	21 05 08	15 15 39	0♏36 52	7♏14 30	11 14.8	11 28.9	11 26.4	14 09.1	14 05.8	3 06.0	2 40.2	27 52.7	4R 40.1	9 20.5	6 26.3	5 44.0
9 M	21 09 04	16 13 10	13 46 03	20 11 51	11 11.6	11D 28.8	13 30.8	15 23.2	14 42.7	3 33.2	2 52.9	27R 52.8	4 40.0	9 22.3	6 25.4	5 42.7
10 Tu	21 13 01	17 10 42	26 32 22	2♐48 03	11 08.4	11 28.9	15 34.8	16 37.3	15 19.7	4 00.4	3 05.6	27 52.8	4 40.0	9 24.1	6 24.5	5 41.3
11 W	21 16 57	18 08 14	8♐59 23	15 06 53	11 05.3	11 29.3	17 38.2	17 51.4	15 56.8	4 27.7	3 18.4	27 52.7	4 39.8	9 25.9	6 23.6	5 39.9
12 Th	21 20 54	19 05 47	21 11 04	27 12 25	11 02.1	11 29.9	19 40.7	19 05.5	16 34.0	4 55.0	3 31.2	27 52.6	4 39.7	9 27.6	6 22.6	5 38.6
13 F	21 24 50	20 03 21	3♑11 25	9♑08 32	10 58.9	11 30.7	21 42.3	20 19.7	17 11.3	5 22.3	3 44.1	27 52.3	4 39.4	9 29.3	6 21.6	5 37.2
14 Sa	21 28 47	21 00 56	15 04 13	20 58 52	10 55.7	11 31.6	23 42.8	21 33.8	17 48.7	5 49.6	3 56.9	27 51.9	4 39.1	9 30.9	6 20.5	5 35.9
15 Su	21 32 44	21 58 33	26 52 54	2♒46 39	10 52.6	11 32.3	25 42.2	22 48.0	18 26.2	6 16.9	4 09.8	27 51.4	4 38.8	9 32.5	6 19.5	5 34.6
16 M	21 36 40	22 56 10	8♒40 29	14 34 42	10 49.4	11R 32.7	27 40.3	24 02.1	19 03.8	6 44.3	4 22.7	27 50.8	4 38.4	9 34.0	6 18.4	5 33.2
17 Tu	21 40 37	23 53 48	20 29 36	26 25 28	10 46.2	11 32.6	29 37.1	25 16.3	19 41.5	7 11.6	4 35.6	27 50.1	4 37.9	9 35.5	6 17.3	5 31.9
18 W	21 44 33	24 51 28	2♓22 35	8♓21 11	10 43.0	11 31.8	1♍32.5	26 30.5	20 19.3	7 39.0	4 48.5	27 49.3	4 37.4	9 36.9	6 16.2	5 30.6
19 Th	21 48 30	25 49 09	14 21 32	20 23 52	10 39.8	11 30.3	3 26.6	27 44.7	20 57.1	8 06.4	5 01.4	27 48.4	4 36.9	9 38.3	6 15.0	5 29.3
20 F	21 52 26	26 46 51	26 28 28	2♈35 34	10 36.7	11 28.3	5 19.4	28 59.0	21 35.1	8 33.8	5 14.4	27 47.4	4 36.2	9 39.6	6 13.8	5 28.0
21 Sa	21 56 23	27 44 35	8♈45 26	14 58 21	10 33.5	11 25.9	7 10.7	0♍13.2	22 13.1	9 01.3	5 27.3	27 46.3	4 35.6	9 40.9	6 12.6	5 26.8
22 Su	22 00 19	28 42 20	21 14 36	27 34 27	10 30.3	11 23.5	9 00.6	1 27.5	22 51.3	9 28.7	5 40.3	27 45.1	4 34.9	9 42.2	6 11.4	5 25.5
23 M	22 04 16	29 40 07	3♉58 13	10♉26 12	10 27.1	11 21.5	10 49.2	2 41.7	23 29.5	9 56.2	5 53.3	27 43.8	4 34.1	9 43.4	6 10.2	5 24.2
24 Tu	22 08 13	0♍37 55	16 58 40	23 35 53	10 23.9	11 20.1	12 36.3	3 56.0	24 07.8	10 23.7	6 06.3	27 42.3	4 33.3	9 44.5	6 08.9	5 23.0
25 W	22 12 09	1 35 46	0♊18 07	7♊05 34	10 20.8	11D 19.5	14 22.1	5 10.3	24 46.2	10 51.2	6 19.3	27 40.8	4 32.4	9 45.7	6 07.6	5 21.8
26 Th	22 16 06	2 33 38	13 58 22	20 56 36	10 17.6	11 19.8	16 06.6	6 24.6	25 24.7	11 18.7	6 32.3	27 39.2	4 31.4	9 46.7	6 06.3	5 20.6
27 F	22 20 02	3 31 32	28 00 14	5♋09 10	10 14.4	11 20.9	17 49.6	7 39.0	26 03.4	11 46.2	6 45.4	27 37.5	4 30.5	9 47.7	6 05.0	5 19.4
28 Sa	22 23 59	4 29 28	12♋23 09	19 41 47	10 11.2	11 22.3	19 31.4	8 53.3	26 42.1	12 13.8	6 58.4	27 35.7	4 29.4	9 48.7	6 03.7	5 18.2
29 Su	22 27 55	5 27 26	27 04 32	4♌30 45	10 08.1	11R 23.4	21 11.9	10 07.7	27 20.8	12 41.3	7 11.4	27 33.8	4 28.3	9 49.6	6 02.3	5 17.0
30 M	22 31 52	6 25 25	11♌59 36	19 30 11	10 04.9	11 23.9	22 51.0	11 22.1	27 59.7	13 08.9	7 24.5	27 31.8	4 27.2	9 50.5	6 00.9	5 15.8
31 Tu	22 35 48	7♍23 26	27 01 28	4♍32 20	10♒01.7	11♒23.2	24♍28.9	12♍36.5	28♎38.7	13♍36.4	7♍37.5	27♈29.7	4♉26.0	9♊51.3	5♈59.5	5♒14.7

1st of Month

Julian Day # 2461618.5
Obliquity 23°26'■4"
SVP 4♓52'■4"
GC 27♐13.5
Eris 26♈11.3R

Day	⚴	⚵	⚶
1	20♋37.6	16♊37.6	9♋12.3
6	23 35.4	19 21.0	11 16.8
11	26 32.5	22 03.0	13 20.2
16	29 28.5	24 43.1	15 22.5
21	2♌23.4	27 21.4	17 23.6
26	5 17.1	29 57.4	19 23.3
31	8 09.4	2♋31.0	21 21.5

DECLINATION and LATITUDE

Day	☉ Decl	☽ Decl	☽ Lat	☽ 12h Decl	☿ Decl	☿ Lat	♀ Decl	♀ Lat	♂ Decl	♂ Lat	⚳ Decl	⚳ Lat	♃ Decl	♃ Lat	♄ Decl	♄ Lat
1 Su	18N07	24N14	2N05	22N21	21N32	0N49	19N51	0N59	3S45	0N09	18N36	7N37	11N54	0N54	8N19	2S33
2 M	17 52	20 05	0 44	17 28	21 17	0 58	19 34	1 01	4 01	0 08	18 26	7 37	11 49	0 54	8 19	2 33
3 Tu	17 37	14 35	0S40	11 29	20 59	1 06	19 17	1 02	4 16	0 07	18 17	7 37	11 45	0 54	8 19	2 34
4 W	17 21	8 15	2 01	4 56	20 39	1 14	18 59	1 04	4 31	0 06	18 07	7 36	11 40	0 54	8 19	2 34
5 Th	17 05	1 34	3 12	1S45	20 16	1 21	18 40	1 06	4 46	0 06	17 57	7 36	11 36	0 54	8 19	2 34
6 F	16 49	5S00	4 09	8 09	19 51	1 27	18 21	1 07	5 01	0 05	17 47	7 36	11 31	0 54	8 19	2 34
7 Sa	16 32	11 09	4 49	13 57	19 23	1 32	18 02	1 08	5 16	0 04	17 36	7 36	11 27	0 54	8 19	2 35
8 Su	16 15	16 33	5 12	18 55	18 53	1 36	17 42	1 10	5 31	0 03	17 26	7 36	11 22	0 54	8 18	2 35
9 M	15 58	21 01	5 17	22 50	18 21	1 39	17 21	1 11	5 46	0 02	17 16	7 36	11 18	0 54	8 18	2 35
10 Tu	15 41	24 21	5 07	25 33	17 47	1 42	17 00	1 12	6 01	0 01	17 06	7 36	11 13	0 54	8 18	2 35
11 W	15 24	26 26	4 42	26 59	17 12	1 44	16 39	1 14	6 16	0 00	16 56	7 36	11 08	0 55	8 18	2 36
12 Th	15 06	27 13	4 05	27 07	16 35	1 45	16 17	1 15	6 31	0S00	16 46	7 36	11 04	0 55	8 17	2 36
13 F	14 48	26 41	3 17	25 57	15 56	1 46	15 54	1 16	6 46	0 01	16 35	7 35	10 59	0 55	8 17	2 36
14 Sa	14 29	24 56	2 22	23 38	15 16	1 46	15 32	1 17	7 01	0 02	16 25	7 35	10 54	0 55	8 17	2 37
15 Su	14 11	22 06	1 20	20 19	14 36	1 45	15 08	1 18	7 16	0 03	16 15	7 35	10 50	0 55	8 16	2 37
16 M	13 52	18 21	0 16	16 11	13 54	1 43	14 45	1 19	7 31	0 04	16 04	7 35	10 45	0 55	8 16	2 37
17 Tu	13 33	13 53	0N49	11 26	13 11	1 41	14 21	1 20	7 46	0 04	15 54	7 35	10 40	0 55	8 15	2 37
18 W	13 14	8 52	1 53	6 13	12 28	1 39	13 56	1 20	8 01	0 05	15 44	7 35	10 36	0 55	8 15	2 38
19 Th	12 55	3 31	2 52	0 45	11 44	1 36	13 32	1 21	8 16	0 06	15 33	7 35	10 31	0 55	8 14	2 38
20 F	12 35	2N01	3 44	4N48	10 59	1 32	13 06	1 22	8 31	0 07	15 23	7 35	10 26	0 55	8 14	2 38
21 Sa	12 15	7 33	4 26	10 15	10 14	1 28	12 41	1 22	8 46	0 08	15 12	7 35	10 22	0 55	8 13	2 38
22 Su	11 55	12 52	4 57	15 22	9 29	1 23	12 15	1 23	9 01	0 08	15 02	7 35	10 17	0 55	8 12	2 39
23 M	11 35	17 45	5 13	19 56	8 43	1 19	11 49	1 24	9 16	0 09	14 51	7 35	10 12	0 55	8 11	2 39
24 Tu	11 15	21 55	5 14	23 39	7 58	1 13	11 22	1 24	9 31	0 10	14 41	7 35	10 07	0 55	8 11	2 39
25 W	10 54	25 04	4 59	26 10	7 12	1 08	10 55	1 24	9 45	0 11	14 30	7 35	10 03	0 55	8 10	2 39
26 Th	10 34	26 53	4 26	27 11	6 26	1 02	10 28	1 25	10 00	0 11	14 19	7 35	9 58	0 55	8 09	2 40
27 F	10 13	27 02	3 37	26 27	5 40	0 56	10 01	1 25	10 15	0 12	14 09	7 35	9 53	0 55	8 08	2 40
28 Sa	9 52	25 24	2 33	23 55	4 54	0 50	9 33	1 25	10 30	0 13	13 58	7 35	9 48	0 55	8 07	2 40
29 Su	9 31	22 01	1 18	19 45	4 09	0 43	9 05	1 25	10 44	0 14	13 47	7 35	9 43	0 55	8 07	2 40
30 M	9 09	17 08	0S03	14 16	3 23	0 36	8 37	1 25	10 59	0 14	13 37	7 35	9 39	0 55	8 06	2 41
31 Tu	8N48	11N10	1S25	7N55	2N38	0N29	8N08	1N25	11S14	0S15	13N26	7N35	9N34	0N55	8N05	2S41

Day	⚷ Decl	⚷ Lat	♅ Decl	♅ Lat	♆ Decl	♆ Lat	♇ Decl	♇ Lat
1	12N52	0S13	21N43	0S06	1N17	1S26	23S26	4S47
6	12 52	0 13	21 44	0 06	1 15	1 26	23 28	4 47
11	12 52	0 14	21 46	0 06	1 13	1 27	23 30	4 48
16	12 51	0 14	21 47	0 06	1 11	1 27	23 32	4 48
21	12 49	0 14	21 48	0 06	1 08	1 27	23 33	4 48
26	12 48	0 15	21 49	0 06	1 05	1 27	23 35	4 48
31	12N45	0S15	21N50	0S06	1N03	1S27	23S37	4S48

Day	⚴ Decl	⚴ Lat	⚵ Decl	⚵ Lat	⚶ Decl	⚶ Lat	Eris Decl	Eris Lat
1	1S35	23S41	13N25	9S24	21N38	1S30	0N32	10S16
6	1 53	23 35	13 20	9 43	21 33	1 24	0 31	10 16
11	2 14	23 28	13 11	10 02	21 28	1 19	0 31	10 16
16	2 36	23 20	12 59	10 22	21 20	1 13	0 30	10 17
21	3 01	23 11	12 43	10 42	21 11	1 08	0 29	10 17
26	3 27	23 02	12 24	11 02	21 01	1 02	0 28	10 17
31	3S56	22S53	12N02	11S23	20N49	0S56	0N28	10S18

Moon Phenomena

Max/0 Decl
dy hr mn
5 5:40 0 S
12 2:08 27S13
19 15:16 0 N
26 14:17 27N11

Max/0 Lat
dy hr mn
2 12:35 0 S
8 19:46 5S18
16 5:50 0 N
23 13:40 5N16
29 23:02 0 S

Perigee/Apogee
dy hr m kilometers
2 6:26 p 357365
15 14:24 a 406085
30 15:43 p 359210

PH dy hr mn
● 2 10:06 9♌55
● 2 607:50T 06■23"
☽ 9 4:55 16♏25
○ 17 7:30 24♒12
● 17 7:15 A 0.545
☾ 25 2:28 1♊42
● 31 17:42 8♍06

Void of Course Moon

Last Aspect	☽ Ingress
1 15:55 ☿ ☌	♌ 1 18:26
3 14:32 ♄ △	♍ 3 17:58
4 8:47 ♅ □	♎ 5 18:56
7 19:06 ♄ ☍	♏ 7 22:54
9 4:55 ☉ □	♐ 10 6:37
12 13:20 ♄ △	♑ 12 17:36
15 1:59 ♄ □	♒ 15 6:21
17 14:50 ♄ ⚹	♓ 17 19:13
18 14:33 ♅ □	♈ 20 6:56
22 15:17 ☉ △	♉ 22 16:34
23 14:44 ☿ △	♊ 24 23:28
26 23:22 ♄ ⚹	♋ 27 3:22
29 0:47 ♄ □	♌ 29 4:44
31 2:42 ♂ ⚹	♍ 31 4:45

DAILY ASPECTARIAN

1 Su: ⚳ ♍ 3:21; ☽ # ♇ 5:29; ♀ ☍ ♇ 7:15; ☿ □ ♄ 8:49; ☽ ∠ ♅ 9:07; ☉ ⚹ ♅ 14:19; ☽ □ ♄ 14:59; ☽ ∥ ♅ 15:33; ☽ ☌ ☿ 15:55; ☽ ∥ ☿ 17:31; ☽ ⊻ ⚳ 18:54; ♀ △ ♆ 19:34; ☽ ⊻ ♃ 20:37

2 M: ☽ □ ⚷ 1:47; ☽ ∥ ♀ 2:38; ☽ ☍ ♇ 3:43; ☽ △ ♆ 4:44; ☽ ☌ ♀ 5:33; ☽ ∥ ⚳ 7:56; ☽ ⚹ ♅ 8:54; ☉ ☌ ☽ 10:06; ☉ ∥ ☽ 10:45; ☿ ♌ 10:54; ☽ ⚹ ♂ 11:23; ☊ D 12:21; ☿ ⊻ ⚳ 19:55

3 Tu: ☽ ⚼ ♆ 4:27; ☿ ⊻ ♃ 6:40; ☽ ∥ ⚷ 6:44; ☽ ∥ ♃ 11:10; ☽ ∠ ♂ 12:09; ☽ △ ♄ 14:32; ☽ ☌ ⚳ 19:55; ☽ ☌ ♃ 20:51; ☽ ⊻ ☿ 22:52; ☽ ∥ ♄ 23:46; ♀ ⚹ ♅ 23:55

4 W: ☽ △ ⚷ 1:26; ☊ R 1:47; ☽ ⊼ ♇ 3:18; ☽ ⊼ ♆ 4:23; ☽ □ ♅ 8:47; ☽ ⊻ ♀ 9:34; ☽ # ♂ 13:01; ☉ ⊻ ☽ 13:13; ☽ ⊻ ♂ 13:16; ☽ ⚼ ♄ 14:41; ☉ ⚹ ♂ 15:17; ☿ □ ⚷ 17:36

5 Th: ☽ ∥ ♆ 1:09; ☽ ⚼ ⚷ 1:47; ☽ ∠ ☿ 3:08; ☽ ⚼ ♇ 3:40; ☿ ☍ ♇ 6:46; ☽ # ♆ 10:11; ☽ ∠ ♀ 12:24; ☿ △ ♆ 14:36; ☽ ⊼ ♄ 15:22; ☉ ∠ ☽ 15:36; ☽ ⊻ ⚳ 22:34; ☽ ⊻ ♃ 22:41

6 F: ☽ ∥ ♂ 0:01; ☽ ⊼ ⚷ 2:47; ☽ △ ♇ 4:40; ⚳ ☌ ♃ 5:11; ☽ ☍ ♆ 5:50; ☽ ⚹ ☿ 8:29; ☽ △ ♅ 10:39; ☽ # ♄ 12:38; ☽ ⚹ ♀ 16:11; ☽ ☌ ♂ 17:34; ☉ ⚹ ☽ 18:55; ☿ ⚹ ♅ 23:24

7 Sa: ☽ ∠ ♃ 0:45; ☽ ∠ ⚳ 1:06; ☽ # ♃ 1:14; ☽ # ⚷ 7:16; ☽ ⚼ ♅ 12:47; ☽ ☍ ♄ 19:06; ♀ ⚹ ♂ 21:49; ☉ # ☽ 22:40

8 Su: ⚷ R 2:56; ☽ ⚹ ♃ 3:46; ☽ # ⚳ 4:13; ☽ ⚹ ⚳ 4:38; ☽ # ♀ 5:17; ☽ ☍ ⚷ 7:19; ☽ □ ♇ 9:14; ☽ ⊼ ♆ 10:32; ☽ # ☿ 10:37; ☽ ⊼ ♅ 15:53; ☽ □ ☿ 23:26

9 M: ☽ ⊻ ♂ 1:50; ☽ □ ♀ 3:19; ☊ D 4:24; ☽ # ♅ 4:42; ☉ □ ☽ 4:55; ♀ ∥ ⚳ 11:06; ☽ ⚼ ♆ 14:17; ☽ ∥ ♇ 16:55; ♄ R 18:07; ☿ ⚹ ♂ 19:49

10 Tu: ☽ ⊼ ♄ 2:33; ☽ ∠ ♂ 7:37; ☽ □ ♃ 12:47; ☽ □ ⚳ 14:52; ☽ ⊼ ⚷ 15:36; ☽ ⚹ ♇ 17:33; ☽ △ ♆ 18:57

11 W: ☽ ☍ ♅ 0:52; ☿ ☌ ♀ 6:31; ☽ ⚼ ♄ 7:36; ⚳ △ ⚷ 10:37; ☉ ☌ ☿ 11:03; ☽ ⚹ ♂ 14:22; ☿ ∥ ⚳ 14:27; ☽ △ ♀ 19:23; ☉ △ ☽ 19:30; ☽ △ ☿ 20:25; ☽ ⚼ ⚷ 20:59; ☽ ∠ ♇ 22:56

12 Th: ☉ ☌ ♀ 0:22; ☽ △ ♄ 13:20; ☿ ⚼ ♆ 19:56

13 F: ☽ △ ♃ 1:07; ☿ ∥ ♀ 2:33; ☽ △ ⚷ 2:57; ☉ ⚼ ☽ 4:05; ☽ △ ⚳ 4:34; ☽ ⚼ ♀ 4:48; ☽ ⊻ ♇ 4:53; ☽ □ ♆ 6:22; ☽ ⚼ ☿ 8:31; ⚳ ⊼ ♇ 12:33; ☽ ⊼ ♅ 12:44; ♀ ⚼ ♆ 19:46

14 Sa: ☽ □ ♂ 5:52; ☽ ⚼ ♃ 8:01; ☉ ⚼ ♆ 8:01; ☽ ⚼ ⚳ 12:09; ☽ ∥ ♇ 13:00; ☉ ⊼ ☽ 13:08; ☽ ⊼ ♀ 14:43; ☽ ⚼ ♅ 19:14; ☽ ⊼ ☿ 21:07

15 Su: ☽ □ ♄ 1:59; ⚳ ⊼ ♆ 2:11; ☽ # ♅ 2:14; ☽ ⊼ ♃ 15:06; ☽ □ ⚷ 15:48; ☽ ☌ ♇ 17:40; ☽ ⚹ ♆ 19:11; ☽ ⊼ ⚳ 19:54

16 M: ☉ ∥ ☿ 1:34; ☽ △ ♅ 1:49; ☿ △ ♄ 2:08; ☊ R 5:49; ☽ # ⚳ 13:08; ♂ ∠ ♃ 18:17; ☽ # ♀ 21:24; ⚴ ♌ 21:34; ☽ △ ♂ 22:17

17 Tu: ☽ ∠ ♆ 1:36; ☉ # ☽ 1:43; ☽ # ☿ 4:03; ♃ △ ⚷ 4:13; ☿ ♍ 4:44; ☽ # ⚷ 5:08; ☉ ☍ ☽ 7:30; ☽ ☍ ♀ 10:48; ☿ ∥ ⚷ 11:25; ☽ ⚹ ♄ 14:50; ☽ # ♃ 15:50; ☽ ☍ ☿ 22:00

18 W: ☽ # ♄ 2:52; ☽ ∥ ♂ 3:43; ☽ ⚹ ⚷ 4:31; ☽ ☍ ♃ 4:59; ☽ ⚼ ♂ 6:15; ☽ ⊻ ♇ 6:17; ☽ ⊻ ♆ 7:49; ☽ ☍ ⚳ 11:01; ☽ □ ♅ 14:33; ♂ # ♄ 20:53; ☽ ∠ ♄ 20:55

19 Th: ♀ △ ♄ 1:10; ☉ ∥ ⚷ 5:49; ☽ # ♆ 10:18; ☽ ∠ ⚷ 10:26; ☽ ∠ ♇ 12:10; ☽ ⊼ ♂ 13:49; ☿ △ ⚷ 14:50; ☽ ∥ ♆ 20:13; ☿ ☌ ♃ 22:48

20 F: ☉ ⊼ ☽ 0:39; ☿ ⊼ ♇ 1:50; ☽ ⊻ ♄ 2:35; ☽ ⊼ ♀ 5:29; ☿ ⊼ ♆ 11:35; ♀ ∥ ⚷ 15:46; ☽ ⊻ ⚷ 15:55; ☽ ⊼ ♃ 17:28; ☽ ⚹ ♇ 17:35; ☽ ☌ ♆ 19:04; ☿ ∥ ♃ 19:34; ♀ ♍ 19:44; ☽ ⊼ ☿ 20:24; ♃ ⊼ ♇ 23:01

21 Sa: ☽ ⊼ ⚳ 0:32; ☉ △ ♄ 0:42; ☿ ∠ ♂ 0:48; ☽ ⚹ ♅ 1:48; ☽ ∥ ♄ 2:56; ☽ # ♂ 5:39; ☉ ⚼ ☽ 8:21; ☽ ∥ ☿ 10:29; ☽ ∥ ♃ 12:20; ☽ ⚼ ♀ 13:51; ☉ ∥ ☽ 19:54; ☽ ∥ ♀ 21:22; ☽ ⚼ ♃ 22:54; ☽ ∥ ⚷ 23:48

22 Su: ☽ ☍ ♂ 3:14; ☽ ⚼ ☿ 6:08; ☽ ⚼ ⚳ 6:23; ☽ ∠ ♅ 6:35; ☿ ☌ ⚳ 8:16; ☿ □ ♅ 9:16; ☽ ∥ ⚳ 9:57; ☿ # ♂ 11:06; ⚳ □ ♅ 12:19; ☽ ☌ ♄ 12:19; ☉ △ ☽ 15:17; ☽ △ ♀ 21:22

23 M: ☽ ☌ ⚷ 1:07; ☽ □ ♇ 2:40; ☽ △ ♃ 3:38; ☽ ⊻ ♆ 4:05; ☉ ♍ 8:15; ☽ ⊻ ♅ 10:42; ☽ △ ⚳ 11:29; ☽ △ ☿ 14:44; ☿ ∥ ♄ 16:59; ☽ ∥ ♅ 23:19

24 Tu: ☿ ⚼ ♄ 1:20; ♃ ⊼ ♆ 4:22; ☽ ∠ ♆ 7:34; ☽ # ♇ 11:29; ♀ △ ⚷ 11:53; ☽ ⊼ ♂ 13:37; ☽ ⊻ ♄ 19:20; ♂ ⚼ ♅ 23:38

25 W: ☉ □ ☽ 2:28; ☊ D 2:29; ☉ ∥ ♀ 3:23; ♀ ⊼ ♇ 3:38; ☽ ⊻ ⚷ 7:30; ☽ △ ♇ 8:57; ☽ □ ♀ 9:29; ☽ ⚹ ♆ 10:17; ☽ □ ♃ 10:49; ☽ ☌ ♅ 16:42; ☽ ⚼ ♂ 17:30; ♀ ⊼ ♆ 18:11; ☽ □ ⚳ 19:13; ♂ # ♃ 20:57; ☽ ∠ ♄ 21:43

26 Th: ⚵ ♋ 1:59; ♀ ☌ ♃ 3:01; ☽ □ ☿ 4:13; ☽ ∠ ⚷ 9:33; ☽ ⚼ ♇ 10:57; ♀ # ♂ 15:54; ☽ △ ♂ 20:33; ☉ # ♂ 22:33; ☽ ⚹ ♄ 23:22

27 F: ♀ ∥ ♃ 8:09; ☉ ⚹ ☽ 9:57; ☽ ⚹ ⚷ 10:55; ☽ ⊼ ♇ 12:16; ☽ □ ♆ 13:32; ☽ ⚹ ♃ 14:54; ☽ ⚹ ♀ 17:40; ☽ ⊻ ♅ 19:44; ☿ ⚼ ⚷ 23:32; ☽ ⚹ ⚳ 23:44; ☉ △ ⚷ 23:59

28 Sa: ☉ ∥ ♃ 5:20; ☿ ⚼ ♇ 11:00; ☉ ∠ ☽ 12:29; ☽ ⚹ ☿ 13:14; ☽ # ♇ 14:11; ☽ ∠ ♃ 15:57; ⚳ ⚼ ♄ 17:53; ♀ □ ♅ 18:05; ☉ ⊼ ♇ 19:46; ☽ ∠ ♅ 20:21; ☽ ∠ ♀ 20:33

29 Su: ☽ □ ♂ 0:28; ☽ □ ♄ 0:47; ☽ ∠ ⚳ 1:01; ☽ ∥ ♅ 1:06; ♂ ☍ ♄ 7:37; ☽ □ ⚷ 11:55; ☽ ☍ ♇ 13:13; ☉ ⊼ ♆ 14:06; ☽ △ ♆ 14:26; ☉ ⊻ ☽ 14:27; ☽ ∠ ☿ 16:32; ☽ ⊻ ♃ 16:33; ☽ ⚹ ♅ 20:33; ☽ ⊻ ♀ 22:54; ☊ R 23:03

30 M: ☽ ⊻ ⚳ 1:54; ☽ ⚼ ♆ 14:23; ☽ ∥ ⚳ 15:02; ☽ ∥ ⚷ 17:56; ♂ ∠ ⚳ 19:16; ☽ ⊻ ☿ 19:27; ♀ ⚼ ♄ 21:53; ☽ # ♂ 23:48

31 Tu: ☽ △ ♄ 0:45; ☽ ⚹ ♂ 2:42; ♀ ∥ ♄ 3:12; ☽ ∥ ♃ 6:05; ☉ ☌ ♃ 7:31; ☉ ∥ ☽ 9:20; ☽ ∥ ♄ 11:28; ☽ △ ⚷ 11:49; ☽ ∥ ♀ 12:05; ☽ ⊼ ♇ 13:07; ☽ ⊼ ♆ 14:18; ☽ ☌ ♃ 17:11; ☉ ☌ ☽ 17:42; ☽ □ ♅ 20:32

LONGITUDE

September 2027

Day	Sid.Time	☉	☽	☽ 12 hour	Mean ☊	True ☊	☿	♀	♂	⚳	♃	♄	⚷	♅	♆	♇
	h m s	° ' "	° ' "	° ' "	° '	° '	° '	° '	° '	° '	° '	° '	° '	° '	° '	° '
1 W	22 39 45	8♍21 29	12♍01 43	19♍28 30	9♒58.5	11♒21.3	26♍05.5	13♍50.8	29♎17.8	14♍04.0	7♍50.6	27♈27.5	4♉24.8	9♊52.0	5♈58.1	5♒13.6
2 Th	22 43 42	9 19 33	26 51 39	4♎10 16	9 55.4	11R 18.0	27 40.8	15 05.3	29 56.9	14 31.6	8 03.6	27R 25.2	4R 23.5	9 52.7	5R 56.7	5R 12.5
3 F	22 47 38	10 17 39	11♎23 31	18 30 49	9 52.2	11 14.0	29 14.9	16 19.7	0♏36.2	14 59.2	8 16.6	27 22.8	4 22.2	9 53.4	5 55.2	5 11.4
4 Sa	22 51 35	11 15 46	25 31 40	2♏25 46	9 49.0	11 09.6	0♎47.7	17 34.1	1 15.5	15 26.8	8 29.7	27 20.3	4 20.8	9 54.0	5 53.7	5 10.3
5 Su	22 55 31	12 13 55	9♏13 02	15 53 28	9 45.8	11 05.7	2 19.2	18 48.5	1 54.9	15 54.4	8 42.7	27 17.8	4 19.3	9 54.6	5 52.2	5 09.2
6 M	22 59 28	13 12 06	22 27 17	28 54 45	9 42.6	11 02.7	3 49.5	20 03.0	2 34.4	16 22.0	8 55.7	27 15.1	4 17.8	9 55.1	5 50.8	5 08.2
7 Tu	23 03 24	14 10 17	5♐16 17	11♐32 22	9 39.5	11D 00.9	5 18.5	21 17.4	3 14.0	16 49.7	9 08.7	27 12.3	4 16.3	9 55.5	5 49.2	5 07.2
8 W	23 07 21	15 08 31	17 43 32	23 50 23	9 36.3	11 00.6	6 46.3	22 31.9	3 53.7	17 17.3	9 21.8	27 09.5	4 14.7	9 55.9	5 47.7	5 06.2
9 Th	23 11 17	16 06 45	29 53 31	5♑53 33	9 33.1	11 01.4	8 12.8	23 46.3	4 33.4	17 44.9	9 34.8	27 06.6	4 13.1	9 56.3	5 46.2	5 05.2
10 F	23 15 14	17 05 02	11♑51 06	17 46 48	9 29.9	11 03.0	9 38.0	25 00.8	5 13.3	18 12.5	9 47.7	27 03.6	4 11.4	9 56.6	5 44.6	5 04.2
11 Sa	23 19 11	18 03 19	23 41 13	29 34 56	9 26.8	11 04.6	11 01.8	26 15.2	5 53.2	18 40.1	10 00.7	27 00.5	4 09.7	9 56.9	5 43.1	5 03.3
12 Su	23 23 07	19 01 39	5♒28 28	11♒22 20	9 23.6	11R 05.8	12 24.4	27 29.7	6 33.2	19 07.8	10 13.7	26 57.3	4 08.0	9 57.1	5 41.5	5 02.3
13 M	23 27 04	20 00 00	17 16 58	23 12 48	9 20.4	11 05.7	13 45.5	28 44.2	7 13.3	19 35.4	10 26.6	26 54.1	4 06.2	9 57.2	5 39.9	5 01.4
14 Tu	23 31 00	20 58 22	29 10 12	5♓09 29	9 17.2	11 04.0	15 05.3	29 58.7	7 53.5	20 03.0	10 39.6	26 50.8	4 04.3	9 57.3	5 38.3	5 00.6
15 W	23 34 57	21 56 47	11♓10 56	17 14 47	9 14.0	11 00.4	16 23.6	1♎13.1	8 33.7	20 30.6	10 52.5	26 47.4	4 02.4	9R 57.3	5 36.7	4 59.7
16 Th	23 38 53	22 55 13	23 21 13	29 30 24	9 10.9	10 54.9	17 40.3	2 27.6	9 14.1	20 58.3	11 05.4	26 43.9	4 00.5	9 57.3	5 35.1	4 58.8
17 F	23 42 50	23 53 41	5♈42 27	11♈57 28	9 07.7	10 47.9	18 55.6	3 42.1	9 54.5	21 25.9	11 18.3	26 40.3	3 58.5	9 57.3	5 33.5	4 58.0
18 Sa	23 46 46	24 52 11	18 15 29	24 36 36	9 04.5	10 40.1	20 09.1	4 56.6	10 35.0	21 53.5	11 31.1	26 36.7	3 56.5	9 57.2	5 31.9	4 57.2
19 Su	23 50 43	25 50 43	1♉00 49	7♉28 11	9 01.3	10 32.2	21 21.0	6 11.1	11 15.5	22 21.1	11 43.9	26 33.0	3 54.5	9 57.0	5 30.2	4 56.5
20 M	23 54 40	26 49 17	13 58 45	20 32 34	8 58.2	10 25.1	22 31.0	7 25.6	11 56.2	22 48.7	11 56.8	26 29.3	3 52.4	9 56.8	5 28.6	4 55.7
21 Tu	23 58 36	27 47 53	27 09 41	3♊50 11	8 55.0	10 19.4	23 39.2	8 40.1	12 36.9	23 16.3	12 09.6	26 25.4	3 50.3	9 56.5	5 26.9	4 55.0
22 W	0 02 33	28 46 32	10♊34 08	17 21 36	8 51.8	10 15.8	24 45.3	9 54.7	13 17.7	23 43.9	12 22.3	26 21.6	3 48.1	9 56.2	5 25.3	4 54.3
23 Th	0 06 29	29 45 12	24 12 41	1♋07 26	8 48.6	10D 14.2	25 49.3	11 09.2	13 58.7	24 11.5	12 35.1	26 17.6	3 45.9	9 55.9	5 23.6	4 53.6
24 F	0 10 26	0♎43 56	8♋05 54	15 08 03	8 45.4	10 14.3	26 50.9	12 23.7	14 39.6	24 39.1	12 47.8	26 13.6	3 43.7	9 55.5	5 22.0	4 52.9
25 Sa	0 14 22	1 42 41	22 13 50	29 23 06	8 42.3	10 15.2	27 50.1	13 38.3	15 20.7	25 06.7	13 00.5	26 09.5	3 41.4	9 55.0	5 20.3	4 52.3
26 Su	0 18 19	2 41 29	6♌35 37	13♌51 02	8 39.1	10R 16.0	28 46.6	14 52.8	16 01.9	25 34.3	13 13.2	26 05.4	3 39.1	9 54.5	5 18.7	4 51.7
27 M	0 22 15	3 40 18	21 08 54	28 28 38	8 35.9	10 15.6	29 40.3	16 07.4	16 43.1	26 01.9	13 25.8	26 01.2	3 36.8	9 53.9	5 17.0	4 51.1
28 Tu	0 26 12	4 39 10	5♍49 34	13♍10 53	8 32.7	10 13.1	0♏30.8	17 21.9	17 24.4	26 29.4	13 38.4	25 57.0	3 34.4	9 53.3	5 15.3	4 50.5
29 W	0 30 09	5 38 04	20 31 45	27 51 13	8 29.6	10 08.2	1 18.0	18 36.5	18 05.8	26 57.0	13 50.9	25 52.7	3 32.0	9 52.7	5 13.7	4 50.0
30 Th	0 34 05	6♎37 00	5♎08 22	12♎22 19	8♒26.4	10♒01.0	2♏01.6	19♎51.0	18♏47.3	27♍24.5	14♍03.5	25♈48.3	3♉29.6	9♊51.9	5♈12.0	4♒49.5

1st of Month

Julian Day #
2461649.5
Obliquity
23°26′5″
SVP 4♓52′0″
GC 27♐13.5
Eris 26♈03.7R

Day	⚴
1	8♌43.7
6	11 34.0
11	14 22.6
16	17 09.2
21	19 53.7
26	22 35.9

Day	⚵
1	3♋01.4
6	5 31.6
11	7 58.6
16	10 22.0
21	12 41.6
26	14 56.9

Day	⚶
1	21♋44.9
6	23 41.1
11	25 35.2
16	27 27.3
21	29 17.1
26	1♌04.4

DECLINATION and LATITUDE

Day	☉ Decl	☽ Decl	☽ Lat	☽ 12h Decl	☿ Decl	☿ Lat	♀ Decl	♀ Lat	♂ Decl	♂ Lat	⚳ Decl	⚳ Lat	♃ Decl	♃ Lat	♄ Decl	♄ Lat
1 W	8N26	4N35	2S41	1N11	1N53	0N22	7N40	1N25	11S28	0S16	13N15	7N35	9N29	0N55	8N04	2S41
2 Th	8 04	2S11	3 44	5S29	1 08	0 14	7 11	1 25	11 43	0 16	13 05	7 35	9 24	0 55	8 03	2 41
3 F	7 42	8 40	4 32	11 47	0 24	0 07	6 42	1 25	11 57	0 17	12 54	7 35	9 19	0 55	8 02	2 42
4 Sa	7 20	14 33	5 02	17 09	0S20	0S01	6 12	1 24	12 11	0 18	12 43	7 35	9 14	0 55	8 00	2 42
5 Su	6 58	19 30	5 13	21 34	1 03	0 09	5 43	1 24	12 26	0 19	12 32	7 35	9 10	0 55	7 59	2 42
6 M	6 36	23 19	5 07	24 45	1 47	0 17	5 13	1 24	12 40	0 19	12 22	7 35	9 05	0 56	7 58	2 42
7 Tu	6 14	25 52	4 46	26 37	2 29	0 25	4 44	1 23	12 54	0 20	12 11	7 35	8 60	0 56	7 57	2 42
8 W	5 51	27 02	4 11	27 07	3 11	0 33	4 14	1 23	13 08	0 21	11 60	7 35	8 55	0 56	7 56	2 43
9 Th	5 29	26 52	3 26	26 19	3 53	0 41	3 44	1 22	13 23	0 21	11 49	7 35	8 50	0 56	7 55	2 43
10 F	5 06	25 27	2 33	24 18	4 34	0 49	3 14	1 21	13 37	0 22	11 38	7 35	8 45	0 56	7 53	2 43
11 Sa	4 43	22 54	1 34	21 15	5 15	0 57	2 43	1 21	13 50	0 23	11 28	7 35	8 41	0 56	7 52	2 43
12 Su	4 21	19 24	0 31	17 21	5 55	1 06	2 13	1 20	14 04	0 23	11 17	7 36	8 36	0 56	7 51	2 43
13 M	3 58	15 07	0N34	12 45	6 34	1 14	1 43	1 19	14 18	0 24	11 06	7 36	8 31	0 56	7 49	2 44
14 Tu	3 35	10 15	1 37	7 39	7 12	1 22	1 12	1 18	14 32	0 25	10 55	7 36	8 26	0 56	7 48	2 44
15 W	3 12	4 58	2 36	2 13	7 50	1 30	0 42	1 17	14 45	0 25	10 44	7 36	8 21	0 56	7 47	2 44
16 Th	2 49	0N34	3 29	3N21	8 27	1 38	0 11	1 16	14 59	0 26	10 34	7 36	8 16	0 56	7 45	2 44
17 F	2 25	6 08	4 13	8 53	9 03	1 47	0S20	1 15	15 12	0 27	10 23	7 36	8 12	0 56	7 44	2 44
18 Sa	2 02	11 33	4 45	14 07	9 39	1 55	0 50	1 14	15 26	0 27	10 12	7 36	8 07	0 56	7 42	2 44
19 Su	1 39	16 34	5 04	18 51	10 13	2 02	1 21	1 12	15 39	0 28	10 01	7 36	8 02	0 56	7 41	2 45
20 M	1 16	20 55	5 07	22 45	10 47	2 10	1 51	1 11	15 52	0 29	9 50	7 36	7 57	0 57	7 39	2 45
21 Tu	0 53	24 18	4 55	25 32	11 19	2 18	2 22	1 10	16 05	0 29	9 39	7 37	7 52	0 57	7 38	2 45
22 W	0 29	26 25	4 26	26 55	11 50	2 25	2 53	1 08	16 18	0 30	9 28	7 37	7 47	0 57	7 36	2 45
23 Th	0 06	27 01	3 42	26 41	12 21	2 33	3 23	1 07	16 31	0 31	9 18	7 37	7 43	0 57	7 35	2 45
24 F	0S17	25 55	2 44	24 45	12 50	2 40	3 54	1 05	16 44	0 31	9 07	7 37	7 38	0 57	7 33	2 45
25 Sa	0 41	23 11	1 36	21 14	13 18	2 47	4 24	1 04	16 57	0 32	8 56	7 37	7 33	0 57	7 32	2 46
26 Su	1 04	18 57	0 20	16 22	13 44	2 53	4 54	1 02	17 09	0 32	8 45	7 37	7 28	0 57	7 30	2 46
27 M	1 28	13 32	0S58	10 30	14 09	2 59	5 25	1 01	17 22	0 33	8 34	7 38	7 24	0 57	7 28	2 46
28 Tu	1 51	7 19	2 13	4 02	14 32	3 05	5 55	0 59	17 34	0 34	8 24	7 38	7 19	0 57	7 27	2 46
29 W	2 14	0 43	3 19	2S37	14 54	3 11	6 25	0 57	17 46	0 34	8 13	7 38	7 14	0 57	7 25	2 46
30 Th	2S38	5S53	4S11	9S02	15S14	3S16	6S54	0N55	17S58	0S35	8N02	7N38	7N09	0N57	7N23	2S46

Day	⚷ Decl	⚷ Lat	♅ Decl	♅ Lat	♆ Decl	♆ Lat	♇ Decl	♇ Lat
1	12N45	0S15	21N50	0S06	1N02	1S27	23S37	4S48
6	12 42	0 16	21 50	0 06	0 59	1 27	23 38	4 48
11	12 39	0 16	21 51	0 06	0 56	1 28	23 39	4 48
16	12 35	0 17	21 51	0 06	0 53	1 28	23 40	4 48
21	12 32	0 17	21 51	0 06	0 49	1 28	23 41	4 48
26	12 27	0 18	21 50	0 06	0 46	1 28	23 42	4 48

Day	⚴ Decl	⚴ Lat	⚵ Decl	⚵ Lat	⚶ Decl	⚶ Lat	Eris Decl	Eris Lat
1	4S02	22S51	11N58	11S27	20N47	0S55	0N27	10S18
6	4 32	22 40	11 32	11 48	20 34	0 48	0 26	10 18
11	5 04	22 29	11 04	12 09	20 20	0 42	0 25	10 18
16	5 37	22 18	10 33	12 31	20 05	0 36	0 25	10 18
21	6 11	22 06	10 00	12 53	19 50	0 29	0 24	10 18
26	6 46	21 53	9 25	13 16	19 34	0 22	0 23	10 18

Moon Phenomena

Max/0 Decl dy hr mn
1 16:13 0 S
8 8:56 27S08
15 21:35 0 N
22 20:37 27N02
29 2:33 0 S

Max/0 Lat dy hr mn
5 3:20 5S13
12 11:26 0 N
19 17:30 5N08
26 6:05 0 S

Perigee/Apogee dy hr m kilometers
11 23:39 a 405383
27 20:12 p 363454

PH dy hr mn
☽ 7 18:32 14♐55
○ 15 23:05 22♓53
☾ 23 10:22 0♋11
● 30 2:37 6♎43

Void of Course Moon

Last Aspect	☽ Ingress
2 1:30 ☿ ☌	♎ 2 5:08
4 3:07 ♄ ☍	♏ 4 7:45
5 19:07 ♀ ⚹	♐ 6 14:02
8 18:30 ♄ △	♑ 9 0:13
11 6:44 ♄ □	♒ 11 12:51
13 19:21 ♄ ⚹	♓ 14 1:40
15 23:05 ☉ ☍	♈ 16 12:57
18 15:41 ♄ ☌	♉ 18 22:06
21 1:14 ☉ △	♊ 21 5:07
23 3:36 ♄ ⚹	♋ 23 10:03
25 10:05 ☿ □	♌ 25 13:02
27 7:57 ♄ △	♍ 27 14:29
28 19:50 ♂ ⚹	♎ 29 15:32

DAILY ASPECTARIAN

1 W: ☽⚼♄ 0:41; ☽☌♀ 3:11; ☽☌⚳ 3:23; ☽∠♂ 3:49; ♀☌⚳ 6:45; ☽∥☿ 10:43; ☽⚼⚷ 11:53; ☽∥♆ 12:34; ☽⚼♇ 13:12; ♀∠♂ 18:19; ☽#♆ 19:52; ☿⚻♄ 20:09; ☽#☿ 20:39

2 Th: ☽⚻♄ 0:55; ☽☌☿ 1:30; ♂ ♏ 1:53; ☉∥♄ 1:58; ☿∥♆ 3:51; ☽⚺♂ 5:17; ☽⚻⚷ 12:21; ☽△♇ 13:42; ☉□♅ 13:52; ☽☍♆ 14:55; ☽#♀ 17:02; ☽⚺♃ 18:44; ☉#☽ 20:31; ☽△♅ 21:29; ☽#♄ 21:32; ☉⚺☽ 22:02

3 F: ☽#♃ 2:28; ☽⚺⚳ 6:14; ☽⚺♀ 9:06; ☿ ♎ 11:38; ☽∥♂ 13:34; ☽#⚷ 16:12; ☽#⚳ 16:25; ☽∠♃ 20:27; ☽⚼♅ 22:55; ⚳∥⚷ 23:30

4 Sa: ☉∠☽ 1:22; ☽☍♄ 3:07; ☽∠⚳ 8:50; ☽⚺☿ 10:17; ☽☌♂ 10:27; ☿⚺♂ 12:44; ☽∠♀ 13:28; ☽☍⚷ 15:21; ☽□♇ 16:48; ☽⚻♆ 18:04; ☿#♆ 21:55; ☽⚹♃ 23:05

5 Su: ☽⚻♅ 1:14; ☉⚼♄ 1:31; ☉⚹☽ 5:49; ♂#⚳ 6:16; ♀⚼⚷ 9:44; ☽⚹⚳ 12:28; ☽#♅ 13:45; ☽∠☿ 16:29; ☽⚹♀ 19:07; ☽⚼♆ 21:03

6 M: ♀⚼♇ 1:40; ☽∥♇ 2:25; ♂#⚷ 3:24; ☿⚻⚷ 7:29; ☽⚻♄ 8:52; ☽⚺♂ 19:55; ☿△♇ 20:57; ☽⚻⚷ 22:06; ☽⚹♇ 23:43

7 Tu: ☽⚹☿ 0:05; ☽△♆ 1:03; ☽□♃ 7:32; ☿☍♆ 8:13; ☽☍♅ 8:54; ☽⚼♄ 13:14; ☊ D 18:19; ☉□☽ 18:32; ☽□⚳ 23:07

8 W: ☽∠♂ 2:25; ☽⚼⚷ 2:58; ☽∠♇ 4:39; ☽□♀ 10:29; ♂☍⚷ 12:13; ☽△♄ 18:30; ☿#♀ 20:49

9 Th: ☽△⚷ 8:37; ☽⚹♂ 9:52; ☽⚺♇ 10:22; ☽□♆ 11:44; ♂□♇ 18:40; ☽□☿ 18:55; ☽△♃ 19:46; ☽⚻♅ 20:09

10 F: ☿⚺♃ 3:17; ☿△♅ 5:19; ☉△☽ 11:32; ☉#☿ 12:03; ☽△⚳ 13:23; ♃□♅ 16:42; ☽∥♇ 17:47; ♂⚻♆ 18:09

11 Sa: ☽⚼♅ 2:34; ☽⚼♃ 2:45; ☽△♀ 5:50; ☽□♄ 6:44; ☽#♅ 7:53; ♀⚻♄ 14:00; ☉⚼☽ 20:47; ☽⚼⚳ 21:09; ☽□⚷ 21:17; ☽☌♇ 23:07

12 Su: ⚳⚼⚷ 0:10; ☽⚹♆ 0:26; ☽□♂ 2:20; ☉⚼⚷ 2:32; ☉☌⚳ 4:47; ☽△♅ 9:07; ☽⚻♃ 9:51; ☊ R 11:25; ☽△☿ 15:56; ☽⚼♀ 15:58

13 M: ☉⚼♇ 0:35; ☽∥♂ 4:01; ☽⚻⚳ 4:52; ☉⚻☽ 6:00; ☽∠♆ 6:50; ☽#⚷ 12:37; ☽⚹♄ 19:21; ☽#⚳ 20:43; ⚳⚼♇ 21:56

14 Tu: ♀ ♎ 0:26; ☽⚻♀ 1:49; ☽⚼☿ 2:04; ☽#♃ 8:33; ☽⚹⚷ 9:48; ☽#♄ 11:21; ☽⚺♇ 11:41; ☽∥☿ 12:31; ☽⚺♆ 12:56; ♀∥♆ 14:36; ☽△♂ 18:29; ☽□♅ 21:34; ☿#♄ 21:52; ☽☍♃ 23:23

15 W: ☽∠♄ 1:12; ☉#☽ 8:20; ♅ R 9:10; ☽⚻☿ 11:32; ☽∠⚷ 15:30; ☽∠♇ 17:23; ☽#♆ 17:48; ☿#♃ 17:48; ☽☍⚳ 19:09; ☽#♀ 20:28; ☽∥♀ 22:31; ☉☍☽ 23:05

16 Th: ☽∥♆ 1:21; ☽⚼♂ 1:49; ☽⚺♄ 6:34; ☉∥☽ 9:02; ☽☍♀ 19:42; ☽⚺⚷ 20:40; ☽⚹♇ 22:34; ☽☌♆ 23:43

17 F: ♂⚻♅ 1:40; ♀⚻⚷ 5:09; ☽∥♄ 6:55; ☽⚹♅ 8:10; ☽⚻♂ 8:32; ☽∥♃ 8:51; ☽⚻♃ 10:56; ☽#☿ 14:22; ☽∥⚳ 18:05

18 Sa: ♀△♇ 0:12; ♀#♆ 0:51; ☽☍☿ 3:58; ☽∥⚷ 4:40; ☽⚻⚳ 7:08; ♃⚼♄ 8:10; ♀☍♆ 11:07; ☽∠♅ 12:39; ☉⚻☽ 13:31; ☽☌♄ 15:41; ☽⚼♃ 15:51; ☿#⚳ 17:30; ☽#♂ 19:12

19 Su: ☽☌⚷ 5:23; ☽□♇ 7:18; ☉#♀ 8:09; ☽⚺♆ 8:20; ☽⚻♀ 10:38; ☽⚼⚳ 12:13; ☉⚻♄ 16:18; ☽⚺♅ 16:35; ☉⚼☽ 19:43; ☽☍♂ 20:02; ☽△♃ 20:12

20 M: ♂⚹♃ 0:30; ☽∥♅ 5:51; ☉∠♂ 9:16; ☿⚺⚳ 10:20; ☽∠♆ 11:51; ☽△⚳ 16:42; ☽⚼♀ 17:02; ☽⚻☿ 17:04; ☽#♇ 18:57; ☽⚺♄ 22:40

21 Tu: ☉△☽ 1:14; ☉∥♆ 3:25; ☽⚺⚷ 11:58; ☽△♇ 13:55; ☽⚹♆ 14:51; ☽⚼☿ 22:26; ☽△♀ 22:43; ☽☌♅ 22:53

22 W: ♀△♅ 0:30; ☽∠♄ 1:24; ☽□♃ 3:15; ☿⚼♅ 4:02; ☽⚻♂ 5:05; ☽∠⚷ 14:30; ☽⚼♇ 16:27; ⚶ ♌ 23:37; ☽□⚳ 23:58

23 Th: ☽△☿ 3:02; ☽⚹♄ 3:36; ☉ ♎ 6:03; ☿#⚷ 7:17; ☽⚼♂ 8:43; ☿☍♄ 10:15; ☉□☽ 10:22; ☊ D 10:27; ☽⚹⚷ 16:31; ☽⚻♇ 18:29; ☽□♆ 19:19

24 F: ☽⚺♅ 3:07; ☽□♀ 8:03; ☽⚹♃ 8:09; ♀⚺♃ 9:20; ☽△♂ 11:46; ☽#♇ 20:20

25 Sa: ☽∠♅ 4:31; ☽⚹⚳ 5:00; ☿∠♃ 5:33; ☉#♆ 5:49; ☽□♄ 6:34; ☽∥♅ 8:26; ☽∠♃ 9:51; ☽□☿ 10:05; ♃∥♄ 11:27; ☉⚹☽ 17:02; ☽□⚷ 19:08; ☽☍♇ 21:08; ☽△♆ 21:53

26 Su: ☽⚹♅ 5:29; ☊ R 6:05; ☽∠⚳ 6:48; ☽#♂ 8:08; ☽⚺♃ 11:07; ☽⚹♀ 14:58; ☽□♂ 16:22; ☉∠☽ 19:38; ☽#☿ 21:36; ☽⚼♆ 22:35; ☉⚻⚷ 22:37; ⚳⚻♄ 23:29

27 M: ☽∥⚷ 4:24; ☽△♄ 7:57; ☽⚺⚳ 8:15; ☿ ♏ 9:11; ☽⚹☿ 14:49; ☽∠♀ 17:50; ☽∥⚳ 19:52; ☽△⚷ 20:20; ☉⚺☽ 21:57; ☽⚻♇ 22:24; ☽⚻♆ 23:04; ☽∥♄ 23:31

28 Tu: ☽∥♃ 0:00; ♀⚺♂ 1:48; ☉△♇ 4:35; ☽#♀ 4:48; ☽□♅ 6:37; ☽⚼♄ 8:19; ☽☌♃ 12:56; ☉☍♆ 14:20; ☽∠☿ 16:43; ☉#☽ 18:48; ☽⚹♂ 19:50; ☽⚺♀ 20:34; ☽⚼⚷ 20:45; ☽⚼♇ 22:52; ☽∥♆ 23:55

29 W: ☽#♆ 5:11; ☽⚻♄ 8:43; ☽☌⚳ 10:51; ☉∥☽ 11:19; ☽⚺☿ 18:36; ☽⚻⚷ 21:17; ☽∠♂ 21:39; ☽△♇ 23:29

30 Th: ☽☍♆ 0:06; ☉☌☽ 2:37; ☽∥♀ 4:11; ☽#♃ 4:44; ☽#♄ 5:40; ☽△♅ 7:49; ☽#⚳ 7:54; ♀#♃ 10:20; ☽⚺♃ 15:02; ♀#♄ 22:06; ☽⚺♂ 23:54

October 2027

LONGITUDE

Day	Sid.Time	☉	☽	☽ 12 hour	Mean ☊	True ☊	☿	♀	♂	⚳	♃	♄	⚷	♅	♆	♇
	h m s	° ' "	° ' "	° ' "	° '	° '	° '	° '	° '	° '	° '	° '	° '	° '	° '	° '
1 F	0 38 02	7♎35 59	19♎32 12	26♎37 17	8♒23.2	9♒52.0	2♏41.2	21♎05.6	19♏28.8	27♍52.1	14♍16.0	25♈43.9	3♉27.1	9♊51.2	5♈10.3	4♒49.0
2 Sa	0 41 58	8 34 59	3♏36 57	10♏30 43	8 20.0	9R 42.3	3 16.5	22 20.2	20 10.5	28 19.6	14 28.4	25R 39.5	3R 24.6	9R 50.4	5R 08.7	4R 48.5
3 Su	0 45 55	9 34 01	17 18 16	23 59 26	8 16.8	9 32.9	3 47.1	23 34.7	20 52.2	28 47.1	14 40.8	25 35.0	3 22.1	9 49.5	5 07.0	4 48.1
4 M	0 49 51	10 33 05	0♐34 14	7♐02 48	8 13.7	9 24.9	4 12.6	24 49.3	21 34.0	29 14.6	14 53.2	25 30.5	3 19.5	9 48.6	5 05.3	4 47.7
5 Tu	0 53 48	11 32 11	13 25 24	19 42 26	8 10.5	9 19.0	4 32.7	26 03.9	22 15.9	29 42.1	15 05.5	25 26.0	3 17.0	9 47.6	5 03.7	4 47.3
6 W	0 57 44	12 31 18	25 54 21	2♑01 44	8 07.3	9 15.4	4 46.7	27 18.4	22 57.8	0♎09.5	15 17.8	25 21.4	3 14.4	9 46.6	5 02.0	4 47.0
7 Th	1 01 41	13 30 28	8♑05 09	14 05 17	8 04.1	9D 13.9	4R 54.4	28 33.0	23 39.8	0 37.0	15 30.0	25 16.8	3 11.8	9 45.6	5 00.4	4 46.7
8 F	1 05 37	14 29 39	20 02 47	25 58 21	8 01.0	9 13.9	4 55.1	29 47.6	24 21.9	1 04.4	15 42.2	25 12.2	3 09.1	9 44.5	4 58.7	4 46.4
9 Sa	1 09 34	15 28 52	1♒52 40	7♒46 25	7 57.8	9R 14.4	4 48.6	1♏02.1	25 04.1	1 31.8	15 54.4	25 07.5	3 06.5	9 43.4	4 57.1	4 46.1
10 Su	1 13 31	16 28 06	13 40 14	19 34 46	7 54.6	9 14.5	4 34.3	2 16.7	25 46.3	1 59.2	16 06.5	25 02.8	3 03.8	9 42.2	4 55.5	4 45.9
11 M	1 17 27	17 27 23	25 30 35	1♓28 15	7 51.4	9 13.2	4 12.1	3 31.2	26 28.7	2 26.5	16 18.5	24 58.1	3 01.1	9 40.9	4 53.9	4 45.6
12 Tu	1 21 24	18 26 41	7♓28 14	13 30 59	7 48.2	9 09.6	3 41.6	4 45.8	27 11.1	2 53.9	16 30.5	24 53.4	2 58.4	9 39.6	4 52.2	4 45.4
13 W	1 25 20	19 26 01	19 36 52	25 46 10	7 45.1	9 03.3	3 02.9	6 00.3	27 53.5	3 21.2	16 42.4	24 48.7	2 55.7	9 38.3	4 50.6	4 45.3
14 Th	1 29 17	20 25 23	1♈59 07	8♈15 51	7 41.9	8 54.5	2 16.1	7 14.9	28 36.1	3 48.5	16 54.3	24 43.9	2 52.9	9 37.0	4 49.0	4 45.2
15 F	1 33 13	21 24 47	14 36 26	21 00 53	7 38.7	8 43.4	1 21.8	8 29.4	29 18.7	4 15.7	17 06.1	24 39.1	2 50.2	9 35.5	4 47.5	4 45.0
16 Sa	1 37 10	22 24 13	27 29 06	4♉00 58	7 35.5	8 31.0	0 20.7	9 43.9	0♐01.3	4 43.0	17 17.9	24 34.4	2 47.4	9 34.1	4 45.9	4 45.0
17 Su	1 41 06	23 23 41	10♉36 18	17 14 53	7 32.4	8 18.4	29♎13.9	10 58.5	0 44.1	5 10.2	17 29.6	24 29.6	2 44.6	9 32.6	4 44.3	4 44.9
18 M	1 45 03	24 23 11	23 56 28	0♊40 50	7 29.2	8 06.9	28 02.8	12 13.0	1 26.9	5 37.4	17 41.2	24 24.8	2 41.8	9 31.1	4 42.8	4D 44.9
19 Tu	1 49 00	25 22 44	7♊27 42	14 16 53	7 26.0	7 57.4	26 49.2	13 27.5	2 09.8	6 04.6	17 52.8	24 20.0	2 39.0	9 29.5	4 41.2	4 44.9
20 W	1 52 56	26 22 18	21 08 11	28 01 26	7 22.8	7 50.7	25 35.2	14 42.1	2 52.8	6 31.7	18 04.3	24 15.3	2 36.2	9 27.9	4 39.7	4 45.0
21 Th	1 56 53	27 21 55	4♋56 30	11♋53 18	7 19.6	7 46.8	24 22.9	15 56.6	3 35.8	6 58.9	18 15.8	24 10.5	2 33.4	9 26.2	4 38.2	4 45.0
22 F	2 00 49	28 21 34	18 51 46	25 51 51	7 16.5	7D 45.2	23 14.5	17 11.1	4 18.9	7 25.9	18 27.2	24 05.7	2 30.5	9 24.5	4 36.7	4 45.1
23 Sa	2 04 46	29 21 16	2♌53 31	9♌56 42	7 13.3	7R 45.1	22 12.1	18 25.7	5 02.1	7 53.0	18 38.5	24 01.0	2 27.7	9 22.8	4 35.2	4 45.2
24 Su	2 08 42	0♏21 00	17 01 19	24 07 14	7 10.1	7 44.9	21 17.4	19 40.2	5 45.4	8 20.0	18 49.7	23 56.2	2 24.9	9 21.0	4 33.8	4 45.4
25 M	2 12 39	1 20 46	1♍14 14	8♍22 05	7 06.9	7 43.5	20 32.0	20 54.7	6 28.7	8 47.0	19 00.9	23 51.5	2 22.0	9 19.2	4 32.3	4 45.6
26 Tu	2 16 35	2 20 34	15 30 25	22 38 48	7 03.8	7 39.7	19 57.0	22 09.3	7 12.1	9 14.0	19 12.0	23 46.8	2 19.2	9 17.4	4 30.9	4 45.8
27 W	2 20 32	3 20 24	29 46 43	6♎53 35	7 00.6	7 33.0	19 33.1	23 23.8	7 55.6	9 40.9	19 23.1	23 42.1	2 16.3	9 15.5	4 29.4	4 46.0
28 Th	2 24 29	4 20 16	13♎58 48	21 01 43	6 57.4	7 23.3	19D 20.7	24 38.3	8 39.1	10 07.8	19 34.0	23 37.4	2 13.5	9 13.6	4 28.0	4 46.3
29 F	2 28 25	5 20 11	28 01 39	4♏58 01	6 54.2	7 11.5	19 19.7	25 52.8	9 22.8	10 34.7	19 44.9	23 32.8	2 10.7	9 11.6	4 26.7	4 46.6
30 Sa	2 32 22	6 20 08	11♏50 14	18 37 51	6 51.0	6 58.6	19 29.7	27 07.4	10 06.5	11 01.5	19 55.7	23 28.2	2 07.8	9 09.6	4 25.3	4 46.9
31 Su	2 36 18	7♏20 06	25 20 28	1♐57 51	6♒47.9	6♒45.9	19♎50.2	28♏21.9	10♐50.2	11♎28.3	20♍06.4	23♈23.6	2♉05.0	9♊07.6	4♈24.0	4♒47.2

1st of Month

Julian Day #
2461679.5
Obliquity
23°26'15"
SVP 4♓52'07"
GC 27♐13.6
Eris 25♈49.0R

Day	⚴	⚵	⚶
1	25♌15.8	17♋07.3	2♌48.8
6	27 52.9	19 12.5	4 30.1
11	0♍27.2	21 11.7	6 07.9
16	2 58.5	23 04.5	7 41.9
21	5 26.6	24 50.3	9 11.7
26	7 51.3	26 28.3	10 37.0
31	10 12.2	27 57.8	11 57.1

DECLINATION and LATITUDE

Day	☉ Decl	☽ Decl	☽ Lat	☽ 12h Decl	☿ Decl	☿ Lat	♀ Decl	♀ Lat	♂ Decl	♂ Lat	⚳ Decl	⚳ Lat	♃ Decl	♃ Lat	♄ Decl	♄ Lat
1 F	3S01	12S03	4S46	14S52	15S32	3S20	7S24	0N53	18S10	0S35	7N51	7N38	7N05	0N58	7N22	2S46
2 Sa	3 24	17 28	5 03	19 47	15 48	3 24	7 54	0 52	18 22	0 36	7 40	7 39	6 60	0 58	7 20	2 46
3 Su	3 47	21 49	5 02	23 32	16 02	3 28	8 23	0 50	18 34	0 37	7 30	7 39	6 55	0 58	7 18	2 46
4 M	4 11	24 54	4 45	25 55	16 13	3 30	8 52	0 48	18 45	0 37	7 19	7 39	6 51	0 58	7 17	2 46
5 Tu	4 34	26 36	4 13	26 54	16 21	3 32	9 21	0 46	18 57	0 38	7 08	7 39	6 46	0 58	7 15	2 47
6 W	4 57	26 52	3 30	26 30	16 27	3 33	9 50	0 43	19 08	0 38	6 58	7 40	6 41	0 58	7 13	2 47
7 Th	5 20	25 50	2 38	24 51	16 29	3 32	10 19	0 41	19 19	0 39	6 47	7 40	6 37	0 58	7 11	2 47
8 F	5 43	23 36	1 41	22 06	16 28	3 31	10 47	0 39	19 30	0 39	6 36	7 40	6 32	0 58	7 10	2 47
9 Sa	6 06	20 23	0 39	18 27	16 24	3 29	11 15	0 37	19 41	0 40	6 26	7 40	6 27	0 58	7 08	2 47
10 Su	6 28	16 21	0N24	14 05	16 15	3 25	11 43	0 35	19 51	0 41	6 15	7 41	6 23	0 59	7 06	2 47
11 M	6 51	11 40	1 26	9 09	16 02	3 19	12 11	0 32	20 02	0 41	6 04	7 41	6 18	0 59	7 05	2 47
12 Tu	7 14	6 32	2 24	3 50	15 45	3 12	12 38	0 30	20 12	0 42	5 54	7 41	6 14	0 59	7 03	2 47
13 W	7 36	1 05	3 17	1N42	15 23	3 03	13 05	0 28	20 22	0 42	5 43	7 41	6 09	0 59	7 01	2 47
14 Th	7 59	4N29	4 02	7 16	14 57	2 52	13 32	0 25	20 32	0 43	5 33	7 42	6 05	0 59	6 59	2 47
15 F	8 21	9 59	4 35	12 38	14 27	2 40	13 58	0 23	20 42	0 43	5 22	7 42	6 00	0 59	6 58	2 47
16 Sa	8 43	15 10	4 56	17 34	13 52	2 25	14 24	0 21	20 52	0 44	5 12	7 42	5 56	0 59	6 56	2 47
17 Su	9 05	19 46	5 01	21 44	13 13	2 09	14 50	0 18	21 01	0 44	5 01	7 43	5 51	0 60	6 54	2 47
18 M	9 27	23 26	4 50	24 49	12 31	1 52	15 15	0 16	21 11	0 45	4 51	7 43	5 47	0 60	6 52	2 47
19 Tu	9 49	25 52	4 23	26 32	11 47	1 33	15 40	0 13	21 20	0 45	4 41	7 43	5 42	0 60	6 51	2 47
20 W	10 11	26 48	3 40	26 39	11 01	1 13	16 05	0 11	21 29	0 46	4 30	7 44	5 38	0 60	6 49	2 47
21 Th	10 32	26 05	2 44	25 06	10 16	0 52	16 29	0 08	21 38	0 46	4 20	7 44	5 34	1 00	6 47	2 47
22 F	10 53	23 44	1 38	21 60	9 31	0 32	16 52	0 06	21 46	0 47	4 10	7 44	5 29	1 00	6 45	2 47
23 Sa	11 15	19 56	0 26	17 34	8 49	0 11	17 16	0 03	21 55	0 47	3 59	7 45	5 25	1 00	6 44	2 47
24 Su	11 36	14 57	0S49	12 08	8 10	0N09	17 39	0 00	22 03	0 48	3 49	7 45	5 21	1 01	6 42	2 47
25 M	11 56	9 09	2 01	6 03	7 36	0 27	18 01	0S02	22 11	0 48	3 39	7 45	5 17	1 01	6 40	2 47
26 Tu	12 17	2 52	3 05	0S21	7 06	0 45	18 23	0 05	22 19	0 49	3 29	7 46	5 12	1 01	6 39	2 47
27 W	12 38	3S33	3 58	6 42	6 42	1 01	18 44	0 07	22 26	0 49	3 19	7 46	5 08	1 01	6 37	2 47
28 Th	12 58	9 45	4 36	12 39	6 24	1 16	19 05	0 10	22 34	0 50	3 09	7 47	5 04	1 01	6 35	2 47
29 F	13 18	15 23	4 56	17 53	6 12	1 28	19 26	0 13	22 41	0 50	2 59	7 47	4 60	1 01	6 34	2 47
30 Sa	13 38	20 07	4 59	22 04	6 06	1 39	19 46	0 15	22 48	0 50	2 49	7 47	4 56	1 01	6 32	2 46
31 Su	13S58	23S42	4S45	24S59	6S05	1N49	20S05	0S18	22S54	0S51	2N39	7N48	4N52	1N02	6N30	2S46

Day	⚷ Decl	⚷ Lat	♅ Decl	♅ Lat	♆ Decl	♆ Lat	♇ Decl	♇ Lat
1	12N23	0S18	21N50	0S06	0N43	1S28	23S42	4S48
6	12 18	0 19	21 49	0 06	0 39	1 28	23 43	4 47
11	12 13	0 19	21 48	0 06	0 36	1 28	23 43	4 47
16	12 08	0 19	21 47	0 06	0 33	1 28	23 43	4 47
21	12 03	0 20	21 46	0 06	0 30	1 28	23 42	4 46
26	11 58	0 20	21 45	0 06	0 27	1 28	23 42	4 46
31	11N52	0S21	21N44	0S06	0N25	1S28	23S41	4S46

Day	⚴ Decl	⚴ Lat	⚵ Decl	⚵ Lat	⚶ Decl	⚶ Lat	Eris Decl	Eris Lat
1	7S21	21S40	8N48	13S39	19N18	0S14	0N21	10S18
6	7 57	21 26	8 09	14 02	19 02	0 06	0 20	10 18
11	8 34	21 12	7 29	14 26	18 46	0N02	0 20	10 18
16	9 10	20 57	6 49	14 51	18 30	0 10	0 19	10 18
21	9 46	20 41	6 08	15 16	18 16	0 19	0 18	10 18
26	10 21	20 25	5 26	15 41	18 02	0 29	0 17	10 18
31	10S56	20S09	4N45	16S07	17N49	0N38	0N16	10S18

Moon Phenomena

Max/0 Decl
dy hr mn
5 16:50 26S56
13 4:42 0 N
20 1:41 26N48
26 10:41 0 S

Max/0 Lat
dy hr mn
2 10:27 5S05
9 14:59 0 N
16 19:53 5N01
23 8:16 0 S
29 15:37 5S00

Perigee/Apogee
dy hr m kilometers
9 15:48 a 404529
25 5:36 p 368652

PH dy hr mn
☽ 7 11:49 14♑00
○ 15 13:48 21♈59
☾ 22 17:30 29♋05
● 29 13:38 5♏54

Void of Course Moon

Last Aspect	☽ Ingress
1 10:26 ♄ ☍	♏ 1 17:47
3 6:44 ♂ ☌	♐ 3 22:57
6 3:03 ♀ ⚹	♑ 6 8:01
8 10:22 ♄ □	♒ 8 20:11
11 2:05 ♂ □	♓ 11 9:03
13 17:05 ♂ △	♈ 13 20:11
15 18:39 ♄ ☌	♉ 16 4:38
17 12:37 ♃ △	♊ 18 10:48
20 9:50 ☉ △	♋ 20 15:26
22 17:30 ☉ □	♌ 22 19:04
24 11:38 ♄ △	♍ 24 21:55
26 12:14 ♀ ⚹	♎ 27 0:22
28 16:21 ♄ ☍	♏ 29 3:24
31 6:01 ♀ ☌	♐ 31 8:25

DAILY ASPECTARIAN

1 F ☽⋕⚷ 1:21, ☽☌♀ 2:53, ☽⚼♅ 8:59, ☽☍♄ 10:26, ☽⊻⚳ 14:36, ☽∥☿ 15:47, ♀⋕⚳ 16:03, ☽∠♃ 16:46, ♂⚼♆ 23:00, ☽☌☿ 23:23, ☽☍⚷ 23:39

2 Sa ☽□♇ 2:04, ☽⚻♆ 2:38, ☽∥♂ 4:40, ☿☍⚷ 5:34, ☉⊻☽ 9:18, ☽⚻♅ 10:49, ☽∠⚳ 17:33, ☽⚹♃ 19:16

3 Su ☽⋕♅ 0:03, ☽⚼♆ 5:01, ☉△♅ 6:12, ☽☌♂ 6:44, ☽⊻♀ 12:25, ☽∥♇ 13:25, ☉∠☽ 14:06, ☽⚻♄ 14:48, ☽⚹⚳ 21:29, ♀⚼♅ 23:46

4 M ☽⚻⚷ 5:04, ⚳∥♄ 6:20, ☽⊻☿ 6:55, ☽⚹♇ 7:48, ☽△♆ 8:20, ♀☍♄ 12:31, ☽☍♅ 17:09, ☽⚼♄ 18:23, ☽∠♀ 19:03, ☉⚹☽ 20:08

5 Tu ☽□♃ 3:13, ☽⚼⚷ 9:14, ☽∠☿ 11:56, ☽∠♇ 12:09, ⚳ ♎ 15:40, ☽⊻♂ 17:57, ☽△♄ 22:56

6 W ☿□♇ 0:35, ☽⚹♀ 3:03, ☽□⚳ 8:39, ☽△⚷ 14:20, ☽⊻♇ 17:26, ☽⚹☿ 17:38, ☽□♆ 17:54

7 Th ☽∠♂ 1:13, ☽⚻♅ 3:20, ☊ D 11:39, ☉□☽ 11:49, ☿ R 14:38, ☽△♃ 15:06, ☽∥♇ 23:01

8 F ♀ ♏ 4:00, ☽⚹♂ 9:18, ☽⚼♅ 9:29, ☽□♄ 10:22, ☽⋕♅ 14:07, ⚳∥♃ 17:14, ♀∠♃ 21:01, ☽⚼♃ 21:59, ☽□♀ 22:05, ☽△⚳ 23:16

9 Sa ♂⚻♄ 1:45, ☽□⚷ 2:30, ☽∥♂ 4:18, ☿□♇ 5:25, ☽□☿ 5:52, ☽☌♇ 5:53, ☽⚹♆ 6:14, ☉⊻♃ 12:59, ☉⋕⚳ 14:23, ☊ R 14:58, ♀⊻⚳ 15:06, ☽△♅ 15:56, ☉⋕♃ 19:03

10 Su ☽∥☿ 0:31, ⚴ ♍ 2:38, ☽⚻♃ 5:02, ☉△☽ 6:12, ☽⚼⚳ 7:00, ☽∠♆ 12:40, ♀☍⚷ 14:39, ☽⋕⚷ 21:19, ☽∥♀ 21:44, ☽⚹♄ 22:55

11 M ☽□♂ 2:05, ♀⋕⚷ 2:06, ☿☌♀ 9:33, ☉⋕♄ 13:10, ☽⚻⚳ 14:30, ☽⚹⚷ 15:03, ☉⚼☽ 15:14, ☽△☿ 16:47, ☽△♀ 17:58, ☽⊻♇ 18:35, ☽⊻♆ 18:49, ☉∥☽ 21:03, ☽⋕♄ 21:40, ♀□♇ 23:54

12 Tu ☽⋕♃ 1:23, ♀⚻♆ 2:02, ☽⋕⚳ 2:57, ⚳⚻⚷ 3:37, ☽□♅ 4:21, ☽∠♄ 4:47, ☿⊻⚳ 17:38, ☽☍♃ 18:12, ☽∠⚷ 20:42, ☽⚼☿ 21:06, ☉⚻☽ 23:37

13 W ☽∠♇ 0:16, ☽⋕♆ 2:12, ☽⚼♀ 3:02, ☿☍⚷ 4:15, ☽∥♆ 7:12, ☽⊻♄ 10:04, ☽△♂ 17:05

14 Th ☽⚻☿ 0:31, ☽⊻⚷ 1:43, ☽☍⚳ 3:38, ☽∥⚳ 4:26, ☽⚹♇ 5:18, ☽☌♆ 5:25, ☽∥♃ 6:47, ☿∠♃ 8:13, ☽∥♄ 10:46, ☽⚻♀ 11:10, ☽⚹♅ 14:32, ☉⋕☽ 16:14, ☽⚼♂ 23:25

15 F ☽⚻♃ 4:46, ☽∥⚷ 9:45, ☿∥♀ 11:24, ☉☍☽ 13:48, ☽⋕☿ 18:24, ☽∠♅ 18:37, ☽☌♄ 18:39, ☽⋕♀ 19:57, ♀⚻♅ 20:54, ♂ ♐ 23:15

16 Sa ⚳△♇ 1:45, ♄∠♅ 2:06, ⚳☍♆ 2:25, ☿⊻♂ 4:19, ☽☍☿ 4:52, ☽⚻♂ 4:57, ☿R♎ 7:37, ☽⚼♃ 8:59, ☽☌⚷ 9:43, ☽□♇ 13:20, ☽⊻♆ 13:21, ☽⚻⚳ 13:45, ♆⚹♇ 14:29, ☽⊻♅ 22:05

17 Su ☽☍♀ 0:44, ☽⋕♂ 7:50, ☽∥♅ 12:21, ☽△♃ 12:37, ☽∠♆ 16:27, ☽⚼⚳ 17:51

18 M ☉☍♄ 0:37, ☽⊻♄ 0:50, ☉⚻☽ 0:52, ♃⚼⚷ 0:59, ☽⋕♇ 2:11, ☉⚼♅ 3:06, ♇ D 3:52, ☽⚻☿ 6:43, ☿⋕⚷ 14:00, ☽☍♂ 14:06, ☽⊻⚷ 15:31, ☽⚹♆ 19:06, ☽△♇ 19:12, ☽△⚳ 21:28

19 Tu ☽∠♄ 3:17, ☽☌♅ 3:34, ☉⚼☽ 5:33, ☽⚼☿ 7:02, ☽⚻♀ 11:37, ♂⚻⚷ 15:18, ☉☌☿ 15:32, ☽∠⚷ 17:51, ☽□♃ 18:34, ☽⚼♇ 21:35

20 W ☽⚹♄ 5:25, ☽△☿ 7:08, ☉△☽ 9:50, ☽⚼♀ 16:23, ☉∥☿ 18:10, ☽⚹⚷ 19:53, ☽⚻♂ 21:33, ☿⚼♅ 22:52, ☽□♆ 23:28, ☽⚻♇ 23:40

21 Th ☽□⚳ 3:39, ☿☍♄ 4:33, ☽⊻♅ 7:45, ☽△♀ 20:50, ☽⚹♃ 23:17, ♂⋕♅ 23:36

22 F ☽⋕♇ 0:12, ☽⚼♂ 0:49, ☽□☿ 6:58, ☽□♄ 8:55, ☽∠♅ 9:29, ♂△♆ 9:33, ☽⋕♂ 12:55, ☽∥♅ 13:25, ♂⚹♇ 14:36, ☉□☽ 17:30, ☊ D 17:39, ☽□⚷ 23:16

23 Sa ☽∠♃ 1:18, ☽△♆ 2:53, ☽☍♇ 3:10, ☽△♂ 3:51, ♀⚹♃ 4:52, ☊ R 8:17, ☽⚹⚳ 8:47, ☽⚹♅ 11:01, ☽⋕♀ 12:30, ☉ ♏ 15:34, ♀⚼♆ 21:58

24 Su ☽⊻♃ 3:06, ☽⚼♆ 4:17, ☽□♀ 4:55, ☽⚹☿ 6:50, ☿∠♂ 8:21, ☽∠⚳ 11:01, ☽△♄ 11:38, ☽∥⚷ 12:36, ☉⋕☽ 13:26, ☿⊻♀ 19:18

25 M ☉⚹☽ 0:12, ☽△⚷ 1:54, ☉⋕⚷ 2:32, ☽⚻♆ 5:33, ☽⚻♇ 5:56, ☽⋕☿ 6:37, ☽∠☿ 6:55, ☽□♂ 9:18, ☽∥♄ 9:39, ☽⚼♄ 12:45, ☽⊻⚳ 13:07, ☽□♅ 13:34, ☽∥♃ 15:05, ☽∥⚳ 21:37, ☉☍⚷ 23:28

26 Tu ⚳△♅ 2:47, ☽⚼⚷ 3:02, ☉∠☽ 3:19, ☽☌♃ 6:17, ☽⚼♇ 7:09, ☽⊻☿ 7:14, ☽∥♆ 9:01, ☽⚹♀ 12:14, ☽⋕♆ 12:22, ☽⚻♄ 13:50, ☽⋕⚳ 23:07

27 W ☽⚻⚷ 4:11, ♀⚻♄ 5:33, ☽⋕♃ 5:56, ☉⊻☽ 6:27, ☿⋕♄ 6:51, ☽☍♆ 7:56, ☽△♇ 8:25, ☿⊻♃ 8:58, ☽∥☿ 11:25, ☽⋕♄ 11:37, ☽⚹♂ 14:29, ☽∠♀ 15:56, ☽△♅ 15:58, ☽☌⚳ 17:16, ♂⚼♄ 23:09

28 Th ☉⚻♆ 3:03, ☉∠♃ 6:44, ☽⋕⚷ 8:54, ☽☌☿ 9:05, ☽⊻♃ 9:38, ☉□♇ 10:28, ☉∥☽ 14:10, ☿ D 14:12, ♀∠⚳ 14:52, ☽☍♄ 16:21, ☽∠♂ 17:23, ☽⚼♅ 17:26, ♂☍♅ 18:08, ☽⊻♀ 19:57

29 F ♃⚼♇ 3:51, ☽☍⚷ 7:08, ☽⚻♆ 11:04, ☽□♇ 11:40, ☽∠♃ 11:46, ☉☌☽ 13:38, ☽⚻♅ 19:19, ☽⊻♂ 20:48, ☽∥♀ 21:47, ☽⊻⚳ 22:32

30 Sa ☽⋕♅ 9:45, ☽⚼♆ 13:23, ☽⊻☿ 13:51, ☽⚹♃ 14:30, ☽∥♂ 17:38, ☽⚻♄ 20:31, ☽∥♇ 23:53

31 Su ☽∠⚳ 2:07, ☽☌♀ 6:01, ☽⚻⚷ 12:10, ☽△♆ 16:26, ☽⚹♇ 17:10, ☽∠☿ 17:55, ☿⊻♃ 20:25, ☽⚼♄ 23:40, ☉⊻☽ 23:41

LONGITUDE

November 2027

Day	Sid.Time	☉	☽	☽ 12 hour	Mean☊	True☊	☿	♀	♂	⚳	♃	♄	⚷	♅	♆	♇
	h m s	° ' "	° ' "	° ' "	° '	° '	° '	° '	° '	° '	° '	° '	° '	° '	° '	° '
1 M	2 40 15	8♏20 06	8♐29 51	14♐56 27	6♒44.7	6♒34.7	20♎20.6	29♏36.4	11♐34.0	11♎55.1	20♍17.0	23♈19.1	2♉02.2	9♊05.6	4♈22.6	4♒47.6
2 Tu	2 44 11	9 20 09	21 17 46	27 34 02	6 41.5	6R 25.9	20 59.9	0♐50.9	12 17.9	12 21.8	20 27.6	23R 14.6	1R 59.3	9R 03.5	4R 21.3	4 48.0
3 W	2 48 08	10 20 12	3♑45 35	9♑52 50	6 38.3	6 19.8	21 47.3	2 05.5	13 01.9	12 48.4	20 38.0	23 10.1	1 56.5	9 01.4	4 20.1	4 48.5
4 Th	2 52 04	11 20 18	15 56 17	21 56 31	6 35.2	6 16.5	22 42.0	3 20.0	13 45.9	13 15.1	20 48.4	23 05.7	1 53.7	8 59.2	4 18.8	4 48.9
5 F	2 56 01	12 20 25	27 54 08	3♒49 47	6 32.0	6D 15.2	23 43.1	4 34.5	14 30.0	13 41.6	20 58.7	23 01.3	1 50.9	8 57.1	4 17.6	4 49.4
6 Sa	2 59 58	13 20 33	9♒44 11	15 38 00	6 28.8	6R 15.0	24 49.8	5 49.0	15 14.2	14 08.2	21 08.9	22 57.0	1 48.2	8 54.9	4 16.3	4 50.0
7 Su	3 03 54	14 20 43	21 31 57	27 26 44	6 25.6	6 14.9	26 01.3	7 03.4	15 58.4	14 34.7	21 18.9	22 52.7	1 45.4	8 52.7	4 15.2	4 50.5
8 M	3 07 51	15 20 55	3♓23 02	9♓21 30	6 22.5	6 13.7	27 17.0	8 17.9	16 42.7	15 01.1	21 28.9	22 48.5	1 42.7	8 50.4	4 14.0	4 51.1
9 Tu	3 11 47	16 21 08	15 22 45	21 27 21	6 19.3	6 10.4	28 36.2	9 32.4	17 27.0	15 27.5	21 38.8	22 44.3	1 39.9	8 48.2	4 12.8	4 51.7
10 W	3 15 44	17 21 23	27 35 47	3♈48 31	6 16.1	6 04.6	29 58.4	10 46.8	18 11.4	15 53.8	21 48.6	22 40.1	1 37.2	8 45.9	4 11.7	4 52.3
11 Th	3 19 40	18 21 39	10♈05 52	16 28 06	6 12.9	5 56.0	1♏23.1	12 01.3	18 55.9	16 20.1	21 58.3	22 36.1	1 34.5	8 43.6	4 10.6	4 53.0
12 F	3 23 37	19 21 56	22 55 20	29 27 38	6 09.7	5 45.2	2 50.0	13 15.7	19 40.4	16 46.3	22 07.9	22 32.1	1 31.8	8 41.2	4 09.6	4 53.7
13 Sa	3 27 33	20 22 15	6♉04 55	12♉47 00	6 06.6	5 33.0	4 18.6	14 30.2	20 25.0	17 12.5	22 17.4	22 28.1	1 29.2	8 38.9	4 08.5	4 54.4
14 Su	3 31 30	21 22 36	19 33 34	26 24 16	6 03.4	5 20.4	5 48.6	15 44.6	21 09.7	17 38.6	22 26.8	22 24.3	1 26.5	8 36.5	4 07.5	4 55.1
15 M	3 35 27	22 22 59	3♊18 37	10♊16 07	6 00.2	5 08.8	7 19.8	16 59.0	21 54.4	18 04.7	22 36.1	22 20.5	1 23.9	8 34.1	4 06.5	4 55.9
16 Tu	3 39 23	23 23 23	17 16 14	24 18 24	5 57.0	4 59.3	8 51.9	18 13.4	22 39.1	18 30.7	22 45.3	22 16.7	1 21.3	8 31.7	4 05.6	4 56.7
17 W	3 43 20	24 23 49	1♋22 06	8♋26 50	5 53.9	4 52.5	10 24.8	19 27.8	23 24.0	18 56.7	22 54.3	22 13.0	1 18.7	8 29.3	4 04.6	4 57.5
18 Th	3 47 16	25 24 17	15 32 08	22 37 38	5 50.7	4 48.7	11 58.2	20 42.2	24 08.9	19 22.6	23 03.3	22 09.5	1 16.2	8 26.9	4 03.7	4 58.4
19 F	3 51 13	26 24 47	29 43 00	6♌48 00	5 47.5	4D 47.3	13 32.1	21 56.6	24 53.8	19 48.4	23 12.1	22 05.9	1 13.7	8 24.4	4 02.9	4 59.2
20 Sa	3 55 09	27 25 18	13♌52 25	20 56 07	5 44.3	4 47.3	15 06.4	23 11.0	25 38.8	20 14.2	23 20.9	22 02.5	1 11.2	8 22.0	4 02.0	5 00.1
21 Su	3 59 06	28 25 52	27 58 59	5♍00 54	5 41.2	4R 47.7	16 40.9	24 25.4	26 23.9	20 39.9	23 29.5	21 59.1	1 08.7	8 19.5	4 01.2	5 01.1
22 M	4 03 02	29 26 27	12♍01 49	19 01 36	5 38.0	4 47.0	18 15.5	25 39.7	27 09.0	21 05.6	23 38.0	21 55.8	1 06.3	8 17.0	4 00.4	5 02.0
23 Tu	4 06 59	0♐27 03	26 00 08	2♎57 17	5 34.8	4 44.3	19 50.3	26 54.1	27 54.2	21 31.2	23 46.3	21 52.6	1 03.9	8 14.5	3 59.7	5 03.0
24 W	4 10 56	1 27 42	9♎52 51	16 46 36	5 31.6	4 39.0	21 25.1	28 08.5	28 39.4	21 56.7	23 54.6	21 49.5	1 01.5	8 12.0	3 58.9	5 04.0
25 Th	4 14 52	2 28 22	23 38 15	0♏27 33	5 28.4	4 31.2	22 59.9	29 22.8	29 24.7	22 22.2	24 02.7	21 46.5	0 59.2	8 09.5	3 58.2	5 05.0
26 F	4 18 49	3 29 04	7♏14 10	13 57 46	5 25.3	4 21.3	24 34.8	0♑37.1	0♑10.1	22 47.5	24 10.7	21 43.5	0 56.9	8 07.0	3 57.6	5 06.1
27 Sa	4 22 45	4 29 47	20 38 05	27 14 49	5 22.1	4 10.4	26 09.5	1 51.5	0 55.5	23 12.9	24 18.5	21 40.6	0 54.6	8 04.4	3 56.9	5 07.1
28 Su	4 26 42	5 30 32	3♐47 44	10♐16 39	5 18.9	3 59.6	27 44.3	3 05.8	1 41.0	23 38.1	24 26.2	21 37.9	0 52.4	8 01.9	3 56.3	5 08.2
29 M	4 30 38	6 31 18	16 41 27	23 02 07	5 15.7	3 50.0	29 18.9	4 20.1	2 26.5	24 03.3	24 33.8	21 35.2	0 50.2	7 59.4	3 55.8	5 09.4
30 Tu	4 34 35	7♐32 05	29 18 39	5♑31 11	5♒12.6	3♒42.4	0♐53.6	5♑34.4	3♑12.1	24♎28.4	24♍41.3	21♈32.6	0♉48.0	7♊56.8	3♈55.2	5♒10.5

1st of Month

Julian Day #
2461710.5
Obliquity
23°26'[illegible]4"
SVP 4♓52'[illegible]4"
GC 27♐13.7
Eris 25♈30.7R

Day	⚴	Day	⚵	Day	⚶
1	10♍40.0	1	28♋14.6	1	12♌12.5
6	12 56.1	6	29 32.6	6	13 25.8
11	15 07.9	11	0♌40.4	11	14 32.9
16	17 15.0	16	1 37.0	16	15 33.1
21	19 17.2	21	2 21.7	21	16 25.8
26	21 14.1	26	2 53.7	26	17 10.4

DECLINATION and LATITUDE

Day	☉ Decl	☽ Decl	☽ Lat	☽12h Decl	☿ Decl	☿ Lat	♀ Decl	♀ Lat	♂ Decl	♂ Lat	⚳ Decl	⚳ Lat	♃ Decl	♃ Lat	♄ Decl	♄ Lat
1 M	14S17	25S55	4S16	26S30	6S09	1N56	20S24	0S20	23S01	0S51	2N29	7N48	4N48	1N02	6N29	2S46
2 Tu	14 36	26 43	3 34	26 34	6 18	2 02	20 42	0 23	23 07	0 52	2 19	7 49	4 44	1 02	6 27	2 46
3 W	14 55	26 06	2 43	25 19	6 32	2 07	20 60	0 26	23 13	0 52	2 09	7 49	4 40	1 02	6 26	2 46
4 Th	15 14	24 14	1 45	22 53	6 49	2 10	21 17	0 28	23 19	0 53	1 59	7 50	4 36	1 02	6 24	2 46
5 F	15 32	21 18	0 44	19 30	7 09	2 12	21 33	0 31	23 25	0 53	1 49	7 50	4 32	1 02	6 23	2 46
6 Sa	15 51	17 31	0N19	15 21	7 33	2 13	21 49	0 33	23 30	0 53	1 40	7 51	4 28	1 03	6 21	2 46
7 Su	16 09	13 04	1 20	10 38	7 59	2 13	22 05	0 36	23 35	0 54	1 30	7 51	4 24	1 03	6 20	2 46
8 M	16 26	8 07	2 19	5 30	8 27	2 12	22 19	0 39	23 40	0 54	1 20	7 52	4 21	1 03	6 18	2 46
9 Tu	16 44	2 49	3 12	0 05	8 57	2 10	22 33	0 41	23 45	0 55	1 11	7 52	4 17	1 03	6 17	2 45
10 W	17 01	2N40	3 57	5N25	9 29	2 07	22 47	0 44	23 49	0 55	1 01	7 53	4 13	1 03	6 16	2 45
11 Th	17 18	8 10	4 32	10 51	10 01	2 03	22 60	0 46	23 54	0 55	0 52	7 53	4 09	1 04	6 14	2 45
12 F	17 34	13 27	4 54	15 57	10 35	1 60	23 12	0 49	23 58	0 56	0 42	7 54	4 06	1 04	6 13	2 45
13 Sa	17 50	18 17	5 01	20 25	11 09	1 55	23 23	0 51	24 01	0 56	0 33	7 54	4 02	1 04	6 12	2 45
14 Su	18 06	22 18	4 52	23 54	11 43	1 50	23 34	0 54	24 05	0 56	0 24	7 55	3 59	1 04	6 10	2 45
15 M	18 22	25 10	4 26	26 03	12 18	1 45	23 44	0 56	24 08	0 57	0 14	7 55	3 55	1 04	6 09	2 44
16 Tu	18 37	26 33	3 44	26 36	12 53	1 39	23 53	0 58	24 11	0 57	0 05	7 56	3 52	1 05	6 08	2 44
17 W	18 52	26 25	2 48	25 25	13 28	1 34	24 02	1 01	24 14	0 57	0S04	7 56	3 48	1 05	6 07	2 44
18 Th	19 07	24 12	1 40	22 36	14 02	1 27	24 10	1 03	24 16	0 58	0 13	7 57	3 45	1 05	6 05	2 44
19 F	19 21	20 39	0 27	18 24	14 37	1 21	24 17	1 06	24 18	0 58	0 22	7 58	3 42	1 05	6 04	2 44
20 Sa	19 35	15 53	0S48	13 10	15 11	1 15	24 23	1 08	24 20	0 58	0 31	7 58	3 39	1 05	6 03	2 44
21 Su	19 49	10 17	2 00	7 17	15 44	1 08	24 29	1 10	24 22	0 59	0 40	7 59	3 35	1 06	6 02	2 43
22 M	20 02	4 12	3 05	1 05	16 17	1 01	24 34	1 12	24 23	0 59	0 49	7 59	3 32	1 06	6 01	2 43
23 Tu	20 15	2S03	3 58	5S08	16 49	0 54	24 38	1 14	24 25	0 59	0 58	8 00	3 29	1 06	6 00	2 43
24 W	20 27	8 09	4 36	11 03	17 21	0 48	24 42	1 16	24 26	0 60	1 06	8 01	3 26	1 06	5 59	2 43
25 Th	20 39	13 48	4 58	16 21	17 52	0 41	24 45	1 19	24 26	1 00	1 15	8 01	3 23	1 06	5 58	2 43
26 F	20 51	18 42	5 03	20 47	18 22	0 34	24 47	1 21	24 27	1 00	1 24	8 02	3 20	1 07	5 57	2 42
27 Sa	21 02	22 35	4 52	24 05	18 52	0 27	24 48	1 23	24 27	1 01	1 32	8 03	3 17	1 07	5 56	2 42
28 Su	21 13	25 14	4 24	26 02	19 20	0 20	24 48	1 24	24 26	1 01	1 41	8 03	3 14	1 07	5 56	2 42
29 M	21 24	26 29	3 44	26 35	19 48	0 13	24 48	1 26	24 26	1 01	1 49	8 04	3 11	1 07	5 55	2 42
30 Tu	21S34	26S19	2S53	25S44	20S14	0N06	24S47	1S28	24S25	1S01	1S58	8N05	3N09	1N08	5N54	2S41

Day	⚷ Decl	⚷ Lat	♅ Decl	♅ Lat	♆ Decl	♆ Lat	♇ Decl	♇ Lat
1	11N51	0S21	21N43	0S06	0N24	1S28	23S41	4S46
6	11 46	0 21	21 42	0 06	0 22	1 27	23 40	4 46
11	11 41	0 21	21 40	0 05	0 20	1 27	23 39	4 45
16	11 36	0 22	21 38	0 05	0 18	1 27	23 38	4 45
21	11 32	0 22	21 36	0 05	0 16	1 27	23 37	4 45
26	11 27	0 22	21 34	0 05	0 15	1 27	23 35	4 45

Day	⚴ Decl	⚴ Lat	⚵ Decl	⚵ Lat	⚶ Decl	⚶ Lat	Eris Decl	Eris Lat
1	11S02	20S05	4N37	16S12	17N47	0N41	0N16	10S18
6	11 36	19 48	3 57	16 38	17 36	0 51	0 15	10 17
11	12 08	19 30	3 19	17 04	17 28	1 02	0 14	10 17
16	12 38	19 11	2 43	17 29	17 21	1 14	0 14	10 16
21	13 06	18 51	2 09	17 55	17 18	1 27	0 13	10 16
26	13 31	18 30	1 39	18 19	17 17	1 41	0 13	10 16

Moon Phenomena

Max/0 Decl (dy hr mn)
2 1:13 26S43
9 12:23 0 N
16 7:36 26N38
22 16:08 0 S
29 9:06 26S35

Max/0 Lat (dy hr mn)
5 16:54 0 N
12 23:03 5N01
19 8:35 0 S
25 18:57 5S04

Perigee/Apogee (dy hr m kilometers)
6 11:39 a 404179
19 0:11 p 369360

PH (dy hr mn)
☽ 6 8:01 13♒41
○ 14 3:27 21♉31
☾ 21 0:49 28♌28
● 28 3:26 5♐39

Void of Course Moon

Last Aspect	☽ Ingress
2 3:41 ♄ △	♑ 2 16:42
4 14:45 ☿ □	♒ 5 4:14
7 10:11 ♅ △	♓ 7 17:10
9 12:33 ♃ ☍	♈ 10 4:40
11 23:17 ♄ ☌	♉ 12 12:59
14 5:08 ♃ △	♊ 14 18:16
16 9:42 ♂ ☍	♋ 16 21:41
18 17:59 ☉ △	♌ 19 0:29
21 0:49 ☉ □	♍ 21 3:26
23 3:28 ♂ □	♎ 23 6:54
25 11:06 ♀ ⚹	♏ 25 11:11
27 11:23 ☿ ☌	♐ 27 17:02
29 15:04 ♃ □	♑ 30 1:20

DAILY ASPECTARIAN

1 M ☽☍♅ 1:06; ☽☌♂ 6:02; ☽⚹⚳ 6:35; ♀ ♐ 7:36; ☽⚼⚷ 15:53; ☉⊼♅ 17:34; ☽∠♇ 21:10; ☽□♃ 22:23; ☽⚹☿ 23:24

2 Tu ☽△♄ 3:41; ♂⚹⚳ 5:20; ☉∠☽ 6:18; ☿#♄ 15:32; ☽⚺♀ 20:23; ☽△⚷ 20:29; ♀⊼⚷ 21:14

3 W ☽□♆ 1:07; ☽⚺♇ 2:03; ☽⊼♅ 10:17; ☉⚹☽ 14:03; ☽□⚳ 18:28; ☽⚺♂ 19:24

4 Th ☽∥♇ 5:13; ☽∠♀ 5:19; ☽∥♂ 8:05; ☿☍♄ 8:56; ☽△♃ 9:52; ☽□♄ 14:14; ☽□☿ 14:45; ☽⚼♅ 16:04; ♀△♆ 18:39; ☽#♅ 21:08; ☽∥♀ 22:18

5 F ☽∠♂ 3:27; ♀⚹♇ 4:51; ☿⚼♅ 5:02; ☽□⚷ 7:57; ♀#♅ 12:22; ☽⚹♆ 12:55; ☽☌♇ 14:02; ☽⚹♀ 15:06; ☽⚼♃ 16:36; ☊ D 16:54; ☽△♅ 22:20

6 Sa ☊ R 7:53; ☉□☽ 8:01; ☉∥☽ 8:47; ☽△⚳ 9:18; ☽⚹♂ 11:56; ☽∠♆ 19:22; ☽⊼♃ 23:33

7 Su ☽⚹♄ 2:43; ☽#⚷ 6:34; ☉⚺⚳ 9:55; ☽△☿ 10:11; ♀⚼♄ 15:01; ☽⚼⚳ 16:57; ☽⚹⚷ 20:38; ♂∥♇ 21:42; ⚵ ♌ 22:16; ☽∥☿ 22:31; ♂⚼⚷ 23:59

8 M ☽⚺♆ 1:42; ☽⚺♇ 2:57; ☽#♄ 8:21; ☽∠♄ 8:50; ♀☍♅ 10:10; ☽□♅ 10:56; ☽□♀ 11:01; ☽#♃ 17:24; ☽⚼☿ 20:02

9 Tu ☽⊼⚳ 0:10; ☉△☽ 2:06; ☽∠⚷ 2:32; ☽□♂ 4:22; ☽#⚳ 7:26; ☽∠♇ 8:52; ☽#♆ 10:55; ☽☍♃ 12:33; ☽∥♆ 13:51; ☽⚺♄ 14:26; ☽∥⚳ 17:03

10 W ☿ ♏ 0:27; ☽⊼☿ 5:12; ☽∥♃ 6:41; ☽⚺⚷ 7:46; ☉⚼☽ 10:01; ☽☌♆ 12:43; ☽⚹♇ 14:03; ☽∥♄ 15:35; ☽⚹♅ 21:24

11 Th ☿☍⚷ 3:04; ☽△♀ 4:02; ☽#☿ 9:14; ☽☍⚳ 12:10; ☽∥⚷ 15:45; ☉⊼☽ 16:51; ☽△♂ 17:37; ☉⚼♆ 19:10; ☽⊼♃ 22:31; ☽☌♄ 23:17

12 F ☽∠♅ 1:24; ♂∠♇ 7:15; ☽⚼♀ 10:50; ☽☌⚷ 15:43; ☽☍☿ 20:24; ☽⚺♆ 20:30; ☿⊼♆ 21:20; ☉#☽ 21:31; ☽□♇ 21:53; ☽⚼♂ 22:44

13 Sa ☽⚼♃ 2:12; ☉⚺♂ 4:12; ☽⚺♅ 4:36; ☿□♇ 9:40; ☽⊼♀ 16:35; ♃⊼♄ 19:22; ☽∥♅ 19:39; ☽⊼⚳ 20:30; ☿#⚷ 20:31; ☽∠♆ 23:14

14 Su ☽⊼♂ 2:59; ☉☍☽ 3:27; ☽⚺♄ 4:59; ☽△♃ 5:08; ☽#♀ 9:49; ☽#♇ 9:52; ♀∥♇ 10:49; ☿∠♂ 10:56; ♀⚼⚷ 13:04; ☽#♂ 13:48; ⚳∥♆ 14:24; ☽⚺⚷ 20:42; ☉⊼♄ 23:03; ☽⚼⚳ 23:35

15 M ☽⚹♆ 1:23; ☽△♇ 2:48; ☿∠♃ 4:45; ☉⚹♃ 6:09; ☽∠♄ 6:56; ☽⊼☿ 7:48; ☽☌♅ 9:03; ♂△♄ 12:54; ☿⊼♅ 18:54; ☽∠⚷ 22:26

16 Tu ☽☍♀ 1:47; ☽△⚳ 2:11; ♂□♃ 4:08; ☽⚼♇ 4:34; ☽⚹♄ 8:31; ♀⚹⚳ 8:34; ☽□♃ 9:28; ☽☍♂ 9:42; ☉⊼☽ 11:15; ☽⚼☿ 12:38; ☽⚹⚷ 23:54

17 W ☽□♆ 4:35; ☽⊼♇ 6:06; ♀∠♇ 9:41; ☽⚺♅ 12:02; ☉⚼☽ 14:39; ☽△☿ 17:13; ☽#♂ 23:22

18 Th ☽#♀ 0:16; ☽#♇ 4:36; ☽□⚳ 6:42; ☽⊼♀ 9:35; ⚳#♆ 10:09; ☽□♄ 11:10; ☽⚹♃ 12:52; ☽∠♅ 13:21; ☽⊼♂ 15:23; ☉△☽ 17:59; ☽∥♅ 18:16

19 F ☽□⚷ 2:33; ♀△♄ 2:52; ☉#☽ 6:45; ☽△♆ 7:20; ♀∥♂ 7:46; ☊ D 8:33; ☽☍♇ 8:56; ☽⚼♀ 13:25; ☽∠♃ 14:32; ☽⚹♅ 14:41; ☽⚼♂ 18:13

20 Sa ☽□☿ 2:21; ☽#☿ 2:56; ♀□♃ 3:36; ☽⚼♆ 8:45; ☽⚹⚳ 11:09; ☽△♄ 13:50; ☽⚺♃ 16:16; ☽△♀ 17:21; ☽∥⚷ 18:55; ☽△♂ 21:09

21 Su ☉□☽ 0:49; ☊ R 1:01; ☽△⚷ 5:23; ☽⊼♆ 10:17; ☽⊼♇ 12:01; ☽∠⚳ 13:31; ☽⚼♄ 15:18; ☽∥♄ 16:57; ☽□♅ 17:36

22 M ☽∥♃ 2:35; ☽⚼⚷ 6:58; ☿⚼♆ 11:17; ☽⚹☿ 12:02; ☽#⚳ 12:43; ☉ ♐ 13:17; ☽⚼♇ 13:45; ☽∥♆ 15:08; ☽⚺⚳ 16:02; ☽⊼♄ 16:56; ☽#♆ 17:08; ☽∥⚳ 19:43; ☽☌♃ 20:07

23 Tu ☽□♀ 1:42; ☽□♂ 3:28; ☽#♃ 5:31; ☉⚹☽ 8:16; ☽⊼⚷ 8:43; ☽☍♆ 13:47; ☉⊼⚷ 14:02; ☽#♄ 15:23; ☽△♇ 15:39; ☽∠☿ 17:13; ⚳☍♄ 17:57; ☽△♅ 21:06

24 W ☿⊼♄ 5:59; ☿⚺⚳ 10:56; ☉∠☽ 12:22; ☽#⚷ 13:49; ☽☍♄ 20:45; ☽☌⚳ 21:42; ☽⚺☿ 22:44; ☽⚼♅ 23:10

25 Th ☽⚺♃ 0:43; ♀☌♂ 1:37; ☽⚹♂ 10:45; ☽⚹♀ 11:06; ♀ ♑ 12:01; ☽☍⚷ 12:54; ☉⚺☽ 16:49; ☿⚹♃ 17:21; ☽⊼♆ 18:12; ♂ ♑ 18:39; ☽□♇ 20:12; ☽∥☿ 22:00

26 F ☽⊼♅ 1:34; ☽∠♃ 3:29; ♀△⚷ 6:11; ☉△♆ 11:09; ☉∥☽ 13:02; ☽∠♂ 15:01; ☽∠♀ 16:30; ⚳⚼♅ 16:44; ☽#♅ 16:57; ☽⚼♆ 20:58; ♂△⚷ 23:33

27 Sa ☽⊼♄ 1:53; ☽⚺⚳ 4:49; ☽⚹♃ 6:43; ☽∥♇ 7:42; ☽☌☿ 11:23; ☉⚹♇ 15:02; ☽∥♂ 15:27; ☽⊼⚷ 18:39; ☽∥♀ 19:10; ☽⚺♂ 19:53; ☽⚺♀ 22:35

28 Su ☽△♆ 0:16; ☽⚹♇ 2:29; ☉☌☽ 3:26; ☽⚼♄ 5:13; ☽☍♅ 7:48; ☽∠⚳ 9:15; ♀□♆ 16:12; ☽⚼⚷ 22:24

29 M ☉⚼♄ 1:29; ☽∠♇ 6:33; ☽△♄ 9:13; ☿ ♐ 10:25; ☽⚹⚳ 14:25; ☽□♃ 15:04; ♀⚺♇ 16:10; ☉#♅ 21:10; ☿⊼⚷ 22:38

30 Tu ☽△⚷ 2:52; ☽⚺☿ 3:29; ☽☌♂ 8:00; ☽□♆ 8:53; ☉☍♅ 9:23; ☽⚺♇ 11:21; ☽☌♀ 13:27; ☽⊼♅ 16:40; ☉⚺☽ 17:21; ⚳⚺♃ 17:33; ♂□♆ 22:25

December 2027

LONGITUDE

Day	Sid.Time	☉	☽	☽ 12 hour	Mean☊	True☊	☿	♀	♂	⚳	♃	♄	⚷	♅	♆	♇
	h m s	° ' "	° ' "	° ' "	° '	° '	° '	° '	° '	° '	° '	° '	° '	° '	° '	° '
1 W	4 38 32	8♐32 53	11♑39 55	17♑45 08	5♒09.4	3♒37.3	2♐28.1	6♑48.7	3♑57.8	24♎53.4	24♍48.6	21♈30.1	0♉45.9	7♊54.3	3♈54.7	5♒11.7
2 Th	4 42 28	9 33 43	23 47 10	29 46 28	5 06.2	3D 34.7	4 02.5	8 03.0	4 43.4	25 18.3	24 55.8	21R 27.7	0R 43.9	7R 51.8	3R 54.2	5 12.9
3 F	4 46 25	10 34 33	5♒43 28	11♒38 45	5 03.0	3 34.1	5 36.9	9 17.2	5 29.2	25 43.2	25 02.9	21 25.4	0 41.8	7 49.3	3 53.8	5 14.1
4 Sa	4 50 21	11 35 25	17 32 51	23 26 25	4 59.9	3 34.9	7 11.3	10 31.5	6 15.0	26 07.9	25 09.7	21 23.2	0 39.8	7 46.7	3 53.4	5 15.4
5 Su	4 54 18	12 36 17	29 20 05	5♓14 31	4 56.7	3 36.2	8 45.5	11 45.7	7 00.8	26 32.6	25 16.5	21 21.1	0 37.9	7 44.2	3 53.0	5 16.6
6 M	4 58 14	13 37 10	11♓10 23	17 08 23	4 53.5	3R 37.0	10 19.8	12 59.9	7 46.7	26 57.2	25 23.1	21 19.1	0 36.0	7 41.7	3 52.7	5 17.9
7 Tu	5 02 11	14 38 03	23 09 09	29 13 22	4 50.3	3 36.6	11 54.0	14 14.1	8 32.6	27 21.7	25 29.6	21 17.2	0 34.1	7 39.2	3 52.4	5 19.2
8 W	5 06 07	15 38 58	5♈21 37	11♈34 29	4 47.2	3 34.3	13 28.2	15 28.2	9 18.6	27 46.1	25 35.9	21 15.4	0 32.3	7 36.7	3 52.1	5 20.5
9 Th	5 10 04	16 39 53	17 52 27	24 15 56	4 44.0	3 30.0	15 02.4	16 42.4	10 04.6	28 10.4	25 42.0	21 13.8	0 30.5	7 34.2	3 51.9	5 21.9
10 F	5 14 01	17 40 49	0♉45 17	7♉20 41	4 40.8	3 23.9	16 36.6	17 56.5	10 50.7	28 34.7	25 48.0	21 12.2	0 28.8	7 31.7	3 51.7	5 23.3
11 Sa	5 17 57	18 41 46	14 02 13	20 49 50	4 37.6	3 16.6	18 10.8	19 10.6	11 36.8	28 58.8	25 53.9	21 10.7	0 27.1	7 29.2	3 51.5	5 24.6
12 Su	5 21 54	19 42 43	27 43 20	4♊42 23	4 34.4	3 08.9	19 45.1	20 24.7	12 22.9	29 22.8	25 59.6	21 09.3	0 25.5	7 26.8	3 51.4	5 26.1
13 M	5 25 50	20 43 42	11♊46 30	18 55 04	4 31.3	3 01.7	21 19.4	21 38.7	13 09.1	29 46.8	26 05.1	21 08.0	0 23.9	7 24.3	3 51.3	5 27.5
14 Tu	5 29 47	21 44 41	26 07 24	3♋22 43	4 28.1	2 55.9	22 53.8	22 52.7	13 55.4	0♏10.6	26 10.5	21 06.9	0 22.3	7 21.9	3 51.2	5 28.9
15 W	5 33 43	22 45 41	10♋40 10	17 58 55	4 24.9	2 51.9	24 28.4	24 06.7	14 41.7	0 34.4	26 15.8	21 05.8	0 20.9	7 19.5	3D 51.2	5 30.4
16 Th	5 37 40	23 46 42	25 18 09	2♌37 04	4 21.8	2D 50.1	26 03.0	25 20.7	15 28.0	0 58.0	26 20.8	21 04.9	0 19.4	7 17.1	3 51.2	5 31.9
17 F	5 41 36	24 47 43	9♌54 59	17 11 15	4 18.6	2 50.0	27 37.7	26 34.7	16 14.4	1 21.5	26 25.7	21 04.0	0 18.0	7 14.7	3 51.2	5 33.4
18 Sa	5 45 33	25 48 46	24 25 22	1♍36 53	4 15.4	2 51.2	29 12.6	27 48.6	17 00.8	1 45.0	26 30.5	21 03.3	0 16.7	7 12.3	3 51.3	5 34.9
19 Su	5 49 30	26 49 49	8♍45 29	15 50 54	4 12.2	2 52.7	0♑47.6	29 02.5	17 47.2	2 08.3	26 35.0	21 02.7	0 15.4	7 10.0	3 51.4	5 36.5
20 M	5 53 26	27 50 53	22 52 59	29 51 39	4 09.0	2R 53.7	2 22.7	0♒16.3	18 33.7	2 31.5	26 39.4	21 02.2	0 14.2	7 07.6	3 51.5	5 38.0
21 Tu	5 57 23	28 51 58	6♎46 49	13♎38 29	4 05.9	2 53.5	3 58.1	1 30.2	19 20.3	2 54.6	26 43.6	21 01.8	0 13.0	7 05.3	3 51.7	5 39.6
22 W	6 01 19	29 53 04	20 26 41	27 11 26	4 02.7	2 51.8	5 33.6	2 44.0	20 06.8	3 17.6	26 47.7	21 01.5	0 11.9	7 03.0	3 51.9	5 41.2
23 Th	6 05 16	0♑54 11	3♏52 46	10♏30 43	3 59.5	2 48.5	7 09.2	3 57.8	20 53.5	3 40.5	26 51.6	21 01.3	0 10.8	7 00.8	3 52.1	5 42.8
24 F	6 09 12	1 55 19	17 05 21	23 36 39	3 56.3	2 44.0	8 45.1	5 11.5	21 40.1	4 03.2	26 55.3	21D 01.2	0 09.8	6 58.5	3 52.4	5 44.4
25 Sa	6 13 09	2 56 27	0♐04 41	6♐29 28	3 53.2	2 38.9	10 21.1	6 25.3	22 26.8	4 25.8	26 58.8	21 01.3	0 08.8	6 56.3	3 52.7	5 46.1
26 Su	6 17 05	3 57 36	12 51 02	19 09 25	3 50.0	2 33.7	11 57.3	7 39.0	23 13.5	4 48.3	27 02.2	21 01.4	0 07.9	6 54.1	3 53.1	5 47.7
27 M	6 21 02	4 58 45	25 24 41	1♑36 53	3 46.8	2 29.1	13 33.6	8 52.6	24 00.3	5 10.7	27 05.3	21 01.7	0 07.1	6 52.0	3 53.5	5 49.4
28 Tu	6 24 59	5 59 55	7♑46 09	13 52 36	3 43.6	2 25.7	15 10.1	10 06.2	24 47.1	5 32.9	27 08.3	21 02.1	0 06.3	6 49.9	3 53.9	5 51.1
29 W	6 28 55	7 01 04	19 56 23	25 57 44	3 40.5	2 23.6	16 46.7	11 19.8	25 33.9	5 55.0	27 11.1	21 02.6	0 05.5	6 47.8	3 54.4	5 52.8
30 Th	6 32 52	8 02 14	1♒56 53	7♒54 08	3 37.3	2D 22.9	18 23.3	12 33.4	26 20.8	6 17.0	27 13.7	21 03.2	0 04.9	6 45.7	3 54.8	5 54.5
31 F	6 36 48	9♑03 25	13 49 48	19 44 16	3♒34.1	2♒23.4	20♑00.0	13♒46.9	27♑07.7	6♏38.9	27♍16.2	21♈03.9	0♉04.2	6♊43.7	3♈55.4	5♒56.2

1st of Month		
Julian Day #		
2461740.5		
Obliquity		
23°26'13"		
SVP 4♓51'58"		
GC 27♐13.8		
Eris 25♈15.1R		
Day	⚴	
1	23♍	05.2
6	24	49.9
11	26	27.9
16	27	58.5
21	29	21.3
26	0♎	35.5
31	1	40.3
	⚵	
1	3♌	12.1
6	3	16.5R
11	3	06.9R
16	2	43.5R
21	2	06.7R
26	1	17.5R
31	0	17.6R
	⚶	
1	17♌	46.1
6	18	12.3
11	18	28.3
16	18	33.6R
21	18	27.8R
26	18	10.5R
31	17	41.6R

DECLINATION and LATITUDE

Day	☉ Decl	☽ Decl	☽ Lat	☽ 12h Decl	☿ Decl	☿ Lat	♀ Decl	♀ Lat	♂ Decl	♂ Lat	⚳ Decl	⚳ Lat	♃ Decl	♃ Lat	♄ Decl	♄ Lat
1 W	21S44	24S50	1S55	23S39	20S40	0S01	24S45	1S30	24S24	1S02	2S06	8N05	3N06	1N08	5N53	2S41
2 Th	21 53	22 12	0 52	20 32	21 05	0 08	24 43	1 32	24 23	1 02	2 14	8 06	3 03	1 08	5 53	2 41
3 F	22 02	18 39	0N12	16 36	21 29	0 15	24 40	1 33	24 22	1 02	2 22	8 07	3 01	1 08	5 52	2 41
4 Sa	22 10	14 23	1 15	12 03	21 51	0 21	24 36	1 35	24 20	1 02	2 30	8 08	2 58	1 09	5 52	2 40
5 Su	22 18	9 36	2 14	7 04	22 13	0 28	24 31	1 36	24 18	1 03	2 38	8 08	2 56	1 09	5 51	2 40
6 M	22 26	4 28	3 09	1 48	22 34	0 34	24 26	1 38	24 15	1 03	2 46	8 09	2 53	1 09	5 50	2 40
7 Tu	22 33	0N53	3 55	3N36	22 53	0 41	24 19	1 39	24 13	1 03	2 54	8 10	2 51	1 09	5 50	2 40
8 W	22 40	6 18	4 32	8 58	23 11	0 47	24 12	1 41	24 10	1 03	3 02	8 11	2 49	1 09	5 50	2 39
9 Th	22 46	11 35	4 57	14 08	23 28	0 53	24 05	1 42	24 07	1 04	3 10	8 11	2 47	1 10	5 49	2 39
10 F	22 52	16 33	5 08	18 48	23 44	0 59	23 56	1 43	24 03	1 04	3 17	8 12	2 44	1 10	5 49	2 39
11 Sa	22 57	20 52	5 03	22 41	23 59	1 05	23 47	1 44	23 59	1 04	3 25	8 13	2 42	1 10	5 48	2 39
12 Su	23 02	24 13	4 41	25 24	24 12	1 10	23 37	1 45	23 55	1 04	3 32	8 14	2 40	1 10	5 48	2 38
13 M	23 07	26 11	4 02	26 33	24 25	1 16	23 27	1 46	23 51	1 04	3 40	8 15	2 38	1 11	5 48	2 38
14 Tu	23 11	26 29	3 06	25 57	24 36	1 21	23 16	1 47	23 47	1 04	3 47	8 16	2 36	1 11	5 48	2 38
15 W	23 14	24 58	1 58	23 33	24 45	1 26	23 04	1 48	23 42	1 05	3 55	8 16	2 35	1 11	5 48	2 38
16 Th	23 17	21 45	0 41	19 36	24 53	1 31	22 51	1 49	23 37	1 05	4 02	8 17	2 33	1 12	5 48	2 37
17 F	23 20	17 09	0S39	14 27	25 00	1 35	22 38	1 50	23 31	1 05	4 09	8 18	2 31	1 12	5 48	2 37
18 Sa	23 22	11 34	1 55	8 33	25 06	1 40	22 24	1 50	23 26	1 05	4 16	8 19	2 29	1 12	5 47	2 37
19 Su	23 24	5 27	3 03	2 18	25 10	1 44	22 09	1 51	23 20	1 05	4 23	8 20	2 28	1 12	5 48	2 37
20 M	23 25	0S51	3 60	3S57	25 13	1 48	21 54	1 51	23 14	1 05	4 30	8 21	2 26	1 13	5 48	2 36
21 Tu	23 26	6 59	4 41	9 55	25 14	1 52	21 38	1 52	23 07	1 05	4 37	8 22	2 25	1 13	5 48	2 36
22 W	23 26	12 42	5 05	15 18	25 14	1 55	21 22	1 52	23 01	1 06	4 43	8 23	2 24	1 13	5 48	2 36
23 Th	23 26	17 42	5 12	19 52	25 13	1 58	21 05	1 52	22 54	1 06	4 50	8 24	2 22	1 13	5 48	2 35
24 F	23 25	21 46	5 03	23 23	25 10	2 01	20 47	1 52	22 47	1 06	4 56	8 25	2 21	1 14	5 48	2 35
25 Sa	23 24	24 41	4 38	25 39	25 05	2 03	20 29	1 53	22 39	1 06	5 03	8 26	2 20	1 14	5 49	2 35
26 Su	23 23	26 17	3 59	26 34	24 59	2 06	20 10	1 53	22 31	1 06	5 09	8 27	2 19	1 14	5 49	2 35
27 M	23 21	26 31	3 09	26 07	24 51	2 07	19 51	1 52	22 23	1 06	5 16	8 28	2 18	1 14	5 49	2 34
28 Tu	23 18	25 24	2 11	24 22	24 42	2 09	19 31	1 52	22 15	1 06	5 22	8 29	2 17	1 15	5 50	2 34
29 W	23 15	23 05	1 08	21 32	24 32	2 10	19 10	1 52	22 07	1 06	5 28	8 30	2 16	1 15	5 50	2 34
30 Th	23 12	19 46	0 02	17 48	24 19	2 10	18 49	1 52	21 58	1 06	5 34	8 31	2 15	1 15	5 51	2 33
31 F	23S08	15S40	1N03	13S24	24S06	2S10	18S28	1S51	21S49	1S06	5S40	8N32	2N14	1N16	5N51	2S33

Day	⚷ Decl	⚷ Lat	♅ Decl	♅ Lat	♆ Decl	♆ Lat	♇ Decl	♇ Lat
1	11N23	0S23	21N32	0S05	0N14	1S27	23S34	4S44
6	11 19	0 23	21 30	0 05	0 13	1 26	23 32	4 44
11	11 16	0 23	21 28	0 05	0 13	1 26	23 30	4 44
16	11 13	0 24	21 26	0 05	0 13	1 26	23 28	4 44
21	11 10	0 24	21 24	0 05	0 13	1 26	23 26	4 44
26	11 08	0 24	21 23	0 05	0 14	1 26	23 24	4 44
31	11N07	0S25	21N21	0S05	0N15	1S25	23S22	4S44

Day	⚴ Decl	⚴ Lat	⚵ Decl	⚵ Lat	⚶ Decl	⚶ Lat	Eris Decl	Eris Lat
1	13S54	18S09	1N13	18S42	17N20	1N55	0N13	10S15
6	14 13	17 45	0 52	19 02	17 26	2 10	0 13	10 14
11	14 29	17 21	0 36	19 20	17 36	2 26	0 12	10 14
16	14 41	16 54	0 27	19 35	17 50	2 42	0 12	10 13
21	14 48	16 26	0 24	19 45	18 08	2 60	0 13	10 13
26	14 49	15 56	0 29	19 50	18 31	3 17	0 13	10 12
31	14S45	15S23	0N42	19S49	18N57	3N36	0N13	10S11

Moon Phenomena

Max/0 Decl
dy hr mn
6 20:03 0 N
13 15:59 26N35
19 20:46 0 S
26 15:50 26S35

Max/0 Lat
dy hr mn
2 19:38 0 N
10 4:47 5N09
16 12:21 0 S
22 22:04 5S12
30 0:52 0 N

Perigee/Apogee
dy hr m kilometers
4 8:42 a 404657
16 2:27 p 364028

PH dy hr mn
☽ 6 5:23 13♓51
○ 13 16:10 21♊25
☾ 20 9:12 28♍14
● 27 20:13 5♑50

Void of Course Moon

Last Aspect			☽ Ingress		
2 2:19	♃	△	♒	2	12:27
4 7:48	♄	⚹	♓	5	1:21
7 4:41	♃	☍	♈	7	13:32
9 6:18	♄	☌	♉	9	22:37
11 20:59	♃	△	♊	12	3:56
14 0:05	♃	□	♋	14	6:25
16 1:43	♃	⚹	♌	16	7:42
18 8:58	☿	△	♍	18	9:18
20 9:12	☉	□	♎	20	12:14
22 1:02	♄	☍	♏	22	17:02
24 18:13	♃	⚹	♐	24	23:51
27 3:15	♃	□	♑	27	8:52
29 14:30	♃	△	♒	29	20:05

DAILY ASPECTARIAN

1 W
☽∥♀ 0:52
☽∥♂ 4:42
☽∥♇ 12:48
☽∠☿ 13:09
☽□♄ 19:23
♀⚻♅ 20:30
☿△♆ 21:54
☽⚼♅ 22:10

2 Th
☉∠☽ 1:42
☽△♃ 2:19
☉∥☽ 2:19
☽□⚳ 3:09
☽#♅ 5:01
☽∥☿ 7:20
☽□⚷ 13:53
♂⚺♇ 15:53
☿⚹♇ 18:07
☊ D 19:37
☿⚺♂ 20:11
☽⚹♆ 20:19
☽☌♇ 23:01
☽⚺♂ 23:29
☽⚹☿ 23:45

3 F
☿#♅ 2:49
☽△♅ 4:14
☉∠⚳ 5:44
☽⚺♀ 8:03
☽⚼♃ 8:51
☉⚹☽ 10:45
☿⚼♄ 12:03

4 Sa
☽∠♆ 2:44
☽⚹♄ 7:48
☽∠♂ 8:04
☿☍♅ 8:48
☽#⚷ 15:33
☽⚻♃ 15:39
☽△⚳ 18:07
☽∠♀ 18:09

5 Su
⚵ R 2:05
☽⚹⚷ 2:38
☽⚺♆ 9:14
☉∥☿ 9:39
☽⚺♇ 12:06
☽∠♄ 14:13
☽⚹♂ 16:40
☽□♅ 17:00
☽#♄ 17:41
♂⚻♅ 21:31
☽□☿ 22:02

6 M
☽⚼⚳ 1:38
☽⚹♀ 4:06
☊ R 5:15
☉□☽ 5:23
☽#♃ 7:11
☽∥⚳ 7:28
☽∠⚷ 8:53
⚳#♃ 16:36
☽∠♇ 18:21
☽#♆ 19:05
☽⚺♄ 20:18
☽∥♆ 21:02

7 Tu
☽☍♃ 4:41
☽⚻⚳ 8:37
☽∥♃ 8:38
☽#⚳ 9:09
☿∠⚳ 9:32
☽⚺⚷ 14:36
☽☌♆ 21:06
☉⚼⚷ 21:27
☽∥♄ 21:54
☽⚹♇ 23:58

8 W
☽⚹♅ 4:21
☽□♂ 8:09
♀∥♂ 14:10
☽△☿ 17:51
☉⚺♀ 19:28
☉△☽ 21:31
☽□♀ 21:33
☽∥⚷ 22:35

9 Th
☿∥♇ 3:35
☽☌♄ 6:18
☿⚼⚷ 7:02
☽∠♅ 8:48
☽⚻♃ 14:47
☽☍⚳ 19:52
☽☌⚷ 23:30

10 F
☽⚼☿ 1:47
☉⚼☽ 3:49
☽⚺♆ 5:41
☽□♇ 8:28
☿∥♀ 12:00
☽⚺♅ 12:18
☽⚼♃ 18:21
☽△♂ 19:25

11 Sa
☿∥♂ 0:34
☽∥♅ 3:46
☽⚻☿ 8:18
☽∠♆ 8:32
☉⚻☽ 8:55
☽△♀ 10:00
☽⚺♄ 12:35
☉#☽ 14:18
☽#♇ 18:04
☽#♀ 19:19
☽△♃ 20:59
☽#♂ 21:35
☉☌☿ 22:18
☽⚼♂ 23:23
☽#☿ 23:58

12 Su
☽⚻⚳ 2:57
☽⚺⚷ 4:39
☽⚹♆ 10:33
☿∠♇ 10:35
☽△♇ 13:16
♀□♄ 14:13
☽∠♄ 14:27
☽⚼♀ 14:28
☽☌♅ 16:37
☉∠♇ 17:28
♀∥♇ 17:59
☿△♄ 21:09

13 M
☽⚻♂ 2:27
☽⚼⚳ 5:12
☽∠⚷ 6:05
☉△♄ 9:24
⚳ ♏ 13:18
♀⚼♅ 14:19
☽⚼♇ 14:36
☽⚹♄ 15:41
☉☍☽ 16:10
☽☍☿ 17:59
☽⚻♀ 18:06
☿⚺♀ 22:43

14 Tu
☽□♃ 0:05
☽△⚳ 6:54
☽⚹⚷ 7:01
☉∥♀ 7:31
⚳☍⚷ 11:08
☽□♆ 12:47
☽⚻♇ 15:30
☽⚺♅ 18:31

15 W
☽#☿ 1:54
☽☍♂ 6:59
♆ D 9:08
☽#♂ 11:09
☽#♇ 12:32
☉#☽ 14:01
☽#♀ 16:28
☽□♄ 17:05
☽∠♅ 19:04
☉⚻☽ 21:19
⚶ R 22:27

16 Th
☽☍♀ 0:05
☽⚻☿ 1:22
☽⚹♃ 1:43
☽∥♅ 1:49
☿□♃ 4:47
☽□⚷ 8:13
☽□⚳ 9:33
☊ D 12:19
☽△♆ 14:02
☽☍♇ 16:49
☽⚹♅ 19:37
♀△♃ 20:54
☉⚼☽ 23:47

17 F
☽∠♃ 2:30
☽⚼☿ 5:01
☽⚻♂ 11:01
☽⚼♆ 14:46
♂∥♇ 16:26
☽△♄ 18:25

18 Sa
☽∥⚷ 1:31
☉△☽ 2:29
☽⚺♃ 3:29
☽⚻♀ 6:10
☽△☿ 8:58
☽△⚷ 9:45
☉∥♂ 11:16
☿ ♑ 11:59
☽⚹⚳ 12:34
☽⚼♂ 13:23
☽⚻♆ 15:45
☿△⚷ 15:59
☉□♃ 17:43
☽⚻♇ 18:41
☽⚼♄ 19:26
☽□♅ 21:20
☽∥♄ 22:41

19 Su
☽#⚳ 4:01
☽⚼♀ 9:47
☽⚼⚷ 10:59
☽∥♃ 11:26
☽∠⚳ 14:36
☽△♂ 16:11
♀ ♒ 18:41
☽∥♆ 19:56
☽⚼♇ 20:09
☽⚻♄ 20:51
☽#♆ 21:37
♀□⚷ 23:19

20 M
☿⚹⚳ 2:55
☽#♃ 6:06
☽☌♃ 6:31
☉□☽ 9:12
☊ R 9:21
☽⚻⚷ 12:38
☽△♀ 13:57
☽∥⚳ 14:23
☽⚺⚳ 17:05
☽□☿ 18:29
☽☍♆ 18:55
☽#♄ 19:14
☽△♇ 22:03
☿□♆ 22:23

21 Tu
☽△♅ 0:32
☉∥♇ 11:03
☽#⚷ 17:20
♀#♅ 20:45
☽□♂ 23:23

22 W
☽☍♄ 1:02
☿⚺♇ 1:57
☉ ♑ 2:43
☽⚼♅ 2:50
☉△⚷ 7:16
☽⚺♃ 11:21
♀□⚳ 15:50
☽☍⚷ 17:22
☉⚹☽ 18:12
☿⚻♅ 21:55
♀⚹♆ 22:10
☽☌⚳ 23:37
☽⚻♆ 23:59

23 Th
☽□♀ 0:10
☽□♇ 3:19
♂□♄ 4:02
☽⚻♅ 5:38
☽⚹☿ 6:43
⚳⚻♆ 12:28
⚴ ♎ 12:47
☽∠♃ 14:31
☽∥♀ 18:03
☽#♅ 21:27
☉∠☽ 23:40

24 F
♄ D 2:48
☽⚼♆ 3:16
☽∥♂ 6:57
☽⚻♄ 7:13
☽⚹♂ 8:57
♂⚼♅ 9:03
♀☌♇ 10:57
☉∥♇ 11:48
☉∥☽ 12:16
☽∥♇ 12:16
☽∠☿ 13:59
☽⚹♃ 18:13

25 Sa
☽⚻⚷ 0:08
☽∥☿ 4:16
☉⚺☽ 5:48
☽△♆ 7:06
☽⚺⚳ 8:23
♀△♅ 9:49
☽⚹♇ 10:40
☽⚼♄ 11:07
☽☍♅ 12:48
☽⚹♀ 13:08
☽∠♂ 14:42
☽⚺☿ 22:04
☉□♆ 22:13

26 Su
☽⚼⚷ 4:19
☽∠⚳ 13:39
☽∠♇ 15:10
☽△♄ 15:35
☽∠♀ 20:43
☽⚺♂ 21:07

27 M
☽□♃ 3:15
☉⚹⚳ 7:23
☽△⚷ 9:05
☽□♆ 16:26
☽⚹⚳ 19:32
☉☌☽ 20:13
☽⚺♇ 20:14
☉⚺♇ 20:26
☽⚻♅ 22:10

28 Tu
☽⚺♀ 5:05
☽∥☿ 9:09
☽☌☿ 16:46
☉⚻♅ 18:57
⚳□♇ 21:18
☽∥♇ 21:21
☉∥☽ 22:29

29 W
☽□♄ 2:12
☽⚼♅ 3:41
☽∥♂ 8:04
☽☌♂ 11:59
☽#♅ 13:15
☽△♃ 14:30
♀⚼♃ 17:22
☽□⚷ 20:15

30 Th
☊ D 0:50
☽⚹♆ 3:58
☽∥♀ 6:29
☽☌♇ 8:00
☽□⚳ 9:01
☽△♅ 9:40
☉⚺☽ 13:26
☽⚼♃ 20:50
☽☌♀ 23:53

31 F
♂△♃ 4:34
⚳⚻♅ 4:51
☽∠♆ 10:21
☽⚺☿ 14:31
☽⚹♄ 14:43
☿□♄ 16:01
☉∠☽ 22:46
☽#⚷ 23:32

LONGITUDE

Day	Sid.Time	☉	☽	☽ 12 hour	Mean☊	True☊	☿	♀	♂	⚳	♃	♄	⚷	♅	♆	♇
	h m s	° ' "	° ' "	° ' "	° '	° '	° '	° '	° '	° '	° '	° '	° '	° '	° '	° '
1 Sa	6 40 45	10♑04 35	25♒37 57	1♓31 19	3♒30.9	2♒24.8	21♑36.6	15♒00.3	27♑54.6	7♏00.5	27♍18.4	21♈04.7	0♉03.7	6♊41.7	3♈55.9	5♒57.9
2 Su	6 44 41	11 05 45	7♓24 52	13 19 08	3 27.8	2 26.5	23 13.1	16 13.7	28 41.6	7 22.1	27 20.5	21 05.6	0R 03.1	6R 39.7	3 56.5	5 59.7
3 M	6 48 38	12 06 54	19 14 40	25 12 04	3 24.6	2 28.2	24 49.5	17 27.1	29 28.6	7 43.5	27 22.4	21 06.7	0 02.7	6 37.7	3 57.1	6 01.4
4 Tu	6 52 34	13 08 04	1♈11 55	7♈14 51	3 21.4	2 29.5	26 25.6	18 40.4	0♒15.6	8 04.8	27 24.0	21 07.8	0 02.3	6 35.8	3 57.8	6 03.2
5 W	6 56 31	14 09 13	13 21 28	19 32 21	3 18.2	2R 30.0	28 01.3	19 53.7	1 02.6	8 25.9	27 25.5	21 09.1	0 02.0	6 34.0	3 58.5	6 05.0
6 Th	7 00 28	15 10 22	25 48 06	2♉09 14	3 15.0	2 29.6	29 36.4	21 06.9	1 49.7	8 46.8	27 26.9	21 10.5	0 01.7	6 32.1	3 59.2	6 06.7
7 F	7 04 24	16 11 31	8♉36 13	15 09 29	3 11.9	2 28.4	1♒10.8	22 20.1	2 36.8	9 07.6	27 28.0	21 12.0	0 01.5	6 30.3	4 00.0	6 08.5
8 Sa	7 08 21	17 12 39	21 49 17	28 35 51	3 08.7	2 26.7	2 44.3	23 33.2	3 23.9	9 28.3	27 28.9	21 13.6	0 01.3	6 28.6	4 00.8	6 10.3
9 Su	7 12 17	18 13 48	5♊29 13	12♊29 18	3 05.5	2 24.7	4 16.7	24 46.2	4 11.0	9 48.7	27 29.6	21 15.3	0 01.2	6 26.9	4 01.6	6 12.2
10 M	7 16 14	19 14 55	19 35 49	26 48 21	3 02.3	2 22.8	5 47.6	25 59.2	4 58.2	10 09.1	27 30.2	21 17.1	0D 01.1	6 25.2	4 02.5	6 14.0
11 Tu	7 20 10	20 16 03	4♋06 19	11♋28 58	2 59.2	2 21.4	7 16.8	27 12.1	5 45.3	10 29.2	27 30.5	21 19.0	0 01.1	6 23.6	4 03.4	6 15.8
12 W	7 24 07	21 17 10	18 55 24	26 24 38	2 56.0	2D 20.5	8 43.8	28 24.9	6 32.5	10 49.2	27R 30.7	21 21.0	0 01.2	6 22.0	4 04.3	6 17.7
13 Th	7 28 04	22 18 16	3♌55 35	11♌27 09	2 52.8	2 20.3	10 08.2	29 37.7	7 19.8	11 09.0	27 30.7	21 23.2	0 01.3	6 20.4	4 05.3	6 19.5
14 F	7 32 00	23 19 23	18 58 15	26 27 48	2 49.6	2 20.6	11 29.6	0♓50.4	8 07.0	11 28.7	27 30.5	21 25.4	0 01.5	6 18.9	4 06.3	6 21.4
15 Sa	7 35 57	24 20 29	3♍54 51	11♍18 33	2 46.5	2 21.2	12 47.3	2 03.1	8 54.3	11 48.2	27 30.1	21 27.7	0 01.8	6 17.5	4 07.3	6 23.2
16 Su	7 39 53	25 21 35	18 38 09	25 53 05	2 43.3	2 21.9	14 00.7	3 15.6	9 41.5	12 07.5	27 29.5	21 30.2	0 02.1	6 16.0	4 08.3	6 25.1
17 M	7 43 50	26 22 40	3♎02 54	10♎07 19	2 40.1	2 22.5	15 09.2	4 28.1	10 28.8	12 26.6	27 28.7	21 32.7	0 02.4	6 14.7	4 09.4	6 26.9
18 Tu	7 47 46	27 23 46	17 06 11	23 59 26	2 36.9	2R 22.8	16 11.9	5 40.6	11 16.1	12 45.5	27 27.7	21 35.4	0 02.8	6 13.3	4 10.5	6 28.8
19 W	7 51 43	28 24 51	0♏47 09	7♏29 28	2 33.7	2 22.9	17 08.1	6 52.9	12 03.5	13 04.2	27 26.5	21 38.1	0 03.3	6 12.0	4 11.7	6 30.7
20 Th	7 55 39	29 25 56	14 06 37	20 38 51	2 30.6	2 22.8	17 56.8	8 05.2	12 50.8	13 22.8	27 25.1	21 41.0	0 03.8	6 10.8	4 12.9	6 32.6
21 F	7 59 36	0♒27 01	27 06 28	3♐29 47	2 27.4	2 22.6	18 37.3	9 17.4	13 38.2	13 41.2	27 23.5	21 43.9	0 04.4	6 09.6	4 14.1	6 34.5
22 Sa	8 03 33	1 28 05	9♐49 08	16 04 50	2 24.2	2D 22.4	19 08.6	10 29.5	14 25.6	13 59.3	27 21.8	21 47.0	0 05.1	6 08.4	4 15.3	6 36.3
23 Su	8 07 29	2 29 10	22 17 12	28 26 34	2 21.0	2 22.4	19 30.0	11 41.6	15 13.0	14 17.3	27 19.8	21 50.1	0 05.8	6 07.3	4 16.6	6 38.2
24 M	8 11 26	3 30 13	4♑33 13	10♑37 25	2 17.9	2 22.4	19R 40.7	12 53.6	16 00.4	14 35.0	27 17.7	21 53.4	0 06.6	6 06.3	4 17.9	6 40.1
25 Tu	8 15 22	4 31 16	16 39 28	22 39 37	2 14.7	2 22.6	19 40.2	14 05.4	16 47.8	14 52.5	27 15.4	21 56.7	0 07.4	6 05.3	4 19.2	6 42.0
26 W	8 19 19	5 32 18	28 38 06	4♒35 11	2 11.5	2R 22.7	19 28.3	15 17.2	17 35.2	15 09.9	27 12.9	22 00.2	0 08.3	6 04.3	4 20.6	6 43.9
27 Th	8 23 15	6 33 20	10♒31 06	16 26 06	2 08.3	2 22.7	19 04.9	16 28.9	18 22.7	15 27.0	27 10.2	22 03.7	0 09.2	6 03.4	4 21.9	6 45.8
28 F	8 27 12	7 34 20	22 20 26	28 14 22	2 05.2	2 22.3	18 30.3	17 40.5	19 10.1	15 43.8	27 07.3	22 07.4	0 10.2	6 02.6	4 23.4	6 47.7
29 Sa	8 31 08	8 35 20	4♓08 12	10♓02 14	2 02.0	2 21.7	17 45.3	18 52.0	19 57.6	16 00.5	27 04.2	22 11.1	0 11.2	6 01.8	4 24.8	6 49.6
30 Su	8 35 05	9 36 18	15 56 48	21 52 15	1 58.8	2 20.8	16 51.0	20 03.4	20 45.0	16 16.9	27 00.9	22 14.9	0 12.3	6 01.0	4 26.3	6 51.5
31 M	8 39 02	10♒37 16	27 48 59	3♈47 24	1♒55.6	2♒19.6	15♒48.8	21♓14.7	21♒32.5	16♏33.1	26♍57.5	22♈18.8	0♉13.5	6♊00.3	4♈27.7	6♒53.4

1st of Month

Julian Day # 2461771.5
Obliquity 23°26'13"
SVP 4♓51'52"
GC 27♐13.8
Eris 25♈06.1R

Day	⚴	Day	⚵	Day	⚶
1	1♒52.1	1	0♌04.5R	1	17♌34.4R
6	2 44.6	6	28♋55.0R	6	16 52.0R
11	3 26.3	11	27 40.5R	11	15 59.3R
16	3 56.2	16	26 24.1R	16	14 57.4R
21	4 13.6	21	25 08.7R	21	13 47.7R
26	4 17.8R	26	23 57.3R	26	12 32.2R
31	4 08.2R	31	22 52.7R	31	11 13.3R

DECLINATION and LATITUDE

Day	☉ Decl	☽ Decl	☽ Lat	☽ 12h Decl	☿ Decl	☿ Lat	♀ Decl	♀ Lat	♂ Decl	♂ Lat	⚳ Decl	⚳ Lat	♃ Decl	♃ Lat	♄ Decl	♄ Lat
1 Sa	23S03	11S01	2N05	8S32	23S50	2S10	18S06	1S51	21S40	1S06	5S46	8N33	2N14	1N16	5N52	2S33
2 Su	22 58	5 58	3 02	3 22	23 34	2 09	17 43	1 50	21 30	1 06	5 52	8 34	2 13	1 16	5 52	2 33
3 M	22 53	0 43	3 51	1N57	23 15	2 08	17 20	1 49	21 21	1 07	5 57	8 35	2 13	1 16	5 53	2 32
4 Tu	22 47	4N37	4 31	7 16	22 56	2 06	16 57	1 49	21 11	1 07	6 03	8 36	2 12	1 17	5 54	2 32
5 W	22 41	9 52	4 59	12 24	22 34	2 03	16 33	1 48	21 00	1 07	6 09	8 37	2 12	1 17	5 54	2 32
6 Th	22 34	14 51	5 14	17 10	22 11	2 00	16 09	1 47	20 50	1 07	6 14	8 38	2 12	1 17	5 55	2 31
7 F	22 27	19 20	5 15	21 18	21 47	1 57	15 44	1 46	20 39	1 07	6 19	8 39	2 12	1 18	5 56	2 31
8 Sa	22 20	23 01	4 59	24 28	21 22	1 52	15 19	1 44	20 28	1 07	6 25	8 40	2 11	1 18	5 57	2 31
9 Su	22 12	25 34	4 26	26 18	20 55	1 47	14 53	1 43	20 17	1 07	6 30	8 41	2 11	1 18	5 58	2 31
10 M	22 03	26 37	3 36	26 28	20 27	1 41	14 27	1 42	20 06	1 07	6 35	8 43	2 11	1 18	5 59	2 30
11 Tu	21 54	25 53	2 30	24 49	19 58	1 34	14 01	1 40	19 54	1 07	6 40	8 44	2 12	1 19	5 60	2 30
12 W	21 45	23 19	1 14	21 24	19 28	1 27	13 34	1 39	19 43	1 07	6 45	8 45	2 12	1 19	6 01	2 30
13 Th	21 35	19 08	0S09	16 32	18 58	1 18	13 07	1 37	19 31	1 07	6 49	8 46	2 12	1 19	6 02	2 29
14 F	21 25	13 41	1 31	10 39	18 26	1 09	12 40	1 36	19 18	1 06	6 54	8 47	2 12	1 19	6 03	2 29
15 Sa	21 15	7 29	2 47	4 14	17 55	0 59	12 13	1 34	19 06	1 06	6 59	8 48	2 13	1 20	6 04	2 29
16 Su	21 04	0 58	3 50	2S17	17 23	0 47	11 44	1 32	18 53	1 06	7 03	8 50	2 13	1 20	6 05	2 29
17 M	20 53	5S27	4 37	8 31	16 51	0 35	11 16	1 30	18 40	1 06	7 08	8 51	2 14	1 20	6 06	2 28
18 Tu	20 41	11 26	5 07	14 10	16 20	0 22	10 48	1 28	18 27	1 06	7 12	8 52	2 15	1 21	6 07	2 28
19 W	20 29	16 42	5 18	18 60	15 49	0 08	10 19	1 26	18 14	1 06	7 16	8 53	2 15	1 21	6 09	2 28
20 Th	20 16	21 01	5 11	22 46	15 20	0N07	9 50	1 24	18 01	1 06	7 21	8 55	2 16	1 21	6 10	2 28
21 F	20 03	24 12	4 49	25 18	14 53	0 23	9 20	1 21	17 47	1 06	7 25	8 56	2 17	1 21	6 11	2 27
22 Sa	19 50	26 05	4 13	26 31	14 27	0 40	8 51	1 19	17 33	1 06	7 29	8 57	2 18	1 22	6 13	2 27
23 Su	19 36	26 37	3 25	26 23	14 04	0 57	8 21	1 16	17 19	1 06	7 32	8 58	2 19	1 22	6 14	2 27
24 M	19 22	25 50	2 29	24 58	13 44	1 15	7 51	1 14	17 05	1 06	7 36	8 60	2 20	1 22	6 16	2 27
25 Tu	19 08	23 50	1 26	22 25	13 27	1 33	7 21	1 11	16 51	1 06	7 40	9 01	2 21	1 22	6 17	2 26
26 W	18 53	20 46	0 21	18 55	13 13	1 51	6 51	1 08	16 36	1 05	7 43	9 02	2 22	1 23	6 19	2 26
27 Th	18 38	16 53	0N45	14 41	13 04	2 08	6 20	1 06	16 21	1 05	7 47	9 04	2 24	1 23	6 20	2 26
28 F	18 23	12 21	1 49	9 55	12 58	2 25	5 50	1 03	16 06	1 05	7 50	9 05	2 25	1 23	6 22	2 25
29 Sa	18 07	7 23	2 48	4 48	12 57	2 41	5 19	0 60	15 51	1 05	7 54	9 06	2 27	1 24	6 23	2 25
30 Su	17 51	2 10	3 39	0N29	12 59	2 56	4 48	0 57	15 36	1 05	7 57	9 08	2 28	1 24	6 25	2 25
31 M	17S34	3N08	4N22	5N46	13S05	3N09	4S17	0S53	15S21	1S05	8S00	9N09	2N30	1N24	6N27	2S25

Day	⚷ Decl	⚷ Lat	♅ Decl	♅ Lat	♆ Decl	♆ Lat	♇ Decl	♇ Lat
1	11N06	0S25	21N21	0S05	0N16	1S25	23S22	4S44
6	11 06	0 25	21 19	0 05	0 17	1 25	23 20	4 44
11	11 05	0 25	21 18	0 05	0 19	1 25	23 17	4 44
16	11 05	0 25	21 16	0 05	0 21	1 25	23 15	4 45
21	11 06	0 26	21 15	0 05	0 23	1 24	23 13	4 45
26	11 07	0 26	21 15	0 05	0 26	1 24	23 11	4 45
31	11N08	0S26	21N14	0S05	0N29	1S24	23S09	4S46

Day	⚴ Decl	⚴ Lat	⚵ Decl	⚵ Lat	⚶ Decl	⚶ Lat	Eris Decl	Eris Lat
1	14S43	15S16	0N45	19S48	19N03	3N39	0N13	10S11
6	14 31	14 40	1 07	19 39	19 34	3 58	0 14	10 10
11	14 11	13 60	1 36	19 23	20 07	4 17	0 14	10 10
16	13 43	13 16	2 11	19 00	20 43	4 35	0 15	10 09
21	13 07	12 29	2 52	18 31	21 21	4 52	0 16	10 08
26	12 20	11 36	3 37	17 57	21 59	5 09	0 17	10 07
31	11S24	10S38	4N26	17S17	22N36	5N24	0N18	10S07

Moon Phenomena

Max/0 Decl

dy	hr mn	
3	3:13	0 N
10	2:27	26N37
16	3:34	0 S
22	21:34	26S38
30	9:50	0 N

Max/0 Lat

dy	hr mn	
6	12:37	5N17
12	21:27	0 S
19	2:50	5S18
26	7:32	0 N

Perigee/Apogee

dy	hr m		kilometers
1	3:53	a	405631
13	7:47	p	359050
28	15:32	a	406388

PH	dy	hr mn	
☽	5	1:42	14♈14
○	12	4:04	21♋28
(lunar eclipse)	12	4:14	P 0.066
☾	18	19:27	28♎13
●	26	15:14	6♒11
(solar eclipse)	26	908:59	A 10'27"

Void of Course Moon

Last Aspect			☽ Ingress		
31	14:43	♄ ⚹	♓	1	8:54
3	16:24	♃ ☍	♈	3	21:37
5	15:08	♄ ☌	♉	6	7:57
8	10:03	♃ △	♊	8	14:28
10	13:09	♃ □	♋	10	17:16
12	13:46	♃ ⚹	♌	12	17:44
14	3:56	♄ △	♍	14	17:41
16	14:40	♃ ☌	♎	16	18:53
18	19:27	☉ □	♏	18	22:36
21	0:32	♃ ⚹	♐	21	5:25
23	9:48	♃ □	♑	23	15:03
25	21:09	♃ △	♒	26	2:45
27	23:33	♄ ⚹	♓	28	15:35
30	22:17	♃ ☍	♈	31	4:24

DAILY ASPECTARIAN

1 Sa: ☿⚼♅ 1:14; ☽⚻♃ 3:25; ☽⚺♂ 4:58; ⚵R♋ 8:13; ☽⚹⚷ 9:01; ☽⚺♆ 16:55; ☽⚺♇ 21:06; ☽∠♄ 21:19; ☽□♅ 22:28; ☽△⚳ 23:54

2 Su: ☽⋕♄ 0:29; ☽∥⚳ 0:31; ☽∠☿ 1:54; ⚳⋕♄ 2:43; ☉⚹☽ 8:12; ☽∠♂ 13:40; ☽∠⚷ 15:30; ☿∥♇ 16:46; ☽⋕♃ 17:13; ☽⚺♀ 19:58

3 M: ♂⋕♅ 1:23; ☽⋕♆ 2:01; ☽∠♇ 3:36; ☽⚺♄ 3:46; ☽∥♆ 4:26; ☽⚼⚳ 7:14; ☽⚹☿ 12:59; ☽∥♃ 13:10; ♂ ♒ 16:03; ☽☍♃ 16:24; ♂□⚷ 17:16; ☽⚺⚷ 21:41; ☽⚹♂ 22:00

4 Tu: ☽∠♀ 5:29; ☽☌♆ 5:30; ♀∠♆ 5:45; ☽∥♄ 5:48; ☽⋕⚳ 6:36; ☽⚹♇ 9:40; ☽⚹♅ 10:41; ☉∥☿ 13:15; ☽⚻⚳ 14:03; ☿△♃ 14:54

5 W: ☊R 1:34; ☉□☽ 1:42; ☽∥⚷ 5:47; ☽⚹♀ 14:04; ☽☌♄ 15:08; ☽∠♅ 15:52

6 Th: ♀⚹♄ 1:12; ☽⚻♃ 3:08; ☿ ♒ 5:59; ☽⋕♀ 6:05; ☿□⚷ 6:23; ☽☌⚷ 8:00; ☽□☿ 8:14; ☽□♂ 12:08; ☽⚺♆ 15:27; ☽□♇ 19:26; ☽⚺♅ 20:08

7 F: ☽☍⚳ 0:59; ☽⚼♃ 7:06; ☽⋕♂ 7:34; ☽∥♅ 12:05; ☽⋕☿ 13:39; ☉△☽ 15:02; ☽∠♆ 18:58; ☉⋕☽ 19:08; ☽⚺♄ 22:56

8 Sa: ☽⋕♇ 2:13; ☿⋕♅ 3:04; ☽□♀ 3:23; ☽△♃ 10:03; ☽⚺⚷ 14:30; ♂⚹♆ 19:08; ☉⚼☽ 19:47; ☿⚹♆ 20:01; ☿☌♂ 20:57; ☽⚹♆ 21:28; ☽△♂ 21:37; ☽△☿ 21:39

9 Su: ☽△♇ 1:14; ☽∠♄ 1:20; ☽☌♅ 1:39; ☽⚻⚳ 7:37; ☽∠⚷ 16:17; ☉⚻☽ 23:22

10 M: ☽⚼♂ 0:40; ☽⚼☿ 2:14; ☽⚼♇ 2:45; ☽⚹♄ 2:50; ⚷D 6:42; ☿☌♇ 7:11; ☽⚼⚳ 9:29; ☿△♅ 9:52; ☽△♀ 11:37; ☽□♃ 13:09; ☽⚹⚷ 17:18; ☽□♆ 23:55

11 Tu: ☽⚻♂ 2:51; ☽⚻♇ 3:32; ☽⚺♅ 3:44; ☿∥♂ 5:05; ☽⚻☿ 5:45; ♀⚻♃ 6:06; ☽△⚳ 10:38; ☽⚼♀ 14:20; ♂☌♇ 16:07; ♂△♅ 18:48

12 W: ☽⋕♇ 0:15; ☉□♄ 1:34; ☉⚼♅ 1:51; ☽□♄ 3:54; ☽∠♅ 3:55; ☉☍☽ 4:04; ♄∠♅ 6:19; ♃R 8:55; ☉⋕☽ 10:23; ☽∥♅ 12:39; ☽⚹♃ 13:46; ☽⚻♀ 16:32; ☽□⚷ 17:46; ☊D 21:23; ☽⋕♂ 22:01

13 Th: ☽△♆ 0:15; ☽⋕☿ 0:55; ☽☍♇ 3:50; ☽⚹♅ 3:51; ☽☍♂ 5:44; ♅△♇ 6:40; ♀ ♓ 7:21; ♀⚹⚷ 7:49; ☽☍☿ 10:54; ☽□⚳ 11:47; ☽∠♃ 13:41; ☿□⚳ 23:39

14 F: ☽⚼♆ 0:13; ☽△♄ 3:56; ☽⋕♀ 4:28; ☉⚻☽ 7:28; ☽∥⚷ 10:20; ☽⚺♃ 13:40; ☽△⚷ 17:44; ☿⚼♃ 18:36; ☉⋕♅ 19:40; ☽☍♀ 20:44

15 Sa: ☽⚻♆ 0:20; ☽⋕⚳ 1:51; ☽□♅ 3:50; ☽⚻♇ 4:01; ☽⚼♄ 4:08; ☽∥♄ 5:15; ☽⚻♂ 8:33; ☉⚼☽ 9:27; ☽⚹⚳ 13:06; ☽⚻☿ 15:44; ☽⚼⚷ 18:05; ☽∥♃ 19:24

16 Su: ☽∥♆ 2:16; ☽⚼♇ 4:36; ☽⚻♄ 4:45; ☽⋕♆ 4:51; ☽⚼♂ 10:36; ☽⋕♃ 11:49; ☉△☽ 11:58; ☽∠⚳ 14:23; ☽☌♃ 14:40; ♀⚺♆ 17:42; ☽⚼☿ 18:44; ☽⚻⚷ 18:57

17 M: ☽☍♆ 1:52; ⚳∠♃ 2:31; ☽⋕♄ 2:31; ☽⚻♀ 2:37; ☽△♅ 5:24; ☽△♇ 5:46; ☽∥⚳ 6:35; ♀⋕⚷ 9:04; ☽△♂ 13:22; ☽⚺⚳ 16:21; ☽∥♀ 21:30; ☽△☿ 22:19; ☽⋕⚷ 22:33

18 Tu: ☉△♃ 1:30; ☽⚼♀ 6:48; ☽⚼♅ 7:09; ☽☍♄ 7:49; ♀□♅ 10:40; ♀⚺♇ 16:26; ☽⚺♃ 18:05; ♀∠♄ 18:53; ☉□☽ 19:27; ☊R 19:50; ☽∥☿ 20:06; ☽☍⚷ 22:42

19 W: ☽⚻♆ 6:05; ☽∥♂ 7:31; ☽⚻♅ 9:40; ☽□♇ 10:16; ♂⚼♃ 11:21; ☽△♀ 11:59; ☉∥☽ 19:36; ☽∠♃ 20:55; ☽□♂ 21:33; ☽☌⚳ 22:38

20 Th: ☽⋕♅ 1:33; ☽□☿ 7:26; ☽⚼♆ 9:22; ☉ ♒ 13:23; ☽⚻♄ 13:58; ☉□⚷ 15:02; ☽∥♇ 15:37

21 F: ☽⚹♃ 0:32; ♂□⚳ 2:27; ☽⚻⚷ 5:34; ☉⚹☽ 6:48; ☽△♆ 13:25; ☽☍♅ 17:01; ☽⚹♇ 17:52; ☽⚼♄ 18:12

22 Sa: ☽□♀ 1:25; ☿∠♆ 6:44; ☽⚺⚳ 8:10; ☽⚹♂ 9:25; ☽⚼⚷ 10:06; ☉∠☽ 13:53; ☽⚹☿ 18:28; ☊D 20:15; ☽∠♇ 22:44; ☽△♄ 23:07

23 Su: ☽□♃ 9:48; ☽∠⚳ 14:00; ☽△⚷ 15:15; ☽∠♂ 16:32; ☉⚺☽ 21:45; ☽□♆ 23:30

24 M: ☽∠☿ 0:15; ☽⚻♅ 3:03; ☽⚺♇ 4:11; ♀∥⚳ 10:43; ☿R 11:04; ☽⚹♀ 18:19; ☉⚹♆ 19:09; ☽⚹⚳ 20:22

25 Tu: ☽⚺♂ 0:18; ⚴R 0:52; ☽∥♇ 5:41; ☽⚺☿ 5:57; ☽⚼♅ 8:50; ☽□♄ 10:37; ☽⋕♅ 20:43; ♀△⚳ 20:45; ♀∠⚷ 20:58; ☽△♃ 21:09

26 W: ☽□⚷ 3:02; ☽∠♀ 3:42; ☊R 7:37; ☿∠♆ 8:47; ☽⚹♆ 11:32; ☉△♅ 12:24; ☉∥☽ 13:01; ☽△♅ 14:59; ☉☌☽ 15:14; ☽☌♇ 16:23

27 Th: ♀⋕♄ 0:10; ☽∥♂ 3:06; ☽⚼♃ 3:20; ☉☌♇ 5:04; ☽□⚳ 10:15; ☿☌♂ 12:45; ☽⚺♀ 13:27; ☽☌☿ 16:36; ☽☌♂ 17:05; ☽∠♆ 17:59; ☽∥☿ 20:48; ☽⚹♄ 23:33

28 F: ☽⋕⚷ 6:05; ♂∠♆ 6:54; ☽⚻♃ 9:41; ☿⚺♀ 10:30; ☽⚹⚷ 15:57; ☽∥⚳ 21:39

29 Sa: ☽⚺♆ 0:34; ☽□♅ 3:51; ☽⋕♄ 4:38; ☽⚺♇ 5:29; ☽∠♄ 6:14; ☉⚺☽ 9:55; ☽∥♀ 10:41; ☽∠⚷ 22:30; ☽⋕♃ 22:40

30 Su: ☽△⚳ 0:42; ☽⚺☿ 1:41; ☽⋕♆ 7:40; ☽☌♀ 9:16; ☽⚺♂ 10:26; ☿□⚳ 10:41; ☽∠♇ 12:00; ☽∥♆ 12:01; ☽⚺♄ 12:50; ☉∠☽ 19:10; ☽∥♃ 21:06; ☽☍♃ 22:17

31 M: ☽⋕♀ 4:46; ☽⚺⚷ 4:51; ☽∠☿ 5:31; ☽⚼⚳ 7:41; ☽☌♆ 13:23; ♀∠♇ 13:23; ☽∥♄ 15:11; ☽⚹♅ 16:25; ♀⚺♂ 17:59; ☽⚹♇ 18:15; ☽∠♂ 18:44; ☽⋕⚳ 22:30; ♀⚺♄ 22:54

February 2028

LONGITUDE

Day	Sid.Time	☉	☽	☽ 12 hour	Mean ☊	True ☊	☿	♀	♂	⚳	♃	♄	⚷	♅	♆	♇
	h m s	° ' "	° ' "	° ' "	° '	° '	° '	° '	° '	° '	° '	° '	° '	° '	° '	° '
1 Tu	8 42 58	11♒38 12	9♈47 56	15♈51 04	1♒52.5	2♒18.3	14♒40.7	22♓25.9	22♒20.0	16♏49.1	26♍53.9	22♈22.8	0♉14.7	5♊59.6	4♈29.3	6♒55.3
2 W	8 46 55	12 39 07	21 57 16	28 07 03	1 49.3	2R 17.2	13R 28.5	23 37.0	23 07.5	17 04.8	26R 50.1	22 26.9	0 16.0	5R 59.0	4 30.8	6 57.2
3 Th	8 50 51	13 40 00	4♉20 55	10♉39 23	1 46.1	2D 16.5	12 14.5	24 47.9	23 54.9	17 20.2	26 46.1	22 31.1	0 17.3	5 58.5	4 32.4	6 59.0
4 F	8 54 48	14 40 53	17 02 56	23 32 04	1 42.9	2 16.4	11 00.9	25 58.8	24 42.4	17 35.5	26 42.0	22 35.4	0 18.7	5 58.0	4 34.0	7 00.9
5 Sa	8 58 44	15 41 44	0♊07 10	6♊48 38	1 39.7	2 16.8	9 49.5	27 09.5	25 29.9	17 50.4	26 37.7	22 39.8	0 20.1	5 57.5	4 35.6	7 02.8
6 Su	9 02 41	16 42 34	13 36 44	20 31 37	1 36.6	2 17.7	8 42.2	28 20.1	26 17.4	18 05.2	26 33.2	22 44.2	0 21.6	5 57.1	4 37.2	7 04.7
7 M	9 06 37	17 43 22	27 33 22	4♋41 51	1 33.4	2 19.0	7 40.4	29 30.6	27 04.9	18 19.6	26 28.6	22 48.7	0 23.1	5 56.8	4 38.9	7 06.6
8 Tu	9 10 34	18 44 09	11♋56 48	19 17 46	1 30.2	2 20.1	6 45.3	0♈40.9	27 52.3	18 33.8	26 23.8	22 53.4	0 24.7	5 56.5	4 40.6	7 08.4
9 W	9 14 31	19 44 54	26 44 06	4♌14 58	1 27.0	2R 20.8	5 57.7	1 51.1	28 39.8	18 47.8	26 18.9	22 58.1	0 26.3	5 56.3	4 42.3	7 10.3
10 Th	9 18 27	20 45 38	11♌49 23	19 26 13	1 23.9	2 20.7	5 18.0	3 01.1	29 27.3	19 01.5	26 13.8	23 02.9	0 28.0	5 56.1	4 44.1	7 12.1
11 F	9 22 24	21 46 21	27 04 13	4♍42 06	1 20.7	2 19.5	4 46.4	4 11.0	0♓14.7	19 14.9	26 08.5	23 07.7	0 29.8	5 56.0	4 45.8	7 14.0
12 Sa	9 26 20	22 47 02	12♍18 34	19 52 22	1 17.5	2 17.4	4 23.1	5 20.8	1 02.2	19 28.0	26 03.1	23 12.7	0 31.5	5D 55.9	4 47.6	7 15.8
13 Su	9 30 17	23 47 42	27 22 22	4♎47 33	1 14.3	2 14.6	4 07.7	6 30.4	1 49.6	19 40.8	25 57.6	23 17.7	0 33.4	5 55.9	4 49.4	7 17.7
14 M	9 34 13	24 48 21	12♎07 06	19 20 22	1 11.1	2 11.5	4D 00.1	7 39.9	2 37.1	19 53.4	25 51.9	23 22.8	0 35.3	5 55.9	4 51.2	7 19.5
15 Tu	9 38 10	25 48 58	26 26 55	3♏26 29	1 08.0	2 08.7	3 59.9	8 49.1	3 24.5	20 05.7	25 46.1	23 27.9	0 37.2	5 56.0	4 53.1	7 21.3
16 W	9 42 06	26 49 35	10♏19 01	17 04 36	1 04.8	2 06.6	4 06.7	9 58.3	4 12.0	20 17.6	25 40.1	23 33.2	0 39.2	5 56.1	4 55.0	7 23.1
17 Th	9 46 03	27 50 10	23 43 27	0♐15 54	1 01.6	2D 05.6	4 19.9	11 07.3	4 59.4	20 29.3	25 34.0	23 38.5	0 41.2	5 56.3	4 56.8	7 24.9
18 F	9 50 00	28 50 44	6♐42 22	13 03 21	0 58.4	2 05.8	4 39.3	12 16.1	5 46.8	20 40.7	25 27.8	23 43.9	0 43.3	5 56.5	4 58.7	7 26.7
19 Sa	9 53 56	29 51 17	19 19 20	25 30 52	0 55.3	2 06.9	5 04.3	13 24.7	6 34.3	20 51.8	25 21.4	23 49.4	0 45.4	5 56.8	5 00.7	7 28.5
20 Su	9 57 53	0♓51 49	1♑38 30	7♑42 46	0 52.1	2 08.7	5 34.5	14 33.2	7 21.7	21 02.5	25 15.0	23 54.9	0 47.6	5 57.2	5 02.6	7 30.3
21 M	10 01 49	1 52 20	13 44 12	19 43 18	0 48.9	2 10.4	6 09.5	15 41.5	8 09.1	21 13.0	25 08.4	24 00.5	0 49.8	5 57.6	5 04.6	7 32.0
22 Tu	10 05 46	2 52 49	25 40 30	1♒36 17	0 45.7	2R 11.6	6 49.0	16 49.6	8 56.5	21 23.1	25 01.7	24 06.2	0 52.1	5 58.1	5 06.6	7 33.8
23 W	10 09 42	3 53 16	7♒31 02	13 25 07	0 42.6	2 11.7	7 32.5	17 57.6	9 43.8	21 32.9	24 54.9	24 11.9	0 54.4	5 58.6	5 08.6	7 35.5
24 Th	10 13 39	4 53 42	19 18 52	25 12 35	0 39.4	2 10.2	8 19.9	19 05.3	10 31.2	21 42.3	24 48.0	24 17.7	0 56.8	5 59.1	5 10.6	7 37.3
25 F	10 17 35	5 54 07	1♓06 33	7♓01 01	0 36.2	2 06.9	9 10.7	20 12.8	11 18.6	21 51.5	24 41.0	24 23.6	0 59.2	5 59.7	5 12.6	7 39.0
26 Sa	10 21 32	6 54 30	12 56 12	18 52 21	0 33.0	2 02.0	10 04.8	21 20.2	12 05.9	22 00.2	24 33.9	24 29.5	1 01.6	6 00.4	5 14.6	7 40.7
27 Su	10 25 29	7 54 51	24 49 39	0♈48 20	0 29.8	1 55.7	11 01.8	22 27.3	12 53.2	22 08.7	24 26.8	24 35.5	1 04.1	6 01.1	5 16.7	7 42.4
28 M	10 29 25	8 55 10	6♈48 37	12 50 43	0 26.7	1 48.6	12 01.7	23 34.2	13 40.5	22 16.8	24 19.5	24 41.6	1 06.6	6 01.9	5 18.8	7 44.0
29 Tu	10 33 22	9♓55 27	18 54 53	25 01 23	0♒23.5	1♒41.4	13♒04.1	24♈40.9	14♓27.8	22♏24.5	24♍12.2	24♈47.7	1♉09.2	6♊02.7	5♈20.9	7♒45.7

1st of Month

Julian Day # 2461802.5
Obliquity 23°26'[illegible]3"
SVP 4♓51'[illegible]7"
GC 27♐13.9
Eris 25♈07.3

Day	⚴
1	4♎04.5R
6	3 38.0R
11	2 57.5R
16	2 03.5R
21	0 56.9R
26	29♍39.0R

Day	⚵
1	22♋40.8R
6	21 47.2R
11	21 04.4R
16	20 33.3R
21	20 14.2R
26	20 07.2R

Day	⚶
1	10♌57.4R
6	9 37.9R
11	8 20.9R
16	7 08.6R
21	6 03.2R
26	5 06.5R

DECLINATION and LATITUDE

Day	☉ Decl	☽ Decl	☽ Lat	☽ 12h Decl	☿ Decl	☿ Lat	♀ Decl	♀ Lat	♂ Decl	♂ Lat	⚳ Decl	⚳ Lat	♃ Decl	♃ Lat	♄ Decl	♄ Lat
1 Tu	17S18	8N22	4N53	10N55	13S15	3N20	3S46	0S50	15S05	1S05	8S03	9N10	2N31	1N24	6N28	2S24
2 W	17 01	13 22	5 12	15 43	13 27	3 28	3 15	0 47	14 49	1 04	8 06	9 12	2 33	1 25	6 30	2 24
3 Th	16 43	17 56	5 17	19 59	13 42	3 34	2 44	0 43	14 33	1 04	8 09	9 13	2 35	1 25	6 32	2 24
4 F	16 26	21 49	5 07	23 25	13 58	3 38	2 13	0 40	14 17	1 04	8 12	9 15	2 37	1 25	6 34	2 24
5 Sa	16 08	24 44	4 41	25 44	14 16	3 39	1 41	0 36	14 01	1 04	8 14	9 16	2 39	1 25	6 36	2 23
6 Su	15 50	26 23	3 58	26 37	14 34	3 38	1 10	0 33	13 45	1 04	8 17	9 17	2 41	1 26	6 38	2 23
7 M	15 31	26 26	3 01	25 48	14 53	3 35	0 38	0 29	13 29	1 03	8 19	9 19	2 43	1 26	6 39	2 23
8 Tu	15 12	24 44	1 51	23 14	15 12	3 29	0 07	0 25	13 12	1 03	8 22	9 20	2 45	1 26	6 41	2 23
9 W	14 54	21 19	0 31	19 01	15 31	3 22	0N24	0 22	12 55	1 03	8 24	9 22	2 47	1 26	6 43	2 23
10 Th	14 34	16 24	0S52	13 31	15 48	3 14	0 56	0 18	12 39	1 03	8 26	9 23	2 49	1 26	6 45	2 22
11 F	14 15	10 25	2 13	7 09	16 05	3 04	1 27	0 14	12 22	1 03	8 28	9 24	2 52	1 27	6 47	2 22
12 Sa	13 55	3 49	3 23	0 26	16 21	2 54	1 59	0 10	12 05	1 02	8 30	9 26	2 54	1 27	6 49	2 22
13 Su	13 35	2S55	4 19	6S11	16 35	2 43	2 30	0 06	11 47	1 02	8 32	9 27	2 56	1 27	6 51	2 22
14 M	13 15	9 20	4 56	12 18	16 48	2 31	3 01	0 01	11 30	1 02	8 34	9 29	2 59	1 27	6 53	2 21
15 Tu	12 55	15 04	5 14	17 35	17 00	2 19	3 32	0N03	11 13	1 02	8 36	9 30	3 01	1 27	6 55	2 21
16 W	12 34	19 50	5 12	21 48	17 11	2 07	4 04	0 07	10 55	1 01	8 37	9 32	3 04	1 28	6 58	2 21
17 Th	12 13	23 26	4 53	24 44	17 20	1 54	4 35	0 11	10 38	1 01	8 39	9 33	3 06	1 28	6 60	2 21
18 F	11 52	25 41	4 20	26 18	17 27	1 42	5 05	0 16	10 20	1 01	8 40	9 34	3 09	1 28	7 02	2 21
19 Sa	11 31	26 34	3 34	26 30	17 33	1 29	5 36	0 20	10 02	1 00	8 42	9 36	3 12	1 28	7 04	2 20
20 Su	11 10	26 06	2 40	25 23	17 38	1 17	6 07	0 25	9 44	1 00	8 43	9 37	3 14	1 28	7 06	2 20
21 M	10 48	24 23	1 40	23 07	17 41	1 05	6 38	0 29	9 26	0 60	8 44	9 39	3 17	1 29	7 09	2 20
22 Tu	10 27	21 35	0 36	19 51	17 43	0 53	7 08	0 34	9 08	0 60	8 45	9 40	3 20	1 29	7 11	2 20
23 W	10 05	17 55	0N29	15 49	17 43	0 42	7 38	0 39	8 50	0 59	8 46	9 42	3 23	1 29	7 13	2 20
24 Th	9 43	13 34	1 32	11 11	17 42	0 30	8 08	0 43	8 32	0 59	8 47	9 43	3 26	1 29	7 15	2 19
25 F	9 21	8 43	2 32	6 10	17 39	0 19	8 38	0 48	8 14	0 59	8 48	9 44	3 29	1 29	7 18	2 19
26 Sa	8 58	3 33	3 24	0 55	17 35	0 08	9 08	0 53	7 55	0 58	8 49	9 46	3 32	1 29	7 20	2 19
27 Su	8 36	1N45	4 08	4N23	17 29	0S02	9 38	0 57	7 37	0 58	8 50	9 47	3 35	1 30	7 22	2 19
28 M	8 13	7 01	4 41	9 35	17 23	0 12	10 07	1 02	7 18	0 58	8 50	9 49	3 38	1 30	7 25	2 19
29 Tu	7S51	12N04	5N03	14N27	17S14	0S22	10N36	1N07	6S60	0S57	8S51	9N50	3N41	1N30	7N27	2S18

Day	⚷ Decl	⚷ Lat	♅ Decl	♅ Lat	♆ Decl	♆ Lat	♇ Decl	♇ Lat
1	11N09	0S26	21N14	0S05	0N30	1S24	23S09	4S46
6	11 11	0 26	21 13	0 04	0 33	1 24	23 07	4 46
11	11 14	0 27	21 13	0 04	0 37	1 24	23 05	4 47
16	11 17	0 27	21 13	0 04	0 40	1 24	23 03	4 47
21	11 20	0 27	21 14	0 04	0 44	1 24	23 01	4 48
26	11N24	0S28	21N14	0S04	0N48	1S23	22S60	4S49

Day	⚴ Decl	⚴ Lat	⚵ Decl	⚵ Lat	⚶ Decl	⚶ Lat	Eris Decl	Eris Lat
1	11S11	10S26	4N36	17S09	22N43	5N27	0N18	10S07
6	10 01	9 21	5 27	16 25	23 18	5 40	0 19	10 06
11	8 41	8 11	6 19	15 39	23 49	5 51	0 20	10 05
16	7 10	6 55	7 10	14 51	24 18	6 01	0 21	10 05
21	5 28	5 33	8 00	14 03	24 42	6 08	0 22	10 04
26	3S38	4S07	8N49	13S15	25N01	6N14	0N24	10S03

Moon Phenomena

Max/0 Decl
dy hr mn
6 12:54 26N37
12 13:33 0 S
19 3:23 26S35
26 16:08 0 N

Max/0 Lat
dy hr mn
2 20:01 5N17
9 8:58 0 S
15 9:43 5S15
22 13:12 0 N

Perigee/Apogee
dy hr m kilometers
10 19:57 p 356682
24 16:29 a 406562

PH dy hr mn
☽ 3 19:12 14♉29
○ 10 15:05 21♌24
☾ 17 8:09 28♏11
● 25 10:39 6♓21

Void of Course Moon

Last Aspect	☽ Ingress
2 2:27 ♂ ⚹	♉ 2 15:38
4 18:06 ♀ ⚹	♊ 4 23:47
7 3:36 ♀ □	♋ 7 4:08
8 23:20 ♃ ⚹	♌ 9 5:14
10 17:46 ♄ △	♍ 11 4:36
12 21:45 ♃ ☌	♎ 13 4:14
14 22:51 ☉ △	♏ 15 6:04
17 8:09 ☉ □	♐ 17 11:31
19 11:36 ♃ □	♑ 19 20:46
21 22:42 ♃ △	♒ 22 8:45
24 10:13 ♄ ⚹	♓ 24 21:45
26 23:14 ♃ ☍	♈ 27 10:23
29 12:28 ♀ ☌	♉ 29 21:43

DAILY ASPECTARIAN

1 Tu ♂⚹♄ 1:35; ☉⚹☽ 3:59; ☉⚼♃ 5:50; ☽⚹☿ 8:49; ☽∥⚷ 13:08; ☽⚻⚳ 14:13; ☽∠♅ 22:06

2 W ☽#☿ 0:24; ☽☌♄ 0:58; ☽⚹♂ 2:27; ☽⊻♀ 3:36; ☽#♂ 6:56; ☉☌☿ 8:48; ☽⚻♃ 9:28; ☽☌⚷ 16:11; ☉#☽ 17:43

3 Th ☽⊻♆ 0:22; ☽⊻♅ 3:06; ☽□♇ 5:03; ♀#♃ 6:29; ☿⚼♃ 9:45; ☽∠♀ 11:27; ☽□☿ 13:40; ☽⚼♃ 14:02; ☊ D 18:54; ☉□☽ 19:12; ☽∥♅ 19:58

4 F ☿∠♀ 0:21; ☽☍⚳ 1:02; ☽∠♆ 4:41; ☽#♇ 9:35; ☽⊻♄ 10:19; ☿∥♂ 13:48; ♀☍♃ 13:50; ☽□♂ 15:04; ☽△♃ 17:42; ☽⚹♀ 18:06

5 Sa ☽⊻⚷ 0:23; ☽⚹♆ 8:04; ☽☌♅ 10:29; ☽△♇ 12:27; ☽∠♄ 13:35; ☽△☿ 16:00

6 Su ☽∠⚷ 3:03; ☉△☽ 5:50; ♂⚻♃ 7:19; ☽⚻⚳ 7:55; ☽⚼♇ 14:42; ☽⚹♄ 15:53; ☽⚼☿ 16:14; ☽□♃ 22:11; ☽△♂ 23:09

7 M ♀#♆ 3:25; ☽□♀ 3:36; ☽⚹⚷ 4:47; ☉⚼☽ 9:22; ☽⚼⚳ 9:52; ♀ ♈ 10:02; ☽□♆ 11:56; ☿☌♇ 13:55; ☽⊻♅ 14:04; ☽⚻☿ 15:55; ☽⚻♇ 16:03; ♀⊻⚷ 18:20; ☉□⚳ 18:42

8 Tu ☉∥☿ 0:10; ☽⚼♂ 1:36; ☽△⚳ 10:59; ☉⚻☽ 11:54; ☽#♇ 12:55; ☽∠♅ 14:40; ☽□♄ 17:54; ☉∠♆ 22:57; ☽⚹♃ 23:20

9 W ☽∥♅ 0:31; ☿△♅ 0:46; ☽⚻♂ 3:16; ☽□⚷ 5:56; ♀∥♆ 8:26; ☽△♀ 8:52; ☊ R 9:00; ☽△♆ 12:45; ☽☍☿ 14:05; ☽⚹♅ 14:41; ☽☍♇ 16:40; ☽∠♃ 23:04

10 Th ☽#☿ 2:27; ☉#☽ 8:10; ☽⚼♀ 10:35; ☽□⚳ 11:31; ☽⚼♆ 12:29; ☉☍☽ 15:05; ☽#♂ 16:11; ♂ ♓ 16:33; ☽△♄ 17:46; ☽∥⚷ 20:55; ☽⊻♃ 22:33

11 F ☿⚹♆ 0:29; ♀⚼⚳ 1:37; ☽☍♂ 5:16; ☽△⚷ 5:24; ☽#⚳ 7:10; ♂⚹⚷ 7:53; ☿⚹♀ 8:52; ☽⚻☿ 11:47; ☽⚻♀ 12:07; ☽⚻♆ 12:07; ♀☌♆ 12:17; ☽∥♄ 13:16; ☽□♅ 13:56; ☽⚻♇ 16:01; ☽⚼♄ 17:30

12 Sa ☽∥♃ 3:14; ☽⚼⚷ 5:06; ☽∥♀ 6:03; ☽⚼☿ 11:01; ☉⚹♄ 11:03; ☽∥♆ 11:19; ☽⚹⚳ 11:31; ♀⚹♅ 12:05; ☽#♆ 15:48; ☽⚼♇ 15:51; ☽⚻♄ 17:25; ☉⚻☽ 17:51; ☽☌♃ 21:45; ☽#♀ 22:22; ♅ D 23:51

13 Su ☽#♃ 0:05; ☽⚻⚷ 5:09; ☽⚻♂ 7:36; ☽△☿ 10:48; ☽∠⚳ 11:59; ☽☍♆ 12:05; ☽△♅ 13:51; ☽#♄ 14:36; ☽☍♀ 16:04; ☽△♇ 16:07; ♀⚹♇ 16:46; ⚳⚼♆ 19:08; ☉⚼☽ 19:55; ☽∥⚳ 21:01; ♀∥♃ 21:57

14 M ☽#⚷ 7:42; ☽∥♂ 8:17; ☽⚼♂ 9:39; ☿ D 12:39; ☽⊻⚳ 13:07; ☽⚼♅ 14:40; ☉∥☽ 15:06; ☽☍♄ 18:55; ♂#⚷ 19:33; ☉△☽ 22:51; ☽⊻♃ 22:51; ☉⚻♃ 22:57

15 Tu ☽☍⚷ 7:09; ☽∥☿ 9:26; ☽△♂ 12:40; ☽□☿ 13:03; ☽⚻♆ 14:32; ☽⚻♅ 16:20; ☽□♇ 18:51; ☿⊻♂ 20:38; ☽⚻♀ 23:20

16 W ☽∠♃ 0:37; ☽#♅ 8:19; ☽⚼♆ 17:09; ☽☌⚳ 18:03; ☽∥♇ 20:57; ♂⊻♆ 22:39; ☽⚻♄ 23:51

17 Th ☽⚹♃ 3:20; ☽⚼♀ 4:48; ☉□☽ 8:09; ☊ D 8:13; ☽⚻⚷ 12:49; ☽⚹☿ 20:03; ☽△♆ 20:45; ☽□♂ 22:09; ☽☍♅ 22:34

18 F ☽⚹♇ 1:23; ☽⚼♄ 3:50; ♂□♅ 4:57; ☽△♀ 11:33; ☽⚼⚷ 17:08; ☿⚹♆ 20:35

19 Sa ☽∠☿ 1:30; ☽⊻⚳ 3:01; ☉ ♓ 3:27; ☽∠♇ 6:06; ☽△♄ 8:46; ☽□♃ 11:36; ☉#⚷ 13:44; ☉⚹⚷ 22:16; ☽△⚷ 22:20; ☉⚹☽ 22:20

20 Su ♂⊻♇ 4:31; ☽□♆ 6:44; ☽⊻☿ 8:08; ☽⚻♅ 8:31; ☽∠⚳ 8:49; ☽⊻♇ 11:37; ☽⚹♂ 12:06; ☿△♅ 16:05

21 M ☽□♀ 4:19; ☉∠☽ 6:51; ☽∥♇ 12:47; ☽⚼♅ 14:30; ☽⚹⚳ 15:13; ☽∠♂ 20:15; ☽□♄ 20:48; ☽△♃ 22:42

22 Tu ♀∥♄ 2:24; ☽#♅ 2:37; ♂∠♄ 5:36; ☽□⚷ 10:32; ☊ R 13:11; ☉⊻☽ 15:57; ☽⚹♆ 19:10; ☽△♅ 20:52

23 W ☽☌☿ 0:03; ☽☌♇ 0:09; ☽∥☿ 1:13; ☿☌♇ 1:38; ♂∥⚳ 4:32; ☽⊻♂ 4:49; ☽⚼♃ 4:50; ☽⚹♀ 23:29

24 Th ☽∠♆ 1:46; ☽□⚳ 4:56; ☉⊻♆ 6:56; ☽⚹♄ 10:13; ☽⚻♃ 11:03; ☽#⚷ 11:04; ♀#♂ 11:40; ⚴ R♍ 17:08; ☉∥☽ 20:45; ☽∥⚳ 23:35; ☽⚹⚷ 23:45

25 F ☽#♀ 0:20; ☉□♅ 2:15; ☽∥♂ 2:29; ☽#♄ 6:40; ♀#⚳ 8:12; ☽⊻♆ 8:21; ☽∠♀ 9:13; ☽□♅ 9:56; ☉☌☽ 10:39; ☿⚼♃ 12:03; ☽⊻♇ 13:19; ♀∠♅ 16:52; ☽∠♄ 16:58; ☽⊻☿ 17:43; ☉#♀ 19:33; ☽☌♂ 22:11

26 Sa ☽#♃ 0:08; ☽∠⚷ 6:16; ♃⚻♄ 8:01; ⚵ D 9:23; ☉∥⚳ 9:48; ☽#♆ 12:27; ♀⚻⚳ 16:23; ☽△⚳ 18:32; ☽⊻♀ 18:44; ☉⊻♇ 18:53; ☽∠♇ 19:43; ☽∥♆ 19:50; ☽☍♃ 23:14; ☽⊻♄ 23:31

27 Su ☽∠☿ 2:38; ☽∥♃ 8:23; ☽⊻⚷ 12:34; ♂#♄ 16:33; ☽☌♆ 21:00; ☽⚹♅ 22:27

28 M ☽⚼⚳ 0:57; ☽#♂ 1:17; ☽⚹♇ 1:51; ☽∥♄ 1:53; ☉⊻☽ 4:35; ☉#☽ 5:15; ☽#⚳ 8:32; ☽⚹☿ 11:21; ☽⊻♂ 14:36; ♀⚻♃ 14:40; ☽∥♀ 16:07; ☉∠♄ 20:34; ☽∥⚷ 20:56

29 Tu ♀☌♄ 2:42; ☽∠♅ 4:12; ☽⚻⚳ 6:57; ☽⚻♃ 10:17; ☽☌♄ 11:39; ☽☌♀ 12:28; ☉∠☽ 12:52; ☽∠♂ 22:05; ☉#♄ 22:30

March 2028

LONGITUDE

Day	Sid.Time	☉	☽	☽ 12 hour	Mean ☊	True ☊	☿	♀	♂	⚳	♃	♄	⚷	♅	♆	♇
	h m s	° ' "	° ' "	° ' "	° '	° '	° '	° '	° '	° '	° '	° '	° '	° '	° '	° '
1 W	10 37 18	10♓55 43	1♉10 31	7♉22 35	0♒20.3	1♒34.9	14♒09.0	25♈47.4	15♓15.1	22♏31.9	24♍04.8	24♈53.9	1♉11.8	6♊03.6	5♈23.0	7♒47.3
2 Th	10 41 15	11 55 56	13 37 56	19 55 55	0 17.1	1R 29.8	15 16.1	26 53.6	16 02.3	22 38.9	23R 57.3	25 00.1	1 14.4	6 04.5	5 25.1	7 49.0
3 F	10 45 11	12 56 08	26 19 54	2♊47 18	0 13.9	1 26.4	16 25.4	27 59.6	16 49.5	22 45.6	23 49.8	25 06.4	1 17.1	6 05.5	5 27.2	7 50.6
4 Sa	10 49 08	13 56 17	9♊19 30	15 56 51	0 10.8	1D 25.0	17 36.6	29 05.3	17 36.7	22 51.9	23 42.2	25 12.8	1 19.8	6 06.5	5 29.3	7 52.2
5 Su	10 53 04	14 56 25	22 39 44	29 28 25	0 07.6	1 25.1	18 49.8	0♉10.8	18 23.9	22 57.8	23 34.6	25 19.2	1 22.6	6 07.6	5 31.5	7 53.8
6 M	10 57 01	15 56 30	6♋23 07	13♋24 00	0 04.4	1 26.3	20 04.8	1 16.0	19 11.1	23 03.4	23 26.9	25 25.7	1 25.4	6 08.7	5 33.6	7 55.4
7 Tu	11 00 58	16 56 33	20 31 04	27 44 10	0 01.2	1R 27.5	21 21.5	2 20.9	19 58.2	23 08.5	23 19.2	25 32.2	1 28.2	6 09.9	5 35.8	7 56.9
8 W	11 04 54	17 56 34	5♌03 01	12♌27 07	29♑58.1	1 27.8	22 39.8	3 25.6	20 45.3	23 13.4	23 11.5	25 38.7	1 31.1	6 11.2	5 38.0	7 58.5
9 Th	11 08 51	18 56 33	19 55 48	27 28 11	29 54.9	1 26.4	23 59.7	4 29.9	21 32.4	23 17.8	23 03.7	25 45.3	1 34.0	6 12.4	5 40.2	8 00.0
10 F	11 12 47	19 56 30	5♍03 15	12♍39 49	29 51.7	1 22.9	25 21.2	5 34.0	22 19.5	23 21.8	22 56.0	25 52.0	1 36.9	6 13.8	5 42.4	8 01.5
11 Sa	11 16 44	20 56 24	20 16 35	27 52 14	29 48.5	1 17.1	26 44.1	6 37.7	23 06.5	23 25.5	22 48.2	25 58.7	1 39.9	6 15.2	5 44.6	8 03.0
12 Su	11 20 40	21 56 17	5♎25 26	12♎54 57	29 45.4	1 09.7	28 08.4	7 41.2	23 53.5	23 28.7	22 40.4	26 05.5	1 42.9	6 16.6	5 46.8	8 04.4
13 M	11 24 37	22 56 08	20 19 39	27 38 35	29 42.2	1 01.5	29 34.2	8 44.3	24 40.5	23 31.6	22 32.6	26 12.2	1 45.9	6 18.1	5 49.0	8 05.9
14 Tu	11 28 33	23 55 57	4♏51 00	11♏56 21	29 39.0	0 53.5	1♓01.3	9 47.0	25 27.4	23 34.1	22 24.7	26 19.1	1 49.0	6 19.6	5 51.3	8 07.3
15 W	11 32 30	24 55 45	18 54 19	25 44 47	29 35.8	0 46.8	2 29.8	10 49.4	26 14.3	23 36.1	22 16.9	26 26.0	1 52.1	6 21.1	5 53.5	8 08.7
16 Th	11 36 26	25 55 30	2♐27 49	9♐03 39	29 32.6	0 42.0	3 59.6	11 51.5	27 01.2	23 37.8	22 09.2	26 32.9	1 55.2	6 22.8	5 55.7	8 10.1
17 F	11 40 23	26 55 14	15 32 39	21 55 18	29 29.5	0D 39.4	5 30.8	12 53.2	27 48.1	23 39.1	22 01.4	26 39.8	1 58.4	6 24.4	5 58.0	8 11.5
18 Sa	11 44 20	27 54 57	28 12 10	4♑23 50	29 26.3	0 38.6	7 03.2	13 54.6	28 34.9	23 39.9	21 53.6	26 46.8	2 01.6	6 26.1	6 00.2	8 12.8
19 Su	11 48 16	28 54 38	10♑30 58	16 34 13	29 23.1	0 39.2	8 36.9	14 55.5	29 21.8	23R 40.4	21 45.9	26 53.9	2 04.8	6 27.9	6 02.5	8 14.2
20 M	11 52 13	29 54 16	22 34 15	28 31 44	29 19.9	0R 40.0	10 11.9	15 56.1	0♈08.5	23 40.4	21 38.2	27 01.0	2 08.0	6 29.7	6 04.8	8 15.5
21 Tu	11 56 09	0♈53 54	4♒27 16	10♒21 28	29 16.8	0 40.2	11 48.1	16 56.3	0 55.3	23 40.0	21 30.6	27 08.1	2 11.3	6 31.5	6 07.0	8 16.8
22 W	12 00 06	1 53 29	16 14 53	22 08 01	29 13.6	0 38.8	13 25.7	17 56.0	1 42.0	23 39.2	21 23.0	27 15.2	2 14.6	6 33.4	6 09.3	8 18.0
23 Th	12 04 02	2 53 02	28 01 22	3♓55 18	29 10.4	0 35.1	15 04.5	18 55.4	2 28.7	23 38.0	21 15.4	27 22.4	2 17.9	6 35.4	6 11.6	8 19.3
24 F	12 07 59	3 52 34	9♓50 14	15 46 28	29 07.2	0 28.7	16 44.7	19 54.2	3 15.4	23 36.4	21 07.9	27 29.6	2 21.2	6 37.3	6 13.8	8 20.5
25 Sa	12 11 55	4 52 03	21 44 15	27 43 50	29 04.0	0 19.6	18 26.1	20 52.6	4 02.0	23 34.3	21 00.5	27 36.9	2 24.6	6 39.4	6 16.1	8 21.7
26 Su	12 15 52	5 51 31	3♈45 23	9♈49 04	29 00.9	0 08.5	20 08.8	21 50.6	4 48.6	23 31.8	20 53.1	27 44.1	2 28.0	6 41.4	6 18.4	8 22.9
27 M	12 19 49	6 50 56	15 54 59	22 03 14	28 57.7	29♑56.1	21 52.9	22 48.0	5 35.1	23 29.0	20 45.8	27 51.4	2 31.4	6 43.5	6 20.7	8 24.0
28 Tu	12 23 45	7 50 20	28 13 55	4♉27 06	28 54.5	29 43.4	23 38.3	23 45.0	6 21.6	23 25.7	20 38.6	27 58.8	2 34.8	6 45.7	6 22.9	8 25.2
29 W	12 27 42	8 49 41	10♉42 53	17 01 22	28 51.3	29 31.6	25 25.0	24 41.4	7 08.1	23 22.0	20 31.5	28 06.1	2 38.3	6 47.9	6 25.2	8 26.3
30 Th	12 31 38	9 49 01	23 22 39	29 46 54	28 48.1	29 21.8	27 13.1	25 37.3	7 54.6	23 17.9	20 24.4	28 13.5	2 41.7	6 50.1	6 27.5	8 27.4
31 F	12 35 35	10♈48 18	6♊14 17	12♊44 59	28♑45.0	29♑14.6	29♓02.5	26♉32.6	8♈41.0	23♏13.4	20♍17.5	28♈20.9	2♉45.2	6♊52.4	6♈29.7	8♒28.4

1st of Month

Julian Day # 2461831.5
Obliquity 23°26'33"
SVP 4♓51'34"
GC 27♐14.0
Eris 25♈17.5

Day	⚴	Day	⚵	Day	⚶
1	28♍30.1R	1	20♋10.3	1	4♌28.5R
6	26 57.8R	6	20 24.4	6	3 51.0R
11	25 21.6R	11	20 49.4	11	3 25.1R
16	23 44.3R	16	21 24.4	16	3 10.8R
21	22 09.2R	21	22 08.7	21	3 08.3
26	20 39.1R	26	23 01.5	26	3 17.2
31	19 16.8R	31	24 02.0	31	3 37.2

DECLINATION and LATITUDE

Day	☉ Decl	☽ Decl	☽ Lat	☽ 12h Decl	☿ Decl	☿ Lat	♀ Decl	♀ Lat	♂ Decl	♂ Lat	⚳ Decl	⚳ Lat	♃ Decl	♃ Lat	♄ Decl	♄ Lat
1 W	7S28	16N43	5N10	18N50	17S05	0S31	11N05	1N12	6S41	0S57	8S51	9N51	3N44	1N30	7N30	2S18
2 Th	7 05	20 45	5 03	22 27	16 54	0 40	11 34	1 17	6 23	0 57	8 52	9 53	3 47	1 30	7 32	2 18
3 F	6 42	23 53	4 42	25 03	16 41	0 49	12 02	1 22	6 04	0 56	8 52	9 54	3 50	1 30	7 34	2 18
4 Sa	6 19	25 53	4 05	26 22	16 27	0 57	12 30	1 27	5 45	0 56	8 52	9 56	3 53	1 30	7 37	2 18
5 Su	5 56	26 28	3 15	26 11	16 12	1 05	12 58	1 32	5 26	0 55	8 52	9 57	3 56	1 30	7 39	2 18
6 M	5 33	25 28	2 12	24 22	15 56	1 12	13 26	1 37	5 07	0 55	8 52	9 58	3 59	1 30	7 42	2 17
7 Tu	5 09	22 50	0 59	20 56	15 38	1 19	13 53	1 42	4 49	0 55	8 52	9 59	4 02	1 31	7 44	2 17
8 W	4 46	18 41	0S19	16 07	15 19	1 26	14 20	1 47	4 30	0 54	8 52	10 01	4 05	1 31	7 47	2 17
9 Th	4 23	13 17	1 38	10 13	14 59	1 32	14 46	1 52	4 11	0 54	8 52	10 02	4 08	1 31	7 49	2 17
10 F	3 59	7 00	2 51	3 40	14 37	1 38	15 13	1 57	3 52	0 53	8 52	10 03	4 12	1 31	7 52	2 17
11 Sa	3 35	0 17	3 52	3S05	14 14	1 44	15 39	2 02	3 33	0 53	8 52	10 04	4 15	1 31	7 55	2 17
12 Su	3 12	6S23	4 37	9 34	13 50	1 49	16 04	2 07	3 14	0 53	8 51	10 06	4 18	1 31	7 57	2 17
13 M	2 48	12 35	5 01	15 24	13 24	1 54	16 30	2 12	2 55	0 52	8 51	10 07	4 21	1 31	7 60	2 16
14 Tu	2 25	17 56	5 06	20 11	12 57	1 58	16 55	2 17	2 36	0 52	8 50	10 08	4 24	1 31	8 02	2 16
15 W	2 01	22 07	4 52	23 42	12 29	2 02	17 19	2 22	2 17	0 51	8 50	10 09	4 27	1 31	8 05	2 16
16 Th	1 37	24 55	4 21	25 46	11 60	2 06	17 43	2 27	1 58	0 51	8 49	10 10	4 30	1 31	8 07	2 16
17 F	1 13	26 16	3 38	26 24	11 29	2 09	18 07	2 32	1 39	0 51	8 48	10 11	4 33	1 31	8 10	2 16
18 Sa	0 50	26 11	2 45	25 38	10 57	2 11	18 31	2 37	1 20	0 50	8 48	10 12	4 37	1 31	8 13	2 16
19 Su	0 26	24 47	1 46	23 39	10 24	2 14	18 54	2 42	1 01	0 50	8 47	10 13	4 40	1 31	8 15	2 16
20 M	0 02	22 16	0 43	20 38	9 50	2 16	19 16	2 47	0 42	0 49	8 46	10 14	4 43	1 31	8 18	2 16
21 Tu	0N21	18 49	0N20	16 49	9 15	2 17	19 38	2 52	0 23	0 49	8 45	10 15	4 46	1 31	8 21	2 15
22 W	0 45	14 39	1 22	12 22	8 38	2 18	20 00	2 57	0 04	0 48	8 44	10 15	4 49	1 31	8 23	2 15
23 Th	1 09	9 57	2 21	7 28	8 00	2 18	20 22	3 02	0N15	0 48	8 43	10 16	4 52	1 31	8 26	2 15
24 F	1 32	4 54	3 13	2 17	7 21	2 18	20 42	3 07	0 34	0 47	8 42	10 17	4 55	1 31	8 29	2 15
25 Sa	1 56	0N21	3 57	3N00	6 41	2 18	21 03	3 11	0 53	0 47	8 41	10 18	4 57	1 31	8 31	2 15
26 Su	2 20	5 38	4 31	8 14	6 00	2 17	21 23	3 16	1 12	0 46	8 40	10 18	5 00	1 31	8 34	2 15
27 M	2 43	10 46	4 53	13 13	5 18	2 16	21 42	3 21	1 31	0 46	8 39	10 19	5 03	1 31	8 37	2 15
28 Tu	3 07	15 32	5 02	17 43	4 34	2 14	22 01	3 25	1 50	0 45	8 37	10 19	5 06	1 31	8 39	2 15
29 W	3 30	19 43	4 56	21 31	3 50	2 11	22 20	3 30	2 09	0 45	8 36	10 20	5 09	1 31	8 42	2 15
30 Th	3 53	23 04	4 36	24 21	3 04	2 08	22 38	3 34	2 28	0 44	8 35	10 20	5 11	1 31	8 45	2 15
31 F	4N17	25N19	4N02	25N57	2S18	2S05	22N56	3N39	2N46	0S44	8S33	10N20	5N14	1N31	8N47	2S15

Day	⚷ Decl	⚷ Lat	♅ Decl	♅ Lat	♆ Decl	♆ Lat	♇ Decl	♇ Lat
1	11N27	0S28	21N15	0S04	0N52	1S23	22S58	4S49
6	11 32	0 28	21 16	0 04	0 56	1 23	22 57	4 50
11	11 37	0 28	21 17	0 04	1 00	1 23	22 56	4 51
16	11 42	0 29	21 18	0 04	1 05	1 23	22 55	4 52
21	11 47	0 29	21 20	0 04	1 09	1 23	22 54	4 52
26	11 52	0 29	21 22	0 04	1 14	1 23	22 53	4 53
31	11N58	0S29	21N24	0S04	1N18	1S23	22S52	4S54

Day	⚴ Decl	⚴ Lat	⚵ Decl	⚵ Lat	⚶ Decl	⚶ Lat	Eris Decl	Eris Lat
1	2S05	2S55	9N26	12S38	25N14	6N17	0N25	10S03
6	0 03	1 23	10 09	11 52	25 26	6 20	0 26	10 02
11	2N01	0N11	10 49	11 08	25 33	6 21	0 28	10 02
16	4 05	1 44	11 26	10 25	25 37	6 21	0 29	10 01
21	6 06	3 15	11 59	9 45	25 37	6 21	0 30	10 01
26	8 01	4 42	12 29	9 07	25 33	6 19	0 32	10 01
31	9N49	6N04	12N55	8S30	25N27	6N17	0N33	10S00

Moon Phenomena

Max/0 Decl

dy	hr mn	
4	21:13	26N29
11	1:02	0 S
17	10:25	26S24
24	22:23	0 N

Perigee/Apogee

dy	hr m		kilometers
10	8:23	p	357602
22	23:24	a	406093

Max/0 Lat

dy	hr mn	
1	0:47	5N10
7	18:07	0 S
13	17:26	5S07
20	16:19	0 N
28	2:50	5N02

PH

PH	dy	hr mn	
☽	4	9:04	14♊19
○	11	1:07	20♍59
☾	17	23:24	27♐53
●	26	4:32	6♈03

Void of Course Moon

Last Aspect			☽ Ingress		
2	19:21	♃ △	♊	3	6:50
5	4:44	♄ ✱	♋	5	12:55
7	8:25	♄ □	♌	7	15:44
9	9:21	♄ △	♍	9	16:01
11	4:43	♂ ☍	♎	11	15:23
13	9:42	♄ ☍	♏	13	15:54
15	13:40	♂ △	♐	15	19:34
18	0:47	♂ □	♑	18	3:28
20	9:02	♄ □	♒	20	14:58
22	22:40	♄ ✱	♓	23	4:02
24	22:33	♃ ☍	♈	25	16:32
27	23:30	♄ ☌	♉	28	3:25
30	8:24	☿ ✱	♊	30	12:24

DAILY ASPECTARIAN

1 W: ☽☌⚷ 0:02; ☽#☿ 1:53; ☽⚺♆ 8:11; ☽⚺♅ 9:28; ☽□♇ 12:49; ☽⚼♃ 15:08; ♀∥⚷ 19:18; ☉✱☽ 20:28

2 Th: ☽∥♅ 3:25; ☽□☿ 3:26; ☽✱♂ 4:53; ♂∠⚷ 6:31; ☉∠♀ 9:34; ☽∠♆ 12:55; ☽#♇ 16:04; ☽☍⚳ 17:15; ☽△♃ 19:21; ☽⚺♄ 21:41

3 F: ☽⚺♀ 3:23; ☽⚺⚷ 9:15; ☽✱♆ 16:57; ☽☌♅ 18:06; ☽△♇ 21:20

4 Sa: ☿⚺♂ 0:07; ☽∠♄ 1:38; ☊ D 8:52; ☉□☽ 9:04; ☽∠♀ 9:25; ☽∠⚷ 12:44; ☽□♂ 15:56; ☽△☿ 16:29; ♀ ♉ 20:02

5 Su: ☽⚼♇ 0:25; ☽⚻⚳ 0:32; ☽□♃ 1:36; ☽✱♄ 4:44; ☽✱♀ 14:22; ☽✱⚷ 15:22; ☽⚼☿ 21:31; ☽□♆ 22:34; ☽⚺♅ 23:35

6 M: ☽⚻♇ 2:39; ☽⚼⚳ 2:54; ♀☌⚷ 3:37; ☿∠♆ 9:22; ☉∠⚷ 12:07; ☉△☽ 17:32; ☽△♂ 23:02; ☽#♇ 23:16

7 Tu: ☽∠♅ 1:05; ☽⚻☿ 1:33; ☽△⚳ 4:24; ☽✱♃ 4:38; ☽□♄ 8:25; ☽∥♅ 10:04; ☊ R 18:08; ☽□⚷ 18:12; ☉⚼☽ 20:18; ⚳✱♃ 20:24; ☽□♀ 21:08

8 W: ☽△♆ 0:57; ☽⚼♂ 1:13; ☽✱♅ 1:51; ☽☍♇ 4:46; ☽∠♃ 5:04; ☿⚻♃ 8:44; ☿□⚳ 10:45; ☽#☿ 16:30; ☽∥♀ 18:16; ☉⚻☽ 22:19

9 Th: ☽⚼♆ 1:11; ♂#♃ 2:30; ☽⚻♂ 2:43; ☽⚺♃ 4:57; ☽□⚳ 5:24; ☿#♀ 6:03; ☽∥⚷ 6:46; ☽☍☿ 7:07; ☽△♄ 9:21; ♃⚼♇ 9:44; ☉#♃ 12:37; ☽#⚳ 17:07; ☽△⚷ 18:33; ☽∥♄ 20:51

10 F: ☽△♀ 0:52; ☽⚻♆ 1:02; ☽□♅ 1:51; ♀⚺♆ 3:16; ☽⚻♇ 4:42; ☽⚼♄ 9:14; ☿✱♄ 9:46; ☽∥♃ 10:03; ☉#☽ 11:34; ☽#♂ 11:52; ♀⚺♅ 15:18; ♂☍♃ 15:59; ☽⚼⚷ 18:17; ☽∥♆ 21:28; ♂∠♇ 22:08

11 Sa: ☉☍☽ 1:07; ☽⚼♀ 2:18; ☽☌♃ 3:57; ☽⚼♇ 4:23; ☽#♆ 4:37; ☽☍♂ 4:43; ☽✱⚳ 4:59; ☽⚻♄ 9:04; ♂△⚳ 10:26; ☽⚻☿ 11:14; ☽∥♂ 13:04; ☉∥☽ 13:04; ☉∥♂ 13:24; ☽#♃ 16:20; ☽⚻⚷ 18:05; ♀⚼♃ 23:44

12 Su: ☽☍♆ 0:34; ☽△♅ 1:22; ☽⚻♀ 3:53; ☽△♇ 4:14; ☽∠⚳ 4:54; ☽#♄ 5:52; ♀□♇ 9:03; ☽∥⚳ 9:14; ☽⚼☿ 13:40; ☉☍♃ 15:38; ☽#⚷ 20:08

13 M: ☽⚼♅ 1:35; ☽∥☿ 3:07; ☽⚺♃ 3:35; ☉∠♇ 4:00; ☉⚻☽ 4:34; ☽⚺⚳ 5:15; ☿ ♓ 7:09; ☽⚻♂ 7:31; ☽☍♄ 9:42; ☉△⚳ 14:51; ☽△☿ 16:53; ☽#♀ 18:34; ☽☍⚷ 18:55

14 Tu: ☽⚻♆ 1:42; ☽⚻♅ 2:29; ☽∠♃ 4:17; ☽□♇ 5:31; ☉⚼☽ 7:25; ☽☍♀ 9:00; ☽⚼♂ 10:02; ☿✱⚷ 13:26; ☽#♅ 18:42

15 W: ☽⚼♆ 3:28; ☽∥♇ 5:45; ☽✱♃ 5:51; ♂⚺♄ 6:59; ☽☌⚳ 8:14; ☉△☽ 11:24; ☽⚻♄ 13:20; ☽△♂ 13:40; ☽⚻⚷ 23:01

16 Th: ☽□☿ 3:07; ☽△♆ 6:18; ☽☍♅ 7:07; ☽✱♇ 10:23; ☿#⚷ 13:51; ♀∠♂ 15:38; ☽⚼♄ 16:44; ☉⚺♄ 17:00; ☽⚻♀ 18:38

17 F: ☽⚼⚷ 2:41; ☿⚺♆ 7:17; ☉#♆ 7:34; ☽□♃ 12:04; ☿□♅ 14:14; ☽∠♇ 14:26; ☽⚺⚳ 15:18; ☽△♄ 21:15; ☉□☽ 23:24; ☊ D 23:33

18 Sa: ☽□♂ 0:47; ☽⚼♀ 1:29; ☽△⚷ 7:25; ☽□♆ 15:11; ♂#♆ 15:51; ☽⚻♅ 16:01; ☿⚺♇ 18:08; ☽⚺♇ 19:30; ☽✱☿ 19:42; ☽∠⚳ 20:22

19 Su: ☽△♀ 9:32; ⚳ R 13:48; ⚶ D 14:08; ☽∥♇ 18:44; ♂ ♈ 19:37; ☽⚼♅ 21:50; ☽△♃ 22:09

20 M: ☽✱⚳ 2:13; ☉ ♈ 2:18; ☽∠☿ 6:06; ☽#♅ 7:06; ☽□♄ 9:02; ☉✱☽ 16:08; ☊ R 16:19; ☽✱♂ 16:20; ☽#♀ 19:13; ☽□⚷ 19:23

21 Tu: ☉#♂ 0:43; ☉☌♂ 2:37; ☽✱♆ 3:23; ☽⚼♃ 4:08; ☽△♅ 4:13; ☿∠♄ 5:19; ☽☌♇ 7:47; ☽⚺☿ 17:20; ☿∥⚳ 19:58

22 W: ☽∠♂ 0:59; ☉∠☽ 1:26; ☽□♀ 3:45; ☿#♄ 8:52; ☉⚺⚷ 9:00; ☽∠♆ 10:02; ☽⚻♃ 10:21; ☽#⚷ 14:48; ☽□⚳ 15:04; ♂⚺⚷ 18:01; ☽✱♄ 22:40

23 Th: ☉∥♆ 2:24; ☽∥⚳ 6:02; ☽#♄ 7:19; ☽✱⚷ 8:44; ☽⚺♂ 9:42; ☉⚺☽ 10:48; ☽∥☿ 10:48; ☽⚺♆ 16:40; ☽□♅ 17:28; ☽⚺♇ 20:58; ☽#♃ 23:57

24 F: ☽∠♄ 5:26; ☿∠⚷ 8:59; ☉#☽ 14:19; ☽∠⚷ 15:15; ☽☌☿ 16:15; ☽#♆ 16:53; ☽#♂ 18:41; ☽✱♀ 22:07; ☽☍♃ 22:33

25 Sa: ☽∥♂ 2:33; ♀△♃ 2:52; ☽∠♇ 3:16; ☽△⚳ 3:40; ☽∥♆ 3:54; ☉∥☽ 7:43; ♀∠♆ 10:05; ☽⚺♄ 11:53; ☽∥♃ 21:04; ☽⚺⚷ 21:25; ♀∥♅ 22:39

26 Su: ☽#☿ 1:28; ♂∥♆ 2:10; ☽☌♂ 2:14; ☉☌☽ 4:32; ☽☌♆ 5:04; ☽✱♅ 5:50; ☽∠♀ 6:39; ☽✱♇ 9:11; ☽⚼⚳ 9:25; ☿☍♃ 9:34; ☉☌♆ 11:17; ☽∥♄ 13:40; ☽#⚳ 13:57; ☊R♑ 16:32; ☉✱♅ 20:54

27 M: ☽∥⚷ 5:28; ☿#♃ 7:39; ☽⚻♃ 9:23; ☽∠♅ 11:24; ⚳#♄ 11:35; ☽⚺☿ 13:36; ☽⚺♀ 14:35; ☽⚻⚳ 14:43; ♀☍⚳ 16:18; ☿∠♇ 21:00; ☿△⚳ 21:14; ☽☌♄ 23:30

28 Tu: ♂☌♆ 0:42; ☿✱♀ 3:15; ☽☌⚷ 8:26; ♂✱♅ 13:01; ☉⚼⚳ 13:28; ☽⚼♃ 14:09; ☉✱♇ 14:21; ☽⚺♆ 15:45; ☽⚺♅ 16:29; ☽⚺♂ 16:42; ☽□♇ 19:38; ☉⚺☽ 20:05; ☽∠☿ 23:20

29 W: ☉#☿ 6:57; ☽∥♅ 11:03; ☽△♃ 18:27; ☽∥♀ 20:02; ☽∠♆ 20:22; ☽#♇ 22:24; ☽∠♂ 23:04; ☽☍⚳ 23:51

30 Th: ☉∠☽ 2:56; ☽☌♀ 4:33; ☽✱☿ 8:24; ☽⚺♄ 9:11; ♂⚼⚳ 11:01; ☿#♂ 13:33; ☿⚺♄ 14:15; ♂✱♇ 17:21; ☽⚺⚷ 17:30; ♀#♇ 19:43

31 F: ☽✱♆ 0:29; ☽☌♅ 1:11; ☽△♇ 4:08; ☽✱♂ 4:48; ☉✱☽ 9:07; ☿ ♈ 12:29; ☽∠♄ 13:13; ☽∠⚷ 21:15

April 2028

LONGITUDE

Day	Sid.Time	☉	☽	☽ 12 hour	Mean☊	True☊	☿	♀	♂	⚳	♃	♄	⚷	♅	♆	♇
	h m s	° ' "	° ' "	° ' "	° '	° '	° '	° '	° '	° '	° '	° '	° '	° '	° '	° '
1 Sa	12 39 31	11♈47 33	19♊19 14	25♊57 16	28♑41.8	29♑10.1	0♈53.4	27♉27.3	9♈27.3	23♏08.5	20♍10.6	28♈28.3	2♉48.7	6♊54.7	6♈32.0	8♒29.5
2 Su	12 43 28	12 46 45	2♋39 20	9♋25 40	28 38.6	29D 08.2	2 45.6	28 21.4	10 13.7	23R 03.2	20R 03.8	28 35.8	2 52.3	6 57.0	6 34.3	8 30.5
3 M	12 47 24	13 45 55	16 16 31	23 12 02	28 35.4	29R 07.9	4 39.1	29 14.9	11 00.0	22 57.5	19 57.2	28 43.3	2 55.8	6 59.4	6 36.5	8 31.5
4 Tu	12 51 21	14 45 03	0♌12 20	7♌17 28	28 32.3	29 08.0	6 34.1	0♊07.7	11 46.2	22 51.4	19 50.6	28 50.8	2 59.4	7 01.9	6 38.8	8 32.4
5 W	12 55 18	15 44 08	14 27 19	21 41 42	28 29.1	29 07.3	8 30.4	0 59.8	12 32.4	22 44.9	19 44.2	28 58.3	3 02.9	7 04.3	6 41.1	8 33.4
6 Th	12 59 14	16 43 11	29 00 14	6♍22 23	28 25.9	29 04.7	10 28.0	1 51.3	13 18.6	22 38.1	19 37.9	29 05.8	3 06.5	7 06.8	6 43.3	8 34.3
7 F	13 03 11	17 42 12	13♍47 27	21 14 34	28 22.7	28 59.4	12 27.0	2 42.0	14 04.7	22 30.8	19 31.7	29 13.3	3 10.1	7 09.3	6 45.5	8 35.2
8 Sa	13 07 07	18 41 11	28 42 46	6♎10 56	28 19.6	28 51.4	14 27.2	3 31.9	14 50.7	22 23.2	19 25.6	29 20.9	3 13.7	7 11.9	6 47.8	8 36.0
9 Su	13 11 04	19 40 07	13♎37 55	21 02 35	28 16.4	28 41.1	16 28.7	4 21.0	15 36.8	22 15.3	19 19.7	29 28.4	3 17.4	7 14.5	6 50.0	8 36.9
10 M	13 15 00	20 39 01	28 23 48	5♏40 34	28 13.2	28 29.7	18 31.3	5 09.4	16 22.8	22 07.0	19 13.9	29 36.0	3 21.0	7 17.1	6 52.2	8 37.7
11 Tu	13 18 57	21 37 54	12♏52 01	19 57 25	28 10.0	28 18.3	20 35.0	5 56.8	17 08.7	21 58.4	19 08.2	29 43.6	3 24.6	7 19.8	6 54.5	8 38.5
12 W	13 22 53	22 36 44	26 56 16	3♐48 14	28 06.8	28 08.3	22 39.6	6 43.4	17 54.6	21 49.4	19 02.7	29 51.2	3 28.3	7 22.5	6 56.7	8 39.2
13 Th	13 26 50	23 35 33	10♐33 12	17 11 12	28 03.7	28 00.6	24 45.1	7 29.1	18 40.5	21 40.0	18 57.3	29 58.8	3 32.0	7 25.3	6 58.9	8 40.0
14 F	13 30 47	24 34 20	23 42 27	0♑07 17	28 00.5	27 55.4	26 51.1	8 13.9	19 26.3	21 30.4	18 52.1	0♉06.5	3 35.6	7 28.0	7 01.1	8 40.7
15 Sa	13 34 43	25 33 05	6♑26 08	12 39 35	27 57.3	27 52.7	28 57.6	8 57.7	20 12.1	21 20.5	18 47.0	0 14.1	3 39.3	7 30.8	7 03.3	8 41.4
16 Su	13 38 40	26 31 49	18 48 13	24 52 42	27 54.1	27 51.8	1♉04.3	9 40.5	20 57.8	21 10.2	18 42.0	0 21.7	3 43.0	7 33.7	7 05.4	8 42.0
17 M	13 42 36	27 30 31	0♒53 42	6♒51 54	27 51.0	27 51.7	3 11.0	10 22.2	21 43.5	20 59.6	18 37.2	0 29.4	3 46.7	7 36.5	7 07.6	8 42.6
18 Tu	13 46 33	28 29 11	12 48 02	18 42 44	27 47.8	27 51.3	5 17.4	11 02.8	22 29.1	20 48.8	18 32.6	0 37.0	3 50.4	7 39.4	7 09.7	8 43.2
19 W	13 50 29	29 27 49	24 36 41	0♓30 30	27 44.6	27 49.6	7 23.1	11 42.4	23 14.7	20 37.7	18 28.1	0 44.7	3 54.1	7 42.3	7 11.9	8 43.8
20 Th	13 54 26	0♉26 26	6♓24 45	12 20 00	27 41.4	27 45.5	9 27.9	12 20.7	24 00.3	20 26.3	18 23.8	0 52.3	3 57.8	7 45.3	7 14.0	8 44.4
21 F	13 58 22	1 25 01	18 16 43	24 15 20	27 38.2	27 38.8	11 31.5	12 57.9	24 45.8	20 14.7	18 19.6	0 59.9	4 01.6	7 48.2	7 16.1	8 44.9
22 Sa	14 02 19	2 23 34	0♈16 12	6♈19 39	27 35.1	27 29.3	13 33.6	13 33.7	25 31.3	20 02.8	18 15.6	1 07.6	4 05.3	7 51.2	7 18.2	8 45.4
23 Su	14 06 16	3 22 05	12 25 54	18 35 08	27 31.9	27 17.5	15 33.7	14 08.3	26 16.7	19 50.8	18 11.8	1 15.2	4 09.0	7 54.3	7 20.3	8 45.8
24 M	14 10 12	4 20 35	24 47 29	1♉02 59	27 28.7	27 04.3	17 31.6	14 41.5	27 02.1	19 38.5	18 08.1	1 22.9	4 12.7	7 57.3	7 22.4	8 46.3
25 Tu	14 14 09	5 19 02	7♉21 40	13 43 29	27 25.5	26 50.8	19 27.0	15 13.3	27 47.4	19 26.0	18 04.6	1 30.5	4 16.4	8 00.4	7 24.5	8 46.7
26 W	14 18 05	6 17 29	20 08 24	26 36 19	27 22.4	26 38.2	21 19.7	15 43.6	28 32.7	19 13.3	18 01.3	1 38.2	4 20.1	8 03.5	7 26.5	8 47.1
27 Th	14 22 02	7 15 53	3♊07 10	9♊40 51	27 19.2	26 27.6	23 09.3	16 12.4	29 17.9	19 00.5	17 58.2	1 45.8	4 23.9	8 06.6	7 28.6	8 47.4
28 F	14 25 58	8 14 15	16 17 18	22 56 28	27 16.0	26 19.7	24 55.6	16 39.6	0♉03.1	18 47.6	17 55.2	1 53.4	4 27.6	8 09.8	7 30.6	8 47.8
29 Sa	14 29 55	9 12 35	29 38 20	6♋22 54	27 12.8	26 14.8	26 38.5	17 05.2	0 48.2	18 34.5	17 52.4	2 01.0	4 31.3	8 12.9	7 32.6	8 48.1
30 Su	14 33 51	10♉10 53	13♋10 10	20 00 13	27♑09.7	26♑12.4	28♉17.8	17♊29.1	1♉33.3	18♏21.3	17♍49.8	2♉08.7	4♉35.0	8♊16.1	7♈34.6	8♒48.3

1st of Month

Julian Day # 2461862.5
Obliquity 23°26'[illegible]3"
SVP 4♓51'[illegible]0"
GC 27♐14.0
Eris 25♈35.2

Day	⚴
1	19♍01.4R
6	17 51.1R
11	16 52.4R
16	16 06.0R
21	15 32.2R
26	15 11.2R

Day	⚵
1	24♋15.0
6	25 23.9
11	26 38.9
16	27 59.4
21	29 24.9
26	0♌54.8

Day	⚶
1	3♌42.5
6	4 14.9
11	4 57.0
16	5 48.1
21	6 47.5
26	7 54.7

DECLINATION and LATITUDE

Day	☉ Decl	☽ Decl	☽ Lat	☽ 12h Decl	☿ Decl	☿ Lat	♀ Decl	♀ Lat	♂ Decl	♂ Lat	⚳ Decl	⚳ Lat	♃ Decl	♃ Lat	♄ Decl	♄ Lat
1 Sa	4N40	26N14	3N14	26N09	1S30	2S01	23N13	3N43	3N05	0S43	8S32	10N20	5N17	1N31	8N50	2S14
2 Su	5 03	25 40	2 16	24 48	0 41	1 57	23 29	3 48	3 24	0 43	8 31	10 21	5 19	1 30	8 53	2 14
3 M	5 26	23 34	1 08	21 58	0N08	1 52	23 45	3 52	3 42	0 42	8 29	10 21	5 22	1 30	8 56	2 14
4 Tu	5 49	20 01	0S06	17 45	0 58	1 47	24 01	3 56	4 01	0 42	8 28	10 21	5 24	1 30	8 58	2 14
5 W	6 12	15 13	1 20	12 26	1 50	1 41	24 16	4 00	4 19	0 41	8 26	10 21	5 27	1 30	9 01	2 14
6 Th	6 34	9 27	2 31	6 20	2 42	1 34	24 31	4 04	4 38	0 41	8 25	10 20	5 29	1 30	9 04	2 14
7 F	6 57	3 06	3 33	0S11	3 35	1 27	24 45	4 08	4 56	0 40	8 23	10 20	5 31	1 30	9 06	2 14
8 Sa	7 19	3S28	4 21	6 42	4 28	1 20	24 58	4 12	5 14	0 40	8 22	10 20	5 34	1 30	9 09	2 14
9 Su	7 42	9 50	4 51	12 49	5 22	1 12	25 12	4 15	5 33	0 39	8 20	10 20	5 36	1 30	9 12	2 14
10 M	8 04	15 35	5 01	18 06	6 17	1 04	25 24	4 19	5 51	0 39	8 19	10 19	5 38	1 30	9 14	2 14
11 Tu	8 26	20 19	4 51	22 13	7 11	0 55	25 36	4 22	6 09	0 38	8 17	10 18	5 40	1 30	9 17	2 14
12 W	8 48	23 45	4 24	24 55	8 06	0 46	25 48	4 26	6 27	0 37	8 15	10 18	5 42	1 29	9 20	2 14
13 Th	9 10	25 42	3 42	26 06	9 01	0 36	25 59	4 29	6 45	0 37	8 14	10 17	5 44	1 29	9 23	2 14
14 F	9 31	26 07	2 50	25 47	9 57	0 26	26 09	4 32	7 03	0 36	8 12	10 16	5 46	1 29	9 25	2 14
15 Sa	9 53	25 08	1 51	24 09	10 51	0 16	26 19	4 35	7 21	0 36	8 11	10 15	5 48	1 29	9 28	2 14
16 Su	10 14	22 54	0 48	21 25	11 46	0 05	26 28	4 38	7 38	0 35	8 09	10 14	5 50	1 29	9 31	2 14
17 M	10 35	19 42	0N16	17 47	12 39	0N05	26 37	4 40	7 56	0 35	8 08	10 13	5 52	1 29	9 33	2 14
18 Tu	10 56	15 43	1 18	13 30	13 32	0 16	26 46	4 43	8 13	0 34	8 06	10 12	5 53	1 29	9 36	2 14
19 W	11 17	11 10	2 17	8 44	14 24	0 27	26 53	4 45	8 31	0 33	8 05	10 10	5 55	1 28	9 39	2 14
20 Th	11 38	6 14	3 09	3 40	15 15	0 38	27 01	4 47	8 48	0 33	8 03	10 09	5 56	1 28	9 41	2 14
21 F	11 58	1 03	3 53	1N34	16 04	0 49	27 07	4 49	9 05	0 32	8 02	10 07	5 58	1 28	9 44	2 14
22 Sa	12 18	4N12	4 27	6 48	16 51	0 60	27 14	4 50	9 22	0 32	8 01	10 06	5 59	1 28	9 47	2 14
23 Su	12 38	9 22	4 50	11 51	17 37	1 10	27 19	4 52	9 39	0 31	7 59	10 04	6 01	1 28	9 49	2 14
24 M	12 58	14 15	4 60	16 30	18 21	1 20	27 25	4 53	9 56	0 31	7 58	10 02	6 02	1 27	9 52	2 14
25 Tu	13 18	18 37	4 55	20 31	19 02	1 30	27 29	4 54	10 13	0 30	7 57	9 60	6 03	1 27	9 55	2 14
26 W	13 37	22 12	4 36	23 37	19 41	1 39	27 33	4 55	10 30	0 29	7 56	9 58	6 04	1 27	9 57	2 14
27 Th	13 56	24 44	4 02	25 31	20 18	1 48	27 37	4 55	10 46	0 29	7 54	9 56	6 05	1 27	9 60	2 14
28 F	14 15	25 57	3 14	26 01	20 52	1 56	27 40	4 55	11 03	0 28	7 53	9 53	6 06	1 27	10 02	2 14
29 Sa	14 34	25 42	2 16	24 60	21 24	2 03	27 43	4 55	11 19	0 28	7 52	9 51	6 07	1 27	10 05	2 14
30 Su	14N52	23N55	1N08	22N29	21N54	2N10	27N44	4N55	11N35	0S27	7S51	9N48	6N08	1N26	10N08	2S14

Day	⚷ Decl	⚷ Lat	♅ Decl	♅ Lat	♆ Decl	♆ Lat	♇ Decl	♇ Lat
1	11N59	0S30	21N24	0S04	1N19	1S23	22S52	4S55
6	12 05	0 30	21 26	0 04	1 24	1 23	22 52	4 56
11	12 11	0 30	21 28	0 04	1 28	1 23	22 52	4 57
16	12 17	0 30	21 31	0 04	1 32	1 24	22 52	4 58
21	12 23	0 31	21 33	0 04	1 36	1 24	22 52	4 59
26	12 28	0 31	21 36	0 03	1 40	1 24	22 53	4 60

Day	⚴ Decl	⚴ Lat	⚵ Decl	⚵ Lat	⚶ Decl	⚶ Lat	Eris Decl	Eris Lat
1	10N10	6N20	12N60	8S23	25N25	6N16	0N34	10S00
6	11 47	7 35	13 21	7 50	25 14	6 14	0 35	9 60
11	13 13	8 44	13 39	7 18	25 01	6 11	0 36	9 60
16	14 29	9 47	13 54	6 48	24 45	6 08	0 38	9 60
21	15 33	10 43	14 05	6 19	24 27	6 05	0 39	9 59
26	16 28	11 33	14 13	5 52	24 06	6 02	0 40	9 59

Moon Phenomena

Max/0 Decl
dy hr mn
1 3:05 26N15
7 11:19 0 S
13 18:49 26S09
21 4:50 0 N
28 8:01 26N02

Max/0 Lat
dy hr mn
3 22:10 0 S
10 0:09 5S01
16 17:56 0 N
24 4:18 5N00
30 22:48 0 S

Perigee/Apogee
dy hr m kilometers
7 16:08 p 361363
19 15:14 a 405101

PH dy hr mn
☽ 2 19:17 13♋34
○ 9 10:28 20♎06
☾ 16 16:38 27♑13
● 24 19:48 5♉09

Void of Course Moon

Last Aspect	☽ Ingress
1 16:41 ♄ ⚹	♋ 1 19:16
3 21:40 ♄ □	♌ 3 23:39
6 0:09 ♄ △	♍ 6 1:38
7 9:11 ♃ ☌	♎ 8 2:04
10 2:00 ♄ ☍	♏ 10 2:38
11 10:32 ♃ ⚹	♐ 12 5:20
14 7:01 ☿ △	♑ 14 11:46
16 16:38 ☉ □	♒ 16 22:13
19 10:46 ☉ ⚹	♓ 19 10:58
21 0:06 ♃ ☍	♈ 21 23:28
24 4:35 ♂ ☌	♉ 24 10:00
26 2:35 ☿ ☌	♊ 26 18:16
28 2:56 ♃ □	♋ 29 0:39

DAILY ASPECTARIAN

1 Sa: ☽□♃ 1:33; ☿⋕♆ 5:21; ☽⚻⚳ 6:53; ☽⚼♇ 7:34; ☽⚺♀ 15:46; ☽⚹♄ 16:41

2 Su: ☽□☿ 0:13; ☽⚹⚷ 0:23; ☿⚺⚷ 1:28; ☽□♆ 6:58; ♀⚺♄ 7:28; ☽⚺♅ 7:39; ☽⚼⚳ 9:30; ☽⚻♇ 10:23; ☽□♂ 14:13; ☊ D 19:08; ☉□☽ 19:17; ☉∥♃ 19:18; ☽∠♀ 20:13; ☽∥♀ 22:29

3 M: ☽⋕♇ 5:30; ☽⚹♃ 6:20; ☽∠♅ 9:56; ☽△⚳ 11:30; ☽∥♅ 15:32; ♀ ♊ 20:29; ☽□♄ 21:40; ☊ R 22:11; ☽⚹♀ 23:52

4 Tu: ☿☌♆ 1:00; ☽□⚷ 4:45; ☿⚹♅ 5:53; ☽∠♃ 7:49; ☽△♆ 10:57; ☿∥♆ 11:08; ☽⚹♅ 11:36; ☽△☿ 12:28; ☽☍♇ 14:07; ☿⚼⚳ 15:09; ☽△♂ 20:37

5 W: ☿⚹♇ 0:37; ☉△☽ 2:17; ☽⚺♃ 8:42; ☽⚼♆ 12:01; ☽∥⚷ 13:29; ☽□⚳ 13:38; ☽⚼☿ 17:18; ☽⚼♂ 22:48

6 Th: ☽△♄ 0:09; ☽∥♄ 1:32; ☽⋕⚳ 4:05; ☉⚼☽ 4:45; ☽□♀ 4:56; ☽△⚷ 6:43; ☉∥☽ 10:28; ☽⚻♆ 12:36; ☽□♅ 13:14; ☽∥♃ 15:04; ☽⚻♇ 15:35; ☽∥♂ 17:31; ☽⚻☿ 21:30; ☽∥☿ 22:27; ☉∠♀ 23:20

7 F: ☽⚻♂ 0:29; ☽⚼♄ 0:42; ☽∥♆ 6:11; ☉⚻☽ 6:45; ☽⚼⚷ 7:05; ☽☌♃ 9:11; ☽⚹⚳ 13:56; ♀⚺⚷ 14:33; ☽⚼♇ 15:47; ☽⋕♆ 16:29

8 Sa: ☽⚻♄ 1:02; ☽⋕☿ 4:15; ☽⋕♂ 6:50; ☽⚻⚷ 7:17; ☿☌♂ 7:31; ☽⋕♃ 7:46; ☽△♀ 8:11; ☽☍♆ 13:01; ☽△♅ 13:40; ☽∠⚳ 13:49; ☉⋕☽ 15:13; ☽△♇ 15:54; ☉⚻♃ 16:26; ☽∥⚳ 18:12; ☽⋕♄ 21:29

9 Su: ☽☍♂ 3:22; ♂∥♃ 5:04; ☽☍☿ 5:20; ☿∥♃ 6:25; ☿∥♂ 7:01; ☽⚺♃ 9:09; ☽⋕⚷ 9:15; ☽⚼♀ 9:47; ☉☍☽ 10:28; ☽⚺⚳ 13:51; ☽⚼♅ 14:00

10 M: ☽☍♄ 2:00; ☿⚻♃ 7:55; ☽☍⚷ 8:11; ☽∠♃ 9:33; ☽⚻♀ 11:47; ☽⚻♆ 14:01; ☽⚻♅ 14:43; ☉⋕⚳ 15:01; ☽□♇ 16:55

11 Tu: ☿∠♀ 6:46; ☽⋕♅ 7:04; ☉⚻⚳ 7:15; ☽⚻♂ 7:38; ⚳⚼♆ 8:26; ☽⚹♃ 10:32; ☿⚻⚳ 15:00; ☽☌⚳ 15:17; ☽⚻☿ 15:20; ☽⚼♆ 15:23; ☉⚻☽ 15:59; ☽∥♇ 16:47; ☉∠♅ 17:55; ☿∠♅ 20:39; ☉☌☿ 22:57

12 W: ☿⋕⚳ 3:52; ☽⚻♄ 5:07; ♀⚹♆ 7:15; ☽⚼♂ 11:03; ☽⚻⚷ 11:28; ☽△♆ 17:36; ☽☍♀ 18:12; ☽☍♅ 18:23; ☉⚼☽ 20:13; ☽⚹♇ 20:37; ♀☌♅ 21:48; ☽⚼☿ 22:18

13 Th: ♄ ♉ 3:41; ☉∥☿ 5:49; ♂⚻♃ 7:54; ☽⚼♄ 8:04; ☿∥♄ 9:39; ☽⚼⚷ 14:32; ☽□♃ 15:08; ☽△♂ 15:38; ☉∥♄ 16:24; ☽⚺⚳ 19:59; ☽⋕♀ 22:19; ☽⋕♀ 22:19; ☽∠♇ 23:57

14 F: ☉△☽ 1:44; ☽△☿ 7:01; ☽△♄ 12:06; ♀△♇ 14:51; ☽△⚷ 18:40; ☽∠⚳ 23:49

15 Sa: ☽□♆ 1:11; ☽⚻♅ 2:04; ☽⚺♇ 4:20; ☽⚻♀ 5:09; ☿ ♉ 11:49; ☿☌♄ 15:25; ♃⚼⚷ 21:10; ☽△♃ 23:48

16 Su: ☽∥♇ 0:20; ☽□♂ 4:32; ☽⚹⚳ 4:36; ♂⚻⚳ 5:18; ☽⚼♅ 7:26; ☽⋕♅ 11:14; ☽⚼♀ 12:18; ☿∥⚷ 14:05; ☉□☽ 16:38; ☽□♄ 23:11

17 M: ☿⚼♃ 4:48; ☽⚼♃ 5:26; ☽□☿ 5:34; ☽□⚷ 5:49; ☿☌⚷ 6:59; ☽⚹♆ 12:34; ☽△♅ 13:33; ♂⋕⚳ 15:12; ☽☌♇ 15:44; ☽△♀ 20:14

18 Tu: ♂∠♅ 5:46; ☽⋕☿ 9:55; ☽⚻♃ 11:35; ☽□⚳ 16:01; ☽⋕⚷ 18:06; ☽∠♆ 19:04; ☽⚹♂ 21:02; ☿⚺♆ 21:49; ☉⋕☽ 23:29

19 W: ☿⚺♅ 3:46; ☽⋕♄ 7:31; ☉⚹☽ 10:46; ☽⋕♂ 12:23; ☽⚹♄ 12:37; ☉ ♉ 13:11; ☽∥⚳ 15:15; ☿□♇ 15:34; ☽⚹⚷ 19:00

20 Th: ☽⋕♃ 1:22; ☽⚺♆ 1:40; ☽□♅ 2:44; ☽⚺♇ 4:43; ☽∠♂ 5:37; ☽⚹☿ 7:30; ☉☌♄ 12:11; ☽□♀ 12:41; ☽∠♄ 19:21; ☉∠☽ 19:55; ☽⋕♆ 21:30

21 F: ☽☍♃ 0:06; ☽∠⚷ 1:31; ☽△⚳ 3:53; ☽∠♇ 10:59; ☽∥♆ 12:11; ☽⚺♂ 13:54; ☽∠☿ 19:54

22 Sa: ☿⚺♀ 0:03; ☽⚺♄ 1:43; ☉⚺☽ 4:35; ☉∥⚷ 7:04; ☽⚺⚷ 7:37; ☽∥♃ 8:16; ☽⚼⚳ 9:19; ☽☌♆ 13:58; ☽⚹♅ 15:04; ☽⚹♇ 16:48; ☽⋕⚳ 17:33; ☉⚼♃ 20:02; ⚵ ♌ 23:34

23 Su: ☽∥♂ 1:29; ☽∥♄ 2:12; ☽⚹♀ 3:30; ☽⚺☿ 7:17; ☽⚻♃ 11:11; ☽⚻⚳ 14:13; ☽∥⚷ 14:50; ♂∥♄ 16:25; ☉∥☽ 17:02; ☽∠♅ 20:27; ☉☌⚷ 20:33

24 M: ☽☌♂ 4:35; ☿△♃ 7:19; ☽∠♀ 9:49; ☽☌♄ 12:46; ☽⚼♃ 15:54; ☽☌⚷ 18:07; ☉☌☽ 19:48; ☿☍⚳ 23:48

25 Tu: ☽⚺♆ 0:05; ☽⚺♅ 1:14; ☽□♇ 2:41; ☽∥☿ 3:04; ☽⚺♀ 15:25; ☽∥♅ 19:27; ☽△♃ 20:04; ☽☍⚳ 22:19

26 W: ☽☌☿ 2:35; ☽∠♆ 4:18; ☽⋕♇ 5:29; ☿∠♆ 14:50; ☽⚺♂ 16:32; ☽⚺♄ 21:29

27 Th: ☽⚺⚷ 2:21; ☉⚺♆ 5:25; ☽⚹♆ 8:00; ☉⚺☽ 8:12; ☽☌♅ 9:10; ☽△♇ 10:23; ☽∠♂ 21:37; ☉⚺♅ 22:03; ♂ ♉ 22:22

28 F: ☽☌♀ 0:42; ☽∠♄ 1:06; ☽□♃ 2:56; ☽⚻⚳ 4:27; ☽∠⚷ 5:45; ☉∠☽ 13:31; ☽⚼♇ 13:32; ☉□♇ 13:51; ☽⚺☿ 17:52; ♀∠♄ 18:14

29 Sa: ☽⚹♂ 2:12; ☽⚹♄ 4:17; ☽⚼⚳ 6:54; ☽⚹⚷ 8:44; ☿∥♅ 10:25; ☽□♆ 14:06; ☽⚺♅ 15:19; ☽⚻♇ 16:18; ☉⚹☽ 18:19

30 Su: ☽∠☿ 0:15; ☽⚺♀ 7:48; ☽⚹♃ 8:10; ☽⋕♇ 8:54; ☽△⚳ 8:58; ☽∥☿ 14:20; ☽∠♅ 17:46; ☽∥♅ 18:03; ♀□♃ 20:12; ♂☌♄ 22:42; ☊ D 22:46

LONGITUDE

Day	Sid.Time	☉	☽	☽ 12 hour	Mean☊	True☊	☿	♀	♂	⚳	♃	♄	⚷	♅	♆	♇
	h m s	° ' "	° ' "	° ' "	° '	° '	° '	° '	° '	° '	° '	° '	° '	° '	° '	° '
1 M	14 37 48	11♉09 10	26♋53 06	3♌48 52	27♑06.5	26♑11.9	29♉53.3	17♊51.2	2♉18.3	18♏08.0	17♍47.4	2♉16.3	4♉38.7	8♊19.4	7♈36.6	8♒48.6
2 Tu	14 41 45	12 07 24	10♌47 32	17 49 09	27 03.3	26R 12.1	1♊24.9	18 11.4	3 03.3	17R 54.6	17R 45.2	2 23.8	4 42.4	8 22.6	7 38.6	8 48.8
3 W	14 45 41	13 05 35	24 53 37	2♍00 51	27 00.1	26 11.7	2 52.4	18 29.8	3 48.2	17 41.2	17 43.1	2 31.4	4 46.1	8 25.8	7 40.5	8 49.0
4 Th	14 49 38	14 03 45	9♍10 36	16 22 34	26 56.9	26 09.5	4 15.9	18 46.2	4 33.0	17 27.7	17 41.2	2 39.0	4 49.8	8 29.1	7 42.4	8 49.1
5 F	14 53 34	15 01 53	23 36 20	0♎51 22	26 53.8	26 05.0	5 35.1	19 00.6	5 17.8	17 14.2	17 39.5	2 46.5	4 53.5	8 32.4	7 44.3	8 49.3
6 Sa	14 57 31	15 59 59	8♎07 00	15 22 32	26 50.6	25 57.9	6 50.1	19 12.9	6 02.6	17 00.6	17 38.0	2 54.0	4 57.1	8 35.7	7 46.2	8 49.4
7 Su	15 01 27	16 58 03	22 37 10	29 50 03	26 47.4	25 48.7	8 00.7	19 23.0	6 47.3	16 47.1	17 36.7	3 01.6	5 00.8	8 39.0	7 48.1	8 49.5
8 M	15 05 24	17 56 05	7♏00 24	14♏07 24	26 44.2	25 38.4	9 06.8	19 31.0	7 32.0	16 33.6	17 35.5	3 09.0	5 04.5	8 42.4	7 49.9	8 49.5
9 Tu	15 09 20	18 54 06	21 10 19	28 08 33	26 41.1	25 28.0	10 08.5	19 36.7	8 16.6	16 20.1	17 34.5	3 16.5	5 08.1	8 45.7	7 51.8	8R 49.5
10 W	15 13 17	19 52 05	5♐01 34	11♐49 00	26 37.9	25 18.8	11 05.6	19R 40.1	9 01.1	16 06.6	17 33.8	3 24.0	5 11.7	8 49.1	7 53.6	8 49.5
11 Th	15 17 14	20 50 02	18 30 39	25 06 24	26 34.7	25 11.6	11 58.1	19 41.2	9 45.6	15 53.3	17 33.2	3 31.4	5 15.4	8 52.5	7 55.4	8 49.5
12 F	15 21 10	21 47 59	1♑36 19	8♑00 34	26 31.5	25 06.7	12 46.0	19 39.9	10 30.1	15 40.0	17 32.7	3 38.8	5 19.0	8 55.9	7 57.1	8 49.4
13 Sa	15 25 07	22 45 53	14 19 28	20 33 23	26 28.4	25D 04.3	13 29.0	19 36.2	11 14.5	15 26.7	17D 32.5	3 46.2	5 22.6	8 59.3	7 58.9	8 49.4
14 Su	15 29 03	23 43 47	26 42 48	2♒48 16	26 25.2	25 03.7	14 07.3	19 30.2	11 58.8	15 13.6	17 32.4	3 53.6	5 26.2	9 02.7	8 00.6	8 49.2
15 M	15 33 00	24 41 39	8♒50 21	14 49 41	26 22.0	25 04.3	14 40.8	19 21.6	12 43.1	15 00.7	17 32.5	4 00.9	5 29.7	9 06.1	8 02.3	8 49.1
16 Tu	15 36 56	25 39 30	20 46 56	26 42 45	26 18.8	25R 05.0	15 09.3	19 10.7	13 27.4	14 47.8	17 32.8	4 08.2	5 33.3	9 09.6	8 04.0	8 48.9
17 W	15 40 53	26 37 19	2♓37 48	8♓32 44	26 15.6	25 04.9	15 33.0	18 57.3	14 11.6	14 35.1	17 33.3	4 15.5	5 36.8	9 13.0	8 05.7	8 48.7
18 Th	15 44 49	27 35 08	14 28 12	20 24 48	26 12.5	25 03.3	15 51.7	18 41.6	14 55.7	14 22.6	17 34.0	4 22.8	5 40.3	9 16.5	8 07.3	8 48.5
19 F	15 48 46	28 32 55	26 23 07	2♈23 41	26 09.3	24 59.6	16 05.5	18 23.5	15 39.8	14 10.2	17 34.8	4 30.0	5 43.8	9 20.0	8 08.9	8 48.3
20 Sa	15 52 43	29 30 41	8♈26 59	14 33 25	26 06.1	24 53.7	16 14.5	18 03.1	16 23.8	13 58.1	17 35.9	4 37.2	5 47.3	9 23.5	8 10.5	8 48.0
21 Su	15 56 39	0♊28 26	20 43 21	26 57 04	26 02.9	24 45.9	16R 18.6	17 40.5	17 07.8	13 46.1	17 37.1	4 44.4	5 50.8	9 26.9	8 12.1	8 47.7
22 M	16 00 36	1 26 10	3♉14 47	9♉36 37	25 59.8	24 36.9	16 17.9	17 15.7	17 51.7	13 34.4	17 38.4	4 51.6	5 54.3	9 30.4	8 13.6	8 47.4
23 Tu	16 04 32	2 23 53	16 02 36	22 32 43	25 56.6	24 27.6	16 12.7	16 48.9	18 35.6	13 22.9	17 40.0	4 58.7	5 57.7	9 33.9	8 15.1	8 47.0
24 W	16 08 29	3 21 34	29 06 53	5♊44 55	25 53.4	24 18.9	16 03.0	16 20.3	19 19.4	13 11.6	17 41.8	5 05.7	6 01.1	9 37.5	8 16.6	8 46.6
25 Th	16 12 25	4 19 14	12♊26 36	19 11 41	25 50.2	24 11.6	15 49.2	15 49.8	20 03.2	13 00.6	17 43.7	5 12.8	6 04.5	9 41.0	8 18.1	8 46.2
26 F	16 16 22	5 16 53	25 59 53	2♋50 54	25 47.0	24 06.3	15 31.4	15 17.7	20 46.9	12 49.9	17 45.8	5 19.8	6 07.9	9 44.5	8 19.5	8 45.8
27 Sa	16 20 18	6 14 31	9♋44 27	16 40 12	25 43.9	24 03.4	15 10.0	14 44.2	21 30.6	12 39.5	17 48.0	5 26.7	6 11.2	9 48.0	8 20.9	8 45.3
28 Su	16 24 15	7 12 08	23 37 55	0♌37 20	25 40.7	24D 02.5	14 45.4	14 09.4	22 14.2	12 29.3	17 50.5	5 33.7	6 14.5	9 51.5	8 22.3	8 44.9
29 M	16 28 12	8 09 43	7♌38 14	14 40 24	25 37.5	24 03.0	14 18.0	13 33.6	22 57.8	12 19.5	17 53.1	5 40.6	6 17.8	9 55.1	8 23.7	8 44.4
30 Tu	16 32 08	9 07 16	21 43 39	28 47 48	25 34.3	24 04.2	13 48.3	12 56.9	23 41.2	12 09.9	17 55.9	5 47.4	6 21.1	9 58.6	8 25.0	8 43.8
31 W	16 36 05	10♊04 48	5♍52 40	12♍58 04	25♑31.2	24♑05.1	13♊16.7	12♊19.7	24♉24.7	12♏00.7	17♍58.9	5♉54.2	6♉24.3	10♊02.1	8♈26.3	8♒43.3

1st of Month

Julian Day #
2461892.5
Obliquity
23°26'52"
SVP 4♓51'36"
GC 27♐14.1
Eris 25♈54.7

Day	⚴	⚵	⚶
1	15♍02.6R	2♌28.7	9♌09.0
6	15 06.0	4 06.2	10 29.9
11	15 20.6	5 46.8	11 56.7
16	15 45.6	7 30.1	13 29.1
21	16 20.3	9 15.9	15 06.5
26	17 04.0	11 03.9	16 48.6
31	17 56.0	12 53.9	18 35.1

DECLINATION and LATITUDE

Day	☉ Decl	☽ Decl	☽ Lat	☽ 12h Decl	☿ Decl	☿ Lat	♀ Decl	♀ Lat	♂ Decl	♂ Lat	⚳ Decl	⚳ Lat	♃ Decl	♃ Lat	♄ Decl	♄ Lat
1 M	15N10	20N43	0S04	18N39	22N20	2N16	27N46	4N54	11N52	0S26	7S50	9N46	6N09	1N26	10N10	2S14
2 Tu	15 28	16 18	1 17	13 43	22 45	2 21	27 47	4 53	12 08	0 26	7 49	9 43	6 10	1 26	10 13	2 14
3 W	15 46	10 56	2 26	7 59	23 07	2 26	27 47	4 52	12 23	0 25	7 49	9 40	6 10	1 26	10 15	2 14
4 Th	16 03	4 56	3 27	1 48	23 26	2 29	27 47	4 50	12 39	0 25	7 48	9 37	6 11	1 26	10 18	2 14
5 F	16 21	1S22	4 16	4S32	23 43	2 32	27 46	4 48	12 55	0 24	7 47	9 34	6 11	1 25	10 20	2 14
6 Sa	16 37	7 38	4 48	10 37	23 58	2 33	27 45	4 46	13 10	0 23	7 47	9 31	6 12	1 25	10 23	2 14
7 Su	16 54	13 28	5 02	16 07	24 11	2 34	27 43	4 43	13 25	0 23	7 46	9 27	6 12	1 25	10 25	2 14
8 M	17 10	18 31	4 56	20 38	24 21	2 34	27 40	4 40	13 41	0 22	7 46	9 24	6 12	1 25	10 28	2 14
9 Tu	17 26	22 26	4 33	23 53	24 29	2 32	27 37	4 36	13 56	0 21	7 45	9 21	6 12	1 25	10 30	2 14
10 W	17 42	24 58	3 53	25 39	24 35	2 30	27 33	4 32	14 10	0 21	7 45	9 17	6 13	1 24	10 33	2 14
11 Th	17 58	25 57	3 02	25 53	24 39	2 27	27 28	4 27	14 25	0 20	7 45	9 13	6 13	1 24	10 35	2 14
12 F	18 13	25 27	2 02	24 41	24 41	2 23	27 23	4 22	14 40	0 20	7 45	9 10	6 13	1 24	10 38	2 14
13 Sa	18 28	23 37	0 57	22 16	24 41	2 17	27 17	4 16	14 54	0 19	7 45	9 06	6 12	1 24	10 40	2 14
14 Su	18 42	20 40	0N09	18 52	24 40	2 11	27 11	4 10	15 08	0 18	7 45	9 02	6 12	1 23	10 43	2 14
15 M	18 56	16 52	1 13	14 44	24 36	2 03	27 03	4 04	15 22	0 18	7 45	8 58	6 12	1 23	10 45	2 14
16 Tu	19 10	12 28	2 13	10 05	24 31	1 55	26 55	3 57	15 36	0 17	7 46	8 54	6 12	1 23	10 47	2 14
17 W	19 24	7 37	3 07	5 06	24 24	1 45	26 47	3 49	15 50	0 16	7 46	8 50	6 11	1 23	10 50	2 14
18 Th	19 37	2 32	3 53	0N04	24 16	1 35	26 37	3 41	16 04	0 16	7 46	8 45	6 11	1 23	10 52	2 14
19 F	19 50	2N41	4 29	5 16	24 06	1 23	26 27	3 32	16 17	0 15	7 47	8 41	6 10	1 22	10 55	2 14
20 Sa	20 03	7 50	4 53	10 21	23 54	1 11	26 16	3 22	16 31	0 14	7 48	8 37	6 10	1 22	10 57	2 15
21 Su	20 15	12 48	5 05	15 08	23 41	0 58	26 04	3 13	16 44	0 14	7 49	8 32	6 09	1 22	10 59	2 15
22 M	20 27	17 19	5 02	19 21	23 27	0 43	25 51	3 02	16 57	0 13	7 50	8 28	6 08	1 22	11 01	2 15
23 Tu	20 38	21 10	4 45	22 45	23 12	0 28	25 37	2 51	17 09	0 12	7 51	8 23	6 07	1 22	11 04	2 15
24 W	20 49	24 03	4 12	25 02	22 55	0 13	25 23	2 40	17 22	0 12	7 52	8 18	6 07	1 21	11 06	2 15
25 Th	21 00	25 40	3 25	25 56	22 37	0S04	25 08	2 28	17 34	0 11	7 53	8 14	6 06	1 21	11 08	2 15
26 F	21 11	25 48	2 25	25 16	22 19	0 20	24 52	2 16	17 47	0 11	7 54	8 09	6 05	1 21	11 10	2 15
27 Sa	21 21	24 21	1 16	23 03	21 59	0 38	24 36	2 03	17 59	0 10	7 56	8 04	6 04	1 21	11 13	2 15
28 Su	21 31	21 24	0 02	19 26	21 39	0 55	24 19	1 50	18 11	0 09	7 58	7 60	6 02	1 20	11 15	2 15
29 M	21 40	17 11	1S13	14 41	21 19	1 13	24 01	1 37	18 22	0 09	7 59	7 55	6 01	1 20	11 17	2 15
30 Tu	21 49	11 59	2 24	9 08	20 58	1 30	23 43	1 23	18 34	0 08	8 01	7 50	5 60	1 20	11 19	2 15
31 W	21N58	6N09	3S27	3N05	20N37	1S47	23N25	1N09	18N45	0S07	8S03	7N45	5N59	1N20	11N21	2S16

Day	⚷ Decl	⚷ Lat	♅ Decl	♅ Lat	♆ Decl	♆ Lat	♇ Decl	♇ Lat
1	12N34	0S32	21N38	0S03	1N44	1S24	22S53	5S01
6	12 40	0 32	21 41	0 03	1 48	1 24	22 54	5 02
11	12 46	0 32	21 43	0 03	1 51	1 24	22 55	5 03
16	12 51	0 33	21 46	0 03	1 54	1 24	22 56	5 04
21	12 57	0 33	21 49	0 03	1 57	1 25	22 58	5 05
26	13 02	0 34	21 51	0 03	2 00	1 25	22 59	5 06
31	13N07	0S34	21N54	0S03	2N03	1S25	23S01	5S07

Day	⚴ Decl	⚴ Lat	⚵ Decl	⚵ Lat	⚶ Decl	⚶ Lat	Eris Decl	Eris Lat
1	17N12	12N18	14N17	5S27	23N43	5N58	0N41	9S59
6	17 48	12 58	14 19	5 03	23 18	5 55	0 43	9 59
11	18 15	13 34	14 17	4 41	22 50	5 52	0 44	9 59
16	18 34	14 06	14 12	4 20	22 20	5 49	0 45	9 59
21	18 46	14 34	14 05	3 60	21 48	5 46	0 45	9 59
26	18 52	14 60	13 55	3 40	21 14	5 43	0 46	9 60
31	18N52	15N23	13N42	3S22	20N38	5N40	0N47	9S60

Moon Phenomena

Max/0 Decl

dy	hr mn	
4	18:48	0 S
11	3:41	25S58
18	11:41	0 N
25	14:02	25N56
31	23:59	0 S

Max/0 Lat

dy	hr mn	
7	5:14	5S02
13	20:46	0 N
21	7:42	5N06
28	0:42	0 S

Perigee/Apogee

dy	hr m		kilometers
5	10:32	p	366534
17	9:56	a	404277
31	6:37	p	369760

PH	dy	hr mn	
☽	2	2:27	12♌13
○	8	19:50	18♏44
☾	16	10:44	26♒05
●	24	8:17	3♊41
☽	31	7:38	10♍23

Void of Course Moon

Last Aspect				☽ Ingress		
30	8:10	♃	⚹	♌	1	5:24
2	12:55	♀	⚹	♍	3	8:37
4	16:15	♀	□	♎	5	10:35
6	18:35	♀	△	♏	7	12:17
8	19:50	☉	☍	♐	9	15:13
11	2:08	♀	☍	♑	11	21:01
13	17:40	☉	△	♒	14	6:28
16	10:44	☉	□	♓	16	18:40
19	4:42	☉	⚹	♈	19	7:14
20	18:16	♀	⚹	♉	21	17:50
23	5:00	♂	☌	♊	24	1:36
25	9:25	♃	□	♋	26	7:01
27	21:28	♂	⚹	♌	28	10:56
30	3:31	♂	□	♍	30	14:02

DAILY ASPECTARIAN

1 M: ☿ ♊ 1:43; ☽⚹☿ 5:52; ☽□♄ 9:25; ☽□♂ 9:56; ☽∠♃ 10:12; ☽∠♀ 10:36; ♀⚻⚳ 11:51; ☽□⚷ 13:30; ♂⚼♃ 14:48; ☽△♆ 18:35; ☽⚹♅ 19:50; ☽☍♇ 20:36

2 Tu: ♀ D 0:43; ☊ R 2:24; ☉□☽ 2:27; ☉∥☽ 3:43; ♀∠♂ 7:35; ☿#♇ 9:19; ☽⚺♃ 11:51; ☽□⚳ 11:58; ☽⚹♀ 12:55; ☽∥⚷ 16:52; ☿⚺♄ 17:34; ☽∥♂ 18:05; ⚳⚹♃ 19:57; ☽⚼♆ 20:14

3 W: ☽∥♄ 2:47; ☽#⚳ 12:44; ☽△♄ 12:58; ☽□☿ 14:54; ☽△♂ 15:50; ☽△⚷ 16:42; ☽∥♃ 19:09; ☽⚻♆ 21:32; ♂∥⚷ 21:59; ☽□♅ 22:50; ☽⚻♇ 23:24

4 Th: ♃⚼♄ 5:49; ☉△☽ 8:44; ♂☌⚷ 9:47; ☿⚺⚷ 10:36; ☿⚺♂ 11:35; ☽∥♆ 12:04; ☽⚹⚳ 13:35; ☽☌♃ 14:09; ☽⚼♄ 14:14; ☽□♀ 16:15; ☽⚼⚷ 17:49; ☽⚼♂ 18:13

5 F: ☽⚼♇ 0:21; ☽#♆ 1:33; ☉⚼☽ 11:24; ☽∠⚳ 14:04; ☽⚻♄ 15:18; ☽#♃ 18:24; ☽⚻⚷ 18:45; ☽⚻♂ 20:23; ☽△☿ 21:41; ☽☍♆ 23:26

6 Sa: ☽∥⚳ 0:35; ☽△♅ 0:48; ☽△♇ 1:10; ☽#♄ 11:06; ☉⚻☽ 13:58; ☽⚺⚳ 14:29; ☽⚺♃ 15:43; ☽△♀ 18:35; ☿⚹♆ 19:29; ☉☍⚳ 20:20; ☽#⚷ 20:39; ☽#♂ 23:49

7 Su: ☽⚼☿ 0:42; ☽⚼♅ 1:43; ☿☌♅ 14:27; ☉△♃ 15:39; ☽∠♃ 16:37; ☉#☽ 16:45; ☽☍♄ 17:29; ☿△♇ 17:33; ☽⚼♀ 19:47; ☽☍⚷ 20:45

8 M: ☽☍♂ 0:56; ☽⚻♆ 1:23; ☽⚻♅ 2:52; ☽□♇ 3:03; ☽⚻☿ 3:50; ♂⚺♆ 10:05; ☽☌⚳ 15:53; ☽⚹♃ 17:52; ☽#♅ 18:52; ☉☍☽ 19:50; ☽⚻♀ 21:19

9 Tu: ☽⚼♆ 2:54; ☽∥♇ 3:41; ♇ R 9:34; ♂⚺♅ 16:59; ♂□♇ 17:45; ☉⚺♀ 18:49; ☽#☿ 19:07; ☽⚻♄ 21:07

10 W: ☽⚻⚷ 0:18; ♅△♇ 3:08; ☽△♆ 5:03; ☽⚹♇ 6:42; ☽☍♅ 6:43; ☽⚻♂ 7:27; ☽☍☿ 11:29; ☽⚺⚳ 19:21; ☽□♃ 22:16; ♀ R 23:04

11 Th: ☽⚼♄ 0:01; ☽☍♀ 2:08; ☽⚼⚷ 3:10; ☉⚻☽ 4:32; ☽∠♇ 9:39; ☽⚼♂ 12:03; ☽∠⚳ 22:17

12 F: ☽△♄ 3:51; ☽△⚷ 6:58; ☉⚼☽ 10:31; ☽□♆ 11:55; ☽#☿ 11:58; ☽⚺♇ 13:32; ☽⚻♅ 13:48; ☽△♂ 17:45; ☽⚻☿ 22:18

13 Sa: ☽⚹⚳ 2:07; ☉∠♆ 5:33; ☽△♃ 6:10; ☽∥♇ 6:21; ☽⚻♀ 10:05; ☽#♅ 16:04; ☉△☽ 17:40; ☽⚼♅ 18:46; ♃ D 20:01; ☊ D 20:44

14 Su: ☽⚼☿ 4:58; ☽⚼♃ 11:29; ☉#☽ 12:13; ☽□♄ 14:18; ☽⚼♀ 15:12; ☽□⚷ 17:18; ☽⚹♆ 22:24; ☽☌♇ 23:58

15 M: ☽△♅ 0:32; ☽#♂ 8:03; ☽□♂ 8:16; ☿⚻⚳ 11:09; ☽□⚳ 12:09; ☽△☿ 12:13; ☽⚻♃ 17:28; ☽△♀ 20:49; ☽#⚷ 21:57

16 Tu: ♀∠♄ 3:00; ☽∠♆ 4:38; ☽#♄ 8:25; ☉□☽ 10:44; ☊ R 10:58; ☽∥⚳ 23:20

17 W: ☽⚹♄ 3:20; ☽⚹⚷ 6:05; ☽#♃ 6:52; ♂☍⚳ 9:58; ☽⚺♆ 11:07; ☽⚺♇ 12:32; ☽□♅ 13:26; ☽△⚳ 23:49

18 Th: ☽⚹♂ 0:59; ☽#♆ 2:48; ☽□☿ 2:53; ☽☍♃ 6:16; ☽□♀ 8:20; ☽∠♄ 10:01; ☽∠⚷ 12:35; ☽∠♇ 18:49; ☽∥♆ 20:35

19 F: ☉⚹☽ 4:42; ☽⚼⚳ 5:29; ☽∠♂ 9:06; ☽∥♃ 16:09; ☽⚺♄ 16:21; ☿⚺♂ 17:55; ☽⚺⚷ 18:43; ☽☌♆ 23:27; ☽#⚳ 23:47

20 Sa: ☽⚹♇ 0:41; ☽⚹♅ 1:52; ☽⚻⚳ 10:40; ☉ ♊ 12:11; ☉∠☽ 12:55; ☽∥♄ 14:59; ☽⚹☿ 15:24; ☽⚺♂ 16:35; ☽⚻♃ 17:58; ☽⚹♀ 18:16

21 Su: ☽∥⚷ 0:46; ♀□♃ 3:16; ☽∠♅ 7:14; ☿ R 8:44; ♀⚺♂ 11:30; ♂△♃ 16:29; ☉⚺☽ 20:17; ☽∠☿ 20:19; ☽∥♂ 21:45; ☽∠♀ 22:12; ☽⚼♃ 22:51

22 M: ☽☌♄ 3:05; ☽☌⚷ 5:03; ☽⚺♆ 9:25; ☽□♇ 10:27; ☽⚺♅ 11:52; ☽☍⚳ 19:07; ☉∥☽ 20:06

23 Tu: ☽⚺☿ 0:19; ☽⚺♀ 1:23; ☽△♃ 3:01; ☽∥♅ 4:46; ☽☌♂ 5:00; ☽∠♆ 13:19; ☽#♇ 13:54; ☽∥☿ 14:21; ☿#♇ 18:45

24 W: ☉☌☽ 8:17; ☽⚺♄ 10:55; ☽⚺⚷ 12:32; ☽∥♀ 15:08; ☽⚹♆ 16:34; ☽△♇ 17:26; ☽☌♅ 19:03

25 Th: ☿☌♀ 0:55; ☽⚻⚳ 1:00; ☽☌♀ 5:48; ☽☌☿ 5:54; ☽□♃ 9:25; ☽∠♄ 13:55; ☽⚺♂ 14:17; ☽∠⚷ 15:23; ☽⚼♇ 20:04

26 F: ☉⚺♄ 1:22; ☽⚼⚳ 3:11; ☽⚹♄ 16:28; ☉⚺☽ 17:28; ☽⚹⚷ 17:48; ☽∠♂ 18:04; ☽∥♀ 20:41; ☽□♆ 21:35; ☽⚻♇ 22:17; ☉⚺⚷ 22:32

27 Sa: ☽⚺♅ 0:06; ☽△⚳ 5:00; ☽⚺♀ 8:19; ☿∥♅ 8:37; ☽⚺☿ 9:09; ☽#♇ 12:25; ☽⚹♃ 14:00; ☽∥♅ 20:50; ☉∠☽ 21:21; ☽⚹♂ 21:28; ☽∥☿ 22:10; ☉∥☽ 23:20

28 Su: ☊ D 0:40; ☽∠♅ 2:07; ☉∥☿ 6:52; ☽∠♀ 9:06; ☽∠☿ 10:12; ☽∠♃ 15:51; ☽∥♂ 18:06; ☽□♄ 20:37; ☽□⚷ 21:42

29 M: ☉⚹☽ 0:58; ☽△♆ 1:18; ☽☍♇ 1:53; ☽⚹♅ 3:55; ☉⚹♆ 5:58; ☽□⚳ 7:54; ☽⚹♀ 9:41; ☽⚹☿ 10:59; ☉△♇ 14:19; ♂∠♆ 14:46; ☽⚺♃ 17:31; ☽∥⚷ 19:10

30 Tu: ☽∥♄ 2:50; ☽⚼♆ 2:53; ☽□♂ 3:31; ☉∥♅ 13:16; ☽#⚳ 16:25; ☉☌♅ 22:47

31 W: ☽△♄ 0:03; ☽∥♃ 0:41; ☽△⚷ 0:54; ☽⚻♆ 4:21; ☽⚻♇ 4:49; ☽□♅ 7:04; ☊ R 7:33; ☉□☽ 7:38; ☽⚹⚳ 10:16; ☽□♀ 10:27; ☽□☿ 12:04; ♀⚻⚳ 15:55; ☽∥♆ 16:03; ☽☌♃ 20:33

LONGITUDE

Day	Sid.Time	☉	☽	☽ 12 hour	Mean ☊	True ☊	☿	♀	♂	⚳	♃	♄	⚷	♅	♆	♇
	h m s	° ' "	° ' "	° ' "	° '	° '	° '	° '	° '	° '	° '	° '	° '	° '	° '	° '
1 Th	16 40 01	11 ♊ 02 19	20 ♍ 03 48	27 ♍ 09 36	25 ♑ 28.0	24 ♑ 04.8	12 ♊ 43.9	11 ♊ 42.1	25 ♉ 08.0	11 ♏ 51.8	18 ♍ 02.0	6 ♉ 01.0	6 ♉ 27.6	10 ♊ 05.6	8 ♈ 27.6	8 ♒ 42.7
2 F	16 43 58	11 59 48	4 ♎ 15 12	11 ♎ 20 18	25 24.8	24R 02.8	12R 10.4	11R 04.4	25 51.4	11R 43.3	18 05.3	6 07.7	6 30.8	10 09.2	8 28.9	8R 42.1
3 Sa	16 47 54	12 57 16	18 24 31	25 27 28	25 21.6	23 59.2	11 36.8	10 26.8	26 34.6	11 35.0	18 08.7	6 14.4	6 33.9	10 12.7	8 30.1	8 41.4
4 Su	16 51 51	13 54 43	2 ♏ 28 44	9 ♏ 27 51	25 18.5	23 54.0	11 03.6	9 49.5	27 17.8	11 27.1	18 12.4	6 21.0	6 37.1	10 16.2	8 31.3	8 40.8
5 M	16 55 47	14 52 08	16 24 24	23 17 57	25 15.3	23 48.1	10 31.5	9 12.9	28 01.0	11 19.6	18 16.2	6 27.6	6 40.2	10 19.7	8 32.5	8 40.1
6 Tu	16 59 44	15 49 33	0 ♐ 08 04	6 ♐ 54 24	25 12.1	23 42.0	10 01.0	8 37.2	28 44.1	11 12.4	18 20.1	6 34.1	6 43.3	10 23.3	8 33.6	8 39.4
7 W	17 03 41	16 46 57	13 36 39	20 14 36	25 08.9	23 36.7	9 32.5	8 02.5	29 27.1	11 05.6	18 24.2	6 40.6	6 46.3	10 26.8	8 34.7	8 38.7
8 Th	17 07 37	17 44 20	26 48 03	3 ♑ 16 57	25 05.8	23 32.6	9 06.7	7 29.1	0 ♊ 10.1	10 59.2	18 28.5	6 47.0	6 49.3	10 30.3	8 35.8	8 38.0
9 F	17 11 34	18 41 42	9 ♑ 41 18	16 01 13	25 02.6	23 30.1	8 43.8	6 57.2	0 53.0	10 53.1	18 32.9	6 53.4	6 52.3	10 33.8	8 36.8	8 37.2
10 Sa	17 15 30	19 39 03	22 16 51	28 28 28	24 59.4	23D 29.2	8 24.3	6 26.9	1 35.9	10 47.3	18 37.5	6 59.7	6 55.3	10 37.3	8 37.9	8 36.4
11 Su	17 19 27	20 36 24	4 ♒ 36 23	10 ♒ 41 01	24 56.2	23 29.7	8 08.5	5 58.5	2 18.7	10 42.0	18 42.2	7 06.0	6 58.2	10 40.8	8 38.9	8 35.6
12 M	17 23 23	21 33 44	16 42 47	22 42 10	24 53.1	23 31.1	7 56.6	5 32.0	3 01.5	10 37.0	18 47.1	7 12.2	7 01.1	10 44.3	8 39.8	8 34.8
13 Tu	17 27 20	22 31 03	28 39 44	4 ♓ 36 02	24 49.9	23 32.8	7 48.9	5 07.6	3 44.2	10 32.4	18 52.2	7 18.4	7 04.0	10 47.7	8 40.8	8 33.9
14 W	17 31 16	23 28 22	10 ♓ 31 39	16 27 12	24 46.7	23 34.3	7D 45.6	4 45.4	4 26.9	10 28.2	18 57.4	7 24.5	7 06.8	10 51.2	8 41.7	8 33.0
15 Th	17 35 13	24 25 41	22 23 17	28 20 30	24 43.5	23R 35.0	7 46.7	4 25.4	5 09.5	10 24.3	19 02.7	7 30.6	7 09.6	10 54.7	8 42.5	8 32.1
16 F	17 39 10	25 22 59	4 ♈ 19 29	10 ♈ 20 48	24 40.3	23 34.6	7 52.3	4 07.7	5 52.0	10 20.8	19 08.2	7 36.6	7 12.3	10 58.1	8 43.4	8 31.2
17 Sa	17 43 06	26 20 17	16 25 00	22 32 38	24 37.2	23 33.1	8 02.6	3 52.4	6 34.5	10 17.7	19 13.8	7 42.5	7 15.1	11 01.6	8 44.2	8 30.3
18 Su	17 47 03	27 17 34	28 44 08	4 ♉ 59 57	24 34.0	23 30.5	8 17.4	3 39.5	7 17.0	10 15.0	19 19.6	7 48.4	7 17.7	11 05.0	8 45.0	8 29.3
19 M	17 50 59	28 14 51	11 ♉ 20 25	17 45 47	24 30.8	23 27.1	8 36.9	3 28.9	7 59.4	10 12.7	19 25.6	7 54.2	7 20.4	11 08.4	8 45.7	8 28.4
20 Tu	17 54 56	29 12 09	24 16 16	0 ♊ 51 57	24 27.6	23 23.4	9 00.9	3 20.8	8 41.7	10 10.8	19 31.6	8 00.0	7 23.0	11 11.8	8 46.4	8 27.4
21 W	17 58 52	0 ♋ 09 25	7 ♊ 32 48	14 18 43	24 24.5	23 19.9	9 29.5	3 15.1	9 24.0	10 09.2	19 37.8	8 05.7	7 25.6	11 15.2	8 47.1	8 26.4
22 Th	18 02 49	1 06 42	21 09 30	28 04 49	24 21.3	23 17.1	10 02.5	3D 11.8	10 06.2	10 08.0	19 44.2	8 11.3	7 28.1	11 18.6	8 47.8	8 25.3
23 F	18 06 46	2 03 58	5 ♋ 04 17	12 ♋ 07 26	24 18.1	23 15.2	10 40.0	3 10.8	10 48.4	10 07.3	19 50.7	8 16.9	7 30.6	11 21.9	8 48.4	8 24.3
24 Sa	18 10 42	3 01 14	19 13 45	26 22 38	24 14.9	23D 14.4	11 21.9	3 12.1	11 30.5	10D 06.9	19 57.3	8 22.4	7 33.1	11 25.3	8 49.0	8 23.2
25 Su	18 14 39	3 58 29	3 ♌ 33 30	10 ♌ 45 45	24 11.8	23 14.6	12 08.0	3 15.7	12 12.6	10 06.8	20 04.1	8 27.8	7 35.5	11 28.6	8 49.5	8 22.2
26 M	18 18 35	4 55 44	17 58 47	25 12 02	24 08.6	23 15.5	12 58.4	3 21.5	12 54.6	10 07.2	20 11.0	8 33.2	7 37.9	11 31.9	8 50.1	8 21.1
27 Tu	18 22 32	5 52 58	2 ♍ 24 58	9 ♍ 37 06	24 05.4	23 16.7	13 53.0	3 29.5	13 36.5	10 07.9	20 18.0	8 38.5	7 40.2	11 35.2	8 50.5	8 19.9
28 W	18 26 28	6 50 12	16 47 59	23 57 14	24 02.2	23 17.8	14 51.6	3 39.5	14 18.4	10 09.0	20 25.2	8 43.7	7 42.5	11 38.5	8 51.0	8 18.8
29 Th	18 30 25	7 47 25	1 ♎ 04 31	8 ♎ 09 33	23 59.0	23R 18.4	15 54.3	3 51.7	15 00.2	10 10.5	20 32.4	8 48.9	7 44.7	11 41.8	8 51.4	8 17.7
30 F	18 34 21	8 ♋ 44 37	15 12 05	22 11 54	23 ♑ 55.9	23 ♑ 18.4	17 ♊ 01.1	4 ♊ 05.8	15 ♊ 42.0	10 ♏ 12.3	20 ♍ 39.9	8 ♉ 54.0	7 ♉ 46.9	11 ♊ 45.0	8 ♈ 51.8	8 ♒ 16.5

1st of Month

Julian Day # 2461923.5
Obliquity 23°26'32"
SVP 4♓51'32"
GC 27♐14.2
Eris 26♈12.5

Day	⚴	⚵	⚶
1	18♍07.3	13♌16.2	18♌56.9
6	19 08.2	15 08.2	20 48.1
11	20 15.8	17 01.6	22 42.8
16	21 29.5	18 56.4	24 40.9
21	22 48.8	20 52.3	26 42.0
26	24 13.2	22 49.2	28 46.1

DECLINATION and LATITUDE

Day	☉ Decl	☽ Decl	☽ Lat	☽ 12h Decl	☿ Decl	☿ Lat	♀ Decl	♀ Lat	♂ Decl	♂ Lat	⚳ Decl	⚳ Lat	♃ Decl	♃ Lat	♄ Decl	♄ Lat
1 Th	22N06	0S00	4S17	3S06	20N16	2S04	23N06	0N55	18N56	0S07	8S05	7N40	5N57	1N20	11N23	2S16
2 F	22 14	6 09	4 51	9 07	19 55	2 21	22 46	0 41	19 07	0 06	8 07	7 35	5 56	1 19	11 26	2 16
3 Sa	22 21	11 58	5 08	14 38	19 36	2 36	22 27	0 27	19 18	0 05	8 10	7 30	5 54	1 19	11 28	2 16
4 Su	22 28	17 07	5 06	19 21	19 16	2 51	22 08	0 12	19 29	0 05	8 12	7 25	5 52	1 19	11 30	2 16
5 M	22 35	21 18	4 46	22 57	18 58	3 05	21 48	0S02	19 39	0 04	8 15	7 20	5 51	1 19	11 32	2 16
6 Tu	22 41	24 14	4 10	25 11	18 41	3 18	21 29	0 16	19 49	0 03	8 17	7 15	5 49	1 19	11 34	2 16
7 W	22 47	25 44	3 20	25 55	18 25	3 30	21 09	0 30	19 59	0 03	8 20	7 10	5 47	1 18	11 36	2 16
8 Th	22 52	25 44	2 20	25 12	18 11	3 40	20 51	0 43	20 09	0 02	8 23	7 05	5 45	1 18	11 38	2 16
9 F	22 57	24 19	1 15	23 09	17 59	3 49	20 32	0 57	20 19	0 01	8 26	6 60	5 43	1 18	11 40	2 17
10 Sa	23 02	21 42	0 07	20 01	17 48	3 57	20 14	1 10	20 28	0 01	8 29	6 55	5 41	1 18	11 42	2 17
11 Su	23 06	18 08	1N00	16 04	17 39	4 04	19 57	1 23	20 37	0N00	8 32	6 50	5 39	1 18	11 43	2 17
12 M	23 10	13 52	2 04	11 32	17 32	4 09	19 40	1 35	20 46	0 01	8 36	6 44	5 37	1 17	11 45	2 17
13 Tu	23 14	9 07	3 01	6 37	17 26	4 13	19 24	1 47	20 55	0 01	8 39	6 39	5 35	1 17	11 47	2 17
14 W	23 17	4 05	3 50	1 30	17 23	4 16	19 09	1 59	21 04	0 02	8 43	6 34	5 33	1 17	11 49	2 17
15 Th	23 19	1N06	4 29	3N41	17 22	4 18	18 54	2 10	21 12	0 03	8 46	6 29	5 31	1 17	11 51	2 17
16 F	23 21	6 15	4 56	8 46	17 23	4 18	18 40	2 20	21 20	0 03	8 50	6 24	5 28	1 17	11 53	2 18
17 Sa	23 23	11 14	5 11	13 37	17 25	4 17	18 27	2 30	21 28	0 04	8 54	6 19	5 26	1 16	11 54	2 18
18 Su	23 25	15 53	5 12	18 00	17 29	4 15	18 16	2 40	21 36	0 05	8 58	6 14	5 23	1 16	11 56	2 18
19 M	23 25	19 57	4 59	21 42	17 35	4 12	18 05	2 49	21 44	0 05	9 02	6 09	5 21	1 16	11 58	2 18
20 Tu	23 26	23 11	4 30	24 24	17 43	4 08	17 54	2 58	21 51	0 06	9 06	6 04	5 18	1 16	11 60	2 18
21 W	23 26	25 16	3 45	25 48	17 52	4 03	17 45	3 06	21 58	0 07	9 10	5 59	5 16	1 16	12 01	2 18
22 Th	23 26	25 56	2 48	25 40	18 02	3 57	17 37	3 14	22 05	0 07	9 15	5 54	5 13	1 15	12 03	2 19
23 F	23 25	24 59	1 38	23 54	18 14	3 51	17 30	3 21	22 12	0 08	9 19	5 49	5 10	1 15	12 04	2 19
24 Sa	23 24	22 25	0 22	20 35	18 27	3 43	17 23	3 28	22 18	0 09	9 23	5 45	5 08	1 15	12 06	2 19
25 Su	23 23	18 26	0S57	16 00	18 41	3 35	17 18	3 35	22 25	0 09	9 28	5 40	5 05	1 15	12 08	2 19
26 M	23 21	13 20	2 12	10 29	18 56	3 26	17 13	3 41	22 31	0 10	9 33	5 35	5 02	1 15	12 09	2 19
27 Tu	23 18	7 30	3 20	4 26	19 12	3 17	17 09	3 46	22 36	0 11	9 38	5 30	4 59	1 14	12 11	2 19
28 W	23 16	1 18	4 14	1S49	19 29	3 07	17 06	3 51	22 42	0 11	9 42	5 25	4 56	1 14	12 12	2 20
29 Th	23 12	4S54	4 53	7 54	19 46	2 57	17 03	3 56	22 48	0 12	9 47	5 21	4 53	1 14	12 14	2 20
30 F	23N09	10S48	5S13	13S31	20N03	2S46	17N02	4S00	22N53	0N13	9S53	5N16	4N50	1N14	12N15	2S20

Day	⚷ Decl	⚷ Lat	♅ Decl	♅ Lat	♆ Decl	♆ Lat	♇ Decl	♇ Lat
1	13N08	0S34	21N55	0S03	2N03	1S25	23S01	5S08
6	13 13	0 35	21 57	0 03	2 05	1 25	23 03	5 09
11	13 17	0 35	21 60	0 03	2 07	1 26	23 05	5 10
16	13 21	0 36	22 02	0 03	2 08	1 26	23 07	5 11
21	13 25	0 36	22 05	0 03	2 10	1 26	23 09	5 11
26	13 29	0 37	22 07	0 03	2 11	1 26	23 12	5 12

Day	⚴ Decl	⚴ Lat	⚵ Decl	⚵ Lat	⚶ Decl	⚶ Lat	Eris Decl	Eris Lat
1	18N52	15N27	13N39	3S19	20N31	5N40	0N47	9S60
6	18 46	15 48	13 24	3 02	19 52	5 37	0 48	10 00
11	18 37	16 06	13 06	2 45	19 12	5 34	0 48	10 00
16	18 23	16 23	12 46	2 30	18 30	5 32	0 49	10 01
21	18 06	16 39	12 24	2 15	17 46	5 29	0 49	10 01
26	17 46	16 54	12 00	2 01	17 00	5 27	0 49	10 01

Moon Phenomena

Max/0 Decl
dy hr mn
7 11:54 25S55
14 18:57 0 N
21 22:04 25N56
28 5:00 0 S

Max/0 Lat
dy hr mn
3 9:26 5S10
10 2:19 0 N
17 13:54 5N14
24 6:44 0 S
30 13:54 5S16

Perigee/Apogee
dy hr m kilometers
14 4:47 a 404220
26 4:25 p 366530

PH dy hr mn
○ 7 6:10 17♐02
☾ 15 4:29 24♓36
● 22 18:29 1♋51
☽ 29 12:12 8♎16

Void of Course Moon

Last Aspect				☽ Ingress	
1	9:02	♂	△	♎ 1	16:48
2	14:04	☉	△	♏ 3	19:45
5	21:24	♂	☍	♐ 5	23:46
7	8:42	♃	□	♑ 8	5:54
9	16:56	♃	△	♒ 10	14:58
12	10:33	☉	△	♓ 13	2:42
15	4:29	☉	□	♈ 15	15:20
17	20:59	☉	✶	♉ 18	2:26
19	15:12	♃	△	♊ 20	10:26
21	21:30	♃	□	♋ 22	15:18
24	1:14	♃	✶	♌ 24	18:04
25	15:09	☿	✶	♍ 26	19:59
28	6:07	♃	☌	♎ 28	22:11

DAILY ASPECTARIAN

1 Th
☽⚼♄ 1:37
☽⚼⚷ 2:22
♀#♇ 5:14
☽⚼♇ 6:10
☽#♆ 7:56
☽△♂ 9:02
☉☌♀ 10:01
☽∠⚳ 11:23
☉⚻⚳ 17:59
☽#♃ 23:08

2 F
☉☌☿ 2:47
☽⚻♄ 3:12
☽⚻⚷ 3:50
☽☍♆ 7:10
☽△♇ 7:32
☽∥⚳ 8:00
☽△♅ 10:02
☽△♀ 11:04
☽⚼♂ 11:47
☽⚺⚳ 12:32
☽△☿ 12:54
☉△☽ 14:04
☽#♄ 21:50
☽⚺♃ 23:33

3 Sa
☿⚻⚳ 1:39
☽#⚷ 5:19
☉∥♀ 5:27
♀☌♅ 8:15
☽⚼♀ 11:28
☽⚼♅ 11:38
☽⚼☿ 13:26
☿∥♂ 13:55
☽⚻♂ 14:40
☉⚼☽ 17:27

4 Su
☽∠♃ 1:15
☽☍♄ 6:42
☽☍⚷ 7:08
☽⚻♆ 10:23
☽□♇ 10:38
☽#☿ 10:46
☽⚻♀ 12:05
☽#♂ 13:18
☽⚻♅ 13:27
♀∥♅ 13:43
☽⚻☿ 14:12
☽☌⚳ 15:17
☉⚻☽ 21:08

5 M
☽#♀ 3:06
☽✶♃ 3:15
☽#♅ 4:25
☿☌♅ 8:08
☉#☽ 9:27
☽⚼♆ 12:26
☽∥♇ 12:55
☽☍♂ 21:24
♀△♇ 22:27

6 Tu
♀✶♆ 2:22
☽⚻♄ 11:29
☽⚻⚷ 11:43
☽☍♀ 14:26
☽△♆ 14:58
☽✶♇ 15:06
☽☍☿ 16:57
☽☍♅ 18:18
☽⚺⚳ 19:31

7 W
☉☍☽ 6:10
☽□♃ 8:42
☽⚼♄ 14:44
☽⚼⚷ 14:51
☽∠♇ 18:11
♂ ♊ 18:21
☽∠⚳ 22:31

8 Th
☽⚻♂ 6:35
♄☌⚷ 16:26
☽△⚷ 18:41
☽△♄ 18:42
☽⚻♀ 19:04
☉□♃ 20:01
☽□♆ 21:59
☽⚺♇ 21:59
☽⚻☿ 22:15

9 F
☽⚻♅ 1:39
☽✶⚳ 2:14
♀⚺♄ 2:27
♀⚺⚷ 3:27
☿✶♇ 4:38
☿✶♆ 7:40
☿△♇ 7:57
♀∥♂ 11:42
☽⚼♂ 12:27
☽∥♇ 12:38
☉#☽ 13:20
☽△♃ 16:56
☉⚻☽ 18:32
☽#♅ 21:48
☽⚼♀ 22:28

10 Sa
☽⚼☿ 2:07
☊ D 2:17
☽⚼♅ 6:29
☽#♂ 8:34
☽#♀ 11:29
☉#♇ 17:31
☽△♂ 19:13
☽⚼♃ 22:13

11 Su
☉⚼☽ 2:08
☽△♀ 2:36
☽#☿ 3:00
⚳⚻♅ 3:20
☽□⚷ 4:40
☽□♄ 4:57
☽△☿ 6:51
☽☌♇ 7:51
☽✶♆ 7:59
☽□⚳ 11:57
☽△♅ 12:03

12 M
☽#⚷ 2:55
☽⚻♃ 4:10
☉△☽ 10:33
☽#♄ 10:48
☉∠⚷ 12:04
☽∠♆ 13:57
☉∠♄ 18:04

13 Tu
☽∥⚳ 2:13
☽□♂ 10:54
☽□♀ 12:40
☽#♃ 17:02
☽✶⚷ 17:03
☽✶♄ 17:38
☽□☿ 18:24
☽⚺♇ 20:00
☽⚺♆ 20:17
☽△⚳ 23:53

14 W
☽□♅ 0:40
☉⚼♇ 1:56
☿ D 6:07
♀☌♂ 6:59
☽#♆ 9:03
☽☍♃ 17:12
☽∠⚷ 23:32

15 Th
☽∠♄ 0:15
☽∠♇ 2:19
☉□☽ 4:29
☊ R 4:40
☽∥♆ 4:50
☽⚼⚳ 6:03
☽∥♃ 20:23
☉⚼⚳ 23:09
☽✶♀ 23:37

16 F
☽✶♂ 3:16
☽⚺⚷ 5:46
☽⚺♄ 6:37
☽✶☿ 7:10
☽✶♇ 8:22
☽☌♆ 8:47
☽⚻⚳ 11:57
☽#⚳ 12:26
☽✶♅ 13:18

17 Sa
☽∥♄ 3:20
☽∠♀ 4:44
☽⚻♃ 5:34
☽∠♂ 10:44
☽∥⚷ 10:45
☽∠☿ 13:13
☽∠♅ 18:51
☉✶☽ 20:59

18 Su
♂⚺⚷ 0:28
☽∥☿ 9:10
☽⚺♀ 9:18
☽⚼♃ 10:48
☽∥♀ 12:53
☿△♇ 14:40
☽☌⚷ 16:25
☽⚺♂ 17:18
☽☌♄ 17:28
☽□♇ 18:36
☽⚺☿ 18:43
☽⚺♆ 19:08
♂⚺♄ 20:37
☽☍⚳ 21:53
☽⚺♅ 23:37

19 M
☉∠☽ 3:52
☿✶♆ 9:40
☽∥♂ 12:42
☽∥♅ 14:46
☽△♃ 15:12
♂△♇ 16:04
☽∠♆ 23:05
☽#♇ 23:40

20 Tu
☉∥☽ 2:14
♂✶♆ 2:43
☉⚺☽ 9:41
☿∥♀ 15:24
☽☌♀ 16:21
☉ ♋ 20:03
☽⚺⚷ 23:47

21 W
☽⚺♄ 0:59
☽△♇ 1:35
☽✶♆ 2:13
☽☌♂ 3:29
☽☌☿ 3:36
☽⚻⚳ 4:38
☽☌♅ 6:37
☿☌♂ 12:52
☽□♃ 21:30

22 Th
♂∥♅ 0:08
♂⚻⚳ 1:01
☽∠⚷ 2:17
☽∠♄ 3:33
☿⚻⚳ 3:37
☽⚼♇ 3:56
☽⚼⚳ 6:54
☉☌☽ 18:29
☽⚺♀ 20:46
♀ D 22:14

23 F
☽✶⚷ 4:10
☽✶♄ 5:31
☽⚻♇ 5:41
☽□♆ 6:22
☽△⚳ 8:36
☽⚺☿ 10:00
☽⚺♂ 10:17
☽⚺♅ 10:45
☉∥☽ 16:17
☽#♇ 18:12
♂☌♅ 20:46
☽∠♀ 22:16

24 Sa
☽∥♂ 0:49
☽✶♃ 1:14
☿☌♅ 2:00
☽∥♅ 2:17
♄□♇ 3:03
☉⚺♀ 4:47
☊ D 6:40
☽∠♅ 12:07
☽∠☿ 12:39
☽∠♂ 12:51
⚳ D 13:31
☽∥☿ 22:45
☽✶♀ 23:30

25 Su
☉⚺☽ 0:45
☽∠♃ 2:32
☽∥♀ 5:54
☽□⚷ 6:44
☽☍♇ 8:00
☽□♄ 8:14
☽△♆ 8:47
☽□⚳ 10:55
☽✶♅ 13:14
☿☌♂ 14:28
☽✶♂ 15:09
☽✶☿ 15:09
☽∥⚷ 23:24

26 M
☉∠☽ 3:28
☽⚺♃ 3:41
☽∥♄ 5:04
☽⚼♆ 9:44
☽#⚳ 15:38

27 Tu
☽□♀ 1:49
☉✶☽ 6:11
☽△⚷ 8:46
☽⚻♇ 9:51
☽∥♃ 9:56
☽△♄ 10:26
☽⚻♆ 10:43
☽✶⚳ 12:52
☽□♅ 15:21
☽□♂ 19:37
☽□☿ 20:31
☽∥♆ 20:38

28 W
☽☌♃ 6:07
☽⚼⚷ 9:56
☽⚼♇ 10:55
☽⚼♄ 11:42
☽#♆ 13:24
☽∠⚳ 14:02
☉#♇ 20:04
⚶ ♍ 22:15
☉✶⚷ 22:50
☽#♃ 23:55

29 Th
☽△♀ 4:47
☽⚻⚷ 11:20
☊ R 12:04
☉□☽ 12:12
☽△♇ 12:13
☉⚻♇ 12:26
♄⚺♆ 12:59
☽☍♆ 13:12
☽⚻♄ 13:12
☽⚺⚳ 15:28
☽△♅ 18:05
☽∥⚳ 20:04

30 F
☽△♂ 0:54
☉□♆ 3:02
☽△☿ 3:23
☉✶♄ 4:18
☽#♄ 6:20
☽⚼♀ 6:48
☽⚺♃ 9:27
☽#⚷ 12:01
☽⚼♅ 19:56

July 2028

LONGITUDE

Day	Sid.Time	☉	☽	☽ 12 hour	Mean☊	True☊	☿	♀	♂	⚳	♃	♄	⚷	♅	♆	♇
	h m s	° ' "	° ' "	° ' "	° '	° '	° '	° '	° '	° '	° '	° '	° '	° '	° '	° '
1 Sa	18 38 18	9♋41 50	29♎08 49	6♏02 43	23♑52.7	23♑17.8	18♊11.7	4♊21.9	16♊23.7	10♏14.6	20♍47.4	8♉59.0	7♉49.1	11♊48.2	8♈52.2	8♒15.3
2 Su	18 42 15	10 39 01	12♏53 28	19 40 56	23 49.5	23R 16.6	19 26.3	4 39.9	17 05.4	10 17.1	20 55.0	9 03.9	7 51.2	11 51.4	8 52.5	8R 14.1
3 M	18 46 11	11 36 13	26 25 04	3♐05 47	23 46.3	23 15.2	20 44.7	4 59.7	17 47.0	10 20.1	21 02.8	9 08.8	7 53.3	11 54.6	8 52.8	8 12.9
4 Tu	18 50 08	12 33 24	9♐43 00	16 16 43	23 43.2	23 13.8	22 06.9	5 21.2	18 28.5	10 23.3	21 10.7	9 13.6	7 55.3	11 57.8	8 53.1	8 11.7
5 W	18 54 04	13 30 36	22 46 53	29 13 31	23 40.0	23 12.6	23 32.9	5 44.5	19 10.0	10 27.0	21 18.7	9 18.3	7 57.3	12 00.9	8 53.3	8 10.5
6 Th	18 58 01	14 27 47	5♑36 39	11♑56 19	23 36.8	23 11.8	25 02.5	6 09.5	19 51.4	10 31.0	21 26.9	9 22.9	7 59.2	12 04.0	8 53.5	8 09.3
7 F	19 01 57	15 24 58	18 12 37	24 25 40	23 33.6	23D 11.4	26 35.8	6 36.1	20 32.8	10 35.3	21 35.1	9 27.5	8 01.1	12 07.1	8 53.7	8 08.0
8 Sa	19 05 54	16 22 09	0♒35 38	6♒42 41	23 30.5	23 11.4	28 12.7	7 04.2	21 14.1	10 40.0	21 43.5	9 32.0	8 03.0	12 10.2	8 53.8	8 06.8
9 Su	19 09 50	17 19 20	12 47 05	18 49 04	23 27.3	23 11.7	29 53.0	7 33.8	21 55.4	10 45.0	21 51.9	9 36.4	8 04.8	12 13.2	8 53.9	8 05.5
10 M	19 13 47	18 16 31	24 48 59	0♓47 10	23 24.1	23 12.2	1♋36.7	8 04.8	22 36.6	10 50.3	22 00.5	9 40.7	8 06.5	12 16.2	8 54.0	8 04.2
11 Tu	19 17 44	19 13 43	6♓44 01	12 39 57	23 20.9	23 12.7	3 23.7	8 37.2	23 17.8	10 56.0	22 09.2	9 44.9	8 08.2	12 19.2	8R 54.0	8 02.9
12 W	19 21 40	20 10 55	18 35 26	24 30 57	23 17.8	23 13.1	5 13.7	9 11.0	23 58.9	11 01.9	22 18.0	9 49.1	8 09.9	12 22.2	8 54.0	8 01.6
13 Th	19 25 37	21 08 08	0♈27 00	6♈24 10	23 14.6	23 13.3	7 06.7	9 46.0	24 39.9	11 08.2	22 26.9	9 53.1	8 11.5	12 25.1	8 54.0	8 00.3
14 F	19 29 33	22 05 21	12 22 57	18 23 57	23 11.4	23 13.4	9 02.4	10 22.3	25 20.9	11 14.9	22 35.9	9 57.1	8 13.0	12 28.1	8 53.9	7 59.0
15 Sa	19 33 30	23 02 35	24 27 42	0♉34 48	23 08.2	23 13.5	11 00.6	10 59.8	26 01.9	11 21.8	22 45.0	10 01.0	8 14.5	12 30.9	8 53.8	7 57.6
16 Su	19 37 26	23 59 49	6♉45 46	13 01 06	23 05.0	23 13.5	13 01.1	11 38.4	26 42.8	11 29.0	22 54.2	10 04.8	8 16.0	12 33.8	8 53.7	7 56.3
17 M	19 41 23	24 57 04	19 21 19	25 46 49	23 01.9	23 13.6	15 03.6	12 18.1	27 23.6	11 36.6	23 03.5	10 08.6	8 17.4	12 36.6	8 53.5	7 55.0
18 Tu	19 45 19	25 54 19	2♊17 58	8♊55 02	22 58.7	23 13.8	17 07.7	12 58.9	28 04.4	11 44.5	23 12.9	10 12.2	8 18.7	12 39.4	8 53.3	7 53.6
19 W	19 49 16	26 51 36	15 38 11	22 27 30	22 55.5	23 14.1	19 13.1	13 40.6	28 45.1	11 52.6	23 22.4	10 15.8	8 20.1	12 42.2	8 53.1	7 52.3
20 Th	19 53 13	27 48 53	29 22 54	6♋24 11	22 52.3	23 14.5	21 19.7	14 23.4	29 25.8	12 01.1	23 32.1	10 19.2	8 21.3	12 44.9	8 52.9	7 50.9
21 F	19 57 09	28 46 11	13♋31 02	20 42 56	22 49.2	23R 14.8	23 26.9	15 07.1	0♋06.5	12 09.8	23 41.8	10 22.6	8 22.5	12 47.6	8 52.6	7 49.5
22 Sa	20 01 06	29 43 29	27 59 18	5♌19 23	22 46.0	23 14.8	25 34.6	15 51.7	0 47.0	12 18.9	23 51.6	10 25.9	8 23.7	12 50.3	8 52.3	7 48.2
23 Su	20 05 02	0♌40 48	12♌42 20	20 07 15	22 42.8	23 14.5	27 42.4	16 37.1	1 27.5	12 28.2	24 01.4	10 29.1	8 24.8	12 53.0	8 51.9	7 46.8
24 M	20 08 59	1 38 07	27 33 10	4♍59 08	22 39.6	23 13.9	29 50.1	17 23.4	2 08.0	12 37.8	24 11.4	10 32.2	8 25.8	12 55.6	8 51.5	7 45.4
25 Tu	20 12 55	2 35 26	12♍24 11	19 47 27	22 36.5	23 12.9	1♌57.4	18 10.5	2 48.4	12 47.7	24 21.5	10 35.2	8 26.8	12 58.1	8 51.1	7 44.0
26 W	20 16 52	3 32 46	27 08 08	4♎25 31	22 33.3	23 11.8	4 04.0	18 58.4	3 28.7	12 57.8	24 31.6	10 38.1	8 27.7	13 00.7	8 50.7	7 42.6
27 Th	20 20 48	4 30 07	11♎39 02	18 48 14	22 30.1	23 10.8	6 09.9	19 47.0	4 09.0	13 08.2	24 41.9	10 40.9	8 28.6	13 03.2	8 50.2	7 41.2
28 F	20 24 45	5 27 28	25 52 48	2♏52 30	22 26.9	23D 10.1	8 14.7	20 36.3	4 49.3	13 18.9	24 52.2	10 43.6	8 29.4	13 05.6	8 49.7	7 39.9
29 Sa	20 28 42	6 24 49	9♏47 16	16 37 04	22 23.7	23 10.0	10 18.4	21 26.3	5 29.4	13 29.9	25 02.6	10 46.2	8 30.2	13 08.1	8 49.1	7 38.5
30 Su	20 32 38	7 22 11	23 22 01	0♐02 14	22 20.6	23 10.5	12 20.9	22 17.0	6 09.5	13 41.5	25 13.1	10 48.7	8 30.9	13 10.5	8 48.6	7 37.1
31 M	20 36 35	8♌19 33	6♐37 55	13 09 17	22♑17.4	23♑11.4	14♌22.0	23♊08.3	6♋49.6	13♏52.5	25♍23.6	10♉51.2	8♉31.6	13♊12.8	8♈48.0	7♒35.7

1st of Month

Julian Day #
2461953.5
Obliquity
23°26'[illegible]1"
SVP 4♓51'26"
GC 27♐14.2
Eris 26♈23.3

Day	⚴	⚵	⚶
1	25♍42.3	24♌46.9	0♍52.9
6	27 15.6	26 45.3	3 02.0
11	28 52.7	28 44.3	5 13.5
16	0♎33.4	0♍43.8	7 27.1
21	2 17.3	2 43.7	9 42.8
26	4 04.3	4 44.0	12 00.4
31	5 53.9	6 44.4	14 19.7

DECLINATION and LATITUDE

Day	☉ Decl	☽ Decl	☽ Lat	☽12h Decl	☿ Decl	☿ Lat	♀ Decl	♀ Lat	♂ Decl	♂ Lat	⚳ Decl	⚳ Lat	♃ Decl	♃ Lat	♄ Decl	♄ Lat
1 Sa	23N05	16S04	5S14	18S23	20N21	2S34	17N01	4S04	22N58	0N13	9S58	5N11	4N47	1N14	12N16	2S20
2 Su	23 01	20 26	4 58	22 12	20 39	2 23	17 01	4 08	23 03	0 14	10 03	5 06	4 44	1 14	12 18	2 20
3 M	22 56	23 38	4 25	24 45	20 56	2 11	17 01	4 11	23 07	0 15	10 08	5 02	4 40	1 13	12 19	2 21
4 Tu	22 51	25 30	3 38	25 53	21 14	1 58	17 02	4 14	23 12	0 15	10 14	4 57	4 37	1 13	12 21	2 21
5 W	22 45	25 55	2 41	25 35	21 31	1 46	17 03	4 16	23 16	0 16	10 19	4 53	4 34	1 13	12 22	2 21
6 Th	22 39	24 55	1 36	23 56	21 47	1 33	17 06	4 18	23 20	0 17	10 24	4 48	4 30	1 13	12 23	2 21
7 F	22 33	22 39	0 28	21 07	22 03	1 21	17 08	4 20	23 23	0 17	10 30	4 44	4 27	1 13	12 24	2 21
8 Sa	22 26	19 21	0N41	17 24	22 18	1 08	17 11	4 22	23 27	0 18	10 36	4 39	4 24	1 13	12 26	2 22
9 Su	22 19	15 16	1 47	13 00	22 31	0 55	17 15	4 23	23 30	0 19	10 41	4 35	4 20	1 12	12 27	2 22
10 M	22 11	10 38	2 47	8 10	22 43	0 42	17 19	4 24	23 33	0 19	10 47	4 31	4 17	1 12	12 28	2 22
11 Tu	22 03	5 39	3 39	3 05	22 54	0 30	17 23	4 25	23 36	0 20	10 53	4 26	4 13	1 12	12 29	2 22
12 W	21 55	0 30	4 21	2N05	23 02	0 18	17 27	4 25	23 39	0 21	10 59	4 22	4 09	1 12	12 30	2 22
13 Th	21 47	4N39	4 53	7 11	23 09	0 06	17 32	4 25	23 41	0 21	11 05	4 18	4 06	1 12	12 31	2 23
14 F	21 38	9 40	5 12	12 05	23 14	0N06	17 37	4 25	23 43	0 22	11 11	4 13	4 02	1 12	12 32	2 23
15 Sa	21 28	14 23	5 17	16 35	23 16	0 17	17 43	4 25	23 45	0 23	11 17	4 09	3 58	1 11	12 33	2 23
16 Su	21 18	18 37	5 08	20 29	23 16	0 28	17 48	4 25	23 47	0 23	11 23	4 05	3 54	1 11	12 34	2 23
17 M	21 08	22 08	4 45	23 32	23 13	0 38	17 54	4 24	23 49	0 24	11 29	4 01	3 51	1 11	12 35	2 24
18 Tu	20 58	24 39	4 07	25 26	23 08	0 48	17 60	4 23	23 50	0 25	11 36	3 57	3 47	1 11	12 36	2 24
19 W	20 47	25 52	3 14	25 56	23 00	0 57	18 06	4 22	23 51	0 25	11 42	3 53	3 43	1 11	12 37	2 24
20 Th	20 36	25 35	2 09	24 49	22 49	1 05	18 12	4 21	23 52	0 26	11 48	3 49	3 39	1 11	12 38	2 24
21 F	20 24	23 38	0 54	22 06	22 36	1 13	18 18	4 20	23 53	0 27	11 55	3 45	3 35	1 11	12 39	2 24
22 Sa	20 12	20 08	0S26	17 52	22 20	1 20	18 24	4 18	23 53	0 27	12 01	3 41	3 31	1 10	12 39	2 25
23 Su	20 00	15 18	1 46	12 30	22 01	1 26	18 31	4 16	23 54	0 28	12 08	3 37	3 27	1 10	12 40	2 25
24 M	19 48	9 31	2 59	6 24	21 40	1 31	18 37	4 15	23 54	0 29	12 14	3 33	3 23	1 10	12 41	2 25
25 Tu	19 35	3 13	3 60	0S01	21 17	1 36	18 43	4 13	23 54	0 29	12 21	3 30	3 19	1 10	12 42	2 25
26 W	19 22	3S13	4 44	6 21	20 51	1 39	18 49	4 10	23 53	0 30	12 27	3 26	3 15	1 10	12 42	2 26
27 Th	19 08	9 22	5 10	12 14	20 23	1 42	18 55	4 08	23 53	0 31	12 34	3 22	3 10	1 10	12 43	2 26
28 F	18 54	14 54	5 16	17 21	19 53	1 45	19 01	4 06	23 52	0 31	12 41	3 18	3 06	1 10	12 44	2 26
29 Sa	18 40	19 32	5 03	21 26	19 21	1 46	19 07	4 03	23 51	0 32	12 47	3 15	3 02	1 10	12 44	2 26
30 Su	18 26	23 01	4 34	24 17	18 48	1 47	19 13	4 00	23 50	0 33	12 54	3 11	2 58	1 09	12 45	2 27
31 M	18N11	25S11	3S50	25S45	18N13	1N47	19N18	3S58	23N49	0N33	13S01	3N08	2N53	1N09	12N45	2S27

Day	⚷ Decl	⚷ Lat	♅ Decl	♅ Lat	♆ Decl	♆ Lat	♇ Decl	♇ Lat
1	13N32	0S37	22N09	0S03	2N11	1S27	23S14	5S13
6	13 35	0 38	22 11	0 03	2 11	1 27	23 16	5 14
11	13 37	0 38	22 13	0 03	2 11	1 27	23 19	5 14
16	13 39	0 39	22 15	0 03	2 11	1 28	23 21	5 15
21	13 41	0 39	22 17	0 03	2 10	1 28	23 23	5 16
26	13 42	0 40	22 19	0 03	2 09	1 28	23 25	5 16
31	13N42	0S40	22N20	0S03	2N08	1S28	23S28	5S17

Day	⚴ Decl	⚴ Lat	⚵ Decl	⚵ Lat	⚶ Decl	⚶ Lat	Eris Decl	Eris Lat
1	17N23	17N08	11N35	1S47	16N13	5N25	0N49	10S01
6	16 57	17 21	11 08	1 34	15 24	5 23	0 49	10 02
11	16 30	17 33	10 39	1 21	14 34	5 21	0 49	10 02
16	16 01	17 45	10 09	1 09	13 42	5 19	0 49	10 03
21	15 30	17 56	9 37	0 57	12 49	5 17	0 49	10 03
26	14 59	18 07	9 04	0 45	11 55	5 15	0 49	10 03
31	14N26	18N18	8N31	0S34	10N59	5N14	0N48	10S04

Moon Phenomena

Max/0 Decl
dy hr mn
4 18:50 25S57
12 2:20 0 N
19 7:39 25N57
25 11:57 0 S

Max/0 Lat
dy hr mn
7 9:36 0 N
14 21:33 5N17
21 16:11 0 S
27 19:23 5S16

Perigee/Apogee
dy hr m kilometers
11 22:26 a 404943
23 22:19 p 361636

PH dy hr mn
○ 6 18:12 15♑11
● 6 18:21 P 0.389
☾ 14 20:58 22♈55
● 22 3:03 29♋51
● 22 176:40T 05[illegible]0"
☽ 28 17:41 6♏10

Void of Course Moon

Last Aspect			☽ Ingress	
30 3:23	♀	△	♏	1 1:29
2 14:20	♃	⚹	♐	3 6:25
5 1:36	♀	☍	♑	5 13:27
7 6:34	♃	△	♒	7 22:50
9 19:19	♂	☍	♓	10 10:25
12 11:35	☉	□	♈	12 23:05
15 3:16	♂	⚹	♉	15 10:52
17 11:18	☉	⚹	♊	17 19:47
20 0:05	☉	☌	♋	20 1:04
22 3:03	☉	☌	♌	22 3:18
23 6:41	♀	⚹	♍	24 3:57
25 19:41	♃	☌	♎	26 4:42
27 14:29	♀	□	♏	28 7:03
30 3:22	♃	⚹	♐	30 11:56

DAILY ASPECTARIAN

1 Sa	☽⚼♂	4:06
	☽⋕♀	4:46
	☽⚼☿	7:43
	☽⚻♀	9:16
	☽∠♃	11:40
	☉△⚳	14:22
	☽☍⚷	15:08
	☽□♇	15:50
	☽⚻♆	16:57
	☽☍♄	17:15
	☉∥♂	18:43
	☽☌⚳	19:24
	☉△☽	19:46
	☽⚻♅	22:10
2 Su	☽⋕☿	1:29
	☽⚻♂	7:48
	☽⋕♅	11:47
	☽⚻☿	12:47
	☽⚹♃	14:20
	☉⋕☽	17:57
	☽⋕♂	19:14
	☽⚼♆	19:28
	☽∥♇	20:28
3 M	☉⚼☽	0:21
	☿□♃	5:58
	☉⚺♅	8:10
	☽☍♀	15:51
	☽⚻⚷	20:44
	☽⚹♇	21:14
	☽△♆	22:29
	☽⚻♄	23:06
4 Tu	☽⚺⚳	1:14
	☽☍♅	4:07
	☉⚻☽	5:35
	☿∠⚷	13:58
	☽☍♂	16:56
	☿⚼♇	17:57
	☽□♃	21:15
5 W	☽⚼⚷	0:19
	☽∠♇	0:44
	♂⋕♇	1:06
	☽☍☿	1:36
	☽⚼♄	2:51
	☽∠⚳	4:59
	☿∠♄	12:57
6 Th	☽⚻♀	1:04
	☽△⚷	4:30
	☽⚺♇	4:48
	☽□♆	6:13
	☽△♄	7:11
	☿⚼⚳	7:46
	☽⚹⚳	9:21
	☽⚻♅	12:18
	☽⋕♂	17:33
	☉☍☽	18:12
	☽∥♇	18:26
7 F	☉⋕☽	0:57
	☽⋕♅	3:47
	☽⋕☿	4:34
	☽⚻♂	4:46
	☽△♃	6:34
	☽⚼♀	6:47
	☊ D	9:30
	☿∥♅	14:33
	☽⚼♅	17:18
	☽⚻☿	18:38
8 Sa	☉∥☿	9:42
	☽⚼♂	11:44
	☽⚼♃	12:10
	☽⋕♀	13:02
	☽△♀	13:14
	☽□⚷	14:40
	☽☌♇	14:44
	☽⚹♆	16:19
	☽□♄	17:40
	☽□⚳	19:56
	♂□♃	21:28
	☽△♅	22:53
9 Su	☿ ♋	1:39
	☽⚼☿	4:51
	♇□⚷	5:45
	☽⋕⚷	8:53
	☉⚻☽	9:48
	☽⋕♄	14:49
	☽⚻♃	18:18
	☽△♂	19:19
	☉∥♅	19:24
	☽∠♆	22:10
	☽∥⚳	23:14
	♀△♇	23:34
10 M	♀⚺⚷	1:22
	♂⚼♇	15:36
	☽△☿	16:03
	♂∠⚷	18:11
	☉⚼☽	18:30
11 Tu	☽⚺♇	2:39
	☽⚹⚷	2:51
	☽□♀	4:00
	☽⚺♆	4:23
	☽⚹♄	6:08
	☽⋕♃	6:49
	☽△⚳	8:34
	☽□♅	11:21
	♀⚹♆	12:03
	♆ R	13:05
	☽⋕♆	16:11
12 W	☉△☽	3:30
	☽☍♃	7:37
	☽∠♇	8:58
	☽∠⚷	9:17
	☽□♂	11:35
	☽∥♆	12:30
	☽∠♄	12:41
	☽⚼⚳	15:12
	☽∥♃	21:25
13 Th	♀⚺♄	5:23
	♂∠♄	8:34
	☿⚻♇	11:03
	☿⚹⚷	13:41
	☽⚹♇	15:12
	☽⚺⚷	15:38
	☽□☿	16:00
	☽☌♆	17:01
	☽⚺♄	19:06
	☽⚹♀	19:45
	☽⚻⚳	21:42
	☿□♆	22:15
14 F	☽⚹♅	0:10
	⚵ ♍	4:03
	☽⋕⚳	7:38
	⚴ ♎	8:38
	☿⚹♄	11:33
	☽∥♄	14:23
	☉⚹♃	15:14
	☽∥⚷	20:03
	☽⚻♃	20:35
	☉□☽	20:58
	☿⚺♀	23:44
15 Sa	☽∠♀	3:11
	☽⚹♂	3:16
	☿△⚳	4:31
	☽∠♅	6:02
	♂⚼⚳	14:11
	♀⚻⚳	16:56
	☿⚺♅	18:28
	☽∥♀	18:58
16 Su	☽⚼♃	2:14
	☽□♇	2:16
	☽☌⚷	2:54
	☽⚺♆	4:06
	♃⚼♇	4:44
	☽☌♄	6:25
	☽☍⚳	9:10
	☽⚺♀	9:53
	☽∠♂	10:03
	☽⚺♅	11:10
	☽⚹☿	14:19
	☉∥☽	16:56
17 M	☽∥♅	1:02
	☽△♃	7:01
	☽∠♆	8:29
	☽∥☿	8:55
	☽⋕♇	10:25
	☉⚹☽	11:18
	♀☌♅	11:48
	☽∥♂	14:54
	☽⚺♂	15:49
	☽∠☿	23:38
18 Tu	☽△♇	10:08
	☽⚺⚷	10:56
	☽⚹♆	11:57
	☽⚺♄	14:22
	☉∠☽	16:46
	♃⚼⚷	17:02
	☽⚻⚳	17:14
	☽☌♅	18:46
	☽☌♀	20:20
19 W	☽⚺☿	7:28
	☽⚼♇	12:42
	☽∠⚷	13:33
	☽□♃	13:45
	☽∠♄	16:57
	☽⚼⚳	19:53
	☉⚺☽	21:06
	☉∠♅	22:16
20 Th	☽☌♂	0:05
	☽⚻♇	14:26
	☽⚹⚷	15:20
	☽□♆	16:11
	☽⚹♄	18:42
	♂ ♋	20:11
	☽△⚳	21:42
	☽∥♂	21:50
	☽⚺♅	22:47
21 F	☽⋕♇	2:08
	☽⚺♀	2:49
	☿⚹♃	3:01
	☽∥☿	8:55
	☽∥♅	10:29
	☊ R	16:20
	☽⚹♃	17:07
	☽☌☿	19:21
	☉∥☽	23:33
	☽∠♅	23:45
22 Sa	☉☌☽	3:03
	☿∥♅	3:27
	☽⚺♂	4:48
	☽∠♀	4:58
	☉ ♌	6:55
	☽∥♀	9:03
	☽☍♇	16:01
	☽□⚷	17:01
	☽△♆	17:46
	☽∠♃	17:57
	☽□♄	20:23
	☽□⚳	23:37
23 Su	☽⚹♅	0:17
	☿∠♅	2:01
	☽∠♂	6:22
	☽⚹♀	6:41
	☽∥⚷	7:02
	☽∥♄	11:17
	☽⋕⚳	13:18
	☽⚼♆	18:02
	☽⚺♃	18:31
24 M	☿ ♌	1:52
	☽⚺☿	4:18
	☉⚺☽	7:03
	☽⚹♂	7:45
	☽⚻♇	16:27
	☽△⚷	17:35
	☽⚻♆	18:15
	☽△♄	21:03
	☽∥♃	23:36
25 Tu	☽⚹⚳	0:38
	☽□♅	0:55
	☽∥♆	3:55
	☽∠☿	8:38
	☉∠☽	9:00
	☽□♀	9:54
	☉☌☿	13:09
	☿⚺♂	14:10
	☽⚼♇	16:46
	☽⚼⚷	17:59
	☉⚺♂	18:19
	☽☌♃	19:41
	☽⋕♆	20:01
	☽⚼♄	21:32
	☿∠♀	22:15
26 W	☽⋕♃	0:07
	☽∠⚳	1:22
	⚳⚻♅	8:46
	☽□♂	10:57
	☉⚹☽	11:17
	☽⚹☿	13:20
	☽△♇	17:25
	☽⚻⚷	18:43
	☽☍♆	19:19
	☽⚻♄	22:23
27 Th	☽△♅	2:21
	☽⚺⚳	2:31
	☽∥⚳	13:46
	☽⋕♄	14:10
	☽△♀	14:29
	☉∥♀	15:31
	☿☍♇	17:21
	☽⋕⚷	18:30
	☽⚺♃	22:15
28 F	☿□⚷	2:52
	☽⚼♅	3:48
	☿△♆	6:44
	⚳⋕♄	11:34
	☽△♂	16:09
	☊ D	17:26
	☉□☽	17:41
	☽⚼♀	17:48
	☉⋕☽	19:19
	☽□♇	20:16
	☿∠♃	20:38
	☽⋕♀	21:32
	☽☍⚷	21:45
	☽⚻♆	22:19
	☽⋕☿	23:05
29 Sa	☽∠♃	0:27
	☽□☿	1:04
	☽☍♄	1:43
	☉∠♀	5:02
	☿□♄	5:33
	☽⚻♅	5:53
	☽☌⚳	6:35
	☿∥♀	8:54
	☽⋕♅	18:28
	☽⚼♂	19:51
	☽⚻♀	21:56
30 Su	☽⚼♆	0:47
	☽⚹♃	3:22
	☽∥♇	3:48
	☉☍♇	6:05
	☽⋕♂	7:20
	♀⚼♇	9:12
	☿⚹♅	9:59
	☿□⚳	17:31
31 M	☽⚻♂	0:23
	☽⚹♇	1:46
	☉∥☿	2:44
	☉△☽	3:21
	☽⚻⚷	3:29
	☽△♆	3:58
	☉□⚷	5:06
	☽⚻♄	7:46
	♀∠⚷	10:56
	☉△♆	11:45
	☽☍♅	12:09
	☽⚺⚳	13:32
	☽△☿	16:51

August 2028

LONGITUDE

Day	Sid.Time	☉	☽	☽ 12 hour	Mean ☊	True ☊	☿	♀	♂	⚳	♃	♄	⚷	♅	♆	♇
	h m s	° ' "	° ' "	° ' "	° '	° '	° '	° '	° '	° '	° '	° '	° '	° '	° '	° '
1 Tu	20 40 31	9♌16 56	19♐36 36	26♐00 06	22♑14.2	23♑12.7	16♌21.7	24♊00.2	7♋29.6	14♏04.2	25♍34.3	10♉53.5	8♉32.2	13♊15.1	8♈47.3	7♒34.3
2 W	20 44 28	10 14 20	2♑20 03	8♑36 43	22 11.0	23 13.9	18 19.9	24 52.8	8 09.5	14 16.2	25 45.0	10 55.7	8 32.8	13 17.4	8R 46.7	7R 32.9
3 Th	20 48 24	11 11 44	14 50 21	21 01 11	22 07.9	23R 14.7	20 16.6	25 46.0	8 49.4	14 28.3	25 55.8	10 57.8	8 33.3	13 19.7	8 46.0	7 31.5
4 F	20 52 21	12 09 10	27 09 27	3♒15 23	22 04.7	23 14.9	22 11.7	26 39.7	9 29.3	14 40.8	26 06.6	10 59.9	8 33.7	13 21.9	8 45.3	7 30.1
5 Sa	20 56 17	13 06 36	9♒19 12	15 21 06	22 01.5	23 14.1	24 05.3	27 34.0	10 09.1	14 53.4	26 17.6	11 01.8	8 34.1	13 24.0	8 44.5	7 28.7
6 Su	21 00 14	14 04 02	21 21 20	27 20 05	21 58.3	23 12.3	25 57.4	28 28.8	10 48.8	15 06.3	26 28.6	11 03.6	8 34.5	13 26.2	8 43.8	7 27.4
7 M	21 04 11	15 01 30	3♓17 38	9♓14 11	21 55.2	23 09.5	27 47.8	29 24.1	11 28.5	15 19.4	26 39.6	11 05.4	8 34.7	13 28.3	8 43.0	7 26.0
8 Tu	21 08 07	15 58 59	15 10 03	21 05 30	21 52.0	23 06.0	29 36.7	0♋19.9	12 08.1	15 32.7	26 50.8	11 07.0	8 35.0	13 30.3	8 42.1	7 24.6
9 W	21 12 04	16 56 29	27 00 51	2♈56 27	21 48.8	23 02.1	1♍24.0	1 16.3	12 47.6	15 46.2	27 02.0	11 08.5	8 35.1	13 32.3	8 41.3	7 23.2
10 Th	21 16 00	17 54 01	8♈52 42	14 49 59	21 45.6	22 58.3	3 09.8	2 13.0	13 27.2	15 59.9	27 13.3	11 09.9	8 35.3	13 34.3	8 40.4	7 21.9
11 F	21 19 57	18 51 33	20 48 45	26 49 28	21 42.4	22 55.0	4 54.0	3 10.3	14 06.6	16 13.9	27 24.6	11 11.2	8R 35.3	13 36.2	8 39.5	7 20.5
12 Sa	21 23 53	19 49 08	2♉52 38	8♉58 46	21 39.3	22 52.6	6 36.7	4 08.0	14 46.0	16 28.1	27 36.0	11 12.4	8 35.3	13 38.1	8 38.5	7 19.2
13 Su	21 27 50	20 46 43	15 08 23	21 22 02	21 36.1	22D 51.4	8 17.9	5 06.1	15 25.4	16 42.4	27 47.5	11 13.5	8 35.3	13 39.9	8 37.6	7 17.8
14 M	21 31 46	21 44 20	27 40 15	4♊03 32	21 32.9	22 51.4	9 57.5	6 04.7	16 04.7	16 57.0	27 59.0	11 14.5	8 35.2	13 41.7	8 36.6	7 16.5
15 Tu	21 35 43	22 41 59	10♊32 23	17 07 14	21 29.7	22 52.4	11 35.7	7 03.6	16 43.9	17 11.8	28 10.6	11 15.4	8 35.0	13 43.4	8 35.5	7 15.1
16 W	21 39 40	23 39 39	23 48 26	0♋36 16	21 26.6	22 53.9	13 12.4	8 03.0	17 23.1	17 26.7	28 22.1	11 16.2	8 34.8	13 45.2	8 34.5	7 13.8
17 Th	21 43 36	24 37 21	7♋30 55	14 32 22	21 23.4	22 55.3	14 47.6	9 02.7	18 02.3	17 41.9	28 34.0	11 16.9	8 34.5	13 46.8	8 33.4	7 12.5
18 F	21 47 33	25 35 04	21 40 30	28 55 00	21 20.2	22R 56.0	16 21.3	10 02.8	18 41.3	17 57.2	28 45.7	11 17.5	8 34.2	13 48.4	8 32.3	7 11.2
19 Sa	21 51 29	26 32 49	6♌15 22	13♌40 53	21 17.0	22 55.4	17 53.6	11 03.2	19 20.4	18 12.8	28 57.5	11 18.0	8 33.8	13 50.0	8 31.2	7 09.9
20 Su	21 55 26	27 30 35	21 10 42	28 43 46	21 13.9	22 53.2	19 24.3	12 04.0	19 59.3	18 28.5	29 09.4	11 18.4	8 33.4	13 51.5	8 30.1	7 08.6
21 M	21 59 22	28 28 22	6♍18 54	13♍54 51	21 10.7	22 49.4	20 53.6	13 05.1	20 38.2	18 44.4	29 21.3	11 18.6	8 32.9	13 53.0	8 28.9	7 07.3
22 Tu	22 03 19	29 26 11	21 30 20	29 04 04	21 07.5	22 44.5	22 21.3	14 06.5	21 17.1	19 00.5	29 33.3	11R 18.8	8 32.4	13 54.4	8 27.7	7 06.0
23 W	22 07 15	0♍24 01	6♎34 53	14♎01 42	21 04.3	22 39.1	23 47.6	15 08.3	21 55.9	19 16.7	29 45.3	11 18.8	8 31.8	13 55.8	8 26.5	7 04.8
24 Th	22 11 12	1 21 52	21 23 37	28 39 55	21 01.1	22 34.0	25 12.3	16 10.3	22 34.6	19 33.2	29 57.4	11 18.8	8 31.1	13 57.1	8 25.3	7 03.5
25 F	22 15 09	2 19 45	5♏50 05	12♏53 48	20 58.0	22 30.0	26 35.4	17 12.7	23 13.3	19 49.8	0♎09.5	11 18.6	8 30.4	13 58.4	8 24.0	7 02.3
26 Sa	22 19 05	3 17 39	19 50 53	26 41 24	20 54.8	22 27.5	27 57.0	18 15.3	23 51.9	20 06.5	0 21.7	11 18.3	8 29.6	13 59.7	8 22.7	7 01.1
27 Su	22 23 02	4 15 34	3♐25 29	10♐03 25	20 51.6	22D 26.6	29 16.9	19 18.3	24 30.5	20 23.4	0 33.9	11 17.9	8 28.8	14 00.9	8 21.4	6 59.9
28 M	22 26 58	5 13 30	16 35 32	23 02 18	20 48.4	22 27.2	0♎35.2	20 21.5	25 09.0	20 40.5	0 46.1	11 17.5	8 27.9	14 02.0	8 20.1	6 58.7
29 Tu	22 30 55	6 11 28	29 24 08	5♑41 32	20 45.3	22 28.5	1 51.7	21 24.9	25 47.4	20 57.8	0 58.4	11 16.9	8 27.0	14 03.1	8 18.8	6 57.5
30 W	22 34 51	7 09 27	11♑55 00	18 04 59	20 42.1	22R 29.8	3 06.4	22 28.7	26 25.8	21 15.2	1 10.8	11 16.2	8 26.0	14 04.1	8 17.4	6 56.3
31 Th	22 38 48	8♍07 27	24 11 58	0♒16 22	20♑38.9	22♑30.2	4♎19.3	23♋32.7	27♋04.1	21♏32.7	1♎23.1	11♉15.4	8♉25.0	14♊05.1	8♈16.1	6♒55.2

1st of Month

Julian Day # 2461984.5
Obliquity 23°26'31"
SVP 4♓51'21"
GC 27♐14.3
Eris 26♈25.2R

Day	⚴	Day	⚵	Day	⚶
1	6♎16.2	1	7♍08.5	1	14♍47.8
6	8 08.7	6	9 09.1	6	17 09.1
11	10 03.5	11	11 09.7	11	19 31.9
16	12 00.4	16	13 10.3	16	21 56.3
21	13 59.3	21	15 10.8	21	24 22.0
26	15 59.9	26	17 11.1	26	26 49.0
31	18 02.0	31	19 11.1	31	29 17.2

DECLINATION and LATITUDE

Day	☉ Decl	☽ Decl	☽ Lat	☽ 12h Decl	☿ Decl	☿ Lat	♀ Decl	♀ Lat	♂ Decl	♂ Lat	⚳ Decl	⚳ Lat	♃ Decl	♃ Lat	♄ Decl	♄ Lat
1 Tu	17N56	25S57	2S55	25S47	17N37	1N46	19N24	3S55	23N47	0N34	13S08	3N04	2N49	1N09	12N46	2S27
2 W	17 40	25 18	1 53	24 29	16 60	1 45	19 29	3 52	23 46	0 35	13 15	3 01	2 45	1 09	12 46	2 27
3 Th	17 25	23 23	0 46	21 60	16 21	1 43	19 34	3 48	23 44	0 35	13 21	2 57	2 40	1 09	12 47	2 28
4 F	17 09	20 22	0N22	18 32	15 42	1 41	19 39	3 45	23 42	0 36	13 28	2 54	2 36	1 09	12 47	2 28
5 Sa	16 53	16 31	1 28	14 20	15 01	1 38	19 43	3 42	23 39	0 37	13 35	2 50	2 32	1 09	12 47	2 28
6 Su	16 36	12 02	2 29	9 38	14 20	1 34	19 47	3 38	23 37	0 37	13 42	2 47	2 27	1 09	12 48	2 28
7 M	16 20	7 09	3 23	4 36	13 39	1 30	19 51	3 35	23 34	0 38	13 49	2 44	2 23	1 09	12 48	2 29
8 Tu	16 03	2 02	4 08	0N33	12 57	1 26	19 55	3 31	23 31	0 39	13 56	2 40	2 18	1 08	12 48	2 29
9 W	15 45	3N08	4 42	5 40	12 14	1 21	19 58	3 28	23 28	0 39	14 03	2 37	2 14	1 08	12 48	2 29
10 Th	15 28	8 11	5 04	10 37	11 31	1 16	20 01	3 24	23 25	0 40	14 10	2 34	2 09	1 08	12 49	2 29
11 F	15 10	12 57	5 13	15 12	10 48	1 10	20 04	3 20	23 22	0 41	14 17	2 31	2 04	1 08	12 49	2 29
12 Sa	14 52	17 18	5 09	19 14	10 05	1 04	20 06	3 16	23 18	0 41	14 24	2 27	1 60	1 08	12 49	2 30
13 Su	14 34	20 60	4 50	22 32	9 21	0 58	20 08	3 12	23 14	0 42	14 31	2 24	1 55	1 08	12 49	2 30
14 M	14 16	23 49	4 18	24 49	8 37	0 51	20 10	3 08	23 10	0 43	14 38	2 21	1 50	1 08	12 49	2 30
15 Tu	13 57	25 31	3 31	25 51	7 54	0 44	20 11	3 04	23 06	0 43	14 45	2 18	1 46	1 08	12 49	2 30
16 W	13 38	25 50	2 33	25 25	7 10	0 37	20 12	2 60	23 02	0 44	14 52	2 15	1 41	1 08	12 49	2 31
17 Th	13 19	24 37	1 23	23 24	6 27	0 30	20 12	2 56	22 57	0 45	14 60	2 12	1 36	1 08	12 49	2 31
18 F	12 59	21 48	0 07	19 50	5 43	0 22	20 12	2 51	22 53	0 45	15 07	2 09	1 32	1 08	12 49	2 31
19 Sa	12 40	17 32	1S12	14 57	5 00	0 14	20 12	2 47	22 48	0 46	15 14	2 06	1 27	1 07	12 49	2 31
20 Su	12 20	12 06	2 28	9 03	4 17	0 06	20 11	2 43	22 43	0 47	15 21	2 03	1 22	1 07	12 49	2 32
21 M	12 00	5 52	3 34	2 36	3 35	0S02	20 10	2 39	22 38	0 47	15 28	2 00	1 17	1 07	12 49	2 32
22 Tu	11 40	0S42	4 26	3S59	2 52	0 10	20 08	2 34	22 32	0 48	15 35	1 57	1 12	1 07	12 49	2 32
23 W	11 20	7 11	4 58	10 15	2 10	0 19	20 06	2 30	22 27	0 49	15 42	1 55	1 07	1 07	12 48	2 32
24 Th	10 59	13 08	5 10	15 48	1 29	0 28	20 03	2 25	22 21	0 49	15 49	1 52	1 03	1 07	12 48	2 33
25 F	10 39	18 12	5 02	20 19	0 48	0 36	20 00	2 21	22 15	0 50	15 57	1 49	0 58	1 07	12 48	2 33
26 Sa	10 18	22 08	4 36	23 35	0 07	0 45	19 56	2 16	22 09	0 51	16 04	1 46	0 53	1 07	12 47	2 33
27 Su	9 57	24 40	3 55	25 25	0S33	0 54	19 52	2 12	22 03	0 51	16 11	1 44	0 48	1 07	12 47	2 33
28 M	9 36	25 47	3 02	25 48	1 12	1 03	19 48	2 07	21 57	0 52	16 18	1 41	0 43	1 07	12 47	2 34
29 Tu	9 14	25 28	2 02	24 49	1 51	1 12	19 43	2 03	21 51	0 52	16 25	1 38	0 38	1 07	12 46	2 34
30 W	8 53	23 51	0 57	22 37	2 29	1 22	19 37	1 58	21 44	0 53	16 32	1 36	0 33	1 07	12 46	2 34
31 Th	8N31	21S07	0N09	19S24	3S06	1S31	19N31	1S54	21N37	0N54	16S39	1N33	0N28	1N07	12N45	2S34

Day	⚷ Decl	⚷ Lat	♅ Decl	♅ Lat	♆ Decl	♆ Lat	♇ Decl	♇ Lat
1	13N42	0S40	22N21	0S03	2N08	1S28	23S28	5S17
6	13 43	0 41	22 22	0 03	2 06	1 29	23 30	5 17
11	13 42	0 42	22 23	0 03	2 04	1 29	23 32	5 17
16	13 42	0 42	22 24	0 03	2 02	1 29	23 34	5 17
21	13 40	0 43	22 25	0 03	1 60	1 29	23 36	5 18
26	13 39	0 43	22 26	0 02	1 57	1 30	23 38	5 18
31	13N37	0S44	22N27	0S02	1N54	1S30	23S40	5S18

Day	⚴ Decl	⚴ Lat	⚵ Decl	⚵ Lat	⚶ Decl	⚶ Lat	Eris Decl	Eris Lat
1	14N19	18N20	8N24	0S32	10N48	5N13	0N48	10S04
6	13 45	18 30	7 49	0 21	9 51	5 12	0 47	10 04
11	13 11	18 40	7 13	0 10	8 54	5 10	0 47	10 04
16	12 36	18 51	6 37	0 00	7 55	5 08	0 46	10 05
21	12 01	19 01	5 60	0N10	6 56	5 07	0 45	10 05
26	11 25	19 11	5 22	0 20	5 56	5 06	0 45	10 05
31	10N50	19N22	4N45	0N30	4N56	5N04	0N44	10S06

Moon Phenomena

Max/0 Decl
dy hr mn
1 0:43 25S57
8 9:27 0 N
15 17:16 25N53
21 21:26 0 S
28 6:28 25S50

Perigee/Apogee
dy hr m kilometers
8 12:54 a 405892
21 4:14 p 358078

Max/0 Lat
dy hr mn
3 16:20 0 N
11 4:11 5N13
18 2:05 0 S
24 1:54 5S10
30 20:39 0 N

PH dy hr mn
○ 5 8:11 13♒26
◐ 13 11:46 21♉15
● 20 10:45 27♌56
☽ 27 1:37 4♐19

Void of Course Moon

Last Aspect		☽ Ingress
1 11:21	♃ □	♑ 1 19:34
3 21:55	♃ △	♒ 4 5:35
6 15:30	♀ △	♓ 6 17:22
9 0:02	♃ ☍	♈ 9 6:03
10 19:45	☉ △	♉ 11 18:18
14 0:36	♃ △	♊ 14 4:24
16 8:12	♃ □	♋ 16 10:56
18 11:54	♃ ✱	♌ 18 13:47
20 10:45	☉ ☌	♍ 20 14:01
22 12:57	♃ ☌	♎ 22 13:29
24 2:02	♂ □	♏ 24 14:13
26 15:48	☿ ✱	♐ 26 17:52
27 19:16	♅ ☍	♑ 29 1:08
31 5:58	♂ ☍	♒ 31 11:28

DAILY ASPECTARIAN

1 Tu ♂⊼♇ 2:43
☽∠♇ 5:32
☽⚼⚷ 7:22
☽☍♀ 8:51
☉⚼☽ 9:28
☽□♃ 11:21
☽⚼♄ 11:50
☽∠⚳ 18:05

2 W ☽⚼☿ 2:15
☽⊻♇ 9:56
☽☍♂ 11:45
☽△⚷ 11:53
☽□♆ 12:18
♂✱⚷ 14:09
☉∠♃ 15:46
☉⊼☽ 16:23
☽△♄ 16:30
☉□♄ 17:58
☽#♂ 20:26
☽⊼♅ 21:04
♂□♆ 21:58
☽∥♇ 22:57
☽✱⚳ 23:17

3 Th ♀□♃ 5:31
♀∠♄ 5:33
♃⚼♄ 5:41
☽#♅ 9:05
☽⊼☿ 12:30
☊ R 16:22
☽△♃ 21:55
☽⊼♀ 22:57

4 F ☽⚼♅ 2:23
☽#♀ 4:49
☿⚼♆ 19:36
☽☌♇ 20:21
☉#☽ 21:45
☽□⚷ 22:31
☽✱♆ 22:51

5 Sa ☽⊼♂ 1:45
☽□♄ 3:24
☽⚼♃ 3:59
☽⚼♀ 6:59
☉✱♅ 7:35
☽△♅ 8:08
☉☍☽ 8:11
☽#☿ 9:48
☽□⚳ 11:17
☽#⚷ 15:19
☽∥⚳ 15:35
☽#♄ 20:06
☿∠♂ 21:08

6 Su ⚳#⚷ 1:39
☽∠♆ 4:45
☿⊻♃ 7:30
♂✱♄ 9:23
☽⚼♂ 9:28
☽⊼♃ 10:26
☽☍☿ 10:55
☽△♀ 15:30
☿#⚳ 18:57
☿∥⚷ 21:51

7 M ☽⊻♇ 8:20
☉□⚳ 9:41
☽✱⚷ 10:41
☽⊻♆ 10:56
♀ ♋ 15:27
☽✱♄ 15:47
☽△♂ 17:30
☽□♅ 20:38
☽#♃ 22:44
☽#♆ 23:44

8 Tu ☽△⚳ 0:47
♂#♇ 1:21
☉⊼☽ 1:48
☿∥♄ 4:47
☿ ♍ 5:11
♀⚼⚳ 7:10
☽∠♇ 14:39
☽∠⚷ 17:03
☽∥♆ 19:08
☽∥♃ 19:51
☿✱♀ 20:17
☽∠♄ 22:14

9 W ☽☍♃ 0:02
☽⚼⚳ 7:45
☽□♀ 9:22
☽⊼☿ 10:26
☉⚼☽ 10:51
☽✱♇ 20:57
☽⊻⚷ 23:25
☽☌♆ 23:35

10 Th ♂⊻♅ 4:33
☽⊻♄ 4:37
☽✱♅ 9:29
☽□♂ 9:46
☽∥☿ 14:24
☽⊼⚳ 14:38
☉△☽ 19:45
☽⚼☿ 21:52
☽∥♄ 23:15

11 F ♃∥♆ 0:49
☽∥⚷ 3:57
☽#⚳ 7:14
☉∥☽ 11:06
☽⊼♃ 13:23
⚷ R 15:13
☽∠♅ 15:35

12 Sa ☽✱♀ 2:42
☽△☿ 8:32
☽□♇ 8:44
☿⊼♇ 9:54
☽☌⚷ 11:14
☽⊻♆ 11:19
☽☌♄ 16:23
☽∥♀ 17:55
☽⚼♃ 19:22
☽⊻♅ 21:08

13 Su ☽✱♂ 0:35
☉#⚳ 2:34
☽☍⚳ 3:06
☿△⚷ 4:10
☿⊼♆ 4:40
☽∠♀ 10:23
☽∥♅ 10:52
☉□☽ 11:46
☊ D 11:51
☽∠♆ 16:18
☽∥♂ 17:50
☽#♇ 21:23

14 M ☽△♃ 0:36
☽∠♂ 6:46
☽⊻♀ 17:03
☽△♇ 17:57
☿△♄ 18:58
☽⊻⚷ 20:24
☽✱♆ 20:25

15 Tu ☽⊻♄ 1:19
☽□☿ 2:13
♀⊼♇ 4:34
☽☌♅ 5:51
☽⊻♂ 11:53
☽⊼⚳ 12:22
♆⊻⚷ 14:45
☉∥⚷ 19:15
☽⚼♇ 21:11
☉⚼♆ 21:54
☽∠⚷ 23:36
☉✱☽ 23:43

16 W ♂△⚳ 3:37
☽∠♄ 4:23
☽□♃ 8:12
☿□♅ 8:22
♀□♆ 12:28
♀✱⚷ 12:46
☽⚼⚳ 15:30
☽⊼♇ 23:28

17 Th ☽□♆ 1:47
☽✱⚷ 1:49
☽☌♀ 2:50
☉∠☽ 3:53
☽✱♄ 6:28
☽#♇ 10:23
☽⊻♅ 10:44
☽✱☿ 13:58
☽∥♂ 16:01
☽△⚳ 17:39
☽☌♂ 18:46
☽∥♅ 19:45

18 F ☊ R 2:07
☉⊻☽ 6:58
☽∥♀ 9:55
☽∠♅ 11:50
☽✱♃ 11:54
☉∥♄ 12:49
☽∠☿ 17:53

19 Sa ☽☍♇ 1:28
☽△♆ 3:40
☽□⚷ 3:44
♀✱♄ 5:53
☿✱⚳ 6:06
☽□♄ 8:10
☽⊻♀ 8:20
☽#⚳ 10:30
☽✱♅ 12:16
☽∠♃ 12:37
☽∥⚷ 17:27
☽□⚳ 19:36
☽⊻☿ 20:51
☽∥♄ 21:04
☽⊻♂ 22:01
☉∥☽ 22:59

20 Su ☽⚼♆ 3:42
☽∠♀ 10:02
☉☌☽ 10:45
☽⊻♃ 12:51
☿✱♂ 16:37
☽∠♂ 22:53

21 M ☽⊼♇ 1:16
☽⊼♆ 3:25
☽△⚷ 3:32
☽△♄ 7:53
☽∥☿ 9:27
☽✱♀ 11:28
☽□♅ 11:58
☽∥♆ 14:13
☽∥♃ 16:59
♀⊻♅ 19:10
☿⚼♇ 19:51
☽✱⚳ 19:59
☽✱♂ 23:38

22 Tu ☽⚼♇ 0:56
☽☌☿ 1:29
☽#♃ 1:48
☽⚼⚷ 3:13
☉⊻♃ 3:44
☽#♆ 4:40
☽#☿ 7:09
☽⚼♄ 7:37
☽☌♃ 12:57
☉⊻☽ 13:27
☉ ♍ 14:02
☿⚼⚷ 19:36
☽∠⚳ 20:15
♄ R 22:18

23 W ☽△♇ 0:48
☽☍♆ 2:59
☽⊼⚷ 3:08
♂∥♅ 5:18
☿∥♆ 6:52
☽⊼♄ 7:37
☽△♅ 11:52
☽□♀ 14:50
☉∠☽ 15:13
☉#☽ 15:31
☽⊻⚳ 20:56
☽#♄ 22:35

24 Th ☽□♂ 2:02
☽#⚷ 2:17
♃ ♎ 5:09
☽⊻☿ 6:56
☽∥⚳ 12:25
☽⚼♅ 12:30
☽⊻♃ 14:21
☿∥♃ 17:25
☉✱☽ 17:41
☿⚼♄ 19:07

25 F ☽□♇ 2:02
☽⊼♆ 4:20
☽☍⚷ 4:31
☽☍♄ 9:17
☽#♀ 9:55
☽∠☿ 10:49
☽⊼♅ 13:52
☽∠♃ 16:07
☽△♀ 21:01

26 Sa ☽#♂ 0:16
☽☌⚳ 0:28
☽#♅ 2:23
☽⚼♆ 6:10
☽△♂ 7:22
☉∠♀ 11:14
☽∥♇ 12:36
☽✱☿ 15:48
☽✱♃ 18:48

27 Su ☊ D 1:25
☉□☽ 1:37
☽⚼♀ 1:43
☽✱♇ 6:26
☿#♃ 8:12
☽△♆ 8:54
☽⊼⚷ 9:07
☽⚼♂ 11:34
☿ ♎ 13:09
☽⊼♄ 14:16
☽☍♅ 19:16

28 M ☿☌♃ 4:03
☽⊼♀ 7:37
☽⊻⚳ 7:45
♀△⚳ 9:54
☽∠♇ 10:00
☽⚼⚷ 12:47
☽⊼♂ 16:49
☽⚼♄ 18:06

29 Tu ☿#♆ 2:47
☽□♃ 3:02
☽□☿ 5:12
☽∠⚳ 12:49
☉△☽ 14:03
☽⊻♇ 14:25
☽□♆ 17:00
☽△⚷ 17:17
☉⊼♇ 18:41
☽△♄ 22:45

30 W ☽∥♇ 2:04
☽⊼♅ 4:11
☽#♅ 13:25
☽✱⚳ 18:39
☽#♂ 20:01
☊ R 20:40
☉⚼☽ 21:42
☽☍♀ 22:35

31 Th ☉⊼♆ 3:29
☽☍♂ 5:58
☉△⚷ 7:08
☽⚼♅ 9:40
☽#♀ 11:37
☽△♃ 14:27
☽△☿ 22:13

LONGITUDE

September 2028

Day	Sid.Time	☉	☽	☽ 12 hour	Mean ☊	True ☊	☿	♀	♂	⚳	♃	♄	⚷	♅	♆	♇
	h m s	° ' "	° ' "	° ' "	° '	° '	° '	° '	° '	° '	° '	° '	° '	° '	° '	° '
1 F	22 42 44	9♍05 29	6♒18 36	12♒19 02	20♑35.7	22♑29.1	5♎30.3	24♋36.9	27♋42.4	21♏50.4	1♎35.5	11♉14.5	8♉23.9	14♊06.1	8♈14.7	6♒54.1
2 Sa	22 46 41	10 03 32	18 17 59	24 15 47	20 32.5	22R 26.0	6 39.3	25 41.4	28 20.6	22 08.2	1 48.0	11R 13.5	8R 22.8	14 07.0	8R 13.3	6R 52.9
3 Su	22 50 38	11 01 37	0♓12 42	6♓08 58	20 29.4	22 20.6	7 46.2	26 46.2	28 58.7	22 26.2	2 00.5	11 12.4	8 21.6	14 07.8	8 11.8	6 51.8
4 M	22 54 34	11 59 43	12 04 49	18 00 28	20 26.2	22 13.2	8 50.8	27 51.2	29 36.8	22 44.3	2 13.0	11 11.2	8 20.4	14 08.6	8 10.4	6 50.7
5 Tu	22 58 31	12 57 51	23 56 08	29 51 59	20 23.0	22 04.1	9 53.2	28 56.4	0♌14.9	23 02.6	2 25.5	11 09.8	8 19.1	14 09.4	8 08.9	6 49.7
6 W	23 02 27	13 56 01	5♈48 15	11♈45 09	20 19.8	21 54.2	10 53.0	0♌01.9	0 52.8	23 21.0	2 38.1	11 08.4	8 17.7	14 10.1	8 07.5	6 48.6
7 Th	23 06 24	14 54 13	17 42 54	23 41 48	20 16.6	21 44.3	11 50.3	1 07.5	1 30.7	23 39.5	2 50.7	11 06.9	8 16.4	14 10.7	8 06.0	6 47.6
8 F	23 10 20	15 52 26	29 42 08	5♉44 13	20 13.5	21 35.4	12 44.8	2 13.5	2 08.6	23 58.2	3 03.3	11 05.3	8 14.9	14 11.3	8 04.5	6 46.6
9 Sa	23 14 17	16 50 42	11♉48 24	17 55 07	20 10.3	21 28.1	13 36.3	3 19.6	2 46.4	24 17.0	3 16.0	11 03.6	8 13.4	14 11.8	8 02.9	6 45.6
10 Su	23 18 13	17 48 59	24 04 45	0♊17 48	20 07.1	21 23.0	14 24.7	4 25.9	3 24.2	24 35.9	3 28.7	11 01.7	8 11.9	14 12.3	8 01.4	6 44.6
11 M	23 22 10	18 47 19	6♊34 43	12 56 02	20 03.9	21 20.3	15 09.6	5 32.5	4 01.8	24 54.9	3 41.4	10 59.8	8 10.3	14 12.8	7 59.9	6 43.6
12 Tu	23 26 07	19 45 40	19 22 13	25 53 48	20 00.8	21D 19.4	15 51.0	6 39.2	4 39.5	25 14.1	3 54.1	10 57.8	8 08.7	14 13.2	7 58.3	6 42.7
13 W	23 30 03	20 44 04	2♋31 13	9♋14 53	19 57.6	21 19.9	16 28.5	7 46.2	5 17.0	25 33.4	4 06.9	10 55.7	8 07.0	14 13.5	7 56.8	6 41.8
14 Th	23 34 00	21 42 30	16 05 08	23 02 13	19 54.4	21R 20.5	17 01.4	8 53.3	5 54.5	25 52.8	4 19.7	10 53.5	8 05.3	14 13.8	7 55.2	6 40.9
15 F	23 37 56	22 40 59	0♌06 12	7♌17 01	19 51.2	21 20.3	17 30.5	10 00.6	6 32.0	26 12.4	4 32.5	10 51.2	8 03.5	14 14.0	7 53.6	6 40.0
16 Sa	23 41 53	23 39 29	14 34 25	21 57 55	19 48.1	21 18.3	17 54.5	11 08.2	7 09.4	26 32.0	4 45.4	10 48.7	8 01.7	14 14.2	7 52.0	6 39.1
17 Su	23 45 49	24 38 01	29 26 49	7♍00 13	19 44.9	21 13.8	18 13.4	12 15.9	7 46.7	26 51.8	4 58.2	10 46.2	7 59.9	14 14.4	7 50.4	6 38.3
18 M	23 49 46	25 36 35	14♍36 59	22 15 52	19 41.7	21 06.9	18 26.7	13 23.7	8 24.0	27 11.7	5 11.1	10 43.6	7 58.0	14 14.4	7 48.8	6 37.5
19 Tu	23 53 42	26 35 12	29 55 26	7♎34 15	19 38.5	20 57.9	18R 34.1	14 31.8	9 01.2	27 31.7	5 24.0	10 41.0	7 56.0	14R 14.5	7 47.1	6 36.7
20 W	23 57 39	27 33 50	15♎10 54	22 44 01	19 35.3	20 48.0	18 35.3	15 40.0	9 38.3	27 51.8	5 36.9	10 38.2	7 54.0	14 14.4	7 45.5	6 35.9
21 Th	0 01 36	28 32 30	0♏12 24	7♏35 04	19 32.2	20 38.4	18 30.0	16 48.3	10 15.3	28 12.0	5 49.8	10 35.3	7 52.0	14 14.4	7 43.9	6 35.1
22 F	0 05 32	29 31 12	14 51 12	22 00 16	19 29.0	20 30.2	18 17.8	17 56.9	10 52.3	28 32.3	6 02.7	10 32.4	7 49.9	14 14.2	7 42.2	6 34.4
23 Sa	0 09 29	0♎29 55	29 01 56	5♐56 07	19 25.8	20 24.2	17 58.5	19 05.6	11 29.3	28 52.7	6 15.7	10 29.3	7 47.8	14 14.1	7 40.6	6 33.7
24 Su	0 13 25	1 28 41	12♐42 53	19 22 30	19 22.6	20 20.7	17 31.9	20 14.4	12 06.1	29 13.2	6 28.6	10 26.2	7 45.7	14 13.8	7 38.9	6 33.0
25 M	0 17 22	2 27 28	25 55 20	2♑21 52	19 19.5	20D 19.3	16 58.1	21 23.4	12 42.9	29 33.8	6 41.6	10 23.0	7 43.5	14 13.5	7 37.3	6 32.4
26 Tu	0 21 18	3 26 17	8♑42 40	14 58 20	19 16.3	20R 19.2	16 17.1	22 32.5	13 19.6	29 54.6	6 54.6	10 19.7	7 41.3	14 13.2	7 35.6	6 31.8
27 W	0 25 15	4 25 07	21 09 27	27 16 41	19 13.1	20 19.4	15 29.3	23 41.8	13 56.3	0♐15.4	7 07.5	10 16.3	7 39.0	14 12.8	7 33.9	6 31.2
28 Th	0 29 11	5 23 59	3♒20 37	9♒21 51	19 09.9	20 18.7	14 35.3	24 51.2	14 32.9	0 36.3	7 20.5	10 12.9	7 36.7	14 12.4	7 32.3	6 30.6
29 F	0 33 08	6 22 53	15 20 56	21 18 24	19 06.7	20 16.1	13 35.7	26 00.8	15 09.4	0 57.3	7 33.5	10 09.4	7 34.4	14 11.9	7 30.6	6 30.0
30 Sa	0 37 05	7♎21 49	27 14 42	3♓10 18	19♑03.6	20♑11.0	12♎31.8	27♌10.5	15♌45.8	1♐18.4	7♎46.5	10♉05.8	7♉32.0	14♊11.4	7♈28.9	6♒29.5

1st of Month

Julian Day # 2462015.5
Obliquity 23°26'32"
SVP 4♓51'37"
GC 27♐14.4
Eris 26♈17.4R

Day	⚴
1	18♎26.6
6	20 30.5
11	22 35.7
16	24 42.1
21	26 49.6
26	28 58.0

Day	⚵
1	19♍35.1
6	21 34.6
11	23 33.8
16	25 32.5
21	27 30.6
26	29 28.0

Day	⚶
1	29♍46.9
6	2♎16.4
11	4 47.0
16	7 18.5
21	9 51.0
26	12 24.3

DECLINATION and LATITUDE

Day	☉ Decl	☽ Decl	☽ Lat	☽12h Decl	☿ Decl	☿ Lat	♀ Decl	♀ Lat	♂ Decl	♂ Lat	⚳ Decl	⚳ Lat	♃ Decl	♃ Lat	♄ Decl	♄ Lat
1 F	8N10	17S30	1N14	15S25	3S43	1S40	19N25	1S49	21N30	0N54	16S46	1N30	0N23	1N07	12N45	2S35
2 Sa	7 48	13 12	2 15	10 52	4 19	1 49	19 17	1 44	21 23	0 55	16 53	1 28	0 18	1 07	12 44	2 35
3 Su	7 26	8 27	3 09	5 57	4 53	1 58	19 10	1 40	21 16	0 56	17 00	1 25	0 13	1 07	12 44	2 35
4 M	7 04	3 25	3 54	0 51	5 27	2 07	19 02	1 35	21 09	0 56	17 07	1 23	0 08	1 06	12 43	2 35
5 Tu	6 41	1N43	4 30	4N17	5 60	2 16	18 53	1 31	21 01	0 57	17 14	1 20	0 03	1 06	12 43	2 36
6 W	6 19	6 48	4 54	9 15	6 32	2 25	18 44	1 26	20 54	0 58	17 21	1 18	0S02	1 06	12 42	2 36
7 Th	5 57	11 38	5 05	13 55	7 02	2 33	18 35	1 22	20 46	0 58	17 28	1 15	0 07	1 06	12 41	2 36
8 F	5 34	16 04	5 02	18 05	7 31	2 42	18 25	1 17	20 38	0 59	17 35	1 13	0 12	1 06	12 41	2 36
9 Sa	5 12	19 55	4 47	21 33	7 59	2 50	18 14	1 13	20 30	0 60	17 42	1 10	0 17	1 06	12 40	2 36
10 Su	4 49	22 57	4 17	24 05	8 25	2 58	18 03	1 08	20 22	1 00	17 49	1 08	0 22	1 06	12 39	2 37
11 M	4 26	24 57	3 36	25 30	8 50	3 06	17 51	1 04	20 14	1 01	17 56	1 06	0 27	1 06	12 38	2 37
12 Tu	4 03	25 42	2 42	25 34	9 13	3 14	17 39	0 59	20 06	1 02	18 03	1 03	0 32	1 06	12 37	2 37
13 W	3 40	25 04	1 39	24 11	9 34	3 21	17 27	0 55	19 57	1 02	18 10	1 01	0 37	1 06	12 37	2 38
14 Th	3 17	22 56	0 28	21 19	9 53	3 27	17 13	0 50	19 49	1 03	18 17	0 59	0 43	1 06	12 36	2 38
15 F	2 54	19 22	0S47	17 06	10 10	3 34	16 60	0 46	19 40	1 04	18 23	0 56	0 48	1 06	12 35	2 38
16 Sa	2 31	14 32	2 01	11 44	10 24	3 39	16 46	0 42	19 31	1 04	18 30	0 54	0 53	1 06	12 34	2 38
17 Su	2 08	8 43	3 08	5 34	10 36	3 44	16 31	0 37	19 22	1 05	18 37	0 52	0 58	1 06	12 33	2 38
18 M	1 45	2 18	4 04	1S00	10 45	3 48	16 16	0 33	19 13	1 06	18 44	0 49	1 03	1 06	12 32	2 38
19 Tu	1 21	4S18	4 43	7 31	10 51	3 52	16 01	0 29	19 04	1 06	18 50	0 47	1 08	1 06	12 31	2 39
20 W	0 58	10 36	5 01	13 31	10 54	3 54	15 45	0 24	18 55	1 07	18 57	0 45	1 13	1 06	12 30	2 39
21 Th	0 35	16 12	4 58	18 36	10 53	3 56	15 28	0 20	18 45	1 08	19 04	0 43	1 18	1 06	12 29	2 39
22 F	0 11	20 41	4 36	22 25	10 48	3 56	15 12	0 16	18 36	1 08	19 10	0 41	1 23	1 06	12 28	2 39
23 Sa	0S12	23 48	3 57	24 47	10 40	3 54	14 54	0 12	18 26	1 09	19 17	0 39	1 29	1 06	12 27	2 39
24 Su	0 35	25 23	3 06	25 37	10 27	3 52	14 37	0 08	18 17	1 10	19 23	0 36	1 34	1 06	12 25	2 39
25 M	0 59	25 28	2 06	24 59	10 10	3 48	14 18	0 04	18 07	1 10	19 30	0 34	1 39	1 06	12 24	2 40
26 Tu	1 22	24 10	1 01	23 04	9 49	3 42	13 60	0 00	17 57	1 11	19 36	0 32	1 44	1 06	12 23	2 40
27 W	1 45	21 42	0N04	20 06	9 23	3 34	13 41	0N04	17 47	1 12	19 43	0 30	1 49	1 06	12 22	2 40
28 Th	2 09	18 18	1 09	16 19	8 53	3 24	13 21	0 08	17 37	1 12	19 49	0 28	1 54	1 06	12 21	2 40
29 F	2 32	14 11	2 08	11 56	8 19	3 12	13 02	0 11	17 27	1 13	19 55	0 26	1 59	1 06	12 20	2 40
30 Sa	2S55	9S34	3N02	7S08	7S42	2S59	12N41	0N15	17N17	1N14	20S02	0N24	2S04	1N06	12N18	2S40

Day	⚷ Decl	⚷ Lat	♅ Decl	♅ Lat	♆ Decl	♆ Lat	♇ Decl	♇ Lat
1	13N36	0S44	22N27	0S02	1N54	1S30	23S40	5S18
6	13 34	0 45	22 27	0 02	1 51	1 30	23 41	5 18
11	13 31	0 45	22 28	0 02	1 48	1 30	23 42	5 18
16	13 28	0 46	22 28	0 02	1 44	1 30	23 43	5 17
21	13 24	0 46	22 28	0 02	1 41	1 30	23 44	5 17
26	13 20	0 47	22 28	0 02	1 38	1 30	23 45	5 17

Day	⚴ Decl	⚴ Lat	⚵ Decl	⚵ Lat	⚶ Decl	⚶ Lat	Eris Decl	Eris Lat
1	10N43	19N24	4N37	0N32	4N44	5N04	0N43	10S06
6	10 08	19 34	3 59	0 42	3 43	5 02	0 43	10 06
11	9 34	19 45	3 21	0 52	2 42	5 01	0 42	10 06
16	9 00	19 56	2 42	1 01	1 42	4 60	0 41	10 06
21	8 27	20 07	2 04	1 11	0 41	4 59	0 40	10 06
26	7 55	20 19	1 27	1 20	0S20	4 57	0 39	10 06

Moon Phenomena

Max/0 Decl
dy hr mn
4 15:57 0 N
12 1:19 25N42
18 8:22 0 S
24 13:14 25S37

Perigee/Apogee
dy hr m kilometers
4 20:04 a 406398
18 14:21 p 357051

PH dy hr mn
○ 3 23:49 11♓59
☾ 12 0:47 19♊48
● 18 18:25 26♍22
☽ 25 13:11 3♑00

Max/0 Lat
dy hr mn
7 7:58 5N05
14 9:05 0 S
20 8:49 5S03
26 22:22 0 N

Void of Course Moon

Last Aspect	☽ Ingress
1 15:36 ♅ △	♓ 2 23:34
5 11:09 ♀ △	♈ 5 12:16
6 16:53 ♅ ⚹	♉ 8 0:36
9 10:45 ☉ △	♊ 10 11:26
12 0:47 ☉ □	♋ 12 19:27
14 10:27 ☉ ⚹	♌ 14 23:50
16 5:34 ☿ ⚹	♍ 17 0:53
18 18:25 ☉ ☌	♎ 19 0:07
20 5:23 ☿ ☌	♏ 20 23:40
22 5:37 ♀ □	♐ 23 1:40
24 14:52 ♀ △	♑ 25 7:34
26 13:41 ☿ □	♒ 27 17:22
29 23:51 ♀ ☍	♓ 30 5:35

DAILY ASPECTARIAN

1 F ☽☌♇ 1:11 · ☽⚹♆ 3:51 · ☽□⚷ 4:10 · ☽∥⚳ 4:12 · ☉⊼☽ 6:02 · ☽□♄ 9:50 · ⚶ ♎ 10:32 · ☽△♅ 15:36 · ☽⚼♃ 20:56 · ☽⋕⚷ 21:56

2 Sa ☽⋕♄ 2:27 · ☿△♇ 4:45 · ☽⚼☿ 7:27 · ☽□⚳ 7:55 · ☽∠♆ 9:53 · ☿∠⚳ 14:05 · ☽⊼♀ 16:22 · ☽⊼♂ 21:22

3 Su ☽⊼♃ 3:42 · ☉△♄ 4:21 · ☉⋕☽ 5:20 · ♂∠♅ 5:51 · ☿☍♆ 9:14 · ☿⊼⚷ 12:49 · ☽⊻♇ 13:25 · ☽∥☿ 15:21 · ☽⊻♆ 16:07 · ☽⚹⚷ 16:27 · ☽⊼☿ 16:49 · ☽⚹♄ 22:12 · ☉☍☽ 23:49

4 M ☽⚼♀ 1:43 · ☽□♅ 4:11 · ☽⚼♂ 5:25 · ☽⋕♆ 7:16 · ♂ ♌ 14:37 · ☽⋕♃ 15:35 · ☽∥♃ 16:19 · ☽∠♇ 19:44 · ☽△⚳ 22:09 · ☽∠⚷ 22:45

5 Tu ☽∥♆ 0:37 · ☽∠♄ 4:30 · ♀∠♅ 4:49 · ⚳⚼♆ 7:40 · ☽△♀ 11:09 · ☽△♂ 13:29 · ☽☍♃ 17:29 · ☉⋕☿ 18:27 · ☉∥☽ 21:52 · ☽⋕☿ 22:33 · ♀ ♌ 23:19

6 W ☽⚹♇ 2:02 · ☽☌♆ 4:40 · ☽⊻⚷ 5:01 · ☽⚼⚳ 5:17 · ☉□♅ 5:52 · ☿⊼♄ 6:11 · ☽⊻♄ 10:45 · ☽☍☿ 11:09 · ☽⚹♅ 16:53 · ☉⊼☽ 17:51

7 Th ☽∥♄ 5:26 · ☽∥⚷ 10:01 · ☽⊼⚳ 12:14 · ♀☌♂ 19:52 · ☽∠♅ 22:58

8 F ☉⚼☽ 2:32 · ☽□♂ 5:08 · ☽□♀ 5:32 · ☽⊼♃ 6:48 · ☽⋕⚳ 9:13 · ☽∥♀ 13:26 · ☽□♇ 14:02 · ☽⊻♆ 16:36 · ☽☌⚷ 16:56 · ♀⚹♃ 22:23 · ☽☌♄ 22:32

9 Sa ☽⊼☿ 3:48 · ☽∥♂ 4:01 · ☽⊻♅ 4:42 · ☉△☽ 10:45 · ☽⚼♃ 12:54 · ☿△♅ 17:40 · ☽∥♅ 19:37 · ☽∠♆ 21:57

10 Su ☽☍⚳ 1:02 · ♂⚹♃ 4:21 · ☽⋕♇ 7:39 · ☽⚼☿ 10:58 · ♀⋕⚳ 17:53 · ☽△♃ 18:24 · ☽⚹♂ 18:54 · ☽⚹♀ 21:50

11 M ☽△♇ 0:17 · ☽⚹♆ 2:41 · ☽⊻⚷ 3:01 · ☽⊻♄ 8:20 · ☽☌♅ 14:24 · ☉∠♂ 16:50 · ☽△☿ 17:06

12 Tu ☽∠♂ 0:34 · ☉□☽ 0:47 · ☊ D 0:54 · ♀☍♇ 1:14 · ☽⚼♇ 4:19 · ☽∠♀ 4:37 · ☽∠⚷ 6:57 · ☽⊼⚳ 11:04 · ☽∠♄ 12:05

13 W ☽□♃ 2:54 · ♀△♆ 3:42 · ☽⊻♂ 5:12 · ♀□⚷ 7:17 · ☽⊼♇ 7:28 · ☽□♆ 9:40 · ☽⚹⚷ 9:58 · ☽⊻♀ 10:13 · ☽⚼⚳ 14:40 · ☽⚹♄ 14:56 · ☽⋕♇ 16:52 · ☽⊻♅ 20:46 · ☉⚼♇ 23:20

14 Th ☽□☿ 1:42 · ☽∥♅ 3:45 · ☊ R 9:06 · ☉⚹☽ 10:27 · ☽△⚳ 17:15 · ☽∥♂ 22:13 · ☽∠♅ 22:32

15 F ♂☍♇ 5:00 · ☽⋕⚳ 5:13 · ☽⚹♃ 7:33 · ☉⚼⚷ 8:59 · ☽☍♇ 10:58 · ☽☌♂ 11:14 · ☽△♆ 12:59 · ☽∥♀ 13:05 · ☽□⚷ 13:15 · ☉∠☽ 13:34 · ♀□♄ 17:21 · ☽□♄ 17:51 · ☽☌♀ 17:53 · ☽⚹♅ 23:27

16 Sa ☽∥⚷ 4:43 · ☽⚹☿ 5:34 · ☽∥♄ 8:33 · ☽∠♃ 8:33 · ☽⚼♆ 13:26 · ☉⊻☽ 15:45 · ☽⋕☿ 16:49 · ☽□⚳ 19:47

17 Su ♂△♆ 2:16 · ☽∠☿ 6:07 · ♂□⚷ 8:03 · ☽⊻♃ 8:54 · ☽⊼♇ 11:25 · ☽⊼♆ 13:18 · ☽△⚷ 13:32 · ☽⊻♂ 13:47 · ☽△♄ 17:54 · ☽⊻♀ 21:56 · ☽□♅ 23:25

18 M ☉∥♆ 1:40 · ☽∥♆ 2:08 · ☉∥☽ 2:09 · ☉⚼♄ 2:46 · ☽⋕♃ 4:30 · ☽⊻☿ 6:04 · ☽⚼♇ 10:59 · ☽∥♃ 12:20 · ☽⚼⚷ 13:04 · ☉⋕☽ 13:53 · ☽∠♂ 14:22 · ☽⋕♆ 14:35 · ☽⚼♄ 17:22 · ♀⚹♅ 17:54 · ☉☌☽ 18:25 · ☽⚹⚳ 20:10 · ☽∠♀ 23:20

19 Tu ♅ R 0:03 · ☽☌♃ 8:43 · ☽△♇ 10:29 · ☉⋕♃ 11:15 · ☽☍♆ 12:19 · ☽⊼⚷ 12:33 · ☽⚹♂ 14:53 · ☿ R 16:35 · ☽⊼♄ 16:51 · ☽∠⚳ 20:15 · ♂⋕⚳ 20:31 · ☽△♅ 22:31

20 W ☽⚹♀ 0:50 · ☽∥☿ 1:09 · ☽☌☿ 5:23 · ☽⋕♄ 7:41 · ☉⚹⚳ 11:11 · ☽⋕⚷ 11:32 · ☽⊻⚳ 20:41 · ☽⋕♀ 20:50 · ☉⊻☽ 21:08 · ☽⚼♅ 22:26

21 Th ☽⊻♃ 9:16 · ☽□♇ 10:22 · ♂□♄ 12:00 · ☽⊼♆ 12:13 · ☽⋕♂ 12:25 · ☽☍⚷ 12:26 · ☽∥⚳ 14:54 · ☽☍♄ 16:53 · ☽□♂ 17:07 · ☽⊼♅ 22:59 · ☉∠☽ 23:24

22 F ☽□♀ 5:37 · ☽⊻☿ 5:39 · ☿⚹♀ 5:53 · ☽∠♃ 10:32 · ☉ ♎ 11:46 · ☽⋕♅ 12:22 · ☽⚼♆ 13:10 · ☽∥♇ 23:29 · ☽☌⚳ 23:44

23 Sa ☉⚹☽ 2:43 · ☽∠☿ 6:38 · ☽⚹♃ 12:47 · ☽⚹♇ 13:05 · ☽△♆ 15:02 · ☽⊼⚷ 15:14 · ☽⊼♄ 19:58 · ☽△♂ 22:51

24 Su ☽☍♅ 2:43 · ♃△♇ 7:48 · ☽⚹☿ 8:20 · ☽△♀ 14:52 · ☽∠♇ 15:57 · ☽⚼⚷ 18:08 · ♃⋕♆ 22:29 · ☽⚼♄ 23:01

25 M ☽⚼♂ 3:29 · ☽⊻⚳ 6:57 · ♀∠♃ 7:47 · ☊ D 13:02 · ☉□☽ 13:11 · ☽⊻♇ 19:52 · ☽□♃ 20:31 · ☽⚼♀ 21:33 · ☽□♆ 21:53 · ☽△⚷ 22:04

26 Tu ♀⚼♆ 1:02 · ☽△♄ 3:04 · ☽∥♇ 4:56 · ⚳ ♐ 6:17 · ☽⊼♂ 9:17 · ☽⊼♅ 10:33 · ☽∠⚳ 12:13 · ☽□☿ 13:41 · ☉⋕♆ 15:48 · ☽⋕♅ 17:32 · ☊ R 22:22

27 W ☿∠⚳ 4:37 · ☉∥♃ 4:55 · ☽⊼♀ 5:29 · ⚵ ♎ 8:51 · ♂⚹♅ 10:44 · ☽∥⚳ 14:15 · ☽⚼♅ 15:49 · ☽⚹⚳ 18:24

28 Th ☿⚹♂ 0:37 · ♀∥⚷ 3:54 · ☽⋕♂ 4:24 · ☉△☽ 4:27 · ☽☌♇ 6:18 · ☽△♃ 8:06 · ☽⚹♆ 8:20 · ☽□⚷ 8:28 · ☿△♅ 9:32 · ♀ ♏ 9:35 · ☽□♄ 13:38 · ♃☍♆ 19:17 · ☽△☿ 20:45 · ☽△♅ 21:41 · ☽☍♂ 23:36

29 F ♃⊼⚷ 1:24 · ☉△♇ 2:53 · ☽⋕⚷ 4:51 · ☽⋕♀ 6:45 · ☽⋕♄ 9:59 · ☉⚼☽ 13:15 · ☽∠♆ 14:24 · ☽⚼♃ 14:48 · ☽☍♀ 23:51

30 Sa ☽⚼☿ 0:32 · ☉☍♆ 2:49 · ☿∠♀ 3:46 · ☉⊼⚷ 3:59 · ☽□⚳ 8:28 · ☽∥☿ 10:44 · ☉☌♃ 12:52 · ☽⊻♇ 18:43 · ☽⊻♆ 20:41 · ☽⚹⚷ 20:46 · ☽⊼♃ 21:44 · ☉⊼☽ 22:21

October 2028

LONGITUDE

Day	Sid.Time	☉	☽	☽ 12 hour	Mean ☊	True ☊	☿	♀	♂	⚳	♃	♄	⚷	♅	♆	♇
	h m s	° ' "	° ' "	° ' "	° '	° '	° '	° '	° '	° '	° '	° '	° '	° '	° '	° '
1 Su	0 41 01	8♎20 46	9♓05 32	15♓00 46	19♑00.4	20♑03.0	11♎24.8	28♌20.4	16♌22.2	1♐39.5	7♎59.4	10♉02.1	7♉29.6	14♊10.8	7♈27.3	6♒29.0
2 M	0 44 58	9 19 45	20 56 16	26 52 18	18 57.2	19R 52.2	10R 16.3	29 30.3	16 58.5	2 00.8	8 12.4	9R 58.3	7R 27.2	14R 10.1	7R 25.6	6R 28.5
3 Tu	0 48 54	10 18 47	2♈49 04	8♈46 44	18 54.0	19 39.3	9 08.1	0♍40.5	17 34.7	2 22.1	8 25.4	9 54.5	7 24.7	14 09.5	7 23.9	6 28.0
4 W	0 52 51	11 17 50	14 45 29	20 45 27	18 50.8	19 25.2	8 01.8	1 50.7	18 10.9	2 43.5	8 38.4	9 50.7	7 22.2	14 08.7	7 22.3	6 27.6
5 Th	0 56 47	12 16 55	26 46 47	2♉49 36	18 47.7	19 11.1	6 59.5	3 01.1	18 47.0	3 05.0	8 51.4	9 46.7	7 19.7	14 07.9	7 20.6	6 27.2
6 F	1 00 44	13 16 03	8♉54 04	15 00 21	18 44.5	18 58.1	6 02.8	4 11.6	19 23.0	3 26.6	9 04.3	9 42.7	7 17.2	14 07.1	7 18.9	6 26.8
7 Sa	1 04 40	14 15 13	21 08 38	27 19 11	18 41.3	18 47.3	5 13.3	5 22.2	19 59.0	3 48.3	9 17.3	9 38.6	7 14.6	14 06.2	7 17.3	6 26.5
8 Su	1 08 37	15 14 24	3♊32 13	9♊48 05	18 38.1	18 39.2	4 32.4	6 33.0	20 34.9	4 10.0	9 30.3	9 34.5	7 12.0	14 05.3	7 15.6	6 26.2
9 M	1 12 33	16 13 39	16 07 05	22 29 36	18 35.0	18 34.1	4 01.0	7 43.9	21 10.7	4 31.9	9 43.2	9 30.3	7 09.4	14 04.3	7 14.0	6 25.9
10 Tu	1 16 30	17 12 55	28 56 02	5♋26 48	18 31.8	18 31.6	3 40.1	8 54.9	21 46.4	4 53.8	9 56.2	9 26.1	7 06.7	14 03.3	7 12.3	6 25.6
11 W	1 20 27	18 12 14	12♋02 18	18 42 56	18 28.6	18 30.9	3D 29.9	10 06.0	22 22.1	5 15.7	10 09.1	9 21.8	7 04.1	14 02.2	7 10.7	6 25.4
12 Th	1 24 23	19 11 35	25 29 04	2♌21 01	18 25.4	18 30.8	3 30.6	11 17.3	22 57.7	5 37.8	10 22.0	9 17.4	7 01.4	14 01.1	7 09.1	6 25.2
13 F	1 28 20	20 10 59	9♌18 59	16 23 03	18 22.3	18 30.1	3 42.0	12 28.6	23 33.2	5 59.9	10 34.9	9 13.0	6 58.7	13 59.9	7 07.5	6 25.0
14 Sa	1 32 16	21 10 24	23 33 11	0♍49 09	18 19.1	18 27.6	4 03.8	13 40.1	24 08.6	6 22.1	10 47.8	9 08.6	6 55.9	13 58.7	7 05.9	6 24.8
15 Su	1 36 13	22 09 52	8♍10 32	15 36 41	18 15.9	18 22.4	4 35.5	14 51.7	24 44.0	6 44.4	11 00.7	9 04.1	6 53.2	13 57.5	7 04.3	6 24.7
16 M	1 40 09	23 09 23	23 06 47	0♎39 48	18 12.7	18 14.5	5 16.3	16 03.3	25 19.2	7 06.7	11 13.6	8 59.6	6 50.4	13 56.2	7 02.7	6 24.6
17 Tu	1 44 06	24 08 55	8♎14 31	15 49 41	18 09.5	18 04.3	6 05.6	17 15.1	25 54.4	7 29.1	11 26.4	8 55.0	6 47.6	13 54.8	7 01.1	6 24.5
18 W	1 48 02	25 08 30	23 23 53	0♏55 49	18 06.4	17 52.9	7 02.5	18 27.0	26 29.5	7 51.5	11 39.3	8 50.4	6 44.8	13 53.4	6 59.5	6 24.4
19 Th	1 51 59	26 08 06	8♏24 10	15 47 50	18 03.2	17 41.6	8 06.3	19 39.0	27 04.5	8 14.1	11 52.1	8 45.8	6 42.0	13 52.0	6 57.9	6D 24.4
20 F	1 55 56	27 07 45	23 05 49	0♐17 21	18 00.0	17 31.7	9 16.0	20 51.0	27 39.5	8 36.7	12 04.8	8 41.1	6 39.2	13 50.5	6 56.4	6 24.4
21 Sa	1 59 52	28 07 25	7♐21 56	14 19 13	17 56.8	17 24.1	10 31.0	22 03.2	28 14.3	8 59.3	12 17.6	8 36.4	6 36.3	13 49.0	6 54.9	6 24.5
22 Su	2 03 49	29 07 08	21 09 07	27 51 42	17 53.7	17 19.3	11 50.6	23 15.4	28 49.1	9 22.0	12 30.3	8 31.7	6 33.5	13 47.4	6 53.3	6 24.5
23 M	2 07 45	0♏06 52	4♑27 14	10♑56 05	17 50.5	17D 17.0	13 14.0	24 27.8	29 23.7	9 44.8	12 43.0	8 26.9	6 30.6	13 45.8	6 51.8	6 24.6
24 Tu	2 11 42	1 06 38	17 18 45	23 35 48	17 47.3	17 16.5	14 40.7	25 40.2	29 58.3	10 07.6	12 55.7	8 22.1	6 27.7	13 44.2	6 50.3	6 24.8
25 W	2 15 38	2 06 25	29 47 50	5♒55 32	17 44.1	17R 16.6	16 10.2	26 52.7	0♍32.8	10 30.5	13 08.4	8 17.4	6 24.9	13 42.5	6 48.9	6 24.9
26 Th	2 19 35	3 06 14	11♒59 34	18 00 34	17 40.9	17 16.3	17 41.9	28 05.3	1 07.1	10 53.5	13 21.0	8 12.6	6 22.0	13 40.8	6 47.4	6 25.1
27 F	2 23 31	4 06 05	23 59 13	29 56 07	17 37.8	17 14.5	19 15.4	29 17.9	1 41.4	11 16.5	13 33.6	8 07.7	6 19.1	13 39.0	6 46.0	6 25.3
28 Sa	2 27 28	5 05 58	5♓51 53	11♓47 03	17 34.6	17 10.3	20 50.4	0♎30.7	2 15.6	11 39.5	13 46.1	8 02.9	6 16.2	13 37.2	6 44.5	6 25.5
29 Su	2 31 25	6 05 52	17 42 07	23 37 34	17 31.4	17 03.4	22 26.5	1 43.5	2 49.7	12 02.6	13 58.6	7 58.1	6 13.3	13 35.4	6 43.1	6 25.8
30 M	2 35 21	7 05 47	29 33 47	5♈31 07	17 28.2	16 53.9	24 03.6	2 56.4	3 23.7	12 25.7	14 11.1	7 53.2	6 10.5	13 33.5	6 41.7	6 26.1
31 Tu	2 39 18	8♏05 45	11♈29 52	17 30 17	17♑25.1	16♑42.4	25♎41.3	4♎09.4	3♍57.6	12♐48.9	14♎23.6	7♉48.4	6♉07.6	13♊31.6	6♈40.4	6♒26.4

1st of Month

Julian Day # 2462045.5
Obliquity 23°26'32"
SVP 4♓51'34"
GC 27♐14.5
Eris 26♈02.7R

Day	⚴	Day	⚵	Day	⚶
1	1♏07.3	1	1♎24.6	1	14♎58.4
6	3 17.4	6	3 20.3	6	17 33.1
11	5 28.1	11	5 15.2	11	20 08.5
16	7 39.4	16	7 08.9	16	22 44.6
21	9 51.2	21	9 01.5	21	25 21.1
26	12 03.3	26	10 52.8	26	27 58.0
31	14 15.6	31	12 42.6	31	0♏35.3

DECLINATION and LATITUDE

Day	☉ Decl	☽ Decl	☽ Lat	☽ 12h Decl	☿ Decl	☿ Lat	♀ Decl	♀ Lat	♂ Decl	♂ Lat	⚳ Decl	⚳ Lat	♃ Decl	♃ Lat	♄ Decl	♄ Lat
1 Su	3S19	4S39	3N48	2S07	7S01	2S43	12N21	0N19	17N07	1N14	20S08	0N22	2S10	1N06	12N17	2S41
2 M	3 42	0N26	4 23	2N59	6 19	2 27	11 60	0 22	16 56	1 15	20 14	0 20	2 15	1 06	12 16	2 41
3 Tu	4 05	5 31	4 47	7 59	5 35	2 08	11 38	0 26	16 46	1 16	20 20	0 18	2 20	1 06	12 14	2 41
4 W	4 28	10 24	4 59	12 43	4 51	1 49	11 17	0 29	16 35	1 16	20 27	0 16	2 25	1 06	12 13	2 41
5 Th	4 51	14 56	4 57	17 00	4 08	1 29	10 54	0 33	16 25	1 17	20 33	0 14	2 30	1 06	12 12	2 41
6 F	5 14	18 55	4 42	20 38	3 27	1 08	10 32	0 36	16 14	1 18	20 39	0 12	2 35	1 06	12 10	2 41
7 Sa	5 37	22 07	4 14	23 22	2 48	0 48	10 09	0 40	16 03	1 18	20 45	0 10	2 40	1 06	12 09	2 41
8 Su	6 00	24 21	3 33	25 02	2 14	0 28	9 46	0 43	15 53	1 19	20 51	0 08	2 45	1 06	12 08	2 41
9 M	6 23	25 24	2 42	25 26	1 43	0 08	9 23	0 46	15 42	1 20	20 57	0 06	2 50	1 06	12 06	2 41
10 Tu	6 46	25 07	1 41	24 28	1 18	0N10	8 59	0 49	15 31	1 20	21 02	0 04	2 55	1 06	12 05	2 42
11 W	7 08	23 27	0 34	22 07	0 58	0 28	8 35	0 52	15 20	1 21	21 08	0 02	3 00	1 06	12 03	2 42
12 Th	7 31	20 26	0S37	18 27	0 44	0 44	8 11	0 55	15 09	1 22	21 14	0 00	3 05	1 06	12 02	2 42
13 F	7 53	16 12	1 48	13 40	0 35	0 58	7 46	0 58	14 58	1 23	21 20	0S01	3 10	1 06	12 00	2 42
14 Sa	8 16	10 56	2 54	8 01	0 31	1 11	7 21	1 01	14 47	1 23	21 25	0 03	3 15	1 06	11 59	2 42
15 Su	8 38	4 57	3 50	1 47	0 33	1 23	6 56	1 03	14 36	1 24	21 31	0 05	3 20	1 06	11 57	2 42
16 M	8 60	1S26	4 32	4S39	0 41	1 33	6 31	1 06	14 24	1 25	21 37	0 07	3 25	1 06	11 56	2 42
17 Tu	9 22	7 48	4 56	10 50	0 52	1 41	6 05	1 08	14 13	1 25	21 42	0 09	3 30	1 06	11 54	2 42
18 W	9 44	13 43	4 59	16 22	1 08	1 48	5 39	1 11	14 02	1 26	21 47	0 11	3 35	1 06	11 53	2 42
19 Th	10 05	18 44	4 41	20 48	1 28	1 54	5 13	1 13	13 50	1 27	21 53	0 12	3 40	1 06	11 51	2 42
20 F	10 27	22 30	4 05	23 49	1 52	1 58	4 47	1 16	13 39	1 27	21 58	0 14	3 45	1 06	11 50	2 42
21 Sa	10 48	24 44	3 14	25 15	2 18	2 01	4 21	1 18	13 28	1 28	22 03	0 16	3 50	1 07	11 48	2 42
22 Su	11 10	25 22	2 14	25 06	2 48	2 03	3 54	1 20	13 16	1 29	22 09	0 18	3 55	1 07	11 47	2 42
23 M	11 31	24 29	1 07	23 33	3 19	2 04	3 27	1 22	13 05	1 29	22 14	0 20	4 00	1 07	11 45	2 42
24 Tu	11 52	22 19	0N00	20 50	3 53	2 04	3 00	1 24	12 53	1 30	22 19	0 21	4 05	1 07	11 44	2 42
25 W	12 12	19 07	1 06	17 13	4 28	2 03	2 33	1 26	12 42	1 31	22 24	0 23	4 10	1 07	11 42	2 42
26 Th	12 33	15 09	2 07	12 58	5 04	2 02	2 06	1 28	12 30	1 32	22 29	0 25	4 15	1 07	11 41	2 42
27 F	12 53	10 40	3 02	8 17	5 42	1 59	1 39	1 29	12 19	1 32	22 34	0 27	4 19	1 07	11 39	2 42
28 Sa	13 13	5 50	3 48	3 20	6 20	1 56	1 11	1 31	12 07	1 33	22 39	0 28	4 24	1 07	11 38	2 42
29 Su	13 33	0 49	4 24	1N43	6 59	1 53	0 44	1 33	11 55	1 34	22 44	0 30	4 29	1 07	11 36	2 42
30 M	13 53	4N14	4 48	6 43	7 39	1 49	0 16	1 34	11 44	1 34	22 48	0 32	4 34	1 07	11 35	2 42
31 Tu	14S12	9N09	5N00	11N31	8S18	1N45	0S11	1N36	11N32	1N35	22S53	0S33	4S39	1N07	11N33	2S42

Day	⚷ Decl	⚷ Lat	♅ Decl	♅ Lat	♆ Decl	♆ Lat	♇ Decl	♇ Lat
1	13N16	0S47	22N28	0S02	1N34	1S30	23S45	5S17
6	13 11	0 48	22 27	0 02	1 31	1 30	23 46	5 16
11	13 06	0 48	22 27	0 02	1 28	1 30	23 46	5 16
16	13 02	0 49	22 26	0 02	1 25	1 30	23 46	5 16
21	12 56	0 49	22 25	0 02	1 22	1 30	23 45	5 15
26	12 51	0 50	22 24	0 02	1 19	1 30	23 45	5 15
31	12N46	0S50	22N23	0S02	1N16	1S30	23S44	5S15

Day	⚴ Decl	⚴ Lat	⚵ Decl	⚵ Lat	⚶ Decl	⚶ Lat	Eris Decl	Eris Lat
1	7N24	20N31	0N49	1N30	1S21	4N56	0N38	10S06
6	6 55	20 43	0 12	1 40	2 11	4 55	0 37	10 06
11	6 26	20 55	0S25	1 49	3 20	4 54	0 36	10 06
16	5 59	21 08	1 01	1 59	4 19	4 53	0 35	10 06
21	5 33	21 22	1 36	2 09	5 17	4 51	0 34	10 06
26	5 10	21 36	2 10	2 20	6 14	4 50	0 33	10 06
31	4N48	21N50	2S43	2N30	7S09	4N49	0N32	10S05

Moon Phenomena

Max/0 Decl
dy hr mn
1 21:56 0 N
9 7:13 25N27
15 18:39 0 S
21 21:38 25S22
29 3:52 0 N

Max/0 Lat
dy hr mn
4 9:08 5N00
11 11:38 0 S
17 15:21 5S00
23 23:55 0 N
31 10:13 5N02

Perigee/Apogee
dy hr m kilometers
1 21:40 a 406242
17 0:41 p 359013
29 6:56 a 405554

PH dy hr mn
○ 3 16:26 10♈59
☾ 11 11:58 18♋42
● 18 2:58 25♎16
☽ 25 4:54 2♒19

Void of Course Moon

Last Aspect	☽ Ingress
1 10:18 ♅ □	♈ 2 18:19
4 7:13 ♂ △	♉ 5 6:24
6 21:37 ♂ □	♊ 7 17:11
9 10:00 ♂ ✶	♋ 10 1:58
11 11:58 ☉ □	♌ 12 7:55
14 1:01 ♂ ☌	♍ 14 10:39
15 11:44 ♀ ☌	♎ 16 10:57
18 5:07 ♂ ✶	♏ 18 10:31
20 7:55 ♂ □	♐ 20 11:31
22 15:26 ☉ ✶	♑ 22 15:52
24 17:43 ♀ △	♒ 25 0:24
26 13:04 ☿ △	♓ 27 12:08
28 15:41 ♅ □	♈ 30 0:53

DAILY ASPECTARIAN

1 Su
☽✶♄ 1:54
☽⊼☿ 4:18
♀∥♄ 4:31
☉∥☽ 5:53
☽□♅ 10:18
☽∥♃ 11:35
☽#♆ 14:33
☽⊼♂ 15:33

2 M
☽∠♇ 1:05
☽∠⚷ 3:03
☽∥♆ 5:17
☿⊼♄ 6:40
☽∠♄ 8:07
☽#♃ 8:39
♀ ♍ 10:09
☉☌☿ 10:39
☉⊼♄ 14:45
☉#☽ 16:38
☽⊼♀ 19:12
☽△⚳ 23:04
☽⚼♂ 23:30

3 Tu
☽#☿ 0:19
☽✶♇ 7:21
☽☌♆ 9:12
☽⊻⚷ 9:13
☽☍♃ 11:30
☽☍☿ 11:38
☿☌♃ 12:49
☽⊻♄ 14:12
☉☍☽ 16:26
☽✶♅ 22:46
♆⊻⚷ 23:15

4 W
☽∥♀ 4:08
☽⚼♀ 4:38
☽⚼⚳ 6:07
☽△♂ 7:13
☉∥☿ 8:19
☽∥♄ 9:17
☽∥⚷ 14:34
☿☍♆ 15:26
☿⊼⚷ 15:40

5 Th
♀□⚳ 1:56
☽∠♅ 4:40
☽∥♂ 8:08
☽⊼⚳ 12:54
☿△♇ 13:25
☽△♀ 13:42
☽⊼☿ 18:45
☽□♇ 19:10
☽☌⚷ 20:50
☽⊻♆ 20:53

6 F
☽⊼♃ 0:21
☽☌♄ 1:35
☉⊼☽ 9:21
☽⊻♅ 10:15
☽#⚳ 12:32
☉△♅ 20:25
☽□♂ 21:37
☿⊻♀ 22:09
☽⚼☿ 22:18

7 Sa
☽∠♆ 2:13
☽∥♅ 2:58
☿∠♂ 4:16
☿∥♃ 4:49
☽⚼♃ 6:14
☽#♇ 16:23
☉⚼☽ 17:06
♀⊼♇ 21:41

8 Su
☽☍⚳ 1:15
☽△☿ 1:50
☽△♇ 5:34
♃⊼♄ 5:56
☽□♀ 6:23
☽⊻⚷ 7:00
☽✶♆ 7:08
☿✶⚳ 9:33
☽⊻♄ 11:30
☽△♃ 11:38
♀△⚷ 12:44
♀⊼♆ 14:06
☽☌♅ 20:08

9 M
☉△☽ 0:13
☽✶♂ 10:00
☽⚼♇ 10:00
☽∠⚷ 11:20
☿#♆ 13:08
☽∠♄ 15:41

10 Tu
☽□☿ 8:35
♀△♄ 9:55
☽⊼⚳ 11:18
☽⊼♇ 13:47
☽✶⚷ 15:00
☽∠♂ 15:07
☽□♆ 15:11
♂⚼♆ 16:41
☽✶♄ 19:10
☽✶♀ 20:09
☽□♃ 20:31
☽#♇ 20:46

11 W
♀⊻♃ 1:16
☽⊻♅ 3:36
☽∥♅ 9:16
☿ D 10:29
☉□☽ 11:58
☽⚼⚳ 15:10
☽#⚳ 18:43
☽⊻♂ 19:21

12 Th
☽∠♀ 1:33
☽∠♅ 6:11
☽✶☿ 14:10
☽△⚳ 18:09
☽☍♇ 19:02
☽□⚷ 20:00
☽△♆ 20:15
☉#♀ 20:19
☽□♄ 23:50

13 F
☽✶♃ 2:12
☽⊻♀ 5:53
☽∥♂ 6:13
☽✶♅ 7:57
☽∥⚷ 14:44
☽∠☿ 16:17
☽∥♄ 19:29
☉✶☽ 19:44
☽⚼♆ 21:35

14 Sa
☽☌♂ 1:01
⚳✶♇ 2:54
☽∠♃ 3:47
♀□♅ 6:09
☉∠⚳ 7:32
☉#☽ 10:21
☽∥♀ 15:41
☽⊻☿ 17:56
☽⊼♇ 21:08
☽□⚳ 21:36
☽△⚷ 21:55
☽⊼♆ 22:13
☉∠☽ 22:14

15 Su
☽△♄ 1:26
☽⊻♃ 4:39
☽#♃ 6:02
⚳⊼⚷ 8:26
☽□♅ 9:20
☽☌♀ 11:44
☽∥♆ 13:21
☽#☿ 16:18
⚳△♆ 19:58
☽∥☿ 21:06
☽⚼♇ 21:17
☽⚼⚷ 21:59
☽#♆ 23:55

16 M
☉⊻☽ 0:04
☽⚼♄ 1:24
☽⊻♂ 3:39
☽∥♃ 7:31
☽#♀ 17:51
☽☌☿ 20:23
☽△♇ 21:06
☽⊼⚷ 21:43
☽☍♆ 22:04
☽✶⚳ 22:46

17 Tu
☽⊼♄ 1:04
☽∠♂ 4:23
☽☌♃ 5:08
☉∥☽ 6:30
☿△♇ 8:18
☽△♅ 8:57
☽⊻♀ 15:29
☽#♄ 16:18
☿⊼⚷ 17:10
☽#⚷ 20:56
☿☍♆ 22:50
☽∠⚳ 23:07

18 W
☽#♂ 1:21
☉☌☽ 2:58
☽✶♂ 5:07
☽⚼♅ 8:44
♂∠♃ 10:31
☽∠♀ 17:26
☿#♆ 18:11
☽□♇ 20:47
☽☍⚷ 21:16
☽⊼♆ 21:41
☽⊻☿ 23:29
☽⊻⚳ 23:43

19 Th
☽☍♄ 0:35
♇ D 3:44
☿✶⚳ 4:11
☽⊻♃ 5:41
☽⊼♅ 8:50
☿⊼♄ 12:58
☽∥⚳ 19:55
☽✶♀ 19:57
☽⚼♆ 22:05
☽#♅ 23:28

20 F
☽∠☿ 2:07
⚳⊼♄ 3:53
☽∠♃ 6:44
☉⊻☽ 7:12
☽□♂ 7:55
♀⚼♇ 11:07
☽∥♇ 11:27
♀⚼⚷ 15:24
☽✶♇ 22:22
☽⊼⚷ 22:42
☽△♆ 23:14

21 Sa
☽⊼♄ 2:07
☽☌⚳ 2:52
☽✶☿ 5:58
☉✶♂ 6:38
☽✶♃ 8:37
☉∠☽ 10:42
☽☍♅ 11:06
☉⚼♅ 16:17
♀#♃ 23:11

22 Su
☽∠♇ 0:27
☽⚼⚷ 0:43
☽□♀ 4:07
☽⚼♄ 4:12
♀⚼♄ 5:03
☿☌♃ 13:38
☽△♂ 14:21
☉✶☽ 15:26
☉ ♏ 21:14

23 M
☿#♀ 3:18
☽⊻♇ 3:36
☽△⚷ 3:46
☽□♆ 4:26
☽△♄ 7:20
☿△♅ 8:44
☽∥♇ 9:39
☽⊻⚳ 10:05
☽□♃ 15:36
☉#♄ 15:40
☽⊼♅ 17:16
☽□☿ 18:23
☽⚼♂ 19:22
☽#♅ 23:07
♂∥⚷ 23:36
☊ D 23:53
☽∥⚳ 23:58

24 Tu
♂ ♍ 1:12
☿∠♂ 7:47
☿∥♃ 9:54
☽∠⚳ 15:25
☽△♀ 17:43
☽⚼♅ 21:53
♇□⚷ 23:42

25 W
☽⊼♂ 1:32
⚳#♅ 2:27
☊ R 4:49
☉□☽ 4:54
☽□⚷ 12:55
☽☌♇ 12:58
☽✶♆ 13:43
☽□♄ 16:33
☽✶⚳ 21:44
☉#♂ 22:02

26 Th
☽⚼♀ 2:25
☽△♃ 2:45
☽△♅ 3:21
☽#⚷ 12:38
☽△☿ 13:04
☉∥☽ 13:15
☽#♂ 15:06
☽#♄ 18:53
☽∠♆ 19:33
☉#⚷ 20:55

27 F
♃△♅ 9:07
☽⚼♃ 9:23
☽⊼♀ 11:56
♀ ♎ 13:53
☽☍♂ 16:20
♀∥♆ 18:16
☽∥☿ 21:50
☉△☽ 22:18
☽⚼☿ 23:56

28 Sa
☽✶⚷ 0:49
☽⊻♇ 1:08
☽⊻♆ 1:46
☽✶♄ 4:24
☽∥♃ 6:46
☽□⚳ 12:08
☽□♅ 15:41
☽⊼♃ 16:19
☽#♆ 21:45

29 Su
☽#♀ 0:26
☉☍⚷ 2:52
☽∥♀ 6:43
☽∠⚷ 7:06
☉⚼☽ 7:31
☽∠♇ 7:33
☉□♇ 8:02
☽∥♆ 9:57
☽∠♄ 10:36
☽⊼☿ 11:07
☉⊼♆ 14:35
⚶ ♏ 21:04

30 M
☽#♃ 1:37
☽☍♀ 7:35
☽⊼♂ 8:07
☽⊻⚷ 13:16
☽✶♇ 13:51
☽☌♆ 14:20
☉⊼☽ 16:33
☽⊻♄ 16:39
♀⊻♂ 16:48
☉☍♄ 17:35
☽#☿ 19:07
♂∥♄ 21:30

31 Tu
☽△⚳ 2:43
☽✶♅ 4:03
☽☍♃ 5:53
☽∥♂ 11:38
☽∥♄ 12:08
☽⚼♂ 15:38
☽∥⚷ 18:32

LONGITUDE

November 2028

Day	Sid.Time	☉	☽	☽ 12 hour	Mean☊	True☊	☿	♀	♂	⚳	♃	♄	⚷	♅	♆	♇
	h m s	° ' "	° ' "	° ' "	° '	° '	° '	° '	° '	° '	° '	° '	° '	° '	° '	° '
1 W	2 43 14	9♏05 44	23♈32 34	29♈36 51	17♑21.9	16♑29.7	27♎19.5	5♎22.4	4♍31.4	13♐12.1	14♎36.0	7♉43.6	6♉04.7	13♊29.7	6♈39.0	6♒26.8
2 Th	2 47 11	10 05 46	5♉43 17	11♉51 55	17 18.7	16R 16.8	28 58.0	6 35.5	5 05.1	13 35.4	14 48.3	7R 38.7	6R 01.8	13R 27.7	6R 37.7	6 27.1
3 F	2 51 07	11 05 49	18 02 51	24 16 08	17 15.5	16 05.0	0♏36.7	7 48.7	5 38.7	13 58.7	15 00.6	7 33.9	5 58.9	13 25.7	6 36.4	6 27.5
4 Sa	2 55 04	12 05 54	0♊31 48	6♊49 56	17 12.3	15 55.2	2 15.4	9 02.0	6 12.3	14 22.1	15 12.9	7 29.1	5 56.1	13 23.7	6 35.1	6 28.0
5 Su	2 59 00	13 06 00	13 10 36	19 33 53	17 09.2	15 48.0	3 54.2	10 15.3	6 45.7	14 45.5	15 25.1	7 24.3	5 53.2	13 21.6	6 33.8	6 28.4
6 M	3 02 57	14 06 09	25 59 54	2♋28 50	17 06.0	15 43.5	5 32.8	11 28.7	7 19.0	15 09.0	15 37.3	7 19.5	5 50.4	13 19.5	6 32.5	6 28.9
7 Tu	3 06 54	15 06 20	9♋00 50	15 36 06	17 02.8	15D 41.7	7 11.4	12 42.2	7 52.2	15 32.5	15 49.5	7 14.7	5 47.5	13 17.4	6 31.3	6 29.5
8 W	3 10 50	16 06 33	22 14 52	28 57 21	16 59.6	15 41.6	8 49.7	13 55.7	8 25.2	15 56.0	16 01.6	7 10.0	5 44.7	13 15.2	6 30.1	6 30.0
9 Th	3 14 47	17 06 48	5♌43 46	12♌34 20	16 56.5	15R 42.4	10 27.8	15 09.3	8 58.2	16 19.6	16 13.6	7 05.2	5 41.9	13 13.0	6 28.9	6 30.6
10 F	3 18 43	18 07 05	19 29 11	26 28 24	16 53.3	15 42.8	12 05.7	16 23.0	9 31.1	16 43.2	16 25.6	7 00.5	5 39.1	13 10.8	6 27.8	6 31.2
11 Sa	3 22 40	19 07 24	3♍32 00	10♍39 52	16 50.1	15 41.8	13 43.3	17 36.7	10 03.8	17 06.9	16 37.5	6 55.8	5 36.3	13 08.6	6 26.7	6 31.8
12 Su	3 26 36	20 07 45	17 51 47	25 07 21	16 46.9	15 38.7	15 20.6	18 50.5	10 36.5	17 30.6	16 49.4	6 51.2	5 33.5	13 06.3	6 25.5	6 32.5
13 M	3 30 33	21 08 07	2♎26 04	9♎47 15	16 43.8	15 33.4	16 57.6	20 04.4	11 09.0	17 54.3	17 01.3	6 46.6	5 30.7	13 04.0	6 24.5	6 33.1
14 Tu	3 34 29	22 08 32	17 10 05	24 33 41	16 40.6	15 26.1	18 34.4	21 18.3	11 41.4	18 18.1	17 13.0	6 42.0	5 28.0	13 01.7	6 23.4	6 33.9
15 W	3 38 26	23 08 59	1♏57 01	9♏19 05	16 37.4	15 17.6	20 10.8	22 32.2	12 13.6	18 41.9	17 24.7	6 37.4	5 25.2	12 59.4	6 22.4	6 34.6
16 Th	3 42 23	24 09 27	16 38 49	23 55 16	16 34.2	15 09.1	21 47.0	23 46.2	12 45.8	19 05.7	17 36.4	6 32.9	5 22.5	12 57.0	6 21.4	6 35.4
17 F	3 46 19	25 09 57	1♐07 32	8♐14 51	16 31.0	15 01.6	23 22.9	25 00.3	13 17.8	19 29.6	17 48.0	6 28.5	5 19.8	12 54.7	6 20.4	6 36.2
18 Sa	3 50 16	26 10 29	15 16 36	22 12 20	16 27.9	14 55.9	24 58.6	26 14.4	13 49.6	19 53.5	17 59.5	6 24.1	5 17.2	12 52.3	6 19.5	6 37.0
19 Su	3 54 12	27 11 02	29 01 46	5♑44 48	16 24.7	14 52.5	26 34.0	27 28.5	14 21.4	20 17.4	18 11.0	6 19.7	5 14.5	12 49.9	6 18.5	6 37.8
20 M	3 58 09	28 11 37	12♑21 27	18 51 53	16 21.5	14D 51.2	28 09.2	28 42.7	14 53.0	20 41.4	18 22.4	6 15.4	5 11.9	12 47.5	6 17.7	6 38.7
21 Tu	4 02 05	29 12 12	25 16 26	1♒35 28	16 18.3	14 51.7	29 44.1	29 57.0	15 24.4	21 05.3	18 33.7	6 11.1	5 09.3	12 45.0	6 16.8	6 39.6
22 W	4 06 02	0♐12 49	7♒49 30	13 59 03	16 15.2	14 53.0	1♐18.9	1♏11.2	15 55.8	21 29.3	18 44.9	6 06.9	5 06.8	12 42.6	6 16.0	6 40.5
23 Th	4 09 58	1 13 27	20 04 43	26 07 07	16 12.0	14 54.4	2 53.4	2 25.5	16 26.9	21 53.4	18 56.1	6 02.8	5 04.3	12 40.1	6 15.2	6 41.5
24 F	4 13 55	2 14 06	2♓06 54	8♓04 42	16 08.8	14R 55.1	4 27.8	3 39.9	16 58.0	22 17.4	19 07.2	5 58.7	5 01.8	12 37.6	6 14.4	6 42.4
25 Sa	4 17 52	3 14 47	14 01 09	19 56 54	16 05.6	14 54.3	6 02.0	4 54.2	17 28.9	22 41.5	19 18.2	5 54.6	4 59.3	12 35.1	6 13.6	6 43.4
26 Su	4 21 48	4 15 28	25 52 31	1♈48 35	16 02.5	14 51.7	7 36.0	6 08.7	17 59.6	23 05.6	19 29.2	5 50.7	4 56.8	12 32.6	6 12.9	6 44.5
27 M	4 25 45	5 16 10	7♈45 37	13 44 07	15 59.3	14 47.4	9 09.9	7 23.1	18 30.2	23 29.7	19 40.0	5 46.8	4 54.4	12 30.1	6 12.3	6 45.5
28 Tu	4 29 41	6 16 54	19 44 31	25 47 11	15 56.1	14 41.5	10 43.7	8 37.6	19 00.6	23 53.9	19 50.8	5 43.0	4 52.1	12 27.6	6 11.6	6 46.6
29 W	4 33 38	7 17 38	1♉52 27	8♉00 36	15 52.9	14 34.8	12 17.5	9 52.1	19 30.9	24 18.0	20 01.5	5 39.2	4 49.7	12 25.1	6 11.0	6 47.7
30 Th	4 37 34	8♐18 24	14 11 50	20 26 18	15♑49.7	14♑27.8	13♐51.1	11♏06.7	20♍01.0	24♐42.2	20♎12.1	5♉35.5	4♉47.4	12♊22.5	6♈10.4	6♒48.8

1st of Month

Julian Day # 2462076.5
Obliquity 23°26[illegible]1"
SVP 4♓51[illegible]1"
GC 27♐14.5
Eris 25♈44.3R

Day	⚴	⚵	⚶
1	14♏42.1	13♎04.4	1♏06.8
6	16 54.7	14 52.3	3 44.4
11	19 07.2	16 38.5	6 22.2
16	21 19.8	18 22.7	9 00.2
21	23 32.1	20 04.9	11 38.2
26	25 44.1	21 44.7	14 16.1

DECLINATION and LATITUDE

Day	☉ Decl	☽ Decl	☽ Lat	☽ 12h Decl	☿ Decl	☿ Lat	♀ Decl	♀ Lat	♂ Decl	♂ Lat	⚳ Decl	⚳ Lat	♃ Decl	♃ Lat	♄ Decl	♄ Lat
1 W	14S32	13N46	4N59	15N55	8S58	1N40	0S39	1N37	11N20	1N36	22S58	0S35	4S43	1N07	11N32	2S42
2 Th	14 51	17 54	4 45	19 42	9 38	1 35	1 07	1 38	11 09	1 37	23 02	0 37	4 48	1 07	11 30	2 42
3 F	15 09	21 19	4 17	22 19	10 18	1 29	1 35	1 39	10 57	1 37	23 07	0 38	4 53	1 07	11 29	2 42
4 Sa	15 28	23 47	3 36	24 35	10 57	1 23	2 03	1 40	10 45	1 38	23 11	0 40	4 57	1 07	11 27	2 42
5 Su	15 46	25 05	2 44	25 16	11 36	1 17	2 31	1 41	10 34	1 39	23 15	0 42	5 02	1 08	11 26	2 42
6 M	16 04	25 06	1 43	24 35	12 15	1 11	2 58	1 42	10 22	1 40	23 20	0 43	5 07	1 08	11 24	2 42
7 Tu	16 22	23 43	0 36	22 32	12 53	1 05	3 26	1 43	10 10	1 40	23 24	0 45	5 11	1 08	11 23	2 42
8 W	16 39	21 01	0S35	19 13	13 31	0 59	3 54	1 44	9 58	1 41	23 28	0 47	5 16	1 08	11 21	2 42
9 Th	16 57	17 08	1 45	14 49	14 08	0 52	4 22	1 44	9 47	1 42	23 32	0 48	5 20	1 08	11 20	2 42
10 F	17 13	12 16	2 51	9 33	14 44	0 45	4 50	1 45	9 35	1 43	23 36	0 50	5 25	1 08	11 18	2 42
11 Sa	17 30	6 41	3 47	3 42	15 20	0 39	5 18	1 45	9 23	1 43	23 40	0 52	5 29	1 08	11 17	2 42
12 Su	17 46	0 38	4 31	2S27	15 55	0 32	5 45	1 45	9 12	1 44	23 44	0 53	5 34	1 08	11 15	2 41
13 M	18 02	5S31	4 58	8 32	16 30	0 25	6 13	1 46	8 60	1 45	23 48	0 55	5 38	1 08	11 14	2 41
14 Tu	18 18	11 27	5 06	14 11	17 03	0 18	6 40	1 46	8 48	1 46	23 52	0 57	5 42	1 08	11 13	2 41
15 W	18 33	16 44	4 53	19 00	17 36	0 12	7 08	1 46	8 37	1 46	23 55	0 58	5 47	1 08	11 11	2 41
16 Th	18 49	20 59	4 21	22 36	18 08	0 05	7 35	1 46	8 25	1 47	23 59	0 60	5 51	1 09	11 10	2 41
17 F	19 03	23 51	3 33	24 42	18 39	0S02	8 02	1 46	8 14	1 48	24 02	1 01	5 56	1 09	11 09	2 41
18 Sa	19 18	25 09	2 32	25 11	19 09	0 09	8 29	1 46	8 02	1 49	24 06	1 03	5 60	1 09	11 07	2 41
19 Su	19 32	24 50	1 24	24 08	19 38	0 15	8 56	1 46	7 50	1 50	24 09	1 05	6 04	1 09	11 06	2 41
20 M	19 45	23 05	0 13	21 45	20 06	0 22	9 22	1 45	7 39	1 50	24 13	1 06	6 08	1 09	11 05	2 40
21 Tu	19 59	20 10	0N56	18 21	20 33	0 28	9 49	1 45	7 27	1 51	24 16	1 08	6 12	1 09	11 03	2 40
22 W	20 12	16 22	2 01	14 13	20 59	0 35	10 15	1 45	7 16	1 52	24 19	1 09	6 17	1 09	11 02	2 40
23 Th	20 24	11 57	2 59	9 36	21 24	0 41	10 41	1 44	7 05	1 53	24 22	1 11	6 21	1 09	11 01	2 40
24 F	20 36	7 10	3 48	4 42	21 49	0 47	11 07	1 43	6 53	1 54	24 25	1 12	6 25	1 09	10 60	2 40
25 Sa	20 48	2 11	4 26	0N20	22 11	0 54	11 32	1 43	6 42	1 54	24 28	1 14	6 29	1 10	10 59	2 40
26 Su	20 60	2N51	4 53	5 20	22 33	0 60	11 58	1 42	6 31	1 55	24 31	1 16	6 33	1 10	10 58	2 39
27 M	21 11	7 47	5 08	10 10	22 54	1 06	12 23	1 41	6 20	1 56	24 34	1 17	6 37	1 10	10 56	2 39
28 Tu	21 21	12 29	5 09	14 41	23 14	1 11	12 47	1 40	6 08	1 57	24 36	1 19	6 41	1 10	10 55	2 39
29 W	21 31	16 45	4 56	18 40	23 32	1 17	13 12	1 39	5 57	1 58	24 39	1 20	6 45	1 10	10 54	2 39
30 Th	21S41	20N23	4N30	21N53	23S49	1S22	13S36	1N38	5N46	1N58	24S42	1S22	6S49	1N10	10N53	2S39

Day	⚷ Decl	⚷ Lat	♅ Decl	♅ Lat	♆ Decl	♆ Lat	♇ Decl	♇ Lat
1	12N45	0S50	22N23	0S02	1N16	1S30	23S44	5S15
6	12 40	0 51	22 22	0 02	1 13	1 30	23 43	5 14
11	12 35	0 51	22 21	0 02	1 11	1 30	23 42	5 14
16	12 30	0 51	22 19	0 02	1 09	1 30	23 41	5 14
21	12 26	0 52	22 18	0 02	1 07	1 29	23 39	5 13
26	12 21	0 52	22 16	0 02	1 06	1 29	23 38	5 13

Day	⚴ Decl	⚴ Lat	⚵ Decl	⚵ Lat	⚶ Decl	⚶ Lat	Eris Decl	Eris Lat
1	4N44	21N53	2S50	2N32	7S20	4N49	0N32	10S05
6	4 24	22 08	3 22	2 43	8 15	4 48	0 31	10 05
11	4 07	22 24	3 52	2 53	9 08	4 47	0 31	10 05
16	3 51	22 41	4 21	3 05	9 59	4 45	0 30	10 04
21	3 38	22 58	4 49	3 16	10 49	4 44	0 30	10 03
26	3 28	23 16	5 15	3 28	11 36	4 43	0 29	10 03

Moon Phenomena

Max/0 Decl

dy	hr mn	
5	12:05	25N16
12	2:29	0 S
18	7:10	25S13
25	10:25	0 N

Max/0 Lat

dy	hr mn	
7	12:09	0 S
13	21:12	5S06
20	4:35	0 N
27	14:00	5N10

Perigee/Apogee

dy	hr m		kilometers
14	5:55	p	363617
26	0:10	a	404729

PH	dy	hr mn	
○	2	9:19	10♉29
☾	9	21:27	18♌01
●	16	13:19	24♏43
☽	24	0:16	2♓15

Void of Course Moon

Last Aspect			☽ Ingress	
1 8:39	☿	☍	♉	1 12:46
2 9:19	☉	☍	♊	3 22:59
5 4:17	♃	△	♋	6 7:25
7 12:36	♃	□	♌	8 13:51
9 21:27	☉	□	♍	10 18:01
12 4:02	☉	✶	♎	12 20:01
14 7:19	♀	☌	♏	14 20:50
16 13:19	☉	☌	♐	16 22:07
18 20:59	♀	✶	♑	19 1:43
21 8:06	☉	✶	♒	21 8:58
22 21:42	♃	△	♓	23 19:46
25 7:19	♂	☍	♈	26 8:21
28 0:13	♃	☍	♉	28 20:19

DAILY ASPECTARIAN

1 W ☉∦☽ 4:28; ☽☍☿ 8:39; ☽⚼⚳ 9:31; ☽∠♅ 9:46; ♀⚻⚷ 13:21; ⚳☍♅ 16:41; ☿⚼♅ 16:47; ☿∠⚳ 16:49; ♀△♇ 21:14; ☽△♂ 22:42

2 Th ☽☌⚷ 0:36; ♀☍♆ 0:42; ☽□♇ 1:26; ☽⚺♆ 1:46; ☽⚻♀ 1:54; ☽☌♄ 3:45; ♀∦♆ 6:59; ☉☍☽ 9:19; ☽⚺♅ 15:04; ☿ ♏ 15:05; ☽⚻⚳ 15:51; ☽⚻♃ 18:01; ♀⚻♄ 19:27

3 F ☽∠♆ 6:52; ☽∥♅ 9:09; ☽⚼♀ 10:12; ♂△⚷ 13:19; ☽∦⚳ 16:57; ☿∦♂ 18:29; ☽∦♇ 23:19; ☽⚼♃ 23:23

4 Sa ☽⚻☿ 3:48; ☽⚺⚷ 10:15; ☽□♂ 11:18; ☽△♇ 11:19; ♂⚻♇ 11:27; ☽✶♆ 11:31; ☽⚺♄ 13:09; ♂⚻♆ 15:47; ☿∦♄ 17:44; ☽△♀ 17:54; ☉⚻☽ 23:51

5 Su ☽☌♅ 0:21; ☽☍⚳ 3:04; ☽△♃ 4:17; ☉⚻♅ 6:01; ☽⚼☿ 12:21; ☽∠⚷ 14:25; ☽⚼♇ 15:35; ☽∠♄ 17:12

6 M ♂△♄ 0:21; ☿☍⚷ 4:09; ☉⚼☽ 6:14; ☿□♇ 13:44; ☿⚻♆ 14:22; ☿∦⚷ 15:25; ☽✶⚷ 18:07; ☽⚻♇ 19:22; ☽□♆ 19:27; ☽△☿ 20:11; ☽✶♄ 20:47; ☽✶♂ 21:49

7 Tu ☽∦♇ 0:06; ☿☍♄ 0:47; ☽∦⚳ 3:29; ☽□♀ 7:25; ☽⚺♅ 7:47; ♀△♅ 11:09; ☉△☽ 12:01; ☊ D 12:08; ☽⚻⚳ 12:15; ☽□♃ 12:36; ☽∥♅ 13:31; ☿✶♂ 15:00; ☉⚺⚳ 17:07; ☉⚺♃ 21:31

8 W ♆✶♇ 1:35; ☽∠♂ 2:12; ☽∠♅ 10:43; ⚳✶♃ 11:34; ☽⚼⚳ 15:59; ☽□⚷ 23:57

9 Th ☉∦☽ 1:00; ☽△♆ 1:19; ☽☍♇ 1:23; ☽□♄ 2:23; ☽⚺♂ 5:56; ☽□☿ 9:26; ☽✶♅ 13:05; ☽∦☿ 13:38; ☽✶♀ 18:06; ☽✶♃ 18:38; ☽△⚳ 19:04; ☉□☽ 21:27; ☊ R 21:40; ☽∥⚷ 22:29

10 F ♀☌♃ 1:00; ☽⚼♆ 3:24; ☽∥♄ 4:22; ♀✶⚳ 9:41; ☽∥♂ 12:16; ☿⚻♅ 15:40; ☽∠♃ 20:43; ☽∠♀ 22:18

11 Sa ☽△⚷ 3:29; ☽∦♃ 4:46; ☽⚻♆ 4:54; ☽⚻♇ 5:04; ☽∦♀ 5:13; ☽△♄ 5:42; ⚳∥♇ 10:22; ☽☌♂ 11:26; ♀∥♃ 12:03; ☽□♅ 16:06; ☽✶☿ 19:17; ☽∥♆ 21:54; ☽⚺♃ 22:15; ☽□⚳ 23:24

12 Su ☽⚺♀ 1:46; ☉✶☽ 4:02; ☽⚼⚷ 4:27; ☽⚼♇ 6:06; ☽⚼♄ 6:34; ☽∦♆ 7:03; ☽∠☿ 23:08

13 M ☽∥♃ 0:27; ☿⚺♃ 1:02; ☽∥♀ 2:57; ☽⚻⚷ 5:01; ☉⚼♆ 6:23; ☽☍♆ 6:29; ☉∠☽ 6:29; ☽△♇ 6:44; ☽⚻♄ 7:03; ☽∦♂ 13:26; ☽⚺♂ 14:45; ☽△♅ 17:17; ☿⚺⚳ 18:38; ☽∦♄ 23:01

14 Tu ☽☌♃ 0:05; ☽✶⚳ 1:53; ☽⚺☿ 2:34; ☽∦⚷ 4:40; ☽☌♀ 7:19; ☉⚺☽ 8:40; ☽∠♂ 16:02; ☽⚼♅ 17:35

15 W ☽∠⚳ 2:55; ☽∥☿ 5:00; ☽☍⚷ 5:38; ☽⚻♆ 7:11; ☽□♇ 7:32; ☽☍♄ 7:34; ☉∥☽ 10:07; ♄□♇ 12:56; ☽✶♂ 17:23; ☿⚼♆ 17:40; ☽⚻♅ 17:57

16 Th ☽⚺♃ 1:36; ☽⚺⚳ 4:08; ☽⚼♆ 7:45; ♂□♅ 7:52; ☽☌☿ 9:31; ☽∦♅ 9:41; ☽⚺♀ 12:51; ☉☌☽ 13:19; ☽∥♇ 22:01

17 F ☽∥⚳ 2:17; ☽∠♃ 2:51; ☽⚻⚷ 7:03; ♀∦♂ 7:12; ☽△♆ 8:46; ☽⚻♄ 8:57; ☽✶♇ 9:14; ☽∠♀ 16:26; ☉⚺♀ 17:06; ☽☍♅ 19:53; ☽□♂ 21:25

18 Sa ☽✶♃ 4:45; ☽☌⚳ 8:13; ☽⚼⚷ 8:38; ☽⚼♄ 10:33; ☽∠♇ 10:59; ☉∥☿ 13:49; ☽⚺☿ 19:04; ☉⚺☽ 20:29; ☽✶♀ 20:59; ⚳⚼⚷ 21:25

19 Su ♀⚼♅ 6:41; ♄⚺♆ 8:01; ☽△⚷ 11:03; ☽∥⚳ 11:15; ☽△♄ 12:59; ☽□♆ 13:00; ☽⚺♇ 13:37; ☽∥♇ 17:48

20 M ☽⚻♅ 0:47; ☽∠☿ 1:39; ☉∠☽ 1:40; ☉☌☿ 1:41; ☊ D 4:33; ☽△♂ 4:50; ☽∦♅ 7:22; ☽□♃ 11:15; ☽⚺⚳ 15:54; ☽∥☿ 21:31

21 Tu ♀ ♏ 0:59; ☉∥☽ 1:12; ☿ ♐ 4:01; ☽⚼♅ 4:40; ⚳⚼♄ 4:54; ☉✶☽ 8:06; ☽✶☿ 9:40; ☽□♀ 9:50; ☽⚼♂ 10:10; ☿⚺♀ 15:00; ♀∠♂ 15:23; ☽□⚷ 18:47; ☉ ♐ 18:56; ☽□♄ 20:43; ☽✶♆ 20:59; ☽∠⚳ 21:20; ☽☌♇ 21:46

22 W ☽△♅ 9:28; ⚳∠♇ 11:37; ☽⚻♂ 16:31; ☽∦⚷ 21:42; ☽△♃ 21:42

23 Th ☽∠♆ 2:19; ☽✶⚳ 3:43; ☽∦♄ 4:51; ☽∥♀ 5:59; ♀∦♄ 17:47; ☿∠♃ 18:04

24 F ☊ R 0:09; ☉□☽ 0:16; ☽∦♂ 1:26; ☽△♀ 3:28; ☽∥♃ 3:39; ☽⚼♃ 4:05; ☽□☿ 5:26; ☽✶⚷ 5:50; ☽✶♄ 7:43; ☽⚺♆ 8:17; ☿⚻⚷ 8:26; ☽⚺♇ 9:15; ☽□♅ 21:07; ☿⚻♄ 22:12

25 Sa ♀☍⚷ 1:34; ☿△♆ 2:57; ☽∦♆ 5:09; ☿∦♅ 5:15; ☽☍♂ 7:19; ☿✶♇ 10:41; ☽⚻♃ 10:52; ☽∠⚷ 12:02; ☽⚼♀ 13:18; ☽∠♄ 13:52; ☽∠♇ 15:37; ☽∥♆ 15:41; ☽□⚳ 18:10; ♀☍♄ 18:30; ♂∦♃ 20:39

26 Su ♀⚻♆ 1:22; ☉∠♃ 6:36; ♀□♇ 11:42; ☉⚻⚷ 15:44; ☽∥♂ 17:05; ☽∦♃ 18:09; ☽⚺⚷ 18:16; ☉△☽ 18:31; ☽⚺♄ 20:02; ☽☌♆ 20:52; ♀∦⚷ 21:44; ☽✶♇ 21:59; ☽⚻♀ 23:09

27 M ☽△☿ 3:15; ☽✶♅ 9:30; ☉⚻♄ 11:23; ☽∥♄ 15:53; ☉△♆ 21:56; ☽⚻♂ 22:29; ☽∥⚷ 23:11

28 Tu ☽☍♃ 0:13; ☽∦♀ 1:50; ☉⚼☽ 3:21; ♀∠⚳ 7:45; ☽△⚳ 8:33; ☉✶♇ 11:56; ☽⚼☿ 13:39; ☽∠♅ 15:15

29 W ☿☍♅ 1:54; ☽⚼♂ 5:24; ☽☌⚷ 5:46; ☿∥♇ 6:23; ☽☌♄ 7:22; ☽⚺♆ 8:26; ☽□♇ 9:39; ☉⚻☽ 11:33; ♂⚼⚷ 13:57; ☽⚼⚳ 15:00; ☽☍♀ 17:22; ☽⚺♅ 20:29; ☽⚻☿ 23:14

30 Th ☉∦☽ 10:54; ☽△♂ 11:39; ☽⚻♃ 11:43; ☽∠♆ 13:24; ♂⚺♃ 13:46; ☽∥♅ 15:09; ☽⚻⚳ 20:48; ♀⚻♅ 23:37

December 2028

LONGITUDE

Day	Sid.Time	☉	☽	☽ 12 hour	Mean ☊	True ☊	☿	♀	♂	⚳	♃	♄	⚷	♅	♆	♇
	h m s	° ' "	° ' "	° ' "	° '	° '	° '	° '	° '	° '	° '	° '	° '	° '	° '	° '
1 F	4 41 31	9♐19 11	26♉44 06	3♊05 17	15♑46.6	14♑21.4	15♐24.6	12♏21.3	20♍30.9	25♐06.4	20♎22.7	5♉31.9	4♉45.2	12♊20.0	6♈09.8	6♒49.9
2 Sa	4 45 27	10 19 59	9♊29 50	15 57 44	15 43.4	14R 16.1	16 58.1	13 35.9	21 00.7	25 30.6	20 33.1	5R 28.4	4R 42.9	12R 17.5	6R 09.3	6 51.1
3 Su	4 49 24	11 20 48	22 28 54	29 03 13	15 40.2	14 12.5	18 31.5	14 50.5	21 30.4	25 54.8	20 43.5	5 25.0	4 40.7	12 14.9	6 08.8	6 52.3
4 M	4 53 21	12 21 39	5♋40 38	12♋20 59	15 37.0	14D 10.7	20 04.9	16 05.2	21 59.8	26 19.0	20 53.8	5 21.6	4 38.6	12 12.4	6 08.4	6 53.5
5 Tu	4 57 17	13 22 30	19 04 10	25 50 06	15 33.9	14 10.5	21 38.2	17 19.9	22 29.1	26 43.3	21 03.9	5 18.3	4 36.5	12 09.9	6 08.0	6 54.7
6 W	5 01 14	14 23 23	2♌38 40	9♌29 46	15 30.7	14 11.5	23 11.5	18 34.7	22 58.2	27 07.6	21 14.0	5 15.1	4 34.4	12 07.3	6 07.6	6 56.0
7 Th	5 05 10	15 24 17	16 23 20	23 19 16	15 27.5	14 13.0	24 44.8	19 49.4	23 27.1	27 31.8	21 24.0	5 12.0	4 32.4	12 04.8	6 07.2	6 57.3
8 F	5 09 07	16 25 12	0♍17 29	7♍17 53	15 24.3	14 14.5	26 18.0	21 04.2	23 55.9	27 56.1	21 33.9	5 09.0	4 30.4	12 02.3	6 06.9	6 58.6
9 Sa	5 13 03	17 26 09	14 20 20	21 24 40	15 21.2	14R 15.3	27 51.1	22 19.1	24 24.4	28 20.4	21 43.7	5 06.1	4 28.5	11 59.7	6 06.6	6 59.9
10 Su	5 17 00	18 27 07	28 30 41	5♎38 07	15 18.0	14 15.0	29 24.3	23 33.9	24 52.8	28 44.7	21 53.4	5 03.2	4 26.6	11 57.2	6 06.3	7 01.2
11 M	5 20 56	19 28 06	12♎46 38	19 55 53	15 14.8	14 13.5	0♑57.3	24 48.8	25 20.9	29 09.0	22 03.0	5 00.5	4 24.7	11 54.7	6 06.1	7 02.6
12 Tu	5 24 53	20 29 06	27 05 23	4♏14 40	15 11.6	14 10.9	2 30.2	26 03.7	25 48.9	29 33.4	22 12.5	4 57.8	4 22.9	11 52.2	6 05.9	7 04.0
13 W	5 28 50	21 30 07	11♏23 11	18 30 22	15 08.4	14 07.7	4 03.0	27 18.6	26 16.6	29 57.7	22 21.9	4 55.2	4 21.2	11 49.7	6 05.8	7 05.4
14 Th	5 32 46	22 31 09	25 35 36	2♐38 20	15 05.3	14 04.3	5 35.7	28 33.6	26 44.2	0♑22.1	22 31.2	4 52.8	4 19.5	11 47.2	6 05.7	7 06.8
15 F	5 36 43	23 32 12	9♐38 00	16 34 06	15 02.1	14 01.4	7 08.1	29 48.5	27 11.5	0 46.4	22 40.3	4 50.4	4 17.8	11 44.7	6 05.6	7 08.2
16 Sa	5 40 39	24 33 16	23 26 10	0♑13 51	14 58.9	13 59.4	8 40.2	1♐03.5	27 38.6	1 10.8	22 49.4	4 48.1	4 16.2	11 42.2	6D 05.5	7 09.7
17 Su	5 44 36	25 34 21	6♑56 50	13 34 58	14 55.8	13D 58.3	10 12.0	2 18.5	28 05.5	1 35.1	22 58.3	4 46.0	4 14.6	11 39.8	6 05.5	7 11.2
18 M	5 48 32	26 35 27	20 08 09	26 36 22	14 52.6	13 58.3	11 43.4	3 33.5	28 32.1	1 59.5	23 07.2	4 43.9	4 13.1	11 37.3	6 05.5	7 12.7
19 Tu	5 52 29	27 36 32	2♒59 45	9♒18 28	14 49.4	13 59.1	13 14.2	4 48.6	28 58.5	2 23.8	23 15.9	4 41.9	4 11.7	11 34.9	6 05.6	7 14.2
20 W	5 56 26	28 37 38	15 32 49	21 43 07	14 46.2	14 00.4	14 44.3	6 03.6	29 24.7	2 48.2	23 24.4	4 40.1	4 10.2	11 32.5	6 05.7	7 15.7
21 Th	6 00 22	29 38 45	27 49 49	3♓53 21	14 43.0	14 01.8	16 13.6	7 18.7	29 50.6	3 12.6	23 32.9	4 38.3	4 08.9	11 30.1	6 05.8	7 17.3
22 F	6 04 19	0♑39 52	9♓54 14	15 53 01	14 39.9	14 03.0	17 41.9	8 33.7	0♎16.2	3 36.9	23 41.3	4 36.7	4 07.6	11 27.8	6 06.0	7 18.8
23 Sa	6 08 15	1 40 58	21 50 17	27 46 37	14 36.7	14R 03.8	19 09.0	9 48.8	0 41.6	4 01.3	23 49.5	4 35.1	4 06.3	11 25.4	6 06.2	7 20.4
24 Su	6 12 12	2 42 05	3♈42 36	9♈38 52	14 33.5	14 04.0	20 34.6	11 03.9	1 06.8	4 25.6	23 57.6	4 33.7	4 05.1	11 23.1	6 06.4	7 22.0
25 M	6 16 08	3 43 13	15 36 00	21 34 35	14 30.3	14 03.7	21 58.5	12 19.0	1 31.7	4 49.9	24 05.5	4 32.4	4 04.0	11 20.8	6 06.7	7 23.6
26 Tu	6 20 05	4 44 20	27 35 10	3♉38 18	14 27.2	14 02.9	23 20.3	13 34.1	1 56.3	5 14.3	24 13.4	4 31.1	4 02.9	11 18.5	6 06.9	7 25.3
27 W	6 24 01	5 45 27	9♉44 28	15 54 07	14 24.0	14 01.9	24 39.7	14 49.2	2 20.6	5 38.6	24 21.1	4 30.0	4 01.9	11 16.3	6 07.3	7 26.9
28 Th	6 27 58	6 46 35	22 07 38	28 25 20	14 20.8	14 00.9	25 56.2	16 04.3	2 44.7	6 02.9	24 28.6	4 29.0	4 00.9	11 14.0	6 07.7	7 28.6
29 F	6 31 55	7 47 42	4♊47 30	11♊14 18	14 17.6	13 59.9	27 09.2	17 19.4	3 08.5	6 27.2	24 36.1	4 28.1	4 00.0	11 11.8	6 08.1	7 30.2
30 Sa	6 35 51	8 48 50	17 45 49	24 22 05	14 14.5	13 59.3	28 18.3	18 34.6	3 32.0	6 51.5	24 43.4	4 27.4	3 59.1	11 09.6	6 08.5	7 31.9
31 Su	6 39 48	9♑49 58	1♋03 01	7♋48 28	14♑11.3	13♑58.9	29♑22.8	19♐49.7	3♎55.2	7♑15.8	24♎50.5	4♉26.7	3♉58.3	11♊07.5	6♈09.0	7♒33.6

1st of Month

Julian Day #
2462106.5
Obliquity
23°26'0"
SVP 4♓51'6"
GC 27♐14.6
Eris 25♈28.7R

Day	⚴
1	27♏55.7
6	0♐06.8
11	2 17.2
16	4 26.9
21	6 35.6
26	8 43.2
31	10 49.6

Day	⚵
1	23♎22.1
6	24 56.7
11	26 28.4
16	27 57.0
21	29 22.0
26	0♏43.2
31	2 00.3

Day	⚶
1	16♏53.8
6	19 31.2
11	22 08.4
16	24 45.1
21	27 21.3
26	29 56.7
31	2♐31.3

DECLINATION and LATITUDE

Day	☉ Decl	☽ Decl	☽ Lat	☽ 12h Decl	☿ Decl	☿ Lat	♀ Decl	♀ Lat	♂ Decl	♂ Lat	⚳ Decl	⚳ Lat	♃ Decl	♃ Lat	♄ Decl	♄ Lat
1 F	21S51	23N09	3N50	24N08	24S05	1S27	13S60	1N37	5N35	1N59	24S44	1S23	6S52	1N10	10N52	2S38
2 Sa	21 60	24 48	2 58	25 09	24 20	1 32	14 23	1 36	5 24	2 00	24 47	1 25	6 56	1 11	10 51	2 38
3 Su	22 08	25 09	1 56	24 48	24 33	1 37	14 47	1 35	5 13	2 01	24 49	1 27	6 60	1 11	10 50	2 38
4 M	22 16	24 05	0 46	23 02	24 46	1 42	15 09	1 34	5 02	2 02	24 51	1 28	7 04	1 11	10 50	2 38
5 Tu	22 24	21 38	0S27	19 56	24 56	1 46	15 32	1 32	4 52	2 03	24 53	1 30	7 07	1 11	10 49	2 38
6 W	22 31	17 57	1 39	15 43	25 06	1 50	15 54	1 31	4 41	2 04	24 56	1 31	7 11	1 11	10 48	2 37
7 Th	22 38	13 16	2 47	10 37	25 14	1 54	16 15	1 29	4 30	2 04	24 58	1 33	7 15	1 11	10 47	2 37
8 F	22 45	7 50	3 46	4 56	25 21	1 58	16 37	1 28	4 20	2 05	24 60	1 34	7 18	1 11	10 46	2 37
9 Sa	22 51	1 58	4 32	1S02	25 26	2 01	16 58	1 26	4 09	2 06	25 01	1 36	7 22	1 12	10 45	2 37
10 Su	22 56	4S02	5 02	6 59	25 30	2 04	17 18	1 24	3 59	2 07	25 03	1 38	7 25	1 12	10 45	2 36
11 M	23 01	9 52	5 14	12 36	25 33	2 07	17 38	1 23	3 48	2 08	25 05	1 39	7 28	1 12	10 44	2 36
12 Tu	23 06	15 11	5 06	17 33	25 34	2 09	17 57	1 21	3 38	2 09	25 07	1 41	7 32	1 12	10 43	2 36
13 W	23 10	19 40	4 39	21 29	25 34	2 11	18 16	1 19	3 28	2 10	25 08	1 42	7 35	1 12	10 43	2 36
14 Th	23 13	22 58	3 56	24 05	25 32	2 13	18 35	1 17	3 18	2 11	25 10	1 44	7 38	1 12	10 42	2 35
15 F	23 17	24 49	2 58	25 10	25 29	2 14	18 53	1 15	3 08	2 11	25 11	1 45	7 42	1 13	10 42	2 35
16 Sa	23 19	25 07	1 51	24 41	25 24	2 15	19 10	1 13	2 58	2 12	25 13	1 47	7 45	1 13	10 41	2 35
17 Su	23 22	23 54	0 39	22 47	25 18	2 16	19 27	1 11	2 48	2 13	25 14	1 48	7 48	1 13	10 41	2 35
18 M	23 24	21 22	0N34	19 42	25 10	2 15	19 44	1 09	2 38	2 14	25 15	1 50	7 51	1 13	10 40	2 34
19 Tu	23 25	17 49	1 43	15 45	25 01	2 15	19 59	1 07	2 29	2 15	25 16	1 52	7 54	1 13	10 40	2 34
20 W	23 26	13 32	2 46	11 12	24 50	2 14	20 15	1 05	2 19	2 16	25 17	1 53	7 57	1 13	10 39	2 34
21 Th	23 26	8 47	3 39	6 19	24 38	2 12	20 30	1 03	2 10	2 17	25 18	1 55	8 00	1 14	10 39	2 34
22 F	23 26	3 48	4 22	1 16	24 24	2 09	20 44	1 01	2 00	2 18	25 19	1 56	8 03	1 14	10 39	2 33
23 Sa	23 26	1N15	4 53	3N46	24 09	2 06	20 57	0 59	1 51	2 19	25 20	1 58	8 06	1 14	10 39	2 33
24 Su	23 24	6 14	5 11	8 39	23 53	2 03	21 10	0 56	1 42	2 20	25 21	1 59	8 09	1 14	10 38	2 33
25 M	23 23	11 00	5 16	13 15	23 35	1 58	21 23	0 54	1 33	2 21	25 22	2 01	8 11	1 14	10 38	2 32
26 Tu	23 21	15 24	5 08	17 24	23 16	1 53	21 34	0 52	1 24	2 22	25 22	2 03	8 14	1 15	10 38	2 32
27 W	23 19	19 14	4 45	20 53	22 56	1 47	21 45	0 49	1 15	2 23	25 23	2 04	8 17	1 15	10 38	2 32
28 Th	23 16	22 19	4 09	23 29	22 35	1 40	21 56	0 47	1 07	2 24	25 23	2 06	8 19	1 15	10 38	2 32
29 F	23 12	24 23	3 21	24 57	22 14	1 32	22 06	0 44	0 58	2 25	25 24	2 07	8 22	1 15	10 38	2 31
30 Sa	23 09	25 12	2 20	25 06	21 51	1 23	22 15	0 42	0 50	2 26	25 24	2 09	8 24	1 15	10 38	2 31
31 Su	23S04	24N37	1N11	23N46	21S28	1S13	22S23	0N40	0N41	2N27	25S24	2S10	8S27	1N16	10N38	2S31

Day	⚷ Decl	⚷ Lat	♅ Decl	♅ Lat	♆ Decl	♆ Lat	♇ Decl	♇ Lat
1	12N17	0S52	22N15	0S02	1N05	1S29	23S36	5S13
6	12 13	0 53	22 13	0 02	1 04	1 29	23 34	5 13
11	12 10	0 53	22 11	0 02	1 04	1 29	23 32	5 12
16	12 07	0 53	22 10	0 02	1 04	1 28	23 30	5 12
21	12 04	0 53	22 08	0 01	1 04	1 28	23 28	5 12
26	12 02	0 53	22 07	0 01	1 05	1 28	23 26	5 12
31	12N00	0S53	22N05	0S01	1N06	1S28	23S24	5S12

Day	⚴ Decl	⚴ Lat	⚵ Decl	⚵ Lat	⚶ Decl	⚶ Lat	Eris Decl	Eris Lat
1	3N20	23N35	5S40	3N40	12S22	4N42	0N29	10S03
6	3 14	23 54	6 02	3 53	13 06	4 41	0 29	10 02
11	3 12	24 15	6 23	4 06	13 48	4 39	0 29	10 02
16	3 11	24 36	6 42	4 20	14 27	4 38	0 29	10 01
21	3 14	24 58	6 58	4 34	15 04	4 37	0 29	10 00
26	3 20	25 22	7 13	4 49	15 39	4 35	0 29	9 60
31	3N28	25N46	7S24	5N04	16S11	4N34	0N29	9S59

Moon Phenomena

Max/0 Decl

dy hr mn
2 18:03 25N11
9 7:53 0 S
15 16:27 25S11
22 18:03 0 N
30 2:21 25N12

Max/0 Lat

dy hr mn
4 15:15 0 S
11 2:25 5S14
17 12:42 0 N
24 20:54 5N17
31 22:51 0 S

Perigee/Apogee

dy hr m kilometers
11 12:32 p 369052
23 21:02 a 404406

PH dy hr mn
○ 2 1:41 10♊24
☾ 9 5:40 17♍41
● 16 2:08 24♐39
☽ 23 21:46 2♈36
○ 31 16:50 10♋33
☍ 31 16:53 T 1.246

Void of Course Moon

Last Aspect			☽ Ingress		
30 11:39	♂	△	♊	1	6:11
2 22:08	♂	□	♋	3	13:43
5 6:18	♂	⚹	♌	5	19:21
7 16:16	☿	△	♍	7	23:30
10 1:41	☿	□	♎	10	2:31
11 15:44	♃	☌	♏	12	4:53
14 5:32	♀	☌	♐	14	7:30
16 7:40	♂	□	♑	16	11:35
18 16:10	♂	△	♒	18	18:21
21 3:55	☉	⚹	♓	21	4:17
22 17:50	☿	⚹	♈	23	16:30
25 17:13	♃	☍	♉	26	4:48
28 8:04	☿	△	♊	28	14:59
30 12:45	♃	△	♋	30	22:07

DAILY ASPECTARIAN

1 F
♂⚼♄ 0:44
☽#♇ 5:08
☽#☿ 13:31
☽⚺⚷ 15:05
☽⚺♄ 16:31
☽⚼♃ 16:31
☽⚹♆ 17:46
☽△♇ 19:03
☽#⚳ 23:25

2 Sa
☉☍☽ 1:41
☽☌♅ 5:11
☽⚻♀ 8:26
☽☍☿ 15:44
☽∠⚷ 18:52
☽∠♄ 20:14
☽△♃ 20:44
☽□♂ 22:08
☽⚼♇ 22:53

3 Su
☽☍⚳ 6:29
☽#⚳ 11:01
☽#☿ 14:21
☽⚼♀ 14:50
☉#♅ 15:47
☿⚼⚷ 17:24
♂⚼♇ 18:38
☉☍♅ 20:30
☽⚹⚷ 22:08
☽⚹♄ 23:26

4 M
☽□♆ 0:50
☽⚻♇ 2:12
☿⚼♄ 4:09
☽#♇ 6:10
☽⚺♅ 11:42
☉⚻☽ 13:00
☿⚹♃ 14:07
☊ D 15:13
☿∥⚳ 15:17
☉#☽ 18:00
☽∥♅ 19:17
☽△♀ 20:35

5 Tu
☽□♃ 3:36
☿∠♇ 4:19
☽⚻☿ 5:09
☽⚹♂ 6:18
☽⚻⚳ 13:59
☽∠♅ 14:18
⚴ ♐ 17:46
☉⚼☽ 17:49
☿□♂ 19:02

6 W
☽□⚷ 3:23
☽□♄ 4:34
☽△♆ 6:06
☽☍♇ 7:32
☽∠♂ 9:40
☽#♀ 10:16
☽⚼☿ 10:58
☽⚹♅ 16:32
☽⚼⚳ 17:05
☉△☽ 22:09

7 Th
☽∥⚷ 4:53
☽□♀ 6:33
☽⚼♆ 8:12
☽⚹♃ 8:47
☽∥♄ 11:18
☽⚺♂ 12:40
☽△☿ 16:16
☽△⚳ 19:50

8 F
♀⚼♆ 0:51
☽#♃ 2:13
☽△⚷ 7:13
☽△♄ 8:18
☽⚻♆ 9:58
☽∠♃ 10:52
♀⚺♃ 10:58
☽⚻♇ 11:28
☽∥♂ 14:57
☽□♅ 20:01

9 Sa
☽∥♆ 3:37
☉□☽ 5:40
☊ R 5:51
☽⚼⚷ 8:42
☽⚼♄ 9:45
☿☌⚳ 10:12
☽#♆ 12:09
☽⚺♃ 12:41
☽⚼♇ 13:01
☽⚹♀ 14:50
☽☌♂ 17:39
☽#♂ 23:48

10 Su
☽□⚳ 0:24
☽□☿ 1:41
☿ ♑ 9:13
☽⚻⚷ 9:58
☽⚻♄ 10:59
☽☍♆ 12:47
☽∥♃ 13:55
☽△♇ 14:21
☽∠♀ 18:33
☽△♅ 22:33
☉⚼⚷ 22:43

11 M
☽#♄ 3:45
☽#⚷ 9:59
☉⚹☽ 12:05
☉⚼♄ 12:12
☽☌♃ 15:44
♀⚹♂ 16:26
☽⚺♂ 21:47
☽⚺♀ 22:07
☽⚼♅ 23:38

12 Tu
☽⚹⚳ 4:15
☽⚹☿ 10:11
☽☍⚷ 12:12
☽☍♄ 13:10
☽⚻♆ 15:07
☉∠☽ 15:10
☽∥♀ 15:16
☽□♇ 16:46
☽∠♂ 23:49

13 W
☽⚻♅ 0:44
⚳ ♑ 2:16
☿△⚷ 4:36
☽∠⚳ 6:12
☿△♄ 13:10
☉∠♇ 14:12
☽∠☿ 14:30
☽⚼♆ 16:23
☽#♅ 17:15
☉⚺☽ 18:23
☽⚺♃ 18:44

14 Th
☉⚹♃ 0:00
☽⚹♂ 2:00
☉∥☽ 2:31
☽∥♇ 5:27
☽☌♀ 5:32
☿□♆ 7:46
☽⚺⚳ 8:22
☽⚻⚷ 14:51
☽⚻♄ 15:47
☽△♆ 17:55
☽⚺☿ 19:10
☽⚹♇ 19:42
☽∠♃ 20:35

15 F
☿⚺♇ 0:02
☽☍♅ 3:38
♀ ♐ 3:40
☽⚼⚷ 16:43
☽⚼♄ 17:39
☽∠♇ 21:46
☽⚹♃ 22:55

16 Sa
☉☌☽ 2:08
♀⚺⚳ 3:26
☽□♂ 7:40
☽☌⚳ 14:07
☽⚺♀ 14:51
☽△⚷ 19:10
☽△♄ 20:06
♆ D 20:45
☽□♆ 22:28

17 Su
☽⚺♇ 0:26
☽∥♇ 4:40
☉∥☽ 6:04
☽☌☿ 6:38
☽⚻♅ 8:29
☿∥⚳ 10:33
☊ D 12:38
☽#♅ 17:36
☽∠♀ 20:48
☿⚻♅ 22:27

18 M
☽□♃ 5:35
☽∥♀ 10:59
☽⚼♅ 12:00
♀⚻⚷ 12:25
☉⚺☽ 13:00
☽△♂ 16:10
♀⚻♄ 21:56
☽⚺⚳ 22:50

19 Tu
☽□⚷ 2:16
☽□♄ 3:13
☽⚹♀ 3:49
☽⚹♆ 5:52
☽☌♇ 8:04
☽△♅ 16:18
☉∠☽ 19:58
☽⚼♂ 21:44
☽⚺☿ 22:13

20 W
♀△♆ 0:40
☽∠⚳ 4:31
☽#⚷ 7:35
☽∠♆ 10:47
☽#♄ 14:46
☽△♃ 15:29
♀⚹♇ 23:33

21 Th
☽∥♃ 3:49
☉⚹☽ 3:55
☽⚻♂ 4:07
☽∠☿ 7:39
☉□♂ 8:01
☉ ♑ 8:21
♂ ♎ 8:47
☽⚹⚳ 11:01
☽⚹⚷ 12:30
☽⚹♄ 13:28
☽⚺♆ 16:24
☽⚺♇ 18:49
☽□♀ 21:00
☽⚼♃ 21:32

22 F
♀∠♃ 2:42
☽□♅ 3:07
☽#♂ 8:49
☽#♆ 12:57
☽⚹☿ 17:50
☽∠⚷ 18:30
☽∠♄ 19:28
☽∥♆ 23:09

23 Sa
☽∠♇ 1:01
☽∥♂ 2:45
☽⚻♃ 4:03
⚳△⚷ 4:47
⚵ ♏ 7:29
☽☍♂ 18:33
☊ R 21:40
☉□☽ 21:46

24 Su
☽⚺⚷ 0:46
☽□⚳ 1:30
☽⚺♄ 1:43
☽☌♆ 4:51
♀☍♅ 5:57
☽⚹♇ 7:25
⚳△♄ 7:33
☽#♃ 9:31
☽⚹♅ 15:27
☽△♀ 16:36
☽∥♄ 22:06

25 M
☽∥⚷ 5:26
☉△⚷ 8:01
☿∥♇ 11:21
☽□☿ 14:27
☽☍♃ 17:13
☉∥☿ 17:27
☉△♄ 18:55
☽∠♅ 21:28

26 Tu
☽⚼♀ 2:11
⚶ ♐ 2:34
☽⚻♂ 8:56
☽☌⚷ 12:47
☽☌♄ 13:43
☉△☽ 15:28
☽△⚳ 15:41
☽⚺♆ 16:53
☿□♃ 17:41
☽□♇ 19:30
☉☌⚳ 19:31

27 W
☽⚺♅ 2:59
☉□♆ 8:37
☽⚻♀ 11:01
☽⚼♂ 15:17
☽#♀ 20:22
☽⚼⚳ 21:52
☽∥♅ 22:05
☽∠♆ 22:05
☉⚼☽ 23:16

28 Th
☽#☿ 2:18
♂∥♆ 3:22
☽⚻♃ 4:32
⚳□♆ 4:46
☿⚼♅ 5:36
☽△☿ 8:04
☉#☽ 9:17
☽#♇ 11:15
☉⚺♇ 16:57
☽△♂ 20:48
☽⚺⚷ 22:31
☽⚺♄ 23:24
♀#♅ 23:57

29 F
☽⚹♆ 2:31
☽⚻⚳ 3:12
☽△♇ 5:05
☿∥♀ 5:59
☉⚻☽ 6:05
☿#♅ 8:38
☽⚼♃ 9:03
☽☌♅ 11:53
☽⚼☿ 15:02

30 Sa
☽☍♀ 1:38
☽∠⚷ 2:14
☽∠♄ 3:05
♀⚼⚷ 7:45
☽⚼♇ 8:42
☽△♃ 12:45
♀⚼♄ 16:42
☽⚻☿ 20:46

31 Su
♂⚻⚷ 3:10
☽⚹⚷ 5:12
☽□♂ 5:16
☽⚹♄ 6:02
☽□♆ 9:04
☽☍⚳ 11:23
☽⚻♇ 11:35
☿ ♒ 14:50
☽#♇ 16:09
☉☍☽ 16:50
☽⚺♅ 17:48
⚳⚺♇ 18:56
☉#☽ 20:02
☊ D 22:30

LONGITUDE

Day	Sid.Time	☉	☽	☽ 12 hour	Mean☊	True☊	☿	♀	♂	⚳	♃	♄	⚷	♅	♆	♇
	h m s	° ′ ″	° ′ ″	° ′ ″	° ′	° ′	° ′	° ′	° ′	° ′	° ′	° ′	° ′	° ′	° ′	° ′
1 M	6 43 44	10♑51 05	14♋38 12	21♋31 53	14♑08.1	13♑58.8	0♒21.9	21♐04.9	4♎18.1	7♑40.1	24♎57.6	4♉26.1	3♉57.6	11♊05.4	6♈09.5	7♒35.3
2 Tu	6 47 41	11 52 13	28 29 09	5♌29 34	14 04.9	13 58.9	1 14.9	22 20.1	4 40.7	8 04.3	25 04.4	4R 25.7	3R 56.9	11R 03.3	6 10.0	7 37.0
3 W	6 51 37	12 53 21	12♌32 39	19 37 56	14 01.8	13 59.0	2 00.9	23 35.2	5 03.0	8 28.6	25 11.2	4 25.4	3 56.3	11 01.2	6 10.6	7 38.8
4 Th	6 55 34	13 54 29	26 44 52	3♍52 58	13 58.6	13R 59.1	2 39.1	24 50.4	5 24.9	8 52.8	25 17.8	4 25.1	3 55.7	10 59.2	6 11.2	7 40.5
5 F	6 59 30	14 55 38	11♍01 44	18 10 42	13 55.4	13 59.0	3 08.5	26 05.6	5 46.5	9 17.1	25 24.2	4D 25.0	3 55.2	10 57.2	6 11.9	7 42.3
6 Sa	7 03 27	15 56 46	25 19 26	2♎27 32	13 52.2	13 58.9	3 28.2	27 20.8	6 07.8	9 41.3	25 30.5	4 25.0	3 54.7	10 55.3	6 12.5	7 44.0
7 Su	7 07 24	16 57 55	9♎34 41	16 40 31	13 49.0	13D 58.8	3R 37.4	28 36.0	6 28.7	10 05.5	25 36.7	4 25.1	3 54.3	10 53.3	6 13.2	7 45.8
8 M	7 11 20	17 59 03	23 44 49	0♏47 18	13 45.9	13 58.8	3 35.5	29 51.2	6 49.3	10 29.6	25 42.7	4 25.3	3 54.0	10 51.4	6 14.0	7 47.6
9 Tu	7 15 17	19 00 12	7♏47 47	14 46 04	13 42.7	13 59.0	3 21.9	1♑06.4	7 09.5	10 53.8	25 48.5	4 25.7	3 53.7	10 49.6	6 14.8	7 49.4
10 W	7 19 13	20 01 21	21 41 59	28 35 23	13 39.5	13 59.4	2 56.4	2 21.7	7 29.4	11 17.9	25 54.2	4 26.1	3 53.4	10 47.8	6 15.6	7 51.2
11 Th	7 23 10	21 02 31	5♐26 07	12♐14 03	13 36.3	14 00.1	2 19.3	3 36.9	7 48.8	11 42.1	25 59.7	4 26.7	3 53.3	10 46.0	6 16.4	7 53.0
12 F	7 27 06	22 03 40	18 59 02	25 40 58	13 33.2	14 00.8	1 31.1	4 52.1	8 07.9	12 06.2	26 05.1	4 27.4	3 53.2	10 44.3	6 17.3	7 54.8
13 Sa	7 31 03	23 04 49	2♑19 41	8♑55 07	13 30.0	14R 01.4	0 33.0	6 07.4	8 26.6	12 30.3	26 10.3	4 28.1	3D 53.1	10 42.6	6 18.2	7 56.7
14 Su	7 35 00	24 05 58	15 27 09	21 55 44	13 26.8	14 01.6	29♑26.5	7 22.6	8 44.8	12 54.3	26 15.4	4 29.0	3 53.1	10 40.9	6 19.2	7 58.5
15 M	7 38 56	25 07 06	28 20 49	4♒42 25	13 23.6	14 01.2	28 13.5	8 37.9	9 02.7	13 18.4	26 20.3	4 30.1	3 53.2	10 39.3	6 20.1	8 00.3
16 Tu	7 42 53	26 08 14	11♒00 32	17 15 16	13 20.5	14 00.2	26 56.5	9 53.1	9 20.1	13 42.4	26 25.0	4 31.2	3 53.4	10 37.7	6 21.2	8 02.2
17 W	7 46 49	27 09 21	23 26 44	29 35 06	13 17.3	13 58.6	25 37.8	11 08.3	9 37.1	14 06.3	26 29.5	4 32.4	3 53.5	10 36.2	6 22.2	8 04.0
18 Th	7 50 46	28 10 28	5♓40 37	11♓43 33	13 14.1	13 56.4	24 19.9	12 23.6	9 53.6	14 30.3	26 33.9	4 33.8	3 53.8	10 34.7	6 23.3	8 05.9
19 F	7 54 42	29 11 33	17 44 13	23 43 00	13 10.9	13 54.0	23 05.0	13 38.8	10 09.7	14 54.2	26 38.1	4 35.2	3 54.1	10 33.2	6 24.4	8 07.7
20 Sa	7 58 39	0♒12 38	29 40 19	5♈36 39	13 07.7	13 51.7	21 55.3	14 54.1	10 25.3	15 18.1	26 42.1	4 36.8	3 54.5	10 31.8	6 25.5	8 09.6
21 Su	8 02 35	1 13 43	11♈32 29	17 28 22	13 04.6	13 49.8	20 52.2	16 09.3	10 40.4	15 42.0	26 46.0	4 38.5	3 54.9	10 30.5	6 26.7	8 11.5
22 M	8 06 32	2 14 46	23 24 51	29 22 31	13 01.4	13D 48.7	19 57.0	17 24.5	10 55.1	16 05.8	26 49.7	4 40.2	3 55.4	10 29.1	6 27.9	8 13.3
23 Tu	8 10 28	3 15 48	5♉21 58	11♉23 48	12 58.2	13 48.4	19 10.4	18 39.8	11 09.2	16 29.6	26 53.2	4 42.1	3 55.9	10 27.9	6 29.1	8 15.2
24 W	8 14 25	4 16 50	17 28 38	23 37 02	12 55.0	13 49.0	18 33.0	19 55.0	11 22.9	16 53.4	26 56.5	4 44.1	3 56.5	10 26.7	6 30.3	8 17.1
25 Th	8 18 22	5 17 50	29 49 33	6♊06 45	12 51.9	13 50.3	18 04.7	21 10.2	11 36.0	17 17.1	26 59.7	4 46.2	3 57.2	10 25.5	6 31.6	8 19.0
26 F	8 22 18	6 18 49	12♊29 04	18 56 54	12 48.7	13 52.0	17 45.4	22 25.4	11 48.7	17 40.8	27 02.7	4 48.5	3 57.9	10 24.4	6 32.9	8 20.8
27 Sa	8 26 15	7 19 48	25 30 36	2♋10 21	12 45.5	13 53.5	17D 34.9	23 40.6	12 00.8	18 04.4	27 05.5	4 50.8	3 58.7	10 23.3	6 34.3	8 22.7
28 Su	8 30 11	8 20 45	8♋56 17	15 48 21	12 42.3	13R 54.4	17 32.7	24 55.8	12 12.4	18 28.1	27 08.1	4 53.2	3 59.6	10 22.3	6 35.7	8 24.6
29 M	8 34 08	9 21 41	22 46 24	29 50 06	12 39.2	13 54.2	17 38.2	26 11.0	12 23.4	18 51.6	27 10.6	4 55.7	4 00.5	10 21.3	6 37.0	8 26.5
30 Tu	8 38 04	10 22 36	6♌58 58	14♌12 24	12 36.0	13 52.7	17 51.0	27 26.2	12 33.8	19 15.2	27 12.8	4 58.4	4 01.4	10 20.3	6 38.5	8 28.4
31 W	8 42 01	11♒23 31	21 29 39	28 49 53	12♑32.8	13♑49.8	18♑10.4	28♑41.4	12♎43.7	19♑38.7	27♎14.9	5♉01.1	4♉02.4	10♊19.5	6♈39.9	8♒30.3

1st of Month

Julian Day #
2462137.5
Obliquity
23°26'[illegible]0"
SVP 4♓51'[illegible]0"
GC 27♐14.7
Eris 25♈19.9R

Day	⚴	Day	⚵	Day	⚶
1	11♐14.7	1	2♏15.2	1	3♐02.1
6	13 19.4	6	3 26.9	6	5 35.6
11	15 22.5	11	4 33.9	11	8 08.1
16	17 23.8	16	5 35.5	16	10 39.3
21	19 23.2	21	6 31.5	21	13 09.1
26	21 20.3	26	7 21.4	26	15 37.4
31	23 15.0	31	8 04.9	31	18 03.9

DECLINATION and LATITUDE

Day	☉ Decl	☽ Decl	☽ Lat	☽ 12h Decl	☿ Decl	☿ Lat	♀ Decl	♀ Lat	♂ Decl	♂ Lat	⚳ Decl	⚳ Lat	♃ Decl	♃ Lat	♄ Decl	♄ Lat
1 M	22S60	22N34	0S04	21N02	21S05	1S02	22S31	0N37	0N33	2N28	25S25	2S12	8S29	1N16	10N38	2S30
2 Tu	22 54	19 10	1 20	17 01	20 41	0 50	22 38	0 35	0 25	2 29	25 25	2 14	8 31	1 16	10 38	2 30
3 W	22 49	14 36	2 32	11 60	20 18	0 36	22 45	0 32	0 17	2 30	25 25	2 15	8 34	1 16	10 38	2 30
4 Th	22 43	9 13	3 36	6 18	19 55	0 22	22 51	0 30	0 10	2 31	25 25	2 17	8 36	1 16	10 39	2 30
5 F	22 36	3 19	4 26	0 17	19 34	0 07	22 56	0 27	0 02	2 32	25 25	2 18	8 38	1 17	10 39	2 29
6 Sa	22 29	2S44	5 01	5S44	19 13	0N10	23 00	0 24	0S06	2 33	25 25	2 20	8 40	1 17	10 39	2 29
7 Su	22 22	8 38	5 16	11 26	18 54	0 27	23 04	0 22	0 13	2 34	25 24	2 22	8 42	1 17	10 39	2 29
8 M	22 14	14 03	5 13	16 29	18 37	0 45	23 07	0 19	0 20	2 35	25 24	2 23	8 44	1 17	10 40	2 28
9 Tu	22 05	18 41	4 50	20 36	18 22	1 04	23 09	0 17	0 27	2 36	25 24	2 25	8 46	1 17	10 40	2 28
10 W	21 57	22 14	4 11	23 13	18 09	1 23	23 11	0 14	0 34	2 37	25 23	2 27	8 48	1 18	10 41	2 28
11 Th	21 47	24 27	3 18	25 01	17 59	1 42	23 11	0 12	0 40	2 38	25 23	2 28	8 50	1 18	10 41	2 28
12 F	21 38	25 13	2 14	25 02	17 51	2 01	23 12	0 09	0 47	2 39	25 23	2 30	8 51	1 18	10 42	2 27
13 Sa	21 28	24 29	1 04	23 36	17 47	2 18	23 11	0 07	0 53	2 40	25 22	2 32	8 53	1 18	10 42	2 27
14 Su	21 17	22 25	0N08	20 56	17 44	2 35	23 10	0 04	0 60	2 42	25 21	2 33	8 55	1 19	10 43	2 27
15 M	21 06	19 12	1 19	17 16	17 45	2 50	23 08	0 01	1 06	2 43	25 20	2 35	8 56	1 19	10 43	2 26
16 Tu	20 55	15 09	2 24	12 54	17 47	3 02	23 05	0S01	1 11	2 44	25 19	2 36	8 58	1 19	10 44	2 26
17 W	20 43	10 32	3 21	8 05	17 51	3 13	23 02	0 04	1 17	2 45	25 19	2 38	8 59	1 19	10 45	2 26
18 Th	20 31	5 35	4 08	3 03	17 57	3 21	22 58	0 06	1 22	2 46	25 18	2 40	9 01	1 20	10 45	2 25
19 F	20 19	0 30	4 43	2N02	18 05	3 26	22 53	0 09	1 28	2 47	25 17	2 42	9 02	1 20	10 46	2 25
20 Sa	20 06	4N33	5 06	7 00	18 13	3 29	22 47	0 11	1 33	2 48	25 16	2 43	9 03	1 20	10 47	2 25
21 Su	19 53	9 24	5 15	11 42	18 22	3 29	22 41	0 14	1 38	2 49	25 15	2 45	9 04	1 20	10 48	2 25
22 M	19 39	13 54	5 11	15 59	18 32	3 28	22 34	0 16	1 42	2 50	25 13	2 47	9 05	1 20	10 49	2 24
23 Tu	19 25	17 55	4 53	19 41	18 42	3 24	22 26	0 18	1 47	2 52	25 12	2 48	9 06	1 21	10 50	2 24
24 W	19 11	21 15	4 23	22 35	18 52	3 19	22 18	0 21	1 51	2 53	25 11	2 50	9 07	1 21	10 50	2 24
25 Th	18 57	23 41	3 39	24 30	19 03	3 12	22 09	0 23	1 55	2 54	25 09	2 52	9 08	1 21	10 51	2 23
26 F	18 42	25 00	2 44	25 11	19 13	3 04	21 60	0 26	1 59	2 55	25 08	2 53	9 09	1 21	10 52	2 23
27 Sa	18 26	25 01	1 39	24 29	19 23	2 55	21 49	0 28	2 03	2 56	25 07	2 55	9 10	1 22	10 54	2 23
28 Su	18 11	23 35	0 27	22 20	19 33	2 46	21 38	0 30	2 06	2 57	25 05	2 57	9 11	1 22	10 55	2 23
29 M	17 55	20 43	0S49	18 46	19 42	2 35	21 27	0 33	2 09	2 58	25 04	2 59	9 11	1 22	10 56	2 22
30 Tu	17 38	16 32	2 03	14 02	19 51	2 25	21 14	0 35	2 12	2 59	25 02	3 01	9 12	1 22	10 57	2 22
31 W	17S22	11N19	3S12	8N25	19S59	2N14	21S01	0S37	2S15	3N01	25S00	3S02	9S12	1N23	10N58	2S22

Day	⚷ Decl	⚷ Lat	♅ Decl	♅ Lat	♆ Decl	♆ Lat	♇ Decl	♇ Lat
1	11N60	0S54	22N05	0S01	1N06	1S28	23S24	5S12
6	11 59	0 54	22 03	0 01	1 08	1 27	23 21	5 12
11	11 58	0 54	22 02	0 01	1 09	1 27	23 19	5 12
16	11 58	0 54	22 01	0 01	1 11	1 27	23 17	5 12
21	11 58	0 54	22 00	0 01	1 14	1 27	23 15	5 13
26	11 59	0 54	21 59	0 01	1 16	1 27	23 13	5 13
31	12N01	0S54	21N59	0S01	1N19	1S26	23S10	5S13

Day	⚴ Decl	⚴ Lat	⚵ Decl	⚵ Lat	⚶ Decl	⚶ Lat	Eris Decl	Eris Lat
1	3N30	25N51	7S26	5N07	16S17	4N34	0N29	9S59
6	3 42	26 17	7 35	5 24	16 46	4 32	0 30	9 58
11	3 57	26 44	7 41	5 41	17 12	4 31	0 30	9 57
16	4 15	27 12	7 45	5 58	17 36	4 29	0 31	9 57
21	4 36	27 41	7 45	6 17	17 57	4 27	0 32	9 56
26	4 60	28 12	7 43	6 36	18 16	4 25	0 33	9 55
31	5N26	28N44	7S37	6N56	18S32	4N23	0N34	9S55

Moon Phenomena

Max/0 Decl
dy hr mn
5 13:09 0 S
12 0:08 25S13
19 2:20 0 N
26 12:17 25N11

Perigee/Apogee
dy hr m kilometers
5 4:17 p 368917
20 18:09 a 404883

Max/0 Lat
dy hr mn
7 7:26 5S17
13 21:22 0 N
21 4:37 5N15
28 8:41 0 S

PH dy hr mn
☾ 7 13:28 17♎32
● 14 17:26 24♑50
• 14 1033:4P 0.871
☽ 22 19:24 3♉04
○ 30 6:05 10♌38

Void of Course Moon

Last Aspect	☽ Ingress
1 18:05 ♃ □	♌ 2 2:36
3 21:32 ♃ ✶	♍ 4 5:28
6 3:44 ♀ □	♎ 6 7:52
8 3:22 ♃ ☌	♏ 8 10:39
9 20:52 ☉ ✶	♐ 10 14:28
12 12:49 ♃ ✶	♑ 12 19:47
14 23:48 ☿ ☌	♒ 15 3:06
17 5:59 ♃ △	♓ 17 12:49
19 9:45 ☿ ✶	♈ 20 0:40
22 6:55 ♃ ☍	♉ 22 13:15
24 5:20 ♀ △	♊ 25 0:20
27 2:52 ♃ △	♋ 27 8:06
29 7:31 ♃ □	♌ 29 12:17
31 9:26 ♃ ✶	♍ 31 13:54

DAILY ASPECTARIAN

1 M: ☽#♀ 0:26; ☽∥♅ 4:06; ☉⊼♅ 5:26; ♂⊼♄ 8:19; ☽⊼♀ 12:20; ☽#☿ 13:07; ☽□♃ 18:05; ☽∠♅ 19:50

2 Tu: ☽☍☿ 5:02; ♀∠♇ 5:33; ☽□⚷ 9:21; ☽□♄ 10:11; ☽✶♂ 10:54; ☽△♆ 13:10; ☽☍♇ 15:39; ☽⚼♀ 16:37; ☽⊼⚳ 16:53; ☽✶♅ 21:25

3 W: ☉⊼☽ 0:38; ☉∥♀ 7:50; ☽∥⚷ 12:02; ☽∠♂ 13:03; ☽⚼♆ 14:37; ☽∥♄ 17:55; ☽⚼⚳ 19:02; ☽△♀ 20:29; ☽✶♃ 21:32

4 Th: ☊R 2:30; ☽#♃ 2:34; ☉⚼☽ 3:55; ♀✶♃ 9:34; ☽⊼☿ 10:19; ☽△⚷ 12:04; ☽△♄ 12:54; ☽⊻♂ 14:57; ☽⊼♆ 15:53; ☽⊼♇ 18:24; ☽△⚳ 20:59; ☽∠♃ 22:57; ☽□♅ 23:52

5 F: ☉△☽ 7:03; ☽∥♆ 8:42; ☽⚼☿ 12:15; ♄D 12:40; ☽#♂ 13:00; ☽⚼⚷ 13:14; ☽∥♂ 13:17; ☽⚼♄ 14:05; ☽#♆ 17:36; ☽⚼♇ 19:38

6 Sa: ☽⊻♃ 0:19; ☽□♀ 3:44; ♂☍♆ 5:34; ☽△☿ 13:53; ☽⊼⚷ 14:26; ☽⊼♄ 15:18; ☽☍♆ 18:20; ☽☌♂ 18:39; ☽△♇ 20:56

7 Su: ☽∥♃ 0:17; ☽□⚳ 0:53; ☽△♅ 2:13; ☿R 7:58; ☽#♄ 8:39; ☊D 13:22; ☉□☽ 13:28; ☽#⚷ 14:27

8 M: ♀♑ 2:48; ☽☌♃ 3:22; ☽⚼♅ 3:35; ☽✶♀ 11:25; ☽□☿ 16:34; ☽☍⚷ 17:19; ☽☍♄ 18:13; ⚳⊼♅ 20:07; ☽⊼♆ 21:20; ☽∥☿ 22:16; ☽⊻♂ 22:53

9 Tu: ☽□♇ 0:03; ♃⚼♅ 3:24; ☽⊼♅ 5:12; ☽✶⚳ 5:29; ☉#♅ 7:46; ☽∠♀ 15:44; ☉✶☽ 20:52; ☉∥☽ 21:50; ☽#♅ 22:30; ☽⚼♆ 23:14

10 W: ☽∠♂ 1:24; ☽⊻♃ 7:22; ☿⊻♀ 7:42; ☽∠⚳ 8:15; ☽∥♀ 8:37; ☽∥♇ 10:01; ☽✶☿ 18:48; ☽⊻♀ 20:29; ☽⊼⚷ 21:17; ☽⊼♄ 22:15

11 Th: ☉∠☽ 1:09; ☽△♆ 1:29; ☽✶♂ 4:17; ☽✶♇ 4:19; ♀△⚷ 5:13; ♂△♇ 5:44; ☽☍♅ 9:23; ☽∠♃ 9:52; ☽⊻⚳ 11:24; ♀△♄ 16:01; ☽∠☿ 19:52; ☽⚼⚷ 23:50

12 F: ☽⚼♄ 0:51; ☉⊻☽ 5:57; ☽∠♇ 7:03; ☽✶♃ 12:49; ☽⊻☿ 21:01

13 Sa: ☽△⚷ 2:50; ♀□♆ 3:30; ☽△♄ 3:53; ⚷D 6:10; ☽□♆ 7:14; ☽☌♀ 7:37; ☽⊻♇ 10:15; ☽□♂ 11:24; ☿R♑ 12:15; ☽⊼♅ 15:15; ☽∥♇ 15:22; ☽∥♀ 16:42; ☽☌⚳ 19:10; ☊R 21:27

14 Su: ☽#♅ 3:21; ☉∥☽ 9:52; ♀⊻♇ 11:44; ☉☌☽ 17:26; ☽⚼♅ 18:58; ☽□♃ 20:12; ☽☌☿ 23:48

15 M: ☽∥☿ 9:07; ♀□♂ 10:19; ☽□⚷ 10:27; ☽□♄ 11:38; ☉⚼♅ 12:19; ☽✶♆ 15:07; ☽☌♇ 18:19; ☽△♂ 20:44; ☽⊻♀ 21:37; ☽△♅ 23:16

16 Tu: ♂#♆ 0:22; ☽⊻⚳ 5:20; ☉□♃ 7:07; ☉☌☿ 8:18; ☿□♃ 9:06; ♀⊼♅ 13:56; ☽#⚷ 16:48; ☽∠♆ 19:58; ☽#♄ 22:58

17 W: ☿⚼♅ 0:30; ☽⚼♂ 2:20; ☽⊻☿ 3:51; ☽∠♀ 5:51; ☽△♃ 5:59; ☽∥♃ 7:35; ☉⊻☽ 7:54; ☽∠⚳ 11:26; ☽✶⚷ 20:29; ☽✶♄ 21:48

18 Th: ☽⊻♆ 1:24; ☽⊻♇ 4:48; ☽∠☿ 6:33; ☽⊼♂ 8:33; ☽□♅ 9:42; ☽⚼♃ 11:45; ☽✶♀ 14:53; ☉∠☽ 16:16; ☽✶⚳ 18:09; ☽∥♂ 19:32; ☽#♆ 20:38

19 F: ☽∠⚷ 2:20; ☽∠♄ 3:43; ☽∥♆ 8:05; ☽#♂ 9:25; ☽✶☿ 9:45; ☽∠♇ 10:51; ☽⊼♃ 17:59; ☉♒ 19:02

20 Sa: ☉✶☽ 1:11; ☽⊻⚷ 8:34; ♂△♅ 9:27; ☽⊻♄ 10:00; ♀☌⚳ 11:14; ☽☌♆ 13:40; ☽✶♇ 17:12; ☽✶♅ 21:55; ☽☍♂ 22:12; ☽#♃ 22:21

21 Su: ☽∥♄ 7:15; ☽□⚳ 8:42; ☽□♀ 10:26; ☽∥⚷ 13:27; ☽□☿ 17:29

22 M: ☽∠♅ 4:10; ☽☍♃ 6:55; ☊D 19:10; ☉□☽ 19:24; ☽☌⚷ 21:08; ☽☌♄ 22:40

23 Tu: ☽⊻♆ 2:14; ☽#☿ 5:27; ☽□♇ 5:46; ☿☌♀ 6:21; ☉#☽ 9:32; ☽⊻♅ 10:08; ☽⊼♂ 11:44; ☉□⚷ 15:56; ☽△⚳ 22:48

24 W: ☽△☿ 2:01; ☽△♀ 5:20; ☽∥♅ 6:25; ☽∠♆ 7:54; ☽#♀ 8:47; ☉□♄ 11:07; ☽⚼♂ 17:40; ☉∥☿ 18:06; ☽⊼♃ 18:31; ☽#♇ 18:33

25 Th: ☽⚼⚳ 4:52; ☽⚼☿ 6:03; ☽⊻⚷ 7:54; ☽⊻♄ 9:29; ☉△☽ 11:22; ☽✶♆ 12:48; ☽⚼♀ 13:26; ☽△♇ 16:13; ☽☌♅ 20:07; ☽△♂ 22:43; ☽⚼♃ 23:10

26 F: ♀#♅ 0:47; ☿☌⚳ 2:57; ☉✶♆ 5:41; ☽⊼☿ 9:38; ☽⊼⚳ 9:58; ☽∠⚷ 12:03; ☽∠♄ 13:37; ☉⚼☽ 17:43; ☽#⚳ 19:52; ☽#⚳ 19:52; ☽⚼♇ 20:07; ☽⊼♀ 20:19

27 Sa: ☽△♃ 2:52; ☽✶⚷ 15:14; ☽✶♄ 16:49; ☿D 18:41; ☽□♆ 19:51; ☉⊼☽ 22:52; ☽⊼♇ 23:04

28 Su: ☉☌♇ 1:34; ☽⊻♅ 2:31; ☽#♇ 4:08; ☽□♂ 5:49; ♀⚼♅ 8:19; ☊R 8:44; ☽∥♅ 14:47; ☽☍☿ 15:05; ☽☍⚳ 17:05; ☽#♀ 18:32

29 M: ☽∠♅ 4:24; ☽#☿ 6:14; ☽☍♀ 6:23; ☽□♃ 7:31; ☉#☽ 17:54; ☽□⚷ 19:03; ♀□♃ 19:35; ☽□♄ 20:38; ☉△♅ 23:07; ☽△♆ 23:26

30 Tu: ☽☍♇ 2:29; ☽✶♅ 5:35; ☉☍☽ 6:05; ☽✶♂ 9:23; ☽⊼☿ 18:24; ☽⊼⚳ 20:53; ☽∥⚷ 20:59

31 W: ☽⚼♆ 0:17; ☽∥♄ 1:27; ☽#♃ 8:45; ☽✶♃ 9:26; ☽∠♂ 10:19; ☽⊼♀ 12:52; ☽⚼☿ 19:38; ☽△⚷ 20:31; ☽⚼⚳ 22:03; ☽△♄ 22:09

February 2029

LONGITUDE

Day	Sid.Time	☉	☽	☽ 12 hour	Mean☊	True☊	☿	♀	♂	⚳	♃	♄	⚷	♅	♆	♇
	h m s	° E "	° E "	° E "	° E	° E	° E	° E	° E	° E	° E	° E	° E	° E	° E	° E
1 Th	8 45 58	12♒24 24	6♍12 08	13♍35 28	12♑29.6	13♑45.9	18♑36.0	29♑56.6	12♎53.0	20♑02.1	27♎16.8	5♉04.0	4♉03.5	10♊18.6	6♈41.4	8♒32.1
2 F	8 49 54	13 25 16	20 58 53	28 21 26	12 26.5	13R 41.5	19 07.2	1♒11.8	13 01.7	20 25.6	27 18.5	5 06.9	4 04.6	10R 17.8	6 42.9	8 34.0
3 Sa	8 53 51	14 26 07	5♎42 17	13♎00 37	12 23.3	13 37.2	19 43.5	2 27.0	13 09.8	20 48.9	27 20.0	5 09.9	4 05.8	10 17.1	6 44.4	8 35.9
4 Su	8 57 47	15 26 58	20 15 48	27 27 19	12 20.1	13 33.8	20 24.5	3 42.2	13 17.3	21 12.3	27 21.4	5 13.1	4 07.0	10 16.4	6 46.0	8 37.7
5 M	9 01 44	16 27 47	4♏34 46	11♏37 53	12 16.9	13D 31.7	21 09.8	4 57.4	13 24.2	21 35.5	27 22.5	5 16.3	4 08.3	10 15.8	6 47.6	8 39.6
6 Tu	9 05 40	17 28 36	18 36 33	25 30 44	12 13.7	13 31.1	21 59.0	6 12.6	13 30.4	21 58.8	27 23.5	5 19.7	4 09.6	10 15.2	6 49.2	8 41.5
7 W	9 09 37	18 29 24	2♐20 28	9♐05 53	12 10.6	13 31.8	22 51.7	7 27.8	13 35.9	22 22.0	27 24.2	5 23.1	4 11.0	10 14.7	6 50.8	8 43.3
8 Th	9 13 33	19 30 11	15 47 10	22 24 30	12 07.4	13 33.3	23 47.7	8 42.9	13 40.8	22 45.1	27 24.8	5 26.6	4 12.5	10 14.2	6 52.5	8 45.2
9 F	9 17 30	20 30 57	28 58 06	5♑28 12	12 04.2	13 34.9	24 46.6	9 58.1	13 45.0	23 08.2	27 25.2	5 30.3	4 14.0	10 13.8	6 54.2	8 47.1
10 Sa	9 21 27	21 31 43	11♑55 01	18 18 45	12 01.0	13R 35.7	25 48.3	11 13.3	13 48.5	23 31.3	27R 25.4	5 34.0	4 15.6	10 13.4	6 55.9	8 48.9
11 Su	9 25 23	22 32 27	24 39 34	0♒57 38	11 57.9	13 35.0	26 52.4	12 28.4	13 51.3	23 54.3	27 25.4	5 37.8	4 17.2	10 13.1	6 57.6	8 50.7
12 M	9 29 20	23 33 09	7♒13 05	13 26 05	11 54.7	13 32.5	27 58.9	13 43.6	13 53.3	24 17.2	27 25.2	5 41.7	4 18.9	10 12.9	6 59.4	8 52.6
13 Tu	9 33 16	24 33 51	19 36 42	25 45 03	11 51.5	13 27.8	29 07.5	14 58.7	13 54.7	24 40.1	27 24.9	5 45.7	4 20.6	10 12.6	7 01.1	8 54.4
14 W	9 37 13	25 34 31	1♓51 16	7♓55 28	11 48.3	13 21.1	0♒18.2	16 13.9	13R 55.3	25 02.9	27 24.3	5 49.8	4 22.3	10 12.5	7 02.9	8 56.2
15 Th	9 41 09	26 35 09	13 57 45	19 58 19	11 45.1	13 13.0	1 30.6	17 29.0	13 55.2	25 25.7	27 23.5	5 54.0	4 24.2	10 12.4	7 04.7	8 58.0
16 F	9 45 06	27 35 46	25 57 20	1♈55 01	11 42.0	13 04.1	2 44.8	18 44.1	13 54.3	25 48.4	27 22.6	5 58.3	4 26.0	10D 12.3	7 06.6	8 59.8
17 Sa	9 49 02	28 36 21	7♈51 39	13 47 32	11 38.8	12 55.3	4 00.7	19 59.3	13 52.7	26 11.1	27 21.4	6 02.6	4 28.0	10 12.3	7 08.4	9 01.6
18 Su	9 52 59	29 36 55	19 43 00	25 38 28	11 35.6	12 47.4	5 18.1	21 14.4	13 50.4	26 33.7	27 20.1	6 07.1	4 29.9	10 12.4	7 10.3	9 03.4
19 M	9 56 55	0♓37 27	1♉34 23	7♉31 13	11 32.4	12 41.2	6 36.9	22 29.5	13 47.2	26 56.2	27 18.6	6 11.6	4 32.0	10 12.5	7 12.2	9 05.2
20 Tu	10 00 52	1 37 57	13 29 31	19 29 49	11 29.3	12 37.1	7 57.2	23 44.5	13 43.3	27 18.6	27 16.9	6 16.2	4 34.0	10 12.7	7 14.1	9 07.0
21 W	10 04 49	2 38 26	25 32 45	1♊38 53	11 26.1	12D 35.1	9 18.8	24 59.6	13 38.6	27 41.0	27 15.0	6 20.9	4 36.2	10 12.9	7 16.0	9 08.7
22 Th	10 08 45	3 38 52	7♊48 53	14 03 21	11 22.9	12 34.9	10 41.6	26 14.7	13 33.2	28 03.4	27 12.9	6 25.7	4 38.3	10 13.2	7 18.0	9 10.5
23 F	10 12 42	4 39 17	20 22 54	26 48 07	11 19.7	12 35.8	12 05.7	27 29.7	13 27.0	28 25.6	27 10.7	6 30.6	4 40.5	10 13.5	7 20.0	9 12.2
24 Sa	10 16 38	5 39 40	3♋19 31	9♋57 32	11 16.5	12R 36.9	13 31.1	28 44.7	13 20.0	28 47.8	27 08.2	6 35.5	4 42.8	10 13.9	7 22.0	9 13.9
25 Su	10 20 35	6 40 01	16 42 32	23 34 44	11 13.4	12 37.1	14 57.5	29 59.8	13 12.2	29 10.0	27 05.6	6 40.6	4 45.1	10 14.3	7 24.0	9 15.7
26 M	10 24 31	7 40 20	0♌34 10	7♌40 43	11 10.2	12 35.6	16 25.2	1♓14.8	13 03.7	29 32.0	27 02.8	6 45.7	4 47.5	10 14.8	7 26.0	9 17.4
27 Tu	10 28 28	8 40 37	14 54 04	22 13 40	11 07.0	12 31.9	17 53.9	2 29.8	12 54.4	29 54.0	26 59.8	6 50.9	4 49.9	10 15.3	7 28.0	9 19.0
28 W	10 32 24	9♓40 52	29 38 46	7♍08 24	11♑03.8	12♑25.7	19♒23.8	3♓44.7	12♎44.3	0♒15.9	26♎56.7	6♉56.1	4♉52.3	10♊15.9	7♈30.1	9♒20.7

1st of Month

Julian Day #
2462168.5
Obliquity
23°26E0"
SVP 4♓50E54"
GC 27♐14.7
Eris 25♈21.3

Day	⚴
1	23♐37.7
6	25 29.2
11	27 17.9
16	29 03.2
21	0♑45.1
26	2 23.0

Day	⚵
1	8♏12.7
6	8 47.9
11	9 15.6
16	9 35.4
21	9 46.9
26	9 50.0R

Day	⚶
1	18♐32.9
6	20 57.2
11	23 19.3
16	25 39.0
21	27 56.1
26	0♑10.3

DECLINATION and LATITUDE

Day	☉ Decl	☽ Decl	☽ Lat	☽12h Decl	☿ Decl	☿ Lat	♀ Decl	♀ Lat	♂ Decl	♂ Lat	⚳ Decl	⚳ Lat	♃ Decl	♃ Lat	♄ Decl	♄ Lat
1 Th	17S05	5N23	4S08	2N17	20S07	2N03	20S48	0S39	2S18	3N02	24S59	3S04	9S13	1N23	10N59	2S21
2 F	16 47	0S51	4 48	3S57	20 14	1 52	20 34	0 41	2 20	3 03	24 57	3 06	9 13	1 23	11 00	2 21
3 Sa	16 30	6 60	5 09	9 56	20 20	1 41	20 19	0 43	2 22	3 04	24 55	3 08	9 14	1 23	11 02	2 21
4 Su	16 12	12 42	5 10	15 17	20 25	1 30	20 04	0 46	2 24	3 05	24 53	3 09	9 14	1 24	11 03	2 21
5 M	15 54	17 37	4 52	19 41	20 29	1 19	19 48	0 48	2 26	3 06	24 51	3 11	9 14	1 24	11 04	2 20
6 Tu	15 36	21 27	4 16	22 54	20 32	1 08	19 31	0 50	2 27	3 07	24 49	3 13	9 14	1 24	11 06	2 20
7 W	15 17	23 59	3 26	24 43	20 34	0 57	19 14	0 52	2 28	3 08	24 47	3 15	9 14	1 24	11 07	2 20
8 Th	14 58	25 06	2 26	25 06	20 35	0 46	18 56	0 53	2 29	3 09	24 45	3 17	9 14	1 25	11 09	2 19
9 F	14 39	24 45	1 19	24 03	20 35	0 36	18 38	0 55	2 30	3 11	24 43	3 19	9 14	1 25	11 10	2 19
10 Sa	14 20	23 03	0 09	21 46	20 33	0 26	18 19	0 57	2 30	3 12	24 41	3 21	9 14	1 25	11 11	2 19
11 Su	13 60	20 12	0N60	18 26	20 31	0 16	18 00	0 59	2 30	3 13	24 39	3 22	9 14	1 25	11 13	2 19
12 M	13 40	16 27	2 05	14 19	20 27	0 06	17 40	1 01	2 30	3 14	24 36	3 24	9 13	1 25	11 15	2 18
13 Tu	13 20	12 02	3 03	9 40	20 23	0S03	17 20	1 02	2 30	3 15	24 34	3 26	9 13	1 26	11 16	2 18
14 W	12 60	7 13	3 51	4 42	20 17	0 12	16 59	1 04	2 29	3 16	24 32	3 28	9 13	1 26	11 18	2 18
15 Th	12 39	2 10	4 29	0N22	20 09	0 21	16 38	1 06	2 28	3 17	24 30	3 30	9 12	1 26	11 19	2 18
16 F	12 18	2N53	4 54	5 23	20 01	0 29	16 16	1 07	2 27	3 18	24 27	3 32	9 12	1 26	11 21	2 17
17 Sa	11 57	7 48	5 06	10 09	19 51	0 37	15 54	1 09	2 25	3 19	24 25	3 34	9 11	1 27	11 23	2 17
18 Su	11 36	12 25	5 05	14 33	19 40	0 45	15 31	1 10	2 24	3 20	24 22	3 36	9 10	1 27	11 24	2 17
19 M	11 15	16 34	4 51	18 25	19 28	0 53	15 08	1 11	2 22	3 20	24 20	3 38	9 10	1 27	11 26	2 17
20 Tu	10 54	20 05	4 24	21 33	19 15	1 00	14 45	1 13	2 19	3 21	24 17	3 40	9 09	1 27	11 28	2 16
21 W	10 32	22 48	3 46	23 47	19 00	1 07	14 21	1 14	2 17	3 22	24 15	3 42	9 08	1 28	11 30	2 16
22 Th	10 10	24 30	2 56	24 55	18 44	1 14	13 57	1 15	2 14	3 23	24 12	3 44	9 07	1 28	11 31	2 16
23 F	9 48	25 02	1 57	24 48	18 27	1 20	13 32	1 16	2 11	3 24	24 10	3 46	9 06	1 28	11 33	2 16
24 Sa	9 26	24 13	0 50	23 18	18 08	1 26	13 07	1 17	2 07	3 24	24 07	3 48	9 05	1 28	11 35	2 15
25 Su	9 04	22 02	0S22	20 25	17 49	1 32	12 42	1 18	2 04	3 25	24 04	3 50	9 04	1 28	11 37	2 15
26 M	8 41	18 29	1 35	16 15	17 27	1 37	12 16	1 19	1 60	3 26	24 02	3 52	9 02	1 29	11 39	2 15
27 Tu	8 19	13 45	2 44	11 01	17 05	1 42	11 50	1 20	1 56	3 26	23 59	3 54	9 01	1 29	11 41	2 15
28 W	7S56	8N06	3S44	5N02	16S41	1S47	11S23	1S21	1S51	3N27	23S56	3S56	8S60	1N29	11N43	2S14

Day	⚷ Decl	⚷ Lat	♅ Decl	♅ Lat	♆ Decl	♆ Lat	♇ Decl	♇ Lat
1	12N01	0S54	21N58	0S01	1N20	1S26	23S10	5S14
6	12 03	0 54	21 58	0 01	1 23	1 26	23 08	5 14
11	12 05	0 55	21 58	0 01	1 27	1 26	23 06	5 14
16	12 08	0 55	21 58	0 01	1 30	1 26	23 04	5 15
21	12 12	0 55	21 58	0 01	1 34	1 26	23 02	5 16
26	12N15	0S55	21N58	0S01	1N38	1S26	23S00	5S16

Day	⚴ Decl	⚴ Lat	⚵ Decl	⚵ Lat	⚶ Decl	⚶ Lat	Eris Decl	Eris Lat
1	5N32	28N51	7S36	7N00	18S34	4N23	0N34	9S55
6	6 02	29 24	7 27	7 21	18 47	4 21	0 35	9 54
11	6 35	29 60	7 15	7 43	18 58	4 19	0 36	9 53
16	7 10	30 36	6 59	8 06	19 06	4 16	0 37	9 53
21	7 49	31 15	6 41	8 29	19 12	4 14	0 39	9 52
26	8N30	31N55	6S19	8N53	19S15	4N11	0N40	9S51

Moon Phenomena

Max/0 Decl
dy hr mn
1 20:46 0 S
8 6:07 25S08
15 10:15 0 N
22 21:49 25N02

Max/0 Lat
dy hr mn
3 12:57 5S12
10 3:08 0 N
17 10:07 5N07
24 16:44 0 S

Perigee/Apogee
dy hr m kilometers
1 12:21 p 363337
17 11:59 a 405810

PH dy hr mn
☾ 5 21:53 17♏23
● 13 10:33 25♒01
☽ 21 15:11 3♊17
○ 28 17:11 10♍24

Void of Course Moon

Last Aspect			☽ Ingress	
1 20:51	☿	△	♎	2 14:41
4 11:51	♃	☌	♏	4 16:16
6 6:14	☿	⚹	♐	6 19:52
8 21:09	♃	⚹	♑	9 1:54
11 5:15	♃	□	♒	11 10:10
13 15:15	♃	△	♓	13 20:21
14 16:32	♅	□	♈	16 8:08
18 15:24	♃	☍	♉	18 20:49
20 22:47	♀	□	♊	21 8:46
23 14:42	♀	△	♋	23 17:54
25 18:00	♃	□	♌	25 23:02
27 19:40	♃	⚹	♍	28 0:34

DAILY ASPECTARIAN

1 Th
☽⚻♆ 0:48
♀ ♒ 1:04
☽⚻♇ 3:48
☽□♅ 6:40
☽∠♃ 9:53
☉⚻☽ 10:49
☽⚺♂ 10:58
☽⋕♂ 11:53
☉△♂ 13:12
☽⚼♀ 15:31
☽∥♆ 15:38
☽△☿ 20:51
☽⚼⚷ 20:54
☽⚼♄ 22:35
☽△⚳ 23:04

2 F
☽⋕♆ 1:55
☽⚼♇ 4:13
☽∥♂ 5:46
☽⚺♃ 10:19
☉⚼☽ 13:00
☽△♀ 18:11
☽⚻⚷ 21:22
☽⚻♄ 23:07
☿∥♀ 23:22

3 Sa
☽☍♆ 1:42
☽△♇ 4:45
☽△♅ 7:31
☽∥♃ 9:05
☽☌♂ 12:22
☉△☽ 15:26
☽⋕♄ 16:45
☽⋕⚷ 21:03

4 Su
☽□☿ 0:15
☽□⚳ 1:36
♀□⚷ 8:03
☽⚼♅ 8:21
☽☌♃ 11:51
☉∥☽ 15:37
☽☍⚷ 23:15

5 M
☽□♀ 0:42
☽☍♄ 1:11
☽⚻♆ 3:46
♀□♄ 6:19
☽□♇ 6:57
☽⚻♅ 9:39
☽∥♀ 11:51
☽⚺♂ 15:09
☽∥☿ 17:23
☉□☽ 21:53
☊ D 21:58
☿☌⚳ 23:50

6 Tu
☽⋕♅ 3:58
☽⚼♆ 5:35
☽⚹⚳ 6:01
☽⚹☿ 6:14
♀⚹♆ 11:57
☽∥♇ 14:15
☽⚺♃ 15:18
☽∠♂ 17:22

7 W
☽⚻⚷ 3:16
☽⚻♄ 5:25
☽△♆ 8:00
☽∠⚳ 9:11
☽⚹♀ 10:01
☽∠☿ 10:31
☽⚹♇ 11:21
☽∥⚳ 13:01
☽☍♅ 14:02
☽∠♃ 17:56
☽⚹♂ 20:11

8 Th
♀☌♇ 0:45
☽⚼⚷ 6:12
☉⚹☽ 7:17
☽⚼♄ 8:28
☽⚺⚳ 13:00
☽∠♇ 14:29
☽⚺☿ 15:41
☽∠♀ 15:54
☽⚹♃ 21:09

9 F
☽∥⚳ 0:41
♀△♅ 4:59
☽△⚷ 9:44
☿⚼♅ 10:39
☽△♄ 12:07
☉∠☽ 13:07
☽□♆ 14:41
☽⚺♇ 18:12
☽⚻♅ 20:50
☽⚺♀ 22:34
☽∥♇ 23:29

10 Sa
☊ R 3:09
☽□♂ 3:33
☉∠♆ 9:50
☽⋕♅ 10:16
♃ R 13:08
☉⚺☽ 19:38
☽∥☿ 21:43
☽☌⚳ 22:31

11 Su
☽⚼♅ 1:04
☽☌☿ 4:36
☽□♃ 5:15
☿□♃ 11:59
☽∥♀ 16:03
☽□⚷ 18:25
☽□♄ 21:03
☽⚹♆ 23:34

12 M
♀△♂ 3:11
☽☌♇ 3:12
☽△♅ 5:46
☽△♂ 12:54
☽☌♀ 13:59
☉∥☽ 16:44
☽⋕⚷ 23:39

13 Tu
☽⋕♄ 3:56
☉⚺⚳ 3:58
☽∠♆ 4:42
☽⚺⚳ 10:12
☉☌☽ 10:33
☽∥♃ 14:14
☽△♃ 15:15
☿ ♒ 17:53
☽⚼♂ 18:13
☽⚺☿ 20:37

14 W
☽⚹⚷ 4:59
☽⚹♄ 7:54
♂ R 8:17
⚳⚼♅ 10:01
☽⚺♆ 10:17
☽⚺♇ 14:03
☽□♅ 16:32
☽∠⚳ 16:44
☽⚼♃ 20:53
☽∥♂ 22:36
☽⚻♂ 23:55

15 Th
☽⋕♆ 3:12
☽∠☿ 5:40
☽⚺♀ 7:51
☽∠⚷ 10:53
☽∠♄ 13:56
☽∥♆ 17:23
☉△♃ 18:52
☽∠♇ 20:03
☽⋕♂ 21:53
☽⚹⚳ 23:42

16 F
☽⚻♃ 2:51
☉⚺☽ 3:36
♅ D 10:53
☉⋕⚷ 11:16
☽⚹☿ 15:18
☽⚺⚷ 17:07
☽∠♀ 17:31
☽⚺♄ 20:18
☽☌♆ 22:32

17 Sa
☽⚹♇ 2:22
☽⚹♅ 4:45
☉⚼♂ 6:16
☽⋕♃ 6:57
☿□⚷ 8:44
☽☍♂ 12:08
☉∠☽ 12:42
☽∥♄ 18:32
☉⋕☽ 19:57
☽∥⚷ 22:36

18 Su
☽⚹♀ 3:27
☉ ♓ 9:09
☽∠♅ 11:07
☉⋕♄ 12:33
☽□⚳ 14:19
☽☍♃ 15:24
☿□♄ 15:52
☽⋕♀ 16:08
♀∠♆ 18:20
⚴ ♑ 18:21
☉⚹☽ 21:54

19 M
☽☌⚷ 6:00
☽☌♄ 9:23
☿⚹♆ 10:51
☽⚺♆ 11:24
☽□☿ 11:28
☽□♇ 15:11
☽⚺♅ 17:25
☽⋕☿ 18:13
⚳□♃ 22:16

20 Tu
☽⚻♂ 0:28
☽∥♅ 15:44
☽∠♆ 17:29
☿☌♇ 21:00
☽□♀ 22:47

21 W
☽⋕♇ 2:39
☽⚻♃ 3:21
☽△⚳ 4:21
☽⚼♂ 6:04
☊ D 14:59
☉□☽ 15:11
☿△♅ 15:46
☽⚺⚷ 17:49
☽⋕⚳ 18:35
☽⚺♄ 21:18
☽⚹♆ 23:00

22 Th
☽△♇ 2:38
☽☌♅ 4:39
☽△☿ 6:15
☽⚼♃ 8:27
☽⚼⚳ 10:24
☽△♂ 10:57
♀△♃ 18:06
☽∠⚷ 22:40

23 F
☉⚹⚷ 0:31
☽∠♄ 2:08
☽⚼♇ 7:11
☽△♃ 12:39
☽⚼☿ 14:05
☽△♀ 14:42
☽⚻⚳ 15:27
♀⚼♂ 16:47
☿△♂ 21:09

24 Sa
♀⚺⚳ 1:24
☽⋕⚳ 1:42
☽⚹⚷ 2:32
☉△☽ 4:36
☽⚹♄ 5:58
☽□♆ 7:21
☽⚻♇ 10:43
☽⚺♅ 12:30
☽⋕♇ 14:59
☊ R 16:46
☽□♂ 17:51
☽⚻☿ 20:32
☽⚼♀ 20:40

25 Su
♀ ♓ 0:05
☉∥♃ 0:11
☉⚹♄ 0:14
☽∥♅ 0:30
⚵ R 6:43
☉⚼☽ 9:22
⚶ ♑ 14:43
☽∠♅ 14:52
☽□♃ 18:00
☉⚺♆ 18:06
☽☍⚳ 22:11

26 M
♀⋕⚷ 0:39
☽⚻♀ 1:16
☽⋕☿ 6:12
☽□⚷ 7:10
☽□♄ 10:31
☽△♆ 11:37
☉⚻☽ 12:53
☽☍♇ 14:43
☽⚹♅ 16:18
☽⚹♂ 20:44

27 Tu
☽☍☿ 5:29
⚳ ♒ 6:34
☽∥⚷ 6:37
♀⋕♄ 7:51
☽∥♄ 9:07
☽⋕♀ 9:14
☽⚼♆ 12:25
☉⚺♇ 15:45
☽⚹♃ 19:40
☽⋕♃ 20:21
☽∠♂ 20:58

28 W
☉⋕☽ 0:40
☽⚻⚳ 1:01
☽☍♀ 7:10
☽△⚷ 8:24
☽△♄ 11:44
☽⚻♆ 12:36
☉□♅ 14:07
☽⚻♇ 15:32
☽□♅ 16:59
☉☍☽ 17:11
☽∠♃ 19:34
☽⚺♂ 20:39
♀⚹⚷ 22:22

LONGITUDE

Day	Sid.Time	☉	☽	☽ 12 hour	Mean☊	True☊	☿	♀	♂	⚳	♃	♄	⚷	♅	♆	♇
	h m s	° ' "	° ' "	° ' "	° '	° '	° '	° '	° '	° '	° '	° '	° '	° '	° '	° '
1 Th	10 36 21	10♓41 05	14♍41 26	22♍16 37	11♑00.7	12♑17.5	20♒54.7	4♓59.7	12♎33.4	0♒37.7	26♎53.4	7♉01.4	4♉54.8	10♊16.6	7♈32.1	9♒22.4
2 F	10 40 18	11 41 17	29 52 35	7♎27 59	10 57.5	12R 08.2	22 26.8	6 14.7	12R 21.8	0 59.5	26R 49.8	7 06.8	4 57.3	10 17.3	7 34.2	9 24.0
3 Sa	10 44 14	12 41 26	15♎01 31	22 31 57	10 54.3	11 59.1	23 59.9	7 29.6	12 09.5	1 21.2	26 46.2	7 12.3	4 59.9	10 18.0	7 36.3	9 25.7
4 Su	10 48 11	13 41 35	29 58 15	7♏19 33	10 51.1	11 51.1	25 34.2	8 44.6	11 56.4	1 42.8	26 42.3	7 17.9	5 02.5	10 18.8	7 38.4	9 27.3
5 M	10 52 07	14 41 41	14♏35 13	21 44 46	10 47.9	11 45.2	27 09.5	9 59.5	11 42.5	2 04.3	26 38.3	7 23.5	5 05.1	10 19.7	7 40.5	9 28.9
6 Tu	10 56 04	15 41 47	28 47 59	5♐44 48	10 44.8	11 41.8	28 45.9	11 14.4	11 27.9	2 25.8	26 34.1	7 29.2	5 07.8	10 20.6	7 42.7	9 30.5
7 W	11 00 00	16 41 50	12♐35 19	19 19 45	10 41.6	11D 40.5	0♓23.4	12 29.3	11 12.7	2 47.1	26 29.8	7 34.9	5 10.6	10 21.5	7 44.8	9 32.0
8 Th	11 03 57	17 41 53	25 58 26	2♑31 44	10 38.4	11 40.6	2 02.0	13 44.2	10 56.7	3 08.4	26 25.3	7 40.7	5 13.3	10 22.5	7 47.0	9 33.6
9 F	11 07 53	18 41 53	9♑00 05	15 23 58	10 35.2	11R 41.1	3 41.7	14 59.1	10 40.0	3 29.6	26 20.6	7 46.6	5 16.1	10 23.6	7 49.1	9 35.2
10 Sa	11 11 50	19 41 52	21 43 48	28 00 04	10 32.1	11 40.7	5 22.5	16 14.0	10 22.7	3 50.7	26 15.8	7 52.6	5 19.0	10 24.7	7 51.3	9 36.7
11 Su	11 15 47	20 41 49	4♒13 09	10♒23 28	10 28.9	11 38.3	7 04.4	17 28.8	10 04.8	4 11.8	26 10.8	7 58.6	5 21.9	10 25.8	7 53.5	9 38.2
12 M	11 19 43	21 41 45	16 31 21	22 37 07	10 25.7	11 33.4	8 47.5	18 43.7	9 46.2	4 32.7	26 05.6	8 04.7	5 24.8	10 27.1	7 55.7	9 39.7
13 Tu	11 23 40	22 41 39	28 41 03	4♓43 22	10 22.5	11 25.4	10 31.9	19 58.5	9 27.1	4 53.5	26 00.4	8 10.8	5 27.7	10 28.3	7 57.9	9 41.1
14 W	11 27 36	23 41 30	10♓44 18	16 44 01	10 19.3	11 14.7	12 17.2	21 13.3	9 07.4	5 14.3	25 54.9	8 17.0	5 30.7	10 29.6	8 00.1	9 42.6
15 Th	11 31 33	24 41 20	22 42 40	28 40 25	10 16.2	11 01.8	14 03.8	22 28.1	8 47.2	5 34.9	25 49.4	8 23.2	5 33.7	10 31.0	8 02.3	9 44.0
16 F	11 35 29	25 41 08	4♈37 24	10♈33 47	10 13.0	10 47.8	15 51.6	23 42.9	8 26.5	5 55.5	25 43.7	8 29.6	5 36.8	10 32.4	8 04.5	9 45.4
17 Sa	11 39 26	26 40 54	16 29 44	22 25 27	10 09.8	10 33.8	17 40.6	24 57.7	8 05.3	6 15.9	25 37.8	8 35.9	5 39.9	10 33.8	8 06.8	9 46.8
18 Su	11 43 22	27 40 38	28 21 09	4♉17 06	10 06.6	10 20.8	19 30.8	26 12.5	7 43.8	6 36.3	25 31.9	8 42.4	5 43.0	10 35.3	8 09.0	9 48.2
19 M	11 47 19	28 40 20	10♉13 36	16 11 00	10 03.5	10 10.1	21 22.2	27 27.2	7 21.8	6 56.5	25 25.8	8 48.8	5 46.2	10 36.9	8 11.3	9 49.6
20 Tu	11 51 16	29 40 00	22 09 43	28 10 10	10 00.3	10 02.0	23 14.8	28 41.9	6 59.6	7 16.7	25 19.5	8 55.4	5 49.4	10 38.5	8 13.5	9 50.9
21 W	11 55 12	0♈39 37	4♊12 51	10♊18 17	9 57.1	9 56.9	25 08.6	29 56.6	6 37.0	7 36.7	25 13.2	9 02.0	5 52.6	10 40.1	8 15.8	9 52.2
22 Th	11 59 09	1 39 12	16 27 03	22 39 44	9 53.9	9 54.3	27 03.7	1♈11.3	6 14.2	7 56.7	25 06.8	9 08.6	5 55.8	10 41.8	8 18.0	9 53.5
23 F	12 03 05	2 38 45	28 56 56	5♋19 16	9 50.7	9 53.6	28 59.9	2 26.0	5 51.2	8 16.5	25 00.2	9 15.3	5 59.1	10 43.6	8 20.3	9 54.8
24 Sa	12 07 02	3 38 16	11♋47 19	18 21 38	9 47.6	9 53.6	0♈57.2	3 40.7	5 28.0	8 36.2	24 53.6	9 22.0	6 02.4	10 45.4	8 22.5	9 56.1
25 Su	12 10 58	4 37 44	25 02 43	1♌50 56	9 44.4	9 53.1	2 55.6	4 55.3	5 04.8	8 55.8	24 46.8	9 28.8	6 05.7	10 47.2	8 24.8	9 57.3
26 M	12 14 55	5 37 10	8♌46 34	15 49 43	9 41.2	9 50.9	4 55.1	6 09.9	4 41.4	9 15.3	24 40.0	9 35.6	6 09.1	10 49.1	8 27.1	9 58.5
27 Tu	12 18 51	6 36 34	23 00 17	0♍18 00	9 38.0	9 46.2	6 55.5	7 24.5	4 18.0	9 34.7	24 33.0	9 42.5	6 12.4	10 51.0	8 29.4	9 59.7
28 W	12 22 48	7 35 56	7♍42 16	15 12 21	9 34.9	9 38.9	8 56.8	8 39.1	3 54.7	9 53.9	24 26.0	9 49.4	6 15.8	10 52.9	8 31.6	10 00.9
29 Th	12 26 45	8 35 15	22 47 11	0♎25 34	9 31.7	9 29.2	10 58.8	9 53.6	3 31.4	10 13.0	24 18.9	9 56.3	6 19.3	10 54.9	8 33.9	10 02.0
30 F	12 30 41	9 34 32	8♎06 05	15 47 15	9 28.5	9 18.1	13 01.4	11 08.1	3 08.2	10 32.0	24 11.7	10 03.3	6 22.7	10 57.0	8 36.2	10 03.1
31 Sa	12 34 38	10♈33 47	23 27 34	1♏05 33	9♑25.3	9♑06.9	15♈04.5	12♈22.7	2♎45.1	10♒50.9	24♎04.5	10♉10.3	6♉26.2	10♊59.1	8♈38.4	10♒04.2

1st of Month

Julian Day # 2462196.5
Obliquity 23°26'30"
SVP 4♓50'51"
GC 27♐14.8
Eris 25♈31.1

Day	⚴	Day	⚵	Day	⚶
1	3♑19.8	1	9♏47.7R	1	1♑29.3
6	4 51.0	6	9 36.7R	6	3 38.4
11	6 17.3	11	9 16.9R	11	5 44.0
16	7 38.5	16	8 48.3R	16	7 45.6
21	8 53.9	21	8 11.3R	21	9 42.9
26	10 03.1	26	7 26.3R	26	11 35.4
31	11 05.7	31	6 34.3R	31	13 22.8

DECLINATION and LATITUDE

Day	☉ Decl	☽ Decl	☽ Lat	☽12h Decl	☿ Decl	☿ Lat	♀ Decl	♀ Lat	♂ Decl	♂ Lat	⚳ Decl	⚳ Lat	♃ Decl	♃ Lat	♄ Decl	♄ Lat
1 Th	7S34	1N53	4S30	1S19	16S17	1S51	10S57	1S22	1S47	3N27	23S53	3S58	8S58	1N29	11N44	2S14
2 F	7 11	4S30	4 57	7 36	15 50	1 55	10 30	1 23	1 42	3 28	23 51	4 01	8 57	1 29	11 46	2 14
3 Sa	6 48	10 35	5 04	13 23	15 23	1 58	10 03	1 23	1 36	3 28	23 48	4 03	8 56	1 30	11 48	2 14
4 Su	6 25	15 58	4 49	18 17	14 54	2 02	9 35	1 24	1 31	3 29	23 45	4 05	8 54	1 30	11 50	2 14
5 M	6 02	20 17	4 16	21 57	14 24	2 04	9 07	1 24	1 25	3 29	23 42	4 07	8 52	1 30	11 52	2 13
6 Tu	5 38	23 16	3 28	24 12	13 53	2 07	8 39	1 25	1 20	3 29	23 39	4 09	8 51	1 30	11 54	2 13
7 W	5 15	24 45	2 28	24 56	13 20	2 09	8 11	1 25	1 13	3 29	23 37	4 11	8 49	1 30	11 57	2 13
8 Th	4 52	24 45	1 23	24 13	12 47	2 10	7 43	1 25	1 07	3 29	23 34	4 14	8 47	1 31	11 59	2 13
9 F	4 28	23 22	0 14	22 13	12 11	2 11	7 14	1 26	1 01	3 29	23 31	4 16	8 45	1 31	12 01	2 13
10 Sa	4 05	20 48	0N53	19 10	11 35	2 12	6 45	1 26	0 54	3 29	23 28	4 18	8 43	1 31	12 03	2 12
11 Su	3 41	17 19	1 57	15 17	10 58	2 12	6 16	1 26	0 47	3 29	23 25	4 20	8 41	1 31	12 05	2 12
12 M	3 18	13 07	2 54	10 50	10 19	2 12	5 47	1 26	0 40	3 29	23 22	4 23	8 39	1 31	12 07	2 12
13 Tu	2 54	8 28	3 42	6 01	9 39	2 12	5 17	1 26	0 33	3 29	23 19	4 25	8 37	1 31	12 09	2 12
14 W	2 30	3 32	4 19	1 02	8 58	2 10	4 48	1 26	0 25	3 28	23 17	4 27	8 35	1 32	12 11	2 12
15 Th	2 07	1N29	4 45	3N58	8 15	2 09	4 18	1 26	0 18	3 28	23 14	4 30	8 33	1 32	12 13	2 11
16 F	1 43	6 24	4 58	8 47	7 31	2 07	3 49	1 26	0 10	3 27	23 11	4 32	8 31	1 32	12 16	2 11
17 Sa	1 19	11 04	4 59	13 16	6 47	2 04	3 19	1 26	0 02	3 27	23 08	4 34	8 29	1 32	12 18	2 11
18 Su	0 55	15 20	4 46	17 15	6 01	2 01	2 49	1 25	0N05	3 26	23 05	4 37	8 26	1 32	12 20	2 11
19 M	0 32	19 00	4 21	20 34	5 14	1 58	2 19	1 25	0 13	3 25	23 02	4 39	8 24	1 32	12 22	2 11
20 Tu	0 08	21 54	3 44	23 01	4 25	1 54	1 49	1 25	0 21	3 25	22 59	4 42	8 22	1 32	12 25	2 10
21 W	0N16	23 53	2 57	24 27	3 36	1 49	1 18	1 24	0 29	3 24	22 56	4 44	8 19	1 33	12 27	2 10
22 Th	0 39	24 45	2 01	24 44	2 46	1 44	0 48	1 23	0 37	3 23	22 53	4 47	8 17	1 33	12 29	2 10
23 F	1 03	24 23	0 58	23 44	1 54	1 39	0 18	1 23	0 46	3 21	22 51	4 49	8 14	1 33	12 31	2 10
24 Sa	1 27	22 45	0S10	21 26	1 02	1 33	0N12	1 22	0 54	3 20	22 48	4 52	8 12	1 33	12 34	2 10
25 Su	1 50	19 49	1 19	17 54	0 09	1 26	0 43	1 21	1 02	3 19	22 45	4 54	8 09	1 33	12 36	2 10
26 M	2 14	15 43	2 26	13 16	0N45	1 19	1 13	1 21	1 09	3 18	22 42	4 57	8 07	1 33	12 38	2 10
27 Tu	2 37	10 36	3 27	7 44	1 40	1 11	1 43	1 20	1 17	3 16	22 39	4 59	8 04	1 33	12 40	2 09
28 W	3 01	4 44	4 15	1 37	2 35	1 03	2 13	1 19	1 25	3 15	22 37	5 02	8 01	1 33	12 43	2 09
29 Th	3 24	1S32	4 48	4S42	3 31	0 54	2 43	1 18	1 33	3 13	22 34	5 05	7 59	1 33	12 45	2 09
30 F	3 48	7 48	4 60	10 48	4 27	0 45	3 14	1 17	1 41	3 11	22 31	5 07	7 56	1 33	12 47	2 09
31 Sa	4N11	13S37	4S51	16S12	5N24	0S35	3N44	1S16	1N48	3N10	22S28	5S10	7S53	1N33	12N50	2S09

Day	⚷ Decl	⚷ Lat	♅ Decl	♅ Lat	♆ Decl	♆ Lat	♇ Decl	♇ Lat
1	12N18	0S55	21N58	0S01	1N41	1S26	22S59	5S17
6	12 22	0 55	21 59	0 01	1 45	1 26	22 58	5 18
11	12 26	0 55	21 60	0 01	1 49	1 26	22 57	5 18
16	12 31	0 56	22 01	0 01	1 54	1 26	22 55	5 19
21	12 36	0 56	22 02	0 01	1 58	1 26	22 55	5 20
26	12 41	0 56	22 03	0 01	2 02	1 26	22 54	5 21
31	12N47	0S56	22N05	0S00	2N07	1S26	22S53	5S22

Day	⚴ Decl	⚴ Lat	⚵ Decl	⚵ Lat	⚶ Decl	⚶ Lat	Eris Decl	Eris Lat
1	8N55	32N19	6S05	9N07	19S17	4N09	0N41	9S51
6	9 40	33 02	5 39	9 31	19 17	4 06	0 42	9 51
11	10 27	33 46	5 10	9 55	19 17	4 02	0 43	9 50
16	11 15	34 31	4 38	10 19	19 14	3 59	0 45	9 50
21	12 06	35 18	4 05	10 42	19 11	3 54	0 46	9 49
26	12 58	36 07	3 30	11 05	19 07	3 50	0 48	9 49
31	13N51	36N57	2S53	11N26	19S02	3N45	0N49	9S48

Moon Phenomena

Max/0 Decl (dy hr mn)	Perigee/Apogee (dy hr m kilometers)
1 7:03 0 S	1 18:30 p 358630
7 11:51 24S56	16 21:34 a 406528
14 16:55 0 N	30 5:41 p 356667
22 5:19 24N46	
28 18:10 0 S	

Max/0 Lat (dy hr mn)	PH dy hr mn
2 19:12 5S04	☾ 7 7:53 17♐02
9 5:01 0 N	● 15 4:20 24♓52
16 12:13 5N00	☽ 23 7:34 2♋58
23 20:29 0 S	○ 30 2:28 9♎41
30 1:51 5S00	

Void of Course Moon

Last Aspect	☽ Ingress
28 17:11 ☉ ☍	♎ 2 0:12
3 18:44 ♃ ☌	♏ 4 0:03
5 23:56 ♀ ☌	♐ 6 2:04
8 0:49 ♃ ✶	♑ 8 7:21
10 8:36 ♃ □	♒ 10 15:51
12 18:44 ♃ △	♓ 13 2:37
15 4:20 ☉ ☌	♈ 15 14:40
17 18:20 ♃ ☍	♉ 18 3:20
20 14:33 ☉ ✶	♊ 20 15:39
23 0:07 ♀ □	♋ 23 1:59
24 23:32 ♃ □	♌ 25 8:46
27 2:32 ♃ ✶	♍ 27 11:31
28 5:07 ♅ □	♎ 29 11:20
31 0:57 ♃ ☌	♏ 31 10:17

DAILY ASPECTARIAN

1 Th
☽#♂ 0:23
☽∥♆ 0:45
☽⚼⚳ 1:31
☽⚼⚷ 8:17
☽⚻☿ 10:57
☽⚼♄ 11:40
☽#♆ 13:23
☽∥♂ 13:33
☽⚼♇ 15:20
☽⊻♃ 19:13

2 F
♂#♆ 0:44
☽△⚳ 1:48
☿∠♆ 1:58
☉⚼♃ 3:13
☽⚻⚷ 8:03
☉∥☽ 9:45
☽⚻♀ 10:58
☽⚻♄ 11:31
☽☍♆ 12:12
☽⚼☿ 13:20
☉⚻♂ 13:27
☽△♇ 15:06
☽△♅ 16:29
☽∥♃ 17:18
♀✶♄ 18:01
☽☌♂ 19:30
☉⚻☽ 20:01
☽∥♀ 21:57

3 Sa
♀⊻♆ 2:12
☽#♄ 5:11
☽#⚷ 7:22
☽⚼♀ 13:02
☽△☿ 16:03
☽⚼♅ 16:28
☽☌♃ 18:44
☽∥☿ 19:22
☉⚼☽ 21:47

4 Su
☽□⚳ 2:54
☽☍⚷ 8:17
☽☍♄ 12:02
☽⚻♆ 12:33
♀⊻♇ 13:59
☽□♇ 15:32
☽△♀ 15:40
☿△♃ 16:30
☽⚻♅ 16:56
☿⚼♂ 18:07
☽⊻♂ 19:18

5 M
☉△☽ 0:12
♀□♅ 6:32
☽#♅ 12:17
☽⚼♆ 13:36
♀∥♃ 13:42
☽∠♂ 20:05
☽⊻♃ 20:12
☽∥♇ 20:59
☽□☿ 23:56

6 Tu
♀⚻♂ 3:37
☽∥⚳ 4:25
♀⚼♃ 5:58
☽✶⚳ 6:25
☽⚻⚷ 10:58
☽⚻♄ 15:08
☽△♆ 15:28
☿ ♓ 18:16
☽✶♇ 18:37
☽☍♅ 20:04
☽✶♂ 21:37
☽∠♃ 22:05
☽□♀ 23:48

7 W
☉□☽ 7:53
☊ D 8:00
☽∠⚳ 9:29
☽⚼⚷ 13:34
☽⚼♄ 17:59
☽∠♇ 21:26

8 Th
☽✶♃ 0:49
☽✶☿ 12:42
☽⊻⚳ 13:30
☿#⚷ 15:28
☉∠⚳ 16:25
☽△⚷ 17:02
☿⊻⚳ 20:21
☽△♄ 21:42
☽□♆ 21:47
☽∥⚳ 22:09

9 F
☽⊻♇ 1:06
☽⚻♅ 2:36
☽□♂ 3:03
☽∥♇ 4:42
☊ R 5:02
☿#♄ 6:49
☽✶♀ 12:26
☽#♅ 14:04
♄⊻♆ 15:59
☉✶☽ 19:48
☽∠☿ 21:01
♂△♅ 21:29
☿✶⚷ 23:09

10 Sa
☽⚼♅ 7:03
☽□♃ 8:36
☉∠⚷ 15:36
☽∠♀ 20:16
☽☌⚳ 23:57

11 Su
☽□⚷ 2:14
☉∠☽ 3:07
☽⊻☿ 6:26
☽✶♆ 7:09
☽□♄ 7:21
☽☌♇ 10:33
☽△♂ 11:07
☿⊻♆ 11:42
☽△♅ 12:06
☿✶♄ 13:26

12 M
☽#⚷ 3:33
☽⊻♀ 4:50
☽#♄ 5:18
♂△♇ 7:41
☉⊻☽ 11:05
☿⚻♂ 11:27
☿⊻♇ 12:13
☽∠♆ 12:39
☽⚼♂ 15:50
☽∥☿ 17:05
☽△♃ 18:44
♀∠⚳ 21:47
☽∥♃ 23:11
☿□♅ 23:12

13 Tu
☿⚼♃ 6:13
♀∠⚷ 9:46
☽⊻⚳ 12:42
☉∠♄ 13:02
☽✶⚷ 13:32
☽∥♀ 17:15
☽⊻♆ 18:31
☽✶♄ 19:03
☽⚻♂ 20:52
☽⊻♇ 21:56
☽□♅ 23:31

14 W
☽⚼♃ 0:21
☽☌☿ 3:38
☉∥☽ 5:22
☽#♆ 7:59
☿∥♃ 13:23
☽∥♂ 15:17
☽#♂ 18:29
☽∠⚳ 19:36
☽∠⚷ 19:40
⚳□⚷ 22:23
☽☌♀ 23:27

15 Th
☉∠♇ 1:06
☽∠♄ 1:22
☽∥♆ 1:56
☉#☽ 2:49
☽∠♇ 4:05
☉☌☽ 4:20
☽⚻♃ 6:13
☽#♀ 12:26
☉#♆ 13:34
♀∠♄ 19:19
♂⚻♄ 21:16

16 F
☉⚻♃ 0:55
☽⊻⚷ 2:00
☽✶⚳ 2:42
☽#☿ 4:52
☽☌♆ 7:00
☽☍♂ 7:29
☽⊻♄ 7:53
☽✶♇ 10:24
☽#♃ 10:33
☽✶♅ 11:59
♀∠♇ 20:27
♂☍♆ 22:31

17 Sa
☽⊻☿ 2:49
☽∥♄ 6:41
☽∥⚷ 7:57
♀⚻♃ 11:56
♃⚼♅ 12:52
☽☍♃ 18:20
☽∠♅ 18:24
☽⊻♀ 19:09
☉⊻☽ 22:31

18 Su
☽∠☿ 14:46
☽☌⚷ 14:58
☿∠⚷ 16:03
☽□⚳ 17:11
☽⚻♂ 18:24
☽⊻♆ 19:52
☽☌♄ 21:07
☽□♇ 23:11

19 M
☽⊻♅ 0:47
☽∠♀ 5:01
☉∠☽ 7:35
☿∠⚳ 8:57
☉#♂ 13:49
♂△⚳ 14:19
♀#♆ 17:26
☽⚼♂ 23:40

20 Tu
☽∥♅ 1:12
☽∠♆ 2:08
☽✶☿ 2:35
☽⚻♃ 6:16
☉ ♈ 8:03
☿∠♄ 9:06
☽#♇ 10:42
☽#⚳ 11:20
☽✶♀ 14:33
☉✶☽ 16:19
☿∠♇ 20:31

21 W
☿⚻♃ 0:55
♀ ♈ 1:05
☽⊻⚷ 3:18
☽△♂ 4:36
☽△⚳ 6:54
☽✶♆ 8:01
☽⊻♄ 9:35
☽△♇ 11:10
☽⚼♃ 11:44
☽☌♅ 12:45
⚳∥♇ 15:54
☉∥♂ 20:57

22 Th
☉#♀ 3:55
♀#♂ 6:45
☽∠⚷ 8:42
☽⚼⚳ 12:53
☽∠♄ 14:58
☽⚼♇ 16:18
☽△♃ 16:33
♂⚻⚷ 16:49
☿#♆ 21:34

23 F
☽□☿ 0:07
⚳✶♆ 5:13
☽□♀ 7:18
☉□☽ 7:34
☿ ♈ 12:20
☽□♂ 12:37
☽✶⚷ 13:18
☉#☿ 16:15
☽□♆ 17:40
☽⚻⚳ 17:58
☽✶♄ 19:29
☉☌♀ 20:13
☽⚻♇ 20:34
☽⊻♅ 22:06
☽#♇ 22:21
☽#⚳ 23:28

24 Sa
☿#♂ 3:24
☽∥♅ 6:46
☿#♀ 14:23
☽□♃ 23:32

25 Su
☽∠♅ 1:19
♀☍♂ 2:19
☉☍♂ 7:50
☉∥♆ 11:51
☽△☿ 16:13
☽✶♂ 17:08
☉△☽ 18:08
☽△♀ 19:04
☽□⚷ 19:28
♀∥♂ 20:32
☿☍♂ 21:43
☽△♆ 23:26
♀⊻⚷ 23:43

26 M
☽☍⚳ 0:50
☽□♄ 1:25
☽☍♇ 2:03
☽✶♅ 3:30
☿∥♂ 12:41
☉⊻⚷ 13:39
☽∥⚷ 14:37
☽∥♄ 14:47
☿⊻⚷ 15:11
☉☌☿ 16:35
☽∠♂ 18:00
☉⚼☽ 21:31
☽⚼☿ 21:55
☽⚼♀ 22:55

27 Tu
☽⚼♆ 0:48
☽✶♃ 2:32
☿∥♀ 3:17
☿∥♆ 10:29
☽#♃ 10:43
☿☌♀ 14:56
⚳□♄ 15:10
♀∥♆ 16:37
☽⊻♂ 18:02
☿☌♆ 18:56
♀☌♆ 21:32
☽△⚷ 21:40
☉⚻☽ 23:49

28 W
☽⚻♆ 1:20
☽⚻♀ 1:40
☽⚻☿ 2:19
☽∠♃ 2:45
☽△♄ 3:26
☽⚻⚳ 3:36
☽⚻♇ 3:43
☽□♅ 5:07
☉∥☽ 6:15
☽∥☿ 7:14
☽∥♀ 8:58
⚳☌♇ 9:16
☽∥♆ 10:15
☿⊻♄ 10:59
♄∥⚷ 11:54
☽∥♂ 12:30
☿✶♇ 12:44
☿✶⚳ 13:21
☉∥☿ 19:11
☽⚼⚷ 21:41
☿✶♅ 23:14
☉☌♆ 23:26

29 Th
☽#♂ 0:02
♀⊻♄ 0:58
☽#♆ 2:04
☽⊻♃ 2:23
♀✶♇ 2:45
☽⚼♄ 3:25
☽⚼♇ 3:32
☽⚼⚳ 3:54
☽#♀ 4:52
☉#☽ 7:31
♀✶⚳ 8:24
☽#☿ 8:47
☽☌♂ 16:26
♀✶♅ 20:18
☽⚻⚷ 21:18
♄□♇ 23:13

30 F
☽∥♃ 0:30
☽☍♆ 0:47
☉☍☽ 2:28
☽△♇ 3:03
☽⚻♄ 3:04
☽△⚳ 3:53
☽△♅ 4:27
☽☍♀ 5:09
☽☍☿ 8:52
☉✶♇ 11:48
☉⊻♄ 13:14
☽#⚷ 20:21
☽#♄ 20:34

31 Sa
☽☌♃ 0:57
☽⚼♅ 3:58
☉✶⚳ 10:11
☉✶♅ 10:38
⚳△♅ 11:42
☽⊻♂ 14:16
☽☍⚷ 20:32

April 2029

LONGITUDE

Day	Sid.Time h m s	☉ ° ' "	☽ ° ' "	☽ 12 hour ° ' "	Mean ☊ ° '	True ☊ ° '	☿ ° '	♀ ° '	♂ ° '	⚳ ° '	♃ ° '	♄ ° '	⚷ ° '	♅ ° '	♆ ° '	♇ ° '
1 Su	12 38 34	11♈33 00	8♏39 50	16♏09 17	9♑22.1	8♑57.0	17♈07.7	13♈37.2	2♎22.3	11♒09.7	23♎57.2	10♉17.4	6♉29.7	11♊01.2	8♈40.7	10♒05.3
2 M	12 42 31	12 32 11	23 32 53	0♐49 57	9 19.0	8R 49.3	19 10.9	14 51.6	1R 59.7	11 28.4	23R 49.8	10 24.5	6 33.2	11 03.4	8 43.0	10 06.3
3 Tu	12 46 27	13 31 20	7♐59 59	15 02 44	9 15.8	8 44.3	21 13.9	16 06.1	1 37.3	11 46.9	23 42.4	10 31.7	6 36.7	11 05.6	8 45.2	10 07.4
4 W	12 50 24	14 30 28	21 58 10	28 46 25	9 12.6	8 41.9	23 16.3	17 20.6	1 15.2	12 05.3	23 34.9	10 38.8	6 40.3	11 07.8	8 47.5	10 08.4
5 Th	12 54 20	15 29 34	5♑27 45	12♑02 34	9 09.4	8 41.2	25 17.7	18 35.0	0 53.5	12 23.5	23 27.4	10 46.1	6 43.8	11 10.1	8 49.8	10 09.4
6 F	12 58 17	16 28 38	18 31 21	24 54 38	9 06.3	8 41.2	27 18.0	19 49.4	0 32.2	12 41.6	23 19.8	10 53.3	6 47.4	11 12.5	8 52.0	10 10.3
7 Sa	13 02 14	17 27 41	1♒12 59	7♒26 58	9 03.1	8 40.6	29 16.6	21 03.8	0 11.3	12 59.6	23 12.2	11 00.6	6 51.0	11 14.8	8 54.3	10 11.3
8 Su	13 06 10	18 26 41	13 37 08	19 44 03	8 59.9	8 38.4	1♉13.3	22 18.2	29♍50.8	13 17.5	23 04.6	11 07.9	6 54.7	11 17.3	8 56.6	10 12.2
9 M	13 10 07	19 25 40	25 48 13	1♓50 07	8 56.7	8 33.6	3 07.6	23 32.6	29 30.9	13 35.2	22 56.9	11 15.2	6 58.3	11 19.7	8 58.8	10 13.0
10 Tu	13 14 03	20 24 37	7♓50 11	13 48 48	8 53.5	8 26.0	4 59.2	24 46.9	29 11.5	13 52.7	22 49.2	11 22.6	7 01.9	11 22.2	9 01.0	10 13.9
11 W	13 18 00	21 23 32	19 46 19	25 43 02	8 50.4	8 15.7	6 47.8	26 01.2	28 52.6	14 10.1	22 41.5	11 30.0	7 05.6	11 24.7	9 03.3	10 14.7
12 Th	13 21 56	22 22 25	1♈39 15	7♈35 09	8 47.2	8 03.2	8 33.0	27 15.6	28 34.3	14 27.4	22 33.8	11 37.4	7 09.3	11 27.3	9 05.5	10 15.5
13 F	13 25 53	23 21 17	13 30 58	19 26 53	8 44.0	7 49.6	10 14.5	28 29.9	28 16.7	14 44.5	22 26.1	11 44.9	7 13.0	11 29.8	9 07.7	10 16.3
14 Sa	13 29 49	24 20 06	25 23 04	1♉19 40	8 40.8	7 35.8	11 52.1	29 44.1	27 59.7	15 01.5	22 18.4	11 52.3	7 16.7	11 32.5	9 09.9	10 17.0
15 Su	13 33 46	25 18 54	7♉16 53	13 14 53	8 37.7	7 23.2	13 25.3	0♉58.4	27 43.4	15 18.3	22 10.7	11 59.8	7 20.4	11 35.1	9 12.1	10 17.8
16 M	13 37 42	26 17 39	19 13 52	25 14 04	8 34.5	7 12.5	14 54.2	2 12.6	27 27.7	15 34.9	22 03.0	12 07.4	7 24.1	11 37.8	9 14.3	10 18.5
17 Tu	13 41 39	27 16 23	1♊15 45	7♊19 13	8 31.3	7 04.6	16 18.3	3 26.9	27 12.8	15 51.4	21 55.4	12 14.9	7 27.9	11 40.6	9 16.5	10 19.1
18 W	13 45 36	28 15 04	13 24 48	19 32 53	8 28.1	6 59.5	17 37.6	4 41.1	26 58.6	16 07.7	21 47.7	12 22.4	7 31.6	11 43.3	9 18.7	10 19.8
19 Th	13 49 32	29 13 43	25 43 52	1♋58 14	8 24.9	6D 57.0	18 51.9	5 55.2	26 45.1	16 23.9	21 40.1	12 30.0	7 35.4	11 46.1	9 20.9	10 20.4
20 F	13 53 29	0♉12 20	8♋16 27	14 39 01	8 21.8	6 56.4	20 01.0	7 09.4	26 32.4	16 39.8	21 32.6	12 37.6	7 39.1	11 48.9	9 23.0	10 21.0
21 Sa	13 57 25	1 10 55	21 06 25	27 39 09	8 18.6	6R 56.8	21 04.9	8 23.5	26 20.5	16 55.7	21 25.0	12 45.2	7 42.9	11 51.8	9 25.2	10 21.6
22 Su	14 01 22	2 09 28	4♌17 41	11♌02 25	8 15.4	6 57.1	22 03.3	9 37.7	26 09.4	17 11.3	21 17.6	12 52.8	7 46.7	11 54.7	9 27.3	10 22.1
23 M	14 05 18	3 07 58	17 53 39	24 51 35	8 12.2	6 56.1	22 56.4	10 51.8	25 59.0	17 26.8	21 10.1	13 00.5	7 50.4	11 57.6	9 29.5	10 22.6
24 Tu	14 09 15	4 06 27	1♍56 18	9♍07 39	8 09.1	6 53.1	23 43.8	12 05.8	25 49.4	17 42.0	21 02.8	13 08.1	7 54.2	12 00.5	9 31.6	10 23.1
25 W	14 13 11	5 04 53	16 25 22	23 48 53	8 05.9	6 47.9	24 25.7	13 19.9	25 40.6	17 57.1	20 55.5	13 15.8	7 58.0	12 03.5	9 33.7	10 23.6
26 Th	14 17 08	6 03 16	1♎17 28	8♎50 11	8 02.7	6 40.6	25 01.9	14 33.9	25 32.6	18 12.0	20 48.2	13 23.4	8 01.8	12 06.5	9 35.7	10 24.0
27 F	14 21 05	7 01 38	16 25 54	24 03 18	7 59.5	6 32.0	25 32.4	15 47.9	25 25.4	18 26.8	20 41.0	13 31.1	8 05.6	12 09.5	9 37.8	10 24.4
28 Sa	14 25 01	7 59 58	1♏41 03	9♏17 44	7 56.3	6 23.1	25 57.3	17 01.9	25 19.0	18 41.3	20 34.0	13 38.8	8 09.4	12 12.5	9 39.9	10 24.8
29 Su	14 28 58	8 58 16	16 52 01	24 22 38	7 53.2	6 15.2	26 16.4	18 15.8	25 13.4	18 55.7	20 26.9	13 46.5	8 13.2	12 15.6	9 41.9	10 25.1
30 M	14 32 54	9♉56 33	1♐48 28	9♐08 37	7♑50.0	6♑09.1	26♉29.9	19♉29.8	25♍08.5	19♒09.8	20♎20.0	13♉54.2	8♉17.0	12♊18.7	9♈44.0	10♒25.4

1st of Month

Julian Day # 2462227.5
Obliquity 23°26'0"
SVP 4♓50'8"
GC 27♐14.9
Eris 25♈48.8

Day	⚴	⚵	⚶
1	11♑17.4	6♏23.1R	13♑43.6
6	12 11.3	5 23.9R	15 24.3
11	12 57.3	4 19.9R	16 58.8
16	13 34.7	3 12.7R	18 26.4
21	14 03.1	2 03.9R	19 46.7
26	14 21.8	0 55.1R	20 58.9

DECLINATION and LATITUDE

Day	☉ Decl	☽ Decl	☽ Lat	☽ 12h Decl	☿ Decl	☿ Lat	♀ Decl	♀ Lat	♂ Decl	♂ Lat	⚳ Decl	⚳ Lat	♃ Decl	♃ Lat	♄ Decl	♄ Lat
1 Su	4N34	18S30	4S21	20S29	6N20	0S25	4N14	1S15	1N56	3N08	22S26	5S13	7S51	1N34	12N52	2S09
2 M	4 57	22 07	3 34	23 21	7 17	0 15	4 44	1 13	2 03	3 06	22 23	5 15	7 48	1 34	12 54	2 09
3 Tu	5 20	24 11	2 34	24 36	8 13	0 04	5 13	1 12	2 10	3 04	22 20	5 18	7 45	1 34	12 57	2 08
4 W	5 43	24 39	1 27	24 18	9 09	0N07	5 43	1 11	2 17	3 02	22 18	5 21	7 42	1 34	12 59	2 08
5 Th	6 06	23 36	0 17	22 36	10 04	0 18	6 13	1 09	2 24	2 60	22 15	5 24	7 39	1 34	13 01	2 08
6 F	6 29	21 18	0N52	19 45	10 58	0 29	6 42	1 08	2 30	2 57	22 13	5 26	7 37	1 34	13 04	2 08
7 Sa	6 51	17 60	1 56	16 03	11 51	0 41	7 11	1 07	2 36	2 55	22 10	5 29	7 34	1 34	13 06	2 08
8 Su	7 14	13 58	2 53	11 45	12 43	0 52	7 40	1 05	2 42	2 53	22 08	5 32	7 31	1 34	13 08	2 08
9 M	7 36	9 26	3 42	7 03	13 33	1 04	8 09	1 03	2 48	2 51	22 05	5 35	7 28	1 34	13 11	2 08
10 Tu	7 58	4 37	4 19	2 09	14 22	1 15	8 38	1 02	2 54	2 48	22 03	5 38	7 25	1 34	13 13	2 08
11 W	8 20	0N19	4 45	2N47	15 08	1 26	9 07	1 00	2 59	2 46	22 00	5 41	7 22	1 34	13 16	2 07
12 Th	8 42	5 13	4 58	7 36	15 52	1 36	9 35	0 58	3 04	2 43	21 58	5 44	7 20	1 34	13 18	2 07
13 F	9 04	9 55	4 59	12 09	16 34	1 47	10 03	0 57	3 09	2 41	21 56	5 47	7 17	1 34	13 20	2 07
14 Sa	9 26	14 15	4 46	16 14	17 14	1 56	10 31	0 55	3 13	2 38	21 53	5 50	7 14	1 34	13 23	2 07
15 Su	9 48	18 03	4 21	19 41	17 51	2 05	10 59	0 53	3 17	2 36	21 51	5 53	7 11	1 34	13 25	2 07
16 M	10 09	21 08	3 44	22 20	18 26	2 14	11 26	0 51	3 21	2 33	21 49	5 56	7 08	1 34	13 27	2 07
17 Tu	10 30	23 18	2 57	23 60	18 58	2 21	11 53	0 49	3 25	2 31	21 47	5 59	7 06	1 34	13 30	2 07
18 W	10 51	24 25	2 02	24 32	19 27	2 28	12 20	0 47	3 28	2 28	21 45	6 02	7 03	1 34	13 32	2 07
19 Th	11 12	24 21	0 59	23 52	19 54	2 34	12 47	0 45	3 31	2 26	21 43	6 05	6 60	1 33	13 34	2 07
20 F	11 33	23 04	0S07	21 57	20 18	2 39	13 13	0 43	3 34	2 23	21 41	6 08	6 57	1 33	13 37	2 07
21 Sa	11 53	20 33	1 15	18 52	20 39	2 43	13 39	0 41	3 36	2 20	21 39	6 12	6 54	1 33	13 39	2 07
22 Su	12 13	16 55	2 20	14 43	20 58	2 47	14 05	0 39	3 38	2 18	21 37	6 15	6 52	1 33	13 42	2 07
23 M	12 33	12 17	3 20	9 40	21 14	2 49	14 30	0 37	3 40	2 15	21 36	6 18	6 49	1 33	13 44	2 06
24 Tu	12 53	6 54	4 10	3 59	21 27	2 50	14 55	0 35	3 41	2 12	21 34	6 21	6 46	1 33	13 46	2 06
25 W	13 13	0 58	4 45	2S05	21 37	2 50	15 19	0 33	3 42	2 10	21 32	6 25	6 44	1 33	13 49	2 06
26 Th	13 32	5S09	5 03	8 09	21 45	2 49	15 43	0 30	3 43	2 07	21 31	6 28	6 41	1 33	13 51	2 06
27 F	13 51	11 04	4 60	13 49	21 50	2 46	16 07	0 28	3 43	2 04	21 29	6 31	6 39	1 33	13 53	2 06
28 Sa	14 10	16 21	4 35	18 37	21 53	2 43	16 30	0 26	3 43	2 02	21 28	6 35	6 36	1 33	13 56	2 06
29 Su	14 29	20 34	3 52	22 09	21 52	2 38	16 53	0 23	3 43	1 59	21 27	6 38	6 34	1 33	13 58	2 06
30 M	14N48	23S20	2S53	24S06	21N50	2N32	17N16	0S21	3N43	1N56	21S25	6S42	6S31	1N32	14N00	2S06

Day	⚷ Decl	⚷ Lat	♅ Decl	♅ Lat	♆ Decl	♆ Lat	♇ Decl	♇ Lat
1	12N48	0S56	22N05	0S00	2N08	1S26	22S53	5S22
6	12 53	0 57	22 07	0 00	2 12	1 26	22 53	5 23
11	12 59	0 57	22 08	0 00	2 17	1 26	22 52	5 25
16	13 05	0 57	22 10	0 00	2 21	1 26	22 52	5 26
21	13 10	0 58	22 12	0 00	2 25	1 26	22 53	5 27
26	13 16	0 58	22 14	0 00	2 29	1 26	22 53	5 28

Day	⚴ Decl	⚴ Lat	⚵ Decl	⚵ Lat	⚶ Decl	⚶ Lat	Eris Decl	Eris Lat
1	14N02	37N07	2S46	11N30	19S01	3N44	0N49	9S48
6	14 57	37 58	2 09	11 49	18 56	3 38	0 51	9 48
11	15 52	38 50	1 33	12 06	18 51	3 32	0 52	9 48
16	16 47	39 42	0 57	12 21	18 46	3 26	0 54	9 48
21	17 41	40 35	0 23	12 33	18 42	3 18	0 55	9 48
26	18 35	41 28	0N09	12 43	18 40	3 10	0 56	9 47

Moon Phenomena

Max/0 Decl
dy hr mn
3 19:02 24S40
10 22:26 0 N
18 10:49 24N32
25 3:50 0 S

Max/0 Lat
dy hr mn
5 5:51 0 N
12 12:42 5N00
19 21:28 0 S
26 8:29 5S04

Perigee/Apogee
dy hr m kilometers
12 23:06 a 406670
27 16:24 p 357835

PH dy hr mn
☾ 5 19:53 16♑18
● 13 21:41 24♈14
☽ 21 19:51 1♌59
○ 28 10:38 8♏26

Void of Course Moon

Last Aspect			☽ Ingress		
1	2:37	♄ ☍	♐	2	10:37
4	2:48	♃ ⚹	♑	4	14:11
6	19:36	☿ □	♒	6	21:40
8	19:01	♀ ⚹	♓	9	8:20
11	17:55	♂ ☍	♈	11	20:39
13	21:41	☉ ☌	♉	14	9:19
16	16:06	♂ △	♊	16	21:29
19	7:19	☉ ⚹	♋	19	8:13
21	9:28	♂ ⚹	♌	21	16:16
23	9:15	☿ □	♍	23	20:44
25	14:52	♂ ☌	♎	25	21:56
27	6:39	♃ ☌	♏	27	21:21
29	15:18	☿ ☍	♐	29	21:04

DAILY ASPECTARIAN

1 Su
☽⚻♆ 0:01
☽□♇ 2:16
☽☍♄ 2:37
☽⚻♅ 3:46
☽□⚳ 4:04
☉⚻☽ 4:56
☽⚻♀ 8:39
☽∠♂ 13:37
☽⚻☿ 15:45
☽#♅ 23:50

2 M
☽⚼♆ 0:17
☽⚺♃ 0:27
☽∥⚳ 2:19
☉⚼☽ 7:01
☽∥♇ 7:04
☽⚼♀ 11:22
☿#♃ 12:36
☽⚹♂ 13:35
☽⚼☿ 20:31
☽⚻⚷ 21:39
♂∥♆ 22:26

3 Tu
☽∠♃ 1:11
☽△♆ 1:17
☽⚹♇ 3:36
☽⚻♄ 4:19
☽☍♅ 5:15
☽⚹⚳ 6:34
☉△☽ 10:06
☽△♀ 15:10
☽⚼⚷ 23:29

4 W
☉∥♀ 0:10
☽△☿ 2:41
☽⚹♃ 2:48
☿☍♃ 3:27
☽∠♇ 5:34
☽⚼♄ 6:31
☽∠⚳ 9:13
☽□♂ 16:00

5 Th
☽△⚷ 2:18
☽□♆ 6:08
☽⚺♇ 8:33
☽∥♇ 8:59
☽△♄ 9:45
☽⚻♅ 10:26
☿∠♅ 10:38
☽⚺⚳ 12:57
☽∥⚳ 15:43
☽#♅ 16:47
☉□☽ 19:53

6 F
☽□♀ 2:41
☽□♃ 8:56
☽⚼♅ 14:30
☽□☿ 19:36
☽△♂ 22:05

7 Sa
☿ ♉ 8:53
☿⚻♂ 9:31
☽□⚷ 10:54
♂R♍ 13:11
☽⚹♆ 14:52
♀#♃ 16:50
☽☌♇ 17:20
☽□♄ 19:06
☽△♅ 19:26
☽☌⚳ 23:21

8 Su
⚳#♅ 1:05
☽⚼♂ 2:20
☽#♄ 4:30
☽#⚷ 5:41
☽#☿ 5:45
☿∥⚷ 6:04
☉⚹☽ 10:17
☿∥♄ 12:41
♀☍♃ 13:34
☉#♃ 16:23
☽△♃ 18:24
☽⚹♀ 19:01
☽∠♆ 20:22

9 M
☽#♀ 5:53
☽⚻♂ 7:11
☉#☽ 8:36
☽∥♃ 10:02
☽⚹☿ 17:16
☉∠☽ 18:43
♄⚺♅ 21:55
☽⚹⚷ 22:23
☽⚼♃ 23:58

10 Tu
☽⚺♆ 2:22
☽∠♀ 4:21
☽⚺♇ 4:49
☽□♅ 7:07
☽⚹♄ 7:11
☽#♂ 8:15
☽#♆ 11:26
♂⚼⚳ 12:20
☽⚺⚳ 12:26

11 W
☉⚺☽ 3:34
☿☌⚷ 4:09
☽∠⚷ 4:42
☽∠☿ 4:48
☽⚻♃ 5:50
♀∠♅ 7:51
☽∥♆ 9:32
☽∠♇ 11:04
☽∥♂ 13:12
☽∠♄ 13:43
☽⚺♀ 14:05
☽☍♂ 17:55
☽∠⚳ 19:27

12 Th
☉☍♃ 4:06
☿⚺♆ 7:45
☽#♃ 10:29
☽⚺⚷ 11:11
☽☌♆ 15:06
☽⚺☿ 16:17
☽⚹♇ 17:26
☉∥☽ 19:11
☽⚹♅ 19:54
☽⚺♄ 20:23
♀⚻♂ 20:33

13 F
☿□♇ 0:26
☽∥♀ 0:48
☽⚹⚳ 2:32
☽∥⚷ 16:59
☽☍♃ 17:51
☽∥♄ 18:53
☿⚺♅ 18:58
☉☌☽ 21:41

14 Sa
☿☌♄ 0:05
☽∠♅ 2:21
♀ ♉ 5:07
☽⚻♂ 5:09
☽☌♀ 9:48
☿⚼♂ 14:40
☽∥☿ 22:23

15 Su
☽☌⚷ 0:07
☽⚺♆ 3:53
☽□♇ 6:04
☽⚺♅ 8:42
☽☌♄ 9:35
☽⚼♂ 10:42
☽☌☿ 14:07
☽□⚳ 16:31

16 M
☽⚻♃ 5:35
☽#⚳ 6:30
☉∠♅ 8:39
☽∠♆ 10:03
☽∥♅ 10:15
☿□⚳ 14:16
☉⚺☽ 15:22
☽△♂ 16:06
☽#♇ 18:18
♂⚼♄ 21:43
☉⚻♂ 22:49

17 Tu
☽⚺♀ 4:50
☽⚼♃ 11:06
☽⚺⚷ 12:21
☽⚹♆ 15:54
☽△♇ 17:56
☽☌♅ 20:40
☽⚺♄ 21:56
☉∠☽ 23:39

18 W
☽△⚳ 5:27
☽⚺☿ 9:12
☽∠♀ 13:38
☽△♃ 16:12
☽∠⚷ 17:53
☽⚼♇ 23:15

19 Th
☽□♂ 1:56
☽∠♄ 3:27
☉⚹☽ 7:19
☽⚼⚳ 11:08
☽∠☿ 17:13
☉ ♉ 18:57
♀∥⚷ 20:16
☊ D 21:26
☽⚹♀ 21:39
☽⚹⚷ 22:49

20 F
☽□♆ 2:06
☽#♇ 2:13
☽⚻♇ 3:56
☽⚺♅ 6:42
☽⚹♄ 8:17
☽∥♅ 9:34
♀☌⚷ 10:08
☽#⚳ 14:38
☽⚻⚳ 16:05
☽∥☿ 23:16
☽⚹☿ 23:57

21 Sa
♀∥♄ 0:07
☽□♃ 0:34
☿⚻♃ 7:08
☽⚹♂ 9:28
☽∠♅ 10:36
☊ R 19:48
☉□☽ 19:51
♀⚺♆ 20:33

22 Su
☽□⚷ 6:15
☽△♆ 9:13
☽□♀ 10:27
☽☍♇ 10:49
☽∠♂ 12:03
☽⚹♅ 13:35
☽∥♀ 13:59
♀□♇ 14:30
☽□♄ 15:23
☽∥♄ 17:02
☽∥⚷ 19:34
☉∥☽ 22:49
☽☍⚳ 23:12

23 M
♀⚼♂ 2:04
☽⚹♃ 5:37
☽□☿ 9:15
☽⚼♆ 11:24
☽⚺♂ 13:45
♀⚺♅ 22:12

24 Tu
☽#♃ 0:30
☉△☽ 3:54
☽∠♃ 6:49
☽△⚷ 10:01
☽⚻♆ 12:41
☽∥♂ 13:09
☿#⚳ 14:05
☽⚻♇ 14:05
☽□♅ 16:49
☽∥♆ 18:04
☽△♀ 18:28
☽△♄ 18:47
♀☌♄ 22:31

25 W
☽⚻⚳ 2:32
☉∥⚷ 2:51
☿∠♆ 5:15
☉⚼☽ 6:23
☽⚺♃ 7:16
☽⚼⚷ 10:40
☽#♆ 13:33
☽△☿ 13:33
☽⚼♇ 14:33
☽☌♂ 14:52
☽#♂ 18:22
☽⚼♄ 19:19
☽⚼♀ 20:59

26 Th
☽⚼⚳ 3:06
☽∥♃ 6:04
☉⚻☽ 8:06
☽⚻⚷ 10:46
☽☍♆ 13:14
☽⚼☿ 14:24
☽△♇ 14:29
☽△♅ 17:14
☿△♂ 19:12
☽⚻♄ 19:22
☽⚻♀ 22:55

27 F
☉∥♄ 2:35
☽△⚳ 3:14
♂⚼♇ 3:24
☽☌♃ 6:39
☽#⚷ 9:39
☽#♄ 12:24
☉#☽ 12:57
☽⚺♂ 14:03
☽⚻☿ 14:45
☽⚼♅ 16:56

28 Sa
☽#♀ 0:49
☉☌⚷ 4:08
☽☍⚷ 10:15
☉☍☽ 10:38
☽⚻♆ 12:37
☽∠♂ 13:32
☽□♇ 13:46
☽⚻♅ 16:40
☽☍♄ 19:03

29 Su
☽☍♀ 2:25
☽□⚳ 3:20
☽⚺♃ 5:40
☽∥⚳ 6:16
☽#☿ 9:35
☽⚼♆ 12:33
☽#♅ 12:59
☽⚹♂ 13:17
☽☍☿ 15:18
♀□⚳ 16:00
☉⚺♆ 18:38
☽∥♇ 19:01

30 M
⚵R♎ 2:03
☉⚼♂ 4:36
☽∠♃ 5:42
☽⚻⚷ 10:38
☉□♇ 11:58
☽△♆ 13:00
☽⚹♇ 14:07
☉⚻☽ 14:16
♀⚻♃ 14:56
☽☍♅ 17:18
☽⚻♄ 20:04

LONGITUDE

Day	Sid.Time	☉	☽	☽ 12 hour	Mean☊	True☊	☿	♀	♂	⚳	♃	♄	⚷	♅	♆	♇
	h m s	° ' "	° ' "	° ' "	° '	° '	° '	° '	° '	° '	° '	° '	° '	° '	° '	° '
1 Tu	14 36 51	10♉54 48	16♐22 23	23♐29 16	7♑46.8	6♑05.3	26♉37.9	20♉43.7	25♍04.5	19♒23.8	20♎13.2	14♉01.9	8♉20.7	12♊21.8	9♈46.0	10♒25.7
2 W	14 40 47	11 53 01	0♑29 01	7♑21 33	7 43.6	6D 03.6	26R 40.3	21 57.6	25R 01.2	19 37.6	20R 06.4	14 09.6	8 24.5	12 25.0	9 48.0	10 26.0
3 Th	14 44 44	12 51 13	14 06 56	20 45 27	7 40.5	6 03.7	26 37.5	23 11.5	24 58.7	19 51.1	19 59.8	14 17.3	8 28.3	12 28.1	9 50.0	10 26.3
4 F	14 48 40	13 49 23	27 17 27	3♒43 23	7 37.3	6 04.7	26 29.6	24 25.4	24 57.0	20 04.5	19 53.3	14 25.0	8 32.1	12 31.3	9 51.9	10 26.5
5 Sa	14 52 37	14 47 32	10♒03 45	16 19 08	7 34.1	6R 05.6	26 16.9	25 39.2	24D 56.0	20 17.6	19 46.8	14 32.8	8 35.9	12 34.5	9 53.9	10 26.7
6 Su	14 56 34	15 45 39	22 30 06	28 37 16	7 30.9	6 05.4	25 59.6	26 53.1	24 55.8	20 30.6	19 40.5	14 40.5	8 39.7	12 37.8	9 55.8	10 26.8
7 M	15 00 30	16 43 45	4♓41 11	10♓42 28	7 27.8	6 03.6	25 38.2	28 06.9	24 56.3	20 43.3	19 34.3	14 48.2	8 43.4	12 41.0	9 57.7	10 26.9
8 Tu	15 04 27	17 41 49	16 41 37	22 39 11	7 24.6	5 59.8	25 13.0	29 20.7	24 57.6	20 55.8	19 28.2	14 55.9	8 47.2	12 44.3	9 59.6	10 27.0
9 W	15 08 23	18 39 53	28 35 37	4♈31 23	7 21.4	5 54.0	24 44.6	0♊34.5	24 59.6	21 08.1	19 22.2	15 03.6	8 50.9	12 47.6	10 01.5	10 27.1
10 Th	15 12 20	19 37 54	10♈26 52	16 22 25	7 18.2	5 46.5	24 13.5	1 48.2	25 02.3	21 20.1	19 16.3	15 11.3	8 54.7	12 50.9	10 03.4	10 27.2
11 F	15 16 16	20 35 54	22 18 22	28 15 00	7 15.0	5 38.2	23 40.3	3 02.0	25 05.8	21 31.9	19 10.6	15 19.0	8 58.4	12 54.2	10 05.2	10R 27.2
12 Sa	15 20 13	21 33 53	4♉12 34	10♉11 17	7 11.9	5 29.7	23 05.5	4 15.7	25 10.0	21 43.5	19 05.0	15 26.7	9 02.2	12 57.5	10 07.0	10 27.2
13 Su	15 24 09	22 31 50	16 11 21	22 12 57	7 08.7	5 21.9	22 29.8	5 29.4	25 14.8	21 54.9	18 59.6	15 34.4	9 05.9	13 00.9	10 08.8	10 27.1
14 M	15 28 06	23 29 46	28 16 15	4♊21 26	7 05.5	5 15.4	21 53.8	6 43.1	25 20.4	22 06.0	18 54.3	15 42.1	9 09.6	13 04.3	10 10.6	10 27.1
15 Tu	15 32 03	24 27 41	10♊28 39	16 38 06	7 02.3	5 10.8	21 18.2	7 56.8	25 26.7	22 16.8	18 49.1	15 49.7	9 13.3	13 07.6	10 12.4	10 27.0
16 W	15 35 59	25 25 34	22 49 59	29 04 30	6 59.2	5D 08.2	20 43.6	9 10.5	25 33.6	22 27.5	18 44.1	15 57.4	9 17.0	13 11.0	10 14.1	10 26.9
17 Th	15 39 56	26 23 25	5♋21 53	11♋42 23	6 56.0	5 07.4	20 10.5	10 24.1	25 41.2	22 37.8	18 39.2	16 05.0	9 20.7	13 14.5	10 15.8	10 26.7
18 F	15 43 52	27 21 14	18 06 18	24 33 53	6 52.8	5 08.0	19 39.5	11 37.7	25 49.5	22 47.9	18 34.5	16 12.7	9 24.3	13 17.9	10 17.5	10 26.6
19 Sa	15 47 49	28 19 02	1♌05 27	7♌41 18	6 49.6	5 09.4	19 11.0	12 51.3	25 58.4	22 57.8	18 29.9	16 20.3	9 28.0	13 21.3	10 19.2	10 26.4
20 Su	15 51 45	29 16 49	14 21 41	21 06 52	6 46.5	5 10.9	18 45.6	14 04.9	26 07.9	23 07.4	18 25.5	16 27.9	9 31.6	13 24.8	10 20.9	10 26.1
21 M	15 55 42	0♊14 33	27 57 03	4♍52 20	6 43.3	5R 11.6	18 23.6	15 18.4	26 18.0	23 16.7	18 21.2	16 35.5	9 35.2	13 28.2	10 22.5	10 25.9
22 Tu	15 59 38	1 12 16	11♍52 46	18 58 18	6 40.1	5 11.2	18 05.4	16 32.0	26 28.8	23 25.8	18 17.2	16 43.0	9 38.8	13 31.7	10 24.1	10 25.6
23 W	16 03 35	2 09 57	26 08 42	3♎23 39	6 36.9	5 09.3	17 51.0	17 45.5	26 40.1	23 34.6	18 13.2	16 50.6	9 42.4	13 35.2	10 25.7	10 25.3
24 Th	16 07 32	3 07 37	10♎42 49	18 05 04	6 33.7	5 06.2	17 40.9	18 59.0	26 52.0	23 43.1	18 09.5	16 58.1	9 46.0	13 38.7	10 27.2	10 25.0
25 F	16 11 28	4 05 15	25 30 08	2♏56 55	6 30.6	5 02.2	17D 35.1	20 12.4	27 04.5	23 51.4	18 05.9	17 05.6	9 49.5	13 42.2	10 28.7	10 24.6
26 Sa	16 15 25	5 02 52	10♏24 27	17 51 41	6 27.4	4 57.9	17 33.7	21 25.9	27 17.6	23 59.3	18 02.4	17 13.1	9 53.0	13 45.7	10 30.2	10 24.2
27 Su	16 19 21	6 00 27	25 17 33	2♐41 01	6 24.2	4 54.1	17 36.9	22 39.3	27 31.2	24 07.0	17 59.2	17 20.6	9 56.5	13 49.2	10 31.7	10 23.8
28 M	16 23 18	6 58 02	10♐01 07	17 16 59	6 21.0	4 51.3	17 44.5	23 52.7	27 45.3	24 14.4	17 56.1	17 28.0	10 00.0	13 52.7	10 33.2	10 23.4
29 Tu	16 27 14	7 55 35	24 27 53	1♑33 14	6 17.9	4D 49.7	17 56.6	25 06.1	27 59.9	24 21.6	17 53.2	17 35.4	10 03.5	13 56.2	10 34.6	10 22.9
30 W	16 31 11	8 53 07	8♑32 37	15 25 44	6 14.7	4 49.4	18 13.2	26 19.4	28 15.1	24 28.4	17 50.4	17 42.8	10 07.0	13 59.8	10 36.0	10 22.5
31 Th	16 35 08	9♊50 38	22 12 30	28 52 57	6♑11.5	4♑50.2	18♉34.2	27♊32.8	28♍30.8	24♒34.9	17♎47.8	17♉50.2	10♉10.4	14♊03.3	10♈37.4	10♒22.0

1st of Month

Julian Day #
2462257.5
Obliquity
23°26'[illegible]9"
SVP 4♓50'[illegible]4"
GC 27♐14.9
Eris 26♈08.3

Day	⚴	⚵	⚶
1	14♑30.3	29♒47.9R	22♑02.5
6	14 28.2R	28 43.8R	22 56.8
11	14 15.1R	27 44.2R	23 41.0
16	13 50.7R	26 50.2R	24 14.4
21	13 15.1R	26 02.9R	24 36.4
26	12 28.6R	25 23.1R	24 46.7
31	11 31.9R	24 51.1R	24 44.9R

DECLINATION and LATITUDE

Day	☉ Decl	☽ Decl	☽ Lat	☽ 12h Decl	☿ Decl	☿ Lat	♀ Decl	♀ Lat	♂ Decl	♂ Lat	⚳ Decl	⚳ Lat	♃ Decl	♃ Lat	♄ Decl	♄ Lat
1 Tu	15N06	24S27	1S43	24S23	21N44	2N24	17N38	0S19	3N42	1N54	21S24	6S45	6S29	1N32	14N03	2S06
2 W	15 24	23 56	0 30	23 07	21 37	2 16	17 59	0 16	3 41	1 51	21 23	6 49	6 26	1 32	14 05	2 06
3 Th	15 42	21 58	0N43	20 33	21 27	2 06	18 21	0 14	3 39	1 49	21 22	6 52	6 24	1 32	14 07	2 06
4 F	15 59	18 52	1 52	16 60	21 14	1 55	18 41	0 12	3 38	1 46	21 21	6 56	6 22	1 32	14 09	2 06
5 Sa	16 16	14 57	2 52	12 47	20 59	1 43	19 01	0 09	3 36	1 43	21 20	6 60	6 19	1 32	14 12	2 06
6 Su	16 33	10 29	3 43	8 08	20 42	1 30	19 21	0 07	3 34	1 41	21 20	7 03	6 17	1 31	14 14	2 06
7 M	16 50	5 43	4 23	3 15	20 24	1 16	19 40	0 04	3 31	1 38	21 19	7 07	6 15	1 31	14 16	2 06
8 Tu	17 06	0 48	4 50	1N40	20 03	1 01	19 59	0 02	3 28	1 36	21 18	7 11	6 13	1 31	14 19	2 06
9 W	17 23	4N06	5 05	6 30	19 41	0 45	20 17	0N01	3 25	1 33	21 18	7 14	6 11	1 31	14 21	2 06
10 Th	17 38	8 50	5 06	11 05	19 17	0 28	20 34	0 03	3 22	1 31	21 17	7 18	6 09	1 31	14 23	2 06
11 F	17 54	13 14	4 55	15 16	18 52	0 11	20 51	0 06	3 18	1 29	21 17	7 22	6 07	1 31	14 25	2 06
12 Sa	18 09	17 09	4 30	18 52	18 27	0S06	21 08	0 08	3 14	1 26	21 17	7 26	6 05	1 30	14 28	2 06
13 Su	18 24	20 24	3 53	21 43	18 01	0 24	21 23	0 11	3 10	1 24	21 17	7 30	6 03	1 30	14 30	2 06
14 M	18 39	22 48	3 06	23 37	17 35	0 41	21 39	0 13	3 06	1 21	21 17	7 34	6 01	1 30	14 32	2 06
15 Tu	18 53	24 09	2 10	24 24	17 09	0 58	21 53	0 16	3 01	1 19	21 17	7 37	5 59	1 30	14 34	2 06
16 W	19 07	24 21	1 06	23 59	16 43	1 16	22 07	0 18	2 56	1 17	21 17	7 41	5 57	1 30	14 36	2 06
17 Th	19 21	23 18	0S01	22 20	16 18	1 32	22 20	0 20	2 51	1 15	21 17	7 45	5 56	1 29	14 39	2 06
18 F	19 34	21 03	1 10	19 30	15 55	1 48	22 33	0 23	2 46	1 12	21 18	7 49	5 54	1 29	14 41	2 06
19 Sa	19 47	17 41	2 17	15 38	15 32	2 03	22 45	0 25	2 40	1 10	21 18	7 54	5 53	1 29	14 43	2 06
20 Su	19 60	13 22	3 17	10 55	15 11	2 18	22 57	0 28	2 35	1 08	21 19	7 58	5 51	1 29	14 45	2 06
21 M	20 12	8 17	4 09	5 32	14 52	2 31	23 08	0 30	2 29	1 06	21 19	8 02	5 50	1 29	14 47	2 06
22 Tu	20 24	2 41	4 47	0S14	14 35	2 44	23 18	0 33	2 22	1 04	21 20	8 06	5 48	1 28	14 49	2 06
23 W	20 35	3S11	5 08	6 07	14 20	2 55	23 27	0 35	2 16	1 01	21 21	8 10	5 47	1 28	14 51	2 06
24 Th	20 47	8 60	5 10	11 46	14 08	3 06	23 36	0 37	2 09	0 59	21 22	8 14	5 46	1 28	14 53	2 06
25 F	20 58	14 24	4 52	16 49	13 57	3 15	23 44	0 40	2 02	0 57	21 23	8 19	5 45	1 28	14 56	2 06
26 Sa	21 08	18 58	4 15	20 49	13 49	3 23	23 51	0 42	1 55	0 55	21 25	8 23	5 44	1 27	14 58	2 06
27 Su	21 18	22 19	3 20	23 25	13 43	3 30	23 58	0 44	1 48	0 53	21 26	8 27	5 43	1 27	14 60	2 06
28 M	21 28	24 07	2 12	24 24	13 39	3 36	24 04	0 47	1 41	0 51	21 28	8 32	5 42	1 27	15 02	2 06
29 Tu	21 38	24 16	0 57	23 43	13 38	3 41	24 10	0 49	1 33	0 49	21 29	8 36	5 41	1 27	15 04	2 06
30 W	21 47	22 49	0N20	21 35	13 39	3 45	24 14	0 51	1 25	0 47	21 31	8 40	5 40	1 26	15 06	2 06
31 Th	21N55	20S03	1N34	18S17	13N42	3S48	24N18	0N53	1N17	0N45	21S33	8S45	5S39	1N26	15N08	2S06

Day	⚷ Decl	⚷ Lat	♅ Decl	♅ Lat	♆ Decl	♆ Lat	♇ Decl	♇ Lat
1	13N22	0S58	22N16	0S00	2N33	1S26	22S54	5S29
6	13 28	0 59	22 18	0 00	2 37	1 26	22 55	5 30
11	13 33	0 59	22 20	0 00	2 40	1 26	22 56	5 31
16	13 39	0 60	22 23	0 00	2 43	1 27	22 57	5 32
21	13 44	1 00	22 25	0N00	2 47	1 27	22 58	5 34
26	13 49	1 00	22 27	0 00	2 49	1 27	23 00	5 35
31	13N54	1S01	22N29	0N00	2N52	1S27	23S01	5S36

Day	⚴ Decl	⚴ Lat	⚵ Decl	⚵ Lat	⚶ Decl	⚶ Lat	Eris Decl	Eris Lat
1	19N27	42N19	0N38	12N50	18S39	3N01	0N57	9S47
6	20 18	43 10	1 03	12 54	18 40	2 52	0 58	9 47
11	21 05	43 59	1 25	12 55	18 43	2 41	0 60	9 47
16	21 49	44 45	1 43	12 54	18 49	2 29	1 01	9 47
21	22 29	45 28	1 57	12 52	18 58	2 16	1 01	9 47
26	23 05	46 06	2 06	12 47	19 10	2 02	1 02	9 48
31	23N34	46N40	2N12	12N41	19S26	1N46	1N03	9S48

Moon Phenomena

Max/0 Decl
dy hr mn
1 4:04 24S29
8 3:52 0 N
15 15:49 24N25
22 11:02 0 S
28 13:58 24S24

Max/0 Lat
dy hr mn
2 9:43 0 N
9 14:38 5N07
16 23:32 0 S
23 14:51 5S12
29 17:35 0 N

Perigee/Apogee
dy hr m kilometers
10 7:00 a 406121
25 22:27 p 361589

PH dy hr mn
☾ 5 9:49 15♒11
● 13 13:43 23♉05
☽ 21 4:17 0♍25
○ 27 18:39 6♐45

Void of Course Moon

Last Aspect	☽ Ingress
1 14:39 ♂ □	♑ 1 23:10
3 22:33 ☿ △	♒ 4 5:02
6 9:33 ♀ □	♓ 6 14:43
8 16:42 ♂ ☍	♈ 9 2:51
10 17:43 ♃ ☍	♉ 11 15:32
13 18:09 ♂ △	♊ 14 3:25
16 5:18 ♂ □	♋ 16 13:46
18 18:31 ☉ ⚹	♌ 18 22:00
20 7:37 ☿ □	♍ 21 3:34
23 0:53 ♂ ☌	♎ 23 6:24
24 14:40 ♀ △	♏ 25 7:15
27 3:40 ♂ ⚹	♐ 27 7:38
29 6:04 ♂ □	♑ 29 9:21
31 11:34 ♂ △	♒ 31 14:02

DAILY ASPECTARIAN

1 Tu
☽⚹⚳ 5:10
☽⚹♃ 6:25
☽⚻♀ 8:01
☽⚼⚷ 11:49
☽□♂ 14:39
☽∠♇ 15:19
☉⚼☽ 17:20
☽⚻☿ 17:26
☽⚼♄ 21:42
☿ R 23:07

2 W
☽∠⚳ 7:20
☊ D 9:40
☽⚼♀ 12:25
⚴ R 13:14
☽△⚷ 13:55
☉⚺♅ 13:56
☽∥♇ 14:32
☽□♆ 16:21
☽⚺♇ 17:26
☽⚼☿ 19:35
☽#♅ 21:01
☽⚻♅ 21:03
☉△☽ 21:34

3 Th
☽△♄ 0:19
☽#☿ 5:04
☽∥⚳ 5:23
☿#⚳ 9:46
⚳△♃ 10:25
☽□♃ 10:32
☽⚺⚳ 10:32
☽△♀ 18:10
☽△♂ 19:41
☽△☿ 22:33

4 F
☽⚼♅ 0:26
☽#♀ 1:09
♀∠♆ 8:52
♀△♂ 10:06
☉#☽ 16:52
☉☌♄ 16:58
☽□⚷ 21:12
☽⚹♆ 23:41
☽⚼♂ 23:45

5 Sa
☽☌♇ 0:44
☽#♄ 4:13
☽△♅ 4:49
☽#⚷ 8:22
☽□♄ 8:40
☉□☽ 9:49
☿☌♀ 10:03
☊ R 10:03
☽△♃ 18:33
♂ D 19:01
☽☌⚳ 20:03

6 Su
☽⚻♂ 4:45
☽∠♆ 4:46
☽□☿ 6:39
☽□♀ 9:33
☽∥♃ 21:20
☽⚼♃ 23:46

7 M
☽⚹⚷ 8:05
☽⚺♆ 10:32
☽#♂ 10:50
☽⚺♇ 11:29
☽#♆ 15:04
☽□♅ 16:02
☽⚹♄ 20:25

8 Tu
☉⚹☽ 2:12
☿∥♀ 2:30
☽⚻♃ 5:32
☽⚺⚳ 8:40
☿∠♆ 10:54
☿△♂ 12:34
♀ ♊ 12:47
☽∠⚷ 14:22
☽⚹☿ 16:32
☽☍♂ 16:42
☽∥♆ 16:47
☽∠♇ 17:39
☽∥♂ 20:40

9 W
☽∠♄ 3:00
☽⚹♀ 4:28
☽#♃ 10:19
☉∠☽ 11:10
☽∠⚳ 15:32
☉⚻♃ 15:54
☽⚺⚷ 20:52
☽∠☿ 21:38
☽☌♆ 23:12

10 Th
☽⚹♇ 0:01
☽⚹♅ 4:53
☽⚺♄ 9:42
☽∠♀ 14:22
☽☍♃ 17:43
☉⚺☽ 20:14
☽⚹⚳ 22:25

11 F
☽∥⚷ 1:51
☽⚺☿ 2:38
♇ R 4:19
☽⚻♂ 5:40
☽∥♄ 6:59
☽∠♅ 11:21
♀⚼♃ 20:46

12 Sa
☽⚺♀ 0:07
☉□⚳ 4:58
☉∥☽ 7:22
☽∥☿ 7:53
☽☌⚷ 9:44
☉∥☿ 10:21
☽⚺♆ 11:53
☽⚼♂ 12:02
☽□♇ 12:32
♀#⚳ 13:49
☽⚺♅ 17:38
☽☌♄ 22:45
☉☌☿ 23:28

13 Su
☽⚻♃ 5:33
☽#⚳ 7:45
☽∥♀ 9:49
☽□⚳ 11:35
☽☌☿ 11:58
☉☌☽ 13:43
☿□⚳ 17:47
☽∠♆ 17:52
☽△♂ 18:09
☽∥♅ 18:50

14 M
☽#♇ 1:50
☽⚼♃ 11:02
☽☌♀ 18:30
☽⚺⚷ 21:32
☽⚹♆ 23:28
☽△♇ 23:57

15 Tu
♂⚼♇ 1:07
☽☌♅ 5:12
☽⚺♄ 10:33
☽△♃ 16:08
☉∠♆ 19:07
☽⚺☿ 20:06
☽△⚳ 23:16

16 W
♀⚺⚷ 2:14
☽∠⚷ 2:49
☉△♂ 3:49
☽⚼♇ 5:02
☽□♂ 5:18
☉⚺☽ 5:25
☽∠♄ 15:46
♀⚹♆ 21:15
☊ D 23:30
☽∠☿ 23:39

17 Th
♀△♇ 0:51
☽⚼⚳ 4:21
☽#♇ 4:47
♀∥♅ 4:56
☽⚹⚷ 7:35
☽□♆ 9:18
☽⚻♇ 9:37
☽⚺♀ 10:33
☽∥♀ 10:46
☽∥♅ 11:19
☉∠☽ 12:20
☽⚺♅ 14:57
☽⚹♄ 20:25
☽#⚳ 21:56

18 F
☽□♃ 0:52
☽⚹☿ 2:47
♂∥♆ 4:57
☽⚻⚳ 8:51
☉∥☽ 10:50
☽⚹♂ 14:29
☽∠♀ 17:27
☉⚹☽ 18:31
☽∠♅ 18:58

19 Sa
♀☌♅ 10:16
☽∥☿ 13:39
☽□⚷ 15:17
☽△♆ 16:47
☽∥♄ 16:52
☽☍♇ 16:58
☽∠♂ 18:08
☽∥⚷ 22:14
☽⚹♅ 22:18
☽⚹♀ 23:27

20 Su
♀#♇ 2:13
☽□♄ 3:47
☽⚹♃ 7:12
☽□☿ 7:37
☽☍⚳ 15:43
☉ ♊ 17:57
☽⚼♆ 19:29
☽⚺♂ 21:05

21 M
☿⚻♃ 3:38
☊ R 4:14
☉□☽ 4:17
☿∥♄ 6:23
☽∠♃ 9:20
☽#♃ 10:47
☽△⚷ 20:11
☽⚻♆ 21:29
☽⚻♇ 21:31
☽∥♆ 23:35

22 Tu
☽∥♂ 1:19
☽□♅ 2:49
♀⚺♄ 4:02
☽△♄ 8:16
☽□♀ 8:38
☽△☿ 10:20
☽⚺♃ 10:48
♆⚹♇ 19:28
☽⚻⚳ 19:40
☽#♂ 20:20
☽⚼⚷ 21:36
☽#♆ 22:25
☽⚼♇ 22:48

23 W
☽☌♂ 0:53
☿⚺♀ 1:34
♀△♃ 8:37
☽⚼♄ 9:31
☽∥♃ 10:36
☉△☽ 10:41
☽⚼☿ 10:58
☽⚼⚳ 20:43
☽⚻⚷ 22:27
☽△♇ 23:31
☽☍♆ 23:35

24 Th
☉⚼♃ 0:43
☽△♅ 4:48
☽⚻♄ 10:16
☽⚻☿ 11:15
☽☌♃ 12:04
☉⚼☽ 12:54
☽△♀ 14:40
☽#⚷ 21:12
☽△⚳ 21:19
☽#☿ 21:58

25 F
☽#♄ 2:34
☽⚺♂ 2:34
☽⚼♅ 5:11
☉⚻☽ 14:47
☽⚼♀ 17:02
☿ D 19:22
☿∥⚷ 22:59
☽☍⚷ 23:09
☽□♇ 24:00

26 Sa
☽⚻♆ 0:09
☽∠♂ 3:05
☽⚻♅ 5:25
☽☍♄ 11:03
☽☍☿ 11:33
☽⚺♃ 12:15
☉#☽ 15:11
☽∥⚳ 16:36
☽⚻♀ 19:21
☽□⚳ 22:05

27 Su
☽⚼♆ 0:23
☽#♅ 1:22
☽⚹♂ 3:40
☽∥♇ 6:58
☽∠♃ 12:27
⚶ R 18:19
☉☍☽ 18:39
☉#⚳ 22:30
☽#♀ 22:44
☽⚻⚷ 23:58

28 M
☽⚹♇ 0:37
☽△♆ 0:53
☽☍♅ 6:23
♀△⚳ 7:54
☽⚻♄ 12:25
☽⚻☿ 12:56
☽⚹♃ 13:02
☿⚻♃ 19:03
♀∠⚷ 23:07
☽⚹⚳ 23:49

29 Tu
☽⚼⚷ 1:00
☽☍♀ 1:10
☽∠♇ 1:33
☽#♀ 2:48
♀⚼♇ 5:29
☽□♂ 6:04
☽⚼♄ 13:54
☽⚼☿ 14:39
☊ D 17:32
☽∥♇ 21:45

30 W
☉⚻☽ 0:38
☽∠⚳ 1:37
☽△⚷ 2:44
☽⚺♇ 3:10
☽□♆ 3:34
☽#♅ 3:38
☽⚻♅ 9:32
☉#☽ 9:45
☽∥⚳ 12:25
☽△♄ 16:10
☽□♃ 16:12
☽△☿ 17:21
♃⚻♄ 18:16

31 Th
☽⚺⚳ 4:17
☉⚼☽ 5:05
☉⚺⚷ 8:45
☽⚻♀ 10:33
☽△♂ 11:34
☽⚼♅ 12:22
☉△♇ 12:57
☉⚹♆ 19:59

June 2029

LONGITUDE

Day	Sid.Time	☉	☽	☽ 12 hour	Mean☊	True☊	☿	♀	♂	⚳	♃	♄	⚷	♅	♆	♇
	h m s	° ' "	° ' "	° ' "	° '	° '	° '	° '	° '	° '	° '	° '	° '	° '	° '	° '
1 F	16 39 04	10♊48 08	5♒27 12	11♒55 33	6♑08.3	4♑51.6	18♉59.5	28♊46.1	28♍46.9	24♒41.2	17♎45.4	17♉57.5	10♉13.8	14♊06.8	10♈38.7	10♒21.4
2 Sa	16 43 01	11 45 38	18 18 21	24 36 01	6 05.2	4 53.1	19 29.1	29 59.4	29 03.6	24 47.1	17R 43.2	18 04.8	10 17.1	14 10.4	10 40.1	10R 20.9
3 Su	16 46 57	12 43 06	0♓49 03	6♓57 59	6 02.0	4 54.3	20 02.9	1♋12.7	29 20.7	24 52.7	17 41.1	18 12.1	10 20.5	14 13.9	10 41.4	10 20.3
4 M	16 50 54	13 40 34	13 03 21	19 05 43	5 58.8	4R 54.8	20 40.7	2 25.9	29 38.3	24 58.0	17 39.3	18 19.4	10 23.8	14 17.4	10 42.6	10 19.7
5 Tu	16 54 50	14 38 01	25 05 42	1♈03 50	5 55.6	4 54.4	21 22.5	3 39.2	29 56.3	25 03.0	17 37.6	18 26.6	10 27.1	14 20.9	10 43.9	10 19.1
6 W	16 58 47	15 35 27	7♈00 41	12 56 48	5 52.4	4 53.1	22 08.1	4 52.4	0♎14.8	25 07.7	17 36.1	18 33.8	10 30.4	14 24.5	10 45.1	10 18.4
7 Th	17 02 43	16 32 53	18 52 41	24 48 49	5 49.3	4 51.0	22 57.5	6 05.6	0 33.7	25 12.1	17 34.7	18 40.9	10 33.6	14 28.0	10 46.3	10 17.7
8 F	17 06 40	17 30 18	0♉45 41	6♉43 40	5 46.1	4 48.6	23 50.7	7 18.8	0 53.1	25 16.1	17 33.6	18 48.0	10 36.9	14 31.6	10 47.4	10 17.0
9 Sa	17 10 36	18 27 43	12 43 09	18 44 29	5 42.9	4 46.0	24 47.4	8 32.0	1 12.9	25 19.8	17 32.6	18 55.1	10 40.0	14 35.1	10 48.5	10 16.3
10 Su	17 14 33	19 25 06	24 47 58	0♊53 51	5 39.7	4 43.7	25 47.6	9 45.1	1 33.2	25 23.2	17 31.8	19 02.2	10 43.2	14 38.6	10 49.6	10 15.6
11 M	17 18 30	20 22 30	7♊02 22	13 13 41	5 36.6	4 41.8	26 51.3	10 58.3	1 53.8	25 26.2	17 31.2	19 09.2	10 46.3	14 42.2	10 50.7	10 14.8
12 Tu	17 22 26	21 19 52	19 27 59	25 45 23	5 33.4	4 40.7	27 58.4	12 11.4	2 14.8	25 29.0	17 30.7	19 16.1	10 49.4	14 45.7	10 51.8	10 14.0
13 W	17 26 23	22 17 14	2♋05 58	8♋29 49	5 30.2	4D 40.2	29 08.8	13 24.5	2 36.3	25 31.3	17D 30.5	19 23.1	10 52.5	14 49.2	10 52.8	10 13.2
14 Th	17 30 19	23 14 35	14 57 00	21 27 32	5 27.0	4 40.4	0♊22.5	14 37.6	2 58.1	25 33.4	17 30.4	19 30.0	10 55.6	14 52.7	10 53.7	10 12.4
15 F	17 34 16	24 11 55	28 01 29	4♌38 50	5 23.9	4 41.0	1 39.4	15 50.6	3 20.3	25 35.0	17 30.5	19 36.8	10 58.6	14 56.3	10 54.7	10 11.5
16 Sa	17 38 12	25 09 15	11♌19 37	18 03 49	5 20.7	4 41.8	2 59.5	17 03.7	3 42.9	25 36.4	17 30.8	19 43.6	11 01.5	14 59.8	10 55.6	10 10.7
17 Su	17 42 09	26 06 33	24 51 25	1♍42 24	5 17.5	4 42.6	4 22.7	18 16.7	4 05.9	25 37.4	17 31.3	19 50.4	11 04.5	15 03.3	10 56.5	10 09.8
18 M	17 46 06	27 03 51	8♍36 41	15 34 12	5 14.3	4 43.2	5 49.1	19 29.7	4 29.2	25 38.0	17 31.9	19 57.1	11 07.4	15 06.7	10 57.4	10 08.9
19 Tu	17 50 02	28 01 08	22 34 49	29 38 22	5 11.2	4R 43.5	7 18.5	20 42.6	4 52.9	25R 38.3	17 32.8	20 03.7	11 10.2	15 10.2	10 58.2	10 07.9
20 W	17 53 59	28 58 24	6♎44 37	13♎53 18	5 08.0	4 43.5	8 51.1	21 55.6	5 16.9	25 38.2	17 33.8	20 10.3	11 13.1	15 13.7	10 59.0	10 07.0
21 Th	17 57 55	29 55 39	21 04 03	28 16 29	5 04.8	4 43.3	10 26.7	23 08.5	5 41.3	25 37.8	17 35.0	20 16.9	11 15.9	15 17.1	10 59.7	10 06.0
22 F	18 01 52	0♋52 54	5♏30 07	12♏44 24	5 01.6	4 42.9	12 05.3	24 21.3	6 06.0	25 37.1	17 36.3	20 23.4	11 18.6	15 20.6	11 00.5	10 05.0
23 Sa	18 05 48	1 50 07	19 58 46	27 12 36	4 58.4	4 42.6	13 46.8	25 34.2	6 31.0	25 36.0	17 37.9	20 29.9	11 21.3	15 24.0	11 01.2	10 04.0
24 Su	18 09 45	2 47 21	4♐25 15	11♐36 04	4 55.3	4 42.3	15 31.3	26 47.0	6 56.3	25 34.5	17 39.6	20 36.3	11 24.0	15 27.4	11 01.8	10 03.0
25 M	18 13 41	3 44 34	18 44 25	25 49 43	4 52.1	4 42.2	17 18.7	27 59.8	7 21.9	25 32.7	17 41.5	20 42.7	11 26.7	15 30.9	11 02.5	10 01.9
26 Tu	18 17 38	4 41 46	2♑51 23	9♑48 58	4 48.9	4 42.2	19 08.9	29 12.6	7 47.9	25 30.5	17 43.6	20 49.0	11 29.3	15 34.3	11 03.1	10 00.9
27 W	18 21 35	5 38 58	16 42 04	23 30 20	4 45.7	4 42.2	21 01.8	0♌25.3	8 14.1	25 28.0	17 45.8	20 55.2	11 31.9	15 37.6	11 03.7	9 59.8
28 Th	18 25 31	6 36 10	0♒13 35	6♒51 41	4 42.6	4 42.1	22 57.2	1 38.0	8 40.6	25 25.1	17 48.2	21 01.4	11 34.4	15 41.0	11 04.2	9 58.7
29 F	18 29 28	7 33 22	13 24 37	19 52 28	4 39.4	4 41.9	24 55.2	2 50.7	9 07.4	25 21.9	17 50.8	21 07.6	11 36.9	15 44.4	11 04.7	9 57.6
30 Sa	18 33 24	8♋30 34	26 15 24	2♓33 38	4♑36.2	4♑41.5	26♊55.5	4♌03.4	9♎34.5	25♒18.3	17♎53.5	21♉13.7	11♉39.3	15♊47.7	11♈05.2	9♒56.5

1st of Month

Julian Day # 2462288.5
Obliquity 23°26'08"
SVP 4♓50'39"
GC 27♐15.0
Eris 26♈26.2

Day	⚴
1	11♑19.4R
6	10 11.7R
11	8 56.3R
16	7 35.0R
21	6 10.0R
26	4 43.5R

Day	⚵
1	24♎45.6R
6	24 23.4R
11	24 09.4R
16	24 03.7R
21	24 06.0
26	24 16.0

Day	⚶
1	24♑43.0R
6	24 26.5R
11	23 57.7R
16	23 17.5R
21	22 26.9R
26	21 27.5R

DECLINATION and LATITUDE

Day	☉ Decl	☽ Decl	☽ Lat	☽ 12h Decl	☿ Decl	☿ Lat	♀ Decl	♀ Lat	♂ Decl	♂ Lat	⚳ Decl	⚳ Lat	♃ Decl	♃ Lat	♄ Decl	♄ Lat
1 F	22N04	16S19	2N40	14S10	13N47	3S50	24N21	0N56	1N09	0N44	21S35	8S49	5S39	1N26	15N10	2S06
2 Sa	22 12	11 54	3 37	9 32	13 54	3 51	24 24	0 58	1 01	0 42	21 37	8 54	5 38	1 26	15 12	2 06
3 Su	22 19	7 07	4 21	4 38	14 03	3 50	24 26	0 60	0 52	0 40	21 39	8 58	5 37	1 25	15 14	2 06
4 M	22 26	2 09	4 52	0N20	14 14	3 49	24 27	1 02	0 44	0 38	21 42	9 03	5 37	1 25	15 16	2 06
5 Tu	22 33	2N48	5 10	5 14	14 26	3 47	24 27	1 04	0 35	0 36	21 44	9 07	5 37	1 25	15 17	2 06
6 W	22 39	7 36	5 15	9 54	14 41	3 45	24 27	1 06	0 26	0 34	21 47	9 12	5 36	1 25	15 19	2 06
7 Th	22 45	12 06	5 06	14 12	14 56	3 41	24 25	1 08	0 17	0 33	21 50	9 16	5 36	1 24	15 21	2 06
8 F	22 51	16 09	4 43	17 58	15 13	3 37	24 24	1 10	0 07	0 31	21 53	9 21	5 36	1 24	15 23	2 06
9 Sa	22 56	19 36	4 09	21 02	15 32	3 32	24 21	1 12	0S02	0 29	21 56	9 26	5 36	1 24	15 25	2 06
10 Su	23 01	22 14	3 23	23 12	15 52	3 26	24 18	1 13	0 12	0 28	21 59	9 30	5 36	1 24	15 27	2 07
11 M	23 05	23 54	2 27	24 18	16 12	3 20	24 14	1 15	0 21	0 26	22 02	9 35	5 36	1 23	15 29	2 07
12 Tu	23 09	24 24	1 23	24 11	16 34	3 13	24 09	1 17	0 31	0 24	22 06	9 40	5 36	1 23	15 30	2 07
13 W	23 13	23 39	0 14	22 49	16 57	3 06	24 04	1 19	0 41	0 23	22 10	9 45	5 36	1 23	15 32	2 07
14 Th	23 16	21 40	0S57	20 13	17 20	2 58	23 58	1 20	0 51	0 21	22 13	9 49	5 36	1 22	15 34	2 07
15 F	23 18	18 30	2 06	16 32	17 44	2 49	23 51	1 22	1 02	0 19	22 17	9 54	5 36	1 22	15 36	2 07
16 Sa	23 21	14 21	3 09	11 57	18 08	2 40	23 43	1 23	1 12	0 18	22 21	9 59	5 37	1 22	15 38	2 07
17 Su	23 23	9 24	4 03	6 43	18 33	2 30	23 35	1 25	1 23	0 16	22 25	10 04	5 37	1 22	15 39	2 07
18 M	23 24	3 56	4 45	1 05	18 58	2 20	23 26	1 26	1 33	0 15	22 29	10 08	5 38	1 21	15 41	2 07
19 Tu	23 25	1S48	5 10	4S41	19 23	2 10	23 17	1 27	1 44	0 13	22 34	10 13	5 38	1 21	15 43	2 07
20 W	23 26	7 31	5 17	10 17	19 48	1 59	23 07	1 29	1 55	0 12	22 38	10 18	5 39	1 21	15 44	2 07
21 Th	23 26	12 55	5 04	15 23	20 13	1 49	22 56	1 30	2 06	0 10	22 43	10 23	5 40	1 21	15 46	2 07
22 F	23 26	17 38	4 32	19 37	20 38	1 37	22 44	1 31	2 17	0 09	22 48	10 28	5 40	1 20	15 48	2 08
23 Sa	23 25	21 19	3 43	22 40	21 02	1 26	22 32	1 32	2 28	0 08	22 53	10 33	5 41	1 20	15 49	2 08
24 Su	23 24	23 39	2 40	24 14	21 25	1 14	22 19	1 33	2 40	0 06	22 58	10 37	5 42	1 20	15 51	2 08
25 M	23 23	24 25	1 27	24 11	21 48	1 02	22 06	1 34	2 51	0 05	23 03	10 42	5 43	1 19	15 52	2 08
26 Tu	23 21	23 34	0 10	22 36	22 09	0 51	21 52	1 35	3 02	0 03	23 08	10 47	5 44	1 19	15 54	2 08
27 W	23 19	21 18	1N06	19 46	22 29	0 39	21 37	1 36	3 14	0 02	23 13	10 52	5 45	1 19	15 55	2 08
28 Th	23 16	17 52	2 17	15 50	22 48	0 27	21 22	1 37	3 26	0 01	23 19	10 57	5 46	1 19	15 57	2 08
29 F	23 13	13 37	3 18	11 17	23 05	0 15	21 06	1 37	3 38	0S01	23 25	11 01	5 48	1 18	15 58	2 08
30 Sa	23N10	8S52	4N08	6S23	23N20	0S04	20N50	1N38	3S49	0S02	23S30	11S06	5S49	1N18	15N60	2S08

Day	⚷ Decl	⚷ Lat	♅ Decl	♅ Lat	♆ Decl	♆ Lat	♇ Decl	♇ Lat
1	13N55	1S01	22N30	0N00	2N52	1S27	23S02	5S36
6	13 60	1 02	22 32	0 00	2 55	1 28	23 03	5 37
11	14 04	1 02	22 34	0 00	2 57	1 28	23 05	5 38
16	14 08	1 03	22 36	0 00	2 58	1 28	23 08	5 39
21	14 12	1 03	22 38	0 00	2 60	1 28	23 10	5 40
26	14 16	1 04	22 40	0 00	3 01	1 29	23 12	5 41

Day	⚴ Decl	⚴ Lat	⚵ Decl	⚵ Lat	⚶ Decl	⚶ Lat	Eris Decl	Eris Lat
1	23N40	46N46	2N12	12N39	19S30	1N43	1N03	9S48
6	24 02	47 12	2 13	12 32	19 50	1 25	1 04	9 48
11	24 17	47 31	2 10	12 23	20 13	1 07	1 04	9 48
16	24 26	47 43	2 03	12 14	20 39	0 47	1 05	9 49
21	24 27	47 47	1 53	12 04	21 08	0 26	1 05	9 49
26	24 20	47 43	1 41	11 54	21 39	0 05	1 05	9 49

Moon Phenomena

Max/0 Decl

dy	hr mn	
4	10:23	0 N
11	21:54	24N24
18	16:31	0 S
24	23:19	24S25

Perigee/Apogee

dy	hr m		kilometers
6	22:10	a	405102
22	15:34	p	366597

Max/0 Lat

dy	hr mn	
5	19:42	5N15
13	4:49	0 S
19	20:35	5S17
26	3:10	0 N

PH	dy	hr mn	
☾	4	1:20	13♓44
●	12	3:52	21♊29
●	12	246:08P	0.458
☽	19	9:55	28♍25
○	26	3:24	4♑50
●	26	3:23	T 1.844

Void of Course Moon

Last Aspect				☽ Ingress		
2	2:20	☿	□	♓	2	22:25
4	16:05	☿	⚹	♈	5	9:51
6	21:23	♃	☍	♉	7	22:28
10	2:09	☿	☌	♊	10	10:14
12	3:52	☉	☌	♋	12	20:02
14	8:28	♄	⚹	♌	15	3:35
17	2:22	☉	⚹	♍	17	9:01
19	9:55	☉	□	♎	19	12:37
21	3:46	♀	□	♏	21	14:52
23	10:08	♀	△	♐	23	16:38
24	22:14	♃	⚹	♑	25	19:07
27	7:29	♄	△	♒	27	23:36
30	1:30	☿	△	♓	30	7:07

DAILY ASPECTARIAN

1 F: ♀□♂ 0:21; ☽⋕♄ 6:29; ☽□⚷ 8:53; ☽☌♇ 9:04; ☽⚹♆ 9:38; ☉△☽ 10:42; ☽⋕⚷ 13:19; ☽⋕☿ 13:46; ☽⚼♂ 15:49; ☽△♅ 16:10; ☽⚼♀ 17:05; ☽△♃ 22:54; ☽□♄ 23:34

2 Sa: ♀ ♋ 0:12; ☽□☿ 2:20; ☿∥⚷ 6:45; ☽☌⚳ 12:27; ☽∠♆ 14:05; ☽⚻♂ 21:05; ♇□⚷ 22:46

3 Su: ☽△♀ 0:51; ☽⚼♃ 3:37; ☽∥♃ 7:15; ☽⚺♇ 18:37; ☽⚹⚷ 18:43; ☽⚺♆ 19:21; ☽⋕♆ 20:25

4 M: ☉□☽ 1:20; ☊ R 1:33; ☽□♅ 2:27; ☽⋕♂ 7:05; ☽⚻♃ 9:06; ☽⚹♄ 10:34; ☽∥♂ 13:30; ☽⚹☿ 16:05; ☉☌♅ 16:24; ☉∥♅ 16:55; ♀∠♄ 19:25; ☽⚺⚳ 23:55

5 Tu: ☽∠♇ 0:27; ☽∥♆ 0:31; ☽∠⚷ 0:43; ♂ ♎ 4:50; ☽☍♂ 9:59; ☽⋕♃ 13:54; ☽∠♄ 16:58; ☽□♀ 19:11

6 W: ☽∠☿ 0:16; ☽∠⚳ 6:20; ☽⚹♇ 6:39; ☽⚺⚷ 7:06; ☽☌♆ 7:34; ☽⚹♅ 15:02; ☉⚹☽ 18:52; ☽☍♃ 21:23; ☽⚺♄ 23:36

7 Th: ☽⚺☿ 8:54; ☽∥⚷ 10:58; ☽⚹⚳ 12:51; ☽∥☿ 17:43; ☽∥♄ 19:09; ☽∠♅ 21:30

8 F: ☽⚻♂ 0:15; ☉△♃ 1:20; ☉∠☽ 3:49; ☿∥♄ 14:14; ☽⚹♀ 14:40; ☽□♇ 19:07; ☽☌⚷ 19:53; ☽⚺♆ 20:10

9 Sa: ☽⚺♅ 3:45; ☽⚼♂ 7:10; ☽⚻♃ 9:36; ☉⚺☽ 12:26; ☽☌♄ 12:28; ☉⚺♄ 13:04; ☿□⚳ 13:53; ☽⋕⚳ 21:12; ☽∠♀ 23:54

10 Su: ☿∠♆ 0:48; ☽□⚳ 1:10; ☽∠♆ 2:02; ☽☌☿ 2:09; ☽∥♅ 3:37; ☉∥☽ 9:49; ♀⚻♇ 9:53; ☽⋕♇ 10:24; ♀⚼⚳ 13:03; ☽△♂ 13:40; ☽⚼♃ 15:11; ♀⚹⚷ 19:54; ♀□♆ 21:29

11 M: ☉⋕♇ 1:50; ☽△♇ 6:13; ☽⚺⚷ 7:17; ☽⚹♆ 7:24; ☽∥♀ 8:22; ☽⚺♀ 8:28; ☽☌♅ 14:55; ☽△♃ 20:15; ☽⚺♄ 23:37

12 Tu: ☉☌☽ 3:52; ☽⚼♇ 11:00; ☽△⚳ 11:31; ☽∠⚷ 12:11; ☽∥♀ 14:28; ☽⚺☿ 17:51

13 W: ☽□♂ 0:59; ♆⚺⚷ 2:59; ☽∠♄ 4:20; ☊ D 4:44; ☉∥☽ 6:37; ☽⋕♇ 8:14; ☽∥♅ 14:40; ☽⚻♇ 15:12; ☽⚼⚳ 15:49; ☽□♆ 16:28; ☽⚹⚷ 16:30; ☿ ♊ 16:48; ☽⋕⚳ 18:40; ♃ D 21:08; ☽☌♀ 23:20; ☽⚺♅ 23:52

14 Th: ☽∠☿ 0:52; ☽□♃ 4:44; ♀⚺♅ 5:14; ☽⚹♄ 8:28; ☉⚺☽ 16:28; ☽⚻⚳ 19:33

15 F: ☽∠♅ 3:30; ☽∥☿ 4:25; ☽⚹☿ 7:19; ☽⚹♂ 9:55; ☿⚼♃ 15:29; ☽∥♄ 17:09; ☉∠☽ 21:44; ☽☍♇ 21:57; ☽△♆ 23:17; ☽□⚷ 23:28

16 Sa: ☉⚼♇ 0:35; ☽∥⚷ 1:04; ☽⚹♅ 6:35; ♀□♃ 8:59; ☽⚹♃ 11:02; ☽⚺♀ 11:14; ☉△⚳ 11:35; ☽∠♂ 13:32; ☽□♄ 15:04; ☿△♂ 17:25; ☉∠⚷ 23:05

17 Su: ⚵ D 1:05; ☽☍⚳ 1:21; ☽⚼♆ 1:55; ☉⚹☽ 2:22; ☽∠♃ 13:26; ☽∠♀ 16:10; ☽⚺♂ 16:38; ☽⋕♃ 16:46; ☽□☿ 18:35

18 M: ☽⚻♇ 2:39; ☽∥♆ 4:03; ☽⚻♆ 4:03; ☽△⚷ 4:21; ☉∥♀ 5:02; ☽⋕♂ 9:44; ♀⚹♄ 9:55; ☽□♅ 11:16; ☽⚺♃ 15:23; ☽△♄ 19:40; ☽⚹♀ 20:30; ☽∥♂ 23:43

19 Tu: ☽⚼♇ 4:21; ☽⋕♆ 4:56; ☽⚻⚳ 5:13; ☽⚼⚷ 6:08; ⚳ R 8:03; ☊ R 9:52; ☉□☽ 9:55; ♂⚼♄ 15:00; ☽∥♃ 16:02; ⚳⋕♅ 17:49; ♀⋕♇ 18:06; ☽⚼♄ 21:20; ☽☌♂ 21:28

20 W: ☽△☿ 3:59; ☽△♇ 5:40; ☽⚼⚳ 6:33; ☽☍♆ 7:08; ☽⚻⚷ 7:33; ☽△♅ 14:18; ☽☌♃ 18:10; ☿△♇ 18:56; ☽⚻♄ 22:41

21 Th: ☉ ♋ 1:49; ☽□♀ 3:46; ☽⋕⚷ 6:11; ☽△⚳ 7:36; ☿⚹♆ 8:12; ☽⚼☿ 8:13; ☿⚺⚷ 12:25; ☽⋕♄ 14:04; ☽⚼♅ 15:24; ☉△☽ 15:47; ♀⋕⚳ 18:54

22 F: ☽⚺♂ 1:01; ☽□♇ 7:35; ☽⚻♆ 9:08; ☽☍⚷ 9:40; ♀∥♅ 11:59; ☽⚻☿ 12:21; ☽⚻♅ 16:23; ☉⚼☽ 18:25; ☽⚺♃ 20:06; ☽⋕☿ 21:31

23 Sa: ♀⚻⚳ 0:35; ☽☍♄ 0:52; ☽∠♂ 2:37; ☽□⚳ 9:19; ☽⋕♀ 9:52; ☽⚼♆ 10:02; ☽△♀ 10:08; ☽⋕♅ 11:49; ☽∥⚳ 14:51; ☽∥♇ 17:47; ☉⋕☽ 20:39; ☽∠♃ 21:04; ☉⚻☽ 21:05; ☿☌♅ 23:06

24 Su: ☽⚹♂ 4:20; ☽⚹♇ 9:23; ☽△♆ 11:03; ☽⚻⚷ 11:42; ☽⚼♀ 13:27; ☽☍♅ 18:33; ☽☍☿ 21:15; ☽⚹♃ 22:14

25 M: ☽⚻♄ 3:21; ☿△♃ 5:07; ☽∠♇ 10:38; ☽⚹⚳ 11:29; ☿∥♀ 12:18; ☽⚼⚷ 13:05; ☽⚻♀ 17:10; ♂⋕♆ 20:22

26 Tu: ☉⋕☽ 3:13; ☉☍☽ 3:24; ☽∥♇ 5:06; ☽⚼♄ 5:08; ☽∥⚳ 5:41; ☽□♂ 8:47; ☽⋕♅ 11:20; ☽⚺♇ 12:20; ☽∠⚳ 13:10; ☽□♆ 14:09; ☽⋕☿ 14:29; ☽△⚷ 14:57; ♀ ♌ 15:39; ⚳∥♇ 19:19; ☽⋕♀ 21:01; ☽⚻♅ 22:07; ☿⚺♄ 22:33

27 W: ☽□♃ 1:52; ♀∠♅ 4:16; ☽△♄ 7:29; ☉∠♄ 7:39; ☽⚻☿ 8:52; ☿∥♅ 13:52; ☽⚺⚳ 15:26; ☉⋕⚳ 16:14

28 Th: ☽⚼♅ 0:50; ☽☍♀ 2:47; ☽⋕♄ 11:16; ☉⚻☽ 12:26; ☽△♂ 15:51; ☽⚼☿ 16:27; ☽☌♇ 17:40; ☽⚹♆ 19:42; ☽⋕⚷ 20:25; ☽□⚷ 20:41; ☉⋕♇ 22:38

29 F: ☿⚼♇ 0:29; ☽△♅ 4:19; ☿△⚳ 5:12; ☽△♃ 8:15; ☉∥☿ 10:29; ☿⋕♇ 13:33; ☽□♄ 14:27; ☉⚼☽ 18:24; ☽⚼♂ 20:42; ☿∠⚷ 20:44; ☽☌⚳ 22:13; ☽∠♆ 23:41

30 Sa: ☽△☿ 1:30; ☽⚼♃ 12:41; ☽∥♃ 14:39; ☽⚻♀ 16:28; ♂△♇ 18:32; ☽∥♂ 23:17

LONGITUDE

Day	Sid.Time	⊙	☽	☽ 12 hour	Mean ☊	True ☊	☿	♀	♂	⚳	♃	♄	⚷	♅	♆	♇
	h m s	° ' "	° ' "	° ' "	° '	° '	° '	° '	° '	° '	° '	° '	° '	° '	° '	° '
1 Su	18 37 21	9♋27 45	8♓47 31	14♓57 26	4♑33.0	4♑41.0	28♊57.9	5♌16.0	10♎01.9	25♒14.3	17♎56.5	21♉19.7	11♉41.7	15♊51.0	11♈05.6	9♒55.4
2 M	18 41 17	10 24 57	21 03 49	27 07 10	4 29.9	4R40.5	1♋02.1	6 28.7	10 29.5	25R10.0	17 59.5	21 25.7	11 44.1	15 54.3	11 06.1	9R54.2
3 Tu	18 45 14	11 22 09	3♈07 58	9♈06 48	4 26.7	4D40.2	3 08.1	7 41.2	10 57.4	25 05.3	18 02.8	21 31.6	11 46.4	15 57.6	11 06.4	9 53.0
4 W	18 49 10	12 19 21	15 04 13	21 00 48	4 23.5	4 40.1	5 15.5	8 53.8	11 25.6	25 00.3	18 06.2	21 37.4	11 48.7	16 00.9	11 06.8	9 51.9
5 Th	18 53 07	13 16 34	26 57 08	2♉53 46	4 20.3	4 40.3	7 23.9	10 06.3	11 54.0	24 55.0	18 09.8	21 43.2	11 50.9	16 04.1	11 07.1	9 50.7
6 F	18 57 04	14 13 46	8♉51 16	14 50 12	4 17.1	4 41.0	9 33.3	11 18.8	12 22.7	24 49.3	18 13.5	21 48.9	11 53.1	16 07.4	11 07.4	9 49.4
7 Sa	19 01 00	15 10 59	20 51 03	26 54 20	4 14.0	4 41.9	11 43.1	12 31.3	12 51.7	24 43.2	18 17.4	21 54.6	11 55.2	16 10.6	11 07.6	9 48.2
8 Su	19 04 57	16 08 12	3♊00 28	9♊09 52	4 10.8	4 43.0	13 53.2	13 43.8	13 20.9	24 36.8	18 21.5	22 00.2	11 57.3	16 13.8	11 07.9	9 47.0
9 M	19 08 53	17 05 26	15 22 52	21 39 46	4 07.6	4 43.9	16 03.3	14 56.2	13 50.4	24 30.1	18 25.7	22 05.7	11 59.4	16 16.9	11 08.0	9 45.8
10 Tu	19 12 50	18 02 40	28 00 47	4♋26 04	4 04.4	4R44.5	18 13.1	16 08.6	14 20.1	24 23.0	18 30.1	22 11.2	12 01.4	16 20.1	11 08.2	9 44.5
11 W	19 16 46	18 59 54	10♋55 43	17 29 44	4 01.3	4 44.5	20 22.3	17 21.0	14 50.0	24 15.6	18 34.7	22 16.6	12 03.4	16 23.2	11 08.3	9 43.2
12 Th	19 20 43	19 57 08	24 08 05	0♌50 36	3 58.1	4 43.8	22 30.7	18 33.4	15 20.2	24 07.9	18 39.4	22 21.9	12 05.3	16 26.3	11 08.4	9 42.0
13 F	19 24 39	20 54 23	7♌37 06	14 27 20	3 54.9	4 42.3	24 38.2	19 45.7	15 50.6	23 59.8	18 44.3	22 27.1	12 07.1	16 29.4	11 08.5	9 40.7
14 Sa	19 28 36	21 51 38	21 20 59	28 17 42	3 51.7	4 40.3	26 44.6	20 57.9	16 21.2	23 51.5	18 49.3	22 32.3	12 09.0	16 32.4	11R08.5	9 39.4
15 Su	19 32 33	22 48 52	5♍17 06	12♍18 46	3 48.6	4 38.0	28 49.6	22 10.2	16 52.1	23 42.8	18 54.4	22 37.4	12 10.7	16 35.4	11 08.5	9 38.1
16 M	19 36 29	23 46 07	19 22 19	26 27 19	3 45.4	4 35.7	0♌53.2	23 22.4	17 23.2	23 33.8	18 59.7	22 42.4	12 12.4	16 38.4	11 08.4	9 36.7
17 Tu	19 40 26	24 43 22	3♎33 24	10♎40 09	3 42.2	4 33.9	2 55.3	24 34.6	17 54.5	23 24.6	19 05.2	22 47.4	12 14.1	16 41.4	11 08.3	9 35.4
18 W	19 44 22	25 40 37	17 47 13	24 54 17	3 39.0	4D32.8	4 55.8	25 46.7	18 26.0	23 15.0	19 10.8	22 52.3	12 15.7	16 44.3	11 08.2	9 34.1
19 Th	19 48 19	26 37 52	2♏01 02	9♏07 11	3 35.8	4 32.8	6 54.7	26 58.8	18 57.7	23 05.2	19 16.6	22 57.1	12 17.3	16 47.3	11 08.1	9 32.8
20 F	19 52 15	27 35 07	16 12 27	23 16 34	3 32.7	4 33.5	8 51.8	28 10.9	19 29.7	22 55.1	19 22.5	23 01.8	12 18.8	16 50.1	11 07.9	9 31.4
21 Sa	19 56 12	28 32 23	0♐19 19	7♐20 25	3 29.5	4 34.8	10 47.3	29 22.9	20 01.8	22 44.8	19 28.5	23 06.4	12 20.3	16 53.0	11 07.7	9 30.1
22 Su	20 00 08	29 29 39	14 19 39	21 16 45	3 26.3	4 36.2	12 41.0	0♍34.9	20 34.2	22 34.2	19 34.7	23 11.0	12 21.7	16 55.8	11 07.5	9 28.7
23 M	20 04 05	0♌26 55	28 11 27	5♑03 31	3 23.1	4R37.1	14 32.9	1 46.8	21 06.7	22 23.4	19 41.1	23 15.5	12 23.1	16 58.6	11 07.2	9 27.4
24 Tu	20 08 02	1 24 12	11♑52 42	18 38 44	3 20.0	4 37.1	16 23.1	2 58.7	21 39.4	22 12.3	19 47.5	23 19.9	12 24.4	17 01.4	11 06.9	9 26.0
25 W	20 11 58	2 21 29	25 21 25	2♒00 32	3 16.8	4 35.7	18 11.5	4 10.6	22 12.3	22 01.0	19 54.1	23 24.2	12 25.6	17 04.1	11 06.6	9 24.6
26 Th	20 15 55	3 18 46	8♒35 55	15 07 27	3 13.6	4 33.0	19 58.2	5 22.4	22 45.4	21 49.5	20 00.9	23 28.5	12 26.8	17 06.9	11 06.2	9 23.3
27 F	20 19 51	4 16 05	21 35 03	27 58 40	3 10.4	4 29.0	21 43.1	6 34.2	23 18.7	21 37.8	20 07.7	23 32.6	12 28.0	17 09.5	11 05.8	9 21.9
28 Sa	20 23 48	5 13 24	4♓18 23	10♓34 16	3 07.3	4 24.2	23 26.2	7 45.9	23 52.2	21 25.9	20 14.7	23 36.7	12 29.1	17 12.2	11 05.4	9 20.5
29 Su	20 27 44	6 10 43	16 46 29	22 55 17	3 04.1	4 19.0	25 07.7	8 57.6	24 25.8	21 13.8	20 21.9	23 40.7	12 30.1	17 14.8	11 04.9	9 19.1
30 M	20 31 41	7 08 04	29 00 56	5♈03 49	3 00.9	4 14.1	26 47.4	10 09.2	24 59.6	21 01.6	20 29.1	23 44.6	12 31.1	17 17.3	11 04.4	9 17.7
31 Tu	20 35 37	8♌05 26	11♈04 19	17 02 55	2♑57.7	4♑10.0	28♌25.3	11♍20.8	25♎33.6	20♒49.2	20♎36.5	23♉48.4	12♉32.1	17♊19.9	11♈03.9	9♒16.3

1st of Month

Julian Day # 2462318.5
Obliquity 23°26'08"
SVP 4♓50'34"
GC 27♐15.1
Eris 26♈37.1

Day	⚴	Day	⚵	Day	⚶
1	3♑17.8R	1	24♎33.5	1	20♑21.3R
6	1 55.1R	6	24 57.9	6	19 10.5R
11	0 37.4R	11	25 29.0	11	17 57.7R
16	29♐26.6R	16	26 06.3	16	16 45.7R
21	28 24.3R	21	26 49.6	21	15 37.3R
26	27 31.3R	26	27 38.3	26	14 34.9R
31	26 48.4R	31	28 31.9	31	13 40.5R

DECLINATION and LATITUDE

Day	⊙ Decl	☽ Decl	☽ Lat	☽ 12h Decl	☿ Decl	☿ Lat	♀ Decl	♀ Lat	♂ Decl	♂ Lat	⚳ Decl	⚳ Lat	♃ Decl	♃ Lat	♄ Decl	♄ Lat
1 Su	23N06	3S52	4N45	1S20	23N33	0N07	20N33	1N39	4S01	0S03	23S36	11S11	5S50	1N18	16N01	2S09
2 M	23 02	1N11	5 08	3N39	23 44	0 18	20 15	1 39	4 13	0 04	23 42	11 16	5 52	1 18	16 03	2 09
3 Tu	22 57	6 05	5 17	8 27	23 53	0 29	19 57	1 40	4 25	0 06	23 48	11 20	5 53	1 17	16 04	2 09
4 W	22 52	10 43	5 12	12 53	23 59	0 39	19 38	1 40	4 38	0 07	23 54	11 25	5 55	1 17	16 05	2 09
5 Th	22 46	14 56	4 53	16 51	24 02	0 48	19 19	1 40	4 50	0 08	24 00	11 30	5 56	1 17	16 07	2 09
6 F	22 41	18 35	4 22	20 09	24 02	0 57	18 59	1 40	5 02	0 09	24 07	11 34	5 58	1 17	16 08	2 09
7 Sa	22 34	21 30	3 40	22 37	24 00	1 05	18 39	1 41	5 15	0 11	24 13	11 39	5 60	1 16	16 09	2 09
8 Su	22 28	23 29	2 47	24 04	23 55	1 13	18 18	1 41	5 27	0 12	24 20	11 43	6 01	1 16	16 11	2 10
9 M	22 21	24 22	1 45	24 22	23 48	1 20	17 57	1 41	5 40	0 13	24 26	11 48	6 03	1 16	16 12	2 10
10 Tu	22 13	24 02	0 37	23 23	23 37	1 26	17 36	1 40	5 52	0 14	24 33	11 52	6 05	1 16	16 13	2 10
11 W	22 05	22 25	0S34	21 08	23 24	1 32	17 13	1 40	6 05	0 15	24 40	11 57	6 07	1 15	16 14	2 10
12 Th	21 57	19 33	1 45	17 42	23 09	1 36	16 51	1 40	6 17	0 16	24 46	12 01	6 09	1 15	16 16	2 10
13 F	21 49	15 36	2 52	13 16	22 50	1 40	16 28	1 40	6 30	0 18	24 53	12 06	6 11	1 15	16 17	2 10
14 Sa	21 40	10 45	3 49	8 05	22 30	1 44	16 04	1 39	6 43	0 19	25 00	12 10	6 13	1 15	16 18	2 10
15 Su	21 30	5 19	4 35	2 27	22 07	1 46	15 40	1 39	6 56	0 20	25 07	12 14	6 15	1 14	16 19	2 11
16 M	21 21	0S27	5 04	3S21	21 43	1 48	15 16	1 38	7 09	0 21	25 14	12 18	6 18	1 14	16 20	2 11
17 Tu	21 11	6 14	5 15	9 01	21 16	1 49	14 51	1 37	7 22	0 22	25 21	12 22	6 20	1 14	16 21	2 11
18 W	21 00	11 42	5 06	14 13	20 48	1 49	14 26	1 37	7 35	0 23	25 28	12 26	6 22	1 14	16 22	2 11
19 Th	20 50	16 32	4 39	18 38	20 18	1 49	14 01	1 36	7 48	0 24	25 35	12 30	6 25	1 13	16 23	2 11
20 F	20 38	20 26	3 55	21 57	19 46	1 48	13 35	1 35	8 01	0 25	25 42	12 34	6 27	1 13	16 24	2 11
21 Sa	20 27	23 06	2 57	23 54	19 13	1 46	13 09	1 34	8 14	0 26	25 49	12 38	6 30	1 13	16 25	2 12
22 Su	20 15	24 19	1 49	24 21	18 39	1 44	12 43	1 33	8 27	0 27	25 56	12 42	6 32	1 13	16 26	2 12
23 M	20 03	24 01	0 35	23 18	18 04	1 41	12 16	1 32	8 40	0 28	26 04	12 45	6 35	1 12	16 27	2 12
24 Tu	19 51	22 15	0N40	20 53	17 28	1 37	11 49	1 31	8 53	0 29	26 11	12 49	6 38	1 12	16 28	2 12
25 W	19 38	19 14	1 51	17 22	16 51	1 34	11 22	1 29	9 07	0 30	26 18	12 52	6 40	1 12	16 29	2 12
26 Th	19 25	15 17	2 55	13 03	16 14	1 29	10 54	1 28	9 20	0 31	26 25	12 56	6 43	1 12	16 30	2 12
27 F	19 11	10 41	3 49	8 15	15 36	1 24	10 26	1 26	9 33	0 32	26 32	12 59	6 46	1 11	16 31	2 13
28 Sa	18 58	5 44	4 30	3 12	14 57	1 19	9 58	1 25	9 46	0 33	26 39	13 02	6 49	1 11	16 32	2 13
29 Su	18 44	0 39	4 57	1N52	14 18	1 13	9 30	1 23	9 59	0 34	26 46	13 05	6 52	1 11	16 33	2 13
30 M	18 29	4N21	5 10	6 47	13 38	1 07	9 01	1 22	10 13	0 35	26 53	13 08	6 54	1 11	16 33	2 13
31 Tu	18N14	9N07	5N09	11N22	12N58	1N00	8N32	1N20	10S26	0S36	26S60	13S11	6S57	1N11	16N34	2S13

Day	⚷ Decl	⚷ Lat	♅ Decl	♅ Lat	♆ Decl	♆ Lat	♇ Decl	♇ Lat
1	14N19	1S05	22N41	0N00	3N01	1S29	23S14	5S42
6	14 22	1 05	22 43	0 00	3 02	1 29	23 17	5 43
11	14 24	1 06	22 45	0 00	3 02	1 29	23 19	5 43
16	14 26	1 07	22 46	0 01	3 02	1 30	23 22	5 44
21	14 28	1 07	22 48	0 01	3 01	1 30	23 24	5 44
26	14 30	1 08	22 49	0 01	3 00	1 30	23 26	5 45
31	14N30	1S09	22N51	0N01	2N59	1S31	23S29	5S45

Day	⚴ Decl	⚴ Lat	⚵ Decl	⚵ Lat	⚶ Decl	⚶ Lat	Eris Decl	Eris Lat
1	24N06	47N31	1N25	11N44	22S11	0S17	1N05	9S49
6	23 45	47 10	1 07	11 34	22 43	0 40	1 05	9 50
11	23 17	46 43	0 47	11 24	23 15	1 02	1 05	9 50
16	22 42	46 08	0 25	11 14	23 46	1 24	1 05	9 50
21	22 02	45 28	0 01	11 05	24 15	1 44	1 05	9 51
26	21 17	44 42	0S24	10 56	24 42	2 04	1 05	9 51
31	20N27	43N52	0S51	10N47	25S06	2S22	1N04	9S52

Moon Phenomena

Max/0 Decl

dy	hr mn	
1	18:22	0 N
9	5:42	24N24
15	22:08	0 S
22	7:03	24S23
29	3:06	0 N

Max/0 Lat

dy	hr mn	
3	3:04	5N17
10	12:34	0 S
17	1:41	5S15
23	11:14	0 N
30	10:17	5N12

Perigee/Apogee

dy	hr m		kilometers
4	16:05	a	404311
18	11:22	p	369670

PH	dy	hr mn	
☾	3	17:59	12♈05
●	11	15:52	19♋38
☛	11	937:20P	0.230
☽	18	14:16	26♎15
○	25	13:37	2♒54

Void of Course Moon

Last Aspect			☽ Ingress		
2	0:43	♄ ✶	♈	2	17:44
4	6:09	♃ ☍	♉	5	6:09
7	2:07	♄ ☌	♊	7	18:06
9	5:52	♃ △	♋	10	3:44
11	20:48	♄ ✶	♌	12	10:30
14	2:04	♄ □	♍	14	14:56
16	7:59	⊙ ✶	♎	16	18:00
18	14:43	♀ ✶	♏	18	20:36
20	22:15	♀ □	♐	20	23:27
22	11:13	♂ ✶	♑	23	3:09
24	20:29	♄ △	♒	25	8:22
27	3:41	♄ □	♓	27	15:49
29	13:33	♄ ✶	♈	30	1:57

DAILY ASPECTARIAN

1 Su	⊙△☽	1:24
	☽⚺♇	2:11
	☽⚻♂	2:30
	☽⋕♆	3:59
	☽⚺♆	4:28
	☽✶⚷	5:39
	♂⚼⚳	9:24
	⊙⚻♇	11:21
	☿ ♋	12:03
	☿⋕⚳	12:45
	☽□♅	13:49
	☽⚻♃	17:56
	⊙⚼⚳	18:11
2 M	☽✶♄	0:43
	☽⚼♀	0:54
	⊙□♂	3:43
	☽∠♇	7:35
	☽⚺⚳	8:04
	☽∥♆	8:56
	☽∠⚷	11:16
	☽⋕♂	15:24
	⊙□♆	17:22
	☽⋕♃	22:59
3 Tu	☽□☿	0:00
	☽∠♄	6:51
	♂☍♆	7:48
	☽△♀	10:10
	⊙✶⚷	10:36
	☽✶♇	13:32
	☽∠⚳	13:52
	☽☌♆	16:01
	☽☍♂	16:21
	☽⚺⚷	17:25
	⊙□☽	17:59
	☊ D	18:04
4 W	☽✶♅	1:55
	☽☍♃	6:09
	☽⚺♄	13:21
	☿∠♄	16:03
	♀☍♇	18:54
	☽✶⚳	19:55
	☽∥⚷	20:30
	♂⚻⚷	21:09
5 Th	☽∥♄	7:20
	☿⋕⚳	7:23
	☽∠♅	8:21
	⊙∥♅	14:02
	♀△♆	20:11
6 F	☽✶☿	1:43
	☽□♇	1:57
	☽∥♀	2:42
	☿⚼⚳	2:50
	☿⚻♇	2:58
	☽⚺♆	4:34
	☽□♀	5:30
	☽☌⚷	6:06
	☽⚻♂	7:22
	♀□⚷	11:41
	⊙✶☽	11:43
	☽⚺♅	14:38
	☿□♆	17:26
	☽⚻♃	18:52
7 Sa	☽☌♄	2:07
	☿✶⚷	2:17
	☽□⚳	7:37
	☽∠♆	10:28
	⊙∥☽	10:55
	♀✶♂	11:17
	☽∥♅	13:25
	☽∠☿	14:09
	☽⚼♂	14:28
	☿□♂	16:18
	⊙∠☽	20:01
	☿⚺♀	20:05
	☽⋕♇	21:05
8 Su	☽⚼♃	0:41
	⊙⚺♅	2:28
	☽∥☿	7:35
	☽△♇	13:11
	☽✶♆	15:49
	☽⚺⚷	17:27
	☽△♂	20:55
	☽✶♀	23:03
9 M	☽⚺☿	1:34
	☽☌♅	1:44
	☿⚺♅	2:35
	⊙⚺☽	3:33
	☽△♃	5:52
	☽⚺♄	12:55
	☽△⚳	17:13
	☽⚼♇	17:51
	⊙☌☿	20:33
	☽∠⚷	22:08
10 Tu	☿□♃	3:16
	♀✶♅	3:58
	☽∠♀	6:29
	☽∥☿	9:40
	⊙□♃	12:30
	☊ R	12:38
	☽⋕♇	13:02
	☽∠♄	17:13
	☽∥♅	20:21
	☽⚼⚳	20:58
	☽⚻♇	21:47
11 W	☽□♆	0:23
	☽✶⚷	2:04
	⊙∥☽	3:33
	♂∥♃	5:15
	☽□♂	7:26
	☿⋕♇	7:54
	☽⚺♅	10:01
	☽⚺♀	12:55
	☽□♃	14:03
	⊙☌☽	15:52
	☽☌☿	20:31
	☽✶♄	20:48
	☿✶♄	22:16
	☽⚻⚳	24:00
12 Th	♀✶♃	2:09
	☽∠♅	13:06
	☿⚻⚳	17:11
	☽∥♀	18:44
	☽∥♄	20:15
13 F	☽☍♇	3:37
	☿∥♅	5:53
	☽∥⚷	6:11
	☽△♆	6:12
	☽□⚷	7:56
	♀∥♄	10:40
	⚴ R♐	13:47
	☽✶♂	14:59
	☽✶♅	15:36
	☽✶♃	19:35
	☽☌♀	23:16
14 Sa	⊙⚺☽	0:57
	☽□♄	2:04
	♆ R	2:11
	☽☍⚳	4:18
	☽⚼♆	8:17
	♂△♅	9:40
	☽⚺☿	10:58
	☽⋕♂	17:19
	☽∠♂	17:55
	⊙✶♄	18:44
	☽⋕♃	19:59
	☽∠♃	21:38
15 Su	⊙∠☽	4:38
	☽⚻♇	7:25
	☽∥♆	9:35
	♀□♄	9:44
	☽⚻♆	10:00
	☽△⚷	11:48
	☿ ♌	13:38
	☽∠☿	17:04
	☽□♅	19:21
	⊙⚻⚳	19:33
	☽⚺♂	20:30
	☽⚺♃	23:21
16 M	♀☍⚳	3:22
	☽△♄	5:41
	☽⚻⚳	7:02
	☽⚺♀	7:25
	⊙✶☽	7:59
	☽⚼♇	8:52
	☿∠♅	9:05
	☽⋕♆	10:38
	☽⚼⚷	13:18
	☽✶☿	22:45
17 Tu	☽∥♃	0:28
	☽∥♂	5:02
	☽⚼♄	7:11
	⊙∥☿	7:17
	☽⚼⚳	8:06
	☽△♇	10:10
	☽∠♀	11:06
	☽☍♆	12:47
	⊙⚺♀	14:09
	☽⚻⚷	14:40
	☽△♅	22:14
	♀∥⚷	23:18
18 W	☽☌♂	1:08
	☽☌♃	2:22
	♀⚼♆	7:08
	☽⚻♄	8:37
	☽△⚳	9:06
	☽⋕♀	12:04
	☽⋕⚷	13:12
	☊ D	14:04
	⊙□☽	14:16
	☽✶♀	14:43
	☽⋕♄	23:12
	☽⚼♅	23:37
19 Th	☽□☿	9:36
	☽□♇	12:42
	⚳□♄	13:13
	☽⚻♆	15:24
	♂☌♃	17:23
	☽☍⚷	17:24
	☽⋕☿	19:57
20 F	☽⚻♅	1:04
	⊙⋕☽	1:24
	☽⚺♃	5:25
	☽⚺♂	5:48
	☿☍♇	8:05
	☽□⚳	11:15
	☽☍♄	11:39
	☽⚼♆	16:51
	☽⋕♅	20:28
	⊙△☽	20:44
	☽□♀	22:15
21 Sa	☽∥♇	3:52
	☿△♆	4:16
	☽∠♃	7:09
	☽∠♂	8:22
	♀ ♍	12:22
	☽✶♇	15:41
	☽△♆	18:30
	☿□⚷	19:51
	☽⚻⚷	20:37
	☽△☿	20:44
22 Su	⊙⚼☽	0:18
	☽☍♅	4:30
	☽✶♃	9:08
	☽✶♂	11:13
	⊙ ♌	12:43
	☽✶⚳	14:03
	☽⚻♄	15:23
	☽∠♇	17:31
	☽⚼⚷	22:36
23 M	☽⚼☿	2:44
	⊙⚻☽	4:14
	☽△♀	6:52
	☽∥♇	10:18
	☊ R	11:16
	☽∠⚳	15:53
	☽⚼♄	17:43
	☽⋕♅	17:59
	☽⚺♇	19:42
	☽□♆	22:39
24 Tu	☽△⚷	0:56
	☿✶♅	8:39
	☽⚻♅	9:09
	☽⚻☿	9:13
	☽⚼♀	11:52
	☽□♃	14:09
	⊙∠♅	16:23
	♂△⚳	17:52
	☽⚺⚳	18:06
	☽□♂	18:07
	☽△♄	20:29
	⊙⋕☽	21:07
25 W	☽⚼♅	12:09
	⊙☍☽	13:37
	☿∥♄	13:58
	♀∠♃	16:03
	☽⋕♄	17:08
	☽⚻♀	17:32
	☽⋕☿	17:43
26 Th	☿✶♃	0:39
	☽☌♇	1:27
	☽⋕⚷	4:21
	☽✶♆	4:35
	☽□⚷	7:04
	☽△♅	15:44
	☽△♃	21:16
	☿☍⚳	22:54
27 F	☽☌⚳	0:05
	☽☍☿	0:17
	☽⋕♀	1:24
	☽△♂	3:23
	☽□♄	3:41
	☽∥♂	5:24
	☽∠♆	8:27
	♂⚻♄	11:24
	☽∥♃	18:56
28 Sa	☽⚼♃	1:49
	⊙⚻☽	1:54
	☿□♄	2:33
	♀⋕♂	6:52
	☽☍♀	7:19
	☿✶♂	9:06
	☽⚼♂	9:08
	☽⚺♇	9:37
	☽⋕♆	12:57
	☽⚺♆	12:59
	☽✶⚷	15:43
	☿∥⚷	16:24
29 Su	☽□♅	0:55
	☽⚻♃	7:04
	♀⚻♇	7:04
	☽⚺⚳	8:33
	⊙⚼☽	9:19
	☽✶♄	13:33
	☿⚼♆	13:40
	☽∠♇	14:43
	☽⚻♂	15:41
	☽∥♆	17:24
	♀∠♂	17:52
	☽⚻☿	18:55
	☽∠⚷	21:02
30 M	☽⋕♃	12:48
	☽∠⚳	13:41
	⊙△☽	17:31
	♀⚻♆	18:21
	☽∠♄	19:27
	☽✶♇	20:24
	☽∥♀	21:15
	☽☌♆	23:59
31 Tu	☽⚻♀	0:37
	☽⚺⚷	2:56
	☽⚼☿	5:27
	☽⋕♂	7:18
	☽✶♅	12:37
	⚳△♃	15:13
	☽∥☿	18:04
	☽✶⚳	19:16
	☽☍♃	19:23
	☿ ♍	23:36

August 2029

LONGITUDE

Day	Sid.Time	☉	☽	☽ 12 hour	Mean ☊	True ☊	☿	♀	♂	⚳	♃	♄	⚷	♅	♆	♇
	h m s	° ′ ″	° ′ ″	° ′ ″	° ′	° ′	° ′	° ′	° ′	° ′	° ′	° ′	° ′	° ′	° ′	° ′
1 W	20 39 34	9♌02 49	23♈00 06	28♈56 24	2♑54.5	4♑07.2	0♍01.6	12♍32.4	26♎07.8	20♒36.6	20♎44.0	23♉52.1	12♉32.9	17♊22.4	11♈03.3	9♒15.0
2 Th	20 43 31	10 00 13	4♉52 24	10♉48 42	2 51.4	4D 05.8	1 36.1	13 43.9	26 42.1	20R 24.0	20 51.7	23 55.8	12 33.8	17 24.8	11R 02.8	9R 13.6
3 F	20 47 27	10 57 38	16 45 54	22 44 38	2 48.2	4 05.8	3 08.9	14 55.4	27 16.6	20 11.2	20 59.4	23 59.3	12 34.6	17 27.3	11 02.1	9 12.2
4 Sa	20 51 24	11 55 04	28 45 30	4♊49 06	2 45.0	4 06.9	4 40.0	16 06.8	27 51.3	19 58.2	21 07.3	24 02.8	12 35.3	17 29.7	11 01.5	9 10.8
5 Su	20 55 20	12 52 32	10♊56 03	17 06 53	2 41.8	4 08.4	6 09.3	17 18.2	28 26.2	19 45.2	21 15.3	24 06.1	12 35.9	17 32.0	11 00.8	9 09.4
6 M	20 59 17	13 50 00	23 22 05	29 42 09	2 38.7	4R 09.8	7 36.9	18 29.6	29 01.2	19 32.2	21 23.4	24 09.4	12 36.5	17 34.4	11 00.1	9 08.0
7 Tu	21 03 13	14 47 30	6♋07 24	12♋38 09	2 35.5	4 10.2	9 02.8	19 40.9	29 36.4	19 19.0	21 31.7	24 12.6	12 37.1	17 36.6	10 59.4	9 06.7
8 W	21 07 10	15 45 01	19 14 35	25 56 44	2 32.3	4 09.2	10 26.8	20 52.1	0♏11.7	19 05.8	21 40.0	24 15.7	12 37.6	17 38.9	10 58.6	9 05.3
9 Th	21 11 07	16 42 34	2♌44 35	9♌37 54	2 29.1	4 06.3	11 49.0	22 03.3	0 47.2	18 52.6	21 48.5	24 18.6	12 38.0	17 41.1	10 57.9	9 03.9
10 F	21 15 03	17 40 07	16 36 22	23 39 32	2 26.0	4 01.5	13 09.4	23 14.5	1 22.9	18 39.3	21 57.1	24 21.5	12 38.4	17 43.3	10 57.0	9 02.6
11 Sa	21 19 00	18 37 42	0♍46 48	7♍57 30	2 22.8	3 55.2	14 27.8	24 25.6	1 58.7	18 26.0	22 05.8	24 24.3	12 38.8	17 45.4	10 56.2	9 01.2
12 Su	21 22 56	19 35 17	15 10 52	22 26 06	2 19.6	3 48.2	15 44.4	25 36.6	2 34.7	18 12.8	22 14.6	24 27.0	12 39.0	17 47.5	10 55.3	8 59.8
13 M	21 26 53	20 32 54	29 42 23	6♎58 55	2 16.4	3 41.3	16 58.9	26 47.6	3 10.8	17 59.5	22 23.5	24 29.6	12 39.2	17 49.5	10 54.4	8 58.5
14 Tu	21 30 49	21 30 31	14♎14 55	21 29 44	2 13.2	3 35.4	18 11.3	27 58.6	3 47.1	17 46.3	22 32.6	24 32.1	12 39.4	17 51.5	10 53.5	8 57.1
15 W	21 34 46	22 28 10	28 42 46	5♏53 32	2 10.1	3 31.2	19 21.6	29 09.5	4 23.6	17 33.1	22 41.7	24 34.5	12 39.5	17 53.5	10 52.5	8 55.8
16 Th	21 38 42	23 25 49	13♏01 38	20 06 49	2 06.9	3D 29.0	20 29.6	0♎20.3	5 00.2	17 20.0	22 50.9	24 36.8	12R 39.5	17 55.4	10 51.5	8 54.5
17 F	21 42 39	24 23 30	27 08 52	4♐07 43	2 03.7	3 28.5	21 35.4	1 31.1	5 36.9	17 07.0	23 00.3	24 39.0	12 39.5	17 57.3	10 50.5	8 53.1
18 Sa	21 46 35	25 21 11	11♐03 19	17 55 41	2 00.5	3 29.2	22 38.7	2 41.8	6 13.8	16 54.1	23 09.7	24 41.1	12 39.4	17 59.1	10 49.5	8 51.8
19 Su	21 50 32	26 18 54	24 44 53	1♑30 57	1 57.4	3R 30.2	23 39.5	3 52.4	6 50.8	16 41.3	23 19.2	24 43.1	12 39.3	18 00.9	10 48.5	8 50.5
20 M	21 54 29	27 16 38	8♑13 59	14 54 01	1 54.2	3 30.4	24 37.7	5 03.0	7 28.0	16 28.6	23 28.9	24 45.0	12 39.1	18 02.6	10 47.4	8 49.2
21 Tu	21 58 25	28 14 22	21 31 09	28 05 22	1 51.0	3 28.8	25 33.0	6 13.5	8 05.3	16 16.0	23 38.6	24 46.8	12 38.9	18 04.3	10 46.3	8 47.9
22 W	22 02 22	29 12 08	4♒36 44	11♒05 12	1 47.8	3 25.0	26 25.4	7 23.9	8 42.7	16 03.6	23 48.4	24 48.5	12 38.6	18 06.0	10 45.1	8 46.6
23 Th	22 06 18	0♍09 55	17 30 47	23 53 28	1 44.7	3 18.8	27 14.7	8 34.3	9 20.2	15 51.3	23 58.4	24 50.1	12 38.3	18 07.6	10 44.0	8 45.4
24 F	22 10 15	1 07 44	0♓13 14	6♓30 04	1 41.5	3 10.2	28 00.7	9 44.6	9 57.9	15 39.2	24 08.4	24 51.5	12 37.8	18 09.1	10 42.8	8 44.1
25 Sa	22 14 11	2 05 34	12 43 59	18 55 03	1 38.3	3 00.0	28 43.1	10 54.9	10 35.8	15 27.2	24 18.5	24 52.9	12 37.4	18 10.6	10 41.6	8 42.8
26 Su	22 18 08	3 03 25	25 03 20	1♈08 58	1 35.1	2 49.1	29 21.9	12 05.0	11 13.7	15 15.5	24 28.6	24 54.2	12 36.9	18 12.1	10 40.4	8 41.6
27 M	22 22 04	4 01 18	7♈12 07	13 13 02	1 31.9	2 38.4	29 56.8	13 15.1	11 51.8	15 03.9	24 38.9	24 55.3	12 36.3	18 13.5	10 39.1	8 40.4
28 Tu	22 26 01	4 59 13	19 11 58	25 09 18	1 28.8	2 28.9	0♎27.5	14 25.2	12 30.0	14 52.6	24 49.3	24 56.4	12 35.7	18 14.9	10 37.9	8 39.2
29 W	22 29 58	5 57 10	1♉05 23	7♉00 42	1 25.6	2 21.3	0 53.7	15 35.1	13 08.3	14 41.5	24 59.7	24 57.4	12 35.0	18 16.2	10 36.6	8 38.0
30 Th	22 33 54	6 55 08	12 55 45	18 51 03	1 22.4	2 16.1	1 15.3	16 45.0	13 46.8	14 30.6	25 10.3	24 58.2	12 34.2	18 17.5	10 35.3	8 36.8
31 F	22 37 51	7♍53 08	24 47 12	0♊44 48	1♑19.2	2♑13.2	1♎31.9	17♎54.8	14♏25.4	14♒19.9	25♎20.9	24♉58.9	12♉33.4	18♊18.7	10♈34.0	8♒35.6

1st of Month

Julian Day #
2462349.5
Obliquity
23°26′08″
SVP 4♓50′29″
GC 27♐15.1
Eris 26♈39.2R

Day	⚴
1	26♐41.0R
6	26 10.5R
11	25 50.6R
16	25 41.0R
21	25 41.4
26	25 51.3
31	26 10.2

Day	⚵
1	28♎43.3
6	29 42.6
11	0♏46.2
16	1 53.8
21	3 05.2
26	4 19.8
31	5 37.6

Day	⚶
1	13♑30.7R
6	12 47.9R
11	12 16.1R
16	11 56.1R
21	11 48.1R
26	11 52.0
31	12 07.4

DECLINATION and LATITUDE

Day	☉ Decl	☽ Decl	☽ Lat	☽ 12h Decl	☿ Decl	☿ Lat	♀ Decl	♀ Lat	♂ Decl	♂ Lat	⚳ Decl	⚳ Lat	♃ Decl	♃ Lat	♄ Decl	♄ Lat
1 W	17N60	13N30	4N55	15N30	12N18	0N54	8N03	1N18	10S39	0S36	27S06	13S14	7S00	1N10	16N35	2S14
2 Th	17 44	17 21	4 28	19 01	11 37	0 46	7 34	1 16	10 52	0 37	27 13	13 16	7 03	1 10	16 36	2 14
3 F	17 29	20 30	3 49	21 47	10 57	0 39	7 04	1 14	11 06	0 38	27 20	13 19	7 07	1 10	16 36	2 14
4 Sa	17 13	22 49	3 01	23 36	10 17	0 31	6 35	1 12	11 19	0 39	27 26	13 21	7 10	1 10	16 37	2 14
5 Su	16 57	24 06	2 03	24 20	9 36	0 23	6 05	1 10	11 32	0 40	27 33	13 24	7 13	1 10	16 37	2 14
6 M	16 40	24 14	0 58	23 50	8 56	0 14	5 35	1 07	11 46	0 41	27 39	13 26	7 16	1 09	16 38	2 14
7 Tu	16 24	23 07	0S11	22 05	8 16	0 06	5 05	1 05	11 59	0 42	27 46	13 28	7 19	1 09	16 39	2 15
8 W	16 07	20 43	1 21	19 04	7 36	0S03	4 35	1 03	12 12	0 42	27 52	13 30	7 23	1 09	16 39	2 15
9 Th	15 50	17 08	2 28	14 57	6 56	0 12	4 04	1 00	12 25	0 43	27 58	13 32	7 26	1 09	16 40	2 15
10 F	15 32	12 32	3 29	9 56	6 17	0 22	3 34	0 58	12 38	0 44	28 04	13 33	7 29	1 08	16 40	2 15
11 Sa	15 14	7 10	4 18	4 18	5 38	0 31	3 03	0 55	12 52	0 45	28 10	13 35	7 33	1 08	16 41	2 15
12 Su	14 56	1 21	4 52	1S37	4 60	0 41	2 33	0 52	13 05	0 46	28 15	13 36	7 36	1 08	16 41	2 16
13 M	14 38	4S34	5 07	7 28	4 22	0 51	2 02	0 50	13 18	0 46	28 21	13 38	7 40	1 08	16 42	2 16
14 Tu	14 20	10 16	5 02	12 54	3 44	1 01	1 31	0 47	13 31	0 47	28 26	13 39	7 43	1 08	16 42	2 16
15 W	14 01	15 21	4 39	17 34	3 07	1 11	1 00	0 44	13 44	0 48	28 32	13 40	7 47	1 08	16 42	2 16
16 Th	13 42	19 31	3 58	21 10	2 31	1 21	0 30	0 41	13 57	0 49	28 37	13 41	7 51	1 07	16 43	2 16
17 F	13 23	22 29	3 03	23 27	1 56	1 31	0S01	0 38	14 10	0 49	28 42	13 42	7 54	1 07	16 43	2 17
18 Sa	13 04	24 02	1 58	24 16	1 22	1 42	0 32	0 35	14 23	0 50	28 47	13 42	7 58	1 07	16 43	2 17
19 Su	12 45	24 07	0 47	23 36	0 48	1 52	1 03	0 32	14 36	0 51	28 51	13 43	8 01	1 07	16 44	2 17
20 M	12 25	22 45	0N25	21 36	0 16	2 02	1 34	0 29	14 49	0 51	28 56	13 43	8 05	1 07	16 44	2 17
21 Tu	12 05	20 09	1 35	18 27	0S16	2 13	2 05	0 25	15 01	0 52	28 60	13 44	8 09	1 06	16 44	2 18
22 W	11 45	16 32	2 39	14 27	0 46	2 23	2 36	0 22	15 14	0 53	29 04	13 44	8 13	1 06	16 44	2 18
23 Th	11 25	12 12	3 33	9 51	1 15	2 33	3 07	0 19	15 27	0 54	29 08	13 44	8 17	1 06	16 45	2 18
24 F	11 04	7 24	4 15	4 55	1 42	2 43	3 38	0 15	15 39	0 54	29 12	13 44	8 20	1 06	16 45	2 18
25 Sa	10 44	2 23	4 45	0N08	2 08	2 53	4 08	0 12	15 52	0 55	29 15	13 44	8 24	1 06	16 45	2 18
26 Su	10 23	2N38	5 01	5 06	2 33	3 03	4 39	0 08	16 04	0 55	29 19	13 43	8 28	1 06	16 45	2 19
27 M	10 02	7 29	5 03	9 48	2 55	3 12	5 10	0 05	16 17	0 56	29 22	13 43	8 32	1 05	16 45	2 19
28 Tu	9 41	11 60	4 51	14 05	3 16	3 21	5 40	0 01	16 29	0 57	29 25	13 42	8 36	1 05	16 45	2 19
29 W	9 20	16 01	4 27	17 47	3 34	3 30	6 10	0S03	16 41	0 57	29 28	13 42	8 40	1 05	16 45	2 19
30 Th	8 58	19 23	3 51	20 47	3 51	3 39	6 41	0 06	16 54	0 58	29 31	13 41	8 44	1 05	16 45	2 19
31 F	8N37	21N57	3N05	22N54	4S04	3S47	7S11	0S10	17S06	0S59	29S33	13S40	8S48	1N05	16N45	2S20

Day	⚷ Decl	⚷ Lat	♅ Decl	♅ Lat	♆ Decl	♆ Lat	♇ Decl	♇ Lat
1	14N31	1S09	22N51	0N01	2N59	1S31	23S29	5S46
6	14 31	1 10	22 52	0 01	2 58	1 31	23 31	5 46
11	14 31	1 10	22 53	0 01	2 56	1 31	23 33	5 46
16	14 30	1 11	22 54	0 01	2 54	1 31	23 35	5 46
21	14 30	1 12	22 55	0 01	2 51	1 32	23 37	5 47
26	14 28	1 12	22 56	0 01	2 49	1 32	23 39	5 47
31	14N26	1S13	22N56	0N01	2N46	1S32	23S41	5S47

Day	⚴ Decl	⚴ Lat	⚵ Decl	⚵ Lat	⚶ Decl	⚶ Lat	Eris Decl	Eris Lat
1	20N17	43N41	0S56	10N46	25S10	2S26	1N04	9S52
6	19 23	42 47	1 24	10 38	25 31	2 42	1 04	9 52
11	18 27	41 50	1 53	10 30	25 49	2 57	1 03	9 52
16	17 29	40 52	2 22	10 23	26 04	3 11	1 02	9 53
21	16 30	39 53	2 52	10 16	26 17	3 23	1 02	9 53
26	15 30	38 53	3 23	10 10	26 27	3 33	1 01	9 53
31	14N30	37N54	3S53	10N04	26S35	3S43	0N60	9S53

Moon Phenomena

Max/0 Decl
dy hr mn
5 14:41 24N20
12 5:28 0 S
18 13:09 24S16
25 11:21 0 N

Max/0 Lat
dy hr mn
6 20:21 0 S
13 6:31 5S08
19 15:33 0 N
26 15:04 5N03

Perigee/Apogee
dy hr m kilometers
1 10:43 a 404306
13 10:04 p 366375
29 4:45 a 405066

PH dy hr mn
☾ 2 11:17 10♉27
● 10 1:57 17♌45
☽ 16 18:57 24♏11
○ 24 1:52 1♓12

Void of Course Moon

Last Aspect	☽ Ingress
1 6:38 ♂ ☍	♉ 1 14:09
3 14:34 ♄ ☌	♊ 4 2:28
6 11:14 ♂ △	♋ 6 12:34
8 9:02 ♄ ⚹	♌ 8 19:11
10 13:14 ♄ □	♍ 10 22:41
12 18:46 ♀ ☌	♎ 13 0:29
14 13:53 ♃ ☌	♏ 15 2:09
16 19:43 ♄ ☍	♐ 17 4:54
19 2:59 ☉ △	♑ 19 9:18
21 7:53 ☿ △	♒ 21 15:30
23 13:49 ♄ □	♓ 23 23:35
26 8:55 ☿ ☍	♈ 26 9:44
28 11:30 ♃ ☍	♉ 28 21:48
31 0:24 ♄ ☌	♊ 31 10:30

DAILY ASPECTARIAN

1 W
♀△⚷ 0:11
☽⚺♄ 1:46
☉☍♇ 4:58
☽∥⚷ 5:57
☽☍♂ 6:38
☽⚼♀ 10:12
☽△☿ 16:23
☽∥♄ 18:57
☽∠♅ 19:01

2 Th
☉∥☽ 2:30
☽□♇ 8:47
☉□☽ 11:17
☊ D 11:24
☽⚺♆ 12:28
☽☌⚷ 15:33
☽△♀ 19:53
☿#♂ 20:07
♀#♃ 22:26

3 F
☽⚺♅ 1:24
☉△♆ 1:52
☽□⚳ 6:45
☽⚻♃ 8:35
☽☌♄ 14:34
☽∠♆ 18:34
☽⚻♂ 22:07

4 Sa
☽∥♅ 0:36
☽#♇ 10:26
☽□☿ 13:20
☽⚼♃ 14:44
☉□⚷ 17:00
☽△♇ 20:32

5 Su
☽⚹♆ 0:09
☿∠♃ 1:47
☽⚺⚷ 3:15
☉⚹☽ 4:06
♀□♅ 4:48
☽⚼♂ 5:07
☽☌♅ 12:51
☽□♀ 13:40
☽△⚳ 16:47
☽△♃ 20:11

6 M
☽⚼♇ 1:27
☽⚺♄ 1:31
☉∥♄ 3:08
☽∠⚷ 8:03
☉∠☽ 11:12
☽△♂ 11:14
♀⚻⚳ 17:48
☽#♇ 17:50
☊ R 20:23
☽⚼⚳ 20:42

7 Tu
☿⚻♇ 1:05
☽∥♅ 3:11
☽⚻♇ 5:31
☽∠♄ 5:44
☽⚹☿ 6:04
☽□♆ 8:58
⚵ ♏ 9:41
☽⚹⚷ 11:58
♂ ♏ 16:04
☉⚺☽ 17:11
☽⚺♅ 21:07
☽⚻⚳ 23:44

8 W
☽⚹♀ 3:13
☽□♃ 4:24
☿#♃ 7:18
☽⚹♄ 9:02
☿⚻♆ 9:08
☽∠☿ 12:22
♀⚺♃ 18:20
☽□♂ 20:24
☽∠♅ 23:54

9 Th
☽∥♄ 2:41
☉∥☽ 7:50
☽∠♀ 8:14
☽☍♇ 11:00
☽∥⚷ 14:12
☽△♆ 14:17
☿△⚷ 14:39
☽□⚷ 17:11
☽⚺☿ 17:28
☽#♂ 23:30

10 F
☉⚹♅ 1:22
☽⚹♅ 1:55
☉☌☽ 1:57
☽☍⚳ 3:27
☽⚹♃ 9:12
☽⚺♀ 12:19
☽□♄ 13:14
☽⚼♆ 15:51
♀⚼♇ 15:56
☉☍⚳ 20:03
☽#♃ 22:24
♀△♄ 23:34

11 Sa
☽⚹♂ 2:06
♀∥♆ 6:05
☽∥☿ 7:16
☽∠♃ 10:40
☽⚻♇ 13:45
☽⚻♆ 16:56
☽∥♆ 17:37
☽∥♀ 18:42
☽△⚷ 19:48

12 Su
☽☌☿ 1:01
☽∠♂ 4:09
☽□♅ 4:20
☽⚻⚳ 4:57
☉⚺☽ 7:49
♂⚼♅ 9:00
☽⚺♃ 11:48
☽#♀ 14:30
☽⚼♇ 14:33
☽△♄ 15:22
☽#♆ 17:15
☽☌♀ 18:46
☽⚼⚷ 20:37
☽#☿ 23:12

13 M
☽⚼⚳ 5:20
☽⚺♂ 5:59
☉∥⚷ 9:56
☉∠☽ 10:19
☽∥♃ 12:57
☽△♇ 15:16
⚳△♅ 15:45
☽⚼♄ 16:12
☿⚻⚳ 16:56
☿□♅ 17:11
♀⚼⚷ 17:30
☽☍♆ 18:28
☽⚻⚷ 21:22

14 Tu
☽△⚳ 5:45
☽△♅ 5:59
☽⚺☿ 7:06
☉⚹☽ 12:53
☽☌♃ 13:53
☽∥♂ 15:36
☽⚻♄ 17:06
☉#☽ 17:46
☽#⚷ 19:46

15 W
☽⚺♀ 0:48
☿∠♂ 1:28
☉⚹♃ 6:42
☽⚼♅ 7:00
☽#♄ 7:12
☿∥♆ 8:53
☽☌♂ 9:55
☽∠☿ 10:15
☉#♂ 13:01
☽□♇ 17:04
♀ ♎ 17:08
☽⚻♆ 20:21
☽☍⚷ 23:23

16 Th
☽∠♀ 4:16
⚷ R 6:30
☽□⚳ 7:10
☽⚻♅ 8:18
☽⚹☿ 13:43
☽⚺♃ 16:51
☊ D 18:46
☉□☽ 18:57
☽☍♄ 19:43
☽⚼♆ 21:46

17 F
☽#♅ 4:46
☉□♄ 6:42
☽⚹♀ 8:12
♀⚼⚳ 10:19
☽∥♇ 14:36
☽⚺♂ 15:15
☽∠♃ 18:55
☽⚹♇ 20:12
☽△♆ 23:36

18 Sa
☽⚻⚷ 2:47
⚴ D 6:25
☽⚹⚳ 10:03
☉⚼♆ 11:34
☽☍♅ 12:08
♂#⚷ 13:10
☿⚺♃ 14:21
☿#♀ 18:24
☽∠♂ 18:38
☽⚹♃ 21:27
☽□☿ 21:56
☽∠♇ 22:24
☽⚻♄ 23:57

19 Su
☉△☽ 2:59
☿⚼♇ 4:21
☽⚼⚷ 5:09
☽∥♇ 11:48
☽∠⚳ 12:07
☊ R 15:34
☽□♀ 17:45
☽#♅ 22:07
☽⚹♂ 22:34

20 M
☽⚺♇ 1:03
☽⚼♄ 2:44
☿△♄ 3:13
☽□♆ 4:35
☉⚼☽ 7:50
☽△⚷ 7:57
☽⚺⚳ 14:37
☽⚻♅ 17:44

21 Tu
☽□♃ 3:55
☽△♄ 5:57
☽△☿ 7:53
☉⚻☽ 13:15
⚶ D 20:11
☽⚼♅ 21:12
☽#♄ 22:48

22 W
♂□♇ 2:27
☽△♀ 5:40
☽∥♂ 7:13
☽☌♇ 7:42
☽□♂ 7:58
☽⚹♆ 11:22
♀#♆ 11:34
☽#⚷ 11:46
☽⚼☿ 13:30
☽□⚷ 14:54
☉ ♍ 19:53
☽☌⚳ 20:57

23 Th
☽△♅ 1:09
♀△♇ 3:42
☉#☽ 4:24
☿⚼⚷ 11:59
☽△♃ 12:19
☽⚼♀ 12:33
☽□♄ 13:49
☽∠♆ 15:28
☽∥♃ 19:30
☽⚻☿ 19:32

24 F
☉☍☽ 1:52
♀⚼♄ 2:25
♀⚺♂ 9:50
☽⚺♇ 16:16
☽∥♀ 16:27
☽⚼♃ 17:18
♀☍♆ 19:33
☽△♂ 19:39
☽⚺♆ 20:04
☽⚻♀ 20:07
☽#♆ 21:55
☽⚹⚷ 23:47

25 Sa
☽∥☿ 1:06
♂⚻♆ 3:36
☽⚺⚳ 5:11
☽□♅ 10:35
☽∠♇ 21:20
☽⚻♃ 22:51
☽#☿ 23:30
☽⚹♄ 23:42

26 Su
☽∥♆ 0:52
☽⚼♂ 2:26
☽∠⚷ 5:01
☽☍☿ 8:55
☽∠⚳ 10:05
♀⚻⚷ 10:49
☽#♀ 10:57
☿#♆ 16:55
☉⚻☽ 17:08

27 M
☿ ♎ 2:22
☽⚹♇ 2:55
☿⚼⚳ 3:54
☽∠♄ 5:26
☽#♃ 5:28
☽☌♆ 6:52
☽⚻♂ 9:49
☽⚺⚷ 10:46
☉∥☽ 12:19
☽☍♀ 13:22
☽⚹⚳ 15:27
☽⚹♅ 22:05

28 Tu
☉⚼☽ 1:43
♂☍⚷ 3:29
♀△⚳ 8:07
☽☍♃ 11:30
☽⚺♄ 11:35
☽∥⚷ 14:17
♃⚻♄ 18:03
☽⚻☿ 23:36

29 W
☽∠♅ 4:25
☽#♂ 4:43
☽∥♄ 4:51
♂#♄ 7:00
☉△☽ 10:44
☽□♇ 15:16
☽⚺♆ 19:16
☽☌⚷ 23:16

30 Th
☽☍♂ 1:49
☽□⚳ 3:09
☽⚼☿ 6:55
☽⚻♀ 8:35
☽⚺♅ 10:53
☉#♃ 13:27
♂□⚳ 21:21

31 F
☽☌♄ 0:24
☽⚻♃ 1:09
☽∠♆ 1:34
♀△♅ 8:23
☽∥♅ 12:35
☽△☿ 13:49
☉⚻♇ 17:13
☽⚼♀ 18:06

LONGITUDE — September 2029

Day	Sid.Time	☉	☽	☽ 12 hour	Mean☊	True☊	☿	♀	♂	⚳	♃	♄	⚷	♅	♆	♇
	h m s	° ' "	° ' "	° ' "	° '	° '	° '	° '	° '	° '	° '	° '	° '	° '	° '	° '
1 Sa	22 41 47	8♍51 10	6♊44 32	12♊47 01	1♑16.0	2♑12.3	1♎43.2	19♎04.5	15♏04.1	14♒09.6	25♎31.6	24♉59.6	12♉32.6	18♊19.9	10♈32.6	8♒34.4
2 Su	22 45 44	9 49 14	18 52 56	25 02 56	1 12.9	2D 12.5	1R 49.1	20 14.2	15 43.0	13R 59.4	25 42.3	25 00.1	12R 31.7	18 21.1	10R 31.3	8R 33.3
3 M	22 49 40	10 47 20	1♋17 39	7♋37 41	1 09.7	2R 12.9	1 49.2	21 23.8	16 21.9	13 49.6	25 53.2	25 00.5	12 30.7	18 22.1	10 29.9	8 32.2
4 Tu	22 53 37	11 45 28	14 03 35	20 35 47	1 06.5	2 12.3	1 43.2	22 33.3	17 01.0	13 40.0	26 04.1	25 00.8	12 29.7	18 23.2	10 28.5	8 31.1
5 W	22 57 33	12 43 38	27 14 38	4♌00 23	1 03.3	2 09.9	1 31.1	23 42.7	17 40.2	13 30.7	26 15.1	25 01.0	12 28.6	18 24.2	10 27.1	8 30.0
6 Th	23 01 30	13 41 50	10♌53 04	17 52 36	1 00.2	2 05.0	1 12.6	24 52.1	18 19.6	13 21.7	26 26.2	25R 01.1	12 27.5	18 25.1	10 25.6	8 28.9
7 F	23 05 27	14 40 03	24 58 40	2♍10 48	0 57.0	1 57.6	0 47.7	26 01.3	18 59.0	13 13.0	26 37.4	25 01.1	12 26.3	18 26.0	10 24.2	8 27.8
8 Sa	23 09 23	15 38 19	9♍28 19	16 50 20	0 53.8	1 48.0	0 16.4	27 10.5	19 38.6	13 04.6	26 48.6	25 01.0	12 25.1	18 26.8	10 22.7	8 26.8
9 Su	23 13 20	16 36 36	24 15 50	1♎43 43	0 50.6	1 37.3	29♍39.0	28 19.6	20 18.3	12 56.5	26 59.9	25 00.8	12 23.8	18 27.6	10 21.2	8 25.7
10 M	23 17 16	17 34 55	9♎12 47	16 41 51	0 47.4	1 26.6	28 55.6	29 28.6	20 58.1	12 48.8	27 11.2	25 00.4	12 22.5	18 28.3	10 19.7	8 24.7
11 Tu	23 21 13	18 33 16	24 09 47	1♏35 30	0 44.3	1 17.1	28 06.8	0♏37.5	21 38.1	12 41.3	27 22.7	25 00.0	12 21.1	18 29.0	10 18.2	8 23.7
12 W	23 25 09	19 31 38	8♏58 08	16 16 55	0 41.1	1 09.9	27 13.3	1 46.4	22 18.1	12 34.2	27 34.2	24 59.4	12 19.7	18 29.6	10 16.7	8 22.7
13 Th	23 29 06	20 30 02	23 31 17	0♐40 49	0 37.9	1 05.4	26 15.8	2 55.1	22 58.3	12 27.5	27 45.7	24 58.7	12 18.2	18 30.2	10 15.1	8 21.8
14 F	23 33 02	21 28 27	7♐45 18	14 44 39	0 34.7	1 03.3	25 15.5	4 03.7	23 38.6	12 21.1	27 57.4	24 58.0	12 16.6	18 30.8	10 13.6	8 20.9
15 Sa	23 36 59	22 26 54	21 38 54	28 28 11	0 31.6	1 02.8	24 13.6	5 12.2	24 18.9	12 15.0	28 09.0	24 57.1	12 15.0	18 31.2	10 12.0	8 19.9
16 Su	23 40 56	23 25 23	5♑12 45	11♑52 50	0 28.4	1 02.8	23 11.3	6 20.6	24 59.4	12 09.3	28 20.8	24 56.1	12 13.4	18 31.7	10 10.4	8 19.1
17 M	23 44 52	24 23 53	18 28 44	25 00 45	0 25.2	1 02.0	22 10.3	7 28.9	25 40.0	12 04.0	28 32.6	24 55.0	12 11.7	18 32.0	10 08.9	8 18.2
18 Tu	23 48 49	25 22 25	1♒29 11	7♒54 20	0 22.0	0 59.3	21 12.0	8 37.1	26 20.7	11 59.0	28 44.5	24 53.8	12 10.0	18 32.4	10 07.3	8 17.3
19 W	23 52 45	26 20 59	14 16 24	20 35 39	0 18.9	0 53.9	20 17.8	9 45.2	27 01.6	11 54.3	28 56.4	24 52.5	12 08.2	18 32.6	10 05.7	8 16.5
20 Th	23 56 42	27 19 34	26 52 16	3♓06 24	0 15.7	0 45.5	19 29.2	10 53.1	27 42.5	11 50.0	29 08.3	24 51.1	12 06.4	18 32.8	10 04.0	8 15.7
21 F	0 00 38	28 18 11	9♓18 10	15 27 42	0 12.5	0 34.4	18 47.4	12 00.9	28 23.5	11 46.1	29 20.4	24 49.6	12 04.5	18 33.0	10 02.4	8 14.9
22 Sa	0 04 35	29 16 50	21 35 06	27 40 27	0 09.3	0 21.3	18 13.5	13 08.6	29 04.6	11 42.5	29 32.4	24 48.0	12 02.6	18 33.1	10 00.8	8 14.1
23 Su	0 08 31	0♎15 30	3♈43 50	9♈45 24	0 06.1	0 07.2	17 48.4	14 16.2	29 45.8	11 39.3	29 44.6	24 46.3	12 00.7	18R 33.2	9 59.2	8 13.4
24 M	0 12 28	1 14 13	15 45 14	21 43 32	0 03.0	29♐53.3	17 32.7	15 23.6	0♐27.1	11 36.5	29 56.7	24 44.5	11 58.7	18 33.2	9 57.5	8 12.7
25 Tu	0 16 24	2 12 58	27 40 28	3♉36 18	29♐59.8	29 40.8	17D 26.9	16 30.9	1 08.5	11 34.0	0♏09.0	24 42.6	11 56.6	18 33.2	9 55.9	8 12.0
26 W	0 20 21	3 11 44	9♉31 17	15 25 48	29 56.6	29 30.4	17 31.0	17 38.1	1 50.0	11 31.9	0 21.2	24 40.5	11 54.5	18 33.1	9 54.2	8 11.3
27 Th	0 24 18	4 10 33	21 20 11	27 14 55	29 53.4	29 22.9	17 45.2	18 45.1	2 31.7	11 30.1	0 33.5	24 38.4	11 52.4	18 32.9	9 52.5	8 10.6
28 F	0 28 14	5 09 25	3♊10 28	9♊07 22	29 50.2	29 18.1	18 09.2	19 52.0	3 13.4	11 28.8	0 45.9	24 36.2	11 50.3	18 32.7	9 50.9	8 10.0
29 Sa	0 32 11	6 08 18	15 06 12	21 07 35	29 47.1	29 15.9	18 42.7	20 58.7	3 55.2	11 27.7	0 58.3	24 33.9	11 48.1	18 32.5	9 49.2	8 09.4
30 Su	0 36 07	7♎07 14	27 12 08	3♋20 33	29♐43.9	29♐15.3	19♍25.2	22♏05.3	4♐37.1	11♒27.0	1♏10.8	24♉31.5	11♉45.8	18♊32.2	9♈47.6	8♒08.8

1st of Month

Julian Day # 2462380.5
Obliquity 23°26'08"
SVP 4♓50'26"
GC 27♐15.2
Eris 26♈31.5R

Day	⚴
1	26♐15.0
6	26 43.8
11	27 20.4
16	28 04.2
21	28 54.6
26	29 50.9

Day	⚵
1	5♏53.6
6	7 14.8
11	8 38.8
16	10 05.1
21	11 33.6
26	13 04.1

Day	⚶
1	12♑11.9
6	12 40.5
11	13 19.6
16	14 08.5
21	15 06.6
26	16 12.9

DECLINATION and LATITUDE

Day	☉ Decl	☽ Decl	☽ Lat	☽12h Decl	☿ Decl	☿ Lat	♀ Decl	♀ Lat	♂ Decl	♂ Lat	⚳ Decl	⚳ Lat	♃ Decl	♃ Lat	♄ Decl	♄ Lat
1 Sa	8N15	23N35	2N11	24N00	4S16	3S54	7S41	0S14	17S18	0S59	29S36	13S39	8S52	1N05	16N45	2S20
2 Su	7 53	24 08	1 10	23 59	4 24	4 00	8 11	0 18	17 30	0 60	29 38	13 38	8 56	1 04	16 45	2 20
3 M	7 31	23 31	0 05	22 44	4 29	4 06	8 41	0 22	17 42	1 00	29 40	13 37	9 00	1 04	16 45	2 20
4 Tu	7 09	21 39	1S03	20 16	4 31	4 11	9 10	0 26	17 53	1 01	29 42	13 36	9 04	1 04	16 45	2 20
5 W	6 47	18 36	2 09	16 39	4 30	4 15	9 40	0 30	18 05	1 01	29 43	13 35	9 08	1 04	16 45	2 21
6 Th	6 25	14 27	3 10	12 01	4 25	4 18	10 09	0 34	18 17	1 02	29 45	13 33	9 12	1 04	16 44	2 21
7 F	6 02	9 24	4 01	6 37	4 16	4 19	10 38	0 38	18 28	1 03	29 46	13 32	9 17	1 04	16 44	2 21
8 Sa	5 40	3 42	4 39	0 43	4 04	4 19	11 07	0 42	18 39	1 03	29 47	13 30	9 21	1 04	16 44	2 21
9 Su	5 17	2S18	4 59	5S17	3 47	4 17	11 35	0 46	18 51	1 04	29 48	13 28	9 25	1 03	16 44	2 21
10 M	4 54	8 13	4 58	11 02	3 27	4 14	12 04	0 50	19 02	1 04	29 48	13 27	9 29	1 03	16 43	2 22
11 Tu	4 32	13 40	4 38	16 05	3 03	4 08	12 32	0 54	19 13	1 05	29 49	13 25	9 33	1 03	16 43	2 22
12 W	4 09	18 15	3 59	20 06	2 35	4 01	12 60	0 58	19 24	1 05	29 49	13 23	9 38	1 03	16 43	2 22
13 Th	3 46	21 38	3 04	22 47	2 04	3 52	13 27	1 02	19 34	1 06	29 49	13 21	9 42	1 03	16 42	2 22
14 F	3 23	23 34	1 60	23 58	1 30	3 41	13 55	1 06	19 45	1 06	29 49	13 19	9 46	1 03	16 42	2 22
15 Sa	2 60	23 60	0 50	23 39	0 54	3 28	14 22	1 11	19 55	1 07	29 49	13 17	9 50	1 03	16 42	2 23
16 Su	2 37	22 58	0N22	21 57	0 16	3 14	14 48	1 15	20 06	1 07	29 49	13 14	9 55	1 02	16 41	2 23
17 M	2 13	20 40	1 31	19 06	0N23	2 57	15 15	1 19	20 16	1 08	29 48	13 12	9 59	1 02	16 41	2 23
18 Tu	1 50	17 20	2 33	15 22	1 02	2 40	15 41	1 23	20 26	1 08	29 47	13 10	10 03	1 02	16 40	2 23
19 W	1 27	13 14	3 27	10 59	1 41	2 21	16 07	1 27	20 36	1 08	29 47	13 08	10 08	1 02	16 40	2 23
20 Th	1 04	8 38	4 10	6 13	2 18	2 02	16 32	1 32	20 46	1 09	29 46	13 05	10 12	1 02	16 39	2 24
21 F	0 40	3 46	4 40	1 17	2 52	1 42	16 57	1 36	20 55	1 09	29 44	13 03	10 16	1 02	16 39	2 24
22 Sa	0 17	1N12	4 56	3N39	3 24	1 22	17 22	1 40	21 05	1 10	29 43	13 00	10 21	1 02	16 38	2 24
23 Su	0S06	6 03	4 59	8 23	3 52	1 02	17 46	1 44	21 14	1 10	29 42	12 58	10 25	1 02	16 38	2 24
24 M	0 30	10 38	4 48	12 46	4 16	0 42	18 10	1 48	21 24	1 11	29 40	12 55	10 29	1 02	16 37	2 24
25 Tu	0 53	14 46	4 25	16 37	4 36	0 24	18 34	1 52	21 33	1 11	29 38	12 52	10 34	1 01	16 36	2 25
26 W	1 16	18 18	3 51	19 48	4 51	0 05	18 57	1 57	21 41	1 11	29 36	12 50	10 38	1 01	16 36	2 25
27 Th	1 40	21 05	3 06	22 09	5 01	0N11	19 20	2 01	21 50	1 12	29 34	12 47	10 43	1 01	16 35	2 25
28 F	2 03	22 58	2 13	23 32	5 06	0 27	19 42	2 05	21 59	1 12	29 32	12 44	10 47	1 01	16 34	2 25
29 Sa	2 26	23 50	1 14	23 51	5 06	0 42	20 04	2 09	22 07	1 12	29 30	12 42	10 51	1 01	16 34	2 25
30 Su	2S50	23N35	0N11	23N02	5N02	0N55	20S26	2S13	22S15	1S13	29S27	12S39	10S56	1N01	16N33	2S25

Day	⚷ Decl	⚷ Lat	♅ Decl	♅ Lat	♆ Decl	♆ Lat	♇ Decl	♇ Lat
1	14N26	1S13	22N56	0N01	2N46	1S32	23S41	5S47
6	14 24	1 14	22 57	0 01	2 43	1 32	23 43	5 47
11	14 21	1 15	22 57	0 01	2 40	1 32	23 44	5 46
16	14 18	1 16	22 58	0 01	2 37	1 32	23 45	5 46
21	14 15	1 16	22 58	0 01	2 33	1 33	23 46	5 46
26	14 11	1 17	22 58	0 01	2 30	1 33	23 46	5 46

Day	⚴ Decl	⚴ Lat	⚵ Decl	⚵ Lat	⚶ Decl	⚶ Lat	Eris Decl	Eris Lat
1	14N18	37N42	3S59	10N03	26S36	3S44	0N60	9S53
6	13 19	36 43	4 30	9 57	26 41	3 52	0 59	9 54
11	12 21	35 45	5 01	9 53	26 44	3 59	0 58	9 54
16	11 24	34 49	5 31	9 48	26 44	4 05	0 57	9 54
21	10 28	33 54	6 01	9 44	26 43	4 10	0 56	9 54
26	9 35	33 01	6 31	9 41	26 39	4 14	0 55	9 54

Moon Phenomena

Max/0 Decl
dy hr mn
1 23:29 24N08
8 14:53 0 S
14 18:44 24S02
21 18:11 0 N
29 6:52 23N53

Perigee/Apogee
dy hr m kilometers
10 4:29 p 361351
25 19:42 a 405999

Max/0 Lat
dy hr mn
3 1:45 0 S
9 11:41 5S01
15 16:34 0 N
22 16:58 4N59
30 4:01 0 S

PH dy hr mn
☾ 1 4:34 9♊02
● 8 10:45 16♍04
☽ 15 1:30 22♐31
○ 22 16:30 29♓57
☾ 30 20:58 7♋59

Void of Course Moon

Last Aspect	☽ Ingress
2 13:28 ♃ △	♋ 2 21:32
4 22:12 ♃ □	♌ 5 4:55
7 2:47 ♃ ✶	♍ 7 8:23
9 8:17 ☿ ☌	♎ 9 9:14
11 5:15 ♃ ☌	♏ 11 9:25
13 4:17 ☿ ✶	♐ 13 10:51
15 11:36 ♃ ✶	♑ 15 14:43
17 18:49 ♃ □	♒ 17 21:14
20 4:26 ♃ △	♓ 20 6:01
22 16:30 ☉ ☍	♈ 22 16:36
24 5:37 ♅ ✶	♉ 25 4:42
27 6:41 ♄ ☌	♊ 27 17:35
29 7:37 ☿ □	♋ 30 5:29

DAILY ASPECTARIAN

1 Sa
☽⋕♇ 2:13
☽△♇ 3:39
☉□☽ 4:34
☊D 4:43
☽✶♆ 7:33
☽⚼♃ 7:38
☽⊻⚷ 11:31
☽△⚳ 14:31
☉⋕♀ 15:45
☽⊼♂ 17:26
☽☌♅ 22:57

2 Su
☽△♀ 2:55
☽⚼♇ 9:06
☽⊻♄ 11:55
☿R 12:19
☽△♃ 13:28
☽∠⚷ 16:46
☉⊼♆ 16:57
☽⚼⚳ 19:20
☽⋕♇ 20:07

3 M
☽⚼♂ 0:09
☽□☿ 1:00
☊R 1:46
☉∠♃ 2:58
☽∥♅ 9:11
☽⊼♇ 13:41
☿∠♂ 14:54
☽∠♄ 16:28
☽□♆ 17:21
♀∥♃ 18:14
☉✶☽ 19:23
☽✶⚷ 21:06
☽⊼⚳ 23:17

4 Tu
☽△♂ 5:44
☽⊻♅ 7:58
☽□♀ 17:03
☉△⚷ 17:55
☽✶♄ 20:00
☽□♃ 22:12

5 W
☉∠☽ 0:56
☽⋕♂ 3:12
☽✶☿ 7:27
☽∠♅ 10:57
☽∥♄ 11:29
☉⊼⚳ 16:48
☽☍♇ 19:50
☽△♆ 23:13

6 Th
☽∥⚷ 0:17
☽□⚷ 2:43
♀⊼♄ 3:09
♂⊼♅ 3:27
☽☍⚳ 4:14
☉⊻☽ 5:13
♄R 8:36
☽∠☿ 8:55
☽✶♅ 12:56
☽□♂ 13:23
☽⋕♀ 18:55

7 F
☽□♄ 0:04
☽⋕♃ 0:32
☽⚼♆ 0:43
☽✶♀ 1:54
☽✶♃ 2:47
☽⊻☿ 9:23
♀☌♃ 14:55
☉∥☽ 15:25
☽⊼♇ 22:19
☽⋕☿ 22:29

8 Sa
☽⊼♆ 1:29
☽∠♃ 3:52
☽∥♆ 4:06
☽∠♀ 4:47
☽△⚷ 4:48
☽⊼⚳ 5:50
☉☌☽ 10:45
☿R♍ 11:01
☽□♅ 14:37
☽✶♂ 17:19
☽⚼♇ 22:39

9 Su
☽△♄ 1:12
☽⋕♆ 1:33
☽⊻♃ 4:27
☽⚼⚷ 5:02
☽∥☿ 5:41
☽⚼⚳ 5:52
☽⊻♀ 7:05
☽☌☿ 8:17
☉⋕☽ 11:15
☿⊻♀ 17:04
☽∠♂ 18:34
☽△♇ 22:43

10 M
☽⚼♄ 1:16
☽☍♆ 1:47
☽⊼⚷ 5:04
☽∥♃ 5:24
☽△⚳ 5:43
♀ ♏ 10:56
☉⊻☽ 14:21
☽△♅ 14:52
☽∥♀ 18:12
☽⊻♂ 19:44
☉□♅ 22:14

11 Tu
☽⊼♄ 1:21
☽⋕⚷ 3:16
☽☌♃ 5:15
☽⊻☿ 6:01
☽☌♀ 11:19
☿⚼⚳ 13:27
☽⚼♅ 15:05
☽⋕♄ 15:19
☉∠☽ 16:15
☿⊻♃ 16:27
☿⋕♆ 20:35
☿⚼⚷ 21:09
☽□♇ 23:02

12 W
☽⊼♆ 2:08
☽∠☿ 5:00
☽☍⚷ 5:29
☽□⚳ 5:51
☽∥♂ 7:31
☽⊼♅ 15:40
☉✶☽ 18:37
☽☌♂ 23:02

13 Th
☽☍♄ 2:26
☽⚼♆ 2:53
☽✶☿ 4:17
☽⊻♃ 7:11
♀⚼♅ 12:23
☽⋕♅ 14:14
☽⊻♀ 17:10

14 F
☽✶♇ 1:01
☽∥♇ 3:54
☽△♆ 4:13
☿△♄ 6:55
☽⊼⚷ 7:44
☽✶⚳ 7:49
☽∠♃ 9:03
☽☍♅ 18:33
☽∠♀ 21:15
♀⋕⚷ 21:27
☿✶♂ 22:44
⚳□⚷ 23:54

15 Sa
☉□☽ 1:30
☽∠♇ 2:57
☽□☿ 4:12
☽⊻♂ 4:55
☽⊼♄ 5:47
☽∥♇ 9:40
☽∠⚳ 9:47
☽⚼⚷ 9:50
☽✶♃ 11:36
☿⚼♇ 20:58
☉☌☿ 21:12
☉⚼♇ 21:26
♂☍♄ 22:05
☉∥♆ 23:58

16 Su
☽⋕♅ 0:06
☽✶♀ 2:13
☽⊻♇ 5:34
♂⚼♆ 6:16
☽⚼♄ 8:28
☽□♆ 8:54
☽∠♂ 9:03
☽⊻⚳ 12:25
☽△⚷ 12:36
☿∠♀ 20:31

17 M
☽⊼♅ 0:06
☽∥♂ 3:04
☽△☿ 6:17
☉△☽ 11:45
☽△♄ 11:48
☉△♄ 12:31
☽✶♂ 13:56
♀□♇ 17:07
☽□♃ 18:49

18 Tu
☽⚼♅ 3:50
☽⋕♄ 4:10
☽⚼☿ 8:12
☽∥♀ 9:09
☽☌♇ 12:42
☽□♀ 14:38
☽✶♆ 16:08
☉⚼☽ 18:01
☽⋕⚷ 18:16
☉∥☿ 18:39
☽☌⚳ 19:33
☽□⚷ 19:58

19 W
♀⊼♆ 7:04
☽△♅ 8:06
☽⊼☿ 10:43
☉⚼⚳ 12:43
☽∥♃ 16:12
☉⚼⚷ 18:47
☽□♄ 20:08
☽∠♆ 20:33

20 Th
☉⊼☽ 0:57
☽□♂ 1:42
☽△♃ 4:26
♀⋕♄ 6:29
☿∥♆ 11:00
♀□⚳ 19:02
☽⊻♇ 21:57

21 F
♀☍⚷ 1:15
☽⊻♆ 1:26
☽⋕☿ 3:52
☽⊻⚳ 4:46
☽✶⚷ 5:23
☽△♀ 5:49
☽⋕♆ 5:50
☉✶♂ 7:14
☿□♅ 9:28
☽⚼♃ 9:58
☉⋕☽ 16:11
☽☍☿ 17:40
☽□♅ 18:03
☉∥☽ 19:53

22 Sa
☽∠♇ 3:15
☽✶♄ 6:19
☽∥♆ 6:34
☉⊻♃ 8:03
☽∠⚳ 10:03
☽∠⚷ 10:44
☽∥☿ 11:57
☽⚼♀ 14:15
☽△♂ 15:40
☽⊼♃ 15:57
☉☍☽ 16:30
☉ ♎ 17:40
♂⊻♃ 22:59

23 Su
♂ ♐ 8:15
☽✶♇ 8:56
☽∠♄ 12:00
☊R♐ 12:19
☽☌♆ 12:26
☽✶⚳ 15:44
♅R 16:23
☽⊻⚷ 16:28
☽⊼♀ 23:12
☽⋕♃ 23:13
☽⚼♂ 23:21

24 M
☽⊼☿ 3:33
☽✶♅ 5:37
♃ ♏ 6:25
☽⊻♄ 18:02
☽∥⚷ 20:31

25 Tu
☿D 2:03
☽☍♃ 5:06
☽⊼♂ 7:27
☽⚼☿ 9:40
☉⊼☽ 10:01
☽∥♄ 11:53
☽∠♅ 11:54
☿✶♀ 21:07
☽□♇ 21:18

26 W
☽⊻♆ 0:46
☽□⚳ 4:04
☽☌⚷ 4:50
☽⋕♀ 5:46
☽△☿ 16:32
☽☍♀ 18:12
⚴ ♑ 18:16
☽⊻♅ 18:20
☉⚼☽ 19:13
♀⊼♅ 19:39

27 Th
☽☌♄ 6:41
☽∠♆ 7:10
☽⋕♂ 8:49
☽⊼♃ 19:02
☽∥♅ 23:55

28 F
☽☍♂ 0:06
☉△☽ 4:22
☽△♇ 10:04
☽✶♆ 13:26
☽△⚳ 16:43
☿□♅ 17:22
☽⊻⚷ 17:24
☽⋕♇ 20:45
☽⋕♇ 20:48

29 Sa
☽⚼♃ 1:46
☉⋕♆ 1:57
☽☌♅ 6:52
☽□☿ 7:37
☽⊼♀ 12:53
☽⚼♇ 16:01
☽⊻♄ 18:45
☽⚼⚳ 22:31
☽∠⚷ 23:08

30 Su
☉∠♀ 6:10
☽△♃ 7:55
☽∥♅ 13:09
☽⊼♂ 15:21
☉□☽ 20:58
☽⚼♀ 21:08
☽⊼♇ 21:16
☽⋕♂ 21:42
☽∠♄ 23:51

October 2029

LONGITUDE

Day	Sid.Time	☉	☽	☽ 12 hour	Mean ☊	True ☊	☿	♀	♂	⚳	♃	♄	⚷	♅	♆	♇
	h m s	° ' "	° ' "	° ' "	° '	° '	° '	° '	° '	° '	° '	° '	° '	° '	° '	° '
1 M	0 40 04	8♎06 12	9♋33 28	15♋51 33	29♐40.7	29♐15.3	20♍16.1	23♏11.7	5♐19.1	11♒26.7	1♏23.3	24♉29.0	11♉43.5	18♊31.8	9♈45.9	8♒08.3
2 Tu	0 44 00	9 05 13	22 15 25	28 45 38	29 37.5	29R 14.8	21 14.8	24 18.0	6 01.2	11D 26.8	1 35.8	24R 26.4	11R 41.2	18R 31.4	9R 44.2	8R 07.8
3 W	0 47 57	10 04 15	5♌22 43	12♌07 03	29 34.4	29 12.7	22 20.6	25 24.1	6 43.4	11 27.2	1 48.4	24 23.7	11 38.9	18 31.0	9 42.6	8 07.3
4 Th	0 51 53	11 03 20	18 58 52	25 58 16	29 31.2	29 08.2	23 32.7	26 30.1	7 25.7	11 28.0	2 01.0	24 20.9	11 36.5	18 30.5	9 40.9	8 06.8
5 F	0 55 50	12 02 27	3♍05 08	10♍19 08	29 28.0	29 01.1	24 50.5	27 35.9	8 08.1	11 29.1	2 13.6	24 18.0	11 34.1	18 29.9	9 39.2	8 06.3
6 Sa	0 59 47	13 01 37	17 39 43	25 06 05	29 24.8	28 51.7	26 13.2	28 41.5	8 50.6	11 30.6	2 26.3	24 15.1	11 31.6	18 29.3	9 37.5	8 05.9
7 Su	1 03 43	14 00 48	2♎37 14	10♎11 58	29 21.6	28 41.0	27 40.2	29 46.9	9 33.2	11 32.4	2 39.0	24 12.0	11 29.1	18 28.6	9 35.9	8 05.5
8 M	1 07 40	15 00 02	17 48 57	25 26 48	29 18.5	28 30.2	29 10.8	0♐52.2	10 15.8	11 34.6	2 51.8	24 08.9	11 26.6	18 27.9	9 34.2	8 05.1
9 Tu	1 11 36	15 59 18	3♏04 06	10♏39 29	29 15.3	28 20.6	0♎44.5	1 57.2	10 58.6	11 37.1	3 04.5	24 05.6	11 24.0	18 27.2	9 32.5	8 04.8
10 W	1 15 33	16 58 35	18 11 45	25 39 48	29 12.1	28 13.1	2 20.7	3 02.1	11 41.4	11 40.0	3 17.4	24 02.3	11 21.4	18 26.4	9 30.9	8 04.5
11 Th	1 19 29	17 57 55	3♐02 46	10♐20 01	29 08.9	28 08.4	3 58.9	4 06.7	12 24.4	11 43.2	3 30.2	23 58.9	11 18.8	18 25.5	9 29.2	8 04.2
12 F	1 23 26	18 57 17	17 31 06	24 35 46	29 05.8	28D 06.2	5 38.8	5 11.2	13 07.4	11 46.8	3 43.1	23 55.5	11 16.2	18 24.6	9 27.6	8 03.9
13 Sa	1 27 22	19 56 40	1♑33 58	8♑25 48	29 02.6	28 05.9	7 20.0	6 15.4	13 50.6	11 50.7	3 56.0	23 51.9	11 13.5	18 23.7	9 26.0	8 03.7
14 Su	1 31 19	20 56 05	15 11 28	21 51 18	28 59.4	28R 06.3	9 02.1	7 19.4	14 33.8	11 54.9	4 08.9	23 48.3	11 10.9	18 22.7	9 24.3	8 03.5
15 M	1 35 16	21 55 32	28 25 39	4♒54 58	28 56.2	28 06.2	10 44.9	8 23.1	15 17.1	11 59.5	4 21.8	23 44.6	11 08.1	18 21.6	9 22.7	8 03.3
16 Tu	1 39 12	22 55 00	11♒19 40	17 40 12	28 53.1	28 04.5	12 28.1	9 26.6	16 00.4	12 04.4	4 34.8	23 40.8	11 05.4	18 20.5	9 21.1	8 03.1
17 W	1 43 09	23 54 30	23 57 00	0♓10 29	28 49.9	28 00.6	14 11.5	10 29.8	16 43.9	12 09.6	4 47.7	23 37.0	11 02.7	18 19.4	9 19.5	8 03.0
18 Th	1 47 05	24 54 02	6♓21 01	12 28 58	28 46.7	27 54.0	15 55.1	11 32.8	17 27.4	12 15.1	5 00.7	23 33.0	10 59.9	18 18.2	9 17.9	8 02.9
19 F	1 51 02	25 53 36	18 34 38	24 38 19	28 43.5	27 45.0	17 38.5	12 35.5	18 11.0	12 21.0	5 13.8	23 29.1	10 57.1	18 16.9	9 16.3	8 02.8
20 Sa	1 54 58	26 53 11	0♈40 15	6♈40 39	28 40.3	27 34.2	19 21.9	13 37.9	18 54.7	12 27.1	5 26.8	23 25.0	10 54.3	18 15.7	9 14.7	8 02.8
21 Su	1 58 55	27 52 48	12 39 44	18 37 40	28 37.2	27 22.5	21 04.9	14 40.0	19 38.4	12 33.6	5 39.8	23 20.9	10 51.4	18 14.3	9 13.1	8D 02.7
22 M	2 02 51	28 52 28	24 34 38	0♉30 48	28 34.0	27 10.9	22 47.7	15 41.8	20 22.3	12 40.4	5 52.9	23 16.7	10 48.6	18 13.0	9 11.6	8 02.8
23 Tu	2 06 48	29 52 09	6♉26 22	12 21 30	28 30.8	27 00.4	24 30.0	16 43.2	21 06.2	12 47.5	6 06.0	23 12.5	10 45.7	18 11.6	9 10.0	8 02.8
24 W	2 10 45	0♏51 53	18 16 27	24 11 26	28 27.6	26 51.9	26 12.0	17 44.4	21 50.2	12 54.9	6 19.0	23 08.2	10 42.9	18 10.1	9 08.5	8 02.9
25 Th	2 14 41	1 51 38	0♊06 44	6♊02 41	28 24.4	26 45.8	27 53.5	18 45.2	22 34.3	13 02.5	6 32.1	23 03.9	10 40.0	18 08.6	9 07.0	8 03.0
26 F	2 18 38	2 51 26	11 59 37	17 57 57	28 21.3	26 42.2	29 34.5	19 45.7	23 18.4	13 10.5	6 45.2	22 59.5	10 37.1	18 07.1	9 05.5	8 03.1
27 Sa	2 22 34	3 51 15	23 58 07	0♋00 35	28 18.1	26D 40.9	1♏15.0	20 45.8	24 02.6	13 18.8	6 58.4	22 55.1	10 34.2	18 05.5	9 04.0	8 03.2
28 Su	2 26 31	4 51 07	6♋05 52	12 14 32	28 14.9	26 41.2	2 55.0	21 45.5	24 46.9	13 27.3	7 11.5	22 50.6	10 31.3	18 03.9	9 02.6	8 03.4
29 M	2 30 27	5 51 01	18 27 07	24 44 13	28 11.7	26 42.4	4 34.6	22 44.8	25 31.3	13 36.1	7 24.6	22 46.0	10 28.4	18 02.2	9 01.1	8 03.6
30 Tu	2 34 24	6 50 58	1♌06 25	7♌34 15	28 08.6	26R 43.4	6 13.6	23 43.8	26 15.7	13 45.3	7 37.7	22 41.5	10 25.4	18 00.5	8 59.7	8 03.9
31 W	2 38 20	7♏50 56	14 08 13	20 48 47	28♐05.4	26♐43.3	7♏52.1	24♐42.3	27♐00.2	13♒54.6	7♏50.9	22♉36.8	10♉22.5	17♊58.7	8♈58.2	8♒04.1

1st of Month

Julian Day # 2462410.5
Obliquity 23°26'08"
SVP 4♓50'22"
GC 27♐15.3
Eris 26♈16.8R

Day	⚴	⚵	⚶
1	0♑52.8	14♏36.5	17♑27.0
6	1 59.8	16 10.6	18 48.1
11	3 11.4	17 46.2	20 15.8
16	4 27.3	19 23.1	21 49.4
21	5 47.0	21 01.3	23 28.5
26	7 10.1	22 40.5	25 12.5
31	8 36.4	24 20.6	27 00.9

DECLINATION and LATITUDE

Day	☉ Decl	☽ Decl	☽ Lat	☽12h Decl	☿ Decl	☿ Lat	♀ Decl	♀ Lat	♂ Decl	♂ Lat	⚳ Decl	⚳ Lat	♃ Decl	♃ Lat	♄ Decl	♄ Lat
1 M	3S13	22N11	0S54	21N03	4N53	1N07	20S47	2S17	22S23	1S13	29S25	12S36	11S00	1N01	16N32	2S26
2 Tu	3 36	19 39	1 59	17 58	4 40	1 18	21 07	2 21	22 31	1 13	29 22	12 33	11 05	1 01	16 31	2 26
3 W	3 59	16 02	2 59	13 51	4 22	1 27	21 27	2 25	22 38	1 14	29 19	12 30	11 09	1 01	16 30	2 26
4 Th	4 22	11 28	3 51	8 53	4 01	1 35	21 47	2 29	22 46	1 14	29 16	12 28	11 14	1 01	16 30	2 26
5 F	4 46	6 09	4 32	3 17	3 36	1 41	22 06	2 33	22 53	1 14	29 13	12 25	11 18	1 00	16 29	2 26
6 Sa	5 09	0 20	4 56	2S39	3 08	1 47	22 24	2 36	23 00	1 15	29 10	12 22	11 22	1 00	16 28	2 26
7 Su	5 32	5S38	5 01	8 34	2 37	1 51	22 43	2 40	23 07	1 15	29 07	12 19	11 27	1 00	16 27	2 26
8 M	5 55	11 22	4 45	14 01	2 04	1 54	23 00	2 44	23 14	1 15	29 03	12 16	11 31	1 00	16 26	2 27
9 Tu	6 17	16 25	4 08	18 33	1 29	1 56	23 17	2 48	23 20	1 16	28 60	12 13	11 36	1 00	16 25	2 27
10 W	6 40	20 22	3 15	21 49	0 52	1 57	23 34	2 51	23 26	1 16	28 56	12 10	11 40	1 00	16 24	2 27
11 Th	7 03	22 52	2 09	23 32	0 13	1 57	23 50	2 55	23 32	1 16	28 52	12 07	11 44	0 60	16 23	2 27
12 F	7 25	23 47	0 56	23 38	0S27	1 57	24 05	2 58	23 38	1 16	28 49	12 04	11 49	0 60	16 22	2 27
13 Sa	7 48	23 07	0N18	22 15	1 08	1 56	24 20	3 02	23 44	1 17	28 45	12 01	11 53	0 60	16 21	2 27
14 Su	8 10	21 05	1 30	19 38	1 50	1 54	24 34	3 05	23 49	1 17	28 40	11 58	11 58	0 60	16 20	2 27
15 M	8 32	17 57	2 34	16 05	2 33	1 51	24 48	3 08	23 54	1 17	28 36	11 55	12 02	0 60	16 19	2 27
16 Tu	8 55	14 02	3 29	11 51	3 16	1 48	25 01	3 11	23 59	1 17	28 32	11 52	12 07	0 60	16 18	2 28
17 W	9 17	9 34	4 12	7 13	3 60	1 44	25 14	3 14	24 04	1 17	28 28	11 49	12 11	0 60	16 17	2 28
18 Th	9 38	4 48	4 43	2 22	4 43	1 40	25 25	3 17	24 08	1 18	28 23	11 47	12 15	0 59	16 16	2 28
19 F	10 00	0N05	4 60	2N30	5 27	1 36	25 37	3 20	24 12	1 18	28 19	11 44	12 20	0 59	16 15	2 28
20 Sa	10 22	4 54	5 03	7 14	6 10	1 31	25 48	3 23	24 16	1 18	28 14	11 41	12 24	0 59	16 14	2 28
21 Su	10 43	9 30	4 53	11 39	6 54	1 26	25 58	3 26	24 20	1 18	28 09	11 38	12 29	0 59	16 13	2 28
22 M	11 04	13 42	4 30	15 37	7 37	1 21	26 07	3 29	24 23	1 18	28 05	11 35	12 33	0 59	16 12	2 28
23 Tu	11 25	17 22	3 56	18 57	8 20	1 15	26 16	3 31	24 27	1 19	27 60	11 32	12 37	0 59	16 11	2 28
24 W	11 46	20 19	3 11	21 29	9 02	1 09	26 25	3 34	24 30	1 19	27 55	11 29	12 42	0 59	16 10	2 28
25 Th	12 07	22 25	2 18	23 06	9 44	1 03	26 33	3 36	24 32	1 19	27 50	11 26	12 46	0 59	16 09	2 28
26 F	12 28	23 31	1 18	23 40	10 26	0 57	26 40	3 38	24 35	1 19	27 45	11 23	12 50	0 59	16 07	2 28
27 Sa	12 48	23 32	0 15	23 08	11 07	0 51	26 46	3 40	24 37	1 19	27 39	11 20	12 55	0 59	16 06	2 28
28 Su	13 08	22 27	0S51	21 30	11 47	0 44	26 52	3 42	24 39	1 19	27 34	11 18	12 59	0 59	16 05	2 28
29 M	13 28	20 16	1 55	18 47	12 27	0 38	26 58	3 44	24 41	1 19	27 29	11 15	13 03	0 59	16 04	2 28
30 Tu	13 48	17 04	2 55	15 07	13 06	0 31	27 03	3 46	24 42	1 19	27 23	11 12	13 07	0 59	16 03	2 28
31 W	14S07	12N57	3S48	10N36	13S45	0N24	27S07	3S47	24S44	1S20	27S18	11S09	13S12	0N59	16N02	2S28

Day	⚷ Decl	⚷ Lat	♅ Decl	♅ Lat	♆ Decl	♆ Lat	♇ Decl	♇ Lat
1	14N07	1S18	22N58	0N01	2N27	1S33	23S47	5S45
6	14 03	1 18	22 58	0 01	2 24	1 33	23 47	5 45
11	13 58	1 19	22 57	0 01	2 20	1 33	23 47	5 45
16	13 54	1 19	22 57	0 01	2 17	1 33	23 47	5 44
21	13 49	1 20	22 56	0 02	2 14	1 33	23 47	5 44
26	13 44	1 20	22 56	0 02	2 11	1 33	23 47	5 43
31	13N39	1S21	22N55	0N02	2N08	1S32	23S46	5S43

Day	⚴ Decl	⚴ Lat	⚵ Decl	⚵ Lat	⚶ Decl	⚶ Lat	Eris Decl	Eris Lat
1	8N44	32N10	6S60	9N38	26S34	4S18	0N54	9S54
6	7 55	31 20	7 28	9 36	26 26	4 21	0 53	9 54
11	7 08	30 32	7 56	9 33	26 16	4 24	0 52	9 54
16	6 24	29 47	8 23	9 32	26 03	4 27	0 51	9 54
21	5 43	29 03	8 49	9 31	25 48	4 29	0 50	9 54
26	5 05	28 21	9 14	9 30	25 31	4 30	0 49	9 54
31	4N29	27N41	9S38	9N30	25S12	4S32	0N48	9S53

Moon Phenomena

Max/0 Decl

dy	hr mn	
6	1:21	0 S
12	1:34	23S47
18	23:36	0 N
26	12:35	23N40

Perigee/Apogee

dy	hr m		kilometers
8	11:32	p	357745
23	2:04	a	406432

Max/0 Lat

dy	hr mn	
6	17:48	5S01
12	18:00	0 N
19	17:55	5N03
27	5:23	0 S

PH	dy	hr mn	
●	7	19:16	14♎48
☽	14	11:10	21♑24
○	22	9:29	29♈16
☾	30	11:33	7♌20

Void of Course Moon

Last Aspect				☽ Ingress		
2	4:09	♀	△	♌	2	14:16
4	13:59	♀	□	♍	4	18:49
6	19:08	♀	⚹	♎	6	19:50
8	1:01	♅	△	♏	8	19:10
10	9:21	♄	☍	♐	10	19:02
12	2:36	☉	⚹	♑	12	21:17
14	15:28	♄	△	♒	15	2:54
16	23:55	☉	△	♓	17	11:40
19	9:39	♄	⚹	♈	19	22:40
22	9:29	☉	☍	♉	22	10:58
24	9:48	♄	☌	♊	24	23:46
27	0:10	♂	☍	♋	27	11:59
29	8:12	♄	⚹	♌	29	21:56

DAILY ASPECTARIAN

1 M	☽ □ ♆	0:24
	☉ △ ♇	0:50
	☽ ⚻ ⚳	3:37
	☽ ⚹ ⚷	4:08
	⚳ D	8:43
	☽ # ♀	12:53
	☽ ⚺ ♅	17:01
	☽ ⚼ ♂	21:34
	☽ ⚹ ☿	21:57
2 Tu	♀ ☍ ♄	2:55
	☽ ⚹ ♄	4:02
	☽ △ ♀	4:09
	☉ ⚼ ♄	8:15
	♀ ⚼ ♆	9:16
	☉ ☍ ♆	15:25
	☽ □ ♃	17:27
	☽ ∠ ♅	20:39
	☽ ∥ ♄	21:09
3 W	☽ △ ♂	2:33
	☽ ∠ ☿	3:51
	☽ ☍ ♇	4:54
	☽ △ ♆	7:43
	☉ ⚹ ☽	9:02
	☽ ∥ ⚷	10:47
	☽ ☍ ⚳	10:50
	☽ □ ⚷	11:08
	☉ # ☿	12:31
	☿ ⚼ ♇	15:39
	☽ ⚹ ♅	23:11
4 Th	☽ # ♃	1:08
	☽ ⚺ ☿	8:38
	☽ □ ♄	9:12
	☽ ⚼ ♆	9:47
	☉ △ ⚳	10:10
	☉ ⚻ ⚷	12:56
	☉ ∠ ☽	13:03
	☽ □ ♀	13:59
	☿ △ ♄	14:33
	☽ ⚹ ♃	22:32
	♂ ⚹ ♇	23:01
5 F	☉ # ☽	5:30
	☽ ⚻ ♇	8:21
	☽ □ ♂	8:49
	☽ ⚻ ♆	10:53
	☽ ∥ ☿	11:36
	☽ ⚻ ⚳	13:56
	☽ △ ⚷	14:01
	♂ # ♅	15:14
	☽ ∥ ♆	15:38
	☉ ⚺ ☽	15:54
	☽ ∠ ♃	23:38
6 Sa	☽ □ ♅	1:20
	☿ ⚼ ⚳	4:59
	☿ ⚼ ⚷	5:02
	⚳ □ ⚷	5:59
	☽ ⚼ ♇	8:47
	☽ △ ♄	10:36
	☽ # ♆	10:55
	☽ # ☿	12:50
	☽ ⚼ ⚷	14:15
	☽ ⚼ ⚳	14:17
	☽ ☌ ☿	15:15
	☽ ⚹ ♀	19:08
	☉ ∥ ☽	23:31
7 Su	☽ ⚺ ♃	0:03
	♂ △ ♆	1:28
	♀ ♐	4:49
	☽ △ ♇	8:40
	☽ ⚼ ♄	10:23
	☿ ∥ ♆	10:49
	☽ ☍ ♆	11:02
	☽ ⚹ ♂	11:31
	☽ ⚻ ⚷	13:59
	☽ △ ⚳	14:09
	☉ ☌ ☽	19:16
	♀ # ♅	20:23
	☽ ∠ ♀	20:42
8 M	☽ ∥ ♃	0:40
	☽ △ ♅	1:01
	☽ ⚻ ♄	9:55
	☽ # ⚷	12:01
	☽ ∠ ♂	12:17
	☿ ♎	12:42
	☽ ⚺ ☿	19:55
	☽ ⚺ ♀	22:07
9 Tu	☽ # ♄	0:00
	☽ ☌ ♃	0:01
	☽ ⚼ ♅	0:36
	♀ ∥ ♂	6:36
	☽ □ ♇	7:55
	☽ ⚻ ♆	10:13
	☽ ⚺ ♂	13:08
	☽ ☍ ⚷	13:09
	♂ ⚻ ⚷	13:26
	☽ □ ⚳	13:34
	☉ ⚺ ☽	21:55
	☽ ∠ ☿	22:29
	♂ ⚹ ⚳	23:06
10 W	☽ ⚻ ♅	0:23
	♀ ⚺ ♃	7:04
	☽ ☍ ♄	9:21
	☽ ⚼ ♆	10:08
	♃ ⚼ ♅	15:49
	☿ ⚺ ♃	15:59
	♀ ∥ ♇	20:37
	☉ ∠ ☽	23:51
11 Th	☽ ⚺ ♃	0:46
	☽ # ♅	1:13
	☽ ⚹ ☿	1:44
	☽ ☌ ♀	1:53
	☿ ⚹ ♀	5:22
	☽ ⚹ ♇	8:15
	☽ △ ♆	10:35
	☉ △ ♅	11:00
	☽ ⚻ ⚷	13:35
	☽ ∥ ♂	14:01
	☽ ⚹ ⚳	14:22
	☽ ☌ ♂	16:15
12 F	☽ ☍ ♅	1:30
	☽ ∠ ♃	2:03
	☉ ⚹ ☽	2:36
	☽ ∠ ♇	9:23
	☽ ∥ ♂	10:24
	☽ ⚻ ♄	10:49
	☽ ⚼ ⚷	14:49
	☽ ∠ ⚳	15:49
	☊ D	17:58
13 Sa	☽ # ♅	2:43
	☽ ⚹ ♃	4:11
	☽ ⚺ ♀	8:52
	☿ △ ♇	10:16
	☽ ⚺ ♇	11:21
	☽ □ ☿	11:30
	☽ ⚼ ♄	12:43
	☽ □ ♆	13:45
	☽ △ ⚷	16:53
	♂ ∥ ♇	16:57
	☽ ⚺ ⚳	18:08
	☿ ⚼ ♄	20:53
	☽ ⚺ ♂	22:49
14 Su	☿ ☍ ♆	5:07
	☽ ⚻ ♅	5:43
	☊ R	11:07
	☉ □ ☽	11:10
	☽ ∠ ♀	13:58
	☽ △ ♄	15:28
	☿ # ♆	15:35
	♀ ⚹ ♇	16:32
15 M	☽ ∠ ♂	3:37
	☿ ⚻ ⚷	5:17
	☽ ⚼ ♅	9:06
	☽ # ♄	10:32
	☽ □ ♃	11:10
	☽ ☌ ♇	17:51
	☿ △ ⚳	18:13
	☽ ⚹ ♀	20:08
	☽ ⚹ ♆	20:18
	♀ △ ♆	21:58
	☽ □ ⚷	23:33
16 Tu	☽ # ⚷	0:45
	☽ ☌ ⚳	1:25
	☽ △ ☿	2:29
	☽ ⚹ ♂	9:23
	☽ ∥ ♃	10:26
	☽ △ ♅	13:16
	☉ ⚻ ♄	17:21
	☽ □ ♄	23:22
	☉ △ ☽	23:55
17 W	☽ ∠ ♆	0:43
	☉ ∥ ☽	1:24
	☽ ⚼ ☿	11:44
	♀ ⚻ ⚷	11:58
	☽ △ ♃	21:21
18 Th	☽ ∥ ☿	0:21
	☽ ⚺ ♇	3:19
	☽ ⚺ ♆	5:45
	☉ ⚼ ☽	7:33
	☽ ⚹ ⚷	9:03
	☽ □ ♀	11:07
	☽ ⚺ ⚳	11:38
	☽ # ♆	12:30
	♀ ⚹ ⚳	17:51
	☽ ⚻ ☿	21:51
	☽ □ ♂	23:10
	☽ □ ♅	23:25
19 F	♂ ☍ ♅	3:10
	☽ ⚼ ♃	3:19
	☿ △ ♅	8:48
	☽ ∠ ♇	8:51
	☽ ⚹ ♄	9:39
	☽ ∥ ♆	10:43
	☿ ⚹ ♂	13:03
	☽ ∠ ⚷	14:33
	☉ ⚻ ☽	15:47
	☽ ∠ ⚳	17:32
20 Sa	☽ # ☿	7:42
	☽ ⚻ ♃	9:43
	☽ ⚹ ♇	14:44
	☽ ∠ ♄	15:24
	☽ ☌ ♆	17:06
	☽ ⚺ ⚷	20:23
	☽ ⚹ ⚳	23:48
21 Su	♇ D	3:55
	☽ △ ♀	4:25
	☉ # ☽	7:19
	☽ ⚹ ♅	11:12
	☽ △ ♂	14:58
	☽ # ♃	17:00
	☽ ☍ ☿	19:48
	☽ ⚺ ♄	21:24
22 M	☽ ∥ ⚷	0:34
	☿ ⚻ ♄	6:32
	☉ ☍ ☽	9:29
	☽ ⚼ ♀	13:32
	☽ ∥ ♄	15:48
	☽ ∠ ♅	17:26
	☽ ⚼ ♂	23:16
	☽ ☍ ♃	23:18
	♂ ∠ ♃	23:48
23 Tu	☉ ♏	3:09
	☽ □ ♇	3:15
	☽ ⚺ ♆	5:31
	☽ ☌ ⚷	8:44
	☽ □ ⚳	13:01
	☽ ⚻ ♀	22:49
	☽ ⚺ ♅	23:47
24 W	☽ ⚻ ♂	7:42
	☽ ☌ ♄	9:48
	♀ ☍ ♅	9:53
	☽ ∠ ♆	11:53
	☽ ⚻ ☿	18:45
25 Th	☉ ⚻ ☽	3:52
	☽ ∥ ♅	8:43
	☽ ⚻ ♃	13:14
	♂ ⚻ ♄	14:39
	♂ ∠ ♇	15:39
	☽ △ ♇	16:03
	☽ ⚹ ♆	18:10
	☽ ⚺ ⚷	21:14
26 F	☽ △ ⚳	2:24
	☽ ⚼ ☿	6:03
	☿ ♏	6:05
	☉ ⚼ ♅	6:07
	☽ ☌ ♅	12:17
	☉ ⚼ ☽	12:51
	☽ ☍ ♀	17:01
	☽ ⚼ ♃	19:57
	☽ ⚺ ♄	21:55
	☽ ⚼ ♇	22:11
27 Sa	☽ ☍ ♂	0:10
	☽ ∠ ⚷	3:11
	☊ D	5:22
	☽ ⚼ ⚳	8:44
	☉ ∥ ♃	9:52
	☽ ∥ ♅	16:13
	☽ △ ☿	16:45
	☉ △ ☽	21:20
28 Su	☿ ⚼ ♅	2:05
	☽ △ ♃	2:11
	☽ ∠ ♄	3:24
	☽ ⚻ ♇	3:50
	☽ □ ♆	5:45
	☽ ⚹ ⚷	8:37
	♀ ∠ ♃	13:28
	☽ ⚻ ⚳	14:32
	♂ ⚼ ⚷	22:31
	☽ ⚺ ♅	23:12
29 M	♀ ⚻ ♄	0:27
	♀ ∠ ♇	7:40
	☽ ⚹ ♄	8:12
	☽ ⚻ ♀	8:55
	☽ ⚻ ♂	14:19
	☉ # ⚷	14:49
30 Tu	☿ ∥ ♃	0:43
	☽ ∠ ♅	3:32
	☽ ∥ ♄	6:27
	☽ □ ☿	10:54
	☉ □ ☽	11:33
	☊ R	11:48
	☽ □ ♃	12:19
	☽ ☍ ♇	12:55
	☽ △ ♆	14:35
	☽ ⚼ ♀	15:16
	☽ □ ⚷	17:10
	☉ # ☽	18:03
	☽ ⚼ ♂	19:53
	☽ ∥ ⚷	20:12
	☽ # ☿	20:14
	☿ # ⚷	20:23
	☽ # ♃	22:42
	☉ ☌ ☿	23:15
	☽ ☍ ⚳	23:35
	☿ ☌ ♃	23:39
	☉ ☌ ♃	23:58
31 W	☿ □ ♇	2:56
	☉ □ ♇	5:18
	☽ ⚹ ♅	6:55
	☽ □ ♄	15:07
	♀ ⚼ ⚷	15:47
	☿ ⚻ ♆	15:56
	☽ ⚼ ♆	17:34
	☽ △ ♀	20:21

LONGITUDE

Day	Sid.Time	☉	☽	☽ 12 hour	Mean ☊	True ☊	☿	♀	♂	⚳	♃	♄	⚷	♅	♆	♇
	h m s	° ′ ″	° ′ ″	° ′ ″	° ′	° ′	° ′	° ′	° ′	° ′	° ′	° ′	° ′	° ′	° ′	° ′
1 Th	2 42 17	8♏50 57	27♌36 18	4♍30 59	28♐02.2	26♐41.6	9♏30.2	25♐40.4	27♐44.8	14♒04.3	8♏04.0	22♉32.2	10♉19.6	17♊57.0	8♈56.8	8♒04.4
2 F	2 46 14	9 50 59	11♍32 55	18 42 00	27 59.0	26R 37.9	11 07.8	26 38.1	28 29.5	14 14.2	8 17.2	22R 27.5	10R 16.6	17R 55.1	8R 55.5	8 04.7
3 Sa	2 50 10	10 51 04	25 57 56	3♎20 11	27 55.8	26 32.4	12 44.9	27 35.3	29 14.2	14 24.4	8 30.3	22 22.8	10 13.7	17 53.3	8 54.1	8 05.1
4 Su	2 54 07	11 51 11	10♎48 00	18 20 27	27 52.7	26 25.7	14 21.6	28 32.0	29 59.0	14 34.8	8 43.4	22 18.0	10 10.8	17 51.4	8 52.7	8 05.5
5 M	2 58 03	12 51 20	25 56 24	3♏34 33	27 49.5	26 18.8	15 57.8	29 28.2	0♑43.8	14 45.5	8 56.6	22 13.3	10 07.8	17 49.5	8 51.4	8 05.9
6 Tu	3 02 00	13 51 31	11♏13 33	18 52 00	27 46.3	26 12.5	17 33.6	0♑23.9	1 28.8	14 56.5	9 09.7	22 08.5	10 04.9	17 47.5	8 50.1	8 06.3
7 W	3 05 56	14 51 43	26 28 32	4♐01 54	27 43.1	26 07.8	19 09.0	1 19.1	2 13.8	15 07.7	9 22.8	22 03.6	10 02.0	17 45.5	8 48.8	8 06.8
8 Th	3 09 53	15 51 58	11♐30 59	18 54 50	27 40.0	26D 05.0	20 44.1	2 13.7	2 58.8	15 19.1	9 35.9	21 58.8	9 59.0	17 43.5	8 47.6	8 07.2
9 F	3 13 49	16 52 14	26 12 43	3♑24 06	27 36.8	26 04.2	22 18.8	3 07.8	3 44.0	15 30.8	9 49.1	21 53.9	9 56.1	17 41.4	8 46.3	8 07.8
10 Sa	3 17 46	17 52 32	10♑28 41	17 26 18	27 33.6	26 04.8	23 53.1	4 01.2	4 29.2	15 42.8	10 02.2	21 49.1	9 53.2	17 39.3	8 45.1	8 08.3
11 Su	3 21 43	18 52 51	24 17 01	1♒00 59	27 30.4	26 06.3	25 27.0	4 54.0	5 14.4	15 55.0	10 15.2	21 44.2	9 50.3	17 37.2	8 43.9	8 08.9
12 M	3 25 39	19 53 12	7♒38 29	14 09 54	27 27.3	26 07.7	27 00.7	5 46.1	5 59.7	16 07.4	10 28.3	21 39.3	9 47.4	17 35.1	8 42.8	8 09.5
13 Tu	3 29 36	20 53 33	20 35 42	26 56 20	27 24.1	26R 08.4	28 34.0	6 37.5	6 45.1	16 20.0	10 41.4	21 34.4	9 44.5	17 32.9	8 41.6	8 10.1
14 W	3 33 32	21 53 57	3♓12 20	9♓24 13	27 20.9	26 07.7	0♐07.1	7 28.2	7 30.6	16 32.9	10 54.4	21 29.5	9 41.7	17 30.7	8 40.5	8 10.8
15 Th	3 37 29	22 54 21	15 32 29	21 37 40	27 17.7	26 05.4	1 39.8	8 18.2	8 16.0	16 46.0	11 07.4	21 24.6	9 38.8	17 28.4	8 39.4	8 11.5
16 F	3 41 25	23 54 47	27 40 13	3♈40 36	27 14.5	26 01.6	3 12.3	9 07.3	9 01.6	16 59.3	11 20.4	21 19.8	9 36.0	17 26.2	8 38.3	8 12.2
17 Sa	3 45 22	24 55 14	9♈39 15	15 36 33	27 11.4	25 56.7	4 44.5	9 55.7	9 47.2	17 12.8	11 33.4	21 14.9	9 33.2	17 23.9	8 37.3	8 12.9
18 Su	3 49 18	25 55 43	21 32 52	27 28 30	27 08.2	25 51.2	6 16.4	10 43.1	10 32.8	17 26.5	11 46.4	21 10.0	9 30.4	17 21.6	8 36.3	8 13.7
19 M	3 53 15	26 56 13	3♉23 48	9♉19 00	27 05.0	25 45.6	7 48.1	11 29.7	11 18.5	17 40.5	11 59.3	21 05.2	9 27.6	17 19.3	8 35.3	8 14.4
20 Tu	3 57 12	27 56 45	15 14 22	21 10 08	27 01.8	25 40.7	9 19.6	12 15.4	12 04.3	17 54.6	12 12.2	21 00.3	9 24.8	17 16.9	8 34.3	8 15.3
21 W	4 01 08	28 57 18	27 06 32	3♊03 47	26 58.7	25 36.8	10 50.8	13 00.1	12 50.1	18 08.9	12 25.1	20 55.5	9 22.1	17 14.5	8 33.4	8 16.1
22 Th	4 05 05	29 57 52	9♊02 07	15 01 45	26 55.5	25 34.3	12 21.7	13 43.8	13 35.9	18 23.5	12 38.0	20 50.7	9 19.4	17 12.2	8 32.5	8 17.0
23 F	4 09 01	0♐58 29	21 02 55	27 05 52	26 52.3	25D 33.1	13 52.4	14 26.5	14 21.9	18 38.2	12 50.8	20 45.9	9 16.7	17 09.8	8 31.6	8 17.9
24 Sa	4 12 58	1 59 06	3♋10 54	9♋18 17	26 49.1	25 33.3	15 22.8	15 08.0	15 07.8	18 53.2	13 03.6	20 41.2	9 14.1	17 07.3	8 30.8	8 18.8
25 Su	4 16 54	2 59 45	15 28 21	21 41 27	26 46.0	25 34.4	16 52.9	15 48.5	15 53.8	19 08.3	13 16.4	20 36.4	9 11.4	17 04.9	8 30.0	8 19.7
26 M	4 20 51	4 00 26	27 57 55	4♌18 08	26 42.8	25 35.9	18 22.7	16 27.7	16 39.9	19 23.6	13 29.2	20 31.8	9 08.8	17 02.4	8 29.2	8 20.7
27 Tu	4 24 47	5 01 08	10♌42 29	17 11 20	26 39.6	25 37.5	19 52.2	17 05.8	17 26.0	19 39.1	13 41.9	20 27.1	9 06.2	17 00.0	8 28.4	8 21.7
28 W	4 28 44	6 01 52	23 45 04	0♍23 59	26 36.4	25 38.7	21 21.2	17 42.5	18 12.1	19 54.7	13 54.6	20 22.5	9 03.7	16 57.5	8 27.7	8 22.7
29 Th	4 32 41	7 02 37	7♍08 23	13 58 29	26 33.2	25R 39.2	22 49.9	18 18.0	18 58.3	20 10.6	14 07.2	20 17.9	9 01.2	16 55.0	8 27.0	8 23.7
30 F	4 36 37	8♐03 24	20 54 25	27 56 12	26♐30.1	25♐38.7	24♐18.0	18♑52.0	19♑44.5	20♒26.6	14♏19.8	20♉13.3	8♉58.7	16♊52.5	8♈26.3	8♒24.8

1st of Month

Julian Day # 2462441.5
Obliquity 23°26'07"
SVP 4♓50'09"
GC 27♐15.4
Eris 25♈58.4R

Day	⚴	Day	⚵	Day	⚶
1	8♑54.0	1	24♏40.7	1	27♑23.1
6	10 23.8	6	26 21.8	6	29 16.5
11	11 56.1	11	28 03.6	11	1♒13.6
16	13 30.6	16	29 45.8	16	3 14.0
21	15 07.2	21	1♐28.3	21	5 17.4
26	16 45.5	26	3 11.1	26	7 23.6

DECLINATION and LATITUDE

Day	☉ Decl	☽ Decl	☽ Lat	☽ 12h Decl	☿ Decl	☿ Lat	♀ Decl	♀ Lat	♂ Decl	♂ Lat	⚳ Decl	⚳ Lat	♃ Decl	♃ Lat	♄ Decl	♄ Lat
1 Th	14S27	8N04	4S30	5N25	14S23	0N18	27S10	3S48	24S45	1S20	27S12	11S06	13S16	0N59	16N00	2S29
2 F	14 46	2 38	4 58	0S13	14 60	0 11	27 13	3 50	24 45	1 20	27 07	11 04	13 20	0 59	15 59	2 29
3 Sa	15 05	3S07	5 09	6 01	15 36	0 04	27 16	3 51	24 46	1 20	27 01	11 01	13 25	0 59	15 58	2 29
4 Su	15 23	8 51	4 59	11 36	16 11	0S03	27 17	3 52	24 46	1 20	26 55	10 58	13 29	0 59	15 57	2 29
5 M	15 42	14 11	4 29	16 34	16 46	0 09	27 19	3 53	24 46	1 20	26 49	10 55	13 33	0 59	15 56	2 29
6 Tu	15 60	18 40	3 39	20 26	17 20	0 16	27 19	3 53	24 46	1 20	26 43	10 53	13 37	0 59	15 54	2 29
7 W	16 18	21 51	2 34	22 52	17 52	0 23	27 19	3 54	24 45	1 20	26 37	10 50	13 41	0 59	15 53	2 29
8 Th	16 35	23 27	1 18	23 37	18 24	0 29	27 19	3 54	24 44	1 20	26 31	10 47	13 46	0 59	15 52	2 29
9 F	16 52	23 22	0N01	22 44	18 55	0 36	27 18	3 54	24 43	1 20	26 25	10 45	13 50	0 59	15 51	2 28
10 Sa	17 09	21 44	1 18	20 25	19 26	0 42	27 16	3 54	24 42	1 20	26 19	10 42	13 54	0 59	15 50	2 28
11 Su	17 26	18 50	2 28	17 01	19 55	0 49	27 14	3 53	24 40	1 20	26 12	10 40	13 58	0 59	15 48	2 28
12 M	17 42	15 01	3 27	12 52	20 23	0 55	27 11	3 53	24 38	1 20	26 06	10 37	14 02	0 59	15 47	2 28
13 Tu	17 59	10 36	4 14	8 15	20 50	1 01	27 08	3 52	24 36	1 20	25 60	10 34	14 06	0 59	15 46	2 28
14 W	18 14	5 51	4 48	3 25	21 16	1 07	27 04	3 51	24 33	1 20	25 53	10 32	14 10	0 58	15 45	2 28
15 Th	18 30	0 59	5 07	1N27	21 41	1 13	27 00	3 50	24 30	1 20	25 47	10 29	14 14	0 58	15 44	2 28
16 F	18 45	3N51	5 12	6 11	22 05	1 19	26 56	3 49	24 27	1 20	25 40	10 27	14 18	0 58	15 42	2 28
17 Sa	18 60	8 28	5 03	10 40	22 28	1 25	26 50	3 47	24 24	1 20	25 34	10 24	14 22	0 58	15 41	2 28
18 Su	19 14	12 45	4 42	14 43	22 50	1 30	26 45	3 45	24 21	1 20	25 27	10 22	14 26	0 58	15 40	2 28
19 M	19 28	16 32	4 08	18 11	23 10	1 35	26 39	3 43	24 17	1 20	25 20	10 19	14 30	0 58	15 39	2 28
20 Tu	19 42	19 39	3 23	20 54	23 30	1 40	26 32	3 41	24 13	1 20	25 13	10 17	14 34	0 58	15 38	2 28
21 W	19 55	21 56	2 30	22 44	23 48	1 45	26 25	3 38	24 08	1 20	25 06	10 15	14 38	0 58	15 36	2 28
22 Th	20 08	23 17	1 30	23 33	24 05	1 50	26 18	3 35	24 04	1 20	24 59	10 12	14 42	0 58	15 35	2 28
23 F	20 21	23 33	0 25	23 16	24 21	1 54	26 10	3 32	23 59	1 20	24 53	10 10	14 46	0 58	15 34	2 28
24 Sa	20 33	22 42	0S42	21 52	24 36	1 59	26 02	3 29	23 53	1 19	24 45	10 08	14 50	0 58	15 33	2 27
25 Su	20 45	20 45	1 48	19 24	24 49	2 03	25 54	3 25	23 48	1 19	24 38	10 05	14 53	0 58	15 32	2 27
26 M	20 57	17 48	2 49	15 58	25 01	2 06	25 45	3 21	23 42	1 19	24 31	10 03	14 57	0 58	15 31	2 27
27 Tu	21 08	13 57	3 44	11 44	25 12	2 10	25 36	3 17	23 36	1 19	24 24	10 01	15 01	0 58	15 30	2 27
28 W	21 19	9 22	4 29	6 52	25 21	2 13	25 26	3 12	23 30	1 19	24 17	9 59	15 05	0 58	15 29	2 27
29 Th	21 29	4 15	4 60	1 32	25 30	2 15	25 16	3 07	23 24	1 19	24 10	9 56	15 09	0 59	15 27	2 27
30 F	21S39	1S14	5S15	4S01	25S36	2S18	25S06	3S02	23S17	1S19	24S02	9S54	15S12	0N59	15N26	2S27

Day	⚷ Decl	⚷ Lat	♅ Decl	♅ Lat	♆ Decl	♆ Lat	♇ Decl	♇ Lat
1	13N38	1S21	22N55	0N02	2N08	1S32	23S46	5S43
6	13 33	1 21	22 54	0 02	2 05	1 32	23 45	5 42
11	13 28	1 22	22 53	0 02	2 03	1 32	23 44	5 42
16	13 23	1 22	22 52	0 02	2 01	1 32	23 42	5 42
21	13 19	1 22	22 51	0 02	1 59	1 32	23 41	5 41
26	13 14	1 23	22 50	0 02	1 58	1 32	23 39	5 41

Day	⚴ Decl	⚴ Lat	⚵ Decl	⚵ Lat	⚶ Decl	⚶ Lat	Eris Decl	Eris Lat
1	4N22	27N34	9S43	9N30	25S08	4S32	0N48	9S53
6	3 50	26 56	10 05	9 30	24 45	4 34	0 48	9 53
11	3 21	26 20	10 27	9 31	24 21	4 35	0 47	9 53
16	2 54	25 46	10 46	9 32	23 54	4 36	0 46	9 52
21	2 31	25 14	11 05	9 33	23 25	4 37	0 46	9 52
26	2 10	24 43	11 22	9 36	22 53	4 38	0 45	9 51

Moon Phenomena

Max/0 Decl (dy hr mn)

dy hr mn	
2 11:04	0 S
8 10:41	23S37
15 4:50	0 N
22 17:50	23N35
29 18:41	0 S

Max/0 Lat (dy hr mn)

dy hr mn	
3 0:56	5S09
8 23:45	0 N
15 20:44	5N12
23 8:56	0 S
30 8:05	5S16

Perigee/Apogee

dy hr m		kilometers
5 23:09	p	356900
19 2:54	a	406241

PH	dy hr mn	
●	6 4:25	14♏03
☽	13 0:36	20♒55
○	21 4:04	29♉08
☾	28 23:49	7♍02

Void of Course Moon

Last Aspect		☽ Ingress
1 0:16	♂ △	♍ 1 4:11
3 5:38	♂ □	♎ 3 6:35
5 5:55	♀ ⚹	♏ 5 6:23
6 17:04	♄ ☍	♐ 7 5:35
8 10:02	♅ ☍	♑ 9 6:18
11 2:20	♅ ⚹	♒ 11 10:11
13 17:14	☿ □	♓ 13 17:51
15 15:51	☉ △	♈ 16 4:39
17 15:34	♅ ⚹	♉ 18 17:07
21 4:04	☉ ☍	♊ 21 5:50
22 16:17	♅ ☌	♋ 23 17:44
25 9:51	♄ ⚹	♌ 26 3:52
27 19:05	☿ △	♍ 28 11:17
30 6:29	☿ □	♎ 30 15:29

DAILY ASPECTARIAN

1 Th ☽△♂ 0:16; ♃□♇ 0:45; ☉⚻♆ 2:18; ♀∥⚳ 5:16; ☉∥☿ 5:27; ☿☍⚷ 11:47; ☽⚻♇ 18:06; ☽⚹♃ 18:22; ☽⚻♆ 19:33; ☉⚹☽ 20:54; ☽△⚷ 21:51; ☽⚹☿ 23:12

2 F ☽∥♆ 2:10; ☽⚻⚳ 4:35; ☉☍⚷ 9:46; ☽□♅ 10:40; ☽△♄ 18:08; ☿∠♀ 18:13; ☽⚼♇ 19:16; ☽#♆ 19:51; ☽∠♃ 19:54; ☽⚼⚷ 22:48; ☉∠☽ 23:48

3 Sa ☽□♀ 2:50; ☽∠☿ 3:17; ☽□♂ 5:38; ☽⚼⚳ 5:41; ♂∠⚳ 7:07; ☿#♄ 14:28; ☽⚼♄ 18:25; ☽△♇ 19:39; ☽⚺♃ 20:38; ☽☍♆ 20:56; ☽⚻⚷ 23:01

4 Su ♂ ♑ 0:33; ☉⚺☽ 1:48; ☿□⚳ 3:42; ☽△⚳ 6:06; ☽⚺☿ 6:21; ☽△♅ 11:12; ♃⚻♆ 15:27; ☿∠♂ 17:27; ☽⚻♄ 18:10; ☽∥♃ 20:55; ☽#⚷ 21:03

5 M ♃#⚷ 4:58; ☽⚹♀ 5:55; ☽⚹♂ 7:55; ☉∥☽ 8:00; ☽#♄ 8:39; ♀∠⚳ 9:14; ☽⚼♅ 10:48; ♀ ♑ 13:40; ☽∥☿ 15:02; ☉#♄ 17:20; ☽□♇ 19:06; ☽⚻♆ 20:15; ☽☌♃ 20:43; ☽☍⚷ 22:13

6 Tu ☿⚻♅ 3:25; ☉☌☽ 4:25; ☽□⚳ 5:54; ☽∠♀ 6:58; ☽∠♂ 8:40; ☽⚻♅ 10:17; ☽☌☿ 11:06; ☽☍♄ 17:04; ☽⚼♆ 19:48

7 W ☉□⚳ 7:50; ☽⚺♀ 8:11; ☽⚺♂ 9:37; ☽#♅ 12:37; ☽⚹♇ 18:32; ☽△♆ 19:38; ☽⚺♃ 20:52; ⚶ ♒ 21:02; ☽⚻⚷ 21:32

8 Th ☽⚹⚳ 6:14; ☉⚺☽ 7:33; ☽☍♅ 10:02; ☽⚺☿ 16:47; ☽⚻♄ 16:56; ☿☍♄ 18:00; ☽∠♇ 18:55; ☽∠♃ 21:40; ☽⚼⚷ 21:54; ☊ D 23:43

9 F ☽∠⚳ 7:16; ☽#♅ 9:27; ☉∠☽ 10:09; ♃☍⚷ 10:35; ☽☌♀ 12:19; ☽☌♂ 13:16; ☽⚼♄ 17:48; ☉⚻♅ 18:55; ☽⚺♇ 20:01; ☽∠☿ 20:56; ☽□♆ 21:04; ☿⚼♆ 22:00; ☽△⚷ 23:00; ☽⚹♃ 23:14

10 Sa ☽⚺⚳ 9:08; ☽⚻♅ 12:21; ☉⚹☽ 13:46; ☽∥☿ 17:07; ☽△♄ 19:32

11 Su ☽⚹☿ 2:20; ☉∥☽ 8:43; ☽⚼♅ 14:51; ☽#♄ 19:29; ☽⚺♀ 20:21; ☽⚺♂ 20:49

12 M ☽☌♇ 0:57; ☽⚹♆ 1:57; ☽□⚷ 3:55; ☽□♃ 5:16; ☽∥♃ 5:29; ☽#⚷ 8:50; ☽☌⚳ 15:54; ☽△♅ 18:19; ♂⚼♄ 18:54; ♀⚼♄ 22:41

13 Tu ☊ R 0:33; ☉□☽ 0:36; ☽□♄ 1:50; ☽∠♀ 2:05; ☽∠♂ 2:19; ☽∠♆ 5:50; ☉☍♄ 15:02; ☽□☿ 17:14; ☿ ♐ 22:11

14 W ☽⚹♀ 8:50; ☽⚹♂ 8:52; ☽⚺♇ 9:38; ☽⚺♆ 10:34; ♀☌♂ 12:03; ☽⚹⚷ 12:31; ☽△♃ 15:12; ☽#♆ 18:52; ♀⚺♇ 20:43; ♂⚺♇ 21:33

15 Th ☽⚺⚳ 2:27; ☽□♅ 3:47; ♀□♆ 10:06; ☽⚹♄ 11:30; ♂□♆ 12:02; ☽∥♆ 14:50; ☽∠♇ 15:07; ☉△☽ 15:51; ☉⚼♆ 17:35; ☽∠⚷ 17:55; ☽⚼♃ 21:18

16 F ☽∠⚳ 8:47; ☉∠♂ 10:58; ☽△☿ 12:41; ♀△⚷ 13:25; ⚵ ♐ 16:40; ♂△⚷ 17:04; ☽∠♄ 17:12; ☽⚹♇ 21:06; ☽☌♆ 21:56; ☽⚺⚷ 23:48

17 Sa ☽□♂ 0:17; ☉⚼☽ 0:35; ☽□♀ 0:35; ☉∠♀ 0:47; ☽⚻♃ 3:54; ☽⚹⚳ 15:32; ☽⚹♅ 15:34; ⚳△♅ 16:39; ☽⚺♄ 23:14; ☽⚼☿ 23:22

18 Su ☿#♅ 2:20; ☽∥⚷ 3:38; ☉⚻☽ 9:42; ☽#♃ 10:28; ☽∥♄ 18:06; ☽∠♅ 21:50

19 M ☿⚹♇ 6:57; ☽□♇ 9:50; ☽⚻☿ 10:15; ☽⚺♆ 10:31; ☿△♆ 12:14; ☽☌⚷ 12:15; ☽△♂ 17:08; ☽△♀ 17:33; ☽☍♃ 17:44; ♀⚹♃ 21:39

20 Tu ☉#☽ 0:32; ☿⚻⚷ 1:20; ☽⚺♅ 4:07; ☽□⚳ 5:31; ♂⚹♃ 5:48; ☽☌♄ 11:35; ☿∥♇ 14:16; ☽∠♆ 16:50

21 W ☽⚼♂ 1:34; ☽⚼♀ 1:55; ☉☍☽ 4:04; ☽∥♅ 14:09; ☿∥♂ 21:58; ☽△♇ 22:29; ☽⚹♆ 23:01

22 Th ☽⚺⚷ 0:35; ☉ ♐ 0:51; ☿⚺♃ 5:01; ☽⚻♃ 7:20; ☽☍☿ 7:38; ☽⚻♂ 9:46; ☽⚻♀ 10:00; ☽☌♅ 16:17; ☽△⚳ 19:06; ☽⚺♄ 23:26

23 F ☽⚼♇ 4:28; ☽∠⚷ 6:24; ☊ D 8:53; ☽⚼♃ 13:43; ☿⚺♂ 15:53; ☿⚺♀ 16:47; ☽∥♅ 21:23; ☉⚻☽ 21:26

24 Sa ♀☌♂ 1:05; ☽⚼⚳ 1:25; ☽∠♄ 4:53; ☽⚻♇ 10:05; ☽□♆ 10:26; ☿∥⚳ 11:06; ☽⚹⚷ 11:49; ☽△♃ 19:39

25 Su ☉#☽ 0:00; ☽☍♀ 0:41; ☽☍♂ 0:53; ☽⚻☿ 3:06; ☽⚺♅ 3:06; ☿☍♅ 3:07; ☉⚼☽ 5:19; ☽⚻⚳ 7:14; ☽⚹♄ 9:51

26 M ☽∠♅ 7:42; ♂⚻♅ 11:10; ☽⚼☿ 11:37; ☉△☽ 12:26; ♂∥♇ 12:51; ☽∥♄ 14:54; ☽#♃ 17:54; ☽☍♇ 19:37; ☿⚹⚳ 19:44; ☽△♆ 19:50; ♀⚻♅ 20:31; ☽□⚷ 21:01

27 Tu ☽∥⚷ 4:04; ☽□♃ 5:39; ☿⚻♄ 8:56; ☽⚹♅ 11:37; ☽⚻♀ 12:25; ☽⚻♂ 13:14; ☽☍⚳ 16:51; ☽□♄ 17:53; ☽△☿ 19:05; ☽⚼♆ 23:28

28 W ☿∥♀ 6:16; ☽⚼♀ 16:52; ☽⚼♂ 18:02; ☉□☽ 23:49

29 Th ☊ R 0:03; ☽⚻♇ 2:13; ☽⚻♆ 2:19; ☽△⚷ 3:18; ⚳□♄ 8:35; ☿∠♇ 9:19; ☽∥♆ 10:11; ☽⚹♃ 12:27; ☽□♅ 17:04; ☿⚼⚷ 18:52; ☽△♀ 20:20; ☽△♂ 21:53; ☽△♄ 22:50; ☽⚻⚳ 23:11

30 F ☽#♆ 3:06; ☽⚼♇ 4:18; ☽⚼⚷ 5:15; ☽□☿ 6:29; ☉⚹♇ 8:36; ☉△♆ 8:57; ♂△♄ 13:37; ☽∠♃ 14:34; ☉⚻⚷ 20:58; ♆⚹♇ 20:58

December 2029

LONGITUDE

Day	Sid.Time	☉	☽	☽ 12 hour	Mean☊	True☊	☿	♀	♂	⚳	♃	♄	⚷	♅	♆	♇
	h m s	° ' "	° ' "	° ' "	° '	° '	° '	° '	° '	° '	° '	° '	° '	° '	° '	° '
1 Sa	4 40 34	9♐04 12	5♎03 43	12♎16 43	26♐26.9	25♐37.5	25♐45.6	19♑24.7	20♑30.8	20♒42.8	14♏32.4	20♉08.8	8♉56.2	16♊50.0	8♈25.7	8♒25.9
2 Su	4 44 30	10 05 02	19 34 47	26 57 21	26 23.7	25R 35.7	27 12.6	19 55.8	21 17.1	20 59.1	14 44.9	20R 04.4	8R 53.8	16R 47.5	8R 25.1	8 27.0
3 M	4 48 27	11 05 53	4♏23 41	11♏52 54	26 20.5	25 33.7	28 38.8	20 25.5	22 03.5	21 15.7	14 57.4	20 00.0	8 51.4	16 44.9	8 24.5	8 28.2
4 Tu	4 52 23	12 06 46	19 23 59	26 55 53	26 17.4	25 32.0	0♑04.2	20 53.5	22 49.9	21 32.3	15 09.9	19 55.6	8 49.0	16 42.4	8 24.0	8 29.3
5 W	4 56 20	13 07 40	4♐27 25	11♐57 29	26 14.2	25 30.8	1 28.7	21 19.8	23 36.4	21 49.2	15 22.3	19 51.3	8 46.7	16 39.8	8 23.5	8 30.5
6 Th	5 00 16	14 08 35	19 24 57	26 48 50	26 11.0	25D 30.2	2 51.9	21 44.4	24 22.9	22 06.2	15 34.6	19 47.1	8 44.5	16 37.3	8 23.0	8 31.7
7 F	5 04 13	15 09 32	4♑08 12	11♑22 18	26 07.8	25 30.2	4 13.9	22 07.3	25 09.4	22 23.4	15 47.0	19 42.9	8 42.2	16 34.7	8 22.6	8 32.9
8 Sa	5 08 10	16 10 29	18 30 33	25 32 29	26 04.7	25 30.8	5 34.3	22 28.2	25 56.0	22 40.7	15 59.2	19 38.8	8 40.0	16 32.2	8 22.2	8 34.2
9 Su	5 12 06	17 11 26	2♒27 53	9♒16 36	26 01.5	25 31.5	6 53.0	22 47.2	26 42.6	22 58.2	16 11.4	19 34.8	8 37.9	16 29.6	8 21.8	8 35.5
10 M	5 16 03	18 12 25	15 58 42	22 34 22	25 58.3	25 32.3	8 09.5	23 04.2	27 29.3	23 15.9	16 23.6	19 30.8	8 35.8	16 27.1	8 21.4	8 36.8
11 Tu	5 19 59	19 13 24	29 03 52	5♓27 34	25 55.1	25 32.9	9 23.6	23 19.2	28 16.0	23 33.6	16 35.7	19 26.9	8 33.7	16 24.5	8 21.1	8 38.1
12 W	5 23 56	20 14 24	11♓45 55	17 59 26	25 52.0	25R 33.3	10 34.9	23 32.0	29 02.7	23 51.5	16 47.7	19 23.0	8 31.7	16 22.0	8 20.9	8 39.4
13 Th	5 27 52	21 15 24	24 08 38	0♈14 05	25 48.8	25 33.4	11 43.0	23 42.6	29 49.4	24 09.6	16 59.7	19 19.2	8 29.7	16 19.5	8 20.6	8 40.8
14 F	5 31 49	22 16 24	6♈16 22	12 16 03	25 45.6	25 33.2	12 47.2	23 50.9	0♒36.2	24 27.8	17 11.6	19 15.5	8 27.7	16 16.9	8 20.4	8 42.1
15 Sa	5 35 45	23 17 26	18 13 41	24 09 51	25 42.4	25 33.0	13 47.1	23 56.9	1 23.0	24 46.1	17 23.5	19 11.9	8 25.9	16 14.4	8 20.2	8 43.5
16 Su	5 39 42	24 18 27	0♉05 02	5♉59 46	25 39.2	25 32.8	14 42.0	24R 00.5	2 09.8	25 04.6	17 35.3	19 08.4	8 24.0	16 11.9	8 20.1	8 44.9
17 M	5 43 39	25 19 29	11 54 31	17 49 42	25 36.1	25D 32.7	15 31.2	24 01.7	2 56.7	25 23.2	17 47.0	19 04.9	8 22.2	16 09.4	8 20.0	8 46.4
18 Tu	5 47 35	26 20 32	23 45 44	29 42 59	25 32.9	25 32.7	16 13.9	24 00.5	3 43.5	25 41.9	17 58.7	19 01.6	8 20.5	16 06.9	8 19.9	8 47.8
19 W	5 51 32	27 21 35	5♊41 46	11♊42 24	25 29.7	25 32.9	16 49.2	23 56.7	4 30.4	26 00.7	18 10.3	18 58.3	8 18.8	16 04.4	8D 19.9	8 49.3
20 Th	5 55 28	28 22 39	17 45 07	23 50 09	25 26.5	25R 33.0	17 16.3	23 50.5	5 17.4	26 19.7	18 21.8	18 55.1	8 17.1	16 01.9	8 19.9	8 50.8
21 F	5 59 25	29 23 44	29 57 42	6♋07 56	25 23.4	25 33.0	17 34.2	23 41.7	6 04.3	26 38.8	18 33.3	18 52.0	8 15.6	15 59.4	8 20.0	8 52.3
22 Sa	6 03 21	0♑24 48	12♋20 59	18 37 01	25 20.2	25 32.8	17R 42.1	23 30.4	6 51.3	26 58.0	18 44.7	18 48.9	8 14.0	15 57.0	8 20.0	8 53.8
23 Su	6 07 18	1 25 54	24 56 06	1♌18 21	25 17.0	25 32.3	17 39.3	23 16.7	7 38.3	27 17.3	18 56.0	18 46.0	8 12.5	15 54.5	8 20.1	8 55.4
24 M	6 11 15	2 26 59	7♌43 52	14 12 43	25 13.8	25 31.5	17 25.0	23 00.5	8 25.3	27 36.8	19 07.3	18 43.1	8 11.1	15 52.1	8 20.3	8 56.9
25 Tu	6 15 11	3 28 06	20 45 00	27 20 47	25 10.7	25 30.5	16 59.1	22 41.8	9 12.3	27 56.3	19 18.5	18 40.4	8 09.7	15 49.7	8 20.5	8 58.5
26 W	6 19 08	4 29 13	4♍00 08	10♍43 07	25 07.5	25 29.4	16 21.3	22 20.9	9 59.4	28 16.0	19 29.6	18 37.7	8 08.4	15 47.3	8 20.7	9 00.1
27 Th	6 23 04	5 30 20	17 29 48	24 20 11	25 04.3	25 28.5	15 32.2	21 57.7	10 46.4	28 35.8	19 40.6	18 35.2	8 07.1	15 45.0	8 20.9	9 01.7
28 F	6 27 01	6 31 28	1♎14 17	8♎12 05	25 01.1	25D 28.1	14 32.7	21 32.4	11 33.5	28 55.6	19 51.5	18 32.7	8 05.9	15 42.6	8 21.2	9 03.3
29 Sa	6 30 57	7 32 37	15 13 28	22 18 20	24 58.0	25 28.1	13 24.4	21 05.1	12 20.6	29 15.6	20 02.4	18 30.3	8 04.7	15 40.3	8 21.5	9 04.9
30 Su	6 34 54	8 33 46	29 26 27	6♏37 33	24 54.8	25 28.7	12 09.0	20 36.0	13 07.7	29 35.7	20 13.2	18 28.1	8 03.6	15 38.0	8 21.9	9 06.6
31 M	6 38 50	9♑34 55	13♏51 15	21 07 07	24♐51.6	25♐29.8	10♑49.2	20♑05.2	13♒54.9	29♒55.9	20♏23.9	18♉25.9	8♉02.5	15♊35.7	8♈22.3	9♒08.2

1st of Month

Julian Day # 2462471.5
Obliquity 23°26'07"
SVP 4♓50'5"
GC 27♐15.4
Eris 25♈42.8R

Day	⚴	⚵	⚶
1	18♑25.4	4♐54.0	9♒32.2
6	20 06.8	6 36.9	11 43.1
11	21 49.4	8 19.6	13 56.1
16	23 33.0	10 01.9	16 10.9
21	25 17.5	11 43.8	18 27.3
26	27 02.6	13 25.1	20 45.1
31	28 48.3	15 05.6	23 04.2

DECLINATION and LATITUDE

Day	☉ Decl	☽ Decl	☽ Lat	☽12h Decl	☿ Decl	☿ Lat	♀ Decl	♀ Lat	♂ Decl	♂ Lat	⚳ Decl	⚳ Lat	♃ Decl	♃ Lat	♄ Decl	♄ Lat
1 Sa	21S48	6S47	5S12	9S30	25S41	2S20	24S56	2S56	23S10	1S18	23S55	9S52	15S16	0N59	15N25	2S27
2 Su	21 57	12 07	4 49	14 35	25 45	2 21	24 46	2 50	23 02	1 18	23 47	9 50	15 20	0 59	15 24	2 26
3 M	22 06	16 51	4 07	18 52	25 48	2 22	24 35	2 44	22 55	1 18	23 40	9 48	15 23	0 59	15 23	2 26
4 Tu	22 14	20 34	3 07	21 56	25 49	2 23	24 24	2 37	22 47	1 18	23 32	9 46	15 27	0 59	15 22	2 26
5 W	22 22	22 54	1 54	23 27	25 48	2 23	24 12	2 30	22 39	1 18	23 25	9 44	15 30	0 59	15 21	2 26
6 Th	22 30	23 34	0 34	23 16	25 47	2 22	24 01	2 22	22 31	1 18	23 17	9 42	15 34	0 59	15 20	2 26
7 F	22 37	22 34	0N48	21 30	25 43	2 21	23 50	2 14	22 22	1 17	23 09	9 40	15 37	0 59	15 19	2 26
8 Sa	22 43	20 06	2 04	18 25	25 39	2 20	23 38	2 06	22 13	1 17	23 02	9 38	15 41	0 59	15 19	2 25
9 Su	22 49	16 30	3 11	14 24	25 33	2 17	23 26	1 57	22 04	1 17	22 54	9 36	15 44	0 59	15 18	2 25
10 M	22 55	12 08	4 05	9 47	25 25	2 14	23 14	1 48	21 55	1 17	22 46	9 34	15 48	0 59	15 17	2 25
11 Tu	22 60	7 21	4 44	4 53	25 17	2 11	23 02	1 38	21 45	1 16	22 38	9 32	15 51	0 59	15 16	2 25
12 W	23 05	2 23	5 09	0N05	25 06	2 06	22 50	1 28	21 35	1 16	22 30	9 30	15 55	0 59	15 15	2 25
13 Th	23 09	2N32	5 18	4 56	24 55	2 01	22 38	1 18	21 25	1 16	22 22	9 28	15 58	0 59	15 14	2 24
14 F	23 13	7 16	5 12	9 31	24 43	1 54	22 26	1 07	21 15	1 16	22 14	9 26	16 01	0 59	15 13	2 24
15 Sa	23 16	11 40	4 53	13 41	24 29	1 47	22 13	0 55	21 04	1 15	22 06	9 24	16 05	0 59	15 13	2 24
16 Su	23 19	15 35	4 22	17 19	24 15	1 38	22 01	0 44	20 54	1 15	21 58	9 22	16 08	0 59	15 12	2 24
17 M	23 21	18 53	3 40	20 15	23 60	1 29	21 49	0 31	20 43	1 15	21 50	9 20	16 11	0 59	15 11	2 24
18 Tu	23 23	21 25	2 48	22 21	23 44	1 18	21 37	0 19	20 31	1 15	21 42	9 19	16 14	0 59	15 11	2 23
19 W	23 25	23 01	1 48	23 27	23 28	1 06	21 24	0 06	20 20	1 14	21 33	9 17	16 17	0 59	15 10	2 23
20 Th	23 26	23 35	0 43	23 27	23 11	0 52	21 12	0N08	20 08	1 14	21 25	9 15	16 21	0 59	15 09	2 23
21 F	23 26	23 02	0S25	22 19	22 54	0 38	21 00	0 22	19 56	1 14	21 17	9 13	16 24	0 59	15 09	2 23
22 Sa	23 26	21 20	1 32	20 05	22 38	0 22	20 48	0 36	19 44	1 13	21 08	9 12	16 27	0 59	15 08	2 22
23 Su	23 26	18 35	2 36	16 51	22 21	0 05	20 36	0 50	19 32	1 13	20 60	9 10	16 30	0 59	15 07	2 22
24 M	23 25	14 54	3 33	12 45	22 05	0N13	20 24	1 05	19 20	1 13	20 51	9 08	16 33	0 59	15 07	2 22
25 Tu	23 23	10 27	4 21	8 00	21 50	0 32	20 12	1 20	19 07	1 12	20 43	9 07	16 36	0 60	15 06	2 22
26 W	23 22	5 27	4 55	2 49	21 35	0 51	20 00	1 36	18 54	1 12	20 34	9 05	16 39	0 60	15 06	2 21
27 Th	23 19	0 07	5 14	2S36	21 21	1 11	19 49	1 51	18 41	1 12	20 26	9 03	16 42	0 60	15 05	2 21
28 F	23 16	5S19	5 15	7 59	21 08	1 31	19 37	2 07	18 27	1 11	20 17	9 02	16 44	0 60	15 05	2 21
29 Sa	23 13	10 35	4 58	13 03	20 56	1 50	19 26	2 22	18 14	1 11	20 09	9 00	16 47	0 60	15 05	2 21
30 Su	23 10	15 22	4 23	17 29	20 46	2 08	19 15	2 38	18 00	1 11	20 00	8 59	16 50	0 60	15 04	2 20
31 M	23S05	19S21	3S31	20S55	20S36	2N24	19S04	2N54	17S46	1S10	19S51	8S57	16S53	0N60	15N04	2S20

Day	⚷ Decl	⚷ Lat	♅ Decl	♅ Lat	♆ Decl	♆ Lat	♇ Decl	♇ Lat
1	13N10	1S23	22N49	0N02	1N56	1S31	23S38	5S41
6	13 06	1 23	22 48	0 02	1 56	1 31	23 36	5 40
11	13 03	1 23	22 47	0 02	1 55	1 31	23 34	5 40
16	12 59	1 23	22 45	0 02	1 55	1 31	23 32	5 40
21	12 57	1 23	22 44	0 02	1 55	1 31	23 30	5 40
26	12 54	1 23	22 43	0 02	1 56	1 30	23 27	5 40
31	12N52	1S23	22N42	0N02	1N56	1S30	23S25	5S39

Day	⚴ Decl	⚴ Lat	⚵ Decl	⚵ Lat	⚶ Decl	⚶ Lat	Eris Decl	Eris Lat
1	1N52	24N14	11S37	9N38	22S20	4S38	0N45	9S51
6	1 37	23 47	11 51	9 41	21 44	4 39	0 45	9 50
11	1 24	23 21	12 04	9 45	21 06	4 40	0 45	9 50
16	1 15	22 56	12 14	9 49	20 26	4 40	0 45	9 49
21	1 08	22 33	12 23	9 54	19 44	4 41	0 45	9 48
26	1 03	22 11	12 30	9 59	19 01	4 41	0 45	9 48
31	1N01	21N50	12S35	10N04	18S15	4S42	0N45	9S47

Moon Phenomena

Max/0 Decl
dy hr mn
5 21:29 23S35
12 11:35 0 N
20 0:11 23N35
27 0:31 0 S

Max/0 Lat
dy hr mn
6 9:52 0 N
13 2:46 5N18
20 15:21 0 S
27 13:58 5S17

Perigee/Apogee
dy hr m kilometers
4 10:40 p 359279
16 14:00 a 405519

PH dy hr mn
● 5 14:53 13♐45
5 903:54P 0.891
☽ 12 17:51 21♓00
○ 20 22:48 29♊21
20 22:43 T 1.117
☾ 28 9:50 6♎57

Void of Course Moon

Last Aspect			☽ Ingress		
2 13:45	☿	✶	♏	2	16:55
4 5:46	♂	✶	♐	4	16:53
5 19:30	♅	☍	♑	6	17:12
8 13:25	♂	☌	♒	8	19:42
10 6:23	♄	□	♓	11	1:45
12 23:08	♀	✶	♈	13	11:32
15 11:38	♀	□	♉	15	23:50
18 0:30	♀	△	♊	18	12:34
20 22:48	☉	☍	♋	21	0:04
22 20:55	♀	☍	♌	23	9:33
24 21:19	♃	□	♍	25	16:48
27 7:37	♀	△	♎	27	21:51
29 9:37	♀	□	♏	30	0:56

DAILY ASPECTARIAN

1 Sa
☽⚼♄ 0:09
☽⚼⚳ 1:07
☽☍♆ 5:37
☽△♇ 5:38
☽⊼⚷ 6:27
☉✶☽ 7:11
♂⊻⚳ 9:33
☽⊻♃ 15:58
☽△♅ 19:27

2 Su
☽□♀ 0:36
☽⊼♄ 0:48
☽△⚳ 2:20
☽□♂ 2:56
☽⋕⚷ 4:56
♀△♄ 5:55
☉∠☽ 9:37
☽✶☿ 13:45
☽∥♃ 16:01
☽⋕♄ 16:10
☽⚼♅ 19:45

3 M
♃⋕♄ 0:39
☽⊼♆ 6:26
☽□♇ 6:33
☽☍⚷ 7:08
⚳∥♇ 9:56
☉⊻☽ 11:32
☽∠☿ 16:22
☽☌♃ 17:09
☽⊼♅ 19:43
♂⋕♅ 20:04
☿ ♑ 22:48

4 Tu
☽☍♄ 0:50
☿∠♃ 1:52
☽✶♀ 2:27
☽□⚳ 3:28
☽✶♂ 5:46
☽⚼♆ 6:22
☉∥☽ 16:26
☽⊻☿ 18:46
☽∥♂ 20:40
☽⋕♅ 22:32

5 W
☽∠♀ 3:05
☽△♆ 6:17
☽✶♇ 6:29
☽⊼⚷ 6:53
☽∠♂ 7:00
☽∥⚳ 9:26
☉☌☽ 14:53
☽⊻♃ 17:44
☽☍♅ 19:30

6 Th
☽⊼♄ 0:36
☉∥♂ 1:28
☽⊻♀ 3:52
☽✶⚳ 4:26
☽∠♇ 6:40
☽⚼⚷ 6:59
☽⊻♂ 8:29
☊D 9:44
☽∥⚳ 13:20
☽∠♃ 18:25
☽⋕♅ 20:52
☉∥☽ 23:33

7 F
☽☌☿ 0:10
☽⚼♄ 0:57
☽∥♂ 2:53
☽∠⚳ 5:29
☽□♆ 7:01
☽⊻♇ 7:19
☽△⚷ 7:32
☿⚼♄ 8:11
☉⊻♃ 18:27
☽✶♃ 19:41
☉⊻☽ 19:45
☽⊼♅ 20:41

8 Sa
☽△♄ 1:55
♀∥♇ 6:05
☽☌♀ 6:54
☽⊻⚳ 7:15
☉☍♅ 8:13
☽☌♂ 13:25
☉⋕♅ 15:52
☽⚼♅ 22:19
☉∠☽ 23:29

9 Su
☽∥♃ 4:23
☽⋕♄ 7:01
☉∥⚳ 8:12
☽⊻☿ 8:34
☽✶♆ 10:23
☽☌♇ 10:48
☽□⚷ 10:50
♇□⚷ 16:56
☽⋕⚷ 19:13
⚳⋕♅ 21:15

10 M
☽□♃ 0:46
☽△♅ 0:51
☿∠⚳ 2:39
☿□♆ 3:47
☉✶☽ 4:22
♃⊼♅ 5:46
☽□♄ 6:23
⚳∠♆ 7:26
☿△⚷ 8:10
☿⊻♇ 8:53
☽⊻♀ 13:10
☽∠♆ 13:26
☽☌⚳ 13:35
☽∠☿ 14:27
☽⊻♂ 22:25

11 Tu
☉∥♀ 3:04
☉⊼♄ 4:59
☽⊻♆ 17:29
☽∠♀ 17:44
☽✶⚷ 17:50
☽⊻♇ 18:03
☽✶☿ 21:30

12 W
☽⋕♆ 2:17
☽∠♂ 4:40
♀⋕♅ 7:22
☽□♅ 8:50
☽△♃ 9:51
☽✶♄ 14:38
☉□☽ 17:51
☊R 17:51
☽∥♆ 20:57
☽∠⚷ 22:44
☽∠♇ 23:05
☽✶♀ 23:08

13 Th
☽⊻⚳ 0:02
♂ ♒ 5:26
☽✶♂ 11:57
☽⚼♃ 15:45
☽∠♄ 20:00

14 F
☽☌♆ 4:08
☽⊻⚷ 4:22
☽✶♇ 4:52
☽∠⚳ 6:33
☽□☿ 14:15
♂⚼♅ 19:49
☽✶♅ 20:00
☽⊼♃ 22:17

15 Sa
☽⊻♄ 1:57
☉⚼⚷ 3:13
☽∥⚷ 7:49
☉∠♇ 10:30
☉△☽ 11:11
☽□♀ 11:38
☽✶⚳ 13:35
☉⊻♀ 16:36
☽∥♄ 21:30

16 Su
☽∠♅ 2:15
☽⋕♃ 3:44
☽□♂ 4:31
☽⊻♆ 16:45
☽☌⚷ 16:50
☽□♇ 17:37
♀∥⚳ 18:28
☉⚼☽ 20:29
♀R 23:49

17 M
☉✶⚳ 2:05
☊D 4:16
☽△☿ 7:49
☽⊻♅ 8:35
☽☍♃ 12:06
☽☌♄ 14:28
☽⋕♂ 15:16
☿⊼♅ 20:00
☽∠♆ 23:08

18 Tu
☽△♀ 0:30
☽⋕♀ 2:04
☽⋕⚳ 3:04
☽□⚳ 4:01
☉⊼☽ 5:41
♆⊻⚷ 7:38
☽⚼☿ 15:51
☽∥♅ 18:29
☿∥♇ 20:06
☽△♂ 21:27

19 W
☉∥☿ 4:29
☽⊻⚷ 5:13
☽✶♆ 5:16
☽△♇ 6:16
☽⚼♀ 6:27
♆D 8:25
☽⋕☿ 8:56
☉⋕☽ 10:59
☽⋕♇ 14:55
☽☌♅ 20:36
☽⊼☿ 23:01

20 Th
☽⊼♃ 1:14
☽⊻♄ 2:18
☽⚼♂ 5:22
☽⋕♇ 9:41
☽∠⚷ 10:54
☽⊼♀ 11:53
☽⚼♇ 12:03
☉⋕☽ 12:43
☊R 15:38
☽△⚳ 17:21
☉☍☽ 22:48

21 F
☽⋕☿ 3:05
☽∥♅ 5:33
☽⚼♃ 7:07
☽∠♄ 7:34
☽⊼♂ 12:41
☉ ♑ 14:15
☿⋕♅ 15:07
☽✶⚷ 16:05
☽□♆ 16:16
☽⊼♇ 17:20
☽⚼⚳ 23:15

22 Sa
☽⋕⚳ 2:11
☿R 5:52
☽⋕♀ 5:55
☽⊻♅ 6:53
♃☍♄ 7:04
☽☍☿ 10:16
☽✶♄ 12:20
☽△♃ 12:26
☽⋕♂ 16:03
☽☍♀ 20:55

23 Su
☽⊼⚳ 4:34
☽∠♅ 11:13
☉⊼☽ 13:18
☽⋕♃ 14:02
♂□⚷ 16:58
♂✶♆ 21:27
☽∥♄ 22:41

24 M
☽□⚷ 0:51
☽△♆ 1:08
☽☍♂ 1:22
☽☍♇ 2:16
☽∥⚷ 11:08
☽✶♅ 15:00
♂☌♇ 16:42
☽⊼☿ 17:21
☉⚼☽ 19:28
☽□♄ 20:13
☽□♃ 21:19

25 Tu
☽⊼♀ 3:28
☉⚼♄ 4:38
☽⚼♆ 4:44
☽☍⚳ 13:24
☽⚼☿ 19:29

26 W
☉∠♃ 0:10
☉△☽ 0:56
☽⚼♀ 5:50
☽△⚷ 7:24
☽⊼♆ 7:46
☽⊼♇ 8:58
☽⊼♂ 11:22
☽∥♆ 15:58
☿⊼♅ 17:58
☽△☿ 20:45
☽□♅ 20:56

27 Th
☽△♄ 1:55
☽✶♃ 3:53
☽△♀ 7:37
☽⋕♆ 9:02
☽⚼⚷ 9:51
☽⚼♇ 11:29
☽⚼♂ 15:23
☽⊼⚳ 19:54

28 F
☽⚼♄ 3:59
☽∠♃ 6:20
☉□☽ 9:50
☊D 9:55
☿∠⚳ 10:21
☽⊼⚷ 11:48
☽☍♆ 12:16
☽△♇ 13:29
☽△♂ 18:48
☽□☿ 21:09
☽⚼⚳ 22:19

29 Sa
☽△♅ 0:45
☽⊼♄ 5:33
☽⊻♃ 8:17
☽□♀ 9:37
☽⋕⚷ 11:07
☉△⚷ 12:22
☿⊻♂ 12:38
☉□♆ 19:18
☽⋕♄ 22:24

30 Su
☽△⚳ 0:16
☽⚼♅ 1:59
☽∥♃ 8:16
☉⊻♇ 13:14
♀✶♃ 13:18
☽∥♂ 14:19
☽☍⚷ 14:22
☽⊼♆ 14:54
☽□♇ 16:10
☉✶☽ 16:23
☽✶☿ 19:24
☽∥♀ 22:11

31 M
☽□♂ 0:06
☽⊼♅ 2:52
☽∥⚳ 3:30
⚳ ♓ 4:51
☽☍♄ 7:33
☽∥☿ 8:57
☽✶♀ 9:56
☽☌♃ 10:57
☉☌☿ 12:29
☽⚼♆ 15:43
☽∠☿ 18:03
☉∠☽ 19:02

LONGITUDE

January 2030

Day	Sid.Time	☉	☽	☽ 12 hour	Mean ☊	True ☊	☿	♀	♂	⚳	♃	♄	⚷	♅	♆	♇
	h m s	° ' "	° ' "	° ' "	° '	° '	° '	° '	° '	° '	° '	° '	° '	° '	° '	° '
1 Tu	6 42 47	10♑36 06	28♏24 36	5♐43 04	24♐48.4	25♐30.9	9♑27.5	19♑32.9	14♒42.0	0♓16.2	20♏34.5	18♉23.9	8♉01.5	15♊33.5	8♈22.7	9♒09.9
2 W	6 46 44	11 37 16	13♐01 51	20 20 12	24 45.2	25R 31.9	8R 06.6	18R 59.2	15 29.2	0 36.6	20 45.0	18R 21.9	8R 00.6	15R 31.2	8 23.1	9 11.6
3 Th	6 50 40	12 38 27	27 37 21	4♑52 29	24 42.1	25 32.1	6 49.1	18 24.5	16 16.4	0 57.1	20 55.4	18 20.1	7 59.7	15 29.0	8 23.6	9 13.3
4 F	6 54 37	13 39 38	12♑04 51	19 13 43	24 38.9	25 31.5	5 37.2	17 49.0	17 03.6	1 17.7	21 05.7	18 18.3	7 58.9	15 26.9	8 24.2	9 15.0
5 Sa	6 58 33	14 40 49	26 18 26	3♒18 25	24 35.7	25 29.9	4 32.7	17 12.8	17 50.8	1 38.4	21 16.0	18 16.7	7 58.1	15 24.7	8 24.7	9 16.7
6 Su	7 02 30	15 41 59	10♒13 13	17 02 29	24 32.5	25 27.3	3 37.1	16 36.3	18 38.0	1 59.1	21 26.1	18 15.2	7 57.4	15 22.6	8 25.3	9 18.5
7 M	7 06 26	16 43 10	23 46 00	0♓23 41	24 29.4	25 24.0	2 51.1	15 59.6	19 25.3	2 20.0	21 36.2	18 13.8	7 56.8	15 20.5	8 26.0	9 20.2
8 Tu	7 10 23	17 44 20	6♓55 34	13 21 47	24 26.2	25 20.6	2 15.1	15 23.0	20 12.5	2 41.0	21 46.1	18 12.4	7 56.2	15 18.5	8 26.6	9 22.0
9 W	7 14 19	18 45 29	19 42 36	25 58 22	24 23.0	25 17.5	1 49.2	14 46.9	20 59.7	3 02.0	21 55.9	18 11.2	7 55.6	15 16.5	8 27.3	9 23.7
10 Th	7 18 16	19 46 38	2♈09 31	8♈16 31	24 19.8	25 15.1	1 33.1	14 11.4	21 47.0	3 23.1	22 05.7	18 10.2	7 55.2	15 14.5	8 28.0	9 25.5
11 F	7 22 13	20 47 47	14 19 56	20 20 20	24 16.7	25D 13.9	1D 26.5	13 36.7	22 34.2	3 44.3	22 15.3	18 09.2	7 54.8	15 12.5	8 28.8	9 27.3
12 Sa	7 26 09	21 48 55	26 18 20	2♉14 34	24 13.5	25 13.8	1 28.7	13 03.2	23 21.5	4 05.6	22 24.8	18 08.3	7 54.4	15 10.6	8 29.6	9 29.1
13 Su	7 30 06	22 50 03	8♉09 39	14 04 14	24 10.3	25 14.7	1 39.1	12 30.9	24 08.7	4 26.9	22 34.2	18 07.6	7 54.1	15 08.7	8 30.4	9 30.9
14 M	7 34 02	23 51 10	19 58 54	25 54 17	24 07.1	25 16.4	1 57.1	12 00.2	24 56.0	4 48.4	22 43.5	18 06.9	7 53.9	15 06.9	8 31.3	9 32.7
15 Tu	7 37 59	24 52 16	1♊50 56	7♊49 23	24 04.0	25 18.3	2 22.0	11 31.2	25 43.2	5 09.9	22 52.7	18 06.4	7 53.7	15 05.1	8 32.2	9 34.5
16 W	7 41 55	25 53 22	13 50 08	19 53 39	24 00.8	25R 19.9	2 53.1	11 04.1	26 30.5	5 31.4	23 01.8	18 06.0	7 53.6	15 03.3	8 33.1	9 36.3
17 Th	7 45 52	26 54 27	26 00 17	2♋10 25	23 57.6	25 20.4	3 29.9	10 39.0	27 17.7	5 53.1	23 10.8	18 05.7	7D 53.6	15 01.6	8 34.1	9 38.1
18 F	7 49 48	27 55 32	8♋24 17	14 42 05	23 54.4	25 19.6	4 11.8	10 16.0	28 04.9	6 14.8	23 19.6	18 05.5	7 53.6	14 59.9	8 35.1	9 40.0
19 Sa	7 53 45	28 56 36	21 03 57	27 29 57	23 51.2	25 17.0	4 58.3	9 55.3	28 52.2	6 36.6	23 28.3	18D 05.4	7 53.6	14 58.3	8 36.1	9 41.8
20 Su	7 57 42	29 57 39	4♌00 02	10♌34 09	23 48.1	25 12.8	5 48.9	9 37.0	29 39.4	6 58.4	23 36.9	18 05.5	7 53.8	14 56.7	8 37.2	9 43.7
21 M	8 01 38	0♒58 41	17 12 07	23 53 45	23 44.9	25 07.2	6 43.2	9 21.1	0♓26.6	7 20.3	23 45.4	18 05.6	7 54.0	14 55.1	8 38.3	9 45.5
22 Tu	8 05 35	1 59 43	0♍38 48	7♍26 58	23 41.7	25 00.9	7 40.9	9 07.6	1 13.8	7 42.3	23 53.8	18 05.9	7 54.2	14 53.6	8 39.4	9 47.4
23 W	8 09 31	3 00 45	14 17 57	21 11 28	23 38.5	24 54.6	8 41.7	8 56.6	2 01.0	8 04.4	24 02.0	18 06.3	7 54.5	14 52.1	8 40.5	9 49.2
24 Th	8 13 28	4 01 46	28 07 10	5♎04 47	23 35.4	24 49.0	9 45.2	8 48.1	2 48.2	8 26.5	24 10.1	18 06.7	7 54.9	14 50.7	8 41.7	9 51.1
25 F	8 17 24	5 02 46	12♎04 03	19 04 42	23 32.2	24 45.0	10 51.2	8 42.1	3 35.4	8 48.6	24 18.1	18 07.3	7 55.3	14 49.3	8 42.9	9 52.9
26 Sa	8 21 21	6 03 46	26 06 30	3♏09 17	23 29.0	24D 42.8	11 59.4	8D 38.7	4 22.6	9 10.9	24 26.0	18 08.0	7 55.8	14 48.0	8 44.1	9 54.8
27 Su	8 25 17	7 04 45	10♏12 52	17 17 05	23 25.8	24 42.3	13 09.8	8 37.7	5 09.8	9 33.1	24 33.7	18 08.9	7 56.4	14 46.7	8 45.4	9 56.7
28 M	8 29 14	8 05 44	24 21 45	1♐26 42	23 22.7	24 43.2	14 22.0	8 39.2	5 56.9	9 55.5	24 41.3	18 09.8	7 57.0	14 45.4	8 46.7	9 58.5
29 Tu	8 33 11	9 06 43	8♐31 45	15 36 39	23 19.5	24 44.5	15 36.0	8 43.0	6 44.1	10 17.9	24 48.7	18 10.9	7 57.7	14 44.2	8 48.0	10 00.4
30 W	8 37 07	10 07 41	22 41 09	29 44 56	23 16.3	24R 45.4	16 51.5	8 49.3	7 31.2	10 40.3	24 56.0	18 12.0	7 58.4	14 43.1	8 49.4	10 02.3
31 Th	8 41 04	11♒08 38	6♑47 39	13♑48 54	23♐13.1	24♐44.7	18♑08.6	8♑57.8	8♓18.4	11♓02.8	25♏03.2	18♉13.3	7♉59.2	14♊42.0	8♈50.8	10♒04.1

1st of Month

Julian Day # 2462502.5
Obliquity 23°26'06"
SVP 4♓50'09"
GC 27♐15.5
Eris 25♈33.8R

Day	⚴
1	29♑09.5
6	0♒55.7
11	2 42.1
16	4 28.5
21	6 14.8
26	8 01.0
31	9 46.8
	⚵
1	15♐25.6
6	17 05.0
11	18 43.3
16	20 20.2
21	21 55.6
26	23 29.4
31	25 01.4
	⚶
1	23♒32.2
6	25 52.7
11	28 14.2
16	0♓36.6
21	2 59.5
26	5 23.1
31	7 47.1

DECLINATION and LATITUDE

Day	☉ Decl	☽ Decl	☽ Lat	☽ 12h Decl	☿ Decl	☿ Lat	♀ Decl	♀ Lat	♂ Decl	♂ Lat	⚳ Decl	⚳ Lat	♃ Decl	♃ Lat	♄ Decl	♄ Lat
1 Tu	23S01	22S09	2S25	23S01	20S28	2N39	18S53	3N09	17S32	1S10	19S43	8S56	16S56	1N00	15N04	2S20
2 W	22 56	23 30	1 09	23 34	20 21	2 51	18 43	3 25	17 18	1 10	19 34	8 54	16 58	1 00	15 03	2 20
3 Th	22 50	23 13	0N12	22 29	20 15	3 01	18 32	3 40	17 03	1 09	19 25	8 53	17 01	1 00	15 03	2 19
4 F	22 44	21 23	1 30	19 57	20 11	3 08	18 22	3 55	16 49	1 09	19 16	8 51	17 04	1 00	15 03	2 19
5 Sa	22 38	18 14	2 42	16 16	20 08	3 13	18 13	4 09	16 34	1 08	19 07	8 50	17 06	1 00	15 03	2 19
6 Su	22 31	14 06	3 42	11 48	20 08	3 16	18 03	4 23	16 19	1 08	18 58	8 49	17 09	1 00	15 03	2 18
7 M	22 23	9 22	4 28	6 52	20 08	3 16	17 54	4 36	16 04	1 07	18 49	8 47	17 11	1 00	15 02	2 18
8 Tu	22 16	4 20	4 59	1 48	20 11	3 14	17 45	4 49	15 48	1 07	18 40	8 46	17 14	1 01	15 02	2 18
9 W	22 07	0N44	5 13	3N13	20 14	3 11	17 37	5 02	15 33	1 07	18 31	8 44	17 16	1 01	15 02	2 18
10 Th	21 59	5 38	5 12	7 59	20 19	3 06	17 29	5 13	15 17	1 06	18 22	8 43	17 19	1 01	15 02	2 17
11 F	21 50	10 13	4 58	12 21	20 25	3 00	17 22	5 24	15 01	1 06	18 13	8 42	17 21	1 01	15 02	2 17
12 Sa	21 40	14 20	4 30	16 11	20 32	2 53	17 15	5 34	14 46	1 05	18 04	8 40	17 23	1 01	15 02	2 17
13 Su	21 30	17 52	3 51	19 21	20 40	2 45	17 08	5 44	14 29	1 05	17 55	8 39	17 26	1 01	15 02	2 16
14 M	21 20	20 39	3 02	21 44	20 48	2 37	17 02	5 53	14 13	1 04	17 46	8 38	17 28	1 01	15 03	2 16
15 Tu	21 09	22 34	2 05	23 10	20 57	2 28	16 57	6 01	13 57	1 04	17 37	8 37	17 30	1 01	15 03	2 16
16 W	20 58	23 30	1 03	23 33	21 06	2 19	16 52	6 08	13 40	1 04	17 27	8 35	17 32	1 01	15 03	2 16
17 Th	20 46	23 19	0S04	22 48	21 14	2 09	16 47	6 14	13 24	1 03	17 18	8 34	17 34	1 01	15 03	2 15
18 F	20 34	21 59	1 11	20 54	21 23	1 59	16 43	6 20	13 07	1 03	17 09	8 33	17 37	1 02	15 03	2 15
19 Sa	20 22	19 33	2 16	17 56	21 31	1 50	16 40	6 25	12 50	1 02	16 60	8 32	17 39	1 02	15 04	2 15
20 Su	20 09	16 05	3 15	14 01	21 39	1 40	16 37	6 29	12 33	1 02	16 50	8 31	17 41	1 02	15 04	2 14
21 M	19 56	11 46	4 05	9 22	21 46	1 30	16 35	6 33	12 16	1 01	16 41	8 30	17 43	1 02	15 04	2 14
22 Tu	19 43	6 50	4 43	4 11	21 53	1 20	16 33	6 35	11 59	1 01	16 32	8 28	17 45	1 02	15 04	2 14
23 W	19 29	1 29	5 05	1S15	21 59	1 10	16 31	6 38	11 41	1 00	16 22	8 27	17 47	1 02	15 05	2 14
24 Th	19 15	3S59	5 10	6 41	22 05	1 00	16 30	6 39	11 24	0 60	16 13	8 26	17 48	1 02	15 05	2 13
25 F	19 00	9 19	4 56	11 50	22 09	0 50	16 30	6 40	11 06	0 59	16 03	8 25	17 50	1 02	15 06	2 13
26 Sa	18 45	14 12	4 25	16 22	22 13	0 41	16 30	6 40	10 49	0 59	15 54	8 24	17 52	1 02	15 06	2 13
27 Su	18 30	18 19	3 38	20 01	22 16	0 32	16 30	6 40	10 31	0 58	15 44	8 23	17 54	1 02	15 07	2 12
28 M	18 14	21 24	2 37	22 27	22 17	0 23	16 30	6 40	10 13	0 58	15 35	8 22	17 56	1 03	15 07	2 12
29 Tu	17 58	23 09	1 27	23 29	22 18	0 14	16 31	6 38	9 55	0 57	15 25	8 21	17 57	1 03	15 08	2 12
30 W	17 42	23 25	0 11	22 59	22 17	0 05	16 33	6 37	9 37	0 56	15 16	8 20	17 59	1 03	15 08	2 11
31 Th	17S26	22S11	1N05	21S02	22S16	0S04	16S34	6N35	9S19	0S56	15S06	8S19	18S00	1N03	15N09	2S11

Day	⚷ Decl	⚷ Lat	♅ Decl	♅ Lat	♆ Decl	♆ Lat	♇ Decl	♇ Lat
1	12N52	1S23	22N41	0N02	1N57	1S30	23S25	5S39
6	12 51	1 23	22 40	0 02	1 58	1 30	23 22	5 40
11	12 50	1 23	22 39	0 02	1 59	1 30	23 20	5 40
16	12 49	1 23	22 38	0 02	2 01	1 29	23 18	5 40
21	12 49	1 23	22 37	0 02	2 04	1 29	23 15	5 40
26	12 50	1 23	22 37	0 02	2 06	1 29	23 13	5 40
31	12N51	1S23	22N36	0N02	2N09	1S29	23S11	5S41

Day	⚴ Decl	⚴ Lat	⚵ Decl	⚵ Lat	⚶ Decl	⚶ Lat	Eris Decl	Eris Lat
1	1N01	21N46	12S36	10N06	18S06	4S42	0N46	9S47
6	1 02	21 27	12 39	10 12	17 19	4 43	0 46	9 46
11	1 06	21 10	12 41	10 19	16 30	4 43	0 47	9 45
16	1 11	20 53	12 40	10 26	15 40	4 44	0 47	9 45
21	1 19	20 37	12 38	10 35	14 49	4 44	0 48	9 44
26	1 28	20 23	12 34	10 43	13 57	4 45	0 49	9 43
31	1N40	20N09	12S28	10N53	13S04	4S46	0N50	9S43

Moon Phenomena

Max/0 Decl dy hr mn	
2 7:58	23S35
8 20:31	0 N
16 8:13	23N33
23 6:31	0 S
29 16:14	23S30

Max/0 Lat dy hr mn	
2 20:33	0 N
9 10:38	5N15
16 22:41	0 S
23 18:19	5S10
30 3:30	0 N

Perigee/Apogee dy hr m		kilometers
1 15:35	p	364254
13 8:52	a	404643
28 16:01	p	369545

PH	dy hr mn	
●	4 2:51	13♑47
☽	11 14:07	21♈24
○	19 15:55	29♋37
☾	26 18:16	6♏50

Void of Course Moon

Last Aspect			☽ Ingress		
31 10:57	♃	☌	♐	1	2:37
2 4:16	♂	⚹	♑	3	3:56
4 15:20	♃	⚹	♒	5	6:19
6 20:04	♃	□	♓	7	11:17
9 4:18	♃	△	♈	9	19:48
11 17:39	♂	⚹	♉	12	7:28
14 10:45	♂	□	♊	14	20:16
17 2:41	♂	△	♋	17	7:47
19 15:55	☉	☍	♌	19	16:38
21 11:53	♃	□	♍	21	22:51
23 17:06	♃	⚹	♎	24	3:15
25 4:43	♅	△	♏	26	6:38
28 0:33	♃	☌	♐	28	9:33
29 10:30	♅	☍	♑	30	12:26

DAILY ASPECTARIAN

1 Tu: ☽□⚳ 3:08; ☿⚺♇ 5:04; ☽⋕♅ 6:49; ☽∠♀ 9:43; ☉∥☽ 11:16; ☽⚻⚷ 15:46; ☽△♆ 16:22; ☽⚺☿ 16:36; ☽⚹♇ 17:41; ☿□♆ 19:03; ☽∥♇ 20:47; ☉⚺☽ 21:31

2 W: ♂△♅ 0:59; ☿△⚷ 1:50; ☽☍♅ 4:05; ☽⚹♂ 4:16; ☽⚻♄ 8:44; ☽⚺♀ 9:25; ☽⚺♃ 12:50; ☽⚼⚷ 16:23; ☽∠♇ 18:23; ☽∥♇ 19:22; ☊R 20:38

3 Th: ♀△♄ 3:12; ♂∥♃ 3:17; ☽⚹⚳ 5:38; ☽∠♂ 6:23; ☉∥☽ 7:30; ⚴ ♒ 9:07; ☽⋕♅ 9:20; ☽⚼♄ 9:26; ☽∠♃ 13:54; ☽☌☿ 14:02; ☿∠♃ 15:26; ☽△⚷ 17:10; ☽□♆ 17:52; ☽⚺♇ 19:16

4 F: ☉☌☽ 2:51; ☽⚻♅ 5:38; ☽∠⚳ 7:14; ☽⚺♂ 8:50; ☽☌♀ 9:14; ☽∥☿ 10:25; ☽△♄ 10:25; ♀⚺♂ 13:05; ☉⋕♅ 13:10; ☽⚹♃ 15:20; ☽∥⚳ 17:47

5 Sa: ☽∥♀ 0:10; ☽∥♃ 7:00; ☽⚼♅ 7:00; ☽⚺⚳ 9:22; ☽∥♂ 10:57; ♂□♄ 12:44; ☽⚺☿ 13:13; ♀∠⚳ 14:26; ☉⚻♅ 16:39; ☽⋕♄ 18:56; ☽□⚷ 20:03; ☽⚹♆ 20:52; ☽☌♇ 22:24; ☿∠♂ 23:46

6 Su: ☽⋕⚷ 6:39; ☽△♅ 9:02; ☉⚺☽ 10:25; ☽⚺♀ 10:45; ☿⚼♄ 11:09; ☉☌♀ 13:19; ☽∠☿ 13:58; ☽□♄ 14:08; ☽☌♂ 15:45; ☽□♃ 20:04; ☽∠♆ 23:24

7 M: ☽∠♀ 12:31; ☿⚹⚳ 12:34; ☉∠☽ 15:38; ☽⚹☿ 15:44; ☽☌⚳ 15:58; ☉∠⚳ 21:59

8 Tu: ☽⚹⚷ 1:52; ☽⚺♆ 2:49; ♀⚻♅ 3:11; ☽⚺♇ 4:32; ☉△♄ 10:49; ☽⋕♆ 11:09; ☽⚹♀ 15:05; ☽□♅ 15:37; ☽⚹♄ 21:07; ☉⚹☽ 22:02

9 W: ☽⚺♂ 2:37; ☽△♃ 4:18; ☽∥♆ 6:01; ☽∠⚷ 6:08; ☽∠♇ 8:59; ☽□☿ 22:50

10 Th: ☽∠♄ 1:58; ☽⚺⚳ 2:28; ☽∠♂ 9:41; ☽⚼♃ 9:48; ☽⚺⚷ 11:18; ♂□♃ 11:55; ☽☌♆ 12:24; ☽⚹♇ 14:18; ☽□♀ 22:38; ♂⋕♄ 22:43

11 F: ☽⚹♅ 1:44; ♀∥♃ 1:56; ☿D 5:47; ☽⚺♄ 7:37; ☽∠⚳ 9:04; ☊D 13:55; ☉□☽ 14:07; ☽∥⚷ 14:50; ☽⚻♃ 16:04; ☽⚹♂ 17:39

12 Sa: ☽⋕♂ 2:29; ♂∠♆ 4:12; ☽∥♄ 4:27; ☽∠♅ 7:48; ☽△☿ 10:34; ☽⚹⚳ 16:14; ☉⚹♃ 16:40; ☽⋕♀ 18:50; ☽⋕♃ 20:44; ☽☌⚷ 23:28

13 Su: ☽⋕⚳ 0:24; ☽⚺♆ 0:42; ☽□♇ 2:45; ☽△♀ 8:28; ☽⚺♅ 14:09; ☽⚼☿ 17:40; ☽☌♄ 20:13

14 M: ☽⋕☿ 1:39; ☽☍♃ 5:38; ☉⋕☽ 6:41; ☽∠♆ 7:11; ☉△☽ 8:35; ☽□♂ 10:45; ☽⚼♀ 13:39; ⚶ ♓ 17:14

15 Tu: ☽⚻☿ 1:05; ☽∥♅ 1:07; ☽□⚳ 6:52; ☽⚺⚷ 12:09; ☽⚹♆ 13:27; ⚳∥♃ 13:45; ☉∥☿ 14:51; ♀∠♂ 15:25; ☽△♇ 15:33; ☽⋕♇ 15:45; ☉⚼☽ 17:35; ☽⚻♀ 18:41

16 W: ☽☌♅ 2:25; ☽⚺♄ 8:27; ☿⚼♄ 8:44; ☽∠⚷ 17:54; ☽⚻♃ 18:24; ☽⚼♇ 21:19; ☊R 22:43

17 Th: ☽⋕♇ 0:51; ☉⚻☽ 1:55; ☽△♂ 2:41; ⚷D 6:40; ☽∠♄ 13:47; ☽∥♅ 14:46; ☽☍☿ 15:24; ☽△⚳ 19:44; ☽⚹⚷ 23:01; ☽⚼♃ 23:51

18 F: ☽□♆ 0:21; ☽⚻♇ 2:25; ☽☍♀ 3:28; ☽⋕☿ 6:39; ☽⚼♂ 9:31; ☽⚺♅ 12:32; ☉⚺♂ 16:19; ☉⋕☽ 16:24; ☽⚹♄ 18:24

19 Sa: ☽⚼⚳ 1:03; ♂⋕⚷ 1:05; ♄D 3:55; ☽△♃ 4:33; ☽⋕♃ 13:51; ☽⚻♂ 15:29; ♀⚺♇ 15:46; ☉☍☽ 15:55; ☽∠♅ 16:33; ☽⋕⚳ 19:05; ☽⋕♀ 20:38; ☉⚼♅ 23:38

20 Su: ♃⚼♆ 0:45; ☉ ♒ 0:56; ☽⚻☿ 3:34; ☽⚻⚳ 5:36; ☽∥♄ 6:05; ☽□⚷ 7:08; ☽△♆ 8:28; ☽⚻♀ 10:03; ♂ ♓ 10:29; ☽☍♇ 10:30; ☽∥⚷ 18:31; ☽⚹♅ 19:53; ☽⋕♂ 21:17

21 M: ☽□♄ 1:36; ☽⚼☿ 8:44; ☽⚼♆ 11:33; ☽□♃ 11:53; ☽⚼♀ 12:36; ♀∥⚳ 20:04

22 Tu: ☿⚹⚳ 0:53; ☽☍♂ 1:06; ☉⚻☽ 2:35; ☿△⚷ 5:22; ☽☍⚳ 12:48; ☽△⚷ 12:48; ⚳⚹⚷ 13:09; ☽△☿ 13:24; ☽⚻♆ 14:08; ☽△♀ 14:44; ☽⚻♇ 16:09; ♀∠♃ 16:52; ☽∥♆ 21:24; ☿□♆ 23:32

23 W: ☽□♅ 1:00; ☿☌♀ 4:58; ☽△♄ 6:38; ☉⚼☽ 6:59; ☿∠♃ 8:57; ☽⚼⚷ 14:59; ☽⋕♆ 15:37; ☽⚹♃ 17:06; ☽⚼♇ 18:20

24 Th: ☿⚺♇ 2:14; ☽⚻♂ 8:34; ☽⚼♄ 8:37; ☉△☽ 11:00; ☽⚻⚷ 16:53; ⚳⚺♆ 17:26; ☽☍♆ 18:14; ☽⚻⚳ 18:16; ☽□♀ 18:16; ♀⚹⚳ 18:17; ☽∠♃ 19:13; ☽△♇ 20:15; ♀□♆ 21:01; ☽□☿ 21:44

25 F: ☽△♅ 4:43; ☽∥♂ 8:01; ☽⚻♄ 10:22; ☽⚼♂ 11:50; ☽⋕⚷ 17:00; ☽⚼⚳ 20:37; ☽⚺♃ 21:07

26 Sa: ☽⋕♄ 4:53; ☽⚼♅ 6:17; ☽∥⚳ 8:57; ☽∥♀ 12:43; ☽△♂ 14:55; ☉□☽ 18:16; ☊D 18:21; ☽☍⚷ 20:08; ☽∥♃ 21:13; ☽⚹♀ 21:18; ☽⚻♆ 21:31; ♀D 21:34; ☽△⚳ 22:51; ☽□♇ 23:32

27 Su: ☉∥☽ 1:06; ☽⚹☿ 5:28; ☽⚻♅ 7:44; ☽☍♄ 13:29; ☉□⚷ 20:31; ☽∠♀ 22:48; ☽⚼♆ 23:01

28 M: ☽☌♃ 0:33; ⚳⚺♇ 3:33; ☿⚻♅ 7:33; ☽∠☿ 9:17; ☽∥☿ 9:58; ☉⚺♀ 13:56; ☽⋕♅ 14:12; ☉⚹♆ 16:29; ☽□♂ 20:47; ☽⚻⚷ 23:02

29 Tu: ☽⚺♀ 0:19; ☽△♆ 0:28; ☽∥♇ 1:04; ☉⚹☽ 1:04; ☉∥♃ 1:41; ☽⚹♇ 2:30; ☽□⚳ 3:05; ☽☍♅ 10:30; ☽⚺☿ 13:09; ☽⚻♄ 16:23; ☉☌♇ 21:48

30 W: ☽⚼⚷ 0:29; ♀□♆ 0:33; ☊R 3:32; ☽⚺♃ 3:51; ☽∠♇ 4:00; ☉∠☽ 4:28; ☽∥♇ 7:36; ♂⚹⚷ 14:04; ⚳⋕♄ 17:14; ☽⚼♄ 17:54; ☽⋕♅ 18:24; ☉⚺⚳ 20:23; ☽∥☿ 22:56

31 Th: ☿△♄ 1:29; ☽△⚷ 2:02; ☽⚹♂ 2:44; ☽□♆ 3:31; ☽☌♀ 3:45; ☽⚺♇ 5:36; ☽∠♃ 5:37; ☽⚹⚳ 7:28; ☉⚺☽ 8:00; ☽⚻♅ 13:30; ♂⚺♆ 17:01; ☽△♄ 19:35; ☽☌☿ 21:26

February 2030

LONGITUDE

Day	Sid.Time	☉	☽	☽ 12 hour	Mean☊	True☊	☿	♀	♂	⚳	♃	♄	⚷	♅	♆	♇
	h m s	° ' "	° ' "	° ' "	° '	° '	° '	° '	° '	° '	° '	° '	° '	° '	° '	° '
1 F	8 45 00	12♒09 34	20♑48 14	27♑45 14	23♐09.9	24♐41.9	19♑27.0	9♑08.5	9♓05.5	11♓25.4	25♏10.2	18♉14.7	8♉00.1	14♊40.9	8♈52.2	10♒06.0
2 Sa	8 48 57	13 10 29	4♒39 26	11♒30 22	23 06.8	24R 36.8	20 46.8	9 21.5	9 52.6	11 48.0	25 17.1	18 16.2	8 01.0	14R 39.9	8 53.6	10 07.9
3 Su	8 52 53	14 11 24	18 17 37	25 00 51	23 03.6	24 29.4	22 07.8	9 36.5	10 39.7	12 10.7	25 23.9	18 17.8	8 01.9	14 39.0	8 55.1	10 09.7
4 M	8 56 50	15 12 17	1♓39 43	8♓14 02	23 00.4	24 20.3	23 29.9	9 53.6	11 26.8	12 33.4	25 30.5	18 19.5	8 03.0	14 38.0	8 56.6	10 11.6
5 Tu	9 00 46	16 13 08	14 43 38	21 08 29	22 57.2	24 10.6	24 53.1	10 12.6	12 13.8	12 56.1	25 36.9	18 21.4	8 04.0	14 37.2	8 58.1	10 13.5
6 W	9 04 43	17 13 59	27 28 39	3♈44 17	22 54.1	24 01.3	26 17.4	10 33.6	13 00.9	13 18.9	25 43.2	18 23.3	8 05.2	14 36.4	8 59.7	10 15.3
7 Th	9 08 40	18 14 48	9♈55 38	16 03 02	22 50.9	23 53.2	27 42.7	10 56.4	13 47.9	13 41.8	25 49.3	18 25.3	8 06.4	14 35.6	9 01.2	10 17.2
8 F	9 12 36	19 15 36	22 06 53	28 07 40	22 47.7	23 47.1	29 09.0	11 21.0	14 34.9	14 04.6	25 55.3	18 27.5	8 07.6	14 34.9	9 02.8	10 19.0
9 Sa	9 16 33	20 16 22	4♉05 57	10♉02 17	22 44.5	23 43.2	0♒36.2	11 47.3	15 21.9	14 27.6	26 01.2	18 29.8	8 09.0	14 34.2	9 04.4	10 20.9
10 Su	9 20 29	21 17 07	15 57 19	21 51 42	22 41.3	23D 41.6	2 04.3	12 15.3	16 08.8	14 50.5	26 06.8	18 32.1	8 10.3	14 33.6	9 06.1	10 22.7
11 M	9 24 26	22 17 50	27 46 07	3♊41 14	22 38.2	23 41.6	3 33.4	12 44.8	16 55.8	15 13.5	26 12.3	18 34.6	8 11.8	14 33.1	9 07.8	10 24.5
12 Tu	9 28 22	23 18 32	9♊37 45	15 36 19	22 35.0	23 42.4	5 03.4	13 16.0	17 42.7	15 36.5	26 17.7	18 37.2	8 13.2	14 32.6	9 09.5	10 26.4
13 W	9 32 19	24 19 12	21 37 35	27 42 10	22 31.8	23R 43.0	6 34.2	13 48.5	18 29.6	15 59.6	26 22.9	18 39.9	8 14.8	14 32.1	9 11.2	10 28.2
14 Th	9 36 15	25 19 51	3♋50 37	10♋03 28	22 28.6	23 42.5	8 05.9	14 22.6	19 16.4	16 22.7	26 27.9	18 42.7	8 16.4	14 31.7	9 12.9	10 30.0
15 F	9 40 12	26 20 27	16 21 07	22 43 55	22 25.5	23 40.0	9 38.5	14 57.9	20 03.2	16 45.8	26 32.8	18 45.6	8 18.0	14 31.4	9 14.7	10 31.8
16 Sa	9 44 09	27 21 03	29 12 06	5♌45 48	22 22.3	23 34.9	11 12.0	15 34.7	20 50.0	17 09.0	26 37.5	18 48.5	8 19.7	14 31.1	9 16.5	10 33.6
17 Su	9 48 05	28 21 36	12♌25 01	19 09 38	22 19.1	23 27.2	12 46.4	16 12.6	21 36.8	17 32.2	26 42.1	18 51.6	8 21.5	14 30.9	9 18.3	10 35.4
18 M	9 52 02	29 22 08	25 59 23	2♍53 53	22 15.9	23 17.4	14 21.7	16 51.8	22 23.6	17 55.4	26 46.4	18 54.8	8 23.3	14 30.7	9 20.1	10 37.2
19 Tu	9 55 58	0♓22 39	9♍52 39	16 55 05	22 12.8	23 06.3	15 57.8	17 32.2	23 10.3	18 18.7	26 50.6	18 58.1	8 25.1	14 30.6	9 21.9	10 39.0
20 W	9 59 55	1 23 07	24 00 33	1♎08 19	22 09.6	22 55.1	17 34.9	18 13.7	23 57.0	18 42.0	26 54.7	19 01.5	8 27.0	14D 30.5	9 23.8	10 40.8
21 Th	10 03 51	2 23 35	8♎17 42	15 27 59	22 06.4	22 45.0	19 12.9	18 56.3	24 43.6	19 05.3	26 58.5	19 05.0	8 29.0	14 30.5	9 25.7	10 42.5
22 F	10 07 48	3 24 01	22 38 31	29 48 44	22 03.2	22 37.0	20 51.8	19 39.9	25 30.2	19 28.6	27 02.2	19 08.6	8 31.0	14 30.5	9 27.6	10 44.3
23 Sa	10 11 44	4 24 25	6♏58 07	14♏06 16	22 00.0	22 31.6	22 31.6	20 24.6	26 16.8	19 52.0	27 05.7	19 12.2	8 33.1	14 30.6	9 29.5	10 46.0
24 Su	10 15 41	5 24 49	21 12 51	28 17 40	21 56.9	22 28.9	24 12.5	21 10.2	27 03.4	20 15.4	27 09.1	19 16.0	8 35.2	14 30.7	9 31.5	10 47.8
25 M	10 19 38	6 25 11	5♐20 32	12♐21 24	21 53.7	22D 28.2	25 54.2	21 56.7	27 50.0	20 38.8	27 12.3	19 19.9	8 37.3	14 30.9	9 33.4	10 49.5
26 Tu	10 23 34	7 25 32	19 20 11	26 16 55	21 50.5	22R 28.4	27 37.0	22 44.1	28 36.5	21 02.2	27 15.2	19 23.8	8 39.5	14 31.2	9 35.4	10 51.2
27 W	10 27 31	8 25 51	3♑11 35	10♑04 10	21 47.3	22 28.1	29 20.8	23 32.4	29 23.0	21 25.7	27 18.1	19 27.9	8 41.8	14 31.4	9 37.4	10 52.9
28 Th	10 31 27	9♓26 09	16 54 39	23 43 00	21♐44.2	22♐26.0	1♓05.5	24♑21.5	0♈09.4	21♓49.2	27♏20.7	19♉32.0	8♉44.1	14♊31.8	9♈39.4	10♒54.6

1st of Month

Julian Day # 2462533.5
Obliquity 23°26'06"
SVP 4♓50'04"
GC 27♐15.6
Eris 25♈35.1

Day	⚴
1	10♒07.9
6	11 53.2
11	13 37.8
16	15 21.6
21	17 04.4
26	18 46.3

Day	⚵
1	25♐19.5
6	26 48.9
11	28 15.9
16	29 40.3
21	1♑01.8
26	2 20.3

Day	⚶
1	8♓16.0
6	10 40.5
11	13 05.3
16	15 30.1
21	17 55.0
26	20 19.8

DECLINATION and LATITUDE

Day	☉ Decl	☽ Decl	☽ Lat	☽12h Decl	☿ Decl	☿ Lat	♀ Decl	♀ Lat	♂ Decl	♂ Lat	⚳ Decl	⚳ Lat	♃ Decl	♃ Lat	♄ Decl	♄ Lat
1 F	17S09	19S35	2N16	17S51	22S13	0S12	16S36	6N32	9S01	0S55	14S57	8S18	18S02	1N03	15N10	2S11
2 Sa	16 52	15 53	3 18	13 43	22 10	0 20	16 38	6 30	8 43	0 55	14 47	8 17	18 04	1 03	15 10	2 11
3 Su	16 34	11 24	4 08	8 59	22 05	0 28	16 40	6 27	8 24	0 54	14 37	8 16	18 05	1 03	15 11	2 10
4 M	16 16	6 28	4 43	3 55	21 59	0 36	16 42	6 23	8 06	0 54	14 28	8 15	18 06	1 03	15 12	2 10
5 Tu	15 58	1 22	5 02	1N10	21 51	0 43	16 44	6 19	7 47	0 53	14 18	8 15	18 08	1 04	15 13	2 10
6 W	15 40	3N40	5 06	6 06	21 43	0 50	16 47	6 15	7 29	0 53	14 08	8 14	18 09	1 04	15 14	2 09
7 Th	15 21	8 26	4 54	10 40	21 33	0 57	16 49	6 11	7 10	0 52	13 59	8 13	18 11	1 04	15 14	2 09
8 F	15 03	12 47	4 30	14 45	21 22	1 03	16 52	6 07	6 52	0 51	13 49	8 12	18 12	1 04	15 15	2 09
9 Sa	14 44	16 33	3 54	18 11	21 09	1 10	16 54	6 02	6 33	0 51	13 39	8 11	18 13	1 04	15 16	2 09
10 Su	14 24	19 37	3 08	20 50	20 56	1 16	16 57	5 57	6 14	0 50	13 30	8 10	18 14	1 04	15 17	2 08
11 M	14 05	21 50	2 14	22 36	20 41	1 22	16 59	5 52	5 55	0 50	13 20	8 09	18 15	1 04	15 18	2 08
12 Tu	13 45	23 07	1 15	23 23	20 24	1 27	17 01	5 47	5 37	0 49	13 10	8 09	18 17	1 04	15 19	2 08
13 W	13 25	23 21	0 11	23 04	20 07	1 32	17 04	5 41	5 18	0 49	13 00	8 08	18 18	1 05	15 20	2 07
14 Th	13 05	22 29	0S54	21 37	19 48	1 37	17 06	5 36	4 59	0 48	12 51	8 07	18 19	1 05	15 21	2 07
15 F	12 44	20 29	1 58	19 05	19 28	1 41	17 08	5 30	4 40	0 47	12 41	8 06	18 20	1 05	15 22	2 07
16 Sa	12 23	17 25	2 57	15 31	19 06	1 46	17 09	5 24	4 21	0 47	12 31	8 06	18 21	1 05	15 23	2 07
17 Su	12 03	13 24	3 49	11 06	18 43	1 50	17 11	5 18	4 02	0 46	12 21	8 05	18 22	1 05	15 24	2 06
18 M	11 41	8 38	4 29	6 01	18 19	1 53	17 12	5 12	3 43	0 46	12 12	8 04	18 22	1 05	15 25	2 06
19 Tu	11 20	3 19	4 54	0 33	17 54	1 56	17 14	5 06	3 24	0 45	12 02	8 04	18 23	1 05	15 27	2 06
20 W	10 59	2S15	5 02	5S02	17 27	1 59	17 14	4 60	3 05	0 44	11 52	8 03	18 24	1 06	15 28	2 05
21 Th	10 37	7 45	4 51	10 23	16 59	2 02	17 15	4 54	2 46	0 44	11 42	8 02	18 25	1 06	15 29	2 05
22 F	10 15	12 52	4 22	15 10	16 29	2 04	17 15	4 47	2 27	0 43	11 32	8 02	18 25	1 06	15 30	2 05
23 Sa	9 54	17 15	3 37	19 04	15 59	2 05	17 15	4 41	2 08	0 42	11 23	8 01	18 26	1 06	15 31	2 05
24 Su	9 31	20 36	2 38	21 48	15 26	2 07	17 15	4 34	1 49	0 42	11 13	8 00	18 27	1 06	15 33	2 04
25 M	9 09	22 39	1 30	23 09	14 53	2 08	17 14	4 28	1 30	0 41	11 03	7 60	18 27	1 06	15 34	2 04
26 Tu	8 47	23 17	0 17	23 03	14 18	2 08	17 13	4 21	1 10	0 41	10 53	7 59	18 28	1 06	15 35	2 04
27 W	8 24	22 27	0N57	21 32	13 42	2 08	17 12	4 15	0 51	0 40	10 43	7 59	18 28	1 07	15 37	2 04
28 Th	8S02	20S17	2N06	18S46	13S04	2S08	17S10	4N08	0S32	0S39	10S33	7S58	18S29	1N07	15N38	2S03

Day	⚷ Decl	⚷ Lat	♅ Decl	♅ Lat	♆ Decl	♆ Lat	♇ Decl	♇ Lat
1	12N51	1S23	22N36	0N03	2N09	1S29	23S10	5S41
6	12 53	1 23	22 35	0 03	2 12	1 29	23 08	5 41
11	12 55	1 23	22 35	0 03	2 16	1 28	23 06	5 42
16	12 58	1 23	22 35	0 03	2 19	1 28	23 04	5 42
21	13 01	1 23	22 35	0 03	2 23	1 28	23 02	5 43
26	13N04	1S23	22N35	0N03	2N27	1S28	23S00	5S43

Day	⚴ Decl	⚴ Lat	⚵ Decl	⚵ Lat	⚶ Decl	⚶ Lat	Eris Decl	Eris Lat
1	1N43	20N06	12S27	10N55	12S53	4S46	0N50	9S43
6	1 57	19 54	12 19	11 05	11 59	4 47	0 51	9 42
11	2 12	19 43	12 09	11 16	11 04	4 48	0 52	9 41
16	2 30	19 32	11 58	11 28	10 09	4 49	0 53	9 41
21	2 48	19 23	11 45	11 41	9 13	4 50	0 55	9 40
26	3N08	19N14	11S31	11N54	8S17	4S51	0N56	9S39

Moon Phenomena

Max/0 Decl
dy hr mn
5 6:26 0 N
12 17:11 23N24
19 14:21 0 S
25 22:11 23S17

Perigee/Apogee
dy hr m kilometers
10 6:07 a 404288
22 10:12 p 368405

PH dy hr mn
● 2 16:09 13♒51
☽ 10 11:51 21♉47
○ 18 6:21 29♌38
☾ 25 1:59 6♐30

Max/0 Lat
dy hr mn
5 17:30 5N06
13 4:08 0 S
19 22:10 5S02
26 5:24 0 N

Void of Course Moon

Last Aspect	☽ Ingress
1 7:36 ♃ ✶	♒ 1 15:54
3 12:48 ♃ □	♓ 3 20:59
5 21:27 ☿ ✶	♈ 6 4:49
7 17:49 ☉ ✶	♉ 8 15:45
10 20:48 ♃ ☍	♊ 11 4:32
13 5:49 ☉ △	♋ 13 16:30
15 19:13 ♃ △	♌ 16 1:28
18 6:21 ☉ ☍	♍ 18 6:59
20 4:55 ♃ ✶	♎ 20 10:05
21 20:38 ☿ △	♏ 22 12:19
24 10:28 ♂ △	♐ 24 14:54
26 16:59 ♂ □	♑ 26 18:27
28 18:29 ♃ ✶	♒ 28 23:08

DAILY ASPECTARIAN

1 F	♀✶♂ 2:04; ☽∠♂ 6:00; ☽✶♃ 7:36; ☽∠⚳ 9:58; ☽∥♃ 10:45; ☽⚼♅ 15:19; ☉∥☽ 17:46; ☽∥♀ 19:41
2 Sa	☽#♄ 4:03; ☽□⚷ 5:53; ☽∥⚳ 6:29; ☽✶♆ 7:25; ♂⚺♇ 8:06; ☽⚺♀ 8:22; ☽☌♇ 9:36; ☽⚺♂ 9:42; ☽⚺⚳ 12:52; ☉☌☽ 16:09; ☽#⚷ 16:32; ☉∥♀ 17:20; ☽△♅ 17:33
3 Su	☽□♄ 0:00; ☽⚺☿ 7:36; ☽∠♆ 10:03; ☉△♅ 10:42; ☽∠♀ 11:31; ☽□♃ 12:48; ☽∥♂ 15:45
4 M	☽✶⚷ 11:41; ☽⚺♆ 13:20; ☽∠☿ 13:58; ☽✶♀ 15:25; ☽⚺♇ 15:39; ☽☌♂ 19:04; ☽#♆ 20:06; ☽☌⚳ 20:34; ☽□♅ 23:48
5 Tu	♀⚺♇ 1:06; ☉⚺☽ 3:01; ☽✶♄ 6:47; ☿✶♃ 13:31; ☽∠⚷ 15:39; ☽∥♆ 16:56; ☽∠♇ 19:46; ☽△♃ 20:38; ☽✶☿ 21:27
6 W	☉∠☽ 9:54; ☽∠♄ 11:21; ♀∠♃ 14:11; ☽#♂ 17:50; ♂☌⚳ 17:54; ☽⚺⚷ 20:27; ☽☌♆ 22:14
7 Th	☽✶♇ 0:42; ☽⚼♃ 1:46; ☽□♀ 2:03; ☉□♄ 4:19; ☽⚺⚳ 7:37; ☽⚺♂ 8:05; ☉#♄ 8:42; ☽✶♅ 9:08; ☽⚺♄ 16:44; ☉✶☽ 17:49; ☿∠⚳ 22:22
8 F	♂□♅ 0:00; ☽∥⚷ 0:41; ☽#⚳ 5:58; ☿⚼♅ 7:07; ☽⚻♃ 7:39; ☉#☽ 12:49; ☿ ♒ 14:05; ☽∠⚳ 14:22; ☽∠♅ 14:54; ☽∥♄ 15:20; ☿∠♂ 15:32; ☽∠♂ 15:58; ☽□☿ 15:59
9 Sa	☽#♀ 2:31; ⚳□♅ 6:49; ☽☌⚷ 8:12; ☽⚺♆ 10:04; ☽#♃ 12:25; ☽□♇ 12:40; ☽△♀ 16:11; ☽⚺♅ 21:10; ☽✶⚳ 21:40
10 Su	☽✶♂ 0:25; ☽☌♄ 5:16; ☊ D 11:39; ☽#☿ 11:41; ☉□☽ 11:51; ☽∠♆ 16:35; ☽☍♃ 20:48; ☽⚼♀ 23:57
11 M	☽∥♅ 11:34; ☽△☿ 13:26; ☽⚺⚷ 21:09; ☽✶♆ 23:03; ☽#♇ 23:08
12 Tu	☽△♇ 1:38; ☽⚻♀ 7:39; ☽☌♅ 9:52; ☽□⚳ 12:24; ☽□♂ 17:20; ☽⚺♄ 18:05; ☉∠♆ 20:44; ☽⚼☿ 23:52
13 W	☽∠⚷ 3:13; ☊ R 4:09; ♂✶♄ 5:37; ☉△☽ 5:49; ☽⚼♇ 7:37; ☽⚻♃ 9:28; ⚳#⚷ 10:00; ☽#♇ 11:17; ☽∥♅ 22:16; ☽∠♄ 23:44
14 Th	☿□⚷ 2:46; ♀⚻♅ 6:15; ☽✶⚷ 8:35; ☉#⚷ 9:00; ☽⚻☿ 9:24; ☽□♆ 10:24; ☽⚻♇ 12:53; ☉⚼☽ 13:37; ☽⚼♃ 14:48; ☿✶♆ 17:43; ☽⚺♅ 20:32; ☽☍♀ 21:14
15 F	☽△⚳ 0:48; ☽✶♄ 4:34; ☉□♃ 5:19; ☉∥⚳ 6:57; ☽△♂ 7:26; ☽#☿ 10:07; ☿☌♇ 13:59; ☽#♃ 17:34; ☽△♃ 19:13; ☉⚻☽ 20:18
16 Sa	☽∠♅ 0:35; ☽#♀ 1:44; ☽⚼⚳ 5:35; ☽∥♄ 12:45; ☽⚼♂ 12:53; ☽□⚷ 16:41; ☽△♆ 18:24; ☽☍♇ 20:43
17 Su	☽☍☿ 0:43; ☽∥⚷ 2:20; ☽✶♅ 3:45; ⚵ ♑ 4:35; ☽#⚳ 5:47; ☽⚻♀ 7:07; ☉#☽ 7:47; ☽⚻⚳ 9:24; ☽□♄ 11:31; ☽⚻♂ 17:19; ☽⚼♆ 21:06; ☿∥♃ 21:08
18 M	☽□♃ 1:23; ☿△♅ 2:16; ☉☍☽ 6:21; ☽⚼♀ 10:44; ☉ ♓ 15:01; ☽△⚷ 21:30; ☽⚻♆ 23:07; ☽#♂ 23:37
19 Tu	☽⚻♇ 1:19; ☽∥♆ 4:09; ☽□♅ 7:54; ♂∠⚷ 7:57; ☽⚻☿ 11:43; ☽△♀ 13:43; ☽☍⚳ 14:46; ☽△♄ 15:32; ☽⚼⚷ 23:03; ☽☍♂ 23:54
20 W	☽#♆ 0:32; ☽⚼♇ 2:49; ☽∥♂ 3:23; ☽✶♃ 4:55; ☿∥♀ 10:41; ☉⚻☽ 13:21; ☽⚼☿ 16:17; ☿⚺♀ 16:49; ☽⚼♄ 16:55; ☿⚺⚳ 21:34; ☿□♄ 22:00; ♅ D 23:24; ⚳✶♄ 23:38
21 Th	☽⚻⚷ 0:19; ☽☍♆ 1:54; ☽△♇ 4:03; ♀△♄ 5:15; ☽∠♃ 6:11; ☽△♅ 10:24; ♀✶⚳ 10:45; ☉∥☽ 12:17; ☉⚼☽ 16:22; ☽∥⚳ 17:44; ☽⚻♄ 18:07; ☽⚻⚳ 18:34; ☽□♀ 18:45; ☽△☿ 20:38
22 F	☽#⚷ 0:49; ♂#♆ 3:26; ☽⚻♂ 5:04; ☽⚺♃ 7:23; ♂∠♇ 7:31; ☽⚼♅ 11:30; ☽#♄ 13:56; ☽∥☿ 17:21; ☉△☽ 19:23; ☽⚼⚳ 20:22
23 Sa	☽∥♀ 0:03; ☽☍⚷ 2:40; ☽⚻♆ 4:15; ☽□♇ 6:24; ☽∥♃ 7:39; ☽⚼♂ 7:40; ☽⚻♅ 12:41; ☿#♄ 19:38; ☽☍♄ 20:42; ☽△⚳ 22:20; ☽✶♀ 23:55
24 Su	♂△♃ 3:09; ☿∠♆ 4:35; ☽⚼♆ 5:37; ☽□☿ 5:45; ☽☌♃ 10:06; ☽△♂ 10:28; ☽#♅ 22:41
25 M	☉□☽ 1:59; ☊ D 2:05; ☽∠♀ 2:54; ☽⚻⚷ 5:37; ☽△♆ 7:13; ☽∥♇ 7:32; ☽✶♇ 9:24; ☽☍♅ 15:43; ☿□♃ 18:47
26 Tu	☽⚻♄ 0:06; ☽□⚳ 3:01; ☊ R 5:27; ☽⚺♀ 6:13; ☽⚼⚷ 7:29; ☽∠♇ 11:17; ☽∥♇ 13:08; ☽⚺♃ 13:44; ☽✶☿ 16:21; ☽□♂ 16:59; ☽#♅ 21:54
27 W	☿⚺♂ 0:54; ☽⚼♄ 2:14; ☉✶⚷ 6:36; ☿ ♓ 9:01; ☽△⚷ 9:38; ☉✶☽ 9:51; ☽□♆ 11:15; ☽⚺♇ 13:27; ☉∠♀ 13:47; ☽∠♃ 15:58; ♂ ♈ 19:08; ☽⚻♅ 19:49; ☽∠☿ 22:21; ☿#⚷ 23:23
28 Th	☽△♄ 4:38; ☉⚺♆ 5:28; ☽✶⚳ 8:54; ☽☌♀ 13:59; ☽∥♃ 14:02; ☉∠☽ 14:20; ☽✶♃ 18:29; ☽⚼♅ 22:19; ☽∥♀ 23:10

LONGITUDE

March 2030

Day	Sid.Time	☉	☽	☽ 12 hour	Mean ☊	True ☊	☿	♀	♂	⚳	♃	♄	⚷	♅	♆	♇
	h m s	° ' "	° ' "	° ' "	° '	° '	° '	° '	° '	° '	° '	° '	° '	° '	° '	° '
1 F	10 35 24	10♓26 26	0♒29 08	7♒12 55	21♐41.0	22♐21.4	2♓51.3	25♑11.3	0♈55.8	22♓12.7	27♏23.1	19♉36.3	8♉46.5	14♊32.2	9♈41.4	10♒56.3
2 Sa	10 39 20	11 26 40	13 54 13	20 32 51	21 37.8	22R 13.6	4 38.2	26 01.9	1 42.2	22 36.2	27 25.4	19 40.6	8 48.9	14 32.7	9 43.5	10 57.9
3 Su	10 43 17	12 26 54	27 08 39	3♓41 23	21 34.6	22 03.0	6 26.0	26 53.2	2 28.6	22 59.7	27 27.5	19 45.0	8 51.3	14 33.2	9 45.5	10 59.6
4 M	10 47 13	13 27 05	10♓10 55	16 37 03	21 31.4	21 50.3	8 15.0	27 45.2	3 14.9	23 23.3	27 29.4	19 49.5	8 53.8	14 33.7	9 47.6	11 01.2
5 Tu	10 51 10	14 27 15	22 59 40	29 18 42	21 28.3	21 36.4	10 04.9	28 37.9	4 01.2	23 46.9	27 31.1	19 54.1	8 56.3	14 34.4	9 49.7	11 02.8
6 W	10 55 07	15 27 22	5♈34 08	11♈46 01	21 25.1	21 22.8	11 55.9	29 31.2	4 47.4	24 10.5	27 32.6	19 58.7	8 58.9	14 35.0	9 51.8	11 04.4
7 Th	10 59 03	16 27 28	17 54 28	23 59 41	21 21.9	21 10.6	13 48.0	0♒25.1	5 33.6	24 34.1	27 33.9	20 03.5	9 01.5	14 35.7	9 53.9	11 06.0
8 F	11 03 00	17 27 32	0♉01 56	6♉01 33	21 18.7	21 00.7	15 41.0	1 19.5	6 19.8	24 57.7	27 35.1	20 08.3	9 04.2	14 36.5	9 56.0	11 07.6
9 Sa	11 06 56	18 27 34	11 58 57	17 54 37	21 15.5	20 53.7	17 35.0	2 14.6	7 05.9	25 21.3	27 36.0	20 13.2	9 06.9	14 37.3	9 58.2	11 09.2
10 Su	11 10 53	19 27 33	23 49 04	29 42 53	21 12.4	20 49.4	19 30.0	3 10.2	7 52.0	25 44.9	27 36.8	20 18.2	9 09.6	14 38.2	10 00.3	11 10.7
11 M	11 14 49	20 27 31	5♊36 41	11♊31 07	21 09.2	20 47.5	21 25.9	4 06.3	8 38.0	26 08.6	27 37.4	20 23.3	9 12.4	14 39.2	10 02.5	11 12.2
12 Tu	11 18 46	21 27 26	17 26 54	23 24 42	21 06.0	20 47.1	23 22.6	5 02.9	9 24.1	26 32.2	27 37.8	20 28.4	9 15.2	14 40.1	10 04.6	11 13.8
13 W	11 22 42	22 27 20	29 25 14	5♋29 11	21 02.8	20 47.0	25 20.1	5 59.9	10 10.0	26 55.9	27R 38.0	20 33.7	9 18.1	14 41.2	10 06.8	11 15.2
14 Th	11 26 39	23 27 11	11♋37 15	17 50 03	20 59.7	20 46.1	27 18.2	6 57.5	10 56.0	27 19.5	27 38.0	20 39.0	9 21.0	14 42.3	10 09.0	11 16.7
15 F	11 30 36	24 26 59	24 08 10	0♌32 06	20 56.5	20 43.5	29 16.8	7 55.5	11 41.8	27 43.2	27 37.8	20 44.4	9 23.9	14 43.4	10 11.2	11 18.2
16 Sa	11 34 32	25 26 46	7♌02 17	13 39 00	20 53.3	20 38.4	1♈15.8	8 53.9	12 27.7	28 06.9	27 37.5	20 49.8	9 26.9	14 44.6	10 13.4	11 19.6
17 Su	11 38 29	26 26 30	20 22 24	27 12 30	20 50.1	20 30.6	3 14.9	9 52.8	13 13.5	28 30.5	27 36.9	20 55.3	9 29.9	14 45.8	10 15.6	11 21.0
18 M	11 42 25	27 26 13	4♍09 06	11♍11 53	20 47.0	20 20.4	5 14.0	10 52.0	13 59.2	28 54.2	27 36.2	21 00.9	9 33.0	14 47.1	10 17.9	11 22.4
19 Tu	11 46 22	28 25 53	18 20 18	25 33 39	20 43.8	20 08.8	7 12.8	11 51.7	14 44.9	29 17.9	27 35.3	21 06.6	9 36.0	14 48.4	10 20.1	11 23.8
20 W	11 50 18	29 25 31	2♎51 07	10♎11 44	20 40.6	19 57.0	9 10.9	12 51.7	15 30.6	29 41.6	27 34.2	21 12.3	9 39.2	14 49.8	10 22.3	11 25.2
21 Th	11 54 15	0♈25 07	17 34 28	24 58 17	20 37.4	19 46.1	11 08.2	13 52.1	16 16.2	0♈05.3	27 32.9	21 18.1	9 42.3	14 51.3	10 24.6	11 26.5
22 F	11 58 11	1 24 41	2♏22 10	9♏45 07	20 34.2	19 37.5	13 04.1	14 52.9	17 01.8	0 28.9	27 31.4	21 24.0	9 45.5	14 52.7	10 26.8	11 27.9
23 Sa	12 02 08	2 24 13	17 06 18	24 24 58	20 31.1	19 31.6	14 58.5	15 54.0	17 47.3	0 52.6	27 29.7	21 29.9	9 48.7	14 54.3	10 29.1	11 29.2
24 Su	12 06 04	3 23 44	1♐40 31	8♐52 30	20 27.9	19 28.4	16 50.8	16 55.4	18 32.8	1 16.3	27 27.9	21 35.9	9 51.9	14 55.8	10 31.3	11 30.5
25 M	12 10 01	4 23 13	16 00 37	23 04 40	20 24.7	19D 27.5	18 40.6	17 57.2	19 18.3	1 40.0	27 25.9	21 41.9	9 55.2	14 57.5	10 33.6	11 31.7
26 Tu	12 13 58	5 22 40	0♑04 36	7♑00 26	20 21.5	19R 27.6	20 27.5	18 59.3	20 03.7	2 03.7	27 23.7	21 48.1	9 58.5	14 59.1	10 35.8	11 33.0
27 W	12 17 54	6 22 05	13 52 14	20 40 10	20 18.4	19 27.4	22 11.0	20 01.7	20 49.0	2 27.3	27 21.3	21 54.2	10 01.9	15 00.9	10 38.1	11 34.2
28 Th	12 21 51	7 21 29	27 24 22	4♒05 02	20 15.2	19 25.9	23 50.8	21 04.3	21 34.3	2 51.0	27 18.7	22 00.5	10 05.2	15 02.6	10 40.4	11 35.4
29 F	12 25 47	8 20 51	10♒42 18	17 16 20	20 12.0	19 22.0	25 26.5	22 07.3	22 19.6	3 14.7	27 15.9	22 06.8	10 08.6	15 04.4	10 42.6	11 36.6
30 Sa	12 29 44	9 20 11	23 47 17	0♓15 13	20 08.8	19 15.3	26 57.5	23 10.5	23 04.8	3 38.3	27 13.0	22 13.1	10 12.0	15 06.3	10 44.9	11 37.7
31 Su	12 33 40	10♈19 29	6♓40 15	13 02 25	20♐05.6	19♐06.0	28♈23.6	24♒14.0	23♈50.0	4♈02.0	27♏09.9	22♉19.5	10♉15.5	15♊08.2	10♈47.2	11♒38.8

1st of Month

Julian Day #
2462561.5
Obliquity
23°26'06"
SVP 4♓50'00"
GC 27♐15.6
Eris 25♈44.8

Day	⚴	Day	⚵	Day	⚶
1	19♒46.8	1	3♑05.7	1	21♓46.7
6	21 26.7	6	4 18.5	6	24 11.4
11	23 05.2	11	5 27.4	11	26 35.8
16	24 42.0	16	6 32.0	16	28 59.8
21	26 17.1	21	7 31.9	21	1♈23.4
26	27 50.3	26	8 26.9	26	3 46.5
31	29 21.5	31	9 16.6	31	6 09.2

DECLINATION and LATITUDE

Day	☉ Decl	☽ Decl	☽ Lat	☽ 12h Decl	☿ Decl	☿ Lat	♀ Decl	♀ Lat	♂ Decl	♂ Lat	⚳ Decl	⚳ Lat	♃ Decl	♃ Lat	♄ Decl	♄ Lat
1 F	7S39	17S00	3N07	15S02	12S26	2S07	17S08	4N02	0S13	0S39	10S24	7S57	18S29	1N07	15N39	2S03
2 Sa	7 16	12 52	3 57	10 35	11 46	2 06	17 05	3 55	0N06	0 38	10 14	7 57	18 30	1 07	15 41	2 03
3 Su	6 53	8 11	4 33	5 43	11 04	2 04	17 02	3 48	0 25	0 37	10 04	7 56	18 30	1 07	15 42	2 03
4 M	6 30	3 12	4 54	0 41	10 21	2 02	16 59	3 42	0 44	0 37	9 54	7 56	18 30	1 07	15 44	2 02
5 Tu	6 07	1N49	5 00	4N16	9 37	1 59	16 55	3 35	1 03	0 36	9 44	7 55	18 31	1 07	15 45	2 02
6 W	5 44	6 40	4 51	8 58	8 52	1 56	16 51	3 28	1 22	0 36	9 34	7 55	18 31	1 07	15 46	2 02
7 Th	5 21	11 10	4 29	13 13	8 06	1 52	16 46	3 22	1 40	0 35	9 25	7 54	18 31	1 08	15 48	2 02
8 F	4 57	15 08	3 54	16 53	7 18	1 48	16 41	3 15	1 59	0 34	9 15	7 54	18 31	1 08	15 50	2 01
9 Sa	4 34	18 26	3 10	19 48	6 29	1 43	16 36	3 08	2 18	0 34	9 05	7 54	18 31	1 08	15 51	2 01
10 Su	4 10	20 57	2 18	21 52	5 39	1 38	16 30	3 02	2 37	0 33	8 55	7 53	18 31	1 08	15 53	2 01
11 M	3 47	22 32	1 19	22 58	4 48	1 32	16 23	2 55	2 56	0 32	8 46	7 53	18 31	1 08	15 54	2 01
12 Tu	3 23	23 08	0 18	23 02	3 56	1 25	16 16	2 49	3 14	0 32	8 36	7 52	18 31	1 08	15 56	2 00
13 W	2 60	22 40	0S46	22 02	3 03	1 18	16 09	2 42	3 33	0 31	8 26	7 52	18 31	1 08	15 57	2 00
14 Th	2 36	21 08	1 48	19 58	2 09	1 11	16 01	2 35	3 52	0 30	8 16	7 52	18 31	1 09	15 59	1 60
15 F	2 12	18 33	2 47	16 53	1 15	1 03	15 53	2 29	4 10	0 30	8 06	7 51	18 31	1 09	16 01	1 60
16 Sa	1 49	14 59	3 39	12 52	0 19	0 54	15 44	2 23	4 29	0 29	7 57	7 51	18 31	1 09	16 02	1 60
17 Su	1 25	10 34	4 21	8 06	0N36	0 45	15 35	2 16	4 47	0 28	7 47	7 50	18 30	1 09	16 04	1 59
18 M	1 01	5 30	4 49	2 47	1 33	0 35	15 25	2 10	5 05	0 28	7 37	7 50	18 30	1 09	16 06	1 59
19 Tu	0 37	0S00	5 01	2S49	2 29	0 25	15 15	2 03	5 24	0 27	7 28	7 50	18 30	1 09	16 07	1 59
20 W	0 14	5 37	4 53	8 22	3 25	0 14	15 05	1 57	5 42	0 26	7 18	7 49	18 29	1 09	16 09	1 59
21 Th	0N10	10 60	4 27	13 29	4 22	0 03	14 53	1 51	6 00	0 26	7 08	7 49	18 29	1 09	16 11	1 58
22 F	0 34	15 46	3 42	17 48	5 17	0N09	14 42	1 45	6 18	0 25	6 59	7 49	18 28	1 10	16 12	1 58
23 Sa	0 57	19 32	2 42	20 57	6 13	0 20	14 30	1 39	6 36	0 24	6 49	7 49	18 28	1 10	16 14	1 58
24 Su	1 21	22 00	1 33	22 42	7 07	0 32	14 17	1 33	6 54	0 24	6 39	7 48	18 27	1 10	16 16	1 58
25 M	1 45	23 00	0 18	22 56	8 00	0 44	14 04	1 27	7 12	0 23	6 30	7 48	18 27	1 10	16 17	1 58
26 Tu	2 08	22 30	0N56	21 43	8 52	0 57	13 51	1 21	7 30	0 22	6 20	7 48	18 26	1 10	16 19	1 57
27 W	2 32	20 38	2 06	19 15	9 42	1 09	13 37	1 15	7 47	0 22	6 10	7 48	18 26	1 10	16 21	1 57
28 Th	2 55	17 37	3 07	15 46	10 30	1 21	13 23	1 09	8 05	0 21	6 01	7 47	18 25	1 10	16 23	1 57
29 F	3 19	13 45	3 57	11 34	11 17	1 33	13 08	1 03	8 22	0 20	5 51	7 47	18 24	1 10	16 25	1 57
30 Sa	3 42	9 17	4 33	6 55	12 01	1 44	12 53	0 57	8 40	0 20	5 42	7 47	18 23	1 11	16 26	1 57
31 Su	4N05	4S29	4N55	2S02	12N42	1N56	12S38	0N52	8N57	0S19	5S32	7S47	18S23	1N11	16N28	1S57

Day	⚷ Decl	⚷ Lat	♅ Decl	♅ Lat	♆ Decl	♆ Lat	♇ Decl	♇ Lat
1	13N06	1S23	22N35	0N03	2N29	1S28	22S59	5S44
6	13 10	1 24	22 35	0 03	2 34	1 28	22 58	5 45
11	13 14	1 24	22 36	0 03	2 38	1 28	22 56	5 45
16	13 19	1 24	22 37	0 03	2 42	1 28	22 55	5 46
21	13 24	1 24	22 37	0 03	2 47	1 28	22 54	5 47
26	13 29	1 24	22 38	0 03	2 51	1 28	22 53	5 48
31	13N34	1S24	22N39	0N03	2N55	1S28	22S52	5S49

Day	⚴ Decl	⚴ Lat	⚵ Decl	⚵ Lat	⚶ Decl	⚶ Lat	Eris Decl	Eris Lat
1	3N21	19N09	11S22	12N02	7S43	4S51	0N57	9S39
6	3 43	19 02	11 05	12 17	6 47	4 52	0 58	9 39
11	4 06	18 55	10 48	12 32	5 50	4 54	0 59	9 38
16	4 30	18 50	10 29	12 49	4 54	4 55	1 01	9 38
21	4 55	18 45	10 09	13 06	3 59	4 56	1 02	9 37
26	5 21	18 40	9 48	13 24	3 03	4 58	1 04	9 37
31	5N47	18N37	9S26	13N42	2S08	4S59	1N05	9S36

Moon Phenomena

Max/0 Decl
dy hr mn
4 15:17 0 N
12 1:39 23N08
18 23:59 0 S
25 3:46 23S01
31 21:55 0 N

Max/0 Lat
dy hr mn
4 21:25 5N00
12 6:43 0 S
19 2:58 5S01
25 5:50 0 N
31 23:09 5N02

Perigee/Apogee
dy hr m kilometers
10 2:24 a 404746
21 22:02 p 362976

PH dy hr mn
● 4 6:36 13♓44
☽ 12 8:49 21♊49
○ 19 17:58 29♍11
☾ 26 9:53 5♑47

Void of Course Moon

Last Aspect			☽ Ingress		
3 0:34	♃	□	♓	3	5:13
5 11:31	♀	⚹	♈	5	13:19
6 17:31	♅	⚹	♉	7	23:56
10 7:44	♃	☍	♊	10	12:35
12 14:16	☿	□	♋	13	1:09
15 6:34	♃	△	♌	15	11:00
17 12:42	♃	□	♍	17	16:51
19 17:58	☉	☍	♎	19	19:19
20 21:46	♂	☍	♏	21	20:09
23 17:03	♃	☌	♐	23	21:13
25 5:54	♂	△	♑	25	23:52
27 23:50	♃	⚹	♒	28	4:39
30 6:37	☿	⚹	♓	30	11:32

DAILY ASPECTARIAN

1 F
☽⚹♂ 0:50
☽⚺☿ 4:51
☽⋕♄ 8:15
☉⚺♇ 12:14
☽∠⚳ 12:21
☽□⚷ 14:50
☽⚹♆ 16:28
☽☌♇ 18:42
☉⚺☽ 19:13
☽⋕⚷ 22:42

2 Sa
☽△♅ 1:09
☽∠♂ 5:21
☽∥☿ 6:57
☽□♄ 10:29
☽∥⚳ 14:17
☽⚺⚳ 16:13
☽∠♆ 19:38
☽⚺♀ 23:30

3 Su
☽□♃ 0:34
☉∥☽ 6:52
☽⚺♂ 10:23
♀⚹♃ 16:26
☽☌☿ 19:50
☽⚹⚷ 21:36
☽⚺♆ 23:17

4 M
☽⚺♇ 1:34
☽⋕♆ 3:13
☽∠♀ 5:08
☉☌☽ 6:36
☽□♅ 8:10
☿⚹⚷ 8:42
☽⋕♂ 11:07
☽⚹♄ 18:08
☿∥⚳ 19:15
☽∥♂ 20:03
☿⚺♆ 20:38

5 Tu
☽☌⚳ 1:32
☽∠⚷ 1:48
☉□♅ 2:52
☽∥♆ 3:33
☽∠♇ 5:48
☽△♃ 8:36
⚳∠⚷ 10:47
☽⚹♀ 11:31
☿⚺♇ 12:44
☉⋕☽ 19:38
☽☌♂ 22:24
☽∠♄ 22:51

6 W
♀⚼♅ 1:45
♂∠♄ 6:33
☽⚺⚷ 6:37
☽☌♆ 8:20
☽⋕☿ 9:49
☽⚹♇ 10:41
♀ ♒ 12:52
☽⚼♃ 13:32
☽⚺☿ 14:31
☽⋕⚳ 14:43
☽⚹♅ 17:31
☉⚺☽ 20:54

7 Th
☽⚺♄ 4:15
☿□♅ 10:14
☽∥⚷ 11:49
☽⚺⚳ 13:35
☽⚻♃ 19:07
☽∠♅ 23:09

8 F
☽∠☿ 1:33
☽□♀ 2:48
☽∥♄ 4:39
☉∠☽ 5:17
☽⋕♀ 10:22
☽⚺♂ 13:29
☿∠♀ 15:42
☽☌⚷ 18:12
☽⚺♆ 19:56
☽∠⚳ 20:36
☽□♇ 22:19

9 Sa
☽⋕♃ 0:40
☽⚺♅ 5:21
☽⚹☿ 13:32
☉⚹☽ 14:20
☽☌♄ 16:48
☽∠♂ 21:56
☉☌☿ 22:56

10 Su
♂∥♆ 0:03
☽∠♆ 2:25
☽⚹⚳ 4:04
☽☍♃ 7:44
☿⚹♄ 10:27
☽△♀ 20:40
☉⚹♄ 22:09

11 M
☽∥♅ 1:18
⚳∠♇ 3:59
☽⚹♂ 6:34
☽⚺⚷ 7:20
☽⚹♆ 9:02
☽⋕♇ 10:52
☽△♇ 11:23
☽☌♅ 18:22
♂⚺⚷ 19:05

12 Tu
☉⋕♂ 5:00
☽⚼♀ 5:42
☽⚺♄ 6:09
☉□☽ 8:49
☿∠⚷ 11:02
☽∠⚷ 13:45
☿⋕♂ 14:00
☽□☿ 14:16
☽⋕♇ 16:31
☽⚼♇ 17:41
☽□⚳ 18:52
☽⚻♃ 20:26
♂☌♆ 22:15

13 W
☽∥♅ 1:37
☉∥☿ 2:49
☿⋕♆ 10:21
☿∠♇ 11:22
☽∠♄ 12:14
☽⚻♀ 14:07
♃ R 14:35
☽⚹⚷ 19:33
☉⋕♆ 19:35
☽□♆ 21:08
☽□♂ 22:34
☽⚻♇ 23:20

14 Th
☿☌⚳ 0:20
☽⚼♃ 1:58
☿△♃ 4:00
♀⋕♄ 5:48
☽⚺♅ 5:59
♂⚹♇ 11:13
☽⚹♄ 17:30
⚳△♃ 18:36
☉∠⚷ 22:42

15 F
☽⋕♃ 0:14
☉△☽ 0:39
☽△♃ 6:34
☽△⚳ 6:57
☿ ♈ 8:43
☽∠♅ 10:30
☽△☿ 11:25
☽∥♄ 17:32
☽⋕♀ 19:11

16 Sa
☽☍♀ 3:40
☽□⚷ 4:25
♂⚼♃ 5:05
☽△♆ 5:49
☉⚼☽ 6:43
☽☍♇ 7:49
☽∥⚷ 9:31
☽△♂ 10:27
☽⚼⚳ 11:22
☽⚹♅ 13:59
♀□⚷ 14:12
☽⚼☿ 19:35
☉∠♇ 21:45

17 Su
☽□♄ 0:59
☽⚼♆ 8:37
♀⚹♆ 9:39
☉⚻☽ 11:30
☽□♃ 12:42
☽⋕⚳ 13:56
☉⋕☿ 14:33
☽⚼♂ 14:34
☽⚻⚳ 14:41

18 M
☽∥♂ 1:43
☽⚻☿ 2:09
⚶ ♈ 2:15
☉△♃ 3:57
☽△⚷ 9:14
☿∠♄ 9:57
☽⚻♆ 10:30
☽∥♆ 12:10
☽⚻♀ 12:18
☽⚻♇ 12:19
♀☌♇ 12:33
☽∥☿ 14:51
☽⚻♂ 17:39
☽□♅ 18:04
☉⋕☽ 21:07

19 Tu
♂⚹♅ 1:54
☉∥☽ 2:29
☽△♄ 4:39
☿∥♆ 6:49
☽⚼⚷ 10:27
☽⋕♆ 11:44
☽⋕☿ 12:42
☽⚼♇ 13:24
☽⚼♀ 15:11
☽⚹♃ 15:20
☉☍☽ 17:58
☽☍⚳ 18:40

20 W
☽⋕♂ 0:22
☽⚼♄ 5:31
☿⚺⚷ 5:55
☽∥⚳ 7:06
☉☌⚳ 10:44
☽⚻⚷ 11:09
☽☍☿ 11:56
☽☍♆ 12:19
☉ ♈ 13:53
☽△♇ 14:01
☿☌♆ 14:52
☽∠♃ 15:51
☽△♀ 17:32
⚳ ♈ 18:40
☽△♅ 19:34
☽☍♂ 21:46

21 Th
☿⚹♇ 3:50
☽⚻♄ 6:05
☽⋕⚷ 11:36
☽⚺♃ 16:09
☿⚼♃ 17:17
☽∥♀ 18:29
☽⚼♅ 19:57
☽⚻⚳ 20:51
☉⚻☽ 22:20
♀△♅ 23:56

22 F
☽⋕♄ 2:30
☽☍⚷ 12:03
☽⚻♆ 13:10
☽□♇ 14:49
☽∥♃ 16:25
☽⚻☿ 20:00
☽⚻♅ 20:24
☽□♀ 21:53
☽⚼⚳ 21:56
☿⚹♅ 23:06
♀∠⚳ 23:07

23 Sa
☉⚼☽ 0:31
☽⚻♂ 1:11
☽☍♄ 7:15
♂⋕⚳ 11:03
☿⋕⚳ 13:34
☽⚼♆ 13:48
☿∥♂ 15:29
☽☌♃ 17:03
☽△⚳ 23:19

24 Su
☽⚼☿ 0:20
☿⚹♀ 2:17
☉△☽ 3:04
☽⚼♂ 3:17
☽⋕♅ 10:39
☽⚻⚷ 13:43
☽△♆ 14:48
☽⚹♇ 16:26
☽∥♇ 17:50
☽☍♅ 22:13

25 M
☽⚹♀ 3:33
☽△☿ 5:10
☊ D 5:47
☽△♂ 5:54
☽⚻♄ 9:43
☽∥♇ 13:52
☿☌♂ 14:34
☽⚼⚷ 15:12
☽∠♇ 17:56
☽⚺♃ 19:24
☽⋕♅ 21:05

26 Tu
☽□⚳ 3:31
☽∠♀ 7:18
☉□☽ 9:53
☊ R 10:07
☽⚼♄ 11:44
☽△⚷ 17:15
☽□♆ 18:19
☿⚺♄ 19:48
☽⚺♇ 19:58
☽∠♃ 21:21

27 W
☽⚻♅ 2:01
☽⚺♀ 11:46
♀⋕⚷ 12:07
☽□♂ 12:59
☽△♄ 14:18
☉∠♄ 14:31
☽□☿ 16:46
☽∥♃ 18:20
☉∥♆ 21:27
☽⚹♃ 23:50

28 Th
☽⚼♅ 4:44
☽⋕♄ 8:08
☽⚹⚳ 10:04
♂⚺♄ 16:05
☉⚹☽ 19:22
☽□⚷ 22:58
♀□♄ 23:47

29 F
☽⚹♆ 0:01
☽⋕⚷ 1:14
☽☌♇ 1:39
☽∥♀ 3:39
☽△♅ 7:59
☽⋕☿ 11:39
☽∠⚳ 14:13
♀⚹♂ 16:29
☽□♄ 21:05
☽⚹♂ 22:37
☽☌♀ 22:46

30 Sa
☉∠☽ 1:06
☽⋕♂ 3:00
☽∠♆ 3:38
☿⚻♃ 4:05
☽□♃ 6:20
☽⚹☿ 6:37
☽∥⚳ 18:39
☽⚺⚳ 18:54
☿⋕♀ 22:04
☉⚺⚷ 22:17

31 Su
☉⋕☽ 1:48
☽∠♂ 4:19
☽⚹⚷ 6:47
☉⚺☽ 7:27
☽⋕♆ 7:37
☽⚺♆ 7:46
☽⚺♇ 9:23
☉☌♆ 11:40
☽∠☿ 14:12
☽□♅ 16:01

April 2030

LONGITUDE

Day	Sid.Time	☉	☽	☽ 12 hour	Mean ☊	True ☊	☿	♀	♂	⚳	♃	♄	⚷	♅	♆	♇
	h m s	° ' "	° ' "	° ' "	° '	° '	° '	° '	° '	° '	° '	° '	° '	° '	° '	° '
1 M	12 37 37	11♈18 46	19♓21 46	25♓38 21	20♐02.5	18♐54.7	29♈44.5	25♒17.7	24♈35.2	4♈25.6	27♏06.6	22♉26.0	10♉19.0	15♊10.1	10♈49.5	11♒40.0
2 Tu	12 41 33	12 18 00	1♈52 11	8♈03 18	19 59.3	18R 42.4	0♉59.8	26 21.6	25 20.3	4 49.3	27R 03.1	22 32.5	10 22.4	15 12.1	10 51.7	11 41.0
3 W	12 45 30	13 17 12	14 11 46	20 17 39	19 56.1	18 30.2	2 09.2	27 25.8	26 05.3	5 12.9	26 59.5	22 39.1	10 26.0	15 14.1	10 54.0	11 42.1
4 Th	12 49 27	14 16 23	26 21 05	2♉22 12	19 52.9	18 19.2	3 12.6	28 30.2	26 50.3	5 36.5	26 55.7	22 45.7	10 29.5	15 16.2	10 56.3	11 43.1
5 F	12 53 23	15 15 31	8♉21 13	14 18 22	19 49.7	18 10.3	4 09.7	29 34.8	27 35.2	6 00.1	26 51.7	22 52.4	10 33.1	15 18.3	10 58.5	11 44.2
6 Sa	12 57 20	16 14 37	20 13 58	26 08 21	19 46.6	18 03.9	5 00.4	0♓39.6	28 20.1	6 23.7	26 47.6	22 59.1	10 36.7	15 20.5	11 00.8	11 45.2
7 Su	13 01 16	17 13 41	2♊01 56	7♊55 10	19 43.4	18 00.1	5 44.4	1 44.7	29 05.0	6 47.3	26 43.3	23 05.9	10 40.3	15 22.7	11 03.1	11 46.1
8 M	13 05 13	18 12 43	13 48 34	19 42 40	19 40.2	17D 58.6	6 21.8	2 49.9	29 49.8	7 10.9	26 38.8	23 12.7	10 43.9	15 24.9	11 05.3	11 47.1
9 Tu	13 09 09	19 11 43	25 38 05	1♋35 24	19 37.0	17 58.8	6 52.5	3 55.3	0♉34.6	7 34.4	26 34.2	23 19.6	10 47.5	15 27.2	11 07.6	11 48.0
10 W	13 13 06	20 10 40	7♋35 17	13 38 24	19 33.9	17 59.7	7 16.4	5 00.9	1 19.3	7 57.9	26 29.5	23 26.5	10 51.2	15 29.5	11 09.8	11 48.9
11 Th	13 17 02	21 09 35	19 45 25	25 57 00	19 30.7	18R 00.3	7 33.5	6 06.6	2 03.9	8 21.4	26 24.5	23 33.4	10 54.9	15 31.9	11 12.1	11 49.8
12 F	13 20 59	22 08 28	2♌13 45	8♌36 17	19 27.5	17 59.7	7 44.0	7 12.5	2 48.5	8 44.9	26 19.5	23 40.4	10 58.6	15 34.3	11 14.3	11 50.6
13 Sa	13 24 56	23 07 18	15 05 08	21 40 42	19 24.3	17 57.3	7R 47.9	8 18.6	3 33.1	9 08.4	26 14.3	23 47.5	11 02.3	15 36.7	11 16.6	11 51.4
14 Su	13 28 52	24 06 07	28 23 21	5♍13 14	19 21.1	17 52.9	7 45.5	9 24.9	4 17.6	9 31.8	26 08.9	23 54.5	11 06.0	15 39.2	11 18.8	11 52.2
15 M	13 32 49	25 04 53	12♍10 22	19 14 37	19 18.0	17 46.5	7 36.8	10 31.3	5 02.0	9 55.3	26 03.4	24 01.7	11 09.8	15 41.7	11 21.0	11 53.0
16 Tu	13 36 45	26 03 36	26 25 36	3♎42 46	19 14.8	17 38.8	7 22.4	11 37.9	5 46.4	10 18.7	25 57.8	24 08.8	11 13.5	15 44.2	11 23.2	11 53.7
17 W	13 40 42	27 02 18	11♎05 20	18 32 23	19 11.6	17 30.8	7 02.6	12 44.6	6 30.7	10 42.1	25 52.0	24 16.0	11 17.3	15 46.8	11 25.4	11 54.4
18 Th	13 44 38	28 00 57	26 02 50	3♏35 30	19 08.4	17 23.4	6 37.8	13 51.4	7 15.0	11 05.4	25 46.1	24 23.2	11 21.1	15 49.4	11 27.6	11 55.1
19 F	13 48 35	28 59 35	11♏09 09	18 42 33	19 05.3	17 17.5	6 08.6	14 58.4	7 59.3	11 28.8	25 40.1	24 30.5	11 24.9	15 52.0	11 29.8	11 55.8
20 Sa	13 52 31	29 58 11	26 14 33	3♐44 03	19 02.1	17 13.7	5 35.6	16 05.6	8 43.5	11 52.1	25 34.0	24 37.7	11 28.7	15 54.7	11 32.0	11 56.4
21 Su	13 56 28	0♉56 45	11♐10 08	18 32 01	18 58.9	17D 12.1	4 59.4	17 12.9	9 27.6	12 15.4	25 27.8	24 45.1	11 32.5	15 57.4	11 34.2	11 57.0
22 M	14 00 25	1 55 17	25 49 06	3♑00 56	18 55.7	17 12.2	4 20.8	18 20.3	10 11.7	12 38.6	25 21.4	24 52.4	11 36.3	16 00.2	11 36.4	11 57.6
23 Tu	14 04 21	2 53 48	10♑07 16	17 07 57	18 52.5	17 13.3	3 40.5	19 27.9	10 55.7	13 01.9	25 14.9	24 59.8	11 40.2	16 03.0	11 38.5	11 58.2
24 W	14 08 18	3 52 18	24 03 00	0♒52 30	18 49.4	17R 14.4	2 59.3	20 35.5	11 39.7	13 25.1	25 08.4	25 07.2	11 44.0	16 05.8	11 40.7	11 58.7
25 Th	14 12 14	4 50 45	7♒36 39	14 15 41	18 46.2	17 14.8	2 18.0	21 43.3	12 23.7	13 48.3	25 01.7	25 14.6	11 47.9	16 08.6	11 42.8	11 59.2
26 F	14 16 11	5 49 11	20 49 54	27 19 34	18 43.0	17 13.7	1 37.2	22 51.3	13 07.6	14 11.4	24 54.9	25 22.1	11 51.7	16 11.5	11 44.9	11 59.7
27 Sa	14 20 07	6 47 35	3♓45 03	10♓06 37	18 39.8	17 10.7	0 57.8	23 59.3	13 51.4	14 34.6	24 48.0	25 29.6	11 55.6	16 14.4	11 47.0	12 00.2
28 Su	14 24 04	7 45 58	16 24 36	22 39 17	18 36.7	17 06.1	0 20.4	25 07.4	14 35.2	14 57.7	24 41.1	25 37.1	11 59.4	16 17.3	11 49.1	12 00.6
29 M	14 28 00	8 44 19	28 50 57	4♈59 51	18 33.5	17 00.1	29♈45.5	26 15.7	15 19.0	15 20.7	24 34.1	25 44.6	12 03.3	16 20.3	11 51.2	12 01.0
30 Tu	14 31 57	9♉42 39	11♈06 14	17 10 18	18♐30.3	16♐53.4	29♈13.7	27♓24.0	16♉02.7	15♈43.8	24♏26.9	25♉52.2	12♉07.2	16♊23.3	11♈53.3	12♒01.3

1st of Month

Julian Day # 2462592.5
Obliquity 23°26'06"
SVP 4♓49'57"
GC 27♐15.7
Eris 26♈02.3

Day	⚴		Day	⚵		Day	⚶
1	29♒39.4		1	9♑25.8		1	6♈37.6
6	1♓07.8		6	10 08.3		6	8 59.5
11	2 33.7		11	10 44.6		11	11 20.7
16	3 56.8		16	11 14.0		16	13 41.0
21	5 17.0		21	11 36.4		21	16 00.5
26	6 34.1		26	11 51.3		26	18 19.1

DECLINATION and LATITUDE

Day	☉ Decl	☽ Decl	☽ Lat	☽ 12h Decl	☿ Decl	☿ Lat	♀ Decl	♀ Lat	♂ Decl	♂ Lat	⚳ Decl	⚳ Lat	♃ Decl	♃ Lat	♄ Decl	♄ Lat
1 M	4N28	0N26	5N02	2N52	13N21	2N06	12S22	0N46	9N14	0S18	5S23	7S47	18S22	1N11	16N30	1S56
2 Tu	4 52	5 15	4 54	7 34	13 57	2 17	12 05	0 41	9 31	0 18	5 13	7 47	18 21	1 11	16 32	1 56
3 W	5 15	9 47	4 33	11 54	14 30	2 26	11 48	0 35	9 48	0 17	5 04	7 46	18 20	1 11	16 34	1 56
4 Th	5 38	13 53	3 59	15 42	15 00	2 35	11 31	0 30	10 05	0 16	4 54	7 46	18 19	1 11	16 35	1 56
5 F	6 00	17 22	3 15	18 50	15 27	2 43	11 14	0 25	10 22	0 16	4 45	7 46	18 18	1 11	16 37	1 56
6 Sa	6 23	20 05	2 23	21 08	15 51	2 49	10 56	0 20	10 39	0 15	4 36	7 46	18 17	1 11	16 39	1 55
7 Su	6 46	21 56	1 24	22 30	16 11	2 55	10 37	0 15	10 55	0 14	4 26	7 46	18 16	1 11	16 41	1 55
8 M	7 08	22 49	0 22	22 53	16 28	3 00	10 19	0 10	11 12	0 14	4 17	7 46	18 15	1 11	16 43	1 55
9 Tu	7 31	22 41	0S41	22 13	16 42	3 04	9 60	0 05	11 28	0 13	4 08	7 46	18 14	1 11	16 45	1 55
10 W	7 53	21 30	1 43	20 32	16 52	3 06	9 40	0S00	11 44	0 12	3 58	7 46	18 12	1 12	16 47	1 55
11 Th	8 15	19 18	2 42	17 51	16 59	3 07	9 21	0 05	12 00	0 12	3 49	7 46	18 11	1 12	16 48	1 55
12 F	8 37	16 10	3 35	14 17	17 02	3 07	9 01	0 09	12 16	0 11	3 40	7 46	18 10	1 12	16 50	1 55
13 Sa	8 59	12 11	4 18	9 55	17 02	3 06	8 40	0 14	12 32	0 10	3 31	7 46	18 09	1 12	16 52	1 54
14 Su	9 21	7 30	4 50	4 57	16 58	3 03	8 19	0 19	12 48	0 10	3 22	7 46	18 07	1 12	16 54	1 54
15 M	9 42	2 17	5 05	0S27	16 51	2 58	7 58	0 23	13 03	0 09	3 13	7 46	18 06	1 12	16 56	1 54
16 Tu	10 04	3S13	5 03	5 59	16 41	2 52	7 37	0 27	13 19	0 08	3 03	7 46	18 05	1 12	16 58	1 54
17 W	10 25	8 42	4 42	11 19	16 27	2 45	7 16	0 31	13 34	0 08	2 54	7 46	18 03	1 12	16 60	1 54
18 Th	10 46	13 47	4 00	16 03	16 11	2 36	6 54	0 36	13 49	0 07	2 45	7 46	18 02	1 12	17 02	1 54
19 F	11 07	18 03	3 02	19 45	15 51	2 25	6 32	0 40	14 04	0 07	2 36	7 46	18 00	1 12	17 03	1 54
20 Sa	11 28	21 06	1 51	22 05	15 29	2 14	6 09	0 43	14 19	0 06	2 27	7 46	17 59	1 12	17 05	1 53
21 Su	11 48	22 39	0 33	22 49	15 05	2 01	5 46	0 47	14 34	0 05	2 18	7 46	17 57	1 12	17 07	1 53
22 M	12 08	22 36	0N47	21 59	14 39	1 47	5 24	0 51	14 48	0 05	2 10	7 46	17 56	1 12	17 09	1 53
23 Tu	12 28	21 02	2 01	19 46	14 11	1 32	5 00	0 55	15 02	0 04	2 01	7 46	17 54	1 12	17 11	1 53
24 W	12 48	18 14	3 06	16 28	13 42	1 16	4 37	0 58	15 17	0 03	1 52	7 46	17 53	1 12	17 13	1 53
25 Th	13 08	14 30	3 59	12 23	13 13	1 00	4 14	1 02	15 31	0 03	1 43	7 46	17 51	1 12	17 15	1 53
26 F	13 28	10 09	4 38	7 49	12 43	0 43	3 50	1 05	15 45	0 02	1 34	7 46	17 50	1 12	17 17	1 53
27 Sa	13 47	5 26	5 02	3 01	12 13	0 26	3 26	1 08	15 58	0 01	1 26	7 46	17 48	1 12	17 19	1 53
28 Su	14 06	0 36	5 10	1N49	11 44	0 09	3 02	1 11	16 12	0 01	1 17	7 46	17 46	1 12	17 20	1 52
29 M	14 25	4N11	5 04	6 30	11 16	0S08	2 37	1 14	16 26	0N00	1 08	7 47	17 45	1 12	17 22	1 52
30 Tu	14N43	8N44	4N43	10N52	10N49	0S25	2S13	1S17	16N39	0N01	0S60	7S47	17S43	1N12	17N24	1S52

Day	⚷ Decl	⚷ Lat	♅ Decl	♅ Lat	♆ Decl	♆ Lat	♇ Decl	♇ Lat
1	13N35	1S24	22N40	0N03	2N56	1S28	22S52	5S49
6	13 40	1 24	22 41	0 03	3 01	1 28	22 52	5 51
11	13 45	1 25	22 42	0 03	3 05	1 28	22 52	5 52
16	13 51	1 25	22 43	0 03	3 09	1 28	22 52	5 53
21	13 57	1 25	22 45	0 03	3 14	1 28	22 52	5 54
26	14 02	1 25	22 46	0 03	3 18	1 28	22 52	5 55

Day	⚴ Decl	⚴ Lat	⚵ Decl	⚵ Lat	⚶ Decl	⚶ Lat	Eris Decl	Eris Lat
1	5N52	18N36	9S22	13N46	1S57	4S60	1N05	9S36
6	6 19	18 33	8 59	14 06	1 03	5 01	1 07	9 36
11	6 46	18 31	8 37	14 26	0 10	5 03	1 08	9 36
16	7 12	18 30	8 14	14 47	0N43	5 05	1 09	9 36
21	7 39	18 29	7 51	15 08	1 34	5 07	1 11	9 36
26	8 06	18 29	7 28	15 30	2 25	5 09	1 12	9 35

Moon Phenomena

Max/0 Decl

dy	hr mn	
8	8:42	22N53
15	10:02	0 S
21	11:05	22S49
28	2:57	0 N

Perigee/Apogee

dy	hr m		kilometers
6	18:47	a	405655
19	3:47	p	358708

Max/0 Lat

dy	hr mn	
8	8:28	0 S
15	9:26	5S07
21	9:49	0 N
28	1:18	5N10

PH	dy	hr mn	
●	2	22:04	13♈12
☽	11	2:58	21♋17
○	18	3:21	28♎09
☾	24	18:40	4♒38

Void of Course Moon

Last Aspect			☽ Ingress		
1 14:45	♃	△	♈	1	20:23
4 4:42	♀	⚹	♉	4	7:16
6 13:15	♃	☍	♊	6	19:52
8 9:46	☉	⚹	♋	9	8:48
11 12:48	♃	△	♌	11	19:46
13 20:03	♃	□	♍	14	2:51
15 23:14	♃	⚹	♎	16	5:54
18 3:21	☉	☍	♏	18	6:18
19 22:56	♃	☌	♐	20	6:01
21 10:40	♀	□	♑	22	6:57
24 1:53	♃	⚹	♒	24	10:27
26 8:27	♄	□	♓	26	16:59
28 18:28	♀	☌	♈	29	2:14

DAILY ASPECTARIAN

1 M: ☿ ♉ 4:48; ☽⚹♄ 5:55; ☿∠♅ 8:11; ☉⚹♇ 8:45; ☿∥⚷ 9:14; ☽⚺♂ 10:37; ☽∠⚷ 11:26; ♀∠♆ 12:23; ☽⚺♀ 12:24; ☽∥♆ 12:26; ☽∠♇ 14:00; ☽△♃ 14:45; ☉⚼♃ 18:19; ☉∥☽ 21:52; ☽⚺☿ 22:08; ☽#⚳ 23:53

2 Tu: ⚴ ♓ 3:39; ☽☌⚳ 5:54; ☽∠♄ 11:06; ♀□♃ 14:42; ☉#⚳ 16:01; ☽⚺⚷ 16:36; ☽☌♆ 17:32; ☽⚹♇ 19:07; ☽⚼♃ 19:42; ☽∠♀ 20:13; ☉☌☽ 22:04

3 W: ☽∥♂ 0:07; ☽⚹♅ 2:03; ☽#♀ 10:43; ☽⚺♄ 16:49; ☽∥⚷ 22:26

4 Th: ☽☌♂ 1:02; ☽⚻♃ 1:08; ♂⚻♃ 2:39; ☽⚹♀ 4:42; ☽∠♅ 7:50; ☽∥☿ 8:20; ☽☌☿ 14:53; ☽∥♄ 18:25; ☽⚺⚳ 19:07

5 F: ☉⚹♅ 1:11; ☽☌⚷ 4:27; ☽⚺♆ 5:18; ☽□♇ 6:49; ☽#♃ 7:26; ♀ ♓ 9:20; ☽⚺♅ 14:04; ☉⚺☽ 15:11

6 Sa: ☽∠⚳ 2:26; ☽☌♄ 5:39; ♀#♂ 11:44; ☽∠♆ 11:47; ☽☍♃ 13:15; ☽⚺♂ 17:35; ☽□♀ 23:21

7 Su: ☉∠☽ 0:26; ☽⚺☿ 8:01; ☽⚹⚳ 10:02; ☽∥♅ 17:35; ☽⚺⚷ 17:42; ☽⚹♆ 18:27; ☽△♇ 19:52

8 M: ☽∠♂ 2:13; ☽#♇ 3:10; ☽☌♅ 3:17; ♂ ♉ 5:28; ☊ D 8:27; ☉⚹☽ 9:46; ☽#♇ 14:13; ☽∠☿ 16:04; ☽⚺♄ 19:17; ♂∠♅ 19:50; ☽∥♅ 23:36

9 Tu: ☽∠⚷ 0:19; ☽⚻♃ 1:53; ☽⚼♇ 2:21; ☿∥♄ 6:44; ☽⚹♂ 10:38; ☽△♀ 18:21; ☽⚹☿ 23:21

10 W: ☽□⚳ 0:47; ☽∠♄ 1:43; ☽⚹⚷ 6:31; ☽□♆ 7:08; ☽⚼♃ 7:42; ☽⚻♇ 8:24; ☽⚺♅ 15:42

11 Th: ☽⚼♀ 2:54; ☊ R 2:54; ☉□☽ 2:58; ☽⚹♄ 7:27; ☽#♃ 9:27; ☉∠♀ 10:14; ☽△♃ 12:48; ⚳∠♄ 17:27; ☽∥☿ 18:04; ☽∥♄ 19:27; ☽∠♅ 20:50

12 F: ☽□♂ 1:10; ☽⚻♀ 10:16; ☽□☿ 10:27; ☿⚹♀ 12:28; ☽△⚳ 12:39; ☉#♀ 13:16; ☽∥⚷ 14:55; ☽□⚷ 16:30; ♃⚼♆ 16:34; ☽△♆ 16:57; ☽☍♇ 18:02; ☽∥♂ 22:12

13 Sa: ☽⚹♅ 0:58; ☿ R 2:35; ☉∥☽ 15:33; ☉△☽ 15:45; ☽□♄ 15:56; ☽⚼⚳ 16:55; ☉⚺♄ 18:38; ☽#♀ 19:41; ☽□♃ 20:03; ☽⚼♆ 20:18

14 Su: ♀⚺⚳ 3:54; ☽△♂ 10:58; ☿∥♄ 12:18; ☽△☿ 16:15; ☽#⚳ 19:45; ☽⚻⚳ 20:01; ☉⚼☽ 20:08; ☽∥♆ 20:11; ☽☍♀ 20:55; ☽△⚷ 22:16; ☽⚻♆ 22:35; ☽⚻♇ 23:30

15 M: ☽□♅ 6:01; ⚳#♆ 9:45; ☽⚼♂ 14:03; ♀⚹⚷ 14:43; ☽⚼☿ 17:23; ♀⚺♆ 18:33; ☽△♄ 20:11; ☉⚻♃ 21:50; ☽⚹♃ 23:14; ☽∥⚳ 23:19; ☉⚻☽ 23:21; ☽⚼⚷ 23:40; ☽#♆ 23:43

16 Tu: ☽⚼♇ 0:47; ♀⚺♇ 5:46; ☽⚻♂ 16:11; ☽⚻☿ 17:35; ☽∥♀ 17:59; ☽⚼♄ 21:01; ☽☍⚳ 23:21; ☽∠♃ 23:39

17 W: ☽⚻⚷ 0:19; ☽☍♆ 0:33; ☽△♇ 1:19; ☽⚻♀ 2:53; ☽△♅ 7:35; ⚳⚼♃ 8:11; ☉#☽ 8:21; ☿☌♂ 11:16; ☽⚻♄ 21:20; ☽⚺♃ 23:34

18 Th: ☽#♂ 0:09; ☽#⚷ 0:30; ☉☍☽ 3:21; ☽⚼♀ 4:50; ♂∥⚷ 7:14; ☽⚼♅ 7:37; ☽#☿ 11:51; ☽☍☿ 16:19; ☽#♄ 17:47; ☽☍♂ 18:43; ⚳⚺⚷ 19:13; ☽∥♃ 23:42

19 F: ☽☍⚷ 0:25; ☽⚻⚳ 0:32; ☽⚻♆ 0:33; ⚳☌♆ 1:13; ☽□♇ 1:14; ☽△♀ 6:33; ☽⚻♅ 7:30; ♀□♅ 19:58; ☽☍♄ 21:24; ☽☌♃ 22:56

20 Sa: ☽⚼♆ 0:28; ☉ ♉ 0:45; ☽⚼⚳ 1:02; ⚳⚹♇ 4:36; ☉⚻☽ 6:23; ☽⚻☿ 14:25; ☽⚻♂ 21:05

21 Su: ☉∠♅ 0:18; ☽⚻⚷ 0:36; ☽△♆ 0:39; ☽⚹♇ 1:16; ☽△⚳ 1:49; ☽#♅ 3:53; ☽☍♅ 7:49; ☉⚼☽ 8:19; ☊ D 9:47; ☽□♀ 10:40; ☽⚼☿ 13:47; ☽#♅ 18:08; ☿∥♂ 18:33; ☽⚻♄ 22:25; ☽⚼♂ 22:55; ☽⚺♃ 23:14

22 M: ♆⚺⚷ 0:35; ☽⚼⚷ 1:19; ☽∠♇ 1:54; ☉△☽ 10:55; ☿∠♀ 13:30; ☽△☿ 13:36; ☽⚼♄ 23:47

23 Tu: ☽∠♃ 0:13; ☽△♂ 1:27; ☽□♆ 2:36; ☽△⚷ 2:39; ☽⚺♇ 3:09; ☽□⚳ 5:06; ☿∥⚷ 9:52; ☽⚻♅ 10:10; ☉☌☿ 11:16; ☽⚹♀ 17:27

24 W: ♂⚺♆ 0:32; ☽△♄ 1:53; ☽⚹♃ 1:53; ♃☍♄ 1:58; ♂☌⚷ 2:33; ☽∥♃ 2:34; ☽#♄ 7:03; ♂□♇ 10:29; ☽⚼♅ 12:26; ☽□☿ 14:59; ☽#♂ 18:19; ☉□☽ 18:40; ☊ R 18:55; ☽∠♀ 22:16

25 Th: ☉∥☿ 2:12; ☽#⚷ 2:50; ☉#☽ 7:18; ☽⚹♆ 7:24; ☽□⚷ 7:34; ☽☌♇ 7:53; ☽#☿ 8:25; ☽□♂ 9:07; ☽⚹⚳ 11:30; ☽△♅ 15:29

26 F: ☽⚺♀ 4:05; ☽□♃ 7:28; ☽□♄ 8:27; ☽∠♆ 10:57; ☿∠♅ 14:29; ☽∠⚳ 15:57; ☽⚹☿ 19:02

27 Sa: ☉⚹☽ 6:12; ♀#♆ 7:08; ☽#♆ 10:33; ☽∥♀ 10:52; ☽⚺♆ 15:13; ☽⚹⚷ 15:32; ♀△♃ 15:35; ☽⚺♇ 15:36; ☽⚹♂ 20:18; ☽∥⚳ 20:30; ☽⚺⚳ 21:09; ☉∥⚷ 21:59; ☽∠☿ 22:03; ☽□♅ 23:46

28 Su: ♇□⚷ 7:53; ☽#⚳ 9:04; ♀⚹♄ 11:44; ☉∠☽ 13:15; ☿R♈ 13:46; ☽△♃ 15:46; ☽#♀ 16:42; ☽⚹♄ 17:55; ☽☌♀ 18:28; ☽∥♆ 19:39; ☽∠♇ 20:26; ☽∠⚷ 20:30

29 M: ☽⚺☿ 1:41; ♂⚺⚳ 2:03; ☽∠♂ 3:02; ♀∠♇ 16:00; ♀∠⚷ 17:44; ☽⚼♃ 20:46; ☉⚺☽ 21:01; ☽∠♄ 23:32

30 Tu: ☽☌♆ 1:33; ☽⚹♇ 1:49; ☽⚺⚷ 2:01; ☽☌⚳ 9:26; ☽⚺♂ 10:23; ☽⚹♅ 10:29; ☽∥☿ 10:34; ♂⚺♅ 12:10

LONGITUDE

May 2030

Day	Sid.Time	☉	☽	☽ 12 hour	Mean☊	True☊	☿	♀	♂	⚳	♃	♄	⚷	♅	♆	♇
	h m s	° ′ ″	° ′ ″	° ′ ″	° ′	° ′	° ′	° ′	° ′	° ′	° ′	° ′	° ′	° ′	° ′	° ′
1 W	14 35 53	10♉40 57	23♈12 17	29♈12 23	18♐27.1	16♐46.7	28♈45.4	28♓32.5	16♉46.3	16♈06.8	24♏19.8	25♉59.8	12♉11.1	16♊26.3	11♈55.3	12♒01.7
2 Th	14 39 50	11 39 13	5♉10 48	11♉07 46	18 23.9	16R 40.7	28R 21.1	29 41.0	17 29.9	16 29.7	24R 12.5	26 07.4	12 14.9	16 29.3	11 57.4	12 02.0
3 F	14 43 47	12 37 27	17 03 30	22 58 13	18 20.8	16 35.9	28 01.0	0♈49.6	18 13.5	16 52.7	24 05.2	26 15.0	12 18.8	16 32.4	11 59.4	12 02.3
4 Sa	14 47 43	13 35 40	28 52 13	4♊45 44	18 17.6	16 32.8	27 45.3	1 58.4	18 57.0	17 15.6	23 57.8	26 22.6	12 22.7	16 35.5	12 01.4	12 02.5
5 Su	14 51 40	14 33 51	10♊39 07	16 32 42	18 14.4	16D 31.3	27 34.3	3 07.2	19 40.4	17 38.4	23 50.4	26 30.3	12 26.6	16 38.6	12 03.4	12 02.8
6 M	14 55 36	15 32 00	22 26 52	28 22 02	18 11.2	16 31.3	27D 27.9	4 16.1	20 23.8	18 01.2	23 42.9	26 38.0	12 30.5	16 41.7	12 05.4	12 03.0
7 Tu	14 59 33	16 30 08	4♋18 39	10♋17 11	18 08.1	16 32.4	27 26.2	5 25.0	21 07.1	18 24.0	23 35.4	26 45.7	12 34.3	16 44.9	12 07.3	12 03.2
8 W	15 03 29	17 28 13	16 18 09	22 22 05	18 04.9	16 34.0	27 29.3	6 34.1	21 50.4	18 46.7	23 27.9	26 53.3	12 38.2	16 48.1	12 09.3	12 03.3
9 Th	15 07 26	18 26 17	28 29 32	4♌41 03	18 01.7	16 35.7	27 37.2	7 43.2	22 33.7	19 09.4	23 20.3	27 01.1	12 42.1	16 51.3	12 11.2	12 03.4
10 F	15 11 23	19 24 18	10♌57 13	17 18 34	17 58.5	16R 36.8	27 49.6	8 52.4	23 16.8	19 32.1	23 12.7	27 08.8	12 45.9	16 54.5	12 13.1	12 03.5
11 Sa	15 15 19	20 22 18	23 45 36	0♍18 46	17 55.4	16 37.1	28 06.6	10 01.7	24 00.0	19 54.7	23 05.1	27 16.5	12 49.8	16 57.8	12 15.0	12 03.6
12 Su	15 19 16	21 20 16	6♍58 28	13 45 00	17 52.2	16 36.2	28 28.0	11 11.0	24 43.0	20 17.2	22 57.5	27 24.2	12 53.6	17 01.0	12 16.9	12R 03.6
13 M	15 23 12	22 18 12	20 38 31	27 39 04	17 49.0	16 34.3	28 53.8	12 20.4	25 26.1	20 39.7	22 49.8	27 32.0	12 57.5	17 04.3	12 18.7	12 03.7
14 Tu	15 27 09	23 16 06	4♎46 30	12♎00 31	17 45.8	16 31.6	29 23.7	13 29.9	26 09.0	21 02.2	22 42.2	27 39.7	13 01.3	17 07.6	12 20.5	12 03.6
15 W	15 31 05	24 13 59	19 20 35	26 46 03	17 42.6	16 28.6	29 57.7	14 39.5	26 52.0	21 24.6	22 34.5	27 47.5	13 05.2	17 10.9	12 22.4	12 03.6
16 Th	15 35 02	25 11 50	4♏16 00	11♏49 27	17 39.5	16 25.8	0♉35.7	15 49.1	27 34.8	21 47.0	22 26.9	27 55.2	13 09.0	17 14.3	12 24.1	12 03.5
17 F	15 38 58	26 09 39	19 25 15	27 02 09	17 36.3	16 23.6	1 17.4	16 58.8	28 17.6	22 09.3	22 19.3	28 03.0	13 12.8	17 17.6	12 25.9	12 03.4
18 Sa	15 42 55	27 07 27	4♐38 56	12♐14 20	17 33.1	16D 22.4	2 02.8	18 08.5	29 00.4	22 31.6	22 11.7	28 10.8	13 16.6	17 21.0	12 27.7	12 03.3
19 Su	15 46 52	28 05 13	19 47 13	27 16 32	17 29.9	16 22.1	2 51.8	19 18.4	29 43.1	22 53.8	22 04.1	28 18.5	13 20.4	17 24.4	12 29.4	12 03.2
20 M	15 50 48	29 02 59	4♑41 21	12♑00 55	17 26.8	16 22.7	3 44.2	20 28.2	0♊25.8	23 16.0	21 56.5	28 26.3	13 24.2	17 27.8	12 31.1	12 03.0
21 Tu	15 54 45	0♊00 43	19 14 40	26 22 13	17 23.6	16 23.8	4 39.9	21 38.2	1 08.4	23 38.1	21 49.0	28 34.1	13 27.9	17 31.2	12 32.8	12 02.8
22 W	15 58 41	0 58 26	3♒23 18	10♒17 51	17 20.4	16 24.9	5 38.9	22 48.2	1 51.0	24 00.1	21 41.5	28 41.8	13 31.7	17 34.6	12 34.4	12 02.6
23 Th	16 02 38	1 56 07	17 05 55	23 47 40	17 17.2	16 25.9	6 41.0	23 58.3	2 33.5	24 22.1	21 34.1	28 49.6	13 35.4	17 38.1	12 36.1	12 02.3
24 F	16 06 34	2 53 48	0♓23 21	6♓53 18	17 14.1	16R 26.3	7 46.1	25 08.4	3 16.0	24 44.1	21 26.7	28 57.4	13 39.2	17 41.5	12 37.7	12 02.1
25 Sa	16 10 31	3 51 28	13 17 55	19 37 37	17 10.9	16 26.1	8 54.2	26 18.6	3 58.4	25 06.0	21 19.3	29 05.1	13 42.9	17 45.0	12 39.3	12 01.8
26 Su	16 14 27	4 49 07	25 52 51	2♈04 04	17 07.7	16 25.4	10 05.1	27 28.9	4 40.7	25 27.8	21 12.1	29 12.9	13 46.6	17 48.5	12 40.9	12 01.4
27 M	16 18 24	5 46 44	8♈11 43	14 16 15	17 04.5	16 24.3	11 18.9	28 39.2	5 23.1	25 49.6	21 04.8	29 20.6	13 50.2	17 52.0	12 42.4	12 01.1
28 Tu	16 22 21	6 44 21	20 18 06	26 17 41	17 01.3	16 22.9	12 35.5	29 49.6	6 05.3	26 11.3	20 57.7	29 28.3	13 53.9	17 55.5	12 43.9	12 00.7
29 W	16 26 17	7 41 57	2♉15 24	8♉11 36	16 58.2	16 21.6	13 54.8	1♉00.0	6 47.6	26 33.0	20 50.6	29 36.1	13 57.5	17 59.0	12 45.4	12 00.3
30 Th	16 30 14	8 39 32	14 06 40	20 00 55	16 55.0	16 20.6	15 16.7	2 10.4	7 29.7	26 54.6	20 43.6	29 43.8	14 01.2	18 02.5	12 46.9	11 59.8
31 F	16 34 10	9♊37 06	25 54 41	1♊48 15	16♐51.8	16♐19.8	16♉41.3	3♉20.9	8♊11.9	27♈16.1	20♏36.6	29♉51.5	14♉04.8	18♊06.0	12♈48.3	11♒59.4

1st of Month

Julian Day #
2462622.5
Obliquity
23°26′06″
SVP 4♓49′54″
GC 27♐15.8
Eris 26♈21.9

Day	⚴
1	7♓47.8
6	8 57.7
11	10 03.7
16	11 05.3
21	12 02.3
26	12 54.3
31	13 41.0

Day	⚵
1	11♑58.2
6	11 56.8R
11	11 47.0R
16	11 28.7R
21	11 01.8R
26	10 26.7R
31	9 43.6R

Day	⚶
1	20♈36.7
6	22 53.2
11	25 08.6
16	27 22.6
21	29 35.4
26	1♉46.8
31	3 56.7

DECLINATION and LATITUDE

Day	☉ Decl	☽ Decl	☽ Lat	☽ 12h Decl	☿ Decl	☿ Lat	♀ Decl	♀ Lat	♂ Decl	♂ Lat	⚳ Decl	⚳ Lat	♃ Decl	♃ Lat	♄ Decl	♄ Lat
1 W	15N02	12N53	4N10	14N46	10N23	0S41	1S48	1S20	16N52	0N01	0S51	7S47	17S41	1N12	17N26	1S52
2 Th	15 20	16 29	3 27	18 02	9 60	0 57	1 24	1 23	17 05	0 02	0 43	7 47	17 39	1 12	17 28	1 52
3 F	15 37	19 23	2 34	20 32	9 38	1 13	0 59	1 25	17 18	0 03	0 34	7 47	17 38	1 12	17 30	1 52
4 Sa	15 55	21 27	1 35	22 08	9 19	1 28	0 34	1 28	17 30	0 03	0 26	7 48	17 36	1 12	17 32	1 52
5 Su	16 12	22 34	0 32	22 45	9 02	1 42	0 09	1 30	17 43	0 04	0 17	7 48	17 34	1 12	17 33	1 52
6 M	16 29	22 41	0S33	22 21	8 47	1 55	0N17	1 33	17 55	0 05	0 09	7 48	17 32	1 12	17 35	1 52
7 Tu	16 46	21 46	1 36	20 56	8 35	2 07	0 42	1 35	18 07	0 05	0 01	7 48	17 30	1 12	17 37	1 52
8 W	17 03	19 51	2 36	18 33	8 25	2 18	1 07	1 37	18 19	0 06	0N08	7 48	17 29	1 12	17 39	1 52
9 Th	17 19	17 01	3 31	15 17	8 18	2 29	1 33	1 39	18 31	0 06	0 16	7 49	17 27	1 12	17 41	1 51
10 F	17 35	13 22	4 16	11 17	8 14	2 38	1 58	1 41	18 42	0 07	0 24	7 49	17 25	1 12	17 43	1 51
11 Sa	17 50	9 02	4 50	6 38	8 12	2 47	2 24	1 43	18 54	0 08	0 32	7 49	17 23	1 12	17 44	1 51
12 Su	18 06	4 08	5 11	1 33	8 12	2 55	2 49	1 45	19 05	0 08	0 40	7 50	17 21	1 12	17 46	1 51
13 M	18 21	1S06	5 14	3S48	8 15	3 02	3 15	1 46	19 16	0 09	0 48	7 50	17 19	1 12	17 48	1 51
14 Tu	18 35	6 28	4 59	9 06	8 20	3 07	3 40	1 48	19 27	0 10	0 56	7 50	17 18	1 11	17 50	1 51
15 W	18 50	11 39	4 25	14 03	8 27	3 12	4 06	1 49	19 37	0 10	1 04	7 50	17 16	1 11	17 52	1 51
16 Th	19 04	16 16	3 32	18 13	8 36	3 16	4 31	1 51	19 48	0 11	1 12	7 51	17 14	1 11	17 53	1 51
17 F	19 17	19 53	2 23	21 12	8 48	3 20	4 57	1 52	19 58	0 11	1 20	7 51	17 12	1 11	17 55	1 51
18 Sa	19 31	22 07	1 04	22 38	9 01	3 22	5 22	1 53	20 08	0 12	1 28	7 51	17 10	1 11	17 57	1 51
19 Su	19 44	22 44	0N19	22 24	9 16	3 24	5 48	1 54	20 18	0 13	1 35	7 52	17 08	1 11	17 59	1 51
20 M	19 57	21 41	1 40	20 37	9 33	3 25	6 13	1 55	20 27	0 13	1 43	7 52	17 06	1 11	18 00	1 51
21 Tu	20 09	19 13	2 52	17 32	9 51	3 25	6 39	1 56	20 37	0 14	1 51	7 53	17 05	1 11	18 02	1 51
22 W	20 21	15 38	3 52	13 33	10 11	3 24	7 04	1 57	20 46	0 15	1 58	7 53	17 03	1 11	18 04	1 51
23 Th	20 33	11 19	4 36	8 59	10 33	3 23	7 29	1 57	20 55	0 15	2 06	7 53	17 01	1 10	18 06	1 51
24 F	20 44	6 35	5 05	4 08	10 56	3 21	7 54	1 58	21 04	0 16	2 13	7 54	16 59	1 10	18 07	1 51
25 Sa	20 55	1 41	5 16	0N45	11 20	3 18	8 19	1 58	21 12	0 16	2 21	7 54	16 57	1 10	18 09	1 51
26 Su	21 06	3N09	5 13	5 29	11 45	3 15	8 44	1 59	21 21	0 17	2 28	7 55	16 56	1 10	18 11	1 51
27 M	21 16	7 45	4 54	9 56	12 12	3 11	9 08	1 59	21 29	0 18	2 35	7 55	16 54	1 10	18 12	1 50
28 Tu	21 26	11 60	4 23	13 55	12 40	3 06	9 33	1 59	21 37	0 18	2 43	7 56	16 52	1 10	18 14	1 50
29 W	21 35	15 43	3 41	17 20	13 08	3 01	9 57	1 59	21 45	0 19	2 50	7 56	16 51	1 10	18 16	1 50
30 Th	21 45	18 46	2 50	20 00	13 38	2 55	10 22	1 59	21 52	0 19	2 57	7 57	16 49	1 09	18 17	1 50
31 F	21N53	21N02	1N51	21N49	14N08	2S49	10N46	1S59	21N60	0N20	3N04	7S57	16S47	1N09	18N19	1S50

Day	⚷ Decl	⚷ Lat	♅ Decl	♅ Lat	♆ Decl	♆ Lat	♇ Decl	♇ Lat
1	14N08	1S26	22N48	0N03	3N22	1S28	22S53	5S56
6	14 13	1 26	22 49	0 03	3 25	1 28	22 53	5 58
11	14 19	1 27	22 51	0 03	3 29	1 29	22 54	5 59
16	14 24	1 27	22 53	0 03	3 32	1 29	22 56	5 60
21	14 29	1 27	22 54	0 03	3 35	1 29	22 57	6 01
26	14 34	1 28	22 56	0 03	3 38	1 29	22 58	6 02
31	14N39	1S29	22N57	0N03	3N41	1S29	23S00	6S03

Day	⚴ Decl	⚴ Lat	⚵ Decl	⚵ Lat	⚶ Decl	⚶ Lat	Eris Decl	Eris Lat
1	8N32	18N29	7S06	15N52	3N14	5S11	1N13	9S35
6	8 58	18 30	6 44	16 13	4 03	5 13	1 14	9 35
11	9 23	18 32	6 24	16 35	4 49	5 16	1 15	9 35
16	9 47	18 33	6 05	16 55	5 35	5 18	1 16	9 35
21	10 09	18 36	5 47	17 15	6 19	5 21	1 17	9 35
26	10 31	18 38	5 32	17 33	7 01	5 24	1 18	9 36
31	10N50	18N41	5S18	17N49	7N42	5S27	1N19	9S36

Moon Phenomena

Max/0 Decl
dy hr mn
5 14:34 22N45
12 19:01 0 S
18 20:41 22S44
25 8:19 0 N

Max/0 Lat
dy hr mn
5 11:56 0 S
12 16:57 5S15
18 18:33 0 N
25 5:55 5N17

Perigee/Apogee
dy hr m kilometers
4 3:39 a 406361
17 13:49 p 357024
31 6:16 a 406466

PH dy hr mn
● 2 14:13 12♉14
☽ 10 17:13 20♌06
○ 17 11:20 26♏37
☾ 24 4:59 3♓06

Void of Course Moon

Last Aspect	☽ Ingress
1 10:43 ☿ ☌	♉ 1 13:35
3 18:52 ♄ ☌	♊ 4 2:18
6 10:08 ☿ ⚹	♋ 6 15:18
8 22:16 ☿ □	♌ 9 2:56
11 8:12 ☿ △	♍ 11 11:26
13 11:54 ♄ △	♎ 13 15:59
14 20:28 ♅ △	♏ 15 17:11
17 14:40 ♂ ☍	♐ 17 16:40
18 23:10 ♀ △	♑ 19 16:24
21 15:53 ♄ △	♒ 21 18:11
23 21:21 ♄ □	♓ 23 23:17
26 6:31 ♄ ⚹	♈ 26 7:59
27 19:14 ♅ ⚹	♉ 28 19:27
31 8:08 ♄ ☌	♊ 31 8:20

DAILY ASPECTARIAN

1 W
☽⚻♃ 2:13
☿⚺♀ 3:17
☽⚺♄ 5:38
☽∥⚷ 7:51
☽☌☿ 10:43
☽⚺♀ 11:47
☉∥☽ 15:01
☽∠♅ 16:33
⚳⚹♅ 23:29

2 Th
☽∥♂ 4:46
♀ ♈ 6:39
☽∥♄ 7:29
☉⚺♆ 7:45
☽⋕♃ 8:50
☉□♇ 9:26
☽⚺♆ 13:43
☽□♇ 13:50
☉☌☽ 14:13
☽☌⚷ 14:20
☉☌⚷ 15:46
⚵ R 16:40
☽∠♀ 21:14
☽⚺♅ 22:57
☽⚺⚳ 23:37

3 F
☽☌♂ 2:31
☽☍♃ 14:07
☽☌♄ 18:52
☽∠♆ 20:14
☽⚺☿ 21:46

4 Sa
♂∥♄ 2:53
☽⚹♀ 7:00
☽∠⚳ 7:08
♂⋕♃ 9:13
♀∥⚳ 11:30
♆⚹♇ 15:42

5 Su
☽△♇ 2:50
☽⚹♆ 2:52
☽⚺⚷ 3:40
♃⋕♄ 3:43
☽∠☿ 3:52
☉⚺☽ 8:41
☊ D 11:55
☽☌♅ 12:15
☽⚹⚳ 14:42
♀⋕⚳ 18:34
☽⚺♂ 19:34

6 M
☽⚻♃ 2:33
☽⚺♄ 8:35
☽⚼♇ 9:20
☽⚹☿ 10:08
☽∠⚷ 10:19
☉∠☽ 17:50
☿ D 20:16

7 Tu
☽□♀ 2:28
☽∠♂ 3:52
☉⚺♅ 6:27
☽⚼♃ 8:31
☽∠♄ 15:07
☽⚻♇ 15:32
☽□♆ 15:43
☽⚹⚷ 16:40

8 W
☽⚺♅ 1:00
☉⚹☽ 2:31
☽□⚳ 5:04
☽⚹♂ 11:39
☽∥♂ 13:02
☽△♃ 14:01
♀∠♂ 15:10
☽∥♄ 19:04
☽⋕♃ 20:47
☽⚹♄ 21:06
☉∥☽ 22:00
☽□☿ 22:16

9 Th
☽∠♅ 6:34
☉⋕♃ 10:47
♀⚼♃ 11:36
☽∥⚷ 18:24
☽△♀ 19:38
♂☍♃ 22:03

10 F
☽☍♇ 2:06
☽△♆ 2:24
☽□⚷ 3:27
☉⚺⚳ 5:16
☽⚹♅ 11:18
☉∥♄ 13:50
☽△⚳ 16:39
☊ R 17:11
☉□☽ 17:13
♄∠♆ 17:48
☽□♃ 22:46

11 Sa
☽□♂ 0:28
☽⚼♀ 2:34
☽∥☿ 4:14
☽⚼♆ 6:26
☽□♄ 6:31
☽△☿ 8:12
☽⚼⚳ 20:54

12 Su
☽∥♆ 3:01
☽∥♀ 5:41
☽⚻♀ 8:10
☽⚻♇ 9:02
☽⚻♆ 9:26
☽△⚷ 10:33
☽⚼☿ 11:51
☽∥⚳ 15:35
☽□♅ 17:47
♀⚹♇ 18:12
☽⋕⚳ 22:36
♇ R 23:14
♀☌♆ 23:23

13 M
☽⚻⚳ 0:02
☉△☽ 3:04
☽⚹♃ 3:44
♀∠♄ 4:29
☽△♂ 8:40
☽⋕♀ 10:22
☽⋕♆ 10:44
☽⚼♇ 11:00
☉☍♃ 11:34
☽△♄ 11:54
☽⚼⚷ 12:35
♀⚺⚷ 13:33
☽⚻☿ 14:37
♀∥♆ 15:07

14 Tu
☽∠♃ 4:50
☉⚼☽ 6:14
☽⋕☿ 8:37
☽⚼♂ 11:08
☽△♇ 12:05
☽☍♆ 12:34
☽⚼♄ 13:11
☽⚻⚷ 13:44
☽☍♀ 15:42
☽△♅ 20:28

15 W
☿ ♉ 1:31
☽☍⚳ 3:26
☽⚺♃ 5:12
☉⚻☽ 8:28
☽⚻♂ 12:46
☽⋕⚷ 13:46
☽⚻♄ 13:46
♂∠♆ 17:45
☽☍☿ 17:52
☽⚼♅ 20:45

16 Th
☽∥♃ 5:41
☽⋕♄ 9:56
☽□♇ 12:22
☽⚻♆ 12:56
♂☌♄ 13:58
☽☍⚷ 14:09
☉⋕☽ 19:06
☽⚻♀ 19:50
☽⚻♅ 20:38

17 F
☽⋕♂ 0:42
☽⚻⚳ 4:25
☽☌♃ 4:32
♀⚹♅ 6:49
⚳⚻♃ 8:00
☉☍☽ 11:20
☽⚼♆ 12:39
☽☍♄ 13:43
☽☍♂ 14:40
☽⚻☿ 19:40
☽⚼♀ 21:26

18 Sa
☽⚼⚳ 4:39
☉∠♆ 8:39
☿∠♅ 9:48
☽⚹♇ 11:43
☽△♆ 12:23
☽⚻⚷ 13:42
☊ D 18:29
☽☍♅ 20:12
☽⚼☿ 20:45
☽△♀ 23:10

19 Su
☽⚺♃ 3:37
☽△⚳ 5:06
☉☌♄ 6:23
♂ ♊ 9:30
☽∠♇ 11:38
☽⚼⚷ 13:46
☽⚻♄ 13:47
☉⚻☽ 14:14
☽⚻♂ 16:45
☽△☿ 22:21

20 M
☽∠♃ 3:39
☽⚺♇ 12:03
☽⋕♂ 12:42
☽□♆ 12:51
☽△⚷ 14:21
☽⚼♄ 14:29
☉⚼☽ 16:27
☉⋕☽ 16:48
☽⚼♂ 18:34
☽⚻♅ 21:07
☉ ♊ 23:42

21 Tu
♀⚻♃ 3:21
☽⚹♃ 4:16
☽□♀ 4:22
☽□⚳ 7:34
☽⋕♄ 8:32
☽∥♃ 15:09
☽△♄ 15:53
☉△☽ 19:33
☽△♂ 21:13
⚶ ♉ 22:21
☽⚼♅ 22:36

22 W
☽□☿ 4:13
☽⋕⚷ 6:35
☽☌♇ 15:04
☽⚹♆ 16:02
☽□⚷ 17:46

23 Th
☽△♅ 0:58
☽⋕☿ 3:41
☽□♃ 7:55
♀☌⚳ 11:53
☽⚹⚳ 13:25
☽⚹♀ 13:31
☽⋕♀ 17:57
☽∠♆ 18:57
☽□♄ 21:21

24 F
☉□☽ 4:59
☊ R 5:15
☽□♂ 5:36
☽⋕♆ 14:30
☽⚹☿ 14:57
☽∠⚳ 17:49
☽∠♀ 19:53
☽⋕⚳ 20:52
☽⚺♇ 21:37
☽⚺♆ 22:47

25 Sa
☽⚹⚷ 0:47
☽□♅ 8:28
☉☌♂ 10:51
☽△♃ 15:06
☽∥⚳ 20:30
☽∠☿ 22:18
☽⚺⚳ 23:10

26 Su
☽∠♇ 2:12
☽∥♆ 2:31
☽⚺♀ 3:25
☽∠⚷ 5:38
☽⚹♄ 6:31
☽⚹♂ 18:09
☉⚹☽ 18:51
☽⚼♃ 19:53

27 M
☽⚺☿ 6:52
☽⚹♇ 7:32
☽∥♀ 8:22
☽☌♆ 8:55
☽⚺⚷ 11:12
☽∠♄ 12:16
☿□♇ 13:15
♀⚺♄ 15:52
☽⚹♅ 19:14

28 Tu
☽⚻♃ 1:18
☽∠♂ 1:40
☿⚺♆ 2:39
☉∠☽ 3:07
♀ ♉ 3:34
☽∥☿ 4:36
☽☌⚳ 12:09
☽∥⚷ 16:31
☽⚺♄ 18:35
☽☌♀ 21:11

29 W
☿☌⚷ 0:52
☽∠♅ 1:28
☽⋕♃ 8:11
☽⚺♂ 9:45
☉⚺☽ 11:58
☽□♇ 19:43
☽∥♄ 19:49
☽⚺♆ 21:18
☽☌⚷ 23:49

30 Th
☽☌☿ 2:41
☽⚺♅ 8:01
☽☍♃ 13:19
♀∠♅ 18:39

31 F
☽⚺⚳ 2:51
☽∠♆ 3:52
☽☌♄ 8:08
☉∥☽ 14:54
☽⚺♀ 16:49
☽∥♂ 17:03

June 2030

LONGITUDE

Day	Sid.Time	☉	☽	☽ 12 hour	Mean☊	True☊	☿	♀	♂	⚳	♃	♄	⚷	♅	♆	♇
	h m s	° ' "	° ' "	° ' "	° '	° '	° '	° '	° '	° '	° '	° '	° '	° '	° '	° '
1 Sa	16 38 07	10♊34 39	7♊41 54	13♊35 57	16♐48.6	16♐19.4	18♉08.6	4♉31.5	8♊54.0	27♈37.5	20♏29.8	29♉59.2	14♉08.4	18♊09.5	12♈49.7	11♒58.9
2 Su	16 42 03	11 32 11	19 30 39	25 26 18	16 45.5	16D 19.4	19 38.4	5 42.1	9 36.0	27 58.9	20R 23.1	0♊06.9	14 11.9	18 13.0	12 51.1	11R 58.4
3 M	16 46 00	12 29 41	1♋23 11	7♋21 35	16 42.3	16 19.5	21 10.8	6 52.8	10 18.0	28 20.3	20 16.4	0 14.5	14 15.5	18 16.6	12 52.5	11 57.9
4 Tu	16 49 56	13 27 11	13 21 50	19 24 14	16 39.1	16 19.8	22 45.7	8 03.5	10 59.9	28 41.5	20 09.9	0 22.2	14 19.0	18 20.1	12 53.8	11 57.3
5 W	16 53 53	14 24 40	25 29 08	1♌36 52	16 35.9	16 20.1	24 23.2	9 14.2	11 41.8	29 02.7	20 03.4	0 29.8	14 22.5	18 23.7	12 55.2	11 56.7
6 Th	16 57 50	15 22 07	7♌47 50	14 02 22	16 32.8	16 20.2	26 03.3	10 25.0	12 23.6	29 23.8	19 57.1	0 37.4	14 25.9	18 27.2	12 56.4	11 56.1
7 F	17 01 46	16 19 33	20 20 53	26 43 44	16 29.6	16R 20.3	27 45.8	11 35.8	13 05.4	29 44.8	19 50.9	0 45.0	14 29.4	18 30.8	12 57.7	11 55.5
8 Sa	17 05 43	17 16 58	3♍11 19	9♍43 58	16 26.4	16 20.3	29 30.9	12 46.7	13 47.1	0♉05.8	19 44.8	0 52.6	14 32.8	18 34.3	12 58.9	11 54.8
9 Su	17 09 39	18 14 22	16 22 00	23 05 41	16 23.2	16D 20.2	1♊18.5	13 57.6	14 28.8	0 26.6	19 38.8	1 00.1	14 36.2	18 37.9	13 00.1	11 54.2
10 M	17 13 36	19 11 45	29 55 14	6♎50 45	16 20.0	16 20.3	3 08.5	15 08.5	15 10.5	0 47.4	19 32.9	1 07.7	14 39.6	18 41.4	13 01.3	11 53.5
11 Tu	17 17 32	20 09 07	13♎52 16	20 59 38	16 16.9	16 20.5	5 01.0	16 19.5	15 52.0	1 08.2	19 27.2	1 15.2	14 42.9	18 45.0	13 02.4	11 52.7
12 W	17 21 29	21 06 27	28 12 39	5♏30 54	16 13.7	16 20.8	6 55.8	17 30.5	16 33.6	1 28.8	19 21.6	1 22.7	14 46.2	18 48.5	13 03.5	11 52.0
13 Th	17 25 25	22 03 47	12♏53 51	20 20 48	16 10.5	16 21.3	8 53.0	18 41.6	17 15.1	1 49.3	19 16.1	1 30.1	14 49.5	18 52.1	13 04.6	11 51.2
14 F	17 29 22	23 01 06	27 50 54	5♐23 12	16 07.3	16 21.7	10 52.3	19 52.7	17 56.5	2 09.8	19 10.8	1 37.6	14 52.8	18 55.6	13 05.7	11 50.5
15 Sa	17 33 19	23 58 24	12♐56 40	20 30 09	16 04.2	16R 22.0	12 53.8	21 03.8	18 37.9	2 30.2	19 05.6	1 45.0	14 56.0	18 59.2	13 06.7	11 49.7
16 Su	17 37 15	24 55 41	28 02 32	5♑32 41	16 01.0	16 21.9	14 57.3	22 15.0	19 19.2	2 50.5	19 00.6	1 52.3	14 59.2	19 02.7	13 07.7	11 48.8
17 M	17 41 12	25 52 58	12♑59 35	20 22 14	15 57.8	16 21.3	17 02.5	23 26.2	20 00.5	3 10.7	18 55.7	1 59.7	15 02.4	19 06.2	13 08.7	11 48.0
18 Tu	17 45 08	26 50 14	27 39 51	4♒51 43	15 54.6	16 20.3	19 09.4	24 37.5	20 41.8	3 30.8	18 50.9	2 07.0	15 05.5	19 09.8	13 09.6	11 47.1
19 W	17 49 05	27 47 30	11♒57 22	18 56 26	15 51.5	16 19.0	21 17.7	25 48.8	21 23.0	3 50.9	18 46.3	2 14.3	15 08.6	19 13.3	13 10.5	11 46.2
20 Th	17 53 01	28 44 46	25 48 46	2♓34 18	15 48.3	16 17.6	23 27.2	27 00.2	22 04.2	4 10.8	18 41.9	2 21.6	15 11.7	19 16.8	13 11.4	11 45.3
21 F	17 56 58	29 42 01	9♓13 11	15 45 38	15 45.1	16 16.4	25 37.7	28 11.6	22 45.3	4 30.6	18 37.6	2 28.8	15 14.7	19 20.3	13 12.2	11 44.4
22 Sa	18 00 54	0♋39 16	22 12 00	28 32 41	15 41.9	16D 15.7	27 48.8	29 23.0	23 26.3	4 50.4	18 33.4	2 36.0	15 17.7	19 23.8	13 13.1	11 43.4
23 Su	18 04 51	1 36 30	4♈48 11	10♈59 00	15 38.8	16 15.5	0♋00.2	0♊34.5	24 07.4	5 10.0	18 29.5	2 43.1	15 20.6	19 27.3	13 13.8	11 42.5
24 M	18 08 48	2 33 45	17 05 42	23 08 51	15 35.6	16 16.0	2 11.8	1 46.1	24 48.3	5 29.6	18 25.7	2 50.3	15 23.6	19 30.8	13 14.6	11 41.5
25 Tu	18 12 44	3 31 00	29 09 01	5♉06 46	15 32.4	16 17.1	4 23.2	2 57.6	25 29.3	5 49.0	18 22.0	2 57.3	15 26.5	19 34.3	13 15.3	11 40.5
26 W	18 16 41	4 28 14	11♉02 39	16 57 12	15 29.2	16 18.6	6 34.2	4 09.2	26 10.2	6 08.4	18 18.5	3 04.4	15 29.3	19 37.8	13 16.0	11 39.5
27 Th	18 20 37	5 25 29	22 50 55	28 44 18	15 26.0	16 20.0	8 44.4	5 20.9	26 51.0	6 27.6	18 15.2	3 11.4	15 32.1	19 41.2	13 16.6	11 38.4
28 F	18 24 34	6 22 43	4♊37 45	10♊31 44	15 22.9	16R 21.2	10 53.8	6 32.6	27 31.8	6 46.8	18 12.1	3 18.4	15 34.9	19 44.7	13 17.3	11 37.4
29 Sa	18 28 30	7 19 57	16 26 36	22 22 42	15 19.7	16 21.6	13 02.0	7 44.3	28 12.6	7 05.8	18 09.1	3 25.3	15 37.7	19 48.1	13 17.9	11 36.3
30 Su	18 32 27	8♋17 11	28 20 20	4♋19 48	15♐16.5	16♐21.1	15♋08.9	8♊56.0	28♊53.3	7♉24.7	18♏06.3	3♊32.2	15♉40.4	19♊51.5	13♈18.4	11♒35.2

1st of Month

Julian Day # 2462653.5
Obliquity 23°26'05"
SVP 4♓49'50"
GC 27♐15.8
Eris 26♈39.8

Day	⚴
1	13♓49.7
6	14 29.4
11	15 02.9
16	15 29.7
21	15 49.5
26	16 01.9

Day	⚵
1	9♑34.0R
6	8 42.2R
11	7 44.2R
16	6 41.2R
21	5 34.5R
26	4 25.7R

Day	⚶
1	4♉22.5
6	6 30.4
11	8 36.5
16	10 40.7
21	12 42.9
26	14 42.9

DECLINATION and LATITUDE

Day	☉ Decl	☽ Decl	☽ Lat	☽ 12h Decl	☿ Decl	☿ Lat	♀ Decl	♀ Lat	♂ Decl	♂ Lat	⚳ Decl	⚳ Lat	♃ Decl	♃ Lat	♄ Decl	♄ Lat
1 Sa	22N02	22N22	0N48	22N41	14N38	2S42	11N10	1S59	22N07	0N21	3N11	7S58	16S46	1N09	18N21	1S50
2 Su	22 10	22 44	0S18	22 31	15 10	2 34	11 33	1 59	22 14	0 21	3 18	7 58	16 44	1 09	18 22	1 50
3 M	22 17	22 03	1 23	21 20	15 42	2 26	11 57	1 58	22 20	0 22	3 25	7 59	16 42	1 09	18 24	1 50
4 Tu	22 25	20 22	2 25	19 10	16 14	2 18	12 20	1 58	22 27	0 22	3 32	7 59	16 41	1 09	18 26	1 50
5 W	22 31	17 45	3 21	16 07	16 47	2 09	12 43	1 57	22 34	0 23	3 39	7 60	16 39	1 08	18 27	1 50
6 Th	22 38	14 18	4 09	12 19	17 19	1 60	13 06	1 57	22 40	0 23	3 45	8 00	16 38	1 08	18 29	1 50
7 F	22 44	10 11	4 46	7 54	17 52	1 50	13 28	1 56	22 46	0 24	3 52	8 01	16 36	1 08	18 30	1 50
8 Sa	22 50	5 31	5 10	3 02	18 24	1 40	13 50	1 55	22 51	0 25	3 59	8 02	16 35	1 08	18 32	1 50
9 Su	22 55	0 30	5 18	2S06	18 57	1 30	14 12	1 55	22 57	0 25	4 05	8 02	16 33	1 08	18 33	1 50
10 M	22 60	4S42	5 09	7 16	19 29	1 20	14 34	1 54	23 02	0 26	4 12	8 03	16 32	1 07	18 35	1 50
11 Tu	23 04	9 48	4 42	12 14	19 60	1 09	14 55	1 53	23 07	0 26	4 18	8 03	16 31	1 07	18 36	1 50
12 W	23 08	14 31	3 57	16 38	20 31	0 58	15 16	1 52	23 12	0 27	4 25	8 04	16 29	1 07	18 38	1 50
13 Th	23 12	18 30	2 56	20 04	21 00	0 47	15 37	1 51	23 17	0 27	4 31	8 05	16 28	1 07	18 39	1 50
14 F	23 15	21 19	1 41	22 11	21 29	0 36	15 57	1 49	23 21	0 28	4 37	8 05	16 27	1 07	18 41	1 50
15 Sa	23 18	22 40	0 19	22 43	21 56	0 25	16 17	1 48	23 25	0 29	4 43	8 06	16 26	1 06	18 42	1 50
16 Su	23 20	22 21	1N04	21 35	22 22	0 14	16 36	1 47	23 29	0 29	4 49	8 07	16 24	1 06	18 44	1 50
17 M	23 22	20 26	2 23	18 58	22 46	0 02	16 56	1 45	23 33	0 30	4 55	8 07	16 23	1 06	18 45	1 50
18 Tu	23 24	17 12	3 30	15 12	23 08	0N08	17 14	1 44	23 37	0 30	5 01	8 08	16 22	1 06	18 47	1 50
19 W	23 25	13 00	4 22	10 41	23 28	0 19	17 33	1 42	23 40	0 31	5 07	8 09	16 21	1 06	18 48	1 50
20 Th	23 26	8 04	4 57	5 46	23 46	0 29	17 51	1 41	23 43	0 31	5 13	8 10	16 20	1 05	18 49	1 50
21 F	23 26	3 15	5 15	0 44	24 01	0 39	18 09	1 39	23 46	0 32	5 19	8 10	16 19	1 05	18 51	1 50
22 Sa	23 26	1N44	5 15	4N09	24 14	0 49	18 26	1 37	23 49	0 32	5 25	8 11	16 18	1 05	18 52	1 51
23 Su	23 25	6 30	5 01	8 46	24 24	0 58	18 42	1 36	23 51	0 33	5 30	8 12	16 18	1 05	18 54	1 51
24 M	23 25	10 54	4 32	12 55	24 31	1 06	18 59	1 34	23 54	0 34	5 36	8 13	16 17	1 04	18 55	1 51
25 Tu	23 23	14 47	3 53	16 30	24 36	1 14	19 14	1 32	23 56	0 34	5 41	8 13	16 16	1 04	18 56	1 51
26 W	23 22	18 02	3 03	19 23	24 37	1 21	19 30	1 30	23 57	0 35	5 47	8 14	16 15	1 04	18 57	1 51
27 Th	23 19	20 37	2 06	21 26	24 36	1 27	19 45	1 28	23 59	0 35	5 52	8 15	16 14	1 04	18 59	1 51
28 F	23 17	22 07	1 04	22 33	24 32	1 33	19 59	1 26	24 00	0 36	5 57	8 16	16 14	1 03	19 00	1 51
29 Sa	23 14	22 44	0S00	22 40	24 26	1 38	20 13	1 24	24 02	0 36	6 03	8 17	16 13	1 03	19 01	1 51
30 Su	23N11	22N20	1S06	21N44	24N16	1N42	20N26	1S22	24N03	0N37	6N08	8S18	16S13	1N03	19N03	1S51

Day	⚷ Decl	⚷ Lat	♅ Decl	♅ Lat	♆ Decl	♆ Lat	♇ Decl	♇ Lat
1	14N40	1S29	22N58	0N03	3N42	1S29	23S01	6S04
6	14 45	1 29	22 59	0 03	3 44	1 30	23 02	6 05
11	14 49	1 30	23 01	0 03	3 46	1 30	23 04	6 06
16	14 53	1 30	23 02	0 04	3 48	1 30	23 07	6 07
21	14 57	1 31	23 04	0 04	3 49	1 30	23 09	6 08
26	15 01	1 32	23 05	0 04	3 51	1 31	23 11	6 09

Day	⚴ Decl	⚴ Lat	⚵ Decl	⚵ Lat	⚶ Decl	⚶ Lat	Eris Decl	Eris Lat
1	10N54	18N41	5S16	17N52	7N50	5S27	1N19	9S36
6	11 11	18 44	5 06	18 05	8 29	5 31	1 20	9 36
11	11 26	18 47	4 59	18 15	9 05	5 34	1 20	9 36
16	11 39	18 50	4 55	18 22	9 40	5 37	1 21	9 36
21	11 48	18 52	4 54	18 26	10 14	5 41	1 21	9 37
26	11 54	18 54	4 57	18 25	10 45	5 45	1 21	9 37

Moon Phenomena

Max/0 Decl
dy hr mn
1 20:13 22N44
9 2:18 0 S
15 7:28 22S44
21 15:35 0 N
29 2:36 22N45

Max/0 Lat
dy hr mn
1 17:31 0 S
8 23:56 5S18
15 5:26 0 N
21 12:56 5N17
28 23:49 0 S

Perigee/Apogee
dy hr m kilometers
14 23:34 p 358185
27 14:16 a 405877

PH dy hr mn
● 1 6:23 10♊50
• 1 389:11A 05'21"
☽ 9 3:37 18♍23
○ 15 18:42 24♐43
• 15 18:35 P 0.502
☾ 22 17:21 1♈21
● 30 21:36 9♋09

Void of Course Moon

Last Aspect	☽ Ingress
1 21:22 ♅ ☌	♋ 2 21:12
4 21:30 ☿ ⚹	♌ 5 8:51
7 16:07 ☿ □	♍ 7 18:06
9 5:50 ♃ ⚹	♎ 10 0:08
11 11:21 ☉ △	♏ 12 2:57
13 10:12 ♃ ☌	♐ 14 3:26
15 18:42 ☉ ☍	♑ 16 3:07
17 18:32 ♀ △	♒ 18 3:53
20 5:35 ☉ △	♓ 20 7:25
22 12:50 ☿ □	♈ 22 14:47
24 16:14 ♂ ⚹	♉ 25 1:42
26 14:41 ♃ ☍	♊ 27 14:34
30 1:10 ♂ ☌	♋ 30 3:20

DAILY ASPECTARIAN

1 Sa
☿⚺♅ 0:16
☿∥⚷ 1:15
♄ ♊ 2:35
☽☌♂ 2:36
☉☌☽ 6:23
☽△♇ 8:42
☽∠⚳ 10:20
☽⚹♆ 10:27
☽⚺⚷ 13:10
☊ D 17:22
☽☌♅ 21:22

2 Su
☽⚺☿ 0:18
☽⚻♃ 1:45
☽∠♀ 2:41
☉△♇ 10:50
☿☍♃ 10:54
☽⚼♇ 15:05
☽⚹⚳ 17:40
☽∥♂ 17:51
☉∥☽ 19:12
☽∠⚷ 19:41
☽⚺♄ 21:40

3 M
☽⚼♃ 7:45
☉⚹♆ 9:45
☽∠☿ 11:05
☽⚹♀ 12:15
☽⚺♂ 18:59
☽⚻♇ 21:12
☽□♆ 23:04

4 Tu
☉⚺☽ 0:12
☽⚹⚷ 1:54
☽∠♄ 4:02
☉∠⚳ 9:29
☽⚺♅ 9:56
☽△♃ 13:23
☽∥♄ 18:17
☿#♃ 18:52
☽⚹☿ 21:30
☉⚺⚷ 23:02

5 W
☽∠♂ 2:31
☽∥☿ 6:17
☽□⚳ 7:11
☽#♃ 8:16
☉∠☽ 8:21
♂△♇ 8:27
☽⚹♄ 9:55
☽∠♅ 15:32
⚳∥♆ 18:40
☽∥⚷ 21:12

6 Th
☽□♀ 5:35
☽∥♀ 6:48
☽☍♇ 7:58
☽⚹♂ 9:22
☽△♆ 9:55
☽□⚷ 12:49
☉⚹☽ 15:44
♂⚹♆ 19:26
☽⚹♅ 20:30
☽□♃ 23:04

7 F
☊ R 1:46
☿∠♆ 2:46
♀□♇ 6:37
☽⚼♆ 14:19
☽□☿ 16:07
⚳ ♉ 17:23
☽△⚳ 18:07
☽□♄ 19:41

8 Sa
♀⚺♆ 4:13
☿∥♄ 5:46
☿ ♊ 6:32
☽∥⚳ 7:20
☽∥♆ 8:36
☿⚺⚳ 9:44
☽⚻♇ 15:57
☽⚻♆ 17:56
☽△♀ 19:14
☿☌♄ 19:38
☽□♂ 20:25
☽△⚷ 20:49
☽⚼⚳ 22:18

9 Su
☊ D 3:06
☉□☽ 3:37
☽□♅ 4:05
♂⚺⚷ 4:38
☽⚹♃ 5:50
☉☌♅ 10:29
♀☌⚷ 13:44
♂∥♅ 16:17
☽⚼♇ 18:42
☽#♆ 19:42
☽#⚳ 21:39
☽⚼⚷ 23:33

10 M
☽⚼♀ 0:25
☽⚻⚳ 1:33
♀⚺♂ 1:36
☽△♄ 2:07
☉∥♅ 5:19
☽△☿ 6:28
☽∠♃ 7:59
☉⚻♃ 8:03
♂#♇ 8:58
♀∥⚷ 17:02
☽△♇ 20:37
☽☍♆ 22:35

11 Tu
☽⚻⚷ 1:26
☉#♇ 1:37
☽△♂ 3:33
☽⚼♄ 4:04
☽⚻♀ 4:32
☽△♅ 8:16
☽⚺♃ 9:21
☉△☽ 11:21
☽⚼☿ 11:57
⚳⚺♄ 12:48
♂∠⚳ 18:30

12 W
☽#⚷ 1:42
☽#♀ 4:28
☽⚻♄ 5:16
☽☍⚳ 5:31
☽⚼♂ 5:48
☽⚼♅ 9:15
☽∥♃ 11:07
☉⚼☽ 13:52
☽⚻☿ 16:29
☽□♇ 22:19

13 Th
☽⚻♆ 0:17
☽#♄ 1:09
☽☍⚷ 3:08
♀⚺♅ 3:44
☽⚻♂ 7:22
☽⚻♅ 9:40
☽☍♀ 10:09
☽☌♃ 10:12
♀☍♃ 10:51
☉⚻☽ 15:45

14 F
☽⚼♆ 0:24
☽#☿ 2:27
☽☍♄ 6:04
☽⚻⚳ 7:02
☿△♇ 11:28
☽⚹♇ 22:14
☽☍☿ 23:55

15 Sa
☽△♆ 0:16
☿⚹♆ 2:33
☽⚻⚷ 3:10
☊ R 5:37
☽⚼⚳ 7:24
☽☍♂ 9:28
☽☍♅ 9:38
☽⚺♃ 9:42
♀#♃ 10:07
♂☌♅ 13:30
☽⚻♀ 13:59
♂⚻♃ 14:20
♃⚻♅ 18:00
☉☍☽ 18:42
☽∠♇ 22:03
☽#☿ 23:45

16 Su
☿⚺⚷ 0:23
☽⚼⚷ 3:07
☽⚻♄ 6:10
☽△⚳ 7:51
☽∠♃ 9:29
☽⚼♀ 16:01
☽⚺♇ 22:04

17 M
☽□♆ 0:15
☽△⚷ 3:20
☽⚼♄ 6:33
☽⚻☿ 7:40
☽⚹♃ 9:36
☽⚻♅ 9:58
☽⚻♂ 11:58
☽#♄ 13:23
☿∠⚳ 15:22
☿∥♅ 18:32
☽△♀ 18:32
☿⚻♃ 20:39
☉⚻☽ 22:32
☉⚼♇ 22:43
☿#♇ 23:26
☽#♀ 23:44

18 Tu
☿☌♅ 0:04
☽∥♃ 5:08
☽△♄ 7:28
☽□⚳ 9:58
☽⚼♅ 10:52
☽⚼☿ 12:43
☽#⚷ 13:34
☽⚼♂ 14:05
☉∥☿ 20:08
☽☌♇ 23:41

19 W
☿☌♂ 1:26
☉⚼☽ 1:32
☽⚹♆ 2:05
☽□⚷ 5:28
☽□♃ 11:39
☽△♅ 12:32
☽△♂ 17:06
☽△☿ 19:05
☿∥♂ 19:41

20 Th
☽□♀ 2:18
☽∠♆ 4:12
☉△☽ 5:35
⚳∠♅ 8:50
☽□♄ 11:44
☽#⚳ 14:20
☽⚹⚳ 15:16
☽#♆ 21:16

21 F
♀∠♆ 0:13
☽⚺♇ 4:36
☽⚺♆ 7:18
☉ ♋ 7:32
☽⚹⚷ 11:05
☿⚼♇ 12:08
☉∠⚷ 14:27
☽△♃ 17:14
☽□♅ 18:44
☽∠⚳ 19:28

22 Sa
☽□♂ 2:28
☽∠♇ 8:32
☽∥♆ 10:22
♀ ♊ 12:25
☽□☿ 12:50
☽⚹♀ 15:01
☽∠⚷ 15:24
☉□☽ 17:21
☊ D 17:28
☽∥⚳ 18:44
☽⚹♄ 19:57
☽⚼♃ 21:29
☿ ♋ 23:58

23 Su
☽⚺⚳ 0:43
☿∠⚷ 3:49
☽⚹♇ 13:24
☿⚺♀ 13:42
☽☌♆ 16:25
♀∥♄ 17:47
☽⚺⚷ 20:38
☽∠♀ 23:17

24 M
☽∠♄ 1:29
☽⚻♃ 2:37
☽⚹♅ 4:48
☉☌☿ 7:06
☿⚺♄ 7:25
☉⚺♄ 7:54
☿⚼♃ 13:07
☽⚹♂ 16:14
☉⚼♃ 20:27
♀☌♄ 23:54

25 Tu
☽∥⚷ 1:24
☽⚺♄ 7:44
☽⚺♀ 8:31
☉⚹☽ 9:33
☽#♃ 10:14
☽∠♅ 10:58
☽⚹☿ 12:54
☽☌⚳ 13:48
☿⚹⚳ 18:27

26 W
☽∠♂ 0:16
☽□♇ 1:15
☽⚺♆ 4:31
☽∥♄ 8:05
☽☌⚷ 9:03
☽∥♀ 14:38
☽☍♃ 14:41
♂⚼♇ 16:46
☽⚺♅ 17:32
☉∠☽ 18:38

27 Th
☽∠☿ 2:13
☉⚺♀ 7:39
☽⚺♂ 8:39
☽∠♆ 11:04
☽☌♄ 21:17

28 F
☉⚺☽ 3:52
☽☌♀ 4:20
☽⚺⚳ 4:30
♀⚺⚳ 6:29
☿⚻♇ 8:04
☽△♇ 14:12
☉⚹⚳ 15:07
☽⚺☿ 15:34
☽⚹♆ 17:37
☽⚺⚷ 22:20
☊ R 23:52

29 Sa
☿□♆ 3:00
☽⚻♃ 3:27
☽☌♅ 6:50
☉#♇ 9:20
☽∠⚳ 11:45
☽⚼♇ 20:29

30 Su
☽☌♂ 1:10
☽∠⚷ 4:42
☿⚹⚷ 6:07
☽⚼♃ 9:31
☽⚺♄ 10:31
☽⚹⚳ 18:38
☉☌☽ 21:36
☽⚺♀ 23:30

LONGITUDE

Day	Sid.Time	☉	☽	☽ 12 hour	Mean☊	True☊	☿	♀	♂	⚳	♃	♄	⚷	♅	♆	♇
	h m s	° ' "	° ' "	° ' "	° '	° '	° '	° '	° '	° '	° '	° '	° '	° '	° '	° '
1 M	18 36 23	9♋14 25	10♋21 21	16♋25 12	15♐13.3	16♐19.5	17♋14.4	10♊07.8	29♊34.0	7♉43.5	18♏03.7	3♊39.0	15♉43.0	19♊54.9	13♈19.0	11♒34.1
2 Tu	18 40 20	10 11 39	22 31 33	28 40 36	15 10.2	16R 16.7	19 18.3	11 19.7	0♋14.6	8 02.2	18R 01.2	3 45.8	15 45.7	19 58.3	13 19.5	11R 33.0
3 W	18 44 17	11 08 53	4♌52 30	11♌07 25	15 07.0	16 13.2	21 20.5	12 31.6	0 55.2	8 20.8	17 58.9	3 52.6	15 48.2	20 01.7	13 19.9	11 31.9
4 Th	18 48 13	12 06 06	17 25 30	23 46 54	15 03.8	16 09.1	23 20.9	13 43.5	1 35.8	8 39.2	17 56.8	3 59.3	15 50.8	20 05.1	13 20.3	11 30.7
5 F	18 52 10	13 03 19	0♍11 45	6♍40 12	15 00.6	16 05.1	25 19.4	14 55.4	2 16.3	8 57.6	17 54.9	4 05.9	15 53.3	20 08.4	13 20.7	11 29.5
6 Sa	18 56 06	14 00 32	13 12 24	19 48 28	14 57.5	16 01.6	27 16.1	16 07.4	2 56.7	9 15.7	17 53.2	4 12.5	15 55.7	20 11.7	13 21.1	11 28.4
7 Su	19 00 03	14 57 45	26 28 34	3♎12 49	14 54.3	15 59.1	29 10.9	17 19.4	3 37.1	9 33.8	17 51.6	4 19.1	15 58.1	20 15.1	13 21.4	11 27.2
8 M	19 03 59	15 54 58	10♎01 18	16 54 07	14 51.1	15D 57.9	1♌03.7	18 31.4	4 17.5	9 51.8	17 50.3	4 25.6	16 00.5	20 18.3	13 21.7	11 26.0
9 Tu	19 07 56	16 52 10	23 51 16	0♏52 45	14 47.9	15 58.0	2 54.5	19 43.5	4 57.8	10 09.6	17 49.1	4 32.0	16 02.8	20 21.6	13 22.0	11 24.8
10 W	19 11 52	17 49 22	7♏58 29	15 08 16	14 44.7	15 59.0	4 43.4	20 55.6	5 38.1	10 27.3	17 48.1	4 38.4	16 05.1	20 24.9	13 22.2	11 23.5
11 Th	19 15 49	18 46 34	22 21 51	29 38 50	14 41.6	16 00.4	6 30.3	22 07.7	6 18.3	10 44.8	17 47.2	4 44.8	16 07.3	20 28.1	13 22.4	11 22.3
12 F	19 19 46	19 43 46	6♐58 46	14♐21 00	14 38.4	16R 01.5	8 15.2	23 19.9	6 58.5	11 02.2	17 46.6	4 51.0	16 09.5	20 31.3	13 22.6	11 21.0
13 Sa	19 23 42	20 40 58	21 44 51	29 09 31	14 35.2	16 01.6	9 58.1	24 32.2	7 38.7	11 19.5	17 46.1	4 57.3	16 11.7	20 34.5	13 22.7	11 19.8
14 Su	19 27 39	21 38 10	6♑34 05	13♑57 40	14 32.0	16 00.3	11 39.1	25 44.4	8 18.8	11 36.6	17 45.9	5 03.5	16 13.7	20 37.7	13 22.9	11 18.5
15 M	19 31 35	22 35 22	21 19 17	28 38 01	14 28.9	15 57.2	13 18.1	26 56.7	8 58.8	11 53.6	17D 45.8	5 09.6	16 15.8	20 40.9	13 22.9	11 17.2
16 Tu	19 35 32	23 32 35	5♒52 59	13♒03 25	14 25.7	15 52.6	14 55.0	28 09.0	9 38.8	12 10.4	17 45.8	5 15.6	16 17.8	20 44.0	13R 23.0	11 15.9
17 W	19 39 28	24 29 48	20 08 38	27 08 06	14 22.5	15 46.9	16 30.1	29 21.4	10 18.8	12 27.1	17 46.1	5 21.6	16 19.7	20 47.1	13 23.0	11 14.6
18 Th	19 43 25	25 27 01	4♓01 26	10♓48 23	14 19.3	15 40.9	18 03.1	0♋33.8	10 58.7	12 43.7	17 46.5	5 27.6	16 21.6	20 50.2	13 22.9	11 13.3
19 F	19 47 22	26 24 15	17 28 54	24 03 01	14 16.2	15 35.3	19 34.1	1 46.3	11 38.6	13 00.1	17 47.1	5 33.5	16 23.5	20 53.2	13 22.9	11 12.0
20 Sa	19 51 18	27 21 29	0♈30 58	6♈53 02	14 13.0	15 30.8	21 03.1	2 58.8	12 18.5	13 16.3	17 47.9	5 39.3	16 25.3	20 56.2	13 22.8	11 10.7
21 Su	19 55 15	28 18 44	13 09 37	19 21 14	14 09.8	15 27.8	22 30.1	4 11.3	12 58.3	13 32.4	17 48.9	5 45.0	16 27.0	20 59.2	13 22.7	11 09.4
22 M	19 59 11	29 16 00	25 28 25	1♉31 46	14 06.6	15D 26.5	23 55.0	5 23.9	13 38.1	13 48.3	17 50.1	5 50.7	16 28.7	21 02.2	13 22.5	11 08.0
23 Tu	20 03 08	0♌13 17	7♉31 54	13 29 28	14 03.4	15 26.7	25 17.9	6 36.5	14 17.9	14 04.1	17 51.4	5 56.3	16 30.4	21 05.2	13 22.3	11 06.7
24 W	20 07 04	1 10 35	19 25 07	25 19 29	14 00.3	15 27.8	26 38.7	7 49.2	14 57.6	14 19.7	17 52.9	6 01.9	16 32.0	21 08.1	13 22.1	11 05.3
25 Th	20 11 01	2 07 53	1♊13 13	7♊06 54	13 57.1	15 29.2	27 57.3	9 01.9	15 37.2	14 35.1	17 54.6	6 07.4	16 33.5	21 11.0	13 21.9	11 04.0
26 F	20 14 57	3 05 13	13 01 07	18 56 25	13 53.9	15R 30.0	29 13.7	10 14.6	16 16.9	14 50.3	17 56.5	6 12.8	16 35.0	21 13.8	13 21.6	11 02.6
27 Sa	20 18 54	4 02 33	24 53 18	0♋52 13	13 50.7	15 29.6	0♍27.8	11 27.4	16 56.5	15 05.4	17 58.5	6 18.1	16 36.5	21 16.7	13 21.3	11 01.3
28 Su	20 22 51	4 59 54	6♋53 33	12 57 40	13 47.6	15 27.2	1 39.6	12 40.2	17 36.0	15 20.3	18 00.8	6 23.4	16 37.9	21 19.5	13 20.9	10 59.9
29 M	20 26 47	5 57 16	19 04 50	25 15 17	13 44.4	15 22.7	2 49.1	13 53.1	18 15.5	15 35.0	18 03.2	6 28.6	16 39.2	21 22.3	13 20.5	10 58.5
30 Tu	20 30 44	6 54 39	1♌29 11	7♌46 37	13 41.2	15 16.1	3 56.0	15 06.0	18 55.0	15 49.5	18 05.7	6 33.7	16 40.5	21 25.0	13 20.1	10 57.2
31 W	20 34 40	7♌52 02	14 07 39	20 32 16	13♐38.0	15♐07.8	5♍00.4	16♋18.9	19♋34.4	16♉03.8	18♏08.5	6♊38.8	16♉41.7	21♊27.7	13♈19.7	10♒55.8

1st of Month

Julian Day #
2462683.5
Obliquity
23°26[illegible]4"
SVP 4♓49[illegible]4"
GC 27♐15.9
Eris 26♈50.8

Day	⚴
1	16♓06.3
6	16 02.6R
11	15 50.3R
16	15 29.5R
21	15 00.0R
26	14 22.0R
31	13 35.6R

Day	⚵
1	3♑16.2R
6	2 08.0R
11	1 02.6R
16	0 01.6R
21	29♐06.2R
26	28 17.5R
31	27 36.5R

Day	⚶
1	16♉40.6
6	18 35.8
11	20 28.2
16	22 17.7
21	24 04.0
26	25 47.0
31	27 26.2

DECLINATION and LATITUDE

Day	☉	☽		☽ 12h	☿		♀		♂		⚳		♃		♄	
	Decl	Decl	Lat	Decl	Decl	Lat	Decl	Lat	Decl	Lat	Decl	Lat	Decl	Lat	Decl	Lat
1 M	23N07	20N54	2S09	19N48	24N05	1N46	20N39	1S20	24N03	0N37	6N13	8S18	16S12	1N03	19N04	1S51
2 Tu	23 03	18 29	3 06	16 57	23 50	1 49	20 51	1 18	24 04	0 38	6 18	8 19	16 12	1 02	19 05	1 51
3 W	22 58	15 13	3 56	13 18	23 34	1 51	21 03	1 15	24 04	0 38	6 23	8 20	16 11	1 02	19 06	1 51
4 Th	22 53	11 14	4 35	9 01	23 15	1 52	21 14	1 13	24 04	0 39	6 28	8 21	16 11	1 02	19 07	1 51
5 F	22 48	6 41	5 02	4 16	22 55	1 53	21 25	1 11	24 04	0 39	6 32	8 22	16 11	1 02	19 09	1 51
6 Sa	22 42	1 46	5 13	0S46	22 32	1 53	21 35	1 08	24 04	0 40	6 37	8 23	16 11	1 01	19 10	1 51
7 Su	22 36	3S19	5 08	5 51	22 08	1 52	21 44	1 06	24 04	0 40	6 42	8 24	16 10	1 01	19 11	1 51
8 M	22 29	8 21	4 46	10 47	21 43	1 50	21 53	1 03	24 03	0 41	6 46	8 25	16 10	1 01	19 12	1 51
9 Tu	22 22	13 05	4 08	15 15	21 16	1 48	22 01	1 01	24 02	0 41	6 51	8 26	16 10	1 01	19 13	1 51
10 W	22 15	17 13	3 13	18 56	20 47	1 45	22 09	0 59	24 01	0 42	6 55	8 27	16 10	1 00	19 14	1 51
11 Th	22 07	20 23	2 06	21 31	20 17	1 42	22 16	0 56	23 59	0 42	6 60	8 28	16 10	1 00	19 15	1 52
12 F	21 59	22 17	0 49	22 40	19 47	1 38	22 23	0 53	23 58	0 43	7 04	8 29	16 10	0 60	19 16	1 52
13 Sa	21 51	22 39	0N31	22 15	19 15	1 34	22 28	0 51	23 56	0 43	7 08	8 30	16 10	0 60	19 17	1 52
14 Su	21 42	21 27	1 50	20 16	18 43	1 29	22 34	0 48	23 54	0 44	7 12	8 31	16 10	0 59	19 18	1 52
15 M	21 33	18 46	3 01	16 59	18 09	1 23	22 38	0 46	23 52	0 44	7 16	8 32	16 11	0 59	19 19	1 52
16 Tu	21 23	14 56	3 59	12 43	17 35	1 17	22 42	0 43	23 50	0 45	7 20	8 33	16 11	0 59	19 20	1 52
17 W	21 13	10 20	4 40	7 44	17 01	1 11	22 46	0 40	23 47	0 45	7 24	8 34	16 11	0 59	19 21	1 52
18 Th	21 03	5 18	5 04	2 44	16 26	1 04	22 48	0 38	23 45	0 46	7 28	8 35	16 12	0 58	19 22	1 52
19 F	20 52	0 11	5 10	2N20	15 51	0 57	22 50	0 35	23 42	0 46	7 32	8 36	16 12	0 58	19 23	1 52
20 Sa	20 41	4N47	4 60	7 09	15 15	0 49	22 52	0 32	23 39	0 47	7 35	8 37	16 13	0 58	19 24	1 52
21 Su	20 30	9 25	4 35	11 33	14 39	0 41	22 52	0 30	23 35	0 47	7 39	8 38	16 13	0 58	19 25	1 52
22 M	20 18	13 32	3 58	15 22	14 03	0 32	22 52	0 27	23 32	0 48	7 42	8 39	16 14	0 57	19 26	1 53
23 Tu	20 06	17 02	3 11	18 30	13 27	0 24	22 52	0 24	23 28	0 48	7 46	8 40	16 14	0 57	19 27	1 53
24 W	19 54	19 46	2 17	20 49	12 51	0 14	22 51	0 22	23 24	0 49	7 49	8 41	16 15	0 57	19 28	1 53
25 Th	19 41	21 39	1 17	22 14	12 16	0 05	22 49	0 19	23 20	0 49	7 52	8 43	16 16	0 57	19 28	1 53
26 F	19 28	22 35	0 13	22 40	11 40	0S05	22 46	0 16	23 16	0 50	7 56	8 44	16 16	0 56	19 29	1 53
27 Sa	19 14	22 30	0S51	22 04	11 04	0 15	22 43	0 14	23 12	0 50	7 59	8 45	16 17	0 56	19 30	1 53
28 Su	19 01	21 23	1 53	20 26	10 29	0 25	22 39	0 11	23 07	0 51	8 02	8 46	16 18	0 56	19 31	1 53
29 M	18 47	19 15	2 51	17 51	9 54	0 36	22 34	0 08	23 02	0 51	8 05	8 47	16 19	0 56	19 32	1 53
30 Tu	18 32	16 13	3 42	14 24	9 20	0 47	22 29	0 06	22 57	0 52	8 08	8 49	16 20	0 55	19 32	1 53
31 W	18N18	12N24	4S23	10N14	8N47	0S58	22N23	0S03	22N52	0N52	8N10	8S50	16S21	0N55	19N33	1S53

Day	⚷		♅		♆		♇	
	Decl	Lat	Decl	Lat	Decl	Lat	Decl	Lat
1	15N04	1S33	23N07	0N04	3N52	1S31	23S13	6S10
6	15 07	1 33	23 08	0 04	3 52	1 31	23 16	6 11
11	15 09	1 34	23 09	0 04	3 52	1 32	23 18	6 11
16	15 12	1 35	23 10	0 04	3 52	1 32	23 21	6 12
21	15 13	1 36	23 12	0 04	3 52	1 32	23 23	6 13
26	15 15	1 37	23 13	0 04	3 51	1 32	23 26	6 13
31	15N16	1S37	23N14	0N04	3N50	1S33	23S28	6S14

Day	⚴		⚵		⚶		Eris	
	Decl	Lat	Decl	Lat	Decl	Lat	Decl	Lat
1	11N57	18N55	5S03	18N21	11N14	5S49	1N22	9S37
6	11 55	18 55	5 12	18 13	11 41	5 53	1 22	9 38
11	11 50	18 53	5 25	18 01	12 06	5 58	1 22	9 38
16	11 39	18 50	5 40	17 46	12 30	6 03	1 21	9 38
21	11 23	18 45	5 59	17 27	12 51	6 08	1 21	9 39
26	11 02	18 37	6 19	17 07	13 10	6 13	1 21	9 39
31	10N35	18N27	6S41	16N43	13N26	6S18	1N20	9S39

Moon Phenomena

Max/0 Decl
dy hr mn
6 8:24 0 S
12 17:41 22S43
19 0:51 0 N
26 10:03 22N40

Perigee/Apogee
dy hr m kilometers
13 5:16 p 361798
25 4:55 a 404886

Max/0 Lat
dy hr mn
6 5:07 5S14
12 14:43 0 N
18 20:35 5N10
26 5:02 0 S

PH dy hr mn
☽ 8 11:03 16♎21
○ 15 2:13 22♑41
☾ 22 8:09 29♈35
● 30 11:12 7♌21

Void of Course Moon

Last Aspect	☽ Ingress
1 16:24 ☿ ☌	♌ 2 14:34
4 5:03 ♅ ⚹	♍ 4 23:38
7 5:37 ☿ ⚹	♎ 7 6:18
8 17:58 ♅ △	♏ 9 10:30
10 17:38 ☉ △	♐ 11 12:35
13 4:55 ♀ ☍	♑ 13 13:22
15 2:13 ☉ ☍	♒ 15 14:15
17 1:06 ♅ △	♓ 17 16:58
19 17:39 ☉ △	♈ 19 23:02
22 8:09 ☉ □	♉ 22 8:58
24 16:32 ☿ □	♊ 24 21:31
26 16:42 ♅ ☌	♋ 27 10:16
28 22:18 ♂ ☌	♌ 29 21:09

DAILY ASPECTARIAN

1 M
☉∥♅ 0:05
☿∥♂ 2:03
☽⚻♇ 2:24
☽∥♀ 2:41
⚴ R 5:51
☽□♆ 5:52
☿△♃ 9:19
☽⚹⚷ 10:39
☽△♃ 15:11
♂ ♋ 15:21
☽☌☿ 16:24
☽∠♄ 16:33
☿∠♄ 17:19
☽∥♄ 18:53
☽⚺♅ 18:58

2 Tu
♀△♇ 4:23
☿⚺♅ 8:03
☽∠♀ 8:14
☽⚺♂ 15:55
☽#♃ 17:26
♂∠⚷ 19:35
☽⚹♄ 22:03

3 W
☽∠♅ 0:18
☽∥⚷ 0:54
☽□⚳ 6:51
☉⚻♇ 9:27
☽☍♇ 12:46
☉⚺☽ 13:02
☽⚹♀ 16:13
☽△♆ 16:14
♀⚹♆ 16:15
☽□⚷ 21:00
☽∠♂ 22:20

4 Th
☿#♇ 0:38
☽□♃ 0:59
☽⚹♅ 5:03
☿∥♅ 9:19
☽⚺☿ 13:14
☉∠☽ 19:41
☽⚼♆ 20:33

5 F
☽∥⚳ 0:44
☽⚹♂ 4:04
☽□♄ 7:19
☉□♆ 7:21
☉∥☿ 10:39
☽∥♆ 13:56
☽△⚳ 16:36
♀⚺⚷ 19:59
☽⚻♇ 20:50
♂⚼♃ 21:59
☽∠☿ 21:59

6 Sa
☽⚻♆ 0:16
☉⚹☽ 1:35
☽△⚷ 4:59
☽□♀ 5:51
☽⚹♃ 8:30
☽□♅ 12:45
☽⚼⚳ 20:30
☽⚼♇ 23:57

7 Su
☽#♆ 2:36
☽⚹☿ 5:37
☽⚼⚷ 8:02
☿ ♌ 10:24
♀⚻♃ 10:33
☽∠♃ 11:21
☽□♂ 13:23
☽△♄ 14:04
☽#⚳ 16:14
☿∥♀ 16:48
☽⚻⚳ 23:43

8 M
☉⚹⚷ 2:25
☽△♇ 2:28
♂⚺♄ 5:43
☽☍♆ 5:51
☽⚻⚷ 10:29
☊ D 10:54
☉□☽ 11:03
☽⚺♃ 13:36
☽△♀ 16:13
☽⚼♄ 16:30
☽△♅ 17:58

9 Tu
☽#⚷ 11:23
♀☌♅ 13:18
☽∥♃ 17:28
☽□☿ 17:43
☽⚻♄ 18:20
☽⚼♅ 19:40
☽△♂ 19:52
☽⚼♀ 20:14
☿⚹♄ 22:49
☉△♃ 23:28

10 W
☽☍⚳ 4:15
☽□♇ 5:44
☽⚻♆ 9:03
☉∥♀ 9:22
☿∠♅ 9:33
☽☍⚷ 13:37
☽#♄ 14:22
☽☌♃ 16:25
☉△☽ 17:38
☿⚺♂ 19:38
☽⚻♅ 20:51
☽⚼♂ 22:10
☽#☿ 23:16
☽⚻♀ 23:35

11 Th
☽⚼♆ 9:55
☉#☽ 19:09
☉⚼☽ 20:04
☽☍♄ 20:30
☽⚻♂ 24:00

12 F
☽△☿ 2:21
☽#♀ 2:22
☉∠♄ 3:26
☿∠♀ 3:35
☽⚻⚳ 6:45
☽⚹♇ 7:07
☽△♆ 10:25
☊ R 14:46
☽⚻⚷ 14:58
☽⚺♃ 17:33
☉⚺♅ 21:08
☽☍♅ 22:06
☉⚻☽ 22:09
☿∥♄ 22:27

13 Sa
⚳□♇ 0:23
☽☍♀ 4:55
☽⚼☿ 5:53
☽#♀ 6:01
☽∠♇ 7:25
☽⚼⚳ 7:33
☽⚼⚷ 15:20
☽∠♃ 17:50
☿☍♇ 19:08
☉#☽ 20:26
☽⚻♄ 21:32
☿□⚳ 23:17

14 Su
☽☍♂ 2:58
☽⚺♇ 7:41
☽△⚳ 8:20
☽⚻☿ 9:17
☽□♆ 11:03
♀⚼♇ 11:07
☽△⚷ 15:44
☽⚹♃ 18:11
☽#♄ 19:54
☽⚼♄ 22:05
♀∠⚳ 22:39
☽⚻♅ 22:57

15 M
☿△♆ 1:12
♃ D 1:28
☉☍☽ 2:13
☽#☿ 5:08
☽⚻♀ 10:03
☽∥♃ 16:51
☽#⚷ 22:35
☽△♄ 22:57
☽⚼♅ 23:45

16 Tu
⚵ R♐ 3:19
☽⚻♂ 6:35
☽☌♇ 8:59
☽□⚳ 10:44
☽⚹♆ 12:33
☽⚼♀ 13:17
♆ R 16:29
☽☍☿ 17:03
☽□⚷ 17:30
☽□♃ 19:58
☿□⚷ 21:19

17 W
☽△♅ 1:06
☉⚻☽ 8:00
☽⚼♂ 9:18
♀ ♋ 12:47
☽#⚳ 13:57
☽∠♆ 14:10
☽△♀ 17:22
☿□♃ 19:40

18 Th
☽□♄ 2:33
☽#♆ 6:43
♂⚻♇ 8:29
☿#♃ 9:42
☉⚼☽ 12:14
☽⚺♇ 12:43
☽△♂ 12:57
☽⚹⚳ 15:46
♀∠⚷ 16:15
☽⚺♆ 16:37
☽⚹⚷ 22:01

19 F
☽△♃ 0:33
☽⚻☿ 4:17
☽□♅ 6:13
☽∠♇ 15:57
☉△☽ 17:39
☽∥♆ 19:26
☽∠⚳ 19:44
♀⚼♃ 20:22
☿⚹♅ 22:04

20 Sa
☿∥⚷ 1:23
☽∠⚷ 1:42
☽⚼♃ 4:17
☽□♀ 5:06
⚳⚺♆ 9:34
☽⚹♄ 9:45
☽⚼☿ 11:47
☽∥⚳ 14:26
☽⚹♇ 20:09
☽□♂ 23:37

21 Su
☽☌♆ 0:25
☽⚺⚳ 0:45
☽⚺⚷ 6:22
☽⚻♃ 9:01
♂□♆ 14:38
☽∠♄ 14:50
☽⚹♅ 15:15
☽△☿ 20:32

22 M
☽∥☿ 2:49
☉□☽ 8:09
☊ D 8:17
♀⚺♄ 9:36
♂⚹⚳ 10:14
☽∥⚷ 11:02
☽#♃ 18:04
☉ ♌ 18:26
☽⚺♄ 20:47
☽∠♅ 21:05
☽⚹♀ 21:56

23 Tu
☽□♇ 7:11
☽⚺♆ 11:45
☽☌⚳ 13:28
☽⚹♂ 14:26
☽☌⚷ 18:08
☽∥♄ 20:51
☽☍♃ 20:53
♂#♇ 21:58

24 W
☉∥☽ 1:10
☽⚺♅ 3:30
☽∠♀ 7:42
☽□☿ 16:32
☽∠♆ 18:11
☽∠♂ 22:42

25 Th
☉⚹☽ 2:01
☿⚼♆ 7:37
☽☌♄ 10:03
☽⚺♀ 17:43
☽△♇ 20:00
☉∥♄ 21:39

26 F
☽⚹♆ 0:41
☽⚺⚳ 3:46
☊ R 5:03
☽⚺♂ 7:00
☽⚺⚷ 7:15
☽⚻♃ 10:00
☉∠☽ 11:10
♂⚹⚷ 11:27
☿ ♍ 14:55
♀⚻♇ 15:33
☽☌♅ 16:42
♂∥♅ 17:36

27 Sa
☽⚼♇ 2:16
☽∠⚳ 10:40
☽⚹☿ 12:26
☽∠⚷ 13:30
☽⚼♃ 16:15
☉⚺☽ 19:55
☽⚺♄ 23:00

28 Su
☽⚻♇ 8:07
☽☌♀ 12:41
☽□♆ 12:45
♀□♆ 13:20
♂△♃ 16:00
☽⚹⚳ 17:01
☽⚹⚷ 19:15
☽∠☿ 21:17
☽∥♄ 21:28
☽△♃ 21:59
☽☌♂ 22:18

29 M
☽⚺♅ 4:29
☉∥☽ 4:40
☽∠♄ 4:42
☉∠♅ 10:59
☉⚹♄ 14:23
☿∠♂ 23:03
☽#♃ 23:13

30 Tu
☽⚺☿ 5:08
☽∥⚷ 6:26
☽∠♅ 9:27
☽⚹♄ 9:45
☉☌☽ 11:12
♀⚹⚳ 17:50
☽☍♇ 17:59
☽△♆ 22:30

31 W
☽□⚳ 3:42
☽⚺♀ 4:32
☽□⚷ 4:50
☽□♃ 7:33
♀⚹⚷ 7:38
☽⚺♂ 10:45
☽⚹♅ 13:46
☽∥☿ 22:23
☽∥⚳ 22:37

August 2030

LONGITUDE

Day	Sid.Time	☉	☽	☽ 12 hour	Mean☊	True☊	☿	♀	♂	⚳	♃	♄	⚷	♅	♆	♇
	h m s	° ' "	° ' "	° ' "	° '	° '	° '	° '	° '	° '	° '	° '	° '	° '	° '	° '
1 Th	20 38 37	8♌49 27	27♌00 26	3♍32 02	13♐34.9	14♐58.6	6♍02.2	17♋31.9	20♋13.8	16♉17.9	18♏11.4	6♊43.7	16♉42.9	21♊30.4	13♈19.2	10♒54.4
2 F	20 42 33	9 46 52	10♍06 59	16 45 08	13 31.7	14R 49.3	7 01.2	18 44.9	20 53.2	16 31.8	18 14.5	6 48.6	16 44.0	21 33.0	13R 18.7	10R 53.0
3 Sa	20 46 30	10 44 17	23 26 21	0♎10 30	13 28.5	14 41.0	7 57.3	19 57.9	21 32.5	16 45.6	18 17.8	6 53.5	16 45.1	21 35.6	13 18.1	10 51.6
4 Su	20 50 26	11 41 44	6♎57 27	13 47 04	13 25.3	14 34.4	8 50.3	21 11.0	22 11.8	16 59.1	18 21.2	6 58.2	16 46.1	21 38.2	13 17.6	10 50.3
5 M	20 54 23	12 39 11	20 39 17	27 34 00	13 22.1	14 30.2	9 40.3	22 24.1	22 51.0	17 12.4	18 24.8	7 02.9	16 47.0	21 40.7	13 17.0	10 48.9
6 Tu	20 58 19	13 36 38	4♏31 09	11♏30 40	13 19.0	14D 28.1	10 26.9	23 37.2	23 30.2	17 25.5	18 28.6	7 07.4	16 47.9	21 43.2	13 16.4	10 47.5
7 W	21 02 16	14 34 07	18 32 28	25 36 28	13 15.8	14 27.8	11 10.0	24 50.4	24 09.4	17 38.4	18 32.5	7 11.9	16 48.8	21 45.7	13 15.7	10 46.1
8 Th	21 06 13	15 31 36	2♐42 34	9♐50 33	13 12.6	14R 28.4	11 49.5	26 03.6	24 48.5	17 51.1	18 36.6	7 16.4	16 49.6	21 48.1	13 15.0	10 44.8
9 F	21 10 09	16 29 06	17 00 14	24 11 17	13 09.4	14 28.7	12 25.1	27 16.8	25 27.6	18 03.5	18 40.9	7 20.7	16 50.3	21 50.5	13 14.3	10 43.4
10 Sa	21 14 06	17 26 37	1♑23 21	8♑35 56	13 06.3	14 27.6	12 56.7	28 30.1	26 06.6	18 15.8	18 45.3	7 24.9	16 51.0	21 52.9	13 13.6	10 42.0
11 Su	21 18 02	18 24 09	15 48 31	23 00 30	13 03.1	14 24.3	13 24.0	29 43.4	26 45.6	18 27.8	18 49.9	7 29.1	16 51.6	21 55.2	13 12.8	10 40.7
12 M	21 21 59	19 21 41	0♒11 11	7♒19 53	12 59.9	14 18.4	13 46.9	0♌56.8	27 24.6	18 39.5	18 54.7	7 33.2	16 52.1	21 57.5	13 12.0	10 39.3
13 Tu	21 25 55	20 19 15	14 25 55	21 28 34	12 56.7	14 10.1	14 05.1	2 10.2	28 03.5	18 51.1	18 59.6	7 37.2	16 52.6	21 59.7	13 11.2	10 38.0
14 W	21 29 52	21 16 49	28 27 14	5♓21 20	12 53.6	14 00.1	14 18.5	3 23.6	28 42.4	19 02.4	19 04.6	7 41.1	16 53.1	22 02.0	13 10.3	10 36.6
15 Th	21 33 49	22 14 25	12♓10 26	18 54 12	12 50.4	13 49.2	14 26.7	4 37.1	29 21.3	19 13.5	19 09.8	7 44.9	16 53.5	22 04.1	13 09.4	10 35.3
16 F	21 37 45	23 12 02	25 32 23	2♈04 57	12 47.2	13 38.8	14R 29.7	5 50.6	0♌00.1	19 24.3	19 15.2	7 48.6	16 53.8	22 06.2	13 08.5	10 33.9
17 Sa	21 41 42	24 09 41	8♈31 54	14 53 25	12 44.0	13 29.8	14 27.3	7 04.1	0 38.9	19 34.9	19 20.7	7 52.3	16 54.1	22 08.3	13 07.6	10 32.6
18 Su	21 45 38	25 07 21	21 09 47	27 21 21	12 40.8	13 23.0	14 19.3	8 17.7	1 17.6	19 45.2	19 26.4	7 55.8	16 54.3	22 10.4	13 06.6	10 31.3
19 M	21 49 35	26 05 02	3♉28 37	9♉32 05	12 37.7	13 18.5	14 05.6	9 31.3	1 56.3	19 55.3	19 32.2	7 59.3	16 54.4	22 12.3	13 05.6	10 29.9
20 Tu	21 53 31	27 02 46	15 32 20	21 30 02	12 34.5	13 16.3	13 46.3	10 45.0	2 35.0	20 05.1	19 38.2	8 02.6	16 54.5	22 14.3	13 04.6	10 28.6
21 W	21 57 28	28 00 30	27 25 48	3♊20 21	12 31.3	13D 15.7	13 21.3	11 58.7	3 13.7	20 14.6	19 44.3	8 05.9	16R 54.6	22 16.2	13 03.5	10 27.3
22 Th	22 01 24	28 58 17	9♊14 22	15 08 30	12 28.1	13R 15.9	12 50.8	13 12.4	3 52.3	20 23.9	19 50.5	8 09.1	16 54.6	22 18.1	13 02.5	10 26.0
23 F	22 05 21	29 56 05	21 03 28	26 59 53	12 25.0	13 15.7	12 15.0	14 26.2	4 30.9	20 32.9	19 56.9	8 12.1	16 54.5	22 19.9	13 01.4	10 24.7
24 Sa	22 09 17	0♍53 55	2♋58 23	8♋59 32	12 21.8	13 14.2	11 34.3	15 40.0	5 09.4	20 41.6	20 03.5	8 15.1	16 54.3	22 21.7	13 00.3	10 23.5
25 Su	22 13 14	1 51 47	15 03 51	21 11 48	12 18.6	13 10.5	10 49.2	16 53.8	5 47.9	20 50.0	20 10.2	8 18.0	16 54.2	22 23.4	12 59.1	10 22.2
26 M	22 17 11	2 49 40	27 23 45	3♌40 01	12 15.4	13 04.3	10 00.3	18 07.7	6 26.4	20 58.2	20 17.0	8 20.8	16 53.9	22 25.1	12 58.0	10 21.0
27 Tu	22 21 07	3 47 35	10♌00 48	16 26 14	12 12.2	12 55.4	9 08.3	19 21.6	7 04.8	21 06.0	20 24.0	8 23.5	16 53.6	22 26.8	12 56.8	10 19.7
28 W	22 25 04	4 45 31	22 56 20	29 31 00	12 09.1	12 44.3	8 14.1	20 35.6	7 43.2	21 13.6	20 31.1	8 26.1	16 53.2	22 28.4	12 55.6	10 18.5
29 Th	22 29 00	5 43 29	6♍10 05	12♍53 18	12 05.9	12 32.0	7 18.9	21 49.5	8 21.6	21 20.8	20 38.3	8 28.6	16 52.8	22 29.9	12 54.3	10 17.3
30 F	22 32 57	6 41 28	19 40 20	26 30 48	12 02.7	12 19.5	6 23.6	23 03.6	8 59.9	21 27.8	20 45.7	8 30.9	16 52.3	22 31.4	12 53.1	10 16.0
31 Sa	22 36 53	7♍39 30	3♎24 15	10♎20 16	11♐59.5	12♐08.3	5♍29.4	24♌17.6	9♌38.2	21♉34.4	20♏53.2	8♊33.2	16♉51.8	22♊32.9	12♈51.8	10♒14.8

1st of Month

Julian Day # 2462714.5
Obliquity 23°26'35"
SVP 4♓49'39"
GC 27♐16.0
Eris 26♈53.1R

Day	⚴	Day	⚵	Day	⚶
1	13♓25.3R	1	27♐29.3R	1	27♉45.5
6	12 29.6R	6	26 58.4R	6	29 19.8
11	11 27.2R	11	26 36.4R	11	0♊49.6
16	10 19.0R	16	26 23.2R	16	2 14.5
21	9 06.3R	21	26 19.1	21	3 34.2
26	7 50.5R	26	26 23.8	26	4 48.2
31	6 33.3R	31	26 37.1	31	5 55.8

DECLINATION and LATITUDE

Day	☉ Decl	☽ Decl	☽ Lat	☽12h Decl	☿ Decl	☿ Lat	♀ Decl	♀ Lat	♂ Decl	♂ Lat	⚳ Decl	⚳ Lat	♃ Decl	♃ Lat	♄ Decl	♄ Lat
1 Th	18N03	7N57	4S51	5N33	8N13	1S09	22N17	0S00	22N47	0N53	8N13	8S51	16S22	0N55	19N34	1S54
2 F	17 48	3 04	5 05	0 32	7 41	1 21	22 10	0N02	22 41	0 53	8 16	8 52	16 23	0 55	19 34	1 54
3 Sa	17 32	2S01	5 02	4S34	7 10	1 32	22 02	0 05	22 35	0 54	8 18	8 53	16 24	0 54	19 35	1 54
4 Su	17 16	7 05	4 43	9 32	6 39	1 44	21 53	0 08	22 30	0 54	8 21	8 55	16 25	0 54	19 36	1 54
5 M	17 00	11 53	4 07	14 05	6 10	1 55	21 44	0 10	22 24	0 54	8 23	8 56	16 27	0 54	19 36	1 54
6 Tu	16 44	16 07	3 17	17 56	5 41	2 07	21 35	0 13	22 17	0 55	8 25	8 57	16 28	0 54	19 37	1 54
7 W	16 28	19 29	2 14	20 46	5 14	2 19	21 24	0 15	22 11	0 55	8 28	8 58	16 29	0 53	19 38	1 54
8 Th	16 11	21 43	1 03	22 20	4 48	2 31	21 13	0 18	22 05	0 56	8 30	8 60	16 31	0 53	19 38	1 54
9 F	15 54	22 35	0N14	22 27	4 24	2 43	21 02	0 20	21 58	0 56	8 32	9 01	16 32	0 53	19 39	1 55
10 Sa	15 36	21 57	1 29	21 05	4 01	2 54	20 50	0 23	21 51	0 57	8 34	9 02	16 33	0 53	19 39	1 55
11 Su	15 19	19 52	2 39	18 21	3 40	3 06	20 37	0 25	21 44	0 57	8 36	9 04	16 35	0 52	19 40	1 55
12 M	15 01	16 33	3 38	14 31	3 21	3 17	20 23	0 28	21 37	0 58	8 38	9 05	16 36	0 52	19 40	1 55
13 Tu	14 43	12 17	4 24	9 55	3 04	3 28	20 10	0 30	21 30	0 58	8 39	9 06	16 38	0 52	19 41	1 55
14 W	14 24	7 26	4 52	4 54	2 49	3 38	19 55	0 32	21 22	0 58	8 41	9 08	16 40	0 52	19 41	1 55
15 Th	14 06	2 20	5 03	0N14	2 36	3 48	19 40	0 35	21 14	0 59	8 43	9 09	16 41	0 51	19 42	1 55
16 F	13 47	2N46	4 56	5 13	2 26	3 58	19 24	0 37	21 07	0 59	8 44	9 10	16 43	0 51	19 42	1 56
17 Sa	13 28	7 35	4 35	9 51	2 19	4 07	19 08	0 39	20 59	0 60	8 46	9 12	16 45	0 51	19 43	1 56
18 Su	13 09	11 58	4 00	13 56	2 15	4 15	18 51	0 41	20 51	1 00	8 47	9 13	16 46	0 51	19 43	1 56
19 M	12 49	15 43	3 15	17 20	2 13	4 22	18 34	0 43	20 42	1 01	8 48	9 14	16 48	0 51	19 44	1 56
20 Tu	12 30	18 45	2 22	19 57	2 15	4 28	18 16	0 46	20 34	1 01	8 49	9 16	16 50	0 50	19 44	1 56
21 W	12 10	20 56	1 23	21 41	2 20	4 33	17 58	0 48	20 26	1 01	8 51	9 17	16 52	0 50	19 44	1 56
22 Th	11 50	22 11	0 21	22 26	2 28	4 37	17 39	0 50	20 17	1 02	8 52	9 18	16 54	0 50	19 45	1 56
23 F	11 30	22 27	0S41	22 12	2 40	4 39	17 19	0 52	20 08	1 02	8 53	9 20	16 56	0 50	19 45	1 57
24 Sa	11 09	21 41	1 43	20 56	2 55	4 40	16 59	0 54	19 59	1 03	8 53	9 21	16 58	0 49	19 45	1 57
25 Su	10 49	19 56	2 40	18 41	3 13	4 38	16 39	0 56	19 50	1 03	8 54	9 22	16 60	0 49	19 46	1 57
26 M	10 28	17 13	3 31	15 33	3 34	4 35	16 18	0 57	19 41	1 03	8 55	9 24	17 02	0 49	19 46	1 57
27 Tu	10 07	13 40	4 13	11 37	3 58	4 31	15 57	0 59	19 32	1 04	8 56	9 25	17 04	0 49	19 46	1 57
28 W	9 46	9 24	4 43	7 04	4 24	4 24	15 35	1 01	19 22	1 04	8 56	9 27	17 06	0 49	19 47	1 57
29 Th	9 25	4 37	4 59	2 05	4 52	4 15	15 13	1 03	19 13	1 05	8 57	9 28	17 08	0 48	19 47	1 57
30 F	9 03	0S29	4 58	3S04	5 22	4 04	14 50	1 04	19 03	1 05	8 57	9 29	17 10	0 48	19 47	1 58
31 Sa	8N42	5S39	4S40	8S09	5N54	3S52	14N27	1N06	18N53	1N06	8N57	9S31	17S12	0N48	19N47	1S58

Day	⚷ Decl	⚷ Lat	♅ Decl	♅ Lat	♆ Decl	♆ Lat	♇ Decl	♇ Lat
1	15N16	1S38	23N14	0N04	3N50	1S33	23S28	6S14
6	15 17	1 39	23 15	0 04	3 49	1 33	23 31	6 14
11	15 17	1 39	23 15	0 04	3 47	1 33	23 33	6 14
16	15 17	1 40	23 16	0 04	3 45	1 33	23 35	6 15
21	15 16	1 41	23 17	0 04	3 43	1 34	23 37	6 15
26	15 15	1 42	23 17	0 04	3 41	1 34	23 39	6 15
31	15N13	1S43	23N18	0N04	3N38	1S34	23S41	6S15

Day	⚴ Decl	⚴ Lat	⚵ Decl	⚵ Lat	⚶ Decl	⚶ Lat	Eris Decl	Eris Lat
1	10N29	18N24	6S46	16N39	13N30	6S19	1N20	9S39
6	9 56	18 10	7 11	16 14	13 44	6 25	1 20	9 40
11	9 17	17 52	7 36	15 47	13 56	6 31	1 19	9 40
16	8 32	17 31	8 03	15 21	14 07	6 37	1 19	9 40
21	7 42	17 05	8 30	14 53	14 16	6 44	1 18	9 41
26	6 48	16 36	8 58	14 26	14 21	6 51	1 17	9 41
31	5N50	16N03	9S25	13N59	14N26	6S58	1N16	9S41

Moon Phenomena

Max/0 Decl

dy	hr mn	
2	14:31	0 S
9	1:53	22S35
15	10:53	0 N
22	18:13	22N28
29	21:45	0 S

Max/0 Lat

dy	hr mn	
2	8:25	5S06
8	19:46	0 N
15	2:52	5N03
22	8:11	0 S
29	11:11	5S01

Perigee/Apogee

dy	hr m		kilometers
9	22:46	p	366740
21	22:50	a	404172

PH	dy	hr mn	
☽	6	16:44	14♏17
○	13	10:46	20♒45
☾	21	1:17	28♉04
●	28	23:09	5♍41

Void of Course Moon

Last Aspect				☽ Ingress		
31	13:46	♅	✶	♍	1	5:31
2	20:41	♅	□	♎	3	11:41
5	4:01	♂	□	♏	5	16:12
7	11:42	♀	△	♐	7	19:26
9	8:06	♅	△	♑	9	21:41
11	19:08	♂	☍	♒	11	23:41
13	12:55	♅	△	♓	14	2:41
15	17:45	♅	□	♈	16	8:10
18	8:18	☉	△	♉	18	17:10
21	1:17	☉	□	♊	21	5:13
23	2:35	♅	☌	♋	23	18:02
25	10:05	♃	△	♌	26	5:00
27	23:09	♅	✶	♍	28	12:53
30	5:01	♅	□	♎	30	18:05

DAILY ASPECTARIAN

1 Th: ☿∥⚳ 0:14; ☽⚼♆ 2:25; ☽∠♀ 11:12; ♀△♃ 13:35; ☽∠♂ 15:54; ☽☌☿ 17:55; ☽□♄ 17:57; ☿□♄ 18:20; ☽∥♆ 20:21; ☉⚺☽ 23:21

2 F: ☽⚻♇ 1:23; ☽⚻♆ 5:47; ☽△⚳ 11:48; ☽△⚷ 11:59; ☽✶♃ 14:44; ☽✶♀ 17:09; ☽✶♂ 20:26; ☽□♅ 20:41; ⚳☌⚷ 23:05

3 Sa: ♂⚺♅ 2:03; ☉☍♇ 3:00; ☽⚼♇ 4:19; ☉∠☽ 4:25; ☽∦♆ 8:28; ♂∠♄ 14:34; ☽⚼⚷ 14:49; ☽⚼⚳ 15:04; ☽∠♃ 17:36; ☽∦☿ 22:05

4 Su: ☽△♄ 0:01; ☽⚺☿ 3:32; ☽∦⚳ 6:09; ☽△♇ 6:49; ☉✶☽ 8:58; ♀⚺♅ 9:16; ☽☍♆ 11:08; ♀∠♄ 16:34; ☽⚻⚷ 17:14; ☽⚻⚳ 17:53; ☽⚺♃ 20:05

5 M: ☽△♅ 1:47; ☽⚼♄ 2:26; ☽□♀ 3:20; ☽□♂ 4:01; ☽∠☿ 7:24; ☉△♆ 15:37; ☽∦⚷ 18:55; ♀☌♂ 19:04

6 Tu: ☽∥♃ 2:14; ☉∦☽ 3:41; ☽⚼♅ 3:48; ☽⚻♄ 4:30; ☽✶☿ 10:45; ☽□♇ 10:45; ☿⚻♇ 10:54; ☽⚻♆ 15:00; ☊ D 16:34; ☉□☽ 16:44; ☽☍⚷ 21:03; ☉∦♃ 21:49; ☽☍⚳ 22:26

7 W: ☽☌♃ 0:00; ☽∦♄ 1:12; ☽⚻♅ 5:30; ☽△♂ 10:00; ☽△♀ 11:42; ☽⚼♆ 16:29; ☽∦♀ 17:52

8 Th: ⚶ ♊ 4:59; ☽∦♂ 5:40; ☽☍♄ 7:43; ☽⚼♂ 12:31; ☽✶♇ 13:30; ☽⚼♀ 15:21; ☽□☿ 16:00; ☽△♆ 17:42; ☊ R 19:48; ☉△☽ 23:04; ☽⚻⚷ 23:43

9 F: ☽⚻⚳ 1:47; ☽⚺♃ 2:49; ☿∠♀ 4:56; ☽☍♅ 8:06; ☉□⚷ 8:57; ☽∠♇ 14:32; ☽⚻♂ 14:47; ☽⚻♀ 18:45

10 Sa: ☽⚼⚷ 0:46; ☽∦♂ 1:40; ☉⚼☽ 1:53; ☽⚼⚳ 3:10; ☽∠♃ 3:58; ☽⚻♄ 10:05; ☿⚻♆ 13:58; ☽⚺♇ 15:28; ☿∥♆ 15:28; ☽∦♀ 16:14; ☽□♆ 19:41; ☽△☿ 19:52

11 Su: ☽∦♄ 1:43; ☽△⚷ 1:45; ☉□⚳ 1:54; ☉∥⚷ 2:24; ☽△⚳ 4:29; ☉⚻☽ 4:38; ☽✶♃ 5:04; ♀ ♌ 5:25; ☽⚻♅ 10:13; ☽⚼♄ 11:11; ☉□♃ 11:42; ☽☍♂ 19:08; ☽⚼☿ 21:35; ☽∥♃ 23:38

12 M: ☽☍♀ 1:24; ☽∦⚷ 7:38; ☉∦☽ 9:53; ☽⚼♅ 11:24; ☽△♄ 12:26; ☽☌♇ 17:35; ☽✶♆ 21:53; ☽⚻☿ 23:24

13 Tu: ☽□⚷ 4:09; ☽□⚳ 7:37; ☽□♃ 7:48; ☉☍☽ 10:46; ☽△♅ 12:55; ☽∦⚳ 18:04; ☽∠♆ 23:31

14 W: ☽⚻♂ 0:28; ⚳☍♃ 8:54; ☽⚻♀ 9:25; ☽□♄ 16:10; ☽∦♆ 17:19; ☉✶♅ 19:32; ♀∥♄ 20:50; ☽⚺♇ 21:12; ☽∦☿ 22:39

15 Th: ☽⚺♆ 1:44; ☿∠♂ 3:55; ☽☍☿ 4:04; ☽⚼♂ 4:04; ☽✶⚷ 8:24; ☽△♃ 12:33; ☽✶⚳ 12:45; ☽⚼♀ 14:38; ☽□♅ 17:45; ☉⚻☽ 19:25; ☽∥☿ 22:30; ♂ ♌ 23:57

16 F: ☽∠♇ 0:03; ☿ R 1:21; ☽∥♆ 4:47; ☽△♂ 8:35; ☽∠⚷ 11:40; ☽⚼♃ 16:08; ☽∠⚳ 16:32; ☽△♀ 20:58; ☽✶♄ 22:45

17 Sa: ☉⚼☽ 1:17; ♀∠♅ 1:24; ☽✶♇ 3:46; ☽∥⚳ 6:11; ☽☌♆ 8:39; ☽⚻☿ 11:05; ☽⚺⚷ 15:50; ♀✶♄ 16:30; ☽⚻♃ 20:40; ☽⚺⚳ 21:15

18 Su: ☽✶♅ 1:57; ☽∠♄ 3:26; ☉∥☽ 6:34; ☉△☽ 8:18; ☽⚼☿ 15:34; ☽□♂ 20:48; ☽∥⚷ 20:51

19 M: ☽∠♅ 7:24; ☽∦♃ 7:56; ☽⚺♄ 8:58; ☽□♀ 13:20; ☽□♇ 13:54; ♀☍♇ 18:46; ☽⚺♆ 19:04; ☽∥♀ 20:07; ☽△☿ 20:34

20 Tu: ☽☌⚷ 2:45; ☽☍♃ 8:19; ☽☌⚳ 9:16; ☽∥♄ 9:41; ☽⚺♅ 13:32; ☽∥♂ 17:55; ⚵ D 20:12

21 W: ☉⚼♆ 1:14; ☽∠♆ 1:16; ☉□☽ 1:17; ☊ D 1:26; ⚷ R 4:53; ☽✶♂ 12:27; ☿⚻♆ 15:00; ☿⚺♀ 19:08; ♀△♆ 20:49; ☽☌♄ 21:47

22 Th: ☽△♇ 2:26; ☽□☿ 7:00; ☽✶♆ 7:43; ☊ R 8:12; ☽✶♀ 9:00; ☽⚺⚷ 15:35; ☽∠♂ 20:42; ☽⚻♃ 21:44; ☽⚺⚳ 22:57

23 F: ☉ ♍ 1:38; ☽☌♅ 2:35; ☽⚼♇ 8:47; ☽∠♀ 18:51; ☉✶☽ 19:29; ☽∠⚷ 21:52

24 Sa: ♀∦♃ 2:01; ☽⚼♃ 4:12; ☽⚺♂ 4:37; ☽∠⚳ 5:30; ☽⚺♄ 10:34; ☽⚻♇ 14:45; ☽✶☿ 16:08; ☽□♆ 19:55

25 Su: ♀□⚷ 0:06; ☽∥♂ 1:03; ☽∥♄ 1:45; ☽✶⚷ 3:37; ☉∠☽ 3:50; ☽⚺♀ 4:00; ☽△♃ 10:05; ♂∥♄ 11:17; ☽✶⚳ 11:25; ☿⚻♇ 13:48; ☽⚺♅ 14:21; ☽∠♄ 16:09; ☽∠☿ 19:41

26 M: ☽∦♃ 1:28; ☿∥♆ 7:05; ☽∥♀ 7:31; ☉⚺☽ 11:16; ☽∥⚷ 13:59; ☽☌♂ 18:11; ☽∠♅ 19:09; ☽✶♄ 20:56; ☽⚺☿ 22:28

27 Tu: ☽☍♇ 0:35; ☽△♆ 5:29; ☽□⚷ 12:50; ♂∠♅ 14:19; ☿□♄ 19:00; ☽☌♀ 19:14; ☽□♃ 19:30; ☽□⚳ 20:49; ☉∥☽ 21:56; ♀□♃ 22:23; ☽✶♅ 23:09

28 W: ☽∥⚳ 2:26; ☿⚺♂ 7:56; ☽⚼♆ 9:06; ♀□⚳ 13:41; ☽∥☿ 22:52; ♀∥⚷ 22:55; ☉☌☽ 23:09

29 Th: ☽☌☿ 1:55; ☽⚺♂ 4:07; ☽□♄ 4:09; ☽∥♆ 4:37; ♂✶♄ 4:38; ☽⚻♇ 7:22; ☽⚻♆ 12:01; ♀✶♅ 13:22; ☽△⚷ 19:04; ☉☌☿ 20:12

30 F: ☽✶♃ 1:56; ☽△⚳ 3:11; ☽□♅ 5:01; ☽⚺♀ 6:33; ☉∥⚳ 6:48; ☽∠♂ 7:58; ☽⚼♇ 9:48; ☽∦♆ 14:38; ☽⚼⚷ 21:19

31 Sa: ☽∦☿ 1:20; ☽⚺☿ 3:24; ☽∠♃ 4:21; ☽⚼⚳ 5:32; ☉⚺☽ 7:55; ☽△♄ 8:57; ☽∠♀ 11:11; ☽✶♂ 11:19; ☽△♇ 11:50; ☉∦☽ 13:37; ☽∦⚳ 15:55; ☽☍♆ 16:20; ♂☍♇ 22:16; ☉□♄ 23:05; ☽⚻⚷ 23:13

LONGITUDE

Day	Sid.Time	☉	☽	☽ 12 hour	Mean ☊	True ☊	☿	♀	♂	⚳	♃	♄	⚷	♅	♆	♇
	h m s	° ' "	° ' "	° ' "	° '	° '	° '	° '	° '	° '	° '	° '	° '	° '	° '	° '
1 Su	22 40 50	8♍37 32	17♎18 23	24♎18 11	11♐56.3	11♐59.2	4♍37.5	25♌31.7	10♌16.5	21♉40.8	21♏00.8	8♊35.4	16♉51.2	22♊34.3	12♈50.5	10♒13.7
2 M	22 44 46	9 35 36	1♏19 16	8♏21 19	11 53.2	11R 52.8	3R 49.1	26 45.8	10 54.7	21 46.8	21 08.6	8 37.5	16R 50.5	22 35.7	12R 49.2	10R 12.5
3 Tu	22 48 43	10 33 41	15 24 01	22 27 09	11 50.0	11 49.3	3 05.3	27 59.9	11 32.9	21 52.5	21 16.5	8 39.4	16 49.8	22 37.0	12 47.8	10 11.3
4 W	22 52 40	11 31 48	29 30 31	6♐34 00	11 46.8	11 48.0	2 27.2	29 14.1	12 11.1	21 57.8	21 24.5	8 41.3	16 49.0	22 38.3	12 46.5	10 10.2
5 Th	22 56 36	12 29 57	13♐37 26	20 40 46	11 43.6	11 47.8	1 55.6	0♍28.3	12 49.2	22 02.9	21 32.7	8 43.1	16 48.2	22 39.5	12 45.1	10 09.1
6 F	23 00 33	13 28 06	27 43 51	4♑46 36	11 40.5	11 47.5	1 31.3	1 42.5	13 27.3	22 07.6	21 40.9	8 44.7	16 47.3	22 40.7	12 43.7	10 08.0
7 Sa	23 04 29	14 26 18	11♑48 50	18 50 23	11 37.3	11 45.8	1 15.0	2 56.7	14 05.3	22 12.0	21 49.3	8 46.3	16 46.4	22 41.8	12 42.3	10 06.9
8 Su	23 08 26	15 24 30	25 51 00	2♒50 23	11 34.1	11 41.7	1D 07.2	4 11.0	14 43.3	22 16.0	21 57.8	8 47.7	16 45.4	22 42.9	12 40.9	10 05.8
9 M	23 12 22	16 22 44	9♒48 13	16 44 06	11 30.9	11 34.8	1 08.1	5 25.3	15 21.3	22 19.7	22 06.5	8 49.1	16 44.4	22 43.9	12 39.4	10 04.8
10 Tu	23 16 19	17 21 00	23 37 39	0♓28 25	11 27.8	11 25.2	1 18.0	6 39.6	15 59.2	22 23.1	22 15.2	8 50.3	16 43.3	22 44.9	12 38.0	10 03.7
11 W	23 20 15	18 19 17	7♓16 01	14 00 02	11 24.6	11 13.6	1 36.9	7 54.0	16 37.1	22 26.1	22 24.1	8 51.4	16 42.1	22 45.8	12 36.5	10 02.7
12 Th	23 24 12	19 17 36	20 40 08	27 16 03	11 21.4	11 01.1	2 04.7	9 08.3	17 14.9	22 28.8	22 33.0	8 52.5	16 40.9	22 46.7	12 35.0	10 01.7
13 F	23 28 09	20 15 57	3♈47 33	10♈14 31	11 18.2	10 48.9	2 41.2	10 22.8	17 52.8	22 31.1	22 42.1	8 53.4	16 39.6	22 47.5	12 33.5	10 00.7
14 Sa	23 32 05	21 14 19	16 36 55	22 54 49	11 15.0	10 38.2	3 26.2	11 37.2	18 30.6	22 33.0	22 51.3	8 54.2	16 38.3	22 48.3	12 32.0	9 59.7
15 Su	23 36 02	22 12 44	29 08 22	5♉17 50	11 11.9	10 29.7	4 19.1	12 51.7	19 08.3	22 34.6	23 00.6	8 54.9	16 36.9	22 49.0	12 30.4	9 58.8
16 M	23 39 58	23 11 11	11♉23 32	17 25 53	11 08.7	10 23.9	5 19.6	14 06.1	19 46.0	22 35.8	23 10.0	8 55.5	16 35.5	22 49.6	12 28.9	9 57.9
17 Tu	23 43 55	24 09 39	23 22 31	29 22 22	11 05.5	10 20.7	6 27.1	15 20.7	20 23.7	22 36.7	23 19.5	8 55.9	16 34.0	22 50.3	12 27.3	9 57.0
18 W	23 47 51	25 08 10	5♊17 55	11♊12 12	11 02.3	10D 19.5	7 41.1	16 35.2	21 01.4	22R 37.2	23 29.1	8 56.3	16 32.5	22 50.8	12 25.8	9 56.1
19 Th	23 51 48	26 06 44	17 06 02	23 00 06	10 59.1	10R 19.5	9 00.9	17 49.8	21 39.0	22 37.3	23 38.9	8 56.6	16 30.9	22 51.4	12 24.2	9 55.2
20 F	23 55 44	27 05 19	28 55 04	4♋51 38	10 56.0	10 19.7	10 26.0	19 04.4	22 16.6	22 37.1	23 48.7	8R 56.7	16 29.3	22 51.8	12 22.6	9 54.3
21 Sa	23 59 41	28 03 57	10♋50 29	16 52 17	10 52.8	10 18.9	11 55.7	20 19.0	22 54.2	22 36.4	23 58.6	8 56.8	16 27.6	22 52.2	12 21.0	9 53.5
22 Su	0 03 38	29 02 36	22 57 39	29 07 09	10 49.6	10 16.4	13 29.4	21 33.7	23 31.7	22 35.4	24 08.6	8 56.7	16 25.9	22 52.6	12 19.4	9 52.7
23 M	0 07 34	0♎01 18	5♌21 19	11♌40 34	10 46.4	10 11.5	15 06.6	22 48.4	24 09.2	22 34.0	24 18.7	8 56.5	16 24.1	22 52.9	12 17.8	9 51.9
24 Tu	0 11 31	1 00 02	18 05 15	24 35 36	10 43.3	10 04.1	16 46.7	24 03.1	24 46.7	22 32.2	24 29.0	8 56.2	16 22.3	22 53.2	12 16.1	9 51.2
25 W	0 15 27	1 58 49	1♍11 44	7♍53 38	10 40.1	9 54.7	18 29.1	25 17.8	25 24.1	22 30.1	24 39.3	8 55.8	16 20.4	22 53.4	12 14.5	9 50.4
26 Th	0 19 24	2 57 37	14 41 09	21 34 00	10 36.9	9 43.9	20 13.5	26 32.5	26 01.5	22 27.5	24 49.7	8 55.3	16 18.5	22 53.5	12 12.9	9 49.7
27 F	0 23 20	3 56 27	28 31 45	5♎33 53	10 33.7	9 32.9	21 59.3	27 47.3	26 38.8	22 24.6	25 00.2	8 54.7	16 16.6	22 53.6	12 11.2	9 49.0
28 Sa	0 27 17	4 55 20	12♎39 46	19 48 42	10 30.5	9 22.9	23 46.3	29 02.1	27 16.1	22 21.2	25 10.8	8 54.0	16 14.5	22R 53.7	12 09.6	9 48.4
29 Su	0 31 13	5 54 14	26 59 57	4♏12 46	10 27.4	9 14.9	25 34.1	0♎16.9	27 53.4	22 17.5	25 21.4	8 53.2	16 12.5	22 53.6	12 07.9	9 47.7
30 M	0 35 10	6♎53 10	11♏26 24	18 40 12	10♐24.2	9♐09.4	27♍22.3	1♎31.7	28♌30.6	22♉13.4	25♏32.2	8♊52.2	16♉10.4	22♊53.6	12♈06.2	9♒47.1

1st of Month

Julian Day #
2462745.5
Obliquity
23°26'05"
SVP 4♓49'36"
GC 27♐16.1
Eris 26♈45.6R

Day	⚴
1	6♓17.8R
6	5 01.2R
11	3 47.0R
16	2 36.6R
21	1 31.5R
26	0 32.9R

Day	⚵
1	26♐40.8
6	27 04.1
11	27 35.4
16	28 14.0
21	28 59.8
26	29 52.2

Day	⚶
1	6♊08.5
6	7 07.9
11	7 59.8
16	8 43.7
21	9 19.0
26	9 44.8

DECLINATION and LATITUDE

Day	☉ Decl	☽ Decl	☽ Lat	☽12h Decl	☿ Decl	☿ Lat	♀ Decl	♀ Lat	♂ Decl	♂ Lat	⚳ Decl	⚳ Lat	♃ Decl	♃ Lat	♄ Decl	♄ Lat
1 Su	8N20	10S35	4S06	12S52	6N25	3S38	14N04	1N07	18N43	1N06	8N58	9S32	17S14	0N48	19N47	1S58
2 M	7 58	15 00	3 17	16 55	6 57	3 23	13 40	1 09	18 33	1 06	8 58	9 33	17 17	0 48	19 48	1 58
3 Tu	7 36	18 36	2 15	19 60	7 29	3 06	13 16	1 10	18 23	1 07	8 58	9 35	17 19	0 47	19 48	1 58
4 W	7 14	21 06	1 05	21 51	7 59	2 48	12 51	1 12	18 13	1 07	8 58	9 36	17 21	0 47	19 48	1 58
5 Th	6 52	22 16	0N10	22 20	8 27	2 30	12 26	1 13	18 02	1 08	8 58	9 37	17 23	0 47	19 48	1 59
6 F	6 30	22 02	1 23	21 23	8 53	2 11	12 01	1 14	17 52	1 08	8 58	9 39	17 26	0 47	19 48	1 59
7 Sa	6 07	20 24	2 32	19 06	9 17	1 52	11 36	1 15	17 41	1 08	8 58	9 40	17 28	0 47	19 48	1 59
8 Su	5 45	17 31	3 30	15 42	9 38	1 33	11 10	1 16	17 31	1 09	8 57	9 41	17 31	0 46	19 48	1 59
9 M	5 22	13 40	4 16	11 28	9 55	1 14	10 43	1 18	17 20	1 09	8 57	9 42	17 33	0 46	19 48	1 59
10 Tu	4 60	9 08	4 47	6 42	10 09	0 55	10 17	1 19	17 09	1 09	8 57	9 44	17 35	0 46	19 48	1 59
11 W	4 37	4 12	4 60	1 40	10 19	0 37	9 50	1 20	16 58	1 10	8 56	9 45	17 38	0 46	19 48	1 59
12 Th	4 14	0N51	4 56	3N20	10 26	0 20	9 23	1 20	16 47	1 10	8 56	9 46	17 40	0 46	19 48	1 60
13 F	3 51	5 45	4 37	8 04	10 28	0 03	8 56	1 21	16 35	1 11	8 55	9 47	17 43	0 45	19 48	1 60
14 Sa	3 28	10 17	4 04	12 22	10 26	0N12	8 28	1 22	16 24	1 11	8 54	9 49	17 45	0 45	19 48	1 60
15 Su	3 05	14 17	3 20	16 01	10 21	0 27	8 00	1 23	16 13	1 11	8 54	9 50	17 48	0 45	19 48	2 00
16 M	2 42	17 35	2 27	18 55	10 11	0 40	7 32	1 23	16 01	1 12	8 53	9 51	17 50	0 45	19 48	2 00
17 Tu	2 19	20 03	1 29	20 57	9 57	0 52	7 04	1 24	15 50	1 12	8 52	9 52	17 53	0 45	19 48	2 00
18 W	1 56	21 37	0 27	22 02	9 40	1 04	6 35	1 24	15 38	1 12	8 51	9 53	17 55	0 44	19 48	2 01
19 Th	1 33	22 13	0S36	22 08	9 19	1 13	6 07	1 25	15 26	1 13	8 50	9 54	17 58	0 44	19 48	2 01
20 F	1 09	21 48	1 37	21 19	8 55	1 22	5 38	1 25	15 14	1 13	8 49	9 55	18 01	0 44	19 48	2 01
21 Sa	0 46	20 25	2 35	19 22	8 28	1 29	5 09	1 25	15 02	1 14	8 48	9 56	18 03	0 44	19 48	2 01
22 Su	0 23	18 05	3 26	16 35	7 58	1 36	4 39	1 26	14 50	1 14	8 47	9 57	18 06	0 44	19 47	2 01
23 M	0S01	14 53	4 10	13 00	7 25	1 41	4 10	1 26	14 38	1 14	8 45	9 58	18 08	0 44	19 47	2 01
24 Tu	0 24	10 56	4 41	8 43	6 50	1 45	3 41	1 26	14 26	1 15	8 44	9 59	18 11	0 43	19 47	2 01
25 W	0 47	6 22	4 60	3 55	6 13	1 48	3 11	1 26	14 14	1 15	8 43	9 60	18 14	0 43	19 47	2 02
26 Th	1 11	1 23	5 02	1S12	5 34	1 51	2 41	1 26	14 01	1 15	8 41	10 00	18 16	0 43	19 47	2 02
27 F	1 34	3S48	4 47	6 23	4 53	1 52	2 11	1 26	13 49	1 16	8 40	10 01	18 19	0 43	19 46	2 02
28 Sa	1 57	8 54	4 14	11 19	4 12	1 52	1 42	1 26	13 37	1 16	8 38	10 02	18 22	0 43	19 46	2 02
29 Su	2 21	13 35	3 25	15 40	3 29	1 52	1 12	1 25	13 24	1 17	8 37	10 03	18 25	0 43	19 46	2 02
30 M	2S44	17S31	2S22	19S05	2N45	1N51	0N42	1N25	13N11	1N17	8N35	10S03	18S27	0N42	19N46	2S02

Day	⚷ Decl	⚷ Lat	♅ Decl	♅ Lat	♆ Decl	♆ Lat	♇ Decl	♇ Lat
1	15N13	1S43	23N18	0N04	3N38	1S34	23S41	6S15
6	15 11	1 44	23 18	0 04	3 35	1 34	23 42	6 15
11	15 09	1 45	23 19	0 05	3 32	1 34	23 44	6 15
16	15 06	1 46	23 19	0 05	3 29	1 35	23 45	6 14
21	15 03	1 47	23 19	0 05	3 26	1 35	23 46	6 14
26	14 60	1 48	23 19	0 05	3 22	1 35	23 47	6 14

Day	⚴ Decl	⚴ Lat	⚵ Decl	⚵ Lat	⚶ Decl	⚶ Lat	Eris Decl	Eris Lat
1	5N38	15N56	9S30	13N53	14N27	6S59	1N16	9S41
6	4 36	15 18	9 58	13 27	14 29	7 06	1 15	9 41
11	3 32	14 38	10 24	13 01	14 30	7 14	1 14	9 42
16	2 28	13 55	10 50	12 35	14 29	7 21	1 13	9 42
21	1 23	13 10	11 15	12 11	14 27	7 29	1 12	9 42
26	0 20	12 23	11 39	11 47	14 23	7 36	1 11	9 42

Moon Phenomena

Max/0 Decl
dy hr mn
5 7:55 22S21
11 19:57 0 N
19 2:18 22N13
26 6:26 0 S

Perigee/Apogee
dy hr m kilometers
4 17:00 p 369881
18 18:11 a 404254
30 15:38 p 366352

PH dy hr mn
☽ 4 21:57 12♐25
○ 11 21:19 19♓11
☾ 19 19:58 26♊55
● 27 9:56 4♎21

Max/0 Lat
dy hr mn
4 20:53 0 N
11 6:56 5N01
18 10:12 0 S
25 15:22 5S03

Void of Course Moon

Last Aspect	☽ Ingress
1 15:27 ♀ ⚹	♏ 1 21:45
3 23:29 ♀ □	♐ 4 0:50
5 15:23 ♅ ☍	♑ 6 3:52
7 17:17 ♃ ⚹	♒ 8 7:07
9 22:28 ♅ △	♓ 10 11:10
12 3:50 ♅ □	♈ 12 17:01
14 11:48 ♅ ⚹	♉ 15 1:40
17 1:37 ☉ △	♊ 17 13:16
19 19:58 ☉ □	♋ 20 2:11
22 12:52 ☉ ⚹	♌ 22 13:42
24 12:57 ♂ ☌	♍ 24 21:50
26 22:36 ♀ ☌	♎ 27 2:31
29 1:33 ♂ ⚹	♏ 29 5:00

DAILY ASPECTARIAN

1 Su ☽∠☿ 3:45; ☽⊻♃ 6:25; ☽⊼⚳ 7:34; ☽△♅ 9:03; ☽Q♄ 10:48; ☉∠☽ 11:39; ☽⚹♀ 15:27; ☽#♀ 17:01

2 M ☽#⚷ 1:15; ☽⚹☿ 4:03; ☽Q♅ 10:43; ☽⊼♄ 12:29; ☽∥♃ 14:34; ☉⊼♇ 14:57; ☽□♇ 15:08; ☉⚹☽ 15:09; ☽□♂ 17:08; ☽⊼♆ 19:35; ♀Q♆ 20:10; ☽#♂ 22:27

3 Tu ☽☍⚷ 2:26; ☉∥☿ 3:34; ☽☌♃ 10:06; ☽#♄ 10:08; ☽☍⚳ 11:05; ☽⊼♅ 12:18; ☽Q♆ 21:03; ☽□♀ 23:29

4 W ☽□☿ 4:49; ♀ ♍ 14:52; ☽☍♄ 15:38; ☽⚹♇ 18:06; ♂△♆ 21:32; ☉□☽ 21:57; ☽△♆ 22:31; ☽△♂ 22:34

5 Th ☽⊼⚷ 5:24; ☉⊼♆ 6:07; ☽⊻♃ 13:36; ☽⊼⚳ 14:25; ☽☍♅ 15:23; ☽∠♇ 19:35; ☿☌♀ 21:11; ☉⊻♂ 22:59

6 F ☽Q♂ 1:17; ☿∥⚳ 4:14; ☽△☿ 6:19; ☽Q⚷ 6:54; ☽△♀ 7:25; ☽∠♃ 15:24; ☽Q⚳ 16:05; ☽⊼♄ 18:48; ☽⊻♇ 21:06

7 Sa ☽□♆ 1:31; ☽⊼♂ 4:04; ☉△☽ 4:49; ☽#♄ 5:48; ☽Q☿ 7:29; ☽△⚷ 8:27; ☽Q♀ 11:29; ☽⚹♃ 17:17; ☽△⚳ 17:50; ☽⊼♅ 18:37; ☽Q♄ 20:28

8 Su ♂#♃ 0:02; ☽∥♃ 0:06; ☽#♂ 0:06; ☉Q☽ 8:24; ☽⊼☿ 9:01; ☿ D 9:29; ☽#⚷ 15:17; ☽⊼♀ 15:42; ☽Q♅ 20:25; ☽△♄ 22:18

9 M ☽☌♇ 0:29; ☽⚹♆ 4:55; ☉△⚷ 8:45; ☽☍♂ 10:04; ☽□⚷ 11:59; ☉⊼☽ 12:14; ☽#♀ 17:33; ☽#☿ 19:02; ☽□♃ 21:35; ☽□⚳ 21:49; ☽△♅ 22:28

10 Tu ☽#⚳ 0:56; ☿∥♀ 4:48; ☽∠♆ 7:00; ☽☍☿ 13:44; ☉#☽ 21:49

11 W ☽☍♀ 1:14; ☽□♄ 2:50; ♂□⚷ 3:05; ☽#♆ 3:10; ☽⊻♇ 4:56; ⚳☍♃ 7:56; ☽⊻♆ 9:30; ☽⚹⚷ 16:49; ☽⊼♂ 17:31; ♀□♄ 18:48; ☉☍☽ 21:19

12 Th ☽⚹⚳ 3:17; ☽△♃ 3:27; ☽□♅ 3:50; ☽∠♇ 7:54; ☽∥♆ 12:55; ☉∥☽ 15:16; ♀⊼♇ 16:59; ☽∠⚷ 20:04; ☽⊼☿ 21:51; ☽Q♂ 22:14

13 F ♀∥⚳ 0:33; ☽∠⚳ 6:56; ☽Q♃ 7:21; ☽⚹♄ 9:29; ☽⚹♇ 11:33; ☽⊼♀ 13:34; ☽∥♀ 15:01; ♃⊼♅ 15:22; ☽☌♆ 16:19; ☽∥⚳ 16:27; ☉∥♆ 22:18

14 Sa ☽⊻⚷ 0:03; ☽∥☿ 0:50; ☽Q☿ 3:42; ☽△♂ 3:47; ☉⊼☽ 9:32; ☽⊻⚳ 11:20; ☽⚹♅ 11:48; ☽⊼♃ 12:02; ☽∠♄ 13:55; ♀⊼♆ 17:18; ☽Q♀ 21:15

15 Su ☽∥⚷ 5:33; ☉△⚳ 9:12; ☽△☿ 10:57; ☽∥♂ 12:38; ☉□♅ 15:04; ☽∠♅ 16:58; ☉Q☽ 17:08; ☽⊻♄ 19:07; ☽□♇ 21:11; ☉⚹♃ 23:25

16 M ☽⊻♆ 2:09; ☽#♃ 2:13; ☽△♀ 5:59; ☽☌⚷ 10:18; ☽□♂ 17:35; ☽∥♄ 21:06; ☽☌⚳ 22:22; ☽⊻♅ 22:49; ☽☍♃ 23:48

17 Tu ☉△☽ 1:37; ☽∠♆ 8:06; ☉Q♇ 19:06; ♀△⚷ 23:09

18 W ☽□☿ 5:27; ☽☌♄ 7:24; ☽△♇ 9:24; ☊ D 10:12; ☽⚹♆ 14:28; ⚳ R 19:43; ☿□♄ 22:44; ☽⊻⚷ 22:49

19 Th ☽□♀ 1:40; ☽⚹♂ 9:46; ☽⊻⚳ 11:14; ☽☌♅ 11:43; ☽⊼♃ 13:30; ☿⊼♇ 15:19; ☽Q♇ 15:53; ☉□☽ 19:58; ☊ R 20:12

20 F ☽∠⚷ 5:11; ☿∥⚳ 5:56; ♂□⚳ 12:52; ☽∠⚳ 17:32; ☽∠♂ 17:47; ☽⊻♄ 20:12; ☽Q♃ 20:13; ♄ R 21:31; ☽⊼♇ 22:06; ♂∥⚷ 22:30; ♂⚹♅ 22:44

21 Sa ☽⚹☿ 2:29; ☽□♆ 3:00; ☿⊼♆ 6:28; ☽∥♄ 7:26; ☽⚹⚷ 11:10; ☽⚹♀ 20:56; ☽⚹⚳ 23:16; ☽⊻♅ 23:50; ☽#♃ 23:55

22 Su ☽⊻♂ 1:10; ☽∠♄ 1:56; ☽△♃ 2:21; ☽∠☿ 12:23; ☉⚹☽ 12:52; ♀△⚳ 19:29; ☽∥⚷ 23:04; ☉ ♎ 23:28

23 M ♀□♅ 1:28; ☽∥♂ 1:47; ☽∠♅ 4:49; ☽∠♀ 5:11; ☽⚹♄ 6:50; ♂□♃ 8:24; ☽☍♇ 8:34; ☽△♆ 13:08; ☿△⚷ 18:19; ☉∠☽ 19:48; ☽□⚷ 20:49; ☽⊻☿ 21:12

24 Tu ☽□⚳ 8:12; ☉Q⚷ 8:49; ☽⚹♅ 8:52; ♀⚹♃ 9:39; ☽□♃ 11:57; ☽∥⚳ 11:59; ☽⊻♀ 12:10; ☽☌♂ 12:57; ♀∥♆ 14:03; ♀Q♇ 15:18; ☽Q♆ 16:51

25 W ☽∥☿ 0:55; ☉⊻☽ 1:32; ♀⊻♂ 4:03; ☽□♄ 13:50; ☽∥♆ 14:35; ☽⊼♇ 15:26; ☽∥♀ 17:12; ☽⊼♆ 19:40

26 Th ☉#☽ 0:54; ☽△⚷ 2:50; ☽☌☿ 11:05; ☉∥☽ 12:51; ☽△⚳ 13:30; ☽□♅ 14:18; ⚵ ♑ 16:47; ☽#♀ 17:12; ☽Q♇ 17:37; ☽⚹♃ 17:52; ☽⊻♂ 20:37; ☽#♆ 21:58; ☽☌♀ 22:36

27 F ☽#☿ 4:27; ☽Q⚷ 4:41; ☿△⚳ 5:31; ☉☌☽ 9:56; ☿□♅ 12:13; ☽Q⚳ 15:04; ☉#♀ 16:53; ☽△♄ 17:39; ☽△♇ 19:11; ☽∠♃ 19:46; ♂Q♆ 19:58; ☽#⚳ 22:45; ☽☍♆ 23:09; ☽∠♂ 23:18

28 Sa ☽⊼⚷ 6:00; ♅ R 8:28; ☿Q♇ 13:45; ☽⊼⚳ 16:11; ☽△♅ 17:09; ♀ ♎ 18:35; ☽Q♄ 18:49; ☿⚹♃ 20:53; ☽⊻♃ 21:14; ☽⊻☿ 21:16; ☽#♂ 23:02

29 Su ☽⚹♂ 1:33; ⚴ R♒ 2:52; ☿∥♆ 4:35; ☽⊻♀ 5:59; ☽#⚷ 7:46; ☉⊻☽ 15:53; ♀Q⚷ 17:21; ☽Q♅ 18:07; ☽⊼♄ 19:44; ☽□♇ 21:15

30 M ☉#☿ 0:13; ☽⊼♆ 1:06; ☽∠☿ 1:46; ☽∥♃ 7:01; ☉Q⚳ 7:41; ☽☍⚷ 7:50; ☽∠♀ 9:15; ☽☍⚳ 17:49; ☽#♄ 17:56; ☉∠☽ 18:36; ☽⊼♅ 19:01; ☿⊻♂ 22:58; ☽☌♃ 23:42

October 2030

LONGITUDE

Day	Sid.Time	☉	☽	☽ 12 hour	Mean☊	True☊	☿	♀	♂	⚳	♃	♄	⚷	♅	♆	♇
	h m s	° ' "	° ' "	° ' "	° '	° '	° '	° '	° '	° '	° '	° '	° '	° '	° '	° '
1 Tu	0 39 06	7♎52 09	25♏53 33	3♐05 53	10♐21.0	9♐06.6	29♍10.9	2♎46.6	29♌07.8	22♉09.0	25♏43.0	8♊51.2	16♉08.2	22♊53.5	12♈04.6	9♒46.5
2 W	0 43 03	8 51 09	10♐16 48	17 25 55	10 17.8	9D 05.9	0♎59.5	4 01.4	29 45.0	22R 04.1	25 54.0	8R 50.0	16R 06.1	22R 53.3	12R 02.9	9R 45.9
3 Th	0 47 00	9 50 11	24 32 59	1♑37 49	10 14.7	9 06.5	2 48.0	5 16.3	0♍22.1	21 58.9	26 05.0	8 48.7	16 03.8	22 53.1	12 01.2	9 45.4
4 F	0 50 56	10 49 14	8♑40 15	15 40 14	10 11.5	9R 07.0	4 36.3	6 31.2	0 59.2	21 53.3	26 16.1	8 47.4	16 01.6	22 52.8	11 59.6	9 44.8
5 Sa	0 54 53	11 48 20	22 37 42	29 32 35	10 08.3	9 06.5	6 24.1	7 46.1	1 36.2	21 47.3	26 27.3	8 45.9	15 59.3	22 52.5	11 57.9	9 44.4
6 Su	0 58 49	12 47 27	6♒24 54	13♒14 33	10 05.1	9 04.1	8 11.5	9 01.0	2 13.2	21 40.9	26 38.5	8 44.3	15 56.9	22 52.1	11 56.2	9 43.9
7 M	1 02 46	13 46 35	20 01 32	26 45 44	10 01.9	8 59.3	9 58.4	10 15.9	2 50.1	21 34.2	26 49.9	8 42.6	15 54.6	22 51.7	11 54.6	9 43.4
8 Tu	1 06 42	14 45 46	3♓27 06	10♓05 29	9 58.8	8 52.3	11 44.7	11 30.9	3 27.1	21 27.1	27 01.3	8 40.8	15 52.2	22 51.2	11 52.9	9 43.0
9 W	1 10 39	15 44 58	16 40 49	23 12 58	9 55.6	8 43.7	13 30.3	12 45.8	4 03.9	21 19.7	27 12.7	8 38.9	15 49.7	22 50.7	11 51.2	9 42.6
10 Th	1 14 35	16 44 12	29 41 49	6♈07 17	9 52.4	8 34.2	15 15.3	14 00.8	4 40.8	21 11.9	27 24.3	8 36.9	15 47.2	22 50.1	11 49.6	9 42.2
11 F	1 18 32	17 43 28	12♈29 18	18 47 51	9 49.2	8 25.0	16 59.6	15 15.8	5 17.6	21 03.7	27 35.9	8 34.8	15 44.7	22 49.5	11 47.9	9 41.9
12 Sa	1 22 29	18 42 46	25 02 56	1♉14 37	9 46.1	8 16.9	18 43.1	16 30.8	5 54.3	20 55.2	27 47.6	8 32.6	15 42.1	22 48.8	11 46.2	9 41.6
13 Su	1 26 25	19 42 07	7♉23 01	13 28 20	9 42.9	8 10.6	20 26.0	17 45.8	6 31.1	20 46.4	27 59.3	8 30.3	15 39.6	22 48.1	11 44.6	9 41.3
14 M	1 30 22	20 41 29	19 30 46	25 30 38	9 39.7	8 06.5	22 08.1	19 00.8	7 07.8	20 37.2	28 11.2	8 27.9	15 37.0	22 47.3	11 42.9	9 41.0
15 Tu	1 34 18	21 40 54	1♊28 17	7♊24 08	9 36.5	8D 04.6	23 49.6	20 15.9	7 44.4	20 27.8	28 23.1	8 25.4	15 34.3	22 46.5	11 41.3	9 40.8
16 W	1 38 15	22 40 21	13 18 38	19 12 16	9 33.3	8 04.5	25 30.3	21 30.9	8 21.0	20 18.0	28 35.0	8 22.9	15 31.6	22 45.6	11 39.7	9 40.6
17 Th	1 42 11	23 39 50	25 05 37	0♋59 16	9 30.2	8 05.6	27 10.3	22 46.0	8 57.6	20 07.8	28 47.0	8 20.2	15 28.9	22 44.7	11 38.0	9 40.4
18 F	1 46 08	24 39 21	6♋53 48	12 49 53	9 27.0	8 07.1	28 49.7	24 01.1	9 34.1	19 57.4	28 59.1	8 17.4	15 26.2	22 43.7	11 36.4	9 40.3
19 Sa	1 50 04	25 38 55	18 48 09	24 49 17	9 23.8	8R 08.4	0♏28.4	25 16.2	10 10.6	19 46.7	29 11.3	8 14.5	15 23.5	22 42.7	11 34.8	9 40.1
20 Su	1 54 01	26 38 31	0♌53 54	7♌02 38	9 20.6	8 08.5	2 06.5	26 31.3	10 47.1	19 35.7	29 23.4	8 11.6	15 20.7	22 41.7	11 33.2	9 40.0
21 M	1 57 58	27 38 09	13 16 06	19 34 51	9 17.5	8 07.1	3 43.9	27 46.4	11 23.5	19 24.4	29 35.7	8 08.5	15 17.9	22 40.5	11 31.6	9 40.0
22 Tu	2 01 54	28 37 49	25 59 21	2♍30 00	9 14.3	8 04.0	5 20.7	29 01.5	11 59.9	19 12.9	29 48.0	8 05.4	15 15.1	22 39.4	11 30.0	9 39.9
23 W	2 05 51	29 37 32	9♍07 05	15 50 47	9 11.1	7 59.4	6 57.0	0♏16.7	12 36.2	19 01.1	0♐00.4	8 02.1	15 12.2	22 38.2	11 28.4	9D 39.9
24 Th	2 09 47	0♏37 17	22 41 08	29 37 58	9 07.9	7 53.7	8 32.6	1 31.8	13 12.5	18 49.1	0 12.8	7 58.8	15 09.4	22 36.9	11 26.9	9 39.9
25 F	2 13 44	1 37 04	6♎41 01	13♎49 50	9 04.7	7 47.7	10 07.7	2 47.0	13 48.7	18 36.8	0 25.3	7 55.4	15 06.5	22 35.6	11 25.3	9 39.9
26 Sa	2 17 40	2 36 53	21 03 47	28 22 07	9 01.6	7 42.2	11 42.2	4 02.1	14 24.9	18 24.3	0 37.8	7 51.9	15 03.6	22 34.3	11 23.8	9 40.0
27 Su	2 21 37	3 36 44	5♏43 58	13♏08 23	8 58.4	7 37.9	13 16.2	5 17.3	15 01.1	18 11.6	0 50.4	7 48.4	15 00.7	22 32.9	11 22.2	9 40.1
28 M	2 25 33	4 36 37	20 34 21	28 00 52	8 55.2	7 35.2	14 49.7	6 32.5	15 37.2	17 58.8	1 03.0	7 44.7	14 57.8	22 31.4	11 20.7	9 40.2
29 Tu	2 29 30	5 36 32	5♐26 58	12♐51 43	8 52.0	7D 34.2	16 22.7	7 47.7	16 13.2	17 45.7	1 15.7	7 41.0	14 54.8	22 29.9	11 19.2	9 40.4
30 W	2 33 27	6 36 29	20 14 19	27 34 03	8 48.9	7 34.6	17 55.2	9 02.9	16 49.3	17 32.5	1 28.4	7 37.2	14 51.9	22 28.4	11 17.8	9 40.6
31 Th	2 37 23	7♏36 28	4♑50 20	12♑02 42	8♐45.7	7♐35.9	19♏27.2	10♏18.1	17♍25.2	17♉19.2	1♐41.2	7♊33.4	14♉48.9	22♊26.9	11♈16.3	9♒40.8

1st of Month

Julian Day #
2462775.5
Obliquity
23°26'04"
SVP 4♓49'53"
GC 27♐16.1
Eris 26♈31.0R

Day	⚴
1	29♒41.7R
6	28 58.8R
11	28 24.6R
16	27 59.3R
21	27 43.0R
26	27 35.6R
31	27 37.0

Day	⚵
1	0♑50.9
6	1 55.5
11	3 05.5
16	4 20.7
21	5 40.6
26	7 05.0
31	8 33.6

Day	⚶
1	10♊00.8
6	10 06.3
11	10 01.0R
16	9 44.7R
21	9 17.2R
26	8 38.7R
31	7 49.9R

DECLINATION and LATITUDE

Day	☉ Decl	☽ Decl	☽ Lat	☽ 12h Decl	☿ Decl	☿ Lat	♀ Decl	♀ Lat	♂ Decl	♂ Lat	⚳ Decl	⚳ Lat	♃ Decl	♃ Lat	♄ Decl	♄ Lat
1 Tu	3S07	20S22	1S10	21S18	1N60	1N49	0N11	1N25	12N59	1N17	8N34	10S04	18S30	0N42	19N45	2S02
2 W	3 31	21 53	0N06	22 06	1 15	1 47	0S19	1 24	12 46	1 18	8 32	10 04	18 33	0 42	19 45	2 03
3 Th	3 54	21 58	1 22	21 28	0 29	1 44	0 49	1 24	12 33	1 18	8 30	10 05	18 35	0 42	19 45	2 03
4 F	4 17	20 38	2 32	19 29	0S17	1 41	1 19	1 23	12 20	1 18	8 29	10 05	18 38	0 42	19 44	2 03
5 Sa	4 40	18 04	3 31	16 23	1 03	1 37	1 49	1 23	12 08	1 19	8 27	10 05	18 41	0 42	19 44	2 03
6 Su	5 03	14 30	4 18	12 26	1 49	1 33	2 19	1 22	11 55	1 19	8 25	10 06	18 44	0 41	19 44	2 03
7 M	5 26	10 13	4 50	7 54	2 35	1 29	2 49	1 21	11 42	1 19	8 23	10 06	18 46	0 41	19 43	2 03
8 Tu	5 49	5 30	5 05	3 03	3 21	1 24	3 19	1 20	11 29	1 20	8 21	10 06	18 49	0 41	19 43	2 03
9 W	6 12	0 36	5 03	1N51	4 07	1 19	3 49	1 19	11 16	1 20	8 19	10 06	18 52	0 41	19 42	2 04
10 Th	6 35	4N15	4 46	6 35	4 53	1 13	4 19	1 19	11 02	1 20	8 18	10 06	18 55	0 41	19 42	2 04
11 F	6 57	8 50	4 14	10 58	5 38	1 08	4 49	1 18	10 49	1 21	8 16	10 06	18 58	0 41	19 42	2 04
12 Sa	7 20	12 58	3 31	14 48	6 23	1 02	5 19	1 17	10 36	1 21	8 14	10 06	19 00	0 41	19 41	2 04
13 Su	7 42	16 28	2 38	17 56	7 07	0 56	5 48	1 15	10 23	1 21	8 12	10 05	19 03	0 40	19 41	2 04
14 M	8 05	19 11	1 39	20 14	7 51	0 50	6 18	1 14	10 09	1 22	8 10	10 05	19 06	0 40	19 40	2 04
15 Tu	8 27	21 02	0 36	21 36	8 35	0 43	6 47	1 13	9 56	1 22	8 08	10 05	19 09	0 40	19 40	2 04
16 W	8 49	21 55	0S28	21 60	9 17	0 37	7 17	1 12	9 43	1 22	8 06	10 04	19 11	0 40	19 39	2 04
17 Th	9 11	21 50	1 31	21 25	9 60	0 30	7 46	1 10	9 29	1 23	8 04	10 04	19 14	0 40	19 39	2 04
18 F	9 33	20 45	2 30	19 52	10 41	0 23	8 15	1 09	9 16	1 23	8 02	10 03	19 17	0 40	19 38	2 05
19 Sa	9 55	18 46	3 23	17 26	11 22	0 17	8 43	1 08	9 02	1 23	7 60	10 02	19 20	0 40	19 37	2 05
20 Su	10 16	15 55	4 08	14 12	12 03	0 10	9 12	1 06	8 49	1 24	7 58	10 01	19 22	0 40	19 37	2 05
21 M	10 38	12 19	4 43	10 16	12 42	0 03	9 40	1 05	8 35	1 24	7 56	10 00	19 25	0 39	19 36	2 05
22 Tu	10 59	8 04	5 04	5 45	13 21	0S04	10 09	1 03	8 22	1 24	7 54	9 59	19 28	0 39	19 36	2 05
23 W	11 20	3 20	5 11	0 50	13 60	0 10	10 36	1 01	8 08	1 25	7 52	9 58	19 31	0 39	19 35	2 05
24 Th	11 41	1S42	5 01	4S17	14 37	0 17	11 04	0 60	7 54	1 25	7 50	9 57	19 33	0 39	19 35	2 05
25 F	12 02	6 50	4 33	9 20	15 14	0 24	11 32	0 58	7 41	1 25	7 48	9 55	19 36	0 39	19 34	2 05
26 Sa	12 23	11 43	3 47	13 58	15 50	0 31	11 59	0 56	7 27	1 26	7 46	9 54	19 39	0 39	19 33	2 05
27 Su	12 43	16 02	2 45	17 50	16 25	0 37	12 26	0 54	7 13	1 26	7 45	9 52	19 41	0 39	19 33	2 05
28 M	13 03	19 22	1 32	20 34	16 59	0 44	12 52	0 53	6 60	1 26	7 43	9 51	19 44	0 39	19 32	2 05
29 Tu	13 23	21 24	0 12	21 51	17 32	0 51	13 18	0 51	6 46	1 27	7 41	9 49	19 47	0 38	19 31	2 05
30 W	13 43	21 56	1N09	21 37	18 05	0 57	13 44	0 49	6 32	1 27	7 39	9 47	19 50	0 38	19 31	2 06
31 Th	14S03	20S57	2N24	19S56	18S37	1S04	14S10	0N47	6N19	1N27	7N38	9S45	19S52	0N38	19N30	2S06

Day	⚷ Decl	⚷ Lat	♅ Decl	♅ Lat	♆ Decl	♆ Lat	♇ Decl	♇ Lat
1	14N56	1S48	23N19	0N05	3N19	1S35	23S47	6S13
6	14 52	1 49	23 19	0 05	3 16	1 35	23 47	6 13
11	14 48	1 50	23 19	0 05	3 13	1 35	23 48	6 13
16	14 43	1 51	23 19	0 05	3 09	1 35	23 48	6 12
21	14 39	1 51	23 19	0 05	3 06	1 35	23 47	6 12
26	14 34	1 52	23 19	0 05	3 03	1 35	23 47	6 11
31	14N29	1S52	23N18	0N05	3N00	1S35	23S46	6S11

Day	⚴ Decl	⚴ Lat	⚵ Decl	⚵ Lat	⚶ Decl	⚶ Lat	Eris Decl	Eris Lat
1	0S41	11N36	12S02	11N24	14N18	7S43	1N10	9S42
6	1 40	10 49	12 23	11 02	14 13	7 50	1 09	9 42
11	2 36	10 02	12 43	10 41	14 06	7 56	1 08	9 42
16	3 28	9 15	13 02	10 20	13 58	8 01	1 07	9 42
21	4 17	8 30	13 18	10 01	13 50	8 06	1 06	9 42
26	5 01	7 45	13 33	9 42	13 41	8 09	1 06	9 41
31	5S40	7N03	13S46	9N24	13N33	8S10	1N05	9S41

Moon Phenomena

Max/0 Decl
dy hr mn
2 13:16 22S06
9 2:56 0 N
16 9:38 22N00
23 15:58 0 S
29 20:14 21S57

Max/0 Lat
dy hr mn
1 22:01 0 N
8 9:41 5N06
15 13:21 0 S
22 21:59 5S11
29 3:25 0 N

Perigee/Apogee
dy hr m kilometers
16 13:23 a 405075
28 12:05 p 361126

PH dy hr mn
☽ 4 3:57 10♑59
○ 11 10:48 18♈10
☾ 19 14:52 26♋16
● 26 20:18 3♏28

Void of Course Moon

Last Aspect	☽ Ingress
1 6:16 ☿ ✶	♐ 1 6:50
2 21:11 ♅ ☍	♑ 3 9:14
5 6:43 ♃ ✶	♒ 5 12:48
7 12:18 ♃ □	♓ 7 17:48
9 19:41 ♃ △	♈ 10 0:34
11 19:42 ♅ ✶	♉ 12 9:35
14 17:40 ♃ ☍	♊ 14 21:02
17 4:56 ♀ △	♋ 17 9:59
19 20:59 ♃ △	♌ 19 22:14
22 7:10 ♃ □	♍ 22 7:25
23 23:53 ♅ □	♎ 24 12:38
26 2:29 ♅ △	♏ 26 14:40
27 15:40 ♂ ✶	♐ 28 15:12
30 3:39 ♅ ☍	♑ 30 16:00

DAILY ASPECTARIAN

1 Tu
☽⚼♆ 1:58
☽□♂ 5:38
☽✶☿ 6:16
☿ ♎ 10:51
☉⋕♆ 11:48
☽✶♀ 12:33
☉✶☽ 21:26
☽☍♄ 21:35
☊ D 22:00
☽✶♇ 23:08
☉△♄ 23:32

2 W
☿⚼⚷ 1:25
☽△♆ 2:57
♂ ♍ 9:43
☽⚻⚷ 9:44
☿⋕♀ 17:46
☽⚻⚳ 19:41
☽☍♅ 21:11
☉△♇ 22:04

3 Th
☽∠♇ 0:21
☽⚺♃ 2:38
☽△♂ 10:18
☽⚼⚷ 11:01
☽□☿ 16:03
☽□♀ 19:58
☽⚼⚳ 20:58

4 F
☽⚻♄ 0:12
☽⚺♇ 1:50
☊ R 3:56
☉□☽ 3:57
☽∠♃ 4:30
☽□♆ 5:41
♀⚼⚳ 6:34
☽⋕♄ 9:36
☽△⚷ 12:35
☽⚼♂ 13:07
☉∠♃ 13:27
☽∥♃ 19:06
☽△⚳ 22:33

5 Sa
☽⚻♅ 0:26
☽⚼♄ 1:58
☉☍♆ 3:47
☿⚼⚳ 4:53
☽✶♃ 6:43
☽⚻♂ 16:19
♀△♄ 18:46
☽⋕⚷ 21:43

6 Su
⚶ R 1:43
☽⚼♅ 2:33
☽△☿ 3:35
☽△♄ 4:04
☽△♀ 5:01
☽☌♇ 5:49
☿△♄ 7:14
☽✶♆ 9:41
☉△☽ 12:05
♀△♇ 13:39
☽⋕♂ 15:39
☽□⚷ 16:44
☿△♇ 20:39

7 M
☽□⚳ 2:43
☽△♅ 5:02
♃⚼♆ 8:39
☽⋕⚳ 9:34
☽⚼☿ 10:09
☽⚼♀ 10:17
☽∠♆ 12:14
☽□♃ 12:18
☿☌♀ 13:22
☉⚼☽ 16:51
♀⋕♆ 20:16
☿⋕♆ 20:26
☿∥♀ 20:45
☉∥☽ 22:32
☽☍♂ 24:00

8 Tu
☿☍♆ 1:50
☿∠♃ 4:13
♀☍♆ 6:54
☽∥☿ 9:07
☽□♄ 9:25
☽∥♀ 9:43
☽⋕♆ 11:07
☽⚺♇ 11:19
♀∠♃ 11:29
☽⚺♆ 15:13
☽⚻♀ 16:07
☽⚻☿ 17:19
☉⚻☽ 22:10
☽✶⚷ 22:27

9 W
☉⚻⚷ 1:51
☽✶⚳ 8:26
☽□♅ 11:19
☽∠♇ 14:45
☽∥♆ 18:50
☽△♃ 19:41

10 Th
☽⋕♀ 0:23
☽∠⚷ 2:01
☽⋕☿ 3:48
☿⚻⚷ 7:10
☽⚻♂ 9:46
☽∠⚳ 12:01
☉⋕☽ 13:01
☽✶♄ 16:39
☽✶♇ 18:44
☽∥⚳ 20:54
☽☌♆ 22:42

11 F
☽⚼♃ 0:13
☽☍♀ 5:51
☽⚺⚷ 6:10
♀⚻⚷ 8:57
☽☍☿ 9:55
☽∥♂ 10:36
☉☍☽ 10:48
☽⚼♂ 15:38
☽⚺⚳ 16:09
☽✶♅ 19:42
☽∠♄ 21:07
☉☌☿ 23:49

12 Sa
☽⚻♃ 5:23
☽∥⚷ 11:50
☽△♂ 22:13

13 Su
☽∠♅ 0:49
☽⚺♄ 2:12
☿⚻⚳ 4:24
☽□♇ 4:32
☽⚺♆ 8:34
☽☌⚷ 16:17
☉⚻⚳ 22:31
☽⚻♀ 22:53
☽⋕♃ 23:01
☿∠♂ 23:52

14 M
☽☌⚳ 2:11
☉⚻☽ 2:34
☉⋕⚳ 5:03
☽∥♄ 5:12
☽⚻☿ 6:06
☽⚺♅ 6:32
☿△♅ 9:11
☿⋕⚳ 9:49
☽∠♆ 14:23
☉∥☿ 15:18
☽☍♃ 17:40
☿⚼♄ 18:25

15 Tu
♀⚻⚳ 3:22
☽⚼♀ 8:34
☉⚼☽ 11:30
☊ D 13:21
☽□♂ 13:23
☽☌♄ 14:01
☽△♇ 16:37
☽⚼☿ 17:21
☽✶♆ 20:39

16 W
♂□♄ 1:07
☉△♅ 2:06
☽⚺⚷ 4:30
☿⋕♂ 10:49
☽⚺⚳ 14:02
☉⚼♄ 16:25
☽△♀ 18:42
☽☌♅ 19:13
☉△☽ 20:49
☽⚼♇ 23:09
♀△♅ 23:36

17 Th
☽△☿ 4:56
☽⚻♃ 7:39
♀⚼♄ 10:33
☽∠⚷ 10:56
☉⋕♂ 12:16
♀⋕⚳ 14:02
☉∠♂ 18:34
☽∠⚳ 20:07

18 F
☿⚺♃ 2:36
☽⚺♄ 2:49
♂⚻♇ 4:01
☽⚻♇ 5:37
☽✶♂ 5:42
☽□♆ 9:30
☽⚼♃ 14:34
☽∥♄ 14:49
☿ ♏ 17:04
☽✶⚷ 17:11
☽⋕♃ 18:17
♀∠♂ 20:34

19 Sa
☽✶⚳ 1:55
☽⚺♅ 7:48
☽∠♄ 8:50
♀⋕♂ 10:42
☽∠♂ 13:23
☽□♀ 14:22
☉□☽ 14:52
☊ R 15:08
☽△♃ 20:59

20 Su
☽□☿ 2:44
☽∥⚷ 8:55
☉☌♀ 11:14
☽∠♅ 13:14
☽✶♄ 14:10
☽☍♇ 17:04
☽⚺♂ 20:13
☽△♆ 20:40
☽⋕☿ 21:55

21 M
☽□⚷ 3:52
♂⚻♆ 5:07
☉⋕☽ 9:08
☽□⚳ 11:30
☽⋕♀ 13:48
☽✶♅ 17:47
☽∥♂ 22:23

22 Tu
☽∥⚳ 0:56
☽⚼♆ 0:57
☉✶☽ 5:18
☽✶♀ 6:13
☽□♃ 7:10
♀⚺♃ 17:47
♀ ♏ 18:41
☽✶☿ 19:33
☽□♄ 22:04
♃ ♐ 23:15

23 W
☽⚻♇ 0:59
☽∥♆ 1:15
♇ D 3:07
☽⚻♆ 4:13
☽☌♂ 6:32
☉ ♏ 9:02
☿⚼♅ 10:11
☉∠☽ 10:37
☽△⚷ 10:49
☉⚺♃ 11:35
☽∠♀ 12:07
☿⚻♄ 15:48
☽△⚳ 17:20
☿⋕⚷ 23:16
☽□♅ 23:53

24 Th
☽∠☿ 1:41
☽⚼♇ 3:26
☽⋕♆ 6:22
♂∥⚳ 8:42
♃⋕♄ 8:53
☽⚼⚷ 12:51
☽✶♃ 13:11
☉⚺☽ 14:44
☽⚺♀ 16:44
☿□♇ 16:59
☽⚼⚳ 18:52

25 F
☽△♄ 2:05
☽⋕♂ 3:52
☽⋕⚳ 4:37
☽△♇ 5:02
☽⚺☿ 6:31
☽☍♆ 7:57
☽⚺♂ 12:30
☽⚻⚷ 14:05
☽∠♃ 14:52
☿⚻♆ 19:23
☽⚻⚳ 19:40

26 Sa
☽∥♀ 1:28
☽△♅ 2:29
☽⚼♄ 2:58
☉∥☽ 3:41
☽∠♂ 14:18
☽⋕⚷ 15:18
☽⚺♃ 15:55
☉☌☽ 20:18
☽☌♀ 23:13
♂△⚷ 23:46

27 Su
☽∥☿ 2:52
☽⚼♅ 2:56
☽⚻♄ 3:21
☽□♇ 6:23
☽⚻♆ 9:07
☽☌☿ 13:39
☽☍⚷ 14:59
☽✶♂ 15:40
⚴ D 16:51
☽☍⚳ 19:53

28 M
☽⋕♄ 1:31
☿☍⚷ 2:00
☽⚻♅ 3:09
☽∥♃ 3:28
☽⚼♆ 9:18
☽☌♃ 17:08
♀⚼♅ 18:26
☿✶♂ 19:59
♀⚻♄ 21:58

29 Tu
☉⚺☽ 0:17
☊ D 3:24
☽☍♄ 3:36
☽⚺♀ 4:09
☽✶♇ 6:50
☽△♆ 9:29
☽⚻⚷ 15:17
☽□♂ 18:12
☿☍⚳ 18:50
☉∥♀ 19:20
☽⚻⚳ 19:40
☽⚺☿ 19:47

30 W
☉∠☽ 2:24
☽☍♅ 3:39
☽∠♀ 6:49
☽∠♇ 7:15
♀□♇ 12:03
☽⚼⚷ 15:44
☽⚺♃ 18:42
☽⚼⚳ 19:54
☉⚼♅ 20:15
♂△⚳ 21:04
☉⚻♄ 22:50
☽∠☿ 23:17

31 Th
☽⚻♄ 4:30
☉✶☽ 4:56
☽⚺♇ 8:03
☽✶♀ 9:57
☽□♆ 10:41
☽∥♃ 12:23
☽⋕♄ 16:18
☽△⚷ 16:35
♀⋕⚷ 17:47
♀⚻♆ 18:13
☽∠♃ 20:06
☽∥☿ 20:21
☽△⚳ 20:32
☽△♂ 21:57

Day	Sid.Time	☉	☽	☽ 12 hour	Mean ☊	True ☊	☿	♀	♂	⚳	♃	♄	⚷	♅	♆	♇
	h m s	° ' "	° ' "	° ' "	° '	° '	° '	° '	° '	° '	° '	° '	° '	° '	° '	° '
1 F	2 41 20	8♏36 28	19♑10 50	26♑14 29	8♐42.5	7♐37.4	20♏58.8	11♏33.3	18♍01.1	17♉05.7	1♐54.0	7♊29.4	14♉46.0	22♊25.3	11♈14.9	9♒41.0
2 Sa	2 45 16	9 36 30	3♒13 34	10♒08 01	8 39.3	7R 38.4	22 29.8	12 48.5	18 37.0	16R 52.1	2 06.8	7R 25.4	14R 43.0	22R 23.6	11R 13.4	9 41.3
3 Su	2 49 13	10 36 33	16 57 54	23 43 18	8 36.1	7 38.4	24 00.4	14 03.8	19 12.8	16 38.4	2 19.7	7 21.4	14 40.0	22 21.9	11 12.0	9 41.6
4 M	2 53 09	11 36 38	0♓24 20	7♓01 11	8 33.0	7 37.2	25 30.5	15 19.0	19 48.6	16 24.7	2 32.6	7 17.2	14 37.0	22 20.2	11 10.6	9 41.9
5 Tu	2 57 06	12 36 44	13 34 00	20 02 59	8 29.8	7 34.7	27 00.2	16 34.2	20 24.3	16 10.8	2 45.6	7 13.0	14 34.0	22 18.4	11 09.3	9 42.3
6 W	3 01 02	13 36 52	26 28 19	2♈50 11	8 26.6	7 31.4	28 29.4	17 49.4	20 59.9	15 57.0	2 58.6	7 08.8	14 31.0	22 16.6	11 07.9	9 42.6
7 Th	3 04 59	14 37 01	9♈08 46	15 24 12	8 23.4	7 27.6	29 58.1	19 04.7	21 35.5	15 43.0	3 11.6	7 04.5	14 28.0	22 14.8	11 06.6	9 43.0
8 F	3 08 56	15 37 12	21 36 42	27 46 24	8 20.3	7 23.9	1♐26.3	20 19.9	22 11.1	15 29.1	3 24.6	7 00.1	14 25.0	22 12.9	11 05.2	9 43.5
9 Sa	3 12 52	16 37 25	3♉53 29	9♉58 07	8 17.1	7 20.7	2 53.9	21 35.1	22 46.6	15 15.2	3 37.7	6 55.7	14 22.1	22 11.0	11 04.0	9 43.9
10 Su	3 16 49	17 37 40	16 00 29	22 00 47	8 13.9	7 18.4	4 21.1	22 50.3	23 22.0	15 01.2	3 50.8	6 51.2	14 19.1	22 09.0	11 02.7	9 44.4
11 M	3 20 45	18 37 56	27 59 15	3♊56 06	8 10.7	7D 17.1	5 47.7	24 05.6	23 57.4	14 47.3	4 04.0	6 46.7	14 16.1	22 07.1	11 01.4	9 44.9
12 Tu	3 24 42	19 38 14	9♊51 37	15 46 06	8 07.5	7 16.8	7 13.6	25 20.8	24 32.8	14 33.5	4 17.2	6 42.1	14 13.1	22 05.0	11 00.2	9 45.5
13 W	3 28 38	20 38 34	21 39 52	27 33 17	8 04.4	7 17.4	8 39.0	26 36.1	25 08.1	14 19.7	4 30.4	6 37.5	14 10.1	22 03.0	10 59.0	9 46.0
14 Th	3 32 35	21 38 56	3♋26 45	9♋20 43	8 01.2	7 18.6	10 03.6	27 51.3	25 43.3	14 06.0	4 43.6	6 32.9	14 07.1	22 00.9	10 57.8	9 46.6
15 F	3 36 31	22 39 19	15 15 37	21 11 57	7 58.0	7 20.0	11 27.4	29 06.6	26 18.5	13 52.4	4 56.9	6 28.2	14 04.2	21 58.8	10 56.7	9 47.3
16 Sa	3 40 28	23 39 45	27 10 16	3♌11 05	7 54.8	7 21.4	12 50.5	0♐21.8	26 53.7	13 38.8	5 10.1	6 23.5	14 01.2	21 56.7	10 55.5	9 47.9
17 Su	3 44 25	24 40 12	9♌14 58	15 22 30	7 51.7	7 22.4	14 12.5	1 37.1	27 28.8	13 25.5	5 23.4	6 18.7	13 58.3	21 54.5	10 54.4	9 48.6
18 M	3 48 21	25 40 41	21 34 15	27 50 45	7 48.5	7R 22.9	15 33.5	2 52.4	28 03.8	13 12.2	5 36.8	6 13.9	13 55.4	21 52.3	10 53.3	9 49.3
19 Tu	3 52 18	26 41 12	4♍12 34	10♍40 10	7 45.3	7 22.8	16 53.4	4 07.7	28 38.7	12 59.1	5 50.1	6 09.1	13 52.5	21 50.1	10 52.3	9 50.0
20 W	3 56 14	27 41 45	17 13 59	23 54 22	7 42.1	7 22.3	18 11.9	5 22.9	29 13.7	12 46.1	6 03.4	6 04.3	13 49.6	21 47.8	10 51.3	9 50.8
21 Th	4 00 11	28 42 19	0♎41 33	7♎35 40	7 39.0	7 21.4	19 29.0	6 38.2	29 48.5	12 33.4	6 16.8	5 59.4	13 46.7	21 45.5	10 50.3	9 51.6
22 F	4 04 07	29 42 55	14 36 40	21 44 23	7 35.8	7 20.4	20 44.4	7 53.5	0♎23.3	12 20.8	6 30.2	5 54.5	13 43.8	21 43.2	10 49.3	9 52.4
23 Sa	4 08 04	0♐43 33	28 58 28	6♏18 21	7 32.6	7 19.5	21 57.9	9 08.8	0 58.0	12 08.5	6 43.6	5 49.7	13 41.0	21 40.9	10 48.3	9 53.2
24 Su	4 12 00	1 44 13	13♏43 20	21 12 32	7 29.4	7 18.9	23 09.2	10 24.1	1 32.7	11 56.4	6 57.0	5 44.7	13 38.1	21 38.6	10 47.4	9 54.1
25 M	4 15 57	2 44 54	28 44 56	6♐19 25	7 26.2	7D 18.6	24 18.0	11 39.4	2 07.3	11 44.5	7 10.5	5 39.8	13 35.3	21 36.2	10 46.5	9 55.0
26 Tu	4 19 54	3 45 36	13♐54 48	21 29 52	7 23.1	7 18.6	25 24.0	12 54.7	2 41.8	11 32.8	7 23.9	5 34.9	13 32.6	21 33.8	10 45.7	9 55.9
27 W	4 23 50	4 46 20	29 03 27	6♑34 26	7 19.9	7 18.8	26 26.8	14 10.0	3 16.2	11 21.5	7 37.3	5 30.0	13 29.8	21 31.4	10 44.8	9 56.8
28 Th	4 27 47	5 47 06	14♑01 49	21 24 44	7 16.7	7 18.9	27 25.9	15 25.3	3 50.6	11 10.4	7 50.8	5 25.0	13 27.1	21 29.0	10 44.0	9 57.8
29 F	4 31 43	6 47 52	28 42 29	5♒54 33	7 13.5	7R 19.1	28 20.8	16 40.6	4 24.9	10 59.6	8 04.3	5 20.1	13 24.4	21 26.6	10 43.3	9 58.8
30 Sa	4 35 40	7♐48 39	13♒00 33	20 00 17	7♐10.4	7♐19.1	29♐11.0	17♐55.9	4♎59.2	10♉49.1	8♐17.7	5♊15.2	13♉21.7	21♊24.1	10♈42.5	9♒59.8

1st of Month

Julian Day #
2462806.5
Obliquity
23°26[illegible]4"
SVP 4♓49[illegible]0"
GC 27♐16.2
Eris 26♈12.6R

Day	⚴
1	27♒38.3
6	27 49.8
11	28 09.2
16	28 36.2
21	29 10.3
26	29 51.1

Day	⚵
1	8♑51.9
6	10 25.1
11	12 01.9
16	13 42.0
21	15 25.2
26	17 11.3

Day	⚶
1	7♊38.9R
6	6 39.0R
11	5 31.4R
16	4 17.9R
21	3 00.5R
26	1 41.7R

DECLINATION and LATITUDE

Day	☉ Decl	☽ Decl	☽ Lat	☽ 12h Decl	☿ Decl	☿ Lat	♀ Decl	♀ Lat	♂ Decl	♂ Lat	⚳ Decl	⚳ Lat	♃ Decl	♃ Lat	♄ Decl	♄ Lat
1 F	14S22	18S37	3N29	17S02	19S07	1S10	14S35	0N45	6N05	1N28	7N36	9S43	19S55	0N38	19N29	2S06
2 Sa	14 41	15 13	4 20	13 13	19 37	1 16	15 00	0 43	5 51	1 28	7 34	9 41	19 58	0 38	19 29	2 06
3 Su	15 00	11 04	4 54	8 48	20 06	1 22	15 25	0 41	5 37	1 28	7 33	9 39	20 00	0 38	19 28	2 06
4 M	15 19	6 27	5 12	4 04	20 34	1 28	15 49	0 39	5 24	1 29	7 31	9 36	20 03	0 38	19 27	2 06
5 Tu	15 37	1 39	5 13	0N46	21 00	1 34	16 12	0 36	5 10	1 29	7 30	9 34	20 05	0 38	19 26	2 06
6 W	15 55	3N09	4 58	5 29	21 26	1 39	16 36	0 34	4 56	1 29	7 29	9 31	20 08	0 38	19 26	2 06
7 Th	16 13	7 44	4 28	9 53	21 51	1 45	16 58	0 32	4 42	1 30	7 27	9 28	20 11	0 37	19 25	2 06
8 F	16 31	11 55	3 46	13 48	22 14	1 50	17 21	0 30	4 29	1 30	7 26	9 26	20 13	0 37	19 24	2 06
9 Sa	16 48	15 33	2 54	17 06	22 37	1 55	17 43	0 28	4 15	1 30	7 25	9 23	20 16	0 37	19 24	2 06
10 Su	17 05	18 28	1 55	19 37	22 58	1 60	18 04	0 25	4 01	1 30	7 24	9 20	20 18	0 37	19 23	2 06
11 M	17 22	20 32	0 51	21 14	23 19	2 05	18 25	0 23	3 47	1 31	7 23	9 17	20 21	0 37	19 22	2 06
12 Tu	17 38	21 41	0S14	21 54	23 38	2 09	18 46	0 21	3 34	1 31	7 22	9 14	20 24	0 37	19 21	2 06
13 W	17 55	21 52	1 19	21 35	23 56	2 13	19 06	0 18	3 20	1 31	7 22	9 10	20 26	0 37	19 20	2 06
14 Th	18 10	21 03	2 20	20 18	24 12	2 17	19 25	0 16	3 06	1 32	7 21	9 07	20 29	0 37	19 20	2 06
15 F	18 26	19 19	3 15	18 08	24 28	2 20	19 44	0 14	2 52	1 32	7 20	9 03	20 31	0 37	19 19	2 06
16 Sa	18 41	16 45	4 03	15 10	24 42	2 23	20 02	0 11	2 39	1 32	7 20	8 60	20 33	0 37	19 18	2 06
17 Su	18 56	13 26	4 40	11 32	24 55	2 26	20 20	0 09	2 25	1 33	7 20	8 56	20 36	0 36	19 17	2 06
18 M	19 10	9 29	5 06	7 19	25 06	2 28	20 37	0 06	2 11	1 33	7 19	8 53	20 38	0 36	19 17	2 06
19 Tu	19 25	5 02	5 17	2 40	25 17	2 30	20 54	0 04	1 58	1 33	7 19	8 49	20 41	0 36	19 16	2 06
20 W	19 39	0 14	5 13	2S15	25 25	2 31	21 10	0 02	1 44	1 33	7 19	8 45	20 43	0 36	19 15	2 06
21 Th	19 52	4S44	4 52	7 13	25 33	2 32	21 26	0S01	1 31	1 34	7 19	8 41	20 46	0 36	19 14	2 06
22 F	20 05	9 39	4 13	11 59	25 39	2 33	21 40	0 03	1 17	1 34	7 19	8 37	20 48	0 36	19 13	2 06
23 Sa	20 18	14 11	3 18	16 12	25 44	2 32	21 55	0 06	1 03	1 34	7 20	8 33	20 50	0 36	19 13	2 06
24 Su	20 30	17 59	2 08	19 29	25 47	2 32	22 08	0 08	0 50	1 35	7 20	8 29	20 53	0 36	19 12	2 06
25 M	20 42	20 39	0 47	21 27	25 49	2 30	22 21	0 10	0 37	1 35	7 20	8 24	20 55	0 36	19 11	2 06
26 Tu	20 54	21 51	0N37	21 52	25 49	2 28	22 33	0 13	0 23	1 35	7 21	8 20	20 57	0 36	19 10	2 06
27 W	21 05	21 28	1 58	20 41	25 48	2 25	22 45	0 15	0 10	1 36	7 22	8 16	20 59	0 36	19 09	2 05
28 Th	21 16	19 32	3 11	18 05	25 45	2 21	22 56	0 18	0S04	1 36	7 23	8 11	21 02	0 36	19 09	2 05
29 F	21 26	16 21	4 09	14 24	25 41	2 16	23 06	0 20	0 17	1 36	7 24	8 07	21 04	0 35	19 08	2 05
30 Sa	21S36	12S16	4N50	9S60	25S36	2S10	23S16	0S23	0S30	1N36	7N25	8S03	21S06	0N35	19N07	2S05

Day	⚷ Decl	⚷ Lat	♅ Decl	♅ Lat	♆ Decl	♆ Lat	♇ Decl	♇ Lat
1	14N28	1S52	23N18	0N05	2N60	1S35	23S46	6S11
6	14 24	1 53	23 18	0 05	2 57	1 35	23 45	6 10
11	14 19	1 53	23 17	0 05	2 55	1 34	23 44	6 10
16	14 14	1 54	23 17	0 05	2 53	1 34	23 43	6 09
21	14 09	1 54	23 16	0 05	2 51	1 34	23 41	6 09
26	14 05	1 54	23 15	0 06	2 49	1 34	23 40	6 08

Day	⚴ Decl	⚴ Lat	⚵ Decl	⚵ Lat	⚶ Decl	⚶ Lat	Eris Decl	Eris Lat
1	5S48	6N54	13S49	9N21	13N31	8S10	1N05	9S41
6	6 23	6 13	13 59	9 04	13 23	8 09	1 04	9 41
11	6 53	5 34	14 08	8 48	13 15	8 06	1 03	9 40
16	7 19	4 56	14 14	8 32	13 07	8 01	1 03	9 40
21	7 42	4 20	14 19	8 17	13 01	7 53	1 02	9 40
26	7 60	3 46	14 21	8 03	12 56	7 42	1 02	9 39

Moon Phenomena

Max/0 Decl
dy hr mn
5 8:10 0 N
12 16:10 21N55
20 1:09 0 S
26 6:05 21S54

Perigee/Apogee
dy hr m kilometers
13 5:01 a 405993
25 21:10 p 357521

PH dy hr mn
☽ 2 11:57 10♒06
○ 10 3:31 17♉47
☾ 18 8:33 26♌02
● 25 6:48 3♐02
✔ 25 411:36T 03[illegible]4"

Max/0 Lat
dy hr mn
4 13:03 5N14
11 18:46 0 S
19 5:54 5S18
25 13:33 0 N

Void of Course Moon

Last Aspect	☽ Ingress
1 3:25 ☿ ⚹	♒ 1 18:26
3 14:05 ☿ □	♓ 3 23:16
6 4:17 ☿ △	♈ 6 6:38
8 1:10 ♅ ⚹	♉ 8 16:21
10 15:29 ♂ △	♊ 11 4:03
13 7:26 ♂ □	♋ 13 16:59
15 23:25 ♂ ⚹	♌ 16 5:39
18 8:33 ☉ □	♍ 18 16:05
20 22:23 ♂ ☌	♎ 20 22:47
22 11:56 ♅ △	♏ 23 1:41
23 17:50 ♇ □	♐ 25 1:59
26 19:33 ☿ ☌	♑ 27 1:30
27 18:41 ♆ □	♒ 29 2:08

DAILY ASPECTARIAN

1 F
☽⚹☿ 3:25
☽⚻♅ 5:29
☽⚼♄ 5:35
☉⋕⚷ 7:29
☿⋕♄ 17:19
☽⚹♃ 22:03
☿⚻♅ 22:23

2 Sa
☽⚼♂ 0:42
☽∥♀ 1:14
☉□♇ 1:56
☉∥☽ 3:02
☽⋕⚷ 4:42
☽⚼♅ 7:13
☽△♄ 7:14
☽☌♇ 11:14
☉□☽ 11:57
☊R 11:57
☽⚹♆ 13:53
☽□♀ 18:22
☿∥♃ 18:49
☽□⚷ 19:58
☽□⚳ 23:26

3 Su
☽⚻♂ 4:10
☽△♅ 9:34
♀☍⚷ 11:08
☉⚻♆ 13:51
☽□☿ 14:05
☽∠♆ 16:24
☽⋕⚳ 18:33

4 M
☽□♃ 3:56
☽⋕♂ 5:37
☿⚼♆ 10:33
☽□♄ 12:25
☽⚺♇ 16:54
☽⋕♆ 17:27
♀☍⚳ 17:42
☽⚺♆ 19:34
☉△☽ 22:06

5 Tu
☽⚹⚷ 1:50
☽⚹⚳ 4:44
☽△♀ 6:08
☽☍♂ 13:16
☽□♅ 16:10
☽∠♇ 20:42
☽∥♆ 23:00

6 W
☽△☿ 4:17
☉⚼☽ 4:22
☽∠⚷ 5:42
☽∠⚳ 8:17
☽∥♂ 8:44
☽△♃ 12:29
☽⚼♀ 13:17
☽⚹♄ 20:04
☉☍⚷ 20:35
☽∥⚳ 22:32

7 Th
☿ ♐ 0:32
☽⚹♇ 1:06
☽☌♆ 3:45
☽⚺⚷ 10:09
☉⚻☽ 11:24
☽⚺⚳ 12:22
☽⚼☿ 12:39
☽⚼♃ 17:41
☽⚻♀ 21:14
☉☍⚳ 21:22

8 F
☽∠♄ 0:45
♂□♅ 1:10
☽⚹♅ 1:10
☽⚻♂ 1:10
☽∥⚷ 15:38
☽⚻☿ 21:47
☽⚻♃ 23:28

9 Sa
☽⚺♄ 5:57
☽∠♅ 6:28
☽⚼♂ 8:03
☉⋕☽ 10:38
♀⚻♅ 11:09
☽□♇ 11:32
☽⚺♆ 14:09
☿☌♃ 14:10
☽⋕♀ 19:49
☽☌⚷ 20:39
☽☌⚳ 22:04

10 Su
☉☍☽ 3:31
☽∥♄ 9:21
☽⚺♅ 12:15
☽☍♀ 15:15
☽△♂ 15:29
♀⚹♂ 19:06
☽∠♆ 20:03
☽⋕♃ 21:14
☿⋕♅ 22:24

11 M
☽☍♃ 12:30
☿☍♄ 15:38
☽☌♄ 17:38
☽☍☿ 17:56
☊D 18:44
☽△♇ 23:48

12 Tu
☽⚹♆ 2:19
☿∥♇ 7:37
♂⚼♇ 8:45
☽⚺⚷ 8:49
☽⚺⚳ 9:21
♀⚼♆ 12:22
☉⚻☽ 21:44

13 W
☽☌♅ 0:47
☽⚼♇ 6:20
☽□♂ 7:26
☽⚻♀ 11:15
☽∠⚷ 15:13
☽∠⚳ 15:19
♀⋕♄ 17:36
☿⚹♇ 19:09
⚳☌⚷ 21:24

14 Th
☽⚻♃ 2:39
☽⚺♄ 6:16
☉⚼☽ 7:08
☉⚻♅ 8:27
☽⋕♃ 9:17
☽⚻♇ 12:53
☽⚻☿ 15:16
☽□♆ 15:16
☿△♆ 15:17
☽⋕♀ 19:55
☽⚹⚳ 21:15
☽⚼♀ 21:24
☽⚹⚷ 21:36
♂∥♆ 22:49

15 F
☽∥♄ 0:05
☉⋕☽ 8:20
☽⚼♃ 9:39
☽∠♄ 12:28
☽⚺♅ 13:32
☉△☽ 16:19
♀ ♐ 17:02
☽⚹♂ 23:25

16 Sa
☽⚼☿ 1:31
☽△♀ 7:08
☿⚻⚳ 12:08
☽△♃ 16:14
☽⚹♄ 18:14
☽∥⚷ 18:40
☽∠♅ 19:24
☿⚻⚷ 19:58

17 Su
☽☍♇ 1:06
☽△♆ 3:15
☽∠♂ 6:40
☽□⚳ 8:03
☽□⚷ 9:14
☽△☿ 10:56

18 M
☽⚹♅ 0:35
♀∥♃ 1:38
♂⚼⚳ 4:12
☉⚼♆ 4:56
☽⚼♆ 8:16
☉□☽ 8:33
☊R 8:54
☉⋕♄ 9:42
☽∥⚳ 11:57
☽⚺♂ 13:01
☽□♀ 23:50

19 Tu
☽□♃ 3:05
☽□♄ 3:36
♂⚼⚷ 8:42
☽⚻♇ 10:28
☽∥♆ 11:04
☽⚻♆ 12:21
☽△⚳ 15:59
☽∥♂ 16:16
☽△⚷ 17:49

20 W
♃☍♄ 1:07
☽□☿ 1:56
☽□♅ 8:12
☽⋕♂ 9:08
♀☍♄ 12:23
☽⚼♇ 13:41
☽⋕♆ 14:54
♀☌♃ 15:42
☽⚼⚳ 18:34
☉⚹☽ 20:14
☽⚼⚷ 20:39
☽☌♂ 22:23

21 Th
♂ ♎ 7:56
☽△♄ 9:10
☽⚹♃ 9:53
☽⚹♀ 11:22
☽⋕⚳ 12:30
☽△♇ 15:55
☽☍♆ 17:33
☽⚻⚳ 20:12
☽⚻⚷ 22:31

22 F
☉∠☽ 0:11
☉ ♐ 6:46
☽⚼♄ 10:33
☽⚹☿ 11:18
☽∠♃ 11:47
☽△♅ 11:56
☽∠♀ 15:15
☿☍♅ 18:35
☽⋕⚷ 23:41

23 Sa
☉⚺☽ 3:06
☽⚺♂ 3:25
☽⚻♄ 11:09
☽⚼♅ 12:35
☽⚺♃ 12:53
☉⚹♂ 13:21
☽∠☿ 14:13
♀⚹♇ 14:20
☽□♇ 17:50
☽⚺♀ 18:09
☽⚻♆ 19:16
☽☍⚳ 21:10
☽☍⚷ 23:52

24 Su
☽∠♂ 4:43
♀△♆ 7:21
☽⋕♄ 9:31
☽⚻♅ 12:40
☽⚺☿ 16:21
☽⚼♆ 19:17

25 M
☉∥☽ 0:47
♀⚻⚳ 1:24
☽∥♃ 3:32
☽⚹♂ 5:33
☉☌☽ 6:48
☽☍♄ 10:54
☊D 13:17
☿∠♇ 13:30
☽☌♃ 13:33
☽⚹♇ 17:42
☽△♆ 19:01
☽⚻⚳ 20:18
☽☌♀ 22:16
☽⚻⚷ 23:25

26 Tu
☉∥♃ 8:44
♀⚻⚷ 11:39
☽☍♅ 12:04
☽∠♇ 17:28
☽☌☿ 19:33
☽⚼⚳ 19:46
☿⚼⚳ 22:14
☽⚼⚷ 23:07
⚴ ♓ 23:53

27 W
☉∥☽ 5:45
☽□♂ 6:59
☽∥♃ 7:37
☉⚺☽ 9:47
☽⚻♄ 10:13
☽⚺♃ 13:53
☉☍♄ 15:57
☽⚺♇ 17:26
☽□♆ 18:41
☽△⚳ 19:27
☽△⚷ 23:04

28 Th
☽⚺♀ 2:28
☽⋕♄ 3:29
☽⚼♄ 10:19
☉∠☽ 11:47
☽⚻♅ 12:05
☽∠♃ 14:34
☽⚺☿ 23:22

29 F
☿⚼⚷ 1:33
☽∠♀ 5:24
☽△♂ 9:54
☽△♄ 10:59
☽⚼♅ 12:52
☽⋕⚷ 14:07
☊R 14:20
☉⚹☽ 14:32
☽⚹♃ 15:53
☽☌♇ 18:53
☽⚹♆ 20:06
☽□⚳ 20:19
♀⋕♅ 22:06

30 Sa
☽□⚷ 0:36
☽∠☿ 2:07
☽⚹♀ 9:16
♂△♄ 9:50
☽⚼♂ 12:29
☽△♅ 14:23
☉☌♃ 14:44
⚳⚺♆ 16:32
☽∠♆ 21:54

December 2030

LONGITUDE

Day	Sid.Time	☉	☽	☽ 12 hour	Mean☊	True☊	☿	♀	♂	⚳	♃	♄	⚷	♅	♆	♇
	h m s	° ' "	° ' "	° ' "	° '	° '	° '	° '	° '	° '	° '	° '	° '	° '	° '	° '
1 Su	4 39 36	8♐49 27	26♒53 42	3♓40 51	7♐07.2	7♐19.0	29♐55.7	19♐11.2	5♎33.3	10♉38.9	8♐31.2	5♊10.3	13♉19.1	21♊21.6	10♈41.8	10♒00.9
2 M	4 43 33	9 50 16	10♓21 56	16 57 11	7 04.0	7D 19.0	0♑34.4	20 26.4	6 07.4	10R 29.0	8 44.6	5R 05.4	13R 16.5	21R 19.1	10R 41.1	10 01.9
3 Tu	4 47 29	10 51 06	23 26 58	29 51 39	7 00.8	7 19.1	1 06.1	21 41.7	6 41.4	10 19.5	8 58.1	5 00.5	13 13.9	21 16.6	10 40.5	10 03.0
4 W	4 51 26	11 51 56	6♈11 38	12♈27 21	6 57.7	7 19.4	1 30.1	22 57.0	7 15.4	10 10.3	9 11.6	4 55.6	13 11.3	21 14.1	10 39.9	10 04.1
5 Th	4 55 23	12 52 48	18 39 15	24 47 43	6 54.5	7 19.9	1 45.7	24 12.3	7 49.2	10 01.4	9 25.0	4 50.7	13 08.8	21 11.6	10 39.3	10 05.2
6 F	4 59 19	13 53 40	0♉53 12	6♉56 05	6 51.3	7 20.6	1R 51.8	25 27.5	8 23.0	9 52.9	9 38.5	4 45.9	13 06.3	21 09.1	10 38.7	10 06.4
7 Sa	5 03 16	14 54 33	12 56 45	18 55 32	6 48.1	7 21.3	1 47.8	26 42.8	8 56.7	9 44.7	9 51.9	4 41.1	13 03.9	21 06.6	10 38.2	10 07.6
8 Su	5 07 12	15 55 28	24 52 48	0♊48 51	6 44.9	7 21.9	1 33.0	27 58.1	9 30.3	9 36.9	10 05.3	4 36.3	13 01.5	21 04.0	10 37.7	10 08.8
9 M	5 11 09	16 56 23	6♊43 58	12 38 26	6 41.8	7R 22.2	1 07.0	29 13.3	10 03.9	9 29.5	10 18.8	4 31.5	12 59.1	21 01.5	10 37.3	10 10.0
10 Tu	5 15 05	17 57 19	18 32 32	24 26 30	6 38.6	7 21.9	0 29.5	0♑28.6	10 37.3	9 22.4	10 32.2	4 26.8	12 56.8	20 58.9	10 36.8	10 11.3
11 W	5 19 02	18 58 16	0♋20 36	6♋15 06	6 35.4	7 21.1	29♐40.9	1 43.8	11 10.7	9 15.8	10 45.6	4 22.1	12 54.5	20 56.4	10 36.4	10 12.5
12 Th	5 22 58	19 59 14	12 10 16	18 06 23	6 32.2	7 19.6	28 41.9	2 59.1	11 44.0	9 09.5	10 59.0	4 17.4	12 52.2	20 53.8	10 36.1	10 13.8
13 F	5 26 55	21 00 12	24 03 43	0♌02 37	6 29.1	7 17.6	27 33.7	4 14.3	12 17.2	9 03.6	11 12.4	4 12.8	12 50.0	20 51.2	10 35.8	10 15.1
14 Sa	5 30 52	22 01 12	6♌03 23	12 06 24	6 25.9	7 15.3	26 18.2	5 29.6	12 50.4	8 58.0	11 25.8	4 08.2	12 47.8	20 48.7	10 35.5	10 16.4
15 Su	5 34 48	23 02 13	18 12 01	24 20 40	6 22.7	7 12.9	24 57.6	6 44.8	13 23.4	8 52.9	11 39.1	4 03.7	12 45.7	20 46.1	10 35.2	10 17.8
16 M	5 38 45	24 03 15	0♍32 44	6♍48 41	6 19.5	7 11.0	23 34.7	8 00.1	13 56.4	8 48.2	11 52.5	3 59.2	12 43.6	20 43.6	10 35.0	10 19.2
17 Tu	5 42 41	25 04 17	13 08 57	19 33 58	6 16.4	7 09.7	22 12.3	9 15.3	14 29.2	8 43.8	12 05.8	3 54.8	12 41.6	20 41.0	10 34.8	10 20.5
18 W	5 46 38	26 05 21	26 04 09	2♎39 54	6 13.2	7D 09.2	20 53.0	10 30.6	15 02.0	8 39.9	12 19.1	3 50.4	12 39.6	20 38.5	10 34.7	10 21.9
19 Th	5 50 34	27 06 25	9♎21 35	16 09 28	6 10.0	7 09.6	19 39.5	11 45.8	15 34.7	8 36.3	12 32.4	3 46.1	12 37.7	20 35.9	10 34.5	10 23.4
20 F	5 54 31	28 07 30	23 03 46	0♏04 33	6 06.8	7 10.8	18 33.7	13 01.0	16 07.3	8 33.2	12 45.6	3 41.8	12 35.8	20 33.4	10 34.5	10 24.8
21 Sa	5 58 27	29 08 37	7♏11 47	14 25 17	6 03.7	7 12.2	17 37.2	14 16.2	16 39.7	8 30.5	12 58.9	3 37.6	12 33.9	20 30.9	10D 34.4	10 26.3
22 Su	6 02 24	0♑09 44	21 44 41	29 09 26	6 00.5	7 13.5	16 51.0	15 31.5	17 12.1	8 28.2	13 12.1	3 33.4	12 32.1	20 28.3	10 34.4	10 27.8
23 M	6 06 21	1 10 52	6♐38 49	14♐11 54	5 57.3	7R 14.1	16 15.7	16 46.7	17 44.4	8 26.2	13 25.3	3 29.4	12 30.4	20 25.8	10 34.4	10 29.3
24 Tu	6 10 17	2 12 00	21 47 39	29 24 53	5 54.1	7 13.5	15 51.2	18 01.9	18 16.5	8 24.7	13 38.4	3 25.4	12 28.7	20 23.3	10 34.5	10 30.8
25 W	6 14 14	3 13 09	7♑02 18	14♑38 38	5 51.0	7 11.6	15D 37.3	19 17.1	18 48.6	8 23.6	13 51.6	3 21.4	12 27.1	20 20.9	10 34.6	10 32.3
26 Th	6 18 10	4 14 19	22 12 35	29 42 58	5 47.8	7 08.3	15 33.5	20 32.3	19 20.5	8 22.9	14 04.7	3 17.5	12 25.5	20 18.4	10 34.7	10 33.9
27 F	6 22 07	5 15 28	7♒08 42	14♒28 52	5 44.6	7 04.2	15 39.2	21 47.5	19 52.3	8D 22.6	14 17.7	3 13.7	12 23.9	20 15.9	10 34.9	10 35.4
28 Sa	6 26 03	6 16 38	21 42 44	28 49 47	5 41.4	6 59.9	15 53.6	23 02.7	20 24.0	8 22.7	14 30.7	3 10.0	12 22.5	20 13.5	10 35.1	10 37.0
29 Su	6 30 00	7 17 47	5♓49 42	12♓42 20	5 38.2	6 56.0	16 16.0	24 17.9	20 55.6	8 23.2	14 43.7	3 06.4	12 21.0	20 11.1	10 35.3	10 38.6
30 M	6 33 56	8 18 57	19 27 44	26 06 06	5 35.1	6 53.1	16 45.6	25 33.1	21 27.1	8 24.1	14 56.7	3 02.8	12 19.7	20 08.7	10 35.6	10 40.2
31 Tu	6 37 53	9♑20 06	2♈37 47	9♈03 10	5♐31.9	6♐51.5	17♐21.7	26♑48.2	21♎58.4	8♉25.4	15♐09.6	2♊59.3	12♉18.3	20♊06.3	10♈35.9	10♒41.8

1st of Month

Julian Day # 2462836.5
Obliquity 23°26'03"
SVP 4♓49'25"
GC 27♐16.3
Eris 25♈56.9R

Day	⚴	⚵	⚶
1	0♓38.2	19♑00.2	0♊23.9R
6	1 31.2	20 51.5	29♉09.7R
11	2 29.6	22 45.2	28 01.1R
16	3 33.0	24 41.0	27 00.0R
21	4 41.0	26 38.8	26 07.9R
26	5 53.4	28 38.6	25 26.0R
31	7 09.8	0♒40.1	24 54.9R

DECLINATION and LATITUDE

Day	☉ Decl	☽ Decl	☽ Lat	☽12h Decl	☿ Decl	☿ Lat	♀ Decl	♀ Lat	♂ Decl	♂ Lat	⚳ Decl	⚳ Lat	♃ Decl	♃ Lat	♄ Decl	♄ Lat
1 Su	21S46	7S38	5N13	5S13	25S29	2S03	23S24	0S25	0S44	1N37	7N26	7S58	21S08	0N35	19N06	2S05
2 M	21 55	2 46	5 18	0 20	25 21	1 55	23 33	0 27	0 57	1 37	7 27	7 53	21 11	0 35	19 06	2 05
3 Tu	22 04	2N05	5 06	4N26	25 12	1 46	23 40	0 30	1 10	1 37	7 29	7 49	21 13	0 35	19 05	2 05
4 W	22 12	6 43	4 39	8 55	25 01	1 35	23 47	0 32	1 23	1 38	7 31	7 44	21 15	0 35	19 04	2 05
5 Th	22 20	10 60	3 59	12 56	24 49	1 23	23 53	0 34	1 36	1 38	7 32	7 40	21 17	0 35	19 03	2 05
6 F	22 28	14 44	3 09	16 22	24 35	1 10	23 58	0 37	1 49	1 38	7 34	7 35	21 19	0 35	19 02	2 05
7 Sa	22 35	17 49	2 12	19 04	24 21	0 55	24 02	0 39	2 02	1 38	7 36	7 30	21 21	0 35	19 02	2 05
8 Su	22 41	20 06	1 09	20 55	24 05	0 39	24 06	0 41	2 15	1 39	7 38	7 25	21 23	0 35	19 01	2 04
9 M	22 48	21 29	0 04	21 49	23 47	0 22	24 09	0 43	2 28	1 39	7 41	7 21	21 25	0 35	19 00	2 04
10 Tu	22 53	21 55	1S02	21 46	23 29	0 03	24 12	0 46	2 41	1 39	7 43	7 16	21 27	0 35	18 60	2 04
11 W	22 59	21 22	2 04	20 44	23 10	0N16	24 13	0 48	2 54	1 39	7 45	7 11	21 29	0 35	18 59	2 04
12 Th	23 03	19 52	3 01	18 47	22 49	0 36	24 14	0 50	3 07	1 40	7 48	7 06	21 31	0 35	18 58	2 04
13 F	23 08	17 30	3 51	16 02	22 28	0 57	24 14	0 52	3 19	1 40	7 51	7 01	21 33	0 34	18 57	2 04
14 Sa	23 12	14 23	4 31	12 34	22 06	1 17	24 13	0 54	3 32	1 40	7 54	6 57	21 35	0 34	18 57	2 04
15 Su	23 15	10 37	4 59	8 33	21 45	1 36	24 12	0 56	3 44	1 41	7 57	6 52	21 37	0 34	18 56	2 03
16 M	23 18	6 22	5 14	4 06	21 23	1 54	24 10	0 58	3 57	1 41	7 60	6 47	21 38	0 34	18 55	2 03
17 Tu	23 21	1 46	5 15	0S36	21 03	2 10	24 07	1 00	4 09	1 41	8 03	6 42	21 40	0 34	18 55	2 03
18 W	23 23	3S01	4 59	5 26	20 44	2 24	24 03	1 02	4 22	1 41	8 06	6 37	21 42	0 34	18 54	2 03
19 Th	23 24	7 42	4 28	10 08	20 26	2 36	23 59	1 04	4 34	1 42	8 10	6 33	21 44	0 34	18 53	2 03
20 F	23 25	12 22	3 40	14 29	20 12	2 45	23 53	1 06	4 46	1 42	8 13	6 28	21 46	0 34	18 53	2 03
21 Sa	23 26	16 24	2 38	18 07	19 60	2 53	23 47	1 08	4 59	1 42	8 17	6 23	21 47	0 34	18 52	2 02
22 Su	23 26	19 33	1 24	20 41	19 51	2 57	23 41	1 09	5 11	1 42	8 21	6 18	21 49	0 34	18 52	2 02
23 M	23 26	21 28	0 03	21 52	19 44	2 60	23 33	1 11	5 23	1 43	8 25	6 13	21 51	0 34	18 51	2 02
24 Tu	23 25	21 52	1N19	21 27	19 41	2 60	23 25	1 13	5 35	1 43	8 29	6 09	21 52	0 34	18 50	2 02
25 W	23 24	20 38	2 37	19 27	19 41	2 60	23 16	1 14	5 47	1 43	8 33	6 04	21 54	0 34	18 50	2 02
26 Th	23 22	17 56	3 43	16 08	19 43	2 57	23 07	1 16	5 58	1 43	8 37	5 59	21 56	0 34	18 49	2 01
27 F	23 20	14 05	4 32	11 51	19 47	2 53	22 57	1 17	6 10	1 44	8 42	5 54	21 57	0 34	18 49	2 01
28 Sa	23 17	9 29	5 03	7 01	19 54	2 48	22 46	1 19	6 22	1 44	8 46	5 50	21 59	0 34	18 48	2 01
29 Su	23 14	4 30	5 14	1 59	20 02	2 43	22 34	1 20	6 33	1 44	8 51	5 45	22 00	0 34	18 48	2 01
30 M	23 10	0N31	5 06	2N59	20 11	2 36	22 22	1 21	6 45	1 44	8 55	5 40	22 02	0 34	18 47	2 01
31 Tu	23S06	5N22	4N43	7N39	20S22	2N29	22S09	1S23	6S56	1N45	9N00	5S36	22S03	0N33	18N47	2S00

Day	⚷ Decl	⚷ Lat	♅ Decl	♅ Lat	♆ Decl	♆ Lat	♇ Decl	♇ Lat
1	14N01	1S54	23N15	0N06	2N48	1S34	23S38	6S08
6	13 57	1 55	23 14	0 06	2 47	1 33	23 36	6 07
11	13 53	1 55	23 13	0 06	2 46	1 33	23 34	6 07
16	13 50	1 55	23 12	0 06	2 46	1 33	23 32	6 07
21	13 47	1 55	23 11	0 06	2 46	1 33	23 30	6 07
26	13 45	1 55	23 11	0 06	2 46	1 33	23 27	6 06
31	13N42	1S55	23N10	0N06	2N47	1S32	23S25	6S06

Day	⚴ Decl	⚴ Lat	⚵ Decl	⚵ Lat	⚶ Decl	⚶ Lat	Eris Decl	Eris Lat
1	8S14	3N13	14S21	7N49	12N53	7S30	1N01	9S39
6	8 25	2 41	14 18	7 36	12 53	7 15	1 01	9 38
11	8 33	2 11	14 14	7 23	12 54	6 59	1 01	9 37
16	8 38	1 41	14 07	7 10	12 58	6 41	1 01	9 37
21	8 39	1 13	13 58	6 59	13 04	6 23	1 01	9 36
26	8 38	0 46	13 47	6 47	13 13	6 04	1 01	9 36
31	8S34	0N20	13S33	6N36	13N25	5S44	1N02	9S35

Moon Phenomena

Max/0 Decl

dy	hr mn	
2	13:39	0 N
9	22:28	21N55
17	8:57	0 S
23	17:50	21S54
29	21:29	0 N

Max/0 Lat

dy	hr mn	
1	18:30	5N18
9	1:17	0 S
16	12:40	5S16
23	0:56	0 N
29	1:54	5N14

Perigee/Apogee

dy	hr m		kilometers
10	10:06	a	406368
24	10:10	p	356932

PH	dy	hr mn	
☽	1	22:58	9♓48
○	9	22:42	17♊54
(eclipse)	9	22:29	A 0.941
☾	18	0:02	26♍05
●	24	17:33	2♑57
☽	31	13:37	9♈55

Void of Course Moon

Last Aspect			☽ Ingress	
30 14:23	♅	△	♓	1 5:28
2 20:24	♀	□	♈	3 12:16
5 12:05	♀	△	♉	5 22:15
6 18:21	♇	□	♊	8 10:21
10 22:45	☿	☍	♋	10 23:18
11 23:04	♂	□	♌	13 11:55
15 11:52	☿	△	♍	15 22:57
18 0:02	☉	□	♎	18 7:10
20 9:21	☉	✶	♏	20 11:52
21 12:51	♀	✶	♐	22 13:21
23 21:47	♅	☍	♑	24 12:55
25 21:06	♀	☌	♒	26 12:27
27 21:44	♂	△	♓	28 14:00
30 12:09	♀	✶	♈	30 19:09

DAILY ASPECTARIAN

1 Su: ☽⋕⚳ 1:01 · ☿ ♑ 2:28 · ☽✶☿ 5:38 · ☽□♄ 14:34 · ☽⚻♂ 16:02 · ☽□♃ 21:01 · ☊ D 22:20 · ☉□☽ 22:58 · ☽⚺♇ 23:24 · ☽⋕♆ 23:54

2 M: ☽✶⚳ 0:13 · ☽⚺♆ 0:35 · ☉✶♇ 4:41 · ☽✶⚷ 5:16 · ☽∥♂ 8:35 · ☉⚻⚳ 13:12 · ⚶R♉ 13:51 · ♀∥♇ 14:30 · ♀☍♅ 16:16 · ☽⋕♂ 19:13 · ☉△♆ 19:51 · ☽□♅ 19:59 · ☽□♀ 20:24

3 Tu: ☽∠♇ 2:59 · ☽∠⚳ 3:27 · ☽∥♆ 3:34 · ☽∠⚷ 8:54 · ☽□☿ 14:50 · ☽✶♄ 21:36

4 W: ☽☍♂ 2:07 · ☽∥⚳ 4:16 · ☽△♃ 5:50 · ☽✶♇ 7:25 · ☽⚺⚳ 7:31 · ☽☌♆ 8:33 · ☉△☽ 11:50 · ☽⚺⚷ 13:22 · ⚳□♇ 14:38

5 Th: ☽∠♄ 2:18 · ☽✶♅ 4:56 · ☉⚻⚷ 6:04 · ☽⚼♃ 11:28 · ☽△♀ 12:05 · ♀⚼⚳ 14:03 · ♀∠♇ 17:09 · ☽∥⚷ 18:38 · ☉⚼☽ 19:42

6 F: ☽△☿ 1:56 · ☿ R 2:49 · ☽⚺♄ 7:38 · ☽∠♅ 10:24 · ☽⚻♂ 15:37 · ⚳⚻♃ 15:58 · ☽☌⚳ 17:40 · ☽⚻♃ 17:43 · ☽□♇ 18:21 · ☽⚺♆ 19:23 · ☽⚼♀ 21:15

7 Sa: ☽☌⚷ 0:14 · ☉⚻☽ 4:18 · ☽⚼☿ 7:36 · ☽∥♄ 11:37 · ☽⚺♅ 16:20 · ☿∥♀ 22:03 · ☽⚼♂ 23:12

8 Su: ♀⚼⚷ 1:03 · ☽∠♆ 1:31 · ♂⚻⚳ 3:51 · ♃✶♇ 6:45 · ☽⚻♀ 6:59 · ☽⚻☿ 13:04 · ☽☌♄ 19:33 · ☽⋕♃ 22:12

9 M: ☊ R 1:21 · ♂△♇ 4:34 · ☽⚺⚳ 5:33 · ☽△♇ 6:59 · ☽△♂ 7:06 · ☽☍♃ 7:25 · ☽✶♆ 7:53 · ☽⚺⚷ 12:39 · ♀ ♑ 14:53 · ☿∥♇ 17:15 · ♂✶♃ 17:50 · ☉☍☽ 22:42 · ♂☍♆ 23:38

10 Tu: ☿☌♀ 0:11 · ☽☌♅ 4:57 · ♃△♆ 8:03 · ♂⋕♆ 9:40 · ☽∠⚳ 11:45 · ☽⚼♇ 13:32 · ☿R♐ 15:12 · ☽∠⚷ 19:04 · ☿⋕♅ 19:46 · ☽⋕♃ 21:09 · ☽☍☿ 22:45

11 W: ☽☍♀ 3:09 · ☽⚺♄ 8:07 · ☉∥☿ 10:37 · ☽✶⚳ 17:57 · ☽⚻♇ 20:04 · ☽□♆ 20:49 · ☽⚻♃ 21:33 · ☽□♂ 23:04

12 Th: ☽✶⚷ 1:25 · ☽∥♄ 10:10 · ☽∠♄ 14:18 · ☉⚻☽ 17:16 · ☽⚺♅ 17:34 · ☿⚼⚷ 18:20 · ☉☍♅ 20:37 · ♀⚻♄ 23:32

13 F: ☽⚼♃ 4:23 · ☽⚻☿ 6:23 · ☽✶♄ 20:12 · ♂⚻⚷ 22:17 · ☽⚻♀ 22:45 · ☽∠♅ 23:31

14 Sa: ☉⚼☽ 2:06 · ☽∥⚷ 3:35 · ☽□⚳ 5:45 · ☉⋕♅ 6:24 · ☽☍♇ 8:23 · ☽△♆ 9:00 · ☽⚼☿ 9:23 · ☽△♃ 10:52 · ☽□⚷ 13:20 · ☽✶♂ 14:05 · ☿∠♇ 18:11

15 Su: ☽✶♅ 5:01 · ☽⚼♀ 7:44 · ☿∥♃ 8:10 · ☉△☽ 10:18 · ☽△☿ 11:52 · ☽⚼♆ 14:25 · ☽∥⚳ 15:13 · ☉⚼⚳ 18:29 · ☉☌☿ 19:15 · ☿⚼⚳ 19:54 · ☽∠♂ 20:46

16 M: ☽□♄ 6:34 · ☽⋕♂ 12:16 · ♀△⚳ 14:29 · ☽△⚳ 15:42 · ☽△♀ 15:50 · ☽⚻♇ 18:42 · ☽∥♆ 18:57 · ☽⚻♆ 19:09 · ☽□♃ 21:59 · ☽△⚷ 23:09

17 Tu: ☽⚺♂ 2:38 · ☉∠♇ 6:32 · ☽□♅ 14:02 · ☽□☿ 15:19 · ☽⚼⚳ 19:36 · ♀⚺♇ 21:12 · ☽⚼♇ 22:42 · ☽⋕♆ 22:44

18 W: ☉□☽ 0:02 · ☊ D 0:10 · ♀□♆ 1:19 · ☽⚼⚷ 2:54 · ☿☍♅ 4:45 · ☽∥♂ 6:59 · ☽△♄ 14:03 · ☽⚻⚳ 22:40

19 Th: ☽⋕⚳ 1:49 · ☽△♇ 1:50 · ☽☍♆ 2:10 · ☽□♀ 4:42 · ☽✶♃ 5:44 · ☽⚻⚷ 5:47 · ♃⚻⚷ 8:22 · ☽☌♂ 11:26 · ☉⚼⚷ 11:55 · ♀△⚷ 16:09 · ☽⚼♄ 16:28 · ☽✶☿ 16:45 · ♀⚺♃ 18:03 · ☽△♅ 19:41

20 F: ☽⋕⚷ 7:59 · ☽∠♃ 8:11 · ☉✶☽ 9:21 · ☽∠☿ 16:45 · ☽⚻♄ 18:02 · ☽⚼♅ 21:11

21 Sa: ☽☍⚳ 2:11 · ☽□♇ 5:25 · ☽⚻♆ 5:38 · ☽☍⚷ 8:55 · ☽⚺♃ 9:46 · ☉∠☽ 12:24 · ☽✶♀ 12:51 · ☽⚺♂ 16:17 · ☽⚺☿ 16:22 · ☿✶♂ 17:14 · ☽⋕♄ 17:56 · ☉ ♑ 20:11 · ♆ D 20:41 · ☽⚻♅ 21:56

22 Su: ☽∥☿ 2:36 · ☽⚼♆ 6:13 · ☉⚺☽ 14:37 · ☽∠♀ 15:30 · ☿⚺♀ 17:01 · ☽∠♂ 17:31 · ☽☍♄ 18:59

23 M: ☊ R 0:59 · ☽⚻⚳ 2:51 · ☽✶♇ 6:07 · ☽△♆ 6:15 · ☽⚻⚷ 9:18 · ☽☌♃ 10:56 · ☽☌☿ 14:50 · ♀∥♇ 15:13 · ☽⚺♀ 17:32 · ☽✶♂ 18:15 · ☽☍♅ 21:47 · ☽∥♃ 23:08 · ☽∥♃ 23:08

24 Tu: ☉∥♀ 1:05 · ☽⚼⚳ 2:33 · ☽∠♇ 5:52 · ♂⚼♄ 5:52 · ♀⚼♄ 7:06 · ♀□♂ 8:08 · ☽⚼⚷ 8:56 · ☉☌☽ 17:33 · ☽⚻♄ 18:14

25 W: ☽△⚳ 2:08 · ☉⚻♄ 3:03 · ☽⚺♇ 5:32 · ☽□♆ 5:35 · ☽△⚷ 8:31 · ☽∥☿ 9:50 · ☽⚺♃ 10:55 · ☽⚺☿ 13:28 · ♀⋕♅ 14:48 · ☽⋕♄ 17:17 · ☽⚼♄ 17:48 · ☽□♂ 19:17 · ♀⚻♅ 19:42 · ☽⚻♅ 20:59 · ☽☌♀ 21:06 · ☿ D 21:15

26 Th: ☽∠♃ 11:08 · ☽∠☿ 13:25 · ♆✶♇ 14:22 · ☽△♄ 17:41 · ☉⚺☽ 20:43 · ☽⚼♅ 20:58

27 F: ☽⋕⚷ 1:59 · ☽□⚳ 2:00 · ☽✶♆ 5:36 · ☽☌♇ 5:38 · ⚳ D 5:38 · ☽□⚷ 8:34 · ☽✶♃ 11:52 · ☽✶☿ 14:08 · ♂△♅ 16:35 · ☽△♅ 21:31 · ☽△♂ 21:44 · ☉∠☽ 23:13

28 Sa: ☽⚺♀ 2:27 · ☽⋕⚳ 3:29 · ☽∠♆ 6:30 · ☽∥♂ 14:36 · ☽□♄ 19:20

29 Su: ☽⚼♂ 0:11 · ☉✶☽ 2:45 · ☽✶⚳ 4:27 · ☽∠♀ 6:38 · ☽⋕♆ 8:14 · ☽⚺♆ 8:17 · ☽⚺♇ 8:24 · ⚵ ♒ 8:37 · ☽✶⚷ 11:21 · ☽□♃ 15:50 · ☽□☿ 18:59

30 M: ☽□♅ 1:13 · ☉△⚳ 2:05 · ☉⋕♅ 2:59 · ☽⚻♂ 3:43 · ☽∠⚳ 7:06 · ☽∥♆ 11:00 · ☽∠♇ 11:14 · ☽✶♀ 12:09 · ☽∠⚷ 14:13

31 Tu: ☽✶♄ 0:40 · ☽⋕♂ 8:33 · ♀∥♃ 9:13 · ☽⚺⚳ 10:50 · ☊ D 13:27 · ☉□☽ 13:37 · ☽☌♆ 14:55 · ☽✶♇ 15:08 · ☽⚺⚷ 18:07 · ☽∥⚳ 19:44 · ☽△♃ 23:59

Haumea and Makemake
Longitudes and Declinations

Haumea

Makemake

1900	♇ Haumea 136108	♇ Makemake 136472
JAN 1	27R50.3	16R59.6
11	27♊37.7	16♉53.6
21	27 26.2	16 50.2
31	27 16.2	16D49.4
FEB 10	27 08.1	16 51.4
20	27 02.2	16 56.1
MAR 2	26 58.8	17 03.4
12	26D57.9	17 13.1
22	26 59.5	17 24.9
APR 1	27 03.7	17 38.5
11	27 10.3	17 53.7
21	27 19.2	18 10.0
MAY 1	27 30.2	18 27.0
11	27 42.8	18 44.4
21	27 57.0	19 01.7
31	28 12.2	19 18.7
JUN 10	28 28.2	19 34.8
20	28 44.6	19 49.7
30	29 01.0	20 03.2
JUL 10	29 17.1	20 14.9
20	29 32.5	20 24.5
30	29 46.8	20 31.8
AUG 9	29 59.7	20 36.7
19	0♋11.0	20 39.0
29	0 20.3	20R38.7
SEP 8	0 27.4	20 35.9
18	0 32.1	20 30.6
28	0 34.4	20 23.0
OCT 8	0R34.1	20 13.4
18	0 31.3	20 02.1
28	0 26.1	19 49.6
NOV 7	0 18.6	19 36.3
17	0 09.2	19 22.7
27	29♊58.2	19 09.4
DEC 7	29 46.0	18 56.8
17	29 33.0	18 45.5
27	29 19.8	18 35.9
JAN 6	29♊06.8	18♉28.4
JAN 1	08N51.9	03N40.0
21	08 56.1	03 45.7
FEB 10	09 02.5	03 54.8
MAR 2	09 10.4	04 06.5
22	09 19.2	04 19.5
APR 11	09 27.8	04 32.9
MAY 1	09 35.5	04 45.5
21	09 41.7	04 56.2
JUN 10	09 46.0	05 04.4
30	09 48.0	05 09.5
JUL 20	09 47.8	05 11.3
AUG 9	09 45.5	05 10.0
29	09 41.7	05 05.8
SEP 18	09 36.7	04 59.7
OCT 8	09 31.6	04 52.5
28	09 26.9	04 45.6
NOV 17	09 23.5	04 40.2
DEC 7	09 22.1	04 37.5
27	09N23.1	04N38.1
	3/10.31 10/1.67	1/28.54 8/22.72

1901	♇ Haumea 136108	♇ Makemake 136472
JAN 1	29R13.2	18R31.9
11	29♊00.6	18♉25.5
21	28 48.9	18 21.6
31	28 38.8	18D20.4
FEB 10	28 30.4	18 21.9
20	28 24.2	18 26.0
MAR 2	28 20.3	18 32.8
12	28 19.0	18 42.0
22	28D20.2	18 53.4
APR 1	28 23.9	19 06.7
11	28 30.1	19 21.5
21	28 38.6	19 37.6
MAY 1	28 49.1	19 54.4
11	29 01.4	20 11.7
21	29 15.2	20 29.0
31	29 30.2	20 45.9
JUN 10	29 46.0	21 02.1
20	0♋02.2	21 17.2
30	0 18.5	21 30.9
JUL 10	0 34.6	21 42.8
20	0 50.0	21 52.8
30	1 04.4	22 00.5
AUG 9	1 17.4	22 05.8
19	1 28.9	22 08.5
29	1 38.4	22R08.7
SEP 8	1 45.9	22 06.3
18	1 50.9	22 01.4
28	1 53.6	21 54.3
OCT 8	1R53.7	21 45.0
18	1 51.3	21 34.1
28	1 46.4	21 21.8
NOV 7	1 39.4	21 08.7
17	1 30.3	20 55.1
27	1 19.6	20 41.8
DEC 7	1 07.6	20 29.1
17	0 54.7	20 17.6
27	0 41.6	20 07.7
JAN 6	0♋28.6	19♉59.8
JAN 1	09N23.8	04N38.8
21	09 27.9	04 44.0
FEB 10	09 34.1	04 52.6
MAR 2	09 41.8	05 03.6
22	09 50.2	05 16.3
APR 11	09 58.5	05 29.3
MAY 1	10 06.0	05 41.6
21	10 11.9	05 52.3
JUN 10	10 15.9	06 00.5
30	10 17.8	06 05.9
JUL 20	10 17.6	06 08.1
AUG 9	10 15.4	06 07.2
29	10 11.6	06 03.5
SEP 18	10 07.0	05 57.9
OCT 8	10 02.0	05 51.1
28	09 57.6	05 44.5
NOV 17	09 54.4	05 39.2
DEC 7	09 53.2	05 36.3
27	09N54.3	05N36.6
	3/12.01 10/3.23	1/30.30 8/24.45

1902	♇ Haumea 136108	♇ Makemake 136472
JAN 1	0R35.1	20R03.5
11	0♋22.4	19♉56.7
21	0 10.6	19 52.4
31	0 00.2	19 50.7
FEB 10	29♊51.6	19D51.7
20	29 45.1	19 55.4
MAR 2	29 40.8	20 01.7
12	29 39.1	20 10.4
22	29D39.9	20 21.4
APR 1	29 43.2	20 34.3
11	29 48.9	20 48.8
21	29 57.0	21 04.5
MAY 1	0♋07.1	21 21.2
11	0 19.1	21 38.3
21	0 32.6	21 55.5
31	0 47.3	22 12.5
JUN 10	1 02.8	22 28.8
20	1 18.9	22 44.0
30	1 35.1	22 57.9
JUL 10	1 51.1	23 10.1
20	2 06.5	23 20.4
30	2 21.0	23 28.4
AUG 9	2 34.2	23 34.1
19	2 45.8	23 37.3
29	2 55.6	23R38.0
SEP 8	3 03.3	23 36.0
18	3 08.7	23 31.6
28	3 11.7	23 24.8
OCT 8	3R12.2	23 15.9
18	3 10.2	23 05.3
28	3 05.8	22 53.3
NOV 7	2 59.1	22 40.3
17	2 50.3	22 26.8
27	2 39.9	22 13.5
DEC 7	2 28.1	22 00.7
17	2 15.5	21 49.0
27	2 02.4	21 38.8
JAN 6	1♋49.5	21♉30.6
JAN 1	09N55.0	05N37.2
21	09 59.0	05 42.0
FEB 10	10 05.1	05 50.0
MAR 2	10 12.5	06 00.5
22	10 20.7	06 12.6
APR 11	10 28.7	06 25.2
MAY 1	10 35.8	06 37.3
21	10 41.5	06 47.9
JUN 10	10 45.3	06 56.2
30	10 47.0	07 01.8
JUL 20	10 46.7	07 04.3
AUG 9	10 44.6	07 03.9
29	10 41.0	07 00.7
SEP 18	10 36.5	06 55.5
OCT 8	10 31.8	06 49.2
28	10 27.6	06 42.9
NOV 17	10 24.7	06 37.7
DEC 7	10 23.7	06 34.7
27	10N24.8	06N34.7
	3/13.62 10/4.74	2/1.11 8/26.22

1903	♇ Haumea 136108	♇ Makemake 136472
JAN 1	1R55.9	21R34.4
11	1♋43.2	21♉27.3
21	1 31.3	21 22.5
31	1 20.8	21 20.4
FEB 10	1 11.9	21D20.9
20	1 05.0	21 24.1
MAR 2	1 00.5	21 29.9
12	0 58.3	21 38.2
22	0D58.7	21 48.8
APR 1	1 01.6	22 01.3
11	1 06.9	22 15.5
21	1 14.6	22 30.9
MAY 1	1 24.3	22 47.4
11	1 35.9	23 04.3
21	1 49.0	23 21.5
31	2 03.5	23 38.4
JUN 10	2 18.8	23 54.8
20	2 34.7	24 10.1
30	2 50.8	24 24.2
JUL 10	3 06.7	24 36.7
20	3 22.1	24 47.3
30	3 36.7	24 55.7
AUG 9	3 50.0	25 01.8
19	4 01.8	25 05.4
29	4 11.9	25R06.5
SEP 8	4 19.8	25 05.0
18	4 25.6	25 01.0
28	4 28.9	24 54.6
OCT 8	4R29.8	24 46.1
18	4 28.2	24 35.8
28	4 24.1	24 24.0
NOV 7	4 17.8	24 11.2
17	4 09.4	23 57.9
27	3 59.2	23 44.5
DEC 7	3 47.7	23 31.6
17	3 35.2	23 19.7
27	3 22.3	23 09.3
JAN 6	3♋09.4	23♉00.8
JAN 1	10N25.5	06N35.3
21	10 29.5	06 39.5
FEB 10	10 35.4	06 47.0
MAR 2	10 42.7	06 57.0
22	10 50.5	07 08.6
APR 11	10 58.2	07 20.8
MAY 1	11 05.0	07 32.6
21	11 10.4	07 43.0
JUN 10	11 14.0	07 51.4
30	11 15.6	07 57.2
JUL 20	11 15.3	08 00.0
AUG 9	11 13.2	08 00.0
29	11 09.7	07 57.4
SEP 18	11 05.3	07 52.7
OCT 8	11 00.9	07 46.8
28	10 56.9	07 40.8
NOV 17	10 54.3	07 35.7
DEC 7	10 53.4	07 32.7
27	10N54.7	07N32.5
	3/15.24 10/6.27	2/2.84 8/27.90

1904	♇ Haumea 136108	♇ Makemake 136472
JAN 1	3R15.8	23R04.8
11	3♋03.1	22♉57.3
21	2 51.1	22 52.1
31	2 40.4	22 49.5
FEB 10	2 31.3	22D49.5
20	2 24.2	22 52.3
MAR 1	2 19.3	22 57.6
11	2 16.7	23 05.5
21	2D16.7	23 15.6
31	2 19.2	23 27.7
APR 10	2 24.1	23 41.5
20	2 31.3	23 56.7
30	2 40.7	24 12.9
MAY 10	2 51.9	24 29.7
20	3 04.7	24 46.8
30	3 18.9	25 03.7
JUN 9	3 34.0	25 20.1
19	3 49.7	25 35.6
29	4 05.7	25 49.9
JUL 9	4 21.5	26 02.6
19	4 36.9	26 13.4
29	4 51.5	26 22.2
AUG 8	5 05.0	26 28.7
18	5 17.0	26 32.7
28	5 27.2	26 34.2
SEP 7	5 35.5	26R33.1
17	5 41.6	26 29.6
27	5 45.2	26 23.6
OCT 7	5R46.5	26 15.5
17	5 45.2	26 05.5
27	5 41.6	25 54.0
NOV 6	5 35.6	25 41.4
16	5 27.5	25 28.1
26	5 17.7	25 14.8
DEC 6	5 06.4	25 01.8
16	4 54.1	24 49.8
26	4 41.3	24 39.1
JAN 5	4♋28.4	24♉30.3
JAN 1	10N55.3	07N32.9
21	10 59.3	07 36.7
FEB 10	11 05.1	07 43.7
MAR 1	11 12.2	07 53.1
21	11 19.7	08 04.2
APR 10	11 27.1	08 16.0
30	11 33.6	08 27.5
MAY 20	11 38.8	08 37.8
JUN 9	11 42.2	08 46.1
29	11 43.6	08 52.1
JUL 19	11 43.2	08 55.2
AUG 8	11 41.1	08 55.6
28	11 37.7	08 53.5
SEP 17	11 33.5	08 49.3
OCT 7	11 29.3	08 43.9
27	11 25.6	08 38.2
NOV 16	11 23.2	08 33.3
DEC 6	11 22.5	08 30.2
26	11N23.9	08N29.8
	3/15.84 10/6.78	2/4.60 8/28.65

1905	Haumea 136108	Makemake 136472
JAN 1	4R33.5	24R33.6
11	4♋20.9	24♉25.9
21	4 09.0	24 20.6
31	3 58.2	24 17.8
FEB 10	3 49.1	24D17.7
20	3 41.9	24 20.2
MAR 2	3 36.8	24 25.3
12	3 34.2	24 32.9
22	3D34.0	24 42.8
APR 1	3 36.3	24 54.7
11	3 41.1	25 08.4
21	3 48.1	25 23.4
MAY 1	3 57.3	25 39.5
11	4 08.3	25 56.2
21	4 21.0	26 13.1
31	4 34.9	26 30.0
JUN 10	4 49.9	26 46.3
20	5 05.5	27 01.8
30	5 21.3	27 16.1
JUL 10	5 37.1	27 28.9
20	5 52.4	27 39.8
30	6 07.0	27 48.7
AUG 9	6 20.4	27 55.3
19	6 32.4	27 59.5
29	6 42.7	28 01.2
SEP 8	6 51.0	28R00.3
18	6 57.1	27 56.9
28	7 00.9	27 51.1
OCT 8	7 02.3	27 43.2
18	7R01.2	27 33.3
28	6 57.6	27 22.0
NOV 7	6 51.8	27 09.5
17	6 43.9	26 56.3
27	6 34.2	26 43.0
DEC 7	6 23.0	26 30.0
17	6 10.8	26 18.0
27	5 58.1	26 07.2
JAN 6	5♋45.3	25♉58.2
JAN 1	11N24.7	08N30.2
21	11 28.8	08 33.8
FEB 10	11 34.5	08 40.3
MAR 2	11 41.4	08 49.3
22	11 48.7	09 00.0
APR 11	11 55.8	09 11.3
MAY 1	12 02.0	09 22.5
21	12 06.8	09 32.5
JUN 10	12 09.8	09 40.8
30	12 11.0	09 46.7
JUL 20	12 10.4	09 50.0
AUG 9	12 08.3	09 50.7
29	12 04.9	09 48.9
SEP 18	12 00.9	09 45.1
OCT 8	11 56.9	09 40.1
28	11 53.5	09 34.8
NOV 17	11 51.3	09 30.1
DEC 7	11 50.9	09 27.2
27	11N52.5	09N26.7
	3/17.41	2/5.35
	10/8.23	8/30.32

1906	Haumea 136108	Makemake 136472
JAN 1	5R51.7	26R02.5
11	5♋39.0	25♉54.5
21	5 27.0	25 48.8
31	5 16.1	25 45.6
FEB 10	5 06.8	25D44.9
20	4 59.3	25 47.0
MAR 2	4 53.9	25 51.6
12	4 50.9	25 58.8
22	4D50.4	26 08.3
APR 1	4 52.3	26 19.8
11	4 56.6	26 33.1
21	5 03.2	26 47.8
MAY 1	5 12.0	27 03.6
11	5 22.7	27 20.2
21	5 35.1	27 37.0
31	5 48.8	27 53.8
JUN 10	6 03.5	28 10.2
20	6 18.8	28 25.8
30	6 34.6	28 40.2
JUL 10	6 50.3	28 53.2
20	7 05.6	29 04.5
30	7 20.2	29 13.7
AUG 9	7 33.7	29 20.6
19	7 45.9	29 25.2
29	7 56.4	29 27.3
SEP 8	8 04.9	29R26.8
18	8 11.4	29 23.9
28	8 15.5	29 18.5
OCT 8	8 17.2	29 10.9
18	8R16.4	29 01.4
28	8 13.2	28 50.3
NOV 7	8 07.8	28 38.0
17	8 00.2	28 24.9
27	7 50.8	28 11.7
DEC 7	7 39.9	27 58.7
17	7 27.9	27 46.4
27	7 15.2	27 35.5
JAN 6	7♋02.5	27♉26.2
JAN 1	11N53.3	09N27.0
21	11 57.3	09 30.2
FEB 10	12 03.0	09 36.2
MAR 2	12 09.7	09 44.7
22	12 16.8	09 54.8
APR 11	12 23.6	10 05.7
MAY 1	12 29.5	10 16.5
21	12 34.0	10 26.4
JUN 10	12 36.8	10 34.6
30	12 37.9	10 40.6
JUL 20	12 37.2	10 44.2
AUG 9	12 35.0	10 45.3
29	12 31.7	10 43.9
SEP 18	12 27.9	10 40.6
OCT 8	12 24.0	10 36.1
28	12 20.9	10 31.1
NOV 17	12 19.0	10 26.6
DEC 7	12 18.8	10 23.7
27	12N20.5	10N23.0
	3/19.01	2/7.09
	10/9.72	8/31.98

1907	Haumea 136108	Makemake 136472
JAN 1	7R08.9	27R30.6
11	6♋56.2	27♉22.3
21	6 44.1	27 16.2
31	6 33.1	27 12.6
FEB 10	6 23.6	27D11.5
20	6 15.8	27 13.1
MAR 2	6 10.1	27 17.2
12	6 06.8	27 23.9
22	6D05.8	27 33.0
APR 1	6 07.3	27 44.1
11	6 11.3	27 57.0
21	6 17.5	28 11.5
MAY 1	6 25.9	28 27.1
11	6 36.3	28 43.4
21	6 48.3	29 00.2
31	7 01.7	29 16.9
JUN 10	7 16.2	29 33.3
20	7 31.4	29 49.0
30	7 47.0	0♊03.6
JUL 10	8 02.6	0 16.8
20	8 17.9	0 28.2
30	8 32.5	0 37.8
AUG 9	8 46.1	0 45.1
19	8 58.4	0 50.1
29	9 09.1	0 52.5
SEP 8	9 17.9	0R52.5
18	9 24.6	0 50.0
28	9 29.0	0 45.0
OCT 8	9 31.1	0 37.8
18	9R30.7	0 28.6
28	9 27.9	0 17.8
NOV 7	9 22.7	0 05.6
17	9 15.5	29♉52.7
27	9 06.4	29 39.5
DEC 7	8 55.7	29 26.5
17	8 43.9	29 14.1
27	8 31.4	29 03.0
JAN 6	8♋18.7	28♉53.4
JAN 1	12N21.3	10N23.3
21	12 25.3	10 26.1
FEB 10	12 30.9	10 31.6
MAR 2	12 37.5	10 39.5
22	12 44.3	10 49.1
APR 11	12 50.9	10 59.6
MAY 1	12 56.5	11 10.1
21	13 00.7	11 19.7
JUN 10	13 03.3	11 27.8
30	13 04.2	11 34.0
JUL 20	13 03.4	11 37.8
AUG 9	13 01.2	11 39.2
29	12 58.0	11 38.3
SEP 18	12 54.3	11 35.5
OCT 8	12 50.6	11 31.4
28	12 47.7	11 26.8
NOV 17	12 46.0	11 22.6
DEC 7	12 46.0	11 19.7
27	12N47.9	11N18.8
	3/20.55	2/8.85
	10/11.13	9/2.65

1908	Haumea 136108	Makemake 136472
JAN 1	8R25.0	28R57.9
11	8♋12.4	28♉49.3
21	8 00.3	28 42.9
31	7 49.2	28 38.8
FEB 10	7 39.4	28 37.3
20	7 31.4	28D38.4
MAR 1	7 25.4	28 42.1
11	7 21.7	28 48.4
21	7 20.4	28 57.0
31	7D21.5	29 07.7
APR 10	7 25.1	29 20.3
20	7 30.9	29 34.4
30	7 39.0	29 49.7
MAY 10	7 49.0	0♊05.9
20	8 00.6	0 22.5
30	8 13.8	0 39.2
JUN 9	8 28.0	0 55.6
19	8 43.0	1 11.3
29	8 58.5	1 26.1
JUL 9	9 14.0	1 39.4
19	9 29.3	1 51.2
29	9 43.9	2 01.0
AUG 8	9 57.6	2 08.7
18	10 10.0	2 14.0
28	10 20.9	2 16.9
SEP 7	10 29.9	2R17.3
17	10 36.9	2 15.1
27	10 41.6	2 10.6
OCT 7	10 44.0	2 03.7
17	10R43.9	1 54.9
27	10 41.5	1 44.3
NOV 6	10 36.7	1 32.4
16	10 29.8	1 19.7
26	10 20.9	1 06.5
DEC 6	10 10.5	0 53.4
16	9 58.9	0 41.0
26	9 46.6	0 29.6
JAN 5	9♋33.9	0♊19.8
JAN 1	12N48.6	11N19.0
21	12 52.8	11 21.5
FEB 10	12 58.3	11 26.5
MAR 1	13 04.7	11 33.9
21	13 11.3	11 43.0
APR 10	13 17.6	11 53.0
30	13 22.9	12 03.1
MAY 20	13 26.9	12 12.5
JUN 9	13 29.3	12 20.5
29	13 30.0	12 26.7
JUL 19	13 29.1	12 30.8
AUG 8	13 26.9	12 32.5
28	13 23.7	12 32.0
SEP 17	13 20.1	12 29.7
OCT 7	13 16.6	12 26.0
27	13 13.9	12 21.8
NOV 16	13 12.4	12 17.8
DEC 6	13 12.6	12 15.0
26	13N14.7	12N14.1
	3/21.14	2/10.53
	10/11.56	9/3.25

1909	Haumea 136108	Makemake 136472
JAN 1	9R39.0	0R23.5
11	9♋26.4	0♊14.8
21	9 14.3	0 08.2
31	9 03.2	0 04.0
FEB 10	8 53.4	0 02.3
20	8 45.3	0D03.2
MAR 2	8 39.3	0 06.7
12	8 35.5	0 12.8
22	8 34.1	0 21.2
APR 1	8D35.1	0 31.7
11	8 38.4	0 44.1
21	8 44.1	0 58.1
MAY 1	8 52.0	1 13.2
11	9 01.8	1 29.3
21	9 13.3	1 45.8
31	9 26.3	2 02.4
JUN 10	9 40.4	2 18.8
20	9 55.3	2 34.5
30	10 10.6	2 49.2
JUL 10	10 26.0	3 02.6
20	10 41.2	3 14.4
30	10 55.8	3 24.3
AUG 9	11 09.5	3 32.1
19	11 21.9	3 37.6
29	11 32.8	3 40.6
SEP 8	11 41.8	3R41.1
18	11 48.8	3 39.2
28	11 53.6	3 34.8
OCT 8	11 56.1	3 28.1
18	11R56.1	3 19.4
28	11 53.8	3 08.9
NOV 7	11 49.1	2 57.2
17	11 42.3	2 44.5
27	11 33.6	2 31.3
DEC 7	11 23.3	2 18.3
17	11 11.8	2 05.8
27	10 59.5	1 54.4
JAN 6	10♋46.9	1♊44.5
JAN 1	13N15.6	12N14.2
21	13 19.8	12 16.4
FEB 10	13 25.4	12 21.2
MAR 2	13 31.7	12 28.1
22	13 38.1	12 36.8
APR 11	13 44.1	12 46.3
MAY 1	13 49.1	12 56.0
21	13 52.7	13 05.1
JUN 10	13 54.8	13 12.9
30	13 55.2	13 19.1
JUL 20	13 54.1	13 23.2
AUG 9	13 51.8	13 25.1
29	13 48.7	13 25.0
SEP 18	13 45.1	13 23.0
OCT 8	13 41.9	13 19.8
28	13 39.4	13 15.9
NOV 17	13 38.2	13 12.2
DEC 7	13 38.7	13 09.6
27	13N41.0	13N08.6
	3/22.67	2/11.28
	10/12.95	9/4.90

1910	Haumea 136108	Makemake 136472
JAN 1	10R53.2	1R49.3
11	10♋40.7	1♊40.3
21	10 28.5	1 33.3
31	10 17.3	1 28.7
FEB 10	10 07.3	1 26.6
20	9 59.1	1D27.1
MAR 2	9 52.7	1 30.1
12	9 48.6	1 35.7
22	9 46.8	1 43.7
APR 1	9D47.4	1 53.8
11	9 50.4	2 05.9
21	9 55.8	2 19.6
MAY 1	10 03.2	2 34.5
11	10 12.7	2 50.3
21	10 23.9	3 06.7
31	10 36.6	3 23.2
JUN 10	10 50.5	3 39.6
20	11 05.1	3 55.3
30	11 20.3	4 10.2
JUL 10	11 35.7	4 23.8
20	11 50.8	4 35.8
30	12 05.4	4 46.0
AUG 9	12 19.2	4 54.1
19	12 31.7	4 59.9
29	12 42.7	5 03.4
SEP 8	12 52.0	5R04.3
18	12 59.3	5 02.7
28	13 04.4	4 58.7
OCT 8	13 07.1	4 52.4
18	13R07.5	4 44.0
28	13 05.5	4 33.9
NOV 7	13 01.2	4 22.3
17	12 54.7	4 09.8
27	12 46.2	3 56.8
DEC 7	12 36.2	3 43.7
17	12 24.9	3 31.2
27	12 12.7	3 19.6
JAN 6	12♋00.2	3♊09.4
JAN 1	13N41.8	13N08.7
21	13 46.1	13 10.6
FEB 10	13 51.6	13 14.9
MAR 2	13 57.7	13 21.4
22	14 04.0	13 29.4
APR 11	14 09.7	13 38.5
MAY 1	14 14.4	13 47.8
21	14 17.8	13 56.6
JUN 10	14 19.6	14 04.3
30	14 19.9	14 10.5
JUL 20	14 18.7	14 14.7
AUG 9	14 16.3	14 17.0
29	14 13.2	14 17.2
SEP 18	14 09.8	14 15.7
OCT 8	14 06.7	14 12.9
28	14 04.4	14 09.5
NOV 17	14 03.4	14 06.1
DEC 7	14 04.1	14 03.5
27	14N06.5	14N02.5
	3/24.18 10/14.32	2/12.95 9/6.48

1911	Haumea 136108	Makemake 136472
JAN 1	12R06.5	3R14.3
11	11♋54.0	3♊05.0
21	11 41.9	2 57.8
31	11 30.5	2 52.8
FEB 10	11 20.4	2 50.2
20	11 11.9	2D50.2
MAR 2	11 05.3	2 52.9
12	11 00.8	2 58.1
22	10 58.7	3 05.6
APR 1	10D58.9	3 15.3
11	11 01.6	3 27.1
21	11 06.5	3 40.4
MAY 1	11 13.7	3 55.1
11	11 22.8	4 10.7
21	11 33.7	4 26.9
31	11 46.1	4 43.4
JUN 10	11 59.7	4 59.7
20	12 14.2	5 15.5
30	12 29.2	5 30.5
JUL 10	12 44.5	5 44.3
20	12 59.6	5 56.5
30	13 14.2	6 07.0
AUG 9	13 28.0	6 15.4
19	13 40.6	6 21.6
29	13 51.8	6 25.4
SEP 8	14 01.3	6 26.7
18	14 08.8	6R25.5
28	14 14.2	6 21.9
OCT 8	14 17.3	6 16.0
18	14R18.0	6 08.0
28	14 16.3	5 58.1
NOV 7	14 12.3	5 46.8
17	14 06.1	5 34.4
27	13 58.0	5 21.5
DEC 7	13 48.2	5 08.4
17	13 37.1	4 55.8
27	13 25.1	4 44.1
JAN 6	13♋12.7	4♊33.7
JAN 1	14N07.4	14N02.6
21	14 11.7	14 04.2
FEB 10	14 17.2	14 08.0
MAR 2	14 23.2	14 13.9
22	14 29.3	14 21.5
APR 11	14 34.7	14 30.1
MAY 1	14 39.2	14 38.9
21	14 42.3	14 47.5
JUN 10	14 43.9	14 55.0
30	14 44.0	15 01.2
JUL 20	14 42.7	15 05.6
AUG 9	14 40.2	15 08.1
29	14 37.1	15 08.7
SEP 18	14 33.8	15 07.6
OCT 8	14 30.8	15 05.3
28	14 28.7	15 02.2
NOV 17	14 28.0	14 59.1
DEC 7	14 28.8	14 56.7
27	14N31.4	14N55.6
	3/25.71 10/15.72	2/14.62 9/8.10

1912	Haumea 136108	Makemake 136472
JAN 1	13R18.9	4R38.7
11	13♋06.4	4♊29.2
21	12 54.3	4 21.6
31	12 42.8	4 16.2
FEB 10	12 32.6	4 13.2
20	12 23.8	4D12.8
MAR 1	12 17.0	4 15.1
11	12 12.2	4 19.8
21	12 09.8	4 26.9
31	12D09.7	4 36.3
APR 10	12 11.9	4 47.6
20	12 16.5	5 00.6
30	12 23.3	5 15.0
MAY 10	12 32.1	5 30.5
20	12 42.7	5 46.6
30	12 54.8	6 02.9
JUN 9	13 08.2	6 19.2
19	13 22.5	6 35.1
29	13 37.3	6 50.1
JUL 9	13 52.5	7 04.0
19	14 07.5	7 16.5
29	14 22.1	7 27.2
AUG 8	14 36.0	7 36.0
18	14 48.7	7 42.5
28	15 00.1	7 46.7
SEP 7	15 09.8	7 48.4
17	15 17.5	7R47.6
27	15 23.2	7 44.4
OCT 7	15 26.6	7 38.9
17	15R27.6	7 31.2
27	15 26.2	7 21.6
NOV 6	15 22.6	7 10.5
16	15 16.7	6 58.3
26	15 08.8	6 45.5
DEC 6	14 59.3	6 32.5
16	14 48.4	6 19.8
26	14 36.6	6 07.9
JAN 5	14♋24.2	5♊57.4
JAN 1	14N32.3	14N55.7
21	14 36.7	14 57.0
FEB 10	14 42.1	15 00.4
MAR 1	14 48.1	15 05.9
21	14 53.9	15 12.9
APR 10	14 59.2	15 20.9
30	15 03.4	15 29.4
MAY 20	15 06.3	15 37.6
JUN 9	15 07.6	15 45.0
29	15 07.5	15 51.1
JUL 19	15 06.0	15 55.6
AUG 8	15 03.5	15 58.3
28	15 00.4	15 59.3
SEP 17	14 57.1	15 58.7
OCT 7	14 54.3	15 56.8
27	14 52.4	15 54.2
NOV 16	14 51.8	15 51.4
DEC 6	14 52.9	15 49.1
26	14N55.6	15N48.0
	3/26.16 10/16.05	2/16.28 9/8.71

1913	Haumea 136108	Makemake 136472
JAN 1	14R29.2	6R01.4
11	14♋16.8	5♊51.8
21	14 04.7	5 44.1
31	13 53.3	5 38.6
FEB 10	13 43.0	5 35.5
20	13 34.2	5D35.0
MAR 2	13 27.3	5 37.0
12	13 22.5	5 41.5
22	13 19.9	5 48.5
APR 1	13D19.7	5 57.7
11	13 21.9	6 08.8
21	13 26.3	6 21.7
MAY 1	13 33.0	6 36.0
11	13 41.6	6 51.3
21	13 52.1	7 07.2
31	14 04.0	7 23.5
JUN 10	14 17.3	7 39.8
20	14 31.4	7 55.6
30	14 46.2	8 10.6
JUL 10	15 01.3	8 24.6
20	15 16.2	8 37.1
30	15 30.8	8 47.9
AUG 9	15 44.6	8 56.7
19	15 57.3	9 03.3
29	16 08.7	9 07.6
SEP 8	16 18.4	9 09.5
18	16 26.2	9R08.9
28	16 31.9	9 05.8
OCT 8	16 35.3	9 00.4
18	16R36.4	8 52.9
28	16 35.1	8 43.5
NOV 7	16 31.6	8 32.5
17	16 25.8	8 20.4
27	16 18.1	8 07.6
DEC 7	16 08.6	7 54.6
17	15 57.8	7 42.0
27	15 46.1	7 30.1
JAN 6	15♋33.8	7♊19.4
JAN 1	14N56.7	15N48.0
21	15 01.3	15 49.2
FEB 10	15 06.7	15 52.3
MAR 2	15 12.6	15 57.4
22	15 18.3	16 04.0
APR 11	15 23.3	16 11.5
MAY 1	15 27.2	16 19.6
21	15 29.7	16 27.4
JUN 10	15 30.7	16 34.5
30	15 30.3	16 40.5
JUL 20	15 28.6	16 45.0
AUG 9	15 26.0	16 47.9
29	15 22.9	16 49.2
SEP 18	15 19.7	16 48.9
OCT 8	15 17.0	16 47.4
28	15 15.3	16 45.1
NOV 17	15 15.0	16 42.7
DEC 7	15 16.4	16 40.6
27	15N19.3	16N39.6
	3/27.65 10/17.44	2/16.90 9/10.27

1914	Haumea 136108	Makemake 136472
JAN 1	15R40.0	7R24.6
11	15♋27.6	7♊14.7
21	15 15.5	7 06.7
31	15 04.0	7 00.9
FEB 10	14 53.6	6 57.4
20	14 44.7	6D56.4
MAR 2	14 37.5	6 58.0
12	14 32.4	7 02.2
22	14 29.5	7 08.7
APR 1	14D29.0	7 17.5
11	14 30.8	7 28.3
21	14 34.9	7 40.9
MAY 1	14 41.2	7 54.9
11	14 49.5	8 09.9
21	14 59.6	8 25.8
31	15 11.4	8 42.0
JUN 10	15 24.3	8 58.2
20	15 38.3	9 14.0
30	15 52.9	9 29.1
JUL 10	16 07.9	9 43.2
20	16 22.8	9 55.9
30	16 37.3	10 07.0
AUG 9	16 51.2	10 16.1
19	17 04.0	10 23.1
29	17 15.5	10 27.7
SEP 8	17 25.4	10 30.0
18	17 33.4	10R29.8
28	17 39.4	10 27.1
OCT 8	17 43.1	10 22.0
18	17 44.5	10 14.9
28	17R43.6	10 05.7
NOV 7	17 40.4	9 55.0
17	17 34.9	9 43.1
27	17 27.5	9 30.5
DEC 7	17 18.3	9 17.5
17	17 07.7	9 04.8
27	16 56.1	8 52.8
JAN 6	16♋43.9	8♊42.0
JAN 1	15N20.3	16N39.6
21	15 24.9	16 40.5
FEB 10	15 30.4	16 43.3
MAR 2	15 36.1	16 47.9
22	15 41.7	16 53.9
APR 11	15 46.5	17 01.0
MAY 1	15 50.1	17 08.6
21	15 52.4	17 16.1
JUN 10	15 53.2	17 23.0
30	15 52.6	17 28.9
JUL 20	15 50.7	17 33.5
AUG 9	15 48.0	17 36.6
29	15 44.9	17 38.1
SEP 18	15 41.7	17 38.3
OCT 8	15 39.1	17 37.2
28	15 37.6	17 35.4
NOV 17	15 37.5	17 33.3
DEC 7	15 39.0	17 31.4
27	15N42.1	17N30.4
	3/29.08 10/18.78	2/18.56 9/11.88

1915	♀ Haumea 136108	♀ Makemake 136472
JAN 1	16R50.1	8R47.2
11	16♋37.8	8♊37.2
21	16 25.7	8 28.9
31	16 14.1	8 22.7
FEB 10	16 03.6	8 18.8
20	15 54.5	8 17.5
MAR 2	15 47.1	8D18.6
12	15 41.7	8 22.3
22	15 38.5	8 28.5
APR 1	15D37.6	8 36.9
11	15 39.1	8 47.3
21	15 42.8	8 59.6
MAY 1	15 48.8	9 13.3
11	15 56.8	9 28.2
21	16 06.6	9 43.8
31	16 18.1	9 59.9
JUN 10	16 30.8	10 16.1
20	16 44.6	10 31.9
30	16 59.1	10 47.1
JUL 10	17 13.9	11 01.3
20	17 28.7	11 14.2
30	17 43.3	11 25.5
AUG 9	17 57.2	11 34.9
19	18 10.1	11 42.2
29	18 21.7	11 47.2
SEP 8	18 31.8	11 49.9
18	18 40.0	11R50.0
28	18 46.3	11 47.7
OCT 8	18 50.3	11 43.1
18	18 52.0	11 36.3
28	18R51.4	11 27.4
NOV 7	18 48.5	11 17.0
17	18 43.3	11 05.3
27	18 36.2	10 52.8
DEC 7	18 27.3	10 39.9
17	18 16.9	10 27.1
27	18 05.5	10 15.0
JAN 6	17♋53.4	10♊04.0
JAN 1	15N43.1	17N30.4
21	15 47.8	17 31.1
FEB 10	15 53.3	17 33.5
MAR 2	15 59.0	17 37.6
22	16 04.4	17 43.2
APR 11	16 09.0	17 49.8
MAY 1	16 12.4	17 56.9
21	16 14.4	18 04.0
JUN 10	16 15.0	18 10.7
30	16 14.2	18 16.5
JUL 20	16 12.2	18 21.1
AUG 9	16 09.4	18 24.4
29	16 06.2	18 26.3
SEP 18	16 03.1	18 26.8
OCT 8	16 00.6	18 26.2
28	15 59.2	18 24.8
NOV 17	15 59.3	18 23.0
DEC 7	16 01.0	18 21.3
27	16N04.2	18N20.4
	3/30.51 10/20.12	2/20.13 9/13.43

1916	♀ Haumea 136108	♀ Makemake 136472
JAN 1	17R59.5	10R09.4
11	17♋47.3	9♊59.1
21	17 35.2	9 50.5
31	17 23.6	9 44.0
FEB 10	17 12.9	9 39.8
20	17 03.7	9 38.0
MAR 1	16 56.1	9D38.8
11	16 50.4	9 42.1
21	16 46.9	9 47.8
31	16D45.7	9 55.8
APR 10	16 46.8	10 05.9
20	16 50.2	10 17.8
30	16 55.9	10 31.3
MAY 10	17 03.5	10 45.9
20	17 13.1	11 01.4
30	17 24.2	11 17.4
JUN 9	17 36.7	11 33.5
19	17 50.3	11 49.3
29	18 04.6	12 04.6
JUL 9	18 19.3	12 18.9
19	18 34.1	12 32.0
29	18 48.7	12 43.5
AUG 8	19 02.6	12 53.2
18	19 15.6	13 00.8
28	19 27.4	13 06.2
SEP 7	19 37.6	13 09.2
17	19 46.1	13R09.7
27	19 52.5	13 07.8
OCT 7	19 56.9	13 03.6
17	19 58.9	12 57.1
27	19R58.6	12 48.6
NOV 6	19 56.0	12 38.4
16	19 51.1	12 26.9
26	19 44.3	12 14.5
DEC 6	19 35.6	12 01.6
16	19 25.5	11 48.9
26	19 14.2	11 36.7
JAN 5	19♋02.3	11♊25.5
JAN 1	16N05.3	18N20.3
21	16 10.1	18 20.9
FEB 10	16 15.6	18 23.0
MAR 1	16 21.2	18 26.7
21	16 26.5	18 31.7
APR 10	16 30.9	18 37.8
30	16 34.1	18 44.5
MAY 20	16 35.9	18 51.2
JUN 9	16 36.2	18 57.6
29	16 35.2	19 03.3
JUL 19	16 33.0	19 07.9
AUG 8	16 30.1	19 11.4
28	16 26.9	19 13.5
SEP 17	16 23.8	19 14.4
OCT 7	16 21.4	19 14.2
27	16 20.2	19 13.3
NOV 16	16 20.4	19 11.8
DEC 6	16 22.3	19 10.4
26	16N25.7	19N09.6
	3/30.95 10/20.48	2/21.77 9/14.02

1917	♀ Haumea 136108	♀ Makemake 136472
JAN 1	19R07.1	11R29.9
11	18♋55.0	11♊19.5
21	18 42.9	11 10.9
31	18 31.3	11 04.3
FEB 10	18 20.7	10 59.9
20	18 11.4	10 58.0
MAR 2	18 03.8	10D58.6
12	17 58.1	11 01.7
22	17 54.5	11 07.3
APR 1	17 53.2	11 15.1
11	17D54.2	11 25.1
21	17 57.5	11 36.8
MAY 1	18 03.0	11 50.1
11	18 10.6	12 04.6
21	18 20.0	12 20.0
31	18 31.0	12 35.9
JUN 10	18 43.4	12 51.9
20	18 56.9	13 07.8
30	19 11.1	13 23.0
JUL 10	19 25.7	13 37.3
20	19 40.4	13 50.5
30	19 54.9	14 02.0
AUG 9	20 08.8	14 11.8
19	20 21.7	14 19.5
29	20 33.5	14 25.0
SEP 8	20 43.7	14 28.1
18	20 52.2	14R28.8
28	20 58.8	14 27.0
OCT 8	21 03.1	14 22.9
18	21 05.2	14 16.5
28	21R05.0	14 08.1
NOV 7	21 02.5	13 58.1
17	20 57.7	13 46.7
27	20 50.9	13 34.3
DEC 7	20 42.4	13 21.6
17	20 32.3	13 08.8
27	20 21.1	12 56.6
JAN 6	20♋09.3	12♊45.4
JAN 1	16N27.0	19N09.5
21	16 31.9	19 10.0
FEB 10	16 37.5	19 11.8
MAR 2	16 43.1	19 15.1
22	16 48.2	19 19.8
APR 11	16 52.4	19 25.4
MAY 1	16 55.3	19 31.6
21	16 56.8	19 38.0
JUN 10	16 56.8	19 44.1
30	16 55.5	19 49.6
JUL 20	16 53.2	19 54.1
AUG 9	16 50.1	19 57.6
29	16 46.8	20 00.0
SEP 18	16 43.8	20 01.2
OCT 8	16 41.5	20 01.4
28	16 40.5	20 00.8
NOV 17	16 41.0	19 59.7
DEC 7	16 43.1	19 58.6
27	16N46.7	19N57.9
	4/1.31 10/21.79	2/22.37 9/15.57

1918	♀ Haumea 136108	♀ Makemake 136472
JAN 1	20R15.3	12R50.9
11	20♋03.2	12♊40.3
21	19 51.2	12 31.4
31	19 39.6	12 24.5
FEB 10	19 28.8	12 19.8
20	19 19.4	12 17.5
MAR 2	19 11.5	12D17.7
12	19 05.6	12 20.4
22	19 01.7	12 25.5
APR 1	19 00.1	12 33.0
11	19D00.8	12 42.6
21	19 03.8	12 54.0
MAY 1	19 08.9	13 07.0
11	19 16.2	13 21.3
21	19 25.3	13 36.5
31	19 36.0	13 52.3
JUN 10	19 48.2	14 08.2
20	20 01.5	14 24.1
30	20 15.5	14 39.4
JUL 10	20 30.0	14 53.8
20	20 44.7	15 07.1
30	20 59.1	15 18.8
AUG 9	21 13.0	15 28.9
19	21 26.1	15 36.9
29	21 37.9	15 42.7
SEP 8	21 48.4	15 46.2
18	21 57.0	15R47.2
28	22 03.8	15 45.8
OCT 8	22 08.4	15 42.1
18	22 10.8	15 36.1
28	22R10.9	15 28.0
NOV 7	22 08.7	15 18.2
17	22 04.2	15 07.0
27	21 57.8	14 54.8
DEC 7	21 49.4	14 42.1
17	21 39.6	14 29.4
27	21 28.6	14 17.1
JAN 6	21♋16.8	14♊05.8
JAN 1	16N47.9	19N57.8
21	16 52.9	19 58.2
FEB 10	16 58.5	19 59.7
MAR 2	17 04.1	20 02.6
22	17 09.1	20 06.8
APR 11	17 13.1	20 11.9
MAY 1	17 15.8	20 17.6
21	17 17.1	20 23.6
JUN 10	17 16.9	20 29.4
30	17 15.4	20 34.7
JUL 20	17 12.8	20 39.3
AUG 9	17 09.7	20 42.9
29	17 06.3	20 45.5
SEP 18	17 03.3	20 47.1
OCT 8	17 01.1	20 47.7
28	17 00.2	20 47.5
NOV 17	17 00.8	20 46.8
DEC 7	17 03.1	20 45.9
27	17N07.0	20N45.3
	4/2.76 10/23.12	2/23.95 9/17.10

1919	♀ Haumea 136108	♀ Makemake 136472
JAN 1	21R22.8	14R11.3
11	21♋10.8	14♊00.6
21	20 58.8	13 51.4
31	20 47.1	13 44.2
FEB 10	20 36.3	13 39.1
20	20 26.7	13 36.4
MAR 2	20 18.7	13D36.2
12	20 12.5	13 38.5
22	20 08.3	13 43.2
APR 1	20 06.4	13 50.3
11	20D06.8	13 59.5
21	20 09.4	14 10.6
MAY 1	20 14.2	14 23.4
11	20 21.2	14 37.4
21	20 30.0	14 52.4
31	20 40.5	15 08.1
JUN 10	20 52.4	15 23.9
20	21 05.4	15 39.7
30	21 19.3	15 55.1
JUL 10	21 33.7	16 09.6
20	21 48.3	16 23.1
30	22 02.7	16 35.0
AUG 9	22 16.6	16 45.3
19	22 29.7	16 53.6
29	22 41.7	16 59.8
SEP 8	22 52.3	17 03.6
18	23 01.2	17 05.0
28	23 08.2	17R04.0
OCT 8	23 13.1	17 00.6
18	23 15.7	16 54.9
28	23R16.1	16 47.2
NOV 7	23 14.2	16 37.6
17	23 10.1	16 26.7
27	23 03.8	16 14.6
DEC 7	22 55.8	16 02.0
17	22 46.2	15 49.3
27	22 35.3	15 36.9
JAN 6	22♋23.7	15♊25.4
JAN 1	17N08.1	20N45.2
21	17 13.3	20 45.5
FEB 10	17 19.0	20 46.8
MAR 2	17 24.5	20 49.3
22	17 29.4	20 53.0
APR 11	17 33.3	20 57.6
MAY 1	17 35.8	21 02.8
21	17 36.8	21 08.4
JUN 10	17 36.4	21 13.9
30	17 34.7	21 19.0
JUL 20	17 32.0	21 23.6
AUG 9	17 28.7	21 27.3
29	17 25.3	21 30.1
SEP 18	17 22.3	21 32.0
OCT 8	17 20.2	21 33.0
28	17 19.3	21 33.2
NOV 17	17 20.1	21 32.9
DEC 7	17 22.6	21 32.3
27	17N26.6	21N31.8
	4/4.13 10/24.41	2/25.57 9/18.65

1920	Haumea 136108	Makemake 136472
JAN 1	22R29.6	15R31.0
11	22♋17.7	15♊20.2
21	22 05.7	15 10.8
31	21 54.0	15 03.2
FEB 10	21 43.1	14 57.8
20	21 33.4	14 54.7
MAR 1	21 25.1	14D54.1
11	21 18.7	14 56.0
21	21 14.3	15 00.4
31	21 12.1	15 07.1
APR 10	21D12.1	15 15.9
20	21 14.4	15 26.7
30	21 18.9	15 39.1
MAY 10	21 25.5	15 52.9
20	21 34.0	16 07.8
30	21 44.2	16 23.2
JUN 9	21 55.9	16 39.1
19	22 08.8	16 54.8
29	22 22.5	17 10.2
JUL 9	22 36.7	17 24.8
19	22 51.2	17 38.4
29	23 05.6	17 50.6
AUG 8	23 19.5	18 01.1
18	23 32.7	18 09.7
28	23 44.8	18 16.1
SEP 7	23 55.5	18 20.3
17	24 04.6	18 22.1
27	24 11.8	18R21.5
OCT 7	24 17.0	18 18.4
17	24 19.9	18 13.1
27	24R20.6	18 05.7
NOV 6	24 19.0	17 56.4
16	24 15.2	17 45.6
26	24 09.2	17 33.8
DEC 6	24 01.4	17 21.2
16	23 52.0	17 08.5
26	23 41.3	16 56.1
JAN 5	23♋29.8	16♊44.5
JAN 1	17N27.8	21N31.8
21	17 33.1	21 31.9
FEB 10	17 38.8	21 33.0
MAR 1	17 44.4	21 35.1
21	17 49.2	21 38.3
APR 10	17 52.9	21 42.4
30	17 55.2	21 47.2
MAY 20	17 56.1	21 52.4
JUN 9	17 55.4	21 57.6
29	17 53.5	22 02.5
JUL 19	17 50.6	22 06.9
AUG 8	17 47.2	22 10.7
28	17 43.7	22 13.7
SEP 17	17 40.7	22 15.9
OCT 7	17 38.6	22 17.3
27	17 37.9	22 17.9
NOV 16	17 38.9	22 18.0
DEC 6	17 41.5	22 17.7
26	17N45.7	22N17.4
	4/4.53 10/24.69	2/27.13 9/19.13

1921	Haumea 136108	Makemake 136472
JAN 1	23R34.5	16R49.0
11	23♋22.7	16♊38.1
21	23 10.8	16 28.6
31	22 59.1	16 21.0
FEB 10	22 48.2	16 15.5
20	22 38.4	16 12.3
MAR 2	22 30.2	16D11.5
12	22 23.7	16 13.3
22	22 19.2	16 17.5
APR 1	22 16.9	16 24.0
11	22D16.9	16 32.7
21	22 19.1	16 43.3
MAY 1	22 23.5	16 55.6
11	22 30.0	17 09.3
21	22 38.4	17 24.0
31	22 48.5	17 39.4
JUN 10	23 00.0	17 55.1
20	23 12.8	18 10.9
30	23 26.4	18 26.2
JUL 10	23 40.6	18 40.8
20	23 55.0	18 54.4
30	24 09.3	19 06.6
AUG 9	24 23.2	19 17.2
19	24 36.3	19 25.9
29	24 48.4	19 32.4
SEP 8	24 59.1	19 36.7
18	25 08.2	19 38.6
28	25 15.5	19R38.1
OCT 8	25 20.7	19 35.2
18	25 23.7	19 30.0
28	25R24.4	19 22.7
NOV 7	25 22.8	19 13.5
17	25 19.1	19 02.8
27	25 13.2	18 51.0
DEC 7	25 05.5	18 38.6
17	24 56.1	18 25.9
27	24 45.6	18 13.5
JAN 6	24♋34.1	18♊01.8
JAN 1	17N47.1	22N17.3
21	17 52.6	22 17.5
FEB 10	17 58.4	22 18.4
MAR 2	18 03.9	22 20.2
22	18 08.7	22 23.0
APR 11	18 12.2	22 26.7
MAY 1	18 14.2	22 31.0
21	18 14.8	22 35.7
JUN 10	18 13.8	22 40.6
30	18 11.7	22 45.3
JUL 20	18 08.6	22 49.6
AUG 9	18 05.0	22 53.4
29	18 01.5	22 56.5
SEP 18	17 58.5	22 59.0
OCT 8	17 56.5	23 00.7
28	17 56.0	23 01.7
NOV 17	17 57.1	23 02.1
DEC 7	18 00.0	23 02.1
27	18N04.4	23N02.0
	4/5.92 10/25.98	2/27.74 9/20.66

1922	Haumea 136108	Makemake 136472
JAN 1	24R39.9	18R07.5
11	24♋28.2	17♊56.4
21	24 16.3	17 46.7
31	24 04.6	17 38.8
FEB 10	23 53.6	17 33.0
20	23 43.7	17 29.4
MAR 2	23 35.3	17D28.3
12	23 28.6	17 29.6
22	23 23.8	17 33.4
APR 1	23 21.2	17 39.6
11	23D20.9	17 47.9
21	23 22.8	17 58.2
MAY 1	23 26.9	18 10.2
11	23 33.0	18 23.6
21	23 41.1	18 38.1
31	23 51.0	18 53.4
JUN 10	24 02.3	19 09.1
20	24 14.8	19 24.7
30	24 28.3	19 40.1
JUL 10	24 42.3	19 54.8
20	24 56.7	20 08.5
30	25 11.0	20 20.9
AUG 9	25 24.9	20 31.7
19	25 38.1	20 40.7
29	25 50.2	20 47.5
SEP 8	26 01.1	20 52.1
18	26 10.4	20 54.4
28	26 17.8	20R54.2
OCT 8	26 23.3	20 51.7
18	26 26.5	20 46.8
28	26R27.6	20 39.8
NOV 7	26 26.3	20 31.0
17	26 22.8	20 20.5
27	26 17.2	20 08.9
DEC 7	26 09.7	19 56.5
17	26 00.6	19 43.9
27	25 50.2	19 31.4
JAN 6	25♋38.9	19♊19.7
JAN 1	18N05.7	23N02.0
21	18 11.3	23 02.1
FEB 10	18 17.1	23 02.8
MAR 2	18 22.7	23 04.3
22	18 27.4	23 06.6
APR 11	18 30.7	23 09.8
MAY 1	18 32.6	23 13.7
21	18 33.0	23 18.0
JUN 10	18 31.8	23 22.5
30	18 29.4	23 26.9
JUL 20	18 26.2	23 31.1
AUG 9	18 22.5	23 34.9
29	18 18.8	23 38.2
SEP 18	18 15.8	23 40.9
OCT 8	18 13.9	23 43.0
28	18 13.4	23 44.4
NOV 17	18 14.7	23 45.3
DEC 7	18 17.8	23 45.6
27	18N22.3	23N45.7
	4/7.28 10/27.21	3/1.28 9/22.14

1923	Haumea 136108	Makemake 136472
JAN 1	25R44.6	19R25.4
11	25♋33.0	19♊14.2
21	25 21.2	19 04.3
31	25 09.5	18 56.1
FEB 10	24 58.4	18 49.9
20	24 48.4	18 46.0
MAR 2	24 39.7	18 44.5
12	24 32.8	18D45.5
22	24 27.8	18 48.9
APR 1	24 24.9	18 54.6
11	24D24.3	19 02.6
21	24 25.9	19 12.6
MAY 1	24 29.6	19 24.3
11	24 35.5	19 37.5
21	24 43.3	19 51.8
31	24 52.9	20 06.9
JUN 10	25 04.0	20 22.4
20	25 16.3	20 38.1
30	25 29.6	20 53.5
JUL 10	25 43.5	21 08.3
20	25 57.8	21 22.1
30	26 12.0	21 34.7
AUG 9	26 25.9	21 45.7
19	26 39.2	21 54.9
29	26 51.4	22 02.1
SEP 8	27 02.4	22 07.0
18	27 11.9	22 09.6
28	27 19.5	22R09.8
OCT 8	27 25.2	22 07.6
18	27 28.8	22 03.1
28	27 30.0	21 56.4
NOV 7	27R29.1	21 47.8
17	27 25.9	21 37.6
27	27 20.6	21 26.2
DEC 7	27 13.3	21 13.9
17	27 04.4	21 01.3
27	26 54.2	20 48.8
JAN 6	26♋43.0	20♊36.9
JAN 1	18N23.6	23N45.7
21	18 29.3	23 45.8
FEB 10	18 35.3	23 46.3
MAR 2	18 40.9	23 47.4
22	18 45.5	23 49.4
APR 11	18 48.8	23 52.1
MAY 1	18 50.5	23 55.5
21	18 50.6	23 59.3
JUN 10	18 49.3	24 03.4
30	18 46.7	24 07.6
JUL 20	18 43.2	24 11.7
AUG 9	18 39.4	24 15.5
29	18 35.7	24 18.9
SEP 18	18 32.6	24 21.9
OCT 8	18 30.7	24 24.3
28	18 30.3	24 26.2
NOV 17	18 31.7	24 27.4
DEC 7	18 34.9	24 28.0
27	18N39.6	24N28.3
	4/8.67 10/28.50	3/2.84 9/23.63

1924	Haumea 136108	Makemake 136472
JAN 1	26R48.7	20R42.8
11	26♋37.2	20♊31.4
21	26 25.4	20 21.3
31	26 13.7	20 12.8
FEB 10	26 02.6	20 06.3
20	25 52.4	20 02.1
MAR 1	25 43.6	20 00.2
11	25 36.5	20D00.8
21	25 31.2	20 03.8
31	25 28.1	20 09.2
APR 10	25D27.1	20 16.8
20	25 28.4	20 26.5
30	25 31.8	20 37.9
MAY 10	25 37.4	20 50.8
20	25 45.0	21 04.9
30	25 54.3	21 19.9
JUN 9	26 05.1	21 35.3
19	26 17.2	21 50.9
29	26 30.3	22 06.3
JUL 9	26 44.1	22 21.2
19	26 58.3	22 35.1
29	27 12.5	22 47.9
AUG 8	27 26.4	22 59.1
18	27 39.7	23 08.6
28	27 52.1	23 16.0
SEP 7	28 03.2	23 21.3
17	28 12.8	23 24.2
27	28 20.7	23R24.8
OCT 7	28 26.6	23 23.0
17	28 30.4	23 18.8
27	28 32.0	23 12.5
NOV 6	28R31.3	23 04.2
16	28 28.4	22 54.2
26	28 23.3	22 42.9
DEC 6	28 16.3	22 30.8
16	28 07.7	22 18.2
26	27 57.6	22 05.7
JAN 5	27♋46.6	21♊53.8
JAN 1	18N41.0	24N28.3
21	18 46.8	24 28.5
FEB 10	18 52.9	24 28.8
MAR 1	18 58.5	24 29.7
21	19 03.1	24 31.2
APR 10	19 06.2	24 33.5
30	19 07.8	24 36.4
MAY 20	19 07.7	24 39.8
JUN 9	19 06.2	24 43.5
29	19 03.4	24 47.5
JUL 19	18 59.8	24 51.4
AUG 8	18 55.8	24 55.1
28	18 51.9	24 58.7
SEP 17	18 48.8	25 01.9
OCT 7	18 46.9	25 04.7
27	18 46.6	25 06.9
NOV 16	18 48.2	25 08.5
DEC 6	18 51.5	25 09.5
26	18N56.3	25N10.0
	4/8.98 10/28.73	3/3.40 9/24.13

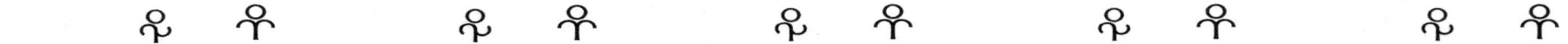

1925	Haumea 136108	Makemake 136472
JAN 1	27R51.1	21R58.4
11	27♋39.6	21♊47.0
21	27 27.9	21 36.9
31	27 16.2	21 28.3
FEB 10	27 05.1	21 21.8
20	26 54.9	21 17.4
MAR 2	26 46.1	21 15.4
12	26 38.9	21D15.9
22	26 33.7	21 18.8
APR 1	26 30.5	21 24.0
11	26D29.4	21 31.5
21	26 30.6	21 41.0
MAY 1	26 34.0	21 52.3
11	26 39.5	22 05.1
21	26 46.9	22 19.1
31	26 56.1	22 34.0
JUN 10	27 06.9	22 49.3
20	27 18.9	23 04.9
30	27 31.9	23 20.3
JUL 10	27 45.7	23 35.1
20	27 59.7	23 49.0
30	28 13.9	24 01.8
AUG 9	28 27.7	24 13.1
19	28 41.0	24 22.6
29	28 53.3	24 30.2
SEP 8	29 04.5	24 35.5
18	29 14.1	24 38.6
28	29 22.0	24R39.3
OCT 8	29 27.9	24 37.6
18	29 31.8	24 33.5
28	29 33.4	24 27.3
NOV 7	29R32.8	24 19.1
17	29 29.9	24 09.2
27	29 25.0	23 58.0
DEC 7	29 18.0	23 46.0
17	29 09.4	23 33.4
27	28 59.4	23 20.9
JAN 6	28♋48.5	23♊09.0
JAN 1	18N58.0	25N10.1
21	19 04.0	25 10.2
FEB 10	19 10.2	25 10.5
MAR 2	19 15.8	25 11.1
22	19 20.3	25 12.3
APR 11	19 23.3	25 14.1
MAY 1	19 24.6	25 16.6
21	19 24.3	25 19.5
JUN 10	19 22.4	25 22.9
30	19 19.4	25 26.5
JUL 20	19 15.6	25 30.3
AUG 9	19 11.4	25 34.0
29	19 07.5	25 37.6
SEP 18	19 04.4	25 41.0
OCT 8	19 02.6	25 44.1
28	19 02.4	25 46.7
NOV 17	19 04.1	25 48.6
DEC 7	19 07.7	25 49.9
27	19N12.8	25N50.7
	4/10.34 10/29.97	3/4.90 9/25.58

1926	Haumea 136108	Makemake 136472
JAN 1	28R54.1	23R14.9
11	28♋42.7	23♊03.3
21	28 31.0	22 53.0
31	28 19.3	22 44.2
FEB 10	28 08.2	22 37.4
20	27 57.9	22 32.7
MAR 2	27 48.9	22 30.3
12	27 41.6	22D30.4
22	27 36.0	22 32.9
APR 1	27 32.6	22 37.8
11	27 31.3	22 44.9
21	27D32.2	22 54.1
MAY 1	27 35.2	23 05.1
11	27 40.4	23 17.7
21	27 47.6	23 31.5
31	27 56.5	23 46.2
JUN 10	28 07.1	24 01.4
20	28 18.9	24 16.9
30	28 31.7	24 32.3
JUL 10	28 45.3	24 47.2
20	28 59.3	25 01.2
30	29 13.4	25 14.2
AUG 9	29 27.3	25 25.7
19	29 40.6	25 35.5
29	29 53.0	25 43.3
SEP 8	0♌04.3	25 49.0
18	0 14.1	25 52.4
28	0 22.1	25R53.4
OCT 8	0 28.3	25 52.0
18	0 32.4	25 48.3
28	0 34.3	25 42.4
NOV 7	0R34.0	25 34.5
17	0 31.4	25 24.9
27	0 26.7	25 13.9
DEC 7	0 20.1	25 02.0
17	0 11.7	24 49.5
27	0 01.9	24 37.0
JAN 6	29♋51.0	24♊25.0
JAN 1	19N14.2	25N50.8
21	19 20.4	25 51.0
FEB 10	19 26.6	25 51.2
MAR 2	19 32.3	25 51.5
22	19 36.7	25 52.3
APR 11	19 39.6	25 53.7
MAY 1	19 40.8	25 55.7
21	19 40.3	25 58.2
JUN 10	19 38.3	26 01.2
30	19 35.0	26 04.5
JUL 20	19 31.0	26 08.1
AUG 9	19 26.7	26 11.7
29	19 22.7	26 15.4
SEP 18	19 19.5	26 19.0
OCT 8	19 17.7	26 22.4
28	19 17.6	26 25.3
NOV 17	19 19.4	26 27.7
DEC 7	19 23.1	26 29.4
27	19N28.3	26N30.3
	4/11.66 10/31.23	3/6.45 9/27.09

1927	Haumea 136108	Makemake 136472
JAN 1	29R56.6	24R30.9
11	29♋45.3	24♊19.3
21	29 33.7	24 08.8
31	29 22.0	23 59.8
FEB 10	29 10.8	23 52.6
20	29 00.5	23 47.6
MAR 2	28 51.4	23 44.9
12	28 43.8	23D44.6
22	28 38.0	23 46.8
APR 1	28 34.3	23 51.3
11	28 32.7	23 58.1
21	28D33.3	24 06.9
MAY 1	28 36.1	24 17.6
11	28 41.0	24 29.9
21	28 47.9	24 43.5
31	28 56.6	24 58.0
JUN 10	29 06.9	25 13.2
20	29 18.5	25 28.6
30	29 31.2	25 44.0
JUL 10	29 44.6	25 58.9
20	29 58.6	26 13.1
30	0♌12.6	26 26.2
AUG 9	0 26.5	26 37.9
19	0 39.8	26 47.9
29	0 52.3	26 56.0
SEP 8	1 03.7	27 02.0
18	1 13.6	27 05.8
28	1 21.9	27 07.1
OCT 8	1 28.3	27R06.1
18	1 32.7	27 02.8
28	1 34.8	26 57.2
NOV 7	1R34.8	26 49.6
17	1 32.5	26 40.2
27	1 28.1	26 29.4
DEC 7	1 21.7	26 17.6
17	1 13.5	26 05.3
27	1 03.9	25 52.8
JAN 6	0♌53.2	25♊40.7
JAN 1	19N29.8	26N30.5
21	19 36.1	26 30.8
FEB 10	19 42.4	26 30.9
MAR 2	19 48.1	26 31.0
22	19 52.6	26 31.5
APR 11	19 55.4	26 32.4
MAY 1	19 56.5	26 33.9
21	19 55.8	26 36.0
JUN 10	19 53.6	26 38.6
30	19 50.1	26 41.6
JUL 20	19 45.9	26 44.9
AUG 9	19 41.5	26 48.5
29	19 37.3	26 52.2
SEP 18	19 34.1	26 56.0
OCT 8	19 32.2	26 59.6
28	19 32.1	27 02.9
NOV 17	19 34.1	27 05.7
DEC 7	19 37.9	27 07.7
27	19N43.2	27N09.0
	4/12.94 11/1.44	3/7.93 9/28.54

1928	Haumea 136108	Makemake 136472
JAN 1	0R58.7	25R46.7
11	0♌47.6	25♊34.9
21	0 36.0	25 24.3
31	0 24.3	25 15.0
FEB 10	0 13.1	25 07.6
20	0 02.7	25 02.3
MAR 1	29♋53.4	24 59.3
11	29 45.6	24D58.6
21	29 39.7	25 00.4
31	29 35.7	25 04.5
APR 10	29 33.8	25 11.0
20	29D34.1	25 19.5
30	29 36.7	25 29.9
MAY 10	29 41.3	25 41.9
20	29 47.9	25 55.3
30	29 56.3	26 09.7
JUN 9	0♌06.4	26 24.7
19	0 17.8	26 40.1
29	0 30.3	26 55.4
JUL 9	0 43.6	27 10.4
19	0 57.5	27 24.7
29	1 11.4	27 37.9
AUG 8	1 25.3	27 49.8
18	1 38.7	28 00.1
28	1 51.3	28 08.5
SEP 7	2 02.7	28 14.8
17	2 12.9	28 18.9
27	2 21.3	28 20.6
OCT 7	2 28.0	28R19.9
17	2 32.6	28 16.9
27	2 35.0	28 11.7
NOV 6	2R35.2	28 04.4
16	2 33.2	27 55.3
26	2 29.1	27 44.7
DEC 6	2 22.9	27 33.0
16	2 15.0	27 20.8
26	2 05.6	27 08.3
JAN 5	1♌55.0	26♊56.1
JAN 1	19N44.8	27N09.2
21	19 51.2	27 09.6
FEB 10	19 57.7	27 09.6
MAR 1	20 03.4	27 09.5
21	20 07.9	27 09.6
APR 10	20 10.7	27 10.2
30	20 11.6	27 11.2
MAY 20	20 10.8	27 12.8
JUN 9	20 08.3	27 15.0
29	20 04.7	27 17.7
JUL 19	20 00.3	27 20.8
AUG 8	19 55.7	27 24.2
28	19 51.4	27 28.0
SEP 17	19 48.1	27 31.9
OCT 7	19 46.2	27 35.8
27	19 46.2	27 39.4
NOV 16	19 48.1	27 42.6
DEC 6	19 52.1	27 45.0
26	19N57.6	27N46.5
	4/13.27 11/1.70	3/8.44 9/29.02

1929	Haumea 136108	Makemake 136472
JAN 1	1R59.4	27R00.9
11	1♌48.3	26♊49.2
21	1 36.8	26 38.5
31	1 25.2	26 29.2
FEB 10	1 14.0	26 21.7
20	1 03.5	26 16.3
MAR 2	0 54.3	26 13.2
12	0 46.5	26D12.4
22	0 40.5	26 14.1
APR 1	0 36.5	26 18.1
11	0 34.6	26 24.4
21	0D34.8	26 32.8
MAY 1	0 37.3	26 43.1
11	0 41.8	26 55.0
21	0 48.3	27 08.3
31	0 56.7	27 22.5
JUN 10	1 06.6	27 37.5
20	1 18.0	27 52.8
30	1 30.4	28 08.2
JUL 10	1 43.7	28 23.1
20	1 57.5	28 37.4
30	2 11.4	28 50.6
AUG 9	2 25.2	29 02.6
19	2 38.6	29 12.9
29	2 51.1	29 21.4
SEP 8	3 02.6	29 27.8
18	3 12.7	29 31.9
28	3 21.2	29 33.8
OCT 8	3 27.9	29R33.2
18	3 32.5	29 30.3
28	3 35.0	29 25.2
NOV 7	3R35.3	29 18.0
17	3 33.3	29 09.0
27	3 29.2	28 58.5
DEC 7	3 23.1	28 46.9
17	3 15.3	28 34.7
27	3 05.9	28 22.3
JAN 6	2♌55.4	28♊10.1
JAN 1	19N59.5	27N46.8
21	20 06.1	27 47.3
FEB 10	20 12.6	27 47.3
MAR 2	20 18.4	27 47.0
22	20 22.8	27 46.8
APR 11	20 25.4	27 47.0
MAY 1	20 26.1	27 47.6
21	20 25.1	27 48.8
JUN 10	20 22.4	27 50.5
30	20 18.5	27 52.9
JUL 20	20 13.9	27 55.8
AUG 9	20 09.1	27 59.1
29	20 04.7	28 02.9
SEP 18	20 01.4	28 06.9
OCT 8	19 59.5	28 11.1
28	19 59.6	28 15.0
NOV 17	20 01.8	28 18.5
DEC 7	20 05.9	28 21.2
27	20N11.6	28N23.0
	4/14.53 11/2.92	3/9.93 9/30.50

1930	♇ Haumea 136108	♈ Makemake 136472
JAN 1	3R00.8	28R16.1
11	2♌49.9	28♊04.3
21	2 38.4	27 53.4
31	2 26.9	27 44.0
FEB 10	2 15.6	27 36.2
20	2 05.1	27 30.5
MAR 2	1 55.7	27 27.0
12	1 47.8	27D25.9
22	1 41.5	27 27.2
APR 1	1 37.3	27 30.8
11	1 35.1	27 36.8
21	1D35.1	27 44.9
MAY 1	1 37.2	27 54.9
11	1 41.5	28 06.5
21	1 47.7	28 19.6
31	1 55.8	28 33.7
JUN 10	2 05.6	28 48.5
20	2 16.7	29 03.8
30	2 29.0	29 19.1
JUL 10	2 42.1	29 34.1
20	2 55.8	29 48.4
30	3 09.7	0♋01.8
AUG 9	3 23.5	0 14.0
19	3 36.8	0 24.5
29	3 49.5	0 33.2
SEP 8	4 01.1	0 39.9
18	4 11.3	0 44.4
28	4 20.0	0 46.6
OCT 8	4 26.9	0R46.4
18	4 31.8	0 43.9
28	4 34.5	0 39.1
NOV 7	4R35.0	0 32.1
17	4 33.4	0 23.4
27	4 29.6	0 13.1
DEC 7	4 23.7	0 01.7
17	4 16.1	29♊49.6
27	4 06.9	29 37.2
JAN 6	3♌56.6	29♊25.0

1930	Haumea	Makemake
JAN 1	20N13.2	28N23.3
21	20 20.0	28 24.0
FEB 10	20 26.7	28 24.0
MAR 2	20 32.5	28 23.5
22	20 36.9	28 23.0
APR 11	20 39.5	28 22.7
MAY 1	20 40.1	28 22.9
21	20 38.9	28 23.6
JUN 10	20 36.0	28 24.9
30	20 31.9	28 26.9
JUL 20	20 27.1	28 29.5
AUG 9	20 22.2	28 32.8
29	20 17.7	28 36.5
SEP 18	20 14.2	28 40.7
OCT 8	20 12.4	28 45.0
28	20 12.5	28 49.3
NOV 17	20 14.7	28 53.1
DEC 7	20 18.9	28 56.2
27	20N24.8	28N58.3
	4/15.82 11/4.15	3/11.39 10/1.93

1931	♇ Haumea 136108	♈ Makemake 136472
JAN 1	4R01.9	29R31.0
11	3♌51.1	29♊19.1
21	3 39.7	29 08.1
31	3 28.2	28 58.4
FEB 10	3 16.9	28 50.4
20	3 06.3	28 44.4
MAR 2	2 56.8	28 40.6
12	2 48.7	28 39.1
22	2 42.2	28D40.0
APR 1	2 37.8	28 43.4
11	2 35.3	28 49.0
21	2D35.0	28 56.7
MAY 1	2 36.9	29 06.4
11	2 40.9	29 17.8
21	2 46.8	29 30.6
31	2 54.7	29 44.6
JUN 10	3 04.2	29 59.3
20	3 15.1	0♋14.4
30	3 27.2	0 29.7
JUL 10	3 40.2	0 44.7
20	3 53.8	0 59.2
30	4 07.6	1 12.7
AUG 9	4 21.4	1 25.0
19	4 34.8	1 35.8
29	4 47.5	1 44.7
SEP 8	4 59.2	1 51.7
18	5 09.6	1 56.5
28	5 18.5	1 59.1
OCT 8	5 25.6	1R59.2
18	5 30.7	1 57.0
28	5 33.7	1 52.5
NOV 7	5R34.5	1 45.9
17	5 33.1	1 37.4
27	5 29.5	1 27.4
DEC 7	5 23.9	1 16.1
17	5 16.5	1 04.1
27	5 07.6	0 51.7
JAN 6	4♌57.4	0♋39.5

1931	Haumea	Makemake
JAN 1	20N26.4	28N58.7
21	20 33.3	28 59.5
FEB 10	20 40.1	28 59.5
MAR 2	20 46.0	28 58.9
22	20 50.5	28 58.1
APR 11	20 53.0	28 57.5
MAY 1	20 53.6	28 57.2
21	20 52.2	28 57.4
JUN 10	20 49.1	28 58.3
30	20 44.9	28 59.9
JUL 20	20 39.9	29 02.3
AUG 9	20 34.7	29 05.3
29	20 30.1	29 09.0
SEP 18	20 26.6	29 13.2
OCT 8	20 24.6	29 17.8
28	20 24.7	29 22.4
NOV 17	20 27.0	29 26.6
DEC 7	20 31.4	29 30.1
27	20N37.3	29N32.5
	4/17.10 11/5.38	3/12.92 10/3.41

1932	♇ Haumea 136108	♈ Makemake 136472
JAN 1	5R02.6	0R45.5
11	4♌52.0	0♋33.6
21	4 40.7	0 22.4
31	4 29.2	0 12.6
FEB 10	4 17.9	0 04.3
20	4 07.2	29♊58.0
MAR 1	3 57.5	29 53.9
11	3 49.3	29 52.0
21	3 42.6	29D52.6
31	3 37.9	29 55.6
APR 10	3 35.2	0♋00.8
20	3D34.6	0 08.2
30	3 36.2	0 17.6
MAY 10	3 39.9	0 28.7
20	3 45.6	0 41.3
30	3 53.2	0 55.1
JUN 9	4 02.5	1 09.7
19	4 13.2	1 24.7
29	4 25.1	1 40.0
JUL 9	4 38.0	1 55.0
19	4 51.5	2 09.5
29	5 05.2	2 23.2
AUG 8	5 19.0	2 35.6
18	5 32.4	2 46.6
28	5 45.2	2 55.8
SEP 7	5 57.0	3 03.1
17	6 07.5	3 08.2
27	6 16.6	3 11.1
OCT 7	6 23.9	3R11.6
17	6 29.2	3 09.7
27	6 32.5	3 05.6
NOV 6	6R33.5	2 59.3
16	6 32.4	2 51.0
26	6 29.1	2 41.2
DEC 6	6 23.8	2 30.1
16	6 16.6	2 18.2
26	6 07.8	2 05.8
JAN 5	5♌57.8	1♋53.6

1932	Haumea	Makemake
JAN 1	20N39.0	29N32.9
21	20 46.0	29 33.9
FEB 10	20 53.0	29 33.9
MAR 1	20 59.0	29 33.2
21	21 03.5	29 32.2
APR 10	21 06.0	29 31.1
30	21 06.4	29 30.4
MAY 20	21 04.9	29 30.2
JUN 9	21 01.7	29 30.6
29	20 57.2	29 31.9
JUL 19	20 52.1	29 33.9
AUG 8	20 46.8	29 36.8
28	20 42.0	29 40.4
SEP 17	20 38.3	29 44.7
OCT 7	20 36.4	29 49.4
27	20 36.4	29 54.3
NOV 16	20 38.8	29 58.9
DEC 6	20 43.2	30 02.7
26	20N49.3	30N05.5
	4/17.36 11/5.54	3/13.37 10/3.81

1933	♇ Haumea 136108	♈ Makemake 136472
JAN 1	6R01.9	1R58.5
11	5♌51.3	1♋46.5
21	5 40.1	1 35.3
31	5 28.6	1 25.4
FEB 10	5 17.3	1 17.1
20	5 06.7	1 10.7
MAR 2	4 57.0	1 06.5
12	4 48.7	1 04.5
22	4 42.1	1D05.0
APR 1	4 37.3	1 07.8
11	4 34.5	1 12.9
21	4D33.9	1 20.2
MAY 1	4 35.4	1 29.5
11	4 39.1	1 40.5
21	4 44.7	1 53.0
31	4 52.2	2 06.7
JUN 10	5 01.4	2 21.2
20	5 12.1	2 36.2
30	5 23.9	2 51.4
JUL 10	5 36.7	3 06.4
20	5 50.1	3 20.9
30	6 03.8	3 34.5
AUG 9	6 17.6	3 47.0
19	6 30.9	3 58.1
29	6 43.7	4 07.4
SEP 8	6 55.5	4 14.7
18	7 06.0	4 19.9
28	7 15.1	4 22.9
OCT 8	7 22.4	4R23.4
18	7 27.8	4 21.7
28	7 31.1	4 17.6
NOV 7	7R32.2	4 11.4
17	7 31.1	4 03.3
27	7 27.8	3 53.5
DEC 7	7 22.5	3 42.5
17	7 15.4	3 30.6
27	7 06.7	3 18.3
JAN 6	6♌56.7	3♋06.1

1933	Haumea	Makemake
JAN 1	20N51.4	30N06.0
21	20 58.6	30 07.2
FEB 10	21 05.6	30 07.2
MAR 2	21 11.6	30 06.4
22	21 16.0	30 05.0
APR 11	21 18.5	30 03.7
MAY 1	21 18.7	30 02.5
21	21 17.0	30 01.9
JUN 10	21 13.5	30 01.9
30	21 08.8	30 02.8
JUL 20	21 03.5	30 04.6
AUG 9	20 58.0	30 07.3
29	20 53.1	30 10.9
SEP 18	20 49.4	30 15.2
OCT 8	20 47.5	30 20.2
28	20 47.7	30 25.3
NOV 17	20 50.1	30 30.2
DEC 7	20 54.8	30 34.3
27	21N01.1	30N37.4
	4/18.66 11/6.78	3/14.87 10/5.26

1934	♇ Haumea 136108	♈ Makemake 136472
JAN 1	7R01.9	3R12.2
11	6♌51.4	3♋00.1
21	6 40.2	2 48.8
31	6 28.8	2 38.7
FEB 10	6 17.5	2 30.2
20	6 06.7	2 23.5
MAR 2	5 57.0	2 19.0
12	5 48.5	2 16.7
22	5 41.7	2D16.8
APR 1	5 36.6	2 19.2
11	5 33.6	2 24.0
21	5D32.7	2 31.0
MAY 1	5 34.0	2 39.9
11	5 37.3	2 50.7
21	5 42.7	3 02.9
31	5 50.0	3 16.4
JUN 10	5 59.0	3 30.8
20	6 09.4	3 45.7
30	6 21.1	4 00.8
JUL 10	6 33.7	4 15.9
20	6 47.0	4 30.4
30	7 00.7	4 44.2
AUG 9	7 14.4	4 56.8
19	7 27.8	5 08.1
29	7 40.6	5 17.6
SEP 8	7 52.5	5 25.2
18	8 03.2	5 30.7
28	8 12.4	5 34.0
OCT 8	8 19.9	5R34.9
18	8 25.5	5 33.5
28	8 29.0	5 29.8
NOV 7	8 30.4	5 23.8
17	8R29.5	5 16.0
27	8 26.6	5 06.5
DEC 7	8 21.5	4 55.6
17	8 14.6	4 43.8
27	8 06.1	4 31.6
JAN 6	7♌56.3	4♋19.3

1934	Haumea	Makemake
JAN 1	21N02.8	30N37.9
21	21 10.1	30 39.3
FEB 10	21 17.3	30 39.4
MAR 2	21 23.4	30 38.5
22	21 27.9	30 36.9
APR 11	21 30.3	30 35.2
MAY 1	21 30.5	30 33.6
21	21 28.7	30 32.6
JUN 10	21 25.0	30 32.2
30	21 20.2	30 32.6
JUL 20	21 14.6	30 34.1
AUG 9	21 09.0	30 36.5
29	21 03.9	30 40.0
SEP 18	21 00.1	30 44.4
OCT 8	20 58.1	30 49.5
28	20 58.3	30 54.9
NOV 17	21 00.8	31 00.1
DEC 7	21 05.5	31 04.7
27	21N11.9	31N08.0
	4/19.89 11/7.94	3/16.35 10/6.67

1935	Haumea 136108	Makemake 136472
JAN 1	8R01.3	4R25.4
11	7♌51.0	4♋13.3
21	7 39.9	4 01.9
31	7 28.5	3 51.6
FEB 10	7 17.2	3 42.9
20	7 06.4	3 35.9
MAR 2	6 56.5	3 31.0
12	6 47.9	3 28.4
22	6 40.8	3D28.2
APR 1	6 35.6	3 30.3
11	6 32.4	3 34.7
21	6 31.2	3 41.3
MAY 1	6D32.2	3 50.0
11	6 35.2	4 00.5
21	6 40.4	4 12.5
31	6 47.4	4 25.8
JUN 10	6 56.1	4 40.0
20	7 06.3	4 54.8
30	7 17.8	5 09.9
JUL 10	7 30.3	5 24.9
20	7 43.5	5 39.5
30	7 57.1	5 53.4
AUG 9	8 10.8	6 06.2
19	8 24.2	6 17.6
29	8 37.0	6 27.4
SEP 8	8 49.0	6 35.3
18	8 59.8	6 41.1
28	9 09.2	6 44.7
OCT 8	9 16.9	6 45.9
18	9 22.7	6R44.8
28	9 26.5	6 41.4
NOV 7	9 28.1	6 35.8
17	9R27.6	6 28.2
27	9 24.8	6 18.9
DEC 7	9 20.0	6 08.2
17	9 13.4	5 56.6
27	9 05.0	5 44.4
JAN 6	8♌55.4	5♋32.1

1935	Haumea 136108	Makemake 136472
JAN 1	21N13.7	31N08.7
21	21 21.2	31 10.3
FEB 10	21 28.5	31 10.4
MAR 2	21 34.7	31 09.5
22	21 39.2	31 07.7
APR 11	21 41.6	31 05.7
MAY 1	21 41.8	31 03.7
21	21 39.8	31 02.2
JUN 10	21 36.1	31 01.4
30	21 31.0	31 01.4
JUL 20	21 25.3	31 02.5
AUG 9	21 19.4	31 04.8
29	21 14.3	31 08.1
SEP 18	21 10.3	31 12.5
OCT 8	21 08.2	31 17.7
28	21 08.4	31 23.4
NOV 17	21 10.9	31 28.9
DEC 7	21 15.7	31 33.8
27	21N22.2	31N37.6
	4/21.18 11/9.11	3/17.81 10/8.05

1936	Haumea 136108	Makemake 136472
JAN 1	9R00.3	5R38.2
11	8♌50.1	5♋26.1
21	8 39.1	5 14.6
31	8 27.8	5 04.1
FEB 10	8 16.5	4 55.1
20	8 05.6	4 47.9
MAR 1	7 55.6	4 42.7
11	7 46.8	4 39.8
21	7 39.6	4D39.2
31	7 34.2	4 41.0
APR 10	7 30.6	4 45.0
20	7 29.2	4 51.3
30	7D29.9	4 59.7
MAY 10	7 32.7	5 09.9
20	7 37.6	5 21.7
30	7 44.3	5 34.7
JUN 9	7 52.8	5 48.8
19	8 02.9	6 03.5
29	8 14.2	6 18.5
JUL 9	8 26.6	6 33.6
19	8 39.6	6 48.2
29	8 53.1	7 02.2
AUG 8	9 06.8	7 15.1
18	9 20.2	7 26.7
28	9 33.1	7 36.7
SEP 7	9 45.2	7 44.9
17	9 56.1	7 51.0
27	10 05.6	7 54.9
OCT 7	10 13.5	7 56.4
17	10 19.6	7R55.7
27	10 23.6	7 52.6
NOV 6	10 25.4	7 47.3
16	10R25.1	7 40.0
26	10 22.6	7 30.9
DEC 6	10 18.1	7 20.4
16	10 11.7	7 08.9
26	10 03.5	6 56.8
JAN 5	9♌54.0	6♋44.5

1936	Haumea 136108	Makemake 136472
JAN 1	21N24.0	31N38.3
21	21 31.7	31 40.1
FEB 10	21 39.1	31 40.4
MAR 1	21 45.5	31 39.4
21	21 50.1	31 37.5
APR 10	21 52.5	31 35.1
30	21 52.6	31 32.8
MAY 20	21 50.5	31 30.8
JUN 9	21 46.6	31 29.6
29	21 41.4	31 29.2
JUL 19	21 35.4	31 30.0
AUG 8	21 29.5	31 32.0
28	21 24.1	31 35.2
SEP 17	21 20.1	31 39.6
OCT 7	21 17.9	31 44.9
27	21 18.0	31 50.8
NOV 16	21 20.6	31 56.6
DEC 6	21 25.4	32 01.9
26	21N32.0	32N06.0
	4/21.43 11/9.31	3/18.29 10/8.50

1937	Haumea 136108	Makemake 136472
JAN 1	9R58.0	6R49.4
11	9♌47.8	6♋37.3
21	9 36.8	6 25.7
31	9 25.5	6 15.2
FEB 10	9 14.2	6 06.2
20	9 03.4	5 58.9
MAR 2	8 53.4	5 53.6
12	8 44.6	5 50.6
22	8 37.3	5D49.9
APR 1	8 31.8	5 51.5
11	8 28.3	5 55.5
21	8 26.8	6 01.7
MAY 1	8D27.5	6 09.9
11	8 30.2	6 20.0
21	8 35.0	6 31.7
31	8 41.7	6 44.7
JUN 10	8 50.1	6 58.7
20	9 00.1	7 13.3
30	9 11.4	7 28.3
JUL 10	9 23.7	7 43.3
20	9 36.7	7 57.9
30	9 50.1	8 11.9
AUG 9	10 03.7	8 24.9
19	10 17.1	8 36.5
29	10 30.0	8 46.6
SEP 8	10 42.1	8 54.8
18	10 53.0	9 01.0
28	11 02.5	9 04.9
OCT 8	11 10.4	9 06.6
18	11 16.5	9R05.9
28	11 20.5	9 02.9
NOV 7	11 22.4	8 57.7
17	11R22.2	8 50.5
27	11 19.7	8 41.5
DEC 7	11 15.2	8 31.1
17	11 08.8	8 19.6
27	11 00.7	8 07.5
JAN 6	10♌51.3	7♋55.3

1937	Haumea 136108	Makemake 136472
JAN 1	21N34.3	32N06.9
21	21 42.0	32 08.9
FEB 10	21 49.6	32 09.3
MAR 2	21 56.0	32 08.2
22	22 00.6	32 06.1
APR 11	22 02.9	32 03.5
MAY 1	22 02.8	32 00.7
21	22 00.5	31 58.4
JUN 10	21 56.4	31 56.7
30	21 51.0	31 56.0
JUL 20	21 44.9	31 56.5
AUG 9	21 38.7	31 58.3
29	21 33.3	32 01.4
SEP 18	21 29.2	32 05.8
OCT 8	21 27.0	32 11.2
28	21 27.2	32 17.3
NOV 17	21 29.9	32 23.5
DEC 7	21 34.9	32 29.1
27	21N41.7	32N33.4
	4/22.66 11/10.46	3/19.71 10/9.87

1938	Haumea 136108	Makemake 136472
JAN 1	10R56.1	8R01.4
11	10♌46.1	7♋49.2
21	10 35.3	7 37.6
31	10 24.0	7 27.0
FEB 10	10 12.7	7 17.7
20	10 01.8	7 10.2
MAR 2	9 51.7	7 04.6
12	9 42.8	7 01.3
22	9 35.3	7D00.2
APR 1	9 29.6	7 01.5
11	9 25.8	7 05.2
21	9 24.1	7 11.0
MAY 1	9D24.5	7 18.9
11	9 27.0	7 28.7
21	9 31.5	7 40.2
31	9 37.9	7 53.0
JUN 10	9 46.1	8 06.8
20	9 55.9	8 21.3
30	10 07.0	8 36.3
JUL 10	10 19.1	8 51.2
20	10 32.0	9 05.9
30	10 45.4	9 20.0
AUG 9	10 59.0	9 33.1
19	11 12.4	9 44.9
29	11 25.3	9 55.2
SEP 8	11 37.5	10 03.6
18	11 48.5	10 10.1
28	11 58.2	10 14.4
OCT 8	12 06.3	10 16.4
18	12 12.6	10R16.1
28	12 16.8	10 13.4
NOV 7	12 19.0	10 08.5
17	12R19.0	10 01.5
27	12 16.8	9 52.8
DEC 7	12 12.5	9 42.6
17	12 06.3	9 31.2
27	11 58.5	9 19.2
JAN 6	11♌49.2	9♋07.0

1938	Haumea 136108	Makemake 136472
JAN 1	21N43.6	32N34.3
21	21 51.5	32 36.6
FEB 10	21 59.2	32 37.1
MAR 2	22 05.8	32 36.0
22	22 10.4	32 33.8
APR 11	22 12.8	32 30.9
MAY 1	22 12.7	32 27.8
21	22 10.3	32 25.0
JUN 10	22 06.1	32 22.9
30	22 00.5	32 21.8
JUL 20	21 54.2	32 21.9
AUG 9	21 47.9	32 23.4
29	21 42.3	32 26.3
SEP 18	21 38.0	32 30.7
OCT 8	21 35.8	32 36.2
28	21 35.9	32 42.5
NOV 17	21 38.6	32 49.0
DEC 7	21 43.7	32 54.9
27	21N50.6	32N59.6
	4/23.93 11/11.65	3/21.19 10/11.30

1939	Haumea 136108	Makemake 136472
JAN 1	11R54.0	9R13.1
11	11♌44.1	9♋00.9
21	11 33.3	8 49.2
31	11 22.1	8 38.4
FEB 10	11 10.8	8 29.0
20	10 59.8	8 21.2
MAR 2	10 49.7	8 15.4
12	10 40.6	8 11.7
22	10 33.0	8 10.3
APR 1	10 27.1	8D11.3
11	10 23.1	8 14.6
21	10 21.1	8 20.1
MAY 1	10D21.2	8 27.7
11	10 23.4	8 37.2
21	10 27.7	8 48.4
31	10 33.9	9 01.0
JUN 10	10 41.9	9 14.7
20	10 51.4	9 29.1
30	11 02.3	9 44.0
JUL 10	11 14.3	9 58.9
20	11 27.1	10 13.6
30	11 40.5	10 27.8
AUG 9	11 54.0	10 41.0
19	12 07.4	10 53.0
29	12 20.3	11 03.5
SEP 8	12 32.5	11 12.2
18	12 43.7	11 19.0
28	12 53.6	11 23.6
OCT 8	13 01.8	11 25.9
18	13 08.3	11R25.9
28	13 12.8	11 23.5
NOV 7	13 15.2	11 19.0
17	13R15.5	11 12.3
27	13 13.5	11 03.8
DEC 7	13 09.5	10 53.8
17	13 03.6	10 42.6
27	12 55.9	10 30.7
JAN 6	12♌46.8	10♋18.5

1939	Haumea 136108	Makemake 136472
JAN 1	21N52.5	33N00.6
21	22 00.6	33 03.1
FEB 10	22 08.4	33 03.8
MAR 2	22 15.1	33 02.8
22	22 19.8	33 00.4
APR 11	22 22.2	32 57.3
MAY 1	22 22.1	32 53.9
21	22 19.6	32 50.7
JUN 10	22 15.3	32 48.1
30	22 09.5	32 46.6
JUL 20	22 03.1	32 46.3
AUG 9	21 56.6	32 47.5
29	21 50.8	32 50.3
SEP 18	21 46.5	32 54.5
OCT 8	21 44.1	33 00.1
28	21 44.2	33 06.6
NOV 17	21 46.9	33 13.3
DEC 7	21 52.0	33 19.6
27	21N59.0	33N24.7
	4/25.13 11/12.82	3/22.60 10/12.71

1940	♌ Haumea 136108	♈ Makemake 136472
JAN 1	12R51.5	10R24.6
11	12♌41.8	10♋12.4
21	12 31.1	10 00.6
31	12 19.9	9 49.7
FEB 10	12 08.6	9 40.1
20	11 57.7	9 32.0
MAR 1	11 47.4	9 25.9
11	11 38.2	9 21.9
21	11 30.4	9 20.2
31	11 24.3	9D20.9
APR 10	11 20.0	9 23.8
20	11 17.8	9 29.0
30	11D17.7	9 36.3
MAY 10	11 19.6	9 45.6
20	11 23.7	9 56.5
30	11 29.6	10 08.9
JUN 9	11 37.4	10 22.4
19	11 46.7	10 36.7
29	11 57.4	10 51.5
JUL 9	12 09.3	11 06.4
19	12 22.0	11 21.2
29	12 35.2	11 35.4
AUG 8	12 48.7	11 48.7
18	13 02.1	12 00.9
28	13 15.1	12 11.6
SEP 7	13 27.4	12 20.6
17	13 38.7	12 27.7
27	13 48.7	12 32.6
OCT 7	13 57.2	12 35.2
17	14 03.8	12R35.5
27	14 08.6	12 33.5
NOV 6	14 11.2	12 29.3
16	14R11.7	12 22.9
26	14 10.0	12 14.6
DEC 6	14 06.3	12 04.8
16	14 00.6	11 53.8
26	13 53.1	11 42.0
JAN 5	13♌44.1	11♋29.8
JAN 1	22N01.0	33N25.7
21	22 09.2	33 28.6
FEB 10	22 17.1	33 29.5
MAR 1	22 23.9	33 28.5
21	22 28.7	33 26.0
APR 10	22 31.2	33 22.6
30	22 31.0	33 18.9
MAY 20	22 28.5	33 15.3
JUN 9	22 24.1	33 12.3
29	22 18.2	33 10.3
JUL 19	22 11.5	33 09.7
AUG 8	22 04.9	33 10.5
28	21 58.9	33 13.1
SEP 17	21 54.4	33 17.3
OCT 7	21 52.0	33 22.9
27	21 52.0	33 29.5
NOV 16	21 54.7	33 36.5
DEC 6	21 59.9	33 43.1
26	22N06.9	33N48.5
	4/25.36 11/13.00	3/23.02 10/13.12

1941	♌ Haumea 136108	♈ Makemake 136472
JAN 1	13R47.9	11R34.7
11	13♌38.2	11♋22.5
21	13 27.6	11 10.8
31	13 16.4	10 59.8
FEB 10	13 05.2	10 50.1
20	12 54.2	10 42.1
MAR 2	12 43.9	10 35.9
12	12 34.8	10 31.8
22	12 27.0	10 30.0
APR 1	12 20.8	10D30.5
11	12 16.6	10 33.4
21	12 14.3	10 38.5
MAY 1	12D14.1	10 45.7
11	12 16.0	10 54.9
21	12 20.0	11 05.7
31	12 25.9	11 18.0
JUN 10	12 33.6	11 31.4
20	12 42.9	11 45.7
30	12 53.6	12 00.4
JUL 10	13 05.4	12 15.3
20	13 18.0	12 30.1
30	13 31.2	12 44.3
AUG 9	13 44.7	12 57.7
19	13 58.0	13 09.9
29	14 11.0	13 20.6
SEP 8	14 23.3	13 29.7
18	14 34.6	13 36.8
28	14 44.6	13 41.8
OCT 8	14 53.1	13 44.5
18	14 59.8	13R45.0
28	15 04.6	13 43.1
NOV 7	15 07.2	13 38.9
17	15R07.8	13 32.6
27	15 06.2	13 24.5
DEC 7	15 02.4	13 14.7
17	14 56.8	13 03.8
27	14 49.3	12 52.0
JAN 6	14♌40.4	12♋39.8
JAN 1	22N09.3	33N49.8
21	22 17.7	33 52.9
FEB 10	22 25.7	33 53.9
MAR 2	22 32.6	33 52.9
22	22 37.4	33 50.3
APR 11	22 39.7	33 46.7
MAY 1	22 39.5	33 42.6
21	22 36.8	33 38.6
JUN 10	22 32.1	33 35.2
30	22 26.0	33 32.9
JUL 20	22 19.2	33 31.9
AUG 9	22 12.3	33 32.5
29	22 06.3	33 34.9
SEP 18	22 01.7	33 39.1
OCT 8	21 59.3	33 44.8
28	21 59.4	33 51.5
NOV 17	22 02.2	33 58.8
DEC 7	22 07.5	34 05.6
27	22N14.7	34N11.4
	4/26.56 11/14.20	3/24.46 10/14.56

1942	♌ Haumea 136108	♈ Makemake 136472
JAN 1	14R45.0	12R45.9
11	14♌35.5	12♋33.8
21	14 25.0	12 21.9
31	14 13.9	12 10.9
FEB 10	14 02.7	12 01.0
20	13 51.7	11 52.7
MAR 2	13 41.4	11 46.3
12	13 32.0	11 41.9
22	13 24.1	11 39.8
APR 1	13 17.8	11D40.0
11	13 13.3	11 42.5
21	13 10.8	11 47.3
MAY 1	13D10.3	11 54.2
11	13 12.0	12 03.0
21	13 15.7	12 13.7
31	13 21.4	12 25.7
JUN 10	13 28.8	12 39.0
20	13 37.9	12 53.1
30	13 48.4	13 07.8
JUL 10	14 00.1	13 22.7
20	14 12.6	13 37.4
30	14 25.8	13 51.7
AUG 9	14 39.2	14 05.2
19	14 52.5	14 17.6
29	15 05.6	14 28.6
SEP 8	15 17.9	14 37.9
18	15 29.3	14 45.3
28	15 39.5	14 50.6
OCT 8	15 48.1	14 53.6
18	15 55.1	14R54.4
28	16 00.0	14 52.8
NOV 7	16 03.0	14 48.9
17	16R03.8	14 43.0
27	16 02.4	14 35.1
DEC 7	15 58.9	14 25.5
17	15 53.5	14 14.7
27	15 46.3	14 03.1
JAN 6	15♌37.5	13♋51.0
JAN 1	22N16.8	34N12.5
21	22 25.2	34 16.0
FEB 10	22 33.4	34 17.2
MAR 2	22 40.4	34 16.2
22	22 45.3	34 13.6
APR 11	22 47.7	34 09.7
MAY 1	22 47.4	34 05.3
21	22 44.7	34 01.0
JUN 10	22 39.9	33 57.2
30	22 33.6	33 54.4
JUL 20	22 26.6	33 53.0
AUG 9	22 19.6	33 53.3
29	22 13.4	33 55.5
SEP 18	22 08.7	33 59.5
OCT 8	22 06.2	34 05.1
28	22 06.2	34 12.0
NOV 17	22 08.9	34 19.5
DEC 7	22 14.3	34 26.7
27	22N21.6	34N32.8
	4/27.76 11/15.35	3/25.85 10/15.94

1943	♌ Haumea 136108	♈ Makemake 136472
JAN 1	15R42.1	13R57.0
11	15♌32.7	13♋44.9
21	15 22.3	13 33.0
31	15 11.3	13 21.9
FEB 10	15 00.1	13 11.8
20	14 49.1	13 03.3
MAR 2	14 38.7	12 56.6
12	14 29.2	12 51.9
22	14 21.1	12 49.5
APR 1	14 14.6	12D49.3
11	14 09.9	12 51.5
21	14 07.1	12 56.0
MAY 1	14D06.5	13 02.6
11	14 07.9	13 11.2
21	14 11.3	13 21.5
31	14 16.7	13 33.4
JUN 10	14 24.0	13 46.5
20	14 32.9	14 00.5
30	14 43.2	14 15.0
JUL 10	14 54.7	14 29.9
20	15 07.1	14 44.7
30	15 20.2	14 59.0
AUG 9	15 33.5	15 12.6
19	15 46.9	15 25.2
29	16 00.0	15 36.3
SEP 8	16 12.4	15 45.9
18	16 23.9	15 53.5
28	16 34.3	15 59.1
OCT 8	16 43.1	16 02.5
18	16 50.2	16R03.6
28	16 55.4	16 02.3
NOV 7	16 58.6	15 58.8
17	16R59.6	15 53.1
27	16 58.5	15 45.5
DEC 7	16 55.3	15 36.2
17	16 50.1	15 25.5
27	16 43.1	15 14.0
JAN 6	16♌34.5	15♋01.9
JAN 1	22N23.6	34N34.0
21	22 32.2	34 37.7
FEB 10	22 40.5	34 39.2
MAR 2	22 47.6	34 38.4
22	22 52.7	34 35.7
APR 11	22 55.1	34 31.7
MAY 1	22 54.9	34 27.0
21	22 52.1	34 22.2
JUN 10	22 47.2	34 18.0
30	22 40.8	34 14.8
JUL 20	22 33.6	34 13.0
AUG 9	22 26.4	34 13.0
29	22 20.0	34 14.8
SEP 18	22 15.2	34 18.7
OCT 8	22 12.5	34 24.3
28	22 12.4	34 31.3
NOV 17	22 15.1	34 39.0
DEC 7	22 20.5	34 46.5
27	22N27.9	34N52.9
	4/28.99 11/16.56	3/27.30 10/17.37

1944	♌ Haumea 136108	♈ Makemake 136472
JAN 1	16R39.0	15R08.0
11	16♌29.8	14♋55.9
21	16 19.5	14 43.9
31	16 08.6	14 32.7
FEB 10	15 57.4	14 22.5
20	15 46.3	14 13.7
MAR 1	15 35.8	14 06.7
11	15 26.3	14 01.8
21	15 18.0	13 59.0
31	15 11.3	13D58.5
APR 10	15 06.4	14 00.4
20	15 03.4	14 04.5
30	15D02.5	14 10.8
MAY 10	15 03.6	14 19.1
20	15 06.8	14 29.2
30	15 12.0	14 40.9
JUN 9	15 19.1	14 53.8
19	15 27.7	15 07.6
29	15 37.9	15 22.1
JUL 9	15 49.2	15 36.9
19	16 01.5	15 51.7
29	16 14.5	16 06.1
AUG 8	16 27.8	16 19.8
18	16 41.2	16 32.5
28	16 54.3	16 43.9
SEP 7	17 06.8	16 53.6
17	17 18.4	17 01.6
27	17 28.9	17 07.5
OCT 7	17 37.9	17 11.2
17	17 45.2	17 12.5
27	17 50.6	17R11.6
NOV 6	17 54.1	17 08.4
16	17 55.3	17 03.0
26	17R54.5	16 55.6
DEC 6	17 51.5	16 46.6
16	17 46.5	16 36.1
26	17 39.7	16 24.7
JAN 5	17♌31.3	16♋12.7
JAN 1	22N29.9	34N54.3
21	22 38.6	34 58.3
FEB 10	22 47.1	35 00.0
MAR 1	22 54.4	34 59.3
21	22 59.5	34 56.6
APR 10	23 02.0	34 52.5
30	23 01.8	34 47.5
MAY 20	22 58.9	34 42.4
JUN 9	22 53.9	34 37.7
29	22 47.4	34 34.1
JUL 19	22 40.1	34 31.9
AUG 8	22 32.7	34 31.5
28	22 26.2	34 33.1
SEP 17	22 21.1	34 36.8
OCT 7	22 18.3	34 42.4
27	22 18.2	34 49.4
NOV 16	22 20.8	34 57.3
DEC 6	22 26.2	35 05.1
26	22N33.6	35N11.9
	4/29.15 11/16.70	3/27.70 10/17.74

1945	Haumea 136108	Makemake 136472
JAN 1	17R34.9	16R17.5
11	17♌25.7	16♋05.4
21	17 15.5	15 53.5
31	17 04.6	15 42.2
FEB 10	16 53.4	15 31.9
20	16 42.4	15 23.1
MAR 2	16 31.9	15 16.1
12	16 22.3	15 11.1
22	16 14.1	15 08.2
APR 1	16 07.3	15D07.6
11	16 02.4	15 09.4
21	15 59.4	15 13.4
MAY 1	15D58.4	15 19.6
11	15 59.5	15 27.8
21	16 02.7	15 37.8
31	16 07.8	15 49.4
JUN 10	16 14.8	16 02.2
20	16 23.4	16 16.0
30	16 33.5	16 30.4
JUL 10	16 44.8	16 45.2
20	16 57.1	17 00.0
30	17 10.0	17 14.4
AUG 9	17 23.3	17 28.1
19	17 36.6	17 40.8
29	17 49.7	17 52.2
SEP 8	18 02.2	18 02.1
18	18 13.9	18 10.1
28	18 24.3	18 16.0
OCT 8	18 33.3	18 19.8
18	18 40.7	18 21.3
28	18 46.1	18R20.4
NOV 7	18 49.6	18 17.3
17	18 50.9	18 12.0
27	18R50.1	18 04.7
DEC 7	18 47.1	17 55.7
17	18 42.2	17 45.3
27	18 35.4	17 33.9
JAN 6	18♌27.1	17♋21.9
JAN 1	22N36.1	35N13.6
21	22 45.0	35 17.9
FEB 10	22 53.6	35 19.7
MAR 2	23 00.8	35 19.1
22	23 06.0	35 16.3
APR 11	23 08.4	35 11.9
MAY 1	23 08.1	35 06.7
21	23 05.1	35 01.2
JUN 10	22 59.9	34 56.2
30	22 53.2	34 52.2
JUL 20	22 45.7	34 49.7
AUG 9	22 38.2	34 49.0
29	22 31.5	34 50.4
SEP 18	22 26.4	34 54.0
OCT 8	22 23.6	34 59.6
28	22 23.4	35 06.8
NOV 17	22 26.2	35 14.8
DEC 7	22 31.7	35 22.9
27	22N39.3	35N30.0
	4/30.39	3/29.14
	11/17.85	10/19.11

1946	Haumea 136108	Makemake 136472
JAN 1	18R31.4	17R28.0
11	18♌22.4	17♋15.9
21	18 12.3	17 03.9
31	18 01.5	16 52.5
FEB 10	17 50.3	16 42.1
20	17 39.3	16 33.1
MAR 2	17 28.8	16 25.8
12	17 19.1	16 20.5
22	17 10.7	16 17.3
APR 1	17 03.8	16D16.4
11	16 58.6	16 17.9
21	16 55.4	16 21.6
MAY 1	16 54.1	16 27.4
11	16D55.0	16 35.4
21	16 57.9	16 45.1
31	17 02.8	16 56.4
JUN 10	17 09.5	17 09.1
20	17 18.0	17 22.7
30	17 27.9	17 37.1
JUL 10	17 39.0	17 51.8
20	17 51.2	18 06.5
30	18 04.0	18 21.0
AUG 9	18 17.3	18 34.8
19	18 30.6	18 47.7
29	18 43.7	18 59.3
SEP 8	18 56.3	19 09.3
18	19 08.0	19 17.6
28	19 18.6	19 23.8
OCT 8	19 27.8	19 27.9
18	19 35.3	19 29.7
28	19 41.0	19R29.2
NOV 7	19 44.7	19 26.3
17	19 46.3	19 21.3
27	19R45.7	19 14.3
DEC 7	19 43.0	19 05.5
17	19 38.3	18 55.3
27	19 31.7	18 44.0
JAN 6	19♌23.5	18♋32.1
JAN 1	22N41.4	35N31.5
21	22 50.3	35 36.1
FEB 10	22 59.1	35 38.2
MAR 2	23 06.5	35 37.7
22	23 11.7	35 35.0
APR 11	23 14.3	35 30.5
MAY 1	23 13.9	35 25.0
21	23 10.9	35 19.2
JUN 10	23 05.7	35 13.8
30	22 58.8	35 09.4
JUL 20	22 51.2	35 06.5
AUG 9	22 43.5	35 05.4
29	22 36.6	35 06.5
SEP 18	22 31.4	35 09.9
OCT 8	22 28.4	35 15.4
28	22 28.2	35 22.6
NOV 17	22 30.9	35 30.9
DEC 7	22 36.4	35 39.2
27	22N44.0	35N46.6
	5/1.59	3/30.57
	11/19.03	10/20.50

1947	Haumea 136108	Makemake 136472
JAN 1	19R27.8	18R38.1
11	19♌19.0	18♋26.1
21	19 09.0	18 14.1
31	18 58.2	18 02.6
FEB 10	18 47.1	17 52.0
20	18 36.0	17 42.8
MAR 2	18 25.4	17 35.3
12	18 15.7	17 29.7
22	18 07.1	17 26.2
APR 1	18 00.0	17D25.0
11	17 54.6	17 26.1
21	17 51.1	17 29.5
MAY 1	17 49.7	17 35.0
11	17D50.3	17 42.6
21	17 53.0	17 52.1
31	17 57.6	18 03.2
JUN 10	18 04.1	18 15.7
20	18 12.3	18 29.2
30	18 22.1	18 43.4
JUL 10	18 33.1	18 58.1
20	18 45.1	19 12.8
30	18 57.9	19 27.3
AUG 9	19 11.0	19 41.2
19	19 24.4	19 54.2
29	19 37.5	20 06.0
SEP 8	19 50.1	20 16.2
18	20 01.9	20 24.7
28	20 12.7	20 31.3
OCT 8	20 22.0	20 35.6
18	20 29.7	20 37.8
28	20 35.6	20R37.5
NOV 7	20 39.6	20 35.0
17	20 41.4	20 30.3
27	20R41.0	20 23.6
DEC 7	20 38.6	20 15.0
17	20 34.1	20 05.0
27	20 27.7	19 53.8
JAN 6	20♌19.8	19♋42.0
JAN 1	22N46.1	35N48.2
21	22 55.2	35 53.2
FEB 10	23 04.1	35 55.6
MAR 2	23 11.6	35 55.3
22	23 17.0	35 52.6
APR 11	23 19.6	35 48.0
MAY 1	23 19.4	35 42.3
21	23 16.3	35 36.2
JUN 10	23 11.0	35 30.4
30	23 04.0	35 25.6
JUL 20	22 56.2	35 22.2
AUG 9	22 48.4	35 20.8
29	22 41.3	35 21.6
SEP 18	22 35.9	35 24.8
OCT 8	22 32.8	35 30.2
28	22 32.5	35 37.4
NOV 17	22 35.1	35 45.8
DEC 7	22 40.6	35 54.4
27	22N48.3	36N02.2
	5/2.78	3/31.96
	11/20.14	10/21.83

1948	Haumea 136108	Makemake 136472
JAN 1	20R23.9	19R48.0
11	20♌15.2	19♋36.0
21	20 05.4	19 23.9
31	19 54.7	19 12.4
FEB 10	19 43.6	19 01.7
20	19 32.6	18 52.3
MAR 1	19 21.9	18 44.5
11	19 12.0	18 38.6
21	19 03.3	18 34.8
31	18 56.0	18 33.3
APR 10	18 50.4	18D34.0
20	18 46.7	18 37.1
30	18 45.0	18 42.4
MAY 10	18D45.4	18 49.7
20	18 47.8	18 58.9
30	18 52.2	19 09.7
JUN 9	18 58.5	19 22.0
19	19 06.5	19 35.3
29	19 16.1	19 49.5
JUL 9	19 26.9	20 04.1
19	19 38.8	20 18.8
29	19 51.5	20 33.3
AUG 8	20 04.6	20 47.3
18	20 17.9	21 00.4
28	20 31.0	21 12.4
SEP 7	20 43.7	21 22.8
17	20 55.6	21 31.6
27	21 06.5	21 38.4
OCT 7	21 16.0	21 43.1
17	21 23.9	21 45.5
27	21 30.0	21R45.6
NOV 6	21 34.2	21 43.4
16	21 36.2	21 39.0
26	21R36.1	21 32.5
DEC 6	21 33.9	21 24.2
16	21 29.7	21 14.3
26	21 23.5	21 03.3
JAN 5	21♌15.7	20♋51.6
JAN 1	22N50.4	36N03.8
21	22 59.6	36 09.2
FEB 10	23 08.6	36 11.9
MAR 1	23 16.3	36 11.8
21	23 21.8	36 09.2
APR 10	23 24.6	36 04.5
30	23 24.3	35 58.6
MAY 20	23 21.3	35 52.2
JUN 9	23 15.9	35 46.0
29	23 08.8	35 40.8
JUL 19	23 00.8	35 37.0
AUG 8	22 52.8	35 35.2
28	22 45.6	35 35.7
SEP 17	22 40.0	35 38.6
OCT 7	22 36.8	35 43.9
27	22 36.3	35 51.2
NOV 16	22 38.9	35 59.7
DEC 6	22 44.4	36 08.5
26	22N52.1	36N16.6
	5/3.02	4/1.42
	11/20.30	10/22.21

1949	Haumea 136108	Makemake 136472
JAN 1	21R19.0	20R56.3
11	21♌10.3	20♋44.3
21	21 00.5	20 32.3
31	20 49.9	20 20.7
FEB 10	20 38.8	20 10.0
20	20 27.7	20 00.6
MAR 2	20 17.1	19 52.7
12	20 07.2	19 46.8
22	19 58.5	19 42.9
APR 1	19 51.2	19 41.3
11	19 45.6	19D41.9
21	19 41.8	19 44.9
MAY 1	19 40.1	19 50.0
11	19D40.4	19 57.3
21	19 42.8	20 06.4
31	19 47.1	20 17.2
JUN 10	19 53.4	20 29.3
20	20 01.3	20 42.6
30	20 10.8	20 56.7
JUL 10	20 21.7	21 11.3
20	20 33.5	21 26.0
30	20 46.1	21 40.5
AUG 9	20 59.2	21 54.5
19	21 12.5	22 07.6
29	21 25.6	22 19.6
SEP 8	21 38.3	22 30.1
18	21 50.2	22 38.9
28	22 01.1	22 45.8
OCT 8	22 10.6	22 50.5
18	22 18.5	22 53.0
28	22 24.7	22R53.2
NOV 7	22 28.8	22 51.1
17	22 30.9	22 46.8
27	22R30.9	22 40.4
DEC 7	22 28.7	22 32.1
17	22 24.5	22 22.3
27	22 18.3	22 11.4
JAN 6	22♌10.6	21♋59.6
JAN 1	22N54.7	36N18.7
21	23 04.0	36 24.3
FEB 10	23 13.1	36 27.2
MAR 2	23 20.9	36 27.2
22	23 26.5	36 24.5
APR 11	23 29.1	36 19.7
MAY 1	23 28.8	36 13.6
21	23 25.6	36 06.9
JUN 10	23 20.1	36 00.4
30	23 12.8	35 54.8
JUL 20	23 04.7	35 50.7
AUG 9	22 56.5	35 48.6
29	22 49.2	35 48.9
SEP 18	22 43.6	35 51.7
OCT 8	22 40.3	35 57.0
28	22 39.9	36 04.3
NOV 17	22 42.6	36 13.0
DEC 7	22 48.1	36 22.0
27	22N56.0	36N30.4
	5/4.19	4/2.81
	11/21.42	10/23.55

1950	Haumea 136108	Makemake 136472
JAN 1	22R14.6	22R05.6
11	22♌06.1	21♋53.6
21	21 56.4	21 41.6
31	21 45.9	21 29.9
FEB 10	21 34.8	21 19.1
20	21 23.8	21 09.5
MAR 2	21 13.1	21 01.4
12	21 03.1	20 55.2
22	20 54.2	20 51.0
APR 1	20 46.7	20 49.1
11	20 40.9	20D49.4
21	20 37.0	20 52.0
MAY 1	20 35.0	20 56.9
11	20D35.1	21 03.8
21	20 37.2	21 12.7
31	20 41.3	21 23.2
JUN 10	20 47.3	21 35.2
20	20 55.1	21 48.3
30	21 04.4	22 02.3
JUL 10	21 15.0	22 16.8
20	21 26.8	22 31.5
30	21 39.3	22 46.0
AUG 9	21 52.3	23 00.1
19	22 05.6	23 13.3
29	22 18.8	23 25.5
SEP 8	22 31.5	23 36.2
18	22 43.5	23 45.2
28	22 54.5	23 52.4
OCT 8	23 04.1	23 57.4
18	23 12.3	24 00.2
28	23 18.6	24R00.7
NOV 7	23 23.0	23 58.9
17	23 25.3	23 54.9
27	23R25.5	23 48.7
DEC 7	23 23.5	23 40.7
17	23 19.5	23 31.1
27	23 13.6	23 20.3
JAN 6	23♌06.1	23♋08.7
JAN 1	22N58.2	36N32.2
21	23 07.6	36 38.1
FEB 10	23 16.9	36 41.3
MAR 2	23 24.8	36 41.5
22	23 30.5	36 39.0
APR 11	23 33.3	36 34.2
MAY 1	23 33.0	36 27.9
21	23 29.8	36 20.9
JUN 10	23 24.2	36 14.0
30	23 16.9	36 08.0
JUL 20	23 08.6	36 03.5
AUG 9	23 00.3	36 01.0
29	22 52.8	36 01.0
SEP 18	22 47.0	36 03.5
OCT 8	22 43.6	36 08.6
28	22 43.1	36 15.9
NOV 17	22 45.6	36 24.7
DEC 7	22 51.2	36 34.0
27	22N59.1	36N42.6
	5/5.40	4/4.21
	11/22.55	10/24.92

1951	Haumea 136108	Makemake 136472
JAN 1	23R10.0	23R14.6
11	23♌01.7	23♋02.7
21	22 52.1	22 50.7
31	22 41.7	22 39.0
FEB 10	22 30.7	22 28.0
20	22 19.6	22 18.2
MAR 2	22 08.8	22 09.9
12	21 58.8	22 03.4
22	21 49.8	21 59.0
APR 1	21 42.1	21 56.7
11	21 36.1	21D56.7
21	21 31.9	21 59.1
MAY 1	21 29.7	22 03.6
11	21D29.5	22 10.2
21	21 31.4	22 18.8
31	21 35.3	22 29.1
JUN 10	21 41.1	22 40.9
20	21 48.6	22 53.9
30	21 57.8	23 07.7
JUL 10	22 08.3	23 22.1
20	22 19.9	23 36.8
30	22 32.3	23 51.4
AUG 9	22 45.3	24 05.5
19	22 58.5	24 18.9
29	23 11.7	24 31.2
SEP 8	23 24.5	24 42.1
18	23 36.5	24 51.4
28	23 47.6	24 58.8
OCT 8	23 57.5	25 04.1
18	24 05.8	25 07.2
28	24 12.3	25R08.1
NOV 7	24 16.9	25 06.6
17	24 19.5	25 02.8
27	24R19.9	24 57.0
DEC 7	24 18.2	24 49.2
17	24 14.5	24 39.8
27	24 08.8	24 29.2
JAN 6	24♌01.4	24♋17.6
JAN 1	23N01.3	36N44.5
21	23 10.8	36 50.8
FEB 10	23 20.2	36 54.3
MAR 2	23 28.3	36 54.8
22	23 34.1	36 52.4
APR 11	23 37.0	36 47.5
MAY 1	23 36.8	36 41.1
21	23 33.6	36 33.8
JUN 10	23 28.0	36 26.6
30	23 20.5	36 20.2
JUL 20	23 12.1	36 15.3
AUG 9	23 03.7	36 12.4
29	22 56.0	36 12.0
SEP 18	22 50.0	36 14.3
OCT 8	22 46.5	36 19.3
28	22 45.8	36 26.5
NOV 17	22 48.3	36 35.4
DEC 7	22 53.8	36 44.8
27	23N01.8	36N53.8
	5/6.58	4/5.61
	11/23.70	10/26.30

1952	Haumea 136108	Makemake 136472
JAN 1	24R05.3	24R23.5
11	23♌57.1	24♋11.7
21	23 47.6	23 59.7
31	23 37.3	23 47.9
FEB 10	23 26.3	23 36.8
20	23 15.3	23 26.8
MAR 1	23 04.5	23 18.3
11	22 54.3	23 11.6
21	22 45.2	23 06.9
31	22 37.4	23 04.3
APR 10	22 31.2	23D04.0
20	22 26.8	23 06.0
30	22 24.3	23 10.3
MAY 10	22D23.9	23 16.6
20	22 25.5	23 24.9
30	22 29.2	23 35.0
JUN 9	22 34.8	23 46.6
19	22 42.1	23 59.3
29	22 51.0	24 13.1
JUL 9	23 01.4	24 27.4
19	23 12.8	24 42.1
29	23 25.2	24 56.6
AUG 8	23 38.1	25 10.8
18	23 51.3	25 24.3
28	24 04.5	25 36.8
SEP 7	24 17.3	25 47.9
17	24 29.5	25 57.4
27	24 40.7	26 05.1
OCT 7	24 50.7	26 10.7
17	24 59.2	26 14.1
27	25 05.9	26R15.3
NOV 6	25 10.8	26 14.1
16	25 13.6	26 10.7
26	25R14.2	26 05.1
DEC 6	25 12.8	25 57.6
16	25 09.2	25 48.4
26	25 03.8	25 37.9
JAN 5	24♌56.6	25♋26.5
JAN 1	23N04.0	36N55.8
21	23 13.6	37 02.4
FEB 10	23 23.1	37 06.2
MAR 1	23 31.4	37 06.9
21	23 37.3	37 04.6
APR 10	23 40.4	36 59.8
30	23 40.2	36 53.2
MAY 20	23 37.1	36 45.7
JUN 9	23 31.4	36 38.2
29	23 23.8	36 31.4
JUL 19	23 15.3	36 26.0
AUG 8	23 06.7	36 22.8
28	22 58.9	36 22.0
SEP 17	22 52.7	36 24.0
OCT 7	22 49.0	36 28.7
27	22 48.2	36 35.9
NOV 16	22 50.6	36 44.8
DEC 6	22 56.1	36 54.5
26	23N04.0	37N03.7
	5/6.74	4/5.96
	11/23.82	10/26.64

1953	Haumea 136108	Makemake 136472
JAN 1	24R59.6	25R31.2
11	24♌51.5	25♋19.4
21	24 42.1	25 07.4
31	24 31.7	24 55.7
FEB 10	24 20.8	24 44.6
20	24 09.8	24 34.5
MAR 2	23 59.0	24 26.0
12	23 48.8	24 19.2
22	23 39.7	24 14.4
APR 1	23 31.9	24 11.8
11	23 25.6	24D11.4
21	23 21.2	24 13.3
MAY 1	23 18.8	24 17.5
11	23D18.3	24 23.7
21	23 19.9	24 31.9
31	23 23.5	24 41.9
JUN 10	23 29.0	24 53.4
20	23 36.3	25 06.2
30	23 45.3	25 19.9
JUL 10	23 55.6	25 34.2
20	24 07.0	25 48.8
30	24 19.3	26 03.4
AUG 9	24 32.2	26 17.6
19	24 45.4	26 31.1
29	24 58.6	26 43.6
SEP 8	25 11.4	26 54.7
18	25 23.6	27 04.3
28	25 34.8	27 12.1
OCT 8	25 44.8	27 17.8
18	25 53.3	27 21.3
28	26 00.1	27 22.5
NOV 7	26 04.9	27R21.4
17	26 07.8	27 18.1
27	26R08.5	27 12.6
DEC 7	26 07.1	27 05.1
17	26 03.6	26 56.0
27	25 58.1	26 45.6
JAN 6	25♌50.9	26♋34.2
JAN 1	23N06.8	37N06.1
21	23 16.5	37 13.0
FEB 10	23 26.1	37 17.0
MAR 2	23 34.4	37 17.8
22	23 40.3	37 15.5
APR 11	23 43.3	37 10.6
MAY 1	23 43.1	37 03.8
21	23 39.8	36 56.0
JUN 10	23 34.0	36 48.2
30	23 26.3	36 41.1
JUL 20	23 17.6	36 35.4
AUG 9	23 08.8	36 31.8
29	23 00.9	36 30.8
SEP 18	22 54.7	36 32.7
OCT 8	22 50.9	36 37.3
28	22 50.1	36 44.5
NOV 17	22 52.6	36 53.5
DEC 7	22 58.2	37 03.4
27	23N06.2	37N12.8
	5/7.93	4/7.36
	11/25.01	10/28.06

1954	Haumea 136108	Makemake 136472
JAN 1	25R54.7	26R40.0
11	25♌46.8	26♋28.3
21	25 37.5	26 16.4
31	25 27.2	26 04.5
FEB 10	25 16.4	25 53.3
20	25 05.4	25 43.2
MAR 2	24 54.5	25 34.4
12	24 44.3	25 27.4
22	24 35.0	25 22.3
APR 1	24 27.1	25 19.4
11	24 20.7	25D18.7
21	24 16.0	25 20.3
MAY 1	24 13.3	25 24.1
11	24D12.6	25 30.1
21	24 14.0	25 38.1
31	24 17.4	25 47.8
JUN 10	24 22.7	25 59.1
20	24 29.8	26 11.7
30	24 38.5	26 25.2
JUL 10	24 48.6	26 39.4
20	24 59.9	26 54.0
30	25 12.2	27 08.6
AUG 9	25 25.0	27 22.9
19	25 38.2	27 36.5
29	25 51.4	27 49.1
SEP 8	26 04.2	28 00.5
18	26 16.5	28 10.3
28	26 27.8	28 18.3
OCT 8	26 38.0	28 24.3
18	26 46.7	28 28.1
28	26 53.6	28 29.6
NOV 7	26 58.7	28R28.9
17	27 01.8	28 25.8
27	27R02.8	28 20.6
DEC 7	27 01.6	28 13.4
17	26 58.3	28 04.6
27	26 53.1	27 54.3
JAN 6	26♌46.1	27♋43.0
JAN 1	23N08.5	37N14.9
21	23 18.3	37 22.1
FEB 10	23 28.1	37 26.4
MAR 2	23 36.5	37 27.5
22	23 42.6	37 25.4
APR 11	23 45.7	37 20.5
MAY 1	23 45.5	37 13.6
21	23 42.3	37 05.6
JUN 10	23 36.4	36 57.5
30	23 28.6	36 49.9
JUL 20	23 19.8	36 43.9
AUG 9	23 10.9	36 39.9
29	23 02.8	36 38.5
SEP 18	22 56.4	36 40.0
OCT 8	22 52.5	36 44.5
28	22 51.6	36 51.6
NOV 17	22 53.9	37 00.6
DEC 7	22 59.4	37 10.6
27	23N07.5	37N20.3
	5/9.05	4/8.70
	11/26.14	10/29.40

1955	Haumea 136108	Makemake 136472
JAN 1	26R49.8	27R48.8
11	26♌42.0	27♋37.2
21	26 32.9	27 25.2
31	26 22.8	27 13.4
FEB 10	26 12.0	27 02.1
20	26 00.9	26 51.8
MAR 2	25 50.1	26 42.8
12	25 39.8	26 35.5
22	25 30.4	26 30.2
APR 1	25 22.3	26 27.0
11	25 15.7	26D26.0
21	25 10.8	26 27.3
MAY 1	25 07.9	26 30.8
11	25D07.0	26 36.5
21	25 08.1	26 44.1
31	25 11.3	26 53.6
JUN 10	25 16.3	27 04.7
20	25 23.2	27 17.1
30	25 31.8	27 30.5
JUL 10	25 41.7	27 44.7
20	25 52.9	27 59.2
30	26 05.0	28 13.8
AUG 9	26 17.8	28 28.1
19	26 31.0	28 41.8
29	26 44.1	28 54.6
SEP 8	26 57.0	29 06.1
18	27 09.4	29 16.1
28	27 20.9	29 24.4
OCT 8	27 31.2	29 30.7
18	27 40.0	29 34.8
28	27 47.2	29 36.6
NOV 7	27 52.5	29R36.2
17	27 55.8	29 33.5
27	27 57.0	29 28.5
DEC 7	27R56.1	29 21.6
17	27 53.1	29 13.0
27	27 48.1	29 02.9
JAN 6	27♌41.3	28♋51.7
JAN 1	23N09.8	37N22.5
21	23 19.6	37 30.0
FEB 10	23 29.5	37 34.7
MAR 2	23 38.1	37 36.0
22	23 44.3	37 34.1
APR 11	23 47.6	37 29.2
MAY 1	23 47.5	37 22.3
21	23 44.2	37 14.1
JUN 10	23 38.3	37 05.6
30	23 30.5	36 57.7
JUL 20	23 21.6	36 51.3
AUG 9	23 12.5	36 46.9
29	23 04.2	36 45.1
SEP 18	22 57.6	36 46.3
OCT 8	22 53.5	36 50.5
28	22 52.5	36 57.5
NOV 17	22 54.7	37 06.5
DEC 7	23 00.1	37 16.7
27	23N08.2	37N26.6
	5/10.24	4/10.10
	11/27.29	10/30.77

1956	Haumea 136108	Makemake 136472
JAN 1	27R44.9	28R57.4
11	27♌37.3	28♋45.9
21	27 28.3	28 34.0
31	27 18.3	28 22.1
FEB 10	27 07.5	28 10.7
20	26 56.5	28 00.3
MAR 1	26 45.6	27 51.1
11	26 35.2	27 43.6
21	26 25.8	27 38.0
31	26 17.5	27 34.5
APR 10	26 10.7	27 33.2
20	26 05.7	27D34.1
30	26 02.5	27 37.3
MAY 10	26 01.3	27 42.7
20	26D02.2	27 50.1
30	26 05.1	27 59.3
JUN 9	26 10.0	28 10.2
19	26 16.7	28 22.4
29	26 25.0	28 35.7
JUL 9	26 34.8	28 49.7
19	26 45.9	29 04.2
29	26 57.9	29 18.8
AUG 8	27 10.6	29 33.1
18	27 23.7	29 46.9
28	27 36.9	29 59.8
SEP 7	27 49.8	0♌11.6
17	28 02.3	0 21.8
27	28 13.8	0 30.3
OCT 7	28 24.3	0 36.8
17	28 33.3	0 41.3
27	28 40.7	0 43.4
NOV 6	28 46.2	0R43.3
16	28 49.8	0 40.8
26	28 51.2	0 36.2
DEC 6	28R50.5	0 29.6
16	28 47.7	0 21.1
26	28 42.9	0 11.2
JAN 5	28♌36.4	0♌00.2
JAN 1	23N10.5	37N28.9
21	23 20.4	37 36.7
FEB 10	23 30.4	37 41.7
MAR 1	23 39.1	37 43.4
21	23 45.5	37 41.6
APR 10	23 48.9	37 36.9
30	23 48.9	37 29.9
MAY 20	23 45.7	37 21.5
JUN 9	23 39.8	37 12.7
29	23 31.9	37 04.5
JUL 19	23 22.8	36 57.6
AUG 8	23 13.6	36 52.9
28	23 05.1	36 50.7
SEP 17	22 58.4	36 51.6
OCT 7	22 54.1	36 55.6
27	22 52.9	37 02.4
NOV 16	22 55.0	37 11.4
DEC 6	23 00.4	37 21.7
26	23N08.5	37N31.8
	5/10.40	4/10.48
	11/27.47	10/31.13

1957	Haumea 136108	Makemake 136472
JAN 1	28R39.2	0R04.7
11	28♌31.6	29♋53.2
21	28 22.7	29 41.3
31	28 12.6	29 29.5
FEB 10	28 01.9	29 18.1
20	27 50.9	29 07.6
MAR 2	27 40.0	28 58.4
12	27 29.7	28 50.8
22	27 20.2	28 45.1
APR 1	27 11.9	28 41.5
11	27 05.1	28 40.1
21	27 00.0	28D41.0
MAY 1	26 56.8	28 44.1
11	26 55.6	28 49.4
21	26D56.5	28 56.7
31	26 59.3	29 05.9
JUN 10	27 04.1	29 16.6
20	27 10.8	29 28.8
30	27 19.1	29 42.0
JUL 10	27 28.9	29 56.0
20	27 39.9	0♌10.4
30	27 51.9	0 25.0
AUG 9	28 04.6	0 39.4
19	28 17.6	0 53.2
29	28 30.8	1 06.1
SEP 8	28 43.8	1 17.9
18	28 56.2	1 28.1
28	29 07.8	1 36.7
OCT 8	29 18.3	1 43.3
18	29 27.3	1 47.8
28	29 34.7	1 50.0
NOV 7	29 40.3	1R50.0
17	29 43.9	1 47.6
27	29 45.3	1 43.1
DEC 7	29R44.7	1 36.5
17	29 41.9	1 28.1
27	29 37.2	1 18.2
JAN 6	29♌30.6	1♌07.3
JAN 1	23N11.2	37N34.6
21	23 21.3	37 42.7
FEB 10	23 31.3	37 47.9
MAR 2	23 40.1	37 49.7
22	23 46.5	37 48.0
APR 11	23 49.9	37 43.2
MAY 1	23 49.8	37 36.1
21	23 46.5	37 27.5
JUN 10	23 40.5	37 18.5
30	23 32.4	37 10.0
JUL 20	23 23.2	37 02.8
AUG 9	23 13.8	36 57.7
29	23 05.3	36 55.3
SEP 18	22 58.4	36 56.0
OCT 8	22 54.1	36 59.9
28	22 52.9	37 06.7
NOV 17	22 55.1	37 15.8
DEC 7	23 00.6	37 26.2
27	23N08.7	37N36.6
	5/11.55	4/11.85
	11/28.57	11/1.46

1958	Haumea 136108	Makemake 136472
JAN 1	29R34.1	1R12.9
11	29♌26.7	1♌01.5
21	29 17.9	0 49.6
31	29 08.0	0 37.7
FEB 10	28 57.3	0 26.3
20	28 46.3	0 15.6
MAR 2	28 35.4	0 06.3
12	28 25.0	29♋58.5
22	28 15.4	29 52.5
APR 1	28 06.9	29 48.6
11	27 59.9	29 46.9
21	27 54.7	29D47.4
MAY 1	27 51.2	29 50.2
11	27 49.8	29 55.2
21	27D50.4	0♌02.2
31	27 53.0	0 11.1
JUN 10	27 57.6	0 21.7
20	28 04.1	0 33.6
30	28 12.2	0 46.7
JUL 10	28 21.8	1 00.6
20	28 32.7	1 15.0
30	28 44.5	1 29.5
AUG 9	28 57.2	1 43.9
19	29 10.2	1 57.8
29	29 23.4	2 10.9
SEP 8	29 36.4	2 22.8
18	29 48.9	2 33.3
28	0♍00.6	2 42.1
OCT 8	0 11.2	2 48.9
18	0 20.4	2 53.7
28	0 28.0	2 56.2
NOV 7	0 33.8	2R56.5
17	0 37.6	2 54.4
27	0 39.3	2 50.2
DEC 7	0R38.8	2 43.9
17	0 36.3	2 35.7
27	0 31.8	2 26.0
JAN 6	0♍25.4	2♌15.2
JAN 1	23N11.1	37N39.0
21	23 21.1	37 47.4
FEB 10	23 31.3	37 52.9
MAR 2	23 40.3	37 55.0
22	23 46.8	37 53.6
APR 11	23 50.3	37 48.9
MAY 1	23 50.4	37 41.7
21	23 47.1	37 33.0
JUN 10	23 41.1	37 23.7
30	23 32.9	37 14.9
JUL 20	23 23.6	37 07.3
AUG 9	23 14.1	37 01.9
29	23 05.4	36 59.1
SEP 18	22 58.4	36 59.5
OCT 8	22 53.9	37 03.1
28	22 52.6	37 09.8
NOV 17	22 54.6	37 18.8
DEC 7	23 00.0	37 29.3
27	23N08.1	37N39.9
	5/12.77	4/13.29
	11/29.73	11/2.81

1959	Haumea 136108	Makemake 136472
JAN 1	0R28.8	2R20.7
11	0♍21.6	2♌09.4
21	0 12.9	1 57.6
31	0 03.1	1 45.7
FEB 10	29♌52.6	1 34.2
20	29 41.6	1 23.4
MAR 2	29 30.7	1 13.8
12	29 20.1	1 05.8
22	29 10.4	0 59.6
APR 1	29 01.8	0 55.4
11	28 54.7	0 53.4
21	28 49.2	0D53.6
MAY 1	28 45.6	0 56.1
11	28 43.9	1 00.8
21	28D44.2	1 07.5
31	28 46.6	1 16.1
JUN 10	28 51.0	1 26.5
20	28 57.2	1 38.2
30	29 05.1	1 51.1
JUL 10	29 14.6	2 04.9
20	29 25.3	2 19.2
30	29 37.0	2 33.7
AUG 9	29 49.6	2 48.1
19	0♍02.6	3 02.1
29	0 15.8	3 15.3
SEP 8	0 28.8	3 27.3
18	0 41.3	3 38.0
28	0 53.1	3 47.1
OCT 8	1 03.9	3 54.2
18	1 13.3	3 59.3
28	1 21.1	4 02.1
NOV 7	1 27.1	4R02.7
17	1 31.1	4 00.9
27	1 33.0	3 56.9
DEC 7	1R32.9	3 50.9
17	1 30.6	3 42.9
27	1 26.2	3 33.5
JAN 6	1♍20.1	3♌22.7
JAN 1	23N10.5	37N42.3
21	23 20.6	37 51.1
FEB 10	23 30.9	37 57.0
MAR 2	23 40.0	37 59.4
22	23 46.8	37 58.2
APR 11	23 50.4	37 53.6
MAY 1	23 50.5	37 46.5
21	23 47.4	37 37.6
JUN 10	23 41.3	37 28.1
30	23 33.2	37 19.0
JUL 20	23 23.8	37 11.1
AUG 9	23 14.1	37 05.2
29	23 05.2	37 02.1
SEP 18	22 58.0	37 02.1
OCT 8	22 53.4	37 05.4
28	22 51.9	37 11.9
NOV 17	22 53.8	37 20.9
DEC 7	22 59.1	37 31.5
27	23N07.2	37N42.3
	5/13.92	4/14.65
	11/30.85	11/4.11

1960	Haumea 136108	Makemake 136472
JAN 1	1R23.4	3R28.2
11	1♍16.4	3♌17.1
21	1 07.8	3 05.3
31	0 58.2	2 53.4
FEB 10	0 47.6	2 41.8
20	0 36.7	2 30.9
MAR 1	0 25.7	2 21.1
11	0 15.2	2 12.9
21	0 05.3	2 06.4
31	29♌56.6	2 01.9
APR 10	29 49.3	1 59.6
20	29 43.6	1D59.5
30	29 39.7	2 01.7
MAY 10	29 37.8	2 06.1
20	29D37.9	2 12.5
30	29 40.1	2 20.9
JUN 9	29 44.2	2 31.0
19	29 50.2	2 42.5
29	29 57.9	2 55.3
JUL 9	0♍07.2	3 08.9
19	0 17.8	3 23.2
29	0 29.4	3 37.7
AUG 8	0 41.9	3 52.1
18	0 54.8	4 06.1
28	1 08.0	4 19.4
SEP 7	1 21.0	4 31.6
17	1 33.7	4 42.5
27	1 45.6	4 51.8
OCT 7	1 56.4	4 59.2
17	2 06.0	5 04.5
27	2 14.0	5 07.7
NOV 6	2 20.2	5R08.5
16	2 24.4	5 07.1
26	2 26.6	5 03.4
DEC 6	2R26.7	4 57.6
16	2 24.6	4 49.9
26	2 20.5	4 40.6
JAN 5	2♍14.5	4♌30.0
JAN 1	23N09.6	37N44.8
21	23 19.8	37 53.8
FEB 10	23 30.2	38 00.1
MAR 1	23 39.4	38 02.9
21	23 46.3	38 01.9
APR 10	23 50.1	37 57.5
30	23 50.4	37 50.3
MAY 20	23 47.3	37 41.4
JUN 9	23 41.3	37 31.7
29	23 33.0	37 22.2
JUL 19	23 23.6	37 14.0
AUG 8	23 13.8	37 07.7
28	23 04.7	37 04.2
SEP 17	22 57.4	37 03.9
OCT 7	22 52.5	37 06.9
27	22 50.9	37 13.2
NOV 16	22 52.7	37 22.2
DEC 6	22 57.9	37 32.8
26	23N06.0	37N43.8
	5/14.12 11/30.96	4/15.06 11/4.45

1961	Haumea 136108	Makemake 136472
JAN 1	2R17.1	4R34.4
11	2♍10.1	4♌23.2
21	2 01.6	4 11.5
31	1 52.0	3 59.6
FEB 10	1 41.5	3 48.0
20	1 30.5	3 37.1
MAR 2	1 19.6	3 27.3
12	1 09.0	3 19.0
22	0 59.1	3 12.4
APR 1	0 50.4	3 07.9
11	0 43.0	3 05.5
21	0 37.3	3D05.3
MAY 1	0 33.4	3 07.4
11	0 31.5	3 11.7
21	0D31.6	3 18.0
31	0 33.7	3 26.3
JUN 10	0 37.7	3 36.3
20	0 43.7	3 47.8
30	0 51.4	4 00.5
JUL 10	1 00.6	4 14.1
20	1 11.2	4 28.3
30	1 22.8	4 42.8
AUG 9	1 35.3	4 57.2
19	1 48.2	5 11.2
29	2 01.4	5 24.5
SEP 8	2 14.4	5 36.8
18	2 27.0	5 47.7
28	2 38.9	5 57.0
OCT 8	2 49.8	6 04.5
18	2 59.4	6 09.9
28	3 07.4	6 13.1
NOV 7	3 13.6	6R14.0
17	3 17.9	6 12.7
27	3 20.1	6 09.1
DEC 7	3R20.2	6 03.3
17	3 18.2	5 55.7
27	3 14.1	5 46.5
JAN 6	3♍08.1	5♌35.9
JAN 1	23N08.8	37N46.9
21	23 19.1	37 56.1
FEB 10	23 29.6	38 02.6
MAR 2	23 38.9	38 05.5
22	23 45.9	38 04.6
APR 11	23 49.6	38 00.2
MAY 1	23 49.9	37 53.0
21	23 46.7	37 43.9
JUN 10	23 40.5	37 33.9
30	23 32.2	37 24.2
JUL 20	23 22.6	37 15.7
AUG 9	23 12.7	37 09.2
29	23 03.6	37 05.4
SEP 18	22 56.1	37 04.9
OCT 8	22 51.3	37 07.9
28	22 49.6	37 14.2
NOV 17	22 51.5	37 23.1
DEC 7	22 56.8	37 33.9
27	23N05.0	37N45.0
	5/15.30 12/2.10	4/16.44 11/5.77

1962	Haumea 136108	Makemake 136472
JAN 1	3R11.3	5R41.3
11	3♍04.5	5♌30.3
21	2 56.2	5 18.6
31	2 46.6	5 06.7
FEB 10	2 36.2	4 55.1
20	2 25.3	4 44.0
MAR 2	2 14.3	4 34.1
12	2 03.7	4 25.6
22	1 53.7	4 18.8
APR 1	1 44.8	4 13.9
11	1 37.3	4 11.2
21	1 31.4	4D10.8
MAY 1	1 27.3	4 12.5
11	1 25.1	4 16.5
21	1D24.9	4 22.6
31	1 26.8	4 30.6
JUN 10	1 30.7	4 40.4
20	1 36.4	4 51.7
30	1 43.9	5 04.2
JUL 10	1 52.9	5 17.7
20	2 03.4	5 31.8
30	2 14.9	5 46.3
AUG 9	2 27.2	6 00.7
19	2 40.1	6 14.8
29	2 53.3	6 28.2
SEP 8	3 06.3	6 40.6
18	3 19.0	6 51.7
28	3 31.0	7 01.3
OCT 8	3 42.0	7 09.0
18	3 51.8	7 14.7
28	4 00.0	7 18.2
NOV 7	4 06.4	7 19.4
17	4 10.9	7R18.3
27	4 13.3	7 15.0
DEC 7	4R13.7	7 09.6
17	4 11.9	7 02.2
27	4 08.0	6 53.2
JAN 6	4♍02.3	6♌42.8
JAN 1	23N07.4	37N47.6
21	23 17.7	37 57.1
FEB 10	23 28.3	38 03.9
MAR 2	23 37.8	38 07.2
22	23 44.9	38 06.6
APR 11	23 48.8	38 02.3
MAY 1	23 49.2	37 55.1
21	23 46.0	37 46.0
JUN 10	23 39.9	37 35.9
30	23 31.6	37 25.8
JUL 20	23 21.9	37 17.0
AUG 9	23 11.9	37 10.1
29	23 02.6	37 06.0
SEP 18	22 55.0	37 05.1
OCT 8	22 49.9	37 07.8
28	22 48.1	37 13.8
NOV 17	22 49.9	37 22.7
DEC 7	22 55.1	37 33.4
27	23N03.2	37N44.7
	5/16.47 12/3.19	4/17.80 11/7.08

1963	Haumea 136108	Makemake 136472
JAN 1	4R05.4	6R48.1
11	3♍58.8	6♌37.2
21	3 50.6	6 25.6
31	3 41.1	6 13.7
FEB 10	3 30.8	6 02.0
20	3 19.9	5 50.9
MAR 2	3 08.9	5 40.8
12	2 58.2	5 32.1
22	2 48.2	5 25.0
APR 1	2 39.2	5 19.9
11	2 31.5	5 17.0
21	2 25.3	5D16.2
MAY 1	2 21.0	5 17.7
11	2 18.6	5 21.3
21	2D18.2	5 27.1
31	2 19.9	5 34.9
JUN 10	2 23.5	5 44.4
20	2 29.0	5 55.5
30	2 36.3	6 07.9
JUL 10	2 45.2	6 21.2
20	2 55.5	6 35.3
30	3 06.9	6 49.7
AUG 9	3 19.1	7 04.1
19	3 32.0	7 18.3
29	3 45.1	7 31.8
SEP 8	3 58.2	7 44.3
18	4 10.9	7 55.6
28	4 23.0	8 05.4
OCT 8	4 34.2	8 13.4
18	4 44.1	8 19.3
28	4 52.4	8 23.1
NOV 7	4 59.1	8 24.7
17	5 03.8	8R23.9
27	5 06.5	8 20.9
DEC 7	5R07.1	8 15.7
17	5 05.5	8 08.6
27	5 01.9	7 59.8
JAN 6	4♍56.4	7♌49.6
JAN 1	23N05.6	37N47.4
21	23 16.0	37 57.2
FEB 10	23 26.7	38 04.4
MAR 2	23 36.3	38 07.9
22	23 43.6	38 07.6
APR 11	23 47.7	38 03.5
MAY 1	23 48.2	37 56.4
21	23 45.2	37 47.2
JUN 10	23 39.1	37 36.9
30	23 30.7	37 26.6
JUL 20	23 20.9	37 17.4
AUG 9	23 10.8	37 10.1
29	23 01.3	37 05.6
SEP 18	22 53.6	37 04.4
OCT 8	22 48.4	37 06.7
28	22 46.4	37 12.5
NOV 17	22 48.0	37 21.3
DEC 7	22 53.1	37 32.1
27	23N01.2	37N43.5
	5/17.66 12/4.35	4/19.18 11/8.46

1964	Haumea 136108	Makemake 136472
JAN 1	4R59.4	7R54.8
11	4♍52.9	7♌44.1
21	4 44.9	7 32.6
31	4 35.6	7 20.7
FEB 10	4 25.3	7 09.0
20	4 14.5	6 57.7
MAR 1	4 03.5	6 47.5
11	3 52.8	6 38.6
21	3 42.6	6 31.3
31	3 33.5	6 26.0
APR 10	3 25.6	6 22.7
20	3 19.3	6D21.6
30	3 14.8	6 22.8
MAY 10	3 12.2	6 26.2
20	3D11.5	6 31.7
30	3 12.9	6 39.2
JUN 9	3 16.3	6 48.5
19	3 21.7	6 59.4
29	3 28.8	7 11.6
JUL 9	3 37.5	7 24.8
19	3 47.6	7 38.8
29	3 58.9	7 53.1
AUG 8	4 11.0	8 07.6
18	4 23.8	8 21.8
28	4 37.0	8 35.4
SEP 7	4 50.1	8 48.1
17	5 02.9	8 59.6
27	5 15.1	9 09.5
OCT 7	5 26.3	9 17.8
17	5 36.4	9 24.0
27	5 45.0	9 28.1
NOV 6	5 51.8	9 30.0
16	5 56.8	9R29.5
26	5 59.7	9 26.8
DEC 6	6R00.5	9 21.9
16	5 59.2	9 15.1
26	5 55.8	9 06.5
JAN 5	5♍50.5	8♌56.4
JAN 1	23N03.6	37N46.2
21	23 14.0	37 56.3
FEB 10	23 24.8	38 03.8
MAR 1	23 34.6	38 07.7
21	23 42.0	38 07.6
APR 10	23 46.2	38 03.7
30	23 46.8	37 56.7
MAY 20	23 43.9	37 47.4
JUN 9	23 37.9	37 36.9
29	23 29.5	37 26.4
JUL 19	23 19.6	37 16.8
AUG 8	23 09.3	37 09.2
28	22 59.7	37 04.3
SEP 17	22 51.8	37 02.7
OCT 7	22 46.4	37 04.7
27	22 44.2	37 10.3
NOV 16	22 45.7	37 18.9
DEC 6	22 50.7	37 29.6
26	22N58.7	37N41.1
	5/17.78 12/4.47	4/19.49 11/8.78

1965	Haumea 136108	Makemake 136472
JAN 1	5R52.9	9R00.6
11	5♍46.4	8♌49.9
21	5 38.5	8 38.4
31	5 29.2	8 26.6
FEB 10	5 18.9	8 14.8
20	5 08.1	8 03.6
MAR 2	4 57.1	7 53.4
12	4 46.4	7 44.4
22	4 36.2	7 37.1
APR 1	4 27.1	7 31.7
11	4 19.2	7 28.4
21	4 12.9	7D27.2
MAY 1	4 08.3	7 28.3
11	4 05.7	7 31.6
21	4D05.0	7 37.0
31	4 06.4	7 44.5
JUN 10	4 09.8	7 53.7
20	4 15.1	8 04.5
30	4 22.1	8 16.7
JUL 10	4 30.8	8 29.9
20	4 40.9	8 43.8
30	4 52.2	8 58.2
AUG 9	5 04.4	9 12.6
19	5 17.2	9 26.8
29	5 30.3	9 40.4
SEP 8	5 43.4	9 53.2
18	5 56.2	10 04.7
28	6 08.4	10 14.7
OCT 8	6 19.7	10 23.0
18	6 29.8	10 29.3
28	6 38.4	10 33.5
NOV 7	6 45.3	10 35.5
17	6 50.3	10R35.1
27	6 53.3	10 32.5
DEC 7	6R54.1	10 27.7
17	6 52.8	10 20.9
27	6 49.5	10 12.3
JAN 6	6♍44.2	10♌02.4

1965	Haumea	Makemake
JAN 1	23N01.6	37N44.5
21	23 12.1	37 54.7
FEB 10	23 23.0	38 02.4
MAR 2	23 32.8	38 06.4
22	23 40.2	38 06.4
APR 11	23 44.5	38 02.5
MAY 1	23 45.0	37 55.4
21	23 42.0	37 46.0
JUN 10	23 35.9	37 35.4
30	23 27.3	37 24.6
JUL 20	23 17.3	37 14.8
AUG 9	23 06.9	37 06.9
29	22 57.2	37 01.8
SEP 18	22 49.2	36 59.9
OCT 8	22 43.8	37 01.8
28	22 41.6	37 07.3
NOV 17	22 43.1	37 15.9
DEC 7	22 48.2	37 26.7
27	22N56.3	37N38.3
	5/18.95 12/5.62	4/20.86 11/10.15

1966	Haumea 136108	Makemake 136472
JAN 1	6R47.0	10R07.5
11	6♍40.8	9♌57.0
21	6 33.0	9 45.6
31	6 23.9	9 33.8
FEB 10	6 13.7	9 22.0
20	6 03.0	9 10.7
MAR 2	5 52.0	9 00.3
12	5 41.2	8 51.2
22	5 31.0	8 43.7
APR 1	5 21.7	8 38.0
11	5 13.7	8 34.4
21	5 07.2	8 32.9
MAY 1	5 02.4	8D33.7
11	4 59.5	8 36.7
21	4D58.6	8 41.9
31	4 59.8	8 49.0
JUN 10	5 03.0	8 58.0
20	5 08.0	9 08.6
30	5 14.9	9 20.6
JUL 10	5 23.4	9 33.7
20	5 33.4	9 47.5
30	5 44.5	10 01.8
AUG 9	5 56.6	10 16.3
19	6 09.4	10 30.5
29	6 22.5	10 44.2
SEP 8	6 35.6	10 57.1
18	6 48.5	11 08.8
28	7 00.8	11 19.1
OCT 8	7 12.2	11 27.6
18	7 22.5	11 34.2
28	7 31.2	11 38.7
NOV 7	7 38.3	11 40.9
17	7 43.6	11R40.9
27	7 46.8	11 38.5
DEC 7	7R47.9	11 34.0
17	7 46.8	11 27.5
27	7 43.7	11 19.2
JAN 6	7♍38.6	11♌09.4

1966	Haumea	Makemake
JAN 1	22N58.7	37N41.2
21	23 09.2	37 51.6
FEB 10	23 20.2	37 59.6
MAR 2	23 30.1	38 03.9
22	23 37.7	38 04.2
APR 11	23 42.1	38 00.6
MAY 1	23 42.8	37 53.6
21	23 39.8	37 44.1
JUN 10	23 33.7	37 33.3
30	23 25.1	37 22.3
JUL 20	23 15.1	37 12.2
AUG 9	23 04.6	37 04.0
29	22 54.7	36 58.4
SEP 18	22 46.5	36 56.2
OCT 8	22 40.9	36 57.8
28	22 38.5	37 03.0
NOV 17	22 39.8	37 11.4
DEC 7	22 44.8	37 22.2
27	22N52.8	37N33.9
	5/20.07 12/6.81	4/22.18 11/11.49

1967	Haumea 136108	Makemake 136472
JAN 1	7R41.4	11R14.4
11	7♍35.4	11♌04.1
21	7 27.8	10 52.8
31	7 18.8	10 41.0
FEB 10	7 08.7	10 29.2
20	6 58.0	10 17.9
MAR 2	6 47.0	10 07.3
12	6 36.2	9 58.0
22	6 25.9	9 50.3
APR 1	6 16.5	9 44.4
11	6 08.3	9 40.5
21	6 01.7	9 38.7
MAY 1	5 56.7	9D39.2
11	5 53.6	9 41.9
21	5 52.5	9 46.8
31	5D53.4	9 53.7
JUN 10	5 56.3	10 02.4
20	6 01.2	10 12.8
30	6 07.9	10 24.6
JUL 10	6 16.2	10 37.5
20	6 26.0	10 51.3
30	6 37.0	11 05.5
AUG 9	6 49.0	11 20.0
19	7 01.7	11 34.3
29	7 14.8	11 48.0
SEP 8	7 28.0	12 01.0
18	7 40.9	12 12.9
28	7 53.3	12 23.4
OCT 8	8 04.9	12 32.2
18	8 15.3	12 39.0
28	8 24.2	12 43.8
NOV 7	8 31.6	12 46.3
17	8 37.0	12R46.6
27	8 40.4	12 44.6
DEC 7	8 41.8	12 40.3
17	8R41.0	12 34.1
27	8 38.1	12 26.0
JAN 6	8♍33.2	12♌16.4

1967	Haumea	Makemake
JAN 1	22N55.2	37N36.8
21	23 05.8	37 47.5
FEB 10	23 16.8	37 55.7
MAR 2	23 26.9	38 00.4
22	23 34.6	38 01.0
APR 11	23 39.1	37 57.6
MAY 1	23 40.0	37 50.7
21	23 37.1	37 41.3
JUN 10	23 31.1	37 30.3
30	23 22.5	37 19.1
JUL 20	23 12.4	37 08.7
AUG 9	23 01.7	37 00.1
29	22 51.7	36 54.1
SEP 18	22 43.3	36 51.6
OCT 8	22 37.5	36 52.8
28	22 35.0	36 57.7
NOV 17	22 36.1	37 06.0
DEC 7	22 40.9	37 16.7
27	22N48.9	37N28.5
	5/21.19 12/7.92	4/23.52 11/12.82

1968	Haumea 136108	Makemake 136472
JAN 1	8R35.9	12R21.3
11	8♍30.1	12♌11.1
21	8 22.7	11 59.9
31	8 13.8	11 48.2
FEB 10	8 03.8	11 36.4
20	7 53.2	11 25.0
MAR 1	7 42.3	11 14.4
11	7 31.4	11 04.9
21	7 21.0	10 56.9
31	7 11.5	10 50.7
APR 10	7 03.2	10 46.6
20	6 56.3	10 44.6
30	6 51.1	10D44.7
MAY 10	6 47.8	10 47.1
20	6 46.5	10 51.7
30	6D47.2	10 58.3
JUN 9	6 49.9	11 06.8
19	6 54.5	11 17.0
29	7 01.0	11 28.6
JUL 9	7 09.2	11 41.4
19	7 18.8	11 55.0
29	7 29.7	12 09.2
AUG 8	7 41.6	12 23.6
18	7 54.2	12 37.9
28	8 07.3	12 51.8
SEP 7	8 20.5	13 04.9
17	8 33.5	13 16.9
27	8 46.0	13 27.6
OCT 7	8 57.6	13 36.6
17	9 08.2	13 43.7
27	9 17.3	13 48.8
NOV 6	9 24.8	13 51.6
16	9 30.5	13R52.2
26	9 34.2	13 50.5
DEC 6	9 35.8	13 46.5
16	9R35.3	13 40.5
26	9 32.6	13 32.7
JAN 5	9♍28.0	13♌23.2

1968	Haumea	Makemake
JAN 1	22N51.3	37N31.4
21	23 01.8	37 42.3
FEB 10	23 12.9	37 50.9
MAR 1	23 23.1	37 55.9
21	23 31.0	37 56.8
APR 10	23 35.7	37 53.6
30	23 36.7	37 46.9
MAY 20	23 34.0	37 37.5
JUN 9	23 27.9	37 26.5
29	23 19.3	37 15.0
JUL 19	23 09.2	37 04.3
AUG 8	22 58.4	36 55.3
28	22 48.2	36 49.1
SEP 17	22 39.7	36 46.1
OCT 7	22 33.7	36 47.0
27	22 30.9	36 51.6
NOV 16	22 31.9	36 59.7
DEC 6	22 36.6	37 10.3
26	22N44.5	37N22.2
	5/21.38 12/8.10	4/23.91 11/13.17

1969	Haumea 136108	Makemake 136472
JAN 1	9R30.1	13R27.2
11	9♍24.3	13♌17.0
21	9 16.9	13 05.9
31	9 08.0	12 54.2
FEB 10	8 58.1	12 42.4
20	8 47.4	12 31.0
MAR 2	8 36.5	12 20.3
12	8 25.6	12 10.8
22	8 15.3	12 02.7
APR 1	8 05.7	11 56.5
11	7 57.4	11 52.3
21	7 50.5	11 50.2
MAY 1	7 45.3	11D50.3
11	7 42.0	11 52.6
21	7 40.6	11 57.1
31	7D41.2	12 03.6
JUN 10	7 43.9	12 12.0
20	7 48.5	12 22.1
30	7 55.0	12 33.7
JUL 10	8 03.1	12 46.4
20	8 12.7	13 00.0
30	8 23.6	13 14.1
AUG 9	8 35.5	13 28.5
19	8 48.1	13 42.9
29	9 01.2	13 56.7
SEP 8	9 14.4	14 09.9
18	9 27.4	14 21.9
28	9 39.9	14 32.6
OCT 8	9 51.6	14 41.7
18	10 02.2	14 48.9
28	10 11.3	14 54.0
NOV 7	10 18.9	14 56.9
17	10 24.6	14R57.6
27	10 28.3	14 55.9
DEC 7	10 29.9	14 52.0
17	10R29.4	14 46.1
27	10 26.8	14 38.3
JAN 6	10♍22.2	14♌28.9

1969	Haumea	Makemake
JAN 1	22N47.4	37N25.8
21	22 58.0	37 36.8
FEB 10	23 09.1	37 45.5
MAR 2	23 19.4	37 50.7
22	23 27.3	37 51.7
APR 11	23 32.0	37 48.6
MAY 1	23 32.9	37 41.8
21	23 30.1	37 32.3
JUN 10	23 24.0	37 21.2
30	23 15.3	37 09.5
JUL 20	23 05.0	36 58.6
AUG 9	22 54.1	36 49.4
29	22 43.9	36 42.9
SEP 18	22 35.2	36 39.8
OCT 8	22 29.2	36 40.5
28	22 26.4	36 45.1
NOV 17	22 27.4	36 53.1
DEC 7	22 32.2	37 03.8
27	22N40.1	37N15.7
	5/22.50 12/9.23	4/25.24 11/14.45

1970	Haumea 136108	Makemake 136472
JAN 1	10R24.7	14R33.8
11	10♍19.2	14♌23.8
21	10 11.9	14 12.7
31	10 03.2	14 01.1
FEB 10	9 53.4	13 49.3
20	9 42.8	13 37.8
MAR 2	9 31.9	13 27.0
12	9 21.0	13 17.4
22	9 10.5	13 09.1
APR 1	9 00.9	13 02.6
11	8 52.4	12 58.1
21	8 45.3	12 55.7
MAY 1	8 39.9	12D55.5
11	8 36.3	12 57.5
21	8 34.7	13 01.7
31	8D35.2	13 08.0
JUN 10	8 37.6	13 16.1
20	8 42.0	13 26.0
30	8 48.2	13 37.3
JUL 10	8 56.2	13 49.9
20	9 05.6	14 03.4
30	9 16.4	14 17.5
AUG 9	9 28.2	14 31.8
19	9 40.8	14 46.2
29	9 53.8	15 00.1
SEP 8	10 07.0	15 13.4
18	10 20.0	15 25.6
28	10 32.6	15 36.5
OCT 8	10 44.4	15 45.8
18	10 55.1	15 53.2
28	11 04.5	15 58.6
NOV 7	11 12.3	16 01.8
17	11 18.2	16R02.7
27	11 22.1	16 01.4
DEC 7	11 24.0	15 57.8
17	11R23.7	15 52.1
27	11 21.3	15 44.5
JAN 6	11♍16.9	15♌35.4

1970	Haumea 136108	Makemake 136472
JAN 1	22N42.5	37N18.7
21	22 53.2	37 30.0
FEB 10	23 04.4	37 39.0
MAR 2	23 14.7	37 44.5
22	23 22.8	37 45.8
APR 11	23 27.7	37 42.9
MAY 1	23 28.8	37 36.3
21	23 26.1	37 26.9
JUN 10	23 20.0	37 15.7
30	23 11.3	37 03.9
JUL 20	23 01.0	36 52.7
AUG 9	22 50.0	36 43.2
29	22 39.6	36 36.3
SEP 18	22 30.8	36 32.8
OCT 8	22 24.6	36 33.2
28	22 21.7	36 37.5
NOV 17	22 22.5	36 45.3
DEC 7	22 27.1	36 55.9
27	22N35.0	37N07.9

5/23.69 4/26.64
12/10.36 11/15.78

1971	Haumea 136108	Makemake 136472
JAN 1	11R19.4	15R40.1
11	11♍14.0	15♌30.3
21	11 06.9	15 19.4
31	10 58.4	15 07.8
FEB 10	10 48.7	14 56.0
20	10 38.1	14 44.5
MAR 2	10 27.2	14 33.5
12	10 16.3	14 23.7
22	10 05.8	14 15.3
APR 1	9 56.0	14 08.5
11	9 47.4	14 03.7
21	9 40.1	14 01.1
MAY 1	9 34.5	14D00.6
11	9 30.7	14 02.3
21	9 28.9	14 06.1
31	9D29.1	14 12.1
JUN 10	9 31.3	14 20.0
20	9 35.4	14 29.6
30	9 41.5	14 40.8
JUL 10	9 49.2	14 53.2
20	9 58.5	15 06.5
30	10 09.1	15 20.6
AUG 9	10 20.8	15 34.9
19	10 33.3	15 49.2
29	10 46.3	16 03.2
SEP 8	10 59.5	16 16.6
18	11 12.6	16 28.9
28	11 25.3	16 40.0
OCT 8	11 37.2	16 49.5
18	11 48.0	16 57.2
28	11 57.6	17 02.9
NOV 7	12 05.5	17 06.4
17	12 11.7	17 07.6
27	12 15.9	17R06.5
DEC 7	12 18.0	17 03.2
17	12R17.9	16 57.8
27	12 15.8	16 50.5
JAN 6	12♍11.6	16♌41.5

1971	Haumea 136108	Makemake 136472
JAN 1	22N37.4	37N10.9
21	22 48.0	37 22.4
FEB 10	22 59.3	37 31.7
MAR 2	23 09.8	37 37.5
22	23 18.0	37 39.2
APR 11	23 23.0	37 36.6
MAY 1	23 24.3	37 30.2
21	23 21.7	37 20.8
JUN 10	23 15.7	37 09.5
30	23 07.1	36 57.6
JUL 20	22 56.7	36 46.1
AUG 9	22 45.6	36 36.3
29	22 35.1	36 29.1
SEP 18	22 26.1	36 25.2
OCT 8	22 19.7	36 25.2
28	22 16.6	36 29.2
NOV 17	22 17.3	36 36.9
DEC 7	22 21.7	36 47.4
27	22N29.5	36N59.4

5/24.86 4/27.99
12/11.51 11/17.07

1972	Haumea 136108	Makemake 136472
JAN 1	12R13.9	16R46.2
11	12♍08.8	16♌36.5
21	12 01.9	16 25.7
31	11 53.5	16 14.2
FEB 10	11 43.8	16 02.4
20	11 33.4	15 50.8
MAR 1	11 22.5	15 39.8
11	11 11.6	15 29.8
21	11 01.0	15 21.2
31	10 51.1	15 14.2
APR 10	10 42.3	15 09.1
20	10 34.9	15 06.1
30	10 29.0	15D05.3
MAY 10	10 25.0	15 06.7
20	10 23.0	15 10.3
30	10D22.9	15 16.0
JUN 9	10 24.9	15 23.6
19	10 28.8	15 33.1
29	10 34.6	15 44.0
JUL 9	10 42.2	15 56.2
19	10 51.3	16 09.4
29	11 01.8	16 23.4
AUG 8	11 13.4	16 37.7
18	11 25.8	16 52.0
28	11 38.8	17 06.0
SEP 7	11 52.0	17 19.5
17	12 05.1	17 32.0
27	12 17.8	17 43.2
OCT 7	12 29.8	17 52.9
17	12 40.8	18 00.9
27	12 50.5	18 06.8
NOV 6	12 58.7	18 10.6
16	13 05.0	18 12.1
26	13 09.5	18R11.4
DEC 6	13 11.8	18 08.3
16	13R12.0	18 03.2
26	13 10.1	17 56.1
JAN 5	13♍06.1	17♌47.3

1972	Haumea 136108	Makemake 136472
JAN 1	22N31.9	37N02.4
21	22 42.6	37 14.1
FEB 10	22 53.9	37 23.7
MAR 1	23 04.5	37 29.8
21	23 12.9	37 31.8
APR 10	23 18.1	37 29.5
30	23 19.6	37 23.3
MAY 20	23 17.1	37 14.0
JUN 9	23 11.2	37 02.7
29	23 02.6	36 50.6
JUL 19	22 52.1	36 38.9
AUG 8	22 41.0	36 28.8
28	22 30.4	36 21.2
SEP 17	22 21.2	36 17.0
OCT 7	22 14.6	36 16.7
27	22 11.3	36 20.4
NOV 16	22 11.8	36 27.8
DEC 6	22 16.2	36 38.2
26	22N23.9	36N50.2

5/25.02 4/28.36
12/11.61 11/17.34

1973	Haumea 136108	Makemake 136472
JAN 1	13R07.9	17R51.0
11	13♍02.8	17♌41.4
21	12 55.9	17 30.6
31	12 47.5	17 19.1
FEB 10	12 37.9	17 07.3
20	12 27.5	16 55.7
MAR 2	12 16.6	16 44.7
12	12 05.6	16 34.7
22	11 55.0	16 26.0
APR 1	11 45.1	16 19.0
11	11 36.3	16 13.8
21	11 28.8	16 10.8
MAY 1	11 23.0	16D09.9
11	11 18.9	16 11.2
21	11 16.8	16 14.7
31	11D16.7	16 20.3
JUN 10	11 18.7	16 27.9
20	11 22.6	16 37.2
30	11 28.4	16 48.1
JUL 10	11 35.9	17 00.2
20	11 45.0	17 13.4
30	11 55.5	17 27.3
AUG 9	12 07.0	17 41.6
19	12 19.4	17 55.9
29	12 32.4	18 10.0
SEP 8	12 45.6	18 23.4
18	12 58.7	18 35.9
28	13 11.5	18 47.2
OCT 8	13 23.5	18 57.0
18	13 34.5	19 05.0
28	13 44.3	19 10.9
NOV 7	13 52.4	19 14.8
17	13 58.8	19 16.4
27	14 03.3	19R15.7
DEC 7	14 05.6	19 12.7
17	14R05.9	19 07.7
27	14 04.0	19 00.6
JAN 6	14♍00.0	18♌51.9

1973	Haumea 136108	Makemake 136472
JAN 1	22N26.7	36N53.9
21	22 37.4	37 05.7
FEB 10	22 48.9	37 15.4
MAR 2	22 59.5	37 21.7
22	23 08.0	37 23.8
APR 11	23 13.2	37 21.5
MAY 1	23 14.6	37 15.3
21	23 12.1	37 06.0
JUN 10	23 06.1	36 54.6
30	22 57.4	36 42.4
JUL 20	22 46.9	36 30.5
AUG 9	22 35.6	36 20.2
29	22 24.9	36 12.5
SEP 18	22 15.7	36 08.1
OCT 8	22 09.1	36 07.6
28	22 05.8	36 11.2
NOV 17	22 06.3	36 18.6
DEC 7	22 10.7	36 28.9
27	22N18.5	36N41.0

5/26.22 4/29.74
12/12.75 11/18.68

1974	Haumea 136108	Makemake 136472
JAN 1	14R02.3	18R56.4
11	13♍57.3	18♌47.0
21	13 50.6	18 36.4
31	13 42.4	18 24.9
FEB 10	13 32.9	18 13.2
20	13 22.5	18 01.6
MAR 2	13 11.6	17 50.4
12	13 00.6	17 40.2
22	12 50.0	17 31.4
APR 1	12 40.0	17 24.1
11	12 31.0	17 18.7
21	12 23.4	17 15.4
MAY 1	12 17.3	17 14.2
11	12 13.0	17D15.2
21	12 10.7	17 18.4
31	12D10.4	17 23.7
JUN 10	12 12.1	17 31.0
20	12 15.7	17 40.1
30	12 21.3	17 50.8
JUL 10	12 28.7	18 02.8
20	12 37.6	18 15.9
30	12 47.9	18 29.6
AUG 9	12 59.4	18 43.9
19	13 11.7	18 58.2
29	13 24.6	19 12.3
SEP 8	13 37.8	19 25.8
18	13 51.0	19 38.5
28	14 03.8	19 49.9
OCT 8	14 15.9	19 59.9
18	14 27.1	20 08.1
28	14 37.0	20 14.4
NOV 7	14 45.3	20 18.5
17	14 51.9	20 20.4
27	14 56.6	20R20.0
DEC 7	14 59.2	20 17.4
17	14R59.7	20 12.5
27	14 58.0	20 05.7
JAN 6	14♍54.3	19♌57.2

1974	Haumea 136108	Makemake 136472
JAN 1	22N20.9	36N44.1
21	22 31.6	36 56.1
FEB 10	22 43.1	37 06.0
MAR 2	22 53.8	37 12.6
22	23 02.4	37 15.1
APR 11	23 07.8	37 13.1
MAY 1	23 09.4	37 07.1
21	23 07.1	36 57.8
JUN 10	23 01.2	36 46.4
30	22 52.5	36 34.1
JUL 20	22 41.9	36 22.0
AUG 9	22 30.7	36 11.5
29	22 19.8	36 03.4
SEP 18	22 10.4	35 58.6
OCT 8	22 03.6	35 57.8
28	22 00.2	36 01.1
NOV 17	22 00.5	36 08.2
DEC 7	22 04.7	36 18.4
27	22N12.4	36N30.5

5/27.37 5/1.05
12/13.87 11/19.95

1975	Haumea 136108	Makemake 136472
JAN 1	14R56.4	20R01.7
11	14♍51.7	19♌52.4
21	14 45.2	19 41.9
31	14 37.1	19 30.6
FEB 10	14 27.7	19 18.9
20	14 17.4	19 07.2
MAR 2	14 06.6	18 56.0
12	13 55.6	18 45.7
22	13 44.8	18 36.6
APR 1	13 34.8	18 29.2
11	13 25.6	18 23.5
21	13 17.8	18 19.9
MAY 1	13 11.6	18 18.4
11	13 07.1	18D19.1
21	13 04.5	18 22.1
31	13D04.0	18 27.1
JUN 10	13 05.4	18 34.1
20	13 08.8	18 43.0
30	13 14.2	18 53.4
JUL 10	13 21.4	19 05.3
20	13 30.1	19 18.2
30	13 40.3	19 31.9
AUG 9	13 51.6	19 46.0
19	14 03.9	20 00.4
29	14 16.8	20 14.5
SEP 8	14 30.0	20 28.1
18	14 43.2	20 40.9
28	14 56.0	20 52.5
OCT 8	15 08.3	21 02.7
18	15 19.6	21 11.2
28	15 29.6	21 17.7
NOV 7	15 38.2	21 22.1
17	15 45.0	21 24.3
27	15 49.9	21R24.2
DEC 7	15 52.8	21 21.8
17	15R53.5	21 17.3
27	15 52.1	21 10.8
JAN 6	15♍48.6	21♌02.5
JAN 1	22N14.8	36N33.6
21	22 25.5	36 45.7
FEB 10	22 37.1	36 55.9
MAR 2	22 47.9	37 02.8
22	22 56.7	37 05.6
APR 11	23 02.3	37 03.9
MAY 1	23 04.0	36 58.1
21	23 01.8	36 49.0
JUN 10	22 56.0	36 37.6
30	22 47.4	36 25.1
JUL 20	22 36.8	36 12.9
AUG 9	22 25.4	36 02.0
29	22 14.5	35 53.6
SEP 18	22 05.0	35 48.5
OCT 8	21 58.0	35 47.3
28	21 54.3	35 50.2
NOV 17	21 54.5	35 57.1
DEC 7	21 58.6	36 07.2
27	22N06.2	36N19.2
	5/28.56 12/15.01	5/2.43 11/21.29

1976	Haumea 136108	Makemake 136472
JAN 1	15R50.6	21R06.8
11	15♍46.1	20♌57.7
21	15 39.8	20 47.4
31	15 31.8	20 36.2
FEB 10	15 22.6	20 24.5
20	15 12.3	20 12.8
MAR 1	15 01.5	20 01.5
11	14 50.5	19 51.1
21	14 39.7	19 41.9
31	14 29.6	19 34.2
APR 10	14 20.3	19 28.3
20	14 12.3	19 24.4
30	14 05.9	19 22.6
MAY 10	14 01.2	19D23.1
20	13 58.4	19 25.7
30	13D57.6	19 30.4
JUN 9	13 58.8	19 37.2
19	14 02.0	19 45.8
29	14 07.2	19 56.1
JUL 9	14 14.1	20 07.7
19	14 22.7	20 20.5
29	14 32.8	20 34.1
AUG 8	14 44.0	20 48.2
18	14 56.2	21 02.5
28	15 09.0	21 16.7
SEP 7	15 22.2	21 30.4
17	15 35.4	21 43.3
27	15 48.3	21 55.1
OCT 7	16 00.7	22 05.5
17	16 12.1	22 14.2
27	16 22.3	22 21.0
NOV 6	16 31.1	22 25.7
16	16 38.1	22 28.2
26	16 43.3	22R28.4
DEC 6	16 46.4	22 26.3
16	16R47.3	22 22.0
26	16 46.2	22 15.8
JAN 5	16♍42.9	22♌07.7
JAN 1	22N08.5	36N22.4
21	22 19.2	36 34.6
FEB 10	22 30.8	36 45.0
MAR 1	22 41.8	36 52.3
21	22 50.7	36 55.3
APR 10	22 56.5	36 53.9
30	22 58.4	36 48.3
MAY 20	22 56.3	36 39.3
JUN 9	22 50.6	36 27.9
29	22 42.0	36 15.4
JUL 19	22 31.4	36 02.9
AUG 8	22 20.0	35 51.8
28	22 08.8	35 43.0
SEP 17	21 59.2	35 37.5
OCT 7	21 52.0	35 36.0
27	21 48.2	35 38.6
NOV 16	21 48.1	35 45.3
DEC 6	21 52.1	35 55.2
26	21N59.6	36N07.2
	5/28.71 12/15.20	5/2.73 11/21.61

1977	Haumea 136108	Makemake 136472
JAN 1	16R44.5	22R11.1
11	16♍40.0	22♌02.1
21	16 33.7	21 51.8
31	16 25.8	21 40.6
FEB 10	16 16.5	21 29.0
20	16 06.3	21 17.3
MAR 2	15 55.5	21 06.0
12	15 44.5	20 55.6
22	15 33.7	20 46.3
APR 1	15 23.5	20 38.6
11	15 14.3	20 32.6
21	15 06.3	20 28.7
MAY 1	14 59.8	20 26.8
11	14 55.1	20D27.2
21	14 52.2	20 29.8
31	14D51.4	20 34.4
JUN 10	14 52.6	20 41.1
20	14 55.8	20 49.7
30	15 00.9	20 59.9
JUL 10	15 07.9	21 11.5
20	15 16.4	21 24.2
30	15 26.5	21 37.8
AUG 9	15 37.7	21 51.9
19	15 49.9	22 06.2
29	16 02.7	22 20.4
SEP 8	16 15.9	22 34.1
18	16 29.1	22 47.0
28	16 42.1	22 58.8
OCT 8	16 54.5	23 09.3
18	17 05.9	23 18.0
28	17 16.2	23 24.9
NOV 7	17 25.0	23 29.7
17	17 32.1	23 32.2
27	17 37.3	23R32.5
DEC 7	17 40.4	23 30.5
17	17R41.4	23 26.3
27	17 40.3	23 20.1
JAN 6	17♍37.0	23♌12.1
JAN 1	22N02.4	36N10.9
21	22 13.1	36 23.2
FEB 10	22 24.8	36 33.7
MAR 2	22 35.8	36 41.1
22	22 44.7	36 44.2
APR 11	22 50.4	36 42.9
MAY 1	22 52.3	36 37.4
21	22 50.2	36 28.3
JUN 10	22 44.4	36 16.9
30	22 35.7	36 04.2
JUL 20	22 25.0	35 51.6
AUG 9	22 13.5	35 40.3
29	22 02.3	35 31.3
SEP 18	21 52.6	35 25.7
OCT 8	21 45.4	35 24.0
28	21 41.5	35 26.5
NOV 17	21 41.5	35 33.0
DEC 7	21 45.4	35 42.9
27	21N53.0	35N54.9
	5/29.83 12/16.33	5/4.05 11/22.93

1978	Haumea 136108	Makemake 136472
JAN 1	17R38.9	23R16.3
11	17♍34.7	23♌07.5
21	17 28.6	22 57.4
31	17 20.8	22 46.3
FEB 10	17 11.7	22 34.7
20	17 01.6	22 23.0
MAR 2	16 50.8	22 11.7
12	16 39.9	22 01.1
22	16 29.0	21 51.7
APR 1	16 18.7	21 43.8
11	16 09.3	21 37.6
21	16 01.2	21 33.4
MAY 1	15 54.5	21 31.2
11	15 49.6	21D31.3
21	15 46.5	21 33.6
31	15 45.5	21 38.0
JUN 10	15D46.4	21 44.4
20	15 49.4	21 52.7
30	15 54.3	22 02.7
JUL 10	16 01.1	22 14.1
20	16 09.5	22 26.7
30	16 19.3	22 40.1
AUG 9	16 30.5	22 54.2
19	16 42.6	23 08.5
29	16 55.4	23 22.7
SEP 8	17 08.5	23 36.5
18	17 21.8	23 49.5
28	17 34.8	24 01.5
OCT 8	17 47.3	24 12.1
18	17 58.9	24 21.1
28	18 09.4	24 28.2
NOV 7	18 18.4	24 33.3
17	18 25.7	24 36.2
27	18 31.1	24R36.7
DEC 7	18 34.5	24 35.1
17	18 35.7	24 31.2
27	18R34.8	24 25.2
JAN 6	18♍31.8	24♌17.4
JAN 1	21N55.3	35N58.1
21	22 06.0	36 10.4
FEB 10	22 17.7	36 21.2
MAR 2	22 28.8	36 28.8
22	22 37.9	36 32.3
APR 11	22 43.8	36 31.3
MAY 1	22 45.8	36 25.9
21	22 43.8	36 17.0
JUN 10	22 38.1	36 05.6
30	22 29.5	35 52.8
JUL 20	22 18.7	35 40.1
AUG 9	22 07.1	35 28.5
29	21 55.8	35 19.2
SEP 18	21 45.9	35 13.2
OCT 8	21 38.5	35 11.2
28	21 34.4	35 13.4
NOV 17	21 34.2	35 19.6
DEC 7	21 38.0	35 29.3
27	21N45.4	35N41.3
	5/31.01 12/17.54	5/5.39 11/24.28

1979	Haumea 136108	Makemake 136472
JAN 1	18R33.6	24R21.5
11	18♍29.6	24♌12.9
21	18 23.7	24 03.0
31	18 16.1	23 52.0
FEB 10	18 07.2	23 40.5
20	17 57.1	23 28.8
MAR 2	17 46.4	23 17.4
12	17 35.4	23 06.7
22	17 24.6	22 57.1
APR 1	17 14.2	22 49.0
11	17 04.7	22 42.6
21	16 56.4	22 38.1
MAY 1	16 49.5	22 35.7
11	16 44.4	22D35.5
21	16 41.1	22 37.4
31	16 39.8	22 41.6
JUN 10	16D40.6	22 47.7
20	16 43.3	22 55.8
30	16 48.0	23 05.5
JUL 10	16 54.5	23 16.8
20	17 02.8	23 29.2
30	17 12.5	23 42.5
AUG 9	17 23.5	23 56.5
19	17 35.5	24 10.8
29	17 48.2	24 25.0
SEP 8	18 01.4	24 38.9
18	18 14.7	24 52.0
28	18 27.8	25 04.1
OCT 8	18 40.4	25 15.0
18	18 52.1	25 24.2
28	19 02.7	25 31.6
NOV 7	19 11.9	25 36.9
17	19 19.4	25 40.1
27	19 25.1	25R40.9
DEC 7	19 28.7	25 39.6
17	19 30.3	25 35.9
27	19R29.6	25 30.2
JAN 6	19♍26.9	25♌22.7
JAN 1	21N47.7	35N44.4
21	21 58.4	35 56.9
FEB 10	22 10.1	36 07.8
MAR 2	22 21.3	36 15.7
22	22 30.5	36 19.5
APR 11	22 36.6	36 18.8
MAY 1	22 38.8	36 13.7
21	22 36.9	36 05.0
JUN 10	22 31.4	35 53.6
30	22 22.7	35 40.8
JUL 20	22 12.0	35 27.8
AUG 9	22 00.3	35 16.0
29	21 48.9	35 06.5
SEP 18	21 38.8	35 00.1
OCT 8	21 31.2	34 57.7
28	21 27.0	34 59.6
NOV 17	21 26.6	35 05.6
DEC 7	21 30.2	35 15.1
27	21N37.4	35N26.9
	6/1.12 12/18.71	5/6.69 11/25.56

1980	♇ Haumea 136108	♇ Makemake 136472
JAN 1	19R28.5	25R26.7
11	19♍24.7	25♌18.3
21	19 19.0	25 08.5
31	19 11.6	24 57.7
FEB 10	19 02.8	24 46.2
20	18 52.9	24 34.5
MAR 1	18 42.3	24 23.1
11	18 31.3	24 12.3
21	18 20.4	24 02.6
31	18 09.9	23 54.2
APR 10	18 00.3	23 47.6
20	17 51.8	23 42.8
30	17 44.8	23 40.1
MAY 10	17 39.5	23D39.6
20	17 36.0	23 41.3
30	17 34.4	23 45.1
JUN 9	17D34.9	23 51.0
19	17 37.4	23 58.8
29	17 41.9	24 08.3
JUL 9	17 48.3	24 19.4
19	17 56.3	24 31.6
29	18 05.9	24 44.9
AUG 8	18 16.8	24 58.8
18	18 28.7	25 13.0
28	18 41.4	25 27.2
SEP 7	18 54.5	25 41.2
17	19 07.9	25 54.4
27	19 21.0	26 06.7
OCT 7	19 33.7	26 17.7
17	19 45.5	26 27.1
27	19 56.3	26 34.8
NOV 6	20 05.7	26 40.4
16	20 13.4	26 43.8
26	20 19.3	26R45.0
DEC 6	20 23.2	26 43.9
16	20 25.0	26 40.6
26	20R24.6	26 35.2
JAN 5	20♍22.1	26♌27.8
JAN 1	21N39.7	35N30.1
21	21 50.3	35 42.6
FEB 10	22 02.0	35 53.8
MAR 1	22 13.3	36 02.0
21	22 22.7	36 06.1
APR 10	22 28.9	36 05.7
30	22 31.3	36 00.8
MAY 20	22 29.6	35 52.2
JUN 9	22 24.2	35 40.9
29	22 15.6	35 28.1
JUL 19	22 04.9	35 15.0
AUG 8	21 53.1	35 03.0
28	21 41.5	34 53.1
SEP 17	21 31.3	34 46.4
OCT 7	21 23.5	34 43.7
27	21 19.1	34 45.2
NOV 16	21 18.5	34 50.9
DEC 6	21 21.9	35 00.2
26	21N29.0	35N12.0
	6/1.30	5/7.07
	12/18.86	11/25.90

1981	♇ Haumea 136108	♇ Makemake 136472
JAN 1	20R23.3	26R31.0
11	20♍19.6	26♌22.7
21	20 13.9	26 12.9
31	20 06.6	26 02.1
FEB 10	19 57.8	25 50.6
20	19 47.9	25 39.0
MAR 2	19 37.2	25 27.5
12	19 26.2	25 16.7
22	19 15.3	25 07.0
APR 1	19 04.9	24 58.6
11	18 55.2	24 51.9
21	18 46.7	24 47.1
MAY 1	18 39.7	24 44.3
11	18 34.3	24D43.7
21	18 30.8	24 45.3
31	18 29.2	24 49.1
JUN 10	18D29.7	24 54.9
20	18 32.1	25 02.6
30	18 36.6	25 12.1
JUL 10	18 42.9	25 23.0
20	18 50.9	25 35.3
30	19 00.5	25 48.4
AUG 9	19 11.4	26 02.3
19	19 23.3	26 16.5
29	19 36.0	26 30.8
SEP 8	19 49.1	26 44.7
18	20 02.5	26 57.9
28	20 15.6	27 10.3
OCT 8	20 28.3	27 21.3
18	20 40.2	27 30.8
28	20 51.0	27 38.5
NOV 7	21 00.5	27 44.1
17	21 08.3	27 47.6
27	21 14.2	27 48.9
DEC 7	21 18.1	27R47.9
17	21 19.9	27 44.6
27	21R19.6	27 39.2
JAN 6	21♍17.1	27♌32.0
JAN 1	21N31.8	35N15.8
21	21 42.4	35 28.4
FEB 10	21 54.2	35 39.6
MAR 2	22 05.5	35 47.9
22	22 14.9	35 52.1
APR 11	22 21.1	35 51.8
MAY 1	22 23.5	35 47.0
21	22 21.7	35 38.4
JUN 10	22 16.2	35 27.1
30	22 07.5	35 14.2
JUL 20	21 56.7	35 01.0
AUG 9	21 44.9	34 48.8
29	21 33.3	34 38.8
SEP 18	21 23.0	34 32.0
OCT 8	21 15.2	34 29.1
28	21 10.7	34 30.5
NOV 17	21 10.1	34 36.1
DEC 7	21 13.6	34 45.4
27	21N20.7	34N57.1
	6/2.48	5/8.40
	12/20.05	11/27.17

1982	♇ Haumea 136108	♇ Makemake 136472
JAN 1	21R18.6	27R35.8
11	21♍15.1	27♌27.7
21	21 09.6	27 18.1
31	21 02.4	27 07.5
FEB 10	20 53.8	26 56.1
20	20 44.0	26 44.4
MAR 2	20 33.4	26 32.9
12	20 22.4	26 22.0
22	20 11.5	26 12.1
APR 1	20 00.9	26 03.6
11	19 51.2	25 56.6
21	19 42.5	25 51.5
MAY 1	19 35.3	25 48.5
11	19 29.7	25D47.6
21	19 25.9	25 48.9
31	19 24.1	25 52.4
JUN 10	19D24.4	25 57.9
20	19 26.6	26 05.4
30	19 30.8	26 14.6
JUL 10	19 36.9	26 25.4
20	19 44.8	26 37.4
30	19 54.2	26 50.5
AUG 9	20 04.9	27 04.3
19	20 16.8	27 18.4
29	20 29.4	27 32.7
SEP 8	20 42.5	27 46.6
18	20 55.9	28 00.0
28	21 09.1	28 12.4
OCT 8	21 21.9	28 23.7
18	21 33.9	28 33.3
28	21 44.9	28 41.3
NOV 7	21 54.5	28 47.2
17	22 02.5	28 51.0
27	22 08.6	28 52.5
DEC 7	22 12.8	28R51.8
17	22 14.9	28 48.8
27	22R14.8	28 43.7
JAN 6	22♍12.5	28♌36.7
JAN 1	21N23.0	35N00.3
21	21 33.6	35 13.0
FEB 10	21 45.4	35 24.4
MAR 2	21 56.8	35 32.9
22	22 06.3	35 37.5
APR 11	22 12.7	35 37.5
MAY 1	22 15.2	35 32.9
21	22 13.7	35 24.6
JUN 10	22 08.3	35 13.3
30	21 59.7	35 00.4
JUL 20	21 48.9	34 47.1
AUG 9	21 37.0	34 34.7
29	21 25.3	34 24.4
SEP 18	21 14.8	34 17.3
OCT 8	21 06.8	34 14.0
28	21 02.1	34 15.1
NOV 17	21 01.4	34 20.5
DEC 7	21 04.6	34 29.5
27	21N11.7	34N41.2
	6/3.63	5/9.77
	12/21.18	11/28.44

1983	♇ Haumea 136108	♇ Makemake 136472
JAN 1	22R13.9	28R40.4
11	22♍10.7	28♌32.6
21	22 05.4	28 23.1
31	21 58.4	28 12.6
FEB 10	21 49.9	28 01.3
20	21 40.2	27 49.6
MAR 2	21 29.7	27 38.1
12	21 18.7	27 27.1
22	21 07.7	27 17.1
APR 1	20 57.1	27 08.3
11	20 47.2	27 01.1
21	20 38.4	26 55.8
MAY 1	20 31.0	26 52.5
11	20 25.2	26 51.3
21	20 21.2	26D52.3
31	20 19.2	26 55.5
JUN 10	20D19.2	27 00.7
20	20 21.2	27 08.0
30	20 25.2	27 16.9
JUL 10	20 31.1	27 27.5
20	20 38.7	27 39.4
30	20 48.0	27 52.3
AUG 9	20 58.6	28 06.0
19	21 10.3	28 20.1
29	21 22.9	28 34.3
SEP 8	21 36.0	28 48.4
18	21 49.3	29 01.8
28	22 02.6	29 14.4
OCT 8	22 15.5	29 25.7
18	22 27.6	29 35.6
28	22 38.7	29 43.8
NOV 7	22 48.5	29 50.0
17	22 56.7	29 54.1
27	23 03.1	29 55.9
DEC 7	23 07.5	29R55.5
17	23 09.8	29 52.8
27	23R10.0	29 47.9
JAN 6	23♍08.0	29♌41.1
JAN 1	21N13.9	34N44.3
21	21 24.5	34 57.1
FEB 10	21 36.3	35 08.6
MAR 2	21 47.8	35 17.5
22	21 57.4	35 22.3
APR 11	22 04.0	35 22.6
MAY 1	22 06.7	35 18.4
21	22 05.3	35 10.2
JUN 10	22 00.0	34 59.0
30	21 51.5	34 46.1
JUL 20	21 40.7	34 32.7
AUG 9	21 28.8	34 20.1
29	21 17.0	34 09.6
SEP 18	21 06.4	34 02.1
OCT 8	20 58.2	33 58.6
28	20 53.4	33 59.3
NOV 17	20 52.4	34 04.4
DEC 7	20 55.5	34 13.2
27	21N02.4	34N24.8
	6/4.85	5/11.13
	12/22.35	11/29.74

1984	♇ Haumea 136108	♇ Makemake 136472
JAN 1	23R09.3	29R44.8
11	23♍06.2	29♌37.1
21	23 01.2	29 27.9
31	22 54.4	29 17.4
FEB 10	22 46.0	29 06.2
20	22 36.4	28 54.6
MAR 1	22 26.0	28 43.0
11	22 15.0	28 32.0
21	22 04.0	28 21.8
31	21 53.3	28 12.8
APR 10	21 43.3	28 05.4
20	21 34.4	27 59.9
30	21 26.8	27 56.3
MAY 10	21 20.8	27 54.8
20	21 16.6	27D55.5
30	21 14.3	27 58.4
JUN 9	21D14.0	28 03.4
19	21 15.8	28 10.3
29	21 19.5	28 19.0
JUL 9	21 25.2	28 29.4
19	21 32.7	28 41.1
29	21 41.8	28 53.9
AUG 8	21 52.2	29 07.5
18	22 03.8	29 21.5
28	22 16.3	29 35.8
SEP 7	22 29.4	29 49.8
17	22 42.8	0♍03.3
27	22 56.1	0 16.0
OCT 7	23 09.0	0 27.6
17	23 21.3	0 37.6
27	23 32.6	0 46.0
NOV 6	23 42.5	0 52.5
16	23 51.0	0 56.8
26	23 57.6	0 59.0
DEC 6	24 02.2	0R58.8
16	24 04.8	0 56.4
26	24R05.2	0 51.8
JAN 5	24♍03.4	0♍45.3
JAN 1	21N04.6	34N27.9
21	21 15.1	34 40.7
FEB 10	21 26.9	34 52.4
MAR 1	21 38.5	35 01.5
21	21 48.3	35 06.7
APR 10	21 55.1	35 07.3
30	21 58.0	35 03.3
MAY 20	21 56.8	34 55.3
JUN 9	21 51.6	34 44.3
29	21 43.2	34 31.4
JUL 19	21 32.4	34 17.9
AUG 8	21 20.5	34 05.1
28	21 08.5	33 54.3
SEP 17	20 57.8	33 46.6
OCT 7	20 49.5	33 42.7
27	20 44.4	33 43.1
NOV 16	20 43.2	33 47.8
DEC 6	20 46.2	33 56.5
26	20N52.9	34N07.9
	12/22.35	5/11.45
	12/22.48	11/29.98

1985	Haumea 136108	Makemake 136472
JAN 1	24R04.4	0R48.1
11	24♍01.4	0♍40.5
21	23 56.4	0 31.3
31	23 49.6	0 20.9
FEB 10	23 41.2	0 09.7
20	23 31.6	29♌58.1
MAR 2	23 21.2	29 46.6
12	23 10.2	29 35.5
22	22 59.2	29 25.3
APR 1	22 48.5	29 16.3
11	22 38.5	29 08.8
21	22 29.5	29 03.2
MAY 1	22 21.8	28 59.6
11	22 15.8	28 58.0
21	22 11.5	28D58.6
31	22 09.2	29 01.4
JUN 10	22D08.9	29 06.3
20	22 10.7	29 13.2
30	22 14.4	29 21.9
JUL 10	22 20.0	29 32.2
20	22 27.5	29 43.8
30	22 36.5	29 56.6
AUG 9	22 47.0	0♍10.1
19	22 58.6	0 24.1
29	23 11.1	0 38.4
SEP 8	23 24.2	0 52.4
18	23 37.5	1 05.9
28	23 50.9	1 18.6
OCT 8	24 03.9	1 30.2
18	24 16.2	1 40.3
28	24 27.4	1 48.7
NOV 7	24 37.5	1 55.3
17	24 45.9	1 59.7
27	24 52.6	2 01.8
DEC 7	24 57.2	2R01.7
17	24 59.8	1 59.4
27	25R00.3	1 54.9
JAN 6	24♍58.5	1♍48.4
JAN 1	20N55.6	34N11.7
21	21 06.1	34 24.5
FEB 10	21 18.0	34 36.3
MAR 2	21 29.6	34 45.4
22	21 39.4	34 50.7
APR 11	21 46.2	34 51.4
MAY 1	21 49.1	34 47.5
21	21 47.8	34 39.5
JUN 10	21 42.6	34 28.5
30	21 34.2	34 15.5
JUL 20	21 23.3	34 01.9
AUG 9	21 11.3	33 49.1
29	20 59.3	33 38.1
SEP 18	20 48.6	33 30.3
OCT 8	20 40.2	33 26.2
28	20 35.1	33 26.5
NOV 17	20 34.0	33 31.2
DEC 7	20 36.9	33 39.8
27	20N43.8	33N51.2
	12/22.49	5/12.84
	12/23.62	12/1.27

1986	Haumea 136108	Makemake 136472
JAN 1	24R59.7	1R51.9
11	24♍56.9	1♍44.5
21	24 52.1	1 35.5
31	24 45.5	1 25.2
FEB 10	24 37.3	1 14.1
20	24 27.8	1 02.6
MAR 2	24 17.4	0 51.0
12	24 06.5	0 39.8
22	23 55.5	0 29.5
APR 1	23 44.7	0 20.3
11	23 34.5	0 12.7
21	23 25.4	0 06.8
MAY 1	23 17.6	0 02.9
11	23 11.3	0 01.1
21	23 06.8	0D01.4
31	23 04.3	0 03.9
JUN 10	23D03.7	0 08.5
20	23 05.2	0 15.1
30	23 08.7	0 23.6
JUL 10	23 14.2	0 33.6
20	23 21.4	0 45.1
30	23 30.3	0 57.7
AUG 9	23 40.6	1 11.2
19	23 52.1	1 25.1
29	24 04.5	1 39.3
SEP 8	24 17.6	1 53.4
18	24 30.9	2 07.0
28	24 44.3	2 19.8
OCT 8	24 57.4	2 31.5
18	25 09.8	2 41.8
28	25 21.2	2 50.5
NOV 7	25 31.4	2 57.3
17	25 40.0	3 01.9
27	25 46.9	3 04.4
DEC 7	25 51.9	3R04.6
17	25 54.7	3 02.5
27	25R55.4	2 58.3
JAN 6	25♍53.9	2♍52.1
JAN 1	20N46.0	33N54.3
21	20 56.4	34 07.2
FEB 10	21 08.3	34 19.1
MAR 2	21 20.0	34 28.5
22	21 30.0	34 34.0
APR 11	21 36.9	34 35.0
MAY 1	21 40.0	34 31.4
21	21 38.9	34 23.7
JUN 10	21 33.9	34 12.7
30	21 25.5	33 59.8
JUL 20	21 14.7	33 46.1
AUG 9	21 02.6	33 33.1
29	20 50.6	33 22.0
SEP 18	20 39.7	33 13.8
OCT 8	20 31.2	33 09.4
28	20 25.9	33 09.4
NOV 17	20 24.5	33 13.8
DEC 7	20 27.3	33 22.1
27	20N34.0	33N33.4
	12/23.61	5/14.14
	12/24.79	12/2.52

1987	Haumea 136108	Makemake 136472
JAN 1	25R54.9	2R55.4
11	25♍52.4	2♍48.2
21	25 47.8	2 39.4
31	25 41.4	2 29.4
FEB 10	25 33.3	2 18.3
20	25 24.0	2 06.8
MAR 2	25 13.6	1 55.2
12	25 02.8	1 44.0
22	24 51.7	1 33.6
APR 1	24 40.8	1 24.2
11	24 30.6	1 16.4
21	24 21.3	1 10.3
MAY 1	24 13.3	1 06.1
11	24 06.9	1 04.0
21	24 02.2	1D04.1
31	23 59.4	1 06.3
JUN 10	23D58.6	1 10.6
20	23 59.8	1 17.0
30	24 03.1	1 25.2
JUL 10	24 08.3	1 35.0
20	24 15.4	1 46.3
30	24 24.1	1 58.8
AUG 9	24 34.3	2 12.1
19	24 45.6	2 26.0
29	24 58.0	2 40.2
SEP 8	25 11.0	2 54.3
18	25 24.4	3 08.0
28	25 37.8	3 20.9
OCT 8	25 50.9	3 32.8
18	26 03.4	3 43.3
28	26 15.0	3 52.2
NOV 7	26 25.4	3 59.2
17	26 34.2	4 04.1
27	26 41.4	4 06.9
DEC 7	26 46.5	4R07.4
17	26 49.6	4 05.6
27	26R50.5	4 01.6
JAN 6	26♍49.3	3♍55.6
JAN 1	20N36.2	33N36.5
21	20 46.6	33 49.3
FEB 10	20 58.5	34 01.4
MAR 2	21 10.3	34 11.0
22	21 20.4	34 16.8
APR 11	21 27.5	34 18.1
MAY 1	21 30.8	34 14.8
21	21 29.8	34 07.3
JUN 10	21 24.9	33 56.5
30	21 16.6	33 43.6
JUL 20	21 05.8	33 29.8
AUG 9	20 53.8	33 16.7
29	20 41.6	33 05.3
SEP 18	20 30.6	32 56.8
OCT 8	20 21.9	32 52.1
28	20 16.4	32 51.7
NOV 17	20 14.9	32 55.8
DEC 7	20 17.5	33 03.9
27	20N24.0	33N15.0
	12/24.79	5/15.46
	12/25.92	12/3.82

1988	Haumea 136108	Makemake 136472
JAN 1	26R50.2	3R58.9
11	26♍47.9	3♍51.9
21	26 43.5	3 43.3
31	26 37.3	3 33.4
FEB 10	26 29.4	3 22.5
20	26 20.2	3 11.0
MAR 1	26 10.0	2 59.5
11	25 59.1	2 48.2
21	25 48.1	2 37.6
31	25 37.2	2 28.2
APR 10	25 26.8	2 20.1
20	25 17.4	2 13.8
30	25 09.2	2 09.3
MAY 10	25 02.6	2 07.0
20	24 57.7	2D06.7
30	24 54.6	2 08.7
JUN 9	24D53.6	2 12.7
19	24 54.6	2 18.8
29	24 57.7	2 26.8
JUL 9	25 02.7	2 36.4
19	25 09.5	2 47.5
29	25 18.1	2 59.9
AUG 8	25 28.1	3 13.1
18	25 39.3	3 26.9
28	25 51.6	3 41.1
SEP 7	26 04.6	3 55.2
17	26 17.9	4 08.9
27	26 31.4	4 22.0
OCT 7	26 44.6	4 34.0
17	26 57.2	4 44.7
27	27 09.0	4 53.8
NOV 6	27 19.5	5 01.0
16	27 28.6	5 06.3
26	27 35.9	5 09.3
DEC 6	27 41.3	5R10.1
16	27 44.7	5 08.6
26	27 45.9	5 04.9
JAN 5	27R44.9	4♍59.2
JAN 1	20N26.2	33N18.1
21	20 36.5	33 30.9
FEB 10	20 48.4	33 43.1
MAR 1	21 00.2	33 52.9
21	21 10.5	33 59.0
APR 10	21 17.7	34 00.6
30	21 21.2	33 57.6
MAY 20	21 20.4	33 50.2
JUN 9	21 15.7	33 39.6
29	21 07.4	33 26.7
JUL 19	20 56.7	33 12.9
AUG 8	20 44.6	32 59.6
28	20 32.4	32 48.0
SEP 17	20 21.2	32 39.2
OCT 7	20 12.3	32 34.2
27	20 06.7	32 33.5
NOV 16	20 04.9	32 37.3
DEC 6	20 07.4	32 45.1
26	20N13.7	32N56.0
	12/25.92	5/15.77
	12/26.13	12/4.12

1989	Haumea 136108	Makemake 136472
JAN 1	27R45.5	5R01.7
11	27♍43.3	4♍54.9
21	27 38.9	4 46.3
31	27 32.7	4 36.4
FEB 10	27 24.9	4 25.6
20	27 15.7	4 14.1
MAR 2	27 05.4	4 02.6
12	26 54.6	3 51.3
22	26 43.5	3 40.7
APR 1	26 32.6	3 31.2
11	26 22.2	3 23.1
21	26 12.8	3 16.8
MAY 1	26 04.6	3 12.3
11	25 57.9	3 09.9
21	25 53.0	3D09.6
31	25 49.9	3 11.4
JUN 10	25D48.9	3 15.4
20	25 49.8	3 21.4
30	25 52.8	3 29.3
JUL 10	25 57.8	3 38.9
20	26 04.7	3 50.0
30	26 13.2	4 02.3
AUG 9	26 23.2	4 15.5
19	26 34.5	4 29.3
29	26 46.7	4 43.4
SEP 8	26 59.7	4 57.5
18	27 13.1	5 11.3
28	27 26.6	5 24.3
OCT 8	27 39.8	5 36.4
18	27 52.5	5 47.1
28	28 04.3	5 56.3
NOV 7	28 14.9	6 03.6
17	28 24.0	6 08.9
27	28 31.3	6 12.0
DEC 7	28 36.8	6R12.8
17	28 40.2	6 11.4
27	28 41.4	6 07.8
JAN 6	28R40.5	6♍02.1
JAN 1	20N16.3	32N59.7
21	20 26.7	33 12.5
FEB 10	20 38.6	33 24.7
MAR 2	20 50.4	33 34.6
22	21 00.6	33 40.8
APR 11	21 07.9	33 42.4
MAY 1	21 11.3	33 39.4
21	21 10.6	33 32.1
JUN 10	21 05.7	33 21.5
30	20 57.4	33 08.6
JUL 20	20 46.6	32 54.7
AUG 9	20 34.5	32 41.3
29	20 22.2	32 29.6
SEP 18	20 11.0	32 20.7
OCT 8	20 02.0	32 15.6
28	19 56.4	32 14.8
NOV 17	19 54.6	32 18.4
DEC 7	19 57.0	32 26.2
27	20N03.5	32N37.1
	12/26.12	5/17.05
	12/27.31	12/5.39

1990		♀ Haumea 136108	♀ Makemake 136472
JAN	1	28R41.2	6R05.2
	11	28♍39.2	5♍58.6
	21	28 35.1	5 50.2
	31	28 29.1	5 40.5
FEB	10	28 21.5	5 29.8
	20	28 12.4	5 18.4
MAR	2	28 02.3	5 06.9
	12	27 51.5	4 55.6
	22	27 40.4	4 44.9
APR	1	27 29.4	4 35.2
	11	27 19.0	4 27.0
	21	27 09.4	4 20.4
MAY	1	27 01.1	4 15.7
	11	26 54.2	4 13.0
	21	26 49.0	4D12.4
	31	26 45.7	4 14.0
JUN	10	26 44.4	4 17.7
	20	26D45.2	4 23.4
	30	26 47.9	4 31.1
JUL	10	26 52.7	4 40.5
	20	26 59.3	4 51.3
	30	27 07.7	5 03.4
AUG	9	27 17.6	5 16.5
	19	27 28.7	5 30.3
	29	27 40.9	5 44.4
SEP	8	27 53.8	5 58.5
	18	28 07.2	6 12.3
	28	28 20.7	6 25.5
OCT	8	28 34.0	6 37.6
	18	28 46.8	6 48.6
	28	28 58.7	6 57.9
NOV	7	29 09.5	7 05.5
	17	29 18.8	7 11.0
	27	29 26.4	7 14.4
DEC	7	29 32.1	7R15.6
	17	29 35.8	7 14.4
	27	29 37.3	7 11.1
JAN	6	29R36.6	7♍05.7
JAN	1	20N05.6	32N40.1
	21	20 15.8	32 52.9
FEB	10	20 27.7	33 05.2
MAR	2	20 39.6	33 15.3
	22	20 50.0	33 21.7
APR	11	20 57.4	33 23.6
MAY	1	21 01.0	33 20.9
	21	21 00.4	33 13.9
JUN	10	20 55.7	33 03.4
	30	20 47.5	32 50.5
JUL	20	20 36.7	32 36.6
AUG	9	20 24.5	32 23.1
	29	20 12.1	32 11.2
SEP	18	20 00.8	32 02.0
OCT	8	19 51.7	31 56.6
	28	19 45.8	31 55.4
NOV	17	19 43.9	31 58.8
DEC	7	19 46.1	32 06.3
	27	19N52.3	32N17.0
		12/27.31	5/18.38
		12/28.49	12/6.72

1991		♀ Haumea 136108	♀ Makemake 136472
JAN	1	29R37.2	7R08.7
	11	29♍35.5	7♍02.3
	21	29 31.6	6 54.2
	31	29 25.8	6 44.6
FEB	10	29 18.3	6 34.0
	20	29 09.4	6 22.7
MAR	2	28 59.4	6 11.2
	12	28 48.6	5 59.8
	22	28 37.5	5 49.0
APR	1	28 26.5	5 39.3
	11	28 16.0	5 30.8
	21	28 06.3	5 24.0
MAY	1	27 57.8	5 19.0
	11	27 50.7	5 16.1
	21	27 45.3	5D15.2
	31	27 41.8	5 16.5
JUN	10	27 40.3	5 19.9
	20	27D40.8	5 25.4
	30	27 43.3	5 32.8
JUL	10	27 47.9	5 42.0
	20	27 54.3	5 52.6
	30	28 02.5	6 04.6
AUG	9	28 12.2	6 17.6
	19	28 23.2	6 31.2
	29	28 35.3	6 45.3
SEP	8	28 48.2	6 59.4
	18	29 01.6	7 13.3
	28	29 15.1	7 26.5
OCT	8	29 28.5	7 38.8
	18	29 41.4	7 49.9
	28	29 53.5	7 59.5
NOV	7	0♎04.4	8 07.3
	17	0 13.9	8 13.1
	27	0 21.8	8 16.8
DEC	7	0 27.7	8 18.2
	17	0 31.6	8R17.4
	27	0 33.4	8 14.3
JAN	6	0R33.0	8♍09.2
JAN	1	19N54.5	32N20.0
	21	20 04.6	32 32.8
FEB	10	20 16.4	32 45.1
MAR	2	20 28.4	32 55.4
	22	20 38.9	33 02.1
APR	11	20 46.4	33 04.3
MAY	1	20 50.2	33 01.9
	21	20 49.8	32 55.1
JUN	10	20 45.2	32 44.7
	30	20 37.1	32 32.0
JUL	20	20 26.4	32 18.1
AUG	9	20 14.2	32 04.4
	29	20 01.7	31 52.3
SEP	18	19 50.3	31 42.9
OCT	8	19 41.0	31 37.1
	28	19 34.9	31 35.6
NOV	17	19 32.7	31 38.7
DEC	7	19 34.8	31 45.9
	27	19N40.8	31N56.4
		12/28.50	5/19.65
		12/29.73	12/7.98

1992		♀ Haumea 136108	♀ Makemake 136472
JAN	1	0R33.5	8R12.0
	11	0♎31.9	8♍05.9
	21	0 28.3	7 58.0
	31	0 22.8	7 48.6
FEB	10	0 15.4	7 38.1
	20	0 06.7	7 26.9
MAR	1	29♍56.7	7 15.4
	11	29 46.0	7 04.0
	21	29 35.0	6 53.1
	31	29 23.9	6 43.2
APR	10	29 13.3	6 34.6
	20	29 03.5	6 27.6
	30	28 54.8	6 22.3
MAY	10	28 47.6	6 19.1
	20	28 42.0	6 18.0
	30	28 38.2	6D19.0
JUN	9	28 36.4	6 22.1
	19	28D36.7	6 27.4
	29	28 39.0	6 34.5
JUL	9	28 43.3	6 43.4
	19	28 49.6	6 53.9
	29	28 57.5	7 05.7
AUG	8	29 07.1	7 18.5
	18	29 18.0	7 32.1
	28	29 30.0	7 46.1
SEP	7	29 42.9	8 00.2
	17	29 56.2	8 14.1
	27	0♎09.8	8 27.4
OCT	7	0 23.2	8 39.9
	17	0 36.2	8 51.1
	27	0 48.4	9 00.9
NOV	6	0 59.5	9 08.9
	16	1 09.2	9 15.0
	26	1 17.3	9 18.9
DEC	6	1 23.5	9 20.7
	16	1 27.7	9R20.1
	26	1 29.7	9 17.3
JAN	5	1R29.5	9♍12.4
JAN	1	19N42.9	31N59.4
	21	19 53.0	32 12.1
FEB	10	20 04.8	32 24.6
MAR	1	20 16.8	32 35.0
	21	20 27.3	32 42.0
APR	10	20 35.1	32 44.5
	30	20 39.0	32 42.4
MAY	20	20 38.8	32 35.8
JUN	9	20 34.4	32 25.6
	29	20 26.4	32 13.0
JUL	19	20 15.7	31 59.1
AUG	8	20 03.5	31 45.3
	28	19 50.9	31 33.0
SEP	17	19 39.3	31 23.3
OCT	7	19 29.9	31 17.2
	27	19 23.6	31 15.5
NOV	16	19 21.3	31 18.2
DEC	6	19 23.1	31 25.2
	26	19N29.0	31N35.5
		12/29.72	5/20.00
		12/29.89	12/8.25

1993		♀ Haumea 136108	♀ Makemake 136472
JAN	1	1R29.9	9R14.6
	11	1♎28.4	9♍08.6
	21	1 24.8	9 00.7
	31	1 19.3	8 51.4
FEB	10	1 12.0	8 40.9
	20	1 03.2	8 29.8
MAR	2	0 53.3	8 18.2
	12	0 42.6	8 06.9
	22	0 31.5	7 56.0
APR	1	0 20.5	7 46.1
	11	0 09.8	7 37.4
	21	0 00.0	7 30.3
MAY	1	29♍51.3	7 25.1
	11	29 44.0	7 21.8
	21	29 38.3	7 20.6
	31	29 34.5	7D21.5
JUN	10	29 32.7	7 24.6
	20	29D32.9	7 29.7
	30	29 35.2	7 36.8
JUL	10	29 39.5	7 45.6
	20	29 45.7	7 56.0
	30	29 53.7	8 07.8
AUG	9	0♎03.2	8 20.6
	19	0 14.1	8 34.1
	29	0 26.1	8 48.1
SEP	8	0 39.0	9 02.2
	18	0 52.3	9 16.1
	28	1 05.9	9 29.4
OCT	8	1 19.4	9 41.9
	18	1 32.4	9 53.2
	28	1 44.6	10 03.0
NOV	7	1 55.8	10 11.0
	17	2 05.6	10 17.2
	27	2 13.7	10 21.1
DEC	7	2 19.9	10 22.9
	17	2 24.2	10R22.4
	27	2 26.2	10 19.7
JAN	6	2R26.1	10♍14.9
JAN	1	19N31.5	31N39.1
	21	19 41.5	31 51.8
FEB	10	19 53.4	32 04.2
MAR	2	20 05.4	32 14.7
	22	20 16.0	32 21.7
APR	11	20 23.7	32 24.3
MAY	1	20 27.6	32 22.2
	21	20 27.3	32 15.7
JUN	10	20 22.9	32 05.6
	30	20 14.8	31 52.9
JUL	20	20 04.1	31 39.0
AUG	9	19 51.8	31 25.2
	29	19 39.2	31 12.8
SEP	18	19 27.6	31 03.0
OCT	8	19 18.2	30 56.9
	28	19 11.9	30 55.0
NOV	17	19 09.5	30 57.6
DEC	7	19 11.4	31 04.5
	27	19N17.3	31N14.8
		12/29.89	5/21.32
		12/31.11	12/9.53

1994		♀ Haumea 136108	♀ Makemake 136472
JAN	1	2R26.4	10R17.6
	11	2♎25.2	10♍11.7
	21	2 21.9	10 04.1
	31	2 16.5	9 55.0
FEB	10	2 09.4	9 44.6
	20	2 00.8	9 33.5
MAR	2	1 51.0	9 22.0
	12	1 40.4	9 10.6
	22	1 29.3	8 59.7
APR	1	1 18.2	8 49.6
	11	1 07.5	8 40.8
	21	0 57.5	8 33.5
MAY	1	0 48.7	8 28.0
	11	0 41.2	8 24.4
	21	0 35.3	8 22.9
	31	0 31.3	8D23.6
JUN	10	0 29.2	8 26.4
	20	0D29.2	8 31.2
	30	0 31.2	8 38.1
JUL	10	0 35.3	8 46.7
	20	0 41.3	8 56.9
	30	0 49.0	9 08.4
AUG	9	0 58.4	9 21.1
	19	1 09.2	9 34.5
	29	1 21.1	9 48.4
SEP	8	1 33.9	10 02.5
	18	1 47.2	10 16.4
	28	2 00.8	10 29.8
OCT	8	2 14.3	10 42.4
	18	2 27.4	10 53.9
	28	2 39.8	11 03.9
NOV	7	2 51.1	11 12.2
	17	3 01.1	11 18.5
	27	3 09.4	11 22.8
DEC	7	3 15.9	11 24.8
	17	3 20.4	11R24.6
	27	3 22.7	11 22.2
JAN	6	3R22.9	11♍17.6
JAN	1	19N19.3	31N17.8
	21	19 29.3	31 30.4
FEB	10	19 41.1	31 42.9
MAR	2	19 53.1	31 53.6
	22	20 03.8	32 00.8
APR	11	20 11.7	32 03.8
MAY	1	20 15.9	32 02.0
	21	20 15.7	31 55.7
JUN	10	20 11.5	31 45.8
	30	20 03.5	31 33.2
JUL	20	19 52.9	31 19.3
AUG	9	19 40.6	31 05.4
	29	19 27.9	30 52.8
SEP	18	19 16.2	30 42.8
OCT	8	19 06.6	30 36.4
	28	19 00.1	30 34.2
NOV	17	18 57.5	30 36.5
DEC	7	18 59.2	30 43.2
	27	19N05.0	30N53.3
		12/31.11	5/22.63
		1/1.28	12/10.75

1995	Haumea 136108	Makemake 136472
JAN 1	3♎23.1	11R20.2
11	3R22.1	11♍14.6
21	3 19.0	11 07.2
31	3 13.9	10 58.2
FEB 10	3 07.0	10 48.0
20	2 58.5	10 37.0
MAR 2	2 48.8	10 25.5
12	2 38.2	10 14.1
22	2 27.2	10 03.1
APR 1	2 16.1	9 52.9
11	2 05.3	9 43.9
21	1 55.2	9 36.4
MAY 1	1 46.1	9 30.6
11	1 38.5	9 26.8
21	1 32.4	9 25.0
31	1 28.1	9D25.4
JUN 10	1 25.8	9 27.9
20	1D25.5	9 32.5
30	1 27.3	9 39.0
JUL 10	1 31.1	9 47.4
20	1 36.9	9 57.4
30	1 44.4	10 08.8
AUG 9	1 53.7	10 21.3
19	2 04.3	10 34.6
29	2 16.1	10 48.5
SEP 8	2 28.8	11 02.5
18	2 42.1	11 16.5
28	2 55.7	11 29.9
OCT 8	3 09.3	11 42.6
18	3 22.5	11 54.2
28	3 35.0	12 04.4
NOV 7	3 46.5	12 12.9
17	3 56.6	12 19.5
27	4 05.2	12 24.1
DEC 7	4 11.9	12 26.4
17	4 16.6	12R26.5
27	4 19.2	12 24.3
JAN 6	4R19.6	12♍20.0

1995	Haumea 136108	Makemake 136472
JAN 1	19N07.0	30N56.2
21	19 16.8	31 08.8
FEB 10	19 28.6	31 21.3
MAR 2	19 40.7	31 32.1
22	19 51.5	31 39.6
APR 11	19 59.5	31 42.8
MAY 1	20 03.9	31 41.4
21	20 03.9	31 35.4
JUN 10	19 59.8	31 25.6
30	19 52.0	31 13.1
JUL 20	19 41.4	30 59.3
AUG 9	19 29.1	30 45.3
29	19 16.4	30 32.6
SEP 18	19 04.6	30 22.4
OCT 8	18 54.8	30 15.6
28	18 48.2	30 13.1
NOV 17	18 45.4	30 15.2
DEC 7	18 46.9	30 21.5
27	18N52.5	30N31.4
	1/1.28	5/24.00
	1/2.46	12/12.02

1996	Haumea 136108	Makemake 136472
JAN 1	4♎19.7	12R22.4
11	4R19.0	12♍17.1
21	4 16.2	12 09.9
31	4 11.3	12 01.1
FEB 10	4 04.5	11 51.0
20	3 56.2	11 40.1
MAR 1	3 46.6	11 28.7
11	3 36.1	11 17.2
21	3 25.1	11 06.2
31	3 14.0	10 55.9
APR 10	3 03.1	10 46.7
20	2 52.9	10 39.0
30	2 43.7	10 33.0
MAY 10	2 35.8	10 28.9
20	2 29.5	10 26.8
30	2 25.0	10D26.9
JUN 9	2 22.4	10 29.1
19	2D21.9	10 33.5
29	2 23.4	10 39.7
JUL 9	2 27.0	10 47.9
19	2 32.5	10 57.6
29	2 39.9	11 08.8
AUG 8	2 48.9	11 21.2
18	2 59.4	11 34.4
28	3 11.1	11 48.2
SEP 7	3 23.8	12 02.2
17	3 37.0	12 16.2
27	3 50.7	12 29.7
OCT 7	4 04.3	12 42.5
17	4 17.5	12 54.2
27	4 30.2	13 04.6
NOV 6	4 41.8	13 13.3
16	4 52.1	13 20.2
26	5 00.9	13 25.0
DEC 6	5 07.9	13 27.6
16	5 12.9	13R27.9
26	5 15.7	13 26.0
JAN 5	5R16.4	13♍22.0

1996	Haumea 136108	Makemake 136472
JAN 1	18N54.4	30N34.3
21	19 04.2	30 46.8
FEB 10	19 15.9	30 59.4
MAR 1	19 28.1	31 10.4
21	19 39.0	31 18.1
APR 10	19 47.2	31 21.6
30	19 51.7	31 20.4
MAY 20	19 52.0	31 14.7
JUN 9	19 48.0	31 05.2
29	19 40.3	30 52.8
JUL 19	19 29.8	30 39.0
AUG 8	19 17.5	30 24.9
28	19 04.8	30 12.1
SEP 17	18 52.9	30 01.6
OCT 7	18 42.9	29 54.6
27	18 36.1	29 51.8
NOV 16	18 33.1	29 53.6
DEC 6	18 34.4	29 59.6
26	18N39.8	30N09.3
	1/2.45	5/24.29
	1/2.66	12/12.24

1997	Haumea 136108	Makemake 136472
JAN 1	5♎16.4	13R23.9
11	5R15.7	13♍18.6
21	5 12.9	13 11.4
31	5 08.0	13 02.7
FEB 10	5 01.3	12 52.7
20	4 53.0	12 41.8
MAR 2	4 43.4	12 30.4
12	4 32.9	12 18.9
22	4 21.9	12 07.9
APR 1	4 10.7	11 57.5
11	3 59.8	11 48.3
21	3 49.6	11 40.6
MAY 1	3 40.4	11 34.5
11	3 32.4	11 30.4
21	3 26.1	11 28.3
31	3 21.5	11D28.3
JUN 10	3 18.9	11 30.4
20	3D18.4	11 34.7
30	3 19.8	11 40.9
JUL 10	3 23.4	11 49.0
20	3 28.9	11 58.7
30	3 36.2	12 09.8
AUG 9	3 45.2	12 22.1
19	3 55.7	12 35.3
29	4 07.4	12 49.0
SEP 8	4 20.0	13 03.1
18	4 33.3	13 17.0
28	4 46.9	13 30.5
OCT 8	5 00.6	13 43.3
18	5 13.9	13 55.1
28	5 26.6	14 05.5
NOV 7	5 38.2	14 14.2
17	5 48.6	14 21.1
27	5 57.4	14 26.0
DEC 7	6 04.5	14 28.6
17	6 09.5	14R29.0
27	6 12.4	14 27.2
JAN 6	6R13.1	14♍23.2

1997	Haumea 136108	Makemake 136472
JAN 1	18N42.2	30N12.8
21	18 52.0	30 25.2
FEB 10	19 03.7	30 37.9
MAR 2	19 15.9	30 48.8
22	19 26.8	30 56.6
APR 11	19 35.0	31 00.2
MAY 1	19 39.5	30 59.0
21	19 39.7	30 53.4
JUN 10	19 35.7	30 43.8
30	19 28.0	30 31.5
JUL 20	19 17.5	30 17.6
AUG 9	19 05.2	30 03.6
29	18 52.4	29 50.7
SEP 18	18 40.4	29 40.1
OCT 8	18 30.5	29 33.1
28	18 23.6	29 30.2
NOV 17	18 20.7	29 31.8
DEC 7	18 22.0	29 37.8
27	18N27.4	29N47.5
	1/2.66	5/25.64
	1/3.80	12/13.49

1998	Haumea 136108	Makemake 136472
JAN 1	6♎13.0	14R25.5
11	6R12.6	14♍20.4
21	6 10.0	14 13.5
31	6 05.4	14 05.0
FEB 10	5 58.9	13 55.1
20	5 50.7	13 44.3
MAR 2	5 41.2	13 33.0
12	5 30.8	13 21.5
22	5 19.8	13 10.4
APR 1	5 08.6	12 59.9
11	4 57.7	12 50.6
21	4 47.3	12 42.6
MAY 1	4 37.9	12 36.4
11	4 29.8	12 32.0
21	4 23.2	12 29.6
31	4 18.5	12D29.3
JUN 10	4 15.6	12 31.2
20	4D14.8	12 35.1
30	4 16.0	12 41.1
JUL 10	4 19.3	12 48.9
20	4 24.6	12 58.4
30	4 31.7	13 09.4
AUG 9	4 40.5	13 21.5
19	4 50.9	13 34.6
29	5 02.4	13 48.3
SEP 8	5 15.0	14 02.3
18	5 28.2	14 16.2
28	5 41.9	14 29.8
OCT 8	5 55.6	14 42.7
18	6 09.0	14 54.6
28	6 21.7	15 05.2
NOV 7	6 33.5	15 14.1
17	6 44.1	15 21.3
27	6 53.2	15 26.4
DEC 7	7 00.4	15 29.3
17	7 05.7	15R30.0
27	7 08.9	15 28.4
JAN 6	7R09.8	15♍24.7

1998	Haumea 136108	Makemake 136472
JAN 1	18N29.4	29N50.3
21	18 39.0	30 02.7
FEB 10	18 50.8	30 15.3
MAR 2	19 02.9	30 26.4
22	19 13.9	30 34.4
APR 11	19 22.3	30 38.3
MAY 1	19 27.0	30 37.4
21	19 27.4	30 32.0
JUN 10	19 23.6	30 22.7
30	19 16.1	30 10.5
JUL 20	19 05.6	29 56.7
AUG 9	18 53.3	29 42.5
29	18 40.5	29 29.5
SEP 18	18 28.4	29 18.8
OCT 8	18 18.3	29 11.4
28	18 11.3	29 08.2
NOV 17	18 08.1	29 09.6
DEC 7	18 09.2	29 15.3
27	18N14.5	29N24.7
	1/3.81	5/26.94
	1/5.03	12/14.75

1999	Haumea 136108	Makemake 136472
JAN 1	7♎09.6	15R26.8
11	7R09.5	15♍22.1
21	7 07.1	15 15.4
31	7 02.7	15 07.0
FEB 10	6 56.4	14 57.3
20	6 48.4	14 46.6
MAR 2	6 39.1	14 35.3
12	6 28.8	14 23.9
22	6 17.8	14 12.7
APR 1	6 06.6	14 02.2
11	5 55.6	13 52.7
21	5 45.1	13 44.6
MAY 1	5 35.5	13 38.1
11	5 27.3	13 33.4
21	5 20.5	13 30.8
31	5 15.5	13D30.3
JUN 10	5 12.4	13 31.8
20	5D11.3	13 35.5
30	5 12.3	13 41.2
JUL 10	5 15.3	13 48.8
20	5 20.4	13 58.1
30	5 27.3	14 08.9
AUG 9	5 36.0	14 20.9
19	5 46.1	14 33.8
29	5 57.6	14 47.4
SEP 8	6 10.1	15 01.4
18	6 23.3	15 15.3
28	6 36.9	15 29.0
OCT 8	6 50.6	15 42.0
18	7 04.1	15 54.0
28	7 17.0	16 04.7
NOV 7	7 29.0	16 13.9
17	7 39.7	16 21.3
27	7 49.0	16 26.6
DEC 7	7 56.5	16 29.9
17	8 02.0	16R30.8
27	8 05.5	16 29.6
JAN 6	8♎06.7	16♍26.1

1999	Haumea 136108	Makemake 136472
JAN 1	18N16.4	29N27.5
21	18 26.0	29 39.8
FEB 10	18 37.6	29 52.4
MAR 2	18 49.8	30 03.7
22	19 00.9	30 11.9
APR 11	19 09.5	30 16.0
MAY 1	19 14.3	30 15.4
21	19 15.0	30 10.2
JUN 10	19 11.3	30 01.1
30	19 03.9	29 49.1
JUL 20	18 53.5	29 35.3
AUG 9	18 41.2	29 21.1
29	18 28.3	29 07.9
SEP 18	18 16.2	28 57.0
OCT 8	18 05.9	28 49.4
28	17 58.7	28 45.9
NOV 17	17 55.4	28 46.9
DEC 7	17 56.3	28 52.4
27	18N01.4	29N01.6
	1/5.02	5/28.22
	6/19.93	12/15.98

2000	Haumea 136108	Makemake 136472
JAN 1	8♎06.3	16R28.1
11	8R06.5	16♍23.6
21	8 04.4	16 17.2
31	8 00.2	16 09.0
FEB 10	7 54.1	15 59.5
20	7 46.3	15 48.9
MAR 1	7 37.1	15 37.7
11	7 26.9	15 26.2
21	7 15.9	15 15.0
31	7 04.7	15 04.4
APR 10	6 53.6	14 54.8
20	6 43.1	14 46.5
30	6 33.4	14 39.8
MAY 10	6 24.9	14 34.9
20	6 18.0	14 32.0
30	6 12.7	14D31.2
JUN 9	6 09.4	14 32.5
19	6 08.1	14 36.0
29	6D08.8	14 41.4
JUL 9	6 11.6	14 48.7
19	6 16.4	14 57.8
29	6 23.1	15 08.4
AUG 8	6 31.6	15 20.2
18	6 41.6	15 33.0
28	6 53.0	15 46.6
SEP 7	7 05.4	16 00.5
17	7 18.6	16 14.5
27	7 32.2	16 28.2
OCT 7	7 45.9	16 41.3
17	7 59.5	16 53.4
27	8 12.5	17 04.3
NOV 6	8 24.6	17 13.7
16	8 35.6	17 21.3
26	8 45.1	17 26.9
DEC 6	8 52.8	17 30.4
16	8 58.6	17 31.7
26	9 02.3	17R30.7
JAN 5	9♎03.8	17♍27.5
JAN 1	18N03.2	29N04.3
21	18 12.7	29 16.5
FEB 10	18 24.3	29 29.1
MAR 1	18 36.5	29 40.4
21	18 47.7	29 48.8
APR 10	18 56.3	29 53.2
30	19 01.4	29 52.9
MAY 20	19 02.2	29 48.0
JUN 9	18 58.7	29 39.1
29	18 51.4	29 27.2
JUL 19	18 41.1	29 13.5
AUG 8	18 28.8	28 59.3
28	18 15.9	28 46.0
SEP 17	18 03.6	28 34.8
OCT 7	17 53.3	28 27.0
27	17 45.9	28 23.2
NOV 16	17 42.3	28 23.9
DEC 6	17 43.0	28 29.0
26	17N47.9	28N38.0
	1/6.21 6/20.16	5/28.53 12/16.29

2001	Haumea 136108	Makemake 136472
JAN 1	9♎03.5	17R29.0
11	9R03.6	17♍24.6
21	9 01.6	17 18.2
31	8 57.5	17 10.1
FEB 10	8 51.4	17 00.6
20	8 43.6	16 50.1
MAR 2	8 34.5	16 38.9
12	8 24.2	16 27.5
22	8 13.3	16 16.3
APR 1	8 02.1	16 05.7
11	7 51.0	15 56.1
21	7 40.4	15 47.7
MAY 1	7 30.7	15 41.0
11	7 22.2	15 36.1
21	7 15.2	15 33.1
31	7 09.9	15D32.3
JUN 10	7 06.5	15 33.5
20	7 05.1	15 36.9
30	7D05.9	15 42.3
JUL 10	7 08.6	15 49.6
20	7 13.4	15 58.6
30	7 20.1	16 09.1
AUG 9	7 28.6	16 20.9
19	7 38.6	16 33.7
29	7 49.9	16 47.2
SEP 8	8 02.3	17 01.1
18	8 15.5	17 15.1
28	8 29.2	17 28.8
OCT 8	8 43.0	17 41.9
18	8 56.6	17 54.1
28	9 09.6	18 05.0
NOV 7	9 21.8	18 14.4
17	9 32.8	18 22.1
27	9 42.4	18 27.7
DEC 7	9 50.2	18 31.3
17	9 56.0	18 32.6
27	9 59.8	18R31.7
JAN 6	10♎01.3	18♍28.6
JAN 1	17N50.1	28N41.3
21	17 59.5	28 53.3
FEB 10	18 11.1	29 05.9
MAR 2	18 23.4	29 17.3
22	18 34.5	29 25.7
APR 11	18 43.2	29 30.1
MAY 1	18 48.2	29 29.8
21	18 49.0	29 25.0
JUN 10	18 45.4	29 16.1
30	18 38.1	29 04.2
JUL 20	18 27.7	28 50.5
AUG 9	18 15.4	28 36.3
29	18 02.4	28 22.9
SEP 18	17 50.1	28 11.7
OCT 8	17 39.7	28 03.8
28	17 32.3	27 59.9
NOV 17	17 28.7	28 00.5
DEC 7	17 29.4	28 05.6
27	17N34.3	28N14.5
	1/6.43 6/21.34	5/29.76 12/17.53

2002	Haumea 136108	Makemake 136472
JAN 1	10♎00.8	18R30.4
11	10R01.3	18♍26.2
21	9 59.5	18 20.1
31	9 55.6	18 12.2
FEB 10	9 49.8	18 02.9
20	9 42.2	17 52.5
MAR 2	9 33.2	17 41.4
12	9 23.0	17 30.0
22	9 12.1	17 18.8
APR 1	9 00.9	17 08.1
11	8 49.8	16 58.3
21	8 39.1	16 49.9
MAY 1	8 29.3	16 42.9
11	8 20.6	16 37.8
21	8 13.4	16 34.6
31	8 07.9	16 33.5
JUN 10	8 04.3	16D34.4
20	8 02.7	16 37.5
30	8D03.2	16 42.7
JUL 10	8 05.7	16 49.7
20	8 10.3	16 58.5
30	8 16.7	17 08.8
AUG 9	8 25.0	17 20.5
19	8 34.9	17 33.1
29	8 46.1	17 46.5
SEP 8	8 58.4	18 00.4
18	9 11.6	18 14.4
28	9 25.2	18 28.1
OCT 8	9 39.1	18 41.3
18	9 52.7	18 53.6
28	10 05.9	19 04.7
NOV 7	10 18.2	19 14.3
17	10 29.4	19 22.2
27	10 39.2	19 28.1
DEC 7	10 47.2	19 32.0
17	10 53.3	19 33.6
27	10 57.4	19R32.9
JAN 6	10♎59.2	19♍30.1
JAN 1	17N36.2	28N17.2
21	17 45.5	28 29.1
FEB 10	17 57.0	28 41.7
MAR 2	18 09.2	28 53.1
22	18 20.4	29 01.7
APR 11	18 29.2	29 06.4
MAY 1	18 34.4	29 06.4
21	18 35.4	29 01.8
JUN 10	18 32.0	28 53.2
30	18 24.8	28 41.4
JUL 20	18 14.5	28 27.8
AUG 9	18 02.2	28 13.5
29	17 49.2	28 00.1
SEP 18	17 36.8	27 48.7
OCT 8	17 26.2	27 40.5
28	17 18.7	27 36.4
NOV 17	17 14.9	27 36.7
DEC 7	17 15.3	27 41.5
27	17N20.0	27N50.1
	1/7.68 6/22.51	5/31.07 12/18.80

2003	Haumea 136108	Makemake 136472
JAN 1	10♎58.6	19R31.8
11	10R59.3	19♍27.9
21	10 57.8	19 22.0
31	10 54.2	19 14.3
FEB 10	10 48.5	19 05.2
20	10 41.1	18 54.9
MAR 2	10 32.3	18 43.9
12	10 22.2	18 32.6
22	10 11.4	18 21.3
APR 1	10 00.2	18 10.5
11	9 49.1	18 00.7
21	9 38.3	17 52.0
MAY 1	9 28.3	17 44.9
11	9 19.5	17 39.5
21	9 12.1	17 36.1
31	9 06.4	17 34.7
JUN 10	9 02.5	17D35.4
20	9 00.7	17 38.2
30	9D00.9	17 43.1
JUL 10	9 03.2	17 49.9
20	9 07.5	17 58.4
30	9 13.8	18 08.6
AUG 9	9 21.9	18 20.0
19	9 31.6	18 32.6
29	9 42.7	18 45.9
SEP 8	9 54.9	18 59.7
18	10 08.0	19 13.7
28	10 21.6	19 27.4
OCT 8	10 35.5	19 40.7
18	10 49.2	19 53.1
28	11 02.5	20 04.4
NOV 7	11 15.0	20 14.2
17	11 26.4	20 22.3
27	11 36.4	20 28.5
DEC 7	11 44.6	20 32.6
17	11 51.0	20 34.5
27	11 55.3	20R34.1
JAN 6	11♎57.4	20♍31.5
JAN 1	17N21.8	27N52.7
21	17 31.0	28 04.6
FEB 10	17 42.4	28 17.1
MAR 2	17 54.6	28 28.6
22	18 06.0	28 37.4
APR 11	18 14.9	28 42.3
MAY 1	18 20.2	28 42.6
21	18 21.3	28 38.3
JUN 10	18 18.2	28 29.9
30	18 11.1	28 18.3
JUL 20	18 00.8	28 04.7
AUG 9	17 48.6	27 50.5
29	17 35.6	27 36.9
SEP 18	17 23.1	27 25.4
OCT 8	17 12.4	27 16.9
28	17 04.6	27 12.5
NOV 17	17 00.6	27 12.5
DEC 7	17 00.9	27 17.0
27	17N05.4	27N25.4
	1/8.89 6/23.74	6/1.33 12/20.07

2004	Haumea 136108	Makemake 136472
JAN 1	11♎56.7	20R33.1
11	11R57.7	20♍29.5
21	11 56.5	20 23.8
31	11 53.1	20 16.4
FEB 10	11 47.7	20 07.4
20	11 40.5	19 57.3
MAR 1	11 31.8	19 46.4
11	11 21.8	19 35.1
21	11 11.1	19 23.8
31	10 59.9	19 13.0
APR 10	10 48.7	19 03.0
20	10 37.9	18 54.2
30	10 27.8	18 46.8
MAY 10	10 18.8	18 41.2
20	10 11.2	18 37.5
30	10 05.2	18 35.9
JUN 9	10 01.2	18D36.3
19	9 59.0	18 38.9
29	9D59.0	18 43.5
JUL 9	10 01.0	18 50.0
19	10 05.1	18 58.3
29	10 11.2	19 08.3
AUG 8	10 19.1	19 19.6
18	10 28.6	19 32.0
28	10 39.6	19 45.2
SEP 7	10 51.7	19 59.0
17	11 04.8	20 12.9
27	11 18.4	20 26.7
OCT 7	11 32.3	20 40.0
17	11 46.1	20 52.6
27	11 59.5	21 04.0
NOV 6	12 12.1	21 14.0
16	12 23.7	21 22.3
26	12 33.8	21 28.7
DEC 6	12 42.4	21 33.1
16	12 49.0	21 35.2
26	12 53.6	21R35.2
JAN 5	12♎56.0	21♍32.9
JAN 1	17N07.1	27N28.0
21	17 16.1	27 39.7
FEB 10	17 27.5	27 52.2
MAR 1	17 39.7	28 03.8
21	17 51.1	28 12.7
APR 10	18 00.1	28 17.9
30	18 05.6	28 18.4
MAY 20	18 07.0	28 14.4
JUN 9	18 03.9	28 06.2
29	17 57.0	27 54.8
JUL 19	17 46.9	27 41.3
AUG 8	17 34.6	27 27.1
28	17 21.6	27 13.4
SEP 17	17 09.0	27 01.7
OCT 7	16 58.2	26 53.1
27	16 50.2	26 48.3
NOV 16	16 46.0	26 48.1
DEC 6	16 46.1	26 52.3
26	16N50.4	27N00.4
	1/10.16 6/23.93	6/1.62 12/20.29

2005	Haumea 136108	Makemake 136472
JAN 1	12♎55.3	21R34.1
11	12R56.4	21♍30.5
21	12 55.2	21 24.9
31	12 51.8	21 17.5
FEB 10	12 46.5	21 08.6
20	12 39.3	20 58.5
MAR 2	12 30.6	20 47.6
12	12 20.7	20 36.3
22	12 10.0	20 25.1
APR 1	11 58.8	20 14.2
11	11 47.6	20 04.2
21	11 36.7	19 55.4
MAY 1	11 26.6	19 48.0
11	11 17.6	19 42.4
21	11 09.9	19 38.6
31	11 03.9	19 36.9
JUN 10	10 59.8	19D37.3
20	10 57.6	19 39.8
30	10D57.5	19 44.3
JUL 10	10 59.5	19 50.8
20	11 03.6	19 59.0
30	11 09.6	20 08.9
AUG 9	11 17.5	20 20.2
19	11 27.0	20 32.5
29	11 38.0	20 45.7
SEP 8	11 50.1	20 59.4
18	12 03.2	21 13.4
28	12 16.8	21 27.2
OCT 8	12 30.7	21 40.5
18	12 44.6	21 53.0
28	12 58.0	22 04.5
NOV 7	13 10.7	22 14.5
17	13 22.3	22 22.9
27	13 32.5	22 29.3
DEC 7	13 41.1	22 33.7
17	13 47.8	22 35.9
27	13 52.4	22R35.9
JAN 6	13♎54.9	22♍33.7
JAN 1	16N52.5	27N03.5
21	17 01.5	27 15.1
FEB 10	17 12.9	27 27.6
MAR 2	17 25.0	27 39.2
22	17 36.4	27 48.2
APR 11	17 45.4	27 53.3
MAY 1	17 50.9	27 53.9
21	17 52.2	27 50.0
JUN 10	17 49.2	27 41.8
30	17 42.2	27 30.4
JUL 20	17 32.0	27 17.0
AUG 9	17 19.8	27 02.7
29	17 06.7	26 49.1
SEP 18	16 54.1	26 37.3
OCT 8	16 43.3	26 28.6
28	16 35.3	26 23.8
NOV 17	16 31.1	26 23.5
DEC 7	16 31.2	26 27.6
27	16N35.5	26N35.7
	1/10.38	6/2.95
	6/25.17	12/21.55

2006	Haumea 136108	Makemake 136472
JAN 1	13♎54.0	22R35.1
11	13 55.3	22♍31.7
21	13R54.4	22 26.4
31	13 51.3	22 19.2
FEB 10	13 46.2	22 10.5
20	13 39.2	22 00.5
MAR 2	13 30.7	21 49.7
12	13 20.9	21 38.5
22	13 10.2	21 27.2
APR 1	12 59.1	21 16.3
11	12 47.8	21 06.2
21	12 36.9	20 57.2
MAY 1	12 26.6	20 49.7
11	12 17.4	20 43.8
21	12 09.6	20 39.8
31	12 03.4	20 37.8
JUN 10	11 59.0	20D37.9
20	11 56.6	20 40.1
30	11D56.2	20 44.4
JUL 10	11 58.0	20 50.6
20	12 01.8	20 58.6
30	12 07.6	21 08.3
AUG 9	12 15.3	21 19.4
19	12 24.6	21 31.6
29	12 35.4	21 44.7
SEP 8	12 47.5	21 58.3
18	13 00.4	22 12.2
28	13 14.0	22 26.0
OCT 8	13 28.0	22 39.4
18	13 41.9	22 52.1
28	13 55.4	23 03.6
NOV 7	14 08.2	23 13.8
17	14 20.0	23 22.4
27	14 30.5	23 29.1
DEC 7	14 39.3	23 33.8
17	14 46.2	23 36.2
27	14 51.1	23R36.5
JAN 6	14♎53.9	23♍34.5
JAN 1	16N37.2	26N38.3
21	16 46.1	26 49.7
FEB 10	16 57.4	27 02.2
MAR 2	17 09.5	27 13.8
22	17 21.0	27 23.0
APR 11	17 30.1	27 28.3
MAY 1	17 35.8	27 29.2
21	17 37.2	27 25.5
JUN 10	17 34.4	27 17.7
30	17 27.5	27 06.4
JUL 20	17 17.5	26 53.1
AUG 9	17 05.3	26 38.9
29	16 52.2	26 25.1
SEP 18	16 39.5	26 13.2
OCT 8	16 28.6	26 04.3
28	16 20.5	25 59.3
NOV 17	16 16.1	25 58.6
DEC 7	16 15.9	26 02.5
27	16N20.1	26N10.3
	1/11.61	6/4.21
	6/26.40	12/22.74

2007	Haumea 136108	Makemake 136472
JAN 1	14♎52.8	23R35.8
11	14 54.4	23♍32.7
21	14R53.8	23 27.6
31	14 50.9	23 20.7
FEB 10	14 46.0	23 12.1
20	14 39.3	23 02.3
MAR 2	14 30.9	22 51.6
12	14 21.2	22 40.4
22	14 10.6	22 29.1
APR 1	13 59.5	22 18.2
11	13 48.2	22 08.0
21	13 37.2	21 58.8
MAY 1	13 26.8	21 51.1
11	13 17.5	21 45.0
21	13 09.5	21 40.7
31	13 03.0	21 38.5
JUN 10	12 58.4	21D38.3
20	12 55.7	21 40.3
30	12D55.1	21 44.2
JUL 10	12 56.6	21 50.2
20	13 00.2	21 58.0
30	13 05.7	22 07.5
AUG 9	13 13.2	22 18.3
19	13 22.3	22 30.4
29	13 33.0	22 43.4
SEP 8	13 44.9	22 57.0
18	13 57.8	23 10.8
28	14 11.4	23 24.6
OCT 8	14 25.3	23 38.1
18	14 39.3	23 50.8
28	14 52.9	24 02.5
NOV 7	15 05.9	24 12.9
17	15 17.8	24 21.7
27	15 28.5	24 28.6
DEC 7	15 37.5	24 33.5
17	15 44.7	24 36.2
27	15 49.9	24R36.7
JAN 6	15♎52.9	24♍35.0
JAN 1	16N21.7	26N12.8
21	16 30.4	26 24.2
FEB 10	16 41.6	26 36.5
MAR 2	16 53.8	26 48.2
22	17 05.3	26 57.5
APR 11	17 14.6	27 03.2
MAY 1	17 20.4	27 04.3
21	17 22.1	27 00.9
JUN 10	17 19.4	26 53.3
30	17 12.7	26 42.2
JUL 20	17 02.8	26 29.0
AUG 9	16 50.6	26 14.8
29	16 37.5	26 01.0
SEP 18	16 24.8	25 49.0
OCT 8	16 13.7	25 39.8
28	16 05.5	25 34.5
NOV 17	16 00.9	25 33.6
DEC 7	16 00.5	25 37.2
27	16N04.5	25N44.8
	1/12.86	12/22.74
	6/27.64	12/23.96

2008	Haumea 136108	Makemake 136472
JAN 1	15♎51.7	24R36.2
11	15 53.6	24♍33.4
21	15R53.2	24 28.5
31	15 50.6	24 21.8
FEB 10	15 46.0	24 13.4
20	15 39.4	24 03.8
MAR 1	15 31.2	23 53.1
11	15 21.7	23 42.0
21	15 11.2	23 30.7
31	15 00.0	23 19.7
APR 10	14 48.7	23 09.4
20	14 37.6	23 00.1
30	14 27.2	22 52.2
MAY 10	14 17.6	22 45.8
20	14 09.4	22 41.4
30	14 02.8	22 38.8
JUN 9	13 57.9	22D38.4
19	13 55.0	22 40.1
29	13D54.1	22 43.8
JUL 9	13 55.3	22 49.5
19	13 58.6	22 57.0
29	14 03.9	23 06.3
AUG 8	14 11.2	23 17.0
18	14 20.2	23 28.9
28	14 30.7	23 41.7
SEP 7	14 42.5	23 55.2
17	14 55.3	24 09.1
27	15 08.8	24 22.9
OCT 7	15 22.8	24 36.4
17	15 36.7	24 49.2
27	15 50.5	25 01.0
NOV 6	16 03.5	25 11.6
16	16 15.7	25 20.5
26	16 26.5	25 27.7
DEC 6	16 35.8	25 32.8
16	16 43.2	25 35.8
26	16 48.7	25R36.6
JAN 5	16♎51.9	25♍35.2
JAN 1	16N06.1	25N47.2
21	16 14.7	25 58.4
FEB 10	16 25.8	26 10.7
MAR 1	16 37.9	26 22.4
21	16 49.5	26 31.9
APR 10	16 58.9	26 37.7
30	17 04.9	26 39.2
MAY 20	17 06.8	26 36.0
JUN 9	17 04.3	26 28.6
29	16 57.8	26 17.8
JUL 19	16 47.9	26 04.7
AUG 8	16 35.8	25 50.5
28	16 22.7	25 36.7
SEP 17	16 10.0	25 24.5
OCT 7	15 58.8	25 15.2
27	15 50.3	25 09.6
NOV 16	15 45.6	25 08.4
DEC 6	15 45.0	25 11.7
26	15N48.8	25N19.0
	1/14.05	12/23.96
	6/27.94	12/24.18

2009	Haumea 136108	Makemake 136472
JAN 1	16♎50.9	25R36.0
11	16 52.9	25♍33.3
21	16R52.5	25 28.5
31	16 50.0	25 21.8
FEB 10	16 45.4	25 13.4
20	16 38.9	25 03.8
MAR 2	16 30.7	24 53.2
12	16 21.2	24 42.1
22	16 10.6	24 30.8
APR 1	15 59.5	24 19.8
11	15 48.2	24 09.5
21	15 37.1	24 00.2
MAY 1	15 26.5	23 52.2
11	15 17.0	23 45.8
21	15 08.7	23 41.3
31	15 02.0	23 38.7
JUN 10	14 57.0	23D38.2
20	14 54.0	23 39.8
30	14D53.1	23 43.5
JUL 10	14 54.3	23 49.1
20	14 57.5	23 56.6
30	15 02.8	24 05.8
AUG 9	15 10.0	24 16.4
19	15 19.0	24 28.3
29	15 29.5	24 41.1
SEP 8	15 41.3	24 54.6
18	15 54.1	25 08.4
28	16 07.7	25 22.2
OCT 8	16 21.6	25 35.6
18	16 35.6	25 48.5
28	16 49.4	26 00.3
NOV 7	17 02.5	26 10.9
17	17 14.7	26 19.9
27	17 25.6	26 27.0
DEC 7	17 34.9	26 32.2
17	17 42.4	26 35.3
27	17 47.9	26R36.1
JAN 6	17♎51.2	26♍34.7
JAN 1	15N50.7	25N21.9
21	15 59.3	25 33.0
FEB 10	16 10.4	25 45.3
MAR 2	16 22.5	25 57.0
22	16 34.1	26 06.4
APR 11	16 43.5	26 12.3
MAY 1	16 49.4	26 13.8
21	16 51.3	26 10.7
JUN 10	16 48.8	26 03.3
30	16 42.2	25 52.5
JUL 20	16 32.4	25 39.4
AUG 9	16 20.3	25 25.3
29	16 07.2	25 11.4
SEP 18	15 54.4	24 59.3
OCT 8	15 43.2	24 49.9
28	15 34.7	24 44.3
NOV 17	15 30.0	24 43.0
DEC 7	15 29.4	24 46.2
27	15N33.2	24N53.5
	1/14.30	12/24.18
	6/29.15	12/25.35

2010	Haumea 136108	Makemake 136472
JAN 1	17≏49.8	26R35.7
11	17 52.1	26♍33.2
21	17R52.0	26 28.6
31	17 49.8	26 22.2
FEB 10	17 45.4	26 14.0
20	17 39.1	26 04.5
MAR 2	17 31.0	25 54.1
12	17 21.7	25 43.0
22	17 11.2	25 31.7
APR 1	17 00.1	25 20.7
11	16 48.8	25 10.3
21	16 37.6	25 00.8
MAY 1	16 26.9	24 52.7
11	16 17.2	24 46.1
21	16 08.7	24 41.3
31	16 01.8	24 38.5
JUN 10	15 56.6	24D37.7
20	15 53.4	24 39.1
30	15 52.2	24 42.5
JUL 10	15D53.1	24 47.8
20	15 56.1	24 55.1
30	16 01.1	25 04.0
AUG 9	16 08.1	25 14.5
19	16 16.9	25 26.2
29	16 27.2	25 38.9
SEP 8	16 38.9	25 52.3
18	16 51.6	26 06.0
28	17 05.1	26 19.8
OCT 8	17 19.1	26 33.3
18	17 33.1	26 46.2
28	17 47.0	26 58.2
NOV 7	18 00.2	27 08.9
17	18 12.5	27 18.1
27	18 23.6	27 25.5
DEC 7	18 33.2	27 30.9
17	18 40.9	27 34.2
27	18 46.7	27R35.3
JAN 6	18≏50.3	27♍34.2
JAN 1	15N34.8	24N55.9
21	15 43.2	25 06.8
FEB 10	15 54.3	25 19.1
MAR 2	16 06.4	25 30.8
22	16 18.0	25 40.4
APR 11	16 27.5	25 46.4
MAY 1	16 33.7	25 48.2
21	16 35.7	25 45.3
JUN 10	16 33.4	25 38.2
30	16 27.0	25 27.6
JUL 20	16 17.3	25 14.6
AUG 9	16 05.2	25 00.5
29	15 52.1	24 46.7
SEP 18	15 39.2	24 34.4
OCT 8	15 27.9	24 24.8
28	15 19.4	24 18.9
NOV 17	15 14.4	24 17.4
DEC 7	15 13.7	24 20.3
27	15N17.2	24N27.4

1/15.51 12/25.36
6/30.45 12/26.61

2011	Haumea 136108	Makemake 136472
JAN 1	18≏48.8	27R35.0
11	18 51.3	27♍32.8
21	18R51.5	27 28.5
31	18 49.5	27 22.3
FEB 10	18 45.4	27 14.3
20	18 39.3	27 05.0
MAR 2	18 31.4	26 54.7
12	18 22.2	26 43.7
22	18 11.8	26 32.4
APR 1	18 00.8	26 21.3
11	17 49.4	26 10.8
21	17 38.2	26 01.3
MAY 1	17 27.4	25 52.9
11	17 17.5	25 46.2
21	17 08.9	25 41.2
31	17 01.7	25 38.1
JUN 10	16 56.3	25D37.1
20	16 52.8	25 38.1
30	16 51.3	25 41.2
JUL 10	16D52.0	25 46.4
20	16 54.7	25 53.4
30	16 59.6	26 02.1
AUG 9	17 06.3	26 12.4
19	17 14.9	26 23.9
29	17 25.0	26 36.5
SEP 8	17 36.6	26 49.8
18	17 49.2	27 03.5
28	18 02.7	27 17.3
OCT 8	18 16.6	27 30.9
18	18 30.7	27 43.8
28	18 44.6	27 55.9
NOV 7	18 58.0	28 06.8
17	19 10.5	28 16.2
27	19 21.8	28 23.8
DEC 7	19 31.5	28 29.4
17	19 39.5	28 33.0
27	19 45.6	28 34.4
JAN 6	19≏49.5	28R33.5
JAN 1	15N18.8	24N29.7
21	15 27.1	24 40.4
FEB 10	15 38.0	24 52.6
MAR 2	15 50.1	25 04.3
22	16 01.7	25 14.0
APR 11	16 11.4	25 20.3
MAY 1	16 17.7	25 22.3
21	16 19.9	25 19.7
JUN 10	16 17.8	25 12.8
30	16 11.5	25 02.4
JUL 20	16 01.9	24 49.6
AUG 9	15 50.0	24 35.5
29	15 36.8	24 21.6
SEP 18	15 23.9	24 09.2
OCT 8	15 12.5	23 59.4
28	15 03.8	23 53.3
NOV 17	14 58.6	23 51.5
DEC 7	14 57.7	23 54.2
27	15N01.1	24N00.9

1/16.73 12/26.60
7/1.69 12/27.80

2012	Haumea 136108	Makemake 136472
JAN 1	19≏47.8	28R34.2
11	19 50.6	28♍32.3
21	19R51.1	28 28.2
31	19 49.4	28 22.2
FEB 10	19 45.5	28 14.5
20	19 39.6	28 05.4
MAR 1	19 32.0	27 55.1
11	19 22.8	27 44.2
21	19 12.6	27 33.0
31	19 01.6	27 21.9
APR 10	18 50.2	27 11.3
20	18 38.9	27 01.6
30	18 28.1	26 53.1
MAY 10	18 18.1	26 46.2
20	18 09.2	26 40.9
30	18 01.9	26 37.6
JUN 9	17 56.2	26 36.3
19	17 52.5	26D37.1
29	17 50.7	26 40.0
JUL 9	17D51.1	26 44.9
19	17 53.6	26 51.6
29	17 58.2	27 00.2
AUG 8	18 04.7	27 10.2
18	18 13.1	27 21.6
28	18 23.1	27 34.1
SEP 7	18 34.5	27 47.2
17	18 47.0	28 00.9
27	19 00.5	28 14.7
OCT 7	19 14.4	28 28.3
17	19 28.5	28 41.3
27	19 42.5	28 53.5
NOV 6	19 56.0	29 04.6
16	20 08.6	29 14.1
26	20 20.1	29 22.0
DEC 6	20 30.1	29 27.9
16	20 38.4	29 31.7
26	20 44.7	29 33.4
JAN 5	20≏48.8	29R32.8
JAN 1	15N02.6	24N03.2
21	15 10.7	24 13.8
FEB 10	15 21.5	24 25.8
MAR 1	15 33.6	24 37.6
21	15 45.2	24 47.4
APR 10	15 55.0	24 53.9
30	16 01.4	24 56.1
MAY 20	16 03.8	24 53.8
JUN 9	16 01.9	24 47.2
29	15 55.8	24 37.0
JUL 19	15 46.3	24 24.2
AUG 8	15 34.4	24 10.2
28	15 21.3	23 56.3
SEP 17	15 08.3	23 43.8
OCT 7	14 56.8	23 33.8
27	14 47.9	23 27.5
NOV 16	14 42.6	23 25.4
DEC 6	14 41.4	23 27.8
26	14N44.6	23N34.3

1/18.00 12/27.81
7/1.92 12/28.05

2013	Haumea 136108	Makemake 136472
JAN 1	20≏47.4	29R33.3
11	20 50.3	29♍31.4
21	20R50.9	29 27.4
31	20 49.2	29 21.4
FEB 10	20 45.4	29 13.7
20	20 39.5	29 04.6
MAR 2	20 31.9	28 54.4
12	20 22.8	28 43.6
22	20 12.6	28 32.4
APR 1	20 01.6	28 21.3
11	19 50.2	28 10.7
21	19 38.9	28 01.0
MAY 1	19 28.0	27 52.5
11	19 18.0	27 45.5
21	19 09.1	27 40.3
31	19 01.7	27 36.9
JUN 10	18 56.0	27 35.6
20	18 52.2	27D36.3
30	18 50.4	27 39.1
JUL 10	18D50.7	27 43.9
20	18 53.2	27 50.6
30	18 57.7	27 59.1
AUG 9	19 04.2	28 09.1
19	19 12.5	28 20.5
29	19 22.5	28 32.9
SEP 8	19 33.9	28 46.0
18	19 46.5	28 59.7
28	19 59.9	29 13.5
OCT 8	20 13.8	29 27.0
18	20 28.0	29 40.1
28	20 42.0	29 52.3
NOV 7	20 55.6	0≏03.4
17	21 08.3	0 12.9
27	21 19.8	0 20.8
DEC 7	21 29.9	0 26.8
17	21 38.2	0 30.7
27	21 44.6	0 32.4
JAN 6	21≏48.8	0R31.8
JAN 1	14N46.4	23N36.9
21	14 54.5	23 47.4
FEB 10	15 05.3	23 59.4
MAR 2	15 17.3	24 11.1
22	15 29.0	24 20.9
APR 11	15 38.7	24 27.4
MAY 1	15 45.1	24 29.6
21	15 47.5	24 27.4
JUN 10	15 45.5	24 20.8
30	15 39.4	24 10.6
JUL 20	15 29.8	23 57.9
AUG 9	15 17.9	23 44.0
29	15 04.8	23 30.1
SEP 18	14 51.8	23 17.5
OCT 8	14 40.3	23 07.6
28	14 31.4	23 01.2
NOV 17	14 26.1	22 59.0
DEC 7	14 24.9	23 01.3
27	14N28.1	23N07.8

1/18.23 12/28.05
7/3.19 12/29.30

2014	Haumea 136108	Makemake 136472
JAN 1	21≏47.0	0R32.4
11	21 50.1	0≏30.7
21	21R51.0	0 27.0
31	21 49.6	0 21.3
FEB 10	21 46.0	0 13.8
20	21 40.4	0 04.9
MAR 2	21 33.0	29♍54.8
12	21 24.1	29 44.0
22	21 14.0	29 32.9
APR 1	21 03.0	29 21.8
11	20 51.7	29 11.1
21	20 40.3	29 01.3
MAY 1	20 29.4	28 52.7
11	20 19.2	28 45.5
21	20 10.1	28 40.0
31	20 02.5	28 36.4
JUN 10	19 56.6	28 34.8
20	19 52.5	28D35.3
30	19 50.5	28 37.9
JUL 10	19D50.5	28 42.4
20	19 52.7	28 48.9
30	19 57.0	28 57.2
AUG 9	20 03.3	29 07.0
19	20 11.4	29 18.2
29	20 21.2	29 30.4
SEP 8	20 32.5	29 43.5
18	20 45.0	29 57.1
28	20 58.3	0≏10.8
OCT 8	21 12.3	0 24.5
18	21 26.5	0 37.6
28	21 40.6	0 49.9
NOV 7	21 54.2	1 01.1
17	22 07.1	1 10.9
27	22 18.8	1 19.0
DEC 7	22 29.1	1 25.2
17	22 37.7	1 29.3
27	22 44.3	1 31.3
JAN 6	22≏48.9	1R31.0
JAN 1	14N29.5	23N09.9
21	14 37.5	23 20.3
FEB 10	14 48.2	23 32.1
MAR 2	15 00.1	23 43.9
22	15 11.8	23 53.7
APR 11	15 21.6	24 00.4
MAY 1	15 28.2	24 02.9
21	15 30.7	24 00.9
JUN 10	15 28.9	23 54.6
30	15 23.0	23 44.6
JUL 20	15 13.6	23 32.1
AUG 9	15 01.7	23 18.2
29	14 48.6	23 04.2
SEP 18	14 35.6	22 51.6
OCT 8	14 23.9	22 41.5
28	14 14.9	22 34.9
NOV 17	14 09.3	22 32.4
DEC 7	14 08.0	22 34.5
27	14N10.9	22N40.6

1/19.54 12/29.30
7/4.39 12/30.51

2015	Haumea 136108	Makemake 136472
JAN 1	22≏46.9	1R31.4
11	22 50.3	1≏30.1
21	22R51.5	1 26.6
31	22 50.4	1 21.1
FEB 10	22 47.1	1 13.8
20	22 41.7	1 05.1
MAR 2	22 34.5	0 55.2
12	22 25.7	0 44.4
22	22 15.7	0 33.3
APR 1	22 04.9	0 22.2
11	21 53.5	0 11.5
21	21 42.2	0 01.6
MAY 1	21 31.1	29♍52.8
11	21 20.8	29 45.5
21	21 11.6	29 39.8
31	21 03.7	29 35.9
JUN 10	20 57.6	29 34.1
20	20 53.3	29D34.3
30	20 51.0	29 36.6
JUL 10	20D50.8	29 40.9
20	20 52.7	29 47.1
30	20 56.7	29 55.2
AUG 9	21 02.8	0≏04.8
19	21 10.7	0 15.8
29	21 20.4	0 27.9
SEP 8	21 31.5	0 40.9
18	21 43.8	0 54.4
28	21 57.1	1 08.2
OCT 8	22 11.1	1 21.8
18	22 25.3	1 35.0
28	22 39.4	1 47.4
NOV 7	22 53.2	1 58.7
17	23 06.2	2 08.7
27	23 18.1	2 17.0
DEC 7	23 28.6	2 23.4
17	23 37.5	2 27.8
27	23 44.4	2 30.0
JAN 6	23≏49.2	2R30.1
JAN 1	14N12.3	22N42.7
21	14 20.1	22 52.9
FEB 10	14 30.7	23 04.6
MAR 2	14 42.6	23 16.4
22	14 54.3	23 26.3
APR 11	15 04.2	23 33.2
MAY 1	15 10.9	23 35.9
21	15 13.6	23 34.2
JUN 10	15 12.0	23 28.1
30	15 06.2	23 18.4
JUL 20	14 56.9	23 06.0
AUG 9	14 45.2	22 52.1
29	14 32.1	22 38.2
SEP 18	14 19.0	22 25.5
OCT 8	14 07.2	22 15.2
28	13 58.0	22 08.4
NOV 17	13 52.3	22 05.7
DEC 7	13 50.8	22 07.4
27	13N53.5	22N13.3
	1/20.81 7/5.67	12/30.51 12/31.76

2016	Haumea 136108	Makemake 136472
JAN 1	23≏47.1	2R30.3
11	23 50.8	2≏29.3
21	23 52.3	2 26.0
31	23R51.5	2 20.8
FEB 10	23 48.4	2 13.7
20	23 43.3	2 05.2
MAR 1	23 36.3	1 55.4
11	23 27.7	1 44.8
21	23 17.9	1 33.7
31	23 07.1	1 22.6
APR 10	22 55.8	1 11.8
20	22 44.4	1 01.8
30	22 33.2	0 52.9
MAY 10	22 22.8	0 45.4
20	22 13.4	0 39.4
30	22 05.4	0 35.4
JUN 9	21 59.0	0 33.3
19	21 54.4	0D33.2
29	21 51.9	0 35.2
JUL 9	21D51.4	0 39.3
19	21 53.1	0 45.3
29	21 56.8	0 53.1
AUG 8	22 02.6	1 02.5
18	22 10.4	1 13.3
28	22 19.8	1 25.3
SEP 7	22 30.8	1 38.2
17	22 43.0	1 51.7
27	22 56.3	2 05.4
OCT 7	23 10.2	2 19.0
17	23 24.4	2 32.3
27	23 38.6	2 44.8
NOV 6	23 52.5	2 56.3
16	24 05.6	3 06.4
26	24 17.7	3 14.9
DEC 6	24 28.5	3 21.6
16	24 37.6	3 26.2
26	24 44.8	3 28.7
JAN 5	24≏49.9	3R29.0
JAN 1	13N54.9	22N15.4
21	14 02.5	22 25.3
FEB 10	14 12.9	22 37.0
MAR 1	14 24.8	22 48.7
21	14 36.5	22 58.7
APR 10	14 46.4	23 05.8
30	14 53.3	23 08.7
MAY 20	14 56.2	23 07.2
JUN 9	14 54.8	23 01.4
29	14 49.2	22 51.9
JUL 19	14 40.0	22 39.7
AUG 8	14 28.3	22 25.9
28	14 15.2	22 12.0
SEP 17	14 02.1	21 59.2
OCT 7	13 50.3	21 48.7
27	13 40.9	21 41.7
NOV 16	13 35.1	21 38.7
DEC 6	13 33.3	21 40.2
26	13N35.8	21N45.8
	1/22.09 7/5.91	12/31.77 12/31.94

2017	Haumea 136108	Makemake 136472
JAN 1	24≏48.1	3R29.1
11	24 51.9	3≏28.1
21	24 53.4	3 24.9
31	24R52.7	3 19.7
FEB 10	24 49.7	3 12.7
20	24 44.6	3 04.2
MAR 2	24 37.7	2 54.4
12	24 29.1	2 43.9
22	24 19.3	2 32.8
APR 1	24 08.5	2 21.7
11	23 57.2	2 11.0
21	23 45.8	2 00.9
MAY 1	23 34.6	1 52.0
11	23 24.1	1 44.4
21	23 14.7	1 38.5
31	23 06.6	1 34.4
JUN 10	23 00.2	1 32.2
20	22 55.5	1D32.1
30	22 52.9	1 34.1
JUL 10	22D52.4	1 38.1
20	22 54.0	1 44.0
30	22 57.7	1 51.7
AUG 9	23 03.5	2 01.1
19	23 11.2	2 11.9
29	23 20.6	2 23.8
SEP 8	23 31.6	2 36.7
18	23 43.8	2 50.1
28	23 57.0	3 03.8
OCT 8	24 11.0	3 17.4
18	24 25.2	3 30.7
28	24 39.5	3 43.2
NOV 7	24 53.4	3 54.7
17	25 06.6	4 04.8
27	25 18.8	4 13.3
DEC 7	25 29.6	4 20.0
17	25 38.7	4 24.7
27	25 46.0	4 27.2
JAN 6	25≏51.2	4R27.5
JAN 1	13N37.4	21N48.2
21	13 45.0	21 58.1
FEB 10	13 55.4	22 09.7
MAR 2	14 07.3	22 21.3
22	14 19.0	22 31.4
APR 11	14 28.9	22 38.4
MAY 1	14 35.7	22 41.4
21	14 38.6	22 39.9
JUN 10	14 37.1	22 34.1
30	14 31.5	22 24.7
JUL 20	14 22.3	22 12.5
AUG 9	14 10.6	21 58.8
29	13 57.5	21 44.9
SEP 18	13 44.4	21 32.1
OCT 8	13 32.6	21 21.7
28	13 23.2	21 14.6
NOV 17	13 17.4	21 11.6
DEC 7	13 15.6	21 13.0
27	13N18.2	21N18.6
	1/22.40 7/7.19	12/31.94 1/2.16

2018	Haumea 136108	Makemake 136472
JAN 1	25≏48.9	4≏27.7
11	25 53.0	4R26.9
21	25 54.8	4 24.0
31	25R54.3	4 19.0
FEB 10	25 51.6	4 12.2
20	25 46.8	4 03.9
MAR 2	25 40.1	3 54.3
12	25 31.7	3 43.8
22	25 22.0	3 32.8
APR 1	25 11.3	3 21.7
11	25 00.0	3 10.9
21	24 48.5	3 00.8
MAY 1	24 37.3	2 51.7
11	24 26.7	2 43.9
21	24 17.1	2 37.8
31	24 08.8	2 33.4
JUN 10	24 02.1	2 31.0
20	23 57.3	2D30.7
30	23 54.4	2 32.4
JUL 10	23D53.6	2 36.1
20	23 54.9	2 41.8
30	23 58.4	2 49.3
AUG 9	24 03.9	2 58.4
19	24 11.4	3 09.0
29	24 20.6	3 20.8
SEP 8	24 31.4	3 33.6
18	24 43.5	3 46.9
28	24 56.7	4 00.6
OCT 8	25 10.6	4 14.2
18	25 24.8	4 27.5
28	25 39.2	4 40.1
NOV 7	25 53.2	4 51.7
17	26 06.5	5 02.0
27	26 18.9	5 10.7
DEC 7	26 29.9	5 17.7
17	26 39.3	5 22.6
27	26 46.8	5 25.4
JAN 6	26≏52.3	5R25.9
JAN 1	13N19.4	21N20.5
21	13 26.9	21 30.2
FEB 10	13 37.2	21 41.7
MAR 2	13 49.0	21 53.3
22	14 00.6	22 03.4
APR 11	14 10.6	22 10.6
MAY 1	14 17.6	22 13.8
21	14 20.7	22 12.6
JUN 10	14 19.4	22 07.1
30	14 13.9	21 57.8
JUL 20	14 04.9	21 45.8
AUG 9	13 53.3	21 32.2
29	13 40.2	21 18.3
SEP 18	13 27.1	21 05.5
OCT 8	13 15.2	20 54.9
28	13 05.7	20 47.6
NOV 17	12 59.7	20 44.3
DEC 7	12 57.7	20 45.5
27	13N00.0	20N50.8
	1/23.65 7/8.50	1/2.15 1/3.34

2019	Haumea 136108	Makemake 136472
JAN 1	26≏49.8	5≏25.9
11	26 54.2	5R25.4
21	26 56.3	5 22.7
31	26R56.1	5 18.0
FEB 10	26 53.7	5 11.5
20	26 49.2	5 03.3
MAR 2	26 42.7	4 53.9
12	26 34.4	4 43.4
22	26 24.9	4 32.5
APR 1	26 14.3	4 21.4
11	26 03.0	4 10.6
21	25 51.5	4 00.4
MAY 1	25 40.3	3 51.1
11	25 29.5	3 43.2
21	25 19.8	3 36.9
31	25 11.3	3 32.3
JUN 10	25 04.4	3 29.6
20	24 59.3	3D29.0
30	24 56.1	3 30.4
JUL 10	24D55.0	3 33.9
20	24 56.1	3 39.3
30	24 59.3	3 46.6
AUG 9	25 04.5	3 55.5
19	25 11.8	4 06.0
29	25 20.8	4 17.6
SEP 8	25 31.5	4 30.2
18	25 43.4	4 43.5
28	25 56.5	4 57.1
OCT 8	26 10.4	5 10.7
18	26 24.6	5 24.0
28	26 39.0	5 36.7
NOV 7	26 53.1	5 48.5
17	27 06.6	5 58.9
27	27 19.1	6 07.8
DEC 7	27 30.3	6 15.0
17	27 40.0	6 20.1
27	27 47.8	6 23.2
JAN 6	27≏53.5	6R24.0
JAN 1	13N01.3	20N52.7
21	13 08.5	21 02.2
FEB 10	13 18.7	21 13.5
MAR 2	13 30.4	21 25.1
22	13 42.1	21 35.3
APR 11	13 52.2	21 42.6
MAY 1	13 59.3	21 46.0
21	14 02.6	21 45.1
JUN 10	14 01.5	21 39.8
30	13 56.2	21 30.8
JUL 20	13 47.3	21 19.0
AUG 9	13 35.8	21 05.4
29	13 22.8	20 51.6
SEP 18	13 09.6	20 38.6
OCT 8	12 57.6	20 27.9
28	12 48.0	20 20.4
NOV 17	12 41.8	20 16.9
DEC 7	12 39.6	20 17.8
27	12N41.8	20N22.8
	1/24.95 7/9.75	1/3.35 1/4.50

2020	♇ Haumea 136108	♇ Makemake 136472
JAN 1	27≏50.9	6≏23.9
11	27 55.6	6R23.6
21	27 58.0	6 21.2
31	27R58.1	6 16.7
FEB 10	27 56.0	6 10.4
20	27 51.7	6 02.4
MAR 1	27 45.4	5 53.1
11	27 37.4	5 42.8
21	27 27.9	5 31.9
31	27 17.4	5 20.8
APR 10	27 06.2	5 09.9
20	26 54.7	4 59.6
30	26 43.4	4 50.3
MAY 10	26 32.5	4 42.2
20	26 22.6	4 35.6
30	26 13.9	4 30.8
JUN 9	26 06.8	4 27.9
19	26 01.4	4D27.0
29	25 58.0	4 28.2
JUL 9	25 56.6	4 31.4
19	25D57.4	4 36.6
29	26 00.3	4 43.6
AUG 8	26 05.3	4 52.4
18	26 12.3	5 02.6
28	26 21.2	5 14.1
SEP 7	26 31.6	5 26.6
17	26 43.5	5 39.7
27	26 56.5	5 53.3
OCT 7	27 10.2	6 06.9
17	27 24.5	6 20.3
27	27 38.9	6 33.1
NOV 6	27 53.1	6 44.9
16	28 06.7	6 55.5
26	28 19.4	7 04.6
DEC 6	28 30.8	7 12.0
16	28 40.7	7 17.4
26	28 48.8	7 20.6
JAN 5	28≏54.8	7R21.7
JAN 1	12N43.0	20N24.7
21	12 50.0	20 33.9
FEB 10	13 00.1	20 45.2
MAR 1	13 11.7	20 56.7
21	13 23.4	21 07.0
APR 10	13 33.6	21 14.5
30	13 40.9	21 18.1
MAY 20	13 44.3	21 17.4
JUN 9	13 43.4	21 12.4
29	13 38.3	21 03.6
JUL 19	13 29.5	20 51.9
AUG 8	13 18.1	20 38.5
28	13 05.1	20 24.6
SEP 17	12 51.9	20 11.7
OCT 7	12 39.9	20 00.8
27	12 30.1	19 53.1
NOV 16	12 23.7	19 49.4
DEC 6	12 21.4	19 50.0
26	12N23.3	19N54.8
	1/26.21	1/4.50
	7/10.10	1/4.71

2021	♇ Haumea 136108	♇ Makemake 136472
JAN 1	28≏52.7	7≏21.6
11	28 57.4	7R21.3
21	28 59.9	7 19.0
31	29R00.0	7 14.5
FEB 10	28 58.0	7 08.2
20	28 53.7	7 00.3
MAR 2	28 47.5	6 51.0
12	28 39.5	6 40.8
22	28 30.0	6 29.9
APR 1	28 19.5	6 18.8
11	28 08.3	6 07.9
21	27 56.8	5 57.6
MAY 1	27 45.5	5 48.3
11	27 34.6	5 40.1
21	27 24.6	5 33.6
31	27 15.9	5 28.7
JUN 10	27 08.6	5 25.8
20	27 03.2	5D24.8
30	26 59.7	5 25.9
JUL 10	26 58.3	5 29.1
20	26D59.0	5 34.2
30	27 01.9	5 41.2
AUG 9	27 06.8	5 49.9
19	27 13.8	6 00.0
29	27 22.6	6 11.5
SEP 8	27 33.0	6 23.9
18	27 44.9	6 37.1
28	27 57.8	6 50.6
OCT 8	28 11.6	7 04.2
18	28 25.9	7 17.6
28	28 40.4	7 30.3
NOV 7	28 54.6	7 42.2
17	29 08.2	7 52.8
27	29 21.0	8 01.9
DEC 7	29 32.5	8 09.3
17	29 42.4	8 14.7
27	29 50.6	8 18.0
JAN 6	29≏56.7	8R19.2
JAN 1	12N24.7	19N56.9
21	12 31.8	20 06.1
FEB 10	12 41.8	20 17.2
MAR 2	12 53.5	20 28.7
22	13 05.1	20 38.9
APR 11	13 15.3	20 46.4
MAY 1	13 22.5	20 50.0
21	13 25.8	20 49.4
JUN 10	13 24.9	20 44.4
30	13 19.8	20 35.6
JUL 20	13 11.1	20 24.0
AUG 9	12 59.6	20 10.7
29	12 46.6	19 56.8
SEP 18	12 33.5	19 43.9
OCT 8	12 21.4	19 33.0
28	12 11.7	19 25.3
NOV 17	12 05.3	19 21.6
DEC 7	12 03.0	19 22.1
27	12N05.0	19N26.8
	1/26.47	1/4.70
	7/11.40	1/5.84

2022	♇ Haumea 136108	♇ Makemake 136472
JAN 1	29≏53.9	8≏18.9
11	29 58.9	8R18.9
21	0♏01.7	8 16.8
31	0R02.1	8 12.6
FEB 10	0 00.3	8 06.5
20	29≏56.3	7 58.7
MAR 2	29 50.3	7 49.6
12	29 42.5	7 39.5
22	29 33.2	7 28.7
APR 1	29 22.8	7 17.6
11	29 11.7	7 06.7
21	29 00.2	6 56.3
MAY 1	28 48.7	6 46.8
11	28 37.8	6 38.6
21	28 27.6	6 31.8
31	28 18.7	6 26.7
JUN 10	28 11.2	6 23.5
20	28 05.5	6 22.3
30	28 01.8	6D23.2
JUL 10	28 00.1	6 26.1
20	28D00.5	6 31.0
30	28 03.1	6 37.7
AUG 9	28 07.8	6 46.2
19	28 14.5	6 56.2
29	28 23.1	7 07.4
SEP 8	28 33.4	7 19.8
18	28 45.1	7 32.8
28	28 58.0	7 46.3
OCT 8	29 11.7	7 59.9
18	29 26.0	8 13.3
28	29 40.4	8 26.1
NOV 7	29 54.7	8 38.1
17	0♏08.5	8 48.9
27	0 21.4	8 58.1
DEC 7	0 33.1	9 05.7
17	0 43.3	9 11.4
27	0 51.7	9 14.9
JAN 6	0♏58.1	9≏16.3
JAN 1	12N06.1	19N28.6
21	12 13.0	19 37.6
FEB 10	12 22.9	19 48.5
MAR 2	12 34.4	20 00.0
22	12 46.1	20 10.2
APR 11	12 56.3	20 17.8
MAY 1	13 03.7	20 21.7
21	13 07.2	20 21.2
JUN 10	13 06.4	20 16.5
30	13 01.5	20 08.0
JUL 20	12 52.9	19 56.5
AUG 9	12 41.6	19 43.3
29	12 28.6	19 29.5
SEP 18	12 15.5	19 16.5
OCT 8	12 03.3	19 05.5
28	11 53.5	18 57.7
NOV 17	11 47.0	18 53.6
DEC 7	11 44.4	18 53.9
27	11N46.2	18N58.4
	1/27.75	1/5.85
	7/12.69	6/20.59

2023	♇ Haumea 136108	♇ Makemake 136472
JAN 1	0♏55.1	9≏15.9
11	1 00.5	9R16.2
21	1 03.5	9 14.3
31	1R04.3	9 10.4
FEB 10	1 02.8	9 04.5
20	0 59.1	8 57.0
MAR 2	0 53.3	8 48.0
12	0 45.7	8 38.0
22	0 36.6	8 27.2
APR 1	0 26.3	8 16.2
11	0 15.2	8 05.3
21	0 03.6	7 54.8
MAY 1	29≏52.2	7 45.2
11	29 41.1	7 36.8
21	29 30.8	7 29.8
31	29 21.7	7 24.6
JUN 10	29 14.0	7 21.2
20	29 08.1	7 19.7
30	29 04.0	7D20.3
JUL 10	29 02.0	7 23.0
20	29D02.2	7 27.6
30	29 04.5	7 34.1
AUG 9	29 09.0	7 42.4
19	29 15.5	7 52.2
29	29 23.8	8 03.3
SEP 8	29 33.9	8 15.5
18	29 45.5	8 28.4
28	29 58.2	8 41.9
OCT 8	0♏11.9	8 55.5
18	0 26.2	9 08.9
28	0 40.7	9 21.8
NOV 7	0 55.0	9 33.9
17	1 08.9	9 44.8
27	1 22.0	9 54.2
DEC 7	1 33.9	10 02.0
17	1 44.3	10 07.9
27	1 53.0	10 11.7
JAN 6	1♏59.6	10≏13.4
JAN 1	11N47.3	19N00.1
21	11 54.0	19 08.8
FEB 10	12 03.7	19 19.7
MAR 2	12 15.2	19 31.1
22	12 26.9	19 41.3
APR 11	12 37.1	19 49.1
MAY 1	12 44.6	19 53.1
21	12 48.3	19 52.9
JUN 10	12 47.7	19 48.4
30	12 43.0	19 40.1
JUL 20	12 34.5	19 28.9
AUG 9	12 23.3	19 15.7
29	12 10.4	19 02.0
SEP 18	11 57.2	18 49.0
OCT 8	11 45.0	18 37.9
28	11 35.1	18 29.8
NOV 17	11 28.4	18 25.6
DEC 7	11 25.6	18 25.6
27	11N27.2	18N29.7
	1/29.00	1/7.04
	7/14.02	6/21.79

2024	♇ Haumea 136108	♇ Makemake 136472
JAN 1	1♏56.6	10≏12.8
11	2 02.2	10R13.4
21	2 05.5	10 11.8
31	2R06.6	10 08.1
FEB 10	2 05.4	10 02.4
20	2 01.9	9 55.1
MAR 1	1 56.4	9 46.3
11	1 49.0	9 36.4
21	1 40.1	9 25.7
31	1 29.9	9 14.7
APR 10	1 18.8	9 03.8
20	1 07.3	8 53.3
30	0 55.8	8 43.6
MAY 10	0 44.6	8 35.0
20	0 34.2	8 27.9
30	0 24.9	8 22.4
JUN 9	0 17.0	8 18.8
19	0 10.8	8 17.1
29	0 06.5	8D17.4
JUL 9	0 04.3	8 19.8
19	0D04.2	8 24.2
29	0 06.2	8 30.5
AUG 8	0 10.4	8 38.5
18	0 16.7	8 48.2
28	0 24.8	8 59.1
SEP 7	0 34.7	9 11.2
17	0 46.1	9 24.1
27	0 58.8	9 37.5
OCT 7	1 12.4	9 51.0
17	1 26.6	10 04.5
27	1 41.2	10 17.4
NOV 6	1 55.6	10 29.6
16	2 09.6	10 40.7
26	2 22.8	10 50.3
DEC 6	2 34.9	10 58.3
16	2 45.6	11 04.4
26	2 54.5	11 08.5
JAN 5	3♏01.5	11≏10.4
JAN 1	11N28.2	18N31.4
21	11 34.8	18 39.9
FEB 10	11 44.3	18 50.6
MAR 1	11 55.7	19 01.9
21	12 07.4	19 12.2
APR 10	12 17.7	19 20.1
30	12 25.3	19 24.3
MAY 20	12 29.1	19 24.4
JUN 9	12 28.7	19 20.1
29	12 24.1	19 12.1
JUL 19	12 15.8	19 01.0
AUG 8	12 04.7	18 48.0
28	11 51.9	18 34.3
SEP 17	11 38.7	18 21.2
OCT 7	11 26.4	18 10.0
27	11 16.3	18 01.8
NOV 16	11 09.5	17 57.3
DEC 6	11 06.6	17 57.0
26	11N07.9	18N00.9
	1/30.33	1/8.23
	7/14.27	6/22.01

2025	♀ Haumea 136108	♀ Makemake 136472
JAN 1	2♏58.9	11♎09.9
11	3 04.6	11R10.5
21	3 08.0	11 08.9
31	3R09.2	11 05.3
FEB 10	3 08.0	10 59.7
20	3 04.6	10 52.4
MAR 2	2 59.2	10 43.6
12	2 51.8	10 33.8
22	2 42.9	10 23.1
APR 1	2 32.7	10 12.2
11	2 21.7	10 01.3
21	2 10.2	9 50.8
MAY 1	1 58.7	9 41.1
11	1 47.5	9 32.5
21	1 37.0	9 25.3
31	1 27.7	9 19.8
JUN 10	1 19.7	9 16.1
20	1 13.5	9 14.4
30	1 09.1	9D14.7
JUL 10	1 06.8	9 17.1
20	1D06.6	9 21.4
30	1 08.6	9 27.7
AUG 9	1 12.7	9 35.7
19	1 18.9	9 45.2
29	1 27.1	9 56.2
SEP 8	1 37.0	10 08.2
18	1 48.4	10 21.0
28	2 01.0	10 34.4
OCT 8	2 14.6	10 48.0
18	2 28.9	11 01.4
28	2 43.4	11 14.4
NOV 7	2 57.9	11 26.5
17	3 12.0	11 37.6
27	3 25.3	11 47.3
DEC 7	3 37.5	11 55.3
17	3 48.2	12 01.4
27	3 57.2	12 05.5
JAN 6	4♏04.2	12♎07.5
JAN 1	11N09.1	18N02.9
21	11 15.6	18 11.3
FEB 10	11 25.2	18 21.9
MAR 2	11 36.6	18 33.2
22	11 48.1	18 43.4
APR 11	11 58.4	18 51.2
MAY 1	12 05.9	18 55.5
21	12 09.7	18 55.5
JUN 10	12 09.3	18 51.3
30	12 04.7	18 43.3
JUL 20	11 56.4	18 32.3
AUG 9	11 45.2	18 19.3
29	11 32.4	18 05.7
SEP 18	11 19.2	17 52.6
OCT 8	11 07.0	17 41.5
28	10 56.9	17 33.2
NOV 17	10 50.1	17 28.7
DEC 7	10 47.2	17 28.4
27	10N48.5	17N32.3
	1/30.61 7/15.58	1/8.41 6/23.23

2026	♀ Haumea 136108	♀ Makemake 136472
JAN 1	4♏00.9	12♎06.8
11	4 06.9	12R07.7
21	4 10.7	12 06.4
31	4 12.1	12 03.0
FEB 10	4R11.2	11 57.6
20	4 08.1	11 50.5
MAR 2	4 02.9	11 41.9
12	3 55.8	11 32.2
22	3 47.1	11 21.7
APR 1	3 37.0	11 10.7
11	3 26.1	10 59.8
21	3 14.6	10 49.3
MAY 1	3 03.0	10 39.5
11	2 51.8	10 30.8
21	2 41.2	10 23.4
31	2 31.7	10 17.7
JUN 10	2 23.5	10 13.8
20	2 17.0	10 11.9
30	2 12.4	10D11.9
JUL 10	2 09.8	10 14.0
20	2D09.4	10 18.1
30	2 11.1	10 24.1
AUG 9	2 14.9	10 31.9
19	2 20.9	10 41.3
29	2 28.8	10 52.1
SEP 8	2 38.5	11 04.0
18	2 49.7	11 16.7
28	3 02.3	11 30.0
OCT 8	3 15.8	11 43.6
18	3 30.1	11 57.0
28	3 44.6	12 10.0
NOV 7	3 59.2	12 22.3
17	4 13.4	12 33.5
27	4 26.8	12 43.4
DEC 7	4 39.2	12 51.6
17	4 50.1	12 57.9
27	4 59.4	13 02.3
JAN 6	5♏06.7	13♎04.5
JAN 1	10N49.5	17N33.9
21	10 55.8	17 42.1
FEB 10	11 05.2	17 52.5
MAR 2	11 16.5	18 03.7
22	11 28.1	18 14.0
APR 11	11 38.3	18 21.9
MAY 1	11 46.0	18 26.3
21	11 49.9	18 26.6
JUN 10	11 49.7	18 22.6
30	11 45.2	18 14.9
JUL 20	11 37.1	18 04.0
AUG 9	11 26.0	17 51.2
29	11 13.3	17 37.6
SEP 18	11 00.1	17 24.6
OCT 8	10 47.8	17 13.3
28	10 37.6	17 04.9
NOV 17	10 30.6	17 00.2
DEC 7	10 27.6	16 59.6
27	10N28.7	17N03.2
	1/31.93 7/16.84	1/9.65 6/24.41

2027	♀ Haumea 136108	♀ Makemake 136472
JAN 1	5♏03.3	13♎03.7
11	5 09.6	13R04.8
21	5 13.6	13 03.7
31	5 15.4	13 00.6
FEB 10	5R14.8	12 55.5
20	5 12.0	12 48.6
MAR 2	5 07.0	12 40.2
12	5 00.2	12 30.6
22	4 51.6	12 20.1
APR 1	4 41.7	12 09.3
11	4 30.9	11 58.3
21	4 19.4	11 47.8
MAY 1	4 07.8	11 37.9
11	3 56.5	11 29.0
21	3 45.8	11 21.5
31	3 36.1	11 15.6
JUN 10	3 27.7	11 11.5
20	3 21.0	11 09.3
30	3 16.1	11D09.1
JUL 10	3 13.3	11 11.0
20	3D12.5	11 14.8
30	3 14.0	11 20.6
AUG 9	3 17.6	11 28.2
19	3 23.3	11 37.3
29	3 30.9	11 47.9
SEP 8	3 40.4	11 59.7
18	3 51.5	12 12.3
28	4 03.9	12 25.6
OCT 8	4 17.4	12 39.1
18	4 31.6	12 52.6
28	4 46.2	13 05.6
NOV 7	5 00.8	13 18.0
17	5 15.1	13 29.4
27	5 28.7	13 39.4
DEC 7	5 41.3	13 47.8
17	5 52.4	13 54.4
27	6 01.9	13 58.9
JAN 6	6♏09.5	14♎01.4
JAN 1	10N29.6	17N04.7
21	10 35.8	17 12.7
FEB 10	10 45.0	17 23.0
MAR 2	10 56.2	17 34.1
22	11 07.7	17 44.4
APR 11	11 18.0	17 52.4
MAY 1	11 25.8	17 57.0
21	11 29.9	17 57.5
JUN 10	11 29.8	17 53.8
30	11 25.5	17 46.3
JUL 20	11 17.5	17 35.6
AUG 9	11 06.6	17 22.9
29	10 53.9	17 09.4
SEP 18	10 40.7	16 56.4
OCT 8	10 28.4	16 45.0
28	10 18.1	16 36.4
NOV 17	10 11.0	16 31.5
DEC 7	10 07.7	16 30.7
27	10N08.6	16N34.0
	2/2.28 7/18.14	1/10.81 6/25.66

2028	♀ Haumea 136108	♀ Makemake 136472
JAN 1	6♏06.0	14♎00.4
11	6 12.6	14 01.8
21	6 16.9	14R01.0
31	6 19.0	13 58.1
FEB 10	6R18.7	13 53.2
20	6 16.2	13 46.6
MAR 1	6 11.5	13 38.3
11	6 04.9	13 28.9
21	5 56.5	13 18.5
31	5 46.8	13 07.7
APR 10	5 36.0	12 56.8
20	5 24.6	12 46.2
30	5 13.0	12 36.2
MAY 10	5 01.6	12 27.2
20	4 50.8	12 19.6
30	4 40.9	12 13.4
JUN 9	4 32.4	12 09.1
19	4 25.4	12 06.7
29	4 20.2	12D06.2
JUL 9	4 17.1	12 07.8
19	4D16.1	12 11.4
29	4 17.2	12 17.0
AUG 8	4 20.6	12 24.3
18	4 26.0	12 33.3
28	4 33.4	12 43.7
SEP 7	4 42.7	12 55.3
17	4 53.6	13 07.9
27	5 05.9	13 21.0
OCT 7	5 19.3	13 34.5
17	5 33.5	13 48.0
27	5 48.1	14 01.1
NOV 6	6 02.7	14 13.6
16	6 17.1	14 25.0
26	6 30.9	14 35.2
DEC 6	6 43.6	14 43.8
16	6 55.0	14 50.6
26	7 04.8	14 55.4
JAN 5	7♏12.7	14♎58.1
JAN 1	10N09.5	16N35.5
21	10 15.5	16 43.2
FEB 10	10 24.6	16 53.3
MAR 1	10 35.6	17 04.3
21	10 47.1	17 14.6
APR 10	10 57.5	17 22.8
30	11 05.3	17 27.5
MAY 20	11 09.6	17 28.3
JUN 9	11 09.7	17 24.8
29	11 05.6	17 17.5
JUL 19	10 57.7	17 07.1
AUG 8	10 46.9	16 54.5
28	10 34.3	16 41.1
SEP 17	10 21.2	16 28.0
OCT 7	10 08.8	16 16.6
27	09 58.4	16 07.8
NOV 16	09 51.1	16 02.7
DEC 6	09 47.6	16 01.7
26	09N48.4	16N04.7
	2/3.58 7/18.47	1/12.01 6/25.86

2029	♀ Haumea 136108	♀ Makemake 136472
JAN 1	7♏09.7	14♎57.3
11	7 16.4	14 58.7
21	7 20.8	14R58.0
31	7 23.0	14 55.1
FEB 10	7R22.8	14 50.3
20	7 20.3	14 43.6
MAR 2	7 15.7	14 35.4
12	7 09.1	14 26.0
22	7 00.8	14 15.7
APR 1	6 51.1	14 04.9
11	6 40.3	13 54.0
21	6 29.0	13 43.4
MAY 1	6 17.3	13 33.4
11	6 05.9	13 24.4
21	5 55.0	13 16.7
31	5 45.1	13 10.6
JUN 10	5 36.5	13 06.2
20	5 29.5	13 03.7
30	5 24.3	13D03.3
JUL 10	5 21.0	13 04.8
20	5D19.9	13 08.3
30	5 21.0	13 13.8
AUG 9	5 24.3	13 21.1
19	5 29.7	13 30.1
29	5 37.1	13 40.4
SEP 8	5 46.3	13 52.0
18	5 57.2	14 04.5
28	6 09.5	14 17.6
OCT 8	6 22.9	14 31.1
18	6 37.1	14 44.6
28	6 51.7	14 57.7
NOV 7	7 06.4	15 10.1
17	7 20.8	15 21.6
27	7 34.6	15 31.8
DEC 7	7 47.4	15 40.4
17	7 58.9	15 47.2
27	8 08.7	15 52.1
JAN 6	8♏16.7	15♎54.8
JAN 1	09N49.4	16N06.4
21	09 55.3	16 14.1
FEB 10	10 04.4	16 24.1
MAR 2	10 15.4	16 35.0
22	10 26.8	16 45.3
APR 11	10 37.1	16 53.3
MAY 1	10 44.9	16 58.1
21	10 49.1	16 58.9
JUN 10	10 49.2	16 55.4
30	10 45.1	16 48.2
JUL 20	10 37.2	16 37.8
AUG 9	10 26.4	16 25.3
29	10 13.9	16 11.9
SEP 18	10 00.7	15 58.9
OCT 8	09 48.4	15 47.5
28	09 38.0	15 38.8
NOV 17	09 30.8	15 33.7
DEC 7	09 27.3	15 32.6
27	09N28.1	15N35.6
	2/3.94 7/19.74	1/12.20 6/27.12

2030	Haumea 136108	Makemake 136472
JAN 1	8♏13.0	15♎53.7
11	8 19.9	15 55.4
21	8 24.7	15R54.9
31	8 27.1	15 52.3
FEB 10	8R27.3	15 47.6
20	8 25.1	15 41.2
MAR 2	8 20.7	15 33.2
12	8 14.4	15 23.9
22	8 06.2	15 13.7
APR 1	7 56.7	15 03.0
11	7 46.0	14 52.1
21	7 34.7	14 41.4
MAY 1	7 23.1	14 31.3
11	7 11.6	14 22.2
21	7 00.6	14 14.4
31	6 50.5	14 08.0
JUN 10	6 41.7	14 03.4
20	6 34.4	14 00.7
30	6 28.9	14D00.0
JUL 10	6 25.4	14 01.3
20	6 24.1	14 04.6
30	6D24.9	14 09.8
AUG 9	6 27.8	14 16.9
19	6 33.0	14 25.6
29	6 40.1	14 35.8
SEP 8	6 49.2	14 47.2
18	6 59.9	14 59.6
28	7 12.0	15 12.7
OCT 8	7 25.3	15 26.1
18	7 39.4	15 39.5
28	7 54.0	15 52.7
NOV 7	8 08.8	16 05.2
17	8 23.3	16 16.8
27	8 37.2	16 27.1
DEC 7	8 50.2	16 35.9
17	9 01.9	16 43.0
27	9 12.0	16 48.0
JAN 6	9♏20.2	16♎51.0
JAN 1	09N28.9	15N36.9
21	09 34.7	15 44.4
FEB 10	09 43.6	15 54.3
MAR 2	09 54.4	16 05.1
22	10 05.8	16 15.3
APR 11	10 16.2	16 23.5
MAY 1	10 24.0	16 28.4
21	10 28.4	16 29.4
JUN 10	10 28.7	16 26.2
30	10 24.7	16 19.2
JUL 20	10 17.0	16 09.0
AUG 9	10 06.4	15 56.7
29	09 53.8	15 43.4
SEP 18	09 40.7	15 30.4
OCT 8	09 28.3	15 18.9
28	09 17.9	15 10.0
NOV 17	09 10.5	15 04.7
DEC 7	09 06.9	15 03.3
27	09N07.5	15N06.1
	2/5.25 7/21.12	1/13.34 6/28.36

2031	Haumea 136108	Makemake 136472
JAN 1	9♏16.4	16♎49.8
11	9 23.6	16 51.7
21	9 28.6	16R51.5
31	9 31.4	16 49.1
FEB 10	9R31.8	16 44.7
20	9 30.0	16 38.5
MAR 2	9 25.9	16 30.6
12	9 19.8	16 21.5
22	9 11.9	16 11.4
APR 1	9 02.5	16 00.7
11	8 51.9	15 49.8
21	8 40.6	15 39.1
MAY 1	8 29.0	15 28.9
11	8 17.4	15 19.7
21	8 06.3	15 11.7
31	7 56.1	15 05.2
JUN 10	7 47.1	15 00.4
20	7 39.6	14 57.4
30	7 33.8	14D56.4
JUL 10	7 30.0	14 57.5
20	7 28.4	15 00.5
30	7D28.9	15 05.5
AUG 9	7 31.6	15 12.3
19	7 36.4	15 20.9
29	7 43.3	15 30.9
SEP 8	7 52.1	15 42.1
18	8 02.6	15 54.4
28	8 14.6	16 07.4
OCT 8	8 27.8	16 20.7
18	8 41.9	16 34.2
28	8 56.5	16 47.4
NOV 7	9 11.3	17 00.0
17	9 25.9	17 11.7
27	9 39.9	17 22.1
DEC 7	9 53.1	17 31.1
17	10 05.0	17 38.4
27	10 15.3	17 43.6
JAN 6	10♏23.8	17♎46.9
JAN 1	09N08.3	15N07.4
21	09 13.8	15 14.6
FEB 10	09 22.5	15 24.3
MAR 2	09 33.3	15 35.0
22	09 44.7	15 45.2
APR 11	09 55.0	15 53.5
MAY 1	10 03.0	15 58.6
21	10 07.5	15 59.7
JUN 10	10 07.9	15 56.8
30	10 04.2	15 50.0
JUL 20	09 56.6	15 40.0
AUG 9	09 46.1	15 27.9
29	09 33.7	15 14.6
SEP 18	09 20.6	15 01.6
OCT 8	09 08.2	14 50.1
28	08 57.6	14 41.1
NOV 17	08 50.1	14 35.6
DEC 7	08 46.3	14 34.0
27	08N46.7	14N36.5
	2/6.59 7/22.44	1/14.53 6/29.57

2032	Haumea 136108	Makemake 136472
JAN 1	10♏19.8	17♎45.5
11	10 27.3	17 47.7
21	10 32.7	17R47.7
31	10 35.8	17 45.6
FEB 10	10R36.5	17 41.4
20	10 34.9	17 35.4
MAR 1	10 31.1	17 27.7
11	10 25.3	17 18.7
21	10 17.6	17 08.7
31	10 08.3	16 58.1
APR 10	9 57.9	16 47.2
20	9 46.7	16 36.5
30	9 35.0	16 26.2
MAY 10	9 23.4	16 16.9
20	9 12.2	16 08.7
30	9 01.8	16 02.0
JUN 9	8 52.6	15 57.0
19	8 44.9	15 53.8
29	8 38.9	15 52.6
JUL 9	8 34.8	15D53.3
19	8 32.8	15 56.1
29	8D33.0	16 00.9
AUG 8	8 35.4	16 07.5
18	8 40.0	16 15.8
28	8 46.6	16 25.6
SEP 7	8 55.2	16 36.7
17	9 05.6	16 48.9
27	9 17.4	17 01.8
OCT 7	9 30.4	17 15.1
17	9 44.4	17 28.5
27	9 59.0	17 41.7
NOV 6	10 13.8	17 54.4
16	10 28.5	18 06.2
26	10 42.7	18 16.8
DEC 6	10 56.0	18 25.9
16	11 08.1	18 33.4
26	11 18.7	18 38.9
JAN 5	11♏27.5	18♎42.4
JAN 1	08N47.4	14N37.7
21	08 52.8	14 44.7
FEB 10	09 01.4	14 54.2
MAR 1	09 12.0	15 04.8
21	09 23.3	15 15.0
APR 10	09 33.7	15 23.3
30	09 41.7	15 28.6
MAY 20	09 46.4	15 30.0
JUN 9	09 47.0	15 27.3
29	09 43.4	15 20.7
JUL 19	09 36.0	15 10.9
AUG 8	09 25.6	14 58.9
28	09 13.3	14 45.8
SEP 17	09 00.2	14 32.8
OCT 7	08 47.8	14 21.2
27	08 37.2	14 12.1
NOV 16	08 29.5	14 06.3
DEC 6	08 25.6	14 04.5
26	08N25.7	14N06.8
	2/7.92 7/22.79	1/15.66 6/29.86

2033	Haumea 136108	Makemake 136472
JAN 1	11♏24.2	18♎41.2
11	11 31.8	18 43.4
21	11 37.2	18R43.4
31	11 40.4	18 41.3
FEB 10	11R41.2	18 37.2
20	11 39.7	18 31.2
MAR 2	11 36.0	18 23.6
12	11 30.1	18 14.6
22	11 22.5	18 04.6
APR 1	11 13.3	17 54.0
11	11 02.8	17 43.2
21	10 51.6	17 32.4
MAY 1	10 40.0	17 22.2
11	10 28.3	17 12.8
21	10 17.1	17 04.6
31	10 06.6	16 57.9
JUN 10	9 57.3	16 52.8
20	9 49.5	16 49.6
30	9 43.4	16 48.3
JUL 10	9 39.3	16D49.1
20	9 37.2	16 51.8
30	9D37.4	16 56.5
AUG 9	9 39.7	17 03.1
19	9 44.2	17 11.3
29	9 50.8	17 21.1
SEP 8	9 59.3	17 32.2
18	10 09.6	17 44.3
28	10 21.4	17 57.1
OCT 8	10 34.5	18 10.4
18	10 48.5	18 23.8
28	11 03.1	18 37.0
NOV 7	11 17.9	18 49.7
17	11 32.6	19 01.5
27	11 46.9	19 12.1
DEC 7	12 00.2	19 21.3
17	12 12.4	19 28.7
27	12 23.1	19 34.3
JAN 6	12♏31.9	19♎37.8
JAN 1	08N26.6	14N08.2
21	08 31.9	14 15.1
FEB 10	08 40.5	14 24.5
MAR 2	08 51.1	14 35.0
22	09 02.3	14 45.1
APR 11	09 12.6	14 53.4
MAY 1	09 20.6	14 58.6
21	09 25.2	15 00.0
JUN 10	09 25.7	14 57.3
30	09 22.1	14 50.8
JUL 20	09 14.8	14 41.1
AUG 9	09 04.4	14 29.2
29	08 52.1	14 16.1
SEP 18	08 39.0	14 03.2
OCT 8	08 26.6	13 51.6
28	08 16.1	13 42.5
NOV 17	08 08.4	13 36.8
DEC 7	08 04.5	13 34.9
27	08N04.7	13N37.1
	2/8.22 7/24.17	1/15.81 7/1.06

2034	Haumea 136108	Makemake 136472
JAN 1	12♏27.7	19♎36.3
11	12 35.6	19 38.7
21	12 41.3	19R39.0
31	12 44.8	19 37.1
FEB 10	12R45.9	19 33.2
20	12 44.8	19 27.4
MAR 2	12 41.3	19 20.0
12	12 35.7	19 11.2
22	12 28.3	19 01.3
APR 1	12 19.2	18 50.8
11	12 09.0	18 39.9
21	11 57.8	18 29.2
MAY 1	11 46.1	18 18.9
11	11 34.5	18 09.4
21	11 23.1	18 01.1
31	11 12.5	17 54.1
JUN 10	11 03.0	17 48.9
20	10 55.0	17 45.4
30	10 48.7	17 43.9
JUL 10	10 44.2	17D44.4
20	10 41.9	17 46.9
30	10D41.7	17 51.4
AUG 9	10 43.7	17 57.7
19	10 48.0	18 05.7
29	10 54.3	18 15.3
SEP 8	11 02.6	18 26.2
18	11 12.7	18 38.2
28	11 24.3	18 51.0
OCT 8	11 37.3	19 04.2
18	11 51.2	19 17.6
28	12 05.7	19 30.8
NOV 7	12 20.6	19 43.6
17	12 35.4	19 55.5
27	12 49.7	20 06.2
DEC 7	13 03.3	20 15.5
17	13 15.6	20 23.2
27	13 26.5	20 29.0
JAN 6	13♏35.7	20♎32.7
JAN 1	08N05.4	13N38.3
21	08 10.5	13 44.9
FEB 10	08 18.9	13 54.1
MAR 2	08 29.4	14 04.5
22	08 40.6	14 14.6
APR 11	08 50.9	14 23.0
MAY 1	08 58.9	14 28.3
21	09 03.6	14 29.9
JUN 10	09 04.4	14 27.5
30	09 00.9	14 21.2
JUL 20	08 53.7	14 11.7
AUG 9	08 43.5	13 59.9
29	08 31.2	13 46.9
SEP 18	08 18.2	13 34.0
OCT 8	08 05.8	13 22.4
28	07 55.2	13 13.2
NOV 17	07 47.4	13 07.3
DEC 7	07 43.3	13 05.2
27	07N43.3	13N07.1
	2/9.58 7/25.49	1/16.96 7/2.28

2035	Haumea 136108	Makemake 136472
JAN 1	13♏31.3	20♎31.1
11	13 39.5	20 33.8
21	13 45.5	20R34.3
31	13 49.3	20 32.7
FEB 10	13 50.8	20 29.0
20	13R49.9	20 23.4
MAR 2	13 46.7	20 16.2
12	13 41.4	20 07.5
22	13 34.2	19 57.8
APR 1	13 25.3	19 47.3
11	13 15.1	19 36.5
21	13 04.1	19 25.7
MAY 1	12 52.4	19 15.4
11	12 40.7	19 05.8
21	12 29.3	18 57.3
31	12 18.6	18 50.2
JUN 10	12 08.9	18 44.8
20	12 00.6	18 41.1
30	11 54.0	18 39.3
JUL 10	11 49.3	18D39.6
20	11 46.7	18 41.9
30	11D46.2	18 46.1
AUG 9	11 47.9	18 52.2
19	11 51.9	19 00.0
29	11 57.9	19 09.4
SEP 8	12 06.0	19 20.2
18	12 15.9	19 32.0
28	12 27.4	19 44.7
OCT 8	12 40.2	19 57.9
18	12 54.0	20 11.3
28	13 08.5	20 24.5
NOV 7	13 23.4	20 37.3
17	13 38.3	20 49.3
27	13 52.7	21 00.2
DEC 7	14 06.4	21 09.7
17	14 19.0	21 17.6
27	14 30.1	21 23.5
JAN 6	14♏39.5	21♎27.5
JAN 1	07N44.0	13N08.2
21	07 48.9	13 14.6
FEB 10	07 57.1	13 23.6
MAR 2	08 07.5	13 33.9
22	08 18.5	13 44.0
APR 11	08 28.9	13 52.4
MAY 1	08 37.0	13 57.8
21	08 41.8	13 59.6
JUN 10	08 42.7	13 57.4
30	08 39.4	13 51.4
JUL 20	08 32.4	13 42.1
AUG 9	08 22.3	13 30.5
29	08 10.1	13 17.6
SEP 18	07 57.2	13 04.7
OCT 8	07 44.7	12 53.1
28	07 34.0	12 43.7
NOV 17	07 26.2	12 37.6
DEC 7	07 21.9	12 35.3
27	07N21.7	12N37.0
	2/10.87 7/26.88	1/18.09 7/3.49

2036	Haumea 136108	Makemake 136472
JAN 1	14♏35.1	21♎25.8
11	14 43.5	21 28.7
21	14 49.8	21R29.5
31	14 54.0	21 28.1
FEB 10	14 55.7	21 24.7
20	14R55.1	21 19.3
MAR 1	14 52.3	21 12.3
11	14 47.2	21 03.8
21	14 40.2	20 54.2
31	14 31.6	20 43.8
APR 10	14 21.6	20 33.0
20	14 10.6	20 22.3
30	13 59.0	20 11.9
MAY 10	13 47.2	20 02.2
20	13 35.7	19 53.6
30	13 24.9	19 46.3
JUN 9	13 15.0	19 40.7
19	13 06.5	19 36.8
29	12 59.7	19 34.8
JUL 9	12 54.7	19D34.8
19	12 51.8	19 36.8
29	12D51.0	19 40.8
AUG 8	12 52.5	19 46.7
18	12 56.1	19 54.3
28	13 01.9	20 03.6
SEP 7	13 09.7	20 14.2
17	13 19.4	20 25.9
27	13 30.7	20 38.5
OCT 7	13 43.4	20 51.6
17	13 57.1	21 05.0
27	14 11.6	21 18.3
NOV 6	14 26.5	21 31.1
16	14 41.4	21 43.2
26	14 56.0	21 54.2
DEC 6	15 09.9	22 03.9
16	15 22.6	22 11.9
26	15 34.0	22 18.2
JAN 5	15♏43.7	22♎22.4
JAN 1	07N22.3	12N38.0
21	07 27.0	12 44.2
FEB 10	07 35.0	12 53.0
MAR 1	07 45.2	13 03.2
21	07 56.3	13 13.2
APR 10	08 06.6	13 21.6
30	08 14.8	13 27.2
MAY 20	08 19.7	13 29.2
JUN 9	08 20.7	13 27.2
29	08 17.6	13 21.4
JUL 19	08 10.8	13 12.3
AUG 8	08 00.8	13 00.9
28	07 48.7	12 48.1
SEP 17	07 35.8	12 35.3
OCT 7	07 23.4	12 23.6
27	07 12.6	12 14.2
NOV 16	07 04.6	12 07.9
DEC 6	07 00.2	12 05.4
26	06N59.8	12N06.8
	2/12.23 7/27.18	1/19.30 7/3.65

2037	Haumea 136108	Makemake 136472
JAN 1	15♏40.0	22♎20.9
11	15 48.6	22 23.9
21	15 55.0	22R24.7
31	15 59.2	22 23.4
FEB 10	16 01.0	22 20.0
20	16R00.5	22 14.7
MAR 2	15 57.7	22 07.7
12	15 52.8	21 59.2
22	15 45.9	21 49.6
APR 1	15 37.2	21 39.3
11	15 27.3	21 28.6
21	15 16.3	21 17.8
MAY 1	15 04.7	21 07.4
11	14 52.9	20 57.7
21	14 41.4	20 49.1
31	14 30.5	20 41.9
JUN 10	14 20.6	20 36.2
20	14 12.1	20 32.3
30	14 05.2	20 30.3
JUL 10	14 00.1	20D30.2
20	13 57.1	20 32.2
30	13D56.3	20 36.2
AUG 9	13 57.6	20 42.0
19	14 01.2	20 49.6
29	14 07.0	20 58.8
SEP 8	14 14.7	21 09.4
18	14 24.4	21 21.1
28	14 35.7	21 33.6
OCT 8	14 48.3	21 46.7
18	15 02.1	22 00.1
28	15 16.6	22 13.4
NOV 7	15 31.5	22 26.2
17	15 46.5	22 38.3
27	16 01.1	22 49.4
DEC 7	16 15.0	22 59.0
17	16 27.9	23 07.1
27	16 39.3	23 13.3
JAN 6	16♏49.1	23♎17.6
JAN 1	07N00.5	12N08.0
21	07 05.2	12 14.1
FEB 10	07 13.2	12 22.8
MAR 2	07 23.3	12 32.8
22	07 34.2	12 42.8
APR 11	07 44.5	12 51.1
MAY 1	07 52.6	12 56.7
21	07 57.4	12 58.7
JUN 10	07 58.4	12 56.7
30	07 55.3	12 50.9
JUL 20	07 48.4	12 41.9
AUG 9	07 38.4	12 30.6
29	07 26.4	12 17.9
SEP 18	07 13.6	12 05.1
OCT 8	07 01.2	11 53.5
28	06 50.4	11 44.1
NOV 17	06 42.5	11 37.8
DEC 7	06 38.1	11 35.2
27	06N37.7	11N36.6
	2/12.60 7/28.53	1/19.44 7/4.87

2038	Haumea 136108	Makemake 136472
JAN 1	16♏44.4	23♎15.7
11	16 53.2	23 18.9
21	17 00.0	23R20.0
31	17 04.5	23 18.9
FEB 10	17 06.7	23 15.8
20	17R06.5	23 10.7
MAR 2	17 04.0	23 03.9
12	16 59.3	22 55.6
22	16 52.7	22 46.2
APR 1	16 44.3	22 35.9
11	16 34.4	22 25.2
21	16 23.6	22 14.5
MAY 1	16 12.0	22 04.0
11	16 00.3	21 54.3
21	15 48.7	21 45.6
31	15 37.6	21 38.1
JUN 10	15 27.6	21 32.3
20	15 18.8	21 28.1
30	15 11.7	21 25.9
JUL 10	15 06.3	21D25.6
20	15 03.1	21 27.4
30	15D01.9	21 31.1
AUG 9	15 03.0	21 36.7
19	15 06.3	21 44.1
29	15 11.8	21 53.1
SEP 8	15 19.3	22 03.5
18	15 28.7	22 15.1
28	15 39.9	22 27.6
OCT 8	15 52.4	22 40.6
18	16 06.0	22 54.0
28	16 20.5	23 07.2
NOV 7	16 35.4	23 20.2
17	16 50.5	23 32.3
27	17 05.2	23 43.5
DEC 7	17 19.2	23 53.4
17	17 32.3	24 01.6
27	17 44.0	24 08.1
JAN 6	17♏54.0	24♎12.5
JAN 1	06N38.2	11N37.6
21	06 42.8	11 43.4
FEB 10	06 50.6	11 51.9
MAR 2	07 00.6	12 01.9
22	07 11.4	12 11.7
APR 11	07 21.6	12 20.1
MAY 1	07 29.8	12 25.8
21	07 34.8	12 28.0
JUN 10	07 35.9	12 26.2
30	07 33.0	12 20.7
JUL 20	07 26.2	12 11.9
AUG 9	07 16.4	12 00.7
29	07 04.5	11 48.2
SEP 18	06 51.7	11 35.5
OCT 8	06 39.3	11 23.8
28	06 28.5	11 14.3
NOV 17	06 20.4	11 07.8
DEC 7	06 15.9	11 05.1
27	06N15.3	11N06.2
	2/13.96 7/29.87	1/20.64 7/6.02

2039	Haumea 136108	Makemake 136472
JAN 1	17♏49.2	24♎10.6
11	17 58.3	24 14.0
21	18 05.4	24 15.3
31	18 10.2	24R14.5
FEB 10	18 12.7	24 11.6
20	18R12.9	24 06.8
MAR 2	18 10.7	24 00.1
12	18 06.3	23 52.0
22	17 59.9	23 42.7
APR 1	17 51.7	23 32.6
11	17 42.0	23 21.9
21	17 31.3	23 11.2
MAY 1	17 19.8	23 00.7
11	17 08.1	22 50.9
21	16 56.4	22 42.0
31	16 45.3	22 34.5
JUN 10	16 35.1	22 28.4
20	16 26.1	22 24.1
30	16 18.7	22 21.6
JUL 10	16 13.1	22D21.1
20	16 09.5	22 22.6
30	16 08.1	22 26.1
AUG 9	16D08.9	22 31.5
19	16 11.9	22 38.7
29	16 17.1	22 47.5
SEP 8	16 24.4	22 57.7
18	16 33.6	23 09.2
28	16 44.5	23 21.6
OCT 8	16 56.9	23 34.5
18	17 10.5	23 47.8
28	17 24.9	24 01.1
NOV 7	17 39.8	24 14.1
17	17 54.9	24 26.4
27	18 09.7	24 37.7
DEC 7	18 23.9	24 47.7
17	18 37.1	24 56.1
27	18 49.1	25 02.8
JAN 6	18♏59.4	25♎07.5
JAN 1	06N15.8	11N07.1
21	06 20.1	11 12.7
FEB 10	06 27.7	11 21.0
MAR 2	06 37.6	11 30.8
22	06 48.4	11 40.6
APR 11	06 58.5	11 49.0
MAY 1	07 06.7	11 54.8
21	07 11.8	11 57.2
JUN 10	07 13.1	11 55.7
30	07 10.3	11 50.4
JUL 20	07 03.8	11 41.8
AUG 9	06 54.1	11 30.8
29	06 42.3	11 18.3
SEP 18	06 29.6	11 05.7
OCT 8	06 17.2	10 54.0
28	06 06.3	10 44.4
NOV 17	05 58.2	10 37.8
DEC 7	05 53.5	10 34.8
27	05N52.7	10N35.7
	2/15.37 7/31.18	1/21.83 7/7.23

2040	Haumea 136108	Makemake 136472
JAN 1	18♏54.4	25♎05.4
11	19 03.8	25 09.1
21	19 11.2	25 10.6
31	19 16.3	25R10.1
FEB 10	19 19.2	25 07.4
20	19R19.7	25 02.8
MAR 1	19 17.8	24 56.4
11	19 13.7	24 48.5
21	19 07.5	24 39.3
31	18 59.6	24 29.2
APR 10	18 50.1	24 18.6
20	18 39.4	24 07.9
30	18 28.0	23 57.4
MAY 10	18 16.3	23 47.5
20	18 04.6	23 38.5
30	17 53.4	23 30.8
JUN 9	17 43.0	23 24.5
19	17 33.8	23 20.0
29	17 26.2	23 17.3
JUL 9	17 20.3	23D16.6
19	17 16.4	23 17.8
29	17 14.7	23 21.1
AUG 8	17D15.2	23 26.2
18	17 17.9	23 33.2
28	17 22.8	23 41.8
SEP 7	17 29.9	23 51.9
17	17 38.9	24 03.2
27	17 49.6	24 15.5
OCT 7	18 01.8	24 28.4
17	18 15.3	24 41.7
27	18 29.6	24 55.0
NOV 6	18 44.5	25 08.0
16	18 59.6	25 20.3
26	19 14.6	25 31.8
DEC 6	19 28.9	25 41.9
16	19 42.3	25 50.5
26	19 54.5	25 57.4
JAN 5	20♏05.1	26♎02.4
JAN 1	05N53.2	10N36.5
21	05 57.3	10 41.9
FEB 10	06 04.7	10 50.0
MAR 1	06 14.4	10 59.6
21	06 25.1	11 09.4
APR 10	06 35.2	11 17.8
30	06 43.5	11 23.7
MAY 20	06 48.7	11 26.2
JUN 9	06 50.1	11 24.9
29	06 47.5	11 19.9
JUL 19	06 41.1	11 11.5
AUG 8	06 31.6	11 00.7
28	06 19.9	10 48.4
SEP 17	06 07.2	10 35.8
OCT 7	05 54.8	10 24.1
27	05 44.0	10 14.4
NOV 16	05 35.7	10 07.6
DEC 6	05 30.9	10 04.4
26	05N29.9	10N05.1
	2/16.73 7/31.58	1/22.96 7/7.43

2041	Haumea 136108	Makemake 136472
JAN 1	20♏01.0	26♎00.6
11	20 10.5	26 04.3
21	20 18.0	26 05.9
31	20 23.2	26R05.4
FEB 10	20 26.2	26 02.8
20	20R26.7	25 58.2
MAR 2	20 25.0	25 51.8
12	20 20.9	25 43.9
22	20 14.8	25 34.8
APR 1	20 06.9	25 24.7
11	19 57.5	25 14.2
21	19 46.9	25 03.5
MAY 1	19 35.5	24 53.0
11	19 23.7	24 43.0
21	19 12.0	24 34.1
31	19 00.7	24 26.3
JUN 10	18 50.3	24 20.0
20	18 41.1	24 15.5
30	18 33.4	24 12.8
JUL 10	18 27.4	24D12.0
20	18 23.5	24 13.2
30	18 21.7	24 16.4
AUG 9	18D22.1	24 21.5
19	18 24.7	24 28.5
29	18 29.6	24 37.0
SEP 8	18 36.5	24 47.1
18	18 45.5	24 58.3
28	18 56.2	25 10.6
OCT 8	19 08.4	25 23.5
18	19 21.8	25 36.7
28	19 36.2	25 50.0
NOV 7	19 51.1	26 03.0
17	20 06.3	26 15.4
27	20 21.2	26 26.8
DEC 7	20 35.6	26 37.0
17	20 49.1	26 45.6
27	21 01.4	26 52.5
JAN 6	21♏12.0	26♎57.5
JAN 1	05N30.4	10N06.0
21	05 34.6	10 11.3
FEB 10	05 42.0	10 19.3
MAR 2	05 51.6	10 28.8
22	06 02.2	10 38.5
APR 11	06 12.2	10 46.8
MAY 1	06 20.4	10 52.7
21	06 25.5	10 55.2
JUN 10	06 26.9	10 53.9
30	06 24.2	10 48.9
JUL 20	06 17.8	10 40.6
AUG 9	06 08.3	10 29.9
29	05 56.7	10 17.7
SEP 18	05 44.1	10 05.1
OCT 8	05 31.7	09 53.5
28	05 20.9	09 43.8
NOV 17	05 12.7	09 37.1
DEC 7	05 07.9	09 33.9
27	05N07.0	09N34.5
	2/17.14 8/1.92	1/23.15 7/8.61

2042	Haumea 136108	Makemake 136472
JAN 1	21♏06.9	26♎55.2
11	21 16.7	26 59.2
21	21 24.4	27 01.0
31	21 30.0	27R00.7
FEB 10	21 33.3	26 58.3
20	21R34.2	26 54.0
MAR 2	21 32.7	26 47.8
12	21 29.0	26 40.1
22	21 23.2	26 31.1
APR 1	21 15.5	26 21.1
11	21 06.2	26 10.6
21	20 55.7	25 59.9
MAY 1	20 44.4	25 49.4
11	20 32.7	25 39.4
21	20 20.9	25 30.3
31	20 09.5	25 22.4
JUN 10	19 58.9	25 15.9
20	19 49.5	25 11.2
30	19 41.6	25 08.2
JUL 10	19 35.4	25D07.2
20	19 31.1	25 08.2
30	19 29.0	25 11.1
AUG 9	19D29.1	25 16.0
19	19 31.4	25 22.7
29	19 36.0	25 31.1
SEP 8	19 42.7	25 41.0
18	19 51.4	25 52.1
28	20 01.9	26 04.2
OCT 8	20 13.9	26 17.0
18	20 27.3	26 30.2
28	20 41.5	26 43.5
NOV 7	20 56.5	26 56.6
17	21 11.6	27 09.0
27	21 26.7	27 20.5
DEC 7	21 41.2	27 30.8
17	21 54.9	27 39.7
27	22 07.3	27 46.8
JAN 6	22♏18.2	27♎51.9
JAN 1	05N07.4	09N35.2
21	05 11.4	09 40.3
FEB 10	05 18.6	09 48.1
MAR 2	05 28.1	09 57.4
22	05 38.5	10 07.0
APR 11	05 48.6	10 15.4
MAY 1	05 56.7	10 21.4
21	06 02.0	10 24.0
JUN 10	06 03.5	10 22.9
30	06 01.0	10 18.2
JUL 20	05 54.8	10 10.1
AUG 9	05 45.4	09 59.5
29	05 33.9	09 47.4
SEP 18	05 21.3	09 35.0
OCT 8	05 09.0	09 23.4
28	04 58.2	09 13.6
NOV 17	04 49.9	09 06.7
DEC 7	04 45.0	09 03.3
27	04N43.9	09N03.7
	2/18.52 8/3.31	1/24.26 7/9.87

2043	Haumea 136108	Makemake 136472
JAN 1	22♏13.0	27♎49.6
11	22 23.0	27 53.8
21	22 31.1	27 55.8
31	22 37.0	27R55.8
FEB 10	22 40.6	27 53.6
20	22R41.8	27 49.5
MAR 2	22 40.7	27 43.5
12	22 37.2	27 36.0
22	22 31.7	27 27.1
APR 1	22 24.2	27 17.3
11	22 15.2	27 06.8
21	22 04.8	26 56.1
MAY 1	21 53.6	26 45.6
11	21 41.8	26 35.5
21	21 30.0	26 26.3
31	21 18.6	26 18.2
JUN 10	21 07.8	26 11.6
20	20 58.2	26 06.6
30	20 50.0	26 03.4
JUL 10	20 43.5	26 02.2
20	20 39.0	26D02.9
30	20 36.6	26 05.6
AUG 9	20D36.4	26 10.3
19	20 38.4	26 16.8
29	20 42.7	26 25.0
SEP 8	20 49.1	26 34.7
18	20 57.5	26 45.6
28	21 07.8	26 57.6
OCT 8	21 19.7	27 10.4
18	21 32.9	27 23.5
28	21 47.1	27 36.8
NOV 7	22 02.0	27 49.9
17	22 17.2	28 02.4
27	22 32.3	28 14.0
DEC 7	22 46.9	28 24.5
17	23 00.8	28 33.4
27	23 13.4	28 40.7
JAN 6	23♏24.6	28♎46.1
JAN 1	04N44.3	09N04.3
21	04 48.0	09 09.2
FEB 10	04 55.0	09 16.7
MAR 2	05 04.4	09 25.9
22	05 14.8	09 35.4
APR 11	05 24.7	09 43.8
MAY 1	05 32.9	09 49.9
21	05 38.2	09 52.7
JUN 10	05 39.9	09 51.8
30	05 37.6	09 47.3
JUL 20	05 31.5	09 39.4
AUG 9	05 22.3	09 29.0
29	05 10.9	09 17.1
SEP 18	04 58.4	09 04.7
OCT 8	04 46.2	08 53.1
28	04 35.3	08 43.3
NOV 17	04 27.0	08 36.2
DEC 7	04 21.9	08 32.6
27	04N20.7	08N32.8
	2/19.88 8/4.70	1/25.40 7/11.04

2044	Haumea 136108	Makemake 136472
JAN 1	23♏19.2	28♎43.7
11	23 29.5	28 48.1
21	23 37.9	28 50.4
31	23 44.1	28R50.6
FEB 10	23 48.0	28 48.6
20	23 49.6	28 44.7
MAR 1	23R48.7	28 39.0
11	23 45.6	28 31.6
21	23 40.3	28 22.8
31	23 33.1	28 13.1
APR 10	23 24.2	28 02.7
20	23 14.0	27 52.0
30	23 02.9	27 41.4
MAY 10	22 51.2	27 31.3
20	22 39.3	27 22.0
30	22 27.8	27 13.8
JUN 9	22 16.9	27 07.0
19	22 07.1	27 01.8
29	21 58.6	26 58.4
JUL 9	21 51.9	26 56.9
19	21 47.1	26D57.4
29	21 44.3	26 59.9
AUG 8	21D43.8	27 04.3
18	21 45.5	27 10.6
28	21 49.5	27 18.5
SEP 7	21 55.6	27 28.1
17	22 03.8	27 38.9
27	22 13.9	27 50.7
OCT 7	22 25.6	28 03.4
17	22 38.6	28 16.5
27	22 52.8	28 29.8
NOV 6	23 07.6	28 42.8
16	23 22.8	28 55.4
26	23 38.0	29 07.2
DEC 6	23 52.7	29 17.7
16	24 06.7	29 26.9
26	24 19.6	29 34.4
JAN 5	24♏31.0	29♎40.0
JAN 1	04N21.0	08N33.4
21	04 24.5	08 37.9
FEB 10	04 31.4	08 45.3
MAR 1	04 40.5	08 54.3
21	04 50.8	09 03.7
APR 10	05 00.7	09 12.1
30	05 09.0	09 18.3
MAY 20	05 14.3	09 21.3
JUN 9	05 16.1	09 20.6
29	05 14.0	09 16.2
JUL 19	05 08.1	09 08.6
AUG 8	04 59.0	08 58.4
28	04 47.7	08 46.6
SEP 17	04 35.4	08 34.3
OCT 7	04 23.1	08 22.7
27	04 12.2	08 12.8
NOV 16	04 03.8	08 05.6
DEC 6	03 58.6	08 01.8
26	03N57.2	08N01.7
	2/21.29 8/5.09	1/26.53 7/11.27

2045	Haumea 136108	Makemake 136472
JAN 1	24♏26.6	29♎38.0
11	24 37.0	29 42.4
21	24 45.4	29 44.7
31	24 51.7	29R44.9
FEB 10	24 55.8	29 43.0
20	24 57.4	29 39.1
MAR 2	24R56.7	29 33.4
12	24 53.6	29 26.0
22	24 48.4	29 17.3
APR 1	24 41.3	29 07.6
11	24 32.4	28 57.2
21	24 22.2	28 46.6
MAY 1	24 11.1	28 36.0
11	23 59.4	28 25.8
21	23 47.5	28 16.5
31	23 35.9	28 08.3
JUN 10	23 25.0	28 01.5
20	23 15.1	27 56.2
30	23 06.6	27 52.8
JUL 10	22 59.7	27 51.3
20	22 54.8	27D51.7
30	22 52.0	27 54.2
AUG 9	22D51.4	27 58.5
19	22 53.0	28 04.8
29	22 56.9	28 12.7
SEP 8	23 03.0	28 22.2
18	23 11.1	28 33.0
28	23 21.1	28 44.8
OCT 8	23 32.7	28 57.4
18	23 45.8	29 10.5
28	23 59.9	29 23.8
NOV 7	24 14.7	29 36.8
17	24 30.0	29 49.4
27	24 45.2	0♏01.1
DEC 7	25 00.0	0 11.7
17	25 14.1	0 20.9
27	25 27.0	0 28.4
JAN 6	25♏38.5	0♏34.0
JAN 1	03N57.6	08N02.4
21	04 01.1	08 06.9
FEB 10	04 07.9	08 14.2
MAR 2	04 17.0	08 23.1
22	04 27.2	08 32.4
APR 11	04 37.0	08 40.7
MAY 1	04 45.1	08 46.8
21	04 50.4	08 49.7
JUN 10	04 52.1	08 49.1
30	04 49.9	08 44.8
JUL 20	04 44.0	08 37.2
AUG 9	04 35.0	08 27.1
29	04 23.8	08 15.4
SEP 18	04 11.4	08 03.2
OCT 8	03 59.3	07 51.6
28	03 48.5	07 41.8
NOV 17	03 40.1	07 34.7
DEC 7	03 35.0	07 30.9
27	03N33.6	07N30.7
	2/21.62 8/6.53	1/26.62 7/12.49

2046	Haumea 136108	Makemake 136472
JAN 1	25♏32.9	0♏31.4
11	25 43.6	0 36.1
21	25 52.3	0 38.6
31	25 58.9	0R39.1
FEB 10	26 03.3	0 37.4
20	26 05.2	0 33.7
MAR 2	26R04.8	0 28.2
12	26 02.1	0 21.0
22	25 57.1	0 12.4
APR 1	25 50.2	0 02.8
11	25 41.6	29♎52.5
21	25 31.6	29 41.9
MAY 1	25 20.5	29 31.3
11	25 08.8	29 21.1
21	24 56.9	29 11.6
31	24 45.2	29 03.3
JUN 10	24 34.2	28 56.3
20	24 24.1	28 50.9
30	24 15.3	28 47.2
JUL 10	24 08.2	28 45.5
20	24 03.0	28D45.7
30	23 59.9	28 47.9
AUG 9	23D59.0	28 52.0
19	24 00.3	28 58.0
29	24 03.9	29 05.8
SEP 8	24 09.6	29 15.0
18	24 17.5	29 25.7
28	24 27.3	29 37.4
OCT 8	24 38.7	29 49.9
18	24 51.6	0♏03.0
28	25 05.6	0 16.2
NOV 7	25 20.4	0 29.3
17	25 35.7	0 41.9
27	25 50.9	0 53.8
DEC 7	26 05.8	1 04.5
17	26 20.1	1 13.8
27	26 33.2	1 21.5
JAN 6	26♏44.9	1♏27.3
JAN 1	03N33.9	07N31.2
21	03 37.3	07 35.5
FEB 10	03 43.9	07 42.5
MAR 2	03 52.8	07 51.3
22	04 02.8	08 00.5
APR 11	04 12.6	08 08.8
MAY 1	04 20.7	08 14.9
21	04 26.1	08 18.0
JUN 10	04 27.9	08 17.6
30	04 25.9	08 13.5
JUL 20	04 20.1	08 06.2
AUG 9	04 11.2	07 56.3
29	04 00.1	07 44.7
SEP 18	03 47.9	07 32.6
OCT 8	03 35.8	07 21.0
28	03 25.0	07 11.2
NOV 17	03 16.5	07 03.9
DEC 7	03 11.3	06 59.9
27	03N09.8	06N59.5
	2/23.01 8/7.90	1/27.77 7/13.64

2047	Haumea 136108	Makemake 136472
JAN 1	26♏39.2	1♏24.6
11	26 50.1	1 29.5
21	26 59.1	1 32.3
31	27 06.1	1R33.0
FEB 10	27 10.7	1 31.5
20	27 13.1	1 28.1
MAR 2	27R13.0	1 22.8
12	27 10.5	1 15.8
22	27 05.9	1 07.4
APR 1	26 59.2	0 57.9
11	26 50.8	0 47.6
21	26 40.9	0 37.0
MAY 1	26 30.0	0 26.4
11	26 18.3	0 16.1
21	26 06.4	0 06.6
31	25 54.7	29♎58.1
JUN 10	25 43.5	29 51.0
20	25 33.2	29 45.3
30	25 24.2	29 41.5
JUL 10	25 16.9	29 39.5
20	25 11.4	29D39.5
30	25 07.9	29 41.4
AUG 9	25 06.7	29 45.4
19	25D07.7	29 51.2
29	25 11.0	29 58.7
SEP 8	25 16.4	0♏07.8
18	25 24.0	0 18.3
28	25 33.6	0 29.9
OCT 8	25 44.9	0 42.3
18	25 57.6	0 55.3
28	26 11.5	1 08.5
NOV 7	26 26.2	1 21.7
17	26 41.4	1 34.3
27	26 56.8	1 46.3
DEC 7	27 11.8	1 57.1
17	27 26.2	2 06.6
27	27 39.5	2 14.5
JAN 6	27♏51.4	2♏20.5
JAN 1	03N10.0	07N00.0
21	03 13.2	07 04.0
FEB 10	03 19.6	07 10.8
MAR 2	03 28.4	07 19.4
22	03 38.3	07 28.5
APR 11	03 48.0	07 36.8
MAY 1	03 56.1	07 43.0
21	04 01.5	07 46.2
JUN 10	04 03.4	07 46.0
30	04 01.5	07 42.1
JUL 20	03 56.0	07 35.0
AUG 9	03 47.3	07 25.3
29	03 36.3	07 13.9
SEP 18	03 24.1	07 01.9
OCT 8	03 12.1	06 50.4
28	03 01.2	06 40.4
NOV 17	02 52.8	06 33.0
DEC 7	02 47.4	06 28.9
27	02N45.7	06N28.3
	2/24.39 8/9.33	1/28.87 7/14.84

2048	Haumea 136108	Makemake 136472
JAN 1	27♏45.7	2♏17.7
11	27 56.8	2 22.8
21	28 06.1	2 25.9
31	28 13.3	2R26.8
FEB 10	28 18.3	2 25.6
20	28 21.0	2 22.4
MAR 1	28R21.2	2 17.2
11	28 19.1	2 10.4
21	28 14.8	2 02.2
31	28 08.4	1 52.8
APR 10	28 00.2	1 42.7
20	27 50.4	1 32.1
30	27 39.6	1 21.5
MAY 10	27 28.0	1 11.2
20	27 16.1	1 01.6
30	27 04.3	0 52.9
JUN 9	26 53.0	0 45.6
19	26 42.5	0 39.8
29	26 33.4	0 35.8
JUL 9	26 25.8	0 33.6
19	26 20.0	0D33.3
29	26 16.2	0 35.0
AUG 8	26 14.7	0 38.7
18	26D15.3	0 44.3
28	26 18.3	0 51.6
SEP 7	26 23.5	1 00.6
17	26 30.8	1 10.9
27	26 40.1	1 22.4
OCT 7	26 51.2	1 34.7
17	27 03.8	1 47.7
27	27 17.6	2 00.9
NOV 6	27 32.3	2 14.0
16	27 47.5	2 26.8
26	28 02.8	2 38.8
DEC 6	28 17.9	2 49.8
16	28 32.5	2 59.4
26	28 46.0	3 07.5
JAN 5	28♏58.2	3♏13.7
JAN 1	02N45.9	06N28.7
21	02 48.9	06 32.5
FEB 10	02 55.1	06 39.0
MAR 1	03 03.7	06 47.5
21	03 13.5	06 56.5
APR 10	03 23.1	07 04.7
30	03 31.2	07 11.0
MAY 20	03 36.7	07 14.4
JUN 9	03 38.8	07 14.3
29	03 37.0	07 10.7
JUL 19	03 31.6	07 03.8
AUG 8	03 23.0	06 54.3
28	03 12.2	06 43.1
SEP 17	03 00.2	06 31.1
OCT 7	02 48.1	06 19.7
27	02 37.3	06 09.7
NOV 16	02 28.8	06 02.2
DEC 6	02 23.3	05 57.8
26	02N21.5	05N57.0
	2/25.77 8/9.71	1/30.03 7/14.97

2049	Haumea 136108	Makemake 136472
JAN 1	28♏53.5	3♏11.5
11	29 04.7	3 16.6
21	29 14.1	3 19.6
31	29 21.4	3R20.6
FEB 10	29 26.5	3 19.4
20	29 29.3	3 16.2
MAR 2	29R29.6	3 11.2
12	29 27.6	3 04.4
22	29 23.3	2 56.2
APR 1	29 17.0	2 46.8
11	29 08.9	2 36.7
21	28 59.2	2 26.1
MAY 1	28 48.4	2 15.5
11	28 36.8	2 05.2
21	28 24.9	1 55.6
31	28 13.0	1 47.0
JUN 10	28 01.7	1 39.7
20	27 51.2	1 33.9
30	27 42.0	1 29.8
JUL 10	27 34.3	1 27.5
20	27 28.4	1D27.2
30	27 24.6	1 28.9
AUG 9	27 22.9	1 32.6
19	27D23.5	1 38.1
29	27 26.4	1 45.4
SEP 8	27 31.5	1 54.4
18	27 38.8	2 04.7
28	27 48.0	2 16.1
OCT 8	27 59.1	2 28.5
18	28 11.6	2 41.4
28	28 25.4	2 54.6
NOV 7	28 40.1	3 07.7
17	28 55.3	3 20.4
27	29 10.7	3 32.5
DEC 7	29 25.9	3 43.5
17	29 40.5	3 53.1
27	29 54.1	4 01.2
JAN 6	0♐06.3	4♏07.5
JAN 1	02N21.7	05N57.5
21	02 24.7	06 01.2
FEB 10	02 30.9	06 07.7
MAR 2	02 39.4	06 16.0
22	02 49.1	06 24.8
APR 11	02 58.6	06 33.0
MAY 1	03 06.5	06 39.2
21	03 11.9	06 42.6
JUN 10	03 13.8	06 42.5
30	03 12.1	06 38.9
JUL 20	03 06.6	06 32.1
AUG 9	02 58.1	06 22.7
29	02 47.3	06 11.6
SEP 18	02 35.4	05 59.7
OCT 8	02 23.4	05 48.4
28	02 12.7	05 38.5
NOV 17	02 04.2	05 31.0
DEC 7	01 58.9	05 26.6
27	01N57.1	05N25.8
	2/26.21 8/11.07	1/30.20 7/16.14

2050		♇ Haumea 136108	♇ Makemake 136472
JAN	1	0♐00.4	4♏04.6
	11	0 11.9	4 09.9
	21	0 21.6	4 13.2
	31	0 29.2	4 14.4
FEB	10	0 34.6	4R13.5
	20	0 37.7	4 10.5
MAR	2	0R38.4	4 05.7
	12	0 36.7	3 59.1
	22	0 32.8	3 51.0
APR	1	0 26.7	3 41.8
	11	0 18.8	3 31.8
	21	0 09.3	3 21.3
MAY	1	29♏58.6	3 10.6
	11	29 47.1	3 00.3
	21	29 35.2	2 50.6
	31	29 23.3	2 41.9
JUN	10	29 11.9	2 34.4
	20	29 01.2	2 28.4
	30	28 51.8	2 24.1
JUL	10	28 43.8	2 21.7
	20	28 37.7	2D21.2
	30	28 33.6	2 22.6
AUG	9	28 31.6	2 26.0
	19	28D31.9	2 31.4
	29	28 34.4	2 38.5
SEP	8	28 39.3	2 47.2
	18	28 46.3	2 57.3
	28	28 55.3	3 08.7
OCT	8	29 06.1	3 20.9
	18	29 18.5	3 33.8
	28	29 32.2	3 47.0
NOV	7	29 46.8	4 00.1
	17	0♐02.0	4 12.9
	27	0 17.4	4 25.0
DEC	7	0 32.7	4 36.1
	17	0 47.4	4 46.0
	27	1 01.2	4 54.2
JAN	6	1♐13.7	5♏00.7
JAN	1	01N57.2	05N26.1
	21	02 00.0	05 29.6
FEB	10	02 06.0	05 35.8
MAR	2	02 14.4	05 44.0
	22	02 23.9	05 52.7
APR	11	02 33.3	06 00.9
MAY	1	02 41.3	06 07.1
	21	02 46.7	06 10.6
JUN	10	02 48.8	06 10.7
	30	02 47.1	06 07.4
JUL	20	02 41.8	06 00.8
AUG	9	02 33.5	05 51.6
	29	02 22.8	05 40.6
SEP	18	02 11.0	05 28.9
OCT	8	01 59.1	05 17.5
	28	01 48.4	05 07.6
NOV	17	01 39.9	05 00.0
DEC	7	01 34.4	04 55.5
	27	01N32.5	04N54.5
		2/27.61 8/12.49	1/31.32 7/17.30

2051		♇ Haumea 136108	♇ Makemake 136472
JAN	1	1♐07.6	4♏57.7
	11	1 19.4	5 03.3
	21	1 29.3	5 06.8
	31	1 37.3	5 08.2
FEB	10	1 43.1	5R07.6
	20	1 46.5	5 04.8
MAR	2	1R47.5	5 00.2
	12	1 46.2	4 53.8
	22	1 42.6	4 45.9
APR	1	1 36.8	4 36.8
	11	1 29.1	4 26.9
	21	1 19.8	4 16.4
MAY	1	1 09.3	4 05.8
	11	0 57.8	3 55.4
	21	0 46.0	3 45.7
	31	0 34.0	3 36.8
JUN	10	0 22.5	3 29.2
	20	0 11.7	3 23.0
	30	0 02.0	3 18.5
JUL	10	29♏53.8	3 15.8
	20	29 47.4	3D15.1
	30	29 43.0	3 16.3
AUG	9	29 40.7	3 19.5
	19	29D40.7	3 24.6
	29	29 42.9	3 31.5
SEP	8	29 47.4	3 40.1
	18	29 54.2	3 50.1
	28	0♐02.9	4 01.2
OCT	8	0 13.5	4 13.4
	18	0 25.8	4 26.2
	28	0 39.3	4 39.3
NOV	7	0 53.8	4 52.5
	17	1 09.0	5 05.3
	27	1 24.5	5 17.6
DEC	7	1 39.8	5 28.8
	17	1 54.7	5 38.8
	27	2 08.7	5 47.2
JAN	6	2♐21.4	5♏53.9
JAN	1	01N32.6	04N54.8
	21	01 35.3	04 58.0
FEB	10	01 41.1	05 04.0
MAR	2	01 49.2	05 11.9
	22	01 58.6	05 20.6
APR	11	02 08.0	05 28.7
MAY	1	02 15.9	05 35.0
	21	02 21.3	05 38.6
JUN	10	02 23.5	05 38.9
	30	02 22.0	05 35.7
JUL	20	02 16.8	05 29.3
AUG	9	02 08.6	05 20.3
	29	01 58.1	05 09.5
SEP	18	01 46.4	04 57.9
OCT	8	01 34.6	04 46.6
	28	01 23.9	04 36.7
NOV	17	01 15.4	04 29.0
DEC	7	01 09.9	04 24.3
	27	01N07.8	04N23.1
		3/1.07 8/13.86	2/1.51 7/18.44

2052		♇ Haumea 136108	♇ Makemake 136472
JAN	1	2♐15.2	5♏50.8
	11	2 27.2	5 56.6
	21	2 37.5	6 00.3
	31	2 45.8	6 02.0
FEB	10	2 51.9	6R01.6
	20	2 55.6	5 59.1
MAR	1	2 57.0	5 54.6
	11	2R56.0	5 48.4
	21	2 52.7	5 40.7
	31	2 47.2	5 31.8
APR	10	2 39.7	5 21.9
	20	2 30.7	5 11.5
	30	2 20.3	5 00.9
MAY	10	2 08.9	4 50.5
	20	1 57.1	4 40.7
	30	1 45.1	4 31.7
JUN	9	1 33.5	4 23.9
	19	1 22.5	4 17.6
	29	1 12.7	4 12.9
JUL	9	1 04.3	4 10.0
	19	0 57.6	4D09.0
	29	0 52.8	4 10.0
AUG	8	0 50.2	4 13.0
	18	0D49.9	4 17.9
	28	0 51.8	4 24.5
SEP	7	0 56.0	4 32.9
	17	1 02.5	4 42.7
	27	1 11.0	4 53.8
OCT	7	1 21.4	5 05.8
	17	1 33.4	5 18.6
	27	1 46.8	5 31.7
NOV	6	2 01.3	5 44.8
	16	2 16.4	5 57.7
	26	2 31.9	6 10.0
DEC	6	2 47.3	6 21.4
	16	3 02.3	6 31.5
	26	3 16.5	6 40.1
JAN	5	3♐29.4	6♏47.0
JAN	1	01N07.9	04N23.3
	21	01 10.3	04 26.3
FEB	10	01 15.9	04 32.1
MAR	1	01 23.9	04 39.8
	21	01 33.2	04 48.3
APR	10	01 42.4	04 56.3
	30	01 50.3	05 02.7
MAY	20	01 55.8	05 06.4
JUN	9	01 58.0	05 06.9
	29	01 56.6	05 03.9
JUL	19	01 51.7	04 57.8
AUG	8	01 43.6	04 49.0
	28	01 33.3	04 38.4
SEP	17	01 21.7	04 26.9
OCT	7	01 09.9	04 15.6
	27	00 59.3	04 05.7
NOV	16	00 50.7	03 57.9
DEC	6	00 45.1	03 53.1
	26	00N42.9	03N51.6
		3/1.49 8/14.29	2/2.63 7/18.66

2053		♇ Haumea 136108	♇ Makemake 136472
JAN	1	3♐24.4	6♏44.5
	11	3 36.5	6 50.3
	21	3 46.8	6 54.1
	31	3 55.2	6 55.8
FEB	10	4 01.4	6R55.4
	20	4 05.3	6 52.9
MAR	2	4 06.8	6 48.5
	12	4R05.9	6 42.3
	22	4 02.7	6 34.6
APR	1	3 57.3	6 25.7
	11	3 49.9	6 15.9
	21	3 40.9	6 05.5
MAY	1	3 30.5	5 54.9
	11	3 19.2	5 44.5
	21	3 07.4	5 34.6
	31	2 55.4	5 25.7
JUN	10	2 43.7	5 17.9
	20	2 32.7	5 11.5
	30	2 22.8	5 06.8
JUL	10	2 14.3	5 03.8
	20	2 07.5	5D02.8
	30	2 02.7	5 03.8
AUG	9	2 00.0	5 06.7
	19	1D59.5	5 11.6
	29	2 01.4	5 18.2
SEP	8	2 05.5	5 26.6
	18	2 11.9	5 36.3
	28	2 20.3	5 47.4
OCT	8	2 30.6	5 59.4
	18	2 42.6	6 12.1
	28	2 56.0	6 25.2
NOV	7	3 10.5	6 38.4
	17	3 25.7	6 51.3
	27	3 41.2	7 03.6
DEC	7	3 56.6	7 14.9
	17	4 11.7	7 25.1
	27	4 25.9	7 33.7
JAN	6	4♐38.9	7♏40.6
JAN	1	00N43.0	03N51.8
	21	00 45.4	03 54.7
FEB	10	00 51.0	04 00.4
MAR	2	00 58.9	04 08.0
	22	01 08.1	04 16.4
APR	11	01 17.1	04 24.3
MAY	1	01 24.9	04 30.6
	21	01 30.3	04 34.2
JUN	10	01 32.4	04 34.7
	30	01 30.9	04 31.8
JUL	20	01 26.0	04 25.7
AUG	9	01 17.9	04 17.0
	29	01 07.6	04 06.5
SEP	18	00 56.1	03 55.1
OCT	8	00 44.5	03 44.0
	28	00 34.0	03 34.1
NOV	17	00 25.5	03 26.3
DEC	7	00 20.0	03 21.5
	27	00N17.9	03N20.0
		3/2.93 8/15.69	2/2.77 7/19.80

2054		♇ Haumea 136108	♇ Makemake 136472
JAN	1	4♐32.6	7♏37.4
	11	4 44.9	7 43.4
	21	4 55.5	7 47.4
	31	5 04.2	7 49.3
FEB	10	5 10.8	7R49.2
	20	5 15.0	7 46.9
MAR	2	5 16.9	7 42.7
	12	5R16.3	7 36.8
	22	5 13.4	7 29.2
APR	1	5 08.3	7 20.4
	11	5 01.2	7 10.7
	21	4 52.4	7 00.3
MAY	1	4 42.2	6 49.8
	11	4 30.9	6 39.3
	21	4 19.1	6 29.4
	31	4 07.1	6 20.3
JUN	10	3 55.4	6 12.4
	20	3 44.2	6 05.8
	30	3 34.1	6 00.9
JUL	10	3 25.4	5 57.8
	20	3 18.3	5 56.5
	30	3 13.2	5D57.3
AUG	9	3 10.2	6 00.0
	19	3D09.4	6 04.6
	29	3 10.9	6 11.0
SEP	8	3 14.7	6 19.1
	18	3 20.8	6 28.8
	28	3 29.0	6 39.7
OCT	8	3 39.1	6 51.6
	18	3 50.9	7 04.2
	28	4 04.1	7 17.3
NOV	7	4 18.5	7 30.4
	17	4 33.6	7 43.4
	27	4 49.1	7 55.7
DEC	7	5 04.7	8 07.2
	17	5 19.8	8 17.5
	27	5 34.2	8 26.3
JAN	6	5♐47.4	8♏33.4
JAN	1	00N17.9	03N20.2
	21	00 20.2	03 22.8
FEB	10	00 25.6	03 28.3
MAR	2	00 33.3	03 35.7
	22	00 42.3	03 43.9
APR	11	00 51.3	03 51.8
MAY	1	00 59.0	03 58.1
	21	01 04.3	04 01.9
JUN	10	01 06.5	04 02.5
	30	01 05.2	03 59.8
JUL	20	01 00.4	03 53.9
AUG	9	00 52.5	03 45.4
	29	00 42.4	03 35.1
SEP	18	00 31.0	03 23.8
OCT	8	00 19.5	03 12.7
	28	00 09.0	03 02.8
NOV	17	00 00.5	02 55.0
DEC	7	00S05.1	02 50.0
	27	00S07.3	02N48.3
		3/4.39 8/17.12	2/3.91 7/21.01

Titles by Neil F. Michelsen

The American Ephemeris 1931-1980 & Book of Tables
The American Ephemeris 1901-1930
The American Ephemeris 1941-1950
The American Ephemeris1951-1960
The American Ephemeris1961-1970
The American Ephemeris1971-1980
The American Ephemeris1971-1980
The American Ephemeris1981-1990
The American Ephemeris1991-2000
The American Ephemeris for the 20th Century, 1900 to 2000 at Noon
The American Ephemeris for the 20th Century, 1900 to 2000 at Midnight
The American Ephemeris for the 21st Century, 2000 to2050 at Noon
The American Ephemeris for the 21st Century, 2000 to2050 at Midnight
The American Sidereal Ephemeris 1976-2000
The American Sidereal Ephemeris 2001-2025
The American Heliocentric Ephemeris 1901-2000
The American Heliocentric Ephemeris 2001-2050
The American Midpoint Ephemeris 1986-1990
The American Midpoint Ephemeris 1990-1995
The American Midpoint Ephemeris 1996-2000
The American Midpoint Ephemeris 2001-2005
The American Book of Tables
The Koch Book of Tables
The Michelsen Book of Tables
The Uranian Transneptune Ephemeris 1901-1996
Comet Halley Ephemeris 1901-1996
Search for the Christmas Star (with Maria K. Simms)
The Asteroid Ephemeris (with Zipporah Dobyns and Rique Pottenger)
Tables of Planetary Phenomena

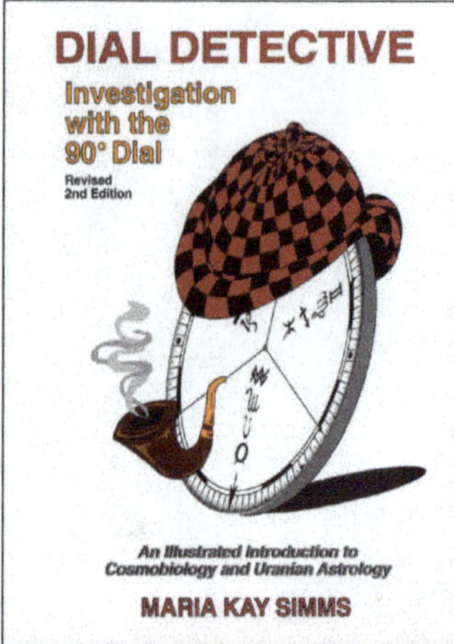

Dial Detective
Investigation with the 90 degree dial, revised 2nd edition

An Illustrated Introduction to Cosmobiology and Uranian Astrology. Since its original publication in 1989, Dial Detective has become the most frequently recommended book among students, practitioners and teachers of Cosmobiology and Uranian Astrology as the best book of instruction in 90 degree dial techniques.

An interesting variety of case studies lead you through the practice of dial techniques as they apply to: natal analysis, solar arc directions, transits, chart comparison, composite charts, relocation astrology, solar returns, mundane astrology, karmic astrology.

Added in this new edition: Sixteen additional pages of illustrated instruction, Expanded section on Cosmobiology, Updated references, Dial techniques for rectification Also: a 90 degree dial to cut out and use for practice, an appendix of planetary pictures, listed alphabetically by delineations, an appendix of "grim" planetary pictures with alternative delineations, an appendix of Uranian tips and terminology, featuring 360 degree dial techniques and the Uranian houses.

Titles by Maria Kay Simms

Twelve Wings of the Eagle
Our Spiritual Evolution through the Ages of the Zodiac.

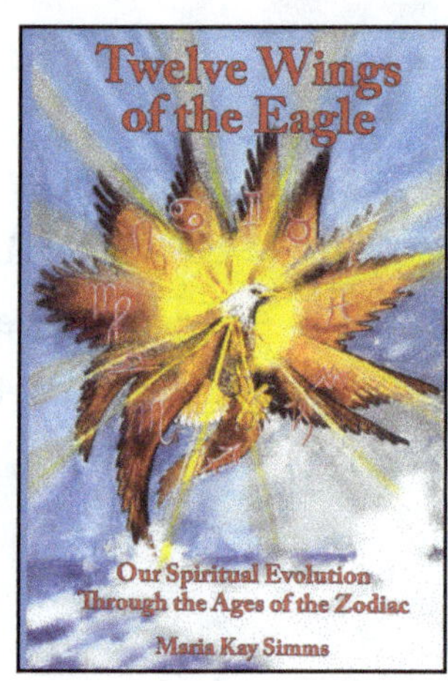

In a light, conversational style, the author has traced the spiritual evolution of western civilization through the precessional ages of history and a detailed study of the biblical Genesis. Her narrative along with lively dialogue, with her students, and interspersed with stories from Genesis, Exodus, and the gospels that are retold from class discussions that emphasize the zodiacal and numerological symbolism that can be found in the stories.

The use of astrology is seen here as a synthesis of such apparent opposites as faith (religion) and reason (science). The astrology of the Great Ages is shown to reflect the matriarchal roots of humanity through the dominance of the patriarchy to the current and future reemergence of the Goddess.

The vision of Esdras, from the Apocrypha, of an eagle with twelve wings brings this story of the ages to a close, but with hope and inspiration for a future for humanity that extends and will likely continue to extend far beyond the fabled Age of Aquarius.

Little has changed in the text in regard to the history of the past ages, though there is commentary and at least an estimate on when the new age might actually arrive, when we might once again be hearing a new revival of that popular song of years past that began with the lyrics, "It is the dawning of the Age of Aquarius... Aquarius...Aquarius!"

More Titles by Maria Kay Simms

Astrology and the Power of Eight

What is Eight...8? A doubled four? A double cross? Or a symbol of balance?

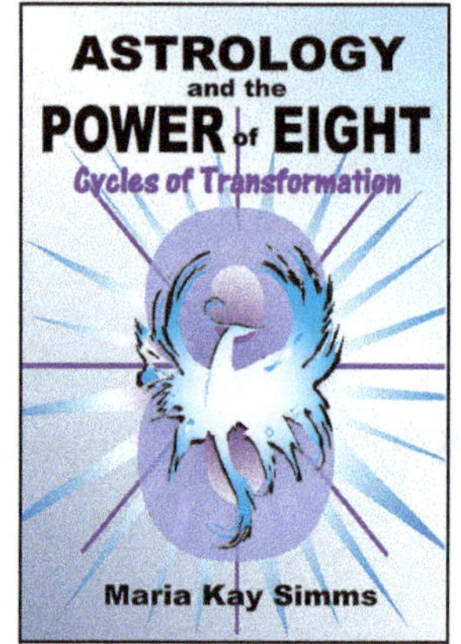

In numerology it is a symbol of power. In astrology it is the 8th sign of Scorpio, and the 8th house of shared resources that we share in partnership.

Eight aspects of astrology have been deemed hard or challenging, conjunction, opposition, 2 squares, 4 semi-squares. In this book they are called active, the aspects on which the most important events in our lives happen! We experience them all within repeated cycles of 29-30 years each. Three cycles are formed by the hard aspects of transiting Saturn to natal Saturn, to the Ascendant, and as transiting Saturn begins moving upward and around your chart from the IC, a point of endings and new beginnings.

Many examples are provided throughout, including chapters that are devoted to full lifetime phases cycles for one private person and four well known public figures, each of whom lived enough to experience at least part of their third phase cycles. Who knows...with this book, you may gain appreciation for, and even learn to look forward to those hard aspects.

We have software for a personal Power of Eight report. The book explains the report. Be sure to include your birth data when you order. When ordering through the ACS website, the birth data can be listed in the Comments box which appears towards the end of the order process.

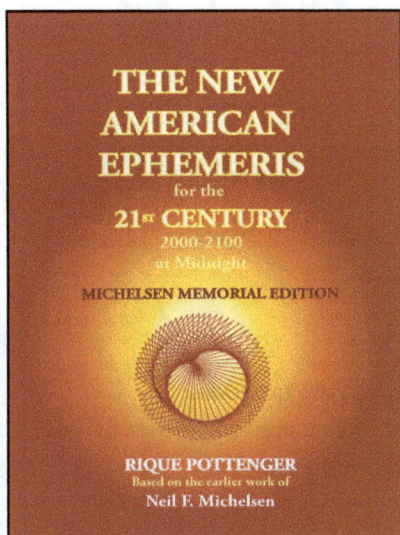

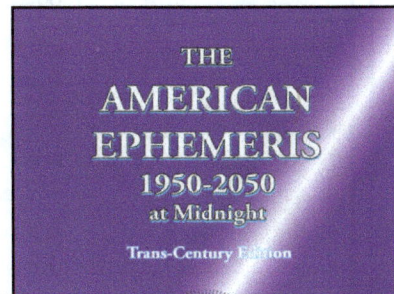

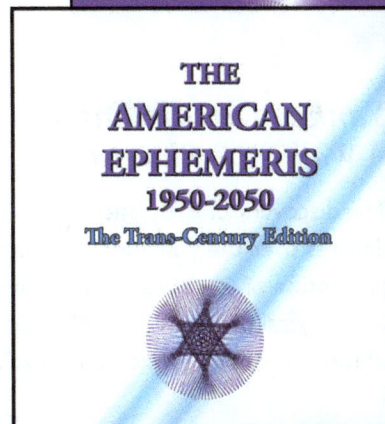

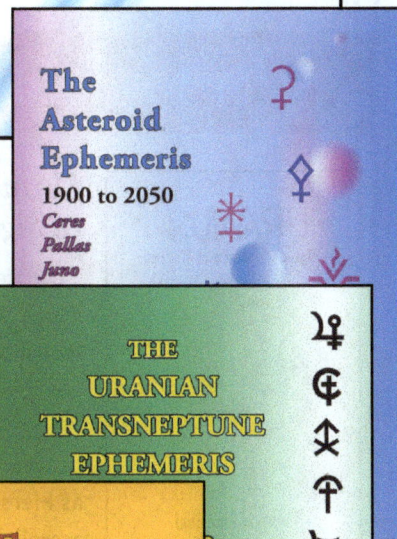

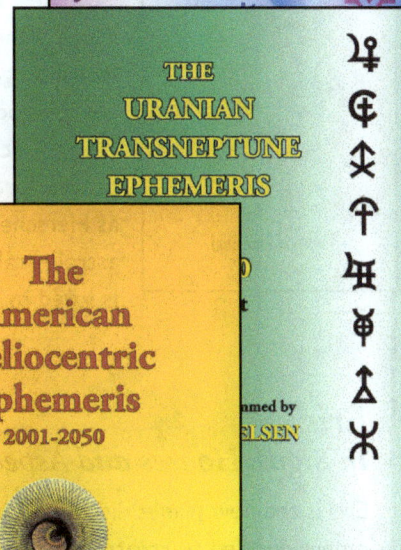

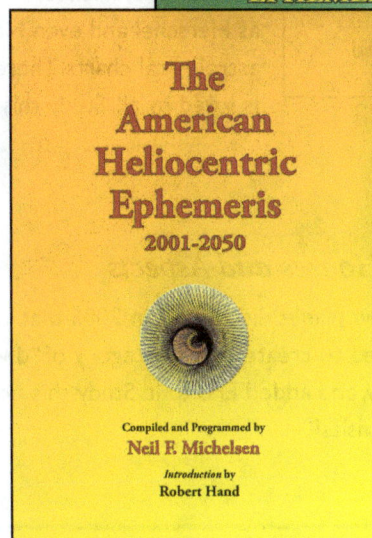

Brother Pluto, Sister Eris

Aspects Between the Dwarf Planets Through 800 Years of History
Written as a follow-up to Yankee Doodle Discord, this book examines the Eris Frenemy principle in regard to Pluto. Covering 800 years of major Pluto aspects with Eris, the chapters take you from one historical event to another, pointing out that the deadliest wars have taken place with Eris and Pluto in cooperative aspects (semi-sextile, sextile, trine), and the least discord has taken place under challenging aspects (square, quincunx, opposition.) Eris-Pluto conjunctions tell a tale of treachery, which may have repercussions later on. Follow the history and the aspects, and you will see a pattern emerging with these two dwarf planets. If this were a criminal investigation, these two would be considered "persons of interest."

Yankee Doodle Discord

A Walk With Planet Eris Through USA History

The discovery of the planet Eris in 2005 created discord in the Astronomical community with debates over the definition of what was a "planet", leading to the demotion of Pluto and the promotion of Ceres to "dwarf planet" status. Now, Thomas Canfield takes that discord to the Astrological community. "Yankee Doodle Discord" examines the role of planet Eris in the charts of the United States, the Founding Fathers, and major events of upheaval in American history.

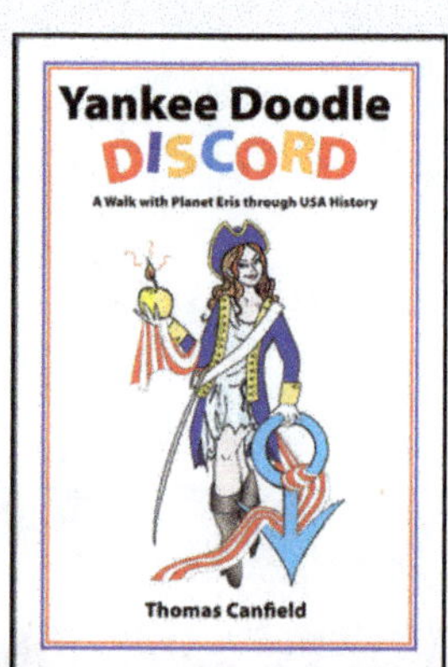

Titles by Thomas Canfield

Uranus

In Signs, Houses and Aspects

The latest booklet in the All About Astrology series. This booklet raises the questions:
Can a planet named George find happiness as the ruler of Aquarius, after being fought over by the British Angels? Should astronomers be allowed to name the planets they discovered?
Do sky-gods have the right to lock up their children in caves?

For these and other questions, and possible answers, look through this booklet for the history, lore, science, and astrological interpretations of Uranus (aka George, and also known as Herschel and even Neptune.) It has been less than 200 years since Uranus has been used in astrological charts. There once was a time when astrologers did not like Uranus, but now Uranus is loved by all. Study this book as a means of loving Uranus!

Eris

In Signs, Houses and Aspects

Eris is the new planet discovered in 2005 that was found to be larger than Pluto. The astronomers decided to create a new category of "dwarf planets." Then they demoted Pluto to the new category, and added Eris to it. Study this booklet to find out what Eris is doing in your natal chart and transits!

Midpoints

Unleashing the Power of the Planets

Michael Munkasey

Since the first edition of this book by Michael Munkasey was published in 1991, it has been a widely used reference book for many astrologers and their students who have recognized the value and importance in horoscope interpretation of the midpoints--the halfway point between any two planets, or a planet and a highly significant point such as Midheaven, Ascendant or North or South Node of the Moon. The format of this edition is very similar to the first edition, but you will find that the author has updated the interpretive text. So do read it carefully...and if you have not used midpoints routinely before, you will soon realize how significant they can be in chart interpretation!

This book is filled with interpretive material. It is a "must have" addition to the library of anyone who works with the dial techniques of Cosmobiology and Uranian Astrology.

Table of Planetary Phenomena

Neil F. Michelsen

This amazing volume has a wealth of information for every astrological researcher, teacher and student! Whether you are interested in history, mundane astrology, planetary patterns, cycles, sunspots or other solar system activity, this book has something for you.

Tables are provided for planetary ingresses from 501 BC through AD 2100. Eclipse data are given from 1700 through 2050. Perihelions and aphelions are also listed from 1700 through 2050. Aspects between outer planets (Jupiter through Pluto) are provided from 1700 through 2050 (with conjunctions back to 501 BC and up to AD 2100).

Planetary stations in longitude are listed from 1700 through 2050 along with times when five or more planets were within a 20 degree arc. The eight lunar phases between 1900 and 2020 are also included. Other tables provide yearly mean sunspot numbers, daily sunspot numbers and major magnetic storms.

Each table is preceded by an explanatory article, giving tips on how to use the tabular information and examples from astrological practice and tradition.

An artistic masterpiece within this work is provided by the planetary mandalas. These striking figures show orbital patterns involving various planetary (and asteroid) combinations (Look for the Venus-Earth mandala which forms a valentine!) The infinite designs of our universe are incredible.

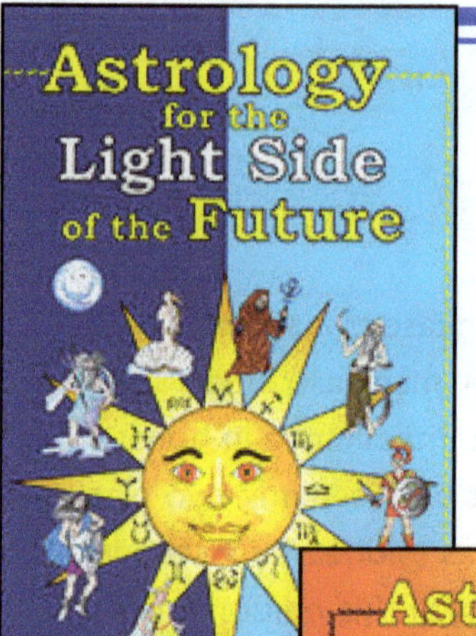

Astrology for the Light Side of the Future

Kim takes you on a unique tour of the planets - with a kit for each one. Your Mars kit includes a sword, a copy of Rambo, a Swiss army knife, a chip for your shoulder and health insurance for yourself and your victims!

Learn to create the future by understanding each of the planets and how their current positions relate to the patterns in the sky when you were born.

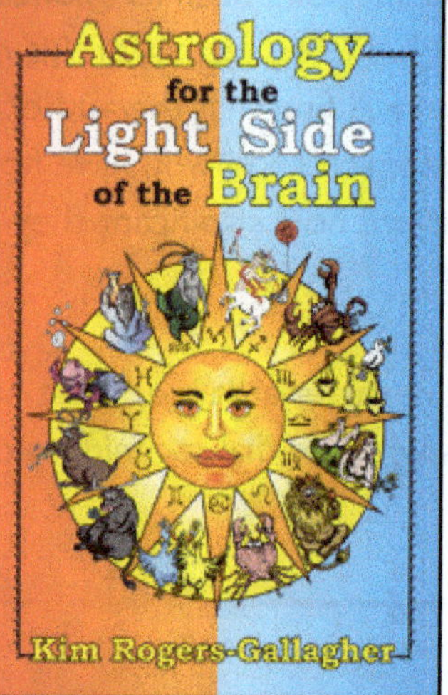

Astrology for the Light Side of the Brain

Laugh while you learn astrology! Kim has written a unique, FUN book. Inside, you'll meet Pluto as Darth Vader, Venus in Aries as a flamenco dancer, the Sun as CEO of your horoscope, and much more. Her colorful, humorous descriptions help you capture the essence of a person. Laughter lurks throughout these pages. Have a great time!

Amidst all your chuckles, you'll learn a lot of astrology--from the Four Basic Food Groups (planets, houses, signs, and aspects)-to remedies, suggestions and antidotes for aspects with "bad" reputations.

Kim covers personality basics, predictive tools, relationship insights, and more!

More Titles by Starcrafts Publishing

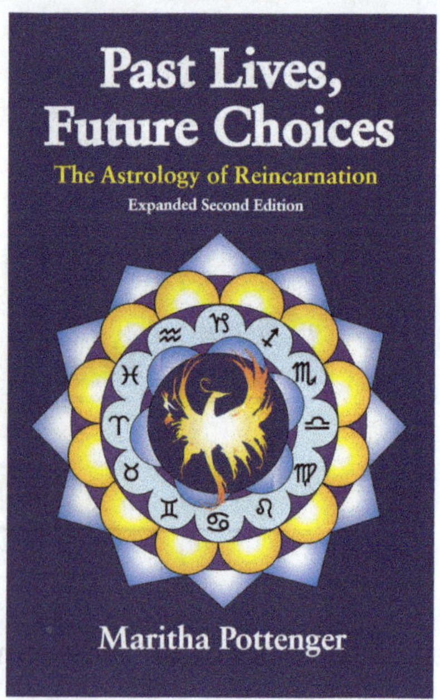

Past Lives, Future Choices

The Astrology of Reincarnation

Reincarnation helps to explain many phobias, dysfunctional family patterns, eating disorders, chronic pain, and other long-term problems. Using the ancient art of astrology, the reader can get instant access to possible past lives. Important, repetitive issues can be addressed - and solved! By looking backward, people are able to move forward to fulfillment.

Within the pages of Past Lives, Future Choices:

*Readers can get an "instant" past life reading for themselves.

*Karmic issues and blocks are discussed with suggested paths for resolution.

*Painful relationships, addictions, and other long-term problems are explained through reincarnation.

The Only Way to learn Astrology series

Here are all the basics of natal astrology— how to analyze and understand, how to look ahead, how to compare charts for relationship potential, and how to answer questions! Generations of astrologers have learned from March & McEvers.

Now you can learn from these master teachers , too!

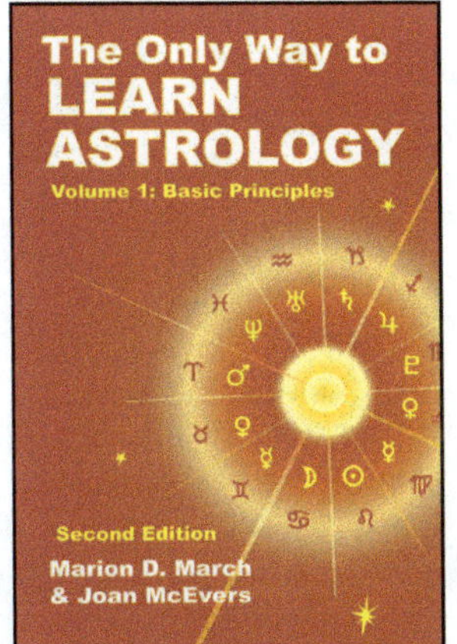

Book 1 of the series

Basic Principles

Here are the basics that we all must learn when we begin to study astrology — the planets, the signs, the houses and the aspects . Before we can make sense of a total horoscope, we need to first learn the meaning of each of its separate parts.

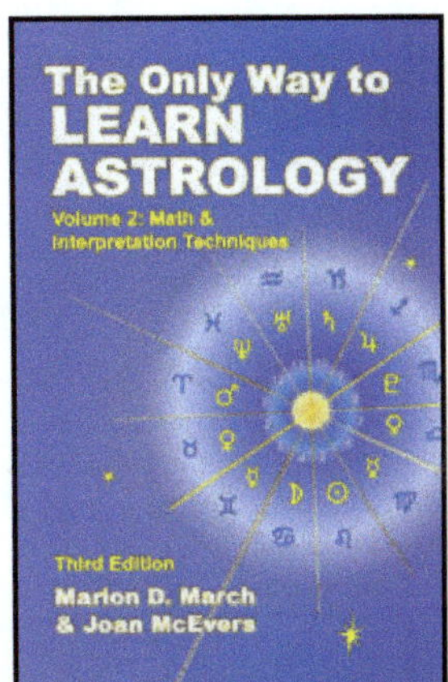

Book 2 of the series

Math and Interpretation Techniques

Yes, the math—even with a computer chart we need to know the basics, else we risk "garbage in, garbage out." With no idea how a chart is calculated, we won't know if we've made an error in data entry. Besides, this book has great info on interpretation, too!

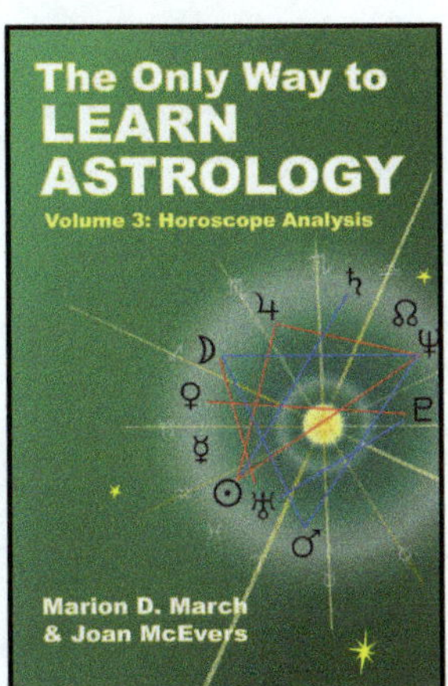

Book 3 of the series

Horoscope Analysis

Now we get into much greater depth in how to look a chart and analyze what all of its planets, their placements and aspects means, and most significantly, how to make sense of what all of them together say about each chart. In this book, we learn how to synthesize.

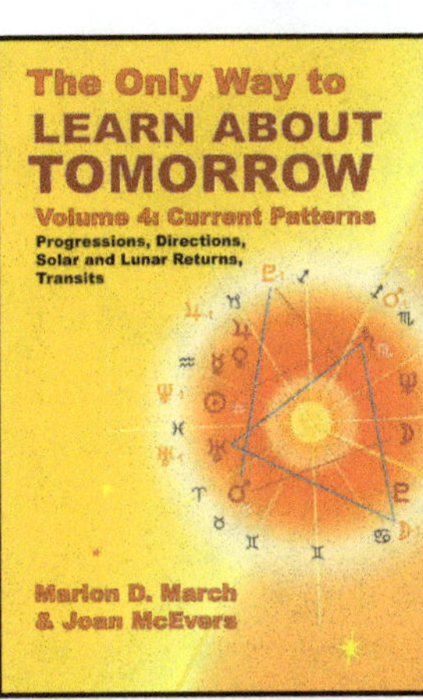

Book 4 of the series

Current Patterns

Now, at last, we've learned the basics, so now we are ready to begin to learn how to use astrology to look ahead. We can learn how to anticipate what might be happening in the future, and use that knowledge to make choices that could improve it! **Progressions, Directions, Solar Returns and Transits** are covered in this book.

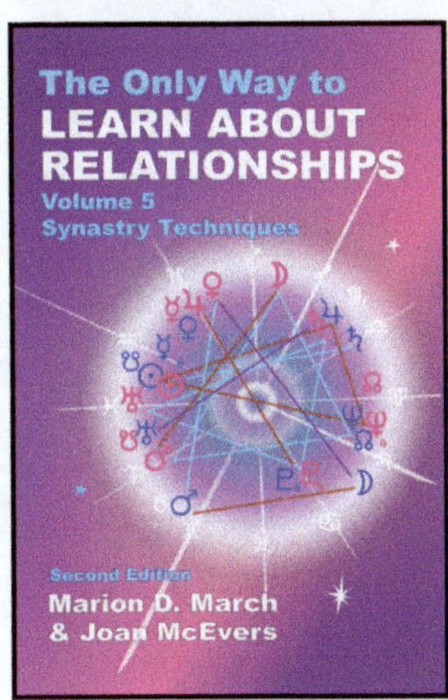

Book 5 of the series

Synastry Techniques

In this book we learn about how to compare charts to analyze how they do, or do not,blend together well. This is valuable for understanding romantic relationships, but also for many other types of personal or business relationships. Learn how to analyze comparison and composite charts.

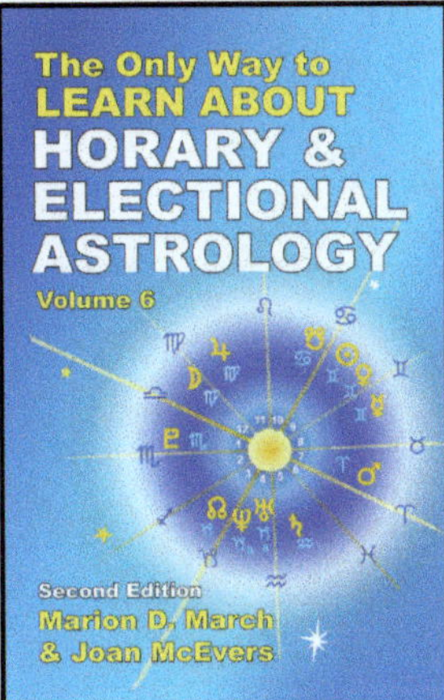

Book 6 of the series

Horary & Electional Astrology

In this book we learn how to use the exact moment when a question is asked (or first comes to mind, if it's our own question) to calculate a chart that can answer the question (Horary)—and we also learn how we can choose the time for just the right chart to begin something important (Electional Astrology).

www.ingramcontent.com/pod-product-compliance
Lightning Source LLC
Chambersburg PA
CBHW050500110426
42742CB00018B/3323

* 9 7 8 1 9 3 4 9 7 6 6 8 5 *